PETERSON'S
NURSING
PROGRAMS
2011

PETERSON'S

A **nelnet** COMPANY

About Peterson's

To succeed on your lifelong educational journey, you will need accurate, dependable, and practical tools and resources. That is why Peterson's is everywhere education happens. Because whenever and however you need education content delivered, you can rely on Peterson's to provide the information, know-how, and guidance to help you reach your goals. Tools to match the right students with the right school. It's here. Personalized resources and expert guidance. It's here. Comprehensive and dependable education content—delivered whenever and however you need it. It's all here.

For more information, contact Peterson's, 2000 Lenox Drive, Lawrenceville, NJ 08648; 800-338-3282; or find us on the World Wide Web at www.petersons.com/about.

© 2010 Peterson's, a Nelnet company

Previous editions © 1994, 1996, 1997, 1998, 1999, 2000, 2001, 2002, 2003, 2004, 2005, 2006, 2007, 2008, 2009

Stephen Clemente, Managing Director, Publishing and Institutional Research; Bernadette Webster, Director of Publishing; Jill C. Schwartz, Editor; Christine Lucas, Research Project Manager; Amy Weber, Research Associate; Phyllis Johnson, Programmer; Ray Golaszewski, Manufacturing Manager; Linda M. Williams, Composition Manager; Karen Mount, Danielle Vreeland, Shannon White, Client Service Representatives

Peterson's makes every reasonable effort to obtain accurate, complete, and timely data from reliable sources. Nevertheless, Peterson's and the third-party data suppliers make no representation or warranty, either expressed or implied, as to the accuracy, timeliness, or completeness of the data or the results to be obtained from using the data, including, but not limited to, its quality, performance, merchantability, or fitness for a particular purpose, non-infringement or otherwise.

Neither Peterson's nor the third-party data suppliers warrant, guarantee, or make any representations that the results from using the data will be successful or will satisfy users' requirements. The entire risk to the results and performance is assumed by the user.

ISSN 1552-7743
ISBN-13: 978-0-7689-2836-5
ISBN-10: 0-7689-2836-2

Printed in the United States of America

10 9 8 7 6 5 4 3 2 1   12 11 10

Sixteenth Edition

By producing this book on recycled paper (40% post-consumer waste) 73 trees were saved.

Sustainability—Its Importance to Peterson's, a Nelnet company

What does sustainability mean to Peterson's? As a leading publisher, we are aware that our business has a direct impact on vital resources—most especially the trees that are used to make our books. Peterson's is proud that its products are certified by the Sustainable Forestry Initiative (SFI) and that all of its books are printed on paper that is 40 percent post-consumer waste.

Being a part of the Sustainable Forestry Initiative (SFI) means that all of our vendors—from paper suppliers to printers—have undergone rigorous audits to demonstrate that they are maintaining a sustainable environment.

Peterson's continually strives to find new ways to incorporate sustainability throughout all aspects of its business.

CONTENTS

FOREWORD

The American Association of Colleges of Nursing (AACN) is proud to collaborate on *Peterson's Nursing Programs 2011*.

According to the Bureau of Labor Statistics, more than 1 million new and replacement registered nurses will be needed by the year 2012 to fill new positions and vacancies. Nursing schools are working hard to find creative solutions to expand capacity and recruit new students during this nursing shortage.

As registered nurses find employment beyond hospitals in such areas as home care, community health, and long-term care, newly licensed RNs must have the proper education and training to work in these settings. It is vital that those seeking to enter or advance in a nursing career find the appropriate nursing program. This guide allows readers to find the program that best fits their needs, whether beginning a new career in nursing or attempting to advance one.

According to AACN's most recent annual institutional survey, enrollment in entry-level B.S.N. programs continues to climb. Gains were reported in all parts of the country in 2009, with an overall 3.6 percent increase in enrollments nationwide. In addition, the number of entry-level baccalaureate students has increased by 19.2 percent in the past five years, jumping from 117,453 in 2005 to 140,039 in 2009.

Although the health-care environment is complex and dynamic, there continues to be a significant demand for professional-level nurses. The primary route into professional-level nursing is the four-year baccalaureate degree. The professional nurse with a baccalaureate degree is the only basic nursing graduate prepared to practice in all health-care settings, including critical care, public health, primary care, and mental health. In addition, advanced practice nurses (APNs) deliver essential services as nurse practitioners, certified nurse-midwives, clinical nurse specialists, and nurse anesthetists. APNs typically are prepared in master's degree programs, and the demand for their services is expected to increase substantially.

Higher education in nursing expands the gateway to a variety of career opportunities in the health-care field. In addition to providing primary care to patients, graduates can work as case managers for the growing numbers of managed-care companies or can assume administrative or managerial roles in hospitals, clinics, insurance companies, and other diverse settings.

The Nursing School Adviser section of this guide is instructive and invaluable. Whether you are a high school student looking for a four-year program, an RN returning to school, or a professional in another field contemplating a career change, this section will address your concerns. This information presents various nursing perspectives to benefit students from diverse backgrounds.

Peterson's effort in making this guide well organized and convenient to read cannot be overstated. Peterson's has worked with AACN in producing a publication that is comprehensive and user-friendly. Like the previous editions, this edition is a genuine collaborative work, as AACN provided input from start to finish.

AACN's dedication and achievements in advancing the quality of baccalaureate and graduate nursing education are appreciated by Peterson's. We at AACN are fortunate to work with an organization that prides itself on being the leading publisher of education search and selection.

Furthermore, this publication would not be possible without the cooperation of the institutions included in this guide. We acknowledge the time and effort of those who undertook the task of completing and returning the surveys regarding their programs. We certainly appreciate their contribution.

Peterson's Nursing Programs 2011 is the only comprehensive and concise guide to baccalaureate and graduate nursing education programs in the United States and Canada. We hope its contents will serve as the impetus for those looking for a rewarding and satisfying career in health care. AACN is proud to present this publication to the nursing profession and to those who seek to enter it.

—Kathleen Potempa, DNSc, RN, FAAN
President, AACN

—Geraldine D. Bednash, Ph.D., RN, FAAN
Executive Director, AACN

A NOTE FROM THE PETERSON'S EDITORS

For more than forty years, Peterson's has given students and parents the most comprehensive, up-to-date information on undergraduate and graduate institutions in the United States, Canada, and abroad.

Peterson's Nursing Programs 2011 provides prospective nursing students with the most comprehensive information on baccalaureate and graduate nursing education in the United States and Canada. Our goal is to help students find the best nursing program for them.

To this end, Peterson's has joined forces with the American Association of Colleges of Nursing (AACN), the national voice for America's baccalaureate- and higher-degree nursing education programs. AACN's educational, research, governmental advocacy, data collection, publications, and other programs work to establish high-quality standards for bachelor's- and graduate-degree nursing education, assist deans and directors to implement those standards, influence the nursing profession to improve health care, and promote public support of baccalaureate and graduate education, research, and practice in nursing—the nation's largest health-care profession.

For those seeking to enter the nursing profession or to further their nursing careers, *Peterson's Nursing Programs 2011* includes information needed to make important nursing program decisions and to approach the admissions process with knowledge and confidence.

The Nursing School Adviser section contains useful articles to help guide nursing education choices, with information on nursing careers today, selecting a nursing program, financing nursing education, returning to school, and more. It also includes listings that provide valuable contact information for financial aid resources and specialty nursing organizations. And if you are one of the many people interested in accelerated nursing programs, there is an article that offers an in-depth look at this increasingly popular approach to nursing education. It is a must-read for those wishing to enter an accelerated baccalaureate or generic master's degree program.

At the end of **The Nursing School Adviser** is the "How to Use This Guide" article, which explains some of the key factors to consider when choosing a nursing program. In addition, it explains how the book is organized and shows you how to maximize your use of *Peterson's Nursing Programs 2011* to its full potential.

If you already have specifics in mind, such as a particular program or location, turn to the **Quick-Reference Chart.** Here you can search through "Nursing Programs At-a-Glance" for particular degree options offered by schools, listed alphabetically by state.

In the **Profiles of Nursing Programs** section you'll find expanded and updated nursing program descriptions, arranged alphabetically by state. Each profile provides all of the need-to-know information about accredited nursing programs in the United States and Canada.

If you are looking for additional information, you can turn to the **Close-Ups of Nursing Programs** section. Here you will find two-page narrative descriptions written by admissions deans who chose to provide additional information about their schools and nursing programs.

Finally, turn to the back of the book to find eight **Indexes** listing institutions offering *baccalaureate, master's degree, concentrations within master's degree, doctoral, postdoctoral, online,* and *continuing education* programs. The last index lists every college and university contained in the guide along with its corresponding page reference.

Peterson's publishes a full line of resources to help guide you and your family through the admission process. Peterson's publications can be found at high school guidance offices, college and university libraries and career centers, and your local bookstore or library.

Peterson's guides are also available as e-books. Continue to check our Web site, www.petersons.com for more information about our e-book program. In addition, at www.petersons.com, you'll find Peterson's Nursing Programs Search—a comprehensive information resource that will help you with your nursing program search and selection process, with up-to-date information about prospective schools.

We welcome any comments or suggestions you may have about this publication and invite you to complete our online survey at **www.petersons.com/booksurvey.** Or you can fill out the survey at the back of this book, tear it out, and mail it to us at:

Publishing Department
Peterson's, a Nelnet company
2000 Lenox Drive
Lawrenceville, NJ 08648

Your feedback will help us make your educational dreams possible. The editors at Peterson's wish you great success in your nursing program search.

THE NURSING
SCHOOL ADVISER

NURSING FACT SHEET

Misconceptions about nursing have contributed to misinformation about the profession in the media. Here are the real facts:

- **Nursing is the nation's largest health-care profession, with more than 2.9 million registered nurses nationwide.** Of all licensed RNs, 2.42 million, or 83.2 percent, are employed in nursing.[1]

- **Nursing students account for more than one-half (52 percent) of all health profession students in the United States.**[2]

- **Registered Nurses compose one of the largest segments of the U.S. workforce as a whole, and nursing is among the highest-paying large occupations.** Nearly 59 percent of RNs worked in general medical and surgical hospitals where RN salaries averaged $58,550 per year. With 2.5 million nurses in the workforce in 2007, RNs composed the largest segment of professionals (28 percent) working in the health-care industry.[3]

- **Nurses compose the largest single component of hospital staff.** They are the primary providers of hospital patient care, and they deliver most of the nation's long-term care.

- **Most health-care services involve some form of care by nurses.** In 1980, 66 percent of all employed RNs worked in hospitals. By 2004, that number had declined to 56.2 percent as more health care moved to sites outside of hospitals and nurses increased their ranks in a wide range of other settings, including private practices, health maintenance organizations, public health agencies, primary-care clinics, home health care, nursing homes, outpatient surgicenters, nursing-school–operated nursing centers, insurance and managed care companies, schools, mental health agencies, hospices, the military, industry, nursing education, and health-care research.[4]

- **Though often working collaboratively, nursing does not "assist" medicine or other fields.** Nursing operates independent of—not as an auxiliary to—medicine and other disciplines. Nurses' roles range from direct patient care and case management to establishing nursing practice standards, developing quality assurance procedures, and directing complex nursing care systems.

- **With more than four times as many RNs in the United States as physicians, nursing delivers an extended array of health-care services.** These services include primary and preventive care by advanced nurse practitioners in such areas as pediatrics, family health, women's health, and gerontological care. Nursing's scope also includes services by certified nurse-midwives and nurse anesthetists, as well as care in cardiac, oncology, neonatal, neurological, and obstetric/gynecological nursing and other advanced clinical specialties.

- **The primary pathway to professional nursing, as compared to technical-level practice, is the four-year Bachelor of Science in Nursing (B.S.N.) degree.** Registered nurses are prepared through a B.S.N. program, a three-year associate degree in nursing, or a three-year hospital training program, receiving a hospital diploma. All take the same state licensing exam. *(The number of diploma programs has declined steadily, to less than 10 percent of all basic RN education programs, as nursing education has shifted from hospital-operated instruction into the college and university system.)*

- **To meet the more complex demands of today's health-care environment, the National Advisory Council on Nurse Education and Practice recommended that at least two thirds of the basic nurse workforce hold baccalaureate or higher degrees in nursing by 2010.**[5] Aware of the need, RNs are seeking the B.S.N. degree in increasing numbers. In 1980, almost 55 percent of employed registered nurses held a hospital diploma as their highest educational credential, 22 percent held a bachelor's degree, and 18 percent an associate degree. By 2004, a diploma was the highest educational credential for only 17.5 percent of RNs, while the number with bachelor's degrees had climbed to 34.2 percent (with 33.7 percent holding an associate degree as their top academic preparation).[6] In 2005, 13,232 RNs with diplomas or associate degrees graduated from B.S.N. programs.[7]

- **In 2004, 13 percent of the nation's registered nurses held either a master's or doctoral degree as their highest educational credential.**[8] The current demand for master's-prepared and doctorally prepared nurses for advanced practice, clinical specialties, teaching, and research roles far outstrips the supply.

- **According to the U.S. Bureau of Labor Statistics, registered nursing is among the occupations with the greatest job growth from 2006–16.**[9] Other federal projections indicate that by 2020, the U.S. nursing shortage will expand to more than 800,000 registered nursing positions.[10] Even as health care continues to shift beyond the hospital to more community-based primary care sites and other outpatient sites, federal projections say the rising complexity of acute care will cause demand for RNs in hospitals to climb by 36 percent by 2020.[11]

---

1. Health Resources and Services Administration. (February 2007). *The Registered Nurse Population: Findings From the March 2004 National Sample Survey of Registered Nurses*. Washington, DC: U.S. Department of Health and Human Services.

2. Health Resources and Services Administration. (September 1992). *Health Personnel in the United States,*

1991: Eighth Report to Congress. Washington, DC: U.S. Department of Health and Human Services, p. 215 and other tables.

3. U.S. Bureau of Labor Statistics. (May 2008). Occupational Employment and Wages for 2007. Access online at http://www.bls.gov/news.release/pdf/ocwage.pdf.

4. Ibid.

5. Health Resources and Services Administration. (February 2007). *The Registered Nurse Population.*

6. National Advisory Council on Nurse Education and Practice. (October 1996). *Report to the Secretary of the Department of Health and Human Services on the Basic Registered Nurse Workforce.* Washington, DC: U.S. Department of Health and Human Services, Division of Nursing.

7. Health Resources and Services Administration. (February 2007). *The Registered Nurse Population.*

8. American Association of Colleges of Nursing (2007). *2006-07 Enrollment and Graduations in Baccalaureate and Graduate Programs in Nursing.* Washington, DC.

9. U.S. Bureau of Labor Statistics. (May 2008). *Occupational Employment and Wages for 2007.*

10. Hecker, D.E. (2004). *Occupational Employment Projections to 2012.* Washington, DC: U.S. Department of Labor, Bureau of Labor Statistics.

11. Health Resources and Services Administration, Bureau of Health Professions. (2002). *Projected Supply, Demand and Shortages of Registered Nurses: 2000-2020.* Washington, DC: U.S. Department of Health and Human Services.

Counselors of Care in the Modern Health-Care System

Geraldine Bednash, Ph.D., RN, FAAN
Executive Director
American Association of Colleges of Nursing

A Different Era

The nursing profession is alive and reshaping itself. The role of nurses as those who minister exclusively to a patient's basic-care needs has changed. Much of the effectiveness and productivity of the future health-care industry will derive from the training of and services provided by nurses.

Modern nurses take a proactive role in health care by addressing health issues before they develop into problems. They oversee the continued care of patients who have left the health-care facility. Nurses are expected to make complex decisions in areas ranging from patient screening to diagnosis and education. They explore and document the effects of alternative therapies (e.g., guided imagery) and address public health problems, such as teen pregnancy. They explore and understand new technology and how it relates both to patient care and to their own job performance. They work in a variety of settings and are held accountable for their decisions. In today's health-care environment, health-care administrators must recruit nurses with a broad, well-rounded education.

Health-care providers must change the way they administer care. Instead of focusing on the treatment of illness, they must promote wellness. Nurses will oversee patient treatment and medication and must understand the repercussions of these health-care processes for the patient and his or her family.

Cost is the driving force behind this industry-wide transformation. Insurance companies have, for the most part, instigated changes in the way health-care benefits are paid. The old fee-for-service system is no longer the only option. The trend toward managed care, in which a fixed amount of money is allocated for the care of each patient, is changing the way care is provided. It seems that employers of the future will recruit nurses who understand the overall structure of the health-care industry, who possess highly developed critical-thinking skills, and who bring to their positions a well-rounded understanding of the risks and benefits of every health-care decision.

Counselors of Care

Job prospects for graduates of nursing programs are positive. Although many graduates receive associate degrees as registered nurses (RNs), hospital administrators and other employers want applicants with at least a Bachelor of Science in Nursing degree.

To practice in a fast-changing health system, entry-level RNs must understand community-based primary care and emphasize health promotion and cost-effective coordinated care—all hallmarks of baccalaureate education. In addition to its broad scientific curriculum and focus on leadership and clinical decision-making skills, a Bachelor of Science in Nursing degree education provides specific preparation in community-based care not typically included in associate degree or hospital diploma programs. Moreover, the nurse with a baccalaureate degree is the only basic nursing graduate prepared for all health-care settings—critical care, outpatient care, public health, and mental health—and so has the flexibility to practice in outpatient centers, private homes, and neighborhood clinics where demand is fast expanding as health care moves beyond the hospital to more primary and preventive care throughout the community.

Health-care administrators realize that patients are becoming more sophisticated about the care they receive, requiring an explanation and understanding of their health needs. Nurses will have to be knowledgeable care providers, working with physicians, pharmacists, and public health officials in interdisciplinary settings to satisfy these requirements.

Broader training enables graduates of baccalaureate programs to provide improved and varying types of care, and ensures stability and security in an industry now noted for its instability.

Promising Opportunities

One of the rewards of a baccalaureate education can be a competitive salary. Graduates of four-year degree programs can expect salaries starting around $37,000 per year, a figure that might fluctuate depending on geographic area and, more specifically, by the demand in that area. Obviously, the greater the need for nurses, the higher their salaries.

The baccalaureate degree also serves as a foundation for the pursuit of a master's degree in nursing, which prepares students for the role of advanced practice nurse (APN). Students can earn degrees as clinical nurse specialists in neonatology, oncology, cardiology, and other specialties or as nurse practitioners, nurse-midwives, or nurse anesthetists. Master's-prepared nurses can also enjoy rewarding careers in nursing administration and education.

These programs generally span one to two years. Graduates can expect starting salaries of approximately $50,000 annually in advanced practice nursing settings, and demand for these graduates is expected to be high over the next fifteen years. In some localities, for example, the nurse practitioner may be the sole provider of health care to a family.

Overall Transformation

The nursing field must be transformed to be compatible with the overall changes in the health-care industry. According to 2004 statistics, the average age of nurses was 46.8, with only 16.6 percent of nurses under the age of 35. It is projected that over the next ten years much of the nursing population will retire. Employment is projected to increase 23 percent by 2016.

The traditional career path of nurses is expected to change. More nurses will enter master's programs directly from baccalaureate programs, and more master's degree graduates will pursue doctoral degrees at a younger age. Since nurses will play a critical role in providing health care, a four-year baccalaureate degree is a crucial first step in preparing nurses to assume increased patient responsibilities within the health-care system.

RNs Returning to School: Choosing a Nursing Program

Marilyn Oermann, Ph.D., RN, FAAN, ANEF
Professor and Adult/Geriatric Health Chair
College of Nursing
The University of North Carolina at Chapel Hill

If you are thinking about returning to school to complete your baccalaureate degree or to pursue a graduate degree in nursing, you are not alone. Registered nurses (RNs) are returning to school in record numbers, many seeking advancement or transition to new roles in nursing. Over the last two decades, the number of RNs prepared initially in diploma and associate degree in nursing programs who have graduated from baccalaureate nursing degree programs has more than doubled, according to the AACN. There are expanded opportunities for nurses with baccalaureate degrees in nursing. Although the decision to return to school means considerable investment of time, financial resources, and effort, the benefits can be overwhelmingly positive.

Higher education in nursing opens doors to many opportunities for career growth not otherwise available. By continuing your education, you can do the following:

- Update your knowledge and skills, critical today in light of rapid advances in health care

- Move more easily into a new role within your organization or in other health-care settings

- Pursue a different career path within nursing

Moreover, returning to school brings personal fulfillment and satisfaction gained through learning more about nursing and the changing health-care system and using that knowledge in the delivery and management of patient care.

More Skills and Flexibility Needed

If you are contemplating returning to school, here are some facts to consider. The health-care system continues to undergo dramatic changes. These changes include hospitalized patients who are more acutely ill; an aging population; technological advances that require highly skilled nursing care; a greater role for nurses in primary care, health promotion, and health education; and the need for nurses to care for patients and families in multiple settings, such as schools, workplaces, homes, clinics, and outpatient facilities, as well as hospitals. With the nursing shortage, nurses are in great demand in hospitals. Moreover, as hospitals continue to become centers for acute and critical care, the nurse's role in both patient care and management of other health-care providers in the hospital has become more complex, requiring advanced knowledge and skills.

Because of the complexity of today's health-care environment, AACN and other leading nursing organizations have called for the baccalaureate degree in nursing as the minimum educational requirement for professional nursing practice. In fact, nurse executives in hospitals have indicated their desire for the majority of nurses on staff to be prepared at least at the baccalaureate level to handle the increasingly complex demands of patient care and management of health-care delivery. The baccalaureate nursing degree is essential for nurses to function in different management roles, move across employment settings, have the flexibility to change positions within nursing, and advance in their career. Baccalaureate nursing degree programs prepare the nurse for a broad role within the health-care system and for practice in hospitals, community settings, home health care, neighborhood clinics, and other outpatient settings where opportunities are expanding. Continuing education provides the means for nurses to prepare themselves for a future role in nursing.

The demand for nurses with baccalaureate and more advanced degrees will continue to grow. There is an excess of nurses prepared at the associate degree level, a mounting shortage of baccalaureate-prepared nurses, and only half as many nurses prepared at master's and doctoral levels as needed. Nurses with baccalaureate nursing degrees are needed in all areas of health care, and the demand for nurses with master's and doctoral preparation for advanced practice, management, teaching, and research will continue.

Identifying Strategies

The decision to return to school marks the beginning of a new phase in your career development. It is essential for you to plan this future carefully. Why are you thinking about returning to school, and what do you want to accomplish by doing so? Understanding why you want to go back to school will help you select the best program for you. Knowing what you want to accomplish will help you to focus on your goals and overcome the obstacles that could prevent you from achieving your full potential.

Even if you decide that additional education will help you reach your professional goals, you may also have a list of reasons why you think you cannot return to school—no time, limited financial resources, fear of failure, and concerns about meeting family responsibilities, among others. If you are concerned about the demands of school combined with existing responsibilities, begin by identifying strategies for incorporating classes and study time into your present schedule or consider taking an online course. Remember, you can start your program with one course and reevaluate your time at the end of the term.

Research and anecdotal evidence from adults returning to college indicate that, despite their need to balance school work with a career and often with family responsibilities, these adult learners experience less stress and manage their lives better than they had thought possible. Many of these adult learners report that the satisfaction gained from their education more than compensates for any added stress. Furthermore, studies of nurses who have returned to school suggest that while their education may create stress for them, most nurses cope effectively with the demands of advanced education.

If costs are of concern, it is best to investigate tuition-reimbursement opportunities where you are employed, scholarships from the nursing program and other nursing organizations, and loans. The financial aid officer at the program you are considering is probably the best available resource to answer your financial assistance questions.

If you are unsure of what to expect when returning to school, remember that such feelings are natural for anyone facing a new situation. If you are motivated and committed to pursuing your degree, you will succeed. Most nursing programs offer resources, such as test-taking skills, study skills, and time-management workshops, as well as assistance with academic problems. You can combine school, work, family, and other responsibilities. Even with these greater demands, the benefits of education outweigh the difficulties.

Clarifying Career Goals

Nursing, unlike many other professions, has a variety of educational paths for those who return for advanced education. You should decide if baccalaureate- or graduate-level work is congruent with your career goals. The next step in this process is to reexamine your specific career goals, both immediate and long-term, to determine the level and type of nursing education you will need to meet them. Ask yourself what you want to be doing in the next five to ten years. Discuss your ideas with a counselor in a nursing education program, nurses who are practicing in roles you are considering, and others who are enrolled in a nursing program or who have recently completed a nursing degree.

Baccalaureate degree nursing programs prepare nurses as generalists for practice in all health-care settings. Graduate nursing education occurs at two levels— master's and doctoral. Master's programs vary in length, typically between one and two years. Preparation for roles in advanced practice as nurse practitioners, certified nurse midwives, clinical nurse specialists, certified registered nurse anesthetists, nursing administrators, and nursing educators requires a master's degree in nursing. Many programs meet the needs of RNs by offering options such as accelerated course work, advanced placement, evening and weekend classes, and distance learning courses.

A trend in education for RNs is accelerated programs that combine baccalaureate and master's nursing programs. These combined programs are designed for RNs without degrees whose career goals involve advanced nursing practice and other roles requiring a master's degree. Nurses who complete these combined programs may be awarded both a baccalaureate and a master's degree in nursing or a master's degree only.

At the doctoral level, nurses are prepared for a variety of roles, including research and teaching. Doctoral programs generally consist of three years of full-time study beyond the master's degree, although some programs admit baccalaureate graduates and include the master's-level requirements and degree within the doctoral program.

Matching a Program to Your Needs

Once you have defined your career goals and the level of nursing education they will require, the next step is matching your needs with the offerings and characteristics of specific nursing programs. Some of the criteria you may want to consider in evaluating potential schools of nursing include the types of programs offered, the length of the program and its specific requirements, the availability of full- and part-time study and number of credits required for part-time study, the flexibility of the program, whether distance education courses are available, and the days, times, and sites at which classes and clinical experiences are offered as they relate to your work schedule. Take into consideration the program's accreditation status; faculty qualifications in terms of research, teaching, and practice; and the resources of the school of nursing and of the college/university, such as library holdings, computer services, and statistical consultants. You should also consider the clinical settings used in the curriculum and their relationship to your career goals, as well as the availability of financial aid for nursing students.

Carefully review the admission criteria, including minimum grade point average requirements; scores required on any admission tests, such as the Graduate Record Examinations (GRE) for master's and doctoral programs; and any requirements in terms of work experience. For students returning for a baccalaureate degree, prior nursing knowledge may be validated through testing, transfer of courses, and other mechanisms. Review these options prior to applying to a program.

While the intrinsic quality and characteristics of the program are important, your own personal goals and needs have to be included in your decision. Consider commuting distance, whether courses are offered online, costs in relation to your financial resources, program design, and flexibility of the curriculum in relation to your work, family, and personal responsibilities. While the majority of nursing programs offer part-time study, many programs also schedule classes to accommodate work situations.

Many schools offer nursing courses online, and in some places, the entire baccalaureate and master's programs are available through distance learning. The largest enrollment in nursing distance learning is in baccalaureate programs for RNs. Distance learning allows RNs to further their education no matter where they live. Many nurses prefer online courses because they can learn at times convenient for them, especially considering competing demands associated with their jobs, families, and other commitments.

Ensure Your Success

Once you have made the decision to return to school and have chosen the program that best meets your needs, take an additional step to ensure your success. Identify the support you will need, both academic and personal, to be successful in the nursing program. Academic support is provided by the institution and may include tutoring services, learning resource centers, computer facilities, and other resources to support your learning. You should take advantage of available support services and seek out resources for areas in which you are weak or need review. Academic support services, however, need to be complemented by personal support through family, friends, and peers. With a firm commitment to pursuing advanced education, a clear choice of a nursing program to meet your goals, and support from others, you are certain to find success in returning to school.

BACCALAUREATE PROGRAMS

Linda K. Amos, Ed.D., RN, FAAN
*Former Associate Vice President for Health
   Sciences*
Dean Emerita
University of Utah

The health-care industry has continued to change dramatically over the past few years, transforming the roles of nurses and escalating their opportunities. The current shortage of nurses is caused by an increasing number of hospitalized patients who are older and more acutely ill, a growing elderly population with multiple chronic health problems, and expanded opportunities in HMOs, home care, occupational health, surgical centers, and other primary-care settings. Expanding technological advances that prolong life also require more highly skilled personnel.

The increasing scope of nursing opportunities will grow immensely as nurses become the frontline providers of health care. They are assuming important roles in the provision of managed care, and they will be responsible for coordinating and continuing the care outside traditional health-care facilities. Nurses will play a major role in educating the public and addressing the social and economic factors that impact quality of care.

Worldwide Standards

Nursing students of the future will receive a wealth of information. Understanding the technology used to manage that information will be essential to their ability to track and assess care. In this area, nurses will be able to provide care over great distances. In some areas, care is being managed by the nurse via tele-home health over the Internet. Use of the Internet and other computer-oriented systems is now an integral tool used by nurses. Nurses of the future, therefore, will have to become aware of worldwide standards of care. Nevertheless, the primary job of a nurse will be making sure that the right person is providing the right care at the right cost.

This goal will be accomplished as the industry turns away from the hospital as the center of operation. Nurses will work in a broad array of locations, including clinics, outpatient facilities, community centers, schools, and even places of business.

Much of the emphasis in health care will shift to preventive care and the promotion of health. In this system, nurses will take on a broader and more diverse role than they have in the past.

Unlimited Opportunities, Expanded Responsibilities

The four-year baccalaureate programs in today's nursing colleges provide the educational and experiential base not only for entry-level professional practice, but also as the platform on which to build a career through graduate-level study for advanced practice nursing, including careers as nurse practitioners, nurse-midwives, clinical specialists, and nurse administrators and educators. Nurses at this level can be expected to specialize in oncology, pediatrics, neonatology, obstetrics and gynecology, critical care, infection control, psychiatry, women's health, community health, and neuroscience. The potential and responsibilities at this level are great. Increasingly, many families use the nurse practitioner for all health-care needs. In almost all U.S. states, the nurse practitioner can prescribe medications and provide health care for the management of chronic non-acute illnesses and preventive care.

The health-care system demands a lot from nurses. The education of a nurse must transcend the traditional areas of study, such as chemistry and anatomy, to include health promotion, disease prevention, screening, genetic counseling, and immunization. Nurses should understand how health problems may have a social cause, such as poverty and environmental contamination, and they must develop insight into human psychology, behavior, and cultural mores and values.

The transformation of the health-care system offers unlimited opportunities for nurses at the baccalaureate and graduate levels as care in urban and rural settings becomes more accessible. According to the U.S. Bureau of Labor Statistics, employment of RNs will grow more quickly than the average employment for all occupations through 2012, due largely to growing demand in settings such as health maintenance organizations, community health centers, home care, and long-term care. The increased complexity of health problems and increased management of health problems outside of hospitals require highly educated and well-prepared nurses at the baccalaureate and graduate levels. It is an exciting era in nursing that holds exceptional promise for nurses with a baccalaureate nursing degree.

The compensation for new nurses is once again becoming competitive with that of other industries. Entry-level nurses with baccalaureate degrees in nursing can expect a salary range of about $31,000 to $46,000 per year, depending on geographic location and experience. Five years into their careers, the national average for nurses with four-year degrees is more than $50,000 per year, with many earning more than $65,000. The current shortage has prompted some employers to offer sign-on bonuses and other incentives to attract and retain staff.

Applying to College

Meeting your chosen school's general entrance requirements is the first step toward a university or college degree in nursing. Admission requirements may vary, but a high school diploma or equivalent is necessary. Most accredited colleges consider SAT scores along with high school grade point average. A strong preparatory class load in science and mathematics is generally preferred among nursing schools. Students may obtain specific admission information by writing to a school's nursing department.

To apply to a nursing school, contact the admission offices of the colleges or universities you are interested in and request the appropriate application forms. With limited spaces in nursing schools, programs are competitive, and early submission of an application is recommended.

Accreditation

Accreditation of the nursing program is very important, and it should be considered on two levels—the accreditation of the university or college and the accreditation of the nursing program itself. Accreditation is a voluntary process in which the school or the program asks for an external review of its programs, facilities, and faculty. For nursing programs, the review is performed by peers in nursing education to ensure program quality and integrity.

Baccalaureate nursing programs in the United States undergo two types of regular systematic reviews. First, the school must be approved by the state board of nursing. This approval is necessary to ensure that the graduates of the program may sit for the licensing examinations offered through the National Council of State Boards of Nursing, Inc. The second is accreditation administered by a nursing accreditation agency that is recognized by the U.S. Department of Education.

Although accreditation is a voluntary process, access to federal loans and scholarships requires it, and most graduate schools accept only students who have earned degrees from accredited schools. Further, accreditation ensures an ongoing process of quality improvement based on national standards. Canadian nursing school programs are accredited by the Canadian Association of University Schools of Nursing, and the Canadian programs listed in this book must hold this accreditation. There are two recognized accreditation agencies for baccalaureate nursing programs in the United States: the Commission on Collegiate Nursing Education (CCNE) and the National League for Nursing Accrediting Commission (NLNAC).

Focusing Your Education

Academic performance is not the sole basis of acceptance into the upper level of the nursing program. Admission officers also weigh such factors as student activities, employment, and references. Moreover, many require an interview and/or essay in which the nursing candidate offers a goal statement. This part of the admission process can be completed prior to a student's entrance into the college or university or prior to the student's entrance into the school of nursing itself, depending on the program.

In the interview or essay, students may list career preferences and reasons for their choices. This allows admission officers to assess the goals of students and gain insights into their values, integrity, and honesty. One would expect that a goal statement from a student who is just entering college would be more general than that of a student who has had two years of preprofessional nursing studies. The more experienced student would be likely to have a more focused idea of what is to be gained by an education in nursing; there would be more evidence of the student's values and the ways in which she or he relates them to the knowledge gained from preprofessional nursing classes.

Baccalaureate Curriculum

A standard basic or generic baccalaureate program in nursing is a four-year college or university education that incorporates a variety of liberal arts courses with professional education and training. It is designed for high school graduates with no previous nursing experience.

Currently, there are more than 700 baccalaureate programs in the United States. Of the 583 programs that responded to a 2008 survey conducted by the American Association of Colleges of Nursing, total enrollment in all nursing programs leading to a baccalaureate degree was 201,407. A report from the National Advisory Council on Nursing Education recommends that at least two-thirds of the nursing workforce holds a baccalaureate degree or higher by 2010, compared to the current 40 percent.

The baccalaureate curriculum is designed to prepare students for work in the growing and changing health-care environment. As nurses take a more active role in all facets of health care, they are expected to develop critical thinking and communication skills in addition to receiving standard nurse training in clinics and hospitals. In a university or college setting, the first two years include classes in the humanities, social sciences, basic sciences, business, psychology, technology, sociology, ethics, and nutrition.

In some programs, nursing classes begin in the sophomore year; others begin in the junior year. Many schools require satisfactory grade point averages before students advance into professional nursing classes. On a 4.0 scale, admission into the last two years of the nursing program may require a minimum GPA of 2.5 to 3.0 in preprofessional nursing classes. The national average is about 2.8, but the cutoff level varies with each program.

In the junior and senior years, the curriculum focuses on the nursing sciences, and emphasis moves from the classroom to health facilities. This is where students are exposed to clinical skills, nursing theory, and the varied roles nurses play in the health-care system. Courses include nurse leadership, health promotion, family planning, mental health, environmental and occupational health, adult and pediatric care, medical and surgical care, psychiatric care, community health, management, and home health care.

This level of education comes in a variety of settings: community hospitals, clinics, social service agencies, schools, and health-maintenance organizations. Training in diverse settings is the best preparation for becoming a vital player in the growing health-care field.

Reentry Programs

Practicing nurses who return to school to earn a baccalaureate degree will have to meet requirements that may include possession of a valid RN license and an associate degree or hospital diploma from an accredited institution. Again, it is best to check with the school's admissions department to determine specifics.

Nurses returning to school will have to consider the rapid rate of change in health care and science. A nurse who passed an undergraduate-level chemistry class ten years ago would probably not receive credit for that class today because of the growth of knowledge in that and all other scientific fields. The need to reeducate applies not only to practicing nurses returning to school, but also to all nurses throughout their careers.

In the same vein, nurses with diplomas from hospital programs who want to work toward a baccalaureate degree must meet the common requirements for more clinical practice, and must develop a deeper understanding of community-based nursing practices such as health prevention and promotion.

Colleges and universities available to the RN in search of a baccalaureate give credit for previous nurse training. These programs are designed to accommodate the needs and career goals of the practicing nurse by providing flexible course schedules and credit for previous experience and education. Some programs lead to a master's-level degree, a process that can take up to three years. Licensed practical nurses (LPNs) can also continue their education through baccalaureate programs.

Nurses considering reentering school may also consider other specialized programs. For example, some programs are aimed at enabling nurses with A.D.N. degrees or LPN/LVN licenses to earn B.S.N.'s. Also, accelerated B.S.N. programs are available for students with degrees in other fields.

RN-to-Baccalaureate Programs Fact Sheet

More than 620 RN-to-baccalaureate programs are available nationwide, including programs offered in a more intense, accelerated format. Program length varies from one to two years depending upon the school's requirements, program type, and the student's previous academic achievement.

Concerns about the limited availability of RN-to-baccalaureate programs are unfounded. In fact, there are more RN-to-baccalaureate programs available than there are four-year nursing programs or accelerated bachelor's degree programs for non-nursing college graduates. Access to RN-to-baccalaureate programs is further enhanced when programs are offered completely online or on-site at various health-care facilities.

Enrollment in RN-to-baccalaureate programs is increasing in response to calls for a more highly educated nursing workforce. From 2004 to 2005, enrollments increased by 8.3 percent, or by 2,772 students, marking the third year of increases in RN-to-baccalaureate programs.

Hundreds of articulation agreements between A.D.N. and diploma programs and four-year institutions exist nationwide (including some statewide agreements), to help students who are seeking baccalaureate-level nursing education. Before enrolling in diploma and A.D.N. programs, students are encouraged to check with school administrators to see what articulation agreements exist with baccalaureate degree–granting schools and to determine which course work will be transferable.

Choosing a Program

With more than 700 baccalaureate programs in the United States, the prospective student must do research to determine which programs match his or her needs and career objectives.

If you have no health-care experience, it might be best to gain some insight into the field by volunteering or working part-time in a care facility such as a hospital or an outpatient clinic. Talking to nurse professionals about their work will also help you determine how your attributes may apply to the nursing field.

When considering a nursing education, consider your personal needs. Is it best for you to work in a heavily structured environment or one that offers more flexibility in terms of, say, integrating a part-time work schedule into studies? Do you need to stay close to home? Do you prefer to work in a large health-care system such as a health maintenance organization or a medical center, or do you prefer smaller, community-based operations?

As for nursing programs, ask the following questions: How involved is the faculty in developing students for today's health-care industry? How strong is the school's affiliation with clinics and hospitals? Is there assurance that a student will gain an up-to-date educational experience for the current job market? Are a variety of care settings available? How much time in clinics is required for graduation? What are the program's resources in terms of computer and science laboratories? Does the school work with hospitals and community-based centers to provide health care? How available is the faculty to oversee a student's curriculum? What kind of student support is available in terms of study groups and audiovisual aids? Moreover, what kind of counseling from faculty members and administrators is available to help students develop well-rounded, effective progress through the program?

Visiting a school and talking to the program's guidance counselors will give you a better understanding of how a particular program or school will fit your needs. You can get a closer look at the faculty, its members' credentials, and the focus of the program. It's also not too early to consider what each program can offer in terms of job placement.

MASTER'S PROGRAMS

Kathleen Dracup, D.N.Sc., RN, FNP, FAAN
Professor and Dean
School of Nursing
University of California, San Francisco

The transformation of the health-care system is taking place as you read this, and it can be seen even today in the most common areas:

• A mother brings her child into a clinic for treatment of an earache. Instead of a physician, a nurse practitioner provides the care.

• A patient is readied for surgery. A variety of specialists move around the surgery room, but it's not a specially trained physician administering the anesthetic—it's a certified nurse anesthetist.

• During a patient's recovery from an acute illness, it's decided that the patient no longer needs to stay in the hospital but isn't well enough to return home. The best place to continue the recovery is an intermediate-care facility. Who makes that decision? A clinical nurse specialist. Who oversees the physical and emotional rehabilitation programs at this facility? Another clinical nurse specialist.

These health-care professionals are all advanced practice nurses (APNs). All have graduate-level degrees, and they serve as proof that the demand for nurses with master's and doctoral degrees for advanced practice, clinical specialties, teaching, and research will double the supply.

Another study estimated that the U.S. could save as much as $8.75 billion annually if APNs were used appropriately in place of physicians. As more and more of the restrictions on APNs succumb to legislative or economic forces, the demand for graduate-level nurses is expected to remain high.

Educational Core for APN

A master's degree in nursing is the educational core that allows advanced practice nurses to work as nurse practitioners, certified nurse-midwives, clinical nurse specialists, and certified nurse anesthetists.

Nurse practitioners conduct physical exams, diagnose and treat common acute illnesses and injuries, administer immunizations, manage chronic problems such as high blood pressure and diabetes, and order lab services and X-rays.

Nurse-midwives provide prenatal and gynecological care, deliver babies in hospitals and private settings such as homes, and follow up with postpartum care.

Clinical nurse specialists provide a range of care in specialty areas, such as oncology, pediatrics, and cardiac, neonatal, obstetric/gynecological, neurological, and psychiatric nursing.

Nurse anesthetists administer anesthesia for all types of surgery in operating rooms, dental offices, and outpatient surgical centers.

Master's degrees in nursing administration or nursing education are also available.

There are more than 340 master's degree programs accredited by the Commission on Collegiate Nursing Education (CCNE) or by the National League for Nursing Accrediting Commission (NLNAC). The wide spectrum of programs includes the Master of Science in Nursing (M.S.N.) degree, Master of Nursing (M.N.) degree, Master of Science (M.S.) degree with a nursing major, or Master of Arts (M.A.) degree with a nursing major. The specific degrees depend on the requirements set by the college or university or by the faculty of the nursing program. There are accelerated programs for RNs, which allow the nurse with a hospital diploma or associate degree to earn both a baccalaureate and a master's degree in a condensed program. Some schools offer accelerated master's degree programs for nurses with non-nursing degrees and for non-nursing college graduates. There are joint-degree programs, such as a master's in nursing combined with a Master of Business Administration, Master of Public Health, or Master of Hospital Administration.

Master's Curriculum

The master's degree builds on the baccalaureate degree to enable the student to develop expertise in one area. That specialty can range from running a hospital to providing care for prematurely born babies, from researching the effectiveness of alternative therapies to tackling social and economic causes of health problems. It is an opportunity for the student who has assessed his or her personal career goals and matched them to individual, community, and industry needs. What students can do with their APN degrees is limited only by their imagination.

Full-time master's programs consist of eighteen to twenty-four months of uninterrupted study. Many graduate school students, however, fit their master's-level studies around their work schedules, which can extend the time it takes to graduate.

Master's-level study incorporates theories and concepts of nursing science and their applications, along with the management of health care. Research provides a foundation for the improvement of health-care techniques. Students also have the opportunity to develop the knowledge, leadership skills, and interpersonal skills that will enable them to improve the health-care system.

Classroom and clinical work are involved throughout the master's program. In class, students spend less time listening to lectures and taking notes and more time participating in student- and faculty-led seminars and roundtable discussions. Extended clinical work is generally required.

Graduate-level education in many programs includes courses in statistics, research management, health economics, health policy, health-care ethics, health promotion, nutrition, family planning, mental health, and the prevention of family and social violence. When students begin to concentrate their study in their clinical areas, any number of courses that support their chosen specialty may be included. For example, a nurse wanting to specialize in pediatrics may take courses in child development.

A clinical nurse specialist can focus on acute care, geriatrics, adult health, community health, critical care, gerontology, rehabilitation, and cardiovascular, surgical, oncology, maternity/newborn, pediatric, mental/psychiatric, and women's health nursing. Areas of specialization in nurse practitioner programs include acute care, adult health, child care, community health, emergency care, geriatric care, neonatal health, occupational health, and primary care.

Admission Requirements

The admission requirements for master's programs in nursing vary greatly. Generally, a bachelor's degree from a school accredited by the Commission on Collegiate Nursing Education or by the National League for Nursing Accrediting Commission and a state RN license are required. Scores from the Graduate Record Examinations (GRE) or the Miller Analogies Test (MAT), college transcripts, letters of reference, and an essay are also typically required. Non-nurses and nurses with non-nursing degrees have special requirements. The profiles and in-depth descriptions of colleges and universities in this publication will give you an idea of each school's specific requirements.

It is important to remember that admissions officers look at a student's transcripts, clinical work, and letters of reference together. A low grade point average is not an automatic knockout—admissions officers are after a composite package. Also, some specialties require specific courses. Students in the nurse anesthetist program, for instance, must have taken an upper-level college course in biochemistry.

A Master's That's Best for You

Most nurses who think of entering a master's program are already practicing nurses. They have a good idea of what they want to specialize in before they apply for admission. It is crucial to know what you want to study before you enter a master's program.

The best way to ensure success in a master's program is to understand your individual strengths and career desires and then find the faculty and college setting that are best suited to help you develop those strengths. Students must make an effort to educate themselves as to the strength of the faculty in each college's master's program. That's the best thing to look for: a strong faculty in one specialty.

This can be tricky. One university's master's program may be rated reasonably high in all fields. Another program might not be rated as high overall, but its cardiovascular program, for example, may be one of the best because of its access to facilities or the fact that its faculty is in the process of developing an innovative new treatment.

This type of information is not hard for the master's candidate to discover; it just takes time. Such information is available from each school's admissions office, which should be more than happy to promote its nursing faculty and support its opinion with proof, such as the research papers that faculty members have published in journals or the number of degrees each faculty member holds.

This type of research is the best way to find a program that meets your needs. The profiles of master's nursing programs in this book should help. If you can, narrow the list to three or four graduate schools, and then write each school's admissions department for catalogs and other information. Visit the schools and take time to talk to a guidance counselor from the nursing program in each one.

Other key questions to consider when applying for a master's program are: Does the school offer financial aid, such as loans, scholarships, fellowships, or teaching posts? How much clinical work is needed? Does the clinical work meet your needs, and does the type of clinical work involved match what you understand the health-care system will be using when you graduate? Is the course work flexible? Can you work part-time and still progress toward a master's degree? This is important to know. A majority of master's program students continue to work while they pursue the degree. Therefore, master's degree programs may present a flexible offering of short courses to meet the student's schedule demands.

Some programs require a thesis, whereas others provide another type of culminating experience, such as a comprehensive examination.

The Master's Trends

Today's master's programs have increased the amount of clinical practice required by students so that graduates enter the job market ready for certification. There is also a greater emphasis on applying new research findings to methods of patient care. This might involve students' reading literature about new treatments and then incorporating the appropriate changes.

All master's program candidates should consider courses in cost-benefit analysis. As managed-care systems become more predominant in the industry, health-care workers will be asked to justify the expense of each treatment, as well as its effectiveness. This leads to the crucial issue of quality. There will always be a strong effort to minimize costs in every health-care procedure, but that cannot compromise the quality of care. It's safe to say that discharging a newborn too soon from a hospital due to shortsightedness can be quite costly.

Depending on the specialty, master's candidates entering the job market may be expected to oversee auxiliary-care providers, such as nurse aides or other unlicensed employees. They may work in a team structure, and in this capacity, the nurse specialist may be expected to manage, motivate, and steer the group. This requires team-building and other management techniques.

While everyone in the health-care facility will have a part in ensuring patient satisfaction, nurses—particularly advanced practice nurses—will shoulder a great deal of this load. Developing interpersonal and communication skills and having an understanding of human behavior will make it easier for the advanced practice nurse to help patients to understand modern health-care procedures, which will no doubt improve their feelings of satisfaction.

Finally, nurses at all levels should be aware of the need for flexibility. Many health-care organizations are reducing the number of beds in hospitals and transferring the care of a growing number of patients to other types of facilities or settings. In light of this trend, it's best for the master's program student to gain experience in a variety of settings, including homes, clinics, and community-based facilities.

The demand for high-quality care will continue to grow. Medical innovations and technological advances will continue. The quality and effectiveness of health care will continue to improve, and nurses with graduate degrees will play an active role in this trend.

The Hot Employment Spots

The health-care industry has undergone such radical transformation in the last five years that administrators feel they cannot predict whether any one geographic region will have more hirings than another. Generally, nurses with master's degrees will be in demand in all regions of the country, in both the United States and Canada.

Industry trends indicate that, along with continuing opportunities in hospitals, more and more nurses will also work outside the hospital in outpatient clinics and community settings—and even in businesses. As patients spend less time in hospitals, the need grows for nurse specialists to oversee home-care settings and ensure that the quality of care is high. In this vein, some nurses are taking the initiative and running their own businesses as

RN-to-Master's Degree Programs Fact Sheet

Currently, there are 160 programs available nationwide to transition RNs with diplomas and associate degrees to the master's degree level. These programs prepare nurses to assume positions requiring graduate preparation, including the advanced practice roles of nurse practitioner, clinical nurse specialist, certified nurse-midwife, and certified registered nurse anesthetist. Master's degree-prepared nurses are in high demand as expert clinicians, nurse executives, clinical educators, health policy consultants, and research assistants.

RN-to-master's degree programs generally take about three years to complete; specific requirements vary by institution and the student's previous course work. Although the majority of these programs are offered in traditional classroom settings, some RN-to-master's programs are offered largely online or in a blended classroom/online format.

The baccalaureate-level content missing from diploma and A.D.N. programs is built into the front end of the RN-to-master's degree program. Mastery of this upper-level basic nursing content is necessary for students to move on to graduate study. Upon completion, programs award both a baccalaureate and a master's degree.

The number of RN-to-master's degree programs in the United States has doubled within the past ten years, from seventy programs in 2000 to more than 160 programs today.

health-care providers, offering services as they see fit in whatever locations are appropriate.

Immediate Rewards

Advanced practice nurses right out of school can expect annual salaries ranging from $60,000 to $90,000, depending on geographic location and previous experience. However, some rural county health clinics start their nurse practitioners at salaries as low as $40,000 per year.

Certified nurse anesthetists and certified nurse-midwives, however, draw higher salaries. Nurse-midwives, for example, can draw first-year salaries as high as $90,000 per year. Areas such as the Northeast and the West Coast tend to have nurses in these fields at the higher end of the salary scale. After five years of practice, the salary range for APNs stretches from $60,000 to $100,000 a year. Again, it depends on location. After five years, nurse-midwives earn salaries ranging from $65,000 to $120,000 annually.

THE CLINICAL NURSE LEADER

The Clinical Nurse Leader or CNL® is a rapidly emerging nursing role developed by the American Association of Colleges of Nursing (AACN) in collaboration with leaders from the nursing education and practice arenas. The national movement to advance the CNL is fueled by the critical need to improve the quality of patient care and better prepare nurses to thrive across the health-care system. The CNL role was developed following research and discussion with stakeholder groups as a way to engage highly skilled clinicians as leaders in outcome-based practices.

CNL provide lateral integration at the point of care and combine evidence-based practice with the following:

- Microsystems-level advocacy
- Centralized care coordination
- Outcomes measurement
- Risk assessment
- Quality improvement
- Interprofessional communication

In practice, the CNL oversees the care coordination of a distinct group of patients and actively provides direct patient care in complex situations. CNLs have master's degrees and are advanced generalists, evaluating patient outcomes, assessing risks, and using their authority to change care plans when necessary. CNLs are leaders in the health-care delivery system; the implementation of their roles will vary across settings.

Connecting Nursing Practice and Education

To support the creation of this new nursing role, AACN launched a national initiative involving more than 100 education-practice partnerships across the nation. Partners from schools of nursing and nursing practice sites are working together to transform care delivery by educating new CNLs and integrating them into the health delivery system.

More than seventy schools of nursing are now preparing CNLs for advanced generalist programs offered at the graduate level. Students may choose from traditional post-baccalaureate master's programs, degree completion programs for registered nurses (RNs), and accelerated programs for those seeking to make the transition into nursing. Most CNL programs are directly connected with practice sites interested in employing graduates to enhance care delivery, patient safety, and quality outcomes.

The Veterans Health Administration, the nation's largest employer of RNs, has embraced the CNL role and is planning to introduce it into all Veterans Affairs hospitals nationwide. Support for the clinical role is gaining momentum as many practice sites are reporting on the pioneering outcomes of the CNL staff.

The Key to Positive Patient Outcomes

CNLs provide efficient and cost-effective patient care services, as well as the leadership needed to repair fragmented health-care delivery systems. CNLs are having a measurable impact on the quality of nursing services with practice sites reporting that CNLs

- are quickly making significant progress on raising patient, nurse, and physician satisfaction; improving care outcomes; and realizing sizable cost-savings.
- are elevating the level of practice for all nurses on the unit by promoting critical thinking and innovation in nursing care.
- are constructively managing change and promoting a team-based approach to care.
- are understanding the bigger picture, including outcomes and patient satisfaction, when considering next steps, needed changes, and improvements to the practice setting.

The CNL Mark of Excellence

The CNL Mark of Excellence certification is a unique credential that recognizes graduates of master's and post-master's CNL programs who have demonstrated accepted standards of practice. The CNL Mark of Excellence promotes safe, quality practice through its ongoing requirements for personal and professional growth. In 2007, AACN established a new certification commission—the Commission on Nurse Certification (CNC)—to oversee all aspects of the CNL certification program.

Becoming a CNL

Those interested in becoming a CNL are encouraged to visit the AACN Web site, www.aacn.nche.edu/CNL, to find out more about this nursing career option. Detailed information is available online, including frequently asked questions, the white paper on the CNL role, and a directory of Web links for related programs.

ACCELERATED PROGRAMS

With the Bureau of Labor Statistics projecting the need for more than one million new and replacement registered nurses by the year 2016, nursing schools across North America are exploring creative ways to increase student capacity and reach out to new student populations. The challenge inherent in these efforts is to quickly produce competent nurses while maintaining the integrity and quality of the nursing education provided.

One innovative approach to nursing education that is gaining momentum nationwide is the accelerated degree program for non-nursing graduates. Offered at the baccalaureate and master's degree levels, these programs build on previous learning experiences and transition individuals with undergraduate degrees in other disciplines into nursing.

Shifts in the economy and the desire of many adults to make a post–September 11 difference in their work have increased interest in the nursing profession among "second-degree" students. For those with a prior degree, accelerated baccalaureate programs offer the quickest route to becoming a registered nurse, with programs generally running 12-18 months. Generic master's degrees, also accelerated and geared to non-nursing graduates, generally take three years to finish. Students in these programs usually complete baccalaureate-level nursing courses in the first year, followed by two years of graduate study.

Though not new to nursing education, accelerated programs have proliferated over the past twenty years. In 1990, thirty-one accelerated baccalaureate (B.S.N.) programs and twelve generic master's (M.S.N.) programs were offered around the country.

Today, 205 accelerated baccalaureate nursing programs are operating, and the number of generic master's programs has increased to fifty-six. According to AACN's database on enrollment and graduations, which is based on responses from 645 of 751 institutions (86 percent), thirty-seven new accelerated B.S.N. programs are now in the planning stages. This number far outpaces all other types of entry-level nursing programs currently being considered at four-year nursing schools. Thirteen new generic master's programs are also taking shape.

Graduates of accelerated programs are prized by nurse employers, who value the many layers of skill and education these graduates bring to the workplace. Employers report that these graduates are more mature, possess strong clinical skills, and are quick studies on the job. Many practice settings are partnering with schools and offering tuition repayment to graduates as a mechanism to recruit highly qualified nurses.

Changing Gears: Second-Degree Students

The typical second-degree nursing student is motivated, older, and has higher academic expectations than high school–entry baccalaureate students. Accelerated students excel in class and are eager to gain clinical experiences. Faculty members see them as excellent learners who are not afraid to challenge their instructors.

"Our accelerated students are a remarkable group," said Nancy DeBasio, Ph.D., RN, Dean of the Research College of Nursing in Kansas City. "Their mean GPA is 3.3, they come from a wide array of backgrounds, and the experiences they bring with them enrich their nursing." The compressed program format is a key motivator for this group of students. "Our exit surveys indicate that the one-year program completion time is a primary reason for enrollment in our program," Dr. DeBasio explained.

Second-degree students bring new dimensions to nursing and a rich history of prior learning. "We are seeing a steady increase in applicants to our accelerated program this year, and those accepted come with backgrounds that are varied and impressive," said Janet B. Younger, Ph.D., RN, CPNP, Professor and Associate Dean of the School of Nursing at Virginia Commonwealth University. "We welcomed several Ph.D.'s, some M.D.'s from other countries, and a few fine arts majors. These students excel in class and perform very well post-graduation."

Students in accelerated programs are competitive, maintain high grade point averages, and almost always pass the NCLEX-RN licensure exam on the first attempt. "Second-degree candidates are excellent students and are very likely to see the program through to graduation," said Afaf Meleis, Ph.D., RN, FAAN, Dean of the University of Pennsylvania School of Nursing. "These students are committed to their studies, actively engaged in research, and very often involved in university organizations."

Susan M. Di Biase, M.S.N., CRNP, a faculty member at Jacksonville State University in Alabama, knows a thing or two about second-degree students. She was one. "As a nurse educator, I have taught dozens of second-degree students who often distinguish themselves as class leaders," explained Di Biase. "When I was taking classes, I thought the students were strong academically, and many said nursing was harder than their first degree. My first employer made a custom of hiring second-degree students because she thought they were good thinkers and strong patient advocates."

Accelerated Baccalaureate Programs

Accelerated baccalaureate programs accomplish programmatic objectives in a shorter time frame than traditional four-year programs, usually through a combination of bridge courses and core content. Instruction is intense, with courses offered full-time with no breaks between sessions. Students receive the same number of clinical hours as their counterparts in traditional programs. Admission standards are high, with programs typically requiring a minimum of a 3.0 GPA and a thorough prescreening process. Typically, students with a prior degree are not required to take the liberal arts content included in a four-year B.S.N. program. Accelerated programs do have prerequisites, many of which may have been completed during the student's initial degree program. "Before students can begin our program, their college transcripts are reviewed to assure that all prerequisites are met," stated Maureen C. Creegan, Ed.D., RN, Nursing Program Director at Dominican College (NY). "Almost all students meet the arts and social sciences requirements; most do not meet the natural sciences requirements, including anatomy and microbiology. To assist students, we offer back-to-back prerequisite courses just prior to the start of the accelerated program."

Accelerated programs require a heavy credit load and intense clinical experiences. Identifying students who will flourish in this environment is a priority for administrators. "Due to the intensity of the program, an interview was added to the admission process to better screen students," explained Maryann O. Forbes, Ph.D., RN, Associate Professor at Adelphi University. "Faculty members feel that the interview and ongoing mentoring are key components to student success. The most successful accelerated students are bright, inquisitive, and sophisticated consumers of higher education who actively pursue learning opportunities," said Harriet Feldman, Ph.D., RN, FAAN, Dean and Professor at the Lienhard School of Nursing at Pace University (NY), whose Combined Degree Program (B.S.N./M.S.) has been in existence since 1984. "As adults, these students tend to know what they need and aggressively pursue programs that best meet their needs: fast-tracked, competitive, and well respected. While some students do attend part-time, most are full-time students who want to reach their career objective as quickly and efficiently as possible."

"Our accelerated B.S.N. program attracts second-career seekers who are unable to make the time and financial commitment to a generic master's program," explained Elizabeth F. McGann, D.N.Sc., RN, BC, Professor and Former Chair of the Department of Nursing at Quinnipiac University (CT). "Our program gives students the option of entering basic nursing practice now with graduate education as a potential future step."

Generic Master's Degree Programs

Having already completed a degree at the baccalaureate or graduate level, many second-degree students are attracted to the generic master's program as the natural next step in their higher education. "Why would a bachelor's-prepared applicant, thinking about a career in health care, want to get a second bachelor's in nursing when they can get a professional master's or doctorate in every other health-care field?," asked Melanie Dreher, Ph.D., RN, FAAN, Dean of the Rush University College of Nursing. Recently approved by the state board, Iowa's professional Master's Degree in Nursing and Healthcare Practice may be completed in four semesters, including a semester-long clinical internship that occurs five days a week for three months.

"In 1974, Yale University was the first school to open its door to college graduates who were not yet nurses and instituted the Graduate Entry Prespecialty in Nursing (GEPN)," explained Sharon Sanderson, Director of Student Recruitment for Yale's School of Nursing. "We recognized that bright, committed people without a background in nursing could be prepared as advanced practice nurses." At Marquette University in Wisconsin, students admitted into the direct-entry M.S.N. program are high achievers. "Our students are self-motivated, have definite goals, demonstrate good study habits, and succeed," explained Judith Fitzgerald Miller, Ph.D., RN, FAAN, former Interim Dean of the College of Nursing.

"Our generic M.S.N. students bring a wonderful expertise to the class," said Arlene Lowenstein Ph.D., RN, Professor Emerita, and former Director of the Graduate Program in Nursing at MGH Institute of Health Professions in Boston. "We run the gamut from a 53-year-old male lawyer, students holding Ph.D.'s and master's degrees in other fields, and students fresh out of a liberal arts program. One of my past students was a horticulture major who wrote a paper on therapeutic gardens for health-care settings. As they learn from us, we also learn from them, and they learn from each other. Second-degree students are a challenging, exciting group with the potential to make significant contributions to nursing as well as to their patients, families, and communities."

Interest in generic M.S.N. programs is running high. In Chicago, the DePaul University program grew from 20 students two years ago to 48 students last fall with a minimal amount of advertising. "With little more than a one-sentence notice about the program on the school's Web site when the program was announced, we received more than 100 inquiries and more than forty applications in short order," said Kathryn Anderson, Ph.D., RN, Graduate Program Director at the Seattle University School of Nursing. "Based on this initial response, it's obvious that the most effective marketing tool is the program itself."

Many universities offer both accelerated baccalaureate and generic master's programs with opportunities for students to apply credits to both degree programs. New York University, for example, offers a dual-degree program that enables B.S.N. students to take a maximum of 9 credits at the graduate level while completing the bachelor's degree, thus accelerating the completion of an M.S.N.

Education-Practice Setting Partnerships

Nurse employers recognize the value and skills that second-degree students bring to the work setting, as evidenced by the growing number of partnerships forming to support these graduates. "Our cooperative relationship with Poudre Valley Hospital brings the educational and practice settings closer together with clinical nurses at the hospital serving in faculty roles," explained Sandra Baird, Ed.D., B.S.N., Director of the School of Nursing at the University of North Colorado. The school is working to branch out and establish cooperative relationships with a wider network of health-care settings. "Second-degree students are a very attractive catch for any health-care institution and many are willing to fund them in exchange for work commitments after graduation," said Donna Ayers Snelson, M.S.N., RN, Chair of the Nursing Department at College Misericordia (PA). Although Creighton University (NE) is a private institution with a significantly higher tuition than that of public institutions, the reputation of its program led two Omaha health systems and four rural hospitals to offer full-tuition scholarships to accelerated nursing students in exchange for employment commitments. "More than half of the students in the accelerated baccalaureate program accepted tuition scholarships from area hospitals in return for a commitment to work in basic practice prior to going on for a master's degree," added Linda Cronenwett, Ph.D., RN, FAAN, Dean of the School of Nursing at University of North Carolina–Chapel Hill. Research College of Nursing uses grant-funded initiatives and clinical connections to build student capacity. "Recently we received a $100,000 grant from the Helene Fuld Health Trust to support financial aid for our accelerated students," said Dean Nancy DeBasio. "Fuld had never supported this type of student before, but we were able to demonstrate that these students were economically disadvantaged, not always eligible for traditional undergraduate funding, and unable to work due to the program's intensity." The school also partners with a local health-care system to secure educational debt repayment for accelerated students in exchange for work commitments. It is projected that this arrangement will save the health system more than $3 million in nurse recruitment costs over three years.

Nursing Education in the Fast Lane

Although accelerated programs have proven to produce highly qualified nurses, the programs do present some

unique challenges to nursing education. "Teaching accelerated students can be challenging because of their experience, age, and high level of inquiry," said Mary E. Pike, M.S.N., RN, faculty member at Bellarmine University (KY). "Some students struggle with the transition from being a competent, worldly adult to returning to life as an undergraduate student." One key to facilitating this transition and encouraging student success is using experienced faculty members who are comfortable teaching adults. In instances where employers are not repaying educational debt, the cost of an accelerated program can be prohibitive. "I receive many inquiries about our accelerated program, but the lack of financial aid is the major deterrent," said Arlene G. Wiens, Ph.D., RN, Nursing Department Chair at Eastern Mennonite University (VA). Some find the pace of accelerated programs too intense, and they opt for more regularly paced programs offered for second-degree nursing students. "The accelerated format is taxing, and some find it too difficult to assimilate into their daily routines," said Louann Zinsmeister, D.N.Sc., M.S.N., RN, instructor at Messiah College (PA). "These students often transfer into a more traditionally paced two-year B.S.N. program that permits them to continue working and attend to family responsibilities while completing a nursing degree." For students who cannot accommodate full-time study, schools are looking for creative alternatives. "We are opening a part-time evening program so second-degree students and adult learners can obtain a degree while working full-time," added Donna Ayers Snelson of College Misericordia. "Students attend classes two nights a week and are still able to obtain a nursing degree in two years and one semester."

Post-Graduation Success

In addition to nursing skills, second-degree students bring additional layers of education and significant work experience to their role as nurses, which enhances their clinical practice. "Initially when we began our program in 1991, our clinical partners were quite doubtful about what we could produce in one year," explained Dr. DeBasio of the Research College of Nursing. "Now they are at our doorstep each year to snap up students as they graduate." The college has tracked students through their careers and found that accelerated students move into management positions more quickly and generally excel in their roles." Employers of advanced practice nurses (APN) are equally pleased with graduates from both our traditional and generic M.S.N. programs," stated Linda D. Norman, D.S.N., RN, Senior Associate Dean for Academics at Vanderbilt University School of Nursing. Employers rated Vanderbilt's M.S.N. graduates who did not have a nursing background equally high in terms of level of preparation for APN positions as those who entered with a B.S.N. degree. "We know that employers love hiring accelerated graduates because they are bright, have a track record of success, and possess an understanding of the work world not always found in younger students," said Patricia Ladewig, Ph.D., RN, Dean of the School of Health Care Professions at Regis University in Denver. "We have found that second-degree students are readily accepted by employers who understand that these graduates lacked only vacation during their academic program," confirmed Sandra S. Angell, M.L.A., RN, Associate Dean for Academic and Student Support Services at The Johns Hopkins University School of Nursing.

Growing Demand for Accelerated Programs

With a greater number of second-degree students turning to nursing, the demand for accelerated programs is growing. At the University of Pennsylvania, application trends showed a 34 percent increase from 1995 to 2001. "Within two weeks of the program's approval by the state board and without any public announcement, we received more than fifty requests for applications almost immediately," explained Marianne W. Rogers, Ed.D., RN, Chairperson for Nursing at the University of Southern Maine. "Our program is growing very quickly, and we have seen almost a 100 percent increase in applications compared to last year," said Linda A. Bernhard, Ph.D., RN, Associate Dean for Undergraduate Studies at The Ohio State University. The 16-month Second Career/ Second Degree program in nursing at Wayne State University in Michigan experienced a 25 percent increase in enrollment from fall 2000 to fall 2001, making it one of the school's most popular degree offerings. Enrollment in the University of Virginia's second-degree program has doubled since it was introduced in 1988. "At this time, we are seeing an enormous increase in the numbers of applicants with bachelor's degrees applying for our new

12-month accelerated pathway to the B.S.N.," reports Christena Langley, Ph.D., RN, Assistant Dean for Undergraduate Programs at the College of Nursing and Health Science at George Mason University (VA). "Many of them are recent college graduates who are looking for the quickest route to the B.S.N. They are confident that they can adapt to the accelerated pace given their past success in college."

Supporting Accelerated Nursing Programs

Second-degree students bring a wealth of knowledge, experience, and energy to the nursing workforce and are highly skilled clinicians. With calls for nursing schools to produce more graduates in response to the nursing shortage, a similar call should go out to employers and legislators to increase support for accelerated nursing programs. Hospitals, health-care systems, and other practice settings are encouraged to form partnerships with schools offering accelerated programs to remove the student's financial burden in exchange for a steady stream of new nurse recruits. Legislators on the state and federal levels are encouraged to increase scholarship and grant funding for these programs that produce entry-level nurses faster than any other basic nursing education program. These programs are ideal career transition vehicles for those segments of the labor force impacted by recent fluctuations in the economy." The overwhelming response to our accelerated programs demonstrates the existence of a deep pool of career changers available to nursing," said Gloria F. Donnelly, Ph.D., RN, FAAN, Dean of the College of Nursing and Health Professions at Drexel University (PA). "We need to do more to remove barriers and attract more second-degree students to the nursing profession."

"Accelerated Programs: The Fast-Track to Careers in Nursing," updated April 2008. Reprinted with permission of the American Association of Colleges of Nursing.

THE DOCTOR OF NURSING PRACTICE

In October 2004, the American Association of Colleges of Nursing (AACN) endorsed the Position Statement on the Practice Doctorate in Nursing, which called for moving the level of preparation necessary for advanced nursing practice roles from the master's degree to the doctorate level by the year 2015. The AACN position statement calls for educating advanced practice nurses (APNs) and other nurses seeking top clinical positions in Doctor of Nursing Practice (DNP) programs. The following points explain this evolutionary step forward for nursing education.

The Need for Change in Graduate Nursing Education

- The changing demands of the nation's complex health-care environment require that nurses serving in specialty positions have the highest level of scientific knowledge and practice expertise possible. Research from Drs. Linda Aiken, Carole Estabrooks, and others have established a clear link between higher levels of nursing education and better patient outcomes.
- Some of the many factors that are emerging to build momentum for change in nursing education at the graduate level include the rapid expansion of knowledge underlying practice, increased complexity of patient care, national concerns about the quality of care and patient safety, shortages of nursing personnel that demand a higher level of preparation for leaders who can design and assess care, shortages of doctorally prepared nursing faculty, and increasing educational expectations for the preparation of other health professionals.
- The Institute of Medicine, Joint Commission on the Accreditation of Healthcare Organizations, and other authorities have called for reconceptualizing health professions education to meet the needs of the health-care delivery system. Nursing is answering that call by moving to prepare APNs for an evolving practice.
- In a 2005 report titled "Advancing the Nation's Health Needs: NIH Research Training Programs," the National Academy of Sciences called for nursing to develop a non-research clinical doctorate to prepare expert practitioners who can also serve as clinical faculty. AACN's work to advance the DNP is consistent with this call to action.

- Nursing is moving in the direction of other health professions in the transition to the DNP. Medicine (MD), Dentistry (DDS), Pharmacy (PharmD), Psychology (PsyD), Physical Therapy (DPT), and Audiology (AudD) all offer practice doctorates.

Impact on Nursing Education and Practice

- Currently, advanced practice nurses, including nurse practitioners, clinical nurse specialists, nurse midwives, and nurse-anesthetists, are typically prepared in master's degree programs, some of which carry a credit load equivalent to doctoral degrees in the other health professions.
- DNP curricula build on current master's programs by providing education in evidence-based practice, quality improvement, and systems thinking, among other key areas.
- Transitioning to the DNP will not alter the current scope of practice for APNs. State Nurse Practice Acts describes the scope of practice allowed, and it differs from state to state. (These requirements would likely remain unchanged.) The transition to the DNP will better prepare APNs for their current roles, given the calls for new models of education and the growing complexity of health care.
- The DNP is designed for nurses seeking a terminal degree in nursing practice and offers an alternative to research-focused doctoral programs. DNP-prepared nurses will be well-equipped to fully implement the science developed by nurse researchers prepared in PhD, DNSc, and other research-focused nursing doctorates.
- The title of doctor is common to many disciplines and is not the domain of any one health profession. Many APNs currently hold doctoral degrees and are addressed as doctors, which is similar to the way in which clinical psychologists, dentists, podiatrists, and other experts are addressed. Like other providers, DNPs would be expected to display their credentials to insure that patients understand their preparation as a nursing provider.
- Nursing and medicine are distinct health disciplines that prepare clinicians to assume different roles and meet different practice expectations. DNP programs will prepare nurses for the highest level of nursing practice.

THE NURSE PH.D.: A VITAL PROFESSION NEEDS LEADERS

Carole A. Anderson, Ph.D., RN, FAAN
Vice Provost for Academic Administration and Interim Dean of the Graduate School
The Ohio State University

There is no doubt that education is the path for a nurse to achieve greater clinical expertise. At the same time, however, the nursing profession needs more nurses educated at the doctoral level to replenish the supply of faculty and researchers. The national shortage of faculty will soon reach critical proportions, making a significant impact on educational programs and their capacity to educate future generations of nursing students.

Although the number of doctorate programs has continued to increase, the total enrollment of students in these programs has remained fairly constant, resulting in a shortage of newly trained Ph.D.'s to renew faculty ranks. As a result, approximately 50 percent of nursing faculty possess the doctorate as a terminal degree. Furthermore, with many advances being made in the treatment of chronic illnesses, there is a continuing need for research that assists patients in living with their illness. This research requires individual investigators who are prepared on the doctoral level.

One reason there is a lack of nurses prepared at the doctoral level is that, compared to other professions, nurses have more interruptions in their careers. Many in the profession are women who work as nurses while fulfilling responsibilities as wives and mothers. As a result, many pursue their education on a part-time basis. Also, the nursing profession traditionally has viewed clinical experience as being a prerequisite to graduate education. This career path results in fewer individuals completing the doctorate at an earlier stage in their career, thereby truncating their productivity as academics, researchers, and administrators. To reverse this trend, many nursing schools have developed programs that admit students into graduate (doctoral and master's) programs directly from their undergraduate or master's programs.

Nursing Research

When nurses do research for their doctorates, many people tend to think that it focuses primarily on nurses and nursing care. In reality, nurses carry out clinical research in a variety of areas, such as diabetes care, cancer care, and eating disorders.

In the last twenty years advances in medicine have involved, for the most part, advancing treatment, not cures. In other words, no cure for the illness has been discovered, but treatment for that illness has improved. However, sometimes the treatment itself causes problems for patients, such as the unwelcome side effects of chemotherapy. Nurses have opportunities to devise solutions to problems like these through research, such as studies on how to manage the illness and its treatment, thereby allowing individuals to lead happy and productive lives.

The Curricula

Doctoral programs in nursing are aimed at preparing students for careers in health administration, education, clinical research, and advanced clinical practice. Basically, doctoral programs prepare nurses to be experts within the profession, prepared to assume leadership roles in a variety of academic and clinical settings, course work, and research. Students are trained as researchers and scholars to tackle complex health-care questions. Program emphasis may vary from a focus on health education to a concentration on policy research. The majority of doctoral programs confer the Doctor of Philosophy (Ph.D.) degree, but some award the Doctor of Nursing Science (D.N.S. or D.N.Sc.), the Doctor of Science in Nursing (D.S.N.), the Nursing Doctorate (N.D.), and the Doctor of Education (Ed.D.).

Doctoral nursing programs traditionally offer courses on the history and philosophy of nursing and the development and testing of nursing and other health-care techniques, as well as the social, economic, political, and ethical issues important to the field. Data management and research methodology are also areas of instruction. Students are expected to work individually on research projects and complete a dissertation.

Doctoral programs allow study on a full- or part-time basis. For graduate students who are employed and therefore seek flexibility in their schedules, many programs offer courses on weekends and in the evenings.

Admission Requirements

Admission requirements for doctoral programs vary. Generally, a master's degree is necessary, but in some schools a master's degree is completed in conjunction with fulfillment of the doctoral degree requirements. Standard requirements include an RN license, Graduate Record Examinations (GRE) scores, college transcripts, letters of recommendation, and an essay. Students applying for doctoral-level study should have a solid foundation in nursing and an interest in research. Programs are usually the equivalent of three to five years of full-time study.

Selecting a Doctoral Program

Selecting a doctoral program comes down to personal choice. Students work closely with professors, and thus the support and mentoring you receive while pursuing your degree is as vital as the quality of the facilities. The most important question is whether there is a "match" between your research interest and faculty research. Many of the same questions you would ask about baccalaureate and master's degree programs apply to doctoral programs. However, in a doctoral program, the contact with professors, the use of research equipment and facilities, and the program's flexibility in allowing you to choose your course of study are critical.

Other questions to consider include: Does the university consider research a priority? Does the university have adequate funding for student research? Many nurses with doctoral degrees make the natural transition into an academic career, but there are many other career options available for nurses prepared at this level. For example, nurses prepared at the doctoral level are often hired by large consulting firms to work with others in designing solutions to health-care delivery problems.

Others are hired by large hospital chains to manage various divisions, and some nurses with doctoral degrees are hired to manage complex health-care systems at the executive level. On another front, they conduct research and formulate national and international health-care policy. In short, because of the high level of education and a shortage of nurses prepared at this level, there are a number of options.

Needless to say, a doctoral education does provide individuals with a wide range of opportunities, with salaries commensurate with the type and level of responsibilities. Are there opportunities to present research findings at professional meetings? Is scholarship of faculty, alumni, and students presented at regional and national nursing meetings and subsequently published? Has the body of research done at a university enhanced the knowledge of nursing and health care?

Salaries are related to the various positions. Faculty salaries vary by the type of institution and by faculty rank, typically ranging from approximately $50,000 at the assistant professor level to above $100,000 at the professor level. Salaries of nurse executives also vary, with the lowest salaries being in small rural hospitals and the highest being in complex university medical centers. In the latter, average salaries are well above $100,000 and often reach close to $200,000 annually. Consultant salaries are wide-ranging but often consist of a base plus some percentage of work contracted. Clinical and research positions vary considerably by the type of institution and the nature of the work.

AACN INDICATORS OF QUALITY IN RESEARCH-FOCUSED DOCTORAL PROGRAMS IN NURSING

Schools of nursing must consider the indicators of quality in evaluating their ability to mount research-focused doctoral programs. High-quality programs require a large number of increasingly scarce resources and a critical mass of faculty members and students. The "AACN Indicators of Quality in Research-Focused Doctoral Programs in Nursing" represent those indicators that should be present in a research-focused program.

There is considerable consensus within the discipline that while there are differences in the purpose and curricula of Ph.D. and Doctor of Nursing/Doctor of Nursing Science programs; most programs emphasize preparation for research. Therefore, AACN recommends continuing with a single set of quality indicators for research-focused doctoral programs in nursing, whether the program leads to a Ph.D. or to a Doctor of Nursing or Doctor of Nursing Science degree.

The following indicators apply to the Doctor of Philosophy (Ph.D.) in nursing, Doctor of Nursing Science (D.N.S. or D.N.Sc.), and Doctor of Nursing (N.D.) degrees.

Faculty

I. Represent and value a diversity of backgrounds and intellectual perspectives.

II. Meet the requirements of the parent institution for graduate research and doctoral education; a substantial proportion of faculty hold earned doctorates in nursing.

III. Conceptualize and implement productive programs of research and scholarship that are developed over time and build upon previous work, are at the cutting edge of the field of inquiry, are congruent with research priorities within nursing and its constituent communities, include a substantial proportion of extramural funding, and attract and engage students.

IV. Create an environment in which mentoring, socialization of students, and the existence of a community of scholars is evident.

V. Assist students in understanding the value of programs of research and scholarship that continue over time and build upon previous work.

VI. Identify, generate, and utilize resources within the university and the broader community to support program goals.

VII. Devote a significant proportion of time to dissertation advisement. Generally, each faculty member should serve as the major adviser/chair for no more than 3 to 5 students during the dissertation phase.

Programs of Study

The emphasis of the program of study is consistent with the mission of the parent institution, the discipline of nursing, and the degree awarded. The faculty's areas of expertise and scholarship determine specific foci in the program of study. Requirements and their sequence for progression in the program are clear and available to students in writing. Common elements of the program of study are outlined below.

I. Core and related course content—the distribution between nursing and supporting content is consistent with the mission and goals of the program, and the student's area of focus and course work are included in the following:

A. Historical and philosophical foundations to the development of nursing knowledge

B. Existing and evolving substantive nursing knowledge

C. Methods and processes of theory/knowledge development

D. Research methods and scholarship appropriate to inquiry

E. Development related to roles in academic, research, practice, or policy environments

II. Elements for formal and informal teaching and learning focus on the following:

A. Analytical and leadership strategies for dealing with social, ethical, cultural, economic, and political issues related to nursing, health care, and research

B. Progressive and guided student scholarship research experiences, including exposure to faculty's interdisciplinary research programs

C. Immersion experiences that foster the student's development as a nursing leader, scholarly practitioner, educator, and/or nurse scientist

D. Socialization opportunities for scholarly development in roles that complement students' career goals

III. Outcome indicators for the programs of study include the following:

A. Advancement to candidacy requires faculty's satisfactory evaluation (e.g., comprehensive exam) of the student's basic knowledge of elements I-A through I-E identified above

B. Dissertations represent original contributions to the scholarship of the field

C. Systematic evaluation of graduate outcomes is conducted at regular intervals

D. Within three to five years of completion, graduates have designed and secured funding for a research study, or, within two years of completion, graduates have utilized the research process to address an issue of importance to the discipline of nursing or health care within their employment setting

E. Employers report satisfaction with graduates' leadership and scholarship at regular intervals

F. Graduates' scholarship and leadership are recognized through awards, honors, or external funding within three to five years of completion

Resources

I. Sufficient human, financial, and institutional resources are available to accomplish the goals of the unit for doctoral education and faculty research.

A. The parent institution exhibits the following characteristics:

1) Research is an explicit component of the mission of the parent institution

2) An office of research administration

3) A record of peer-reviewed external funding

4) Postdoctoral programs

5) Internal research funds

6) Mechanisms that value, support, and reward faculty and student scholarship and role preparation

7) A university environment that fosters interdisciplinary research and collaboration

B. The nursing doctoral program exhibits the following characteristics:

1) Research-active faculty as well as other faculty experts to mentor students in other role preparations

2) Provide technical support for the following:

(a) Peer review of proposals and manuscripts in their development phases

(b) Research design expertise

(c) Data management and analysis support

(d) Hardware and software availability

(e) Expertise in grant proposal development and management

3) Procure space sufficient for the following:

(a) Faculty research needs

(b) Doctoral student study, meeting, and socializing

(c) Seminars

(d) Small-group work

C. Schools of exceptional quality also have the following:

1) Centers of research excellence

2) Endowed professorships

3) Mechanisms for financial support to allow full-time study

4) Master teachers capable of preparing graduates for faculty roles

II. State-of-the-art technical and support services are available and accessible to faculty, students, and staff for state-of-the-science information acquisition, communication, and management.

III. Library and database resources are sufficient to support the scholarly endeavors of faculty and students.

Students

I. Students are selected from a pool of highly qualified and motivated applicants who represent diverse populations.

II. Students' research goals and objectives are congruent with faculty research expertise and scholarship and institutional resources.

III. Students are successful in obtaining financial support through competitive intramural and extramural academic and research awards.

IV. Students commit a significant portion of their time to the program and complete the program in a timely fashion.

V. Students establish a pattern of productive scholarship, collaborating with researchers in nursing and other disciplines in scientific endeavors that result in the presentation and publication of scholarly work that continues after graduation.

Evaluation

The evaluation plan includes the following:

I. Is systematic, ongoing, comprehensive, and focuses on the university's and program's specific mission and goals.

II. Includes both process and outcome data related to these indicators of quality in research-focused doctoral programs.

III. Adheres to established ethical and process standards for formal program evaluation, e.g., confidentiality and rigorous quantitative and qualitative analyses.

IV. Involves students and graduates in evaluation activities.

V. Includes data from a variety of internal and external constituencies.

VI. Provides for comparison of program processes and outcomes to the standards of its parent graduate school/university and selected peer groups within nursing.

VII. Includes ongoing feedback to program faculty, administrators, and external constituents to promote program improvement.

VIII. Provides comprehensive data in order to determine patterns and trends and recommend future directions at regular intervals.

IX. Is supported with adequate human, financial, and institutional resources.

Approved by AACN Membership, November 2001.

WHAT YOU NEED TO KNOW ABOUT ONLINE LEARNING

Rosalee C. Yeaworth, Ph.D., RN, FAAN
Professor and Dean Emerita
College of Nursing
University of Nebraska Medical Center

Sue Schmidt, M.A. in Education and Human
Development
Director Web Management
MediaOne

Half a century ago, young women who graduated from high school and chose to enter a nursing program were expected to move into a "nurses' home," which housed not only dormitory-style rooms but also classrooms and faculty offices. Most of the clinical learning was done in apprenticeship style in a single hospital setting. There was no such thing as distance learning.

However, over the course of the past half-century, nursing education, like health care and education in general, has changed dramatically, creating a need for educators to implement distance education programs. The demographics of nursing students have changed. Not only is the nursing student far more likely to be a man than fifty years ago, but also the student who once was referred to as "nontraditional" is now becoming the traditional student. These students are mature, employed individuals who have complex family responsibilities and often live or work some distance from the university offering the courses they wish to take. The rapid advances in health-care knowledge and technology have increased the demand for nurses with graduate degrees. All nurses are faced with the need to enhance their knowledge through lifelong education as their roles and expectations change. In addition, a much greater effort is being made to provide education and training to residents in rural settings in the hope that they will continue to live and work in these areas.

Universities are addressing these changing educational needs by using advanced technologies and new communication capabilities. Distance learning offerings are continually enhanced by using new technologies and delivery systems such as the Internet and desktop videoconferencing. These technologies enable universities to reach beyond the boundaries imposed on them by traditional classrooms to deliver educational material to students located in different, noncentralized locations, thus allowing instruction and learning to occur independently of time and place. This model, known as "distributive learning," can be used in combination with traditional classroom-based courses and with traditional distance learning courses, or to create wholly virtual classrooms.

Tools used for distance education include the following:

E-mail: This is one of the most commonly used communication tools. It allows for a one-to-one exchange of information between the sender and receiver of the e-mail message. Course papers and draft materials may be sent, commented on, and returned as attached documents.

Listservs: This is a one-to-many communication exchange. People subscribe to listservs based on discussion topics that interest them. When a participant on a listserv sends an e-mail to the listserv, the message is copied and sent to all people who have subscribed to it. Listservs are generally free; there is no charge to subscribe.

Discussion Groups: This is a many-to-many communication exchange. E-mail and listservs deliver the messages directly to your electronic mailbox. Discussion groups, on the other hand, are retained in a specified area on the Internet. You must go to the discussion group to post your comments and read and reply to the comments of others. The advantage of a discussion group over e-mail or listservs is that the comments can be viewed easily by all and the sequence of comments and replies posted is readily apparent in its structure.

Chat Rooms: Chat is synchronous communication; the participants are online at the same time talking to each other. E-mail, listservs, and discussion groups, on the other hand, are asynchronous communication. With moderated chat, a moderator views the questions and comments posed by the participants and selects those that will be seen by all participants. After posting the comment or question, the moderator answers it. In a regular chat room, there is no management over what is or is not posted.

Streaming Video: Entire lectures can be delivered using streaming video technology. Even students accessing the material with slower modems can receive clear audio and good video images.

Desktop Videoconferencing: With a small camera mounted on top of the computer, students and faculty members are able to see and talk with each other using desktop videoconferencing software.

Virtual Reality: Student lounges can be constructed visually using virtual reality software. When students want to have a discussion with other students, they literally walk into the lounge as an avatar (a visual image of themselves they have selected) and hold live chat sessions with their fellow classmates.

Web Sites: Components of or the entire course content can be delivered via the Internet through the creation of a Web site. Any or all of the technology tools noted above can be linked through an educational Web site. Among other things, a Web site includes the syllabus, discussion groups, assignments, student lounges, faculty information, resources (including links to Web documents that enrich the course content), lecture notes, and other course components. Traditional distance education tools, such as satellite transmission, videotapes, telephone conferences, correspondence material, and CD-ROM interactive instruction, are also frequently used in conjunction with Web-delivered course material.

The key to using technology successfully is to define your goals and objectives and then decide which technology or combination of technologies will be most effective. Keep in mind that faculty members and students must have the appropriate computer equipment and user knowledge to participate in distance learning.

Even though computers today are much more user-friendly, it is important to allot some time for students to become accustomed to using the new technologies necessary for transmitting their course material. Campus information technology services should work closely with the faculty to prepare introductory manuals or self-help materials for students. Information technology specialists should be available to answer technology questions or solve problems so that faculty members can concentrate on the course content questions. Enthusiasm can be dampened if too much time must be devoted to learning the technology or dealing with technology problems.

When deciding to take distance-learning courses, other factors must be considered. What you need to participate in distance learning varies with the sophistication of the tools used by the course instructor. Sending and receiving e-mail, participating in discussion groups, and viewing online syllabi require fairly simple technology. You need a computer with a modem and an Internet service provider (ISP). When selecting an ISP, participants should consider cost, reliability of access, and speed. World Wide Web access provided through your cable provider is generally more expensive but provides significantly faster access to documents.

Video streaming and desktop videoconferencing require more sophisticated computer systems. Sometimes, in rural areas, the local telephone company or the Internet or TV provider may provide only limited services. Students may find, for example, that they have to use a teleconference line for sound with desktop videoconferencing. It is important to investigate the technology issues in your area before undertaking a course, because technical limitations can add to the cost and decrease your satisfaction and learning.

Access to the campus bookstore and library may also be a concern for students who are at considerable distance from the school offering the course. Books and supplies may be ordered online from the bookstore, and journal articles can be made available from the library through electronic reserve. Courses that use electronic reserve usually require a fee to cover copyright costs.

Some advantages of distance learning are the following:

Student-Centered versus Instructor-Directed Learning: Students take an active role in their own learning experience. They are able to select what material they need to cover more extensively and are given the opportunity for exploration through accessing linked material provided by their instructor. They are also given more opportunity to learn at their own pace and select the time when they are more prepared to effectively view the course material.

Flexibility: Students may work at their own computers on a weekend or the middle of the night, without having to worry about library hours or driving in bad weather. Valuable time can be focused on learning rather than on the logistics of getting to class.

Accessibility: Students who would not be able to attend classes because of geographic proximity or time constraints are now able to participate.

Student Interaction Increases: Interaction increases in a distance learning environment. Students not only listen and take notes, but they also pose ideas to and ask questions of the instructor as well as other students in discussion groups. Interaction is encouraged, and the instructor has a better understanding of what and how the student is learning. In most classroom settings, it is very difficult to get students to discuss a topic. They may ask a question of or make a comment to the instructor, but they seldom interact with classmates about course topics.

Collaboration and Team Problem Solving: Using asynchronous and synchronous communication tools, students can work together on projects much more easily. It has always been difficult to bring a group together face-to-face to discuss what needs to be done. Through these new communication channels, information can be easily passed among a group, and resources such as research documents and drafts of works in progress can be distributed instantly.

Increased Sharing of Knowledge: In the traditional classroom, the instructor is the primary source of information. In distance learning, using tools such as a discussion group, students have a greater opportunity to share their knowledge and experience, allowing the members of the group to learn from each other. In addition, access to the Internet allows students to access the experience and knowledge of others outside their immediate classroom setting.

Immediate Access to Updated Material: Any material or announcements that have been changed can be distributed instantly, reducing distribution costs and providing students with access to the most current information.

Developing Needed Technology Skills: Students are learning technology skills that they can apply later in their work setting.

Some important factors should be considered when deciding whether a distance education model is right for you. It has been shown that students can learn course content by distance methods as well as or better than in the traditional classroom setting. Less information is available on socialization issues related to the nurse generalist, specialist, or practitioner roles. Socialization involves internalizing attitudes, values, and norms. The role modeling, mentoring, and collegial friendships may or may not be as adaptable to distance methods. Careful selection of clinical settings for experience, on-site preceptors, requirements for certain on-campus experiences, and group attendance of students and faculty members at regional or national meetings are some methods used to assist socialization.

Distance learning will not suffice for the "college experience" of joining sororities and fraternities and of participating in athletic and social activities that many young undergraduate students desire. On the other hand, for the adult learner with job and family responsibilities,

the distance education methodologies can provide the opportunity to participate in educational experiences that might otherwise have been beyond consideration.

When selecting your educational program, you should clearly define your goals for your educational experiences. If you want to have clinical experience in a particular setting, to be a research or teaching assistant to a certain person, or to be mentored by a selected expert, then your choice would be an on-site educational environment in a particular setting. However, if you want a degree from a particular institution but do not want to move or travel there, explore the distance learning opportunities offered. You need to remember that it is not an either-or proposition. You may be able to combine traditional classroom-based courses with distance learning for selected courses to optimize your overall educational program.

Distance learning is used by more and more educational institutions to provide both degree and continuing education. Many schools collaborate to offer students a selection of courses taught by different colleges and universities. A recent collaborative effort is the Western Governors University, a virtual university that is a partnership involving eighteen states and approximately 100 participating colleges and universities.

As noted above, the world is changing and so is the way we deliver nursing education. Distance education has opened a world of opportunities to students and faculty members. Students now have the ability to further their education by removing many of the time and access barriers they previously faced. Faculty members are presented with new and exciting challenges as they begin to use innovative technologies in their course delivery. With careful consideration and planning, the outcome will enhance the overall learning experience of both learner and teacher.

THE INTERNATIONAL NURSING STUDENT

For many international students completing baccalaureate, master's, or doctoral nursing programs, their choice of learning institutions is obvious. U.S. and Canadian colleges and universities are thought to offer the finest programs of nursing education available anywhere in the world. U.S. and Canadian nursing programs are renowned for their breadth and flexibility, for the excellence of their basic curriculum structure, and for their commitment to extensive on-site clinical training. Nursing study in the U.S. and Canada also affords students the opportunity for hands-on learning and practice in the world's most technologically advanced health-care systems. For many international nursing students, and especially for students from countries that are medically underserved, these features make U.S. and Canadian nursing programs unsurpassed.

Applying to Nursing School

The application process for international students often involves the completion of two separate written applications. Many colleges screen international candidates with a brief preliminary application requesting basic biographical and educational information. This document helps the admission officer determine whether the student has the minimum credentials for admission before requiring him or her to begin the lengthy process of completing and submitting final application forms.

Final applications to U.S. and Canadian colleges and universities vary widely in length and complexity, just as specific admission requirements vary from institution to institution. However, international nursing students must typically have a satisfactory scholastic record and demonstrated proficiency in English. To be admitted to any postsecondary institution in the United States or Canada, you must have satisfactorily completed a minimum of twelve years of elementary and secondary education. The customary cycle for this education includes a six-year elementary program, a three-year intermediate program, and a three-year postsecondary program, generally referred to as high school in the U.S. In addition, nursing school programs generally require successful completion of several years of high school-level mathematics and science.

The documentation of satisfactory completion of secondary schooling (and university education, in the case of graduate-level applicants) is achieved through submission of school reports, transcripts, and teacher recommendations. Because academic records and systems of evaluation differ widely from one educational system to the next, request that your school include a guide to grading standards. If you have received your secondary education at a school in which English is not the language of instruction, be certain to include official translations of all documents.

International students who have completed some university-level course work in their native country may be eligible to receive credit for equivalent courses at the U.S. or Canadian institution in which they enroll. Under special circumstances, practical nursing experience may also qualify for university credit. Policies regarding the transfer of or qualification for credits based on education or nursing experience outside the U.S. (or Canada for Canadian schools) vary widely, so be certain to inquire about these policies at the universities or colleges that interest you.

Language skills are a key to scholastic success. "The ability to speak, write, and understand English is an important determinant of success," says Joann Weiss, former Director of the Nursing and Latin American Studies dual-degree programs at the University of New Mexico in Albuquerque. Her advice for potential international applicants is simple: "Develop a true command of written and spoken English." English proficiency for students who have not received formal education in English-speaking schools is usually demonstrated via the Test of English as a Foreign Language (TOEFL); minimum test scores of 550 to 580 are commonly required. This policy, as well as the level of proficiency required, varies from school to school, so be sure to investigate each college's policies.

In addition, most universities offer some form of English language instruction for international students, often under the rubric ESL (English as a second language). Students who require additional language study to meet admission requirements or students who wish to deepen their skills in written or verbal English should inquire about ESL program availability.

Many colleges and universities also require that all undergraduate applicants take a standardized test—either the SAT and three SAT Subject Tests or the ACT. Like their U.S. and Canadian counterparts, international applicants to graduate-level nursing programs are required by most institutions to take the standardized Graduate Record Examinations (GRE).

Applicants should also be aware that financial assistance for international students is usually quite limited. To spare international students economic hardship during their schooling in the U.S. or Canada, many colleges and universities require them to demonstrate the availability of sufficient financial resources for tuition and minimum living expenses and supplies. As with so many admission requirements, policies regarding financial aid vary considerably; find out early what the policies are at the colleges that interest you.

Attending School in the U.S. or Canada

Once you are accepted by the college or university of your choice, take full advantage of the academic and personal advising systems offered to international students. Most institutions of higher education in the U.S. and Canada maintain an international student advisory office staffed with trained counselors. In addition to general academic counseling and planning, an international adviser can assist in a broad range of matters ranging from immigration and visa concerns to employment opportunities and health-care issues.

With few exceptions, all university students also obtain specialized academic counseling from an assigned faculty adviser. Faculty advisers monitor academic performance and progress and try to ensure that students meet the institutional requirements for their degree. Faculty advisers are excellent sources of information regarding course selection, and some advisers offer tutorials or special language or educational support to international students.

Although all university students face academic challenges, international students often find life outside the classroom equally demanding. Suddenly introduced into a new culture where the way of life may be dramatically different from that of their native country, international students often face a variety of social, domestic, medical, religious, or emotional concerns. Questions about social conventions, meal preparation, or other personal concerns can often be addressed by your international or faculty adviser.

Lorraine Rudowski, Assistant Professor and Coordinator of the International Health Program at the College of Health and Human Services at George Mason University in Fairfax, Virginia, emphasizes the benefits of a strong relationship with your advisers: "My job as an adviser is to provide comprehensive support to my students—from academic counseling and opportunities for language development to emotional support and guidance to attending parties or other informal social events to ease the sense of social and personal isolation often experienced by foreign students."

Dr. Rudowski says that international students would do well to find a sponsor or confidant within the university who understands the conventions of the student's native country. "A culturally sensitive sponsor is better equipped to understand the unique needs of each international student and is much more likely to help students obtain the assistance they need, whether we're talking about religious issues, help with study methods or social skills, or simply knowing how to deal with such everyday chores as cooking and cleaning. All of these matters can be sources of deep concern to international students."

Yet for all the academic, social, and personal challenges facing international nursing students, there is good news. Deans of nursing, professors, and advisers typically praise the motivation and determination of their international students, and international nursing students often boast matriculation rates that match or exceed those of their U.S. and Canadian counterparts.

For more information about the rules and regulations governing international students' entrance to U.S. schools, log on to educationUSA, part of the U.S. Department of State's Web site, at http://exchanges.state.gov/education/educationusa.

SPECIALTY NURSING ORGANIZATIONS

Academy of Medical-Surgical Nurses
East Holly Avenue
Box 56
Pitman, NJ 08071-0056
866-877-AMSN (2676) (toll-free)
E-mail: amsn@ajj.com
www.medsurgnurse.org

Air & Surface Transport Nurses Association
7995 East Prentice Avenue
Suite 100
Greenwood Village, CO 80111
800-897-NFNA (6362) (toll-free)
Fax: 303-770-1614
E-mail: astna@gwami.com
www.astna.org

American Academy of Ambulatory Care Nursing
East Holly Avenue
Box 56
Pitman, NJ 08071-0056
800-262-6877 (toll-free)
E-mail: aaacn@ajj.com
www.aaacn.org

American Association of Critical-Care Nurses
101 Columbia
Aliso Viejo, CA 92656-4109
949-362-2000
800-899-2226 (toll-free)
E-mail: info@aacn.org
www.aacn.org

American Association of Diabetes Educators
200 West Madison Street
Suite 800
Chicago, IL 60606
800-338-3633 (toll-free)
Fax: 312-424-2427
E-mail: aade@aadenet.org
www.aadenet.org

The American Association of Legal Nurse Consultants
401 North Michigan Avenue
Chicago, IL 60611
877-402-2562 (toll-free)
Fax: 312-673-6655
E-mail: info@aalnc.org
www.aalnc.org

American Association of Neuroscience Nurses
4700 West Lake Avenue
Glenview, IL 60025
847-375-4733
888-557-2266 (toll-free in the U.S. only)
Fax: 847-375-6430
E-mail: info@aann.org
www.aann.org

American Association of Nurse Anesthetists
222 South Prospect Avenue
Park Ridge, IL 60068-4001
847-692-7050
Fax: 847-692-6968
E-mail: info@aana.com
www.aana.com

American Association of Nurse Attorneys
P.O. Box 14218
Lenexa, KS 66285-4218
877-538-2262 (toll-free)
Fax: 913-895-4652
E-mail: taana@taana.org
www.taana.org

American Association of Occupational Health Nurses, Inc.
7794 Grow Drive
Pensacola, FL 32514
850-474-6963
Fax: 850-484-8762
E-mail: aaohn@aaohn.org
www.aaohn.org

American Association of Spinal Cord Injury Nurses
801 18th Street, NW
Washington, DC 20006
202-416-7704
Fax: 202-416-7641
E-mail: aascin@pva.org
www.aascin.org

American College of Nurse-Midwives
8403 Colesville Road
Suite 1550
Silver Spring, MD 20910
240-485-1800
Fax: 240-485-1818
www.midwife.org

American College of Nurse Practitioners (ACNP)
1501 Wilson Boulevard
Suite 509
Arlington, VA 22209
703-740-2529
Fax: 703-740-2533
E-mail: acnp@acnpweb.org
www.acnpweb.org

American Holistic Nurses Association
323 N. San Francisco Street
Suite 201
Flagstaff, AZ 86001
800-278-2462 (toll-free)
928-526-2196
Fax: 928-526-2752
E-mail: info@ahna.org
www.ahna.org

American Nephrology Nurses' Association
East Holly Avenue
Box 56
Pitman, NJ 08071-0056
856-256-2320
888-600-ANNA (2662) (toll-free)
E-mail: anna@ajj.com
www.annanurse.org

American Psychiatric Nurses Association
1555 Wilson Boulevard
Suite 530
Arlington, VA 22209
866-243-2443 (toll-free)
703-243-2443
Fax: 703-243-3390
E-mail: inform@apna.org
www.apna.org

American Public Health Association
800 I Street, NW
Washington, DC 20001-3710
202-777-APHA
Fax: 202-777-2534
E-mail: comments@apha.org
www.apha.org

American Society for Pain Management Nursing
P.O. Box 15473
Lenexa, KS 66285-5473
888-342-7766 (toll-free)
913-895-4606
Fax: 913-895-4652
E-mail: aspmn@goamp.org
www.aspmn.org

American Society of Ophthalmic Registered Nurses
P.O. Box 193030
San Francisco, CA 94119-3030
415-561-8513
Fax: 415-561-8531
E-mail: asorn@aao.org
http://webeye.ophth.uiowa.edu/ASORN

American Society of PeriAnesthesia Nurses
90 Frontage Road
Cherry Hill, NJ 08034-1412
877-737-9696 (toll-free)
856-616-9600
Fax: 856-616-9601
E-mail: aspan@aspan.org
www.aspan.org

American Society of Plastic Surgical Nurses
7794 Grow Drive
Pensacola, FL 32514
800-272-0136 (toll-free)
Fax: 850-484-8762
E-mail: aspsn@dancyamc.com
www.aspsn.org

Association for Death Education and Counseling
111 Deer Lake Road
Suite 100
Deerfield, IL 60015
847-509-0403
Fax: 847-480-9282
E-mail: info@adec.org
www.adec.org

Association for Professionals in Infection Control and Epidemiology, Inc.
1275 K Street, NW
Suite 1000
Washington, DC 20005-4006
202-789-1890
Fax: 202-789-1899
E-mail: apicinfo@apic.org
www.apic.org

Association for Radiologic and Imaging Nurses
7794 Grow Drive
Pensacola, FL 32514
866-486-2762 (toll-free)
850-474-7292
Fax: 850-484-8762
E-mail: arin@dancyamc.com
www.arinursing.org

Association of Nurses in AIDS Care
3538 Ridgewood Road
Akron, OH 44333-3122
800-260-6780 (toll-free)
330-670-0101
Fax: 330-670-0109
E-mail: anac@anacnet.org
www.anacnet.org

Association of Pediatric Oncology Nurses
4700 West Lake Avenue
Glenview, IL 60025-1485
847-375-4724
Fax: 877-375-6478
E-mail: info@apon.org
www.aphon.org

Association of Perioperative Registered Nurses
2170 South Parker Road
Suite 300
Denver, CO 80231
800-755-2676 (toll-free)
303-755-6304
E-mail: custsvc@aorn.org
www.aorn.org

Association of Rehabilitation Nurses
4700 West Lake Avenue
Glenview, IL 60025
800-229-7530 (toll-free)
E-mail: info@rehabnurse.org
www.rehabnurse.org

Association of Women's Health, Obstetric, and Neonatal Nurses
2000 L Street, NW
Suite 740
Washington, DC 20036
202-261-2400
800-673-8499 (toll-free in the U.S.)
800-245-0231 (toll-free in Canada)
Fax: 202-728-0575
E-mail: customerservice@awhonn.org
www.awhonn.org

Dermatology Nurses' Association
15000 Commerce Parkway
Suite C
Mount Laurel, NJ 08054
800-454-4362 (toll-free)
E-mail: dna@dnanurse.org
www.dnanurse.org

Developmental Disabilities Nurses Association
P.O. Box 536489
Orlando, FL 32853-6489
800-888-6733 (toll-free)
407-835-0642
Fax: 407-426-7440
www.ddna.org

SPECIALTY NURSING ORGANIZATIONS

Emergency Nurses Association
915 Lee Street
Des Plaines, IL 60016-6569
800-900-9659 (toll-free)
Fax: 847-460-4001
E-mail: enainfo@ena.org
www.ena.org

Hospice and Palliative Nurses Association
One Penn Center West
Suite 229
Pittsburgh, PA 15276-0100
412-787-9301
Fax: 412-787-9305
E-mail: hpna@hpna.org
www.hpna.org

Infusion Nurses Society
315 Norwood Park South
Norwood, MA 02062
781-440-9408
Fax: 781-440-9409
E-mail: ins@ins1.org
www.ins1.org

International Nurses Society on Addictions
P.O. Box 14846
Lenexa, KS 66285-4846
877-646-8672 (toll-free)
Fax: 913-895-4652
E-mail: intnsa@intnsa.org
www.intnsa.org

National Association for Home Care & Hospice
228 Seventh Street, SE
Washington, DC 20003
202-547-7424
Fax: 202-547-3540
E-mail: exec@nahc.org
www.nahc.org

National Association of Clinical Nurse Specialists
2090 Linglestown Road
Suite 107
Harrisburg, PA 17110
717-234-6799
Fax: 717-234-6798
E-mail: nacnsorg@nacns.org
www.nacns.org

**National Association of Directors of Nursing
Administration in Long-Term Care**
11353 Reed Hartman Highway
Suite 210
Cincinnati, OH 45241
800-222-0539 (toll-free)
513-791-3679
Fax: 513-791-3699
www.nadona.org

National Association of Neonatal Nurses
4700 West Lake Avenue
Glenview, IL 60025-1485
800-451-3795 (toll-free)
Fax: 888-477-6266
E-mail: info@nann.org
www.nann.org

**National Association of Nurse Practitioners in
Women's Health**
505 C Street, NE
Washington, DC 20002
202-543-9693, Ext. 1
Fax: 202-543-9858
E-mail: info@npwh.org
www.npwh.org

National Association of Orthopaedic Nurses
401 North Michigan Avenue
Suite 2200
Chicago, IL 60611
800-289-6266 (toll-free)
Fax: 312-527-6658
E-mail: naon@smithbucklin.com
www.orthonurse.org

National Association of Pediatric Nurse Practitioners
20 Brace Road
Suite 200
Cherry Hill, NJ 08034-2634
856-857-9700
Fax: 856-857-1600
E-mail: info@napnap.org
www.napnap.org

National Association of School Nurses
8484 Georgia Avenue
Suite 420
Silver Spring, MD 20910
240-821-1130
E-mail: nasn@nasn.org
www.nasn.org

National Gerontological Nursing Association
7794 Grow Drive
Pensacola, FL 32514
800-723-0560 (toll-free)
Fax: 850-484-8762
E-mail: ngna@dancyamc.com
www.ngna.org

National Organization of Nurse Practitioner Faculties
900 19th Street, NW
Suite 200B
Washington, DC 20006
202-289-8044
Fax: 202-384-1444
E-mail: nonpf@nonpf.org
www.nonpf.com

Oncology Nursing Society
125 Enterprise Drive
Pittsburgh, PA 15275
866-257-4ONS (4667) (toll-free)
412-859-6100
Fax: 877-369-5497 (toll-free)
E-mail: customer.service@ons.org
www.ons.org

Preventive Cardiovascular Nurses Association
613 Williamson Street
Suite 205
Madison, WI 53703
608-250-2440
Fax: 608-250-2410
E-mail: info@pcna.net
www.pcna.net

Respiratory Nursing Society
c/o Donna Bond, Secretary
309 E. Lee Avenue
Vinton, VA 24179
E-mail: DMHCRRN@aol.com
www.respiratorynursingsociety.org

Society for Vascular Nursing
203 Washington Street
PMB 311
Salem, MA 01970
888-536-4SVN (4786) (toll-free)
978-744-5005
Fax: 978-744-5029
E-mail: svn@administrare.com
www.svnnet.org

Society of Gastroenterology Nurses and Associates
401 North Michigan Avenue
Chicago, IL 60611-4267
800-245-7462 (toll-free)
312-321-5165 (in Illinois)
Fax: 312-673-6694
E-mail: sgna@smithbucklin.com
www.sgna.org

Society of Otorhinolaryngology and Head-Neck Nurses, Inc.
202 Julia Street
New Smyrna Beach, FL 32168
386-428-1695
Fax: 386-423-7566
E-mail: info@sohnnurse.com
www.sohnnurse.com

Society of Urologic Nurses and Associates
East Holly Avenue
Box 56
Pitman, NJ 08071-0056
888-827-7862 (toll-free)
E-mail: suna@ajj.com
www.suna.org

Wound, Ostomy and Continence Nurses Society
15000 Commerce Parkway, Suite C
Mt. Laurel, NJ 08054
888-224-WOCN (9626) (toll-free)
E-mail: wocn_info@wocn.org
www.wocn.org

Paying for Your Nursing Education

Whether you are considering a baccalaureate degree in nursing or have completed your undergraduate education and are planning to attend graduate school, finding a way to pay for that education is essential.

The cost to attend college is considerable and is increasing each year at a rate faster than most other products and services. In fact, the cost of a nursing education at a public four-year college can be more than $14,000 per year, including tuition, fees, books, room and board, transportation, and miscellaneous expenses. The cost at a private college or university, at either the graduate or undergraduate level, can be more than $30,000 per year.

This is where financial aid comes in. Financial aid is money made available by the government and other sources to help students who otherwise would be unable to attend college. More than $143 billion in aid is provided to students each year (College Board, *Trends in Student Aid 2008*). Most college students in this country receive some form of aid, and all prospective students should investigate what may be available. Most of this aid is given to students because neither they nor their families have sufficient personal resources to pay for college. This type of aid is referred to as need-based aid. Recipients of need-based aid include traditional students just out of high school or college and older, nontraditional students who are returning to college or graduate school.

There is also merit-based aid, which is awarded to students who display a particular ability. Merit scholarships are based primarily on academic merit, but may include other special talents. Many colleges and graduate schools offer merit-based aid in addition to need-based aid to their students.

Types and Sources of Financial Aid

There are four types of aid:

1 Scholarships

2 Grants

3 Loans

4 Student employment (including fellowships and assistantships)

Scholarships and grants are outright gifts and do not have to be repaid. Loans are borrowed money that must be repaid with interest, usually after graduation. Student employment provides jobs during the academic year for which students are paid. For graduate students, student employment may include fellowships and assistantships in which students work, receive free or reduced tuition, and may be paid a stipend for living expenses.

Most of the aid available to students is need-based and comes from the federal government through nine financial aid programs. Four of these programs are grant-based and are only available to undergraduate students:

1 Federal Pell Grants

2 Academic Competitive Grants

3 SMART Grants

4 Federal Supplemental Educational Opportunity Grants

Four are loan programs:

1 Federal Perkins Loan

2 Federal Stafford Student/Direct Loans (subsidized and unsubsidized)

3 Federal Graduate PLUS loans

4 Federal PLUS Loans

The final program is a student employment program called the Federal Work-Study Program, which is also awarded to undergraduate and graduate students based on financial need.

The federal government also offers a number of programs especially for nursing students. For example, the U.S. Department of Health and Human Services offers Nursing Student Scholarships, Nursing Student Loans, the Nursing Education Loan Repayment Program, and the Scholarship for Disadvantaged Students (SDS) program. Some of these programs require that the student work in a designated nursing shortage area for a period of time. These programs are administered by the nursing school's financial aid office. For more information, log on to http://bhpr.hrsa.gov/dsa.

The second-largest source of aid is from the colleges and universities themselves. Almost all colleges have aid programs from institutional resources, most of which are grants, scholarships, and fellowships. These can be either need- or merit-based.

Federal Financial Aid Programs

Program	Who Benefits?	Maximum/Year
Federal Pell Grants	Undergraduate students	$5550
Federal Supplemental Educational Opportunity Grants (FSEOG)	Undergraduate students	$4000
Academic Competitivess Grants	Undergraduate students who are eligible for Federal Pell Grants	$750 (first-year students) $1300 (second-year students)
SMART Grants	Undergraduate students who are eligible for Federal Pell Grants	$4000 (third- and fourth-year students)
Federal Perkins Loans	Undergraduate students	$4000
	Graduate students	$6000
Federal Stafford Student/Direct Loans (subsidized)	Undergraduate students	$3500 (first-year students) $4500 (second-year students) $5500 (third-year students and above)
	Graduate students	$8500
Federal Stafford Student/Direct Loans (unsubsidized)	Dependent undergraduate students	$2000
	Independent undergraduate students	$6000 (first- and second-year students) $7000 (third-year students and above)
	Graduate students	$12,000
Federal PLUS Loans	Dependent undergraduate students	Up to cost of attendance (less other financial aid received)
Federal Graduate PLUS loans	Graduate and professional students	Up to cost of attendance (less other financial aid received)

The unsubsidized Federal Stafford Student/Direct Loan amounts provided are in addition to the subsidized Federal Stafford/Direct Loan amounts.

A third source of aid is from state governments. Nearly every state provides aid for students attending college in their home state, although most only have programs for undergraduates. Most state aid programs are scholarships and grants, but many states now have low-interest loan and work-study programs. Most state grants and scholarships are not "portable," meaning that they cannot be used outside of your home state of residence.

A fourth source of aid is from private sources such as corporations, hospitals, civic associations, unions, fraternal organizations, foundations, and religious groups that give scholarships, grants, and fellowships to students. Most of these are not based on need, although the amount of the scholarship may vary depending upon financial need. The competition for these scholarships can be formidable, but the rewards are well worth the process. Many companies also offer tuition reimbursement to employees and their dependents. Check with the personnel or human resources department at your or your parents' place of employment for benefit and eligibility information.

Eligibility for Financial Aid

Since most of the financial aid that college students receive is need-based, colleges employ a process called "need analysis" to determine student awards. For most applicants, the student and parents (if the student is a dependent) fill out one form on which family income, assets, and household information are reported. This form is the Free Application for Federal Student Aid (FAFSA). The end result of this need analysis is the student's "Expected Family Contribution," or EFC, representing the amount a family should be able to contribute toward education expenses.

Dependent or Independent

The basic principle of financial aid is that the primary responsibility for paying college expenses resides with the family. In determining your EFC, you will first need to know who makes up your "family." That will tell you whose income is counted when the need analysis is done.

Graduate Students: By definition, all graduate nursing students are considered independent for federal aid purposes. Therefore, only your income and assets (and your spouse's if you are married) count in determining your expected family contribution.

Undergraduate Students: If you are financially dependent upon your parents, their income and assets, as well as yours, are counted toward the family contribution. If you are financially independent of your parents, only your income (and your spouse's if you are married) counts in the calculation.

According to the U.S. Department of Education, in order to be considered independent for financial aid for 2010–11, you must meet any ONE of the following:

- You were born before January 1, 1987.
- You are or will be enrolled in a master's or doctoral program (beyond a bachelor's degree) during the 2010–11 school year.
- You are married on the day you apply (even if you are separated but not divorced).
- You have children who receive more than half their support from you.
- You have dependents (other than your children or spouse) who live with you and who receive more than half of their support from you and will continue to receive more than half their support from you through June 30, 2011.
- Both your parents are deceased, or you are an orphan or ward of the court (or were a ward of the court until age 18).
- You are engaged in active duty in the U.S. Armed Forces or are a National Guard or Reserves enlistee and are called to active duty for purposes other than training.
- You are a veteran of the U.S. Armed Forces. ("Veteran" includes students who attended a U.S. service academy and who were released under a condition other than dishonorable. Contact your financial aid office for more information.)

If you meet any one of these conditions, you are considered independent and only your income and assets (and your spouse's if you are married) count toward your family contribution. Remember, if you are attending school as a graduate student, you are automatically independent for federal aid consideration.

If there are extraordinary circumstances, the financial aid administrator at the college you will be attending has the authority to make a change to your dependency status. You will need to provide extensive documentation of your family situation.

Whether you are dependent or independent, check out www.petersons.com/finaid/efcsimplecalc.asp to determine your estimated EFC.

Determining Cost and Need

Now that you know approximately how much you and your family will be expected to contribute toward your college expenses, you can subtract the EFC from the total cost of attending a college or graduate school to determine the amount of need-based financial aid for which you will be eligible. The average cost listed assumes that you will be attending nursing school full-time. If you will be attending part-time, you should adjust costs accordingly. For a more accurate estimate of the cost of attendance at a particular college, check the financial aid information usually available on the college's Web site or in its publications.

Applying for Financial Aid

After you have subtracted your EFC from the cost of your education and determined your financial need, you will have a better understanding of how much assistance you will need. Even if you do not demonstrate financial need, you are still encouraged to file the FAFSA, as you may be eligible for assistance that is not based on need. The process for applying for aid can be confusing if you are not familiar with completing these types of applications. If you need assistance, you should contact the financial aid office for help.

Undergraduate and graduate students applying for aid must fill out the FAFSA. This application is available in high school guidance offices, college financial aid offices, state education department offices, and many local libraries. You are strongly encouraged to file the FAFSA online at www.fafsa.ed.gov. If you file online, you will need to have a Personal Identification Number (PIN). The PIN can easily be obtained at www.pin.ed.gov. Dependent students will need a PIN for themselves and one parent. When you file online, your application is processed more rapidly, and you are far less likely to make major errors. The FAFSA, whether you file a paper application or online, becomes available in November or December, almost a year before the fall term in which you will enroll, but you cannot complete it until after January 1.

If you file a paper application, you and your parents (if appropriate) must sign your completed FAFSA and mail it to a processing center in the envelope provided. Do not send any additional materials, but do make copies of everything you filled out.

The processing center enters the data into a computer that runs the federal methodology of need analysis to calculate your EFC. This center then distributes the information to the schools and agencies you listed on the FAFSA. The actual determination of need and the awarding of aid are handled by each college financial aid office.

It is generally recommended that you complete the FAFSA as soon as possible after January 1. You should check with each college to which you are applying to determine its filing deadline. It is important to meet all college deadlines for financial aid, since there is a limited amount of funds available. However, students who procrastinate can still file for federal aid any time during the year.

What Happens After You Submit the FAFSA?

Two to four weeks after you send in your completed FAFSA, you will receive a Student Aid Report (SAR) that shows the information you reported and your official EFC. This is an opportunity for you to make corrections or to have the information sent to any new school you are considering that you did not list on the original FAFSA. The SAR contains instructions on how to make corrections or to designate additional schools. If you provided an e-mail address on the FAFSA, this information will be sent to this address rather than through conventional mail.

At the same time that you receive the SAR, the college(s) you specified also receive the information. The financial aid office at the school may request additional information from you or may ask you to provide documentation verifying the information you reported on the FAFSA. For example, they may ask you for a copy of your (and your parents') income tax return or official forms verifying any untaxed income you or your parents received (e.g., Social Security, disability, or welfare benefits).

Once the financial aid office is satisfied that the information is correct, you will receive a financial aid offer. Many colleges like to make this offer in the spring prior to the fall enrollment so that students have ample opportunity to make their plans. However, some colleges will wait until summer to notify you.

Other Applications

The FAFSA is the required form for applying for federal and most state financial aid programs. Most schools also use the FASFA to determine eligibility for institutional aid; however, some colleges and graduate schools require additional information to determine eligibility for institutional aid. Nearly 500 colleges and universities, plus more than 200 private scholarship programs, employ a form called the Financial Aid PROFILE® from the College Scholarship Service (CSS). While the form is similar to the FAFSA, several additional questions must be answered for colleges that award their own funds. You begin the process in October or November by completing a PROFILE Registration form on which you designate the schools to which you are applying. A few weeks later, you will receive a customized, individualized application that you complete and send back to CSS, which, in turn, forwards your application information to the schools you selected. There is a fee charged for each school listed on the application.

Financial Aid Offer

If you qualify for need-based aid, a college will typically offer a combination of different types of assistance—scholarship, grant, loan, and work-study—to meet this need. An offer of aid usually is made after you have been admitted to the college or program. You may accept all or part of the financial aid package. If you will be enrolling part-time (fewer than 12 credits per term), be sure to contact the financial aid office in advance since this may have impact on your overall aid eligibility.

If you are awarded Federal Work-Study Program aid, the amount you are awarded represents your earnings limit for the academic year under the program. In general, schools assume you will earn this money on an hourly basis, so it cannot be used to pay your term bill charges. On most campuses there are many jobs available for students. Not all of these are limited to students in the Federal Work-Study Program. Check with your placement office or financial aid office for more information.

Keep in mind that the student budget used to establish eligibility for financial aid is based on averages. It may not reflect your actual expenses. Student budgets usually reflect most expenses for categories of students (for example, single students living in their parents' home, campus-provided housing, or living in an apartment or house near campus, etc.). But if you have unusual expenses that are not included, you should consult with your school's financial aid office regarding a budget adjustment.

If Your Family or Job Situation Changes

Because a family contribution is based on the previous year's income, many nursing students find they do not qualify for need-based aid (or not enough to pay their full expenses). This is particularly true of older students who were working full-time last year but are no longer doing so or who will not work during the academic year. If this is your situation, you should speak to a counselor in the financial aid office about making an adjustment in your family contribution need analysis. Financial aid administrators may make changes to any of the elements that go into the need analysis if there are conditions that merit a change. Contact the financial aid office for more information.

Don't Qualify for Need-Based Aid?

If you don't qualify for need-based aid but feel you do not have the resources necessary to pay for college or graduate school, you still have several options available.

First, there are two student loan programs for which need is not a consideration. These two programs are the Federal Stafford Student Loan (unsubsidized) program and the Direct Loan (unsubsidized) program. There are also non-need-based loan programs for parents of dependent students or for graduate or professional students called the Federal PLUS Loans and the Direct PLUS Loan program. If you or your parents are interested in borrowing through one of these programs, you should check with the financial aid office for more information. There are also numerous private or alternative loan sources available. For many students, borrowing to pay for a nursing education can be an excellent investment in one's future. At the same time, be sure that you do not overburden yourself when it comes to paying back the loans. Before you accept a federal student loan, the financial aid office will schedule a counseling session to make certain that you know the terms of the loan and that you understand the ramifications of borrowing. If you can do without, it is often suggested that you postpone student loans until they are absolutely necessary.

For graduate nursing students, Federal PLUS Loans are now available to graduate and professional students. Students who are looking into alternative loan programs should be sure to compare any terms and conditions with this federal program. Students should borrow through the Federal Graduate PLUS loans (or other alternative loan) program only after they have used the Federal Stafford Student Loan or Direct Loan program. You can borrow Federal Graduate PLUS loans and alternative loan funds up to the cost of attendance less any other financial aid received.

A second option if you do not qualify for need-based aid is to search for scholarships. Be wary of scholarship search companies that promise to find you scholarships but require you to pay a fee. There are many resources that provide lists of scholarships, including the annually published *Peterson's Scholarships, Grants & Prizes,* which are available in libraries, counselors' offices, and bookstores. Non-need scholarships require application forms and are extremely competitive; only a handful of students from thousands of applicants receive awards. Check out opportunities on our site, www.petersons.com.

Another option is to work more hours at an existing job or to find a paying position if you do not already have one. The student employment or placement office at your college should be able to help you find a job, either on or off campus. Many colleges have vacancies remaining after they have placed Federal Work-Study Program eligible students in their jobs.

You should always contact the financial aid office at the school you plan to attend for advice concerning sources of college-based and private aid.

Employer-Paid Financial Aid

Bob Atwater is a certified personnel consultant and certified medical staff recruiter and founder of Atwater Consulting & Recruiting in Lilburn, Georgia, a consulting firm for the employment and recruitment of physician assistants, nurse practitioners, certified nurse midwives, nurses, and nursing managers.

Health-care administrators, Atwater says, have coined a phrase to characterize their efforts to meet the growing demand for nurses with better skills and training: "Grow your own."

"Constant training through the course of a nursing career is the only way to keep pace with the technological and medical advances, but it can be a financial burden on the nurse," Atwater says.

That is why many employers now give qualified employees a benefits package that includes a continuing education allowance.

For the employer, this type of benefits package can help to recruit candidates willing to further their careers through education. Administrators feel it is the best way to build a staff of nurses with up-to-date certifications in all areas.

In a constantly expanding field, nurses should be required to continue and update their education. The nurses get a paid education, can keep their job, and work flexible hours while they are going to school. Inquiries about these allowances should be made during an interview with the company's human resources department. Additional information can be obtained from the nursing school, local hospitals in the area, or from other health-care professionals. There are many attractive options available because of the nationwide shortage of qualified nurses. Check with a number of potential employers before agreeing to any long-term contract.

Sources of Financial Aid for Nursing Students

The largest proportion of financial aid for college expenses comes from the federal government and is given on the basis of financial need. Beyond this federal need-based aid—which should always be the primary source of financial aid that a prospective student investigates and which is given regardless of one's field of study—a sizable amount of scholarship assistance specifically meant to help students in nursing programs is also available from government agencies, associations, civic or fraternal organizations, and corporations. These sources of aid can be particularly attractive for students who may not be eligible for need-based aid. The following list presents some of the major sources of financial aid specifically for nursing students. Not listed are scholarships that are specific to individual colleges and universities or are limited to residents of a particular place or to individuals who have relatively unusual qualifications. Students seeking financial aid should investigate all appropriate possibilities, including sources not listed here. You can find this information in libraries, bookstores, and guidance offices guides, including two of Peterson's annually updated publications: *Peterson's How to Get Money for College: Financing Your Future Beyond Federal Aid,* for information about undergraduate awards given by the federal government, state governments, and specific colleges, and *Peterson's Scholarships, Grants & Prizes,* for information about awards from private sources.

Students should also check out the many scholarship search engines available on the Web, especially www.petersons.com/finaid and www.aacn.nche.edu/Education/Financialaid.htm.

Air Force Institute of Technology
Award Name: Air Force Active Duty Health Professions Loan Repayment Program
Program Description: Program provides up to $40,000 (2009) to repay qualified educational loans in exchange for active duty service in the U.S. armed forces.
Application Contact: Air Force Institute of Technology
AFIT/ENEM
Attn: Ms. Patricia Faustman
2950 Hobson Way
Wright Patterson AFB, OH 45433-7765
800-543-3490, Ext. 3015 (toll-free)
E-mail: enem.adhplrp@afit.edu
www.afit.edu/adhplrp

American Association of Colleges of Nursing (AACN)
Award Name: AfterCollege/AACN Scholarship Fund
Program Description: This scholarship program supports students who are seeking a baccalaureate, master's, or doctoral degree in nursing. Special consideration will be given to students enrolled in a master's or doctoral program with the goal of pursuing a nursing faculty career, completing an RN to baccalaureate program (B.S.N.), or enrolled in an accelerated baccalaureate or master's degree nursing program.
Application Contact: American Association of Colleges of Nursing
One Dupont Circle, NW
Suite 530
Washington, DC 20036
202-463-6930
Fax: 202-785-8320
E-mail: scholarship@aacn.nche.edu
http://go.aftercollege.com/events/AACN/2006/index.cfm

American Association of Critical-Care Nurses
Award Name: AACN Educational Advancement Scholarships
Program Description: Nonrenewable scholarships for AACN members who are RNs currently enrolled in undergraduate or graduate NLNAC-accredited programs. The undergraduate award is for use in the junior or senior year. Minimum 3.0 GPA.
Application Contact: American Association of Critical-Care Nurses Scholarships
101 Columbia
Aliso Viejo, CA 92656-4109
800-899-2226 (toll-free)
E-mail: info@aacn.org
www.aacn.org

American Cancer Society
Award Name: Scholarships in Cancer Nursing
Program Description: Renewable awards for graduate students in nursing pursuing advanced preparation in cancer nursing: research, education, administration, or clinical practice. Must be U.S. citizen.
Application Contact: American Cancer Society
Extramural Grants Program
250 Williams Street
Atlanta, GA 30303-1002
800-ACS-2345 (toll-free)
Fax: 404-321-4669
E-mail: grants@cancer.org
www.cancer.org

American Holistic Nurses' Association (AHNA)
Award Name: Charlotte McGuire Scholarship Program
Program Description: Open to any licensed nurse or nursing student pursuing holistic education. Experience in holistic health care or alternative health practices is preferred. Must be an AHNA member with a minimum 3.0 GPA.
Application Contact: Charlotte McGuire Scholarships
American Holistic Nurses' Association
323 N. San Francisco Street
Suite 201
Flagstaff, AZ 86001
800-278-2462 (toll-free)
E-mail: info@ahna.org
www.ahna.org/edu/assist.html

American Indian Graduate Center (AIGC)
Award Name: AIGC Fellowships
Program Description: Graduate fellowships available for American Indian and Alaska Native students from federally recognized U.S. tribes. Applicants must be pursuing a postbaccalaureate graduate

or professional degree as a full-time student at an accredited institution in the U.S., demonstrate financial need, and be enrolled in a federally recognized American Indian tribe or Alaska Native group or provide documentation of Indian descent.

Application Contact: American Indian Graduate Center Fellowships
American Indian Graduate Center
4520 Montgomery Boulevard, NE
Suite 1B
Albuquerque, NM 87109
800-628-1920 (toll-free)
505-881-4584
E-mail: web@aigcs.org
www.aigc.com

Association of Perioperative Registered Nurses (AORN)

Award Name: AORN Foundation Scholarships
Program Description: Applicant must be an active RN and a member of AORN for twelve consecutive months prior to application. Reapplication for each period is required. For baccalaureate, master's of nursing, or doctoral degree at an accredited institution. Minimum 3.0 GPA required.
Application Contact: AORN Foundation Scholarship Program
2170 South Parker Road
Suite 400
Denver, CO 80231-5711
800-755-2676 (toll-free)
E-mail: foundation@aorn.org
www.aorn.org/AORNFoundation/Scholarships

Bethesda Lutheran Homes and Services, Inc.

Award Name: Nursing Scholastic Achievement Scholarship
Program Description: Award for college nursing students with a minimum 3.0 GPA who are Lutheran and have completed their sophomore year of a four-year nursing program or one year of a two-year program. Must be interested in working with people with developmental disabilities.
Application Contact: Bethesda Lutheran Homes and Services, Inc.
Coordinator, Outreach Programs and Services
600 Hoffmann Drive
Watertown, WI 53094
800-369-4636, Ext. 4449 (toll-free)
E-mail: bethesda.institute@mailblc.org
www.blhs.org/youth/scholarships

Foundation of the National Student Nurses' Association, Inc.

Award Names: Scholarship Program
Program Description: One-time awards available to nursing students in various educational situations: enrolled in programs leading to an RN license, RNs enrolled in programs leading to a bachelor's or master's degree in nursing, enrolled in a state-approved school in a specialty area of nursing, and minority students enrolled in nursing or prenursing programs. High school students are not eligible. Funds for graduate study are available only for a first degree in nursing. Based on financial need, academic ability, and health-related nursing and community activities. Application fee of $10. Send self-addressed stamped envelope with two stamps along with application request.
Application Contact: Scholarship Chairperson
Foundation of the National Student Nurses' Association, Inc.
45 Main Street
Suite 606
Brooklyn, NY 11201
718-210-0705
E-mail: nsna@nsna.org
www.nsna.org/foundation

Heart and Stroke Foundation of Canada

Award Name: Nursing Research Fellowships
Program Description: In-training awards for study in an area of cardiovascular or cerebrovascular nursing. Award is directed toward preparing nurses who have completed their doctoral degree and who intend to undertake independent research programs. For master's degree candidates, the programs must include a thesis or project requirement.
Application Contact: Heart and Stroke Foundation of Canada
1402-222 Queen Street
Ottawa, Ontario K1P-5V9
Canada
613-569-4361, Ext. 275
E-mail: research@hsf.ca
www.hsf.ca/research/en/general/home.html

International Order of the King's Daughters and Sons, Inc.

Award Name: International Order of King's Daughters and Sons Health Scholarships
Program Description: For study in the health fields. B.A./B.S. students are eligible in junior year. Application must be for at least third year of college. RN students must have completed first year of schooling. Send #10 self-addressed stamped envelope for application and information.
Application Contact: Director
Health Careers Scholarship Department
P.O. Box 1040
Chautauqua, NY 14722-1040
716-357-4951
E-mail: iokds5@windstream.net
www.iokds.org/scholarship.html

March of Dimes

Award Name: Graduate Scholarships
Program Description: Scholarships for registered nurses enrolled in graduate programs in maternal-child nursing. Must be a member of the Association of Women's Health, Obstetric and Neonatal Nurses; the American College of Nurse-Midwives; or the National Association of Neonatal Nurses (NANN).
Application Contact: Education Services
March of Dimes
1275 Mamaroneck Avenue
White Plains, NY 10605
914-997-4555
E-mail: mlavan@marchofdimes.com
www.marchofdimes.com/professionals/685.asp

National Alaska Native American Indian Nurses Association (NANAINA)

Award Name: NANAINA Merit Awards
Program Description: Annual $500 awards presented to NANAINA members who are enrolled in a U.S. federally or state-recognized tribe and are enrolled as a full-time undergraduate or graduate nursing student in an accredited or state-approved school of nursing.
Application Contact: Audrey Koertvelyessy
NANAINA Treasurer
11911 Parkelawn Drive, #101
Rockville, MD 20852
888-566-8773 (toll-free)
E-mail: akoertvelyessy@hrsa.gov
www.nanainanurses.org/Scholarships/index.php

National Association of Hispanic Nurses (NAHN)

Award Name: National Scholarship Awards

Program Description: One-time award to an outstanding Hispanic nursing student. Must have at least a 3.0 GPA and be a member of NAHN. Based on academic merit, potential contribution to nursing, and financial need.

Application Contact: Juan F. Perez, RN-B.S.N., Chair
Awards/Scholarship Committee
1455 Pennsylvania Avenue, NW
Suite 400
Washington, DC 20004
202-387-2477
E-mail: info@thehispanicnurses.org
www.thehispanicnurses.org

National Black Nurses Association, Inc. (NBNA)

Award Names: NBNA Scholarships

Program Description: Scholarships available to nursing students who are members of NBNA and are enrolled in an accredited school of nursing. Must demonstrate involvement in African-American community and present letter of recommendation from local chapter of NBNA.

Application Contact: National Black Nurses Association, Inc.
Scholarship Committee
8630 Fenton Street, Suite 330
Silver Spring, MD 20910-3803
301-589-3200
E-mail: contact@nbna.org
www.nbna.org/scholarship.htm

National Student Nurses' Association (NSNA)

Award Name: Educational Advancement Scholarships

Program Description: Scholarships are awarded based on academic achievement and demonstrated commitment to nursing through involvement in student organizations and school and community activities related to health care.

Application Contact: National Student Nurses' Association Foundation
45 Main Street
Suite 606
Brooklyn, NY 11201
718-210-0705
E-mail: nsna@nsna.org
www.nsna.org

Nurses' Educational Funds, Inc.

Award Name: Nurses' Educational Fund Scholarships

Program Description: Awards for full-time students at master's level, full-time or part-time at doctoral level, or RNs who are U.S. citizens and members of a national professional nursing association. Application fee: $10.

Application Contact: Nurses' Educational Funds, Inc.
304 Park Avenue South
11th Floor
New York, NY 10010
212-590-2443
E-mail: info@n-e-f.org
www.n-e-f.org

Oncology Nursing Society

Award Name: Scholarships

Program Description: ONF offers nearly a dozen one-time scholarships and awards at all levels of study, with various requirements and purposes, to nursing students who are interested in pursuing oncology nursing. Contact the foundation for details about appropriate awards. Application fee: $5.

Application Contact: Oncology Nursing Society
Development Coordinator
125 Enterprise Drive
RIDC Park West
Pittsburgh, PA 15275-1214
866-257-4667 (toll-free)
E-mail: customer.service@ons.org
www.ons.org/awards

United States Air Force Reserve Officer Training Corps

Award Name: Air Force ROTC Nursing Scholarships

Program Description: One- to four-year programs available to students of nursing and high school seniors. Nursing graduates agree to accept a commission in the Air Force Nurse Corps and serve four years on active duty after successfully completing their licensing examination. Must have at least a 2.5 GPA for one- and four-year scholarships or at least a 2.65 GPA for two- and three-year scholarships. Two exam failures result in a four-year assignment as an Air Force line officer.

Application Contact: Air Force ROTC
551 East Maxwell Boulevard
Maxwell AFB, AL 36112-6106
866-423-7682 (toll-free)
www.afrotc.com/scholarships/index.htm

United States Army Reserve Officers' Training Corps

Award Name: Army ROTC Nursing Scholarships

Program Description: Two- to four-year programs available to students of nursing and high school seniors. Nursing graduates agree to accept a commission in the Army Nurse Corps and serve in the military for a period of eight years. This may be fulfilled by serving on active duty for two to four years, followed by service in the Army National Guard or the United States Army Reserve or in the Inactive Ready Reserve for the remainder of the eight-year obligation.

Application Contact: Army ROTC Cadet Command
Army ROTC Scholarship
Fort Monroe, VA 23651-1052
800-USA-ROTC (toll-free)
www.goarmy.com/rotc/scholarships.jsp

United States Department of Health and Human Services, Bureau of Health Professions

Award Names: Nursing Scholarship

Program Description: Awards for U.S. citizens enrolled or accepted for enrollment as a full- or part-time student in an accredited school of nursing in a professional registered nurse program (baccalaureate, graduate, associate degree, or diploma)

Application Contact: Division of Nursing
U.S. Dept. of Health and Human Services
5600 Fishers Lane, Room 9-35
Parklawn Building
Rockville, MD 20857
301-443-5688
www.bhpr.hrsa.gov/dsa

How to Use This Guide

The following includes an overview of the various components of *Peterson's Nursing Programs 2011,* along with background information on the criteria used for including institutions and nursing programs in the guide, and explanatory material to help users interpret details presented within the guide.

Profiles of Nursing Programs

The **Profiles of Nursing Programs** section contains detailed profiles of schools that responded to our online survey and the nursing programs they offer. This section is organized geographically; U.S. schools are listed alphabetically by state or territory, followed by Canadian schools listed alphabetically by province.

The profiles contain basic information about the colleges and universities, along with details specific to the nursing school or department, the nursing student body, and the nursing programs offered.

Schools that are members of a consortium appear with an abbreviated profile. The abbreviated profile lists only the school heading and the specific college or university information, followed by a reference line that refers readers to the consortium profile, which contains detailed program information.

An outline of the profile follows. The items of information found under each section heading are defined and displayed. Any item discussed below that is omitted from an individual profile either does not apply to that particular college or university or is one for which no information was supplied. Each profile begins with a heading with the name of the institution (the college or university), the nursing college or unit, the location of the nursing facilities, the school's Web address, and the institution's founding date, specifically the year in which it was chartered or the year when instruction actually began, whichever date is earlier. In most cases, the location is identical to the main campus of the institution. However, in a few instances, the nursing facilities are not located in the same city or state as the main campus of the college or university.

Basic information about the college follows:

Nursing Program Faculty: The total number of full-time and part-time faculty members, followed by, if provided, the percentage of faculty members holding doctoral degrees.

Baccalaureate Enrollment: The total number of matriculated full-time and part-time baccalaureate program students as of fall 2009 is given. This snapshot of the nursing student body indicates the total number of matriculated students, both full-time and part-time, in the baccalaureate-level nursing program; the school's estimate of the percentage of nursing students in each of the following categories is provided, if applicable: **Women, Men, Minority, International,** and **Part-time.**

Graduate Enrollment: The total number of matriculated full-time and part-time students in graduate programs in fall 2009 and the percentages of **Women, Men, Minority, International,** and **Part-time** students are given.

Distance Learning Courses: This section appears if distance learning courses are available.

Nursing Student Activities: This section lists organizations open only to nursing students, including nursing clubs, Sigma Theta Tau (the international honor society for nursing), recruiter clubs, and Student Nurses' Association.

Nursing Student Resources: This section lists special learning resources available for nursing students within the nursing school's (or unit's) facilities.

Library Facilities: Figures are provided for the total number of bound volumes held by the college or university, the number of those volumes in health-related subjects, and the number in nursing and the number of periodical subscriptions held and the number of those in health-related subjects.

BACCALAUREATE PROGRAMS

Degree: Baccalaureate degree or degrees awarded are specified.

Available Programs: If, in addition to a generic baccalaureate program in nursing, a school has other baccalaureate nursing programs (e.g., accelerated programs or programs for RNs, LPNs, or college graduates with non-nursing degrees) they are specified here.

Site Options: Locations other than the nursing program's main campus at which baccalaureate programs may be taken are listed. Off-campus classes generally are held in health-care facilities or other educational facilities that are part of or affiliated with the college or nursing school.

Study Options: Lists full-time and part-time options.

Online Degree Options: This section appears if online baccalaureate degrees are available. It also specifies if the distance learning options are only available online.

Program Entrance Requirements: Lists special requirements typically required to enter a program of nursing leading to a baccalaureate degree, including completion of a specific program of prerequisite courses, sometimes called prenursing courses. These are specific course credits that must be earned by students who wish to enter the generic baccalaureate program. Students entering into other tracks may be required to prove that they have completed analogous courses. Often the minimum GPA requirement for prerequisite courses differs from that expected for general college courses. Other requirements are generally self-explanatory. This paragraph also indicates if transfer students are accepted into the program. Special tracks will require appropriate proof of experience, diplomas, or other credentials. Finally, application deadlines and fees are given.

Advanced Placement: This entry indicates that program credits may be granted on the basis of examinations or evaluations of earned credits at other facilities by the program's faculty and administrators.

Expenses: In this section, figures are provided for tuition, mandatory and other fees, and room and board, as well as an estimate of costs for books and supplies, based on the 2009–10 academic year. If a school did not return a survey, expenses for the 2007–08 or 2008–09 academic year are listed. Unless otherwise indicated, tuition is for one full academic year. If applicable, distinct tuition figures are given for state residents and nonresidents. Part-time, summer, and evening tuition is expressed in terms of the per-unit rate (per credit, per semester hour, etc.) specified by the institution. The tuition structure at some institutions is very complex, with different rates for freshmen and sophomores than for juniors and seniors or with part-time tuition prorated on a sliding scale according to the number of credit hours taken. Mandatory fees include such items as activity fees, health insurance, and malpractice insurance.

Financial Aid: This section combines data from our online nursing survey with data received on available financial aid programs. It provides information on college-administered aid for baccalaureate-level students, including the percentage of undergraduate nursing students receiving financial aid, all types of aid offered, and application deadlines. Financial aid programs are organized into these categories: gift aid (need-based), awards based on a student's formally designated inability to pay some or all of the cost of education; gift aid (non-need-based), scholarships given on the basis of a student's special achievements, abilities, or personal characteristics; loans, subsidized low-interest student loans that can be need-based or not; and work-study, a need-based program of part-time work offered to help pay educational expenditures. The application deadline is the deadline by which application forms and need calculations, such as the FAFSA, must be submitted to the institution in order to qualify for need-based and institutional aid.

Contact: This section lists the name, title, mailing address, telephone number, and, if available, fax number and e-mail address of the person to contact for admission information about the baccalaureate program.

GRADUATE PROGRAMS

The first three paragraphs provide information that is common to the college's graduate programs in nursing.

Expenses: In this section, figures are provided for tuition, room and board, and required fees based on the 2009–10 academic year. If a school did not return a survey, expenses for the 2007–08 or 2008–09 academic year are listed. Unless otherwise indicated, tuition is for one full academic year. If applicable, distinct tuition figures are given for state residents and nonresidents. Part-time, summer, and evening tuition is expressed in terms of the per-unit rate (per credit, per semester hour, etc.) specified by the institution.

Financial Aid: This section combines data from our online nursing survey with data received on available financial aid programs. It provides information on college-administered aid including the percentage of graduate nursing students receiving financial aid, all types of aid offered, and application deadlines. The major kinds of aid available are listed, including traineeships, low-interest student loans, fellowships, research assistantships, teaching assistantships, and full and partial tuition waivers. If aid is available to part-time students, this is indicated. The application deadline is the deadline by which application forms must be submitted to the college's financial aid office.

Contact: Lists the name, title, mailing address, telephone number, and, if available, fax number and e-mail address of the person to contact for admission information about graduate programs.

MASTER'S DEGREE PROGRAM

Degree(s): Master's degree or degrees awarded are specified. Joint degrees specify which two degrees are given, e.g., M.S.N./Ed. D., M.S.N./M.B.A., M.S./M.H.A., M.S.N./M.P.H., in programs that combine a master's degree (or doctorate) in nursing with a master's degree in another discipline, such as business administration, hospital administration, or public health.

Available Programs: If a college has special tracks that give credit, accelerated programs, or advanced courses designed for students with previous nursing experience or higher education credentials that enable students to complete programs in less time than regularly required, these are specified here in three categories:

1 For RNs—programs that admit registered nurses with associate degrees or diplomas in nursing and award a master's degree. These include RN-to-master's programs that combine the baccalaureate and master's degrees into one program for nurses who are graduates of associate or hospital diploma programs and programs that admit registered nurses with non-nursing baccalaureate degrees.

② For LPNs—programs that admit licensed practical nurses and award a master's degree.

③ For College Graduates with Non-Nursing Degrees—programs that admit students with baccalaureate or master's degrees in areas other than nursing and award a master's degree in nursing.

Concentrations Available: Specific areas of study and concentrations offered by the school are listed. Areas of specialization in case management, health-care administration, legal nurse consultant, nurse anesthesia, nurse-midwifery, nursing administration, nursing education, and nursing informatics are noted. Clinical nurse specialist and nurse practitioner programs and areas of specialization within them are noted.

Site Options: Locations other than the nursing program's main campus at which the master's degree programs are offered are listed. Off-campus classes generally are held in health-care facilities or other educational facilities that are part of or affiliated with the nursing school.

Study Options: Lists full-time and part-time options.

Online Degree Options: This section appears if online master's degrees are available. It also specifies if the distance learning options are only available online.

Program Entrance Requirements: Lists generally self-explanatory requirements.

Advanced Placement: Indicates that program credits may be granted on the basis of examinations or evaluations of earned credits at other facilities by the program's faculty and administrators.

Degree Requirements: Indicates the number of master's program credit hours required to earn the master's degree and the need for a thesis or qualifying score on a comprehensive examination.

POST-MASTER'S PROGRAM

Areas of Study: Listed here are the specific areas of clinical nurse specialist programs, nurse practitioner programs, and other specializations offered as post-master's programs.

DOCTORAL DEGREE PROGRAM

Degree: Doctoral degree awarded is specified.

Areas of Study: Lists specific areas of study and concentration offered by the school.

Program Entrance Requirements: Lists generally self-explanatory requirements.

Degree Requirements: Indicates the number of program credit hours required to earn the doctorate and the need for a dissertation, oral examination, written examination, or residency.

POSTDOCTORAL PROGRAM

Areas of Study: Lists areas of study currently reported. These may change, dependent upon the individuals in the program.

Postdoctoral Program Contact: Lists the name, title, mailing address, telephone number, and, if available, fax number and e-mail address of the person to contact for information about postdoctoral programs.

CONTINUING EDUCATION PROGRAM

Contact: The appearance of this heading indicates that the nursing school has a program of continuing education. If provided, the name, title, mailing address, telephone number, fax number, and e-mail address of the person to contact regarding the program are given.

Announcements

Announcements, which appear within some institutions' profiles, have been written by those colleges or universities that wished to supplement the profile data with timely or important information about their institutions or nursing programs. Some chose to mention degree programs that are not yet accredited.

Close-Ups of Nursing Programs

The **Close-Ups of Nursing Programs** section is an open forum for nursing schools to communicate their particular message to prospective students. The absence of any college or university from this section does not constitute an editorial decision on the part of Peterson's. Those who have chosen to write these inclusions are responsible for the accuracy of the content. Statements regarding a school's objectives and accomplishments represent its own beliefs and are not the opinions of the editors. The **Close-Ups of Nursing Programs** are arranged alphabetically by the official institution name.

Indexes

Indexes at the back of the book provide references to profiles by baccalaureate, master's, doctoral, post-doctoral, online, and continuing education programs offered; for master's-level programs, by area of study or concentration; and by institution name.

Abbreviations Used in This Guide

AACN	American Association of Colleges of Nursing
AACSB	AACSB International—The Association to Advance Collegiate Schools of Business
AAHC	Association of Academic Health Centers
AAS	Associate in Applied Science
ABSN	Accelerated Bachelor of Science in Nursing
ACT	American College Testing, Inc.
ACT ASSET	American College Testing Assessment of Skills for Successful Entry and Transfer
ACT COMP	American College Testing College Outcomes Measures Program
ACT PEP	American College Testing Proficiency Examination Program
AD	Associate Degree
ADN	Associate Degree in Nursing
AHNP	Adult Health Nurse Practitioner
ALE	American Language Exam
AMEDD	Army Medical Department
ANA	American Nurses Association
ANP	Adult Nurse Practitioner
APN	Advanced Practice Nurse
ARNP	Advanced Registered Nurse Practitioner
AS	Associate of Science
ASN	Associate of Science in Nursing
BA	Bachelor of Arts
BAA	Bachelor of Applied Arts
BN	Bachelor of Nursing
BNSc	Bachelor of Nursing Science
BRN	Baccalaureate for the Registered Nurse
BS	Bachelor of Science
BScMH	Bachelor of Science in Mental Health
BScN	Bachelor of Science in Nursing
BSEd	Bachelor of Science in Education
BSN	Bachelor of Science in Nursing
CAI	computer-assisted instruction
CAUSN	Canadian Association of University Schools of Nursing
CCNE	Commission on Collegiate Nursing Education
CCRN	Critical-Care Registered Nurse
CFNP	Certified Family Nurse Practitioner
CGFNS	Commission on Graduates of Foreign Nursing Schools
CINAHL	Cumulative Index to Nursing and Allied Health Literature
CLAST	College-Level Academic Skills Test
CLEP	College-Level Examination Program
CNA	Certified Nurse Assistant, Certified Nursing Assistant, Certified Nurses' Aide
CNAT	Canadian Nurses Association Testing
CNL	Clinical Nurse Leader
CNM	Certified Nurse-Midwife
CNS	Clinical Nurse Specialist
CODEC	coder/decoder
CPR	cardiopulmonary resuscitation
CRNA	Certified Registered Nurse Anesthetist
CS	Certified Specialist
CSS	College Scholarship Service
DNP	Doctor of Nursing Practice
DNS	Doctor of Nursing Science
DNSc	Doctor of Nursing Science
DOE	U.S. Department of Education
DrPH	Doctor of Public Health
DSN	Doctor of Science in Nursing
EdD	Doctor of Education
EFC	expected family contribution
ERIC	Educational Resources Information Center
ESL	English as a second language
ETN	Enterostomal Nurse
FAAN	Fellow in the American Academy of Nursing
FAF	Financial Aid Form
FAFSA	Free Application for Federal Student Aid
FC	family contribution
FNP	Family Nurse Practitioner
FSEOG	Federal Supplemental Educational Opportunity Grants
GED	General Educational Development test
GMAT	Graduate Management Admission Test
GPA	grade point average
GPO	Government Printing Office
GRE	Graduate Record Examinations
Gyn	gynecology
HIV	human immunodeficiency virus
HMO	health maintenance organization
ICEOP	Illinois Consortium for Educational Opportunities Program
ICU	intensive care unit
ISP	Internet service provider
ITV	interactive television
LD	Licensed Dietician
LPN	Licensed Practical Nurse
LVN	Licensed Vocational Nurse
MA	Master of Arts
MAEd	Master of Arts in Education
MAT	Miller Analogies Test
MBA	Master of Business Administration
MCSc	Master of Clinical Science
MDiv	Master of Divinity
MEd	Master of Education
MEDLINE	MEDLARS On-Line
MELAB	Michigan English Language Assessment Battery
MHA	Master of Hospital Administration Master of Health Administration
MHD	Master of Human Development
MHSA	Master of Health Services Administration
MN	Master of Nursing
MNSc	Master of Nursing Science
MOM	Master of Organizational Management

MPA	Master of Public Affairs
MPH	Master of Public Health
MPS	Master of Public Service
MS	Master of Science
MSBA	Master of Science in Business Administration
M Sc	Master of Science
MSc(A)	Master of Science (Applied)
MScN	Master of Science in Nursing
MTS	Master of Theological Studies
MSEd	Master of Science in Education
MSN	Master of Science in Nursing
MSOB	Master of Science in Organizational Behavior
NCAA	National Collegiate Athletic Association
NCLEX-RN	National Council Licensure Examination for Registered Nurses
ND	Doctor of Nursing
NLN	National League for Nursing
NNP	Neonatal Nurse Practitioner
NP	Nurse Practitioner
NSNA	National Student Nurses' Association
OB	Organizational Behavior
OB/GYN	obstetrics/gynecology
OCLC	Online Computer Library Center
OM	Organizational Management
PEP	Proficiency Examination Program
PhD	Doctor of Philosophy
PHEAA	Pennsylvania Higher Education Assistance Agency
PHS	Public Health Service
PLUS	Parents' Loan for Undergraduate Students
PNNP	Perinatal Nurse Practitioner
PNP	Pediatric Nurse Practitioner
PSAT	Preliminary SAT
RD	Registered Dietician
RN	Registered Nurse
RN, C	Registered Nurse, Certified
RN, CAN	Registered Nurse, Certified in Nursing Administration
RN, CNAA	Registered Nurse, Certified in Nursing Administration, Advanced
RN, CS	Registered Nurse, Certified Specialist
ROTC	Reserve Officers' Training Corps
RPN	Registered Psychiatric Nurse
SAR	Student Aid Report
SAT	SAT and SAT Subject Tests
SLS	Supplemental Loans to Students
SNA	Student Nurses' Association
SNAP	Student Nurses Acting for Progress
SNO	Student Nurses Organization
SUNY	State University of New York
TAP	Tuition Assistance Program
TB	tuberculosis
TOEFL	Test of English as a Foreign Language
TSE	Test of Spoken English
TWE	Test of Written English
USIS	United States Information Service
WHNP	Women's Health Nurse Practitioner

Data Collection Procedures

The data contained in the preponderant number of nursing college profiles, as well as in the indexes to them, were collected through *Peterson's Survey of Nursing Programs* during winter 2009-10. Questionnaires were posted online for more than 700 colleges and universities with baccalaureate and graduate programs in nursing. With minor exceptions, data for those colleges or schools of nursing that responded to the questionnaires were submitted by officials at the schools themselves. All usable information received in time for publication has been included. The omission of a particular item from a profile means that it is either not applicable to that institution or was not available or usable. In the handful of instances in which no information regarding an eligible nursing program was submitted and research of reliable secondary sources was unable to elicit the desired information, the name, location, and some general information regarding the nursing program appear in the profile section to indicate the existence of the program. Because of the extensive system of checks performed on the data collected by Peterson's, we believe that the information presented in this guide is accurate. Nonetheless, errors and omissions are possible in a data collection and processing endeavor of this scope. Also, facts and figures, such as tuition and fees, can suddenly change. Therefore, students should check with a specific college or university at the time of application to verify all pertinent information.

Criteria for Inclusion in This Book

Peterson's Nursing Programs 2011 covers accredited institutions in the U.S., U.S. territories, and Canada that grant baccalaureate and graduate degrees. The institutions that sponsor the nursing programs must be accredited by accrediting agencies approved by the U.S. Department of Education (USDE) or the Council for Higher Education Accreditation (CHEA) or be candidates for accreditation with an agency recognized by the USDE for its preaccreditation category. Canadian schools may be provincially chartered instead of accredited.

Baccalaureate-level and master's-level nursing programs represented by a profile within the guide are accredited by the National League for Nursing Accrediting Commission (NLNAC) or the Commission on Collegiate Nursing Education (CCNE). Canadian nursing schools are members of the Canadian Association of University Schools of Nursing (CAUSN).

Doctoral, postdoctoral, continuing education, and other nursing programs included in the profiles are offered by nursing schools or departments affiliated with colleges or universities that meet the criteria outlined above.

QUICK-REFERENCE CHART

Nursing Programs At-a-Glance

	Baccalaureate	Master's	Accelerated	Joint Degree	Post-Master's	Doctoral	Postdoctoral	Continuing Education
UNITED STATES								
Alabama								
Auburn University	•	•						
Auburn University Montgomery	•	•						
Jacksonville State University	•	•						•
Oakwood University	•							
Samford University	•	•		•	•	•		•
Spring Hill College	•	•	M					
Troy University	•	•			•			
Tuskegee University	•							
The University of Alabama	•	•			•	•		
The University of Alabama at Birmingham	•	•	M	•	•	•		
The University of Alabama in Huntsville	•	•			•	•		•
University of Mobile	•	•						•
University of North Alabama	•	•						•
University of South Alabama	•	•	B,M		•			
Alaska								
University of Alaska Anchorage	•	•						
Arizona								
Arizona State University at the Downtown Phoenix Campus	•	•	B	•	•	•		•
Grand Canyon University	•	•	B	•	•			•
Northern Arizona University	•	•	B		•			
The University of Arizona	•		B			•	•	
University of Phoenix	•	•	B	•	•	•		•
University of Phoenix-Phoenix Campus	•	•	B	•	•			•
University of Phoenix-Southern Arizona Campus	•	•	B		•			•
Arkansas								
Arkansas State University	•	•						
Arkansas Tech University	•	•						
Harding University	•							•
Henderson State University	•							
Southern Arkansas University-Magnolia	•							
University of Arkansas	•	•						•
University of Arkansas at Fort Smith	•							
University of Arkansas at Monticello	•							
University of Arkansas at Pine Bluff	•							
University of Arkansas for Medical Sciences	•	•	B			•	•	•
University of Central Arkansas	•	•			•			
California								
Azusa Pacific University	•	•	B,M		•	•		•
Biola University	•							
California Baptist University	•		B					
California State University, Bakersfield	•							•
California State University Channel Islands	•							
California State University, Chico	•	•			•			•
California State University, Dominguez Hills	•	•			•			•

B = Baccalaureate; M = Master's

California (continued)	Baccalaureate	Master's	Accelerated	Joint Degree	Post-Master's	Doctoral	Postdoctoral	Continuing Education
California State University, East Bay	•		B					
California State University, Fresno	•	•	M		•			•
California State University, Fullerton	•	•	M					•
California State University, Long Beach	•	•	M	•	•			
California State University, Los Angeles	•	•	M		•			
California State University, Northridge	•		B					
California State University, Sacramento	•	•						
California State University, San Bernardino	•	•						
California State University, San Marcos	•		B					
California State University, Stanislaus	•							
Dominican University of California	•	•						•
Fresno Pacific University	•							
Holy Names University	•	•		•	•			
Humboldt State University	•							
Loma Linda University	•	•	B,M	•	•	•		
Mount St. Mary's College	•	•	B					
National University	•		B					
Pacific Union College	•							•
Point Loma Nazarene University	•	•			•			•
Samuel Merritt University	•	•	B		•			
San Diego State University	•	•	B		•			•
San Francisco State University	•	•	B,M		•			•
San Jose State University	•	•						
Sonoma State University	•	•	M		•			
University of California, Irvine	•							
University of California, Los Angeles	•	•		•	•	•	•	•
University of California, San Francisco		•			•	•	•	
University of Phoenix-Bay Area Campus	•	•	B	•				
University of Phoenix-Central Valley Campus	•							
University of Phoenix-Sacramento Valley Campus	•	•	B,M		•			•
University of Phoenix-San Diego Campus	•	•	B					
University of Phoenix-Southern California Campus	•	•	B	•	•			•
University of San Diego		•	M	•		•		
University of San Francisco	•	•	M			•		
West Coast University	•		B					
Western University of Health Sciences		•	M		•	•		
Colorado								
Adams State College	•							
Colorado State University-Pueblo	•	•	B		•			
Mesa State College	•							
Metropolitan State College of Denver	•							
Platt College	•		B					
Regis University	•	•	B					
University of Colorado at Colorado Springs	•	•	B		•	•		•
University of Colorado Denver	•	•			•	•	•	•
University of Northern Colorado	•	•	B		•	•		
University of Phoenix-Denver Campus	•	•	B					
University of Phoenix-Southern Colorado Campus								
Connecticut								
Central Connecticut State University	•							
Fairfield University	•	•	B		•			•

B = Baccalaureate; M = Master's

	Baccalaureate	Master's	Accelerated	Joint Degree	Post-Master's	Doctoral	Postdoctoral	Continuing Education
Connecticut *(continued)*								
Quinnipiac University	•	•	B		•			•
Sacred Heart University	•	•		•	•	•		
Saint Joseph College	•	•	B		•			
Southern Connecticut State University	•	•	B		•			
University of Connecticut	•	•	M	•	•	•		•
University of Hartford	•	•		•	•			•
Western Connecticut State University	•	•			•			
Yale University		•		•	•	•	•	
Delaware								
Delaware State University	•							
University of Delaware	•	•	B		•			
Wesley College	•	•	M		•			•
Wilmington University	•	•	B,M	•	•			
District of Columbia								
The Catholic University of America	•	•	B	•	•	•		
Georgetown University	•	•	B		•			
The George Washington University								
Howard University	•	•	B		•			
Trinity (Washington) University	•							
University of the District of Columbia	•							
Florida								
Barry University	•	•	B	•	•	•		
Bethune-Cookman University	•							
Florida Agricultural and Mechanical University	•	•			•	•		•
Florida Atlantic University	•	•	B	•	•	•		•
Florida Gulf Coast University	•	•			•			•
Florida Hospital College of Health Sciences	•							
Florida International University	•	•	B,M		•	•		
Florida Southern College	•	•	M		•			•
Florida State University	•	•	B		•	•		
Indian River State College	•							
Jacksonville University	•	•	B	•	•			
Nova Southeastern University	•	•		•				
Palm Beach Atlantic University	•							
St. Petersburg College	•							•
South University	•	•						
University of Central Florida	•	•	B		•	•		
University of Florida	•	•	B	•	•	•		
University of Miami	•	•	B		•	•		•
University of North Florida	•	•	B		•			
University of Phoenix–Central Florida Campus	•	•	B					
University of Phoenix–North Florida Campus	•	•	B					
University of Phoenix–South Florida Campus	•	•		•				
University of Phoenix–West Florida Campus	•		B					
University of South Florida	•	•	B	•	•	•		•
The University of Tampa	•	•			•			•
University of West Florida	•							
Georgia								
Albany State University	•	•	B,M		•			
Armstrong Atlantic State University	•	•		•	•			

B = Baccalaureate; M = Master's

	Baccalaureate	Master's	Accelerated	Joint Degree	Post-Master's	Doctoral	Postdoctoral	Continuing Education
Georgia (*continued*)								
Brenau University	•	•	M		•			•
Clayton State University	•	•						
Columbus State University	•							
Emory University	•	•		•	•	•		
Georgia Baptist College of Nursing of Mercer University	•	•			•	•		
Georgia College & State University	•	•		•	•			
Georgia Southern University	•	•	·		•	•		
Georgia Southwestern State University	•		B					
Georgia State University	•	•			•	•		
Kennesaw State University	•	•	B					•
LaGrange College	•							
Macon State College	•							
Medical College of Georgia	•	•	M		•	•		
North Georgia College & State University	•	•			•			
Piedmont College	•							
Shorter College	•							
Thomas University	•	•	B	•	•			
University of Phoenix–Atlanta Campus								
University of West Georgia	•	•			•			
Valdosta State University	•	•						•
Guam								
University of Guam	•							
Hawaii								
Hawai'i Pacific University	•	•		•	•			
University of Hawaii at Hilo	•							
University of Hawaii at Manoa	•	•	M	•	•	•		
University of Phoenix–Hawaii Campus	•	•	B					
Idaho								
Boise State University	•	•	B					
Idaho State University	•	•	B,M		•			
Lewis-Clark State College	•							
Northwest Nazarene University	•	•						
Illinois								
Aurora University	•	•						
Benedictine University	•	•	B,M					
Blessing-Rieman College of Nursing	•	•	B					
Bradley University	•	•	M					
Chicago State University	•							
DePaul University	•	•	B		•			
Eastern Illinois University	•							
Elmhurst College	•	•		•				
Governors State University	•	•			•			
Illinois State University	•	•	B		•	•		
Illinois Wesleyan University	•							
Lakeview College of Nursing	•		B					
Lewis University	•	•	B,M	•	•			•
Loyola University Chicago	•	•	B	•		•		
MacMurray College	•							
McKendree University	•	•						
Methodist College of Nursing	•		B					

B = Baccalaureate; M = Master's

Illinois (continued)	Baccalaureate	Master's	Accelerated	Joint Degree	Post-Master's	Doctoral	Postdoctoral	Continuing Education
Millikin University	•	•	M					
Northern Illinois University	•	•		•	•			
North Park University	•	•		•	•			
Olivet Nazarene University	•	•	B					
Rockford College	•							
Rush University		•			•	•		•
Saint Anthony College of Nursing	•	•			•			
Saint Francis Medical Center College of Nursing	•	•	B			•		
St. John's College	•							
Saint Xavier University	•	•		•	•			•
Southern Illinois University Edwardsville	•	•	B		•			•
Trinity Christian College	•							
Trinity College of Nursing and Health Sciences	•		B					
University of Illinois at Chicago	•	•		•	•	•	•	•
University of St. Francis	•	•	B		•	•		
Western Illinois University	•							
West Suburban College of Nursing	•	•	B,M		•			
Indiana								
Anderson University	•	•		•	•			
Ball State University	•	•	B		•	•		
Bethel College	•	•			•			
Goshen College	•							
Huntington University	•							
Indiana State University	•	•			•			•
Indiana University Bloomington	•							
Indiana University East	•							
Indiana University Kokomo	•		B					•
Indiana University Northwest	•							
Indiana University–Purdue University Fort Wayne	•	•			•			•
Indiana University–Purdue University Indianapolis	•	•	B	•	•	•	•	•
Indiana University South Bend	•	•	B					
Indiana University Southeast	•							
Indiana Wesleyan University	•	•	B		•			
Marian University	•		B					
Purdue University	•	•	B		•	•		•
Purdue University Calumet	•	•	B,M		•			
Purdue University North Central	•							
Saint Mary's College	•		B					
University of Evansville	•							
University of Indianapolis	•	•	B,M	•	•			•
University of Saint Francis	•	•			•			
University of Southern Indiana	•	•			•	•		•
Valparaiso University	•		B	•	•			•
Vincennes University	•							
Iowa								
Allen College	•	•	B		•			•
Briar Cliff University	•	•						•
Clarke College	•	•			•			•
Coe College	•							
Dordt College	•							
Grand View University	•							•

B = Baccalaureate; M = Master's

	Baccalaureate	Master's	Accelerated	Joint Degree	Post-Master's	Doctoral	Postdoctoral	Continuing Education
Iowa (*continued*)								
Iowa Wesleyan College	•							
Luther College	•							•
Mercy College of Health Sciences	•							
Morningside College	•							
Mount Mercy College	•		B					•
Northwestern College	•							
St. Ambrose University	•	•						
University of Dubuque	•							
The University of Iowa	•	•	M	•	•	•	•	•
Upper Iowa University	•							
Kansas								
Baker University	•							
Bethel College	•							
Emporia State University	•							
Fort Hays State University	•	•			•			
Kansas Wesleyan University	•							
MidAmerica Nazarene University	•		B					•
Newman University	•							
Pittsburg State University	•	•			•			•
Southwestern College	•		B					
Tabor College	•		B					
The University of Kansas	•	•	M	•	•	•	•	•
University of Saint Mary	•							
Washburn University	•	•			•			•
Wichita State University	•	•	B	•	•	•		
Kentucky								
Bellarmine University	•	•	B	•	•			•
Berea College	•							•
Eastern Kentucky University	•	•	B					
Frontier School of Midwifery and Family Nursing		•	M			•		
Kentucky Christian University	•							
Kentucky State University	•							
Midway College	•		B					•
Morehead State University	•							
Murray State University	•	•			•			•
Northern Kentucky University	•	•	B		•			
Spalding University	•	•	B,M		•			•
Thomas More College	•							
University of Kentucky	•	•			•	•		•
University of Louisville	•	•	B		•	•	•	•
Western Kentucky University	•	•			•			•
Louisiana								
Dillard University	•							
Grambling State University	•	•			•			
Louisiana College	•							
Louisiana State University Health Sciences Center	•	•	B			•		•
Loyola University New Orleans	•	•			•			
McNeese State University	•	•			•			•
Nicholls State University	•							•
Northwestern State University of Louisiana	•	•			•			•
Our Lady of Holy Cross College	•							

B = Baccalaureate; M = Master's

Louisiana *(continued)*	Baccalaureate	Master's	Accelerated	Joint Degree	Post-Master's	Doctoral	Postdoctoral	Continuing Education
Our Lady of the Lake College	•	•						•
Southeastern Louisiana University	•	•	B					
Southern University and Agricultural and Mechanical College	•	•			•	•		
University of Louisiana at Lafayette	•	•	B		•			•
University of Louisiana at Monroe	•		B					•
University of Phoenix–Louisiana Campus	•		B					
Maine								
Husson University	•	•			•			
Saint Joseph's College of Maine	•	•						•
University of Maine	•	•						
University of Maine at Fort Kent	•		B					
University of New England	•		B					•
University of Southern Maine	•	•	B	•				•
Maryland								
Bowie State University	•	•	B					
College of Notre Dame of Maryland	•		B					
Columbia Union College	•		B					
Coppin State University	•	•	B		•			
The Johns Hopkins University	•	•	B	•	•	•	•	
Salisbury University	•	•	B		•			
Stevenson University	•		B					
Towson University	•	•						
University of Maryland, Baltimore	•	•	M	•	•	•		•
Massachusetts								
American International College	•	•						
Anna Maria College	•							•
Atlantic Union College	•							
Boston College	•	•	M	•	•	•		•
Curry College	•	•	B					
Elms College	•	•						
Emmanuel College	•							
Endicott College	•	•						•
Fitchburg State College	•	•			•			
Framingham State College	•	•						•
Massachusetts College of Pharmacy and Health Sciences	•		B					•
MGH Institute of Health Professions	•	•	B		•	•		
Northeastern University	•	•	M	•	•	•		•
Regis College	•	•	B,M		•	•		•
Salem State College	•	•	B,M	•				•
Simmons College	•	•	B,M		•	•		•
University of Massachusetts Amherst	•	•	B			•		•
University of Massachusetts Boston	•	•	B		•	•		•
University of Massachusetts Dartmouth	•	•			•	•		•
University of Massachusetts Lowell	•	•	M			•		
University of Massachusetts Worcester		•	M		•	•		•
Worcester State College	•	•						
Michigan								
Andrews University	•	•			•			
Calvin College	•							
Davenport University	•							

B = Baccalaureate; M = Master's

Michigan *(continued)*	Baccalaureate	Master's	Accelerated	Joint Degree	Post-Master's	Doctoral	Postdoctoral	Continuing Education
Eastern Michigan University	•	•						
Ferris State University	•	•	B,M	•				
Finlandia University	•							
Grand Valley State University	•	•	B		•	•		•
Hope College	•							
Lake Superior State University	•							
Madonna University	•	•	M	•	•			•
Michigan State University	•	•	B		•	•		•
Northern Michigan University	•	•	B		•			•
Oakland University	•	•			•			•
Saginaw Valley State University	•	•	B		•			•
Spring Arbor University	•	•		•				
University of Detroit Mercy	•	•	B,M		•			
University of Michigan	•	•	B,M	•	•	•	•	
University of Michigan–Flint	•		B			•		•
University of Phoenix–Metro Detroit Campus	•	•	B					
University of Phoenix–West Michigan Campus								
Wayne State University	•	•	B		•	•	•	•
Western Michigan University	•							
Minnesota								
Augsburg College	•	•						
Bemidji State University	•							•
Bethel University	•	•						
College of Saint Benedict	•							
The College of St. Scholastica	•	•	B		•	•		
Concordia College	•	•	B					
Crown College	•							
Globe University	•							
Gustavus Adolphus College	•							
Metropolitan State University	•	•			•			
Minnesota Intercollegiate Nursing Consortium	•							
Minnesota State University Mankato	•	•	B,M		•	•		•
Minnesota State University Moorhead	•	•				•		
St. Catherine University	•	•			•	•		
St. Cloud State University	•							
St. Olaf College	•							
University of Minnesota, Twin Cities Campus	•	•		•		•		•
Winona State University	•	•			•	•		
Mississippi								
Alcorn State University	•	•			•			
Delta State University	•	•	M		•			
Mississippi College	•							
Mississippi University for Women	•	•			•			
University of Mississippi Medical Center	•	•	B,M		•	•		•
University of Southern Mississippi	•	•			•	•		
William Carey University	•	•						
Missouri								
Avila University	•							
Central Methodist University	•	•						
Chamberlain College of Nursing	•		B					
College of the Ozarks	•							

B = Baccalaureate; M = Master's

	Baccalaureate	Master's	Accelerated	Joint Degree	Post-Master's	Doctoral	Postdoctoral	Continuing Education
Missouri *(continued)*								
Cox College of Nursing and Health Sciences	•		B					•
Goldfarb School of Nursing at Barnes-Jewish College	•	•	B		•	•		
Graceland University	•	•	B		•			
Lincoln University	•							
Maryville University of Saint Louis	•	•	B,M					
Missouri Southern State University	•	•						
Missouri State University	•	•	B,M		•			•
Missouri Western State University	•							
Research College of Nursing	•	•	B					
Saint Louis University	•	•	B	•	•	•		•
Saint Luke's College	•							
Southeast Missouri State University	•	•			•			
Southwest Baptist University	•							
Truman State University	•							
University of Central Missouri	•	•			•			
University of Missouri–Columbia	•	•	B	•	•	•		•
University of Missouri–Kansas City	•	•	B		•	•		•
University of Missouri–St. Louis	•	•	B		•	•		•
Webster University	•	•						
William Jewell College	•		B					
Montana								
Carroll College	•							
Montana State University	•	•			•			
Montana State University–Northern	•							
Salish Kootenai College	•							
Nebraska								
BryanLGH College of Health Sciences	•	•						
Clarkson College	•	•	B		•			•
College of Saint Mary	•							
Creighton University	•	•	B		•	•		
Midland Lutheran College	•							
Nebraska Methodist College	•	•	B		•			•
Nebraska Wesleyan University	•	•	B,M		•			
Union College	•							
University of Nebraska Medical Center	•	•	B		•	•	•	•
Nevada								
Great Basin College	•							
Nevada State College at Henderson	•		B					
Touro University	•	•	B		•	•		•
University of Nevada, Las Vegas	•	•	B		•	•		
University of Nevada, Reno	•	•	B	•	•			
University of Southern Nevada	•							
New Hampshire								
Colby-Sawyer College	•							
Franklin Pierce University	•	•						
Rivier College	•	•			•			
Saint Anselm College	•							•
University of New Hampshire	•	•			•			
New Jersey								
Bloomfield College	•							

B = Baccalaureate; M = Master's

	Baccalaureate	Master's	Accelerated	Joint Degree	Post-Master's	Doctoral	Postdoctoral	Continuing Education
New Jersey (continued)								
The College of New Jersey	•	•			•			
College of Saint Elizabeth	•		B					•
Fairleigh Dickinson University, Metropolitan Campus	•	•	B,M		•	•		•
Felician College	•	•	M	•	•			
Kean University	•	•	M	•				•
Monmouth University	•	•	M		•			•
New Jersey City University	•		B					
Ramapo College of New Jersey	•	•			•			•
The Richard Stockton College of New Jersey	•	•						
Rutgers, The State University of New Jersey, Camden College of Arts and Sciences	•		B					
Rutgers, The State University of New Jersey, College of Nursing	•	•	B	•	•	•		•
Saint Peter's College	•	•			•			
Seton Hall University	•	•	B,M	•	•	•		•
Thomas Edison State College	•	•						
University of Medicine and Dentistry of New Jersey	•	•	B	•	•	•		•
William Paterson University of New Jersey	•	•	B		•			
New Mexico								
Eastern New Mexico University	•							
New Mexico State University	•	•	B					•
University of New Mexico	•	•	B	•	•	•		
University of Phoenix-New Mexico Campus	•	•	B					
Western New Mexico University	•							
New York								
Adelphi University		•	B	•	•	•		•
The College at Brockport, State University of New York	•		B					
College of Mount Saint Vincent	•	•			•			
The College of New Rochelle	•	•	B		•			
College of Staten Island of the City University of New York	•	•			•			
Columbia University	•	•	B,M	•	•	•	•	•
Concordia College-New York	•							
Daemen College	•	•	B,M		•	•		
Dominican College	•	•	B					
D'Youville College	•	•			•			
Elmira College	•							•
Excelsior College	•	•				•		
Hartwick College	•		B					
Hunter College of the City University of New York	•	•		•	•			•
Keuka College	•		B					
Lehman College of the City University of New York	•		B			•		
Le Moyne College	•	•			•			
Long Island University, Brooklyn Campus	•	•			•			
Long Island University, C.W. Post Campus	•	•		•	•			
Medgar Evers College of the City University of New York	•		B					
Mercy College	•	•	B,M		•			
Molloy College	•	•	B		•			•
Mount Saint Mary College	•	•	B		•			
Nazareth College of Rochester	•	•			•			•
New York City College of Technology of the City University of New York	•							
New York University	•	•	B	•	•	•		•
Niagara University	•							

B = Baccalaureate; M = Master's

	Baccalaureate	Master's	Accelerated	Joint Degree	Post-Master's	Doctoral	Postdoctoral	Continuing Education
New York *(continued)*								
Pace University	•	•	B		•	•		
Roberts Wesleyan College	•	•	B,M		•			
The Sage Colleges	•	•	B,M		•	•		•
St. Francis College	•							
St. John Fisher College	•	•	B		•	•		
St. Joseph's College, New York	•	•						
State University of New York at Binghamton	•	•	B		•	•		•
State University of New York at Plattsburgh	•							
State University of New York College of Agriculture and Technology at Morrisville	•							
State University of New York Downstate Medical Center	•	•	B	•	•			•
State University of New York Empire State College	•							
State University of New York Institute of Technology	•	•	B,M		•			•
State University of New York Upstate Medical University	•	•	M		•			•
Stony Brook University, State University of New York	•	•	B		•			•
Teachers College, Columbia University						•		
University at Buffalo, the State University of New York	•	•	B		•	•		
University of Rochester	•	•	B,M	•	•	•	•	•
Utica College	•							
Wagner College	•	•			•			
York College of the City University of New York	•							
North Carolina								
Appalachian State University	•							
Barton College	•							
Cabarrus College of Health Sciences	•							
Duke University	•	•	B	•	•	•		
East Carolina University	•	•	M		•	•		
Fayetteville State University	•							
Gardner-Webb University	•	•		•				
Lees-McRae College	•							
Lenoir-Rhyne University	•							
North Carolina Agricultural and Technical State University	•							
North Carolina Central University	•							
Queens University of Charlotte	•	•	B,M	•	•			•
The University of North Carolina at Chapel Hill	•	•	B		•	•	•	•
The University of North Carolina at Charlotte	•	•			•			
The University of North Carolina at Greensboro	•	•		•	•	•		
The University of North Carolina at Pembroke	•							
The University of North Carolina Wilmington	•	•			•			•
Western Carolina University	•	•	B		•			
Winston-Salem State University	•	•	B					•
North Dakota								
Dickinson State University	•							
Jamestown College	•							
Medcenter One College of Nursing	•							
Minot State University	•							
North Dakota State University	•	•				•		
University of Mary	•	•		•				
University of North Dakota	•	•	B		•	•		
Ohio								
Ashland University	•		B					

B = Baccalaureate; M = Master's

	Baccalaureate	Master's	Accelerated	Joint Degree	Post-Master's	Doctoral	Postdoctoral	Continuing Education
Ohio (continued)								
Capital University	•	•	B	•	•			
Case Western Reserve University	•	•	M	•	•	•	•	•
Cedarville University	•							
Cleveland State University	•	•	B	•	•			•
College of Mount St. Joseph	•	•	B,M					
Franciscan University of Steubenville	•	•						
Kent State University	•	•	B,M	•	•	•		•
Kettering College of Medical Arts	•							
Lourdes College	•							
Malone University	•	•						
MedCentral College of Nursing	•		B					
Mercy College of Northwest Ohio	•							•
Miami University	•							
Mount Carmel College of Nursing	•	•	B		•			
Mount Vernon Nazarene University	•							
Muskingum University	•							
Notre Dame College	•							
Ohio Northern University	•							
The Ohio State University	•	•	B,M	•	•	•		
Ohio University	•	•						
Otterbein College	•	•	B		•			•
Shawnee State University	•							•
The University of Akron	•	•	B		•	•		•
University of Cincinnati	•	•	B,M	•	•	•		•
University of Phoenix–Cleveland Campus	•	•	B					
University of Rio Grande	•							
The University of Toledo	•	•			•	•		•
Urbana University	•	•						
Ursuline College	•	•	B,M		•			
Walsh University	•		B					
Wright State University	•	•	B	•	•	•		•
Xavier University	•	•		•				
Youngstown State University	•	•						
Oklahoma								
Bacone College	•		B					
East Central University	•							
Langston University	•							
Northeastern State University	•		B					
Northwestern Oklahoma State University	•		B					
Oklahoma Baptist University	•	•						
Oklahoma Christian University	•							
Oklahoma City University	•	•	B	•		•		•
Oklahoma Panhandle State University	•							
Oklahoma Wesleyan University	•		B					
Oral Roberts University	•							
Rogers State University	•							
Southern Nazarene University	•	•	M					
Southwestern Oklahoma State University	•							
University of Central Oklahoma	•							
University of Oklahoma Health Sciences Center	•	•	B		•	•		•
University of Phoenix–Oklahoma City Campus								
University of Phoenix–Tulsa Campus								

B = Baccalaureate; M = Master's

	Baccalaureate	Master's	Accelerated	Joint Degree	Post-Master's	Doctoral	Postdoctoral	Continuing Education
Oklahoma (*continued*)								
University of Tulsa	•							
Oregon								
Concordia University	•							
George Fox University	•							
Linfield College	•		B					•
Oregon Health & Science University	•	•	B	•	•	•	•	•
University of Portland	•	•				•		
Pennsylvania								
Alvernia University	•							•
Bloomsburg University of Pennsylvania	•	•		•	•			•
California University of Pennsylvania	•							
Carlow University	•	•	B,M		•			•
Cedar Crest College	•	•						
Chatham University	•	•				•		
Clarion University of Pennsylvania	•	•			•			
DeSales University	•	•	B,M	•	•			•
Drexel University	•	•	B		•	•		•
Duquesne University	•	•	B		•	•		•
Eastern University	•		B					
East Stroudsburg University of Pennsylvania	•							
Edinboro University of Pennsylvania	•		B					
Gannon University	•	•	M					
Gwynedd-Mercy College	•	•	B		•			
Holy Family University	•	•	B					•
Immaculata University	•	•	B					
Indiana University of Pennsylvania	•	•				•		
Kutztown University of Pennsylvania	•	•						
La Roche College	•	•	B					•
La Salle University	•	•		•	•			•
Mansfield University of Pennsylvania	•	•						
Marywood University	•	•		•				•
Messiah College	•							
Millersville University of Pennsylvania	•	•				•		•
Misericordia University	•	•	B		•			
Moravian College	•	•						•
Mount Aloysius College	•		B					•
Neumann University	•	•			•			
Penn State University Park	•	•		•	•	•	•	•
Pennsylvania College of Technology	•							
Robert Morris University	•	•				•		
Saint Francis University	•							
Slippery Rock University of Pennsylvania	•							
Temple University	•	•	B		•			
Thomas Jefferson University	•	•	B,M		•	•		•
University of Pennsylvania	•	•	B,M	•	•	•	•	•
University of Pittsburgh	•	•	B		•	•		•
University of Pittsburgh at Bradford	•							
The University of Scranton	•	•	B,M		•			
Villanova University	•	•	B,M		•			•
Waynesburg University	•	•	B,M	•		•		
West Chester University of Pennsylvania	•	•	B					

B = Baccalaureate; M = Master's

	Baccalaureate	Master's	Accelerated	Joint Degree	Post-Master's	Doctoral	Postdoctoral	Continuing Education
Pennsylvania (*continued*)								
Widener University	•	•		•	•	•		
Wilkes University	•	•	B,M		•			•
York College of Pennsylvania	•	•			•			
Puerto Rico								
Inter American University of Puerto Rico, Arecibo Campus	•							
Inter American University of Puerto Rico, Metropolitan Campus	•		B					
Pontifical Catholic University of Puerto Rico	•							
Universidad Adventista de las Antillas	•							•
Universidad del Turabo	•							
Universidad Metropolitana	•							
University of Puerto Rico at Arecibo	•							
University of Puerto Rico at Humacao	•							
University of Puerto Rico, Mayagüez Campus	•							•
University of Puerto Rico, Medical Sciences Campus	•	•						•
University of the Sacred Heart	•	•						
Rhode Island								
Rhode Island College	•							
Salve Regina University	•							•
University of Rhode Island	•	•			•	•		
South Carolina								
Charleston Southern University	•	•						
Clemson University	•	•			•			•
Francis Marion University	•							
Lander University	•		B					
Medical University of South Carolina	•	•	B		•	•	•	•
South Carolina State University	•							
University of South Carolina	•	•		•	•	•		•
University of South Carolina Aiken	•							•
University of South Carolina Beaufort	•							
University of South Carolina Upstate	•							
South Dakota								
Augustana College	•	•						
Mount Marty College	•		B					
National American University	•							
Presentation College	•							
South Dakota State University	•	•	B		•	•		•
Tennessee								
Aquinas College	•							
Austin Peay State University	•							
Baptist College of Health Sciences	•							
Belmont University	•	•	B		•			
Bethel University	•							
Carson-Newman College	•	•	B		•			
Cumberland University	•		B					
East Tennessee State University	•	•	B		•	•		
King College	•	•	B,M	•				
Lincoln Memorial University	•							
Lipscomb University	•							
Martin Methodist College	•							
Middle Tennessee State University	•	•	M		•			

B = Baccalaureate; M = Master's

	Baccalaureate	Master's	Accelerated	Joint Degree	Post-Master's	Doctoral	Postdoctoral	Continuing Education
Tennessee *(continued)*								
Milligan College	•							
South College	•							
Southern Adventist University	•	•	M	•				•
Tennessee State University	•	•			•			
Tennessee Technological University	•	•						
Tennessee Wesleyan College	•							
Union University	•	•	B		•			•
University of Memphis	•	•	B,M		•			
The University of Tennessee	•	•	B,M		•	•		•
The University of Tennessee at Chattanooga	•	•			•			•
The University of Tennessee at Martin	•							•
The University of Tennessee Health Science Center		•	M		•	•		
Vanderbilt University		•	M	•	•	•	•	•
Texas								
Angelo State University	•	•						
Baylor University	•	•	B		•	•		
East Texas Baptist University	•							
Houston Baptist University	•							
Lamar University	•	•		•	•			•
Lubbock Christian University	•							
Midwestern State University	•	•			•			•
Patty Hanks Shelton School of Nursing	•	•			•			•
Prairie View A&M University	•	•			•			
Southwestern Adventist University	•		B					
Stephen F. Austin State University	•							
Tarleton State University	•							•
Texas A&M International University	•	•						
Texas A&M University–Corpus Christi	•	•	B,M		•			•
Texas A&M University–Texarkana	•	•						
Texas Christian University	•	•	B		•	•		•
Texas Tech University Health Sciences Center	•	•	B		•	•		•
Texas Woman's University	•	•	B		•	•		
University of Houston–Victoria	•	•	B					
University of Mary Hardin-Baylor	•	•						•
The University of Texas at Arlington	•	•	B	•	•	•		•
The University of Texas at Austin	•	•		•	•	•	•	
The University of Texas at Brownsville	•	•						
The University of Texas at El Paso	•	•	B		•			
The University of Texas at Tyler	•	•	B,M	•	•	•		•
The University of Texas Health Science Center at Houston	•	•	B	•	•	•		
The University of Texas Health Science Center at San Antonio	•	•	B	•	•	•		
The University of Texas Medical Branch	•	•	B	•	•	•		
The University of Texas–Pan American	•	•			•			
University of the Incarnate Word	•	•		•	•			
West Texas A&M University	•	•			•			
Utah								
Brigham Young University	•					•		
Southern Utah University	•							
University of Phoenix–Utah Campus						•		
University of Utah	•	•	B		•	•	•	
Utah Valley University	•							

B = Baccalaureate; M = Master's

	Baccalaureate	Master's	Accelerated	Joint Degree	Post-Master's	Doctoral	Postdoctoral	Continuing Education
Utah (continued)								
Weber State University	•	•	B					
Westminster College	•	•			•			
Vermont								
Norwich University	•							
Southern Vermont College	•							
University of Vermont	•	•			•			
Virgin Islands								
University of the Virgin Islands	•							
Virginia								
Eastern Mennonite University	•							
ECPI College of Technology	•							
George Mason University	•	•	B	•	•	•		•
Hampton University	•	•	B		•	•		
James Madison University	•	•	B		•			
Jefferson College of Health Sciences	•	•						•
Liberty University	•	•						
Lynchburg College	•							
Marymount University	•	•	B		•	•		
Norfolk State University	•		B					
Old Dominion University	•	•	B		•	•		•
Radford University	•	•			•	•		
Shenandoah University	•	•	B		•			•
Stratford University	•							
University of Virginia	•	•		•	•	•	•	
The University of Virginia's College at Wise	•							
Virginia Commonwealth University	•	•	B,M		•	•	•	
Washington								
Gonzaga University	•	•	M		•			•
Intercollegiate College of Nursing/Washington State University	•	•	M		•	•		•
Northwest University	•							
Pacific Lutheran University	•	•	M	•				•
Seattle Pacific University	•	•			•			
Seattle University	•	•	M		•			
University of Washington	•	•	B	•	•	•	•	•
Walla Walla University	•							
West Virginia								
Alderson-Broaddus College	•							
Bluefield State College	•							
Fairmont State University	•		B					•
Marshall University	•	•	B		•			
Mountain State University	•	•	B		•			
Shepherd University	•							•
University of Charleston	•							
West Liberty University	•		B					
West Virginia University	•	•	B		•	•		•
West Virginia Wesleyan College	•	•						
Wheeling Jesuit University	•	•						
Wisconsin								
Alverno College	•	•						•

B = Baccalaureate; M = Master's

	Baccalaureate	Master's	Accelerated	Joint Degree	Post-Master's	Doctoral	Postdoctoral	Continuing Education
Wisconsin *(continued)*								
Bellin College	•	•	B					
Cardinal Stritch University	•	•	M					
Carroll University	•							
Columbia College of Nursing/Mount Mary College Nursing Program	•							
Concordia University Wisconsin	•	•			•	•		
Edgewood College	•	•	B	•				
Maranatha Baptist Bible College	•							
Marian University	•	•			•			
Marquette University	•	•	M	•	•	•		
Milwaukee School of Engineering	•							
Silver Lake College	•							
University of Wisconsin-Eau Claire	•	•	B					•
University of Wisconsin-Green Bay	•							
University of Wisconsin-Madison	•					•	•	•
University of Wisconsin-Milwaukee	•	•	M	•	•	•		
University of Wisconsin-Oshkosh	•	•	B		•			•
Viterbo University	•	•			•			•
Wisconsin Lutheran College	•							•
Wyoming								
University of Wyoming	•	•	B		•			
CANADA								
Alberta								
Athabasca University	•	•		•	•			
University of Alberta	•	•	B		•	•		
University of Calgary	•	•	B		•	•		
University of Lethbridge	•	•	B					
British Columbia								
British Columbia Institute of Technology	•							•
Kwantlen University College	•							
Thompson Rivers University	•							•
Trinity Western University	•							
The University of British Columbia	•	•	B	•		•	•	
University of Northern British Columbia	•	•					•	
University of Victoria	•	•				•		
Vancouver Island University	•							
Manitoba								
Brandon University	•							
University of Manitoba	•	•				•		•
New Brunswick								
Université de Moncton	•	•						•
University of New Brunswick Fredericton	•	•	B					•
Newfoundland and Labrador								
Memorial University of Newfoundland	•	•	B					
Nova Scotia								
Dalhousie University	•	•	B		•	•		
St. Francis Xavier University	•		B					•

B = Baccalaureate; M = Master's

	Baccalaureate	Master's	Accelerated	Joint Degree	Post-Master's	Doctoral	Postdoctoral	Continuing Education
Ontario								
Brock University	•							
Lakehead University	•		B					
Laurentian University	•							•
McMaster University	•	•		•		•		
Nipissing University	•							
Queen's University at Kingston	•	•	B			•		
Ryerson University	•	•						•
Trent University	•		B					
University of Ottawa	•	•				•	•	
University of Toronto	•	•	B		•	•		
The University of Western Ontario	•	•	B			•	•	
University of Windsor	•	•						•
York University	•							•
Prince Edward Island								
University of Prince Edward Island	•							
Quebec								
McGill University	•	•	B			•	•	
Université de Montréal	•	•			•	•	•	•
Université de Sherbrooke	•	•				•	•	
Université du Québec à Chicoutimi	•	•	B,M					
Université du Québec à Rimouski	•	•						•
Université du Québec à Trois-Rivières	•	•						
Université du Québec en Abitibi-Témiscamingue	•							
Université du Québec en Outaouais	•	•						
Université Laval	•	•	B,M		•	•	•	•
Saskatchewan								
University of Saskatchewan	•	•	B		•	•		•

B = Baccalaureate; M = Master's

PROFILES OF
NURSING PROGRAMS

U.S. AND U.S. TERRITORIES

ALABAMA

Auburn University

School of Nursing
Auburn University, Alabama

http://www.auburn.edu/academic/nursing/au_nursing.html

Founded in 1856

DEGREES • BSN • MSN

Nursing Program Faculty 15 (85% with doctorates).

Baccalaureate Enrollment 181
Women 90% **Men** 10% **Minority** 3%

Nursing Student Activities Nursing Honor Society, Sigma Theta Tau, Student Nurses' Association, nursing club.

Nursing Student Resources Academic advising; academic or career counseling; assistance for students with disabilities; bookstore; campus computer network; career placement assistance; computer lab; computer-assisted instruction; e-mail services; employment services for current students; interactive nursing skills videos; Internet; library services; nursing audiovisuals; placement services for program completers; remedial services; resume preparation assistance; skills, simulation, or other laboratory; tutoring.

Library Facilities 3 million volumes; 29,355 periodical subscriptions.

BACCALAUREATE PROGRAMS

Degree BSN

Available Programs Generic Baccalaureate.

Study Options Full-time.

Program Entrance Requirements Minimum overall college GPA of 2.5, transcript of college record, CPR certification, health exam, health insurance, immunizations, interview, minimum GPA in nursing prerequisites of 2.5, professional liability insurance/malpractice insurance, prerequisite course work. Transfer students are accepted. *Application deadline:* 2/1 (fall).

Expenses (2009–10) *Tuition, area resident:* full-time $21,776. *Tuition, nonresident:* full-time $34,256.

Financial Aid 75% of baccalaureate students in nursing programs received some form of financial aid in 2008–09.

Contact Pam Hennessey, Academic Advisor, School of Nursing, Auburn University, 118 Miller Hall, Auburn University, AL 36849. *Telephone:* 334-844-5665. *Fax:* 334-844-4177. *E-mail:* hennepp@auburn.edu.

GRADUATE PROGRAMS

Contact Dr. Anita All, Director, MSN Program, School of Nursing, Auburn University, 118 Miller Hall, Auburn University, AL 36849. *Telephone:* 334-844-5665. *E-mail:* aca0001@auburn.edu.

MASTER'S DEGREE PROGRAM

Degree MSN

Available Programs Master's.

Concentrations Available Nursing education. *Clinical nurse specialist programs in:* adult health, gerontology, pediatric.

Study Options Full-time and part-time.

Program Entrance Requirements Minimum overall college GPA of 3.0, transcript of college record, nursing research course, statistics course.

Degree Requirements 51 total credit hours, thesis or project.

Auburn University Montgomery

School of Nursing
Montgomery, Alabama

http://www.aum.edu/academics/schools/nursing/index.cfm

Founded in 1967

DEGREES • BSN • MSN

Nursing Program Faculty 20 (60% with doctorates).

Baccalaureate Enrollment 600
Women 80% **Men** 20% **Minority** 33% **International** 1% **Part-time** 20%

Graduate Enrollment 6

Nursing Student Activities Nursing Honor Society, Sigma Theta Tau, Student Nurses' Association.

Nursing Student Resources Academic advising; academic or career counseling; assistance for students with disabilities; bookstore; campus computer network; career placement assistance; computer lab; computer-assisted instruction; daycare for children of students; e-mail services; housing assistance; interactive nursing skills videos; Internet; learning resource lab; library services; nursing audiovisuals; remedial services; resume preparation assistance; skills, simulation, or other laboratory; tutoring.

Library Facilities 331,513 volumes (9,568 in nursing); 2,280 periodical subscriptions (273 health-care related).

BACCALAUREATE PROGRAMS

Degree BSN

Available Programs Generic Baccalaureate; RN Baccalaureate.

Study Options Full-time.

Program Entrance Requirements Transcript of college record, CPR certification, health exam, high school transcript, immunizations, interview, minimum GPA in nursing prerequisites of 2.5, professional liability insurance/malpractice insurance, prerequisite course work. Transfer students are accepted. *Application deadline:* 2/1 (fall), 5/1 (spring).

Expenses (2009–10) *Tuition, state resident:* part-time $183 per credit hour. *Tuition, nonresident:* part-time $531 per credit hour. *Required fees:* part-time $45 per term.

Financial Aid 75% of baccalaureate students in nursing programs received some form of financial aid in 2008–09. *Gift aid (need-based):* Federal Pell, FSEOG, state, private, college/university gift aid from institutional funds. *Loans:* FFEL (Subsidized and Unsubsidized Stafford PLUS), Perkins. *Work-study:* Federal Work-Study. *Financial aid application deadline (priority):* 3/1.

Contact Mrs. Lorinda Brewer Stutheit RNC, MSN, Admissions Chair Coordinator, Advising/Recruiting, School of Nursing, Auburn University Montgomery, PO Box 244023, Montgomery, AL 36124-4023. *Telephone:* 334-244-3431. *Fax:* 334-244-3243. *E-mail:* Lorinda.Stutheit@aum.edu.

GRADUATE PROGRAMS

Financial Aid 10% of graduate students in nursing programs received some form of financial aid in 2008–09.

Contact Dr. Anita C. All, Professor and Director, School of Nursing, Auburn University Montgomery, 213 Miller Hall, Auburn University, AL 36849-5055. *Telephone:* 334-844-5613. *Fax:* 334-844-4177. *E-mail:* msnnurse@auburn.edu.

MASTER'S DEGREE PROGRAM

Degree MSN

Available Programs Master's.

Auburn University Montgomery (continued)

Concentrations Available Nursing education. *Clinical nurse specialist programs in:* adult health, gerontology, pediatric.

Study Options Full-time and part-time.

Program Entrance Requirements Clinical experience, minimum overall college GPA of 3.0, written essay, 3 letters of recommendation, resume, statistics course.

Advanced Placement Credit given for nursing courses completed elsewhere dependent upon specific evaluations.

Degree Requirements 42 total credit hours, thesis or project, comprehensive exam.

Jacksonville State University
College of Nursing and Health Sciences
Jacksonville, Alabama

http://www.jsu.edu/depart/nursing

Founded in 1883

DEGREES • BSN • MSN

Nursing Program Faculty 28 (36% with doctorates).

Baccalaureate Enrollment 401
Women 82% **Men** 18% **Minority** 25% **International** 1% **Part-time** 21%

Graduate Enrollment 56
Women 89% **Men** 11% **Minority** 25% **Part-time** 88%

Distance Learning Courses Available.

Nursing Student Activities Sigma Theta Tau, Student Nurses' Association.

Nursing Student Resources Academic advising; academic or career counseling; campus computer network; computer lab; computer-assisted instruction; e-mail services; Internet; learning resource lab; nursing audiovisuals; remedial services; skills, simulation, or other laboratory; tutoring.

Library Facilities 685,991 volumes (27,462 in health, 1,837 in nursing); 14,376 periodical subscriptions (1,462 health-care related).

BACCALAUREATE PROGRAMS

Degree BSN

Available Programs Generic Baccalaureate; RN Baccalaureate.

Study Options Full-time and part-time.

Online Degree Options Yes.

Program Entrance Requirements Transcript of college record, CPR certification, health exam, health insurance, high school transcript, immunizations, minimum GPA in nursing prerequisites, professional liability insurance/malpractice insurance, prerequisite course work. Transfer students are accepted. *Application deadline:* 6/1 (fall), 10/1 (spring).

Expenses (2009–10) *Tuition, area resident:* full-time $4992; part-time $208 per credit hour. *Tuition, state resident:* full-time $6192; part-time $258 per credit hour. *Tuition, nonresident:* full-time $9984; part-time $416 per credit hour. *International tuition:* $9984 full-time. *Room and board:* $5800; room only: $2572 per academic year.

Financial Aid 70% of baccalaureate students in nursing programs received some form of financial aid in 2008–09.

Contact Mr. David Hofland, Student Services Coordinator, College of Nursing and Health Sciences, Jacksonville State University, 700 Pelham Road North, Jacksonville, AL 36265-1602. *Telephone:* 256-782-5276. *Fax:* 256-782-5406. *E-mail:* hofland@jsu.edu.

GRADUATE PROGRAMS

Expenses (2009–10) *Tuition, state resident:* full-time $5832; part-time $324 per credit hour. *Tuition, nonresident:* full-time $5832; part-time $324 per credit hour. *International tuition:* $5832 full-time. *Room and board:* $5800; room only: $2572 per academic year.

Financial Aid 60% of graduate students in nursing programs received some form of financial aid in 2008–09.

Contact Dr. Beth Hembree, Director, Graduate Studies, College of Nursing and Health Sciences, Jacksonville State University, 700 Pelham Road North, Jacksonville, AL 36265-1602. *Telephone:* 256-782-5431. *Fax:* 256-782-5406. *E-mail:* bhembree@jsu.edu.

MASTER'S DEGREE PROGRAM

Degree MSN

Available Programs Master's.

Concentrations Available *Clinical nurse specialist programs in:* community health.

Study Options Full-time and part-time.

Online Degree Options Yes (online only).

Program Entrance Requirements Minimum overall college GPA of 3.0, transcript of college record, written essay, interview, 3 letters of recommendation, nursing research course, physical assessment course, statistics course. *Application deadline:* Applications may be processed on a rolling basis for some programs.

Advanced Placement Credit given for nursing courses completed elsewhere dependent upon specific evaluations.

Degree Requirements 36 total credit hours, thesis or project, comprehensive exam.

CONTINUING EDUCATION PROGRAM

Contact Mr. David Hofland, Student Services Coordinator, College of Nursing and Health Sciences, Jacksonville State University, 700 Pelham Road North, Jacksonville, AL 36265-1602. *Telephone:* 256-782-5276. *Fax:* 256-782-5406. *E-mail:* hofland@jsu.edu.

Oakwood University
Department of Nursing
Huntsville, Alabama

Founded in 1896

DEGREE • BS

Baccalaureate Enrollment 77
Women 92% **Men** 8% **Minority** 100% **International** 2%

Nursing Student Activities Nursing club.

Nursing Student Resources Academic advising; academic or career counseling; assistance for students with disabilities; bookstore; campus computer network; career placement assistance; computer lab; computer-assisted instruction; e-mail services; employment services for current students; externships; interactive nursing skills videos; Internet; learning resource lab; library services; nursing audiovisuals; paid internships; placement services for program completers; remedial services; resume preparation assistance; skills, simulation, or other laboratory; tutoring; unpaid internships.

Library Facilities 133,106 volumes (5,147 in health, 3,474 in nursing); 726 periodical subscriptions (47 health-care related).

BACCALAUREATE PROGRAMS

Degree BS

Available Programs Generic Baccalaureate; RN Baccalaureate.

Study Options Full-time and part-time.

Program Entrance Requirements Minimum overall college GPA of 3.00, transcript of college record, written essay, health exam, health insurance, high school transcript, immunizations, 3 letters of recommendation. Transfer students are accepted. *Application deadline:* 11/16 (fall).

Expenses (2009–10) *Tuition:* part-time $6521 per semester. *Room and board:* $4200; room only: $2000 per academic year. *Required fees:* part-time $400 per term.

Financial Aid 95% of baccalaureate students in nursing programs received some form of financial aid in 2008–09.

Contact Mrs. Denise Finley, Secretary, Department of Nursing, Oakwood University, 7000 Adventist Boulevard, Huntsville, AL 35896. *Telephone:* 256-726-7287. *Fax:* 256-726-8338. *E-mail:* dfinley@oakwood.edu.

Samford University
Ida V. Moffett School of Nursing
Birmingham, Alabama

http://www.samford.edu

Founded in 1841

DEGREES • BSN • DNP • MSN • MSN/MBA

Nursing Program Faculty 33 (54% with doctorates).

Baccalaureate Enrollment 300
Women 97% **Men** 3% **Minority** 5% **International** 2% **Part-time** 10%

Graduate Enrollment 125
Women 88% **Men** 12% **Minority** 32% **Part-time** 5%

Nursing Student Activities Sigma Theta Tau, Student Nurses' Association, nursing club.

Nursing Student Resources Academic advising; academic or career counseling; assistance for students with disabilities; bookstore; campus computer network; career placement assistance; computer lab; computer-assisted instruction; e-mail services; externships; interactive nursing skills videos; Internet; learning resource lab; library services; nursing audiovisuals; paid internships; placement services for program completers; remedial services; resume preparation assistance; skills, simulation, or other laboratory; tutoring; unpaid internships.

Library Facilities 439,760 volumes (7,000 in health, 2,500 in nursing); 3,724 periodical subscriptions (100 health-care related).

BACCALAUREATE PROGRAMS

Degree BSN

Available Programs Baccalaureate for Second Degree; Generic Baccalaureate.

Study Options Full-time and part-time.

Program Entrance Requirements Minimum overall college GPA of 2.7, transcript of college record, CPR certification, written essay, health exam, health insurance, high school biology, high school chemistry, 2 years high school math, 2 years high school science, high school transcript, immunizations, minimum high school GPA of 3.0, minimum GPA in nursing prerequisites of 2.0, professional liability insurance/malpractice insurance, prerequisite course work. Transfer students are accepted.

Advanced Placement Credit given for nursing courses completed elsewhere dependent upon specific evaluations.

Expenses (2008–09) *Tuition:* full-time $19,300; part-time $645 per credit. *Room and board:* $5962; room only: $3070 per academic year. *Required fees:* full-time $1530; part-time $765 per term.

Financial Aid 80% of baccalaureate students in nursing programs received some form of financial aid in 2007–08.

Contact Mrs. Janice G. Paine, Director, Undergraduate Student Services, Ida V. Moffett School of Nursing, Samford University, 800 Lakeshore Drive, Birmingham, AL 35229. *Telephone:* 205-726-2872 Ext. 2746. *Fax:* 205-726-4269. *E-mail:* jgpaine@samford.edu.

GRADUATE PROGRAMS

Expenses (2008–09) *Tuition:* full-time $12,500; part-time $575 per credit hour. *Required fees:* full-time $600.

Financial Aid 80% of graduate students in nursing programs received some form of financial aid in 2007–08. Institutionally sponsored loans, scholarships, and traineeships available. *Financial aid application deadline:* 3/1.

Contact Mrs. Marian W. Carter, Director, Graduate Student Services, Ida V. Moffett School of Nursing, Samford University, 800 Lakeshore Drive, Birmingham, AL 35229. *Telephone:* 205-726-2047. *Fax:* 205-726-4269. *E-mail:* mwcarter@samford.edu.

MASTER'S DEGREE PROGRAM

Degrees MSN; MSN/MBA

Available Programs Master's; RN to Master's.

Concentrations Available Nurse anesthesia; nursing administration; nursing education. *Nurse practitioner programs in:* family health, primary care.

Study Options Full-time and part-time.

Program Entrance Requirements Clinical experience, computer literacy, minimum overall college GPA of 3.0, transcript of college record, CPR certification, immunizations, interview, 3 letters of recommendation, nursing research course, physical assessment course, professional liability insurance/malpractice insurance, prerequisite course work, statistics course, GRE General Test or MAT. *Application deadline:* 7/7 (fall), 11/1 (spring), 4/15 (summer). Applications may be processed on a rolling basis for some programs. *Application fee:* $35.

Advanced Placement Credit given for nursing courses completed elsewhere dependent upon specific evaluations.

Degree Requirements 38 total credit hours.

POST-MASTER'S PROGRAM

Areas of Study Nurse anesthesia; nursing administration; nursing education. *Nurse practitioner programs in:* family health, primary care.

DOCTORAL DEGREE PROGRAM

Degree DNP

Available Programs Doctorate.

Areas of Study Advanced practice nursing, faculty preparation, family health, health-care systems, nursing administration, nursing education.

Program Entrance Requirements Minimum overall college GPA of 3.5, interview by faculty committee, interview, 3 letters of recommendation, MSN or equivalent, statistics course, vita, writing sample. Application deadline: 1/31 (spring). Application fee: $35.

Degree Requirements 38 total credit hours.

CONTINUING EDUCATION PROGRAM

Contact Mrs. Suzanne Scharf, Coordinator, Ida V. Moffett School of Nursing, Samford University, 800 Lakeshore Drive, Birmingham, AL 35229. *Telephone:* 205-726-2045. *Fax:* 205-726-2219. *E-mail:* shscharf@samford.edu.

Spring Hill College
Division of Nursing
Mobile, Alabama

http://faculty.shc.edu/nursing

Founded in 1830

DEGREES • BSN • MSN

Nursing Program Faculty 8 (84% with doctorates).

Baccalaureate Enrollment 124
Women 86% **Men** 14% **Minority** 12%

Graduate Enrollment 62
Women 95% **Men** 5% **Minority** 45% **Part-time** 40%

Distance Learning Courses Available.

Nursing Student Activities Nursing Honor Society, Sigma Theta Tau, Student Nurses' Association.

Nursing Student Resources Academic advising; academic or career counseling; assistance for students with disabilities; bookstore; campus computer network; career placement assistance; computer lab; computer-assisted instruction; e-mail services; employment services for current students; externships; interactive nursing skills videos; Internet; learning resource lab; library services; nursing audiovisuals; placement services for program completers; resume preparation assistance; skills, simulation, or other laboratory; tutoring; unpaid internships.

Library Facilities 185,926 volumes (330 in health, 300 in nursing); 889 periodical subscriptions (58 health-care related).

BACCALAUREATE PROGRAMS

Degree BSN

Available Programs Baccalaureate for Second Degree; Generic Baccalaureate.

Study Options Full-time.

Spring Hill College (continued)

Program Entrance Requirements Minimum overall college GPA of 2.75, transcript of college record, CPR certification, written essay, health exam, health insurance, high school transcript, immunizations, 1 letter of recommendation, minimum GPA in nursing prerequisites of 2.75, prerequisite course work. Transfer students are accepted. *Application deadline:* 3/1 (spring).

Advanced Placement Credit by examination available.

Expenses (2008–09) *Tuition:* full-time $22,770; part-time $850 per hour. *Room and board:* $7200; room only: $5000 per academic year. *Required fees:* full-time $300; part-time $50 per credit.

Financial Aid 80% of baccalaureate students in nursing programs received some form of financial aid in 2007–08. *Gift aid (need-based):* Federal Pell, FSEOG, state, private, college/university gift aid from institutional funds, Academic Competitiveness Grant, National Smart Grant. *Loans:* FFEL (Subsidized and Unsubsidized Stafford PLUS), Perkins, alternative loans. *Work-study:* Federal Work-Study, part-time campus jobs. *Financial aid application deadline (priority):* 3/1.

Contact Dr. Carol Harrison, Chair/Professor, Division of Nursing, Spring Hill College, 4000 Dauphin Street, Mobile, AL 36608. *Telephone:* 334-380-4492. *Fax:* 334-380-4495. *E-mail:* charrison@shc.edu.

GRADUATE PROGRAMS

Expenses (2008–09) *Tuition:* full-time $5400; part-time $450 per credit.

Financial Aid 25% of graduate students in nursing programs received some form of financial aid in 2007–08.

Contact Ms. Donna Tarasavage, Director of Marketing and Recruiting, Division of Nursing, Spring Hill College, Division of Graduate Studies, 4000 Dauphin Street, Mobile, AL 36608. *Telephone:* 251-380-3067. *Fax:* 251-460-2190. *E-mail:* dtarasavage@shc.edu.

MASTER'S DEGREE PROGRAM

Degree MSN

Available Programs Accelerated AD/RN to Master's; Master's; RN to Master's.

Concentrations Available Clinical nurse leader.

Study Options Full-time and part-time.

Online Degree Options Yes (online only).

Program Entrance Requirements Clinical experience, minimum overall college GPA of 3.0, transcript of college record, immunizations, professional liability insurance/malpractice insurance, prerequisite course work, resume, statistics course. *Application deadline:* Applications may be processed on a rolling basis for some programs.

Advanced Placement Credit by examination available. Credit given for nursing courses completed elsewhere dependent upon specific evaluations.

Degree Requirements 36 total credit hours, thesis or project.

Troy University

School of Nursing
Troy, Alabama

Founded in 1887

DEGREES • BSN • MSN

Nursing Program Faculty 40 (47% with doctorates).

Baccalaureate Enrollment 550
Women 88% **Men** 12% **Minority** 35% **International** 4% **Part-time** 10%

Graduate Enrollment 120
Women 97% **Men** 3% **Minority** 23% **Part-time** 29%

Nursing Student Activities Sigma Theta Tau, Student Nurses' Association.

Nursing Student Resources Academic advising; academic or career counseling; assistance for students with disabilities; bookstore; campus computer network; career placement assistance; computer lab; computer-assisted instruction; daycare for children of students; e-mail services; employment services for current students; externships; housing assistance; interactive nursing skills videos; Internet; learning resource lab; library

services; nursing audiovisuals; placement services for program completers; remedial services; resume preparation assistance; skills, simulation, or other laboratory; tutoring; unpaid internships.

Library Facilities 571,172 volumes (45,006 in health, 3,843 in nursing); 3,309 periodical subscriptions (703 health-care related).

BACCALAUREATE PROGRAMS

Degree BSN

Available Programs ADN to Baccalaureate; Generic Baccalaureate.

Study Options Full-time and part-time.

Program Entrance Requirements Minimum overall college GPA of 2.5, transcript of college record, CPR certification, health exam, health insurance, high school transcript, immunizations, professional liability insurance/malpractice insurance, prerequisite course work. Transfer students are accepted.

Advanced Placement Credit by examination available. Credit given for nursing courses completed elsewhere dependent upon specific evaluations.

Contact *Telephone:* 334-670-3428. *Fax:* 334-670-3744.

GRADUATE PROGRAMS

Contact *Telephone:* 334-834-2320. *Fax:* 334-241-8627.

MASTER'S DEGREE PROGRAM

Degree MSN

Available Programs Master's; RN to Master's.

Concentrations Available Nursing administration; nursing education; nursing informatics. *Clinical nurse specialist programs in:* adult health, maternity-newborn. *Nurse practitioner programs in:* family health.

Study Options Full-time and part-time.

Program Entrance Requirements Minimum overall college GPA of 3.0, transcript of college record, CPR certification, immunizations, 3 letters of recommendation, physical assessment course, professional liability insurance/malpractice insurance.

Advanced Placement Credit given for nursing courses completed elsewhere dependent upon specific evaluations.

Degree Requirements 39 total credit hours, thesis or project, comprehensive exam.

POST-MASTER'S PROGRAM

Areas of Study *Nurse practitioner programs in:* family health.

Tuskegee University

Program in Nursing
Tuskegee, Alabama

http://www.tusk.edu

Founded in 1881

DEGREE • BSN

Nursing Program Faculty 9 (40% with doctorates).

Baccalaureate Enrollment 156
Women 93% **Men** 7% **Minority** 100%

Nursing Student Activities Nursing Honor Society, Student Nurses' Association, nursing club.

Nursing Student Resources Academic advising; academic or career counseling; assistance for students with disabilities; bookstore; campus computer network; career placement assistance; computer lab; computer-assisted instruction; e-mail services; interactive nursing skills videos; Internet; learning resource lab; library services; nursing audiovisuals; placement services for program completers; remedial services; resume preparation assistance; skills, simulation, or other laboratory; tutoring; unpaid internships.

Library Facilities 623,824 volumes (3,500 in health, 1,279 in nursing); 81,157 periodical subscriptions (250 health-care related).

BACCALAUREATE PROGRAMS

Degree BSN

Available Programs ADN to Baccalaureate; Generic Baccalaureate; RN Baccalaureate.

Study Options Full-time.

Program Entrance Requirements Minimum overall college GPA of 3.0, transcript of college record, CPR certification, written essay, health exam, health insurance, high school biology, high school chemistry, 2 years high school math, 1 year of high school science, high school transcript, immunizations, interview, minimum high school GPA of 3.0, minimum GPA in nursing prerequisites of 3.0, professional liability insurance/malpractice insurance, prerequisite course work. Transfer students are accepted. *Application deadline:* 3/30 (fall), 10/30 (spring), 4/30 (summer). Applications may be processed on a rolling basis for some programs. *Application fee:* $35.

Advanced Placement Credit given for nursing courses completed elsewhere dependent upon specific evaluations.

Expenses (2008–09) *Tuition:* full-time $14,740; part-time $815 per credit. *Room and board:* $4350 per academic year. *Required fees:* full-time $1370.

Financial Aid 85% of baccalaureate students in nursing programs received some form of financial aid in 2007–08.

Contact Dr. Doris S. Holeman, Associate Dean and Director, Program in Nursing, Tuskegee University, 209 Basil O'Connor Hall, Tuskegee, AL 36083. *Telephone:* 334-727-8382. *Fax:* 334-727-5461. *E-mail:* dholeman@tuskegee.edu.

The University of Alabama
Capstone College of Nursing
Tuscaloosa, Alabama

http://nursing.ua.edu

Founded in 1831

DEGREES • BSN • DNP • MSN • MSN/ED D • MSN/MA

Nursing Program Faculty 42 (57% with doctorates).

Baccalaureate Enrollment 1,283
Women 88% **Men** 12% **Minority** 14% **International** .4% **Part-time** 4%

Graduate Enrollment 170
Women 92% **Men** 8% **Minority** 34% **Part-time** 67%

Distance Learning Courses Available.

Nursing Student Activities Sigma Theta Tau, Student Nurses' Association.

Nursing Student Resources Academic advising; academic or career counseling; assistance for students with disabilities; bookstore; campus computer network; career placement assistance; computer lab; computer-assisted instruction; e-mail services; interactive nursing skills videos; Internet; learning resource lab; library services; nursing audiovisuals; paid internships; placement services for program completers; skills, simulation, or other laboratory; tutoring; unpaid internships.

Library Facilities 2.8 million volumes (21,000 in health, 400 in nursing); 47,486 periodical subscriptions (1,500 health-care related).

BACCALAUREATE PROGRAMS

Degree BSN

Available Programs Baccalaureate for Second Degree; Generic Baccalaureate; RN Baccalaureate.

Study Options Full-time and part-time.

Program Entrance Requirements Minimum overall college GPA of 3.0, transcript of college record, CPR certification, health exam, health insurance, 4 years high school math, 4 years high school science, high school transcript, immunizations, minimum high school GPA of 2.5, minimum GPA in nursing prerequisites of 3.0, professional liability insurance/malpractice insurance, prerequisite course work. Transfer students are accepted. *Application deadline:* 6/15 (fall), 3/15 (summer). *Application fee:* $25.

Expenses (2009–10) *Tuition, state resident:* full-time $7000; part-time $375 per credit hour. *Tuition, nonresident:* full-time $19,200; part-time $895 per credit hour. *Room and board:* $7470; room only: $4400 per academic year. *Required fees:* full-time $700; part-time $30 per credit; part-time $350 per term.

Financial Aid 31% of baccalaureate students in nursing programs received some form of financial aid in 2008–09.

Contact Ms. Rebekah Welch, Director of Nursing Student Services, Capstone College of Nursing, The University of Alabama, Box 870358, Tuscaloosa, AL 35487-0358. *Telephone:* 205-348-6639. *Fax:* 205-348-5559. *E-mail:* rebekah.welch@ua.edu.

GRADUATE PROGRAMS

Expenses (2009–10) *Tuition, state resident:* full-time $10,608; part-time $312 per credit hour. *Tuition, nonresident:* full-time $10,608; part-time $312 per credit hour.

Financial Aid 70% of graduate students in nursing programs received some form of financial aid in 2008–09.

Contact Dr. Mariettta Stanton, Director, Graduate Program, Capstone College of Nursing, The University of Alabama, Box 870358, Tuscaloosa, AL 35487-0358. *Telephone:* 205-348-6639. *Fax:* 205-348-5559. *E-mail:* MStanton@bama.ua.edu.

MASTER'S DEGREE PROGRAM

Degrees MSN; MSN/Ed D; MSN/MA

Available Programs Master's; RN to Master's.

Concentrations Available Clinical nurse leader; nurse case management; nursing administration; nursing education.

Study Options Full-time and part-time.

Online Degree Options Yes (online only).

Program Entrance Requirements Minimum overall college GPA of 3.0, transcript of college record, written essay. *Application deadline:* 7/1 (fall), 12/1 (spring), 3/1 (summer). Applications may be processed on a rolling basis for some programs. *Application fee:* $25.

Degree Requirements 35 total credit hours.

POST-MASTER'S PROGRAM

Areas of Study Clinical nurse leader; nurse case management.

DOCTORAL DEGREE PROGRAM

Degree DNP

Available Programs Doctorate.

Areas of Study Advanced practice nursing, nursing administration.

Online Degree Options Yes (online only).

Program Entrance Requirements Minimum overall college GPA of 3.0, interview, 2 letters of recommendation, MSN or equivalent, writing sample. Application deadline: 7/1 (fall). Applications may be processed on a rolling basis for some programs. Application fee: $25.

Degree Requirements 34 total credit hours, residency.

The University of Alabama at Birmingham
School of Nursing
Birmingham, Alabama

http://www.uab.edu/son/

Founded in 1969

DEGREES • BSN • DNP • MSN • MSN/MPH • PHD

Nursing Program Faculty 48 (100% with doctorates).

Baccalaureate Enrollment 505
Women 85% **Men** 15% **Minority** 23% **International** 2% **Part-time** 32%

Graduate Enrollment 973
Women 91% **Men** 9% **Minority** 21% **International** 2% **Part-time** 74%

Distance Learning Courses Available.

Nursing Student Activities Sigma Theta Tau, Student Nurses' Association, nursing club.

Nursing Student Resources Academic advising; academic or career counseling; assistance for students with disabilities; bookstore; campus computer network; career placement assistance; computer lab; computer-assisted instruction; e-mail services; housing assistance; interactive nursing skills videos; Internet; learning resource lab; library services; nursing

The University of Alabama at Birmingham (continued)
audiovisuals; paid internships; placement services for program completers; resume preparation assistance; skills, simulation, or other laboratory; tutoring.

Library Facilities 1.4 million volumes (318,000 in health, 6,862 in nursing); 67,902 periodical subscriptions (2,566 health-care related).

BACCALAUREATE PROGRAMS

Degree BSN

Available Programs Baccalaureate for Second Degree; Generic Baccalaureate; RN Baccalaureate.
Study Options Full-time.
Program Entrance Requirements Minimum overall college GPA of 2.75, transcript of college record, CPR certification, written essay, health exam, health insurance, high school biology, high school transcript, immunizations, minimum high school GPA of 2.0, minimum GPA in nursing prerequisites of 2.75, prerequisite course work. Transfer students are accepted. *Application deadline:* 4/23 (fall), 9/3 (spring).
Expenses (2009–10) *Tuition, state resident:* full-time $4680; part-time $195 per credit hour. *Tuition, nonresident:* full-time $11,712; part-time $488 per credit hour. *International tuition:* $11,712 full-time. *Room and board:* $8142; room only: $4492 per academic year. *Required fees:* full-time $848.
Financial Aid *Gift aid (need-based):* Federal Pell, FSEOG, state, private, college/university gift aid from institutional funds, United Negro College Fund. *Loans:* Federal Direct (Subsidized and Unsubsidized Stafford PLUS), Perkins, state, college/university. *Work-study:* Federal Work-Study. *Financial aid application deadline (priority):* 4/1.
Contact Mr. Peter Tofani, Assistant Dean for Student Affairs, School of Nursing, The University of Alabama at Birmingham, Nursing Building, 1530 3rd Avenue South, Room 208A, Birmingham, AL 35294-1210. *Telephone:* 205-975-7529. *Fax:* 205-934-5490. *E-mail:* tofanip@uab.edu.

GRADUATE PROGRAMS

Expenses (2009–10) *Tuition, state resident:* full-time $4968; part-time $276 per credit hour. *Tuition, nonresident:* full-time $12,420; part-time $690 per credit hour. *International tuition:* $12,420 full-time. *Room and board:* $8142; room only: $4492 per academic year. *Required fees:* full-time $662.
Financial Aid 29% of graduate students in nursing programs received some form of financial aid in 2008–09. 3 fellowships (averaging $12,833 per year), 1 research assistantship, teaching assistantships (averaging $6,760 per year) were awarded; Federal Work-Study also available. Aid available to part-time students.
Contact Mr. Peter Tofani, Assistant Dean for Student Affairs, School of Nursing, The University of Alabama at Birmingham, NB 208A, 1530 3rd Avenue South, Birmingham, AL 35294-1210. *Telephone:* 205-975-7529. *Fax:* 205-934-5490. *E-mail:* tofanip@uab.edu.

MASTER'S DEGREE PROGRAM

Degrees MSN; MSN/MPH

Available Programs Accelerated Master's for Non-Nursing College Graduates; Master's; RN to Master's.
Concentrations Available Clinical nurse leader; health-care administration; nursing administration; nursing informatics. *Clinical nurse specialist programs in:* adult health. *Nurse practitioner programs in:* acute care, adult health, family health, gerontology, neonatal health, occupational health, pediatric, primary care, psychiatric/mental health, women's health.
Study Options Full-time and part-time.
Online Degree Options Yes (online only).
Program Entrance Requirements Clinical experience, minimum overall college GPA of 3.0, transcript of college record, CPR certification, written essay, immunizations, 3 letters of recommendation, prerequisite course work, statistics course, GRE General Test. *Application deadline:* 5/29 (fall), 9/25 (spring), 2/26 (summer). *Application fee:* $35.
Advanced Placement Credit given for nursing courses completed elsewhere dependent upon specific evaluations.
Degree Requirements 30 total credit hours, comprehensive exam.

POST-MASTER'S PROGRAM

Areas of Study *Nurse practitioner programs in:* acute care, adult health, family health, gerontology, neonatal health, pediatric, psychiatric/mental health.

DOCTORAL DEGREE PROGRAM

Degree DNP, PhD

Available Programs Doctorate; Post-Baccalaureate Doctorate.
Areas of Study Nursing research, nursing science, clinical nurse specialist, certified registered nurse anesthetist, executive nurse leadership, nurse practitioner.
Program Entrance Requirements Clinical experience, minimum overall college GPA of 3.0, interview by faculty committee, interview, 3 letters of recommendation, scholarly papers, statistics course, vita, writing sample, MSN degree, goal statement. Application deadline: 1/15 (fall). Application fee: $35.
Degree Requirements 34–66 total credit hours, dissertation, oral exam, written exam, residency.

The University of Alabama in Huntsville
College of Nursing
Huntsville, Alabama

http://www.uab.edu/nursing
Founded in 1950
DEGREES • BSN • DNP • MSN

Nursing Program Faculty 46 (30% with doctorates).
Baccalaureate Enrollment 662
Women 90% **Men** 10% **Minority** 14% **International** 1% **Part-time** 22%
Graduate Enrollment 106
Women 92% **Men** 8% **Minority** 15% **International** 1% **Part-time** 65%
Distance Learning Courses Available.
Nursing Student Activities Sigma Theta Tau, Student Nurses' Association.
Nursing Student Resources Academic advising; academic or career counseling; assistance for students with disabilities; bookstore; campus computer network; career placement assistance; computer lab; computer-assisted instruction; e-mail services; employment services for current students; housing assistance; interactive nursing skills videos; Internet; learning resource lab; library services; nursing audiovisuals; placement services for program completers; remedial services; resume preparation assistance; skills, simulation, or other laboratory; tutoring.
Library Facilities 334,612 volumes (13,004 in health, 3,480 in nursing); 926 periodical subscriptions (3,200 health-care related).

BACCALAUREATE PROGRAMS

Degree BSN

Available Programs Baccalaureate for Second Degree; Generic Baccalaureate; RN Baccalaureate.
Study Options Full-time and part-time.
Program Entrance Requirements Minimum overall college GPA of 2.0, transcript of college record, CPR certification, health exam, health insurance, immunizations, minimum GPA in nursing prerequisites of 2.0, professional liability insurance/malpractice insurance, prerequisite course work. Transfer students are accepted. *Application deadline:* 3/1 (fall), 9/1 (spring).
Advanced Placement Credit by examination available. Credit given for nursing courses completed elsewhere dependent upon specific evaluations.
Financial Aid 75% of baccalaureate students in nursing programs received some form of financial aid in 2008–09. *Gift aid (need-based):* Federal Pell, FSEOG, state, private, college/university gift aid from institutional funds, Federal Nursing. *Loans:* Federal Direct (Subsidized and Unsubsidized Stafford PLUS). *Work-study:* Federal Work-Study. *Financial aid application deadline:* 7/31 (priority: 4/1).
Contact Mrs. Laura Mann, Director, Nursing Undergraduate Programs, College of Nursing, The University of Alabama in Huntsville, 207 Nursing Building, Huntsville, AL 35899. *Telephone:* 256-824-6742. *Fax:* 256-824-2850. *E-mail:* laura.mann@uah.edu.

GRADUATE PROGRAMS

Financial Aid 65% of graduate students in nursing programs received some form of financial aid in 2008–09. 8 teaching assistantships with full and partial tuition reimbursements available (averaging $6,123 per year) were awarded; career-related internships or fieldwork, Federal Work-Study, institutionally sponsored loans, scholarships, traineeships, and unspecified assistantships also available. Aid available to part-time students. *Financial aid application deadline:* 4/1.

Contact Mr. Charles Davis, Director of Nursing Graduate Program Student Affairs, College of Nursing, The University of Alabama in Huntsville, Huntsville, AL 35899. *Telephone:* 256-824-6742. *Fax:* 256-824-6026. *E-mail:* charles.davis@uah.edu.

MASTER'S DEGREE PROGRAM

Degree MSN

Available Programs Master's; RN to Master's.

Concentrations Available Clinical nurse leader; health-care administration. *Clinical nurse specialist programs in:* adult health. *Nurse practitioner programs in:* acute care, family health.

Study Options Full-time and part-time.

Online Degree Options Yes.

Program Entrance Requirements Minimum overall college GPA of 3.0, transcript of college record, CPR certification, immunizations, 3 letters of recommendation, professional liability insurance/malpractice insurance, statistics course, MAT or GRE. *Application deadline:* 4/15 (fall).

Advanced Placement Credit given for nursing courses completed elsewhere dependent upon specific evaluations.

Degree Requirements 42 total credit hours, thesis or project, comprehensive exam.

POST-MASTER'S PROGRAM

Areas of Study Nursing education. *Nurse practitioner programs in:* family health.

DOCTORAL DEGREE PROGRAM

Degree DNP

Available Programs Doctorate.

Areas of Study Advanced practice nursing, nursing administration.

Online Degree Options Yes (online only).

Program Entrance Requirements interview by faculty committee, letters of recommendation, MSN or equivalent, vita, writing sample. Application deadline: 4/15 (fall). Application fee: $40.

Degree Requirements 34 total credit hours, oral exam, written exam.

CONTINUING EDUCATION PROGRAM

Contact Mrs. Ina Warboys, Director of Continuing Education, College of Nursing, The University of Alabama in Huntsville, Huntsville, AL 35899. *Telephone:* 256-824-2456. *Fax:* 256-824-6026. *E-mail:* ina.warboys@uah.edu.

University of Mobile
School of Nursing
Mobile, Alabama

http://www.umobile.edu

Founded in 1961

DEGREES • BSN • MSN

Nursing Program Faculty 14 (22% with doctorates).

Baccalaureate Enrollment 84
Women 89% **Men** 11% **Minority** 25%

Graduate Enrollment 22
Women 91% **Men** 9% **Minority** 45% **Part-time** 50%

Nursing Student Activities Sigma Theta Tau, Student Nurses' Association.

Nursing Student Resources Academic advising; academic or career counseling; assistance for students with disabilities; bookstore; campus computer network; career placement assistance; computer lab; computer-assisted instruction; e-mail services; employment services for current

students; interactive nursing skills videos; Internet; learning resource lab; library services; nursing audiovisuals; remedial services; resume preparation assistance; skills, simulation, or other laboratory; tutoring; unpaid internships.

Library Facilities 107,563 volumes (7,846 in health, 6,500 in nursing); 325 periodical subscriptions (109 health-care related).

BACCALAUREATE PROGRAMS

Degree BSN

Available Programs ADN to Baccalaureate; Generic Baccalaureate; RN Baccalaureate.

Study Options Full-time.

Program Entrance Requirements Minimum overall college GPA of 2.75, transcript of college record, CPR certification, health exam, health insurance, high school transcript, immunizations, minimum GPA in nursing prerequisites of 2.75, prerequisite course work. Transfer students are accepted.

Advanced Placement Credit given for nursing courses completed elsewhere dependent upon specific evaluations.

Contact *Telephone:* 251-442-2337. *Fax:* 251-442-2520.

GRADUATE PROGRAMS

Contact *Telephone:* 251-442-2446. *Fax:* 251-442-2520.

MASTER'S DEGREE PROGRAM

Degree MSN

Available Programs Master's.

Concentrations Available Nursing administration; nursing education.

Study Options Full-time and part-time.

Program Entrance Requirements Minimum overall college GPA of 3.0, transcript of college record, CPR certification, immunizations, 3 letters of recommendation, statistics course.

Advanced Placement Credit given for nursing courses completed elsewhere dependent upon specific evaluations.

Degree Requirements 39 total credit hours, thesis or project, comprehensive exam.

CONTINUING EDUCATION PROGRAM

Contact *Telephone:* 251-442-2227. *Fax:* 251-442-2520.

University of North Alabama
College of Nursing and Allied Health
Florence, Alabama

http://www2.una.edu/nursing/

Founded in 1830

DEGREES • BSN • MSN

Nursing Program Faculty 37 (22% with doctorates).

Baccalaureate Enrollment 390
Women 87% **Men** 13% **Minority** 20.5% **International** 1% **Part-time** 31%

Graduate Enrollment 36
Women 97% **Men** 3% **Minority** 17% **Part-time** 25%

Distance Learning Courses Available.

Nursing Student Activities Sigma Theta Tau, Student Nurses' Association.

Nursing Student Resources Academic advising; academic or career counseling; assistance for students with disabilities; bookstore; campus computer network; career placement assistance; computer lab; e-mail services; employment services for current students; housing assistance; interactive nursing skills videos; Internet; learning resource lab; library services; nursing audiovisuals; remedial services; resume preparation assistance; skills, simulation, or other laboratory; tutoring.

Library Facilities 393,457 volumes; 3,742 periodical subscriptions.

BACCALAUREATE PROGRAMS

Degree BSN

Available Programs Generic Baccalaureate; RN Baccalaureate.

University of North Alabama (continued)

Study Options Full-time and part-time.

Online Degree Options Yes (online only).

Program Entrance Requirements Transcript of college record, CPR certification, health exam, health insurance, high school transcript, immunizations, minimum GPA in nursing prerequisites of 2.5, professional liability insurance/malpractice insurance, prerequisite course work. Transfer students are accepted.

Contact *Telephone:* 256-765-4984. *Fax:* 256-765-4935.

GRADUATE PROGRAMS

Contact *Telephone:* 256-765-4931. *Fax:* 256-765-4701.

MASTER'S DEGREE PROGRAM

Degree MSN

Available Programs Master's.

Concentrations Available Nursing administration; nursing education.

Study Options Full-time and part-time.

Online Degree Options Yes (online only).

Program Entrance Requirements Clinical experience, minimum overall college GPA of 3.0, transcript of college record, written essay, 3 letters of recommendation, professional liability insurance/malpractice insurance.

Degree Requirements 42 total credit hours, thesis or project.

CONTINUING EDUCATION PROGRAM

Contact *Telephone:* 256-765-4787. *Fax:* 256-765-4872.

University of South Alabama

College of Nursing
Mobile, Alabama

http://www.southalabama.edu/nursing/

Founded in 1963

DEGREES • BSN • MSN

Nursing Program Faculty 57 (30% with doctorates).

Baccalaureate Enrollment 316
Women 82% **Men** 18% **Minority** 24% **International** 3% **Part-time** 11%

Graduate Enrollment 368
Women 86% **Men** 14% **Minority** 19% **Part-time** 22%

Nursing Student Activities Sigma Theta Tau, Student Nurses' Association.

Nursing Student Resources Academic advising; academic or career counseling; assistance for students with disabilities; bookstore; campus computer network; career placement assistance; computer lab; learning resource lab; library services; nursing audiovisuals; resume preparation assistance.

Library Facilities 1.1 million volumes (2,406 in health, 2,300 in nursing); 7,344 periodical subscriptions (299 health-care related).

BACCALAUREATE PROGRAMS

Degree BSN

Available Programs ADN to Baccalaureate; Accelerated Baccalaureate; Generic Baccalaureate; RN Baccalaureate.

Site Options Fairhope, AL.

Study Options Full-time and part-time.

Program Entrance Requirements Minimum overall college GPA of 2.5, transcript of college record, CPR certification, health exam, health insurance, immunizations, minimum GPA in nursing prerequisites of 2.5, professional liability insurance/malpractice insurance, prerequisite course work. Transfer students are accepted.

Advanced Placement Credit given for nursing courses completed elsewhere dependent upon specific evaluations.

Contact *Telephone:* 251-434-3410. *Fax:* 251-434-3413.

GRADUATE PROGRAMS

Contact *Telephone:* 251-434-3410. *Fax:* 251-434-3413.

MASTER'S DEGREE PROGRAM

Degree MSN

Available Programs Accelerated Master's; Master's; Master's for Nurses with Non-Nursing Degrees.

Concentrations Available Nursing administration; nursing education. *Clinical nurse specialist programs in:* acute care, community health, family health, gerontology, maternity-newborn, pediatric, psychiatric/mental health, women's health. *Nurse practitioner programs in:* acute care, family health, gerontology, neonatal health, pediatric, psychiatric/mental health, women's health.

Study Options Full-time and part-time.

Program Entrance Requirements Computer literacy, minimum overall college GPA of 3.0, transcript of college record, immunizations, nursing research course, physical assessment course, resume.

Advanced Placement Credit given for nursing courses completed elsewhere dependent upon specific evaluations.

Degree Requirements 30 total credit hours, thesis or project.

POST-MASTER'S PROGRAM

Areas of Study Nursing administration; nursing education. *Clinical nurse specialist programs in:* acute care, community health, family health, gerontology, maternity-newborn, pediatric, psychiatric/mental health, women's health. *Nurse practitioner programs in:* acute care, family health, gerontology, neonatal health, pediatric, psychiatric/mental health, women's health.

ALASKA

University of Alaska Anchorage

School of Nursing
Anchorage, Alaska

http://www.son.uaa.alaska.edu

Founded in 1954

DEGREES • BS • MS

Nursing Program Faculty 26 (42% with doctorates).

Baccalaureate Enrollment 224
Women 80% **Men** 20% **Minority** 31% **International** 3% **Part-time** 18%

Graduate Enrollment 60
Women 94% **Men** 6% **Minority** 9% **Part-time** 12%

Nursing Student Activities Sigma Theta Tau, Student Nurses' Association.

Nursing Student Resources Academic advising; academic or career counseling; assistance for students with disabilities; bookstore; campus computer network; career placement assistance; computer lab; computer-assisted instruction; daycare for children of students; e-mail services; interactive nursing skills videos; Internet; learning resource lab; library services; nursing audiovisuals; placement services for program completers; remedial services; resume preparation assistance; skills, simulation, or other laboratory; tutoring.

Library Facilities 894,080 volumes (23,000 in health, 150 in nursing); 3,833 periodical subscriptions (780 health-care related).

BACCALAUREATE PROGRAMS

Degree BS

Available Programs Generic Baccalaureate; RN Baccalaureate.

Study Options Full-time and part-time.

Program Entrance Requirements Minimum overall college GPA of 2.7, transcript of college record, CPR certification, written essay, immunizations, 3 letters of recommendation, minimum GPA in nursing prerequisites of 2.7, professional liability insurance/malpractice insurance, prerequisite course work. Transfer students are accepted.

Advanced Placement Credit given for nursing courses completed elsewhere dependent upon specific evaluations.

Contact *Telephone:* 907-786-4550. *Fax:* 907-786-4558.

GRADUATE PROGRAMS

Contact *Telephone:* 907-786-4570. *Fax:* 907-786-4559.

MASTER'S DEGREE PROGRAM

Degree MS

Available Programs Master's.

Concentrations Available Health-care administration; nursing education. *Clinical nurse specialist programs in:* community health, psychiatric/mental health. *Nurse practitioner programs in:* family health, psychiatric/mental health.

Study Options Full-time and part-time.

Program Entrance Requirements Clinical experience, minimum overall college GPA of 3.0, transcript of college record, written essay, 3 letters of recommendation, nursing research course, prerequisite course work, statistics course, GRE or MAT.

Advanced Placement Credit given for nursing courses completed elsewhere dependent upon specific evaluations.

Degree Requirements 50 total credit hours, thesis or project.

ARIZONA

Arizona State University at the Downtown Phoenix Campus
College of Nursing
Phoenix, Arizona

http://nursing.asu.edu

Founded in 2006

DEGREES • BSN • DNP • MS • MS/MPH

Nursing Program Faculty 119 (44% with doctorates).

Baccalaureate Enrollment 1,625
Women 89% **Men** 11% **Minority** 29% **International** 1% **Part-time** 18%

Graduate Enrollment 179
Women 91% **Men** 9% **Minority** 7% **Part-time** 46%

Distance Learning Courses Available.

Nursing Student Activities Nursing Honor Society, Sigma Theta Tau, Student Nurses' Association, nursing club.

Nursing Student Resources Academic advising; academic or career counseling; assistance for students with disabilities; bookstore; campus computer network; career placement assistance; computer lab; computer-assisted instruction; daycare for children of students; e-mail services; employment services for current students; housing assistance; interactive nursing skills videos; Internet; learning resource lab; library services; nursing audiovisuals; paid internships; placement services for program completers; remedial services; resume preparation assistance; skills, simulation, or other laboratory; tutoring; unpaid internships.

Library Facilities 77,814 volumes in health, 7,501 volumes in nursing; 755 periodical subscriptions health-care related.

BACCALAUREATE PROGRAMS

Degree BSN

Available Programs Accelerated Baccalaureate for Second Degree; Accelerated RN Baccalaureate; Baccalaureate for Second Degree; Generic Baccalaureate; RN Baccalaureate.

Site Options Scottsdale, AZ; Phoenix, AZ.

Study Options Full-time.

Program Entrance Requirements Minimum overall college GPA of 2.75, transcript of college record, CPR certification, health exam, high school biology, high school chemistry, high school foreign language, 4 years high school math, 3 years high school science, high school transcript, immunizations, minimum high school GPA of 3.0, minimum high school rank 25%, minimum GPA in nursing prerequisites of 3.25, prerequisite course work. *Application deadline:* 5/1 (fall); 9/1 (spring); 2/1 (summer).

Financial Aid 70% of baccalaureate students in nursing programs received some form of financial aid in 2008–09.

Contact Ms. Maurine Lee, Senior Student Support Specialist, College of Nursing, Arizona State University at the Downtown Phoenix Campus, 500 North 3rd Street, Phoenix, AZ 85004. *Telephone:* 602-496-0888. *Fax:* 602-496-0705. *E-mail:* maurine.lee@asu.edu.

GRADUATE PROGRAMS

Financial Aid 75% of graduate students in nursing programs received some form of financial aid in 2008–09.

Contact Ms. Eula Bradley, Academic Success Coordinator, College of Nursing, Arizona State University at the Downtown Phoenix Campus, 550 North 3rd Street, Phoenix, AZ 85004. *Telephone:* 602-496-0703. *E-mail:* eula.bradley@asu.edu.

MASTER'S DEGREE PROGRAM

Degrees MS; MS/MPH

Available Programs Master's.

Concentrations Available *Clinical nurse specialist programs in:* acute care, adult health, community health, pediatric, psychiatric/mental health. *Nurse practitioner programs in:* acute care, adult health, family health, neonatal health, pediatric, psychiatric/mental health, women's health.

Site Options Phoenix, AZ.

Study Options Full-time and part-time.

Program Entrance Requirements Clinical experience, minimum overall college GPA of 3.0, transcript of college record, immunizations, interview, 3 letters of recommendation, physical assessment course, prerequisite course work, resume, statistics course, GRE.

Advanced Placement Credit given for nursing courses completed elsewhere dependent upon specific evaluations.

Degree Requirements 40 total credit hours, thesis or project.

POST-MASTER'S PROGRAM

Areas of Study *Clinical nurse specialist programs in:* acute care, adult health, community health, pediatric, psychiatric/mental health. *Nurse practitioner programs in:* acute care, adult health, family health, neonatal health, pediatric, psychiatric/mental health, women's health.

DOCTORAL DEGREE PROGRAM

Degree DNP

Available Programs Doctorate.

Areas of Study Advanced practice nursing.

Site Options Phoenix, AZ.

CONTINUING EDUCATION PROGRAM

Contact Daniel Weberg, Faculty Associate, College of Nursing, Arizona State University at the Downtown Phoenix Campus, 550 North 3rd Stret, Phoenix, AZ 85004. *Telephone:* 602-496-0878. *E-mail:* Daniel.Weberg@asu.edu.

Grand Canyon University
College of Nursing and Health Sciences
Phoenix, Arizona

Founded in 1949

DEGREES • BSN • MS • MS/MBA

Nursing Program Faculty 122 (3% with doctorates).

Baccalaureate Enrollment 1,067
Women 90% **Men** 10% **International** .01% **Part-time** 58%

Graduate Enrollment 297
Women 93% **Men** 7% **Part-time** 89%

Distance Learning Courses Available.

Nursing Student Activities Sigma Theta Tau, Student Nurses' Association.

Nursing Student Resources Academic advising; academic or career counseling; assistance for students with disabilities; bookstore; campus computer network; career placement assistance; computer lab; computer-assisted instruction; e-mail services; employment services for current

Grand Canyon University (continued)

students; housing assistance; Internet; learning resource lab; library services; nursing audiovisuals; other; paid internships; remedial services; resume preparation assistance; skills, simulation, or other laboratory; tutoring; unpaid internships.

Library Facilities 9,663 volumes in health; 177 periodical subscriptions health-care related.

BACCALAUREATE PROGRAMS

Degree BSN

Available Programs ADN to Baccalaureate; Accelerated Baccalaureate; Generic Baccalaureate; RN Baccalaureate.

Site Options Phoenix, AZ; Tucson, AZ.

Study Options Full-time.

Online Degree Options Yes.

Program Entrance Requirements Minimum overall college GPA of 3.0, transcript of college record, CPR certification, health exam, health insurance, high school transcript, immunizations, minimum GPA in nursing prerequisites of 3.0, prerequisite course work. Transfer students are accepted.

Advanced Placement Credit by examination available. Credit given for nursing courses completed elsewhere dependent upon specific evaluations.

Contact Denise Tolitsky, Associate Director of Enrollment, College of Nursing and Health Sciences, College of Nursing and Health Sciences, Grand Canyon University, 3300 West Camelback Road, Phoenix, AZ 85017. *Telephone:* 602-639-6478. *E-mail:* dtolitsky@gcu.edu.

GRADUATE PROGRAMS

Contact Denise Tolitsky, Associate Director of Enrollment, College of Nursing and Health Sciences, College of Nursing and Health Sciences, Grand Canyon University, 3300 West Camelback Road, Phoenix, AZ 85017. *Telephone:* 602-639-6478. *E-mail:* dtolitsky@gcu.edu.

MASTER'S DEGREE PROGRAM

Degrees MS; MS/MBA

Available Programs Master's; RN to Master's.

Concentrations Available Health-care administration; nursing education. *Clinical nurse specialist programs in:* adult health. *Nurse practitioner programs in:* family health.

Site Options Phoenix, AZ; Tucson, AZ.

Study Options Full-time and part-time.

Online Degree Options Yes.

Program Entrance Requirements Computer literacy, minimum overall college GPA of 3.0, transcript of college record, CPR certification, immunizations, nursing research course, physical assessment course, professional liability insurance/malpractice insurance, prerequisite course work, statistics course.

Advanced Placement Credit given for nursing courses completed elsewhere dependent upon specific evaluations.

Degree Requirements 52 total credit hours, thesis or project.

POST-MASTER'S PROGRAM

Areas of Study Nursing education. *Clinical nurse specialist programs in:* adult health. *Nurse practitioner programs in:* family health.

CONTINUING EDUCATION PROGRAM

Contact Mrs. Nancy Webber, RN, Director of Continuing Education, College of Nursing and Health Sciences, Grand Canyon University, 3300 West Camelback Road, Phoenix, AZ 85017. *Telephone:* 623-639-6164. *Fax:* 602-639-7816. *E-mail:* nwebber@gcu.edu.

See full description on page 496.

Northern Arizona University

School of Nursing
Flagstaff, Arizona

http://www.nau.edu/hp/dept/nurse

Founded in 1899

DEGREES • BSN • MS

Nursing Program Faculty 60 (22% with doctorates).

Baccalaureate Enrollment 450
Women 89% **Men** 11% **Minority** 18% **International** 1% **Part-time** 17%

Graduate Enrollment 65
Women 98% **Men** 2% **Minority** 21% **Part-time** 40%

Distance Learning Courses Available.

Nursing Student Activities Nursing Honor Society, Sigma Theta Tau, Student Nurses' Association.

Nursing Student Resources Academic advising; academic or career counseling; bookstore; campus computer network; computer lab; computer-assisted instruction; e-mail services; externships; interactive nursing skills videos; Internet; learning resource lab; library services; nursing audiovisuals; paid internships; remedial services; skills, simulation, or other laboratory; tutoring.

Library Facilities 1.1 million volumes; 43,560 periodical subscriptions.

BACCALAUREATE PROGRAMS

Degree BSN

Available Programs Accelerated Baccalaureate for Second Degree; Generic Baccalaureate; RN Baccalaureate.

Site Options St. Michaels/Window Rock, AZ; Tucson, AZ; Yuma, AZ.

Study Options Full-time.

Online Degree Options Yes (online only).

Program Entrance Requirements Transcript of college record, CPR certification, written essay, health exam, health insurance, high school transcript, immunizations, 2 letters of recommendation, minimum GPA in nursing prerequisites of 2.75, professional liability insurance/malpractice insurance, prerequisite course work. Transfer students are accepted. *Application deadline:* 3/15 (fall), 9/15 (spring).

Advanced Placement Credit given for nursing courses completed elsewhere dependent upon specific evaluations.

Financial Aid 75% of baccalaureate students in nursing programs received some form of financial aid in 2008–09. *Gift aid (need-based):* Federal Pell, FSEOG, state, private, college/university gift aid from institutional funds, Federal Nursing. *Loans:* Federal Nursing Student Loans, Federal Direct (Subsidized and Unsubsidized Stafford PLUS), Perkins, state, college/university. *Work-study:* Federal Work-Study, part-time campus jobs. *Financial aid application deadline (priority):* 2/14.

Contact Mr. Gregg Schneider, Senior Academic Advisor, School of Nursing, Northern Arizona University, Box 15035, Flagstaff, AZ 86011. *Telephone:* 928-523-6717. *Fax:* 928-523-7171. *E-mail:* gregg.schneider@nau.edu.

GRADUATE PROGRAMS

Financial Aid 75% of graduate students in nursing programs received some form of financial aid in 2008–09. 1 research assistantship was awarded.

Contact Mr. Gregg Schneider, Senior Academic Advisor, School of Nursing, Northern Arizona University, Box 15035, Flagstaff, AZ 86011. *Telephone:* 928-523-6717. *Fax:* 928-523-7171. *E-mail:* gregg.schneider@nau.edu.

MASTER'S DEGREE PROGRAM

Degree MS

Available Programs Master's.

Concentrations Available Nursing education. *Nurse practitioner programs in:* family health.

Site Options St. Michaels/Window Rock, AZ; Tucson, AZ; Yuma, AZ.

Study Options Full-time and part-time.

Online Degree Options Yes (online only).

Program Entrance Requirements Clinical experience, minimum overall college GPA of 3.0, transcript of college record, CPR certification, written essay, immunizations, interview, 3 letters of recommendation, nursing research course, physical assessment course, professional liability insurance/malpractice insurance, prerequisite course work, resume, statistics course, GRE General Test.

Degree Requirements 39 total credit hours, thesis or project.

POST-MASTER'S PROGRAM

Areas of Study *Nurse practitioner programs in:* family health.

The University of Arizona
College of Nursing
Tucson, Arizona

http://www.nursing.arizona.edu

Founded in 1885

DEGREES • BSN • PHD

Nursing Program Faculty 64 (58% with doctorates).

Baccalaureate Enrollment 268
Women 89.5% **Men** 10.5% **Minority** 27.6% **International** 1.5%

Graduate Enrollment 126
Women 86.5% **Men** 13.5% **Minority** 26.2% **International** 4% **Part-time** 5%

Distance Learning Courses Available.

Nursing Student Activities Nursing Honor Society, Sigma Theta Tau, Student Nurses' Association, nursing club.

Nursing Student Resources Academic advising; academic or career counseling; assistance for students with disabilities; bookstore; campus computer network; career placement assistance; computer lab; computer-assisted instruction; e-mail services; externships; housing assistance; interactive nursing skills videos; Internet; learning resource lab; library services; nursing audiovisuals; other; placement services for program completers; skills, simulation, or other laboratory; tutoring.

Library Facilities 5.3 million volumes (112,500 in health, 5,400 in nursing); 62,468 periodical subscriptions (10,785 health-care related).

BACCALAUREATE PROGRAMS

Degree BSN

Available Programs Accelerated Baccalaureate for Second Degree; Generic Baccalaureate.

Study Options Full-time.

Program Entrance Requirements Minimum overall college GPA of 3.0, transcript of college record, written essay, interview, minimum GPA in nursing prerequisites of 3.0, prerequisite course work. Transfer students are accepted. *Application deadline:* 2/1 (fall), 9/1 (spring), 1/15 (summer).

Advanced Placement Credit by examination available. Credit given for nursing courses completed elsewhere dependent upon specific evaluations.

Expenses (2009–10) *Tuition, area resident:* full-time $7774. *Tuition, nonresident:* full-time $22,982. *International tuition:* $2982 full-time. *Room and board:* $7934 per academic year. *Required fees:* full-time $1080.

Financial Aid 75% of baccalaureate students in nursing programs received some form of financial aid in 2008–09.

Contact Ms. Vickie Radoye, Assistant Dean for Student Affairs, College of Nursing, The University of Arizona, 1305 North Martin, PO Box 210203, Tucson, AZ 85721-0203. *Telephone:* 520-626-3808. *Fax:* 520-626-6424. *E-mail:* vradoye@nursing.arizona.edu.

GRADUATE PROGRAMS

Expenses (2009–10) *Tuition, area resident:* full-time $11,764. *Tuition, nonresident:* full-time $26,476. *International tuition:* $26,476 full-time. *Room and board:* $11,234 per academic year. *Required fees:* full-time $1082.

Financial Aid 76% of graduate students in nursing programs received some form of financial aid in 2008–09. 6 research assistantships with full tuition reimbursements available (averaging $16,201 per year), 34 teaching assistantships with full tuition reimbursements available (averaging $14,342 per year) were awarded; career-related internships or fieldwork, institutionally sponsored loans, scholarships, traineeships, tuition waivers (full), and unspecified assistantships also available. *Financial aid application deadline:* 6/1.

Contact Sue Rawley, Senior Academic Advisor, College of Nursing, The University of Arizona, 1305 North Martin, PO Box 210203, Tucson, AZ 85721-0203. *Telephone:* 520-626-3808. *Fax:* 520-626-6424. *E-mail:* srawley@nursing.arizona.edu.

MASTER'S DEGREE PROGRAM

Site Options Tucson, AZ.

Program Entrance Requirements *Application deadline:* 3/1 (fall).

DOCTORAL DEGREE PROGRAM

Degree PhD

Available Programs Doctorate; Post-Baccalaureate Doctorate.

Areas of Study Aging, bio-behavioral research, biology of health and illness, health promotion/disease prevention, health-care systems, information systems, nursing research, nursing science.

Site Options Tucson, AZ.

Online Degree Options Yes (online only).

Program Entrance Requirements Minimum overall college GPA of 3.0, interview by faculty committee, interview, 3 letters of recommendation, statistics course, vita. Application deadline: 12/15 (fall).

Degree Requirements 64 total credit hours, dissertation, oral exam, written exam, residency.

POSTDOCTORAL PROGRAM

Areas of Study Nursing research.

Postdoctoral Program Contact Ms. Vickie Radoye, Assistant Dean for Student Affairs, College of Nursing, The University of Arizona, 1305 North Martin, PO Box 210203, Tucson, AZ 85721-0203. *Telephone:* 520-626-3808. *Fax:* 520-626-6424. *E-mail:* vradoye@nursing.arizona.edu.

University of Phoenix
Online Campus
Phoenix, Arizona

Founded in 1989

DEGREES • BSN • MSN • MSN/MBA • MSN/MHA • PHD

Nursing Program Faculty 444 (29% with doctorates).

Baccalaureate Enrollment 5,644
Women 92.2% **Men** 7.8% **Minority** 18.1%

Graduate Enrollment 5,878
Women 92.5% **Men** 7.5% **Minority** 23%

Distance Learning Courses Available.

Nursing Student Activities Sigma Theta Tau.

Nursing Student Resources Academic advising; academic or career counseling; assistance for students with disabilities; bookstore; campus computer network; computer lab; computer-assisted instruction; e-mail services; interactive nursing skills videos; Internet; learning resource lab; library services; nursing audiovisuals; remedial services; skills, simulation, or other laboratory; tutoring.

Library Facilities 16,781 periodical subscriptions (1,300 health-care related).

BACCALAUREATE PROGRAMS

Degree BSN

Available Programs Accelerated Baccalaureate.

Study Options Full-time.

Online Degree Options Yes.

Program Entrance Requirements Transcript of college record, CPR certification, immunizations, 1 letter of recommendation, RN licensure. Transfer students are accepted. *Application deadline:* Applications may be processed on a rolling basis for some programs.

Advanced Placement Credit by examination available. Credit given for nursing courses completed elsewhere dependent upon specific evaluations.

Expenses (2009–10) *Tuition:* full-time $10,800. *International tuition:* $10,800 full-time. *Required fees:* full-time $600.

Contact Program Chair, Healthcare, Online Campus, University of Phoenix, CF-A101, 3157 East Elwood Street, Phoenix, AZ 85034-7209. *Telephone:* 602-387-7000.

GRADUATE PROGRAMS

Expenses (2009–10) *Tuition:* full-time $13,200. *International tuition:* $13,200 full-time. *Required fees:* full-time $760.

Contact Program Chair, Healthcare, Online Campus, University of Phoenix, Phoenix, AZ 85034-7209. *Telephone:* 602-387-7000.

University of Phoenix (continued)

MASTER'S DEGREE PROGRAM

Degrees MSN; MSN/MBA; MSN/MHA

Available Programs Master's; Master's for Nurses with Non-Nursing Degrees.

Concentrations Available Health-care administration; nursing administration; nursing education. *Nurse practitioner programs in:* family health.

Study Options Full-time.

Online Degree Options Yes.

Program Entrance Requirements Clinical experience, computer literacy, minimum overall college GPA of 3.0, transcript of college record, CPR certification. *Application deadline:* Applications may be processed on a rolling basis for some programs.

Advanced Placement Credit given for nursing courses completed elsewhere dependent upon specific evaluations.

Degree Requirements 39 total credit hours, thesis or project.

POST-MASTER'S PROGRAM

Areas of Study *Nurse practitioner programs in:* family health.

DOCTORAL DEGREE PROGRAM

Degree PhD

Available Programs Doctorate.

Areas of Study Nursing administration, nursing education.

Online Degree Options Yes (online only).

Program Entrance Requirements Minimum overall college GPA of 3.0, MSN or equivalent. Application deadline: Applications may be processed on a rolling basis for some programs. Application fee: $45.

Degree Requirements 62 total credit hours, dissertation, residency.

CONTINUING EDUCATION PROGRAM

Contact Program Chair, Healthcare, Online Campus, University of Phoenix, Phoenix, AZ 85034. *Telephone:* 602-387-7000.

See full description on page 524.

University of Phoenix–Phoenix Campus
College of Health and Human Services
Phoenix, Arizona

Founded in 1976

DEGREES • BSN • MSN • MSN/MBA • MSN/MHA

Nursing Program Faculty 38 (32% with doctorates).

Baccalaureate Enrollment 239
Women 89.5% **Men** 10.5% **Minority** 23.4%

Graduate Enrollment 148
Women 91.9% **Men** 8.1% **Minority** 14.86%

Nursing Student Activities Sigma Theta Tau.

Nursing Student Resources Academic advising; academic or career counseling; assistance for students with disabilities; bookstore; campus computer network; computer lab; computer-assisted instruction; interactive nursing skills videos; Internet; learning resource lab; library services; nursing audiovisuals; skills, simulation, or other laboratory; tutoring.

Library Facilities 16,781 periodical subscriptions (1,300 health-care related).

BACCALAUREATE PROGRAMS

Degree BSN

Available Programs Accelerated Baccalaureate; LPN to Baccalaureate.
Site Options Scottsdale, AZ; Mesa, AZ; Chandler, AZ.
Study Options Full-time.
Online Degree Options Yes.

Program Entrance Requirements Transcript of college record, CPR certification, immunizations, 1 letter of recommendation, RN licensure. Transfer students are accepted. *Application deadline:* Applications may be processed on a rolling basis for some programs.

Advanced Placement Credit by examination available. Credit given for nursing courses completed elsewhere dependent upon specific evaluations.

Expenses (2009–10) *Tuition:* full-time $9300. *Required fees:* full-time $600.

Contact Campus College Chair, Nursing, College of Health and Human Services, University of Phoenix–Phoenix Campus, 4635 East Elwood Street, Phoenix, AZ 85040-1958. *Telephone:* 480-804-7600.

GRADUATE PROGRAMS

Expenses (2009–10) *Tuition:* full-time $10,560. *Required fees:* full-time $760.

Financial Aid Institutionally sponsored loans and scholarships available.

Contact Campus College Chair, Nursing, College of Health and Human Services, University of Phoenix–Phoenix Campus, 4635 East Elwood Street, Phoenix, AZ 85040-1958. *Telephone:* 480-804-7600.

MASTER'S DEGREE PROGRAM

Degrees MSN; MSN/MBA; MSN/MHA

Available Programs Master's.

Concentrations Available Health-care administration; nursing administration; nursing education. *Nurse practitioner programs in:* family health.

Site Options Scottsdale, AZ; Mesa, AZ; Chandler, AZ.

Study Options Full-time.

Online Degree Options Yes.

Program Entrance Requirements Clinical experience, computer literacy, minimum overall college GPA of 2.5, transcript of college record. *Application deadline:* Applications may be processed on a rolling basis for some programs. *Application fee:* $45.

Advanced Placement Credit given for nursing courses completed elsewhere dependent upon specific evaluations.

Degree Requirements 39 total credit hours, thesis or project.

POST-MASTER'S PROGRAM

Areas of Study *Nurse practitioner programs in:* family health.

CONTINUING EDUCATION PROGRAM

Contact Campus College Chair, Nursing, College of Health and Human Services, University of Phoenix–Phoenix Campus, Mail Stop CJ A101, 4635 East Elwood Street, Phoenix, AZ 85040-1958. *Telephone:* 480-557-2279. *Fax:* 480-557-2338.

University of Phoenix–Southern Arizona Campus
College of Health and Human Services
Tucson, Arizona

Founded in 1979

DEGREES • BSN • MSN

Nursing Program Faculty 19 (32% with doctorates).

Baccalaureate Enrollment 67
Women 85.1% **Men** 14.9% **Minority** 33.8%

Graduate Enrollment 97
Women 80.4% **Men** 19.6% **Minority** 18.56%

Nursing Student Activities Sigma Theta Tau.

Nursing Student Resources Academic advising; academic or career counseling; assistance for students with disabilities; bookstore; campus computer network; computer lab; computer-assisted instruction; e-mail services; interactive nursing skills videos; Internet; learning resource lab; library services; nursing audiovisuals; remedial services; skills, simulation, or other laboratory; tutoring.

Library Facilities 16,781 periodical subscriptions (1,300 health-care related).

BACCALAUREATE PROGRAMS

Degree BSN

Available Programs Accelerated Baccalaureate; LPN to Baccalaureate.

Site Options Sierra Vista, AZ; Yuma, AZ; Nogales, AZ.

Study Options Full-time.

Online Degree Options Yes.

Program Entrance Requirements Transcript of college record, CPR certification, immunizations, 1 letter of recommendation, RN licensure. Transfer students are accepted. *Application deadline:* Applications may be processed on a rolling basis for some programs.

Advanced Placement Credit by examination available. Credit given for nursing courses completed elsewhere dependent upon specific evaluations.

Expenses (2009–10) *Tuition:* full-time $9300. *Required fees:* full-time $600.

Contact Campus College Chair, Nursing, College of Health and Human Services, University of Phoenix–Southern Arizona Campus, 300 South Craycroft Road, Tucson, AZ 85711-4574. *Telephone:* 520-881-6512.

GRADUATE PROGRAMS

Expenses (2009–10) *Tuition:* full-time $10,560. *Required fees:* full-time $760.

Financial Aid Institutionally sponsored loans and scholarships available.

Contact Campus College Chair, Nursing, College of Health and Human Services, University of Phoenix–Southern Arizona Campus, 300 South Craycroft Road, Tucson, AZ 85711-4574. *Telephone:* 520-881-6512.

MASTER'S DEGREE PROGRAM

Degree MSN

Available Programs Master's.

Concentrations Available Health-care administration; nursing administration; nursing education. *Nurse practitioner programs in:* family health.

Site Options Sierra Vista, AZ; Yuma, AZ; Nogales, AZ.

Study Options Full-time.

Online Degree Options Yes.

Program Entrance Requirements Clinical experience, computer literacy, minimum overall college GPA of 2.5, transcript of college record. *Application deadline:* Applications may be processed on a rolling basis for some programs. *Application fee:* $45.

Advanced Placement Credit given for nursing courses completed elsewhere dependent upon specific evaluations.

Degree Requirements 39 total credit hours, thesis or project.

POST-MASTER'S PROGRAM

Areas of Study *Nurse practitioner programs in:* family health.

CONTINUING EDUCATION PROGRAM

Contact Campus College Chair, Nursing, College of Health and Human Services, University of Phoenix–Southern Arizona Campus, 300 South Craycroft Road, Tucson, AZ 85711-4574. *Telephone:* 520-881-6512.

ARKANSAS

Arkansas State University

Department of Nursing

Jonesboro, State University, Arkansas

http://www.conhp.astate.edu/Nursing/

Founded in 1909

DEGREES • BSN • MSN

Nursing Program Faculty 35 (20% with doctorates).

Baccalaureate Enrollment 245

Graduate Enrollment 91

Nursing Student Activities Nursing Honor Society, Sigma Theta Tau.

Library Facilities 620,610 volumes; 2,764 periodical subscriptions.

BACCALAUREATE PROGRAMS

Degree BSN

Available Programs Generic Baccalaureate; LPN to Baccalaureate; RN Baccalaureate.

Site Options Mountain Home, AR; Melbourne, AR; Beebe, AR.

Study Options Full-time.

Program Entrance Requirements Minimum overall college GPA of 2.5, transcript of college record, CPR certification, health exam, immunizations, minimum GPA in nursing prerequisites of 3.5, prerequisite course work. Transfer students are accepted.

Advanced Placement Credit given for nursing courses completed elsewhere dependent upon specific evaluations.

Contact *Telephone:* 870-972-3074. *Fax:* 870-972-2954.

GRADUATE PROGRAMS

Contact *Telephone:* 870-972-3074. *Fax:* 870-972-2954.

MASTER'S DEGREE PROGRAM

Degree MSN

Available Programs Master's.

Concentrations Available Nurse anesthesia; nursing education. *Clinical nurse specialist programs in:* adult health. *Nurse practitioner programs in:* primary care.

Site Options Mountain Home, AR; Melbourne, AR; Beebe, AR.

Study Options Full-time and part-time.

Program Entrance Requirements Clinical experience, minimum overall college GPA of 2.75, transcript of college record, CPR certification, written essay, immunizations, interview, letters of recommendation, physical assessment course, professional liability insurance/malpractice insurance, statistics course.

Degree Requirements 39 total credit hours, thesis or project, comprehensive exam.

Arkansas Tech University

Program in Nursing

Russellville, Arkansas

http://nursing.atu.edu

Founded in 1909

DEGREES • BSN • MSN

Nursing Program Faculty 26 (20% with doctorates).

Baccalaureate Enrollment 205

Women 84% **Men** 16% **Minority** 11% **Part-time** 14%

Graduate Enrollment 8

Women 87% **Men** 13% **Part-time** 13%

Distance Learning Courses Available.

Nursing Student Activities Nursing Honor Society, Sigma Theta Tau, Student Nurses' Association.

Nursing Student Resources Academic advising; academic or career counseling; assistance for students with disabilities; bookstore; campus computer network; career placement assistance; computer lab; computer-assisted instruction; e-mail services; employment services for current students; housing assistance; interactive nursing skills videos; Internet; learning resource lab; library services; nursing audiovisuals; other; paid internships; placement services for program completers; remedial services; resume preparation assistance; skills, simulation, or other laboratory; tutoring.

Library Facilities 278,540 volumes (16,900 in health, 2,100 in nursing); 1,069 periodical subscriptions (130 health-care related).

BACCALAUREATE PROGRAMS

Degree BSN

Available Programs ADN to Baccalaureate; Generic Baccalaureate; LPN to Baccalaureate; RN Baccalaureate.

Site Options Russellville, AR.

Arkansas Tech University (continued)

Study Options Full-time and part-time.

Online Degree Options Yes.

Program Entrance Requirements Transcript of college record, CPR certification, health exam, immunizations, minimum GPA in nursing prerequisites of 2.75, professional liability insurance/malpractice insurance, prerequisite course work. Transfer students are accepted. *Application deadline:* 6/30 (fall), 10/30 (spring).

Advanced Placement Credit by examination available. Credit given for nursing courses completed elsewhere dependent upon specific evaluations.

Expenses (2009–10) *Room and board:* $5665; room only: $3665 per academic year.

Financial Aid 80% of baccalaureate students in nursing programs received some form of financial aid in 2008–09.

Contact Dr. Rebecca F. Burris, Professor and Department Chair, Program in Nursing, Arkansas Tech University, 402 West O Street, Russellville, AR 72801. *Telephone:* 479-968-0383. *Fax:* 479-968-0219. *E-mail:* rburris@atu. edu.

GRADUATE PROGRAMS

Expenses (2009–10) *Tuition, state resident:* part-time $175 per credit hour. *Tuition, nonresident:* part-time $350 per credit hour. *Required fees:* part-time $8 per credit; part-time $120 per term.

Financial Aid 75% of graduate students in nursing programs received some form of financial aid in 2008–09.

Contact Dr. Eldon Clarey, Dean of Graduate School, Program in Nursing, Arkansas Tech University, Tomlinson Graduate School, Russellville, AR 72801. *Telephone:* 479-968-0398. *E-mail:* eclarey@atu.edu.

MASTER'S DEGREE PROGRAM

Degree MSN

Available Programs Master's; Master's for Nurses with Non-Nursing Degrees; RN to Master's.

Concentrations Available Nursing administration.

Site Options Russellville, AR.

Study Options Full-time and part-time.

Program Entrance Requirements Clinical experience, computer literacy, minimum overall college GPA of 3.0, transcript of college record, statistics course. *Application deadline:* 3/1 (fall).

Advanced Placement Credit given for nursing courses completed elsewhere dependent upon specific evaluations.

Degree Requirements 39 total credit hours, thesis or project.

Harding University
College of Nursing
Searcy, Arkansas

http://www.harding.edu/nursing

Founded in 1924

DEGREE ● BSN

Nursing Program Faculty 19 (25% with doctorates).

Baccalaureate Enrollment 89
Women 83% **Men** 17% **Minority** 1% **International** 1% **Part-time** 1%

Nursing Student Activities Nursing Honor Society, Sigma Theta Tau, Student Nurses' Association.

Nursing Student Resources Academic advising; academic or career counseling; assistance for students with disabilities; bookstore; campus computer network; career placement assistance; computer lab; computer-assisted instruction; e-mail services; employment services for current students; externships; housing assistance; interactive nursing skills videos; Internet; learning resource lab; library services; nursing audiovisuals; placement services for program completers; remedial services; resume preparation assistance; skills, simulation, or other laboratory; tutoring.

Library Facilities 237,892 volumes (5,000 in health, 1,729 in nursing); 22,180 periodical subscriptions (120 health-care related).

BACCALAUREATE PROGRAMS

Degree BSN

Available Programs ADN to Baccalaureate; Generic Baccalaureate; LPN to Baccalaureate; LPN to RN Baccalaureate; RN Baccalaureate.

Site Options Searcy, AR.

Study Options Full-time and part-time.

Program Entrance Requirements Minimum overall college GPA of 2.0, transcript of college record, CPR certification, health exam, high school transcript, immunizations, 3 letters of recommendation, minimum GPA in nursing prerequisites of 2.5, prerequisite course work. Transfer students are accepted. *Application deadline:* 3/1 (fall), 10/1 (spring).

Advanced Placement Credit by examination available. Credit given for nursing courses completed elsewhere dependent upon specific evaluations.

Expenses (2009–10) *Tuition:* full-time $6352; part-time $4600 per semester. *International tuition:* $6352 full-time. *Room and board:* $3051; room only: $1412 per academic year.

Financial Aid 95% of baccalaureate students in nursing programs received some form of financial aid in 2008–09. *Gift aid (need-based):* Federal Pell, FSEOG, state, private, college/university gift aid from institutional funds. *Loans:* Federal Nursing Student Loans, FFEL (Subsidized and Unsubsidized Stafford PLUS), Perkins, state, college/university. *Work-study:* Federal Work-Study, part-time campus jobs. *Financial aid application deadline (priority):* 4/15.

Contact Ms. Jeanne L. Castleberry, Assistant to the Dean, College of Nursing, Harding University, Box 12265, 914 East Market Avenue, Searcy, AR 72149-2265. *Telephone:* 501-279-4682. *Fax:* 501-305-8902. *E-mail:* nursing@harding.edu.

CONTINUING EDUCATION PROGRAM

Contact Dr. Cathleen M. Shultz, Dean and Professor, College of Nursing, Harding University, Box 12265, Searcy, AR 72149-2265. *Telephone:* 501-279-4476. *Fax:* 501-279-4669. *E-mail:* nursing@harding.edu.

Henderson State University
Department of Nursing
Arkadelphia, Arkansas

http://www.hsu.edu/dept/nsg/index.html

Founded in 1890

DEGREE ● BSN

Nursing Program Faculty 7 (14% with doctorates).

Baccalaureate Enrollment 80
Women 96% **Men** 4% **Minority** 35% **International** 2%

Nursing Student Activities Student Nurses' Association.

Nursing Student Resources Academic advising; academic or career counseling; assistance for students with disabilities; bookstore; campus computer network; career placement assistance; computer lab; computer-assisted instruction; e-mail services; interactive nursing skills videos; Internet; learning resource lab; library services; nursing audiovisuals; remedial services; resume preparation assistance; skills, simulation, or other laboratory; tutoring.

Library Facilities 264,367 volumes (1,000 in health, 200 in nursing); 216,738 periodical subscriptions (40 health-care related).

BACCALAUREATE PROGRAMS

Degree BSN

Available Programs ADN to Baccalaureate; Generic Baccalaureate.

Study Options Full-time and part-time.

Program Entrance Requirements Minimum overall college GPA of 2.5, transcript of college record, CPR certification, immunizations, prerequisite course work. Transfer students are accepted. *Application deadline:* 2/15 (fall). *Application fee:* $57.

Advanced Placement Credit given for nursing courses completed elsewhere dependent upon specific evaluations.

Expenses (2009–10) *Tuition, area resident:* full-time $4920; part-time $170 per hour. *Tuition, nonresident:* full-time $9840; part-time $340 per hour. *International tuition:* $9840 full-time. *Room and board:* $5400; room only: $3270 per academic year. *Required fees:* full-time $1544.

Financial Aid 80% of baccalaureate students in nursing programs received some form of financial aid in 2008–09. *Gift aid (need-based):* Federal Pell, FSEOG, state, private, college/university gift aid from institutional funds. *Loans:* FFEL (Subsidized and Unsubsidized Stafford PLUS), Perkins. *Work-study:* Federal Work-Study, part-time campus jobs. *Financial aid application deadline (priority):* 6/1.

Contact Dr. Barbara J. Landrum, Professor and Department Chair, Department of Nursing, Henderson State University, Box 7803, 1100 Henderson Street, Arkadelphia, AR 71999-0001. *Telephone:* 870-230-5508. *Fax:* 870-230-5390. *E-mail:* landrub@hsu.edu.

Southern Arkansas University–Magnolia

Department of Nursing
Magnolia, Arkansas

http://www.saumag.edu/academics/science_and_technology/nursing/

Founded in 1909

DEGREE • BSN

Nursing Program Faculty 12 (17% with doctorates).
Baccalaureate Enrollment 63
Women 95% **Men** 5% **Minority** 10% **Part-time** 90%
Distance Learning Courses Available.
Nursing Student Activities Student Nurses' Association.
Nursing Student Resources Academic advising; academic or career counseling; assistance for students with disabilities; bookstore; campus computer network; career placement assistance; computer lab; computer-assisted instruction; e-mail services; employment services for current students; housing assistance; interactive nursing skills videos; Internet; learning resource lab; library services; nursing audiovisuals; remedial services; resume preparation assistance; skills, simulation, or other laboratory; tutoring.
Library Facilities 151,166 volumes (800 in health, 200 in nursing); 1,065 periodical subscriptions (2,000 health-care related).

BACCALAUREATE PROGRAMS

Degree BSN

Available Programs ADN to Baccalaureate; Generic Baccalaureate; RN Baccalaureate.
Study Options Full-time and part-time.
Program Entrance Requirements Minimum overall college GPA of 2.5, transcript of college record, CPR certification, immunizations, minimum GPA in nursing prerequisites of 2.5, prerequisite course work. Transfer students are accepted. *Application deadline:* 3/1 (fall). Applications may be processed on a rolling basis for some programs.
Advanced Placement Credit given for nursing courses completed elsewhere dependent upon specific evaluations.
Expenses (2009–10) *Tuition, state resident:* full-time $5100; part-time $170 per credit hour. *Tuition, nonresident:* full-time $7740; part-time $258 per credit hour. *Room and board:* $4450; room only: $2236 per academic year. *Required fees:* full-time $244; part-time $12 per credit.
Financial Aid 40% of baccalaureate students in nursing programs received some form of financial aid in 2008–09. *Gift aid (need-based):* Federal Pell, FSEOG, state, private, college/university gift aid from institutional funds. *Loans:* FFEL (Subsidized and Unsubsidized Stafford PLUS), Perkins. *Work-study:* Federal Work-Study, part-time campus jobs. *Financial aid application deadline (priority):* 7/1.
Contact Dr. Shari Kist, PhD, BSN Program Director, Department of Nursing, Southern Arkansas University–Magnolia, 100 East University, Magnolia, AR 71753-5000. *Telephone:* 870-235-4331. *Fax:* 870-235-5058. *E-mail:* ShariKist@saumag.edu.

University of Arkansas

Eleanor Mann School of Nursing
Fayetteville, Arkansas

http://www.uark.edu/coehp

Founded in 1871

DEGREES • BSN • MSN

Nursing Program Faculty 25 (26% with doctorates).
Baccalaureate Enrollment 220
Women 95% **Men** 5% **Minority** 7%
Graduate Enrollment 20
Nursing Student Activities Sigma Theta Tau, Student Nurses' Association.
Nursing Student Resources Academic advising; academic or career counseling; assistance for students with disabilities; bookstore; campus computer network; career placement assistance; computer lab; computer-assisted instruction; e-mail services; employment services for current students; housing assistance; interactive nursing skills videos; Internet; learning resource lab; library services; nursing audiovisuals; other; placement services for program completers; remedial services; resume preparation assistance; skills, simulation, or other laboratory; tutoring.
Library Facilities 1.8 million volumes (60,000 in health, 20,000 in nursing); 18,576 periodical subscriptions (130,000 health-care related).

BACCALAUREATE PROGRAMS

Degree BSN

Available Programs Generic Baccalaureate; LPN to Baccalaureate; LPN to RN Baccalaureate; RN Baccalaureate.
Study Options Full-time and part-time.
Program Entrance Requirements Minimum overall college GPA of 2.75, transcript of college record, CPR certification, health insurance, immunizations, minimum GPA in nursing prerequisites of 2.75, professional liability insurance/malpractice insurance, prerequisite course work. Transfer students are accepted.
Advanced Placement Credit by examination available. Credit given for nursing courses completed elsewhere dependent upon specific evaluations.
Contact *Telephone:* 479-575-3907. *Fax:* 479-575-3218.

GRADUATE PROGRAMS

Contact *Telephone:* 479-575-3907. *Fax:* 479-575-3218.

MASTER'S DEGREE PROGRAM

Degree MSN

Available Programs Master's.
Concentrations Available Nursing education. *Clinical nurse specialist programs in:* acute care, medical-surgical.
Study Options Full-time and part-time.
Online Degree Options Yes.
Program Entrance Requirements Computer literacy, minimum overall college GPA of 3.0, transcript of college record, CPR certification, immunizations, nursing research course, physical assessment course, statistics course.
Degree Requirements 42 total credit hours, thesis or project, comprehensive exam.

CONTINUING EDUCATION PROGRAM

Contact *Telephone:* 479-575-3907. *Fax:* 479-575-3218.

University of Arkansas at Fort Smith

Carol McKelvey Moore School of Nursing
Fort Smith, Arkansas

Founded in 1928

University of Arkansas at Fort Smith (continued)
DEGREE • BSN

Nursing Program Faculty 18

Baccalaureate Enrollment 20
Women 60% **Men** 40% **Minority** 5%

Distance Learning Courses Available.

Nursing Student Activities Student Nurses' Association.

Nursing Student Resources Academic advising; academic or career counseling; assistance for students with disabilities; bookstore; campus computer network; career placement assistance; computer lab; computer-assisted instruction; e-mail services; housing assistance; interactive nursing skills videos; Internet; learning resource lab; library services; nursing audiovisuals; remedial services; resume preparation assistance; skills, simulation, or other laboratory; tutoring.

Library Facilities 84,427 volumes (2,231 in health, 1,183 in nursing); 1,868 periodical subscriptions (5,350 health-care related).

BACCALAUREATE PROGRAMS

Degree BSN

Available Programs ADN to Baccalaureate; Generic Baccalaureate.
Study Options Full-time.
Online Degree Options Yes (online only).
Program Entrance Requirements Minimum overall college GPA of 2.5, transcript of college record, CPR certification, health exam, health insurance, immunizations, interview, minimum GPA in nursing prerequisites of 2.5, prerequisite course work. Transfer students are accepted.
Advanced Placement Credit given for nursing courses completed elsewhere dependent upon specific evaluations.
Contact *Telephone:* 479-788-7840. *Fax:* 479-788-7869.

University of Arkansas at Monticello

School of Nursing
Monticello, Arkansas

http://www.uamont.edu/Nursing/
Founded in 1909
DEGREE • BSN

Nursing Program Faculty 9 (11% with doctorates).

Baccalaureate Enrollment 70
Women 87% **Men** 13% **Minority** 6%

Distance Learning Courses Available.

Nursing Student Activities Student Nurses' Association.

Nursing Student Resources Academic advising; academic or career counseling; assistance for students with disabilities; bookstore; campus computer network; computer lab; computer-assisted instruction; e-mail services; interactive nursing skills videos; Internet; learning resource lab; library services; nursing audiovisuals; skills, simulation, or other laboratory; tutoring.

Library Facilities 241,822 volumes (3,961 in health, 478 in nursing); 956 periodical subscriptions (239 health-care related).

BACCALAUREATE PROGRAMS

Degree BSN

Available Programs ADN to Baccalaureate; Generic Baccalaureate; LPN to Baccalaureate; RN Baccalaureate.
Study Options Full-time.
Program Entrance Requirements Transcript of college record, health exam, immunizations, minimum GPA in nursing prerequisites of 2.5, professional liability insurance/malpractice insurance, prerequisite course work. Transfer students are accepted. *Application deadline:* 4/1 (spring).
Advanced Placement Credit by examination available. Credit given for nursing courses completed elsewhere dependent upon specific evaluations.

Expenses (2009–10) *Tuition, state resident:* full-time $3510; part-time $114 per credit hour. *Tuition, nonresident:* full-time $7770; part-time $139 per credit hour. *Room and board:* $4350; room only: $1850 per academic year. *Required fees:* full-time $1240; part-time $46 per credit; part-time $620 per term.
Financial Aid 89% of baccalaureate students in nursing programs received some form of financial aid in 2008–09.
Contact Ms. Pamela D. Gouner, RN, Dean, School of Nursing, University of Arkansas at Monticello, PO Box 3606, Monticello, AR 71656. *Telephone:* 870-460-1069. *Fax:* 870-460-1969. *E-mail:* gouner@uamont.edu.

University of Arkansas at Pine Bluff

Department of Nursing
Pine Bluff, Arkansas

http://www.uapb.com
Founded in 1873
DEGREE • BSN

Nursing Program Faculty 7

Baccalaureate Enrollment 51
Women 94% **Men** 6% **Minority** 96%

Nursing Student Activities Student Nurses' Association.

Nursing Student Resources Academic advising; academic or career counseling; assistance for students with disabilities; bookstore; campus computer network; career placement assistance; computer lab; computer-assisted instruction; e-mail services; housing assistance; interactive nursing skills videos; Internet; learning resource lab; library services; nursing audiovisuals; remedial services; resume preparation assistance; skills, simulation, or other laboratory; tutoring.

Library Facilities 287,857 volumes (2,600 in health, 1,550 in nursing); 3,041 periodical subscriptions (60 health-care related).

BACCALAUREATE PROGRAMS

Degree BSN

Available Programs Generic Baccalaureate.
Study Options Full-time and part-time.
Program Entrance Requirements Minimum overall college GPA of 2.5, transcript of college record, CPR certification, written essay, health exam, immunizations, 3 letters of recommendation, minimum GPA in nursing prerequisites of 2.5, professional liability insurance/malpractice insurance, prerequisite course work. Transfer students are accepted.
Advanced Placement Credit by examination available. Credit given for nursing courses completed elsewhere dependent upon specific evaluations.
Contact *Telephone:* 870-575-8220. *Fax:* 870-575-8229.

University of Arkansas for Medical Sciences

College of Nursing
Little Rock, Arkansas

http://www.nursing.uams.edu/
Founded in 1879
DEGREES • BSN • MN SC • PHD

Nursing Program Faculty 85 (38% with doctorates).

Baccalaureate Enrollment 299

Graduate Enrollment 217

Distance Learning Courses Available.

Nursing Student Activities Nursing Honor Society, Sigma Theta Tau, Student Nurses' Association.

Nursing Student Resources Academic advising; academic or career counseling; assistance for students with disabilities; bookstore; campus computer network; computer lab; computer-assisted instruction; e-mail services; externships; interactive nursing skills videos; Internet; learning resource lab; library services; nursing audiovisuals; remedial services; skills, simulation, or other laboratory; tutoring.

Library Facilities 183,975 volumes (183,975 in health); 1,567 periodical subscriptions (1,567 health-care related).

BACCALAUREATE PROGRAMS

Degree BSN

Available Programs ADN to Baccalaureate; Accelerated Baccalaureate for Second Degree; Accelerated RN Baccalaureate; Baccalaureate for Second Degree; Generic Baccalaureate; LPN to Baccalaureate; RN Baccalaureate.

Site Options Texarkana, AR; Helena, AR; Jonesboro, AR; Hope, AR; Fayetteville, AR; El Dorado, AR.

Study Options Full-time.

Online Degree Options Yes.

Program Entrance Requirements Minimum overall college GPA of 2.5, transcript of college record, CPR certification, health insurance, immunizations, minimum high school GPA of 2.5, prerequisite course work. Transfer students are accepted. *Application deadline:* 2/1 (summer).

Advanced Placement Credit by examination available. Credit given for nursing courses completed elsewhere dependent upon specific evaluations.

Expenses (2009–10) *Tuition, state resident:* part-time $208 per hour. *Tuition, nonresident:* part-time $519 per hour.

Contact Dr. Donna Middaugh, Associate Dean for Service, College of Nursing, University of Arkansas for Medical Sciences, 4301 West Markham, #529, Little Rock, AR 72205-7199. *Telephone:* 501-686-5374. *Fax:* 501-686-8350. *E-mail:* middaughdonnaj@uams.edu.

GRADUATE PROGRAMS

Expenses (2009–10) *Tuition, area resident:* part-time $295 per hour. *Tuition, state resident:* part-time $219 per hour. *Tuition, nonresident:* part-time $633 per hour.

Financial Aid Career-related internships or fieldwork and traineeships available.

Contact Dr. Donna Middaugh, Associate Dean for Service, College of Nursing, University of Arkansas for Medical Sciences, 4301 West Markham, #529, Little Rock, AR 72205-7199. *Telephone:* 501-686-8349. *Fax:* 501-686-8350. *E-mail:* middaughdonnaj@uams.edu.

MASTER'S DEGREE PROGRAM

Degree MN Sc

Available Programs Master's; RN to Master's.

Concentrations Available Nursing administration; nursing education. *Clinical nurse specialist programs in:* acute care, adult health, pediatric. *Nurse practitioner programs in:* acute care, family health, gerontology, pediatric, psychiatric/mental health, women's health.

Site Options Texarkana, AR; Helena, AR; Jonesboro, AR; Fayetteville, AR; El Dorado, AR.

Study Options Full-time and part-time.

Program Entrance Requirements Clinical experience, minimum overall college GPA of 2.85, transcript of college record, CPR certification, immunizations, physical assessment course, professional liability insurance/malpractice insurance, statistics course. *Application deadline:* 4/1 (fall), 9/1 (spring).

Advanced Placement Credit given for nursing courses completed elsewhere dependent upon specific evaluations.

Degree Requirements 39 total credit hours, thesis or project, comprehensive exam.

DOCTORAL DEGREE PROGRAM

Degree PhD

Available Programs Doctorate; Doctorate for Nurses with Non-Nursing Degrees; Post-Baccalaureate Doctorate.

Areas of Study Advanced practice nursing, clinical practice, gerontology, health-care systems, nursing administration, nursing education, nursing research, nursing science, oncology, women's health.

Program Entrance Requirements Minimum overall college GPA of 3.65, interview by faculty committee, interview, 4 letters of recommendation, MSN or equivalent, scholarly papers, statistics course, writing sample. Application deadline: 12/31 (spring).

Degree Requirements 60 total credit hours, dissertation, oral exam, written exam.

POSTDOCTORAL PROGRAM

Areas of Study Aging, cancer care, gerontology, nursing research, nursing science.

Postdoctoral Program Contact Postdoctoral Contact, College of Nursing, University of Arkansas for Medical Sciences, 4301 West Markham, #529, Little Rock, AR 72205-7199. *Telephone:* 501-686-5374. *Fax:* 501-686-8350.

CONTINUING EDUCATION PROGRAM

Contact Dr. Claudia P. Barone, Dean and Professor, College of Nursing, University of Arkansas for Medical Sciences, 4301 West Markham, #529, Little Rock, AR 72205-7199. *Telephone:* 501-686-5374. *Fax:* 501-686-8350. *E-mail:* BaroneClaudiaP@uams.edu.

University of Central Arkansas
Department of Nursing
Conway, Arkansas

http://www.uca.edu/divisions/academic/nursing/
Founded in 1907

DEGREES • BSN • MSN

Nursing Program Faculty 32 (28% with doctorates).

Baccalaureate Enrollment 245
Women 84.9% **Men** 15.1% **Minority** 12.65% **International** 2.04% **Part-time** 23.67%

Graduate Enrollment 136
Women 95.59% **Men** 4.41% **Minority** 11.76% **International** .74% **Part-time** 95.59%

Distance Learning Courses Available.

Nursing Student Activities Sigma Theta Tau, Student Nurses' Association.

Nursing Student Resources Academic advising; academic or career counseling; assistance for students with disabilities; bookstore; campus computer network; career placement assistance; computer lab; computer-assisted instruction; e-mail services; employment services for current students; externships; housing assistance; interactive nursing skills videos; Internet; learning resource lab; library services; nursing audiovisuals; paid internships; placement services for program completers; remedial services; resume preparation assistance; skills, simulation, or other laboratory; tutoring; unpaid internships.

Library Facilities 600,084 volumes; 804 periodical subscriptions.

BACCALAUREATE PROGRAMS

Degree BSN

Available Programs ADN to Baccalaureate; Generic Baccalaureate; LPN to Baccalaureate; LPN to RN Baccalaureate; RN Baccalaureate.

Study Options Full-time and part-time.

Program Entrance Requirements Minimum overall college GPA of 2.5, transcript of college record, health exam, health insurance, immunizations, minimum GPA in nursing prerequisites, prerequisite course work. Transfer students are accepted. *Application deadline:* 3/1 (fall). *Application fee:* $50.

Advanced Placement Credit given for nursing courses completed elsewhere dependent upon specific evaluations.

Expenses (2009–10) *Tuition, area resident:* full-time $12,578; part-time $6289 per semester. *Room and board:* $4880 per academic year.

Contact Ms. Ann Mattison, Education Counselor, Department of Nursing, University of Central Arkansas, Doyne Health Science Center, 201 South Donaghey Avenue, Conway, AR 72035. *Telephone:* 501-450-5526. *Fax:* 501-450-5560. *E-mail:* annm@uca.edu.

University of Central Arkansas (continued)

GRADUATE PROGRAMS

Financial Aid Federal Work-Study, traineeships, and unspecified assistantships available.

Contact Ms. Rose Schlosser, Education Counselor, Department of Nursing, University of Central Arkansas, Doyne Health Science Center, 201 South Donaghey Avenue, Conway, AR 72035. *Telephone:* 501-450-5532. *Fax:* 501-450-5560. *E-mail:* RSchlosser@uca.edu.

MASTER'S DEGREE PROGRAM

Degree MSN

Available Programs Master's; RN to Master's.

Concentrations Available Nursing education. *Clinical nurse specialist programs in:* medical-surgical. *Nurse practitioner programs in:* adult health, family health.

Site Options Russelville, AR; Pine Bluff, AR; Fort Smith, AR.

Study Options Full-time and part-time.

Online Degree Options Yes (online only).

Program Entrance Requirements Clinical experience, minimum overall college GPA of 2.7, transcript of college record, CPR certification, immunizations, professional liability insurance/malpractice insurance, prerequisite course work, resume, statistics course, GRE General Test. *Application deadline:* 4/1 (fall), 8/1 (spring). *Application fee:* $50.

Degree Requirements 39 total credit hours, comprehensive exam.

POST-MASTER'S PROGRAM

Areas of Study Nursing education. *Clinical nurse specialist programs in:* medical-surgical. *Nurse practitioner programs in:* adult health, family health.

CALIFORNIA

Azusa Pacific University
School of Nursing
Azusa, California

http://www.apu.edu/nursing/grad

Founded in 1899

DEGREES • BSN • MSN • PHD

Nursing Program Faculty 77 (22% with doctorates).

Baccalaureate Enrollment 236
Women 90% **Men** 10% **Minority** 44% **International** 11% **Part-time** 2%

Graduate Enrollment 110
Women 89% **Men** 11% **Minority** 37%

Nursing Student Activities Sigma Theta Tau, Student Nurses' Association, nursing club.

Nursing Student Resources Academic advising; academic or career counseling; bookstore; campus computer network; career placement assistance; computer lab; computer-assisted instruction; e-mail services; employment services for current students; housing assistance; interactive nursing skills videos; Internet; learning resource lab; library services; nursing audiovisuals; remedial services; resume preparation assistance; skills, simulation, or other laboratory; tutoring.

Library Facilities 185,708 volumes (14,206 in health, 4,712 in nursing); 14,031 periodical subscriptions (432 health-care related).

BACCALAUREATE PROGRAMS

Degree BSN

Available Programs ADN to Baccalaureate; Accelerated Baccalaureate; Accelerated RN Baccalaureate; Generic Baccalaureate.

Study Options Full-time and part-time.

Program Entrance Requirements Minimum overall college GPA of 3.0, transcript of college record, CPR certification, written essay, health exam, high school biology, high school chemistry, 2 years high school math, high school transcript, immunizations, 3 letters of recommendation, minimum high school GPA of 3.0, minimum GPA in nursing prerequisites of 3.0. Transfer students are accepted.

Advanced Placement Credit by examination available. Credit given for nursing courses completed elsewhere dependent upon specific evaluations.

Contact *Telephone:* 626-815-6000 Ext. 5501. *Fax:* 626-815-5414.

GRADUATE PROGRAMS

Contact *Telephone:* 626-815-5386. *Fax:* 626-815-5414.

MASTER'S DEGREE PROGRAM

Degree MSN

Available Programs Accelerated Master's for Non-Nursing College Graduates; Accelerated Master's for Nurses with Non-Nursing Degrees; Master's.

Concentrations Available Nursing administration; nursing education. *Clinical nurse specialist programs in:* adult health, medical-surgical, parent-child, pediatric, school health. *Nurse practitioner programs in:* adult health, family health, pediatric, primary care.

Study Options Full-time and part-time.

Program Entrance Requirements Clinical experience, computer literacy, minimum overall college GPA of 3.0, transcript of college record, CPR certification, written essay, immunizations, 3 letters of recommendation, nursing research course, physical assessment course, professional liability insurance/malpractice insurance, prerequisite course work, resume, statistics course.

Advanced Placement Credit by examination available. Credit given for nursing courses completed elsewhere dependent upon specific evaluations.

Degree Requirements 42 total credit hours, thesis or project, comprehensive exam.

POST-MASTER'S PROGRAM

Areas of Study Nursing administration; nursing education. *Clinical nurse specialist programs in:* adult health, medical-surgical, parent-child, pediatric, school health. *Nurse practitioner programs in:* adult health, family health, pediatric, primary care.

DOCTORAL DEGREE PROGRAM

Degree PhD

Available Programs Doctorate.

Areas of Study Community health, family health, nursing education.

Program Entrance Requirements Clinical experience, minimum overall college GPA of 3.5, interview by faculty committee, interview, 3 letters of recommendation, MSN or equivalent, scholarly papers, statistics course, vita, writing sample.

Degree Requirements 64 total credit hours, dissertation, oral exam, written exam.

CONTINUING EDUCATION PROGRAM

Contact *Telephone:* 626-815-5385. *Fax:* 626-815-5414.

Biola University
Department of Nursing
La Mirada, California

http://www.biola.edu

Founded in 1908

DEGREE • BSN

Nursing Program Faculty 16 (31% with doctorates).

Baccalaureate Enrollment 243
Women 91% **Men** 9% **Minority** 23% **International** 1%

Nursing Student Activities Student Nurses' Association.

Nursing Student Resources Academic advising; academic or career counseling; assistance for students with disabilities; bookstore; campus computer network; career placement assistance; computer lab; computer-assisted instruction; e-mail services; employment services for current students; housing assistance; Internet; learning resource lab; library services; nursing audiovisuals; placement services for program completers; remedial services; resume preparation assistance; skills, simulation, or other laboratory; tutoring.

Library Facilities 301,956 volumes (20,000 in health, 10,000 in nursing); 17,876 periodical subscriptions (500 health-care related).

BACCALAUREATE PROGRAMS
Degree BSN

Available Programs ADN to Baccalaureate; Generic Baccalaureate; LPN to Baccalaureate; RN Baccalaureate.
Study Options Full-time.
Program Entrance Requirements Minimum overall college GPA of 3.0, transcript of college record, CPR certification, written essay, health exam, health insurance, high school biology, high school chemistry, high school foreign language, 2 years high school math, high school transcript, immunizations, interview, 2 letters of recommendation, minimum high school GPA of 3.5, minimum GPA in nursing prerequisites of 3.0, professional liability insurance/malpractice insurance, prerequisite course work. Transfer students are accepted. *Application deadline:* 1/15 (fall), 1/15 (winter), 1/15 (spring), 1/15 (summer). *Application fee:* $50.
Advanced Placement Credit given for nursing courses completed elsewhere dependent upon specific evaluations.
Expenses (2009–10) *Tuition:* full-time $27,744; part-time $1156 per unit. *International tuition:* $27,744 full-time. *Room and board:* $8520; room only: $4338 per academic year. *Required fees:* full-time $1200.
Financial Aid 95% of baccalaureate students in nursing programs received some form of financial aid in 2008–09. *Gift aid (need-based):* Federal Pell, FSEOG, state, private, college/university gift aid from institutional funds. *Loans:* Federal Nursing Student Loans, FFEL (Subsidized and Unsubsidized Stafford PLUS), Perkins, college/university, alternative loans. *Work-study:* Federal Work-Study. *Financial aid application deadline:* Continuous.
Contact Dr. Anne L. Gewe, Associate Chair/Associate Professor, Department of Nursing, Biola University, 13800 Biola Avenue, La Mirada, CA 90639. *Telephone:* 562-903-4850. *Fax:* 562-903-4803. *E-mail:* anne.gewe@biola.edu.

California Baptist University
School of Nursing
Riverside, California

Founded in 1950
DEGREE • BSN

Nursing Program Faculty 26 (8% with doctorates).
Baccalaureate Enrollment 168
Women 92% **Men** 8% **Minority** 37% **International** 1.2%
Graduate Enrollment 25
Women 88% **Men** 12% **Minority** 52% **International** .04%
Nursing Student Activities Student Nurses' Association.
Nursing Student Resources Academic advising; bookstore; campus computer network; career placement assistance; computer lab; e-mail services; employment services for current students; interactive nursing skills videos; Internet; learning resource lab; library services; nursing audiovisuals; resume preparation assistance; skills, simulation, or other laboratory; tutoring.
Library Facilities 180,946 volumes (335 in health, 236 in nursing); 11,166 periodical subscriptions (286 health-care related).

BACCALAUREATE PROGRAMS
Degree BSN
Available Programs ADN to Baccalaureate; Accelerated RN Baccalaureate; Generic Baccalaureate.

Program Entrance Requirements Minimum overall college GPA of 2.7, CPR certification, written essay, health exam, health insurance, immunizations, 2 letters of recommendation, minimum GPA in nursing prerequisites of 2.7, prerequisite course work. *Application deadline:* 4/7 (fall), 8/26 (spring). *Application fee:* $50.
Expenses (2009–10) *Tuition:* full-time $21,866. *International tuition:* $35,206 full-time. *Room and board:* $8170; room only: $3960 per academic year. *Required fees:* full-time $2600.
Financial Aid 100% of baccalaureate students in nursing programs received some form of financial aid in 2008–09. *Gift aid (need-based):* Federal Pell, FSEOG, state, private, college/university gift aid from institutional funds. *Loans:* FFEL (Subsidized and Unsubsidized Stafford PLUS), Perkins, alternative loans. *Work-study:* Federal Work-Study. *Financial aid application deadline (priority):* 3/2.
Contact Beth Wagner, Program Specialist, School of Nursing, California Baptist University, 8432 Magnolia Avenue, Riverside, CA 92504. *Telephone:* 951-343-4336. *E-mail:* bwagner@calbaptist.edu.

GRADUATE PROGRAMS
Expenses (2009–10) *Tuition:* full-time $30,180; part-time $560 per unit. *International tuition:* $32,365 full-time. *Room and board:* $8170; room only: $3960 per academic year. *Required fees:* full-time $510; part-time $125 per credit; part-time $255 per term.
Financial Aid 92% of graduate students in nursing programs received some form of financial aid in 2008–09.
Contact Beth Wagner, Program Specialist, School of Nursing, California Baptist University, 8432 Magnolia Avenue, Riverside, CA 92504. *Telephone:* 951-343-4336. *Fax:* 951-343-4703. *E-mail:* bwagner@calbaptist.edu.

California State University, Bakersfield
Program in Nursing
Bakersfield, California

http://www.csub.edu/nursing
Founded in 1970
DEGREE • BSN

Baccalaureate Enrollment 222
Women 88% **Men** 12% **Minority** 62% **International** 6% **Part-time** 8%
Distance Learning Courses Available.
Nursing Student Activities Sigma Theta Tau, Student Nurses' Association.
Nursing Student Resources Academic advising; academic or career counseling; assistance for students with disabilities; bookstore; campus computer network; career placement assistance; computer lab; computer-assisted instruction; daycare for children of students; e-mail services; employment services for current students; externships; housing assistance; interactive nursing skills videos; Internet; learning resource lab; library services; nursing audiovisuals; paid internships; placement services for program completers; remedial services; resume preparation assistance; skills, simulation, or other laboratory; tutoring; unpaid internships.
Library Facilities 354,016 volumes (20,000 in health, 1,850 in nursing); 2,260 periodical subscriptions (255 health-care related).

BACCALAUREATE PROGRAMS
Degree BSN
Available Programs Generic Baccalaureate; RN Baccalaureate.
Site Options Visalia, CA; Lancaster, CA.
Study Options Full-time.
Program Entrance Requirements Minimum overall college GPA of 2.0, transcript of college record, CPR certification, health exam, health insurance, high school transcript, immunizations, interview, minimum GPA in nursing prerequisites of 2.8, professional liability insurance/malpractice insurance, prerequisite course work. Transfer students are accepted. *Application deadline:* 4/30 (fall), 12/31 (spring). *Application fee:* $25.
Advanced Placement Credit by examination available. Credit given for nursing courses completed elsewhere dependent upon specific evaluations.

CALIFORNIA

California State University, Bakersfield (continued)

Expenses (2009–10) *Tuition, area resident:* full-time $4026. *Tuition, nonresident:* full-time $8928. *Required fees:* full-time $1065.

Financial Aid 78% of baccalaureate students in nursing programs received some form of financial aid in 2008–09.

Contact Mrs. Kathy Lewis, Pre-Nursing Advisor, Program in Nursing, California State University, Bakersfield, 9001 Stockdale Highway, Romberg Nursing Education Center, Bakersfield, CA 93311-1022. *Telephone:* 661-654-2508. *Fax:* 661-654-6347. *E-mail:* klewis3@csub.edu.

CONTINUING EDUCATION PROGRAM

Contact Dr. Craig Kelsey, Dean, Extended University, Program in Nursing, California State University, Bakersfield, 9001 Stockdale Highway, Bakersfield, CA 93311-1099. *Telephone:* 661-654-2446. *Fax:* 661-664-2447. *E-mail:* ckelsey@csub.edu.

California State University Channel Islands
Nursing Program
Camarillo, California

Founded in 2002

DEGREE • BSN

Nursing Program Faculty 13 (20% with doctorates).

Baccalaureate Enrollment 120

Nursing Student Activities Student Nurses' Association.

Nursing Student Resources Academic advising; academic or career counseling; assistance for students with disabilities; bookstore; campus computer network; career placement assistance; computer lab; e-mail services; housing assistance; interactive nursing skills videos; Internet; learning resource lab; library services; nursing audiovisuals; remedial services; skills, simulation, or other laboratory; tutoring.

BACCALAUREATE PROGRAMS

Degree BSN

Available Programs Generic Baccalaureate; RN Baccalaureate.

Contact Nursing Program, Nursing Program, California State University Channel Islands, One University Drive, Camarillo, CA 93012. *Telephone:* 805-437-3307. *E-mail:* nursing@csuci.edu.

California State University, Chico
School of Nursing
Chico, California

http://www.csuchico.edu/nurs/nurs.html

Founded in 1887

DEGREES • BSN • MSN

Nursing Program Faculty 33 (21% with doctorates).

Baccalaureate Enrollment 336
Women 86% **Men** 14% **Minority** 25% **Part-time** 30%

Graduate Enrollment 25
Women 95% **Men** 5% **Minority** 15% **Part-time** 100%

Distance Learning Courses Available.

Nursing Student Activities Sigma Theta Tau, Student Nurses' Association, nursing club.

Nursing Student Resources Academic advising; academic or career counseling; assistance for students with disabilities; bookstore; campus computer network; career placement assistance; computer lab; computer-assisted instruction; daycare for children of students; e-mail services; employment services for current students; externships; housing assistance; interactive nursing skills videos; Internet; learning resource lab; library services; nursing audiovisuals; paid internships; placement services for program completers; remedial services; resume preparation assistance; skills, simulation, or other laboratory; tutoring; unpaid internships.

Library Facilities 953,632 volumes (17,727 in health, 1,467 in nursing); 20,000 periodical subscriptions (133 health-care related).

BACCALAUREATE PROGRAMS

Degree BSN

Available Programs ADN to Baccalaureate; Baccalaureate for Second Degree; Generic Baccalaureate; LPN to Baccalaureate; RN Baccalaureate.

Study Options Full-time.

Program Entrance Requirements Minimum overall college GPA of 3.0, transcript of college record, CPR certification, health exam, health insurance, immunizations, minimum GPA in nursing prerequisites of 3.0, professional liability insurance/malpractice insurance, prerequisite course work. Transfer students are accepted. *Application deadline:* 11/30 (fall), 8/30 (spring). *Application fee:* $55.

Advanced Placement Credit given for nursing courses completed elsewhere dependent upon specific evaluations.

Expenses (2009–10) *Tuition, state resident:* full-time $5336; part-time $1822 per semester. *Tuition, nonresident:* full-time $14,264; part-time $4054 per semester. *International tuition:* $14,264 full-time. *Room and board:* $9404; room only: $6398 per academic year. *Required fees:* full-time $250; part-time $125 per term.

Financial Aid 75% of baccalaureate students in nursing programs received some form of financial aid in 2008–09. *Gift aid (need-based):* Federal Pell, FSEOG, state, private, college/university gift aid from institutional funds, United Negro College Fund. *Loans:* Federal Direct (Subsidized and Unsubsidized Stafford PLUS), Perkins, college/university. *Work-study:* Federal Work-Study. *Financial aid application deadline:* Continuous.

Contact Sherry D. Fox, Director, School of Nursing, California State University, Chico, Holt Hall 369, Chico, CA 95929-0200. *Telephone:* 530-898-5891. *Fax:* 530-898-4363. *E-mail:* sdfox@csuchico.edu.

GRADUATE PROGRAMS

Expenses (2009–10) *Tuition, state resident:* full-time $6272; part-time $2095 per semester. *Tuition, nonresident:* full-time $15,200; part-time $4327 per semester. *International tuition:* $15,200 full-time.

Financial Aid 25% of graduate students in nursing programs received some form of financial aid in 2008–09. Career-related internships or fieldwork available.

Contact Irene Morgan, Graduate Coordinator, School of Nursing, California State University, Chico, 400 West 1st Street, Chico, CA 95929-0200. *Telephone:* 530-898-5891. *Fax:* 530-898-6709. *E-mail:* imorgan@csuchico.edu.

MASTER'S DEGREE PROGRAM

Degree MSN

Available Programs Master's.

Concentrations Available Nursing education. *Clinical nurse specialist programs in:* adult health.

Site Options Chico, CA.

Study Options Part-time.

Online Degree Options Yes (online only).

Program Entrance Requirements Clinical experience, minimum overall college GPA of 3.0, transcript of college record, CPR certification, written essay, immunizations, physical assessment course, professional liability insurance/malpractice insurance, statistics course, GRE. *Application deadline:* 11/30 (fall), 8/30 (spring). *Application fee:* $55.

Advanced Placement Credit given for nursing courses completed elsewhere dependent upon specific evaluations.

Degree Requirements 30 total credit hours, thesis or project.

POST-MASTER'S PROGRAM

Areas of Study Nursing education.

CONTINUING EDUCATION PROGRAM

Contact Ms. Clare Robe, School of Nursing, California State University, Chico, 400 West 1st Street, Chico, CA 95929-0250. *Telephone:* 530-898-6105. *E-mail:* rce@csuchico.edu.

California State University, Dominguez Hills
Program in Nursing
Carson, California

http://www.csudh.edu/bhs/son/index.htm

Founded in 1960

DEGREES • BSN • MS

Nursing Program Faculty 87 (80% with doctorates).

Baccalaureate Enrollment 770
Women 90.5% **Men** 9.5% **Minority** 55.2% **Part-time** 91.3%

Graduate Enrollment 536
Women 90.1% **Men** 9.9% **Minority** 53.9% **Part-time** 76.7%

Distance Learning Courses Available.

Nursing Student Activities Nursing Honor Society, Sigma Theta Tau, Student Nurses' Association, nursing club.

Nursing Student Resources Academic advising; academic or career counseling; assistance for students with disabilities; bookstore; campus computer network; career placement assistance; computer lab; computer-assisted instruction; daycare for children of students; e-mail services; externships; housing assistance; interactive nursing skills videos; Internet; learning resource lab; library services; nursing audiovisuals; remedial services; skills, simulation, or other laboratory; tutoring.

Library Facilities 438,746 volumes (10,000 in nursing); 70,691 periodical subscriptions (215 health-care related).

BACCALAUREATE PROGRAMS

Degree BSN

Available Programs Baccalaureate for Second Degree; RN Baccalaureate.

Site Options Salinas, CA; Whittier, CA; Ventura, CA.

Online Degree Options Yes.

Program Entrance Requirements Minimum overall college GPA of 2.0, transcript of college record, minimum GPA in nursing prerequisites of 2.0, prerequisite course work, RN licensure. Transfer students are accepted. *Application deadline:* 8/3 (fall), 1/9 (spring), 5/15 (summer). Applications may be processed on a rolling basis for some programs. *Application fee:* $55.

Expenses (2008–09) *Tuition, state resident:* full-time $3048; part-time $1770 per semester. *Tuition, nonresident:* full-time $11,187; part-time $3804 per semester. *International tuition:* $11,795 full-time. *Required fees:* full-time $620; part-time $310 per term.

Financial Aid 95% of baccalaureate students in nursing programs received some form of financial aid in 2007–08.

Contact Dr. Kathleen T. Chai, BSN Coordinator, Program in Nursing, California State University, Dominguez Hills, 1000 East Victoria Street, WH 335, Carson, CA 90747. *Telephone:* 310-243-2005. *Fax:* 310-516-3542. *E-mail:* kchai@csudh.edu.

GRADUATE PROGRAMS

Expenses (2008–09) *Tuition, state resident:* full-time $3756; part-time $2178 per semester. *Tuition, nonresident:* full-time $11,892; part-time $6246 per semester. *International tuition:* $11,892 full-time. *Required fees:* full-time $620; part-time $310 per term.

Financial Aid 95% of graduate students in nursing programs received some form of financial aid in 2007–08.

Contact Dr. Rose Aguilar Welch, MSN Coordinator, Program in Nursing, California State University, Dominguez Hills, 1000 East Victoria Street, WH A320, Carson, CA 90747. *Telephone:* 310-243-2112. *Fax:* 310-516-3542. *E-mail:* rwelch@csudh.edu.

MASTER'S DEGREE PROGRAM

Degree MS

Available Programs Master's; Master's for Non-Nursing College Graduates; Master's for Nurses with Non-Nursing Degrees.

Concentrations Available Clinical nurse leader; nursing administration; nursing education. *Clinical nurse specialist programs in:* gerontology, parent-child. *Nurse practitioner programs in:* family health.

Site Options Salinas, CA; Whittier, CA.

Study Options Full-time.

Online Degree Options Yes.

Program Entrance Requirements Clinical experience, minimum overall college GPA of 3.0, transcript of college record, written essay, nursing research course, physical assessment course, prerequisite course work, resume, statistics course. *Application deadline:* 8/3 (fall), 1/9 (spring), 5/15 (summer). Applications may be processed on a rolling basis for some programs. *Application fee:* $55.

Advanced Placement Credit given for nursing courses completed elsewhere dependent upon specific evaluations.

Degree Requirements 45 total credit hours, comprehensive exam.

POST-MASTER'S PROGRAM

Areas of Study Nursing administration; nursing education. *Clinical nurse specialist programs in:* gerontology, parent-child. *Nurse practitioner programs in:* family health.

CONTINUING EDUCATION PROGRAM

Contact Cathy Crandall, School of Nursing Staff, Program in Nursing, California State University, Dominguez Hills, School of Nursing, 1000 East Victoria Street, Carson, CA 90747. *Telephone:* 310-243-3426. *Fax:* 310-516-3542. *E-mail:* ccrandall@csudh.edu.

California State University, East Bay
Department of Nursing and Health Sciences
Hayward, California

Founded in 1957

DEGREE • BS

Nursing Program Faculty 39 (30% with doctorates).

Baccalaureate Enrollment 360
Women 80% **Men** 20% **Minority** 40% **International** 5% **Part-time** 1%

Distance Learning Courses Available.

Nursing Student Activities Sigma Theta Tau, Student Nurses' Association.

Nursing Student Resources Academic advising; academic or career counseling; assistance for students with disabilities; campus computer network; career placement assistance; computer lab; computer-assisted instruction; daycare for children of students; e-mail services; employment services for current students; externships; interactive nursing skills videos; Internet; learning resource lab; library services; nursing audiovisuals; other; paid internships; placement services for program completers; remedial services; resume preparation assistance; skills, simulation, or other laboratory; tutoring; unpaid internships.

BACCALAUREATE PROGRAMS

Degree BS

Available Programs ADN to Baccalaureate; Accelerated Baccalaureate; Generic Baccalaureate.

Site Options Concord, CA.

Study Options Full-time and part-time.

Program Entrance Requirements Minimum overall college GPA of 3.0, transcript of college record, health exam, minimum GPA in nursing prerequisites of 3.0, prerequisite course work. Transfer students are accepted. *Application deadline:* 11/30 (fall).

Advanced Placement Credit given for nursing courses completed elsewhere dependent upon specific evaluations.

Financial Aid *Gift aid (need-based):* Federal Pell, FSEOG, state, private, college/university gift aid from institutional funds. *Loans:* FFEL (Subsidized and Unsubsidized Stafford PLUS), Perkins, college/university. *Work-study:* Federal Work-Study. *Financial aid application deadline (priority):* 3/2.

Contact Lara Dungan, Preadmission Student Advisor, Department of Nursing and Health Sciences, California State University, East Bay, 25800 Carlos Bee Boulevard, Hayward, CA 94542. *Telephone:* 510-885-3481. *Fax:* 510-885-2156. *E-mail:* lara.dungan@csueastbay.edu.

California State University, Fresno
Department of Nursing
Fresno, California

http://www.csufresno.edu/nursing/
Founded in 1911
DEGREES • BSN • MSN

Nursing Program Faculty 56 (20% with doctorates).
Baccalaureate Enrollment 450
Women 80% **Men** 20% **Minority** 49% **Part-time** 5%
Graduate Enrollment 114
Women 84% **Men** 16% **Minority** 53% **International** 4% **Part-time** 36%
Distance Learning Courses Available.
Nursing Student Activities Sigma Theta Tau, Student Nurses' Association.
Nursing Student Resources Academic advising; academic or career counseling; assistance for students with disabilities; bookstore; campus computer network; career placement assistance; computer lab; computer-assisted instruction; daycare for children of students; e-mail services; externships; housing assistance; interactive nursing skills videos; Internet; learning resource lab; library services; nursing audiovisuals; paid internships; placement services for program completers; remedial services; skills, simulation, or other laboratory; tutoring.
Library Facilities 23,961 volumes in health, 1,287 volumes in nursing; 2,617 periodical subscriptions (1,260 health-care related).

BACCALAUREATE PROGRAMS
Degree BSN

Available Programs ADN to Baccalaureate; Generic Baccalaureate.
Study Options Full-time.
Program Entrance Requirements Transcript of college record, CPR certification, health exam, immunizations, minimum GPA in nursing prerequisites of 3.0, professional liability insurance/malpractice insurance, prerequisite course work. Transfer students are accepted. *Application deadline:* 3/31 (fall), 8/31 (spring).
Advanced Placement Credit by examination available. Credit given for nursing courses completed elsewhere dependent upon specific evaluations.
Expenses (2009–10) *Tuition, state resident:* full-time $4672; part-time $1490 per semester. *Tuition, nonresident:* full-time $11,160. *International tuition:* $11,160 full-time. *Room and board:* $8495; room only: $4200 per academic year. *Required fees:* full-time $80.
Financial Aid 65% of baccalaureate students in nursing programs received some form of financial aid in 2008–09. *Gift aid (need-based):* Federal Pell, FSEOG, state, private, college/university gift aid from institutional funds. *Loans:* Federal Nursing Student Loans, FFEL (Subsidized and Unsubsidized Stafford PLUS), Perkins, college/university, alternative loans. *Work-study:* Federal Work-Study. *Financial aid application deadline (priority):* 3/2.
Contact Dr. Michael F. Russler, Chair, Department of Nursing, California State University, Fresno, 2345 East San Ramon Avenue, MH25, Fresno, CA 93740-8031. *Telephone:* 559-278-2429. *Fax:* 559-278-6360. *E-mail:* michaelr@csufresno.edu.

GRADUATE PROGRAMS
Expenses (2009–10) *Tuition, state resident:* full-time $5608; part-time $2804 per semester. *Tuition, nonresident:* full-time $11,160; part-time $5580 per semester. *International tuition:* $11,160 full-time. *Room and board:* $8495; room only: $4200 per academic year. *Required fees:* full-time $40.
Financial Aid 30% of graduate students in nursing programs received some form of financial aid in 2008–09. 2 teaching assistantships were awarded; career-related internships or fieldwork, Federal Work-Study, scholarships, and traineeships also available. Aid available to part-time students. *Financial aid application deadline:* 3/1.
Contact Dr. Robert Fire, Graduate Coordinator, Department of Nursing, California State University, Fresno, 2345 East San Ramon Avenue, MH25, Fresno, CA 93740-8031. *Telephone:* 559-278-8852. *Fax:* 559-278-6360. *E-mail:* rfire@csufresno.edu.

MASTER'S DEGREE PROGRAM
Degree MSN
Available Programs Accelerated Master's; Master's; Master's for Nurses with Non-Nursing Degrees.
Concentrations Available Nursing education. *Clinical nurse specialist programs in:* acute care, community health, critical care, pediatric, psychiatric/mental health, public health. *Nurse practitioner programs in:* family health, pediatric.
Study Options Full-time and part-time.
Program Entrance Requirements Computer literacy, minimum overall college GPA of 3.0, transcript of college record, CPR certification, written essay, 3 letters of recommendation, nursing research course, physical assessment course, professional liability insurance/malpractice insurance, prerequisite course work, resume, statistics course, GRE General Test. *Application deadline:* 4/1 (fall).
Advanced Placement Credit given for nursing courses completed elsewhere dependent upon specific evaluations.
Degree Requirements 38 total credit hours, thesis or project, comprehensive exam.

POST-MASTER'S PROGRAM
Areas of Study *Nurse practitioner programs in:* family health, pediatric.

CONTINUING EDUCATION PROGRAM
Contact Dr. Berta Gonzalez, Associate Vice President, Department of Nursing, California State University, Fresno, 5005 North Maple Avenue, ED76, Fresno, CA 93740-0076. *Telephone:* 559-278-0333. *Fax:* 559-278-0395. *E-mail:* bertag@csufresno.edu.

California State University, Fullerton
Department of Nursing
Fullerton, California

http://nursing.fullerton.edu/
Founded in 1957
DEGREES • BSN • MSN

Nursing Program Faculty 75 (32% with doctorates).
Baccalaureate Enrollment 456
Women 86% **Men** 14% **Minority** 69% **International** 4% **Part-time** 76%
Graduate Enrollment 393
Women 82% **Men** 18% **Minority** 57% **International** 1% **Part-time** 53%
Distance Learning Courses Available.
Nursing Student Activities Nursing Honor Society, Sigma Theta Tau, Student Nurses' Association.
Nursing Student Resources Academic advising; academic or career counseling; assistance for students with disabilities; bookstore; campus computer network; computer lab; computer-assisted instruction; daycare for children of students; e-mail services; housing assistance; Internet; learning resource lab; library services; resume preparation assistance; skills, simulation, or other laboratory; tutoring.
Library Facilities 1.3 million volumes (17,340 in health, 837 in nursing); 10,902 periodical subscriptions (8,145 health-care related).

BACCALAUREATE PROGRAMS
Degree BSN

Available Programs ADN to Baccalaureate; Baccalaureate for Second Degree; Generic Baccalaureate.
Site Options Riverside, CA; Los Angeles, CA; Mission Viejo, CA.
Study Options Full-time and part-time.
Program Entrance Requirements Minimum overall college GPA of 2.5, transcript of college record, CPR certification, immunizations, 2 letters of recommendation, professional liability insurance/malpractice insurance, prerequisite course work, RN licensure. Transfer students are accepted. *Application deadline:* 6/1 (fall), 10/1 (spring). Applications may be processed on a rolling basis for some programs. *Application fee:* $55.

Advanced Placement Credit given for nursing courses completed elsewhere dependent upon specific evaluations.

Expenses (2009–10) *Tuition, state resident:* full-time $4662; part-time $2970 per semester. *Tuition, nonresident:* full-time $6795; part-time $3717 per semester. *International tuition:* $6795 full-time. *Room and board:* $9082 per academic year.

Contact Ms. Jennifer Crum, Advisor, Department of Nursing, California State University, Fullerton, EC-182, PO Box 6868, Fullerton, CA 92834-6868. *Telephone:* 657-278-7648. *Fax:* 657-278-3338. *E-mail:* jcrum@fullerton.edu.

GRADUATE PROGRAMS

Expenses (2009–10) *Tuition, state resident:* full-time $5598; part-time $1758 per semester. *Tuition, nonresident:* full-time $12,294; part-time $2502 per semester. *International tuition:* $12,294 full-time. *Room and board:* room only: $5775 per academic year. *Required fees:* full-time $500; part-time $250 per term.

Financial Aid 44% of graduate students in nursing programs received some form of financial aid in 2008–09.

Contact Ms. Mary Lehn-Mooney, Advisor, Department of Nursing, California State University, Fullerton, EC-182, PO Box 6868, Fullerton, CA 92834-6868. *Telephone:* 714-278-3217. *Fax:* 714-278-3338. *E-mail:* mlehn-mooney@fullerton.edu.

MASTER'S DEGREE PROGRAM

Degree MSN

Available Programs Accelerated AD/RN to Master's; Accelerated Master's for Non-Nursing College Graduates; Master's.

Concentrations Available Nurse anesthesia; nurse-midwifery; nursing administration; nursing education. *Clinical nurse specialist programs in:* school health. *Nurse practitioner programs in:* women's health.

Study Options Full-time and part-time.

Online Degree Options Yes.

Program Entrance Requirements Clinical experience, minimum overall college GPA of 3.0, transcript of college record, CPR certification, written essay, immunizations, interview, 3 letters of recommendation, nursing research course, professional liability insurance/malpractice insurance, prerequisite course work, statistics course. *Application deadline:* 11/30 (fall). Applications may be processed on a rolling basis for some programs. *Application fee:* $55.

Advanced Placement Credit given for nursing courses completed elsewhere dependent upon specific evaluations.

Degree Requirements 71 total credit hours, thesis or project, comprehensive exam.

CONTINUING EDUCATION PROGRAM

Contact Ms. Debra Day, Department of Nursing, California State University, Fullerton, 800 North State College Boulevard, Extended Ed CP-920, Fullerton, CA 92834-9480. *Telephone:* 657-278-4280. *E-mail:* dday@fullerton.edu.

California State University, Long Beach
Department of Nursing
Long Beach, California

http://www.csulb.edu/depts/nursing/
Founded in 1949

DEGREES • BSN • MSN • MSN/MPH

Nursing Program Faculty 82 (25% with doctorates).

Baccalaureate Enrollment 548
Women 80.47% **Men** 19.53% **Minority** 73.18% **International** .01%

Graduate Enrollment 343
Women 89.8% **Men** 10.2% **Minority** 68.22% **International** .01% **Part-time** 50%

Nursing Student Activities Nursing Honor Society, Sigma Theta Tau, Student Nurses' Association.

Nursing Student Resources Academic advising; Internet; library services; skills, simulation, or other laboratory; tutoring.

Library Facilities 1.2 million volumes; 39,682 periodical subscriptions.

BACCALAUREATE PROGRAMS

Degree BSN

Available Programs ADN to Baccalaureate; Baccalaureate for Second Degree; Generic Baccalaureate; LPN to Baccalaureate.

Site Options Long Beach, CA.

Study Options Full-time.

Program Entrance Requirements Transcript of college record, CPR certification, health exam, health insurance, immunizations, interview, minimum GPA in nursing prerequisites of 2.5, professional liability insurance/malpractice insurance, prerequisite course work. Transfer students are accepted. *Application deadline:* 2/15 (fall), 9/15 (spring).

Advanced Placement Credit given for nursing courses completed elsewhere dependent upon specific evaluations.

Expenses (2009–10) *Tuition, area resident:* full-time $2185; part-time $1600 per semester. *Tuition, state resident:* full-time $2185; part-time $1660 per semester. *Tuition, nonresident:* full-time $8000; part-time $5000 per semester. *International tuition:* $8000 full-time. *Room and board:* $9000; room only: $7600 per academic year. *Required fees:* full-time $1362.

Financial Aid 50% of baccalaureate students in nursing programs received some form of financial aid in 2008–09. *Gift aid (need-based):* Federal Pell, FSEOG, state, private, college/university gift aid from institutional funds. *Loans:* FFEL (Subsidized and Unsubsidized Stafford PLUS), Perkins. *Work-study:* Federal Work-Study. *Financial aid application deadline (priority):* 3/2.

Contact Dr. Beth R. Keely, Assistant Director, Undergraduate Nursing Programs, Department of Nursing, California State University, Long Beach, 1250 Bellflower Boulevard, Long Beach, CA 90840. *Telephone:* 562-985-4478. *Fax:* 562-985-2382. *E-mail:* bkeely@csulb.edu.

GRADUATE PROGRAMS

Expenses (2009–10) *Tuition, state resident:* full-time $2185; part-time $1800 per semester. *Tuition, nonresident:* full-time $10,000; part-time $7000 per semester. *International tuition:* $10,000 full-time. *Room and board:* $9000; room only: $7600 per academic year. *Required fees:* full-time $2000.

Financial Aid 25% of graduate students in nursing programs received some form of financial aid in 2008–09. Federal Work-Study, institutionally sponsored loans, and scholarships available. *Financial aid application deadline:* 3/2.

Contact Alison Kliachko-Trafas, Administrative Assistant, Department of Nursing, California State University, Long Beach, 1250 Bellflower Boulevard, Long Beach, CA 90840. *Telephone:* 562-985-4473. *Fax:* 562-985-2382. *E-mail:* akliachk@csulb.edu.

MASTER'S DEGREE PROGRAM

Degrees MSN; MSN/MPH

Available Programs Accelerated Master's; Master's; Master's for Non-Nursing College Graduates.

Concentrations Available Health-care administration; nursing education. *Clinical nurse specialist programs in:* adult health. *Nurse practitioner programs in:* adult health, family health, gerontology, pediatric, psychiatric/mental health, women's health.

Study Options Full-time and part-time.

Program Entrance Requirements Clinical experience, minimum overall college GPA of 2.75, transcript of college record, written essay, 3 letters of recommendation, physical assessment course, prerequisite course work, resume, statistics course. *Application deadline:* 3/15 (fall), 10/15 (spring).

Advanced Placement Credit given for nursing courses completed elsewhere dependent upon specific evaluations.

Degree Requirements 37 total credit hours, thesis or project, comprehensive exam.

POST-MASTER'S PROGRAM

Areas of Study *Clinical nurse specialist programs in:* adult health. *Nurse practitioner programs in:* adult health, family health, gerontology, pediatric, psychiatric/mental health, women's health.

California State University, Los Angeles

School of Nursing
Los Angeles, California

http://www.calstatela.edu/dept/nursing/

Founded in 1947

DEGREES • BSN • MSN

Nursing Program Faculty 31 (39% with doctorates).

Baccalaureate Enrollment 300

Graduate Enrollment 100

Nursing Student Resources Academic advising.

Library Facilities 1.2 million volumes; 24,031 periodical subscriptions.

BACCALAUREATE PROGRAMS

Degree BSN

Available Programs Generic Baccalaureate; LPN to RN Baccalaureate; RN Baccalaureate.

Study Options Full-time.

Program Entrance Requirements Minimum overall college GPA of 2.75, CPR certification, health exam, health insurance, high school biology, immunizations, minimum GPA in nursing prerequisites of 2.75, professional liability insurance/malpractice insurance, prerequisite course work. Transfer students are accepted. *Application deadline:* 12/1 (fall).

Advanced Placement Credit given for nursing courses completed elsewhere dependent upon specific evaluations.

Financial Aid 50% of baccalaureate students in nursing programs received some form of financial aid in 2007–08. *Gift aid (need-based):* Federal Pell, FSEOG, state, private, college/university gift aid from institutional funds. *Loans:* Federal Nursing Student Loans, Federal Direct (Subsidized and Unsubsidized Stafford PLUS), FFEL, Perkins. *Work-study:* Federal Work-Study. *Financial aid application deadline (priority):* 3/2.

Contact Dr. Lorie Judson, Undergraduate Coordinator, School of Nursing, California State University, Los Angeles, 5151 State University Drive, Los Angeles, CA 90032-8171. *Telephone:* 323-343-4700. *Fax:* 323-343-6454. *E-mail:* ljudson@calstatela.edu.

GRADUATE PROGRAMS

Expenses (2008–09) *Tuition, nonresident:* full-time $10,170; part-time $226 per credit. *Required fees:* full-time $808.

Financial Aid 50% of graduate students in nursing programs received some form of financial aid in 2007–08. Federal Work-Study available. Aid available to part-time students. *Financial aid application deadline:* 3/1.

Contact Dr. Cynthia B. Hughes, RN, Acting Director, School of Nursing, School of Nursing, California State University, Los Angeles, 5151 State University Drive, Los Angeles, CA 90032. *Telephone:* 323-343-4700. *Fax:* 323-343-6454. *E-mail:* chughes2@calstatela.edu.

MASTER'S DEGREE PROGRAM

Degree MSN

Available Programs Accelerated Master's for Nurses with Non-Nursing Degrees; Accelerated RN to Master's; Master's; Master's for Non-Nursing College Graduates.

Concentrations Available Nursing administration; nursing education. *Clinical nurse specialist programs in:* psychiatric/mental health. *Nurse practitioner programs in:* acute care, adult health, family health, pediatric, primary care, psychiatric/mental health.

Study Options Full-time and part-time.

Program Entrance Requirements Clinical experience, minimum overall college GPA of 3.0, transcript of college record, written essay, immunizations, letters of recommendation, nursing research course, physical assessment course, professional liability insurance/malpractice insurance, resume, statistics course. *Application deadline:* 11/15 (fall), 5/15 (spring).

Advanced Placement Credit given for nursing courses completed elsewhere dependent upon specific evaluations.

Degree Requirements 45 total credit hours, comprehensive exam.

POST-MASTER'S PROGRAM

Areas of Study *Nurse practitioner programs in:* acute care, adult health, family health, pediatric, primary care.

California State University, Northridge

Nursing Program
Northridge, California

http://www.csun.edu/~nursing/

Founded in 1958

DEGREE • BSN

Nursing Program Faculty 15 (27% with doctorates).

Baccalaureate Enrollment 106

Women 92% **Men** 8% **Minority** 60% **International** 12% **Part-time** 66%

Nursing Student Activities Sigma Theta Tau, Student Nurses' Association.

Nursing Student Resources Academic advising; academic or career counseling; assistance for students with disabilities; bookstore; campus computer network; career placement assistance; computer lab; computer-assisted instruction; daycare for children of students; e-mail services; housing assistance; interactive nursing skills videos; Internet; learning resource lab; library services; nursing audiovisuals; remedial services; resume preparation assistance; skills, simulation, or other laboratory; tutoring.

Library Facilities 1.4 million volumes (61,848 in health, 1,401 in nursing); 1,584 periodical subscriptions (303 health-care related).

BACCALAUREATE PROGRAMS

Degree BSN

Available Programs ADN to Baccalaureate; Accelerated Baccalaureate.

Study Options Full-time.

Program Entrance Requirements Minimum overall college GPA of 3.0, transcript of college record, CPR certification, written essay, health exam, health insurance, immunizations, interview, 3 letters of recommendation, minimum GPA in nursing prerequisites of 3.0, professional liability insurance/malpractice insurance, prerequisite course work, RN licensure. Transfer students are accepted. *Application deadline:* 12/4 (fall), 12/4 (summer). *Application fee:* $55.

Advanced Placement Credit by examination available. Credit given for nursing courses completed elsewhere dependent upon specific evaluations.

Contact Health Sciences Dept Staff, Nursing Program, California State University, Northridge, Health Sciences Department, 18111 Nordhoff Street, Northridge, CA 91330-8285. *Telephone:* 818-677-3101. *Fax:* 818-677-2045. *E-mail:* hsci@csun.edu.

California State University, Sacramento

Division of Nursing
Sacramento, California

http://www.hhs.csus.edu/nrs

Founded in 1947

DEGREES • BSN • MS

Nursing Program Faculty 64 (50% with doctorates).

Baccalaureate Enrollment 286

Women 89% **Men** 11%

Graduate Enrollment 180

Women 95% **Men** 5% **Part-time** 100%

Distance Learning Courses Available.

Nursing Student Activities Sigma Theta Tau, Student Nurses' Association.

Nursing Student Resources Academic advising; academic or career counseling; assistance for students with disabilities; bookstore; campus computer network; computer lab; computer-assisted instruction; daycare for children of students; e-mail services; externships; housing assistance; interactive nursing skills videos; Internet; learning resource lab; library services; nursing audiovisuals; paid internships; placement services for program completers; remedial services; resume preparation assistance; skills, simulation, or other laboratory; tutoring.

Library Facilities 1.4 million volumes (33,000 in health); 2,171 periodical subscriptions (327 health-care related).

BACCALAUREATE PROGRAMS

Degree BSN

Available Programs ADN to Baccalaureate; Baccalaureate for Second Degree; Generic Baccalaureate; LPN to RN Baccalaureate.

Study Options Full-time.

Program Entrance Requirements Transcript of college record, CPR certification, health exam, health insurance, high school biology, high school math, immunizations, minimum GPA in nursing prerequisites of 3.3, professional liability insurance/malpractice insurance, prerequisite course work. Transfer students are accepted. *Application deadline:* 3/1 (fall), 10/1 (spring).

Advanced Placement Credit by examination available. Credit given for nursing courses completed elsewhere dependent upon specific evaluations.

Expenses (2009–10) *Tuition, area resident:* full-time $4900.

Financial Aid 60% of baccalaureate students in nursing programs received some form of financial aid in 2008–09.

Contact Nancy Beers, Administrative Support Coordinator, Division of Nursing, California State University, Sacramento, 6000 J Street, Sacramento, CA 95819-6096. *Telephone:* 916-278-6525. *E-mail:* beersnj@csus.edu.

GRADUATE PROGRAMS

Expenses (2009–10) *Tuition, area resident:* full-time $5836; part-time $1877 per semester.

Financial Aid 10% of graduate students in nursing programs received some form of financial aid in 2008–09. Research assistantships, teaching assistantships, career-related internships or fieldwork and Federal Work-Study available. Aid available to part-time students. *Financial aid application deadline:* 3/1.

Contact Dr. Kelly Tobar, Graduate Coordinator, Division of Nursing, California State University, Sacramento, 6000 J Street, Sacramento, CA 95819-6096. *Telephone:* 916-278-7298. *Fax:* 916-278-6311. *E-mail:* tobark@csus.edu.

MASTER'S DEGREE PROGRAM

Degree MS

Available Programs Master's; Master's for Nurses with Non-Nursing Degrees.

Concentrations Available Nursing administration; nursing education. *Clinical nurse specialist programs in:* adult health, community health, family health, parent-child, pediatric, perinatal, psychiatric/mental health, school health. *Nurse practitioner programs in:* family health, primary care.

Study Options Part-time.

Online Degree Options Yes (online only).

Program Entrance Requirements Clinical experience, computer literacy, minimum overall college GPA of 3.0, transcript of college record, CPR certification, immunizations, nursing research course, professional liability insurance/malpractice insurance, prerequisite course work, statistics course, GRE. *Application deadline:* 11/30 (fall).

Advanced Placement Credit given for nursing courses completed elsewhere dependent upon specific evaluations.

Degree Requirements 33 total credit hours, comprehensive exam.

California State University, San Bernardino
Department of Nursing
San Bernardino, California

http://nursing.csusb.edu
Founded in 1965

DEGREES • BSN • MSN

Nursing Program Faculty 42 (19% with doctorates).

Baccalaureate Enrollment 457
Women 81% **Men** 19% **Minority** 59%

Graduate Enrollment 19
Women 89% **Men** 11% **Minority** 47%

Distance Learning Courses Available.

Nursing Student Activities Sigma Theta Tau, Student Nurses' Association.

Nursing Student Resources Academic advising; academic or career counseling; assistance for students with disabilities; bookstore; campus computer network; computer lab; computer-assisted instruction; daycare for children of students; e-mail services; Internet; learning resource lab; library services; nursing audiovisuals; remedial services; skills, simulation, or other laboratory.

Library Facilities 731,259 volumes (1,500 in health, 1,000 in nursing); 2,028 periodical subscriptions (5,000 health-care related).

BACCALAUREATE PROGRAMS

Degree BSN

Available Programs Generic Baccalaureate; LPN to Baccalaureate; RN Baccalaureate.

Site Options Palm Desert, CA.

Study Options Full-time.

Program Entrance Requirements Minimum overall college GPA of 2.5, transcript of college record, 3 letters of recommendation, minimum GPA in nursing prerequisites of 2.5, prerequisite course work. Transfer students are accepted. *Application deadline:* 3/1 (fall), 10/1 (winter).

Advanced Placement Credit given for nursing courses completed elsewhere dependent upon specific evaluations.

Financial Aid 80% of baccalaureate students in nursing programs received some form of financial aid in 2008–09. *Gift aid (need-based):* Federal Pell, FSEOG, state, private, college/university gift aid from institutional funds. *Loans:* Federal Direct (Subsidized and Unsubsidized Stafford PLUS), Perkins. *Work-study:* Federal Work-Study. *Financial aid application deadline (priority):* 3/2.

Contact Dr. Jean Nix, BSN Coordinator, Department of Nursing, California State University, San Bernardino, 5500 University Parkway, HP 231 Nursing, San Bernardino, CA 92407. *Telephone:* 909-537-5381. *E-mail:* pjnix@csusb.edu.

GRADUATE PROGRAMS

Financial Aid 60% of graduate students in nursing programs received some form of financial aid in 2008–09.

Contact Dr. Mary Molle, MSN Coordinator and Professor, Department of Nursing, California State University, San Bernardino, 5500 University Parkway, San Bernardino, CA 92407. *Telephone:* 909-537-7241. *E-mail:* mmolle@csusb.edu.

MASTER'S DEGREE PROGRAM

Degree MSN

Available Programs Master's.

Concentrations Available Nursing administration; nursing education. *Clinical nurse specialist programs in:* community health.

Study Options Full-time and part-time.

Program Entrance Requirements Clinical experience, minimum overall college GPA of 3.0, transcript of college record, letters of recommendation, prerequisite course work, resume, statistics course. *Application deadline:* 6/10 (fall).

Advanced Placement Credit given for nursing courses completed elsewhere dependent upon specific evaluations.

California State University, San Bernardino (continued)
Degree Requirements 65 total credit hours, thesis or project, comprehensive exam.

California State University, San Marcos
School of Nursing
San Marcos, California

Founded in 1990
DEGREE • BSN

Nursing Student Activities Student Nurses' Association.
Library Facilities 280,492 volumes; 2,868 periodical subscriptions.

BACCALAUREATE PROGRAMS
Degree BSN

Available Programs Accelerated Baccalaureate; Generic Baccalaureate.

Contact Baccalaureate programs, School of Nursing, California State University, San Marcos, 333 South Twin Oaks Valley Road, San Marcos, CA 92096-0001. *Telephone:* 706-750-7550. *Fax:* 706-750-3646.

California State University, Stanislaus
Department of Nursing
Turlock, California

http://www.csustan.edu/Nursing/index.htm
Founded in 1957
DEGREE • BSN

Nursing Program Faculty 17 (24% with doctorates).
Baccalaureate Enrollment 164
Women 88% **Men** 12% **Minority** 42% **Part-time** 30%
Nursing Student Activities Sigma Theta Tau, Student Nurses' Association.
Nursing Student Resources Academic advising; academic or career counseling; assistance for students with disabilities; bookstore; campus computer network; career placement assistance; computer lab; computer-assisted instruction; daycare for children of students; e-mail services; employment services for current students; externships; interactive nursing skills videos; Internet; learning resource lab; library services; nursing audiovisuals; resume preparation assistance; skills, simulation, or other laboratory; tutoring.
Library Facilities 372,636 volumes (12,642 in health, 1,338 in nursing); 10,539 periodical subscriptions (93 health-care related).

BACCALAUREATE PROGRAMS
Degree BSN

Available Programs ADN to Baccalaureate; Generic Baccalaureate; LPN to Baccalaureate.
Study Options Full-time.
Program Entrance Requirements Minimum overall college GPA of 3.0, transcript of college record, CPR certification, health exam, immunizations, minimum GPA in nursing prerequisites of 3.0, professional liability insurance/malpractice insurance, prerequisite course work. Transfer students are accepted.
Advanced Placement Credit given for nursing courses completed elsewhere dependent upon specific evaluations.
Contact *Telephone:* 209-667-3141. *Fax:* 209-667-3690.

Dominican University of California
Program in Nursing
San Rafael, California

Founded in 1890
DEGREES • BSN • MSN

Nursing Program Faculty 43 (15% with doctorates).
Baccalaureate Enrollment 436
Women 93% **Men** 7% **Minority** 62% **International** 2% **Part-time** 12%
Graduate Enrollment 5
Women 95% **Men** 5% **Minority** 20%
Nursing Student Activities Nursing Honor Society, Sigma Theta Tau, Student Nurses' Association, nursing club.
Nursing Student Resources Academic advising; academic or career counseling; assistance for students with disabilities; bookstore; campus computer network; career placement assistance; computer lab; computer-assisted instruction; e-mail services; housing assistance; interactive nursing skills videos; Internet; learning resource lab; library services; nursing audiovisuals; resume preparation assistance; skills, simulation, or other laboratory; tutoring.
Library Facilities 118,375 volumes (1,200 in health, 1,000 in nursing); 57,534 periodical subscriptions (1,300 health-care related).

BACCALAUREATE PROGRAMS
Degree BSN

Available Programs Baccalaureate for Second Degree; Generic Baccalaureate; LPN to Baccalaureate; LPN to RN Baccalaureate; RN Baccalaureate.
Study Options Full-time and part-time.
Program Entrance Requirements Minimum overall college GPA of 2.5, transcript of college record, CPR certification, written essay, health exam, health insurance, high school biology, high school chemistry, 2 years high school math, high school transcript, immunizations, 1 letter of recommendation, minimum high school GPA of 2.7, minimum GPA in nursing prerequisites of 3.0, prerequisite course work. Transfer students are accepted.
Advanced Placement Credit given for nursing courses completed elsewhere dependent upon specific evaluations.
Expenses (2008–09) *Tuition:* part-time $32,090 per degree program. *Room and board:* $11,800; room only: $7250 per academic year.
Financial Aid 97% of baccalaureate students in nursing programs received some form of financial aid in 2007–08. *Gift aid (need-based):* Federal Pell, FSEOG, state, private, college/university gift aid from institutional funds. *Loans:* FFEL (Subsidized and Unsubsidized Stafford PLUS), Perkins, private loans. *Work-study:* Federal Work-Study, part-time campus jobs. *Financial aid application deadline (priority):* 3/2.
Contact Rebecca Finn, Director of Admissions, Program in Nursing, Dominican University of California, 50 Acacia Avenue, San Rafael, CA 94901-2298. *Telephone:* 415-257-1376. *Fax:* 415-485-3214. *E-mail:* rfinn@dominican.edu.

GRADUATE PROGRAMS
Expenses (2008–09) *Tuition:* part-time $810 per unit.
Financial Aid 65% of graduate students in nursing programs received some form of financial aid in 2007–08. 10 fellowships (averaging $3,200 per year) were awarded; scholarships also available. Aid available to part-time students.
Contact Dr. Barbara Ganley, RN, Director of Graduate Nursing, Program in Nursing, Dominican University of California, 50 Acacia Avenue, San Rafael, CA 94901-2298. *Telephone:* 415-482-1829. *Fax:* 415-482-1829. *E-mail:* bganley@dominican.edu.

MASTER'S DEGREE PROGRAM
Degree MSN

Available Programs Master's; Master's for Nurses with Non-Nursing Degrees.
Concentrations Available Nursing education. *Clinical nurse specialist programs in:* gerontology.
Study Options Full-time and part-time.

Program Entrance Requirements Clinical experience, minimum overall college GPA of 3.0, transcript of college record, CPR certification, written essay, interview, 2 letters of recommendation, nursing research course, prerequisite course work, statistics course. *Application deadline:* Applications may be processed on a rolling basis for some programs. *Application fee:* $45.

Advanced Placement Credit given for nursing courses completed elsewhere dependent upon specific evaluations.

Degree Requirements 45 total credit hours, thesis or project.

CONTINUING EDUCATION PROGRAM

Contact Ms. Sandy Baker, Director of Adult and Extended Education, Program in Nursing, Dominican University of California, 50 Acacia Avenue, San Rafael, CA 94901-2298. *Telephone:* 415-458-3255. *Fax:* 415-482-3575. *E-mail:* sbaker@dominican.edu.

Fresno Pacific University

RN to BSN Program
Fresno, California

Founded in 1944

DEGREE • BSN

Library Facilities 196,000 volumes; 16,000 periodical subscriptions.

BACCALAUREATE PROGRAMS

Degree BSN

Available Programs RN Baccalaureate.

Contact RN to BSN Program, RN to BSN Program, Fresno Pacific University, 1717 South Chestnut Avenue, Fresno, CA 93702-4709. *Telephone:* 559-453-2000.

Holy Names University

Department of Nursing
Oakland, California

http://www.hnu.edu/academics/
adultBaccalaureateDegreePrograms/
registeredNurse.html

Founded in 1868

DEGREES • BSN • MSN • MSN/MBA

Nursing Program Faculty 44 (8.8% with doctorates).

Baccalaureate Enrollment 68
Women 90% **Men** 10% **Minority** 52% **International** 1% **Part-time** 100%

Graduate Enrollment 70
Women 85% **Men** 15% **Minority** 60% **International** 2% **Part-time** 10%

Distance Learning Courses Available.

Nursing Student Activities Nursing Honor Society, Sigma Theta Tau, nursing club.

Nursing Student Resources Academic advising; academic or career counseling; assistance for students with disabilities; bookstore; campus computer network; career placement assistance; computer lab; computer-assisted instruction; e-mail services; employment services for current students; externships; housing assistance; interactive nursing skills videos; Internet; learning resource lab; library services; nursing audiovisuals; placement services for program completers; remedial services; resume preparation assistance; skills, simulation, or other laboratory; tutoring.

Library Facilities 117,760 volumes (500 in health, 200 in nursing); 8,003 periodical subscriptions (200 health-care related).

BACCALAUREATE PROGRAMS

Degree BSN

Available Programs RN Baccalaureate.

Site Options Stanford, CA; CHW hospitals, CA.

Study Options Full-time and part-time.

Program Entrance Requirements Minimum overall college GPA of 2.7, transcript of college record, written essay, prerequisite course work, RN licensure. Transfer students are accepted. *Application deadline:* Applications may be processed on a rolling basis for some programs. *Application fee:* $50.

Advanced Placement Credit given for nursing courses completed elsewhere dependent upon specific evaluations.

Expenses (2009–10) *Tuition:* part-time $530 per unit. *Room and board:* $12,000; room only: $9000 per academic year.

Financial Aid 95% of baccalaureate students in nursing programs received some form of financial aid in 2008–09.

Contact Ms. Lisa Marie Gibson, Admission Counselor, Department of Nursing, Holy Names University, 3500 Mountain Boulevard, Oakland, CA 94619-1699. *Telephone:* 510-436-1317. *Fax:* 510-436-1376. *E-mail:* lgibson@hnu.edu.

GRADUATE PROGRAMS

Expenses (2009–10) *Tuition:* part-time $730 per unit. *Room and board:* $12,000; room only: $9000 per academic year.

Financial Aid 95% of graduate students in nursing programs received some form of financial aid in 2008–09. Scholarships available. Aid available to part-time students. *Financial aid application deadline:* 3/2.

Contact Ms. Lisa Marie Gibson, Admission Counselor, Department of Nursing, Holy Names University, 3500 Mountain Boulevard, Oakland, CA 94619-1699. *Telephone:* 510-436-1317. *Fax:* 510-436-1376. *E-mail:* lgibson@hnu.edu.

MASTER'S DEGREE PROGRAM

Degrees MSN; MSN/MBA

Available Programs Master's; Master's for Nurses with Non-Nursing Degrees.

Concentrations Available Nursing administration; nursing education. *Nurse practitioner programs in:* family health.

Site Options CHW hospitals, CA.

Study Options Full-time and part-time.

Program Entrance Requirements Minimum overall college GPA of 2.8, transcript of college record, written essay, 2 letters of recommendation, resume. *Application deadline:* Applications may be processed on a rolling basis for some programs. *Application fee:* $65.

Degree Requirements 45 total credit hours, thesis or project.

POST-MASTER'S PROGRAM

Areas of Study Nursing administration; nursing education. *Nurse practitioner programs in:* family health.

Humboldt State University

Department of Nursing
Arcata, California

http://www.humboldt.edu/~nurs

Founded in 1913

DEGREE • BSN

Nursing Program Faculty 21 (14% with doctorates).

Baccalaureate Enrollment 150
Women 85% **Men** 15% **Minority** 21%

Distance Learning Courses Available.

Nursing Student Activities Nursing Honor Society, Sigma Theta Tau, Student Nurses' Association.

Nursing Student Resources Academic advising; academic or career counseling; assistance for students with disabilities; bookstore; campus computer network; career placement assistance; computer lab; computer-assisted instruction; daycare for children of students; e-mail services; employment services for current students; housing assistance; interactive nursing skills videos; Internet; learning resource lab; library services; nursing audiovisuals; placement services for program completers; remedial services; resume preparation assistance; skills, simulation, or other laboratory; tutoring.

Humboldt State University (continued)
Library Facilities 1 million volumes (16,000 in health, 750 in nursing); 1,737 periodical subscriptions (152 health-care related).

BACCALAUREATE PROGRAMS

Degree BSN

Available Programs ADN to Baccalaureate; Baccalaureate for Second Degree; Generic Baccalaureate; RN Baccalaureate.

Site Options Fortuna, CA; Eureka, CA; Arcata, CA.

Study Options Full-time.

Program Entrance Requirements Minimum overall college GPA of 2.5, transcript of college record, CPR certification, health exam, high school foreign language, 2 years high school math, 1 year of high school science, high school transcript, immunizations, minimum GPA in nursing prerequisites of 2.5, prerequisite course work. Transfer students are accepted. *Application deadline:* 2/1 (fall), 10/1 (spring).

Advanced Placement Credit given for nursing courses completed elsewhere dependent upon specific evaluations.

Expenses (2009–10) *Tuition, state resident:* full-time $4496; part-time $1437 per term. *Tuition, nonresident:* full-time $12,632. *Room and board:* $9510; room only: $9088 per academic year. *Required fees:* full-time $868; part-time $36 per credit; part-time $434 per term.

Financial Aid 75% of baccalaureate students in nursing programs received some form of financial aid in 2008–09. *Gift aid (need-based):* Federal Pell, FSEOG, state, private, college/university gift aid from institutional funds. *Loans:* Federal Direct (Subsidized and Unsubsidized Stafford PLUS), Perkins. *Work-study:* Federal Work-Study. *Financial aid application deadline (priority):* 3/2.

Contact Miss Marcie Evans, Administrative Support Assistant, Department of Nursing, Humboldt State University, 1 Harpst Street, Arcata, CA 95521-8299. *Telephone:* 707-826-3839. *Fax:* 707-826-5141. *E-mail:* naac@humboldt.edu.

Loma Linda University
School of Nursing
Loma Linda, California

http://nursing.llu.edu
Founded in 1905
DEGREES • BS • DNP • MS • MS/MA • MS/MPH • PHD

Nursing Program Faculty 47 (55% with doctorates).

Baccalaureate Enrollment 496
Women 81% **Men** 19% **Minority** 62% **International** 19% **Part-time** 22%

Graduate Enrollment 128
Women 98% **Men** 2% **Minority** 40% **International** 8% **Part-time** 73%

Nursing Student Activities Nursing Honor Society, Sigma Theta Tau, Student Nurses' Association, nursing club.

Nursing Student Resources Academic advising; academic or career counseling; assistance for students with disabilities; bookstore; campus computer network; computer lab; computer-assisted instruction; e-mail services; employment services for current students; externships; housing assistance; interactive nursing skills videos; Internet; learning resource lab; library services; nursing audiovisuals; paid internships; remedial services; resume preparation assistance; skills, simulation, or other laboratory; tutoring.

Library Facilities 338,418 volumes (73,702 in health, 4,965 in nursing); 1,671 periodical subscriptions (6,516 health-care related).

BACCALAUREATE PROGRAMS

Degree BS

Available Programs ADN to Baccalaureate; Accelerated Baccalaureate for Second Degree; Accelerated RN Baccalaureate; Generic Baccalaureate; LPN to Baccalaureate; LPN to RN Baccalaureate; RN Baccalaureate.

Study Options Full-time and part-time.

Program Entrance Requirements Minimum overall college GPA of 3.0, transcript of college record, CPR certification, written essay, health exam, high school transcript, immunizations, interview, 3 letters of recommendation, minimum GPA in nursing prerequisites of 3.0, prerequisite course work. Transfer students are accepted. *Application deadline:* 3/31 (fall), 8/15 (winter), 11/1 (spring). Applications may be processed on a rolling basis for some programs. *Application fee:* $120.

Advanced Placement Credit by examination available. Credit given for nursing courses completed elsewhere dependent upon specific evaluations.

Expenses (2009–10) *Tuition:* part-time $525 per quarter hour. *Room and board:* room only: $4000 per academic year. *Required fees:* part-time $520 per term.

Financial Aid 95% of baccalaureate students in nursing programs received some form of financial aid in 2008–09.

Contact Mrs. Heather Krause, Director of Admissions, Marketing and Recruitment, School of Nursing, Loma Linda University, Loma Linda, CA 92350. *Telephone:* 909-558-4923. *Fax:* 909-558-0175. *E-mail:* hkrause@llu.edu.

GRADUATE PROGRAMS

Expenses (2009–10) *Tuition:* part-time $605 per quarter hour. *Required fees:* part-time $520 per term.

Financial Aid 26% of graduate students in nursing programs received some form of financial aid in 2008–09.

Contact Mrs. Tiny Loftis, Administrative Assistant, School of Nursing, Loma Linda University, Loma Linda, CA 92350. *Telephone:* 909-558-8061. *Fax:* 909-558-4134. *E-mail:* nursing@llu.edu.

MASTER'S DEGREE PROGRAM

Degrees MS; MS/MA; MS/MPH

Available Programs Accelerated Master's for Non-Nursing College Graduates; Master's; RN to Master's.

Concentrations Available Health-care administration; nursing administration; nursing education. *Clinical nurse specialist programs in:* adult health, family health, maternity-newborn, medical-surgical, parent-child, pediatric. *Nurse practitioner programs in:* adult health, family health, pediatric, primary care, psychiatric/mental health.

Study Options Full-time and part-time.

Program Entrance Requirements Clinical experience, minimum overall college GPA of 3.0, transcript of college record, written essay, immunizations, interview, 3 letters of recommendation, nursing research course, prerequisite course work, statistics course. *Application deadline:* 8/1 (fall), 11/1 (winter), 2/1 (spring). *Application fee:* $60.

Degree Requirements Comprehensive exam.

POST-MASTER'S PROGRAM

Areas of Study *Clinical nurse specialist programs in:* adult health, family health, maternity-newborn, medical-surgical, parent-child, pediatric. *Nurse practitioner programs in:* adult health, family health, pediatric, primary care, psychiatric/mental health.

DOCTORAL DEGREE PROGRAM

Degree DNP, PhD

Available Programs Doctorate.

Areas of Study Ethics, faculty preparation, gerontology, health policy, health promotion/disease prevention, human health and illness, nursing education, nursing research.

Program Entrance Requirements Clinical experience, minimum overall college GPA of 3.5, interview by faculty committee, interview, 3 letters of recommendation, MSN or equivalent, scholarly papers, statistics course, vita, writing sample. Application deadline: 8/1 (fall), 11/1 (winter), 2/1 (spring), 4/15 (summer). Application fee: $60.

Degree Requirements 90 total credit hours, dissertation, oral exam, written exam, residency.

Mount St. Mary's College
Department of Nursing
Los Angeles, California

http://www.msmc.la.edu/nursing/

Founded in 1925

DEGREES • BSN • BSC PN • MSN

Nursing Program Faculty 112 (10% with doctorates).

Baccalaureate Enrollment 326
Women 87% **Men** 13% **Minority** 80%

Graduate Enrollment 51
Women 91% **Men** 9% **Minority** 54%

Distance Learning Courses Available.

Nursing Student Activities Nursing Honor Society, Student Nurses' Association, nursing club.

Nursing Student Resources Academic advising; academic or career counseling; assistance for students with disabilities; bookstore; campus computer network; career placement assistance; computer lab; computer-assisted instruction; daycare for children of students; e-mail services; employment services for current students; housing assistance; interactive nursing skills videos; Internet; learning resource lab; library services; nursing audiovisuals; remedial services; resume preparation assistance; skills, simulation, or other laboratory; tutoring.

Library Facilities 4,000 volumes in health, 1,000 volumes in nursing; 150 periodical subscriptions health-care related.

BACCALAUREATE PROGRAMS

Degrees BSN; BSc PN

Available Programs ADN to Baccalaureate; Accelerated Baccalaureate; Generic Baccalaureate.

Study Options Full-time.

Program Entrance Requirements Minimum overall college GPA of 2.7, transcript of college record, CPR certification, written essay, health exam, high school chemistry, high school transcript, immunizations, 1 letter of recommendation, minimum GPA in nursing prerequisites of 2.5, professional liability insurance/malpractice insurance, prerequisite course work. Transfer students are accepted. *Application deadline:* 2/1 (fall). *Application fee:* $20.

Advanced Placement Credit by examination available. Credit given for nursing courses completed elsewhere dependent upon specific evaluations.

Expenses (2009–10) *Tuition:* full-time $27,840. *Room and board:* $8810 per academic year. *Required fees:* full-time $705.

Financial Aid 95% of baccalaureate students in nursing programs received some form of financial aid in 2008–09. *Gift aid (need-based):* Federal Pell, FSEOG, state, private, college/university gift aid from institutional funds. *Loans:* Federal Nursing Student Loans, FFEL (Subsidized and Unsubsidized Stafford PLUS), college/university. *Work-study:* Federal Work-Study, part-time campus jobs. *Financial aid application deadline:* 5/15 (priority: 3/2).

Contact Anne Tumbarello, Director, Department of Nursing, Mount St. Mary's College, 12001 Chalon Road, Los Angeles, CA 90049-1599. *Telephone:* 310-954-4279. *Fax:* 310-954-4229. *E-mail:* atumbarello@msmc.la. edu.

GRADUATE PROGRAMS

Expenses (2009–10) *Tuition:* part-time $708 per unit.

Financial Aid 95% of graduate students in nursing programs received some form of financial aid in 2008–09.

Contact Dr. Marsha Sato, Program Director, Department of Nursing, Mount St. Mary's College, 10 Chester Place, Los Angeles, CA 90007. *Telephone:* 213-477-2980. *Fax:* 213-477-2639. *E-mail:* msato@msmc.la.edu.

MASTER'S DEGREE PROGRAM

Degree MSN

Available Programs Master's; RN to Master's.

Concentrations Available Nursing administration; nursing education. *Clinical nurse specialist programs in:* adult health, community health.

Study Options Full-time and part-time.

Program Entrance Requirements Minimum overall college GPA of 3.0, transcript of college record, CPR certification, written essay, immunizations, interview, professional liability insurance/malpractice insurance, statistics course. *Application deadline:* Applications may be processed on a rolling basis for some programs. *Application fee:* $50.

Advanced Placement Credit given for nursing courses completed elsewhere dependent upon specific evaluations.

Degree Requirements 39 total credit hours, thesis or project.

National University
Department of Nursing
La Jolla, California

http://www.nu.edu/Academics/Schools/SOHHS/nursing.html

Founded in 1971

DEGREE • BSN

Nursing Program Faculty 65 (9% with doctorates).

Baccalaureate Enrollment 188
Women 88% **Men** 12% **Minority** 27% **International** 2%

Distance Learning Courses Available.

Nursing Student Activities Student Nurses' Association.

Nursing Student Resources Academic advising; academic or career counseling; assistance for students with disabilities; bookstore; campus computer network; computer lab; Internet; library services; nursing audiovisuals; other; remedial services; resume preparation assistance; tutoring.

Library Facilities 303,000 volumes (14,446 in health, 1,167 in nursing); 22,700 periodical subscriptions (2,047 health-care related).

BACCALAUREATE PROGRAMS

Degree BSN

Available Programs Accelerated Baccalaureate; Generic Baccalaureate; LPN to Baccalaureate; RN Baccalaureate.

Study Options Full-time.

Program Entrance Requirements Minimum overall college GPA of 2.0, transcript of college record, CPR certification, written essay, health exam, health insurance, immunizations, minimum GPA in nursing prerequisites of 2.75, professional liability insurance/malpractice insurance, prerequisite course work. Transfer students are accepted.

Advanced Placement Credit given for nursing courses completed elsewhere dependent upon specific evaluations.

Contact *Telephone:* 800-628-8648 Ext. 8211. *Fax:* 858-642-8709.

Pacific Union College
Department of Nursing
Angwin, California

http://www.puc.edu/PUC/academics/Academic_Departments/Nursing_Dept/

Founded in 1882

DEGREE • BSN

Nursing Program Faculty 16 (14% with doctorates).

Baccalaureate Enrollment 56
Women 77% **Men** 23% **Minority** 39% **Part-time** 59%

Nursing Student Activities Student Nurses' Association.

Nursing Student Resources Academic advising; academic or career counseling; assistance for students with disabilities; bookstore; campus computer network; career placement assistance; computer lab; daycare for children of students; e-mail services; employment services for current students; externships; housing assistance; Internet; learning resource lab; library services; nursing audiovisuals; skills, simulation, or other laboratory; tutoring.

Pacific Union College (continued)
Library Facilities 125 volumes in health, 75 volumes in nursing; 109 periodical subscriptions health-care related.

BACCALAUREATE PROGRAMS

Degree BSN

Available Programs ADN to Baccalaureate.

Site Options Napa, CA.

Study Options Full-time and part-time.

Program Entrance Requirements Transcript of college record, CPR certification, health exam, health insurance, immunizations, interview, 2 letters of recommendation, minimum GPA in nursing prerequisites of 2.0, professional liability insurance/malpractice insurance, prerequisite course work, RN licensure. Transfer students are accepted.

Advanced Placement Credit given for nursing courses completed elsewhere dependent upon specific evaluations.

Expenses (2009–10) *Tuition:* full-time $23,844; part-time $695 per quarter hour. *Room and board:* $6750; room only: $3975 per academic year. *Required fees:* part-time $7948 per term.

Financial Aid 93% of baccalaureate students in nursing programs received some form of financial aid in 2008–09. *Gift aid (need-based):* Federal Pell, FSEOG, state, private, college/university gift aid from institutional funds. *Loans:* FFEL (Subsidized and Unsubsidized Stafford PLUS), Perkins, college/university. *Work-study:* Federal Work-Study. *Financial aid application deadline (priority):* 3/2.

Contact Mrs. Nancy Tucker, PhD, Coordinator, BSN Program, Department of Nursing, Pacific Union College, One Angwin Avenue, Angwin, CA 94508. *Telephone:* 707-965-7618. *Fax:* 707-965-6499. *E-mail:* ntucker@puc.edu.

CONTINUING EDUCATION PROGRAM

Contact Dr. Shana L. Ruggenberg, Chair, Department of Nursing, Pacific Union College, One Angwin Avenue, Angwin, CA 94508. *Telephone:* 707-965-7262. *Fax:* 707-965-6499. *E-mail:* sruggenberg@puc.edu.

Point Loma Nazarene University
School of Nursing
San Diego, California

http://www.ptloma.edu/nursing
Founded in 1902
DEGREES • BSN • MSN

Nursing Program Faculty 28 (40% with doctorates).

Baccalaureate Enrollment 170
Women 90% **Men** 10% **Minority** 23% **International** 1% **Part-time** 2%

Graduate Enrollment 43
Women 92% **Men** 8% **Minority** 45% **Part-time** 5%

Nursing Student Activities Sigma Theta Tau, Student Nurses' Association.

Nursing Student Resources Academic advising; academic or career counseling; bookstore; campus computer network; computer lab; computer-assisted instruction; daycare for children of students; e-mail services; employment services for current students; externships; housing assistance; interactive nursing skills videos; Internet; learning resource lab; library services; nursing audiovisuals; paid internships; resume preparation assistance; skills, simulation, or other laboratory; tutoring; unpaid internships.

BACCALAUREATE PROGRAMS

Degree BSN

Available Programs ADN to Baccalaureate; Generic Baccalaureate; LPN to RN Baccalaureate; RN Baccalaureate.

Site Options San Diego, CA.

Study Options Full-time.

Program Entrance Requirements Minimum overall college GPA of 2.7, transcript of college record, CPR certification, written essay, health exam, health insurance, 2 years high school math, immunizations, 1 letter of recommendation, minimum GPA in nursing prerequisites of 2.7, prerequisite course work. Transfer students are accepted. *Application deadline:* 2/1 (fall), 2/1 (winter).

Advanced Placement Credit by examination available. Credit given for nursing courses completed elsewhere dependent upon specific evaluations.

Expenses (2009–10) *Tuition:* full-time $30,000. *Room and board:* $12,000 per academic year. *Required fees:* full-time $700.

Financial Aid 90% of baccalaureate students in nursing programs received some form of financial aid in 2008–09. *Gift aid (need-based):* Federal Pell, FSEOG, state, private, college/university gift aid from institutional funds. *Loans:* Federal Nursing Student Loans, FFEL (Subsidized and Unsubsidized Stafford PLUS), Perkins. *Work-study:* Federal Work-Study. *Financial aid application deadline (priority):* 3/2.

Contact Ms. Marsha Reece, Program Assistant, School of Nursing, Point Loma Nazarene University, 3900 Lomaland Drive, San Diego, CA 92106-2899. *Telephone:* 619-849-7055. *Fax:* 619-849-2672. *E-mail:* mreece@pointloma.edu.

GRADUATE PROGRAMS

Expenses (2009–10) *Tuition:* full-time $15,000.

Financial Aid 80% of graduate students in nursing programs received some form of financial aid in 2008–09.

Contact Prof. Larry Rankin, PhD, MSN Director/Associate Dean, School of Nursing, Point Loma Nazarene University, 4007 Camino Del Rio South, San Diego, CA 92108. *Telephone:* 619-849-2863. *Fax:* 619-849-2672. *E-mail:* lrankin@pointloma.edu.

MASTER'S DEGREE PROGRAM

Degree MSN

Available Programs Master's; RN to Master's.

Concentrations Available Nursing education. *Clinical nurse specialist programs in:* family health, gerontology, medical-surgical, psychiatric/mental health.

Site Options San Diego, CA.

Study Options Full-time and part-time.

Program Entrance Requirements Clinical experience, computer literacy, minimum overall college GPA of 3.0, transcript of college record, CPR certification, written essay, immunizations, interview, 3 letters of recommendation, professional liability insurance/malpractice insurance, resume. *Application deadline:* 8/1 (fall), 12/1 (winter), 8/1 (summer). *Application fee:* $40.

Degree Requirements 43 total credit hours, thesis or project.

POST-MASTER'S PROGRAM

Areas of Study Nursing education. *Clinical nurse specialist programs in:* family health, gerontology, medical-surgical, psychiatric/mental health.

CONTINUING EDUCATION PROGRAM

Contact Ms. Marsha Reece, Program Assistant, School of Nursing, Point Loma Nazarene University, 3900 Lomaland Drive, San Diego, CA 92106-2899. *Telephone:* 619-849-7055. *Fax:* 619-849-2672. *E-mail:* mreece@pointloma.edu.

Samuel Merritt University
School of Nursing
Oakland, California

http://www.samuelmerritt.edu/nursing
Founded in 1909
DEGREES • BSN • MSN

Nursing Program Faculty 171 (24% with doctorates).

Baccalaureate Enrollment 513
Women 86% **Men** 14% **Minority** 63% **Part-time** 1%

Graduate Enrollment 350
Women 79% **Men** 21% **Minority** 59% **Part-time** 29%

Distance Learning Courses Available.

Nursing Student Activities Sigma Theta Tau, Student Nurses' Association.

Nursing Student Resources Academic advising; academic or career counseling; assistance for students with disabilities; bookstore; campus computer network; computer lab; computer-assisted instruction; e-mail services; housing assistance; interactive nursing skills videos; Internet; learning resource lab; library services; nursing audiovisuals; remedial services; skills, simulation, or other laboratory; tutoring; unpaid internships.

Library Facilities 36,995 volumes (11,000 in health, 3,550 in nursing); 4,018 periodical subscriptions (9,064 health-care related).

BACCALAUREATE PROGRAMS

Degree BSN

Available Programs Accelerated Baccalaureate; Generic Baccalaureate.

Site Options Sacramento, CA; San Francisco, CA; San Mateo, CA.

Study Options Full-time and part-time.

Program Entrance Requirements Minimum overall college GPA of 3.0, transcript of college record, health exam, high school biology, high school chemistry, high school foreign language, 2 years high school math, 3 years high school science, high school transcript, immunizations, 1 letter of recommendation, minimum high school GPA of 2.5, minimum GPA in nursing prerequisites of 3.0, prerequisite course work. Transfer students are accepted. *Application deadline:* 3/1 (fall), 9/1 (spring). *Application fee:* $50.

Advanced Placement Credit by examination available. Credit given for nursing courses completed elsewhere dependent upon specific evaluations.

Expenses (2009–10) *Tuition:* full-time $34,148; part-time $1439 per credit. *International tuition:* $34,148 full-time. *Required fees:* full-time $1323; part-time $1323 per term.

Financial Aid 79% of baccalaureate students in nursing programs received some form of financial aid in 2008–09.

Contact Ms. Anne E. Seed, Director of Admissions, School of Nursing, Samuel Merritt University, 370 Hawthorne Avenue, Office of Admissions, Oakland, CA 94609. *Telephone:* 510-869-6610. *Fax:* 510-869-6525. *E-mail:* admission@samuelmerritt.edu.

GRADUATE PROGRAMS

Expenses (2009–10) *Tuition:* full-time $35,617; part-time $967 per credit. *International tuition:* $35,617 full-time. *Required fees:* full-time $690; part-time $690 per term.

Financial Aid 89% of graduate students in nursing programs received some form of financial aid in 2008–09. Career-related internships or fieldwork, Federal Work-Study, scholarships, and traineeships available. Aid available to part-time students. *Financial aid application deadline:* 3/2.

Contact Ms. Anne E. Seed, Director of Admissions, School of Nursing, Samuel Merritt University, 370 Hawthorne Avenue, Office of Admissions, Oakland, CA 94609. *Telephone:* 510-869-6610. *Fax:* 510-869-6525. *E-mail:* aseed@samuelmerritt.edu.

MASTER'S DEGREE PROGRAM

Degree MSN

Available Programs Master's; Master's for Non-Nursing College Graduates; Master's for Nurses with Non-Nursing Degrees.

Concentrations Available Nurse anesthesia; nurse case management. *Nurse practitioner programs in:* family health.

Site Options Sacramento, CA.

Study Options Full-time and part-time.

Online Degree Options Yes.

Program Entrance Requirements Clinical experience, computer literacy, minimum overall college GPA of 3.0, transcript of college record, CPR certification, written essay, immunizations, interview, 2 letters of recommendation, prerequisite course work, statistics course. *Application deadline:* 1/15 (fall), 7/1 (spring). *Application fee:* $50.

Advanced Placement Credit by examination available. Credit given for nursing courses completed elsewhere dependent upon specific evaluations.

Degree Requirements 49 total credit hours, thesis or project, comprehensive exam.

POST-MASTER'S PROGRAM

Areas of Study Nurse anesthesia; nurse case management. *Nurse practitioner programs in:* family health.

San Diego State University
School of Nursing
San Diego, California

http://nursing.sdsu.edu

Founded in 1897

DEGREES • BSN • MSN

Nursing Program Faculty 66 (36% with doctorates).

Baccalaureate Enrollment 540
Women 95% **Men** 5% **Minority** 60% **International** 1%

Graduate Enrollment 79
Women 95% **Men** 5% **Minority** 5% **Part-time** 75%

Distance Learning Courses Available.

Nursing Student Activities Sigma Theta Tau, Student Nurses' Association.

Nursing Student Resources Academic advising; academic or career counseling; assistance for students with disabilities; bookstore; campus computer network; career placement assistance; computer lab; daycare for children of students; e-mail services; housing assistance; Internet; learning resource lab; library services; nursing audiovisuals; paid internships; placement services for program completers; remedial services; resume preparation assistance; skills, simulation, or other laboratory; unpaid internships.

Library Facilities 1.3 million volumes (36,000 in health, 14,000 in nursing); 8,245 periodical subscriptions (335 health-care related).

BACCALAUREATE PROGRAMS

Degree BSN

Available Programs ADN to Baccalaureate; Accelerated Baccalaureate for Second Degree; Generic Baccalaureate; RN Baccalaureate.

Study Options Full-time.

Online Degree Options Yes.

Program Entrance Requirements Minimum overall college GPA of 2.5, transcript of college record, CPR certification, health exam, health insurance, high school biology, high school chemistry, high school foreign language, 3 years high school math, 2 years high school science, high school transcript, immunizations, minimum high school GPA of 2.5, minimum GPA in nursing prerequisites of 2.5, professional liability insurance/malpractice insurance, prerequisite course work. Transfer students are accepted. *Application deadline:* 11/30 (fall), 4/5 (spring). Applications may be processed on a rolling basis for some programs. *Application fee:* $45.

Advanced Placement Credit by examination available. Credit given for nursing courses completed elsewhere dependent upon specific evaluations.

Expenses (2009–10) *Tuition, state resident:* full-time $4228; part-time $1323 per semester. *Room and board:* $11,485; room only: $7675 per academic year. *Required fees:* part-time $1800 per credit; part-time $900 per term.

Financial Aid 75% of baccalaureate students in nursing programs received some form of financial aid in 2008–09. *Gift aid (need-based):* Federal Pell, FSEOG, state, private, college/university gift aid from institutional funds, Federal Nursing. *Loans:* Federal Direct (Subsidized and Unsubsidized Stafford PLUS), Perkins, college/university. *Work-study:* Federal Work-Study. *Financial aid application deadline:* 3/2.

Contact Nursing Contact, School of Nursing, San Diego State University, 5500 Campanile Drive, San Diego, CA 92182-0254. *Telephone:* 619-594-2540. *Fax:* 619-594-2765. *E-mail:* nursing@mail.sdsu.edu.

GRADUATE PROGRAMS

Expenses (2009–10) *Tuition, state resident:* full-time $4632; part-time $1464 per semester. *Tuition, nonresident:* full-time $5085. *International tuition:* $5085 full-time. *Room and board:* $11,485; room only: $7675 per academic year. *Required fees:* full-time $1000; part-time $500 per credit; part-time $500 per term.

San Diego State University (continued)

Financial Aid 90% of graduate students in nursing programs received some form of financial aid in 2008–09. Career-related internships or fieldwork, scholarships, traineeships, and unspecified assistantships available.

Contact Dr. Charlie A. Nicodemus, Graduate Adviser, School of Nursing, San Diego State University, 5500 Campanile Drive, San Diego, CA 92182-0254. *Telephone:* 619-594-5117. *Fax:* 619-594-2765. *E-mail:* cnicodem@mail.sdsu.ede.

MASTER'S DEGREE PROGRAM

Degree MSN

Available Programs Master's.

Concentrations Available Nurse-midwifery; nursing administration; nursing education. *Clinical nurse specialist programs in:* adult health, community health, critical care, gerontology, maternity-newborn, school health, women's health. *Nurse practitioner programs in:* acute care, adult health, gerontology, women's health.

Site Options La Jolla, CA.

Study Options Full-time and part-time.

Program Entrance Requirements Clinical experience, minimum overall college GPA of 3.0, transcript of college record, written essay, 3 letters of recommendation, nursing research course, physical assessment course, professional liability insurance/malpractice insurance, resume, statistics course, GRE General Test. *Application deadline:* 2/1 (fall), 2/1 (spring). Applications may be processed on a rolling basis for some programs. *Application fee:* $45.

Advanced Placement Credit by examination available. Credit given for nursing courses completed elsewhere dependent upon specific evaluations.

Degree Requirements 39 total credit hours, thesis or project, comprehensive exam.

POST-MASTER'S PROGRAM

Areas of Study Nurse-midwifery.

CONTINUING EDUCATION PROGRAM

Contact Dr. Charlie A. Nicodemus, Nursing Contact, School of Nursing, San Diego State University, 5500 Campanile Drive, San Diego, CA 92182-0254. *Telephone:* 619-594-5117. *Fax:* 619-594-2765. *E-mail:* cnicodem@mail.sdsu.edu.

San Francisco State University
School of Nursing
San Francisco, California

Founded in 1899

DEGREES • BSN • MSN

Nursing Program Faculty 40 (50% with doctorates).

Baccalaureate Enrollment 250
Women 88% **Men** 12% **Minority** 53% **International** 2% **Part-time** 5%

Graduate Enrollment 180
Women 80% **Men** 20% **Minority** 80% **International** 10% **Part-time** 20%

Nursing Student Activities Sigma Theta Tau, Student Nurses' Association.

Nursing Student Resources Academic advising; academic or career counseling; assistance for students with disabilities; bookstore; campus computer network; career placement assistance; computer lab; computer-assisted instruction; daycare for children of students; e-mail services; employment services for current students; externships; housing assistance; interactive nursing skills videos; Internet; learning resource lab; library services; nursing audiovisuals; other; placement services for program completers; remedial services; resume preparation assistance; skills, simulation, or other laboratory; tutoring.

Library Facilities 1.2 million volumes (11,000 in health, 1,500 in nursing); 20,796 periodical subscriptions (200 health-care related).

BACCALAUREATE PROGRAMS

Degree BSN

Available Programs ADN to Baccalaureate; Accelerated LPN to Baccalaureate; Generic Baccalaureate; RN Baccalaureate.

Study Options Full-time.

Program Entrance Requirements Minimum overall college GPA of 2.5, transcript of college record, CPR certification, health exam, health insurance, immunizations, minimum GPA in nursing prerequisites of 2.5, professional liability insurance/malpractice insurance, prerequisite course work. Transfer students are accepted.

Advanced Placement Credit by examination available. Credit given for nursing courses completed elsewhere dependent upon specific evaluations.

Contact *Telephone:* 415-338-2315 Ext. 1. *Fax:* 415-338-0555.

GRADUATE PROGRAMS

Contact *Telephone:* 415-338-1802. *Fax:* 415-338-0555.

MASTER'S DEGREE PROGRAM

Degree MSN

Available Programs Accelerated Master's for Non-Nursing College Graduates; Accelerated Master's for Nurses with Non-Nursing Degrees; Master's; Master's for Non-Nursing College Graduates; Master's for Nurses with Non-Nursing Degrees.

Concentrations Available Nurse case management; nursing administration. *Clinical nurse specialist programs in:* adult health, perinatal, public health. *Nurse practitioner programs in:* family health.

Study Options Full-time and part-time.

Program Entrance Requirements Minimum overall college GPA of 3.0, transcript of college record, CPR certification, written essay, immunizations, 3 letters of recommendation, nursing research course, professional liability insurance/malpractice insurance, resume, statistics course.

Advanced Placement Credit by examination available. Credit given for nursing courses completed elsewhere dependent upon specific evaluations.

Degree Requirements 36 total credit hours, thesis or project.

POST-MASTER'S PROGRAM

Areas of Study Nursing administration. *Nurse practitioner programs in:* family health.

CONTINUING EDUCATION PROGRAM

Contact *Telephone:* 415-405-3660. *Fax:* 415-338-0555.

San Jose State University
School of Nursing
San Jose, California

Founded in 1857

DEGREES • BS • MS

Nursing Program Faculty 55 (52% with doctorates).

Baccalaureate Enrollment 550
Women 92% **Men** 8% **Minority** 76% **Part-time** 20%

Graduate Enrollment 101
Women 92% **Men** 8% **Minority** 46% **Part-time** 83%

Nursing Student Activities Sigma Theta Tau, Student Nurses' Association, nursing club.

Nursing Student Resources Academic advising; academic or career counseling; assistance for students with disabilities; bookstore; career placement assistance; computer lab; computer-assisted instruction; housing assistance; interactive nursing skills videos; Internet; learning resource lab; library services; nursing audiovisuals; skills, simulation, or other laboratory; tutoring.

Library Facilities 1.8 million volumes (280 in health, 250 in nursing); 35,390 periodical subscriptions (80 health-care related).

BACCALAUREATE PROGRAMS

Degree BS

Available Programs Generic Baccalaureate; RPN to Baccalaureate.

Site Options Salinas, CA; Gilroy, CA.

Study Options Full-time and part-time.

Program Entrance Requirements Transcript of college record, health insurance, 3 years high school math, minimum high school GPA of 2.0, minimum GPA in nursing prerequisites of 2.0, professional liability insurance/malpractice insurance, prerequisite course work. Transfer students are accepted.

Advanced Placement Credit by examination available. Credit given for nursing courses completed elsewhere dependent upon specific evaluations.

Contact *Telephone:* 408-924-3131. *Fax:* 408-924-3135.

GRADUATE PROGRAMS

Contact *Telephone:* 408-924-3144. *Fax:* 408-924-3135.

MASTER'S DEGREE PROGRAM

Degree MS

Available Programs Master's.

Concentrations Available Nursing administration; nursing education. *Clinical nurse specialist programs in:* gerontology, school health. *Nurse practitioner programs in:* family health.

Study Options Full-time and part-time.

Program Entrance Requirements Minimum overall college GPA of 3.0, transcript of college record, CPR certification, written essay, immunizations, 3 letters of recommendation, nursing research course, physical assessment course, professional liability insurance/malpractice insurance, resume, statistics course.

Degree Requirements 36 total credit hours, thesis or project.

Sonoma State University
Department of Nursing
Rohnert Park, California

http://www.sonoma.edu/nursing

Founded in 1960

DEGREES • BSN • MSN

Nursing Program Faculty 37 (22% with doctorates).

Baccalaureate Enrollment 129
Women 86% **Men** 14% **Minority** 25% **Part-time** 27%

Graduate Enrollment 116
Women 91% **Men** 9% **Minority** 29% **Part-time** 59%

Distance Learning Courses Available.

Nursing Student Activities Nursing Honor Society, Sigma Theta Tau, Student Nurses' Association, nursing club.

Nursing Student Resources Academic advising; academic or career counseling; assistance for students with disabilities; bookstore; campus computer network; career placement assistance; computer lab; computer-assisted instruction; daycare for children of students; e-mail services; employment services for current students; externships; housing assistance; interactive nursing skills videos; Internet; learning resource lab; library services; nursing audiovisuals; remedial services; resume preparation assistance; skills, simulation, or other laboratory; tutoring; unpaid internships.

Library Facilities 678,474 volumes (26,700 in health, 1,400 in nursing); 21,117 periodical subscriptions (64 health-care related).

BACCALAUREATE PROGRAMS

Degree BSN

Available Programs ADN to Baccalaureate; Baccalaureate for Second Degree; Generic Baccalaureate; RN Baccalaureate.

Study Options Full-time.

Program Entrance Requirements Minimum overall college GPA of 3.0, transcript of college record, CPR certification, written essay, health exam, high school biology, high school chemistry, high school foreign language, 3 years high school math, 2 years high school science, high school transcript, immunizations, minimum high school GPA of 3.0, minimum GPA in nursing prerequisites of 3.0, professional liability insurance/malpractice insurance, prerequisite course work. Transfer students are accepted. *Application deadline:* 2/28 (fall). *Application fee:* $25.

Financial Aid 53% of baccalaureate students in nursing programs received some form of financial aid in 2008–09. *Gift aid (need-based):* Federal Pell, FSEOG, state, private, college/university gift aid from institutional funds, Academic Competitiveness Grant, National Smart Grant. *Loans:* Federal Direct (Subsidized and Unsubsidized Stafford PLUS), Perkins. *Work-study:* Federal Work-Study, part-time campus jobs. *Financial aid application deadline (priority):* 1/31.

Contact Ms. Eileen P. O'Brien, Administrative Coordinator, Department of Nursing, Sonoma State University, 1801 East Cotati Avenue, Rohnert Park, CA 94928. *Telephone:* 707-664-2465. *Fax:* 707-664-2653. *E-mail:* nursing@sonoma.edu.

GRADUATE PROGRAMS

Financial Aid 70% of graduate students in nursing programs received some form of financial aid in 2008–09.

Contact Ms. Eileen P. O'Brien, Administrative Coordinator, Department of Nursing, Sonoma State University, 1801 East Cotati Avenue, Rohnert Park, CA 94928. *Telephone:* 707-664-2465. *Fax:* 707-664-2653. *E-mail:* nursing@sonoma.edu.

MASTER'S DEGREE PROGRAM

Degree MSN

Available Programs Accelerated Master's for Non-Nursing College Graduates; Master's; Master's for Nurses with Non-Nursing Degrees.

Concentrations Available Clinical nurse leader; nursing administration; nursing education. *Nurse practitioner programs in:* family health.

Site Options Turlock, CA; Chico, CA.

Study Options Full-time and part-time.

Online Degree Options Yes.

Program Entrance Requirements Clinical experience, computer literacy, minimum overall college GPA of 3.0, transcript of college record, CPR certification, written essay, immunizations, 3 letters of recommendation, physical assessment course, professional liability insurance/malpractice insurance, prerequisite course work, statistics course. *Application deadline:* 3/31 (fall). *Application fee:* $25.

Advanced Placement Credit given for nursing courses completed elsewhere dependent upon specific evaluations.

Degree Requirements 32 total credit hours, thesis or project, comprehensive exam.

POST-MASTER'S PROGRAM

Areas of Study *Nurse practitioner programs in:* family health.

University of California, Irvine
Program in Nursing Science
Irvine, California

Founded in 1965

DEGREE • BS

Nursing Program Faculty 30 (27% with doctorates).

Baccalaureate Enrollment 171

Nursing Student Activities Student Nurses' Association.

Nursing Student Resources Academic advising; academic or career counseling; assistance for students with disabilities; bookstore; campus computer network; computer lab; computer-assisted instruction; daycare for children of students; e-mail services; employment services for current students; housing assistance; interactive nursing skills videos; Internet; learning resource lab; library services; nursing audiovisuals; skills, simulation, or other laboratory; tutoring.

Library Facilities 2.7 million volumes (365,965 in health, 6,047 in nursing); 47,000 periodical subscriptions.

BACCALAUREATE PROGRAMS

Degree BS

Available Programs Generic Baccalaureate.

Contact Baccalaureate Program, Program in Nursing Science, University of California, Irvine, 31 Irvine Hall, Irvine, CA 92697-3959. *Telephone:* 949-824-3580. *Fax:* 949-824-0470.

University of California, Los Angeles

School of Nursing
Los Angeles, California

http://www.nursing.ucla.edu

Founded in 1919

DEGREES • BS • MSN • MSN/MBA • PHD

Nursing Program Faculty 63 (80% with doctorates).

Baccalaureate Enrollment 244
Women 91% **Men** 9% **Minority** 66% **International** 1%

Graduate Enrollment 343
Women 91% **Men** 9% **Minority** 50% **International** 1%

Nursing Student Activities Nursing Honor Society, Sigma Theta Tau, Student Nurses' Association, nursing club.

Nursing Student Resources Academic advising; academic or career counseling; assistance for students with disabilities; bookstore; campus computer network; computer lab; daycare for children of students; e-mail services; housing assistance; Internet; library services; nursing audiovisuals; skills, simulation, or other laboratory.

Library Facilities 8.2 million volumes (760,000 in health, 8,000 in nursing); 77,509 periodical subscriptions (600,000 health-care related).

BACCALAUREATE PROGRAMS

Degree BS

Available Programs ADN to Baccalaureate; Generic Baccalaureate.
Study Options Full-time.
Program Entrance Requirements Transcript of college record, written essay, high school transcript, 2 letters of recommendation, minimum high school GPA, prerequisite course work. Transfer students are accepted. *Application deadline:* 11/30 (fall). *Application fee:* $60.
Expenses (2009–10) *Tuition, state resident:* full-time $8814. *Tuition, nonresident:* full-time $31,820. *International tuition:* $31,820 full-time. *Room and board:* $13,314 per academic year.
Financial Aid 72% of baccalaureate students in nursing programs received some form of financial aid in 2008–09. *Gift aid (need-based):* Federal Pell, FSEOG, state, private, college/university gift aid from institutional funds, United Negro College Fund, Federal Nursing. *Loans:* Federal Nursing Student Loans, FFEL (Subsidized and Unsubsidized Stafford PLUS), Perkins, state, college/university. *Work-study:* Federal Work-Study, part-time campus jobs. *Financial aid application deadline:* Continuous.

Contact Ms. Rhonda Flenoy-Younger, Director of Recruitment, Outreach and Admissions, School of Nursing, University of California, Los Angeles, Box 951702, Los Angeles, CA 90095-1702. *Telephone:* 310-825-9193. *Fax:* 310-206-7433. *E-mail:* rflenoy@sonnet.ucla.edu.

GRADUATE PROGRAMS

Expenses (2009–10) *Tuition, state resident:* full-time $12,714. *Tuition, nonresident:* full-time $27,408. *International tuition:* $27,408 full-time. *Room and board:* $13,968 per academic year.
Financial Aid 82% of graduate students in nursing programs received some form of financial aid in 2008–09. 209 fellowships with full and partial tuition reimbursements available, 11 research assistantships with full and partial tuition reimbursements available, 28 teaching assistantships with full and partial tuition reimbursements available were awarded; Federal Work-Study, institutionally sponsored loans, scholarships, tuition waivers (full and partial), and unspecified assistantships also available. *Financial aid application deadline:* 3/1.
Contact Ms. Rhonda Flenoy-Younger, Director of Recruitment, Outreach and Admissions, School of Nursing, University of California, Los Angeles, Box 951702, Los Angeles, CA 90095-1702. *Telephone:* 310-825-9193. *Fax:* 310-267-0330. *E-mail:* rflenoy@sonnet.ucla.edu.

MASTER'S DEGREE PROGRAM

Degrees MSN; MSN/MBA

Available Programs Master's; Master's for Non-Nursing College Graduates.

Concentrations Available Clinical nurse leader; nursing administration. *Clinical nurse specialist programs in:* acute care, adult health, gerontology, oncology, pediatric. *Nurse practitioner programs in:* acute care, adult health, family health, gerontology, occupational health, oncology, pediatric.
Study Options Full-time.
Program Entrance Requirements Minimum overall college GPA of 3.0, transcript of college record, written essay, 3 letters of recommendation, nursing research course, physical assessment course, prerequisite course work, statistics course. *Application deadline:* 11/1 (fall). *Application fee:* $70.
Degree Requirements 72 total credit hours, comprehensive exam.

POST-MASTER'S PROGRAM

Areas of Study Nursing administration. *Nurse practitioner programs in:* acute care, adult health, family health, gerontology, oncology, pediatric.

DOCTORAL DEGREE PROGRAM

Degree PhD
Available Programs Doctorate; Post-Baccalaureate Doctorate.
Areas of Study Addiction/substance abuse, advanced practice nursing, aging, bio-behavioral research, biology of health and illness, clinical practice, community health, critical care, family health, gerontology, health policy, health promotion/disease prevention, health-care systems, human health and illness, illness and transition, neuro-behavior, nursing administration, nursing research, nursing science, oncology, women's health.
Program Entrance Requirements Minimum overall college GPA of 3.5, 4 letters of recommendation, MSN or equivalent, scholarly papers, statistics course, vita, writing sample, GRE General Test. Application deadline: 12/1 (fall). Application fee: $70.
Degree Requirements 127 total credit hours, dissertation, oral exam, written exam, residency.

POSTDOCTORAL PROGRAM

Areas of Study Addiction/substance abuse, adolescent health, aging, cancer care, gerontology, health promotion/disease prevention, nursing research, vulnerable population, women's health.
Postdoctoral Program Contact Dr. Peggy Compton, Acting Associate Dean for Academic Affairs, School of Nursing, University of California, Los Angeles, Box 951702, Los Angeles, CA 90095-1702. *Telephone:* 310-206-2825. *Fax:* 310-206-7433. *E-mail:* pcompton@sonnet.ucla.edu.

CONTINUING EDUCATION PROGRAM

Contact Ms. Salpy Akaragian, Education Specialist, School of Nursing, University of California, Los Angeles, Box 951701, Los Angeles, CA 90095-1701. *Telephone:* 310-206-9581. *E-mail:* nssa@mednet.ucla.edu.

University of California, San Francisco

School of Nursing
San Francisco, California

http://www.nurseweb.ucsf.edu

Founded in 1864

DEGREES • MS • PHD

Nursing Program Faculty 151 (72% with doctorates).

Graduate Enrollment 721
Women 87% **Men** 13% **Minority** 30% **International** 10% **Part-time** 1%

Distance Learning Courses Available.

Nursing Student Activities Nursing Honor Society, Sigma Theta Tau, Student Nurses' Association, nursing club.

Nursing Student Resources Academic advising; academic or career counseling; assistance for students with disabilities; bookstore; campus computer network; career placement assistance; computer lab; computer-assisted instruction; daycare for children of students; e-mail services; employment services for current students; housing assistance; interactive nursing skills videos; Internet; learning resource lab; library services; nursing audiovisuals; other; paid internships; placement services for program completers; remedial services; resume preparation assistance; skills, simulation, or other laboratory; tutoring; unpaid internships.

Library Facilities 856,169 volumes in health, 131,046 volumes in nursing; 3,270 periodical subscriptions health-care related.

GRADUATE PROGRAMS

Expenses (2009–10) *Tuition, state resident:* full-time $14,695. *Tuition, nonresident:* full-time $26,940. *International tuition:* $26,940 full-time.

Financial Aid 59% of graduate students in nursing programs received some form of financial aid in 2008–09. Fellowships, career-related internships or fieldwork and Federal Work-Study available. Aid available to part-time students.

Contact Mr. Terry Linton, Admissions and Progression Officer, School of Nursing, University of California, San Francisco, Room N319X, 2 Koret Way, San Francisco, CA 94143-0602. *Telephone:* 415-476-1435. *Fax:* 415-476-9707. *E-mail:* terry.linton@nursing.ucsf.edu.

MASTER'S DEGREE PROGRAM

Degree MS

Available Programs Master's; Master's for Non-Nursing College Graduates; Master's for Nurses with Non-Nursing Degrees.

Concentrations Available Nurse-midwifery; nursing administration. *Clinical nurse specialist programs in:* cardiovascular, community health, critical care, gerontology, occupational health, oncology, pediatric, perinatal, psychiatric/mental health. *Nurse practitioner programs in:* acute care, adult health, family health, gerontology, neonatal health, occupational health, pediatric, psychiatric/mental health.

Study Options Full-time.

Program Entrance Requirements Clinical experience, computer literacy, minimum overall college GPA of 3.0, transcript of college record, written essay, immunizations, 4 letters of recommendation, statistics course, GRE General Test. *Application deadline:* 2/1 (fall). *Application fee:* $60.

Advanced Placement Credit given for nursing courses completed elsewhere dependent upon specific evaluations.

Degree Requirements 44 total credit hours, comprehensive exam.

POST-MASTER'S PROGRAM

Areas of Study *Clinical nurse specialist programs in:* cardiovascular, community health, critical care, gerontology, occupational health, oncology, pediatric, perinatal, psychiatric/mental health. *Nurse practitioner programs in:* acute care, adult health, family health, gerontology, neonatal health, occupational health, pediatric, psychiatric/mental health.

DOCTORAL DEGREE PROGRAM

Degree PhD

Available Programs Doctorate; Post-Baccalaureate Doctorate.

Areas of Study Addiction/substance abuse, aging, bio-behavioral research, biology of health and illness, community health, critical care, ethics, family health, gerontology, health policy, health promotion/disease prevention, health-care systems, human health and illness, illness and transition, individualized study, information systems, maternity-newborn, nursing administration, nursing policy, nursing research, nursing science, oncology, urban health, women's health.

Program Entrance Requirements Minimum overall college GPA of 3.0, 4 letters of recommendation, statistics course, writing sample, GRE General Test. Application deadline: 12/15 (fall). Application fee: $60.

Degree Requirements Dissertation, oral exam, written exam, residency.

POSTDOCTORAL PROGRAM

Areas of Study Individualized study.

Postdoctoral Program Contact Mr. Jeff Kilmer, Director, Office of Student and Curricular Affairs, School of Nursing, University of California, San Francisco, Room N319X, 2 Koret Way, San Francisco, CA 94143-0602. *Telephone:* 415-476-1435. *Fax:* 415-476-9707. *E-mail:* jeff.kilmer@nursing.ucsf.edu.

University of Phoenix–Bay Area Campus
College of Health and Human Services
Pleasanton, California

DEGREES • BSN • MSN • MSN/MBA • MSN/MHA

Nursing Program Faculty 12 (58% with doctorates).

Baccalaureate Enrollment 39
Women 92.3% **Men** 7.7% **Minority** 35.9%

Graduate Enrollment 22
Women 86.4% **Men** 13.6% **Minority** 40.91%

Nursing Student Activities Sigma Theta Tau.

Nursing Student Resources Academic advising; academic or career counseling; assistance for students with disabilities; bookstore; campus computer network; computer lab; computer-assisted instruction; e-mail services; interactive nursing skills videos; Internet; learning resource lab; library services; nursing audiovisuals; remedial services; skills, simulation, or other laboratory; tutoring.

Library Facilities 16,781 periodical subscriptions (1,300 health-care related).

BACCALAUREATE PROGRAMS

Degree BSN

Available Programs Accelerated Baccalaureate.

Site Options Oakland, CA; San Francisco, CA; Novato, CA.

Study Options Full-time.

Program Entrance Requirements Transcript of college record, CPR certification, immunizations, 1 letter of recommendation, RN licensure. Transfer students are accepted. *Application deadline:* Applications may be processed on a rolling basis for some programs.

Advanced Placement Credit by examination available. Credit given for nursing courses completed elsewhere dependent upon specific evaluations.

Expenses (2009–10) *Tuition:* full-time $9300. *Required fees:* full-time $600.

Contact Campus College Chair, Nursing, College of Health and Human Services, University of Phoenix–Bay Area Campus, 7901 Stoneridge Drive, Suite #130, Pleasanton, CA 94588-3677. *Telephone:* 877-416-4100.

GRADUATE PROGRAMS

Expenses (2009–10) *Tuition:* full-time $10,560. *Required fees:* full-time $760.

Financial Aid Institutionally sponsored loans and scholarships available.

Contact Campus College Chair, Nursing, College of Health and Human Services, University of Phoenix–Bay Area Campus, 7901 Stoneridge Drive, Suite #130, Pleasanton, CA 94588-3677. *Telephone:* 877-416-4100.

MASTER'S DEGREE PROGRAM

Degrees MSN; MSN/MBA; MSN/MHA

Available Programs Master's.

Concentrations Available Health-care administration; nursing administration; nursing education.

Site Options Oakland, CA; San Francisco, CA; Novato, CA.

Study Options Full-time.

Program Entrance Requirements Clinical experience, computer literacy, minimum overall college GPA of 2.5, transcript of college record. *Application deadline:* Applications may be processed on a rolling basis for some programs. *Application fee:* $45.

Advanced Placement Credit given for nursing courses completed elsewhere dependent upon specific evaluations.

Degree Requirements 39 total credit hours, thesis or project.

University of Phoenix–Central Valley Campus

College of Health and Human Services
Fresno, California

Founded in 2004

DEGREE • BSN

Nursing Program Faculty 8 (13% with doctorates).

Baccalaureate Enrollment 53
Women 94.3% **Men** 5.7% **Minority** 30.2%

Nursing Student Activities Sigma Theta Tau.

Nursing Student Resources Academic advising; academic or career counseling; bookstore; campus computer network; computer lab; computer-assisted instruction; e-mail services; interactive nursing skills videos; Internet; learning resource lab; library services; nursing audiovisuals; remedial services; skills, simulation, or other laboratory; tutoring.

Library Facilities 1,300 periodical subscriptions health-care related.

BACCALAUREATE PROGRAMS

Degree BSN

Available Programs RN Baccalaureate.

Site Options Fresno, CA; Visalia, CA; Bakersfield, CA.

Study Options Full-time.

Program Entrance Requirements Transcript of college record, CPR certification, immunizations, 1 letter of recommendation, RN licensure. Transfer students are accepted.

Advanced Placement Credit by examination available. Credit given for nursing courses completed elsewhere dependent upon specific evaluations.

Contact Campus College Chair, Nursing, College of Health and Human Services, University of Phoenix–Central Valley Campus, 4900 California Avenue, Tower A, Suite 300, Bakersfield, CA 93309-7018. *Telephone:* 661-663-0300. *Fax:* 661-633-2711.

University of Phoenix–Sacramento Valley Campus

College of Health and Human Services
Sacramento, California

Founded in 1993

DEGREES • BSN • MSN • MSN/MHA

Nursing Program Faculty 29 (28% with doctorates).

Baccalaureate Enrollment 250
Women 88.8% **Men** 11.2% **Minority** 32%

Graduate Enrollment 53
Women 90.6% **Men** 9.4% **Minority** 15.09%

Nursing Student Activities Sigma Theta Tau.

Nursing Student Resources Academic advising; academic or career counseling; assistance for students with disabilities; bookstore; campus computer network; computer lab; computer-assisted instruction; e-mail services; interactive nursing skills videos; Internet; learning resource lab; library services; nursing audiovisuals; skills, simulation, or other laboratory; tutoring.

Library Facilities 16,781 periodical subscriptions (1,300 health-care related).

BACCALAUREATE PROGRAMS

Degree BSN

Available Programs Accelerated Baccalaureate; LPN to Baccalaureate.

Site Options Lathrop, CA; Modesto, CA; Fairfield, CA.

Study Options Full-time.

Online Degree Options Yes.

Program Entrance Requirements Transcript of college record, CPR certification, immunizations, 1 letter of recommendation, RN licensure. Transfer students are accepted. *Application deadline:* Applications may be processed on a rolling basis for some programs.

Advanced Placement Credit by examination available. Credit given for nursing courses completed elsewhere dependent upon specific evaluations.

Expenses (2009–10) *Tuition:* full-time $11,100. *Required fees:* full-time $600.

Contact Campus College Chair, Nursing, College of Health and Human Services, University of Phoenix–Sacramento Valley Campus, 1760 Creekside Oaks Drive, #100, Sacramento, CA 95833-3632. *Telephone:* 800-266-2107.

GRADUATE PROGRAMS

Expenses (2009–10) *Tuition:* full-time $13,200. *Required fees:* full-time $760.

Financial Aid Institutionally sponsored loans and scholarships available.

Contact Campus College Chair, Nursing, College of Health and Human Services, University of Phoenix–Sacramento Valley Campus, 1760 Creekside Oaks Drive, #100, Sacramento, CA 95833-3632. *Telephone:* 800-266-2107.

MASTER'S DEGREE PROGRAM

Degrees MSN; MSN/MHA

Available Programs Accelerated Master's.

Concentrations Available Health-care administration; nursing administration; nursing education. *Nurse practitioner programs in:* family health.

Site Options Lathrop, CA; Modesto, CA; Fairfield, CA.

Study Options Full-time and part-time.

Program Entrance Requirements Clinical experience, computer literacy, minimum overall college GPA of 2.5, transcript of college record. *Application deadline:* Applications may be processed on a rolling basis for some programs. *Application fee:* $45.

Advanced Placement Credit given for nursing courses completed elsewhere dependent upon specific evaluations.

Degree Requirements 39 total credit hours, thesis or project.

POST-MASTER'S PROGRAM

Areas of Study *Nurse practitioner programs in:* family health.

CONTINUING EDUCATION PROGRAM

Contact Campus College Chair, College of Health and Human Services, University of Phoenix–Sacramento Valley Campus, 1760 Creekside Oaks Drive, #100, Scaramento, CA 95833-3632. *Telephone:* 800-266-2107.

University of Phoenix–San Diego Campus

College of Health and Human Services
San Diego, California

Founded in 1988

DEGREES • BSN • MSN • MSN/ED D

Nursing Program Faculty 30 (37% with doctorates).

Baccalaureate Enrollment 103
Women 81.6% **Men** 18.4% **Minority** 29.1%

Graduate Enrollment 46
Women 89.1% **Men** 10.9% **Minority** 58.7%

Nursing Student Activities Sigma Theta Tau.

Nursing Student Resources Academic advising; academic or career counseling; assistance for students with disabilities; bookstore; campus computer network; computer lab; computer-assisted instruction; e-mail services; interactive nursing skills videos; Internet; learning resource lab; library services; nursing audiovisuals; skills, simulation, or other laboratory; tutoring.

Library Facilities 16,781 periodical subscriptions (1,300 health-care related).

BACCALAUREATE PROGRAMS

Degree BSN

Available Programs Accelerated Baccalaureate.

Site Options Chula Vista, CA; Imperial, CA; Palm Desert, CA.

Study Options Full-time.

Program Entrance Requirements Transcript of college record, CPR certification, immunizations, 1 letter of recommendation, RN licensure. Transfer students are accepted. *Application deadline:* Applications may be processed on a rolling basis for some programs.

Advanced Placement Credit by examination available. Credit given for nursing courses completed elsewhere dependent upon specific evaluations.

Expenses (2009–10) *Tuition:* full-time $10,560. *Required fees:* full-time $600.

Contact Campus College Chair, Nursing, College of Health and Human Services, University of Phoenix–San Diego Campus, 3870 Murphy Canyon Road, #100, San Diego, CA 92123-4403. *Telephone:* 888-867-4636.

GRADUATE PROGRAMS

Expenses (2009–10) *Tuition:* full-time $13,200. *Required fees:* full-time $760.

Financial Aid Institutionally sponsored loans and scholarships available.

Contact Campus College Chair, Nursing, College of Health and Human Services, University of Phoenix–San Diego Campus, 3870 Murphy Canyon Road, #100, San Diego, CA 92123-4403. *Telephone:* 888-867-4636.

MASTER'S DEGREE PROGRAM

Degrees MSN; MSN/Ed D

Available Programs Master's.

Concentrations Available Health-care administration; nursing administration; nursing education.

Site Options Chula Vista, CA; Imperial, CA; Palm Desert, CA.

Study Options Full-time.

Program Entrance Requirements Clinical experience, computer literacy, minimum overall college GPA of 2.5, transcript of college record. *Application deadline:* Applications may be processed on a rolling basis for some programs. *Application fee:* $45.

Advanced Placement Credit given for nursing courses completed elsewhere dependent upon specific evaluations.

Degree Requirements 39 total credit hours, thesis or project.

University of Phoenix–Southern California Campus

College of Health and Human Services
Costa Mesa, California

Founded in 1980

DEGREES • BSN • MSN • MSN/MBA • MSN/MHA

Nursing Program Faculty 109 (23% with doctorates).

Baccalaureate Enrollment 563
Women 89.2% **Men** 10.8% **Minority** 36.8%

Graduate Enrollment 379
Women 90.2% **Men** 9.8% **Minority** 40.9%

Nursing Student Activities Sigma Theta Tau.

Nursing Student Resources Academic advising; academic or career counseling; assistance for students with disabilities; bookstore; campus computer network; computer lab; computer-assisted instruction; e-mail services; interactive nursing skills videos; Internet; learning resource lab; library services; nursing audiovisuals; remedial services; skills, simulation, or other laboratory; tutoring.

Library Facilities 16,781 periodical subscriptions (1,300 health-care related).

BACCALAUREATE PROGRAMS

Degree BSN

Available Programs Accelerated Baccalaureate.

Site Options Diamond Bar, CA; La Marada, CA; Lancaster, CA.

Study Options Full-time.

Program Entrance Requirements Transcript of college record, CPR certification, immunizations, 1 letter of recommendation, RN licensure. Transfer students are accepted. *Application deadline:* Applications may be processed on a rolling basis for some programs.

Advanced Placement Credit by examination available. Credit given for nursing courses completed elsewhere dependent upon specific evaluations.

Expenses (2009–10) *Tuition:* full-time $11,400. *Required fees:* full-time $600.

Contact Campus College Chair, Nursing, College of Health and Human Services, University of Phoenix–Southern California Campus, 10540 Talbert Avenue, West Tower, Suite 120, Fountain Valley, CA 92708-6027. *Telephone:* 800-697-8223.

GRADUATE PROGRAMS

Expenses (2009–10) *Tuition:* full-time $15,120. *Required fees:* full-time $760.

Financial Aid Institutionally sponsored loans and scholarships available.

Contact Campus College Chair, Nursing, College of Health and Human Services, University of Phoenix–Southern California Campus, 10540 Talbert Avenue, West Tower, Suite 120, Fountain Valley, CA 92708-6027. *Telephone:* 800-697-8223.

MASTER'S DEGREE PROGRAM

Degrees MSN; MSN/MBA; MSN/MHA

Available Programs Master's.

Concentrations Available Health-care administration; nursing administration; nursing education. *Nurse practitioner programs in:* family health.

Site Options Diamond Bar, CA; La Marada, CA; Lancaster, CA.

Study Options Full-time.

Program Entrance Requirements Clinical experience, computer literacy, minimum overall college GPA of 2.5, transcript of college record, 1 letter of recommendation. *Application deadline:* Applications may be processed on a rolling basis for some programs. *Application fee:* $45.

Advanced Placement Credit given for nursing courses completed elsewhere dependent upon specific evaluations.

Degree Requirements 39 total credit hours, thesis or project.

POST-MASTER'S PROGRAM

Areas of Study *Nurse practitioner programs in:* family health.

CONTINUING EDUCATION PROGRAM

Contact Campus College Chair, College of Health and Human Services, University of Phoenix–Southern California Campus, 3100 Bristol Street, Costa Mesa, CA 92626-3099. *Telephone:* 714-338-1720.

University of San Diego

Hahn School of Nursing and Health Science
San Diego, California

http://www.sandiego.edu/academics/nursing

Founded in 1949

DEGREES • MSN • MSN/MBA • PHD

Nursing Program Faculty 44 (75% with doctorates).

Baccalaureate Enrollment 326

Graduate Enrollment 326
Women 86% **Men** 14% **Minority** 35% **International** 1% **Part-time** 35%

Nursing Student Activities Nursing Honor Society, Sigma Theta Tau, Student Nurses' Association.

Nursing Student Resources Academic advising; academic or career counseling; assistance for students with disabilities; bookstore; campus computer network; career placement assistance; computer lab; computer-assisted instruction; daycare for children of students; e-mail services; employment services for current students; externships; interactive nursing

University of San Diego (continued)

skills videos; Internet; learning resource lab; library services; nursing audiovisuals; resume preparation assistance; skills, simulation, or other laboratory; tutoring.

Library Facilities 704,887 volumes (44,000 in health, 23,500 in nursing); 38,488 periodical subscriptions (1,850 health-care related).

GRADUATE PROGRAMS

Expenses (2009–10) *Tuition:* full-time $21,150; part-time $1175 per credit hour. *International tuition:* $21,150 full-time. *Required fees:* full-time $450.

Financial Aid 90% of graduate students in nursing programs received some form of financial aid in 2008–09. Scholarships and traineeships available. Aid available to part-time students. *Financial aid application deadline:* 4/1.

Contact Ms. Cathleen Mumper, Director of Student Services and Admissions Officer, Hahn School of Nursing and Health Science, University of San Diego, 5998 Alcala Park, San Diego, CA 92110-2492. *Telephone:* 619-260-4548. *Fax:* 619-260-6814. *E-mail:* cmm@sandiego.edu.

MASTER'S DEGREE PROGRAM

Degrees MSN; MSN/MBA

Available Programs Accelerated Master's for Non-Nursing College Graduates; Master's; Master's for Nurses with Non-Nursing Degrees.

Concentrations Available Clinical nurse leader; nursing administration; nursing education. *Clinical nurse specialist programs in:* acute care, adult health, medical-surgical. *Nurse practitioner programs in:* adult health, family health, pediatric.

Study Options Full-time and part-time.

Program Entrance Requirements Clinical experience, computer literacy, minimum overall college GPA of 3.0, transcript of college record, CPR certification, written essay, immunizations, interview, 3 letters of recommendation, professional liability insurance/malpractice insurance, prerequisite course work, resume, statistics course, GRE General Test (for entry-level nursing). *Application deadline:* 3/1 (fall), 11/1 (spring). *Application fee:* $45.

Advanced Placement Credit by examination available. Credit given for nursing courses completed elsewhere dependent upon specific evaluations.

DOCTORAL DEGREE PROGRAM

Degree PhD

Available Programs Doctorate.

Areas of Study Advanced practice nursing, aging, clinical practice, community health, ethics, faculty preparation, family health, health policy, health promotion/disease prevention, health-care systems, human health and illness, illness and transition, individualized study, maternity-newborn, nursing administration, nursing education, nursing research, nursing science, oncology, women's health.

Program Entrance Requirements Clinical experience, minimum overall college GPA of 3.5, interview by faculty committee, interview, 3 letters of recommendation, MSN or equivalent, scholarly papers, statistics course, vita, writing sample. Application deadline: 3/1 (fall).

Degree Requirements 48 total credit hours, dissertation, oral exam, residency.

University of San Francisco
School of Nursing
San Francisco, California

http://www.usfca.edu/nursing/

Founded in 1855

DEGREES • BSN • DNP • MSN

Nursing Program Faculty 75 (80% with doctorates).

Baccalaureate Enrollment 599

Women 86% **Men** 14% **Minority** 57% **International** 1% **Part-time** 1%

Graduate Enrollment 225

Women 84% **Men** 16% **Minority** 40% **Part-time** 1%

Distance Learning Courses Available.

Nursing Student Activities Nursing Honor Society, Sigma Theta Tau, Student Nurses' Association, nursing club.

Nursing Student Resources Academic advising; academic or career counseling; assistance for students with disabilities; bookstore; campus computer network; career placement assistance; computer lab; computer-assisted instruction; e-mail services; employment services for current students; housing assistance; interactive nursing skills videos; Internet; learning resource lab; library services; nursing audiovisuals; placement services for program completers; remedial services; resume preparation assistance; skills, simulation, or other laboratory; tutoring; unpaid internships.

Library Facilities 1.1 million volumes; 5,560 periodical subscriptions (200 health-care related).

BACCALAUREATE PROGRAMS

Degree BSN

Available Programs Baccalaureate for Second Degree; Generic Baccalaureate.

Study Options Full-time.

Program Entrance Requirements Minimum overall college GPA of 3.0, transcript of college record, written essay, health insurance, high school biology, high school chemistry, 3 years high school math, 2 years high school science, high school transcript, immunizations, 2 letters of recommendation, minimum high school GPA of 3.0, prerequisite course work. Transfer students are accepted.

Advanced Placement Credit given for nursing courses completed elsewhere dependent upon specific evaluations.

Expenses (2009–10) *Tuition:* full-time $34,430; part-time $1225 per unit. *International tuition:* $34,430 full-time. *Room and board:* $11,540; room only: $7730 per academic year. *Required fees:* full-time $1658; part-time $829 per term.

Financial Aid 95% of baccalaureate students in nursing programs received some form of financial aid in 2008–09.

Contact Office of Undergraduate Admissions, School of Nursing, University of San Francisco, 2130 Fulton Street, San Francisco, CA 94117. *Telephone:* 800-422-6563. *Fax:* 415-422-6877. *E-mail:* admission@usfca.edu.

GRADUATE PROGRAMS

Expenses (2009–10) *Tuition:* part-time $995 per unit. *Required fees:* part-time $400 per term.

Financial Aid 95% of graduate students in nursing programs received some form of financial aid in 2008–09. Institutionally sponsored loans available. *Financial aid application deadline:* 3/2.

Contact Ms. Megan McDrew, Graduate Programs Outreach, School of Nursing, University of San Francisco, 2130 Fulton Street, Cowell Hall, San Francisco, CA 94117-1080. *Telephone:* 415-422-6681. *Fax:* 415-422-6877. *E-mail:* msmcdrew@usfca.edu.

MASTER'S DEGREE PROGRAM

Degree MSN

Available Programs Accelerated AD/RN to Master's; Accelerated Master's for Non-Nursing College Graduates; Master's for Nurses with Non-Nursing Degrees; RN to Master's.

Concentrations Available Clinical nurse leader.

Site Options San Ramon, CA; Santa Rosa, CA; Cupertino, CA.

Study Options Full-time and part-time.

Program Entrance Requirements Clinical experience, minimum overall college GPA of 3.5, transcript of college record, written essay, 2 letters of recommendation, prerequisite course work, resume, statistics course.

Advanced Placement Credit given for nursing courses completed elsewhere dependent upon specific evaluations.

Degree Requirements 30 total credit hours, thesis or project, comprehensive exam.

DOCTORAL DEGREE PROGRAM

Degree DNP

Available Programs Doctorate.

Areas of Study Advanced practice nursing, family health, health-care systems.

Program Entrance Requirements Clinical experience, minimum overall college GPA of 3.0, 3 letters of recommendation, statistics course, vita, writing sample.

Degree Requirements 96 total credit hours, dissertation, oral exam, residency.

West Coast University
Nursing Programs
North Hollywood, California

Founded in 1909

DEGREE • BSN

BACCALAUREATE PROGRAMS

Degree BSN

Available Programs Accelerated RN Baccalaureate; RN Baccalaureate.

Contact Nursing Program, Nursing Programs, West Coast University, 4021 Rosewood Avenue, Los Angeles, CA 90004. *Telephone:* 866-508-2684.

Western University of Health Sciences
College of Graduate Nursing
Pomona, California

http://www.westernu.edu/cogn.html

Founded in 1977

DEGREES • DNP • MSN

Nursing Program Faculty 25 (65% with doctorates).

Graduate Enrollment 285
Women 85% **Men** 15% **Minority** 54% **International** 1% **Part-time** 5%

Distance Learning Courses Available.

Nursing Student Activities Nursing Honor Society, Sigma Theta Tau, Student Nurses' Association, nursing club.

Nursing Student Resources Academic advising; academic or career counseling; assistance for students with disabilities; bookstore; campus computer network; career placement assistance; computer lab; computer-assisted instruction; e-mail services; interactive nursing skills videos; Internet; learning resource lab; library services; nursing audiovisuals; other; remedial services; resume preparation assistance; skills, simulation, or other laboratory; tutoring.

Library Facilities 17,171 volumes in health, 322 volumes in nursing; 5,000 periodical subscriptions health-care related.

GRADUATE PROGRAMS

Expenses (2009–10) *Tuition:* full-time $20,000; part-time $673 per unit. *International tuition:* $20,000 full-time. *Required fees:* full-time $1800; part-time $600 per term.

Financial Aid 80% of graduate students in nursing programs received some form of financial aid in 2008–09. Institutionally sponsored loans, scholarships, and veterans educational benefits available. *Financial aid application deadline:* 3/2.

Contact Ms. Mitzi McKay, Assistant Dean of Student Affairs, College of Graduate Nursing, Western University of Health Sciences, 309 East Second Street, Pomona, CA 91766-1854. *Telephone:* 909-469-5255. *Fax:* 909-469-5521. *E-mail:* mmckay@westernu.edu.

MASTER'S DEGREE PROGRAM

Degree MSN

Available Programs Accelerated AD/RN to Master's; Accelerated Master's; Accelerated Master's for Non-Nursing College Graduates; Master's.

Concentrations Available Clinical nurse leader; nursing administration. *Nurse practitioner programs in:* family health.

Study Options Full-time and part-time.

Online Degree Options Yes (online only).

Program Entrance Requirements Computer literacy, minimum overall college GPA of 3.0, transcript of college record, CPR certification, written essay, immunizations, interview, 3 letters of recommendation, prerequisite course work, resume, statistics course, GRE General Test. *Application deadline:* 3/1 (fall). Applications may be processed on a rolling basis for some programs. *Application fee:* $60.

Advanced Placement Credit given for nursing courses completed elsewhere dependent upon specific evaluations.

Degree Requirements 50 total credit hours, thesis or project.

POST-MASTER'S PROGRAM

Areas of Study *Nurse practitioner programs in:* family health.

DOCTORAL DEGREE PROGRAM

Degree DNP

Available Programs Doctorate.

Online Degree Options Yes (online only).

Program Entrance Requirements Minimum overall college GPA of 3.0, 3 letters of recommendation, MSN or equivalent, scholarly papers, statistics course, vita, writing sample. Application deadline: 3/1 (fall). Applications may be processed on a rolling basis for some programs. Application fee: $60.

Degree Requirements 30 total credit hours, dissertation.

COLORADO

Adams State College
Nursing Program
Alamosa, Colorado

Founded in 1921

DEGREE • BSN

Nursing Program Faculty 4 (25% with doctorates).

Distance Learning Courses Available.

Library Facilities 169,525 volumes; 20,153 periodical subscriptions.

BACCALAUREATE PROGRAMS

Degree BSN

Available Programs RN Baccalaureate.

Site Options Salida, CO; Trinidad, CO.

Program Entrance Requirements RN licensure.

Contact *Telephone:* 719-587-8134. *Fax:* 719-587-7522.

Colorado State University–Pueblo
Department of Nursing
Pueblo, Colorado

Founded in 1933

DEGREES • BSN • MS

Nursing Program Faculty 30 (10% with doctorates).

Baccalaureate Enrollment 134
Women 90% **Men** 10% **Minority** 42% **International** 1% **Part-time** 2%

Graduate Enrollment 26
Women 73% **Men** 27% **Minority** 50% **Part-time** 92%

Nursing Student Activities Sigma Theta Tau, Student Nurses' Association.

Nursing Student Resources Academic advising; academic or career counseling; assistance for students with disabilities; bookstore; campus computer network; computer lab; computer-assisted instruction; daycare for children of students; e-mail services; employment services for current

Colorado State University–Pueblo (continued)

students; housing assistance; Internet; learning resource lab; library services; nursing audiovisuals; remedial services; resume preparation assistance; skills, simulation, or other laboratory; tutoring.

Library Facilities 274,890 volumes (2,891 in health, 1,168 in nursing); 14,672 periodical subscriptions (101 health-care related).

BACCALAUREATE PROGRAMS

Degree BSN

Available Programs ADN to Baccalaureate; Accelerated Baccalaureate for Second Degree; Accelerated RN Baccalaureate; Baccalaureate for Second Degree; Generic Baccalaureate; LPN to Baccalaureate; LPN to RN Baccalaureate; RN Baccalaureate.

Study Options Full-time.

Program Entrance Requirements Minimum overall college GPA of 2.75, transcript of college record, CPR certification, health exam, immunizations, minimum GPA in nursing prerequisites of 2.75, professional liability insurance/malpractice insurance, prerequisite course work. Transfer students are accepted. *Application deadline:* 5/25 (fall), 10/1 (summer). *Application fee:* $25.

Advanced Placement Credit by examination available. Credit given for nursing courses completed elsewhere dependent upon specific evaluations.

Expenses (2008–09) *Tuition, state resident:* full-time $3852; part-time $143 per credit hour. *Tuition, nonresident:* full-time $13,973. *International tuition:* $13,973 full-time. *Room and board:* $7890; room only: $4790 per academic year. *Required fees:* full-time $1434; part-time $42 per credit; part-time $498 per term.

Financial Aid 80% of baccalaureate students in nursing programs received some form of financial aid in 2007–08. *Gift aid (need-based):* Federal Pell, FSEOG, state, private, college/university gift aid from institutional funds, Academic Competitiveness Grant, National Smart Grant, TEACH Grant. *Loans:* Federal Direct (Subsidized and Unsubsidized Stafford PLUS), FFEL (Subsidized and Unsubsidized Stafford PLUS), Perkins. *Work-study:* Federal Work-Study, part-time campus jobs. *Financial aid application deadline (priority):* 3/1.

Contact Ruth DePalma, RN, Nursing Undergraduate Coordinator, MSN, Department of Nursing, Colorado State University–Pueblo, 2200 Bonforte Boulevard, Pueblo, CO 81001. *Telephone:* 719-549-2422. *Fax:* 719-549-2113. *E-mail:* ruth.depalma@colostate-pueblo.edu.

GRADUATE PROGRAMS

Expenses (2008–09) *Tuition, state resident:* full-time $4022; part-time $168 per credit hour. *Tuition, nonresident:* full-time $10,800; part-time $564 per credit hour. *Room and board:* $7890; room only: $4790 per academic year. *Required fees:* part-time $47 per credit.

Financial Aid 50% of graduate students in nursing programs received some form of financial aid in 2007–08.

Contact Mrs. Karen De la Cruz, RN, Nursing Graduate Coordinator, Department of Nursing, Colorado State University–Pueblo, 2200 Bonforte Boulevard, Pueblo, CO 81001. *Telephone:* 719-549-2502. *Fax:* 719-549-2949. *E-mail:* karen.delcruz@colostate-pueblo.edu.

MASTER'S DEGREE PROGRAM

Degree MS

Available Programs Master's.

Concentrations Available Nursing education. *Clinical nurse specialist programs in:* acute care, psychiatric/mental health. *Nurse practitioner programs in:* acute care, family health, pediatric.

Study Options Full-time and part-time.

Program Entrance Requirements Clinical experience, computer literacy, minimum overall college GPA of 3.0, transcript of college record, CPR certification, written essay, immunizations, 3 letters of recommendation, nursing research course, professional liability insurance/malpractice insurance, prerequisite course work, resume, statistics course. *Application deadline:* 5/25 (fall). *Application fee:* $35.

Advanced Placement Credit given for nursing courses completed elsewhere dependent upon specific evaluations.

Degree Requirements 46 total credit hours, thesis or project, comprehensive exam.

POST-MASTER'S PROGRAM

Areas of Study Nursing education. *Clinical nurse specialist programs in:* acute care, psychiatric/mental health. *Nurse practitioner programs in:* acute care, family health, pediatric.

Mesa State College
Department of Nursing and Radiologic Sciences
Grand Junction, Colorado

http://www.mesastate.edu/schools/sbps/nars/index.htm

Founded in 1925

DEGREE • BSN

Nursing Program Faculty 40 (7% with doctorates).

Baccalaureate Enrollment 190

Women 88% **Men** 12% **Minority** 11% **International** 4% **Part-time** 8%

Distance Learning Courses Available.

Nursing Student Activities Sigma Theta Tau, Student Nurses' Association.

Nursing Student Resources Academic advising; academic or career counseling; assistance for students with disabilities; bookstore; campus computer network; career placement assistance; computer lab; computer-assisted instruction; daycare for children of students; e-mail services; employment services for current students; housing assistance; interactive nursing skills videos; Internet; learning resource lab; library services; nursing audiovisuals; placement services for program completers; resume preparation assistance; skills, simulation, or other laboratory; tutoring; unpaid internships.

Library Facilities 260,784 volumes (7,500 in health, 6,576 in nursing); 31,992 periodical subscriptions (100 health-care related).

BACCALAUREATE PROGRAMS

Degree BSN

Available Programs ADN to Baccalaureate; Generic Baccalaureate; LPN to Baccalaureate; LPN to RN Baccalaureate; RN Baccalaureate.

Study Options Full-time and part-time.

Online Degree Options Yes.

Program Entrance Requirements Minimum overall college GPA of 2.0, transcript of college record, CPR certification, health exam, immunizations, minimum GPA in nursing prerequisites of 2.0, professional liability insurance/malpractice insurance, prerequisite course work. Transfer students are accepted. *Application deadline:* 3/1 (fall), 10/1 (spring).

Advanced Placement Credit by examination available. Credit given for nursing courses completed elsewhere dependent upon specific evaluations.

Expenses (2009–10) *Tuition, state resident:* full-time $5509; part-time $230 per credit hour. *Tuition, nonresident:* full-time $11,707; part-time $488 per credit hour. *Room and board:* $8515 per academic year. *Required fees:* full-time $591; part-time $25 per credit.

Financial Aid 90% of baccalaureate students in nursing programs received some form of financial aid in 2008–09.

Contact Dr. Alma Jackson, Program Director, Department of Nursing and Radiologic Sciences, Mesa State College, 1100 North Avenue, Grand Junction, CO 81501. *Telephone:* 970-248-1840. *Fax:* 970-248-1133. *E-mail:* ajackson@mesastate.edu.

Metropolitan State College of Denver
Department of Health Professions
Denver, Colorado

http://www.mscd.edu/~nursing

Founded in 1963

DEGREE • BS

Nursing Program Faculty 10 (10% with doctorates).

Baccalaureate Enrollment 124

Women 89% **Men** 11% **Minority** 17% **International** 2% **Part-time** 63%

Distance Learning Courses Available.

Nursing Student Activities Nursing club.

Nursing Student Resources Academic advising; academic or career counseling; assistance for students with disabilities; bookstore; campus computer network; computer lab; computer-assisted instruction; daycare for children of students; e-mail services; interactive nursing skills videos; Internet; library services; nursing audiovisuals; remedial services; resume preparation assistance; skills, simulation, or other laboratory.

Library Facilities 607,971 volumes (21,503 in health); 2,380 periodical subscriptions (204 health-care related).

BACCALAUREATE PROGRAMS

Degree BS

Available Programs ADN to Baccalaureate; RN Baccalaureate.

Study Options Full-time and part-time.

Program Entrance Requirements Transcript of college record, CPR certification, written essay, immunizations, minimum GPA in nursing prerequisites of 2.5, professional liability insurance/malpractice insurance, prerequisite course work, RN licensure. Transfer students are accepted.

Advanced Placement Credit given for nursing courses completed elsewhere dependent upon specific evaluations.

Financial Aid 35% of baccalaureate students in nursing programs received some form of financial aid in 2007–08.

Contact Linda Stroup, Chair of the Nursing Department. *Telephone:* 303-556-4391. *Fax:* 303-556-5165. *E-mail:* lstroup@mscd.edu.

Platt College
School of Nursing
Aurora, Colorado

Founded in 1986

DEGREE • BSN

Nursing Program Faculty 8 (2% with doctorates).

Baccalaureate Enrollment 134

Women 90% **Men** 10% **Minority** 2.5%

Nursing Student Activities Student Nurses' Association.

Nursing Student Resources Academic advising; academic or career counseling; assistance for students with disabilities; campus computer network; career placement assistance; housing assistance; Internet; learning resource lab; library services; nursing audiovisuals; resume preparation assistance; skills, simulation, or other laboratory; tutoring; unpaid internships.

Library Facilities 1,000 volumes in health, 888 volumes in nursing; 12 periodical subscriptions health-care related.

BACCALAUREATE PROGRAMS

Degree BSN

Available Programs Accelerated Baccalaureate.

Study Options Full-time.

Program Entrance Requirements Transcript of college record, CPR certification, written essay, health exam, health insurance, high school transcript, interview, letters of recommendation, minimum GPA in nursing prerequisites. Transfer students are accepted. *Application deadline:* 7/15 (fall), 11/15 (winter), 2/15 (spring), 5/15 (summer). Applications may be processed on a rolling basis for some programs. *Application fee:* $50.

Advanced Placement Credit by examination available. Credit given for nursing courses completed elsewhere dependent upon specific evaluations.

Expenses (2009–10) *Tuition:* full-time $15,500; part-time $338 per quarter hour.

Financial Aid 98% of baccalaureate students in nursing programs received some form of financial aid in 2008–09. *Gift aid (need-based):* Federal Pell, FSEOG. *Loans:* FFEL (Subsidized and Unsubsidized Stafford PLUS), Perkins. *Financial aid application deadline:* Continuous.

Contact Ms. Barb Jones, BSN Coordinator, School of Nursing, Platt College, 3100 South Parker Road, Aurora, CO 80014. *Telephone:* 303-369-5151. *E-mail:* BarbJones@plattcolorado.edu.

Regis University
School of Nursing
Denver, Colorado

Founded in 1877

DEGREES • BSN • MS

Nursing Program Faculty 18 (55% with doctorates).

Distance Learning Courses Available.

Nursing Student Activities Nursing Honor Society, Sigma Theta Tau, Student Nurses' Association.

Nursing Student Resources Academic advising; academic or career counseling; assistance for students with disabilities; bookstore; campus computer network; computer lab; computer-assisted instruction; e-mail services; interactive nursing skills videos; Internet; learning resource lab; library services; nursing audiovisuals; resume preparation assistance; skills, simulation, or other laboratory; tutoring; unpaid internships.

Library Facilities 350,000 volumes; 20,800 periodical subscriptions.

BACCALAUREATE PROGRAMS

Degree BSN

Available Programs Accelerated Baccalaureate; Generic Baccalaureate; RN Baccalaureate.

Site Options Cheyenne, WY.

Study Options Full-time.

Program Entrance Requirements Minimum overall college GPA of 2.5, transcript of college record, written essay, 2 letters of recommendation, prerequisite course work. Transfer students are accepted.

Advanced Placement Credit by examination available.

Contact Kristal Watson, Assistant Director of Admissions, School of Nursing, Regis University, 3333 Regis Boulevard G-9, Denver, CO 80221-1099. *Telephone:* 303-964-5178. *Fax:* 303-964-5400. *E-mail:* kwatson@regis.edu.

GRADUATE PROGRAMS

Contact Amy Beaudoin, Admissions Counselor, School of Nursing, Regis University, 3333 Regis Boulevard, G-9, Denver, CO 80221-1099. *Telephone:* 303-458-3534. *Fax:* 303-964-5400. *E-mail:* abeaudoi@regis.edu.

MASTER'S DEGREE PROGRAM

Degree MS

Available Programs Master's; RN to Master's.

Concentrations Available Health-care administration; nursing administration; nursing education. *Nurse practitioner programs in:* family health, neonatal health.

Study Options Full-time and part-time.

Online Degree Options Yes.

Program Entrance Requirements Minimum overall college GPA of 2.75, transcript of college record, written essay, 3 letters of recommendation, prerequisite course work, statistics course.

Advanced Placement Credit by examination available.

Degree Requirements 42 total credit hours, thesis or project.

University of Colorado at Colorado Springs
Beth-El College of Nursing and Health Sciences
Colorado Springs, Colorado

http://www.uccs.edu/~bethel/

Founded in 1965

DEGREES • BSN • DNP • MSN

Nursing Program Faculty 43 (32% with doctorates).

Baccalaureate Enrollment 332
Women 92% **Men** 8% **Minority** 6.5% **Part-time** 5%

Graduate Enrollment 155
Women 94% **Men** 6% **Minority** 8% **Part-time** 38%

Distance Learning Courses Available.

Nursing Student Activities Nursing Honor Society, Sigma Theta Tau, Student Nurses' Association, nursing club.

Nursing Student Resources Academic advising; academic or career counseling; assistance for students with disabilities; bookstore; campus computer network; career placement assistance; computer lab; computer-assisted instruction; daycare for children of students; e-mail services; employment services for current students; externships; housing assistance; interactive nursing skills videos; Internet; learning resource lab; library services; nursing audiovisuals; resume preparation assistance; skills, simulation, or other laboratory; tutoring; unpaid internships.

Library Facilities 391,638 volumes (10,454 in health, 1,040 in nursing); 2,201 periodical subscriptions (331 health-care related).

BACCALAUREATE PROGRAMS

Degree BSN

Available Programs Accelerated Baccalaureate for Second Degree; Generic Baccalaureate; RN Baccalaureate.

Study Options Full-time.

Online Degree Options Yes.

Program Entrance Requirements Minimum overall college GPA of 3.3, transcript of college record, CPR certification, health insurance, high school biology, high school chemistry, high school foreign language, 3 years high school math, 1 year of high school science, high school transcript, immunizations, minimum high school GPA of 3.3, minimum GPA in nursing prerequisites of 3.0. Transfer students are accepted. *Application deadline:* Applications may be processed on a rolling basis for some programs. *Application fee:* $50.

Advanced Placement Credit given for nursing courses completed elsewhere dependent upon specific evaluations.

Expenses (2009–10) *Tuition, area resident:* full-time $6312; part-time $263 per credit hour. *Tuition, nonresident:* full-time $7800; part-time $780 per credit hour. *Room and board:* $4330; room only: $3745 per academic year. *Required fees:* full-time $1004; part-time $501 per term.

Financial Aid 68% of baccalaureate students in nursing programs received some form of financial aid in 2008–09. *Gift aid (need-based):* Federal Pell, FSEOG, state, private, college/university gift aid from institutional funds. *Loans:* FFEL (Subsidized and Unsubsidized Stafford PLUS), Perkins, college/university. *Work-study:* Federal Work-Study, part-time campus jobs. *Financial aid application deadline (priority):* 4/1.

Contact Linda Goodwin, Advisor, Baccalaureate Nursing and Health Sciences, Beth-El College of Nursing and Health Sciences, University of Colorado at Colorado Springs, 1420 Austin Bluffs Parkway, Colorado Springs, CO 80918. *Telephone:* 719-255-3867. *Fax:* 719-255-3645. *E-mail:* lgoodwin@uccs.edu.

GRADUATE PROGRAMS

Expenses (2009–10) *Tuition, area resident:* full-time $5883; part-time $684 per credit hour. *Tuition, nonresident:* full-time $9686; part-time $1154 per credit hour. *Required fees:* full-time $2019.

Financial Aid 27% of graduate students in nursing programs received some form of financial aid in 2008–09.

Contact Diane Busch, Program Assistant, Nursing Department, Beth-El College of Nursing and Health Sciences, University of Colorado at Colorado Springs, 1420 Austin Bluffs Parkway, Colorado Springs, CO 80918. *Telephone:* 719-255-4424. *Fax:* 719-255-4496. *E-mail:* dbusch@uccs.edu.

MASTER'S DEGREE PROGRAM

Degree MSN

Available Programs Master's.

Concentrations Available *Clinical nurse specialist programs in:* adult health. *Nurse practitioner programs in:* adult health, family health.

Study Options Full-time and part-time.

Online Degree Options Yes (online only).

Program Entrance Requirements Clinical experience, computer literacy, minimum overall college GPA of 3.0, transcript of college record, CPR certification, immunizations, 4 letters of recommendation, nursing research course, physical assessment course, professional liability insurance/malpractice insurance, prerequisite course work, resume, statistics course. *Application deadline:* 7/1 (fall), 11/1 (spring). *Application fee:* $60.

Advanced Placement Credit given for nursing courses completed elsewhere dependent upon specific evaluations.

Degree Requirements 47 total credit hours, thesis or project, comprehensive exam.

POST-MASTER'S PROGRAM

Areas of Study Nursing education. *Clinical nurse specialist programs in:* adult health. *Nurse practitioner programs in:* adult health, family health.

DOCTORAL DEGREE PROGRAM

Degree DNP

Available Programs Doctorate.

Areas of Study Forensic nursing, gerontology, individualized study.

Online Degree Options Yes (online only).

Program Entrance Requirements Clinical experience, minimum overall college GPA of 3.3, interview, 3 letters of recommendation, MSN or equivalent, statistics course, vita. Application deadline: 3/1 (summer). Application fee: $60.

Degree Requirements 36 total credit hours, written exam, residency.

CONTINUING EDUCATION PROGRAM

Contact Dr. William Crouch, Director, Extended Studies, Beth-El College of Nursing and Health Sciences, University of Colorado at Colorado Springs, 1420 Austin Bluffs Parkway, Colorado Springs, CO 80918. *Telephone:* 719-255-4651. *Fax:* 719-255-4284. *E-mail:* wcrouch@uccs.edu.

University of Colorado Denver
College of Nursing
Denver, Colorado

http://www.uchsc.edu/nursing

Founded in 1912

DEGREES • BS • MS • PHD

Nursing Program Faculty 75 (66% with doctorates).

Baccalaureate Enrollment 416
Women 92% **Men** 8% **Minority** 16% **Part-time** 9%

Graduate Enrollment 230
Women 93% **Men** 7% **Minority** 13% **International** 1% **Part-time** 18%

Distance Learning Courses Available.

Nursing Student Activities Sigma Theta Tau, Student Nurses' Association, nursing club.

Nursing Student Resources Academic advising; academic or career counseling; assistance for students with disabilities; bookstore; campus computer network; computer lab; computer-assisted instruction; e-mail services; externships; interactive nursing skills videos; Internet; learning resource lab; library services; nursing audiovisuals; paid internships; remedial services; skills, simulation, or other laboratory; tutoring; unpaid internships.

Library Facilities 1,000 volumes in health, 40 volumes in nursing; 200 periodical subscriptions health-care related.

BACCALAUREATE PROGRAMS
Degree BS
Available Programs Generic Baccalaureate; RN Baccalaureate.
Site Options Aurora, CO.
Study Options Full-time and part-time.
Online Degree Options Yes.
Program Entrance Requirements Minimum overall college GPA of 3.0, transcript of college record, written essay, health exam, health insurance, immunizations, minimum GPA in nursing prerequisites of 3.0, prerequisite course work. Transfer students are accepted. *Application deadline:* 6/15 (spring), 9/15 (summer). *Application fee:* $65.
Advanced Placement Credit given for nursing courses completed elsewhere dependent upon specific evaluations.
Expenses (2009–10) *Tuition, area resident:* full-time $10,860; part-time $362 per credit hour. *Tuition, state resident:* full-time $10,860. *Tuition, nonresident:* full-time $24,570. *International tuition:* $24,570 full-time. *Required fees:* full-time $1500; part-time $1500 per term.
Financial Aid 60% of baccalaureate students in nursing programs received some form of financial aid in 2008–09.
Contact Mr. Pete Wolfe, Assistant Dean and Director of Student Services and Diversity, College of Nursing, University of Colorado Denver, 13120 East 19th Avenue, Box C288-6, Aurora, CO 80045. *Telephone:* 303-724-1450. *Fax:* 303-724-1710. *E-mail:* Pete.Wolfe@ucdenver.edu.

GRADUATE PROGRAMS
Expenses (2009–10) *Tuition, state resident:* full-time $9775; part-time $425 per credit hour. *Tuition, nonresident:* full-time $22,517; part-time $979 per credit hour. *International tuition:* $22,517 full-time. *Required fees:* full-time $1925.
Financial Aid 35% of graduate students in nursing programs received some form of financial aid in 2008–09. Fellowships, research assistantships, teaching assistantships, career-related internships or fieldwork, Federal Work-Study, and institutionally sponsored loans available. Aid available to part-time students. *Financial aid application deadline:* 3/15.
Contact Mr. Pete Wolfe, Assistant Dean and Director of Student Services and Diversity, College of Nursing, University of Colorado Denver, 13120 East 19th Avenue, Box C288-6, Aurora, CO 80045. *Telephone:* 303-724-1450. *Fax:* 303-724-1710. *E-mail:* Pete.Wolfe@ucdenver.edu.

MASTER'S DEGREE PROGRAM
Degree MS
Available Programs Master's; RN to Master's.
Concentrations Available Nurse-midwifery; nursing informatics. *Clinical nurse specialist programs in:* adult health. *Nurse practitioner programs in:* adult health, family health, pediatric, psychiatric/mental health, women's health.
Site Options Aurora, CO.
Study Options Full-time and part-time.
Online Degree Options Yes.
Program Entrance Requirements Computer literacy, minimum overall college GPA of 3.0, transcript of college record, written essay, immunizations, 4 letters of recommendation, nursing research course, resume, statistics course. *Application deadline:* 9/1 (fall), 4/1 (spring). *Application fee:* $65.
Advanced Placement Credit given for nursing courses completed elsewhere dependent upon specific evaluations.
Degree Requirements 35 total credit hours, comprehensive exam.

POST-MASTER'S PROGRAM
Areas of Study Nurse-midwifery; nursing informatics. *Clinical nurse specialist programs in:* adult health. *Nurse practitioner programs in:* adult health, family health, pediatric, psychiatric/mental health, women's health.

DOCTORAL DEGREE PROGRAM
Degree PhD
Available Programs Doctorate; Post-Baccalaureate Doctorate.
Areas of Study Health-care systems, human health and illness, illness and transition, individualized study, nursing research, nursing science.
Site Options Aurora, CO.

Program Entrance Requirements Minimum overall college GPA of 3.0, interview by faculty committee, interview, 4 letters of recommendation, MSN or equivalent, statistics course, vita, writing sample. Application deadline: 12/1 (winter). Application fee: $65.
Degree Requirements 75 total credit hours, dissertation, oral exam, written exam.

POSTDOCTORAL PROGRAM
Areas of Study Adolescent health, cancer care, community health, gerontology, individualized study, information systems, nursing informatics, nursing interventions, nursing research, nursing science, outcomes, vulnerable population.
Postdoctoral Program Contact Mr. Pete Wolfe, Assistant Dean and Director of Student Services and Diversity, College of Nursing, University of Colorado Denver, 13120 East 19th Avenue, Box C288-6, Aurora, CO 80045. *Telephone:* 303-724-1450. *Fax:* 303-724-1450. *E-mail:* Pete.Wolfe@ucdenver.edu.

CONTINUING EDUCATION PROGRAM
Contact Ms. Jennifer Disabato, Manager, Extended Studies, College of Nursing, University of Colorado Denver, 13120 East 19th Avenue, Box C288-6, Aurora, CO 80045. *Telephone:* 303-724-1529. *Fax:* 303-724-1372. *E-mail:* jennifer.disabato@ucdenver.edu.

University of Northern Colorado
School of Nursing
Greeley, Colorado

http://www.unco.edu/nursing
Founded in 1890
DEGREES • BS • MS • PHD
Nursing Program Faculty 52 (60% with doctorates).
Baccalaureate Enrollment 216
Women 94% **Men** 6% **Minority** 18%
Graduate Enrollment 57
Women 98% **Men** 2% **Minority** 10% **Part-time** 60%
Distance Learning Courses Available.
Nursing Student Activities Sigma Theta Tau, Student Nurses' Association.
Nursing Student Resources Academic advising; academic or career counseling; assistance for students with disabilities; bookstore; campus computer network; career placement assistance; computer lab; computer-assisted instruction; e-mail services; employment services for current students; housing assistance; interactive nursing skills videos; Internet; learning resource lab; library services; nursing audiovisuals; paid internships; placement services for program completers; resume preparation assistance; skills, simulation, or other laboratory; tutoring.
Library Facilities 1 million volumes (43,602 in health, 25,700 in nursing); 3,417 periodical subscriptions (140 health-care related).

BACCALAUREATE PROGRAMS
Degree BS
Available Programs Accelerated Baccalaureate; Generic Baccalaureate; RN Baccalaureate.
Site Options Greeley, CO.
Study Options Full-time.
Program Entrance Requirements Minimum overall college GPA of 3.0, transcript of college record, CPR certification, health exam, immunizations, 2 letters of recommendation, minimum GPA in nursing prerequisites of 3.0, professional liability insurance/malpractice insurance, prerequisite course work. Transfer students are accepted.
Advanced Placement Credit given for nursing courses completed elsewhere dependent upon specific evaluations.
Financial Aid 70% of baccalaureate students in nursing programs received some form of financial aid in 2008–09.
Contact Dr. Audrey Bopp, Assistant Director, School of Nursing, University of Northern Colorado, Gunter Hall, Box 125, Greeley, CO 80639. *Telephone:* 970-351-2293. *Fax:* 970-351-1707. *E-mail:* Audrey.Bopp@unco.edu.

University of Northern Colorado (continued)

GRADUATE PROGRAMS

Financial Aid 80% of graduate students in nursing programs received some form of financial aid in 2008–09. 7 research assistantships (averaging $6,183 per year), 1 teaching assistantship (averaging $2,849 per year) were awarded; fellowships, unspecified assistantships also available. *Financial aid application deadline:* 3/1.

Contact Dr. Janice Hayes, Graduate Program Assistant Director and Professor, School of Nursing, University of Northern Colorado, Gunter Hall, Box 125, Greeley, CO 80639. *Telephone:* 970-351-2293. *Fax:* 970-351-1707. *E-mail:* janice.hayes@unco.edu.

MASTER'S DEGREE PROGRAM

Degree MS

Available Programs Master's.

Concentrations Available Nursing education. *Clinical nurse specialist programs in:* family health. *Nurse practitioner programs in:* family health.

Site Options Greeley, CO.

Study Options Full-time and part-time.

Online Degree Options Yes (online only).

Program Entrance Requirements Clinical experience, minimum overall college GPA of 3.0, transcript of college record, CPR certification, immunizations, 2 letters of recommendation, GRE General Test.

Advanced Placement Credit given for nursing courses completed elsewhere dependent upon specific evaluations.

Degree Requirements 45 total credit hours, thesis or project, comprehensive exam.

POST-MASTER'S PROGRAM

Areas of Study Nursing education. *Nurse practitioner programs in:* family health.

DOCTORAL DEGREE PROGRAM

Degree PhD

Available Programs Doctorate.

Areas of Study Nursing education.

Site Options Greeley, CO.

Online Degree Options Yes (online only).

Program Entrance Requirements Clinical experience, minimum overall college GPA of 3.0, 2 letters of recommendation, MSN or equivalent, vita, writing sample, GRE General Test.

Degree Requirements 60 total credit hours, dissertation.

University of Phoenix–Denver Campus

College of Health and Human Services
Lone Tree, Colorado

DEGREES • BSN • MSN • MSN/ED D • MSN/MHA

Nursing Program Faculty 19 (5% with doctorates).

Baccalaureate Enrollment 330
Women 86.7% **Men** 13.3% **Minority** 23.3%

Graduate Enrollment 19
Women 78.9% **Men** 21.1% **Minority** 21.05%

Nursing Student Activities Sigma Theta Tau.

Nursing Student Resources Academic advising; academic or career counseling; assistance for students with disabilities; bookstore; campus computer network; computer lab; computer-assisted instruction; e-mail services; interactive nursing skills videos; Internet; learning resource lab; library services; nursing audiovisuals; remedial services; skills, simulation, or other laboratory; tutoring.

Library Facilities 16,781 periodical subscriptions (1,300 health-care related).

BACCALAUREATE PROGRAMS

Degree BSN

Available Programs Accelerated Baccalaureate; LPN to Baccalaureate.

Site Options Westminister, CO; Aurora, CO; Ft. Collins, CO.

Study Options Full-time.

Program Entrance Requirements Transcript of college record, CPR certification, immunizations, 1 letter of recommendation, RN licensure. Transfer students are accepted. *Application deadline:* Applications may be processed on a rolling basis for some programs.

Advanced Placement Credit by examination available. Credit given for nursing courses completed elsewhere dependent upon specific evaluations.

Expenses (2009–10) *Tuition:* full-time $8820. *Required fees:* full-time $600.

Contact Campus College Chair, Nursing, College of Health and Human Services, University of Phoenix–Denver Campus, 10004 Park Meadow Drive, Lone Tree, CO 80124-5453. *Telephone:* 303-694-9093.

GRADUATE PROGRAMS

Expenses (2009–10) *Tuition:* full-time $12,480. *Required fees:* full-time $760.

Financial Aid Institutionally sponsored loans and scholarships available.

Contact Campus College Chair, Nursing, College of Health and Human Services, University of Phoenix–Denver Campus, 10004 Park Meadow Drive, Lone Tree, CO 80124-5453. *Telephone:* 303-694-9003.

MASTER'S DEGREE PROGRAM

Degrees MSN; MSN/Ed D; MSN/MHA

Available Programs Master's.

Concentrations Available Nursing administration; nursing education.

Site Options Westminister, CO; Aurora, CO.

Study Options Full-time.

Program Entrance Requirements Clinical experience, computer literacy, minimum overall college GPA of 2.5, transcript of college record. *Application deadline:* Applications may be processed on a rolling basis for some programs. *Application fee:* $45.

Advanced Placement Credit given for nursing courses completed elsewhere dependent upon specific evaluations.

Degree Requirements 39 total credit hours, thesis or project.

University of Phoenix–Southern Colorado Campus

College of Health and Human Services
Colorado Springs, Colorado

Founded in 1999.

Nursing Program Faculty 2

Nursing Student Activities Sigma Theta Tau.

Nursing Student Resources Academic advising; academic or career counseling; assistance for students with disabilities; bookstore; campus computer network; computer lab; computer-assisted instruction; e-mail services; interactive nursing skills videos; Internet; learning resource lab; library services; nursing audiovisuals; remedial services; skills, simulation, or other laboratory; tutoring.

Library Facilities 16,781 periodical subscriptions (1,300 health-care related).

CONNECTICUT

Central Connecticut State University
Department of Nursing
New Britain, Connecticut

Founded in 1849

DEGREE • BSN

Nursing Program Faculty 4 (100% with doctorates).

Nursing Student Activities Sigma Theta Tau, nursing club.

Nursing Student Resources Academic advising; academic or career counseling; assistance for students with disabilities; bookstore; campus computer network; career placement assistance; computer lab; computer-assisted instruction; e-mail services; employment services for current students; externships; Internet; learning resource lab; library services; nursing audiovisuals; resume preparation assistance; skills, simulation, or other laboratory; tutoring.

Library Facilities 717,553 volumes; 31,195 periodical subscriptions.

BACCALAUREATE PROGRAMS

Degree BSN

Available Programs Generic Baccalaureate; RN Baccalaureate.

Site Options New Britain, CT.

Study Options Full-time and part-time.

Program Entrance Requirements Minimum overall college GPA of 2.7, CPR certification, health exam, high school transcript, immunizations, minimum GPA in nursing prerequisites of 2.7, prerequisite course work. Transfer students are accepted.

Advanced Placement Credit given for nursing courses completed elsewhere dependent upon specific evaluations.

Contact Dr. Linda D. Wagner, Associate Professor and Department Chairperson, Department of Nursing, Central Connecticut State University, 1615 Stanley Street, New Britain, CT 06050-4010. *Telephone:* 860-832-2147. *Fax:* 860-832-2188. *E-mail:* wagnerlid@ccsu.edu.

Fairfield University
School of Nursing
Fairfield, Connecticut

http://www.fairfield.edu/academic/nursing/
Founded in 1942

DEGREES • BS • MSN

Nursing Program Faculty 24 (50% with doctorates).

Baccalaureate Enrollment 389
Women 93% **Men** 7% **Minority** 22% **International** 1% **Part-time** 22%

Graduate Enrollment 127
Women 88% **Men** 12% **Minority** 20% **International** 2% **Part-time** 93%

Nursing Student Activities Nursing Honor Society, Sigma Theta Tau, Student Nurses' Association.

Nursing Student Resources Academic advising; academic or career counseling; assistance for students with disabilities; bookstore; campus computer network; career placement assistance; computer lab; computer-assisted instruction; daycare for children of students; e-mail services; interactive nursing skills videos; Internet; learning resource lab; library services; nursing audiovisuals; placement services for program completers; resume preparation assistance; skills, simulation, or other laboratory; tutoring; unpaid internships.

Library Facilities 351,091 volumes (5,643 in health, 4,282 in nursing); 31,424 periodical subscriptions (270 health-care related).

BACCALAUREATE PROGRAMS

Degree BS

Available Programs Accelerated Baccalaureate for Second Degree; Generic Baccalaureate; RN Baccalaureate.

Study Options Full-time.

Program Entrance Requirements Written essay, health exam, health insurance, high school biology, high school chemistry, high school foreign language, 3 years high school math, 3 years high school science, high school transcript, immunizations, 1 letter of recommendation, minimum high school GPA of 3.0. Transfer students are accepted. *Application deadline:* 1/15 (fall). *Application fee:* $60.

Advanced Placement Credit given for nursing courses completed elsewhere dependent upon specific evaluations.

Expenses (2009–10) *Tuition:* full-time $36,900. *International tuition:* $36,900 full-time. *Room and board:* $11,270; room only: $6730 per academic year.

Financial Aid 75% of baccalaureate students in nursing programs received some form of financial aid in 2008–09. *Gift aid (need-based):* Federal Pell, FSEOG, state, private, college/university gift aid from institutional funds, United Negro College Fund. *Loans:* FFEL (Subsidized and Unsubsidized Stafford PLUS), Perkins, alternative loans. *Work-study:* Federal Work-Study. *Financial aid application deadline:* 2/15.

Contact Ms. Karen Pellegrino, Director of Admission, School of Nursing, Fairfield University, 1073 North Benson Road, Kelley Center, Fairfield, CT 06824-5195. *Telephone:* 203-254-4100. *Fax:* 203-254-4199. *E-mail:* admis@fairfield.edu.

GRADUATE PROGRAMS

Expenses (2009–10) *Tuition:* part-time $545 per credit hour. *International tuition:* $4930 full-time. *Required fees:* part-time $665 per term.

Financial Aid 11% of graduate students in nursing programs received some form of financial aid in 2008–09. Traineeships, unspecified assistantships, and Traineeships is a federally funded grant program available.

Contact Ms. Marianne Gumpper, Director of Graduate and Continuing Studies Admission, School of Nursing, Fairfield University, 1073 North Benson Road, Kelley Center, Fairfield, CT 06824-5195. *Telephone:* 203-254-4184. *Fax:* 203-254-4073. *E-mail:* gradadmis@fairfield.edu.

MASTER'S DEGREE PROGRAM

Degree MSN

Available Programs Master's; Master's for Nurses with Non-Nursing Degrees.

Concentrations Available Clinical nurse leader; health-care administration; nurse anesthesia. *Nurse practitioner programs in:* family health, psychiatric/mental health.

Study Options Full-time and part-time.

Program Entrance Requirements Computer literacy, minimum overall college GPA of 3.0, transcript of college record, written essay, immunizations, interview, 2 letters of recommendation, resume, statistics course, GRE (nurse anesthesia applicants only). *Application deadline:* Applications may be processed on a rolling basis for some programs. *Application fee:* $60.

Advanced Placement Credit given for nursing courses completed elsewhere dependent upon specific evaluations.

Degree Requirements Thesis or project.

POST-MASTER'S PROGRAM

Areas of Study *Nurse practitioner programs in:* family health, psychiatric/mental health.

CONTINUING EDUCATION PROGRAM

Contact Carol A. Pomarico, Adult Program Director, School of Nursing, Fairfield University, 1073 North Benson Road, Fairfield, CT 06824. *Telephone:* 203-254-4000 Ext. 2711. *Fax:* 203-254-4126. *E-mail:* capomarico@fairfield.edu.

Quinnipiac University
Department of Nursing
Hamden, Connecticut

Founded in 1929

Quinnipiac University (continued)

DEGREES • BSN • MSN

Nursing Program Faculty 50 (90% with doctorates).

Baccalaureate Enrollment 445
Women 98% **Men** 2% **Minority** 7% **International** 2%

Graduate Enrollment 98
Women 98% **Men** 2% **Minority** 6% **International** 1% **Part-time** 60%

Nursing Student Activities Sigma Theta Tau, Student Nurses' Association.

Nursing Student Resources Academic advising; academic or career counseling; bookstore; campus computer network; career placement assistance; computer lab; computer-assisted instruction; e-mail services; employment services for current students; externships; housing assistance; interactive nursing skills videos; Internet; learning resource lab; library services; nursing audiovisuals; paid internships; placement services for program completers; resume preparation assistance; skills, simulation, or other laboratory; tutoring; unpaid internships.

Library Facilities 285,000 volumes (1,700 in nursing); 5,500 periodical subscriptions.

BACCALAUREATE PROGRAMS

Degree BSN

Available Programs Accelerated Baccalaureate for Second Degree; Generic Baccalaureate.

Site Options North Haven, CT.

Study Options Full-time.

Program Entrance Requirements Minimum overall college GPA of 3.0, transcript of college record, written essay, health exam, high school biology, high school chemistry, 4 years high school math, 4 years high school science, high school transcript, immunizations, 1 letter of recommendation, minimum high school GPA of 3.0, minimum high school rank 50%, minimum GPA in nursing prerequisites of 3.0. Transfer students are accepted. *Application deadline:* 11/1 (fall), 12/1 (spring). Applications may be processed on a rolling basis for some programs. *Application fee:* $45.

Advanced Placement Credit given for nursing courses completed elsewhere dependent upon specific evaluations.

Expenses (2009–10) *Tuition:* full-time $31,100; part-time $750 per credit. *International tuition:* $31,100 full-time. *Room and board:* $12,380 per academic year. *Required fees:* full-time $1300; part-time $35 per credit.

Financial Aid 72% of baccalaureate students in nursing programs received some form of financial aid in 2008–09. *Gift aid (need-based):* Federal Pell, FSEOG, state, private, college/university gift aid from institutional funds. *Loans:* Federal Nursing Student Loans, Federal Direct (Subsidized and Unsubsidized Stafford PLUS), FFEL (Subsidized and Unsubsidized Stafford PLUS), Perkins. *Work-study:* Federal Work-Study, part-time campus jobs. *Financial aid application deadline (priority):* 3/1.

Contact Ms. Carla Knowlton, Director of Undergraduate Admissions, Department of Nursing, Quinnipiac University, 275 Mount Carmel Avenue, Hamden, CT 06518. *Telephone:* 203-582-8600. *Fax:* 203-582-8906. *E-mail:* admissions@quinnipiac.edu.

GRADUATE PROGRAMS

Expenses (2009–10) *Tuition:* full-time $15,400; part-time $770 per credit. *International tuition:* $15,400 full-time. *Required fees:* full-time $630; part-time $35 per credit; part-time $315 per term.

Financial Aid 30% of graduate students in nursing programs received some form of financial aid in 2008–09.

Contact Jennifer Boutin, Assistant Director of Graduate Admissions, Department of Nursing, Quinnipiac University, 275 Mount Carmel Avenue, Hamden, CT 06518. *Telephone:* 203-582-8672. *Fax:* 203-582-3443. *E-mail:* graduate@quinnipiac.edu.

MASTER'S DEGREE PROGRAM

Degree MSN

Available Programs Master's.

Concentrations Available Health-care administration. *Nurse practitioner programs in:* adult health, family health.

Site Options North Haven, CT.

Study Options Full-time and part-time.

Program Entrance Requirements Clinical experience, minimum overall college GPA of 3.0, transcript of college record, CPR certification, written essay, immunizations, interview, 3 letters of recommendation, prerequisite course work, resume. *Application deadline:* 6/1 (fall), 12/15 (spring). Applications may be processed on a rolling basis for some programs. *Application fee:* $45.

Advanced Placement Credit given for nursing courses completed elsewhere dependent upon specific evaluations.

Degree Requirements 47 total credit hours, thesis or project.

POST-MASTER'S PROGRAM

Areas of Study *Nurse practitioner programs in:* adult health, family health.

CONTINUING EDUCATION PROGRAM

Contact Ms. Mary Wargo, Director of Transfer and Part-Time Admissions, Department of Nursing, Quinnipiac University, 275 Mount Carmel Avenue, Hamden, CT 06518. *Telephone:* 203-582-8612. *Fax:* 203-582-8906. *E-mail:* mary.wargo@quinnipiac.edu.

Sacred Heart University
Program in Nursing
Fairfield, Connecticut

http://nursing.sacredheart.edu/

Founded in 1963

DEGREES • BS • DNP • MSN • MSN/MBA

Nursing Program Faculty 43 (27% with doctorates).

Baccalaureate Enrollment 260
Women 95% **Men** 5% **Minority** 7% **International** 1% **Part-time** 32%

Graduate Enrollment 166
Women 96% **Men** 4% **Minority** 16% **International** 1% **Part-time** 95%

Distance Learning Courses Available.

Nursing Student Activities Nursing Honor Society, Sigma Theta Tau, Student Nurses' Association.

Nursing Student Resources Academic advising; academic or career counseling; assistance for students with disabilities; bookstore; campus computer network; career placement assistance; computer lab; computer-assisted instruction; e-mail services; employment services for current students; externships; housing assistance; interactive nursing skills videos; Internet; learning resource lab; library services; nursing audiovisuals; paid internships; placement services for program completers; remedial services; resume preparation assistance; skills, simulation, or other laboratory; tutoring; unpaid internships.

Library Facilities 147,098 volumes (5,000 in health, 649 in nursing); 1,698 periodical subscriptions (328 health-care related).

BACCALAUREATE PROGRAMS

Degree BS

Available Programs ADN to Baccalaureate; Generic Baccalaureate; RN Baccalaureate.

Study Options Full-time and part-time.

Online Degree Options Yes.

Program Entrance Requirements Minimum overall college GPA of 2.8, transcript of college record, written essay, high school biology, high school chemistry, high school foreign language, 3 years high school math, 3 years high school science, high school transcript, interview, 1 letter of recommendation, minimum high school GPA of 3.2, minimum high school rank 30%, minimum GPA in nursing prerequisites of 3.0, prerequisite course work. Transfer students are accepted. *Application deadline:* 2/1 (fall), 12/1 (spring). Applications may be processed on a rolling basis for some programs. *Application fee:* $50.

Advanced Placement Credit given for nursing courses completed elsewhere dependent upon specific evaluations.

Expenses (2009–10) *Tuition:* full-time $30,090; part-time $460 per credit. *International tuition:* $30,090 full-time. *Room and board:* $11,605; room only: $9015 per academic year. *Required fees:* full-time $2346; part-time $1163 per term.

Financial Aid 83% of baccalaureate students in nursing programs received some form of financial aid in 2008–09. *Gift aid (need-based):* Federal Pell, FSEOG, state, private, college/university gift aid from institutional funds. *Loans:* Federal Direct (Subsidized and Unsubsidized Stafford PLUS), FFEL (Subsidized and Unsubsidized Stafford PLUS), Perkins, state. *Work-study:* Federal Work-Study, part-time campus jobs. *Financial aid application deadline (priority):* 2/15.

Contact Office of Undergraduate Admissions, Program in Nursing, Sacred Heart University, 5151 Park Avenue, Fairfield, CT 06825-1000. *Telephone:* 203-371-7880. *E-mail:* enroll@sacredheart.edu.

GRADUATE PROGRAMS

Expenses (2009–10) *Tuition:* full-time $9900; part-time $550 per credit. *International tuition:* $9900 full-time. *Required fees:* full-time $248; part-time $124 per term.

Contact Mr. Duke Thompson, Admissions Manager, Program in Nursing, Sacred Heart University, 5151 Park Avenue, Fairfield, CT 06825-1000. *Telephone:* 877-791-7181 Ext. 5316. *Fax:* 877-791-7183. *E-mail:* thompsond3@sacredheart.edu.

MASTER'S DEGREE PROGRAM

Degrees MSN; MSN/MBA

Available Programs Master's; RN to Master's.

Concentrations Available Clinical nurse leader; nursing administration. *Nurse practitioner programs in:* family health.

Study Options Full-time and part-time.

Online Degree Options Yes.

Program Entrance Requirements Clinical experience, minimum overall college GPA of 3.0, transcript of college record, written essay, interview, 2 letters of recommendation, prerequisite course work, statistics course. *Application deadline:* Applications may be processed on a rolling basis for some programs. *Application fee:* $50.

Advanced Placement Credit given for nursing courses completed elsewhere dependent upon specific evaluations.

Degree Requirements 38 total credit hours, thesis or project.

POST-MASTER'S PROGRAM

Areas of Study *Nurse practitioner programs in:* family health.

DOCTORAL DEGREE PROGRAM

Degree DNP

Available Programs Doctorate.

Areas of Study Clinical practice, nursing administration.

Program Entrance Requirements Minimum overall college GPA of 3.2, interview by faculty committee, 2 letters of recommendation, MSN or equivalent, statistics course, writing sample. Application deadline: 4/1 (fall). Application fee: $50.

Degree Requirements 39 total credit hours, dissertation.

Saint Joseph College
Department of Nursing
West Hartford, Connecticut

http://www.sjc.edu

Founded in 1932

DEGREES • BS • MS

Nursing Program Faculty 23 (44% with doctorates).

Baccalaureate Enrollment 173

Women 98% **Men** 2% **Minority** 21% **International** 2% **Part-time** 38%

Graduate Enrollment 40

Women 98% **Men** 2% **Minority** 25% **International** 1% **Part-time** 66%

Distance Learning Courses Available.

Nursing Student Activities Sigma Theta Tau, Student Nurses' Association, nursing club.

Nursing Student Resources Academic advising; academic or career counseling; assistance for students with disabilities; bookstore; campus computer network; career placement assistance; computer lab; computer-assisted instruction; daycare for children of students; e-mail services;

employment services for current students; externships; housing assistance; interactive nursing skills videos; Internet; learning resource lab; library services; nursing audiovisuals; paid internships; placement services for program completers; remedial services; resume preparation assistance; skills, simulation, or other laboratory; tutoring; unpaid internships.

Library Facilities 7,058 volumes in health, 1,949 volumes in nursing; 1,495 periodical subscriptions health-care related.

BACCALAUREATE PROGRAMS

Degree BS

Available Programs Accelerated Baccalaureate for Second Degree; Baccalaureate for Second Degree; Generic Baccalaureate.

Site Options Middletown, CT.

Study Options Full-time.

Program Entrance Requirements Minimum overall college GPA of 2.8, transcript of college record, CPR certification, written essay, health exam, health insurance, high school biology, high school chemistry, high school transcript, immunizations, minimum GPA in nursing prerequisites of 2.8, prerequisite course work. Transfer students are accepted. *Application deadline:* 4/1 (fall), 12/1 (spring). *Application fee:* $50.

Advanced Placement Credit given for nursing courses completed elsewhere dependent upon specific evaluations.

Expenses (2008–09) *Tuition:* full-time $26,420; part-time $540 per credit. *Room and board:* $6414; room only: $3162 per academic year. *Required fees:* full-time $700.

Financial Aid 85% of baccalaureate students in nursing programs received some form of financial aid in 2007–08.

Contact Dr. Joyce Fontana, Chairperson, Department of Nursing, Saint Joseph College, 1678 Asylum Avenue, West Hartford, CT 06117. *Telephone:* 860-231-5304. *E-mail:* tbosworth@sjc.edu.

GRADUATE PROGRAMS

Expenses (2008–09) *Tuition:* part-time $550 per credit hour.

Financial Aid 75% of graduate students in nursing programs received some form of financial aid in 2007–08.

Contact Dr. Marylouise Welch, Director, Department of Nursing, Saint Joseph College, 1678 Asylum Avenue, West Hartford, CT 06117-2700. *Telephone:* 860-231-5211. *Fax:* 860-231-8396. *E-mail:* mwelch@sjc.edu.

MASTER'S DEGREE PROGRAM

Degree MS

Available Programs Master's; Master's for Nurses with Non-Nursing Degrees.

Concentrations Available Nursing education. *Clinical nurse specialist programs in:* family health, psychiatric/mental health. *Nurse practitioner programs in:* family health.

Site Options Middletown, CT.

Study Options Full-time and part-time.

Program Entrance Requirements Clinical experience, minimum overall college GPA of 3.0, transcript of college record, CPR certification, written essay, immunizations, interview, 2 letters of recommendation, nursing research course, physical assessment course, professional liability insurance/malpractice insurance, resume, statistics course. *Application deadline:* Applications may be processed on a rolling basis for some programs. *Application fee:* $50.

Degree Requirements 47 total credit hours, thesis or project.

POST-MASTER'S PROGRAM

Areas of Study Nursing education. *Clinical nurse specialist programs in:* family health, psychiatric/mental health. *Nurse practitioner programs in:* family health.

Southern Connecticut State University
Department of Nursing
New Haven, Connecticut

http://www.southernct.edu/departments/nursing

Founded in 1893

CONNECTICUT

Southern Connecticut State University (continued)
DEGREES • BS • MSN

Nursing Program Faculty 18 (65% with doctorates).

Baccalaureate Enrollment 220
Women 85% **Men** 15% **Minority** 20% **Part-time** 5%

Graduate Enrollment 40
Women 97% **Men** 3% **Part-time** 97%

Distance Learning Courses Available.

Nursing Student Activities Nursing Honor Society, Sigma Theta Tau, Student Nurses' Association.

Nursing Student Resources Academic advising; academic or career counseling; assistance for students with disabilities; bookstore; campus computer network; career placement assistance; computer lab; daycare for children of students; e-mail services; employment services for current students; housing assistance; Internet; learning resource lab; library services; nursing audiovisuals; resume preparation assistance; skills, simulation, or other laboratory; tutoring.

Library Facilities 495,660 volumes (35,540 in health, 2,279 in nursing); 3,549 periodical subscriptions (318 health-care related).

BACCALAUREATE PROGRAMS

Degree BS

Available Programs ADN to Baccalaureate; Accelerated Baccalaureate; Generic Baccalaureate; RN Baccalaureate.

Study Options Full-time and part-time.

Program Entrance Requirements Minimum overall college GPA of 2.8, transcript of college record, CPR certification, health exam, high school transcript, minimum GPA in nursing prerequisites, prerequisite course work. Transfer students are accepted. *Application deadline:* 2/1 (spring).

Advanced Placement Credit given for nursing courses completed elsewhere dependent upon specific evaluations.

Expenses (2009–10) *Tuition, state resident:* full-time $7578. *Tuition, nonresident:* full-time $17,270. *Room and board:* $9469; room only: $6000 per academic year. *Required fees:* full-time $600.

Financial Aid *Gift aid (need-based):* Federal Pell, FSEOG, state, college/university gift aid from institutional funds. *Loans:* FFEL (Subsidized and Unsubsidized Stafford PLUS), Perkins. *Work-study:* Federal Work-Study, part-time campus jobs. *Financial aid application deadline:* 3/9.

Contact Dr. Barbara Aronson, RN, Coordinator, BSN Program in Nursing, Department of Nursing, Southern Connecticut State University, 501 Crescent Street, New Haven, CT 06515-1355. *Telephone:* 203-392-6496. *Fax:* 203-392-6493. *E-mail:* aronsonb1@southernct.edu.

GRADUATE PROGRAMS

Expenses (2009–10) *Tuition, area resident:* full-time $8756; part-time $500 per credit. *Tuition, state resident:* full-time $8756. *Tuition, nonresident:* full-time $17,852.

Contact Dr. Antonia Nelson, RN, Coordinator, Graduate Programs in Nursing, Department of Nursing, Southern Connecticut State University, 501 Crescent Street, New Haven, CT 06515. *Telephone:* 203-392-6480. *Fax:* 203-392-6493. *E-mail:* nelsona13@southernct.edu.

MASTER'S DEGREE PROGRAM

Degree MSN

Available Programs Master's; RN to Master's.

Concentrations Available Clinical nurse leader; nursing education. *Nurse practitioner programs in:* family health.

Study Options Full-time and part-time.

Program Entrance Requirements Clinical experience, minimum overall college GPA of 3.0, transcript of college record, CPR certification, immunizations, interview, 2 letters of recommendation, nursing research course, physical assessment course, professional liability insurance/malpractice insurance, prerequisite course work, resume, statistics course, GRE, MAT. *Application deadline:* Applications may be processed on a rolling basis for some programs.

Advanced Placement Credit given for nursing courses completed elsewhere dependent upon specific evaluations.

Degree Requirements 42 total credit hours, thesis or project.

POST-MASTER'S PROGRAM

Areas of Study Nursing education. *Nurse practitioner programs in:* family health.

University of Connecticut
School of Nursing
Storrs, Connecticut

http://www.nursing.uconn.edu
Founded in 1881
DEGREES • BS • MS • MS/MBA • PHD

Nursing Program Faculty 68 (24% with doctorates).

Baccalaureate Enrollment 537
Women 89.7% **Men** 10.3% **Minority** 15.3%

Graduate Enrollment 198
Women 89.4% **Men** 10.6% **Minority** 15.2% **International** 1% **Part-time** 58.6%

Distance Learning Courses Available.

Nursing Student Activities Sigma Theta Tau, Student Nurses' Association.

Nursing Student Resources Academic advising; academic or career counseling; assistance for students with disabilities; bookstore; campus computer network; career placement assistance; computer lab; e-mail services; externships; housing assistance; interactive nursing skills videos; Internet; learning resource lab; library services; nursing audiovisuals; remedial services; resume preparation assistance; skills, simulation, or other laboratory; tutoring; unpaid internships.

Library Facilities 3 million volumes (46,250 in health, 1,170 in nursing); 17,378 periodical subscriptions (4,553 health-care related).

BACCALAUREATE PROGRAMS

Degree BS

Available Programs Generic Baccalaureate.

Site Options Waterbury, CT; Stamford, CT; West Hartford, CT; Avery Point, CT.

Study Options Full-time and part-time.

Program Entrance Requirements Minimum overall college GPA of 3.0, transcript of college record, written essay, health exam, health insurance, high school chemistry, high school foreign language, 3 years high school math, 2 years high school science, high school transcript, immunizations, minimum high school GPA of 3.0, minimum GPA in nursing prerequisites of 2.0, prerequisite course work. Transfer students are accepted. *Application deadline:* 2/1 (fall). *Application fee:* $70.

Advanced Placement Credit by examination available. Credit given for nursing courses completed elsewhere dependent upon specific evaluations.

Expenses (2009–10) *Tuition, area resident:* full-time $7632; part-time $318 per credit. *Tuition, nonresident:* full-time $23,232; part-time $968 per credit. *International tuition:* $23,232 full-time. *Room and board:* $10,120; room only: $5396 per academic year. *Required fees:* full-time $2254; part-time $1127 per term.

Financial Aid 77% of baccalaureate students in nursing programs received some form of financial aid in 2008–09. *Gift aid (need-based):* Federal Pell, FSEOG, state, private, college/university gift aid from institutional funds. *Loans:* FFEL (Subsidized and Unsubsidized Stafford PLUS), Perkins, state. *Work-study:* Federal Work-Study, part-time campus jobs. *Financial aid application deadline (priority):* 3/1.

Contact Mrs. Dorine Nagy, Admissions Coordinator, School of Nursing, University of Connecticut, 231 Glenbrook Road, Unit 2026, Storrs, CT 06269-2026. *Telephone:* 860-486-1937. *Fax:* 860-486-0906. *E-mail:* Dorine.Nagy@uconn.edu.

GRADUATE PROGRAMS

Expenses (2009–10) *Tuition, area resident:* full-time $4725; part-time $525 per credit. *Tuition, nonresident:* full-time $12,267; part-time $1363 per credit. *International tuition:* $12,267 full-time. *Room and board:* $11,180; room only: $6356 per academic year.

Financial Aid 24% of graduate students in nursing programs received some form of financial aid in 2008–09. 7 research assistantships with full tuition reimbursements available, 20 teaching assistantships with full tuition reimbursements available were awarded; fellowships, Federal Work-Study, scholarships, and unspecified assistantships also available. *Financial aid application deadline:* 2/1.

Contact Mrs. Dorine Nagy, Admission Coordinator, School of Nursing, University of Connecticut, 231 Glenbrook Road, Unit 2026, Storrs, CT 06269-2026. *Telephone:* 860-486-1937. *Fax:* 860-486-0906. *E-mail:* Dorine.Nagy@uconn.edu.

MASTER'S DEGREE PROGRAM

Degrees MS; MS/MBA

Available Programs Accelerated Master's for Nurses with Non-Nursing Degrees; Master's; RN to Master's.

Concentrations Available Clinical nurse leader; nursing administration. *Clinical nurse specialist programs in:* acute care, community health, maternity-newborn. *Nurse practitioner programs in:* acute care, neonatal health, primary care.

Site Options West Hartford, CT.

Study Options Full-time and part-time.

Program Entrance Requirements Clinical experience, computer literacy, minimum overall college GPA of 3.0, transcript of college record, CPR certification, immunizations, interview, 3 letters of recommendation, nursing research course, physical assessment course, professional liability insurance/malpractice insurance, resume, statistics course. *Application deadline:* Applications may be processed on a rolling basis for some programs. *Application fee:* $55.

Advanced Placement Credit given for nursing courses completed elsewhere dependent upon specific evaluations.

Degree Requirements 24 total credit hours, comprehensive exam.

POST-MASTER'S PROGRAM

Areas of Study Nursing administration. *Nurse practitioner programs in:* acute care, neonatal health, primary care.

DOCTORAL DEGREE PROGRAM

Degree PhD

Available Programs Doctorate; Post-Baccalaureate Doctorate.

Areas of Study Nursing research, nursing science.

Program Entrance Requirements Minimum overall college GPA of 3.25, interview by faculty committee, interview, 3 letters of recommendation, MSN or equivalent, statistics course, vita, writing sample. Application deadline: 2/1 (fall). Application fee: $55.

Degree Requirements 60 total credit hours, dissertation, oral exam, written exam.

CONTINUING EDUCATION PROGRAM

Contact Dorine Nagy, SON Admission and Enrollment Services, School of Nursing, University of Connecticut, 231 Glenbrook Road, Unit 2026, Storrs, CT 06269-2026. *Telephone:* 860-486-1937. *Fax:* 860-486-0906. *E-mail:* Dorine.Nagy@uconn.edu.

University of Hartford

College of Education, Nursing, and Health Professions

West Hartford, Connecticut

http://www.hartford.edu/enhp

Founded in 1877

DEGREES • BSN • MSN • MSN/MSOB

Nursing Program Faculty 8 (70% with doctorates).

Baccalaureate Enrollment 111

Women 96% **Men** 4% **Minority** 32% **Part-time** 100%

Graduate Enrollment 182

Women 97% **Men** 3% **Minority** 27% **Part-time** 100%

Nursing Student Activities Sigma Theta Tau.

Nursing Student Resources Academic advising; academic or career counseling; assistance for students with disabilities; bookstore; computer lab; e-mail services; Internet; library services; resume preparation assistance; tutoring.

Library Facilities 481,685 volumes; 2,424 periodical subscriptions.

BACCALAUREATE PROGRAMS

Degree BSN

Available Programs ADN to Baccalaureate; RN Baccalaureate.

Study Options Part-time.

Program Entrance Requirements Transcript of college record, professional liability insurance/malpractice insurance, RN licensure. Transfer students are accepted. *Application deadline:* Applications may be processed on a rolling basis for some programs. *Application fee:* $45.

Advanced Placement Credit by examination available. Credit given for nursing courses completed elsewhere dependent upon specific evaluations.

Expenses (2009–10) *Tuition:* part-time $410 per credit hour.

Financial Aid 50% of baccalaureate students in nursing programs received some form of financial aid in 2008–09. *Gift aid (need-based):* Federal Pell, FSEOG, state, private, college/university gift aid from institutional funds. *Loans:* FFEL (Subsidized and Unsubsidized Stafford PLUS), Perkins. *Work-study:* Federal Work-Study, part-time campus jobs. *Financial aid application deadline (priority):* 2/1.

Contact Dr. Mary Jane Williams, RN, Chair, Department of Nursing, College of Education, Nursing, and Health Professions, University of Hartford, 200 Bloomfield Avenue, West Hartford, CT 06117-1599. *Telephone:* 860-768-4213. *Fax:* 860-768-5346. *E-mail:* mjwilliam@hartford.edu.

GRADUATE PROGRAMS

Expenses (2009–10) *Tuition:* part-time $430 per credit hour. *Required fees:* part-time $439 per credit.

Financial Aid 50% of graduate students in nursing programs received some form of financial aid in 2008–09. 4 research assistantships (averaging $4,500 per year) were awarded; teaching assistantships, institutionally sponsored loans and unspecified assistantships also available. *Financial aid application deadline:* 6/1.

Contact Ms. Marlene J. Hall, Director of Communication and Recruitment, ENHP, College of Education, Nursing, and Health Professions, University of Hartford, 200 Bloomfield Avenue, West Hartford, CT 06117-1599. *Telephone:* 860-768-5116. *Fax:* 860-768-5346. *E-mail:* mhall@hartford.edu.

MASTER'S DEGREE PROGRAM

Degrees MSN; MSN/MSOB

Available Programs Master's; Master's for Nurses with Non-Nursing Degrees.

Concentrations Available Nursing administration; nursing education. *Clinical nurse specialist programs in:* public health.

Study Options Part-time.

Program Entrance Requirements Clinical experience, minimum overall college GPA of 3.0, transcript of college record, written essay, immunizations, 2 letters of recommendation, professional liability insurance/malpractice insurance, resume. *Application deadline:* 4/15 (fall), 11/15 (spring). *Application fee:* $45.

Advanced Placement Credit given for nursing courses completed elsewhere dependent upon specific evaluations.

Degree Requirements 34 total credit hours, thesis or project.

POST-MASTER'S PROGRAM

Areas of Study Nursing education.

CONTINUING EDUCATION PROGRAM

Contact Ms. Marlene J. Hall, Director of Communication and Recruitment, ENHP, College of Education, Nursing, and Health Professions, University of Hartford, 200 Bloomfield Avenue, West Hartford, CT 06117-1599. *Telephone:* 860-768-5116. *Fax:* 860-768-5346. *E-mail:* mhall@hartford.edu.

Western Connecticut State University
Department of Nursing
Danbury, Connecticut

Founded in 1903
DEGREES • BS • MS

Nursing Program Faculty 18 (50% with doctorates).

Baccalaureate Enrollment 160
Women 95% **Men** 5% **Minority** 20%

Graduate Enrollment 35
Women 100% **Minority** 2% **Part-time** 100%

Distance Learning Courses Available.

Nursing Student Activities Sigma Theta Tau, Student Nurses' Association.

Nursing Student Resources Academic advising; academic or career counseling; assistance for students with disabilities; bookstore; campus computer network; career placement assistance; computer lab; computer-assisted instruction; daycare for children of students; e-mail services; employment services for current students; externships; housing assistance; interactive nursing skills videos; Internet; learning resource lab; library services; nursing audiovisuals; paid internships; remedial services; resume preparation assistance; skills, simulation, or other laboratory; tutoring.

Library Facilities 216,284 volumes; 1,010 periodical subscriptions.

BACCALAUREATE PROGRAMS

Degree BS

Available Programs Generic Baccalaureate; RN Baccalaureate.
Site Options Waterbury, CT.
Study Options Full-time.
Program Entrance Requirements Minimum overall college GPA of 2.5, transcript of college record, CPR certification, health exam, health insurance, high school biology, high school chemistry, high school foreign language, 3 years high school math, 2 years high school science, high school transcript, immunizations, minimum GPA in nursing prerequisites of 2.5, prerequisite course work. Transfer students are accepted. *Application deadline:* Applications may be processed on a rolling basis for some programs.
Advanced Placement Credit by examination available. Credit given for nursing courses completed elsewhere dependent upon specific evaluations.
Expenses (2008–09) *Tuition, state resident:* full-time $3346. *Tuition, nonresident:* full-time $10,831. *Room and board:* $8750; room only: $5095 per academic year. *Required fees:* full-time $3278.
Financial Aid *Gift aid (need-based):* Federal Pell, FSEOG, state, private, college/university gift aid from institutional funds. *Loans:* Federal Direct (Subsidized and Unsubsidized Stafford PLUS), FFEL (Subsidized and Unsubsidized Stafford PLUS), Perkins. *Work-study:* Federal Work-Study, part-time campus jobs. *Financial aid application deadline:* 3/30 (priority: 3/1).
Contact Karen Crouse, EdD, Chair, Department of Nursing, Western Connecticut State University, 181 White Street, Danbury, CT 06810. *Telephone:* 203-837-8556. *Fax:* 203-837-8550. *E-mail:* crousek@wcsu.edu.

GRADUATE PROGRAMS

Expenses (2008–09) *Tuition, state resident:* part-time $363 per credit hour. *Tuition, nonresident:* part-time $363 per credit hour.
Contact Karen Daley, PhD, Graduate Program Coordinator, Department of Nursing, Western Connecticut State University, 181 White Street, Danbury, CT 06810. *Telephone:* 203-837-8556. *Fax:* 203-837-8550. *E-mail:* daleyk@wcsu.edu.

MASTER'S DEGREE PROGRAM

Degree MS
Available Programs Master's.
Concentrations Available *Clinical nurse specialist programs in:* adult health. *Nurse practitioner programs in:* adult health.
Study Options Part-time.

Program Entrance Requirements Clinical experience, computer literacy, minimum overall college GPA of 3.0, transcript of college record, CPR certification, immunizations, interview, 2 letters of recommendation, nursing research course, physical assessment course, professional liability insurance/malpractice insurance, prerequisite course work, resume, statistics course.
Advanced Placement Credit by examination available. Credit given for nursing courses completed elsewhere dependent upon specific evaluations.
Degree Requirements 36 total credit hours, thesis or project.

POST-MASTER'S PROGRAM

Areas of Study *Clinical nurse specialist programs in:* adult health. *Nurse practitioner programs in:* adult health.

Yale University
School of Nursing
New Haven, Connecticut

http://www.nursing.yale.edu
Founded in 1701
DEGREES • MSN • MSN/MDIV • MSN/MPH • PHD

Nursing Program Faculty 149 (50% with doctorates).
Graduate Enrollment 340
Women 94% **Men** 6% **Minority** 17% **International** 5% **Part-time** 12%
Distance Learning Courses Available.
Nursing Student Activities Nursing Honor Society, Sigma Theta Tau.
Nursing Student Resources Academic advising; academic or career counseling; assistance for students with disabilities; bookstore; campus computer network; career placement assistance; computer lab; computer-assisted instruction; daycare for children of students; e-mail services; employment services for current students; housing assistance; interactive nursing skills videos; Internet; learning resource lab; library services; nursing audiovisuals; placement services for program completers; remedial services; resume preparation assistance; skills, simulation, or other laboratory; tutoring; unpaid internships.
Library Facilities 12 million volumes (400,000 in health); 85,000 periodical subscriptions (2,900 health-care related).

GRADUATE PROGRAMS

Expenses (2009–10) *Tuition:* full-time $30,185. *International tuition:* $30,185 full-time. *Required fees:* full-time $325.
Financial Aid 90% of graduate students in nursing programs received some form of financial aid in 2008–09. 197 fellowships (averaging $5,650 per year), 18 research assistantships with tuition reimbursements available (averaging $25,333 per year) were awarded; Federal Work-Study, institutionally sponsored loans, scholarships, and traineeships also available. Aid available to part-time students. *Financial aid application deadline:* 2/1.
Contact Dr. Frank A. Grosso, Assistant Dean for Student Affairs, School of Nursing, Yale University, PO Box 9740, New Haven, CT 06536-0740. *Telephone:* 203-737-2257. *Fax:* 203-737-5409. *E-mail:* frank.grosso@yale.edu.

MASTER'S DEGREE PROGRAM

Degrees MSN; MSN/MDIV; MSN/MPH
Available Programs Master's; Master's for Non-Nursing College Graduates; Master's for Nurses with Non-Nursing Degrees.
Concentrations Available Nurse-midwifery; nursing administration. *Clinical nurse specialist programs in:* cardiovascular, critical care, oncology, psychiatric/mental health. *Nurse practitioner programs in:* acute care, adult health, family health, gerontology, oncology, pediatric, primary care, psychiatric/mental health, women's health.
Study Options Full-time.
Online Degree Options Yes.
Program Entrance Requirements Minimum overall college GPA of 3.0, transcript of college record, CPR certification, written essay, immunizations, interview, 3 letters of recommendation, resume, GRE General Test. *Application deadline:* 11/1 (fall). *Application fee:* $65.

Advanced Placement Credit by examination available. Credit given for nursing courses completed elsewhere dependent upon specific evaluations.

Degree Requirements 40 total credit hours, thesis or project.

POST-MASTER'S PROGRAM

Areas of Study *Clinical nurse specialist programs in:* psychiatric/mental health. *Nurse practitioner programs in:* acute care, adult health, gerontology, oncology, pediatric.

DOCTORAL DEGREE PROGRAM

Degree PhD

Available Programs Doctorate.

Areas of Study Aging, critical care, family health, gerontology, health policy, health promotion/disease prevention, health-care systems, human health and illness, maternity-newborn, neuro-behavior, nursing policy, nursing research, oncology.

Program Entrance Requirements Minimum overall college GPA of 3.0, interview by faculty committee, interview, 3 letters of recommendation, MSN or equivalent, statistics course, vita, writing sample, GRE General Test. Application deadline: 1/2 (fall). Application fee: $90.

Degree Requirements 60 total credit hours, dissertation, oral exam, written exam.

POSTDOCTORAL PROGRAM

Areas of Study Adolescent health, chronic illness.

Postdoctoral Program Contact Ms. Sarah Zaino, Assistant Director, Research Activities, School of Nursing, Yale University, PO Box 9740, New Haven, CT 06536-0740. *Telephone:* 203-737-2420. *Fax:* 203-737-4480. *E-mail:* sarah.zaino@yale.edu.

DELAWARE

Delaware State University

Department of Nursing
Dover, Delaware

http://www.dsc.edu/schools/professional_studies/ nursing

Founded in 1891

DEGREE • BSN

Nursing Program Faculty 11

Nursing Student Activities Sigma Theta Tau, Student Nurses' Association.

Library Facilities 187,045 volumes; 74,881 periodical subscriptions.

BACCALAUREATE PROGRAMS

Degree BSN

Available Programs Generic Baccalaureate; LPN to Baccalaureate.

Study Options Full-time and part-time.

Program Entrance Requirements High school biology, high school chemistry, high school transcript, minimum high school GPA of 2.0, prerequisite course work. Transfer students are accepted.

Advanced Placement Credit by examination available. Credit given for nursing courses completed elsewhere dependent upon specific evaluations.

Contact *Telephone:* 302-857-6750. *Fax:* 302-857-6755.

University of Delaware

School of Nursing
Newark, Delaware

http://www.udel.edu/nursing/udnursing.html

Founded in 1743

DEGREES • BSN • MSN

Nursing Program Faculty 58 (48% with doctorates).

Baccalaureate Enrollment 674
Women 90% **Men** 10% **Minority** 17% **International** 1% **Part-time** 18%

Graduate Enrollment 121
Women 92% **Men** 8% **Minority** 21% **Part-time** 93%

Distance Learning Courses Available.

Nursing Student Activities Sigma Theta Tau, Student Nurses' Association.

Nursing Student Resources Academic advising; academic or career counseling; assistance for students with disabilities; bookstore; campus computer network; career placement assistance; computer lab; computer-assisted instruction; e-mail services; employment services for current students; housing assistance; interactive nursing skills videos; Internet; learning resource lab; library services; nursing audiovisuals; resume preparation assistance; skills, simulation, or other laboratory; tutoring.

Library Facilities 2.7 million volumes (2.7 million in health, 40,000 in nursing); 12,532 periodical subscriptions (240 health-care related).

BACCALAUREATE PROGRAMS

Degree BSN

Available Programs Accelerated Baccalaureate for Second Degree; Generic Baccalaureate; RN Baccalaureate.

Study Options Full-time.

Program Entrance Requirements CPR certification, written essay, high school biology, high school chemistry, high school foreign language, 3 years high school math, 4 years high school science, high school transcript, immunizations, 1 letter of recommendation, minimum high school GPA of 3.0. Transfer students are accepted.

Advanced Placement Credit given for nursing courses completed elsewhere dependent upon specific evaluations.

Contact *Telephone:* 302-831-1117. *Fax:* 302-831-2382.

GRADUATE PROGRAMS

Contact *Telephone:* 302-831-8386. *Fax:* 302-831-2382.

MASTER'S DEGREE PROGRAM

Degree MSN

Available Programs Master's; Master's for Nurses with Non-Nursing Degrees; RN to Master's.

Concentrations Available Health-care administration. *Clinical nurse specialist programs in:* adult health, pediatric, psychiatric/mental health, school health. *Nurse practitioner programs in:* adult health, family health.

Study Options Full-time and part-time.

Program Entrance Requirements Clinical experience, minimum overall college GPA of 3.0, transcript of college record, CPR certification, written essay, immunizations, interview, 3 letters of recommendation, professional liability insurance/malpractice insurance, resume.

Advanced Placement Credit given for nursing courses completed elsewhere dependent upon specific evaluations.

Degree Requirements 34 total credit hours.

POST-MASTER'S PROGRAM

Areas of Study Health-care administration. *Clinical nurse specialist programs in:* adult health, pediatric, psychiatric/mental health. *Nurse practitioner programs in:* adult health, family health.

Wesley College

Nursing Program
Dover, Delaware

http://www.wesley.edu

Founded in 1873

DEGREES • BSN • MSN

Nursing Program Faculty 10 (80% with doctorates).

Baccalaureate Enrollment 240
Women 85% **Men** 15% **Minority** 35% **International** 1% **Part-time** 2%

Wesley College (continued)
Graduate Enrollment 87
Women 90% **Men** 10% **Minority** 25% **Part-time** 10%

Nursing Student Activities Sigma Theta Tau, Student Nurses' Association.

Nursing Student Resources Academic advising; academic or career counseling; assistance for students with disabilities; bookstore; campus computer network; career placement assistance; computer lab; computer-assisted instruction; e-mail services; employment services for current students; externships; housing assistance; interactive nursing skills videos; Internet; learning resource lab; library services; nursing audiovisuals; placement services for program completers; remedial services; resume preparation assistance; skills, simulation, or other laboratory; tutoring; unpaid internships.

Library Facilities 104,636 volumes (15,000 in health, 1,500 in nursing); 252 periodical subscriptions (40 health-care related).

BACCALAUREATE PROGRAMS

Degree BSN

Available Programs Generic Baccalaureate; International Nurse to Baccalaureate; LPN to Baccalaureate.

Study Options Full-time and part-time.

Program Entrance Requirements Transcript of college record, CPR certification, written essay, health exam, high school biology, high school chemistry, 2 years high school math, 2 years high school science, high school transcript, immunizations, minimum high school GPA of 2.75, minimum GPA in nursing prerequisites of 2.0, professional liability insurance/malpractice insurance. Transfer students are accepted. *Application deadline:* Applications may be processed on a rolling basis for some programs. *Application fee:* $40.

Advanced Placement Credit by examination available. Credit given for nursing courses completed elsewhere dependent upon specific evaluations.

Expenses (2009–10) *Tuition:* full-time $17,500; part-time $800 per credit. *International tuition:* $17,500 full-time. *Room and board:* $8500; room only: $4000 per academic year. *Required fees:* full-time $500; part-time $250 per term.

Financial Aid 90% of baccalaureate students in nursing programs received some form of financial aid in 2008–09.

Contact Dr. Nancy D. Rubino, Program Director, Nursing Program, Wesley College, 120 North State Street, Dulany Hall, Dover, DE 19901. *Telephone:* 302-736-2550. *Fax:* 302-736-2548. *E-mail:* rubinona@wesley.edu.

GRADUATE PROGRAMS

Expenses (2009–10) *Tuition:* part-time $400 per credit. *Required fees:* part-time $50 per term.

Financial Aid 100% of graduate students in nursing programs received some form of financial aid in 2008–09. Traineeships available.

Contact Dr. Lucille C. Gambardella, Chairperson, Nursing Program, Wesley College, 120 North State Street, Dover, DE 19901. *Telephone:* 302-736-2512. *Fax:* 302-736-2548. *E-mail:* gambarlu@wesley.edu.

MASTER'S DEGREE PROGRAM

Degree MSN

Available Programs Accelerated AD/RN to Master's; Accelerated RN to Master's; Master's; RN to Master's.

Concentrations Available *Clinical nurse specialist programs in:* community health, women's health.

Site Options New Castle, DE.

Study Options Full-time and part-time.

Online Degree Options Yes.

Program Entrance Requirements Clinical experience, computer literacy, minimum overall college GPA of 3.0, transcript of college record, written essay, interview, 2 letters of recommendation, professional liability insurance/malpractice insurance, resume, statistics course, GRE or MAT. *Application deadline:* Applications may be processed on a rolling basis for some programs. *Application fee:* $35.

Advanced Placement Credit by examination available. Credit given for nursing courses completed elsewhere dependent upon specific evaluations.

Degree Requirements 36 total credit hours, thesis or project.

POST-MASTER'S PROGRAM

Areas of Study Nursing education. *Clinical nurse specialist programs in:* palliative care, women's health.

CONTINUING EDUCATION PROGRAM

Contact Dr. Lucille C. Gambardella, Chairperson, Nursing Program, Wesley College, 120 North State Street, Dover, DE 19901. *Telephone:* 302-736-2512. *Fax:* 302-736-2548. *E-mail:* gambarlu@wesley.edu.

Wilmington University
College of Health Professions
New Castle, Delaware

Founded in 1967

DEGREES • BSN • MSN • MSN/MBA • MSN/MS

Nursing Program Faculty 10 (60% with doctorates).

Baccalaureate Enrollment 400
Women 96% **Men** 4% **Minority** 8% **Part-time** 90%

Graduate Enrollment 180
Women 92% **Men** 8% **Minority** 17% **International** 5% **Part-time** 50%

Distance Learning Courses Available.

Nursing Student Activities Sigma Theta Tau.

Nursing Student Resources Academic advising; academic or career counseling; assistance for students with disabilities; bookstore; campus computer network; career placement assistance; computer lab; computer-assisted instruction; e-mail services; employment services for current students; housing assistance; interactive nursing skills videos; learning resource lab; library services; nursing audiovisuals; remedial services; resume preparation assistance; tutoring.

Library Facilities 98,713 volumes (6,000 in health, 3,500 in nursing); 425 periodical subscriptions (60 health-care related).

BACCALAUREATE PROGRAMS

Degree BSN

Available Programs Accelerated RN Baccalaureate; International Nurse to Baccalaureate; RN Baccalaureate.

Site Options Georgetown, DE; Dover, DE.

Study Options Full-time and part-time.

Online Degree Options Yes.

Program Entrance Requirements Transcript of college record, CPR certification, written essay, health exam, immunizations, prerequisite course work, RN licensure. Transfer students are accepted. *Application deadline:* 8/31 (fall), 1/1 (spring), 5/1 (summer). Applications may be processed on a rolling basis for some programs. *Application fee:* $35.

Advanced Placement Credit by examination available. Credit given for nursing courses completed elsewhere dependent upon specific evaluations.

Financial Aid 60% of baccalaureate students in nursing programs received some form of financial aid in 2008–09.

Contact Ms. Denise Westbrook, RN, BSN Program Coordinator, College of Health Professions, Wilmington University, 320 DuPont Highway, New Castle, DE 19720. *Telephone:* 302-856-5780. *Fax:* 302-322-7081. *E-mail:* denise.z.westbrook@wilmu.edu.

GRADUATE PROGRAMS

Financial Aid 65% of graduate students in nursing programs received some form of financial aid in 2008–09. 28 fellowships with tuition reimbursements available (averaging $2,200 per year) were awarded; traineeships also available.

Contact Ms. Kim Christensen, Admissions Associate, College of Health Professions, Wilmington University, Wilson Graduate Center, 31 Read's Way, New Castle, DE 19720. *Telephone:* 302-295-1120. *E-mail:* kimberly.a.christensen@wilmu.edu.

MASTER'S DEGREE PROGRAM

Degrees MSN; MSN/MBA; MSN/MS

Available Programs Accelerated AD/RN to Master's; Master's.

Concentrations Available Legal nurse consultant; nursing administration; nursing education. *Nurse practitioner programs in:* adult health, family health, gerontology.

Site Options Georgetown, DE; New Castle, DE.

Study Options Full-time and part-time.

Program Entrance Requirements Clinical experience, computer literacy, minimum overall college GPA of 3.0, transcript of college record, CPR certification, written essay, immunizations, interview, 2 letters of recommendation, nursing research course, physical assessment course, professional liability insurance/malpractice insurance, prerequisite course work, resume, statistics course. *Application deadline:* 5/15 (fall). Applications may be processed on a rolling basis for some programs. *Application fee:* $35.

Advanced Placement Credit given for nursing courses completed elsewhere dependent upon specific evaluations.

Degree Requirements 42 total credit hours, thesis or project.

POST-MASTER'S PROGRAM

Areas of Study Legal nurse consultant; nursing administration; nursing education. *Nurse practitioner programs in:* adult health, family health, gerontology.

DISTRICT OF COLUMBIA

The Catholic University of America
School of Nursing
Washington, District of Columbia

http://www.nursing.cua.edu

Founded in 1887

DEGREES • BSN • MA/MSM • MSN • PHD

Nursing Program Faculty 30 (75% with doctorates).

Baccalaureate Enrollment 280
Women 91% **Men** 9% **Minority** 18% **International** 2% **Part-time** 3%

Graduate Enrollment 150
Women 98% **Men** 2% **Minority** 22% **International** 9% **Part-time** 69%

Distance Learning Courses Available.

Nursing Student Activities Nursing Honor Society, Sigma Theta Tau, Student Nurses' Association, nursing club.

Nursing Student Resources Academic advising; academic or career counseling; assistance for students with disabilities; bookstore; computer lab; computer-assisted instruction; e-mail services; interactive nursing skills videos; Internet; learning resource lab; library services; nursing audiovisuals; skills, simulation, or other laboratory.

Library Facilities 1.6 million volumes (39,000 in health, 17,500 in nursing); 10,428 periodical subscriptions (250 health-care related).

BACCALAUREATE PROGRAMS

Degree BSN

Available Programs Accelerated Baccalaureate; Accelerated Baccalaureate for Second Degree; Generic Baccalaureate; RN Baccalaureate.

Study Options Full-time and part-time.

Program Entrance Requirements Minimum overall college GPA of 3.0, transcript of college record, written essay, health exam, health insurance, high school chemistry, 3 years high school math, high school transcript, immunizations, 1 letter of recommendation, minimum high school GPA of 3.0, minimum GPA in nursing prerequisites of 2.75, prerequisite course work. Transfer students are accepted. *Application deadline:* 8/1 (fall), 12/1 (spring), 2/28 (summer). *Application fee:* $55.

Advanced Placement Credit given for nursing courses completed elsewhere dependent upon specific evaluations.

Expenses (2009–10) *Tuition:* part-time $1170 per credit hour. *Required fees:* part-time $75 per credit.

Financial Aid 50% of baccalaureate students in nursing programs received some form of financial aid in 2008–09. *Gift aid (need-based):* Federal Pell, FSEOG, state, private, college/university gift aid from institutional funds, Federal Nursing. *Loans:* Federal Nursing Student Loans, FFEL (Subsidized and Unsubsidized Stafford PLUS), Perkins, college/university, commercial loans. *Work-study:* Federal Work-Study. *Financial aid application deadline (priority):* 2/15.

Contact Ms. Lynn Doyle, Administrative Assistant, School of Nursing, The Catholic University of America, 124 Gowan Hall, 620 Michigan Avenue NE, Washington, DC 20064. *Telephone:* 202-319-6457. *Fax:* 202-319-6485. *E-mail:* doyle@cua.edu.

GRADUATE PROGRAMS

Expenses (2009–10) *Tuition:* part-time $1245 per credit hour. *International tuition:* $1245 full-time.

Financial Aid 80% of graduate students in nursing programs received some form of financial aid in 2008–09. Fellowships, research assistantships, teaching assistantships, Federal Work-Study, scholarships, tuition waivers (full and partial), and unspecified assistantships available. *Financial aid application deadline:* 2/1.

Contact Miss Melisa Darby, Graduate Recruitment and Clinical Outreach Coordinator, School of Nursing, The Catholic University of America, 118 Gowan Hall, Washington, DC 20064. *Telephone:* 202-319-6536. *Fax:* 202-319-6485. *E-mail:* darby@cua.edu.

MASTER'S DEGREE PROGRAM

Degrees MA/MSM; MSN

Available Programs Master's.

Concentrations Available Nursing education. *Clinical nurse specialist programs in:* adult health, community health, pediatric. *Nurse practitioner programs in:* acute care, adult health, family health, gerontology, pediatric.

Site Options Washington, DC.

Study Options Full-time and part-time.

Program Entrance Requirements Clinical experience, minimum overall college GPA of 3.0, transcript of college record, written essay, immunizations, 3 letters of recommendation, professional liability insurance/malpractice insurance, prerequisite course work, statistics course. *Application deadline:* 8/1 (fall), 12/1 (spring). Applications may be processed on a rolling basis for some programs. *Application fee:* $55.

Advanced Placement Credit given for nursing courses completed elsewhere dependent upon specific evaluations.

Degree Requirements 44 total credit hours, comprehensive exam.

POST-MASTER'S PROGRAM

Areas of Study Nursing education. *Clinical nurse specialist programs in:* adult health, community health, pediatric. *Nurse practitioner programs in:* acute care, adult health, family health, gerontology, pediatric.

DOCTORAL DEGREE PROGRAM

Degree PhD

Available Programs Doctorate; Post-Baccalaureate Doctorate.

Areas of Study Clinical practice, nursing research, nursing science.

Online Degree Options Yes.

Program Entrance Requirements Clinical experience, minimum overall college GPA of 3.5, interview by faculty committee, interview, 3 letters of recommendation, MSN or equivalent, scholarly papers, statistics course, writing sample, GRE General Test. Application deadline: 8/1 (fall), 12/1 (spring). Applications may be processed on a rolling basis for some programs. Application fee: $55.

Degree Requirements 66 total credit hours, dissertation, oral exam, written exam, residency.

Georgetown University
School of Nursing & Health Studies
Washington, District of Columbia

http://nhs.georgetown.edu

Founded in 1789

Georgetown University (continued)
DEGREES • BSN • MS

Nursing Program Faculty 72 (50% with doctorates).

Baccalaureate Enrollment 480
Women 85% **Men** 15% **Minority** 26% **International** 1% **Part-time** 2%

Graduate Enrollment 235
Women 73% **Men** 27% **Minority** 24% **International** 1% **Part-time** 20%

Nursing Student Activities Nursing Honor Society, Sigma Theta Tau, Student Nurses' Association.

Nursing Student Resources Academic advising; academic or career counseling; assistance for students with disabilities; bookstore; campus computer network; career placement assistance; computer lab; computer-assisted instruction; e-mail services; employment services for current students; housing assistance; interactive nursing skills videos; Internet; learning resource lab; library services; nursing audiovisuals; placement services for program completers; resume preparation assistance; skills, simulation, or other laboratory; tutoring; unpaid internships.

Library Facilities 2.5 million volumes (36,000 in health, 20,000 in nursing); 31,099 periodical subscriptions (92 health-care related).

BACCALAUREATE PROGRAMS

Degree BSN

Available Programs Accelerated Baccalaureate for Second Degree; Generic Baccalaureate.

Study Options Full-time.

Program Entrance Requirements Transcript of college record, CPR certification, written essay, health exam, health insurance, high school biology, 3 years high school math, 4 years high school science, high school transcript, immunizations, interview, 2 letters of recommendation. Transfer students are accepted. *Application deadline:* 1/10 (fall). *Application fee:* $65.

Advanced Placement Credit by examination available.

Expenses (2009–10) *Tuition:* full-time $38,616; part-time $1609 per credit. *International tuition:* $38,616 full-time. *Room and board:* $12,506 per academic year.

Financial Aid 46% of baccalaureate students in nursing programs received some form of financial aid in 2008–09. *Gift aid (need-based):* Federal Pell, FSEOG, state, private, college/university gift aid from institutional funds. *Loans:* Federal Nursing Student Loans, FFEL (Subsidized and Unsubsidized Stafford PLUS), Perkins, alternative loans. *Work-study:* Federal Work-Study. *Financial aid application deadline:* 2/1.

Contact Office of Undergraduate Admissions, School of Nursing & Health Studies, Georgetown University, 37th and O Street NW, Washington, DC 20057. *Telephone:* 202-687-3600.

GRADUATE PROGRAMS

Expenses (2009–10) *Tuition:* full-time $36,744; part-time $1531 per credit hour.

Financial Aid Scholarships and traineeships available.

Contact Office of Graduate Admissions, School of Nursing & Health Studies, Georgetown University, 37th and O Street NW, Washington, DC 20057. *Telephone:* 202-687-5568.

MASTER'S DEGREE PROGRAM

Degree MS

Available Programs Master's; Master's for Non-Nursing College Graduates.

Concentrations Available Health-care administration; nurse anesthesia; nurse-midwifery; nursing education. *Clinical nurse specialist programs in:* acute care, critical care. *Nurse practitioner programs in:* acute care, family health, women's health.

Study Options Full-time and part-time.

Program Entrance Requirements Clinical experience, minimum overall college GPA of 3.0, transcript of college record, CPR certification, written essay, immunizations, interview, 3 letters of recommendation, resume, statistics course, GRE General Test or MAT. *Application deadline:* 6/1 (fall), 11/1 (spring). Applications may be processed on a rolling basis for some programs. *Application fee:* $75.

Advanced Placement Credit given for nursing courses completed elsewhere dependent upon specific evaluations.

Degree Requirements 40 total credit hours, thesis or project.

POST-MASTER'S PROGRAM

Areas of Study Nurse-midwifery; nursing education. *Clinical nurse specialist programs in:* acute care, critical care. *Nurse practitioner programs in:* acute care, family health, women's health.

The George Washington University
Department of Nursing Education
Washington, District of Columbia

Founded in 1821

Library Facilities 2 million volumes; 15,365 periodical subscriptions.

Howard University
Division of Nursing
Washington, District of Columbia

http://www.howard.edu

Founded in 1867

DEGREES • BSN • MSN

Nursing Program Faculty 32 (25% with doctorates).

Graduate Enrollment 22
Women 90% **Men** 10% **Minority** 55% **International** 45% **Part-time** 75%

Nursing Student Activities Sigma Theta Tau, Student Nurses' Association.

Nursing Student Resources Academic advising; academic or career counseling; assistance for students with disabilities; bookstore; campus computer network; career placement assistance; computer lab; computer-assisted instruction; e-mail services; externships; housing assistance; interactive nursing skills videos; Internet; learning resource lab; library services; nursing audiovisuals; paid internships; placement services for program completers; remedial services; resume preparation assistance; skills, simulation, or other laboratory.

Library Facilities 2.5 million volumes (219,448 in health, 4,500 in nursing); 26,382 periodical subscriptions (5,247 health-care related).

BACCALAUREATE PROGRAMS

Degree BSN

Available Programs Accelerated Baccalaureate for Second Degree; Baccalaureate for Second Degree; Generic Baccalaureate; LPN to Baccalaureate; RN Baccalaureate.

Study Options Full-time and part-time.

Program Entrance Requirements Minimum overall college GPA of 2.8, transcript of college record, CPR certification, written essay, health exam, high school biology, high school chemistry, 2 years high school math, 2 years high school science, high school transcript, immunizations, 2 letters of recommendation, minimum high school GPA of 2.8, minimum high school rank 50%, minimum GPA in nursing prerequisites of 2.5. Transfer students are accepted. *Application deadline:* 2/15 (fall), 4/1 (summer). *Application fee:* $45.

Advanced Placement Credit by examination available. Credit given for nursing courses completed elsewhere dependent upon specific evaluations.

Expenses (2008–09) *Tuition:* full-time $14,205; part-time $578 per credit hour. *Room and board:* $14,372; room only: $10,512 per academic year. *Required fees:* full-time $805.

Financial Aid 92% of baccalaureate students in nursing programs received some form of financial aid in 2007–08. *Gift aid (need-based):* Federal Pell, FSEOG, state, private, college/university gift aid from institutional funds, Federal Nursing. *Loans:* Federal Nursing Student Loans, Federal Direct (Subsidized and Unsubsidized Stafford PLUS), FFEL (Subsidized and Unsubsidized Stafford PLUS), Perkins, state, college/university. *Work-study:* Federal Work-Study, part-time campus jobs. *Financial aid application deadline:* 8/15 (priority: 2/15).

Contact Ms. Carolyn Harris, JD, Interim Chairperson, Undergraduate Program, Division of Nursing, Howard University, 501 Bryant Street NW, Room 119, Washington, DC 20059. *Telephone:* 202-806-7854. *Fax:* 202-806-5958. *E-mail:* cjharris@howard.edu.

GRADUATE PROGRAMS

Financial Aid Teaching assistantships (averaging $16,000 per year); career-related internships or fieldwork, institutionally sponsored loans, and scholarships also available.

Contact Mamie Clark Montague, PhD, Interim Associate Dean for Nursing, Division of Nursing, Howard University, 501 Bryant Street NW, Washington, DC 20059. *Telephone:* 202-806-7460. *Fax:* 202-806-5978. *E-mail:* mmontague@howard.edu.

MASTER'S DEGREE PROGRAM

Degree MSN

Available Programs Master's.

Concentrations Available *Nurse practitioner programs in:* family health.

Study Options Full-time and part-time.

Program Entrance Requirements Minimum overall college GPA of 3.0, transcript of college record, CPR certification, written essay, immunizations, interview, 3 letters of recommendation, physical assessment course, professional liability insurance/malpractice insurance, statistics course. *Application deadline:* Applications may be processed on a rolling basis for some programs. *Application fee:* $45.

Advanced Placement Credit given for nursing courses completed elsewhere dependent upon specific evaluations.

Degree Requirements 46 total credit hours, comprehensive exam.

POST-MASTER'S PROGRAM

Areas of Study *Nurse practitioner programs in:* family health.

Trinity (Washington) University
Nursing Program
Washington, District of Columbia

Founded in 1897

DEGREE • BSN

Nursing Program Faculty 9 (4% with doctorates).

Baccalaureate Enrollment 80

Nursing Student Activities Sigma Theta Tau, Student Nurses' Association.

Nursing Student Resources Academic advising; academic or career counseling; assistance for students with disabilities; bookstore; campus computer network; career placement assistance; computer lab; computer-assisted instruction; e-mail services; employment services for current students; housing assistance; Internet; learning resource lab; library services; nursing audiovisuals; paid internships; remedial services; resume preparation assistance; skills, simulation, or other laboratory; tutoring; unpaid internships.

Library Facilities 207,000 volumes (1,200 in health, 200 in nursing); 498 periodical subscriptions (40 health-care related).

BACCALAUREATE PROGRAMS

Degree BSN

Available Programs Generic Baccalaureate; RN Baccalaureate.

Study Options Full-time and part-time.

Program Entrance Requirements Transcript of college record, CPR certification, written essay, health exam, health insurance, high school transcript, immunizations, interview, 1 letter of recommendation, minimum GPA in nursing prerequisites of 2.0, professional liability insurance/malpractice insurance, prerequisite course work, RN licensure. Transfer students are accepted. *Application deadline:* Applications may be processed on a rolling basis for some programs.

Advanced Placement Credit by examination available. Credit given for nursing courses completed elsewhere dependent upon specific evaluations.

Contact Dr. Stephanie Holaday, Director, Nursing Programs, Nursing Program, Trinity (Washington) University, 125 Michigan Avenue NE, Washington, DC 22017. *Telephone:* 202-884-9245. *Fax:* 202-884-9308. *E-mail:* holadays@trinitydc.edu.

University of the District of Columbia
Nursing Education Program
Washington, District of Columbia

Founded in 1976

DEGREE • BSN

Nursing Program Faculty 11 (3% with doctorates).

Baccalaureate Enrollment 26
Women 97% **Men** 3% **Minority** 98% **International** 50% **Part-time** 100%

Nursing Student Activities Student Nurses' Association.

Nursing Student Resources Academic advising; academic or career counseling; assistance for students with disabilities; bookstore; campus computer network; career placement assistance; computer lab; computer-assisted instruction; daycare for children of students; e-mail services; employment services for current students; Internet; learning resource lab; library services; nursing audiovisuals; remedial services; resume preparation assistance; skills, simulation, or other laboratory; tutoring.

Library Facilities 544,412 volumes (500 in health, 250 in nursing); 594 periodical subscriptions (75 health-care related).

BACCALAUREATE PROGRAMS

Degree BSN

Available Programs RN Baccalaureate.

Site Options Washington, DC.

Study Options Full-time and part-time.

Program Entrance Requirements Minimum overall college GPA of 2.5, transcript of college record, CPR certification, written essay, health exam, health insurance, immunizations, letters of recommendation, minimum GPA in nursing prerequisites of 2.5, professional liability insurance/malpractice insurance, prerequisite course work, RN licensure. Transfer students are accepted. *Application deadline:* 4/21 (fall), 10/21 (spring).

Advanced Placement Credit given for nursing courses completed elsewhere dependent upon specific evaluations.

Contact Dr. JoAnne Deborah Joyner, RN, Director, Nursing Program, Nursing Education Program, University of the District of Columbia, Building 44, Room 104A, 4200 Connecticut Avenue NW, Washington, DC 20008. *Telephone:* 202-274-5916. *Fax:* 202-274-5952. *E-mail:* jjoyner@udc.edu.

FLORIDA

Barry University
School of Nursing
Miami Shores, Florida

http://www.barry.edu/nursing

Founded in 1940

DEGREES • BSN • MSN • MSN/MBA • PHD

Nursing Program Faculty 30 (50% with doctorates).

Baccalaureate Enrollment 431
Women 87% **Men** 13% **Minority** 51% **International** 2% **Part-time** 20%

Graduate Enrollment 161
Women 93% **Men** 7% **Minority** 51% **International** 1% **Part-time** 99%

Nursing Student Activities Sigma Theta Tau, Student Nurses' Association.

Barry University (continued)

Nursing Student Resources Academic advising; academic or career counseling; assistance for students with disabilities; bookstore; campus computer network; career placement assistance; computer lab; computer-assisted instruction; e-mail services; employment services for current students; housing assistance; interactive nursing skills videos; Internet; learning resource lab; library services; nursing audiovisuals; paid internships; remedial services; resume preparation assistance; skills, simulation, or other laboratory; tutoring.

Library Facilities 233,938 volumes (15,000 in health, 8,500 in nursing); 2,880 periodical subscriptions (400 health-care related).

BACCALAUREATE PROGRAMS

Degree BSN

Available Programs ADN to Baccalaureate; Accelerated Baccalaureate; Accelerated Baccalaureate for Second Degree; Baccalaureate for Second Degree; Generic Baccalaureate; LPN to Baccalaureate; LPN to RN Baccalaureate; RN Baccalaureate.

Site Options Davie, FL; Kendall, FL.

Study Options Full-time and part-time.

Program Entrance Requirements Minimum overall college GPA of 3.0, transcript of college record, CPR certification, health exam, health insurance, high school biology, high school chemistry, high school math, high school science, high school transcript, immunizations, 2 letters of recommendation, minimum high school GPA of 3.0, minimum GPA in nursing prerequisites of 3.0, professional liability insurance/malpractice insurance. Transfer students are accepted. *Application deadline:* Applications may be processed on a rolling basis for some programs.

Advanced Placement Credit given for nursing courses completed elsewhere dependent upon specific evaluations.

Expenses (2009–10) *Tuition:* full-time $26,400; part-time $790 per credit.

Financial Aid 90% of baccalaureate students in nursing programs received some form of financial aid in 2008–09.

Contact Ms. Rosanne Sonshine, Recruiter and Clinical Coordinator, School of Nursing, Barry University, 11300 NE Second Avenue, Miami Shores, FL 33161-6695. *Telephone:* 305-899-3813. *Fax:* 305-899-3831. *E-mail:* rsonshine@mail.barry.edu.

GRADUATE PROGRAMS

Expenses (2009–10) *Tuition:* part-time $845 per credit.

Financial Aid 90% of graduate students in nursing programs received some form of financial aid in 2008–09. 3 research assistantships (averaging $5,000 per year), 3 teaching assistantships (averaging $5,000 per year) were awarded; scholarships and tuition waivers (full) also available. *Financial aid application deadline:* 5/1.

Contact Rosanne Sonshine, Recruiter and Clinical Coordinator, School of Nursing, Barry University, 11300 NE Second Avenue, Miami Shores, FL 33161-6695. *Telephone:* 305-899-3813. *Fax:* 305-899-3831. *E-mail:* rsonshine@mail.barry.edu.

MASTER'S DEGREE PROGRAM

Degrees MSN; MSN/MBA

Available Programs Master's.

Concentrations Available Nursing administration; nursing education. *Nurse practitioner programs in:* acute care, family health.

Study Options Part-time.

Program Entrance Requirements Clinical experience, computer literacy, minimum overall college GPA of 3.0, transcript of college record, written essay, 2 letters of recommendation, nursing research course, professional liability insurance/malpractice insurance, statistics course, GRE General Test or MAT. *Application deadline:* Applications may be processed on a rolling basis for some programs.

Advanced Placement Credit given for nursing courses completed elsewhere dependent upon specific evaluations.

Degree Requirements 45 total credit hours.

POST-MASTER'S PROGRAM

Areas of Study Nursing administration; nursing education. *Nurse practitioner programs in:* acute care, family health.

DOCTORAL DEGREE PROGRAM

Degree PhD

Available Programs Doctorate.

Areas of Study Nursing research, nursing science.

Program Entrance Requirements Clinical experience, minimum overall college GPA of 3.0, interview, 2 letters of recommendation, MSN or equivalent, statistics course, writing sample, GRE General Test or MAT. *Application deadline:* Applications may be processed on a rolling basis for some programs.

Degree Requirements 45 total credit hours, dissertation, written exam, residency.

Bethune-Cookman University
School of Nursing
Daytona Beach, Florida

http://www.cookman.edu/Nursing

Founded in 1904

DEGREE • BSN

Nursing Program Faculty 11 (2% with doctorates).

Baccalaureate Enrollment 137
Women 93% **Men** 7% **Minority** 95% **International** 2%

Nursing Student Activities Nursing Honor Society, Student Nurses' Association.

Nursing Student Resources Academic advising; bookstore; campus computer network; computer lab; computer-assisted instruction; e-mail services; interactive nursing skills videos; Internet; learning resource lab; library services; nursing audiovisuals; resume preparation assistance; skills, simulation, or other laboratory; tutoring; unpaid internships.

Library Facilities 187,908 volumes; 800 periodical subscriptions.

BACCALAUREATE PROGRAMS

Degree BSN

Available Programs Generic Baccalaureate; RN Baccalaureate.

Study Options Full-time.

Program Entrance Requirements Minimum overall college GPA of 2.8, transcript of college record, CPR certification, written essay, health exam, high school transcript, immunizations, interview, 2 letters of recommendation, minimum GPA in nursing prerequisites of 2.8, prerequisite course work. Transfer students are accepted.

Advanced Placement Credit by examination available. Credit given for nursing courses completed elsewhere dependent upon specific evaluations.

Contact *Telephone:* 386-481-2000.

Florida Agricultural and Mechanical University
School of Nursing
Tallahassee, Florida

http://www.famu.edu/acad/colleges/son

Founded in 1887

DEGREES • BSN • MSN • PHD

Nursing Program Faculty 28 (18% with doctorates).

Baccalaureate Enrollment 161
Women 90% **Men** 10% **Minority** 98%

Graduate Enrollment 17
Women 83% **Men** 17% **Minority** 76% **Part-time** 12%

Nursing Student Activities Sigma Theta Tau, Student Nurses' Association.

Nursing Student Resources Academic advising; academic or career counseling; bookstore; campus computer network; career placement assistance; computer lab; computer-assisted instruction; daycare for children of students; e-mail services; employment services for current students; externships; interactive nursing skills videos; Internet; library services;

nursing audiovisuals; placement services for program completers; remedial services; resume preparation assistance; skills, simulation, or other laboratory; tutoring.

Library Facilities 484,801 volumes (5,000 in health, 4,091 in nursing); 7,672 periodical subscriptions (385 health-care related).

BACCALAUREATE PROGRAMS

Degree BSN

Available Programs Generic Baccalaureate.

Study Options Part-time.

Program Entrance Requirements CPR certification, health exam, immunizations, 3 letters of recommendation, minimum high school GPA of 2.5, prerequisite course work. Transfer students are accepted.

Contact *Telephone:* 850-599-3458. *Fax:* 850-599-3508.

GRADUATE PROGRAMS

Contact *Telephone:* 850-599-3017. *Fax:* 850-599-3508.

MASTER'S DEGREE PROGRAM

Degree MSN

Available Programs Master's.

Concentrations Available *Nurse practitioner programs in:* adult health, gerontology, women's health.

Study Options Full-time and part-time.

Program Entrance Requirements Clinical experience, minimum overall college GPA of 3.0, CPR certification, immunizations, interview, nursing research course, physical assessment course, professional liability insurance/malpractice insurance, statistics course.

Degree Requirements 42 total credit hours, thesis or project.

POST-MASTER'S PROGRAM

Areas of Study *Nurse practitioner programs in:* adult health, gerontology, women's health.

DOCTORAL DEGREE PROGRAM

Degree PhD

Program Entrance Requirements Minimum overall college GPA of 3.5, 3 letters of recommendation, MSN or equivalent.

Degree Requirements 90 total credit hours, dissertation, oral exam, written exam.

CONTINUING EDUCATION PROGRAM

Contact *Telephone:* 850-599-3017. *Fax:* 850-599-3508.

Florida Atlantic University
Christine E. Lynn College of Nursing
Boca Raton, Florida

http://www.fau.edu/nursing
Founded in 1961

DEGREES • BS • MS • MSN/MBA • PHD

Nursing Program Faculty 73 (49% with doctorates).

Baccalaureate Enrollment 528
Women 85% **Men** 15% **Minority** 40% **International** 5% **Part-time** 40%

Graduate Enrollment 515
Women 89% **Men** 11% **Minority** 39% **International** 2% **Part-time** 85%

Distance Learning Courses Available.

Nursing Student Activities Sigma Theta Tau, Student Nurses' Association.

Nursing Student Resources Academic advising; academic or career counseling; assistance for students with disabilities; bookstore; campus computer network; computer lab; computer-assisted instruction; e-mail services; housing assistance; interactive nursing skills videos; Internet; learning resource lab; library services; nursing audiovisuals; remedial services; skills, simulation, or other laboratory; tutoring.

Library Facilities 1.3 million volumes (17,825 in health, 4,889 in nursing); 12,811 periodical subscriptions (333 health-care related).

BACCALAUREATE PROGRAMS

Degree BS

Available Programs Accelerated Baccalaureate for Second Degree; Generic Baccalaureate; RN Baccalaureate.

Site Options Port St. Lucie, FL; Davie, FL.

Study Options Full-time.

Program Entrance Requirements Minimum overall college GPA of 3.0, transcript of college record, CPR certification, health exam, health insurance, high school transcript, immunizations, minimum GPA in nursing prerequisites of 2.0, professional liability insurance/malpractice insurance, prerequisite course work. Transfer students are accepted. *Application deadline:* 11/30 (fall). *Application fee:* $30.

Advanced Placement Credit by examination available. Credit given for nursing courses completed elsewhere dependent upon specific evaluations.

Expenses (2009–10) *Tuition, state resident:* full-time $1680; part-time $840 per semester. *Tuition, nonresident:* full-time $7008; part-time $3500 per semester. *International tuition:* $7008 full-time. *Room and board:* $9500; room only: $5000 per academic year. *Required fees:* full-time $300; part-time $100 per term.

Financial Aid 75% of baccalaureate students in nursing programs received some form of financial aid in 2008–09. *Gift aid (need-based):* Federal Pell, FSEOG, state, private, college/university gift aid from institutional funds, Federal Nursing. *Loans:* FFEL (Subsidized and Unsubsidized Stafford PLUS), Perkins, college/university. *Work-study:* Federal Work-Study, part-time campus jobs. *Financial aid application deadline (priority):* 3/1.

Contact Ms. Mary Ellen Wright, Interim Director, Undergraduate Programs, Christine E. Lynn College of Nursing, Florida Atlantic University, 777 Glades Road, Boca Raton, FL 33431. *Telephone:* 561-297-2535. *Fax:* 561-297-3652. *E-mail:* mehodges@fau.edu.

GRADUATE PROGRAMS

Expenses (2009–10) *Tuition, state resident:* full-time $7055; part-time $294 per credit hour. *Tuition, nonresident:* full-time $22,095; part-time $921 per credit hour. *International tuition:* $22,095 full-time. *Room and board:* $9500; room only: $5000 per academic year. *Required fees:* full-time $1500; part-time $500 per term.

Financial Aid 15% of graduate students in nursing programs received some form of financial aid in 2008–09. Research assistantships with partial tuition reimbursements available, teaching assistantships with partial tuition reimbursements available, career-related internships or fieldwork, Federal Work-Study, institutionally sponsored loans, scholarships, and traineeships available. Aid available to part-time students.

Contact Dr. Shirley Gordon, Masters Program Director, Christine E. Lynn College of Nursing, Florida Atlantic University, 777 Glades Road, Boca Raton, FL 33431. *Telephone:* 561-297-3389. *Fax:* 561-297-3652. *E-mail:* sgordon@fau.edu.

MASTER'S DEGREE PROGRAM

Degrees MS; MSN/MBA

Available Programs Master's; Master's for Nurses with Non-Nursing Degrees; RN to Master's.

Concentrations Available Clinical nurse leader; nursing administration; nursing education. *Nurse practitioner programs in:* adult health, family health, gerontology.

Site Options Port St. Lucie, FL; Davie, FL.

Online Degree Options Yes.

Program Entrance Requirements Minimum overall college GPA of 3.0, transcript of college record, CPR certification, written essay, immunizations, interview, 2 letters of recommendation, nursing research course, physical assessment course, professional liability insurance/malpractice insurance, prerequisite course work, resume, statistics course, GRE General Test. *Application deadline:* 6/1 (fall), 10/1 (spring), 2/1 (summer). *Application fee:* $30.

Degree Requirements 30 total credit hours.

POST-MASTER'S PROGRAM

Areas of Study Clinical nurse leader; nursing administration; nursing education. *Nurse practitioner programs in:* adult health, family health, gerontology.

Florida Atlantic University (continued)

DOCTORAL DEGREE PROGRAM

Degree PhD

Available Programs Doctorate; Post-Baccalaureate Doctorate.

Areas of Study Aging, bio-behavioral research, gerontology, human health and illness, individualized study, nursing administration, nursing research, nursing science.

Program Entrance Requirements Minimum overall college GPA of 3.5, interview by faculty committee, interview, 3 letters of recommendation, MSN or equivalent, scholarly papers, statistics course, vita, writing sample, GRE General Test. Application deadline: 2/28 (fall). Application fee: $30.

Degree Requirements 62 total credit hours, dissertation, oral exam, written exam, residency.

CONTINUING EDUCATION PROGRAM

Contact Dr. Beth King, Director, Christine E. Lynn College of Nursing, Florida Atlantic University, 777 Glades Road, Boca Raton, FL 33431. *Telephone:* 561-297-3887. *Fax:* 561-297-3652. *E-mail:* bking@fau.edu.

Florida Gulf Coast University

School of Nursing
Fort Myers, Florida

http://www.fgcu.edu/chp/nursing/

Founded in 1991

DEGREES • BSN • MSN

Nursing Program Faculty 21 (57% with doctorates).

Baccalaureate Enrollment 192
Women 96.5% **Men** 3.5% **Minority** 29.5% **International** 7%

Graduate Enrollment 48
Women 96% **Men** 4% **Minority** 12.5% **Part-time** 21%

Nursing Student Activities Sigma Theta Tau, Student Nurses' Association.

Nursing Student Resources Academic advising; academic or career counseling; assistance for students with disabilities; bookstore; campus computer network; career placement assistance; computer lab; computer-assisted instruction; e-mail services; employment services for current students; Internet; library services; nursing audiovisuals; skills, simulation, or other laboratory; tutoring.

Library Facilities 387,860 volumes (13,943 in health, 6,742 in nursing); 8,007 periodical subscriptions (471 health-care related).

BACCALAUREATE PROGRAMS

Degree BSN

Available Programs ADN to Baccalaureate; Generic Baccalaureate.

Study Options Full-time.

Online Degree Options Yes.

Program Entrance Requirements Minimum overall college GPA of 3.0, transcript of college record, CPR certification, health insurance, high school foreign language, immunizations, minimum GPA in nursing prerequisites of 3.0, professional liability insurance/malpractice insurance, prerequisite course work. Transfer students are accepted.

Advanced Placement Credit by examination available. Credit given for nursing courses completed elsewhere dependent upon specific evaluations.

Contact *Telephone:* 239-590-7455. *Fax:* 239-590-7474.

GRADUATE PROGRAMS

Contact *Telephone:* 239-590-7518. *Fax:* 239-590-7474.

MASTER'S DEGREE PROGRAM

Degree MSN

Available Programs Master's.

Concentrations Available Nurse anesthesia; nursing education. *Nurse practitioner programs in:* acute care, adult health, family health.

Study Options Full-time and part-time.

Program Entrance Requirements Minimum overall college GPA of 3.0, physical assessment course, resume, statistics course.

Advanced Placement Credit given for nursing courses completed elsewhere dependent upon specific evaluations.

POST-MASTER'S PROGRAM

Areas of Study *Nurse practitioner programs in:* family health.

CONTINUING EDUCATION PROGRAM

Contact *Telephone:* 239-590-7513. *Fax:* 239-590-7474.

Florida Hospital College of Health Sciences

Department of Nursing
Orlando, Florida

http://www.fhchs.edu/

Founded in 1913

DEGREE • BS

Nursing Program Faculty 12 (16% with doctorates).

Nursing Student Resources Campus computer network; computer lab; computer-assisted instruction; Internet; learning resource lab; library services; nursing audiovisuals; skills, simulation, or other laboratory.

Library Facilities 74,581 volumes; 158 periodical subscriptions.

BACCALAUREATE PROGRAMS

Degree BS

Available Programs Generic Baccalaureate; RN Baccalaureate.

Study Options Full-time and part-time.

Program Entrance Requirements Minimum overall college GPA of 2.5, transcript of college record, health exam, 1 letter of recommendation, prerequisite course work, RN licensure. Transfer students are accepted.

Advanced Placement Credit by examination available. Credit given for nursing courses completed elsewhere dependent upon specific evaluations.

Contact *Telephone:* 407-303-9798. *Fax:* 407-303-9408.

Florida International University

Nursing Program
Miami, Florida

http://www.fiu.edu

Founded in 1965

DEGREES • BSN • MSN • PHD

Nursing Program Faculty 77 (29% with doctorates).

Baccalaureate Enrollment 474
Women 73% **Men** 27% **Minority** 88% **International** 1% **Part-time** 25%

Graduate Enrollment 395
Women 82% **Men** 18% **Minority** 74% **International** 1% **Part-time** 60%

Distance Learning Courses Available.

Nursing Student Activities Sigma Theta Tau, Student Nurses' Association.

Nursing Student Resources Academic advising; academic or career counseling; assistance for students with disabilities; bookstore; campus computer network; career placement assistance; computer lab; computer-assisted instruction; daycare for children of students; e-mail services; externships; housing assistance; interactive nursing skills videos; Internet; learning resource lab; library services; nursing audiovisuals; paid internships; remedial services; resume preparation assistance; skills, simulation, or other laboratory; tutoring.

Library Facilities 2 million volumes (25,000 in health, 3,300 in nursing); 40,813 periodical subscriptions (1,500 health-care related).

BACCALAUREATE PROGRAMS

Degree BSN

Available Programs Accelerated Baccalaureate for Second Degree; Generic Baccalaureate; RN Baccalaureate.

Site Options St. Petersburg, FL; North Miami, FL.

Study Options Full-time.

Online Degree Options Yes.

Program Entrance Requirements Minimum overall college GPA of 3.0, transcript of college record, CPR certification, written essay, health exam, health insurance, high school foreign language, high school transcript, immunizations, minimum GPA in nursing prerequisites of 3.0, prerequisite course work. Transfer students are accepted. *Application deadline:* 5/15 (fall), 2/15 (summer). *Application fee:* $30.

Advanced Placement Credit by examination available. Credit given for nursing courses completed elsewhere dependent upon specific evaluations.

Expenses (2009–10) *Tuition, state resident:* full-time $4004; part-time $128 per credit. *Tuition, nonresident:* full-time $16,782; part-time $542 per credit. *International tuition:* $16,782 full-time. *Room and board:* $16,000; room only: $10,000 per academic year. *Required fees:* full-time $1500; part-time $62 per credit; part-time $500 per term.

Financial Aid 75% of baccalaureate students in nursing programs received some form of financial aid in 2008–09.

Contact Diane M. Loffredo, Director for Admissions and Student Services, Nursing Program, Florida International University, 11200 SW 8th Street, Modesto A. Maidique Campus, HLS 2, RM 482, Miami, FL 33199. *Telephone:* 305-348-7717. *Fax:* 305-348-7764. *E-mail:* dloffred@fiu.edu.

GRADUATE PROGRAMS

Expenses (2009–10) *Tuition, state resident:* full-time $9174; part-time $341 per credit. *Tuition, nonresident:* full-time $22,822; part-time $845 per credit. *International tuition:* $22,822 full-time. *Room and board:* $16,000; room only: $10,000 per academic year. *Required fees:* full-time $1600; part-time $65 per credit; part-time $600 per term.

Financial Aid 60% of graduate students in nursing programs received some form of financial aid in 2008–09. Research assistantships, teaching assistantships, institutionally sponsored loans and scholarships available. *Financial aid application deadline:* 3/1.

Contact Diane M. Loffredo, Director for Admissions and Student Services, Nursing Program, Florida International University, 11200 SW 8th Street, Modesto A. Maidique Campus, HLS 2, RM 482, Miami, FL 33199. *Telephone:* 305-348-7717. *Fax:* 305-348-7764. *E-mail:* dloffred@fiu.edu.

MASTER'S DEGREE PROGRAM

Degree MSN

Available Programs Accelerated AD/RN to Master's; Master's; Master's for Nurses with Non-Nursing Degrees.

Concentrations Available Nurse anesthesia; nursing administration; nursing education. *Nurse practitioner programs in:* adult health, family health, pediatric.

Study Options Full-time and part-time.

Program Entrance Requirements Clinical experience, computer literacy, minimum overall college GPA of 3.0, transcript of college record, CPR certification, written essay, immunizations, interview, 3 letters of recommendation, nursing research course, physical assessment course, professional liability insurance/malpractice insurance, prerequisite course work, resume, statistics course. *Application deadline:* 6/1 (fall), 10/1 (spring), 3/1 (summer). *Application fee:* $30.

Advanced Placement Credit given for nursing courses completed elsewhere dependent upon specific evaluations.

Degree Requirements 43 total credit hours.

POST-MASTER'S PROGRAM

Areas of Study Nursing administration; nursing education. *Nurse practitioner programs in:* adult health, family health, pediatric.

DOCTORAL DEGREE PROGRAM

Degree PhD

Available Programs Doctorate.

Areas of Study Faculty preparation, health policy, health-care systems, individualized study, nursing administration, nursing education, nursing policy, nursing research, nursing science.

Program Entrance Requirements Clinical experience, minimum overall college GPA of 3.0, interview by faculty committee, 3 letters of recommendation, MSN or equivalent, statistics course, writing sample, GRE. Application deadline: Applications may be processed on a rolling basis for some programs. Application fee: $30.

Degree Requirements 84 total credit hours, dissertation, oral exam, written exam.

Florida Southern College
Department of Nursing
Lakeland, Florida

http://www.flsouthern.edu/academics/nursing/

Founded in 1885

DEGREES • BSN • MSN

Nursing Program Faculty 6 (100% with doctorates).

Baccalaureate Enrollment 24
Women 87% **Men** 13% **Minority** 22% **International** 8%

Graduate Enrollment 43
Women 90% **Men** 10% **Minority** 20% **Part-time** 98%

Nursing Student Activities Sigma Theta Tau, Student Nurses' Association.

Nursing Student Resources Academic advising; academic or career counseling; assistance for students with disabilities; bookstore; campus computer network; career placement assistance; computer lab; computer-assisted instruction; e-mail services; externships; interactive nursing skills videos; Internet; learning resource lab; library services; nursing audiovisuals; paid internships; placement services for program completers; remedial services; resume preparation assistance; skills, simulation, or other laboratory; tutoring.

Library Facilities 166,595 volumes (4,000 in health, 3,500 in nursing); 31,092 periodical subscriptions (12 health-care related).

BACCALAUREATE PROGRAMS

Degree BSN

Available Programs ADN to Baccalaureate; Generic Baccalaureate.

Study Options Full-time.

Program Entrance Requirements Minimum overall college GPA of 3.2, transcript of college record, CPR certification, health exam, immunizations, minimum high school GPA of 3.2, minimum GPA in nursing prerequisites of 3.0, prerequisite course work. Transfer students are accepted. *Application deadline:* 3/1 (spring).

Advanced Placement Credit given for nursing courses completed elsewhere dependent upon specific evaluations.

Expenses (2008–09) *Tuition:* full-time $22,000; part-time $11,000 per semester. *International tuition:* $22,000 full-time. *Room and board:* $3500 per academic year. *Required fees:* full-time $400; part-time $200 per term.

Financial Aid 100% of baccalaureate students in nursing programs received some form of financial aid in 2007–08. *Gift aid (need-based):* Federal Pell, FSEOG, state, private, college/university gift aid from institutional funds. *Loans:* FFEL (Subsidized and Unsubsidized Stafford PLUS), Perkins. *Work-study:* Federal Work-Study, part-time campus jobs. *Financial aid application deadline:* 7/1 (priority: 3/1).

Contact Dr. Marcia Posey, Undergraduate Coordinator, Department of Nursing, Florida Southern College, 111 Lake Hollingsworth Drive, Lakeland, FL 33801. *Telephone:* 863-680-4315. *Fax:* 863-680-3860. *E-mail:* mposey@flsouthern.edu.

GRADUATE PROGRAMS

Expenses (2008–09) *Tuition:* full-time $13,850; part-time $355 per credit hour. *International tuition:* $13,850 full-time.

Financial Aid 40% of graduate students in nursing programs received some form of financial aid in 2007–08.

Contact Dr. Annette Kelly, Graduate Nursing Coordinator, Department of Nursing, Florida Southern College, 111 Lake Hollingsworth Drive, Lakeland, FL 33801. *Telephone:* 863-680-3882. *Fax:* 863-680-3860. *E-mail:* akelly@flsouthern.edu.

Florida Southern College (continued)

MASTER'S DEGREE PROGRAM

Degree MSN

Available Programs Accelerated AD/RN to Master's; Master's; Master's for Nurses with Non-Nursing Degrees.

Concentrations Available Nursing education. *Clinical nurse specialist programs in:* adult health. *Nurse practitioner programs in:* adult health.

Study Options Full-time and part-time.

Program Entrance Requirements Computer literacy, minimum overall college GPA of 3.0, transcript of college record, written essay, immunizations, 3 letters of recommendation, nursing research course, physical assessment course, resume, statistics course. *Application deadline:* 6/1 (fall), 11/1 (spring). *Application fee:* $30.

Advanced Placement Credit given for nursing courses completed elsewhere dependent upon specific evaluations.

Degree Requirements 39 total credit hours, thesis or project.

POST-MASTER'S PROGRAM

Areas of Study Nursing education. *Clinical nurse specialist programs in:* adult health.

CONTINUING EDUCATION PROGRAM

Contact Ms. Deborah Stanley, Assistant Director, Evening Program, Department of Nursing, Florida Southern College, 111 Lake Hollingsworth Drive, Lakeland, FL 33801. *Telephone:* 863-680-4205. *Fax:* 863-680-3872. *E-mail:* dstanley@flsouthern.edu.

Florida State University
College of Nursing
Tallahassee, Florida

http://nursing.fsu.edu

Founded in 1851

DEGREES • BSN • DNP • MSN

Nursing Program Faculty 46 (39% with doctorates).

Baccalaureate Enrollment 331
Women 92% **Men** 8% **Minority** 26% **International** 2% **Part-time** 22%

Graduate Enrollment 118
Women 96% **Men** 4% **Minority** 15% **Part-time** 95%

Distance Learning Courses Available.

Nursing Student Activities Sigma Theta Tau, Student Nurses' Association.

Nursing Student Resources Academic advising; academic or career counseling; assistance for students with disabilities; bookstore; campus computer network; career placement assistance; computer lab; computer-assisted instruction; e-mail services; housing assistance; interactive nursing skills videos; Internet; learning resource lab; library services; nursing audiovisuals; resume preparation assistance; skills, simulation, or other laboratory; tutoring; unpaid internships.

BACCALAUREATE PROGRAMS

Degree BSN

Available Programs Accelerated Baccalaureate; Generic Baccalaureate; RN Baccalaureate.

Site Options Panama City, FL; Marianna, FL.

Study Options Full-time.

Online Degree Options Yes.

Program Entrance Requirements Minimum overall college GPA of 3.0, transcript of college record, CPR certification, health exam, health insurance, high school foreign language, immunizations, minimum GPA in nursing prerequisites of 3.0, professional liability insurance/malpractice insurance, prerequisite course work. Transfer students are accepted. *Application deadline:* 2/1 (fall).

Advanced Placement Credit given for nursing courses completed elsewhere dependent upon specific evaluations.

Expenses (2009–10) *Tuition, state resident:* full-time $3690; part-time $123 per credit hour. *Tuition, nonresident:* full-time $18,120; part-time $604 per credit hour. *International tuition:* $18,120 full-time. *Room and board:* $9000; room only: $6000 per academic year. *Required fees:* full-time $1740; part-time $58 per credit; part-time $870 per term.

Financial Aid 93% of baccalaureate students in nursing programs received some form of financial aid in 2008–09. *Gift aid (need-based):* Federal Pell, FSEOG, state, private, college/university gift aid from institutional funds, Academic Competitiveness Grant, National Smart Grant. *Loans:* FFEL (Subsidized and Unsubsidized Stafford PLUS), Perkins, college/university. *Work-study:* Federal Work-Study, part-time campus jobs. *Financial aid application deadline:* Continuous.

Contact Ms. Brenda Pereira, Director of Student Services, College of Nursing, Florida State University, 98 Varsity Way, 103 SCN, Tallahassee, FL 32306-4310. *Telephone:* 850-644-5638. *Fax:* 850-645-7249. *E-mail:* bpereira@fsu.edu.

GRADUATE PROGRAMS

Expenses (2009–10) *Tuition, state resident:* full-time $7392; part-time $308 per credit hour. *Tuition, nonresident:* full-time $22,560; part-time $940 per credit hour. *International tuition:* $22,560 full-time. *Room and board:* $9000; room only: $6000 per academic year. *Required fees:* full-time $3696.

Financial Aid 97% of graduate students in nursing programs received some form of financial aid in 2008–09. Fellowships with partial tuition reimbursements available (averaging $6,300 per year), research assistantships with partial tuition reimbursements available (averaging $3,000 per year), 3 teaching assistantships with partial tuition reimbursements available (averaging $3,000 per year) were awarded; career-related internships or fieldwork, Federal Work-Study, institutionally sponsored loans, scholarships, traineeships, and tuition waivers (partial) also available. *Financial aid application deadline:* 4/15.

Contact Ms. Brenda Pereira, Director of Student Services, College of Nursing, Florida State University, 98 Varsity Way, 103 SCN, Tallahassee, FL 32306-4310. *Telephone:* 850-644-5638. *Fax:* 850-645-7249. *E-mail:* bpereira@fsu.edu.

MASTER'S DEGREE PROGRAM

Degree MSN

Available Programs Master's.

Concentrations Available Nursing education.

Study Options Full-time and part-time.

Online Degree Options Yes (online only).

Program Entrance Requirements Minimum overall college GPA of 3.0, transcript of college record, CPR certification, immunizations, 2 letters of recommendation, professional liability insurance/malpractice insurance, GRE General Test. *Application deadline:* 7/1 (fall).

Advanced Placement Credit given for nursing courses completed elsewhere dependent upon specific evaluations.

Degree Requirements 38 total credit hours.

POST-MASTER'S PROGRAM

Areas of Study Nursing education.

DOCTORAL DEGREE PROGRAM

Degree DNP

Available Programs Doctorate.

Areas of Study Family health, health-care systems.

Program Entrance Requirements Minimum overall college GPA of 3.0, 2 letters of recommendation. Application deadline: 4/15 (fall).

Degree Requirements 90 total credit hours, residency.

Indian River State College
Bachelor of Science in Nursing Program
Fort Pierce, Florida

Founded in 1960

DEGREE • BSN

Library Facilities 58,657 volumes; 554 periodical subscriptions.

BACCALAUREATE PROGRAMS

Degree BSN

Available Programs RN Baccalaureate.

Contact Nursing Program, Bachelor of Science in Nursing Program, Indian River State College, 3209 Virginia Avenue, Fort Pierce, FL 34981-5596. *Telephone:* 772-462-7415.

Jacksonville University

School of Nursing
Jacksonville, Florida

http://www.jacksonville.edu

Founded in 1934

DEGREES • BSN • MSN • MSN/MBA

Nursing Program Faculty 29 (48% with doctorates).

Baccalaureate Enrollment 714
Women 90% **Men** 10% **Minority** 33% **International** 1% **Part-time** 77%

Graduate Enrollment 63
Women 87% **Men** 13% **Minority** 37%

Distance Learning Courses Available.

Nursing Student Activities Nursing Honor Society, Sigma Theta Tau, Student Nurses' Association, nursing club.

Nursing Student Resources Academic advising; academic or career counseling; assistance for students with disabilities; bookstore; campus computer network; career placement assistance; computer lab; computer-assisted instruction; e-mail services; employment services for current students; externships; interactive nursing skills videos; Internet; learning resource lab; library services; nursing audiovisuals; placement services for program completers; remedial services; resume preparation assistance; skills, simulation, or other laboratory; tutoring; unpaid internships.

Library Facilities 385,016 volumes; 686 periodical subscriptions.

BACCALAUREATE PROGRAMS

Degree BSN

Available Programs ADN to Baccalaureate; Accelerated Baccalaureate; Accelerated Baccalaureate for Second Degree; Baccalaureate for Second Degree; Generic Baccalaureate.

Site Options Jacksonville, FL.

Study Options Full-time.

Online Degree Options Yes.

Program Entrance Requirements Minimum overall college GPA of 2.5, transcript of college record, CPR certification, written essay, health exam, health insurance, immunizations, interview, 3 letters of recommendation, minimum GPA in nursing prerequisites of 2.5, prerequisite course work. Transfer students are accepted. *Application deadline:* 4/1 (fall), 12/1 (summer). *Application fee:* $15.

Advanced Placement Credit given for nursing courses completed elsewhere dependent upon specific evaluations.

Expenses (2009–10) *Tuition:* full-time $25,300; part-time $410 per credit hour. *International tuition:* $25,300 full-time. *Room and board:* $9060; room only: $5300 per academic year.

Financial Aid 92% of baccalaureate students in nursing programs received some form of financial aid in 2008–09. *Gift aid (need-based):* Federal Pell, FSEOG, state, private, college/university gift aid from institutional funds, Academic Competitiveness Grant, National Smart Grant. *Loans:* FFEL (Subsidized and Unsubsidized Stafford PLUS), Perkins, state, college/university. *Work-study:* Federal Work-Study. *Financial aid application deadline (priority):* 3/15.

Contact Mr. Chris Rillstone, Enrollment Coordinator, School of Nursing, Jacksonville University, 2800 University Boulevard North, Jacksonville, FL 32211. *Telephone:* 904-256-7286. *Fax:* 904-256-7287. *E-mail:* crillst@ju.edu.

GRADUATE PROGRAMS

Expenses (2009–10) *Tuition:* full-time $7614; part-time $423 per credit hour. *International tuition:* $7614 full-time. *Room and board:* $9060; room only: $5300 per academic year.

Financial Aid 59% of graduate students in nursing programs received some form of financial aid in 2008–09.

Contact Ms. Laura Winn, Graduate Program Advisor, School of Nursing, Jacksonville University, 2800 University Boulevard North, Jacksonville, FL 32211. *Telephone:* 904-256-7034. *Fax:* 904-256-7287. *E-mail:* lwinn@ju.edu.

MASTER'S DEGREE PROGRAM

Degrees MSN; MSN/MBA

Available Programs Master's; RN to Master's.

Concentrations Available Nursing administration; nursing education. *Nurse practitioner programs in:* family health.

Site Options Jacksonville, FL.

Study Options Full-time and part-time.

Program Entrance Requirements Clinical experience, minimum overall college GPA of 3.0, transcript of college record, CPR certification, written essay, immunizations, interview, 3 letters of recommendation, prerequisite course work, resume. *Application deadline:* 4/30 (fall). Applications may be processed on a rolling basis for some programs. *Application fee:* $30.

Advanced Placement Credit given for nursing courses completed elsewhere dependent upon specific evaluations.

Degree Requirements 46 total credit hours, thesis or project, comprehensive exam.

POST-MASTER'S PROGRAM

Areas of Study *Nurse practitioner programs in:* family health.

Nova Southeastern University

College of Allied Health and Nursing
Fort Lauderdale, Florida

Founded in 1964

DEGREES • BSN • MSN • MSN/MBA

Library Facilities 725,000 volumes; 22,295 periodical subscriptions.

BACCALAUREATE PROGRAMS

Degree BSN

Available Programs Generic Baccalaureate; RN Baccalaureate.

Study Options Full-time.

Program Entrance Requirements Minimum overall college GPA of 2.75, transcript of college record, written essay, health exam, immunizations, 2 letters of recommendation, prerequisite course work.

Contact *Telephone:* 800-356-0026 Ext. 1983. *Fax:* 954-262-1036.

GRADUATE PROGRAMS

Contact *Telephone:* 954-262-1956. *Fax:* 954-262-1036.

MASTER'S DEGREE PROGRAM

Degrees MSN; MSN/MBA

Available Programs Master's.

Concentrations Available Nursing administration; nursing education.

Study Options Full-time and part-time.

Program Entrance Requirements Minimum overall college GPA of 3.0, transcript of college record, 3 letters of recommendation, GRE General Test.

Degree Requirements 42 total credit hours, thesis or project.

DOCTORAL DEGREE PROGRAM

Program Entrance Requirements GRE General Test.

Palm Beach Atlantic University

School of Nursing
West Palm Beach, Florida

Founded in 1968

DEGREE • BSN

Nursing Student Activities Student Nurses' Association.

Palm Beach Atlantic University (continued)
Library Facilities 147,514 volumes; 332 periodical subscriptions.

BACCALAUREATE PROGRAMS

Degree BSN

Available Programs RN Baccalaureate.
Program Entrance Requirements RN licensure.
Contact *Telephone:* 561-803-2825. *Fax:* 561-803-2828.

St. Petersburg College
Department of Nursing
St. Petersburg, Florida

http://www.spcollege.edu
Founded in 1927
DEGREE • BSN

Nursing Program Faculty 20 (60% with doctorates).
Baccalaureate Enrollment 442
Women 88% **Men** 12% **Minority** 26% **International** 6%
Distance Learning Courses Available.
Nursing Student Activities Sigma Theta Tau, Student Nurses' Association, nursing club.
Nursing Student Resources Academic advising; academic or career counseling; assistance for students with disabilities; bookstore; campus computer network; computer lab; computer-assisted instruction; e-mail services; employment services for current students; interactive nursing skills videos; Internet; learning resource lab; library services; nursing audiovisuals; paid internships; remedial services; resume preparation assistance; skills, simulation, or other laboratory; tutoring; unpaid internships.
Library Facilities 222,990 volumes (1,000 in health, 1,000 in nursing); 1,393 periodical subscriptions (375 health-care related).

BACCALAUREATE PROGRAMS

Degree BSN

Available Programs ADN to Baccalaureate; RN Baccalaureate.
Site Options Pinellas Park, FL; Tarpon Springs, FL.
Study Options Full-time.
Online Degree Options Yes.
Program Entrance Requirements Minimum overall college GPA of 2.0, transcript of college record, high school transcript, RN licensure. Transfer students are accepted. *Application deadline:* Applications may be processed on a rolling basis for some programs. *Application fee:* $40.
Advanced Placement Credit given for nursing courses completed elsewhere dependent upon specific evaluations.
Expenses (2009–10) *Tuition, state resident:* part-time $95 per credit hour. *Tuition, nonresident:* part-time $364 per credit hour.
Financial Aid 80% of baccalaureate students in nursing programs received some form of financial aid in 2008–09. *Gift aid (need-based):* Federal Pell, FSEOG, state, private, college/university gift aid from institutional funds. *Loans:* FFEL (Subsidized and Unsubsidized Stafford PLUS), college/university. *Work-study:* Federal Work-Study. *Financial aid application deadline (priority):* 4/15.
Contact Dr. Jean M. Wortock, Dean, Department of Nursing, St. Petersburg College, PO Box 13489, St. Petersburg, FL 33733. *Telephone:* 727-341-3640. *Fax:* 727-341-3646. *E-mail:* Wortock.Jean@spcollege.edu.

CONTINUING EDUCATION PROGRAM

Contact Denise Kerwin, Program Director, Department of Nursing, St. Petersburg College, PO Box 13489, St. Petersburg, FL 33733. *Telephone:* 727-341-3374. *Fax:* 727-341-4197. *E-mail:* kerwin.denise@spcollege.edu.

South University
Nursing Program
West Palm Beach, Florida

http://www.southuniversity.edu/campus/campus_programs.asp?plid=4&id=2
Founded in 1899
DEGREES • BSN • MSN

Nursing Program Faculty 89 (50% with doctorates).
Baccalaureate Enrollment 1,150
Women 93% **Men** 7% **Minority** 40%
Graduate Enrollment 212
Women 93% **Men** 7% **Minority** 40%
Distance Learning Courses Available.
Nursing Student Activities Nursing Honor Society, Student Nurses' Association.
Nursing Student Resources Academic advising; academic or career counseling; assistance for students with disabilities; bookstore; campus computer network; career placement assistance; computer lab; computer-assisted instruction; e-mail services; externships; interactive nursing skills videos; Internet; learning resource lab; library services; nursing audiovisuals; placement services for program completers; remedial services; resume preparation assistance; skills, simulation, or other laboratory; tutoring.
Library Facilities 6,000 volumes in health, 2,000 volumes in nursing; 50 periodical subscriptions health-care related.

BACCALAUREATE PROGRAMS

Degree BSN

Available Programs Generic Baccalaureate; RN Baccalaureate.
Site Options Tampa, FL; West Palm Beach, FL; Columbia, SC.
Study Options Full-time.
Online Degree Options Yes.
Program Entrance Requirements Minimum overall college GPA of 2.5, transcript of college record, health exam, high school transcript, immunizations, minimum GPA in nursing prerequisites of 2.5, prerequisite course work. Transfer students are accepted.
Financial Aid 95% of baccalaureate students in nursing programs received some form of financial aid in 2008–09.
Contact Admissions, Nursing Program, South University, 709 Mall Boulevard, Savannah, GA 31406. *Telephone:* 800-688-0932.

GRADUATE PROGRAMS

Contact Admissions, Nursing Program, South University, 709 Mall Boulevard, Savannah, GA 31406-4805. *Telephone:* 888-444-3404.

MASTER'S DEGREE PROGRAM

Degree MSN

Available Programs Master's; RN to Master's.
Concentrations Available Nursing education.
Site Options West Palm Beach, FL.
Study Options Full-time and part-time.
Online Degree Options Yes.
Program Entrance Requirements Minimum overall college GPA of 2.7, transcript of college record, written essay, 3 letters of recommendation, nursing research course, prerequisite course work, resume, statistics course. *Application deadline:* Applications may be processed on a rolling basis for some programs.
Advanced Placement Credit given for nursing courses completed elsewhere dependent upon specific evaluations.
Degree Requirements 48 total credit hours, thesis or project.

University of Central Florida

School of Nursing
Orlando, Florida

---

http://www.cohpa.ucf.edu/nursing

Founded in 1963

DEGREES • BSN • MSN • PHD

Nursing Program Faculty 56 (43% with doctorates).

Baccalaureate Enrollment 379
Women 91% **Men** 9% **Minority** 25% **Part-time** 32%

Graduate Enrollment 136
Women 87% **Men** 13% **Minority** 10% **Part-time** 75%

Nursing Student Activities Sigma Theta Tau, Student Nurses' Association.

Nursing Student Resources Academic advising; academic or career counseling; assistance for students with disabilities; bookstore; campus computer network; computer lab; computer-assisted instruction; daycare for children of students; e-mail services; employment services for current students; externships; housing assistance; interactive nursing skills videos; Internet; learning resource lab; library services; nursing audiovisuals; skills, simulation, or other laboratory; tutoring.

Library Facilities 1.6 million volumes (38,944 in health, 2,848 in nursing); 18,012 periodical subscriptions (360 health-care related).

BACCALAUREATE PROGRAMS

Degree BSN

Available Programs Accelerated Baccalaureate for Second Degree; Generic Baccalaureate; RN Baccalaureate.

Study Options Full-time and part-time.

Program Entrance Requirements Minimum overall college GPA of 2.5, transcript of college record, CPR certification, health exam, health insurance, high school foreign language, high school math, high school transcript, immunizations, minimum high school GPA of 2.5, prerequisite course work. Transfer students are accepted.

Advanced Placement Credit given for nursing courses completed elsewhere dependent upon specific evaluations.

Contact *Telephone:* 407-823-2744. *Fax:* 407-823-5675.

GRADUATE PROGRAMS

Contact *Telephone:* 407-823-2744. *Fax:* 407-823-5675.

MASTER'S DEGREE PROGRAM

Degree MSN

Available Programs Master's; RN to Master's.

Concentrations Available Nurse case management; nursing administration; nursing education. *Clinical nurse specialist programs in:* acute care, critical care. *Nurse practitioner programs in:* adult health, family health, pediatric.

Study Options Full-time and part-time.

Program Entrance Requirements Clinical experience, minimum overall college GPA of 3.0, transcript of college record, CPR certification, written essay, immunizations, 3 letters of recommendation, physical assessment course, resume, statistics course.

Advanced Placement Credit given for nursing courses completed elsewhere dependent upon specific evaluations.

Degree Requirements 47 total credit hours, thesis or project.

POST-MASTER'S PROGRAM

Areas of Study *Nurse practitioner programs in:* adult health, family health, pediatric.

DOCTORAL DEGREE PROGRAM

Degree PhD

Available Programs Doctorate.

Areas of Study Health policy, health-care systems, individualized study, information systems, nursing research.

Program Entrance Requirements Minimum overall college GPA of 3.5, interview by faculty committee, 3 letters of recommendation, MSN or equivalent, statistics course, vita.

Degree Requirements 57 total credit hours, dissertation.

University of Florida

College of Nursing
Gainesville, Florida

---

http://www.nursing.ufl.edu

Founded in 1853

DEGREES • BSN • MSN • MSN/PHD • PHD

Nursing Program Faculty 62 (50% with doctorates).

Baccalaureate Enrollment 374
Women 94% **Men** 6% **Minority** 23% **International** 1%

Graduate Enrollment 364
Women 97% **Men** 3% **Minority** 17% **International** 1% **Part-time** 56%

Distance Learning Courses Available.

Nursing Student Activities Nursing Honor Society, Sigma Theta Tau, Student Nurses' Association.

Nursing Student Resources Academic advising; academic or career counseling; assistance for students with disabilities; bookstore; campus computer network; career placement assistance; computer lab; computer-assisted instruction; daycare for children of students; e-mail services; employment services for current students; housing assistance; interactive nursing skills videos; Internet; learning resource lab; library services; nursing audiovisuals; placement services for program completers; remedial services; resume preparation assistance; skills, simulation, or other laboratory; tutoring.

Library Facilities 5.3 million volumes (260,000 in health, 3,000 in nursing); 25,342 periodical subscriptions (200 health-care related).

BACCALAUREATE PROGRAMS

Degree BSN

Available Programs Accelerated Baccalaureate for Second Degree; Generic Baccalaureate.

Study Options Full-time.

Program Entrance Requirements Minimum overall college GPA of 2.8, transcript of college record, CPR certification, written essay, health exam, health insurance, high school biology, high school chemistry, high school foreign language, high school transcript, immunizations, 2 letters of recommendation, minimum GPA in nursing prerequisites of 2.8, prerequisite course work. Transfer students are accepted. *Application deadline:* 3/15 (fall), 1/15 (summer). *Application fee:* $30.

Advanced Placement Credit by examination available. Credit given for nursing courses completed elsewhere dependent upon specific evaluations.

Expenses (2009–10) *Tuition, state resident:* part-time $146 per credit hour. *Tuition, nonresident:* part-time $791 per credit hour. *Room and board:* $8330; room only: $7020 per academic year.

Financial Aid 90% of baccalaureate students in nursing programs received some form of financial aid in 2008–09.

Contact Mr. Kenneth H. Foote, Coordinator, Admissions and Registration, College of Nursing, University of Florida, PO Box 100197, HPNP Complex, Gainesville, FL 32610-0197. *Telephone:* 352-273-6383. *Fax:* 352-273-6440. *E-mail:* kfoote@ufl.edu.

GRADUATE PROGRAMS

Expenses (2009–10) *Tuition, state resident:* part-time $395 per credit hour. *Tuition, nonresident:* part-time $1120 per credit hour.

Financial Aid 59% of graduate students in nursing programs received some form of financial aid in 2008–09. 1 research assistantship with partial tuition reimbursement available (averaging $14,942 per year), 1 teaching assistantship with partial tuition reimbursement available (averaging $14,942 per year) were awarded; fellowships with partial tuition reimbursements available, career-related internships or fieldwork and Federal Work-Study also available. Aid available to part-time students.

University of Florida (continued)

Contact Ms. Cecile Kiley, Coordinator, Academic Support Services, College of Nursing, University of Florida, PO Box 100197, HPNP Complex, Gainesville, FL 32610-0197. *Telephone:* 352-273-6331. *Fax:* 352-273-6440. *E-mail:* ckiley@ufl.edu.

MASTER'S DEGREE PROGRAM

Degrees MSN; MSN/PhD

Available Programs Master's.

Concentrations Available Clinical nurse leader; nurse-midwifery. *Clinical nurse specialist programs in:* psychiatric/mental health, public health. *Nurse practitioner programs in:* acute care, adult health, family health, neonatal health, pediatric, psychiatric/mental health.

Site Options Jacksonville, FL.

Study Options Full-time and part-time.

Online Degree Options Yes.

Program Entrance Requirements Minimum overall college GPA of 3.0, transcript of college record, CPR certification, written essay, immunizations, 2 letters of recommendation, resume, GRE General Test. *Application deadline:* 3/15 (fall). Applications may be processed on a rolling basis for some programs. *Application fee:* $30.

Advanced Placement Credit given for nursing courses completed elsewhere dependent upon specific evaluations.

Degree Requirements 46 total credit hours, comprehensive exam.

POST-MASTER'S PROGRAM

Areas of Study Clinical nurse leader; nurse-midwifery. *Clinical nurse specialist programs in:* psychiatric/mental health, public health. *Nurse practitioner programs in:* acute care, adult health, family health, neonatal health, pediatric, psychiatric/mental health.

DOCTORAL DEGREE PROGRAM

Degree PhD

Available Programs Doctorate; Post-Baccalaureate Doctorate.

Areas of Study Aging, bio-behavioral research, health policy, nursing policy, nursing science, oncology, women's health.

Site Options Jacksonville, FL.

Online Degree Options Yes.

Program Entrance Requirements Minimum overall college GPA of 3.5, 3 letters of recommendation, MSN or equivalent, vita, writing sample, GRE General Test. Application deadline: 3/15 (fall). Applications may be processed on a rolling basis for some programs. Application fee: $30.

Degree Requirements 62 total credit hours, dissertation.

University of Miami
School of Nursing and Health Studies
Coral Gables, Florida

http://www.miami.edu/nur

Founded in 1925

DEGREES • BSN • DSN • MSN

Nursing Program Faculty 46 (37% with doctorates).

Baccalaureate Enrollment 405
Women 86.55% **Men** 13.45% **Minority** 55.86% **International** 4.14% **Part-time** 3.45%

Graduate Enrollment 85
Women 72% **Men** 28% **Minority** 53% **International** 1% **Part-time** 26.5%

Distance Learning Courses Available.

Nursing Student Activities Sigma Theta Tau, Student Nurses' Association.

Nursing Student Resources Academic advising; academic or career counseling; assistance for students with disabilities; bookstore; campus computer network; career placement assistance; computer lab; computer-assisted instruction; daycare for children of students; e-mail services; employment services for current students; externships; housing assistance; interactive nursing skills videos; Internet; learning resource lab; library

services; nursing audiovisuals; placement services for program completers; remedial services; resume preparation assistance; skills, simulation, or other laboratory; tutoring; unpaid internships.

Library Facilities 3.2 million volumes (2,000 in nursing); 62,621 periodical subscriptions (89 health-care related).

BACCALAUREATE PROGRAMS

Degree BSN

Available Programs Accelerated Baccalaureate for Second Degree; Baccalaureate for Second Degree; Generic Baccalaureate; RN Baccalaureate.

Study Options Full-time.

Program Entrance Requirements Minimum overall college GPA of 3.3, transcript of college record, health exam, health insurance, immunizations, 2 letters of recommendation, minimum GPA in nursing prerequisites of 3.0, professional liability insurance/malpractice insurance, prerequisite course work. Transfer students are accepted. *Application deadline:* 3/1 (spring). *Application fee:* $65.

Expenses (2009–10) *Tuition:* full-time $35,540; part-time $1480 per credit. *International tuition:* $35,540 full-time. *Room and board:* $11,698; room only: $7408 per academic year. *Required fees:* full-time $1390; part-time $140 per term.

Financial Aid *Gift aid (need-based):* Federal Pell, FSEOG, state, private, college/university gift aid from institutional funds, Federal Nursing, Academic Competitiveness Grant, National Smart Grant. *Loans:* Federal Nursing Student Loans, FFEL (Subsidized and Unsubsidized Stafford PLUS), Perkins, college/university, private alternative loans. *Work-study:* Federal Work-Study, part-time campus jobs. *Financial aid application deadline (priority):* 2/1.

Contact Ms. Deborah Paris, Assistant Dean for the Office of Student Services, School of Nursing and Health Studies, University of Miami, 5030 Brunson Drive, Coral Gables, FL 33143. *Telephone:* 305-284-4325. *Fax:* 305-284-4827. *E-mail:* dparis@miami.edu.

GRADUATE PROGRAMS

Expenses (2009–10) *Tuition:* full-time $26,640; part-time $1480 per credit. *International tuition:* $26,640 full-time. *Room and board:* $17,511; room only: $13,221 per academic year. *Required fees:* full-time $1044; part-time $770 per term.

Financial Aid 95% of graduate students in nursing programs received some form of financial aid in 2008–09. 1 fellowship (averaging $36,000 per year), 6 research assistantships with tuition reimbursements available (averaging $36,000 per year), 4 teaching assistantships with tuition reimbursements available (averaging $36,000 per year) were awarded; Federal Work-Study, institutionally sponsored loans, scholarships, and unspecified assistantships also available. Aid available to part-time students. *Financial aid application deadline:* 3/1.

Contact Mrs. Kathy Del Toro, Director of Graduate Studies, School of Nursing and Health Studies, University of Miami, PO Box 248153, M. Christine Schwartz Center, Room 152, Coral Gables, FL 33124-3850. *Telephone:* 305-284-4732. *Fax:* 305-284-4827. *E-mail:* kdeltoro@miami.edu.

MASTER'S DEGREE PROGRAM

Degree MSN

Available Programs Master's; Master's for Non-Nursing College Graduates.

Concentrations Available Nurse anesthesia; nursing education. *Nurse practitioner programs in:* acute care, family health.

Study Options Full-time and part-time.

Program Entrance Requirements Clinical experience, minimum overall college GPA of 3.0, transcript of college record, CPR certification, written essay, immunizations, interview, 3 letters of recommendation, prerequisite course work, resume, statistics course, GRE General Test. *Application deadline:* 7/15 (fall), 11/1 (spring). Applications may be processed on a rolling basis for some programs.

Degree Requirements 30 total credit hours.

POST-MASTER'S PROGRAM

Areas of Study *Nurse practitioner programs in:* acute care, family health.

DOCTORAL DEGREE PROGRAM

Degree DSN

Available Programs Doctorate; Post-Baccalaureate Doctorate.

Areas of Study Addiction/substance abuse, health policy, health promotion/disease prevention, maternity-newborn, nursing policy, nursing research.

Program Entrance Requirements Minimum overall college GPA of 3.0, interview by faculty committee, interview, 3 letters of recommendation, MSN or equivalent, statistics course, vita, writing sample, GRE General Test. Application deadline: 3/17 (fall). Applications may be processed on a rolling basis for some programs.

Degree Requirements 60 total credit hours, dissertation, written exam, residency.

CONTINUING EDUCATION PROGRAM

Contact Ms. Deborah Paris, Assistant Dean, School of Nursing and Health Studies, University of Miami, PO Box 248153, M. Christine Schwartz Center, Room 152, Coral Gables, FL 33124-3850. *Telephone:* 305-284-4325. *Fax:* 305-284-4827. *E-mail:* dparis@miami.edu.

University of North Florida
School of Nursing
Jacksonville, Florida

http://www.unf.edu/coh/cohnursi.htm

Founded in 1965

DEGREES • BSN • MSN

Nursing Program Faculty 19 (50% with doctorates).

Baccalaureate Enrollment 279
Women 85% **Men** 15% **Minority** 20% **International** 1% **Part-time** 27%

Graduate Enrollment 35
Women 86% **Men** 14% **Minority** 6% **Part-time** 70%

Nursing Student Activities Sigma Theta Tau, Student Nurses' Association.

Nursing Student Resources Academic advising; academic or career counseling; assistance for students with disabilities; bookstore; campus computer network; career placement assistance; computer lab; computer-assisted instruction; e-mail services; interactive nursing skills videos; Internet; learning resource lab; library services; nursing audiovisuals; resume preparation assistance; skills, simulation, or other laboratory.

Library Facilities 957,625 volumes (30,466 in health, 3,000 in nursing); 3,979 periodical subscriptions (200 health-care related).

BACCALAUREATE PROGRAMS

Degree BSN

Available Programs Accelerated Baccalaureate for Second Degree; Generic Baccalaureate; RN Baccalaureate.

Study Options Full-time.

Program Entrance Requirements Minimum overall college GPA of 2.7, CPR certification, written essay, health exam, immunizations, interview, minimum high school GPA, minimum GPA in nursing prerequisites of 3.0, professional liability insurance/malpractice insurance, prerequisite course work. Transfer students are accepted.

Advanced Placement Credit given for nursing courses completed elsewhere dependent upon specific evaluations.

Contact *Telephone:* 904-620-2418.

GRADUATE PROGRAMS

Contact *Telephone:* 904-620-2684. *Fax:* 904-620-2848.

MASTER'S DEGREE PROGRAM

Degree MSN

Available Programs Master's; RN to Master's.

Concentrations Available *Clinical nurse specialist programs in:* adult health, cardiovascular, community health, critical care, gerontology, maternity-newborn, medical-surgical, pediatric, psychiatric/mental health, women's health. *Nurse practitioner programs in:* family health, primary care.

Study Options Full-time and part-time.

Program Entrance Requirements Clinical experience, computer literacy, minimum overall college GPA of 3.0, transcript of college record, CPR certification, written essay, immunizations, 2 letters of recommendation, nursing research course, physical assessment course, professional liability insurance/malpractice insurance, resume, statistics course.

Advanced Placement Credit given for nursing courses completed elsewhere dependent upon specific evaluations.

Degree Requirements 43 total credit hours, thesis or project.

POST-MASTER'S PROGRAM

Areas of Study *Nurse practitioner programs in:* family health, primary care.

University of Phoenix–Central Florida Campus
College of Health and Human Services
Maitland, Florida

Founded in 1996

DEGREES • BSN • MSN • MSN/ED D

Nursing Program Faculty 10 (60% with doctorates).

Baccalaureate Enrollment 35
Women 88.6% **Men** 11.4% **Minority** 45.7%

Graduate Enrollment 18
Women 94.4% **Men** 5.6% **Minority** 50%

Nursing Student Activities Sigma Theta Tau.

Nursing Student Resources Academic advising; academic or career counseling; assistance for students with disabilities; bookstore; campus computer network; computer lab; computer-assisted instruction; e-mail services; interactive nursing skills videos; Internet; learning resource lab; library services; nursing audiovisuals; remedial services; skills, simulation, or other laboratory; tutoring.

Library Facilities 16,781 periodical subscriptions (1,300 health-care related).

BACCALAUREATE PROGRAMS

Degree BSN

Available Programs Accelerated Baccalaureate.

Site Options Orlando, FL; Daytona Beach, FL.

Study Options Full-time.

Program Entrance Requirements Transcript of college record, CPR certification, immunizations, 1 letter of recommendation, RN licensure. Transfer students are accepted. *Application deadline:* Applications may be processed on a rolling basis for some programs.

Advanced Placement Credit by examination available. Credit given for nursing courses completed elsewhere dependent upon specific evaluations.

Expenses (2009–10) *Tuition:* full-time $9300. *Required fees:* full-time $600.

Contact Campus College Chair, Nursing, College of Health and Human Services, University of Phoenix–Central Florida Campus, 2290 Lucien Way, Suite 400, Maitland, FL 32751-7057. *Telephone:* 407-667-0555.

GRADUATE PROGRAMS

Expenses (2009–10) *Tuition:* full-time $11,640. *Required fees:* full-time $760.

Financial Aid Institutionally sponsored loans and scholarships available.

Contact Campus College Chair, Nursing, College of Health and Human Services, University of Phoenix–Central Florida Campus, 2290 Lucien Way, Suite 400, Maitland, FL 32751-7057. *Telephone:* 407-667-0555.

MASTER'S DEGREE PROGRAM

Degrees MSN; MSN/Ed D

Available Programs Master's.

Concentrations Available Nursing administration; nursing education.

Site Options Orlando, FL; Daytona Beach, FL.

Study Options Full-time.

Program Entrance Requirements Clinical experience, computer literacy, minimum overall college GPA of 2.5, transcript of college record. *Application deadline:* Applications may be processed on a rolling basis for some programs. *Application fee:* $45.

University of Phoenix–Central Florida Campus (continued)

Advanced Placement Credit given for nursing courses completed elsewhere dependent upon specific evaluations.

Degree Requirements 39 total credit hours, thesis or project.

University of Phoenix–North Florida Campus

College of Health and Human Services
Jacksonville, Florida

Founded in 1976

DEGREES • BSN • MSN • MSN/ED D • MSN/MHA

Nursing Program Faculty 7 (29% with doctorates).

Baccalaureate Enrollment 13
Women 92.3% **Men** 7.7% **Minority** 38.5%

Graduate Enrollment 10
Women 100% **Minority** 20%

Nursing Student Activities Sigma Theta Tau.

Nursing Student Resources Academic advising; academic or career counseling; assistance for students with disabilities; bookstore; campus computer network; computer lab; computer-assisted instruction; e-mail services; interactive nursing skills videos; Internet; learning resource lab; library services; nursing audiovisuals; remedial services; skills, simulation, or other laboratory; tutoring.

Library Facilities 1,300 periodical subscriptions health-care related.

BACCALAUREATE PROGRAMS

Degree BSN

Available Programs Accelerated Baccalaureate.

Site Options Orange Park, FL.

Study Options Full-time.

Program Entrance Requirements Transcript of college record, CPR certification, immunizations, 1 letter of recommendation, RN licensure. Transfer students are accepted. *Application deadline:* Applications may be processed on a rolling basis for some programs.

Advanced Placement Credit by examination available. Credit given for nursing courses completed elsewhere dependent upon specific evaluations.

Expenses (2009–10) *Tuition:* full-time $9300. *Required fees:* full-time $600.

Contact Campus College Chair, Nursing, College of Health and Human Services, University of Phoenix–North Florida Campus, 4500 Salisbury Road, Suite 200, Jacksonville, FL 32216-0959. *Telephone:* 904-636-6645.

GRADUATE PROGRAMS

Expenses (2009–10) *Tuition:* full-time $11,640. *Required fees:* full-time $760.

Financial Aid Institutionally sponsored loans and scholarships available.

Contact Campus College Chair, Nursing, College of Health and Human Services, University of Phoenix–North Florida Campus, 4500 Salisbury Road, Suite 200, Jacksonville, FL 32216-0959. *Telephone:* 904-636-6645.

MASTER'S DEGREE PROGRAM

Degrees MSN; MSN/Ed D; MSN/MHA

Available Programs Master's.

Concentrations Available Health-care administration; nursing administration; nursing education.

Site Options Orange Park, FL.

Study Options Full-time.

Program Entrance Requirements Clinical experience, computer literacy, minimum overall college GPA of 2.5, transcript of college record. *Application deadline:* Applications may be processed on a rolling basis for some programs. *Application fee:* $45.

Advanced Placement Credit given for nursing courses completed elsewhere dependent upon specific evaluations.

Degree Requirements 39 total credit hours, thesis or project.

University of Phoenix–South Florida Campus

College of Health and Human Services
Fort Lauderdale, Florida

DEGREES • BSN • MSN • MSN/MBA • MSN/MHA

Nursing Program Faculty 24 (21% with doctorates).

Baccalaureate Enrollment 135
Women 96.3% **Men** 3.7% **Minority** 38.5%

Graduate Enrollment 102
Women 91.2% **Men** 8.8% **Minority** 41.18%

Nursing Student Activities Sigma Theta Tau.

Nursing Student Resources Academic advising; academic or career counseling; assistance for students with disabilities; bookstore; campus computer network; computer lab; computer-assisted instruction; e-mail services; interactive nursing skills videos; Internet; learning resource lab; library services; nursing audiovisuals; skills, simulation, or other laboratory; tutoring.

Library Facilities 16,781 periodical subscriptions (1,300 health-care related).

BACCALAUREATE PROGRAMS

Degree BSN

Available Programs RN Baccalaureate.

Site Options Palm Beach Gardens, FL; Ft. Lauderdale, FL; Miramar, FL.

Study Options Full-time.

Online Degree Options Yes.

Program Entrance Requirements Transcript of college record, CPR certification, immunizations, 1 letter of recommendation, RN licensure. Transfer students are accepted. *Application deadline:* Applications may be processed on a rolling basis for some programs.

Advanced Placement Credit by examination available. Credit given for nursing courses completed elsewhere dependent upon specific evaluations.

Expenses (2009–10) *Tuition:* full-time $9420. *Required fees:* full-time $600.

Contact Campus College Chair, Nursing, College of Health and Human Services, University of Phoenix–South Florida Campus, 600 North Pine Island Road, Suite #500, Plantation, FL 33324-1393. *Telephone:* 954-382-5303.

GRADUATE PROGRAMS

Expenses (2009–10) *Tuition:* full-time $11,640.

Financial Aid Institutionally sponsored loans and scholarships available.

Contact Campus College Chair, Nursing, College of Health and Human Services, University of Phoenix–South Florida Campus, 600 North Pine Island Road, Suite #500, Plantation, FL 33324-1393. *Telephone:* 954-382-5303.

MASTER'S DEGREE PROGRAM

Degrees MSN; MSN/MBA; MSN/MHA

Available Programs Master's.

Concentrations Available Health-care administration; nursing administration; nursing education.

Site Options Palm Beach Gardens, FL; Ft. Lauderdale, FL; Miramar, FL.

Study Options Full-time.

Online Degree Options Yes.

Program Entrance Requirements Clinical experience, computer literacy, minimum overall college GPA of 2.5, transcript of college record. *Application deadline:* Applications may be processed on a rolling basis for some programs. *Application fee:* $45.

Advanced Placement Credit given for nursing courses completed elsewhere dependent upon specific evaluations.

Degree Requirements 39 total credit hours, thesis or project.

Peterson's Nursing Programs 2011

University of Phoenix–West Florida Campus

College of Health and Human Services
Temple Terrace, Florida

DEGREE • BSN

Nursing Program Faculty 5 (60% with doctorates).

Baccalaureate Enrollment 8
Women 87.5% **Men** 12.5% **Minority** 12.5%

Nursing Student Activities Sigma Theta Tau.

Nursing Student Resources Academic advising; academic or career counseling; assistance for students with disabilities; bookstore; campus computer network; computer lab; computer-assisted instruction; e-mail services; interactive nursing skills videos; Internet; learning resource lab; library services; nursing audiovisuals; remedial services; skills, simulation, or other laboratory; tutoring.

Library Facilities 16,781 periodical subscriptions (1,300 health-care related).

BACCALAUREATE PROGRAMS

Degree BSN

Available Programs Accelerated Baccalaureate.
Site Options Tampa, FL; Clearwater, FL; Sarasota, FL.
Study Options Full-time.
Online Degree Options Yes.
Program Entrance Requirements Transcript of college record, CPR certification, immunizations, 1 letter of recommendation, RN licensure. Transfer students are accepted. *Application deadline:* Applications may be processed on a rolling basis for some programs.
Advanced Placement Credit by examination available. Credit given for nursing courses completed elsewhere dependent upon specific evaluations.
Expenses (2009–10) *Tuition:* full-time $9300. *Required fees:* full-time $600.
Contact Campus College Chair, Nursing, College of Health and Human Services, University of Phoenix–West Florida Campus, 100 Tampa Oaks Boulevard, Suite #200, Temple Terrace, FL 33637-1920. *Telephone:* 813-626-7911.

University of South Florida

College of Nursing
Tampa, Florida

http://hsc.usf.edu/nursing
Founded in 1956

DEGREES • BS • DNP • MS • MS/MPH • PHD

Nursing Program Faculty 61 (62% with doctorates).

Baccalaureate Enrollment 615
Women 89% **Men** 11% **Minority** 35% **International** 1% **Part-time** 38%
Graduate Enrollment 631
Women 90% **Men** 10% **Minority** 25% **International** 1% **Part-time** 91%

Distance Learning Courses Available.

Nursing Student Activities Nursing Honor Society, Sigma Theta Tau, Student Nurses' Association.

Nursing Student Resources Academic advising; academic or career counseling; assistance for students with disabilities; bookstore; campus computer network; career placement assistance; computer lab; computer-assisted instruction; daycare for children of students; e-mail services; employment services for current students; housing assistance; Internet; learning resource lab; library services; nursing audiovisuals; remedial services; resume preparation assistance; skills, simulation, or other laboratory; tutoring.

Library Facilities 2.2 million volumes (106,028 in health, 3,898 in nursing); 42,049 periodical subscriptions (1,581 health-care related).

BACCALAUREATE PROGRAMS

Degree BS

Available Programs ADN to Baccalaureate; Accelerated Baccalaureate for Second Degree; Generic Baccalaureate.
Site Options Sarasota, FL.
Study Options Full-time.
Program Entrance Requirements Minimum overall college GPA of 3.2, transcript of college record, CPR certification, health insurance, immunizations, prerequisite course work. Transfer students are accepted. *Application deadline:* 6/15 (fall), 3/15 (summer). *Application fee:* $30.
Financial Aid 40% of baccalaureate students in nursing programs received some form of financial aid in 2008–09.
Contact Mrs. Miranda Nerland, Coordinator, Baccalaureate Admissions, College of Nursing, University of South Florida, 12901 Bruce B. Downs Boulevard, MDC Box 22, Tampa, FL 33612-4766. *Telephone:* 813-974-2191. *Fax:* 813-974-3118. *E-mail:* mnerland@health.usf.edu.

GRADUATE PROGRAMS

Financial Aid 40% of graduate students in nursing programs received some form of financial aid in 2008–09. Federal Work-Study, institutionally sponsored loans, scholarships, traineeships, tuition waivers (partial), and unspecified assistantships available. *Financial aid application deadline:* 2/1.
Contact Ms. Michelle Kobus, Coordinator, Academic Advising, College of Nursing, University of South Florida, 12901 Bruce B. Downs Boulevard, MDC Box 22, Tampa, FL 33612-4766. *Telephone:* 813-974-2191. *Fax:* 813-974-5418. *E-mail:* mkobus@health.usf.edu.

MASTER'S DEGREE PROGRAM

Degrees MS; MS/MPH

Available Programs Master's; Master's for Nurses with Non-Nursing Degrees; RN to Master's.
Concentrations Available Clinical nurse leader; nurse anesthesia; nursing education. *Nurse practitioner programs in:* adult health, family health, occupational health, oncology, pediatric, psychiatric/mental health.
Study Options Full-time and part-time.
Program Entrance Requirements Computer literacy, minimum overall college GPA of 3.0, transcript of college record, CPR certification, immunizations, interview, 3 letters of recommendation, resume, GRE General Test. *Application deadline:* 6/1 (fall), 10/1 (spring), 2/15 (summer). *Application fee:* $30.
Advanced Placement Credit given for nursing courses completed elsewhere dependent upon specific evaluations.
Degree Requirements 41 total credit hours, thesis or project, comprehensive exam.

POST-MASTER'S PROGRAM

Areas of Study Clinical nurse leader; nursing education. *Nurse practitioner programs in:* adult health, family health, occupational health, oncology, pediatric, psychiatric/mental health.

DOCTORAL DEGREE PROGRAM

Degree DNP, PhD

Available Programs Doctorate; Post-Baccalaureate Doctorate.
Areas of Study Bio-behavioral research, clinical practice, critical care, ethics, faculty preparation, family health, gerontology, health promotion/disease prevention, human health and illness, illness and transition, maternity-newborn, nursing education, nursing research, nursing science, oncology, women's health.
Program Entrance Requirements Minimum overall college GPA of 3.0, interview by faculty committee, interview, 3 letters of recommendation, MSN or equivalent, vita, writing sample, GRE General Test. *Application deadline:* 2/1 (fall). *Application fee:* $30.
Degree Requirements 52–63 total credit hours, dissertation or residency.

CONTINUING EDUCATION PROGRAM

Contact Dr. Patricia Gorzka, Coordinator of Continuing Medical Education, College of Nursing, University of South Florida, 12901 Bruce B. Downs Boulevard, MDC Box 22, Tampa, FL 33612-4766. *Telephone:* 813-974-4392. *Fax:* 813-974-5418. *E-mail:* pgorzka@hsc.usf.edu.

The University of Tampa
Department of Nursing
Tampa, Florida

http://www.ut.edu

Founded in 1931

DEGREES • BSN • MSN

Nursing Program Faculty 27 (35% with doctorates).

Baccalaureate Enrollment 92
Women 93% **Men** 7% **Minority** 18% **International** 5% **Part-time** 16%

Graduate Enrollment 91
Women 94% **Men** 6% **Minority** 23% **International** 3% **Part-time** 66%

Nursing Student Activities Sigma Theta Tau, Student Nurses' Association.

Nursing Student Resources Academic advising; academic or career counseling; assistance for students with disabilities; bookstore; campus computer network; career placement assistance; computer lab; computer-assisted instruction; e-mail services; employment services for current students; externships; housing assistance; interactive nursing skills videos; Internet; learning resource lab; library services; nursing audiovisuals; paid internships; placement services for program completers; remedial services; resume preparation assistance; skills, simulation, or other laboratory; tutoring; unpaid internships.

Library Facilities 286,521 volumes (252,147 in health); 27,666 periodical subscriptions (10,854 health-care related).

BACCALAUREATE PROGRAMS

Degree BSN

Available Programs ADN to Baccalaureate; Generic Baccalaureate; RN Baccalaureate.

Study Options Full-time.

Program Entrance Requirements Minimum overall college GPA of 3.25, transcript of college record, CPR certification, written essay, health exam, health insurance, high school transcript, immunizations, 1 letter of recommendation, minimum GPA in nursing prerequisites, professional liability insurance/malpractice insurance, prerequisite course work. Transfer students are accepted. *Application deadline:* 10/15 (spring).

Expenses (2009–10) *Tuition:* full-time $21,420; part-time $455 per credit. *International tuition:* $21,420 full-time. *Room and board:* $8296; room only: $4430 per academic year. *Required fees:* full-time $1062; part-time $85 per term.

Financial Aid 85% of baccalaureate students in nursing programs received some form of financial aid in 2008–09. *Gift aid (need-based):* Federal Pell, FSEOG, state, private, college/university gift aid from institutional funds. *Loans:* FFEL (Subsidized and Unsubsidized Stafford PLUS), Perkins, state, college/university. *Work-study:* Federal Work-Study. *Financial aid application deadline:* Continuous.

Contact Admissions Office, Department of Nursing, The University of Tampa, 401 West Kennedy Boulevard, Box F, Tampa, FL 33606. *Telephone:* 813-253-6211. *Fax:* 813-258-7398. *E-mail:* admissions@ut.edu.

GRADUATE PROGRAMS

Expenses (2009–10) *Tuition:* part-time $488 per credit. *Room and board:* $8296; room only: $4430 per academic year. *Required fees:* part-time $120 per term.

Financial Aid 80% of graduate students in nursing programs received some form of financial aid in 2008–09.

Contact Graduate Studies Office, Department of Nursing, The University of Tampa, 401 West Kennedy Boulevard, Tampa, FL 33606. *Telephone:* 813-258-7409. *E-mail:* utgrad@ut.edu.

MASTER'S DEGREE PROGRAM

Degree MSN

Available Programs Master's; RN to Master's.

Concentrations Available *Nurse practitioner programs in:* adult health, family health.

Study Options Full-time and part-time.

Program Entrance Requirements Computer literacy, minimum overall college GPA of 3.0, transcript of college record, CPR certification, written essay, immunizations, interview, 2 letters of recommendation, physical assessment course, professional liability insurance/malpractice insurance, prerequisite course work, resume, statistics course. *Application deadline:* Applications may be processed on a rolling basis for some programs.

Advanced Placement Credit given for nursing courses completed elsewhere dependent upon specific evaluations.

Degree Requirements 48 total credit hours, comprehensive exam.

POST-MASTER'S PROGRAM

Areas of Study *Nurse practitioner programs in:* adult health, family health.

CONTINUING EDUCATION PROGRAM

Contact Dr. Kim Curry, Assistant Professor/Associate Director, Department of Nursing, The University of Tampa, 401 West Kennedy Boulevard, Box 10-F, Tampa, FL 33606-1490. *Telephone:* 813-257-3633. *Fax:* 813-258-7214. *E-mail:* kcurry@ut.edu.

See full description on page 530.

University of West Florida
Department of Nursing
Pensacola, Florida

http://uwf.edu/nursing

Founded in 1963

DEGREE • BSN

Nursing Program Faculty 14 (1% with doctorates).

Baccalaureate Enrollment 134
Women 87% **Men** 13% **Minority** 14% **Part-time** 31%

Distance Learning Courses Available.

Nursing Student Activities Sigma Theta Tau, Student Nurses' Association.

Nursing Student Resources Academic advising; academic or career counseling; assistance for students with disabilities; bookstore; campus computer network; career placement assistance; computer lab; computer-assisted instruction; daycare for children of students; e-mail services; employment services for current students; housing assistance; interactive nursing skills videos; Internet; learning resource lab; library services; nursing audiovisuals; remedial services; resume preparation assistance; skills, simulation, or other laboratory; tutoring.

Library Facilities 996,243 volumes (3,500 in health, 1,950 in nursing); 5,019 periodical subscriptions (54 health-care related).

BACCALAUREATE PROGRAMS

Degree BSN

Available Programs ADN to Baccalaureate; Generic Baccalaureate.

Study Options Full-time.

Online Degree Options Yes.

Program Entrance Requirements Minimum overall college GPA of 2.75, transcript of college record, CPR certification, health exam, health insurance, immunizations, minimum GPA in nursing prerequisites of 2.75, professional liability insurance/malpractice insurance, prerequisite course work. Transfer students are accepted. *Application deadline:* 3/1 (fall).

Advanced Placement Credit by examination available. Credit given for nursing courses completed elsewhere dependent upon specific evaluations.

Expenses (2009–10) *Tuition, state resident:* full-time $3649; part-time $140 per credit hour. *Tuition, nonresident:* full-time $14,813; part-time $570 per credit hour. *International tuition:* $14,813 full-time. *Room and board:* $7576 per academic year. *Required fees:* full-time $102.

Financial Aid 70% of baccalaureate students in nursing programs received some form of financial aid in 2008–09.

Contact Ms. Carol K. Hatcher, Nursing Advisor, Department of Nursing, University of West Florida, 11000 University Parkway, Pensacola, FL 32514. *Telephone:* 850-473-7757. *Fax:* 850-473-7769. *E-mail:* chatcher@uwf.edu.

GEORGIA

Albany State University
College of Sciences and Health Professions
Albany, Georgia

http://asuweb.asurams.edu
Founded in 1903
DEGREES • BSN • MSN

Nursing Program Faculty 17 (41% with doctorates).
Baccalaureate Enrollment 302
Women 94% **Men** 6% **Minority** 94% **International** 1% **Part-time** 21%
Graduate Enrollment 67
Women 93% **Men** 7% **Minority** 47% **International** 4% **Part-time** 49%
Distance Learning Courses Available.
Nursing Student Activities Nursing Honor Society, Student Nurses' Association, nursing club.
Nursing Student Resources Academic advising; academic or career counseling; assistance for students with disabilities; bookstore; campus computer network; career placement assistance; computer lab; computer-assisted instruction; e-mail services; interactive nursing skills videos; Internet; learning resource lab; library services; nursing audiovisuals; paid internships; placement services for program completers; remedial services; resume preparation assistance; skills, simulation, or other laboratory; tutoring; unpaid internships.
Library Facilities 15,000 volumes in health, 7,000 volumes in nursing; 75 periodical subscriptions health-care related.

BACCALAUREATE PROGRAMS
Degree BSN

Available Programs ADN to Baccalaureate; Accelerated Baccalaureate for Second Degree; Accelerated RN Baccalaureate; Generic Baccalaureate; RN Baccalaureate.
Study Options Full-time.
Online Degree Options Yes.
Program Entrance Requirements Minimum overall college GPA of 2.75, transcript of college record, CPR certification, written essay, health exam, health insurance, high school biology, high school foreign language, 4 years high school math, 3 years high school science, high school transcript, immunizations, interview, minimum GPA in nursing prerequisites of 2.75, professional liability insurance/malpractice insurance, prerequisite course work. Transfer students are accepted. *Application deadline:* 7/1 (fall), 11/16 (spring), 4/1 (summer). Applications may be processed on a rolling basis for some programs. *Application fee:* $20.
Advanced Placement Credit given for nursing courses completed elsewhere dependent upon specific evaluations.
Expenses (2009–10) *Tuition, state resident:* full-time $3874; part-time $130 per credit hour. *Tuition, nonresident:* full-time $15,488; part-time $517 per credit hour. *International tuition:* $15,488 full-time. *Room and board:* $6114; room only: $3764 per academic year. *Required fees:* full-time $1032; part-time $35 per term.
Financial Aid 89% of baccalaureate students in nursing programs received some form of financial aid in 2008–09.
Contact Dr. Linda P. Grimsley, RN, Chair, Department of Nursing, College of Sciences and Health Professions, Albany State University, 504 College Drive, Albany, GA 31705. *Telephone:* 229-430-4724. *Fax:* 229-430-3937. *E-mail:* linda.grimsley@asurams.edu.

GRADUATE PROGRAMS
Expenses (2009–10) *Tuition, state resident:* full-time $3345; part-time $350 per credit hour. *Tuition, nonresident:* full-time $3345; part-time $350 per credit hour. *International tuition:* $3345 full-time. *Room and board:* $6114; room only: $3764 per academic year. *Required fees:* full-time $390; part-time $195 per term.
Financial Aid 70% of graduate students in nursing programs received some form of financial aid in 2008–09. Scholarships and traineeships available.
Contact Dr. Linda P. Grimsley, RN, Chair, Department of Nursing, College of Sciences and Health Professions, Albany State University, 504 College Drive, Albany, GA 31705. *Telephone:* 229-430-4724. *Fax:* 229-430-3937. *E-mail:* linda.grimsley@asurams.edu.

MASTER'S DEGREE PROGRAM
Degree MSN
Available Programs Accelerated AD/RN to Master's; Accelerated Master's; Master's; RN to Master's.
Concentrations Available Nursing education. *Nurse practitioner programs in:* family health.
Study Options Full-time and part-time.
Online Degree Options Yes (online only).
Program Entrance Requirements Clinical experience, computer literacy, minimum overall college GPA of 3.0, transcript of college record, CPR certification, immunizations, interview, 2 letters of recommendation, nursing research course, physical assessment course, professional liability insurance/malpractice insurance, prerequisite course work, resume, statistics course, GRE General Test or MAT. *Application deadline:* 7/1 (fall), 11/16 (spring), 4/1 (summer). Applications may be processed on a rolling basis for some programs. *Application fee:* $20.
Advanced Placement Credit given for nursing courses completed elsewhere dependent upon specific evaluations.
Degree Requirements 36 total credit hours, thesis or project, comprehensive exam.

POST-MASTER'S PROGRAM
Areas of Study Nursing education. *Nurse practitioner programs in:* family health.

Armstrong Atlantic State University
Program in Nursing
Savannah, Georgia

http://www.don.armstrong.edu/
Founded in 1935
DEGREES • BSN • MS/MHSA • MSN
Nursing Program Faculty 40 (28% with doctorates).
Baccalaureate Enrollment 350
Women 85% **Men** 15% **Minority** 30% **International** 2% **Part-time** 10%
Graduate Enrollment 39
Women 93% **Men** 7% **Minority** 38% **Part-time** 70%
Distance Learning Courses Available.
Nursing Student Activities Nursing Honor Society, Sigma Theta Tau, Student Nurses' Association.
Nursing Student Resources Academic advising; academic or career counseling; assistance for students with disabilities; bookstore; campus computer network; career placement assistance; computer lab; computer-assisted instruction; e-mail services; employment services for current students; housing assistance; interactive nursing skills videos; Internet; learning resource lab; library services; nursing audiovisuals; placement services for program completers; remedial services; resume preparation assistance; skills, simulation, or other laboratory; tutoring.
Library Facilities 227,439 volumes (8,200 in nursing); 990 periodical subscriptions (171 health-care related).

BACCALAUREATE PROGRAMS
Degree BSN

Armstrong Atlantic State University (continued)

Available Programs ADN to Baccalaureate; Baccalaureate for Second Degree; Generic Baccalaureate; LPN to Baccalaureate; RN Baccalaureate.

Study Options Full-time and part-time.

Program Entrance Requirements Transcript of college record, CPR certification, health exam, health insurance, immunizations, minimum GPA in nursing prerequisites of 2.7, professional liability insurance/malpractice insurance, prerequisite course work. Transfer students are accepted. *Application deadline:* 2/15 (fall), 10/15 (spring).

Advanced Placement Credit by examination available.

Financial Aid 90% of baccalaureate students in nursing programs received some form of financial aid in 2008–09.

Contact Dr. Helen Taggart, Undergraduate Coordinator, Program in Nursing, Armstrong Atlantic State University, 11935 Abercorn Street, Savannah, GA 31419-1997. *Telephone:* 912-344-2667. *Fax:* 912-344-3481. *E-mail:* Helen.Taggart@armstrong.edu.

GRADUATE PROGRAMS

Financial Aid 85% of graduate students in nursing programs received some form of financial aid in 2008–09. Research assistantships with partial tuition reimbursements available (averaging $2,500 per year); Federal Work-Study, scholarships, and unspecified assistantships also available. Aid available to part-time students.

Contact Dr. Anita Nivens, Graduate Program Coordinator, Program in Nursing, Armstrong Atlantic State University, 11935 Abercorn Street, Savannah, GA 31419-1997. *Telephone:* 912-344-2724. *Fax:* 912-344-3481. *E-mail:* Anita.Nivens@armstrong.edu.

MASTER'S DEGREE PROGRAM

Degrees MS/MHSA; MSN

Available Programs Master's; RN to Master's.

Concentrations Available Nursing administration. *Clinical nurse specialist programs in:* adult health. *Nurse practitioner programs in:* adult health.

Study Options Full-time and part-time.

Program Entrance Requirements Clinical experience, minimum overall college GPA of 3.0, transcript of college record, CPR certification, written essay, immunizations, interview, 3 letters of recommendation, nursing research course, physical assessment course, professional liability insurance/malpractice insurance, prerequisite course work, statistics course, GRE General Test or MAT. *Application deadline:* 5/15 (fall), 11/15 (spring).

Advanced Placement Credit by examination available.

Degree Requirements 36 total credit hours, thesis or project.

POST-MASTER'S PROGRAM

Areas of Study Nursing administration. *Clinical nurse specialist programs in:* adult health. *Nurse practitioner programs in:* adult health.

Brenau University

School of Health and Science
Gainesville, Georgia

Founded in 1878

DEGREES • BSN • MSN

Nursing Program Faculty 14 (65% with doctorates).

Baccalaureate Enrollment 300
Women 95% **Men** 5% **Minority** 40% **International** 10% **Part-time** 50%

Graduate Enrollment 55
Women 95% **Men** 5% **Minority** 20% **Part-time** 100%

Distance Learning Courses Available.

Nursing Student Activities Sigma Theta Tau, Student Nurses' Association.

Nursing Student Resources Academic advising; academic or career counseling; assistance for students with disabilities; bookstore; campus computer network; career placement assistance; computer lab; computer-assisted instruction; e-mail services; housing assistance; interactive nursing skills videos; Internet; learning resource lab; library services; nursing audiovisuals; remedial services; skills, simulation, or other laboratory; tutoring.

Library Facilities 86,878 volumes (6,000 in health, 5,000 in nursing); 15,541 periodical subscriptions (275 health-care related).

BACCALAUREATE PROGRAMS

Degree BSN

Available Programs ADN to Baccalaureate; Generic Baccalaureate; RN Baccalaureate.

Study Options Full-time and part-time.

Online Degree Options Yes.

Program Entrance Requirements Minimum overall college GPA of 2.5, transcript of college record, health exam, high school biology, high school chemistry, high school foreign language, 2 years high school math, 1 year of high school science, high school transcript, immunizations, minimum high school GPA of 2.5, minimum GPA in nursing prerequisites of 2.5, professional liability insurance/malpractice insurance, prerequisite course work. Transfer students are accepted. *Application deadline:* 1/15 (fall), 7/15 (spring).

Advanced Placement Credit by examination available. Credit given for nursing courses completed elsewhere dependent upon specific evaluations.

Financial Aid 75% of baccalaureate students in nursing programs received some form of financial aid in 2008–09. *Gift aid (need-based):* Federal Pell, FSEOG, state, private, college/university gift aid from institutional funds, Academic Competitiveness Grant, National Smart Grant. *Loans:* FFEL (Subsidized and Unsubsidized Stafford PLUS), Perkins, state. *Work-study:* Federal Work-Study, part-time campus jobs. *Financial aid application deadline (priority):* 4/1.

Contact Ms. Christina White, Undergraduate Admissions Coordinator for Women's College, School of Health and Science, Brenau University, 500 Washington Street SE, Gainesville, GA 30501. *Telephone:* 770-534-6100. *Fax:* 770-538-4306. *E-mail:* cwhite@brenau.edu.

GRADUATE PROGRAMS

Financial Aid 90% of graduate students in nursing programs received some form of financial aid in 2008–09. Scholarships and traineeships available. Aid available to part-time students. *Financial aid application deadline:* 7/15.

Contact Dr. Cathy Dyches, Coordinator of Graduate Nursing Programs, School of Health and Science, Brenau University, 500 Washington Street SE, Gainesville, GA 30501. *Telephone:* 770-534-6125. *Fax:* 770-534-4666. *E-mail:* cdyches@brenau.edu.

MASTER'S DEGREE PROGRAM

Degree MSN

Available Programs Accelerated AD/RN to Master's; Accelerated RN to Master's; Master's; RN to Master's.

Concentrations Available Clinical nurse leader; nursing education. *Nurse practitioner programs in:* family health.

Site Options Atlanta, GA.

Study Options Part-time.

Program Entrance Requirements Clinical experience, minimum overall college GPA of 3.0, transcript of college record, CPR certification, written essay, immunizations, 3 letters of recommendation, nursing research course, physical assessment course, prerequisite course work, statistics course, GRE General Test or MAT. *Application deadline:* Applications may be processed on a rolling basis for some programs.

Degree Requirements Thesis or project.

POST-MASTER'S PROGRAM

Areas of Study *Nurse practitioner programs in:* family health.

CONTINUING EDUCATION PROGRAM

Contact Dr. Keeta Wilborn, Chair, Department of Nursing, School of Health and Science, Brenau University, 500 Washington Street SE, Gainesville, GA 30501. *Telephone:* 770-534-6206. *Fax:* 770-538-4666. *E-mail:* kwilborn@brenau.edu.

Clayton State University
Department of Nursing
Morrow, Georgia

http://www.healthsci.clayton.edu

Founded in 1969

DEGREES • BSN • MSN

Nursing Program Faculty 38 (32% with doctorates).

Baccalaureate Enrollment 195
Women 83.33% **Men** 16.67% **Minority** 65.79% **International** 2.19%
Part-time 17.98%

Graduate Enrollment 7
Women 94.44% **Men** 5.56% **Minority** 72.22% **Part-time** 66.67%

Distance Learning Courses Available.

Nursing Student Activities Nursing Honor Society, Sigma Theta Tau, Student Nurses' Association.

Nursing Student Resources Academic advising; academic or career counseling; assistance for students with disabilities; bookstore; campus computer network; career placement assistance; computer lab; computer-assisted instruction; e-mail services; employment services for current students; externships; housing assistance; interactive nursing skills videos; Internet; learning resource lab; library services; nursing audiovisuals; paid internships; placement services for program completers; remedial services; resume preparation assistance; skills, simulation, or other laboratory; tutoring.

Library Facilities 77,043 volumes (3,450 in health, 1,800 in nursing); 4,250 periodical subscriptions (151 health-care related).

BACCALAUREATE PROGRAMS
Degree BSN

Available Programs Generic Baccalaureate; RN Baccalaureate.
Study Options Full-time.
Online Degree Options Yes.
Program Entrance Requirements Minimum overall college GPA of 2.5, transcript of college record, CPR certification, health exam, health insurance, immunizations, interview, minimum GPA in nursing prerequisites of 2.5, professional liability insurance/malpractice insurance, prerequisite course work. Transfer students are accepted. *Application deadline:* 3/15 (fall), 9/15 (spring). *Application fee:* $25.
Expenses (2009–10) *Tuition, state resident:* full-time $4858; part-time $130 per credit hour. *Tuition, nonresident:* full-time $16,472; part-time $517 per credit hour. *International tuition:* $16,472 full-time. *Room and board:* $8078; room only: $5100 per academic year. *Required fees:* part-time $12 per credit; part-time $492 per term.
Financial Aid 61% of baccalaureate students in nursing programs received some form of financial aid in 2008–09.
Contact Dr. Sue E. Odom, Associate Dean, Department of Nursing, Clayton State University, 2000 Clayton State Boulevard, Morrow, GA 30260. *Telephone:* 678-466-4959. *Fax:* 678-466-4999. *E-mail:* sueodom@clayton.edu.

GRADUATE PROGRAMS
Expenses (2009–10) *Tuition, area resident:* full-time $3960; part-time $220 per credit hour. *Tuition, nonresident:* full-time $15,840; part-time $880 per credit hour. *Required fees:* full-time $824; part-time $412 per term.
Financial Aid 86% of graduate students in nursing programs received some form of financial aid in 2008–09.
Contact Dr. Katherine Willock, Director of the MSN Program, Department of Nursing, Clayton State University, 2000 Clayton State Boulevard, Morrow, GA 30260. *Telephone:* 678-466-4987. *Fax:* 678-466-4999. *E-mail:* katherinewillock@clayton.edu.

MASTER'S DEGREE PROGRAM
Degree MSN

Available Programs Master's.
Concentrations Available Nursing administration; nursing education.
Study Options Full-time and part-time.

Program Entrance Requirements Computer literacy, minimum overall college GPA of 3.0, transcript of college record, CPR certification, written essay, immunizations, interview, 3 letters of recommendation, professional liability insurance/malpractice insurance. *Application deadline:* 7/1 (fall), 11/1 (spring), 3/1 (summer). *Application fee:* $25.
Advanced Placement Credit given for nursing courses completed elsewhere dependent upon specific evaluations.
Degree Requirements 36 total credit hours, thesis or project.

Columbus State University
Nursing Program
Columbus, Georgia

http://nursing.colstate.edu

Founded in 1958

DEGREE • BSN

Nursing Program Faculty 33 (12% with doctorates).

Baccalaureate Enrollment 194
Women 90% **Men** 10% **Minority** 40%

Distance Learning Courses Available.

Nursing Student Activities Sigma Theta Tau, Student Nurses' Association.

Nursing Student Resources Academic advising; academic or career counseling; assistance for students with disabilities; bookstore; campus computer network; career placement assistance; computer lab; computer-assisted instruction; e-mail services; housing assistance; interactive nursing skills videos; Internet; learning resource lab; library services; nursing audiovisuals; remedial services; resume preparation assistance; skills, simulation, or other laboratory; tutoring.

Library Facilities 382,400 volumes (11,571 in health, 1,759 in nursing); 1,713 periodical subscriptions (79 health-care related).

BACCALAUREATE PROGRAMS
Degree BSN

Available Programs Generic Baccalaureate.
Study Options Full-time.
Program Entrance Requirements Minimum overall college GPA of 2.75, transcript of college record, CPR certification, health exam, health insurance, immunizations, 3 letters of recommendation, minimum GPA in nursing prerequisites of 2.75, professional liability insurance/malpractice insurance, prerequisite course work. Transfer students are accepted. *Application deadline:* 3/31 (fall).
Advanced Placement Credit given for nursing courses completed elsewhere dependent upon specific evaluations.
Expenses (2009–10) *Tuition, state resident:* full-time $3874; part-time $130 per credit hour. *Tuition, nonresident:* full-time $15,488; part-time $517 per credit hour. *International tuition:* $15,488 full-time. *Room and board:* $7090; room only: $3990 per academic year. *Required fees:* full-time $1150.
Financial Aid 95% of baccalaureate students in nursing programs received some form of financial aid in 2008–09. *Gift aid (need-based):* Federal Pell, FSEOG, state, private, college/university gift aid from institutional funds. *Loans:* Federal Direct (Subsidized and Unsubsidized Stafford PLUS), Perkins, state, college/university. *Work-study:* Federal Work-Study. *Financial aid application deadline (priority):* 5/1.
Contact Dr. June S. Goyne, Director, School of Nursing, Nursing Program, Columbus State University, 4225 University Avenue, Columbus, GA 31907. *Telephone:* 706-568-5050. *Fax:* 706-569-3101. *E-mail:* goyne_june@colstate.edu.

Emory University
Nell Hodgson Woodruff School of Nursing
Atlanta, Georgia

http://www.nursing.emory.edu

Founded in 1836

Emory University (continued)
DEGREES • BSN • MSN • MSN/MPH • PHD

Nursing Program Faculty 62 (56% with doctorates).

Baccalaureate Enrollment 218
Women 88% **Men** 12% **Minority** 41% **International** 2%

Graduate Enrollment 163
Women 96% **Men** 4% **Minority** 45% **International** 2% **Part-time** 33%

Nursing Student Activities Sigma Theta Tau, Student Nurses' Association.

Nursing Student Resources Academic advising; academic or career counseling; assistance for students with disabilities; bookstore; campus computer network; career placement assistance; computer lab; computer-assisted instruction; daycare for children of students; e-mail services; employment services for current students; externships; housing assistance; interactive nursing skills videos; Internet; learning resource lab; library services; nursing audiovisuals; other; resume preparation assistance; skills, simulation, or other laboratory; tutoring; unpaid internships.

Library Facilities 3.4 million volumes (250,000 in health); 54,295 periodical subscriptions (1,800 health-care related).

BACCALAUREATE PROGRAMS

Degree BSN

Available Programs Baccalaureate for Second Degree; Generic Baccalaureate.

Study Options Full-time.

Program Entrance Requirements Minimum overall college GPA of 3.0, transcript of college record, written essay, 3 letters of recommendation, minimum GPA in nursing prerequisites of 3.0, prerequisite course work. Transfer students are accepted. *Application deadline:* 1/15 (fall). *Application fee:* $50.

Advanced Placement Credit given for nursing courses completed elsewhere dependent upon specific evaluations.

Expenses (2009–10) *Tuition:* full-time $33,400. *Room and board:* $10,100; room only: $6300 per academic year. *Required fees:* full-time $4800.

Financial Aid 96% of baccalaureate students in nursing programs received some form of financial aid in 2008–09. *Gift aid (need-based):* Federal Pell, FSEOG, state, private, college/university gift aid from institutional funds. *Loans:* Federal Nursing Student Loans, FFEL (Subsidized and Unsubsidized Stafford PLUS), Perkins, state, college/university. *Work-study:* Federal Work-Study, part-time campus jobs. *Financial aid application deadline:* 3/1 (priority: 2/15).

Contact Office of Admission and Student Services, Nell Hodgson Woodruff School of Nursing, Emory University, 1520 Clifton Road NE, Atlanta, GA 30322. *Telephone:* 404-727-7980. *Fax:* 404-727-8509. *E-mail:* admit@nursing.emory.edu.

GRADUATE PROGRAMS

Expenses (2009–10) *Tuition:* full-time $50,100; part-time $1392 per credit hour. *Room and board:* room only: $1236 per academic year. *Required fees:* full-time $5000.

Financial Aid 96% of graduate students in nursing programs received some form of financial aid in 2008–09. Fellowships, career-related internships or fieldwork, Federal Work-Study, institutionally sponsored loans, scholarships, traineeships, and tuition waivers (full and partial) available. Aid available to part-time students. *Financial aid application deadline:* 3/15.

Contact Office of Admission and Student Services, Nell Hodgson Woodruff School of Nursing, Emory University, 1520 Clifton Road NE, Atlanta, GA 30322. *Telephone:* 404-727-7980. *Fax:* 404-727-8509. *E-mail:* admit@nursing.emory.edu.

MASTER'S DEGREE PROGRAM

Degrees MSN; MSN/MPH

Available Programs Master's; RN to Master's.

Concentrations Available Nurse-midwifery. *Clinical nurse specialist programs in:* public health. *Nurse practitioner programs in:* acute care, adult health, family health, gerontology, pediatric, primary care, women's health.

Study Options Full-time and part-time.

Program Entrance Requirements Clinical experience, minimum overall college GPA of 3.0, transcript of college record, written essay, interview, 3 letters of recommendation, physical assessment course, prerequisite course work, resume, statistics course, GRE General Test or MAT. *Application deadline:* 1/15 (fall), 10/1 (spring), 1/15 (summer). Applications may be processed on a rolling basis for some programs. *Application fee:* $50.

Advanced Placement Credit given for nursing courses completed elsewhere dependent upon specific evaluations.

Degree Requirements 41 total credit hours.

POST-MASTER'S PROGRAM

Areas of Study Nurse-midwifery; nursing education. *Clinical nurse specialist programs in:* public health. *Nurse practitioner programs in:* acute care, adult health, family health, gerontology, pediatric, primary care, women's health.

DOCTORAL DEGREE PROGRAM

Degree PhD

Available Programs Doctorate; Post-Baccalaureate Doctorate.

Areas of Study Aging, biology of health and illness, ethics, faculty preparation, gerontology, health policy, human health and illness, illness and transition, individualized study, neuro-behavior, nursing policy, nursing research, nursing science, women's health.

Program Entrance Requirements Minimum overall college GPA of 3.0, interview by faculty committee, 3 letters of recommendation, MSN or equivalent, statistics course, vita, writing sample. Application deadline: 1/3 (fall). Applications may be processed on a rolling basis for some programs.

Degree Requirements 50 total credit hours, dissertation, oral exam, written exam, residency.

POSTDOCTORAL PROGRAM

Postdoctoral Program Contact Ms. Teresa Fosque, Senior Business Manager, Nell Hodgson Woodruff School of Nursing, Emory University, 1520 Clifton Road NE, Atlanta, GA 30322. *E-mail:* tfosque@emory.edu.

See full description on page 494.

Georgia Baptist College of Nursing of Mercer University
Department of Nursing
Atlanta, Georgia

http://nursing.mercer.edu
Founded in 1988
DEGREES • BSN • MSN • PHD

Nursing Program Faculty 334 (47% with doctorates).

Baccalaureate Enrollment 413
Women 95% **Men** 5% **Minority** 51% **International** 3% **Part-time** 16%

Graduate Enrollment 17
Women 94% **Men** 6% **Minority** 29% **Part-time** 41%

Nursing Student Activities Nursing Honor Society, Sigma Theta Tau, Student Nurses' Association, nursing club.

Nursing Student Resources Academic advising; academic or career counseling; assistance for students with disabilities; bookstore; campus computer network; career placement assistance; computer lab; computer-assisted instruction; e-mail services; employment services for current students; housing assistance; interactive nursing skills videos; Internet; learning resource lab; library services; nursing audiovisuals; placement services for program completers; remedial services; resume preparation assistance; skills, simulation, or other laboratory; tutoring.

Library Facilities 12,836 volumes (4,072 in health, 2,805 in nursing); 182 periodical subscriptions (218 health-care related).

BACCALAUREATE PROGRAMS

Degree BSN

Available Programs Generic Baccalaureate; RN Baccalaureate.

Study Options Full-time and part-time.

Program Entrance Requirements Transcript of college record, written essay, health exam, health insurance, high school biology, high school foreign language, 3 years high school math, 3 years high school science, high school transcript, immunizations, prerequisite course work. Transfer students are accepted. *Application deadline:* 5/15 (fall). *Application fee:* $50.

Advanced Placement Credit by examination available. Credit given for nursing courses completed elsewhere dependent upon specific evaluations.

Expenses (2009–10) *Tuition:* full-time $19,215; part-time $801 per credit hour. *International tuition:* $19,215 full-time. *Room and board:* room only: $5400 per academic year. *Required fees:* full-time $430; part-time $9 per credit.

Financial Aid 80% of baccalaureate students in nursing programs received some form of financial aid in 2008–09.

Contact Mrs. Lynn Vines, Director of Admissions, Department of Nursing, Georgia Baptist College of Nursing of Mercer University, 3001 Mercer University Drive, Atlanta, GA 30341. *Telephone:* 678-547-6700. *Fax:* 678-547-6794. *E-mail:* vines_ml@mercer.edu.

GRADUATE PROGRAMS

Expenses (2009–10) *Tuition:* full-time $17,050; part-time $947 per hour. *International tuition:* $17,050 full-time. *Required fees:* full-time $310.

Financial Aid 90% of graduate students in nursing programs received some form of financial aid in 2008–09.

Contact Dr. Linda A. Streit, Associate Dean for the Graduate Program, Department of Nursing, Georgia Baptist College of Nursing of Mercer University, 3001 Mercer University Drive, Atlanta, GA 30341. *Telephone:* 678-547-6774. *Fax:* 678-547-6777. *E-mail:* streit_la@mercer.edu.

MASTER'S DEGREE PROGRAM

Degree MSN

Available Programs Master's.

Concentrations Available Nursing education. *Clinical nurse specialist programs in:* acute care, critical care.

Study Options Full-time and part-time.

Program Entrance Requirements Clinical experience, computer literacy, minimum overall college GPA of 3.0, transcript of college record, CPR certification, written essay, immunizations, interview, 3 letters of recommendation, nursing research course, physical assessment course, statistics course. *Application deadline:* 5/15 (fall), 11/1 (spring). *Application fee:* $50.

Advanced Placement Credit given for nursing courses completed elsewhere dependent upon specific evaluations.

Degree Requirements 40 total credit hours, thesis or project.

POST-MASTER'S PROGRAM

Areas of Study Nursing education.

DOCTORAL DEGREE PROGRAM

Degree PhD

Available Programs Doctorate.

Areas of Study Clinical practice, ethics, nursing education.

Program Entrance Requirements Minimum overall college GPA of 3.2, interview, 3 letters of recommendation, MSN or equivalent, scholarly papers, statistics course, vita, writing sample. Application deadline: 2/28 (fall). Applications may be processed on a rolling basis for some programs. Application fee: $50.

Degree Requirements 52 total credit hours, dissertation, oral exam, written exam, residency.

Georgia College & State University
College of Health Sciences
Milledgeville, Georgia

http://www.gcsu.edu/acad_affairs/ school_healthsci/healthsci
Founded in 1889

DEGREES • BSN • MSN • MSN/MBA

Nursing Program Faculty 36 (25% with doctorates).

Baccalaureate Enrollment 267
Women 85% **Men** 15% **Minority** 12% **International** 1% **Part-time** 30%

Graduate Enrollment 70
Women 80% **Men** 20% **Minority** 16% **International** 1% **Part-time** 100%

Nursing Student Activities Sigma Theta Tau, Student Nurses' Association.

Nursing Student Resources Academic advising; academic or career counseling; assistance for students with disabilities; bookstore; campus computer network; career placement assistance; computer lab; computer-assisted instruction; e-mail services; employment services for current students; housing assistance; interactive nursing skills videos; Internet; learning resource lab; library services; nursing audiovisuals; remedial services; resume preparation assistance; skills, simulation, or other laboratory; tutoring; unpaid internships.

Library Facilities 199,506 volumes (3,095 in health, 1,465 in nursing); 5,625 periodical subscriptions (315 health-care related).

BACCALAUREATE PROGRAMS

Degree BSN

Available Programs Generic Baccalaureate; RN Baccalaureate.

Site Options Macon, GA.

Study Options Full-time and part-time.

Program Entrance Requirements Minimum overall college GPA of 2.5, transcript of college record, CPR certification, health exam, health insurance, high school biology, high school foreign language, 4 years high school math, 3 years high school science, high school transcript, immunizations, minimum GPA in nursing prerequisites of 2.5, professional liability insurance/malpractice insurance, prerequisite course work. Transfer students are accepted.

Advanced Placement Credit by examination available. Credit given for nursing courses completed elsewhere dependent upon specific evaluations.

Contact *Telephone:* 478-445-4004. *Fax:* 478-445-1913.

GRADUATE PROGRAMS

Contact *Telephone:* 478-445-1795. *Fax:* 478-445-1913.

MASTER'S DEGREE PROGRAM

Degrees MSN; MSN/MBA

Available Programs Master's; RN to Master's.

Concentrations Available Nursing administration; nursing education; nursing informatics. *Clinical nurse specialist programs in:* adult health. *Nurse practitioner programs in:* family health.

Site Options Macon, GA.

Study Options Part-time.

Program Entrance Requirements Clinical experience, computer literacy, minimum overall college GPA of 2.75, transcript of college record, CPR certification, immunizations, interview, nursing research course, professional liability insurance/malpractice insurance, resume, statistics course, GRE, GMAT or MAT.

Advanced Placement Credit given for nursing courses completed elsewhere dependent upon specific evaluations.

Degree Requirements 36 total credit hours, thesis or project, comprehensive exam.

POST-MASTER'S PROGRAM

Areas of Study Nursing education; nursing informatics. *Nurse practitioner programs in:* family health.

Georgia Southern University
School of Nursing
Statesboro, Georgia

http://www.georgiasouthern.edu
Founded in 1906

Georgia Southern University (continued)

DEGREES • BSN • DNP • MSN

Nursing Program Faculty 36 (47% with doctorates).

Baccalaureate Enrollment 300
Women 90.3% **Men** 9.7% **Minority** 15.7% **International** .7% **Part-time** 23.7%

Graduate Enrollment 78
Women 93.6% **Men** 6.4% **Minority** 15.4% **Part-time** 6.4%

Distance Learning Courses Available.

Nursing Student Activities Sigma Theta Tau, Student Nurses' Association.

Nursing Student Resources Academic advising; academic or career counseling; assistance for students with disabilities; bookstore; campus computer network; career placement assistance; computer lab; computer-assisted instruction; daycare for children of students; e-mail services; housing assistance; interactive nursing skills videos; Internet; learning resource lab; library services; nursing audiovisuals; placement services for program completers; resume preparation assistance; skills, simulation, or other laboratory; tutoring.

Library Facilities 603,315 volumes (25,000 in health, 12,000 in nursing); 2,484 periodical subscriptions (20,000 health-care related).

BACCALAUREATE PROGRAMS

Degree BSN

Available Programs ADN to Baccalaureate; Generic Baccalaureate; LPN to RN Baccalaureate.

Study Options Full-time.

Online Degree Options Yes.

Program Entrance Requirements Minimum overall college GPA of 3.0, transcript of college record, CPR certification, written essay, health exam, health insurance, high school biology, high school chemistry, high school foreign language, 2 years high school math, 4 years high school science, high school transcript, immunizations, minimum GPA in nursing prerequisites of 3.0, professional liability insurance/malpractice insurance, prerequisite course work. Transfer students are accepted. *Application deadline:* 2/1 (fall), 8/1 (spring).

Advanced Placement Credit by examination available. Credit given for nursing courses completed elsewhere dependent upon specific evaluations.

Expenses (2009–10) *Tuition, state resident:* full-time $3996; part-time $134 per credit hour. *Tuition, nonresident:* full-time $15,972; part-time $533 per credit hour. *International tuition:* $15,972 full-time. *Room and board:* $7850; room only: $5420 per academic year. *Required fees:* full-time $1444; part-time $722 per term.

Financial Aid 94% of baccalaureate students in nursing programs received some form of financial aid in 2008–09.

Contact Dr. Danette Wood, BSN Program Director, School of Nursing, Georgia Southern University, PO Box 8158, Statesboro, GA 30460-8158. *Telephone:* 912-478-5454. *Fax:* 912-478-1159. *E-mail:* danette_wood@georgiasouthern.edu.

GRADUATE PROGRAMS

Expenses (2009–10) *Tuition, state resident:* full-time $5040; part-time $210 per credit hour. *Tuition, nonresident:* full-time $20,136; part-time $839 per credit hour. *International tuition:* $20,136 full-time. *Room and board:* $7850; room only: $5420 per academic year. *Required fees:* full-time $1444; part-time $722 per term.

Financial Aid 39% of graduate students in nursing programs received some form of financial aid in 2008–09. Research assistantships with partial tuition reimbursements available (averaging $6,850 per year), teaching assistantships with partial tuition reimbursements available (averaging $6,850 per year) were awarded; career-related internships or fieldwork, Federal Work-Study, scholarships, traineeships, tuition waivers (partial), and unspecified assistantships also available. Aid available to part-time students. *Financial aid application deadline:* 4/15.

Contact Dr. Donna Hodnicki, Director, Graduate Program, School of Nursing, Georgia Southern University, PO Box 8158, Statesboro, GA 30460-8158. *Telephone:* 912-478-5056. *Fax:* 912-478-1679. *E-mail:* dhodnick@georgiasouthern.edu.

MASTER'S DEGREE PROGRAM

Degree MSN

Available Programs Master's; RN to Master's.

Concentrations Available *Clinical nurse specialist programs in:* community health. *Nurse practitioner programs in:* family health.

Study Options Full-time and part-time.

Program Entrance Requirements Clinical experience, computer literacy, minimum overall college GPA of 3.0, transcript of college record, CPR certification, immunizations, interview, 3 letters of recommendation, professional liability insurance/malpractice insurance, prerequisite course work, statistics course, GRE General Test or MAT. *Application deadline:* 3/15 (fall).

Advanced Placement Credit given for nursing courses completed elsewhere dependent upon specific evaluations.

Degree Requirements 48 total credit hours, comprehensive exam.

POST-MASTER'S PROGRAM

Areas of Study *Clinical nurse specialist programs in:* community health. *Nurse practitioner programs in:* family health.

DOCTORAL DEGREE PROGRAM

Degree DNP

Available Programs Doctorate.

Areas of Study Nursing science.

Online Degree Options Yes (online only).

Program Entrance Requirements Minimum overall college GPA of 3.0, interview by faculty committee, 3 letters of recommendation, MSN or equivalent, vita, writing sample. Application deadline: 3/1 (fall).

Degree Requirements 40 total credit hours, residency.

Georgia Southwestern State University
School of Nursing
Americus, Georgia

http://www.gsw.edu
Founded in 1906

DEGREE • BSN

Nursing Program Faculty 11 (45% with doctorates).

Baccalaureate Enrollment 187
Women 90% **Men** 10% **Minority** 30% **International** 8% **Part-time** 35%

Distance Learning Courses Available.

Nursing Student Activities Sigma Theta Tau, Student Nurses' Association.

Nursing Student Resources Academic advising; academic or career counseling; assistance for students with disabilities; bookstore; campus computer network; career placement assistance; computer lab; computer-assisted instruction; e-mail services; employment services for current students; interactive nursing skills videos; Internet; learning resource lab; library services; nursing audiovisuals; placement services for program completers; remedial services; resume preparation assistance; skills, simulation, or other laboratory; tutoring.

Library Facilities 627 volumes in health, 528 volumes in nursing; 141 periodical subscriptions health-care related.

BACCALAUREATE PROGRAMS

Degree BSN

Available Programs Accelerated Baccalaureate for Second Degree; Baccalaureate for Second Degree; Generic Baccalaureate; LPN to RN Baccalaureate; RN Baccalaureate.

Study Options Full-time and part-time.

Online Degree Options Yes (online only).

Program Entrance Requirements Minimum overall college GPA of 2.8, transcript of college record, CPR certification, written essay, health exam, health insurance, high school foreign language, 4 years high school math, 4 years high school science, high school transcript, immunizations, 2 letters of recommendation, minimum high school GPA of 2.8, minimum GPA in nursing prerequisites of 2.8, professional liability insurance/malpractice insurance, prerequisite course work, RN licensure. Transfer students are accepted. *Application deadline:* 2/15 (fall), 10/15 (spring).

Advanced Placement Credit given for nursing courses completed elsewhere dependent upon specific evaluations.

Expenses (2009–10) *Tuition, state resident:* full-time $3874; part-time $130 per credit hour. *Tuition, nonresident:* full-time $15,488; part-time $517 per credit hour. *International tuition:* $15,488 full-time. *Room and board:* $5950; room only: $3400 per academic year. *Required fees:* full-time $1500.

Financial Aid 91% of baccalaureate students in nursing programs received some form of financial aid in 2008–09. *Gift aid (need-based):* Federal Pell, FSEOG, state, private, college/university gift aid from institutional funds. *Loans:* FFEL (Subsidized and Unsubsidized Stafford PLUS), Perkins, state, college/university. *Work-study:* Federal Work-Study, part-time campus jobs. *Financial aid application deadline (priority):* 4/1.

Contact Dr. Sandra Daniel, Dean and Professor, School of Nursing, Georgia Southwestern State University, 800 Georgia Southwestern State University Drive, Americus, GA 31709. *Telephone:* 229-931-2280. *Fax:* 229-931-2288. *E-mail:* sdd@canes.gsw.edu.

Georgia State University
Byrdine F. Lewis School of Nursing
Atlanta, Georgia

http://chhs.gsu.edu/nursing/

Founded in 1913

DEGREES • BS • MSN • PHD

Nursing Program Faculty 60 (40% with doctorates).

Baccalaureate Enrollment 269
Women 82% **Men** 18% **Minority** 35% **International** 5% **Part-time** 5%

Graduate Enrollment 200
Women 90% **Men** 10% **Minority** 33% **Part-time** 90%

Distance Learning Courses Available.

Nursing Student Activities Sigma Theta Tau, Student Nurses' Association.

Nursing Student Resources Academic advising; academic or career counseling; assistance for students with disabilities; bookstore; campus computer network; career placement assistance; computer lab; computer-assisted instruction; e-mail services; interactive nursing skills videos; Internet; learning resource lab; library services; nursing audiovisuals; remedial services; resume preparation assistance; skills, simulation, or other laboratory; tutoring.

Library Facilities 2.2 million volumes (52,835 in health, 20,856 in nursing); 7,398 periodical subscriptions (725 health-care related).

BACCALAUREATE PROGRAMS

Degree BS

Available Programs Generic Baccalaureate.

Study Options Full-time and part-time.

Program Entrance Requirements Minimum overall college GPA of 3.0, transcript of college record, CPR certification, written essay, health exam, immunizations, 2 letters of recommendation, minimum GPA in nursing prerequisites of 3.0, professional liability insurance/malpractice insurance, prerequisite course work. Transfer students are accepted. *Application deadline:* 3/1 (fall), 10/1 (spring).

Advanced Placement Credit given for nursing courses completed elsewhere dependent upon specific evaluations.

Expenses (2009–10) *Tuition, state resident:* full-time $6000; part-time $203 per credit hour. *Tuition, nonresident:* full-time $24,200; part-time $810 per credit hour. *International tuition:* $24,200 full-time. *Room and board:* room only: $3000 per academic year. *Required fees:* full-time $1500; part-time $203 per credit.

Financial Aid 90% of baccalaureate students in nursing programs received some form of financial aid in 2008–09. *Gift aid (need-based):* Federal Pell, FSEOG, state, private, college/university gift aid from institutional funds. *Loans:* Federal Direct (Subsidized and Unsubsidized Stafford PLUS), FFEL, Perkins, state. *Work-study:* Federal Work-Study. *Financial aid application deadline:* 11/1 (priority: 4/1).

Contact Ms. Denisa Hightower, Admissions Counselor, Byrdine F. Lewis School of Nursing, Georgia State University, College of Health and Human Sciences, Office of Academic Assistance, Atlanta, GA 30303-3083. *Telephone:* 404-413-1000. *Fax:* 404-413-1001. *E-mail:* dhightower@gsu.edu.

GRADUATE PROGRAMS

Expenses (2009–10) *Tuition, state resident:* full-time $26,000; part-time $221 per credit hour. *Room and board:* $12,000; room only: $4000 per academic year. *Required fees:* full-time $2500.

Financial Aid 50% of graduate students in nursing programs received some form of financial aid in 2008–09. Research assistantships with full and partial tuition reimbursements available (averaging $3,108 per year); fellowships with full tuition reimbursements available, teaching assistantships, Federal Work-Study, institutionally sponsored loans, scholarships, traineeships, tuition waivers (partial), and unspecified assistantships also available. Aid available to part-time students. *Financial aid application deadline:* 4/1.

Contact Ms. Barbara Smith, Admissions Counselor, Byrdine F. Lewis School of Nursing, Georgia State University, College of Health and Human Sciences, PO Box 3995, Atlanta, GA 30302-3995. *Telephone:* 404-413-1007. *Fax:* 404-413-1001. *E-mail:* alhbbs@langate.gsu.edu.

MASTER'S DEGREE PROGRAM

Degree MSN

Available Programs Master's; RN to Master's.

Concentrations Available Nursing informatics. *Clinical nurse specialist programs in:* adult health, pediatric, perinatal, psychiatric/mental health, women's health. *Nurse practitioner programs in:* adult health, family health, pediatric, psychiatric/mental health, women's health.

Site Options Alpharetta, GA.

Study Options Full-time and part-time.

Program Entrance Requirements Clinical experience, computer literacy, minimum overall college GPA of 3.0, transcript of college record, CPR certification, written essay, interview, 2 letters of recommendation, professional liability insurance/malpractice insurance, MAT (preferred) or GRE. *Application deadline:* 3/1 (fall), 10/15 (spring), 3/1 (summer). *Application fee:* $50.

Advanced Placement Credit given for nursing courses completed elsewhere dependent upon specific evaluations.

Degree Requirements 48 total credit hours.

POST-MASTER'S PROGRAM

Areas of Study *Clinical nurse specialist programs in:* adult health, pediatric, perinatal, psychiatric/mental health, women's health. *Nurse practitioner programs in:* adult health, family health, pediatric, psychiatric/mental health, women's health.

DOCTORAL DEGREE PROGRAM

Degree PhD

Available Programs Doctorate; Post-Baccalaureate Doctorate.

Areas of Study Bio-behavioral research, health promotion/disease prevention, individualized study, nursing research, nursing science.

Site Options Alpharetta, GA.

Program Entrance Requirements Minimum overall college GPA of 3.0, interview by faculty committee, interview, 3 letters of recommendation, MSN or equivalent, vita, GRE General Test. Application deadline: 3/1 (fall). Application fee: $50.

Degree Requirements 60 total credit hours, dissertation, written exam, residency.

Kennesaw State University
School of Nursing
Kennesaw, Georgia

http://www.kennesaw.edu/chhs/schoolofnursing

Founded in 1963

DEGREES • BSN • MSN

Distance Learning Courses Available.

Nursing Student Activities Sigma Theta Tau, Student Nurses' Association.

Nursing Student Resources Academic advising; academic or career counseling; assistance for students with disabilities; bookstore; campus computer network; career placement assistance; computer lab; computer-assisted instruction; e-mail services; employment services for current

Kennesaw State University (continued)

students; externships; housing assistance; interactive nursing skills videos; Internet; learning resource lab; library services; nursing audiovisuals; paid internships; placement services for program completers; remedial services; resume preparation assistance; skills, simulation, or other laboratory; tutoring.

Library Facilities 645,788 volumes (20,000 in health, 10,000 in nursing); 889 periodical subscriptions (503 health-care related).

BACCALAUREATE PROGRAMS

Degree BSN

Available Programs ADN to Baccalaureate; Accelerated Baccalaureate; Accelerated Baccalaureate for Second Degree; Baccalaureate for Second Degree; Generic Baccalaureate; RN Baccalaureate.

Site Options Rome, GA; Jasper, GA.

Study Options Full-time and part-time.

Program Entrance Requirements Minimum overall college GPA of 2.7, transcript of college record, CPR certification, health exam, health insurance, 2 years high school math, 2 years high school science, high school transcript, immunizations, interview, 1 letter of recommendation, minimum high school GPA of 2.5, minimum GPA in nursing prerequisites of 2.7, professional liability insurance/malpractice insurance, prerequisite course work. Transfer students are accepted.

Advanced Placement Credit by examination available. Credit given for nursing courses completed elsewhere dependent upon specific evaluations.

Contact Fran Herzig, Admissions Coordinator, School of Nursing, Kennesaw State University, 1000 Chastain Road, Kennesaw, GA 30144. *Telephone:* 770-499-3211. *Fax:* 770-423-6627. *E-mail:* fpaul@kennesaw.edu.

GRADUATE PROGRAMS

Contact Dr. Regina Dorman, Coordinator, School of Nursing, Kennesaw State University, 1000 Chastain Road, Kennesaw, GA 30144. *Telephone:* 770-423-6061. *Fax:* 770-423-6627. *E-mail:* gdorman@ksumail.kennesaw.edu.

MASTER'S DEGREE PROGRAM

Degree MSN

Available Programs Master's.

Concentrations Available *Clinical nurse specialist programs in:* adult health. *Nurse practitioner programs in:* adult health, family health, primary care.

Study Options Full-time.

Program Entrance Requirements Clinical experience, minimum overall college GPA of 3.0, transcript of college record, CPR certification, written essay, immunizations, 2 letters of recommendation, nursing research course, physical assessment course, professional liability insurance/malpractice insurance, prerequisite course work, resume.

Advanced Placement Credit given for nursing courses completed elsewhere dependent upon specific evaluations.

Degree Requirements 40 total credit hours, thesis or project.

CONTINUING EDUCATION PROGRAM

Contact Dr. Vanice Wise Roberts, Associate Dean, School of Nursing, Kennesaw State University, 1000 Chastain Road, #1601, Kennesaw, GA 30144. *Telephone:* 770-423-6064. *Fax:* 770-423-6627. *E-mail:* vroberts@kennesaw.edu.

LaGrange College
Department of Nursing
LaGrange, Georgia

http://www.lagrange.edu

Founded in 1831

DEGREE • BSN

Nursing Program Faculty 6 (20% with doctorates).

Baccalaureate Enrollment 65
Women 90% **Men** 10% **Minority** 20%

Nursing Student Activities Nursing Honor Society, Student Nurses' Association.

Nursing Student Resources Academic advising; academic or career counseling; assistance for students with disabilities; bookstore; campus computer network; career placement assistance; computer lab; computer-assisted instruction; e-mail services; employment services for current students; externships; interactive nursing skills videos; Internet; learning resource lab; library services; nursing audiovisuals; paid internships; placement services for program completers; remedial services; resume preparation assistance; skills, simulation, or other laboratory; tutoring; unpaid internships.

Library Facilities 116,300 volumes (19,000 in health, 10,000 in nursing); 374 periodical subscriptions (100 health-care related).

BACCALAUREATE PROGRAMS

Degree BSN

Available Programs Generic Baccalaureate; RN Baccalaureate.

Study Options Full-time.

Program Entrance Requirements Minimum overall college GPA of 2.5, transcript of college record, CPR certification, written essay, health exam, health insurance, immunizations, interview, 2 letters of recommendation, minimum GPA in nursing prerequisites of 2.5, professional liability insurance/malpractice insurance, prerequisite course work. Transfer students are accepted. *Application deadline:* 4/15 (spring).

Advanced Placement Credit given for nursing courses completed elsewhere dependent upon specific evaluations.

Expenses (2009–10) *Tuition:* full-time $10,547; part-time $869 per credit hour. *International tuition:* $10,547 full-time. *Room and board:* $4500; room only: $2511 per academic year. *Required fees:* full-time $300.

Financial Aid 95% of baccalaureate students in nursing programs received some form of financial aid in 2008–09.

Contact Dr. Celia G. Hay, RN, Chair, Department of Nursing, LaGrange College, 601 Broad Street, LaGrange, GA 30240-2999. *Telephone:* 706-880-8220. *Fax:* 706-880-8029. *E-mail:* chay@lagrange.edu.

Macon State College
School of Nursing and Health Sciences
Macon, Georgia

http://www.maconstate.edu/nursing/nursing_introduction.aspx

Founded in 1968

DEGREE • BSN

Nursing Program Faculty 30 (7% with doctorates).

Baccalaureate Enrollment 70
Women 88% **Men** 12% **Minority** 21% **International** 2%

Distance Learning Courses Available.

Nursing Student Activities Sigma Theta Tau, Student Nurses' Association.

Nursing Student Resources Academic advising; academic or career counseling; assistance for students with disabilities; bookstore; campus computer network; career placement assistance; computer lab; computer-assisted instruction; e-mail services; externships; interactive nursing skills videos; Internet; learning resource lab; library services; nursing audiovisuals; resume preparation assistance; skills, simulation, or other laboratory; tutoring.

Library Facilities 80,000 volumes (4,000 in health, 920 in nursing); 513 periodical subscriptions (90 health-care related).

BACCALAUREATE PROGRAMS

Degree BSN

Available Programs ADN to Baccalaureate; Generic Baccalaureate.

Site Options Warner Robins, GA.

Study Options Full-time and part-time.

Program Entrance Requirements Minimum overall college GPA of 2.0, transcript of college record, CPR certification, health exam, health insurance, immunizations, minimum GPA in nursing prerequisites of 2.5, professional liability insurance/malpractice insurance, prerequisite course work, RN licensure. Transfer students are accepted. *Application deadline:* 2/15 (fall).

Advanced Placement Credit given for nursing courses completed elsewhere dependent upon specific evaluations.

Expenses (2009–10) *Tuition, state resident:* full-time $2494; part-time $84 per credit hour. *Tuition, nonresident:* full-time $9976; part-time $233 per credit hour. *International tuition:* $9976 full-time. *Required fees:* full-time $388; part-time $194 per term.

Financial Aid 67% of baccalaureate students in nursing programs received some form of financial aid in 2008–09.

Contact Mrs. Bobbye Wynne, Admissions Coordinator, School of Nursing and Health Sciences, Macon State College, 100 College Station Drive, Macon, GA 31206-5145. *Telephone:* 478-471-2761. *Fax:* 478-471-2983. *E-mail:* bobbye.wynne@maconstate.edu.

Medical College of Georgia
School of Nursing
Augusta, Georgia

http://www.mcg.edu/son

Founded in 1828

DEGREES • BSN • DNP • MSN • PHD

Nursing Program Faculty 73 (40% with doctorates).

Baccalaureate Enrollment 289
Women 94% **Men** 6% **Minority** 14.5% **Part-time** 1%

Graduate Enrollment 298
Women 89.6% **Men** 10.4% **Minority** 21.14% **Part-time** 27.85%

Distance Learning Courses Available.

Nursing Student Activities Nursing Honor Society, Sigma Theta Tau, Student Nurses' Association, nursing club.

Nursing Student Resources Academic advising; academic or career counseling; assistance for students with disabilities; bookstore; campus computer network; career placement assistance; computer lab; computer-assisted instruction; daycare for children of students; e-mail services; employment services for current students; externships; housing assistance; interactive nursing skills videos; Internet; learning resource lab; library services; nursing audiovisuals; paid internships; remedial services; skills, simulation, or other laboratory; tutoring.

Library Facilities 165,433 volumes (178,650 in health, 14,650 in nursing); 1,823 periodical subscriptions (1,307 health-care related).

BACCALAUREATE PROGRAMS

Degree BSN

Available Programs Generic Baccalaureate.

Site Options Columbus, GA; Athens, GA.

Study Options Full-time.

Program Entrance Requirements Minimum overall college GPA of 2.8, transcript of college record, CPR certification, written essay, health insurance, immunizations, 2 letters of recommendation, prerequisite course work. Transfer students are accepted. *Application deadline:* 12/1 (fall). *Application fee:* $30.

Expenses (2009–10) *Tuition, area resident:* full-time $9105; part-time $203 per credit hour. *Tuition, nonresident:* full-time $36,420; part-time $810 per credit hour. *Room and board:* room only: $1500 per academic year. *Required fees:* full-time $842.

Financial Aid 80% of baccalaureate students in nursing programs received some form of financial aid in 2008–09. *Gift aid (need-based):* Federal Pell, FSEOG, state, private, college/university gift aid from institutional funds, Federal Nursing. *Loans:* Federal Nursing Student Loans, FFEL (Subsidized and Unsubsidized Stafford PLUS), Perkins, state, college/university. *Work-study:* Federal Work-Study. *Financial aid application deadline:* Continuous.

Contact Office of Academic Admissions, School of Nursing, Medical College of Georgia, AA-170 Kelly Building, Augusta, GA 30912. *Telephone:* 706-721-2725. *Fax:* 706-721-0186. *E-mail:* underadm@mail.mcg.edu.

GRADUATE PROGRAMS

Expenses (2009–10) *Tuition, area resident:* full-time $11,469; part-time $319 per credit hour. *Tuition, nonresident:* full-time $31,881; part-time $886 per credit hour. *Room and board:* room only: $1500 per academic year. *Required fees:* full-time $607.

Financial Aid 75% of graduate students in nursing programs received some form of financial aid in 2008–09.

Contact Director, Academic Admissions, School of Nursing, Medical College of Georgia, AA-170 Kelly Building, Augusta, GA 30912. *Telephone:* 706-721-2725. *Fax:* 706-721-0186. *E-mail:* gradadm@mail.mcg.edu.

MASTER'S DEGREE PROGRAM

Degree MSN

Available Programs Accelerated Master's; Accelerated Master's for Non-Nursing College Graduates; Master's; RN to Master's.

Concentrations Available Clinical nurse leader; nurse anesthesia. *Nurse practitioner programs in:* family health, pediatric.

Site Options Columbus, GA; Athens, GA.

Study Options Full-time and part-time.

Online Degree Options Yes.

Program Entrance Requirements Clinical experience, computer literacy, minimum overall college GPA of 3.0, transcript of college record, CPR certification, written essay, immunizations, interview, 3 letters of recommendation, professional liability insurance/malpractice insurance, prerequisite course work, resume, statistics course. *Application fee:* $30.

Degree Requirements 46 total credit hours, thesis or project.

POST-MASTER'S PROGRAM

Areas of Study Nurse anesthesia. *Nurse practitioner programs in:* family health, pediatric.

DOCTORAL DEGREE PROGRAM

Degree DNP, PhD

Available Programs Doctorate; Post-Baccalaureate Doctorate.

Areas of Study Bio-behavioral research, nursing research.

Site Options Columbus, GA; Athens, GA.

Program Entrance Requirements Clinical experience, minimum overall college GPA of 3.2, interview by faculty committee, interview, 3 letters of recommendation, MSN or equivalent, scholarly papers, statistics course, vita, writing sample. Application fee: $30.

Expenses (2009–10) *Tuition, state resident:* full-time $11,469–$17,805; part-time $319–$495 per credit hour. *Tuition, nonresident:* full-time $31,881–$37,881; part-time $886–$1052 per credit hour.

Degree Requirements 40–60 total credit hours, dissertation, oral exam, written exam.

See full description on page 510.

North Georgia College & State University
Department of Nursing
Dahlonega, Georgia

http://www.ngcsu.edu

Founded in 1873

DEGREES • BSN • MS

Nursing Program Faculty 42 (17% with doctorates).

Baccalaureate Enrollment 70
Women 90% **Men** 10% **Minority** 12% **International** 4% **Part-time** 40%

Graduate Enrollment 50
Women 90% **Men** 10% **Minority** 10% **International** 2% **Part-time** 5%

Distance Learning Courses Available.

Nursing Student Activities Nursing Honor Society, Sigma Theta Tau, Student Nurses' Association.

North Georgia College & State University (continued)

Nursing Student Resources Academic advising; academic or career counseling; assistance for students with disabilities; bookstore; campus computer network; career placement assistance; computer lab; computer-assisted instruction; e-mail services; externships; interactive nursing skills videos; Internet; learning resource lab; library services; nursing audiovisuals; remedial services; resume preparation assistance; skills, simulation, or other laboratory; tutoring.

Library Facilities 204,045 volumes (6,875 in health, 619 in nursing); 43,943 periodical subscriptions (2,377 health-care related).

BACCALAUREATE PROGRAMS

Degree BSN

Available Programs ADN to Baccalaureate.

Study Options Full-time and part-time.

Online Degree Options Yes (online only).

Program Entrance Requirements Minimum overall college GPA of 2.75, transcript of college record, CPR certification, health exam, health insurance, high school biology, high school chemistry, high school foreign language, 3 years high school math, 2 years high school science, high school transcript, immunizations, 2 letters of recommendation, professional liability insurance/malpractice insurance, prerequisite course work, RN licensure. Transfer students are accepted. *Application deadline:* 2/1 (fall). *Application fee:* $25.

Financial Aid 75% of baccalaureate students in nursing programs received some form of financial aid in 2008–09.

Contact Mrs. Nancy Stahl, RN, Coordinator, BSN Program, Department of Nursing, North Georgia College & State University, 82 College Circle, Dahlonega, GA 30597. *Telephone:* 706-864-1937. *Fax:* 706-864-1845. *E-mail:* nstahl@ngcsu.edu.

GRADUATE PROGRAMS

Financial Aid 100% of graduate students in nursing programs received some form of financial aid in 2008–09.

Contact Dr. Grace Newsome, Coordinator, MS Program, Department of Nursing, North Georgia College & State University, 82 College Circle, Dahlonega, GA 30597. *Telephone:* 706-864-1489. *Fax:* 706-864-1845. *E-mail:* gnewsome@ngsu.edu.

MASTER'S DEGREE PROGRAM

Degree MS

Available Programs Master's.

Concentrations Available Nursing education. *Nurse practitioner programs in:* family health.

Study Options Full-time and part-time.

Program Entrance Requirements Clinical experience, computer literacy, minimum overall college GPA of 2.75, transcript of college record, CPR certification, written essay, immunizations, 3 letters of recommendation, nursing research course, physical assessment course, professional liability insurance/malpractice insurance, prerequisite course work. *Application deadline:* 2/28 (spring). *Application fee:* $25.

Degree Requirements 46 total credit hours, thesis or project, comprehensive exam.

POST-MASTER'S PROGRAM

Areas of Study Nursing education. *Nurse practitioner programs in:* family health.

Piedmont College

School of Nursing
Demorest, Georgia

http://www.piedmont.edu/schools/index. html#nursing

Founded in 1897

DEGREE • BSN

Nursing Program Faculty 8 (25% with doctorates).

Baccalaureate Enrollment 60

Women 99% **Men** 1% **Minority** 10% **International** 1% **Part-time** 20%

Distance Learning Courses Available.

Nursing Student Activities Nursing Honor Society, Student Nurses' Association.

Nursing Student Resources Academic advising; academic or career counseling; assistance for students with disabilities; bookstore; campus computer network; career placement assistance; computer lab; computer-assisted instruction; e-mail services; externships; housing assistance; interactive nursing skills videos; Internet; learning resource lab; library services; nursing audiovisuals; other; paid internships; resume preparation assistance; skills, simulation, or other laboratory; tutoring.

Library Facilities 115,400 volumes (3,000 in health, 500 in nursing); 365 periodical subscriptions (75 health-care related).

BACCALAUREATE PROGRAMS

Degree BSN

Available Programs Generic Baccalaureate; LPN to Baccalaureate; RN Baccalaureate.

Study Options Full-time.

Program Entrance Requirements Transcript of college record, CPR certification, health exam, health insurance, high school foreign language, 2 years high school math, 3 years high school science, high school transcript, immunizations, minimum GPA in nursing prerequisites of 3.0, professional liability insurance/malpractice insurance, prerequisite course work. Transfer students are accepted. *Application deadline:* 10/15 (fall).

Advanced Placement Credit given for nursing courses completed elsewhere dependent upon specific evaluations.

Expenses (2009–10) *Tuition:* full-time $18,000; part-time $9000 per semester. *International tuition:* $18,000 full-time. *Room and board:* $6000 per academic year.

Financial Aid 50% of baccalaureate students in nursing programs received some form of financial aid in 2008–09. *Gift aid (need-based):* Federal Pell, FSEOG, state, private, college/university gift aid from institutional funds. *Loans:* Federal Direct (Subsidized and Unsubsidized Stafford PLUS), state. *Work-study:* Federal Work-Study, part-time campus jobs. *Financial aid application deadline (priority):* 3/1.

Contact Dr. Linda Scott, Dean, School of Nursing, Piedmont College, 165 Central Avenue, Demorest, GA 30535. *Telephone:* 706-776-0116. *Fax:* 706-778-0701. *E-mail:* lscott@piedmont.edu.

Shorter College

School of Nursing
Rome, Georgia

Founded in 1873

DEGREE • BSN

Nursing Program Faculty 5 (20% with doctorates).

Library Facilities 213,297 volumes; 8,511 periodical subscriptions.

BACCALAUREATE PROGRAMS

Degree BSN

Available Programs RN Baccalaureate.

Study Options Full-time.

Program Entrance Requirements Minimum GPA in nursing prerequisites of 2.8. Transfer students are accepted. *Application deadline:* 2/1 (fall).

Expenses (2009–10) *Tuition:* full-time $15,950. *Room and board:* $7975; room only: $4200 per academic year. *Required fees:* full-time $350.

Contact Dr. Vanice W. Roberts, Dean, School of Nursing, Shorter College, 315 Shorter Avenue, Rome, GA 30165. *Telephone:* 706-233-7464. *Fax:* 706-291-4283. *E-mail:* aallen@shorter.edu.

Thomas University

Division of Nursing
Thomasville, Georgia

http://www.thomasu.edu/nursing.htm

Founded in 1950

DEGREES • BSN • MSN • MSN/MBA

Nursing Program Faculty 12 (40% with doctorates).

Baccalaureate Enrollment 85
Women 85% **Men** 15% **Minority** 30%

Graduate Enrollment 30
Women 90% **Men** 10% **Minority** 30% **Part-time** 40%

Distance Learning Courses Available.

Nursing Student Activities Nursing Honor Society, Sigma Theta Tau.

Nursing Student Resources Academic advising; academic or career counseling; assistance for students with disabilities; bookstore; campus computer network; career placement assistance; computer lab; computer-assisted instruction; e-mail services; housing assistance; interactive nursing skills videos; Internet; library services; nursing audiovisuals; resume preparation assistance; skills, simulation, or other laboratory; tutoring.

Library Facilities 41,467 volumes (800 in health, 400 in nursing); 451 periodical subscriptions (60 health-care related).

BACCALAUREATE PROGRAMS

Degree BSN

Available Programs ADN to Baccalaureate; Accelerated RN Baccalaureate; RN Baccalaureate.

Site Options Tallahassee, FL; Moultrie, GA.

Study Options Full-time and part-time.

Program Entrance Requirements Minimum overall college GPA of 2.5, transcript of college record, CPR certification, health exam, health insurance, immunizations, minimum GPA in nursing prerequisites of 2.5, professional liability insurance/malpractice insurance, prerequisite course work, RN licensure. Transfer students are accepted. *Application deadline:* 8/1 (fall), 12/1 (spring), 4/15 (summer). Applications may be processed on a rolling basis for some programs. *Application fee:* $35.

Advanced Placement Credit by examination available. Credit given for nursing courses completed elsewhere dependent upon specific evaluations.

Financial Aid 90% of baccalaureate students in nursing programs received some form of financial aid in 2008–09. *Gift aid (need-based):* Federal Pell, FSEOG, state, private, college/university gift aid from institutional funds. *Loans:* FFEL (Subsidized and Unsubsidized Stafford PLUS), state, alternative loans. *Work-study:* Federal Work-Study. *Financial aid application deadline:* Continuous.

Contact Deryl Ouzts, Associate Director of Enrollment Services, Division of Nursing, Thomas University, 1501 Millpond Road, Thomasville, GA 31792. *Telephone:* 229-227-6884. *Fax:* 229-226-1653. *E-mail:* douzts@thomasu.edu.

GRADUATE PROGRAMS

Financial Aid 90% of graduate students in nursing programs received some form of financial aid in 2008–09.

Contact Deryl Ouzts, Associate Director of Enrollment Management, Division of Nursing, Thomas University, 1501 Millpond Road, Thomasville, GA 31792. *Telephone:* 229-227-6884. *Fax:* 229-226-1653. *E-mail:* douzts@thomasu.edu.

MASTER'S DEGREE PROGRAM

Degrees MSN; MSN/MBA

Available Programs Master's; Master's for Nurses with Non-Nursing Degrees.

Concentrations Available Health-care administration; nursing administration; nursing education.

Study Options Full-time and part-time.

Program Entrance Requirements Computer literacy, minimum overall college GPA of 3.0, transcript of college record, CPR certification, written essay, immunizations, 3 letters of recommendation, professional liability insurance/malpractice insurance, resume, statistics course. *Application deadline:* 8/1 (fall), 12/1 (spring), 4/15 (summer). Applications may be processed on a rolling basis for some programs. *Application fee:* $50.

Advanced Placement Credit given for nursing courses completed elsewhere dependent upon specific evaluations.

Degree Requirements 36 total credit hours, thesis or project.

POST-MASTER'S PROGRAM

Areas of Study Health-care administration; nursing administration; nursing education.

University of Phoenix–Atlanta Campus
College of Health and Human Services
Sandy Springs, Georgia

Nursing Student Activities Sigma Theta Tau.

Nursing Student Resources Academic advising; academic or career counseling; assistance for students with disabilities; bookstore; campus computer network; computer lab; computer-assisted instruction; e-mail services; interactive nursing skills videos; Internet; learning resource lab; library services; nursing audiovisuals; remedial services; skills, simulation, or other laboratory; tutoring.

Library Facilities 16,781 periodical subscriptions (1,300 health-care related).

University of West Georgia
School of Nursing
Carrollton, Georgia

http://www.westga.edu/~nurs/

Founded in 1933

DEGREES • BSN • MSN

Nursing Program Faculty 31 (32% with doctorates).

Baccalaureate Enrollment 346
Women 91% **Men** 9% **Minority** 33% **International** 2% **Part-time** 68%

Graduate Enrollment 25
Women 100% **Minority** 20% **Part-time** 28%

Distance Learning Courses Available.

Nursing Student Activities Sigma Theta Tau, Student Nurses' Association.

Nursing Student Resources Academic advising; academic or career counseling; assistance for students with disabilities; bookstore; campus computer network; career placement assistance; computer lab; computer-assisted instruction; e-mail services; employment services for current students; externships; housing assistance; interactive nursing skills videos; Internet; learning resource lab; library services; nursing audiovisuals; remedial services; resume preparation assistance; skills, simulation, or other laboratory; tutoring.

Library Facilities 536,446 volumes (1,116 in health, 1,042 in nursing); 16,131 periodical subscriptions (58 health-care related).

BACCALAUREATE PROGRAMS

Degree BSN

Available Programs Generic Baccalaureate; RN Baccalaureate.

Site Options Newnan, GA; Rome, GA; Dalton, GA.

Study Options Full-time and part-time.

Program Entrance Requirements Minimum overall college GPA of 2.75, transcript of college record, CPR certification, health exam, health insurance, immunizations, minimum GPA in nursing prerequisites of 2.75, professional liability insurance/malpractice insurance, prerequisite course work. Transfer students are accepted. *Application deadline:* 1/15 (spring).

Advanced Placement Credit given for nursing courses completed elsewhere dependent upon specific evaluations.

Expenses (2009–10) *Tuition, state resident:* full-time $3996; part-time $134 per credit. *Tuition, nonresident:* full-time $15,972; part-time $533 per credit. *Room and board:* $6544; room only: $3340 per academic year. *Required fees:* full-time $371; part-time $185 per term.

University of West Georgia (continued)

Financial Aid 82% of baccalaureate students in nursing programs received some form of financial aid in 2008–09. *Gift aid (need-based):* Federal Pell, FSEOG, state, private, college/university gift aid from institutional funds, Academic Competitiveness Grant, National Smart Grant, LEAP. *Loans:* Federal Direct (Subsidized and Unsubsidized Stafford PLUS), Perkins, state. *Work-study:* Federal Work-Study, part-time campus jobs. *Financial aid application deadline:* 7/1 (priority: 4/1).

Contact Dr. Cynthia D. Epps, Associate Dean and Undergraduate Program Coordinator, School of Nursing, University of West Georgia, 1601 Maple Street, Carrollton, GA 30118. *Telephone:* 678-839-6552. *Fax:* 678-839-6553. *E-mail:* cepps@westga.edu.

GRADUATE PROGRAMS

Expenses (2009–10) *Tuition, state resident:* full-time $3932; part-time $164 per credit hour. *Tuition, nonresident:* full-time $15,736; part-time $656 per credit hour. *Room and board:* $6544; room only: $3340 per academic year. *Required fees:* full-time $200; part-time $100 per term.

Financial Aid 87% of graduate students in nursing programs received some form of financial aid in 2008–09.

Contact Dr. Laurie Jowers Ware, Assistant Dean and Director of Graduate Program, School of Nursing, University of West Georgia, 1601 Maple Street, Carrollton, GA 30118. *Telephone:* 678-839-6552. *Fax:* 678-839-6553. *E-mail:* lware@westga.edu.

MASTER'S DEGREE PROGRAM

Degree MSN

Available Programs Master's.

Concentrations Available Clinical nurse leader; nursing administration; nursing education.

Study Options Full-time and part-time.

Program Entrance Requirements Clinical experience, computer literacy, minimum overall college GPA of 3.0, transcript of college record, CPR certification, immunizations, 3 letters of recommendation, nursing research course, professional liability insurance/malpractice insurance, prerequisite course work, resume, statistics course. *Application deadline:* 7/1 (summer).

Degree Requirements 36 total credit hours, thesis or project, comprehensive exam.

POST-MASTER'S PROGRAM

Areas of Study Clinical nurse leader; nursing administration; nursing education.

Valdosta State University
College of Nursing
Valdosta, Georgia

http://www.valdosta.edu/nursing/

Founded in 1906

DEGREES • BSN • MSN

Nursing Program Faculty 23 (52% with doctorates).

Baccalaureate Enrollment 183
Women 87% **Men** 13% **Minority** 21% **International** 1% **Part-time** 7%

Graduate Enrollment 25
Women 99% **Men** 1% **Minority** 15% **International** 1% **Part-time** 49%

Nursing Student Activities Sigma Theta Tau, Student Nurses' Association.

Nursing Student Resources Academic advising; academic or career counseling; assistance for students with disabilities; bookstore; campus computer network; career placement assistance; computer lab; computer-assisted instruction; e-mail services; employment services for current students; externships; housing assistance; Internet; learning resource lab; library services; nursing audiovisuals; placement services for program completers; resume preparation assistance; skills, simulation, or other laboratory; tutoring; unpaid internships.

Library Facilities 626,173 volumes (21,688 in health); 2,788 periodical subscriptions (75 health-care related).

BACCALAUREATE PROGRAMS

Degree BSN

Available Programs Generic Baccalaureate; RN Baccalaureate.

Study Options Full-time.

Program Entrance Requirements Minimum overall college GPA of 2.8, transcript of college record, CPR certification, health exam, health insurance, immunizations, minimum GPA in nursing prerequisites of 2.8, professional liability insurance/malpractice insurance, prerequisite course work. Transfer students are accepted.

Advanced Placement Credit given for nursing courses completed elsewhere dependent upon specific evaluations.

Contact *Telephone:* 229-333-5959. *Fax:* 229-333-7300.

GRADUATE PROGRAMS

Contact *Telephone:* 229-333-5959. *Fax:* 229-333-7300.

MASTER'S DEGREE PROGRAM

Degree MSN

Available Programs Master's; RN to Master's.

Concentrations Available Nurse case management; nursing administration; nursing education. *Clinical nurse specialist programs in:* adult health, family health, psychiatric/mental health.

Study Options Full-time and part-time.

Program Entrance Requirements Minimum overall college GPA of 2.8, transcript of college record, CPR certification, immunizations, 3 letters of recommendation, physical assessment course, professional liability insurance/malpractice insurance, statistics course, GRE General Test.

Advanced Placement Credit given for nursing courses completed elsewhere dependent upon specific evaluations.

Degree Requirements 36 total credit hours, thesis or project, comprehensive exam.

CONTINUING EDUCATION PROGRAM

Contact *Telephone:* 229-333-5960.

GUAM

University of Guam
College of Nursing and Health Sciences
Mangilao, Guam

http://www.uog.edu/cnhs/index.html

Founded in 1952

DEGREE • BSN

Nursing Program Faculty 10 (30% with doctorates).

Baccalaureate Enrollment 175
Women 97% **Men** 3% **International** 2%

Nursing Student Activities Student Nurses' Association.

Nursing Student Resources Academic advising; academic or career counseling; assistance for students with disabilities; bookstore; campus computer network; career placement assistance; computer lab; daycare for children of students; e-mail services; employment services for current students; interactive nursing skills videos; Internet; learning resource lab; library services; nursing audiovisuals; remedial services; skills, simulation, or other laboratory; tutoring.

Library Facilities 386,539 volumes (5,246 in health, 982 in nursing); 2,276 periodical subscriptions (53 health-care related).

BACCALAUREATE PROGRAMS

Degree BSN

Available Programs ADN to Baccalaureate; Generic Baccalaureate; RN Baccalaureate.

Study Options Full-time and part-time.

Program Entrance Requirements Transcript of college record, CPR certification, written essay, health exam, high school biology, high school chemistry, 1 year of high school math, 1 year of high school science, high school transcript, immunizations, interview, minimum high school GPA of 2.5, minimum GPA in nursing prerequisites of 2.7, prerequisite course work. Transfer students are accepted.

Advanced Placement Credit by examination available. Credit given for nursing courses completed elsewhere dependent upon specific evaluations.

Contact *Telephone:* 671-735-2210. *Fax:* 671-734-4245.

HAWAII

Hawai'i Pacific University
College of Nursing and Health Sciences
Honolulu, Hawaii

http://www.hpu.edu
Founded in 1965

DEGREES • BSN • MSN • MSN/MBA

Nursing Program Faculty 98 (12% with doctorates).

Baccalaureate Enrollment 1,523
Women 83% **Men** 17% **Minority** 80% **International** 2% **Part-time** 32%

Graduate Enrollment 38
Women 92% **Men** 8% **Minority** 47% **International** 3% **Part-time** 32%

Distance Learning Courses Available.

Nursing Student Activities Nursing Honor Society, Sigma Theta Tau, Student Nurses' Association.

Nursing Student Resources Academic advising; academic or career counseling; assistance for students with disabilities; bookstore; campus computer network; career placement assistance; computer lab; computer-assisted instruction; e-mail services; employment services for current students; externships; housing assistance; Internet; learning resource lab; library services; paid internships; placement services for program completers; resume preparation assistance; skills, simulation, or other laboratory; tutoring.

Library Facilities 160,800 volumes (4,325 in health, 971 in nursing); 38,050 periodical subscriptions (5,581 health-care related).

■ Hawai'i Pacific University's Bachelor of Science in Nursing (B.S.N.) program offers hands-on learning in multicultural classroom and clinical settings. While students are accepted directly into the nursing program after being accepted into the University, there is a rank-ordered system for being admitted into entry-level nursing courses. Students are rank-ordered according to four selection categories: (1) Overall GPA (minimum overall 2.75 GPA); (2) GPA in prerequisite science-based courses; (3) Scores on the Test of the Essential Academic Skills (TEAS); and (4) HPU credits (points are awarded based on the number of courses taken at HPU). There are 140 seats offered each fall and spring (280 seats per year). In the sophomore year, HPU students begin their clinical experiences. Small clinical laboratory classes (8–10 students) utilize health-care facilities all over the island of O'ahu for clinical experiences. The Master of Science in Nursing (M.S.N.) is available to registered nurses and offers three concentrations: community clinical nurse specialist (CNS) studies, community clinical nurse specialist educator option (CNS), and family nurse practitioner (FNP) studies. Hawai'i Pacific's B.S.N. and M.S.N. programs are accredited by the National League for Nursing Accrediting Commission and approved by the State of Hawai'i Board of Nursing.

BACCALAUREATE PROGRAMS

Degree BSN

Available Programs Generic Baccalaureate; International Nurse to Baccalaureate; LPN to Baccalaureate; RN Baccalaureate.

Site Options Aiea, HI; Kahuku, HI; Wahiawa, HI; Kailua, HI; Kaneohe, HI; Honolulu, HI.

Study Options Full-time and part-time.

Program Entrance Requirements Minimum overall college GPA of 2.75, transcript of college record, CPR certification, health exam, health insurance, immunizations, minimum GPA in nursing prerequisites of 2.75, prerequisite course work. Transfer students are accepted. *Application deadline:* Applications may be processed on a rolling basis for some programs. *Application fee:* $50.

Advanced Placement Credit given for nursing courses completed elsewhere dependent upon specific evaluations.

Expenses (2009–10) *Tuition:* full-time $14,860; part-time $300 per credit hour. *International tuition:* $14,860 full-time. *Room and board:* $8866 per academic year. *Required fees:* full-time $100.

Financial Aid 79% of baccalaureate students in nursing programs received some form of financial aid in 2008–09. *Gift aid (need-based):* Federal Pell, FSEOG, state, private, college/university gift aid from institutional funds, Federal Nursing. *Loans:* Federal Nursing Student Loans, FFEL (Subsidized and Unsubsidized Stafford PLUS), Perkins. *Work-study:* Federal Work-Study. *Financial aid application deadline (priority):* 3/1.

Contact Miss Sara Sato, Director of Admissions, College of Nursing and Health Sciences, Hawai'i Pacific University, 1164 Bishop Street, Honolulu, HI 96813. *Telephone:* 808-544-0238. *Fax:* 808-544-1136. *E-mail:* ssato@hpu.edu.

GRADUATE PROGRAMS

Expenses (2009–10) *Tuition:* full-time $16,740; part-time $930 per credit hour. *International tuition:* $16,740 full-time.

Financial Aid 50% of graduate students in nursing programs received some form of financial aid in 2008–09. Career-related internships or fieldwork, Federal Work-Study, scholarships, and traineeships available. Aid available to part-time students. *Financial aid application deadline:* 3/1.

Contact Dr. Patricia Burrell, Chair, Department of Graduate and Post-Baccalaureate Nursing Programs, College of Nursing and Health Sciences, Hawai'i Pacific University, 45-045 Kamehameha Highway, Kaneohe, HI 96744-5297. *Telephone:* 808-236-5813. *Fax:* 808-236-5818. *E-mail:* pburrell@hpu.edu.

MASTER'S DEGREE PROGRAM

Degrees MSN; MSN/MBA

Available Programs Master's; RN to Master's.

Concentrations Available Nursing education. *Clinical nurse specialist programs in:* community health. *Nurse practitioner programs in:* family health.

Study Options Full-time and part-time.

Program Entrance Requirements Clinical experience, minimum overall college GPA of 3.0, transcript of college record, written essay, interview, 2 letters of recommendation, nursing research course, prerequisite course work, resume, statistics course. *Application deadline:* Applications may be processed on a rolling basis for some programs. *Application fee:* $50.

Advanced Placement Credit given for nursing courses completed elsewhere dependent upon specific evaluations.

Degree Requirements 48 total credit hours, thesis or project.

POST-MASTER'S PROGRAM

Areas of Study *Nurse practitioner programs in:* family health.

See full description on page 498.

University of Hawaii at Hilo
Department in Nursing
Hilo, Hawaii

http://www.uhh.hawaii.edu

Founded in 1970

DEGREE • BSN

Nursing Program Faculty 13 (38% with doctorates).

Baccalaureate Enrollment 79
Women 84% **Men** 16% **Minority** 70% **Part-time** 18%

Distance Learning Courses Available.

Nursing Student Activities Nursing Honor Society, Sigma Theta Tau, Student Nurses' Association, nursing club.

Nursing Student Resources Academic advising; academic or career counseling; assistance for students with disabilities; bookstore; campus computer network; career placement assistance; computer lab; computer-assisted instruction; daycare for children of students; e-mail services; employment services for current students; externships; housing assistance; interactive nursing skills videos; Internet; learning resource lab; library services; nursing audiovisuals; paid internships; remedial services; resume preparation assistance; skills, simulation, or other laboratory; tutoring.

Library Facilities 250,000 volumes (680 in health, 284 in nursing); 2,500 periodical subscriptions (15,000 health-care related).

BACCALAUREATE PROGRAMS

Degree BSN

Available Programs ADN to Baccalaureate; Generic Baccalaureate; RN Baccalaureate.

Site Options Kona, HI; Lihue, HI; Kahalui, HI.

Study Options Full-time.

Program Entrance Requirements Minimum overall college GPA of 2.7, transcript of college record, CPR certification, written essay, health exam, health insurance, high school biology, high school chemistry, high school foreign language, 1 year of high school math, 3 years high school science, high school transcript, immunizations, 2 letters of recommendation, minimum high school GPA of 3.0, minimum GPA in nursing prerequisites of 2.7, professional liability insurance/malpractice insurance, prerequisite course work. *Application deadline:* 1/15 (spring).

Expenses (2009–10) *Tuition, state resident:* full-time $7242; part-time $213 per credit. *Tuition, nonresident:* full-time $22,100; part-time $650 per credit. *International tuition:* $22,100 full-time. *Room and board:* $8000; room only: $4000 per academic year. *Required fees:* full-time $1000; part-time $500 per term.

Financial Aid 80% of baccalaureate students in nursing programs received some form of financial aid in 2008–09. *Gift aid (need-based):* Federal Pell, FSEOG, state, private, college/university gift aid from institutional funds. *Loans:* FFEL (Subsidized and Unsubsidized Stafford PLUS), Perkins, state. *Work-study:* Federal Work-Study, part-time campus jobs. *Financial aid application deadline (priority):* 3/1.

Contact Dr. Katharyn Daub, Chair and Program Director, Department in Nursing, University of Hawaii at Hilo, 200 West Kawili Street, UCB 235, Hilo, HI 96720. *Telephone:* 808-974-7760. *Fax:* 808-974-7665. *E-mail:* katharyn@hawaii.edu.

University of Hawaii at Manoa
School of Nursing and Dental Hygiene
Honolulu, Hawaii

http://www.nursing.hawaii.edu

Founded in 1907

DEGREES • BSN • MS • MSN/MBA • PHD

Nursing Program Faculty 97 (35% with doctorates).

Baccalaureate Enrollment 336
Women 77% **Men** 23% **Minority** 83% **International** 3% **Part-time** 56%

Graduate Enrollment 170
Women 88% **Men** 12% **Minority** 60% **International** 2% **Part-time** 66%

Distance Learning Courses Available.

Nursing Student Activities Nursing Honor Society, Sigma Theta Tau, Student Nurses' Association, nursing club.

Nursing Student Resources Academic advising; academic or career counseling; assistance for students with disabilities; bookstore; computer lab; computer-assisted instruction; e-mail services; employment services for current students; housing assistance; Internet; learning resource lab; library services; nursing audiovisuals; resume preparation assistance; skills, simulation, or other laboratory.

Library Facilities 2.9 million volumes; 23,511 periodical subscriptions.

BACCALAUREATE PROGRAMS

Degree BSN

Available Programs ADN to Baccalaureate; Generic Baccalaureate; RN Baccalaureate.

Study Options Full-time and part-time.

Program Entrance Requirements Minimum overall college GPA of 2.5, transcript of college record, CPR certification, health exam, health insurance, immunizations, minimum GPA in nursing prerequisites of 2.5, prerequisite course work. Transfer students are accepted. *Application deadline:* 3/1 (fall), 10/1 (spring). *Application fee:* $50.

Advanced Placement Credit by examination available. Credit given for nursing courses completed elsewhere dependent upon specific evaluations.

Expenses (2008–09) *Tuition, state resident:* full-time $2976; part-time $248 per credit. *Tuition, nonresident:* full-time $8304; part-time $692 per credit. *International tuition:* $8304 full-time. *Room and board:* $6000; room only: $4000 per academic year. *Required fees:* full-time $2000.

Contact Ms. Tiana Cho, Academic Advisor, School of Nursing and Dental Hygiene, University of Hawaii at Manoa, 2528 McCarthy Mall, Webster 201, Honolulu, HI 96822. *Telephone:* 808-956-8939. *Fax:* 808-956-5977. *E-mail:* nursing@hawaii.edu.

GRADUATE PROGRAMS

Expenses (2008–09) *Tuition, state resident:* full-time $4168; part-time $521 per credit. *Tuition, nonresident:* full-time $7816; part-time $977 per credit. *International tuition:* $7816 full-time. *Room and board:* $6000; room only: $4000 per academic year. *Required fees:* full-time $320.

Financial Aid 6 fellowships (averaging $1,587 per year), 2 research assistantships (averaging $16,824 per year) were awarded.

Contact Dr. Ray Jarman, Graduate Advisor, School of Nursing and Dental Hygiene, University of Hawaii at Manoa, 2528 McCarthy Mall, Webster 201, Honolulu, HI 96822. *Telephone:* 808-956-3519. *Fax:* 808-956-5977. *E-mail:* jarmanr@hawaii.edu.

MASTER'S DEGREE PROGRAM

Degrees MS; MSN/MBA

Available Programs Accelerated Master's; Master's; Master's for Non-Nursing College Graduates; RN to Master's.

Concentrations Available Nursing administration; nursing education. *Clinical nurse specialist programs in:* psychiatric/mental health. *Nurse practitioner programs in:* adult health, community health, family health, gerontology, pediatric.

Site Options Kahului, HI; Lihue, HI; Kailua Kona, HI.

Study Options Full-time and part-time.

Online Degree Options Yes.

Program Entrance Requirements Minimum overall college GPA of 3.0, transcript of college record, CPR certification, written essay, immunizations, interview, 2 letters of recommendation, resume, statistics course. *Application deadline:* 3/1 (fall). *Application fee:* $60.

Advanced Placement Credit given for nursing courses completed elsewhere dependent upon specific evaluations.

Degree Requirements 52 total credit hours.

POST-MASTER'S PROGRAM

Areas of Study Nursing administration; nursing education. *Clinical nurse specialist programs in:* psychiatric/mental health. *Nurse practitioner programs in:* adult health, community health, family health, gerontology, pediatric.

DOCTORAL DEGREE PROGRAM

Degree PhD

Available Programs Doctorate.

Areas of Study Faculty preparation, nursing education, nursing research, nursing science.

Site Options Kahului, HI; Lihue, HI; Kailua Kona, HI.

Online Degree Options Yes (online only).

Program Entrance Requirements Clinical experience, minimum overall college GPA of 3.0, interview by faculty committee, interview, 3 letters of recommendation, MSN or equivalent, scholarly papers, statistics course, vita, writing sample. Application deadline: 2/1 (fall).

Degree Requirements 46 total credit hours, dissertation, oral exam, residency.

University of Phoenix–Hawaii Campus
College of Health and Human Services
Honolulu, Hawaii

DEGREES • BSN • MSN • MSN/ED D

Nursing Program Faculty 26 (15% with doctorates).

Baccalaureate Enrollment 70
Women 90% **Men** 10% **Minority** 40%

Graduate Enrollment 14
Women 71.4% **Men** 28.6% **Minority** 57.14%

Nursing Student Activities Sigma Theta Tau.

Nursing Student Resources Academic advising; academic or career counseling; assistance for students with disabilities; bookstore; campus computer network; computer lab; computer-assisted instruction; e-mail services; interactive nursing skills videos; Internet; learning resource lab; library services; nursing audiovisuals; remedial services; skills, simulation, or other laboratory; tutoring.

Library Facilities 16,781 periodical subscriptions (1,300 health-care related).

BACCALAUREATE PROGRAMS
Degree BSN

Available Programs Accelerated Baccalaureate; LPN to Baccalaureate.

Site Options Kaneohe, HI; Mililani, HI; Kapolei, HI.

Study Options Full-time.

Program Entrance Requirements Transcript of college record, CPR certification, immunizations, 1 letter of recommendation, RN licensure. Transfer students are accepted. Application deadline: Applications may be processed on a rolling basis for some programs.

Advanced Placement Credit by examination available. Credit given for nursing courses completed elsewhere dependent upon specific evaluations.

Expenses (2009–10) Tuition: full-time $10,560. Required fees: full-time $600.

Contact Campus College Chair, Nursing, College of Health and Human Services, University of Phoenix–Hawaii Campus, 827 Fort Street, Hololulu, HI 96813-4317. Telephone: 808-536-2686.

GRADUATE PROGRAMS
Expenses (2009–10) Tuition: full-time $13,200. Required fees: full-time $760.

Financial Aid Institutionally sponsored loans and scholarships available.

Contact Campus College Chair, Nursing, College of Health and Human Services, University of Phoenix–Hawaii Campus, 827 Fort Street, Hololulu, HI 96813-4317. Telephone: 808-536-2686.

MASTER'S DEGREE PROGRAM
Degrees MSN; MSN/Ed D

Available Programs Master's.

Concentrations Available Health-care administration; nursing administration; nursing education. Nurse practitioner programs in: family health.

Site Options Kaneohe, HI; Mililani, HI; Kapolei, HI.

Study Options Full-time.

Program Entrance Requirements Clinical experience, computer literacy, minimum overall college GPA of 2.5, transcript of college record. Application deadline: Applications may be processed on a rolling basis for some programs. Application fee: $45.

Advanced Placement Credit given for nursing courses completed elsewhere dependent upon specific evaluations.

Degree Requirements 39 total credit hours, thesis or project.

IDAHO

Boise State University
Department of Nursing
Boise, Idaho

http://nursing.boisestate.edu/

Founded in 1932

DEGREES • BS • MSN • MSN/MS

Nursing Program Faculty 55 (25% with doctorates).

Baccalaureate Enrollment 540
Women 75% **Men** 25% **Minority** 1% **International** 1%

Graduate Enrollment 12

Distance Learning Courses Available.

Nursing Student Activities Nursing Honor Society, Sigma Theta Tau, Student Nurses' Association.

Nursing Student Resources Academic advising; academic or career counseling; assistance for students with disabilities; bookstore; campus computer network; career placement assistance; computer lab; computer-assisted instruction; daycare for children of students; e-mail services; employment services for current students; housing assistance; interactive nursing skills videos; Internet; learning resource lab; library services; nursing audiovisuals; placement services for program completers; remedial services; resume preparation assistance; skills, simulation, or other laboratory; tutoring.

Library Facilities 838,932 volumes (27,919 in health, 2,617 in nursing); 5,575 periodical subscriptions (158 health-care related).

BACCALAUREATE PROGRAMS
Degree BS

Available Programs Accelerated RN Baccalaureate; Generic Baccalaureate; LPN to Baccalaureate; RN Baccalaureate.

Site Options Nampa, ID.

Study Options Full-time.

Online Degree Options Yes.

Program Entrance Requirements Transcript of college record, immunizations, minimum GPA in nursing prerequisites of 3.0, professional liability insurance/malpractice insurance, prerequisite course work. Transfer students are accepted. Application deadline: 3/1 (fall), 10/1 (spring). Application fee: $20.

Advanced Placement Credit by examination available. Credit given for nursing courses completed elsewhere dependent upon specific evaluations.

Expenses (2008–09) Tuition, state resident: full-time $4632; part-time $2316 per semester. Tuition, nonresident: full-time $13,208; part-time $6604 per semester. Room and board: $4968; room only: $2339 per academic year.

Financial Aid 81% of baccalaureate students in nursing programs received some form of financial aid in 2007–08. Gift aid (need-based): Federal Pell, FSEOG, state, private, college/university gift aid from institutional funds, Leveraging Educational Assistance Program (LEAP). Loans: Federal Direct (Subsidized and Unsubsidized Stafford PLUS), Perkins, state, college/university, Alaska Loans. Work-study: Federal Work-Study, part-time campus jobs. Financial aid application deadline: 6/1 (priority: 2/15).

Contact Dr. Marty Downey, Associate Chair of Student Affairs, Department of Nursing, Boise State University, 1910 University Drive, Boise, ID 83725-0399. Telephone: 208-426-4143. Fax: 208-426-1370. E-mail: MDowney@boisestate.edu.

Boise State University (continued)
GRADUATE PROGRAMS

Expenses (2008–09) *Tuition, state resident:* full-time $5504; part-time $2752 per semester. *Tuition, nonresident:* full-time $14,080; part-time $7040 per semester.

Financial Aid 20% of graduate students in nursing programs received some form of financial aid in 2007–08.

Contact Dr. Abigail Gerding, Associate Chair of Graduate Studies, Department of Nursing, Boise State University, 1910 University Drive, Boise, ID 83725. *Telephone:* 208-426-4143. *E-mail:* abigailgerding@ boisestate.edu.

MASTER'S DEGREE PROGRAM

Degrees MSN; MSN/MS

Available Programs Master's.

Concentrations Available Clinical nurse leader; health-care administration; nurse case management; nursing administration; nursing education.

Study Options Part-time.

Program Entrance Requirements Minimum overall college GPA of 3.0, transcript of college record, CPR certification, written essay, letters of recommendation, nursing research course, professional liability insurance/malpractice insurance, prerequisite course work, resume, statistics course. *Application deadline:* 3/31 (spring).

Degree Requirements 39 total credit hours, thesis or project.

Idaho State University
Department of Nursing
Pocatello, Idaho

Founded in 1901

DEGREES • BSN • MS

Nursing Program Faculty 22 (36% with doctorates).

Baccalaureate Enrollment 195
Women 76% **Men** 24% **Minority** 14%

Graduate Enrollment 124
Women 85% **Men** 15% **Minority** 6% **Part-time** 58%

Distance Learning Courses Available.

Nursing Student Activities Sigma Theta Tau, Student Nurses' Association.

Nursing Student Resources Academic advising; academic or career counseling; assistance for students with disabilities; bookstore; campus computer network; computer lab; computer-assisted instruction; daycare for children of students; e-mail services; employment services for current students; housing assistance; interactive nursing skills videos; Internet; learning resource lab; library services; nursing audiovisuals; resume preparation assistance; skills, simulation, or other laboratory; tutoring.

Library Facilities 835,638 volumes (35,948 in health, 1,775 in nursing); 4,867 periodical subscriptions (5,312 health-care related).

BACCALAUREATE PROGRAMS

Degree BSN

Available Programs ADN to Baccalaureate; Accelerated Baccalaureate for Second Degree; Generic Baccalaureate; LPN to Baccalaureate.

Site Options Boise, ID; Idaho Falls, ID; Twin Falls, ID.

Study Options Full-time.

Program Entrance Requirements Minimum overall college GPA, transcript of college record, CPR certification, written essay, health exam, health insurance, high school transcript, immunizations, 3 letters of recommendation, minimum high school GPA of 2.0, minimum GPA in nursing prerequisites of 3.0, professional liability insurance/malpractice insurance, prerequisite course work. Transfer students are accepted. *Application deadline:* 9/15 (spring). *Application fee:* $50.

Advanced Placement Credit given for nursing courses completed elsewhere dependent upon specific evaluations.

Expenses (2009–10) *Tuition, state resident:* full-time $4968; part-time $253 per credit. *Tuition, nonresident:* full-time $7385; part-time $393 per credit. *International tuition:* $14,770 full-time. *Room and board:* $4293; room only: $2943 per academic year. *Required fees:* full-time $1200; part-time $600 per term.

Contact Dr. Carol A. Ashton, Associate Dean and Director, School of Nursing, Department of Nursing, Idaho State University, 921 South 8th Avenue, Stop 8101, Pocatello, ID 83209-8101. *Telephone:* 208-282-2443. *Fax:* 208-236-4476. *E-mail:* ashtcaro@isu.edu.

GRADUATE PROGRAMS

Expenses (2009–10) *Tuition, state resident:* full-time $5848; part-time $297 per credit. *Tuition, nonresident:* full-time $7825; part-time $437 per credit. *International tuition:* $15,650 full-time. *Room and board:* $4075; room only: $3375 per academic year. *Required fees:* full-time $1540; part-time $770 per term.

Financial Aid 2 teaching assistantships (averaging $9,401 per year) were awarded; career-related internships or fieldwork, Federal Work-Study, institutionally sponsored loans, scholarships, traineeships, tuition waivers (full and partial), and unspecified assistantships also available.

Contact Dr. Carol A. Ashton, Associate Dean and Director, School of Nursing, Department of Nursing, Idaho State University, 921 South 8th Avenue, Stop 8101, Pocatello, ID 83209-8101. *Telephone:* 208-282-2443. *Fax:* 208-282-4476. *E-mail:* ashtcaro@isu.edu.

MASTER'S DEGREE PROGRAM

Degree MS

Available Programs Accelerated AD/RN to Master's; Master's.

Concentrations Available Clinical nurse leader; nursing administration; nursing education. *Clinical nurse specialist programs in:* adult health. *Nurse practitioner programs in:* family health.

Study Options Full-time and part-time.

Online Degree Options Yes (online only).

Program Entrance Requirements Minimum overall college GPA of 3.0, transcript of college record, CPR certification, immunizations, interview, 3 letters of recommendation, professional liability insurance/malpractice insurance, prerequisite course work, statistics course, GRE General Test. *Application deadline:* 2/2 (fall). *Application fee:* $50.

Advanced Placement Credit given for nursing courses completed elsewhere dependent upon specific evaluations.

Degree Requirements 46 total credit hours, comprehensive exam.

POST-MASTER'S PROGRAM

Areas of Study Nursing administration; nursing education. *Clinical nurse specialist programs in:* adult health. *Nurse practitioner programs in:* family health.

Lewis-Clark State College
Division of Nursing and Health Sciences
Lewiston, Idaho

http://www.lcsc.edu/Nurdiv/

Founded in 1893

DEGREE • BSN

Nursing Program Faculty 22 (23% with doctorates).

Baccalaureate Enrollment 120
Women 85% **Men** 15% **Minority** 10% **International** 5% **Part-time** 20%

Distance Learning Courses Available.

Nursing Student Activities Student Nurses' Association.

Nursing Student Resources Academic advising; academic or career counseling; assistance for students with disabilities; bookstore; campus computer network; career placement assistance; computer lab; computer-assisted instruction; daycare for children of students; e-mail services; employment services for current students; housing assistance; interactive nursing skills videos; Internet; learning resource lab; library services; nursing audiovisuals; remedial services; resume preparation assistance; skills, simulation, or other laboratory; tutoring; unpaid internships.

Library Facilities 139,499 volumes (19,920 in health, 5,101 in nursing); 1,612 periodical subscriptions (12,058 health-care related).

BACCALAUREATE PROGRAMS

Degree BSN

Available Programs ADN to Baccalaureate; Generic Baccalaureate; LPN to Baccalaureate.

Site Options Coeur d'Alene, ID.

Study Options Full-time.

Program Entrance Requirements Minimum overall college GPA of 2.5, transcript of college record, CPR certification, written essay, health insurance, immunizations, 2 letters of recommendation, minimum GPA in nursing prerequisites of 2.5, prerequisite course work. Transfer students are accepted. *Application deadline:* 9/15 (fall), 1/15 (spring). *Application fee:* $35.

Advanced Placement Credit given for nursing courses completed elsewhere dependent upon specific evaluations.

Expenses (2009–10) *Tuition, state resident:* full-time $4596; part-time $234 per credit. *Tuition, nonresident:* full-time $12,786. *International tuition:* $12,786 full-time. *Room and board:* $6100; room only: $3200 per academic year.

Financial Aid 80% of baccalaureate students in nursing programs received some form of financial aid in 2008–09.

Contact Advising Center, Division of Nursing and Health Sciences, Lewis-Clark State College, 500 8th Avenue, Lewiston, ID 83501. *Telephone:* 208-792-2688. *Fax:* 208-792-2062. *E-mail:* NHS@lcsc.edu.

Northwest Nazarene University
School of Health and Science
Nampa, Idaho

http://www.nnu.edu

Founded in 1913

DEGREES • BSN • MSN

Nursing Program Faculty 19

Baccalaureate Enrollment 88
Women 92% **Men** 8% **Minority** 5% **International** 3% **Part-time** 1%

Graduate Enrollment 9
Women 100%

Distance Learning Courses Available.

Nursing Student Activities Student Nurses' Association.

Nursing Student Resources Academic advising; academic or career counseling; assistance for students with disabilities; bookstore; campus computer network; career placement assistance; computer lab; computer-assisted instruction; e-mail services; housing assistance; interactive nursing skills videos; Internet; learning resource lab; library services; nursing audiovisuals; remedial services; resume preparation assistance; skills, simulation, or other laboratory; tutoring; unpaid internships.

Library Facilities 10,026 volumes (1,500 in health, 950 in nursing); 821 periodical subscriptions (218 health-care related).

BACCALAUREATE PROGRAMS

Degree BSN

Available Programs Generic Baccalaureate.

Study Options Full-time.

Program Entrance Requirements Transcript of college record, high school chemistry, minimum GPA in nursing prerequisites of 2.75, prerequisite course work. Transfer students are accepted. *Application deadline:* 4/15 (spring).

Advanced Placement Credit given for nursing courses completed elsewhere dependent upon specific evaluations.

Expenses (2009–10) *Tuition:* full-time $21,930; part-time $950 per credit. *Room and board:* $5790; room only: $2560 per academic year. *Required fees:* full-time $296.

Financial Aid 90% of baccalaureate students in nursing programs received some form of financial aid in 2008–09.

Contact Dr. Patricia D. Kissell, RN, Chair, School of Health and Science, Northwest Nazarene University, 623 Holly Street, Nampa, ID 83686. *Telephone:* 208-467-8650. *Fax:* 208-467-8651. *E-mail:* nursing@nnu.edu.

GRADUATE PROGRAMS

Expenses (2009–10) *Tuition:* full-time $9900.

Contact Mrs. Kathy L. Hanson, Program Administrator, School of Health and Science, Northwest Nazarene University, 623 Holly Street, Nampa, ID 83686. *Telephone:* 208-467-8642. *Fax:* 208-467-8651. *E-mail:* klhanson@nnu.edu.

MASTER'S DEGREE PROGRAM

Degree MSN

Available Programs Master's; RN to Master's.

Concentrations Available Nursing education.

Online Degree Options Yes (online only).

Program Entrance Requirements Computer literacy, minimum overall college GPA of 3.0, transcript of college record, prerequisite course work, resume, statistics course. *Application deadline:* 7/31 (fall). Applications may be processed on a rolling basis for some programs. *Application fee:* $50.

Degree Requirements 36 total credit hours, thesis or project.

ILLINOIS

Aurora University
School of Nursing
Aurora, Illinois

http://www.aurora.edu

Founded in 1893

DEGREES • BSN • MSN

Nursing Program Faculty 15 (27% with doctorates).

Baccalaureate Enrollment 226
Women 94% **Men** 6% **Minority** 27% **Part-time** 49%

Nursing Student Activities Sigma Theta Tau, Student Nurses' Association, nursing club.

Nursing Student Resources Academic advising; academic or career counseling; assistance for students with disabilities; bookstore; campus computer network; career placement assistance; computer lab; computer-assisted instruction; e-mail services; externships; interactive nursing skills videos; Internet; learning resource lab; library services; nursing audiovisuals; remedial services; resume preparation assistance; skills, simulation, or other laboratory; tutoring.

Library Facilities 99,000 volumes (3,791 in health, 620 in nursing); 210 periodical subscriptions (1,700 health-care related).

BACCALAUREATE PROGRAMS

Degree BSN

Available Programs Generic Baccalaureate; RN Baccalaureate.

Site Options Winfield, IL; Williams Bay, WI; Aurora, IL.

Study Options Full-time.

Program Entrance Requirements Minimum overall college GPA of 2.75, transcript of college record, CPR certification, written essay, health exam, health insurance, immunizations, interview, minimum GPA in nursing prerequisites of 2.75, prerequisite course work. Transfer students are accepted. *Application deadline:* 1/15 (fall). *Application fee:* $25.

Advanced Placement Credit given for nursing courses completed elsewhere dependent upon specific evaluations.

Expenses (2009–10) *Tuition:* full-time $18,600; part-time $550 per credit hour. *International tuition:* $18,600 full-time. *Room and board:* $8170 per academic year. *Required fees:* part-time $37 per credit.

Financial Aid 85% of baccalaureate students in nursing programs received some form of financial aid in 2008–09. *Gift aid (need-based):* Federal Pell, FSEOG, state, private, college/university gift aid from institutional funds. *Loans:* FFEL (Subsidized and Unsubsidized Stafford PLUS), Perkins, college/university. *Work-study:* Federal Work-Study. *Financial aid application deadline (priority):* 4/15.

Aurora University (continued)

Contact Dr. Carmella M. Moran, Director and Associate Professor of Nursing, School of Nursing, Aurora University, 347 South Gladstone Avenue, Aurora, IL 60506-4892. *Telephone:* 630-844-5130. *Fax:* 630-844-7822. *E-mail:* cmoran@aurora.edu.

GRADUATE PROGRAMS

Expenses (2009–10) *Tuition:* part-time $615 per credit hour.

Contact Dr. Barbara Lockwood, Coordinator, MSN Program, School of Nursing, Aurora University, 347 South Gladstone Avenue, Aurora, IL 60506-4892. *Telephone:* 630-844-5139. *Fax:* 630-844-7822. *E-mail:* lockwood@aurora.edu.

MASTER'S DEGREE PROGRAM

Degree MSN

Available Programs Master's.

Concentrations Available Nursing administration; nursing education.

Study Options Part-time.

Program Entrance Requirements Computer literacy, minimum overall college GPA of 2.75, transcript of college record, CPR certification, written essay, immunizations, interview, 3 letters of recommendation, professional liability insurance/malpractice insurance, résumé. *Application deadline:* Applications may be processed on a rolling basis for some programs. *Application fee:* $25.

Degree Requirements 36 total credit hours, thesis or project.

Benedictine University
Department of Nursing
Lisle, Illinois

Founded in 1887

DEGREES • BSN • MSN

Nursing Program Faculty 26 (62% with doctorates).

Baccalaureate Enrollment 110
Women 95% **Men** 5% **Minority** 17% **International** 1%

Graduate Enrollment 130
Women 96% **Men** 4% **Minority** 37%

Nursing Student Activities Nursing Honor Society, Sigma Theta Tau.

Nursing Student Resources Academic advising; academic or career counseling; assistance for students with disabilities; bookstore; campus computer network; career placement assistance; computer lab; computer-assisted instruction; e-mail services; interactive nursing skills videos; Internet; learning resource lab; library services; nursing audiovisuals; placement services for program completers; remedial services; résumé preparation assistance; skills, simulation, or other laboratory; tutoring.

Library Facilities 138,000 volumes (1,350 in health, 850 in nursing); 23,906 periodical subscriptions (291 health-care related).

BACCALAUREATE PROGRAMS

Degree BSN

Available Programs Accelerated RN Baccalaureate.

Site Options River Grove, IL; Springfield, IL; Glen Ellyn, IL.

Study Options Full-time.

Program Entrance Requirements Minimum overall college GPA of 2.50, transcript of college record, 1 letter of recommendation, RN licensure. Transfer students are accepted. *Application deadline:* 7/1 (fall), 11/1 (winter), 2/1 (spring), 5/1 (summer). Applications may be processed on a rolling basis for some programs.

Advanced Placement Credit given for nursing courses completed elsewhere dependent upon specific evaluations.

Expenses (2009–10) *Tuition:* full-time $8695; part-time $235 per credit hour. *International tuition:* $8695 full-time.

Financial Aid 50% of baccalaureate students in nursing programs received some form of financial aid in 2008–09.

Contact Dr. Ethel C. Ragland, Chair and Professor, Department of Nursing, Benedictine University, 5700 College Road, Kindlon Hall 249, Lisle, IL 60532-0900. *Telephone:* 630-829-6583. *Fax:* 630-829-1154. *E-mail:* eragland@ben.edu.

GRADUATE PROGRAMS

Expenses (2009–10) *Tuition:* full-time $17,640; part-time $490 per credit hour. *International tuition:* $17,640 full-time.

Contact Dr. Bonnie Beardsley, Associate Professor, Department of Nursing, Benedictine University, 5700 College Road, Kindlon Hall 249, Lisle, IL 60532. *Telephone:* 630-829-1933. *Fax:* 630-829-1154. *E-mail:* bbeardsley@ben.edu.

MASTER'S DEGREE PROGRAM

Degree MSN

Available Programs Accelerated Master's; Master's.

Study Options Full-time and part-time.

Online Degree Options Yes (online only).

Program Entrance Requirements Minimum overall college GPA of 3.00, transcript of college record, written essay, 1 letter of recommendation, resume. *Application deadline:* Applications may be processed on a rolling basis for some programs.

Advanced Placement Credit given for nursing courses completed elsewhere dependent upon specific evaluations.

Degree Requirements 36 total credit hours, thesis or project.

Blessing–Rieman College of Nursing
Blessing–Rieman College of Nursing
Quincy, Illinois

http://www.brcn.edu

DEGREES • BSN • MSN

Nursing Program Faculty 19 (21% with doctorates).

Baccalaureate Enrollment 200
Women 95% **Men** 5% **Minority** 5% **Part-time** 8%

Graduate Enrollment 8
Women 88% **Men** 12% **Part-time** 100%

Distance Learning Courses Available.

Nursing Student Activities Nursing Honor Society, Sigma Theta Tau, Student Nurses' Association.

Nursing Student Resources Academic advising; academic or career counseling; bookstore; campus computer network; computer lab; computer-assisted instruction; daycare for children of students; e-mail services; employment services for current students; externships; interactive nursing skills videos; Internet; learning resource lab; library services; nursing audiovisuals; paid internships; resume preparation assistance; skills, simulation, or other laboratory; tutoring.

Library Facilities 3,752 volumes in health, 3,752 volumes in nursing; 125 periodical subscriptions health-care related.

BACCALAUREATE PROGRAMS

Degree BSN

Available Programs Accelerated Baccalaureate for Second Degree; Generic Baccalaureate; LPN to Baccalaureate; RN Baccalaureate.

Study Options Full-time and part-time.

Online Degree Options Yes.

Program Entrance Requirements Minimum overall college GPA of 2.5, transcript of college record, CPR certification, health insurance, high school biology, high school chemistry, 2 years high school math, 2 years high school science, high school transcript, immunizations, minimum high school GPA of 3.0, minimum GPA in nursing prerequisites of 2.5, prerequisite course work. Transfer students are accepted. *Application deadline:* Applications may be processed on a rolling basis for some programs.

Advanced Placement Credit by examination available. Credit given for nursing courses completed elsewhere dependent upon specific evaluations.

Expenses (2009–10) *Tuition:* full-time $16,275; part-time $543 per credit hour. *Room and board:* room only: $2840 per academic year. *Required fees:* full-time $750.

Financial Aid 90% of baccalaureate students in nursing programs received some form of financial aid in 2008–09.

Contact Mrs. Heather Mutter, Admission Counselor, Blessing–Rieman College of Nursing, Broadway at 11th Street, PO Box 7005, Quincy, IL 62305-7005. *Telephone:* 217-228-5520 Ext. 6949. *Fax:* 217-223-4661. *E-mail:* admissions@brcn.edu.

GRADUATE PROGRAMS

Expenses (2009–10) *Tuition:* part-time $300 per credit hour.

Contact Mrs. Heather Mutter, Admissions Counselor, Blessing–Rieman College of Nursing, Broadway at 11th Street, PO Box 7005, Quincy, IL 62305-7005. *Telephone:* 217-228-5520 Ext. 6949. *Fax:* 217-223-4661. *E-mail:* admissions@brcn.edu.

MASTER'S DEGREE PROGRAM

Degree MSN

Available Programs Master's.

Concentrations Available Nursing administration; nursing education.

Study Options Part-time.

Program Entrance Requirements Clinical experience, computer literacy, minimum overall college GPA of 3.0, transcript of college record, CPR certification, written essay, immunizations, letters of recommendation, nursing research course, physical assessment course, professional liability insurance/malpractice insurance, resume, statistics course. *Application deadline:* 4/15 (spring). Applications may be processed on a rolling basis for some programs.

Advanced Placement Credit given for nursing courses completed elsewhere dependent upon specific evaluations.

Degree Requirements 40 total credit hours, thesis or project.

See full description on page 482.

Bradley University
Department of Nursing
Peoria, Illinois

http://www.bradley.edu/academics/ehs/nur/ nur_index.html
Founded in 1897
DEGREES • BSN • BSC PN • MSN

Nursing Program Faculty 36 (25% with doctorates).
Baccalaureate Enrollment 325
Women 91.1% **Men** 8.9% **Minority** 13.2% **Part-time** 3%
Graduate Enrollment 50
Women 58% **Men** 42% **Minority** 14% **Part-time** 94%
Nursing Student Activities Sigma Theta Tau, Student Nurses' Association.
Nursing Student Resources Academic advising; bookstore; campus computer network; career placement assistance; computer lab; computer-assisted instruction; e-mail services; housing assistance; Internet; learning resource lab; library services; nursing audiovisuals; placement services for program completers; resume preparation assistance; skills, simulation, or other laboratory; tutoring.
Library Facilities 510,297 volumes (11,159 in health, 2,214 in nursing); 29,776 periodical subscriptions (210 health-care related).

BACCALAUREATE PROGRAMS

Degrees BSN; BSc PN

Available Programs Generic Baccalaureate; LPN to Baccalaureate; RN Baccalaureate.

Study Options Full-time and part-time.

Program Entrance Requirements Minimum overall college GPA of 2.5, transcript of college record, health exam, high school biology, high school chemistry, 3 years high school math, 3 years high school science, high school transcript, immunizations, minimum high school GPA of 2.5, minimum GPA in nursing prerequisites of 2.0. Transfer students are accepted.

Advanced Placement Credit by examination available. Credit given for nursing courses completed elsewhere dependent upon specific evaluations.

Contact *Telephone:* 309-677-2530. *Fax:* 309-677-2566.

GRADUATE PROGRAMS

Contact *Telephone:* 309-677-2530. *Fax:* 309-677-2527.

MASTER'S DEGREE PROGRAM

Degree MSN

Available Programs Accelerated Master's for Nurses with Non-Nursing Degrees; Master's.

Concentrations Available Nurse anesthesia; nursing administration.
Site Options Decatur, IL.
Study Options Full-time and part-time.
Program Entrance Requirements Clinical experience, minimum overall college GPA of 3.0, transcript of college record, interview, 3 letters of recommendation, nursing research course, physical assessment course, prerequisite course work, resume, statistics course, GRE General Test or MAT.
Advanced Placement Credit given for nursing courses completed elsewhere dependent upon specific evaluations.
Degree Requirements Thesis or project, comprehensive exam.

Chicago State University
College of Nursing and Allied Health Professions
Chicago, Illinois

http://www.csu.edu
Founded in 1867
DEGREE • BSN

Nursing Program Faculty 23 (60% with doctorates).
Baccalaureate Enrollment 372
Women 90% **Men** 10% **Minority** 97% **International** 15% **Part-time** 24%
Nursing Student Activities Nursing Honor Society, Student Nurses' Association.
Nursing Student Resources Academic advising; academic or career counseling; assistance for students with disabilities; bookstore; campus computer network; computer lab; computer-assisted instruction; daycare for children of students; e-mail services; employment services for current students; externships; interactive nursing skills videos; Internet; learning resource lab; library services; nursing audiovisuals; remedial services; resume preparation assistance; skills, simulation, or other laboratory; tutoring; unpaid internships.
Library Facilities 426,691 volumes; 1,654 periodical subscriptions.

BACCALAUREATE PROGRAMS

Degree BSN

Available Programs Generic Baccalaureate; LPN to Baccalaureate; RN Baccalaureate.
Study Options Full-time.
Program Entrance Requirements Minimum overall college GPA of 2.5, transcript of college record, written essay, health exam, health insurance, 3 years high school math, 3 years high school science, high school transcript, immunizations, interview, 3 letters of recommendation, minimum GPA in nursing prerequisites of 2.5, professional liability insurance/malpractice insurance, prerequisite course work. Transfer students are accepted.
Advanced Placement Credit by examination available.
Contact *Telephone:* 773-995-3992. *Fax:* 773-821-2438.

DePaul University
Department of Nursing
Chicago, Illinois

http://www.depaul.edu/~nursing

Founded in 1898

DEGREES • BS • MS

Nursing Program Faculty 19 (89% with doctorates).

Baccalaureate Enrollment 5

Graduate Enrollment 131
Women 87% **Men** 13% **Minority** 23% **Part-time** 35%

Nursing Student Activities Sigma Theta Tau, Student Nurses' Association.

Nursing Student Resources Academic advising; academic or career counseling; assistance for students with disabilities; bookstore; campus computer network; computer lab; computer-assisted instruction; e-mail services; employment services for current students; externships; housing assistance; interactive nursing skills videos; Internet; learning resource lab; library services; nursing audiovisuals; resume preparation assistance; skills, simulation, or other laboratory; tutoring.

Library Facilities 897,564 volumes; 28,514 periodical subscriptions (193 health-care related).

BACCALAUREATE PROGRAMS

Degree BS

Available Programs Accelerated RN Baccalaureate.

Study Options Full-time and part-time.

Program Entrance Requirements Minimum overall college GPA of 2.5, transcript of college record, CPR certification, health exam, immunizations, professional liability insurance/malpractice insurance, RN licensure. Transfer students are accepted.

Advanced Placement Credit given for nursing courses completed elsewhere dependent upon specific evaluations.

Contact *Telephone:* 773-325-7280. *Fax:* 773-325-7282.

GRADUATE PROGRAMS

Contact *Telephone:* 773-325-7280. *Fax:* 773-325-7282.

MASTER'S DEGREE PROGRAM

Degree MS

Available Programs Master's; Master's for Non-Nursing College Graduates; Master's for Nurses with Non-Nursing Degrees; RN to Master's.

Concentrations Available Nurse anesthesia; nurse case management; nursing administration; nursing education. *Clinical nurse specialist programs in:* community health, medical-surgical. *Nurse practitioner programs in:* adult health, community health, family health, pediatric, women's health.

Study Options Full-time and part-time.

Program Entrance Requirements Computer literacy, minimum overall college GPA of 2.75, transcript of college record, CPR certification, physical assessment course, professional liability insurance/malpractice insurance, prerequisite course work, statistics course, GRE.

Advanced Placement Credit given for nursing courses completed elsewhere dependent upon specific evaluations.

Degree Requirements 52 total credit hours, thesis or project.

POST-MASTER'S PROGRAM

Areas of Study Nurse anesthesia. *Nurse practitioner programs in:* adult health, community health, family health, pediatric, women's health.

Eastern Illinois University
Nursing Program
Charleston, Illinois

Founded in 1895

DEGREE • BSN

Distance Learning Courses Available.

Library Facilities 950,188 volumes; 32,860 periodical subscriptions.

BACCALAUREATE PROGRAMS

Degree BSN

Available Programs RN Baccalaureate.

Study Options Full-time and part-time.

Contact RN to BS in Nursing Program, Nursing Program, Eastern Illinois University, 600 Lincoln Avenue, 2230 McAfee, Charleston, IL 61920. *Telephone:* 217-581-7049. *Fax:* 217-581-7050.

Elmhurst College
Deicke Center for Nursing Education
Elmhurst, Illinois

Founded in 1871

DEGREES • BS • MS • MS/MBA

Nursing Program Faculty 13 (55% with doctorates).

Baccalaureate Enrollment 195

Graduate Enrollment 34

Nursing Student Activities Sigma Theta Tau, Student Nurses' Association.

Nursing Student Resources Academic advising; academic or career counseling; assistance for students with disabilities; bookstore; campus computer network; career placement assistance; computer lab; e-mail services; employment services for current students; housing assistance; Internet; learning resource lab; library services; nursing audiovisuals; resume preparation assistance; skills, simulation, or other laboratory; tutoring.

Library Facilities 225,254 volumes (6,000 in health); 1,414 periodical subscriptions (80 health-care related).

BACCALAUREATE PROGRAMS

Degree BS

Available Programs Generic Baccalaureate; RN Baccalaureate.

Study Options Full-time.

Program Entrance Requirements Minimum overall college GPA of 2.75, transcript of college record, CPR certification, written essay, health insurance, immunizations, 2 letters of recommendation, minimum GPA in nursing prerequisites of 2.75, prerequisite course work. Transfer students are accepted.

Advanced Placement Credit given for nursing courses completed elsewhere dependent upon specific evaluations.

Contact Dr. Jan Strom, Director, Deicke Center for Nursing Education, Elmhurst College, 190 Prospect Avenue, Elmhurst, IL 60126. *Telephone:* 630-617-3344. *Fax:* 630-617-3237. *E-mail:* janstrom@elmhurst.edu.

GRADUATE PROGRAMS

Contact Dr. Mary Oesterle, Deicke Center for Nursing Education, Elmhurst College, 190 Prospect Avenue, Elmhurst, IL 60126. *Fax:* 630-617-3514. *E-mail:* oesterle@elmhurst.edu.

MASTER'S DEGREE PROGRAM

Degrees MS; MS/MBA

Available Programs Master's.

Concentrations Available Clinical nurse leader; nursing education.

Study Options Full-time.

Program Entrance Requirements Clinical experience, computer literacy, transcript of college record, CPR certification, written essay, immunizations, interview, 3 letters of recommendation, nursing research course, physical assessment course, prerequisite course work, resume, statistics course. *Application deadline:* Applications may be processed on a rolling basis for some programs.

Degree Requirements 33 total credit hours.

Governors State University

College of Health and Human Services
University Park, Illinois

http://www.govst.edu/nursing/index.html

Founded in 1969

DEGREES • BS • MS

Nursing Program Faculty 7 (85% with doctorates).

Baccalaureate Enrollment 31
Women 98% **Men** 2% **Minority** 92% **International** 1% **Part-time** 100%

Graduate Enrollment 72
Women 97% **Men** 3% **Minority** 89% **International** 6% **Part-time** 4%

Nursing Student Activities Sigma Theta Tau.

Nursing Student Resources Academic advising; assistance for students with disabilities; bookstore; campus computer network; computer lab; daycare for children of students; e-mail services; Internet; learning resource lab; library services; nursing audiovisuals; tutoring.

Library Facilities 260,000 volumes; 2,200 periodical subscriptions.

BACCALAUREATE PROGRAMS

Degree BS

Available Programs RN Baccalaureate.

Study Options Part-time.

Program Entrance Requirements Transcript of college record, CPR certification, health exam, health insurance, immunizations, minimum GPA in nursing prerequisites of 2.0, professional liability insurance/malpractice insurance, prerequisite course work, RN licensure. Transfer students are accepted.

Contact *Telephone:* 708-534-4053. *Fax:* 708-534-2197.

GRADUATE PROGRAMS

Contact *Telephone:* 708-534-4053. *Fax:* 708-534-2197.

MASTER'S DEGREE PROGRAM

Degree MS

Available Programs Master's.

Concentrations Available *Clinical nurse specialist programs in:* adult health.

Study Options Full-time and part-time.

Program Entrance Requirements Clinical experience, computer literacy, minimum overall college GPA of 3.0, transcript of college record, CPR certification, written essay, immunizations, nursing research course, physical assessment course, professional liability insurance/malpractice insurance, prerequisite course work, statistics course.

Degree Requirements 42 total credit hours, comprehensive exam.

POST-MASTER'S PROGRAM

Areas of Study Nursing education.

Illinois State University

Mennonite College of Nursing
Normal, Illinois

http://www.mcn.ilstu.edu

Founded in 1857

DEGREES • BSN • MSN • PHD

Nursing Program Faculty 51 (29% with doctorates).

Baccalaureate Enrollment 308
Women 94% **Men** 6% **Minority** 7% **International** 1% **Part-time** 12%

Graduate Enrollment 82
Women 93% **Men** 7% **Minority** 11% **International** 3% **Part-time** 78%

Distance Learning Courses Available.

Nursing Student Activities Nursing Honor Society, Sigma Theta Tau, Student Nurses' Association.

Nursing Student Resources Academic advising; academic or career counseling; assistance for students with disabilities; bookstore; campus computer network; career placement assistance; computer lab; computer-assisted instruction; daycare for children of students; e-mail services; employment services for current students; externships; interactive nursing skills videos; Internet; learning resource lab; library services; nursing audiovisuals; placement services for program completers; resume preparation assistance; skills, simulation, or other laboratory; tutoring.

Library Facilities 1.6 million volumes (18,000 in health, 4,000 in nursing); 14,166 periodical subscriptions (700 health-care related).

BACCALAUREATE PROGRAMS

Degree BSN

Available Programs Accelerated Baccalaureate for Second Degree; Generic Baccalaureate; RN Baccalaureate.

Site Options Normal, IL.

Study Options Full-time.

Online Degree Options Yes.

Program Entrance Requirements Minimum overall college GPA of 2.7, transcript of college record, CPR certification, health exam, health insurance, immunizations, minimum GPA in nursing prerequisites of 2.0, prerequisite course work. Transfer students are accepted. *Application deadline:* 1/15 (fall). *Application fee:* $40.

Advanced Placement Credit given for nursing courses completed elsewhere dependent upon specific evaluations.

Expenses (2009–10) *Tuition, state resident:* full-time $4140; part-time $276 per credit hour. *Tuition, nonresident:* full-time $7155; part-time $477 per credit hour. *Room and board:* $7852; room only: $4190 per academic year. *Required fees:* full-time $1929; part-time $64 per credit.

Financial Aid 70% of baccalaureate students in nursing programs received some form of financial aid in 2008–09. *Gift aid (need-based):* Federal Pell, FSEOG, state, private, college/university gift aid from institutional funds, Federal Nursing. *Loans:* Federal Nursing Student Loans, Federal Direct (Subsidized and Unsubsidized Stafford PLUS), Perkins, college/university. *Work-study:* Federal Work-Study, part-time campus jobs. *Financial aid application deadline (priority):* 3/1.

Contact Mrs. Tenna Webb, Academic Advising Secretary, Mennonite College of Nursing, Illinois State University, 5810 Edwards Hall, Normal, IL 61790-5810. *Telephone:* 309-438-2252. *Fax:* 309-438-2620. *E-mail:* tlwebb@ilstu.edu.

GRADUATE PROGRAMS

Expenses (2009–10) *Tuition, state resident:* full-time $3960; part-time $440 per credit hour. *Tuition, nonresident:* full-time $8226; part-time $457 per credit hour. *Required fees:* full-time $579; part-time $64 per credit.

Financial Aid 50% of graduate students in nursing programs received some form of financial aid in 2008–09.

Contact Ms. Melissa K. Moody, Academic Advisor, Mennonite College of Nursing, Illinois State University, 5810 Edwards Hall, Normal, IL 61790-5810. *Telephone:* 309-438-7035. *Fax:* 309-438-2280. *E-mail:* mkmoody@ilstu.edu.

MASTER'S DEGREE PROGRAM

Degree MSN

Available Programs Master's.

Concentrations Available Clinical nurse leader; nursing administration. *Nurse practitioner programs in:* family health, gerontology.

Site Options Normal, IL.

Study Options Full-time and part-time.

Program Entrance Requirements Minimum overall college GPA of 3.0, transcript of college record, CPR certification, written essay, immunizations, 3 letters of recommendation, nursing research course, physical assessment course, prerequisite course work, resume, statistics course. *Application deadline:* 2/1 (fall), 9/1 (spring). Applications may be processed on a rolling basis for some programs. *Application fee:* $40.

Advanced Placement Credit given for nursing courses completed elsewhere dependent upon specific evaluations.

Degree Requirements 44 total credit hours, comprehensive exam.

POST-MASTER'S PROGRAM

Areas of Study Nursing education. *Nurse practitioner programs in:* family health, gerontology.

Illinois State University (continued)
DOCTORAL DEGREE PROGRAM

Degree PhD

Available Programs Doctorate.

Areas of Study Aging.

Site Options Normal, IL.

Program Entrance Requirements Minimum overall college GPA of 3.0, interview by faculty committee, interview, 3 letters of recommendation, MSN or equivalent, statistics course, vita. Application deadline: 2/1 (fall). Applications may be processed on a rolling basis for some programs. Application fee: $40.

Degree Requirements 66 total credit hours, dissertation, oral exam, written exam, residency.

Illinois Wesleyan University
School of Nursing
Bloomington, Illinois

http://www2.iwu.edu/nursing/
Founded in 1850

DEGREE • BSN

Nursing Program Faculty 27 (30% with doctorates).

Baccalaureate Enrollment 131
Women 95% **Men** 5% **Minority** 11%

Nursing Student Activities Nursing Honor Society, Sigma Theta Tau, Student Nurses' Association, nursing club.

Nursing Student Resources Academic advising; academic or career counseling; assistance for students with disabilities; bookstore; campus computer network; career placement assistance; computer lab; computer-assisted instruction; e-mail services; employment services for current students; externships; housing assistance; interactive nursing skills videos; Internet; learning resource lab; library services; nursing audiovisuals; paid internships; placement services for program completers; resume preparation assistance; skills, simulation, or other laboratory; tutoring; unpaid internships.

Library Facilities 330,300 volumes (5,500 in health, 3,000 in nursing); 32,080 periodical subscriptions (200 health-care related).

BACCALAUREATE PROGRAMS

Degree BSN

Available Programs Generic Baccalaureate.

Study Options Full-time and part-time.

Program Entrance Requirements Minimum overall college GPA of 3.0, transcript of college record, written essay, health exam, health insurance, high school biology, high school chemistry, 2 years high school math, 2 years high school science, high school transcript, immunizations, interview, minimum high school GPA of 3.0, minimum high school rank 25%, minimum GPA in nursing prerequisites of 3.0. Transfer students are accepted. *Application deadline:* Applications may be processed on a rolling basis for some programs.

Expenses (2009–10) *Tuition:* full-time $33,808; part-time $4226 per unit. *International tuition:* $33,808 full-time. *Room and board:* $7776; room only: $4800 per academic year. *Required fees:* full-time $174.

Financial Aid 91% of baccalaureate students in nursing programs received some form of financial aid in 2008–09. *Gift aid (need-based):* Federal Pell, FSEOG, state, private, college/university gift aid from institutional funds. *Loans:* Federal Nursing Student Loans, FFEL (Subsidized and Unsubsidized Stafford PLUS), Perkins, college/university. *Work-study:* Federal Work-Study, part-time campus jobs. *Financial aid application deadline:* 3/1.

Contact Dr. Victoria N. Folse, Director and Associate Professor, School of Nursing, Illinois Wesleyan University, PO Box 2900, Bloomington, IL 61702-2900. *Telephone:* 309-556-3051. *Fax:* 309-556-3043. *E-mail:* vfolse@iwu.edu.

Lakeview College of Nursing
Lakeview College of Nursing
Danville, Illinois

http://www.lakeviewcol.edu/
Founded in 1987

DEGREE • BSN

Nursing Program Faculty 20 (3% with doctorates).

Baccalaureate Enrollment 286
Women 87% **Men** 13% **Minority** 20% **Part-time** 8%

Nursing Student Activities Nursing Honor Society, Sigma Theta Tau, Student Nurses' Association.

Nursing Student Resources Academic advising; academic or career counseling; assistance for students with disabilities; bookstore; campus computer network; career placement assistance; computer lab; Internet; library services; nursing audiovisuals; resume preparation assistance; skills, simulation, or other laboratory; tutoring.

Library Facilities 2,000 volumes in health; 41 periodical subscriptions health-care related.

BACCALAUREATE PROGRAMS

Degree BSN

Available Programs Accelerated RN Baccalaureate; Generic Baccalaureate; RN Baccalaureate.

Site Options Charleston, IL.

Study Options Full-time and part-time.

Program Entrance Requirements Minimum overall college GPA of 2.5, transcript of college record, CPR certification, written essay, health exam, immunizations, 2 letters of recommendation, prerequisite course work. Transfer students are accepted. *Application deadline:* 4/1 (fall), 10/1 (spring). *Application fee:* $99.

Advanced Placement Credit given for nursing courses completed elsewhere dependent upon specific evaluations.

Expenses (2008–09) *Tuition:* part-time $320 per credit.

Financial Aid 52% of baccalaureate students in nursing programs received some form of financial aid in 2007–08.

Contact Mrs. Connie Young, Coordinator of Admissions and Records/Registrar, Lakeview College of Nursing, 903 North Logan Avenue, Danville, IL 61832. *Telephone:* 217-554-6899. *Fax:* 217-442-2279. *E-mail:* cyoung@lakeviewcol.edu.

Lewis University
Program in Nursing
Romeoville, Illinois

http://www.lewisu.edu/academics/nursing/index.htm
Founded in 1932

DEGREES • BSN • MSN • MSN/MBA

Nursing Program Faculty 30 (40% with doctorates).

Baccalaureate Enrollment 630
Women 90% **Men** 10% **Minority** 31% **International** 9% **Part-time** 69%

Graduate Enrollment 147
Women 91% **Men** 9% **Minority** 16% **International** 2%

Distance Learning Courses Available.

Nursing Student Activities Sigma Theta Tau, Student Nurses' Association.

Nursing Student Resources Academic advising; academic or career counseling; assistance for students with disabilities; bookstore; campus computer network; career placement assistance; computer lab; computer-assisted instruction; e-mail services; employment services for current students; externships; interactive nursing skills videos; Internet; learning resource lab; library services; nursing audiovisuals; other; placement services for program completers; remedial services; resume preparation assistance; skills, simulation, or other laboratory; tutoring.

Library Facilities 149,870 volumes (3,100 in health, 2,038 in nursing); 1,990 periodical subscriptions (90 health-care related).

BACCALAUREATE PROGRAMS

Degree BSN

Available Programs Accelerated Baccalaureate for Second Degree; Accelerated RN Baccalaureate; Generic Baccalaureate.

Site Options Hickory Hills, IL; Shorewood, IL; Oak Brook, IL; Tinley Park, IL.

Study Options Full-time.

Program Entrance Requirements Minimum overall college GPA of 2.75, transcript of college record, CPR certification, health exam, health insurance, high school biology, high school chemistry, 3 years high school math, high school transcript, immunizations, minimum high school GPA of 2.75, minimum GPA in nursing prerequisites of 2.75, prerequisite course work. Transfer students are accepted.

Advanced Placement Credit given for nursing courses completed elsewhere dependent upon specific evaluations.

Contact *Telephone:* 815-836-5245. *Fax:* 815-838-8306.

GRADUATE PROGRAMS

Contact *Telephone:* 815-836-5878 Ext. 815. *Fax:* 815-836-5806.

MASTER'S DEGREE PROGRAM

Degrees MSN; MSN/MBA

Available Programs Accelerated Master's; Accelerated Master's for Nurses with Non-Nursing Degrees; Accelerated RN to Master's; RN to Master's.

Concentrations Available Nurse case management; nursing administration; nursing education. *Nurse practitioner programs in:* adult health.

Site Options Hickory Hills, IL; Shorewood, IL; Oak Brook, IL; Tinley Park, IL.

Study Options Full-time and part-time.

Online Degree Options Yes (online only).

Program Entrance Requirements Clinical experience, computer literacy, minimum overall college GPA of 3.0, transcript of college record, CPR certification, immunizations, interview, 2 letters of recommendation, nursing research course, physical assessment course, professional liability insurance/malpractice insurance, prerequisite course work, resume, statistics course.

Advanced Placement Credit given for nursing courses completed elsewhere dependent upon specific evaluations.

Degree Requirements 45 total credit hours, thesis or project.

POST-MASTER'S PROGRAM

Areas of Study Nursing administration; nursing education. *Nurse practitioner programs in:* adult health.

CONTINUING EDUCATION PROGRAM

Contact *Telephone:* 815-836-5889. *Fax:* 815-838-8306.

Loyola University Chicago
Marcella Niehoff School of Nursing
Maywood, Illinois

http://www.luc.edu/schools/nursing/
Founded in 1870

DEGREES • BSN • MSN • MSN/MBA • MSN/MDIV • PHD

Nursing Program Faculty 40 (90% with doctorates).

Nursing Student Activities Nursing Honor Society, Sigma Theta Tau, Student Nurses' Association.

Library Facilities 1.4 million volumes (51,674 in health, 4,966 in nursing); 13,939 periodical subscriptions (2,630 health-care related).

BACCALAUREATE PROGRAMS

Degree BSN

Available Programs Accelerated Baccalaureate; Generic Baccalaureate; RN Baccalaureate.

Site Options Maywood, IL; Chicago, IL.

Study Options Full-time and part-time.

Program Entrance Requirements Transcript of college record, CPR certification, written essay, health exam, health insurance, high school biology, high school chemistry, 2 years high school math, high school transcript, immunizations, 2 letters of recommendation, minimum high school GPA of 3.0, minimum high school rank 25%, prerequisite course work. Transfer students are accepted.

Advanced Placement Credit given for nursing courses completed elsewhere dependent upon specific evaluations.

Contact *Telephone:* 773-508-3249. *Fax:* 773-508-3241.

GRADUATE PROGRAMS

Contact *Telephone:* 773-508-3249. *Fax:* 773-508-3241.

MASTER'S DEGREE PROGRAM

Degrees MSN; MSN/MBA; MSN/MDIV

Available Programs Master's; RN to Master's.

Concentrations Available Nurse-midwifery; nursing administration. *Clinical nurse specialist programs in:* acute care, cardiovascular, oncology. *Nurse practitioner programs in:* acute care, adult health, family health, pediatric, women's health.

Site Options Maywood, IL; Chicago, IL.

Study Options Full-time and part-time.

Program Entrance Requirements Clinical experience, minimum overall college GPA of 3.0, transcript of college record, CPR certification, written essay, immunizations, interview, 3 letters of recommendation, physical assessment course, professional liability insurance/malpractice insurance, statistics course.

Advanced Placement Credit given for nursing courses completed elsewhere dependent upon specific evaluations.

Degree Requirements 48 total credit hours, comprehensive exam.

DOCTORAL DEGREE PROGRAM

Degree PhD

Available Programs Post-Baccalaureate Doctorate.

Areas of Study Ethics, nursing education, nursing research, nursing science.

Site Options Maywood, IL; Chicago, IL.

Program Entrance Requirements interview by faculty committee, interview, 3 letters of recommendation, scholarly papers, statistics course, vita, writing sample, GRE General Test.

Degree Requirements 64 total credit hours, dissertation, oral exam, written exam.

MacMurray College
Department of Nursing
Jacksonville, Illinois

http://www.mac.edu/academics/nursing.html
Founded in 1846

DEGREE • BSN

Nursing Program Faculty 10 (25% with doctorates).

Baccalaureate Enrollment 100
Women 90% **Men** 10% **Minority** 8% **International** 1% **Part-time** 5%

Nursing Student Activities Sigma Theta Tau, nursing club.

Nursing Student Resources Academic advising; academic or career counseling; bookstore; campus computer network; career placement assistance; computer lab; computer-assisted instruction; e-mail services; externships; interactive nursing skills videos; Internet; learning resource lab; library services; nursing audiovisuals; paid internships; resume preparation assistance; skills, simulation, or other laboratory; tutoring.

Library Facilities 1.8 million volumes (1,800 in health, 1,300 in nursing); 185 periodical subscriptions (50 health-care related).

MacMurray College (continued)

BACCALAUREATE PROGRAMS

Degree BSN

Available Programs ADN to Baccalaureate; Baccalaureate for Second Degree; Generic Baccalaureate; LPN to RN Baccalaureate; RN Baccalaureate.

Study Options Full-time and part-time.

Program Entrance Requirements Minimum overall college GPA of 2.5, transcript of college record, CPR certification, health exam, health insurance, high school transcript, immunizations, minimum high school GPA of 2.5, minimum GPA in nursing prerequisites of 2.5. Transfer students are accepted. *Application deadline:* 5/30 (fall). Applications may be processed on a rolling basis for some programs.

Expenses (2009–10) *Tuition:* full-time $17,940; part-time $600 per credit hour. *Room and board:* $6394; room only: $3170 per academic year. *Required fees:* full-time $650; part-time $25 per credit.

Financial Aid 98% of baccalaureate students in nursing programs received some form of financial aid in 2008–09. *Gift aid (need-based):* Federal Pell, FSEOG, state, private, college/university gift aid from institutional funds. *Loans:* FFEL (Subsidized and Unsubsidized Stafford PLUS), Perkins. *Work-study:* Federal Work-Study. *Financial aid application deadline (priority):* 5/1.

Contact James Malley, Vice President for Enrollment, Department of Nursing, MacMurray College, 447 East College Avenue, Jacksonville, IL 62650. *Telephone:* 800-252-7485. *Fax:* 217-291-0702. *E-mail:* admissions@mac.edu.

McKendree University
Department of Nursing
Lebanon, Illinois

http://www.mckendree.edu/nursing

Founded in 1828

DEGREES • BSN • MSN

Nursing Program Faculty 27 (30% with doctorates).

Baccalaureate Enrollment 331
Women 90% **Men** 10% **Minority** 8% **Part-time** 76%

Graduate Enrollment 87
Women 94% **Men** 6% **Minority** 7% **International** 1% **Part-time** 100%

Distance Learning Courses Available.

Nursing Student Activities Nursing Honor Society.

Nursing Student Resources Academic advising; academic or career counseling; assistance for students with disabilities; bookstore; campus computer network; career placement assistance; computer lab; computer-assisted instruction; e-mail services; interactive nursing skills videos; Internet; learning resource lab; library services; nursing audiovisuals; resume preparation assistance; tutoring.

Library Facilities 109,000 volumes (1,929 in health, 760 in nursing); 450 periodical subscriptions (100 health-care related).

BACCALAUREATE PROGRAMS

Degree BSN

Available Programs ADN to Baccalaureate.

Site Options Belleville, IL; Louisville, KY; Marion, IL.

Study Options Full-time and part-time.

Program Entrance Requirements Minimum overall college GPA of 2.0, transcript of college record, CPR certification, health exam, high school transcript, immunizations, prerequisite course work, RN licensure. Transfer students are accepted. *Application deadline:* Applications may be processed on a rolling basis for some programs.

Advanced Placement Credit given for nursing courses completed elsewhere dependent upon specific evaluations.

Expenses (2009–10) *Tuition:* part-time $245 per credit.

Financial Aid 90% of baccalaureate students in nursing programs received some form of financial aid in 2008–09. *Gift aid (need-based):* Federal Pell, FSEOG, state, private, college/university gift aid from institutional funds. *Loans:* Federal Direct (Subsidized and Unsubsidized Stafford PLUS), Perkins. *Work-study:* Federal Work-Study, part-time campus jobs. *Financial aid application deadline (priority):* 5/31.

Contact Kim Eichelberger, Director of Nursing Admissions, Department of Nursing, McKendree University, 701 College Road, Lebanon, IL 62254. *Telephone:* 800-232-7228 Ext. 6411. *Fax:* 618-537-6259. *E-mail:* kaeichelberger@mckendree.edu.

GRADUATE PROGRAMS

Expenses (2009–10) *Tuition:* part-time $330 per credit hour.

Financial Aid 90% of graduate students in nursing programs received some form of financial aid in 2008–09.

Contact Kim Eichelberger, Director of Nursing Admissions, Department of Nursing, McKendree University, 701 College Road, Lebanon, IL 62254. *Telephone:* 618-537-6411. *Fax:* 618-537-6410. *E-mail:* kaeichelberger@mckendree.edu.

MASTER'S DEGREE PROGRAM

Degree MSN

Available Programs Master's; RN to Master's.

Concentrations Available Nursing administration; nursing education.

Site Options Belleville, IL; Louisville, KY; Marion, IL.

Study Options Full-time and part-time.

Program Entrance Requirements Minimum overall college GPA of 3.0, transcript of college record, CPR certification, written essay, immunizations, interview, 3 letters of recommendation. *Application deadline:* Applications may be processed on a rolling basis for some programs.

Advanced Placement Credit given for nursing courses completed elsewhere dependent upon specific evaluations.

Degree Requirements 34 total credit hours, thesis or project.

Methodist College of Nursing
Methodist College of Nursing
Peoria, Illinois

DEGREE • BSN

BACCALAUREATE PROGRAMS

Degree BSN

Available Programs Accelerated Baccalaureate for Second Degree; RN Baccalaureate.

Contact Mary Jane Dowling, Methodist College of Nursing, Peoria, IL 60613. *Telephone:* 309-672-5513. *Fax:* 309-671-8303. *E-mail:* mjdowling@mcon.edu.

Millikin University
School of Nursing
Decatur, Illinois

Founded in 1901

DEGREES • BSN • MSN

Nursing Program Faculty 18 (53% with doctorates).

Baccalaureate Enrollment 227
Women 90% **Men** 10% **Minority** 11% **International** 1% **Part-time** 4%

Graduate Enrollment 17
Women 100% **Minority** 6% **Part-time** 25%

Distance Learning Courses Available.

Nursing Student Activities Nursing Honor Society, Sigma Theta Tau, Student Nurses' Association.

Nursing Student Resources Academic advising; academic or career counseling; assistance for students with disabilities; bookstore; campus computer network; career placement assistance; computer lab; computer-assisted instruction; e-mail services; employment services for current students; housing assistance; interactive nursing skills videos; Internet; learning resource lab; library services; nursing audiovisuals; other; placement services for program completers; remedial services; resume preparation assistance; skills, simulation, or other laboratory; tutoring; unpaid internships.

Library Facilities 216,883 volumes (10,000 in health, 6,000 in nursing); 430 periodical subscriptions (64 health-care related).

BACCALAUREATE PROGRAMS

Degree BSN

Available Programs Generic Baccalaureate; RN Baccalaureate.

Study Options Full-time and part-time.

Program Entrance Requirements Minimum overall college GPA of 2.5, transcript of college record, CPR certification, written essay, health exam, high school biology, high school chemistry, 2 years high school math, 2 years high school science, high school transcript, immunizations, minimum high school GPA of 3.0, minimum high school rank 75%, minimum GPA in nursing prerequisites of 2.5. Transfer students are accepted. *Application deadline:* Applications may be processed on a rolling basis for some programs.

Advanced Placement Credit given for nursing courses completed elsewhere dependent upon specific evaluations.

Expenses (2009–10) *Tuition:* full-time $25,750; part-time $860 per credit hour. *International tuition:* $25,750 full-time. *Room and board:* $3560 per academic year. *Required fees:* full-time $695; part-time $100 per term.

Financial Aid 97% of baccalaureate students in nursing programs received some form of financial aid in 2008–09.

Contact Ms. Kim Wenthe, Administrative Assistant, School of Nursing, School of Nursing, Millikin University, 1184 West Main Street, Decatur, IL 62522. *Telephone:* 217-424-6348. *Fax:* 217-420-6731. *E-mail:* kwenthe@mail.millikin.edu.

GRADUATE PROGRAMS

Expenses (2009–10) *Tuition:* part-time $630 per credit hour.

Contact Ms. Michelle Whitehead, Administrative Assistant, Master of Science in Nursing Program, School of Nursing, Millikin University, 1184 West Main Street, Decatur, IL 62522. *Telephone:* 800-373-7733 Ext. 5034. *Fax:* 217-424-5034. *E-mail:* mwhitehead@mail.millikin.edu.

MASTER'S DEGREE PROGRAM

Degree MSN

Available Programs Accelerated Master's for Non-Nursing College Graduates; Master's.

Concentrations Available Clinical nurse leader; nursing education.

Study Options Full-time and part-time.

Program Entrance Requirements Minimum overall college GPA of 3.0, transcript of college record, CPR certification, written essay, immunizations, interview, 3 letters of recommendation, professional liability insurance/malpractice insurance, statistics course. *Application deadline:* Applications may be processed on a rolling basis for some programs.

Advanced Placement Credit given for nursing courses completed elsewhere dependent upon specific evaluations.

Degree Requirements 36 total credit hours, thesis or project.

Northern Illinois University
School of Nursing and Health Studies
De Kalb, Illinois

http://www.nursing.niu.edu

Founded in 1895

DEGREES • BS • MS • MSN/MPH

Nursing Program Faculty 43 (44% with doctorates).

Baccalaureate Enrollment 469

Women 92% **Men** 8% **Minority** 20% **Part-time** 23%

Graduate Enrollment 164

Women 96% **Men** 4% **Minority** 23% **Part-time** 96%

Distance Learning Courses Available.

Nursing Student Activities Nursing Honor Society, Sigma Theta Tau, Student Nurses' Association, nursing club.

Nursing Student Resources Academic advising; academic or career counseling; assistance for students with disabilities; bookstore; campus computer network; career placement assistance; computer lab; computer-assisted instruction; daycare for children of students; e-mail services; employment services for current students; externships; housing assistance; interactive nursing skills videos; Internet; learning resource lab; library services; nursing audiovisuals; paid internships; placement services for program completers; remedial services; resume preparation assistance; skills, simulation, or other laboratory; tutoring; unpaid internships.

Library Facilities 3.1 million volumes (39,869 in health, 7,600 in nursing); 24,696 periodical subscriptions (676 health-care related).

BACCALAUREATE PROGRAMS

Degree BS

Available Programs ADN to Baccalaureate; Generic Baccalaureate; RN Baccalaureate.

Site Options Rockford, IL; Palatine, IL; Aurora, IL.

Study Options Full-time and part-time.

Program Entrance Requirements Transcript of college record, CPR certification, health exam, health insurance, high school transcript, immunizations, minimum high school GPA of 3.25, minimum high school rank 50%, minimum GPA in nursing prerequisites of 2.5, professional liability insurance/malpractice insurance. Transfer students are accepted.

Advanced Placement Credit given for nursing courses completed elsewhere dependent upon specific evaluations.

Contact *Telephone:* 815-753-0665. *Fax:* 815-753-0814.

GRADUATE PROGRAMS

Contact *Telephone:* 815-753-6551. *Fax:* 815-753-0814.

MASTER'S DEGREE PROGRAM

Degrees MS; MSN/MPH

Available Programs Master's.

Concentrations Available Nursing education. *Clinical nurse specialist programs in:* adult health, community health. *Nurse practitioner programs in:* adult health, family health.

Study Options Full-time and part-time.

Program Entrance Requirements Minimum overall college GPA of 3.0, transcript of college record, CPR certification, written essay, immunizations, 2 letters of recommendation, nursing research course, physical assessment course, professional liability insurance/malpractice insurance, statistics course.

Degree Requirements 48 total credit hours.

POST-MASTER'S PROGRAM

Areas of Study Nursing education. *Nurse practitioner programs in:* family health.

North Park University
School of Nursing
Chicago, Illinois

http://www.northpark.edu/nursing/

Founded in 1891

DEGREES • BS • MS • MSN/MA • MSN/MBA • MSN/MM

Nursing Program Faculty 35 (63% with doctorates).

Baccalaureate Enrollment 278

Women 88.4% **Men** 11.6% **Minority** 57% **International** 4% **Part-time** 36%

Graduate Enrollment 189

Women 95% **Men** 5% **Minority** 76% **International** 7% **Part-time** 80%

Nursing Student Activities Sigma Theta Tau, Student Nurses' Association.

North Park University (continued)

Nursing Student Resources Academic advising; academic or career counseling; assistance for students with disabilities; bookstore; campus computer network; career placement assistance; computer lab; computer-assisted instruction; e-mail services; employment services for current students; interactive nursing skills videos; Internet; learning resource lab; library services; nursing audiovisuals; remedial services; skills, simulation, or other laboratory; tutoring.

Library Facilities 260,685 volumes (3,959 in health, 1,791 in nursing); 1,178 periodical subscriptions (239 health-care related).

BACCALAUREATE PROGRAMS

Degree BS

Available Programs Generic Baccalaureate; RN Baccalaureate.

Site Options Evanston, IL; Arlington Heights, IL; Grayslake, IL.

Study Options Full-time.

Program Entrance Requirements Minimum overall college GPA of 2.75, transcript of college record, CPR certification, health exam, health insurance, immunizations, 1 letter of recommendation, minimum GPA in nursing prerequisites of 2.75, prerequisite course work. Transfer students are accepted.

Financial Aid 92% of baccalaureate students in nursing programs received some form of financial aid in 2008–09. *Gift aid (need-based):* Federal Pell, FSEOG, state, private, college/university gift aid from institutional funds. *Loans:* Federal Nursing Student Loans, Federal Direct (Subsidized and Unsubsidized Stafford PLUS), Perkins. *Work-study:* Federal Work-Study. *Financial aid application deadline (priority):* 5/1.

Contact Mr. Robert Berki, Admissions Counselor, School of Nursing, North Park University, 3225 West Foster Avenue, Chicago, IL 60625. *Telephone:* 773-244-5516. *E-mail:* rberki@northpark.edu.

GRADUATE PROGRAMS

Financial Aid 95% of graduate students in nursing programs received some form of financial aid in 2008–09.

Contact Ms. Jennifer Hulting, Assistant Director of Admissions, School of Nursing, North Park University, 3225 West Foster Avenue, Chicago, IL 60625. *Telephone:* 773-244-5508. *Fax:* 773-279-7082. *E-mail:* jhulting@northpark.edu.

MASTER'S DEGREE PROGRAM

Degrees MS; MSN/MA; MSN/MBA; MSN/MM

Available Programs Master's; RN to Master's.

Concentrations Available Nursing administration. *Clinical nurse specialist programs in:* community health. *Nurse practitioner programs in:* adult health, family health.

Site Options Arlington Heights, IL; Grayslake, IL.

Study Options Full-time and part-time.

Program Entrance Requirements Clinical experience, minimum overall college GPA of 3.0, transcript of college record, CPR certification, immunizations, 2 letters of recommendation, nursing research course, physical assessment course, professional liability insurance/malpractice insurance, prerequisite course work, resume, statistics course.

Degree Requirements 37 total credit hours.

POST-MASTER'S PROGRAM

Areas of Study *Nurse practitioner programs in:* adult health, family health.

Olivet Nazarene University

Division of Nursing
Bourbonnais, Illinois

http://web.olivet.edu/nursing/
Founded in 1907

Nursing Program Faculty 14 (36% with doctorates).

Baccalaureate Enrollment 414
Women 94% **Men** 6% **Minority** 26% **Part-time** 2%

Graduate Enrollment 65
Women 95% **Men** 5% **Minority** 35%

Nursing Student Activities Sigma Theta Tau, Student Nurses' Association.

Nursing Student Resources Academic advising; academic or career counseling; assistance for students with disabilities; bookstore; campus computer network; career placement assistance; computer lab; computer-assisted instruction; e-mail services; employment services for current students; externships; housing assistance; interactive nursing skills videos; Internet; learning resource lab; library services; nursing audiovisuals; placement services for program completers; remedial services; resume preparation assistance; skills, simulation, or other laboratory; tutoring.

Library Facilities 160,039 volumes (8,847 in health, 5,489 in nursing); 925 periodical subscriptions (722 health-care related).

BACCALAUREATE PROGRAMS

Degree BSN

Available Programs Accelerated RN Baccalaureate; Generic Baccalaureate.

Site Options Chicago, IL.

Study Options Full-time.

Program Entrance Requirements Minimum overall college GPA of 2.75, transcript of college record, CPR certification, health exam, health insurance, high school biology, high school chemistry, 2 years high school science, high school transcript, immunizations, minimum GPA in nursing prerequisites of 2.75. Transfer students are accepted.

Expenses (2009–10) *Tuition:* full-time $11,375; part-time $576 per credit hour. *Room and board:* $3200 per academic year. *Required fees:* full-time $420.

Financial Aid 98% of baccalaureate students in nursing programs received some form of financial aid in 2008–09. *Gift aid (need-based):* Federal Pell, FSEOG, state, private, college/university gift aid from institutional funds. *Loans:* Federal Direct (Subsidized and Unsubsidized Stafford PLUS), Perkins, alternative loans. *Work-study:* Federal Work-Study, part-time campus jobs. *Financial aid application deadline (priority):* 3/1.

Contact Mrs. Susan Wolff, Director of Admissions, Division of Nursing, Olivet Nazarene University, One University Avenue, Bourbonnais, IL 60914-2345. *Telephone:* 815-939-5203. *Fax:* 815-935-4998. *E-mail:* swolff@olivet.edu.

GRADUATE PROGRAMS

Expenses (2009–10) *Tuition:* full-time $13,877.

Financial Aid 38% of graduate students in nursing programs received some form of financial aid in 2008–09.

Contact Linda Westerberg, Division of Nursing, Olivet Nazarene University, One University Avenue, Bourbonnais, IL 60914-2345. *Telephone:* 815-939-5186. *Fax:* 815-935-4991. *E-mail:* lwester@olivet.edu.

MASTER'S DEGREE PROGRAM

Degree MSN

Available Programs Master's.

Study Options Full-time.

Program Entrance Requirements Computer literacy, minimum overall college GPA of 2.75, transcript of college record, nursing research course, statistics course.

Degree Requirements 32 total credit hours, thesis or project.

Quincy University
Blessing–Rieman College of Nursing
Quincy, Illinois

http://www.quincy.edu/

See description of programs under
Blessing–Rieman College of Nursing (Quincy, Illinois).

Rockford College
Department of Nursing
Rockford, Illinois

http://www.rockford.edu
Founded in 1847
DEGREE • BSN

Nursing Program Faculty 6 (17% with doctorates).
Baccalaureate Enrollment 76
Women 89% **Men** 11% **Minority** 22% **International** 4% **Part-time** 7%
Nursing Student Activities Student Nurses' Association.
Nursing Student Resources Academic advising; academic or career counseling; assistance for students with disabilities; bookstore; campus computer network; career placement assistance; computer lab; computer-assisted instruction; e-mail services; employment services for current students; externships; housing assistance; interactive nursing skills videos; Internet; learning resource lab; library services; nursing audiovisuals; paid internships; placement services for program completers; remedial services; resume preparation assistance; skills, simulation, or other laboratory; tutoring.
Library Facilities 140,000 volumes (655 in health, 600 in nursing); 831 periodical subscriptions (55 health-care related).

BACCALAUREATE PROGRAMS

Degree BSN

Available Programs ADN to Baccalaureate; Generic Baccalaureate; RN Baccalaureate.
Study Options Full-time.
Program Entrance Requirements Minimum overall college GPA of 2.75, transcript of college record, CPR certification, written essay, health exam, health insurance, high school biology, high school chemistry, 4 years high school math, 2 years high school science, high school transcript, immunizations, minimum high school GPA of 2.75, minimum high school rank 50%, minimum GPA in nursing prerequisites of 2.75, prerequisite course work. Transfer students are accepted. *Application deadline:* 9/1 (fall), 9/1 (spring).
Advanced Placement Credit given for nursing courses completed elsewhere dependent upon specific evaluations.
Expenses (2009–10) *Tuition:* full-time $24,350; part-time $650 per credit hour. *International tuition:* $24,350 full-time. *Room and board:* $6630; room only: $3850 per academic year. *Required fees:* full-time $160; part-time $78 per term.
Financial Aid 98% of baccalaureate students in nursing programs received some form of financial aid in 2008–09.
Contact Ms. Jennifer Nordstrom, Associate Vice President for Undergraduate Admissions, Department of Nursing, Rockford College, 5050 East State Street, Rockford, IL 61108-2393. *Telephone:* 815-226-4050. *E-mail:* jnordstrom@rockford.edu.

Rush University
College of Nursing
Chicago, Illinois

http://www.rushu.rush.edu/nursing
Founded in 1969
DEGREES • DNP • MSN

Nursing Program Faculty 93 (66% with doctorates).
Graduate Enrollment 700
Women 91% **Men** 9% **Minority** 16% **Part-time** 68%
Distance Learning Courses Available.
Nursing Student Activities Nursing Honor Society, Sigma Theta Tau, Student Nurses' Association.
Nursing Student Resources Academic advising; academic or career counseling; assistance for students with disabilities; bookstore; campus computer network; computer lab; computer-assisted instruction; e-mail services; employment services for current students; housing assistance; interactive nursing skills videos; Internet; learning resource lab; library services; nursing audiovisuals; remedial services; resume preparation assistance; skills, simulation, or other laboratory; tutoring; unpaid internships.
Library Facilities 120,042 volumes; 1,100 periodical subscriptions (5,228 health-care related).

GRADUATE PROGRAMS

Expenses (2009–10) *Tuition:* full-time $30,696; part-time $674 per credit. *Room and board:* room only: $7848 per academic year.
Financial Aid 88% of graduate students in nursing programs received some form of financial aid in 2008–09. Fellowships, research assistantships with partial tuition reimbursements available, teaching assistantships with partial tuition reimbursements available, Federal Work-Study, institutionally sponsored loans, scholarships, and traineeships available. Aid available to part-time students. *Financial aid application deadline:* 4/15.
Contact Ms. Angela Mason-Johnson, Acting Director of Admissions, College of Nursing, Rush University, 600 South Paulina Street, Armour Academic Center, Room 440, Chicago, IL 60612. *Telephone:* 312-942-7100. *Fax:* 312-942-2219. *E-mail:* Rush_Admissions@rush.edu.

MASTER'S DEGREE PROGRAM

Degree MSN

Available Programs Master's; Master's for Non-Nursing College Graduates; Master's for Nurses with Non-Nursing Degrees; RN to Master's.
Concentrations Available Clinical nurse leader; nurse anesthesia. *Clinical nurse specialist programs in:* community health, critical care, gerontology, medical-surgical, pediatric, psychiatric/mental health, public health. *Nurse practitioner programs in:* acute care, adult health, family health, gerontology, neonatal health, pediatric, psychiatric/mental health.
Study Options Full-time and part-time.
Online Degree Options Yes.
Program Entrance Requirements Minimum overall college GPA of 3.0, transcript of college record, CPR certification, written essay, immunizations, interview, 3 letters of recommendation, resume, GRE General Test (waived if nursing GPA is greater than 3.0 or cumulative GPA is greater than 3.25). *Application deadline:* 4/1 (fall), 5/1 (winter), 10/1 (spring), 1/1 (summer). Applications may be processed on a rolling basis for some programs.
Advanced Placement Credit given for nursing courses completed elsewhere dependent upon specific evaluations.
Degree Requirements 55 total credit hours, thesis or project.

POST-MASTER'S PROGRAM

Areas of Study Nurse anesthesia. *Clinical nurse specialist programs in:* community health, critical care, gerontology, medical-surgical, pediatric, psychiatric/mental health, public health. *Nurse practitioner programs in:* acute care, adult health, family health, gerontology, neonatal health, pediatric, psychiatric/mental health.

DOCTORAL DEGREE PROGRAM

Degree DNP
Available Programs Doctorate; Post-Baccalaureate Doctorate.

Rush University (continued)

Areas of Study Nursing administration.

Online Degree Options Yes (online only).

Program Entrance Requirements Clinical experience, minimum overall college GPA of 3.0, interview, 3 letters of recommendation, MSN or equivalent, statistics course, vita, writing sample, GRE General Test. Application deadline: 7/15 (winter), 1/15 (summer). Applications may be processed on a rolling basis for some programs. Application fee: $40.

Degree Requirements 41 total credit hours, dissertation, oral exam.

POSTDOCTORAL PROGRAM

Postdoctoral Program Contact Dr. Carol Farran, PhD Program Director, College of Nursing, Rush University, 600 South Paulina Street, 1064 AR, Chicago, IL 60612. *Telephone:* 312-942-6955. *Fax:* 312-942-3043. *E-mail:* Carol_J_Farran@rush.edu.

CONTINUING EDUCATION PROGRAM

Contact Dr. Marilyn Wideman, RN, Director of Faculty Practice, College of Nursing, Rush University, 600 South Paulina Street, Suite 1080, Chicago, IL 60612-3832. *Telephone:* 312-942-7013. *Fax:* 312-942-3043. *E-mail:* Marlyn_Wideman@rush.edu.

Saint Anthony College of Nursing

Saint Anthony College of Nursing
Rockford, Illinois

http://www.sacn.edu

Founded in 1915

DEGREES • BSN • MSN

Nursing Program Faculty 21 (9% with doctorates).

Baccalaureate Enrollment 166
Women 94% **Men** 6% **Minority** 18% **Part-time** 20.5%

Graduate Enrollment 18
Women 100% **Minority** 16.7% **Part-time** 100%

Nursing Student Activities Student Nurses' Association.

Nursing Student Resources Academic advising; academic or career counseling; campus computer network; computer lab; computer-assisted instruction; e-mail services; interactive nursing skills videos; Internet; learning resource lab; library services; nursing audiovisuals; paid internships; skills, simulation, or other laboratory; tutoring.

Library Facilities 1,258 volumes (48 in health, 47 in nursing); 3,136 periodical subscriptions (12 health-care related).

BACCALAUREATE PROGRAMS

Degree BSN

Available Programs Baccalaureate for Second Degree; Generic Baccalaureate; RN Baccalaureate.

Site Options Rockford, IL.

Study Options Full-time and part-time.

Program Entrance Requirements Minimum overall college GPA of 2.5, transcript of college record, CPR certification, written essay, health exam, health insurance, immunizations, interview, 3 letters of recommendation, minimum GPA in nursing prerequisites of 2.7, prerequisite course work. Transfer students are accepted. *Application deadline:* 2/15 (fall), 9/15 (spring). *Application fee:* $50.

Advanced Placement Credit by examination available. Credit given for nursing courses completed elsewhere dependent upon specific evaluations.

Expenses (2009–10) *Tuition:* full-time $1886; part-time $590 per credit hour. *Required fees:* full-time $258.

Financial Aid 91% of baccalaureate students in nursing programs received some form of financial aid in 2008–09. *Gift aid (need-based):* Federal Pell, state, private, college/university gift aid from institutional funds. *Loans:* FFEL (Subsidized and Unsubsidized Stafford PLUS), alternative loans. *Financial aid application deadline (priority):* 5/1.

Contact Ms. Cheryl Delgado, Supervisor for Enrollment Management, Saint Anthony College of Nursing, 5658 East State Street, Rockford, IL 61108-2468. *Telephone:* 815-227-2141. *Fax:* 815-227-2730. *E-mail:* cheryldelgado@sacn.edu.

GRADUATE PROGRAMS

Expenses (2009–10) *Tuition:* part-time $701 per credit hour.

Financial Aid 92% of graduate students in nursing programs received some form of financial aid in 2008–09.

Contact Ms. Melissa Wrolstad, Student Affairs Specialist, Graduate Affairs, Saint Anthony College of Nursing, 5658 East State Street, Rockford, IL 61108-2468. *Telephone:* 815-395-5476. *Fax:* 815-395-2275. *E-mail:* melissawrolstad@sacn.edu.

MASTER'S DEGREE PROGRAM

Degree MSN

Available Programs Master's.

Concentrations Available Clinical nurse leader; nursing education. *Clinical nurse specialist programs in:* adult health.

Study Options Part-time.

Program Entrance Requirements Minimum overall college GPA of 2.7, transcript of college record, CPR certification, written essay, immunizations, interview, 3 letters of recommendation, professional liability insurance/malpractice insurance, prerequisite course work, resume, statistics course. *Application deadline:* 4/1 (fall).

Advanced Placement Credit given for nursing courses completed elsewhere dependent upon specific evaluations.

Degree Requirements 39 total credit hours, thesis or project.

POST-MASTER'S PROGRAM

Areas of Study Nursing education.

Saint Francis Medical Center College of Nursing

Baccalaureate Nursing Program
Peoria, Illinois

http://www.sfmccon.edu

Founded in 1986

DEGREES • BSN • DNP • MSN

Nursing Program Faculty 45 (27% with doctorates).

Baccalaureate Enrollment 364
Women 90% **Men** 10% **Minority** 12% **Part-time** 23%

Graduate Enrollment 142
Women 92% **Men** 8% **Minority** 5% **Part-time** 94%

Distance Learning Courses Available.

Nursing Student Activities Sigma Theta Tau, Student Nurses' Association.

Nursing Student Resources Academic advising; academic or career counseling; campus computer network; computer lab; computer-assisted instruction; e-mail services; externships; housing assistance; interactive nursing skills videos; Internet; learning resource lab; library services; nursing audiovisuals; skills, simulation, or other laboratory; tutoring.

Library Facilities 2,032 volumes in nursing; 212 periodical subscriptions health-care related.

BACCALAUREATE PROGRAMS

Degree BSN

Available Programs Accelerated RN Baccalaureate; Generic Baccalaureate.

Study Options Full-time and part-time.

Program Entrance Requirements Transcript of college record, CPR certification, written essay, health exam, high school transcript, immunizations, minimum GPA in nursing prerequisites of 2.5, professional liability insurance/malpractice insurance, prerequisite course work. Transfer students are accepted. *Application deadline:* 9/15 (fall), 2/15 (spring). *Application fee:* $50.

Advanced Placement Credit given for nursing courses completed elsewhere dependent upon specific evaluations.

Expenses (2009–10) *Tuition:* full-time $14,632; part-time $472 per credit hour. *International tuition:* $14,632 full-time. *Room and board:* room only: $2400 per academic year. *Required fees:* full-time $556.

Financial Aid 87% of baccalaureate students in nursing programs received some form of financial aid in 2008–09. *Gift aid (need-based):* Federal Pell, state, private, college/university gift aid from institutional funds. *Loans:* FFEL (Subsidized and Unsubsidized Stafford PLUS), college/university. *Financial aid application deadline (priority):* 3/1.

Contact Ms. Janice E. Farquharson, Director of Admissions/Registrar, Baccalaureate Nursing Program, Saint Francis Medical Center College of Nursing, 511 NE Greenleaf Street, Peoria, IL 61603. *Telephone:* 309-624-8980. *Fax:* 309-624-8973. *E-mail:* janice.farquharson@osfhealthcare.org.

GRADUATE PROGRAMS

Expenses (2009–10) *Tuition:* full-time $8496; part-time $472 per credit hour. *International tuition:* $8496 full-time. *Required fees:* full-time $260.

Financial Aid 91% of graduate students in nursing programs received some form of financial aid in 2008–09.

Contact Dr. Janice F. Boundy, Associate Dean of Graduate Program, Baccalaureate Nursing Program, Saint Francis Medical Center College of Nursing, 511 NE Greenleaf Street, Peoria, IL 61603. *Telephone:* 309-655-2230. *Fax:* 309-655-3648. *E-mail:* janice.f.boundy@osfhealthcare.org.

MASTER'S DEGREE PROGRAM

Degree MSN

Available Programs Master's; Master's for Nurses with Non-Nursing Degrees; RN to Master's.

Concentrations Available Clinical nurse leader; nursing education. *Clinical nurse specialist programs in:* medical-surgical, parent-child. *Nurse practitioner programs in:* neonatal health.

Study Options Full-time and part-time.

Online Degree Options Yes (online only).

Program Entrance Requirements Clinical experience, computer literacy, minimum overall college GPA of 2.8, transcript of college record, CPR certification, written essay, immunizations, interview, 3 letters of recommendation, nursing research course, physical assessment course, professional liability insurance/malpractice insurance, prerequisite course work, resume, statistics course. *Application deadline:* Applications may be processed on a rolling basis for some programs. *Application fee:* $50.

Advanced Placement Credit given for nursing courses completed elsewhere dependent upon specific evaluations.

Degree Requirements 45 total credit hours, thesis or project.

DOCTORAL DEGREE PROGRAM

Degree DNP

Available Programs Doctorate.

Areas of Study Clinical practice.

Online Degree Options Yes (online only).

Program Entrance Requirements Clinical experience, minimum overall college GPA of 3.2, 3 letters of recommendation, scholarly papers, statistics course, vita, writing sample. Application deadline: Applications may be processed on a rolling basis for some programs. Application fee: $50.

Degree Requirements 39 total credit hours, oral exam, residency.

St. John's College
Department of Nursing
Springfield, Illinois

http://www.st-johns.org/collegeofnursing
Founded in 1886
DEGREE • BSN

Nursing Program Faculty 15 (13% with doctorates).

Baccalaureate Enrollment 81
Women 93% **Men** 7% **Minority** 4% **International** 1% **Part-time** 5%

Nursing Student Activities Student Nurses' Association.

Nursing Student Resources Academic advising; computer lab; daycare for children of students; interactive nursing skills videos; Internet; library services; resume preparation assistance; skills, simulation, or other laboratory.

BACCALAUREATE PROGRAMS

Degree BSN

Available Programs Generic Baccalaureate.

Study Options Full-time and part-time.

Program Entrance Requirements Transcript of college record, CPR certification, health exam, high school transcript, immunizations, 2 letters of recommendation, minimum GPA in nursing prerequisites of 2.4, professional liability insurance/malpractice insurance, prerequisite course work. Transfer students are accepted.

Advanced Placement Credit given for nursing courses completed elsewhere dependent upon specific evaluations.

Contact *Telephone:* 217-525-5628. *Fax:* 217-757-6870.

Saint Xavier University
School of Nursing
Chicago, Illinois

http://www.sxu.edu/son
Founded in 1847
DEGREES • BSN • MSN • MSN/MBA

Nursing Program Faculty 38 (54% with doctorates).

Baccalaureate Enrollment 683
Women 91% **Men** 9% **Minority** 37% **International** .1% **Part-time** 20%
Graduate Enrollment 127
Women 93% **Men** 7% **Minority** 38% **Part-time** 33%

Distance Learning Courses Available.

Nursing Student Activities Nursing Honor Society, Sigma Theta Tau, Student Nurses' Association.

Nursing Student Resources Academic advising; academic or career counseling; assistance for students with disabilities; bookstore; campus computer network; career placement assistance; computer lab; computer-assisted instruction; e-mail services; employment services for current students; externships; housing assistance; interactive nursing skills videos; Internet; learning resource lab; library services; nursing audiovisuals; other; placement services for program completers; remedial services; resume preparation assistance; skills, simulation, or other laboratory; tutoring; unpaid internships.

Library Facilities 170,753 volumes (4,704 in health, 2,817 in nursing); 717 periodical subscriptions (4,672 health-care related).

BACCALAUREATE PROGRAMS

Degree BSN

Available Programs Generic Baccalaureate; LPN to RN Baccalaureate; RN Baccalaureate.

Site Options Orland Park, IL; Chicago, IL; Elk Grove Village, IL.

Study Options Full-time and part-time.

Program Entrance Requirements Minimum overall college GPA of 2.75, transcript of college record, CPR certification, written essay, health exam, health insurance, high school biology, high school chemistry, high school foreign language, 3 years high school math, 4 years high school science, high school transcript, immunizations, minimum high school GPA of 2.75, minimum GPA in nursing prerequisites of 2.75, prerequisite course work. Transfer students are accepted. *Application deadline:* 5/1 (fall), 11/1 (spring). Applications may be processed on a rolling basis for some programs.

Advanced Placement Credit by examination available. Credit given for nursing courses completed elsewhere dependent upon specific evaluations.

Expenses (2009–10) *Tuition:* full-time $23,610; part-time $790 per credit hour. *International tuition:* $23,610 full-time. *Room and board:* $8408; room only: $4897 per academic year. *Required fees:* full-time $730; part-time $245 per term.

Saint Xavier University (continued)

Financial Aid 94% of baccalaureate students in nursing programs received some form of financial aid in 2008–09. *Gift aid (need-based):* Federal Pell, FSEOG, state, private, college/university gift aid from institutional funds, United Negro College Fund, Federal Nursing. *Loans:* FFEL (Subsidized and Unsubsidized Stafford PLUS), Perkins. *Work-study:* Federal Work-Study, part-time campus jobs. *Financial aid application deadline (priority):* 3/1.

Contact Brian Hotzfield, Director, Undergraduate Admission, School of Nursing, Saint Xavier University, 3700 West 103rd Street, Chicago, IL 60655. *Telephone:* 773-298-3050. *Fax:* 773-298-3076. *E-mail:* admission@sxu.edu.

GRADUATE PROGRAMS

Expenses (2009–10) *Tuition:* full-time $4248; part-time $708 per credit hour. *International tuition:* $4248 full-time. *Required fees:* full-time $550; part-time $210 per term.

Financial Aid 42% of graduate students in nursing programs received some form of financial aid in 2008–09. Available to part-time students.

Contact Kelly Fox, Assistant Director, Graduate Admission, School of Nursing, Saint Xavier University, 3700 West 103rd Street, Chicago, IL 60655. *Telephone:* 773-298-3053. *Fax:* 773-298-3951. *E-mail:* graduateadmission@sxu.edu.

MASTER'S DEGREE PROGRAM

Degrees MSN; MSN/MBA

Available Programs Master's; Master's for Nurses with Non-Nursing Degrees.

Concentrations Available Clinical nurse leader; nursing administration. *Nurse practitioner programs in:* family health.

Site Options Chicago, IL; Elk Grove Village, IL.

Study Options Full-time and part-time.

Online Degree Options Yes.

Program Entrance Requirements Minimum overall college GPA of 3.0, transcript of college record, written essay, 2 letters of recommendation, prerequisite course work, GRE General Test or MAT. *Application deadline:* 4/15 (fall), 10/15 (spring). Applications may be processed on a rolling basis for some programs.

Advanced Placement Credit given for nursing courses completed elsewhere dependent upon specific evaluations.

Degree Requirements 36 total credit hours, thesis or project.

POST-MASTER'S PROGRAM

Areas of Study Nursing education. *Nurse practitioner programs in:* family health.

CONTINUING EDUCATION PROGRAM

Contact Darlene O'Callaghan, RN, Assistant Dean, Special Initiatives, School of Nursing, Saint Xavier University, 3700 West 103rd Street, Chicago, IL 60655. *Telephone:* 773-298-3742. *Fax:* 773-298-3704. *E-mail:* ocallaghan@sxu.edu.

Southern Illinois University Edwardsville

School of Nursing
Edwardsville, Illinois

http://www.siue.edu/NURSING

Founded in 1957

DEGREES • BS • MS

Nursing Program Faculty 75 (45% with doctorates).

Baccalaureate Enrollment 646
Women 87% **Men** 13% **Minority** 12% **International** 1% **Part-time** 15%

Graduate Enrollment 192
Women 84% **Men** 16% **Minority** 10% **International** 2% **Part-time** 60%

Distance Learning Courses Available.

Nursing Student Activities Sigma Theta Tau, Student Nurses' Association, nursing club.

Nursing Student Resources Academic advising; academic or career counseling; assistance for students with disabilities; bookstore; campus computer network; career placement assistance; computer lab; computer-assisted instruction; daycare for children of students; e-mail services; employment services for current students; housing assistance; interactive nursing skills videos; Internet; learning resource lab; library services; nursing audiovisuals; placement services for program completers; remedial services; resume preparation assistance; skills, simulation, or other laboratory; tutoring.

Library Facilities 847,631 volumes; 24,530 periodical subscriptions.

BACCALAUREATE PROGRAMS

Degree BS

Available Programs ADN to Baccalaureate; Accelerated Baccalaureate; Generic Baccalaureate.

Site Options Carbondale, IL.

Study Options Full-time.

Program Entrance Requirements Minimum overall college GPA of 2.5, transcript of college record, CPR certification, written essay, health exam, health insurance, immunizations, minimum GPA in nursing prerequisites of 2.7, prerequisite course work. Transfer students are accepted. *Application deadline:* 3/1 (fall).

Advanced Placement Credit given for nursing courses completed elsewhere dependent upon specific evaluations.

Expenses (2009–10) *Tuition, state resident:* full-time $6201; part-time $207 per credit hour. *Tuition, nonresident:* full-time $15,502; part-time $517 per credit hour. *International tuition:* $15,502 full-time. *Room and board:* $7460; room only: $4720 per academic year. *Required fees:* full-time $3015.

Financial Aid *Gift aid (need-based):* Federal Pell, FSEOG, state, private, college/university gift aid from institutional funds, Federal Nursing. *Loans:* Federal Nursing Student Loans, Federal Direct (Subsidized and Unsubsidized Stafford PLUS), FFEL (Subsidized and Unsubsidized Stafford PLUS), Perkins, college/university, alternative loans. *Work-study:* Federal Work-Study, part-time campus jobs. *Financial aid application deadline (priority):* 3/1.

Contact Mrs. Karen Montgomery, Coordinator, Academic Advising, School of Nursing, Southern Illinois University Edwardsville, Box 1066, Edwardsville, IL 62026-1066. *Telephone:* 618-650-3956. *Fax:* 618-650-3854. *E-mail:* kmontgo@siue.edu.

GRADUATE PROGRAMS

Expenses (2009–10) *Tuition, state resident:* full-time $4500; part-time $251 per credit hour. *Tuition, nonresident:* full-time $11,272; part-time $626 per credit hour. *International tuition:* $11,272 full-time. *Room and board:* $6410; room only: $3670 per academic year. *Required fees:* full-time $1750.

Financial Aid 1 fellowship (averaging $8,370 per year) was awarded; research assistantships, teaching assistantships, career-related internships or fieldwork, Federal Work-Study, institutionally sponsored loans, scholarships, traineeships, and unspecified assistantships also available.

Contact Mrs. Hailey King, Academic Advisor, School of Nursing, Southern Illinois University Edwardsville, Alumni Hall, Room 2107, Edwardsville, IL 62026-1066. *Telephone:* 618-650-3956. *Fax:* 618-650-3854. *E-mail:* hking@siue.edu.

MASTER'S DEGREE PROGRAM

Degree MS

Available Programs Master's.

Concentrations Available Health-care administration; nurse anesthesia; nursing education. *Nurse practitioner programs in:* family health.

Site Options Springfield, IL; Carbondale, IL.

Study Options Full-time and part-time.

Program Entrance Requirements Clinical experience, minimum overall college GPA of 3.0, transcript of college record, CPR certification, written essay, immunizations, interview, 3 letters of recommendation, prerequisite course work. *Application deadline:* 3/1 (fall), 6/1 (summer).

Advanced Placement Credit given for nursing courses completed elsewhere dependent upon specific evaluations.

Degree Requirements 35 total credit hours, thesis or project.

POST-MASTER'S PROGRAM

Areas of Study Health-care administration; nurse anesthesia; nursing education. *Nurse practitioner programs in:* family health.

CONTINUING EDUCATION PROGRAM

Contact Dr. Karen Kelly, School of Nursing, Southern Illinois University Edwardsville, Box 1066, Edwardsville, IL 62026-1066. *Telephone:* 618-650-3908. *Fax:* 618-650-3854. *E-mail:* kkelly@siue.edu.

Trinity Christian College
Department of Nursing
Palos Heights, Illinois

http://www.trnty/depts/nursing/

Founded in 1959

DEGREE • BSN

Nursing Program Faculty 8 (37% with doctorates).

Baccalaureate Enrollment 145
Women 94.5% **Men** 5.5% **Minority** 14% **International** 3%

Nursing Student Activities Student Nurses' Association.

Nursing Student Resources Academic advising; academic or career counseling; assistance for students with disabilities; bookstore; campus computer network; career placement assistance; computer lab; computer-assisted instruction; e-mail services; interactive nursing skills videos; Internet; learning resource lab; library services; nursing audiovisuals; resume preparation assistance; skills, simulation, or other laboratory; tutoring; unpaid internships.

Library Facilities 75,298 volumes (2,500 in health, 500 in nursing); 284 periodical subscriptions (100 health-care related).

BACCALAUREATE PROGRAMS

Degree BSN

Available Programs Generic Baccalaureate; RN Baccalaureate.

Study Options Full-time.

Program Entrance Requirements Minimum overall college GPA of 2.5, transcript of college record, CPR certification, health exam, health insurance, high school biology, 3 years high school math, 2 years high school science, high school transcript, immunizations, minimum high school GPA of 2.0, minimum GPA in nursing prerequisites of 2.5, prerequisite course work. Transfer students are accepted.

Advanced Placement Credit given for nursing courses completed elsewhere dependent upon specific evaluations.

Contact *Telephone:* 866-874-6463. *Fax:* 708-385-5665.

Trinity College of Nursing and Health Sciences
Trinity College of Nursing and Health Sciences
Rock Island, Illinois

http://www.trinityqc.com/college/default.htm

Founded in 1994

DEGREE • BSN

Nursing Program Faculty 16 (25% with doctorates).

Baccalaureate Enrollment 54
Women 94% **Men** 6% **Minority** 6% **Part-time** 87%

Nursing Student Activities Nursing Honor Society.

Nursing Student Resources Academic advising; academic or career counseling; assistance for students with disabilities; bookstore; campus computer network; computer lab; computer-assisted instruction; daycare for children of students; e-mail services; interactive nursing skills videos; Internet; learning resource lab; library services; nursing audiovisuals; remedial services; skills, simulation, or other laboratory; tutoring.

Library Facilities 8,500 volumes (6,000 in health, 3,400 in nursing); 791 periodical subscriptions (746 health-care related).

BACCALAUREATE PROGRAMS

Degree BSN

Available Programs ADN to Baccalaureate; Accelerated Baccalaureate for Second Degree; RN Baccalaureate.

Study Options Full-time and part-time.

Program Entrance Requirements Transcript of college record, CPR certification, health exam, high school transcript, immunizations, RN licensure. Transfer students are accepted. *Application deadline:* Applications may be processed on a rolling basis for some programs. *Application fee:* $50.

Advanced Placement Credit given for nursing courses completed elsewhere dependent upon specific evaluations.

Financial Aid 95% of baccalaureate students in nursing programs received some form of financial aid in 2008–09. *Gift aid (need-based):* Federal Pell, FSEOG, state, college/university gift aid from institutional funds. *Loans:* Federal Nursing Student Loans, FFEL (Subsidized and Unsubsidized Stafford PLUS). *Financial aid application deadline:* Continuous.

Contact Mrs. Tracy L. Poelvoorde, Dean of Nursing and Health Sciences, Trinity College of Nursing and Health Sciences, 2122 25th Avenue, Rock Island, IL 61201. *Telephone:* 309-779-7708. *Fax:* 309-779-7798. *E-mail:* poelvoordet@ihs.org.

University of Illinois at Chicago
College of Nursing
Chicago, Illinois

http://www.uic.edu/nursing

Founded in 1946

DEGREES • BSN • MS • MS/MBA • MS/MPH • PHD

Nursing Program Faculty 200 (75% with doctorates).

Baccalaureate Enrollment 300
Women 90% **Men** 10% **Minority** 23% **International** 3% **Part-time** 20%
Graduate Enrollment 600
Women 95% **Men** 5% **Minority** 10% **International** 6%

Distance Learning Courses Available.

Nursing Student Activities Sigma Theta Tau, Student Nurses' Association.

Nursing Student Resources Academic advising; academic or career counseling; assistance for students with disabilities; bookstore; campus computer network; computer lab; computer-assisted instruction; daycare for children of students; e-mail services; employment services for current students; externships; Internet; learning resource lab; library services; nursing audiovisuals; resume preparation assistance; skills, simulation, or other laboratory; tutoring.

Library Facilities 3.3 million volumes (500,000 in health); 44,614 periodical subscriptions (5,100 health-care related).

BACCALAUREATE PROGRAMS

Degree BSN

Available Programs ADN to Baccalaureate; Baccalaureate for Second Degree; Generic Baccalaureate; RN Baccalaureate.

Site Options Urbana, IL.

Study Options Full-time and part-time.

Online Degree Options Yes.

Program Entrance Requirements Minimum overall college GPA of 2.5, transcript of college record, written essay, immunizations, 2 letters of recommendation, minimum GPA in nursing prerequisites of 2.5, prerequisite course work. Transfer students are accepted.

Contact Ms. Elizabeth Fern, Undergraduate Program Coordinator, College of Nursing, University of Illinois at Chicago, MC 802, 845 South Damen Avenue, Chicago, IL 60612-7350. *Telephone:* 312-996-5786. *Fax:* 312-996-8066. *E-mail:* efern@uic.edu.

GRADUATE PROGRAMS

Financial Aid 3 fellowships were awarded; research assistantships, teaching assistantships, career-related internships or fieldwork, Federal Work-Study, institutionally sponsored loans, scholarships, traineeships, tuition waivers (full and partial), and unspecified assistantships also available.

University of Illinois at Chicago (continued)

Contact Ms. Dianne L. Yauch, RN, Admissions and Recruitment Counselor/Academic Programs Advisor, College of Nursing, University of Illinois at Chicago, MC 802, 845 South Damen Avenue, Chicago, IL 60612-7350. *Telephone:* 312-996-5786. *Fax:* 312-996-8066. *E-mail:* dyauch@uic.edu.

MASTER'S DEGREE PROGRAM

Degrees MS; MS/MBA; MS/MPH

Available Programs Master's; Master's for Non-Nursing College Graduates; Master's for Nurses with Non-Nursing Degrees.

Concentrations Available Health-care administration; nurse-midwifery; nursing administration; nursing informatics. *Clinical nurse specialist programs in:* acute care, adult health, cardiovascular, community health, family health, gerontology, maternity-newborn, medical-surgical, occupational health, pediatric, perinatal, psychiatric/mental health, public health, school health, women's health. *Nurse practitioner programs in:* acute care, adult health, family health, gerontology, occupational health, pediatric, psychiatric/mental health, school health, women's health.

Site Options Urbana, IL; Rockford, IL; Peoria, IL.

Study Options Full-time and part-time.

Program Entrance Requirements Clinical experience, computer literacy, minimum overall college GPA of 3.0, transcript of college record, CPR certification, written essay, immunizations, interview, 3 letters of recommendation, nursing research course, physical assessment course, prerequisite course work, resume, statistics course, GRE General Test.

Advanced Placement Credit given for nursing courses completed elsewhere dependent upon specific evaluations.

Degree Requirements Thesis or project.

POST-MASTER'S PROGRAM

Areas of Study Health-care administration; nurse-midwifery; nursing administration; nursing education; nursing informatics. *Clinical nurse specialist programs in:* acute care, adult health, cardiovascular, family health, forensic nursing, gerontology, medical-surgical, occupational health, palliative care, pediatric, psychiatric/mental health, public health, school health, women's health. *Nurse practitioner programs in:* acute care, adult health, family health, gerontology, occupational health, pediatric, psychiatric/mental health, school health, women's health.

DOCTORAL DEGREE PROGRAM

Degree PhD

Available Programs Doctorate; Post-Baccalaureate Doctorate.

Areas of Study Advanced practice nursing, aging, bio-behavioral research, clinical practice, community health, faculty preparation, family health, forensic nursing, gerontology, health policy, health-care systems, individualized study, information systems, maternity-newborn, nursing administration, nursing policy, nursing research, nursing science, women's health.

Site Options Urbana, IL; Rockford, IL; Peoria, IL.

Program Entrance Requirements Minimum overall college GPA of 3.0, interview by faculty committee, interview, 3 letters of recommendation, MSN or equivalent, statistics course, vita, writing sample, GRE General Test.

Degree Requirements 96 total credit hours, dissertation.

POSTDOCTORAL PROGRAM

Areas of Study Individualized study, information systems, nursing informatics, nursing interventions, nursing research, nursing science, vulnerable population.

Postdoctoral Program Contact Dr. Julie Johnson Zerwic, Interim Department Head, Medical-Surgical Nursing, College of Nursing, University of Illinois at Chicago, UIC CON 845 South Damen Avenue (MS 802), Department MSN, Chicago, IL 60612-7350. *Telephone:* 312-996-8431. *E-mail:* juljohns@uic.edu.

CONTINUING EDUCATION PROGRAM

Contact Prof. Susan M. Ohlson, RN, Clinical Instructor, College of Nursing, University of Illinois at Chicago, UIC CON 845 South Damen Avenue (MC 802), Department PMA, Chicago, IL 60612-7350. *Telephone:* 312-413-2978. *E-mail:* sohlso1@uic.edu.

University of St. Francis
College of Nursing and Allied Health
Joliet, Illinois

http://www.stfrancis.edu/conah/

Founded in 1920

DEGREES • BSN • DNP • MSN

Nursing Program Faculty 45 (29% with doctorates).

Baccalaureate Enrollment 454
Women 93% **Men** 7% **Minority** 23% **International** 1% **Part-time** 26%

Graduate Enrollment 167
Women 92% **Men** 8% **Minority** 24% **Part-time** 92%

Distance Learning Courses Available.

Nursing Student Activities Sigma Theta Tau, Student Nurses' Association.

Nursing Student Resources Academic advising; academic or career counseling; assistance for students with disabilities; bookstore; campus computer network; career placement assistance; computer lab; computer-assisted instruction; e-mail services; employment services for current students; externships; housing assistance; interactive nursing skills videos; Internet; learning resource lab; library services; nursing audiovisuals; remedial services; resume preparation assistance; skills, simulation, or other laboratory; tutoring.

Library Facilities 117,111 volumes (723 in health, 624 in nursing); 13,500 periodical subscriptions (123 health-care related).

BACCALAUREATE PROGRAMS

Degree BSN

Available Programs Accelerated RN Baccalaureate; Generic Baccalaureate.

Study Options Full-time and part-time.

Online Degree Options Yes.

Program Entrance Requirements Minimum overall college GPA of 2.75, transcript of college record, CPR certification, health exam, high school biology, high school chemistry, 3 years high school math, 2 years high school science, high school transcript, immunizations, minimum high school GPA of 2.5, minimum high school rank 50%, minimum GPA in nursing prerequisites of 2.0, prerequisite course work. Transfer students are accepted. *Application deadline:* Applications may be processed on a rolling basis for some programs. *Application fee:* $30.

Advanced Placement Credit by examination available. Credit given for nursing courses completed elsewhere dependent upon specific evaluations.

Expenses (2009–10) *Tuition:* full-time $22,288; part-time $743 per credit hour. *International tuition:* $22,288 full-time. *Room and board:* $7938 per academic year. *Required fees:* full-time $410.

Financial Aid 81% of baccalaureate students in nursing programs received some form of financial aid in 2008–09. *Gift aid (need-based):* Federal Pell, FSEOG, state, private, college/university gift aid from institutional funds. *Loans:* Federal Direct (Subsidized and Unsubsidized Stafford PLUS), Perkins, alternative loans. *Work-study:* Federal Work-Study, part-time campus jobs. *Financial aid application deadline (priority):* 4/1.

Contact Julie Marlatt, Director, Undergraduate Admissions, College of Nursing and Allied Health, University of St. Francis, 500 Wilcox Street, Joliet, IL 60435. *Telephone:* 800-735-7500. *Fax:* 815-740-5032. *E-mail:* jmarlatt@stfrancis.edu.

GRADUATE PROGRAMS

Expenses (2009–10) *Tuition:* part-time $589 per credit hour.

Financial Aid 42% of graduate students in nursing programs received some form of financial aid in 2008–09.

Contact Ms. Sandee Sloka, Director, Graduate/Degree Completion Admissions, College of Nursing and Allied Health, University of St. Francis, 500 Wilcox Street, Joliet, IL 60435. *Telephone:* 888-890-8329. *Fax:* 815-740-3431. *E-mail:* ssloka@stfrancis.edu.

MASTER'S DEGREE PROGRAM

Degree MSN

Available Programs Master's; Master's for Nurses with Non-Nursing Degrees.

Concentrations Available Nursing education. *Clinical nurse specialist programs in:* adult health. *Nurse practitioner programs in:* adult health, family health.

Site Options Albuquerque, NM.

Study Options Part-time.

Online Degree Options Yes.

Program Entrance Requirements Clinical experience, computer literacy, minimum overall college GPA of 3.0, transcript of college record, CPR certification, written essay, immunizations, interview, 3 letters of recommendation, nursing research course, physical assessment course, professional liability insurance/malpractice insurance, prerequisite course work, resume, statistics course. *Application fee:* $30.

Advanced Placement Credit given for nursing courses completed elsewhere dependent upon specific evaluations.

Degree Requirements 44 total credit hours, thesis or project.

POST-MASTER'S PROGRAM

Areas of Study *Clinical nurse specialist programs in:* adult health. *Nurse practitioner programs in:* adult health, family health.

DOCTORAL DEGREE PROGRAM

Degree DNP

Available Programs Doctorate.

Areas of Study Nursing education.

Program Entrance Requirements Clinical experience, minimum overall college GPA of 3.0, interview by faculty committee, interview, letters of recommendation, MSN or equivalent, statistics course, vita. Application deadline: Applications may be processed on a rolling basis for some programs. Application fee: $50.

Degree Requirements 37 total credit hours, residency.

Western Illinois University
School of Nursing
Macomb, Illinois

Founded in 1899

DEGREE • BSN

Nursing Program Faculty 5 (6% with doctorates).

Baccalaureate Enrollment 29

Women 86% **Men** 14% **Minority** 12% **International** 2%

Distance Learning Courses Available.

Nursing Student Activities Nursing Honor Society, Student Nurses' Association.

Nursing Student Resources Academic advising; academic or career counseling; assistance for students with disabilities; bookstore; campus computer network; career placement assistance; computer lab; computer-assisted instruction; daycare for children of students; e-mail services; housing assistance; interactive nursing skills videos; Internet; learning resource lab; library services; nursing audiovisuals; resume preparation assistance; skills, simulation, or other laboratory.

Library Facilities 998,041 volumes; 3,200 periodical subscriptions.

BACCALAUREATE PROGRAMS

Degree BSN

Available Programs Baccalaureate for Second Degree; Generic Baccalaureate; RN Baccalaureate.

Site Options Moline, IL.

Study Options Full-time.

Online Degree Options Yes.

Program Entrance Requirements Minimum overall college GPA of 2.33, transcript of college record, CPR certification, written essay, health exam, health insurance, immunizations, 2 letters of recommendation, minimum GPA in nursing prerequisites of 2.33, professional liability insurance/malpractice insurance, prerequisite course work. Transfer students are accepted. *Application deadline:* 3/1 (fall).

Expenses (2009–10) *Tuition, state resident:* full-time $6778. *Tuition, nonresident:* full-time $8678. *Room and board:* $7642; room only: $4612 per academic year. *Required fees:* full-time $3000.

Financial Aid 90% of baccalaureate students in nursing programs received some form of financial aid in 2008–09. *Gift aid (need-based):* Federal Pell, FSEOG, state, private, college/university gift aid from institutional funds. *Loans:* FFEL (Subsidized and Unsubsidized Stafford PLUS), Perkins, college/university. *Work-study:* Federal Work-Study, part-time campus jobs. *Financial aid application deadline (priority):* 2/15.

Contact Mr. Theo E. Schultz, Academic Advisor, School of Nursing, Western Illinois University, 1 University Circle, Macomb, IL 61455. *Telephone:* 309-298-2571. *E-mail:* t-schultz@wiu.ecu.

West Suburban College of Nursing
West Suburban College of Nursing
Oak Park, Illinois

Founded in 1982

DEGREES • BSN • MSN

Nursing Program Faculty 20 (20% with doctorates).

Baccalaureate Enrollment 237

Women 82.7% **Men** 17.3% **Minority** 64.5% **Part-time** 21.5%

Graduate Enrollment 20

Women 98% **Men** 2% **Minority** 52% **Part-time** 100%

Distance Learning Courses Available.

Nursing Student Activities Student Nurses' Association.

Nursing Student Resources Academic advising; academic or career counseling; bookstore; campus computer network; career placement assistance; computer lab; computer-assisted instruction; e-mail services; employment services for current students; externships; Internet; learning resource lab; library services; nursing audiovisuals; resume preparation assistance; skills, simulation, or other laboratory; tutoring.

Library Facilities 2,400 volumes in health, 1,100 volumes in nursing; 300 periodical subscriptions health-care related.

BACCALAUREATE PROGRAMS

Degree BSN

Available Programs ADN to Baccalaureate; Accelerated Baccalaureate; Accelerated Baccalaureate for Second Degree; Accelerated RN Baccalaureate; Baccalaureate for Second Degree; RN Baccalaureate.

Study Options Full-time and part-time.

Program Entrance Requirements Minimum overall college GPA of 2.75, transcript of college record, CPR certification, written essay, health exam, health insurance, immunizations, 1 letter of recommendation, minimum GPA in nursing prerequisites of 2.75, prerequisite course work. Transfer students are accepted. *Application deadline:* 2/1 (fall), 9/15 (spring), 2/1 (summer). Applications may be processed on a rolling basis for some programs. *Application fee:* $30.

Advanced Placement Credit by examination available. Credit given for nursing courses completed elsewhere dependent upon specific evaluations.

Expenses (2009–10) *Tuition:* full-time $22,000; part-time $711 per credit. *Required fees:* full-time $250.

Financial Aid 90% of baccalaureate students in nursing programs received some form of financial aid in 2008–09.

Contact Mrs. Wilda Tutol-Ortiz, Senior Admissions Counselor, West Suburban College of Nursing, 3 Erie Court, Oak Park, IL 60302. *Telephone:* 708-763-6532. *Fax:* 708-763-1531. *E-mail:* admissions@wscn.edu.

GRADUATE PROGRAMS

Expenses (2009–10) *Tuition:* part-time $550 per credit.

Financial Aid 80% of graduate students in nursing programs received some form of financial aid in 2008–09.

Contact Dr. Cindy Valdez, EdD, Director of Office of Enrollment Management, West Suburban College of Nursing, 3 Erie Court, Oak Park, IL 60302. *Telephone:* 708-763-6532. *Fax:* 708-763-1531. *E-mail:* admissions@wscn.edu.

MASTER'S DEGREE PROGRAM

Degree MSN

West Suburban College of Nursing (continued)

Available Programs Accelerated Master's for Nurses with Non-Nursing Degrees; Master's; Master's for Nurses with Non-Nursing Degrees; RN to Master's.

Concentrations Available Clinical nurse leader; health-care administration; nursing administration; nursing education.

Study Options Part-time.

Program Entrance Requirements Computer literacy, minimum overall college GPA of 3.0, transcript of college record, CPR certification, written essay, immunizations, 3 letters of recommendation, resume. *Application deadline:* 7/1 (fall). Applications may be processed on a rolling basis for some programs. *Application fee:* $30.

Advanced Placement Credit given for nursing courses completed elsewhere dependent upon specific evaluations.

Degree Requirements 32 total credit hours, thesis or project.

POST-MASTER'S PROGRAM

Areas of Study Clinical nurse leader; health-care administration; nursing administration; nursing education.

INDIANA

Anderson University

School of Nursing
Anderson, Indiana

http://www.anderson.edu/academics/nurs/

Founded in 1917

DEGREES • BSN • MSN • MSN/MBA

Nursing Program Faculty 12 (17% with doctorates).

Baccalaureate Enrollment 95
Women 97% **Men** 3% **Minority** 10% **International** 1% **Part-time** 26%

Graduate Enrollment 31
Women 83% **Men** 17% **Minority** 13% **International** 30%

Distance Learning Courses Available.

Nursing Student Activities Nursing Honor Society, Sigma Theta Tau, Student Nurses' Association.

Nursing Student Resources Academic advising; academic or career counseling; assistance for students with disabilities; bookstore; campus computer network; career placement assistance; computer lab; computer-assisted instruction; e-mail services; housing assistance; interactive nursing skills videos; Internet; learning resource lab; library services; nursing audiovisuals; placement services for program completers; remedial services; resume preparation assistance; skills, simulation, or other laboratory; tutoring.

Library Facilities 325,133 volumes (6,954 in health, 1,259 in nursing); 698 periodical subscriptions (818 health-care related).

BACCALAUREATE PROGRAMS

Degree BSN

Available Programs RN Baccalaureate.

Study Options Full-time and part-time.

Program Entrance Requirements Minimum overall college GPA of 3.0, transcript of college record, CPR certification, health exam, high school biology, high school chemistry, 2 years high school math, 3 years high school science, high school transcript, immunizations, minimum high school GPA of 3.5, minimum high school rank 33%, minimum GPA in nursing prerequisites of 3.0, prerequisite course work. Transfer students are accepted. *Application deadline:* 5/31 (spring).

Advanced Placement Credit given for nursing courses completed elsewhere dependent upon specific evaluations.

Expenses (2009–10) *Tuition:* full-time $22,910; part-time $955 per credit hour. *International tuition:* $22,910 full-time. *Room and board:* $7980; room only: $5100 per academic year. *Required fees:* full-time $350.

Financial Aid 98% of baccalaureate students in nursing programs received some form of financial aid in 2008–09.

Contact Dr. Karen S. Williams, Dean, School of Nursing, School of Nursing, Anderson University, 1100 East 5th Street, Anderson, IN 46012-3495. *Telephone:* 765-641-4385. *Fax:* 765-641-3095. *E-mail:* kswilliams@anderson.edu.

GRADUATE PROGRAMS

Expenses (2009–10) *Tuition:* full-time $19,100; part-time $400 per credit hour. *International tuition:* $19,100 full-time.

Financial Aid 90% of graduate students in nursing programs received some form of financial aid in 2008–09.

Contact Dr. Paula Boley, Graduate Coordinator and Professor, School of Nursing, Anderson University, 1100 East 5th Street, Anderson, IN 46012-3495. *Telephone:* 765-641-4387. *Fax:* 765-641-3095. *E-mail:* pboley@anderson.edu.

MASTER'S DEGREE PROGRAM

Degrees MSN; MSN/MBA

Available Programs Master's.

Concentrations Available Nursing administration.

Site Options Indianapolis, IN.

Study Options Full-time and part-time.

Program Entrance Requirements Clinical experience, minimum overall college GPA of 2.75, transcript of college record, CPR certification, written essay, immunizations, 3 letters of recommendation. *Application deadline:* Applications may be processed on a rolling basis for some programs. *Application fee:* $50.

Degree Requirements 55 total credit hours, thesis or project.

POST-MASTER'S PROGRAM

Areas of Study Nursing administration.

Ball State University

School of Nursing
Muncie, Indiana

http://www.bsu.edu/nursing

Founded in 1918

DEGREES • BS • DNP • MS

Nursing Program Faculty 55 (29% with doctorates).

Baccalaureate Enrollment 428
Women 86% **Men** 14% **Minority** 4% **International** .5% **Part-time** 6%

Graduate Enrollment 387
Women 92% **Men** 8% **Minority** 7% **International** 100%

Distance Learning Courses Available.

Nursing Student Activities Nursing Honor Society, Sigma Theta Tau, Student Nurses' Association.

Nursing Student Resources Academic advising; academic or career counseling; assistance for students with disabilities; bookstore; campus computer network; career placement assistance; computer lab; computer-assisted instruction; e-mail services; employment services for current students; housing assistance; interactive nursing skills videos; Internet; learning resource lab; library services; nursing audiovisuals; placement services for program completers; remedial services; resume preparation assistance; skills, simulation, or other laboratory; tutoring.

Library Facilities 1.1 million volumes (16,885 in health, 9,221 in nursing); 3,243 periodical subscriptions (3,713 health-care related).

BACCALAUREATE PROGRAMS

Degree BS

Available Programs Accelerated Baccalaureate for Second Degree; Baccalaureate for Second Degree; Generic Baccalaureate; LPN to Baccalaureate; RN Baccalaureate.

Study Options Full-time and part-time.

Online Degree Options Yes.

Program Entrance Requirements Minimum overall college GPA of 3.00, transcript of college record, CPR certification, health exam, immunizations, prerequisite course work. Transfer students are accepted. *Application deadline:* 8/28 (fall), 1/21 (spring).

Advanced Placement Credit given for nursing courses completed elsewhere dependent upon specific evaluations.

Expenses (2009–10) *Tuition, state resident:* full-time $7228; part-time $1070 per course. *Tuition, nonresident:* full-time $9898; part-time $2628 per course. *International tuition:* $9898 full-time. *Room and board:* $8438; room only: $7390 per academic year. *Required fees:* full-time $900.

Financial Aid 90% of baccalaureate students in nursing programs received some form of financial aid in 2008–09. *Gift aid (need-based):* Federal Pell, FSEOG, state, private, college/university gift aid from institutional funds. *Loans:* Federal Direct (Subsidized and Unsubsidized Stafford PLUS), Perkins. *Work-study:* Federal Work-Study, part-time campus jobs. *Financial aid application deadline (priority):* 3/10.

Contact Dr. Nancy Dillard, RN, Baccalaureate Program Director, School of Nursing, Ball State University, CN 418, Muncie, IN 47306. *Telephone:* 765-285-5589. *Fax:* 765-285-2169. *E-mail:* ndillard@bsu.edu.

GRADUATE PROGRAMS

Expenses (2009–10) *Tuition, state resident:* part-time $256 per credit hour. *Tuition, nonresident:* part-time $454 per credit hour. *Required fees:* part-time $400 per term.

Financial Aid 3 teaching assistantships (averaging $9,874 per year) were awarded; research assistantships, career-related internships or fieldwork also available.

Contact Dr. Marilyn Ryan, RN, Associate Director, Graduate Program, School of Nursing, Ball State University, Muncie, IN 47306. *Telephone:* 765-285-5764. *Fax:* 765-285-2169. *E-mail:* mryan@bsu.edu.

MASTER'S DEGREE PROGRAM

Degree MS

Available Programs Master's; RN to Master's.

Concentrations Available Nursing administration; nursing education. *Clinical nurse specialist programs in:* adult health. *Nurse practitioner programs in:* adult health, family health.

Study Options Part-time.

Online Degree Options Yes (online only).

Program Entrance Requirements Clinical experience, computer literacy, minimum overall college GPA of 2.8, transcript of college record, CPR certification, written essay, immunizations, interview, 1 letter of recommendation, nursing research course, physical assessment course, prerequisite course work, statistics course. *Application deadline:* Applications may be processed on a rolling basis for some programs. *Application fee:* $35.

Advanced Placement Credit given for nursing courses completed elsewhere dependent upon specific evaluations.

POST-MASTER'S PROGRAM

Areas of Study Nursing education. *Nurse practitioner programs in:* adult health, family health.

DOCTORAL DEGREE PROGRAM

Degree DNP

Available Programs Doctorate.

Areas of Study Advanced practice nursing.

Online Degree Options Yes (online only).

Program Entrance Requirements Clinical experience, minimum overall college GPA of 3.2, interview by faculty committee, letters of recommendation, MSN or equivalent, statistics course, writing sample. Application deadline: 4/5 (fall). Application fee: $35.

Degree Requirements 38 total credit hours, residency.

Bethel College

Department of Nursing
Mishawaka, Indiana

http://www.bethelcollege.edu
Founded in 1947

DEGREES • BSN • MSN

Nursing Program Faculty 30 (13% with doctorates).

Baccalaureate Enrollment 138
Women 89% **Men** 11% **Minority** 11% **International** 3% **Part-time** 25%

Graduate Enrollment 29
Women 97% **Men** 3% **Minority** 7% **Part-time** 21%

Nursing Student Activities Sigma Theta Tau, Student Nurses' Association.

Nursing Student Resources Academic advising; academic or career counseling; assistance for students with disabilities; bookstore; campus computer network; career placement assistance; computer lab; computer-assisted instruction; e-mail services; employment services for current students; housing assistance; interactive nursing skills videos; Internet; learning resource lab; library services; nursing audiovisuals; placement services for program completers; remedial services; resume preparation assistance; skills, simulation, or other laboratory; tutoring.

Library Facilities 118,393 volumes (3,000 in health, 2,050 in nursing); 1,496 periodical subscriptions (175 health-care related).

BACCALAUREATE PROGRAMS

Degree BSN

Available Programs ADN to Baccalaureate; Generic Baccalaureate; RN Baccalaureate.

Site Options Winona Lake, IN; St. Joseph, MI; Mishawaka, IN.

Study Options Full-time and part-time.

Program Entrance Requirements Minimum overall college GPA of 2.5, transcript of college record, CPR certification, written essay, health exam, high school chemistry, high school transcript, immunizations, 1 letter of recommendation, minimum high school GPA of 2.5, minimum high school rank 35%, minimum GPA in nursing prerequisites of 2.5. Transfer students are accepted. *Application deadline:* 8/28 (fall). *Application fee:* $25.

Advanced Placement Credit by examination available. Credit given for nursing courses completed elsewhere dependent upon specific evaluations.

Expenses (2009–10) *Tuition:* full-time $21,000; part-time $450 per credit hour. *International tuition:* $21,000 full-time. *Room and board:* $6250; room only: $3150 per academic year. *Required fees:* full-time $274.

Financial Aid 77% of baccalaureate students in nursing programs received some form of financial aid in 2008–09. *Gift aid (need-based):* Federal Pell, FSEOG, state, private, college/university gift aid from institutional funds, Federal Nursing. *Loans:* FFEL (Subsidized and Unsubsidized Stafford PLUS), Perkins, college/university, GATE Loans. *Work-study:* Federal Work-Study, part-time campus jobs. *Financial aid application deadline (priority):* 3/1.

Contact Dr. Karon Schwartz, Interim Dean of Nursing, Department of Nursing, Bethel College, 1001 Bethel Circle, Mishawaka, IN 46545. *Telephone:* 574-257-3382. *Fax:* 574-257-2683. *E-mail:* schwark@bethelcollege. edu.

GRADUATE PROGRAMS

Expenses (2009–10) *Tuition:* full-time $4200; part-time $350 per credit hour. *International tuition:* $4200 full-time. *Required fees:* full-time $185.

Financial Aid 95% of graduate students in nursing programs received some form of financial aid in 2008–09.

Contact Dr. Karon Schwartz, Graduate Nursing Program Director, Department of Nursing, Bethel College, 1001 Bethel Circle, Mishawaka, IN 46545. *Telephone:* 574-257-3382. *Fax:* 574-257-7616. *E-mail:* schwark@ bethelcollege.edu.

MASTER'S DEGREE PROGRAM

Degree MSN

Available Programs Master's.

Concentrations Available Nursing administration; nursing education.

Site Options Mishawaka, IN.

Study Options Full-time and part-time.

Program Entrance Requirements Clinical experience, minimum overall college GPA of 3.0, transcript of college record, CPR certification, immunizations, 3 letters of recommendation, nursing research course, physical assessment course, statistics course. *Application deadline:* 8/28 (fall). Applications may be processed on a rolling basis for some programs. *Application fee:* $25.

Bethel College (continued)

Advanced Placement Credit given for nursing courses completed elsewhere dependent upon specific evaluations.

Degree Requirements 36 total credit hours, thesis or project.

POST-MASTER'S PROGRAM

Areas of Study Nursing administration; nursing education.

Goshen College
Department of Nursing
Goshen, Indiana

http://www.goshen.edu

Founded in 1894

DEGREE • BSN

Nursing Program Faculty 15 (13% with doctorates).

Baccalaureate Enrollment 150
Women 91% **Men** 9% **Minority** 11% **International** 9%

Graduate Enrollment 34
Women 91% **Men** 9% **Minority** 94% **Part-time** 3%

Nursing Student Activities Sigma Theta Tau, Student Nurses' Association.

Nursing Student Resources Academic advising; academic or career counseling; bookstore; campus computer network; career placement assistance; computer lab; e-mail services; employment services for current students; externships; library services; nursing audiovisuals; placement services for program completers; resume preparation assistance.

Library Facilities 137,000 volumes (80 in health, 80 in nursing); 350 periodical subscriptions (68 health-care related).

BACCALAUREATE PROGRAMS

Degree BSN

Available Programs Generic Baccalaureate; RN Baccalaureate.
Site Options Elkhart, IN.
Study Options Full-time and part-time.
Program Entrance Requirements Minimum overall college GPA of 2.5, transcript of college record, CPR certification, health exam, high school chemistry, high school foreign language, 2 years high school math, high school science, high school transcript, immunizations, 2 letters of recommendation, minimum high school GPA of 2.5, minimum high school rank 50%. Transfer students are accepted. *Application deadline:* 3/1 (spring).
Advanced Placement Credit by examination available. Credit given for nursing courses completed elsewhere dependent upon specific evaluations.
Expenses (2009–10) *Tuition:* full-time $23,400; part-time $580 per credit hour. *International tuition:* $23,400 full-time. *Room and board:* $7800; room only: $4150 per academic year. *Required fees:* full-time $500; part-time $500 per credit.
Financial Aid 98% of baccalaureate students in nursing programs received some form of financial aid in 2008–09.
Contact Admissions, Department of Nursing, Goshen College, 1700 South Main Street, Goshen, IN 46526. *Telephone:* 574-535-7535. *Fax:* 574-535-7609. *E-mail:* admissions@goshen.edu.

GRADUATE PROGRAMS

Expenses (2009–10) *Tuition:* full-time $9860; part-time $580 per credit. *International tuition:* $9860 full-time. *Room and board:* $7900; room only: $4150 per academic year. *Required fees:* full-time $300; part-time $300 per credit.
Financial Aid 25% of graduate students in nursing programs received some form of financial aid in 2008–09.
Contact Ms. Brenda Srof, PhD, Director, Masters in Nursing, Department of Nursing, Goshen College, 1700 South Main Street, Goshen, IN 46526. *Telephone:* 574-535-7375. *Fax:* 575-535-7375. *E-mail:* brendajs@goshen.edu.

Huntington University
Department of Nursing
Huntington, Indiana

Founded in 1897

DEGREE • BSN

Nursing Program Faculty 3 (33% with doctorates).

Baccalaureate Enrollment 10
Women 80% **Men** 20% **Minority** 10% **International** 10%

Nursing Student Activities Nursing club.

Nursing Student Resources Academic advising; academic or career counseling; assistance for students with disabilities; bookstore; campus computer network; career placement assistance; computer lab; computer-assisted instruction; daycare for children of students; e-mail services; employment services for current students; externships; housing assistance; interactive nursing skills videos; Internet; learning resource lab; library services; nursing audiovisuals; other; placement services for program completers; remedial services; resume preparation assistance; skills, simulation, or other laboratory; tutoring; unpaid internships.

Library Facilities 176,744 volumes (1,544 in health, 31 in nursing); 114 periodical subscriptions health-care related.

BACCALAUREATE PROGRAMS

Degree BSN

Available Programs Generic Baccalaureate; RN Baccalaureate.
Study Options Full-time.
Program Entrance Requirements Minimum overall college GPA of 2.75, transcript of college record, CPR certification, health exam, high school chemistry, 2 years high school math, 2 years high school science, high school transcript, immunizations, interview, minimum high school GPA of 2.3, minimum high school rank 33%, minimum GPA in nursing prerequisites of 2.5, professional liability insurance/malpractice insurance, prerequisite course work. Transfer students are accepted. *Application deadline:* 3/31 (fall).
Expenses (2009–10) *Tuition:* full-time $20,820. *International tuition:* $20,820 full-time. *Room and board:* $7180 per academic year. *Required fees:* full-time $400.
Financial Aid 95% of baccalaureate students in nursing programs received some form of financial aid in 2008–09. *Gift aid (need-based):* Federal Pell, FSEOG, state, private, college/university gift aid from institutional funds. *Loans:* FFEL (Subsidized and Unsubsidized Stafford PLUS), Perkins. *Work-study:* Federal Work-Study. *Financial aid application deadline (priority):* 3/1.
Contact Dr. Margaret Winter, Director, Department of Nursing, Department of Nursing, Huntington University, 2303 College Avenue, Huntington, IN 46750. *Telephone:* 260-359-4360. *Fax:* 260-359-4133. *E-mail:* mwinter@huntington.edu.

Indiana State University
Department of Nursing
Terre Haute, Indiana

http://www.indstate.edu/nurs/

Founded in 1865

DEGREES • BS • MSN

Nursing Program Faculty 34 (38% with doctorates).

Baccalaureate Enrollment 407
Women 88% **Men** 12% **Minority** 14% **International** 1% **Part-time** 53%

Graduate Enrollment 239
Women 92% **Men** 8% **Minority** 18% **International** 1% **Part-time** 82%

Distance Learning Courses Available.

Nursing Student Activities Sigma Theta Tau, Student Nurses' Association.

Nursing Student Resources Academic advising; academic or career counseling; assistance for students with disabilities; bookstore; campus computer network; career placement assistance; computer lab; computer-assisted instruction; daycare for children of students; e-mail services;

employment services for current students; externships; housing assistance; interactive nursing skills videos; Internet; learning resource lab; library services; nursing audiovisuals; paid internships; placement services for program completers; remedial services; resume preparation assistance; skills, simulation, or other laboratory; tutoring; unpaid internships.

Library Facilities 1.2 million volumes (54,890 in health, 33,560 in nursing); 104 periodical subscriptions health-care related.

BACCALAUREATE PROGRAMS

Degree BS

Available Programs Generic Baccalaureate; LPN to Baccalaureate; LPN to RN Baccalaureate; RN Baccalaureate.

Site Options Terre Haute, IN.

Study Options Full-time and part-time.

Online Degree Options Yes.

Program Entrance Requirements Minimum overall college GPA of 2.25, transcript of college record, CPR certification, health exam, high school chemistry, high school foreign language, 3 years high school math, 3 years high school science, high school transcript, immunizations, minimum high school GPA of 2.5, minimum high school rank 40%, minimum GPA in nursing prerequisites of 2.5, prerequisite course work, RN licensure. Transfer students are accepted. *Application deadline:* 6/1 (fall), 11/1 (spring).

Advanced Placement Credit by examination available. Credit given for nursing courses completed elsewhere dependent upon specific evaluations.

Financial Aid 7.5% of baccalaureate students in nursing programs received some form of financial aid in 2008–09. *Gift aid (need-based):* Federal Pell, FSEOG, state, private, college/university gift aid from institutional funds. *Loans:* FFEL (Subsidized and Unsubsidized Stafford PLUS), Perkins. *Work-study:* Federal Work-Study, part-time campus jobs. *Financial aid application deadline:* 3/1.

Contact Ms. Lynn C. Foster, Director of Student Affairs, Department of Nursing, Indiana State University, 749 Chestnut Street, Terre Haute, IN 47809. *Telephone:* 812-237-2316. *Fax:* 812-237-8022. *E-mail:* lfoster@indstate.edu.

GRADUATE PROGRAMS

Expenses (2009–10) *Tuition, area resident:* part-time $328 per credit hour. *Tuition, nonresident:* part-time $645 per credit hour. *International tuition:* $24,610 full-time. *Room and board:* $3687; room only: $1734 per academic year. *Required fees:* full-time $6500; part-time $5800 per credit; part-time $700 per term.

Financial Aid 7.5% of graduate students in nursing programs received some form of financial aid in 2008–09. 5 research assistantships with partial tuition reimbursements available (averaging $7,500 per year) were awarded; teaching assistantships with partial tuition reimbursements available, career-related internships or fieldwork and Federal Work-Study also available. Aid available to part-time students. *Financial aid application deadline:* 3/1.

Contact Ms. Cherie Howk, Chairperson, Advanced Practice Nursing, Department of Nursing, Indiana State University, 749 Chestnut Street, Terre Haute, IN 47809. *Telephone:* 812-237-2591. *Fax:* 812-237-4300. *E-mail:* cherie.howk@indstate.edu.

MASTER'S DEGREE PROGRAM

Degree MSN

Available Programs Master's.

Concentrations Available Nursing administration; nursing education. *Nurse practitioner programs in:* family health.

Site Options Terre Haute, IN.

Study Options Full-time and part-time.

Online Degree Options Yes (online only).

Program Entrance Requirements Clinical experience, minimum overall college GPA of 3.0, transcript of college record, CPR certification, written essay, immunizations, 3 letters of recommendation, nursing research course, prerequisite course work, statistics course. *Application deadline:* 3/1 (fall), 10/1 (spring).

Advanced Placement Credit given for nursing courses completed elsewhere dependent upon specific evaluations.

Degree Requirements 36 total credit hours, thesis or project.

POST-MASTER'S PROGRAM

Areas of Study Nursing education. *Nurse practitioner programs in:* family health.

CONTINUING EDUCATION PROGRAM

Contact Ms. Deb Bartnick, RN, Director of Continuing Education, Department of Nursing, Indiana State University, Landsbaum Center, LCHE 208, 1433 North 61/2 Street, Terre Haute, IN 47807. *Telephone:* 812-237-3695. *Fax:* 812-237-8248. *E-mail:* deborah.bartnick@indstate.edu.

Indiana University Bloomington
Department of Nursing–Bloomington Division
Bloomington, Indiana

Founded in 1820

DEGREE • BSN

Nursing Program Faculty 19 (3.5% with doctorates).

Baccalaureate Enrollment 187
Women 97% **Men** 3% **Minority** 1%

Distance Learning Courses Available.

Nursing Student Activities Nursing Honor Society, Sigma Theta Tau, Student Nurses' Association.

Nursing Student Resources Academic advising; academic or career counseling; assistance for students with disabilities; campus computer network; computer lab; computer-assisted instruction; e-mail services; employment services for current students; interactive nursing skills videos; Internet; learning resource lab; library services; nursing audiovisuals; remedial services; resume preparation assistance; skills, simulation, or other laboratory; tutoring.

Library Facilities 6.6 million volumes (8,500 in nursing); 1,000 periodical subscriptions health-care related.

BACCALAUREATE PROGRAMS

Degree BSN

Available Programs Baccalaureate for Second Degree; Generic Baccalaureate; RN Baccalaureate.

Site Options Bloomington, IN; Columbus, IN; Bedford, IN.

Study Options Full-time.

Program Entrance Requirements Minimum overall college GPA of 2.5, transcript of college record, CPR certification, written essay, health exam, health insurance, high school chemistry, 3 years high school math, high school transcript, immunizations, interview, minimum GPA in nursing prerequisites of 2.7, prerequisite course work. Transfer students are accepted. *Application deadline:* 3/15 (fall).

Advanced Placement Credit by examination available. Credit given for nursing courses completed elsewhere dependent upon specific evaluations.

Expenses (2009–10) *Tuition, state resident:* full-time $6388; part-time $199 per credit. *Tuition, nonresident:* full-time $32,764; part-time $743 per credit. *Room and board:* $5000 per academic year. *Required fees:* full-time $891; part-time $406 per credit.

Financial Aid 50% of baccalaureate students in nursing programs received some form of financial aid in 2008–09. *Gift aid (need-based):* Federal Pell, FSEOG, state, private, college/university gift aid from institutional funds. *Loans:* Federal Direct (Subsidized and Unsubsidized Stafford PLUS), Perkins, college/university. *Work-study:* Federal Work-Study, part-time campus jobs. *Financial aid application deadline (priority):* 3/1.

Contact Mrs. Deborah Hrisomalos, Academic Advisor, Department of Nursing–Bloomington Division, Indiana University Bloomington, Sycamore Hall, Room 401, Bloomington, IN 47405. *Telephone:* 812-855-2592. *Fax:* 812-855-6986. *E-mail:* dhrisoma@indiana.edu.

Indiana University East
School of Nursing
Richmond, Indiana

http://www.indiana.edu/nursing

Founded in 1971

DEGREE • BSN

Nursing Program Faculty 15 (7% with doctorates).

Baccalaureate Enrollment 201
Women 92.5% **Men** 7.5% **Minority** 5% **International** 1%

Nursing Student Activities Sigma Theta Tau, Student Nurses' Association.

Nursing Student Resources Academic advising; academic or career counseling; assistance for students with disabilities; bookstore; campus computer network; career placement assistance; computer lab; computer-assisted instruction; daycare for children of students; e-mail services; externships; interactive nursing skills videos; Internet; learning resource lab; library services; nursing audiovisuals; placement services for program completers; remedial services; resume preparation assistance; skills, simulation, or other laboratory; tutoring; unpaid internships.

Library Facilities 67,036 volumes (5,039 in health, 3,418 in nursing); 435 periodical subscriptions (70 health-care related).

BACCALAUREATE PROGRAMS

Degree BSN

Available Programs ADN to Baccalaureate; Generic Baccalaureate; RN Baccalaureate.

Study Options Full-time.

Program Entrance Requirements Minimum overall college GPA of 2.7, transcript of college record, CPR certification, high school biology, high school chemistry, 3 years high school math, 3 years high school science, high school transcript, immunizations, minimum high school GPA of 2.0, minimum high school rank 50%, minimum GPA in nursing prerequisites of 2.0, prerequisite course work. Transfer students are accepted. *Application deadline:* 3/1 (fall).

Advanced Placement Credit by examination available. Credit given for nursing courses completed elsewhere dependent upon specific evaluations.

Expenses (2008–09) *Tuition, state resident:* full-time $5178; part-time $173 per credit hour. *Tuition, nonresident:* full-time $13,344; part-time $445 per credit hour. *International tuition:* $13,344 full-time. *Required fees:* full-time $825; part-time $46 per credit; part-time $65 per term.

Financial Aid 80% of baccalaureate students in nursing programs received some form of financial aid in 2007–08. *Gift aid (need-based):* Federal Pell, FSEOG, state, private, college/university gift aid from institutional funds. *Loans:* Federal Direct (Subsidized and Unsubsidized Stafford PLUS), Perkins, college/university. *Work-study:* Federal Work-Study. *Financial aid application deadline (priority):* 3/1.

Contact Dr. Bonnie Hestand, Pre-nursing Advisor, School of Nursing, Indiana University East, Hayes Hall, 2325 Chester Boulevard, Richmond, IN 47374-1289. *Telephone:* 765-973-8353. *Fax:* 765-973-8220. *E-mail:* bhestand@indiana.edu.

Indiana University Kokomo
Indiana University School of Nursing
Kokomo, Indiana

Founded in 1945

DEGREE • BSN

Nursing Program Faculty 14 (43% with doctorates).

Baccalaureate Enrollment 235
Women 95% **Men** 5% **Minority** 1% **International** 1% **Part-time** 32%

Nursing Student Activities Sigma Theta Tau, Student Nurses' Association.

Nursing Student Resources Academic advising; academic or career counseling; assistance for students with disabilities; bookstore; campus computer network; career placement assistance; computer lab; computer-assisted instruction; daycare for children of students; e-mail services; employment services for current students; externships; interactive nursing skills videos; Internet; learning resource lab; library services; nursing audiovisuals; paid internships; remedial services; resume preparation assistance; skills, simulation, or other laboratory; tutoring.

Library Facilities 132,424 volumes (2,881 in health, 1,513 in nursing); 1,513 periodical subscriptions (75 health-care related).

BACCALAUREATE PROGRAMS

Degree BSN

Available Programs Accelerated RN Baccalaureate; Generic Baccalaureate.

Site Options Peru, IN; Marion, IN; Logansport, IN.

Study Options Full-time.

Program Entrance Requirements Minimum overall college GPA of 2.5, transcript of college record, CPR certification, high school biology, high school chemistry, 4 years high school math, high school transcript, immunizations, minimum high school GPA of 2.0, minimum high school rank 50%, minimum GPA in nursing prerequisites of 2.7, prerequisite course work. Transfer students are accepted.

Financial Aid 75% of baccalaureate students in nursing programs received some form of financial aid in 2008–09. *Gift aid (need-based):* Federal Pell, FSEOG, state, private, college/university gift aid from institutional funds. *Loans:* Federal Nursing Student Loans, Federal Direct (Subsidized and Unsubsidized Stafford PLUS), Perkins, college/university. *Work-study:* Federal Work-Study, part-time campus jobs. *Financial aid application deadline:* 3/1.

Contact Mr. Morris S. Starkey, Coordinator, Nursing Student Services, Indiana University School of Nursing, Indiana University Kokomo, 2300 South Washington Street, PO Box 9003, Kokomo, IN 46904-9003. *Telephone:* 765-455-9384. *Fax:* 765-455-9421. *E-mail:* mstarke@iuk.edu.

CONTINUING EDUCATION PROGRAM

Contact Mr. Morris S. Starkey, Advisor, Nursing/Allied Health, Indiana University School of Nursing, Indiana University Kokomo, 2300 South Washington Street, PO Box 9003, Kokomo, IN 46904-9003. *Telephone:* 765-455-9384. *Fax:* 765-455-9421. *E-mail:* mstarke@iuk.edu.

Indiana University Northwest
School of Nursing and Health Professions
Gary, Indiana

http://www.iun.edu/~nurse

Founded in 1959

DEGREE • BSN

Nursing Program Faculty 25 (15% with doctorates).

Baccalaureate Enrollment 178
Women 90% **Men** 10% **Minority** 30% **International** .6% **Part-time** 6%

Nursing Student Activities Sigma Theta Tau, Student Nurses' Association.

Nursing Student Resources Academic advising; academic or career counseling; assistance for students with disabilities; bookstore; campus computer network; career placement assistance; computer lab; computer-assisted instruction; daycare for children of students; e-mail services; externships; interactive nursing skills videos; Internet; learning resource lab; library services; nursing audiovisuals; placement services for program completers; skills, simulation, or other laboratory; tutoring.

Library Facilities 251,508 volumes (42,000 in health, 15,000 in nursing); 1,541 periodical subscriptions (200 health-care related).

BACCALAUREATE PROGRAMS

Degree BSN

Available Programs Baccalaureate for Second Degree; Generic Baccalaureate; RN Baccalaureate.

Study Options Full-time.

Program Entrance Requirements Minimum overall college GPA of 2.5, transcript of college record, CPR certification, health exam, health insurance, high school biology, high school chemistry, high school foreign language, 4 years high school science, high school transcript, immunizations, minimum high school rank 25%, minimum GPA in nursing prerequisites, prerequisite course work. Transfer students are accepted.

Advanced Placement Credit given for nursing courses completed elsewhere dependent upon specific evaluations.

Contact *Telephone:* 219-980-6611. *Fax:* 219-980-6578.

Indiana University–Purdue University Fort Wayne

Department of Nursing
Fort Wayne, Indiana

http://www.ipfw.edu/nursing

Founded in 1917

DEGREES • BS • MS

Nursing Program Faculty 48 (10% with doctorates).

Baccalaureate Enrollment 251
Women 90% **Men** 10% **Minority** 14% **International** 2% **Part-time** 23%

Graduate Enrollment 37
Women 95% **Men** 5% **Minority** 10% **Part-time** 89%

Distance Learning Courses Available.

Nursing Student Activities Sigma Theta Tau.

Nursing Student Resources Academic advising; academic or career counseling; assistance for students with disabilities; bookstore; campus computer network; career placement assistance; computer lab; computer-assisted instruction; daycare for children of students; e-mail services; employment services for current students; housing assistance; interactive nursing skills videos; Internet; learning resource lab; library services; nursing audiovisuals; placement services for program completers; remedial services; resume preparation assistance; skills, simulation, or other laboratory; tutoring.

Library Facilities 455,020 volumes (1,100 in health, 500 in nursing); 22,433 periodical subscriptions (120 health-care related).

BACCALAUREATE PROGRAMS

Degree BS

Available Programs Generic Baccalaureate; LPN to RN Baccalaureate; RN Baccalaureate.

Study Options Full-time and part-time.

Program Entrance Requirements Minimum overall college GPA, transcript of college record, CPR certification, health exam, high school transcript, immunizations, minimum GPA in nursing prerequisites, professional liability insurance/malpractice insurance, prerequisite course work, RN licensure. Transfer students are accepted. *Application deadline:* 5/1 (fall), 12/1 (spring).

Advanced Placement Credit by examination available. Credit given for nursing courses completed elsewhere dependent upon specific evaluations.

Expenses (2009–10) *Tuition, state resident:* full-time $6045; part-time $202 per credit hour. *Tuition, nonresident:* full-time $15,597; part-time $520 per credit hour. *International tuition:* $15,597 full-time. *Room and board:* room only: $4900 per academic year. *Required fees:* full-time $881; part-time $29 per credit.

Financial Aid 60% of baccalaureate students in nursing programs received some form of financial aid in 2008–09.

Contact Ms. Joanne Bauman, Nursing Advisor, Department of Nursing, Indiana University–Purdue University Fort Wayne, 2101 East Coliseum Boulevard, Fort Wayne, IN 46805. *Telephone:* 260-481-6282. *Fax:* 260-481-6482. *E-mail:* baumanj@ipfw.edu.

GRADUATE PROGRAMS

Expenses (2009–10) *Tuition, state resident:* full-time $7658; part-time $255 per credit hour. *Tuition, nonresident:* full-time $18,272; part-time $609 per credit hour. *International tuition:* $18,272 full-time. *Room and board:* room only: $4900 per academic year. *Required fees:* full-time $881; part-time $29 per credit.

Financial Aid 46% of graduate students in nursing programs received some form of financial aid in 2008–09.

Contact Dr. Susan Ahrens, Director of Graduate Programs and Associate Professor, Department of Nursing, Indiana University–Purdue University Fort Wayne, 2101 East Coliseum Boulevard, Fort Wayne, IN 46805. *Telephone:* 260-481-6278. *Fax:* 260-481-6482. *E-mail:* ahrenss@ipfw.edu.

MASTER'S DEGREE PROGRAM

Degree MS

Available Programs Master's.

Concentrations Available Nursing administration; nursing education. *Nurse practitioner programs in:* adult health, women's health.

Study Options Part-time.

Program Entrance Requirements Computer literacy, minimum overall college GPA of 3, transcript of college record, CPR certification, immunizations, 3 letters of recommendation, nursing research course, professional liability insurance/malpractice insurance, prerequisite course work, resume, statistics course. *Application deadline:* 7/15 (fall), 11/15 (spring), 4/1 (summer). *Application fee:* $40.

Advanced Placement Credit by examination available. Credit given for nursing courses completed elsewhere dependent upon specific evaluations.

Degree Requirements 43 total credit hours, thesis or project.

POST-MASTER'S PROGRAM

Areas of Study Nursing administration.

CONTINUING EDUCATION PROGRAM

Contact Mersiha Alic, Registrar, Continuing Studies, Department of Nursing, Indiana University–Purdue University Fort Wayne, 2101 East Coliseum Boulevard, Fort Wayne, IN 46805. *Telephone:* 260-481-6627. *E-mail:* alicm@ipfw.edu.

Indiana University–Purdue University Indianapolis

School of Nursing
Indianapolis, Indiana

http://www.nursing.iupui.edu

Founded in 1969

DEGREES • BSN • MSN • MSN/MPH • PHD

Nursing Program Faculty 182 (37% with doctorates).

Nursing Student Activities Sigma Theta Tau, Student Nurses' Association.

Nursing Student Resources Academic advising; academic or career counseling; assistance for students with disabilities; bookstore; campus computer network; career placement assistance; computer lab; computer-assisted instruction; e-mail services; employment services for current students; externships; housing assistance; interactive nursing skills videos; Internet; learning resource lab; library services; nursing audiovisuals; other; paid internships; remedial services; resume preparation assistance; skills, simulation, or other laboratory; tutoring; unpaid internships.

Library Facilities 1.5 million volumes (318,211 in health, 8,258 in nursing); 14,673 periodical subscriptions (1,951 health-care related).

BACCALAUREATE PROGRAMS

Degree BSN

Available Programs ADN to Baccalaureate; Accelerated Baccalaureate for Second Degree; Generic Baccalaureate; RN Baccalaureate.

Site Options Columbus, IN.

Study Options Full-time and part-time.

Indiana University–Purdue University Indianapolis (continued)

Program Entrance Requirements Minimum overall college GPA of 2.5, transcript of college record, CPR certification, health insurance, 2 years high school math, 1 year of high school science, high school transcript, immunizations, interview, minimum GPA in nursing prerequisites of 2.7, prerequisite course work. Transfer students are accepted.

Advanced Placement Credit by examination available. Credit given for nursing courses completed elsewhere dependent upon specific evaluations.

Contact Associate Dean for Undergraduate Programs, School of Nursing, Indiana University–Purdue University Indianapolis, 1111 Middle Drive, Indianapolis, IN 46202. *Telephone:* 317-274-2806. *Fax:* 317-274-2996. *E-mail:* nursing@iupui.edu.

GRADUATE PROGRAMS

Financial Aid 9 fellowships (averaging $7,039 per year), 7 teaching assistantships (averaging $5,300 per year) were awarded; research assistantships, Federal Work-Study, institutionally sponsored loans, scholarships, and tuition waivers (full) also available.

Contact Associate Dean for Graduate Programs, School of Nursing, Indiana University–Purdue University Indianapolis, 1111 Middle Drive, Indianapolis, IN 46202. *Telephone:* 317-274-2806. *Fax:* 317-274-2996. *E-mail:* nursing@iupui.edu.

MASTER'S DEGREE PROGRAM

Degrees MSN; MSN/MPH

Available Programs Master's; RN to Master's.

Concentrations Available Nursing administration. *Clinical nurse specialist programs in:* acute care, adult health, community health, critical care, oncology, pediatric, psychiatric/mental health. *Nurse practitioner programs in:* acute care, adult health, family health, neonatal health, pediatric, women's health.

Study Options Full-time and part-time.

Program Entrance Requirements Clinical experience, computer literacy, minimum overall college GPA of 3.0, transcript of college record, written essay, immunizations, 3 letters of recommendation, physical assessment course, resume, statistics course.

Advanced Placement Credit given for nursing courses completed elsewhere dependent upon specific evaluations.

Degree Requirements 42 total credit hours, thesis or project.

POST-MASTER'S PROGRAM

Areas of Study Nursing administration. *Clinical nurse specialist programs in:* adult health, community health, pediatric, psychiatric/mental health. *Nurse practitioner programs in:* acute care, adult health, family health, neonatal health, pediatric, women's health.

DOCTORAL DEGREE PROGRAM

Degree PhD

Available Programs Doctorate; Post-Baccalaureate Doctorate.

Areas of Study Aging, bio-behavioral research, faculty preparation, family health, health policy, health promotion/disease prevention, health-care systems, human health and illness, information systems, nursing administration, nursing education, nursing policy, nursing research, nursing science, oncology.

Program Entrance Requirements Minimum overall college GPA of 3.0, interview by faculty committee, 3 letters of recommendation, scholarly papers, statistics course, vita, GRE General Test.

Degree Requirements 90 total credit hours, dissertation, oral exam, written exam, residency.

POSTDOCTORAL PROGRAM

Areas of Study Adolescent health, cancer care, chronic illness, family health, health promotion/disease prevention, individualized study, nursing informatics, nursing research, nursing science.

Postdoctoral Program Contact Center for Academic Affairs, School of Nursing, Indiana University–Purdue University Indianapolis, 1111 Middle Drive, Indianapolis, IN 46202. *Telephone:* 317-274-2806. *Fax:* 317-274-2996. *E-mail:* nursing@iupui.edu.

CONTINUING EDUCATION PROGRAM

Contact Janice Ward, Director, Lifelong Learning, School of Nursing, Indiana University–Purdue University Indianapolis, 1111 Middle Drive, Indianapolis, IN 46202. *Telephone:* 317-274-7779. *Fax:* 317-274-0012. *E-mail:* jaward@iupui.edu.

Indiana University South Bend
Division of Nursing and Health Professions
South Bend, Indiana

http://www.iusb.edu/~health/

Founded in 1922

DEGREES • BSN • MSN

Nursing Program Faculty 24 (25% with doctorates).

Baccalaureate Enrollment 170
Women 94% **Men** 6% **Minority** 11% **International** 1% **Part-time** 36%

Nursing Student Activities Sigma Theta Tau, Student Nurses' Association.

Nursing Student Resources Academic advising; academic or career counseling; assistance for students with disabilities; bookstore; campus computer network; career placement assistance; computer lab; computer-assisted instruction; daycare for children of students; e-mail services; employment services for current students; externships; interactive nursing skills videos; Internet; learning resource lab; library services; nursing audiovisuals; placement services for program completers; resume preparation assistance; skills, simulation, or other laboratory; tutoring.

Library Facilities 300,202 volumes (4,300 in health, 2,300 in nursing); 1,937 periodical subscriptions (145 health-care related).

BACCALAUREATE PROGRAMS

Degree BSN

Available Programs Accelerated Baccalaureate for Second Degree; Generic Baccalaureate; RN Baccalaureate.

Site Options Indianapolis, IN.

Study Options Full-time and part-time.

Program Entrance Requirements Minimum overall college GPA of 2.5, transcript of college record, CPR certification, written essay, health exam, health insurance, high school biology, high school chemistry, high school transcript, immunizations, minimum high school GPA of 2.0, minimum high school rank 50%, minimum GPA in nursing prerequisites of 2.5, prerequisite course work. Transfer students are accepted.

Advanced Placement Credit given for nursing courses completed elsewhere dependent upon specific evaluations.

Contact *Telephone:* 574-520-4571. *Fax:* 574-520-4461.

GRADUATE PROGRAMS

Contact *Telephone:* 574-520-4569. *Fax:* 574-520-4461.

MASTER'S DEGREE PROGRAM

Degree MSN

Available Programs Master's.

Concentrations Available *Nurse practitioner programs in:* family health.

Study Options Part-time.

Program Entrance Requirements Clinical experience, computer literacy, minimum overall college GPA of 3.0, transcript of college record, CPR certification, written essay, immunizations, 3 letters of recommendation, nursing research course, physical assessment course, statistics course.

Advanced Placement Credit given for nursing courses completed elsewhere dependent upon specific evaluations.

Degree Requirements 42 total credit hours, thesis or project.

Indiana University Southeast

Division of Nursing
New Albany, Indiana

http://www.ius.edu/Nursing/homepage1.htm

Founded in 1941

DEGREE • BSN

Nursing Program Faculty 23 (27% with doctorates).

Baccalaureate Enrollment 162
Women 92% **Men** 8% **Minority** 2% **International** 2%

Distance Learning Courses Available.

Nursing Student Activities Sigma Theta Tau, Student Nurses' Association.

Nursing Student Resources Academic advising; academic or career counseling; assistance for students with disabilities; bookstore; campus computer network; career placement assistance; computer lab; computer-assisted instruction; daycare for children of students; e-mail services; externships; housing assistance; interactive nursing skills videos; Internet; learning resource lab; library services; nursing audiovisuals; paid internships; remedial services; resume preparation assistance; skills, simulation, or other laboratory; tutoring.

Library Facilities 215,429 volumes (35 in health, 15 in nursing); 962 periodical subscriptions (35 health-care related).

BACCALAUREATE PROGRAMS

Degree BSN

Available Programs Generic Baccalaureate; RN Baccalaureate.
Study Options Full-time.
Program Entrance Requirements Transcript of college record, CPR certification, immunizations, minimum GPA in nursing prerequisites of 2.5, prerequisite course work. Transfer students are accepted.
Advanced Placement Credit given for nursing courses completed elsewhere dependent upon specific evaluations.
Contact *Telephone:* 812-941-2283. *Fax:* 812-941-2687.

Indiana Wesleyan University

School of Nursing
Marion, Indiana

http://www.indwes.edu/academics/Nursing

Founded in 1920

DEGREES • BSN • MSN

Nursing Program Faculty 210 (21% with doctorates).

Baccalaureate Enrollment 1,581
Women 93% **Men** 7% **Minority** 16% **Part-time** 9%

Graduate Enrollment 427
Women 95% **Men** 5% **Minority** 13% **Part-time** 10%

Distance Learning Courses Available.

Nursing Student Activities Nursing Honor Society, Sigma Theta Tau, Student Nurses' Association, nursing club.

Nursing Student Resources Academic advising; academic or career counseling; assistance for students with disabilities; bookstore; campus computer network; career placement assistance; computer lab; computer-assisted instruction; e-mail services; housing assistance; interactive nursing skills videos; Internet; learning resource lab; library services; nursing audiovisuals; remedial services; resume preparation assistance; skills, simulation, or other laboratory; tutoring.

Library Facilities 164,272 volumes (7,142 in health, 5,672 in nursing); 85,642 periodical subscriptions (160 health-care related).

BACCALAUREATE PROGRAMS

Degree BSN

Available Programs Accelerated Baccalaureate for Second Degree; Generic Baccalaureate; RN Baccalaureate.

Site Options Lexington, KY; Merrillville, IN; Louisville, KY.
Study Options Full-time and part-time.
Program Entrance Requirements Minimum overall college GPA of 2.75, transcript of college record, CPR certification, written essay, health exam, health insurance, high school biology, high school chemistry, high school foreign language, 3 years high school math, 3 years high school science, high school transcript, immunizations, minimum high school GPA of 2.8, minimum GPA in nursing prerequisites of 2.75, prerequisite course work. Transfer students are accepted. *Application deadline:* 5/30 (fall), 12/1 (spring).
Advanced Placement Credit given for nursing courses completed elsewhere dependent upon specific evaluations.
Expenses (2009–10) *Tuition:* full-time $20,496; part-time $436 per credit. *International tuition:* $20,496 full-time. *Room and board:* $6770; room only: $3260 per academic year. *Required fees:* full-time $750.
Financial Aid 92% of baccalaureate students in nursing programs received some form of financial aid in 2008–09. *Gift aid (need-based):* Federal Pell, FSEOG, state, private, college/university gift aid from institutional funds. *Loans:* FFEL (Subsidized and Unsubsidized Stafford PLUS), Perkins, college/university. *Work-study:* Federal Work-Study, part-time campus jobs. *Financial aid application deadline (priority):* 3/1.
Contact Teresa Weaver, Secretary, School of Nursing, Indiana Wesleyan University, 4201 South Washington Street, Marion, IN 46953. *Telephone:* 765-677-2268. *Fax:* 765-677-2284. *E-mail:* teresa.weaver@indwes.edu.

GRADUATE PROGRAMS

Expenses (2009–10) *Tuition:* full-time $9765; part-time $465 per credit. *International tuition:* $9765 full-time. *Required fees:* full-time $323.
Financial Aid 48% of graduate students in nursing programs received some form of financial aid in 2008–09. 15 fellowships were awarded; career-related internships or fieldwork, scholarships, and traineeships also available. Aid available to part-time students. *Financial aid application deadline:* 3/15.
Contact Mr. Steve Evans, Recruitment, School of Nursing, Indiana Wesleyan University, 1900 West 50th Street, Marion, IN 46953. *Telephone:* 765-677-2045. *Fax:* 765-677-2380. *E-mail:* steve.evans@indwes.edu.

MASTER'S DEGREE PROGRAM

Degree MSN

Available Programs Master's.
Concentrations Available Nursing administration; nursing education. *Nurse practitioner programs in:* family health.
Site Options Lexington, KY; Merrillville, IN; Louisville, KY.
Study Options Full-time and part-time.
Online Degree Options Yes.
Program Entrance Requirements Clinical experience, minimum overall college GPA of 3.0, transcript of college record, written essay, immunizations, interview, 3 letters of recommendation, nursing research course, physical assessment course, resume, statistics course.
Advanced Placement Credit given for nursing courses completed elsewhere dependent upon specific evaluations.
Degree Requirements 41 total credit hours, thesis or project.

POST-MASTER'S PROGRAM

Areas of Study Nursing administration; nursing education. *Nurse practitioner programs in:* family health.

Marian University

Department of Nursing and Nutritional Science
Indianapolis, Indiana

http://www.sonak.marian.edu/academ/nursing/index.html

Founded in 1851

DEGREE • BSN

Nursing Program Faculty 16

Marian University (continued)
Baccalaureate Enrollment 225
Women 95% **Men** 5% **Minority** 15% **International** 2% **Part-time** 10%
Nursing Student Activities Nursing Honor Society, Sigma Theta Tau, Student Nurses' Association.

Nursing Student Resources Academic advising; academic or career counseling; assistance for students with disabilities; bookstore; campus computer network; career placement assistance; computer lab; computer-assisted instruction; e-mail services; employment services for current students; interactive nursing skills videos; Internet; learning resource lab; library services; nursing audiovisuals; resume preparation assistance; skills, simulation, or other laboratory; tutoring.

Library Facilities 102,237 volumes (3,250 in health, 2,000 in nursing); 337 periodical subscriptions (116 health-care related).

BACCALAUREATE PROGRAMS

Degree BSN

Available Programs Accelerated Baccalaureate for Second Degree; Generic Baccalaureate; LPN to Baccalaureate; RN Baccalaureate.
Study Options Full-time and part-time.
Program Entrance Requirements Minimum overall college GPA of 2.5, transcript of college record, CPR certification, high school biology, high school chemistry, high school transcript, immunizations, minimum high school GPA of 2.7, minimum GPA in nursing prerequisites of 2.67, prerequisite course work. Transfer students are accepted.
Advanced Placement Credit by examination available. Credit given for nursing courses completed elsewhere dependent upon specific evaluations.
Financial Aid 97% of baccalaureate students in nursing programs received some form of financial aid in 2007–08. *Gift aid (need-based):* Federal Pell, FSEOG, state, private, college/university gift aid from institutional funds. *Loans:* FFEL (Subsidized and Unsubsidized Stafford PLUS), Perkins, college/university. *Work-study:* Federal Work-Study, part-time campus jobs. *Financial aid application deadline (priority):* 3/1.
Contact Ms. Marsha Schuler, Academic Advisor, Department of Nursing and Nutritional Science, Marian University, School of Nursing, 3200 Cold Spring Road, Indianapolis, IN 46222-1997. *Telephone:* 317-955-6157. *Fax:* 317-955-6135. *E-mail:* mschuler@marian.edu.

Purdue University
School of Nursing
West Lafayette, Indiana

http://www.nursing.purdue.edu
Founded in 1869
DEGREES • BS • DNP • MS

Nursing Program Faculty 60 (15% with doctorates).
Baccalaureate Enrollment 552
Women 94% **Men** 6% **Minority** 3% **International** .5% **Part-time** .06%
Graduate Enrollment 48
Women 96% **Men** 4% **Minority** 2% **Part-time** 50%
Nursing Student Activities Sigma Theta Tau, Student Nurses' Association.
Nursing Student Resources Academic advising; academic or career counseling; assistance for students with disabilities; bookstore; campus computer network; career placement assistance; computer lab; computer-assisted instruction; e-mail services; interactive nursing skills videos; Internet; learning resource lab; library services; nursing audiovisuals; remedial services; resume preparation assistance; skills, simulation, or other laboratory; tutoring.
Library Facilities 2.5 million volumes (200,000 in health, 10,000 in nursing); 40,073 periodical subscriptions (1,000 health-care related).

BACCALAUREATE PROGRAMS

Degree BS

Available Programs ADN to Baccalaureate; Accelerated Baccalaureate for Second Degree; Baccalaureate for Second Degree; Generic Baccalaureate; RN Baccalaureate.

Site Options Indianapolis, IN.
Study Options Full-time and part-time.
Program Entrance Requirements Transcript of college record, CPR certification, health exam, health insurance, high school biology, high school chemistry, high school foreign language, 3 years high school math, 3 years high school science, high school transcript, immunizations, letters of recommendation, minimum high school GPA of 3.0. Transfer students are accepted.
Advanced Placement Credit by examination available. Credit given for nursing courses completed elsewhere dependent upon specific evaluations.
Contact *Telephone:* 765-494-1776. *Fax:* 765-494-0544.

GRADUATE PROGRAMS
Contact *Telephone:* 765-494-4015. *Fax:* 765-496-1800.

MASTER'S DEGREE PROGRAM
Degree MS
Available Programs Master's.
Concentrations Available *Nurse practitioner programs in:* adult health, pediatric.
Study Options Full-time and part-time.
Program Entrance Requirements Clinical experience, computer literacy, minimum overall college GPA of 3.0, transcript of college record, CPR certification, written essay, interview, 3 letters of recommendation, professional liability insurance/malpractice insurance, prerequisite course work, resume, statistics course.
Advanced Placement Credit given for nursing courses completed elsewhere dependent upon specific evaluations.
Degree Requirements 46 total credit hours, thesis or project.

POST-MASTER'S PROGRAM
Areas of Study *Nurse practitioner programs in:* adult health, pediatric.

DOCTORAL DEGREE PROGRAM
Degree DNP
Available Programs Doctorate.
Areas of Study Advanced practice nursing, aging, biology of health and illness, clinical practice, critical care, ethics, gerontology, health policy, health promotion/disease prevention, health-care systems, illness and transition, individualized study, information systems, nursing administration, nursing education, nursing policy, nursing research, nursing science, oncology, urban health, women's health.
Program Entrance Requirements Clinical experience, minimum overall college GPA of 3.0, interview by faculty committee, interview, letters of recommendation, MSN or equivalent, statistics course, vita, writing sample.
Degree Requirements 83 total credit hours, oral exam, residency.

CONTINUING EDUCATION PROGRAM
Contact *Telephone:* 765-494-4030. *Fax:* 765-494-6339.

Purdue University Calumet
School of Nursing
Hammond, Indiana

http://www.calumet.purdue.edu/nursing/
Founded in 1951
DEGREES • BS • MS

Nursing Program Faculty 29 (31% with doctorates).
Baccalaureate Enrollment 451
Women 89% **Men** 11% **Minority** 27% **Part-time** 37%
Graduate Enrollment 131
Women 95% **Men** 5% **Minority** 21% **Part-time** 86%
Distance Learning Courses Available.
Nursing Student Activities Sigma Theta Tau, Student Nurses' Association, nursing club.

Nursing Student Resources Academic advising; academic or career counseling; assistance for students with disabilities; bookstore; campus computer network; career placement assistance; computer lab; computer-assisted instruction; daycare for children of students; e-mail services; employment services for current students; externships; housing assistance; interactive nursing skills videos; Internet; learning resource lab; library services; nursing audiovisuals; other; paid internships; placement services for program completers; remedial services; resume preparation assistance; skills, simulation, or other laboratory; tutoring; unpaid internships.

Library Facilities 272,153 volumes (7,900 in health, 1,140 in nursing); 996 periodical subscriptions (204 health-care related).

BACCALAUREATE PROGRAMS

Degree BS

Available Programs Accelerated Baccalaureate for Second Degree; Accelerated RN Baccalaureate; Generic Baccalaureate; RN Baccalaureate.

Study Options Full-time and part-time.

Online Degree Options Yes.

Program Entrance Requirements Minimum overall college GPA of 2.5, transcript of college record, CPR certification, health exam, high school biology, high school chemistry, 3 years high school math, 3 years high school science, high school transcript, immunizations, minimum high school rank, minimum GPA in nursing prerequisites of 2.0, prerequisite course work. Transfer students are accepted. *Application deadline:* 2/1 (fall).

Advanced Placement Credit by examination available. Credit given for nursing courses completed elsewhere dependent upon specific evaluations.

Expenses (2009–10) *Tuition, state resident:* full-time $6166; part-time $193 per credit hour. *Tuition, nonresident:* full-time $14,494; part-time $453 per credit hour. *Room and board:* room only: $4680 per academic year. *Required fees:* full-time $562; part-time $18 per credit.

Financial Aid 35% of baccalaureate students in nursing programs received some form of financial aid in 2008–09.

Contact Prof. Kathleen An Nix, Undergraduate Program Coordinator, School of Nursing, Purdue University Calumet, 2200 169th Street, Hammond, IN 46323-2094. *Telephone:* 219-989-2814. *Fax:* 219-989-2848. *E-mail:* nix@calumet.purdue.edu.

GRADUATE PROGRAMS

Expenses (2009–10) *Tuition, state resident:* full-time $5605; part-time $244 per credit hour. *Tuition, nonresident:* full-time $12,140; part-time $528 per credit hour. *Room and board:* room only: $4680 per academic year. *Required fees:* part-time $12 per credit; part-time $112 per term.

Financial Aid 50% of graduate students in nursing programs received some form of financial aid in 2008–09.

Contact Dr. Jane Walker, Graduate Program Coordinator, School of Nursing, Purdue University Calumet, 2200 169th Street, Hammond, IN 46323-2094. *Telephone:* 219-989-2815. *Fax:* 219-989-2848. *E-mail:* walkerj@calumet.purdue.edu.

MASTER'S DEGREE PROGRAM

Degree MS

Available Programs Accelerated RN to Master's; Master's.

Concentrations Available Nursing administration. *Clinical nurse specialist programs in:* adult health, critical care. *Nurse practitioner programs in:* family health.

Study Options Full-time and part-time.

Online Degree Options Yes.

Program Entrance Requirements Clinical experience, minimum overall college GPA of 3.0, transcript of college record, written essay, 3 letters of recommendation, physical assessment course, resume, statistics course. *Application deadline:* 4/15 (fall), 9/15 (spring), 4/15 (summer). Applications may be processed on a rolling basis for some programs. *Application fee:* $55.

Advanced Placement Credit given for nursing courses completed elsewhere dependent upon specific evaluations.

Degree Requirements 45 total credit hours.

POST-MASTER'S PROGRAM

Areas of Study Nursing education. *Clinical nurse specialist programs in:* adult health, critical care. *Nurse practitioner programs in:* family health.

Purdue University North Central
Department of Nursing
Westville, Indiana

Founded in 1967

DEGREE • BS

Nursing Program Faculty 27 (11% with doctorates).

Baccalaureate Enrollment 52
Women 98% **Men** 2% **Minority** 12% **Part-time** 87%

Nursing Student Activities Nursing Honor Society, Student Nurses' Association.

Nursing Student Resources Academic advising; academic or career counseling; assistance for students with disabilities; bookstore; campus computer network; career placement assistance; computer lab; computer-assisted instruction; daycare for children of students; e-mail services; interactive nursing skills videos; Internet; learning resource lab; library services; nursing audiovisuals; placement services for program completers; resume preparation assistance; skills, simulation, or other laboratory; tutoring.

Library Facilities 87,307 volumes (1,100 in health, 560 in nursing); 222 periodical subscriptions (229 health-care related).

BACCALAUREATE PROGRAMS

Degree BS

Available Programs ADN to Baccalaureate; RN Baccalaureate.

Site Options Valparaiso, IN.

Study Options Full-time and part-time.

Program Entrance Requirements Minimum overall college GPA of 2.5, transcript of college record, high school biology, high school chemistry, 3 years high school math, 3 years high school science, high school transcript, minimum high school GPA of 2.5, minimum high school rank 50%, minimum GPA in nursing prerequisites of 2.5. Transfer students are accepted. *Application deadline:* 1/16 (fall), 8/16 (spring).

Advanced Placement Credit given for nursing courses completed elsewhere dependent upon specific evaluations.

Expenses (2009–10) *Tuition, state resident:* part-time $195 per credit hour. *Tuition, nonresident:* part-time $484 per credit hour. *Required fees:* part-time $16 per credit.

Financial Aid 44% of baccalaureate students in nursing programs received some form of financial aid in 2008–09. *Gift aid (need-based):* Federal Pell, FSEOG, state, private, college/university gift aid from institutional funds. *Loans:* FFEL (Subsidized and Unsubsidized Stafford PLUS), Perkins, alternative loans. *Work-study:* Federal Work-Study, part-time campus jobs. *Financial aid application deadline:* 6/30 (priority: 3/10).

Contact Nursing Contact, Department of Nursing, Purdue University North Central, 1401 South U.S. 421, Westville, IN 46391. *Telephone:* 219-785-5226. *E-mail:* nursing@pnc.edu.

Saint Mary's College
Department of Nursing
Notre Dame, Indiana

http://www.saintmarys.edu

Founded in 1844

DEGREE • BS

Nursing Program Faculty 15 (9% with doctorates).

Baccalaureate Enrollment 235
Women 100% **Minority** 4%

Nursing Student Activities Nursing Honor Society, Sigma Theta Tau, Student Nurses' Association.

Nursing Student Resources Academic advising; academic or career counseling; assistance for students with disabilities; bookstore; campus computer network; career placement assistance; computer lab; computer-assisted instruction; daycare for children of students; e-mail services; employment services for current students; externships; interactive nursing skills videos; Internet; learning resource lab; library services; nursing

Saint Mary's College (continued)

audiovisuals; paid internships; placement services for program completers; remedial services; resume preparation assistance; skills, simulation, or other laboratory; tutoring; unpaid internships.

Library Facilities 268,569 volumes (9,787 in health, 5,149 in nursing); 938 periodical subscriptions (70 health-care related).

BACCALAUREATE PROGRAMS

Degree BS

Available Programs Accelerated Baccalaureate; Generic Baccalaureate.

Site Options South Bend, IN; Goshen, IN.

Study Options Full-time.

Program Entrance Requirements Minimum overall college GPA of 3.0, transcript of college record, CPR certification, written essay, health exam, high school foreign language, 3 years high school math, 2 years high school science, high school transcript, immunizations, 2 letters of recommendation, minimum GPA in nursing prerequisites of 2.75. Transfer students are accepted. *Application deadline:* Applications may be processed on a rolling basis for some programs. *Application fee:* $30.

Advanced Placement Credit given for nursing courses completed elsewhere dependent upon specific evaluations.

Expenses (2009–10) *Tuition:* full-time $29,400. *Room and board:* $9209 per academic year. *Required fees:* full-time $200.

Financial Aid 75% of baccalaureate students in nursing programs received some form of financial aid in 2008–09. *Gift aid (need-based):* Federal Pell, FSEOG, state, private, college/university gift aid from institutional funds. *Loans:* FFEL (Subsidized and Unsubsidized Stafford PLUS), Perkins. *Work-study:* Federal Work-Study, part-time campus jobs. *Financial aid application deadline (priority):* 3/1.

Contact Mr. Daniel L. Meyer, Vice President for Enrollment Management, Department of Nursing, Saint Mary's College, 124 LeMans, Notre Dame, IN 46556. *Telephone:* 574-284-4587. *Fax:* 574-284-4716. *E-mail:* dmeyer@saintmarys.edu.

University of Evansville
Department of Nursing
Evansville, Indiana

http://nursing.evansville.edu

Founded in 1854

DEGREE • BSN

Nursing Program Faculty 9 (22% with doctorates).

Baccalaureate Enrollment 164
Women 90% **Men** 10% **Minority** 10% **International** 1%

Distance Learning Courses Available.

Nursing Student Activities Sigma Theta Tau, Student Nurses' Association.

Nursing Student Resources Academic advising; academic or career counseling; assistance for students with disabilities; bookstore; campus computer network; career placement assistance; computer lab; computer-assisted instruction; e-mail services; employment services for current students; externships; housing assistance; interactive nursing skills videos; Internet; learning resource lab; library services; nursing audiovisuals; paid internships; placement services for program completers; remedial services; resume preparation assistance; skills, simulation, or other laboratory; tutoring; unpaid internships.

Library Facilities 274,174 volumes (11,000 in nursing); 845 periodical subscriptions (155 health-care related).

BACCALAUREATE PROGRAMS

Degree BSN

Available Programs Generic Baccalaureate; RN Baccalaureate.
Study Options Full-time.

Program Entrance Requirements CPR certification, health exam, health insurance, high school chemistry, 3 years high school math, 2 years high school science, high school transcript, immunizations, minimum high school rank 67%, professional liability insurance/malpractice insurance. Transfer students are accepted. *Application deadline:* Applications may be processed on a rolling basis for some programs. *Application fee:* $35.

Advanced Placement Credit given for nursing courses completed elsewhere dependent upon specific evaluations.

Expenses (2009–10) *Tuition:* full-time $26,010; part-time $725 per credit hour. *International tuition:* $26,010 full-time. *Room and board:* $3930 per academic year. *Required fees:* full-time $850; part-time $800 per term.

Financial Aid 100% of baccalaureate students in nursing programs received some form of financial aid in 2008–09. *Gift aid (need-based):* Federal Pell, FSEOG, state, private, college/university gift aid from institutional funds. *Loans:* Federal Nursing Student Loans, FFEL (Subsidized and Unsubsidized Stafford PLUS), Perkins. *Work-study:* Federal Work-Study, part-time campus jobs. *Financial aid application deadline (priority):* 3/10.

Contact Dr. Amy M. Hall, Chair/Professor of Nursing, Department of Nursing, University of Evansville, 1800 Lincoln Avenue, Evansville, IN 47722. *Telephone:* 812-488-2414. *Fax:* 812-488-2717. *E-mail:* ah169@evansville.edu.

University of Indianapolis
School of Nursing
Indianapolis, Indiana

http://www.uindy.edu

Founded in 1902

DEGREES • BSN • MSN • MSN/MBA

Nursing Program Faculty 46 (26% with doctorates).

Baccalaureate Enrollment 259
Women 96.5% **Men** 3.5% **Minority** 7% **International** 1% **Part-time** 54%

Graduate Enrollment 148
Women 82.4% **Men** 17.6% **Minority** 12% **International** 1% **Part-time** 90%

Distance Learning Courses Available.

Nursing Student Activities Nursing Honor Society, Sigma Theta Tau, Student Nurses' Association.

Nursing Student Resources Academic advising; academic or career counseling; assistance for students with disabilities; bookstore; campus computer network; career placement assistance; computer lab; computer-assisted instruction; e-mail services; employment services for current students; housing assistance; interactive nursing skills videos; Internet; learning resource lab; library services; nursing audiovisuals; other; paid internships; placement services for program completers; remedial services; resume preparation assistance; skills, simulation, or other laboratory; tutoring.

Library Facilities 173,363 volumes (15,600 in health, 1,000 in nursing); 1,015 periodical subscriptions (600 health-care related).

BACCALAUREATE PROGRAMS

Degree BSN

Available Programs ADN to Baccalaureate; Accelerated Baccalaureate for Second Degree; Generic Baccalaureate.

Site Options Indianapolis, IN.

Study Options Full-time.

Program Entrance Requirements Minimum overall college GPA of 2.82, transcript of college record, CPR certification, health exam, health insurance, high school biology, high school chemistry, 2 years high school math, 2 years high school science, high school transcript, immunizations, minimum GPA in nursing prerequisites of 2.0, prerequisite course work. Transfer students are accepted. *Application deadline:* 4/15 (fall).

Advanced Placement Credit by examination available. Credit given for nursing courses completed elsewhere dependent upon specific evaluations.

Expenses (2008–09) *Tuition:* full-time $21,000; part-time $815 per credit hour. *Room and board:* $4175; room only: $2130 per academic year. *Required fees:* full-time $200; part-time $100 per term.

Financial Aid 88% of baccalaureate students in nursing programs received some form of financial aid in 2007–08.

Contact Dr. Cheryl M. Martin, Director, BSN Program, School of Nursing, University of Indianapolis, 1400 East Hanna Avenue, Indianapolis, IN 46227-3697. *Telephone:* 317-788-3324. *Fax:* 317-788-3542. *E-mail:* martincm@uindy.edu.

GRADUATE PROGRAMS

Expenses (2008–09) *Tuition:* part-time $540 per credit hour.

Financial Aid 90% of graduate students in nursing programs received some form of financial aid in 2007–08.

Contact Dr. Anne Thomas, Director, MSN Program, School of Nursing, University of Indianapolis, 1400 East Hanna Avenue, Indianapolis, IN 46227-3697. *Telephone:* 317-788-3543. *Fax:* 317-788-3542. *E-mail:* athomas@uindy.edu.

MASTER'S DEGREE PROGRAM

Degrees MSN; MSN/MBA

Available Programs Accelerated Master's for Non-Nursing College Graduates; Master's.

Concentrations Available Nurse-midwifery; nursing administration; nursing education. *Nurse practitioner programs in:* family health, gerontology, women's health.

Site Options Indianapolis, IN.

Study Options Full-time and part-time.

Online Degree Options Yes.

Program Entrance Requirements Clinical experience, minimum overall college GPA of 3.0, transcript of college record, CPR certification, written essay, immunizations, interview, 3 letters of recommendation. *Application deadline:* Applications may be processed on a rolling basis for some programs. *Application fee:* $60.

Advanced Placement Credit given for nursing courses completed elsewhere dependent upon specific evaluations.

Degree Requirements Thesis or project, comprehensive exam.

POST-MASTER'S PROGRAM

Areas of Study Nurse-midwifery; nursing administration; nursing education. *Nurse practitioner programs in:* family health, gerontology, women's health.

CONTINUING EDUCATION PROGRAM

Contact Tondra Crum, Graduate Academic Advisor, School of Nursing, University of Indianapolis, School of Nursing, 1400 East Hanna Avenue, Indianapolis, IN 46227. *Telephone:* 317-788-2128. *E-mail:* tcrum@uindy.edu.

University of Saint Francis
Department of Nursing
Fort Wayne, Indiana

http://www.sf.edu
Founded in 1890
DEGREES • BSN • MSN

Nursing Program Faculty 62 (8% with doctorates).

Baccalaureate Enrollment 254
Women 96% **Men** 4% **Minority** 4% **Part-time** 4%

Graduate Enrollment 88
Women 100% **Minority** 8% **Part-time** 74%

Distance Learning Courses Available.

Nursing Student Activities Sigma Theta Tau, Student Nurses' Association.

Nursing Student Resources Academic advising; academic or career counseling; assistance for students with disabilities; bookstore; campus computer network; career placement assistance; computer lab; computer-assisted instruction; e-mail services; employment services for current students; externships; housing assistance; interactive nursing skills videos; Internet; learning resource lab; library services; nursing audiovisuals; paid internships; remedial services; resume preparation assistance; skills, simulation, or other laboratory; tutoring; unpaid internships.

Library Facilities 95,991 volumes (7,826 in health, 1,746 in nursing); 567 periodical subscriptions (142 health-care related).

BACCALAUREATE PROGRAMS

Degree BSN

Available Programs Generic Baccalaureate.

Study Options Full-time and part-time.

Program Entrance Requirements Minimum overall college GPA of 2.7, transcript of college record, CPR certification, health exam, high school biology, high school chemistry, 1 year of high school math, high school transcript, immunizations, minimum high school GPA of 2.7, minimum GPA in nursing prerequisites of 2.7, prerequisite course work. Transfer students are accepted.

Advanced Placement Credit given for nursing courses completed elsewhere dependent upon specific evaluations.

Expenses (2009–10) *Room and board:* $7908 per academic year.

Financial Aid 96% of baccalaureate students in nursing programs received some form of financial aid in 2008–09. *Gift aid (need-based):* Federal Pell, FSEOG, state, private, college/university gift aid from institutional funds. *Loans:* FFEL (Subsidized and Unsubsidized Stafford PLUS), Perkins. *Work-study:* Federal Work-Study, part-time campus jobs. *Financial aid application deadline:* 6/30 (priority: 3/10).

Contact Mindy Yoder, BSN/MSN Program Director, Department of Nursing, University of Saint Francis, 2701 Spring Street, Fort Wayne, IN 46808. *Telephone:* 260-399-7700 Ext. 8510. *Fax:* 260-434-7404. *E-mail:* myoder@sf.edu.

GRADUATE PROGRAMS

Expenses (2009–10) *Tuition:* part-time $625 per term. *Room and board:* $7908 per academic year. *Required fees:* part-time $19 per credit; part-time $186 per term.

Financial Aid 82% of graduate students in nursing programs received some form of financial aid in 2008–09. Federal Work-Study and unspecified assistantships available.

Contact Mindy Yoder, BSN/MSN Program Director, Department of Nursing, University of Saint Francis, 2701 Spring Street, Fort Wayne, IN 46808. *Telephone:* 260-399-7700 Ext. 8510. *Fax:* 260-434-7404. *E-mail:* myoder@sf.edu.

MASTER'S DEGREE PROGRAM

Degree MSN

Available Programs Master's; Master's for Nurses with Non-Nursing Degrees.

Concentrations Available *Nurse practitioner programs in:* community health, family health.

Study Options Full-time and part-time.

Program Entrance Requirements Computer literacy, minimum overall college GPA of 3.2, transcript of college record, CPR certification, written essay, immunizations, interview, 3 letters of recommendation, nursing research course, physical assessment course, resume, statistics course, GRE.

Advanced Placement Credit given for nursing courses completed elsewhere dependent upon specific evaluations.

Degree Requirements 48 total credit hours.

POST-MASTER'S PROGRAM

Areas of Study *Nurse practitioner programs in:* family health.

University of Southern Indiana
College of Nursing and Health Professions
Evansville, Indiana

http://health.usi.edu
Founded in 1965
DEGREES • BSN • DNP • MSN

Nursing Program Faculty 30 (50% with doctorates).

University of Southern Indiana (continued)
Baccalaureate Enrollment 276
Women 90% **Men** 10% **Minority** 7% **International** 1% **Part-time** 18%

Graduate Enrollment 283
Women 96% **Men** 4% **Minority** 6% **Part-time** 70%

Distance Learning Courses Available.

Nursing Student Activities Sigma Theta Tau, Student Nurses' Association.

Nursing Student Resources Academic advising; academic or career counseling; assistance for students with disabilities; bookstore; campus computer network; career placement assistance; computer lab; computer-assisted instruction; daycare for children of students; e-mail services; employment services for current students; housing assistance; interactive nursing skills videos; Internet; learning resource lab; library services; nursing audiovisuals; placement services for program completers; remedial services; resume preparation assistance; skills, simulation, or other laboratory; tutoring; unpaid internships.

Library Facilities 336,457 volumes (9,200 in health, 1,500 in nursing); 22,135 periodical subscriptions (2,000 health-care related).

BACCALAUREATE PROGRAMS

Degree BSN

Available Programs Generic Baccalaureate; RN Baccalaureate.

Study Options Full-time.

Online Degree Options Yes.

Program Entrance Requirements Minimum overall college GPA of 3.0, transcript of college record, CPR certification, written essay, health exam, health insurance, high school transcript, immunizations, minimum GPA in nursing prerequisites of 2.0, professional liability insurance/malpractice insurance, prerequisite course work. Transfer students are accepted. *Application deadline:* 8/15 (fall).

Advanced Placement Credit given for nursing courses completed elsewhere dependent upon specific evaluations.

Expenses (2009–10) *Tuition, state resident:* full-time $2640; part-time $176 per credit hour. *Tuition, nonresident:* full-time $3960; part-time $265 per credit hour. *International tuition:* $12,600 full-time. *Room and board:* $6700; room only: $3450 per academic year. *Required fees:* full-time $300; part-time $10 per credit; part-time $150 per term.

Financial Aid 70% of baccalaureate students in nursing programs received some form of financial aid in 2008–09. *Gift aid (need-based):* Federal Pell, FSEOG, state, private, college/university gift aid from institutional funds, Federal Nursing. *Loans:* Federal Direct (Subsidized and Unsubsidized Stafford PLUS). *Work-study:* Federal Work-Study. *Financial aid application deadline:* 3/1.

Contact Dr. Ann H. White, Assistant Dean for Nursing, College of Nursing and Health Professions, University of Southern Indiana, 8600 University Boulevard, Evansville, IN 47712. *Telephone:* 812-465-1173. *Fax:* 812-465-7092. *E-mail:* awhite@usi.edu.

GRADUATE PROGRAMS

Expenses (2009–10) *Tuition, state resident:* full-time $6120; part-time $255 per credit hour. *Tuition, nonresident:* full-time $6120; part-time $255 per credit hour. *International tuition:* $12,600 full-time. *Room and board:* $6700; room only: $3450 per academic year. *Required fees:* full-time $300; part-time $10 per credit; part-time $150 per term.

Financial Aid 45% of graduate students in nursing programs received some form of financial aid in 2008–09. Federal Work-Study, scholarships, tuition waivers (full and partial), and unspecified assistantships available. *Financial aid application deadline:* 3/1.

Contact Dr. Ann H. White, Assistant Dean for Nursing, College of Nursing and Health Professions, University of Southern Indiana, 8600 University Boulevard, Evansville, IN 47712. *Telephone:* 812-465-1173. *Fax:* 812-465-7092. *E-mail:* awhite@usi.edu.

MASTER'S DEGREE PROGRAM

Degree MSN

Available Programs Master's; RN to Master's.

Concentrations Available Nursing administration; nursing education. *Nurse practitioner programs in:* acute care, family health.

Study Options Full-time and part-time.

Online Degree Options Yes (online only).

Program Entrance Requirements Computer literacy, minimum overall college GPA of 3.0, transcript of college record, CPR certification, written essay, immunizations, 2 letters of recommendation, professional liability insurance/malpractice insurance, resume, statistics course. *Application deadline:* 2/15 (fall). *Application fee:* $25.

Advanced Placement Credit given for nursing courses completed elsewhere dependent upon specific evaluations.

Degree Requirements 42 total credit hours.

POST-MASTER'S PROGRAM

Areas of Study Nursing administration; nursing education. *Nurse practitioner programs in:* acute care, family health.

DOCTORAL DEGREE PROGRAM

Degree DNP

Available Programs Doctorate.

Areas of Study Clinical practice, nursing administration.

Program Entrance Requirements Clinical experience, minimum overall college GPA of 3.25, 3 letters of recommendation, MSN or equivalent, vita, writing sample. Application deadline: 1/15 (fall). Application fee: $25.

Degree Requirements 78 total credit hours.

CONTINUING EDUCATION PROGRAM

Contact Peggy Graul, Coordinator of Continuing Education for Nursing and Health Professions, College of Nursing and Health Professions, University of Southern Indiana, 8600 University Boulevard, Evansville, IN 47712. *Telephone:* 812-465-1161. *Fax:* 812-465-7092. *E-mail:* pgraul@usi.edu.

See full description on page 528.

Valparaiso University
College of Nursing
Valparaiso, Indiana

http://www.valpo.edu/nursing
Founded in 1859

DEGREES • BSN • MSN • MSN/MBA

Nursing Program Faculty 13 (38% with doctorates).

Baccalaureate Enrollment 310
Women 92% **Men** 8% **Minority** 12% **International** 2% **Part-time** 6%

Graduate Enrollment 34
Women 91% **Men** 9% **Minority** 12% **Part-time** 59%

Nursing Student Activities Sigma Theta Tau, Student Nurses' Association.

Nursing Student Resources Academic advising; academic or career counseling; assistance for students with disabilities; bookstore; campus computer network; career placement assistance; computer lab; computer-assisted instruction; e-mail services; employment services for current students; externships; housing assistance; interactive nursing skills videos; Internet; learning resource lab; library services; nursing audiovisuals; placement services for program completers; remedial services; resume preparation assistance; skills, simulation, or other laboratory; tutoring; unpaid internships.

Library Facilities 506,437 volumes (9,500 in health, 995 in nursing); 50,199 periodical subscriptions (1,000 health-care related).

BACCALAUREATE PROGRAMS

Degree BSN

Available Programs Accelerated Baccalaureate; Generic Baccalaureate; RN Baccalaureate.

Study Options Full-time and part-time.

Program Entrance Requirements Minimum overall college GPA of 3.0, transcript of college record, written essay, high school biology, high school chemistry, 2 years high school math, 4 years high school science, high school transcript, immunizations, minimum high school GPA of 2.0, minimum GPA in nursing prerequisites of 2.5. Transfer students are accepted.

Advanced Placement Credit by examination available. Credit given for nursing courses completed elsewhere dependent upon specific evaluations.

Contact *Telephone:* 219-464-5011. *Fax:* 219-464-6888.

GRADUATE PROGRAMS

Contact *Telephone:* 219-464-5289. *Fax:* 219-464-5425.

MASTER'S DEGREE PROGRAM

Degrees MSN; MSN/MBA

Available Programs Master's; RN to Master's.

Concentrations Available *Clinical nurse specialist programs in:* adult health, gerontology, women's health.

Study Options Full-time and part-time.

Program Entrance Requirements Minimum overall college GPA of 3.0, transcript of college record, CPR certification, written essay, immunizations, 2 letters of recommendation, nursing research course, physical assessment course, statistics course.

Advanced Placement Credit given for nursing courses completed elsewhere dependent upon specific evaluations.

Degree Requirements 36 total credit hours, thesis or project.

POST-MASTER'S PROGRAM

Areas of Study *Nurse practitioner programs in:* family health.

CONTINUING EDUCATION PROGRAM

Contact *Telephone:* 219-464-5291. *Fax:* 219-464-5425.

Vincennes University
Department of Nursing
Vincennes, Indiana

Founded in 1801

DEGREE • BSN

BACCALAUREATE PROGRAMS

Degree BSN

Available Programs RN Baccalaureate.

Contact Nursing Program, Department of Nursing, Vincennes University, 1002 North First Street, Vincennes, IN 47591. *Telephone:* 812-888-8888.

IOWA

Allen College
Program in Nursing
Waterloo, Iowa

http://www.allencollege.edu

Founded in 1989

DEGREES • BSN • MSN

Nursing Program Faculty 31 (19% with doctorates).

Baccalaureate Enrollment 314

Women 93% **Men** 7% **Minority** 4% **Part-time** 20%

Graduate Enrollment 140

Women 96% **Men** 4% **Minority** 4% **Part-time** 74%

Distance Learning Courses Available.

Nursing Student Activities Sigma Theta Tau, Student Nurses' Association, nursing club.

Nursing Student Resources Academic advising; academic or career counseling; campus computer network; career placement assistance; computer lab; computer-assisted instruction; daycare for children of students; e-mail services; employment services for current students; externships; housing assistance; interactive nursing skills videos; Internet; library services; nursing audiovisuals; other; paid internships; placement services for program completers; resume preparation assistance; skills, simulation, or other laboratory; tutoring.

Library Facilities 3,200 volumes (3,200 in health, 3,200 in nursing); 199 periodical subscriptions (185 health-care related).

BACCALAUREATE PROGRAMS

Degree BSN

Available Programs ADN to Baccalaureate; Accelerated Baccalaureate; Accelerated Baccalaureate for Second Degree; Accelerated RN Baccalaureate; Baccalaureate for Second Degree; Generic Baccalaureate; LPN to Baccalaureate; RN Baccalaureate.

Study Options Full-time.

Program Entrance Requirements Minimum overall college GPA of 2.7, transcript of college record, CPR certification, health exam, immunizations, 1 letter of recommendation, prerequisite course work. Transfer students are accepted. *Application deadline:* Applications may be processed on a rolling basis for some programs. *Application fee:* $50.

Advanced Placement Credit given for nursing courses completed elsewhere dependent upon specific evaluations.

Expenses (2009–10) *Tuition:* part-time $481 per credit hour. *Room and board:* $6816; room only: $3408 per academic year.

Financial Aid 97% of baccalaureate students in nursing programs received some form of financial aid in 2008–09. *Gift aid (need-based):* Federal Pell, FSEOG, state, private, college/university gift aid from institutional funds, Federal Nursing, Federal Scholarships for Disadvantaged Students. *Loans:* Federal Nursing Student Loans, Federal Direct (Subsidized and Unsubsidized Stafford PLUS), Perkins, state, college/university. *Work-study:* Federal Work-Study, part-time campus jobs. *Financial aid application deadline:* Continuous.

Contact Dina Dowden, Student Services Education Secretary, Program in Nursing, Allen College, 1825 Logan Avenue, Waterloo, IA 50703. *Telephone:* 319-226-2000. *Fax:* 319-226-2051. *E-mail:* AllenCollegeAdmissions@ihs.org.

GRADUATE PROGRAMS

Expenses (2009–10) *Tuition:* part-time $651 per credit hour. *International tuition:* $651 full-time. *Room and board:* $6816; room only: $3408 per academic year. *Required fees:* part-time $65 per credit.

Financial Aid 94% of graduate students in nursing programs received some form of financial aid in 2008–09. Teaching assistantships, institutionally sponsored loans, scholarships, and traineeships available. Aid available to part-time students. *Financial aid application deadline:* 8/15.

Contact Dina Dowden, Student Services Education Secretary, Program in Nursing, Allen College, 1825 Logan Avenue, Waterloo, IA 50703. *Telephone:* 319-226-2000. *Fax:* 319-226-2051. *E-mail:* AllenCollegeAdmissions@ihs.org.

MASTER'S DEGREE PROGRAM

Degree MSN

Available Programs Master's; Master's for Nurses with Non-Nursing Degrees; RN to Master's.

Concentrations Available Nursing administration; nursing education. *Nurse practitioner programs in:* acute care, adult health, family health, gerontology, psychiatric/mental health.

Study Options Full-time and part-time.

Online Degree Options Yes.

Program Entrance Requirements Clinical experience, computer literacy, minimum overall college GPA of 3.0, transcript of college record, CPR certification, written essay, immunizations, interview, 3 letters of recommendation, nursing research course, professional liability insurance/malpractice insurance, prerequisite course work, resume, statistics course. *Application deadline:* Applications may be processed on a rolling basis for some programs. *Application fee:* $50.

Advanced Placement Credit given for nursing courses completed elsewhere dependent upon specific evaluations.

Degree Requirements 44 total credit hours, thesis or project.

Allen College (continued)

POST-MASTER'S PROGRAM

Areas of Study Nursing administration; nursing education. *Nurse practitioner programs in:* acute care, adult health, family health, gerontology, psychiatric/mental health.

POSTDOCTORAL PROGRAM

Postdoctoral Program Contact Dr. Diane Young, Department Chair, MSN Program, Program in Nursing, Allen College, 1825 Logan Avenue, Waterloo, IA 50703. *Telephone:* 319-226-2047. *Fax:* 319-226-2070. *E-mail:* YoungDM@ihs.org.

CONTINUING EDUCATION PROGRAM

Contact Mrs. Mary Kay Frost, Continuing Education Coordinator, Program in Nursing, Allen College, 1825 Logan Avenue, Waterloo, IA 50703. *Telephone:* 319-226-2028. *Fax:* 319-226-2051. *E-mail:* FrostMK@ihs.org.

Briar Cliff University
Department of Nursing
Sioux City, Iowa

http://www.briarcliff.edu/nursing

Founded in 1930

DEGREES • BSN • MSN

Nursing Program Faculty 8 (38% with doctorates).

Baccalaureate Enrollment 150
Women 90% **Men** 10% **Minority** 5% **Part-time** 25%

Graduate Enrollment 32
Women 95% **Men** 5% **Minority** 5% **Part-time** 75%

Distance Learning Courses Available.

Nursing Student Activities Sigma Theta Tau, Student Nurses' Association.

Nursing Student Resources Academic advising; academic or career counseling; assistance for students with disabilities; bookstore; campus computer network; career placement assistance; computer lab; computer-assisted instruction; e-mail services; employment services for current students; externships; interactive nursing skills videos; Internet; learning resource lab; library services; nursing audiovisuals; placement services for program completers; remedial services; resume preparation assistance; skills, simulation, or other laboratory; tutoring.

Library Facilities 76,339 volumes; 164 periodical subscriptions.

BACCALAUREATE PROGRAMS

Degree BSN

Available Programs ADN to Baccalaureate; Generic Baccalaureate; LPN to Baccalaureate; RN Baccalaureate.

Study Options Full-time and part-time.

Program Entrance Requirements Minimum overall college GPA of 2.75, transcript of college record, CPR certification, written essay, health exam, high school transcript, immunizations, minimum GPA in nursing prerequisites of 2.75, prerequisite course work. Transfer students are accepted. *Application deadline:* 6/15 (fall), 7/1 (winter), 10/31 (spring), 4/1 (summer). Applications may be processed on a rolling basis for some programs. *Application fee:* $25.

Advanced Placement Credit given for nursing courses completed elsewhere dependent upon specific evaluations.

Expenses (2009–10) *Tuition:* full-time $21,867; part-time $729 per credit. *International tuition:* $21,867 full-time. *Room and board:* $6357; room only: $3357 per academic year.

Financial Aid 99% of baccalaureate students in nursing programs received some form of financial aid in 2008–09.

Contact Dr. Richard A. Petersen, Department Chair and Associate Professor, Department of Nursing, Briar Cliff University, 3303 Rebecca Street, Sioux City, IA 51104. *Telephone:* 712-279-1662. *E-mail:* rick. petersen@briarcliff.edu.

GRADUATE PROGRAMS

Expenses (2009–10) *Tuition:* part-time $479 per credit.

Financial Aid 60% of graduate students in nursing programs received some form of financial aid in 2008–09.

Contact Dr. Richard A. Petersen, Department Chair and Associate Professor, Department of Nursing, Briar Cliff University, 3303 Rebecca Street, Sioux City, IA 51104. *Telephone:* 712-279-1662. *E-mail:* rick. petersen@briarcliff.edu.

MASTER'S DEGREE PROGRAM

Degree MSN

Available Programs Master's.

Concentrations Available Nursing education. *Nurse practitioner programs in:* family health.

Study Options Part-time.

Program Entrance Requirements Clinical experience, computer literacy, minimum overall college GPA of 3.0, transcript of college record, CPR certification, written essay, immunizations, 2 letters of recommendation, nursing research course, physical assessment course, resume, statistics course. *Application deadline:* 6/15 (fall). Applications may be processed on a rolling basis for some programs. *Application fee:* $25.

Advanced Placement Credit given for nursing courses completed elsewhere dependent upon specific evaluations.

Degree Requirements 40 total credit hours, thesis or project, comprehensive exam.

CONTINUING EDUCATION PROGRAM

Contact Dr. Richard A. Petersen, Chair and Associate Professor, Department of Nursing, Briar Cliff University, 3303 Rebecca Street, Sioux City, IA 51104. *Telephone:* 712-279-1662. *Fax:* 712-279-5463. *E-mail:* rick.petersen@ briarcliff.edu.

Clarke College
Department of Nursing and Health
Dubuque, Iowa

Founded in 1843

DEGREES • BS • MSN

Nursing Program Faculty 18 (3% with doctorates).

Baccalaureate Enrollment 104
Women 92% **Men** 8% **Minority** 1% **International** 1% **Part-time** 9%

Graduate Enrollment 52
Women 99% **Men** 1% **Part-time** 35%

Nursing Student Activities Nursing Honor Society, Sigma Theta Tau, Student Nurses' Association.

Nursing Student Resources Academic advising; academic or career counseling; assistance for students with disabilities; bookstore; campus computer network; career placement assistance; computer lab; computer-assisted instruction; e-mail services; employment services for current students; externships; housing assistance; interactive nursing skills videos; Internet; learning resource lab; library services; nursing audiovisuals; paid internships; placement services for program completers; remedial services; resume preparation assistance; skills, simulation, or other laboratory; tutoring; unpaid internships.

Library Facilities 120,000 volumes (7,000 in health, 2,856 in nursing); 9,600 periodical subscriptions (124 health-care related).

BACCALAUREATE PROGRAMS

Degree BS

Available Programs Baccalaureate for Second Degree; Generic Baccalaureate; RN Baccalaureate.

Site Options Dubuque, IA.

Study Options Full-time and part-time.

Program Entrance Requirements Minimum overall college GPA of 2.75, transcript of college record, CPR certification, written essay, health exam, health insurance, high school chemistry, high school foreign language, high school math, high school transcript, immunizations, interview, 2 letters of recommendation, minimum high school GPA of 2.0, minimum GPA in nursing prerequisites of 1.67, professional liability insurance/malpractice insurance, prerequisite course work. Transfer students are accepted. *Application deadline:* Applications may be processed on a rolling basis for some programs.

Advanced Placement Credit given for nursing courses completed elsewhere dependent upon specific evaluations.

Expenses (2009–10) *Tuition:* full-time $22,800; part-time $578 per credit. *Room and board:* $6840; room only: $3360 per academic year. *Required fees:* full-time $10,000.

Financial Aid 98% of baccalaureate students in nursing programs received some form of financial aid in 2008–09.

Contact Keith Tackett, Interim Chairperson, Department of Nursing and Health, Clarke College, 1550 Clarke Drive, Dubuque, IA 52001. *Telephone:* 563-588-8109. *Fax:* 563-588-8684. *E-mail:* keith.tackett@clarke.edu.

GRADUATE PROGRAMS

Expenses (2009–10) *Tuition:* part-time $602 per credit.

Financial Aid 30% of graduate students in nursing programs received some form of financial aid in 2008–09. Career-related internships or fieldwork available. Aid available to part-time students.

Contact Keith Tackett, Interim Chairperson, Department of Nursing and Health, Clarke College, 1550 Clarke Drive, Dubuque, IA 52001. *Telephone:* 563-588-8109. *Fax:* 563-588-8684. *E-mail:* keith.tackett@clarke.edu.

MASTER'S DEGREE PROGRAM

Degree MSN

Available Programs Master's.

Concentrations Available Nursing education. *Nurse practitioner programs in:* family health.

Study Options Full-time and part-time.

Program Entrance Requirements Computer literacy, minimum overall college GPA of 3.0, transcript of college record, CPR certification, written essay, immunizations, interview, 3 letters of recommendation, nursing research course, physical assessment course, prerequisite course work, resume, statistics course, GRE General Test or MAT. *Application deadline:* Applications may be processed on a rolling basis for some programs. *Application fee:* $35.

Advanced Placement Credit given for nursing courses completed elsewhere dependent upon specific evaluations.

Degree Requirements 37 total credit hours, thesis or project.

POST-MASTER'S PROGRAM

Areas of Study *Nurse practitioner programs in:* family health.

CONTINUING EDUCATION PROGRAM

Contact Scott Schneider, Director of Adult Education and Timesaver Programs, Department of Nursing and Health, Clarke College, 1550 Clarke Drive, Dubuque, IA 52001. *Telephone:* 563-588-6378. *Fax:* 563-588-8684. *E-mail:* scott.schneider@clarke.edu.

Coe College
Department of Nursing
Cedar Rapids, Iowa

Founded in 1851

DEGREE • BSN

Nursing Program Faculty 9 (33% with doctorates).

Baccalaureate Enrollment 45
Women 98% **Men** 2%

Nursing Student Activities Student Nurses' Association.

Nursing Student Resources Academic advising; academic or career counseling; assistance for students with disabilities; bookstore; campus computer network; career placement assistance; computer lab; e-mail services; employment services for current students; housing assistance; Internet; learning resource lab; library services; nursing audiovisuals; remedial services; resume preparation assistance; skills, simulation, or other laboratory; tutoring; unpaid internships.

Library Facilities 2,929 volumes in health, 492 volumes in nursing; 34 periodical subscriptions health-care related.

BACCALAUREATE PROGRAMS

Degree BSN

Available Programs Generic Baccalaureate; RN Baccalaureate.

Study Options Full-time and part-time.

Program Entrance Requirements Minimum overall college GPA of 2.7, transcript of college record, CPR certification, written essay, health exam, health insurance, high school chemistry, high school transcript, immunizations, minimum high school GPA of 2.0, minimum GPA in nursing prerequisites of 2.7, prerequisite course work. Transfer students are accepted.

Advanced Placement Credit given for nursing courses completed elsewhere dependent upon specific evaluations.

Expenses (2008–09) *Tuition:* full-time $27,400; part-time $3475 per course. *International tuition:* $27,400 full-time. *Room and board:* $6890; room only: $3120 per academic year. *Required fees:* full-time $320.

Financial Aid 100% of baccalaureate students in nursing programs received some form of financial aid in 2007–08. *Gift aid (need-based):* Federal Pell, FSEOG, state, private, college/university gift aid from institutional funds, ROTC. *Loans:* Federal Direct (Subsidized and Unsubsidized Stafford PLUS), Perkins, college/university. *Work-study:* Federal Work-Study, part-time campus jobs. *Financial aid application deadline (priority):* 3/1.

Contact Dr. H. Jule Ohrt, RN, Associate Professor and Chairperson, Department of Nursing, Coe College, 1220 First Avenue NE, Cedar Rapids, IA 52402. *Telephone:* 319-399-8120. *Fax:* 319-399-8121. *E-mail:* johrt@coe.edu.

Dordt College
Nursing Program
Sioux Center, Iowa

Founded in 1955

DEGREE • BSN

Nursing Program Faculty 3

Library Facilities 170,000 volumes; 6,597 periodical subscriptions.

BACCALAUREATE PROGRAMS

Degree BSN

Available Programs Generic Baccalaureate.

Contact *Telephone:* 712-722-6000.

Grand View University
Division of Nursing
Des Moines, Iowa

http://www.gvc.edu/academics/nursing/

Founded in 1896

DEGREE • BSN

Nursing Program Faculty 16 (25% with doctorates).

Nursing Student Activities Student Nurses' Association.

Library Facilities 109,386 volumes (3,868 in health); 25,431 periodical subscriptions (91 health-care related).

BACCALAUREATE PROGRAMS

Degree BSN

Available Programs Generic Baccalaureate; RN Baccalaureate.

Study Options Full-time and part-time.

Program Entrance Requirements Minimum overall college GPA of 2.2, transcript of college record, CPR certification, health exam, high school chemistry, high school transcript, immunizations, 3 letters of recommendation, minimum GPA in nursing prerequisites of 2.2, prerequisite course work. Transfer students are accepted.

Grand View University (continued)

Advanced Placement Credit by examination available. Credit given for nursing courses completed elsewhere dependent upon specific evaluations.

Contact *Telephone:* 515-263-2866. *Fax:* 515-263-6077.

CONTINUING EDUCATION PROGRAM

Contact *Telephone:* 515-263-2912. *Fax:* 515-263-6190.

Iowa Wesleyan College
Division of Health and Natural Sciences
Mount Pleasant, Iowa

http://www.iwc.edu

Founded in 1842

DEGREE • BSN

Nursing Program Faculty 6 (17% with doctorates).

Baccalaureate Enrollment 80
Women 93% **Men** 7% **Minority** 7% **Part-time** 2%

Distance Learning Courses Available.

Nursing Student Activities Student Nurses' Association.

Nursing Student Resources Academic advising; academic or career counseling; assistance for students with disabilities; bookstore; campus computer network; career placement assistance; computer lab; computer-assisted instruction; e-mail services; interactive nursing skills videos; Internet; learning resource lab; library services; nursing audiovisuals; remedial services; resume preparation assistance; skills, simulation, or other laboratory; tutoring; unpaid internships.

Library Facilities 102,356 volumes (500 in health, 300 in nursing); 9,452 periodical subscriptions (40 health-care related).

BACCALAUREATE PROGRAMS

Degree BSN

Available Programs ADN to Baccalaureate; Baccalaureate for Second Degree; Generic Baccalaureate; LPN to Baccalaureate; LPN to RN Baccalaureate; RN Baccalaureate.

Study Options Full-time and part-time.

Program Entrance Requirements Minimum overall college GPA of 2.25, transcript of college record, CPR certification, health exam, health insurance, high school transcript, immunizations, interview, minimum high school GPA of 2.25, minimum high school rank 50%, minimum GPA in nursing prerequisites of 2.0, professional liability insurance/malpractice insurance, prerequisite course work. Transfer students are accepted. *Application deadline:* 8/1 (fall).

Financial Aid 98% of baccalaureate students in nursing programs received some form of financial aid in 2008–09.

Contact Mr. Mark Petty, Director, Enrollment Management, Division of Health and Natural Sciences, Iowa Wesleyan College, 601 North Main Street, Mount Pleasant, IA 52641. *Telephone:* 800-582-2383 Ext. 6231. *Fax:* 319-385-6296. *E-mail:* mpetty@iwc.edu.

Luther College
Department of Nursing
Decorah, Iowa

http://nursing.luther.edu/

Founded in 1861

DEGREE • BA

Nursing Program Faculty 17 (31% with doctorates).

Baccalaureate Enrollment 130
Women 96% **Men** 4% **Minority** 3% **International** 2% **Part-time** 1%

Nursing Student Activities Nursing club.

Nursing Student Resources Academic advising; academic or career counseling; assistance for students with disabilities; bookstore; campus computer network; career placement assistance; computer lab; computer-assisted instruction; e-mail services; Internet; learning resource lab; library services; nursing audiovisuals; placement services for program completers; remedial services; resume preparation assistance; skills, simulation, or other laboratory; tutoring; unpaid internships.

Library Facilities 327,019 volumes (4,324 in health, 3,337 in nursing); 831 periodical subscriptions (35 health-care related).

BACCALAUREATE PROGRAMS

Degree BA

Available Programs ADN to Baccalaureate; Generic Baccalaureate.

Site Options Rochester, MN.

Study Options Full-time and part-time.

Program Entrance Requirements Minimum overall college GPA of 2.5, transcript of college record, written essay, health exam, health insurance, 3 years high school math, 2 years high school science, high school transcript, immunizations, minimum high school rank 50%, minimum GPA in nursing prerequisites of 2.3, prerequisite course work. Transfer students are accepted.

Advanced Placement Credit given for nursing courses completed elsewhere dependent upon specific evaluations.

Expenses (2008–09) *Tuition:* full-time $30,920; part-time $1104 per credit. *Room and board:* $5040; room only: $2420 per academic year. *Required fees:* full-time $465.

Financial Aid 98% of baccalaureate students in nursing programs received some form of financial aid in 2007–08. *Gift aid (need-based):* Federal Pell, FSEOG, state, private, college/university gift aid from institutional funds. *Loans:* Federal Direct (Subsidized and Unsubsidized Stafford PLUS), Perkins, college/university. *Work-study:* Federal Work-Study, part-time campus jobs. *Financial aid application deadline (priority):* 3/1.

Contact Ms. Ruth Green, Administrative Assistant, Department of Nursing, Luther College, 700 College Drive, Decorah, IA 52101. *Telephone:* 563-387-1057. *Fax:* 563-387-2149. *E-mail:* greenru@luther.edu.

CONTINUING EDUCATION PROGRAM

Contact Ms. Ruth Green, Administrative Assistant, Department of Nursing, Luther College, 700 College Drive, Decorah, IA 52101. *Telephone:* 563-387-1057. *Fax:* 563-387-2149. *E-mail:* greenru@luther.edu.

See full description on page 506.

Mercy College of Health Sciences
Division of Nursing
Des Moines, Iowa

http://www.mchs.edu/divnurs.html

Founded in 1995

DEGREE • BSN

Nursing Program Faculty 22 (2% with doctorates).

Baccalaureate Enrollment 76
Women 98% **Men** 2% **Minority** 1% **Part-time** 98%

Nursing Student Activities Sigma Theta Tau, Student Nurses' Association.

Nursing Student Resources Academic advising; academic or career counseling; assistance for students with disabilities; campus computer network; career placement assistance; computer lab; computer-assisted instruction; daycare for children of students; e-mail services; employment services for current students; interactive nursing skills videos; Internet; learning resource lab; library services; nursing audiovisuals; placement services for program completers; skills, simulation, or other laboratory.

Library Facilities 15,964 volumes; 165 periodical subscriptions.

BACCALAUREATE PROGRAMS

Degree BSN

Available Programs ADN to Baccalaureate.

Study Options Full-time and part-time.

Program Entrance Requirements Minimum overall college GPA of 2.7, transcript of college record, CPR certification, health exam, high school biology, high school chemistry, high school transcript, immunizations, minimum GPA in nursing prerequisites of 2.7, prerequisite course work, RN licensure. Transfer students are accepted. *Application deadline:* Applications may be processed on a rolling basis for some programs. *Application fee:* $25.

Advanced Placement Credit given for nursing courses completed elsewhere dependent upon specific evaluations.

Expenses (2008–09) *Tuition:* full-time $13,000; part-time $440 per credit hour.

Financial Aid 10% of baccalaureate students in nursing programs received some form of financial aid in 2007–08.

Contact General Information, Division of Nursing, Mercy College of Health Sciences, 928 6th Avenue, Des Moines, IA 50309. *Telephone:* 515-643-3180. *Fax:* 515-643-6698. *E-mail:* information@mchs.edu.

Morningside College
Department of Nursing Education
Sioux City, Iowa

http://www.morningside.edu/
academicdepartments/nursing.htm

Founded in 1894

DEGREE • BSN

Nursing Program Faculty 10 (20% with doctorates).

Baccalaureate Enrollment 74
Women 95% **Men** 5% **Minority** 8% **Part-time** 5%

Nursing Student Activities Sigma Theta Tau, Student Nurses' Association.

Nursing Student Resources Academic advising; academic or career counseling; assistance for students with disabilities; bookstore; campus computer network; computer lab; computer-assisted instruction; e-mail services; employment services for current students; externships; housing assistance; interactive nursing skills videos; Internet; learning resource lab; library services; nursing audiovisuals; remedial services; resume preparation assistance; skills, simulation, or other laboratory; tutoring; unpaid internships.

Library Facilities 94,775 volumes (2,500 in health, 2,500 in nursing); 325 periodical subscriptions (125 health-care related).

BACCALAUREATE PROGRAMS

Degree BSN

Available Programs Baccalaureate for Second Degree; Generic Baccalaureate; International Nurse to Baccalaureate; LPN to Baccalaureate; RN Baccalaureate.

Study Options Full-time and part-time.

Program Entrance Requirements Minimum overall college GPA of 2.75, transcript of college record, CPR certification, high school transcript, immunizations, interview, minimum GPA in nursing prerequisites of 2.75, prerequisite course work. Transfer students are accepted. *Application deadline:* 8/15 (fall).

Advanced Placement Credit given for nursing courses completed elsewhere dependent upon specific evaluations.

Expenses (2009–10) *Tuition:* full-time $22,020; part-time $390 per credit hour. *International tuition:* $22,020 full-time. *Room and board:* $6740 per academic year. *Required fees:* full-time $195; part-time $100 per term.

Financial Aid 99% of baccalaureate students in nursing programs received some form of financial aid in 2008–09. *Gift aid (need-based):* Federal Pell, FSEOG, state, private, college/university gift aid from institutional funds. *Loans:* FFEL (Subsidized and Unsubsidized Stafford PLUS), Perkins, state, college/university, private loans. *Work-study:* Federal Work-Study, part-time campus jobs. *Financial aid application deadline (priority):* 3/1.

Contact Dr. Mary Kovarna, EdD, Professor and Chair, Department of Nursing Education, Morningside College, 1501 Morningside Avenue, Sioux City, IA 51106-1751. *Telephone:* 712-274-5154. *Fax:* 712-274-5101. *E-mail:* kovarna@morningside.edu.

Mount Mercy College
Department of Nursing
Cedar Rapids, Iowa

http://www.mtmercy.edu

Founded in 1928

DEGREE • BSN

Nursing Program Faculty 41 (15% with doctorates).

Baccalaureate Enrollment 267
Women 97% **Men** 3% **Minority** 2% **Part-time** 30%

Nursing Student Activities Sigma Theta Tau, Student Nurses' Association.

Nursing Student Resources Academic advising; academic or career counseling; assistance for students with disabilities; bookstore; campus computer network; career placement assistance; computer lab; computer-assisted instruction; e-mail services; employment services for current students; externships; housing assistance; interactive nursing skills videos; Internet; learning resource lab; library services; nursing audiovisuals; paid internships; placement services for program completers; remedial services; resume preparation assistance; skills, simulation, or other laboratory; tutoring; unpaid internships.

Library Facilities 138,043 volumes (5,100 in health, 1,475 in nursing); 10,900 periodical subscriptions (130 health-care related).

BACCALAUREATE PROGRAMS

Degree BSN

Available Programs Accelerated RN Baccalaureate; Generic Baccalaureate.

Study Options Full-time and part-time.

Program Entrance Requirements Minimum overall college GPA of 2.7, transcript of college record, CPR certification, health exam, health insurance, high school chemistry, 2 years high school math, 2 years high school science, high school transcript, immunizations, minimum high school rank 75%, minimum GPA in nursing prerequisites of 2.5, prerequisite course work. Transfer students are accepted. *Application deadline:* 4/15 (spring).

Advanced Placement Credit by examination available. Credit given for nursing courses completed elsewhere dependent upon specific evaluations.

Expenses (2009–10) *Tuition:* full-time $22,100; part-time $610 per credit hour. *Room and board:* $6980; room only: $1675 per academic year. *Required fees:* full-time $300; part-time $150 per term.

Financial Aid 90% of baccalaureate students in nursing programs received some form of financial aid in 2008–09. *Gift aid (need-based):* Federal Pell, FSEOG, state, college/university gift aid from institutional funds. *Loans:* Federal Direct (Subsidized and Unsubsidized Stafford PLUS), Perkins, state, college/university. *Work-study:* Federal Work-Study, part-time campus jobs. *Financial aid application deadline (priority):* 3/1.

Contact Dr. Mary P. Tarbox, Professor and Chair, Department of Nursing, Mount Mercy College, 1330 Elmhurst Drive NE, Cedar Rapids, IA 52402. *Telephone:* 800-248-4504 Ext. 6460. *Fax:* 319-368-6479. *E-mail:* mtarbox@mtmercy.edu.

CONTINUING EDUCATION PROGRAM

Contact Dr. Mary P. Tarbox, Professor and Chair, Department of Nursing, Mount Mercy College, 1330 Elmhurst Drive NE, Cedar Rapids, IA 52402. *Telephone:* 319-368-6471. *Fax:* 319-368-6479. *E-mail:* mtarbox@mtmercy.edu.

Northwestern College
Nursing Program
Orange City, Iowa

Founded in 1882

DEGREE • BSN

Nursing Program Faculty 8

Baccalaureate Enrollment 58

Nursing Student Resources Academic advising; assistance for students with disabilities; bookstore; campus computer network; career placement assistance; computer lab; e-mail services; housing assistance; interactive nursing skills videos; Internet; learning resource lab; library services; nursing audiovisuals; placement services for program completers; remedial services; resume preparation assistance; skills, simulation, or other laboratory; tutoring.

Library Facilities 125,000 volumes; 615 periodical subscriptions.

BACCALAUREATE PROGRAMS

Degree BSN

Available Programs Generic Baccalaureate.

Contact Dr. Ruth Daumer, Associate Professor of Nursing, Nursing Program, Northwestern College, 101 7th Street SW, Orange City, IA 51041. *Telephone:* 712-707-7086. *E-mail:* rdaumer@nwciowa.edu.

St. Ambrose University
Program in Nursing (BSN)
Davenport, Iowa

Founded in 1882

DEGREES • BSN • MSN

Nursing Program Faculty 15 (27% with doctorates).

Baccalaureate Enrollment 204
Women 94% **Men** 6% **Minority** 8% **Part-time** 2%

Graduate Enrollment 15
Women 100% **Part-time** 100%

Nursing Student Activities Student Nurses' Association.

Nursing Student Resources Academic advising; academic or career counseling; assistance for students with disabilities; bookstore; campus computer network; career placement assistance; computer lab; e-mail services; employment services for current students; housing assistance; interactive nursing skills videos; Internet; learning resource lab; library services; nursing audiovisuals; resume preparation assistance; skills, simulation, or other laboratory; tutoring; unpaid internships.

Library Facilities 169,549 volumes (1,793 in health, 674 in nursing); 728 periodical subscriptions (157 health-care related).

BACCALAUREATE PROGRAMS

Degree BSN

Available Programs Generic Baccalaureate; RN Baccalaureate.

Study Options Full-time and part-time.

Program Entrance Requirements Minimum overall college GPA of 3.0, transcript of college record, CPR certification, health exam, health insurance, high school biology, high school chemistry, high school foreign language, 3 years high school math, high school transcript, immunizations, minimum GPA in nursing prerequisites of 2.0, prerequisite course work. Transfer students are accepted. *Application deadline:* 4/1 (fall), 11/30 (spring), 4/29 (summer). Applications may be processed on a rolling basis for some programs. *Application fee:* $25.

Advanced Placement Credit by examination available. Credit given for nursing courses completed elsewhere dependent upon specific evaluations.

Expenses (2009–10) *Tuition:* full-time $22,590; part-time $702 per credit. *International tuition:* $22,590 full-time. *Room and board:* $4925; room only: $2725 per academic year. *Required fees:* full-time $310.

Financial Aid 95% of baccalaureate students in nursing programs received some form of financial aid in 2008–09. *Gift aid (need-based):* Federal Pell, FSEOG, state, private, college/university gift aid from institutional funds. *Loans:* FFEL (Subsidized and Unsubsidized Stafford PLUS), Perkins, private loans. *Work-study:* Federal Work-Study, part-time campus jobs. *Financial aid application deadline (priority):* 3/15.

Contact Nursing Department, Program in Nursing (BSN), St. Ambrose University, 518 West Locust Street, Davenport, IA 52803. *Telephone:* 563-333-6076. *E-mail:* nursing@sau.edu.

GRADUATE PROGRAMS

Expenses (2009–10) *Tuition:* full-time $22,590; part-time $702 per contact hour. *International tuition:* $22,590 full-time. *Room and board:* $4675; room only: $2725 per academic year. *Required fees:* full-time $150; part-time $150 per credit.

Financial Aid 100% of graduate students in nursing programs received some form of financial aid in 2008–09.

Contact Ms. Kathryn M. McKnight, RN, Director of MSN Program, Program in Nursing (BSN), St. Ambrose University, 518 West Locust Street, Davenport, IA 52803. *Telephone:* 563-333-6069. *Fax:* 563-333-6063. *E-mail:* Mc KnightKathrynM@sau.edu.

MASTER'S DEGREE PROGRAM

Degree MSN

Available Programs Master's.

Concentrations Available Nursing administration.

Study Options Part-time.

Program Entrance Requirements Clinical experience, minimum overall college GPA of 3.0, transcript of college record, CPR certification, immunizations, 3 letters of recommendation, physical assessment course, resume, statistics course. *Application deadline:* 4/15 (fall). Applications may be processed on a rolling basis for some programs. *Application fee:* $25.

Advanced Placement Credit given for nursing courses completed elsewhere dependent upon specific evaluations.

Degree Requirements 40 total credit hours, thesis or project.

University of Dubuque
School of Professional Programs
Dubuque, Iowa

http://www.dbq.edu/academics/nursing

Founded in 1852

DEGREE • BSN

Nursing Program Faculty 8 (1% with doctorates).

Baccalaureate Enrollment 58
Women 86% **Men** 14% **Minority** 2%

Nursing Student Activities Student Nurses' Association.

Nursing Student Resources Academic advising; academic or career counseling; assistance for students with disabilities; bookstore; campus computer network; career placement assistance; computer lab; daycare for children of students; e-mail services; employment services for current students; interactive nursing skills videos; Internet; learning resource lab; library services; nursing audiovisuals; resume preparation assistance; skills, simulation, or other laboratory; tutoring; unpaid internships.

Library Facilities 168,579 volumes; 484 periodical subscriptions.

BACCALAUREATE PROGRAMS

Degree BSN

Available Programs RN Baccalaureate.

Study Options Full-time.

Program Entrance Requirements Transcript of college record, CPR certification, health exam, health insurance, immunizations, 2 letters of recommendation, minimum GPA in nursing prerequisites of 2.75, professional liability insurance/malpractice insurance, prerequisite course work. Transfer students are accepted.

Contact BSN Program, School of Professional Programs, University of Dubuque, 2000 University Avenue, Dubuque, IA 52001. *Telephone:* 563-589-3000.

The University of Iowa
College of Nursing
Iowa City, Iowa

http://www.nursing.uiowa.edu
Founded in 1847
DEGREES • BSN • MSN • MSN/MBA • MSN/MPH • PHD

Nursing Program Faculty 67 (63% with doctorates).
Baccalaureate Enrollment 618
Women 93% **Men** 7% **Minority** 6% **Part-time** 25%
Graduate Enrollment 258
Women 89% **Men** 11% **Minority** 4% **International** 7% **Part-time** 50%
Nursing Student Activities Sigma Theta Tau, Student Nurses' Association.
Nursing Student Resources Academic advising; academic or career counseling; assistance for students with disabilities; campus computer network; career placement assistance; computer lab; computer-assisted instruction; e-mail services; employment services for current students; Internet; learning resource lab; nursing audiovisuals; placement services for program completers; resume preparation assistance; skills, simulation, or other laboratory; tutoring.
Library Facilities 4.1 million volumes (273,469 in health); 49,279 periodical subscriptions (2,500 health-care related).

BACCALAUREATE PROGRAMS
Degree BSN
Available Programs Generic Baccalaureate; RN Baccalaureate.
Study Options Full-time and part-time.
Program Entrance Requirements Minimum overall college GPA of 2.7, transcript of college record, CPR certification, written essay, health exam, health insurance, high school biology, high school chemistry, high school foreign language, 3 years high school math, 3 years high school science, high school transcript, immunizations, minimum GPA in nursing prerequisites of 2.7, professional liability insurance/malpractice insurance, prerequisite course work. Transfer students are accepted.
Advanced Placement Credit given for nursing courses completed elsewhere dependent upon specific evaluations.
Contact *Telephone:* 319-335-7016. *Fax:* 319-384-4423.

GRADUATE PROGRAMS
Contact *Telephone:* 319-335-7021. *Fax:* 319-335-9990.

MASTER'S DEGREE PROGRAM
Degrees MSN; MSN/MBA; MSN/MPH
Available Programs Accelerated RN to Master's; Master's; Master's for Nurses with Non-Nursing Degrees.
Concentrations Available Nurse anesthesia; nursing administration; nursing education; nursing informatics. *Clinical nurse specialist programs in:* adult health, community health, gerontology, occupational health, psychiatric/mental health. *Nurse practitioner programs in:* adult health, family health, gerontology, neonatal health, pediatric, psychiatric/mental health.
Study Options Full-time and part-time.
Program Entrance Requirements Computer literacy, minimum overall college GPA of 3.0, transcript of college record, written essay, immunizations, 3 letters of recommendation, nursing research course, physical assessment course, professional liability insurance/malpractice insurance, prerequisite course work, resume, statistics course.
Advanced Placement Credit given for nursing courses completed elsewhere dependent upon specific evaluations.
Degree Requirements 33 total credit hours, thesis or project.

POST-MASTER'S PROGRAM
Areas of Study Nursing informatics. *Clinical nurse specialist programs in:* adult health, psychiatric/mental health. *Nurse practitioner programs in:* adult health, family health, gerontology, pediatric, psychiatric/mental health.

DOCTORAL DEGREE PROGRAM
Degree PhD
Available Programs Doctorate; Post-Baccalaureate Doctorate.
Areas of Study Aging, family health, gerontology, individualized study, information systems, nursing administration.
Program Entrance Requirements Minimum overall college GPA of 3.0, interview, 3 letters of recommendation, statistics course, vita, GRE General Test.
Degree Requirements 60 total credit hours, dissertation, oral exam, written exam, residency.

POSTDOCTORAL PROGRAM
Areas of Study Family health, nursing informatics, nursing interventions, outcomes.
Postdoctoral Program Contact *Telephone:* 319-335-7021. *Fax:* 319-335-9990.

CONTINUING EDUCATION PROGRAM
Contact *Telephone:* 319-335-7075. *Fax:* 319-335-9990.

Upper Iowa University
RN-BSN Nursing Program
Fayette, Iowa

Founded in 1857
DEGREE • BSN
Nursing Program Faculty 10
Library Facilities 64,043 volumes; 3,241 periodical subscriptions.

BACCALAUREATE PROGRAMS
Degree BSN
Available Programs RN Baccalaureate.
Site Options Cedar Rapids, IA; West Des Moines, IA.
Program Entrance Requirements Minimum overall college GPA of 2.5, transcript of college record, CPR certification, health exam, high school transcript, RN licensure. Transfer students are accepted.
Expenses (2008–09) *Tuition:* part-time $312 per credit hour.
Contact Dr. Margaret Wimmer Johnson, Associate Professor of Nursing. *Telephone:* 563-425-5357. *E-mail:* wimmerm@uiu.edu.

KANSAS

Baker University
School of Nursing
Topeka, Kansas

http://www.bakeru.edu
Founded in 1858
DEGREE • BSN
Nursing Program Faculty 15 (13% with doctorates).
Baccalaureate Enrollment 161
Women 91% **Men** 9% **Minority** 15% **Part-time** 1.2%
Nursing Student Activities Sigma Theta Tau, Student Nurses' Association.

Baker University (continued)

Nursing Student Resources Academic advising; assistance for students with disabilities; campus computer network; computer lab; computer-assisted instruction; e-mail services; Internet; learning resource lab; library services; nursing audiovisuals; resume preparation assistance; skills, simulation, or other laboratory; tutoring.

Library Facilities 107,255 volumes (5,000 in health, 2,716 in nursing); 676 periodical subscriptions (414 health-care related).

BACCALAUREATE PROGRAMS

Degree BSN

Available Programs Generic Baccalaureate; RN Baccalaureate.

Study Options Full-time and part-time.

Program Entrance Requirements Transcript of college record, CPR certification, written essay, health exam, health insurance, high school transcript, immunizations, interview, minimum GPA in nursing prerequisites of 2.7, prerequisite course work. Transfer students are accepted. *Application deadline:* 12/1 (fall), 8/1 (spring).

Advanced Placement Credit given for nursing courses completed elsewhere dependent upon specific evaluations.

Expenses (2009–10) *Tuition:* full-time $13,470; part-time $450 per credit hour. *Required fees:* full-time $563; part-time $196 per term.

Financial Aid 89% of baccalaureate students in nursing programs received some form of financial aid in 2008–09. *Gift aid (need-based):* Federal Pell, FSEOG, state, private, college/university gift aid from institutional funds. *Loans:* FFEL (Subsidized and Unsubsidized Stafford PLUS), Perkins, alternative loans. *Work-study:* Federal Work-Study, part-time campus jobs. *Financial aid application deadline (priority):* 3/1.

Contact Ms. Janet Creager, Student Affairs Specialist, School of Nursing, Baker University, 1500 SW 10th Street, Topeka, KS 66604-1353. *Telephone:* 785-354-5850. *Fax:* 785-354-5832. *E-mail:* janet.creager@bakeru.edu.

Bethel College
Department of Nursing
North Newton, Kansas

http://www.bethelks.edu
Founded in 1887

DEGREE • BSN

Nursing Program Faculty 9

Baccalaureate Enrollment 100
Women 75% **Men** 25% **Minority** 30% **International** 25% **Part-time** 1%

Nursing Student Activities Nursing Honor Society, Sigma Theta Tau, Student Nurses' Association.

Nursing Student Resources Academic advising; academic or career counseling; assistance for students with disabilities; bookstore; computer lab; e-mail services; employment services for current students; housing assistance; Internet; learning resource lab; library services; nursing audiovisuals; resume preparation assistance; skills, simulation, or other laboratory; tutoring.

Library Facilities 176,002 volumes (5,690 in health, 3,150 in nursing); 33,498 periodical subscriptions (445 health-care related).

BACCALAUREATE PROGRAMS

Degree BSN

Available Programs Generic Baccalaureate; LPN to Baccalaureate; RN Baccalaureate.

Study Options Full-time and part-time.

Program Entrance Requirements Minimum overall college GPA of 3.0, transcript of college record, CPR certification, written essay, health exam, health insurance, high school transcript, immunizations, interview, 2 letters of recommendation, minimum high school GPA of 3.0, minimum GPA in nursing prerequisites of 2.0, prerequisite course work. Transfer students are accepted.

Advanced Placement Credit given for nursing courses completed elsewhere dependent upon specific evaluations.

Contact *Telephone:* 316-283-2500 Ext. 377. *Fax:* 316-284-5286.

Emporia State University
Newman Division of Nursing
Emporia, Kansas

http://www.emporia.edu/ndn
Founded in 1863

DEGREE • BSN

Nursing Program Faculty 13 (31% with doctorates).

Baccalaureate Enrollment 122
Women 92% **Men** 8% **Minority** 12% **International** 3% **Part-time** 3%

Nursing Student Activities Student Nurses' Association.

Nursing Student Resources Academic advising; academic or career counseling; assistance for students with disabilities; bookstore; campus computer network; career placement assistance; computer lab; computer-assisted instruction; daycare for children of students; e-mail services; employment services for current students; housing assistance; interactive nursing skills videos; Internet; learning resource lab; library services; nursing audiovisuals; placement services for program completers; remedial services; resume preparation assistance; skills, simulation, or other laboratory; tutoring.

Library Facilities 2.4 million volumes (52,426 in health, 2,360 in nursing); 37,675 periodical subscriptions (179 health-care related).

BACCALAUREATE PROGRAMS

Degree BSN

Available Programs ADN to Baccalaureate; Generic Baccalaureate; LPN to Baccalaureate; RN Baccalaureate.

Study Options Full-time and part-time.

Program Entrance Requirements Transcript of college record, written essay, minimum GPA in nursing prerequisites of 2.5, prerequisite course work. Transfer students are accepted. *Application deadline:* 5/1 (fall). *Application fee:* $25.

Advanced Placement Credit given for nursing courses completed elsewhere dependent upon specific evaluations.

Expenses (2009–10) *Tuition, area resident:* full-time $3426; part-time $114 per credit hour. *Tuition, state resident:* full-time $5140; part-time $171 per credit hour. *Tuition, nonresident:* full-time $12,630; part-time $421 per credit hour. *International tuition:* $12,630 full-time. *Room and board:* $6146 per academic year. *Required fees:* full-time $948; part-time $58 per credit.

Financial Aid 90% of baccalaureate students in nursing programs received some form of financial aid in 2008–09. *Gift aid (need-based):* Federal Pell, FSEOG, state, private, college/university gift aid from institutional funds, Jones Foundation Grants, grants from outside sources. *Loans:* FFEL (Subsidized and Unsubsidized Stafford PLUS), Perkins, Alaska Loans, alternative loans. *Work-study:* Federal Work-Study, part-time campus jobs. *Financial aid application deadline (priority):* 3/15.

Contact Dr. Judith E. Calhoun, RN, Division Chair, Newman Division of Nursing, Emporia State University, 1127 Chestnut Street, Emporia, KS 66801. *Telephone:* 620-343-6800 Ext. 5641. *Fax:* 620-341-7871. *E-mail:* jcalhoun@emporia.edu.

Fort Hays State University
Department of Nursing
Hays, Kansas

http://www.fhsu.edu/nursing/
Founded in 1902

DEGREES • BSN • MSN

Nursing Program Faculty 21 (19% with doctorates).

Baccalaureate Enrollment 115
Women 92% **Men** 8% **Minority** 3% **Part-time** 44%

Graduate Enrollment 78
Women 99% **Men** 1% **Minority** 1% **Part-time** 99%

Distance Learning Courses Available.

Nursing Student Activities Sigma Theta Tau, Student Nurses' Association, nursing club.

Nursing Student Resources Academic advising; academic or career counseling; assistance for students with disabilities; bookstore; campus computer network; career placement assistance; computer lab; computer-assisted instruction; daycare for children of students; e-mail services; employment services for current students; housing assistance; interactive nursing skills videos; Internet; learning resource lab; library services; nursing audiovisuals; paid internships; placement services for program completers; remedial services; resume preparation assistance; skills, simulation, or other laboratory; tutoring.

Library Facilities 624,637 volumes (11,390 in health, 1,750 in nursing); 1,689 periodical subscriptions (205 health-care related).

BACCALAUREATE PROGRAMS

Degree BSN

Available Programs Generic Baccalaureate; RN Baccalaureate.

Study Options Full-time and part-time.

Online Degree Options Yes.

Program Entrance Requirements Minimum overall college GPA of 2.5, transcript of college record, CPR certification, written essay, health exam, health insurance, high school transcript, immunizations, 2 letters of recommendation, minimum GPA in nursing prerequisites of 2.0, professional liability insurance/malpractice insurance, prerequisite course work. Transfer students are accepted. *Application deadline:* 3/1 (fall), 10/1 (spring).

Advanced Placement Credit by examination available. Credit given for nursing courses completed elsewhere dependent upon specific evaluations.

Expenses (2009–10) *Tuition, area resident:* full-time $1881; part-time $125 per credit hour. *Tuition, state resident:* full-time $2618; part-time $175 per credit hour. *Tuition, nonresident:* full-time $5957; part-time $397 per credit hour. *International tuition:* $5957 full-time. *Room and board:* $6560; room only: $3335 per academic year.

Financial Aid 96% of baccalaureate students in nursing programs received some form of financial aid in 2008–09.

Contact Ms. Rebecca Sander, Coordinator of Quality and Advising, Department of Nursing, Fort Hays State University, 600 Park Street, Stroup Hall, Room 139, Hays, KS 67601-4099. *Telephone:* 785-628-5561. *Fax:* 785-628-4080. *E-mail:* rsander@fhsu.edu.

GRADUATE PROGRAMS

Expenses (2009–10) *Tuition, area resident:* full-time $2087; part-time $174 per credit hour. *Tuition, state resident:* full-time $2968; part-time $247 per credit hour. *Tuition, nonresident:* full-time $5545; part-time $462 per credit hour. *International tuition:* $462 full-time. *Room and board:* $6560; room only: $3335 per academic year.

Financial Aid 94% of graduate students in nursing programs received some form of financial aid in 2008–09. 1 teaching assistantship (averaging $5,000 per year) was awarded; research assistantships.

Contact Dr. Liane Connelly, Chair, Department of Nursing, Fort Hays State University, 600 Park Street, Stroup Hall, Room 127, Hays, KS 67601-4099. *Telephone:* 785-628-4511. *Fax:* 785-628-4080. *E-mail:* lconnell@fhsu.edu.

MASTER'S DEGREE PROGRAM

Degree MSN

Available Programs Master's.

Concentrations Available Nursing administration; nursing education. *Nurse practitioner programs in:* family health.

Study Options Full-time and part-time.

Online Degree Options Yes.

Program Entrance Requirements Clinical experience, computer literacy, minimum overall college GPA of 3.0, transcript of college record, CPR certification, written essay, immunizations, 2 letters of recommendation, physical assessment course, professional liability insurance/malpractice insurance, prerequisite course work, statistics course, GRE General Test or MAT. *Application deadline:* 2/1 (fall), 9/1 (spring), 2/1 (summer).

Advanced Placement Credit given for nursing courses completed elsewhere dependent upon specific evaluations.

Degree Requirements 34 total credit hours, thesis or project, comprehensive exam.

POST-MASTER'S PROGRAM

Areas of Study Nursing administration; nursing education. *Nurse practitioner programs in:* family health.

Kansas Wesleyan University
Department of Nursing Education
Salina, Kansas

http://www.kwu.edu/nursing

Founded in 1886

DEGREE • BSN

Nursing Program Faculty 8 (13% with doctorates).

Baccalaureate Enrollment 69
Women 91% **Men** 9% **Minority** 12% **International** 3% **Part-time** 2%

Nursing Student Activities Nursing club.

Nursing Student Resources Academic advising; academic or career counseling; assistance for students with disabilities; bookstore; campus computer network; career placement assistance; computer lab; computer-assisted instruction; e-mail services; employment services for current students; housing assistance; Internet; learning resource lab; library services; nursing audiovisuals; resume preparation assistance; skills, simulation, or other laboratory; tutoring.

Library Facilities 97,060 volumes (15,921 in health, 8,700 in nursing); 188 periodical subscriptions (1,123 health-care related).

BACCALAUREATE PROGRAMS

Degree BSN

Available Programs ADN to Baccalaureate; Generic Baccalaureate; RN Baccalaureate.

Study Options Full-time and part-time.

Program Entrance Requirements Minimum overall college GPA of 2.6, transcript of college record, health exam, high school transcript, immunizations, minimum GPA in nursing prerequisites of 2.6, prerequisite course work. Transfer students are accepted. *Application deadline:* Applications may be processed on a rolling basis for some programs.

Advanced Placement Credit by examination available. Credit given for nursing courses completed elsewhere dependent upon specific evaluations.

Expenses (2009–10) *Tuition:* full-time $19,200; part-time $220 per credit hour. *International tuition:* $19,200 full-time. *Room and board:* $5600; room only: $2400 per academic year. *Required fees:* full-time $500; part-time $50 per credit; part-time $250 per term.

Financial Aid 100% of baccalaureate students in nursing programs received some form of financial aid in 2008–09.

Contact Ms. Connie Sue Neuburger, RN, Chair and Interim Director of Nursing Education Division, Department of Nursing Education, Kansas Wesleyan University, 100 East Claflin Avenue, Campus Box 39, Salina, KS 67401-6196. *Telephone:* 785-827-5541 Ext. 2311. *Fax:* 785-827-0927. *E-mail:* cnuburgr@kwu.edu.

MidAmerica Nazarene University
Division of Nursing
Olathe, Kansas

http://www.mnu.edu

Founded in 1966

DEGREE • BSN

Nursing Program Faculty 14 (36% with doctorates).

Baccalaureate Enrollment 63
Women 81% **Men** 19% **Minority** 16% **International** 17%

Nursing Student Activities Student Nurses' Association, nursing club.

MidAmerica Nazarene University (continued)

Nursing Student Resources Academic advising; academic or career counseling; assistance for students with disabilities; bookstore; campus computer network; career placement assistance; computer lab; computer-assisted instruction; e-mail services; employment services for current students; housing assistance; Internet; learning resource lab; library services; nursing audiovisuals; resume preparation assistance; skills, simulation, or other laboratory; tutoring; unpaid internships.

Library Facilities 132,991 volumes (1,903 in health, 547 in nursing); 1,250 periodical subscriptions (115 health-care related).

BACCALAUREATE PROGRAMS

Degree BSN

Available Programs ADN to Baccalaureate; Accelerated Baccalaureate; Accelerated Baccalaureate for Second Degree; Accelerated LPN to Baccalaureate; Accelerated RN Baccalaureate; Generic Baccalaureate; RN Baccalaureate.

Study Options Full-time.

Program Entrance Requirements Minimum overall college GPA of 2.6, transcript of college record, CPR certification, written essay, health exam, health insurance, high school transcript, immunizations, 2 letters of recommendation, minimum GPA in nursing prerequisites of 2.6, prerequisite course work. Transfer students are accepted.

Advanced Placement Credit by examination available. Credit given for nursing courses completed elsewhere dependent upon specific evaluations.

Contact *Telephone:* 913-971-3698. *Fax:* 913-971-3408.

CONTINUING EDUCATION PROGRAM

Contact *Telephone:* 913-971-3696. *Fax:* 913-971-3408.

Newman University
Division of Nursing
Wichita, Kansas

http://www.newmanu.edu

Founded in 1933

DEGREE • BSN

Nursing Program Faculty 12 (17% with doctorates).

Baccalaureate Enrollment 104
Women 85% **Men** 15% **Minority** 24% **International** 6% **Part-time** 4%

Graduate Enrollment 37
Women 51% **Men** 49% **Minority** 7%

Nursing Student Activities Sigma Theta Tau, nursing club.

Nursing Student Resources Academic advising; academic or career counseling; assistance for students with disabilities; bookstore; campus computer network; computer lab; computer-assisted instruction; e-mail services; Internet; learning resource lab; library services; nursing audiovisuals; remedial services; resume preparation assistance; skills, simulation, or other laboratory; tutoring.

Library Facilities 110,167 volumes (2,904 in health, 720 in nursing); 156 periodical subscriptions (769 health-care related).

BACCALAUREATE PROGRAMS

Degree BSN

Available Programs Generic Baccalaureate; LPN to Baccalaureate; RN Baccalaureate.

Study Options Full-time and part-time.

Program Entrance Requirements Minimum overall college GPA of 2.75, transcript of college record, CPR certification, written essay, health exam, health insurance, immunizations, interview, 2 letters of recommendation, minimum GPA in nursing prerequisites of 2.75, professional liability insurance/malpractice insurance, prerequisite course work. Transfer students are accepted. *Application deadline:* Applications may be processed on a rolling basis for some programs.

Advanced Placement Credit given for nursing courses completed elsewhere dependent upon specific evaluations.

Expenses (2009–10) *Tuition:* full-time $19,200; part-time $640 per credit hour. *International tuition:* $19,200 full-time. *Room and board:* $3400 per academic year. *Required fees:* full-time $595; part-time $10 per credit.

Financial Aid 97% of baccalaureate students in nursing programs received some form of financial aid in 2008–09. *Gift aid (need-based):* Federal Pell, FSEOG, state, private, college/university gift aid from institutional funds. *Loans:* FFEL (Subsidized and Unsubsidized Stafford PLUS), Perkins. *Work-study:* Federal Work-Study, part-time campus jobs. *Financial aid application deadline (priority):* 3/1.

Contact Dr. Bernadette M. Fetterolf, RN, Director, School of Nursing and Allied Health, Division of Nursing, Newman University, 3100 McCormick Avenue, Wichita, KS 67213-2097. *Telephone:* 316-942-4291 Ext. 2244. *Fax:* 316-942-4483. *E-mail:* fetterolfb@newmanu.edu.

GRADUATE PROGRAMS

Expenses (2009–10) *Tuition:* full-time $20,000. *International tuition:* $20,000 full-time. *Room and board:* $4900 per academic year. *Required fees:* full-time $300.

Financial Aid 100% of graduate students in nursing programs received some form of financial aid in 2008–09. *Application deadline:* 8/15.

Contact Ms. Sharon Niemann, Director, Master of Science in Nurse Anesthesia Program, Division of Nursing, Newman University, 3100 McCormick Avenue, Wichita, KS 67213-2097. *Telephone:* 316-942-4291 Ext. 2272. *Fax:* 316-942-4483. *E-mail:* niemanns@newmanu.edu.

MASTER'S DEGREE PROGRAM

Program Entrance Requirements MAT.

Pittsburg State University
Department of Nursing
Pittsburg, Kansas

http://www.pittstate.edu/nurs

Founded in 1903

DEGREES • BSN • MSN

Nursing Program Faculty 23 (25% with doctorates).

Baccalaureate Enrollment 130
Women 90% **Men** 10% **Minority** 1% **International** 1%

Graduate Enrollment 85
Women 95% **Men** 5% **Minority** 1% **International** 1%

Distance Learning Courses Available.

Nursing Student Activities Nursing Honor Society, Sigma Theta Tau, Student Nurses' Association.

Nursing Student Resources Academic advising; academic or career counseling; assistance for students with disabilities; bookstore; career placement assistance; computer lab; computer-assisted instruction; e-mail services; employment services for current students; externships; housing assistance; interactive nursing skills videos; Internet; learning resource lab; library services; nursing audiovisuals; placement services for program completers; resume preparation assistance; skills, simulation, or other laboratory; tutoring; unpaid internships.

Library Facilities 741,835 volumes (3,400 in nursing); 15,338 periodical subscriptions.

BACCALAUREATE PROGRAMS

Degree BSN

Available Programs Generic Baccalaureate; RN Baccalaureate.

Study Options Full-time and part-time.

Online Degree Options Yes.

Program Entrance Requirements Minimum overall college GPA of 2.5, transcript of college record, CPR certification, health exam, immunizations, 3 letters of recommendation, minimum GPA in nursing prerequisites of 2.5, professional liability insurance/malpractice insurance, prerequisite course work. Transfer students are accepted. *Application deadline:* 12/15 (fall). *Application fee:* $25.

Advanced Placement Credit by examination available. Credit given for nursing courses completed elsewhere dependent upon specific evaluations.

Expenses (2009–10) *Tuition, area resident:* full-time $2296; part-time $165 per credit hour. *Tuition, nonresident:* full-time $6558; part-time $449 per credit hour. *Required fees:* full-time $2296; part-time $165 per credit.

Financial Aid 95% of baccalaureate students in nursing programs received some form of financial aid in 2008–09. *Gift aid (need-based):* Federal Pell, FSEOG, state, private, college/university gift aid from institutional funds. *Loans:* Federal Nursing Student Loans, Federal Direct (Subsidized and Unsubsidized Stafford PLUS), FFEL (Subsidized and Unsubsidized Stafford PLUS), Perkins, college/university. *Work-study:* Federal Work-Study, part-time campus jobs. *Financial aid application deadline (priority):* 3/1.

Contact Dr. Barbara Ruth McClaskey, Coordinator of Bachelor of Science in Nursing Program, Department of Nursing, Pittsburg State University, 1701 South Broadway, Pittsburg, KS 66762. *Telephone:* 620-235-4437. *Fax:* 620-235-4449. *E-mail:* bmcclask@pittstate.edu.

GRADUATE PROGRAMS

Expenses (2009–10) *Tuition, area resident:* full-time $2576; part-time $219 per credit hour. *Tuition, nonresident:* full-time $6235; part-time $523 per credit hour. *Required fees:* full-time $2576; part-time $219 per credit.

Financial Aid 80% of graduate students in nursing programs received some form of financial aid in 2008–09.

Contact Dr. Mary Carol Pomatto, Master of Science Coordinator, Department of Nursing, Pittsburg State University, 1701 South Broadway, Pittsburg, KS 66762. *Telephone:* 316-235-4431. *Fax:* 316-235-4449. *E-mail:* mpomatto@pittstate.edu.

MASTER'S DEGREE PROGRAM

Degree MSN

Available Programs Master's.

Concentrations Available Clinical nurse leader; nursing administration; nursing education. *Clinical nurse specialist programs in:* family health. *Nurse practitioner programs in:* family health.

Study Options Full-time and part-time.

Program Entrance Requirements Clinical experience, minimum overall college GPA of 3.0, transcript of college record, CPR certification, written essay, immunizations, 3 letters of recommendation, nursing research course, physical assessment course, professional liability insurance/malpractice insurance, prerequisite course work, statistics course, GRE General Test. *Application deadline:* 2/1 (fall), 10/1 (spring), 10/1 (summer). *Application fee:* $50.

Advanced Placement Credit given for nursing courses completed elsewhere dependent upon specific evaluations.

Degree Requirements 47 total credit hours, thesis or project, comprehensive exam.

POST-MASTER'S PROGRAM

Areas of Study Clinical nurse leader; nursing administration; nursing education. *Clinical nurse specialist programs in:* family health. *Nurse practitioner programs in:* family health.

CONTINUING EDUCATION PROGRAM

Contact Ms. Kristy L. Frisbee, Coordinator of Continuing Nursing Education, Department of Nursing, Pittsburg State University, 1701 South Broadway, McPherson Hall, RM 121, Pittsburg, KS 66762. *Telephone:* 620-235-4434. *Fax:* 620-235-4449. *E-mail:* kfrisbee@pittstate.edu.

Southwestern College
Nursing Program
Winfield, Kansas

Founded in 1885

DEGREE • BSN

Nursing Program Faculty 6 (33% with doctorates).

Baccalaureate Enrollment 79

Nursing Student Activities Nursing Honor Society, Sigma Theta Tau, Student Nurses' Association, nursing club.

Nursing Student Resources Academic advising; academic or career counseling; assistance for students with disabilities; bookstore; campus computer network; career placement assistance; computer lab; computer-assisted instruction; e-mail services; externships; housing assistance; interactive nursing skills videos; Internet; learning resource lab; library services; nursing audiovisuals; paid internships; placement services for program completers; remedial services; resume preparation assistance; skills, simulation, or other laboratory; tutoring; unpaid internships.

Library Facilities 81,621 volumes; 33,234 periodical subscriptions.

BACCALAUREATE PROGRAMS

Degree BSN

Available Programs Accelerated RN Baccalaureate; Generic Baccalaureate; LPN to Baccalaureate; RN Baccalaureate.

Site Options Wichita, KS.

Study Options Full-time and part-time.

Online Degree Options Yes.

Program Entrance Requirements Transcript of college record, CPR certification, written essay, health exam, health insurance, high school transcript, immunizations, interview, minimum high school GPA of 2.75, minimum GPA in nursing prerequisites of 2.75, professional liability insurance/malpractice insurance, prerequisite course work. Transfer students are accepted.

Advanced Placement Credit given for nursing courses completed elsewhere dependent upon specific evaluations.

Contact *Telephone:* 620-229-6207. *Fax:* 620-229-6152 Ext. 6152.

Tabor College
Department of Nursing
Hillsboro, Kansas

http://www.tabor.edu/adult-graduate

Founded in 1908

DEGREE • BSN

Nursing Program Faculty 12

Baccalaureate Enrollment 71
Women 90% **Men** 10% **Minority** 10% **Part-time** 100%

Distance Learning Courses Available.

Nursing Student Activities Sigma Theta Tau.

Nursing Student Resources Academic advising; academic or career counseling; bookstore; campus computer network; computer lab; e-mail services; Internet; learning resource lab; library services; nursing audiovisuals; remedial services; resume preparation assistance; skills, simulation, or other laboratory; tutoring.

Library Facilities 80,099 volumes (240 in health, 140 in nursing); 265 periodical subscriptions (600 health-care related).

BACCALAUREATE PROGRAMS

Degree BSN

Available Programs ADN to Baccalaureate; Accelerated RN Baccalaureate.

Site Options Wichita, KS; Colby, KS; Larned, KS.

Study Options Full-time and part-time.

Online Degree Options Yes (online only).

Program Entrance Requirements Minimum overall college GPA of 2.5, transcript of college record, RN licensure. Transfer students are accepted. *Application deadline:* 8/31 (fall), 12/31 (spring), 4/30 (summer). Applications may be processed on a rolling basis for some programs. *Application fee:* $30.

Advanced Placement Credit by examination available. Credit given for nursing courses completed elsewhere dependent upon specific evaluations.

Expenses (2009–10) *Tuition:* part-time $340 per credit hour.

Tabor College (continued)

Financial Aid 90% of baccalaureate students in nursing programs received some form of financial aid in 2008–09. *Gift aid (need-based):* Federal Pell, FSEOG, state, private, college/university gift aid from institutional funds. *Loans:* FFEL (Subsidized and Unsubsidized Stafford PLUS), Perkins. *Work-study:* Federal Work-Study, part-time campus jobs. *Financial aid application deadline:* 8/15 (priority: 3/1).

Contact Ms. Tona L. Leiker, Dean, Nursing Department, Department of Nursing, Tabor College, 7348 West 21st Street, Suite 117, Wichita, KS 67205. *Telephone:* 316-729-6333 Ext. 206. *Fax:* 316-773-5436. *E-mail:* tonal@tabor. edu.

The University of Kansas
School of Nursing
Kansas City, Kansas

http://www2.kumc.edu/son
Founded in 1866
DEGREES • BSN • MS • MS/MHSA • MS/MPH • PHD

Nursing Program Faculty 74 (58% with doctorates).

Baccalaureate Enrollment 308
Women 91% **Men** 9% **Minority** 15% **International** 1% **Part-time** 20%

Graduate Enrollment 384
Women 92% **Men** 8% **Minority** 16% **International** 2% **Part-time** 92%

Distance Learning Courses Available.

Nursing Student Activities Nursing Honor Society, Sigma Theta Tau, Student Nurses' Association, nursing club.

Nursing Student Resources Academic advising; academic or career counseling; assistance for students with disabilities; bookstore; campus computer network; computer lab; computer-assisted instruction; e-mail services; employment services for current students; interactive nursing skills videos; Internet; learning resource lab; library services; nursing audiovisuals; remedial services; resume preparation assistance; skills, simulation, or other laboratory.

Library Facilities 3.5 million volumes (180,000 in health, 5,050 in nursing); 62,016 periodical subscriptions (6,500 health-care related).

BACCALAUREATE PROGRAMS

Degree BSN

Available Programs ADN to Baccalaureate; Generic Baccalaureate; RN Baccalaureate.

Study Options Full-time and part-time.

Program Entrance Requirements Minimum overall college GPA of 2.5, transcript of college record, CPR certification, written essay, health exam, health insurance, immunizations, 3 letters of recommendation, minimum GPA in nursing prerequisites of 2.5, prerequisite course work. Transfer students are accepted. *Application deadline:* 10/15 (fall). *Application fee:* $60.

Advanced Placement Credit given for nursing courses completed elsewhere dependent upon specific evaluations.

Financial Aid 65% of baccalaureate students in nursing programs received some form of financial aid in 2008–09.

Contact Dr. Rita Clifford, Associate Dean of Student Affairs, School of Nursing, The University of Kansas, 3901 Rainbow Boulevard, Mail Stop 2029, Kansas City, KS 66160. *Telephone:* 913-588-1619. *Fax:* 913-588-1615. *E-mail:* soninfo@kumc.edu.

GRADUATE PROGRAMS

Financial Aid 52% of graduate students in nursing programs received some form of financial aid in 2008–09. 7 research assistantships (averaging $24,000 per year), 23 teaching assistantships with full and partial tuition reimbursements available (averaging $24,000 per year) were awarded; traineeships also available. *Financial aid application deadline:* 2/14.

Contact Dr. Rita Clifford, Associate Dean, Student Affairs, School of Nursing, The University of Kansas, 3901 Rainbow Boulevard, Mail Stop 2029, Kansas City, KS 66160. *Telephone:* 913-588-1619. *Fax:* 913-588-1615. *E-mail:* soninfo@kumc.edu.

MASTER'S DEGREE PROGRAM

Degrees MS; MS/MHSA; MS/MPH

Available Programs Accelerated AD/RN to Master's; Master's; RN to Master's.

Concentrations Available Health-care administration; nurse-midwifery; nursing administration; nursing informatics. *Clinical nurse specialist programs in:* adult health, gerontology. *Nurse practitioner programs in:* adult health, family health, gerontology, psychiatric/mental health.

Site Options Garden City, KS.

Study Options Full-time and part-time.

Online Degree Options Yes.

Program Entrance Requirements Clinical experience, minimum overall college GPA of 3.0, transcript of college record, CPR certification, immunizations, interview, 3 letters of recommendation, physical assessment course, resume, statistics course, GRE General Test. *Application deadline:* 4/1 (fall), 9/1 (spring). *Application fee:* $60.

Degree Requirements 37 total credit hours, thesis or project, comprehensive exam.

POST-MASTER'S PROGRAM

Areas of Study Health-care administration; nurse-midwifery; nursing administration; nursing informatics. *Clinical nurse specialist programs in:* adult health, gerontology. *Nurse practitioner programs in:* adult health, family health, gerontology, psychiatric/mental health.

DOCTORAL DEGREE PROGRAM

Degree PhD

Available Programs Doctorate; Post-Baccalaureate Doctorate.

Areas of Study Advanced practice nursing, nursing administration, nursing research.

Online Degree Options Yes.

Program Entrance Requirements Minimum overall college GPA of 3.5, interview by faculty committee, interview, 3 letters of recommendation, statistics course, vita, writing sample, GRE General Test. Application deadline: 3/1 (fall), 12/1 (summer). Application fee: $60.

Degree Requirements 65 total credit hours, dissertation, oral exam, written exam, residency.

POSTDOCTORAL PROGRAM

Areas of Study Gerontology, nursing research, outcomes, self-care.

Postdoctoral Program Contact Dr. Marjorie J. Bott, Associate Dean, Research, School of Nursing, The University of Kansas, 3901 Rainbow Boulevard, Mail Stop 4043, Kansas City, KS 66160. *Telephone:* 913-588-1692. *E-mail:* mbott@kumc.edu.

CONTINUING EDUCATION PROGRAM

Contact Mary Gambino, PhD, Assistant Dean, Community Affairs, School of Nursing, The University of Kansas, 3901 Rainbow Boulevard, Mail Stop 4001, Kansas City, KS 66160. *Telephone:* 913-588-4488. *Fax:* 913-588-4486. *E-mail:* ceinfo@kumc.edu.

University of Saint Mary
Bachelor of Science in Nursing Program
Leavenworth, Kansas

Founded in 1923
DEGREE • BSN

Nursing Program Faculty 22 (9% with doctorates).

Baccalaureate Enrollment 168
Women 93% **Men** 7% **Minority** 12.5% **International** 3.5% **Part-time** 39%

Distance Learning Courses Available.

Nursing Student Activities Student Nurses' Association.

Nursing Student Resources Academic advising; academic or career counseling; bookstore; campus computer network; e-mail services; employment services for current students; Internet; learning resource lab; library services; nursing audiovisuals; placement services for program completers; resume preparation assistance; skills, simulation, or other laboratory; tutoring.

Library Facilities 120,753 volumes; 157 periodical subscriptions.

BACCALAUREATE PROGRAMS

Degree BSN

Available Programs Generic Baccalaureate; RN Baccalaureate.
Site Options Overland Park, KS.
Study Options Full-time.
Online Degree Options Yes (online only).
Program Entrance Requirements Minimum overall college GPA of 2.5, transcript of college record, CPR certification, written essay, health exam, health insurance, immunizations, 2 letters of recommendation, minimum GPA in nursing prerequisites of 2.5, prerequisite course work. Transfer students are accepted. *Application deadline:* 3/1 (fall). Applications may be processed on a rolling basis for some programs.

Contact Michelle Johnson, Nursing Program Specialist, Bachelor of Science in Nursing Program, University of Saint Mary, 4100 South 4th Street, Leavenworth, KS 66007. *Telephone:* 913-758-4381. *Fax:* 913-758-4356. *E-mail:* johnsonm@stmary.edu.

Washburn University
School of Nursing
Topeka, Kansas

http://www.washburn.edu/sonu/index.html
Founded in 1865
DEGREES • BSN • MSN

Nursing Program Faculty 29 (24% with doctorates).
Baccalaureate Enrollment 315
Women 89% **Men** 11% **Minority** 10% **International** 1% **Part-time** 1%
Graduate Enrollment 51
Women 90% **Men** 10% **Minority** 1% **Part-time** 70%
Nursing Student Activities Sigma Theta Tau, Student Nurses' Association, nursing club.
Nursing Student Resources Academic advising; academic or career counseling; assistance for students with disabilities; bookstore; campus computer network; career placement assistance; computer lab; computer-assisted instruction; e-mail services; employment services for current students; interactive nursing skills videos; Internet; learning resource lab; library services; nursing audiovisuals; remedial services; resume preparation assistance; skills, simulation, or other laboratory; tutoring; unpaid internships.
Library Facilities 345,642 volumes (12,880 in health, 1,612 in nursing); 1,672 periodical subscriptions (84 health-care related).

BACCALAUREATE PROGRAMS

Degree BSN

Available Programs ADN to Baccalaureate; Baccalaureate for Second Degree; Generic Baccalaureate; LPN to Baccalaureate; RN Baccalaureate.
Study Options Full-time.
Program Entrance Requirements Minimum overall college GPA of 2.7, transcript of college record, CPR certification, written essay, health exam, health insurance, immunizations, interview, 2 letters of recommendation, minimum GPA in nursing prerequisites of 2.0, professional liability insurance/malpractice insurance, prerequisite course work. Transfer students are accepted.
Advanced Placement Credit by examination available. Credit given for nursing courses completed elsewhere dependent upon specific evaluations.
Financial Aid 60% of baccalaureate students in nursing programs received some form of financial aid in 2007–08.
Contact Ms. Mary V. Allen, Director of Student Services, School of Nursing, Washburn University, 1700 SW College Avenue, Topeka, KS 66621-1117. *Telephone:* 785-231-1032 Ext. 1525. *Fax:* 785-231-1032. *E-mail:* mary.allen@washburn.edu.

GRADUATE PROGRAMS

Contact Ms. Mary V. Allen, Director of Student Services, School of Nursing, Washburn University, 1700 SW College Avenue, Topeka, KS 66621-1117. *Telephone:* 785-231-1010 Ext. 1533. *Fax:* 785-213-1032. *E-mail:* mary.allen@washburn.edu.

MASTER'S DEGREE PROGRAM

Degree MSN

Available Programs Master's.
Concentrations Available Nursing administration. *Nurse practitioner programs in:* adult health, family health.
Study Options Full-time and part-time.
Program Entrance Requirements Computer literacy, transcript of college record, CPR certification, written essay, immunizations, 2 letters of recommendation, nursing research course, physical assessment course, professional liability insurance/malpractice insurance, prerequisite course work, resume, statistics course. *Application deadline:* 3/15 (fall). *Application fee:* $35.
Degree Requirements 42 total credit hours, thesis or project.

POST-MASTER'S PROGRAM

Areas of Study Nursing education.

CONTINUING EDUCATION PROGRAM

Contact Dr. Cynthia Ann Hornberger, Dean, School of Nursing, Washburn University, 1700 SW College Avenue, Topeka, KS 66621-1117. *Telephone:* 785-231-1010 Ext. 1526. *Fax:* 785-231-1032. *E-mail:* cynthia.hornberger@washburn.edu.

Wichita State University
School of Nursing
Wichita, Kansas

http://www.wichita.edu/nurs
Founded in 1895
DEGREES • BSN • DNP • MSN • MSN/MBA

Nursing Program Faculty 51 (25% with doctorates).
Baccalaureate Enrollment 251
Women 90% **Men** 10% **Minority** 21% **International** 4% **Part-time** 1%
Graduate Enrollment 150
Women 94% **Men** 6% **Minority** 6% **International** 1% **Part-time** 66%
Distance Learning Courses Available.
Nursing Student Activities Sigma Theta Tau, Student Nurses' Association.
Nursing Student Resources Academic advising; academic or career counseling; assistance for students with disabilities; bookstore; campus computer network; career placement assistance; computer lab; computer-assisted instruction; daycare for children of students; e-mail services; employment services for current students; housing assistance; interactive nursing skills videos; Internet; learning resource lab; library services; nursing audiovisuals; resume preparation assistance; skills, simulation, or other laboratory.
Library Facilities 1.7 million volumes (31,320 in health, 2,746 in nursing); 3,697 periodical subscriptions (406 health-care related).

BACCALAUREATE PROGRAMS

Degree BSN

Available Programs ADN to Baccalaureate; Accelerated Baccalaureate; Accelerated Baccalaureate for Second Degree; Generic Baccalaureate; LPN to RN Baccalaureate; RN Baccalaureate.
Site Options Derby, KS.
Study Options Full-time.
Online Degree Options Yes.
Program Entrance Requirements Minimum overall college GPA of 2.75, transcript of college record, CPR certification, written essay, health exam, health insurance, immunizations, interview, minimum GPA in nursing prerequisites of 2.0, professional liability insurance/malpractice insurance, prerequisite course work. Transfer students are accepted. *Application deadline:* 2/1 (fall), 9/1 (spring).

Wichita State University (continued)

Advanced Placement Credit given for nursing courses completed elsewhere dependent upon specific evaluations.

Expenses (2009–10) *Tuition, area resident:* full-time $5325; part-time $178 per credit hour. *Tuition, nonresident:* full-time $13,359; part-time $445 per credit hour. *Room and board:* $6000; room only: $3350 per academic year. *Required fees:* full-time $212.

Financial Aid 80% of baccalaureate students in nursing programs received some form of financial aid in 2008–09.

Contact Ms. Courtney Fleetwood, Senior Academic Advisor, School of Nursing, Wichita State University, 1845 Fairmount Street, Wichita, KS 67260-0041. *Telephone:* 316-978-5732. *Fax:* 316-978-3094. *E-mail:* courtney.fleetwood@wichita.edu.

GRADUATE PROGRAMS

Expenses (2009–10) *Tuition, area resident:* full-time $4247; part-time $236 per credit hour. *Tuition, nonresident:* full-time $11,170; part-time $621 per credit hour. *Room and board:* $6400; room only: $3700 per academic year. *Required fees:* full-time $600.

Financial Aid 60% of graduate students in nursing programs received some form of financial aid in 2008–09. 3 teaching assistantships with full tuition reimbursements available (averaging $8,243 per year) were awarded; fellowships, research assistantships, Federal Work-Study, institutionally sponsored loans, scholarships, traineeships, and unspecified assistantships also available. Aid available to part-time students. *Financial aid application deadline:* 4/1.

Contact Dr. Alicia Huckstadt, Director, Graduate Program, School of Nursing, Wichita State University, 1845 Fairmount Street, Wichita, KS 67260-0041. *Telephone:* 316-978-3610. *Fax:* 316-978-3094. *E-mail:* alicia.huckstadt@wichita.edu.

MASTER'S DEGREE PROGRAM

Degrees MSN; MSN/MBA

Available Programs Master's; Master's for Nurses with Non-Nursing Degrees; RN to Master's.

Concentrations Available Nurse-midwifery. *Clinical nurse specialist programs in:* acute care. *Nurse practitioner programs in:* acute care, family health, pediatric, psychiatric/mental health.

Study Options Full-time and part-time.

Program Entrance Requirements Clinical experience, computer literacy, minimum overall college GPA of 3.0, transcript of college record, CPR certification, immunizations, physical assessment course, professional liability insurance/malpractice insurance, resume, statistics course, GRE. *Application deadline:* Applications may be processed on a rolling basis for some programs. *Application fee:* $35.

Advanced Placement Credit given for nursing courses completed elsewhere dependent upon specific evaluations.

Degree Requirements 49 total credit hours, comprehensive exam.

POST-MASTER'S PROGRAM

Areas of Study *Clinical nurse specialist programs in:* acute care. *Nurse practitioner programs in:* acute care, family health, pediatric, psychiatric/mental health.

DOCTORAL DEGREE PROGRAM

Degree DNP

Available Programs Doctorate; Post-Baccalaureate Doctorate.

Areas of Study Advanced practice nursing, clinical practice, critical care, faculty preparation, family health, health policy, health promotion/disease prevention, health-care systems, human health and illness, nursing administration, nursing education, nursing policy, nursing research, nursing science.

Program Entrance Requirements Clinical experience, minimum overall college GPA of 3.0, interview by faculty committee, interview, 2 letters of recommendation, statistics course, vita. Application deadline: 2/15 (fall), 10/15 (spring). Application fee: $35.

Degree Requirements 74 total credit hours, written exam, residency.

KENTUCKY

Bellarmine University
Donna and Allan Lansing School of Nursing and Health Sciences
Louisville, Kentucky

http://www.bellarmine.edu
Founded in 1950
DEGREES • BSN • MSN • MSN/MBA

Nursing Program Faculty 64 (6.4% with doctorates).

Baccalaureate Enrollment 210
Women 90% **Men** 10% **Minority** 10% **International** 5% **Part-time** 20%

Graduate Enrollment 79
Women 95% **Men** 5% **Minority** 5% **Part-time** 100%

Nursing Student Activities Sigma Theta Tau, Student Nurses' Association.

Nursing Student Resources Academic advising; academic or career counseling; assistance for students with disabilities; bookstore; campus computer network; career placement assistance; computer lab; computer-assisted instruction; e-mail services; employment services for current students; externships; housing assistance; interactive nursing skills videos; Internet; learning resource lab; library services; nursing audiovisuals; paid internships; placement services for program completers; remedial services; resume preparation assistance; skills, simulation, or other laboratory; tutoring; unpaid internships.

Library Facilities 126,164 volumes (1,795 in health, 1,395 in nursing); 514 periodical subscriptions (93 health-care related).

BACCALAUREATE PROGRAMS

Degree BSN

Available Programs Accelerated Baccalaureate for Second Degree; Accelerated RN Baccalaureate; Baccalaureate for Second Degree; Generic Baccalaureate; RN Baccalaureate.

Study Options Full-time and part-time.

Program Entrance Requirements Minimum overall college GPA of 2.5, transcript of college record, CPR certification, written essay, health exam, health insurance, high school biology, high school chemistry, 2 years high school math, 2 years high school science, high school transcript, immunizations, interview, minimum high school GPA of 2.75, minimum GPA in nursing prerequisites of 2.75, prerequisite course work. Transfer students are accepted. *Application deadline:* 8/15 (fall), 1/3 (winter), 1/3 (spring), 5/3 (summer). Applications may be processed on a rolling basis for some programs. *Application fee:* $25.

Advanced Placement Credit by examination available. Credit given for nursing courses completed elsewhere dependent upon specific evaluations.

Expenses (2009–10) *Tuition:* full-time $28,900; part-time $660 per credit hour. *International tuition:* $28,900 full-time. *Required fees:* full-time $1100.

Financial Aid 77% of baccalaureate students in nursing programs received some form of financial aid in 2008–09. *Gift aid (need-based):* Federal Pell, FSEOG, state, private, college/university gift aid from institutional funds. *Loans:* Federal Direct (Subsidized and Unsubsidized Stafford PLUS), FFEL (Subsidized and Unsubsidized Stafford PLUS), Perkins, state, college/university. *Work-study:* Federal Work-Study, part-time campus jobs. *Financial aid application deadline (priority):* 3/1.

Contact Dr. Beverley Holland, BSN Department Chairperson, Donna and Allan Lansing School of Nursing and Health Sciences, Bellarmine University, 2001 Newburg Road, Miles Hall, #202, Louisville, KY 40205-0671. *Telephone:* 502-452-8279. *Fax:* 502-452-8058. *E-mail:* bholland@bellarmine.edu.

GRADUATE PROGRAMS

Financial Aid 77% of graduate students in nursing programs received some form of financial aid in 2008–09. Career-related internships or fieldwork and scholarships available.

Contact Ms. Julie Armstrong-Binnix, Lansing School Marketing/Recruiter, Donna and Allan Lansing School of Nursing and Health Sciences, Bellarmine University, 2001 Newburg Road, Miles Hall, #201, Louisville, KY 40205-0671. *Telephone:* 502-452-8364. *Fax:* 502-452-8058. *E-mail:* julieab@bellarmine.edu.

MASTER'S DEGREE PROGRAM

Degrees MSN; MSN/MBA

Available Programs Master's; Master's for Nurses with Non-Nursing Degrees; RN to Master's.

Concentrations Available Nursing administration; nursing education.

Study Options Part-time.

Program Entrance Requirements Minimum overall college GPA of 2.75, transcript of college record, professional liability insurance/malpractice insurance, GRE General Test. *Application deadline:* 8/20 (fall), 1/5 (winter), 1/5 (spring), 5/1 (summer). Applications may be processed on a rolling basis for some programs. *Application fee:* $25.

Advanced Placement Credit given for nursing courses completed elsewhere dependent upon specific evaluations.

Degree Requirements 38 total credit hours, thesis or project.

POST-MASTER'S PROGRAM

Areas of Study *Nurse practitioner programs in:* family health.

DOCTORAL DEGREE PROGRAM

Program Entrance Requirements GRE General Test.

CONTINUING EDUCATION PROGRAM

Contact Ms. Linda Bailey, Director, Continuing Education, Donna and Allan Lansing School of Nursing and Health Sciences, Bellarmine University, 2001 Newburg Road, Continuing Education Office, Louisville, KY 40205-0671. *Telephone:* 502-452-8161. *Fax:* 502-452-8203. *E-mail:* lbailey@bellarmine.edu.

Berea College
Department of Nursing
Berea, Kentucky

http://www.berea.edu

Founded in 1855

DEGREE • BS

Nursing Program Faculty 8 (25% with doctorates).

Baccalaureate Enrollment 80
Women 90% **Men** 10% **Minority** 20% **International** 15%

Nursing Student Activities Student Nurses' Association.

Nursing Student Resources Academic advising; academic or career counseling; assistance for students with disabilities; bookstore; campus computer network; career placement assistance; computer lab; computer-assisted instruction; daycare for children of students; e-mail services; employment services for current students; externships; housing assistance; interactive nursing skills videos; Internet; learning resource lab; library services; nursing audiovisuals; paid internships; placement services for program completers; remedial services; resume preparation assistance; skills, simulation, or other laboratory; tutoring; unpaid internships.

Library Facilities 386,252 volumes (5,760 in health, 4,871 in nursing); 2,020 periodical subscriptions (95 health-care related).

BACCALAUREATE PROGRAMS

Degree BS

Available Programs Generic Baccalaureate.

Study Options Full-time.

Program Entrance Requirements Transcript of college record, written essay, high school transcript, immunizations, 3 letters of recommendation, minimum high school rank 20%. Transfer students are accepted.

Advanced Placement Credit given for nursing courses completed elsewhere dependent upon specific evaluations.

Contact *Telephone:* 859-985-3384. *Fax:* 859-985-3917.

CONTINUING EDUCATION PROGRAM

Contact *Telephone:* 859-985-3384. *Fax:* 859-985-3917.

Eastern Kentucky University
Department of Baccalaureate and Graduate Nursing
Richmond, Kentucky

http://www.bsn-gn.eku.edu

Founded in 1906

DEGREES • BSN • MSN

Nursing Program Faculty 42 (40% with doctorates).

Baccalaureate Enrollment 500

Graduate Enrollment 200

Distance Learning Courses Available.

Nursing Student Activities Sigma Theta Tau, Student Nurses' Association.

Nursing Student Resources Academic advising; academic or career counseling; assistance for students with disabilities; bookstore; campus computer network; computer lab; computer-assisted instruction; e-mail services; housing assistance; interactive nursing skills videos; Internet; learning resource lab; library services; nursing audiovisuals; skills, simulation, or other laboratory.

Library Facilities 799,496 volumes; 2,901 periodical subscriptions.

BACCALAUREATE PROGRAMS

Degree BSN

Available Programs Accelerated RN Baccalaureate; Baccalaureate for Second Degree; Generic Baccalaureate; RN Baccalaureate.

Site Options Hazard, KY; Corbin, KY; Danville, KY.

Study Options Full-time and part-time.

Program Entrance Requirements Minimum overall college GPA of 2.5, CPR certification, immunizations, professional liability insurance/malpractice insurance, prerequisite course work. Transfer students are accepted.

Advanced Placement Credit given for nursing courses completed elsewhere dependent upon specific evaluations.

Contact *Telephone:* 859-622-1827. *Fax:* 859-622-1972.

GRADUATE PROGRAMS

Contact *Telephone:* 859-622-1838. *Fax:* 859-622-1972.

MASTER'S DEGREE PROGRAM

Degree MSN

Available Programs Master's.

Concentrations Available Nursing education. *Clinical nurse specialist programs in:* public health. *Nurse practitioner programs in:* family health, psychiatric/mental health.

Site Options Hazard, KY; Corbin, KY; Danville, KY.

Study Options Full-time and part-time.

Program Entrance Requirements Minimum overall college GPA of 2.75, transcript of college record, written essay, 3 letters of recommendation, statistics course.

Advanced Placement Credit given for nursing courses completed elsewhere dependent upon specific evaluations.

Degree Requirements 48 total credit hours, thesis or project, comprehensive exam.

Frontier School of Midwifery and Family Nursing
Nursing Degree Programs
Hyden, Kentucky

Founded in 1939

Frontier School of Midwifery and Family Nursing (continued)
DEGREES • DNP • MSN

GRADUATE PROGRAMS

Contact Doctorate and Master in Nursing Programs, Nursing Degree Programs, Frontier School of Midwifery and Family Nursing, PO Box 528, 195 School Street, Hyden, KY 41749. *Telephone:* 606-672-2312. *E-mail:* fsmfn@midwives.org.

MASTER'S DEGREE PROGRAM

Degree MSN

Available Programs Accelerated AD/RN to Master's.

DOCTORAL DEGREE PROGRAM

Degree DNP

Available Programs Doctorate.

Kentucky Christian University

School of Nursing
Grayson, Kentucky

Founded in 1919

DEGREE • BSN

Nursing Program Faculty 6 (20% with doctorates).

Baccalaureate Enrollment 63

Women 90% **Men** 10% **Minority** 1% **International** 1%

Nursing Student Activities Student Nurses' Association.

Nursing Student Resources Academic advising; assistance for students with disabilities; bookstore; campus computer network; computer lab; e-mail services; housing assistance; interactive nursing skills videos; Internet; learning resource lab; library services; nursing audiovisuals; other; remedial services; skills, simulation, or other laboratory.

Library Facilities 103,323 volumes (400 in health, 300 in nursing); 395 periodical subscriptions (200 health-care related).

BACCALAUREATE PROGRAMS

Degree BSN

Available Programs Generic Baccalaureate.

Study Options Full-time.

Program Entrance Requirements Transcript of college record, written essay, health exam, health insurance, high school transcript, immunizations, minimum GPA in nursing prerequisites of 2.5, prerequisite course work. Transfer students are accepted.

Contact *Telephone:* 606-474-3255. *Fax:* 606-474-3342.

CONTINUING EDUCATION PROGRAM

Contact *Telephone:* 606-474-3271. *Fax:* 606-474-3342.

Kentucky State University

School of Nursing
Frankfort, Kentucky

Founded in 1886

DEGREE • BSN

Nursing Program Faculty 18 (11% with doctorates).

Baccalaureate Enrollment 25

Nursing Student Activities Student Nurses' Association.

Nursing Student Resources Academic advising; academic or career counseling; assistance for students with disabilities; bookstore; campus computer network; career placement assistance; computer lab; computer-assisted instruction; e-mail services; externships; housing assistance; interactive nursing skills videos; Internet; learning resource lab; library services; nursing audiovisuals; other; placement services for program completers; remedial services; resume preparation assistance; skills, simulation, or other laboratory; tutoring.

Library Facilities 462,703 volumes; 922 periodical subscriptions.

BACCALAUREATE PROGRAMS

Degree BSN

Available Programs ADN to Baccalaureate.

Program Entrance Requirements Transfer students are accepted.

Contact *Telephone:* 502-597-6963. *Fax:* 502-597-5818.

Midway College

Program in Nursing (Baccalaureate)
Midway, Kentucky

http://www.midway.edu/degreeprograms/nursing.html

Founded in 1847

DEGREE • BSN

Nursing Program Faculty 12 (25% with doctorates).

Baccalaureate Enrollment 20

Women 100% **Minority** 30% **Part-time** 10%

Distance Learning Courses Available.

Nursing Student Activities Student Nurses' Association, nursing club.

Nursing Student Resources Academic advising; academic or career counseling; assistance for students with disabilities; bookstore; campus computer network; career placement assistance; computer lab; computer-assisted instruction; e-mail services; externships; interactive nursing skills videos; Internet; learning resource lab; library services; nursing audiovisuals; placement services for program completers; remedial services; resume preparation assistance; skills, simulation, or other laboratory; tutoring; unpaid internships.

Library Facilities 96,236 volumes (1,200 in health, 800 in nursing); 250 periodical subscriptions (102 health-care related).

BACCALAUREATE PROGRAMS

Degree BSN

Available Programs ADN to Baccalaureate; Accelerated RN Baccalaureate; RN Baccalaureate.

Site Options Lexington, KY; Lexington, NT.

Study Options Full-time and part-time.

Program Entrance Requirements Minimum overall college GPA of 2.8, transcript of college record, CPR certification, health exam, health insurance, high school chemistry, 2 years high school math, high school transcript, immunizations, interview, 1 letter of recommendation, minimum high school GPA of 3.0, minimum GPA in nursing prerequisites of 3.0, professional liability insurance/malpractice insurance, prerequisite course work, RN licensure. Transfer students are accepted. *Application deadline:* Applications may be processed on a rolling basis for some programs. *Application fee:* $25.

Advanced Placement Credit given for nursing courses completed elsewhere dependent upon specific evaluations.

Expenses (2009–10) *Tuition:* full-time $12,360; part-time $515 per credit hour. *International tuition:* $12,360 full-time.

Financial Aid 95% of baccalaureate students in nursing programs received some form of financial aid in 2008–09.

Contact Dr. Barbara R. Kitchen, RN, Chair, Nursing and Science Programs, Program in Nursing (Baccalaureate), Midway College, 512 East Stephens Street, Midway, KY 40347. *Telephone:* 859-846-5335. *Fax:* 859-846-5876. *E-mail:* bkitchen@midway.edu.

CONTINUING EDUCATION PROGRAM

Contact Dr. Barbara R. Kitchen, RN, Chair, Nursing and Science Programs, Program in Nursing (Baccalaureate), Midway College, 512 East Stephens Street, Midway, KY 40347. *Telephone:* 859-846-5335. *Fax:* 859-846-5876. *E-mail:* bkitchen@midway.edu.

Morehead State University
Department of Nursing
Morehead, Kentucky

http://www.moreheadstate.edu/colleges/science/nahs/

Founded in 1922

DEGREE • BSN

Nursing Program Faculty 31 (13% with doctorates).

Baccalaureate Enrollment 139
Women 88% **Men** 12% **Part-time** 33%

Distance Learning Courses Available.

Nursing Student Activities Student Nurses' Association.

Nursing Student Resources Academic advising; academic or career counseling; assistance for students with disabilities; bookstore; campus computer network; career placement assistance; computer lab; computer-assisted instruction; e-mail services; interactive nursing skills videos; Internet; learning resource lab; library services; nursing audiovisuals; remedial services; resume preparation assistance; skills, simulation, or other laboratory; tutoring.

Library Facilities 529,130 volumes (500,000 in health, 850 in nursing); 2,006 periodical subscriptions (286 health-care related).

BACCALAUREATE PROGRAMS

Degree BSN

Available Programs ADN to Baccalaureate; Generic Baccalaureate; RN Baccalaureate.

Site Options Ashland, KY; Prestonsburg, KY; Mt. Sterling, KY.

Study Options Full-time.

Online Degree Options Yes.

Program Entrance Requirements Minimum overall college GPA of 2.0, transcript of college record, CPR certification, immunizations, minimum GPA in nursing prerequisites of 2.5, prerequisite course work. Transfer students are accepted. *Application deadline:* 3/15 (fall).

Advanced Placement Credit by examination available. Credit given for nursing courses completed elsewhere dependent upon specific evaluations.

Expenses (2009–10) *Tuition, state resident:* full-time $6036; part-time $234 per credit hour. *Tuition, nonresident:* full-time $15,096; part-time $585 per credit hour. *International tuition:* $15,096 full-time. *Room and board:* $6134; room only: $3310 per academic year. *Required fees:* full-time $500.

Financial Aid 80% of baccalaureate students in nursing programs received some form of financial aid in 2008–09.

Contact Ms. Carla June Aagaard, Academic Counseling Coordinator, Department of Nursing, Morehead State University, Reed Hall 234, Morehead, KY 40351. *Telephone:* 606-783-2641. *Fax:* 606-783-9104. *E-mail:* c.aagaard@moreheadstate.edu.

Murray State University
Program in Nursing
Murray, Kentucky

http://www.murraystate.edu/

Founded in 1922

DEGREES • BSN • MSN

Nursing Program Faculty 16 (47% with doctorates).

Baccalaureate Enrollment 206
Women 94% **Men** 6% **Minority** 3%

Graduate Enrollment 48
Women 85% **Men** 15%

Distance Learning Courses Available.

Nursing Student Activities Sigma Theta Tau, Student Nurses' Association.

Nursing Student Resources Academic advising; academic or career counseling; assistance for students with disabilities; bookstore; campus computer network; career placement assistance; computer lab; computer-assisted instruction; daycare for children of students; e-mail services; employment services for current students; externships; housing assistance; interactive nursing skills videos; Internet; learning resource lab; library services; nursing audiovisuals; placement services for program completers; remedial services; resume preparation assistance; skills, simulation, or other laboratory; tutoring; unpaid internships.

Library Facilities 518,450 volumes (4,060 in health, 2,160 in nursing); 1,381 periodical subscriptions (124 health-care related).

BACCALAUREATE PROGRAMS

Degree BSN

Available Programs Generic Baccalaureate; RN Baccalaureate.

Site Options Hopkinsville, KY; Paducah, KY; Madisonville, KY.

Study Options Full-time.

Program Entrance Requirements Transcript of college record, CPR certification, immunizations, minimum GPA in nursing prerequisites of 2.5, professional liability insurance/malpractice insurance, prerequisite course work. Transfer students are accepted. *Application deadline:* 5/1 (fall), 11/22 (spring).

Advanced Placement Credit by examination available. Credit given for nursing courses completed elsewhere dependent upon specific evaluations.

Expenses (2009–10) *Tuition, state resident:* full-time $3200; part-time $300 per credit hour. *Tuition, nonresident:* full-time $7000; part-time $600 per credit hour. *Room and board:* $2400; room only: $1400 per academic year. *Required fees:* full-time $300.

Financial Aid 70% of baccalaureate students in nursing programs received some form of financial aid in 2008–09. *Gift aid (need-based):* Federal Pell, FSEOG, state, private, college/university gift aid from institutional funds. *Loans:* Federal Nursing Student Loans, FFEL (Subsidized and Unsubsidized Stafford PLUS), Perkins, state, college/university. *Work-study:* Federal Work-Study, part-time campus jobs. *Financial aid application deadline (priority):* 4/1.

Contact Dr. Michael B. Perlow, Chair, Program in Nursing, Murray State University, 120 Mason Hall, Murray, KY 42071-0009. *Telephone:* 270-809-2193. *Fax:* 270-809-6662. *E-mail:* michael.perlow@murraystate.edu.

GRADUATE PROGRAMS

Expenses (2009–10) *Tuition, state resident:* full-time $4000; part-time $400 per credit hour. *Tuition, nonresident:* full-time $8000; part-time $800 per credit hour. *International tuition:* $4000 full-time. *Room and board:* $2000; room only: $900 per academic year. *Required fees:* full-time $400.

Financial Aid 70% of graduate students in nursing programs received some form of financial aid in 2008–09. Traineeships available. *Financial aid application deadline:* 4/1.

Contact Dr. Nancey E.M. France, RN, Graduate Coordinator, Program in Nursing, Murray State University, 120 Mason Hall, Murray, KY 42071-0009. *Telephone:* 270-809-6671. *Fax:* 270-809-6662. *E-mail:* nancey.france@murraystate.edu.

MASTER'S DEGREE PROGRAM

Degree MSN

Available Programs Master's.

Concentrations Available Nurse anesthesia. *Clinical nurse specialist programs in:* adult health, critical care, medical-surgical. *Nurse practitioner programs in:* family health.

Site Options Hopkinsville, KY; Paducah, KY; Madisonville, KY.

Study Options Full-time and part-time.

Program Entrance Requirements Clinical experience, minimum overall college GPA of 3.0, transcript of college record, CPR certification, immunizations, interview, 3 letters of recommendation, nursing research course, physical assessment course, professional liability insurance/malpractice insurance, prerequisite course work, statistics course, GRE General Test. *Application deadline:* 11/1 (fall).

Advanced Placement Credit given for nursing courses completed elsewhere dependent upon specific evaluations.

Degree Requirements 46 total credit hours.

Murray State University (continued)
POST-MASTER'S PROGRAM
Areas of Study Nurse anesthesia. *Clinical nurse specialist programs in:* adult health, critical care, medical-surgical. *Nurse practitioner programs in:* family health.

CONTINUING EDUCATION PROGRAM
Contact Michele Hack, Program in Nursing, Murray State University, 120 Mason Hall, Murray, KY 42071-0009. *Telephone:* 270-809-6674. *Fax:* 270-809-6662. *E-mail:* mhack@murraystate.edu.

Northern Kentucky University
Department of Nursing
Highland Heights, Kentucky

http://www.nku.edu/~nursing/
Founded in 1968
DEGREES • BSN • MSN

Nursing Program Faculty 125 (8% with doctorates).
Baccalaureate Enrollment 1,000
Women 95% **Men** 5% **Minority** 2% **International** 1% **Part-time** 50%
Graduate Enrollment 247
Women 95% **Men** 5% **Minority** 1% **Part-time** 90%
Distance Learning Courses Available.
Nursing Student Activities Sigma Theta Tau, Student Nurses' Association.
Nursing Student Resources Academic advising; academic or career counseling; assistance for students with disabilities; bookstore; campus computer network; career placement assistance; computer lab; computer-assisted instruction; daycare for children of students; e-mail services; employment services for current students; housing assistance; interactive nursing skills videos; Internet; learning resource lab; library services; nursing audiovisuals; resume preparation assistance; skills, simulation, or other laboratory; tutoring.
Library Facilities 850,752 volumes (6,380 in health, 3,500 in nursing); 1,579 periodical subscriptions (100 health-care related).

BACCALAUREATE PROGRAMS
Degree BSN

Available Programs Accelerated Baccalaureate for Second Degree; Generic Baccalaureate; RN Baccalaureate.
Study Options Full-time.
Program Entrance Requirements Minimum overall college GPA of 2.5, transcript of college record, CPR certification, health exam, health insurance, high school biology, high school chemistry, 3 years high school math, high school transcript, immunizations, minimum GPA in nursing prerequisites of 2.5, prerequisite course work. Transfer students are accepted. *Application deadline:* 1/15 (fall), 8/15 (spring).
Advanced Placement Credit by examination available. Credit given for nursing courses completed elsewhere dependent upon specific evaluations.
Expenses (2009–10) *Tuition, area resident:* full-time $4063. *Tuition, state resident:* full-time $6247. *Tuition, nonresident:* full-time $7179. *International tuition:* $7179 full-time. *Room and board:* $2835; room only: $1590 per academic year. *Required fees:* full-time $230.
Contact Dr. Carrie McCoy, Chair, Department of Nursing, Department of Nursing, Northern Kentucky University, Nunn Drive, AHC 303, Highland Heights, KY 41099. *Telephone:* 859-572-5248. *Fax:* 859-572-6098. *E-mail:* mccoy@nku.edu.

GRADUATE PROGRAMS
Expenses (2009–10) *Tuition, state resident:* part-time $384 per credit. *Tuition, nonresident:* part-time $675 per credit.
Financial Aid 10% of graduate students in nursing programs received some form of financial aid in 2008–09.

Contact Dr. Marilyn Schleyer, Chair of Advanced Nursing Studies, Department of Nursing, Northern Kentucky University, HC 206, Highland Heights, KY 41099. *Telephone:* 859-572-5579. *Fax:* 859-572-1934. *E-mail:* schleyerm1@nku.edu.

MASTER'S DEGREE PROGRAM
Degree MSN

Available Programs Master's.
Concentrations Available Nursing administration; nursing education. *Nurse practitioner programs in:* adult health, family health, gerontology, pediatric.
Study Options Full-time and part-time.
Online Degree Options Yes.
Program Entrance Requirements Clinical experience, minimum overall college GPA of 3.0, transcript of college record, CPR certification, immunizations, 1 letter of recommendation, nursing research course, physical assessment course, professional liability insurance/malpractice insurance, prerequisite course work, resume, statistics course. *Application deadline:* 2/15 (fall), 10/15 (spring).
Advanced Placement Credit by examination available. Credit given for nursing courses completed elsewhere dependent upon specific evaluations.
Degree Requirements 44 total credit hours, thesis or project.

POST-MASTER'S PROGRAM
Areas of Study Nursing administration; nursing education. *Nurse practitioner programs in:* adult health, family health, gerontology, pediatric, psychiatric/mental health.

Spalding University
School of Nursing
Louisville, Kentucky

http://www.spalding.edu/nursing
Founded in 1814
DEGREES • BSN • MSN

Nursing Program Faculty 33 (18% with doctorates).
Baccalaureate Enrollment 170
Women 94% **Men** 6% **Minority** 10% **International** 6%
Graduate Enrollment 56
Women 99.5% **Men** .5% **Minority** 2% **International** 3.4% **Part-time** 50%
Nursing Student Activities Sigma Theta Tau, Student Nurses' Association.
Nursing Student Resources Academic advising; academic or career counseling; assistance for students with disabilities; bookstore; campus computer network; career placement assistance; computer lab; computer-assisted instruction; e-mail services; employment services for current students; externships; interactive nursing skills videos; Internet; learning resource lab; library services; nursing audiovisuals; remedial services; resume preparation assistance; skills, simulation, or other laboratory; tutoring; unpaid internships.
Library Facilities 87,856 volumes (2,875 in health, 1,125 in nursing); 367 periodical subscriptions health-care related.

BACCALAUREATE PROGRAMS
Degree BSN

Available Programs Accelerated Baccalaureate for Second Degree; Accelerated RN Baccalaureate; Generic Baccalaureate.
Study Options Full-time and part-time.
Program Entrance Requirements Minimum overall college GPA of 2.5, transcript of college record, CPR certification, health exam, health insurance, high school transcript, immunizations, minimum GPA in nursing prerequisites of 2.5, professional liability insurance/malpractice insurance, prerequisite course work. Transfer students are accepted.
Advanced Placement Credit given for nursing courses completed elsewhere dependent upon specific evaluations.
Contact *Telephone:* 502-585-7125. *Fax:* 502-588-7175.

GRADUATE PROGRAMS

Contact *Telephone:* 502-585-9911 Ext. 2332. *Fax:* 502-588-7175.

MASTER'S DEGREE PROGRAM

Degree MSN

Available Programs Accelerated RN to Master's; Master's.

Concentrations Available Nursing administration; nursing education. *Nurse practitioner programs in:* adult health, family health, pediatric.

Study Options Full-time and part-time.

Program Entrance Requirements Computer literacy, minimum overall college GPA of 3.0, transcript of college record, CPR certification, written essay, immunizations, interview, 2 letters of recommendation, physical assessment course, professional liability insurance/malpractice insurance, prerequisite course work, resume, statistics course, GRE General Test.

Advanced Placement Credit by examination available. Credit given for nursing courses completed elsewhere dependent upon specific evaluations.

Degree Requirements 53 total credit hours, thesis or project.

POST-MASTER'S PROGRAM

Areas of Study Nursing administration; nursing education. *Nurse practitioner programs in:* adult health, family health, pediatric.

CONTINUING EDUCATION PROGRAM

Contact *Telephone:* 502-585-9911 Ext. 2332. *Fax:* 502-588-7175.

Thomas More College
Program in Nursing
Crestview Hills, Kentucky

---

http://www.thomasmore.edu

Founded in 1921

DEGREE • BSN

Nursing Program Faculty 7 (29% with doctorates).

Baccalaureate Enrollment 121
Women 90% **Men** 10% **Minority** 1% **Part-time** 5%

Nursing Student Activities Student Nurses' Association, nursing club.

Nursing Student Resources Academic advising; academic or career counseling; assistance for students with disabilities; bookstore; campus computer network; career placement assistance; computer lab; computer-assisted instruction; e-mail services; employment services for current students; externships; interactive nursing skills videos; Internet; learning resource lab; library services; nursing audiovisuals; other; placement services for program completers; remedial services; resume preparation assistance; skills, simulation, or other laboratory; tutoring.

Library Facilities 116,839 volumes (350 in health, 200 in nursing); 479 periodical subscriptions (50 health-care related).

BACCALAUREATE PROGRAMS

Degree BSN

Available Programs Generic Baccalaureate.

Study Options Full-time.

Program Entrance Requirements CPR certification, health exam, health insurance, immunizations, minimum GPA in nursing prerequisites of 2.5, professional liability insurance/malpractice insurance, prerequisite course work. Transfer students are accepted. *Application deadline:* 5/1 (fall).

Advanced Placement Credit given for nursing courses completed elsewhere dependent upon specific evaluations.

Expenses (2009–10) *Tuition:* full-time $22,500; part-time $530 per credit hour.

Financial Aid 90% of baccalaureate students in nursing programs received some form of financial aid in 2008–09. *Gift aid (need-based):* Federal Pell, FSEOG, state, private, college/university gift aid from institutional funds. *Loans:* Federal Nursing Student Loans, FFEL (Subsidized and Unsubsidized Stafford PLUS), Perkins, college/university. *Work-study:* Federal Work-Study, part-time campus jobs. *Financial aid application deadline (priority):* 3/15.

Contact Dr. Lisa Spangler Torok, Chair, Program in Nursing, Thomas More College, 333 Thomas More Parkway, Crestview Hills, KY 41017. *Telephone:* 859-344-3413. *Fax:* 859-344-3537. *E-mail:* Lisa.spangler-torok@ thomasmore.edu.

University of Kentucky
Graduate School Programs in the College of Nursing
Lexington, Kentucky

---

http://www.mc.uky.edu/nursing

Founded in 1865

DEGREES • BSN • MSN • PHD

Nursing Program Faculty 65 (54% with doctorates).

Baccalaureate Enrollment 260
Women 97% **Men** 3% **Minority** 6% **Part-time** 14%

Graduate Enrollment 221
Women 92% **Men** 8% **Minority** 9% **International** 5% **Part-time** 35%

Nursing Student Activities Sigma Theta Tau, Student Nurses' Association.

Nursing Student Resources Academic advising; academic or career counseling; assistance for students with disabilities; bookstore; campus computer network; career placement assistance; computer lab; computer-assisted instruction; e-mail services; interactive nursing skills videos; Internet; learning resource lab; library services; nursing audiovisuals; skills, simulation, or other laboratory.

Library Facilities 3.1 million volumes (105,793 in health); 29,633 periodical subscriptions (3,347 health-care related).

BACCALAUREATE PROGRAMS

Degree BSN

Available Programs Baccalaureate for Second Degree; Generic Baccalaureate; RN Baccalaureate.

Study Options Full-time and part-time.

Program Entrance Requirements Minimum overall college GPA of 2.5, transcript of college record, CPR certification, written essay, high school transcript, immunizations, minimum GPA in nursing prerequisites of 2.5, prerequisite course work. Transfer students are accepted.

Advanced Placement Credit by examination available. Credit given for nursing courses completed elsewhere dependent upon specific evaluations.

Contact *Telephone:* 859-323-5108. *Fax:* 859-323-1057.

GRADUATE PROGRAMS

Contact *Telephone:* 859-323-5108. *Fax:* 859-323-1057.

MASTER'S DEGREE PROGRAM

Degree MSN

Available Programs Master's; RN to Master's.

Concentrations Available Nurse case management; nursing administration. *Clinical nurse specialist programs in:* acute care, adult health, community health, critical care, gerontology, medical-surgical, oncology, parent-child, pediatric, perinatal, psychiatric/mental health, public health, women's health. *Nurse practitioner programs in:* acute care, adult health, family health, gerontology, pediatric, psychiatric/mental health.

Site Options Morehead, KY.

Study Options Full-time and part-time.

Program Entrance Requirements Clinical experience, minimum overall college GPA of 2.75, transcript of college record, written essay, interview, 3 letters of recommendation, physical assessment course, statistics course, GRE General Test.

Advanced Placement Credit given for nursing courses completed elsewhere dependent upon specific evaluations.

Degree Requirements 40 total credit hours, comprehensive exam.

University of Kentucky (continued)

POST-MASTER'S PROGRAM

Areas of Study Nurse case management. *Nurse practitioner programs in:* acute care, adult health, family health, gerontology, pediatric, psychiatric/mental health.

DOCTORAL DEGREE PROGRAM

Degree PhD

Available Programs Doctorate.

Areas of Study Nursing research.

Program Entrance Requirements Minimum overall college GPA of 3.3, interview, 3 letters of recommendation, MSN or equivalent, statistics course, writing sample, GRE General Test.

Degree Requirements 63 total credit hours, dissertation, oral exam, written exam, residency.

CONTINUING EDUCATION PROGRAM

Contact *Telephone:* 859-323-3851. *Fax:* 859-323-1057.

University of Louisville
School of Nursing
Louisville, Kentucky

http://www.louisville.edu/nursing
Founded in 1798

DEGREES • BSN • MSN • PHD

Nursing Program Faculty 53 (50% with doctorates).

Baccalaureate Enrollment 276
Women 87% **Men** 13% **Minority** 12% **International** 1% **Part-time** 1%

Graduate Enrollment 129
Women 91% **Men** 9% **Minority** 16% **International** 1% **Part-time** 55%

Distance Learning Courses Available.

Nursing Student Activities Sigma Theta Tau, Student Nurses' Association.

Nursing Student Resources Academic advising; academic or career counseling; assistance for students with disabilities; bookstore; campus computer network; career placement assistance; computer lab; computer-assisted instruction; e-mail services; employment services for current students; housing assistance; interactive nursing skills videos; Internet; learning resource lab; library services; nursing audiovisuals; skills, simulation, or other laboratory; tutoring.

Library Facilities 2.2 million volumes (253,595 in health, 2,806 in nursing); 47,062 periodical subscriptions (4,329 health-care related).

BACCALAUREATE PROGRAMS

Degree BSN

Available Programs Accelerated Baccalaureate for Second Degree; Generic Baccalaureate; RN Baccalaureate.

Study Options Full-time.

Program Entrance Requirements Minimum overall college GPA of 2.8, transcript of college record, CPR certification, written essay, health insurance, high school foreign language, 3 years high school math, 3 years high school science, high school transcript, immunizations, minimum high school GPA of 2.8, minimum GPA in nursing prerequisites of 2.8, professional liability insurance/malpractice insurance, prerequisite course work. Transfer students are accepted. *Application deadline:* 3/1 (fall), 9/15 (spring). *Application fee:* $40.

Advanced Placement Credit by examination available. Credit given for nursing courses completed elsewhere dependent upon specific evaluations.

Expenses (2009–10) *Tuition, area resident:* full-time $7944; part-time $331 per credit hour. *Tuition, nonresident:* full-time $19,272; part-time $803 per credit hour. *Room and board:* $6100 per academic year. *Required fees:* full-time $2000; part-time $75 per term.

Financial Aid 85% of baccalaureate students in nursing programs received some form of financial aid in 2008–09. *Gift aid (need-based):* Federal Pell, FSEOG, state, private, college/university gift aid from institutional funds. *Loans:* Federal Nursing Student Loans, FFEL (Subsidized and Unsubsidized Stafford PLUS), Perkins, college/university. *Work-study:* Federal Work-Study. *Financial aid application deadline (priority):* 3/15.

Contact Trish Hart, Director of Student Services, School of Nursing, University of Louisville, 555 South Floyd Street, Louisville, KY 40202. *Telephone:* 502-852-8298. *Fax:* 502-852-8783. *E-mail:* p0hart01@louisville.edu.

GRADUATE PROGRAMS

Expenses (2009–10) *Tuition, area resident:* full-time $8622; part-time $479 per credit hour. *Tuition, nonresident:* full-time $18,504; part-time $1028 per credit hour. *Room and board:* $7000 per academic year. *Required fees:* full-time $2000.

Financial Aid 85% of graduate students in nursing programs received some form of financial aid in 2008–09. 2 fellowships with full tuition reimbursements available (averaging $20,000 per year), 5 research assistantships with full tuition reimbursements available (averaging $18,000 per year), 5 teaching assistantships with full tuition reimbursements available (averaging $18,000 per year) were awarded; institutionally sponsored loans, scholarships, traineeships, and unspecified assistantships also available. Aid available to part-time students. *Financial aid application deadline:* 4/15.

Contact Dr. Rosalie Mainous, Associate Dean for Graduate Academic Affairs, School of Nursing, University of Louisville, 555 South Floyd Street, Louisville, KY 40292. *Telephone:* 502-852-8387. *Fax:* 502-852-8783. *E-mail:* rosalie.mainous@louisville.edu.

MASTER'S DEGREE PROGRAM

Degree MSN

Available Programs Master's.

Concentrations Available *Clinical nurse specialist programs in:* psychiatric/mental health. *Nurse practitioner programs in:* adult health, family health, neonatal health, psychiatric/mental health.

Study Options Full-time and part-time.

Program Entrance Requirements Clinical experience, minimum overall college GPA of 3.0, transcript of college record, CPR certification, written essay, immunizations, 2 letters of recommendation, professional liability insurance/malpractice insurance, GRE General Test.

Advanced Placement Credit given for nursing courses completed elsewhere dependent upon specific evaluations.

Degree Requirements 45 total credit hours.

POST-MASTER'S PROGRAM

Areas of Study *Clinical nurse specialist programs in:* psychiatric/mental health. *Nurse practitioner programs in:* adult health, family health, neonatal health, psychiatric/mental health.

DOCTORAL DEGREE PROGRAM

Degree PhD

Available Programs Doctorate; Post-Baccalaureate Doctorate.

Areas of Study Faculty preparation, health policy, individualized study, nursing research, nursing science.

Program Entrance Requirements Minimum overall college GPA of 3.0, interview by faculty committee, 3 letters of recommendation, vita, writing sample, GRE General Test. Application deadline: 2/1 (fall). Application fee: $50.

Degree Requirements Dissertation, written exam.

POSTDOCTORAL PROGRAM

Areas of Study Family health.

Postdoctoral Program Contact Dr. Rosalie Mainous, Associate Dean for Graduate Academic Affairs, School of Nursing, University of Louisville, 555 South Floyd Street, Louisville, KY 40292. *Telephone:* 502-852-8387. *Fax:* 502-852-8783. *E-mail:* rosalie.mainous@louisville.edu.

CONTINUING EDUCATION PROGRAM

Contact Dr. Deborah Thomas, Director, School of Nursing, University of Louisville, 555 South Floyd Street, K-3019, Louisville, KY 40292. *Telephone:* 502-852-8392. *Fax:* 502-852-8783. *E-mail:* dvthom01@louisville.edu.

Western Kentucky University
Department of Nursing
Bowling Green, Kentucky

http://www.wku.edu

Founded in 1906

DEGREES • BSN • MSN

Nursing Program Faculty 18 (58% with doctorates).

Baccalaureate Enrollment 163
Women 89% **Men** 11% **Minority** 3% **Part-time** 40%

Graduate Enrollment 34
Women 89% **Men** 11% **Minority** 2%

Nursing Student Activities Nursing Honor Society, Sigma Theta Tau, Student Nurses' Association.

Nursing Student Resources Academic advising; academic or career counseling; assistance for students with disabilities; bookstore; campus computer network; career placement assistance; computer lab; computer-assisted instruction; e-mail services; employment services for current students; externships; housing assistance; interactive nursing skills videos; Internet; learning resource lab; library services; nursing audiovisuals; paid internships; placement services for program completers; remedial services; resume preparation assistance; skills, simulation, or other laboratory; tutoring; unpaid internships.

Library Facilities 1.8 million volumes (17,880 in health, 1,697 in nursing); 3,931 periodical subscriptions (217 health-care related).

BACCALAUREATE PROGRAMS

Degree BSN

Study Options Full-time.

Program Entrance Requirements Minimum overall college GPA of 2.75, transcript of college record, CPR certification, health exam, health insurance, high school transcript, immunizations, professional liability insurance/malpractice insurance. Transfer students are accepted.

Advanced Placement Credit given for nursing courses completed elsewhere dependent upon specific evaluations.

Contact *Telephone:* 270-745-3391. *Fax:* 270-745-3392.

GRADUATE PROGRAMS

Contact *Telephone:* 270-745-3490. *Fax:* 270-745-3392.

MASTER'S DEGREE PROGRAM

Degree MSN

Concentrations Available Nursing administration; nursing education. *Nurse practitioner programs in:* primary care.

Study Options Full-time and part-time.

Program Entrance Requirements Computer literacy, minimum overall college GPA of 2.75, transcript of college record, CPR certification, written essay, immunizations, interview, 3 letters of recommendation, nursing research course, physical assessment course, professional liability insurance/malpractice insurance, statistics course, GRE General Test.

Advanced Placement Credit given for nursing courses completed elsewhere dependent upon specific evaluations.

Degree Requirements 45 total credit hours, thesis or project, comprehensive exam.

POST-MASTER'S PROGRAM

Areas of Study *Nurse practitioner programs in:* primary care.

CONTINUING EDUCATION PROGRAM

Contact *Telephone:* 270-745-3762. *Fax:* 270-745-3392.

LOUISIANA

Dillard University
Division of Nursing
New Orleans, Louisiana

http://www.dillard.edu/academic/nursing

Founded in 1869

DEGREE • BSN

Nursing Program Faculty 14 (5% with doctorates).

Baccalaureate Enrollment 58
Women 98% **Men** 2% **Minority** 99% **International** 2%

Distance Learning Courses Available.

Nursing Student Activities Nursing Honor Society, Sigma Theta Tau, Student Nurses' Association.

Nursing Student Resources Academic advising; academic or career counseling; assistance for students with disabilities; bookstore; campus computer network; career placement assistance; computer lab; computer-assisted instruction; e-mail services; externships; interactive nursing skills videos; Internet; learning resource lab; library services; nursing audiovisuals; paid internships; placement services for program completers; remedial services; resume preparation assistance; skills, simulation, or other laboratory; tutoring.

Library Facilities 21 periodical subscriptions health-care related.

BACCALAUREATE PROGRAMS

Degree BSN

Available Programs Generic Baccalaureate; LPN to RN Baccalaureate; RN Baccalaureate.

Study Options Full-time.

Program Entrance Requirements Minimum overall college GPA of 2.5, transcript of college record, CPR certification, health exam, health insurance, high school transcript, immunizations, minimum high school GPA of 2.5, minimum GPA in nursing prerequisites of 2.5, professional liability insurance/malpractice insurance, prerequisite course work. Transfer students are accepted. *Application deadline:* 5/15 (spring). Applications may be processed on a rolling basis for some programs.

Expenses (2009–10) *Tuition:* full-time $13,000; part-time $542 per credit. *Room and board:* $2995 per academic year.

Financial Aid 80% of baccalaureate students in nursing programs received some form of financial aid in 2008–09. *Gift aid (need-based):* Federal Pell, FSEOG, state, private, college/university gift aid from institutional funds, United Negro College Fund. *Loans:* Federal Nursing Student Loans, FFEL (Subsidized and Unsubsidized Stafford PLUS), Perkins, alternative loans. *Work-study:* Federal Work-Study, part-time campus jobs. *Financial aid application deadline (priority):* 5/1.

Contact Division of Nursing, Division of Nursing, Dillard University, 2601 Gentilly Boulevard, New Orleans, LA 70122. *Telephone:* 504-816-4717. *Fax:* 504-816-4861.

Grambling State University
School of Nursing
Grambling, Louisiana

Founded in 1901

DEGREES • BSN • MSN

Nursing Program Faculty 23 (20% with doctorates).

Baccalaureate Enrollment 600
Women 85% **Men** 15% **Minority** 68% **International** 9% **Part-time** 5%

Graduate Enrollment 41
Women 86% **Men** 14% **Minority** 66% **International** 12%

Distance Learning Courses Available.

Nursing Student Activities Student Nurses' Association.

Grambling State University (continued)

Nursing Student Resources Academic advising; academic or career counseling; assistance for students with disabilities; bookstore; campus computer network; career placement assistance; computer lab; computer-assisted instruction; e-mail services; employment services for current students; interactive nursing skills videos; Internet; learning resource lab; library services; nursing audiovisuals; skills, simulation, or other laboratory; tutoring.

Library Facilities 230,243 volumes (10,000 in health, 5,000 in nursing); 65 periodical subscriptions health-care related.

BACCALAUREATE PROGRAMS

Degree BSN

Available Programs Generic Baccalaureate; LPN to RN Baccalaureate; RN Baccalaureate.

Study Options Full-time.

Program Entrance Requirements Transcript of college record, CPR certification, health exam, high school foreign language, 3 years high school math, 3 years high school science, high school transcript, immunizations, minimum high school GPA of 2.0, minimum GPA in nursing prerequisites of 2.75, professional liability insurance/malpractice insurance, prerequisite course work. Transfer students are accepted. *Application deadline:* 6/1 (fall), 12/1 (spring). *Application fee:* $20.

Advanced Placement Credit given for nursing courses completed elsewhere dependent upon specific evaluations.

Expenses (2008–09) *Tuition, area resident:* part-time $190 per credit. *Tuition, state resident:* full-time $2306. *Tuition, nonresident:* full-time $5304. *International tuition:* $5304 full-time. *Room and board:* $2601 per academic year. *Required fees:* full-time $650; part-time $250 per term.

Financial Aid 86% of baccalaureate students in nursing programs received some form of financial aid in 2007–08.

Contact Dr. Afua O. Arhin, RN, Associate Dean, School of Nursing, Grambling State University, PO Box 1192, 1 Cole Street, Grambling, LA 71245. *Telephone:* 318-274-2528. *Fax:* 318-274-3491. *E-mail:* arhina@gram.edu.

GRADUATE PROGRAMS

Expenses (2008–09) *Tuition, state resident:* full-time $2303. *Tuition, nonresident:* full-time $4978. *Required fees:* full-time $650.

Financial Aid 35% of graduate students in nursing programs received some form of financial aid in 2007–08. Tuition waivers (full and partial) available. *Financial aid application deadline:* 5/31.

Contact Dr. Rhonda Hensley, NP, Director, MSN Program, School of Nursing, Grambling State University, PO Box 4272, 1 Cole Street, Grambling, LA 71245. *Telephone:* 318-274-2897. *Fax:* 318-274-3491. *E-mail:* hensleyr@gram.edu.

MASTER'S DEGREE PROGRAM

Degree MSN

Available Programs Master's.

Concentrations Available Nursing education. *Clinical nurse specialist programs in:* adult health, maternity-newborn, pediatric. *Nurse practitioner programs in:* family health, pediatric.

Study Options Full-time and part-time.

Program Entrance Requirements Clinical experience, minimum overall college GPA of 3.0, transcript of college record, CPR certification, immunizations, interview, 3 letters of recommendation, physical assessment course, professional liability insurance/malpractice insurance, prerequisite course work, statistics course, GRE. *Application deadline:* 6/1 (fall). *Application fee:* $20.

Advanced Placement Credit given for nursing courses completed elsewhere dependent upon specific evaluations.

Degree Requirements 49 total credit hours, thesis or project, comprehensive exam.

POST-MASTER'S PROGRAM

Areas of Study *Nurse practitioner programs in:* family health.

Louisiana College
Department of Nursing
Pineville, Louisiana

http://www.lacollege.edu

Founded in 1906

DEGREE • BSN

Nursing Program Faculty 6 (17% with doctorates).

Baccalaureate Enrollment 100

Nursing Student Activities Sigma Theta Tau, Student Nurses' Association.

Nursing Student Resources Academic advising; academic or career counseling; assistance for students with disabilities; bookstore; campus computer network; career placement assistance; computer lab; computer-assisted instruction; e-mail services; employment services for current students; externships; Internet; learning resource lab; library services; nursing audiovisuals; skills, simulation, or other laboratory; tutoring; unpaid internships.

Library Facilities 135,566 volumes (3,426 in health, 500 in nursing); 380 periodical subscriptions (142 health-care related).

BACCALAUREATE PROGRAMS

Degree BSN

Available Programs Generic Baccalaureate.

Study Options Full-time.

Program Entrance Requirements Minimum overall college GPA of 2.6, transcript of college record, CPR certification, health exam, health insurance, immunizations, interview, minimum high school GPA of 2.0, minimum high school rank 50%, minimum GPA in nursing prerequisites of 2.6, professional liability insurance/malpractice insurance, prerequisite course work. Transfer students are accepted.

Advanced Placement Credit given for nursing courses completed elsewhere dependent upon specific evaluations.

Contact *Telephone:* 318-487-7127. *Fax:* 318-487-7488.

Louisiana State University Health Sciences Center
School of Nursing
New Orleans, Louisiana

http://nursing.lsuhsc.edu

Founded in 1931

DEGREES • BSN • DNS • MN

Nursing Program Faculty 70 (33% with doctorates).

Baccalaureate Enrollment 632
Women 84.9% **Men** 15.1% **Minority** 17% **International** .55% **Part-time** 25.5%

Graduate Enrollment 261
Women 23% **Men** 77% **Minority** 21.9% **Part-time** 39.08%

Nursing Student Activities Nursing Honor Society, Sigma Theta Tau, Student Nurses' Association.

Nursing Student Resources Academic advising; academic or career counseling; assistance for students with disabilities; bookstore; campus computer network; computer lab; computer-assisted instruction; e-mail services; housing assistance; interactive nursing skills videos; Internet; learning resource lab; library services; nursing audiovisuals; skills, simulation, or other laboratory.

Library Facilities 232,617 volumes (69,200 in health, 4,471 in nursing); 2,359 periodical subscriptions (7,600 health-care related).

BACCALAUREATE PROGRAMS

Degree BSN

Available Programs Accelerated Baccalaureate for Second Degree; Generic Baccalaureate; RN Baccalaureate.

Study Options Full-time and part-time.

Program Entrance Requirements Minimum overall college GPA of 2.8, transcript of college record, interview, prerequisite course work. Transfer students are accepted. *Application deadline:* 2/2 (fall), 9/1 (spring). *Application fee:* $50.

Expenses (2009–10) *Tuition, state resident:* full-time $2636. *Tuition, nonresident:* full-time $2636. *International tuition:* $2636 full-time. *Room and board:* room only: $1066 per academic year. *Required fees:* full-time $724.

Financial Aid 75% of baccalaureate students in nursing programs received some form of financial aid in 2008–09.

Contact Ms. Pamela Mathews, Nurse Recruiter, School of Nursing, Louisiana State University Health Sciences Center, 1900 Gravier Street, New Orleans, LA 70112. *Telephone:* 504-568-5198. *Fax:* 504-568-5711. *E-mail:* pmath1@lsuhsc.edu.

GRADUATE PROGRAMS

Expenses (2009–10) *Tuition, state resident:* part-time $184 per hour. *Tuition, nonresident:* part-time $184 per hour. *Room and board:* room only: $1066 per academic year.

Financial Aid 75% of graduate students in nursing programs received some form of financial aid in 2008–09. 12 fellowships, 1 research assistantship were awarded; teaching assistantships, Federal Work-Study, institutionally sponsored loans, and unspecified assistantships also available. Aid available to part-time students.

Contact Ms. Pamela Mathews, Nurse Recruiter, School of Nursing, Louisiana State University Health Sciences Center, 1900 Gravier Street, New Orleans, LA 70112. *Telephone:* 504-568-5198. *Fax:* 504-568-5711. *E-mail:* pmath1@lsuhsc.edu.

MASTER'S DEGREE PROGRAM

Degree MN

Available Programs Master's.

Concentrations Available Health-care administration; nurse anesthesia; nursing administration; nursing education. *Clinical nurse specialist programs in:* adult health, community health, parent-child, psychiatric/mental health. *Nurse practitioner programs in:* neonatal health, primary care.

Study Options Full-time and part-time.

Program Entrance Requirements Clinical experience, minimum overall college GPA of 3.0, transcript of college record, CPR certification, interview, 3 letters of recommendation, statistics course, GRE General Test, MAT. *Application deadline:* 2/1 (fall), 9/1 (spring). *Application fee:* $50.

Degree Requirements 38 total credit hours.

DOCTORAL DEGREE PROGRAM

Degree DNS

Available Programs Doctorate.

Areas of Study Clinical practice, nursing education.

Program Entrance Requirements Clinical experience, minimum overall college GPA of 3.5, 3 letters of recommendation, MSN or equivalent, scholarly papers, writing sample, GRE General Test. Application deadline: 2/1 (fall), 9/1 (spring). Application fee: $50.

Degree Requirements 54 total credit hours, dissertation, oral exam.

POSTDOCTORAL PROGRAM

Postdoctoral Program Contact Dr. Anita Hufft, Associate Dean, School of Nursing, Louisiana State University Health Sciences Center, 1900 Gravier Street, New Orleans, LA 70112. *Telephone:* 504-568-4107. *Fax:* 504-568-5853. *E-mail:* ahufft@lsuhsc.edu.

CONTINUING EDUCATION PROGRAM

Contact Dr. Demetrius J. Porche, RN, Dean, School of Nursing, Louisiana State University Health Sciences Center, 1900 Gravier Street, New Orleans, LA 70112. *Telephone:* 504-568-4106. *Fax:* 504-568-5853. *E-mail:* dporch@lsuhsc.edu.

Loyola University New Orleans
School of Nursing
New Orleans, Louisiana

http://www.loyno.edu/~nursing

Founded in 1912

DEGREES • BSN • MSN

Nursing Program Faculty 10 (80% with doctorates).

Baccalaureate Enrollment 98
Women 93% **Men** 7% **Minority** 26% **Part-time** 100%

Graduate Enrollment 519
Women 91% **Men** 9% **Minority** 20% **Part-time** 90%

Distance Learning Courses Available.

Nursing Student Activities Sigma Theta Tau.

Nursing Student Resources Academic advising; academic or career counseling; assistance for students with disabilities; bookstore; campus computer network; career placement assistance; computer lab; computer-assisted instruction; e-mail services; Internet; library services; skills, simulation, or other laboratory; tutoring.

Library Facilities 612,163 volumes; 40,662 periodical subscriptions.

BACCALAUREATE PROGRAMS

Degree BSN

Available Programs RN Baccalaureate.

Site Options Baton Rouge, LA.

Study Options Part-time.

Program Entrance Requirements Minimum overall college GPA of 2.5, transcript of college record, written essay, immunizations, minimum GPA in nursing prerequisites of 2.0, professional liability insurance/malpractice insurance, RN licensure. Transfer students are accepted.

Advanced Placement Credit by examination available. Credit given for nursing courses completed elsewhere dependent upon specific evaluations.

Expenses (2008–09) *Tuition:* part-time $321 per credit hour.

Financial Aid 98% of baccalaureate students in nursing programs received some form of financial aid in 2007–08. *Gift aid (need-based):* Federal Pell, FSEOG, state, private, college/university gift aid from institutional funds. *Loans:* FFEL (Subsidized and Unsubsidized Stafford PLUS), Perkins. *Work-study:* Federal Work-Study. *Financial aid application deadline:* 6/1 (priority: 2/15).

Contact Dr. Ann H. Cary, RN, Director, School of Nursing, School of Nursing, Loyola University New Orleans, 6363 St. Charles Avenue, Campus Box 45, New Orleans, LA 70118. *Telephone:* 504-865-3142. *Fax:* 504-865-3254. *E-mail:* nursing@loyno.edu.

GRADUATE PROGRAMS

Expenses (2008–09) *Tuition:* part-time $407 per credit hour.

Financial Aid 100% of graduate students in nursing programs received some form of financial aid in 2007–08. Traineeships and Incumbent Workers Training Program grants available. *Financial aid application deadline:* 5/1.

Contact Dr. Ann H. Cary, RN, Director, School of Nursing, School of Nursing, Loyola University New Orleans, 6363 St. Charles Avenue, Campus Box 45, New Orleans, LA 70118. *Telephone:* 504-865-3142. *Fax:* 504-865-3254. *E-mail:* nursing@loyno.edu.

MASTER'S DEGREE PROGRAM

Degree MSN

Available Programs Master's; Master's for Nurses with Non-Nursing Degrees; RN to Master's.

Concentrations Available Health-care administration; nurse case management. *Nurse practitioner programs in:* adult health, family health.

Study Options Full-time and part-time.

Program Entrance Requirements Clinical experience, minimum overall college GPA of 2.8, transcript of college record, written essay, immunizations, interview, 3 letters of recommendation, nursing research course, professional liability insurance/malpractice insurance, prerequisite course work, statistics course.

Loyola University New Orleans (continued)

Advanced Placement Credit given for nursing courses completed elsewhere dependent upon specific evaluations.

Degree Requirements 39 total credit hours, comprehensive exam.

POST-MASTER'S PROGRAM

Areas of Study *Nurse practitioner programs in:* adult health, family health.

McNeese State University

College of Nursing
Lake Charles, Louisiana

http://www.mcneese.edu

Founded in 1939

DEGREES • BSN • MSN

Nursing Program Faculty 51 (8% with doctorates).

Baccalaureate Enrollment 1,019
Women 78% **Men** 22% **Minority** 25% **International** 6% **Part-time** 12%

Graduate Enrollment 88
Women 82% **Men** 18% **Minority** 10% **Part-time** 70%

Distance Learning Courses Available.

Nursing Student Activities Sigma Theta Tau, Student Nurses' Association.

Nursing Student Resources Academic advising; academic or career counseling; assistance for students with disabilities; bookstore; campus computer network; career placement assistance; computer lab; computer-assisted instruction; daycare for children of students; e-mail services; employment services for current students; housing assistance; interactive nursing skills videos; Internet; learning resource lab; library services; nursing audiovisuals; placement services for program completers; resume preparation assistance; skills, simulation, or other laboratory; tutoring.

Library Facilities 332,521 volumes (41,000 in health, 27,500 in nursing); 22,177 periodical subscriptions (120 health-care related).

BACCALAUREATE PROGRAMS

Degree BSN

Available Programs ADN to Baccalaureate; Generic Baccalaureate; LPN to Baccalaureate; LPN to RN Baccalaureate.

Study Options Full-time and part-time.

Program Entrance Requirements Minimum overall college GPA of 2.7, transcript of college record, CPR certification, health exam, health insurance, high school transcript, immunizations, minimum high school GPA of 2.5, minimum GPA in nursing prerequisites of 2.7, prerequisite course work. Transfer students are accepted. *Application deadline:* 10/15 (fall), 3/10 (spring). *Application fee:* $30.

Advanced Placement Credit by examination available. Credit given for nursing courses completed elsewhere dependent upon specific evaluations.

Expenses (2009–10) *Tuition, state resident:* full-time $3600; part-time $1800 per semester. *Tuition, nonresident:* full-time $6200; part-time $3100 per semester. *International tuition:* $9500 full-time. *Room and board:* $4600; room only: $3900 per academic year. *Required fees:* full-time $1120; part-time $68 per credit; part-time $560 per term.

Financial Aid 81% of baccalaureate students in nursing programs received some form of financial aid in 2008–09.

Contact Dr. Peggy L. Wolfe, Dean and Professor, College of Nursing, McNeese State University, PO Box 90415, Lake Charles, LA 70609-0415. *Telephone:* 337-475-5820. *Fax:* 337-475-5924. *E-mail:* pwolfe@mail. mcneese.edu.

GRADUATE PROGRAMS

Expenses (2009–10) *Tuition, state resident:* full-time $3256; part-time $493 per credit. *Tuition, nonresident:* full-time $9322; part-time $493 per credit. *International tuition:* $9322 full-time. *Required fees:* full-time $728; part-time $364 per term.

Financial Aid 40% of graduate students in nursing programs received some form of financial aid in 2008–09. *Application deadline:* 5/1.

Contact Dr. Valarie Waldmeier, MSN Coordinator, College of Nursing, McNeese State University, PO Box 90415, Lake Charles, LA 70609-0415. *Telephone:* 337-475-5753. *Fax:* 337-475-5702. *E-mail:* vwaldmei@mcneese. edu.

MASTER'S DEGREE PROGRAM

Degree MSN

Available Programs Master's.

Concentrations Available Health-care administration; nursing administration; nursing education. *Clinical nurse specialist programs in:* adult health, psychiatric/mental health. *Nurse practitioner programs in:* adult health, psychiatric/mental health.

Site Options Lafayette, LA; Baton Rouge, LA; Lake Charles, LA.

Study Options Full-time and part-time.

Online Degree Options Yes (online only).

Program Entrance Requirements Minimum overall college GPA of 3.2, transcript of college record, CPR certification, immunizations, physical assessment course, statistics course, GRE. *Application deadline:* 6/23 (fall), 11/18 (spring). *Application fee:* $20.

Advanced Placement Credit given for nursing courses completed elsewhere dependent upon specific evaluations.

Degree Requirements 42 total credit hours, thesis or project.

POST-MASTER'S PROGRAM

Areas of Study Health-care administration; nursing administration; nursing education. *Clinical nurse specialist programs in:* adult health, psychiatric/mental health. *Nurse practitioner programs in:* adult health, psychiatric/mental health.

CONTINUING EDUCATION PROGRAM

Contact Mrs. Patsy Trahan, Continuing Education Coordinator, College of Nursing, McNeese State University, PO Box 90415, Lake Charles, LA 70609-0415. *Telephone:* 337-475-5832. *Fax:* 337-475-5924. *E-mail:* ptrahan@mcneese.edu.

Nicholls State University

Department of Nursing
Thibodaux, Louisiana

http://www.nicholls.edu/nursing/

Founded in 1948

DEGREE • BSN

Nursing Program Faculty 19 (21% with doctorates).

BACCALAUREATE PROGRAMS

Degree BSN

Available Programs Generic Baccalaureate; LPN to Baccalaureate; RN Baccalaureate.

Program Entrance Requirements Minimum overall college GPA of 2.75, transcript of college record, minimum GPA in nursing prerequisites of 2.0, prerequisite course work. Transfer students are accepted.

Contact *Telephone:* 985-448-4696. *Fax:* 985-448-4932.

CONTINUING EDUCATION PROGRAM

Contact *Telephone:* 985-448-4696. *Fax:* 985-448-4932.

Northwestern State University of Louisiana

College of Nursing
Shreveport, Louisiana

http://www.nsula.edu

Founded in 1884

DEGREES • BSN • MSN

Nursing Program Faculty 60 (22% with doctorates).

Baccalaureate Enrollment 1,234
Women 85% **Men** 15% **Minority** 35% **Part-time** 37%

Graduate Enrollment 204
Women 91% **Men** 9% **Minority** 20% **Part-time** 97%

Distance Learning Courses Available.

Nursing Student Activities Sigma Theta Tau, Student Nurses' Association.

Nursing Student Resources Academic advising; academic or career counseling; assistance for students with disabilities; bookstore; campus computer network; computer lab; computer-assisted instruction; e-mail services; employment services for current students; interactive nursing skills videos; Internet; learning resource lab; library services; nursing audiovisuals; remedial services; skills, simulation, or other laboratory; tutoring.

Library Facilities 778,085 volumes (4,443 in health, 3,047 in nursing); 1,183 periodical subscriptions (1,359 health-care related).

BACCALAUREATE PROGRAMS

Degree BSN

Available Programs ADN to Baccalaureate; Generic Baccalaureate; LPN to Baccalaureate; RN Baccalaureate.

Site Options Alexandria, LA; Ferriday, LA.

Study Options Full-time and part-time.

Online Degree Options Yes.

Program Entrance Requirements Minimum overall college GPA of 2.0, transcript of college record, CPR certification, health exam, health insurance, high school transcript, immunizations, minimum GPA in nursing prerequisites of 2.7, prerequisite course work, RN licensure. Transfer students are accepted. *Application deadline:* 5/31 (fall), 8/31 (spring). *Application fee:* $20.

Advanced Placement Credit by examination available. Credit given for nursing courses completed elsewhere dependent upon specific evaluations.

Expenses (2009–10) *Tuition, state resident:* full-time $5580; part-time $170 per credit hour. *Tuition, nonresident:* full-time $10,020; part-time $325 per credit hour. *International tuition:* $10,020 full-time. *Required fees:* full-time $1275; part-time $213 per term.

Financial Aid 80% of baccalaureate students in nursing programs received some form of financial aid in 2008–09.

Contact Mrs. Shirley Cashio, Director, Undergraduate Studies in Nursing, College of Nursing, Northwestern State University of Louisiana, 1800 Line Avenue, Shreveport, LA 71101. *Telephone:* 318-677-3100. *Fax:* 318-677-3127. *E-mail:* cashios@nsula.edu.

GRADUATE PROGRAMS

Expenses (2009–10) *Tuition, state resident:* full-time $6507; part-time $200 per credit hour. *Tuition, nonresident:* full-time $10,029; part-time $670 per credit hour. *International tuition:* $10,029 full-time. *Required fees:* full-time $1275; part-time $213 per term.

Financial Aid 20% of graduate students in nursing programs received some form of financial aid in 2008–09. Career-related internships or fieldwork and Federal Work-Study available. Aid available to part-time students. *Financial aid application deadline:* 7/15.

Contact Dr. Sally Cook, Director, Graduate Studies and Research in Nursing, College of Nursing, Northwestern State University of Louisiana, 1800 Line Avenue, Shreveport, LA 71101. *Telephone:* 318-677-3100. *Fax:* 318-677-3127. *E-mail:* cooks@nsula.edu.

MASTER'S DEGREE PROGRAM

Degree MSN

Available Programs Master's.

Concentrations Available Nursing administration; nursing education. *Clinical nurse specialist programs in:* adult health, critical care. *Nurse practitioner programs in:* acute care, family health, neonatal health, pediatric, women's health.

Site Options Alexandria, LA; Ferriday, LA.

Study Options Full-time and part-time.

Program Entrance Requirements Clinical experience, minimum overall college GPA of 3.0, transcript of college record, written essay, immunizations, 2 letters of recommendation, nursing research course, physical assessment course, professional liability insurance/malpractice insurance, statistics course, GRE General Test. *Application deadline:* 3/15 (fall), 10/15 (spring). *Application fee:* $20.

Advanced Placement Credit given for nursing courses completed elsewhere dependent upon specific evaluations.

Degree Requirements 42 total credit hours, thesis or project, comprehensive exam.

POST-MASTER'S PROGRAM

Areas of Study *Nurse practitioner programs in:* acute care, family health, neonatal health, pediatric, women's health.

CONTINUING EDUCATION PROGRAM

Contact Ms. Diane Graham Webb, Director, Non-Traditional Studies in Nursing, College of Nursing, Northwestern State University of Louisiana, 1800 Line Avenue, Shreveport, LA 71101. *Telephone:* 318-677-3100. *Fax:* 318-677-3127. *E-mail:* grahamd@nsula.edu.

Our Lady of Holy Cross College
Division of Nursing
New Orleans, Louisiana

http://www.olhcc.edu
Founded in 1916

DEGREE • BSN

Nursing Program Faculty 16 (32% with doctorates).

Baccalaureate Enrollment 168
Women 90% **Men** 10% **Minority** 15% **Part-time** 11%

Nursing Student Activities Sigma Theta Tau, Student Nurses' Association, nursing club.

Nursing Student Resources Academic advising; academic or career counseling; assistance for students with disabilities; bookstore; campus computer network; career placement assistance; computer lab; computer-assisted instruction; e-mail services; interactive nursing skills videos; Internet; learning resource lab; library services; nursing audiovisuals; remedial services; resume preparation assistance; skills, simulation, or other laboratory; tutoring.

Library Facilities 83,631 volumes (5,000 in health, 3,100 in nursing); 1,002 periodical subscriptions (103 health-care related).

BACCALAUREATE PROGRAMS

Degree BSN

Available Programs Generic Baccalaureate.

Study Options Full-time.

Program Entrance Requirements Minimum overall college GPA of 2.5, transcript of college record, CPR certification, written essay, health exam, health insurance, high school transcript, immunizations, 3 letters of recommendation, minimum high school GPA of 2.0, minimum GPA in nursing prerequisites of 2.5, professional liability insurance/malpractice insurance, prerequisite course work. Transfer students are accepted.

Advanced Placement Credit by examination available. Credit given for nursing courses completed elsewhere dependent upon specific evaluations.

Contact *Telephone:* 504-398-2215. *Fax:* 504-391-2421.

Our Lady of the Lake College
Division of Nursing
Baton Rouge, Louisiana

http://www.ololcollege.edu
Founded in 1990

Our Lady of the Lake College (continued)
DEGREES • BSN • MSN

Nursing Program Faculty 44 (14% with doctorates).

Baccalaureate Enrollment 90
Women 90% **Men** 10% **Minority** 5% **Part-time** 45%

Graduate Enrollment 94
Women 55% **Men** 45% **Minority** 3%

Nursing Student Activities Nursing Honor Society, Student Nurses' Association.

Nursing Student Resources Academic advising; academic or career counseling; assistance for students with disabilities; bookstore; campus computer network; career placement assistance; computer lab; computer-assisted instruction; e-mail services; employment services for current students; interactive nursing skills videos; Internet; learning resource lab; library services; nursing audiovisuals; paid internships; remedial services; resume preparation assistance; skills, simulation, or other laboratory; tutoring.

Library Facilities 10,000 volumes in health, 1,000 volumes in nursing; 200 periodical subscriptions health-care related.

BACCALAUREATE PROGRAMS

Degree BSN

Available Programs RN Baccalaureate.

Site Options New Orleans, LA.

Study Options Full-time and part-time.

Program Entrance Requirements Minimum overall college GPA of 2.0, transcript of college record, CPR certification, written essay, health exam, health insurance, immunizations, minimum high school GPA of 2.0, professional liability insurance/malpractice insurance, prerequisite course work, RN licensure. Transfer students are accepted. *Application deadline:* 1/15 (fall), 8/15 (spring). *Application fee:* $35.

Advanced Placement Credit by examination available.

Expenses (2009–10) *Tuition:* full-time $7904; part-time $304 per credit hour. *Required fees:* full-time $775; part-time $12 per credit; part-time $125 per term.

Financial Aid 90% of baccalaureate students in nursing programs received some form of financial aid in 2008–09.

Contact Dr. Phyllis LeBlanc, RN-BSN Program Coordinator, Division of Nursing, Our Lady of the Lake College, 7434 Perkins Road, Baton Rouge, LA 70808. *Telephone:* 225-768-1793. *Fax:* 225-768-1760. *E-mail:* pleblanc@ololcollege.edu.

GRADUATE PROGRAMS

Expenses (2009–10) *Tuition:* full-time $23,220; part-time $645 per credit hour. *International tuition:* $23,220 full-time. *Required fees:* full-time $1392; part-time $12 per credit; part-time $475 per term.

Financial Aid 95% of graduate students in nursing programs received some form of financial aid in 2008–09.

Contact Dr. Melanie Green, Dean, School of Nursing, Division of Nursing, Our Lady of the Lake College, 7500 Hennessy Boulevard, Baton Rouge, LA 70808. *Telephone:* 225-768-1751. *Fax:* 225-768-1760. *E-mail:* Melanie.Green@ololcollege.edu.

MASTER'S DEGREE PROGRAM

Degree MSN

Available Programs Master's.

Concentrations Available Nurse anesthesia; nursing administration; nursing education.

Study Options Full-time and part-time.

Program Entrance Requirements Clinical experience, minimum overall college GPA of 3.3, transcript of college record, interview, letters of recommendation, nursing research course, physical assessment course, statistics course. *Application deadline:* 1/15 (fall), 8/15 (spring). *Application fee:* $35.

Advanced Placement Credit given for nursing courses completed elsewhere dependent upon specific evaluations.

Degree Requirements 42 total credit hours, thesis or project.

CONTINUING EDUCATION PROGRAM

Contact Mrs. Marie Kelley, Vice President, HCI, Division of Nursing, Our Lady of the Lake College, 7434 Perkins Road, Baton Rouge, LA 70808. *Telephone:* 225-768-1789. *Fax:* 225-214-1940. *E-mail:* mkelley@ololcollege.edu.

Southeastern Louisiana University
School of Nursing
Hammond, Louisiana

http://www.selu.edu/acad_research/depts/nurs
Founded in 1925
DEGREES • BS • MSN

Nursing Program Faculty 65 (29% with doctorates).

Baccalaureate Enrollment 1,764
Women 86.3% **Men** 13.7% **Minority** 23.1% **International** .6% **Part-time** 18.5%

Graduate Enrollment 88
Women 83% **Men** 17% **Minority** 11.4% **International** 1.1% **Part-time** 92%

Distance Learning Courses Available.

Nursing Student Activities Nursing Honor Society, Sigma Theta Tau, Student Nurses' Association.

Nursing Student Resources Academic advising; academic or career counseling; assistance for students with disabilities; bookstore; campus computer network; career placement assistance; computer lab; computer-assisted instruction; e-mail services; employment services for current students; interactive nursing skills videos; Internet; learning resource lab; library services; nursing audiovisuals; other; placement services for program completers; remedial services; resume preparation assistance; skills, simulation, or other laboratory; tutoring.

Library Facilities 716,268 volumes (11,862 in health, 6,804 in nursing); 4,008 periodical subscriptions (338 health-care related).

BACCALAUREATE PROGRAMS

Degree BS

Available Programs Accelerated Baccalaureate for Second Degree; Accelerated RN Baccalaureate; Generic Baccalaureate; LPN to Baccalaureate; RN Baccalaureate.

Site Options Baton Rouge, LA.

Study Options Full-time and part-time.

Online Degree Options Yes.

Program Entrance Requirements Health exam, immunizations, minimum GPA in nursing prerequisites of 3.0. Transfer students are accepted. *Application deadline:* 7/15 (fall), 12/1 (spring), 5/1 (summer). Applications may be processed on a rolling basis for some programs. *Application fee:* $20.

Advanced Placement Credit by examination available. Credit given for nursing courses completed elsewhere dependent upon specific evaluations.

Expenses (2009–10) *Tuition, state resident:* full-time $2546; part-time $187 per credit hour. *Tuition, nonresident:* full-time $9802. *International tuition:* $9802 full-time. *Room and board:* $6450; room only: $4020 per academic year. *Required fees:* full-time $1386; part-time $116 per credit.

Financial Aid 77% of baccalaureate students in nursing programs received some form of financial aid in 2008–09.

Contact Dr. Cynthia Logan, Interim Director, School of Nursing, School of Nursing, Southeastern Louisiana University, SLU 10835, Hammond, LA 70402. *Telephone:* 985-549-2156. *Fax:* 985-549-2869. *E-mail:* nursing@selu.edu.

GRADUATE PROGRAMS

Expenses (2009–10) *Tuition, state resident:* full-time $3086; part-time $225 per credit hour. *Tuition, nonresident:* full-time $10,342; part-time $529 per credit hour. *International tuition:* $10,342 full-time. *Room and board:* $6450; room only: $4020 per academic year. *Required fees:* full-time $1195; part-time $133 per credit.

Financial Aid 32% of graduate students in nursing programs received some form of financial aid in 2008–09. 1 fellowship with full tuition reimbursement available (averaging $11,400 per year) was awarded; career-related internships or fieldwork, Federal Work-Study, institutionally sponsored loans, scholarships, unspecified assistantships, and administrative assistantship also available. Aid available to part-time students. *Financial aid application deadline:* 5/1.

Contact Dr. Ann Carruth, Graduate Nursing Program Coordinator, School of Nursing, Southeastern Louisiana University, SLU 10835, Hammond, LA 70402. *Telephone:* 985-549-5045. *Fax:* 985-549-2869. *E-mail:* acarruth@selu. edu.

MASTER'S DEGREE PROGRAM

Degree MSN

Available Programs Master's.

Concentrations Available Nursing administration; nursing education. *Clinical nurse specialist programs in:* adult health, psychiatric/mental health. *Nurse practitioner programs in:* adult health, psychiatric/mental health.

Site Options Lake Charles, LA; Lafayette, LA.

Study Options Full-time and part-time.

Program Entrance Requirements Clinical experience, minimum overall college GPA of 2.7, transcript of college record, immunizations, physical assessment course, resume, statistics course, GRE General Test. *Application deadline:* 7/15 (fall), 12/1 (spring), 5/1 (summer). Applications may be processed on a rolling basis for some programs. *Application fee:* $20.

Advanced Placement Credit given for nursing courses completed elsewhere dependent upon specific evaluations.

Degree Requirements 36 total credit hours, thesis or project.

Southern University and Agricultural and Mechanical College

School of Nursing
Baton Rouge, Louisiana

http://www.subr.edu/suson

Founded in 1880

DEGREES • BSN • MSN • PHD

Nursing Program Faculty 36 (3% with doctorates).

Baccalaureate Enrollment 1,020
Women 91% **Men** 9% **Minority** 96% **International** 1% **Part-time** 12%

Nursing Student Activities Nursing Honor Society, Student Nurses' Association, nursing club.

Nursing Student Resources Academic advising; academic or career counseling; assistance for students with disabilities; bookstore; campus computer network; computer lab; computer-assisted instruction; e-mail services; interactive nursing skills videos; Internet; learning resource lab; library services; nursing audiovisuals; resume preparation assistance; skills, simulation, or other laboratory; tutoring.

Library Facilities 880,098 volumes (4,220 in health, 716 in nursing); 8,882 periodical subscriptions (114 health-care related).

BACCALAUREATE PROGRAMS

Degree BSN

Available Programs Generic Baccalaureate.

Study Options Full-time and part-time.

Program Entrance Requirements Minimum overall college GPA of 2.6, CPR certification, health exam, immunizations, minimum GPA in nursing prerequisites, prerequisite course work. Transfer students are accepted.

Contact *Telephone:* 225-771-3416. *Fax:* 225-771-2651.

GRADUATE PROGRAMS

Contact *Telephone:* 225-771-2663. *Fax:* 225-771-3547.

MASTER'S DEGREE PROGRAM

Degree MSN

Available Programs Master's.

Concentrations Available Health-care administration; nursing education. *Clinical nurse specialist programs in:* family health. *Nurse practitioner programs in:* family health.

Study Options Full-time and part-time.

Program Entrance Requirements Minimum overall college GPA of 3.0, transcript of college record, 3 letters of recommendation, physical assessment course, statistics course, GRE General Test.

Degree Requirements 46 total credit hours, thesis or project, comprehensive exam.

POST-MASTER'S PROGRAM

Areas of Study *Nurse practitioner programs in:* family health.

DOCTORAL DEGREE PROGRAM

Degree PhD

Areas of Study Advanced practice nursing, nursing education, nursing research, women's health.

Program Entrance Requirements Clinical experience, minimum overall college GPA of 3.2, interview by faculty committee, 3 letters of recommendation, MSN or equivalent, scholarly papers, statistics course, vita, writing sample, GRE General Test.

Degree Requirements 60 total credit hours, dissertation, written exam.

University of Louisiana at Lafayette

College of Nursing
Lafayette, Louisiana

http://www.nursing.louisiana.edu

Founded in 1898

DEGREES • BSN • MSN

Nursing Program Faculty 47 (13% with doctorates).

Baccalaureate Enrollment 1,354
Women 83% **Men** 17% **Minority** 25% **Part-time** 10%

Distance Learning Courses Available.

Nursing Student Activities Nursing Honor Society, Sigma Theta Tau, Student Nurses' Association.

Nursing Student Resources Academic advising; academic or career counseling; assistance for students with disabilities; bookstore; campus computer network; career placement assistance; computer lab; computer-assisted instruction; daycare for children of students; e-mail services; employment services for current students; externships; housing assistance; interactive nursing skills videos; Internet; learning resource lab; library services; nursing audiovisuals; other; paid internships; placement services for program completers; remedial services; resume preparation assistance; skills, simulation, or other laboratory; tutoring; unpaid internships.

Library Facilities 999,913 volumes (6,883 in health, 4,593 in nursing); 2,851 periodical subscriptions (184 health-care related).

BACCALAUREATE PROGRAMS

Degree BSN

Available Programs ADN to Baccalaureate; Accelerated Baccalaureate for Second Degree; Generic Baccalaureate; LPN to Baccalaureate.

Study Options Full-time and part-time.

Online Degree Options Yes.

Program Entrance Requirements Minimum overall college GPA of 2.8, transcript of college record, CPR certification, health exam, health insurance, high school biology, high school chemistry, high school foreign language, 2 years high school math, 3 years high school science, high school transcript, immunizations, minimum high school GPA of 2.0, minimum high school rank 25%, minimum GPA in nursing prerequisites of 2.0, prerequisite course work. Transfer students are accepted. *Application deadline:* 4/1 (fall), 11/2 (spring).

University of Louisiana at Lafayette (continued)

Advanced Placement Credit by examination available. Credit given for nursing courses completed elsewhere dependent upon specific evaluations.

Expenses (2008–09) *Tuition, state resident:* full-time $3604; part-time $449 per credit hour. *Tuition, nonresident:* full-time $9784; part-time $449 per credit hour. *International tuition:* $9920 full-time. *Room and board:* $4243 per academic year. *Required fees:* full-time $364.

Financial Aid 80% of baccalaureate students in nursing programs received some form of financial aid in 2007–08.

Contact Amanda L. Menard, Administrative Assistant II, College of Nursing, University of Louisiana at Lafayette, PO Box 43810, Lafayette, LA 70504-3810. *Telephone:* 337-482-5604. *Fax:* 337-482-5700. *E-mail:* all4401@louisiana.edu.

GRADUATE PROGRAMS

Expenses (2008–09) *Tuition, state resident:* full-time $3490; part-time $464 per credit hour. *Tuition, nonresident:* full-time $10,031; part-time $464 per credit hour. *International tuition:* $10,166 full-time. *Room and board:* $4690 per academic year. *Required fees:* full-time $214.

Financial Aid 50% of graduate students in nursing programs received some form of financial aid in 2007–08. Fellowships with full tuition reimbursements available available.

Contact Dr. Donna Gauthier, Graduate Coordinator, College of Nursing, University of Louisiana at Lafayette, PO Box 43810, Lafayette, LA 70504-3810. *Telephone:* 337-482-5639. *Fax:* 337-482-5650. *E-mail:* dmg6362@louisiana.edu.

MASTER'S DEGREE PROGRAM

Degree MSN

Available Programs Master's; RN to Master's.

Concentrations Available Health-care administration; nursing administration; nursing education. *Clinical nurse specialist programs in:* adult health, psychiatric/mental health. *Nurse practitioner programs in:* adult health, psychiatric/mental health.

Site Options Hammond, LA; Baton Rouge, LA; Lake Charles, LA.

Study Options Full-time and part-time.

Online Degree Options Yes (online only).

Program Entrance Requirements Minimum overall college GPA of 2.75, transcript of college record, immunizations, 3 letters of recommendation, physical assessment course, statistics course, GRE General Test. *Application deadline:* Applications may be processed on a rolling basis for some programs. *Application fee:* $25.

Advanced Placement Credit given for nursing courses completed elsewhere dependent upon specific evaluations.

Degree Requirements 38 total credit hours, thesis or project.

POST-MASTER'S PROGRAM

Areas of Study *Clinical nurse specialist programs in:* adult health, psychiatric/mental health. *Nurse practitioner programs in:* adult health, psychiatric/mental health.

CONTINUING EDUCATION PROGRAM

Contact Patricia Miller, Director of Continuing Education, College of Nursing, University of Louisiana at Lafayette, PO Box 43810, Lafayette, LA 70504-3810. *Telephone:* 337-482-5648. *Fax:* 337-482-5053.

University of Louisiana at Monroe

Nursing

Monroe, Louisiana

http://www.ulm.edu/nursing

Founded in 1931

DEGREE • BS

Nursing Program Faculty 32 (2% with doctorates).

Baccalaureate Enrollment 220

Women 85% **Men** 15% **Minority** 20% **International** 1% **Part-time** 20%

Nursing Student Activities Sigma Theta Tau, Student Nurses' Association.

Nursing Student Resources Academic advising; academic or career counseling; assistance for students with disabilities; bookstore; campus computer network; computer lab; computer-assisted instruction; daycare for children of students; e-mail services; employment services for current students; interactive nursing skills videos; Internet; learning resource lab; library services; nursing audiovisuals; placement services for program completers; remedial services; resume preparation assistance; skills, simulation, or other laboratory; tutoring.

Library Facilities 647,696 volumes (20,924 in health, 3,000 in nursing); 140 periodical subscriptions (425 health-care related).

BACCALAUREATE PROGRAMS

Degree BS

Available Programs ADN to Baccalaureate; Accelerated Baccalaureate; Generic Baccalaureate; LPN to Baccalaureate; LPN to RN Baccalaureate; RN Baccalaureate.

Study Options Full-time and part-time.

Online Degree Options Yes (online only).

Program Entrance Requirements Transcript of college record, CPR certification, health exam, high school transcript, immunizations, minimum high school GPA of 2.0, minimum high school rank 50%, minimum GPA in nursing prerequisites of 2.8, professional liability insurance/malpractice insurance, prerequisite course work. Transfer students are accepted.

Advanced Placement Credit given for nursing courses completed elsewhere dependent upon specific evaluations.

Contact *Telephone:* 318-342-1640. *Fax:* 318-342-1567.

CONTINUING EDUCATION PROGRAM

Contact *Telephone:* 318-342-1679. *Fax:* 318-342-1567.

University of Phoenix–Louisiana Campus

College of Health and Human Services

Metairie, Louisiana

Founded in 1976

DEGREE • BSN

Nursing Program Faculty 2 (50% with doctorates).

Baccalaureate Enrollment 9

Nursing Student Activities Sigma Theta Tau.

Nursing Student Resources Academic advising; academic or career counseling; assistance for students with disabilities; bookstore; campus computer network; computer lab; computer-assisted instruction; e-mail services; interactive nursing skills videos; Internet; learning resource lab; library services; nursing audiovisuals; remedial services; tutoring.

Library Facilities 16,781 periodical subscriptions (1,300 health-care related).

BACCALAUREATE PROGRAMS

Degree BSN

Available Programs Accelerated Baccalaureate; LPN to Baccalaureate.

Study Options Full-time.

Program Entrance Requirements Transcript of college record, CPR certification, immunizations, 1 letter of recommendation, RN licensure. Transfer students are accepted. *Application deadline:* Applications may be processed on a rolling basis for some programs.

Advanced Placement Credit by examination available. Credit given for nursing courses completed elsewhere dependent upon specific evaluations.

Expenses (2009–10) *Tuition:* full-time $8832. *International tuition:* $8832 full-time.

Contact Campus College Chair, Nursing, College of Health and Human Services, University of Phoenix–Louisiana Campus, One Galleria Boulevard, Suite 725, Metairie, LA 70001-2082. *Telephone:* 504-461-8852.

MAINE

Husson University
School of Nursing
Bangor, Maine

http://www.husson.edu

Founded in 1898

DEGREES • BSN • MSN

Nursing Program Faculty 15 (27% with doctorates).

Baccalaureate Enrollment 245
Women 91% **Men** 9% **Minority** 4% **International** 1%

Graduate Enrollment 42
Women 98% **Men** 2% **Part-time** 21%

Distance Learning Courses Available.

Nursing Student Activities Sigma Theta Tau, Student Nurses' Association, nursing club.

Nursing Student Resources Academic advising; academic or career counseling; assistance for students with disabilities; bookstore; campus computer network; career placement assistance; computer lab; computer-assisted instruction; e-mail services; employment services for current students; externships; interactive nursing skills videos; Internet; learning resource lab; library services; nursing audiovisuals; remedial services; resume preparation assistance; skills, simulation, or other laboratory; tutoring; unpaid internships.

Library Facilities 49,036 volumes (3,450 in health, 1,100 in nursing); 500 periodical subscriptions (183 health-care related).

BACCALAUREATE PROGRAMS

Degree BSN

Available Programs Generic Baccalaureate.

Study Options Full-time and part-time.

Program Entrance Requirements Minimum overall college GPA of 3.0, transcript of college record, written essay, health exam, health insurance, high school biology, high school chemistry, 2 years high school math, 2 years high school science, high school transcript, immunizations, 2 letters of recommendation, minimum high school GPA of 3.0, minimum GPA in nursing prerequisites of 3.0, prerequisite course work. Transfer students are accepted. *Application deadline:* Applications may be processed on a rolling basis for some programs. *Application fee:* $25.

Advanced Placement Credit by examination available. Credit given for nursing courses completed elsewhere dependent upon specific evaluations.

Expenses (2009–10) *Tuition:* full-time $12,690; part-time $423 per credit hour. *International tuition:* $12,690 full-time. *Room and board:* $6994 per academic year. *Required fees:* full-time $275; part-time $50 per credit.

Financial Aid 90% of baccalaureate students in nursing programs received some form of financial aid in 2008–09. *Gift aid (need-based):* Federal Pell, FSEOG, state, private, college/university gift aid from institutional funds. *Loans:* FFEL (Subsidized and Unsubsidized Stafford PLUS), Perkins, state, alternative loans. *Work-study:* Federal Work-Study. *Financial aid application deadline (priority):* 4/15.

Contact Dr. Beth E. Clark, Director, Undergraduate Nursing Program, School of Nursing, Husson University, One College Circle, Bangor, ME 04401-2999. *Telephone:* 207-941-7036. *Fax:* 207-941-7198. *E-mail:* clarkeli@husson.edu.

GRADUATE PROGRAMS

Expenses (2009–10) *Tuition:* full-time $8800; part-time $440 per credit hour. *International tuition:* $8800 full-time. *Room and board:* $6994 per academic year. *Required fees:* full-time $275; part-time $50 per credit.

Financial Aid 57% of graduate students in nursing programs received some form of financial aid in 2008–09.

Contact Ms. Amy Friedenberg, Administrative Coordinator, School of Nursing, Husson University, One College Circle, Bangor, ME 04401. *Telephone:* 207-941-7001. *Fax:* 207-941-7198. *E-mail:* friedenberga@husson.edu.

MASTER'S DEGREE PROGRAM

Degree MSN

Available Programs Master's; Master's for Nurses with Non-Nursing Degrees.

Concentrations Available Nursing education. *Clinical nurse specialist programs in:* psychiatric/mental health. *Nurse practitioner programs in:* family health.

Site Options Presque Isle, ME; South Portland, ME.

Study Options Full-time and part-time.

Program Entrance Requirements Clinical experience, minimum overall college GPA of 3.0, transcript of college record, written essay, immunizations, interview, 3 letters of recommendation, physical assessment course, prerequisite course work, statistics course. *Application deadline:* Applications may be processed on a rolling basis for some programs. *Application fee:* $25.

Advanced Placement Credit by examination available. Credit given for nursing courses completed elsewhere dependent upon specific evaluations.

Degree Requirements 44 total credit hours, thesis or project.

POST-MASTER'S PROGRAM

Areas of Study Nursing education. *Clinical nurse specialist programs in:* psychiatric/mental health. *Nurse practitioner programs in:* family health, psychiatric/mental health.

Saint Joseph's College of Maine
Department of Nursing
Standish, Maine

Founded in 1912

DEGREES • BSN • MSN • MSN/MHA

Nursing Program Faculty 65 (8% with doctorates).

Baccalaureate Enrollment 558
Women 95% **Men** 5% **Minority** 1% **Part-time** 48%

Graduate Enrollment 343
Women 93% **Men** 7% **Minority** 3% **Part-time** 100%

Distance Learning Courses Available.

Nursing Student Activities Sigma Theta Tau, Student Nurses' Association.

Nursing Student Resources Academic advising; academic or career counseling; assistance for students with disabilities; bookstore; campus computer network; computer lab; computer-assisted instruction; e-mail services; interactive nursing skills videos; Internet; learning resource lab; library services; nursing audiovisuals; remedial services; resume preparation assistance; skills, simulation, or other laboratory; tutoring.

Library Facilities 113,453 volumes (4,114 in health, 409 in nursing); 15,646 periodical subscriptions (108 health-care related).

BACCALAUREATE PROGRAMS

Degree BSN

Available Programs Generic Baccalaureate; RN Baccalaureate.

Study Options Full-time and part-time.

Program Entrance Requirements Minimum overall college GPA of 2.0, transcript of college record, written essay, health exam, health insurance, high school biology, high school chemistry, 3 years high school math, 2 years high school science, high school transcript, immunizations, 1 letter of recommendation, minimum high school GPA of 2.0. *Application deadline:* 5/1 (spring). *Application fee:* $250.

Advanced Placement Credit given for nursing courses completed elsewhere dependent upon specific evaluations.

Expenses (2009–10) *Tuition:* full-time $25,150; part-time $835 per credit. *Room and board:* $10,350 per academic year. *Required fees:* full-time $990; part-time $160 per term.

Saint Joseph's College of Maine (continued)

Financial Aid 98% of baccalaureate students in nursing programs received some form of financial aid in 2008–09. *Gift aid (need-based):* Federal Pell, FSEOG, state, private, college/university gift aid from institutional funds, Federal Nursing. *Loans:* Federal Nursing Student Loans, FFEL (Subsidized and Unsubsidized Stafford PLUS), Perkins, state. *Work-study:* Federal Work-Study. *Financial aid application deadline (priority):* 3/1.

Contact Admissions Department, Department of Nursing, Saint Joseph's College of Maine, 278 Whites Bridge Road, Standish, ME 04084-5263. *Telephone:* 207-893-7830. *Fax:* 207-892-7423. *E-mail:* info@sjcme.edu.

GRADUATE PROGRAMS

Expenses (2009–10) *Tuition:* part-time $400 per credit.

Financial Aid 1% of graduate students in nursing programs received some form of financial aid in 2008–09. Institutionally sponsored loans available. Aid available to part-time students.

Contact Dr. Lois Hamel, Director of Distance Nursing Education, Department of Nursing, Saint Joseph's College of Maine, 278 Whites Bridge Road, Standish, ME 04084-5263. *Telephone:* 207-893-7956. *Fax:* 207-893-7520. *E-mail:* lhamel@sjcme.edu.

MASTER'S DEGREE PROGRAM

Degrees MSN; MSN/MHA

Available Programs Master's; Master's for Nurses with Non-Nursing Degrees; RN to Master's.

Concentrations Available Nursing administration; nursing education.

Study Options Full-time and part-time.

Online Degree Options Yes (online only).

Program Entrance Requirements Clinical experience, computer literacy, minimum overall college GPA of 3.0, transcript of college record, prerequisite course work, resume, MAT. *Application deadline:* Applications may be processed on a rolling basis for some programs.

Advanced Placement Credit given for nursing courses completed elsewhere dependent upon specific evaluations.

Degree Requirements 42 total credit hours, thesis or project.

CONTINUING EDUCATION PROGRAM

Contact Dr. Lois Hamel, Director of Distance Nursing Education, Department of Nursing, Saint Joseph's College of Maine, 278 Whites Bridge Road, Standish, ME 04084-5263. *Telephone:* 207-893-7956. *Fax:* 207-893-7520. *E-mail:* lhamel@sjcme.edu.

University of Maine
School of Nursing
Orono, Maine

Founded in 1865

DEGREES • BSN • MSN

Nursing Program Faculty 20 (40% with doctorates).

Baccalaureate Enrollment 407
Women 90% **Men** 10% **Minority** .4% **International** .1% **Part-time** .5%

Graduate Enrollment 27
Women 99% **Men** 1% **Part-time** 50%

Distance Learning Courses Available.

Nursing Student Activities Sigma Theta Tau, Student Nurses' Association.

Nursing Student Resources Academic advising; academic or career counseling; assistance for students with disabilities; bookstore; campus computer network; computer lab; daycare for children of students; e-mail services; employment services for current students; housing assistance; interactive nursing skills videos; Internet; learning resource lab; library services; nursing audiovisuals; skills, simulation, or other laboratory; tutoring.

Library Facilities 20,600 volumes in health, 2,100 volumes in nursing; 3,750 periodical subscriptions health-care related.

BACCALAUREATE PROGRAMS

Degree BSN

Available Programs Generic Baccalaureate; RN Baccalaureate.

Site Options Presque Isle, ME; Augusta, ME; Portland, ME.

Study Options Full-time and part-time.

Program Entrance Requirements Minimum overall college GPA of 2.75, transcript of college record, CPR certification, written essay, health exam, high school biology, high school chemistry, high school foreign language, 3 years high school math, 3 years high school science, high school transcript, immunizations, interview, minimum high school rank 30%. Transfer students are accepted.

Advanced Placement Credit by examination available. Credit given for nursing courses completed elsewhere dependent upon specific evaluations.

Contact *Telephone:* 207-581-2588. *Fax:* 207-581-2585.

GRADUATE PROGRAMS

Contact *Telephone:* 207-581-2605. *Fax:* 207-581-2585.

MASTER'S DEGREE PROGRAM

Degree MSN

Available Programs Master's; RN to Master's.

Concentrations Available Health-care administration; nursing education. *Nurse practitioner programs in:* family health.

Study Options Full-time and part-time.

Program Entrance Requirements Clinical experience, minimum overall college GPA of 3.0, transcript of college record, CPR certification, written essay, immunizations, interview, 3 letters of recommendation, nursing research course, physical assessment course, statistics course, GRE General Test.

Advanced Placement Credit given for nursing courses completed elsewhere dependent upon specific evaluations.

Degree Requirements 47 total credit hours, thesis or project.

University of Maine at Fort Kent
Department of Nursing
Fort Kent, Maine

http://www.umfk.maine.edu/academics/ programs/nursing/

Founded in 1878

DEGREE • BSN

Nursing Program Faculty 6 (16% with doctorates).

Baccalaureate Enrollment 246
Women 90% **Men** 10% **Minority** 2% **International** 2% **Part-time** 63%

Distance Learning Courses Available.

Nursing Student Activities Nursing Honor Society, Student Nurses' Association, nursing club.

Nursing Student Resources Academic advising; academic or career counseling; assistance for students with disabilities; bookstore; campus computer network; career placement assistance; computer lab; computer-assisted instruction; e-mail services; employment services for current students; externships; housing assistance; interactive nursing skills videos; Internet; learning resource lab; library services; nursing audiovisuals; paid internships; placement services for program completers; remedial services; resume preparation assistance; skills, simulation, or other laboratory; tutoring; unpaid internships.

Library Facilities 65,461 volumes (3,386 in health, 2,425 in nursing); 310 periodical subscriptions (73 health-care related).

BACCALAUREATE PROGRAMS

Degree BSN

Available Programs Accelerated Baccalaureate; Generic Baccalaureate; RN Baccalaureate.

Study Options Full-time and part-time.

Online Degree Options Yes.

Program Entrance Requirements Minimum overall college GPA of 2.5, CPR certification, written essay, health exam, health insurance, high school transcript, immunizations, prerequisite course work. Transfer students are accepted.

Advanced Placement Credit given for nursing courses completed elsewhere dependent upon specific evaluations.

Expenses (2009–10) *Tuition, state resident:* full-time $6030; part-time $201 per credit. *Tuition, nonresident:* full-time $15,180; part-time $506 per credit. *International tuition:* $15,180 full-time. *Room and board:* $7080; room only: $4000 per academic year. *Required fees:* full-time $773.

Financial Aid 80% of baccalaureate students in nursing programs received some form of financial aid in 2008–09. *Gift aid (need-based):* Federal Pell, FSEOG, state, private, college/university gift aid from institutional funds. *Loans:* Federal Direct (Subsidized and Unsubsidized Stafford PLUS), FFEL (Subsidized and Unsubsidized Stafford PLUS), Perkins, state. *Work-study:* Federal Work-Study, part-time campus jobs. *Financial aid application deadline (priority):* 3/1.

Contact Ms. Diana White, Chair of Admission, Advisement, and Advancement Committee, Department of Nursing, University of Maine at Fort Kent, 23 University Drive, Fort Kent, ME 04743-1292. *Telephone:* 207-834-8607. *Fax:* 207-834-7577. *E-mail:* dianaw@maine.edu.

University of New England
Department of Nursing
Biddeford, Maine

http://www.une.edu/chp/nursing/

Founded in 1831

DEGREE • BSN

Nursing Program Faculty 16 (26% with doctorates).

Baccalaureate Enrollment 32
Women 73% **Men** 27%

Nursing Student Activities Nursing Honor Society, Sigma Theta Tau, Student Nurses' Association, nursing club.

Nursing Student Resources Academic advising; academic or career counseling; assistance for students with disabilities; bookstore; campus computer network; career placement assistance; computer lab; computer-assisted instruction; e-mail services; employment services for current students; housing assistance; interactive nursing skills videos; Internet; learning resource lab; library services; nursing audiovisuals; placement services for program completers; remedial services; resume preparation assistance; skills, simulation, or other laboratory; tutoring; unpaid internships.

Library Facilities 156,752 volumes (10,000 in health, 5,500 in nursing); 39,705 periodical subscriptions (1,300 health-care related).

BACCALAUREATE PROGRAMS

Degree BSN

Available Programs Accelerated RN Baccalaureate; RN Baccalaureate.
Study Options Full-time and part-time.

Program Entrance Requirements Minimum overall college GPA of 2.5, transcript of college record, CPR certification, health exam, health insurance, high school biology, high school chemistry, 2 years high school math, 2 years high school science, high school transcript, immunizations, minimum high school GPA of 2.5, professional liability insurance/ malpractice insurance. Transfer students are accepted. *Application deadline:* 2/15 (fall). *Application fee:* $100.

Advanced Placement Credit by examination available. Credit given for nursing courses completed elsewhere dependent upon specific evaluations.

Expenses (2009–10) *Tuition:* full-time $26,940; part-time $970 per credit hour. *Room and board:* $10,870 per academic year. *Required fees:* full-time $680.

Financial Aid 88% of baccalaureate students in nursing programs received some form of financial aid in 2008–09. *Gift aid (need-based):* Federal Pell, FSEOG, state, private, college/university gift aid from institutional funds. *Loans:* Federal Nursing Student Loans, FFEL (Subsidized and Unsubsidized Stafford PLUS), Perkins, state, college/university. *Work-study:* Federal Work-Study, part-time campus jobs. *Financial aid application deadline (priority):* 5/1.

Contact Admissions Office, Department of Nursing, University of New England, 716 Stevens Avenue, Portland, ME 04103. *Telephone:* 800-477-4863. *E-mail:* admissions@une.edu.

CONTINUING EDUCATION PROGRAM

Contact Ms. Audrey Gup-Mathews, Department of Nursing, University of New England, 11 Hills Beach Road, Biddeford, ME 04005. *Telephone:* 207-602-2050. *Fax:* 207-602-5973.

University of Southern Maine
College of Nursing and Health Professions
Portland, Maine

http://www.usm.maine.edu/conhp

Founded in 1878

DEGREES • BS • MS • MS/MBA

Nursing Program Faculty 65 (23% with doctorates).

Baccalaureate Enrollment 447
Women 88% **Men** 12% **Minority** 8% **Part-time** 30%
Graduate Enrollment 105
Women 85% **Men** 15% **Minority** 4% **Part-time** 51%

Nursing Student Activities Sigma Theta Tau, Student Nurses' Association.

Nursing Student Resources Academic advising; academic or career counseling; assistance for students with disabilities; bookstore; campus computer network; computer lab; computer-assisted instruction; daycare for children of students; e-mail services; interactive nursing skills videos; Internet; learning resource lab; library services; nursing audiovisuals; remedial services; resume preparation assistance; skills, simulation, or other laboratory; tutoring.

Library Facilities 18,042 volumes in health, 622 volumes in nursing; 230 periodical subscriptions health-care related.

BACCALAUREATE PROGRAMS

Degree BS

Available Programs ADN to Baccalaureate; Accelerated Baccalaureate for Second Degree; Generic Baccalaureate; RN Baccalaureate.
Site Options Lewiston, ME.
Study Options Full-time and part-time.

Program Entrance Requirements Minimum overall college GPA of 3.0, transcript of college record, written essay, high school biology, high school chemistry, 3 years high school math, 2 years high school science, high school transcript, immunizations, 2 letters of recommendation, minimum high school GPA of 3.0. Transfer students are accepted. *Application deadline:* 1/15 (fall). *Application fee:* $40.

Advanced Placement Credit by examination available. Credit given for nursing courses completed elsewhere dependent upon specific evaluations.

Expenses (2009–10) *Tuition, state resident:* full-time $6930; part-time $231 per credit. *Tuition, nonresident:* full-time $19,140; part-time $638 per credit. *International tuition:* $19,140 full-time. *Room and board:* $8762; room only: $4696 per academic year. *Required fees:* full-time $2100; part-time $1000 per term.

Financial Aid 96% of baccalaureate students in nursing programs received some form of financial aid in 2008–09. *Gift aid (need-based):* Federal Pell, FSEOG, state, college/university gift aid from institutional funds. *Loans:* Federal Nursing Student Loans, FFEL (Subsidized and Unsubsidized Stafford PLUS), Perkins, college/university. *Work-study:* Federal Work-Study. *Financial aid application deadline (priority):* 2/15.

Contact Ms. Brenda D. Webster, Coordinator of Nursing Student Services, College of Nursing and Health Professions, University of Southern Maine, PO Box 9300, Portland, ME 04104-9300. *Telephone:* 207-780-4802. *Fax:* 207-780-4997. *E-mail:* bwebster@usm.maine.edu.

GRADUATE PROGRAMS

Expenses (2009–10) *Tuition, state resident:* full-time $6246; part-time $347 per credit. *Tuition, nonresident:* full-time $17,730; part-time $985 per credit. *International tuition:* $17,730 full-time. *Room and board:* $8762; room only: $4696 per academic year. *Required fees:* full-time $878; part-time $439 per term.

University of Southern Maine (continued)

Financial Aid 90% of graduate students in nursing programs received some form of financial aid in 2008–09. 5 research assistantships with tuition reimbursements available (averaging $3,375 per year), 7 teaching assistantships with tuition reimbursements available (averaging $3,375 per year) were awarded; career-related internships or fieldwork, Federal Work-Study, scholarships, traineeships, tuition waivers (full and partial), and unspecified assistantships also available. Aid available to part-time students. *Financial aid application deadline:* 2/15.

Contact Dr. Marjorie Thomas Lawson, Coordinator of Graduate Nursing Programs, College of Nursing and Health Professions, University of Southern Maine, PO Box 9300, Portland, ME 04104-9300. *Telephone:* 207-780-4114. *Fax:* 207-228-8177. *E-mail:* lawson@usm.maine.edu.

MASTER'S DEGREE PROGRAM

Degrees MS; MS/MBA

Available Programs Master's; Master's for Non-Nursing College Graduates; Master's for Nurses with Non-Nursing Degrees; RN to Master's.

Concentrations Available Clinical nurse leader. *Clinical nurse specialist programs in:* medical-surgical, psychiatric/mental health. *Nurse practitioner programs in:* adult health, family health, psychiatric/mental health.

Study Options Full-time and part-time.

Program Entrance Requirements Minimum overall college GPA of 3.0, transcript of college record, written essay, 2 letters of recommendation, physical assessment course, prerequisite course work, statistics course, GRE General Test or MAT. *Application deadline:* 4/1 (fall), 10/1 (spring), 12/1 (summer). *Application fee:* $50.

Advanced Placement Credit given for nursing courses completed elsewhere dependent upon specific evaluations.

Degree Requirements 54 total credit hours.

POST-MASTER'S PROGRAM

Areas of Study Clinical nurse leader. *Clinical nurse specialist programs in:* medical-surgical, psychiatric/mental health. *Nurse practitioner programs in:* adult health, family health, psychiatric/mental health.

CONTINUING EDUCATION PROGRAM

Contact Ms. Molly Morrell, Associate Director for Program Development, College of Nursing and Health Professions, University of Southern Maine, PO Box 9300, Center for Continuing Education, Portland, ME 04104-9300. *Telephone:* 207-780-5931. *Fax:* 207-780-5954. *E-mail:* mmorrell@usm.maine.edu.

MARYLAND

Bowie State University
Department of Nursing
Bowie, Maryland

http://www.bowiestate.edu/academics/nursing.htm

Founded in 1865

DEGREES • BSN • MSN

Nursing Program Faculty 20 (35% with doctorates).

Baccalaureate Enrollment 225
Women 88% **Men** 12% **Minority** 93% **International** 5% **Part-time** 25%

Graduate Enrollment 43
Women 87% **Men** 13% **Minority** 93% **International** 47% **Part-time** 5%

Distance Learning Courses Available.

Nursing Student Activities Nursing Honor Society, Student Nurses' Association.

Nursing Student Resources Academic advising; academic or career counseling; assistance for students with disabilities; bookstore; campus computer network; computer lab; computer-assisted instruction; housing assistance; interactive nursing skills videos; Internet; library services; nursing audiovisuals; skills, simulation, or other laboratory; tutoring.

Library Facilities 331,640 volumes; 3,152 periodical subscriptions.

BACCALAUREATE PROGRAMS

Degree BSN

Available Programs Accelerated Baccalaureate; Generic Baccalaureate; RN Baccalaureate.

Study Options Full-time.

Program Entrance Requirements Minimum overall college GPA of 2.75, transcript of college record, health exam, health insurance, high school biology, high school chemistry, 4 years high school math, 4 years high school science, high school transcript, immunizations, minimum high school GPA of 3.0, minimum GPA in nursing prerequisites of 2.75, prerequisite course work. Transfer students are accepted. *Application deadline:* 3/31 (fall).

Advanced Placement Credit given for nursing courses completed elsewhere dependent upon specific evaluations.

Expenses (2009–10) *Tuition, state resident:* full-time $4286; part-time $189 per credit. *Tuition, nonresident:* full-time $14,724; part-time $620 per credit. *Room and board:* $3342; room only: $1990 per academic year. *Required fees:* full-time $877; part-time $88 per credit.

Financial Aid 90% of baccalaureate students in nursing programs received some form of financial aid in 2008–09.

Contact Mr. Kenneth Dovale, Nursing Academic Adviser, Department of Nursing, Bowie State University, 14000 Jericho Park Road, Center for Learning Technology, Suite 202, Bowie, MD 20715. *Telephone:* 301-860-3202. *Fax:* 301-860-3222. *E-mail:* kdovale@bowiestate.edu.

GRADUATE PROGRAMS

Expenses (2009–10) *Tuition, state resident:* full-time $6030; part-time $335 per credit. *Tuition, nonresident:* full-time $11,520; part-time $640 per credit. *Room and board:* $7185; room only: $4480 per academic year. *Required fees:* full-time $1079; part-time $67 per credit; part-time $540 per term.

Financial Aid 20% of graduate students in nursing programs received some form of financial aid in 2008–09. Institutionally sponsored loans and traineeships available. *Financial aid application deadline:* 4/1.

Contact Mr. Kenneth Dovale, Nursing Academic Adviser, Department of Nursing, Bowie State University, 14000 Jericho Park Road, Center for Learning Technology, Suite 202, Bowie, MD 20715. *Telephone:* 301-860-3202. *Fax:* 301-860-3222. *E-mail:* kdovale@bowiestate.edu.

MASTER'S DEGREE PROGRAM

Degree MSN

Available Programs Master's.

Concentrations Available Nursing education. *Nurse practitioner programs in:* family health.

Study Options Full-time and part-time.

Program Entrance Requirements Clinical experience, minimum overall college GPA of 2.5, CPR certification, written essay, immunizations, 3 letters of recommendation, physical assessment course, professional liability insurance/malpractice insurance, resume, statistics course. *Application deadline:* 11/30 (fall), 4/30 (spring). Applications may be processed on a rolling basis for some programs.

Advanced Placement Credit by examination available. Credit given for nursing courses completed elsewhere dependent upon specific evaluations.

Degree Requirements 45 total credit hours, comprehensive exam.

College of Notre Dame of Maryland

Department of Nursing
Baltimore, Maryland

http://206.205.71.30/academics/departments/nd_aca_nursing.cfm

Founded in 1873

DEGREE • BS

Nursing Program Faculty 5 (60% with doctorates).
Nursing Student Resources Library services.
Library Facilities 999,295 volumes; 42,427 periodical subscriptions.

BACCALAUREATE PROGRAMS

Degree BS

Available Programs Accelerated RN Baccalaureate; RN Baccalaureate.
Site Options Frederick, MD; Aberdeen, MD.
Study Options Full-time and part-time.
Program Entrance Requirements Minimum overall college GPA of 2.5, transcript of college record, interview, minimum GPA in nursing prerequisites of 2.0, prerequisite course work, RN licensure. Transfer students are accepted.
Advanced Placement Credit by examination available. Credit given for nursing courses completed elsewhere dependent upon specific evaluations.
Contact *Telephone:* 410-532-5500.

Columbia Union College

Nursing Department
Takoma Park, Maryland

Founded in 1904

DEGREE • BS

Nursing Program Faculty 8 (14% with doctorates).
Baccalaureate Enrollment 240
Women 90% **Men** 10% **Minority** 75% **International** 1% **Part-time** 10%
Nursing Student Activities Student Nurses' Association, nursing club.
Nursing Student Resources Academic advising; academic or career counseling; bookstore; campus computer network; computer lab; e-mail services; externships; interactive nursing skills videos; Internet; learning resource lab; library services; nursing audiovisuals; remedial services; skills, simulation, or other laboratory; tutoring; unpaid internships.
Library Facilities 141,534 volumes; 9,000 periodical subscriptions.

BACCALAUREATE PROGRAMS

Degree BS

Available Programs Accelerated RN Baccalaureate; Generic Baccalaureate.
Study Options Full-time.
Program Entrance Requirements Minimum overall college GPA of 2.75, transcript of college record, CPR certification, written essay, health exam, immunizations, interview, 2 letters of recommendation, minimum GPA in nursing prerequisites of 2.75, prerequisite course work. Transfer students are accepted.
Advanced Placement Credit given for nursing courses completed elsewhere dependent upon specific evaluations.
Contact *Telephone:* 301-891-4144. *Fax:* 301-891-4191.

Coppin State University

Helene Fuld School of Nursing
Baltimore, Maryland

http://www.coppin.edu/nursing

Founded in 1900

DEGREES • BSN • MSN

Nursing Program Faculty 45 (18% with doctorates).
Baccalaureate Enrollment 529
Women 91% **Men** 9% **Minority** 99% **International** 2% **Part-time** 33%
Graduate Enrollment 32
Women 94% **Men** 6% **Minority** 94% **Part-time** 22%
Distance Learning Courses Available.
Nursing Student Activities Nursing Honor Society, Sigma Theta Tau, Student Nurses' Association.
Nursing Student Resources Academic advising; academic or career counseling; assistance for students with disabilities; bookstore; campus computer network; career placement assistance; computer lab; computer-assisted instruction; e-mail services; externships; interactive nursing skills videos; Internet; learning resource lab; library services; nursing audiovisuals; other; placement services for program completers; remedial services; resume preparation assistance; skills, simulation, or other laboratory; tutoring; unpaid internships.
Library Facilities 134,983 volumes (1,339 in health, 1,298 in nursing); 665 periodical subscriptions (132 health-care related).

BACCALAUREATE PROGRAMS

Degree BSN

Available Programs Accelerated RN Baccalaureate; Baccalaureate for Second Degree; Generic Baccalaureate; RN Baccalaureate.
Site Options Baltimore, MD.
Study Options Full-time and part-time.
Program Entrance Requirements Written essay, health exam, high school biology, high school chemistry, high school foreign language, 3 years high school math, 2 years high school science, high school transcript, immunizations, 3 letters of recommendation, minimum high school GPA of 2.5, minimum GPA in nursing prerequisites of 2.5. Transfer students are accepted.
Contact *Telephone:* 410-951-3988. *Fax:* 410-400-5978.

GRADUATE PROGRAMS

Contact *Telephone:* 410-951-3988. *Fax:* 410-400-5978.

MASTER'S DEGREE PROGRAM

Degree MSN

Available Programs Master's.
Concentrations Available *Nurse practitioner programs in:* family health.
Site Options Baltimore, MD.
Study Options Full-time and part-time.
Program Entrance Requirements Clinical experience, computer literacy, minimum overall college GPA of 3.0, transcript of college record, CPR certification, written essay, immunizations, interview, 3 letters of recommendation, nursing research course, physical assessment course, statistics course.
Advanced Placement Credit given for nursing courses completed elsewhere dependent upon specific evaluations.
Degree Requirements 48 total credit hours, thesis or project, comprehensive exam.

POST-MASTER'S PROGRAM

Areas of Study *Nurse practitioner programs in:* family health.

The Johns Hopkins University
School of Nursing
Baltimore, Maryland

http://www.son.jhmi.edu

Founded in 1876

DEGREES • BS • MSN • MSN/MBA • MSN/MPH • MSN/PHD • PHD

Nursing Program Faculty 250 (45% with doctorates).

Baccalaureate Enrollment 380
Women 90% **Men** 10% **Minority** 26.3% **International** 4% **Part-time** 4.6%

Graduate Enrollment 240
Women 92.9% **Men** 7.1% **Minority** 21.8% **International** 3% **Part-time** 67.6%

Distance Learning Courses Available.

Nursing Student Activities Nursing Honor Society, Sigma Theta Tau, Student Nurses' Association, nursing club.

Nursing Student Resources Academic advising; academic or career counseling; assistance for students with disabilities; bookstore; campus computer network; career placement assistance; computer lab; computer-assisted instruction; e-mail services; employment services for current students; housing assistance; Internet; learning resource lab; library services; nursing audiovisuals; other; resume preparation assistance; skills, simulation, or other laboratory; tutoring.

Library Facilities 2.9 million volumes (412,000 in health); 55,000 periodical subscriptions (6,000 health-care related).

BACCALAUREATE PROGRAMS

Degree BS

Available Programs Accelerated Baccalaureate for Second Degree; Baccalaureate for Second Degree; Generic Baccalaureate; RN Baccalaureate.

Study Options Full-time and part-time.

Program Entrance Requirements Minimum overall college GPA of 3.0, transcript of college record, CPR certification, written essay, health exam, health insurance, immunizations, interview, 3 letters of recommendation, minimum GPA in nursing prerequisites of 3.0, prerequisite course work. Transfer students are accepted. *Application deadline:* 1/15 (fall), 11/15 (summer). *Application fee:* $75.

Advanced Placement Credit by examination available. Credit given for nursing courses completed elsewhere dependent upon specific evaluations.

Expenses (2009–10) *Tuition:* full-time $31,920; part-time $1330 per credit. *International tuition:* $31,920 full-time.

Financial Aid 80% of baccalaureate students in nursing programs received some form of financial aid in 2008–09. *Gift aid (need-based):* Federal Pell, FSEOG, state, private, college/university gift aid from institutional funds. *Loans:* Federal Direct (Subsidized and Unsubsidized Stafford PLUS), Perkins, college/university. *Work-study:* Federal Work-Study. *Financial aid application deadline:* 3/1.

Contact Office of Admissions and Student Services, School of Nursing, The Johns Hopkins University, 525 North Wolfe Street, Baltimore, MD 21205-2110. *Telephone:* 410-955-7548. *Fax:* 410-614-7086. *E-mail:* jhuson@son.jhmi.edu.

GRADUATE PROGRAMS

Expenses (2009–10) *Tuition:* full-time $31,416; part-time $1309 per credit. *International tuition:* $31,416 full-time.

Financial Aid 6 fellowships (averaging $23,272 per year) were awarded; research assistantships, teaching assistantships, career-related internships or fieldwork, Federal Work-Study, scholarships, traineeships, and tuition waivers (partial) also available.

Contact Ms. Mary O'Rourke, Director of Admissions and Student Services, School of Nursing, The Johns Hopkins University, 525 North Wolfe Street, Suite 113, Baltimore, MD 21205-2110. *Telephone:* 410-955-7548. *Fax:* 410-614-7086. *E-mail:* jhuson@son.jhmi.edu.

MASTER'S DEGREE PROGRAM

Degrees MSN; MSN/MBA; MSN/MPH; MSN/PhD

Available Programs Master's.

Concentrations Available Health-care administration; nurse case management; nurse-midwifery; nursing administration. *Clinical nurse specialist programs in:* acute care, adult health, cardiovascular, community health, critical care, family health, forensic nursing, gerontology, maternity-newborn, medical-surgical, oncology, palliative care, parent-child, pediatric, perinatal, public health, women's health. *Nurse practitioner programs in:* acute care, adult health, family health, pediatric, primary care.

Study Options Full-time and part-time.

Program Entrance Requirements Clinical experience, computer literacy, minimum overall college GPA of 3.0, transcript of college record, CPR certification, written essay, immunizations, interview, 3 letters of recommendation, nursing research course, physical assessment course, prerequisite course work, resume, statistics course, GRE. *Application deadline:* 8/1 (fall), 12/1 (winter), 12/1 (spring), 5/1 (summer). Applications may be processed on a rolling basis for some programs. *Application fee:* $75.

Advanced Placement Credit by examination available. Credit given for nursing courses completed elsewhere dependent upon specific evaluations.

Degree Requirements 36 total credit hours, thesis or project.

POST-MASTER'S PROGRAM

Areas of Study Nursing education. *Nurse practitioner programs in:* acute care, adult health, family health, pediatric, primary care.

DOCTORAL DEGREE PROGRAM

Degree PhD

Available Programs Doctorate.

Areas of Study Addiction/substance abuse, advanced practice nursing, aging, bio-behavioral research, biology of health and illness, clinical practice, community health, critical care, family health, forensic nursing, gerontology, health policy, health promotion/disease prevention, health-care systems, human health and illness, illness and transition, individualized study, nurse case management, nursing research, nursing science, oncology, urban health, women's health.

Program Entrance Requirements Clinical experience, minimum overall college GPA of 3.5, interview, 3 letters of recommendation, MSN or equivalent, scholarly papers, statistics course, vita, writing sample, GRE. Application deadline: 1/15 (fall). Applications may be processed on a rolling basis for some programs. Application fee: $100.

Degree Requirements Dissertation, oral exam, written exam.

POSTDOCTORAL PROGRAM

Areas of Study Health promotion/disease prevention, vulnerable population.

Postdoctoral Program Contact Dr. Gayle Page, Director of Center for Nursing Research and Sponsored Projects, School of Nursing, The Johns Hopkins University, 525 North Wolfe Street, Baltimore, MD 21205-2110. *Telephone:* 410-955-7548. *Fax:* 410-614-7086. *E-mail:* gpage@son.jhmi.edu.

CONTINUING EDUCATION PROGRAM

Contact Jane Shivnan, Director, Institute for Johns Hopkins Nursing, School of Nursing, The Johns Hopkins University, 525 North Wolfe Street, Baltimore, MD 21205-2110. *Telephone:* 443-287-4745. *Fax:* 410-614-8972. *E-mail:* ijhn@son.jhmi.edu.

See full description on page 500.

Salisbury University
Program in Nursing
Salisbury, Maryland

http://www.salisbury.edu/nursing

Founded in 1925

DEGREES • BS • MS

Nursing Program Faculty 30 (75% with doctorates).

Baccalaureate Enrollment 475
Women 90% **Men** 10% **Minority** 15% **International** 3% **Part-time** 10%

Graduate Enrollment 28
Women 90% **Men** 10% **Minority** 10% **International** 5% **Part-time** 85%
Distance Learning Courses Available.

Nursing Student Activities Nursing Honor Society, Sigma Theta Tau, Student Nurses' Association.

Nursing Student Resources Academic advising; academic or career counseling; assistance for students with disabilities; bookstore; campus computer network; career placement assistance; computer lab; computer-assisted instruction; e-mail services; employment services for current students; externships; housing assistance; interactive nursing skills videos; Internet; learning resource lab; library services; nursing audiovisuals; paid internships; placement services for program completers; remedial services; resume preparation assistance; skills, simulation, or other laboratory; tutoring; unpaid internships.

Library Facilities 271,328 volumes (6,850 in health, 1,025 in nursing); 1,153 periodical subscriptions (145 health-care related).

BACCALAUREATE PROGRAMS

Degree BS

Available Programs ADN to Baccalaureate; Accelerated Baccalaureate for Second Degree; Generic Baccalaureate; RN Baccalaureate.

Study Options Full-time.

Program Entrance Requirements Minimum overall college GPA of 2.75, transcript of college record, CPR certification, health exam, high school biology, high school chemistry, 2 years high school math, high school transcript, immunizations, minimum GPA in nursing prerequisites of 3.0, prerequisite course work. Transfer students are accepted. *Application deadline:* 2/15 (winter).

Advanced Placement Credit given for nursing courses completed elsewhere dependent upon specific evaluations.

Expenses (2009–10) *Tuition, state resident:* full-time $4814; part-time $200 per credit hour. *Tuition, nonresident:* full-time $13,310; part-time $553 per credit hour. *Room and board:* $8070; room only: $4150 per academic year. *Required fees:* full-time $1804; part-time $61 per credit.

Financial Aid 80% of baccalaureate students in nursing programs received some form of financial aid in 2008–09.

Contact Lisa A. Seldomridge, PhD, Chair and Professor, Department of Nursing, Program in Nursing, Salisbury University, 1101 Camden Avenue, Salisbury, MD 21801. *Telephone:* 410-543-6413. *Fax:* 410-548-3313. *E-mail:* laseldomridge@salisbury.edu.

GRADUATE PROGRAMS

Expenses (2009–10) *Tuition, state resident:* part-time $278 per credit hour. *Tuition, nonresident:* part-time $574 per credit hour. *Room and board:* $8370; room only: $4450 per academic year. *Required fees:* part-time $57 per credit.

Financial Aid Career-related internships or fieldwork, scholarships, and unspecified assistantships available.

Contact Dr. Mary T. Parsons, RN, Director, Graduate and Second Degree Programs, Program in Nursing, Salisbury University, 1101 Camden Avenue, Salisbury, MD 21801. *Telephone:* 410-543-6416. *Fax:* 410-548-3313. *E-mail:* mtparsons@salisbury.edu.

MASTER'S DEGREE PROGRAM

Degree MS

Available Programs Master's; RN to Master's.

Concentrations Available Health-care administration; nursing education. *Nurse practitioner programs in:* family health.

Study Options Full-time and part-time.

Program Entrance Requirements Minimum overall college GPA of 3.0, transcript of college record, CPR certification, written essay, immunizations, interview, 2 letters of recommendation, nursing research course, physical assessment course, resume, statistics course. *Application deadline:* Applications may be processed on a rolling basis for some programs.

Advanced Placement Credit given for nursing courses completed elsewhere dependent upon specific evaluations.

Degree Requirements 43 total credit hours, thesis or project.

POST-MASTER'S PROGRAM

Areas of Study Health-care administration; nursing education. *Nurse practitioner programs in:* family health.

Stevenson University
Nursing Division
Stevenson, Maryland

http://www4.vjc.edu/Nursing
Founded in 1952
DEGREE • BS

Nursing Program Faculty 43 (35% with doctorates).
Baccalaureate Enrollment 428
Women 94% **Men** 6% **Minority** 25% **Part-time** 52%
Distance Learning Courses Available.

Nursing Student Activities Sigma Theta Tau, Student Nurses' Association.

Nursing Student Resources Academic advising; academic or career counseling; assistance for students with disabilities; bookstore; campus computer network; career placement assistance; computer lab; e-mail services; employment services for current students; Internet; learning resource lab; library services; nursing audiovisuals; placement services for program completers; remedial services; resume preparation assistance; skills, simulation, or other laboratory; tutoring.

Library Facilities 81,802 volumes (3,301 in health, 776 in nursing); 1,058 periodical subscriptions (635 health-care related).

BACCALAUREATE PROGRAMS

Degree BS

Available Programs ADN to Baccalaureate; Accelerated Baccalaureate for Second Degree; Accelerated RN Baccalaureate; Generic Baccalaureate; RN Baccalaureate.

Site Options Arnold, MD; Easton, MD; Westminster, MD.

Study Options Full-time and part-time.

Program Entrance Requirements Minimum overall college GPA of 3.0, transcript of college record, written essay, health exam, health insurance, high school biology, high school chemistry, 2 years high school math, high school transcript, immunizations, interview, minimum high school GPA of 3.0, minimum GPA in nursing prerequisites of 3.0. Transfer students are accepted.

Advanced Placement Credit by examination available. Credit given for nursing courses completed elsewhere dependent upon specific evaluations.

Contact Dr. Judith A. Feustle, Director, Nursing Division, Nursing Division, Stevenson University, 1525 Greenspring Valley Road, Stevenson, MD 21153-0641. *Telephone:* 443-334-2312. *Fax:* 443-334-2148. *E-mail:* fac-feus@mail.vjc.edu.

See display on page 220.

Towson University
Department of Nursing
Towson, Maryland

http://www.towson.edu/nursing
Founded in 1866
DEGREES • BS • MS

Nursing Program Faculty 20 (75% with doctorates).
Baccalaureate Enrollment 300
Women 96% **Men** 4% **Minority** 24% **Part-time** 14%
Graduate Enrollment 47
Women 92% **Men** 8% **Minority** 21% **Part-time** 100%
Distance Learning Courses Available.

Nursing Student Activities Sigma Theta Tau, Student Nurses' Association.

Nursing Student Resources Academic advising; academic or career counseling; assistance for students with disabilities; bookstore; campus computer network; career placement assistance; computer lab; computer-assisted instruction; daycare for children of students; e-mail services; employment services for current students; housing assistance; interactive

Towson University (continued)

nursing skills videos; Internet; learning resource lab; library services; nursing audiovisuals; remedial services; resume preparation assistance; skills, simulation, or other laboratory; tutoring.

Library Facilities 578,057 volumes (15,660 in health, 1,409 in nursing); 4,653 periodical subscriptions (550 health-care related).

BACCALAUREATE PROGRAMS

Degree BS

Available Programs Generic Baccalaureate; RN Baccalaureate; RPN to Baccalaureate.

Site Options Hagerstown, MD.

Study Options Full-time and part-time.

Program Entrance Requirements Minimum overall college GPA of 2.5, transcript of college record, CPR certification, health exam, health insurance, immunizations, minimum GPA in nursing prerequisites, prerequisite course work. Transfer students are accepted. *Application deadline:* 1/15 (fall), 8/15 (spring).

Advanced Placement Credit by examination available. Credit given for nursing courses completed elsewhere dependent upon specific evaluations.

Expenses (2008–09) *Tuition, state resident:* full-time $7600; part-time $310 per unit. *Tuition, nonresident:* full-time $18,500; part-time $670 per unit. *International tuition:* $18,500 full-time. *Room and board:* $4200 per academic year.

Financial Aid 89% of baccalaureate students in nursing programs received some form of financial aid in 2007–08. *Gift aid (need-based):* Federal Pell, FSEOG, state, private, college/university gift aid from institutional funds. *Loans:* Federal Direct (Subsidized and Unsubsidized Stafford PLUS), Perkins. *Work-study:* Federal Work-Study. *Financial aid application deadline:* 2/10 (priority: 1/31).

Contact Ms. Brook R. Necker, Admissions and Retention Coordinator, Department of Nursing, Towson University, 8000 York Road, Towson, MD 21252-0001. *Telephone:* 410-704-4170. *E-mail:* bnecker@towson.edu.

GRADUATE PROGRAMS

Contact Dr. Marilyn Halstead, Graduate Program Director, Department of Nursing, Towson University, 8000 York Road, Towson, MD 21252-0001. *E-mail:* mhalstead@towson.edu.

MASTER'S DEGREE PROGRAM

Degree MS

Available Programs Master's.

Concentrations Available Health-care administration; nursing education.

Site Options Hagerstown, MD.

Study Options Part-time.

Program Entrance Requirements Minimum overall college GPA of 3.0, transcript of college record, nursing research course, physical assessment course, resume, statistics course.

Degree Requirements 36 total credit hours.

University of Maryland, Baltimore
Master's Program in Nursing
Baltimore, Maryland

http://nursing.umaryland.edu/

Founded in 1807

DEGREES • BSN • DNP • MS • MSN/JD • MSN/MBA • MSN/MPH

Nursing Program Faculty 191 (82% with doctorates).

Baccalaureate Enrollment 694
Women 83% **Men** 17% **Minority** 48% **International** 6% **Part-time** 38%

Graduate Enrollment 856
Women 88% **Men** 12% **Minority** 39% **International** 1% **Part-time** 62%

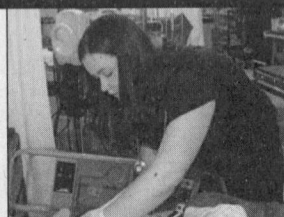
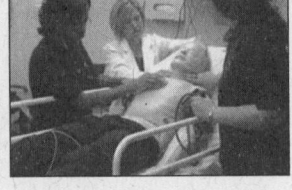

Distance Learning Courses Available.

Nursing Student Activities Nursing Honor Society, Sigma Theta Tau, Student Nurses' Association.

Nursing Student Resources Academic advising; academic or career counseling; assistance for students with disabilities; bookstore; campus computer network; career placement assistance; computer lab; computer-assisted instruction; e-mail services; interactive nursing skills videos; Internet; learning resource lab; library services; nursing audiovisuals; remedial services; skills, simulation, or other laboratory; tutoring.

Library Facilities 360,000 volumes in health, 60 volumes in nursing; 2,400 periodical subscriptions health-care related.

BACCALAUREATE PROGRAMS

Degree BSN

Available Programs Generic Baccalaureate; RN Baccalaureate.

Site Options Baltimore-Shady Grove, MD.

Study Options Full-time and part-time.

Online Degree Options Yes.

Program Entrance Requirements Minimum overall college GPA of 3.0, transcript of college record, CPR certification, written essay, health exam, health insurance, immunizations, 2 letters of recommendation, minimum GPA in nursing prerequisites of 3.0, prerequisite course work. *Application deadline:* 2/1 (fall), 9/1 (spring). *Application fee:* $50.

Expenses (2009–10) *Tuition, area resident:* full-time $6890; part-time $301 per credit hour. *Tuition, nonresident:* full-time $20,629; part-time $484 per credit hour. *International tuition:* $20,629 full-time. *Room and board:* room only: $850 per academic year. *Required fees:* full-time $1366; part-time $823 per term.

Financial Aid 90% of baccalaureate students in nursing programs received some form of financial aid in 2008–09.

Contact Ms. Melissa Egerton, Admissions Counselor, Master's Program in Nursing, University of Maryland, Baltimore, 655 West Lombard Street, Room 102, Student Services, Baltimore, MD 21201. *Telephone:* 410-706-8346. *Fax:* 410-706-7238. *E-mail:* meger002@son.umaryland.edu.

GRADUATE PROGRAMS

Expenses (2009–10) *Tuition, state resident:* part-time $519 per credit hour. *Tuition, nonresident:* part-time $869 per credit hour. *Room and board:* room only: $850 per academic year. *Required fees:* part-time $685 per term.

Financial Aid 50% of graduate students in nursing programs received some form of financial aid in 2008–09. Fellowships, research assistantships, teaching assistantships, career-related internships or fieldwork and traineeships available. Aid available to part-time students. *Financial aid application deadline:* 2/15.

Contact Mr. Kevin Nies, Assistant Director of Admissions, Master's Program in Nursing, University of Maryland, Baltimore, 655 West Lombard Street, Room 102, Baltimore, MD 21201-1579. *Telephone:* 410-706-1281. *Fax:* 410-706-7238. *E-mail:* Knies001@son.umaryland.edu.

MASTER'S DEGREE PROGRAM

Degrees MS; MSN/JD; MSN/MBA; MSN/MPH

Available Programs Accelerated Master's for Non-Nursing College Graduates; Master's; RN to Master's.

Concentrations Available Clinical nurse leader; nurse anesthesia; nursing administration; nursing informatics. *Clinical nurse specialist programs in:* acute care, community health, critical care, pediatric, psychiatric/mental health, public health. *Nurse practitioner programs in:* acute care, adult health, family health, gerontology, pediatric, primary care, psychiatric/mental health.

Site Options Baltimore-Shady Grove, MD.

Study Options Full-time and part-time.

Online Degree Options Yes (online only).

Program Entrance Requirements Minimum overall college GPA of 3.0, transcript of college record, CPR certification, immunizations, interview, 2 letters of recommendation, nursing research course, physical assessment course, professional liability insurance/malpractice insurance, prerequisite course work, resume, statistics course, GRE General Test. *Application deadline:* 2/1 (fall), 9/1 (spring). *Application fee:* $50.

Advanced Placement Credit given for nursing courses completed elsewhere dependent upon specific evaluations.

Degree Requirements 30 total credit hours, comprehensive exam.

POST-MASTER'S PROGRAM

Areas of Study Nursing administration; nursing education; nursing informatics. *Clinical nurse specialist programs in:* community health, pediatric, psychiatric/mental health, public health. *Nurse practitioner programs in:* acute care, adult health, family health, gerontology, pediatric, primary care, psychiatric/mental health.

DOCTORAL DEGREE PROGRAM

Degree DNP

Available Programs Doctorate; Post-Baccalaureate Doctorate.

Areas of Study Addiction/substance abuse, aging, bio-behavioral research, biology of health and illness, community health, critical care, faculty preparation, family health, gerontology, health promotion/disease prevention, health-care systems, human health and illness, information systems, neuro-behavior, nursing administration, nursing education, nursing research, oncology.

Program Entrance Requirements Minimum overall college GPA of 3.0, interview by faculty committee, 3 letters of recommendation, MSN or equivalent, statistics course, vita. Application deadline: 2/15 (fall), 2/15 (winter), 2/15 (spring), 2/15 (summer). Application fee: $50.

Degree Requirements 60 total credit hours, written exam, residency.

CONTINUING EDUCATION PROGRAM

Contact Miss Gail Doerr, Executive Director of Communications, Master's Program in Nursing, University of Maryland, Baltimore, 655 West Lombard Street, Room 311D, Baltimore, MD 21201-1579. *Telephone:* 410-706-4122. *E-mail:* Doerr@son.umaryland.edu.

MASSACHUSETTS

American International College
Division of Nursing
Springfield, Massachusetts

http://www.aic.edu/pages/315.html

Founded in 1885

DEGREES • BSN • MSN

Nursing Program Faculty 11 (10% with doctorates).

Nursing Student Activities Nursing Honor Society, Student Nurses' Association.

Nursing Student Resources Academic advising; academic or career counseling; assistance for students with disabilities; bookstore; campus computer network; career placement assistance; computer lab; e-mail services; employment services for current students; externships; housing assistance; interactive nursing skills videos; Internet; learning resource lab; library services; nursing audiovisuals; other; placement services for program completers; resume preparation assistance; skills, simulation, or other laboratory; tutoring.

Library Facilities 118,000 volumes (750 in health, 275 in nursing); 390 periodical subscriptions (50 health-care related).

BACCALAUREATE PROGRAMS

Degree BSN

Available Programs Generic Baccalaureate; RN Baccalaureate.

Study Options Full-time and part-time.

Program Entrance Requirements Minimum overall college GPA of 2.75, transcript of college record, health exam, health insurance, high school biology, high school chemistry, 3 years high school math, 2 years high school science, high school transcript, immunizations, 1 letter of recommendation, minimum high school GPA of 2.5, minimum GPA in nursing prerequisites of 2.5, professional liability insurance/malpractice insurance. Transfer students are accepted.

Advanced Placement Credit by examination available. Credit given for nursing courses completed elsewhere dependent upon specific evaluations.

American International College (continued)

Contact Admission Services, Division of Nursing, American International College, 1000 State Street, Springfield, MA 01109. *Telephone:* 413-205-3201. *Fax:* 413-205-3051. *E-mail:* peter.miller@aic.edu.

GRADUATE PROGRAMS

Contact Director of Nursing, Division of Nursing, American International College, 1000 State Street, Springfield, MA 01109. *Telephone:* 413-205-3519. *Fax:* 413-205-3957. *E-mail:* anne.glanovsky@aic.edu.

MASTER'S DEGREE PROGRAM

Degree MSN

Available Programs Master's.

Concentrations Available Nursing administration; nursing education.

Study Options Part-time.

Program Entrance Requirements Clinical experience, minimum overall college GPA of 3.0, transcript of college record, CPR certification, immunizations, interview, 2 letters of recommendation, nursing research course, professional liability insurance/malpractice insurance, prerequisite course work, resume, statistics course.

Advanced Placement Credit given for nursing courses completed elsewhere dependent upon specific evaluations.

Degree Requirements 36 total credit hours, thesis or project.

Anna Maria College
Department of Nursing
Paxton, Massachusetts

http://www.annamaria.edu

Founded in 1946

DEGREE • BSN

Nursing Program Faculty 6 (16% with doctorates).

Baccalaureate Enrollment 32
Women 94% **Men** 6% **Minority** 6% **Part-time** 100%

Nursing Student Activities Sigma Theta Tau.

Nursing Student Resources Academic advising; academic or career counseling; assistance for students with disabilities; bookstore; campus computer network; career placement assistance; computer lab; e-mail services; employment services for current students; Internet; learning resource lab; library services; nursing audiovisuals; placement services for program completers; remedial services; resume preparation assistance; skills, simulation, or other laboratory; tutoring; unpaid internships.

Library Facilities 85,117 volumes (3,000 in health, 400 in nursing); 176 periodical subscriptions (22 health-care related).

BACCALAUREATE PROGRAMS

Degree BSN

Available Programs ADN to Baccalaureate; RN Baccalaureate.

Study Options Part-time.

Program Entrance Requirements Minimum overall college GPA of 2.5, transcript of college record, interview, 1 letter of recommendation, minimum high school GPA of 2.5, minimum GPA in nursing prerequisites of 2.5, RN licensure. Transfer students are accepted. *Application deadline:* Applications may be processed on a rolling basis for some programs. *Application fee:* $40.

Advanced Placement Credit by examination available. Credit given for nursing courses completed elsewhere dependent upon specific evaluations.

Expenses (2008–09) *Tuition:* part-time $850 per course.

Financial Aid *Gift aid (need-based):* Federal Pell, FSEOG, state, private, college/university gift aid from institutional funds. *Loans:* FFEL (Subsidized and Unsubsidized Stafford PLUS), Perkins, college/university. *Work-study:* Federal Work-Study. *Financial aid application deadline (priority):* 3/1.

Contact Dr. Audrey Marie Silveri, Director of BSN and Certificate Nursing Programs, Department of Nursing, Anna Maria College, 50 Sunset Lane, Paxton, MA 01612-1198. *Telephone:* 508-829-3316 Ext. 316. *Fax:* 508-849-3343 Ext. 371. *E-mail:* asilveri@annamaria.edu.

CONTINUING EDUCATION PROGRAM

Contact Dr. Audrey Marie Silveri, Director of BSN and Certificate Nursing Programs, Department of Nursing, Anna Maria College, 50 Sunset Lane, Paxton, MA 01612-1198. *Telephone:* 508-849-3316 Ext. 316. *Fax:* 508-849-3343 Ext. 371. *E-mail:* asilveri@annamaria.edu.

Atlantic Union College
Department of Nursing
South Lancaster, Massachusetts

http://www.atlanticuc.edu

Founded in 1882

DEGREE • BS

Nursing Program Faculty 3 (20% with doctorates).

Baccalaureate Enrollment 32
Women 97% **Men** 3% **Minority** 53% **Part-time** 59%

Nursing Student Activities Nursing Honor Society, Sigma Theta Tau.

Nursing Student Resources Academic advising; academic or career counseling; campus computer network; computer lab; computer-assisted instruction; e-mail services; employment services for current students; interactive nursing skills videos; Internet; learning resource lab; library services; nursing audiovisuals; remedial services; skills, simulation, or other laboratory; tutoring.

Library Facilities 153,827 volumes (1,478 in health, 892 in nursing); 76 periodical subscriptions health-care related.

BACCALAUREATE PROGRAMS

Degree BS

Available Programs ADN to Baccalaureate; RN Baccalaureate.

Study Options Full-time and part-time.

Program Entrance Requirements Minimum overall college GPA of 2.75, transcript of college record, CPR certification, written essay, health exam, health insurance, high school biology, high school chemistry, high school foreign language, 3 years high school math, 2 years high school science, high school transcript, immunizations, 2 letters of recommendation, minimum high school GPA of 2.75, minimum GPA in nursing prerequisites of 2.75, professional liability insurance/malpractice insurance, prerequisite course work, RN licensure. Transfer students are accepted. *Application deadline:* 5/25 (fall), 12/15 (winter). Applications may be processed on a rolling basis for some programs.

Advanced Placement Credit by examination available. Credit given for nursing courses completed elsewhere dependent upon specific evaluations.

Expenses (2008–09) *Tuition:* full-time $16,570; part-time $625 per credit hour. *Room and board:* $5000 per academic year. *Required fees:* full-time $1130; part-time $282 per term.

Financial Aid 50% of baccalaureate students in nursing programs received some form of financial aid in 2007–08.

Contact Dr. Lenora D. Follett, Chairperson, Department of Nursing, Atlantic Union College, 338 Main Street, PO Box 1000, South Lancaster, MA 01561-1000. *Telephone:* 978-368-2401. *Fax:* 978-368-2518. *E-mail:* lenora.follett@auc.edu.

Boston College
William F. Connell School of Nursing
Chestnut Hill, Massachusetts

http://www.bc.edu/nursing

Founded in 1863

DEGREES • BS • MS • MSN/MA • MSN/MBA • MSN/PHD • PHD

Nursing Program Faculty 83 (42% with doctorates).

Baccalaureate Enrollment 399
Women 97% **Men** 3% **Minority** 23% **International** 1%

Graduate Enrollment 313

Women 93% **Men** 7% **Minority** 10% **International** 3% **Part-time** 40%

Nursing Student Activities Nursing Honor Society, Sigma Theta Tau, Student Nurses' Association.

Nursing Student Resources Academic advising; academic or career counseling; assistance for students with disabilities; bookstore; campus computer network; career placement assistance; computer lab; computer-assisted instruction; e-mail services; employment services for current students; externships; housing assistance; interactive nursing skills videos; Internet; learning resource lab; library services; nursing audiovisuals; other; placement services for program completers; remedial services; resume preparation assistance; skills, simulation, or other laboratory; tutoring; unpaid internships.

Library Facilities 2.7 million volumes (65,000 in health, 20,000 in nursing); 31,664 periodical subscriptions (5,395 health-care related).

BACCALAUREATE PROGRAMS

Degree BS

Available Programs Generic Baccalaureate.

Study Options Full-time.

Program Entrance Requirements Transcript of college record, written essay, health exam, health insurance, high school biology, high school chemistry, high school foreign language, 4 years high school math, 3 years high school science, high school transcript, immunizations, 2 letters of recommendation. Transfer students are accepted. *Application deadline:* 1/1 (fall), 10/1 (winter). *Application fee:* $70.

Advanced Placement Credit given for nursing courses completed elsewhere dependent upon specific evaluations.

Expenses (2009–10) *Tuition:* full-time $48,340; part-time $1284 per course. *International tuition:* $48,340 full-time. *Room and board:* $14,350; room only: $9810 per academic year. *Required fees:* full-time $2936.

Financial Aid 65% of baccalaureate students in nursing programs received some form of financial aid in 2008–09. *Gift aid (need-based):* Federal Pell, FSEOG, state, private, college/university gift aid from institutional funds. *Loans:* Federal Nursing Student Loans, FFEL (Subsidized and Unsubsidized Stafford PLUS), Perkins, state. *Work-study:* Federal Work-Study. *Financial aid application deadline (priority):* 2/1.

Contact Ms. Christine Murphy, Undergraduate Program Assistant, William F. Connell School of Nursing, Boston College, 140 Commonwealth Avenue, Cushing Hall 202D, Chestnut Hill, MA 02467-3812. *Telephone:* 617-552-4925. *Fax:* 617-552-0745. *E-mail:* christine.murphy.1@bc.edu.

GRADUATE PROGRAMS

Expenses (2009–10) *Tuition:* full-time $12,600; part-time $1050 per credit. *International tuition:* $18,900 full-time. *Room and board:* room only: $8673 per academic year. *Required fees:* full-time $120; part-time $45 per term.

Financial Aid 85% of graduate students in nursing programs received some form of financial aid in 2008–09. 11 fellowships with partial tuition reimbursements available (averaging $12,092 per year), 10 research assistantships (averaging $19,500 per year), 5 teaching assistantships (averaging $13,346 per year) were awarded; Federal Work-Study, institutionally sponsored loans, scholarships, traineeships, and tuition waivers (partial) also available. Aid available to part-time students. *Financial aid application deadline:* 3/1.

Contact Ms. Marybeth Crowley, Graduate Programs Office, William F. Connell School of Nursing, Boston College, 140 Commonwealth Avenue, Cushing Hall, Chestnut Hill, MA 02467-3812. *Telephone:* 617-552-4928. *Fax:* 617-552-2121. *E-mail:* csongrad@bc.edu.

MASTER'S DEGREE PROGRAM

Degrees MS; MSN/MA; MSN/MBA; MSN/PhD

Available Programs Accelerated Master's; Accelerated Master's for Non-Nursing College Graduates; Accelerated Master's for Nurses with Non-Nursing Degrees; Master's; RN to Master's.

Concentrations Available Nurse anesthesia. *Clinical nurse specialist programs in:* adult health, community health, forensic nursing, gerontology, palliative care, pediatric, psychiatric/mental health. *Nurse practitioner programs in:* adult health, family health, gerontology, pediatric, psychiatric/mental health, women's health.

Study Options Full-time and part-time.

Program Entrance Requirements Minimum overall college GPA of 3.0, transcript of college record, written essay, 3 letters of recommendation, statistics course. *Application deadline:* 11/1 (fall), 9/15 (spring). Applications may be processed on a rolling basis for some programs. *Application fee:* $40.

Advanced Placement Credit given for nursing courses completed elsewhere dependent upon specific evaluations.

Degree Requirements 45 total credit hours, comprehensive exam.

POST-MASTER'S PROGRAM

Areas of Study Nurse anesthesia; nursing education. *Clinical nurse specialist programs in:* adult health, community health, forensic nursing, gerontology, palliative care, pediatric, psychiatric/mental health. *Nurse practitioner programs in:* adult health, family health, gerontology, pediatric, psychiatric/mental health, women's health.

DOCTORAL DEGREE PROGRAM

Degree PhD

Available Programs Doctorate; Post-Baccalaureate Doctorate.

Areas of Study Addiction/substance abuse, advanced practice nursing, aging, bio-behavioral research, biology of health and illness, clinical practice, community health, ethics, family health, forensic nursing, gerontology, health promotion/disease prevention, human health and illness, illness and transition, individualized study, maternity-newborn, neuro-behavior, nurse case management, nursing research, nursing science, oncology, urban health, women's health.

Program Entrance Requirements Minimum overall college GPA of 3.0, interview by faculty committee, interview, 3 letters of recommendation, MSN or equivalent, statistics course, vita, writing sample, GRE General Test. Application deadline: 12/31 (fall). Application fee: $40.

Degree Requirements 46 total credit hours, dissertation, oral exam, written exam.

CONTINUING EDUCATION PROGRAM

Contact Dr. Jean Weyman, Assistant Dean, Continuing Education, William F. Connell School of Nursing, Boston College, 140 Commonwealth Avenue, Service Building, 211F, Chestnut Hill, MA 02467-3812. *Telephone:* 617-552-4256. *Fax:* 617-552-0745. *E-mail:* jean.weyman@bc.edu.

Curry College
Division of Nursing
Milton, Massachusetts

http://www.curry.edu

Founded in 1879

DEGREES • BS **•** MSN

Nursing Program Faculty 48 (33% with doctorates).

Baccalaureate Enrollment 611

Women 92% **Men** 8% **Minority** 15% **Part-time** 48%

Graduate Enrollment 31

Women 97% **Men** 3% **Minority** 20% **Part-time** 100%

Nursing Student Activities Sigma Theta Tau, Student Nurses' Association.

Nursing Student Resources Academic advising; academic or career counseling; assistance for students with disabilities; bookstore; campus computer network; career placement assistance; computer lab; computer-assisted instruction; daycare for children of students; e-mail services; employment services for current students; housing assistance; interactive nursing skills videos; Internet; learning resource lab; library services; nursing audiovisuals; placement services for program completers; remedial services; resume preparation assistance; skills, simulation, or other laboratory; tutoring.

Library Facilities 139,000 volumes (5,867 in health, 4,589 in nursing); 29,800 periodical subscriptions (162 health-care related).

BACCALAUREATE PROGRAMS

Degree BS

Available Programs Accelerated Baccalaureate for Second Degree; Generic Baccalaureate; RN Baccalaureate; RPN to Baccalaureate.

Curry College (continued)

Site Options Boston, MA; Plymouth, MA.

Study Options Full-time.

Program Entrance Requirements Written essay, health exam, health insurance, high school biology, high school chemistry, high school foreign language, 4 years high school math, 4 years high school science, high school transcript, immunizations, 1 letter of recommendation, minimum high school GPA of 2.75, minimum GPA in nursing prerequisites of 3.0. Transfer students are accepted. *Application deadline:* 4/1 (fall). Applications may be processed on a rolling basis for some programs. *Application fee:* $50.

Advanced Placement Credit by examination available. Credit given for nursing courses completed elsewhere dependent upon specific evaluations.

Expenses (2009–10) *Tuition:* full-time $28,000; part-time $933 per credit. *Room and board:* $11,960; room only: $6210 per academic year. *Required fees:* full-time $1955.

Financial Aid 70% of baccalaureate students in nursing programs received some form of financial aid in 2008–09. *Gift aid (need-based):* Federal Pell, FSEOG, state, private, college/university gift aid from institutional funds. *Loans:* FFEL (Subsidized and Unsubsidized Stafford PLUS), Perkins, state. *Work-study:* Federal Work-Study. *Financial aid application deadline (priority):* 3/1.

Contact Miss Jane Fidler, Dean of Admission, Division of Nursing, Curry College, 1071 Blue Hill Avenue, Milton, MA 02186. *Telephone:* 800-669-0686. *Fax:* 617-333-2114. *E-mail:* jfidler0803@curry.edu.

GRADUATE PROGRAMS

Expenses (2009–10) *Tuition:* part-time $780 per credit.

Contact Judy Hammond, Division of Nursing, Curry College, 1071 Blue Hill Avenue, Milton, MA 02186. *Telephone:* 617-333-2243. *Fax:* 617-333-6680. *E-mail:* msn@curry.edu.

MASTER'S DEGREE PROGRAM

Degree MSN

Available Programs Master's; RN to Master's.

Concentrations Available Clinical nurse leader.

Site Options Boston, MA.

Program Entrance Requirements Minimum overall college GPA of 3.0, transcript of college record, written essay, immunizations, 2 letters of recommendation, nursing research course, physical assessment course, resume, statistics course. *Application deadline:* Applications may be processed on a rolling basis for some programs. *Application fee:* $50.

Degree Requirements 37 total credit hours, thesis or project.

Elms College
Division of Nursing
Chicopee, Massachusetts

Founded in 1928

DEGREES • BS • MSN

Nursing Program Faculty 13 (46% with doctorates).

Baccalaureate Enrollment 200
Women 87% **Men** 13% **Minority** 11% **Part-time** 35%

Graduate Enrollment 42
Women 97% **Men** 3% **Minority** 5% **Part-time** 50%

Nursing Student Activities Nursing Honor Society, Sigma Theta Tau, Student Nurses' Association.

Nursing Student Resources Academic advising; academic or career counseling; assistance for students with disabilities; bookstore; campus computer network; career placement assistance; computer lab; computer-assisted instruction; e-mail services; employment services for current students; externships; interactive nursing skills videos; Internet; learning resource lab; library services; nursing audiovisuals; resume preparation assistance; skills, simulation, or other laboratory; tutoring.

Library Facilities 111,379 volumes (3,832 in health, 3,000 in nursing); 529 periodical subscriptions (130 health-care related).

BACCALAUREATE PROGRAMS

Degree BS

Available Programs Generic Baccalaureate; RN Baccalaureate.

Study Options Full-time and part-time.

Program Entrance Requirements Minimum overall college GPA of 2.5, transcript of college record, CPR certification, written essay, health exam, health insurance, high school biology, high school chemistry, high school transcript, immunizations, interview, 2 letters of recommendation, minimum high school GPA of 3.3, minimum high school rank 25%, minimum GPA in nursing prerequisites of 2.5, professional liability insurance/malpractice insurance. Transfer students are accepted. *Application deadline:* Applications may be processed on a rolling basis for some programs. *Application fee:* $30.

Advanced Placement Credit given for nursing courses completed elsewhere dependent upon specific evaluations.

Expenses (2009–10) *Tuition:* full-time $24,788. *Room and board:* $9446 per academic year.

Financial Aid 90% of baccalaureate students in nursing programs received some form of financial aid in 2008–09.

Contact Dr. Kathleen B. Scoble, EdD, RN, Director and Chair, Division of Nursing, Division of Nursing, Elms College, 291 Springfield Street, Chicopee, MA 01013. *Telephone:* 413-265-2237. *Fax:* 413-265-2335. *E-mail:* scoblek@elms.edu.

GRADUATE PROGRAMS

Expenses (2009–10) *Tuition:* part-time $588 per credit.

Contact Cynthia Dakin, PhD, RN, Graduate Program Coordinator, Division of Nursing, Elms College, 291 Springfield Street, Chicopee, MA 01013. *Telephone:* 413-265-2455. *E-mail:* dakinc@elms.edu.

MASTER'S DEGREE PROGRAM

Degree MSN

Available Programs Master's; RN to Master's.

Concentrations Available Nursing administration; nursing education.

Program Entrance Requirements Minimum overall college GPA of 3.0, transcript of college record, CPR certification, written essay, immunizations, interview, 2 letters of recommendation, professional liability insurance/malpractice insurance, resume. *Application deadline:* Applications may be processed on a rolling basis for some programs. *Application fee:* $30.

Degree Requirements 36 total credit hours, thesis or project.

Emmanuel College
Department of Nursing
Boston, Massachusetts

http://www.emmanuel.edu/GPP_Programs/ Bachelor_of_Science_in_Nursing_ (BSN).htm.

Founded in 1919

DEGREE • BSN

Nursing Program Faculty 14 (29% with doctorates).

Baccalaureate Enrollment 130
Women 98% **Men** 2% **Minority** 21% **Part-time** 88%

Distance Learning Courses Available.

Nursing Student Activities Sigma Theta Tau.

Nursing Student Resources Academic advising; academic or career counseling; assistance for students with disabilities; bookstore; campus computer network; computer lab; computer-assisted instruction; e-mail services; interactive nursing skills videos; Internet; learning resource lab; library services; nursing audiovisuals; skills, simulation, or other laboratory.

Library Facilities 131,000 volumes (1,705 in health, 1,000 in nursing); 1,063 periodical subscriptions (289 health-care related).

■ The Emmanuel College CCNE-accredited Nursing Program is designed specifically for the registered nurse. The faculty members believe that baccalaureate education builds on the prior educational and practice experiences of the registered nurse. The Nursing Program prepares a professional who thinks critically, communicates effectively, appreciates the diversity of human experience, and uses personal and professional values and standards in responsible, ethical practice. Liberal transfer-credit policies, a strong advisement program, and outstanding individualized clinical placements ensure that the Nursing Program works for practicing nurses. Evening and Saturday courses on two campus locations underpin the commitment to adult learners. Graduates report career and educational advancement.

BACCALAUREATE PROGRAMS
Degree BSN

Available Programs RN Baccalaureate.
Site Options Woburn, MA; Quincy, MA; Lowell, MA.
Program Entrance Requirements Transcript of college record, written essay, interview, 2 letters of recommendation, RN licensure. Transfer students are accepted.
Expenses (2009–10) *Tuition:* part-time $1650 per course.
Financial Aid *Gift aid (need-based):* Federal Pell, FSEOG, state, private, college/university gift aid from institutional funds. *Loans:* FFEL (Subsidized and Unsubsidized Stafford PLUS), Perkins, state, alternative loans. *Work-study:* Federal Work-Study, part-time campus jobs. *Financial aid application deadline (priority):* 4/1.
Contact Dr. Mary Diane Arathuzik, RN, Chair and Associate Professor, Department of Nursing, Department of Nursing, Emmanuel College, 400 The Fenway, Boston, MA 02115. *Telephone:* 617-735-9945. *Fax:* 617-735-9797. *E-mail:* arathuzik@emmanuel.edu.

Endicott College
Major in Nursing
Beverly, Massachusetts

http://www.endicott.edu
Founded in 1939
DEGREES • BS • MSN

Nursing Program Faculty 24 (1% with doctorates).
Baccalaureate Enrollment 120
Women 95% **Men** 5% **Minority** 2%
Nursing Student Activities Nursing Honor Society, Student Nurses' Association.
Nursing Student Resources Academic advising; academic or career counseling; assistance for students with disabilities; bookstore; campus computer network; career placement assistance; computer lab; e-mail services; externships; interactive nursing skills videos; Internet; learning resource lab; library services; nursing audiovisuals; resume preparation assistance; skills, simulation, or other laboratory; tutoring; unpaid internships.
Library Facilities 120,476 volumes (2,828 in health, 624 in nursing); 67,643 periodical subscriptions (55 health-care related).

BACCALAUREATE PROGRAMS
Degree BS

Available Programs Generic Baccalaureate; RN Baccalaureate.
Site Options Beverly, MA.
Study Options Full-time.
Program Entrance Requirements Minimum overall college GPA of 2.5, transcript of college record, written essay, health exam, health insurance, high school biology, high school chemistry, 3 years high school math, 2 years high school science, high school transcript, immunizations, 1 letter of recommendation, minimum high school GPA of 2.5, minimum high school rank 50%, minimum GPA in nursing prerequisites of 2.5. Transfer students are accepted.
Advanced Placement Credit given for nursing courses completed elsewhere dependent upon specific evaluations.

Financial Aid 88% of baccalaureate students in nursing programs received some form of financial aid in 2008–09. *Gift aid (need-based):* Federal Pell, FSEOG, state, private, college/university gift aid from institutional funds. *Loans:* FFEL (Subsidized and Unsubsidized Stafford PLUS), Perkins, college/university. *Work-study:* Federal Work-Study. *Financial aid application deadline (priority):* 3/15.
Contact Mr. Thomas J. Redman, Vice President for Admissions and Financial Aid, Major in Nursing, Endicott College, 376 Hale Street, Beverly, MA 01915. *Telephone:* 978-921-1000. *Fax:* 978-232-2500. *E-mail:* admissio@endicott.edu.

GRADUATE PROGRAMS
Contact Dean Kelly L. Fisher, PhD, Dean, School of Nursing, Major in Nursing, Endicott College, 375 Hale Street, Beverly, MA 01915. *E-mail:* Kfisher@endicott.edu.

MASTER'S DEGREE PROGRAM
Degree MSN

Available Programs Master's.
Concentrations Available Nursing administration; nursing education.
Site Options Beverly, MA.
Program Entrance Requirements Clinical experience, transcript of college record, written essay, letters of recommendation, statistics course.
Degree Requirements 33 total credit hours, thesis or project.

CONTINUING EDUCATION PROGRAM
Contact Kelly Fisher, Dean, School of Nursing and Health Sciences, Major in Nursing, Endicott College, 376 Hale Street, Beverly, MA 01915. *Telephone:* 978-232-2328. *Fax:* 978-232-3100. *E-mail:* kfisher@endicott.edu.

Fitchburg State College
Department of Nursing
Fitchburg, Massachusetts

http://www.fsc.edu/nursing/
Founded in 1894
DEGREES • BS • M SC N

Nursing Program Faculty 18 (27% with doctorates).
Distance Learning Courses Available.
Nursing Student Activities Sigma Theta Tau, Student Nurses' Association.
Nursing Student Resources Academic advising; academic or career counseling; assistance for students with disabilities; bookstore; campus computer network; career placement assistance; computer lab; computer-assisted instruction; e-mail services; employment services for current students; housing assistance; interactive nursing skills videos; Internet; learning resource lab; library services; nursing audiovisuals; remedial services; resume preparation assistance; skills, simulation, or other laboratory; tutoring; unpaid internships.
Library Facilities 259,321 volumes (111 in health, 74 in nursing); 2,967 periodical subscriptions (1,218 health-care related).

BACCALAUREATE PROGRAMS
Degree BS

Available Programs ADN to Baccalaureate; RN Baccalaureate.
Study Options Full-time.
Program Entrance Requirements Minimum overall college GPA of 2.5, transcript of college record, CPR certification, written essay, health exam, health insurance, high school biology, high school chemistry, 3 years high school math, 3 years high school science, high school transcript, immunizations, minimum high school GPA of 3.0, minimum GPA in nursing prerequisites of 2.5, prerequisite course work. Transfer students are accepted. *Application deadline:* 1/1 (fall), 11/1 (spring). *Application fee:* $25.
Financial Aid 76% of baccalaureate students in nursing programs received some form of financial aid in 2008–09. *Gift aid (need-based):* Federal Pell, FSEOG, state, private, college/university gift aid from institutional funds. *Loans:* Federal Nursing Student Loans, Federal Direct (Subsidized and Unsubsidized Stafford PLUS), Perkins, state. *Work-study:* Federal Work-Study. *Financial aid application deadline (priority):* 3/1.

Fitchburg State College (continued)

Contact Office of Admissions, Department of Nursing, Fitchburg State College, 160 Pearl Street, Fitchburg, MA 01420-2697. *Telephone:* 978-665-3144. *Fax:* 978-665-4540. *E-mail:* admissions@fsc.edu.

GRADUATE PROGRAMS

Expenses (2009–10) *Tuition, state resident:* part-time $150 per credit hour. *Tuition, nonresident:* part-time $150 per credit hour. *Required fees:* part-time $192 per credit.

Financial Aid 11% of graduate students in nursing programs received some form of financial aid in 2008–09.

Contact Dr. Rachel Boersma, RN, Chairperson, Department of Nursing, Fitchburg State College, 160 Pearl Street, Fitchburg, MA 01420-2697. *Telephone:* 978-665-3036. *Fax:* 978-665-3658. *E-mail:* rboersma@fsc.edu.

MASTER'S DEGREE PROGRAM

Degree M Sc N

Available Programs Master's.

Concentrations Available *Clinical nurse specialist programs in:* forensic nursing.

Study Options Part-time.

Online Degree Options Yes (online only).

Program Entrance Requirements Clinical experience, computer literacy, minimum overall college GPA of 2.8, transcript of college record, CPR certification, written essay, immunizations, 3 letters of recommendation, nursing research course, physical assessment course, prerequisite course work, resume, statistics course. *Application deadline:* 10/1 (fall), 2/15 (spring). *Application fee:* $25.

Degree Requirements 37 total credit hours, thesis or project.

POST-MASTER'S PROGRAM

Areas of Study *Clinical nurse specialist programs in:* forensic nursing.

Framingham State College
Department of Nursing
Framingham, Massachusetts

http://www.framingham.edu/nursing

Founded in 1839

DEGREES • BS • MSN

Nursing Program Faculty 8 (75% with doctorates).

Baccalaureate Enrollment 74
Women 85% **Men** 15% **Minority** 33% **International** 2% **Part-time** 90%

Graduate Enrollment 58
Women 98% **Men** 2% **Minority** 3% **International** 1% **Part-time** 100%

Nursing Student Activities Sigma Theta Tau.

Nursing Student Resources Academic advising; academic or career counseling; assistance for students with disabilities; bookstore; campus computer network; career placement assistance; computer lab; computer-assisted instruction; daycare for children of students; e-mail services; employment services for current students; housing assistance; interactive nursing skills videos; Internet; learning resource lab; library services; nursing audiovisuals; placement services for program completers; remedial services; resume preparation assistance; skills, simulation, or other laboratory; tutoring.

Library Facilities 5,338 volumes in health, 5,338 volumes in nursing; 1,200 periodical subscriptions health-care related.

BACCALAUREATE PROGRAMS

Degree BS

Available Programs ADN to Baccalaureate.

Study Options Full-time and part-time.

Program Entrance Requirements Minimum overall college GPA of 3.0, transcript of college record, written essay, RN licensure. Transfer students are accepted. *Application deadline:* Applications may be processed on a rolling basis for some programs. *Application fee:* $50.

Advanced Placement Credit by examination available. Credit given for nursing courses completed elsewhere dependent upon specific evaluations.

Expenses (2009–10) *Tuition, state resident:* full-time $970; part-time $162 per course. *Tuition, nonresident:* full-time $7050; part-time $1175 per course. *International tuition:* $7050 full-time. *Room and board:* $8518; room only: $5248 per academic year. *Required fees:* part-time $232 per credit.

Financial Aid 60% of baccalaureate students in nursing programs received some form of financial aid in 2008–09.

Contact Dr. Susan L. Conrad, RN, Chairperson and Professor, Department of Nursing, Framingham State College, 100 State Street, H220, Framingham, MA 01701. *Telephone:* 508-626-4713. *Fax:* 508-626-4746. *E-mail:* sconrad@framingham.edu.

GRADUATE PROGRAMS

Expenses (2009–10) *Tuition, state resident:* part-time $995 per course. *Tuition, nonresident:* part-time $995 per course.

Contact Dr. Susan L. Conrad, RN, Chairperson and Professor, Department of Nursing, Framingham State College, 100 State Street, H220, Framingham, MA 01701. *Telephone:* 508-626-4713. *Fax:* 508-626-4746. *E-mail:* sconrad@framingham.edu.

MASTER'S DEGREE PROGRAM

Degree MSN

Available Programs Master's.

Concentrations Available Nursing administration; nursing education.

Study Options Part-time.

Program Entrance Requirements Minimum overall college GPA of 3.0, transcript of college record, written essay, interview, 3 letters of recommendation, nursing research course, resume, statistics course. *Application deadline:* 6/1 (fall). Applications may be processed on a rolling basis for some programs. *Application fee:* $50.

Degree Requirements 36 total credit hours, thesis or project.

CONTINUING EDUCATION PROGRAM

Contact Dr. Susan L. Conrad, RN, Chairperson and Professor, Department of Nursing, Framingham State College, 100 State Street, H220, Framingham, MA 01701. *Telephone:* 508-626-4713. *Fax:* 508-626-4746. *E-mail:* sconrad@framingham.edu.

Massachusetts College of Pharmacy and Health Sciences
School of Nursing
Boston, Massachusetts

Founded in 1823

DEGREE • BSN

Nursing Program Faculty 16 (44% with doctorates).

Baccalaureate Enrollment 358
Women 66.3% **Men** 33.7% **Minority** 35% **International** 3%

Distance Learning Courses Available.

Nursing Student Activities Nursing Honor Society, Sigma Theta Tau, Student Nurses' Association, nursing club.

Nursing Student Resources Academic advising; academic or career counseling; assistance for students with disabilities; bookstore; campus computer network; career placement assistance; computer lab; computer-assisted instruction; e-mail services; employment services for current students; housing assistance; interactive nursing skills videos; Internet; learning resource lab; library services; nursing audiovisuals; remedial services; resume preparation assistance; skills, simulation, or other laboratory; tutoring.

Library Facilities 17,400 volumes in health, 1,200 volumes in nursing; 10,000 periodical subscriptions health-care related.

BACCALAUREATE PROGRAMS

Degree BSN

Available Programs Accelerated Baccalaureate; Accelerated Baccalaureate for Second Degree.

Site Options Manchester, NH; Worcester, MA.

Study Options Full-time.

Program Entrance Requirements Minimum overall college GPA of 2.5, written essay, high school biology, high school chemistry, 3 years high school math, 2 years high school science, high school transcript, 2 letters of recommendation, prerequisite course work. Transfer students are accepted. *Application deadline:* 2/1 (fall), 10/1 (spring). *Application fee:* $70.

Expenses (2008–09) *Tuition:* full-time $22,900; part-time $840 per credit hour. *Room and board:* $11,600; room only: $7100 per academic year. *Required fees:* full-time $360.

Financial Aid 90% of baccalaureate students in nursing programs received some form of financial aid in 2007–08. *Gift aid (need-based):* Federal Pell, FSEOG, state, private, college/university gift aid from institutional funds. *Loans:* Federal Direct (Subsidized and Unsubsidized Stafford PLUS), FFEL (Subsidized and Unsubsidized Stafford PLUS), Perkins, Health Professions Loan. *Work-study:* Federal Work-Study. *Financial aid application deadline:* 3/15.

Contact Office of Admissions, School of Nursing, Massachusetts College of Pharmacy and Health Sciences, 179 Longwood Avenue, Boston, MA 02115. *Telephone:* 800-225-5506. *E-mail:* admissions@mcphs.edu.

CONTINUING EDUCATION PROGRAM

Contact Dawna Burrus, Director of Continuing Education, School of Nursing, Massachusetts College of Pharmacy and Health Sciences, 179 Longwood Avenue, Boston, MA 02115. *Telephone:* 617-735-1080. *E-mail:* dawna.burrus@mcphs.edu.

MGH Institute of Health Professions
School of Nursing
Boston, Massachusetts

http://www.mghihp.edu

Founded in 1977

DEGREES • BSN • DNP • MS

Nursing Program Faculty 49 (50% with doctorates).

Baccalaureate Enrollment 86
Women 81% **Men** 19% **Minority** 8%

Graduate Enrollment 311
Women 85% **Men** 15% **Minority** 12% **International** 1% **Part-time** 23%

Distance Learning Courses Available.

Nursing Student Activities Nursing Honor Society, Student Nurses' Association.

Nursing Student Resources Academic advising; academic or career counseling; assistance for students with disabilities; bookstore; campus computer network; career placement assistance; computer lab; computer-assisted instruction; daycare for children of students; e-mail services; Internet; learning resource lab; library services; nursing audiovisuals; remedial services; resume preparation assistance; skills, simulation, or other laboratory; tutoring.

Library Facilities 35,000 volumes in health, 13,000 volumes in nursing; 1,400 periodical subscriptions health-care related.

BACCALAUREATE PROGRAMS

Degree BSN

Available Programs Accelerated Baccalaureate.

Site Options Boston, MA.

Study Options Full-time.

Program Entrance Requirements Transcript of college record, written essay, health insurance, immunizations, 3 letters of recommendation, minimum GPA in nursing prerequisites of 3.0, prerequisite course work. Transfer students are accepted. *Application deadline:* 11/1 (summer). *Application fee:* $65.

Advanced Placement Credit by examination available. Credit given for nursing courses completed elsewhere dependent upon specific evaluations.

Expenses (2009–10) *Tuition:* full-time $36,000. *Required fees:* full-time $1575.

Financial Aid 89% of baccalaureate students in nursing programs received some form of financial aid in 2008–09.

Contact Admissions, School of Nursing, MGH Institute of Health Professions, 36 1st Avenue, Boston, MA 02129. *Telephone:* 617-726-3140. *Fax:* 617-726-8010. *E-mail:* admissions@mghihp.edu.

GRADUATE PROGRAMS

Expenses (2009–10) *Tuition:* part-time $943 per credit. *Required fees:* part-time $525 per term.

Financial Aid 73% of graduate students in nursing programs received some form of financial aid in 2008–09. 1 research assistantship (averaging $1,200 per year), 2 teaching assistantships (averaging $1,200 per year) were awarded; career-related internships or fieldwork, scholarships, traineeships, tuition waivers (full and partial), and unspecified assistantships also available. Aid available to part-time students. *Financial aid application deadline:* 3/1.

Contact Office of Student Affairs, School of Nursing, MGH Institute of Health Professions, PO Box 6357, Boston, MA 02114. *Telephone:* 617-726-3140. *Fax:* 617-726-8010. *E-mail:* admissions@mghihp.edu.

MASTER'S DEGREE PROGRAM

Degree MS

Available Programs Master's; Master's for Non-Nursing College Graduates; Master's for Nurses with Non-Nursing Degrees; RN to Master's.

Concentrations Available Nursing education. *Clinical nurse specialist programs in:* acute care, adult health, family health, gerontology, pediatric, psychiatric/mental health. *Nurse practitioner programs in:* acute care, adult health, family health, gerontology, pediatric, primary care, psychiatric/mental health, women's health.

Site Options Boston, MA.

Study Options Full-time and part-time.

Program Entrance Requirements Minimum overall college GPA of 3.0, transcript of college record, CPR certification, written essay, immunizations, 3 letters of recommendation, professional liability insurance/malpractice insurance, prerequisite course work, resume, statistics course, GRE General Test. *Application deadline:* 1/10 (fall). *Application fee:* $65.

Advanced Placement Credit by examination available. Credit given for nursing courses completed elsewhere dependent upon specific evaluations.

Degree Requirements Thesis or project.

POST-MASTER'S PROGRAM

Areas of Study *Clinical nurse specialist programs in:* psychiatric/mental health. *Nurse practitioner programs in:* acute care, adult health, gerontology, pediatric, primary care, psychiatric/mental health, women's health.

DOCTORAL DEGREE PROGRAM

Degree DNP

Available Programs Doctorate; Doctorate for Nurses with Non-Nursing Degrees.

Site Options Boston, MA.

Program Entrance Requirements interview by faculty committee, 3 letters of recommendation, MSN or equivalent, vita. Application deadline: Applications may be processed on a rolling basis for some programs. Application fee: $65.

Degree Requirements 43 total credit hours, residency.

Northeastern University
School of Nursing
Boston, Massachusetts

http://neu.edu/bouve/nursing/

Founded in 1898

Northeastern University (continued)
DEGREES • BSN • MS • MSN/MBA • PHD

Nursing Program Faculty 89 (25% with doctorates).

Baccalaureate Enrollment 433
Women 94% **Men** 6% **Minority** 14% **International** 1%

Graduate Enrollment 460
Women 74% **Men** 26% **Minority** 17% **International** 1% **Part-time** 31%

Nursing Student Activities Nursing Honor Society, Sigma Theta Tau, Student Nurses' Association.

Nursing Student Resources Academic advising; academic or career counseling; assistance for students with disabilities; bookstore; campus computer network; career placement assistance; computer lab; computer-assisted instruction; e-mail services; employment services for current students; externships; housing assistance; interactive nursing skills videos; Internet; learning resource lab; library services; nursing audiovisuals; other; paid internships; placement services for program completers; resume preparation assistance; skills, simulation, or other laboratory; tutoring.

Library Facilities 994,122 volumes (59,933 in health, 3,652 in nursing); 6,773 periodical subscriptions (2,540 health-care related).

BACCALAUREATE PROGRAMS

Degree BSN

Available Programs Generic Baccalaureate; RN Baccalaureate.
Study Options Full-time.

Program Entrance Requirements Transcript of college record, written essay, health exam, high school biology, high school chemistry, 3 years high school math, 2 years high school science, high school transcript, immunizations, 2 letters of recommendation, prerequisite course work. *Application deadline:* 1/15 (fall). *Application fee:* $70.

Advanced Placement Credit given for nursing courses completed elsewhere dependent upon specific evaluations.

Expenses (2009–10) *Tuition:* full-time $34,950. *International tuition:* $34,950 full-time. *Room and board:* $12,350; room only: $6530 per academic year. *Required fees:* full-time $412.

Financial Aid 89% of baccalaureate students in nursing programs received some form of financial aid in 2008–09. *Gift aid (need-based):* Federal Pell, FSEOG, state, private, college/university gift aid from institutional funds, Federal Nursing. *Loans:* Federal Nursing Student Loans, Federal Direct (Subsidized and Unsubsidized Stafford PLUS), Perkins, state, MEFA, TERI, CitiAssist. *Work-study:* Federal Work-Study, part-time campus jobs. *Financial aid application deadline (priority):* 2/15.

Contact Undergraduate Admissions, School of Nursing, Northeastern University, 360 Huntington Avenue, 150 Richards Hall, Boston, MA 02115. *Telephone:* 617-373-2200. *Fax:* 617-373-8780. *E-mail:* admissions@neu.edu.

GRADUATE PROGRAMS

Expenses (2009–10) *Tuition:* full-time $25,560; part-time $1065 per credit hour. *International tuition:* $25,560 full-time. *Required fees:* full-time $256; part-time $37 per term.

Financial Aid 56% of graduate students in nursing programs received some form of financial aid in 2008–09. 7 teaching assistantships with full tuition reimbursements available (averaging $13,958 per year) were awarded; fellowships, research assistantships with full tuition reimbursements available, career-related internships or fieldwork, institutionally sponsored loans, tuition waivers (full and partial), and unspecified assistantships also available. Aid available to part-time students. *Financial aid application deadline:* 7/1.

Contact Ms. Molly Schnabel, Director of Graduate Admissions and Student Services, School of Nursing, Northeastern University, 360 Huntington Avenue, 123 Behrakis Health Sciences Building, Boston, MA 02115. *Telephone:* 617-373-3501. *Fax:* 617-373-4701. *E-mail:* bouvegrad@neu.edu.

MASTER'S DEGREE PROGRAM

Degrees MS; MSN/MBA

Available Programs Accelerated Master's for Non-Nursing College Graduates; Master's; RN to Master's.

Concentrations Available Nurse anesthesia; nursing administration. *Clinical nurse specialist programs in:* psychiatric/mental health. *Nurse practitioner programs in:* acute care, adult health, family health, neonatal health, pediatric, primary care, psychiatric/mental health.

Study Options Full-time and part-time.

Program Entrance Requirements Minimum overall college GPA of 3.0, transcript of college record, written essay, immunizations, 3 letters of recommendation, professional liability insurance/malpractice insurance, resume, statistics course, GRE General Test. *Application deadline:* Applications may be processed on a rolling basis for some programs. *Application fee:* $50.

Advanced Placement Credit given for nursing courses completed elsewhere dependent upon specific evaluations.

Degree Requirements 43 total credit hours.

POST-MASTER'S PROGRAM

Areas of Study Nurse anesthesia; nursing administration. *Clinical nurse specialist programs in:* psychiatric/mental health. *Nurse practitioner programs in:* acute care, adult health, family health, neonatal health, pediatric, primary care, psychiatric/mental health.

DOCTORAL DEGREE PROGRAM

Degree PhD

Available Programs Doctorate; Post-Baccalaureate Doctorate.

Areas of Study Nursing research, nursing science, urban health.

Program Entrance Requirements Minimum overall college GPA of 3.5, interview by faculty committee, interview, 3 letters of recommendation, statistics course, writing sample. Application deadline: 3/1 (fall). Application fee: $50.

Degree Requirements 49 total credit hours, dissertation.

CONTINUING EDUCATION PROGRAM

Contact College of Professional Studies, School of Nursing, Northeastern University, 50 Nightingale Hall, Boston, MA 02115. *Telephone:* 877-668-7727. *E-mail:* cpsadmissions@neu.edu.

Regis College
School of Nursing and Health Professions
Weston, Massachusetts

http://regisnet.regiscollege.edu/nursing/pro_ovrview.htm

Founded in 1927

DEGREES • BSN • DNP • MSN

Nursing Program Faculty 36 (75% with doctorates).

Baccalaureate Enrollment 69
Women 92% **Men** 8%

Graduate Enrollment 292
Women 91% **Men** 9% **Minority** 14% **Part-time** 70%

Distance Learning Courses Available.

Nursing Student Activities Sigma Theta Tau, Student Nurses' Association, nursing club.

Nursing Student Resources Academic advising; academic or career counseling; assistance for students with disabilities; bookstore; campus computer network; computer lab; e-mail services; Internet; learning resource lab; library services; nursing audiovisuals; resume preparation assistance; skills, simulation, or other laboratory; tutoring.

Library Facilities 135,458 volumes (6,300 in health, 4,700 in nursing); 607 periodical subscriptions (228 health-care related).

BACCALAUREATE PROGRAMS

Degree BSN

Available Programs ADN to Baccalaureate; Accelerated Baccalaureate; Accelerated Baccalaureate for Second Degree; Accelerated RN Baccalaureate; Baccalaureate for Second Degree; Generic Baccalaureate; RN Baccalaureate.

Site Options Boston, MA; Medford, MA; Brighton, MA.

Study Options Full-time.

Program Entrance Requirements Written essay, health exam, health insurance, high school foreign language, 3 years high school math, 2 years high school science, high school transcript, immunizations, 2 letters of recommendation, minimum high school GPA of 3.0, minimum high school rank 40%, minimum GPA in nursing prerequisites. Transfer students are accepted. *Application deadline:* Applications may be processed on a rolling basis for some programs. *Application fee:* $50.

Advanced Placement Credit by examination available. Credit given for nursing courses completed elsewhere dependent upon specific evaluations.

Expenses (2009–10) *Tuition:* full-time $28,912.

Financial Aid 85% of baccalaureate students in nursing programs received some form of financial aid in 2008–09. *Gift aid (need-based):* Federal Pell, FSEOG, state, private, college/university gift aid from institutional funds. *Loans:* Federal Direct (Subsidized and Unsubsidized Stafford PLUS), Perkins, state. *Work-study:* Federal Work-Study, part-time campus jobs. *Financial aid application deadline (priority):* 2/15.

Contact Dr. Antionette Hays, Dean, School of Nursing and Health Professions, School of Nursing and Health Professions, Regis College, 235 Wellesley Street, Weston, MA 02493. *Telephone:* 781-768-7090. *Fax:* 781-768-7071. *E-mail:* antoinette.hays@regiscollege.edu.

GRADUATE PROGRAMS

Expenses (2009–10) *Tuition:* full-time $28,912; part-time $800 per credit.

Financial Aid 52% of graduate students in nursing programs received some form of financial aid in 2008–09. 13 research assistantships were awarded; Federal Work-Study, scholarships, traineeships, and unspecified assistantships also available. Aid available to part-time students.

Contact Ms. Claudia C. Pouravelis, Director of Graduate Admission, School of Nursing and Health Professions, Regis College, 235 Wellesley Street, Weston, MA 02493. *Telephone:* 781-768-7058. *Fax:* 781-768-7071. *E-mail:* claudia.pouravelis@regiscollege.edu.

MASTER'S DEGREE PROGRAM

Degree MSN

Available Programs Accelerated AD/RN to Master's; Accelerated Master's; Accelerated Master's for Non-Nursing College Graduates; Accelerated Master's for Nurses with Non-Nursing Degrees; Accelerated RN to Master's; Master's; Master's for Non-Nursing College Graduates; Master's for Nurses with Non-Nursing Degrees; RN to Master's.

Concentrations Available Clinical nurse leader; health-care administration; nurse case management; nursing administration; nursing education. *Clinical nurse specialist programs in:* acute care. *Nurse practitioner programs in:* adult health, family health, pediatric, primary care, psychiatric/mental health, women's health.

Site Options Boston, MA; Medford, MA; Brighton, MA.

Study Options Full-time and part-time.

Program Entrance Requirements Computer literacy, minimum overall college GPA of 3.0, transcript of college record, CPR certification, written essay, immunizations, interview, 3 letters of recommendation, physical assessment course, professional liability insurance/malpractice insurance, prerequisite course work, resume, statistics course, GRE General Test or MAT. *Application deadline:* Applications may be processed on a rolling basis for some programs. *Application fee:* $50.

Advanced Placement Credit by examination available. Credit given for nursing courses completed elsewhere dependent upon specific evaluations.

Degree Requirements 44 total credit hours, thesis or project.

POST-MASTER'S PROGRAM

Areas of Study Clinical nurse leader; health-care administration; nurse case management; nursing administration; nursing education. *Nurse practitioner programs in:* adult health, family health, pediatric, primary care, psychiatric/mental health, women's health.

DOCTORAL DEGREE PROGRAM

Degree DNP

Available Programs Doctorate; Post-Baccalaureate Doctorate.

Areas of Study Nursing administration, nursing education.

Site Options Boston, MA.

Program Entrance Requirements Clinical experience, minimum overall college GPA of 3.5, interview by faculty committee, interview, 2 letters of recommendation, MSN or equivalent, statistics course, vita, writing sample. Application deadline: Applications may be processed on a rolling basis for some programs. Application fee: $50.

Degree Requirements 50 total credit hours.

CONTINUING EDUCATION PROGRAM

Contact Dr. Antoinette Hays, Dean, School of Nursing and Health Professions, School of Nursing and Health Professions, Regis College, 235 Wellesley Street, Weston, MA 02493. *Telephone:* 781-768-7090. *Fax:* 781-768-7089. *E-mail:* antoinette.hays@regiscollege.edu.

See full description on page 514.

Salem State College
Program in Nursing
Salem, Massachusetts

http://www.salemstate.edu
Founded in 1854
DEGREES • BSN • MSN • MSN/MBA

Nursing Program Faculty 90 (25% with doctorates).

Distance Learning Courses Available.

Nursing Student Activities Nursing Honor Society, Sigma Theta Tau, Student Nurses' Association.

Nursing Student Resources Academic advising; academic or career counseling; assistance for students with disabilities; bookstore; campus computer network; career placement assistance; computer lab; computer-assisted instruction; daycare for children of students; e-mail services; employment services for current students; externships; housing assistance; interactive nursing skills videos; Internet; learning resource lab; library services; nursing audiovisuals; paid internships; remedial services; resume preparation assistance; skills, simulation, or other laboratory; tutoring.

Library Facilities 277,985 volumes (2,000 in health, 1,600 in nursing); 1,914 periodical subscriptions (50 health-care related).

BACCALAUREATE PROGRAMS

Degree BSN

Available Programs ADN to Baccalaureate; Accelerated Baccalaureate for Second Degree; Generic Baccalaureate; International Nurse to Baccalaureate; LPN to Baccalaureate; LPN to RN Baccalaureate.

Site Options Haverhill, MA.

Study Options Full-time.

Program Entrance Requirements Minimum overall college GPA of 3.2, transcript of college record, CPR certification, health exam, health insurance, high school biology, high school chemistry, 3 years high school math, 2 years high school science, high school transcript, immunizations, interview, minimum high school GPA of 3.2, professional liability insurance/malpractice insurance. Transfer students are accepted. *Application deadline:* 4/1 (fall), 10/1 (spring), 4/1 (summer). Applications may be processed on a rolling basis for some programs. *Application fee:* $25.

Advanced Placement Credit by examination available. Credit given for nursing courses completed elsewhere dependent upon specific evaluations.

Expenses (2009–10) *Tuition, state resident:* full-time $455; part-time $38 per credit. *Tuition, nonresident:* full-time $3525; part-time $294 per credit. *International tuition:* $3525 full-time. *Room and board:* $11,800; room only: $9000 per academic year. *Required fees:* full-time $3000; part-time $105 per credit.

Financial Aid 60% of baccalaureate students in nursing programs received some form of financial aid in 2008–09.

Contact Dr. Mary Dunn, Assistant Dean of Admissions, Program in Nursing, Salem State College, 352 Lafayette Street, Salem, MA 01970. *Telephone:* 978-542-6200. *E-mail:* admissions@salemstate.edu.

GRADUATE PROGRAMS

Expenses (2009–10) *Tuition, state resident:* full-time $6000; part-time $140 per credit. *Tuition, nonresident:* full-time $7000; part-time $230 per credit. *International tuition:* $7000 full-time. *Required fees:* full-time $2430; part-time $135 per credit.

Financial Aid 25% of graduate students in nursing programs received some form of financial aid in 2008–09.

Salem State College (continued)

Contact Dr. Kathleen Skrabut, Coordinator, Graduate Program, Program in Nursing, Salem State College, 352 Lafayette Street, Salem, MA 01970. *Telephone:* 978-542-7018. *Fax:* 978-542-2016. *E-mail:* kskrabut@salemstate.edu.

MASTER'S DEGREE PROGRAM

Degrees MSN; MSN/MBA

Available Programs Accelerated Master's for Non-Nursing College Graduates; Master's; Master's for Nurses with Non-Nursing Degrees; RN to Master's.

Concentrations Available Clinical nurse leader; nursing administration; nursing education. *Clinical nurse specialist programs in:* community health, public health, rehabilitation.

Study Options Full-time and part-time.

Program Entrance Requirements Clinical experience, computer literacy, minimum overall college GPA of 3.0, transcript of college record, CPR certification, written essay, immunizations, interview, 3 letters of recommendation, professional liability insurance/malpractice insurance, resume, statistics course, GRE General Test, MAT. *Application deadline:* Applications may be processed on a rolling basis for some programs. *Application fee:* $35.

Advanced Placement Credit given for nursing courses completed elsewhere dependent upon specific evaluations.

Degree Requirements 39 total credit hours, thesis or project.

CONTINUING EDUCATION PROGRAM

Contact Ms. Linda A. Frontiero, RN, Director of the Nursing Resource Center, Program in Nursing, Salem State College, 352 Lafayette Street, Salem, MA 01970. *Telephone:* 978-542-6849. *Fax:* 978-542-2016. *E-mail:* lfrontiero@salemstate.edu.

Simmons College
Department of Nursing
Boston, Massachusetts

http://www.simmons.edu/gshs/nursing/

Founded in 1899

DEGREES • BS • DNP • MS

Nursing Program Faculty 135 (15% with doctorates).

Baccalaureate Enrollment 212
Women 100% **Minority** 19% **International** 6% **Part-time** 28%

Graduate Enrollment 170
Women 94% **Men** 6% **Minority** 12% **International** 1% **Part-time** 61%

Distance Learning Courses Available.

Nursing Student Activities Nursing Honor Society, Sigma Theta Tau, Student Nurses' Association, nursing club.

Nursing Student Resources Academic advising; academic or career counseling; assistance for students with disabilities; bookstore; campus computer network; career placement assistance; computer lab; computer-assisted instruction; e-mail services; employment services for current students; housing assistance; interactive nursing skills videos; Internet; learning resource lab; library services; nursing audiovisuals; paid internships; placement services for program completers; remedial services; resume preparation assistance; skills, simulation, or other laboratory; tutoring.

Library Facilities 207,823 volumes (5,005 in health, 1,562 in nursing); 44,734 periodical subscriptions (196 health-care related).

BACCALAUREATE PROGRAMS

Degree BS

Available Programs ADN to Baccalaureate; Accelerated Baccalaureate; Accelerated Baccalaureate for Second Degree; Baccalaureate for Second Degree; Generic Baccalaureate; LPN to Baccalaureate; RN Baccalaureate.
Site Options Winchester, MA; Quincy, MA.
Study Options Full-time and part-time.

Program Entrance Requirements Transcript of college record, written essay, health exam, health insurance, high school biology, high school chemistry, high school foreign language, 4 years high school math, 3 years high school science, high school transcript, immunizations, 2 letters of recommendation, minimum GPA in nursing prerequisites of 3.0, prerequisite course work. Transfer students are accepted. *Application deadline:* 2/1 (fall), 12/1 (spring), 4/1 (summer). *Application fee:* $55.

Advanced Placement Credit given for nursing courses completed elsewhere dependent upon specific evaluations.

Expenses (2009–10) *Tuition:* full-time $33,450; part-time $1045 per credit hour. *International tuition:* $33,450 full-time. *Room and board:* $12,050 per academic year. *Required fees:* full-time $930.

Financial Aid 95% of baccalaureate students in nursing programs received some form of financial aid in 2008–09. *Gift aid (need-based):* Federal Pell, FSEOG, state, private, college/university gift aid from institutional funds. *Loans:* FFEL (Subsidized and Unsubsidized Stafford PLUS), Perkins, state, college/university. *Work-study:* Federal Work-Study. *Financial aid application deadline (priority):* 2/15.

Contact Ms. Catherine C. Capolupo, Director, Undergraduate Admission, Department of Nursing, Simmons College, 300 The Fenway, Boston, MA 02115. *Telephone:* 617-521-2051. *Fax:* 617-521-3190. *E-mail:* ugadm@simmons.edu.

GRADUATE PROGRAMS

Expenses (2009–10) *Tuition:* full-time $28,672; part-time $896 per credit hour. *International tuition:* $28,672 full-time. *Room and board:* $13,500 per academic year. *Required fees:* full-time $800.

Financial Aid 75% of graduate students in nursing programs received some form of financial aid in 2008–09.

Contact Ms. Carmen Fortin, Assistant Dean, Director of Admission, Department of Nursing, Simmons College, 300 The Fenway, Boston, MA 02115. *Telephone:* 617-521-2605. *Fax:* 617-521-3137. *E-mail:* carmen.fortin@simmons.edu.

MASTER'S DEGREE PROGRAM

Degree MS

Available Programs Accelerated AD/RN to Master's; Accelerated Master's; Accelerated Master's for Non-Nursing College Graduates; Accelerated Master's for Nurses with Non-Nursing Degrees; Accelerated RN to Master's; Master's; Master's for Non-Nursing College Graduates; Master's for Nurses with Non-Nursing Degrees; RN to Master's.

Concentrations Available Nursing administration. *Nurse practitioner programs in:* family health, primary care.
Site Options Winchester, MA; Quincy, MA.
Study Options Full-time and part-time.
Online Degree Options Yes.

Program Entrance Requirements Clinical experience, computer literacy, minimum overall college GPA of 3.0, transcript of college record, written essay, letters of recommendation, resume, statistics course. *Application deadline:* 6/1 (fall), 11/1 (spring), 3/1 (summer). *Application fee:* $50.

Advanced Placement Credit given for nursing courses completed elsewhere dependent upon specific evaluations.

Degree Requirements 45 total credit hours, thesis or project.

POST-MASTER'S PROGRAM

Areas of Study Nursing education. *Nurse practitioner programs in:* family health, primary care.

DOCTORAL DEGREE PROGRAM

Degree DNP

Available Programs Doctorate.
Areas of Study Clinical practice, faculty preparation, nursing education.
Online Degree Options Yes (online only).
Program Entrance Requirements Clinical experience, minimum overall college GPA of 3.0, 3 letters of recommendation, MSN or equivalent, statistics course, vita, writing sample. Application deadline: 6/1 (fall), 11/1 (spring). Application fee: $50.
Degree Requirements 32 total credit hours.

University of Massachusetts Amherst

School of Nursing
Amherst, Massachusetts

http://www.umass.edu/nursing

Founded in 1863

DEGREES • BS • MS • PHD

Nursing Program Faculty 65 (30% with doctorates).

Baccalaureate Enrollment 391
Women 90% **Men** 10% **Minority** 24% **International** 1% **Part-time** 1%

Graduate Enrollment 193
Women 93% **Men** 7% **Minority** 31% **International** 1% **Part-time** 72%

Distance Learning Courses Available.

Nursing Student Activities Nursing Honor Society, Sigma Theta Tau, Student Nurses' Association.

Nursing Student Resources Academic advising; academic or career counseling; bookstore; campus computer network; career placement assistance; computer lab; computer-assisted instruction; e-mail services; employment services for current students; housing assistance; interactive nursing skills videos; Internet; learning resource lab; library services; nursing audiovisuals; paid internships; resume preparation assistance; skills, simulation, or other laboratory; tutoring; unpaid internships.

Library Facilities 3.3 million volumes (329,660 in health, 39,833 in nursing); 57,233 periodical subscriptions (4,223 health-care related).

BACCALAUREATE PROGRAMS

Degree BS

Available Programs Accelerated Baccalaureate for Second Degree; Accelerated RN Baccalaureate; Generic Baccalaureate.

Study Options Full-time.

Online Degree Options Yes.

Program Entrance Requirements Minimum overall college GPA of 3.0, transcript of college record, CPR certification, written essay, health exam, health insurance, high school foreign language, 3 years high school math, 3 years high school science, high school transcript, immunizations, 1 letter of recommendation, minimum high school GPA of 3.5, minimum GPA in nursing prerequisites of 2.5, professional liability insurance/malpractice insurance, prerequisite course work. Transfer students are accepted. *Application deadline:* 11/1 (fall), 10/1 (spring). *Application fee:* $40.

Advanced Placement Credit given for nursing courses completed elsewhere dependent upon specific evaluations.

Expenses (2009–10) *Tuition, area resident:* full-time $857. *Tuition, state resident:* full-time $1500. *Tuition, nonresident:* full-time $4969. *Room and board:* $4150; room only: $2160 per academic year.

Financial Aid 78% of baccalaureate students in nursing programs received some form of financial aid in 2008–09.

Contact Miss Elizabeth Theroux, Academic Secretary, Office for the Advancement of Nursing Education, School of Nursing, University of Massachusetts Amherst, 128 Skinner Hall, 651 North Pleasant Street, Amherst, MA 01003-9304. *Telephone:* 413-545-5096. *Fax:* 413-577-2550. *E-mail:* etheroux@acad.umass.edu.

GRADUATE PROGRAMS

Expenses (2009–10) *Tuition, state resident:* full-time $1342. *Tuition, nonresident:* full-time $1877. *Room and board:* $4150; room only: $2160 per academic year.

Financial Aid 41% of graduate students in nursing programs received some form of financial aid in 2008–09. 33 fellowships with full tuition reimbursements available (averaging $4,428 per year), 2 research assistantships with full tuition reimbursements available (averaging $4,290 per year), 20 teaching assistantships with full tuition reimbursements available (averaging $9,155 per year) were awarded; career-related internships or fieldwork, Federal Work-Study, scholarships, traineeships, tuition waivers (full), and unspecified assistantships also available. Aid available to part-time students. *Financial aid application deadline:* 2/1.

Contact Ms. Karen Ayotte, Academic Services Graduate Program Assistant, School of Nursing, University of Massachusetts Amherst, 125 Skinner Hall, 651 North Pleasant Street, Amherst, MA 01003-9299. *Telephone:* 413-545-1302. *Fax:* 413-577-2550. *E-mail:* kayotte@nursing.umass.edu.

MASTER'S DEGREE PROGRAM

Degree MS

Available Programs Master's.

Concentrations Available Clinical nurse leader.

Study Options Full-time and part-time.

Program Entrance Requirements Transcript of college record, CPR certification, written essay, immunizations, 2 letters of recommendation, physical assessment course, professional liability insurance/malpractice insurance, prerequisite course work, statistics course, GRE General Test. *Application deadline:* 2/1 (fall). Applications may be processed on a rolling basis for some programs. *Application fee:* $40.

Advanced Placement Credit given for nursing courses completed elsewhere dependent upon specific evaluations.

Degree Requirements 37 total credit hours.

DOCTORAL DEGREE PROGRAM

Degree PhD

Available Programs Doctorate; Post-Baccalaureate Doctorate.

Areas of Study Health promotion/disease prevention, health-care systems, nursing research, nursing science.

Program Entrance Requirements Minimum overall college GPA of 3.2, interview, 2 letters of recommendation, MSN or equivalent, scholarly papers, statistics course, vita, writing sample, GRE General Test. Application deadline: 2/1 (fall). Applications may be processed on a rolling basis for some programs. Application fee: $40.

Degree Requirements 57 total credit hours, dissertation, oral exam, written exam, residency.

CONTINUING EDUCATION PROGRAM

Contact Ms. Karen Ayotte, Academic Services Graduate Programs Assistant, School of Nursing, University of Massachusetts Amherst, 125 Skinner Hall, 651 North Pleasant Street, Amherst, MA 01003-9299. *Telephone:* 413-545-1302. *Fax:* 413-577-2550. *E-mail:* kayotte@nursing.umass.edu.

University of Massachusetts Boston

College of Nursing and Health Sciences
Boston, Massachusetts

http://www.cnhs.umb.edu/

Founded in 1964

DEGREES • BS • DNP • MS • PHD

Nursing Program Faculty 129 (27% with doctorates).

Baccalaureate Enrollment 1,064
Women 88% **Men** 12% **Minority** 40% **International** .08% **Part-time** 38.5%

Graduate Enrollment 142
Women 78.6% **Men** 21.4% **Minority** 19.7% **International** .7% **Part-time** 85.2%

Distance Learning Courses Available.

Nursing Student Activities Sigma Theta Tau, Student Nurses' Association.

Nursing Student Resources Academic advising; academic or career counseling; assistance for students with disabilities; bookstore; campus computer network; career placement assistance; computer lab; computer-assisted instruction; daycare for children of students; e-mail services; employment services for current students; housing assistance; interactive nursing skills videos; Internet; learning resource lab; library services; nursing audiovisuals; other; paid internships; remedial services; resume preparation assistance; skills, simulation, or other laboratory; tutoring.

University of Massachusetts Boston (continued)

Library Facilities 600,000 volumes (3,700 in health, 1,911 in nursing); 26,500 periodical subscriptions (5,027 health-care related).

BACCALAUREATE PROGRAMS

Degree BS

Available Programs Accelerated Baccalaureate for Second Degree; Generic Baccalaureate; RN Baccalaureate.

Study Options Full-time and part-time.

Online Degree Options Yes.

Program Entrance Requirements Minimum overall college GPA of 2.75, transcript of college record, written essay, health insurance, 3 years high school math, high school transcript, immunizations, 1 letter of recommendation, minimum high school GPA of 2.75, minimum GPA in nursing prerequisites of 3.0. Transfer students are accepted. *Application deadline:* 2/1 (fall), 11/1 (spring). *Application fee:* $40.

Advanced Placement Credit given for nursing courses completed elsewhere dependent upon specific evaluations.

Expenses (2009–10) *Tuition, state resident:* full-time $10,631; part-time $72 per credit. *Tuition, nonresident:* full-time $22,816; part-time $407 per credit. *International tuition:* $22,816 full-time. *Required fees:* full-time $8896; part-time $370 per credit; part-time $250 per term.

Financial Aid 90% of baccalaureate students in nursing programs received some form of financial aid in 2008–09.

Contact Mr. Jon Hutton, Director of Enrollment Information Services, College of Nursing and Health Sciences, University of Massachusetts Boston, 100 Morrissey Boulevard, Boston, MA 02125. *Telephone:* 617-287-6000. *Fax:* 617-265-7173. *E-mail:* enrollment.information@umb.edu.

GRADUATE PROGRAMS

Expenses (2009–10) *Tuition, state resident:* full-time $11,996; part-time $108 per credit. *Tuition, nonresident:* full-time $22,829; part-time $407 per credit. *International tuition:* $22,829 full-time. *Required fees:* full-time $9386; part-time $391 per credit; part-time $250 per term.

Financial Aid 21% of graduate students in nursing programs received some form of financial aid in 2008–09. 3 research assistantships with full tuition reimbursements available (averaging $13,000 per year), 13 teaching assistantships with full tuition reimbursements available (averaging $13,000 per year) were awarded; career-related internships or fieldwork, Federal Work-Study, and unspecified assistantships also available. Aid available to part-time students. *Financial aid application deadline:* 3/1.

Contact Mr. Jon Hutton, Director of Enrollment Information Services, College of Nursing and Health Sciences, University of Massachusetts Boston, 100 Morrissey Boulevard, Boston, MA 02125. *Telephone:* 617-287-6000. *Fax:* 617-265-7173. *E-mail:* enrollment.information@umb.edu.

MASTER'S DEGREE PROGRAM

Degree MS

Available Programs Master's.

Concentrations Available *Clinical nurse specialist programs in:* acute care, critical care. *Nurse practitioner programs in:* adult health, family health, gerontology.

Study Options Full-time and part-time.

Program Entrance Requirements Clinical experience, minimum overall college GPA of 2.75, transcript of college record, CPR certification, written essay, immunizations, 3 letters of recommendation, nursing research course, physical assessment course, professional liability insurance/malpractice insurance, prerequisite course work, statistics course. *Application deadline:* 6/15 (fall), 11/1 (spring). Applications may be processed on a rolling basis for some programs. *Application fee:* $40.

Advanced Placement Credit given for nursing courses completed elsewhere dependent upon specific evaluations.

Degree Requirements 48 total credit hours, thesis or project.

POST-MASTER'S PROGRAM

Areas of Study *Nurse practitioner programs in:* adult health, family health, gerontology.

DOCTORAL DEGREE PROGRAM

Degree DNP, PhD

Available Programs Doctorate; Post-Baccalaureate Doctorate.

Areas of Study Health policy, oncology.

Program Entrance Requirements Clinical experience, minimum overall college GPA of 3.3, interview by faculty committee, interview, 3 letters of recommendation, MSN or equivalent, statistics course, vita, writing sample, GRE General Test. Application deadline: 2/15 (fall). Applications may be processed on a rolling basis for some programs. Application fee: $40.

Degree Requirements 60 total credit hours, dissertation, oral exam, written exam, residency.

CONTINUING EDUCATION PROGRAM

Contact Ms. Wanda Willard, Director of Credit Programs, College of Nursing and Health Sciences, University of Massachusetts Boston, 100 Morrissey Boulevard, Wheatley Building, 2nd Floor, Boston, MA 02125-3393. *Telephone:* 617-287-7874. *Fax:* 617-287-7922. *E-mail:* wanda.willard@umb.edu.

University of Massachusetts Dartmouth

College of Nursing
North Dartmouth, Massachusetts

http://www.umassd.edu/nursing

Founded in 1895

DEGREES • BSN • MS • PHD

Nursing Program Faculty 52 (33% with doctorates).

Nursing Student Activities Sigma Theta Tau, Student Nurses' Association, nursing club.

Nursing Student Resources Academic advising; academic or career counseling; assistance for students with disabilities; bookstore; campus computer network; career placement assistance; computer lab; computer-assisted instruction; daycare for children of students; e-mail services; employment services for current students; externships; housing assistance; interactive nursing skills videos; Internet; learning resource lab; library services; nursing audiovisuals; placement services for program completers; resume preparation assistance; skills, simulation, or other laboratory; tutoring; unpaid internships.

Library Facilities 463,000 volumes; 2,783 periodical subscriptions.

BACCALAUREATE PROGRAMS

Degree BSN

Available Programs Generic Baccalaureate; RN Baccalaureate.

Site Options Fall River, MA.

Study Options Full-time and part-time.

Program Entrance Requirements Transcript of college record, CPR certification, written essay, health exam, health insurance, high school biology, high school chemistry, high school foreign language, 3 years high school math, 3 years high school science, high school transcript, immunizations, letters of recommendation, minimum high school GPA of 3.0, minimum high school rank 66%, professional liability insurance/malpractice insurance. Transfer students are accepted.

Advanced Placement Credit by examination available. Credit given for nursing courses completed elsewhere dependent upon specific evaluations.

Contact Admissions Office, College of Nursing, University of Massachusetts Dartmouth, 285 Old Westport Road, North Dartmouth, MA 02747. *Telephone:* 508-999-8605. *Fax:* 508-999-8755. *E-mail:* admissions@umassd.edu.

GRADUATE PROGRAMS

Financial Aid 8 teaching assistantships (averaging $2,375 per year) were awarded; Federal Work-Study and scholarships also available.

Contact Gail E. Russell, RN, Director of Graduate Program, College of Nursing, University of Massachusetts Dartmouth, 285 Old Westport Road, North Dartmouth, MA 02747-2300. *Telephone:* 508-999-8251. *E-mail:* grussell@umassd.edu.

MASTER'S DEGREE PROGRAM

Degree MS

Available Programs Master's.

Concentrations Available *Clinical nurse specialist programs in:* adult health, community health. *Nurse practitioner programs in:* adult health.
Study Options Full-time and part-time.
Program Entrance Requirements Clinical experience, computer literacy, minimum overall college GPA of 3.0, transcript of college record, CPR certification, written essay, immunizations, interview, 3 letters of recommendation, nursing research course, physical assessment course, professional liability insurance/malpractice insurance, statistics course, GRE General Test.
Advanced Placement Credit given for nursing courses completed elsewhere dependent upon specific evaluations.
Degree Requirements 39 total credit hours, thesis or project.

POST-MASTER'S PROGRAM
Areas of Study *Nurse practitioner programs in:* adult health.

DOCTORAL DEGREE PROGRAM
Degree PhD
Available Programs Doctorate.
Areas of Study Nursing education.
Program Entrance Requirements Clinical experience, minimum overall college GPA of 3.3, 3 letters of recommendation, MSN or equivalent, statistics course, vita, writing sample, GRE General Test.
Degree Requirements 52 total credit hours.

CONTINUING EDUCATION PROGRAM
Contact Program Director, College of Nursing, University of Massachusetts Dartmouth, 285 Old Westport Road, North Dartmouth, MA 02747-2300. *Telephone:* 508-999-8591. *E-mail:* bsantos@umassd.edu.

University of Massachusetts Lowell
Department of Nursing
Lowell, Massachusetts

http://www.uml.edu/dept/nursing
Founded in 1894
DEGREES • BS • MS • PHD
Nursing Program Faculty 35 (100% with doctorates).
Baccalaureate Enrollment 291
Women 90% **Men** 10% **Minority** 13%
Graduate Enrollment 50
Women 90% **Men** 10%
Distance Learning Courses Available.
Nursing Student Activities Sigma Theta Tau, Student Nurses' Association.
Nursing Student Resources Academic advising; academic or career counseling; assistance for students with disabilities; bookstore; campus computer network; career placement assistance; computer lab; computer-assisted instruction; e-mail services; employment services for current students; housing assistance; interactive nursing skills videos; Internet; learning resource lab; library services; nursing audiovisuals; placement services for program completers; resume preparation assistance; skills, simulation, or other laboratory; tutoring.
Library Facilities 11,870 volumes (29,100 in health, 4,465 in nursing); 1,119 periodical subscriptions (350 health-care related).

BACCALAUREATE PROGRAMS
Degree BS
Available Programs Generic Baccalaureate; RN Baccalaureate.
Study Options Full-time.
Program Entrance Requirements Minimum overall college GPA of 2.7, transcript of college record, CPR certification, health exam, health insurance, high school chemistry, high school foreign language, 3 years high school math, 3 years high school science, high school transcript, immunizations, minimum high school GPA of 3.25, minimum GPA in nursing prerequisites of 2.7, professional liability insurance/malpractice insurance. Transfer students are accepted.

Advanced Placement Credit by examination available.
Contact *Telephone:* 800-410-4607.

GRADUATE PROGRAMS
Contact *Telephone:* 978-934-4426. *Fax:* 978-934-3006.

MASTER'S DEGREE PROGRAM
Degree MS
Available Programs Accelerated Master's; Accelerated RN to Master's; Master's.
Concentrations Available *Clinical nurse specialist programs in:* psychiatric/mental health. *Nurse practitioner programs in:* family health, gerontology, psychiatric/mental health.
Study Options Full-time and part-time.
Program Entrance Requirements Computer literacy, minimum overall college GPA of 3.0, transcript of college record, CPR certification, written essay, immunizations, interview, 3 letters of recommendation, professional liability insurance/malpractice insurance, statistics course, GRE General Test.
Advanced Placement Credit given for nursing courses completed elsewhere dependent upon specific evaluations.
Degree Requirements 42 total credit hours, thesis or project.

DOCTORAL DEGREE PROGRAM
Degree PhD
Available Programs Doctorate.
Areas of Study Health promotion/disease prevention.
Program Entrance Requirements Minimum overall college GPA of 3.4, interview by faculty committee, interview, 3 letters of recommendation, MSN or equivalent, scholarly papers, statistics course, writing sample, GRE General Test.
Degree Requirements 60 total credit hours, dissertation, oral exam, written exam.

University of Massachusetts Worcester
Graduate School of Nursing
Worcester, Massachusetts

http://www.umassmed.edu/gsn/
Founded in 1962
DEGREES • MS • PHD
Nursing Program Faculty 51 (40% with doctorates).
Baccalaureate Enrollment 154
Graduate Enrollment 154
Women 85% **Men** 15% **Minority** 17% **Part-time** 4%
Distance Learning Courses Available.
Nursing Student Activities Sigma Theta Tau, Student Nurses' Association.
Nursing Student Resources Academic advising; academic or career counseling; assistance for students with disabilities; bookstore; campus computer network; computer lab; computer-assisted instruction; e-mail services; interactive nursing skills videos; Internet; learning resource lab; library services; nursing audiovisuals; skills, simulation, or other laboratory; unpaid internships.
Library Facilities 207,500 volumes in health, 1,173 volumes in nursing; 5,400 periodical subscriptions health-care related.

GRADUATE PROGRAMS
Financial Aid Scholarships and traineeships available.
Contact Ms. Diane M. Brescia, Admission Coordinator, Graduate School of Nursing, University of Massachusetts Worcester, 55 Lake Avenue North, S1-853, Worcester, MA 01655-0115. *Telephone:* 508-856-3488. *Fax:* 508-856-6552. *E-mail:* GSNAdmissions@umassmed.edu.

MASTER'S DEGREE PROGRAM
Degree MS

University of Massachusetts Worcester (continued)

Available Programs Accelerated Master's for Non-Nursing College Graduates; Master's.

Concentrations Available Nursing education. *Nurse practitioner programs in:* acute care, family health, gerontology, primary care.

Site Options Worcester, MA; Shrewsbury, MA.

Study Options Full-time and part-time.

Program Entrance Requirements Clinical experience, computer literacy, minimum overall college GPA of 3.0, transcript of college record, CPR certification, written essay, immunizations, interview, 3 letters of recommendation, physical assessment course, prerequisite course work, resume, statistics course, GRE General Test. *Application deadline:* 3/15 (fall). Applications may be processed on a rolling basis for some programs.

Degree Requirements 42 total credit hours.

POST-MASTER'S PROGRAM

Areas of Study Nursing education. *Nurse practitioner programs in:* acute care, gerontology, primary care.

DOCTORAL DEGREE PROGRAM

Degree PhD

Available Programs Doctorate; Post-Baccalaureate Doctorate.

Areas of Study Advanced practice nursing, bio-behavioral research, clinical practice, critical care, family health, health promotion/disease prevention, human health and illness, illness and transition, nursing education, nursing research, nursing science, oncology, women's health.

Site Options Worcester, MA.

Program Entrance Requirements Minimum overall college GPA of 3.0, interview by faculty committee, interview, 3 letters of recommendation, MSN or equivalent, scholarly papers, statistics course, vita, writing sample, GRE General Test. Application deadline: 3/15 (fall). Applications may be processed on a rolling basis for some programs.

Degree Requirements 57 total credit hours, dissertation, oral exam, written exam.

CONTINUING EDUCATION PROGRAM

Contact Ms. Diane M. Brescia, Admissions Coordinator, Graduate School of Nursing, University of Massachusetts Worcester, 55 Lake Avenue North, Worcester, MA 01655-0115. *Telephone:* 508-856-3488. *Fax:* 508-856-5851. *E-mail:* GSNAdmissions@umassmed.edu.

Worcester State College
Department of Nursing
Worcester, Massachusetts

http://www.worcester.edu

Founded in 1874

DEGREES • BS • MS

Nursing Program Faculty 25 (20% with doctorates).

Baccalaureate Enrollment 238
Women 95% **Men** 5% **Minority** 13% **International** 1%

Graduate Enrollment 11
Women 100% **Part-time** 100%

Nursing Student Activities Sigma Theta Tau, Student Nurses' Association.

Nursing Student Resources Academic advising; academic or career counseling; assistance for students with disabilities; bookstore; campus computer network; career placement assistance; computer lab; computer-assisted instruction; e-mail services; employment services for current students; housing assistance; interactive nursing skills videos; Internet; learning resource lab; library services; nursing audiovisuals; paid internships; remedial services; resume preparation assistance; skills, simulation, or other laboratory; tutoring; unpaid internships.

Library Facilities 174,299 volumes (5,400 in health, 500 in nursing); 523 periodical subscriptions (85 health-care related).

BACCALAUREATE PROGRAMS

Degree BS

Available Programs Generic Baccalaureate; RN Baccalaureate.

Study Options Full-time.

Program Entrance Requirements Minimum overall college GPA of 3.0, transcript of college record, health exam, health insurance, high school foreign language, 3 years high school math, 3 years high school science, high school transcript, immunizations, minimum high school GPA of 3.0. Transfer students are accepted. *Application deadline:* 1/15 (fall). Applications may be processed on a rolling basis for some programs. *Application fee:* $20.

Advanced Placement Credit by examination available. Credit given for nursing courses completed elsewhere dependent upon specific evaluations.

Expenses (2008–09) *Tuition, state resident:* full-time $970; part-time $40 per credit hour. *Tuition, nonresident:* full-time $7050; part-time $294 per credit hour. *Room and board:* room only: $6000 per academic year. *Required fees:* full-time $5200; part-time $206 per credit; part-time $2600 per term.

Financial Aid 81% of baccalaureate students in nursing programs received some form of financial aid in 2007–08.

Contact Ms. Elizabeth Axelson, Director, Admissions, Department of Nursing, Worcester State College, 486 Chandler Street, Worcester, MA 01602. *Telephone:* 508-929-8040. *Fax:* 508-929-8183. *E-mail:* baxelson@worcester.edu.

GRADUATE PROGRAMS

Expenses (2008–09) *Tuition, state resident:* part-time $150 per credit. *Tuition, nonresident:* part-time $150 per credit. *Required fees:* part-time $95 per credit.

Contact Dr. Stephanie Chalupka, Coordinator, Department of Nursing, Worcester State College, 486 Chandler Street, Worcester, MA 01602. *Telephone:* 508-929-8129. *Fax:* 508-929-8680. *E-mail:* schalupka@worcester.edu.

MASTER'S DEGREE PROGRAM

Degree MS

Available Programs Master's.

Concentrations Available *Clinical nurse specialist programs in:* community health, public health.

Study Options Part-time.

Program Entrance Requirements Clinical experience, minimum overall college GPA of 3.0, transcript of college record, CPR certification, immunizations, interview, 1 letter of recommendation, nursing research course, professional liability insurance/malpractice insurance, prerequisite course work, resume, statistics course. *Application deadline:* Applications may be processed on a rolling basis for some programs.

Advanced Placement Credit by examination available. Credit given for nursing courses completed elsewhere dependent upon specific evaluations.

Degree Requirements 42 total credit hours, comprehensive exam.

MICHIGAN

Andrews University
Department of Nursing
Berrien Springs, Michigan

Founded in 1874

DEGREES • BS • MS

Nursing Program Faculty 11 (50% with doctorates).

Baccalaureate Enrollment 106

Graduate Enrollment 10

Nursing Student Activities Nursing Honor Society, Sigma Theta Tau, Student Nurses' Association.

Nursing Student Resources Academic advising; academic or career counseling; assistance for students with disabilities; bookstore; campus computer network; career placement assistance; computer lab; computer-assisted instruction; daycare for children of students; e-mail services; employment services for current students; externships; housing assistance; interactive nursing skills videos; Internet; learning resource lab; library services; nursing audiovisuals; paid internships; placement services for program completers; remedial services; resume preparation assistance; skills, simulation, or other laboratory; tutoring; unpaid internships.

Library Facilities 615,937 volumes (77,000 in health, 500 in nursing); 39,000 periodical subscriptions (700 health-care related).

BACCALAUREATE PROGRAMS

Degree BS

Available Programs ADN to Baccalaureate; Generic Baccalaureate.
Study Options Full-time.
Program Entrance Requirements Minimum overall college GPA of 2.5, transcript of college record, health exam, high school transcript, immunizations, minimum GPA in nursing prerequisites of 2.5. Transfer students are accepted.
Contact *Telephone:* 269-471-3192. *Fax:* 269-471-3454.

GRADUATE PROGRAMS

Contact *Telephone:* 269-471-3337. *Fax:* 269-471-3454.

MASTER'S DEGREE PROGRAM

Degree MS

Available Programs Master's.
Concentrations Available Nursing education.
Study Options Part-time.
Program Entrance Requirements Minimum overall college GPA of 3.0, transcript of college record, CPR certification, immunizations, 3 letters of recommendation, GRE.
Degree Requirements 38 total credit hours, thesis or project.

POST-MASTER'S PROGRAM

Areas of Study Nursing education.

Calvin College
Department of Nursing
Grand Rapids, Michigan

Founded in 1876
DEGREE • BSN

Nursing Program Faculty 20 (20% with doctorates).
Baccalaureate Enrollment 120
Women 95% **Men** 5% **Minority** 10% **International** 10%
Nursing Student Activities Sigma Theta Tau, Student Nurses' Association, nursing club.
Nursing Student Resources Academic advising; academic or career counseling; assistance for students with disabilities; bookstore; campus computer network; career placement assistance; computer lab; computer-assisted instruction; e-mail services; employment services for current students; externships; housing assistance; interactive nursing skills videos; Internet; learning resource lab; library services; nursing audiovisuals; paid internships; placement services for program completers; remedial services; resume preparation assistance; skills, simulation, or other laboratory; tutoring.
Library Facilities 1 million volumes; 15,697 periodical subscriptions.

BACCALAUREATE PROGRAMS

Degree BSN

Available Programs Generic Baccalaureate.
Site Options Grand Rapids, MI.
Study Options Full-time.

Program Entrance Requirements Minimum overall college GPA of 2.5, transcript of college record, CPR certification, health exam, health insurance, immunizations, 2 letters of recommendation, minimum GPA in nursing prerequisites of 2.5, professional liability insurance/malpractice insurance, prerequisite course work. Transfer students are accepted.
Contact *Telephone:* 616-526-6268. *Fax:* 616-526-8567.

Davenport University
Division of Nursing
Grand Rapids, Michigan

Founded in 1866
DEGREE • BSN

Nursing Program Faculty 40
Baccalaureate Enrollment 215
Women 94% **Men** 6% **Minority** 30% **Part-time** 17%
Distance Learning Courses Available.
Nursing Student Activities Student Nurses' Association.
Nursing Student Resources Academic advising; academic or career counseling; assistance for students with disabilities; bookstore; campus computer network; career placement assistance; computer lab; computer-assisted instruction; e-mail services; employment services for current students; externships; housing assistance; interactive nursing skills videos; Internet; learning resource lab; library services; nursing audiovisuals; placement services for program completers; remedial services; resume preparation assistance; skills, simulation, or other laboratory; tutoring.
Library Facilities 100 volumes in health, 50 volumes in nursing; 20 periodical subscriptions health-care related.

BACCALAUREATE PROGRAMS

Degree BSN

Available Programs ADN to Baccalaureate; Generic Baccalaureate; RN Baccalaureate.
Site Options Midland, MI; Warren, MI.
Study Options Full-time and part-time.
Online Degree Options Yes.
Program Entrance Requirements Minimum overall college GPA of 3.5, transcript of college record, CPR certification, written essay, health exam, health insurance, high school biology, high school chemistry, 2 years high school math, 3 years high school science, high school transcript, immunizations, 2 letters of recommendation, minimum high school GPA of 3.5, minimum GPA in nursing prerequisites. Transfer students are accepted. *Application deadline:* 1/31 (fall).
Advanced Placement Credit by examination available. Credit given for nursing courses completed elsewhere dependent upon specific evaluations.
Expenses (2009–10) *Tuition:* full-time $15,000; part-time $450 per credit hour. *Room and board:* $8500; room only: $6200 per academic year. *Required fees:* full-time $600; part-time $100 per credit.
Financial Aid 70% of baccalaureate students in nursing programs received some form of financial aid in 2008–09. *Gift aid (need-based):* Federal Pell, FSEOG, state, private, college/university gift aid from institutional funds. *Loans:* FFEL (Subsidized and Unsubsidized Stafford PLUS), private/alternative loans. *Work-study:* Federal Work-Study, part-time campus jobs. *Financial aid application deadline (priority):* 3/1.
Contact Division of Nursing, Division of Nursing, Davenport University, 415 Fulton Street East, Grand Rapids, MI 49503-5926. *Telephone:* 616-451-3511. *Fax:* 616-732-1145.

Eastern Michigan University
School of Nursing
Ypsilanti, Michigan

http://www.emich.edu/nursing
Founded in 1849

Eastern Michigan University (continued)
DEGREES • BSN • MSN

Nursing Program Faculty 53 (28% with doctorates).

Baccalaureate Enrollment 338
Women 87% **Men** 13% **Minority** 30% **International** 2% **Part-time** 58%

Graduate Enrollment 40
Women 98% **Men** 2% **Minority** 32% **International** 2% **Part-time** 95%

Nursing Student Activities Sigma Theta Tau, Student Nurses' Association.

Nursing Student Resources Academic advising; academic or career counseling; assistance for students with disabilities; bookstore; campus computer network; career placement assistance; computer lab; computer-assisted instruction; daycare for children of students; e-mail services; employment services for current students; housing assistance; interactive nursing skills videos; Internet; learning resource lab; library services; nursing audiovisuals; placement services for program completers; remedial services; resume preparation assistance; skills, simulation, or other laboratory; tutoring.

Library Facilities 970,268 volumes (24,200 in health, 5,300 in nursing); 2,375 periodical subscriptions (1,600 health-care related).

BACCALAUREATE PROGRAMS

Degree BSN

Available Programs Baccalaureate for Second Degree; Generic Baccalaureate; RN Baccalaureate.

Site Options Livonia, MI; Monroe, MI; Jackson, MI; Brighton, MI; Detroit, MI.

Study Options Full-time and part-time.

Program Entrance Requirements Transcript of college record, CPR certification, health exam, health insurance, immunizations, minimum GPA in nursing prerequisites of 3.0, prerequisite course work, RN licensure. Transfer students are accepted.

Advanced Placement Credit given for nursing courses completed elsewhere dependent upon specific evaluations.

Contact *Telephone:* 734-487-2340. *Fax:* 734-487-6946.

GRADUATE PROGRAMS

Contact *Telephone:* 734-487-3275. *Fax:* 734-487-6946.

MASTER'S DEGREE PROGRAM

Degree MSN

Available Programs Master's.

Concentrations Available *Clinical nurse specialist programs in:* adult health.

Site Options Livonia, MI; Monroe, MI.

Program Entrance Requirements Clinical experience, minimum overall college GPA of 2.5, transcript of college record, CPR certification, written essay, immunizations, interview, 3 letters of recommendation, physical assessment course, statistics course.

Degree Requirements 40 total credit hours, thesis or project.

Ferris State University
School of Nursing
Big Rapids, Michigan

*http://www.ferris.edu/htmls/colleges/alliedhe/
department_desc.cfm?DepartmentID=7*

Founded in 1884

DEGREES • BSN • MSN • MSN/MBA

Nursing Program Faculty 24 (20% with doctorates).

Baccalaureate Enrollment 510
Women 87% **Men** 13% **Minority** 7% **Part-time** 72%

Graduate Enrollment 64
Women 90% **Men** 10% **Part-time** 98%

Distance Learning Courses Available.

Nursing Student Activities Sigma Theta Tau, Student Nurses' Association.

Nursing Student Resources Academic advising; academic or career counseling; assistance for students with disabilities; bookstore; campus computer network; career placement assistance; computer lab; computer-assisted instruction; daycare for children of students; e-mail services; employment services for current students; housing assistance; interactive nursing skills videos; Internet; library services; nursing audiovisuals; resume preparation assistance; skills, simulation, or other laboratory; tutoring.

Library Facilities 410,536 volumes (12,177 in health, 785 in nursing); 36,563 periodical subscriptions (515 health-care related).

BACCALAUREATE PROGRAMS

Degree BSN

Available Programs Accelerated Baccalaureate for Second Degree; Generic Baccalaureate; RN Baccalaureate.

Site Options Midland, MI; Holland, MI; Traverse City, MI.

Study Options Full-time.

Online Degree Options Yes.

Program Entrance Requirements Minimum overall college GPA of 2.7, transcript of college record, CPR certification, health insurance, immunizations, minimum GPA in nursing prerequisites of 2.7, prerequisite course work. Transfer students are accepted. *Application deadline:* 1/15 (fall), 8/15 (spring).

Advanced Placement Credit by examination available. Credit given for nursing courses completed elsewhere dependent upon specific evaluations.

Expenses (2009–10) *Tuition, state resident:* full-time $9480; part-time $316 per credit. *Tuition, nonresident:* full-time $14,235; part-time $475 per credit. *International tuition:* $14,235 full-time. *Room and board:* $8940; room only: $8664 per academic year. *Required fees:* full-time $162; part-time $81 per term.

Financial Aid 87% of baccalaureate students in nursing programs received some form of financial aid in 2008–09.

Contact Dr. Julie A. Coon, Director, School of Nursing, Ferris State University, 200 Ferris Drive, Room 400A, Big Rapids, MI 49307. *Telephone:* 231-591-2267. *Fax:* 231-591-2325. *E-mail:* coonj@ferris.edu.

GRADUATE PROGRAMS

Expenses (2009–10) *Tuition, state resident:* full-time $38,205; part-time $425 per credit. *Tuition, nonresident:* full-time $38,205; part-time $425 per credit. *International tuition:* $38,205 full-time. *Room and board:* $8940; room only: $8664 per academic year.

Financial Aid 20% of graduate students in nursing programs received some form of financial aid in 2008–09.

Contact Dr. Marietta Bell-Scriber, Program Coordinator, School of Nursing, Ferris State University, 200 Ferris Drive, Big Rapids, MI 49307. *Telephone:* 231-591-3987. *Fax:* 231-591-2325. *E-mail:* bellscri@ferris.edu.

MASTER'S DEGREE PROGRAM

Degrees MSN; MSN/MBA

Available Programs Accelerated AD/RN to Master's; Master's.

Concentrations Available Nursing administration; nursing education; nursing informatics.

Study Options Full-time and part-time.

Online Degree Options Yes (online only).

Program Entrance Requirements Clinical experience, minimum overall college GPA of 3.0, transcript of college record, written essay, 3 letters of recommendation, resume. *Application deadline:* 8/1 (fall), 12/1 (winter), 12/2 (spring).

Advanced Placement Credit given for nursing courses completed elsewhere dependent upon specific evaluations.

Degree Requirements 36 total credit hours, thesis or project, comprehensive exam.

Finlandia University
College of Professional Studies
Hancock, Michigan

Founded in 1896

DEGREE • BSN

Nursing Program Faculty 12 (17% with doctorates).

Baccalaureate Enrollment 90
Women 80% **Men** 20% **Minority** 4% **International** 1% **Part-time** 4.4%

Distance Learning Courses Available.

Nursing Student Activities Student Nurses' Association, nursing club.

Nursing Student Resources Academic advising; academic or career counseling; assistance for students with disabilities; bookstore; campus computer network; career placement assistance; computer lab; computer-assisted instruction; e-mail services; interactive nursing skills videos; Internet; learning resource lab; library services; nursing audiovisuals; placement services for program completers; remedial services; resume preparation assistance; skills, simulation, or other laboratory; tutoring.

Library Facilities 68,803 volumes (4,601 in health, 2,316 in nursing); 997 periodical subscriptions (97 health-care related).

BACCALAUREATE PROGRAMS

Degree BSN

Available Programs Generic Baccalaureate; RN Baccalaureate.

Study Options Full-time.

Online Degree Options Yes.

Program Entrance Requirements Minimum overall college GPA of 2.5, transcript of college record, CPR certification, health exam, high school biology, high school chemistry, 1 year of high school math, 2 years high school science, high school transcript, immunizations, minimum high school GPA of 2.5, minimum GPA in nursing prerequisites of 2.5, prerequisite course work. Transfer students are accepted. *Application deadline:* Applications may be processed on a rolling basis for some programs. *Application fee:* $30.

Advanced Placement Credit given for nursing courses completed elsewhere dependent upon specific evaluations.

Expenses (2009–10) *Tuition:* full-time $17,936; part-time $598 per credit hour. *International tuition:* $17,936 full-time. *Room and board:* $5974 per academic year. *Required fees:* full-time $400; part-time $200 per term.

Financial Aid 95% of baccalaureate students in nursing programs received some form of financial aid in 2008–09. *Gift aid (need-based):* Federal Pell, FSEOG, state, private, college/university gift aid from institutional funds. *Loans:* FFEL (Subsidized and Unsubsidized Stafford PLUS), state, private loan program. *Work-study:* Federal Work-Study, part-time campus jobs. *Financial aid application deadline (priority):* 3/1.

Contact Admissions Office, College of Professional Studies, Finlandia University, 601 Quincy Street, Hancock, MI 49930. *Telephone:* 906-487-7274.

Grand Valley State University
Kirkhof College of Nursing
Allendale, Michigan

http://www4.gvsu.edu/kcon
Founded in 1960

DEGREES • BSN • DNP • MSN

Nursing Program Faculty 91 (32% with doctorates).

Baccalaureate Enrollment 411
Women 84% **Men** 16% **Minority** 9% **International** 1% **Part-time** 40%

Graduate Enrollment 75
Women 88% **Men** 12% **Minority** 1% **International** 1% **Part-time** 92%

Distance Learning Courses Available.

Nursing Student Activities Sigma Theta Tau, Student Nurses' Association.

Nursing Student Resources Academic advising; academic or career counseling; assistance for students with disabilities; bookstore; campus computer network; career placement assistance; computer lab; computer-assisted instruction; daycare for children of students; e-mail services; employment services for current students; housing assistance; interactive nursing skills videos; Internet; learning resource lab; library services;

nursing audiovisuals; placement services for program completers; remedial services; resume preparation assistance; skills, simulation, or other laboratory; tutoring.

Library Facilities 664,000 volumes (22,710 in health, 1,704 in nursing); 8,000 periodical subscriptions (937 health-care related).

BACCALAUREATE PROGRAMS

Degree BSN

Available Programs ADN to Baccalaureate; Accelerated Baccalaureate for Second Degree; Baccalaureate for Second Degree; Generic Baccalaureate; RN Baccalaureate.

Site Options Grand Rapids, MI.

Study Options Full-time and part-time.

Program Entrance Requirements Minimum overall college GPA of 2.8, transcript of college record, CPR certification, written essay, health exam, health insurance, immunizations, minimum GPA in nursing prerequisites of 2.0, prerequisite course work. Transfer students are accepted. *Application deadline:* 3/1 (fall), 3/1 (winter), 11/1 (spring).

Advanced Placement Credit given for nursing courses completed elsewhere dependent upon specific evaluations.

Expenses (2009–10) *Tuition, state resident:* full-time $8845; part-time $384 per credit hour. *Tuition, nonresident:* full-time $14,682; part-time $561 per credit hour. *Room and board:* $8693; room only: $6186 per academic year. *Required fees:* part-time $17 per credit.

Financial Aid 93% of baccalaureate students in nursing programs received some form of financial aid in 2008–09. *Gift aid (need-based):* Federal Pell, FSEOG, state, private, college/university gift aid from institutional funds. *Loans:* Federal Nursing Student Loans, Federal Direct (Subsidized and Unsubsidized Stafford PLUS), Perkins. *Work-study:* Federal Work-Study, part-time campus jobs. *Financial aid application deadline (priority):* 3/1.

Contact Ms. Cassonya Carter, Director of Student Services, Kirkhof College of Nursing, Grand Valley State University, Cook-DeVos Center for Health Sciences, 301 Michigan Street NE, Room 320, Grand Rapids, MI 49503-3314. *Telephone:* 616-331-5782. *Fax:* 616-331-2510. *E-mail:* carterc@gvsu.edu.

GRADUATE PROGRAMS

Expenses (2009–10) *Tuition, state resident:* part-time $476 per credit hour. *Tuition, nonresident:* part-time $666 per credit hour. *Room and board:* $6408; room only: $1042 per academic year. *Required fees:* part-time $17 per credit.

Financial Aid 69% of graduate students in nursing programs received some form of financial aid in 2008–09. 9 research assistantships with full and partial tuition reimbursements available (averaging $8,000 per year) were awarded; career-related internships or fieldwork, Federal Work-Study, institutionally sponsored loans, and traineeships also available. *Financial aid application deadline:* 2/15.

Contact Ms. Linda Buck, Student Services Coordinator, Kirkhof College of Nursing, Grand Valley State University, Cook-DeVos Center for Health Sciences, 301 Michigan Street NE, Room 318, Grand Rapids, MI 49503-3314. *Telephone:* 616-331-5785. *Fax:* 616-331-2510. *E-mail:* buckli@gvsu.edu.

MASTER'S DEGREE PROGRAM

Degree MSN

Available Programs Master's.

Concentrations Available Nursing education. *Nurse practitioner programs in:* family health.

Site Options Grand Rapids, MI.

Study Options Full-time and part-time.

Program Entrance Requirements Minimum overall college GPA of 3.0, transcript of college record, CPR certification, written essay, immunizations, 3 letters of recommendation, GRE. *Application deadline:* Applications may be processed on a rolling basis for some programs.

Advanced Placement Credit given for nursing courses completed elsewhere dependent upon specific evaluations.

Degree Requirements 43 total credit hours, thesis or project.

POST-MASTER'S PROGRAM

Areas of Study Nursing education. *Nurse practitioner programs in:* family health.

Grand Valley State University (continued)

DOCTORAL DEGREE PROGRAM

Degree DNP

Available Programs Post-Baccalaureate Doctorate.

Areas of Study Advanced practice nursing, nursing administration.

Site Options Grand Rapids, MI.

Program Entrance Requirements Minimum overall college GPA of 3.0, interview, vita, writing sample. Application deadline: 2/1 (fall). Application fee: $30.

Degree Requirements 93 total credit hours, dissertation.

CONTINUING EDUCATION PROGRAM

Contact Ms. Jan Coye, Academic Community Liaison, Kirkhof College of Nursing, Grand Valley State University, Cook-DeVos Center for Health Sciences, 301 Michigan Street NE, Room 350, Grand Rapids, MI 49503-3314. *Telephone:* 616-331-3558. *Fax:* 616-331-2510. *E-mail:* coyej@gvsu.edu.

Hope College
Department of Nursing
Holland, Michigan

Founded in 1866

DEGREE • BSN

Nursing Program Faculty 14

Baccalaureate Enrollment 100

Nursing Student Activities Sigma Theta Tau, Student Nurses' Association.

Nursing Student Resources Academic advising; academic or career counseling; assistance for students with disabilities; bookstore; campus computer network; career placement assistance; computer lab; computer-assisted instruction; e-mail services; employment services for current students; externships; housing assistance; interactive nursing skills videos; Internet; learning resource lab; library services; nursing audiovisuals; remedial services; resume preparation assistance; skills, simulation, or other laboratory; tutoring; unpaid internships.

Library Facilities 368,864 volumes; 5,771 periodical subscriptions.

BACCALAUREATE PROGRAMS

Degree BSN

Available Programs Generic Baccalaureate.

Study Options Full-time and part-time.

Program Entrance Requirements Minimum overall college GPA of 2.9, transcript of college record, written essay, 2 letters of recommendation, minimum GPA in nursing prerequisites of 2.5. Transfer students are accepted.

Contact *Telephone:* 616-395-7420. *Fax:* 616-395-7163.

Lake Superior State University
Department of Nursing
Sault Sainte Marie, Michigan

http://www.lssu.edu/academics/science/schools/
nursing_health/nursdept/

Founded in 1946

DEGREE • BSN

Nursing Program Faculty 20 (15% with doctorates).

Baccalaureate Enrollment 115
Women 90% **Men** 10% **Minority** 10% **International** 3%

Distance Learning Courses Available.

Nursing Student Activities Nursing Honor Society, Student Nurses' Association, nursing club.

Nursing Student Resources Academic advising; academic or career counseling; assistance for students with disabilities; bookstore; campus computer network; career placement assistance; computer lab; computer-assisted instruction; daycare for children of students; e-mail services; employment services for current students; interactive nursing skills videos; Internet; learning resource lab; library services; nursing audiovisuals; placement services for program completers; remedial services; resume preparation assistance; skills, simulation, or other laboratory; tutoring.

Library Facilities 200,449 volumes (5,246 in health, 942 in nursing); 850 periodical subscriptions (1,196 health-care related).

BACCALAUREATE PROGRAMS

Degree BSN

Available Programs ADN to Baccalaureate; Generic Baccalaureate; LPN to Baccalaureate; LPN to RN Baccalaureate; RN Baccalaureate; RPN to Baccalaureate.

Site Options Escanaba, MI; Petoskey, MI.

Study Options Full-time and part-time.

Program Entrance Requirements Minimum overall college GPA of 2.5, transcript of college record, CPR certification, health exam, health insurance, high school biology, high school chemistry, high school transcript, immunizations, 1 letter of recommendation, minimum high school GPA of 2.0, minimum GPA in nursing prerequisites of 2.5, professional liability insurance/malpractice insurance, prerequisite course work. Transfer students are accepted. *Application deadline:* 2/1 (fall), 10/1 (spring).

Advanced Placement Credit given for nursing courses completed elsewhere dependent upon specific evaluations.

Expenses (2008–09) *Tuition, state resident:* full-time $7824; part-time $326 per credit hour. *Tuition, nonresident:* full-time $15,647; part-time $652 per credit hour. *International tuition:* $15,647 full-time. *Room and board:* $7567 per academic year. *Required fees:* full-time $160.

Financial Aid 76% of baccalaureate students in nursing programs received some form of financial aid in 2007–08.

Contact Dr. Steven E. Merrill, RN, Dean of Nursing and Health Sciences, Department of Nursing, Lake Superior State University, 650 West Easterday Avenue, Sault Sainte Marie, MI 49783. *Telephone:* 906-635-2446. *Fax:* 906-635-2266. *E-mail:* smerrill@lssu.edu.

Madonna University
College of Nursing and Health
Livonia, Michigan

http://www.madonna.edu

Founded in 1947

DEGREES • BSN • MSN • MSN/MBA

Nursing Program Faculty 55 (12% with doctorates).

Baccalaureate Enrollment 373
Women 90% **Men** 10% **Minority** 16% **International** 1% **Part-time** 25%

Graduate Enrollment 52
Women 94% **Men** 6% **Minority** 14% **International** 4% **Part-time** 94%

Nursing Student Activities Sigma Theta Tau, Student Nurses' Association.

Nursing Student Resources Academic advising; academic or career counseling; assistance for students with disabilities; bookstore; campus computer network; career placement assistance; computer lab; computer-assisted instruction; e-mail services; interactive nursing skills videos; Internet; learning resource lab; library services; nursing audiovisuals; remedial services; resume preparation assistance; skills, simulation, or other laboratory; tutoring.

Library Facilities 199,000 volumes (106,387 in health, 6,290 in nursing); 970 periodical subscriptions (891 health-care related).

BACCALAUREATE PROGRAMS

Degree BSN

Available Programs ADN to Baccalaureate; Baccalaureate for Second Degree; Generic Baccalaureate; LPN to Baccalaureate; RN Baccalaureate.

Study Options Full-time and part-time.

Program Entrance Requirements Minimum overall college GPA of 2.5, transcript of college record, CPR certification, health exam, high school biology, high school chemistry, 1 year of high school math, high school transcript, immunizations, minimum high school GPA of 2.75, professional liability insurance/malpractice insurance. Transfer students are accepted.

Advanced Placement Credit by examination available. Credit given for nursing courses completed elsewhere dependent upon specific evaluations.

Contact *Telephone:* 734-432-5718. *Fax:* 734-432-5463.

GRADUATE PROGRAMS

Contact *Telephone:* 734-432-5461. *Fax:* 734-432-5463.

MASTER'S DEGREE PROGRAM

Degrees MSN; MSN/MBA

Available Programs Accelerated AD/RN to Master's; Accelerated RN to Master's; Master's.

Concentrations Available Nursing administration. *Nurse practitioner programs in:* adult health, primary care.

Study Options Full-time and part-time.

Program Entrance Requirements Clinical experience, computer literacy, minimum overall college GPA of 3.0, transcript of college record, written essay, interview, 2 letters of recommendation, nursing research course, physical assessment course, resume, statistics course.

Advanced Placement Credit given for nursing courses completed elsewhere dependent upon specific evaluations.

Degree Requirements 48 total credit hours.

POST-MASTER'S PROGRAM

Areas of Study *Nurse practitioner programs in:* adult health, primary care.

CONTINUING EDUCATION PROGRAM

Contact *Telephone:* 734-432-5863. *Fax:* 734-432-5463.

Michigan State University
College of Nursing
East Lansing, Michigan

http://www.nursing.msu.edu/

Founded in 1855

DEGREES • BSN • MSN • PHD

Nursing Program Faculty 80 (38% with doctorates).

Baccalaureate Enrollment 300
Women 89.18% **Men** 10.82% **Minority** 8.96% **International** .75% **Part-time** 14.18%

Graduate Enrollment 200
Women 94.56% **Men** 5.44% **Minority** 6.67% **Part-time** 82.07%

Distance Learning Courses Available.

Nursing Student Activities Sigma Theta Tau, Student Nurses' Association.

Nursing Student Resources Academic advising; academic or career counseling; assistance for students with disabilities; bookstore; campus computer network; career placement assistance; computer lab; computer-assisted instruction; daycare for children of students; e-mail services; externships; housing assistance; interactive nursing skills videos; Internet; learning resource lab; library services; nursing audiovisuals; placement services for program completers; remedial services; resume preparation assistance; skills, simulation, or other laboratory; tutoring.

Library Facilities 4.9 million volumes (138,556 in health, 3,263 in nursing); 74,177 periodical subscriptions (4,708 health-care related).

BACCALAUREATE PROGRAMS

Degree BSN

Available Programs Accelerated Baccalaureate for Second Degree; Generic Baccalaureate; RN Baccalaureate.

Study Options Full-time.

Online Degree Options Yes.

Program Entrance Requirements Minimum overall college GPA of 2.5, written essay, immunizations, 2 letters of recommendation, prerequisite course work. Transfer students are accepted. *Application deadline:* 10/1 (fall), 3/1 (spring).

Expenses (2008–09) *Tuition, state resident:* full-time $10,283. *Tuition, nonresident:* full-time $25,613. *International tuition:* $25,613 full-time. *Room and board:* $7626; room only: $6218 per academic year. *Required fees:* full-time $1084.

Financial Aid 74% of baccalaureate students in nursing programs received some form of financial aid in 2007–08. *Gift aid (need-based):* Federal Pell, FSEOG, state, private, college/university gift aid from institutional funds, United Negro College Fund. *Loans:* Federal Direct (Subsidized and Unsubsidized Stafford PLUS), Perkins, state, college/university. *Work-study:* Federal Work-Study, part-time campus jobs. *Financial aid application deadline:* Continuous.

Contact Office of Student Support Services, College of Nursing, Michigan State University, A117 Life Sciences Building, East Lansing, MI 48824-1317. *Telephone:* 517-353-4827. *Fax:* 517-432-8251. *E-mail:* nurse@hc.msu.edu.

GRADUATE PROGRAMS

Expenses (2008–09) *Tuition, state resident:* part-time $434 per credit hour. *Tuition, nonresident:* part-time $893 per credit hour. *Required fees:* part-time $337 per term.

Financial Aid 67% of graduate students in nursing programs received some form of financial aid in 2007–08. 2 research assistantships with tuition reimbursements available (averaging $12,636 per year), 3 teaching assistantships with tuition reimbursements available (averaging $12,426 per year) were awarded.

Contact Ms. Nikki O'Brien, Program Advisor, College of Nursing, Michigan State University, A117 Life Sciences Building, East Lansing, MI 48824-1317. *Telephone:* 517-353-4827. *Fax:* 517-432-8251. *E-mail:* obrienni@msu.edu.

MASTER'S DEGREE PROGRAM

Degree MSN

Available Programs Master's.

Concentrations Available Nurse anesthesia; nursing education. *Nurse practitioner programs in:* adult health, family health.

Study Options Full-time and part-time.

Online Degree Options Yes.

Program Entrance Requirements Clinical experience, minimum overall college GPA of 3.0, transcript of college record, CPR certification, written essay, immunizations, interview, 3 letters of recommendation, prerequisite course work, resume, statistics course. *Application deadline:* Applications may be processed on a rolling basis for some programs.

Advanced Placement Credit given for nursing courses completed elsewhere dependent upon specific evaluations.

Degree Requirements 47 total credit hours, comprehensive exam.

POST-MASTER'S PROGRAM

Areas of Study Nursing education. *Nurse practitioner programs in:* adult health, family health.

DOCTORAL DEGREE PROGRAM

Degree PhD

Available Programs Doctorate; Doctorate for Nurses with Non-Nursing Degrees; Post-Baccalaureate Doctorate.

Areas of Study Family health, health promotion/disease prevention, human health and illness, individualized study, nursing research.

Site Options Grand Rapids, MI.

Program Entrance Requirements Minimum overall college GPA of 3.0, interview by faculty committee, interview, 3 letters of recommendation, statistics course, vita, writing sample. Application deadline: Applications may be processed on a rolling basis for some programs.

Degree Requirements 61 total credit hours, dissertation, written exam.

CONTINUING EDUCATION PROGRAM

Contact Katie Kessler, Director of Professional Education, College of Nursing, Michigan State University, A103 Life Sciences Building, East Lansing, MI 48824-1317. *Telephone:* 517-355-8539. *Fax:* 517-432-8131. *E-mail:* kathleen.kessler@hc.msu.edu.

Northern Michigan University
College of Nursing and Allied Health Science
Marquette, Michigan

http://www.nmu.edu/departments/nursing.html
Founded in 1899
DEGREES • BSN • MSN

Nursing Program Faculty 18 (67% with doctorates).
Baccalaureate Enrollment 221
Women 87% **Men** 13% **Minority** 4% **Part-time** 10%
Graduate Enrollment 16
Women 81% **Men** 19% **Part-time** 100%
Distance Learning Courses Available.
Nursing Student Activities Sigma Theta Tau, Student Nurses' Association.
Nursing Student Resources Academic advising; academic or career counseling; assistance for students with disabilities; bookstore; campus computer network; career placement assistance; computer lab; computer-assisted instruction; e-mail services; employment services for current students; housing assistance; interactive nursing skills videos; Internet; learning resource lab; library services; nursing audiovisuals; other; paid internships; remedial services; resume preparation assistance; skills, simulation, or other laboratory; tutoring.
Library Facilities 615,406 volumes (32,879 in health, 2,733 in nursing); 4,573 periodical subscriptions (5,000 health-care related).

BACCALAUREATE PROGRAMS
Degree BSN
Available Programs Accelerated Baccalaureate; Generic Baccalaureate; LPN to Baccalaureate; RN Baccalaureate.
Study Options Full-time and part-time.
Program Entrance Requirements Minimum overall college GPA of 2.75, transcript of college record, CPR certification, health exam, high school transcript, immunizations, minimum GPA in nursing prerequisites of 2.0, prerequisite course work. Transfer students are accepted. *Application deadline:* 2/1 (fall), 10/1 (winter).
Advanced Placement Credit by examination available. Credit given for nursing courses completed elsewhere dependent upon specific evaluations.
Expenses (2009–10) *Tuition, area resident:* full-time $7454; part-time $285 per credit hour. *Tuition, state resident:* full-time $7545; part-time $285 per credit hour. *Tuition, nonresident:* full-time $11,828; part-time $467 per credit hour. *Room and board:* $7846 per academic year. *Required fees:* full-time $614.
Financial Aid 85% of baccalaureate students in nursing programs received some form of financial aid in 2008–09.
Contact Dr. Kerri Durnell Schuiling, RN, Associate Dean for Nursing Education/Department Head, Nursing, College of Nursing and Allied Health Science, Northern Michigan University, 2301 New Science Facility, Marquette, MI 49855. *Telephone:* 906-227-2834. *Fax:* 906-227-1658. *E-mail:* kschuili@nmu.edu.

GRADUATE PROGRAMS
Expenses (2009–10) *Tuition, state resident:* full-time $6050; part-time $340 per credit hour. *Tuition, nonresident:* full-time $8662; part-time $503 per credit hour. *Required fees:* full-time $614.
Financial Aid Career-related internships or fieldwork, Federal Work-Study, institutionally sponsored loans, and unspecified assistantships available.
Contact Prof. Melissa M. Romero, PhD, Coordinator of MSN Program, College of Nursing and Allied Health Science, Northern Michigan University, 2131 New Science Facility, Marquette, MI 49855. *Telephone:* 906-227-2488. *Fax:* 906-227-1658. *E-mail:* mromero@nmu.edu.

MASTER'S DEGREE PROGRAM
Degree MSN
Available Programs Master's.
Concentrations Available *Nurse practitioner programs in:* family health.

Study Options Part-time.
Program Entrance Requirements Clinical experience, computer literacy, minimum overall college GPA of 3.0, transcript of college record, CPR certification, written essay, immunizations, 2 letters of recommendation, physical assessment course, professional liability insurance/malpractice insurance, GRE General Test. *Application deadline:* 2/1 (fall).
Advanced Placement Credit given for nursing courses completed elsewhere dependent upon specific evaluations.
Degree Requirements 45 total credit hours, thesis or project, comprehensive exam.

POST-MASTER'S PROGRAM
Areas of Study *Nurse practitioner programs in:* family health.

CONTINUING EDUCATION PROGRAM
Contact Dr. Cynthia A. Prosen, Associate Provost and Dean of Graduate Studies and Research, College of Nursing and Allied Health Science, Northern Michigan University, 610 Cohodas Hall, Marquette, MI 49855. *Telephone:* 906-227-2300. *E-mail:* cprosen@nmu.edu.

Oakland University
School of Nursing
Rochester, Michigan

http://www2.oakland.edu/nursing
Founded in 1957
DEGREES • BSN • MSN

Nursing Program Faculty 44 (50% with doctorates).
Baccalaureate Enrollment 462
Women 89% **Men** 11% **Minority** 12% **Part-time** 29%
Graduate Enrollment 123
Women 79% **Men** 21% **Minority** 11% **International** 1% **Part-time** 35%
Nursing Student Activities Nursing Honor Society, Sigma Theta Tau, Student Nurses' Association.
Nursing Student Resources Academic advising; academic or career counseling; assistance for students with disabilities; bookstore; campus computer network; career placement assistance; computer lab; computer-assisted instruction; e-mail services; employment services for current students; externships; housing assistance; interactive nursing skills videos; Internet; learning resource lab; library services; nursing audiovisuals; paid internships; placement services for program completers; remedial services; resume preparation assistance; skills, simulation, or other laboratory; tutoring; unpaid internships.
Library Facilities 856,760 volumes (12,652 in health, 2,780 in nursing); 20,490 periodical subscriptions (375 health-care related).

BACCALAUREATE PROGRAMS
Degree BSN
Available Programs Generic Baccalaureate; RN Baccalaureate.
Site Options Royal Oak, MI.
Study Options Full-time and part-time.
Program Entrance Requirements Minimum overall college GPA of 3.0, transcript of college record, CPR certification, health exam, high school biology, high school chemistry, 2 years high school math, 1 year of high school science, high school transcript, immunizations, minimum high school GPA of 3.0, minimum GPA in nursing prerequisites of 3.0, professional liability insurance/malpractice insurance, prerequisite course work. Transfer students are accepted.
Advanced Placement Credit given for nursing courses completed elsewhere dependent upon specific evaluations.
Contact *Telephone:* 248-370-4065. *Fax:* 248-370-4279.

GRADUATE PROGRAMS
Contact *Telephone:* 248-370-4082. *Fax:* 248-370-2996.

MASTER'S DEGREE PROGRAM
Degree MSN
Available Programs Master's.

Concentrations Available Nurse anesthesia; nursing education. *Nurse practitioner programs in:* adult health, family health, gerontology.

Site Options Royal Oak, MI.

Study Options Full-time and part-time.

Program Entrance Requirements Clinical experience, minimum overall college GPA of 3.0, transcript of college record, CPR certification, written essay, immunizations, interview, 2 letters of recommendation, professional liability insurance/malpractice insurance, prerequisite course work, GRE General Test.

Advanced Placement Credit given for nursing courses completed elsewhere dependent upon specific evaluations.

Degree Requirements 45 total credit hours, thesis or project.

POST-MASTER'S PROGRAM

Areas of Study Nurse anesthesia; nursing education. *Nurse practitioner programs in:* adult health, family health, gerontology.

CONTINUING EDUCATION PROGRAM

Contact *Telephone:* 248-370-4013. *Fax:* 248-370-4279.

Saginaw Valley State University
Crystal M. Lange College of Nursing and Health Sciences
University Center, Michigan

http://www.svsu.edu/acadprog/nhs/

Founded in 1963

DEGREES • BSN • MSN

Nursing Program Faculty 12 (50% with doctorates).

Nursing Student Activities Sigma Theta Tau, Student Nurses' Association.

Nursing Student Resources Academic advising; academic or career counseling; assistance for students with disabilities; bookstore; campus computer network; career placement assistance; computer lab; computer-assisted instruction; e-mail services; externships; interactive nursing skills videos; Internet; learning resource lab; library services; nursing audiovisuals; remedial services; resume preparation assistance; skills, simulation, or other laboratory; tutoring.

Library Facilities 241,661 volumes; 23,741 periodical subscriptions.

BACCALAUREATE PROGRAMS

Degree BSN

Available Programs Accelerated Baccalaureate for Second Degree; Baccalaureate for Second Degree; Generic Baccalaureate; RN Baccalaureate.

Study Options Full-time and part-time.

Program Entrance Requirements Minimum overall college GPA of 2.5, transcript of college record, CPR certification, written essay, health exam, immunizations, interview, minimum GPA in nursing prerequisites of 2.5, professional liability insurance/malpractice insurance, prerequisite course work. Transfer students are accepted.

Advanced Placement Credit by examination available. Credit given for nursing courses completed elsewhere dependent upon specific evaluations.

Contact *Telephone:* 989-964-4145 Ext. 4145. *Fax:* 989-964-4024.

GRADUATE PROGRAMS

Contact *Telephone:* 989-964-4145 Ext. 4145. *Fax:* 989-964-4024.

MASTER'S DEGREE PROGRAM

Degree MSN

Available Programs Master's; RN to Master's.

Concentrations Available Nursing administration; nursing education; nursing informatics. *Nurse practitioner programs in:* family health.

Study Options Full-time and part-time.

Program Entrance Requirements Clinical experience, minimum overall college GPA of 3.0, transcript of college record, written essay, interview, 3 letters of recommendation, professional liability insurance/malpractice insurance, resume, statistics course, GRE.

Advanced Placement Credit given for nursing courses completed elsewhere dependent upon specific evaluations.

Degree Requirements 39 total credit hours, thesis or project.

POST-MASTER'S PROGRAM

Areas of Study Nursing administration; nursing education; nursing informatics. *Nurse practitioner programs in:* family health.

CONTINUING EDUCATION PROGRAM

Contact *Telephone:* 989-964-4145.

Spring Arbor University
Program in Nursing
Spring Arbor, Michigan

http://www.arbor.edu/bsn

Founded in 1873

DEGREES • BSN • MSN • MSN/MBA

Nursing Program Faculty 21 (10% with doctorates).

Baccalaureate Enrollment 265
Women 93% **Men** 7% **Minority** 9% **International** 1% **Part-time** 75%

Graduate Enrollment 16
Women 94% **Men** 6%

Nursing Student Resources Academic advising; bookstore; campus computer network; computer-assisted instruction; e-mail services; Internet; library services; nursing audiovisuals; other; tutoring.

Library Facilities 111,736 volumes (1,000 in health, 350 in nursing); 665 periodical subscriptions (25 health-care related).

BACCALAUREATE PROGRAMS

Degree BSN

Available Programs ADN to Baccalaureate.

Site Options Battle Creek, Gaylord, Jackson, Kalamazoo, Lansing, MI; Lambertville, MI.

Program Entrance Requirements Minimum overall college GPA of 2.5, transcript of college record, written essay, high school biology, high school chemistry, 1 year of high school math, 2 years high school science, high school transcript, minimum GPA in nursing prerequisites of 2.5, RN licensure. Transfer students are accepted. *Application deadline:* Applications may be processed on a rolling basis for some programs. *Application fee:* $40.

Expenses (2009–10) *Tuition:* full-time $9135. *Required fees:* full-time $240.

Financial Aid 80% of baccalaureate students in nursing programs received some form of financial aid in 2008–09. *Gift aid (need-based):* Federal Pell, FSEOG, state, private, college/university gift aid from institutional funds. *Loans:* FFEL (Subsidized and Unsubsidized Stafford PLUS), Perkins, Michigan Loan Program and alternative loans. *Work-study:* Federal Work-Study, part-time campus jobs. *Financial aid application deadline (priority):* 3/1.

Contact Mrs. Cindy E. Meredith, RN, Director of Nursing, Program in Nursing, Spring Arbor University, 106 East Main Street, Suite #3, Spring Arbor, MI 49283-9799. *Telephone:* 517-750-6344. *Fax:* 517-750-6602. *E-mail:* cemered@arbor.edu.

GRADUATE PROGRAMS

Expenses (2009–10) *Tuition:* full-time $9465. *Required fees:* full-time $240.

Financial Aid 60% of graduate students in nursing programs received some form of financial aid in 2008–09.

Contact Mr. Jim Madden, Senior Admission Specialist, Program in Nursing, Spring Arbor University, 3497 South 9th Street, Suite A, Kalamazoo, MI 49009-9501. *Telephone:* 800-930-9754 Ext. 4058. *Fax:* 269-372-1840. *E-mail:* jmadden@arbor.edu.

Spring Arbor University (continued)

MASTER'S DEGREE PROGRAM

Degrees MSN; MSN/MBA

Available Programs Master's.

Concentrations Available Nursing education. *Nurse practitioner programs in:* adult health, gerontology.

Study Options Full-time.

Online Degree Options Yes (online only).

Program Entrance Requirements Computer literacy, minimum overall college GPA of 3.0, transcript of college record, written essay, interview, 2 letters of recommendation, nursing research course, prerequisite course work, statistics course. *Application deadline:* 7/1 (fall). *Application fee:* $40.

Degree Requirements 63 total credit hours, thesis or project.

University of Detroit Mercy
McAuley School of Nursing
Detroit, Michigan

http://www.udmercy.edu/healthprof/nursing/
Founded in 1877

DEGREES • BSN • MSN

Nursing Program Faculty 80

Baccalaureate Enrollment 933
Women 88% **Men** 12% **Minority** 24% **International** 6% **Part-time** 46%

Graduate Enrollment 132
Women 95% **Men** 5% **Minority** 27% **International** 2% **Part-time** 96%

Distance Learning Courses Available.

Nursing Student Activities Sigma Theta Tau, Student Nurses' Association.

Nursing Student Resources Academic advising; academic or career counseling; bookstore; campus computer network; career placement assistance; computer lab; computer-assisted instruction; e-mail services; Internet; learning resource lab; library services; nursing audiovisuals; other; paid internships; placement services for program completers; remedial services; resume preparation assistance; skills, simulation, or other laboratory; tutoring.

Library Facilities 32,330 volumes in health, 3,404 volumes in nursing; 2,670 periodical subscriptions health-care related.

BACCALAUREATE PROGRAMS

Degree BSN

Available Programs Accelerated Baccalaureate for Second Degree; Generic Baccalaureate; RN Baccalaureate.

Site Options Dearborn, MI; Grand Rapids, MI; Wayne, MI.

Study Options Full-time and part-time.

Program Entrance Requirements Minimum overall college GPA of 2.5, transcript of college record, CPR certification, health exam, health insurance, high school biology, high school chemistry, 2 years high school math, 2 years high school science, high school transcript, immunizations, minimum high school GPA of 2.5, minimum GPA in nursing prerequisites of 2.5, prerequisite course work. Transfer students are accepted.

Advanced Placement Credit given for nursing courses completed elsewhere dependent upon specific evaluations.

Contact *Telephone:* 313-993-1245. *Fax:* 313-993-3325.

GRADUATE PROGRAMS

Contact *Telephone:* 313-993-6423. *Fax:* 313-993-6175.

MASTER'S DEGREE PROGRAM

Degree MSN

Available Programs Accelerated AD/RN to Master's; Master's; Master's for Nurses with Non-Nursing Degrees.

Concentrations Available Nursing administration; nursing education. *Nurse practitioner programs in:* family health.

Study Options Full-time and part-time.

Program Entrance Requirements Clinical experience, minimum overall college GPA of 3.0, transcript of college record, CPR certification, immunizations, interview, 3 letters of recommendation, resume.

Degree Requirements 50 total credit hours.

POST-MASTER'S PROGRAM

Areas of Study Nursing administration; nursing education. *Nurse practitioner programs in:* family health.

University of Michigan
School of Nursing
Ann Arbor, Michigan

http://www.nursing.umich.edu
Founded in 1817

DEGREES • BSN • MS • MSN/MBA • MSN/MPH • PHD

Nursing Program Faculty 130 (66% with doctorates).

Baccalaureate Enrollment 618
Women 90% **Men** 10% **Minority** 20% **International** 3% **Part-time** 13%

Graduate Enrollment 240
Women 95% **Men** 5% **Minority** 30% **International** 11% **Part-time** 40%

Distance Learning Courses Available.

Nursing Student Activities Nursing Honor Society, Sigma Theta Tau, Student Nurses' Association, nursing club.

Nursing Student Resources Academic advising; academic or career counseling; assistance for students with disabilities; bookstore; campus computer network; career placement assistance; computer lab; computer-assisted instruction; daycare for children of students; e-mail services; employment services for current students; externships; housing assistance; interactive nursing skills videos; Internet; learning resource lab; library services; nursing audiovisuals; paid internships; placement services for program completers; remedial services; resume preparation assistance; skills, simulation, or other laboratory; tutoring; unpaid internships.

Library Facilities 8.2 million volumes (1.2 million in nursing); 74,022 periodical subscriptions.

BACCALAUREATE PROGRAMS

Degree BSN

Available Programs Accelerated Baccalaureate for Second Degree; Generic Baccalaureate; RN Baccalaureate.

Site Options Kalamazoo, MI; Traverse City, MI.

Study Options Full-time and part-time.

Program Entrance Requirements Minimum overall college GPA of 3.0, transcript of college record, written essay, high school chemistry, 2 years high school math, 2 years high school science, high school transcript, minimum high school GPA of 3.0, prerequisite course work. Transfer students are accepted. *Application deadline:* 2/1 (fall). Applications may be processed on a rolling basis for some programs. *Application fee:* $80.

Advanced Placement Credit given for nursing courses completed elsewhere dependent upon specific evaluations.

Expenses (2008–09) *Tuition, state resident:* full-time $10,848; part-time $777 per hour. *Tuition, nonresident:* full-time $32,880; part-time $1695 per hour. *International tuition:* $32,880 full-time. *Room and board:* $8590; room only: $5264 per academic year. *Required fees:* full-time $189.

Contact Sheila Pantlind, Admissions Counselor, School of Nursing, University of Michigan, 1220 Student Activities Building, 515 East Jefferson, Ann Arbor, MI 48109. *Telephone:* 734-647-1443. *Fax:* 734-936-0740. *E-mail:* pantlin@umich.edu.

GRADUATE PROGRAMS

Expenses (2008–09) *Tuition, state resident:* full-time $16,864; part-time $1252 per hour. *Tuition, nonresident:* full-time $34,114; part-time $2210 per hour. *International tuition:* $34,114 full-time. *Required fees:* full-time $189.

Financial Aid 15 research assistantships, 28 teaching assistantships were awarded; fellowships, Federal Work-Study, institutionally sponsored loans, scholarships, traineeships, and tuition waivers (partial) also available.

Contact Dr. Richard Redman, Professor and Executive Associate Dean, Academic Affairs, School of Nursing, University of Michigan, 400 North Ingalls Building, Room 1174, Ann Arbor, MI 48109-5482. *Telephone:* 734-764-7188. *Fax:* 734-647-1419. *E-mail:* RWR@umich.edu.

MASTER'S DEGREE PROGRAM

Degrees MS; MSN/MBA; MSN/MPH

Available Programs Accelerated RN to Master's; Master's; RN to Master's.

Concentrations Available Health-care administration; nurse-midwifery; nursing administration; nursing informatics. *Clinical nurse specialist programs in:* community health, gerontology, home health care, medical-surgical, occupational health, psychiatric/mental health. *Nurse practitioner programs in:* acute care, adult health, family health, gerontology, pediatric, primary care, psychiatric/mental health.

Study Options Full-time and part-time.

Program Entrance Requirements Computer literacy, minimum overall college GPA of 3.0, transcript of college record, written essay, interview, 3 letters of recommendation, resume, GRE General Test (if undergraduate GPA is below 3.25). *Application deadline:* 2/1 (fall). Applications may be processed on a rolling basis for some programs. *Application fee:* $80.

Advanced Placement Credit given for nursing courses completed elsewhere dependent upon specific evaluations.

Degree Requirements 37 total credit hours, thesis or project.

POST-MASTER'S PROGRAM

Areas of Study Health-care administration; nurse-midwifery; nursing administration; nursing informatics. *Clinical nurse specialist programs in:* community health, gerontology, home health care, medical-surgical, occupational health, psychiatric/mental health, women's health. *Nurse practitioner programs in:* acute care, adult health, family health, gerontology, pediatric, primary care, psychiatric/mental health, women's health.

DOCTORAL DEGREE PROGRAM

Degree PhD

Available Programs Doctorate; Post-Baccalaureate Doctorate.

Areas of Study Advanced practice nursing, aging, bio-behavioral research, biology of health and illness, community health, critical care, ethics, family health, gerontology, health policy, health promotion/disease prevention, health-care systems, individualized study, information systems, neuro-behavior, nursing administration, nursing policy, nursing research, nursing science, women's health.

Program Entrance Requirements Minimum overall college GPA of 3.0, interview, 3 letters of recommendation, scholarly papers, vita, writing sample, GRE General Test. Application deadline: 12/11 (fall). Application fee: $80.

Degree Requirements 50 total credit hours, dissertation, oral exam, written exam, residency.

POSTDOCTORAL PROGRAM

Areas of Study Addiction/substance abuse, aging, chronic illness, community health, family health, gerontology, health promotion/disease prevention, individualized study, information systems, neuro-behavior, nursing interventions, nursing research, nursing science, vulnerable population, women's health.

Postdoctoral Program Contact Dr. Richard Redman, Director, Doctoral and Postdoctoral Studies, School of Nursing, University of Michigan, 400 North Ingalls Building, Room 1305, Ann Arbor, MI 48109-0482. *Telephone:* 734-764-9454. *Fax:* 734-763-6668. *E-mail:* rwr@umich.edu.

University of Michigan–Flint

Department of Nursing
Flint, Michigan

http://www.umflint.edu/nur
Founded in 1956
DEGREES • BSN • DNP
Nursing Program Faculty 87 (14% with doctorates).

Baccalaureate Enrollment 1,181
Women 80.44% **Men** 19.56% **Minority** 17.02% **International** 1.02% **Part-time** 48.18%
Graduate Enrollment 82
Women 91.46% **Men** 8.54% **Minority** 10.98% **Part-time** 93.9%
Distance Learning Courses Available.
Nursing Student Activities Nursing Honor Society, Sigma Theta Tau, Student Nurses' Association.
Nursing Student Resources Academic advising; academic or career counseling; assistance for students with disabilities; bookstore; campus computer network; career placement assistance; computer lab; computer-assisted instruction; daycare for children of students; e-mail services; employment services for current students; externships; housing assistance; interactive nursing skills videos; Internet; library services; nursing audio-visuals; remedial services; resume preparation assistance; skills, simulation, or other laboratory; tutoring.
Library Facilities 266,696 volumes (7,436 in health, 4,914 in nursing); 907 periodical subscriptions (6,497 health-care related).

BACCALAUREATE PROGRAMS

Degree BSN

Available Programs Accelerated Baccalaureate for Second Degree; Baccalaureate for Second Degree; Generic Baccalaureate; RN Baccalaureate.

Site Options Lansing, MI; Flint, MI.

Study Options Full-time and part-time.

Online Degree Options Yes.

Program Entrance Requirements Minimum overall college GPA of 2.75, transcript of college record, CPR certification, written essay, health exam, health insurance, immunizations, 2 letters of recommendation, minimum GPA in nursing prerequisites of 2.75, prerequisite course work. Transfer students are accepted. *Application deadline:* 1/20 (fall), 9/1 (winter).

Advanced Placement Credit given for nursing courses completed elsewhere dependent upon specific evaluations.

Expenses (2009–10) *Tuition, state resident:* full-time $9314; part-time $370 per credit hour. *Tuition, nonresident:* full-time $18,232; part-time $740 per credit hour. *International tuition:* $18,232 full-time. *Room and board:* $9474; room only: $6874 per academic year. *Required fees:* full-time $380; part-time $145 per term.

Financial Aid 74% of baccalaureate students in nursing programs received some form of financial aid in 2008–09.

Contact Ms. Marge Hathaway, Administrative Specialist, Department of Nursing, University of Michigan–Flint, 303 East Kearsley, 2180 WSW, Flint, MI 48502-1950. *Telephone:* 810-762-3420. *Fax:* 810-766-6851. *E-mail:* mhath@umflint.edu.

GRADUATE PROGRAMS

Financial Aid 52% of graduate students in nursing programs received some form of financial aid in 2008–09.

Contact Ms. Marge Hathaway, Administrative Specialist, Department of Nursing, University of Michigan–Flint, 303 East Kearsley, Flint, MI 48502-1950. *Telephone:* 810-762-3420. *Fax:* 810-766-6851. *E-mail:* nursing@list.flint.umich.edu.

MASTER'S DEGREE PROGRAM

Site Options Flint, MI.

DOCTORAL DEGREE PROGRAM

Degree DNP

Available Programs Doctorate.

Areas of Study Family health.

Site Options Flint, MI.

Online Degree Options Yes (online only).

Program Entrance Requirements Minimum overall college GPA of 3.2, interview, 3 letters of recommendation, MSN or equivalent, statistics course, vita. Application deadline: 4/1 (fall). Application fee: $55.

Degree Requirements 36 total credit hours.

University of Michigan–Flint (continued)
CONTINUING EDUCATION PROGRAM

Contact Mrs. Carol Hall, Secretary, Nursing Development and Research, Department of Nursing, University of Michigan–Flint, 303 East Kearsley, 2180 WSW, Flint, MI 48502-1950. *Telephone:* 810-762-3420. *Fax:* 810-766-6851. *E-mail:* hallca@umflint.edu.

University of Phoenix–Metro Detroit Campus
College of Health and Human Services
Southfield, Michigan

DEGREES • BSN • MSN

Nursing Program Faculty 15 (33% with doctorates).

Baccalaureate Enrollment 18
Women 94.4% **Men** 5.6% **Minority** 38.9%

Graduate Enrollment 4
Women 100%

Nursing Student Activities Sigma Theta Tau.

Nursing Student Resources Academic advising; academic or career counseling; assistance for students with disabilities; bookstore; campus computer network; computer lab; computer-assisted instruction; e-mail services; interactive nursing skills videos; Internet; learning resource lab; library services; nursing audiovisuals; skills, simulation, or other laboratory; tutoring.

Library Facilities 1,759 volumes; 692 periodical subscriptions (1,300 health-care related).

BACCALAUREATE PROGRAMS
Degree BSN

Available Programs Accelerated Baccalaureate.
Site Options Livonia, MI; Ann Arbor, MI; Southfield, MI.
Study Options Full-time.
Program Entrance Requirements Transcript of college record, CPR certification, immunizations, 1 letter of recommendation, RN licensure. Transfer students are accepted. *Application deadline:* Applications may be processed on a rolling basis for some programs.
Advanced Placement Credit by examination available. Credit given for nursing courses completed elsewhere dependent upon specific evaluations.
Expenses (2009–10) *Tuition:* full-time $10,560. *Required fees:* full-time $600.
Contact Campus College Chair, Nursing, College of Health and Human Services, University of Phoenix–Metro Detroit Campus, 5480 Corporate Drive, Suite 240, Troy, MI 48098-2623. *Telephone:* 800-834-2438.

GRADUATE PROGRAMS
Expenses (2009–10) *Tuition:* full-time $13,200. *Required fees:* full-time $760.
Financial Aid Institutionally sponsored loans and scholarships available.
Contact Campus College Chair, Nursing, College of Health and Human Services, University of Phoenix–Metro Detroit Campus, 5480 Corporate Drive, Suite 240, Troy, MI 48098-2623. *Telephone:* 800-834-2438.

MASTER'S DEGREE PROGRAM
Degree MSN

Available Programs Master's.
Concentrations Available Health-care administration; nursing administration; nursing education.
Site Options Livonia, MI; Ann Arbor, MI; Southfield, MI.
Study Options Full-time.
Program Entrance Requirements Clinical experience, computer literacy, minimum overall college GPA of 2.5, transcript of college record. *Application deadline:* Applications may be processed on a rolling basis for some programs. *Application fee:* $45.

Advanced Placement Credit given for nursing courses completed elsewhere dependent upon specific evaluations.
Degree Requirements 39 total credit hours, thesis or project.

University of Phoenix–West Michigan Campus
College of Health and Human Services
Walker, Michigan

Founded in 2000

Nursing Program Faculty 2
Nursing Student Activities Sigma Theta Tau.

Nursing Student Resources Academic advising; academic or career counseling; assistance for students with disabilities; bookstore; computer lab; computer-assisted instruction; e-mail services; interactive nursing skills videos; Internet; learning resource lab; library services; nursing audiovisuals; remedial services; resume preparation assistance; skills, simulation, or other laboratory.

Library Facilities 16,781 periodical subscriptions (1,300 health-care related).

Wayne State University
College of Nursing
Detroit, Michigan

http://www.nursing.wayne.edu

Founded in 1868

DEGREES • BSN • DNP • MSN • PHD

Nursing Program Faculty 86 (35% with doctorates).

Baccalaureate Enrollment 342
Women 74% **Men** 26% **Minority** 17% **International** 5% **Part-time** 28%

Graduate Enrollment 415
Women 91.5% **Men** 8.5% **Minority** 20% **International** 4.5% **Part-time** 70%

Distance Learning Courses Available.

Nursing Student Activities Nursing Honor Society, Sigma Theta Tau, Student Nurses' Association, nursing club.

Nursing Student Resources Academic advising; academic or career counseling; assistance for students with disabilities; bookstore; campus computer network; career placement assistance; computer lab; computer-assisted instruction; e-mail services; employment services for current students; interactive nursing skills videos; Internet; learning resource lab; library services; nursing audiovisuals; placement services for program completers; resume preparation assistance; skills, simulation, or other laboratory; tutoring.

Library Facilities 3.5 million volumes (156,000 in health, 6,600 in nursing); 45,200 periodical subscriptions (5,000 health-care related).

BACCALAUREATE PROGRAMS
Degree BSN

Available Programs Accelerated Baccalaureate for Second Degree; Generic Baccalaureate.
Study Options Full-time and part-time.
Program Entrance Requirements Minimum overall college GPA of 2.0, transcript of college record, minimum GPA in nursing prerequisites of 2.5, prerequisite course work. Transfer students are accepted. *Application deadline:* 3/31 (fall). *Application fee:* $50.
Expenses (2009–10) *Tuition, area resident:* full-time $8872. *Tuition, nonresident:* full-time $18,711. *International tuition:* $18,711 full-time. *Room and board:* $7659 per academic year. *Required fees:* full-time $2200.
Contact Office of Student Affairs, College of Nursing, Wayne State University, 5557 Cass Avenue, Detroit, MI 48202. *Telephone:* 313-577-4082. *Fax:* 313-577-6949.

GRADUATE PROGRAMS

Expenses (2009–10) *Tuition, area resident:* full-time $6671. *Tuition, nonresident:* full-time $12,188. *Room and board:* $7659 per academic year.

Financial Aid 2 fellowships (averaging $13,901 per year), 2 research assistantships (averaging $16,028 per year), 4 teaching assistantships (averaging $22,997 per year) were awarded; Federal Work-Study, institutionally sponsored loans, scholarships, and traineeships also available.

Contact Office of Student Affairs, College of Nursing, Wayne State University, 5557 Cass Avenue, Detroit, MI 48202: *Telephone:* 313-577-4082. *Fax:* 313-577-6949.

MASTER'S DEGREE PROGRAM

Degree MSN

Available Programs Master's.

Concentrations Available Nurse-midwifery. *Clinical nurse specialist programs in:* acute care, community health, critical care, psychiatric/mental health. *Nurse practitioner programs in:* acute care, gerontology, neonatal health, pediatric, primary care, psychiatric/mental health, women's health.

Study Options Full-time and part-time.

Program Entrance Requirements Minimum overall college GPA of 3.0, transcript of college record, written essay, 3 letters of recommendation, resume. *Application deadline:* 7/1 (fall), 11/1 (winter), 4/1 (spring), 4/1 (summer).

Advanced Placement Credit given for nursing courses completed elsewhere dependent upon specific evaluations.

Degree Requirements 47 total credit hours.

POST-MASTER'S PROGRAM

Areas of Study Nurse-midwifery; nursing education. *Clinical nurse specialist programs in:* psychiatric/mental health. *Nurse practitioner programs in:* acute care, gerontology, pediatric, primary care, psychiatric/mental health, women's health.

DOCTORAL DEGREE PROGRAM

Degree DNP, PhD

Available Programs Doctorate; Post-Baccalaureate Doctorate.

Areas of Study Advanced practice nursing, clinical practice.

Program Entrance Requirements Clinical experience, minimum overall college GPA of 3.0, interview by faculty committee, interview, 2 letters of recommendation, vita, writing sample, GRE General Test. Application deadline: 1/15 (fall). Applications may be processed on a rolling basis for some programs. Application fee: $50.

Degree Requirements 90 total credit hours, written exam, residency.

POSTDOCTORAL PROGRAM

Areas of Study Adolescent health, community health, individualized study, self-care.

Postdoctoral Program Contact Dennis Ross, Academic Services Officer, College of Nursing, Wayne State University, 5557 Cass Avenue, Detroit, MI 48202. *Telephone:* 313-577-4082. *Fax:* 313-577-6949. *E-mail:* nursinginfo@wayne.edu.

CONTINUING EDUCATION PROGRAM

Contact Office of the Dean, College of Nursing, Wayne State University, 5557 Cass Avenue, Detroit, MI 48202. *Telephone:* 313-577-4070. *E-mail:* nursinginfo@wayne.edu.

Western Michigan University
College of Health and Human Services
Kalamazoo, Michigan

Founded in 1903

DEGREE • BSN

Nursing Program Faculty 26 (31% with doctorates).

Baccalaureate Enrollment 377
Women 92% **Men** 8% **Minority** 9% **International** 1% **Part-time** 25%

Nursing Student Activities Nursing Honor Society, Student Nurses' Association.

Nursing Student Resources Academic advising; academic or career counseling; assistance for students with disabilities; bookstore; campus computer network; career placement assistance; computer lab; computer-assisted instruction; daycare for children of students; e-mail services; employment services for current students; externships; housing assistance; interactive nursing skills videos; Internet; learning resource lab; library services; nursing audiovisuals; placement services for program completers; remedial services; resume preparation assistance; skills, simulation, or other laboratory.

Library Facilities 2.5 million volumes (766 in nursing); 12,711 periodical subscriptions (362 health-care related).

BACCALAUREATE PROGRAMS

Degree BSN

Available Programs ADN to Baccalaureate; Baccalaureate for Second Degree; Generic Baccalaureate; RN Baccalaureate.

Site Options St. Joseph, MI.

Study Options Full-time and part-time.

Program Entrance Requirements Minimum overall college GPA of 2.8, transcript of college record, CPR certification, written essay, high school biology, high school chemistry, 3 years high school math, 2 years high school science, high school transcript, immunizations, minimum high school GPA of 2.8, minimum GPA in nursing prerequisites of 2.8, prerequisite course work. Transfer students are accepted. *Application deadline:* Applications may be processed on a rolling basis for some programs.

Advanced Placement Credit given for nursing courses completed elsewhere dependent upon specific evaluations.

Financial Aid 43% of baccalaureate students in nursing programs received some form of financial aid in 2007–08.

Contact Mrs. Marsha Ann Mahan, Student Advisor, College of Health and Human Services, Western Michigan University, 1903 West Michigan Avenue, Kalamazoo, MI 49008. *Telephone:* 269-387-8150. *Fax:* 269-387-8170. *E-mail:* marsha.mahan@wmich.edu.

MINNESOTA

Augsburg College
Program in Nursing
Minneapolis, Minnesota

http://www.augsburg.edu/nursing

Founded in 1869

DEGREES • BS • MA

Nursing Program Faculty 9 (50% with doctorates).

Baccalaureate Enrollment 169
Women 83% **Men** 17% **Part-time** 89%

Graduate Enrollment 42
Women 100% **Minority** 2% **Part-time** 90%

Nursing Student Resources Academic advising; academic or career counseling; assistance for students with disabilities; bookstore; campus computer network; computer lab; computer-assisted instruction; e-mail services; Internet; library services; tutoring.

Library Facilities 146,166 volumes (1,550 in health, 200 in nursing); 754 periodical subscriptions (70 health-care related).

BACCALAUREATE PROGRAMS

Degree BS

Available Programs ADN to Baccalaureate.

Site Options Rochester, MN; Saint Paul, MN.

Study Options Full-time and part-time.

Program Entrance Requirements Minimum overall college GPA of 2.5, transcript of college record, CPR certification, written essay, high school transcript, immunizations, letters of recommendation, prerequisite course work, RN licensure. Transfer students are accepted.

Augsburg College (continued)
Contact *Telephone:* 612-330-1101. *Fax:* 612-330-1784.

GRADUATE PROGRAMS

Contact *Telephone:* 612-330-1101. *Fax:* 612-330-1784.

MASTER'S DEGREE PROGRAM

Degree MA

Available Programs Master's.

Concentrations Available *Clinical nurse specialist programs in:* community health.

Site Options Rochester, MN; Saint Paul, MN.

Study Options Full-time and part-time.

Program Entrance Requirements Computer literacy, minimum overall college GPA of 3.0, transcript of college record, written essay, immunizations, 3 letters of recommendation, prerequisite course work, statistics course.

Advanced Placement Credit given for nursing courses completed elsewhere dependent upon specific evaluations.

Degree Requirements 48 total credit hours, thesis or project.

Bemidji State University

Department of Nursing
Bemidji, Minnesota

http://www.bemidjistate.edu/academics/ departments/nursing/

Founded in 1919

DEGREE • BS

Nursing Program Faculty 5 (60% with doctorates).

Baccalaureate Enrollment 62
Women 95% **Men** 5% **Minority** 3% **Part-time** 68%

Distance Learning Courses Available.

Nursing Student Resources Academic advising; academic or career counseling; assistance for students with disabilities; bookstore; campus computer network; career placement assistance; computer lab; computer-assisted instruction; daycare for children of students; e-mail services; employment services for current students; housing assistance; Internet; library services; nursing audiovisuals; remedial services; tutoring.

Library Facilities 554,087 volumes (9,000 in health, 1,000 in nursing); 991 periodical subscriptions (300 health-care related).

BACCALAUREATE PROGRAMS

Degree BS

Available Programs Generic Baccalaureate; RN Baccalaureate.

Study Options Full-time and part-time.

Program Entrance Requirements Minimum overall college GPA, transcript of college record, immunizations, professional liability insurance/malpractice insurance, RN licensure. Transfer students are accepted.

Contact *Telephone:* 218-755-3892. *Fax:* 218-755-4402.

CONTINUING EDUCATION PROGRAM

Contact *Telephone:* 218-755-3892. *Fax:* 218-755-4402.

Bethel University

Department of Nursing
St. Paul, Minnesota

http://www.bethel.edu/college/dept/nursing/index. html

Founded in 1871

DEGREES • BSN • MA

Nursing Program Faculty 36 (40% with doctorates).

Baccalaureate Enrollment 283
Women 93.6% **Men** 6.4% **Minority** 11%

Graduate Enrollment 66
Women 97% **Men** 3% **Minority** 9.1%

Distance Learning Courses Available.

Nursing Student Activities Sigma Theta Tau, nursing club.

Nursing Student Resources Academic advising; academic or career counseling; assistance for students with disabilities; bookstore; campus computer network; career placement assistance; computer lab; computer-assisted instruction; daycare for children of students; e-mail services; employment services for current students; interactive nursing skills videos; Internet; learning resource lab; library services; nursing audiovisuals; paid internships; placement services for program completers; remedial services; resume preparation assistance; skills, simulation, or other laboratory; tutoring.

Library Facilities 194,000 volumes (4,900 in nursing); 38,080 periodical subscriptions (1,006 health-care related).

BACCALAUREATE PROGRAMS

Degree BSN

Available Programs Generic Baccalaureate; RN Baccalaureate.

Site Options Brooklyn Park, MN.

Study Options Full-time and part-time.

Program Entrance Requirements Minimum overall college GPA of 2.5, transcript of college record, CPR certification, written essay, health exam, health insurance, high school transcript, immunizations, interview, 2 letters of recommendation, minimum GPA in nursing prerequisites of 2.5, professional liability insurance/malpractice insurance, prerequisite course work. Transfer students are accepted. *Application deadline:* 9/15 (fall).

Advanced Placement Credit given for nursing courses completed elsewhere dependent upon specific evaluations.

Expenses (2009–10) *Tuition:* full-time $26,900; part-time $1125 per credit. *International tuition:* $26,900 full-time. *Room and board:* $8920; room only: $5720 per academic year. *Required fees:* full-time $385; part-time $193 per term.

Financial Aid 80% of baccalaureate students in nursing programs received some form of financial aid in 2008–09.

Contact Dr. Elizabeth A. Peterson, RN, Director, Pre-Professional Program, Department of Nursing, Bethel University, 3900 Bethel Drive, St. Paul, MN 55112-6999. *Telephone:* 651-638-6455. *Fax:* 651-635-1965. *E-mail:* e-peterson@bethel.edu.

GRADUATE PROGRAMS

Expenses (2009–10) *Tuition:* part-time $450 per credit.

Financial Aid 50% of graduate students in nursing programs received some form of financial aid in 2008–09. Institutionally sponsored loans and scholarships available.

Contact Ms. Jeanne Shaw, Admissions Advisor, Department of Nursing, Bethel University, 3900 Bethel Drive, PO #2377, St. Paul, MN 55112. *Telephone:* 651-635-8080. *Fax:* 651-635-1965. *E-mail:* jeanne-shaw@bethel. edu.

MASTER'S DEGREE PROGRAM

Degree MA

Available Programs Master's.

Concentrations Available Nursing administration; nursing education.

Study Options Full-time and part-time.

Program Entrance Requirements Clinical experience, computer literacy, minimum overall college GPA of 3.0, transcript of college record, written essay, immunizations, interview, 3 letters of recommendation, professional liability insurance/malpractice insurance, resume, statistics course, MAT. *Application deadline:* Applications may be processed on a rolling basis for some programs. *Application fee:* $25.

Advanced Placement Credit given for nursing courses completed elsewhere dependent upon specific evaluations.

Degree Requirements 43 total credit hours, thesis or project.

College of Saint Benedict
Department of Nursing
Saint Joseph, Minnesota

http://www.csbsju.edu/nursing/

Founded in 1887

DEGREE • BS

Nursing Program Faculty 17 (35% with doctorates).

Baccalaureate Enrollment 136
Women 90.5% **Men** 9.5% **Minority** 1% **International** 1%

Nursing Student Activities Sigma Theta Tau, Student Nurses' Association, nursing club.

Nursing Student Resources Academic advising; academic or career counseling; assistance for students with disabilities; bookstore; campus computer network; career placement assistance; computer lab; computer-assisted instruction; e-mail services; employment services for current students; interactive nursing skills videos; Internet; learning resource lab; library services; nursing audiovisuals; paid internships; placement services for program completers; resume preparation assistance; skills, simulation, or other laboratory; tutoring; unpaid internships.

Library Facilities 749,886 volumes (7,300 in health, 700 in nursing); 13,700 periodical subscriptions (335 health-care related).

BACCALAUREATE PROGRAMS

Degree BS

Available Programs Generic Baccalaureate.
Study Options Full-time.
Program Entrance Requirements Transcript of college record, CPR certification, health exam, health insurance, immunizations, minimum GPA in nursing prerequisites of 2.75, professional liability insurance/malpractice insurance, prerequisite course work. *Application deadline:* 12/1 (fall).

Advanced Placement Credit given for nursing courses completed elsewhere dependent upon specific evaluations.

Expenses (2009–10) *Tuition:* full-time $30,000; part-time $350 per credit. *Required fees:* full-time $700.

Financial Aid 93% of baccalaureate students in nursing programs received some form of financial aid in 2008–09. *Gift aid (need-based):* Federal Pell, FSEOG, state, private, college/university gift aid from institutional funds. *Loans:* Federal Direct (Subsidized and Unsubsidized Stafford PLUS), Perkins, state, private alternative loans. *Work-study:* Federal Work-Study, part-time campus jobs. *Financial aid application deadline (priority):* 3/15.

Contact Dr. Carie Ann Braun, Associate Professor and Chair, Department of Nursing, College of Saint Benedict, 37 College Avenue South, St. Joseph, MN 56374. *Telephone:* 320-363-5223. *Fax:* 320-363-6099. *E-mail:* cbraun@csbsju.edu.

The College of St. Scholastica
Department of Nursing
Duluth, Minnesota

http://www.css.edu

Founded in 1912

DEGREES • BS • DNP • MA

Nursing Program Faculty 31 (32% with doctorates).

Baccalaureate Enrollment 354
Women 87.5% **Men** 12.5% **Minority** 9% **International** 1.4%

Graduate Enrollment 152
Women 94% **Men** 6% **Minority** 4.6% **International** 1.9% **Part-time** 61.1%

Distance Learning Courses Available.

Nursing Student Activities Sigma Theta Tau, Student Nurses' Association.

Nursing Student Resources Academic advising; academic or career counseling; assistance for students with disabilities; bookstore; campus computer network; career placement assistance; computer lab; computer-assisted instruction; e-mail services; Internet; learning resource lab; library services; nursing audiovisuals; paid internships; placement services for program completers; resume preparation assistance; skills, simulation, or other laboratory; tutoring; unpaid internships.

Library Facilities 114,769 volumes (7,280 in health, 1,150 in nursing); 21,656 periodical subscriptions (291 health-care related).

BACCALAUREATE PROGRAMS

Degree BS

Available Programs ADN to Baccalaureate; Accelerated Baccalaureate for Second Degree; Generic Baccalaureate.
Site Options Duluth, MN; Brainerd, MN; St. Cloud, MN.
Study Options Full-time.
Online Degree Options Yes.
Program Entrance Requirements Minimum overall college GPA of 3.0, transcript of college record, CPR certification, health exam, health insurance, high school transcript, immunizations, minimum GPA in nursing prerequisites of 2.0, prerequisite course work. Transfer students are accepted. *Application deadline:* 9/25 (fall).

Expenses (2009–10) *Tuition:* full-time $27,114; part-time $844 per credit hour. *International tuition:* $27,114 full-time. *Room and board:* $7278; room only: $4680 per academic year. *Required fees:* full-time $400; part-time $200 per term.

Financial Aid 98% of baccalaureate students in nursing programs received some form of financial aid in 2008–09. *Gift aid (need-based):* Federal Pell, FSEOG, state, private, college/university gift aid from institutional funds. *Loans:* Federal Nursing Student Loans, FFEL (Subsidized and Unsubsidized Stafford PLUS), Perkins, state, private supplemental loans. *Work-study:* Federal Work-Study, part-time campus jobs. *Financial aid application deadline (priority):* 3/1.

Contact Ms. Paula Byrne, RN, Chair, Department of Traditional Undergraduate Nursing, Department of Nursing, The College of St. Scholastica, 1200 Kenwood Avenue, Duluth, MN 55811. *Telephone:* 218-723-6020. *Fax:* 218-733-2221. *E-mail:* pbyrne@css.edu.

GRADUATE PROGRAMS

Expenses (2009–10) *Tuition:* part-time $675 per credit. *Required fees:* part-time $105 per term.

Financial Aid 90% of graduate students in nursing programs received some form of financial aid in 2008–09. Scholarships and traineeships available. Aid available to part-time students.

Contact Dr. Sally Fauchald, Chair, Graduate Nursing Department, Department of Nursing, The College of St. Scholastica, 1200 Kenwood Avenue, Duluth, MN 55811. *Telephone:* 218-723-6590. *Fax:* 218-733-2221. *E-mail:* sfauchal@css.edu.

MASTER'S DEGREE PROGRAM

Degree MA

Available Programs Master's.
Concentrations Available Nursing administration. *Clinical nurse specialist programs in:* adult health, gerontology. *Nurse practitioner programs in:* adult health, family health, gerontology, pediatric, psychiatric/mental health.
Site Options Duluth, MN.
Study Options Full-time and part-time.
Program Entrance Requirements Clinical experience, computer literacy, minimum overall college GPA of 3.0, transcript of college record, CPR certification, written essay, immunizations, interview, 3 letters of recommendation, nursing research course, physical assessment course, professional liability insurance/malpractice insurance, resume, statistics course, GRE General Test or MAT. *Application deadline:* 3/1 (spring). *Application fee:* $50.

Advanced Placement Credit given for nursing courses completed elsewhere dependent upon specific evaluations.

Degree Requirements 47 total credit hours, thesis or project.

POST-MASTER'S PROGRAM

Areas of Study Nursing administration. *Clinical nurse specialist programs in:* adult health, gerontology. *Nurse practitioner programs in:* adult health, family health, gerontology, pediatric, psychiatric/mental health.

The College of St. Scholastica (continued)

DOCTORAL DEGREE PROGRAM

Degree DNP

Available Programs Doctorate.

Areas of Study Advanced practice nursing, health policy, nursing administration, nursing education, nursing policy.

Site Options Duluth, MN.

Program Entrance Requirements Minimum overall college GPA of 3.0, interview by faculty committee, 3 letters of recommendation, MSN or equivalent, vita, writing sample. Application deadline: 3/1 (spring). Application fee: $50.

Degree Requirements 30 total credit hours, dissertation.

POSTDOCTORAL PROGRAM

Postdoctoral Program Contact Dr. Carleen A. Maynard, Chair, Graduate Nursing Department, Department of Nursing, The College of St. Scholastica, 1200 Kenwood Avenue, Duluth, MN 55811. *Telephone:* 218-723-6452. *Fax:* 218-733-2295. *E-mail:* cmaynard@css.edu.

Concordia College
Department of Nursing
Moorhead, Minnesota

http://www.cord.edu/dept/nursing/index.htm

Founded in 1891

DEGREES • BA • MS

Nursing Program Faculty 6 (33% with doctorates).

Baccalaureate Enrollment 75

Graduate Enrollment 2
Women 100%

Nursing Student Activities Sigma Theta Tau, Student Nurses' Association.

Nursing Student Resources Academic advising; academic or career counseling; assistance for students with disabilities; bookstore; campus computer network; career placement assistance; computer lab; computer-assisted instruction; e-mail services; employment services for current students; externships; housing assistance; interactive nursing skills videos; Internet; learning resource lab; library services; nursing audiovisuals; paid internships; placement services for program completers; remedial services; resume preparation assistance; skills, simulation, or other laboratory; tutoring; unpaid internships.

Library Facilities 340,006 volumes (2,135 in health, 837 in nursing); 3,329 periodical subscriptions (81 health-care related).

BACCALAUREATE PROGRAMS

Degree BA

Available Programs Accelerated Baccalaureate for Second Degree; Generic Baccalaureate.

Study Options Full-time.

Program Entrance Requirements Minimum overall college GPA of 2.9, transcript of college record, CPR certification, health exam, health insurance, immunizations, interview, 2 letters of recommendation, minimum GPA in nursing prerequisites of 2.7, professional liability insurance/malpractice insurance, prerequisite course work. Transfer students are accepted.

Advanced Placement Credit by examination available. Credit given for nursing courses completed elsewhere dependent upon specific evaluations.

Contact *Telephone:* 218-299-3879. *Fax:* 218-299-4309.

GRADUATE PROGRAMS

Contact *Telephone:* 218-299-3879. *Fax:* 218-299-4309.

MASTER'S DEGREE PROGRAM

Degree MS

Available Programs Master's.

Concentrations Available Nursing education.

Study Options Full-time and part-time.

Program Entrance Requirements Computer literacy, minimum overall college GPA of 3.0, transcript of college record, written essay, interview, 3 letters of recommendation.

Advanced Placement Credit given for nursing courses completed elsewhere dependent upon specific evaluations.

Degree Requirements 36 total credit hours, thesis or project, comprehensive exam.

Crown College
Nursing Department
St. Bonifacius, Minnesota

Founded in 1916

DEGREE • BSN

Nursing Program Faculty 6

Baccalaureate Enrollment 20
Women 100% **International** 10%

Distance Learning Courses Available.

Nursing Student Activities Student Nurses' Association.

Nursing Student Resources Academic advising; academic or career counseling; assistance for students with disabilities; bookstore; campus computer network; computer lab; computer-assisted instruction; e-mail services; employment services for current students; housing assistance; interactive nursing skills videos; Internet; learning resource lab; library services; nursing audiovisuals; remedial services; resume preparation assistance; skills, simulation, or other laboratory; tutoring; unpaid internships.

Library Facilities 101,468 volumes; 28,000 periodical subscriptions.

BACCALAUREATE PROGRAMS

Degree BSN

Available Programs Generic Baccalaureate.

Site Options Owatonna, MN.

Study Options Full-time.

Program Entrance Requirements CPR certification, written essay, health exam, immunizations, 2 letters of recommendation, minimum high school GPA, minimum GPA in nursing prerequisites of 2.5, prerequisite course work. Transfer students are accepted. *Application deadline:* 2/1 (spring).

Expenses (2009–10) *Tuition:* full-time $19,870. *Room and board:* $7366 per academic year. *Required fees:* full-time $200.

Financial Aid 90% of baccalaureate students in nursing programs received some form of financial aid in 2008–09. *Gift aid (need-based):* Federal Pell, FSEOG, state, private, college/university gift aid from institutional funds. *Loans:* FFEL (Subsidized and Unsubsidized Stafford PLUS), Perkins, state, SELF Loans, CitiAssist Loans, Signature Loans, U.S. Bank No Fee Educational Loans, Wells Fargo. *Work-study:* Federal Work-Study, part-time campus jobs. *Financial aid application deadline:* 8/1 (priority: 4/5).

Contact Nursing Department, Nursing Department, Crown College, 8700 College View Drive, St. Bonifacius, MN 55375-9001. *Telephone:* 952-446-4482. *E-mail:* nursing@crown.edu.

Globe University
Bachelor of Science in Nursing
Woodbury, Minnesota

Founded in 1885

DEGREE • BS

Nursing Program Faculty 16

Baccalaureate Enrollment 135

Nursing Student Activities Student Nurses' Association.

Nursing Student Resources Academic advising; academic or career counseling; assistance for students with disabilities; bookstore; campus computer network; career placement assistance; computer lab; computer-assisted instruction; e-mail services; employment services for current students; interactive nursing skills videos; Internet; learning resource lab; library services; nursing audiovisuals; placement services for program completers; remedial services; resume preparation assistance; skills, simulation, or other laboratory; tutoring; unpaid internships.

Library Facilities 1,432 volumes; 106 periodical subscriptions.

BACCALAUREATE PROGRAMS

Degree BS

Available Programs Generic Baccalaureate.

Study Options Full-time and part-time.

Program Entrance Requirements Minimum overall college GPA of 2.75, transcript of college record, CPR certification, written essay, health exam, high school biology, high school chemistry, 2 years high school science, high school transcript, immunizations, interview, 2 letters of recommendation, minimum high school GPA of 2.75, minimum high school rank 60%, minimum GPA in nursing prerequisites of 2.75, prerequisite course work. Transfer students are accepted. *Application deadline:* Applications may be processed on a rolling basis for some programs. *Application fee:* $50.

Advanced Placement Credit given for nursing courses completed elsewhere dependent upon specific evaluations.

Contact Karen Miller, Nursing Admissions Representative, Bachelor of Science in Nursing, Globe University, 1401 West 76th Street, Richfield, MN 55423. *Telephone:* 612-798-3762. *E-mail:* kmiller@msbcollege.edu.

Gustavus Adolphus College
Department of Nursing
St. Peter, Minnesota

Founded in 1862

DEGREE • BA

Nursing Program Faculty 9 (20% with doctorates).

Baccalaureate Enrollment 76
Women 92% **Men** 8% **Minority** 8% **International** 4%

Nursing Student Activities Sigma Theta Tau, Student Nurses' Association.

Nursing Student Resources Academic advising; academic or career counseling; assistance for students with disabilities; bookstore; campus computer network; career placement assistance; computer lab; computer-assisted instruction; e-mail services; employment services for current students; housing assistance; interactive nursing skills videos; Internet; learning resource lab; library services; nursing audiovisuals; paid internships; remedial services; resume preparation assistance; skills, simulation, or other laboratory; tutoring; unpaid internships.

Library Facilities 343,448 volumes; 22,931 periodical subscriptions.

BACCALAUREATE PROGRAMS

Degree BA

Available Programs Generic Baccalaureate.

Study Options Full-time.

Program Entrance Requirements Minimum overall college GPA of 2.7, transcript of college record, written essay, high school transcript, immunizations, interview, minimum GPA in nursing prerequisites, prerequisite course work. Transfer students are accepted.

Contact *Telephone:* 507-933-6126. *Fax:* 507-933-6153.

Metropolitan State University
College of Nursing and Health Sciences
St. Paul, Minnesota

http://www.metrostate.edu

Founded in 1971

DEGREES • BSN • MSN

Nursing Program Faculty 22 (18% with doctorates).

Baccalaureate Enrollment 230
Women 91% **Men** 9% **Minority** 9% **Part-time** 96%

Graduate Enrollment 40
Women 95% **Men** 5% **Minority** 8% **Part-time** 23%

Nursing Student Activities Sigma Theta Tau, Student Nurses' Association.

Nursing Student Resources Academic advising; academic or career counseling; assistance for students with disabilities; bookstore; campus computer network; computer lab; e-mail services; externships; Internet; library services; skills, simulation, or other laboratory.

Library Facilities 39,128 volumes; 242 periodical subscriptions.

BACCALAUREATE PROGRAMS

Degree BSN

Site Options Minneapolis, MN.

Study Options Full-time and part-time.

Program Entrance Requirements Minimum overall college GPA of 2.5, transcript of college record, health insurance, immunizations, minimum GPA in nursing prerequisites of 3.0, professional liability insurance/malpractice insurance, prerequisite course work. Transfer students are accepted.

Advanced Placement Credit given for nursing courses completed elsewhere dependent upon specific evaluations.

Contact *Telephone:* 651-793-1379. *Fax:* 651-793-1382.

GRADUATE PROGRAMS

Contact *Telephone:* 651-793-1378. *Fax:* 651-793-1382.

MASTER'S DEGREE PROGRAM

Degree MSN

Available Programs Master's for Nurses with Non-Nursing Degrees; RN to Master's.

Concentrations Available Nursing administration. *Nurse practitioner programs in:* adult health, family health.

Study Options Full-time and part-time.

Program Entrance Requirements Clinical experience, computer literacy, minimum overall college GPA of 3.0, transcript of college record, written essay, immunizations, interview, 3 letters of recommendation, professional liability insurance/malpractice insurance, resume, statistics course, GRE General Test.

Advanced Placement Credit given for nursing courses completed elsewhere dependent upon specific evaluations.

Degree Requirements 42 total credit hours, thesis or project.

POST-MASTER'S PROGRAM

Areas of Study *Nurse practitioner programs in:* adult health, family health.

Minnesota Intercollegiate Nursing Consortium
Minnesota Intercollegiate Nursing Consortium
Northfield, Minnesota

http://www.stolaf.edu/depts/nursing/

DEGREE • BA

Nursing Program Faculty 9 (55% with doctorates).

Baccalaureate Enrollment 99
Women 97% **Men** 3% **Minority** 5%

Nursing Student Activities Sigma Theta Tau, Student Nurses' Association.

Nursing Student Resources Academic advising; academic or career counseling; assistance for students with disabilities; bookstore; campus computer network; career placement assistance; computer lab; computer-assisted instruction; e-mail services; employment services for current

Minnesota Intercollegiate Nursing Consortium (continued)
students; externships; interactive nursing skills videos; Internet; learning resource lab; library services; nursing audiovisuals; paid internships; remedial services; resume preparation assistance; skills, simulation, or other laboratory; tutoring; unpaid internships.

BACCALAUREATE PROGRAMS

Degree BA

Available Programs Generic Baccalaureate.

Site Options Northfield, MN; St. Peter, MN.

Study Options Full-time.

Program Entrance Requirements Minimum overall college GPA of 2.85, transcript of college record, CPR certification, written essay, health exam, health insurance, immunizations, interview, minimum GPA in nursing prerequisites of 2.7, prerequisite course work. Transfer students are accepted. *Application deadline:* 10/31 (fall).

Expenses (2009–10) *Tuition:* full-time $35,500; part-time $4440 per course. *International tuition:* $35,500 full-time. *Room and board:* $8200; room only: $3800 per academic year. *Required fees:* full-time $1100; part-time $550 per term.

Financial Aid 80% of baccalaureate students in nursing programs received some form of financial aid in 2008–09.

Contact Dr. Rita S. Glazebrook, Director, Minnesota Intercollegiate Nursing Consortium, 1520 St. Olaf Avenue, Northfield, MN 55057-1098. *Telephone:* 507-786-3265. *Fax:* 507-786-3733. *E-mail:* glazebro@stolaf.edu.

Minnesota State University Mankato

School of Nursing
Mankato, Minnesota

http://www.mnsu.edu/nursing/

Founded in 1868

DEGREES • BS • DNP • MSN • MSN/MS

Nursing Program Faculty 48 (21% with doctorates).

Baccalaureate Enrollment 292
Women 90% **Men** 10% **Minority** 9% **International** 1% **Part-time** 1%

Graduate Enrollment 60
Women 96% **Men** 4% **Part-time** 48%

Distance Learning Courses Available.

Nursing Student Activities Nursing Honor Society, Sigma Theta Tau, Student Nurses' Association.

Nursing Student Resources Academic advising; academic or career counseling; assistance for students with disabilities; bookstore; campus computer network; career placement assistance; computer lab; computer-assisted instruction; daycare for children of students; e-mail services; employment services for current students; Internet; learning resource lab; library services; nursing audiovisuals; paid internships; placement services for program completers; resume preparation assistance; skills, simulation, or other laboratory; tutoring.

Library Facilities 1.2 million volumes (35,852 in health, 1,500 in nursing); 20,000 periodical subscriptions (156 health-care related).

BACCALAUREATE PROGRAMS

Degree BS

Available Programs Accelerated Baccalaureate for Second Degree; Generic Baccalaureate; RN Baccalaureate.

Study Options Full-time and part-time.

Program Entrance Requirements Minimum overall college GPA of 2.5, transcript of college record, health exam, health insurance, minimum GPA in nursing prerequisites of 2.0, prerequisite course work. Transfer students are accepted.

Advanced Placement Credit by examination available. Credit given for nursing courses completed elsewhere dependent upon specific evaluations.

Contact *Telephone:* 507-389-6828. *Fax:* 507-389-6516.

GRADUATE PROGRAMS

Contact *Telephone:* 507-389-1317. *Fax:* 507-389-6516.

MASTER'S DEGREE PROGRAM

Degrees MSN; MSN/MS

Available Programs Accelerated RN to Master's; Master's; Master's for Nurses with Non-Nursing Degrees; RN to Master's.

Concentrations Available Nursing education. *Clinical nurse specialist programs in:* adult health, family health, pediatric. *Nurse practitioner programs in:* family health.

Study Options Full-time and part-time.

Program Entrance Requirements Clinical experience, computer literacy, minimum overall college GPA of 3.0, transcript of college record, CPR certification, written essay, immunizations, 3 letters of recommendation, nursing research course, professional liability insurance/malpractice insurance, prerequisite course work, resume, statistics course.

Advanced Placement Credit given for nursing courses completed elsewhere dependent upon specific evaluations.

Degree Requirements 53 total credit hours, thesis or project.

POST-MASTER'S PROGRAM

Areas of Study Nursing education. *Clinical nurse specialist programs in:* family health. *Nurse practitioner programs in:* family health.

DOCTORAL DEGREE PROGRAM

Degree DNP

Available Programs Doctorate.

Degree Requirements 36 total credit hours.

CONTINUING EDUCATION PROGRAM

Contact *Telephone:* 507-389-5194. *Fax:* 507-389-6516.

Minnesota State University Moorhead

School of Nursing and Healthcare Leadership
Moorhead, Minnesota

http://www.mnstate.edu/nursing/

Founded in 1885

DEGREES • BSN • DNP • MS

Nursing Program Faculty 11 (36% with doctorates).

Baccalaureate Enrollment 296
Women 95% **Men** 5% **Minority** 3% **International** 3% **Part-time** 50%

Graduate Enrollment 33
Women 94% **Men** 6% **Minority** 6% **Part-time** 42%

Distance Learning Courses Available.

Nursing Student Activities Sigma Theta Tau, Student Nurses' Association.

Nursing Student Resources Academic advising; academic or career counseling; assistance for students with disabilities; bookstore; campus computer network; career placement assistance; computer lab; computer-assisted instruction; daycare for children of students; e-mail services; employment services for current students; Internet; library services; nursing audiovisuals; remedial services; resume preparation assistance; tutoring; unpaid internships.

Library Facilities 634,509 volumes (5,560 in health, 824 in nursing); 164 periodical subscriptions (50 health-care related).

BACCALAUREATE PROGRAMS

Degree BSN

Available Programs ADN to Baccalaureate; Generic Baccalaureate; RN Baccalaureate.

Study Options Full-time.

Program Entrance Requirements CPR certification, written essay, high school biology, high school chemistry, high school transcript, immunizations, 2 letters of recommendation, minimum high school GPA of 3.25. Transfer students are accepted.

Contact *Telephone:* 218-477-4699. *Fax:* 218-477-5990.

GRADUATE PROGRAMS
Contact *Telephone:* 218-477-4699. *Fax:* 218-477-5990.

MASTER'S DEGREE PROGRAM
Degree MS

Available Programs Master's; Master's for Nurses with Non-Nursing Degrees.
Concentrations Available Nursing education. *Clinical nurse specialist programs in:* adult health.
Study Options Full-time and part-time.
Program Entrance Requirements Computer literacy, minimum overall college GPA of 3.0, transcript of college record, written essay, interview, 3 letters of recommendation.
Advanced Placement Credit given for nursing courses completed elsewhere dependent upon specific evaluations.
Degree Requirements 44 total credit hours, thesis or project.

DOCTORAL DEGREE PROGRAM
Degree DNP

Available Programs Doctorate.
Areas of Study Individualized study.
Online Degree Options Yes (online only).
Program Entrance Requirements Minimum overall college GPA of 3.0, interview, letters of recommendation, MSN or equivalent, vita, writing sample.
Degree Requirements 36 total credit hours, dissertation, oral exam.

St. Catherine University
Department of Nursing
St. Paul, Minnesota

http://www.stkate.edu/offices/academic/nursing.nsf

Founded in 1905
DEGREES • BS • DNP • MA

Nursing Program Faculty 47 (36% with doctorates).
Baccalaureate Enrollment 289
Women 97% **Men** 3% **Minority** 22% **International** 1% **Part-time** 6%
Graduate Enrollment 119
Women 94% **Men** 6% **Minority** 15% **Part-time** 50%
Distance Learning Courses Available.
Nursing Student Activities Nursing Honor Society, Sigma Theta Tau, Student Nurses' Association.
Nursing Student Resources Academic advising; academic or career counseling; assistance for students with disabilities; bookstore; campus computer network; career placement assistance; computer lab; computer-assisted instruction; daycare for children of students; e-mail services; employment services for current students; housing assistance; interactive nursing skills videos; Internet; learning resource lab; library services; nursing audiovisuals; paid internships; remedial services; resume preparation assistance; skills, simulation, or other laboratory; tutoring; unpaid internships.
Library Facilities 263,495 volumes (71,297 in health, 18,204 in nursing); 1,141 periodical subscriptions (4,590 health-care related).

BACCALAUREATE PROGRAMS
Degree BS

Available Programs Baccalaureate for Second Degree; Generic Baccalaureate; RN Baccalaureate.
Site Options Minneapolis, MN.
Study Options Full-time.

Program Entrance Requirements Minimum overall college GPA of 2.75, transcript of college record, CPR certification, written essay, health insurance, immunizations, 2 letters of recommendation, minimum GPA in nursing prerequisites of 2.6, prerequisite course work. Transfer students are accepted. *Application deadline:* 3/1 (winter).
Expenses (2009–10) *Tuition:* full-time $28,480; part-time $890 per credit. *International tuition:* $37,509 full-time. *Room and board:* $3905; room only: $2570 per academic year. *Required fees:* full-time $800; part-time $75 per credit; part-time $400 per term.
Financial Aid 81% of baccalaureate students in nursing programs received some form of financial aid in 2008–09. *Gift aid (need-based):* Federal Pell, FSEOG, state, private, college/university gift aid from institutional funds. *Loans:* Federal Nursing Student Loans, Federal Direct (Subsidized and Unsubsidized Stafford PLUS), Perkins, state, alternative loans. *Work-study:* Federal Work-Study, part-time campus jobs. *Financial aid application deadline (priority):* 4/15.
Contact Vicki Schug, PhD, Baccalaureate Program Director, Department of Nursing, St. Catherine University, 2004 Randolph Avenue, St. Paul, MN 55105. *Telephone:* 651-690-6940. *Fax:* 651-690-6941. *E-mail:* vlschug@stkate.edu.

GRADUATE PROGRAMS
Expenses (2009–10) *Tuition:* full-time $12,960; part-time $720 per credit. *International tuition:* $12,960 full-time. *Room and board:* $3905; room only: $2570 per academic year. *Required fees:* full-time $60; part-time $30 per term.
Financial Aid 55% of graduate students in nursing programs received some form of financial aid in 2008–09.
Contact Margaret Dexheimer Pharris, PhD, Graduate Program Director, Department of Nursing, St. Catherine University, 2004 Randolph Avenue, #4250, St. Paul, MN 55105. *Telephone:* 651-690-6572. *Fax:* 651-690-6941. *E-mail:* mdpharris@stkate.edu.

MASTER'S DEGREE PROGRAM
Degree MA

Available Programs Master's.
Concentrations Available Nursing education. *Nurse practitioner programs in:* adult health, gerontology, neonatal health, pediatric.
Study Options Full-time.
Program Entrance Requirements Clinical experience, minimum overall college GPA of 3.0, transcript of college record, CPR certification, written essay, immunizations, interview, 3 letters of recommendation, professional liability insurance/malpractice insurance, resume, statistics course. *Application deadline:* 1/15 (winter). *Application fee:* $35.
Advanced Placement Credit given for nursing courses completed elsewhere dependent upon specific evaluations.
Degree Requirements 38 total credit hours, thesis or project.

POST-MASTER'S PROGRAM
Areas of Study Nursing education. *Nurse practitioner programs in:* adult health, gerontology, neonatal health, pediatric.

DOCTORAL DEGREE PROGRAM
Degree DNP

Available Programs Doctorate.
Areas of Study Advanced practice nursing, health-care systems.
Program Entrance Requirements Minimum overall college GPA of 3.0, interview by faculty committee, 3 letters of recommendation, MSN or equivalent, vita, writing sample. Application deadline: 1/15 (winter). Application fee: $35.
Degree Requirements 28 total credit hours.

St. Cloud State University
Department of Nursing Science
St. Cloud, Minnesota

Founded in 1869
DEGREE • BS

Nursing Program Faculty 12 (25% with doctorates).

St. Cloud State University (continued)
Baccalaureate Enrollment 111
Nursing Student Activities Nursing club.

Nursing Student Resources Academic advising; academic or career counseling; assistance for students with disabilities; bookstore; campus computer network; career placement assistance; computer lab; computer-assisted instruction; daycare for children of students; e-mail services; interactive nursing skills videos; Internet; learning resource lab; library services; nursing audiovisuals; remedial services; resume preparation assistance; skills, simulation, or other laboratory; tutoring; unpaid internships.

Library Facilities 947,787 volumes (18,000 in health, 750 in nursing); 955 periodical subscriptions (100 health-care related).

BACCALAUREATE PROGRAMS

Degree BS
Available Programs Generic Baccalaureate.
Study Options Full-time.
Program Entrance Requirements Minimum overall college GPA of 2.75, transcript of college record, CPR certification, health exam, immunizations, 2 letters of recommendation, minimum GPA in nursing prerequisites of 2.75, prerequisite course work.
Contact *Telephone:* 320-308-1749.

St. Olaf College
Department of Nursing
Northfield, Minnesota

http://www.stolaf.edu/depts/nursing/
Founded in 1874
DEGREE • BA

Nursing Program Faculty 5 (60% with doctorates).
Baccalaureate Enrollment 51
Women 94% **Men** 6% **Minority** 8%
Nursing Student Activities Sigma Theta Tau, Student Nurses' Association.

Nursing Student Resources Academic advising; academic or career counseling; assistance for students with disabilities; bookstore; campus computer network; career placement assistance; computer lab; computer-assisted instruction; e-mail services; employment services for current students; externships; interactive nursing skills videos; Internet; learning resource lab; library services; nursing audiovisuals; paid internships; placement services for program completers; remedial services; resume preparation assistance; skills, simulation, or other laboratory; tutoring; unpaid internships.

Library Facilities 741,478 volumes; 5,935 periodical subscriptions.

BACCALAUREATE PROGRAMS

Degree BA
Available Programs Generic Baccalaureate.
Site Options St. Peter, MN; Northfield, MN.
Study Options Full-time.
Program Entrance Requirements Minimum overall college GPA of 2.85, transcript of college record, CPR certification, written essay, health exam, health insurance, immunizations, interview, minimum GPA in nursing prerequisites of 2.7, prerequisite course work. Transfer students are accepted. *Application deadline:* 10/31 (fall).
Expenses (2009–10) *Tuition:* full-time $35,500; part-time $4440 per course. *International tuition:* $35,500 full-time. *Room and board:* $8200; room only: $3800 per academic year. *Required fees:* full-time $1100; part-time $550 per term.
Financial Aid *Gift aid (need-based):* Federal Pell, FSEOG, state, private, college/university gift aid from institutional funds. *Loans:* Federal Nursing Student Loans, FFEL (Subsidized and Unsubsidized Stafford PLUS), Perkins, state, college/university. *Work-study:* Federal Work-Study, part-time campus jobs. *Financial aid application deadline:* 4/15 (priority: 1/15).

Contact Dr. Rita S. Glazebrook, Chair of the Department of Nursing, Department of Nursing, St. Olaf College, 1520 St. Olaf Avenue, Northfield, MN 55057-1098. *Telephone:* 507-786-3265. *Fax:* 507-786-3733. *E-mail:* glazebro@stolaf.edu.

University of Minnesota, Twin Cities Campus
School of Nursing
Minneapolis, Minnesota

http://www.nursing.umn.edu/
Founded in 1851
DEGREES • BSN • MS • MS/MPH • PHD

Nursing Program Faculty 85 (90% with doctorates).
Baccalaureate Enrollment 392
Women 87% **Men** 13% **Minority** 12% **Part-time** 8%
Graduate Enrollment 343
Women 98% **Men** 2% **Minority** 12% **International** 5% **Part-time** 44%
Nursing Student Activities Nursing Honor Society, Sigma Theta Tau, Student Nurses' Association.

Nursing Student Resources Academic advising; academic or career counseling; assistance for students with disabilities; bookstore; campus computer network; computer lab; computer-assisted instruction; daycare for children of students; e-mail services; employment services for current students; housing assistance; Internet; learning resource lab; library services; skills, simulation, or other laboratory.

Library Facilities 5.7 million volumes (4,000 in health, 1,500 in nursing); 45,000 periodical subscriptions (4,800 health-care related).

BACCALAUREATE PROGRAMS

Degree BSN
Available Programs Generic Baccalaureate.
Site Options Rochester, MN.
Study Options Full-time.
Program Entrance Requirements Minimum overall college GPA of 2.8, transcript of college record, CPR certification, written essay, health exam, health insurance, immunizations, minimum GPA in nursing prerequisites of 2.8, prerequisite course work. Transfer students are accepted.
Contact *Telephone:* 612-625-7980. *Fax:* 612-625-7727.

GRADUATE PROGRAMS

Contact *Telephone:* 612-625-7980. *Fax:* 612-625-7727.

MASTER'S DEGREE PROGRAM

Degrees MS; MS/MPH
Available Programs Master's.
Concentrations Available Nurse anesthesia; nurse-midwifery; nursing administration. *Clinical nurse specialist programs in:* adult health, gerontology, pediatric, psychiatric/mental health. *Nurse practitioner programs in:* family health, gerontology, pediatric, women's health.
Study Options Full-time and part-time.
Program Entrance Requirements Clinical experience, computer literacy, minimum overall college GPA of 3.0, transcript of college record, CPR certification, written essay, immunizations, interview, 2 letters of recommendation, statistics course, GRE General Test.
Degree Requirements 33 total credit hours, thesis or project.

DOCTORAL DEGREE PROGRAM

Degree PhD
Available Programs Doctorate; Doctorate for Nurses with Non-Nursing Degrees; Post-Baccalaureate Doctorate.
Program Entrance Requirements Minimum overall college GPA of 3.0, interview by faculty committee, interview, 2 letters of recommendation, GRE General Test.
Degree Requirements 30 total credit hours, dissertation, oral exam, written exam, residency.

CONTINUING EDUCATION PROGRAM
Contact *Telephone:* 612-625-7980. *Fax:* 612-625-7727.

Winona State University
College of Nursing and Health Sciences
Winona, Minnesota

http://www.winona.edu/nursing/
Founded in 1858
DEGREES • BS • DNP • MS

Nursing Program Faculty 39 (46% with doctorates).

Baccalaureate Enrollment 400
Women 94% **Men** 6% **Minority** 3% **International** 2% **Part-time** 13%

Graduate Enrollment 110
Women 89% **Men** 11% **Minority** 5% **International** 1% **Part-time** 65%

Distance Learning Courses Available.

Nursing Student Activities Sigma Theta Tau, Student Nurses' Association, nursing club.

Nursing Student Resources Academic advising; academic or career counseling; assistance for students with disabilities; bookstore; campus computer network; career placement assistance; computer lab; computer-assisted instruction; daycare for children of students; e-mail services; employment services for current students; externships; housing assistance; Internet; learning resource lab; library services; nursing audiovisuals; paid internships; placement services for program completers; remedial services; resume preparation assistance; skills, simulation, or other laboratory; tutoring.

Library Facilities 350,000 volumes (6,132 in health, 3,920 in nursing); 1,000 periodical subscriptions (413 health-care related).

BACCALAUREATE PROGRAMS
Degree BS
Available Programs Generic Baccalaureate; RN Baccalaureate.
Site Options Rochester, MN.
Study Options Full-time and part-time.
Program Entrance Requirements Minimum overall college GPA of 3.0, transcript of college record, CPR certification, health exam, health insurance, immunizations, minimum GPA in nursing prerequisites of 3.3, professional liability insurance/malpractice insurance, prerequisite course work. Transfer students are accepted. *Application deadline:* 11/1 (fall), 1/31 (spring).
Expenses (2009–10) *Tuition, state resident:* full-time $2971; part-time $196 per credit. *Tuition, nonresident:* full-time $4456; part-time $294 per credit. *International tuition:* $5386 full-time. *Room and board:* $3340; room only: $2435 per academic year. *Required fees:* full-time $1267; part-time $199 per credit; part-time $634 per term.
Financial Aid 70% of baccalaureate students in nursing programs received some form of financial aid in 2008–09.
Contact Nursing Contact, College of Nursing and Health Sciences, Winona State University, PO Box 5838, Winona, MN 55987-5838. *Telephone:* 507-457-5120. *Fax:* 507-457-5550. *E-mail:* nursing@winona.edu.

GRADUATE PROGRAMS
Financial Aid 20% of graduate students in nursing programs received some form of financial aid in 2008–09. 3 research assistantships with partial tuition reimbursements available (averaging $6,000 per year) were awarded; Federal Work-Study, traineeships, and unspecified assistantships also available. Aid available to part-time students. *Financial aid application deadline:* 8/15.
Contact Dr. Julie Ponto, Interim Director, College of Nursing and Health Sciences, Winona State University, 859 SE 30th Avenue, Rochester, MN 55904. *Telephone:* 507-285-7135. *Fax:* 507-292-5127. *E-mail:* jponto@winona.edu.

MASTER'S DEGREE PROGRAM
Degree MS
Available Programs Master's; Master's for Nurses with Non-Nursing Degrees; RN to Master's.
Concentrations Available Nursing administration; nursing education. *Clinical nurse specialist programs in:* adult health. *Nurse practitioner programs in:* adult health, family health.
Site Options Rochester, MN.
Study Options Full-time and part-time.
Program Entrance Requirements Clinical experience, computer literacy, minimum overall college GPA of 3.0, transcript of college record, CPR certification, written essay, immunizations, interview, 3 letters of recommendation, nursing research course, physical assessment course, professional liability insurance/malpractice insurance, statistics course, GRE if GPA is below 3.0. *Application deadline:* 12/1 (fall). *Application fee:* $20.
Advanced Placement Credit given for nursing courses completed elsewhere dependent upon specific evaluations.
Degree Requirements 43 total credit hours, thesis or project.

POST-MASTER'S PROGRAM
Areas of Study Nursing administration; nursing education. *Clinical nurse specialist programs in:* adult health. *Nurse practitioner programs in:* adult health, family health.

DOCTORAL DEGREE PROGRAM
Degree DNP
Available Programs Doctorate.
Areas of Study Advanced practice nursing, faculty preparation, nursing administration.
Site Options Rochester, MN.
Online Degree Options Yes (online only).
Program Entrance Requirements Clinical experience, minimum overall college GPA of 3.0, 2 letters of recommendation, MSN or equivalent, statistics course, vita, writing sample. Application deadline: 3/15 (spring). Application fee: $20.
Degree Requirements 36 total credit hours, oral exam.

MISSISSIPPI

Alcorn State University
School of Nursing
Natchez, Mississippi

http://www.alcorn.edu/academic/academ/nurses.htm
Founded in 1871
DEGREES • BSN • MSN

Nursing Program Faculty 21 (29% with doctorates).

Baccalaureate Enrollment 63
Women 88.8% **Men** 11.2% **Minority** 42.8% **Part-time** 7.9%

Graduate Enrollment 53
Women 89.3% **Men** 10.7% **Minority** 35.7% **Part-time** 78.6%

Distance Learning Courses Available.

Nursing Student Activities Nursing Honor Society, Sigma Theta Tau, Student Nurses' Association.

Nursing Student Resources Academic advising; campus computer network; computer lab; housing assistance; learning resource lab; library services; nursing audiovisuals; paid internships; skills, simulation, or other laboratory.

Library Facilities 335,252 volumes (2,082 in health, 1,385 in nursing); 1,046 periodical subscriptions (30 health-care related).

BACCALAUREATE PROGRAMS
Degree BSN
Available Programs Generic Baccalaureate; RN Baccalaureate.
Study Options Full-time and part-time.
Online Degree Options Yes.

Alcorn State University (continued)

Program Entrance Requirements Minimum overall college GPA of 2.5, transcript of college record, health exam, minimum high school GPA of 2.5, prerequisite course work. Transfer students are accepted.

Advanced Placement Credit given for nursing courses completed elsewhere dependent upon specific evaluations.

Contact *Telephone:* 601-304-4305. *Fax:* 601-304-4398.

GRADUATE PROGRAMS

Contact *Telephone:* 601-304-4303. *Fax:* 601-304-4398.

MASTER'S DEGREE PROGRAM

Degree MSN

Available Programs Master's.

Concentrations Available Nursing education. *Nurse practitioner programs in:* family health.

Study Options Full-time and part-time.

Program Entrance Requirements Computer literacy, minimum overall college GPA of 3.0, transcript of college record, written essay, 2 letters of recommendation, statistics course.

Advanced Placement Credit given for nursing courses completed elsewhere dependent upon specific evaluations.

Degree Requirements 43 total credit hours, thesis or project.

POST-MASTER'S PROGRAM

Areas of Study Nursing education. *Nurse practitioner programs in:* family health.

Delta State University
School of Nursing
Cleveland, Mississippi

http://www.deltastate.edu

Founded in 1924

DEGREES • BSN • MSN

Nursing Program Faculty 17 (41% with doctorates).

Baccalaureate Enrollment 105
Women 91% **Men** 9% **Minority** 20% **Part-time** 7%

Graduate Enrollment 59
Women 90% **Men** 10% **Minority** 31% **Part-time** 34%

Distance Learning Courses Available.

Nursing Student Activities Sigma Theta Tau, Student Nurses' Association.

Nursing Student Resources Academic advising; academic or career counseling; assistance for students with disabilities; bookstore; campus computer network; career placement assistance; computer lab; computer-assisted instruction; daycare for children of students; e-mail services; externships; housing assistance; interactive nursing skills videos; Internet; learning resource lab; library services; nursing audiovisuals; other; remedial services; resume preparation assistance; skills, simulation, or other laboratory; tutoring.

Library Facilities 424,979 volumes (5,000 in health, 1,000 in nursing); 23,184 periodical subscriptions (120 health-care related).

BACCALAUREATE PROGRAMS

Degree BSN

Available Programs ADN to Baccalaureate; Generic Baccalaureate.

Site Options Greenville, MS; Clarksdale, MS.

Study Options Full-time and part-time.

Online Degree Options Yes.

Program Entrance Requirements Transcript of college record, CPR certification, health exam, health insurance, immunizations, interview, 3 letters of recommendation, minimum GPA in nursing prerequisites of 2.5, professional liability insurance/malpractice insurance, prerequisite course work. Transfer students are accepted. *Application deadline:* 3/1 (spring).

Advanced Placement Credit given for nursing courses completed elsewhere dependent upon specific evaluations.

Expenses (2009–10) *Tuition, state resident:* full-time $4450; part-time $185 per credit hour. *Tuition, nonresident:* full-time $7070; part-time $480 per credit hour. *International tuition:* $7070 full-time. *Room and board:* $5650; room only: $3332 per academic year. *Required fees:* full-time $902; part-time $37 per credit; part-time $451 per term.

Financial Aid 95% of baccalaureate students in nursing programs received some form of financial aid in 2008–09.

Contact Dr. Vicki L. Bingham, Chair of Academic Programs, School of Nursing, Delta State University, PO Box 3343, Cleveland, MS 38733. *Telephone:* 662-846-4255. *Fax:* 662-846-4267. *E-mail:* vbingham@deltastate.edu.

GRADUATE PROGRAMS

Expenses (2009–10) *Tuition, state resident:* full-time $2225; part-time $247 per credit hour. *Tuition, nonresident:* full-time $2225; part-time $247 per credit hour. *International tuition:* $2225 full-time. *Room and board:* $5650; room only: $3332 per academic year. *Required fees:* full-time $275; part-time $13 per credit; part-time $138 per term.

Financial Aid 70% of graduate students in nursing programs received some form of financial aid in 2008–09. Research assistantships, career-related internships or fieldwork, Federal Work-Study, and institutionally sponsored loans available. *Financial aid application deadline:* 6/1.

Contact Dr. Vicki L. Bingham, Chair of Academic Programs, School of Nursing, Delta State University, PO Box 3343, Cleveland, MS 38733. *Telephone:* 662-846-4255. *Fax:* 662-846-4267. *E-mail:* vbingham@deltastate.edu.

MASTER'S DEGREE PROGRAM

Degree MSN

Available Programs Accelerated Master's for Nurses with Non-Nursing Degrees; Master's.

Concentrations Available Nursing administration; nursing education. *Nurse practitioner programs in:* family health, gerontology, psychiatric/mental health.

Study Options Full-time and part-time.

Online Degree Options Yes (online only).

Program Entrance Requirements Clinical experience, computer literacy, minimum overall college GPA of 3.0, transcript of college record, CPR certification, written essay, immunizations, interview, 3 letters of recommendation, nursing research course, physical assessment course, professional liability insurance/malpractice insurance, prerequisite course work, statistics course, GRE General Test. *Application deadline:* 4/5 (spring).

Advanced Placement Credit given for nursing courses completed elsewhere dependent upon specific evaluations.

Degree Requirements 44 total credit hours, thesis or project, comprehensive exam.

POST-MASTER'S PROGRAM

Areas of Study Nursing education. *Nurse practitioner programs in:* family health, gerontology, psychiatric/mental health.

Mississippi College
School of Nursing
Clinton, Mississippi

http://www.mc.edu

Founded in 1826

DEGREE • BSN

Nursing Program Faculty 19 (35% with doctorates).

Baccalaureate Enrollment 140
Women 90% **Men** 10% **Minority** 38% **International** 3% **Part-time** 9%

Distance Learning Courses Available.

Nursing Student Activities Sigma Theta Tau, Student Nurses' Association, nursing club.

Nursing Student Resources Academic advising; academic or career counseling; assistance for students with disabilities; bookstore; campus computer network; career placement assistance; computer lab; computer-assisted instruction; e-mail services; employment services for current

students; externships; housing assistance; interactive nursing skills videos; Internet; learning resource lab; library services; nursing audiovisuals; other; paid internships; placement services for program completers; remedial services; resume preparation assistance; skills, simulation, or other laboratory; tutoring; unpaid internships.

Library Facilities 376,719 volumes (40,000 in health, 8,000 in nursing); 290 periodical subscriptions health-care related.

BACCALAUREATE PROGRAMS

Degree BSN

Available Programs Generic Baccalaureate; RN Baccalaureate.

Study Options Full-time and part-time.

Online Degree Options Yes (online only).

Program Entrance Requirements Minimum overall college GPA of 2.5, transcript of college record, CPR certification, health exam, high school biology, high school chemistry, high school transcript, immunizations, 2 letters of recommendation, minimum GPA in nursing prerequisites of 2.5, prerequisite course work. Transfer students are accepted. *Application deadline:* 2/1 (fall), 9/1 (spring), 4/1 (summer).

Advanced Placement Credit given for nursing courses completed elsewhere dependent upon specific evaluations.

Expenses (2009–10) *Tuition:* full-time $12,670; part-time $397 per credit hour. *International tuition:* $12,670 full-time. *Room and board:* $7000 per academic year. *Required fees:* full-time $700; part-time $200 per term.

Financial Aid 93% of baccalaureate students in nursing programs received some form of financial aid in 2008–09. *Gift aid (need-based):* Federal Pell, FSEOG, state, private, college/university gift aid from institutional funds, Federal Nursing. *Loans:* Federal Nursing Student Loans, FFEL (Subsidized and Unsubsidized Stafford PLUS), Perkins, college/university. *Work-study:* Federal Work-Study. *Financial aid application deadline (priority):* 3/1.

Contact Dr. Mary Jean Padgett, RN, Dean, School of Nursing, Mississippi College, Box 4037, 200 South Capitol Street, Clinton, MS 39058. *Telephone:* 601-925-3278. *Fax:* 601-925-3379. *E-mail:* padgett@mc.edu.

Mississippi University for Women
College of Nursing and Speech-Language Pathology
Columbus, Mississippi

http://www.muw.edu/nursing

Founded in 1884

DEGREES • BSN • MSN

Nursing Program Faculty 38 (25% with doctorates).

Baccalaureate Enrollment 166
Women 89% **Men** 11% **Minority** 20% **International** 1% **Part-time** 5%

Graduate Enrollment 42
Women 90% **Men** 10% **Minority** 15% **International** 1% **Part-time** 3%

Distance Learning Courses Available.

Nursing Student Activities Sigma Theta Tau, Student Nurses' Association.

Nursing Student Resources Academic advising; academic or career counseling; assistance for students with disabilities; bookstore; campus computer network; career placement assistance; computer lab; computer-assisted instruction; daycare for children of students; e-mail services; employment services for current students; externships; housing assistance; interactive nursing skills videos; Internet; learning resource lab; library services; nursing audiovisuals; paid internships; placement services for program completers; remedial services; resume preparation assistance; skills, simulation, or other laboratory; tutoring; unpaid internships.

Library Facilities 20,080 volumes (27,348 in health, 26,422 in nursing); 3,255 periodical subscriptions (235 health-care related).

BACCALAUREATE PROGRAMS

Degree BSN

Available Programs ADN to Baccalaureate; Generic Baccalaureate; RN Baccalaureate.

Site Options Tupelo, MS.

Study Options Full-time.

Online Degree Options Yes.

Program Entrance Requirements Minimum overall college GPA of 2.5, transcript of college record, CPR certification, health exam, health insurance, immunizations, minimum GPA in nursing prerequisites of 2.5, professional liability insurance/malpractice insurance, prerequisite course work. Transfer students are accepted. *Application deadline:* 1/15 (fall), 1/15 (winter), 1/15 (summer).

Advanced Placement Credit given for nursing courses completed elsewhere dependent upon specific evaluations.

Expenses (2009–10) *Tuition, area resident:* full-time $4423; part-time $184 per credit hour. *Tuition, nonresident:* full-time $12,051; part-time $502 per credit hour. *International tuition:* $12,051 full-time. *Room and board:* $3088 per academic year. *Required fees:* full-time $500.

Financial Aid 90% of baccalaureate students in nursing programs received some form of financial aid in 2008–09. *Gift aid (need-based):* Federal Pell, FSEOG, state, private, college/university gift aid from institutional funds. *Loans:* FFEL (Subsidized and Unsubsidized Stafford PLUS), Perkins. *Work-study:* Federal Work-Study, part-time campus jobs. *Financial aid application deadline (priority):* 3/1.

Contact Dr. Tammie McCoy, Baccalaureate Nursing Department Chair, College of Nursing and Speech-Language Pathology, Mississippi University for Women, 1100 College Street, MUW-910, Columbus, MS 39701-5800. *Telephone:* 662-329-7301. *Fax:* 662-329-8559. *E-mail:* tmccoy@nsgslp.muw.edu.

GRADUATE PROGRAMS

Expenses (2009–10) *Tuition, area resident:* full-time $4423; part-time $246 per credit hour. *Tuition, nonresident:* full-time $12,051; part-time $246 per credit hour. *International tuition:* $12,051 full-time. *Room and board:* $3088 per academic year. *Required fees:* full-time $500.

Financial Aid 95% of graduate students in nursing programs received some form of financial aid in 2008–09. Fellowships, Federal Work-Study, institutionally sponsored loans, and traineeships available. *Financial aid application deadline:* 4/1.

Contact Dr. Patsy Smyth, Director of Graduate Nursing Program, College of Nursing and Speech-Language Pathology, Mississippi University for Women, 1100 College Street, MUW-910, Columbus, MS 39701-5800. *Telephone:* 662-329-7323. *Fax:* 662-329-7372. *E-mail:* psmyth@nsgslp.muw.edu.

MASTER'S DEGREE PROGRAM

Degree MSN

Available Programs Master's.

Concentrations Available *Nurse practitioner programs in:* family health, gerontology, pediatric, psychiatric/mental health.

Study Options Full-time.

Program Entrance Requirements Clinical experience, computer literacy, minimum overall college GPA of 3.0, transcript of college record, CPR certification, immunizations, interview, 3 letters of recommendation, nursing research course, physical assessment course, professional liability insurance/malpractice insurance, prerequisite course work, statistics course, GRE General Test. *Application deadline:* 4/1 (fall), 4/1 (spring).

Advanced Placement Credit given for nursing courses completed elsewhere dependent upon specific evaluations.

Degree Requirements 39 total credit hours, thesis or project, comprehensive exam.

POST-MASTER'S PROGRAM

Areas of Study *Nurse practitioner programs in:* family health, gerontology, pediatric, psychiatric/mental health.

University of Mississippi Medical Center
Program in Nursing
Jackson, Mississippi

http://son.umc.edu/

Founded in 1955

University of Mississippi Medical Center (continued)
DEGREES • BSN • MSN • PHD

Nursing Program Faculty 67 (47% with doctorates).

Baccalaureate Enrollment 273
Women 87% **Men** 13% **Minority** 17% **Part-time** 10%

Graduate Enrollment 121
Women 93% **Men** 7% **Minority** 26% **Part-time** 66%

Distance Learning Courses Available.

Nursing Student Activities Nursing Honor Society, Sigma Theta Tau, Student Nurses' Association, nursing club.

Nursing Student Resources Academic advising; academic or career counseling; assistance for students with disabilities; bookstore; campus computer network; computer lab; computer-assisted instruction; e-mail services; employment services for current students; externships; interactive nursing skills videos; Internet; learning resource lab; library services; nursing audiovisuals; remedial services; skills, simulation, or other laboratory; tutoring; unpaid internships.

Library Facilities 310,016 volumes (72,557 in health, 8,170 in nursing); 2,732 periodical subscriptions (4,180 health-care related).

BACCALAUREATE PROGRAMS

Degree BSN

Available Programs Accelerated Baccalaureate for Second Degree; Generic Baccalaureate.

Site Options Southaven, MS; Oxford, MS.

Study Options Full-time and part-time.

Program Entrance Requirements Minimum overall college GPA of 2.5, transcript of college record, CPR certification, written essay, health exam, health insurance, immunizations, minimum GPA in nursing prerequisites of 2.5, professional liability insurance/malpractice insurance, prerequisite course work. Transfer students are accepted. *Application deadline:* 1/15 (spring). *Application fee:* $25.

Advanced Placement Credit given for nursing courses completed elsewhere dependent upon specific evaluations.

Expenses (2009–10) *Tuition, area resident:* full-time $7659; part-time $213 per credit hour. *Tuition, state resident:* full-time $7649; part-time $213 per credit hour. *Tuition, nonresident:* full-time $19,659; part-time $520 per credit hour. *Required fees:* full-time $400.

Financial Aid 77% of baccalaureate students in nursing programs received some form of financial aid in 2008–09.

Contact Dr. Patricia A. Waltman, Associate Dean for Academic Affairs, Program in Nursing, University of Mississippi Medical Center, 2500 North State Street, Jackson, MS 39216-4505. *Telephone:* 601-984-6211. *Fax:* 601-815-9309. *E-mail:* pwaltman@son.umsmed.edu.

GRADUATE PROGRAMS

Expenses (2009–10) *Tuition, state resident:* full-time $6759; part-time $284 per credit hour. *Tuition, nonresident:* full-time $19,658; part-time $693 per credit hour. *Required fees:* full-time $300.

Financial Aid 41% of graduate students in nursing programs received some form of financial aid in 2008–09. Institutionally sponsored loans and traineeships available. Aid available to part-time students. *Financial aid application deadline:* 4/1.

Contact Dr. Sharon Lobert, Associate Dean for Graduate Studies, Program in Nursing, University of Mississippi Medical Center, 2500 North State Street, Jackson, MS 39216-4505. *Telephone:* 601-984-6242. *Fax:* 601-984-6206. *E-mail:* slobert@son.umsmed.edu.

MASTER'S DEGREE PROGRAM

Degree MSN

Available Programs Accelerated AD/RN to Master's; Master's; RN to Master's.

Concentrations Available Nursing administration; nursing education. *Nurse practitioner programs in:* acute care, family health, gerontology, psychiatric/mental health.

Site Options Southaven, MS.

Study Options Full-time and part-time.

Program Entrance Requirements Computer literacy, minimum overall college GPA of 3.0, transcript of college record, CPR certification, immunizations, 3 letters of recommendation, professional liability insurance/malpractice insurance, resume, statistics course, GRE. *Application deadline:* 3/31 (spring). Applications may be processed on a rolling basis for some programs. *Application fee:* $25.

Advanced Placement Credit given for nursing courses completed elsewhere dependent upon specific evaluations.

Degree Requirements 40 total credit hours, comprehensive exam.

POST-MASTER'S PROGRAM

Areas of Study Nursing administration; nursing education. *Nurse practitioner programs in:* acute care, family health, gerontology, psychiatric/mental health.

DOCTORAL DEGREE PROGRAM

Degree PhD

Available Programs Doctorate.

Areas of Study Bio-behavioral research, nursing research, nursing science.

Program Entrance Requirements Clinical experience, minimum overall college GPA of 3.0, interview by faculty committee, interview, letters of recommendation, MSN or equivalent, statistics course, vita, writing sample, GRE. Application deadline: 5/1 (fall), 10/1 (spring). Application fee: $25.

Degree Requirements 60 total credit hours, dissertation, oral exam, written exam, residency.

CONTINUING EDUCATION PROGRAM

Contact Dr. Renee Williams, Director of Continuing Education, Program in Nursing, University of Mississippi Medical Center, 2500 North State Street, Jackson, MS 39216-4505. *Telephone:* 601-984-6227. *Fax:* 601-984-6214. *E-mail:* rwilliams@son.umsmed.edu.

University of Southern Mississippi
School of Nursing
Hattiesburg, Mississippi

http://www.usm.edu/nursing/

Founded in 1910

DEGREES • BSN • MSN • PHD

Nursing Program Faculty 47 (47% with doctorates).

Baccalaureate Enrollment 434
Women 82% **Men** 18% **Minority** 20% **Part-time** 4%

Graduate Enrollment 101
Women 91% **Men** 9% **Minority** 21% **Part-time** 39%

Distance Learning Courses Available.

Nursing Student Activities Nursing Honor Society, Sigma Theta Tau, Student Nurses' Association.

Nursing Student Resources Academic advising; academic or career counseling; assistance for students with disabilities; bookstore; campus computer network; career placement assistance; computer lab; computer-assisted instruction; e-mail services; externships; interactive nursing skills videos; Internet; learning resource lab; library services; nursing audiovisuals; remedial services; resume preparation assistance; skills, simulation, or other laboratory.

Library Facilities 1.2 million volumes; 4,570 periodical subscriptions (170 health-care related).

BACCALAUREATE PROGRAMS

Degree BSN

Available Programs ADN to Baccalaureate; Generic Baccalaureate.

Site Options Meridian, MS; Long Beach, MS.

Study Options Full-time and part-time.

Online Degree Options Yes.

Program Entrance Requirements Minimum overall college GPA of 2.5, transcript of college record, CPR certification, written essay, health exam, health insurance, high school transcript, immunizations, minimum GPA in nursing prerequisites of 2.5, professional liability insurance/malpractice insurance, prerequisite course work. Transfer students are accepted. *Application deadline:* 2/1 (fall), 9/1 (spring).

Expenses (2009–10) *Tuition, state resident:* full-time $4916; part-time $213 per hour. *Tuition, nonresident:* full-time $7956; part-time $332 per hour. *International tuition:* $7956 full-time. *Room and board:* $4900; room only: $3200 per academic year. *Required fees:* full-time $300; part-time $10 per credit; part-time $150 per term.

Financial Aid 85% of baccalaureate students in nursing programs received some form of financial aid in 2008–09.

Contact Cindy Sheffield, Coordinator of Student Services, School of Nursing, University of Southern Mississippi, 118 College Drive, Box 5095, Hattiesburg, MS 39406-5095. *Telephone:* 601-266-5394. *Fax:* 601-266-5454. *E-mail:* Cynthia.Sheffield@usm.edu.

GRADUATE PROGRAMS

Expenses (2009–10) *Tuition, state resident:* full-time $5096; part-time $284 per hour. *Tuition, nonresident:* full-time $7956; part-time $442 per hour. *International tuition:* $7956 full-time.

Financial Aid 85% of graduate students in nursing programs received some form of financial aid in 2008–09. 14 research assistantships with full tuition reimbursements available (averaging $12,577 per year) were awarded; teaching assistantships, Federal Work-Study and traineeships also available. *Financial aid application deadline:* 3/15.

Contact Ms. Rosalind Hawthorn, Program Contact, School of Nursing, University of Southern Mississippi, 118 College Drive, Box 5095, Hattiesburg, MS 39406-5095. *Telephone:* 601-266-5457. *Fax:* 601-266-5927. *E-mail:* rosalind.hawthorn@usm.edu.

MASTER'S DEGREE PROGRAM

Degree MSN

Available Programs Master's; RN to Master's.

Concentrations Available Nursing administration. *Clinical nurse specialist programs in:* adult health, community health, psychiatric/mental health. *Nurse practitioner programs in:* family health, psychiatric/mental health.

Site Options Meridian, MS; Long Beach, MS.

Study Options Full-time and part-time.

Program Entrance Requirements Minimum overall college GPA of 3.0, transcript of college record, CPR certification, immunizations, 3 letters of recommendation, professional liability insurance/malpractice insurance, statistics course, GRE General Test. *Application deadline:* 7/15 (fall), 11/15 (spring), 4/15 (summer). *Application fee:* $30.

Degree Requirements 45 total credit hours, thesis or project, comprehensive exam.

POST-MASTER'S PROGRAM

Areas of Study Nursing administration. *Clinical nurse specialist programs in:* adult health, community health, psychiatric/mental health. *Nurse practitioner programs in:* family health, psychiatric/mental health.

DOCTORAL DEGREE PROGRAM

Degree PhD

Available Programs Doctorate.

Areas of Study Ethics, health policy, nursing administration, nursing education.

Program Entrance Requirements Clinical experience, minimum overall college GPA of 3.5, interview by faculty committee, 3 letters of recommendation, MSN or equivalent, statistics course, vita, writing sample, GRE General Test. Application deadline: 3/1 (fall). Application fee: $30.

Degree Requirements 72 total credit hours, dissertation, written exam, residency.

William Carey University
School of Nursing
Hattiesburg, Mississippi

Founded in 1906

DEGREES • BSN • MSN

Nursing Program Faculty 21 (42% with doctorates).

Baccalaureate Enrollment 198
Women 93% **Men** 7% **Minority** 33% **Part-time** 7%

Graduate Enrollment 22
Women 100% **Minority** 26% **Part-time** 11%

Distance Learning Courses Available.

Nursing Student Activities Sigma Theta Tau, Student Nurses' Association.

Nursing Student Resources Academic advising; academic or career counseling; assistance for students with disabilities; bookstore; campus computer network; computer lab; computer-assisted instruction; e-mail services; interactive nursing skills videos; Internet; learning resource lab; library services; nursing audiovisuals; resume preparation assistance; skills, simulation, or other laboratory; tutoring.

Library Facilities 92,290 volumes (450 in health, 450 in nursing); 662 periodical subscriptions (50 health-care related).

BACCALAUREATE PROGRAMS

Degree BSN

Available Programs ADN to Baccalaureate; Generic Baccalaureate.

Site Options Gulfport, MS; New Orleans, LA.

Study Options Full-time and part-time.

Program Entrance Requirements Minimum overall college GPA of 2.5, transcript of college record, CPR certification, health exam, high school transcript, immunizations, minimum GPA in nursing prerequisites of 3.0, prerequisite course work. Transfer students are accepted. *Application deadline:* 4/10 (fall), 10/10 (spring). *Application fee:* $25.

Advanced Placement Credit given for nursing courses completed elsewhere dependent upon specific evaluations.

Expenses (2008–09) *Tuition:* full-time $13,000. *Required fees:* full-time $300.

Financial Aid 90% of baccalaureate students in nursing programs received some form of financial aid in 2007–08. *Gift aid (need-based):* Federal Pell, FSEOG, state, private, college/university gift aid from institutional funds. *Loans:* Federal Nursing Student Loans, FFEL (Subsidized and Unsubsidized Stafford PLUS), Perkins, college/university. *Work-study:* Federal Work-Study, part-time campus jobs. *Financial aid application deadline (priority):* 4/1.

Contact Dr. Nadine T. James, Dean, School of Nursing, William Carey University, 498 Tuscan Avenue, Box 8, Hattiesburg, MS 39401. *Telephone:* 601-318-6478. *Fax:* 601-318-6446. *E-mail:* nadine.james@wmcarey.edu.

GRADUATE PROGRAMS

Expenses (2008–09) *Tuition:* full-time $10,000. *Required fees:* full-time $300.

Financial Aid 50% of graduate students in nursing programs received some form of financial aid in 2007–08.

Contact Dr. Wanda Dubuisson, Director of MSN Program, School of Nursing, William Carey University, Gulfport Campus, 1856 Beach Drive, Gulfport, MS 39507. *Telephone:* 228-897-7200. *E-mail:* wanda.dubuisson@wmcarey.edu.

MASTER'S DEGREE PROGRAM

Degree MSN

Available Programs Master's.

Concentrations Available Nursing education.

Site Options Gulfport, MS.

Study Options Full-time and part-time.

Program Entrance Requirements Computer literacy, minimum overall college GPA of 3.0, transcript of college record, CPR certification, immunizations, nursing research course, professional liability insurance/malpractice insurance, prerequisite course work, statistics course. *Application deadline:* 8/15 (fall), 2/15 (spring). *Application fee:* $25.

Advanced Placement Credit given for nursing courses completed elsewhere dependent upon specific evaluations.

Degree Requirements 35 total credit hours, thesis or project.

MISSOURI

Avila University
School of Nursing
Kansas City, Missouri

http://www.avila.edu/nursing
Founded in 1916

DEGREE • BSN

Nursing Program Faculty 17 (5% with doctorates).

Baccalaureate Enrollment 108
Women 92% **Men** 8% **Minority** 17% **Part-time** 2%

Nursing Student Activities Nursing Honor Society, Sigma Theta Tau, Student Nurses' Association.

Nursing Student Resources Academic advising; academic or career counseling; assistance for students with disabilities; bookstore; campus computer network; career placement assistance; computer lab; computer-assisted instruction; e-mail services; employment services for current students; externships; interactive nursing skills videos; Internet; learning resource lab; library services; nursing audiovisuals; remedial services; resume preparation assistance; skills, simulation, or other laboratory; tutoring.

Library Facilities 80,845 volumes (1,313 in health, 679 in nursing); 22,464 periodical subscriptions (75 health-care related).

BACCALAUREATE PROGRAMS

Degree BSN

Available Programs Generic Baccalaureate.

Study Options Full-time.

Program Entrance Requirements Minimum overall college GPA of 2.7, transcript of college record, CPR certification, written essay, health exam, health insurance, immunizations, interview, minimum GPA in nursing prerequisites of 2.0, prerequisite course work. Transfer students are accepted. *Application deadline:* 1/15 (fall).

Advanced Placement Credit given for nursing courses completed elsewhere dependent upon specific evaluations.

Expenses (2009–10) *Tuition:* full-time $20,250; part-time $515 per credit hour. *Room and board:* $7600; room only: $4500 per academic year. *Required fees:* full-time $1070; part-time $24 per term.

Financial Aid 98% of baccalaureate students in nursing programs received some form of financial aid in 2008–09. *Gift aid (need-based):* Federal Pell, FSEOG, state, private, college/university gift aid from institutional funds, Federal Nursing. *Loans:* FFEL (Subsidized and Unsubsidized Stafford PLUS), Perkins. *Work-study:* Federal Work-Study, part-time campus jobs. *Financial aid application deadline:* Continuous.

Contact Office of Admissions, School of Nursing, Avila University, 11901 Wornall Road, Kansas City, MO 64145-1698. *Telephone:* 816-501-2400. *Fax:* 816-501-2453. *E-mail:* admissions@avila.edu.

Central Methodist University
College of Liberal Arts and Sciences
Fayette, Missouri

Founded in 1854

DEGREES • BN • MSN

Nursing Program Faculty 7

Library Facilities 97,793 volumes; 316 periodical subscriptions.

BACCALAUREATE PROGRAMS

Degree BN

Available Programs Generic Baccalaureate.

Program Entrance Requirements Written essay, health exam, high school biology, high school chemistry, immunizations, minimum high school GPA of 2.75, prerequisite course work. Transfer students are accepted.

Contact *Telephone:* 660-248-6359.

GRADUATE PROGRAMS
Contact *Telephone:* 573-220-1378.

MASTER'S DEGREE PROGRAM
Degree MSN
Available Programs Master's.
Program Entrance Requirements CPR certification, written essay, immunizations, prerequisite course work, statistics course.

Chamberlain College of Nursing
Chamberlain College of Nursing
St. Louis, Missouri

http://www.chamberlain.edu/home.html
Founded in 1889

DEGREE • BSN

Nursing Program Faculty 80 (21% with doctorates).

Distance Learning Courses Available.

Nursing Student Activities Student Nurses' Association.

Nursing Student Resources Academic advising; academic or career counseling; assistance for students with disabilities; bookstore; campus computer network; career placement assistance; computer lab; computer-assisted instruction; e-mail services; employment services for current students; housing assistance; Internet; learning resource lab; library services; nursing audiovisuals; placement services for program completers; skills, simulation, or other laboratory; tutoring.

Library Facilities 8,700 volumes (3,287 in health, 957 in nursing); 233 periodical subscriptions (182 health-care related).

BACCALAUREATE PROGRAMS

Degree BSN

Available Programs ADN to Baccalaureate; Accelerated RN Baccalaureate; Generic Baccalaureate; LPN to RN Baccalaureate; RN Baccalaureate.

Site Options Columbus, OH; Phoenix, AZ; Addison, IL.

Study Options Full-time.

Online Degree Options Yes (online only).

Program Entrance Requirements Minimum overall college GPA of 2.75, transcript of college record, written essay, health exam, health insurance, high school biology, high school chemistry, 3 years high school math, 3 years high school science, high school transcript, immunizations, interview, minimum high school GPA of 2.75, minimum high school rank 33%. Transfer students are accepted.

Advanced Placement Credit by examination available. Credit given for nursing courses completed elsewhere dependent upon specific evaluations.

Contact *Telephone:* 800-942-4310 Ext. 1. *Fax:* 314-768-3044.

College of the Ozarks
Armstrong McDonald School of Nursing
Point Lookout, Missouri

Founded in 1906

DEGREE • BSN

Nursing Program Faculty 8 (38% with doctorates).

Baccalaureate Enrollment 55
Women 92.1% **Men** 7.9%

Nursing Student Activities Nursing club.

Nursing Student Resources Academic advising; academic or career counseling; assistance for students with disabilities; bookstore; campus computer network; career placement assistance; computer lab; computer-assisted instruction; daycare for children of students; e-mail services; employment services for current students; externships; housing assistance;

interactive nursing skills videos; Internet; learning resource lab; library services; nursing audiovisuals; paid internships; placement services for program completers; remedial services; resume preparation assistance; skills, simulation, or other laboratory; tutoring; unpaid internships.

Library Facilities 116,649 volumes (30 in health, 30 in nursing); 549 periodical subscriptions (38 health-care related).

BACCALAUREATE PROGRAMS

Degree BSN

Available Programs RN Baccalaureate.

Study Options Full-time and part-time.

Program Entrance Requirements Minimum overall college GPA of 2.0, transcript of college record, health exam, high school biology, high school chemistry, 2 years high school math, high school transcript, immunizations, interview, 2 letters of recommendation, minimum high school GPA of 2.5, minimum GPA in nursing prerequisites of 2.5, professional liability insurance/malpractice insurance. Transfer students are accepted. *Application deadline:* 3/1 (spring).

Expenses (2009–10) *Tuition:* part-time $295 per credit hour. *Room and board:* $5000; room only: $2450 per academic year.

Financial Aid 100% of baccalaureate students in nursing programs received some form of financial aid in 2008–09.

Contact Mrs. Deborah J. Lyon, Office Manager, Armstrong McDonald School of Nursing, College of the Ozarks, PO Box 17, Point Lookout, MO 65726. *Telephone:* 417-690-2421. *Fax:* 417-690-2422. *E-mail:* dlyon@cofo.edu.

Cox College of Nursing and Health Sciences

Department of Nursing
Springfield, Missouri

Founded in 1994

DEGREE • BSN

Nursing Program Faculty 20 (50% with doctorates).

Baccalaureate Enrollment 250
Women 95% **Men** 5% **Minority** 5% **International** 4% **Part-time** 80%

Nursing Student Activities Nursing Honor Society, Student Nurses' Association, nursing club.

Nursing Student Resources Academic advising; academic or career counseling; assistance for students with disabilities; bookstore; campus computer network; career placement assistance; computer lab; computer-assisted instruction; daycare for children of students; e-mail services; employment services for current students; externships; housing assistance; interactive nursing skills videos; Internet; learning resource lab; library services; nursing audiovisuals; placement services for program completers; remedial services; resume preparation assistance; skills, simulation, or other laboratory; tutoring.

Library Facilities 5,500 volumes in health, 1,900 volumes in nursing; 250 periodical subscriptions health-care related.

BACCALAUREATE PROGRAMS

Degree BSN

Available Programs ADN to Baccalaureate; Accelerated Baccalaureate; Accelerated Baccalaureate for Second Degree; Baccalaureate for Second Degree; Generic Baccalaureate; LPN to Baccalaureate; LPN to RN Baccalaureate; RN Baccalaureate.

Site Options Springfield, MO.

Study Options Full-time and part-time.

Program Entrance Requirements Minimum overall college GPA of 3.0, transcript of college record, CPR certification, written essay, health exam, high school biology, high school chemistry, 2 years high school math, 2 years high school science, high school transcript, immunizations, interview, minimum high school GPA of 3.0, minimum GPA in nursing prerequisites of 3.0, prerequisite course work. Transfer students are accepted.

Advanced Placement Credit given for nursing courses completed elsewhere dependent upon specific evaluations.

Contact *Telephone:* 417-269-3038.

CONTINUING EDUCATION PROGRAM
Contact *Telephone:* 417-269-8450.

Culver-Stockton College

Blessing–Rieman College of Nursing
Canton, Missouri

http://www.culver.edu/

See description of programs under Blessing–Rieman College of Nursing (Quincy, Illinois).

Goldfarb School of Nursing at Barnes-Jewish College

Goldfarb School of Nursing at Barnes-Jewish College
St. Louis, Missouri

Founded in 1902

DEGREES • BSN • DNP • MSN • PHD

Nursing Program Faculty 39 (45% with doctorates).

Baccalaureate Enrollment 499
Women 87% **Men** 13% **Minority** 24% **International** 4% **Part-time** 14%

Graduate Enrollment 109
Women 90% **Men** 10% **Minority** 31% **International** 3% **Part-time** 67%

Distance Learning Courses Available.

Nursing Student Activities Nursing Honor Society, Sigma Theta Tau, Student Nurses' Association.

Nursing Student Resources Academic advising; academic or career counseling; assistance for students with disabilities; bookstore; campus computer network; career placement assistance; computer lab; computer-assisted instruction; e-mail services; employment services for current students; externships; housing assistance; interactive nursing skills videos; Internet; learning resource lab; library services; nursing audiovisuals; placement services for program completers; remedial services; resume preparation assistance; skills, simulation, or other laboratory; tutoring.

Library Facilities 1,100 volumes (11,000 in health, 8,100 in nursing); 44 periodical subscriptions (225 health-care related).

BACCALAUREATE PROGRAMS

Degree BSN

Available Programs ADN to Baccalaureate; Accelerated Baccalaureate; Accelerated Baccalaureate for Second Degree; Generic Baccalaureate; RN Baccalaureate.

Study Options Full-time.

Program Entrance Requirements Minimum overall college GPA of 3.0, transcript of college record, CPR certification, health exam, high school biology, high school transcript, immunizations, 2 letters of recommendation, minimum high school GPA of 3.0, minimum GPA in nursing prerequisites of 3.0, prerequisite course work. Transfer students are accepted. *Application deadline:* 9/1 (fall), 1/2 (spring), 5/1 (summer). Applications may be processed on a rolling basis for some programs. *Application fee:* $50.

Advanced Placement Credit by examination available. Credit given for nursing courses completed elsewhere dependent upon specific evaluations.

Expenses (2009–10) *Tuition:* full-time $20,000; part-time $500 per credit hour. *International tuition:* $20,000 full-time. *Required fees:* full-time $1002; part-time $334 per term.

Goldfarb School of Nursing at Barnes-Jewish College (continued)

Financial Aid 95% of baccalaureate students in nursing programs received some form of financial aid in 2008–09.

Contact Dr. Connie Koch, Associate Dean for Academic Programs, Goldfarb School of Nursing at Barnes-Jewish College, 4483 Duncan, MS #90-36-697, St. Louis, MO 63110-1091. *Telephone:* 314-362-6590. *Fax:* 314-362-0984. *E-mail:* ckoch@bjc.org.

GRADUATE PROGRAMS

Expenses (2009–10) *Tuition:* full-time $12,600; part-time $525 per credit hour. *International tuition:* $12,600 full-time. *Required fees:* full-time $450.

Financial Aid 80% of graduate students in nursing programs received some form of financial aid in 2008–09.

Contact Dr. Connie Koch, Associate Dean for Academic Programs, Goldfarb School of Nursing at Barnes-Jewish College, 4483 Duncan, MS #90-36-697, St. Louis, MO 63110-1091. *Telephone:* 314-362-6590. *Fax:* 314-362-0984. *E-mail:* ckoch@bjc.org.

MASTER'S DEGREE PROGRAM

Degree MSN

Available Programs Master's.

Concentrations Available Nurse anesthesia; nursing administration; nursing education. *Nurse practitioner programs in:* acute care, adult health.

Study Options Full-time and part-time.

Program Entrance Requirements Clinical experience, computer literacy, minimum overall college GPA of 3.0, transcript of college record, CPR certification, immunizations, 2 letters of recommendation, nursing research course, physical assessment course, resume, statistics course. *Application deadline:* 9/1 (fall), 1/2 (spring), 5/1 (summer). Applications may be processed on a rolling basis for some programs. *Application fee:* $50.

Advanced Placement Credit given for nursing courses completed elsewhere dependent upon specific evaluations.

Degree Requirements 34 total credit hours, thesis or project.

POST-MASTER'S PROGRAM

Areas of Study Nursing administration; nursing education. *Nurse practitioner programs in:* acute care, adult health.

DOCTORAL DEGREE PROGRAM

Degree DNP, PhD

Available Programs Doctorate; Doctorate for Nurses with Non-Nursing Degrees; Post-Baccalaureate Doctorate.

Areas of Study Clinical practice, nursing administration, nursing education.

Program Entrance Requirements Minimum overall college GPA of 3, interview by faculty committee, 3 letters of recommendation, statistics course, vita, writing sample. Application deadline: 7/15 (fall). Applications may be processed on a rolling basis for some programs. Application fee: $50.

Degree Requirements 111 total credit hours, dissertation, oral exam, written exam, residency.

Graceland University
School of Nursing
Independence, Missouri

http://www.graceland.edu/nursing

Founded in 1895

DEGREES • BSN • MSN

Nursing Program Faculty 22 (36% with doctorates).

Baccalaureate Enrollment 220
Women 90% **Men** 10% **Minority** 12% **International** 3% **Part-time** 42%

Graduate Enrollment 259
Women 89% **Men** 11% **Minority** 10% **Part-time** 30%

Distance Learning Courses Available.

Nursing Student Activities Nursing Honor Society, Sigma Theta Tau, Student Nurses' Association, nursing club.

Nursing Student Resources Academic advising; academic or career counseling; bookstore; campus computer network; computer lab; computer-assisted instruction; e-mail services; housing assistance; interactive nursing skills videos; Internet; learning resource lab; library services; nursing audiovisuals; resume preparation assistance; skills, simulation, or other laboratory; tutoring.

Library Facilities 124,399 volumes (2,350 in health, 777 in nursing); 559 periodical subscriptions (945 health-care related).

BACCALAUREATE PROGRAMS

Degree BSN

Available Programs ADN to Baccalaureate; Accelerated Baccalaureate; Accelerated Baccalaureate for Second Degree; Accelerated RN Baccalaureate; Generic Baccalaureate; RN Baccalaureate.

Site Options Independence, MO.

Study Options Full-time and part-time.

Program Entrance Requirements Minimum overall college GPA of 2.5, transcript of college record, written essay, health exam, high school chemistry, high school transcript, immunizations, 2 letters of recommendation, minimum high school GPA of 2.0, minimum GPA in nursing prerequisites of 2.0, prerequisite course work. Transfer students are accepted. *Application deadline:* 11/30 (fall). *Application fee:* $50.

Advanced Placement Credit given for nursing courses completed elsewhere dependent upon specific evaluations.

Expenses (2009–10) *Tuition:* part-time $410 per credit hour.

Financial Aid 36% of baccalaureate students in nursing programs received some form of financial aid in 2008–09. *Gift aid (need-based):* Federal Pell, FSEOG, state, private, college/university gift aid from institutional funds. *Loans:* Federal Direct (Subsidized and Unsubsidized Stafford PLUS), Perkins, state, college/university, alternative loans. *Work-study:* Federal Work-Study, part-time campus jobs. *Financial aid application deadline:* Continuous.

Contact Ms. Jennifer Anthony, Program Consultant, School of Nursing, Graceland University, 1401 West Truman Road, Independence, MO 64050-3434. *Telephone:* 800-833-0524 Ext. 4805. *Fax:* 816-833-2990. *E-mail:* janthony@graceland.edu.

GRADUATE PROGRAMS

Expenses (2009–10) *Tuition:* part-time $520 per credit hour.

Financial Aid 72% of graduate students in nursing programs received some form of financial aid in 2008–09.

Contact Ms. Abbey Riley, Program Consultant, School of Nursing, Graceland University, 1401 West Truman Road, Independence, MO 64050-3434. *Telephone:* 816-833-0524 Ext. 4803. *Fax:* 816-833-2990. *E-mail:* ajriley@graceland.edu.

MASTER'S DEGREE PROGRAM

Degree MSN

Available Programs Master's; RN to Master's.

Concentrations Available Nursing education. *Nurse practitioner programs in:* family health.

Site Options Independence, MO.

Study Options Full-time and part-time.

Online Degree Options Yes (online only).

Program Entrance Requirements Clinical experience, minimum overall college GPA of 3.0, transcript of college record, written essay, 3 letters of recommendation, nursing research course, physical assessment course, prerequisite course work, statistics course. *Application deadline:* 6/1 (fall), 10/1 (winter). *Application fee:* $50.

Advanced Placement Credit given for nursing courses completed elsewhere dependent upon specific evaluations.

Degree Requirements 47 total credit hours, thesis or project, comprehensive exam.

POST-MASTER'S PROGRAM

Areas of Study Nursing education. *Nurse practitioner programs in:* family health.

Lincoln University
Department of Nursing
Jefferson City, Missouri

Founded in 1866
DEGREE • BSN

Library Facilities 204,948 volumes; 368 periodical subscriptions.

BACCALAUREATE PROGRAMS

Degree BSN

Available Programs RN Baccalaureate.
Contact *Telephone:* 573-681-5421.

Maryville University of Saint Louis
Nursing Program, School of Health Professions
St. Louis, Missouri

http://www.maryville.edu
Founded in 1872
DEGREES • BSN • MSN

Nursing Program Faculty 46 (17% with doctorates).
Baccalaureate Enrollment 412
Women 97% **Men** 3% **Minority** 10% **Part-time** 40%
Graduate Enrollment 93
Women 94% **Men** 6% **Minority** 10% **Part-time** 99%
Nursing Student Activities Sigma Theta Tau, Student Nurses' Association.

Nursing Student Resources Academic advising; academic or career counseling; assistance for students with disabilities; bookstore; campus computer network; computer lab; computer-assisted instruction; e-mail services; externships; interactive nursing skills videos; Internet; learning resource lab; library services; nursing audiovisuals; resume preparation assistance; skills, simulation, or other laboratory; tutoring.

Library Facilities 156,073 volumes (9,459 in health, 1,521 in nursing); 15,923 periodical subscriptions (2,500 health-care related).

BACCALAUREATE PROGRAMS

Degree BSN

Available Programs Accelerated Baccalaureate; Accelerated RN Baccalaureate; Generic Baccalaureate; LPN to Baccalaureate; RN Baccalaureate.
Study Options Full-time and part-time.
Program Entrance Requirements Minimum overall college GPA of 2.75, transcript of college record, health exam, high school transcript, immunizations, minimum high school GPA of 2.75, minimum GPA in nursing prerequisites of 2.75. Transfer students are accepted.
Advanced Placement Credit given for nursing courses completed elsewhere dependent upon specific evaluations.
Contact *Telephone:* 314-529-9478. *Fax:* 314-529-9139.

GRADUATE PROGRAMS

Contact *Telephone:* 314-529-9453. *Fax:* 314-529-9139.

MASTER'S DEGREE PROGRAM

Degree MSN

Available Programs Accelerated RN to Master's; Master's; RN to Master's.
Concentrations Available Nursing education. *Nurse practitioner programs in:* adult health, family health.
Study Options Full-time and part-time.
Program Entrance Requirements Minimum overall college GPA of 3.0, transcript of college record, 3 letters of recommendation, resume, statistics course.

Advanced Placement Credit by examination available. Credit given for nursing courses completed elsewhere dependent upon specific evaluations.
Degree Requirements 42 total credit hours, thesis or project.

Missouri Southern State University
Department of Nursing
Joplin, Missouri

http://www.mssu.edu/nursing/
Founded in 1937
DEGREES • BSN • MSN

Nursing Program Faculty 10 (20% with doctorates).
Baccalaureate Enrollment 87
Women 85% **Men** 15% **Minority** 10% **International** 2%
Distance Learning Courses Available.
Nursing Student Activities Nursing Honor Society, Student Nurses' Association.

Nursing Student Resources Academic advising; academic or career counseling; assistance for students with disabilities; bookstore; campus computer network; career placement assistance; computer lab; computer-assisted instruction; daycare for children of students; e-mail services; employment services for current students; housing assistance; interactive nursing skills videos; Internet; learning resource lab; library services; nursing audiovisuals; remedial services; resume preparation assistance; skills, simulation, or other laboratory; tutoring.

Library Facilities 4,872 volumes in health, 4,470 volumes in nursing; 4,412 periodical subscriptions health-care related.

BACCALAUREATE PROGRAMS

Degree BSN

Available Programs ADN to Baccalaureate; Baccalaureate for Second Degree; Generic Baccalaureate; LPN to Baccalaureate; RN Baccalaureate.
Study Options Full-time.
Program Entrance Requirements Transcript of college record, CPR certification, health exam, health insurance, immunizations, minimum GPA in nursing prerequisites of 2.5, professional liability insurance/malpractice insurance, prerequisite course work, RN licensure. Transfer students are accepted. *Application deadline:* 1/31 (fall). *Application fee:* $50.
Advanced Placement Credit by examination available. Credit given for nursing courses completed elsewhere dependent upon specific evaluations.
Expenses (2008–09) *Tuition, state resident:* full-time $5555; part-time $143 per credit hour. *Tuition, nonresident:* full-time $7700; part-time $286 per credit hour. *Room and board:* $6000 per academic year.
Financial Aid 83% of baccalaureate students in nursing programs received some form of financial aid in 2007–08. *Gift aid (need-based):* Federal Pell, FSEOG, state, private, college/university gift aid from institutional funds. *Loans:* Federal Direct (Subsidized and Unsubsidized Stafford PLUS), Perkins. *Work-study:* Federal Work-Study, part-time campus jobs. *Financial aid application deadline (priority):* 2/15.
Contact Dr. J. Mari Beth Linder, Director, Department of Nursing, Missouri Southern State University, Justice Center, Room 50, 3950 East Newman Road, Joplin, MO 64801-1595. *Telephone:* 417-625-9322. *Fax:* 417-625-3186. *E-mail:* linder-m@mssu.edu.

GRADUATE PROGRAMS

Expenses (2008–09) *Tuition, state resident:* full-time $3362. *Tuition, nonresident:* full-time $7799. *Room and board:* $6000 per academic year.
Contact Dr. Mari Beth Linder, Director, Department of Nursing, Department of Nursing, Missouri Southern State University, 3950 East Newman Road, Joplin, MO 64801. *Telephone:* 417-625-3149. *Fax:* 417-625-3186. *E-mail:* linder-m@mssu.edu.

MASTER'S DEGREE PROGRAM

Degree MSN
Available Programs Master's.

Missouri Southern State University (continued)
Concentrations Available Nursing education. *Clinical nurse specialist programs in:* family health.
Study Options Full-time.
Program Entrance Requirements Minimum overall college GPA of 3.0. *Application deadline:* 2/1 (spring). *Application fee:* $35.
Degree Requirements 43 total credit hours.

Missouri State University
Department of Nursing
Springfield, Missouri

http://www.smsu.edu/nursing
Founded in 1905
DEGREES • BSN • MSN

Nursing Program Faculty 14 (36% with doctorates).

Baccalaureate Enrollment 118
Women 90% **Men** 10% **Minority** 4% **International** 1% **Part-time** 68%

Graduate Enrollment 36
Women 98% **Men** 2% **Minority** 1% **Part-time** 39%

Distance Learning Courses Available.

Nursing Student Activities Sigma Theta Tau, Student Nurses' Association.

Nursing Student Resources Academic advising; academic or career counseling; assistance for students with disabilities; bookstore; campus computer network; career placement assistance; computer lab; computer-assisted instruction; daycare for children of students; e-mail services; employment services for current students; externships; housing assistance; interactive nursing skills videos; Internet; learning resource lab; library services; nursing audiovisuals; paid internships; placement services for program completers; remedial services; resume preparation assistance; skills, simulation, or other laboratory; tutoring; unpaid internships.

Library Facilities 1.7 million volumes (10,500 in health, 3,516 in nursing); 4,238 periodical subscriptions (370 health-care related).

BACCALAUREATE PROGRAMS
Degree BSN

Available Programs ADN to Baccalaureate; Accelerated RN Baccalaureate; Generic Baccalaureate; LPN to Baccalaureate; RN Baccalaureate.
Study Options Full-time.
Online Degree Options Yes.
Program Entrance Requirements Minimum overall college GPA of 2.75, transcript of college record, CPR certification, health insurance, immunizations, prerequisite course work. Transfer students are accepted. *Application deadline:* 1/31 (summer).
Advanced Placement Credit given for nursing courses completed elsewhere dependent upon specific evaluations.
Expenses (2008–09) *Tuition, state resident:* full-time $5580; part-time $186 per credit hour. *Tuition, nonresident:* full-time $10,860; part-time $362 per credit hour. *Room and board:* $6000; room only: $3970 per academic year. *Required fees:* full-time $963.
Financial Aid 65% of baccalaureate students in nursing programs received some form of financial aid in 2007–08.
Contact Dr. Kathryn L. Hope, Associate Professor, Department of Nursing, Missouri State University, 901 South National Avenue, Springfield, MO 65897. *Telephone:* 417-836-5310. *Fax:* 417-836-5484. *E-mail:* kathrynhope@missouristate.edu.

GRADUATE PROGRAMS
Expenses (2008–09) *Tuition, state resident:* full-time $3852; part-time $214 per credit hour. *Tuition, nonresident:* full-time $7524; part-time $418 per credit hour. *Room and board:* $6000; room only: $3970 per academic year. *Required fees:* full-time $676.
Financial Aid 25% of graduate students in nursing programs received some form of financial aid in 2007–08. Federal Work-Study, institutionally sponsored loans, scholarships, and unspecified assistantships available. *Financial aid application deadline:* 3/31.

Contact Dr. Kathryn L. Hope, Associate Professor, Department of Nursing, Missouri State University, 901 South National Avenue, Springfield, MO 65897. *Telephone:* 417-836-5310. *Fax:* 417-836-5484. *E-mail:* kathrynhope@missouristate.edu.

MASTER'S DEGREE PROGRAM
Degree MSN
Available Programs Accelerated AD/RN to Master's; Master's; RN to Master's.
Concentrations Available Nursing education. *Nurse practitioner programs in:* family health.
Study Options Full-time and part-time.
Online Degree Options Yes (online only).
Program Entrance Requirements Computer literacy, minimum overall college GPA of 3.0, transcript of college record, written essay, immunizations, interview, nursing research course, physical assessment course, professional liability insurance/malpractice insurance, statistics course, GRE General Test. *Application deadline:* 2/15 (fall).
Advanced Placement Credit given for nursing courses completed elsewhere dependent upon specific evaluations.
Degree Requirements 51 total credit hours, thesis or project, comprehensive exam.

POST-MASTER'S PROGRAM
Areas of Study Nursing education. *Nurse practitioner programs in:* family health.

CONTINUING EDUCATION PROGRAM
Contact Virginia Cordova, Program Coordinator, Department of Nursing, Missouri State University, Department of Continuing Education, 901 South National, Springfield, MO 65897. *Telephone:* 417-836-6660. *Fax:* 417-836-7674. *E-mail:* virginiacordova@missouristate.edu.

Missouri Western State University
Department of Nursing
St. Joseph, Missouri

http://www.missouriwestern.edu/nursing
Founded in 1915
DEGREE • BSN

Nursing Program Faculty 35 (23% with doctorates).

Baccalaureate Enrollment 190
Women 90.5% **Men** 9.5% **Minority** 6.3%

Nursing Student Activities Sigma Theta Tau, Student Nurses' Association.

Nursing Student Resources Academic advising; academic or career counseling; assistance for students with disabilities; bookstore; campus computer network; career placement assistance; computer lab; computer-assisted instruction; daycare for children of students; e-mail services; employment services for current students; interactive nursing skills videos; Internet; learning resource lab; library services; nursing audiovisuals; paid internships; placement services for program completers; remedial services; resume preparation assistance; skills, simulation, or other laboratory; tutoring; unpaid internships.

Library Facilities 147,509 volumes (9,441 in health, 8,902 in nursing); 1,068 periodical subscriptions (21 health-care related).

BACCALAUREATE PROGRAMS
Degree BSN
Available Programs Generic Baccalaureate.
Study Options Full-time.
Program Entrance Requirements Minimum overall college GPA of 2.5, transcript of college record, CPR certification, written essay, health insurance, high school transcript, immunizations, minimum GPA in nursing prerequisites of 2.0, prerequisite course work. Transfer students are accepted. *Application deadline:* 1/15 (fall), 8/15 (spring). *Application fee:* $30.
Advanced Placement Credit by examination available. Credit given for nursing courses completed elsewhere dependent upon specific evaluations.

Expenses (2009–10) *Tuition, state resident:* full-time $2780; part-time $215 per credit hour. *Tuition, nonresident:* full-time $4844; part-time $353 per credit hour. *Room and board:* $3981; room only: $2224 per academic year. *Required fees:* full-time $180; part-time $90 per term.

Financial Aid 83% of baccalaureate students in nursing programs received some form of financial aid in 2008–09. *Gift aid (need-based):* Federal Pell, FSEOG, state, private, college/university gift aid from institutional funds. *Loans:* FFEL (Subsidized and Unsubsidized Stafford PLUS), Perkins. *Work-study:* Federal Work-Study, part-time campus jobs. *Financial aid application deadline (priority):* 3/1.

Contact Department of Nursing, Department of Nursing, Missouri Western State University, 4525 Downs Drive, St. Joseph, MO 64507. *Telephone:* 816-271-4415. *Fax:* 816-271-5849. *E-mail:* nursing@missouriwestern.edu.

Research College of Nursing
College of Nursing
Kansas City, Missouri

Founded in 1980

DEGREES • BSN • MSN

Nursing Program Faculty 37 (16% with doctorates).

Baccalaureate Enrollment 359
Women 88% **Men** 12% **Minority** 5% **International** 1%

Graduate Enrollment 101
Women 96% **Men** 4% **Minority** 20% **Part-time** 90%

Distance Learning Courses Available.

Nursing Student Activities Sigma Theta Tau, Student Nurses' Association.

Nursing Student Resources Academic advising; academic or career counseling; bookstore; campus computer network; career placement assistance; computer lab; computer-assisted instruction; daycare for children of students; e-mail services; housing assistance; Internet; learning resource lab; library services; resume preparation assistance; skills, simulation, or other laboratory; tutoring.

Library Facilities 150,000 volumes; 675 periodical subscriptions.

BACCALAUREATE PROGRAMS
Degree BSN

Available Programs Accelerated Baccalaureate; Accelerated Baccalaureate for Second Degree; Baccalaureate for Second Degree; Generic Baccalaureate.

Study Options Full-time.

Program Entrance Requirements Transcript of college record, high school chemistry, 3 years high school math, 2 years high school science, high school transcript, minimum high school rank 50%, minimum GPA in nursing prerequisites of 2.7. Transfer students are accepted. *Application deadline:* Applications may be processed on a rolling basis for some programs.

Advanced Placement Credit given for nursing courses completed elsewhere dependent upon specific evaluations.

Expenses (2009–10) *Tuition:* full-time $24,950; part-time $832 per credit hour. *Room and board:* $7300; room only: $4180 per academic year. *Required fees:* full-time $750; part-time $25 per credit.

Financial Aid 90% of baccalaureate students in nursing programs received some form of financial aid in 2008–09.

Contact Leslie Mendenhall, Director of Transfer and Graduate Admissions, College of Nursing, Research College of Nursing, 2525 East Meyer Boulevard, Kansas City, MO 64132-1199. *Telephone:* 816-995-2820. *Fax:* 816-995-2813. *E-mail:* leslie.mendenhall@researchcollege.edu.

GRADUATE PROGRAMS

Expenses (2009–10) *Tuition:* part-time $380 per credit hour. *Required fees:* part-time $25 per term.

Financial Aid 15% of graduate students in nursing programs received some form of financial aid in 2008–09.

Contact Leslie Mendenhall, Director of Transfer and Graduate Admissions, College of Nursing, Research College of Nursing, 2525 East Meyer Boulevard, Kansas City, MO 64132-1199. *Telephone:* 816-995-2820. *Fax:* 816-995-2813. *E-mail:* leslie.mendenhall@researchcollege.edu.

MASTER'S DEGREE PROGRAM
Degree MSN

Available Programs Master's.

Concentrations Available Nursing administration; nursing education. *Nurse practitioner programs in:* family health.

Study Options Full-time and part-time.

Online Degree Options Yes.

Program Entrance Requirements Minimum overall college GPA of 3.0, transcript of college record, CPR certification, written essay, immunizations, interview, 3 letters of recommendation, physical assessment course, professional liability insurance/malpractice insurance, resume, statistics course. *Application deadline:* 7/1 (fall), 10/1 (spring), 4/1 (summer). *Application fee:* $50.

Advanced Placement Credit given for nursing courses completed elsewhere dependent upon specific evaluations.

Degree Requirements 45 total credit hours, thesis or project.

Saint Louis University
School of Nursing
St. Louis, Missouri

http://nursing.slu.edu

Founded in 1818

DEGREES • BSN • MSN • MSN/MPH • PHD

Nursing Program Faculty 40 (70% with doctorates).

Baccalaureate Enrollment 548
Women 95% **Men** 5% **Minority** 12% **International** 1% **Part-time** 4%

Graduate Enrollment 525
Women 92% **Men** 8% **Minority** 11% **International** 1% **Part-time** 97%

Distance Learning Courses Available.

Nursing Student Activities Sigma Theta Tau, Student Nurses' Association.

Nursing Student Resources Academic advising; assistance for students with disabilities; bookstore; campus computer network; career placement assistance; computer lab; computer-assisted instruction; e-mail services; employment services for current students; housing assistance; interactive nursing skills videos; Internet; learning resource lab; library services; nursing audiovisuals; placement services for program completers; remedial services; resume preparation assistance; skills, simulation, or other laboratory; tutoring; unpaid internships.

Library Facilities 1.9 million volumes (121,994 in health, 6,433 in nursing); 16,067 periodical subscriptions (6,012 health-care related).

BACCALAUREATE PROGRAMS
Degree BSN

Available Programs Accelerated Baccalaureate; Accelerated Baccalaureate for Second Degree; Generic Baccalaureate; RN Baccalaureate.

Site Options St. Louis, MO.

Study Options Full-time and part-time.

Online Degree Options Yes (online only).

Program Entrance Requirements Minimum overall college GPA of 3.0, transcript of college record, health exam, high school biology, high school chemistry, high school transcript, immunizations, minimum high school GPA of 3.0. Transfer students are accepted. *Application deadline:* Applications may be processed on a rolling basis for some programs.

Advanced Placement Credit by examination available. Credit given for nursing courses completed elsewhere dependent upon specific evaluations.

Expenses (2009–10) *Tuition:* full-time $31,660; part-time $1080 per credit hour. *Room and board:* $9000 per academic year. *Required fees:* full-time $390; part-time $75 per term.

Saint Louis University (continued)

Financial Aid 75% of baccalaureate students in nursing programs received some form of financial aid in 2008–09.

Contact Scott Ragsdale, Recruitment Specialist, School of Nursing, Saint Louis University, 3525 Caroline Street, St. Louis, MO 63104. *Telephone:* 314-977-8995. *Fax:* 314-977-8949. *E-mail:* sragsda2@slu.edu.

GRADUATE PROGRAMS

Expenses (2009–10) *Tuition:* part-time $905 per credit hour.

Financial Aid 50% of graduate students in nursing programs received some form of financial aid in 2008–09. 2 research assistantships (averaging $10,250 per year), 5 teaching assistantships with full tuition reimbursements available (averaging $11,000 per year) were awarded; Federal Work-Study, scholarships, traineeships, tuition waivers, and unspecified assistantships also available. Aid available to part-time students. *Financial aid application deadline:* 6/1.

Contact Dr. Mary Lee Barron, MSN/DNP Program Director, School of Nursing, Saint Louis University, 3525 Caroline Street, St. Louis, MO 63104. *Telephone:* 314-977-8978. *Fax:* 314-977-8949. *E-mail:* barronml@slu.edu.

MASTER'S DEGREE PROGRAM

Degrees MSN; MSN/MPH

Available Programs Master's; Master's for Nurses with Non-Nursing Degrees; RN to Master's.

Concentrations Available Nursing education. *Clinical nurse specialist programs in:* adult health, gerontology, pediatric, psychiatric/mental health. *Nurse practitioner programs in:* acute care, adult health, family health, gerontology, pediatric, psychiatric/mental health.

Site Options St. Louis, MO.

Study Options Full-time and part-time.

Online Degree Options Yes (online only).

Program Entrance Requirements Minimum overall college GPA of 3.2, transcript of college record, CPR certification, immunizations, 3 letters of recommendation, resume. *Application deadline:* 7/1 (fall), 11/1 (spring), 4/1 (summer).

Advanced Placement Credit given for nursing courses completed elsewhere dependent upon specific evaluations.

Degree Requirements 44 total credit hours.

POST-MASTER'S PROGRAM

Areas of Study Nursing education. *Clinical nurse specialist programs in:* adult health, gerontology, pediatric, psychiatric/mental health. *Nurse practitioner programs in:* acute care, adult health, family health, gerontology, pediatric, psychiatric/mental health.

DOCTORAL DEGREE PROGRAM

Degree PhD

Available Programs Doctorate.

Areas of Study Nursing education, nursing research.

Site Options St. Louis, MO.

Program Entrance Requirements Minimum overall college GPA of 3.25, 3 letters of recommendation, MSN or equivalent, statistics course, vita, writing sample, GRE General Test. Application deadline: 4/1 (fall), 11/1 (spring), 4/1 (summer). Applications may be processed on a rolling basis for some programs. Application fee: $40.

Degree Requirements 69 total credit hours, dissertation, oral exam, written exam, residency.

CONTINUING EDUCATION PROGRAM

Contact Ms. Kristine M. L'Ecuyer, Continuing Education Director, School of Nursing, Saint Louis University, 3525 Caroline Street, St. Louis, MO 63104. *Telephone:* 314-977-8975. *Fax:* 314-977-8949. *E-mail:* lecuyerk@slu.edu.

Saint Luke's College

Nursing College
Kansas City, Missouri

http://www.saintlukescollege.edu

Founded in 1903

DEGREE • BSN

Nursing Program Faculty 17 (18% with doctorates).

Baccalaureate Enrollment 115
Women 95% **Men** 5% **Minority** 10% **International** 1% **Part-time** 12%

Nursing Student Activities Student Nurses' Association.

Nursing Student Resources Academic advising; assistance for students with disabilities; bookstore; campus computer network; career placement assistance; computer lab; computer-assisted instruction; e-mail services; employment services for current students; interactive nursing skills videos; Internet; learning resource lab; library services; nursing audiovisuals; paid internships; skills, simulation, or other laboratory; tutoring.

BACCALAUREATE PROGRAMS

Degree BSN

Available Programs Generic Baccalaureate.

Site Options Kansas City, MO.

Study Options Full-time and part-time.

Program Entrance Requirements Transcript of college record, CPR certification, written essay, health exam, health insurance, high school transcript, immunizations, interview, 3 letters of recommendation, minimum GPA in nursing prerequisites of 2.7, prerequisite course work. Transfer students are accepted.

Advanced Placement Credit given for nursing courses completed elsewhere dependent upon specific evaluations.

Contact *Telephone:* 816-932-2367.

Southeast Missouri State University

Department of Nursing
Cape Girardeau, Missouri

http://www2.semo.edu/nursing

Founded in 1873

DEGREES • BSN • MSN

Nursing Program Faculty 24 (60% with doctorates).

Baccalaureate Enrollment 408
Women 95% **Men** 5% **Minority** 7% **Part-time** 20%

Graduate Enrollment 37
Women 80% **Men** 20% **Minority** 2% **Part-time** 65%

Nursing Student Activities Sigma Theta Tau, Student Nurses' Association.

Nursing Student Resources Academic advising; academic or career counseling; assistance for students with disabilities; bookstore; campus computer network; computer lab; computer-assisted instruction; daycare for children of students; e-mail services; employment services for current students; housing assistance; interactive nursing skills videos; Internet; learning resource lab; library services; nursing audiovisuals; remedial services; skills, simulation, or other laboratory; tutoring.

Library Facilities 503,242 volumes (450,750 in health, 16,145 in nursing); 49,866 periodical subscriptions (75 health-care related).

BACCALAUREATE PROGRAMS

Degree BSN

Available Programs Generic Baccalaureate; RN Baccalaureate.

Study Options Full-time.

Program Entrance Requirements Minimum overall college GPA of 2.5, transcript of college record, CPR certification, health exam, health insurance, high school transcript, immunizations, professional liability insurance/malpractice insurance, prerequisite course work. Transfer students are accepted.

Contact *Telephone:* 573-651-2585. *Fax:* 573-651-2142.

GRADUATE PROGRAMS

Contact *Telephone:* 573-651-2871. *Fax:* 573-651-2142.

MASTER'S DEGREE PROGRAM

Degree MSN

Available Programs Master's.

Concentrations Available Nursing education. *Clinical nurse specialist programs in:* adult health. *Nurse practitioner programs in:* family health.

Study Options Full-time and part-time.

Program Entrance Requirements Clinical experience, minimum overall college GPA of 3.0, transcript of college record, CPR certification, written essay, immunizations, 2 letters of recommendation, physical assessment course, professional liability insurance/malpractice insurance, prerequisite course work, resume, statistics course.

Degree Requirements 45 total credit hours, thesis or project.

POST-MASTER'S PROGRAM

Areas of Study *Nurse practitioner programs in:* family health.

Southwest Baptist University
College of Nursing
Bolivar, Missouri

http://www.sbuniv.edu/collegeofnursing

Founded in 1878

DEGREE • BSN

Nursing Program Faculty 6 (33% with doctorates).

Baccalaureate Enrollment 130
Women 95% **Men** 5% **Minority** 2% **Part-time** 85%

Distance Learning Courses Available.

Nursing Student Activities Nursing Honor Society, Student Nurses' Association.

Nursing Student Resources Academic advising; bookstore; campus computer network; computer lab; computer-assisted instruction; e-mail services; interactive nursing skills videos; Internet; learning resource lab; library services; nursing audiovisuals; skills, simulation, or other laboratory.

Library Facilities 185,703 volumes; 22,388 periodical subscriptions.

BACCALAUREATE PROGRAMS

Degree BSN

Available Programs RN Baccalaureate.

Site Options Springfield, MO.

Study Options Full-time and part-time.

Online Degree Options Yes.

Program Entrance Requirements Minimum overall college GPA of 2.5, transcript of college record, CPR certification, high school transcript, immunizations, minimum GPA in nursing prerequisites of 2.5, prerequisite course work, RN licensure. Transfer students are accepted. *Application deadline:* 8/15 (fall), 1/1 (winter), 1/15 (spring), 6/1 (summer). Applications may be processed on a rolling basis for some programs. *Application fee:* $25.

Advanced Placement Credit given for nursing courses completed elsewhere dependent upon specific evaluations.

Expenses (2008–09) *Tuition:* part-time $175 per credit hour. *Required fees:* part-time $70 per credit; part-time $105 per term.

Financial Aid 50% of baccalaureate students in nursing programs received some form of financial aid in 2007–08. *Gift aid (need-based):* Federal Pell, FSEOG, state, private, college/university gift aid from institutional funds. *Loans:* Federal Nursing Student Loans, FFEL (Subsidized and Unsubsidized Stafford PLUS), Perkins, state, alternative loans. *Work-study:* Federal Work-Study. *Financial aid application deadline (priority):* 3/15.

Contact Dr. Martha C. Baker, Director, BSN Program, College of Nursing, Southwest Baptist University, 4431 South Fremont Avenue, Springfield, MO 65804. *Telephone:* 417-820-5058. *Fax:* 417-887-4847. *E-mail:* mbaker@sbuniv.edu.

Truman State University
Program in Nursing
Kirksville, Missouri

http://nursing.truman.edu

Founded in 1867

DEGREE • BSN

Nursing Program Faculty 11 (18% with doctorates).

Baccalaureate Enrollment 172
Women 94% **Men** 6% **Minority** 5% **International** 5% **Part-time** 1%

Nursing Student Activities Nursing Honor Society, Sigma Theta Tau, Student Nurses' Association, nursing club.

Nursing Student Resources Academic advising; academic or career counseling; assistance for students with disabilities; bookstore; campus computer network; career placement assistance; computer lab; computer-assisted instruction; e-mail services; employment services for current students; externships; interactive nursing skills videos; Internet; learning resource lab; library services; nursing audiovisuals; paid internships; remedial services; resume preparation assistance; skills, simulation, or other laboratory; tutoring; unpaid internships.

Library Facilities 497,022 volumes (6,923 in health, 1,654 in nursing); 3,942 periodical subscriptions (900 health-care related).

BACCALAUREATE PROGRAMS

Degree BSN

Available Programs Generic Baccalaureate.

Study Options Full-time.

Program Entrance Requirements Minimum overall college GPA of 2.75, transcript of college record, written essay, high school biology, high school chemistry, high school foreign language, 3 years high school math, 3 years high school science, high school transcript, immunizations, minimum high school GPA of 3.3, minimum GPA in nursing prerequisites of 3.0. Transfer students are accepted.

Financial Aid 75% of baccalaureate students in nursing programs received some form of financial aid in 2007–08.

Contact Dr. Stephanie A. Powelson, RN, Department of Nursing Chair, Program in Nursing, Truman State University, 100 East Normal, Barnett 2401, Kirksville, MO 63501. *Telephone:* 660-785-4557. *Fax:* 660-785-7424. *E-mail:* spowelso@truman.edu.

University of Central Missouri
Department of Nursing
Warrensburg, Missouri

http://www.ucmo.edu/nursing

Founded in 1871

DEGREES • BS • MS

Nursing Program Faculty 18 (27% with doctorates).

Baccalaureate Enrollment 141
Women 96% **Men** 4% **Minority** 8% **International** 6%

Graduate Enrollment 116
Women 95% **Men** 5% **Minority** 8% **Part-time** 90%

Distance Learning Courses Available.

Nursing Student Activities Nursing club.

Nursing Student Resources Academic advising; academic or career counseling; assistance for students with disabilities; bookstore; campus computer network; career placement assistance; computer lab; computer-assisted instruction; daycare for children of students; e-mail services; employment services for current students; externships; housing assistance; interactive nursing skills videos; Internet; learning resource lab; library services; nursing audiovisuals; placement services for program completers; remedial services; resume preparation assistance; skills, simulation, or other laboratory; tutoring.

Library Facilities 1.3 million volumes (17,000 in health, 1,000 in nursing); 1,605 periodical subscriptions (300 health-care related).

University of Central Missouri (continued)

BACCALAUREATE PROGRAMS

Degree BS

Available Programs Generic Baccalaureate; RN Baccalaureate.

Site Options Lee's Summit, MO; Warrensburg, MO; Lee's Summit, MO.

Study Options Full-time.

Online Degree Options Yes.

Program Entrance Requirements Minimum overall college GPA of 2.75, minimum GPA in nursing prerequisites of 2.0, prerequisite course work. Transfer students are accepted. *Application deadline:* 1/1 (fall), 7/1 (spring). *Application fee:* $25.

Advanced Placement Credit by examination available. Credit given for nursing courses completed elsewhere dependent upon specific evaluations.

Expenses (2009–10) *Tuition, state resident:* part-time $220 per credit hour. *Tuition, nonresident:* part-time $415 per credit hour. *Room and board:* $5220; room only: $4120 per academic year. *Required fees:* part-time $193 per term.

Financial Aid 86% of baccalaureate students in nursing programs received some form of financial aid in 2008–09.

Contact Dr. Julie Ann Clawson, RN, Chair, Department of Nursing, University of Central Missouri, 600 South College, UHC 106A, Warrensburg, MO 64093. *Telephone:* 660-543-4775. *Fax:* 660-543-8304. *E-mail:* clawson@ucmo.edu.

GRADUATE PROGRAMS

Expenses (2009–10) *Tuition, state resident:* part-time $270 per credit hour. *Tuition, nonresident:* part-time $516 per credit hour. *Room and board:* $5220; room only: $4120 per academic year. *Required fees:* part-time $70 per term.

Financial Aid 70% of graduate students in nursing programs received some form of financial aid in 2008–09.

Contact Dr. Joseph Vaughn, Dean, Department of Nursing, University of Central Missouri, Graduate Studies, WDE 1800, Warrensburg, MO 64093. *Telephone:* 660-543-4621. *E-mail:* vaughn@ucmo.edu.

MASTER'S DEGREE PROGRAM

Degree MS

Available Programs Master's.

Concentrations Available Nursing education. *Nurse practitioner programs in:* family health.

Site Options Lee's Summit, MO; Warrensburg, MO.

Study Options Part-time.

Online Degree Options Yes (online only).

Program Entrance Requirements Clinical experience, minimum overall college GPA of 3.0, transcript of college record, CPR certification, immunizations, professional liability insurance/malpractice insurance. *Application deadline:* Applications may be processed on a rolling basis for some programs. *Application fee:* $25.

Advanced Placement Credit given for nursing courses completed elsewhere dependent upon specific evaluations.

Degree Requirements 32 total credit hours, thesis or project.

POST-MASTER'S PROGRAM

Areas of Study Nursing education. *Nurse practitioner programs in:* family health.

University of Missouri–Columbia

Sinclair School of Nursing
Columbia, Missouri

http://nursing.missouri.edu

Founded in 1839

DEGREES • BSN • MSN • MSN/PHD • PHD

Baccalaureate Enrollment 380
Women 90% **Men** 10% **Minority** 6% **International** 3% **Part-time** 31%

Graduate Enrollment 200
Women 95% **Men** 5% **Minority** 8% **International** 2% **Part-time** 77%

Distance Learning Courses Available.

Nursing Student Activities Nursing Honor Society, Sigma Theta Tau, Student Nurses' Association, nursing club.

Nursing Student Resources Academic advising; academic or career counseling; assistance for students with disabilities; bookstore; campus computer network; career placement assistance; computer lab; computer-assisted instruction; daycare for children of students; e-mail services; employment services for current students; externships; housing assistance; interactive nursing skills videos; Internet; learning resource lab; library services; nursing audiovisuals; paid internships; remedial services; resume preparation assistance; skills, simulation, or other laboratory; tutoring; unpaid internships.

Library Facilities 3.3 million volumes (114,580 in health, 6,416 in nursing); 54,347 periodical subscriptions.

BACCALAUREATE PROGRAMS

Degree BSN

Available Programs ADN to Baccalaureate; Accelerated Baccalaureate; Accelerated Baccalaureate for Second Degree; Generic Baccalaureate; RN Baccalaureate.

Study Options Full-time and part-time.

Online Degree Options Yes.

Program Entrance Requirements Minimum overall college GPA of 2.5, transcript of college record, CPR certification, high school biology, high school chemistry, 4 years high school math, 3 years high school science, high school transcript, immunizations, interview, minimum GPA in nursing prerequisites of 2.5, prerequisite course work. Transfer students are accepted.

Advanced Placement Credit by examination available. Credit given for nursing courses completed elsewhere dependent upon specific evaluations.

Contact *Telephone:* 573-882-0277. *Fax:* 573-884-4544.

GRADUATE PROGRAMS

Contact *Telephone:* 573-882-0277.

MASTER'S DEGREE PROGRAM

Degrees MSN; MSN/PhD

Available Programs Master's.

Concentrations Available Nursing administration; nursing education. *Clinical nurse specialist programs in:* acute care, adult health, cardiovascular, community health, critical care, home health care, maternity-newborn, oncology, palliative care, pediatric, public health, rehabilitation, school health, women's health. *Nurse practitioner programs in:* family health, gerontology, pediatric, primary care, psychiatric/mental health.

Study Options Full-time and part-time.

Online Degree Options Yes (online only).

Program Entrance Requirements Computer literacy, minimum overall college GPA of 3.0, transcript of college record, CPR certification, immunizations, interview, 2 letters of recommendation, nursing research course, prerequisite course work, statistics course, GRE General Test.

Advanced Placement Credit given for nursing courses completed elsewhere dependent upon specific evaluations.

Degree Requirements 43 total credit hours, comprehensive exam.

POST-MASTER'S PROGRAM

Areas of Study Nursing administration; nursing education. *Clinical nurse specialist programs in:* acute care, adult health, cardiovascular, community health, critical care, home health care, maternity-newborn, oncology, palliative care, pediatric, public health, rehabilitation, school health, women's health. *Nurse practitioner programs in:* family health, gerontology, pediatric, primary care, psychiatric/mental health.

DOCTORAL DEGREE PROGRAM

Degree PhD

Available Programs Doctorate; Post-Baccalaureate Doctorate.

Areas of Study Aging, family health, gerontology, health promotion/disease prevention, health-care systems, human health and illness, nursing research, oncology, women's health.

Program Entrance Requirements Minimum overall college GPA of 3.5, interview by faculty committee, 3 letters of recommendation, vita, writing sample.

Degree Requirements 72 total credit hours, dissertation, oral exam, written exam, residency.

CONTINUING EDUCATION PROGRAM

Contact *Telephone:* 573-882-0215. *Fax:* 573-884-4544.

University of Missouri–Kansas City
School of Nursing
Kansas City, Missouri

http://www.umkc.edu/nursing

Founded in 1929

DEGREES • BSN • MSN • PHD

Nursing Program Faculty 48 (52% with doctorates).

Baccalaureate Enrollment 413
Women 89% **Men** 11% **Minority** 21% **International** .01% **Part-time** 28%

Graduate Enrollment 340
Women 92% **Men** 8% **Minority** 11% **Part-time** 83%

Distance Learning Courses Available.

Nursing Student Activities Sigma Theta Tau, Student Nurses' Association.

Nursing Student Resources Academic advising; academic or career counseling; assistance for students with disabilities; bookstore; campus computer network; career placement assistance; computer lab; computer-assisted instruction; e-mail services; employment services for current students; housing assistance; interactive nursing skills videos; Internet; learning resource lab; library services; nursing audiovisuals; other; placement services for program completers; remedial services; resume preparation assistance; skills, simulation, or other laboratory; tutoring.

Library Facilities 1.8 million volumes (111,108 in health, 15,000 in nursing); 30,976 periodical subscriptions (60,000 health-care related).

BACCALAUREATE PROGRAMS

Degree BSN

Available Programs Accelerated Baccalaureate; Generic Baccalaureate; RN Baccalaureate.

Study Options Full-time.

Program Entrance Requirements Minimum overall college GPA of 2.75, transcript of college record, CPR certification, written essay, health insurance, high school foreign language, 4 years high school math, 4 years high school science, high school transcript, immunizations, minimum GPA in nursing prerequisites of 2.75, professional liability insurance/malpractice insurance, prerequisite course work. Transfer students are accepted. *Application deadline:* 1/31 (fall). *Application fee:* $35.

Expenses (2009–10) *Tuition, state resident:* full-time $7368; part-time $246 per credit hour. *Tuition, nonresident:* full-time $18,459; part-time $615 per credit hour. *International tuition:* $27,098 full-time. *Room and board:* $16,320 per academic year. *Required fees:* full-time $636; part-time $18 per credit; part-time $304 per term.

Financial Aid 74% of baccalaureate students in nursing programs received some form of financial aid in 2008–09. *Gift aid (need-based):* Federal Pell, FSEOG, state, private, college/university gift aid from institutional funds, United Negro College Fund. *Loans:* Federal Nursing Student Loans, Federal Direct (Subsidized and Unsubsidized Stafford PLUS), Perkins, state, college/university. *Work-study:* Federal Work-Study. *Financial aid application deadline (priority):* 3/1.

Contact Ms. Judy A. Jellison, Director, Nursing Student Services, School of Nursing, University of Missouri–Kansas City, 2464 Charlotte Street, Kansas City, MO 64108. *Telephone:* 816-235-1740. *Fax:* 816-235-6593. *E-mail:* jellisonj@umkc.edu.

GRADUATE PROGRAMS

Expenses (2009–10) *Tuition, state resident:* full-time $5377; part-time $299 per credit hour. *Tuition, nonresident:* full-time $13,881; part-time $771 per credit hour. *International tuition:* $13,881 full-time. *Room and board:* $16,320 per academic year. *Required fees:* full-time $452; part-time $35 per credit; part-time $342 per term.

Financial Aid 42% of graduate students in nursing programs received some form of financial aid in 2008–09. 10 teaching assistantships with partial tuition reimbursements available (averaging $5,160 per year) were awarded; fellowships, research assistantships, career-related internships or fieldwork, Federal Work-Study, institutionally sponsored loans, and tuition waivers (full and partial) also available. Aid available to part-time students. *Financial aid application deadline:* 3/1.

Contact Ms. Judy A. Jellison, Director, Nursing Student Services, School of Nursing, University of Missouri–Kansas City, 2464 Charlotte Street, Kansas City, MO 64108. *Telephone:* 816-235-1740. *Fax:* 816-235-6593. *E-mail:* jellisonj@umkc.edu.

MASTER'S DEGREE PROGRAM

Degree MSN

Available Programs Master's.

Concentrations Available Nursing education. *Nurse practitioner programs in:* adult health, family health, neonatal health, pediatric, women's health.

Site Options Joplin, MO; St. Joseph, MO.

Study Options Full-time and part-time.

Online Degree Options Yes (online only).

Program Entrance Requirements Clinical experience, computer literacy, minimum overall college GPA of 3.2, transcript of college record, CPR certification, immunizations, physical assessment course, professional liability insurance/malpractice insurance, resume, statistics course. *Application deadline:* 2/1 (fall), 9/1 (winter), 2/1 (summer). *Application fee:* $35.

Degree Requirements 43 total credit hours, thesis or project.

POST-MASTER'S PROGRAM

Areas of Study Nursing education. *Nurse practitioner programs in:* adult health, family health, neonatal health, pediatric, women's health.

DOCTORAL DEGREE PROGRAM

Degree PhD

Available Programs Doctorate; Post-Baccalaureate Doctorate.

Areas of Study Health promotion/disease prevention, health-care systems.

Online Degree Options Yes (online only).

Program Entrance Requirements Minimum overall college GPA of 3.5, interview by faculty committee, interview, 3 letters of recommendation, MSN or equivalent, vita, writing sample, GRE. Application deadline: 2/1 (summer). Application fee: $35.

Degree Requirements 61 total credit hours, dissertation, oral exam, written exam, residency.

CONTINUING EDUCATION PROGRAM

Contact Jodi M. Baker, Continuing Education Coordinator, School of Nursing, University of Missouri–Kansas City, 2464 Charlotte Street, Kansas City, MO 64108. *Telephone:* 816-235-6463. *Fax:* 816-235-1701. *E-mail:* bakerjm@umkc.edu.

University of Missouri–St. Louis
College of Nursing
St. Louis, Missouri

Founded in 1963

DEGREES • BSN • DNP • MSN

Nursing Program Faculty 76 (32% with doctorates).

Baccalaureate Enrollment 630
Women 90% **Men** 10% **Minority** 24% **International** 1% **Part-time** 30%

Graduate Enrollment 225
Women 94% **Men** 6% **Minority** 14% **Part-time** 96%

Distance Learning Courses Available.

Nursing Student Activities Nursing Honor Society, Sigma Theta Tau, Student Nurses' Association.

Nursing Student Resources Academic advising; academic or career counseling; assistance for students with disabilities; bookstore; campus computer network; career placement assistance; computer lab; computer-assisted instruction; daycare for children of students; e-mail services;

University of Missouri–St. Louis (continued)
employment services for current students; externships; interactive nursing skills videos; Internet; learning resource lab; library services; nursing audiovisuals; resume preparation assistance; skills, simulation, or other laboratory; tutoring; unpaid internships.

Library Facilities 1.2 million volumes (85,000 in health, 17,397 in nursing); 3,181 periodical subscriptions (5,400 health-care related).

BACCALAUREATE PROGRAMS

Degree BSN

Available Programs Accelerated Baccalaureate; Generic Baccalaureate; RN Baccalaureate.

Site Options St. Charles, MO; Bridgeton, MO; Creve Coeur, MO.

Study Options Full-time and part-time.

Online Degree Options Yes.

Program Entrance Requirements Minimum overall college GPA of 2.5, transcript of college record, CPR certification, health exam, 4 years high school math, 3 years high school science, high school transcript, immunizations, minimum high school GPA of 2.5, minimum GPA in nursing prerequisites, professional liability insurance/malpractice insurance. Transfer students are accepted. *Application deadline:* 2/1 (fall), 10/1 (spring). *Application fee:* $35.

Advanced Placement Credit given for nursing courses completed elsewhere dependent upon specific evaluations.

Expenses (2009–10) *Tuition, state resident:* full-time $7368; part-time $246 per credit hour. *Tuition, nonresident:* full-time $18,459; part-time $615 per credit hour. *International tuition:* $18,459 full-time. *Room and board:* $8164; room only: $4449 per academic year. *Required fees:* full-time $1227; part-time $47 per credit.

Financial Aid 64% of baccalaureate students in nursing programs received some form of financial aid in 2008–09. *Gift aid (need-based):* Federal Pell, FSEOG, state, private, college/university gift aid from institutional funds, Federal Nursing, Academic Competitiveness Grant, National Smart Grant. *Loans:* Federal Nursing Student Loans, FFEL (Subsidized and Unsubsidized Stafford PLUS), Perkins. *Work-study:* Federal Work-Study. *Financial aid application deadline (priority):* 4/1.

Contact Dr. Sandra J. Lindquist, Associate Dean for the Undergraduate Program, College of Nursing, University of Missouri–St. Louis, One University Boulevard, 233 Nursing Administration Building, St. Louis, MO 63121-4499. *Telephone:* 314-516-6066. *Fax:* 314-516-7519. *E-mail:* Sandy_Lindquist@umsl.edu.

GRADUATE PROGRAMS

Expenses (2009–10) *Tuition, state resident:* full-time $7169; part-time $299 per credit hour. *Tuition, nonresident:* full-time $18,509; part-time $771 per credit hour. *International tuition:* $18,509 full-time. *Room and board:* $8164; room only: $4449 per academic year. *Required fees:* full-time $1154; part-time $47 per credit; part-time $12 per term.

Financial Aid 59% of graduate students in nursing programs received some form of financial aid in 2008–09. 1 research assistantship with full and partial tuition reimbursement available (averaging $12,341 per year), 4 teaching assistantships with full and partial tuition reimbursements available (averaging $6,170 per year) were awarded. *Financial aid application deadline:* 4/1.

Contact Dr. Nancy Magnuson, Acting Associate Dean for Advanced Nursing Education, College of Nursing, University of Missouri–St. Louis, One University Boulevard, Nursing Administration Building, St. Louis, MO 63121-4499. *Telephone:* 314-516-6066. *Fax:* 314-516-7519. *E-mail:* magnusonn@umsl.edu.

MASTER'S DEGREE PROGRAM

Degree MSN

Available Programs Master's.

Concentrations Available Nursing education. *Nurse practitioner programs in:* adult health, family health, neonatal health, pediatric, women's health.

Site Options Park Hill, MO; St. Charles, MO.

Study Options Full-time and part-time.

Online Degree Options Yes.

Program Entrance Requirements Clinical experience, minimum overall college GPA of 3.0, transcript of college record, CPR certification, immunizations, 2 letters of recommendation, physical assessment course, statistics course. *Application deadline:* 4/1 (fall), 10/1 (spring). *Application fee:* $35.

Advanced Placement Credit given for nursing courses completed elsewhere dependent upon specific evaluations.

Degree Requirements 43 total credit hours.

POST-MASTER'S PROGRAM

Areas of Study *Nurse practitioner programs in:* adult health, family health, pediatric, women's health.

DOCTORAL DEGREE PROGRAM

Degree DNP

Available Programs Doctorate.

Areas of Study Advanced practice nursing.

Program Entrance Requirements Minimum overall college GPA of 3.2, interview, 2 letters of recommendation, MSN or equivalent, statistics course, writing sample, GRE General Test. Application deadline: 4/1 (fall). Application fee: $35.

Degree Requirements 41 total credit hours, dissertation.

CONTINUING EDUCATION PROGRAM

Contact Vanessa Loyd, Director of Continuing Education and Outreach, College of Nursing, University of Missouri–St. Louis, One University Boulevard, St. Louis, MO 63121. *Telephone:* 314-516-6066. *Fax:* 314-516-6730. *E-mail:* loydv@umsl.edu.

Webster University
Department of Nursing
St. Louis, Missouri

http://www.webster.edu/depts/artsci/nursing/nursing.html
Founded in 1915

DEGREES • BSN • MSN

Nursing Program Faculty 12 (72% with doctorates).

Baccalaureate Enrollment 150
Women 93% **Men** 7% **Minority** 14% **International** 1% **Part-time** 90%

Graduate Enrollment 75
Women 90% **Men** 10% **Minority** 20% **International** 10% **Part-time** 100%

Nursing Student Activities Nursing Honor Society, Sigma Theta Tau.

Nursing Student Resources Academic advising; academic or career counseling; assistance for students with disabilities; bookstore; campus computer network; career placement assistance; computer lab; e-mail services; employment services for current students; Internet; learning resource lab; library services; nursing audiovisuals; placement services for program completers; remedial services; resume preparation assistance; skills, simulation, or other laboratory; tutoring.

Library Facilities 286,655 volumes (7,030 in health, 3,114 in nursing); 1,821 periodical subscriptions (108 health-care related).

BACCALAUREATE PROGRAMS

Degree BSN

Available Programs ADN to Baccalaureate; RN Baccalaureate.

Site Options Kansas City, MO.

Program Entrance Requirements Minimum overall college GPA of 2.5, transcript of college record, immunizations, interview, prerequisite course work, RN licensure. Transfer students are accepted.

Contact *Telephone:* 314-968-7483. *Fax:* 314-963-6101.

GRADUATE PROGRAMS

Contact *Telephone:* 314-968-7483. *Fax:* 314-963-6101.

MASTER'S DEGREE PROGRAM

Degree MSN

Available Programs Master's; RN to Master's.

Concentrations Available Nursing administration; nursing education. *Clinical nurse specialist programs in:* family health.

Site Options Kansas City, MO.

Study Options Part-time.

Program Entrance Requirements Clinical experience, computer literacy, minimum overall college GPA of 3.0, transcript of college record, written essay, immunizations, interview, 3 letters of recommendation, nursing research course, physical assessment course, resume, statistics course.

Advanced Placement Credit given for nursing courses completed elsewhere dependent upon specific evaluations.

Degree Requirements 36 total credit hours, thesis or project.

William Jewell College
Department of Nursing
Liberty, Missouri

http://www.jewell.edu
Founded in 1849
DEGREE • BS

Nursing Program Faculty 36 (25% with doctorates).

Baccalaureate Enrollment 150
Women 89% **Men** 11% **Minority** 3% **International** 1%

Nursing Student Activities Nursing Honor Society, Sigma Theta Tau, Student Nurses' Association.

Nursing Student Resources Academic advising; academic or career counseling; assistance for students with disabilities; bookstore; campus computer network; career placement assistance; computer lab; computer-assisted instruction; e-mail services; employment services for current students; externships; housing assistance; interactive nursing skills videos; Internet; learning resource lab; library services; nursing audiovisuals; paid internships; placement services for program completers; resume preparation assistance; skills, simulation, or other laboratory; tutoring; unpaid internships.

Library Facilities 236,241 volumes (4,000 in health, 1,000 in nursing); 527 periodical subscriptions (250 health-care related).

BACCALAUREATE PROGRAMS

Degree BS

Available Programs Accelerated Baccalaureate; Generic Baccalaureate.

Study Options Full-time.

Program Entrance Requirements Minimum overall college GPA of 2.5, transcript of college record, CPR certification, written essay, health insurance, high school foreign language, high school transcript, immunizations, interview, 2 letters of recommendation, minimum high school GPA of 3.0, minimum GPA in nursing prerequisites of 2.5, professional liability insurance/malpractice insurance, prerequisite course work. Transfer students are accepted. *Application deadline:* 6/1 (spring), 8/1 (summer). *Application fee:* $25.

Advanced Placement Credit given for nursing courses completed elsewhere dependent upon specific evaluations.

Expenses (2009–10) *Tuition:* full-time $36,240; part-time $750 per credit hour. *International tuition:* $36,240 full-time. *Room and board:* $6700; room only: $4000 per academic year.

Financial Aid 90% of baccalaureate students in nursing programs received some form of financial aid in 2008–09. *Gift aid (need-based):* Federal Pell, FSEOG, state, college/university gift aid from institutional funds. *Loans:* Federal Nursing Student Loans, FFEL (Subsidized and Unsubsidized Stafford PLUS), Perkins, alternative loans. *Work-study:* Federal Work-Study, part-time campus jobs. *Financial aid application deadline (priority):* 3/1.

Contact Ms. Katie A. Stiles, Nursing Admissions Counselor, Department of Nursing, William Jewell College, 500 College Hill, Box 2002, Liberty, MO 64068. *Telephone:* 816-415-5072. *Fax:* 816-415-5024. *E-mail:* stilesk@william.jewell.edu.

MONTANA

Carroll College
Department of Nursing
Helena, Montana

http://www.carroll.edu
Founded in 1909
DEGREE • BA

Nursing Program Faculty 20 (10% with doctorates).

Baccalaureate Enrollment 139
Women 88% **Men** 12% **Minority** 4% **International** 1% **Part-time** 1%

Nursing Student Activities Sigma Theta Tau, Student Nurses' Association.

Nursing Student Resources Academic advising; academic or career counseling; assistance for students with disabilities; bookstore; campus computer network; career placement assistance; computer lab; computer-assisted instruction; e-mail services; employment services for current students; externships; housing assistance; interactive nursing skills videos; Internet; learning resource lab; library services; nursing audiovisuals; paid internships; placement services for program completers; remedial services; resume preparation assistance; skills, simulation, or other laboratory; tutoring; unpaid internships.

Library Facilities 89,003 volumes (1,300 in health, 700 in nursing); 2,721 periodical subscriptions (1,000 health-care related).

BACCALAUREATE PROGRAMS

Degree BA

Available Programs Generic Baccalaureate.

Study Options Full-time.

Program Entrance Requirements Minimum overall college GPA of 2.75, transcript of college record, high school transcript, immunizations, minimum GPA in nursing prerequisites of 2.75, prerequisite course work. Transfer students are accepted. *Application deadline:* 2/15 (spring).

Advanced Placement Credit given for nursing courses completed elsewhere dependent upon specific evaluations.

Expenses (2009–10) *Tuition:* full-time $22,044; part-time $736 per credit. *International tuition:* $22,044 full-time. *Room and board:* $7188; room only: $2100 per academic year. *Required fees:* full-time $620.

Financial Aid 97% of baccalaureate students in nursing programs received some form of financial aid in 2008–09. *Gift aid (need-based):* Federal Pell, FSEOG, state, private, college/university gift aid from institutional funds. *Loans:* FFEL (Subsidized and Unsubsidized Stafford PLUS), Perkins, private loans. *Work-study:* Federal Work-Study, part-time campus jobs. *Financial aid application deadline (priority):* 3/1.

Contact Scott Knickerbocker, Associate Director, Admissions, Department of Nursing, Carroll College, 1601 North Benton Avenue, Helena, MT 59625. *Telephone:* 406-447-4387. *Fax:* 406-447-4533. *E-mail:* sknicker@carroll.edu.

Montana State University
College of Nursing
Bozeman, Montana

http://www.montana.edu/nursing
Founded in 1893
DEGREES • BSN • MN

Nursing Program Faculty 90 (23% with doctorates).

Baccalaureate Enrollment 786
Women 89.7% **Men** 10.3% **Minority** 13.4% **Part-time** 16.8%

Graduate Enrollment 65
Women 98% **Men** 2% **Minority** 8% **Part-time** 38%

Distance Learning Courses Available.

Montana State University (continued)

Nursing Student Activities Sigma Theta Tau, Student Nurses' Association.

Nursing Student Resources Academic advising; academic or career counseling; assistance for students with disabilities; bookstore; campus computer network; career placement assistance; computer lab; computer-assisted instruction; daycare for children of students; e-mail services; employment services for current students; housing assistance; Internet; library services; nursing audiovisuals; paid internships; placement services for program completers; remedial services; resume preparation assistance; skills, simulation, or other laboratory; tutoring; unpaid internships.

Library Facilities 730,422 volumes (80,389 in health, 11,535 in nursing); 9,924 periodical subscriptions (1,690 health-care related).

BACCALAUREATE PROGRAMS

Degree BSN

Available Programs Generic Baccalaureate; LPN to Baccalaureate.

Site Options Billings, MT; Great Falls, MT; Missoula, MT.

Study Options Full-time and part-time.

Program Entrance Requirements Minimum overall college GPA of 2.5, transcript of college record, CPR certification, health exam, health insurance, high school transcript, immunizations, minimum high school GPA of 2.5, minimum high school rank 50%, minimum GPA in nursing prerequisites of 2.5, prerequisite course work. Transfer students are accepted. *Application deadline:* 7/1 (fall), 12/1 (spring), 5/1 (summer). Applications may be processed on a rolling basis for some programs. *Application fee:* $30.

Advanced Placement Credit by examination available. Credit given for nursing courses completed elsewhere dependent upon specific evaluations.

Expenses (2009–10) *Tuition, state resident:* full-time $4696; part-time $196 per credit. *Tuition, nonresident:* full-time $16,272; part-time $678 per credit. *International tuition:* $16,272 full-time. *Room and board:* $6900 per academic year. *Required fees:* full-time $2882; part-time $101 per credit; part-time $1441 per term.

Financial Aid 70% of baccalaureate students in nursing programs received some form of financial aid in 2008–09.

Contact Ms. Patricia Hanson, Undergraduate Student Services Coordinator, College of Nursing, Montana State University, Sherrick Hall, PO Box 173560, Bozeman, MT 59717-3560. *Telephone:* 406-994-3783. *Fax:* 406-994-6020. *E-mail:* phanson@montana.edu.

GRADUATE PROGRAMS

Expenses (2009–10) *Tuition, state resident:* full-time $5635; part-time $235 per credit. *Tuition, nonresident:* full-time $17,211; part-time $717 per credit. *International tuition:* $17,211 full-time. *Room and board:* $6900 per academic year. *Required fees:* full-time $2882; part-time $101 per credit; part-time $1441 per term.

Financial Aid 70% of graduate students in nursing programs received some form of financial aid in 2008–09. 8 teaching assistantships with partial tuition reimbursements available (averaging $7,050 per year) were awarded; institutionally sponsored loans, scholarships, traineeships, and tuition waivers (partial) also available. *Financial aid application deadline:* 3/1.

Contact Ms. Lynn Taylor, Graduate Program Assistant, College of Nursing, Montana State University, Sherrick Hall, PO Box 173560, Bozeman, MT 59717-3560. *Telephone:* 406-994-3500. *Fax:* 406-994-6020. *E-mail:* lynnt@montana.edu.

MASTER'S DEGREE PROGRAM

Degree MN

Available Programs Master's.

Concentrations Available Clinical nurse leader. *Nurse practitioner programs in:* adult health, family health, primary care, psychiatric/mental health.

Site Options Billings, MT; Great Falls, MT; Missoula, MT.

Study Options Full-time and part-time.

Program Entrance Requirements Computer literacy, minimum overall college GPA of 3.0, transcript of college record, CPR certification, written essay, immunizations, interview, 3 letters of recommendation, nursing research course, physical assessment course, prerequisite course work, statistics course, GRE General Test. *Application deadline:* 2/15 (fall). *Application fee:* $50.

Advanced Placement Credit given for nursing courses completed elsewhere dependent upon specific evaluations.

Degree Requirements 35 total credit hours, thesis or project, comprehensive exam.

POST-MASTER'S PROGRAM

Areas of Study Nursing education. *Nurse practitioner programs in:* adult health, family health, primary care, psychiatric/mental health.

Montana State University–Northern
College of Nursing
Havre, Montana

http://www.msun.edu/academics/nursing

Founded in 1929

DEGREE • BSN

Nursing Program Faculty 8 (88% with doctorates).

Baccalaureate Enrollment 53
Women 99% **Men** 1% **Part-time** 92%

Distance Learning Courses Available.

Nursing Student Activities Nursing club.

Nursing Student Resources Academic advising; academic or career counseling; assistance for students with disabilities; bookstore; campus computer network; career placement assistance; computer lab; computer-assisted instruction; e-mail services; employment services for current students; housing assistance; interactive nursing skills videos; Internet; learning resource lab; library services; nursing audiovisuals; remedial services; resume preparation assistance; skills, simulation, or other laboratory; tutoring.

Library Facilities 128,000 volumes (2,600 in health, 1,500 in nursing); 1,729 periodical subscriptions (50 health-care related).

BACCALAUREATE PROGRAMS

Degree BSN

Available Programs ADN to Baccalaureate; RN Baccalaureate.

Site Options Great Falls, MT; Lewistown, MT.

Study Options Full-time and part-time.

Online Degree Options Yes (online only).

Program Entrance Requirements Minimum overall college GPA of 2.25, transcript of college record, CPR certification, health exam, health insurance, immunizations, professional liability insurance/malpractice insurance, prerequisite course work, RN licensure. Transfer students are accepted.

Advanced Placement Credit given for nursing courses completed elsewhere dependent upon specific evaluations.

Contact *Telephone:* 800-446-2698 Ext. 4437. *Fax:* 406-771-4340.

Salish Kootenai College
Nursing Department
Pablo, Montana

Founded in 1977

DEGREE • BS

Nursing Program Faculty 7

Nursing Student Activities Nursing club.

Nursing Student Resources Academic advising; academic or career counseling; bookstore; computer lab; daycare for children of students; employment services for current students; Internet; library services.

Library Facilities 24,000 volumes; 200 periodical subscriptions.

BACCALAUREATE PROGRAMS

Degree BS

Available Programs RN Baccalaureate.

Study Options Full-time and part-time.

Program Entrance Requirements Transcript of college record, CPR certification, health exam, health insurance, high school biology, high school chemistry, 2 years high school math, 2 years high school science, high school transcript, immunizations, minimum high school GPA of 2.5, professional liability insurance/malpractice insurance, prerequisite course work, RN licensure.

Contact *Telephone:* 406-275-4800.

NEBRASKA

BryanLGH College of Health Sciences
School of Nursing
Lincoln, Nebraska

DEGREES • BSC PN • MS

Nursing Program Faculty 29 (10% with doctorates).

Baccalaureate Enrollment 406
Women 92% **Men** 8% **Minority** 5% **Part-time** 44%

Graduate Enrollment 33
Women 52% **Men** 48% **Minority** 9%

Nursing Student Activities Student Nurses' Association.

Nursing Student Resources Academic advising; academic or career counseling; assistance for students with disabilities; bookstore; campus computer network; career placement assistance; computer lab; computer-assisted instruction; e-mail services; employment services for current students; housing assistance; Internet; learning resource lab; library services; nursing audiovisuals; remedial services; resume preparation assistance; skills, simulation, or other laboratory; tutoring.

Library Facilities 4,000 volumes in health, 3,500 volumes in nursing; 95 periodical subscriptions health-care related.

BACCALAUREATE PROGRAMS

Degree BSc PN

Available Programs Generic Baccalaureate; RN Baccalaureate.

Study Options Full-time.

Program Entrance Requirements Minimum overall college GPA of 2.0, written essay, health exam, health insurance, high school transcript, immunizations, interview, 3 letters of recommendation, minimum high school GPA of 2.75. Transfer students are accepted. *Application deadline:* 2/1 (fall), 6/1 (spring). *Application fee:* $40.

Advanced Placement Credit given for nursing courses completed elsewhere dependent upon specific evaluations.

Expenses (2009–10) *Tuition, state resident:* full-time $11,400; part-time $380 per credit hour. *Tuition, nonresident:* full-time $11,400; part-time $380 per credit hour. *Required fees:* full-time $670.

Financial Aid 73% of baccalaureate students in nursing programs received some form of financial aid in 2008–09.

Contact Kelli Backman, Admissions Counselor, School of Nursing, BryanLGH College of Health Sciences, 5035 Everett Street, Lincoln, NE 68505. *Telephone:* 402-481-8698. *Fax:* 402-481-8621. *E-mail:* kelli. backman@bryanlgh.org.

GRADUATE PROGRAMS

Financial Aid 90% of graduate students in nursing programs received some form of financial aid in 2008–09.

Contact Mr. James D. Cuddeford, Program Administrator/Dean of Nurse Anesthesia, School of Nursing, BryanLGH College of Health Sciences, 1600 South 48th Street, Lincoln, NE 68506. *Telephone:* 402-481-3135. *Fax:* 402-481-8404. *E-mail:* james.cuddeford@bryanlgh.org.

MASTER'S DEGREE PROGRAM

Degree MS

Available Programs Master's; Master's for Nurses with Non-Nursing Degrees.

Concentrations Available Nurse anesthesia.

Study Options Full-time.

Program Entrance Requirements Clinical experience, computer literacy, minimum overall college GPA of 3.0, transcript of college record, CPR certification, written essay, immunizations, interview, 4 letters of recommendation, prerequisite course work, resume. *Application deadline:* 10/30 (fall). *Application fee:* $75.

Degree Requirements 71 total credit hours, thesis or project.

Clarkson College
Master of Science in Nursing Program
Omaha, Nebraska

http://www.clarksoncollege.edu/Programs/Nursing/

Founded in 1888

DEGREES • BSN • MSN

Nursing Program Faculty 42 (6% with doctorates).

Baccalaureate Enrollment 415
Women 93% **Men** 7% **Minority** 9% **Part-time** 17%

Graduate Enrollment 121
Women 91% **Men** 9% **Minority** 8% **Part-time** 100%

Distance Learning Courses Available.

Nursing Student Activities Sigma Theta Tau, Student Nurses' Association.

Nursing Student Resources Academic advising; academic or career counseling; assistance for students with disabilities; bookstore; campus computer network; career placement assistance; computer lab; computer-assisted instruction; daycare for children of students; e-mail services; employment services for current students; interactive nursing skills videos; Internet; learning resource lab; library services; nursing audiovisuals; placement services for program completers; resume preparation assistance; skills, simulation, or other laboratory; tutoring.

Library Facilities 8,807 volumes (7,676 in health, 2,758 in nursing); 262 periodical subscriptions (598 health-care related).

BACCALAUREATE PROGRAMS

Degree BSN

Available Programs ADN to Baccalaureate; Accelerated RN Baccalaureate; LPN to Baccalaureate; LPN to RN Baccalaureate; RN Baccalaureate.

Study Options Full-time and part-time.

Online Degree Options Yes.

Program Entrance Requirements Minimum overall college GPA of 2.5, transcript of college record, CPR certification, written essay, health exam, health insurance, 2 years high school math, 2 years high school science, high school transcript, immunizations, minimum high school GPA of 2.5, minimum high school rank 50%. Transfer students are accepted. *Application fee:* $35.

Advanced Placement Credit given for nursing courses completed elsewhere dependent upon specific evaluations.

Expenses (2008–09) *Tuition:* full-time $5992; part-time $399 per credit hour. *International tuition:* $5992 full-time. *Room and board:* room only: $6000 per academic year. *Required fees:* full-time $406; part-time $29 per credit.

Financial Aid 83% of baccalaureate students in nursing programs received some form of financial aid in 2007–08.

Contact Ms. Brooke Clements, Admissions Counselor, Master of Science in Nursing Program, Clarkson College, 101 South 42nd Street, Omaha, NE 68131-2739. *Telephone:* 402-552-3100. *Fax:* 402-552-6057. *E-mail:* admiss@ clarksoncollege.edu.

GRADUATE PROGRAMS

Expenses (2008–09) *Tuition:* part-time $470 per credit hour. *Room and board:* room only: $6000 per academic year. *Required fees:* part-time $25 per credit.

Clarkson College (continued)

Financial Aid 45% of graduate students in nursing programs received some form of financial aid in 2007–08. Federal Work-Study, institutionally sponsored loans, and scholarships available. Aid available to part-time students. *Financial aid application deadline:* 3/1.

Contact Mrs. Denise Work, Director of Admissions, Master of Science in Nursing Program, Clarkson College, 101 South 42nd Street, Omaha, NE 68131-2739. *Telephone:* 800-647-5500. *Fax:* 402-552-6057. *E-mail:* admiss@clarksoncollege.edu.

MASTER'S DEGREE PROGRAM

Degree MSN

Available Programs Master's; RN to Master's.

Concentrations Available Nursing administration; nursing education. *Nurse practitioner programs in:* adult health, family health.

Study Options Full-time and part-time.

Online Degree Options Yes (online only).

Program Entrance Requirements Clinical experience, minimum overall college GPA of 3.0, transcript of college record, written essay, 2 letters of recommendation, resume. *Application deadline:* 7/1 (fall), 11/15 (spring), 4/1 (summer). *Application fee:* $35.

Advanced Placement Credit given for nursing courses completed elsewhere dependent upon specific evaluations.

Degree Requirements 46 total credit hours, thesis or project.

POST-MASTER'S PROGRAM

Areas of Study Nursing administration; nursing education. *Nurse practitioner programs in:* adult health, family health.

CONTINUING EDUCATION PROGRAM

Contact Ms. Denise Work, Director of Admissions, Master of Science in Nursing Program, Clarkson College, 101 South 42nd Street, Omaha, NE 68131-2739. *Telephone:* 402-552-3100. *Fax:* 402-552-6057. *E-mail:* workdenise@clarksoncollege.edu.

College of Saint Mary
Division of Health Care Professions
Omaha, Nebraska

Founded in 1923

DEGREE • BSN

Nursing Program Faculty 18 (6% with doctorates).

Baccalaureate Enrollment 45
Women 100% **Minority** 10% **Part-time** 65%

Graduate Enrollment 8

Nursing Student Activities Nursing Honor Society, Sigma Theta Tau, Student Nurses' Association, nursing club.

Nursing Student Resources Academic advising; academic or career counseling; bookstore; campus computer network; career placement assistance; computer lab; computer-assisted instruction; e-mail services; interactive nursing skills videos; Internet; learning resource lab; library services; nursing audiovisuals; other; placement services for program completers; resume preparation assistance; skills, simulation, or other laboratory; tutoring.

Library Facilities 76,781 volumes; 272 periodical subscriptions (100 health-care related).

BACCALAUREATE PROGRAMS

Degree BSN

Available Programs ADN to Baccalaureate; Generic Baccalaureate.

Study Options Full-time and part-time.

Program Entrance Requirements Minimum overall college GPA of 2.5, transcript of college record, CPR certification, health exam, immunizations, 2 letters of recommendation, minimum high school GPA, minimum GPA in nursing prerequisites of 2.5, prerequisite course work. Transfer students are accepted.

Advanced Placement Credit given for nursing courses completed elsewhere dependent upon specific evaluations.

Contact *Telephone:* 402-399-2658. *Fax:* 402-399-2654.

GRADUATE PROGRAMS

Contact *Telephone:* 402-399-2482. *Fax:* 402-399-2414.

Creighton University
School of Nursing
Omaha, Nebraska

http://www2.creighton.edu/nursing/

Founded in 1878

DEGREES • BSN • DNP • MSN

Nursing Program Faculty 56 (43% with doctorates).

Baccalaureate Enrollment 542
Women 89% **Men** 11% **Minority** 12% **Part-time** 1%

Graduate Enrollment 110
Women 95.5% **Men** 4.5% **Minority** 6% **Part-time** 59%

Distance Learning Courses Available.

Nursing Student Activities Nursing Honor Society, Sigma Theta Tau, Student Nurses' Association.

Nursing Student Resources Academic advising; academic or career counseling; assistance for students with disabilities; bookstore; campus computer network; career placement assistance; computer lab; computer-assisted instruction; daycare for children of students; e-mail services; employment services for current students; Internet; learning resource lab; library services; nursing audiovisuals; remedial services; resume preparation assistance; skills, simulation, or other laboratory; tutoring; unpaid internships.

Library Facilities 925,385 volumes (235,325 in health, 3,421 in nursing); 42,374 periodical subscriptions (4,173 health-care related).

BACCALAUREATE PROGRAMS

Degree BSN

Available Programs Accelerated Baccalaureate for Second Degree; Generic Baccalaureate; RN Baccalaureate.

Site Options Hastings, NE.

Study Options Full-time and part-time.

Online Degree Options Yes.

Program Entrance Requirements Minimum overall college GPA of 2.0, transcript of college record, written essay, health exam, health insurance, high school chemistry, 3 years high school math, 2 years high school science, high school transcript, immunizations, 1 letter of recommendation, minimum high school GPA of 3.0, minimum high school rank 50%. Transfer students are accepted. *Application deadline:* Applications may be processed on a rolling basis for some programs. *Application fee:* $50.

Advanced Placement Credit given for nursing courses completed elsewhere dependent upon specific evaluations.

Expenses (2009–10) *Tuition:* full-time $28,238; part-time $882 per credit hour. *International tuition:* $28,238 full-time. *Room and board:* $8814; room only: $4984 per academic year. *Required fees:* full-time $1306; part-time $252 per term.

Financial Aid 85% of baccalaureate students in nursing programs received some form of financial aid in 2008–09. *Gift aid (need-based):* Federal Pell, FSEOG, state, private, college/university gift aid from institutional funds, Federal Nursing. *Loans:* Federal Nursing Student Loans, FFEL (Subsidized and Unsubsidized Stafford PLUS), Perkins, college/university. *Work-study:* Federal Work-Study. *Financial aid application deadline (priority):* 3/1.

Contact Mrs. Erron M. Holland, Recruitment Counselor, School of Nursing, Creighton University, 2500 California Plaza, Omaha, NE 68178. *Telephone:* 402-280-2067. *Fax:* 402-280-2045. *E-mail:* erronholland@creighton.edu.

GRADUATE PROGRAMS

Expenses (2009–10) *Tuition:* full-time $5850; part-time $650 per credit hour. *International tuition:* $5850 full-time. *Required fees:* full-time $1306; part-time $252 per term.

Financial Aid 85% of graduate students in nursing programs received some form of financial aid in 2008–09. Career-related internships or fieldwork, Federal Work-Study, institutionally sponsored loans, and traineeships available.

Contact Mrs. Erron M. Holland, Recruitment Coordinator, School of Nursing, Creighton University, 2500 California Plaza, Omaha, NE 68178. *Telephone:* 402-280-2067. *Fax:* 402-280-2045. *E-mail:* erronholland@creighton.edu.

MASTER'S DEGREE PROGRAM

Degree MSN

Available Programs Master's.

Concentrations Available Clinical nurse leader; nursing administration; nursing education. *Clinical nurse specialist programs in:* adult health, cardiovascular, family health, gerontology, maternity-newborn, oncology, pediatric. *Nurse practitioner programs in:* acute care, adult health, family health, gerontology, neonatal health, oncology, pediatric, psychiatric/mental health.

Site Options Hastings, NE.

Study Options Full-time and part-time.

Program Entrance Requirements Clinical experience, minimum overall college GPA of 3.0, transcript of college record, CPR certification, written essay, immunizations, 3 letters of recommendation, physical assessment course, prerequisite course work, resume, statistics course. *Application deadline:* Applications may be processed on a rolling basis for some programs. *Application fee:* $50.

Advanced Placement Credit given for nursing courses completed elsewhere dependent upon specific evaluations.

Degree Requirements 36 total credit hours, thesis or project.

POST-MASTER'S PROGRAM

Areas of Study Clinical nurse leader; nursing administration; nursing education. *Clinical nurse specialist programs in:* adult health, cardiovascular, family health, gerontology, maternity-newborn, oncology, pediatric. *Nurse practitioner programs in:* acute care, adult health, family health, gerontology, neonatal health, oncology, pediatric, psychiatric/mental health.

DOCTORAL DEGREE PROGRAM

Degree DNP

Available Programs Doctorate; Post-Baccalaureate Doctorate.

Areas of Study Advanced practice nursing, clinical practice, family health, gerontology, maternity-newborn, nursing administration, nursing education, oncology.

Site Options Hastings, NE.

Program Entrance Requirements Clinical experience, minimum overall college GPA of 3.0, 3 letters of recommendation, statistics course, vita. Application deadline: Applications may be processed on a rolling basis for some programs. Application fee: $50.

Degree Requirements 32 total credit hours, residency.

Midland Lutheran College
Department of Nursing
Fremont, Nebraska

http://www.mlc.edu
Founded in 1883

DEGREE • BSN

Nursing Program Faculty 12 (25% with doctorates).

Baccalaureate Enrollment 130
Women 93% **Men** 7% **Minority** 4% **International** 3% **Part-time** 9%

Distance Learning Courses Available.

Nursing Student Activities Sigma Theta Tau, Student Nurses' Association.

Nursing Student Resources Academic advising; academic or career counseling; assistance for students with disabilities; bookstore; campus computer network; career placement assistance; computer lab; computer-assisted instruction; e-mail services; employment services for current

students; housing assistance; interactive nursing skills videos; Internet; learning resource lab; library services; nursing audiovisuals; paid internships; placement services for program completers; remedial services; resume preparation assistance; skills, simulation, or other laboratory; tutoring; unpaid internships.

Library Facilities 110,000 volumes (4,700 in health, 2,000 in nursing); 900 periodical subscriptions (550 health-care related).

BACCALAUREATE PROGRAMS

Degree BSN

Available Programs ADN to Baccalaureate; Generic Baccalaureate; LPN to RN Baccalaureate; RN Baccalaureate.

Site Options Columbus, NE.

Study Options Full-time and part-time.

Program Entrance Requirements Minimum overall college GPA of 2.5, transcript of college record, CPR certification, written essay, health exam, high school transcript, immunizations, interview, 2 letters of recommendation, minimum GPA in nursing prerequisites of 2.5, prerequisite course work. Transfer students are accepted. *Application deadline:* 3/1 (spring). Applications may be processed on a rolling basis for some programs.

Advanced Placement Credit given for nursing courses completed elsewhere dependent upon specific evaluations.

Expenses (2009–10) *Tuition:* full-time $22,684; part-time $330 per credit hour. *International tuition:* $22,684 full-time. *Room and board:* $5612 per academic year. *Required fees:* full-time $622.

Financial Aid 98% of baccalaureate students in nursing programs received some form of financial aid in 2008–09. *Gift aid (need-based):* Federal Pell, FSEOG, state, private, college/university gift aid from institutional funds. *Loans:* FFEL (Subsidized and Unsubsidized Stafford PLUS), Perkins. *Work-study:* Federal Work-Study, part-time campus jobs. *Financial aid application deadline:* Continuous.

Contact Ms. Amy Poggendorf, Director of Admissions, Department of Nursing, Midland Lutheran College, 900 North Clarkson, Fremont, NE 68025. *Telephone:* 402-941-6505. *Fax:* 402-941-6513. *E-mail:* poggendorf@mlc.edu.

Nebraska Methodist College
Department of Nursing
Omaha, Nebraska

http://www.methodistcollege.edu
Founded in 1891

DEGREES • BSN • MSN

Nursing Program Faculty 48 (21% with doctorates).

Baccalaureate Enrollment 425
Women 91% **Men** 9% **Minority** 87% **Part-time** 33%

Graduate Enrollment 47
Women 98% **Men** 2% **Minority** 7% **Part-time** 51%

Distance Learning Courses Available.

Nursing Student Activities Nursing Honor Society, Sigma Theta Tau, Student Nurses' Association.

Nursing Student Resources Academic advising; academic or career counseling; assistance for students with disabilities; bookstore; campus computer network; career placement assistance; computer lab; computer-assisted instruction; e-mail services; employment services for current students; interactive nursing skills videos; learning resource lab; library services; nursing audiovisuals; remedial services; resume preparation assistance; skills, simulation, or other laboratory; tutoring.

Library Facilities 3,300 volumes in health, 1,200 volumes in nursing; 13,600 periodical subscriptions health-care related.

BACCALAUREATE PROGRAMS

Degree BSN

Available Programs ADN to Baccalaureate; Accelerated Baccalaureate for Second Degree; Generic Baccalaureate; LPN to Baccalaureate.

Study Options Full-time and part-time.

Nebraska Methodist College (continued)

Program Entrance Requirements Minimum overall college GPA of 2.5, transcript of college record, written essay, high school biology, high school chemistry, 2 years high school math, 2 years high school science, high school transcript, interview, minimum high school GPA of 2.5, minimum GPA in nursing prerequisites of 2.5. Transfer students are accepted. *Application deadline:* Applications may be processed on a rolling basis for some programs. *Application fee:* $25.

Advanced Placement Credit given for nursing courses completed elsewhere dependent upon specific evaluations.

Expenses (2009–10) *Tuition:* full-time $11,304; part-time $471 per credit. *Room and board:* room only: $5660 per academic year. *Required fees:* full-time $545; part-time $20 per credit.

Financial Aid 94% of baccalaureate students in nursing programs received some form of financial aid in 2008–09.

Contact Dr. Marilyn Valerio, Chairperson, Department of Nursing, Nebraska Methodist College, 720 North 87th Street, Omaha, NE 68114-3426. *Telephone:* 402-354-7027. *Fax:* 402-354-7020. *E-mail:* Marilyn.Valerio@methodistcollege.edu.

GRADUATE PROGRAMS

Expenses (2009–10) *Tuition:* full-time $6552; part-time $546 per credit hour. *Room and board:* room only: $5660 per academic year. *Required fees:* full-time $300; part-time $25 per credit.

Financial Aid 71% of graduate students in nursing programs received some form of financial aid in 2008–09.

Contact Dr. Linda Foley, Associate Chairperson, Department of Nursing, Nebraska Methodist College, 720 North 87th Street, Omaha, NE 68114-3426. *Telephone:* 402-354-7050. *Fax:* 402-354-7020. *E-mail:* Linda.Foley@methodistcollege.edu.

MASTER'S DEGREE PROGRAM

Degree MSN

Available Programs Master's; Master's for Nurses with Non-Nursing Degrees.

Concentrations Available Nursing administration; nursing education.

Study Options Full-time and part-time.

Online Degree Options Yes (online only).

Program Entrance Requirements Computer literacy, minimum overall college GPA of 3.0, transcript of college record, CPR certification, written essay, immunizations, interview, 2 letters of recommendation, nursing research course, physical assessment course, prerequisite course work, resume, statistics course. *Application deadline:* Applications may be processed on a rolling basis for some programs. *Application fee:* $25.

Advanced Placement Credit given for nursing courses completed elsewhere dependent upon specific evaluations.

Degree Requirements 39 total credit hours, thesis or project.

POST-MASTER'S PROGRAM

Areas of Study Nursing education.

CONTINUING EDUCATION PROGRAM

Contact Ms. Rose Leavitt, Associate Dean for Professional Development, Department of Nursing, Nebraska Methodist College, 720 North 87th Street, Omaha, NE 68114-3426. *Telephone:* 402-354-7137. *Fax:* 402-354-7020. *E-mail:* rose.leavitt@methodistcollege.edu.

Nebraska Wesleyan University
Department of Nursing
Lincoln, Nebraska

http://www.nebrwesleyan.edu

Founded in 1887

DEGREES • BSN • MSN

Nursing Program Faculty 15 (50% with doctorates).

Baccalaureate Enrollment 87
Women 92% **Men** 8% **Minority** 7% **International** 11% **Part-time** 40%

Graduate Enrollment 54
Women 96% **Men** 4% **Minority** 12% **International** 2% **Part-time** 50%

Distance Learning Courses Available.

Nursing Student Activities Sigma Theta Tau.

Nursing Student Resources Academic advising; academic or career counseling; assistance for students with disabilities; bookstore; campus computer network; career placement assistance; computer lab; e-mail services; Internet; library services; nursing audiovisuals; resume preparation assistance; unpaid internships.

Library Facilities 251,909 volumes (5,000 in health, 3,700 in nursing); 597 periodical subscriptions (470 health-care related).

BACCALAUREATE PROGRAMS

Degree BSN

Available Programs ADN to Baccalaureate; Accelerated RN Baccalaureate; International Nurse to Baccalaureate; RN Baccalaureate.

Site Options Omaha, NE.

Study Options Full-time and part-time.

Program Entrance Requirements Transfer students are accepted. *Application deadline:* Applications may be processed on a rolling basis for some programs. *Application fee:* $100.

Advanced Placement Credit by examination available. Credit given for nursing courses completed elsewhere dependent upon specific evaluations.

Expenses (2009–10) *Tuition:* full-time $7350; part-time $245 per credit hour. *International tuition:* $7350 full-time.

Financial Aid 90% of baccalaureate students in nursing programs received some form of financial aid in 2008–09. *Gift aid (need-based):* Federal Pell, FSEOG, state, private, college/university gift aid from institutional funds. *Loans:* FFEL (Subsidized and Unsubsidized Stafford PLUS), Perkins. *Work-study:* Federal Work-Study, part-time campus jobs. *Financial aid application deadline:* Continuous.

Contact Ms. Melissa Green, Recruiter, Department of Nursing, Nebraska Wesleyan University, 5000 St. Paul Avenue, Lincoln, NE 68504. *Telephone:* 800-541-3818 Ext. 2330. *Fax:* 402-465-2479. *E-mail:* jlb@nebrwesleyan.edu.

GRADUATE PROGRAMS

Expenses (2009–10) *Tuition:* full-time $6800; part-time $340 per credit hour. *International tuition:* $6800 full-time.

Financial Aid 60% of graduate students in nursing programs received some form of financial aid in 2008–09.

Contact Dr. Jeri L. Brandt, RN, Program Director, Department of Nursing, Nebraska Wesleyan University, 5000 St. Paul Avenue, Lincoln, NE 68504. *Telephone:* 402-465-2336. *Fax:* 402-465-2179. *E-mail:* jlb@nebrwesleyan.edu.

MASTER'S DEGREE PROGRAM

Degree MSN

Available Programs Accelerated AD/RN to Master's; Accelerated Master's; Accelerated RN to Master's; Master's; RN to Master's.

Concentrations Available Nursing administration; nursing education.

Site Options Omaha, NE.

Study Options Full-time and part-time.

Program Entrance Requirements Clinical experience, computer literacy, minimum overall college GPA of 3.0, transcript of college record, written essay, immunizations, 2 letters of recommendation, nursing research course, resume, statistics course. *Application deadline:* 8/1 (fall), 12/10 (spring). Applications may be processed on a rolling basis for some programs. *Application fee:* $100.

Advanced Placement Credit by examination available. Credit given for nursing courses completed elsewhere dependent upon specific evaluations.

Degree Requirements 40 total credit hours, thesis or project, comprehensive exam.

POST-MASTER'S PROGRAM

Areas of Study Nursing administration; nursing education.

Union College
Division of Health Sciences
Lincoln, Nebraska

http://www.ucollege.edu

Founded in 1891

DEGREE • BSN

Nursing Program Faculty 10

Baccalaureate Enrollment 162
Women 80% **Men** 20% **Minority** 5% **International** 9% **Part-time** 5%

Nursing Student Activities Sigma Theta Tau, nursing club.

Nursing Student Resources Academic advising; academic or career counseling; assistance for students with disabilities; bookstore; campus computer network; career placement assistance; computer lab; computer-assisted instruction; e-mail services; employment services for current students; externships; interactive nursing skills videos; Internet; learning resource lab; library services; nursing audiovisuals; placement services for program completers; remedial services; resume preparation assistance; skills, simulation, or other laboratory; tutoring; unpaid internships.

Library Facilities 147,813 volumes (450 in health, 350 in nursing); 1,357 periodical subscriptions (50 health-care related).

BACCALAUREATE PROGRAMS

Degree BSN

Available Programs ADN to Baccalaureate; Generic Baccalaureate; LPN to Baccalaureate.

Study Options Full-time and part-time.

Program Entrance Requirements Minimum overall college GPA of 2.75, transcript of college record, CPR certification, written essay, health exam, health insurance, high school transcript, immunizations, 3 letters of recommendation, minimum GPA in nursing prerequisites of 2.75, professional liability insurance/malpractice insurance, prerequisite course work. Transfer students are accepted. *Application deadline:* 4/1 (fall), 11/1 (spring). *Application fee:* $25.

Advanced Placement Credit by examination available. Credit given for nursing courses completed elsewhere dependent upon specific evaluations.

Expenses (2009–10) *Tuition:* full-time $16,930; part-time $710 per credit. *International tuition:* $21,930 full-time. *Room and board:* $1645 per academic year. *Required fees:* full-time $465; part-time $465 per term.

Financial Aid 83% of baccalaureate students in nursing programs received some form of financial aid in 2008–09.

Contact Mrs. Stacie Laursen, Office Manager, Division of Health Sciences, Union College, 3800 South 48th Street, Lincoln, NE 68506. *Telephone:* 402-486-2524. *Fax:* 402-486-2559. *E-mail:* stlaurse@ucollege.edu.

University of Nebraska Medical Center
College of Nursing
Omaha, Nebraska

http://www.unmc.edu/nursing/

Founded in 1869

DEGREES • BSN • MSN • PHD

Nursing Program Faculty 112 (60% with doctorates).

Baccalaureate Enrollment 600

Graduate Enrollment 300

Nursing Student Activities Nursing Honor Society, Sigma Theta Tau, Student Nurses' Association, nursing club.

Nursing Student Resources Academic advising; academic or career counseling; assistance for students with disabilities; bookstore; campus computer network; career placement assistance; computer lab; computer-assisted instruction; daycare for children of students; e-mail services; employment services for current students; externships; housing assistance; interactive nursing skills videos; Internet; learning resource lab; library services; nursing audiovisuals; other; paid internships; placement services for program completers; remedial services; resume preparation assistance; skills, simulation, or other laboratory; tutoring.

Library Facilities 238,074 volumes (240,000 in health, 3,500 in nursing); 6,403 periodical subscriptions (2,200 health-care related).

BACCALAUREATE PROGRAMS

Degree BSN

Available Programs ADN to Baccalaureate; Accelerated Baccalaureate; Accelerated Baccalaureate for Second Degree; Accelerated RN Baccalaureate; Baccalaureate for Second Degree; Generic Baccalaureate; International Nurse to Baccalaureate; LPN to Baccalaureate; LPN to RN Baccalaureate; RN Baccalaureate; RPN to Baccalaureate.

Study Options Full-time.

Program Entrance Requirements Minimum overall college GPA of 2.5, transcript of college record, CPR certification, health insurance, high school transcript, immunizations, 2 letters of recommendation, prerequisite course work. Transfer students are accepted.

Advanced Placement Credit by examination available. Credit given for nursing courses completed elsewhere dependent upon specific evaluations.

Contact *Telephone:* 402-559-5184.

GRADUATE PROGRAMS

Contact *Telephone:* 402-559-5184.

MASTER'S DEGREE PROGRAM

Degree MSN

Available Programs Master's; Master's for Non-Nursing College Graduates; RN to Master's.

Concentrations Available Health-care administration; nurse case management; nursing administration; nursing education; nursing informatics. *Clinical nurse specialist programs in:* acute care, adult health, cardiovascular, community health, critical care, family health, gerontology, maternity-newborn, medical-surgical, oncology, parent-child, pediatric, perinatal, psychiatric/mental health, public health, women's health. *Nurse practitioner programs in:* acute care, adult health, community health, family health, gerontology, neonatal health, oncology, pediatric, primary care, psychiatric/mental health, women's health.

Study Options Full-time and part-time.

Program Entrance Requirements Computer literacy, minimum overall college GPA of 3.0, transcript of college record, CPR certification, immunizations, interview, 3 letters of recommendation, nursing research course, statistics course.

Advanced Placement Credit given for nursing courses completed elsewhere dependent upon specific evaluations.

Degree Requirements 45 total credit hours.

POST-MASTER'S PROGRAM

Areas of Study Health-care administration; nurse case management; nursing administration; nursing education; nursing informatics. *Clinical nurse specialist programs in:* acute care, adult health, cardiovascular, community health, critical care, family health, gerontology, maternity-newborn, medical-surgical, oncology, parent-child, pediatric, perinatal, psychiatric/mental health, public health, women's health. *Nurse practitioner programs in:* acute care, adult health, community health, family health, gerontology, neonatal health, oncology, pediatric, primary care, psychiatric/mental health, women's health.

DOCTORAL DEGREE PROGRAM

Degree PhD

Available Programs Doctorate; Doctorate for Nurses with Non-Nursing Degrees; Post-Baccalaureate Doctorate.

Areas of Study Advanced practice nursing, aging, bio-behavioral research, biology of health and illness, clinical practice, community health, critical care, faculty preparation, family health, gerontology, health policy, health promotion/disease prevention, health-care systems, human health and illness, illness and transition, individualized study, information systems, maternity-newborn, neuro-behavior, nurse case management, nursing administration, nursing policy, nursing research, nursing science, oncology, women's health.

University of Nebraska Medical Center (continued)
Program Entrance Requirements Minimum overall college GPA of 3.2, interview by faculty committee, interview, 3 letters of recommendation, scholarly papers, statistics course, vita, writing sample.
Degree Requirements Dissertation, oral exam, written exam.

POSTDOCTORAL PROGRAM

Postdoctoral Program Contact *Telephone:* 402-559-7457. *Fax:* 410-706-0945.

CONTINUING EDUCATION PROGRAM

Contact *Telephone:* 402-559-7487.

NEVADA

Great Basin College
BSN Program
Elko, Nevada

Founded in 1967
DEGREE • BSN

Library Facilities 38,765 volumes.

BACCALAUREATE PROGRAMS

Degree BSN

Available Programs RN Baccalaureate.
Program Entrance Requirements RN licensure.
Contact *Telephone:* 775-738-8493.

Nevada State College at Henderson
Nursing Program
Henderson, Nevada

http://www.nsc.nevada.edu/academics/programs/nursing/
Founded in 2002
DEGREE • BSN

Nursing Program Faculty 27 (26% with doctorates).
Baccalaureate Enrollment 207
Women 88% **Men** 12% **Minority** 34% **Part-time** 28%
Distance Learning Courses Available.
Nursing Student Activities Sigma Theta Tau, Student Nurses' Association.
Nursing Student Resources Academic advising; academic or career counseling; assistance for students with disabilities; bookstore; campus computer network; computer lab; computer-assisted instruction; e-mail services; interactive nursing skills videos; Internet; learning resource lab; library services; nursing audiovisuals; skills, simulation, or other laboratory; tutoring.
Library Facilities 6,800 volumes.

BACCALAUREATE PROGRAMS

Degree BSN

Available Programs Accelerated Baccalaureate for Second Degree; Generic Baccalaureate; RN Baccalaureate.
Study Options Full-time.

Program Entrance Requirements Minimum overall college GPA of 2.5, transcript of college record, CPR certification, health exam, health insurance, high school transcript, immunizations, minimum GPA in nursing prerequisites of 3.0, prerequisite course work. Transfer students are accepted. *Application deadline:* 3/1 (fall), 8/1 (spring).
Advanced Placement Credit given for nursing courses completed elsewhere dependent upon specific evaluations.
Contact School of Nursing, Nursing Program, Nevada State College at Henderson, 1125 Nevada State Drive, Henderson, NV 89002. *Telephone:* 702-992-2850. *Fax:* 702-992-2851. *E-mail:* nursing@nsc.nevada.edu.

Touro University
School of Nursing
Henderson, Nevada

DEGREES • BSN • DNP • MSN

Nursing Program Faculty 20 (7% with doctorates).
Baccalaureate Enrollment 110
Women 70% **Men** 30% **Minority** 68% **International** 6% **Part-time** 6%
Graduate Enrollment 25
Women 84% **Men** 16% **Minority** 40% **International** 4% **Part-time** 100%
Distance Learning Courses Available.
Nursing Student Activities Sigma Theta Tau, Student Nurses' Association.
Nursing Student Resources Academic advising; assistance for students with disabilities; bookstore; campus computer network; computer lab; e-mail services; interactive nursing skills videos; Internet; library services; skills, simulation, or other laboratory; tutoring.

BACCALAUREATE PROGRAMS

Degree BSN

Available Programs Accelerated Baccalaureate; Accelerated Baccalaureate for Second Degree; Accelerated RN Baccalaureate; Baccalaureate for Second Degree; Generic Baccalaureate; RN Baccalaureate.
Study Options Full-time.
Online Degree Options Yes.
Program Entrance Requirements Minimum overall college GPA of 2.5, transcript of college record, CPR certification, health exam, health insurance, immunizations, minimum GPA in nursing prerequisites of 2.5, prerequisite course work. Transfer students are accepted. *Application deadline:* Applications may be processed on a rolling basis for some programs. *Application fee:* $50.
Advanced Placement Credit given for nursing courses completed elsewhere dependent upon specific evaluations.
Financial Aid 90% of baccalaureate students in nursing programs received some form of financial aid in 2008–09.
Contact Gladys Easterling, Admissions Counselor, School of Nursing, Touro University, 874 American Pacific Drive, Henderson, NV 89014. *Telephone:* 702-777-4748. *Fax:* 702-777-1752. *E-mail:* gladys.easterling@tun.touro.edu.

GRADUATE PROGRAMS

Financial Aid 70% of graduate students in nursing programs received some form of financial aid in 2008–09.
Contact Gladys Easterling, Admissions Counselor, School of Nursing, Touro University, 874 American Pacific Drive, Henderson, NV 89014. *Telephone:* 702-777-4748. *Fax:* 702-777-1752. *E-mail:* gladys.easterling@tun.touro.edu.

MASTER'S DEGREE PROGRAM

Degree MSN

Available Programs Master's; Master's for Nurses with Non-Nursing Degrees.
Study Options Part-time.
Online Degree Options Yes (online only).

Program Entrance Requirements Computer literacy, minimum overall college GPA of 3.0, transcript of college record, CPR certification, immunizations, 2 letters of recommendation, statistics course. *Application deadline:* Applications may be processed on a rolling basis for some programs. *Application fee:* $50.

Advanced Placement Credit given for nursing courses completed elsewhere dependent upon specific evaluations.

Degree Requirements 33 total credit hours, thesis or project, comprehensive exam.

POST-MASTER'S PROGRAM

Areas of Study Nursing education.

DOCTORAL DEGREE PROGRAM

Degree DNP

Available Programs Doctorate.

Areas of Study Health policy, health-care systems, individualized study, information systems, nursing administration.

Online Degree Options Yes (online only).

Program Entrance Requirements Minimum overall college GPA of 3.0, interview, 3 letters of recommendation, MSN or equivalent, statistics course. Application deadline: Applications may be processed on a rolling basis for some programs. Application fee: $50.

Degree Requirements 39 total credit hours, dissertation.

CONTINUING EDUCATION PROGRAM

Contact Peggy Taylor, Director, Continuing Professional Education, School of Nursing, Touro University, 874 American Pacific Drive, Henderson, NV 89014. *Telephone:* 702-777-1788. *Fax:* 702-777-4834. *E-mail:* peggy.taylor@tun.touro.edu.

University of Nevada, Las Vegas
School of Nursing
Las Vegas, Nevada

http://nursing.unlv.edu/

Founded in 1957

DEGREES • BSN • MSN • PHD

Nursing Program Faculty 37 (52% with doctorates).

Baccalaureate Enrollment 170
Women 82% **Men** 18% **Minority** 43%

Graduate Enrollment 149
Women 79% **Men** 21% **Minority** 36% **International** 11% **Part-time** 58%

Distance Learning Courses Available.

Nursing Student Activities Sigma Theta Tau, Student Nurses' Association.

Nursing Student Resources Academic advising; academic or career counseling; assistance for students with disabilities; bookstore; campus computer network; career placement assistance; computer lab; computer-assisted instruction; daycare for children of students; e-mail services; employment services for current students; interactive nursing skills videos; Internet; learning resource lab; library services; nursing audiovisuals; remedial services; resume preparation assistance; skills, simulation, or other laboratory; tutoring.

Library Facilities 1.3 million volumes (35,800 in health, 12,000 in nursing); 18,568 periodical subscriptions (305 health-care related).

BACCALAUREATE PROGRAMS

Degree BSN

Available Programs Accelerated Baccalaureate; Generic Baccalaureate.

Study Options Full-time.

Program Entrance Requirements Minimum overall college GPA of 3.0, transcript of college record, CPR certification, health exam, health insurance, high school transcript, immunizations, minimum GPA in nursing prerequisites of 3.0, prerequisite course work. Transfer students are accepted. *Application deadline:* Applications may be processed on a rolling basis for some programs.

Advanced Placement Credit by examination available. Credit given for nursing courses completed elsewhere dependent upon specific evaluations.

Expenses (2009–10) *Tuition, state resident:* full-time $7249. *Tuition, nonresident:* full-time $25,758. *International tuition:* $26,412 full-time. *Room and board:* $12,520; room only: $7280 per academic year. *Required fees:* full-time $1500.

Financial Aid 65% of baccalaureate students in nursing programs received some form of financial aid in 2008–09. *Gift aid (need-based):* Federal Pell, FSEOG, state, private, college/university gift aid from institutional funds. *Loans:* Federal Nursing Student Loans, Federal Direct (Subsidized and Unsubsidized Stafford PLUS), Perkins, state, college/university. *Work-study:* Federal Work-Study, part-time campus jobs. *Financial aid application deadline (priority):* 2/1.

Contact Dr. Nancy York, RN, Undergraduate Coordinator, School of Nursing, University of Nevada, Las Vegas, 4505 Maryland Parkway, Las Vegas, NV 89154-3018. *Telephone:* 702-895-5930. *Fax:* 702-895-4807. *E-mail:* Nancy.York@unlv.edu.

GRADUATE PROGRAMS

Expenses (2009–10) *Tuition, state resident:* full-time $2359. *Tuition, nonresident:* full-time $8529. *International tuition:* $9269 full-time. *Room and board:* $12,520; room only: $7280 per academic year. *Required fees:* full-time $150.

Financial Aid 40% of graduate students in nursing programs received some form of financial aid in 2008–09. 5 research assistantships with partial tuition reimbursements available (averaging $11,750 per year), 2 teaching assistantships (averaging $15,000 per year) were awarded; institutionally sponsored loans, scholarships, and unspecified assistantships also available. *Financial aid application deadline:* 3/1.

Contact Ms. Cheryl Maes, Coordinator, Graduate Programs, School of Nursing, University of Nevada, Las Vegas, Las Vegas, NV 89154-3018. *Telephone:* 702-895-2947. *Fax:* 702-895-4807. *E-mail:* Cheryl.Maes@unlv.edu.

MASTER'S DEGREE PROGRAM

Degree MSN

Available Programs Master's.

Concentrations Available Nursing education. *Nurse practitioner programs in:* family health, pediatric.

Study Options Full-time and part-time.

Online Degree Options Yes (online only).

Program Entrance Requirements Clinical experience, computer literacy, minimum overall college GPA of 3.0, transcript of college record, CPR certification, written essay, immunizations, interview, 2 letters of recommendation, nursing research course, professional liability insurance/malpractice insurance, prerequisite course work, resume, statistics course. *Application deadline:* 3/1 (spring). *Application fee:* $60.

Advanced Placement Credit given for nursing courses completed elsewhere dependent upon specific evaluations.

Degree Requirements 46 total credit hours, thesis or project.

POST-MASTER'S PROGRAM

Areas of Study Nursing education. *Nurse practitioner programs in:* family health, pediatric.

DOCTORAL DEGREE PROGRAM

Degree PhD

Available Programs Doctorate.

Areas of Study Nursing education, urban health.

Online Degree Options Yes (online only).

Program Entrance Requirements Clinical experience, minimum overall college GPA of 3.5, interview by faculty committee, 2 letters of recommendation, MSN or equivalent, statistics course, vita, writing sample, GRE General Test. Application deadline: 3/1 (spring). Application fee: $60.

Degree Requirements 65 total credit hours, dissertation, oral exam, written exam.

CONTINUING EDUCATION PROGRAM

Contact Mrs. Mary Jo Russo, RN, Continuing Education Coordinator, School of Nursing, University of Nevada, Las Vegas, 4505 Maryland Parkway, Las Vegas, NV 89154-3018. *Telephone:* 702-895-4696. *Fax:* 702-895-4807. *E-mail:* MaryJo.Russo@unlv.edu.

University of Nevada, Reno
Orvis School of Nursing
Reno, Nevada

http://www.unr.edu/hcs/osn

Founded in 1874

DEGREES • BSN • MSN • MSN/MPH

Nursing Program Faculty 30 (40% with doctorates).

Baccalaureate Enrollment 144
Women 60% **Men** 40% **Minority** 16% **International** 5%

Graduate Enrollment 67
Women 90% **Men** 10% **Minority** 1% **Part-time** 90%

Distance Learning Courses Available.

Nursing Student Activities Nursing Honor Society, Sigma Theta Tau, Student Nurses' Association.

Nursing Student Resources Academic advising; academic or career counseling; assistance for students with disabilities; bookstore; campus computer network; computer lab; computer-assisted instruction; e-mail services; housing assistance; Internet; learning resource lab; library services; nursing audiovisuals; resume preparation assistance; skills, simulation, or other laboratory.

Library Facilities 1.1 million volumes (5,000 in health, 3,000 in nursing); 24,527 periodical subscriptions (172 health-care related).

BACCALAUREATE PROGRAMS

Degree BSN

Available Programs ADN to Baccalaureate; Accelerated Baccalaureate; Generic Baccalaureate; RN Baccalaureate.

Site Options Reno, NV.

Study Options Full-time.

Program Entrance Requirements Transcript of college record, CPR certification, health exam, health insurance, immunizations, minimum GPA in nursing prerequisites of 3.0, professional liability insurance/malpractice insurance, prerequisite course work. Transfer students are accepted. *Application deadline:* 2/12 (fall), 9/17 (spring).

Advanced Placement Credit given for nursing courses completed elsewhere dependent upon specific evaluations.

Expenses (2009–10) *Tuition, area resident:* full-time $11,299. *Tuition, state resident:* full-time $6589. *Tuition, nonresident:* full-time $19,879. *Room and board:* $10,595; room only: $6100 per academic year.

Financial Aid 50% of baccalaureate students in nursing programs received some form of financial aid in 2008–09.

Contact Mary Ann Lambert, Coordinator, Undergraduate Program, Orvis School of Nursing, University of Nevada, Reno, Mail Stop 134, Reno, NV 89557. *Telephone:* 775-682-7150. *Fax:* 775-784-4262. *E-mail:* lambert@unr.edu.

GRADUATE PROGRAMS

Expenses (2009–10) *Tuition, area resident:* part-time $247 per credit. *Tuition, state resident:* part-time $510 per credit. *Tuition, nonresident:* full-time $13,290; part-time $264 per credit. *Required fees:* full-time $155.

Financial Aid Research assistantships, teaching assistantships, Federal Work-Study, institutionally sponsored loans, scholarships, and unspecified assistantships available.

Contact Elizabeth Amos, PhD, Coordinator, Graduate Program, Orvis School of Nursing, University of Nevada, Reno, 1664 North Virginia Street, Reno, NV 89557-0052. *Telephone:* 775-682-7156. *Fax:* 775-784-4262. *E-mail:* eamos@unr.edu.

MASTER'S DEGREE PROGRAM

Degrees MSN; MSN/MPH

Available Programs Master's.

Concentrations Available Clinical nurse leader; nursing education. *Clinical nurse specialist programs in:* school health. *Nurse practitioner programs in:* family health.

Site Options Reno, NV.

Study Options Full-time and part-time.

Program Entrance Requirements Computer literacy, minimum overall college GPA of 3.0, transcript of college record, CPR certification, written essay, immunizations, 3 letters of recommendation, physical assessment course, professional liability insurance/malpractice insurance, prerequisite course work, resume, statistics course. *Application deadline:* 3/1 (fall).

Advanced Placement Credit given for nursing courses completed elsewhere dependent upon specific evaluations.

Degree Requirements 35 total credit hours, thesis or project, comprehensive exam.

POST-MASTER'S PROGRAM

Areas of Study Clinical nurse leader; nursing education. *Nurse practitioner programs in:* family health.

University of Southern Nevada
College of Nursing
Henderson, Nevada

Founded in 2000

DEGREE • BSN

Nursing Program Faculty 17 (12% with doctorates).

Baccalaureate Enrollment 141
Women 70% **Men** 30% **Minority** 80%

Nursing Student Activities Student Nurses' Association, nursing club.

Nursing Student Resources Academic advising; academic or career counseling; assistance for students with disabilities; bookstore; campus computer network; career placement assistance; computer lab; e-mail services; interactive nursing skills videos; Internet; learning resource lab; library services; nursing audiovisuals; remedial services; resume preparation assistance; skills, simulation, or other laboratory; unpaid internships.

BACCALAUREATE PROGRAMS

Degree BSN

Available Programs Generic Baccalaureate.

Study Options Full-time.

Program Entrance Requirements Transcript of college record, written essay, interview, minimum GPA in nursing prerequisites of 2.75, prerequisite course work. Transfer students are accepted. *Application deadline:* 8/10 (fall), 12/15 (spring). Applications may be processed on a rolling basis for some programs. *Application fee:* $100.

Advanced Placement Credit given for nursing courses completed elsewhere dependent upon specific evaluations.

Expenses (2009–10) *Tuition:* full-time $27,500. *International tuition:* $27,500 full-time. *Required fees:* full-time $2300.

Financial Aid 85% of baccalaureate students in nursing programs received some form of financial aid in 2008–09.

Contact Ms. Imelda C. Revuelto, Recruiter, Admissions and Enrollment Coordinator, College of Nursing, University of Southern Nevada, 11 Sunset Way, Henderson, NV 89014. *Telephone:* 702-968-2075. *Fax:* 702-968-2097. *E-mail:* irevuelto@usn.edu.

NEW HAMPSHIRE

Colby-Sawyer College
Department of Nursing
New London, New Hampshire

http://www.colby-sawyer.edu/academic/nursing

Founded in 1837

DEGREE • BSN

Nursing Program Faculty 14 (.14% with doctorates).

Baccalaureate Enrollment 169
Women 93% **Men** 7% **Minority** 4% **International** 1% **Part-time** 1%
Nursing Student Activities Nursing Honor Society, Student Nurses' Association.

Nursing Student Resources Academic advising; academic or career counseling; assistance for students with disabilities; bookstore; campus computer network; career placement assistance; computer lab; computer-assisted instruction; e-mail services; employment services for current students; housing assistance; interactive nursing skills videos; Internet; learning resource lab; library services; nursing audiovisuals; remedial services; resume preparation assistance; skills, simulation, or other laboratory; tutoring; unpaid internships.

Library Facilities 93,696 volumes (12,050 in health, 760 in nursing); 27,072 periodical subscriptions (135 health-care related).

BACCALAUREATE PROGRAMS

Degree BSN

Available Programs Generic Baccalaureate.

Study Options Full-time and part-time.

Program Entrance Requirements Minimum overall college GPA of 2.7, transcript of college record, CPR certification, written essay, health exam, health insurance, high school biology, high school chemistry, high school foreign language, 3 years high school math, 3 years high school science, high school transcript, immunizations, 2 letters of recommendation, minimum high school GPA of 2.75, minimum GPA in nursing prerequisites of 2.7, prerequisite course work. Transfer students are accepted. *Application deadline:* Applications may be processed on a rolling basis for some programs.

Advanced Placement Credit by examination available. Credit given for nursing courses completed elsewhere dependent upon specific evaluations.

Expenses (2009–10) *Tuition:* full-time $31,090; part-time $1040 per credit hour. *Room and board:* $10,860 per academic year. *Required fees:* full-time $395; part-time $395 per term.

Financial Aid 96% of baccalaureate students in nursing programs received some form of financial aid in 2008–09.

Contact Prof. Susan Anne Reeves, RN, Chair/Director, Nursing Department, Department of Nursing, Colby-Sawyer College, 541 Main Street, New London, NH 03257-7835. *Telephone:* 603-526-3795. *Fax:* 603-526-3159. *E-mail:* sreeves@colby-sawyer.edu.

Franklin Pierce University
Master of Science in Nursing
Rindge, New Hampshire

Founded in 1962
DEGREES • BS • MSN

Nursing Program Faculty 4 (50% with doctorates).

Baccalaureate Enrollment 110
Women 97% **Men** 3% **Minority** 3% **Part-time** 100%

Graduate Enrollment 24
Women 96% **Men** 4% **Minority** 8% **Part-time** 100%

Distance Learning Courses Available.

Nursing Student Resources Academic advising; assistance for students with disabilities; bookstore; campus computer network; computer lab; library services.

Library Facilities 137,458 volumes; 19,414 periodical subscriptions (200 health-care related).

BACCALAUREATE PROGRAMS

Degree BS

Available Programs ADN to Baccalaureate; RN Baccalaureate.
Site Options Concord, NH; Lebanon, NH; Portsmouth, NH.
Study Options Part-time.
Program Entrance Requirements RN licensure. Transfer students are accepted. *Application deadline:* Applications may be processed on a rolling basis for some programs.
Advanced Placement Credit by examination available.

Expenses (2009–10) *Tuition:* full-time $8640; part-time $240 per credit. *International tuition:* $8640 full-time.

Financial Aid 95% of baccalaureate students in nursing programs received some form of financial aid in 2008–09. *Gift aid (need-based):* Federal Pell, FSEOG, state, private, college/university gift aid from institutional funds. *Loans:* FFEL (Subsidized and Unsubsidized Stafford PLUS), Perkins. *Work-study:* Federal Work-Study, part-time campus jobs. *Financial aid application deadline (priority):* 3/1.

Contact Dr. Judith Ann Evans, RN, Director of Nursing. *Telephone:* 603-433-2000 Ext. 2000. *Fax:* 603-899-1067 Ext. 1067. *E-mail:* evansj@franklinpierce.edu.

GRADUATE PROGRAMS

Expenses (2009–10) *Tuition:* full-time $8400; part-time $700 per credit. *International tuition:* $8400 full-time.

Financial Aid 90% of graduate students in nursing programs received some form of financial aid in 2008–09.

Contact Dr. Judith Ann Evans, RN, Director of Nursing, Master of Science in Nursing, Franklin Pierce University, 73 Corporate Drive, Portsmouth, NH 03801. *Telephone:* 603-322-2000. *Fax:* 603-899-1067. *E-mail:* evansj@franklinpierce.edu.

MASTER'S DEGREE PROGRAM

Degree MSN

Available Programs Master's; Master's for Nurses with Non-Nursing Degrees; RN to Master's.
Concentrations Available Nursing administration; nursing education.
Site Options Concord, NH; Lebanon, NH; Portsmouth, NH.
Study Options Part-time.
Program Entrance Requirements Computer literacy, minimum overall college GPA of 2.8, transcript of college record, written essay, interview, 3 letters of recommendation, resume, statistics course. *Application deadline:* Applications may be processed on a rolling basis for some programs.
Degree Requirements 34 total credit hours, thesis or project.

Rivier College
Division of Nursing
Nashua, New Hampshire

Founded in 1933
DEGREES • BS • MS

Nursing Program Faculty 22 (32% with doctorates).

Baccalaureate Enrollment 200
Women 91% **Men** 9% **Minority** 2% **Part-time** 100%

Graduate Enrollment 41
Women 95% **Men** 5% **Part-time** 88%

Distance Learning Courses Available.

Nursing Student Activities Nursing Honor Society, Student Nurses' Association.

Nursing Student Resources Academic advising; academic or career counseling; assistance for students with disabilities; bookstore; campus computer network; career placement assistance; computer lab; computer-assisted instruction; e-mail services; employment services for current students; externships; housing assistance; interactive nursing skills videos; Internet; learning resource lab; library services; nursing audiovisuals; other; placement services for program completers; remedial services; resume preparation assistance; skills, simulation, or other laboratory; tutoring.

Library Facilities 2,584 volumes in health, 1,377 volumes in nursing; 92 periodical subscriptions health-care related.

BACCALAUREATE PROGRAMS

Degree BS

Available Programs ADN to Baccalaureate; RN Baccalaureate.
Study Options Full-time and part-time.
Online Degree Options Yes (online only).

Rivier College (continued)

Program Entrance Requirements Minimum overall college GPA of 2.5, transcript of college record, written essay, health exam, health insurance, high school chemistry, high school foreign language, 2 years high school math, 2 years high school science, high school transcript, immunizations, 2 letters of recommendation, minimum high school GPA of 3.0, minimum high school rank 80%, prerequisite course work. Transfer students are accepted. *Application deadline:* Applications may be processed on a rolling basis for some programs. *Application fee:* $25.

Advanced Placement Credit by examination available. Credit given for nursing courses completed elsewhere dependent upon specific evaluations.

Financial Aid *Gift aid (need-based):* Federal Pell, FSEOG, state, private, college/university gift aid from institutional funds. *Loans:* FFEL (Subsidized and Unsubsidized Stafford PLUS), Perkins, state. *Work-study:* Federal Work-Study, part-time campus jobs. *Financial aid application deadline (priority):* 3/1.

Contact Sarah Martin, Assistant Director, Graduate and Undergraduate Evening Admissions, Division of Nursing, Rivier College, 420 South Main Street, Nashua, NH 03060-5086. *Telephone:* 603-897-8519. *Fax:* 603-897-8808. *E-mail:* smartin@rivier.edu.

GRADUATE PROGRAMS

Expenses (2009–10) *Tuition:* part-time $447 per credit.

Contact Pamela A. Slawinowski, Assistant to Program Director, Division of Nursing, Rivier College, 420 South Main Street, Nashua, NH 03060-5086. *Telephone:* 603-897-8528. *Fax:* 603-897-8884. *E-mail:* pslawinowski@rivier.edu.

MASTER'S DEGREE PROGRAM

Degree MS

Available Programs Master's; Master's for Nurses with Non-Nursing Degrees; RN to Master's.

Concentrations Available Nursing education. *Clinical nurse specialist programs in:* psychiatric/mental health. *Nurse practitioner programs in:* family health, psychiatric/mental health.

Study Options Full-time and part-time.

Program Entrance Requirements Clinical experience, minimum overall college GPA of 3.0, transcript of college record, written essay, immunizations, interview, 2 letters of recommendation, resume, statistics course, GRE, MAT. *Application deadline:* Applications may be processed on a rolling basis for some programs. *Application fee:* $25.

Advanced Placement Credit by examination available. Credit given for nursing courses completed elsewhere dependent upon specific evaluations.

Degree Requirements 43 total credit hours, thesis or project.

POST-MASTER'S PROGRAM

Areas of Study Nursing education. *Clinical nurse specialist programs in:* psychiatric/mental health. *Nurse practitioner programs in:* family health, psychiatric/mental health.

Saint Anselm College

Department of Nursing
Manchester, New Hampshire

http://www.anselm.edu/academics/depts/nursing

Founded in 1889

DEGREE • BSN

Nursing Program Faculty 25 (35% with doctorates).

Baccalaureate Enrollment 250
Women 96% **Men** 4% **Minority** 2% **International** 1% **Part-time** 1%

Nursing Student Activities Sigma Theta Tau, Student Nurses' Association, nursing club.

Nursing Student Resources Academic advising; academic or career counseling; assistance for students with disabilities; bookstore; campus computer network; career placement assistance; computer lab; computer-assisted instruction; e-mail services; employment services for current students; externships; housing assistance; interactive nursing skills videos;

Internet; learning resource lab; library services; nursing audiovisuals; resume preparation assistance; skills, simulation, or other laboratory; tutoring.

Library Facilities 222,000 volumes (7,127 in health); 1,900 periodical subscriptions (292 health-care related).

BACCALAUREATE PROGRAMS

Degree BSN

Available Programs RN Baccalaureate.

Study Options Full-time and part-time.

Program Entrance Requirements Transcript of college record, written essay, health exam, health insurance, high school biology, high school chemistry, high school foreign language, 3 years high school math, 3 years high school science, high school transcript, immunizations, 2 letters of recommendation, professional liability insurance/malpractice insurance. *Application deadline:* 11/15 (fall). *Application fee:* $55.

Advanced Placement Credit by examination available. Credit given for nursing courses completed elsewhere dependent upon specific evaluations.

Expenses (2009–10) *Tuition:* full-time $29,720. *International tuition:* $29,720 full-time. *Room and board:* $11,240 per academic year. *Required fees:* full-time $1200.

Financial Aid 86% of baccalaureate students in nursing programs received some form of financial aid in 2008–09. *Gift aid (need-based):* Federal Pell, FSEOG, state, private, college/university gift aid from institutional funds. *Loans:* FFEL (Subsidized and Unsubsidized Stafford PLUS), Perkins. *Work-study:* Federal Work-Study, part-time campus jobs. *Financial aid application deadline:* 2/1.

Contact Nancy Davis Griffin, Dean of Admission, Department of Nursing, Saint Anselm College, 100 Saint Anselm Drive, Manchester, NH 03102-1310. *Telephone:* 603-641-7500. *Fax:* 603-641-7550. *E-mail:* ngriffin@anselm.edu.

CONTINUING EDUCATION PROGRAM

Contact Sharon George, Dean of Nursing, Department of Nursing, Saint Anselm College, 100 Saint Anselm Drive, #1745, Manchester, NH 03102-1310. *Telephone:* 603-641-7083. *Fax:* 603-641-7089. *E-mail:* sgeorge@ansel.edu.

University of New Hampshire

Department of Nursing
Durham, New Hampshire

http://www.unh.edu/ur-nurs.html

Founded in 1866

DEGREES • BS • MS

Nursing Program Faculty 13 (75% with doctorates).

Baccalaureate Enrollment 268
Women 91% **Men** 9% **Minority** 1%

Graduate Enrollment 54
Women 95% **Men** 5% **Minority** 1%

Nursing Student Activities Nursing Honor Society, Sigma Theta Tau, Student Nurses' Association.

Nursing Student Resources Academic advising; academic or career counseling; assistance for students with disabilities; bookstore; campus computer network; computer lab; computer-assisted instruction; daycare for children of students; e-mail services; housing assistance; interactive nursing skills videos; Internet; learning resource lab; nursing audiovisuals; paid internships; resume preparation assistance; skills, simulation, or other laboratory; tutoring.

Library Facilities 2.2 million volumes; 50,043 periodical subscriptions.

BACCALAUREATE PROGRAMS

Degree BS

Available Programs Generic Baccalaureate; RN Baccalaureate.

Study Options Full-time and part-time.

Program Entrance Requirements High school transcript, prerequisite course work. Transfer students are accepted.

Contact *Telephone:* 603-862-4715. *Fax:* 603-862-4771.

GRADUATE PROGRAMS
Contact *Telephone:* 603-862-2285. *Fax:* 603-862-4771.

MASTER'S DEGREE PROGRAM
Degree MS
Available Programs Master's; Master's for Nurses with Non-Nursing Degrees.
Concentrations Available *Clinical nurse specialist programs in:* adult health. *Nurse practitioner programs in:* adult health, family health.
Program Entrance Requirements GRE General Test or MAT.
Degree Requirements 45 total credit hours, thesis or project, comprehensive exam.

POST-MASTER'S PROGRAM
Areas of Study *Clinical nurse specialist programs in:* adult health. *Nurse practitioner programs in:* adult health, family health.

NEW JERSEY

Bloomfield College
Division of Nursing
Bloomfield, New Jersey

http://www.bloomfield.edu
Founded in 1868
DEGREE • BS

Nursing Program Faculty 18 (33% with doctorates).
Baccalaureate Enrollment 123
Women 88% **Men** 12% **Minority** 67% **International** 2% **Part-time** 17%
Distance Learning Courses Available.
Nursing Student Activities Student Nurses' Association.
Nursing Student Resources Academic advising; academic or career counseling; assistance for students with disabilities; bookstore; campus computer network; career placement assistance; computer lab; e-mail services; employment services for current students; interactive nursing skills videos; Internet; learning resource lab; library services; nursing audiovisuals; placement services for program completers; remedial services; resume preparation assistance; skills, simulation, or other laboratory; tutoring; unpaid internships.
Library Facilities 64,700 volumes (1,500 in health, 1,500 in nursing); 456 periodical subscriptions (44 health-care related).

BACCALAUREATE PROGRAMS
Degree BS
Available Programs Generic Baccalaureate; RN Baccalaureate.
Study Options Full-time and part-time.
Program Entrance Requirements Transcript of college record, CPR certification, health exam, minimum GPA in nursing prerequisites of 2.5, prerequisite course work. Transfer students are accepted. *Application deadline:* 8/1 (fall), 12/15 (spring), 5/1 (summer). Applications may be processed on a rolling basis for some programs. *Application fee:* $40.
Advanced Placement Credit by examination available. Credit given for nursing courses completed elsewhere dependent upon specific evaluations.
Expenses (2009–10) *Tuition:* full-time $20,000; part-time $2040 per course. *International tuition:* $20,000 full-time. *Room and board:* $10,300; room only: $5150 per academic year. *Required fees:* full-time $1000; part-time $250 per term.
Financial Aid 84% of baccalaureate students in nursing programs received some form of financial aid in 2008–09. *Gift aid (need-based):* Federal Pell, FSEOG, state, private, college/university gift aid from institutional funds. *Loans:* FFEL (Subsidized and Unsubsidized Stafford PLUS). *Work-study:* Federal Work-Study, part-time campus jobs. *Financial aid application deadline:* 6/1 (priority: 3/15).

Contact Dr. Neddie Serra, Chair, Division of Nursing, Division of Nursing, Bloomfield College, Bloomfield, NJ 07003. *Telephone:* 973-748-9000 Ext. 120. *Fax:* 973-743-3998. *E-mail:* neddie_serra@bloomfield.edu.

The College of New Jersey
School of Nursing, Health and Exercise Science
Ewing, New Jersey

http://www.tcnj.edu/~nursing
Founded in 1855
DEGREES • BSN • MSN

Nursing Program Faculty 15 (60% with doctorates).
Baccalaureate Enrollment 273
Women 93% **Men** 7% **Minority** 34% **Part-time** 1%
Graduate Enrollment 47
Women 98% **Men** 2% **Minority** 23% **Part-time** 2%
Nursing Student Activities Sigma Theta Tau, Student Nurses' Association.
Nursing Student Resources Academic advising; academic or career counseling; assistance for students with disabilities; bookstore; campus computer network; career placement assistance; computer lab; computer-assisted instruction; daycare for children of students; e-mail services; employment services for current students; externships; interactive nursing skills videos; Internet; learning resource lab; library services; nursing audiovisuals; paid internships; resume preparation assistance; skills, simulation, or other laboratory; tutoring; unpaid internships.
Library Facilities 674,051 volumes (30,000 in health, 18,800 in nursing); 133,506 periodical subscriptions (228 health-care related).

BACCALAUREATE PROGRAMS
Degree BSN
Available Programs Generic Baccalaureate.
Study Options Full-time and part-time.
Program Entrance Requirements Written essay, health exam, high school transcript, immunizations. Transfer students are accepted.
Advanced Placement Credit by examination available. Credit given for nursing courses completed elsewhere dependent upon specific evaluations.
Contact *Telephone:* 609-771-2669. *Fax:* 609-637-5159.

GRADUATE PROGRAMS
Contact *Telephone:* 609-771-2591. *Fax:* 609-637-5159.

MASTER'S DEGREE PROGRAM
Degree MSN
Available Programs Master's; Master's for Nurses with Non-Nursing Degrees; RN to Master's.
Concentrations Available Nursing administration. *Clinical nurse specialist programs in:* adult health. *Nurse practitioner programs in:* family health, neonatal health.
Study Options Full-time and part-time.
Program Entrance Requirements Computer literacy, minimum overall college GPA of 3.0, transcript of college record, written essay, immunizations, interview, 3 letters of recommendation, physical assessment course, statistics course, GRE General Test.
Advanced Placement Credit given for nursing courses completed elsewhere dependent upon specific evaluations.
Degree Requirements 47 total credit hours, comprehensive exam.

POST-MASTER'S PROGRAM
Areas of Study Nursing administration. *Clinical nurse specialist programs in:* adult health. *Nurse practitioner programs in:* family health, neonatal health.

College of Saint Elizabeth
Department of Nursing
Morristown, New Jersey

http://www.cse.edu/sgcs_continuingstudies.htm

Founded in 1899

DEGREE • BSN

Nursing Program Faculty 13 (25% with doctorates).

Baccalaureate Enrollment 231
Women 95% **Men** 5% **Minority** 48% **Part-time** 99%

Nursing Student Activities Nursing Honor Society, Sigma Theta Tau, nursing club.

Nursing Student Resources Academic advising; academic or career counseling; assistance for students with disabilities; bookstore; campus computer network; career placement assistance; computer lab; computer-assisted instruction; e-mail services; employment services for current students; interactive nursing skills videos; Internet; learning resource lab; library services; nursing audiovisuals; other; remedial services; resume preparation assistance; skills, simulation, or other laboratory; tutoring.

Library Facilities 109,352 volumes (4,246 in health, 702 in nursing); 561 periodical subscriptions (194 health-care related).

BACCALAUREATE PROGRAMS

Degree BSN

Available Programs ADN to Baccalaureate; Accelerated RN Baccalaureate; International Nurse to Baccalaureate; RN Baccalaureate.

Site Options Randolph, NJ; Elizabeth, NJ; Hoboken, NJ.

Study Options Part-time.

Program Entrance Requirements Minimum overall college GPA of 2.0, transcript of college record, CPR certification, health exam, immunizations, prerequisite course work, RN licensure. Transfer students are accepted.

Advanced Placement Credit by examination available. Credit given for nursing courses completed elsewhere dependent upon specific evaluations.

Contact *Telephone:* 973-290-4056. *Fax:* 973-290-4177.

CONTINUING EDUCATION PROGRAM

Contact *Telephone:* 973-290-4073. *Fax:* 973-290-4177.

Fairleigh Dickinson University, Metropolitan Campus
Henry P. Becton School of Nursing and Allied Health
Teaneck, New Jersey

http://fduinfo.com/depts/ucnah.php

Founded in 1942

DEGREES • BSN • DNP • MSN

Nursing Program Faculty 17 (41% with doctorates).

Baccalaureate Enrollment 346
Women 94% **Men** 6% **Minority** 63% **International** 3.6% **Part-time** 30%

Graduate Enrollment 156
Women 93.6% **Men** 6.4% **Minority** 41% **Part-time** 100%

Distance Learning Courses Available.

Nursing Student Activities Nursing Honor Society, Sigma Theta Tau, Student Nurses' Association.

Nursing Student Resources Academic advising; academic or career counseling; assistance for students with disabilities; bookstore; campus computer network; career placement assistance; computer lab; computer-assisted instruction; e-mail services; employment services for current students; externships; housing assistance; interactive nursing skills videos; Internet; learning resource lab; library services; nursing audiovisuals; other; placement services for program completers; remedial services; resume preparation assistance; skills, simulation, or other laboratory; tutoring; unpaid internships.

Library Facilities 375,348 volumes (2,166 in nursing); 1,440 periodical subscriptions (118 health-care related).

BACCALAUREATE PROGRAMS

Degree BSN

Available Programs Accelerated Baccalaureate for Second Degree; Generic Baccalaureate; RN Baccalaureate.

Site Options Morristown, NJ; Sewell, NJ; Teaneck, NJ.

Study Options Full-time and part-time.

Program Entrance Requirements Minimum overall college GPA of 3.0, transcript of college record, health exam, health insurance, high school biology, high school chemistry, 2 years high school math, 2 years high school science, high school transcript, immunizations, 2 letters of recommendation. Transfer students are accepted. *Application deadline:* Applications may be processed on a rolling basis for some programs. *Application fee:* $40.

Advanced Placement Credit given for nursing courses completed elsewhere dependent upon specific evaluations.

Expenses (2008–09) *Tuition:* full-time $27,136; part-time $821 per credit. *International tuition:* $27,136 full-time. *Room and board:* $5307; room only: $3500 per academic year. *Required fees:* full-time $1233; part-time $154 per term.

Financial Aid 91% of baccalaureate students in nursing programs received some form of financial aid in 2007–08.

Contact Ms. Sylvia Cabassa, RN, Associate Director, Undergraduate Nursing, Henry P. Becton School of Nursing and Allied Health, Fairleigh Dickinson University, Metropolitan Campus, 1000 River Road, H-DH4-02, Teaneck, NJ 07666-1914. *Telephone:* 201-692-2880. *Fax:* 201-692-2388. *E-mail:* scabassa@fdu.edu.

GRADUATE PROGRAMS

Expenses (2008–09) *Tuition:* part-time $947 per credit. *Room and board:* $5307; room only: $3500 per academic year. *Required fees:* part-time $154 per term.

Financial Aid 91% of graduate students in nursing programs received some form of financial aid in 2007–08.

Contact Dr. Elizabeth S. Parietti, Associate Director of Graduate Programs, Henry P. Becton School of Nursing and Allied Health, Fairleigh Dickinson University, Metropolitan Campus, 1000 River Road, H-DH4-02, H4444, Teaneck, NJ 07666-1914. *Telephone:* 201-692-2881. *Fax:* 201-692-2388. *E-mail:* parietti@fdu.edu.

MASTER'S DEGREE PROGRAM

Degree MSN

Available Programs Accelerated RN to Master's; Master's; Master's for Nurses with Non-Nursing Degrees; RN to Master's.

Concentrations Available Nursing administration; nursing education; nursing informatics. *Clinical nurse specialist programs in:* forensic nursing. *Nurse practitioner programs in:* adult health, family health, psychiatric/mental health.

Site Options Morristown, NJ; Sewell, NJ; Teaneck, NJ.

Study Options Full-time and part-time.

Program Entrance Requirements Computer literacy, minimum overall college GPA of 3.0, transcript of college record, CPR certification, written essay, immunizations, 2 letters of recommendation, nursing research course, physical assessment course, professional liability insurance/malpractice insurance, statistics course. *Application deadline:* Applications may be processed on a rolling basis for some programs. *Application fee:* $40.

Advanced Placement Credit given for nursing courses completed elsewhere dependent upon specific evaluations.

Degree Requirements Thesis or project.

POST-MASTER'S PROGRAM

Areas of Study Nursing administration; nursing education; nursing informatics. *Clinical nurse specialist programs in:* forensic nursing. *Nurse practitioner programs in:* adult health, family health, psychiatric/mental health.

DOCTORAL DEGREE PROGRAM

Degree DNP

Available Programs Doctorate.

Areas of Study Advanced practice nursing, nursing administration, nursing education.

Program Entrance Requirements Minimum overall college GPA of 3.0, interview by faculty committee, 3 letters of recommendation, MSN or equivalent. Application deadline: Applications may be processed on a rolling basis for some programs.

Degree Requirements 40 total credit hours, residency.

CONTINUING EDUCATION PROGRAM

Contact Corinne Ellis, RN, Lecturer, Henry P. Becton School of Nursing and Allied Health, Fairleigh Dickinson University, Metropolitan Campus, 1000 River Road, H-DH4-02, Teaneck, NJ 07666-1914. *Telephone:* 201-692-2343. *Fax:* 201-692-2388. *E-mail:* cellis@fdu.edu.

Felician College

Division of Nursing and Health Management
Lodi, New Jersey

http://www.felician.edu/academics/nahp/nursing. asp

Founded in 1942

DEGREES • BSN • MA/MSM • MSN

Nursing Program Faculty 25 (32% with doctorates).

Baccalaureate Enrollment 487
Women 92% **Men** 8% **Minority** 41% **Part-time** 22%

Graduate Enrollment 82
Women 88% **Men** 12% **Minority** 38% **Part-time** 95%

Distance Learning Courses Available.

Nursing Student Activities Nursing Honor Society, Sigma Theta Tau, Student Nurses' Association.

Nursing Student Resources Academic advising; academic or career counseling; assistance for students with disabilities; bookstore; campus computer network; career placement assistance; computer lab; computer-assisted instruction; daycare for children of students; e-mail services; interactive nursing skills videos; Internet; learning resource lab; library services; nursing audiovisuals; placement services for program completers; remedial services; resume preparation assistance; skills, simulation, or other laboratory; tutoring.

Library Facilities 105,000 volumes (12,519 in health, 12,519 in nursing); 434 periodical subscriptions (21 health-care related).

BACCALAUREATE PROGRAMS

Degree BSN

Available Programs Generic Baccalaureate.

Site Options East Orange, NJ; Long Branch, NJ; Edison, NJ.

Study Options Full-time and part-time.

Program Entrance Requirements Minimum overall college GPA of 3.0, transcript of college record, written essay, health exam, health insurance, high school biology, high school chemistry, 2 years high school math, 2 years high school science, high school transcript, immunizations, minimum high school GPA of 3.0, minimum GPA in nursing prerequisites of 2.8, professional liability insurance/malpractice insurance. Transfer students are accepted. *Application deadline:* 8/15 (fall), 1/10 (spring). Applications may be processed on a rolling basis for some programs. *Application fee:* $30.

Advanced Placement Credit by examination available. Credit given for nursing courses completed elsewhere dependent upon specific evaluations.

Expenses (2009–10) *Tuition:* full-time $23,650; part-time $780 per credit. *International tuition:* $23,650 full-time. *Room and board:* $9700 per academic year. *Required fees:* full-time $1400; part-time $450 per term.

Financial Aid 80% of baccalaureate students in nursing programs received some form of financial aid in 2008–09.

Contact Office of Undergraduate Admissions, Division of Nursing and Health Management, Felician College, 262 South Main Street, Lodi, NJ 07644-2117. *Telephone:* 201-559-6131. *Fax:* 201-559-6138. *E-mail:* admissions@felician.edu.

GRADUATE PROGRAMS

Expenses (2009–10) *Tuition:* part-time $790 per credit. *Room and board:* $9700 per academic year. *Required fees:* part-time $450 per term.

Financial Aid 27% of graduate students in nursing programs received some form of financial aid in 2008–09.

Contact Ms. Wendy Lin-Cook, Dean of Adult and Graduate Admissions, Division of Nursing and Health Management, Felician College, 262 South Main Street, Lodi, NJ 07644-2117. *Telephone:* 201-559-6077. *Fax:* 201-559-6138. *E-mail:* adultandgraduate@felician.edu.

MASTER'S DEGREE PROGRAM

Degrees MA/MSM; MSN

Available Programs Accelerated RN to Master's; Master's.

Concentrations Available Nursing education. *Nurse practitioner programs in:* adult health, family health.

Study Options Full-time and part-time.

Online Degree Options Yes (online only).

Program Entrance Requirements Computer literacy, minimum overall college GPA of 3.0, transcript of college record, CPR certification, written essay, immunizations, 2 letters of recommendation, nursing research course, physical assessment course, professional liability insurance/malpractice insurance, prerequisite course work, statistics course. *Application deadline:* Applications may be processed on a rolling basis for some programs. *Application fee:* $40.

Advanced Placement Credit given for nursing courses completed elsewhere dependent upon specific evaluations.

Degree Requirements 46 total credit hours, thesis or project.

POST-MASTER'S PROGRAM

Areas of Study Nursing education. *Nurse practitioner programs in:* adult health, family health.

Kean University

Department of Nursing
Union, New Jersey

http://www.kean.edu/~nursing/

Founded in 1855

DEGREES • BSN • MSN • MSN/MPA

Nursing Program Faculty 18 (88% with doctorates).

Baccalaureate Enrollment 174
Women 93% **Men** 7% **Minority** 60% **Part-time** 90%

Graduate Enrollment 103
Women 93% **Men** 7% **Minority** 62% **Part-time** 87%

Nursing Student Activities Nursing Honor Society, Sigma Theta Tau, nursing club.

Nursing Student Resources Academic advising; academic or career counseling; assistance for students with disabilities; bookstore; campus computer network; career placement assistance; computer lab; computer-assisted instruction; daycare for children of students; e-mail services; employment services for current students; housing assistance; Internet; learning resource lab; library services; nursing audiovisuals; placement services for program completers; remedial services; resume preparation assistance; skills, simulation, or other laboratory; tutoring; unpaid internships.

Library Facilities 327,883 volumes; 6,198 periodical subscriptions.

BACCALAUREATE PROGRAMS

Degree BSN

Available Programs ADN to Baccalaureate; RN Baccalaureate.

Site Options Raritan, NJ; Plainfield, NJ; Perth Amboy, NJ.

Study Options Full-time and part-time.

Kean University (continued)

Program Entrance Requirements Minimum overall college GPA of 2.0, written essay, 2 letters of recommendation, prerequisite course work, RN licensure. Transfer students are accepted.

Advanced Placement Credit by examination available. Credit given for nursing courses completed elsewhere dependent upon specific evaluations.

Contact *Telephone:* 908-737-3385. *Fax:* 908-737-3393.

GRADUATE PROGRAMS

Contact *Telephone:* 908-737-3386. *Fax:* 908-737-3393.

MASTER'S DEGREE PROGRAM

Degrees MSN; MSN/MPA

Available Programs Accelerated Master's for Nurses with Non-Nursing Degrees; Master's; Master's for Nurses with Non-Nursing Degrees.

Concentrations Available Health-care administration; nursing administration. *Clinical nurse specialist programs in:* community health, school health.

Study Options Full-time and part-time.

Program Entrance Requirements Clinical experience, computer literacy, minimum overall college GPA of 3.0, transcript of college record, written essay, immunizations, interview, 2 letters of recommendation, nursing research course, professional liability insurance/malpractice insurance, statistics course.

Advanced Placement Credit given for nursing courses completed elsewhere dependent upon specific evaluations.

Degree Requirements 36 total credit hours, thesis or project.

CONTINUING EDUCATION PROGRAM

Contact *Telephone:* 908-737-3385. *Fax:* 908-737-3393.

Monmouth University
Marjorie K. Unterberg School of Nursing
West Long Branch, New Jersey

http://www.monmouth.edu

Founded in 1933

DEGREES • BSN • MSN

Nursing Program Faculty 21 (42% with doctorates).

Baccalaureate Enrollment 71
Women 98% **Men** 2% **Minority** 15% **Part-time** 97%

Graduate Enrollment 217
Women 98% **Men** 2% **Minority** 25% **Part-time** 93%

Distance Learning Courses Available.

Nursing Student Activities Sigma Theta Tau, Student Nurses' Association.

Nursing Student Resources Academic advising; academic or career counseling; assistance for students with disabilities; bookstore; campus computer network; career placement assistance; computer lab; computer-assisted instruction; e-mail services; employment services for current students; interactive nursing skills videos; Internet; learning resource lab; library services; nursing audiovisuals; paid internships; remedial services; resume preparation assistance; skills, simulation, or other laboratory; tutoring.

Library Facilities 280,000 volumes (250,000 in health, 25,000 in nursing); 25,196 periodical subscriptions (98 health-care related).

BACCALAUREATE PROGRAMS

Degree BSN

Available Programs ADN to Baccalaureate; RN Baccalaureate.
Site Options Freehold, NJ; Red Bank, NJ.
Study Options Full-time and part-time.

Program Entrance Requirements Transcript of college record, health exam, immunizations, 2 letters of recommendation, minimum GPA in nursing prerequisites of 2.0, professional liability insurance/malpractice insurance, prerequisite course work, RN licensure. Transfer students are accepted. *Application deadline:* Applications may be processed on a rolling basis for some programs. *Application fee:* $50.

Advanced Placement Credit by examination available. Credit given for nursing courses completed elsewhere dependent upon specific evaluations.

Expenses (2009–10) *Tuition:* part-time $706 per credit. *Room and board:* room only: $6000 per academic year.

Financial Aid 80% of baccalaureate students in nursing programs received some form of financial aid in 2008–09. *Gift aid (need-based):* Federal Pell, FSEOG, state, private, college/university gift aid from institutional funds, Federal Nursing. *Loans:* Federal Direct (Subsidized and Unsubsidized Stafford PLUS), FFEL, Perkins, state, college/university, alternative/private loans. *Work-study:* Federal Work-Study. *Financial aid application deadline:* Continuous.

Contact Dr. Cira Fraser, Associate Professor, Marjorie K. Unterberg School of Nursing, Monmouth University, West Long Branch, NJ 07764. *Telephone:* 732-571-3443. *Fax:* 732-263-5131. *E-mail:* cfraser@monmouth.edu.

GRADUATE PROGRAMS

Expenses (2009–10) *Tuition:* part-time $773 per credit. *Room and board:* room only: $6000 per academic year.

Financial Aid 80% of graduate students in nursing programs received some form of financial aid in 2008–09.

Contact Dr. Laura Jannone, EdD, Director of MSN Program, Marjorie K. Unterberg School of Nursing, Monmouth University, 400 Cedar Avenue, West Long Branch, NJ 07764. *Telephone:* 732-571-3443. *Fax:* 732-263-5131. *E-mail:* ljannone@monmouth.edu.

MASTER'S DEGREE PROGRAM

Degree MSN

Available Programs Accelerated RN to Master's; Master's.

Concentrations Available Nursing administration; nursing education. *Clinical nurse specialist programs in:* forensic nursing, school health. *Nurse practitioner programs in:* adult health, family health, psychiatric/mental health.

Site Options Edison, NJ.

Study Options Full-time and part-time.

Program Entrance Requirements Minimum overall college GPA of 2.75, transcript of college record, immunizations, 2 letters of recommendation, professional liability insurance/malpractice insurance. *Application deadline:* Applications may be processed on a rolling basis for some programs. *Application fee:* $50.

Advanced Placement Credit given for nursing courses completed elsewhere dependent upon specific evaluations.

Degree Requirements 42 total credit hours.

POST-MASTER'S PROGRAM

Areas of Study Nursing administration; nursing education. *Clinical nurse specialist programs in:* forensic nursing, school health. *Nurse practitioner programs in:* adult health, family health, psychiatric/mental health.

CONTINUING EDUCATION PROGRAM

Contact Ms. Barbara Paskewich, RN, Special Projects Coordinator, Marjorie K. Unterberg School of Nursing, Monmouth University, 400 Cedar Avenue, West Long Branch, NJ 07764. *Telephone:* 732-571-3694. *Fax:* 732-263-5131. *E-mail:* bpaskewi@monmouth.edu.

New Jersey City University
Department of Nursing
Jersey City, New Jersey

http://www.njcu.edu/dept/ProfStudies/nursing2/rnbsn.htm

Founded in 1927

DEGREE • BSN

Nursing Program Faculty 7 (50% with doctorates).

Baccalaureate Enrollment 110
Women 85% **Men** 15% **Minority** 75% **International** 15% **Part-time** 40%
Nursing Student Activities Nursing Honor Society, Sigma Theta Tau, Student Nurses' Association.

Nursing Student Resources Academic advising; academic or career counseling; assistance for students with disabilities; bookstore; campus computer network; computer lab; computer-assisted instruction; daycare for children of students; e-mail services; interactive nursing skills videos; Internet; learning resource lab; library services; nursing audiovisuals; other; remedial services; skills, simulation, or other laboratory.

Library Facilities 212,786 volumes; 1,260 periodical subscriptions.

BACCALAUREATE PROGRAMS

Degree BSN

Available Programs Accelerated Baccalaureate for Second Degree; RN Baccalaureate.

Site Options Wall Township, NJ; East Orange, NJ.

Study Options Full-time.

Program Entrance Requirements Minimum overall college GPA of 3.0, transcript of college record, CPR certification, written essay, health exam, immunizations, 2 letters of recommendation, professional liability insurance/malpractice insurance, prerequisite course work, RN licensure. Transfer students are accepted. *Application fee:* $35.

Advanced Placement Credit by examination available. Credit given for nursing courses completed elsewhere dependent upon specific evaluations.

Financial Aid 40% of baccalaureate students in nursing programs received some form of financial aid in 2008–09.

Contact Dr. Kevin J. O'Neill, Assistant Professor, Department of Nursing, New Jersey City University, 2039 Kennedy Boulevard, R404, Jersey City, NJ 07305. *Telephone:* 201-200-3157. *Fax:* 201-200-3222. *E-mail:* koneill@njcu.edu.

Ramapo College of New Jersey
Master of Science in Nursing Program
Mahwah, New Jersey

Founded in 1969.

DEGREES • BSN • MSN

Nursing Program Faculty 29 (20% with doctorates).

Baccalaureate Enrollment 435
Women 90% **Men** 10% **Minority** 35% **International** 7% **Part-time** 15%

Graduate Enrollment 41
Women 95% **Men** 5% **Minority** 17% **Part-time** 90%

Distance Learning Courses Available.

Nursing Student Activities Nursing Honor Society, Student Nurses' Association.

Nursing Student Resources Academic advising; academic or career counseling; assistance for students with disabilities; bookstore; campus computer network; career placement assistance; computer lab; computer-assisted instruction; e-mail services; employment services for current students; externships; housing assistance; interactive nursing skills videos; Internet; learning resource lab; library services; nursing audiovisuals; placement services for program completers; remedial services; resume preparation assistance; skills, simulation, or other laboratory; tutoring; unpaid internships.

Library Facilities 265,187 volumes (3,500 in nursing); 600 periodical subscriptions (200 health-care related).

BACCALAUREATE PROGRAMS

Degree BSN

Available Programs Generic Baccalaureate; RN Baccalaureate.

Site Options Englewood, NJ.

Study Options Full-time.

Online Degree Options Yes.

Program Entrance Requirements CPR certification, health exam, 3 years high school science, immunizations, minimum high school GPA of 2.5, minimum high school rank 20%, professional liability insurance/malpractice insurance. Transfer students are accepted. *Application deadline:* 3/1 (fall), 3/1 (spring). Applications may be processed on a rolling basis for some programs. *Application fee:* $60.

Advanced Placement Credit given for nursing courses completed elsewhere dependent upon specific evaluations.

Expenses (2009–10) *Tuition, state resident:* part-time $240 per credit. *Tuition, nonresident:* part-time $480 per credit. *Room and board:* $9950; room only: $7550 per academic year. *Required fees:* part-time $350 per term.

Financial Aid *Gift aid (need-based):* Federal Pell, FSEOG, state, private, college/university gift aid from institutional funds, Federal Nursing. *Loans:* Federal Direct (Subsidized and Unsubsidized Stafford PLUS), Perkins, state. *Work-study:* Federal Work-Study, part-time campus jobs. *Financial aid application deadline (priority):* 3/1.

Contact Kathleen M. Burke, Assistant Dean in Charge of Nursing, Master of Science in Nursing Program, Ramapo College of New Jersey, 505 Ramapo Valley Road, Mahwah, NJ 07430. *Telephone:* 201-684-7737. *Fax:* 201-684-7934. *E-mail:* kmburke@ramapo.edu.

GRADUATE PROGRAMS

Expenses (2009–10) *Tuition, state resident:* part-time $525 per credit. *Tuition, nonresident:* part-time $675 per credit. *Room and board:* $9950; room only: $7550 per academic year. *Required fees:* part-time $100 per term.

Financial Aid Traineeships available.

Contact Kathleen M. Burke, Assistant Dean in Charge of Nursing, Master of Science in Nursing Program, Ramapo College of New Jersey, 505 Ramapo Valley Road, Mahwah, NJ 07430. *Telephone:* 201-684-7737. *Fax:* 201-684-7934. *E-mail:* kmburke@ramapo.edu.

MASTER'S DEGREE PROGRAM

Degree MSN

Available Programs Master's.

Concentrations Available Nursing education.

Study Options Full-time and part-time.

Online Degree Options Yes (online only).

Program Entrance Requirements Clinical experience, computer literacy, minimum overall college GPA of 3.0, transcript of college record, CPR certification, 2 letters of recommendation, nursing research course, professional liability insurance/malpractice insurance, statistics course. *Application deadline:* Applications may be processed on a rolling basis for some programs. *Application fee:* $60.

Advanced Placement Credit given for nursing courses completed elsewhere dependent upon specific evaluations.

Degree Requirements 32 total credit hours.

POST-MASTER'S PROGRAM

Areas of Study Nursing education.

CONTINUING EDUCATION PROGRAM

Contact Dr. Margaret Greene, Associate Professor, Master of Science in Nursing Program, Ramapo College of New Jersey, 505 Ramapo Valley Road, Mahwah, NJ 07430. *Telephone:* 201-684-7206. *Fax:* 201-684-7954. *E-mail:* mgreene1@ramapo.edu.

The Richard Stockton College of New Jersey
Program in Nursing
Pomona, New Jersey

http://talon.stockton.edu/eyos/page.cfm?siteID=14&pageID=48

Founded in 1969

DEGREES • BSN • MSN

Nursing Program Faculty 6 (66% with doctorates).

Baccalaureate Enrollment 69
Women 98% **Men** 2% **Minority** 10% **Part-time** 80%

The Richard Stockton College of New Jersey (continued)
Graduate Enrollment 20
Women 90% **Men** 10% **Minority** 15% **Part-time** 95%
Nursing Student Activities Sigma Theta Tau.

Nursing Student Resources Academic advising; academic or career counseling; assistance for students with disabilities; bookstore; campus computer network; computer lab; computer-assisted instruction; daycare for children of students; e-mail services; housing assistance; Internet; learning resource lab; library services; nursing audiovisuals; resume preparation assistance; skills, simulation, or other laboratory; tutoring.

Library Facilities 283,028 volumes (9,761 in health, 1,258 in nursing); 34,748 periodical subscriptions (83 health-care related).

BACCALAUREATE PROGRAMS

Degree BSN

Available Programs RN Baccalaureate.
Study Options Full-time and part-time.
Program Entrance Requirements Transfer students are accepted.
Advanced Placement Credit given for nursing courses completed elsewhere dependent upon specific evaluations.
Contact *Telephone:* 609-652-4837.

GRADUATE PROGRAMS

Contact *Telephone:* 609-652-4501.

MASTER'S DEGREE PROGRAM

Degree MSN

Concentrations Available *Nurse practitioner programs in:* adult health.
Study Options Full-time and part-time.
Program Entrance Requirements Clinical experience, computer literacy, minimum overall college GPA of 3.0, transcript of college record, CPR certification, written essay, immunizations, 2 letters of recommendation, nursing research course, physical assessment course, professional liability insurance/malpractice insurance, statistics course, GRE General Test.
Advanced Placement Credit given for nursing courses completed elsewhere dependent upon specific evaluations.
Degree Requirements 42 total credit hours, thesis or project.

Rutgers, The State University of New Jersey, Camden College of Arts and Sciences

Department of Nursing
Camden, New Jersey

http://nursing.camden.rutgers.edu
Founded in 1927
DEGREE • BS

Nursing Program Faculty 14 (36% with doctorates).
Baccalaureate Enrollment 86
Nursing Student Activities Sigma Theta Tau, Student Nurses' Association.
Nursing Student Resources Academic advising; academic or career counseling; assistance for students with disabilities; bookstore; campus computer network; career placement assistance; computer lab; computer-assisted instruction; e-mail services; employment services for current students; externships; housing assistance; interactive nursing skills videos; Internet; learning resource lab; library services; nursing audiovisuals; placement services for program completers; remedial services; resume preparation assistance; skills, simulation, or other laboratory; tutoring.
Library Facilities 6.4 million volumes; 28,934 periodical subscriptions.

BACCALAUREATE PROGRAMS

Degree BS

Available Programs Accelerated RN Baccalaureate; Baccalaureate for Second Degree; Generic Baccalaureate; RN Baccalaureate.
Study Options Full-time.
Program Entrance Requirements CPR certification, health exam, immunizations, minimum GPA in nursing prerequisites of 2.5, professional liability insurance/malpractice insurance, prerequisite course work. Transfer students are accepted. *Application deadline:* 2/27 (fall).
Contact Dr. Joanne Robinson, Clinical Associate Professor and Acting Chair, Department of Nursing, Rutgers, The State University of New Jersey, Camden College of Arts and Sciences, 311 North Fifth Street, Armitage Hall, Room 448, Camden, NJ 08102. *Telephone:* 856-225-6226. *Fax:* 856-225-6250. *E-mail:* nursecam@camden.rutgers.edu.

Rutgers, The State University of New Jersey, College of Nursing

Rutgers, The State University of New Jersey, College of Nursing
Newark, New Jersey

http://www.rutgers.edu/
Founded in 1956
DEGREES • BS • DNP • MS • MS/MPH • PHD

Nursing Program Faculty 31 (80% with doctorates).
Baccalaureate Enrollment 567
Women 90% **Men** 10% **Minority** 52% **International** 1% **Part-time** 20%
Graduate Enrollment 176
Women 98% **Men** 2% **Minority** 30% **Part-time** 90%
Distance Learning Courses Available.
Nursing Student Activities Sigma Theta Tau, Student Nurses' Association, nursing club.
Nursing Student Resources Academic advising; academic or career counseling; assistance for students with disabilities; bookstore; campus computer network; career placement assistance; computer lab; computer-assisted instruction; e-mail services; employment services for current students; externships; housing assistance; interactive nursing skills videos; Internet; learning resource lab; library services; nursing audiovisuals; paid internships; remedial services; resume preparation assistance; skills, simulation, or other laboratory; tutoring; unpaid internships.
Library Facilities 6.4 million volumes; 28,934 periodical subscriptions.

BACCALAUREATE PROGRAMS

Degree BS

Available Programs Accelerated Baccalaureate for Second Degree; Baccalaureate for Second Degree; Generic Baccalaureate; RN Baccalaureate.
Site Options Freehold, NJ; New Brunswick, NJ.
Study Options Full-time and part-time.
Program Entrance Requirements Minimum overall college GPA of 3.2, transcript of college record, health exam, high school biology, high school chemistry, 3 years high school math, 2 years high school science, high school transcript, immunizations, minimum high school GPA of 3.2, minimum high school rank, professional liability insurance/malpractice insurance. Transfer students are accepted. *Application deadline:* 12/1 (fall). *Application fee:* $65.
Advanced Placement Credit by examination available. Credit given for nursing courses completed elsewhere dependent upon specific evaluations.
Expenses (2009–10) *Tuition, area resident:* full-time $4773; part-time $307 per credit. *Tuition, nonresident:* full-time $10,089; part-time $654 per credit. *International tuition:* $10,089 full-time. *Room and board:* $10,498; room only: $7064 per academic year. *Required fees:* full-time $925.
Financial Aid 15% of baccalaureate students in nursing programs received some form of financial aid in 2008–09.
Contact Admissions Office, Rutgers, The State University of New Jersey, College of Nursing, 249 University Avenue, Newark, NJ 07102-1803. *Telephone:* 973-353-5205.

GRADUATE PROGRAMS

Expenses (2009–10) *Tuition, area resident:* full-time $7656; part-time $638 per credit. *Tuition, nonresident:* full-time $11,448; part-time $954 per credit. *International tuition:* $11,448 full-time. *Room and board:* $10,399; room only: $6965 per academic year. *Required fees:* full-time $753; part-time $335 per term.

Financial Aid 74% of graduate students in nursing programs received some form of financial aid in 2008–09.

Contact Dr. Mary Ann Scoloveno, Interim Associate Dean for Graduate Education, Rutgers, The State University of New Jersey, College of Nursing, 180 University Avenue, Newark, NJ 07102-1803. *Telephone:* 973-353-5060. *Fax:* 973-353-1277. *E-mail:* scoloven@rutgers.edu.

MASTER'S DEGREE PROGRAM

Degrees MS; MS/MPH

Available Programs Master's.

Concentrations Available *Clinical nurse specialist programs in:* adult health, community health, oncology, parent-child, psychiatric/mental health. *Nurse practitioner programs in:* acute care, adult health, family health, pediatric, psychiatric/mental health, women's health.

Site Options Freehold, NJ; Camden, NJ.

Study Options Full-time and part-time.

Program Entrance Requirements Minimum overall college GPA of 3.0, transcript of college record, written essay, immunizations, 3 letters of recommendation, physical assessment course, professional liability insurance/malpractice insurance, resume, statistics course. *Application deadline:* 6/1 (fall), 10/1 (spring). *Application fee:* $65.

Advanced Placement Credit given for nursing courses completed elsewhere dependent upon specific evaluations.

Degree Requirements 42 total credit hours.

POST-MASTER'S PROGRAM

Areas of Study Nursing education. *Clinical nurse specialist programs in:* adult health, community health, oncology, parent-child, psychiatric/mental health. *Nurse practitioner programs in:* acute care, adult health, family health, pediatric, psychiatric/mental health, women's health.

DOCTORAL DEGREE PROGRAM

Degree DNP, PhD

Available Programs Doctorate.

Areas of Study Nursing research.

Program Entrance Requirements Minimum overall college GPA of 3.2, interview by faculty committee, 3 letters of recommendation, MSN or equivalent, scholarly papers, statistics course, vita, writing sample. *Application deadline:* 3/15 (fall). *Application fee:* $65.

Degree Requirements 59 total credit hours, dissertation, written exam, residency.

CONTINUING EDUCATION PROGRAM

Contact Dr. Gayle Pearson, Assistant Dean, Center for Professional Development, Rutgers, The State University of New Jersey, College of Nursing, 175 University Avenue, Newark, NJ 07102. *Telephone:* 973-353-1061. *Fax:* 973-353-1700. *E-mail:* gaylep@rutgers.edu.

Saint Peter's College
Nursing Program
Jersey City, New Jersey

Founded in 1872

DEGREES • BSN • MSN

Nursing Program Faculty 15 (73% with doctorates).

Baccalaureate Enrollment 161
Women 85% **Men** 15% **Minority** 40%

Graduate Enrollment 55
Women 99% **Men** 1% **Minority** 45%

Distance Learning Courses Available.

Nursing Student Activities Nursing Honor Society, Sigma Theta Tau, Student Nurses' Association.

Nursing Student Resources Academic advising; academic or career counseling; assistance for students with disabilities; bookstore; campus computer network; career placement assistance; computer lab; computer-assisted instruction; e-mail services; externships; interactive nursing skills videos; Internet; learning resource lab; library services; nursing audiovisuals; remedial services; resume preparation assistance; skills, simulation, or other laboratory; tutoring.

Library Facilities 178,587 volumes (7,200 in health); 1,741 periodical subscriptions (1,586 health-care related).

BACCALAUREATE PROGRAMS

Degree BSN

Available Programs ADN to Baccalaureate; Generic Baccalaureate; RN Baccalaureate.

Site Options Englewood Cliffs, NJ.

Study Options Full-time.

Program Entrance Requirements Minimum overall college GPA of 2.7, transcript of college record, written essay, high school biology, high school chemistry, high school foreign language, 3 years high school math, 3 years high school science, high school transcript, immunizations, 2 letters of recommendation, minimum high school GPA of 3.0. Transfer students are accepted. *Application deadline:* Applications may be processed on a rolling basis for some programs.

Expenses (2008–09) *Tuition:* full-time $24,251. *International tuition:* $24,251 full-time. *Room and board:* $9750 per academic year.

Financial Aid 89% of baccalaureate students in nursing programs received some form of financial aid in 2007–08. *Gift aid (need-based):* Federal Pell, FSEOG, state, private, college/university gift aid from institutional funds. *Loans:* FFEL (Subsidized and Unsubsidized Stafford PLUS), state. *Work-study:* Federal Work-Study. *Financial aid application deadline (priority):* 4/15.

Contact Ms. Maryanne Mattson, Assistant Director of Admission, Nursing Program, Saint Peter's College, 2641 Kennedy Boulevard, Jersey City, NJ 07306. *Telephone:* 201-761-7113. *Fax:* 201-761-7105. *E-mail:* mmattson@spc.edu.

GRADUATE PROGRAMS

Financial Aid 25% of graduate students in nursing programs received some form of financial aid in 2007–08. 2 research assistantships with partial tuition reimbursements available were awarded.

Contact Dr. Ann Tritak, Associate Dean of Nursing, Nursing Program, Saint Peter's College, Hudson Terrace, Englewood Cliffs, NJ 07632. *Telephone:* 201-761-6272. *Fax:* 201-761-6271. *E-mail:* atritak@spc.edu.

MASTER'S DEGREE PROGRAM

Degree MSN

Available Programs Master's; Master's for Nurses with Non-Nursing Degrees.

Concentrations Available Nurse case management; nursing administration. *Nurse practitioner programs in:* adult health.

Site Options Englewood Cliffs, NJ.

Study Options Part-time.

Program Entrance Requirements Clinical experience, minimum overall college GPA of 3.0, transcript of college record, written essay, immunizations, 3 letters of recommendation, nursing research course, physical assessment course, professional liability insurance/malpractice insurance, statistics course. *Application deadline:* 8/25 (fall), 10/24 (winter), 12/15 (spring), 5/5 (summer). *Application fee:* $40.

Degree Requirements 39 total credit hours, thesis or project.

POST-MASTER'S PROGRAM

Areas of Study *Nurse practitioner programs in:* adult health.

Seton Hall University
College of Nursing
South Orange, New Jersey

http://nursing.shu.edu/

Founded in 1856

Seton Hall University (continued)

DEGREES • BSN • DNP • MSN • MSN/MA • MSN/MBA • PHD

Nursing Program Faculty 43 (50% with doctorates).

Baccalaureate Enrollment 686
Women 89% **Men** 11% **Minority** 43% **International** 1% **Part-time** 10%

Graduate Enrollment 136
Women 87% **Men** 13% **Minority** 17% **Part-time** 46%

Distance Learning Courses Available.

Nursing Student Activities Sigma Theta Tau, Student Nurses' Association.

Nursing Student Resources Academic advising; academic or career counseling; assistance for students with disabilities; bookstore; campus computer network; career placement assistance; computer lab; computer-assisted instruction; e-mail services; housing assistance; interactive nursing skills videos; Internet; learning resource lab; library services; nursing audiovisuals; paid internships; remedial services; resume preparation assistance; skills, simulation, or other laboratory; tutoring.

Library Facilities 506,042 volumes; 1,475 periodical subscriptions.

BACCALAUREATE PROGRAMS

Degree BSN

Available Programs Accelerated Baccalaureate for Second Degree; Baccalaureate for Second Degree; Generic Baccalaureate; RN Baccalaureate.

Site Options Brick/Toms River, NJ; Lakewood, NJ; Camden, NJ.

Study Options Full-time and part-time.

Program Entrance Requirements Minimum overall college GPA of 3.0, transcript of college record, written essay, high school biology, high school chemistry, high school foreign language, 3 years high school math, 2 years high school science, high school transcript, minimum high school GPA of 2.5. Transfer students are accepted.

Expenses (2009–10) *Tuition:* full-time $30,470; part-time $869 per credit. *Required fees:* full-time $300.

Financial Aid 75% of baccalaureate students in nursing programs received some form of financial aid in 2008–09.

Contact Ms. Kristyn Kent-Wuillermin, Director of Strategic Alliances, Marketing and Enrollment, College of Nursing, Seton Hall University, 400 South Orange Avenue, South Orange, NJ 07079-2697. *Telephone:* 973-761-9291. *Fax:* 973-761-9607. *E-mail:* kristyn.kent@shu.edu.

GRADUATE PROGRAMS

Financial Aid 31% of graduate students in nursing programs received some form of financial aid in 2008–09. Institutionally sponsored loans, traineeships, tuition waivers (partial), and unspecified assistantships available. Aid available to part-time students. *Financial aid application deadline:* 7/15.

Contact Ms. Kristyn Kent-Wuillermin, Director of Strategic Alliances, Marketing and Enrollment, College of Nursing, Seton Hall University, 400 South Orange Avenue, South Orange, NJ 07079-2697. *Telephone:* 973-761-9291. *Fax:* 973-761-9607. *E-mail:* kristyn.kent@shu.edu.

MASTER'S DEGREE PROGRAM

Degrees MSN; MSN/MA; MSN/MBA

Available Programs Accelerated Master's for Nurses with Non-Nursing Degrees; Master's; Master's for Nurses with Non-Nursing Degrees; RN to Master's.

Concentrations Available Clinical nurse leader; health-care administration; nurse case management; nursing administration; nursing education. *Clinical nurse specialist programs in:* school health. *Nurse practitioner programs in:* adult health, gerontology, pediatric, school health.

Study Options Full-time and part-time.

Online Degree Options Yes (online only).

Program Entrance Requirements Computer literacy, minimum overall college GPA of 3.0, transcript of college record, CPR certification, written essay, 2 letters of recommendation, nursing research course, physical assessment course, professional liability insurance/malpractice insurance, resume, statistics course, GRE or MAT. *Application deadline:* Applications may be processed on a rolling basis for some programs.

Degree Requirements 43 total credit hours, thesis or project.

POST-MASTER'S PROGRAM

Areas of Study Health-care administration; nurse case management; nursing administration; nursing education. *Nurse practitioner programs in:* adult health, gerontology, pediatric, school health.

DOCTORAL DEGREE PROGRAM

Degree DNP, PhD

Available Programs Doctorate.

Areas of Study Advanced practice nursing, nursing administration, nursing research.

Online Degree Options Yes (online only).

Program Entrance Requirements Minimum overall college GPA of 3.0, interview, 2 letters of recommendation, MSN or equivalent, scholarly papers, statistics course, vita, writing sample, GRE.

Degree Requirements 46 total credit hours, dissertation.

CONTINUING EDUCATION PROGRAM

Contact Ms. Kristyn Kent-Wuillermin, Director of Strategic Alliances, Marketing and Enrollment, College of Nursing, Seton Hall University, 400 South Orange Avenue, South Orange, NJ 07079-2697. *Telephone:* 973-761-9306. *Fax:* 973-761-9607. *E-mail:* kristyn.kent@shu.edu.

See full description on page 516.

Thomas Edison State College
School of Nursing
Trenton, New Jersey

http://www.tesc.edu/nursing

Nursing program founded in 1983

DEGREES • RN to BSN • RN to BSN/MSN • BSN to MSN

Nursing Student Resources Students in the School of Nursing have the opportunity to earn degrees through traditional and nontraditional methods, which take into consideration the individual needs and interests of each student. All nursing courses are designed and delivered as mentored, independent study courses via the Internet using myEdison®, the College's online course management system that uses the Blackboard platform. Students in these courses communicate with mentors and fellow students using e-mail, and they submit assignments to mentors through the Internet. Students may earn credit toward a degree by demonstrating college-level knowledge through testing and assessment of prior learning; by transfer credit for courses taken through other regionally accredited institutions; through the College's *e*-Pack® courses; and for licenses, certificates, and courses taken at work or through military training, if approved and recommended for academic credit.

School of Nursing Faculty The School employs off-site nurse educators from a variety of nursing education and service settings to develop, implement, and evaluate the program. All nurse educators have a minimum of a master's degree in nursing, with approximately 80 percent prepared at the doctoral level and many tenured at their home institution. With its courses offered by distance learning, the School has the opportunity to draw nurse educators from throughout the United States, resulting in a diverse and experienced group of online nurse educators. The School of Nursing has accreditation through the New Jersey Board of Nursing, the National League for Nursing Accrediting Commission (NLNAC), and, most recently, the Commission on Collegiate Nursing Education (CCNE).

BACCALAUREATE AND MASTER'S DEGREE PROGRAMS

Degrees RN to BSN, RN to BSN/MSN, and BSN to MSN

Certificate Programs A 12–15 credit post-master's Nurse Educator Certificate program is available to RNs with a master's degree in another area of nursing specialty.

Study Options Self-paced programs; online nursing courses offered quarterly; multiple options for credit earning; no time limit for degree completion; no residency requirement with maximum flexibility in transfer credit.

Program Entrance Requirements Admission is open and rolling; RNs can enroll any day of the year. In addition to submitting a notarized copy of their current RN license, valid in the United States, all applicants must submit a completed School of Nursing application with a $75 fee and have official transcripts of completed course work sent to the Office of the Registrar. Applicants to the RN to BSN and RN to BSN/MSN degree programs must also submit a BSN Credential Review fee of $300. All RNs will have 20 credits applied from previous nursing course work toward the 48-credit nursing requirement in the BSN degree. A total of 80 credits may be accepted from a community college, and up to 60 credits, including the 20 credits used in the nursing requirement, will be awarded to diploma graduates based on current licensure. There is no age restriction on credits transferred in to meet general education requirements or lower-division nursing requirements. All upper-division nursing credits must be from an accredited baccalaureate or higher-degree nursing program, and these must be newer than 10 years if completed prior to application to the School of Nursing. All credits used in the nursing requirement must have a grade equivalent of "C" or better. All previously completed credits transferred in to meet MSN degree requirements must be newer than 10 years at the time of application to the School of Nursing, have a grade equivalent of "B" or better and be from an accredited graduate nursing degree program.

Expenses (2009–10) *Tuition, state resident:* $328 per credit. *Tuition, nonresident:* $386 per credit for the BSN degree program; $479 for the MSN degree and Nurse Educator Certificate Programs.

Financial Aid Six percent of the RNs in the undergraduate nursing program and 9 percent in the graduate nursing program received some form of financial aid in 2008–09.

Contact Thomas Edison State College, 101 West State Street, Trenton, NJ 08608-1176. *Telephone:* (888) 442-8372, *E-mail:* nursinginfo@tesc.edu.

See full description on page 518.

University of Medicine and Dentistry of New Jersey

School of Nursing
Newark, New Jersey

http://sn.umdnj.edu/
Founded in 1970
DEGREES • BSN • DNP • MSN • MSN/MPH

Nursing Program Faculty 150 (30% with doctorates).

Baccalaureate Enrollment 266
Women 85% **Men** 15% **Minority** 48% **International** 2%

Graduate Enrollment 573
Women 80% **Men** 20% **Minority** 35% **Part-time** 80%

Distance Learning Courses Available.

Nursing Student Activities Nursing Honor Society, Sigma Theta Tau, Student Nurses' Association.

Nursing Student Resources Academic advising; academic or career counseling; assistance for students with disabilities; bookstore; campus computer network; computer lab; computer-assisted instruction; daycare for children of students; e-mail services; housing assistance; interactive nursing skills videos; Internet; learning resource lab; library services; nursing audiovisuals; remedial services; resume preparation assistance; skills, simulation, or other laboratory; tutoring.

Library Facilities 91,446 volumes in health, 3,273 volumes in nursing; 4,350 periodical subscriptions health-care related.

BACCALAUREATE PROGRAMS

Degree BSN

Available Programs Accelerated Baccalaureate for Second Degree; RN Baccalaureate.
Site Options Glassboro, NJ; Stratford, NJ.

Program Entrance Requirements Minimum overall college GPA of 3.0, transcript of college record, CPR certification, written essay, health exam, health insurance, immunizations, 3 letters of recommendation, minimum GPA in nursing prerequisites of 2.75, prerequisite course work. *Application deadline:* 7/15 (fall), 11/15 (spring), 3/15 (summer). Applications may be processed on a rolling basis for some programs. *Application fee:* $50.

Advanced Placement Credit given for nursing courses completed elsewhere dependent upon specific evaluations.

Expenses (2009–10) *Tuition, state resident:* part-time $345 per credit. *Tuition, nonresident:* part-time $490 per credit.

Financial Aid 88% of baccalaureate students in nursing programs received some form of financial aid in 2008–09.

Contact Denise Tate, EdD, Assistant Dean, Prelicensure Programs, School of Nursing, University of Medicine and Dentistry of New Jersey, 65 Bergen Street, Newark, NJ 07101. *Telephone:* 973-972-0509. *E-mail:* tatedm@umdnj.edu.

GRADUATE PROGRAMS

Expenses (2009–10) *Tuition, state resident:* part-time $486 per credit. *Tuition, nonresident:* part-time $690 per credit. *Required fees:* part-time $200 per term.

Financial Aid 28% of graduate students in nursing programs received some form of financial aid in 2008–09. Teaching assistantships, institutionally sponsored loans and scholarships available. Aid available to part-time students. *Financial aid application deadline:* 5/1.

Contact Mary Kamienski, PhD, Assistant Dean, Graduate Programs, School of Nursing, University of Medicine and Dentistry of New Jersey, 65 Bergen Street, SSB 1130, Newark, NJ 07101. *Telephone:* 973-972-7451. *Fax:* 973-972-7904. *E-mail:* kamienma@umdnj.edu.

MASTER'S DEGREE PROGRAM

Degrees MSN; MSN/MPH

Available Programs Master's; Master's for Nurses with Non-Nursing Degrees.

Concentrations Available Clinical nurse leader; nurse anesthesia; nurse-midwifery; nursing education; nursing informatics. *Clinical nurse specialist programs in:* psychiatric/mental health. *Nurse practitioner programs in:* acute care, adult health, community health, family health, gerontology, psychiatric/mental health, women's health.

Site Options Stratford, NJ.
Study Options Full-time and part-time.
Online Degree Options Yes.

Program Entrance Requirements Clinical experience, minimum overall college GPA of 3.0, transcript of college record, CPR certification, immunizations, interview, 2 letters of recommendation, physical assessment course, statistics course, GRE. *Application deadline:* 7/15 (fall), 11/15 (spring), 3/15 (summer). Applications may be processed on a rolling basis for some programs. *Application fee:* $50.

Advanced Placement Credit given for nursing courses completed elsewhere dependent upon specific evaluations.

Degree Requirements 40 total credit hours.

POST-MASTER'S PROGRAM

Areas of Study Clinical nurse leader; nurse anesthesia; nurse-midwifery; nursing informatics. *Clinical nurse specialist programs in:* psychiatric/mental health. *Nurse practitioner programs in:* acute care, adult health, family health, gerontology, psychiatric/mental health, women's health.

DOCTORAL DEGREE PROGRAM

Degree DNP

Available Programs Doctorate.
Areas of Study Clinical practice, nursing administration.
Site Options Stratford, NJ.

Program Entrance Requirements Clinical experience, minimum overall college GPA of 3.0, interview by faculty committee, interview, 2 letters of recommendation, MSN or equivalent, statistics course, vita, writing sample. Application deadline: 7/15 (fall), 11/15 (spring), 3/15 (summer). Applications may be processed on a rolling basis for some programs. Application fee: $50.

Degree Requirements 32 total credit hours, dissertation.

University of Medicine and Dentistry of New Jersey (continued)
CONTINUING EDUCATION PROGRAM

Contact Dr. Donna Cill, Director of the Center for Lifelong Learning, School of Nursing, University of Medicine and Dentistry of New Jersey, 65 Bergen Street, Room 1132-A, Newark, NJ 07101-1709. *Telephone:* 973-972-9793. *Fax:* 973-972-7904. *E-mail:* cilldm@umdnj.edu.

William Paterson University of New Jersey
Department of Nursing
Wayne, New Jersey

http://www.wpunj.edu/cos/nursing/

Founded in 1855

DEGREES • BSN • MSN

Nursing Program Faculty 27 (48% with doctorates).

Baccalaureate Enrollment 400
Women 82% **Men** 18% **Minority** 55% **International** 5% **Part-time** 25%

Graduate Enrollment 55
Women 100% **Minority** 21% **International** 5% **Part-time** 92%

Distance Learning Courses Available.

Nursing Student Activities Sigma Theta Tau, Student Nurses' Association.

Nursing Student Resources Academic advising; academic or career counseling; assistance for students with disabilities; bookstore; campus computer network; career placement assistance; computer lab; computer-assisted instruction; daycare for children of students; e-mail services; employment services for current students; housing assistance; interactive nursing skills videos; Internet; learning resource lab; library services; nursing audiovisuals; placement services for program completers; remedial services; resume preparation assistance; skills, simulation, or other laboratory; tutoring.

Library Facilities 338,573 volumes (15,000 in health, 12,700 in nursing); 6,569 periodical subscriptions (150 health-care related).

BACCALAUREATE PROGRAMS

Degree BSN

Available Programs ADN to Baccalaureate; Accelerated Baccalaureate for Second Degree; Generic Baccalaureate; LPN to Baccalaureate; RN Baccalaureate.

Study Options Full-time and part-time.

Program Entrance Requirements Minimum overall college GPA of 2.5, transcript of college record, CPR certification, health exam, health insurance, high school biology, high school chemistry, 1 year of high school math, 2 years high school science, high school transcript, immunizations, minimum high school GPA of 3.25, professional liability insurance/malpractice insurance, prerequisite course work. Transfer students are accepted. *Application deadline:* 2/1 (fall), 12/1 (spring). *Application fee:* $50.

Expenses (2009–10) *Tuition, state resident:* full-time $10,838; part-time $210 per credit hour. *Tuition, nonresident:* full-time $17,592; part-time $431 per credit hour. *International tuition:* $17,592 full-time. *Room and board:* $10,000; room only: $6500 per academic year. *Required fees:* full-time $4271; part-time $138 per credit.

Financial Aid 65% of baccalaureate students in nursing programs received some form of financial aid in 2008–09. *Gift aid (need-based):* Federal Pell, FSEOG, state, college/university gift aid from institutional funds. *Loans:* Federal Direct (Subsidized and Unsubsidized Stafford PLUS), FFEL (Subsidized and Unsubsidized Stafford PLUS), Perkins, state. *Work-study:* Federal Work-Study, part-time campus jobs. *Financial aid application deadline (priority):* 4/1.

Contact Dr. Julie Bliss, Chairperson, Department of Nursing, William Paterson University of New Jersey, 300 Pompton Road, W106, Wayne, NJ 07470. *Telephone:* 973-720-2673. *Fax:* 973-720-2668. *E-mail:* blissj@wpunj.edu.

GRADUATE PROGRAMS

Expenses (2009–10) *Tuition, state resident:* part-time $780 per credit. *Tuition, nonresident:* part-time $780 per credit. *Required fees:* part-time $130 per credit.

Financial Aid 15% of graduate students in nursing programs received some form of financial aid in 2008–09. Research assistantships with tuition reimbursements available, unspecified assistantships available. *Financial aid application deadline:* 4/1.

Contact Dr. Kem Louie, Director, Graduate Program, Department of Nursing, William Paterson University of New Jersey, 300 Pompton Road, W240, Wayne, NJ 07470. *Telephone:* 973-720-3511. *Fax:* 973-720-3517. *E-mail:* louiek@wpunj.edu.

MASTER'S DEGREE PROGRAM

Degree MSN

Available Programs Master's; Master's for Nurses with Non-Nursing Degrees.

Concentrations Available Nursing administration; nursing education. *Clinical nurse specialist programs in:* community health. *Nurse practitioner programs in:* adult health, family health.

Study Options Full-time and part-time.

Program Entrance Requirements Computer literacy, minimum overall college GPA of 3.0, transcript of college record, CPR certification, written essay, 2 letters of recommendation, nursing research course, physical assessment course, professional liability insurance/malpractice insurance, resume, statistics course, GRE General Test. *Application deadline:* Applications may be processed on a rolling basis for some programs. *Application fee:* $50.

Advanced Placement Credit given for nursing courses completed elsewhere dependent upon specific evaluations.

Degree Requirements 40 total credit hours, thesis or project.

POST-MASTER'S PROGRAM

Areas of Study *Clinical nurse specialist programs in:* school health. *Nurse practitioner programs in:* adult health.

NEW MEXICO

Eastern New Mexico University
Department of Allied Health–Nursing
Portales, New Mexico

http://www.enmu.edu/academics/undergrad/colleges/las/disorders-nursing

Founded in 1934

DEGREE • BSN

Nursing Program Faculty 5 (2% with doctorates).

Baccalaureate Enrollment 198
Women 90% **Men** 10% **Minority** 45% **International** 5% **Part-time** 95%

Distance Learning Courses Available.

Nursing Student Activities Nursing Honor Society, Student Nurses' Association.

Nursing Student Resources Academic advising; academic or career counseling; assistance for students with disabilities; bookstore; campus computer network; career placement assistance; computer lab; computer-assisted instruction; e-mail services; housing assistance; Internet; library services; other; resume preparation assistance; tutoring.

Library Facilities 325,122 volumes (100 in health, 50 in nursing); 21,537 periodical subscriptions (15 health-care related).

BACCALAUREATE PROGRAMS

Degree BSN

Available Programs RN Baccalaureate.

Study Options Full-time and part-time.

Online Degree Options Yes (online only).

Program Entrance Requirements Minimum overall college GPA of 2.0, transcript of college record, CPR certification, high school biology, high school chemistry, 2 years high school math, 2 years high school science, high school transcript, immunizations, interview, 3 letters of recommendation, minimum high school GPA of 2.5, minimum GPA in nursing prerequisites of 2.0, professional liability insurance/malpractice insurance, prerequisite course work, RN licensure. Transfer students are accepted. *Application deadline:* 9/4 (fall), 9/4 (winter), 1/19 (spring), 6/1 (summer).

Advanced Placement Credit given for nursing courses completed elsewhere dependent upon specific evaluations.

Financial Aid 100% of baccalaureate students in nursing programs received some form of financial aid in 2008–09.

Contact Leslie Denise Paternoster, Program Director, Department of Allied Health–Nursing, Eastern New Mexico University, 1500 South Avenue K, Station 12, Portales, NM 88130. *Telephone:* 575-562-2773. *Fax:* 575-562-2293. *E-mail:* leslie.paternoster@enmu.edu.

New Mexico State University
School of Nursing
Las Cruces, New Mexico

http://www.nmsu.edu/~nursing
Founded in 1888
DEGREES • BSN • MSN

Nursing Program Faculty 36 (37% with doctorates).

Baccalaureate Enrollment 292
Women 84% **Men** 16% **Minority** 49% **International** 1% **Part-time** 15%

Graduate Enrollment 42
Women 88% **Men** 12% **Minority** 24% **International** 1% **Part-time** 69%

Nursing Student Activities Sigma Theta Tau, Student Nurses' Association.

Nursing Student Resources Academic advising; academic or career counseling; assistance for students with disabilities; bookstore; campus computer network; computer lab; computer-assisted instruction; daycare for children of students; e-mail services; housing assistance; interactive nursing skills videos; Internet; learning resource lab; library services; nursing audiovisuals; paid internships; remedial services; skills, simulation, or other laboratory; tutoring.

Library Facilities 1.8 million volumes (33,000 in health, 17,500 in nursing); 4,402 periodical subscriptions (620 health-care related).

BACCALAUREATE PROGRAMS
Degree BSN

Available Programs Accelerated Baccalaureate for Second Degree; Generic Baccalaureate; RN Baccalaureate.

Study Options Full-time.

Program Entrance Requirements Minimum overall college GPA of 3.0, transcript of college record, CPR certification, immunizations, minimum GPA in nursing prerequisites of 2.0, prerequisite course work. Transfer students are accepted.

Advanced Placement Credit given for nursing courses completed elsewhere dependent upon specific evaluations.

Contact *Telephone:* 505-646-3534. *Fax:* 505-646-6166.

GRADUATE PROGRAMS
Contact *Telephone:* 505-646-8170. *Fax:* 505-646-2167.

MASTER'S DEGREE PROGRAM
Degree MSN

Available Programs Master's.

Concentrations Available Nursing administration. *Clinical nurse specialist programs in:* community health, medical-surgical, psychiatric/mental health. *Nurse practitioner programs in:* psychiatric/mental health.

Study Options Full-time and part-time.

Program Entrance Requirements Minimum overall college GPA of 3.0, transcript of college record, CPR certification, written essay, immunizations, 3 letters of recommendation, resume, statistics course.

Advanced Placement Credit given for nursing courses completed elsewhere dependent upon specific evaluations.

Degree Requirements 50 total credit hours, comprehensive exam.

CONTINUING EDUCATION PROGRAM
Contact *Telephone:* 505-646-3812. *Fax:* 505-646-2167.

University of New Mexico
College of Nursing
Albuquerque, New Mexico

http://hsc.unm.edu/consg/
Founded in 1889
DEGREES • BSN • MSN • MSN/MALAS • MSN/MPA • MSN/MPH • PHD

Nursing Program Faculty 48 (60% with doctorates).

Baccalaureate Enrollment 291
Women 86% **Men** 14% **Minority** 53% **Part-time** 44%

Graduate Enrollment 205
Women 93% **Men** 7% **Minority** 32% **Part-time** 73%

Distance Learning Courses Available.

Nursing Student Activities Sigma Theta Tau, Student Nurses' Association.

Nursing Student Resources Academic advising; assistance for students with disabilities; bookstore; campus computer network; career placement assistance; computer lab; computer-assisted instruction; daycare for children of students; e-mail services; housing assistance; interactive nursing skills videos; Internet; learning resource lab; library services; nursing audiovisuals; remedial services; skills, simulation, or other laboratory.

Library Facilities 3.4 million volumes (154,459 in health, 12,629 in nursing); 71,416 periodical subscriptions (2,039 health-care related).

BACCALAUREATE PROGRAMS
Degree BSN

Available Programs Accelerated Baccalaureate for Second Degree; Generic Baccalaureate; RN Baccalaureate.

Study Options Full-time.

Program Entrance Requirements Minimum overall college GPA of 3.0, transcript of college record, written essay, 2 letters of recommendation, minimum GPA in nursing prerequisites of 3.0, prerequisite course work. Transfer students are accepted. *Application deadline:* 2/15 (fall), 9/15 (spring). *Application fee:* $50.

Advanced Placement Credit given for nursing courses completed elsewhere dependent upon specific evaluations.

Financial Aid 70% of baccalaureate students in nursing programs received some form of financial aid in 2008–09.

Contact Ms. Ann Marie Oechsler, Director of Student Services, College of Nursing, University of New Mexico, MSC09 5350, 1 University of New Mexico, Albuquerque, NM 87131-0001. *Telephone:* 505-272-4223. *Fax:* 505-272-3970. *E-mail:* aoechsler@salud.unm.edu.

GRADUATE PROGRAMS
Financial Aid 40% of graduate students in nursing programs received some form of financial aid in 2008–09. 1 research assistantship with partial tuition reimbursement available (averaging $6,000 per year), 9 teaching assistantships with partial tuition reimbursements available (averaging $6,400 per year) were awarded; scholarships and traineeships also available. *Financial aid application deadline:* 3/1.

Contact Ms. Karen Wells, Senior Academic Advisor, College of Nursing, University of New Mexico, MSC09 5350, NRPH Building, Room 152, 1 University of New Mexico, Albuquerque, NM 87131-0001. *Telephone:* 505-272-4223. *Fax:* 505-272-3970. *E-mail:* kwells@salud.unm.edu.

MASTER'S DEGREE PROGRAM
Degrees MSN; MSN/MALAS; MSN/MPA; MSN/MPH

Available Programs Master's.

University of New Mexico (continued)

Concentrations Available Nurse-midwifery; nursing administration; nursing education. *Nurse practitioner programs in:* acute care, family health, pediatric.

Study Options Full-time and part-time.

Online Degree Options Yes (online only).

Program Entrance Requirements Clinical experience, minimum overall college GPA of 3.0, transcript of college record, interview, 3 letters of recommendation, resume, GRE General Test. *Application deadline:* 2/15 (fall), 10/15 (spring). *Application fee:* $50.

Advanced Placement Credit given for nursing courses completed elsewhere dependent upon specific evaluations.

Degree Requirements 32 total credit hours, thesis or project, comprehensive exam.

POST-MASTER'S PROGRAM

Areas of Study Nurse-midwifery; nursing administration; nursing education. *Nurse practitioner programs in:* acute care, family, health, pediatric.

DOCTORAL DEGREE PROGRAM

Degree PhD

Available Programs Doctorate.

Areas of Study Health policy, nursing research.

Program Entrance Requirements Clinical experience, minimum overall college GPA of 3.0, interview by faculty committee, 3 letters of recommendation, MSN or equivalent, vita, writing sample. Application deadline: 2/15 (summer). Application fee: $50.

Degree Requirements 69 total credit hours, dissertation.

University of Phoenix–New Mexico Campus
College of Health and Human Services
Albuquerque, New Mexico

DEGREES • BSN • MSN • MSN/ED D

Nursing Program Faculty 18 (13% with doctorates).

Baccalaureate Enrollment 24
Women 100% **Minority** 33.3%

Graduate Enrollment 14
Women 100% **Minority** 21.43%

Nursing Student Activities Sigma Theta Tau.

Nursing Student Resources Academic advising; academic or career counseling; assistance for students with disabilities; bookstore; campus computer network; computer lab; computer-assisted instruction; e-mail services; interactive nursing skills videos; Internet; learning resource lab; library services; nursing audiovisuals; remedial services; skills, simulation, or other laboratory; tutoring.

Library Facilities 16,781 periodical subscriptions (1,300 health-care related).

BACCALAUREATE PROGRAMS

Degree BSN

Available Programs Accelerated Baccalaureate.

Site Options Santa Fe, NM; Santa Teresa, NM.

Study Options Full-time.

Program Entrance Requirements Transcript of college record, CPR certification, immunizations, 1 letter of recommendation, RN licensure. Transfer students are accepted.

Advanced Placement Credit by examination available. Credit given for nursing courses completed elsewhere dependent upon specific evaluations.

Expenses (2009–10) *Tuition:* full-time $8640. *Required fees:* full-time $600.

Contact Campus College Chair, Nursing, College of Health and Human Services, University of Phoenix–New Mexico Campus, 7471 Pan American Freeway NE, Albuquerque, NM 87109-4645. *Telephone:* 505-821-4800.

GRADUATE PROGRAMS

Expenses (2009–10) *Tuition:* full-time $11,640. *Required fees:* full-time $760.

Financial Aid Institutionally sponsored loans and scholarships available.

Contact Campus College Chair, Nursing, College of Health and Human Services, University of Phoenix–New Mexico Campus, 7471 Pan American Freeway NE, Albuquerque, NM 87109-4645. *Telephone:* 505-821-4800.

MASTER'S DEGREE PROGRAM

Degrees MSN; MSN/Ed D

Available Programs Master's.

Concentrations Available Nursing administration; nursing education.

Site Options Santa Fe, NM; Santa Teresa, NM.

Study Options Full-time.

Online Degree Options Yes.

Program Entrance Requirements Clinical experience, computer literacy, minimum overall college GPA of 2.5, transcript of college record. *Application deadline:* Applications may be processed on a rolling basis for some programs. *Application fee:* $45.

Advanced Placement Credit given for nursing courses completed elsewhere dependent upon specific evaluations.

Degree Requirements 39 total credit hours, thesis or project.

Western New Mexico University
Nursing Department
Silver City, New Mexico

Founded in 1893

DEGREE • BSN

Library Facilities 245,146 volumes; 236 periodical subscriptions.

BACCALAUREATE PROGRAMS

Degree BSN

Available Programs RN Baccalaureate.

Program Entrance Requirements Minimum overall college GPA of 2.75, CPR certification, professional liability insurance/malpractice insurance, RN licensure. Transfer students are accepted.

Contact Gary Cook, Nursing, Nursing Department, Western New Mexico University, PO Box 680, Silver City, NM 88062. *Telephone:* 575-574-5140. *E-mail:* cookg@wnmu.edu.

NEW YORK

Adelphi University
School of Nursing
Garden City, New York

http://www.adelphi.edu

Founded in 1896

DEGREES • BS • MS • MS/MBA • PHD

Nursing Program Faculty 141 (22% with doctorates).

Baccalaureate Enrollment 880
Women 90% **Men** 10% **Minority** 40% **International** 1% **Part-time** 21%

Graduate Enrollment 123
Women 88% **Men** 12% **Minority** 55% **Part-time** 100%

Distance Learning Courses Available.

Nursing Student Activities Nursing Honor Society, Sigma Theta Tau, Student Nurses' Association, nursing club.

Nursing Student Resources Academic advising; academic or career counseling; assistance for students with disabilities; bookstore; campus computer network; career placement assistance; computer lab; computer-assisted instruction; daycare for children of students; e-mail services; employment services for current students; externships; housing assistance; interactive nursing skills videos; Internet; learning resource lab; library services; nursing audiovisuals; paid internships; placement services for program completers; remedial services; resume preparation assistance; skills, simulation, or other laboratory; tutoring; unpaid internships.

Library Facilities 588,987 volumes (29,918 in health, 2,666 in nursing); 32,138 periodical subscriptions (364 health-care related).

BACCALAUREATE PROGRAMS

Degree BS

Available Programs ADN to Baccalaureate; Accelerated Baccalaureate for Second Degree; Baccalaureate for Second Degree; Generic Baccalaureate; LPN to Baccalaureate; LPN to RN Baccalaureate; RN Baccalaureate.

Site Options Manhattan, NY.

Study Options Full-time and part-time.

Program Entrance Requirements Minimum overall college GPA of 3.0, transcript of college record, written essay, health exam, high school foreign language, 3 years high school math, 3 years high school science, high school transcript, immunizations, interview, 2 letters of recommendation, minimum high school GPA of 3.0. Transfer students are accepted. *Application deadline:* Applications may be processed on a rolling basis for some programs. *Application fee:* $50.

Advanced Placement Credit by examination available.

Expenses (2009–10) *Tuition:* full-time $26,500; part-time $780 per credit. *International tuition:* $26,500 full-time. *Room and board:* $9990; room only: $7590 per academic year. *Required fees:* full-time $1250.

Financial Aid 90% of baccalaureate students in nursing programs received some form of financial aid in 2008–09. *Gift aid (need-based):* Federal Pell, FSEOG, state, private, college/university gift aid from institutional funds, United Negro College Fund, endowed-donor scholarships. *Loans:* Federal Nursing Student Loans, FFEL (Subsidized and Unsubsidized Stafford PLUS), Perkins, alternative loans. *Work-study:* Federal Work-Study, part-time campus jobs. *Financial aid application deadline (priority):* 3/1.

Contact Mrs. Christine Murphy, Director of Admissions, School of Nursing, Adelphi University, One South Avenue, Levermore Hall, Garden City, NY 11530. *Telephone:* 516-877-3050. *E-mail:* murphy2@adelphi.edu.

GRADUATE PROGRAMS

Expenses (2009–10) *Tuition:* full-time $12,975; part-time $865 per credit. *International tuition:* $12,975 full-time. *Room and board:* $9990; room only: $7590 per academic year. *Required fees:* full-time $600.

Financial Aid 25% of graduate students in nursing programs received some form of financial aid in 2008–09. 15 teaching assistantships (averaging $4,512 per year) were awarded; career-related internships or fieldwork, unspecified assistantships, and graduate achievement awards also available. Aid available to part-time students. *Financial aid application deadline:* 2/15.

Contact Mrs. Christine Murphy, Director of Admissions, School of Nursing, Adelphi University, One South Avenue, Levermore Hall, Garden City, NY 11530. *Telephone:* 516-877-3050. *Fax:* 516-877-3039. *E-mail:* murphy2@adelphi.edu.

MASTER'S DEGREE PROGRAM

Degrees MS; MS/MBA

Available Programs Master's.

Concentrations Available Health-care administration; nursing administration; nursing education. *Nurse practitioner programs in:* adult health.

Study Options Full-time and part-time.

Program Entrance Requirements Clinical experience, computer literacy, minimum overall college GPA of 3.0, transcript of college record, CPR certification, written essay, immunizations, interview, 2 letters of recommendation, professional liability insurance/malpractice insurance, resume, statistics course. *Application deadline:* Applications may be processed on a rolling basis for some programs. *Application fee:* $50.

Advanced Placement Credit by examination available. Credit given for nursing courses completed elsewhere dependent upon specific evaluations.

Degree Requirements 42 total credit hours, thesis or project.

POST-MASTER'S PROGRAM

Areas of Study Health-care administration; nursing administration; nursing education. *Nurse practitioner programs in:* adult health.

DOCTORAL DEGREE PROGRAM

Degree PhD

Available Programs Doctorate.

Areas of Study Faculty preparation, health-care systems, nursing administration, nursing education, nursing research.

Program Entrance Requirements Minimum overall college GPA of 3.5, interview by faculty committee, interview, 2 letters of recommendation, MSN or equivalent, statistics course, vita, writing sample, GRE. Application deadline: 2/1 (fall). Application fee: $50.

Degree Requirements 54 total credit hours, dissertation, oral exam, written exam.

CONTINUING EDUCATION PROGRAM

Contact Mrs. Karen Pappas, Director, Professional Development and Lifelong Learning, School of Nursing, Adelphi University, One South Avenue, Garden City, NY 11530. *Telephone:* 516-877-4554. *Fax:* 516-877-4558. *E-mail:* pappas@adelphi.edu.

The College at Brockport, State University of New York
Department of Nursing
Brockport, New York

http://www.brockport.edu

Founded in 1867

DEGREE • BSN

Nursing Program Faculty 15 (40% with doctorates).

Baccalaureate Enrollment 148

Women 94% **Men** 6% **Minority** 14% **International** 1% **Part-time** 9%

Distance Learning Courses Available.

Nursing Student Activities Nursing Honor Society, Sigma Theta Tau, Student Nurses' Association.

Nursing Student Resources Academic advising; academic or career counseling; assistance for students with disabilities; bookstore; campus computer network; career placement assistance; computer lab; computer-assisted instruction; e-mail services; interactive nursing skills videos; Internet; learning resource lab; library services; nursing audiovisuals; remedial services; resume preparation assistance; skills, simulation, or other laboratory; tutoring.

Library Facilities 18,952 volumes in health, 1,065 volumes in nursing; 257 periodical subscriptions health-care related.

BACCALAUREATE PROGRAMS

Degree BSN

Available Programs ADN to Baccalaureate; Accelerated RN Baccalaureate; Generic Baccalaureate.

Study Options Full-time and part-time.

Program Entrance Requirements Minimum overall college GPA of 2.75, transcript of college record, CPR certification, health exam, health insurance, high school transcript, immunizations, minimum GPA in nursing prerequisites of 2.0, prerequisite course work. Transfer students are accepted. *Application deadline:* 1/15 (fall).

Advanced Placement Credit given for nursing courses completed elsewhere dependent upon specific evaluations.

Expenses (2009–10) *Tuition, state resident:* full-time $4970; part-time $207 per credit. *Tuition, nonresident:* full-time $12,870; part-time $536 per credit. *International tuition:* $12,870 full-time. *Room and board:* $9200 per academic year. *Required fees:* full-time $1138; part-time $47 per credit.

Financial Aid 66% of baccalaureate students in nursing programs received some form of financial aid in 2008–09. *Gift aid (need-based):* Federal Pell, FSEOG, state, private, college/university gift aid from institutional funds. *Loans:* Federal Nursing Student Loans, Federal Direct

The College at Brockport, State University of New York (continued)
(Subsidized and Unsubsidized Stafford PLUS), Perkins, alternative loans. *Work-study:* Federal Work-Study, part-time campus jobs. *Financial aid application deadline (priority):* 2/15.

Contact Dr. Linda Snell, RN, Chairperson, Department of Nursing, The College at Brockport, State University of New York, 350 New Campus Drive, Brockport, NY 14420-2988. *Telephone:* 585-395-2355. *Fax:* 585-395-5312. *E-mail:* lsnell@brockport.edu.

College of Mount Saint Vincent
Department of Nursing
Riverdale, New York

http://www.mountsaintvincent.edu/academics/ majors_and_programs/nursing2/nursing.htm

Founded in 1911

DEGREES • BS • MSN

Nursing Program Faculty 30 (90% with doctorates).

Baccalaureate Enrollment 490
Women 80% **Men** 20% **Minority** 80% **International** 10% **Part-time** 10%

Graduate Enrollment 80
Women 90% **Men** 10% **Minority** 80% **International** 10% **Part-time** 100%

Nursing Student Activities Sigma Theta Tau, Student Nurses' Association.

Nursing Student Resources Academic advising; academic or career counseling; bookstore; campus computer network; computer lab; computer-assisted instruction; e-mail services; employment services for current students; housing assistance; interactive nursing skills videos; Internet; learning resource lab; library services; nursing audiovisuals; paid internships; remedial services; resume preparation assistance; skills, simulation, or other laboratory; tutoring.

Library Facilities 104,158 volumes (5,304 in nursing).

BACCALAUREATE PROGRAMS
Degree BS

Available Programs ADN to Baccalaureate; Baccalaureate for Second Degree; Generic Baccalaureate; International Nurse to Baccalaureate; LPN to Baccalaureate; LPN to RN Baccalaureate; RN Baccalaureate.

Site Options Manhattan, NY.

Study Options Full-time and part-time.

Program Entrance Requirements Minimum overall college GPA of 2.7, transcript of college record, CPR certification, written essay, health exam, health insurance, high school biology, high school chemistry, high school foreign language, 3 years high school math, 3 years high school science, high school transcript, immunizations, 1 letter of recommendation, minimum high school GPA of 2.7, minimum GPA in nursing prerequisites of 3.0, prerequisite course work. Transfer students are accepted. *Application deadline:* 8/1 (fall), 1/5 (spring). Applications may be processed on a rolling basis for some programs. *Application fee:* $35.

Financial Aid 90% of baccalaureate students in nursing programs received some form of financial aid in 2007–08.

Contact Ms. Harriet Rothman, RN, Recruitment and Advisement Coordinator, Department of Nursing, College of Mount Saint Vincent, 6301 Riverdale Avenue, Riverdale, NY 10471-1093. *Telephone:* 718-405-3365. *Fax:* 718-405-3286. *E-mail:* harriet.rothman@mountsaintvincent.edu.

GRADUATE PROGRAMS
Financial Aid 90% of graduate students in nursing programs received some form of financial aid in 2007–08. Career-related internships or fieldwork available. *Financial aid application deadline:* 6/1.

Contact Dr. Carol Vicino, Chairperson, Graduate Program of Nursing, Department of Nursing, College of Mount Saint Vincent, 6301 Riverdale Avenue, Riverdale, NY 10471-1093. *Telephone:* 718-405-3351. *Fax:* 718-405-3286. *E-mail:* carol.vicino@mountsaintvincent.edu.

MASTER'S DEGREE PROGRAM
Degree MSN

Available Programs Master's; Master's for Nurses with Non-Nursing Degrees.

Concentrations Available Nursing administration; nursing education. *Clinical nurse specialist programs in:* adult health, family health, gerontology. *Nurse practitioner programs in:* adult health, family health.

Study Options Part-time.

Program Entrance Requirements Clinical experience, computer literacy, minimum overall college GPA of 3.0, transcript of college record, CPR certification, written essay, immunizations, interview, 2 letters of recommendation, nursing research course, physical assessment course, professional liability insurance/malpractice insurance, prerequisite course work, statistics course. *Application deadline:* 8/1 (fall), 1/5 (spring). *Application fee:* $35.

Degree Requirements 45 total credit hours, thesis or project.

POST-MASTER'S PROGRAM
Areas of Study Nursing education. *Nurse practitioner programs in:* adult health, family health.

The College of New Rochelle
School of Nursing
New Rochelle, New York

Founded in 1904

DEGREES • BSN • MS

Nursing Program Faculty 15 (75% with doctorates).

Baccalaureate Enrollment 521
Women 90% **Men** 10% **Minority** 67% **International** 1% **Part-time** 50%

Graduate Enrollment 121
Women 90% **Men** 10% **Minority** 18% **International** 1% **Part-time** 100%

Nursing Student Activities Nursing Honor Society, Sigma Theta Tau, Student Nurses' Association, nursing club.

Nursing Student Resources Academic advising; academic or career counseling; assistance for students with disabilities; bookstore; campus computer network; career placement assistance; computer lab; computer-assisted instruction; e-mail services; housing assistance; interactive nursing skills videos; Internet; learning resource lab; library services; nursing audiovisuals; other; remedial services; resume preparation assistance; skills, simulation, or other laboratory; tutoring.

Library Facilities 220,000 volumes (8,700 in health, 8,700 in nursing); 1,450 periodical subscriptions (165 health-care related).

BACCALAUREATE PROGRAMS
Degree BSN

Available Programs Accelerated Baccalaureate for Second Degree; Accelerated RN Baccalaureate; Baccalaureate for Second Degree; Generic Baccalaureate; RN Baccalaureate.

Site Options Bronx, NY.

Study Options Full-time and part-time.

Program Entrance Requirements Transcript of college record, CPR certification, written essay, health exam, health insurance, high school biology, high school chemistry, high school transcript, immunizations. Transfer students are accepted. *Application deadline:* 3/1 (fall), 10/1 (spring). *Application fee:* $35.

Advanced Placement Credit by examination available. Credit given for nursing courses completed elsewhere dependent upon specific evaluations.

Expenses (2008–09) *Tuition:* full-time $24,592; part-time $828 per credit. *Room and board:* $9200 per academic year.

Financial Aid 80% of baccalaureate students in nursing programs received some form of financial aid in 2007–08.

Contact Dr. Mary Alice Donius, Dean, School of Nursing, The College of New Rochelle, 29 Castle Place, New Rochelle, NY 10805-2308. *Telephone:* 914-654-5803. *Fax:* 914-654-5994. *E-mail:* mdonius@cnr.edu.

GRADUATE PROGRAMS
Expenses (2008–09) *Tuition:* part-time $724 per credit.

Financial Aid 75% of graduate students in nursing programs received some form of financial aid in 2007–08.

Contact Dr. Mary Alice Donius, Dean, School of Nursing, The College of New Rochelle, 29 Castle Place, New Rochelle, NY 10805-2308. *Telephone:* 914-654-5803. *Fax:* 914-654-5994. *E-mail:* mdonius@cnr.edu.

MASTER'S DEGREE PROGRAM

Degree MS

Available Programs Master's; RN to Master's.

Concentrations Available Health-care administration; nursing administration; nursing education. *Nurse practitioner programs in:* family health.

Site Options New Rochelle, NY.

Study Options Full-time and part-time.

Program Entrance Requirements Clinical experience, minimum overall college GPA of 3.0, transcript of college record, written essay, immunizations, interview, 2 letters of recommendation, physical assessment course, professional liability insurance/malpractice insurance, resume, statistics course. *Application fee:* $35.

Advanced Placement Credit given for nursing courses completed elsewhere dependent upon specific evaluations.

Degree Requirements 40 total credit hours, thesis or project.

POST-MASTER'S PROGRAM

Areas of Study Health-care administration; nursing administration; nursing education. *Clinical nurse specialist programs in:* palliative care. *Nurse practitioner programs in:* family health.

College of Staten Island of the City University of New York
Department of Nursing
Staten Island, New York

http://www.csi.cuny.edu/nursing

Founded in 1955

DEGREES • BS • MS

Nursing Program Faculty 59 (22% with doctorates).

Baccalaureate Enrollment 123
Women 94% **Men** 6% **Minority** 42% **Part-time** 77%

Graduate Enrollment 56
Women 100% **Minority** 31% **Part-time** 98%

Nursing Student Activities Nursing Honor Society, Sigma Theta Tau.

Nursing Student Resources Academic advising; academic or career counseling; assistance for students with disabilities; bookstore; campus computer network; career placement assistance; computer lab; computer-assisted instruction; daycare for children of students; e-mail services; externships; Internet; learning resource lab; library services; nursing audiovisuals; remedial services; resume preparation assistance; skills, simulation, or other laboratory; tutoring.

Library Facilities 235,000 volumes (3,700 in health, 1,500 in nursing); 28,000 periodical subscriptions (4,900 health-care related).

BACCALAUREATE PROGRAMS

Degree BS

Available Programs ADN to Baccalaureate; RN Baccalaureate.
Site Options Brooklyn, NY.
Study Options Full-time and part-time.
Program Entrance Requirements Minimum overall college GPA of 2.5, transcript of college record, CPR certification, health exam, health insurance, high school transcript, immunizations, minimum GPA in nursing prerequisites, professional liability insurance/malpractice insurance, prerequisite course work, RN licensure. Transfer students are accepted. *Application fee:* $65.
Advanced Placement Credit given for nursing courses completed elsewhere dependent upon specific evaluations.

Expenses (2009–10) *Tuition, area resident:* full-time $4000; part-time $170 per credit. *Tuition, state resident:* part-time $360 per credit. *Tuition, nonresident:* part-time $360 per credit. *Required fees:* full-time $298; part-time $151 per credit.

Financial Aid 40% of baccalaureate students in nursing programs received some form of financial aid in 2008–09. *Gift aid (need-based):* Federal Pell, FSEOG, state, private, college/university gift aid from institutional funds, Federal Nursing. *Loans:* Federal Direct (Subsidized and Unsubsidized Stafford PLUS), Perkins. *Work-study:* Federal Work-Study. *Financial aid application deadline (priority):* 3/31.

Contact Prof. Mary E. O'Donnell, RN, Chairperson, Department of Nursing, College of Staten Island of the City University of New York, 2800 Victory Boulevard, Marcus Hall, 5S-213, Staten Island, NY 10314. *Telephone:* 718-982-3810. *Fax:* 718-982-3813. *E-mail:* odonnellm@mail.csi.cuny.edu.

GRADUATE PROGRAMS

Expenses (2009–10) *Tuition, area resident:* full-time $6400; part-time $500 per credit. *Tuition, state resident:* part-time $500 per credit. *Tuition, nonresident:* part-time $500 per credit. *Required fees:* full-time $298; part-time $151 per credit.

Financial Aid 20% of graduate students in nursing programs received some form of financial aid in 2008–09.

Contact Dr. Margaret Lunney, Director, Graduate Program, Department of Nursing, College of Staten Island of the City University of New York, 2800 Victory Boulevard, Staten Island, NY 10314. *Telephone:* 718-982-3845. *Fax:* 718-982-3813. *E-mail:* lunney@mail.csi.cuny.edu.

MASTER'S DEGREE PROGRAM

Degree MS

Available Programs Master's.
Concentrations Available *Clinical nurse specialist programs in:* adult health, gerontology. *Nurse practitioner programs in:* adult health, gerontology.
Site Options Brooklyn, NY.
Study Options Full-time and part-time.
Program Entrance Requirements Clinical experience, minimum overall college GPA of 3.0, transcript of college record, written essay, immunizations, interview, 2 letters of recommendation, nursing research course, physical assessment course, professional liability insurance/malpractice insurance, prerequisite course work, statistics course. *Application deadline:* Applications may be processed on a rolling basis for some programs. *Application fee:* $65.
Advanced Placement Credit given for nursing courses completed elsewhere dependent upon specific evaluations.
Degree Requirements 48 total credit hours, thesis or project.

POST-MASTER'S PROGRAM

Areas of Study *Nurse practitioner programs in:* adult health, gerontology.

Columbia University
School of Nursing
New York, New York

http://www.nursing.columbia.edu

Founded in 1754

DEGREES • BS • DNP • MS • MSN/MBA • MSN/MPH

Nursing Program Faculty 68 (73% with doctorates).

Baccalaureate Enrollment 194
Women 92% **Men** 8% **Minority** 26% **International** 1%

Graduate Enrollment 343
Women 92% **Men** 8% **Minority** 27% **International** 2% **Part-time** 53%

Nursing Student Activities Sigma Theta Tau, nursing club.

Nursing Student Resources Academic advising; academic or career counseling; assistance for students with disabilities; bookstore; campus computer network; computer lab; computer-assisted instruction; daycare for children of students; e-mail services; employment services for current

Columbia University (continued)

students; housing assistance; interactive nursing skills videos; Internet; learning resource lab; library services; resume preparation assistance; skills, simulation, or other laboratory.

Library Facilities 9.5 million volumes (469,000 in health, 8,220 in nursing); 117,264 periodical subscriptions.

BACCALAUREATE PROGRAMS

Degree BS

Available Programs Accelerated Baccalaureate; Accelerated Baccalaureate for Second Degree; Accelerated RN Baccalaureate.

Study Options Full-time.

Program Entrance Requirements Transcript of college record, written essay, 3 letters of recommendation, prerequisite course work. *Application deadline:* 11/17 (summer). *Application fee:* $65.

Advanced Placement Credit by examination available. Credit given for nursing courses completed elsewhere dependent upon specific evaluations.

Expenses (2009–10) *Tuition:* full-time $66,352. *International tuition:* $66,352 full-time. *Room and board:* room only: $7000 per academic year. *Required fees:* full-time $2500.

Financial Aid 99% of baccalaureate students in nursing programs received some form of financial aid in 2008–09. *Gift aid (need-based):* Federal Pell, FSEOG, state, private, college/university gift aid from institutional funds. *Loans:* FFEL (Subsidized and Unsubsidized Stafford PLUS), Perkins, alternative loans. *Work-study:* Federal Work-Study, part-time campus jobs. *Financial aid application deadline:* 3/1.

Contact Office of Admissions, School of Nursing, Columbia University, 617 West 168th Street, Suite 134, New York, NY 10032. *Telephone:* 212-305-5756. *Fax:* 212-305-3680. *E-mail:* nursing@columbia.edu.

GRADUATE PROGRAMS

Expenses (2009–10) *Tuition:* part-time $1118 per credit. *Required fees:* part-time $400 per term.

Financial Aid 98% of graduate students in nursing programs received some form of financial aid in 2008–09. Research assistantships, teaching assistantships, Federal Work-Study and institutionally sponsored loans available. Aid available to part-time students.

Contact Office of Admissions, School of Nursing, Columbia University, 630 West 168th Street, Box 6, New York, NY 10032. *Telephone:* 212-305-5756. *Fax:* 212-305-3680. *E-mail:* nursing@columbia.edu.

MASTER'S DEGREE PROGRAM

Degrees MS; MSN/MBA; MSN/MPH

Available Programs Accelerated Master's for Non-Nursing College Graduates; Accelerated Master's for Nurses with Non-Nursing Degrees; Master's; Master's for Non-Nursing College Graduates; Master's for Nurses with Non-Nursing Degrees.

Concentrations Available Nurse anesthesia; nurse-midwifery. *Nurse practitioner programs in:* acute care, adult health, family health, gerontology, neonatal health, oncology, pediatric, psychiatric/mental health, women's health.

Study Options Full-time and part-time.

Program Entrance Requirements Transcript of college record, written essay, interview, 3 letters of recommendation, physical assessment course, prerequisite course work, resume, statistics course, GRE General Test. *Application deadline:* 4/15 (fall), 12/15 (summer). *Application fee:* $65.

Advanced Placement Credit by examination available. Credit given for nursing courses completed elsewhere dependent upon specific evaluations.

Degree Requirements 45 total credit hours, thesis or project, comprehensive exam.

POST-MASTER'S PROGRAM

Areas of Study Nurse anesthesia. *Nurse practitioner programs in:* acute care, adult health, family health, gerontology, neonatal health, oncology, pediatric, psychiatric/mental health, women's health.

DOCTORAL DEGREE PROGRAM

Degree DNP

Available Programs Doctorate; Post-Baccalaureate Doctorate.

Areas of Study Advanced practice nursing, clinical practice.

Program Entrance Requirements interview by faculty committee, interview, 3 letters of recommendation, statistics course, vita, writing sample, GRE General Test. Application deadline: 3/1 (fall). Application fee: $75.

Degree Requirements 40 total credit hours, dissertation, written exam, residency.

POSTDOCTORAL PROGRAM

Areas of Study Nursing informatics, nursing research.

Postdoctoral Program Contact Sarah Cook, Vice Dean, School of Nursing, Columbia University, 630 West 168th Street, Box 6, New York, NY 10032. *Telephone:* 212-305-3582. *Fax:* 212-305-1116. *E-mail:* ssc3@columbia.edu.

CONTINUING EDUCATION PROGRAM

Contact Sarah Cook, Vice Dean, School of Nursing, Columbia University, 630 West 168th Street, Box 6, New York, NY 10032. *Telephone:* 212-305-3582. *Fax:* 212-305-1116. *E-mail:* ssc3@columbia.edu.

See full description on page 486.

Concordia College–New York
Nursing Program
Bronxville, New York

Founded in 1881

DEGREE • BSN

Nursing Program Faculty 5 (66% with doctorates).

Baccalaureate Enrollment 36

Nursing Student Activities Nursing club.

Nursing Student Resources Academic advising; academic or career counseling; assistance for students with disabilities; bookstore; campus computer network; career placement assistance; computer lab; e-mail services; housing assistance; interactive nursing skills videos; Internet; learning resource lab; library services; nursing audiovisuals; resume preparation assistance; skills, simulation, or other laboratory; tutoring.

Library Facilities 71,500 volumes; 467 periodical subscriptions.

BACCALAUREATE PROGRAMS

Degree BSN

Available Programs Baccalaureate for Second Degree.

Contact Nursing Program, Nursing Program, Concordia College–New York, 171 White Plains Road, Bronxville, NY 10708. *Telephone:* 914-337-9300.

Daemen College
Department of Nursing
Amherst, New York

http://www.daemen.edu

Founded in 1947

DEGREES • BS • DNP • MS

Nursing Program Faculty 15 (75% with doctorates).

Baccalaureate Enrollment 250

Women 96% **Men** 4% **Minority** 3% **International** 2% **Part-time** 15%

Graduate Enrollment 150

Women 96% **Men** 4% **Minority** 8% **International** 6% **Part-time** 90%

Distance Learning Courses Available.

Nursing Student Activities Sigma Theta Tau, nursing club.

Nursing Student Resources Academic advising; academic or career counseling; assistance for students with disabilities; bookstore; campus computer network; career placement assistance; computer lab; computer-assisted instruction; e-mail services; Internet; learning resource lab; library services; nursing audiovisuals; placement services for program completers; remedial services; resume preparation assistance; skills, simulation, or other laboratory; tutoring.

Library Facilities 152,081 volumes (10,000 in health, 4,000 in nursing); 24,960 periodical subscriptions (250 health-care related).

BACCALAUREATE PROGRAMS

Degree BS

Available Programs ADN to Baccalaureate; Accelerated RN Baccalaureate; International Nurse to Baccalaureate; RN Baccalaureate.

Site Options Jamestown, NY; Olean, NY.

Study Options Full-time and part-time.

Program Entrance Requirements Minimum overall college GPA of 2.0, transcript of college record, immunizations, minimum GPA in nursing prerequisites of 2.0, prerequisite course work. Transfer students are accepted. *Application deadline:* Applications may be processed on a rolling basis for some programs.

Advanced Placement Credit given for nursing courses completed elsewhere dependent upon specific evaluations.

Expenses (2009–10) *Tuition:* full-time $10,125; part-time $340 per credit hour. *International tuition:* $10,125 full-time. *Room and board:* $8800 per academic year. *Required fees:* full-time $160; part-time $80 per term.

Financial Aid 100% of baccalaureate students in nursing programs received some form of financial aid in 2008–09.

Contact Dr. Mary Lou Rusin, Professor and Chair, Department of Nursing, Daemen College, 4380 Main Street, Amherst, NY 14226. *Telephone:* 716-839-8387. *Fax:* 716-839-8403. *E-mail:* mrusin@daemen.edu.

GRADUATE PROGRAMS

Expenses (2009–10) *Tuition:* full-time $13,860; part-time $770 per credit hour. *International tuition:* $13,860 full-time.

Financial Aid 75% of graduate students in nursing programs received some form of financial aid in 2008–09. Institutionally sponsored loans and scholarships available. *Financial aid application deadline:* 2/15.

Contact Dr. Mary Lou Rusin, Professor and Chair, Department of Nursing, Daemen College, 4380 Main Street, Amherst, NY 14226. *Telephone:* 716-839-8387. *Fax:* 716-839-8403. *E-mail:* mrusin@daemen.edu.

MASTER'S DEGREE PROGRAM

Degree MS

Available Programs Accelerated AD/RN to Master's; Accelerated RN to Master's; Master's; RN to Master's.

Concentrations Available Health-care administration; nursing education. *Clinical nurse specialist programs in:* palliative care. *Nurse practitioner programs in:* adult health.

Study Options Full-time and part-time.

Program Entrance Requirements Clinical experience, minimum overall college GPA of 3.25, transcript of college record, written essay, immunizations, interview, 3 letters of recommendation, statistics course. *Application deadline:* Applications may be processed on a rolling basis for some programs. *Application fee:* $25.

Advanced Placement Credit given for nursing courses completed elsewhere dependent upon specific evaluations.

Degree Requirements 30 total credit hours, thesis or project.

POST-MASTER'S PROGRAM

Areas of Study Health-care administration; nursing education. *Clinical nurse specialist programs in:* palliative care. *Nurse practitioner programs in:* adult health.

DOCTORAL DEGREE PROGRAM

Degree DNP

Available Programs Doctorate.

Areas of Study Advanced practice nursing.

Program Entrance Requirements Minimum overall college GPA of 3.25, interview, 3 letters of recommendation, statistics course, vita, writing sample. Application deadline: Applications may be processed on a rolling basis for some programs. Application fee: $25.

Degree Requirements 36 total credit hours, dissertation.

Dominican College
Department of Nursing
Orangeburg, New York

Founded in 1952

DEGREES • BSN • M SC N

Nursing Program Faculty 14 (21% with doctorates).

Baccalaureate Enrollment 182
Women 87% **Men** 13% **Minority** 44% **International** 40% **Part-time** 43%

Graduate Enrollment 37
Women 100% **Minority** 66% **International** 60% **Part-time** 100%

Nursing Student Activities Nursing Honor Society, Sigma Theta Tau, Student Nurses' Association.

Nursing Student Resources Academic advising; academic or career counseling; assistance for students with disabilities; bookstore; campus computer network; career placement assistance; computer lab; computer-assisted instruction; e-mail services; externships; Internet; learning resource lab; library services; nursing audiovisuals; paid internships; remedial services; resume preparation assistance; skills, simulation, or other laboratory; tutoring.

Library Facilities 5,650 volumes in health; 235 periodical subscriptions health-care related.

BACCALAUREATE PROGRAMS

Degree BSN

Available Programs Accelerated Baccalaureate for Second Degree; Accelerated LPN to Baccalaureate; Accelerated RN Baccalaureate; Generic Baccalaureate; LPN to Baccalaureate; RN Baccalaureate.

Study Options Full-time and part-time.

Program Entrance Requirements Minimum overall college GPA of 2.7, transcript of college record, CPR certification, health exam, health insurance, high school transcript, immunizations, minimum GPA in nursing prerequisites of 2.0, professional liability insurance/malpractice insurance, prerequisite course work. Transfer students are accepted.

Advanced Placement Credit by examination available. Credit given for nursing courses completed elsewhere dependent upon specific evaluations.

Contact *Telephone:* 845-848-6051. *Fax:* 845-398-4891.

GRADUATE PROGRAMS

Contact *Telephone:* 845-848-6026. *Fax:* 845-398-4891.

MASTER'S DEGREE PROGRAM

Degree M Sc N

Available Programs Master's.

Concentrations Available *Nurse practitioner programs in:* family health.

Study Options Full-time and part-time.

Program Entrance Requirements Clinical experience, minimum overall college GPA of 3.0, transcript of college record, written essay, immunizations, 3 letters of recommendation, nursing research course, physical assessment course, professional liability insurance/malpractice insurance, prerequisite course work, statistics course.

Degree Requirements 42 total credit hours, thesis or project.

D'Youville College
Department of Nursing
Buffalo, New York

http://www.dyc.edu/academics/nursing/

Founded in 1908

DEGREES • BSN • MS

Nursing Program Faculty 41 (20% with doctorates).

Baccalaureate Enrollment 492
Women 90% **Men** 10% **Minority** 20% **International** 10% **Part-time** 30%

D'Youville College (continued)
Graduate Enrollment 115
Women 96% **Men** 4% **Minority** 10% **International** 35% **Part-time** 40%
Distance Learning Courses Available.

Nursing Student Activities Sigma Theta Tau, Student Nurses' Association.

Nursing Student Resources Academic advising; academic or career counseling; assistance for students with disabilities; bookstore; campus computer network; career placement assistance; computer lab; computer-assisted instruction; e-mail services; externships; interactive nursing skills videos; Internet; learning resource lab; library services; nursing audiovisuals; paid internships; placement services for program completers; remedial services; resume preparation assistance; skills, simulation, or other laboratory; tutoring.

Library Facilities 116,237 volumes (100,000 in health, 17,000 in nursing); 725 periodical subscriptions (171 health-care related).

■ A current worldwide shortage in nursing leaves the door wide open for qualified nurses. D'Youville College has been educating nurses since 1942, and its nursing program is one of the largest four-year, private-college nursing programs in the country. The faculty members are hardworking and dedicated. Classes are small, which permits much individualized attention. Baccalaureate graduates who wish to continue their education can choose from three master's programs at D'Youville College. Registered nurses enrolled in the B.S.N. program have the option of completing some of their major courses via distance learning. D'Youville also offers a combined bachelor's/master's program for RNs and traditional students.

BACCALAUREATE PROGRAMS

Degree BSN

Available Programs Generic Baccalaureate; RN Baccalaureate.
Site Options Buffalo, NY.
Study Options Full-time and part-time.
Program Entrance Requirements Minimum overall college GPA of 2.5, transcript of college record, health exam, health insurance, high school biology, high school chemistry, 1 year of high school math, 1 year of high school science, high school transcript, immunizations, minimum high school GPA of 2.0, minimum high school rank 50%, minimum GPA in nursing prerequisites of 2.0, professional liability insurance/malpractice insurance, prerequisite course work. Transfer students are accepted.
Advanced Placement Credit given for nursing courses completed elsewhere dependent upon specific evaluations.
Financial Aid 90% of baccalaureate students in nursing programs received some form of financial aid in 2007–08. *Gift aid (need-based):* Federal Pell, FSEOG, state, private, college/university gift aid from institutional funds. *Loans:* Federal Nursing Student Loans, FFEL (Subsidized and Unsubsidized Stafford PLUS), Perkins, college/university. *Work-study:* Federal Work-Study, part-time campus jobs. *Financial aid application deadline (priority):* 3/1.
Contact Mr. Ron Dannecker, Director of Admissions, Department of Nursing, D'Youville College, 320 Porter Avenue, Buffalo, NY 14201. *Telephone:* 716-881-7600. *Fax:* 716-515-0679. *E-mail:* admiss@dyc.edu.

GRADUATE PROGRAMS

Financial Aid 1 research assistantship (averaging $3,000 per year) was awarded; Federal Work-Study and scholarships also available.
Contact Miss Linda Fisher, Director of Graduate Admissions, Department of Nursing, D'Youville College, 320 Porter Avenue, Buffalo, NY 14201. *Telephone:* 716-881-7744. *Fax:* 716-515-0679. *E-mail:* fisherl@dyc.edu.

MASTER'S DEGREE PROGRAM

Degree MS

Available Programs Master's; RN to Master's.
Concentrations Available Nursing education. *Clinical nurse specialist programs in:* community health, palliative care. *Nurse practitioner programs in:* family health.
Study Options Full-time and part-time.

Program Entrance Requirements Clinical experience, computer literacy, minimum overall college GPA of 3.0, transcript of college record, CPR certification, written essay, immunizations, interview, 2 letters of recommendation, nursing research course, physical assessment course, professional liability insurance/malpractice insurance, prerequisite course work, resume, statistics course.
Advanced Placement Credit given for nursing courses completed elsewhere dependent upon specific evaluations.
Degree Requirements 41 total credit hours, thesis or project.

POST-MASTER'S PROGRAM

Areas of Study *Nurse practitioner programs in:* family health.

See full description on page 492.

Elmira College
Program in Nursing Education
Elmira, New York

Founded in 1855
DEGREE • BS

Nursing Program Faculty 23 (9% with doctorates).

Baccalaureate Enrollment 160
Women 89% **Men** 11% **Minority** 13% **International** 3% **Part-time** 23%
Nursing Student Activities Sigma Theta Tau, Student Nurses' Association, nursing club.

Nursing Student Resources Academic advising; academic or career counseling; assistance for students with disabilities; bookstore; campus computer network; career placement assistance; computer lab; computer-assisted instruction; e-mail services; housing assistance; interactive nursing skills videos; Internet; learning resource lab; library services; nursing audiovisuals; placement services for program completers; resume preparation assistance; skills, simulation, or other laboratory; tutoring; unpaid internships.

Library Facilities 203,343 volumes (7,461 in health, 5,200 in nursing); 337 periodical subscriptions (72 health-care related).

■ Many features distinguish the Elmira College nursing program. Entering students are admitted directly to the nursing program and do not have to qualify again provided they meet academic standards during their studies. Small classes and clinical groups contribute to the development of close relationships among students and faculty. Clinical experiences begin in the sophomore year and occur in a variety of clinical specialties, including obstetrics, pediatrics, physical rehabilitation, and critical care, at a variety of community-based health-care agencies as well as in acute-care hospitals. Curriculum emphasis is on health maintenance within the community. A 240-hour capstone internship provides excellent preparation for the transition from student to graduate. A strong liberal arts component and a required community service experience ensure a well-rounded graduate. Extracurricular activities are encouraged by the nursing faculty.

BACCALAUREATE PROGRAMS

Degree BS

Available Programs ADN to Baccalaureate; Generic Baccalaureate; RN Baccalaureate.
Study Options Full-time and part-time.
Program Entrance Requirements Minimum overall college GPA of 2.0, transcript of college record, CPR certification, written essay, health exam, health insurance, high school biology, high school chemistry, 3 years high school math, 3 years high school science, high school transcript, immunizations, 2 letters of recommendation, minimum high school GPA of 2.5. Transfer students are accepted. *Application deadline:* Applications may be processed on a rolling basis for some programs. *Application fee:* $100.

Advanced Placement Credit by examination available. Credit given for nursing courses completed elsewhere dependent upon specific evaluations.

Expenses (2009–10) *Tuition:* full-time $33,500; part-time $300 per credit hour. *Room and board:* $10,800 per academic year. *Required fees:* full-time $1600; part-time $100 per term.

Financial Aid 80% of baccalaureate students in nursing programs received some form of financial aid in 2008–09. *Gift aid (need-based):* Federal Pell, FSEOG, state, private, college/university gift aid from institutional funds. *Loans:* FFEL (Subsidized and Unsubsidized Stafford PLUS), Perkins, college/university. *Work-study:* Federal Work-Study, part-time campus jobs. *Financial aid application deadline (priority):* 2/1.

Contact Mrs. Julianna Baumann, Dean, Program in Nursing Education, Elmira College, One Park Place, Elmira, NY 14901. *Telephone:* 607-735-1724. *Fax:* 607-735-1718. *E-mail:* admissions@elmira.edu.

CONTINUING EDUCATION PROGRAM

Contact Dr. Lois Schoener, PhD, Professor of Nursing/Director of Nurse Education, Program in Nursing Education, Elmira College, One Park Place, Elmira, NY 14901. *Telephone:* 607-735-1890. *Fax:* 607-735-1159. *E-mail:* lschoener@elmira.edu.

Excelsior College
School of Nursing
Albany, New York

Founded in 1970
DEGREES • BS • MS

Distance Learning Courses Available.

Nursing Student Activities Sigma Theta Tau.

Nursing Student Resources Academic advising; academic or career counseling; assistance for students with disabilities; bookstore; computer-assisted instruction; e-mail services; Internet; learning resource lab; library services; nursing audiovisuals; other; resume preparation assistance; skills, simulation, or other laboratory; tutoring.

BACCALAUREATE PROGRAMS

Degree BS

Available Programs RN Baccalaureate.

Study Options Part-time.

Program Entrance Requirements Transcript of college record, high school transcript, RN licensure. Transfer students are accepted. *Application deadline:* Applications may be processed on a rolling basis for some programs.

Advanced Placement Credit by examination available. Credit given for nursing courses completed elsewhere dependent upon specific evaluations.

Contact Admissions Office, School of Nursing, Excelsior College, 7 Columbia Circle, Albany, NY 12203. *Telephone:* 518-464-8500. *Fax:* 518-464-8777. *E-mail:* admissions@excelsior.edu.

GRADUATE PROGRAMS

Financial Aid Scholarships and traineeships available.

Contact Admissions Office, School of Nursing, Excelsior College, 7 Columbia Circle, Albany, NY 12203. *Telephone:* 518-464-8500. *Fax:* 518-464-8777. *E-mail:* admissions@excelsior.edu.

MASTER'S DEGREE PROGRAM

Degree MS

Available Programs Master's; RN to Master's.

Concentrations Available Nursing administration; nursing education; nursing informatics.

Study Options Full-time and part-time.

Online Degree Options Yes (online only).

Program Entrance Requirements Computer literacy, minimum overall college GPA of 3, transcript of college record, written essay, resume. *Application deadline:* Applications may be processed on a rolling basis for some programs.

Advanced Placement Credit given for nursing courses completed elsewhere dependent upon specific evaluations.

Degree Requirements 39 total credit hours, thesis or project.

POST-MASTER'S PROGRAM

Areas of Study Nursing education.

Hartwick College
Department of Nursing
Oneonta, New York

http://www.hartwick.edu
Founded in 1797
DEGREE • BS

Nursing Program Faculty 11 (18% with doctorates).

Baccalaureate Enrollment 145
Women 93% **Men** 7% **Minority** 9% **International** 1% **Part-time** 12%

Nursing Student Activities Sigma Theta Tau, Student Nurses' Association.

Nursing Student Resources Academic advising; academic or career counseling; assistance for students with disabilities; bookstore; campus computer network; career placement assistance; computer lab; computer-assisted instruction; e-mail services; employment services for current students; externships; housing assistance; interactive nursing skills videos; Internet; learning resource lab; library services; nursing audiovisuals; placement services for program completers; remedial services; resume preparation assistance; skills, simulation, or other laboratory; tutoring; unpaid internships.

Library Facilities 311,063 volumes (5,697 in health, 1,199 in nursing); 720 periodical subscriptions (30 health-care related).

BACCALAUREATE PROGRAMS

Degree BS

Available Programs Accelerated Baccalaureate; Accelerated Baccalaureate for Second Degree; Generic Baccalaureate; RN Baccalaureate.

Site Options Cooperstown, NY; Albany, NY.

Study Options Full-time and part-time.

Program Entrance Requirements Minimum overall college GPA of 2.5, transcript of college record, CPR certification, written essay, health exam, high school biology, high school chemistry, high school foreign language, 3 years high school math, 2 years high school science, high school transcript, immunizations, 2 letters of recommendation, minimum GPA in nursing prerequisites of 2.5, professional liability insurance/malpractice insurance. Transfer students are accepted. *Application deadline:* Applications may be processed on a rolling basis for some programs. *Application fee:* $35.

Advanced Placement Credit given for nursing courses completed elsewhere dependent upon specific evaluations.

Expenses (2009–10) *Tuition:* full-time $32,550; part-time $1030 per credit. *Room and board:* $9075; room only: $4700 per academic year.

Financial Aid 96% of baccalaureate students in nursing programs received some form of financial aid in 2008–09. *Gift aid (need-based):* Federal Pell, FSEOG, state, private, college/university gift aid from institutional funds. *Loans:* Federal Nursing Student Loans, FFEL (Subsidized and Unsubsidized Stafford PLUS), Perkins, college/university, alternative loans. *Work-study:* Federal Work-Study, part-time campus jobs. *Financial aid application deadline:* 2/15.

Contact Dr. Jeanne-Marie E. Havener, RN, Chair and Associate Professor of Nursing, Department of Nursing, Hartwick College, Johnstone Science Center, 1 Hartwick Drive, Oneonta, NY 13820. *Telephone:* 607-431-4780. *Fax:* 607-431-4850. *E-mail:* havenerj@hartwick.edu.

Hunter College of the City University of New York

Hunter-Bellevue School of Nursing
New York, New York

http://www.hunter.cuny.edu/schoolhp/nursing

Founded in 1870

DEGREES • BS • MS • MS/MPH

Nursing Program Faculty 22 (56% with doctorates).

Nursing Student Activities Sigma Theta Tau.

Nursing Student Resources Academic advising; academic or career counseling; assistance for students with disabilities; bookstore; campus computer network; computer lab; computer-assisted instruction; e-mail services; interactive nursing skills videos; Internet; learning resource lab; library services; nursing audiovisuals.

Library Facilities 789,718 volumes (39,245 in health, 4,295 in nursing); 4,282 periodical subscriptions (375 health-care related).

BACCALAUREATE PROGRAMS

Degree BS

Available Programs Generic Baccalaureate; RN Baccalaureate.
Study Options Full-time.
Program Entrance Requirements Minimum overall college GPA of 2.5, CPR certification, health exam, immunizations, professional liability insurance/malpractice insurance, prerequisite course work. Transfer students are accepted.
Contact *Telephone:* 212-481-7598. *Fax:* 212-481-4427.

GRADUATE PROGRAMS

Contact *Telephone:* 212-481-4465. *Fax:* 212-481-4427.

MASTER'S DEGREE PROGRAM

Degrees MS; MS/MPH

Available Programs Master's.
Concentrations Available *Clinical nurse specialist programs in:* community health, medical-surgical, parent-child, psychiatric/mental health. *Nurse practitioner programs in:* adult health, gerontology, pediatric.
Study Options Full-time and part-time.
Program Entrance Requirements Clinical experience, minimum overall college GPA of 3.0, transcript of college record, written essay, immunizations, 2 letters of recommendation, resume, statistics course.
Degree Requirements 42 total credit hours, thesis or project.

POST-MASTER'S PROGRAM

Areas of Study *Nurse practitioner programs in:* pediatric.

CONTINUING EDUCATION PROGRAM

Contact *Telephone:* 212-650-3850. *Fax:* 212-772-3402.

Keuka College

Division of Nursing
Keuka Park, New York

http://www.keuka.edu/asap/nursing.htm

Founded in 1890

DEGREE • BS

Nursing Program Faculty 5 (20% with doctorates).

Baccalaureate Enrollment 238
Women 94% **Men** 6% **Minority** 4%

Distance Learning Courses Available.

Nursing Student Activities Sigma Theta Tau.

Nursing Student Resources Academic advising; academic or career counseling; assistance for students with disabilities; bookstore; campus computer network; computer lab; computer-assisted instruction; e-mail services; employment services for current students; interactive nursing skills videos; Internet; learning resource lab; library services; nursing audiovisuals; resume preparation assistance; tutoring.

Library Facilities 112,541 volumes (986 in health, 532 in nursing); 384 periodical subscriptions (48 health-care related).

BACCALAUREATE PROGRAMS

Degree BS

Available Programs Accelerated RN Baccalaureate.
Site Options Geneva, NY; Rochester, NY; Canandaigua, NY.
Study Options Full-time and part-time.
Program Entrance Requirements Minimum overall college GPA of 2.5, transcript of college record, CPR certification, health exam, immunizations, minimum GPA in nursing prerequisites of 2.5, prerequisite course work, RN licensure. Transfer students are accepted.
Advanced Placement Credit by examination available. Credit given for nursing courses completed elsewhere dependent upon specific evaluations.
Contact *Telephone:* 315-279-5393. *Fax:* 315-279-5407.

Lehman College of the City University of New York

Department of Nursing
Bronx, New York

http://www.lehman.cuny.edu/departments/

Founded in 1931

DEGREES • BS • DNS • MS

Nursing Program Faculty 43 (35% with doctorates).

Baccalaureate Enrollment 250
Women 80% **Men** 20% **Minority** 85% **International** 40%

Graduate Enrollment 120
Women 90% **Men** 10% **Minority** 75% **Part-time** 75%

Distance Learning Courses Available.

Nursing Student Activities Nursing Honor Society, Sigma Theta Tau, Student Nurses' Association, nursing club.

Nursing Student Resources Academic advising; academic or career counseling; assistance for students with disabilities; bookstore; campus computer network; career placement assistance; computer lab; computer-assisted instruction; daycare for children of students; e-mail services; employment services for current students; externships; interactive nursing skills videos; Internet; learning resource lab; library services; nursing audiovisuals; paid internships; placement services for program completers; resume preparation assistance; skills, simulation, or other laboratory; tutoring; unpaid internships.

Library Facilities 595,952 volumes (1,000 in health, 500 in nursing); 5,738 periodical subscriptions (200 health-care related).

BACCALAUREATE PROGRAMS

Degree BS

Available Programs Accelerated RN Baccalaureate; Baccalaureate for Second Degree; Generic Baccalaureate; International Nurse to Baccalaureate; RN Baccalaureate.
Site Options New York, NY; Queens, NY.
Study Options Full-time.
Online Degree Options Yes.
Program Entrance Requirements Minimum overall college GPA of 2.0, transcript of college record, health exam, high school transcript, immunizations, minimum GPA in nursing prerequisites of 2.75, professional liability insurance/malpractice insurance, prerequisite course work. Transfer students are accepted. *Application deadline:* 3/15 (fall).
Advanced Placement Credit given for nursing courses completed elsewhere dependent upon specific evaluations.

Expenses (2008–09) *Tuition, state resident:* full-time $4000; part-time $170 per credit. *Tuition, nonresident:* part-time $360 per credit. *Required fees:* full-time $290; part-time $88 per term.

Financial Aid 60% of baccalaureate students in nursing programs received some form of financial aid in 2007–08. *Gift aid (need-based):* Federal Pell, FSEOG, state, college/university gift aid from institutional funds. *Loans:* Federal Direct (Subsidized and Unsubsidized Stafford PLUS), Perkins. *Work-study:* Federal Work-Study. *Financial aid application deadline:* Continuous.

Contact Director of Undergraduate Programs, Department of Nursing, Lehman College of the City University of New York, 250 Bedford Park Boulevard West, Bronx, NY 10468. *Telephone:* 718-960-8214. *Fax:* 718-960-8488.

GRADUATE PROGRAMS

Expenses (2008–09) *Tuition, state resident:* full-time $6400; part-time $270 per credit. *Tuition, nonresident:* part-time $500 per credit. *Required fees:* full-time $290.

Financial Aid 25% of graduate students in nursing programs received some form of financial aid in 2007–08. Career-related internships or fieldwork, Federal Work-Study, and tuition waivers (partial) available. Aid available to part-time students. *Financial aid application deadline:* 5/15.

Contact Dr. Catherine Alicia Georges, Graduate Program, Department of Nursing, Lehman College of the City University of New York, 250 Bedford Park Boulevard West, Bronx, NY 10468. *Telephone:* 718-960-8213. *Fax:* 718-960-8488. *E-mail:* nursing@lehman.cuny.edu.

MASTER'S DEGREE PROGRAM

Degree MS

Available Programs Master's; Master's for Nurses with Non-Nursing Degrees.

Concentrations Available Nursing administration; nursing education. *Clinical nurse specialist programs in:* adult health, gerontology, parent-child. *Nurse practitioner programs in:* pediatric.

Site Options New York, NY.

Study Options Full-time and part-time.

Program Entrance Requirements Clinical experience, minimum overall college GPA of 3.0, transcript of college record, written essay, immunizations, interview, 2 letters of recommendation, professional liability insurance/malpractice insurance, prerequisite course work. *Application deadline:* 4/1 (fall), 11/1 (spring). Applications may be processed on a rolling basis for some programs. *Application fee:* $12.

Advanced Placement Credit given for nursing courses completed elsewhere dependent upon specific evaluations.

Degree Requirements 43 total credit hours.

DOCTORAL DEGREE PROGRAM

Degree DNS

Available Programs Doctorate.

Areas of Study Urban health.

Site Options New York, NY.

Program Entrance Requirements Clinical experience, minimum overall college GPA of 3.5, interview by faculty committee, interview, letters of recommendation, MSN or equivalent, statistics course, vita, writing sample. Application deadline: 4/1 (fall).

Degree Requirements 51 total credit hours, dissertation, oral exam, written exam, residency.

Le Moyne College

Nursing Programs
Syracuse, New York

Founded in 1946

DEGREES • BS • MS

Nursing Program Faculty 7 (50% with doctorates).

Baccalaureate Enrollment 150
Women 95% **Men** 5% **Minority** 5% **Part-time** 20%

Graduate Enrollment 40
Women 99% **Men** 1% **Minority** 1% **Part-time** 100%

Distance Learning Courses Available.

Nursing Student Activities Nursing Honor Society.

Nursing Student Resources Academic advising; academic or career counseling; assistance for students with disabilities; bookstore; campus computer network; career placement assistance; computer lab; computer-assisted instruction; e-mail services; employment services for current students; housing assistance; interactive nursing skills videos; Internet; learning resource lab; library services; nursing audiovisuals; placement services for program completers; remedial services; resume preparation assistance; skills, simulation, or other laboratory; tutoring.

Library Facilities 282,975 volumes; 57,438 periodical subscriptions.

BACCALAUREATE PROGRAMS

Degree BS

Available Programs ADN to Baccalaureate; RN Baccalaureate.

Study Options Full-time.

Program Entrance Requirements Minimum overall college GPA of 2.6, transcript of college record, CPR certification, written essay, health exam, health insurance, high school biology, high school chemistry, high school foreign language, high school math, high school science, high school transcript, immunizations, 2 letters of recommendation, minimum high school GPA of 3.0, minimum high school rank, minimum GPA in nursing prerequisites of 2.5, RN licensure. Transfer students are accepted. *Application deadline:* Applications may be processed on a rolling basis for some programs. *Application fee:* $50.

Advanced Placement Credit by examination available. Credit given for nursing courses completed elsewhere dependent upon specific evaluations.

Expenses (2009–10) *Tuition:* part-time $527 per credit.

Financial Aid 90% of baccalaureate students in nursing programs received some form of financial aid in 2008–09. *Gift aid (need-based):* Federal Pell, FSEOG, state, private, college/university gift aid from institutional funds. *Loans:* FFEL (Subsidized and Unsubsidized Stafford PLUS), Perkins. *Work-study:* Federal Work-Study, part-time campus jobs. *Financial aid application deadline (priority):* 2/1.

Contact Dr. Susan B. Bastable, Chair and Professor, Nursing Programs, Le Moyne College, 1419 Salt Springs Road, Syracuse, NY 13214. *Telephone:* 315-445-5435. *Fax:* 315-445-4602. *E-mail:* bastabsb@lemoyne.edu.

GRADUATE PROGRAMS

Expenses (2009–10) *Tuition:* part-time $547 per credit.

Financial Aid 50% of graduate students in nursing programs received some form of financial aid in 2008–09.

Contact Mrs. Kristen P. Trapasso, Director of Graduate Admissions, Nursing Programs, Le Moyne College, 1419 Salt Springs Road, Syracuse, NY 13214. *Telephone:* 315-445-4265. *Fax:* 315-445-6027. *E-mail:* trapaskp@lemoyne.edu.

MASTER'S DEGREE PROGRAM

Degree MS

Available Programs Master's; Master's for Nurses with Non-Nursing Degrees.

Concentrations Available Nursing administration; nursing education.

Study Options Full-time and part-time.

Program Entrance Requirements Computer literacy, minimum overall college GPA of 3.0, transcript of college record, written essay, immunizations, interview, 2 letters of recommendation, nursing research course, physical assessment course, resume, statistics course. *Application deadline:* Applications may be processed on a rolling basis for some programs. *Application fee:* $50.

Advanced Placement Credit given for nursing courses completed elsewhere dependent upon specific evaluations.

Degree Requirements 39 total credit hours, thesis or project.

POST-MASTER'S PROGRAM

Areas of Study Nursing administration; nursing education.

Long Island University, Brooklyn Campus

School of Nursing
Brooklyn, New York

http://www.liunet.edu

Founded in 1926

DEGREES • BS • MS

Nursing Program Faculty 95 (25% with doctorates).

Baccalaureate Enrollment 1,000
Women 88% **Men** 12% **Minority** 85% **Part-time** 20%

Graduate Enrollment 200
Women 90% **Men** 10% **Minority** 85% **Part-time** 83%

Nursing Student Activities Nursing Honor Society, Student Nurses' Association.

Nursing Student Resources Academic advising; academic or career counseling; assistance for students with disabilities; bookstore; campus computer network; computer lab; computer-assisted instruction; daycare for children of students; e-mail services; employment services for current students; interactive nursing skills videos; Internet; learning resource lab; library services; nursing audiovisuals; paid internships; remedial services; skills, simulation, or other laboratory; tutoring.

Library Facilities 314,565 volumes (11,000 in health, 850 in nursing); 329,366 periodical subscriptions (230 health-care related).

BACCALAUREATE PROGRAMS

Degree BS

Available Programs Generic Baccalaureate; International Nurse to Baccalaureate; RN Baccalaureate.

Site Options Brooklyn, NY.

Study Options Full-time and part-time.

Program Entrance Requirements Minimum overall college GPA of 2.75, transcript of college record, CPR certification, health exam, health insurance, high school biology, high school chemistry, 2 years high school math, 2 years high school science, high school transcript, immunizations, interview, minimum high school GPA of 3.0, minimum GPA in nursing prerequisites of 2.75, professional liability insurance/malpractice insurance, prerequisite course work. Transfer students are accepted. *Application deadline:* Applications may be processed on a rolling basis for some programs. *Application fee:* $30.

Advanced Placement Credit given for nursing courses completed elsewhere dependent upon specific evaluations.

Expenses (2009–10) *Tuition:* full-time $30,000; part-time $854 per credit. *International tuition:* $30,000 full-time. *Room and board:* $5000; room only: $3000 per academic year. *Required fees:* full-time $1350; part-time $700 per term.

Financial Aid 94% of baccalaureate students in nursing programs received some form of financial aid in 2008–09. *Gift aid (need-based):* Federal Pell, FSEOG, state, private, college/university gift aid from institutional funds, Scholarships for Disadvantaged Students (Nursing and Pharmacy). *Loans:* Federal Direct (Subsidized and Unsubsidized Stafford PLUS), Perkins, Federal Health Professions Student Loans, alternative loans. *Work-study:* Federal Work-Study, part-time campus jobs. *Financial aid application deadline:* Continuous.

Contact Prof. Dawn F. Kilts, Dean, School of Nursing, Long Island University, Brooklyn Campus, 1 University Plaza, Brooklyn, NY 11201. *Telephone:* 718-488-1509. *Fax:* 718-780-4019. *E-mail:* Dawn.Kilts@liu.edu.

GRADUATE PROGRAMS

Expenses (2009–10) *Tuition:* full-time $10,000; part-time $930 per credit. *International tuition:* $10,000 full-time. *Room and board:* $5000; room only: $3000 per academic year. *Required fees:* full-time $1200; part-time $350 per term.

Financial Aid 75% of graduate students in nursing programs received some form of financial aid in 2008–09. Scholarships and unspecified assistantships available. Aid available to part-time students.

Contact Prof. Susanne Flower, Director, School of Nursing, Long Island University, Brooklyn Campus, 1 University Plaza, Brooklyn, NY 11201. *Telephone:* 718-488-1059. *Fax:* 718-780-4019. *E-mail:* Susanne.Flower@liu.edu.

MASTER'S DEGREE PROGRAM

Degree MS

Available Programs Master's; RN to Master's.

Concentrations Available Nursing administration; nursing education. *Nurse practitioner programs in:* adult health, family health, gerontology.

Site Options Brooklyn, NY.

Study Options Full-time and part-time.

Program Entrance Requirements Clinical experience, minimum overall college GPA of 3.0, transcript of college record, immunizations, interview, 3 letters of recommendation, nursing research course, physical assessment course, professional liability insurance/malpractice insurance, prerequisite course work, resume, statistics course. *Application deadline:* Applications may be processed on a rolling basis for some programs.

Advanced Placement Credit given for nursing courses completed elsewhere dependent upon specific evaluations.

Degree Requirements 43 total credit hours, thesis or project.

POST-MASTER'S PROGRAM

Areas of Study *Nurse practitioner programs in:* adult health, family health, gerontology.

See full description on page 504.

Long Island University, C.W. Post Campus

Department of Nursing
Brookville, New York

http://www.cwpost.liu.edu/cwis/cwp/health/nursing

Founded in 1954

DEGREES • BS • MS • MSN/MA • MSN/MBA

Nursing Program Faculty 9 (22% with doctorates).

Baccalaureate Enrollment 67
Women 97% **Men** 3% **Minority** 30% **Part-time** 100%

Graduate Enrollment 63
Women 97% **Men** 3% **Minority** 25% **Part-time** 100%

Nursing Student Activities Student Nurses' Association.

Nursing Student Resources Academic advising; academic or career counseling; assistance for students with disabilities; bookstore; campus computer network; career placement assistance; computer lab; computer-assisted instruction; e-mail services; employment services for current students; housing assistance; interactive nursing skills videos; Internet; library services; nursing audiovisuals; placement services for program completers; remedial services; resume preparation assistance; skills, simulation, or other laboratory; tutoring.

Library Facilities 177,108 volumes (20,000 in health, 15,000 in nursing); 3,100 periodical subscriptions health-care related.

BACCALAUREATE PROGRAMS

Degree BS

Available Programs RN Baccalaureate.

Site Options Manhasset, NY.

Study Options Part-time.

Program Entrance Requirements Minimum overall college GPA of 2.5, transcript of college record, health exam, health insurance, immunizations, minimum GPA in nursing prerequisites of 2.5, professional liability insurance/malpractice insurance, prerequisite course work, RN licensure. Transfer students are accepted. *Application deadline:* Applications may be processed on a rolling basis for some programs. *Application fee:* $30.

Advanced Placement Credit by examination available. Credit given for nursing courses completed elsewhere dependent upon specific evaluations.

Expenses (2009–10) *Tuition:* full-time $27,368; part-time $854 per credit. *Room and board:* $10,540; room only: $6900 per academic year. *Required fees:* full-time $1400; part-time $7 per credit; part-time $300 per term.

Financial Aid 10% of baccalaureate students in nursing programs received some form of financial aid in 2008–09. *Gift aid (need-based):* Federal Pell, FSEOG, state, private, college/university gift aid from institutional funds. *Loans:* Federal Direct (Subsidized and Unsubsidized Stafford PLUS), Perkins, state, college/university. *Work-study:* Federal Work-Study, part-time campus jobs. *Financial aid application deadline:* 3/1.

Contact Dr. Mary Infantino, Chairperson and Associate Professor, Department of Nursing, Long Island University, C.W. Post Campus, Life Science, Room 270, 720 Northern Boulevard, Brookville, NY 11548-1300. *Telephone:* 516-299-2320. *Fax:* 516-299-2352. *E-mail:* mary.infantino@liu.edu.

GRADUATE PROGRAMS

Expenses (2009–10) *Tuition:* full-time $33,480; part-time $930 per credit. *International tuition:* $33,480 full-time. *Room and board:* $10,540; room only: $6900 per academic year. *Required fees:* full-time $1400; part-time $300 per credit; part-time $7 per term.

Financial Aid 10% of graduate students in nursing programs received some form of financial aid in 2008–09. Federal Work-Study and unspecified assistantships available. Aid available to part-time students. *Financial aid application deadline:* 5/15.

Contact Dr. Mary Infantino, Chairperson and Associate Professor, Department of Nursing, Long Island University, C.W. Post Campus, Life Science, Room 270, 720 Northern Boulevard, Brookville, NY 11548-1300. *Telephone:* 516-299-2320. *Fax:* 516-299-2352. *E-mail:* mary.infantino@liu.edu.

MASTER'S DEGREE PROGRAM

Degrees MS; MSN/MA; MSN/MBA

Available Programs Master's; Master's for Nurses with Non-Nursing Degrees.

Concentrations Available Nursing education. *Clinical nurse specialist programs in:* adult health. *Nurse practitioner programs in:* family health.

Study Options Part-time.

Program Entrance Requirements Clinical experience, minimum overall college GPA of 3.0, transcript of college record, written essay, immunizations, interview, 2 letters of recommendation, physical assessment course, professional liability insurance/malpractice insurance, prerequisite course work. *Application deadline:* Applications may be processed on a rolling basis for some programs. *Application fee:* $30.

Degree Requirements 33–46 total credit hours, thesis or project, comprehensive exam.

POST-MASTER'S PROGRAM

Areas of Study Nursing education. *Nurse practitioner programs in:* family health.

Medgar Evers College of the City University of New York

Department of Nursing
Brooklyn, New York

http://www.mec.cuny.edu/academic_affairs/ science_tech_school/nursing/nurse_home.htm

Founded in 1969

DEGREE • BSN

Nursing Program Faculty 7 (85% with doctorates).

Baccalaureate Enrollment 60
Women 98% **Men** 2% **Minority** 99% **Part-time** 90%

Nursing Student Activities Student Nurses' Association, nursing club.

Nursing Student Resources Academic advising; academic or career counseling; assistance for students with disabilities; bookstore; campus computer network; computer lab; computer-assisted instruction; daycare for children of students; e-mail services; interactive nursing skills videos; Internet; learning resource lab; library services; nursing audiovisuals; remedial services; resume preparation assistance; skills, simulation, or other laboratory; tutoring; unpaid internships.

Library Facilities 111,000 volumes; 24,410 periodical subscriptions.

BACCALAUREATE PROGRAMS

Degree BSN

Available Programs ADN to Baccalaureate; Accelerated RN Baccalaureate.

Study Options Full-time and part-time.

Program Entrance Requirements Minimum overall college GPA of 2.5, transcript of college record, CPR certification, health exam, health insurance, immunizations, professional liability insurance/malpractice insurance, prerequisite course work, RN licensure. Transfer students are accepted.

Advanced Placement Credit given for nursing courses completed elsewhere dependent upon specific evaluations.

Contact *Telephone:* 718-270-6230. *Fax:* 718-270-6235.

Mercy College
Program in Nursing
Dobbs Ferry, New York

Founded in 1951

DEGREES • BS • MS

Nursing Program Faculty 5 (2% with doctorates).

Baccalaureate Enrollment 333
Women 96% **Men** 4% **Minority** 75% **International** 1% **Part-time** 88%

Graduate Enrollment 100
Women 99% **Men** 1% **Minority** 50% **International** 10% **Part-time** 75%

Distance Learning Courses Available.

Nursing Student Activities Sigma Theta Tau, Student Nurses' Association.

Nursing Student Resources Academic advising; academic or career counseling; assistance for students with disabilities; bookstore; campus computer network; career placement assistance; computer lab; computer-assisted instruction; e-mail services; employment services for current students; Internet; learning resource lab; library services; nursing audiovisuals; remedial services; resume preparation assistance; skills, simulation, or other laboratory; tutoring.

Library Facilities 304,396 volumes (10,000 in health, 550 in nursing); 1,820 periodical subscriptions (180 health-care related).

BACCALAUREATE PROGRAMS

Degree BS

Available Programs Accelerated RN Baccalaureate; RN Baccalaureate.

Site Options Dobbs Ferry, NY.

Study Options Full-time and part-time.

Online Degree Options Yes.

Program Entrance Requirements Minimum overall college GPA, transcript of college record, written essay, immunizations, interview, minimum GPA in nursing prerequisites, prerequisite course work, RN licensure. Transfer students are accepted. *Application deadline:* Applications may be processed on a rolling basis for some programs.

Advanced Placement Credit given for nursing courses completed elsewhere dependent upon specific evaluations.

Expenses (2008–09) *Tuition:* full-time $7400; part-time $685 per credit. *International tuition:* $7400 full-time. *Room and board:* $4000; room only: $2000 per academic year. *Required fees:* full-time $240; part-time $120 per term.

Financial Aid 10% of baccalaureate students in nursing programs received some form of financial aid in 2007–08.

Contact Ms. Miriam Ford, Director, Program in Nursing, Mercy College, 555 Broadway, Dobbs Ferry, NY 10522. *Telephone:* 914-674-7865. *Fax:* 914-674-7623. *E-mail:* mford@mercy.edu.

GRADUATE PROGRAMS

Expenses (2008–09) *Tuition:* full-time $8220; part-time $685 per credit. *International tuition:* $8220 full-time. *Room and board:* $4500; room only: $2500 per academic year. *Required fees:* full-time $240; part-time $120 per term.

Mercy College (continued)

Financial Aid 75% of graduate students in nursing programs received some form of financial aid in 2007–08. Career-related internships or fieldwork, Federal Work-Study, scholarships, and unspecified assistantships available. Aid available to part-time students.

Contact Prof. Miriam Ford, RN, Associate Director, Program in Nursing, Mercy College, 555 Broadway, Dobbs Ferry, NY 10522. *Telephone:* 914-674-7867. *Fax:* 914-674-7623. *E-mail:* mford@mercy.edu.

MASTER'S DEGREE PROGRAM

Degree MS

Available Programs Accelerated Master's for Non-Nursing College Graduates; Accelerated Master's for Nurses with Non-Nursing Degrees; Accelerated RN to Master's; Master's; Master's for Non-Nursing College Graduates; Master's for Nurses with Non-Nursing Degrees.

Concentrations Available Health-care administration; nursing administration; nursing education.

Site Options Dobbs Ferry, NY.

Study Options Full-time and part-time.

Online Degree Options Yes.

Program Entrance Requirements Clinical experience, minimum overall college GPA of 3.0, transcript of college record, written essay, immunizations, interview, 2 letters of recommendation, professional liability insurance/malpractice insurance, resume. *Application deadline:* Applications may be processed on a rolling basis for some programs.

Advanced Placement Credit given for nursing courses completed elsewhere dependent upon specific evaluations.

Degree Requirements 36 total credit hours, thesis or project.

POST-MASTER'S PROGRAM

Areas of Study Nursing administration; nursing education.

Molloy College
Department of Nursing
Rockville Centre, New York

Founded in 1955

DEGREES • BS • MS

Nursing Program Faculty 152 (18% with doctorates).

Baccalaureate Enrollment 1,223
Women 90% **Men** 10% **Minority** 44% **International** 1% **Part-time** 38%

Graduate Enrollment 419
Women 93% **Men** 7% **Minority** 51% **International** .07% **Part-time** 98%

Nursing Student Activities Sigma Theta Tau, Student Nurses' Association.

Nursing Student Resources Academic advising; academic or career counseling; assistance for students with disabilities; bookstore; campus computer network; computer lab; computer-assisted instruction; e-mail services; interactive nursing skills videos; Internet; learning resource lab; library services; nursing audiovisuals; tutoring.

Library Facilities 115,000 volumes (2,320 in health, 1,750 in nursing); 680 periodical subscriptions (2,320 health-care related).

■ Undergraduate programs in nursing are designed to prepare the nurse generalist for practice in a variety of health-care settings. Eligible students may pursue one of the following options: baccalaureate degree in nursing, registered nurse baccalaureate completion program, LPN degree completion, and dual-degree programs for both second-degree students and registered nurse students. The Master of Science degree program combines academic, clinical, and research activities that educate graduate nurses for advanced clinical practice and role functions. Preparation as adult, pediatric, psychiatric, and family nurse practitioner is offered in both the master's and post-master's certificate programs. In addition, the post-master's program is available for role functions in education or administration.

BACCALAUREATE PROGRAMS

Degree BS

Available Programs Accelerated RN Baccalaureate; Baccalaureate for Second Degree; Generic Baccalaureate; LPN to Baccalaureate; RN Baccalaureate.

Site Options New Hyde Park, NY; Plainview, NY.

Study Options Full-time and part-time.

Program Entrance Requirements Minimum overall college GPA of 3.0, transcript of college record, written essay, health exam, high school biology, high school chemistry, high school foreign language, 3 years high school math, high school transcript, immunizations, minimum high school GPA of 3.0. Transfer students are accepted.

Advanced Placement Credit given for nursing courses completed elsewhere dependent upon specific evaluations.

Expenses (2009–10) *Tuition:* full-time $15,840; part-time $660 per credit. *Required fees:* full-time $1290.

Financial Aid 81% of baccalaureate students in nursing programs received some form of financial aid in 2008–09. *Gift aid (need-based):* Federal Pell, FSEOG, state, private, college/university gift aid from institutional funds, Academic Competitiveness Grant, National Smart Grant, Trio Grant, TEACH Grant. *Loans:* Federal Nursing Student Loans, FFEL (Subsidized and Unsubsidized Stafford PLUS), Perkins, alternative loans. *Work-study:* Federal Work-Study. *Financial aid application deadline:* 5/1.

Contact Marguerite Lane, Director of Admissions, Department of Nursing, Molloy College, 1000 Hempstead Avenue, PO Box 5002, Rockville Centre, NY 11571-5002. *Telephone:* 516-678-5000 Ext. 6233. *E-mail:* mlane@molloy.edu.

GRADUATE PROGRAMS

Expenses (2009–10) *Tuition:* full-time $13,770; part-time $765 per credit. *Required fees:* full-time $1730.

Financial Aid 10% of graduate students in nursing programs received some form of financial aid in 2008–09. Research assistantships with partial tuition reimbursements available, teaching assistantships with partial tuition reimbursements available, institutionally sponsored loans, scholarships, and unspecified assistantships available. Aid available to part-time students. *Financial aid application deadline:* 4/1.

Contact Ms. Alina Haitz, Assistant Director of Admissions, Department of Nursing, Molloy College, 1000 Hempstead Avenue, PO Box 5002, Rockville Centre, NY 11571-5002. *Telephone:* 516-678-5000 Ext. 6399. *E-mail:* ahaitz@molloy.edu.

MASTER'S DEGREE PROGRAM

Degree MS

Available Programs Master's.

Concentrations Available Nursing administration; nursing education; nursing informatics. *Clinical nurse specialist programs in:* adult health. *Nurse practitioner programs in:* adult health, family health, pediatric, psychiatric/mental health.

Site Options New Hyde Park, NY; Plainview, NY; Farmingdale, NY.

Study Options Full-time and part-time.

Program Entrance Requirements Clinical experience, minimum overall college GPA of 3.0, transcript of college record, written essay, interview, 3 letters of recommendation, nursing research course, prerequisite course work, statistics course. *Application fee:* $30.

Degree Requirements 48 total credit hours, thesis or project.

POST-MASTER'S PROGRAM

Areas of Study Nursing administration; nursing education; nursing informatics. *Clinical nurse specialist programs in:* adult health. *Nurse practitioner programs in:* adult health, family health, pediatric, psychiatric/mental health.

CONTINUING EDUCATION PROGRAM

Contact Anna Jansson, Associate Director, Continuing Education, Department of Nursing, Molloy College, 1000 Hempstead Avenue, Rockville Centre, NY 11571-5002. *Telephone:* 516-678-5000 Ext. 6106. *Fax:* 516-678-7295. *E-mail:* ajansson@molloy.edu.

Mount Saint Mary College
Division of Nursing
Newburgh, New York

Founded in 1960

DEGREES • BSN • MS

Nursing Program Faculty 36 (50% with doctorates).

Nursing Student Activities Sigma Theta Tau, Student Nurses' Association, nursing club.

Nursing Student Resources Academic advising; academic or career counseling; assistance for students with disabilities; bookstore; campus computer network; career placement assistance; computer lab; computer-assisted instruction; e-mail services; employment services for current students; externships; housing assistance; interactive nursing skills videos; Internet; learning resource lab; library services; nursing audiovisuals; paid internships; remedial services; resume preparation assistance; skills, simulation, or other laboratory; tutoring.

Library Facilities 100,031 volumes (2,443 in health, 1,723 in nursing); 25,128 periodical subscriptions (114 health-care related).

BACCALAUREATE PROGRAMS

Degree BSN

Available Programs Accelerated Baccalaureate; Accelerated RN Baccalaureate; Generic Baccalaureate; RN Baccalaureate.

Study Options Full-time and part-time.

Program Entrance Requirements Minimum overall college GPA of 2.75, transcript of college record, CPR certification, health exam, high school biology, high school chemistry, 3 years high school math, high school transcript, immunizations, interview. Transfer students are accepted.

Advanced Placement Credit by examination available. Credit given for nursing courses completed elsewhere dependent upon specific evaluations.

Contact Director of Admissions, Division of Nursing, Mount Saint Mary College, 330 Powell Avenue, Newburgh, NY 12550. *Telephone:* 845-569-3248. *E-mail:* admissions@msmc.edu.

GRADUATE PROGRAMS

Financial Aid Unspecified assistantships and nursing lab assistant available.

Contact Director of Admissions, Division of Nursing, Mount Saint Mary College, 330 Powell Avenue, Newburgh, NY 12550. *Telephone:* 845-569-3248. *E-mail:* admissions@msmc.edu.

MASTER'S DEGREE PROGRAM

Degree MS

Available Programs Master's.

Concentrations Available *Clinical nurse specialist programs in:* adult health. *Nurse practitioner programs in:* adult health.

Study Options Full-time and part-time.

Program Entrance Requirements Clinical experience, computer literacy, minimum overall college GPA of 3.0, transcript of college record, written essay, immunizations, interview, 3 letters of recommendation, nursing research course, physical assessment course, professional liability insurance/malpractice insurance, resume, statistics course.

Degree Requirements 42 total credit hours, thesis or project.

POST-MASTER'S PROGRAM

Areas of Study Nursing administration; nursing education.

Nazareth College of Rochester
Department of Nursing
Rochester, New York

http://www.naz.edu/dept/nursing/

Founded in 1924

DEGREES • BS • MS

Nursing Program Faculty 20 (50% with doctorates).

Baccalaureate Enrollment 173
Women 92% **Men** 8% **Minority** 11% **International** .5% **Part-time** 22%

Graduate Enrollment 20
Women 95% **Men** 5% **Minority** 10% **Part-time** 90%

Distance Learning Courses Available.

Nursing Student Activities Nursing Honor Society, Sigma Theta Tau, nursing club.

Nursing Student Resources Academic advising; academic or career counseling; assistance for students with disabilities; bookstore; campus computer network; career placement assistance; computer lab; computer-assisted instruction; daycare for children of students; e-mail services; employment services for current students; externships; housing assistance; interactive nursing skills videos; Internet; learning resource lab; library services; nursing audiovisuals; resume preparation assistance; skills, simulation, or other laboratory; tutoring.

Library Facilities 283,248 volumes (267,000 in health, 66,000 in nursing); 16,102 periodical subscriptions (44,000 health-care related).

■ Nazareth College in Rochester, New York, offers a four-year B.S. in nursing, an RN-B.S., and an LPN-B.S. program. At the graduate level, Nazareth College offers a post-master's certificate in nursing education. The mission of the Department of Nursing is to educate students in the profession within a transcultural context and to advance students' abilities to integrate the liberal arts and sciences within the discipline. The faculty members are committed to preparing students for culturally competent nursing practice, leadership in service to the community, and commitment to a life informed by intellectual, ethical, and aesthetic values.

BACCALAUREATE PROGRAMS

Degree BS

Available Programs Generic Baccalaureate; LPN to Baccalaureate; RN Baccalaureate.

Site Options Geneva, NY; Rochester, NY.

Study Options Full-time and part-time.

Program Entrance Requirements Minimum overall college GPA of 2.5, transcript of college record, CPR certification, written essay, health exam, high school chemistry, high school transcript, immunizations, minimum high school GPA of 2.5, minimum GPA in nursing prerequisites of 2.5, prerequisite course work. Transfer students are accepted.

Advanced Placement Credit by examination available. Credit given for nursing courses completed elsewhere dependent upon specific evaluations.

Financial Aid *Gift aid (need-based):* Federal Pell, FSEOG, state, private, college/university gift aid from institutional funds, Federal Nursing. *Loans:* Federal Nursing Student Loans, FFEL (Subsidized and Unsubsidized Stafford PLUS), Perkins. *Work-study:* Federal Work-Study. *Financial aid application deadline (priority):* 2/15.

Contact Admissions Office, Department of Nursing, Nazareth College of Rochester, 4245 East Avenue, Rochester, NY 14618-3790. *Telephone:* 585-389-2865. *E-mail:* admissions@naz.edu.

GRADUATE PROGRAMS

Financial Aid Research assistantships, career-related internships or fieldwork available.

Contact Dr. Linda M. Janelli, Director, Masters Nursing Program, Department of Nursing, Nazareth College of Rochester, 4245 East Avenue, Rochester, NY 14618-3790. *Telephone:* 585-389-2713. *Fax:* 585-389-2714. *E-mail:* lmjanell@naz.edu.

MASTER'S DEGREE PROGRAM

Degree MS

Available Programs Master's.

Concentrations Available *Nurse practitioner programs in:* gerontology.

Site Options Rochester, NY.

Nazareth College of Rochester (continued)

Study Options Full-time and part-time.

Program Entrance Requirements Minimum overall college GPA of 3.0, transcript of college record, written essay, immunizations, interview, 2 letters of recommendation, physical assessment course, statistics course.

Advanced Placement Credit given for nursing courses completed elsewhere dependent upon specific evaluations.

Degree Requirements 42 total credit hours, thesis or project.

POST-MASTER'S PROGRAM

Areas of Study Nursing education. *Nurse practitioner programs in:* gerontology.

CONTINUING EDUCATION PROGRAM

Contact Mrs. Helene Lovett, Secretary, Department of Nursing, Nazareth College of Rochester, 4245 East Avenue, Rochester, NY 14618-3790. *Telephone:* 585-389-2709. *Fax:* 585-389-2714. *E-mail:* hlovett8@naz.edu.

New York City College of Technology of the City University of New York

Department of Nursing
Brooklyn, New York

Founded in 1946

DEGREE • BS

Nursing Program Faculty 22

BACCALAUREATE PROGRAMS

Degree BS

Available Programs RN Baccalaureate.

Program Entrance Requirements Minimum overall college GPA of 2.5, immunizations, professional liability insurance/malpractice insurance, RN licensure. Transfer students are accepted.

Expenses (2008–09) *Tuition, state resident:* part-time $170 per credit. *Tuition, nonresident:* part-time $360 per credit.

Contact Prof. Kathryn Richardson, Chair, Department of Nursing, New York City College of Technology of the City University of New York, 300 Jay Street, Pearl 505, Brooklyn, NY 11201. *Telephone:* 718-260-5660. *Fax:* 718-260-5662. *E-mail:* krichardson@citytech.cuny.edu.

New York University

College of Nursing
New York, New York

http://www.nyu.edu/education/nursing/png07

Founded in 1831

DEGREES • BS • MS • MSN/MPH • PHD

Nursing Program Faculty 157 (23% with doctorates).

Baccalaureate Enrollment 323
Women 89.5% **Men** 10.5% **Minority** 54.5%

Graduate Enrollment 260
Women 93% **Men** 7% **Minority** 52% **Part-time** 75%

Distance Learning Courses Available.

Nursing Student Activities Sigma Theta Tau, Student Nurses' Association, nursing club.

Nursing Student Resources Academic advising; academic or career counseling; assistance for students with disabilities; bookstore; campus computer network; computer lab; computer-assisted instruction; e-mail services; employment services for current students; housing assistance; interactive nursing skills videos; Internet; learning resource lab; library services; nursing audiovisuals; resume preparation assistance; skills, simulation, or other laboratory; tutoring.

Library Facilities 5.2 million volumes (102,448 in health, 62,781 in nursing); 48,958 periodical subscriptions (4,658 health-care related).

BACCALAUREATE PROGRAMS

Degree BS

Available Programs Accelerated Baccalaureate; Accelerated Baccalaureate for Second Degree; Baccalaureate for Second Degree; Generic Baccalaureate; RN Baccalaureate.

Study Options Full-time and part-time.

Program Entrance Requirements Minimum overall college GPA of 3.0, transcript of college record, CPR certification, written essay, health exam, health insurance, high school biology, high school chemistry, high school foreign language, 4 years high school math, 4 years high school science, high school transcript, immunizations, 2 letters of recommendation, minimum high school GPA of 3.3, minimum GPA in nursing prerequisites of 2.7. Transfer students are accepted. *Application deadline:* 1/1 (fall), 11/1 (spring). *Application fee:* $75.

Advanced Placement Credit given for nursing courses completed elsewhere dependent upon specific evaluations.

Expenses (2009–10) *Tuition:* full-time $18,293; part-time $1078 per credit. *Room and board:* $13,226 per academic year. *Required fees:* full-time $819; part-time $416 per term.

Financial Aid 80% of baccalaureate students in nursing programs received some form of financial aid in 2008–09. *Gift aid (need-based):* Federal Pell, FSEOG, state, private, college/university gift aid from institutional funds. *Loans:* Federal Nursing Student Loans, Federal Direct (Subsidized and Unsubsidized Stafford PLUS), FFEL (Subsidized and Unsubsidized Stafford PLUS), Perkins. *Work-study:* Federal Work-Study. *Financial aid application deadline (priority):* 2/15.

Contact Ms. Lindsay J. Sutton, Assistant Director of Undergraduate Student Affairs and Admissions, College of Nursing, New York University, 726 Broadway, 10th Floor, New York, NY 10003-6677. *Telephone:* 212-998-5336. *Fax:* 212-995-4302. *E-mail:* ljs333@nyu.edu.

GRADUATE PROGRAMS

Expenses (2009–10) *Tuition:* full-time $29,736; part-time $1239 per credit. *Room and board:* $18,532 per academic year. *Required fees:* full-time $1239; part-time $486 per term.

Financial Aid 54% of graduate students in nursing programs received some form of financial aid in 2008–09. 2 research assistantships with full and partial tuition reimbursements available were awarded; fellowships with full and partial tuition reimbursements available, career-related internships or fieldwork, institutionally sponsored loans, scholarships, and tuition waivers (partial) also available. Aid available to part-time students. *Financial aid application deadline:* 2/1.

Contact Ms. Vida Samuel, Assistant Director of Graduate Student Affairs and Admissions, College of Nursing, New York University, 726 Broadway, New York, NY 10003-6677. *Telephone:* 212-992-9418. *Fax:* 212-995-4302. *E-mail:* nursing.programs@nyu.edu.

MASTER'S DEGREE PROGRAM

Degrees MS; MSN/MPH

Available Programs Master's; RN to Master's.

Concentrations Available Nursing administration; nursing education; nursing informatics. *Nurse practitioner programs in:* acute care, adult health, gerontology, pediatric, primary care, psychiatric/mental health.

Study Options Full-time and part-time.

Program Entrance Requirements Clinical experience, minimum overall college GPA of 3.0, transcript of college record, written essay, 2 letters of recommendation, resume, statistics course. *Application deadline:* 7/1 (fall), 12/1 (spring), 4/1 (summer). Applications may be processed on a rolling basis for some programs. *Application fee:* $75.

Advanced Placement Credit given for nursing courses completed elsewhere dependent upon specific evaluations.

Degree Requirements 48 total credit hours, thesis or project.

POST-MASTER'S PROGRAM

Areas of Study Nursing administration; nursing education; nursing informatics. *Nurse practitioner programs in:* acute care, adult health, gerontology, pediatric, primary care, psychiatric/mental health.

DOCTORAL DEGREE PROGRAM

Degree PhD

Available Programs Doctorate.

Areas of Study Addiction/substance abuse, aging, bio-behavioral research, gerontology, health policy, health-care systems, illness and transition, nursing administration, nursing education, nursing policy, nursing research, oncology, urban health.

Program Entrance Requirements Minimum overall college GPA of 3.0, interview by faculty committee, interview, 3 letters of recommendation, MSN or equivalent, statistics course, vita, writing sample, GRE General Test. Application deadline: 1/15 (fall). Application fee: $75.

Degree Requirements 45 total credit hours, dissertation, oral exam, residency.

CONTINUING EDUCATION PROGRAM

Contact Dr. Hila Richardson, Continuing Education Director, College of Nursing, New York University, 726 Broadway, 10th Floor, New York, NY 10003-6677. *Telephone:* 212-998-5329. *Fax:* 212-995-4302. *E-mail:* nursing.programs@nyu.edu.

See full description on page 512.

Niagara University
Department of Nursing
Niagara Falls, Niagara University, New York

Founded in 1856

DEGREE • BS

Nursing Program Faculty 6

Baccalaureate Enrollment 32
Women 97% **Men** 3% **Minority** 19% **International** 6% **Part-time** 84%

Distance Learning Courses Available.

Nursing Student Activities Sigma Theta Tau.

Nursing Student Resources Academic advising; academic or career counseling; assistance for students with disabilities; bookstore; campus computer network; computer lab; computer-assisted instruction; e-mail services; externships; Internet; library services; nursing audiovisuals; tutoring; unpaid internships.

Library Facilities 297,813 volumes; 164 periodical subscriptions.

BACCALAUREATE PROGRAMS

Degree BS

Available Programs RN Baccalaureate.

Financial Aid *Gift aid (need-based):* Federal Pell, FSEOG, state, private, college/university gift aid from institutional funds. *Loans:* Federal Nursing Student Loans, FFEL (Subsidized and Unsubsidized Stafford PLUS), Perkins, college/university. *Work-study:* Federal Work-Study, part-time campus jobs. *Financial aid application deadline (priority):* 2/15.

Contact Prof. Frances Crosby, Chairperson, Department of Nursing, Niagara University, PO 2203, Niagara University, NY 14109. *Telephone:* 716-286-8155. *Fax:* 716-286-8079. *E-mail:* fcrosby@niagara.edu.

Pace University
Lienhard School of Nursing
New York, New York

http://appserv.pace.edu/execute/page.cfm?doc_id=558

Founded in 1906

DEGREES • BS • DNP • MS

Nursing Program Faculty 69 (32% with doctorates).

Baccalaureate Enrollment 520
Women 88% **Men** 12% **Minority** 37% **International** 1% **Part-time** 14%

Graduate Enrollment 374
Women 91% **Men** 9% **Minority** 38% **International** 3% **Part-time** 89%

Distance Learning Courses Available.

Nursing Student Activities Nursing Honor Society, Sigma Theta Tau, Student Nurses' Association.

Nursing Student Resources Academic advising; academic or career counseling; assistance for students with disabilities; bookstore; campus computer network; career placement assistance; computer lab; computer-assisted instruction; e-mail services; employment services for current students; housing assistance; interactive nursing skills videos; Internet; learning resource lab; library services; nursing audiovisuals; placement services for program completers; resume preparation assistance; skills, simulation, or other laboratory.

Library Facilities 816,086 volumes (17,177 in health, 2,220 in nursing); 31,983 periodical subscriptions (4,231 health-care related).

BACCALAUREATE PROGRAMS

Degree BS

Available Programs Accelerated Baccalaureate for Second Degree; Generic Baccalaureate.

Site Options Pleasantville, NY.

Study Options Full-time and part-time.

Program Entrance Requirements Transcript of college record, CPR certification, written essay, health exam, health insurance, high school biology, high school chemistry, high school foreign language, 4 years high school math, 2 years high school science, high school transcript, immunizations, 2 letters of recommendation, minimum GPA in nursing prerequisites of 2.75. Transfer students are accepted. *Application deadline:* 2/15 (fall). *Application fee:* $50.

Advanced Placement Credit by examination available. Credit given for nursing courses completed elsewhere dependent upon specific evaluations.

Expenses (2009–10) *Tuition:* full-time $31,860; part-time $914 per credit. *International tuition:* $31,860 full-time. *Room and board:* $11,180 per academic year. *Required fees:* full-time $766.

Financial Aid 70% of baccalaureate students in nursing programs received some form of financial aid in 2008–09. *Gift aid (need-based):* Federal Pell, FSEOG, state, private, college/university gift aid from institutional funds, Federal Nursing, endowed and restricted scholarships and grants. *Loans:* Federal Nursing Student Loans, Federal Direct (Subsidized and Unsubsidized Stafford PLUS), Perkins. *Work-study:* Federal Work-Study. *Financial aid application deadline (priority):* 2/15.

Contact Dr. Martha Greenberg, Associate Professor and Chairperson, Undergraduate Department, Lienhard School of Nursing, Pace University, 861 Bedford Road, Pleasantville, NY 10570. *Telephone:* 914-773-3325. *Fax:* 914-773-3345. *E-mail:* mgreenberg@pace.edu.

GRADUATE PROGRAMS

Expenses (2009–10) *Tuition:* part-time $794 per credit. *Room and board:* $11,560 per academic year.

Financial Aid 29% of graduate students in nursing programs received some form of financial aid in 2008–09. Research assistantships, career-related internships or fieldwork, Federal Work-Study, and tuition waivers (partial) available. Aid available to part-time students.

Contact Dr. Rona F. Levin, Professor and Chairperson, Graduate Department, Lienhard School of Nursing, Pace University, 41 Park Row, New York, NY 10038. *Telephone:* 212-346-1632. *Fax:* 212-346-1587. *E-mail:* rlevin@pace.edu.

MASTER'S DEGREE PROGRAM

Degree MS

Available Programs Master's; Master's for Nurses with Non-Nursing Degrees; RN to Master's.

Concentrations Available Nursing education. *Nurse practitioner programs in:* family health.

Site Options Pleasantville, NY.

Study Options Full-time and part-time.

Program Entrance Requirements Computer literacy, minimum overall college GPA of 3.0, transcript of college record, CPR certification, immunizations, 2 letters of recommendation, nursing research course, professional liability insurance/malpractice insurance, prerequisite course work, resume, statistics course, GRE General Test or MAT. *Application deadline:* 8/1 (fall), 12/1 (spring), 5/1 (summer). *Application fee:* $70.

Advanced Placement Credit by examination available. Credit given for nursing courses completed elsewhere dependent upon specific evaluations.

Pace University (continued)

Degree Requirements 42 total credit hours, comprehensive exam.

POST-MASTER'S PROGRAM

Areas of Study Nursing education. *Nurse practitioner programs in:* family health.

DOCTORAL DEGREE PROGRAM

Degree DNP

Available Programs Doctorate.

Areas of Study Family health.

Program Entrance Requirements Clinical experience, minimum overall college GPA of 3.3, 2 letters of recommendation, MSN or equivalent, writing sample. Application deadline: 5/1 (fall). Application fee: $70.

Degree Requirements 37 total credit hours, residency.

Roberts Wesleyan College
Division of Nursing
Rochester, New York

http://www.roberts.edu/Nursing/

Founded in 1866

DEGREES • BSCN • M SC N

Nursing Program Faculty 15 (13% with doctorates).

Baccalaureate Enrollment 278
Women 91% **Men** 9% **Minority** 18% **International** 2% **Part-time** 5%

Graduate Enrollment 47
Women 98% **Men** 2% **Minority** 13%

Nursing Student Activities Sigma Theta Tau, nursing club.

Nursing Student Resources Academic advising; academic or career counseling; assistance for students with disabilities; bookstore; campus computer network; career placement assistance; computer lab; computer-assisted instruction; e-mail services; employment services for current students; externships; housing assistance; interactive nursing skills videos; Internet; learning resource lab; library services; nursing audiovisuals; placement services for program completers; remedial services; resume preparation assistance; skills, simulation, or other laboratory; tutoring; unpaid internships.

Library Facilities 131,477 volumes (7,357 in health, 4,000 in nursing); 785 periodical subscriptions (207 health-care related).

BACCALAUREATE PROGRAMS

Degree BScN

Available Programs Accelerated RN Baccalaureate; Generic Baccalaureate; RN Baccalaureate.

Site Options Buffalo, NY; Rochester, NY; Weedsport, NY; Rochester, NY; Dansville, NY; Clifton Springs, NY, NY.

Study Options Full-time and part-time.

Program Entrance Requirements Minimum overall college GPA of 2.5, transcript of college record, CPR certification, written essay, health exam, health insurance, high school biology, high school chemistry, high school transcript, immunizations, 2 letters of recommendation, minimum GPA in nursing prerequisites of 2.5, prerequisite course work. Transfer students are accepted. *Application deadline:* 2/1 (fall). Applications may be processed on a rolling basis for some programs. *Application fee:* $35.

Expenses (2009–10) *Tuition:* full-time $22,580; part-time $706 per credit. *International tuition:* $22,580 full-time. *Room and board:* $8520; room only: $5816 per academic year. *Required fees:* full-time $866.

Financial Aid 95% of baccalaureate students in nursing programs received some form of financial aid in 2008–09. *Gift aid (need-based):* Federal Pell, FSEOG, state, private, college/university gift aid from institutional funds, Academic Competitiveness Grant, National Smart Grant. *Loans:* FFEL (Subsidized and Unsubsidized Stafford PLUS), Perkins. *Work-study:* Federal Work-Study, part-time campus jobs. *Financial aid application deadline (priority):* 3/15.

Contact Mr. Kirk Kettinger, Director of Admissions, Division of Nursing, Roberts Wesleyan College, 2301 Westside Drive, Office of Admissions, Rochester, NY 14624. *Telephone:* 585-594-6400. *Fax:* 585-549-6371. *E-mail:* admissions@roberts.edu.

GRADUATE PROGRAMS

Expenses (2009–10) *Tuition:* full-time $27,378. *International tuition:* $27,378 full-time. *Required fees:* full-time $260.

Financial Aid 80% of graduate students in nursing programs received some form of financial aid in 2008–09.

Contact Mrs. Laurie Jean Cole, Assistant to Chairperson, Division of Nursing, Roberts Wesleyan College, 2301 Westside Drive, Rochester, NY 14624-1997. *Telephone:* 585-594-6668. *Fax:* 585-594-6593. *E-mail:* cole_laurie@roberts.edu.

MASTER'S DEGREE PROGRAM

Degree M Sc N

Available Programs Accelerated Master's; Accelerated Master's for Nurses with Non-Nursing Degrees.

Concentrations Available Nursing administration; nursing education.

Study Options Full-time.

Program Entrance Requirements Clinical experience, computer literacy, minimum overall college GPA of 3.0, transcript of college record, written essay, immunizations, interview, 2 letters of recommendation, nursing research course, prerequisite course work, resume, statistics course. *Application deadline:* Applications may be processed on a rolling basis for some programs. *Application fee:* $35.

Degree Requirements 39 total credit hours, thesis or project.

POST-MASTER'S PROGRAM

Areas of Study Nursing administration; nursing education.

The Sage Colleges
Department of Nursing
Troy, New York

http://www.sage.edu/departments/nur

DEGREES • BS • DNS • MS

Nursing Program Faculty 16 (31% with doctorates).

Baccalaureate Enrollment 221
Women 99% **Men** 1% **Minority** 21% **Part-time** 24%

Graduate Enrollment 144
Women 96% **Men** 4% **Minority** 10% **International** 7% **Part-time** 85%

Distance Learning Courses Available.

Nursing Student Activities Nursing Honor Society, Sigma Theta Tau, nursing club.

Nursing Student Resources Academic advising; academic or career counseling; assistance for students with disabilities; bookstore; campus computer network; career placement assistance; computer lab; computer-assisted instruction; e-mail services; employment services for current students; externships; interactive nursing skills videos; Internet; learning resource lab; library services; remedial services; resume preparation assistance; skills, simulation, or other laboratory; tutoring.

Library Facilities 4,003 volumes in health, 2,516 volumes in nursing; 400 periodical subscriptions health-care related.

BACCALAUREATE PROGRAMS

Degree BS

Available Programs ADN to Baccalaureate; Accelerated Baccalaureate; Accelerated Baccalaureate for Second Degree; Baccalaureate for Second Degree; Generic Baccalaureate; International Nurse to Baccalaureate; LPN to Baccalaureate; RN Baccalaureate.

Study Options Full-time and part-time.

Program Entrance Requirements Minimum overall college GPA of 2.75, transcript of college record, written essay, health exam, health insurance, high school biology, high school chemistry, 3 years high school math, 3 years high school science, high school transcript, immunizations, interview, 2 letters of recommendation, minimum high school GPA of 2.75, professional liability insurance/malpractice insurance. Transfer students are accepted. *Application deadline:* Applications may be processed on a rolling basis for some programs. *Application fee:* $30.

Advanced Placement Credit by examination available. Credit given for nursing courses completed elsewhere dependent upon specific evaluations.

Expenses (2009–10) *Tuition:* full-time $27,000; part-time $900 per credit hour. *International tuition:* $27,000 full-time. *Room and board:* $9670; room only: $4940 per academic year. *Required fees:* full-time $790.

Financial Aid 84% of baccalaureate students in nursing programs received some form of financial aid in 2008–09.

Contact Michelle Hayward, MS, RN, Program Contact, Department of Nursing, The Sage Colleges, Troy, NY 12180-4115. *Telephone:* 518-244-2231. *Fax:* 518-244-2009. *E-mail:* nursing@sage.edu.

GRADUATE PROGRAMS

Expenses (2009–10) *Tuition:* full-time $10,620; part-time $590 per credit hour. *International tuition:* $10,620 full-time. *Room and board:* $9670; room only: $4940 per academic year.

Financial Aid 81% of graduate students in nursing programs received some form of financial aid in 2008–09. Fellowships, research assistantships, Federal Work-Study, scholarships, and unspecified assistantships available. Aid available to part-time students. *Financial aid application deadline:* 3/1.

Contact Linda Ceriale Peterson, EdD, MS Program, Department of Nursing, The Sage Colleges, Troy, NY 12180-4115. *Telephone:* 518-244-2384. *Fax:* 518-244-2009. *E-mail:* nursing@sage.edu.

MASTER'S DEGREE PROGRAM

Degree MS

Available Programs Accelerated Master's; Accelerated RN to Master's; Master's.

Concentrations Available Health-care administration; nursing administration; nursing education. *Clinical nurse specialist programs in:* acute care, adult health, cardiovascular, community health, critical care, family health, gerontology, medical-surgical, oncology, palliative care, psychiatric/mental health. *Nurse practitioner programs in:* acute care, adult health, community health, family health, gerontology, psychiatric/mental health.

Study Options Full-time and part-time.

Program Entrance Requirements Minimum overall college GPA of 2.75, transcript of college record, CPR certification, written essay, 2 letters of recommendation, physical assessment course, professional liability insurance/malpractice insurance, resume.

Advanced Placement Credit given for nursing courses completed elsewhere dependent upon specific evaluations.

Degree Requirements 42 total credit hours, thesis or project.

POST-MASTER'S PROGRAM

Areas of Study Health-care administration; nursing administration; nursing education. *Clinical nurse specialist programs in:* acute care, adult health, cardiovascular, community health, critical care, family health, gerontology, medical-surgical, oncology, palliative care, psychiatric/mental health. *Nurse practitioner programs in:* acute care, adult health, community health, family health, gerontology, psychiatric/mental health.

DOCTORAL DEGREE PROGRAM

Degree DNS

Available Programs Doctorate.

Areas of Study Faculty preparation, health-care systems, nursing administration, nursing education, nursing policy, nursing research, nursing science.

Program Entrance Requirements Minimum overall college GPA of 3.5, interview by faculty committee, 3 letters of recommendation, MSN or equivalent, statistics course, vita, writing sample.

Degree Requirements 42 total credit hours, dissertation.

CONTINUING EDUCATION PROGRAM

Contact Wendy Nelson, Program Contact. *Telephone:* 518-244-2231. *Fax:* 518-244-2009. *E-mail:* nelsow@sage.edu.

St. Francis College
Department of Nursing
Brooklyn Heights, New York

Founded in 1884

DEGREE • BS

Nursing Program Faculty 6

Baccalaureate Enrollment 76
Women 98% **Men** 2% **Minority** 63% **International** 25% **Part-time** 56%

Nursing Student Resources Academic advising; academic or career counseling; assistance for students with disabilities; bookstore; campus computer network; career placement assistance; computer lab; computer-assisted instruction; e-mail services; employment services for current students; interactive nursing skills videos; learning resource lab; library services; nursing audiovisuals; placement services for program completers; remedial services; resume preparation assistance; skills, simulation, or other laboratory; tutoring.

Library Facilities 116,716 volumes (5,531 in health, 186 in nursing); 31,391 periodical subscriptions (558 health-care related).

BACCALAUREATE PROGRAMS

Degree BS

Available Programs ADN to Baccalaureate; International Nurse to Baccalaureate; RPN to Baccalaureate.

Site Options Brooklyn, NY; New York, NY; Brooklyn, NY.

Study Options Full-time and part-time.

Program Entrance Requirements Minimum overall college GPA of 2.0, transcript of college record, written essay, health exam, health insurance, high school transcript, immunizations, interview, 2 letters of recommendation, professional liability insurance/malpractice insurance, prerequisite course work, RN licensure. Transfer students are accepted.

Advanced Placement Credit by examination available. Credit given for nursing courses completed elsewhere dependent upon specific evaluations.

Contact *Telephone:* 718-489-5267 Ext. 5267. *Fax:* 718-489-5408.

St. John Fisher College
Advanced Practice Nursing Program
Rochester, New York

http://www.sjfc.edu

Founded in 1948

DEGREES • BS • DNP • MS

Nursing Program Faculty 49 (24% with doctorates).

Baccalaureate Enrollment 423
Women 91% **Men** 9% **Minority** 16% **Part-time** 5%

Graduate Enrollment 113
Women 94% **Men** 6% **Minority** 13% **Part-time** 77%

Distance Learning Courses Available.

Nursing Student Activities Sigma Theta Tau, Student Nurses' Association.

Nursing Student Resources Academic advising; academic or career counseling; assistance for students with disabilities; bookstore; campus computer network; career placement assistance; computer lab; computer-assisted instruction; daycare for children of students; e-mail services; employment services for current students; interactive nursing skills videos; Internet; learning resource lab; library services; nursing audiovisuals; resume preparation assistance; skills, simulation, or other laboratory; tutoring.

Library Facilities 214,834 volumes (30,000 in health, 5,000 in nursing); 22,428 periodical subscriptions (200 health-care related).

BACCALAUREATE PROGRAMS

Degree BS

Available Programs ADN to Baccalaureate; Accelerated RN Baccalaureate; Baccalaureate for Second Degree; Generic Baccalaureate; RN Baccalaureate.

Site Options Geneva, NY; Rochester, NY.

Study Options Full-time.

St. John Fisher College (continued)

Program Entrance Requirements Minimum overall college GPA of 2.75, transcript of college record, CPR certification, written essay, health exam, health insurance, high school transcript, immunizations, 2 letters of recommendation, minimum high school GPA of 2.0, minimum GPA in nursing prerequisites of 2.75, prerequisite course work. Transfer students are accepted. *Application deadline:* 3/1 (fall), 10/1 (spring). Applications may be processed on a rolling basis for some programs. *Application fee:* $30.

Advanced Placement Credit given for nursing courses completed elsewhere dependent upon specific evaluations.

Expenses (2009–10) *Tuition:* full-time $23,850; part-time $650 per credit hour. *Room and board:* $10,090; room only: $6550 per academic year. *Required fees:* full-time $205; part-time $25 per term.

Financial Aid 95% of baccalaureate students in nursing programs received some form of financial aid in 2008–09. *Gift aid (need-based):* Federal Pell, FSEOG, state, private, college/university gift aid from institutional funds, Federal Nursing. *Loans:* FFEL (Subsidized and Unsubsidized Stafford PLUS), Perkins, beginning with the 2009-2010 academic year FFEL Stafford & PLUS loans will be replaced by Direct Student & Plus loans. *Work-study:* Federal Work-Study. *Financial aid application deadline (priority):* 2/15.

Contact Dr. Marilyn Dollinger, Chairperson, Advanced Practice Nursing Program, St. John Fisher College, 3690 East Avenue, Rochester, NY 14618. *Telephone:* 585-385-8476. *Fax:* 585-385-8466. *E-mail:* mdollinger@sjfc.edu.

GRADUATE PROGRAMS

Expenses (2009–10) *Tuition:* part-time $680 per credit hour.

Financial Aid 20% of graduate students in nursing programs received some form of financial aid in 2008–09. Federal Work-Study, scholarships, and traineeships available.

Contact Dr. Cynthia Ricci McCloskey, Graduate Program Director, Advanced Practice Nursing Program, St. John Fisher College, 3690 East Avenue, Rochester, NY 14618. *Telephone:* 585-385-8471. *Fax:* 585-385-8466. *E-mail:* cmccloskey@sjfc.edu.

MASTER'S DEGREE PROGRAM

Degree MS

Available Programs Master's; RN to Master's.

Concentrations Available Nursing education. *Clinical nurse specialist programs in:* adult health, gerontology, pediatric, women's health. *Nurse practitioner programs in:* family health.

Study Options Full-time and part-time.

Program Entrance Requirements Computer literacy, minimum overall college GPA of 3.0, transcript of college record, CPR certification, written essay, immunizations, 2 letters of recommendation, nursing research course, physical assessment course, resume, statistics course. *Application deadline:* Applications may be processed on a rolling basis for some programs. *Application fee:* $30.

Advanced Placement Credit given for nursing courses completed elsewhere dependent upon specific evaluations.

Degree Requirements 46 total credit hours, thesis or project.

POST-MASTER'S PROGRAM

Areas of Study Nursing education. *Nurse practitioner programs in:* family health.

DOCTORAL DEGREE PROGRAM

Degree DNP

Available Programs Doctorate; Post-Baccalaureate Doctorate.

Areas of Study Advanced practice nursing.

Program Entrance Requirements Clinical experience, minimum overall college GPA of 3.0, interview by faculty committee, letters of recommendation, scholarly papers, vita, writing sample. Application deadline: Applications may be processed on a rolling basis for some programs. Application fee: $30.

Degree Requirements 48 total credit hours, residency.

St. Joseph's College, New York
Department of Nursing
Brooklyn, New York

http://www.sjcny.edu

Founded in 1916

DEGREES • BSN • MS

Nursing Program Faculty 17 (41% with doctorates).

Baccalaureate Enrollment 225
Women 93% **Men** 7% **Minority** 51% **International** 1% **Part-time** 96%

Graduate Enrollment 67
Women 99% **Men** 1% **Minority** 64% **Part-time** 100%

Nursing Student Activities Nursing Honor Society, nursing club.

Nursing Student Resources Academic advising; academic or career counseling; assistance for students with disabilities; bookstore; campus computer network; computer lab; computer-assisted instruction; e-mail services; Internet; learning resource lab; library services; nursing audiovisuals; remedial services; resume preparation assistance; skills, simulation, or other laboratory; tutoring.

Library Facilities 153,773 volumes (7,069 in health, 686 in nursing); 7,816 periodical subscriptions (2,337 health-care related).

BACCALAUREATE PROGRAMS

Degree BSN

Available Programs RN Baccalaureate.

Site Options Patchogue, NY.

Study Options Full-time and part-time.

Program Entrance Requirements Minimum overall college GPA of 2.5, transcript of college record, CPR certification, written essay, health exam, health insurance, immunizations, 2 letters of recommendation, minimum GPA in nursing prerequisites of 2.5, professional liability insurance/malpractice insurance, prerequisite course work, RN licensure. Transfer students are accepted. *Application deadline:* 8/31 (fall), 1/15 (spring). Applications may be processed on a rolling basis for some programs. *Application fee:* $25.

Advanced Placement Credit by examination available. Credit given for nursing courses completed elsewhere dependent upon specific evaluations.

Expenses (2009–10) *Tuition:* full-time $8100; part-time $530 per credit. *International tuition:* $8100 full-time. *Required fees:* full-time $797; part-time $53 per credit; part-time $425 per term.

Financial Aid 38% of baccalaureate students in nursing programs received some form of financial aid in 2008–09. *Gift aid (need-based):* Federal Pell, FSEOG, state, private, college/university gift aid from institutional funds. *Loans:* FFEL (Subsidized and Unsubsidized Stafford PLUS), Perkins. *Work-study:* Federal Work-Study, part-time campus jobs. *Financial aid application deadline (priority):* 2/25.

Contact Dr. Barbara L. Sands, PhD, Director, Department of Nursing, St. Joseph's College, New York, 245 Clinton Avenue, Brooklyn, NY 11205-3688. *Telephone:* 718-940-5892. *Fax:* 718-638-8839. *E-mail:* bsands@sjcny.edu.

GRADUATE PROGRAMS

Expenses (2009–10) *Tuition:* part-time $625 per credit. *Required fees:* part-time $53 per credit; part-time $130 per term.

Financial Aid 14% of graduate students in nursing programs received some form of financial aid in 2008–09.

Contact Dr. Barbara L. Sands, Director, Department of Nursing, St. Joseph's College, New York, 245 Clinton Avenue, Brooklyn, NY 11205-3688. *Telephone:* 718-940-5892. *Fax:* 718-638-8839. *E-mail:* bsands@sjcny.edu.

MASTER'S DEGREE PROGRAM

Degree MS

Available Programs Master's.

Concentrations Available Nursing education. *Clinical nurse specialist programs in:* adult health.

Site Options Patchogue, NY.

Study Options Part-time.

Program Entrance Requirements Clinical experience, minimum overall college GPA of 3.0, transcript of college record, CPR certification, written essay, immunizations, interview, 2 letters of recommendation, nursing research course, physical assessment course, professional liability insurance/malpractice insurance, prerequisite course work, resume, statistics course. *Application deadline:* 5/15 (fall). Applications may be processed on a rolling basis for some programs. *Application fee:* $25.

Advanced Placement Credit given for nursing courses completed elsewhere dependent upon specific evaluations.

Degree Requirements 38 total credit hours, comprehensive exam.

State University of New York at Binghamton

Decker School of Nursing
Binghamton, New York

http://dson.binghamton.edu

Founded in 1946

DEGREES • BS • MS • PHD

Nursing Program Faculty 43 (40% with doctorates).

Baccalaureate Enrollment 300

Graduate Enrollment 150

Nursing Student Activities Sigma Theta Tau, Student Nurses' Association.

Nursing Student Resources Campus computer network; computer lab; skills, simulation, or other laboratory.

Library Facilities 2.4 million volumes (7,000 in health); 76,166 periodical subscriptions (9,300 health-care related).

BACCALAUREATE PROGRAMS

Degree BS

Available Programs Accelerated RN Baccalaureate; Generic Baccalaureate.

Study Options Full-time and part-time.

Program Entrance Requirements Minimum overall college GPA of 2.7, transcript of college record, CPR certification, written essay, health exam, high school biology, high school chemistry, high school foreign language, 3 years high school math, 2 years high school science, high school transcript, minimum high school GPA of 3.0, prerequisite course work. Transfer students are accepted.

Advanced Placement Credit by examination available. Credit given for nursing courses completed elsewhere dependent upon specific evaluations.

Contact *Telephone:* 607-777-4954. *Fax:* 607-777-4440.

GRADUATE PROGRAMS

Contact *Telephone:* 607-777-4964. *Fax:* 607-777-4440.

MASTER'S DEGREE PROGRAM

Degree MS

Available Programs Master's.

Concentrations Available Nursing administration; nursing education. *Clinical nurse specialist programs in:* community health, family health, gerontology. *Nurse practitioner programs in:* community health, family health, gerontology, primary care.

Study Options Full-time and part-time.

Program Entrance Requirements Minimum overall college GPA of 3.0, transcript of college record, written essay, 2 letters of recommendation, statistics course, GRE General Test.

Advanced Placement Credit given for nursing courses completed elsewhere dependent upon specific evaluations.

Degree Requirements 48 total credit hours, thesis or project, comprehensive exam.

POST-MASTER'S PROGRAM

Areas of Study *Nurse practitioner programs in:* community health, family health, gerontology.

DOCTORAL DEGREE PROGRAM

Degree PhD

Available Programs Doctorate.

Program Entrance Requirements Clinical experience, interview by faculty committee, interview, 3 letters of recommendation, MSN or equivalent, scholarly papers, statistics course, vita, writing sample.

Degree Requirements 66 total credit hours, dissertation, written exam.

CONTINUING EDUCATION PROGRAM

Contact *Telephone:* 607-777-4954. *Fax:* 607-777-4440.

State University of New York at Plattsburgh

Department of Nursing
Plattsburgh, New York

http://www.plattsburgh.edu/nursing

Founded in 1889

DEGREE • BS

Nursing Program Faculty 18 (25% with doctorates).

Baccalaureate Enrollment 280

Women 90% **Men** 10% **Minority** 25% **International** 4% **Part-time** 25%

Distance Learning Courses Available.

Nursing Student Activities Nursing Honor Society, Sigma Theta Tau, Student Nurses' Association.

Nursing Student Resources Academic advising; academic or career counseling; assistance for students with disabilities; bookstore; campus computer network; career placement assistance; computer lab; computer-assisted instruction; e-mail services; employment services for current students; interactive nursing skills videos; Internet; learning resource lab; library services; nursing audiovisuals; remedial services; resume preparation assistance; skills, simulation, or other laboratory; tutoring.

Library Facilities 592,765 volumes (19,450 in health, 200 in nursing); 4,052 periodical subscriptions (174 health-care related).

BACCALAUREATE PROGRAMS

Degree BS

Available Programs ADN to Baccalaureate; Generic Baccalaureate; RN Baccalaureate.

Study Options Full-time and part-time.

Online Degree Options Yes.

Program Entrance Requirements Minimum overall college GPA of 2.5, transcript of college record, CPR certification, health exam, high school biology, high school chemistry, high school foreign language, 3 years high school math, 3 years high school science, high school transcript, immunizations, minimum GPA in nursing prerequisites of 2.5, professional liability insurance/malpractice insurance, prerequisite course work. Transfer students are accepted. *Application deadline:* Applications may be processed on a rolling basis for some programs.

Advanced Placement Credit given for nursing courses completed elsewhere dependent upon specific evaluations.

Expenses (2009–10) *Tuition, state resident:* full-time $4970; part-time $207 per credit hour. *Tuition, nonresident:* full-time $12,870; part-time $536 per credit hour. *Room and board:* $8000; room only: $5500 per academic year. *Required fees:* full-time $1000.

Financial Aid 83% of baccalaureate students in nursing programs received some form of financial aid in 2008–09. *Gift aid (need-based):* Federal Pell, FSEOG, state, private, college/university gift aid from institutional funds. *Loans:* Federal Nursing Student Loans, Federal Direct (Subsidized and Unsubsidized Stafford PLUS), Perkins, alternative loans. *Work-study:* Federal Work-Study. *Financial aid application deadline (priority):* 2/15.

Contact Dr. JoAnn Gleeson-Kreig, Chairperson, Department of Nursing, Department of Nursing, State University of New York at Plattsburgh, 101 Broad Street, Plattsburgh, NY 12901. *Telephone:* 518-564-3124. *Fax:* 518-564-3100. *E-mail:* JoAnn.Gleeson-Kreig@plattsburgh.edu.

State University of New York College of Agriculture and Technology at Morrisville
Division of Nursing
Morrisville, New York

Founded in 1908

DEGREE • BS

Library Facilities 100,000 volumes; 2,500 periodical subscriptions.

BACCALAUREATE PROGRAMS

Degree BS

Available Programs RN Baccalaureate.

Contact Nursing Program, Division of Nursing, State University of New York College of Agriculture and Technology at Morrisville, 80 Eaton Street, PO Box 901, Morrisville, NY 13408. *Telephone:* 800-258-0111.

State University of New York Downstate Medical Center
College of Nursing
Brooklyn, New York

http://sls.downstate.edu/admissions/nursing/index.html

Founded in 1858

DEGREES • BS • MS • MS/MPH

Nursing Program Faculty 17 (53% with doctorates).

Baccalaureate Enrollment 133
Women 93% **Men** 7% **Minority** 80% **Part-time** 77%

Graduate Enrollment 192
Women 83% **Men** 17% **Minority** 79% **Part-time** 74%

Nursing Student Activities Student Nurses' Association, nursing club.

Nursing Student Resources Academic advising; academic or career counseling; assistance for students with disabilities; bookstore; campus computer network; computer lab; computer-assisted instruction; e-mail services; housing assistance; interactive nursing skills videos; Internet; learning resource lab; library services; nursing audiovisuals; paid internships; skills, simulation, or other laboratory.

Library Facilities 357,209 volumes in health, 2,679 volumes in nursing; 619 periodical subscriptions health-care related.

BACCALAUREATE PROGRAMS

Degree BS

Available Programs Accelerated Baccalaureate for Second Degree; RN Baccalaureate.

Study Options Full-time.

Program Entrance Requirements Minimum overall college GPA of 3.0, transcript of college record, written essay, health exam, 2 letters of recommendation, professional liability insurance/malpractice insurance, prerequisite course work. Transfer students are accepted.

Contact *Telephone:* 718-270-7617. *Fax:* 718-270-7641.

GRADUATE PROGRAMS

Contact *Telephone:* 718-270-7605. *Fax:* 718-270-7636.

MASTER'S DEGREE PROGRAM

Degrees MS; MS/MPH

Available Programs Master's.

Concentrations Available Nurse anesthesia; nurse-midwifery. *Clinical nurse specialist programs in:* adult health, maternity-newborn. *Nurse practitioner programs in:* family health, women's health.

Study Options Full-time and part-time.

Program Entrance Requirements Clinical experience, minimum overall college GPA of 3.0, transcript of college record, CPR certification, written essay, interview, 2 letters of recommendation, nursing research course, physical assessment course, professional liability insurance/malpractice insurance, prerequisite course work, resume, statistics course, GRE.

Advanced Placement Credit by examination available. Credit given for nursing courses completed elsewhere dependent upon specific evaluations.

Degree Requirements Thesis or project.

POST-MASTER'S PROGRAM

Areas of Study *Nurse practitioner programs in:* family health, women's health.

CONTINUING EDUCATION PROGRAM

Contact *Telephone:* 718-270-7616. *Fax:* 718-270-7641.

State University of New York Empire State College
Bachelor of Science in Nursing Program
Saratoga Springs, New York

Founded in 1971

DEGREE • BS

Nursing Program Faculty 6 (33% with doctorates).

Baccalaureate Enrollment 92
Women 92.4% **Men** 7.6% **Minority** 17.4% **Part-time** 85.9%

Distance Learning Courses Available.

Nursing Student Resources Academic advising; assistance for students with disabilities; bookstore; computer-assisted instruction; Internet; library services; tutoring.

Library Facilities 50,000 volumes; 24,000 periodical subscriptions.

BACCALAUREATE PROGRAMS

Degree BS

Available Programs RN Baccalaureate.

Study Options Full-time and part-time.

Online Degree Options Yes (online only).

Program Entrance Requirements Minimum overall college GPA of 3.0, transcript of college record, written essay, immunizations, 2 letters of recommendation, RN licensure. Transfer students are accepted. *Application deadline:* 3/1 (fall). *Application fee:* $50.

Advanced Placement Credit given for nursing courses completed elsewhere dependent upon specific evaluations.

Expenses (2009–10) *Tuition, state resident:* full-time $4970; part-time $207 per credit. *Tuition, nonresident:* full-time $12,870; part-time $536 per credit. *Required fees:* full-time $225; part-time $7 per credit; part-time $75 per term.

Financial Aid 27% of baccalaureate students in nursing programs received some form of financial aid in 2008–09.

Contact Ms. Erin White, Student Services Coordinator, Bachelor of Science in Nursing Program, State University of New York Empire State College, 113 West Avenue, Saratoga Springs, NY 12866. *Telephone:* 518-587-2100 Ext. 2812. *Fax:* 518-587-5126. *E-mail:* erin.white@esc.edu.

State University of New York Institute of Technology
School of Nursing and Health Systems
Utica, New York

http://www.sunyit.edu

Founded in 1966

DEGREES • BS • MS

Nursing Program Faculty 8 (70% with doctorates).

Baccalaureate Enrollment 280
Women 96% **Men** 4% **Minority** 5% **Part-time** 82%

Graduate Enrollment 36
Women 96.5% **Men** 3.5% **Minority** 10% **Part-time** 70%

Nursing Student Activities Nursing Honor Society, Sigma Theta Tau, Student Nurses' Association, nursing club.

Nursing Student Resources Academic advising; academic or career counseling; assistance for students with disabilities; bookstore; campus computer network; career placement assistance; computer lab; computer-assisted instruction; e-mail services; employment services for current students; externships; housing assistance; interactive nursing skills videos; Internet; learning resource lab; library services; nursing audiovisuals; other; placement services for program completers; remedial services; resume preparation assistance; skills, simulation, or other laboratory; tutoring; unpaid internships.

Library Facilities 200,730 volumes (14,000 in health, 8,500 in nursing); 372 periodical subscriptions (335 health-care related).

BACCALAUREATE PROGRAMS

Degree BS

Available Programs ADN to Baccalaureate; Accelerated RN Baccalaureate; RN Baccalaureate.

Study Options Full-time and part-time.

Program Entrance Requirements Minimum overall college GPA of 2.0, transcript of college record, CPR certification, minimum GPA in nursing prerequisites of 2.0, prerequisite course work. Transfer students are accepted.

Advanced Placement Credit given for nursing courses completed elsewhere dependent upon specific evaluations.

Contact *Telephone:* 315-792-7500. *Fax:* 315-792-7837.

GRADUATE PROGRAMS

Contact *Telephone:* 315-792-7297. *Fax:* 315-792-7555.

MASTER'S DEGREE PROGRAM

Degree MS

Available Programs Accelerated AD/RN to Master's; Accelerated RN to Master's; Master's.

Concentrations Available Nursing administration. *Nurse practitioner programs in:* adult health, family health.

Study Options Full-time and part-time.

Program Entrance Requirements Clinical experience, computer literacy, minimum overall college GPA of 3.0, transcript of college record, written essay, interview, 2 letters of recommendation, nursing research course, physical assessment course, prerequisite course work, statistics course, GRE General Test if undergraduate GPA is lower than 3.3.

Advanced Placement Credit given for nursing courses completed elsewhere dependent upon specific evaluations.

Degree Requirements 45 total credit hours, thesis or project, comprehensive exam.

POST-MASTER'S PROGRAM

Areas of Study Nursing administration. *Nurse practitioner programs in:* adult health, family health.

CONTINUING EDUCATION PROGRAM

Contact *Telephone:* 315-792-7295. *Fax:* 315-792-7555.

State University of New York Upstate Medical University

College of Nursing
Syracuse, New York

http://www.upstate.edu/con
Founded in 1950

DEGREES • BS • MS

Nursing Program Faculty 21 (35% with doctorates).

Baccalaureate Enrollment 160
Women 99% **Men** 1% **Minority** 1% **Part-time** 75%

Graduate Enrollment 150
Women 99% **Men** 1% **Minority** 1% **International** 1% **Part-time** 75%

Distance Learning Courses Available.

Nursing Student Activities Sigma Theta Tau, Student Nurses' Association.

Nursing Student Resources Academic advising; academic or career counseling; assistance for students with disabilities; bookstore; campus computer network; career placement assistance; computer lab; computer-assisted instruction; daycare for children of students; e-mail services; Internet; learning resource lab; library services; skills, simulation, or other laboratory; tutoring.

Library Facilities 226,060 volumes (220,382 in health, 1,241 in nursing); 3,200 periodical subscriptions (4,928 health-care related).

BACCALAUREATE PROGRAMS

Degree BS

Available Programs ADN to Baccalaureate.

Site Options Ithaca, NY.

Study Options Full-time and part-time.

Program Entrance Requirements Transcript of college record, CPR certification, written essay, health exam, immunizations, 2 letters of recommendation, prerequisite course work, RN licensure. *Application deadline:* 8/15 (fall), 11/25 (spring). *Application fee:* $50.

Advanced Placement Credit by examination available. Credit given for nursing courses completed elsewhere dependent upon specific evaluations.

Expenses (2009–10) *Tuition, state resident:* full-time $4970; part-time $207 per credit. *Tuition, nonresident:* full-time $10,610; part-time $442 per credit. *International tuition:* $10,610 full-time. *Required fees:* full-time $552.

Financial Aid 35% of baccalaureate students in nursing programs received some form of financial aid in 2008–09.

Contact Mrs. Debora E. Kirsch, Director, Undergraduate Program, College of Nursing, State University of New York Upstate Medical University, 750 East Adams Street, Syracuse, NY 13210. *Telephone:* 315-464-4276. *Fax:* 315-464-5168. *E-mail:* kirschde@upstate.edu.

GRADUATE PROGRAMS

Expenses (2009–10) *Tuition, state resident:* full-time $8370; part-time $349 per credit. *Tuition, nonresident:* full-time $10,920; part-time $455 per credit. *International tuition:* $10,920 full-time. *Required fees:* full-time $552.

Financial Aid 30% of graduate students in nursing programs received some form of financial aid in 2008–09. Federal Work-Study, institutionally sponsored loans, scholarships, and traineeships available. Aid available to part-time students. *Financial aid application deadline:* 3/1.

Contact Dr. Carol Gavan, Associate Professor/Associate Dean and Director, Graduate Program, College of Nursing, State University of New York Upstate Medical University, 750 East Adams Street, Syracuse, NY 13210. *Telephone:* 315-464-4276. *Fax:* 315-464-5168. *E-mail:* gavanc@upstate.edu.

MASTER'S DEGREE PROGRAM

Degree MS

Available Programs Accelerated RN to Master's; Master's; Master's for Nurses with Non-Nursing Degrees; RN to Master's.

Concentrations Available *Clinical nurse specialist programs in:* medical-surgical. *Nurse practitioner programs in:* adult health, family health, pediatric, psychiatric/mental health.

Site Options Watertown, NY.

Study Options Full-time and part-time.

Program Entrance Requirements Clinical experience, minimum overall college GPA of 3.0, transcript of college record, CPR certification, written essay, immunizations, 3 letters of recommendation, nursing research course, physical assessment course, statistics course. *Application deadline:* 8/15 (fall), 11/25 (spring). *Application fee:* $50.

State University of New York Upstate Medical University (continued)

Advanced Placement Credit by examination available. Credit given for nursing courses completed elsewhere dependent upon specific evaluations.

Degree Requirements 47 total credit hours, comprehensive exam.

POST-MASTER'S PROGRAM

Areas of Study *Clinical nurse specialist programs in:* medical-surgical. *Nurse practitioner programs in:* adult health, family health, pediatric, psychiatric/mental health.

CONTINUING EDUCATION PROGRAM

Contact Ms. Barbara A. Black, Director, Continuing Nursing Education, College of Nursing, State University of New York Upstate Medical University, 750 East Adams Street, Syracuse, NY 13210. *Telephone:* 315-464-4276. *Fax:* 315-464-5168. *E-mail:* blackb@upstate.edu.

Stony Brook University, State University of New York

School of Nursing
Stony Brook, New York

Founded in 1957

DEGREES • BS • MS

Nursing Program Faculty 79 (50% with doctorates).

Baccalaureate Enrollment 246
Women 82% **Men** 18% **Minority** 44% **International** 17% **Part-time** 57%

Graduate Enrollment 503
Women 91% **Men** 9% **Minority** 25% **International** 9%

Nursing Student Activities Nursing Honor Society, Sigma Theta Tau, Student Nurses' Association, nursing club.

Nursing Student Resources Academic advising; academic or career counseling; assistance for students with disabilities; bookstore; campus computer network; career placement assistance; computer lab; computer-assisted instruction; daycare for children of students; e-mail services; employment services for current students; housing assistance; interactive nursing skills videos; Internet; learning resource lab; library services; nursing audiovisuals; placement services for program completers; resume preparation assistance; skills, simulation, or other laboratory.

Library Facilities 2 million volumes; 59,198 periodical subscriptions.

BACCALAUREATE PROGRAMS

Degree BS

Available Programs Accelerated Baccalaureate; Accelerated RN Baccalaureate; RN Baccalaureate.

Study Options Full-time and part-time.

Program Entrance Requirements Minimum overall college GPA of 2.5, transcript of college record, CPR certification, written essay, health insurance, immunizations, 3 letters of recommendation, minimum GPA in nursing prerequisites of 2.5, professional liability insurance/malpractice insurance. Transfer students are accepted.

Advanced Placement Credit by examination available. Credit given for nursing courses completed elsewhere dependent upon specific evaluations.

Contact *Telephone:* 631-444-3200. *Fax:* 631-444-6628.

GRADUATE PROGRAMS

Contact *Telephone:* 631-444-3200. *Fax:* 631-444-6628.

MASTER'S DEGREE PROGRAM

Degree MS

Available Programs Master's; RN to Master's.

Concentrations Available Nurse-midwifery. *Clinical nurse specialist programs in:* adult health, community health, critical care, family health, parent-child, pediatric, perinatal, psychiatric/mental health, women's health. *Nurse practitioner programs in:* adult health, family health, neonatal health, pediatric, psychiatric/mental health, women's health.

Study Options Full-time and part-time.

Program Entrance Requirements Clinical experience, computer literacy, minimum overall college GPA of 3.0, transcript of college record, CPR certification, written essay, immunizations, interview, 3 letters of recommendation, physical assessment course, professional liability insurance/malpractice insurance, prerequisite course work, resume, statistics course.

Advanced Placement Credit given for nursing courses completed elsewhere dependent upon specific evaluations.

Degree Requirements 45 total credit hours.

POST-MASTER'S PROGRAM

Areas of Study Nurse-midwifery. *Clinical nurse specialist programs in:* adult health, community health, critical care, family health, parent-child, pediatric, perinatal, psychiatric/mental health, women's health. *Nurse practitioner programs in:* adult health, family health, neonatal health, pediatric, psychiatric/mental health, women's health.

CONTINUING EDUCATION PROGRAM

Contact *Telephone:* 631-444-3481. *Fax:* 631-444-6628.

Teachers College, Columbia University

Department of Health and Behavioral Studies
New York, New York

http://www.tc.edu/academic/hbs/nurseed

Founded in 1887

DEGREE • EDD

Nursing Program Faculty 5 (100% with doctorates).

Graduate Enrollment 14
Women 93% **Men** 7% **Minority** 20% **Part-time** 93%

Distance Learning Courses Available.

Nursing Student Activities Sigma Theta Tau.

Nursing Student Resources Academic advising; academic or career counseling; assistance for students with disabilities; bookstore; campus computer network; career placement assistance; computer lab; e-mail services; employment services for current students; housing assistance; Internet; library services; placement services for program completers; resume preparation assistance.

GRADUATE PROGRAMS

Expenses (2009–10) *Tuition:* full-time $27,048; part-time $1127 per credit. *International tuition:* $27,048 full-time. *Room and board:* room only: $10,000 per academic year. *Required fees:* full-time $720; part-time $360 per term.

Financial Aid 70% of graduate students in nursing programs received some form of financial aid in 2008–09. Fellowships, research assistantships, teaching assistantships, career-related internships or fieldwork, Federal Work-Study, institutionally sponsored loans, and tuition waivers (full and partial) available. Aid available to part-time students. *Financial aid application deadline:* 2/1.

Contact Ms. Cynthia Green, Secretary to Nursing Education Program, Department of Health and Behavioral Studies, Teachers College, Columbia University, Box 35, 525 West 120th Street, New York, NY 10027. *Telephone:* 212-678-3950. *Fax:* 212-678-4048. *E-mail:* Green@tc.columbia.edu.

DOCTORAL DEGREE PROGRAM

Degree EdD

Available Programs Doctorate; Doctorate for Nurses with Non-Nursing Degrees.

Areas of Study Addiction/substance abuse, bio-behavioral research, faculty preparation, health promotion/disease prevention, human health and illness, nursing research, women's health.

Program Entrance Requirements Minimum overall college GPA of 3.4, interview, 2 letters of recommendation, MSN or equivalent, vita, writing sample. Application deadline: Applications may be processed on a rolling basis for some programs. Application fee: $65.

Degree Requirements 90 total credit hours, dissertation, written exam.

University at Buffalo, the State University of New York
School of Nursing
Buffalo, New York

http://nursing.buffalo.edu

Founded in 1846

DEGREES • BS • MS • PHD

Nursing Program Faculty 60 (52% with doctorates).

Baccalaureate Enrollment 423
Women 91% **Men** 9% **Minority** 36% **International** 4% **Part-time** 4%

Graduate Enrollment 197
Women 81% **Men** 19% **Minority** 26% **International** 7.6% **Part-time** 35%

Nursing Student Activities Sigma Theta Tau, Student Nurses' Association, nursing club.

Nursing Student Resources Academic advising; academic or career counseling; assistance for students with disabilities; bookstore; campus computer network; career placement assistance; computer lab; computer-assisted instruction; daycare for children of students; e-mail services; employment services for current students; externships; housing assistance; interactive nursing skills videos; Internet; learning resource lab; library services; nursing audiovisuals; paid internships; placement services for program completers; remedial services; resume preparation assistance; skills, simulation, or other laboratory; tutoring.

Library Facilities 3.7 million volumes (250,000 in health, 25,000 in nursing); 71,234 periodical subscriptions (2,500 health-care related).

BACCALAUREATE PROGRAMS
Degree BS

Available Programs Accelerated Baccalaureate for Second. Degree; Generic Baccalaureate.

Study Options Full-time.

Program Entrance Requirements Minimum overall college GPA of 3.0, transcript of college record, CPR certification, health exam, health insurance, high school chemistry, high school transcript, immunizations, minimum high school GPA of 3.0, minimum GPA in nursing prerequisites of 3.0, prerequisite course work. Transfer students are accepted. *Application deadline:* 2/28 (fall).

Advanced Placement Credit by examination available. Credit given for nursing courses completed elsewhere dependent upon specific evaluations.

Expenses (2009–10) *Tuition, state resident:* full-time $4970; part-time $207 per credit hour. *Tuition, nonresident:* part-time $536 per credit hour. *Room and board:* $10,092; room only: $6192 per academic year. *Required fees:* full-time $2043; part-time $90 per credit.

Financial Aid 80% of baccalaureate students in nursing programs received some form of financial aid in 2008–09.

Contact Dr. David J. Lang, Director of Student Affairs, School of Nursing, University at Buffalo, the State University of New York, 103 Wende Hall, 3435 Main Street, Buffalo, NY 14214. *Telephone:* 716-829-2537. *Fax:* 716-829-2067. *E-mail:* nursing@buffalo.edu.

GRADUATE PROGRAMS
Expenses (2009–10) *Tuition, state resident:* full-time $8370; part-time $349 per credit hour. *Tuition, nonresident:* full-time $13,250; part-time $552 per credit hour. *International tuition:* $13,250 full-time. *Room and board:* $10,092; room only: $6192 per academic year. *Required fees:* full-time $1513; part-time $116 per credit.

Financial Aid 65% of graduate students in nursing programs received some form of financial aid in 2008–09. 13 fellowships with full tuition reimbursements available (averaging $7,220 per year), 10 research assistantships with tuition reimbursements available (averaging $17,881 per year), 23 teaching assistantships with full tuition reimbursements available (averaging $11,245 per year) were awarded; Federal Work-Study, scholarships, traineeships, and unspecified assistantships also available. *Financial aid application deadline:* 3/15.

Contact Dr. David J. Lang, Director of Student Affairs, School of Nursing, University at Buffalo, the State University of New York, 103 Wende Hall, 3435 Main Street, Buffalo, NY 14214. *Telephone:* 716-829-2537. *Fax:* 716-829-2067. *E-mail:* nursing@buffalo.edu.

MASTER'S DEGREE PROGRAM
Degree MS

Available Programs Master's.

Concentrations Available Nurse anesthesia. *Clinical nurse specialist programs in:* adult health, medical-surgical. *Nurse practitioner programs in:* adult health, family health, pediatric, psychiatric/mental health, women's health.

Study Options Full-time and part-time.

Program Entrance Requirements Computer literacy, minimum overall college GPA of 3.0, transcript of college record, CPR certification, written essay, immunizations, interview, 3 letters of recommendation, physical assessment course, statistics course, GRE General Test (if overall GPA is below 3.0). *Application deadline:* Applications may be processed on a rolling basis for some programs. *Application fee:* $50.

Advanced Placement Credit given for nursing courses completed elsewhere dependent upon specific evaluations.

Degree Requirements 45 total credit hours, thesis or project, comprehensive exam.

POST-MASTER'S PROGRAM
Areas of Study Nursing education. *Nurse practitioner programs in:* adult health, family health, pediatric, psychiatric/mental health, women's health.

DOCTORAL DEGREE PROGRAM
Degree PhD

Available Programs Doctorate.

Areas of Study Addiction/substance abuse, advanced practice nursing, aging, clinical practice, critical care, ethics, faculty preparation, family health, gerontology, health policy, health promotion/disease prevention, health-care systems, individualized study, information systems, maternity-newborn, nurse case management, nursing administration, nursing education, nursing policy, nursing research, nursing science, oncology, women's health.

Program Entrance Requirements Minimum overall college GPA of 3.25, interview by faculty committee, interview, 3 letters of recommendation, MSN or equivalent, statistics course, vita, writing sample, GRE General Test. Application deadline: Applications may be processed on a rolling basis for some programs. Application fee: $50.

Degree Requirements 60 total credit hours, dissertation, written exam, residency.

University of Rochester
School of Nursing
Rochester, New York

http://www.son.rochester.edu

Founded in 1850

DEGREES • BS • DNP • MS • MSN/PHD • PHD

Nursing Program Faculty 102 (41% with doctorates).

Baccalaureate Enrollment 200
Women 90% **Men** 10% **Minority** 17% **International** 1% **Part-time** 43%

Graduate Enrollment 208
Women 92% **Men** 8% **Minority** 16% **International** 5% **Part-time** 76%

Distance Learning Courses Available.

Nursing Student Activities Sigma Theta Tau, Student Nurses' Association.

Nursing Student Resources Academic advising; academic or career counseling; assistance for students with disabilities; bookstore; campus computer network; career placement assistance; computer lab; computer-assisted instruction; e-mail services; housing assistance; interactive nursing skills videos; Internet; learning resource lab; library services; nursing audiovisuals; resume preparation assistance; skills, simulation, or other laboratory; tutoring.

University of Rochester (continued)

Library Facilities 3.7 million volumes (240,000 in health); 24,240 periodical subscriptions (2,000 health-care related).

BACCALAUREATE PROGRAMS

Degree BS

Available Programs ADN to Baccalaureate; Accelerated Baccalaureate for Second Degree; Accelerated RN Baccalaureate; RN Baccalaureate.

Study Options Full-time.

Program Entrance Requirements Transcript of college record, CPR certification, written essay, health exam, health insurance, immunizations, 2 letters of recommendation, prerequisite course work. *Application deadline:* 7/1 (winter), 11/1 (summer). Applications may be processed on a rolling basis for some programs. *Application fee:* $50.

Advanced Placement Credit by examination available.

Expenses (2009–10) *Tuition:* full-time $33,328; part-time $1070 per credit hour. *International tuition:* $33,328 full-time. *Room and board:* $10,000; room only: $6000 per academic year.

Financial Aid 95% of baccalaureate students in nursing programs received some form of financial aid in 2008–09. *Financial aid application deadline (priority):* 2/1.

Contact Ms. Elaine M. Andolina, MS, RN, Director of Admissions, School of Nursing, University of Rochester, Box SON, 601 Elmwood Avenue, Rochester, NY 14642. *Telephone:* 585-275-2375. *Fax:* 585-756-8299. *E-mail:* son_admissions@urmc.rochester.edu.

GRADUATE PROGRAMS

Expenses (2009–10) *Tuition:* part-time $1070 per credit hour. *Room and board:* $10,000; room only: $6000 per academic year.

Financial Aid 95% of graduate students in nursing programs received some form of financial aid in 2008–09. *Financial aid application deadline:* 6/30.

Contact Ms. Elaine M. Andolina, MS, RN, Director of Admissions, School of Nursing, University of Rochester, Box SON, 601 Elmwood Avenue, Rochester, NY 14642. *Telephone:* 585-275-2375. *Fax:* 585-756-8299. *E-mail:* son_admissions@urmc.rochester.edu.

MASTER'S DEGREE PROGRAM

Degrees MS; MSN/PhD

Available Programs Accelerated AD/RN to Master's; Accelerated Master's for Non-Nursing College Graduates; Accelerated RN to Master's; Master's.

Concentrations Available Clinical nurse leader; health-care administration. *Nurse practitioner programs in:* acute care, adult health, family health, gerontology, neonatal health, pediatric, psychiatric/mental health.

Study Options Full-time and part-time.

Online Degree Options Yes.

Program Entrance Requirements Minimum overall college GPA of 3.0, transcript of college record, CPR certification, written essay, immunizations, interview, 2 letters of recommendation, resume, statistics course. *Application deadline:* Applications may be processed on a rolling basis for some programs. *Application fee:* $50.

Advanced Placement Credit given for nursing courses completed elsewhere dependent upon specific evaluations.

Degree Requirements 42–62 total credit hours, comprehensive exam.

POST-MASTER'S PROGRAM

Areas of Study *Nurse practitioner programs in:* acute care, adult health, family health, gerontology, neonatal health, pediatric, psychiatric/mental health.

DOCTORAL DEGREE PROGRAM

Degree DNP, PhD

Available Programs Doctorate; Post-Baccalaureate Doctorate.

Areas of Study Bio-behavioral research, nursing research.

Program Entrance Requirements Minimum overall college GPA of 3.5, interview, 3 letters of recommendation, MSN or equivalent, statistics course, vita, writing sample, GRE General Test. Application deadline: 2/1 (fall). Application fee: $50.

Degree Requirements 60 total credit hours, dissertation, oral exam, written exam, residency.

POSTDOCTORAL PROGRAM

Areas of Study Addiction/substance abuse, adolescent health, aging, cancer care, chronic illness, community health, family health, gerontology, individualized study, nursing interventions, nursing research, outcomes, vulnerable population.

Postdoctoral Program Contact Dr. Harriet Kitzman, Associate Dean for Research, School of Nursing, University of Rochester, Box SON, 601 Elmwood Avenue, Rochester, NY 14642. *Telephone:* 585-275-8874. *Fax:* 585-273-1258. *E-mail:* harriet_kitzman@urmc.rochester.edu.

CONTINUING EDUCATION PROGRAM

Contact Ms. Nadine Taylor, Administrative Assistant, Center for Lifelong Learning, School of Nursing, University of Rochester, Box SON, 601 Elmwood Avenue, Rochester, NY 14642. *Telephone:* 585-273-0446. *Fax:* 585-461-4488. *E-mail:* nadine_taylor@urmc.rochester.edu.

Utica College
Department of Nursing
Utica, New York

http://www.utica.edu

Founded in 1946

DEGREE • BS

Nursing Program Faculty 33 (1% with doctorates).

Baccalaureate Enrollment 245
Women 90% **Men** 10% **Minority** 21% **International** .01% **Part-time** 40%

Distance Learning Courses Available.

Nursing Student Activities Student Nurses' Association.

Nursing Student Resources Academic advising; academic or career counseling; assistance for students with disabilities; bookstore; campus computer network; career placement assistance; computer lab; computer-assisted instruction; e-mail services; employment services for current students; externships; housing assistance; interactive nursing skills videos; Internet; learning resource lab; library services; nursing audiovisuals; paid internships; placement services for program completers; remedial services; resume preparation assistance; skills, simulation, or other laboratory; tutoring; unpaid internships.

Library Facilities 185,292 volumes (2,652 in health, 1,122 in nursing); 1,093 periodical subscriptions (118 health-care related).

BACCALAUREATE PROGRAMS

Degree BS

Available Programs Generic Baccalaureate; RN Baccalaureate.

Study Options Full-time and part-time.

Program Entrance Requirements Minimum overall college GPA of 2.5, transcript of college record, written essay, health exam, health insurance, high school biology, high school chemistry, 3 years high school math, 3 years high school science, high school transcript, immunizations, 3 letters of recommendation, minimum high school GPA of 2.5, minimum high school rank 25%, minimum GPA in nursing prerequisites of 2.0. Transfer students are accepted. *Application deadline:* Applications may be processed on a rolling basis for some programs. *Application fee:* $40.

Advanced Placement Credit by examination available. Credit given for nursing courses completed elsewhere dependent upon specific evaluations.

Expenses (2009–10) *Tuition:* full-time $26,764; part-time $905 per credit hour. *Room and board:* $10,850 per academic year. *Required fees:* full-time $685; part-time $175 per term.

Financial Aid 97% of baccalaureate students in nursing programs received some form of financial aid in 2008–09. *Gift aid (need-based):* Federal Pell, FSEOG, state, private, college/university gift aid from institutional funds, Federal Nursing. *Loans:* Federal Direct (Subsidized and Unsubsidized Stafford PLUS), Perkins. *Work-study:* Federal Work-Study, part-time campus jobs. *Financial aid application deadline (priority):* 2/15.

Contact Mr. Patrick A. Quinn, Vice President for Enrollment Management, Department of Nursing, Utica College, 1600 Burrstone Road, Utica, NY 13502-4892. *Telephone:* 315-792-3006. *Fax:* 315-792-3003. *E-mail:* pquinn@utica.edu.

Wagner College
Department of Nursing
Staten Island, New York

http://www.wagner.edu/programs/nursing.html

Founded in 1883

DEGREES • BS • MSN

Nursing Program Faculty 17 (90% with doctorates).

Baccalaureate Enrollment 60
Women 82% **Men** 18% **Minority** 20% **International** 10% **Part-time** 5%

Graduate Enrollment 63
Women 90% **Men** 10% **Minority** 10% **Part-time** 95%

Nursing Student Activities Nursing Honor Society, Sigma Theta Tau, Student Nurses' Association.

Nursing Student Resources Academic advising; academic or career counseling; assistance for students with disabilities; bookstore; campus computer network; career placement assistance; computer lab; computer-assisted instruction; e-mail services; externships; housing assistance; interactive nursing skills videos; Internet; learning resource lab; library services; nursing audiovisuals; remedial services; skills, simulation, or other laboratory; tutoring; unpaid internships.

Library Facilities 170,527 volumes (4,505 in health, 859 in nursing); 19,400 periodical subscriptions (87 health-care related).

BACCALAUREATE PROGRAMS

Degree BS

Available Programs Baccalaureate for Second Degree; Generic Baccalaureate.

Study Options Full-time.

Program Entrance Requirements Minimum overall college GPA of 3.0, written essay, health exam, health insurance, high school chemistry, high school transcript, immunizations, letters of recommendation, minimum high school GPA of 2.7, minimum GPA in nursing prerequisites of 3.0, prerequisite course work. Transfer students are accepted.

Advanced Placement Credit by examination available. Credit given for nursing courses completed elsewhere dependent upon specific evaluations.

Contact *Telephone:* 718-390-3452. *Fax:* 718-420-4009.

GRADUATE PROGRAMS

Contact *Telephone:* 718-390-3444. *Fax:* 718-420-4009.

MASTER'S DEGREE PROGRAM

Degree MSN

Concentrations Available Nursing education. *Nurse practitioner programs in:* family health.

Study Options Full-time and part-time.

Program Entrance Requirements Clinical experience, minimum overall college GPA of 2.7, transcript of college record, CPR certification, immunizations, interview, 2 letters of recommendation, nursing research course, professional liability insurance/malpractice insurance, resume.

Degree Requirements 44 total credit hours.

POST-MASTER'S PROGRAM

Areas of Study *Nurse practitioner programs in:* family health.

York College of the City University of New York
Program in Nursing
Jamaica, New York

http://www.york.cuny.edu/~healthsci/nuprogram.html

Founded in 1967

DEGREE • BS

Nursing Program Faculty 5 (60% with doctorates).

Library Facilities 8,714 volumes in health, 567 volumes in nursing.

BACCALAUREATE PROGRAMS

Degree BS

Available Programs ADN to Baccalaureate; RN Baccalaureate.

Program Entrance Requirements Minimum overall college GPA of 2.5, transcript of college record, CPR certification, health exam, immunizations, minimum GPA in nursing prerequisites, professional liability insurance/malpractice insurance, prerequisite course work, RN licensure. Transfer students are accepted.

Advanced Placement Credit by examination available. Credit given for nursing courses completed elsewhere dependent upon specific evaluations.

Contact *Telephone:* 718-262-2165.

NORTH CAROLINA

Appalachian State University
Department of Nursing
Boone, North Carolina

Founded in 1899

DEGREE • BSN

Nursing Program Faculty 5 (80% with doctorates).

Nursing Student Resources Academic advising; academic or career counseling; assistance for students with disabilities; bookstore; campus computer network; career placement assistance; computer lab; computer-assisted instruction; e-mail services; interactive nursing skills videos; Internet; learning resource lab; library services; nursing audiovisuals; remedial services; tutoring.

Library Facilities 1.4 million volumes (3.2 million in health, 541,000 in nursing); 7,383 periodical subscriptions (6,764 health-care related).

BACCALAUREATE PROGRAMS

Degree BSN

Available Programs ADN to Baccalaureate.

Site Options Boone, NC; Hickory, NC; Morganton, NC.

Study Options Full-time and part-time.

Program Entrance Requirements Minimum overall college GPA of 2.5, transcript of college record, CPR certification, immunizations, minimum GPA in nursing prerequisites of 2.5, professional liability insurance/malpractice insurance, prerequisite course work, RN licensure. *Application deadline:* 8/1 (fall), 12/1 (spring). Applications may be processed on a rolling basis for some programs. *Application fee:* $50.

Expenses (2009–10) *Tuition, state resident:* part-time $91 per credit hour. *Tuition, nonresident:* part-time $450 per credit hour.

Financial Aid 50% of baccalaureate students in nursing programs received some form of financial aid in 2008–09. *Gift aid (need-based):* Federal Pell, FSEOG, state, private, college/university gift aid from institutional funds. *Loans:* FFEL (Subsidized and Unsubsidized Stafford PLUS), Perkins. *Work-study:* Federal Work-Study. *Financial aid application deadline (priority):* 3/15.

Contact Ms. Debbie Tabor, Program Manager, Department of Nursing, Appalachian State University, 400 University Hall Drive, Department of Extension and Distance Education, Boone, NC 28608. *Telephone:* 828-262-3113. *Fax:* 828-262-2916. *E-mail:* tabords@appstate.edu.

Barton College
School of Nursing
Wilson, North Carolina

http://www.barton.edu/nursing

Founded in 1902

DEGREE • BSN

Nursing Program Faculty 7 (14% with doctorates).

Baccalaureate Enrollment 98
Women 94.8% **Men** 5.2% **Minority** 17.9% **International** 2.5% **Part-time** 3.8%

Nursing Student Activities Sigma Theta Tau, Student Nurses' Association.

Nursing Student Resources Academic advising; academic or career counseling; assistance for students with disabilities; bookstore; campus computer network; career placement assistance; computer lab; computer-assisted instruction; e-mail services; externships; interactive nursing skills videos; Internet; learning resource lab; library services; nursing audiovisuals; paid internships; placement services for program completers; remedial services; resume preparation assistance; skills, simulation, or other laboratory; tutoring; unpaid internships.

Library Facilities 3,500 volumes in health, 2,250 volumes in nursing; 100 periodical subscriptions health-care related.

BACCALAUREATE PROGRAMS

Degree BSN

Available Programs Generic Baccalaureate; RN Baccalaureate.

Study Options Full-time and part-time.

Program Entrance Requirements Minimum overall college GPA of 2.5, transcript of college record, CPR certification, health exam, health insurance, high school biology, high school chemistry, high school transcript, immunizations, minimum GPA in nursing prerequisites of 2.5, professional liability insurance/malpractice insurance, prerequisite course work. Transfer students are accepted. *Application deadline:* 11/1 (fall).

Advanced Placement Credit given for nursing courses completed elsewhere dependent upon specific evaluations.

Expenses (2009–10) *Tuition:* full-time $19,100; part-time $810 per credit hour. *Room and board:* $7017; room only: $2330 per academic year. *Required fees:* full-time $1548.

Financial Aid 92% of baccalaureate students in nursing programs received some form of financial aid in 2008–09. *Gift aid (need-based):* Federal Pell, FSEOG, state, private, college/university gift aid from institutional funds. *Loans:* FFEL (Subsidized and Unsubsidized Stafford PLUS), Perkins, alternative loans. *Work-study:* Federal Work-Study. *Financial aid application deadline (priority):* 4/1.

Contact Ms. Christine W. Massey, Associate Professor and Interim Dean, School of Nursing, Barton College, PO Box 5000, Wilson, NC 27893-7000. *Telephone:* 252-399-6401. *Fax:* 252-399-6416. *E-mail:* cmassey@barton.edu.

Cabarrus College of Health Sciences
Louise Harkey School of Nursing
Concord, North Carolina

http://www.cabarruscollege.edu

Founded in 1942

DEGREE • BSN

Nursing Program Faculty 3 (25% with doctorates).

Baccalaureate Enrollment 35
Women 90% **Men** 10% **Minority** 10% **Part-time** 50%

Distance Learning Courses Available.

Nursing Student Activities Sigma Theta Tau, Student Nurses' Association, nursing club.

Nursing Student Resources Academic advising; academic or career counseling; assistance for students with disabilities; bookstore; campus computer network; career placement assistance; computer lab; computer-assisted instruction; e-mail services; interactive nursing skills videos; Internet; library services; resume preparation assistance; skills, simulation, or other laboratory.

Library Facilities 500 volumes in health, 300 volumes in nursing; 300 periodical subscriptions health-care related.

BACCALAUREATE PROGRAMS

Degree BSN

Available Programs RN Baccalaureate.

Study Options Full-time and part-time.

Program Entrance Requirements Minimum overall college GPA of 2.5, transcript of college record, CPR certification, written essay, health exam, health insurance, 4 years high school math, immunizations, 2 letters of recommendation, RN licensure. Transfer students are accepted. *Application deadline:* 5/1 (fall), 10/1 (spring). Applications may be processed on a rolling basis for some programs. *Application fee:* $35.

Advanced Placement Credit by examination available.

Financial Aid 80% of baccalaureate students in nursing programs received some form of financial aid in 2007–08.

Contact Mrs. Crystal T. Harris, Chair, Baccalaureate Completion Program, Louise Harkey School of Nursing, Cabarrus College of Health Sciences, 401 Medical Park Drive, Concord, NC 28025-2405. *Telephone:* 704-403-1756. *Fax:* 704-403-2077. *E-mail:* crystal.harris@cabarruscollege.edu.

Duke University
School of Nursing
Durham, North Carolina

http://www.nursing.duke.edu

Founded in 1838

DEGREES • BSN • MSN • MSN/MBA • PHD

Nursing Program Faculty 48 (71% with doctorates).

Baccalaureate Enrollment 138
Women 88% **Men** 12% **Minority** 11% **International** 1%

Graduate Enrollment 360
Women 85% **Men** 15% **Minority** 13% **International** 1% **Part-time** 68%

Distance Learning Courses Available.

Nursing Student Activities Sigma Theta Tau, Student Nurses' Association.

Nursing Student Resources Academic advising; academic or career counseling; assistance for students with disabilities; bookstore; campus computer network; career placement assistance; computer lab; computer-assisted instruction; e-mail services; Internet; library services; nursing audiovisuals; skills, simulation, or other laboratory.

Library Facilities 6 million volumes (280,606 in health, 12,366 in nursing); 61,964 periodical subscriptions (3,948 health-care related).

BACCALAUREATE PROGRAMS

Degree BSN

Available Programs Accelerated Baccalaureate for Second Degree.

Site Options Durham, NC.

Study Options Full-time.

Program Entrance Requirements Minimum overall college GPA of 3.0, transcript of college record, CPR certification, written essay, health exam, health insurance, immunizations, interview, 3 letters of recommendation, prerequisite course work. *Application deadline:* 1/1 (fall). *Application fee:* $50.

Expenses (2008–09) *Room and board:* $13,080 per academic year.

Financial Aid 97% of baccalaureate students in nursing programs received some form of financial aid in 2007–08. *Gift aid (need-based):* Federal Pell, FSEOG, state, private, college/university gift aid from institutional funds. *Loans:* FFEL (Subsidized and Unsubsidized Stafford PLUS), Perkins, college/university, alternative loans from private sources. *Work-study:* Federal Work-Study, part-time campus jobs. *Financial aid application deadline:* 2/1.

Contact Mrs. Melissa Ziberna, Admissions Officer, School of Nursing, Duke University, DUMC 3322 Trent Drive, Durham, NC 27710. *Telephone:* 919-684-9161. *Fax:* 919-668-4693. *E-mail:* ziber001@mc.duke.edu.

GRADUATE PROGRAMS

Expenses (2008–09) *Tuition:* part-time $1025 per credit hour. *Room and board:* $13,080 per academic year. *Required fees:* part-time $158 per credit.

Financial Aid 64% of graduate students in nursing programs received some form of financial aid in 2007–08. Career-related internships or fieldwork, institutionally sponsored loans, scholarships, traineeships, and tuition waivers (partial) available. Aid available to part-time students. *Financial aid application deadline:* 4/1.

Contact Mr. Eric Graham, Admissions Officer, School of Nursing, Duke University, Box 3322, Durham, NC 27710. *Telephone:* 919-684-9163. *Fax:* 919-668-4693. *E-mail:* eric.graham@duke.edu.

MASTER'S DEGREE PROGRAM

Degrees MSN; MSN/MBA

Available Programs Master's; RN to Master's.

Concentrations Available Health-care administration; nurse anesthesia; nurse case management; nursing administration; nursing education; nursing informatics. *Clinical nurse specialist programs in:* critical care, gerontology, maternity-newborn, oncology, pediatric. *Nurse practitioner programs in:* acute care, adult health, family health, gerontology, neonatal health, oncology, pediatric, primary care.

Site Options Durham, NC.

Study Options Full-time and part-time.

Online Degree Options Yes.

Program Entrance Requirements Clinical experience, computer literacy, minimum overall college GPA of 3.0, transcript of college record, CPR certification, written essay, immunizations, interview, 3 letters of recommendation, prerequisite course work, resume, statistics course, GRE General Test or MAT. *Application deadline:* 7/1 (fall), 12/1 (spring), 4/1 (summer). Applications may be processed on a rolling basis for some programs. *Application fee:* $50.

Advanced Placement Credit given for nursing courses completed elsewhere dependent upon specific evaluations.

Degree Requirements 39 total credit hours.

POST-MASTER'S PROGRAM

Areas of Study Health-care administration; nurse anesthesia; nurse case management; nursing administration; nursing education; nursing informatics. *Clinical nurse specialist programs in:* critical care, gerontology, maternity-newborn, oncology, pediatric. *Nurse practitioner programs in:* acute care, adult health, family health, gerontology, neonatal health, oncology, pediatric, primary care.

DOCTORAL DEGREE PROGRAM

Degree PhD

Available Programs Doctorate; Post-Baccalaureate Doctorate.

Areas of Study Health-care systems, illness and transition.

Site Options Durham, NC.

Program Entrance Requirements Minimum overall college GPA of 3.5, interview by faculty committee, interview, 3 letters of recommendation, MSN or equivalent, statistics course, vita. Application deadline: 12/15 (fall). Application fee: $75.

Degree Requirements 54 total credit hours, dissertation, oral exam.

See full description on page 488.

East Carolina University
College of Nursing
Greenville, North Carolina

Founded in 1907

DEGREES • BSN • MSN • PHD

Nursing Program Faculty 102 (45% with doctorates).

Baccalaureate Enrollment 617
Women 90.6% **Men** 9.4% **Minority** 13.4% **International** .4% **Part-time** 16.2%
Graduate Enrollment 464
Women 90.8% **Men** 9.2% **Minority** 14.6% **Part-time** 73.2%
Distance Learning Courses Available.
Nursing Student Activities Sigma Theta Tau, Student Nurses' Association.
Nursing Student Resources Academic advising; academic or career counseling; assistance for students with disabilities; bookstore; campus computer network; career placement assistance; computer lab; computer-assisted instruction; e-mail services; employment services for current students; externships; housing assistance; interactive nursing skills videos; Internet; learning resource lab; library services; nursing audiovisuals; remedial services; resume preparation assistance; skills, simulation, or other laboratory; tutoring; unpaid internships.
Library Facilities 2.1 million volumes (25,790 in health, 2,864 in nursing); 56,896 periodical subscriptions (13,070 health-care related).

BACCALAUREATE PROGRAMS

Degree BSN

Available Programs ADN to Baccalaureate; Generic Baccalaureate.

Study Options Full-time.

Online Degree Options Yes.

Program Entrance Requirements Minimum overall college GPA of 2.5, transcript of college record, CPR certification, health exam, health insurance, immunizations, professional liability insurance/malpractice insurance, prerequisite course work. Transfer students are accepted. *Application deadline:* 2/1 (fall), 9/1 (spring).

Advanced Placement Credit given for nursing courses completed elsewhere dependent upon specific evaluations.

Expenses (2009–10) *Tuition, state resident:* full-time $2491; part-time $311 per semester. *Tuition, nonresident:* full-time $13,325; part-time $1665 per semester. *International tuition:* $13,325 full-time. *Room and board:* $6680; room only: $4190 per academic year. *Required fees:* full-time $1836; part-time $125 per credit; part-time $229 per term.

Financial Aid 60% of baccalaureate students in nursing programs received some form of financial aid in 2008–09.

Contact Ms. Erin Rogers, Assistant Director of Student Services, College of Nursing, East Carolina University, Health Sciences Building, Suite 2150, Greenville, NC 27858-4353. *Telephone:* 252-744-6477. *Fax:* 252-744-6391. *E-mail:* ecunursestudentsvc@ecu.edu.

GRADUATE PROGRAMS

Expenses (2009–10) *Tuition, state resident:* full-time $2995; part-time $374 per semester. *Tuition, nonresident:* full-time $13,311; part-time $1663 per semester. *International tuition:* $13,311 full-time. *Room and board:* $6680; room only: $4190 per academic year. *Required fees:* full-time $1836; part-time $162 per credit; part-time $229 per term.

Financial Aid 45% of graduate students in nursing programs received some form of financial aid in 2008–09. Research assistantships with partial tuition reimbursements available, teaching assistantships with partial tuition reimbursements available, Federal Work-Study available. Aid available to part-time students. *Financial aid application deadline:* 6/1.

Contact Dr. Marie Pokorny, Acting Associate Dean and Professor, College of Nursing, East Carolina University, Health Sciences Building, Room 3166B, Greenville, NC 27858-4353. *Telephone:* 252-744-6422. *Fax:* 252-744-6536. *E-mail:* pokornym@ecu.edu.

MASTER'S DEGREE PROGRAM

Degree MSN

Available Programs Accelerated Master's for Non-Nursing College Graduates; Master's; RN to Master's.

Concentrations Available Nurse anesthesia; nurse-midwifery; nursing administration; nursing education. *Clinical nurse specialist programs in:* adult health. *Nurse practitioner programs in:* adult health, family health, neonatal health.

Study Options Full-time and part-time.

Online Degree Options Yes.

East Carolina University (continued)

Program Entrance Requirements Clinical experience, computer literacy, minimum overall college GPA of 3.0, transcript of college record, CPR certification, written essay, immunizations, interview, 3 letters of recommendation, nursing research course, professional liability insurance/malpractice insurance, prerequisite course work, statistics course, GRE General Test or MAT. *Application deadline:* 3/1 (fall), 10/1 (spring), 3/1 (summer).

Advanced Placement Credit given for nursing courses completed elsewhere dependent upon specific evaluations.

Degree Requirements 52 total credit hours, comprehensive exam.

POST-MASTER'S PROGRAM

Areas of Study Nurse anesthesia; nurse-midwifery; nursing administration; nursing education. *Clinical nurse specialist programs in:* adult health. *Nurse practitioner programs in:* adult health, family health, neonatal health.

DOCTORAL DEGREE PROGRAM

Degree PhD

Available Programs Doctorate; Post-Baccalaureate Doctorate.

Areas of Study Nursing science.

Program Entrance Requirements Minimum overall college GPA of 3.2, interview by faculty committee, 3 letters of recommendation, MSN or equivalent, scholarly papers, statistics course, vita, writing sample. Application deadline: 3/1 (fall).

Degree Requirements 54 total credit hours, dissertation, oral exam, written exam.

Fayetteville State University

Program in Nursing
Fayetteville, North Carolina

Founded in 1867

DEGREE • BS

Library Facilities 334,089 volumes; 2,735 periodical subscriptions.

BACCALAUREATE PROGRAMS

Degree BS

Available Programs Generic Baccalaureate; RN Baccalaureate.

Contact *Telephone:* 910-672-1924.

Gardner-Webb University

School of Nursing
Boiling Springs, North Carolina

http://www.nursing.gardner-webb.edu/index.html

Founded in 1905

DEGREES • BSN • MSN • MSN/MBA

Nursing Student Activities Nursing Honor Society, Student Nurses' Association.

Library Facilities 224,226 volumes; 1,607 periodical subscriptions.

BACCALAUREATE PROGRAMS

Degree BSN

Available Programs RN Baccalaureate.

Site Options Statesville, NC; Charlotte, NC; Cabarrus, NC.

Study Options Full-time and part-time.

Program Entrance Requirements Minimum overall college GPA of 2.5, transcript of college record, minimum GPA in nursing prerequisites of 2.5, prerequisite course work, RN licensure. Transfer students are accepted.

Contact *Telephone:* 704-406-4360. *Fax:* 704-406-3919.

GRADUATE PROGRAMS

Contact *Telephone:* 704-406-4358. *Fax:* 704-406-3919.

MASTER'S DEGREE PROGRAM

Degrees MSN; MSN/MBA

Available Programs Master's; RN to Master's.

Concentrations Available Nursing administration; nursing education.

Program Entrance Requirements Minimum overall college GPA of 2.7, transcript of college record, immunizations, 3 letters of recommendation, statistics course.

Degree Requirements 30 total credit hours.

Lees-McRae College

Nursing Program
Banner Elk, North Carolina

http://www.lmc.edu/sites/Academics/
OffCampusPrograms/nursing.htm

Founded in 1900

DEGREE • BSN

Nursing Program Faculty 3

Baccalaureate Enrollment 51

Women 88% **Men** 12% **Minority** 2% **International** 2%

Distance Learning Courses Available.

Nursing Student Resources Academic advising; academic or career counseling; bookstore; computer lab; computer-assisted instruction; e-mail services; Internet; learning resource lab; library services; nursing audiovisuals; skills, simulation, or other laboratory.

Library Facilities 88,756 volumes; 429 periodical subscriptions.

BACCALAUREATE PROGRAMS

Degree BSN

Available Programs ADN to Baccalaureate.

Site Options Spruce Pine, NC.

Study Options Full-time.

Program Entrance Requirements Transcript of college record, immunizations, 2 letters of recommendation, RN licensure. Transfer students are accepted. *Application deadline:* Applications may be processed on a rolling basis for some programs.

Financial Aid 100% of baccalaureate students in nursing programs received some form of financial aid in 2008–09. *Gift aid (need-based):* Federal Pell, FSEOG, state, private, college/university gift aid from institutional funds, Academic Competitiveness Grant, National Smart Grant. *Loans:* FFEL (Subsidized and Unsubsidized Stafford PLUS), Perkins, college/university, private alternative loans. *Work-study:* Federal Work-Study, part-time campus jobs. *Financial aid application deadline:* Continuous.

Contact Ms. Martha P. Hartley, RN, Director of RN to BSN Completion Program, Nursing Program, Lees-McRae College, 375 College Drive, PO Box 128, Banner Elk, NC 28604. *Telephone:* 828-898-8752. *Fax:* 866-774-4280. *E-mail:* Hartley@lmc.edu.

Lenoir-Rhyne University

Program in Nursing
Hickory, North Carolina

http://www.lrc.edu/nur

Founded in 1891

DEGREE • BS

Nursing Program Faculty 30 (20% with doctorates).

Baccalaureate Enrollment 109

Women 92% **Men** 8% **Minority** 11% **International** 1% **Part-time** 2%

Nursing Student Activities Sigma Theta Tau, Student Nurses' Association.

Nursing Student Resources Academic advising; academic or career counseling; assistance for students with disabilities; bookstore; campus computer network; career placement assistance; computer lab; computer-assisted instruction; e-mail services; employment services for current students; externships; housing assistance; interactive nursing skills videos; Internet; learning resource lab; library services; nursing audiovisuals; placement services for program completers; remedial services; resume preparation assistance; skills, simulation, or other laboratory; tutoring; unpaid internships.

Library Facilities 275,961 volumes (5,000 in health, 4,200 in nursing); 445 periodical subscriptions (220 health-care related).

BACCALAUREATE PROGRAMS

Degree BS

Available Programs ADN to Baccalaureate; Generic Baccalaureate.

Study Options Full-time and part-time.

Program Entrance Requirements Minimum overall college GPA of 3.0, transcript of college record, health exam, high school chemistry, high school foreign language, 3 years high school math, high school transcript, immunizations, minimum high school GPA of 3.0, minimum GPA in nursing prerequisites of 2.7. Transfer students are accepted. *Application deadline:* 3/1 (fall), 11/1 (spring), 4/1 (summer). Applications may be processed on a rolling basis for some programs. *Application fee:* $35.

Advanced Placement Credit by examination available. Credit given for nursing courses completed elsewhere dependent upon specific evaluations.

Expenses (2009–10) *Tuition:* full-time $24,200; part-time $1000 per credit hour. *International tuition:* $24,200 full-time. *Room and board:* $8540; room only: $4350 per academic year.

Financial Aid 100% of baccalaureate students in nursing programs received some form of financial aid in 2008–09.

Contact Dr. Linda W. Reece, Chair, School of Nursing, Program in Nursing, Lenoir-Rhyne University, PO Box 7292, Hickory, NC 28603. *Telephone:* 828-328-7282. *Fax:* 828-328-7284. *E-mail:* reecel@lr.edu.

North Carolina Agricultural and Technical State University

School of Nursing
Greensboro, North Carolina

http://www.ncat.edu/~nursing/index.html

Founded in 1891

DEGREE • BSN

Nursing Program Faculty 28 (32% with doctorates).

Baccalaureate Enrollment 418
Women 99% **Men** 1% **Minority** 91% **Part-time** 1%

Distance Learning Courses Available.

Nursing Student Activities Nursing Honor Society, Sigma Theta Tau, Student Nurses' Association, nursing club.

Nursing Student Resources Academic advising; academic or career counseling; assistance for students with disabilities; bookstore; campus computer network; career placement assistance; computer lab; computer-assisted instruction; e-mail services; employment services for current students; externships; housing assistance; interactive nursing skills videos; Internet; learning resource lab; library services; nursing audiovisuals; other; paid internships; placement services for program completers; remedial services; resume preparation assistance; skills, simulation, or other laboratory; tutoring; unpaid internships.

Library Facilities 597,093 volumes (19,510 in health, 3,232 in nursing); 40,425 periodical subscriptions (85 health-care related).

BACCALAUREATE PROGRAMS

Degree BSN

Available Programs Generic Baccalaureate; LPN to Baccalaureate; LPN to RN Baccalaureate; RN Baccalaureate.

Site Options Greensboro, NC.

Study Options Full-time and part-time.

Program Entrance Requirements Minimum overall college GPA of 2.8, transcript of college record, CPR certification, written essay, health exam, health insurance, high school biology, high school foreign language, 3 years high school math, 3 years high school science, high school transcript, immunizations, minimum high school GPA of 3.0, minimum GPA in nursing prerequisites of 2.8, professional liability insurance/malpractice insurance, prerequisite course work. Transfer students are accepted. *Application deadline:* 2/15 (spring). *Application fee:* $45.

Advanced Placement Credit by examination available. Credit given for nursing courses completed elsewhere dependent upon specific evaluations.

Expenses (2008–09) *Tuition, state resident:* full-time $1994; part-time $748 per semester. *Tuition, nonresident:* full-time $11,436; part-time $4289 per semester. *International tuition:* $11,436 full-time. *Room and board:* $4229; room only: $3079 per academic year. *Required fees:* full-time $1506; part-time $753 per term.

Financial Aid 90% of baccalaureate students in nursing programs received some form of financial aid in 2007–08.

Contact Dr. Dawn F. Murphy, Student Services Director, School of Nursing, North Carolina Agricultural and Technical State University, Noble Hall, 1601 East Market Street, Greensboro, NC 27411. *Telephone:* 336-334-7752. *Fax:* 336-334-7637. *E-mail:* dmurphy@ncat.edu.

North Carolina Central University

Department of Nursing
Durham, North Carolina

http://www.nccu.edu/artsci/nursing/

Founded in 1910

DEGREE • BSN

Nursing Program Faculty 30 (4% with doctorates).

Nursing Student Activities Sigma Theta Tau.

Nursing Student Resources Academic advising; academic or career counseling; assistance for students with disabilities; bookstore; campus computer network; career placement assistance; computer lab; computer-assisted instruction; e-mail services; employment services for current students; externships; housing assistance; interactive nursing skills videos; Internet; learning resource lab; library services; nursing audiovisuals; paid internships; placement services for program completers; resume preparation assistance; skills, simulation, or other laboratory; tutoring.

Library Facilities 573,199 volumes; 1,963 periodical subscriptions.

BACCALAUREATE PROGRAMS

Degree BSN

Available Programs Generic Baccalaureate.

Study Options Full-time.

Program Entrance Requirements Minimum overall college GPA of 2.0, transcript of college record, health exam, immunizations, minimum GPA in nursing prerequisites of 2.5, professional liability insurance/malpractice insurance, prerequisite course work. Transfer students are accepted.

Advanced Placement Credit given for nursing courses completed elsewhere dependent upon specific evaluations.

Contact *Telephone:* 919-530-5336. *Fax:* 919-530-5343.

Queens University of Charlotte
Presbyterian School of Nursing
Charlotte, North Carolina

http://www.queens.edu

Founded in 1857

DEGREES • BSN • MSN • MSN/MBA

Nursing Program Faculty 60 (20% with doctorates).

Baccalaureate Enrollment 260
Women 90% **Men** 10% **Minority** 25% **International** 5% **Part-time** 10%

Graduate Enrollment 55
Women 90% **Men** 10% **Minority** 25% **International** 5% **Part-time** 50%

Distance Learning Courses Available.

Nursing Student Activities Nursing Honor Society, Sigma Theta Tau, Student Nurses' Association.

Nursing Student Resources Academic advising; academic or career counseling; assistance for students with disabilities; bookstore; campus computer network; career placement assistance; computer lab; computer-assisted instruction; e-mail services; employment services for current students; externships; housing assistance; interactive nursing skills videos; Internet; learning resource lab; library services; nursing audiovisuals; placement services for program completers; remedial services; resume preparation assistance; skills, simulation, or other laboratory; tutoring; unpaid internships.

Library Facilities 126,242 volumes (1,703 in health, 713 in nursing); 592 periodical subscriptions (516 health-care related).

BACCALAUREATE PROGRAMS

Degree BSN

Available Programs ADN to Baccalaureate; Accelerated Baccalaureate; Accelerated Baccalaureate for Second Degree; Baccalaureate for Second Degree; Generic Baccalaureate; RN Baccalaureate.

Site Options Charlotte, NC; Gastonia, NC.

Study Options Full-time.

Online Degree Options Yes.

Program Entrance Requirements Minimum overall college GPA of 2.5, transcript of college record, CPR certification, health exam, health insurance, high school biology, high school chemistry, 2 years high school math, 1 year of high school science, high school transcript, immunizations, minimum high school GPA of 3.0, minimum GPA in nursing prerequisites of 2.5, prerequisite course work. Transfer students are accepted. *Application deadline:* 3/15 (fall), 3/15 (spring). *Application fee:* $40.

Advanced Placement Credit given for nursing courses completed elsewhere dependent upon specific evaluations.

Expenses (2009–10) *Tuition:* full-time $22,730; part-time $365 per credit hour. *International tuition:* $22,730 full-time. *Room and board:* $8236 per academic year. *Required fees:* full-time $600; part-time $300 per term.

Financial Aid 85% of baccalaureate students in nursing programs received some form of financial aid in 2008–09.

Contact Danielle Dupree, Director of Admissions, Presbyterian School of Nursing, Queens University of Charlotte, 1900 Selwyn Avenue, Charlotte, NC 28274. *Telephone:* 704-337-2780. *Fax:* 704-337-2477. *E-mail:* dupreed@queens.edu.

GRADUATE PROGRAMS

Expenses (2009–10) *Tuition:* full-time $6570; part-time $365 per credit hour. *International tuition:* $6570 full-time. *Required fees:* full-time $175.

Financial Aid 25% of graduate students in nursing programs received some form of financial aid in 2008–09.

Contact Dr. Janice Janken, RN, Chair and Professor, Presbyterian School of Nursing, Queens University of Charlotte, 1900 Selwyn Avenue, Charlotte, NC 28274. *Telephone:* 704-337-2382. *Fax:* 704-337-2477. *E-mail:* jankenj@queens.edu.

MASTER'S DEGREE PROGRAM

Degrees MSN; MSN/MBA

Available Programs Accelerated RN to Master's; Master's; RN to Master's.

Concentrations Available Clinical nurse leader; nursing administration; nursing education.

Study Options Full-time and part-time.

Program Entrance Requirements Minimum overall college GPA of 3.0, transcript of college record, 2 letters of recommendation, professional liability insurance/malpractice insurance, resume. *Application deadline:* Applications may be processed on a rolling basis for some programs. *Application fee:* $40.

Advanced Placement Credit given for nursing courses completed elsewhere dependent upon specific evaluations.

Degree Requirements 36 total credit hours, thesis or project.

POST-MASTER'S PROGRAM

Areas of Study Clinical nurse leader; nursing administration; nursing education.

CONTINUING EDUCATION PROGRAM

Contact Heather Roberts, RN, Coordinator of Nursing and Health Programs, Presbyterian School of Nursing, Queens University of Charlotte, 1900 Selwyn Avenue, Center for Lifelong Learning, Charlotte, NC 28274. *Telephone:* 704-337-2491. *E-mail:* robertsh@queens.edu.

The University of North Carolina at Chapel Hill
School of Nursing
Chapel Hill, North Carolina

http://nursing.unc.edu/

Founded in 1789

DEGREES • BSN • MSN • MSN/MS • PHD

Nursing Program Faculty 112 (70% with doctorates).

Baccalaureate Enrollment 307
Women 92% **Men** 8% **Minority** 11%

Graduate Enrollment 174
Women 90% **Men** 10% **Minority** 20%

Distance Learning Courses Available.

Nursing Student Activities Nursing Honor Society, Sigma Theta Tau, Student Nurses' Association, nursing club.

Nursing Student Resources Academic advising; academic or career counseling; assistance for students with disabilities; bookstore; campus computer network; career placement assistance; computer lab; computer-assisted instruction; e-mail services; employment services for current students; housing assistance; interactive nursing skills videos; Internet; learning resource lab; library services; nursing audiovisuals; other; remedial services; resume preparation assistance; skills, simulation, or other laboratory; tutoring.

Library Facilities 6.5 million volumes (315,000 in health); 60,713 periodical subscriptions (4,000 health-care related).

BACCALAUREATE PROGRAMS

Degree BSN

Available Programs ADN to Baccalaureate; Accelerated Baccalaureate for Second Degree; Generic Baccalaureate; RN Baccalaureate.

Study Options Full-time.

Program Entrance Requirements Minimum overall college GPA of 2.0, transcript of college record, CPR certification, written essay, health exam, health insurance, high school transcript, immunizations, 2 letters of recommendation, minimum GPA in nursing prerequisites of 2.0, prerequisite course work. Transfer students are accepted.

Advanced Placement Credit by examination available. Credit given for nursing courses completed elsewhere dependent upon specific evaluations.

Financial Aid 40% of baccalaureate students in nursing programs received some form of financial aid in 2008–09.

Contact Ms. Amy Burdette, Assistant Director for Undergraduate Admissions, School of Nursing, The University of North Carolina at Chapel Hill, CB #7460, Chapel Hill, NC 27599-7460. *Telephone:* 919-966-4260. *Fax:* 919-966-3540. *E-mail:* amy_burdette@unc.edu.

GRADUATE PROGRAMS

Financial Aid 8 fellowships, 6 research assistantships (averaging $8,000 per year), 10 teaching assistantships (averaging $8,000 per year) were awarded; scholarships, traineeships, and unspecified assistantships also available.

Contact Ms. Jennifer Moore, Admissions Counselor for Graduate Program and RN Options, School of Nursing, The University of North Carolina at Chapel Hill, CB #7460, Chapel Hill, NC 27599-7460. *Telephone:* 919-966-4260. *Fax:* 919-966-3540. *E-mail:* jennifer.j.moore@unc.edu.

MASTER'S DEGREE PROGRAM

Degrees MSN; MSN/MS

Available Programs Master's for Nurses with Non-Nursing Degrees; RN to Master's.

Concentrations Available Clinical nurse leader; nurse case management; nursing administration; nursing education; nursing informatics. *Clinical nurse specialist programs in:* maternity-newborn, pediatric, psychiatric/mental health, women's health. *Nurse practitioner programs in:* adult health, family health, neonatal health, oncology, pediatric, primary care, psychiatric/mental health, women's health.

Study Options Full-time and part-time.

Program Entrance Requirements Clinical experience, minimum overall college GPA of 3.0, transcript of college record, CPR certification, written essay, immunizations, 3 letters of recommendation, physical assessment course, professional liability insurance/malpractice insurance, resume, statistics course, GRE General Test.

Advanced Placement Credit given for nursing courses completed elsewhere dependent upon specific evaluations.

Degree Requirements 40 total credit hours, thesis or project, comprehensive exam.

POST-MASTER'S PROGRAM

Areas of Study Clinical nurse leader; nurse case management; nursing administration; nursing education; nursing informatics. *Clinical nurse specialist programs in:* maternity-newborn, pediatric, psychiatric/mental health, women's health. *Nurse practitioner programs in:* adult health, family health, neonatal health, oncology, pediatric, primary care, psychiatric/mental health, women's health.

DOCTORAL DEGREE PROGRAM

Degree PhD

Available Programs Doctorate.

Areas of Study Nursing research.

Program Entrance Requirements Minimum overall college GPA of 3.0, interview by faculty committee, 3 letters of recommendation, scholarly papers, statistics course, vita, writing sample, GRE General Test.

Degree Requirements 48 total credit hours, dissertation, oral exam, written exam, residency.

POSTDOCTORAL PROGRAM

Areas of Study Adolescent health, aging, cancer care, chronic illness, community health, family health, gerontology, health promotion/disease prevention, individualized study, information systems, neuro-behavior, nursing informatics, nursing interventions, nursing research, nursing science, outcomes, self-care, vulnerable population, women's health.

Postdoctoral Program Contact Dr. Merle Mishel, Professor, School of Nursing, The University of North Carolina at Chapel Hill, 1002 Carrington Hall, CB #7460, Chapel Hill, NC 27599-7460. *Telephone:* 919-966-5294. *Fax:* 919-966-3540. *E-mail:* mishel@email.unc.edu.

CONTINUING EDUCATION PROGRAM

Contact Dr. Pamela Jenkins, Director, Center for Lifelong Learning, School of Nursing, The University of North Carolina at Chapel Hill, L400 Carrington Hall, CB #7460, Chapel Hill, NC 27599-7460. *Telephone:* 919-966-3638. *Fax:* 919-966-7298. *E-mail:* prjenkin@email.unc.edu.

The University of North Carolina at Charlotte
School of Nursing
Charlotte, North Carolina

http://www.health.uncc.edu

Founded in 1946

DEGREES • BSN • MSN

Nursing Program Faculty 51 (50% with doctorates).

Baccalaureate Enrollment 330
Women 92% **Men** 8% **Minority** 8% **Part-time** 5%

Graduate Enrollment 200
Women 80% **Men** 20% **Minority** 10% **Part-time** 65%

Distance Learning Courses Available.

Nursing Student Activities Sigma Theta Tau, Student Nurses' Association.

Nursing Student Resources Academic advising; academic or career counseling; assistance for students with disabilities; bookstore; campus computer network; career placement assistance; computer lab; computer-assisted instruction; e-mail services; externships; interactive nursing skills videos; Internet; learning resource lab; library services; nursing audiovisuals; resume preparation assistance; skills, simulation, or other laboratory; tutoring.

Library Facilities 1 million volumes (39,000 in health, 2,400 in nursing); 29,174 periodical subscriptions (160 health-care related).

BACCALAUREATE PROGRAMS

Degree BSN

Available Programs ADN to Baccalaureate; Generic Baccalaureate; RN Baccalaureate.

Study Options Full-time.

Program Entrance Requirements Minimum overall college GPA of 2.5, transcript of college record, CPR certification, written essay, health exam, health insurance, high school biology, high school chemistry, high school foreign language, 3 years high school math, 3 years high school science, high school transcript, immunizations, 3 letters of recommendation, minimum GPA in nursing prerequisites of 2.5, prerequisite course work. Transfer students are accepted. *Application deadline:* 1/31 (fall), 8/31 (winter).

Financial Aid 50% of baccalaureate students in nursing programs received some form of financial aid in 2007–08.

Contact Mr. John Sugg, Academic Adviser, School of Nursing, The University of North Carolina at Charlotte, 9201 University City Boulevard, Charlotte, NC 28223-0001. *Telephone:* 704-687-4676. *Fax:* 704-687-3180. *E-mail:* jdsugg@uncc.edu.

GRADUATE PROGRAMS

Financial Aid 75% of graduate students in nursing programs received some form of financial aid in 2007–08.

Contact Dr. Gwen Foss, Associate Director for the Graduate Division, School of Nursing, The University of North Carolina at Charlotte, 9201 University City Boulevard, Charlotte, NC 28223-0001. *Telephone:* 704-687-7992. *Fax:* 704-687-6017. *E-mail:* gffoss@uncc.edu.

MASTER'S DEGREE PROGRAM

Degree MSN

Available Programs Master's; RN to Master's.

Concentrations Available Nurse anesthesia; nursing administration; nursing education. *Clinical nurse specialist programs in:* community health. *Nurse practitioner programs in:* adult health, family health.

Study Options Full-time and part-time.

Online Degree Options Yes.

Program Entrance Requirements Clinical experience, computer literacy, minimum overall college GPA of 3.0, transcript of college record, CPR certification, written essay, immunizations, interview, 3 letters of recommendation, nursing research course, professional liability insurance/malpractice insurance, resume, statistics course.

The University of North Carolina at Charlotte (continued)

POST-MASTER'S PROGRAM

Areas of Study Nurse anesthesia; nursing administration; nursing education. *Nurse practitioner programs in:* family health.

The University of North Carolina at Greensboro
School of Nursing
Greensboro, North Carolina

http://www.uncg.edu/nur/

Founded in 1891

DEGREES • BSN • MSN • MSN/MBA • PHD

Nursing Program Faculty 60 (60% with doctorates).

Baccalaureate Enrollment 1,138
Women 93% **Men** 7% **Minority** 29% **International** 4% **Part-time** 33%

Graduate Enrollment 275
Women 80% **Men** 20% **Minority** 18% **International** 4% **Part-time** 30%

Nursing Student Activities Nursing Honor Society, Sigma Theta Tau, Student Nurses' Association.

Nursing Student Resources Academic advising; academic or career counseling; assistance for students with disabilities; bookstore; campus computer network; career placement assistance; computer lab; computer-assisted instruction; e-mail services; externships; Internet; learning resource lab; library services; nursing audiovisuals; paid internships; placement services for program completers; remedial services; resume preparation assistance; skills, simulation, or other laboratory; tutoring; unpaid internships.

Library Facilities 2 million volumes; 4,648 periodical subscriptions.

BACCALAUREATE PROGRAMS

Degree BSN

Available Programs ADN to Baccalaureate; Baccalaureate for Second Degree; Generic Baccalaureate; LPN to Baccalaureate; LPN to RN Baccalaureate; RN Baccalaureate.

Site Options Hickory, NC; Greensboro, NC.

Study Options Full-time.

Program Entrance Requirements Minimum overall college GPA of 2.7, transcript of college record, CPR certification, health exam, immunizations, minimum GPA in nursing prerequisites of 3.0, professional liability insurance/malpractice insurance, prerequisite course work. Transfer students are accepted.

Contact *Telephone:* 336-334-5280. *Fax:* 336-334-3628.

GRADUATE PROGRAMS

Contact *Telephone:* 336-334-5561. *Fax:* 336-334-3628.

MASTER'S DEGREE PROGRAM

Degrees MSN; MSN/MBA

Available Programs Master's.

Concentrations Available Nurse anesthesia; nursing administration; nursing education. *Nurse practitioner programs in:* adult health, gerontology.

Site Options Hickory, NC.

Study Options Full-time and part-time.

Program Entrance Requirements Clinical experience, minimum overall college GPA of 3.0, transcript of college record, CPR certification, immunizations, 3 letters of recommendation, physical assessment course, professional liability insurance/malpractice insurance, prerequisite course work, statistics course, GRE General Test or MAT.

Advanced Placement Credit given for nursing courses completed elsewhere dependent upon specific evaluations.

Degree Requirements 36 total credit hours, thesis or project, comprehensive exam.

POST-MASTER'S PROGRAM

Areas of Study Nurse anesthesia. *Nurse practitioner programs in:* adult health, gerontology.

DOCTORAL DEGREE PROGRAM

Degree PhD

Available Programs Doctorate.

Areas of Study Aging, faculty preparation, gerontology, health policy, health promotion/disease prevention, nursing administration, nursing education, nursing research, nursing science, women's health.

Program Entrance Requirements Minimum overall college GPA of 3.0, interview by faculty committee, interview, 3 letters of recommendation, MSN or equivalent, writing sample.

Degree Requirements 57 total credit hours, dissertation, oral exam, written exam, residency.

The University of North Carolina at Pembroke
Nursing Program
Pembroke, North Carolina

Founded in 1887

DEGREE • BSN

Nursing Program Faculty 20 (5% with doctorates).

Baccalaureate Enrollment 139

Distance Learning Courses Available.

Nursing Student Activities Student Nurses' Association.

Nursing Student Resources Academic advising; academic or career counseling; assistance for students with disabilities; bookstore; campus computer network; computer lab; computer-assisted instruction; e-mail services; housing assistance; interactive nursing skills videos; Internet; learning resource lab; library services; nursing audiovisuals; remedial services; resume preparation assistance; skills, simulation, or other laboratory; tutoring.

Library Facilities 367,565 volumes; 67,319 periodical subscriptions.

BACCALAUREATE PROGRAMS

Degree BSN

Available Programs Generic Baccalaureate; RN Baccalaureate.

Site Options Southern Pines, NC; Fayetteville, NC; Hamlet, NC.

Study Options Full-time.

Program Entrance Requirements Minimum overall college GPA, health exam, minimum GPA in nursing prerequisites, prerequisite course work, RN licensure. Transfer students are accepted. *Application deadline:* 1/15 (spring).

Advanced Placement Credit given for nursing courses completed elsewhere dependent upon specific evaluations.

Financial Aid 95% of baccalaureate students in nursing programs received some form of financial aid in 2007–08. *Gift aid (need-based):* Federal Pell, FSEOG, state, private, college/university gift aid from institutional funds. *Loans:* FFEL (Subsidized and Unsubsidized Stafford PLUS), Perkins, college/university. *Work-study:* Federal Work-Study, part-time campus jobs. *Financial aid application deadline:* Continuous.

Contact Department of Nursing, Nursing Program, The University of North Carolina at Pembroke, PO Box 1510, Pembroke, NC 28372-1510. *Telephone:* 910-521-6522. *Fax:* 910-521-6178. *E-mail:* nursing@uncp.edu.

The University of North Carolina Wilmington
School of Nursing
Wilmington, North Carolina

http://www.uncwil.edu/inside

Founded in 1947

DEGREES • BS • MSN

Nursing Program Faculty 37 (43% with doctorates).

Baccalaureate Enrollment 227
Women 90% **Men** 10% **Minority** 9% **International** 1% **Part-time** 15%

Graduate Enrollment 57
Women 98% **Men** 2% **Minority** 21% **Part-time** 53%

Distance Learning Courses Available.

Nursing Student Activities Sigma Theta Tau, Student Nurses' Association.

Nursing Student Resources Academic advising; academic or career counseling; assistance for students with disabilities; bookstore; campus computer network; career placement assistance; computer lab; computer-assisted instruction; e-mail services; employment services for current students; externships; housing assistance; interactive nursing skills videos; Internet; learning resource lab; library services; nursing audiovisuals; remedial services; resume preparation assistance; skills, simulation, or other laboratory; tutoring; unpaid internships.

Library Facilities 1 million volumes (16,100 in health, 850 in nursing); 30,000 periodical subscriptions (2,344 health-care related).

BACCALAUREATE PROGRAMS

Degree BS

Available Programs Generic Baccalaureate; RN Baccalaureate.

Site Options Jacksonville, Supply, Elizabethtown, Kenansville, NC; Burgaw, NC; Bolton, NC; Southport, NC; Whiteville, NC.

Study Options Full-time.

Online Degree Options Yes.

Program Entrance Requirements Minimum overall college GPA of 2.5, transcript of college record, CPR certification, written essay, health exam, health insurance, immunizations, minimum GPA in nursing prerequisites of 2.0, professional liability insurance/malpractice insurance, prerequisite course work. Transfer students are accepted. *Application deadline:* 1/10 (fall), 8/10 (spring).

Advanced Placement Credit given for nursing courses completed elsewhere dependent upon specific evaluations.

Expenses (2009–10) *Tuition, state resident:* full-time $2565; part-time $87 per credit hour. *Tuition, nonresident:* full-time $13,447; part-time $454 per credit hour. *Room and board:* $7690 per academic year. *Required fees:* full-time $2146; part-time $227 per term.

Financial Aid 63% of baccalaureate students in nursing programs received some form of financial aid in 2008–09. *Gift aid (need-based):* Federal Pell, FSEOG, state, private, college/university gift aid from institutional funds, Academic Competitiveness Grant, National Smart Grant, TEACH Grant. *Loans:* Federal Direct (Subsidized and Unsubsidized Stafford PLUS), FFEL (Subsidized and Unsubsidized Stafford PLUS), Perkins, state, college/university. *Work-study:* Federal Work-Study. *Financial aid application deadline:* Continuous.

Contact Ms. Marta Medina, Student Service Cordinator, School of Nursing, The University of North Carolina Wilmington, 601 South College Road, Wilmington, NC 28403-5995. *Telephone:* 910-962-7211. *Fax:* 910-962-7656. *E-mail:* medinam@uncw.edu.

GRADUATE PROGRAMS

Expenses (2009–10) *Tuition, state resident:* full-time $2949; part-time $145 per credit hour. *Tuition, nonresident:* full-time $13,663; part-time $670 per credit hour. *Room and board:* $10,775 per academic year. *Required fees:* full-time $2146; part-time $39 per credit.

Financial Aid 25% of graduate students in nursing programs received some form of financial aid in 2008–09. 2 teaching assistantships with full and partial tuition reimbursements available (averaging $9,500 per year) were awarded. *Financial aid application deadline:* 3/15.

Contact Dr. Julie S. Taylor, Graduate Coordinator, School of Nursing, The University of North Carolina Wilmington, 601 South College Road, Wilmington, NC 28403-5995. *Telephone:* 910-962-7927. *Fax:* 910-962-4921. *E-mail:* taylorjs@uncw.edu.

MASTER'S DEGREE PROGRAM

Degree MSN

Available Programs Master's; RN to Master's.

Concentrations Available Nursing education. *Nurse practitioner programs in:* family health.

Site Options Raleigh, NC; Jacksonville, Supply, Elizabethtown, Kenansville, NC; Burgaw, NC; Bolton, NC; Southport, NC; Whiteville, NC.

Study Options Full-time and part-time.

Online Degree Options Yes.

Program Entrance Requirements Clinical experience, computer literacy, minimum overall college GPA of 3.0, transcript of college record, CPR certification, written essay, immunizations, 3 letters of recommendation, nursing research course, physical assessment course, professional liability insurance/malpractice insurance, prerequisite course work, resume, statistics course, GRE General Test. *Application deadline:* 3/1 (fall).

Advanced Placement Credit given for nursing courses completed elsewhere dependent upon specific evaluations.

Degree Requirements 47 total credit hours, thesis or project, comprehensive exam.

POST-MASTER'S PROGRAM

Areas of Study Nursing education. *Nurse practitioner programs in:* family health.

CONTINUING EDUCATION PROGRAM

Contact Ms. Linda Ferrell, Executive Assistant, School of Nursing, The University of North Carolina Wilmington, 601 South College Road, Wilmington, NC 28403-5995. *Telephone:* 910-962-3200. *Fax:* 910-962-3723. *E-mail:* ferrell@uncw.edu.

Western Carolina University
School of Nursing
Cullowhee, North Carolina

Founded in 1889

DEGREES • BSN • MS

Nursing Program Faculty 31 (50% with doctorates).

Baccalaureate Enrollment 200
Women 94% **Men** 6% **Minority** 2%

Graduate Enrollment 122
Women 90% **Men** 10% **Minority** 2%

Distance Learning Courses Available.

Nursing Student Activities Sigma Theta Tau, Student Nurses' Association.

Nursing Student Resources Academic advising; academic or career counseling; assistance for students with disabilities; bookstore; campus computer network; career placement assistance; computer lab; computer-assisted instruction; daycare for children of students; e-mail services; externships; housing assistance; interactive nursing skills videos; Internet; learning resource lab; library services; nursing audiovisuals; resume preparation assistance; skills, simulation, or other laboratory; tutoring.

Library Facilities 634,891 volumes (10,000 in health, 900 in nursing); 47,928 periodical subscriptions (70 health-care related).

BACCALAUREATE PROGRAMS

Degree BSN

Available Programs Accelerated Baccalaureate; Generic Baccalaureate; RN Baccalaureate.

Site Options Enka, NC.

Study Options Full-time.

Online Degree Options Yes.

Program Entrance Requirements Minimum overall college GPA of 3.0, transcript of college record, CPR certification, health exam, high school transcript, immunizations, minimum GPA in nursing prerequisites of 2.0, professional liability insurance/malpractice insurance, prerequisite course work. Transfer students are accepted. *Application deadline:* 2/2 (fall). *Application fee:* $40.

Advanced Placement Credit given for nursing courses completed elsewhere dependent upon specific evaluations.

Western Carolina University (continued)

Financial Aid 75% of baccalaureate students in nursing programs received some form of financial aid in 2008–09. *Gift aid (need-based):* Federal Pell, FSEOG, state, private, college/university gift aid from institutional funds. *Loans:* Federal Direct (Subsidized and Unsubsidized Stafford PLUS), FFEL (Subsidized and Unsubsidized Stafford PLUS), Perkins. *Work-study:* Federal Work-Study. *Financial aid application deadline (priority):* 3/31.

Contact Dr. Vincent P. Hall, RN, Director, School of Nursing, Western Carolina University, 209 Moore Building, Cullowhee, NC 28723. *Telephone:* 828-227-7467. *Fax:* 828-227-7052. *E-mail:* hallv@email.wcu.edu.

GRADUATE PROGRAMS

Financial Aid 75% of graduate students in nursing programs received some form of financial aid in 2008–09.

Contact Ms. Jessica Shirley, Director of Student Services, School of Nursing, School of Nursing, Western Carolina University, 1459 Sand Hill Road, AB Tech Campus, Suite 33, Enka, NC 28715. *Telephone:* 828-670-8810 Ext. 247. *E-mail:* jshirley@email.wcu.edu.

MASTER'S DEGREE PROGRAM

Degree MS

Available Programs Master's.

Concentrations Available Nurse anesthesia; nursing administration; nursing education. *Nurse practitioner programs in:* family health.

Site Options Enka, NC.

Study Options Full-time and part-time.

Online Degree Options Yes.

Program Entrance Requirements Clinical experience, minimum overall college GPA of 3.0, transcript of college record, CPR certification, written essay, immunizations, interview, 3 letters of recommendation, nursing research course, physical assessment course, professional liability insurance/malpractice insurance, resume, statistics course. *Application deadline:* 4/15 (fall), 10/15 (winter). *Application fee:* $40.

Advanced Placement Credit given for nursing courses completed elsewhere dependent upon specific evaluations.

Degree Requirements Thesis or project, comprehensive exam.

POST-MASTER'S PROGRAM

Areas of Study Nursing administration; nursing education. *Nurse practitioner programs in:* family health.

POSTDOCTORAL PROGRAM

Postdoctoral Program Contact Dr. Sandra Grenwicki, Head, School of Nursing, Western Carolina University, Cullowhee, NC 28723. *Telephone:* 828-227-7467. *Fax:* 828-227-7071. *E-mail:* grenwicki@wcu.edu.

Winston-Salem State University
Department of Nursing
Winston-Salem, North Carolina

http://www.wssu.edu
Founded in 1892
DEGREES • BSN • MSN

Nursing Program Faculty 34 (13% with doctorates).

Baccalaureate Enrollment 252
Women 77% **Men** 23% **Minority** 61%

Graduate Enrollment 15

Nursing Student Activities Nursing Honor Society, Sigma Theta Tau, Student Nurses' Association.

Nursing Student Resources Academic advising; academic or career counseling; assistance for students with disabilities; bookstore; campus computer network; computer lab; interactive nursing skills videos; learning resource lab; nursing audiovisuals; skills, simulation, or other laboratory.

Library Facilities 4,381 volumes in health, 2,691 volumes in nursing; 2,205 periodical subscriptions health-care related.

BACCALAUREATE PROGRAMS

Degree BSN

Available Programs ADN to Baccalaureate; Accelerated RN Baccalaureate; Baccalaureate for Second Degree; Generic Baccalaureate; LPN to Baccalaureate; RN Baccalaureate.

Site Options Wilkesboro, NC; Salisbury, NC; Boone, NC.

Study Options Full-time.

Program Entrance Requirements Minimum overall college GPA of 2.6, transcript of college record, CPR certification, health exam, immunizations, professional liability insurance/malpractice insurance, prerequisite course work. Transfer students are accepted.

Advanced Placement Credit by examination available. Credit given for nursing courses completed elsewhere dependent upon specific evaluations.

Contact *Telephone:* 336-750-2560. *Fax:* 336-750-2599.

GRADUATE PROGRAMS

Contact *Telephone:* 336-750-2275. *Fax:* 336-750-2007.

MASTER'S DEGREE PROGRAM

Degree MSN

Available Programs Master's.

Concentrations Available Nursing education. *Nurse practitioner programs in:* family health, psychiatric/mental health.

Study Options Full-time and part-time.

Program Entrance Requirements Clinical experience, transcript of college record, CPR certification, immunizations, interview, 3 letters of recommendation, nursing research course, physical assessment course, professional liability insurance/malpractice insurance, resume, statistics course.

Advanced Placement Credit given for nursing courses completed elsewhere dependent upon specific evaluations.

Degree Requirements 50 total credit hours, thesis or project.

CONTINUING EDUCATION PROGRAM

Contact *Telephone:* 336-750-2665. *Fax:* 336-750-2599.

NORTH DAKOTA

Dickinson State University
Department of Nursing
Dickinson, North Dakota

http://www.dsu.nodak.edu/Catalog/nursing.htm
Founded in 1918
DEGREE • BSN

Nursing Program Faculty 7 (14% with doctorates).

Baccalaureate Enrollment 45
Women 96% **Men** 4% **Minority** 4% **International** 2% **Part-time** 13%

Nursing Student Activities Student Nurses' Association.

Nursing Student Resources Academic advising; academic or career counseling; assistance for students with disabilities; bookstore; campus computer network; career placement assistance; computer lab; computer-assisted instruction; e-mail services; employment services for current students; externships; housing assistance; Internet; learning resource lab; library services; nursing audiovisuals; placement services for program completers; remedial services; resume preparation assistance; skills, simulation, or other laboratory; tutoring; unpaid internships.

Library Facilities 105,713 volumes (7,258 in health, 3,216 in nursing); 823 periodical subscriptions (2,898 health-care related).

BACCALAUREATE PROGRAMS

Degree BSN

Available Programs ADN to Baccalaureate; LPN to Baccalaureate; LPN to RN Baccalaureate; RN Baccalaureate.

Study Options Full-time and part-time.

Program Entrance Requirements Minimum overall college GPA of 2.5, transcript of college record, health exam, immunizations, minimum GPA in nursing prerequisites of 2.5, prerequisite course work. Transfer students are accepted. *Application deadline:* 2/1 (fall).

Advanced Placement Credit given for nursing courses completed elsewhere dependent upon specific evaluations.

Expenses (2009–10) *Tuition, state resident:* full-time $5250; part-time $173 per credit hour. *Tuition, nonresident:* full-time $12,196; part-time $463 per credit hour. *International tuition:* $12,196 full-time. *Room and board:* $4494; room only: $1610 per academic year. *Required fees:* full-time $500; part-time $150 per term.

Financial Aid 85% of baccalaureate students in nursing programs received some form of financial aid in 2008–09.

Contact Dr. Mary Anne Marsh, Chair, Department of Nursing, Dickinson State University, 291 Campus Drive, Dickinson, ND 58601-4896. *Telephone:* 800-279-4295 Ext. 2133. *Fax:* 701-483-2524. *E-mail:* maryanne.marsh@dsu.nodak.edu.

Jamestown College
Department of Nursing
Jamestown, North Dakota

Founded in 1883

DEGREE • BSN

Nursing Program Faculty 11 (9% with doctorates).

Baccalaureate Enrollment 80

Nursing Student Activities Sigma Theta Tau, Student Nurses' Association.

Nursing Student Resources Academic advising; academic or career counseling; bookstore; campus computer network; computer lab; computer-assisted instruction; e-mail services; externships; interactive nursing skills videos; Internet; learning resource lab; library services; nursing audiovisuals; resume preparation assistance; skills, simulation, or other laboratory; tutoring.

Library Facilities 113,572 volumes (990 in health, 983 in nursing); 630 periodical subscriptions (163 health-care related).

BACCALAUREATE PROGRAMS

Degree BSN

Study Options Full-time and part-time.

Program Entrance Requirements Minimum overall college GPA of 3.0, transcript of college record, written essay, high school transcript, immunizations, prerequisite course work. Transfer students are accepted.

Advanced Placement Credit given for nursing courses completed elsewhere dependent upon specific evaluations.

Contact *Telephone:* 701-252-3467 Ext. 2562. *Fax:* 701-253-4318.

Medcenter One College of Nursing
Medcenter One College of Nursing
Bismarck, North Dakota

http://www.medcenterone.com/college of nursing

Founded in 1988

DEGREE • BSN

Nursing Program Faculty 13 (8% with doctorates).

Baccalaureate Enrollment 89

Women 93% **Men** 7% **Minority** 4%

Nursing Student Activities Sigma Theta Tau, Student Nurses' Association.

Nursing Student Resources Academic advising; bookstore; computer lab; computer-assisted instruction; e-mail services; Internet; library services; nursing audiovisuals; paid internships; placement services for program completers; resume preparation assistance; skills, simulation, or other laboratory; tutoring.

Library Facilities 26,078 volumes (2,260 in health, 1,769 in nursing); 446 periodical subscriptions (218 health-care related).

BACCALAUREATE PROGRAMS

Degree BSN

Available Programs RN Baccalaureate.

Study Options Full-time and part-time.

Program Entrance Requirements Minimum overall college GPA of 2.5, transcript of college record, written essay, health exam, high school transcript, immunizations, interview, minimum GPA in nursing prerequisites of 2.5, prerequisite course work. Transfer students are accepted. *Application deadline:* 11/1 (fall). *Application fee:* $40.

Advanced Placement Credit given for nursing courses completed elsewhere dependent upon specific evaluations.

Expenses (2009–10) *Tuition:* full-time $9720; part-time $405 per credit. *Required fees:* full-time $839; part-time $18 per credit; part-time $200 per term.

Financial Aid 99% of baccalaureate students in nursing programs received some form of financial aid in 2008–09. *Gift aid (need-based):* Federal Pell, FSEOG, state, private, college/university gift aid from institutional funds. *Loans:* Federal Nursing Student Loans, FFEL (Subsidized and Unsubsidized Stafford PLUS), Perkins, college/university. *Work-study:* Federal Work-Study. *Financial aid application deadline (priority):* 3/15.

Contact Ms. Mary Smith, RN, Director of Student Services, Medcenter One College of Nursing, 512 North 7th Street, Bismarck, ND 58501. *Telephone:* 701-323-6271. *Fax:* 701-323-6289. *E-mail:* msmith@mohs.org.

Minot State University
Department of Nursing
Minot, North Dakota

http://www.minotstateu.edu/nursing/

Founded in 1913

DEGREE • BSN

Nursing Program Faculty 21 (10% with doctorates).

Baccalaureate Enrollment 118

Women 90% **Men** 10% **Minority** 19% **International** 3% **Part-time** 25%

Distance Learning Courses Available.

Nursing Student Activities Sigma Theta Tau, Student Nurses' Association.

Nursing Student Resources Academic advising; academic or career counseling; assistance for students with disabilities; bookstore; campus computer network; career placement assistance; computer lab; computer-assisted instruction; e-mail services; housing assistance; interactive nursing skills videos; Internet; learning resource lab; library services; nursing audiovisuals; paid internships; remedial services; resume preparation assistance; skills, simulation, or other laboratory; tutoring.

Library Facilities 7,337 volumes in health, 2,842 volumes in nursing; 913 periodical subscriptions health-care related.

BACCALAUREATE PROGRAMS

Degree BSN

Available Programs Generic Baccalaureate; RN Baccalaureate.

Study Options Full-time.

Online Degree Options Yes.

Program Entrance Requirements Minimum overall college GPA of 2.75, transcript of college record, CPR certification, written essay, immunizations, 2 letters of recommendation, minimum GPA in nursing prerequisites of 2.8, prerequisite course work. Transfer students are accepted. *Application deadline:* 10/1 (fall), 2/1 (spring). *Application fee:* $25.

Advanced Placement Credit given for nursing courses completed elsewhere dependent upon specific evaluations.

Minot State University (continued)

Expenses (2009–10) *Tuition, state resident:* full-time $5389. *Tuition, nonresident:* full-time $5389. *International tuition:* $5389 full-time. *Room and board:* $4372 per academic year. *Required fees:* full-time $600.

Financial Aid 91% of baccalaureate students in nursing programs received some form of financial aid in 2008–09. *Gift aid (need-based):* Federal Pell, FSEOG, state, private, college/university gift aid from institutional funds, Federal Nursing. *Loans:* Federal Nursing Student Loans, FFEL (Subsidized and Unsubsidized Stafford PLUS), Perkins, college/university. *Work-study:* Federal Work-Study. *Financial aid application deadline (priority):* 3/15.

Contact Ms. Kelly Buettner-Schmidt, RN, Chair, Department of Nursing, Department of Nursing, Minot State University, 500 University Avenue West, Minot, ND 58707-0002. *Telephone:* 701-858-3101. *Fax:* 701-858-4309. *E-mail:* kelly.schmidt@minotstateu.edu.

North Dakota State University

Department of Nursing
Fargo, North Dakota

http://www.ndsu.edu/ndsu/nursing/

Founded in 1890

DEGREES • BSN • DNP • MS

Nursing Program Faculty 15 (49% with doctorates).

Baccalaureate Enrollment 195
Women 90% **Men** 10% **Minority** 5% **International** 3% **Part-time** 10%

Graduate Enrollment 24
Women 95% **Men** 5% **Minority** 1% **Part-time** 45%

Nursing Student Activities Sigma Theta Tau, Student Nurses' Association.

Nursing Student Resources Academic advising; academic or career counseling; assistance for students with disabilities; bookstore; campus computer network; career placement assistance; computer lab; computer-assisted instruction; daycare for children of students; e-mail services; employment services for current students; interactive nursing skills videos; Internet; learning resource lab; library services; nursing audiovisuals; paid internships; placement services for program completers; remedial services; resume preparation assistance; skills, simulation, or other laboratory; tutoring.

Library Facilities 136,912 volumes (8,631 in health, 1,841 in nursing); 2,499 periodical subscriptions (121 health-care related).

BACCALAUREATE PROGRAMS

Degree BSN

Available Programs ADN to Baccalaureate; Generic Baccalaureate; LPN to Baccalaureate.

Study Options Full-time.

Program Entrance Requirements Minimum overall college GPA of 3.0, transcript of college record, CPR certification, health exam, health insurance, immunizations, 2 letters of recommendation, minimum GPA in nursing prerequisites of 3.0, prerequisite course work. Transfer students are accepted.

Advanced Placement Credit by examination available. Credit given for nursing courses completed elsewhere dependent upon specific evaluations.

Contact *Telephone:* 701-231-7395. *Fax:* 701-231-7606.

GRADUATE PROGRAMS

Contact *Telephone:* 701-231-8355. *Fax:* 701-231-7606.

MASTER'S DEGREE PROGRAM

Degree MS

Available Programs Master's.

Concentrations Available Nursing education. *Clinical nurse specialist programs in:* adult health. *Nurse practitioner programs in:* family health.

Study Options Full-time and part-time.

Program Entrance Requirements Computer literacy, minimum overall college GPA of 3.0, transcript of college record, CPR certification, immunizations, interview, 3 letters of recommendation, nursing research course, physical assessment course, professional liability insurance/malpractice insurance, resume, statistics course.

Advanced Placement Credit given for nursing courses completed elsewhere dependent upon specific evaluations.

Degree Requirements 58 total credit hours, thesis or project, comprehensive exam.

DOCTORAL DEGREE PROGRAM

Degree DNP

Available Programs Post-Baccalaureate Doctorate.

Areas of Study Advanced practice nursing, family health.

Online Degree Options Yes.

Program Entrance Requirements Clinical experience, minimum overall college GPA of 3.0, interview by faculty committee, 2 letters of recommendation, statistics course, vita, writing sample.

Degree Requirements 86 total credit hours, dissertation, oral exam.

University of Mary

Division of Nursing
Bismarck, North Dakota

http://www.umary.edu/AcadInfo/NurDiv

Founded in 1959 ·

DEGREES • BS • MSN • MSN/MBA

Nursing Program Faculty 45 (44% with doctorates).

Baccalaureate Enrollment 127
Women 98% **Men** 2% **Minority** 4%

Graduate Enrollment 198
Women 98% **Men** 2% **Minority** 14% **Part-time** 23%

Distance Learning Courses Available.

Nursing Student Activities Sigma Theta Tau, Student Nurses' Association.

Nursing Student Resources Academic advising; academic or career counseling; assistance for students with disabilities; bookstore; campus computer network; career placement assistance; computer lab; computer-assisted instruction; e-mail services; employment services for current students; externships; housing assistance; interactive nursing skills videos; Internet; library services; nursing audiovisuals; placement services for program completers; resume preparation assistance; skills, simulation, or other laboratory; unpaid internships.

Library Facilities 63,259 volumes (10,425 in health, 3,000 in nursing); 222 periodical subscriptions (125 health-care related).

BACCALAUREATE PROGRAMS

Degree BS

Available Programs Generic Baccalaureate; LPN to Baccalaureate; RN Baccalaureate.

Study Options Full-time and part-time.

Online Degree Options Yes.

Program Entrance Requirements Minimum overall college GPA of 2.75, transcript of college record, CPR certification, written essay, health exam, high school transcript, immunizations, interview, 2 letters of recommendation, minimum GPA in nursing prerequisites of 2.0, professional liability insurance/malpractice insurance, prerequisite course work. Transfer students are accepted. *Application deadline:* 2/27 (spring).

Advanced Placement Credit by examination available. Credit given for nursing courses completed elsewhere dependent upon specific evaluations.

Expenses (2009–10) *Tuition:* full-time $12,360; part-time $390 per credit. *Room and board:* $5000; room only: $3000 per academic year. *Required fees:* full-time $240.

Financial Aid 100% of baccalaureate students in nursing programs received some form of financial aid in 2008–09. *Gift aid (need-based):* Federal Pell, FSEOG, state, private, college/university gift aid from institutional funds, Academic Competitiveness Grant, National Smart Grant,

TEACH Grant. *Loans:* Federal Nursing Student Loans, FFEL (Subsidized and Unsubsidized Stafford PLUS), Perkins, alternative private loans. *Work-study:* Federal Work-Study, part-time campus jobs. *Financial aid application deadline:* Continuous.

Contact Admissions Office, Division of Nursing, University of Mary, 7500 University Drive, Bismarck, ND 58504. *Telephone:* 701-255-7500. *Fax:* 701-255-7687.

GRADUATE PROGRAMS

Expenses (2009–10) *Tuition:* part-time $500 per credit.

Financial Aid 95% of graduate students in nursing programs received some form of financial aid in 2008–09. 14 fellowships with partial tuition reimbursements available, 3 teaching assistantships with partial tuition reimbursements available were awarded; institutionally sponsored loans also available. Aid available to part-time students. *Financial aid application deadline:* 7/1.

Contact Prof. Mariah Dietz, DNS, Graduate Program Director, Division of Nursing, University of Mary, 7500 University Drive, Bismarck, ND 58504. *Telephone:* 701-355-8041. *Fax:* 701-255-7687. *E-mail:* mdietz@umary.edu.

MASTER'S DEGREE PROGRAM

Degrees MSN; MSN/MBA

Available Programs Master's; RN to Master's.

Concentrations Available Nursing administration; nursing education. *Nurse practitioner programs in:* family health.

Site Options Billings, MT; Gillette, WY; Kansas City, MO.

Study Options Full-time and part-time.

Online Degree Options Yes.

Program Entrance Requirements Clinical experience, minimum overall college GPA of 2.75, transcript of college record, CPR certification, written essay, immunizations, interview, 3 letters of recommendation, physical assessment course, statistics course. *Application deadline:* Applications may be processed on a rolling basis for some programs.

Degree Requirements 39 total credit hours, thesis or project, comprehensive exam.

University of North Dakota
College of Nursing
Grand Forks, North Dakota

http://www.nursing.und.edu/

Founded in 1883

DEGREES • BSN • MS • PHD

Nursing Program Faculty 60 (33% with doctorates).

Baccalaureate Enrollment 295
Women 87% **Men** 13% **Minority** 8.81% **International** .33% **Part-time** 13%

Graduate Enrollment 109
Women 88.1% **Men** 11.9% **Minority** 12.8% **Part-time** 52.3%

Distance Learning Courses Available.

Nursing Student Activities Nursing Honor Society, Sigma Theta Tau, Student Nurses' Association.

Nursing Student Resources Academic advising; academic or career counseling; assistance for students with disabilities; bookstore; career placement assistance; computer lab; computer-assisted instruction; daycare for children of students; e-mail services; employment services for current students; externships; housing assistance; interactive nursing skills videos; Internet; learning resource lab; library services; nursing audiovisuals; paid internships; placement services for program completers; remedial services; resume preparation assistance; skills, simulation, or other laboratory; tutoring.

Library Facilities 1.5 million volumes (105,982 in health, 15,000 in nursing); 8,000 periodical subscriptions health-care related.

BACCALAUREATE PROGRAMS

Degree BSN

Available Programs ADN to Baccalaureate; Accelerated Baccalaureate for Second Degree; Accelerated RN Baccalaureate; Baccalaureate for Second Degree; Generic Baccalaureate; International Nurse to Baccalaureate; LPN to Baccalaureate; LPN to RN Baccalaureate; RN Baccalaureate.

Site Options Grand Forks, ND.

Study Options Full-time and part-time.

Online Degree Options Yes.

Program Entrance Requirements Minimum overall college GPA of 2.5, transcript of college record, CPR certification, written essay, health insurance, immunizations, minimum GPA in nursing prerequisites of 2.5, prerequisite course work. Transfer students are accepted. *Application deadline:* 2/1 (fall), 7/1 (spring).

Advanced Placement Credit by examination available. Credit given for nursing courses completed elsewhere dependent upon specific evaluations.

Expenses (2009–10) *Tuition, state resident:* full-time $6726; part-time $280 per credit. *Tuition, nonresident:* full-time $9456; part-time $394 per credit. *International tuition:* $15,845 full-time. *Room and board:* $5660; room only: $5510 per academic year. *Required fees:* full-time $600; part-time $25 per credit.

Financial Aid 81% of baccalaureate students in nursing programs received some form of financial aid in 2008–09.

Contact Ms. Marlys K. Escobar, Director of Student and Alumni Affairs, College of Nursing, University of North Dakota, 430 Oxford Street, Stop 9025, Room 301, Grand Forks, ND 58202-9025. *Telephone:* 701-777-4534. *Fax:* 701-777-4096. *E-mail:* marlysescobar@mail.und.nodak.edu.

GRADUATE PROGRAMS

Expenses (2009–10) *Tuition, state resident:* full-time $12,405; part-time $517 per credit hour. *Tuition, nonresident:* full-time $22,214; part-time $926 per credit hour. *Room and board:* $5702 per academic year. *Required fees:* full-time $1000; part-time $42 per credit; part-time $500 per term.

Financial Aid 75% of graduate students in nursing programs received some form of financial aid in 2008–09. 4 research assistantships with tuition reimbursements available (averaging $10,498 per year), 7 teaching assistantships with full tuition reimbursements available (averaging $10,669 per year) were awarded; fellowships with tuition reimbursements available, Federal Work-Study, institutionally sponsored loans, scholarships, traineeships, and tuition waivers (full and partial) also available. Aid available to part-time students. *Financial aid application deadline:* 3/15.

Contact Dr. Darla J. Adams, Associate Dean for Graduate Studies, College of Nursing, University of North Dakota, PO Box 9025, Room 361, Grand Forks, ND 58202-9025. *Telephone:* 701-777-4543. *Fax:* 701-777-4096. *E-mail:* darlaadams@mail.und.edu.

MASTER'S DEGREE PROGRAM

Degree MS

Available Programs Master's; RN to Master's.

Concentrations Available Nurse anesthesia; nursing education. *Clinical nurse specialist programs in:* community health, gerontology, psychiatric/mental health, public health. *Nurse practitioner programs in:* family health, gerontology, psychiatric/mental health.

Site Options Grand Forks, ND.

Study Options Full-time and part-time.

Online Degree Options Yes.

Program Entrance Requirements Clinical experience, minimum overall college GPA of 3.0, transcript of college record, CPR certification, written essay, immunizations, interview, 3 letters of recommendation, prerequisite course work, resume, statistics course. *Application fee:* $35.

Advanced Placement Credit given for nursing courses completed elsewhere dependent upon specific evaluations.

Degree Requirements 48 total credit hours, thesis or project.

POST-MASTER'S PROGRAM

Areas of Study Nurse anesthesia; nursing education. *Clinical nurse specialist programs in:* psychiatric/mental health. *Nurse practitioner programs in:* family health, psychiatric/mental health.

DOCTORAL DEGREE PROGRAM

Degree PhD

Available Programs Doctorate.

Areas of Study Faculty preparation, health promotion/disease prevention, nursing education, nursing research.

University of North Dakota (continued)
Site Options Grand Forks, ND.
Program Entrance Requirements Minimum overall college GPA of 3.5, interview by faculty committee, interview, 3 letters of recommendation, MSN or equivalent, statistics course, vita, GRE or MAT. Application deadline: 3/15 (fall). Application fee: $35.
Degree Requirements 90 total credit hours, dissertation, oral exam, written exam, residency.

OHIO

Ashland University
Department of Nursing
Ashland, Ohio

http://www.ashland.edu/nursing
Founded in 1878
DEGREE • BSN
Nursing Program Faculty 2 (100% with doctorates).
Baccalaureate Enrollment 50
Women 96% **Men** 4% **Minority** 12% **Part-time** 96%
Distance Learning Courses Available.
Nursing Student Activities Sigma Theta Tau.
Nursing Student Resources Academic advising; academic or career counseling; assistance for students with disabilities; bookstore; campus computer network; career placement assistance; computer lab; computer-assisted instruction; e-mail services; Internet; library services; nursing audiovisuals; remedial services; resume preparation assistance; skills, simulation, or other laboratory; tutoring.
Library Facilities 205,200 volumes; 1,625 periodical subscriptions.

BACCALAUREATE PROGRAMS
Degree BSN
Available Programs ADN to Baccalaureate; Accelerated RN Baccalaureate; Baccalaureate for Second Degree; RN Baccalaureate.
Study Options Full-time and part-time.
Online Degree Options Yes (online only).
Program Entrance Requirements Minimum overall college GPA of 2.0, transcript of college record, CPR certification, minimum GPA in nursing prerequisites of 2.5, professional liability insurance/malpractice insurance, prerequisite course work, RN licensure. Transfer students are accepted. *Application deadline:* Applications may be processed on a rolling basis for some programs.
Advanced Placement Credit by examination available. Credit given for nursing courses completed elsewhere dependent upon specific evaluations.
Expenses (2009–10) *Tuition:* part-time $427 per credit hour.
Financial Aid 90% of baccalaureate students in nursing programs received some form of financial aid in 2008–09. *Gift aid (need-based):* Federal Pell, FSEOG, state, private, college/university gift aid from institutional funds. *Loans:* FFEL (Subsidized and Unsubsidized Stafford PLUS), Perkins, college/university. *Work-study:* Federal Work-Study. *Financial aid application deadline:* Continuous.
Contact Dr. Lori Brohm, Administrator, Department of Nursing, Ashland University, 401 College Avenue, Ashland, OH 44805. *Telephone:* 419-289-5242. *Fax:* 419-289-5989. *E-mail:* lbrohm@ashland.edu.

Capital University
School of Nursing
Columbus, Ohio

http://www.capital.edu/nursing/nurshome.shtml
Founded in 1830

DEGREES • BSN • MN/MBA • MSN • MSN/JD • MSN/MDIV
Nursing Program Faculty 30 (30% with doctorates).
Baccalaureate Enrollment 464
Women 82% **Men** 18% **Minority** 9% **International** 1% **Part-time** 19%
Graduate Enrollment 45
Women 87% **Men** 13% **Minority** 31% **International** 2% **Part-time** 98%
Nursing Student Activities Sigma Theta Tau, Student Nurses' Association.
Nursing Student Resources Academic advising; academic or career counseling; assistance for students with disabilities; bookstore; campus computer network; computer lab; computer-assisted instruction; e-mail services; interactive nursing skills videos; Internet; learning resource lab; library services; nursing audiovisuals; remedial services; resume preparation assistance; skills, simulation, or other laboratory; tutoring; unpaid internships.
Library Facilities 199,011 volumes (6,209 in health); 6,995 periodical subscriptions (82 health-care related).

BACCALAUREATE PROGRAMS
Degree BSN
Available Programs ADN to Baccalaureate; Accelerated Baccalaureate for Second Degree; Generic Baccalaureate; RN Baccalaureate.
Study Options Full-time and part-time.
Program Entrance Requirements Minimum overall college GPA of 3.0, transcript of college record, health exam, high school biology, high school chemistry, high school foreign language, 3 years high school math, 3 years high school science, high school transcript, immunizations, minimum high school GPA of 3.1. Transfer students are accepted. *Application deadline:* Applications may be processed on a rolling basis for some programs.
Advanced Placement Credit by examination available. Credit given for nursing courses completed elsewhere dependent upon specific evaluations.
Expenses (2009–10) *Tuition:* full-time $28,480; part-time $950 per credit hour. *International tuition:* $28,480 full-time.
Financial Aid 100% of baccalaureate students in nursing programs received some form of financial aid in 2008–09.
Contact Dr. Judi Macke, PhD, Program Coordinator, School of Nursing, Capital University, 1 College and Main, Columbus, OH 43209-2394. *Telephone:* 614-236-6339. *Fax:* 614-236-6157. *E-mail:* jmacke@capital.edu.

GRADUATE PROGRAMS
Expenses (2009–10) *Tuition:* full-time $5400; part-time $450 per credit hour.
Financial Aid 30% of graduate students in nursing programs received some form of financial aid in 2008–09. Career-related internships or fieldwork and traineeships available.
Contact Dr. Sharon Stout-Shaffer, PhD, Program Coordinator, School of Nursing, Capital University, 1 College and Main, Columbus, OH 43209-2394. *Telephone:* 614-236-6363. *Fax:* 614-236-6703. *E-mail:* sstoutsh@capital.edu.

MASTER'S DEGREE PROGRAM
Degrees MN/MBA; MSN; MSN/JD; MSN/MDIV
Available Programs Master's; RN to Master's.
Concentrations Available Legal nurse consultant; nursing administration; nursing education.
Study Options Full-time and part-time.
Program Entrance Requirements Computer literacy, minimum overall college GPA of 3.0, transcript of college record, CPR certification, written essay, immunizations, 3 letters of recommendation, nursing research course, physical assessment course, professional liability insurance/malpractice insurance, prerequisite course work, resume, statistics course. *Application deadline:* Applications may be processed on a rolling basis for some programs.
Advanced Placement Credit given for nursing courses completed elsewhere dependent upon specific evaluations.
Degree Requirements 36 total credit hours, thesis or project, comprehensive exam.

POST-MASTER'S PROGRAM

Areas of Study Legal nurse consultant; nursing education.

Case Western Reserve University
Frances Payne Bolton School of Nursing
Cleveland, Ohio

http://fpb.case.edu
Founded in 1826
DEGREES • BSN • MSN • MSN/MA • MSN/MBA • MSN/MPH • PHD

Nursing Program Faculty 108 (54% with doctorates).

Baccalaureate Enrollment 352
Women 91% **Men** 9% **Minority** 26% **International** 2.6% **Part-time** .28%

Graduate Enrollment 533
Women 89% **Men** 11% **Minority** 19% **International** 5.3% **Part-time** 64%

Nursing Student Activities Sigma Theta Tau, Student Nurses' Association.

Nursing Student Resources Academic advising; academic or career counseling; assistance for students with disabilities; bookstore; campus computer network; career placement assistance; computer lab; computer-assisted instruction; e-mail services; employment services for current students; housing assistance; interactive nursing skills videos; Internet; learning resource lab; library services; nursing audiovisuals; other; placement services for program completers; remedial services; resume preparation assistance; skills, simulation, or other laboratory; tutoring.

Library Facilities 2.5 million volumes (475,000 in health); 54,252 periodical subscriptions (2,500 health-care related).

BACCALAUREATE PROGRAMS

Degree BSN

Available Programs ADN to Baccalaureate; Generic Baccalaureate; RN Baccalaureate.

Study Options Full-time.

Program Entrance Requirements Written essay, high school biology, high school chemistry, 2 years high school science, high school transcript, 2 letters of recommendation, minimum high school GPA of 3.0. Transfer students are accepted. *Application deadline:* 1/15 (fall). *Application fee:* $35.

Advanced Placement Credit given for nursing courses completed elsewhere dependent upon specific evaluations.

Financial Aid 100% of baccalaureate students in nursing programs received some form of financial aid in 2007–08. *Gift aid (need-based):* Federal Pell, FSEOG, state, private, college/university gift aid from institutional funds. *Loans:* Federal Nursing Student Loans, FFEL (Subsidized and Unsubsidized Stafford PLUS), Perkins, state, college/university, alternative loans. *Work-study:* Federal Work-Study. *Financial aid application deadline (priority):* 2/15.

Contact Office of Student Services, Frances Payne Bolton School of Nursing, Case Western Reserve University, 10900 Euclid Avenue, Cleveland, OH 44106-4904. *Telephone:* 216-368-2529. *Fax:* 216-368-0124. *E-mail:* admissions@fpb.case.edu.

GRADUATE PROGRAMS

Financial Aid 90% of graduate students in nursing programs received some form of financial aid in 2007–08. 5 research assistantships, 7 teaching assistantships were awarded; fellowships, Federal Work-Study, institutionally sponsored loans, scholarships, and tuition waivers (partial) also available. Aid available to part-time students. *Financial aid application deadline:* 6/30.

Contact Office of Student Services, Frances Payne Bolton School of Nursing, Case Western Reserve University, 10900 Euclid Avenue, Cleveland, OH 44106-4904. *Telephone:* 216-368-2529. *Fax:* 216-368-0124. *E-mail:* admissions@fbp.case.edu.

MASTER'S DEGREE PROGRAM

Degrees MSN; MSN/MA; MSN/MBA; MSN/MPH

Available Programs Accelerated AD/RN to Master's; Master's; RN to Master's.

Concentrations Available Nurse anesthesia; nurse-midwifery; nursing informatics. *Clinical nurse specialist programs in:* gerontology, medical-surgical, psychiatric/mental health, public health. *Nurse practitioner programs in:* acute care, adult health, family health, gerontology, neonatal health, oncology, pediatric, psychiatric/mental health, women's health.

Study Options Full-time and part-time.

Program Entrance Requirements Minimum overall college GPA of 3.0, transcript of college record, written essay, 3 letters of recommendation, resume, statistics course, MAT or GRE General Test. *Application deadline:* 6/1 (fall), 10/1 (spring), 3/1 (summer). Applications may be processed on a rolling basis for some programs. *Application fee:* $75.

Advanced Placement Credit given for nursing courses completed elsewhere dependent upon specific evaluations.

Degree Requirements 40 total credit hours.

POST-MASTER'S PROGRAM

Areas of Study Nurse anesthesia; nurse-midwifery; nursing informatics. *Clinical nurse specialist programs in:* medical-surgical, public health. *Nurse practitioner programs in:* acute care, adult health, family health, gerontology, neonatal health, oncology, pediatric, psychiatric/mental health, women's health.

DOCTORAL DEGREE PROGRAM

Degree PhD

Available Programs Doctorate; Doctorate for Nurses with Non-Nursing Degrees; Post-Baccalaureate Doctorate.

Areas of Study Aging, bio-behavioral research, community health, critical care, ethics, faculty preparation, family health, gerontology, health policy, health promotion/disease prevention, human health and illness, illness and transition, individualized study, maternity-newborn, nursing education, nursing research, nursing science, oncology, women's health.

Program Entrance Requirements Minimum overall college GPA of 3.0, interview by faculty committee, 3 letters of recommendation, statistics course, vita, writing sample, GRE General Test, MAT (DNP). Application deadline: 1/1 (fall), 10/1 (spring), 3/1 (summer). Applications may be processed on a rolling basis for some programs. Application fee: $75.

Degree Requirements 57 total credit hours, dissertation, oral exam, residency.

POSTDOCTORAL PROGRAM

Areas of Study Aging, cancer care, chronic illness, community health, family health, gerontology, health promotion/disease prevention, individualized study, information systems, nursing interventions, nursing research, nursing science, outcomes, self-care, vulnerable population, women's health.

Postdoctoral Program Contact Dr. Shirley M. Moore, Professor and Associate Dean for Research, Frances Payne Bolton School of Nursing, Case Western Reserve University, 10900 Euclid Avenue, Cleveland, OH 44106-4904. *Telephone:* 216-368-5978. *Fax:* 216-368-3542. *E-mail:* shirley.moore@case.edu.

CONTINUING EDUCATION PROGRAM

Contact Ms. Kathleen Montgomery, RN, Instructor in Nursing, Frances Payne Bolton School of Nursing, Case Western Reserve University, 10900 Euclid Avenue, Cleveland, OH 44106-4904. *Telephone:* 216-368-6302. *Fax:* 216-368-5303. *E-mail:* Kathleen.Montgomery@case.edu.

Cedarville University
Department of Nursing
Cedarville, Ohio

http://www.cedarville.edu/academics/nursing
Founded in 1887
DEGREE • BSN

Nursing Program Faculty 21 (38% with doctorates).

Cedarville University (continued)
Baccalaureate Enrollment 346
Women 91.6% **Men** 8.4% **Minority** 5.2% **International** 1.7% **Part-time** .6%

Nursing Student Activities Nursing Honor Society, Student Nurses' Association.

Nursing Student Resources Academic advising; academic or career counseling; assistance for students with disabilities; bookstore; campus computer network; career placement assistance; computer lab; computer-assisted instruction; e-mail services; employment services for current students; housing assistance; interactive nursing skills videos; Internet; library services; nursing audiovisuals; paid internships; resume preparation assistance; skills, simulation, or other laboratory.

Library Facilities 181,053 volumes (5,927 in health, 1,066 in nursing); 21,050 periodical subscriptions (102 health-care related).

BACCALAUREATE PROGRAMS

Degree BSN

Available Programs RN Baccalaureate.

Study Options Full-time.

Program Entrance Requirements Minimum overall college GPA of 2.8, transcript of college record, CPR certification, written essay, health exam, health insurance, high school biology, high school chemistry, high school foreign language, 4 years high school math, 4 years high school science, high school transcript, immunizations, 1 letter of recommendation, minimum high school GPA of 3.0, minimum high school rank 50%, minimum GPA in nursing prerequisites of 2.8, professional liability insurance/malpractice insurance, prerequisite course work. Transfer students are accepted. *Application deadline:* 5/1 (spring).

Advanced Placement Credit given for nursing courses completed elsewhere dependent upon specific evaluations.

Expenses (2009–10) *Tuition:* full-time $22,304. *Room and board:* $4996; room only: $2740 per academic year.

Financial Aid 92% of baccalaureate students in nursing programs received some form of financial aid in 2008–09.

Contact Mr. Scott VanLoo, Admissions, Department of Nursing, Cedarville University, 251 North Main Street, Cedarville, OH 45314-0601. *Telephone:* 800-233-2784. *Fax:* 937-766-7575. *E-mail:* admissions@cedarville.edu.

Cleveland State University
School of Nursing
Cleveland, Ohio

http://www.csuohio.edu
Founded in 1964
DEGREES • BSN • MSN • MSN/MBA

Nursing Program Faculty 34 (34% with doctorates).

Baccalaureate Enrollment 232
Women 78% **Men** 22% **Minority** 16% **International** 1%

Graduate Enrollment 83
Women 95% **Men** 5% **Minority** 18% **International** 1% **Part-time** 100%

Distance Learning Courses Available.

Nursing Student Activities Sigma Theta Tau, Student Nurses' Association.

Nursing Student Resources Academic advising; academic or career counseling; assistance for students with disabilities; bookstore; campus computer network; computer lab; computer-assisted instruction; daycare for children of students; e-mail services; employment services for current students; interactive nursing skills videos; Internet; learning resource lab; library services; nursing audiovisuals; remedial services; resume preparation assistance; skills, simulation, or other laboratory; tutoring.

Library Facilities 847,731 volumes (6,000 in health, 70 in nursing); 7,826 periodical subscriptions (70 health-care related).

BACCALAUREATE PROGRAMS

Degree BSN

Available Programs Accelerated Baccalaureate for Second Degree; Generic Baccalaureate; RN Baccalaureate.

Study Options Full-time.

Online Degree Options Yes.

Program Entrance Requirements Minimum overall college GPA of 2.5, transcript of college record, CPR certification, written essay, health exam, health insurance, high school transcript, immunizations, interview, 2 letters of recommendation, minimum GPA in nursing prerequisites of 2.75, professional liability insurance/malpractice insurance, prerequisite course work. Transfer students are accepted. *Application deadline:* 3/1 (fall). *Application fee:* $15.

Advanced Placement Credit given for nursing courses completed elsewhere dependent upon specific evaluations.

Expenses (2009–10) *Tuition, state resident:* full-time $8196. *Tuition, nonresident:* full-time $12,000. *International tuition:* $12,000 full-time. *Room and board:* $10,250; room only: $6700 per academic year. *Required fees:* full-time $600.

Financial Aid 80% of baccalaureate students in nursing programs received some form of financial aid in 2008–09. *Gift aid (need-based):* Federal Pell, FSEOG, state, private, college/university gift aid from institutional funds. *Loans:* FFEL (Subsidized and Unsubsidized Stafford PLUS), Perkins, state, alternative loans. *Work-study:* Federal Work-Study, part-time campus jobs. *Financial aid application deadline (priority):* 2/15.

Contact Mrs. Mary Leanza Manzuk, Recruiter and Advisor, School of Nursing, Cleveland State University, 2121 Euclid Avenue, RT 915, Cleveland, OH 44115. *Telephone:* 216-687-3810. *Fax:* 216-687-3556. *E-mail:* sonadvising@csuohio.edu.

GRADUATE PROGRAMS

Expenses (2009–10) *Tuition, state resident:* part-time $454 per credit hour. *Tuition, nonresident:* part-time $740 per credit hour. *Room and board:* $10,250; room only: $6700 per academic year. *Required fees:* part-time $25 per credit.

Financial Aid 50% of graduate students in nursing programs received some form of financial aid in 2008–09.

Contact Mrs. Carol Ivan, Recruiter Advisor, School of Nursing, Cleveland State University, 2121 Euclid Avenue, RT 915, Cleveland, OH 44115. *Telephone:* 216-687-5517. *Fax:* 216-687-3556. *E-mail:* sonadvising@csuohio.edu.

MASTER'S DEGREE PROGRAM

Degrees MSN; MSN/MBA

Available Programs Master's.

Concentrations Available Clinical nurse leader; health-care administration; legal nurse consultant; nursing administration; nursing education. *Clinical nurse specialist programs in:* community health, forensic nursing.

Study Options Part-time.

Online Degree Options Yes (online only).

Program Entrance Requirements Clinical experience, computer literacy, minimum overall college GPA of 3.0, transcript of college record, CPR certification, written essay, immunizations, 2 letters of recommendation, professional liability insurance/malpractice insurance, prerequisite course work, resume, statistics course. *Application deadline:* 3/1 (fall).

Advanced Placement Credit given for nursing courses completed elsewhere dependent upon specific evaluations.

Degree Requirements 38 total credit hours, thesis or project.

POST-MASTER'S PROGRAM

Areas of Study Clinical nurse leader; nursing education.

CONTINUING EDUCATION PROGRAM

Contact Jeanine Carroll, Director, Continuing Education Programs for Health Care Professionals, School of Nursing, Cleveland State University, 2121 Euclid Avenue, Division of Continuing Education, Cleveland, OH 44115. *Telephone:* 216-687-4843. *Fax:* 216-687-9399. *E-mail:* j.a.carroll@csuohio.edu.

College of Mount St. Joseph
Department of Nursing
Cincinnati, Ohio

Founded in 1920

DEGREES • BSN • MN

Nursing Program Faculty 32 (4% with doctorates).

Baccalaureate Enrollment 287
Women 97% **Men** 3% **Minority** 5% **Part-time** 60%

Graduate Enrollment 21
Women 90% **Men** 10% **Minority** 5%

Nursing Student Activities Nursing Honor Society, Sigma Theta Tau, Student Nurses' Association.

Nursing Student Resources Academic advising; academic or career counseling; assistance for students with disabilities; bookstore; campus computer network; career placement assistance; computer lab; computer-assisted instruction; daycare for children of students; e-mail services; employment services for current students; externships; housing assistance; interactive nursing skills videos; Internet; learning resource lab; library services; nursing audiovisuals; placement services for program completers; remedial services; resume preparation assistance; skills, simulation, or other laboratory; tutoring.

Library Facilities 97,141 volumes (1,800 in health, 1,200 in nursing); 9,394 periodical subscriptions (300 health-care related).

BACCALAUREATE PROGRAMS

Degree BSN

Available Programs Accelerated RN Baccalaureate; Generic Baccalaureate.
Site Options Cincinnati, OH; Covington, KY.
Study Options Full-time and part-time.
Program Entrance Requirements Minimum overall college GPA of 2.75, transcript of college record, CPR certification, health exam, health insurance, high school chemistry, 2 years high school math, 2 years high school science, high school transcript, immunizations, interview, minimum high school GPA of 2.75, minimum high school rank 60%, minimum GPA in nursing prerequisites of 2.75, professional liability insurance/malpractice insurance, prerequisite course work. Transfer students are accepted. *Application deadline:* Applications may be processed on a rolling basis for some programs. *Application fee:* $25.
Advanced Placement Credit by examination available. Credit given for nursing courses completed elsewhere dependent upon specific evaluations.
Expenses (2008–09) *Tuition:* full-time $21,200; part-time $465 per credit hour. *International tuition:* $21,200 full-time. *Room and board:* $7500; room only: $4000 per academic year. *Required fees:* full-time $1200.
Financial Aid 85% of baccalaureate students in nursing programs received some form of financial aid in 2007–08. *Gift aid (need-based):* Federal Pell, FSEOG, state, private, college/university gift aid from institutional funds. *Loans:* Federal Nursing Student Loans, FFEL (Subsidized and Unsubsidized Stafford PLUS), Perkins, state. *Work-study:* Federal Work-Study, part-time campus jobs. *Financial aid application deadline (priority):* 3/1.
Contact Dr. Darla Vale, Chairperson, Department of Nursing, College of Mount St. Joseph, 5701 Delhi Road, Cincinnati, OH 45233-1670. *Telephone:* 513-244-4511. *Fax:* 513-451-2547. *E-mail:* darla_vale@mail.msj.edu.

GRADUATE PROGRAMS

Expenses (2008–09) *Room and board:* $7500; room only: $4000 per academic year.
Financial Aid 50% of graduate students in nursing programs received some form of financial aid in 2007–08.
Contact Dr. Susan A. Johnson, RN, Nursing Program Director, Department of Nursing, College of Mount St. Joseph, 5701 Delhi Road, Cincinnati, OH 45233-1670. *Telephone:* 513-244-4503. *Fax:* 513-451-2547. *E-mail:* susan_johnson@mail.msj.edu.

MASTER'S DEGREE PROGRAM

Degree MN

Available Programs Accelerated Master's for Non-Nursing College Graduates.
Study Options Full-time.
Program Entrance Requirements Minimum overall college GPA of 3.0, transcript of college record, CPR certification, written essay, immunizations, interview, professional liability insurance/malpractice insurance, prerequisite course work, statistics course. *Application deadline:* Applications may be processed on a rolling basis for some programs. *Application fee:* $50.
Advanced Placement Credit by examination available. Credit given for nursing courses completed elsewhere dependent upon specific evaluations.
Degree Requirements 64 total credit hours, thesis or project.

Franciscan University of Steubenville
Department of Nursing
Steubenville, Ohio

Founded in 1946

DEGREES • BSN • MSN

Nursing Program Faculty 15 (20% with doctorates).

Baccalaureate Enrollment 177
Women 91% **Men** 9% **Minority** 5% **International** 1% **Part-time** 5%

Graduate Enrollment 23
Women 78% **Men** 22% **Minority** 4% **Part-time** 83%

Nursing Student Activities Student Nurses' Association.

Nursing Student Resources Academic advising; academic or career counseling; assistance for students with disabilities; bookstore; campus computer network; computer lab; e-mail services; Internet; learning resource lab; library services; resume preparation assistance; tutoring.

Library Facilities 29,761 volumes in health, 8,946 volumes in nursing; 410 periodical subscriptions (178 health-care related).

BACCALAUREATE PROGRAMS

Degree BSN

Available Programs Generic Baccalaureate; RN Baccalaureate; RPN to Baccalaureate.
Study Options Full-time and part-time.
Program Entrance Requirements Minimum overall college GPA of 2.5, transcript of college record, health exam, health insurance, high school biology, high school chemistry, 2 years high school science, high school transcript, immunizations, 2 letters of recommendation, minimum high school GPA of 2.4, minimum GPA in nursing prerequisites of 2.5, professional liability insurance/malpractice insurance, prerequisite course work. Transfer students are accepted.
Advanced Placement Credit by examination available. Credit given for nursing courses completed elsewhere dependent upon specific evaluations.
Contact *Telephone:* 740-283-6324. *Fax:* 740-283-6449.

GRADUATE PROGRAMS

Contact *Telephone:* 740-284-7245. *Fax:* 740-283-6449.

MASTER'S DEGREE PROGRAM

Degree MSN

Available Programs Master's; RN to Master's.
Concentrations Available Nursing education. *Nurse practitioner programs in:* family health.
Study Options Full-time and part-time.
Program Entrance Requirements Clinical experience, minimum overall college GPA of 3.0, transcript of college record, interview, 2 letters of recommendation, nursing research course, physical assessment course, professional liability insurance/malpractice insurance, prerequisite course work, statistics course.
Advanced Placement Credit given for nursing courses completed elsewhere dependent upon specific evaluations.

Franciscan University of Steubenville (continued)
Degree Requirements 48 total credit hours, thesis or project.

Kent State University
College of Nursing
Kent, Ohio

http://www.kent.edu/nursing
Founded in 1910
DEGREES • BSN • MSN • MSN/MBA • MSN/MPA • PHD

Nursing Program Faculty 120 (20% with doctorates).
Baccalaureate Enrollment 1,150
Women 84% **Men** 16% **Minority** 10% **International** 2% **Part-time** 16%
Graduate Enrollment 300
Women 93% **Men** 7% **Minority** 8% **International** 3% **Part-time** 88%
Distance Learning Courses Available.
Nursing Student Activities Nursing Honor Society, Sigma Theta Tau, Student Nurses' Association.
Nursing Student Resources Academic advising; academic or career counseling; assistance for students with disabilities; bookstore; campus computer network; career placement assistance; computer lab; computer-assisted instruction; e-mail services; employment services for current students; externships; housing assistance; interactive nursing skills videos; Internet; learning resource lab; library services; nursing audiovisuals; other; paid internships; placement services for program completers; remedial services; resume preparation assistance; skills, simulation, or other laboratory; tutoring.
Library Facilities 2.3 million volumes; 12,000 periodical subscriptions (300 health-care related).

BACCALAUREATE PROGRAMS
Degree BSN
Available Programs ADN to Baccalaureate; Accelerated Baccalaureate; Accelerated Baccalaureate for Second Degree; Accelerated RN Baccalaureate; Baccalaureate for Second Degree; Generic Baccalaureate; LPN to Baccalaureate; LPN to RN Baccalaureate; RN Baccalaureate.
Site Options Warren, OH; Canton, OH; Salem, OH; Burton, OH.
Study Options Full-time and part-time.
Program Entrance Requirements Minimum overall college GPA of 2.5, transcript of college record, CPR certification, written essay, health exam, high school biology, high school transcript, immunizations, 2 letters of recommendation, minimum high school GPA of 2.5, minimum GPA in nursing prerequisites of 2.5, prerequisite course work. Transfer students are accepted. *Application deadline:* 3/15 (fall), 11/30 (spring).
Advanced Placement Credit given for nursing courses completed elsewhere dependent upon specific evaluations.
Expenses (2009–10) *Tuition, area resident:* full-time $8726; part-time $397 per credit hour. *Tuition, state resident:* full-time $4938; part-time $225 per credit hour. *Tuition, nonresident:* full-time $16,418; part-time $747 per credit hour. *International tuition:* $16,418 full-time. *Room and board:* $3937; room only: $2203 per academic year.
Financial Aid 91% of baccalaureate students in nursing programs received some form of financial aid in 2008–09. *Gift aid (need-based):* Federal Pell, FSEOG, state, private, college/university gift aid from institutional funds. *Loans:* Federal Nursing Student Loans, Federal Direct (Subsidized and Unsubsidized Stafford PLUS), Perkins, state, college/university, alternative loans. *Work-study:* Federal Work-Study. *Financial aid application deadline (priority):* 3/1.
Contact Mr. Curtis Good, Director of Student Services, College of Nursing, Kent State University, Henderson Hall, Kent, OH 44242-0001. *Telephone:* 330-672-9972. *Fax:* 330-672-7911. *E-mail:* cjgood@kent.edu.

GRADUATE PROGRAMS
Expenses (2009–10) *Tuition, area resident:* full-time $9282; part-time $422 per credit hour. *Tuition, state resident:* full-time $16,542; part-time $752 per credit hour. *Tuition, nonresident:* full-time $16,542; part-time $752 per credit hour. *International tuition:* $16,542 full-time.

Financial Aid 85% of graduate students in nursing programs received some form of financial aid in 2008–09. 10 research assistantships with full tuition reimbursements available, 10 teaching assistantships with full tuition reimbursements available were awarded; Federal Work-Study, institutionally sponsored loans, traineeships, tuition waivers (full), and unspecified assistantships also available. *Financial aid application deadline:* 2/1.
Contact Dr. Karen Budd, Director, Graduate Programs, College of Nursing, Kent State University, PO Box 5190, Kent, OH 44242-0001. *Telephone:* 330-672-8776. *Fax:* 330-672-5003. *E-mail:* kbudd@kent.edu.

MASTER'S DEGREE PROGRAM
Degrees MSN; MSN/MBA; MSN/MPA
Available Programs Accelerated RN to Master's; Master's.
Concentrations Available Health-care administration; nurse case management; nursing administration; nursing education. *Clinical nurse specialist programs in:* acute care, adult health, cardiovascular, critical care, gerontology, medical-surgical, oncology, pediatric, psychiatric/mental health, school health. *Nurse practitioner programs in:* acute care, adult health, family health, gerontology, pediatric, primary care, psychiatric/mental health, women's health.
Study Options Full-time and part-time.
Program Entrance Requirements Computer literacy, minimum overall college GPA of 3.0, transcript of college record, CPR certification, written essay, immunizations, interview, letters of recommendation, nursing research course, professional liability insurance/malpractice insurance, statistics course, GRE (if undergraduate GPA is below 3.0). *Application deadline:* 5/1 (fall), 11/1 (spring), 4/1 (summer). *Application fee:* $30.
Advanced Placement Credit given for nursing courses completed elsewhere dependent upon specific evaluations.
Degree Requirements 36 total credit hours.

POST-MASTER'S PROGRAM
Areas of Study Nursing education. *Nurse practitioner programs in:* acute care, adult health, family health, gerontology, pediatric, primary care, psychiatric/mental health, women's health.

DOCTORAL DEGREE PROGRAM
Degree PhD
Available Programs Doctorate; Post-Baccalaureate Doctorate.
Areas of Study Aging, clinical practice, ethics, gerontology, health policy, health promotion/disease prevention, maternity-newborn, nurse case management, nursing administration, nursing education, nursing research, nursing science, women's health.
Program Entrance Requirements Minimum overall college GPA of 3.0, interview, 3 letters of recommendation, MSN or equivalent, scholarly papers, statistics course, writing sample, GRE. Application deadline: 7/15 (fall). Applications may be processed on a rolling basis for some programs. Application fee: $30.
Degree Requirements 72 total credit hours, dissertation, residency.

CONTINUING EDUCATION PROGRAM
Contact Betty Freund, Coordinator of Continuing Nursing Education, College of Nursing, Kent State University, PO Box 5190, Kent, OH 44242-0001. *Telephone:* 330-672-8810. *Fax:* 330-672-2433. *E-mail:* bfreund@kent.edu.

See full description on page 502.

Kettering College of Medical Arts
Division of Nursing
Kettering, Ohio

http://www.kcma.edu
Founded in 1967
DEGREE • BSN

Nursing Program Faculty 21 (30% with doctorates).
Baccalaureate Enrollment 20
Women 95% **Part-time** 100%
Nursing Student Activities Student Nurses' Association.

Nursing Student Resources Academic advising; academic or career counseling; assistance for students with disabilities; bookstore; campus computer network; computer lab; computer-assisted instruction; e-mail services; externships; interactive nursing skills videos; Internet; learning resource lab; library services; nursing audiovisuals; remedial services; resume preparation assistance; skills, simulation, or other laboratory; tutoring.

Library Facilities 29,390 volumes (4,060 in health, 1,073 in nursing); 266 periodical subscriptions (173 health-care related).

BACCALAUREATE PROGRAMS

Degree BSN

Available Programs RN Baccalaureate.

Study Options Full-time and part-time.

Program Entrance Requirements Transcript of college record, health exam, immunizations, 3 letters of recommendation, RN licensure. Transfer students are accepted.

Advanced Placement Credit given for nursing courses completed elsewhere dependent upon specific evaluations.

Contact *Telephone:* 937-395-8642. *Fax:* 937-395-8810.

Lourdes College
Nursing Department
Sylvania, Ohio

http://www.lourdes.edu
Founded in 1958

DEGREE • BSN

Nursing Program Faculty 15 (20% with doctorates).

Baccalaureate Enrollment 298

Women 95% **Men** 5% **Minority** 17% **Part-time** 24%

Nursing Student Activities Sigma Theta Tau, Student Nurses' Association.

Nursing Student Resources Academic advising; academic or career counseling; assistance for students with disabilities; bookstore; campus computer network; computer lab; computer-assisted instruction; e-mail services; employment services for current students; interactive nursing skills videos; Internet; learning resource lab; library services; nursing audiovisuals; remedial services; resume preparation assistance; skills, simulation, or other laboratory; tutoring.

Library Facilities 64,889 volumes (1,200 in health, 700 in nursing); 226 periodical subscriptions (101 health-care related).

BACCALAUREATE PROGRAMS

Degree BSN

Available Programs Generic Baccalaureate; LPN to Baccalaureate; RN Baccalaureate.

Site Options Sandusky, OH.

Study Options Full-time and part-time.

Program Entrance Requirements Minimum overall college GPA of 2.0, transcript of college record, CPR certification, health exam, health insurance, high school biology, high school chemistry, high school transcript, immunizations, 3 letters of recommendation, minimum GPA in nursing prerequisites of 2.5, professional liability insurance/malpractice insurance, prerequisite course work. Transfer students are accepted.

Advanced Placement Credit by examination available. Credit given for nursing courses completed elsewhere dependent upon specific evaluations.

Contact *Telephone:* 419-824-3793. *Fax:* 419-824-3985.

Malone University
School of Nursing
Canton, Ohio

http://www.malone.edu
Founded in 1892

DEGREES • BSN • MSN

Nursing Program Faculty 32 (25% with doctorates).

Baccalaureate Enrollment 343

Women 85% **Men** 15% **International** .03% **Part-time** 21%

Graduate Enrollment 48

Women 92% **Men** 8% **International** .03% **Part-time** 100%

Nursing Student Activities Sigma Theta Tau, Student Nurses' Association.

Nursing Student Resources Academic advising; academic or career counseling; assistance for students with disabilities; bookstore; campus computer network; career placement assistance; computer lab; computer-assisted instruction; e-mail services; employment services for current students; interactive nursing skills videos; Internet; learning resource lab; library services; nursing audiovisuals; placement services for program completers; remedial services; resume preparation assistance; skills, simulation, or other laboratory; tutoring.

Library Facilities 178,992 volumes (4,013 in health, 1,351 in nursing); 47,942 periodical subscriptions (125 health-care related).

BACCALAUREATE PROGRAMS

Degree BSN

Available Programs ADN to Baccalaureate; Generic Baccalaureate; RN Baccalaureate.

Study Options Full-time and part-time.

Program Entrance Requirements Minimum overall college GPA of 2.5, transcript of college record, CPR certification, written essay, health exam, health insurance, high school biology, high school chemistry, 2 years high school math, 3 years high school science, high school transcript, immunizations, 2 letters of recommendation, minimum high school GPA of 2.5, minimum GPA in nursing prerequisites, professional liability insurance/ malpractice insurance, prerequisite course work. Transfer students are accepted. *Application deadline:* Applications may be processed on a rolling basis for some programs. *Application fee:* $20.

Advanced Placement Credit given for nursing courses completed elsewhere dependent upon specific evaluations.

Expenses (2009–10) *Tuition:* full-time $20,730; part-time $370 per credit hour. *International tuition:* $20,730 full-time. *Room and board:* $7100; room only: $3620 per academic year. *Required fees:* full-time $595; part-time $300 per term.

Financial Aid 100% of baccalaureate students in nursing programs received some form of financial aid in 2008–09. *Gift aid (need-based):* Federal Pell, FSEOG, state, private, college/university gift aid from institutional funds, Academic Competitiveness Grant, National Smart Grant, TEACH Grant. *Loans:* FFEL (Subsidized and Unsubsidized Stafford PLUS), Perkins, state, college/university, alternative loans. *Work-study:* Federal Work-Study, part-time campus jobs. *Financial aid application deadline:* 7/31 (priority: 3/1).

Contact Dr. Brock Schroder, PhD, Vice President for Enrollment Management, School of Nursing, Malone University, 2600 Cleveland Avenue NW, Canton, OH 44709. *Telephone:* 330-471-8145. *Fax:* 330-471-8149. *E-mail:* admissions@malone.edu.

GRADUATE PROGRAMS

Expenses (2009–10) *Tuition:* full-time $15,777. *International tuition:* $15,777 full-time. *Required fees:* full-time $3350.

Financial Aid 100% of graduate students in nursing programs received some form of financial aid in 2008–09.

Contact Ms. Jean Yanok, Administrative Assistant, School of Nursing, Malone University, 2600 Cleveland Avenue NW, Canton, OH 44709. *Telephone:* 330-471-8366. *Fax:* 330-471-8607. *E-mail:* jyanok@malone.edu.

MASTER'S DEGREE PROGRAM

Degree MSN

Available Programs Master's.

Concentrations Available *Clinical nurse specialist programs in:* adult health, medical-surgical. *Nurse practitioner programs in:* family health.

Study Options Full-time and part-time.

Program Entrance Requirements Clinical experience, computer literacy, minimum overall college GPA of 3.0, transcript of college record, CPR certification, written essay, immunizations, interview, 2 letters of recommendation, nursing research course, physical assessment course,

Malone University (continued)

professional liability insurance/malpractice insurance, resume, statistics course. *Application deadline:* Applications may be processed on a rolling basis for some programs. *Application fee:* $25.

Advanced Placement Credit given for nursing courses completed elsewhere dependent upon specific evaluations.

Degree Requirements 56 total credit hours, thesis or project.

MedCentral College of Nursing
MedCentral College of Nursing
Mansfield, Ohio

Founded in 1996
DEGREE • BS

BACCALAUREATE PROGRAMS

Degree BS

Available Programs Accelerated Baccalaureate; LPN to Baccalaureate; RN Baccalaureate.

Contact *Telephone:* 419-520-2600.

Mercy College of Northwest Ohio
Division of Nursing
Toledo, Ohio

http://www.mercycollege.edu
Founded in 1993
DEGREE • BSN

Nursing Program Faculty 14 (20% with doctorates).

Baccalaureate Enrollment 228
Women 88% **Men** 12% **Minority** 12% **Part-time** 13%

Distance Learning Courses Available.

Nursing Student Activities Sigma Theta Tau, Student Nurses' Association.

Nursing Student Resources Academic advising; academic or career counseling; assistance for students with disabilities; campus computer network; career placement assistance; computer lab; computer-assisted instruction; e-mail services; employment services for current students; housing assistance; Internet; learning resource lab; library services; nursing audiovisuals; placement services for program completers; remedial services; resume preparation assistance; skills, simulation, or other laboratory; tutoring.

Library Facilities 8,797 volumes; 171 periodical subscriptions.

BACCALAUREATE PROGRAMS

Degree BSN

Available Programs ADN to Baccalaureate; Generic Baccalaureate; RN Baccalaureate.

Study Options Full-time and part-time.

Online Degree Options Yes.

Program Entrance Requirements Minimum overall college GPA of 2.7, transcript of college record, CPR certification, health exam, high school biology, high school chemistry, 2 years high school math, high school transcript, immunizations, minimum high school GPA of 2.7. Transfer students are accepted. *Application deadline:* 8/1 (fall). *Application fee:* $25.

Advanced Placement Credit by examination available.

Expenses (2009–10) *Tuition:* full-time $8850; part-time $326 per credit hour. *Required fees:* full-time $500.

Financial Aid 80% of baccalaureate students in nursing programs received some form of financial aid in 2008–09.

Contact Susan O'Dell, RN, Program Chair, BS Nursing, Division of Nursing, Mercy College of Northwest Ohio, 2221 Madison Avenue, Toledo, OH 43604. *Telephone:* 888-806-3729. *Fax:* 419-251-1570. *E-mail:* susan. odell@mercycollege.edu.

CONTINUING EDUCATION PROGRAM

Contact Cheryl Nutter, Manager, Continiuing Professional Education, Division of Nursing, Mercy College of Northwest Ohio, 2221 Madison Avenue, Toledo, OH 43606. *Telephone:* 419-251-1519. *E-mail:* Cheryl. Nutter@mercycollege.edu.

Miami University
Department of Nursing
Hamilton, Ohio

http://www.eas.muohio.edu/nsg
Founded in 1809
DEGREE • BSN

Nursing Program Faculty 13 (23% with doctorates).

Baccalaureate Enrollment 106
Women 98% **Men** 2% **Minority** 7% **Part-time** 56%

Distance Learning Courses Available.

Nursing Student Activities Sigma Theta Tau, Student Nurses' Association.

Nursing Student Resources Academic advising; academic or career counseling; assistance for students with disabilities; bookstore; campus computer network; computer lab; daycare for children of students; e-mail services; interactive nursing skills videos; Internet; learning resource lab; library services; nursing audiovisuals; resume preparation assistance; tutoring.

Library Facilities 2.7 million volumes (29,000 in nursing); 14,089 periodical subscriptions (852 health-care related).

BACCALAUREATE PROGRAMS

Degree BSN

Available Programs ADN to Baccalaureate; Generic Baccalaureate; RN Baccalaureate.

Site Options Hamilton, OH; Middletown, OH.

Study Options Full-time and part-time.

Program Entrance Requirements Minimum overall college GPA of 2.5, transcript of college record, health exam, health insurance, high school chemistry, 2 years high school math, 1 year of high school science, high school transcript, immunizations, minimum high school GPA of 3.0, minimum GPA in nursing prerequisites of 2.5, professional liability insurance/malpractice insurance. Transfer students are accepted.

Advanced Placement Credit given for nursing courses completed elsewhere dependent upon specific evaluations.

Contact *Telephone:* 513-785-7751. *Fax:* 513-785-7767.

Mount Carmel College of Nursing
Nursing Programs
Columbus, Ohio

http://www.mccn.edu/index.html
Founded in 1903
DEGREES • BSN • MS

Nursing Program Faculty 60 (17% with doctorates).

Baccalaureate Enrollment 601
Women 91% **Men** 9% **Minority** 12% **Part-time** 18%

Graduate Enrollment 28
Women 88% **Men** 12% **Minority** 3% **Part-time** 64%

Nursing Student Activities Sigma Theta Tau, Student Nurses' Association.

Nursing Student Resources Academic advising; academic or career counseling; assistance for students with disabilities; bookstore; campus computer network; computer lab; computer-assisted instruction; e-mail services; housing assistance; interactive nursing skills videos; Internet;

learning resource lab; library services; nursing audiovisuals; resume preparation assistance; skills, simulation, or other laboratory; tutoring.

Library Facilities 4,713 volumes in health, 1,101 volumes in nursing; 5,577 periodical subscriptions health-care related.

BACCALAUREATE PROGRAMS

Degree BSN

Available Programs Accelerated Baccalaureate for Second Degree; Generic Baccalaureate; RN Baccalaureate.

Study Options Full-time and part-time.

Program Entrance Requirements Minimum overall college GPA of 2.80, transcript of college record, written essay, health exam, high school biology, high school chemistry, high school foreign language, 3 years high school math, 3 years high school science, high school transcript, immunizations, minimum high school GPA of 3.00. Transfer students are accepted.

Advanced Placement Credit given for nursing courses completed elsewhere dependent upon specific evaluations.

Contact Kim M. Campbell, Director, Admissions and Recruitment, Nursing Programs, Mount Carmel College of Nursing, 127 South Davis Avenue, Columbus, OH 43222-1504. *Telephone:* 614-234-5144. *Fax:* 614-234-2875. *E-mail:* kcampbell@mchs.com.

GRADUATE PROGRAMS

Contact Kip Sexton, MS Program Coordinator, Nursing Programs, Mount Carmel College of Nursing, 127 South Davis Avenue, Columbus, OH 43222-1504. *Telephone:* 614-234-5169. *Fax:* 614-234-2875. *E-mail:* esexton@mchs.com.

MASTER'S DEGREE PROGRAM

Degree MS

Available Programs Master's.

Concentrations Available Nursing education. *Clinical nurse specialist programs in:* adult health.

Study Options Full-time and part-time.

Program Entrance Requirements Minimum overall college GPA of 3.0, transcript of college record, CPR certification, written essay, immunizations, 3 letters of recommendation, professional liability insurance/malpractice insurance, resume.

Degree Requirements 42 total credit hours, thesis or project.

POST-MASTER'S PROGRAM

Areas of Study Nursing education.

Mount Vernon Nazarene University

**School of Nursing and Health Sciences
Mount Vernon, Ohio**

Founded in 1964

DEGREE • BSN

Library Facilities 140,093 volumes; 7,541 periodical subscriptions.

BACCALAUREATE PROGRAMS

Degree BSN

Available Programs RN Baccalaureate.

Program Entrance Requirements Transcript of college record, immunizations, professional liability insurance/malpractice insurance, RN licensure.

Contact Nursing Program, School of Nursing and Health Sciences, Mount Vernon Nazarene University, 800 Martinsburg Road, Mount Vernon, OH 43050. *Telephone:* 740-392-6868.

Muskingum University

**Department of Nursing
New Concord, Ohio**

Founded in 1837

DEGREE • BSN

Library Facilities 233,000 volumes; 900 periodical subscriptions.

BACCALAUREATE PROGRAMS

Degree BSN

Available Programs Generic Baccalaureate.

Contact Dr. Elaine Haynes, RN, Director of Nursing, Chair and Professor, Department of Nursing, Muskingum University, New Concord, OH 43762. *Telephone:* 740-826-6151. *E-mail:* ehaynes@muskingum.edu.

Notre Dame College

**Nursing Department
South Euclid, Ohio**

Founded in 1922

DEGREE • BSN

BACCALAUREATE PROGRAMS

Degree BSN

Available Programs Generic Baccalaureate; RN Baccalaureate.

Contact Nursing Division, Nursing Department, Notre Dame College, 4545 College Road, South Euclid, OH 44121-4293. *Telephone:* 216-373-5183.

Ohio Northern University

**Nursing Program
Ada, Ohio**

Founded in 1871

DEGREE • BSN

BACCALAUREATE PROGRAMS

Degree BSN

Available Programs RN Baccalaureate.

Contact Nursing Program, Nursing Program, Ohio Northern University, 525 North Main Street, Ada, OH 45810. *Telephone:* 419-772-2000.

The Ohio State University

**College of Nursing
Columbus, Ohio**

http://www.nursing.osu.edu

Founded in 1870

DEGREES • BSN • DNP • MS • MS/MPH

Nursing Program Faculty 79 (42% with doctorates).

Baccalaureate Enrollment 572
Women 88% **Men** 12% **Minority** 11% **International** 2% **Part-time** 20%

Graduate Enrollment 335
Women 91% **Men** 9% **Minority** 11% **International** 2% **Part-time** 43%

Distance Learning Courses Available.

Nursing Student Activities Nursing Honor Society, Sigma Theta Tau, Student Nurses' Association, nursing club.

The Ohio State University (continued)

Nursing Student Resources Academic advising; academic or career counseling; assistance for students with disabilities; bookstore; campus computer network; career placement assistance; computer lab; computer-assisted instruction; daycare for children of students; e-mail services; employment services for current students; externships; housing assistance; interactive nursing skills videos; Internet; learning resource lab; library services; nursing audiovisuals; other; paid internships; placement services for program completers; remedial services; resume preparation assistance; skills, simulation, or other laboratory; tutoring; unpaid internships.

Library Facilities 6 million volumes (188,602 in health, 4,198 in nursing); 78,903 periodical subscriptions (5,060 health-care related).

BACCALAUREATE PROGRAMS

Degree BSN

Available Programs Accelerated RN Baccalaureate; Generic Baccalaureate.

Site Options Marion, OH; Newark, OH; Lima, OH.

Study Options Full-time.

Program Entrance Requirements Minimum overall college GPA of 2.75, transcript of college record, CPR certification, written essay, health insurance, high school biology, high school chemistry, high school foreign language, 3 years high school math, 2 years high school science, high school transcript, immunizations, minimum GPA in nursing prerequisites of 2.75, professional liability insurance/malpractice insurance, prerequisite course work. Transfer students are accepted. *Application deadline:* 2/1 (fall). *Application fee:* $40.

Advanced Placement Credit by examination available. Credit given for nursing courses completed elsewhere dependent upon specific evaluations.

Expenses (2009–10) *Tuition, state resident:* full-time $9042; part-time $277 per credit hour. *Tuition, nonresident:* full-time $22,614; part-time $653 per credit hour. *International tuition:* $22,614 full-time. *Room and board:* $10,875; room only: $6075 per academic year. *Required fees:* full-time $3122.

Financial Aid 80% of baccalaureate students in nursing programs received some form of financial aid in 2008–09. *Gift aid (need-based):* Federal Pell, FSEOG, state, private, college/university gift aid from institutional funds. *Loans:* Federal Nursing Student Loans, Federal Direct (Subsidized and Unsubsidized Stafford PLUS), Perkins, college/university. *Work-study:* Federal Work-Study, part-time campus jobs. *Financial aid application deadline (priority):* 2/15.

Contact Ms. Jennie Cisar Lawrence, Academic Advising Coordinator, College of Nursing, The Ohio State University, 1585 Neil Avenue, 240 Newton Hall, Columbus, OH 43210-1289. *Telephone:* 614-292-4041. *E-mail:* cisar-lawrence.1@osu.edu.

GRADUATE PROGRAMS

Expenses (2009–10) *Tuition, state resident:* full-time $14,284; part-time $380 per credit hour. *Tuition, nonresident:* full-time $34,604; part-time $888 per credit hour. *International tuition:* $34,604 full-time. *Room and board:* $10,020; room only: $5940 per academic year. *Required fees:* full-time $4747.

Financial Aid 90% of graduate students in nursing programs received some form of financial aid in 2008–09. Fellowships, research assistantships, teaching assistantships, Federal Work-Study, institutionally sponsored loans, and unspecified assistantships available. Aid available to part-time students.

Contact Ms. Jackie Min, Graduate Outreach Coordinator, College of Nursing, The Ohio State University, 1585 Neil Avenue, 212 Newton Hall, Columbus, OH 43210-1289. *Telephone:* 614-688-8145. *Fax:* 614-247-8618. *E-mail:* Min.37@osu.edu.

MASTER'S DEGREE PROGRAM

Degrees MS; MS/MPH

Available Programs Accelerated Master's for Non-Nursing College Graduates; Master's; Master's for Non-Nursing College Graduates; Master's for Nurses with Non-Nursing Degrees.

Concentrations Available Clinical nurse leader; health-care administration; nurse-midwifery; nursing administration. *Clinical nurse specialist programs in:* adult health, cardiovascular, community health, parent-child, psychiatric/mental health, public health. *Nurse practitioner programs in:* adult health, community health, family health, neonatal health, pediatric, primary care, psychiatric/mental health, school health, women's health.

Study Options Full-time and part-time.

Program Entrance Requirements Minimum overall college GPA of 3.0, transcript of college record, written essay, 3 letters of recommendation, prerequisite course work, resume.

Advanced Placement Credit given for nursing courses completed elsewhere dependent upon specific evaluations.

Degree Requirements Thesis or project, comprehensive exam.

POST-MASTER'S PROGRAM

Areas of Study Clinical nurse leader; health-care administration; nurse-midwifery; nursing administration. *Clinical nurse specialist programs in:* adult health, cardiovascular, community health, parent-child, psychiatric/mental health, public health. *Nurse practitioner programs in:* adult health, community health, family health, neonatal health, pediatric, primary care, psychiatric/mental health, school health, women's health.

DOCTORAL DEGREE PROGRAM

Degree DNP

Available Programs Doctorate; Doctorate for Nurses with Non-Nursing Degrees; Post-Baccalaureate Doctorate.

Areas of Study Addiction/substance abuse, aging, bio-behavioral research, biology of health and illness, clinical practice, community health, critical care, ethics, faculty preparation, family health, gerontology, health policy, health promotion/disease prevention, health-care systems, human health and illness, illness and transition, individualized study, information systems, maternity-newborn, neuro-behavior, nursing administration, nursing policy, nursing research, nursing science, oncology, urban health, women's health.

Program Entrance Requirements Clinical experience, minimum overall college GPA of 3.5, interview, 3 letters of recommendation, MSN or equivalent, statistics course, vita, writing sample. Application deadline: 1/15 (fall). Application fee: $40.

Degree Requirements 90 total credit hours, dissertation, oral exam, written exam, residency.

Ohio University
School of Nursing
Athens, Ohio

http://www.ohio.edu/nursing/

Founded in 1804

DEGREES • BSN • MSN

Nursing Program Faculty 9 (89% with doctorates).

Nursing Student Activities Nursing Honor Society, Sigma Theta Tau.

Nursing Student Resources Academic or career counseling; career placement assistance; computer lab; e-mail services; Internet; library services.

Library Facilities 2.9 million volumes; 39,297 periodical subscriptions.

BACCALAUREATE PROGRAMS

Degree BSN

Available Programs Generic Baccalaureate; RN Baccalaureate.

Online Degree Options Yes.

Program Entrance Requirements Transfer students are accepted.

Contact Dr. Deborah Henderson, Associate Director, School of Nursing, Ohio University, E365 Grover Center, Athens, OH 45701. *Telephone:* 740-593-4494. *Fax:* 740-593-0286. *E-mail:* hendersd@ohio.edu.

GRADUATE PROGRAMS

Contact Dr. Kathy Rose-Grippa, Graduate Coordinator, School of Nursing, Ohio University, E365 Grover Center, Athens, OH 45701-2979. *Telephone:* 740-593-4494. *Fax:* 740-593-0144. *E-mail:* grippa@ohio.edu.

MASTER'S DEGREE PROGRAM

Degree MSN

Available Programs Master's.

Concentrations Available Nursing administration; nursing education. *Nurse practitioner programs in:* family health.

Study Options Full-time and part-time.

Program Entrance Requirements Minimum overall college GPA of 3.0, transcript of college record, written essay, 3 letters of recommendation, resume, statistics course.

Advanced Placement Credit given for nursing courses completed elsewhere dependent upon specific evaluations.

Degree Requirements 55 total credit hours.

Otterbein College
Department of Nursing
Westerville, Ohio

http://www.otterbein.edu/dept/NURS

Founded in 1847

DEGREES • BSN • MSN

Nursing Student Activities Nursing Honor Society, Sigma Theta Tau.

Library Facilities 182,629 volumes; 1,012 periodical subscriptions.

BACCALAUREATE PROGRAMS

Degree BSN

Available Programs Accelerated RN Baccalaureate; Generic Baccalaureate; LPN to Baccalaureate; RN Baccalaureate.

Program Entrance Requirements Transfer students are accepted.

Advanced Placement Credit by examination available. Credit given for nursing courses completed elsewhere dependent upon specific evaluations.

Contact *Telephone:* 614-823-1614. *Fax:* 614-823-3131.

GRADUATE PROGRAMS

Contact *Telephone:* 614-823-1614.

MASTER'S DEGREE PROGRAM

Degree MSN

Available Programs Master's.

Concentrations Available Nursing administration; nursing education. *Clinical nurse specialist programs in:* adult health. *Nurse practitioner programs in:* adult health, family health.

Study Options Part-time.

POST-MASTER'S PROGRAM

Areas of Study Nursing education. *Nurse practitioner programs in:* adult health, family health.

CONTINUING EDUCATION PROGRAM

Contact *Telephone:* 614-823-1614.

Shawnee State University
Department of Nursing
Portsmouth, Ohio

http://www.shawnee.edu/acad/hs/bsn/index.html

Founded in 1986

DEGREE • BSN

Nursing Program Faculty 9

Nursing Student Activities Student Nurses' Association.

Nursing Student Resources Academic advising; academic or career counseling; assistance for students with disabilities; bookstore; campus computer network; career placement assistance; computer lab; computer-assisted instruction; daycare for children of students; e-mail services; employment services for current students; housing assistance; interactive nursing skills videos; Internet; learning resource lab; library services; nursing audiovisuals; other; placement services for program completers; remedial services; resume preparation assistance; skills, simulation, or other laboratory; tutoring.

Library Facilities 175,534 volumes (8,273 in health, 870 in nursing); 39,373 periodical subscriptions (1,798 health-care related).

BACCALAUREATE PROGRAMS

Degree BSN

Available Programs ADN to Baccalaureate; RN Baccalaureate.

Study Options Full-time and part-time.

Program Entrance Requirements Minimum overall college GPA of 2.5, transcript of college record, CPR certification, health exam, health insurance, high school transcript, immunizations, professional liability insurance/malpractice insurance, prerequisite course work, RN licensure. Transfer students are accepted.

Advanced Placement Credit given for nursing courses completed elsewhere dependent upon specific evaluations.

Contact *Telephone:* 740-351-3378. *Fax:* 740-351-3354.

CONTINUING EDUCATION PROGRAM

Contact *Telephone:* 740-351-3281.

The University of Akron
College of Nursing
Akron, Ohio

http://www.uakron.edu/nursing

Founded in 1870

DEGREES • BSN • MSN • PHD

Nursing Program Faculty 91 (54% with doctorates).

Baccalaureate Enrollment 602
Women 85% **Men** 15% **Minority** 10% **Part-time** 5%

Graduate Enrollment 331
Women 86% **Men** 14% **Minority** 10% **International** 1% **Part-time** 60%

Distance Learning Courses Available.

Nursing Student Activities Sigma Theta Tau, Student Nurses' Association, nursing club.

Nursing Student Resources Academic advising; academic or career counseling; assistance for students with disabilities; bookstore; campus computer network; career placement assistance; computer lab; computer-assisted instruction; daycare for children of students; e-mail services; employment services for current students; interactive nursing skills videos; Internet; learning resource lab; library services; nursing audiovisuals; remedial services; resume preparation assistance; skills, simulation, or other laboratory; tutoring.

Library Facilities 1.3 million volumes (32,000 in health, 7,286 in nursing); 14,765 periodical subscriptions (1,662 health-care related).

■ The University of Akron College of Nursing is a nationally recognized, comprehensive nursing college offering baccalaureate, master's, and doctoral degrees. Traditional and accelerated BSN options are complemented by programs for RNs to earn a baccalaureate or master's degree as well as for LPNs to earn a BSN. The MSN program offers advanced practice specializations, including the highly ranked Nurse Anesthesia program. This rigorous course of study prepares nurses to become Certified Registered Nurse Anesthetists (CRNAs). Those interested in becoming nurse scholars, can earn the PhD degree offered jointly with Kent State. A Doctor of Nursing Practice degree is being developed.

BACCALAUREATE PROGRAMS

Degree BSN

Available Programs ADN to Baccalaureate; Accelerated Baccalaureate for Second Degree; Generic Baccalaureate; LPN to Baccalaureate; RN Baccalaureate.

Site Options Lorain, OH; Medina, OH; Orville, OH.

Study Options Full-time and part-time.

The University of Akron (continued)

Program Entrance Requirements Transcript of college record, CPR certification, health exam, immunizations, minimum GPA in nursing prerequisites of 2.75, prerequisite course work. Transfer students are accepted. *Application deadline:* Applications may be processed on a rolling basis for some programs. *Application fee:* $30.

Advanced Placement Credit given for nursing courses completed elsewhere dependent upon specific evaluations.

Expenses (2009–10) *Tuition, state resident:* full-time $7471; part-time $311 per credit hour. *Tuition, nonresident:* full-time $17,336; part-time $620 per credit hour. *Room and board:* $8597; room only: $5499 per academic year. *Required fees:* full-time $2466; part-time $68 per credit; part-time $249 per term.

Financial Aid 80% of baccalaureate students in nursing programs received some form of financial aid in 2008–09. *Gift aid (need-based):* Federal Pell, FSEOG, state, college/university gift aid from institutional funds. *Loans:* Federal Nursing Student Loans, FFEL (Subsidized and Unsubsidized Stafford PLUS), Perkins, college/university. *Work-study:* Federal Work-Study, part-time campus jobs. *Financial aid application deadline (priority):* 2/1.

Contact Dr. Rita A. Klein, Director, Nursing Student Affairs, College of Nursing, The University of Akron, Akron, OH 44325-3701. *Telephone:* 330-972-5103. *Fax:* 330-972-5493. *E-mail:* rklein1@uakron.edu.

GRADUATE PROGRAMS

Expenses (2009–10) *Tuition, state resident:* full-time $6570; part-time $365 per credit hour. *Tuition, nonresident:* full-time $11,250; part-time $625 per credit hour. *Room and board:* $8597; room only: $5499 per academic year. *Required fees:* full-time $1186; part-time $52 per credit; part-time $127 per term.

Financial Aid 80% of graduate students in nursing programs received some form of financial aid in 2008–09. 15 fellowships with full tuition reimbursements available, 8 research assistantships with full tuition reimbursements available, 7 teaching assistantships with full tuition reimbursements available were awarded; career-related internships or fieldwork, Federal Work-Study, and tuition waivers (full) also available.

Contact Dr. Marlene Huff, Coordinator, Masters Program, College of Nursing, The University of Akron, Akron, OH 44325-3701. *Telephone:* 330-972-5930. *Fax:* 330-972-5737. *E-mail:* mhuff@uakron.edu.

MASTER'S DEGREE PROGRAM

Degree MSN

Available Programs Master's; RN to Master's.

Concentrations Available Nurse anesthesia; nursing administration. *Clinical nurse specialist programs in:* adult health, gerontology, pediatric, psychiatric/mental health. *Nurse practitioner programs in:* adult health, gerontology, pediatric, psychiatric/mental health.

Site Options Lorain, OH; Orville, OH.

Study Options Full-time and part-time.

Program Entrance Requirements Clinical experience, computer literacy, minimum overall college GPA of 3.0, transcript of college record, CPR certification, written essay, immunizations, interview, 3 letters of recommendation, physical assessment course, professional liability insurance/malpractice insurance, prerequisite course work, resume, statistics course, GRE. *Application deadline:* Applications may be processed on a rolling basis for some programs. *Application fee:* $30.

Advanced Placement Credit given for nursing courses completed elsewhere dependent upon specific evaluations.

Degree Requirements 53 total credit hours.

POST-MASTER'S PROGRAM

Areas of Study Nurse anesthesia. *Clinical nurse specialist programs in:* adult health, gerontology, pediatric, psychiatric/mental health. *Nurse practitioner programs in:* adult health, gerontology, pediatric, psychiatric/mental health.

DOCTORAL DEGREE PROGRAM

Degree PhD

Available Programs Doctorate.

Areas of Study Aging, community health, ethics, gerontology, health policy, health promotion/disease prevention, health-care systems, human health and illness, illness and transition, individualized study, maternity-newborn, nursing administration, nursing policy, nursing research, nursing science, women's health.

Program Entrance Requirements Minimum overall college GPA of 3.0, interview by faculty committee, interview, 3 letters of recommendation, MSN or equivalent, vita, writing sample, GRE. Application deadline: Applications may be processed on a rolling basis for some programs. Application fee: $30.

Degree Requirements 72 total credit hours, dissertation, oral exam, written exam, residency.

CONTINUING EDUCATION PROGRAM

Contact Dr. Marlene Huff, Coordinator, Educational Progression Program, College of Nursing, The University of Akron, Akron, OH 44325-3701. *Telephone:* 330-972-5930. *Fax:* 330-972-5737. *E-mail:* mhuff@uakron.edu.

See full description on page 522.

University of Cincinnati
College of Nursing
Cincinnati, Ohio

http://www.nursing.uc.edu

Founded in 1819

DEGREES • BSN • MSN • MSN/MBA • MSN/PHD • PHD

Nursing Program Faculty 143 (31% with doctorates).

Baccalaureate Enrollment 631
Women 90% **Men** 10% **Minority** 14% **Part-time** 13%

Graduate Enrollment 360
Women 86% **Men** 14% **Minority** 14% **International** 2%

Distance Learning Courses Available.

Nursing Student Activities Sigma Theta Tau, Student Nurses' Association.

Nursing Student Resources Academic advising; academic or career counseling; assistance for students with disabilities; bookstore; campus computer network; computer lab; computer-assisted instruction; e-mail services; employment services for current students; externships; housing assistance; interactive nursing skills videos; Internet; learning resource lab; library services; nursing audiovisuals; paid internships; remedial services; resume preparation assistance; skills, simulation, or other laboratory; tutoring; unpaid internships.

Library Facilities 3 million volumes (221,630 in health, 21,306 in nursing); 16,560 periodical subscriptions (2,384 health-care related).

BACCALAUREATE PROGRAMS

Degree BSN

Available Programs ADN to Baccalaureate; Accelerated Baccalaureate for Second Degree; Generic Baccalaureate; RN Baccalaureate.

Site Options Cincinnati, OH.

Study Options Full-time.

Program Entrance Requirements Minimum overall college GPA of 2.5, transcript of college record, CPR certification, health insurance, high school biology, high school chemistry, 3 years high school math, high school transcript, immunizations, prerequisite course work. Transfer students are accepted. *Application deadline:* 6/30 (fall).

Advanced Placement Credit by examination available. Credit given for nursing courses completed elsewhere dependent upon specific evaluations.

Expenses (2008–09) *Tuition, state resident:* full-time $9399; part-time $262 per credit hour. *Tuition, nonresident:* full-time $23,922; part-time $665 per credit hour. *International tuition:* $23,922 full-time. *Room and board:* $9057; room only: $5523 per academic year. *Required fees:* full-time $1838; part-time $42 per credit; part-time $135 per term.

Financial Aid 65% of baccalaureate students in nursing programs received some form of financial aid in 2007–08. *Gift aid (need-based):* Federal Pell, FSEOG, state, private, college/university gift aid from institutional funds, United Negro College Fund, Federal Nursing, Academic Competitiveness Grant, National Smart Grant, TEACH Grant. *Loans:* Federal Nursing Student Loans, FFEL (Subsidized and Unsubsidized Stafford PLUS), Perkins, state, college/university. *Work-study:* Federal Work-Study. *Financial aid application deadline:* Continuous.

Contact Mr. Aaron Price, Baccalaureate Academic Advisor, College of Nursing, University of Cincinnati, Office of Student Affairs, PO Box 210038, Cincinnati, OH 45221-0038. *Telephone:* 513-558-5070. *Fax:* 513-558-7523. *E-mail:* aaron.price@uc.edu.

GRADUATE PROGRAMS

Expenses (2008–09) *Tuition, state resident:* full-time $12,354; part-time $412 per credit hour. *Tuition, nonresident:* full-time $22,383; part-time $747 per credit hour. *International tuition:* $22,383 full-time. *Room and board:* $7700; room only: $6500 per academic year.

Financial Aid 60% of graduate students in nursing programs received some form of financial aid in 2007–08. 7 fellowships with full tuition reimbursements available (averaging $13,571 per year), research assistantships with full tuition reimbursements available (averaging $12,000 per year), 8 teaching assistantships with full tuition reimbursements available (averaging $12,000 per year) were awarded; career-related internships or fieldwork, scholarships, traineeships, tuition waivers (partial), and unspecified assistantships also available. Aid available to part-time students. *Financial aid application deadline:* 5/1.

Contact Mr. Loren Carter, Graduate Academic Advisor, College of Nursing, University of Cincinnati, PO Box 210038, Cincinnati, OH 45221-0038. *Telephone:* 513-558-5072. *Fax:* 513-558-7523. *E-mail:* loren.carter@uc.edu.

MASTER'S DEGREE PROGRAM

Degrees MSN; MSN/MBA; MSN/PhD

Available Programs Accelerated Master's for Non-Nursing College Graduates; Master's.

Concentrations Available Nurse anesthesia; nurse-midwifery; nursing administration. *Clinical nurse specialist programs in:* adult health, critical care, gerontology, medical-surgical, occupational health, public health. *Nurse practitioner programs in:* adult health, family health, neonatal health, occupational health, pediatric, women's health.

Site Options Cincinnati, OH.

Study Options Full-time and part-time.

Online Degree Options Yes.

Program Entrance Requirements Clinical experience, computer literacy, transcript of college record, CPR certification, written essay, immunizations, interview, 3 letters of recommendation, physical assessment course, professional liability insurance/malpractice insurance, resume, statistics course, GRE General Test. *Application deadline:* 10/1 (fall), 9/1 (winter), 1/1 (spring), 3/1 (summer). Applications may be processed on a rolling basis for some programs. *Application fee:* $40.

Advanced Placement Credit given for nursing courses completed elsewhere dependent upon specific evaluations.

Degree Requirements 65 total credit hours, thesis or project.

POST-MASTER'S PROGRAM

Areas of Study Nursing education. *Nurse practitioner programs in:* adult health, family health, neonatal health, occupational health, pediatric, psychiatric/mental health, women's health.

DOCTORAL DEGREE PROGRAM

Degree PhD

Available Programs Doctorate; Post-Baccalaureate Doctorate.

Areas of Study Addiction/substance abuse, community health, critical care, ethics, faculty preparation, family health, health promotion/disease prevention, health-care systems, human health and illness, illness and transition, individualized study, maternity-newborn, nursing administration, nursing research, nursing science, oncology, women's health.

Site Options Cincinnati, OH.

Program Entrance Requirements Minimum overall college GPA of 3.0, interview by faculty committee, interview, 3 letters of recommendation, statistics course, vita, writing sample, GRE General Test. Application deadline: 8/15 (fall). Applications may be processed on a rolling basis for some programs. Application fee: $40.

Degree Requirements 135 total credit hours, dissertation, oral exam, written exam, residency.

CONTINUING EDUCATION PROGRAM

Contact Ms. Elizabeth Karle, Program Coordinator, Continuing Education, College of Nursing, University of Cincinnati, PO Box 210038, Cincinnati, OH 45221-0038. *Telephone:* 513-558-5311. *Fax:* 513-558-5054. *E-mail:* elizabeth.karle@uc.edu.

University of Phoenix–Cleveland Campus
College of Health and Human Services
Independence, Ohio

Founded in 2000

DEGREES • BSN • MSN

Nursing Program Faculty 10 (20% with doctorates).

Baccalaureate Enrollment 17
Women 82.4% **Men** 17.6% **Minority** 11.8%

Graduate Enrollment 4
Women 100%

Nursing Student Activities Sigma Theta Tau.

Nursing Student Resources Academic advising; academic or career counseling; assistance for students with disabilities; bookstore; campus computer network; computer lab; computer-assisted instruction; e-mail services; interactive nursing skills videos; Internet; learning resource lab; library services; nursing audiovisuals; remedial services; skills, simulation, or other laboratory; tutoring.

Library Facilities 16,781 periodical subscriptions (1,300 health-care related).

BACCALAUREATE PROGRAMS

Degree BSN

Available Programs Accelerated Baccalaureate.

Site Options Beachwood, OH.

Study Options Full-time.

Program Entrance Requirements Transcript of college record, CPR certification, immunizations, 1 letter of recommendation, RN licensure. Transfer students are accepted. *Application deadline:* Applications may be processed on a rolling basis for some programs.

Advanced Placement Credit by examination available. Credit given for nursing courses completed elsewhere dependent upon specific evaluations.

Expenses (2009–10) *Tuition:* full-time $10,560. *Required fees:* full-time $600.

Contact Campus College Chair, Nursing, College of Health and Human Services, University of Phoenix–Cleveland Campus, 5005 Rockside Road, Suite 130, Independence, OH 44131. *Telephone:* 216-447-8807.

GRADUATE PROGRAMS

Expenses (2009–10) *Tuition:* full-time $13,200. *Required fees:* full-time $760.

Financial Aid Institutionally sponsored loans and scholarships available.

Contact Campus College Chair, Nursing, College of Health and Human Services, University of Phoenix–Cleveland Campus, 5005 Rockside Road, Suite 130, Independence, OH 44131. *Telephone:* 216-447-8807.

MASTER'S DEGREE PROGRAM

Degree MSN

Available Programs Master's.

Concentrations Available Nursing administration.

Site Options Beachwood, OH.

Study Options Full-time.

Program Entrance Requirements Clinical experience, computer literacy, minimum overall college GPA of 2.5, transcript of college record. *Application deadline:* Applications may be processed on a rolling basis for some programs. *Application fee:* $45.

Advanced Placement Credit given for nursing courses completed elsewhere dependent upon specific evaluations.

University of Phoenix–Cleveland Campus (continued)
Degree Requirements 39 total credit hours, thesis or project.

University of Rio Grande
Holzer School of Nursing
Rio Grande, Ohio

Founded in 1876
DEGREE • BSN.

Nursing Program Faculty 9
Library Facilities 96,731 volumes; 850 periodical subscriptions.

BACCALAUREATE PROGRAMS

Degree BSN

Available Programs RN Baccalaureate.
Study Options Full-time and part-time.
Contact Donna Mitchell, Director and Professor, Holzer School of Nursing, University of Rio Grande, Holzer School of Nursing 122, Rio Grande, OH 45674. *Telephone:* 800-282-7201 Ext. 7308. *Fax:* 740-245-7177. *E-mail:* mitchell@rio.edu.

The University of Toledo
College of Nursing
Toledo, Ohio

http://www.meduohio.edu/snur/index.html
Founded in 1872

DEGREES • BSN • DNP • MSN

Nursing Program Faculty 45 (40% with doctorates).
Baccalaureate Enrollment 445
Women 90% **Men** 10% **Minority** 8% **International** 2% **Part-time** 23%
Graduate Enrollment 247
Women 89% **Men** 11% **Minority** 7% **Part-time** 77%
Distance Learning Courses Available.
Nursing Student Activities Sigma Theta Tau; Student Nurses' Association, nursing club.
Nursing Student Resources Academic advising; academic or career counseling; assistance for students with disabilities; bookstore; campus computer network; computer lab; computer-assisted instruction; daycare for children of students; e-mail services; interactive nursing skills videos; Internet; learning resource lab; library services; nursing audiovisuals; resume preparation assistance; skills, simulation, or other laboratory; tutoring.
Library Facilities 2 million volumes (33,000 in health, 4,000 in nursing); 76,981 periodical subscriptions (2,400 health-care related).

BACCALAUREATE PROGRAMS

Degree BSN

Available Programs ADN to Baccalaureate; Generic Baccalaureate.
Study Options Full-time and part-time.
Online Degree Options Yes.
Program Entrance Requirements Minimum overall college GPA of 3.0, transcript of college record, CPR certification, health exam, health insurance, high school biology, high school chemistry, high school foreign language, 3 years high school math, 3 years high school science, high school transcript, immunizations, minimum high school GPA of 3.0, professional liability insurance/malpractice insurance, prerequisite course work. Transfer students are accepted. *Application deadline:* 5/1 (fall), 9/1 (spring), 1/1 (summer).
Advanced Placement Credit given for nursing courses completed elsewhere dependent upon specific evaluations.

Expenses (2009–10) *Tuition, state resident:* full-time $7054; part-time $294 per credit hour. *Tuition, nonresident:* full-time $15,866; part-time $661 per credit hour. *Room and board:* $9478 per academic year. *Required fees:* full-time $3402; part-time $111 per credit; part-time $179 per term.
Financial Aid 60% of baccalaureate students in nursing programs received some form of financial aid in 2008–09. *Gift aid (need-based):* Federal Pell, FSEOG, state, private, college/university gift aid from institutional funds. *Loans:* Federal Direct (Subsidized and Unsubsidized Stafford PLUS), Perkins, alternative loans. *Work-study:* Federal Work-Study. *Financial aid application deadline (priority):* 4/1.
Contact Paula Ballmer, RN, Senior Recruiter, College of Nursing, The University of Toledo, 3000 Arlington Avenue, Mail Stop 1026, Health Science Campus, Toledo, OH 43614-2598. *Telephone:* 419-383-5839. *Fax:* 419-383-5894. *E-mail:* paula.ballmer@utoledo.edu.

GRADUATE PROGRAMS

Expenses (2009–10) *Tuition, state resident:* full-time $11,040; part-time $460 per credit hour. *Tuition, nonresident:* full-time $20,928; part-time $872 per credit hour. *Required fees:* full-time $2075; part-time $63 per credit; part-time $162 per term.
Financial Aid 60% of graduate students in nursing programs received some form of financial aid in 2008–09. Federal Work-Study, institutionally sponsored loans, and scholarships available.
Contact Ms. Kathleen Mitchell, RN, Graduate Nursing Advisor, College of Nursing, The University of Toledo, 3000 Arlington Avenue, Toledo, OH 43614-2598. *Telephone:* 419-383-5820. *Fax:* 419-383-5894. *E-mail:* kathleen.mitchell@utoledo.edu.

MASTER'S DEGREE PROGRAM

Degree MSN

Available Programs Master's; Master's for Non-Nursing College Graduates; Master's for Nurses with Non-Nursing Degrees.
Concentrations Available Clinical nurse leader; nursing education. *Clinical nurse specialist programs in:* adult health, psychiatric/mental health. *Nurse practitioner programs in:* adult health, family health, pediatric.
Study Options Full-time and part-time.
Program Entrance Requirements Computer literacy, minimum overall college GPA of 3.0, transcript of college record, written essay, 2 letters of recommendation, resume, GRE General Test. *Application deadline:* 2/1 (fall), 10/1 (spring). *Application fee:* $45.
Advanced Placement Credit given for nursing courses completed elsewhere dependent upon specific evaluations.
Degree Requirements 55 total credit hours, thesis or project, comprehensive exam.

POST-MASTER'S PROGRAM

Areas of Study Nursing education. *Clinical nurse specialist programs in:* psychiatric/mental health. *Nurse practitioner programs in:* adult health, family health, pediatric.

DOCTORAL DEGREE PROGRAM

Degree DNP

Available Programs Doctorate.
Areas of Study Advanced practice nursing, nursing administration.
Online Degree Options Yes (online only).
Program Entrance Requirements Clinical experience, minimum overall college GPA of 3.3, interview by faculty committee, interview, 3 letters of recommendation, MSN or equivalent, statistics course, vita, writing sample. Application deadline: 2/1 (fall). Application fee: $45.
Degree Requirements 36 total credit hours.

CONTINUING EDUCATION PROGRAM

Contact Ms. Deborah Mattin, RN, Director, Continuing Nursing Education, College of Nursing, The University of Toledo, 3000 Arlington Avenue, Toledo, OH 43614-2598. *Telephone:* 419-383-5812. *Fax:* 419-383-5894. *E-mail:* deborah.mattin@utoledo.edu.

Urbana University
BSN Completion Program
Urbana, Ohio

Founded in 1850

DEGREES • BSN • MSN

Nursing Program Faculty 3 (67% with doctorates).

Baccalaureate Enrollment 120
Women 97% **Men** 3% **Minority** 3% **Part-time** 98%

Graduate Enrollment 10

Nursing Student Activities Nursing Honor Society.

Nursing Student Resources Academic advising; academic or career counseling; assistance for students with disabilities; bookstore; campus computer network; career placement assistance; computer lab; e-mail services; Internet; learning resource lab; library services; nursing audiovisuals; placement services for program completers; remedial services; resume preparation assistance; tutoring.

Library Facilities 61,600 volumes; 800 periodical subscriptions.

BACCALAUREATE PROGRAMS

Degree BSN

Available Programs RN Baccalaureate.

Site Options Springfield, OH.

Study Options Full-time and part-time.

Program Entrance Requirements CPR certification, health exam, health insurance, immunizations, professional liability insurance/malpractice insurance, RN licensure. Transfer students are accepted. *Application deadline:* Applications may be processed on a rolling basis for some programs. *Application fee:* $25.

Advanced Placement Credit given for nursing courses completed elsewhere dependent upon specific evaluations.

Expenses (2009–10) *Tuition:* full-time $9960; part-time $415 per credit hour. *Required fees:* part-time $150 per term.

Financial Aid 10% of baccalaureate students in nursing programs received some form of financial aid in 2008–09.

Contact Dr. Nancy Lee Sweeney, Program Director and Professor of Nursing, BSN Completion Program, Urbana University, 101 Miller Hall, 330 South Burnett Road, Springfield, OH 45505. *Telephone:* 937-328-9610. *Fax:* 937-328-8668. *E-mail:* nsweeney@urbana.edu.

GRADUATE PROGRAMS

Expenses (2009–10) *Tuition:* full-time $11,400; part-time $475 per credit hour. *Required fees:* full-time $150.

Financial Aid 10% of graduate students in nursing programs received some form of financial aid in 2008–09.

Contact Dr. Nancy L. Sweeney, Dean, College of Nursing and Allied Health and Professor of Nursing, BSN Completion Program, Urbana University, 579 College Way, Urbana, OH 43078. *Telephone:* 937-328-9610. *Fax:* 937-328-8668. *E-mail:* nsweeney@urbana.edu.

MASTER'S DEGREE PROGRAM

Degree MSN

Available Programs Master's.

Concentrations Available Nursing administration; nursing education.

Site Options Springfield, OH.

Study Options Full-time and part-time.

Program Entrance Requirements Minimum overall college GPA of 3.0, transcript of college record, CPR certification, written essay, immunizations, interview, 3 letters of recommendation, professional liability insurance/malpractice insurance, resume. *Application deadline:* 8/15 (fall), 1/5 (spring), 5/15 (summer). Applications may be processed on a rolling basis for some programs. *Application fee:* $25.

Advanced Placement Credit given for nursing courses completed elsewhere dependent upon specific evaluations.

Degree Requirements 46 total credit hours, thesis or project.

Ursuline College
The Breen School of Nursing
Pepper Pike, Ohio

http://www.ursuline.edu

Founded in 1871

DEGREES • BSN • MSN

Nursing Program Faculty 25 (28% with doctorates).

Nursing Student Activities Sigma Theta Tau, Student Nurses' Association.

Nursing Student Resources Academic advising; academic or career counseling; assistance for students with disabilities; bookstore; campus computer network; career placement assistance; computer lab; computer-assisted instruction; e-mail services; employment services for current students; externships; housing assistance; interactive nursing skills videos; Internet; learning resource lab; library services; nursing audiovisuals; placement services for program completers; remedial services; resume preparation assistance; skills, simulation, or other laboratory; tutoring.

Library Facilities 163,617 volumes; 7,806 periodical subscriptions.

BACCALAUREATE PROGRAMS

Degree BSN

Available Programs Accelerated Baccalaureate for Second Degree; Accelerated LPN to Baccalaureate; Accelerated RN Baccalaureate; Generic Baccalaureate.

Site Options Cleveland, OH.

Study Options Full-time and part-time.

Program Entrance Requirements Minimum overall college GPA of 2.5, transcript of college record, written essay, health exam, health insurance, high school biology, high school chemistry, 2 years high school math, 2 years high school science, high school transcript, immunizations, 1 letter of recommendation, minimum high school GPA of 2.75, minimum GPA in nursing prerequisites of 2.75. Transfer students are accepted.

Advanced Placement Credit given for nursing courses completed elsewhere dependent upon specific evaluations.

Financial Aid 85% of baccalaureate students in nursing programs received some form of financial aid in 2007–08.

Contact Joan Horinka, Director of Admission, The Breen School of Nursing, Ursuline College, 2550 Lander Road, Pepper Pike, OH 44124-4398. *Telephone:* 440-449-4203. *Fax:* 440-684-6138.

GRADUATE PROGRAMS

Contact Dr. M. Murray Mayo, RN, Director, Graduate Program, The Breen School of Nursing, Ursuline College, 2550 Lander Road, Pepper Pike, OH 44124-4398. *Telephone:* 440-646-8127. *Fax:* 440-684-6053. *E-mail:* mmayo@ursuline.edu.

MASTER'S DEGREE PROGRAM

Degree MSN

Available Programs Accelerated Master's; Master's.

Concentrations Available Nurse case management. *Clinical nurse specialist programs in:* adult health, palliative care. *Nurse practitioner programs in:* adult health, family health.

Study Options Full-time and part-time.

Program Entrance Requirements Clinical experience, minimum overall college GPA of 3.0, transcript of college record, CPR certification, immunizations, 3 letters of recommendation.

Advanced Placement Credit given for nursing courses completed elsewhere dependent upon specific evaluations.

Degree Requirements 39 total credit hours.

POST-MASTER'S PROGRAM

Areas of Study Nurse case management. *Clinical nurse specialist programs in:* adult health, palliative care. *Nurse practitioner programs in:* adult health, family health.

See full description on page 534.

Walsh University
Department of Nursing
North Canton, Ohio

http://www.walsh.edu/

Founded in 1958

DEGREE • BSN

Nursing Program Faculty 15

Baccalaureate Enrollment 227
Women 79% **Men** 21% **Minority** 5% **International** 1% **Part-time** 10%
Nursing Student Activities Nursing Honor Society, Student Nurses' Association.

Nursing Student Resources Academic advising; academic or career counseling; assistance for students with disabilities; bookstore; campus computer network; career placement assistance; computer lab; computer-assisted instruction; e-mail services; employment services for current students; housing assistance; interactive nursing skills videos; Internet; learning resource lab; library services; nursing audiovisuals; placement services for program completers; remedial services; resume preparation assistance; skills, simulation, or other laboratory; tutoring.

Library Facilities 241,075 volumes (4,000 in health, 2,000 in nursing); 6,257 periodical subscriptions (114 health-care related).

BACCALAUREATE PROGRAMS

Degree BSN

Available Programs Accelerated Baccalaureate; Accelerated Baccalaureate for Second Degree; Generic Baccalaureate; RN Baccalaureate.

Site Options Medina, OH; Akron, OH; Canton, OH.

Study Options Full-time and part-time.

Program Entrance Requirements Transcript of college record, CPR certification, health exam, health insurance, high school chemistry, high school foreign language, 3 years high school math, 3 years high school science, high school transcript, immunizations, minimum GPA in nursing prerequisites of 2.75, professional liability insurance/malpractice insurance, prerequisite course work. Transfer students are accepted. *Application deadline:* 8/15 (fall), 12/31 (spring), 4/30 (summer). Applications may be processed on a rolling basis for some programs. *Application fee:* $25.

Advanced Placement Credit by examination available. Credit given for nursing courses completed elsewhere dependent upon specific evaluations.

Expenses (2009–10) *Tuition:* full-time $20,500; part-time $675 per contact hour. *International tuition:* $20,500 full-time. *Room and board:* $10,000; room only: $3000 per academic year. *Required fees:* full-time $552; part-time $23 per credit; part-time $276 per term.

Financial Aid 94% of baccalaureate students in nursing programs received some form of financial aid in 2008–09.

Contact Dr. Linda G. Linc, RN, Professor and Chair, Division of Nursing, Department of Nursing, Walsh University, 2020 East Maple Street, North Canton, OH 44720-3336. *Telephone:* 330-490-7251. *Fax:* 330-490-7206. *E-mail:* llinc@walsh.edu.

Wright State University
College of Nursing and Health
Dayton, Ohio

http://www.nursing.wright.edu

Founded in 1964

DEGREES • BSN • DNP • MS • MS/MBA

Nursing Program Faculty 68 (33% with doctorates).

Baccalaureate Enrollment 787
Women 84% **Men** 16% **Minority** 16% **International** 1% **Part-time** 35%

Graduate Enrollment 257
Women 94% **Men** 6% **Minority** 14% **Part-time** 86%

Distance Learning Courses Available.

Nursing Student Activities Nursing Honor Society, Sigma Theta Tau, Student Nurses' Association, nursing club.

Nursing Student Resources Academic advising; academic or career counseling; assistance for students with disabilities; bookstore; campus computer network; career placement assistance; computer lab; computer-assisted instruction; daycare for children of students; e-mail services; employment services for current students; externships; housing assistance; interactive nursing skills videos; Internet; learning resource lab; library services; nursing audiovisuals; remedial services; resume preparation assistance; skills, simulation, or other laboratory; tutoring.

Library Facilities 703,000 volumes (111,826 in health, 7,646 in nursing); 443,200 periodical subscriptions (1,279 health-care related).

BACCALAUREATE PROGRAMS

Degree BSN

Available Programs Accelerated Baccalaureate for Second Degree; Baccalaureate for Second Degree; Generic Baccalaureate; RN Baccalaureate.

Site Options Dayton, OH; Chillicothe, OH; Celina, OH.

Study Options Full-time and part-time.

Program Entrance Requirements Minimum overall college GPA of 2.5, transcript of college record, written essay, high school transcript, minimum GPA in nursing prerequisites of 2.5, prerequisite course work. Transfer students are accepted. *Application deadline:* 6/30 (fall), 12/30 (spring).

Advanced Placement Credit by examination available. Credit given for nursing courses completed elsewhere dependent upon specific evaluations.

Expenses (2009–10) *Tuition, state resident:* full-time $10,044; part-time $227 per quarter hour. *Tuition, nonresident:* full-time $19,460; part-time $443 per quarter hour. *International tuition:* $19,460 full-time. *Room and board:* $7829 per academic year.

Financial Aid 83% of baccalaureate students in nursing programs received some form of financial aid in 2008–09. *Gift aid (need-based):* Federal Pell, FSEOG, state, private, college/university gift aid from institutional funds, United Negro College Fund, Federal Nursing, Choose Ohio First Scholarship. *Loans:* Federal Nursing Student Loans, FFEL (Subsidized and Unsubsidized Stafford PLUS), Perkins, state, college/university, private loans. *Work-study:* Federal Work-Study. *Financial aid application deadline (priority):* 2/15.

Contact Ms. Theresa A. Haghnazarian, Director, Student and Alumni Affairs, College of Nursing and Health, Wright State University, 3640 Colonel Glenn Highway, Dayton, OH 45435. *Telephone:* 937-775-3132. *Fax:* 937-775-4571. *E-mail:* theresa.haghnazarian@wright.edu.

GRADUATE PROGRAMS

Expenses (2009–10) *Tuition, state resident:* full-time $12,984; part-time $335 per quarter hour. *Tuition, nonresident:* full-time $24,760; part-time $572 per quarter hour. *International tuition:* $24,760 full-time. *Room and board:* $7829 per academic year.

Financial Aid 39% of graduate students in nursing programs received some form of financial aid in 2008–09. 15 fellowships with full tuition reimbursements available were awarded; research assistantships, teaching assistantships, Federal Work-Study, institutionally sponsored loans, and unspecified assistantships also available. Aid available to part-time students. *Financial aid application deadline:* 6/1.

Contact Dr. Donna Miles Curry, Associate Dean, Graduate Programs, College of Nursing and Health, Wright State University, 3640 Colonel Glenn Highway, Dayton, OH 45435. *Telephone:* 937-775-3577. *Fax:* 937-775-4571. *E-mail:* donna.curry@wright.edu.

MASTER'S DEGREE PROGRAM

Degrees MS; MS/MBA

Available Programs Master's; Master's for Nurses with Non-Nursing Degrees.

Concentrations Available Clinical nurse leader; health-care administration; nursing administration. *Clinical nurse specialist programs in:* adult health, community health, pediatric, public health, school health. *Nurse practitioner programs in:* acute care, family health, pediatric.

Study Options Full-time and part-time.

Online Degree Options Yes.

Program Entrance Requirements Clinical experience, computer literacy, minimum overall college GPA of 3.0, transcript of college record, written essay, interview, physical assessment course, statistics course, GRE General Test. *Application deadline:* Applications may be processed on a rolling basis for some programs. *Application fee:* $30.

Advanced Placement Credit given for nursing courses completed elsewhere dependent upon specific evaluations.

Degree Requirements 48 total credit hours, thesis or project.

POST-MASTER'S PROGRAM

Areas of Study *Clinical nurse specialist programs in:* school health. *Nurse practitioner programs in:* acute care, family health, pediatric.

DOCTORAL DEGREE PROGRAM

Degree DNP

Available Programs Doctorate.

Areas of Study Advanced practice nursing, biology of health and illness, clinical practice, community health, family health, health policy, health promotion/disease prevention, health-care systems, information systems, nursing administration, nursing policy, nursing science.

Online Degree Options Yes (online only).

Program Entrance Requirements Clinical experience, minimum overall college GPA of 3.3, interview by faculty committee, 3 letters of recommendation, MSN or equivalent, statistics course, vita, writing sample.

Degree Requirements 54 total credit hours, dissertation.

CONTINUING EDUCATION PROGRAM

Contact Ms. Teri Houston, Office Assistant, College of Nursing and Health, Wright State University, 3640 Colonel Glenn Highway, Dayton, OH 45435. *Telephone:* 937-775-3577. *Fax:* 937-775-4571. *E-mail:* teresa.houston@wright.edu.

Xavier University
Department of Nursing
Cincinnati, Ohio

Founded in 1831

DEGREES • BSN • MSN • MSN/MBA

Nursing Program Faculty 68 (8% with doctorates).

Baccalaureate Enrollment 268
Women 90% **Men** 10% **Minority** 11% **Part-time** 1%

Graduate Enrollment 210
Women 94% **Men** 6% **Minority** 10% **Part-time** 70%

Nursing Student Activities Sigma Theta Tau, nursing club.

Nursing Student Resources Academic advising; academic or career counseling; assistance for students with disabilities; bookstore; campus computer network; career placement assistance; computer lab; computer-assisted instruction; e-mail services; employment services for current students; externships; housing assistance; interactive nursing skills videos; Internet; learning resource lab; library services; nursing audiovisuals; paid internships; resume preparation assistance; skills, simulation, or other laboratory; tutoring.

Library Facilities 363,140 volumes (8,900 in health, 1,160 in nursing); 55,934 periodical subscriptions (200 health-care related).

BACCALAUREATE PROGRAMS

Degree BSN

Available Programs Generic Baccalaureate.

Study Options Full-time and part-time.

Program Entrance Requirements Minimum overall college GPA of 2.7, transcript of college record, written essay, high school chemistry, high school foreign language, 3 years high school math, 2 years high school science, high school transcript, minimum high school GPA of 2.8. Transfer students are accepted. *Application deadline:* Applications may be processed on a rolling basis for some programs. *Application fee:* $30.

Advanced Placement Credit given for nursing courses completed elsewhere dependent upon specific evaluations.

Expenses (2009–10) *Tuition:* full-time $27,900. *Room and board:* $9530; room only: $5250 per academic year. *Required fees:* full-time $200.

Financial Aid 90% of baccalaureate students in nursing programs received some form of financial aid in 2008–09. *Gift aid (need-based):* Federal Pell, FSEOG, state, private, college/university gift aid from institutional funds. *Loans:* FFEL (Subsidized and Unsubsidized Stafford PLUS), Perkins. *Work-study:* Federal Work-Study, part-time campus jobs. *Financial aid application deadline (priority):* 2/15.

Contact Ms. Marilyn Volk Gomez, Director of Nursing Student Services, Department of Nursing, Xavier University, 3800 Victory Parkway, Cincinnati, OH 45207-7351. *Telephone:* 513-745-4392. *Fax:* 513-745-1087. *E-mail:* gomez@xavier.edu.

GRADUATE PROGRAMS

Expenses (2009–10) *Tuition:* part-time $555 per credit hour.

Financial Aid 30% of graduate students in nursing programs received some form of financial aid in 2008–09.

Contact Ms. Marilyn Volk Gomez, Director of Nursing Student Services, Department of Nursing, Xavier University, 3800 Victory Parkway, Cincinnati, OH 45207-7351. *Telephone:* 513-745-4392. *Fax:* 513-745-1087. *E-mail:* gomez@xavier.edu.

MASTER'S DEGREE PROGRAM

Degrees MSN; MSN/MBA

Available Programs Master's; Master's for Nurses with Non-Nursing Degrees; RN to Master's.

Concentrations Available Clinical nurse leader; nursing administration; nursing education; nursing informatics. *Clinical nurse specialist programs in:* forensic nursing, school health.

Study Options Full-time and part-time.

Program Entrance Requirements Minimum overall college GPA of 2.8, transcript of college record, written essay, 3 letters of recommendation, statistics course. *Application deadline:* Applications may be processed on a rolling basis for some programs. *Application fee:* $35.

Degree Requirements 36 total credit hours, thesis or project.

Youngstown State University
Department of Nursing
Youngstown, Ohio

Founded in 1908

DEGREES • BSN • MSN

Nursing Program Faculty 22 (18% with doctorates).

Baccalaureate Enrollment 22

Graduate Enrollment 24
Women 75% **Men** 25% **Minority** 13%

Nursing Student Activities Sigma Theta Tau, Student Nurses' Association.

Nursing Student Resources Academic advising; academic or career counseling; assistance for students with disabilities; bookstore; campus computer network; career placement assistance; computer lab; computer-assisted instruction; e-mail services; housing assistance; interactive nursing skills videos; Internet; learning resource lab; library services; nursing audiovisuals; placement services for program completers; resume preparation assistance; skills, simulation, or other laboratory; tutoring.

Library Facilities 873,074 volumes; 41,370 periodical subscriptions.

BACCALAUREATE PROGRAMS

Degree BSN

Site Options Boardman, OH.

Study Options Full-time.

Program Entrance Requirements Minimum overall college GPA of 2.0, transcript of college record, CPR certification, health exam, health insurance, high school biology, high school chemistry, high school foreign language, 3 years high school math, 3 years high school science, high school transcript, immunizations, minimum high school GPA, minimum high school rank, minimum GPA in nursing prerequisites of 2.5, prerequisite course work. Transfer students are accepted.

Youngstown State University (continued)

Advanced Placement Credit by examination available. Credit given for nursing courses completed elsewhere dependent upon specific evaluations.

Contact *Telephone:* 330-941-2328. *Fax:* 330-941-2309.

GRADUATE PROGRAMS

Contact *Telephone:* 330-941-1796. *Fax:* 330-941-2309.

MASTER'S DEGREE PROGRAM

Degree MSN

Concentrations Available Nurse anesthesia; nursing education.

Study Options Full-time and part-time.

Program Entrance Requirements Clinical experience, computer literacy, transcript of college record, CPR certification, written essay, immunizations, nursing research course, physical assessment course, prerequisite course work, resume, GRE General Test.

Advanced Placement Credit given for nursing courses completed elsewhere dependent upon specific evaluations.

Degree Requirements Thesis or project.

OKLAHOMA

Bacone College
Department of Nursing
Muskogee, Oklahoma

Founded in 1880

DEGREE • BSN

Nursing Program Faculty 8

Baccalaureate Enrollment 16
Women 100% **Minority** 65%

Nursing Student Activities Student Nurses' Association, nursing club.

Nursing Student Resources Academic advising; bookstore; campus computer network; computer lab; computer-assisted instruction; interactive nursing skills videos; Internet; learning resource lab; library services; nursing audiovisuals; remedial services; skills, simulation, or other laboratory.

Library Facilities 34,564 volumes; 121 periodical subscriptions.

BACCALAUREATE PROGRAMS

Degree BSN

Available Programs Accelerated RN Baccalaureate.

Program Entrance Requirements Transcript of college record, CPR certification, health exam, health insurance, immunizations, 2 letters of recommendation, minimum GPA in nursing prerequisites of 2.5, prerequisite course work, RN licensure.

Contact *Telephone:* 888-682-5514.

East Central University
Department of Nursing
Ada, Oklahoma

http://www.ecok.edu/dept/nursing

Founded in 1909

DEGREE • BS

Nursing Program Faculty 17 (31% with doctorates).

Baccalaureate Enrollment 495
Women 86% **Men** 14% **Minority** 44% **International** 1% **Part-time** 14%

Distance Learning Courses Available.

Nursing Student Activities Student Nurses' Association.

Nursing Student Resources Academic advising; academic or career counseling; assistance for students with disabilities; bookstore; campus computer network; career placement assistance; computer lab; computer-assisted instruction; daycare for children of students; e-mail services; employment services for current students; externships; housing assistance; interactive nursing skills videos; Internet; learning resource lab; library services; nursing audiovisuals; other; placement services for program completers; resume preparation assistance; skills, simulation, or other laboratory; tutoring.

Library Facilities 182,126 volumes (2,236 in health, 893 in nursing); 25,076 periodical subscriptions (266 health-care related).

BACCALAUREATE PROGRAMS

Degree BS

Available Programs ADN to Baccalaureate; Generic Baccalaureate.

Site Options Ardmore, OK; McAlester, OK; Durant, OK.

Study Options Full-time and part-time.

Program Entrance Requirements Minimum overall college GPA of 2.5, transcript of college record, CPR certification, health exam, immunizations, minimum GPA in nursing prerequisites of 2.5, professional liability insurance/malpractice insurance, prerequisite course work. Transfer students are accepted. *Application deadline:* 9/17 (spring).

Advanced Placement Credit given for nursing courses completed elsewhere dependent upon specific evaluations.

Expenses (2008–09) *Tuition, state resident:* full-time $2000; part-time $105 per credit hour. *Tuition, nonresident:* full-time $6000; part-time $315 per credit hour. *International tuition:* $6000 full-time. *Room and board:* room only: $1400 per academic year. *Required fees:* full-time $800; part-time $100 per credit; part-time $400 per term.

Financial Aid 83% of baccalaureate students in nursing programs received some form of financial aid in 2007–08.

Contact Dr. Joseph T. Catalano, Chair, Department of Nursing, East Central University, 1100 East 14th Street, Ada, OK 74820. *Telephone:* 580-310-5434. *Fax:* 580-310-5785. *E-mail:* jcatalan@mailclerk.ecok.edu.

Langston University
School of Nursing and Health Professions
Langston, Oklahoma

http://www.lunet.ed/nurs5.html

Founded in 1897

DEGREE • BSN

Nursing Program Faculty 16 (13% with doctorates).

Nursing Student Activities Student Nurses' Association, nursing club.

Nursing Student Resources Academic advising; academic or career counseling; assistance for students with disabilities; bookstore; campus computer network; career placement assistance; computer lab; computer-assisted instruction; daycare for children of students; e-mail services; housing assistance; interactive nursing skills videos; Internet; learning resource lab; library services; nursing audiovisuals; remedial services; resume preparation assistance; skills, simulation, or other laboratory; tutoring.

Library Facilities 97,565 volumes (35,397 in health, 2,664 in nursing); 1,235 periodical subscriptions (978 health-care related).

BACCALAUREATE PROGRAMS

Degree BSN

Available Programs Generic Baccalaureate; LPN to Baccalaureate; RN Baccalaureate.

Site Options Tulsa, OK.

Study Options Full-time and part-time.

Program Entrance Requirements Minimum overall college GPA of 2.5, transcript of college record, written essay, health exam, immunizations, minimum GPA in nursing prerequisites of 2.5, professional liability insurance/malpractice insurance, prerequisite course work. Transfer students are accepted.

Advanced Placement Credit by examination available. Credit given for nursing courses completed elsewhere dependent upon specific evaluations.

Contact *Telephone:* 405-466-3411. *Fax:* 405-466-2195.

Northeastern State University
Department of Nursing
Tahlequah, Oklahoma

http://arapaho.nsuok.edu/~nursing

Founded in 1846

DEGREE • BSN

Nursing Program Faculty 4 (25% with doctorates).

Baccalaureate Enrollment 97
Women 88% **Men** 12% **Minority** 31% **Part-time** 96%

Distance Learning Courses Available.

Nursing Student Activities Sigma Theta Tau, Student Nurses' Association.

Nursing Student Resources Academic advising; academic or career counseling; assistance for students with disabilities; bookstore; campus computer network; career placement assistance; computer lab; computer-assisted instruction; e-mail services; employment services for current students; housing assistance; Internet; library services; nursing audiovisuals; placement services for program completers; resume preparation assistance; tutoring.

Library Facilities 415,000 volumes (20,000 in health, 15,293 in nursing); 19,785 periodical subscriptions (1,000 health-care related).

BACCALAUREATE PROGRAMS

Degree BSN

Available Programs Accelerated RN Baccalaureate; RN Baccalaureate.

Site Options Miami, OK; Ponca City, OK; Broken Arrow, OK.

Online Degree Options Yes.

Program Entrance Requirements Minimum overall college GPA of 2.0, transcript of college record, CPR certification, health exam, immunizations, 3 letters of recommendation, minimum GPA in nursing prerequisites of 2.0, professional liability insurance/malpractice insurance, prerequisite course work, RN licensure. Transfer students are accepted.

Expenses (2009–10) *Tuition, state resident:* full-time $4155; part-time $139 per credit hour. *Tuition, nonresident:* full-time $10,245; part-time $342 per credit hour. *International tuition:* $10,245 full-time. *Room and board:* $6034; room only: $2500 per academic year. *Required fees:* full-time $2246; part-time $75 per credit.

Financial Aid 70% of baccalaureate students in nursing programs received some form of financial aid in 2008–09. *Gift aid (need-based):* Federal Pell, FSEOG, state, private, college/university gift aid from institutional funds. *Loans:* FFEL (Subsidized and Unsubsidized Stafford PLUS), Perkins. *Work-study:* Federal Work-Study, part-time campus jobs. *Financial aid application deadline (priority):* 4/1.

Contact Dr. Joyce A. Van Nostrand, Chair, Nursing Program and Department of Health Professions, Department of Nursing, Northeastern State University, PO Box 549, Muskogee, OK 74402-0549. *Telephone:* 918-781-5410. *Fax:* 918-781-5411. *E-mail:* vannostr@nsuok.edu.

Northwestern Oklahoma State University
Division of Nursing
Alva, Oklahoma

http://www.nwosu.edu/nursing

Founded in 1897

DEGREE • BSN

Nursing Program Faculty 12 (.08% with doctorates).

Baccalaureate Enrollment 45
Women 99% **Men** 1% **Minority** 2% **International** 2% **Part-time** 1%

Distance Learning Courses Available.

Nursing Student Activities Nursing Honor Society, Student Nurses' Association.

Nursing Student Resources Academic advising; academic or career counseling; assistance for students with disabilities; bookstore; campus computer network; career placement assistance; computer lab; computer-assisted instruction; e-mail services; housing assistance; interactive nursing skills videos; Internet; learning resource lab; library services; nursing audiovisuals; remedial services; skills, simulation, or other laboratory; tutoring.

Library Facilities 344,640 volumes; 3,990 periodical subscriptions (59 health-care related).

BACCALAUREATE PROGRAMS

Degree BSN

Available Programs ADN to Baccalaureate; Accelerated Baccalaureate; Accelerated LPN to Baccalaureate; Accelerated RN Baccalaureate; Baccalaureate for Second Degree; Generic Baccalaureate; LPN to Baccalaureate; LPN to RN Baccalaureate; RN Baccalaureate.

Site Options Enid, OK; Woodward, OK.

Study Options Full-time and part-time.

Program Entrance Requirements Minimum overall college GPA of 2.5, transcript of college record, CPR certification, health exam, high school transcript, immunizations, 3 letters of recommendation, minimum high school GPA of 2.5, minimum GPA in nursing prerequisites of 2.5, professional liability insurance/malpractice insurance, prerequisite course work. Transfer students are accepted. *Application deadline:* 2/2 (spring).

Advanced Placement Credit by examination available. Credit given for nursing courses completed elsewhere dependent upon specific evaluations.

Financial Aid 74% of baccalaureate students in nursing programs received some form of financial aid in 2007–08.

Contact Dr. Carole McKenzie, Division Director, Division of Nursing, Northwestern Oklahoma State University, 709 Oklahoma Boulevard, Alva, OK 73717-2799. *Telephone:* 580-327-8489. *Fax:* 580-327-8434. *E-mail:* flbuechner@nwosu.edu.

Oklahoma Baptist University
School of Nursing
Shawnee, Oklahoma

http://www.okbu.edu

Founded in 1910

DEGREES • BSN • MSN

Nursing Program Faculty 15 (2.6% with doctorates).

Baccalaureate Enrollment 218
Women 94% **Men** 6% **Minority** 7% **International** 1% **Part-time** 5%

Graduate Enrollment 12

Nursing Student Activities Sigma Theta Tau, Student Nurses' Association.

Nursing Student Resources Academic advising; academic or career counseling; assistance for students with disabilities; bookstore; campus computer network; computer lab; computer-assisted instruction; e-mail services; externships; Internet; learning resource lab; library services; nursing audiovisuals; remedial services; resume preparation assistance; skills, simulation, or other laboratory; tutoring; unpaid internships.

Library Facilities 230,000 volumes (10,000 in health, 5,500 in nursing); 1,800 periodical subscriptions (60 health-care related).

BACCALAUREATE PROGRAMS

Degree BSN

Available Programs ADN to Baccalaureate; Baccalaureate for Second Degree; Generic Baccalaureate; LPN to Baccalaureate; RN Baccalaureate.

Study Options Full-time and part-time.

Program Entrance Requirements Minimum overall college GPA of 2.25, transcript of college record, CPR certification, health exam, high school transcript, immunizations, minimum GPA in nursing prerequisites of 2.3, prerequisite course work. Transfer students are accepted. *Application deadline:* 4/1 (fall), 4/1 (winter), 4/1 (spring), 7/15 (summer).

Oklahoma Baptist University (continued)

Expenses (2008–09) *Tuition:* full-time $15,468; part-time $503 per credit. *International tuition:* $15,468 full-time. *Room and board:* room only: $2600 per academic year. *Required fees:* full-time $1011; part-time $120 per credit; part-time $150 per term.

Financial Aid 93% of baccalaureate students in nursing programs received some form of financial aid in 2007–08. *Gift aid (need-based):* Federal Pell, FSEOG, state, private, college/university gift aid from institutional funds, Academic Competitiveness Grant, National Smart Grant, TEACH Grant. *Loans:* FFEL (Subsidized and Unsubsidized Stafford PLUS), Perkins, college/university. *Work-study:* Federal Work-Study, part-time campus jobs. *Financial aid application deadline:* Continuous.

Contact Dr. Lana Bolhouse, Dean, School of Nursing, School of Nursing, Oklahoma Baptist University, 500 West University, Shawnee, OK 74804. *Telephone:* 405-878-2081. *Fax:* 405-878-2083. *E-mail:* lana.bolhouse@okbu.edu.

GRADUATE PROGRAMS

Expenses (2008–09) *Tuition:* full-time $11,050; part-time $425 per credit. *International tuition:* $11,050 full-time. *Room and board:* room only: $2600 per academic year. *Required fees:* full-time $35.

Financial Aid 100% of graduate students in nursing programs received some form of financial aid in 2007–08.

Contact Dr. Claudine Dickey, Interim Dean, Graduate School, School of Nursing, Oklahoma Baptist University, 111 North Harrison, Oklahoma City, OK 73104. *Telephone:* 405-319-8470. *Fax:* 405-272-1656. *E-mail:* Claudine.Dickey@okbu.edu.

MASTER'S DEGREE PROGRAM

Degree MSN

Available Programs Master's.

Concentrations Available Nursing education.

Site Options Oklahoma City, OK.

Study Options Full-time.

Program Entrance Requirements Clinical experience, transcript of college record, nursing research course, resume, statistics course. *Application deadline:* 7/30 (fall), 12/20 (winter), 7/30 (spring), 7/30 (summer). Applications may be processed on a rolling basis for some programs.

Degree Requirements 39 total credit hours, thesis or project.

Oklahoma Christian University

Nursing Program
Oklahoma City, Oklahoma

Founded in 1950

DEGREE • BSN

Library Facilities 129,324 volumes; 8,694 periodical subscriptions.

BACCALAUREATE PROGRAMS

Degree BSN

Available Programs Generic Baccalaureate.

Program Entrance Requirements Minimum overall college GPA of 2.75, 3 letters of recommendation.

Contact Linda Fly, Director and Assistant Professor of Nursing, Nursing Program, Oklahoma Christian University, Box 11000, Oklahoma City, OK 73136. *Telephone:* 405-425-1921. *E-mail:* linda.fly@oc.edu.

Oklahoma City University

Kramer School of Nursing
Oklahoma City, Oklahoma

http://www.okcu.edu ursing

Founded in 1904

DEGREES • BSN • MSN • MSN/MBA • PHD

Nursing Program Faculty 30 (30% with doctorates).

Baccalaureate Enrollment 212
Women 80% **Men** 20% **Minority** 28% **International** 6% **Part-time** 6%
Graduate Enrollment 39
Women 90% **Men** 10% **Minority** 28% **International** 5% **Part-time** 62%
Distance Learning Courses Available.

Nursing Student Activities Sigma Theta Tau, Student Nurses' Association.

Nursing Student Resources Academic advising; academic or career counseling; assistance for students with disabilities; bookstore; campus computer network; career placement assistance; computer lab; computer-assisted instruction; e-mail services; housing assistance; interactive nursing skills videos; Internet; learning resource lab; library services; nursing audiovisuals; placement services for program completers; remedial services; resume preparation assistance; skills, simulation, or other laboratory; tutoring.

Library Facilities 520,953 volumes (2,714 in health, 590 in nursing); 14,000 periodical subscriptions (234 health-care related).

BACCALAUREATE PROGRAMS

Degree BSN

Available Programs ADN to Baccalaureate; Accelerated Baccalaureate for Second Degree; Generic Baccalaureate.

Study Options Full-time and part-time.

Program Entrance Requirements Minimum overall college GPA of 3.0, transcript of college record, CPR certification, high school transcript, immunizations, minimum GPA in nursing prerequisites of 3.0, prerequisite course work. Transfer students are accepted. *Application deadline:* 8/1 (fall), 12/1 (spring). Applications may be processed on a rolling basis for some programs. *Application fee:* $40.

Advanced Placement Credit by examination available. Credit given for nursing courses completed elsewhere dependent upon specific evaluations.

Expenses (2009–10) *Tuition:* full-time $22,250; part-time $760 per credit hour. *International tuition:* $22,250 full-time. *Room and board:* $7670; room only: $5720 per academic year. *Required fees:* full-time $4430; part-time $145 per credit; part-time $40 per term.

Financial Aid 89% of baccalaureate students in nursing programs received some form of financial aid in 2008–09. *Gift aid (need-based):* Federal Pell, FSEOG, state, private, college/university gift aid from institutional funds, United Negro College Fund, Federal Nursing, Native American Grants. *Loans:* Federal Nursing Student Loans, FFEL (Subsidized and Unsubsidized Stafford PLUS), Perkins. *Work-study:* Federal Work-Study, part-time campus jobs. *Financial aid application deadline (priority):* 3/1.

Contact Ms. Sherri Christian, Traditional BSN Program Specialist, Kramer School of Nursing, Oklahoma City University, 2501 North Blackwelder Avenue, Oklahoma City, OK 73106-1493. *Telephone:* 405-208-5901. *Fax:* 405-208-5914. *E-mail:* schristian@okcu.edu.

GRADUATE PROGRAMS

Expenses (2009–10) *Tuition:* full-time $15,930; part-time $885 per credit hour. *International tuition:* $15,930 full-time. *Room and board:* $6570; room only: $4620 per academic year. *Required fees:* full-time $4430; part-time $145 per credit; part-time $40 per term.

Financial Aid 92% of graduate students in nursing programs received some form of financial aid in 2008–09.

Contact Mr. Christopher Black, Graduate and Continuing Education Specialist, Kramer School of Nursing, Oklahoma City University, 2501 North Blackwelder Avenue, Oklahoma City, OK 73106-1493. *Telephone:* 405-208-5832. *Fax:* 405-208-5914. *E-mail:* cblack@okcu.edu.

MASTER'S DEGREE PROGRAM

Degrees MSN; MSN/MBA

Available Programs Master's.

Concentrations Available Nursing administration; nursing education.

Study Options Full-time and part-time.

Program Entrance Requirements Clinical experience, minimum overall college GPA of 3.0, transcript of college record, physical assessment course, statistics course. *Application deadline:* 8/1 (fall), 12/1 (spring). Applications may be processed on a rolling basis for some programs. *Application fee:* $50.

Advanced Placement Credit given for nursing courses completed elsewhere dependent upon specific evaluations.

Degree Requirements 33 total credit hours, thesis or project.

DOCTORAL DEGREE PROGRAM

Degree PhD

Available Programs Doctorate.

Areas of Study Nursing education.

Program Entrance Requirements Clinical experience, minimum overall college GPA of 3.5, interview by faculty committee, MSN or equivalent, vita. Application deadline: 4/1 (fall). Application fee: $50.

Degree Requirements 90 total credit hours, dissertation, oral exam.

CONTINUING EDUCATION PROGRAM

Contact Mr. Christopher Black, Graduate and Continuing Education Specialist, Kramer School of Nursing, Oklahoma City University, 2501 North Blackwelder Avenue, Oklahoma City, OK 73106-1493. *Telephone:* 405-208-5832. *Fax:* 405-208-5914. *E-mail:* cblack@okcu.edu.

Oklahoma Panhandle State University

Bachelor of Science in Nursing Program
Goodwell, Oklahoma

http://www.opsu.edu
Founded in 1909
DEGREE • BSN

Nursing Program Faculty 4

Baccalaureate Enrollment 57
Women 90% **Men** 10% **Minority** 19% **Part-time** 73%

Distance Learning Courses Available.

Nursing Student Activities Student Nurses' Association.

Nursing Student Resources Academic advising; academic or career counseling; assistance for students with disabilities; bookstore; campus computer network; computer-assisted instruction; e-mail services; Internet; library services.

Library Facilities 1,019 volumes in health, 380 volumes in nursing; 2,032 periodical subscriptions health-care related.

BACCALAUREATE PROGRAMS

Degree BSN

Available Programs ADN to Baccalaureate.

Study Options Full-time and part-time.

Online Degree Options Yes (online only).

Program Entrance Requirements Minimum overall college GPA of 2.0, transcript of college record, CPR certification, immunizations, minimum GPA in nursing prerequisites of 2.0, RN licensure. Transfer students are accepted. *Application deadline:* 8/1 (fall), 1/10 (spring), 5/20 (summer).

Advanced Placement Credit given for nursing courses completed elsewhere dependent upon specific evaluations.

Expenses (2009–10) *Tuition, area resident:* part-time $91 per credit. *Required fees:* part-time $111 per credit.

Financial Aid 34% of baccalaureate students in nursing programs received some form of financial aid in 2008–09. *Gift aid (need-based):* Federal Pell, FSEOG, state, private, college/university gift aid from institutional funds. *Loans:* FFEL (Subsidized and Unsubsidized Stafford PLUS), Perkins. *Work-study:* Federal Work-Study, part-time campus jobs. *Financial aid application deadline (priority):* 3/15.

Contact Lynna Brakhage, RN, Director, RN-BSN Program, Bachelor of Science in Nursing Program, Oklahoma Panhandle State University, PO Box 430, Goodwell, OK 73939. *Telephone:* 580-349-1520. *Fax:* 580-349-1529. *E-mail:* nursing@opsu.edu.

Oklahoma Wesleyan University

Division of Nursing
Bartlesville, Oklahoma

http://nursing.okwu.edu
Founded in 1909
DEGREE • BSN

Nursing Program Faculty 31 (35% with doctorates).

Baccalaureate Enrollment 140
Women 96% **Men** 4% **Minority** 23%

Nursing Student Resources Academic advising; academic or career counseling; assistance for students with disabilities; bookstore; campus computer network; computer lab; computer-assisted instruction; interactive nursing skills videos; Internet; learning resource lab; library services; nursing audiovisuals; skills, simulation, or other laboratory.

Library Facilities 124,722 volumes (946 in health, 483 in nursing); 300 periodical subscriptions (40 health-care related).

BACCALAUREATE PROGRAMS

Degree BSN

Available Programs ADN to Baccalaureate; Accelerated RN Baccalaureate; Baccalaureate for Second Degree; Generic Baccalaureate; International Nurse to Baccalaureate; LPN to Baccalaureate; RN Baccalaureate.

Study Options Full-time.

Program Entrance Requirements Minimum overall college GPA of 2.3, transcript of college record, CPR certification, health exam, health insurance, immunizations, 2 letters of recommendation, minimum GPA in nursing prerequisites of 2.75, professional liability insurance/malpractice insurance, prerequisite course work, RN licensure. Transfer students are accepted.

Advanced Placement Credit by examination available. Credit given for nursing courses completed elsewhere dependent upon specific evaluations.

Contact *Telephone:* 918-335-6254. *Fax:* 918-335-6204.

Oral Roberts University

Anna Vaughn School of Nursing
Tulsa, Oklahoma

http://www.oru.edu
Founded in 1963
DEGREE • BSN

Nursing Program Faculty 14 (14% with doctorates).

Baccalaureate Enrollment 125
Women 89% **Men** 11% **Minority** 31% **International** 8% **Part-time** 6%

Nursing Student Activities Nursing Honor Society, Sigma Theta Tau, Student Nurses' Association.

Nursing Student Resources Academic advising; academic or career counseling; assistance for students with disabilities; bookstore; campus computer network; computer lab; computer-assisted instruction; e-mail services; employment services for current students; externships; housing assistance; interactive nursing skills videos; Internet; learning resource lab; library services; nursing audiovisuals; remedial services; resume preparation assistance; skills, simulation, or other laboratory; tutoring.

Library Facilities 216,691 volumes (9,644 in health, 2,287 in nursing); 600 periodical subscriptions (31,415 health-care related).

BACCALAUREATE PROGRAMS

Degree BSN

Available Programs ADN to Baccalaureate; Generic Baccalaureate; RN Baccalaureate.

Study Options Full-time and part-time.

Oral Roberts University (continued)

Program Entrance Requirements Minimum overall college GPA of 3.3, transcript of college record, CPR certification, health exam, health insurance, high school chemistry, 2 years high school math, 2 years high school science, high school transcript, immunizations, minimum high school GPA of 2.5, minimum GPA in nursing prerequisites of 2.5. Transfer students are accepted. *Application deadline:* 8/1 (fall), 12/1 (spring). *Application fee:* $35.

Expenses (2009–10) *Tuition:* full-time $18,476; part-time $772 per credit hour. *International tuition:* $18,476 full-time. *Room and board:* $7916; room only: $3860 per academic year. *Required fees:* full-time $837; part-time $418 per term.

Financial Aid 98% of baccalaureate students in nursing programs received some form of financial aid in 2008–09.

Contact Dr. Kenda Jezek, Dean, Anna Vaughn School of Nursing, Oral Roberts University, 7777 South Lewis Avenue, Tulsa, OK 74171. *Telephone:* 918-495-6198. *Fax:* 918-495-6020. *E-mail:* kjezek@oru.edu.

Rogers State University

Nursing Program
Claremore, Oklahoma

Founded in 1909

DEGREE • BSN

Baccalaureate Enrollment 18
Women 94% **Men** 6% **Minority** 38% **International** 11%

Distance Learning Courses Available.

Nursing Student Activities Student Nurses' Association.

Nursing Student Resources Academic advising; academic or career counseling; assistance for students with disabilities; bookstore; campus computer network; career placement assistance; computer lab; computer-assisted instruction; daycare for children of students; e-mail services; housing assistance; interactive nursing skills videos; Internet; learning resource lab; library services; nursing audiovisuals; placement services for program completers; remedial services; resume preparation assistance; skills, simulation, or other laboratory.

Library Facilities 77,120 volumes; 355 periodical subscriptions.

BACCALAUREATE PROGRAMS

Degree BSN

Available Programs ADN to Baccalaureate.

Site Options Bartlesville, OK.

Program Entrance Requirements Minimum overall college GPA, CPR certification, health exam, health insurance, immunizations, minimum GPA in nursing prerequisites, RN licensure. Transfer students are accepted.

Expenses (2009–10) *Tuition, state resident:* part-time $91 per credit hour. *Room and board:* room only: $4500 per academic year. *Required fees:* part-time $139 per credit.

Financial Aid 60% of baccalaureate students in nursing programs received some form of financial aid in 2008–09.

Contact Nancy Diede, Department Head, Health Sciences, Nursing Program, Rogers State University, 1701 West Will Rogers Boulevard, Claremore, OK 74017-3252. *Telephone:* 918-343-7885. *Fax:* 918-343-7628. *E-mail:* ndiede@rsu.edu.

Southern Nazarene University

School of Nursing
Bethany, Oklahoma

http://www.snu.edu

Founded in 1899

DEGREES • BS • MS

Nursing Program Faculty 35 (40% with doctorates).

Baccalaureate Enrollment 101
Women 90% **Men** 10% **Minority** 35% **International** 2% **Part-time** 10%

Graduate Enrollment 34
Women 90% **Men** 10% **Minority** 10%

Distance Learning Courses Available.

Nursing Student Activities Sigma Theta Tau, Student Nurses' Association.

Nursing Student Resources Academic advising; academic or career counseling; assistance for students with disabilities; bookstore; campus computer network; career placement assistance; computer lab; computer-assisted instruction; e-mail services; employment services for current students; externships; housing assistance; interactive nursing skills videos; Internet; learning resource lab; library services; nursing audiovisuals; paid internships; remedial services; skills, simulation, or other laboratory; tutoring.

Library Facilities 95,535 volumes; 225 periodical subscriptions.

BACCALAUREATE PROGRAMS

Degree BS

Available Programs ADN to Baccalaureate; Baccalaureate for Second Degree; Generic Baccalaureate; LPN to Baccalaureate.

Study Options Full-time.

Program Entrance Requirements Minimum overall college GPA of 2.75, transcript of college record, CPR certification, health exam, health insurance, immunizations, minimum GPA in nursing prerequisites of 2.75, professional liability insurance/malpractice insurance, prerequisite course work. Transfer students are accepted. *Application deadline:* 12/5 (fall). Applications may be processed on a rolling basis for some programs.

Advanced Placement Credit by examination available. Credit given for nursing courses completed elsewhere dependent upon specific evaluations.

Financial Aid 90% of baccalaureate students in nursing programs received some form of financial aid in 2008–09.

Contact Dr. Carol Jean Dorough, Chair, School of Nursing, Southern Nazarene University, 6729 NW 39th Expressway, Bethany, OK 73008. *Telephone:* 405-717-6217. *Fax:* 405-717-6264. *E-mail:* cdorough@snu.edu.

GRADUATE PROGRAMS

Financial Aid 85% of graduate students in nursing programs received some form of financial aid in 2008–09.

Contact Dr. Carol Jean Dorough, Chair, School of Nursing, Southern Nazarene University, 6729 NW 39th Expressway, Bethany, OK 73008. *Telephone:* 405-717-6217. *Fax:* 405-717-6264. *E-mail:* cdorough@snu.edu.

MASTER'S DEGREE PROGRAM

Degree MS

Available Programs Accelerated Master's; Accelerated Master's for Nurses with Non-Nursing Degrees.

Concentrations Available Nursing administration; nursing education.

Site Options Tulsa, OK.

Study Options Full-time.

Program Entrance Requirements Clinical experience, computer literacy, minimum overall college GPA of 3.0, transcript of college record, immunizations, interview, 3 letters of recommendation, nursing research course, physical assessment course, resume, statistics course. *Application deadline:* Applications may be processed on a rolling basis for some programs.

Advanced Placement Credit given for nursing courses completed elsewhere dependent upon specific evaluations.

Degree Requirements 39 total credit hours, thesis or project.

Southwestern Oklahoma State University

Division of Nursing
Weatherford, Oklahoma

http://www.swosu.edu/academic/nurse

Founded in 1901

DEGREE • BSN

Nursing Program Faculty 8

Baccalaureate Enrollment 84
Women 86% **Men** 14% **Minority** 12% **International** 1%

Distance Learning Courses Available.

Nursing Student Activities Sigma Theta Tau, Student Nurses' Association, nursing club.

Nursing Student Resources Academic advising; academic or career counseling; assistance for students with disabilities; bookstore; campus computer network; computer lab; computer-assisted instruction; e-mail services; externships; housing assistance; interactive nursing skills videos; Internet; learning resource lab; library services; nursing audiovisuals; remedial services; skills, simulation, or other laboratory; tutoring.

Library Facilities 217,051 volumes; 1,230 periodical subscriptions (284 health-care related).

BACCALAUREATE PROGRAMS

Degree BSN

Available Programs ADN to Baccalaureate; Generic Baccalaureate.
Study Options Full-time.
Online Degree Options Yes.
Program Entrance Requirements Minimum overall college GPA of 2.25, transcript of college record, CPR certification, immunizations, 2 letters of recommendation, minimum GPA in nursing prerequisites of 2.25, professional liability insurance/malpractice insurance, prerequisite course work. Transfer students are accepted. *Application deadline:* 2/1 (spring).
Advanced Placement Credit given for nursing courses completed elsewhere dependent upon specific evaluations.
Expenses (2009–10) *Tuition, state resident:* full-time $5490. *Tuition, nonresident:* full-time $10,830. *Room and board:* $3900 per academic year.
Financial Aid 60% of baccalaureate students in nursing programs received some form of financial aid in 2008–09. *Gift aid (need-based):* Federal Pell, FSEOG, state, private, college/university gift aid from institutional funds. *Loans:* FFEL (Subsidized and Unsubsidized Stafford PLUS). *Work-study:* Federal Work-Study. *Financial aid application deadline:* 3/1.
Contact Ms. Debbie Miles, Administrative Assistant, Division of Nursing, Southwestern Oklahoma State University, 100 Campus Drive, Weatherford, OK 73096-3098. *Telephone:* 580-774-3261. *Fax:* 580-774-7075. *E-mail:* debbie.miles@swosu.edu.

University of Central Oklahoma
Department of Nursing
Edmond, Oklahoma

http://nurse.ucok.edu
Founded in 1890

DEGREE • BSN

Nursing Program Faculty 43 (1% with doctorates).

Baccalaureate Enrollment 267
Women 90% **Men** 10% **Minority** 16% **International** 4% **Part-time** 1%

Nursing Student Activities Nursing Honor Society, Sigma Theta Tau, Student Nurses' Association.

Nursing Student Resources Academic advising; academic or career counseling; assistance for students with disabilities; bookstore; campus computer network; career placement assistance; computer lab; computer-assisted instruction; e-mail services; externships; interactive nursing skills videos; Internet; library services; nursing audiovisuals; skills, simulation, or other laboratory; tutoring.

Library Facilities 2,831 volumes in health, 1,733 volumes in nursing.

BACCALAUREATE PROGRAMS

Degree BSN

Available Programs Generic Baccalaureate; LPN to Baccalaureate; RN Baccalaureate.
Site Options Oklahoma City, OK; Midwest City, OK.
Study Options Full-time and part-time.

Program Entrance Requirements Minimum overall college GPA of 2.5, transcript of college record, CPR certification, high school math, immunizations, 3 letters of recommendation, professional liability insurance/malpractice insurance, prerequisite course work. Transfer students are accepted. *Application deadline:* 10/12 (fall), 1/25 (spring). *Application fee:* $25.
Advanced Placement Credit given for nursing courses completed elsewhere dependent upon specific evaluations.
Expenses (2009–10) *Tuition, state resident:* full-time $3378; part-time $141 per credit hour. *Tuition, nonresident:* full-time $8521; part-time $355 per credit hour. *International tuition:* $8521 full-time. *Room and board:* $7776; room only: $4716 per academic year. *Required fees:* full-time $516.
Financial Aid 35% of baccalaureate students in nursing programs received some form of financial aid in 2008–09.
Contact Vicki Addison, Administrative Secretary, Department of Nursing, University of Central Oklahoma, 100 North University Drive, Edmond, OK 73034-5209. *Telephone:* 405-974-5000. *E-mail:* vaddison@ucok.edu.

University of Oklahoma Health Sciences Center
College of Nursing
Oklahoma City, Oklahoma

http://nursing.ouhsc.edu/
Founded in 1890

DEGREES • BSN • MS • PHD

Nursing Program Faculty 185 (16% with doctorates).

Baccalaureate Enrollment 892
Women 85% **Men** 15% **Minority** 37% **International** 1% **Part-time** 4%

Graduate Enrollment 256
Women 93% **Men** 7% **Minority** 26% **International** 1% **Part-time** 71%

Distance Learning Courses Available.

Nursing Student Activities Sigma Theta Tau, Student Nurses' Association.

Nursing Student Resources Academic advising; academic or career counseling; assistance for students with disabilities; bookstore; campus computer network; computer lab; computer-assisted instruction; e-mail services; employment services for current students; housing assistance; Internet; learning resource lab; library services; nursing audiovisuals; skills, simulation, or other laboratory; tutoring.

Library Facilities 300,260 volumes; 4,028 periodical subscriptions.

BACCALAUREATE PROGRAMS

Degree BSN

Available Programs ADN to Baccalaureate; Accelerated Baccalaureate for Second Degree; Generic Baccalaureate; LPN to RN Baccalaureate.
Site Options Lawton, OK; Tulsa, OK.
Study Options Full-time.
Program Entrance Requirements Minimum overall college GPA of 2.5, transcript of college record, high school transcript, minimum GPA in nursing prerequisites of 2.5, prerequisite course work. Transfer students are accepted. *Application deadline:* 1/15 (fall). *Application fee:* $65.
Advanced Placement Credit by examination available. Credit given for nursing courses completed elsewhere dependent upon specific evaluations.
Expenses (2009–10) *Tuition, state resident:* full-time $3537; part-time $118 per credit hour. *Tuition, nonresident:* full-time $13,518; part-time $451 per credit hour. *Room and board:* room only: $7516 per academic year. *Required fees:* full-time $4923; part-time $164 per credit; part-time $2462 per term.
Financial Aid 87% of baccalaureate students in nursing programs received some form of financial aid in 2008–09. *Loans:* Federal Nursing Student Loans, Perkins, college/university.
Contact Rosalyn Alexander, Admissions Coordinator, College of Nursing, University of Oklahoma Health Sciences Center, PO Box 26901, 1100 North Stonewall Avenue, Oklahoma City, OK 73126-0901. *Telephone:* 405-271-2128. *Fax:* 405-271-7341. *E-mail:* Rosalyn-Alexander@ouhsc.edu.

University of Oklahoma Health Sciences Center (continued)

GRADUATE PROGRAMS

Expenses (2009–10) *Tuition, state resident:* full-time $2808; part-time $156 per credit hour. *Tuition, nonresident:* full-time $10,182; part-time $566 per credit hour. *Room and board:* room only: $7516 per academic year.

Financial Aid 30% of graduate students in nursing programs received some form of financial aid in 2008–09. 6 research assistantships (averaging $6,000 per year) were awarded; teaching assistantships, institutionally sponsored loans, scholarships, and traineeships also available. Aid available to part-time students. *Financial aid application deadline:* 8/1.

Contact Trisha Wilhelm, Admissions Coordinator, College of Nursing, University of Oklahoma Health Sciences Center, PO Box 26901, 1100 North Stonewall Avenue, Oklahoma City, OK 73126-0901. *Telephone:* 405-271-2128. *Fax:* 405-271-7341. *E-mail:* patricia-wilhelm@ouhsc.edu.

MASTER'S DEGREE PROGRAM

Degree MS

Available Programs Master's; Master's for Non-Nursing College Graduates.

Concentrations Available Clinical nurse leader; health-care administration; nursing education. *Clinical nurse specialist programs in:* acute care. *Nurse practitioner programs in:* adult health, family health, neonatal health, pediatric.

Site Options Lawton, OK; Tulsa, OK.

Study Options Full-time and part-time.

Online Degree Options Yes.

Program Entrance Requirements Computer literacy, minimum overall college GPA of 3.0, transcript of college record, 3 letters of recommendation, nursing research course, professional liability insurance/malpractice insurance, prerequisite course work, statistics course. *Application deadline:* 3/1 (fall), 8/1 (spring), 1/15 (summer). *Application fee:* $65.

Advanced Placement Credit given for nursing courses completed elsewhere dependent upon specific evaluations.

Degree Requirements 38 total credit hours, thesis or project, comprehensive exam.

POST-MASTER'S PROGRAM

Areas of Study Clinical nurse leader; health-care administration; nursing education. *Nurse practitioner programs in:* adult health, family health, neonatal health, pediatric.

DOCTORAL DEGREE PROGRAM

Degree PhD

Available Programs Doctorate.

Areas of Study Nursing education.

Program Entrance Requirements Minimum overall college GPA of 3.5, interview by faculty committee, 3 letters of recommendation, scholarly papers, statistics course, vita, writing sample. Application deadline: 4/14 (fall). Application fee: $65.

Degree Requirements 90 total credit hours, dissertation, oral exam, written exam.

CONTINUING EDUCATION PROGRAM

Contact Dr. Beverly Bowers, Assistant Dean for Faculty Development and Professional Continuing Education, College of Nursing, University of Oklahoma Health Sciences Center, PO Box 26901, 1100 North Stonewall Avenue, Oklahoma City, OK 73126-0901. *Telephone:* 405-271-2428. *Fax:* 405-271-7341. *E-mail:* Beverly-Bowers@ouhsc.edu.

University of Phoenix–Oklahoma City Campus

College of Health and Human Services
Oklahoma City, Oklahoma

Founded in 1976

Nursing Program Faculty 1

Nursing Student Activities Sigma Theta Tau.

Nursing Student Resources Academic advising; academic or career counseling; assistance for students with disabilities; bookstore; campus computer network; computer lab; computer-assisted instruction; e-mail services; interactive nursing skills videos; Internet; learning resource lab; library services; nursing audiovisuals; skills, simulation, or other laboratory; tutoring.

Library Facilities 16,781 periodical subscriptions (1,300 health-care related).

University of Phoenix–Tulsa Campus

College of Health and Human Services
Tulsa, Oklahoma

Founded in 1998

Nursing Student Activities Sigma Theta Tau.

Nursing Student Resources Academic advising; academic or career counseling; assistance for students with disabilities; bookstore; campus computer network; computer lab; computer-assisted instruction; e-mail services; interactive nursing skills videos; Internet; learning resource lab; library services; nursing audiovisuals; remedial services; skills, simulation, or other laboratory; tutoring.

Library Facilities 16,781 periodical subscriptions (1,300 health-care related).

University of Tulsa

School of Nursing
Tulsa, Oklahoma

http://www.cba.utulsa.edu/depts/nursing

Founded in 1894

DEGREE • BSN

Nursing Program Faculty 12 (33% with doctorates).

Baccalaureate Enrollment 83

Women 93% **Men** 7% **Minority** 25% **Part-time** 2%

Nursing Student Activities Sigma Theta Tau, Student Nurses' Association.

Nursing Student Resources Academic advising; academic or career counseling; assistance for students with disabilities; bookstore; campus computer network; career placement assistance; computer lab; computer-assisted instruction; daycare for children of students; e-mail services; employment services for current students; externships; housing assistance; interactive nursing skills videos; Internet; learning resource lab; library services; nursing audiovisuals; placement services for program completers; remedial services; resume preparation assistance; skills, simulation, or other laboratory; tutoring.

Library Facilities 1.1 million volumes (4,300 in nursing); 27,905 periodical subscriptions (118 health-care related).

BACCALAUREATE PROGRAMS

Degree BSN

Available Programs Generic Baccalaureate; LPN to RN Baccalaureate; RN Baccalaureate.

Study Options Full-time.

Program Entrance Requirements Minimum overall college GPA of 2.5, transcript of college record, CPR certification, written essay, health exam, immunizations, minimum GPA in nursing prerequisites. Transfer students are accepted. *Application deadline:* 2/1 (fall). Applications may be processed on a rolling basis for some programs.

Advanced Placement Credit by examination available. Credit given for nursing courses completed elsewhere dependent upon specific evaluations.

Expenses (2009–10) *Tuition:* full-time $26,722; part-time $899 per credit hour. *International tuition:* $26,722 full-time. *Room and board:* $8544; room only: $4724 per academic year. *Required fees:* full-time $705; part-time $3 per credit.

Financial Aid 90% of baccalaureate students in nursing programs received some form of financial aid in 2008–09.

Contact Dr. Susan Kathleen Gaston, RN, Director, School of Nursing, University of Tulsa, 800 South Tucker Drive, Tulsa, OK 74104-9700. *Telephone:* 918-631-3116. *Fax:* 918-631-2068. *E-mail:* susan-gaston@utulsa.edu.

OREGON

Concordia University
Nursing Program
Portland, Oregon

Founded in 1905

DEGREE • BSN

Nursing Program Faculty 20 (3% with doctorates).

Baccalaureate Enrollment 67

Nursing Student Activities Nursing club.

Nursing Student Resources Academic advising; academic or career counseling; assistance for students with disabilities; bookstore; campus computer network; computer lab; e-mail services; employment services for current students; Internet; learning resource lab; library services; nursing audiovisuals; skills, simulation, or other laboratory; tutoring.

Library Facilities 88,103 volumes; 26,466 periodical subscriptions.

BACCALAUREATE PROGRAMS

Degree BSN

Available Programs Generic Baccalaureate.

Study Options Full-time.

Program Entrance Requirements Transfer students are accepted.

Expenses (2009–10) *Tuition:* full-time $22,900. *International tuition:* $22,900 full-time. *Room and board:* $6700 per academic year.

Financial Aid 100% of baccalaureate students in nursing programs received some form of financial aid in 2008–09.

Contact Mrs. Celeste Krueger, Director of Undergraduate Admissions, Nursing Program, Concordia University, 2811 NE Holman Street, Portland, OR 97211. *Telephone:* 800-321-9371. *E-mail:* admissions@cu-portland.edu.

George Fox University
Nursing Department
Newberg, Oregon

Founded in 1891

DEGREE • BSN

Nursing Program Faculty 9 (44% with doctorates).

Baccalaureate Enrollment 76
Women 89% **Men** 11% **Minority** 11%

Nursing Student Activities Nursing club.

Nursing Student Resources Academic advising; academic or career counseling; assistance for students with disabilities; bookstore; campus computer network; career placement assistance; computer lab; computer-assisted instruction; e-mail services; employment services for current students; housing assistance; interactive nursing skills videos; Internet; learning resource lab; library services; nursing audiovisuals; remedial services; resume preparation assistance; skills, simulation, or other laboratory; tutoring.

Library Facilities 218,240 volumes (378 in health, 87 in nursing); 6,369 periodical subscriptions (4,814 health-care related).

BACCALAUREATE PROGRAMS

Degree BSN

Available Programs Generic Baccalaureate.

Study Options Full-time.

Program Entrance Requirements Minimum overall college GPA of 2.8, transcript of college record, CPR certification, written essay, immunizations, 2 letters of recommendation, minimum GPA in nursing prerequisites of 2.8, prerequisite course work. Transfer students are accepted. *Application deadline:* 10/2 (fall). *Application fee:* $50.

Expenses (2009–10) *Tuition:* full-time $25,860. *International tuition:* $25,860 full-time. *Room and board:* $8320; room only: $4680 per academic year. *Required fees:* full-time $320.

Financial Aid 98% of baccalaureate students in nursing programs received some form of financial aid in 2008–09. *Gift aid (need-based):* Federal Pell, FSEOG, state, private, college/university gift aid from institutional funds, Academic Competitiveness Grant, National Smart Grant. *Loans:* Federal Direct (Subsidized and Unsubsidized Stafford PLUS), FFEL (Subsidized and Unsubsidized Stafford PLUS), Perkins, alternative loans. *Work-study:* Federal Work-Study, part-time campus jobs. *Financial aid application deadline (priority):* 2/1.

Contact Elaine Smith, Nursing Department, George Fox University, 414 North Meridian Street, #6273, Newberg, OR 97132. *Telephone:* 503-554-2950. *Fax:* 503-554-3900. *E-mail:* esmith@georgefox.edu.

Linfield College
School of Nursing
McMinnville, Oregon

http://www.linfield.edu/portland

Founded in 1849

DEGREE • BSN

Nursing Program Faculty 64 (22% with doctorates).

Baccalaureate Enrollment 314
Women 85.4% **Men** 14.6% **Minority** 17.8% **International** .3% **Part-time** 3.5%

Nursing Student Activities Sigma Theta Tau, Student Nurses' Association, nursing club.

Nursing Student Resources Academic advising; academic or career counseling; bookstore; campus computer network; computer lab; e-mail services; Internet; learning resource lab; library services; nursing audiovisuals; resume preparation assistance; skills, simulation, or other laboratory.

Library Facilities 184,931 volumes (7,201 in health, 1,482 in nursing); 958 periodical subscriptions (249 health-care related).

BACCALAUREATE PROGRAMS

Degree BSN

Available Programs ADN to Baccalaureate; Accelerated Baccalaureate for Second Degree; Baccalaureate for Second Degree; Generic Baccalaureate.

Site Options Portland, OR.

Study Options Full-time.

Program Entrance Requirements Minimum overall college GPA of 2.9, transcript of college record, CPR certification, written essay, health exam, health insurance, immunizations, 1 letter of recommendation, minimum GPA in nursing prerequisites of 2.75, professional liability insurance/malpractice insurance, prerequisite course work. Transfer students are accepted.

Advanced Placement Credit given for nursing courses completed elsewhere dependent upon specific evaluations.

Contact *Telephone:* 503-413-8481. *Fax:* 503-413-6283.

CONTINUING EDUCATION PROGRAM

Contact *Telephone:* 503-413-7163. *Fax:* 503-413-6846.

Oregon Health & Science University

School of Nursing
Portland, Oregon

http://www.ohsu.edu/son

Founded in 1974

DEGREES • BS • MS • MSN/MPH • PHD

Nursing Program Faculty 138 (40% with doctorates).

Baccalaureate Enrollment 573
Women 83% **Men** 17% **Minority** 7% **International** 1% **Part-time** 68%

Graduate Enrollment 219
Women 74% **Men** 26% **Minority** 4% **International** 2% **Part-time** 56%

Distance Learning Courses Available.

Nursing Student Activities Nursing Honor Society, Sigma Theta Tau, Student Nurses' Association, nursing club.

Nursing Student Resources Academic advising; assistance for students with disabilities; bookstore; campus computer network; computer lab; e-mail services; externships; interactive nursing skills videos; Internet; learning resource lab; library services; nursing audiovisuals; resume preparation assistance; skills, simulation, or other laboratory.

Library Facilities 275,230 volumes (227,344 in health, 7,666 in nursing); 12,865 periodical subscriptions (2,357 health-care related).

BACCALAUREATE PROGRAMS

Degree BS

Available Programs Accelerated Baccalaureate; Generic Baccalaureate; RN Baccalaureate.

Site Options Klamath Falls, OR; La Grande, OR; Ashland, OR.

Study Options Full-time.

Program Entrance Requirements Transcript of college record, written essay, minimum GPA in nursing prerequisites of 3.0, prerequisite course work. Transfer students are accepted. *Application deadline:* 2/15 (fall).

Advanced Placement Credit given for nursing courses completed elsewhere dependent upon specific evaluations.

Expenses (2008–09) *Tuition, state resident:* full-time $3072; part-time $256 per credit. *Tuition, nonresident:* full-time $6396; part-time $533 per credit. *International tuition:* $6396 full-time. *Required fees:* full-time $4887.

Financial Aid 80% of baccalaureate students in nursing programs received some form of financial aid in 2007–08. *Gift aid (need-based):* Federal Pell, FSEOG, state, private, college/university gift aid from institutional funds, Health Profession Scholarships. *Loans:* Federal Nursing Student Loans, Federal Direct (Subsidized and Unsubsidized Stafford PLUS), Perkins, state, college/university, alternative loans. *Work-study:* Federal Work-Study.

Contact Admissions Counselor, School of Nursing, Oregon Health & Science University, Office of Admissions SN-ADM, 3455 SW U.S. Veterans Hospital Road, Portland, OR 97239-2491. *Telephone:* 503-494-7725. *Fax:* 503-494-6433. *E-mail:* proginfo@ohsu.edu.

GRADUATE PROGRAMS

Expenses (2008–09) *Tuition, state resident:* full-time $4230; part-time $470 per credit. *Tuition, nonresident:* full-time $5625; part-time $625 per credit. *International tuition:* $5625 full-time.

Financial Aid 45% of graduate students in nursing programs received some form of financial aid in 2007–08. Fellowships, research assistantships, teaching assistantships, career-related internships or fieldwork, Federal Work-Study, institutionally sponsored loans, scholarships, and traineeships available. *Financial aid application deadline:* 3/1.

Contact Admissions Counselor, School of Nursing, Oregon Health & Science University, Office of Admissions SN-ADM, 3455 SW U.S. Veterans Hospital Road, Portland, OR 97239-2491. *Telephone:* 503-494-7725. *Fax:* 503-494-4350. *E-mail:* proginfo@ohsu.edu.

MASTER'S DEGREE PROGRAM

Degrees MS; MSN/MPH

Available Programs Master's; Master's for Non-Nursing College Graduates; Master's for Nurses with Non-Nursing Degrees.

Concentrations Available Nurse anesthesia; nurse-midwifery; nursing education. *Nurse practitioner programs in:* family health, psychiatric/mental health.

Site Options Klamath Falls, OR; La Grande, OR; Ashland, OR.

Study Options Full-time and part-time.

Program Entrance Requirements Clinical experience, computer literacy, minimum overall college GPA of 3.0, transcript of college record, CPR certification, written essay, immunizations, interview, 3 letters of recommendation, resume, statistics course, GRE General Test. *Application deadline:* 12/1 (fall). Applications may be processed on a rolling basis for some programs.

Advanced Placement Credit given for nursing courses completed elsewhere dependent upon specific evaluations.

Degree Requirements 45 total credit hours, comprehensive exam.

POST-MASTER'S PROGRAM

Areas of Study Nurse-midwifery; nursing education. *Nurse practitioner programs in:* family health, gerontology, psychiatric/mental health.

DOCTORAL DEGREE PROGRAM

Degree PhD

Available Programs Doctorate; Post-Baccalaureate Doctorate.

Areas of Study Advanced practice nursing, aging, clinical practice, ethics, faculty preparation, family health, gerontology, health policy, health promotion/disease prevention, health-care systems, human health and illness, illness and transition, nursing policy, nursing research, nursing science, women's health.

Program Entrance Requirements Clinical experience, minimum overall college GPA of 3.0, interview by faculty committee, 3 letters of recommendation, MSN or equivalent, scholarly papers, statistics course, vita, writing sample, GRE General Test. Application deadline: 12/1 (fall). Applications may be processed on a rolling basis for some programs.

Degree Requirements 90 total credit hours, dissertation, oral exam, written exam, residency.

POSTDOCTORAL PROGRAM

Areas of Study Adolescent health, aging, chronic illness, family health, gerontology, health promotion/disease prevention, nursing interventions, nursing research, nursing science, outcomes, self-care, vulnerable population, women's health.

Postdoctoral Program Contact Academic Programs Counselor, School of Nursing, Oregon Health & Science University, Office of Admissions SN-ADM, 3455 SW U.S. Veterans Hospital Road, Portland, OR 97239-2491. *Telephone:* 503-494-7725. *Fax:* 503-494-4350. *E-mail:* proginfo@ohsu.edu.

CONTINUING EDUCATION PROGRAM

Contact Paula McNeil, Director of Continuing Education, School of Nursing, Oregon Health & Science University, Office of Continuing Education SN-4N, 3455 SW U.S. Veterans Hospital Road, Portland, OR 97239-2491. *Telephone:* 503-494-6772. *Fax:* 503-494-4350. *E-mail:* snconted@ohsu.edu.

University of Portland

School of Nursing
Portland, Oregon

http://nursing.up.edu

Founded in 1901

DEGREES • BSN • DNP • MS

Nursing Program Faculty 53 (26% with doctorates).

Baccalaureate Enrollment 649
Women 90% **Men** 10% **Minority** 22% **International** 2%

Graduate Enrollment 93
Women 85% **Men** 15% **Minority** 8% **International** 3%

Distance Learning Courses Available.

Nursing Student Activities Sigma Theta Tau, Student Nurses' Association.

Nursing Student Resources Academic advising; academic or career counseling; assistance for students with disabilities; bookstore; campus computer network; career placement assistance; computer lab; computer-assisted instruction; daycare for children of students; e-mail services; employment services for current students; housing assistance; interactive nursing skills videos; Internet; learning resource lab; library services; nursing audiovisuals; remedial services; resume preparation assistance; skills, simulation, or other laboratory; tutoring.

Library Facilities 350,000 volumes (5,690 in health, 1,868 in nursing); 1,400 periodical subscriptions (457 health-care related).

BACCALAUREATE PROGRAMS

Degree BSN

Available Programs Generic Baccalaureate.

Study Options Full-time.

Program Entrance Requirements Minimum overall college GPA of 2.7, transcript of college record, CPR certification, written essay, health exam, health insurance, high school chemistry, high school transcript, immunizations, 1 letter of recommendation, minimum high school GPA of 2.7, minimum GPA in nursing prerequisites of 2.7, prerequisite course work. Transfer students are accepted. *Application deadline:* 1/15 (fall), 2/1 (spring). *Application fee:* $50.

Advanced Placement Credit by examination available. Credit given for nursing courses completed elsewhere dependent upon specific evaluations.

Expenses (2009–10) *Tuition:* full-time $32,046. *Room and board:* $9114 per academic year. *Required fees:* full-time $1560.

Financial Aid 96% of baccalaureate students in nursing programs received some form of financial aid in 2008–09. *Gift aid (need-based):* Federal Pell, FSEOG, state, private, college/university gift aid from institutional funds. *Loans:* Federal Nursing Student Loans, FFEL (Subsidized and Unsubsidized Stafford PLUS), Perkins, college/university. *Work-study:* Federal Work-Study. *Financial aid application deadline (priority):* 3/1.

Contact Mr. Jason McDonald, Dean of Admissions, School of Nursing, University of Portland, 5000 North Willamette Boulevard, Portland, OR 97203-5798. *Telephone:* 503-943-7147. *E-mail:* mcdonaja@up.edu.

GRADUATE PROGRAMS

Expenses (2009–10) *Tuition:* part-time $860 per credit. *Room and board:* $10,270 per academic year. *Required fees:* part-time $35 per credit.

Financial Aid 89% of graduate students in nursing programs received some form of financial aid in 2008–09. Fellowships, research assistantships, Federal Work-Study and scholarships available. Aid available to part-time students. *Financial aid application deadline:* 3/1.

Contact Miss Stacey Boatright, Nursing Program Counselor, School of Nursing, University of Portland, 5000 North Willamette Boulevard, Portland, OR 97203-5798. *Telephone:* 503-943-7423. *Fax:* 503-943-7729. *E-mail:* boatrigh@up.edu.

MASTER'S DEGREE PROGRAM

Degree MS

Available Programs Master's; Master's for Non-Nursing College Graduates; RN to Master's.

Concentrations Available Clinical nurse leader.

Study Options Part-time.

Program Entrance Requirements Computer literacy, minimum overall college GPA of 3.0, transcript of college record, written essay, 2 letters of recommendation, resume, statistics course, GRE General Test or MAT. *Application deadline:* 1/15 (summer). Applications may be processed on a rolling basis for some programs. *Application fee:* $50.

Advanced Placement Credit given for nursing courses completed elsewhere dependent upon specific evaluations.

Degree Requirements 42 total credit hours, thesis or project.

DOCTORAL DEGREE PROGRAM

Degree DNP

Available Programs Doctorate; Post-Baccalaureate Doctorate.

Areas of Study Advanced practice nursing.

Program Entrance Requirements Minimum overall college GPA of 3.0, interview, 3 letters of recommendation, statistics course, vita, writing sample, GRE General Test or MAT. Application deadline: 2/15 (summer). Applications may be processed on a rolling basis for some programs. Application fee: $50.

Degree Requirements 82 total credit hours, residency.

PENNSYLVANIA

Alvernia University
Nursing
Reading, Pennsylvania

http://www.alvernia.edu

Founded in 1958

DEGREE • BSN

Nursing Program Faculty 9 (2% with doctorates).

Baccalaureate Enrollment 203

Women 98% **Men** 2% **Minority** 10% **International** 3% **Part-time** 20%

Nursing Student Activities Nursing Honor Society, Sigma Theta Tau, Student Nurses' Association.

Nursing Student Resources Academic advising; academic or career counseling; bookstore; campus computer network; computer lab; computer-assisted instruction; e-mail services; employment services for current students; externships; interactive nursing skills videos; Internet; learning resource lab; library services; nursing audiovisuals; remedial services; skills, simulation, or other laboratory; tutoring.

Library Facilities 85,635 volumes (2,931 in health, 995 in nursing); 362 periodical subscriptions (89 health-care related).

BACCALAUREATE PROGRAMS

Degree BSN

Available Programs Generic Baccalaureate; LPN to Baccalaureate; LPN to RN Baccalaureate; RN Baccalaureate.

Site Options Reading, PA; Pottsville, PA; Ashland, PA.

Study Options Full-time.

Program Entrance Requirements Minimum overall college GPA of 2.7, transcript of college record, CPR certification, written essay, health exam, health insurance, high school biology, high school chemistry, 2 years high school math, 2 years high school science, high school transcript, immunizations, 2 letters of recommendation, minimum high school GPA of 2.7, minimum GPA in nursing prerequisites of 2.7. Transfer students are accepted.

Advanced Placement Credit by examination available. Credit given for nursing courses completed elsewhere dependent upon specific evaluations.

Contact *Telephone:* 610-796-8460. *Fax:* 610-796-8464.

CONTINUING EDUCATION PROGRAM

Contact *Telephone:* 610-796-5611. *Fax:* 610-796-8464.

Bloomsburg University of Pennsylvania
Department of Nursing
Bloomsburg, Pennsylvania

http://www.bloomu.edu

Founded in 1839

DEGREES • BSN • MSN • MSN/MBA

Nursing Program Faculty 31 (50% with doctorates).

Bloomsburg University of Pennsylvania (continued)

Baccalaureate Enrollment 323
Women 90% **Men** 10% **Minority** 7% **Part-time** 6%

Graduate Enrollment 86
Women 90% **Men** 10% **Minority** 1% **Part-time** 78%

Nursing Student Activities Sigma Theta Tau, Student Nurses' Association, nursing club.

Nursing Student Resources Academic advising; academic or career counseling; assistance for students with disabilities; bookstore; campus computer network; career placement assistance; computer lab; computer-assisted instruction; daycare for children of students; e-mail services; employment services for current students; externships; housing assistance; interactive nursing skills videos; Internet; learning resource lab; library services; nursing audiovisuals; paid internships; placement services for program completers; remedial services; resume preparation assistance; skills, simulation, or other laboratory; tutoring; unpaid internships.

Library Facilities 481,409 volumes (7,603 in health, 2,922 in nursing); 1,744 periodical subscriptions (3,967 health-care related).

BACCALAUREATE PROGRAMS

Degree BSN

Available Programs ADN to Baccalaureate; Baccalaureate for Second Degree; Generic Baccalaureate; LPN to RN Baccalaureate; RN Baccalaureate.

Study Options Full-time and part-time.

Program Entrance Requirements Minimum overall college GPA of 2.5, transcript of college record, CPR certification, health exam, health insurance, high school biology, high school chemistry, 2 years high school math, 3 years high school science, high school transcript, immunizations, interview, 3 letters of recommendation, minimum high school GPA of 3.0, minimum high school rank 80%, minimum GPA in nursing prerequisites of 2.5, professional liability insurance/malpractice insurance, prerequisite course work. Transfer students are accepted. *Application deadline:* 11/15 (fall). *Application fee:* $30.

Advanced Placement Credit by examination available. Credit given for nursing courses completed elsewhere dependent upon specific evaluations.

Expenses (2009–10) *Tuition, state resident:* full-time $5554; part-time $231 per credit. *Tuition, nonresident:* full-time $13,886; part-time $579 per credit. *International tuition:* $13,886 full-time. *Room and board:* $6488; room only: $3882 per academic year. *Required fees:* full-time $1556; part-time $45 per credit; part-time $100–$207 per term.

Financial Aid 78% of baccalaureate students in nursing programs received some form of financial aid in 2008–09. *Gift aid (need-based):* Federal Pell, FSEOG, state, private, college/university gift aid from institutional funds, Academic Competitiveness Grant, National Smart Grant. *Loans:* FFEL (Subsidized and Unsubsidized Stafford PLUS), Perkins, state, alternative loans. *Work-study:* Federal Work-Study, part-time campus jobs. *Financial aid application deadline (priority):* 3/15.

Contact Dr. M. Christine Alichnie, RN, Chairperson, Department of Nursing/Director, School of Health Sciences, Department of Nursing, Bloomsburg University of Pennsylvania, 400 East Second Street, Room 3109, MCHS, Bloomsburg, PA 17815. *Telephone:* 570-389-4426. *Fax:* 570-389-5008. *E-mail:* calichni@bloomu.edu.

GRADUATE PROGRAMS

Expenses (2009–10) *Tuition, state resident:* full-time $6666; part-time $370 per credit. *Tuition, nonresident:* full-time $10,666; part-time $593 per credit. *International tuition:* $10,666 full-time. *Required fees:* full-time $1601; part-time $58 per credit; part-time $100–$115 per term.

Financial Aid 30% of graduate students in nursing programs received some form of financial aid in 2008–09. Unspecified assistantships available.

Contact Dr. Michelle Ficca, Coordinator of Graduate Program, Department of Nursing, Bloomsburg University of Pennsylvania, 400 East Second Street, Room 3136, MCHS, Bloomsburg, PA 17815. *Telephone:* 570-389-4615. *Fax:* 570-389-5008. *E-mail:* mficca@bloomu.edu.

MASTER'S DEGREE PROGRAM

Degrees MSN; MSN/MBA

Available Programs Master's; Master's for Nurses with Non-Nursing Degrees; RN to Master's.

Concentrations Available Nurse anesthesia; nursing administration. *Clinical nurse specialist programs in:* adult health, community health, public health, school health. *Nurse practitioner programs in:* adult health.

Study Options Full-time and part-time.

Program Entrance Requirements Clinical experience, computer literacy, minimum overall college GPA of 3.0, transcript of college record, CPR certification, immunizations, interview, 3 letters of recommendation, nursing research course, physical assessment course, professional liability insurance/malpractice insurance, prerequisite course work, resume, statistics course. *Application deadline:* Applications may be processed on a rolling basis for some programs. *Application fee:* $30.

Advanced Placement Credit by examination available. Credit given for nursing courses completed elsewhere dependent upon specific evaluations.

Degree Requirements 39–56 total credit hours, comprehensive exam.

POST-MASTER'S PROGRAM

Areas of Study Nurse anesthesia. *Clinical nurse specialist programs in:* school health. *Nurse practitioner programs in:* adult health, family health.

CONTINUING EDUCATION PROGRAM

Contact Dr. M. Christine Alichnie, Department Chairperson, Department of Nursing, Bloomsburg University of Pennsylvania, 400 East Second Street, Room 3109, MCHS, Bloomsburg, PA 17815. *Telephone:* 570-389-4426. *Fax:* 570-389-5008. *E-mail:* calichni@bloomu.edu.

California University of Pennsylvania
Department of Nursing
California, Pennsylvania

http://www.cup.edu/eberly/nursing

Founded in 1852

DEGREE • BSN

Nursing Program Faculty 5 (60% with doctorates).

Baccalaureate Enrollment 145
Women 83% **Men** 17% **Minority** 3% **Part-time** 92%

Nursing Student Activities Sigma Theta Tau.

Nursing Student Resources Academic advising; academic or career counseling; assistance for students with disabilities; bookstore; campus computer network; career placement assistance; computer lab; computer-assisted instruction; daycare for children of students; e-mail services; employment services for current students; Internet; library services; nursing audiovisuals; placement services for program completers; remedial services; resume preparation assistance; tutoring.

Library Facilities 437,160 volumes (3,840 in health, 2,010 in nursing); 881 periodical subscriptions (80 health-care related).

BACCALAUREATE PROGRAMS

Degree BSN

Available Programs RN Baccalaureate.

Site Options West Mifflin, PA.

Study Options Full-time and part-time.

Program Entrance Requirements Minimum overall college GPA of 2.0, transcript of college record, CPR certification, health exam, health insurance, immunizations, 2 letters of recommendation, professional liability insurance/malpractice insurance, prerequisite course work, RN licensure. Transfer students are accepted.

Advanced Placement Credit by examination available. Credit given for nursing courses completed elsewhere dependent upon specific evaluations.

Contact *Telephone:* 724-938-5739. *Fax:* 724-938-1612.

Carlow University
School of Nursing
Pittsburgh, Pennsylvania

http://www.carlow.edu/academic/nursing.html

Founded in 1929

DEGREES • BSN • MSN

Nursing Program Faculty 31 (23% with doctorates).

Baccalaureate Enrollment 333
Women 99% **Men** 1% **Minority** 13% **Part-time** 21%

Graduate Enrollment 54
Women 94% **Men** 6% **Minority** 11% **Part-time** 94%

Nursing Student Activities Nursing Honor Society, Sigma Theta Tau, Student Nurses' Association.

Nursing Student Resources Academic advising; academic or career counseling; assistance for students with disabilities; bookstore; campus computer network; career placement assistance; computer lab; computer-assisted instruction; daycare for children of students; e-mail services; employment services for current students; externships; housing assistance; Internet; learning resource lab; library services; nursing audiovisuals; other; paid internships; placement services for program completers; remedial services; resume preparation assistance; skills, simulation, or other laboratory; tutoring; unpaid internships.

Library Facilities 131,831 volumes (14,100 in health, 5,450 in nursing); 363 periodical subscriptions (60 health-care related).

BACCALAUREATE PROGRAMS

Degree BSN

Available Programs Accelerated RN Baccalaureate; Baccalaureate for Second Degree; Generic Baccalaureate.

Site Options Cranberry Township, PA; Greensburg, PA.

Study Options Full-time and part-time.

Program Entrance Requirements Minimum overall college GPA of 3.0, transcript of college record, CPR certification, health exam, health insurance, high school biology, high school chemistry, 2 years high school math, 2 years high school science, high school transcript, immunizations, interview, minimum high school GPA of 3.0, minimum GPA in nursing prerequisites of 2.0, professional liability insurance/malpractice insurance, prerequisite course work. Transfer students are accepted.

Advanced Placement Credit by examination available. Credit given for nursing courses completed elsewhere dependent upon specific evaluations.

Contact *Telephone:* 412-578-6059. *Fax:* 412-578-6668.

GRADUATE PROGRAMS

Contact *Telephone:* 412-578-8764. *Fax:* 412-578-6321.

MASTER'S DEGREE PROGRAM

Degree MSN

Available Programs Accelerated Master's; Master's; RN to Master's.

Concentrations Available Nurse case management; nursing administration; nursing education. *Clinical nurse specialist programs in:* home health care. *Nurse practitioner programs in:* family health.

Site Options Cranberry Township, PA; Greensburg, PA.

Study Options Full-time and part-time.

Program Entrance Requirements Clinical experience, computer literacy, minimum overall college GPA of 3.0, transcript of college record, CPR certification, written essay, immunizations, interview, 3 letters of recommendation, professional liability insurance/malpractice insurance, prerequisite course work, resume, statistics course.

Advanced Placement Credit by examination available. Credit given for nursing courses completed elsewhere dependent upon specific evaluations.

Degree Requirements 56 total credit hours, thesis or project, comprehensive exam.

POST-MASTER'S PROGRAM

Areas of Study *Clinical nurse specialist programs in:* home health care. *Nurse practitioner programs in:* family health.

CONTINUING EDUCATION PROGRAM

Contact *Telephone:* 412-578-8764. *Fax:* 412-578-6321.

Cedar Crest College
Department of Nursing
Allentown, Pennsylvania

http://www.cedarcrest.edu
Founded in 1867

DEGREES • BS • MSN

Nursing Program Faculty 21 (24% with doctorates).

Baccalaureate Enrollment 287
Women 96% **Men** 4% **Minority** 23% **International** 8% **Part-time** 68%

Graduate Enrollment 23
Women 96% **Men** 4% **Minority** 4% **Part-time** 100%

Nursing Student Activities Nursing Honor Society, Sigma Theta Tau, Student Nurses' Association.

Nursing Student Resources Academic advising; academic or career counseling; assistance for students with disabilities; bookstore; campus computer network; career placement assistance; computer lab; computer-assisted instruction; e-mail services; interactive nursing skills videos; Internet; learning resource lab; library services; nursing audiovisuals; remedial services; skills, simulation, or other laboratory; tutoring.

Library Facilities 144,037 volumes; 15,053 periodical subscriptions.

BACCALAUREATE PROGRAMS

Degree BS

Available Programs Baccalaureate for Second Degree; Generic Baccalaureate; LPN to Baccalaureate; RN Baccalaureate.

Study Options Full-time and part-time.

Program Entrance Requirements Minimum overall college GPA of 2.5, CPR certification, written essay, health exam, health insurance, high school biology, high school chemistry, 3 years high school math, 2 years high school science, high school transcript, immunizations, minimum GPA in nursing prerequisites of 2.7, prerequisite course work. Transfer students are accepted. *Application deadline:* Applications may be processed on a rolling basis for some programs.

Advanced Placement Credit given for nursing courses completed elsewhere dependent upon specific evaluations.

Expenses (2008–09) *Tuition:* full-time $26,668; part-time $671 per credit. *International tuition:* $26,668 full-time. *Room and board:* $9009; room only: $4769 per academic year. *Required fees:* full-time $1500; part-time $500 per term.

Financial Aid 93% of baccalaureate students in nursing programs received some form of financial aid in 2007–08. *Gift aid (need-based):* Federal Pell, FSEOG, state, private, college/university gift aid from institutional funds, Federal Nursing. *Loans:* Federal Nursing Student Loans, Federal Direct (Subsidized and Unsubsidized Stafford PLUS), Perkins, college/university. *Work-study:* Federal Work-Study, part-time campus jobs. *Financial aid application deadline (priority):* 5/1.

Contact Office of Admissions, Department of Nursing, Cedar Crest College, 100 College Drive, Allentown, PA 18104. *Telephone:* 610-740-3780. *Fax:* 610-606-4647. *E-mail:* cccadmis@cedarcrest.edu.

GRADUATE PROGRAMS

Expenses (2008–09) *Tuition:* full-time $11,250; part-time $625 per credit. *International tuition:* $11,250 full-time.

Financial Aid 100% of graduate students in nursing programs received some form of financial aid in 2007–08.

Contact Dr. Wendy Robb, Graduate Program Director, Department of Nursing, Cedar Crest College, 100 College Drive, Allentown, PA 18104. *Telephone:* 610-606-4666 Ext. 3480. *E-mail:* wjrobb@cedarcrest.edu.

MASTER'S DEGREE PROGRAM

Degree MSN

Available Programs Master's.

Study Options Part-time.

Program Entrance Requirements Clinical experience, minimum overall college GPA of 3.0, transcript of college record, CPR certification, immunizations, interview, 3 letters of recommendation, nursing research course, physical assessment course, resume, statistics course. *Application deadline:* Applications may be processed on a rolling basis for some programs. *Application fee:* $30.

Cedar Crest College (continued)
Advanced Placement Credit given for nursing courses completed elsewhere dependent upon specific evaluations.
Degree Requirements 38 total credit hours, thesis or project.

Chatham University
Program in Nursing
Pittsburgh, Pennsylvania

Founded in 1869
DEGREES • BSN • DNP • MSN

Nursing Program Faculty 15 (75% with doctorates).

Baccalaureate Enrollment 65
Women 92% **Men** 8% **Minority** 12% **Part-time** 25%

Graduate Enrollment 117
Women 88% **Men** 12% **Minority** 17% **Part-time** 15%

Distance Learning Courses Available.

Nursing Student Resources Academic advising; academic or career counseling; assistance for students with disabilities; bookstore; campus computer network; career placement assistance; computer lab; e-mail services; employment services for current students; housing assistance; Internet; library services; other; placement services for program completers; resume preparation assistance; tutoring.

Library Facilities 90,780 volumes (1,747 in health, 1,732 in nursing); 365 periodical subscriptions (967 health-care related).

BACCALAUREATE PROGRAMS
Degree BSN

Available Programs RN Baccalaureate.

Online Degree Options Yes (online only).

Program Entrance Requirements Transcript of college record, CPR certification, health insurance, immunizations, professional liability insurance/malpractice insurance, prerequisite course work, RN licensure. Transfer students are accepted. *Application deadline:* Applications may be processed on a rolling basis for some programs.

Expenses (2008–09) *Tuition:* part-time $642 per credit. *Required fees:* part-time $160 per term.

Financial Aid 14% of baccalaureate students in nursing programs received some form of financial aid in 2007–08. *Gift aid (need-based):* Federal Pell, FSEOG, state, private, college/university gift aid from institutional funds, United Negro College Fund. *Loans:* FFEL (Subsidized and Unsubsidized Stafford PLUS), Perkins. *Work-study:* Federal Work-Study, part-time campus jobs. *Financial aid application deadline (priority):* 5/1.

Contact Dr. Carol Patton, Program Director, Program in Nursing, Chatham University, 125 Coolidge Hall, Woodland Road, Pittsburgh, PA 15232. *Telephone:* 412-365-2726. *Fax:* 412-365-2439. *E-mail:* cpatton@chatham.edu.

GRADUATE PROGRAMS
Expenses (2008–09) *Tuition:* part-time $686 per credit. *Room and board:* $5000; room only: $4200 per academic year. *Required fees:* part-time $14 per credit.

Financial Aid 79% of graduate students in nursing programs received some form of financial aid in 2007–08.

Contact Dr. Carol Patton, Program Director, Program in Nursing, Chatham University, 125 Coolidge Hall, Woodland Road, Pittsburgh, PA 15232. *Telephone:* 412-365-2726. *Fax:* 412-365-2439. *E-mail:* cpatton@chatham.edu.

MASTER'S DEGREE PROGRAM
Degree MSN

Available Programs Master's.
Concentrations Available Nursing administration; nursing education.
Site Options Pittsburgh, PA.
Study Options Full-time and part-time.
Program Entrance Requirements Minimum overall college GPA of 3.0, transcript of college record, resume. *Application deadline:* 8/15 (fall).

Advanced Placement Credit given for nursing courses completed elsewhere dependent upon specific evaluations.
Degree Requirements 32 total credit hours, thesis or project.

DOCTORAL DEGREE PROGRAM
Degree DNP

Available Programs Doctorate.
Online Degree Options Yes (online only).
Program Entrance Requirements Minimum overall college GPA of 3.0, interview, 2 letters of recommendation, MSN or equivalent, statistics course, vita, writing sample. Application deadline: 5/1 (fall), 10/1 (spring).
Degree Requirements 27 total credit hours, residency.

Clarion University of Pennsylvania
School of Nursing
Oil City, Pennsylvania

Founded in 1867
DEGREES • BSN • MSN

Nursing Program Faculty 20 (25% with doctorates).

Baccalaureate Enrollment 105
Women 90% **Men** 10% **Minority** 2% **International** 1% **Part-time** 88%

Graduate Enrollment 82
Women 98% **Men** 2% **Minority** 3% **Part-time** 80%

Distance Learning Courses Available.

Nursing Student Activities Sigma Theta Tau, nursing club.

Nursing Student Resources Academic advising; academic or career counseling; assistance for students with disabilities; bookstore; campus computer network; career placement assistance; computer lab; computer-assisted instruction; daycare for children of students; e-mail services; employment services for current students; externships; housing assistance; interactive nursing skills videos; Internet; learning resource lab; library services; nursing audiovisuals; placement services for program completers; remedial services; resume preparation assistance; skills, simulation, or other laboratory; tutoring.

Library Facilities 442,871 volumes (12,000 in health, 7,000 in nursing); 20,264 periodical subscriptions (300 health-care related).

BACCALAUREATE PROGRAMS
Degree BSN

Available Programs ADN to Baccalaureate; RN Baccalaureate.

Online Degree Options Yes (online only).

Program Entrance Requirements Minimum overall college GPA of 2.5, transcript of college record, CPR certification, health exam, health insurance, high school transcript, immunizations, minimum GPA in nursing prerequisites of 2.0, professional liability insurance/malpractice insurance, RN licensure. Transfer students are accepted. *Application deadline:* 8/1 (fall), 12/1 (winter). Applications may be processed on a rolling basis for some programs. *Application fee:* $30.

Expenses (2009–10) *Tuition, area resident:* full-time $5554; part-time $231 per credit. *Tuition, nonresident:* full-time $11,108; part-time $462 per credit. *Room and board:* $4000; room only: $2900 per academic year. *Required fees:* full-time $1724.

Financial Aid 70% of baccalaureate students in nursing programs received some form of financial aid in 2008–09.

Contact Dr. Mary L. Zemaitis, Director of Nursing and Allied Health, School of Nursing, Clarion University of Pennsylvania, 1801 West First Street, Oil City, PA 16301. *Telephone:* 814-393-1258. *Fax:* 814-676-0251. *E-mail:* mzemaitis@clarion.edu.

GRADUATE PROGRAMS
Financial Aid 90% of graduate students in nursing programs received some form of financial aid in 2008–09. 2 research assistantships with full tuition reimbursements available (averaging $4,660 per year) were awarded. *Financial aid application deadline:* 3/1.

Contact Dr. Deborah Ciesielka, Coordinator, MSN Family Nurse Practitioner Program, School of Nursing, Clarion University of Pennsylvania, 4900 Friendship Avenue, Pittsburgh, PA 15224. *Telephone:* 412-578-7277. *E-mail:* dciesielka@clarion.edu.

MASTER'S DEGREE PROGRAM

Degree MSN

Available Programs Master's; RN to Master's.

Concentrations Available Nursing education. *Nurse practitioner programs in:* family health.

Site Options Edinboro, PA; Pittsburgh, PA.

Study Options Full-time and part-time.

Program Entrance Requirements Clinical experience, computer literacy, minimum overall college GPA of 3.0, transcript of college record, CPR certification, written essay, immunizations, interview, 3 letters of recommendation, professional liability insurance/malpractice insurance, statistics course. *Application deadline:* 4/1 (fall), 11/1 (winter), 11/1 (spring), 4/1 (summer). *Application fee:* $50.

Advanced Placement Credit given for nursing courses completed elsewhere dependent upon specific evaluations.

Degree Requirements 45 total credit hours, thesis or project, comprehensive exam.

POST-MASTER'S PROGRAM

Areas of Study Nursing education. *Nurse practitioner programs in:* family health.

DeSales University
Department of Nursing and Health
Center Valley, Pennsylvania

http://www.desales.edu

Founded in 1964

DEGREES • BSN • MSN • MSN/MBA

Nursing Program Faculty 74 (23% with doctorates).

Baccalaureate Enrollment 193
Women 88% **Men** 12% **Minority** 4% **International** 2% **Part-time** 23%

Graduate Enrollment 85
Women 93% **Men** 7% **Minority** 2% **Part-time** 95%

Nursing Student Activities Nursing Honor Society, Sigma Theta Tau, Student Nurses' Association.

Nursing Student Resources Academic advising; academic or career counseling; bookstore; campus computer network; career placement assistance; computer lab; computer-assisted instruction; e-mail services; employment services for current students; externships; interactive nursing skills videos; Internet; learning resource lab; library services; nursing audiovisuals; paid internships; placement services for program completers; remedial services; resume preparation assistance; skills, simulation, or other laboratory; tutoring; unpaid internships.

Library Facilities 157,761 volumes (1,215 in health, 100 in nursing); 12,600 periodical subscriptions (100 health-care related).

BACCALAUREATE PROGRAMS

Degree BSN

Available Programs ADN to Baccalaureate; Accelerated Baccalaureate; Accelerated RN Baccalaureate; Baccalaureate for Second Degree; Generic Baccalaureate; RN Baccalaureate.

Study Options Full-time and part-time.

Program Entrance Requirements Minimum overall college GPA of 2.5, transcript of college record, written essay, high school biology, high school chemistry, high school foreign language, 2 years high school math, 3 years high school science, high school transcript, 2 letters of recommendation, minimum high school GPA of 2.5, minimum high school rank 33%, minimum GPA in nursing prerequisites of 2.0. Transfer students are accepted. *Application deadline:* Applications may be processed on a rolling basis for some programs. *Application fee:* $30.

Advanced Placement Credit by examination available. Credit given for nursing courses completed elsewhere dependent upon specific evaluations.

Expenses (2009–10) *Tuition:* full-time $26,000; part-time $1085 per credit. *International tuition:* $26,000 full-time. *Room and board:* $9200 per academic year.

Financial Aid 47% of baccalaureate students in nursing programs received some form of financial aid in 2008–09. *Gift aid (need-based):* Federal Pell, FSEOG, state, private, college/university gift aid from institutional funds, Federal Nursing. *Loans:* Federal Nursing Student Loans, FFEL (Subsidized and Unsubsidized Stafford PLUS), Perkins, alternative loans. *Work-study:* Federal Work-Study, part-time campus jobs. *Financial aid application deadline (priority):* 2/1.

Contact Dr. Margaret M. Slusser, Chair, Nursing and Health Department, Department of Nursing and Health, DeSales University, 2755 Station Avenue, Center Valley, PA 18034-9568. *Telephone:* 610-282-1100 Ext. 1285. *Fax:* 610-282-2091. *E-mail:* Margaret.Slusser@desales.edu.

GRADUATE PROGRAMS

Expenses (2009–10) *Tuition:* part-time $665 per credit. *Required fees:* part-time $200 per credit.

Financial Aid 18% of graduate students in nursing programs received some form of financial aid in 2008–09.

Contact Dr. Carol G. Mest, Director of Graduate Program in Nursing, Department of Nursing and Health, DeSales University, 2755 Station Avenue, Center Valley, PA 18034-9568. *Telephone:* 610-282-1100 Ext. 1664. *Fax:* 610-282-2091. *E-mail:* carol.mest@desales.edu.

MASTER'S DEGREE PROGRAM

Degrees MSN; MSN/MBA

Available Programs Accelerated AD/RN to Master's; Master's; RN to Master's.

Concentrations Available Nursing administration; nursing education. *Clinical nurse specialist programs in:* adult health. *Nurse practitioner programs in:* family health.

Study Options Full-time and part-time.

Program Entrance Requirements Minimum overall college GPA of 3.0, transcript of college record, written essay, interview, 3 letters of recommendation, prerequisite course work, statistics course. *Application deadline:* Applications may be processed on a rolling basis for some programs. *Application fee:* $35.

Advanced Placement Credit given for nursing courses completed elsewhere dependent upon specific evaluations.

Degree Requirements 47 total credit hours.

POST-MASTER'S PROGRAM

Areas of Study Nursing education. *Clinical nurse specialist programs in:* adult health. *Nurse practitioner programs in:* family health.

CONTINUING EDUCATION PROGRAM

Contact Dr. Margaret M. Slusser, Chair, Nursing and Health Department, Department of Nursing and Health, DeSales University, 2755 Station Avenue, Center Valley, PA 18034-9568. *Telephone:* 610-282-1100 Ext. 1271. *Fax:* 610-282-2091. *E-mail:* Margaret.Slusser@desales.edu.

Drexel University
College of Nursing and Health Professions
Philadelphia, Pennsylvania

http://www.drexel.edu

Founded in 1891

DEGREES • BSN • DR NP • MSN

Nursing Program Faculty 73 (49% with doctorates).

Baccalaureate Enrollment 1,100
Women 88% **Men** 12% **Minority** 33% **International** 4% **Part-time** 4%

Graduate Enrollment 800
Women 88% **Men** 12% **Minority** 15% **Part-time** 80%

Distance Learning Courses Available.

Nursing Student Activities Nursing Honor Society, Sigma Theta Tau, Student Nurses' Association.

Nursing Student Resources Academic advising; academic or career counseling; assistance for students with disabilities; bookstore; campus computer network; career placement assistance; computer lab; computer-assisted instruction; e-mail services; housing assistance; interactive nursing skills videos; Internet; learning resource lab; library services; nursing

Drexel University (continued)

audiovisuals; paid internships; placement services for program completers; remedial services; resume preparation assistance; skills, simulation, or other laboratory; tutoring.

Library Facilities 570,335 volumes (51,000 in health, 5,015 in nursing); 8,321 periodical subscriptions (63,000 health-care related).

BACCALAUREATE PROGRAMS

Degree BSN

Available Programs ADN to Baccalaureate; Accelerated Baccalaureate for Second Degree; Generic Baccalaureate; RN Baccalaureate.
Site Options Philadelphia, PA.
Study Options Full-time.

Program Entrance Requirements CPR certification, health insurance, high school biology, high school chemistry, 3 years high school math, 2 years high school science, high school transcript, immunizations. Transfer students are accepted. *Application deadline:* Applications may be processed on a rolling basis for some programs. *Application fee:* $75.

Expenses (2009–10) *Tuition:* full-time $29,800. *Room and board:* $12,681; room only: $7605 per academic year. *Required fees:* full-time $2035.

Financial Aid 93% of baccalaureate students in nursing programs received some form of financial aid in 2008–09. *Gift aid (need-based):* Federal Pell, FSEOG, state, private, college/university gift aid from institutional funds, United Negro College Fund. *Loans:* Federal Nursing Student Loans, FFEL (Subsidized and Unsubsidized Stafford PLUS), Perkins, college/university. *Work-study:* Federal Work-Study. *Financial aid application deadline:* 3/1.

Contact Ms. Margaret Sparzani, Director of Freshman Admissions, College of Nursing and Health Professions, Drexel University, 3141 Chestnut Street, Enrollment Management, Philadelphia, PA 19104. *Telephone:* 215-895-6055. *Fax:* 215-895-5939. *E-mail:* mgts@drexel.edu.

GRADUATE PROGRAMS

Financial Aid Fellowships, research assistantships, teaching assistantships, career-related internships or fieldwork, Federal Work-Study, institutionally sponsored loans, and tuition waivers (partial) available.

Contact Ms. Hannah Brown, Program Coordinator, MSN Programs, College of Nursing and Health Professions, Drexel University, 1505 Race Street, Mail Stop 501, Philadelphia, PA 19102-1192. *Telephone:* 215-762-1336. *Fax:* 215-762-1259. *E-mail:* hmb48@drexel.edu.

MASTER'S DEGREE PROGRAM

Degree MSN

Available Programs Master's; Master's for Nurses with Non-Nursing Degrees; RN to Master's.
Concentrations Available Nurse anesthesia; nursing administration; nursing education. *Clinical nurse specialist programs in:* women's health. *Nurse practitioner programs in:* acute care, family health, pediatric, psychiatric/mental health, women's health.
Site Options Philadelphia, PA.
Study Options Full-time and part-time.
Online Degree Options Yes.
Program Entrance Requirements Clinical experience, computer literacy, minimum overall college GPA of 3.0, transcript of college record, CPR certification, written essay, immunizations, 2 letters of recommendation, resume. *Application deadline:* Applications may be processed on a rolling basis for some programs. *Application fee:* $75.
Advanced Placement Credit given for nursing courses completed elsewhere dependent upon specific evaluations.
Degree Requirements 55 total credit hours, thesis or project, comprehensive exam.

POST-MASTER'S PROGRAM

Areas of Study Nurse anesthesia; nursing administration; nursing education. *Nurse practitioner programs in:* acute care, family health, pediatric, psychiatric/mental health, women's health.

DOCTORAL DEGREE PROGRAM

Degree Dr NP

Available Programs Doctorate; Post-Baccalaureate Doctorate.

Areas of Study Clinical practice, faculty preparation, nursing administration, nursing education, nursing science.
Site Options Philadelphia, PA.
Program Entrance Requirements Clinical experience, minimum overall college GPA of 3.25, interview by faculty committee, 2 letters of recommendation, MSN or equivalent, vita, writing sample, GRE General Test. Application deadline: 3/1 (fall).
Degree Requirements 48 total credit hours, dissertation, oral exam, written exam, residency.

CONTINUING EDUCATION PROGRAM

Contact Mr. Thomas Harkins, Director of Continuing Nursing Education, College of Nursing and Health Professions, Drexel University, 245 North 15th Street, Mail Stop 1002, Philadelphia, PA 19102-1192. *Telephone:* 215-762-2659. *Fax:* 215-762-8171. *E-mail:* tharkins@drexel.edu.

Duquesne University
School of Nursing
Pittsburgh, Pennsylvania

http://www.nursing.duq.edu

Founded in 1878

DEGREES • BSN • MSN • PHD

Nursing Program Faculty 79 (55% with doctorates).
Baccalaureate Enrollment 428
Women 88% **Men** 12% **Minority** 7% **International** 1% **Part-time** 1%
Graduate Enrollment 213
Women 95% **Men** 5% **Minority** 11% **International** 2% **Part-time** 62%
Distance Learning Courses Available.
Nursing Student Activities Nursing Honor Society, Sigma Theta Tau, Student Nurses' Association, nursing club.
Nursing Student Resources Academic advising; academic or career counseling; assistance for students with disabilities; bookstore; campus computer network; career placement assistance; computer lab; computer-assisted instruction; daycare for children of students; e-mail services; employment services for current students; externships; housing assistance; interactive nursing skills videos; Internet; learning resource lab; library services; nursing audiovisuals; paid internships; placement services for program completers; remedial services; resume preparation assistance; skills, simulation, or other laboratory; tutoring; unpaid internships.
Library Facilities 700,245 volumes (27,613 in health, 1,951 in nursing); 30,980 periodical subscriptions (1,779 health-care related).

BACCALAUREATE PROGRAMS

Degree BSN

Available Programs Accelerated Baccalaureate for Second Degree; Generic Baccalaureate.
Study Options Full-time and part-time.
Program Entrance Requirements Minimum overall college GPA of 2.5, transcript of college record, written essay, high school biology, high school chemistry, high school foreign language, 2 years high school math, 3 years high school science, high school transcript, 2 letters of recommendation, minimum high school GPA of 3.0, minimum high school rank 40%. Transfer students are accepted. *Application deadline:* 5/1 (fall), 11/1 (spring). Applications may be processed on a rolling basis for some programs. *Application fee:* $50.
Advanced Placement Credit by examination available.
Expenses (2009–10) *Tuition:* full-time $23,385; part-time $795 per credit. *International tuition:* $23,385 full-time. *Room and board:* $9200 per academic year. *Required fees:* full-time $2083; part-time $81 per credit.
Financial Aid 90% of baccalaureate students in nursing programs received some form of financial aid in 2008–09.
Contact Ms. Susan Hardner, RN, Nursing Recruiter, School of Nursing, Duquesne University, 600 Forbes Avenue, Pittsburgh, PA 15282-1760. *Telephone:* 412-396-4945. *Fax:* 412-396-6346. *E-mail:* hardnersue@duq.edu.

GRADUATE PROGRAMS

Expenses (2009–10) *Tuition:* part-time $873 per course. *Required fees:* part-time $81 per credit.

Financial Aid 55% of graduate students in nursing programs received some form of financial aid in 2008–09. 11 research assistantships with partial tuition reimbursements available (averaging $2,100 per year), 5 teaching assistantships with partial tuition reimbursements available (averaging $1,500 per year) were awarded; institutionally sponsored loans, scholarships, traineeships, tuition waivers (partial), and unspecified assistantships also available.

Contact Ms. Susan Hardner, RN, Nursing Recruiter, School of Nursing, Duquesne University, 600 Forbes Avenue, Pittsburgh, PA 15282-1760. *Telephone:* 412-396-4945. *Fax:* 412-396-6346. *E-mail:* hardnersue@duq.edu.

MASTER'S DEGREE PROGRAM

Degree MSN

Available Programs Master's.

Concentrations Available Nursing education. *Clinical nurse specialist programs in:* forensic nursing. *Nurse practitioner programs in:* family health.

Study Options Full-time and part-time.

Online Degree Options Yes (online only).

Program Entrance Requirements Clinical experience, computer literacy, minimum overall college GPA of 3.0, transcript of college record, written essay, interview, 2 letters of recommendation, nursing research course, physical assessment course, prerequisite course work, resume, statistics course. *Application deadline:* 4/1 (fall).

Advanced Placement Credit given for nursing courses completed elsewhere dependent upon specific evaluations.

Degree Requirements 40 total credit hours, thesis or project.

POST-MASTER'S PROGRAM

Areas of Study Nursing education. *Clinical nurse specialist programs in:* forensic nursing. *Nurse practitioner programs in:* family health.

DOCTORAL DEGREE PROGRAM

Degree PhD

Available Programs Doctorate.

Areas of Study Nursing research.

Online Degree Options Yes (online only).

Program Entrance Requirements Minimum overall college GPA of 3.5, interview by faculty committee, 3 letters of recommendation, MSN or equivalent, scholarly papers, statistics course, vita, writing sample, GRE General Test (PhD). Application deadline: 2/1 (fall).

Degree Requirements 58 total credit hours, dissertation, oral exam, written exam, residency.

CONTINUING EDUCATION PROGRAM

Contact Dr. Shirley P. Smith, Assistant Professor, School of Nursing, Duquesne University, 600 Forbes Avenue, Pittsburgh, PA 15282-1760. *Telephone:* 412-396-6535. *Fax:* 412-396-6346. *E-mail:* smith1@duq.edu.

See full description on page 490.

Eastern University
Program in Nursing
St. Davids, Pennsylvania

http://www.eastern.edu/academics/

Founded in 1952

DEGREE • BSN

Nursing Program Faculty 7 (43% with doctorates).

Baccalaureate Enrollment 100
Women 92% **Men** 8% **Minority** 25% **International** 32%

Distance Learning Courses Available.

Nursing Student Activities Sigma Theta Tau, Student Nurses' Association.

Nursing Student Resources Academic advising; academic or career counseling; assistance for students with disabilities; bookstore; campus computer network; career placement assistance; computer lab; computer-assisted instruction; e-mail services; employment services for current students; Internet; learning resource lab; library services; nursing audio-visuals; placement services for program completers; remedial services; resume preparation assistance; skills, simulation, or other laboratory; tutoring; unpaid internships.

Library Facilities 143,815 volumes (5,858 in health, 3,000 in nursing); 1,215 periodical subscriptions (821 health-care related).

BACCALAUREATE PROGRAMS

Degree BSN

Available Programs Accelerated RN Baccalaureate; Baccalaureate for Second Degree; Generic Baccalaureate; International Nurse to Baccalaureate.

Site Options Wynnewood, PA; West Chester, PA; Harrisburg, PA.

Study Options Full-time.

Program Entrance Requirements Minimum overall college GPA of 3.0, transcript of college record, CPR certification, written essay, health exam, health insurance, high school chemistry, high school transcript, immunizations, interview, 2 letters of recommendation, minimum GPA in nursing prerequisites of 3.0, professional liability insurance/malpractice insurance, prerequisite course work, RN licensure. Transfer students are accepted. *Application deadline:* Applications may be processed on a rolling basis for some programs. *Application fee:* $40.

Expenses (2009–10) *Tuition:* full-time $22,670; part-time $475 per credit hour. *Room and board:* $8870; room only: $4830 per academic year.

Financial Aid 30% of baccalaureate students in nursing programs received some form of financial aid in 2008–09.

Contact Ms. Valerie DiMaio, RN-BSN/BSN TWO Program Advisor, Program in Nursing, Eastern University, 1300 Eagle Road, St. Davids, PA 19087. *Telephone:* 800-732-7669. *Fax:* 610-341-1468. *E-mail:* vdimaio@eastern.edu.

East Stroudsburg University of Pennsylvania
Department of Nursing
East Stroudsburg, Pennsylvania

http://www3.esu/academics/hshp/nurs/home.asp

Founded in 1893

DEGREE • BS

Nursing Program Faculty 14 (44% with doctorates).

Baccalaureate Enrollment 138
Women 91% **Men** 9%

Nursing Student Activities Nursing Honor Society, Sigma Theta Tau, Student Nurses' Association, nursing club.

Nursing Student Resources Academic advising; academic or career counseling; assistance for students with disabilities; bookstore; campus computer network; career placement assistance; computer lab; computer-assisted instruction; daycare for children of students; e-mail services; employment services for current students; externships; housing assistance; interactive nursing skills videos; Internet; learning resource lab; library services; nursing audiovisuals; other; placement services for program completers; remedial services; resume preparation assistance; skills, simulation, or other laboratory; tutoring; unpaid internships.

Library Facilities 554,964 volumes (16,810 in health, 2,035 in nursing); 25,747 periodical subscriptions (495 health-care related).

BACCALAUREATE PROGRAMS

Degree BS

Available Programs Generic Baccalaureate; LPN to Baccalaureate; RN Baccalaureate.

Study Options Full-time and part-time.

East Stroudsburg University of Pennsylvania (continued)

Program Entrance Requirements Minimum overall college GPA of 2.75, transcript of college record, health exam, 2 years high school math, 2 years high school science, high school transcript, minimum high school GPA of 3.0, minimum high school rank 75%, minimum GPA in nursing prerequisites of 2.75. Transfer students are accepted.

Advanced Placement Credit by examination available. Credit given for nursing courses completed elsewhere dependent upon specific evaluations.

Contact *Telephone:* 570-422-3474. *Fax:* 570-422-3848.

Edinboro University of Pennsylvania
Department of Nursing
Edinboro, Pennsylvania

http://www.edinboro.edu/cwis/nursing/nursing.html

Founded in 1857

DEGREE • BS

Nursing Program Faculty 22 (50% with doctorates).

Baccalaureate Enrollment 343
Women 84.5% **Men** 15.5% **Minority** 7.5% **International** 1% **Part-time** 12.8%

Distance Learning Courses Available.

Nursing Student Activities Sigma Theta Tau, Student Nurses' Association, nursing club.

Nursing Student Resources Academic advising; academic or career counseling; assistance for students with disabilities; bookstore; campus computer network; career placement assistance; computer lab; computer-assisted instruction; e-mail services; employment services for current students; housing assistance; interactive nursing skills videos; Internet; learning resource lab; library services; nursing audiovisuals; remedial services; resume preparation assistance; skills, simulation, or other laboratory; tutoring.

Library Facilities 492,293 volumes (500,000 in health, 100 in nursing); 1,315 periodical subscriptions (105 health-care related).

BACCALAUREATE PROGRAMS

Degree BS

Available Programs ADN to Baccalaureate; Accelerated Baccalaureate; Accelerated Baccalaureate for Second Degree; Baccalaureate for Second Degree; Generic Baccalaureate; International Nurse to Baccalaureate.

Site Options Erie, PA.

Study Options Full-time and part-time.

Online Degree Options Yes.

Program Entrance Requirements Minimum overall college GPA of 2.75, transcript of college record, CPR certification, health exam, high school biology, high school chemistry, 2 years high school math, 2 years high school science, high school transcript, immunizations, minimum high school rank 40%, minimum GPA in nursing prerequisites of 2.75, professional liability insurance/malpractice insurance, prerequisite course work. Transfer students are accepted. *Application deadline:* Applications may be processed on a rolling basis for some programs. *Application fee:* $25.

Advanced Placement Credit by examination available.

Expenses (2009–10) *Tuition, state resident:* full-time $5554; part-time $230 per credit. *Tuition, nonresident:* full-time $8332; part-time $345 per credit. *International tuition:* $12,000 full-time. *Room and board:* $9150; room only: $6800 per academic year. *Required fees:* full-time $1762.

Financial Aid 75% of baccalaureate students in nursing programs received some form of financial aid in 2008–09.

Contact Mrs. Patricia Louise Nosel, RN, Chairperson, Department of Nursing, Edinboro University of Pennsylvania, 125 Centennial Hall, Edinboro, PA 16444. *Telephone:* 814-732-1127 Ext. 2900. *Fax:* 814-732-2536. *E-mail:* nosel@edinboro.edu.

Gannon University
Villa Maria School of Nursing
Erie, Pennsylvania

http://www.gannon.edu

Founded in 1925

DEGREES • BSN • MSN

Nursing Program Faculty 15 (20% with doctorates).

Baccalaureate Enrollment 300
Women 88% **Men** 12% **Minority** 4% **International** 3% **Part-time** 5%

Graduate Enrollment 97
Women 68% **Men** 32% **Minority** 6% **Part-time** 38%

Nursing Student Activities Nursing Honor Society, Sigma Theta Tau, nursing club.

Nursing Student Resources Academic advising; academic or career counseling; assistance for students with disabilities; bookstore; campus computer network; career placement assistance; computer lab; computer-assisted instruction; e-mail services; employment services for current students; externships; housing assistance; interactive nursing skills videos; Internet; learning resource lab; library services; nursing audiovisuals; paid internships; placement services for program completers; remedial services; resume preparation assistance; skills, simulation, or other laboratory; tutoring; unpaid internships.

Library Facilities 259,510 volumes (11,604 in health, 1,300 in nursing); 28,463 periodical subscriptions (1,600 health-care related).

BACCALAUREATE PROGRAMS

Degree BSN

Available Programs ADN to Baccalaureate; Baccalaureate for Second Degree; Generic Baccalaureate; International Nurse to Baccalaureate; LPN to RN Baccalaureate; RN Baccalaureate.

Study Options Full-time and part-time.

Program Entrance Requirements Minimum overall college GPA of 2.8, CPR certification, written essay, health exam, health insurance, high school biology, high school chemistry, high school transcript, immunizations, 1 letter of recommendation, minimum high school GPA of 2.5, minimum high school rank 40%, minimum GPA in nursing prerequisites of 2.0. Transfer students are accepted. *Application deadline:* Applications may be processed on a rolling basis for some programs. *Application fee:* $25.

Advanced Placement Credit by examination available.

Expenses (2009–10) *Tuition:* full-time $24,000; part-time $580 per credit. *International tuition:* $24,000 full-time. *Room and board:* $10,000; room only: $6000 per academic year. *Required fees:* full-time $400; part-time $200 per term.

Financial Aid 40% of baccalaureate students in nursing programs received some form of financial aid in 2008–09. *Gift aid (need-based):* Federal Pell, FSEOG, state, private, college/university gift aid from institutional funds, Federal Nursing. *Loans:* Federal Nursing Student Loans, FFEL (Subsidized and Unsubsidized Stafford PLUS), Perkins. *Work-study:* Federal Work-Study, part-time campus jobs. *Financial aid application deadline (priority):* 3/15.

Contact Ms. Patricia Ann Marshall, RN, Director, Undergraduate Programs in Nursing, Villa Maria School of Nursing, Gannon University, 109 University Square, Morosky Academic Center, Erie, PA 16541-0001. *Telephone:* 814-871-5470. *Fax:* 814-871-5662. *E-mail:* marshall001@gannon.edu.

GRADUATE PROGRAMS

Expenses (2009–10) *Tuition:* part-time $680 per credit.

Financial Aid 100% of graduate students in nursing programs received some form of financial aid in 2008–09. Scholarships available. *Financial aid application deadline:* 7/1.

Contact Dr. Kathleen Patterson, PhD, School and Graduate Program Director, Villa Maria School of Nursing, Gannon University, 109 University Square, Erie, PA 16541-0001. *Telephone:* 814-871-5547. *Fax:* 814-871-5662. *E-mail:* patterso018@gannon.edu.

MASTER'S DEGREE PROGRAM

Degree MSN

Available Programs Accelerated AD/RN to Master's; Accelerated RN to Master's; Master's; RN to Master's.

Concentrations Available Health-care administration; nurse anesthesia; nursing administration; nursing education. *Clinical nurse specialist programs in:* medical-surgical. *Nurse practitioner programs in:* family health.

Study Options Full-time and part-time.

Program Entrance Requirements Clinical experience, minimum overall college GPA of 3.0, transcript of college record, CPR certification, written essay, immunizations, interview, 4 letters of recommendation, nursing research course, prerequisite course work, statistics course, GRE General Test. *Application deadline:* Applications may be processed on a rolling basis for some programs. *Application fee:* $25.

Advanced Placement Credit given for nursing courses completed elsewhere dependent upon specific evaluations.

Degree Requirements 46 total credit hours, thesis or project.

Gwynedd-Mercy College

School of Nursing
Gwynedd Valley, Pennsylvania

Founded in 1948

DEGREES • BSN • MSN

Nursing Program Faculty 21 (43% with doctorates).

Baccalaureate Enrollment 85
Women 95% **Men** 5% **Minority** 5% **Part-time** 28%

Graduate Enrollment 40
Women 85% **Men** 15% **Minority** 10% **International** 5% **Part-time** 80%

Nursing Student Activities Sigma Theta Tau, Student Nurses' Association.

Nursing Student Resources Academic advising; bookstore; campus computer network; computer lab; computer-assisted instruction; daycare for children of students; e-mail services; interactive nursing skills videos; learning resource lab; library services; nursing audiovisuals; resume preparation assistance; skills, simulation, or other laboratory; tutoring.

Library Facilities 105,070 volumes; 667 periodical subscriptions.

BACCALAUREATE PROGRAMS

Degree BSN

Available Programs ADN to Baccalaureate; Accelerated RN Baccalaureate; RN Baccalaureate.

Site Options Fort Washington, PA.

Study Options Full-time and part-time.

Program Entrance Requirements Minimum overall college GPA of 2.8, transcript of college record, CPR certification, health exam, health insurance, high school biology, high school chemistry, 2 years high school math, high school transcript, immunizations, letters of recommendation, minimum high school rank 33%, minimum GPA in nursing prerequisites, professional liability insurance/malpractice insurance, RN licensure. Transfer students are accepted.

Advanced Placement Credit by examination available. Credit given for nursing courses completed elsewhere dependent upon specific evaluations.

Contact *Telephone:* 215-646-7300 Ext. 425. *Fax:* 215-641-5556 Ext. 528.

GRADUATE PROGRAMS

Contact *Telephone:* 215-646-7300 Ext. 407. *Fax:* 215-542-5789.

MASTER'S DEGREE PROGRAM

Degree MSN

Available Programs Master's; RN to Master's.

Concentrations Available *Clinical nurse specialist programs in:* gerontology, oncology, pediatric. *Nurse practitioner programs in:* adult health, pediatric.

Study Options Full-time and part-time.

Program Entrance Requirements Clinical experience, minimum overall college GPA of 3.0, transcript of college record, written essay, immunizations, interview, 2 letters of recommendation, physical assessment course, professional liability insurance/malpractice insurance, statistics course, GRE General Test or MAT.

Advanced Placement Credit by examination available. Credit given for nursing courses completed elsewhere dependent upon specific evaluations.

Degree Requirements 43 total credit hours.

POST-MASTER'S PROGRAM

Areas of Study *Nurse practitioner programs in:* adult health, pediatric.

Holy Family University

School of Nursing and Allied Health
Professions
Philadelphia, Pennsylvania

http://www.holyfamily.edu/school_nursing/index.html

Founded in 1954

DEGREES • BSN • MSN

Nursing Program Faculty 40 (28% with doctorates).

Baccalaureate Enrollment 183
Women 90% **Men** 10% **Minority** 25%

Graduate Enrollment 27
Women 97% **Men** 3% **Part-time** 100%

Nursing Student Activities Sigma Theta Tau, Student Nurses' Association.

Nursing Student Resources Academic advising; academic or career counseling; assistance for students with disabilities; bookstore; campus computer network; career placement assistance; computer lab; computer-assisted instruction; daycare for children of students; e-mail services; interactive nursing skills videos; Internet; learning resource lab; library services; nursing audiovisuals; other; resume preparation assistance; skills, simulation, or other laboratory; tutoring.

Library Facilities 135,740 volumes (8,159 in health, 2,177 in nursing); 752 periodical subscriptions (279 health-care related).

BACCALAUREATE PROGRAMS

Degree BSN

Available Programs ADN to Baccalaureate; Accelerated Baccalaureate; Generic Baccalaureate; International Nurse to Baccalaureate; LPN to Baccalaureate; LPN to RN Baccalaureate; RN Baccalaureate.

Site Options Bensalem, PA; Newtown, PA.

Study Options Full-time and part-time.

Program Entrance Requirements Transcript of college record, health exam, high school biology, high school chemistry, high school foreign language, 3 years high school math, 3 years high school science, high school transcript, immunizations, letters of recommendation, minimum high school GPA of 2.5, minimum high school rank 60%, minimum GPA in nursing prerequisites of 2.5. Transfer students are accepted.

Contact *Telephone:* 215-637-3050. *Fax:* 215-281-1022.

GRADUATE PROGRAMS

Contact *Telephone:* 215-637-7203. *Fax:* 215-637-1478.

MASTER'S DEGREE PROGRAM

Degree MSN

Available Programs Master's.

Concentrations Available Health-care administration; nursing education. *Clinical nurse specialist programs in:* community health.

Site Options Newtown, PA.

Study Options Part-time.

Program Entrance Requirements Transcript of college record, written essay, immunizations, 2 letters of recommendation, nursing research course, professional liability insurance/malpractice insurance, prerequisite course work, resume, statistics course.

Holy Family University (continued)

Advanced Placement Credit by examination available. Credit given for nursing courses completed elsewhere dependent upon specific evaluations.

Degree Requirements 39 total credit hours, comprehensive exam.

CONTINUING EDUCATION PROGRAM

Contact *Telephone:* 215-637-7700 Ext. 5002. *Fax:* 215-633-0558.

Immaculata University
Department of Nursing
Immaculata, Pennsylvania

http://www.immaculata.edu/nursing/

Founded in 1920

DEGREES • BSN • MSN

Nursing Program Faculty 30 (50% with doctorates).

Baccalaureate Enrollment 620
Women 92% **Men** 8% **Minority** 13% **Part-time** 100%

Graduate Enrollment 32
Women 87% **Men** 13% **Part-time** 100%

Nursing Student Activities Sigma Theta Tau.

Nursing Student Resources Academic or career counseling; bookstore; campus computer network; career placement assistance; e-mail services; Internet; learning resource lab; library services; nursing audiovisuals; resume preparation assistance.

Library Facilities 143,145 volumes; 604 periodical subscriptions (115 health-care related).

BACCALAUREATE PROGRAMS

Degree BSN

Available Programs Accelerated RN Baccalaureate.

Site Options Abington, PA; Lancaster, PA; Christiana, DE.

Program Entrance Requirements Minimum overall college GPA of 2.0, transcript of college record, CPR certification, health exam, interview, prerequisite course work, RN licensure. Transfer students are accepted.

Contact *Telephone:* 610-647-4400 Ext. 3448. *Fax:* 610-251-1668.

GRADUATE PROGRAMS

Contact *Telephone:* 610-644-4400.

MASTER'S DEGREE PROGRAM

Degree MSN

Available Programs Master's.

Concentrations Available Nursing administration; nursing education.

Study Options Part-time.

Program Entrance Requirements Minimum overall college GPA of 3.0, transcript of college record, interview, 3 letters of recommendation.

Advanced Placement Credit given for nursing courses completed elsewhere dependent upon specific evaluations.

Degree Requirements 36 total credit hours, thesis or project.

Indiana University of Pennsylvania
Department of Nursing and Allied Health
Indiana, Pennsylvania

http://www.hhs.iup.edu/nahp/

Founded in 1875

DEGREES • BSN • MS • PHD

Nursing Program Faculty 38 (39% with doctorates).

Baccalaureate Enrollment 566
Women 89% **Men** 11% **Minority** 12% **International** 5% **Part-time** 29%

Graduate Enrollment 61
Women 93% **Men** 7% **Minority** 2% **Part-time** 97%

Nursing Student Activities Nursing Honor Society, Sigma Theta Tau, Student Nurses' Association, nursing club.

Nursing Student Resources Academic advising; academic or career counseling; assistance for students with disabilities; bookstore; campus computer network; career placement assistance; computer lab; computer-assisted instruction; e-mail services; employment services for current students; housing assistance; interactive nursing skills videos; Internet; learning resource lab; library services; nursing audiovisuals; remedial services; resume preparation assistance; skills, simulation, or other laboratory; tutoring.

Library Facilities 863,626 volumes (5,758 in health, 3,395 in nursing); 16,298 periodical subscriptions (225 health-care related).

BACCALAUREATE PROGRAMS

Degree BSN

Available Programs Baccalaureate for Second Degree; Generic Baccalaureate; LPN to Baccalaureate; RN Baccalaureate.

Site Options Slate Lick, PA.

Study Options Full-time and part-time.

Program Entrance Requirements Minimum overall college GPA of 2.5, transcript of college record, CPR certification, health exam, 2 years high school math, high school transcript, immunizations, minimum high school GPA of 3.0, professional liability insurance/malpractice insurance, prerequisite course work. Transfer students are accepted. *Application deadline:* Applications may be processed on a rolling basis for some programs. *Application fee:* $35.

Expenses (2009–10) *Tuition, state resident:* full-time $5554; part-time $231 per credit. *Tuition, nonresident:* full-time $13,886; part-time $579 per credit. *Room and board:* $8558; room only: $6200 per academic year. *Required fees:* full-time $1671; part-time $265 per credit; part-time $449 per term.

Financial Aid 92% of baccalaureate students in nursing programs received some form of financial aid in 2008–09.

Contact Mr. Mike Husenits, Director of Admissions, Department of Nursing and Allied Health, Indiana University of Pennsylvania, 117 Sutton Hall, Indiana, PA 15705. *E-mail:* admissions-inquiry@iup.edu.

GRADUATE PROGRAMS

Expenses (2009–10) *Tuition, state resident:* full-time $6666; part-time $370 per credit. *Tuition, nonresident:* full-time $10,666; part-time $593 per credit. *Room and board:* $8558; room only: $6200 per academic year. *Required fees:* full-time $1626; part-time $215 per credit; part-time $492 per term.

Financial Aid 44% of graduate students in nursing programs received some form of financial aid in 2008–09. 6 research assistantships with full and partial tuition reimbursements available (averaging $3,117 per year), 1 teaching assistantship (averaging $20,909 per year) were awarded; Federal Work-Study also available. Aid available to part-time students. *Financial aid application deadline:* 3/15.

Contact Dr. Elizabeth A. Palmer, Department Chair, Department of Nursing and Allied Health, Indiana University of Pennsylvania, 1010 Oakland Avenue, Indiana, PA 15705-1087. *Telephone:* 724-357-2557. *Fax:* 724-357-3267. *E-mail:* lpalmer@iup.edu.

MASTER'S DEGREE PROGRAM

Degree MS

Available Programs Master's; Master's for Nurses with Non-Nursing Degrees.

Concentrations Available Nursing administration; nursing education.

Site Options Johnstown, PA; Monroeville, PA; Slate Lick, PA.

Study Options Full-time and part-time.

Program Entrance Requirements Clinical experience, computer literacy, minimum overall college GPA of 3.0, transcript of college record, written essay, 2 letters of recommendation, nursing research course, professional liability insurance/malpractice insurance, resume, statistics course. *Application deadline:* Applications may be processed on a rolling basis for some programs. *Application fee:* $40.

Advanced Placement Credit given for nursing courses completed elsewhere dependent upon specific evaluations.

Degree Requirements 36 total credit hours, thesis or project.

DOCTORAL DEGREE PROGRAM

Degree PhD

Available Programs Doctorate.

Areas of Study Nursing education.

Program Entrance Requirements Minimum overall college GPA of 3.5, interview by faculty committee, 2 letters of recommendation, MSN or equivalent, statistics course, vita, writing sample. Application deadline: Applications may be processed on a rolling basis for some programs. Application fee: $40.

Degree Requirements 60 total credit hours, dissertation, oral exam, written exam, residency.

Kutztown University of Pennsylvania

Department of Nursing
Kutztown, Pennsylvania

http://www.kutztown.edu

Founded in 1866

DEGREES • BSN • MSN

Nursing Program Faculty 7 (57% with doctorates).

Baccalaureate Enrollment 123
Women 92% **Men** 8% **Minority** 1% **International** 1% **Part-time** 95%

Graduate Enrollment 24
Women 100% **Part-time** 100%

Distance Learning Courses Available.

Nursing Student Activities Sigma Theta Tau.

Nursing Student Resources Academic advising; academic or career counseling; assistance for students with disabilities; bookstore; campus computer network; career placement assistance; computer lab; daycare for children of students; e-mail services; employment services for current students; housing assistance; Internet; library services; nursing audiovisuals; placement services for program completers; remedial services; resume preparation assistance; skills, simulation, or other laboratory; tutoring.

Library Facilities 500,484 volumes (38,000 in health, 15,000 in nursing); 15,600 periodical subscriptions (108 health-care related).

BACCALAUREATE PROGRAMS

Degree BSN

Available Programs RN Baccalaureate.

Site Options Reading, PA; Allentown, PA.

Study Options Full-time and part-time.

Online Degree Options Yes.

Program Entrance Requirements Minimum overall college GPA of 2.0, transcript of college record, CPR certification, health exam, high school transcript, immunizations, minimum GPA in nursing prerequisites of 2.0, professional liability insurance/malpractice insurance, prerequisite course work, RN licensure. Transfer students are accepted. *Application deadline:* Applications may be processed on a rolling basis for some programs. *Application fee:* $35.

Advanced Placement Credit by examination available. Credit given for nursing courses completed elsewhere dependent upon specific evaluations.

Expenses (2009–10) *Tuition, state resident:* full-time $7397; part-time $231 per credit. *Tuition, nonresident:* full-time $15,833; part-time $579 per credit.

Contact Mary Ann Dailey, PhD, Chairperson and Assistant Professor, Department of Nursing, Kutztown University of Pennsylvania, Old Main Room 364, PO Box 730, Kutztown, PA 19530. *Telephone:* 610-683-4329. *Fax:* 610-683-4708. *E-mail:* mdailey@kutztown.edu.

GRADUATE PROGRAMS

Expenses (2009–10) *Tuition, area resident:* full-time $6666; part-time $370 per credit. *Tuition, state resident:* part-time $370 per credit. *Tuition, nonresident:* full-time $12,196; part-time $593 per credit. *Required fees:* full-time $1427.

Contact Mary Ann Dailey, PhD, Chairperson and Assistant Professor, Department of Nursing, Kutztown University of Pennsylvania, Old Main Room 364, PO Box 730, Kutztown, PA 19530. *Telephone:* 610-683-4329. *Fax:* 610-683-4708. *E-mail:* mdailey@kutztown.edu.

MASTER'S DEGREE PROGRAM

Degree MSN

Available Programs Master's.

Concentrations Available Clinical nurse leader; nursing education.

Site Options Allentown, PA.

Study Options Full-time and part-time.

Online Degree Options Yes (online only).

Program Entrance Requirements Clinical experience, computer literacy, minimum overall college GPA of 3.0, transcript of college record, written essay, interview, 3 letters of recommendation, nursing research course, resume, statistics course. *Application deadline:* Applications may be processed on a rolling basis for some programs. *Application fee:* $35.

Advanced Placement Credit given for nursing courses completed elsewhere dependent upon specific evaluations.

Degree Requirements 36 total credit hours, thesis or project.

La Roche College

Department of Nursing and Nursing Management
Pittsburgh, Pennsylvania

http://www.laroche.edu

Founded in 1963

DEGREES • BSN • MSN

Nursing Program Faculty 11 (45% with doctorates).

Baccalaureate Enrollment 46
Women 89% **Men** 11% **International** 17% **Part-time** 74%

Graduate Enrollment 18
Women 83% **Men** 17% **International** 5% **Part-time** 94%

Distance Learning Courses Available.

Nursing Student Activities Sigma Theta Tau.

Nursing Student Resources Academic advising; academic or career counseling; assistance for students with disabilities; bookstore; campus computer network; computer lab; e-mail services; externships; Internet; library services; resume preparation assistance; tutoring.

Library Facilities 115,215 volumes; 582 periodical subscriptions (713 health-care related).

BACCALAUREATE PROGRAMS

Degree BSN

Available Programs Accelerated RN Baccalaureate; RN Baccalaureate.

Site Options Pittsburgh, PA.

Study Options Full-time and part-time.

Program Entrance Requirements Minimum overall college GPA of 2.5, transcript of college record, high school transcript, 2 letters of recommendation, professional liability insurance/malpractice insurance, prerequisite course work, RN licensure. Transfer students are accepted. *Application deadline:* Applications may be processed on a rolling basis for some programs. *Application fee:* $50.

Advanced Placement Credit by examination available. Credit given for nursing courses completed elsewhere dependent upon specific evaluations.

Expenses (2009–10) *Tuition:* full-time $10,370; part-time $525 per credit. *International tuition:* $10,370 full-time. *Room and board:* $4000; room only: $2742 per academic year. *Required fees:* full-time $400; part-time $9 per credit.

Financial Aid 87% of baccalaureate students in nursing programs received some form of financial aid in 2008–09. *Gift aid (need-based):* Federal Pell, FSEOG, state, private, college/university gift aid from institutional funds. *Loans:* FFEL (Subsidized and Unsubsidized Stafford PLUS), Perkins, state. *Work-study:* Federal Work-Study. *Financial aid application deadline (priority):* 5/1.

La Roche College (continued)

Contact Ms. Hope A. Schiffgens, Director, Graduate Studies and Adult Education, Department of Nursing and Nursing Management, La Roche College, 9000 Babcock Boulevard, Pittsburgh, PA 15237. *Telephone:* 412-536-1266. *Fax:* 412-536-1283. *E-mail:* hope.schiffgens@laroche.edu.

GRADUATE PROGRAMS

Expenses (2009–10) *Tuition:* part-time $525 per credit hour. *International tuition:* $525 full-time. *Room and board:* $4000; room only: $2742 per academic year. *Required fees:* full-time $200; part-time $9 per credit; part-time $9 per term.

Financial Aid 85% of graduate students in nursing programs received some form of financial aid in 2008–09.

Contact Ms. Hope A. Schiffgens, Director, Graduate Studies and Adult Education, Department of Nursing and Nursing Management, La Roche College, 9000 Babcock Boulevard, Pittsburgh, PA 15237. *Telephone:* 412-536-1262. *Fax:* 412-536-1283. *E-mail:* hope.schiffgens@laroche.edu.

MASTER'S DEGREE PROGRAM

Degree MSN

Available Programs Master's; RN to Master's.

Concentrations Available Health-care administration; nursing administration; nursing education. *Clinical nurse specialist programs in:* community health. *Nurse practitioner programs in:* school health.

Study Options Full-time and part-time.

Online Degree Options Yes (online only).

Program Entrance Requirements Clinical experience, minimum overall college GPA of 3.0, transcript of college record, immunizations, interview, 2 letters of recommendation, professional liability insurance/malpractice insurance, resume. *Application deadline:* Applications may be processed on a rolling basis for some programs. *Application fee:* $50.

Advanced Placement Credit given for nursing courses completed elsewhere dependent upon specific evaluations.

Degree Requirements 41 total credit hours.

CONTINUING EDUCATION PROGRAM

Contact Ms. Hope A. Schiffgens, Director, Graduate Studies and Adult Education, Department of Nursing and Nursing Management, La Roche College, 9000 Babcock Boulevard, Pittsburgh, PA 15237. *Telephone:* 412-536-1262. *Fax:* 412-536-1283. *E-mail:* hope.schiffgens@laroche.edu.

La Salle University
School of Nursing and Health Sciences
Philadelphia, Pennsylvania

http://www.lasalle.edu/academ/nursing
Founded in 1863

DEGREES • BSN • MSN • MSN/MBA

Nursing Program Faculty 45 (32% with doctorates).

Nursing Student Activities Sigma Theta Tau, Student Nurses' Association, nursing club.

Nursing Student Resources Academic advising; academic or career counseling; assistance for students with disabilities; bookstore; campus computer network; career placement assistance; computer lab; computer-assisted instruction; e-mail services; employment services for current students; externships; housing assistance; interactive nursing skills videos; Internet; learning resource lab; library services; nursing audiovisuals; placement services for program completers; remedial services; resume preparation assistance; skills, simulation, or other laboratory; tutoring.

Library Facilities 400,000 volumes (8,350 in nursing); 9,250 periodical subscriptions (310 health-care related).

BACCALAUREATE PROGRAMS

Degree BSN

Available Programs Baccalaureate for Second Degree; Generic Baccalaureate; LPN to Baccalaureate; RN Baccalaureate.

Site Options Newtown, PA.

Study Options Full-time and part-time.

Program Entrance Requirements Minimum overall college GPA of 2.75, transcript of college record, CPR certification, written essay, health exam, health insurance, high school biology, high school chemistry, 3 years high school math, 3 years high school science, high school transcript, immunizations, interview, 2 letters of recommendation, minimum high school GPA of 3.0, minimum high school rank 25%, minimum GPA in nursing prerequisites of 2.75, professional liability insurance/malpractice insurance, prerequisite course work. Transfer students are accepted.

Advanced Placement Credit by examination available. Credit given for nursing courses completed elsewhere dependent upon specific evaluations.

Contact *Telephone:* 215-951-1430. *Fax:* 215-951-1896.

GRADUATE PROGRAMS

Contact *Telephone:* 215-951-1413. *Fax:* 215-951-1896.

MASTER'S DEGREE PROGRAM

Degrees MSN; MSN/MBA

Available Programs Master's; RN to Master's.

Concentrations Available Nurse anesthesia; nursing administration. *Clinical nurse specialist programs in:* adult health, public health. *Nurse practitioner programs in:* adult health, family health.

Site Options Newtown, PA.

Study Options Full-time and part-time.

Program Entrance Requirements Clinical experience, minimum overall college GPA of 3.0, transcript of college record, CPR certification, written essay, immunizations, interview, 2 letters of recommendation, nursing research course, physical assessment course, professional liability insurance/malpractice insurance, resume, statistics course.

Advanced Placement Credit given for nursing courses completed elsewhere dependent upon specific evaluations.

Degree Requirements 41 total credit hours.

POST-MASTER'S PROGRAM

Areas of Study Nurse anesthesia; nursing administration; nursing education. *Clinical nurse specialist programs in:* adult health, public health. *Nurse practitioner programs in:* adult health, family health.

CONTINUING EDUCATION PROGRAM

Contact *Telephone:* 215-951-1432. *Fax:* 215-951-1896.

Mansfield University of Pennsylvania
Robert Packer Department of Health Sciences
Mansfield, Pennsylvania

http://www.mansfield.edu
Founded in 1857

DEGREES • BSN • MSN

Nursing Program Faculty 12 (50% with doctorates).

Baccalaureate Enrollment 187
Women 95% **Men** 5% **Minority** 5% **International** 1% **Part-time** 10%

Graduate Enrollment 42
Women 95% **Men** 5% **Minority** 1% **Part-time** 100%

Distance Learning Courses Available.

Nursing Student Activities Nursing Honor Society, Student Nurses' Association, nursing club.

Nursing Student Resources Academic advising; academic or career counseling; assistance for students with disabilities; bookstore; campus computer network; career placement assistance; computer lab; daycare for children of students; e-mail services; employment services for current students; housing assistance; Internet; learning resource lab; library services; nursing audiovisuals; remedial services; resume preparation assistance; skills, simulation, or other laboratory; tutoring.

Library Facilities 246,141 volumes (1,300 in health, 500 in nursing); 2,948 periodical subscriptions (550 health-care related).

BACCALAUREATE PROGRAMS

Degree BSN

Available Programs Generic Baccalaureate; RN Baccalaureate.

Site Options Sayre, PA.

Study Options Full-time and part-time.

Program Entrance Requirements Minimum overall college GPA of 2.7, transcript of college record, CPR certification, health exam, health insurance, high school biology, high school chemistry, 2 years high school math, 2 years high school science, high school transcript, immunizations, minimum high school GPA of 2.7, minimum high school rank 60%, professional liability insurance/malpractice insurance. Transfer students are accepted. *Application deadline:* Applications may be processed on a rolling basis for some programs. *Application fee:* $25.

Advanced Placement Credit by examination available. Credit given for nursing courses completed elsewhere dependent upon specific evaluations.

Expenses (2009–10) *Tuition, state resident:* full-time $5358; part-time $223 per credit. *Tuition, nonresident:* full-time $13,396; part-time $558 per credit. *International tuition:* $13,396 full-time. *Room and board:* $6396; room only: $4060 per academic year. *Required fees:* full-time $1100; part-time $100 per credit.

Financial Aid 90% of baccalaureate students in nursing programs received some form of financial aid in 2008–09.

Contact Admissions Office, Robert Packer Department of Health Sciences, Mansfield University of Pennsylvania, Alumni Hall, Mansfield, PA 16933. *Telephone:* 570-662-4243. *Fax:* 570-662-4121. *E-mail:* admissions@mansfield.edu.

GRADUATE PROGRAMS

Expenses (2009–10) *Tuition, state resident:* full-time $6666; part-time $370 per credit. *Tuition, nonresident:* full-time $10,666; part-time $593 per credit. *International tuition:* $10,666 full-time. *Required fees:* part-time $111 per credit.

Financial Aid 50% of graduate students in nursing programs received some form of financial aid in 2008–09.

Contact Dr. Janeen Bartlett Sheehe, Department Chair and Nursing Program Director, Robert Packer Department of Health Sciences, Mansfield University of Pennsylvania, 212C Elliott Hall, Mansfield, PA 16933. *Telephone:* 570-662-4522. *Fax:* 570-662-4137. *E-mail:* jsheehe@mansfield.edu.

MASTER'S DEGREE PROGRAM

Degree MSN

Available Programs Master's.

Concentrations Available Nursing administration; nursing education.

Study Options Part-time.

Online Degree Options Yes (online only).

Program Entrance Requirements Minimum overall college GPA of 3.0, transcript of college record, 1 letter of recommendation, nursing research course, prerequisite course work. *Application deadline:* Applications may be processed on a rolling basis for some programs. *Application fee:* $25.

Advanced Placement Credit given for nursing courses completed elsewhere dependent upon specific evaluations.

Degree Requirements 33 total credit hours, thesis or project.

Marywood University
Department of Nursing
Scranton, Pennsylvania

http://www.marywood.edu/uscat/nurs.htm

Founded in 1915

DEGREES • BSN • MSN • MSN/MPH

Nursing Program Faculty 16 (50% with doctorates).

Baccalaureate Enrollment 117

Women 90% **Men** 10% **Minority** 5% **International** 3% **Part-time** 5%

Graduate Enrollment 17

Women 100% **Part-time** 90%

Distance Learning Courses Available.

Nursing Student Activities Sigma Theta Tau, Student Nurses' Association.

Nursing Student Resources Academic advising; academic or career counseling; assistance for students with disabilities; bookstore; campus computer network; computer lab; daycare for children of students; e-mail services; employment services for current students; interactive nursing skills videos; Internet; learning resource lab; library services; nursing audiovisuals; skills, simulation, or other laboratory; tutoring.

Library Facilities 220,365 volumes (7,400 in health, 3,006 in nursing); 15,904 periodical subscriptions (750 health-care related).

BACCALAUREATE PROGRAMS

Degree BSN

Available Programs ADN to Baccalaureate; Generic Baccalaureate; International Nurse to Baccalaureate; LPN to Baccalaureate; RN Baccalaureate.

Study Options Full-time and part-time.

Program Entrance Requirements Transcript of college record, high school biology, high school chemistry, 1 year of high school math, high school transcript, 1 letter of recommendation. Transfer students are accepted.

Advanced Placement Credit given for nursing courses completed elsewhere dependent upon specific evaluations.

Contact *Telephone:* 570-348-6211 Ext. 2374. *Fax:* 570-961-4761.

GRADUATE PROGRAMS

Contact *Telephone:* 570-348-6211 Ext. 2475. *Fax:* 570-961-4761.

MASTER'S DEGREE PROGRAM

Degrees MSN; MSN/MPH

Available Programs Master's.

Concentrations Available Nursing administration.

Study Options Full-time and part-time.

Program Entrance Requirements Clinical experience, minimum overall college GPA of 3.0, transcript of college record, written essay, 2 letters of recommendation, nursing research course, physical assessment course, statistics course.

Degree Requirements 39 total credit hours, thesis or project.

CONTINUING EDUCATION PROGRAM

Contact *Telephone:* 570-340-6060. *Fax:* 570-961-4776.

Messiah College
Department of Nursing
Grantham, Pennsylvania

http://www.messiah.edu

Founded in 1909

DEGREE • BSN

Nursing Program Faculty 18 (22% with doctorates).

Baccalaureate Enrollment 248

Women 96% **Men** 4% **Minority** 8% **International** 1% **Part-time** 1%

Distance Learning Courses Available.

Nursing Student Activities Nursing Honor Society, Sigma Theta Tau, Student Nurses' Association.

Nursing Student Resources Academic advising; academic or career counseling; assistance for students with disabilities; bookstore; campus computer network; career placement assistance; computer lab; computer-assisted instruction; e-mail services; employment services for current students; interactive nursing skills videos; Internet; learning resource lab; library services; nursing audiovisuals; remedial services; resume preparation assistance; skills, simulation, or other laboratory; tutoring.

Library Facilities 259,252 volumes (7,589 in health, 549 in nursing); 27,936 periodical subscriptions (4,530 health-care related).

BACCALAUREATE PROGRAMS

Degree BSN

Messiah College (continued)

Available Programs Generic Baccalaureate.

Study Options Full-time and part-time.

Program Entrance Requirements Minimum overall college GPA of 2.8, transcript of college record, CPR certification, health exam, health insurance, high school foreign language, 2 years high school math, 2 years high school science, high school transcript, immunizations, minimum GPA in nursing prerequisites of 2.5, prerequisite course work. Transfer students are accepted. *Application deadline:* Applications may be processed on a rolling basis for some programs. *Application fee:* $30.

Advanced Placement Credit given for nursing courses completed elsewhere dependent upon specific evaluations.

Expenses (2009–10) *Tuition:* full-time $25,900; part-time $1080 per credit hour. *International tuition:* $25,900 full-time. *Room and board:* $7880; room only: $2085 per academic year. *Required fees:* full-time $440.

Financial Aid 97% of baccalaureate students in nursing programs received some form of financial aid in 2008–09. *Gift aid (need-based):* Federal Pell, FSEOG, state, private, college/university gift aid from institutional funds. *Loans:* Federal Nursing Student Loans, Federal Direct (Subsidized and Unsubsidized Stafford PLUS), FFEL (Subsidized and Unsubsidized Stafford PLUS), Perkins. *Work-study:* Federal Work-Study, part-time campus jobs. *Financial aid application deadline (priority):* 4/1.

Contact Dana Britton, Director of Admissions, Department of Nursing, Messiah College, PO Box 3005, One College Avenue, Grantham, PA 17027. *Telephone:* 800-233-4220. *Fax:* 717-796-5374. *E-mail:* admiss@messiah.edu.

Millersville University of Pennsylvania
Department of Nursing
Millersville, Pennsylvania

http://muweb.millersville.edu/~nursing/

Founded in 1855

DEGREES • BSN • MSN

Nursing Program Faculty 5 (100% with doctorates).

Baccalaureate Enrollment 40
Women 95% **Men** 5% **Minority** 18% **Part-time** 80%

Graduate Enrollment 45
Women 86% **Men** 14% **Minority** 3% **Part-time** 100%

Nursing Student Activities Sigma Theta Tau.

Nursing Student Resources Academic advising; academic or career counseling; assistance for students with disabilities; bookstore; computer lab; e-mail services; interactive nursing skills videos; Internet; library services; nursing audiovisuals.

Library Facilities 564,648 volumes; 16,487 periodical subscriptions (82 health-care related).

BACCALAUREATE PROGRAMS

Degree BSN

Available Programs RN Baccalaureate.

Study Options Full-time and part-time.

Program Entrance Requirements Transcript of college record, CPR certification, health exam, immunizations, professional liability insurance/malpractice insurance, RN licensure. Transfer students are accepted.

Financial Aid 50% of baccalaureate students in nursing programs received some form of financial aid in 2008–09.

Contact Dr. Barbara Zimmerman, Chairperson, Department of Nursing, Millersville University of Pennsylvania, Caputo Hall, PO Box 1002, Millersville, PA 17551-0302. *Telephone:* 717-872-3376. *Fax:* 717-871-4877. *E-mail:* Barbara.Zimmerman@millersville.edu.

GRADUATE PROGRAMS

Financial Aid 5% of graduate students in nursing programs received some form of financial aid jn 2008–09. 1 research assistantship with partial tuition reimbursement available (averaging $2,500 per year) was awarded; institutionally sponsored loans and unspecified assistantships also available. Aid available to part-time students. *Financial aid application deadline:* 3/15.

Contact Dr. Deborah Castellucci, Graduate Program Coordinator, Department of Nursing, Millersville University of Pennsylvania, Caputo Hall, PO Box 1002, Millersville, PA 17551-0302. *Telephone:* 717-871-5341. *Fax:* 717-871-4887. *E-mail:* Deborah.Castellucci@millersville.edu.

MASTER'S DEGREE PROGRAM

Degree MSN

Available Programs Master's.

Concentrations Available Nursing education. *Nurse practitioner programs in:* family health.

Study Options Part-time.

Program Entrance Requirements Clinical experience, minimum overall college GPA of 3.0, transcript of college record, interview, 3 letters of recommendation, nursing research course, physical assessment course, resume, statistics course, GRE or MAT.

Advanced Placement Credit given for nursing courses completed elsewhere dependent upon specific evaluations.

Degree Requirements 42 total credit hours, thesis or project.

POST-MASTER'S PROGRAM

Areas of Study Nursing education. *Nurse practitioner programs in:* family health.

CONTINUING EDUCATION PROGRAM

Contact Ms. Bili Mattes, Director, Professional Training and Education, Department of Nursing, Millersville University of Pennsylvania, Office of Professional Training and Education, PO Box 1002, Millersville, PA 17551-0302. *Telephone:* 717-872-3030. *Fax:* 717-871-2022. *E-mail:* bili.mattes@millersville.edu.

Misericordia University
Department of Nursing
Dallas, Pennsylvania

http://www.misericordia.edu/nursing

Founded in 1924

DEGREES • BSN • MSN

Nursing Program Faculty 35 (3% with doctorates).

Baccalaureate Enrollment 269
Women 87% **Men** 13% **Minority** 3% **Part-time** 38%

Graduate Enrollment 42
Women 95% **Men** 5% **Minority** 1% **Part-time** 100%

Distance Learning Courses Available.

Nursing Student Activities Nursing Honor Society, Sigma Theta Tau, Student Nurses' Association, nursing club.

Nursing Student Resources Academic advising; academic or career counseling; assistance for students with disabilities; bookstore; campus computer network; career placement assistance; computer lab; computer-assisted instruction; e-mail services; employment services for current students; externships; housing assistance; interactive nursing skills videos; Internet; learning resource lab; library services; nursing audiovisuals; placement services for program completers; remedial services; resume preparation assistance; skills, simulation, or other laboratory; tutoring.

Library Facilities 79,612 volumes (5 in health, 5 in nursing); 373 periodical subscriptions (15 health-care related).

BACCALAUREATE PROGRAMS

Degree BSN

Available Programs Accelerated RN Baccalaureate; Baccalaureate for Second Degree; Generic Baccalaureate; RN Baccalaureate.

Site Options Nanticoke, PA.

Study Options Full-time and part-time.

Program Entrance Requirements Minimum overall college GPA of 2.75, transcript of college record, health insurance, high school biology, high school chemistry, 1 year of high school math, high school transcript, immunizations, letters of recommendation, minimum high school GPA of 2.5, minimum high school rank, minimum GPA in nursing prerequisites of 2.75. Transfer students are accepted. *Application deadline:* Applications may be processed on a rolling basis for some programs. *Application fee:* $200.

Advanced Placement Credit by examination available. Credit given for nursing courses completed elsewhere dependent upon specific evaluations.

Expenses (2009–10) *Tuition:* full-time $11,425; part-time $320 per credit. *International tuition:* $11,425 full-time. *Room and board:* $2915; room only: $2260 per academic year. *Required fees:* full-time $925; part-time $275 per term.

Financial Aid 75% of baccalaureate students in nursing programs received some form of financial aid in 2008–09. *Gift aid (need-based):* Federal Pell, FSEOG, state, private, college/university gift aid from institutional funds, Federal Nursing. *Loans:* Federal Nursing Student Loans, FFEL (Subsidized and Unsubsidized Stafford PLUS), Perkins, state. *Work-study:* Federal Work-Study. *Financial aid application deadline (priority):* 3/1.

Contact Glenn Bozinski, Admissions, Department of Nursing, Misericordia University, 301 Lake Street, Dallas, PA 18612. *Telephone:* 570-674-6434. *E-mail:* gbozinsk@misericordia.edu.

GRADUATE PROGRAMS

Expenses (2009–10) *Tuition:* part-time $450 per credit.

Financial Aid 80% of graduate students in nursing programs received some form of financial aid in 2008–09. Teaching assistantships, career-related internships or fieldwork, scholarships, traineeships, tuition waivers (partial), and unspecified assistantships available. Aid available to part-time students. *Financial aid application deadline:* 6/30.

Contact Miss Larree Brown, Adult Education Counselor, Graduate Programs, Department of Nursing, Misericordia University, 301 Lake Street, Dallas, PA 18612. *Telephone:* 570-674-6451. *Fax:* 570-674-8902. *E-mail:* lbrown@misericordia.edu.

MASTER'S DEGREE PROGRAM

Degree MSN

Available Programs Master's; RN to Master's.

Concentrations Available Nursing education. *Clinical nurse specialist programs in:* adult health. *Nurse practitioner programs in:* family health.

Study Options Part-time.

Program Entrance Requirements Clinical experience, computer literacy, minimum overall college GPA of 3.0, transcript of college record, written essay, 3 letters of recommendation, nursing research course, physical assessment course, professional liability insurance/malpractice insurance, statistics course, GRE General Test or MAT in at least 35th percentile. *Application deadline:* Applications may be processed on a rolling basis for some programs. *Application fee:* $200.

Advanced Placement Credit given for nursing courses completed elsewhere dependent upon specific evaluations.

Degree Requirements 45 total credit hours, thesis or project.

POST-MASTER'S PROGRAM

Areas of Study Nursing education. *Clinical nurse specialist programs in:* adult health. *Nurse practitioner programs in:* family health.

Moravian College
St. Luke's School of Nursing
Bethlehem, Pennsylvania

http://www.moravian.edu/academics/ departments/nursing
Founded in 1742

DEGREES • BS • MS

Nursing Program Faculty 29 (34% with doctorates).

Baccalaureate Enrollment 212
Women 95% **Men** 5% **Minority** 3% **International** 1% **Part-time** 49%

Graduate Enrollment 32

Nursing Student Activities Sigma Theta Tau, Student Nurses' Association.

Nursing Student Resources Academic advising; academic or career counseling; assistance for students with disabilities; bookstore; campus computer network; career placement assistance; computer lab; computer-assisted instruction; e-mail services; employment services for current students; externships; housing assistance; interactive nursing skills videos; Internet; learning resource lab; library services; nursing audiovisuals; placement services for program completers; remedial services; resume preparation assistance; skills, simulation, or other laboratory; tutoring.

Library Facilities 260,363 volumes (4,600 in health, 1,900 in nursing); 3,274 periodical subscriptions (275 health-care related).

BACCALAUREATE PROGRAMS

Degree BS

Available Programs Generic Baccalaureate; RN Baccalaureate.

Study Options Full-time.

Program Entrance Requirements CPR certification, written essay, health exam, health insurance, high school biology, high school foreign language, 3 years high school math, 3 years high school science, high school transcript, immunizations, minimum GPA in nursing prerequisites of 2.7, prerequisite course work. Transfer students are accepted. *Application deadline:* 3/1 (fall).

Advanced Placement Credit by examination available. Credit given for nursing courses completed elsewhere dependent upon specific evaluations.

Expenses (2009–10) *Tuition:* full-time $30,368. *Room and board:* $8885; room only: $5061 per academic year. *Required fees:* full-time $515.

Financial Aid 90% of baccalaureate students in nursing programs received some form of financial aid in 2008–09. *Gift aid (need-based):* Federal Pell, FSEOG, state, private, college/university gift aid from institutional funds. *Loans:* FFEL (Subsidized and Unsubsidized Stafford PLUS), Perkins. *Work-study:* Federal Work-Study, part-time campus jobs. *Financial aid application deadline (priority):* 2/14.

Contact Mr. James P. Mackin, Director of Admissions, St. Luke's School of Nursing, Moravian College, 1200 Main Street, Bethlehem, PA 18018. *Telephone:* 800-441-3191. *E-mail:* mejpm01@moravian.edu.

GRADUATE PROGRAMS

Expenses (2009–10) *Tuition:* part-time $1191 per course. *Required fees:* part-time $50 per term.

Contact Dr. Lori Hoffman, RN, MS Program Coordinator, St. Luke's School of Nursing, Moravian College, 1200 Main Street, Bethlehem, PA 18018. *Telephone:* 610-625-7769. *Fax:* 610-625-7861. *E-mail:* lorihoffman@moravian.edu.

MASTER'S DEGREE PROGRAM

Degree MS

Available Programs Master's.

Concentrations Available Clinical nurse leader; nursing administration; nursing education.

Study Options Part-time.

Program Entrance Requirements Computer literacy, minimum overall college GPA of 3.0, transcript of college record, written essay, 2 letters of recommendation, prerequisite course work, resume, statistics course. *Application deadline:* Applications may be processed on a rolling basis for some programs. *Application fee:* $35.

Advanced Placement Credit given for nursing courses completed elsewhere dependent upon specific evaluations.

Degree Requirements 36 total credit hours.

CONTINUING EDUCATION PROGRAM

Contact Mrs. Dawn Goodolf, RN, RN-to-BS Program Coordinator, St. Luke's School of Nursing, Moravian College, 1200 Main Street, Bethlehem, PA 18018. *Telephone:* 610-625-7764. *Fax:* 610-625-7861. *E-mail:* medmg01@moravian.edu.

Mount Aloysius College
Department of Nursing
Cresson, Pennsylvania

http://www.mtaloy.edu

Founded in 1939

DEGREE • BSN

Nursing Program Faculty 8

Baccalaureate Enrollment 72
Women 83% **Men** 17% **Minority** 1% **Part-time** 90%

Nursing Student Activities Student Nurses' Association.

Nursing Student Resources Academic advising; academic or career counseling; assistance for students with disabilities; bookstore; campus computer network; computer lab; computer-assisted instruction; daycare for children of students; e-mail services; interactive nursing skills videos; Internet; learning resource lab; library services; nursing audiovisuals; remedial services; resume preparation assistance; skills, simulation, or other laboratory; tutoring.

Library Facilities 6,999 volumes in health, 1,871 volumes in nursing; 64 periodical subscriptions health-care related.

BACCALAUREATE PROGRAMS

Degree BSN

Available Programs ADN to Baccalaureate; Accelerated RN Baccalaureate.

Site Options Johnstown, PA; Altoona, PA.

Study Options Full-time and part-time.

Program Entrance Requirements Transcript of college record, CPR certification, health exam, high school transcript, immunizations, RN licensure. Transfer students are accepted. *Application deadline:* Applications may be processed on a rolling basis for some programs. *Application fee:* $30.

Advanced Placement Credit by examination available. Credit given for nursing courses completed elsewhere dependent upon specific evaluations.

Expenses (2009–10) *Tuition:* full-time $18,740; part-time $480 per credit. *International tuition:* $18,740 full-time. *Room and board:* $8100; room only: $4550 per academic year. *Required fees:* full-time $700; part-time $105 per term.

Financial Aid 90% of baccalaureate students in nursing programs received some form of financial aid in 2008–09. *Gift aid (need-based):* Federal Pell, FSEOG, state, private, college/university gift aid from institutional funds. *Loans:* Federal Nursing Student Loans, FFEL (Subsidized and Unsubsidized Stafford PLUS), Perkins, alternative loans. *Work-study:* Federal Work-Study. *Financial aid application deadline (priority):* 2/15.

Contact Dr. Nickole M. Tickerhoof George, Chairperson, RN-BSN Program, Department of Nursing, Mount Aloysius College, 7373 Admiral Peary Highway, Cresson, PA 16630. *Telephone:* 814-886-6393. *Fax:* 814-886-6374. *E-mail:* ngeorge@mtaloy.edu.

CONTINUING EDUCATION PROGRAM

Contact Ms. Dawn Hudak, Program Coordinator, Center for Lifelong Learning, Department of Nursing, Mount Aloysius College, 7373 Admiral Peary Highway, Cresson, PA 16630. *Telephone:* 814-886-6537. *Fax:* 814-886-2978. *E-mail:* dhudak@mtaloy.edu.

Neumann University
Program in Nursing and Health Sciences
Aston, Pennsylvania

http://www.neumann.edu

Founded in 1965

DEGREES • BS • MS

Nursing Program Faculty 31 (5% with doctorates).

Baccalaureate Enrollment 503
Women 93% **Men** 7% **Minority** 15% **International** 2% **Part-time** 22%

Graduate Enrollment 22
Women 100% **Minority** 5% **Part-time** 100%

Nursing Student Activities Nursing Honor Society, Sigma Theta Tau, Student Nurses' Association.

Nursing Student Resources Academic advising; academic or career counseling; assistance for students with disabilities; bookstore; campus computer network; career placement assistance; computer lab; computer-assisted instruction; daycare for children of students; e-mail services; employment services for current students; externships; housing assistance; interactive nursing skills videos; Internet; learning resource lab; library services; nursing audiovisuals; paid internships; remedial services; resume preparation assistance; skills, simulation, or other laboratory; tutoring; unpaid internships.

Library Facilities 75,000 volumes (3,956 in health, 1,170 in nursing); 400 periodical subscriptions (155 health-care related).

BACCALAUREATE PROGRAMS

Degree BS

Available Programs Baccalaureate for Second Degree; Generic Baccalaureate; International Nurse to Baccalaureate; RN Baccalaureate.

Study Options Full-time and part-time.

Program Entrance Requirements Minimum overall college GPA of 2.5, transcript of college record, CPR certification, health exam, health insurance, high school biology, high school chemistry, high school foreign language, 2 years high school math, 3 years high school science, high school transcript, immunizations, minimum high school GPA of 2.5, minimum GPA in nursing prerequisites of 2.5, prerequisite course work. Transfer students are accepted. *Application deadline:* Applications may be processed on a rolling basis for some programs. *Application fee:* $25.

Advanced Placement Credit by examination available. Credit given for nursing courses completed elsewhere dependent upon specific evaluations.

Expenses (2009–10) *Tuition:* full-time $10,290; part-time $470 per credit hour. *International tuition:* $10,290 full-time. *Room and board:* $4953; room only: $2866 per academic year. *Required fees:* full-time $1800; part-time $900 per term.

Financial Aid 95% of baccalaureate students in nursing programs received some form of financial aid in 2008–09. *Gift aid (need-based):* Federal Pell, FSEOG, state, private, college/university gift aid from institutional funds. *Loans:* Federal Nursing Student Loans, Federal Direct (Subsidized and Unsubsidized Stafford PLUS), FFEL (Subsidized and Unsubsidized Stafford PLUS), Perkins. *Work-study:* Federal Work-Study, part-time campus jobs. *Financial aid application deadline:* Continuous.

Contact Miss Sarah Reddon, Admissions Counselor, Program in Nursing and Health Sciences, Neumann University, One Neumann Drive, Aston, PA 19014-1298. *Telephone:* 800-963-8626 Ext. 5531. *Fax:* 610-558-5652. *E-mail:* nursediv@neumann.edu.

GRADUATE PROGRAMS

Expenses (2009–10) *Tuition:* part-time $570 per credit hour.

Financial Aid 50% of graduate students in nursing programs received some form of financial aid in 2008–09. Available to part-time students. *Application deadline:* 3/15.

Contact Ms. Kittie Pain, Admissions Counselor, Program in Nursing and Health Sciences, Neumann University, One Neumann Drive, Aston, PA 19014-1298. *Telephone:* 800-963-8626 Ext. 5613. *Fax:* 610-558-5652. *E-mail:* nursediv@neumann.edu.

MASTER'S DEGREE PROGRAM

Degree MS

Available Programs Master's; RN to Master's.

Concentrations Available Nursing education. *Clinical nurse specialist programs in:* gerontology. *Nurse practitioner programs in:* gerontology.

Study Options Full-time and part-time.

Program Entrance Requirements Computer literacy, minimum overall college GPA of 3.0, transcript of college record, CPR certification, immunizations, interview, 2 letters of recommendation, nursing research course, physical assessment course, professional liability insurance/malpractice insurance, prerequisite course work, statistics course, GRE or MAT. *Application deadline:* Applications may be processed on a rolling basis for some programs. *Application fee:* $25.

Advanced Placement Credit by examination available. Credit given for nursing courses completed elsewhere dependent upon specific evaluations.

Degree Requirements 43 total credit hours.

POST-MASTER'S PROGRAM

Areas of Study Nursing education. *Clinical nurse specialist programs in:* gerontology. *Nurse practitioner programs in:* gerontology.

Penn State University Park

School of Nursing
State College, University Park, Pennsylvania

http://www.hhdev.psu.edu/nurs

Founded in 1855

DEGREES • BS • MS • MSN/PHD • PHD

Nursing Program Faculty 110 (20% with doctorates).

Baccalaureate Enrollment 824
Women 95% **Men** 5% **Minority** 7% **Part-time** 43%

Graduate Enrollment 61
Women 92% **Men** 8% **Minority** 10% **Part-time** 59%

Distance Learning Courses Available.

Nursing Student Activities Sigma Theta Tau, Student Nurses' Association.

Nursing Student Resources Academic advising; academic or career counseling; assistance for students with disabilities; bookstore; campus computer network; career placement assistance; computer lab; computer-assisted instruction; daycare for children of students; e-mail services; employment services for current students; externships; housing assistance; interactive nursing skills videos; Internet; learning resource lab; library services; nursing audiovisuals; paid internships; remedial services; resume preparation assistance; skills, simulation, or other laboratory; tutoring.

Library Facilities 5.1 million volumes (244,000 in health); 71,230 periodical subscriptions (3,500 health-care related).

BACCALAUREATE PROGRAMS

Degree BS

Available Programs ADN to Baccalaureate; Generic Baccalaureate; RN Baccalaureate.

Site Options Uniontown, PA; New Kensington, PA; Harrisburg, PA; Hershey, PA; University Park, PA; Altoona, PA; Mont Alto, PA; Sharon, PA; Scranton, PA.

Study Options Full-time.

Online Degree Options Yes.

Program Entrance Requirements Transcript of college record, 3 years high school math, 3 years high school science, high school transcript. Transfer students are accepted. *Application deadline:* 11/30 (fall). *Application fee:* $50.

Advanced Placement Credit given for nursing courses completed elsewhere dependent upon specific evaluations.

Expenses (2008–09) *Tuition, state resident:* part-time $6507 per semester. *Tuition, nonresident:* part-time $12,124 per semester. *Room and board:* $7670; room only: $4110 per academic year.

Financial Aid 80% of baccalaureate students in nursing programs received some form of financial aid in 2007–08.

Contact Ms. Diane Jankura, Academic Advisor for Undergraduate Programs, School of Nursing, Penn State University Park, 210 Health and Human Development East, University Park, PA 16802. *Telephone:* 814-863-8185. *Fax:* 814-863-2925. *E-mail:* dle2@psu.edu.

GRADUATE PROGRAMS

Expenses (2008–09) *Tuition, state resident:* part-time $7388 per semester. *Tuition, nonresident:* part-time $13,196 per semester. *Room and board:* $11,420; room only: $7860 per academic year.

Financial Aid 70% of graduate students in nursing programs received some form of financial aid in 2007–08.

Contact Ms. Xiao Sheng, Graduate Program Staff Assisstant, School of Nursing, Penn State University Park, 210 Health and Human Development East, University Park, PA 16802. *Telephone:* 814-863-2211. *Fax:* 814-865-2925. *E-mail:* xus1@psu.edu.

MASTER'S DEGREE PROGRAM

Degrees MS; MSN/PhD

Available Programs Master's.

Concentrations Available Nursing administration. *Clinical nurse specialist programs in:* adult health, community health, gerontology. *Nurse practitioner programs in:* adult health, family health.

Site Options Hershey, PA; University Park, PA.

Study Options Full-time and part-time.

Online Degree Options Yes.

Program Entrance Requirements Computer literacy, minimum overall college GPA of 3.0, transcript of college record, CPR certification, written essay, immunizations, 2 letters of recommendation, professional liability insurance/malpractice insurance. *Application deadline:* Applications may be processed on a rolling basis for some programs. *Application fee:* $65.

Advanced Placement Credit given for nursing courses completed elsewhere dependent upon specific evaluations.

Degree Requirements 43 total credit hours, thesis or project.

POST-MASTER'S PROGRAM

Areas of Study *Nurse practitioner programs in:* family health.

DOCTORAL DEGREE PROGRAM

Degree PhD

Available Programs Doctorate.

Areas of Study Bio-behavioral research, faculty preparation, gerontology, human health and illness, illness and transition, individualized study, nursing research, nursing science.

Site Options Hershey, PA; University Park, PA.

Program Entrance Requirements Minimum overall college GPA of 3.5, interview, 3 letters of recommendation, MSN or equivalent, writing sample. Application deadline: Applications may be processed on a rolling basis for some programs. Application fee: $65.

Degree Requirements 58 total credit hours, dissertation, oral exam, written exam, residency.

POSTDOCTORAL PROGRAM

Areas of Study Gerontology.

Postdoctoral Program Contact Dr. Janice Penrod, Associate Professor, School of Nursing, Penn State University Park, 306 Health and Human Development East, University Park, PA 16802. *Telephone:* 814-865-9337. *Fax:* 814-865-2925. *E-mail:* jlp198@psu.edu.

CONTINUING EDUCATION PROGRAM

Contact Ms. Madeline Mattern, Coordinator, Outreach Programs, School of Nursing, Penn State University Park, 204 Health and Human Development East, University Park, PA 16802. *Telephone:* 814-865-8469. *Fax:* 814-865-3779. *E-mail:* mfm107@psu.edu.

Pennsylvania College of Technology

School of Health Sciences
Williamsport, Pennsylvania

Founded in 1965

DEGREE • BSN

Nursing Program Faculty 37 (5% with doctorates).

Baccalaureate Enrollment 12
Women 100% **International** 1% **Part-time** 92%

Nursing Student Activities Student Nurses' Association.

Pennsylvania College of Technology (continued)

Nursing Student Resources Academic advising; academic or career counseling; assistance for students with disabilities; bookstore; campus computer network; career placement assistance; computer lab; computer-assisted instruction; daycare for children of students; e-mail services; employment services for current students; externships; housing assistance; interactive nursing skills videos; Internet; learning resource lab; library services; nursing audiovisuals; placement services for program completers; remedial services; resume preparation assistance; skills, simulation, or other laboratory; tutoring.

Library Facilities 126,609 volumes; 16,600 periodical subscriptions.

BACCALAUREATE PROGRAMS

Degree BSN

Available Programs RN Baccalaureate.

Program Entrance Requirements Transfer students are accepted.

Contact *Telephone:* 800-367-9222 Ext. 4525.

Robert Morris University
School of Nursing and Health Sciences
Moon Township, Pennsylvania

http://www.rmu.edu

Founded in 1921

DEGREES • BSN • DNP • MSN

Nursing Program Faculty 2 (60% with doctorates).

Baccalaureate Enrollment 228
Women 84% **Men** 16% **Minority** 6% **Part-time** 18%

Graduate Enrollment 158
Women 88% **Men** 12% **Minority** 6% **International** 1% **Part-time** 100%

Distance Learning Courses Available.

Nursing Student Activities Sigma Theta Tau, Student Nurses' Association.

Nursing Student Resources Academic advising; academic or career counseling; assistance for students with disabilities; bookstore; campus computer network; career placement assistance; computer lab; computer-assisted instruction; e-mail services; employment services for current students; externships; housing assistance; interactive nursing skills videos; Internet; learning resource lab; library services; nursing audiovisuals; paid internships; placement services for program completers; remedial services; resume preparation assistance; skills, simulation, or other laboratory; tutoring; unpaid internships.

Library Facilities 122,650 volumes (4,548 in health, 2,784 in nursing); 582 periodical subscriptions (2,280 health-care related).

BACCALAUREATE PROGRAMS

Degree BSN

Available Programs Baccalaureate for Second Degree; Generic Baccalaureate.

Study Options Full-time.

Program Entrance Requirements Minimum overall college GPA of 3.0, transcript of college record, written essay, health exam, health insurance, high school biology, high school chemistry, 2 years high school math, 2 years high school science, high school transcript, immunizations, 2 letters of recommendation, minimum high school GPA of 3.0, minimum GPA in nursing prerequisites of 2.0, prerequisite course work. Transfer students are accepted. *Application deadline:* 5/1 (fall), 11/1 (spring). Applications may be processed on a rolling basis for some programs. *Application fee:* $30.

Advanced Placement Credit given for nursing courses completed elsewhere dependent upon specific evaluations.

Expenses (2009–10) *Tuition:* full-time $21,940; part-time $730 per credit hour. *International tuition:* $21,940 full-time. *Room and board:* $10,370; room only: $5010 per academic year. *Required fees:* full-time $1202; part-time $30 per credit.

Financial Aid 80% of baccalaureate students in nursing programs received some form of financial aid in 2008–09. *Gift aid (need-based):* Federal Pell, FSEOG, state, private, college/university gift aid from institutional funds. *Loans:* FFEL (Subsidized and Unsubsidized Stafford PLUS), Perkins, alternative private loans. *Work-study:* Federal Work-Study, part-time campus jobs. *Financial aid application deadline:* Continuous.

Contact Enrollment Services, School of Nursing and Health Sciences, Robert Morris University, 6001 University Boulevard, Moon Township, PA 15108-1189. *Telephone:* 412-397-5200. *Fax:* 412-397-2425. *E-mail:* admissionsoffice@rmu.edu.

GRADUATE PROGRAMS

Expenses (2009–10) *Tuition:* full-time $21,945; part-time $740 per credit hour. *Room and board:* $10,370; room only: $5010 per academic year. *Required fees:* part-time $15 per credit.

Financial Aid 80% of graduate students in nursing programs received some form of financial aid in 2008–09. Federal Work-Study, institutionally sponsored loans, and unspecified assistantships available. *Financial aid application deadline:* 5/1.

Contact Enrollment Services, School of Nursing and Health Sciences, Robert Morris University, 6001 University Boulevard, Moon Township, PA 15108-1189. *Telephone:* 412-397-5200. *Fax:* 412-397-2425. *E-mail:* GraduateAdmissions@rmu.edu.

MASTER'S DEGREE PROGRAM

Degree MSN

Available Programs Master's.

Concentrations Available Nursing education.

Site Options Cranberry, PA.

Study Options Part-time.

Program Entrance Requirements Clinical experience, minimum overall college GPA of 3.25, transcript of college record, CPR certification, written essay, 2 letters of recommendation, statistics course. *Application deadline:* Applications may be processed on a rolling basis for some programs. *Application fee:* $35.

Degree Requirements 36 total credit hours, comprehensive exam.

DOCTORAL DEGREE PROGRAM

Degree DNP

Available Programs Doctorate; Post-Baccalaureate Doctorate.

Areas of Study Advanced practice nursing, family health.

Program Entrance Requirements Clinical experience, minimum overall college GPA of 3.25, interview by faculty committee, 2 letters of recommendation, vita, writing sample. Application deadline: Applications may be processed on a rolling basis for some programs. Application fee: $35.

Saint Francis University
Department of Nursing
Loretto, Pennsylvania

http://www.francis.edu/academic/Undergraduate/ Nursing/Nursinghome.shtml

Founded in 1847

DEGREE • BSN

Nursing Program Faculty 7 (2% with doctorates).

Baccalaureate Enrollment 81
Women 90% **Men** 10% **Minority** 2%

Nursing Student Activities Student Nurses' Association, nursing club.

Nursing Student Resources Academic advising; academic or career counseling; assistance for students with disabilities; bookstore; campus computer network; career placement assistance; computer lab; computer-assisted instruction; e-mail services; employment services for current students; externships; interactive nursing skills videos; Internet; learning resource lab; library services; nursing audiovisuals; resume preparation assistance; skills, simulation, or other laboratory; tutoring.

Library Facilities 124,000 volumes (120,000 in nursing); 16,400 periodical subscriptions.

BACCALAUREATE PROGRAMS

Degree BSN

Available Programs Generic Baccalaureate; RN Baccalaureate.

Study Options Full-time and part-time.

Program Entrance Requirements Transcript of college record, high school biology, high school chemistry, 2 years high school math, 2 years high school science, high school transcript, minimum high school GPA of 3.0, minimum high school rank 50%, minimum GPA in nursing prerequisites of 2.0, prerequisite course work. Transfer students are accepted. *Application deadline:* Applications may be processed on a rolling basis for some programs. *Application fee:* $30.

Advanced Placement Credit by examination available. Credit given for nursing courses completed elsewhere dependent upon specific evaluations.

Expenses (2009–10) *Room and board:* $4654; room only: $2190 per academic year.

Financial Aid 100% of baccalaureate students in nursing programs received some form of financial aid in 2008–09.

Contact Dr. Lisa J. Devineni, PhD, Chairperson, Department of Nursing, Saint Francis University, PO Box 600, 117 Evergreen Drive, 103 Schwab Hall, Loretto, PA 15940-0600. *Telephone:* 814-472-3027. *Fax:* 814-472-3849. *E-mail:* ldevineni@francis.edu.

Slippery Rock University of Pennsylvania
Department of Nursing
Slippery Rock, Pennsylvania

http://www.sru.edu/pages/1791.asp

Founded in 1889

DEGREE • BSN

Nursing Program Faculty 7 (86% with doctorates).

Baccalaureate Enrollment 227

Women 95% **Men** 5% **Minority** 1% **Part-time** 95%

Distance Learning Courses Available.

Nursing Student Activities Sigma Theta Tau.

Nursing Student Resources Academic advising; academic or career counseling; assistance for students with disabilities; bookstore; campus computer network; career placement assistance; computer lab; computer-assisted instruction; daycare for children of students; e-mail services; employment services for current students; housing assistance; Internet; library services; nursing audiovisuals; placement services for program completers; resume preparation assistance; tutoring.

Library Facilities 513,194 volumes (7,214 in health, 925 in nursing); 500 periodical subscriptions (1,299 health-care related).

BACCALAUREATE PROGRAMS

Degree BSN

Available Programs ADN to Baccalaureate; RN Baccalaureate.

Study Options Full-time and part-time.

Online Degree Options Yes (online only).

Program Entrance Requirements Minimum overall college GPA of 2.5, transcript of college record, minimum GPA in nursing prerequisites of 2.5, professional liability insurance/malpractice insurance, prerequisite course work, RN licensure. Transfer students are accepted. *Application deadline:* Applications may be processed on a rolling basis for some programs. *Application fee:* $30.

Advanced Placement Credit by examination available. Credit given for nursing courses completed elsewhere dependent upon specific evaluations.

Expenses (2009–10) *Tuition, state resident:* full-time $3617; part-time $937 per course. *Tuition, nonresident:* full-time $3797; part-time $983 per course. *Required fees:* full-time $1840; part-time $141 per credit.

Financial Aid 45% of baccalaureate students in nursing programs received some form of financial aid in 2008–09. *Gift aid (need-based):* Federal Pell, FSEOG, state, private, college/university gift aid from institutional funds. *Loans:* FFEL (Subsidized and Unsubsidized Stafford PLUS), Perkins. *Work-study:* Federal Work-Study, part-time campus jobs. *Financial aid application deadline (priority):* 2/15.

Contact Dr. Judith A. DePalma, RN, Professor and Chair, Department of Nursing, Department of Nursing, Slippery Rock University of Pennsylvania, 119 Behavioral Science Building, Slippery Rock, PA 16057. *Telephone:* 724-738-4921. *Fax:* 724-738-2509. *E-mail:* judith.depalma@sru.edu.

Temple University
Department of Nursing
Philadelphia, Pennsylvania

http://www.temple.edu/nursing

Founded in 1884

DEGREES • BSN • MSN

Nursing Program Faculty 37 (50% with doctorates).

Baccalaureate Enrollment 350

Women 85% **Men** 15% **Minority** 49% **Part-time** 62%

Graduate Enrollment 40

Women 95% **Men** 5% **Minority** 16% **Part-time** 100%

Nursing Student Activities Sigma Theta Tau, Student Nurses' Association.

Nursing Student Resources Academic advising; academic or career counseling; assistance for students with disabilities; bookstore; campus computer network; career placement assistance; computer lab; computer-assisted instruction; e-mail services; externships; housing assistance; interactive nursing skills videos; Internet; learning resource lab; library services; nursing audiovisuals; remedial services; resume preparation assistance; skills, simulation, or other laboratory; tutoring.

Library Facilities 3.2 million volumes (60,374 in health, 1,350 in nursing); 51,198 periodical subscriptions (1,350 health-care related).

BACCALAUREATE PROGRAMS

Degree BSN

Available Programs Accelerated Baccalaureate for Second Degree; Generic Baccalaureate; RN Baccalaureate.

Site Options Ambler, PA; Philadelphia, PA; Bethlehem, PA.

Study Options Full-time.

Program Entrance Requirements Minimum overall college GPA of 3.0, transcript of college record, CPR certification, written essay, health exam, health insurance, high school biology, high school chemistry, high school foreign language, 3 years high school math, 3 years high school science, high school transcript, immunizations, interview, minimum high school GPA of 2.0, minimum GPA in nursing prerequisites of 3.0, prerequisite course work. Transfer students are accepted.

Advanced Placement Credit given for nursing courses completed elsewhere dependent upon specific evaluations.

Contact *Telephone:* 215-707-4688. *Fax:* 215-707-1599.

GRADUATE PROGRAMS

Contact *Telephone:* 215-707-3789. *Fax:* 215-707-1599.

MASTER'S DEGREE PROGRAM

Degree MSN

Available Programs Master's.

Concentrations Available Nursing education. *Clinical nurse specialist programs in:* psychiatric/mental health. *Nurse practitioner programs in:* adult health, family health, pediatric.

Site Options Philadelphia, PA.

Study Options Full-time and part-time.

Program Entrance Requirements Clinical experience, minimum overall college GPA of 3.0, transcript of college record, CPR certification, written essay, immunizations, interview, 2 letters of recommendation, nursing research course, physical assessment course, professional liability insurance/malpractice insurance, statistics course, GRE General Test.

Temple University (continued)

Advanced Placement Credit given for nursing courses completed elsewhere dependent upon specific evaluations.

Degree Requirements 36 total credit hours.

POST-MASTER'S PROGRAM

Areas of Study Nursing education. *Clinical nurse specialist programs in:* psychiatric/mental health. *Nurse practitioner programs in:* adult health, family health, pediatric.

Thomas Jefferson University
Department of Nursing
Philadelphia, Pennsylvania

http://www.tju.edu

Founded in 1824

DEGREES • BSN • DNP • MSN

Nursing Program Faculty 38 (42% with doctorates).

Nursing Student Activities Nursing Honor Society, Sigma Theta Tau, Student Nurses' Association.

Nursing Student Resources Academic advising; academic or career counseling; assistance for students with disabilities; bookstore; campus computer network; career placement assistance; computer lab; computer-assisted instruction; e-mail services; interactive nursing skills videos; Internet; learning resource lab; library services; nursing audiovisuals; paid internships; placement services for program completers; remedial services; resume preparation assistance; skills, simulation, or other laboratory; tutoring.

Library Facilities 170,000 volumes (146,000 in health, 4,700 in nursing); 2,290 periodical subscriptions (2,100 health-care related).

BACCALAUREATE PROGRAMS

Degree BSN

Available Programs ADN to Baccalaureate; Accelerated Baccalaureate; Accelerated Baccalaureate for Second Degree; Accelerated RN Baccalaureate; Baccalaureate for Second Degree; Generic Baccalaureate; RN Baccalaureate.

Site Options Atlantic City, NJ; Philadelphia, PA.

Study Options Full-time and part-time.

Program Entrance Requirements Minimum overall college GPA of 2.9, transcript of college record, CPR certification, written essay, health exam, health insurance, high school transcript, immunizations, 2 letters of recommendation, prerequisite course work. Transfer students are accepted.

Advanced Placement Credit by examination available. Credit given for nursing courses completed elsewhere dependent upon specific evaluations.

Contact Dr. Sandra Krafft, Associate Dean, Undergraduate Programs, Department of Nursing, Thomas Jefferson University, 130 South Ninth Street, Edison Building, Suite 1230B, Philadelphia, PA 19107. *Telephone:* 215-503-8104. *Fax:* 215-503-0376. *E-mail:* Sandra.Krafft@jefferson.edu.

GRADUATE PROGRAMS

Contact Dr. Beth Ann Swan, Associate Dean, Graduate Programs, Department of Nursing, Thomas Jefferson University, 130 South Ninth Street, Suite 1200, Philadelphia, PA 19107. *Telephone:* 215-503-8057. *Fax:* 215-932-1468. *E-mail:* beth.swan@jefferson.edu.

MASTER'S DEGREE PROGRAM

Degree MSN

Available Programs Accelerated Master's; Accelerated RN to Master's; Master's; Master's for Non-Nursing College Graduates; Master's for Nurses with Non-Nursing Degrees; RN to Master's.

Concentrations Available Nurse anesthesia; nursing education; nursing informatics. *Clinical nurse specialist programs in:* acute care, adult health, community health, critical care, home health care, medical-surgical, oncology, pediatric, public health. *Nurse practitioner programs in:* acute care, adult health, family health, neonatal health, oncology, pediatric.

Site Options Philadelphia, PA.

Study Options Full-time and part-time.

Program Entrance Requirements Clinical experience, computer literacy, minimum overall college GPA of 3.0, transcript of college record, CPR certification, written essay, interview, 3 letters of recommendation, nursing research course, physical assessment course, professional liability insurance/malpractice insurance, resume, statistics course.

Advanced Placement Credit given for nursing courses completed elsewhere dependent upon specific evaluations.

Degree Requirements 36 total credit hours.

POST-MASTER'S PROGRAM

Areas of Study Nursing education; nursing informatics. *Nurse practitioner programs in:* acute care, adult health, family health, neonatal health, oncology, pediatric.

DOCTORAL DEGREE PROGRAM

Degree DNP

Available Programs Doctorate.

Areas of Study Advanced practice nursing, clinical practice, individualized study.

Program Entrance Requirements Clinical experience, minimum overall college GPA of 3.2, interview by faculty committee, interview, 3 letters of recommendation, MSN or equivalent, scholarly papers, statistics course, vita, writing sample.

Degree Requirements 36 total credit hours, written exam, residency.

CONTINUING EDUCATION PROGRAM

Contact Dr. Beth Ann Swan, Associate Dean, Graduate Programs, Department of Nursing, Thomas Jefferson University, 130 South Ninth Street, Suite 1200, Philadelphia, PA 19107. *Telephone:* 215-503-8057. *Fax:* 215-503-0376. *E-mail:* beth.swan@jefferson.edu.

See full description on page 520.

University of Pennsylvania
School of Nursing
Philadelphia, Pennsylvania

http://www.nursing.upenn.edu

Founded in 1740

DEGREES • BSN • MSN • MSN/MPH • MSN/PHD • PHD

Nursing Program Faculty 338 (17% with doctorates).

Baccalaureate Enrollment 544
Women 91% **Men** 9% **Minority** 28% **International** 2% **Part-time** 2%

Graduate Enrollment 498
Women 92% **Men** 8% **Minority** 17% **International** 10% **Part-time** 59%

Nursing Student Activities Nursing Honor Society, Sigma Theta Tau, Student Nurses' Association.

Nursing Student Resources Academic advising; academic or career counseling; assistance for students with disabilities; bookstore; campus computer network; career placement assistance; computer lab; computer-assisted instruction; daycare for children of students; e-mail services; employment services for current students; externships; housing assistance; interactive nursing skills videos; Internet; learning resource lab; library services; nursing audiovisuals; other; paid internships; placement services for program completers; remedial services; resume preparation assistance; skills, simulation, or other laboratory; tutoring; unpaid internships.

Library Facilities 5.8 million volumes; 50,252 periodical subscriptions.

BACCALAUREATE PROGRAMS

Degree BSN

Available Programs ADN to Baccalaureate; Accelerated Baccalaureate; Accelerated Baccalaureate for Second Degree; Accelerated RN Baccalaureate; Baccalaureate for Second Degree; Generic Baccalaureate; RN Baccalaureate.

Study Options Full-time and part-time.

Program Entrance Requirements Minimum overall college GPA of 3.0, transcript of college record, written essay, health exam, health insurance, high school biology, high school chemistry, high school foreign language, 4 years high school math, 4 years high school science, high school transcript, immunizations, interview, 2 letters of recommendation, minimum high school GPA of 3.0, minimum high school rank 10%. Transfer students are accepted. *Application deadline:* 1/1 (fall). *Application fee:* $70.

Advanced Placement Credit by examination available. Credit given for nursing courses completed elsewhere dependent upon specific evaluations.

Financial Aid 96% of baccalaureate students in nursing programs received some form of financial aid in 2008–09.

Contact Office of Enrollment Management, School of Nursing, University of Pennsylvania, 418 Curie Boulevard, Philadelphia, PA 19104-4217. *Telephone:* 215-898-4271. *Fax:* 215-573-8439. *E-mail:* admissions@nursing.upenn.edu.

GRADUATE PROGRAMS

Financial Aid 94% of graduate students in nursing programs received some form of financial aid in 2008–09. Fellowships, research assistantships, teaching assistantships, institutionally sponsored loans, scholarships, traineeships, and unspecified assistantships available. *Financial aid application deadline:* 12/15.

Contact Office of Enrollment Management, School of Nursing, University of Pennsylvania, 418 Curie Boulevard, Philadelphia, PA 19104-4217. *Telephone:* 215-898-4271. *Fax:* 215-573-8439. *E-mail:* admissions@nursing.upenn.edu.

MASTER'S DEGREE PROGRAM

Degrees MSN; MSN/MPH; MSN/PhD

Available Programs Accelerated AD/RN to Master's; Accelerated Master's for Non-Nursing College Graduates; Accelerated RN to Master's; Master's.

Concentrations Available Health-care administration; nurse anesthesia; nurse-midwifery; nursing administration. *Clinical nurse specialist programs in:* adult health, pediatric, psychiatric/mental health. *Nurse practitioner programs in:* acute care, adult health, family health, gerontology, neonatal health, primary care, psychiatric/mental health, women's health.

Study Options Full-time and part-time.

Program Entrance Requirements Clinical experience, computer literacy, minimum overall college GPA of 3.0, transcript of college record, CPR certification, written essay, immunizations, interview, 3 letters of recommendation, prerequisite course work, resume, statistics course, GRE General Test. *Application deadline:* 7/1 (fall), 12/1 (winter), 11/1 (spring), 3/1 (summer). Applications may be processed on a rolling basis for some programs. *Application fee:* $70.

Advanced Placement Credit given for nursing courses completed elsewhere dependent upon specific evaluations.

Degree Requirements 36 total credit hours.

POST-MASTER'S PROGRAM

Areas of Study Health-care administration; nurse anesthesia; nurse-midwifery; nursing administration; nursing education. *Clinical nurse specialist programs in:* acute care, adult health, critical care, family health, gerontology, home health care, maternity-newborn, medical-surgical, oncology, pediatric, psychiatric/mental health. *Nurse practitioner programs in:* acute care, adult health, family health, gerontology, neonatal health, oncology, pediatric, primary care, psychiatric/mental health, women's health.

DOCTORAL DEGREE PROGRAM

Degree PhD

Available Programs Doctorate; Post-Baccalaureate Doctorate.

Areas of Study Addiction/substance abuse, aging, bio-behavioral research, biology of health and illness, clinical practice, community health, critical care, ethics, faculty preparation, family health, gerontology, health policy, health promotion/disease prevention, health-care systems, human health and illness, illness and transition, individualized study, information systems, maternity-newborn, neuro-behavior, nursing administration, nursing policy, nursing research, nursing science, oncology, urban health, women's health.

Program Entrance Requirements Minimum overall college GPA of 3.5, interview by faculty committee, interview, 3 letters of recommendation, MSN or equivalent, statistics course, vita, writing sample, GRE General Test. Application deadline: 12/1 (fall). Application fee: $70.

Degree Requirements 39 total credit hours, dissertation, oral exam, written exam, residency.

POSTDOCTORAL PROGRAM

Areas of Study Adolescent health, aging, cancer care, chronic illness, community health, family health, gerontology, health promotion/disease prevention, individualized study, nursing informatics, nursing interventions, nursing research, nursing science, outcomes, self-care, vulnerable population, women's health.

Postdoctoral Program Contact Dr. Linda A. McCauley, Associate Dean for Nursing Research, School of Nursing, University of Pennsylvania, 418 Curie Boulevard, 427 Claire M. Fagan Hall, Philadelphia, PA 19104-4271. *Telephone:* 215-898-3151. *E-mail:* research@nursing.upenn.edu.

CONTINUING EDUCATION PROGRAM

Contact Janet L. Tomcavage, Program Management, School of Nursing, University of Pennsylvania, 418 Curie Boulevard, Philadelphia, PA 19104-4271. *Telephone:* 215-898-5422. *E-mail:* tomcavag@nursing.upenn.edu.

University of Pittsburgh
School of Nursing
Pittsburgh, Pennsylvania

http://www.nursing.pitt.edu/

Founded in 1787

DEGREES • BSN • MSN • PHD

Nursing Program Faculty 106 (61% with doctorates).

Baccalaureate Enrollment 610
Women 89% **Men** 11% **Minority** 10% **International** .3% **Part-time** 4%

Graduate Enrollment 338
Women 86% **Men** 14% **Minority** 9% **International** 3% **Part-time** 53%

Distance Learning Courses Available.

Nursing Student Activities Sigma Theta Tau, Student Nurses' Association.

Nursing Student Resources Academic advising; academic or career counseling; assistance for students with disabilities; bookstore; campus computer network; career placement assistance; computer lab; computer-assisted instruction; daycare for children of students; e-mail services; employment services for current students; externships; housing assistance; interactive nursing skills videos; Internet; learning resource lab; library services; nursing audiovisuals; paid internships; placement services for program completers; remedial services; resume preparation assistance; skills, simulation, or other laboratory; tutoring.

Library Facilities 5.1 million volumes (386,000 in health, 7,000 in nursing); 48,637 periodical subscriptions (4,650 health-care related).

BACCALAUREATE PROGRAMS

Degree BSN

Available Programs Accelerated Baccalaureate for Second Degree; Generic Baccalaureate; RN Baccalaureate.

Site Options Bradford, PA; Johnstown, PA.

Study Options Full-time.

Program Entrance Requirements Minimum overall college GPA of 3.3, transcript of college record, written essay, health insurance, high school biology, high school chemistry, 4 years high school math, 3 years high school science, high school transcript, 2 letters of recommendation, minimum high school GPA of 3.3, minimum GPA in nursing prerequisites of 3.0. Transfer students are accepted. *Application deadline:* Applications may be processed on a rolling basis for some programs. *Application fee:* $50.

Advanced Placement Credit by examination available.

Expenses (2009–10) *Tuition, state resident:* full-time $16,798; part-time $699 per credit. *Tuition, nonresident:* full-time $29,284; part-time $1220 per credit. *International tuition:* $29,284 full-time. *Room and board:* $5600; room only: $2850 per academic year. *Required fees:* full-time $838.

University of Pittsburgh (continued)

Financial Aid 67% of baccalaureate students in nursing programs received some form of financial aid in 2008–09. *Gift aid (need-based):* Federal Pell, FSEOG, state, private, college/university gift aid from institutional funds, Federal Nursing. *Loans:* Federal Nursing Student Loans, FFEL (Subsidized and Unsubsidized Stafford PLUS), Perkins, college/university. *Work-study:* Federal Work-Study. *Financial aid application deadline (priority):* 3/1.

Contact Ms. Mary Rodgers Schubert, Associate Director of Recruitment, School of Nursing, University of Pittsburgh, 239 Victoria Building, 3500 Victoria Street, Pittsburgh, PA 15261. *Telephone:* 412-624-1291. *Fax:* 412-624-2409. *E-mail:* mschuber@pitt.edu.

GRADUATE PROGRAMS

Expenses (2009–10) *Tuition, state resident:* full-time $19,232; part-time $786 per credit. *Tuition, nonresident:* full-time $23,702; part-time $970 per credit. *International tuition:* $23,702 full-time. *Required fees:* full-time $706.

Financial Aid 64% of graduate students in nursing programs received some form of financial aid in 2008–09. 21 research assistantships with full and partial tuition reimbursements available (averaging $8,796 per year), 3 teaching assistantships with full and partial tuition reimbursements available (averaging $8,790 per year) were awarded; institutionally sponsored loans, scholarships, traineeships, and unspecified assistantships also available. Aid available to part-time students. *Financial aid application deadline:* 7/1.

Contact Ms. Mary Rodgers Schubert, Associate Director of Recruitment, School of Nursing, University of Pittsburgh, 239 Victoria Building, 3500 Victoria Street, Pittsburgh, PA 15261. *Telephone:* 412-624-1291. *Fax:* 412-624-2409. *E-mail:* mschuber@pitt.edu.

MASTER'S DEGREE PROGRAM

Degree MSN

Available Programs Master's; RN to Master's.

Concentrations Available Clinical nurse leader; nurse anesthesia; nursing administration; nursing education; nursing informatics. *Clinical nurse specialist programs in:* medical-surgical, psychiatric/mental health. *Nurse practitioner programs in:* acute care, adult health, family health, neonatal health, pediatric, psychiatric/mental health.

Site Options Bradford, PA; Johnstown, PA.

Study Options Full-time and part-time.

Online Degree Options Yes.

Program Entrance Requirements Clinical experience, minimum overall college GPA of 3.0, transcript of college record, written essay, immunizations, interview, 3 letters of recommendation, professional liability insurance/malpractice insurance, prerequisite course work, resume, statistics course, GRE or MAT. *Application deadline:* Applications may be processed on a rolling basis for some programs. *Application fee:* $50.

Advanced Placement Credit by examination available. Credit given for nursing courses completed elsewhere dependent upon specific evaluations.

Degree Requirements 52 total credit hours, comprehensive exam.

POST-MASTER'S PROGRAM

Areas of Study Nursing education; nursing informatics. *Nurse practitioner programs in:* acute care, psychiatric/mental health.

DOCTORAL DEGREE PROGRAM

Degree PhD

Available Programs Doctorate; Post-Baccalaureate Doctorate.

Areas of Study Bio-behavioral research, biology of health and illness, critical care, illness and transition, information systems, nursing research, nursing science, oncology, women's health.

Program Entrance Requirements Minimum overall college GPA of 3.5, interview by faculty committee, interview, 3 letters of recommendation, MSN or equivalent, statistics course, vita, writing sample, GRE. Application deadline: Applications may be processed on a rolling basis for some programs. Application fee: $50.

Degree Requirements 64 total credit hours, dissertation, oral exam, written exam, residency.

POSTDOCTORAL PROGRAM

Areas of Study Chronic illness, individualized study, nursing informatics, nursing research, nursing science, outcomes.

Postdoctoral Program Contact Dr. Judith A. Erlen, PhD Program Coordinator/Associate Director of Center for Research in Chronic Disorders, School of Nursing, University of Pittsburgh, 3500 Victoria Street, Pittsburgh, PA 15261. *Telephone:* 412-624-1905. *Fax:* 412-624-8521. *E-mail:* jae001@pitt.edu.

CONTINUING EDUCATION PROGRAM

Contact Mrs. Susan Albrecht, Interim Director of Continuing Education Program, School of Nursing, University of Pittsburgh, 225 Victoria Building, 3500 Victoria Street, Pittsburgh, PA 15261. *Telephone:* 412-624-3156. *E-mail:* conted@pitt.edu.

See full description on page 526.

University of Pittsburgh at Bradford
Department of Nursing
Bradford, Pennsylvania

http://www.upb.pitt.edu/academics/nursing.aspx

Founded in 1963

DEGREE • BSN

Nursing Program Faculty 7 (29% with doctorates).

Baccalaureate Enrollment 18
Women 78% **Men** 22% **Part-time** 39%

Distance Learning Courses Available.

Nursing Student Activities Nursing club.

Nursing Student Resources Academic advising; academic or career counseling; assistance for students with disabilities; bookstore; campus computer network; career placement assistance; computer lab; computer-assisted instruction; e-mail services; employment services for current students; externships; housing assistance; Internet; learning resource lab; library services; nursing audiovisuals; remedial services; resume preparation assistance; skills, simulation, or other laboratory; tutoring; unpaid internships.

Library Facilities 100,902 volumes (641 in health, 476 in nursing); 246 periodical subscriptions (37 health-care related).

BACCALAUREATE PROGRAMS

Degree BSN

Available Programs Generic Baccalaureate; RN Baccalaureate.

Site Options St. Marys, PA.

Study Options Full-time and part-time.

Program Entrance Requirements Transcript of college record, CPR certification, health exam, health insurance, high school transcript, immunizations, minimum high school GPA of 2.50, minimum GPA in nursing prerequisites of 2.5, professional liability insurance/malpractice insurance, prerequisite course work, RN licensure. Transfer students are accepted. *Application deadline:* Applications may be processed on a rolling basis for some programs. *Application fee:* $45.

Advanced Placement Credit by examination available. Credit given for nursing courses completed elsewhere dependent upon specific evaluations.

Expenses (2009–10) *Tuition, state resident:* full-time $14,104; part-time $587 per credit. *Tuition, nonresident:* full-time $26,236; part-time $1093 per credit. *International tuition:* $26,236 full-time. *Room and board:* $7480; room only: $4540 per academic year. *Required fees:* full-time $722; part-time $117 per term.

Financial Aid 88% of baccalaureate students in nursing programs received some form of financial aid in 2008–09. *Gift aid (need-based):* Federal Pell, FSEOG, state, private, college/university gift aid from institutional funds, Academic Competitiveness Grant, National Smart Grant. *Loans:* FFEL (Subsidized and Unsubsidized Stafford PLUS), Perkins. *Work-study:* Federal Work-Study, part-time campus jobs. *Financial aid application deadline (priority):* 3/1.

Contact Department of Nursing Admissions, Department of Nursing, University of Pittsburgh at Bradford, 300 Campus Drive, Bradford, PA 16701. *Telephone:* 800-872-1787.

The University of Scranton
Department of Nursing
Scranton, Pennsylvania

Founded in 1888
DEGREES • BS • MS

Nursing Program Faculty 40 (85% with doctorates).

Baccalaureate Enrollment 245
Women 94% **Men** 6% **Minority** 8% **Part-time** 7%

Graduate Enrollment 105
Women 70% **Men** 30% **Minority** 6% **Part-time** 50%

Nursing Student Activities Nursing Honor Society, Sigma Theta Tau, Student Nurses' Association, nursing club.

Nursing Student Resources Academic advising; academic or career counseling; bookstore; campus computer network; career placement assistance; computer lab; computer-assisted instruction; e-mail services; employment services for current students; interactive nursing skills videos; Internet; learning resource lab; library services; nursing audiovisuals; placement services for program completers; remedial services; resume preparation assistance; skills, simulation, or other laboratory; tutoring.

Library Facilities 383,984 volumes (28,400 in health, 8,484 in nursing); 23,572 periodical subscriptions (106 health-care related).

BACCALAUREATE PROGRAMS
Degree BS

Available Programs Accelerated LPN to Baccalaureate; Baccalaureate for Second Degree; Generic Baccalaureate; LPN to RN Baccalaureate; RN Baccalaureate.

Study Options Full-time and part-time.

Program Entrance Requirements Minimum overall college GPA of 2.5, transcript of college record, written essay, health exam, health insurance, high school biology, high school chemistry, high school foreign language, 3 years high school math, 3 years high school science, high school transcript, immunizations, minimum high school rank 30%. Transfer students are accepted.

Advanced Placement Credit by examination available. Credit given for nursing courses completed elsewhere dependent upon specific evaluations.

Expenses (2009–10) *Tuition:* full-time $32,824; part-time $693 per credit. *Room and board:* $5914; room only: $3577 per academic year.

Financial Aid 80% of baccalaureate students in nursing programs received some form of financial aid in 2008–09. *Gift aid (need-based):* Federal Pell, FSEOG, state, private, college/university gift aid from institutional funds, TEACH Grant. *Loans:* Federal Nursing Student Loans, Federal Direct (Subsidized and Unsubsidized Stafford PLUS), FFEL (Subsidized and Unsubsidized Stafford PLUS), Perkins. *Work-study:* Federal Work-Study, part-time campus jobs. *Financial aid application deadline (priority):* 2/15.

Contact Dr. Patricia Harrington, Chairperson, Department of Nursing, The University of Scranton, 800 Linden Street, McGurrin Hall, Scranton, PA 18510-4595. *Telephone:* 570-941-7673. *Fax:* 570-941-7903. *E-mail:* harringtonp1@scranton.edu.

GRADUATE PROGRAMS
Expenses (2009–10) *Tuition:* part-time $813 per credit hour.
Financial Aid 90% of graduate students in nursing programs received some form of financial aid in 2008–09. 8 teaching assistantships with full and partial tuition reimbursements available (averaging $5,913 per year) were awarded; career-related internships or fieldwork, Federal Work-Study, and unspecified assistantships also available. Aid available to part-time students. *Financial aid application deadline:* 3/1.

Contact Dr. Mary Jane Hanson, Director, Graduate Nursing Program, Department of Nursing, The University of Scranton, 800 Linden Street, McGurrin Hall, Scranton, PA 18510-4595. *Telephone:* 570-941-4060. *Fax:* 570-941-7093. *E-mail:* hansonm2@scranton.edu.

MASTER'S DEGREE PROGRAM
Degree MS

Available Programs Accelerated AD/RN to Master's; Accelerated RN to Master's; Master's; RN to Master's.

Concentrations Available Nurse anesthesia; nursing education. *Clinical nurse specialist programs in:* adult health. *Nurse practitioner programs in:* family health.

Study Options Full-time and part-time.

Program Entrance Requirements Clinical experience, minimum overall college GPA of 3.0, transcript of college record, CPR certification, written essay, immunizations, interview, 3 letters of recommendation, nursing research course, physical assessment course, professional liability insurance/malpractice insurance, prerequisite course work, statistics course. *Application fee:* $50.

Advanced Placement Credit given for nursing courses completed elsewhere dependent upon specific evaluations.

Degree Requirements 46 total credit hours, comprehensive exam.

POST-MASTER'S PROGRAM
Areas of Study Nurse anesthesia; nursing education. *Clinical nurse specialist programs in:* adult health. *Nurse practitioner programs in:* family health.

Villanova University
College of Nursing
Villanova, Pennsylvania

http://www.nursing.villanova.edu/
Founded in 1842
DEGREES • BSN • MSN • PHD

Nursing Program Faculty 86 (48% with doctorates).

Baccalaureate Enrollment 565
Women 95% **Men** 5% **Minority** 18% **International** 7% **Part-time** 5%

Graduate Enrollment 190
Women 86% **Men** 14% **Minority** 15% **International** 2% **Part-time** 85%

Distance Learning Courses Available.

Nursing Student Activities Nursing Honor Society, Sigma Theta Tau, Student Nurses' Association, nursing club.

Nursing Student Resources Academic advising; academic or career counseling; assistance for students with disabilities; bookstore; campus computer network; career placement assistance; computer lab; computer-assisted instruction; e-mail services; employment services for current students; externships; housing assistance; interactive nursing skills videos; Internet; learning resource lab; library services; nursing audiovisuals; remedial services; resume preparation assistance; skills, simulation, or other laboratory; tutoring.

Library Facilities 720,500 volumes (22,441 in health, 15,574 in nursing); 12,000 periodical subscriptions (1,900 health-care related).

BACCALAUREATE PROGRAMS
Degree BSN

Available Programs ADN to Baccalaureate; Accelerated Baccalaureate for Second Degree; Baccalaureate for Second Degree; Generic Baccalaureate; International Nurse to Baccalaureate; RN Baccalaureate.

Site Options Philadelphia, PA.

Study Options Full-time and part-time.

Program Entrance Requirements Minimum overall college GPA of 2.75, transcript of college record, written essay, health exam, health insurance, high school biology, high school chemistry, high school foreign language, 3 years high school math, 3 years high school science, high school transcript, immunizations, 2 letters of recommendation, minimum high school GPA of 3.0. Transfer students are accepted. *Application deadline:* 11/1 (fall), 1/7 (winter). *Application fee:* $75.

Advanced Placement Credit by examination available. Credit given for nursing courses completed elsewhere dependent upon specific evaluations.

Villanova University (continued)

Expenses (2009–10) *Tuition:* full-time $38,240; part-time $1595 per credit. *International tuition:* $38,240 full-time. *Room and board:* $10,110; room only: $5460 per academic year. *Required fees:* full-time $580; part-time $115 per term.

Financial Aid 66% of baccalaureate students in nursing programs received some form of financial aid in 2008–09. *Gift aid (need-based):* Federal Pell, FSEOG, state, private, college/university gift aid from institutional funds, endowed and restricted grants. *Loans:* Federal Nursing Student Loans, FFEL (Subsidized and Unsubsidized Stafford PLUS), Perkins, Villanova Loan. *Work-study:* Federal Work-Study, part-time campus jobs. *Financial aid application deadline (priority):* 2/7.

Contact Dr. M. Frances Keen, Assistant Dean and Director, Undergraduate Program, College of Nursing, Villanova University, Driscoll Hall, 800 Lancaster Avenue, Villanova, PA 19085-1690. *Telephone:* 610-519-4926. *Fax:* 610-519-7650. *E-mail:* frances.keen@villanova.edu.

GRADUATE PROGRAMS

Expenses (2009–10) *Tuition:* full-time $6120; part-time $680 per credit. *International tuition:* $6120 full-time. *Required fees:* full-time $60; part-time $60 per term.

Financial Aid 52% of graduate students in nursing programs received some form of financial aid in 2008–09. 5 teaching assistantships with full tuition reimbursements available (averaging $12,165 per year) were awarded; institutionally sponsored loans, scholarships, traineeships, tuition waivers (full), and unspecified assistantships also available. *Financial aid application deadline:* 3/1.

Contact Dr. Marguerite K. Schlag, Assistant Dean and Director, Graduate Program, College of Nursing, Villanova University, Driscoll Hall, 800 Lancaster Avenue, Villanova, PA 19085-1690. *Telephone:* 610-519-4934. *Fax:* 610-519-7997. *E-mail:* marguerite.schlag@villanova.edu.

MASTER'S DEGREE PROGRAM

Degree MSN

Available Programs Accelerated Master's; Master's; RN to Master's.

Concentrations Available Health-care administration; nurse anesthesia; nursing education. *Nurse practitioner programs in:* adult health, family health, gerontology, pediatric.

Study Options Full-time and part-time.

Program Entrance Requirements Clinical experience, computer literacy, minimum overall college GPA of 3.0, transcript of college record, CPR certification, written essay, immunizations, 3 letters of recommendation, physical assessment course, professional liability insurance/malpractice insurance, prerequisite course work, resume, statistics course, GRE or MAT. *Application deadline:* 11/1 (fall), 4/1 (spring), 7/1 (summer). Applications may be processed on a rolling basis for some programs. *Application fee:* $50.

Advanced Placement Credit given for nursing courses completed elsewhere dependent upon specific evaluations.

Degree Requirements 45 total credit hours, thesis or project.

POST-MASTER'S PROGRAM

Areas of Study Nurse anesthesia; nursing education. *Nurse practitioner programs in:* adult health, gerontology, pediatric.

DOCTORAL DEGREE PROGRAM

Degree PhD

Available Programs Doctorate.

Areas of Study Faculty preparation, nursing education, nursing research.

Program Entrance Requirements Clinical experience, minimum overall college GPA of 3.5, interview, 3 letters of recommendation, MSN or equivalent, scholarly papers, vita, writing sample, GRE. Application deadline: 1/15 (fall), 1/15 (summer). Application fee: $50.

Degree Requirements 51 total credit hours, dissertation, oral exam, written exam.

CONTINUING EDUCATION PROGRAM

Contact Dr. Lynore DeSilets, RN, Assistant Dean and Director, Continuing Education, College of Nursing, Villanova University, Driscoll Hall, 800 Lancaster Avenue, Villanova, PA 19085-1690. *Telephone:* 610-519-4931. *Fax:* 610-519-6780. *E-mail:* lyn.desilets@villanova.edu.

Waynesburg University
Department of Nursing
Waynesburg, Pennsylvania

http://www.waynesburg.edu

Founded in 1849

DEGREES • BSN • DNP • MSN • MSN/MBA

Nursing Program Faculty 48 (39% with doctorates).

Baccalaureate Enrollment 337
Women 91% **Men** 9% **Minority** 1%

Graduate Enrollment 240
Women 95% **Men** 5% **Minority** 1% **Part-time** 95%

Nursing Student Activities Sigma Theta Tau, Student Nurses' Association.

Nursing Student Resources Academic advising; academic or career counseling; assistance for students with disabilities; bookstore; campus computer network; career placement assistance; computer lab; computer-assisted instruction; e-mail services; employment services for current students; externships; Internet; learning resource lab; library services; nursing audiovisuals; paid internships; placement services for program completers; remedial services; resume preparation assistance; skills, simulation, or other laboratory; tutoring.

Library Facilities 100,000 volumes (4,500 in nursing); 1,206 periodical subscriptions (46 health-care related).

BACCALAUREATE PROGRAMS

Degree BSN

Available Programs Accelerated Baccalaureate; Accelerated Baccalaureate for Second Degree; Generic Baccalaureate; LPN to Baccalaureate.

Site Options Monroeville, PA; Canonsburg, PA; Wexford, PA.

Study Options Full-time.

Program Entrance Requirements Minimum overall college GPA of 3.0, transcript of college record, CPR certification, health exam, high school biology, high school chemistry, 2 years high school math, 2 years high school science, high school transcript, immunizations, minimum high school GPA of 3.0, minimum GPA in nursing prerequisites of 3.0, professional liability insurance/malpractice insurance, prerequisite course work. Transfer students are accepted. *Application deadline:* Applications may be processed on a rolling basis for some programs. *Application fee:* $75.

Advanced Placement Credit by examination available.

Expenses (2009–10) *Tuition:* full-time $17,400. *International tuition:* $17,400 full-time. *Room and board:* $7370; room only: $3750 per academic year. *Required fees:* full-time $400.

Financial Aid 90% of baccalaureate students in nursing programs received some form of financial aid in 2008–09. *Gift aid (need-based):* Federal Pell, FSEOG, state, private, college/university gift aid from institutional funds. *Loans:* Federal Nursing Student Loans, FFEL (Subsidized and Unsubsidized Stafford PLUS), Perkins. *Work-study:* Federal Work-Study. *Financial aid application deadline:* Continuous.

Contact Nancy R. Mosser, EdD, Director/Chairperson, Department of Nursing, Waynesburg University, 51 West College Street, Waynesburg, PA 15370-1222. *Telephone:* 724-852-3356. *Fax:* 724-852-3220. *E-mail:* nmosser@waynesburg.edu.

GRADUATE PROGRAMS

Expenses (2009–10) *Tuition:* part-time $520 per credit hour.

Financial Aid 50% of graduate students in nursing programs received some form of financial aid in 2008–09.

Contact Dr. Lynette Jack, Director of Graduate and Professional Studies Program, Department of Nursing, Waynesburg University, 1001 Corporate Drive, Canonsburg, PA 15317. *Telephone:* 724-743-2256. *Fax:* 724-743-4425. *E-mail:* ljack@waynesburg.edu.

MASTER'S DEGREE PROGRAM

Degrees MSN; MSN/MBA

Available Programs Accelerated Master's; Accelerated Master's for Nurses with Non-Nursing Degrees; Accelerated RN to Master's.

Concentrations Available Nursing administration; nursing education.

Site Options Monroeville, PA; Canonsburg, PA; Wexford, PA.

Study Options Part-time.

Program Entrance Requirements Clinical experience, computer literacy, minimum overall college GPA of 3.0, transcript of college record, 2 letters of recommendation, resume. *Application deadline:* Applications may be processed on a rolling basis for some programs. *Application fee:* $75.

Degree Requirements 36 total credit hours, thesis or project.

DOCTORAL DEGREE PROGRAM

Degree DNP

Available Programs Doctorate; Post-Baccalaureate Doctorate.

Areas of Study Advanced practice nursing, health-care systems, nursing administration.

Site Options Monroeville, PA.

Program Entrance Requirements Minimum overall college GPA of 3.0, interview by faculty committee, interview, letters of recommendation, MSN or equivalent, statistics course, vita, writing sample. Application deadline: Applications may be processed on a rolling basis for some programs.

Degree Requirements 80 total credit hours, oral exam, written exam, residency.

West Chester University of Pennsylvania
Department of Nursing
West Chester, Pennsylvania

http://health-sciences.wcupa.edu/nursing

Founded in 1871

DEGREES • BSN • MSN

Nursing Program Faculty 20 (30% with doctorates).

Baccalaureate Enrollment 332
Women 91.9% **Men** 8.1% **Minority** 12% **International** .3% **Part-time** 20.1%

Graduate Enrollment 39
Women 91.3% **Men** 8.7% **Part-time** 84.6%

Nursing Student Activities Nursing Honor Society, Sigma Theta Tau, Student Nurses' Association.

Nursing Student Resources Academic advising; academic or career counseling; assistance for students with disabilities; bookstore; campus computer network; career placement assistance; computer lab; computer-assisted instruction; daycare for children of students; e-mail services; employment services for current students; externships; housing assistance; interactive nursing skills videos; Internet; learning resource lab; library services; nursing audiovisuals; remedial services; resume preparation assistance; skills, simulation, or other laboratory; tutoring.

Library Facilities 1.3 million volumes (88 in nursing); 8,493 periodical subscriptions (173 health-care related).

BACCALAUREATE PROGRAMS

Degree BSN

Available Programs Accelerated RN Baccalaureate; Generic Baccalaureate.

Study Options Full-time and part-time.

Program Entrance Requirements Minimum overall college GPA, transcript of college record, written essay, health exam, health insurance, high school biology, high school chemistry, 2 years high school math, 2 years high school science, high school transcript, immunizations, minimum high school GPA, minimum high school rank, minimum GPA in nursing prerequisites. Transfer students are accepted.

Advanced Placement Credit given for nursing courses completed elsewhere dependent upon specific evaluations.

Contact *Telephone:* 610-436-2219. *Fax:* 610-436-3083.

GRADUATE PROGRAMS

Contact *Telephone:* 610-436-2258. *Fax:* 610-436-3083.

MASTER'S DEGREE PROGRAM

Degree MSN

Available Programs Master's.

Concentrations Available *Clinical nurse specialist programs in:* community health.

Study Options Full-time and part-time.

Program Entrance Requirements Clinical experience, minimum overall college GPA of 2.5, transcript of college record, interview, 3 letters of recommendation, physical assessment course, professional liability insurance/malpractice insurance, resume, statistics course.

Advanced Placement Credit given for nursing courses completed elsewhere dependent upon specific evaluations.

Degree Requirements 39 total credit hours, thesis or project.

Widener University
School of Nursing
Chester, Pennsylvania

http://www.widener.edu

Founded in 1821

DEGREES • BSN • MSN • MSN/PHD • PHD

Nursing Program Faculty 59 (30% with doctorates).

Baccalaureate Enrollment 546
Women 89% **Men** 11% **Minority** 27% **International** 1% **Part-time** 15%

Graduate Enrollment 122
Women 92% **Men** 8% **Minority** 26% **Part-time** 84%

Distance Learning Courses Available.

Nursing Student Activities Nursing Honor Society, Sigma Theta Tau, Student Nurses' Association.

Nursing Student Resources Academic advising; academic or career counseling; assistance for students with disabilities; bookstore; campus computer network; career placement assistance; computer lab; computer-assisted instruction; e-mail services; employment services for current students; housing assistance; interactive nursing skills videos; Internet; learning resource lab; library services; nursing audiovisuals; placement services for program completers; remedial services; resume preparation assistance; skills, simulation, or other laboratory; tutoring.

Library Facilities 218,284 volumes (18,175 in health, 12,225 in nursing); 2,335 periodical subscriptions (275 health-care related).

BACCALAUREATE PROGRAMS

Degree BSN

Available Programs ADN to Baccalaureate; Generic Baccalaureate; RN Baccalaureate.

Study Options Full-time and part-time.

Program Entrance Requirements Transcript of college record, CPR certification, health exam, health insurance, high school biology, high school chemistry, high school foreign language, 3 years high school math, 3 years high school science, high school transcript, immunizations, 1 letter of recommendation, minimum high school GPA of 2.85, minimum GPA in nursing prerequisites of 2.75, professional liability insurance/malpractice insurance, prerequisite course work. Transfer students are accepted. *Application deadline:* Applications may be processed on a rolling basis for some programs. *Application fee:* $35.

Advanced Placement Credit by examination available. Credit given for nursing courses completed elsewhere dependent upon specific evaluations.

Expenses (2009–10) *Tuition:* full-time $31,340; part-time $1045 per credit. *International tuition:* $31,340 full-time. *Room and board:* $11,900; room only: $6600 per academic year. *Required fees:* full-time $500; part-time $250 per term.

Financial Aid 95% of baccalaureate students in nursing programs received some form of financial aid in 2008–09. *Gift aid (need-based):* Federal Pell, FSEOG, state, private, college/university gift aid from institutional funds, Federal Nursing. *Loans:* FFEL (Subsidized and Unsubsidized Stafford PLUS), Perkins. *Work-study:* Federal Work-Study, part-time campus jobs. *Financial aid application deadline (priority):* 2/15.

Widener University (continued)

Contact Dr. Kathleen Black, Associate Dean, Undergraduate Program, School of Nursing, Widener University, One University Place, Chester, PA 19013-5892. *Telephone:* 610-499-4211. *Fax:* 610-499-4216. *E-mail:* kblack@widener.edu.

GRADUATE PROGRAMS

Expenses (2009–10) *Tuition:* full-time $13,284; part-time $738 per credit. *International tuition:* $13,284 full-time. *Required fees:* full-time $155; part-time $75 per term.

Financial Aid 68% of graduate students in nursing programs received some form of financial aid in 2008–09. Career-related internships or fieldwork, Federal Work-Study, and traineeships available. Aid available to part-time students. *Financial aid application deadline:* 4/1.

Contact Dr. Mary B. Walker, Associate Dean for Graduate Studies, School of Nursing, Widener University, One University Place, Chester, PA 19013-5892. *Telephone:* 610-499-4208. *Fax:* 610-499-4216. *E-mail:* mbwalker@widener.edu.

MASTER'S DEGREE PROGRAM

Degrees MSN; MSN/PhD

Available Programs Master's; Master's for Nurses with Non-Nursing Degrees.

Concentrations Available Nursing education. *Clinical nurse specialist programs in:* adult health, community health, critical care, psychiatric/mental health. *Nurse practitioner programs in:* family health.

Site Options Harrisburg, PA.

Study Options Full-time and part-time.

Program Entrance Requirements Clinical experience, computer literacy, minimum overall college GPA of 3.0, transcript of college record, CPR certification, immunizations, interview, 2 letters of recommendation, nursing research course, physical assessment course, professional liability insurance/malpractice insurance, prerequisite course work, resume, statistics course, GRE General Test. *Application deadline:* 7/15 (fall), 11/15 (spring), 3/16 (summer). Applications may be processed on a rolling basis for some programs. *Application fee:* $35.

Advanced Placement Credit given for nursing courses completed elsewhere dependent upon specific evaluations.

Degree Requirements 42 total credit hours.

POST-MASTER'S PROGRAM

Areas of Study Nursing education. *Clinical nurse specialist programs in:* adult health, community health, critical care, psychiatric/mental health. *Nurse practitioner programs in:* family health.

DOCTORAL DEGREE PROGRAM

Degree PhD

Available Programs Doctorate.

Areas of Study Faculty preparation, nursing education, nursing research, nursing science.

Program Entrance Requirements Minimum overall college GPA of 3.5, interview, 2 letters of recommendation, MSN or equivalent, statistics course, vita, writing sample, GRE General Test. Application deadline: 7/15 (fall), 11/15 (spring), 3/17 (summer). Applications may be processed on a rolling basis for some programs. Application fee: $35.

Degree Requirements 63 total credit hours, dissertation, written exam.

Wilkes University
Department of Nursing
Wilkes-Barre, Pennsylvania

http://www.wilkes.edu

Founded in 1933

DEGREES • BS • MS

Nursing Program Faculty 25 (20% with doctorates).

Baccalaureate Enrollment 300
Women 90% **Men** 10% **Minority** 5% **Part-time** 15%

Graduate Enrollment 65
Women 85% **Men** 15% **Minority** 5% **Part-time** 75%

Distance Learning Courses Available.

Nursing Student Activities Sigma Theta Tau, Student Nurses' Association, nursing club.

Nursing Student Resources Academic advising; academic or career counseling; assistance for students with disabilities; bookstore; campus computer network; career placement assistance; computer lab; computer-assisted instruction; daycare for children of students; e-mail services; employment services for current students; externships; housing assistance; interactive nursing skills videos; Internet; learning resource lab; library services; nursing audiovisuals; paid internships; placement services for program completers; remedial services; resume preparation assistance; skills, simulation, or other laboratory; tutoring; unpaid internships.

Library Facilities 13,450 volumes in health, 13,000 volumes in nursing; 70 periodical subscriptions health-care related.

BACCALAUREATE PROGRAMS

Degree BS

Available Programs ADN to Baccalaureate; Accelerated Baccalaureate for Second Degree; Accelerated LPN to Baccalaureate; Accelerated RN Baccalaureate; Generic Baccalaureate; LPN to RN Baccalaureate; RN Baccalaureate.

Study Options Full-time and part-time.

Program Entrance Requirements Minimum overall college GPA of 2.0, transcript of college record, CPR certification, health exam, health insurance, high school biology, high school chemistry, 2 years high school math, 3 years high school science, high school transcript, immunizations, minimum high school GPA, professional liability insurance/malpractice insurance. Transfer students are accepted.

Advanced Placement Credit by examination available. Credit given for nursing courses completed elsewhere dependent upon specific evaluations.

Contact *Telephone:* 570-408-4074. *Fax:* 570-408-7807.

GRADUATE PROGRAMS

Contact *Telephone:* 570-408-4078. *Fax:* 570-408-7807.

MASTER'S DEGREE PROGRAM

Degree MS

Available Programs Accelerated AD/RN to Master's; Accelerated RN to Master's; Master's; Master's for Non-Nursing College Graduates; RN to Master's.

Concentrations Available Nursing administration; nursing education. *Clinical nurse specialist programs in:* gerontology, psychiatric/mental health.

Study Options Full-time and part-time.

Program Entrance Requirements Clinical experience, minimum overall college GPA of 3.0, transcript of college record, CPR certification, immunizations, interview, 3 letters of recommendation, nursing research course, physical assessment course, professional liability insurance/malpractice insurance, statistics course.

Advanced Placement Credit given for nursing courses completed elsewhere dependent upon specific evaluations.

Degree Requirements 37 total credit hours, thesis or project.

POST-MASTER'S PROGRAM

Areas of Study Nursing administration; nursing education. *Clinical nurse specialist programs in:* gerontology, psychiatric/mental health.

CONTINUING EDUCATION PROGRAM

Contact *Telephone:* 570-408-4462.

York College of Pennsylvania
Department of Nursing
York, Pennsylvania

http://www.ycp.edu/nursing/index.html

Founded in 1787

DEGREES • BS • MS

Nursing Program Faculty 63 (11% with doctorates).

Baccalaureate Enrollment 588
Women 94% **Men** 6% **Minority** 4% **Part-time** 6%

Graduate Enrollment 65
Women 98% **Men** 2% **Minority** 1% **International** 1% **Part-time** 47%

Distance Learning Courses Available.

Nursing Student Activities Nursing Honor Society, Sigma Theta Tau, Student Nurses' Association, nursing club.

Nursing Student Resources Academic advising; academic or career counseling; assistance for students with disabilities; bookstore; campus computer network; career placement assistance; computer lab; computer-assisted instruction; e-mail services; employment services for current students; externships; housing assistance; interactive nursing skills videos; Internet; learning resource lab; library services; nursing audiovisuals; paid internships; placement services for program completers; remedial services; resume preparation assistance; skills, simulation, or other laboratory; tutoring.

Library Facilities 250,642 volumes (6,681 in health, 1,226 in nursing); 31,713 periodical subscriptions (83 health-care related).

BACCALAUREATE PROGRAMS

Degree BS

Available Programs Generic Baccalaureate; LPN to RN Baccalaureate; RN Baccalaureate.

Site Options Chambersburg, PA; Hanover, PA; Harrisburg, PA.

Study Options Full-time and part-time.

Program Entrance Requirements Minimum overall college GPA of 2.8, transcript of college record, CPR certification, written essay, health exam, health insurance, high school biology, high school chemistry, 1 year of high school math, high school science, high school transcript, immunizations, 2 letters of recommendation, minimum high school rank 40%, minimum GPA in nursing prerequisites of 2.8, professional liability insurance/malpractice insurance, prerequisite course work. *Application deadline:* Applications may be processed on a rolling basis for some programs.

Advanced Placement Credit by examination available. Credit given for nursing courses completed elsewhere dependent upon specific evaluations.

Expenses (2009–10) *Tuition:* full-time $14,460; part-time $385 per credit. *International tuition:* $14,460 full-time. *Room and board:* $8080 per academic year. *Required fees:* full-time $1080; part-time $90 per credit.

Financial Aid 90% of baccalaureate students in nursing programs received some form of financial aid in 2008–09. *Gift aid (need-based):* Federal Pell, FSEOG, state, private, college/university gift aid from institutional funds. *Loans:* Federal Nursing Student Loans, Federal Direct (Subsidized and Unsubsidized Stafford PLUS), FFEL (Subsidized and Unsubsidized Stafford PLUS), Perkins, college/university. *Work-study:* Federal Work-Study, part-time campus jobs. *Financial aid application deadline (priority):* 3/1.

Contact Dr. Jacquelin H. Harrington, RN, Chairperson, Department of Nursing, York College of Pennsylvania, York, PA 17405-7199. *Telephone:* 717-815-1420. *Fax:* 717-849-1651. *E-mail:* jharring@ycp.edu.

GRADUATE PROGRAMS

Expenses (2009–10) *Tuition:* part-time $578 per credit. *Room and board:* $8080 per academic year. *Required fees:* part-time $298 per credit.

Financial Aid 8% of graduate students in nursing programs received some form of financial aid in 2008–09.

Contact Dr. Lynn Warner, RN, Coordinator, Department of Nursing, York College of Pennsylvania, York, PA 17405-7199. *Telephone:* 717-815-1212. *Fax:* 717-849-1651.

MASTER'S DEGREE PROGRAM

Degree MS

Available Programs Master's; RN to Master's.

Concentrations Available Nurse anesthesia; nursing administration; nursing education. *Clinical nurse specialist programs in:* adult health. *Nurse practitioner programs in:* adult health.

Site Options Chambersburg, PA; Hanover, PA; Harrisburg, PA.

Study Options Part-time.

Program Entrance Requirements Clinical experience, computer literacy, minimum overall college GPA of 3.0, transcript of college record, CPR certification, written essay, immunizations, 2 letters of recommendation, nursing research course, physical assessment course, professional

liability insurance/malpractice insurance, resume, statistics course. *Application deadline:* 5/30 (fall). Applications may be processed on a rolling basis for some programs. *Application fee:* $75.

Advanced Placement Credit given for nursing courses completed elsewhere dependent upon specific evaluations.

Degree Requirements 41 total credit hours, thesis or project.

POST-MASTER'S PROGRAM

Areas of Study *Clinical nurse specialist programs in:* adult health. *Nurse practitioner programs in:* adult health.

PUERTO RICO

Inter American University of Puerto Rico, Arecibo Campus
Nursing Program
Arecibo, Puerto Rico

Founded in 1957

DEGREE • BS

Library Facilities 73,642 volumes; 640 periodical subscriptions.

BACCALAUREATE PROGRAMS

Degree BS

Available Programs Generic Baccalaureate.

Contact Undergraduate Program, Nursing Program, Inter American University of Puerto Rico, Arecibo Campus, Arecibo, PR 00614-4050. *Telephone:* 787-878-5475.

Inter American University of Puerto Rico, Metropolitan Campus
Carmen Torres de Tiburcio School of Nursing
San Juan, Puerto Rico

http://www.metro.inter.edu/progacad/enfe/ nursing/index.html

Founded in 1960

DEGREE • BSN

Nursing Program Faculty 26 (27% with doctorates).

Baccalaureate Enrollment 312
Women 57% **Men** 43%

Nursing Student Activities Student Nurses' Association.

Nursing Student Resources Academic advising; academic or career counseling; assistance for students with disabilities; bookstore; campus computer network; career placement assistance; computer lab; computer-assisted instruction; daycare for children of students; e-mail services; employment services for current students; externships; interactive nursing skills videos; Internet; learning resource lab; library services; nursing audiovisuals; paid internships; placement services for program completers; remedial services; skills, simulation, or other laboratory; tutoring.

Library Facilities 171,173 volumes (36,000 in health, 21,759 in nursing); 41,660 periodical subscriptions (2,090 health-care related).

BACCALAUREATE PROGRAMS

Degree BSN

Available Programs ADN to Baccalaureate; Accelerated Baccalaureate; Generic Baccalaureate.

Study Options Full-time and part-time.

Inter American University of Puerto Rico, Metropolitan Campus (continued)

Program Entrance Requirements Minimum overall college GPA of 2.0, transcript of college record, CPR certification, health exam, health insurance, high school transcript, immunizations, 2 letters of recommendation, minimum high school rank 4%, minimum GPA in nursing prerequisites of 2. Transfer students are accepted.

Advanced Placement Credit by examination available. Credit given for nursing courses completed elsewhere dependent upon specific evaluations.

Contact *Telephone:* 787-763-3066. *Fax:* 787-250-1242 Ext. 2159.

Pontifical Catholic University of Puerto Rico

Department of Nursing
Ponce, Puerto Rico

http://www.pucpr.edu/catalogo/espanol/ciencias/ dep_enf.htm

Founded in 1948

DEGREE • BSN

Library Facilities 304,693 volumes (1,499 in nursing); 90,588 periodical subscriptions.

BACCALAUREATE PROGRAMS

Degree BSN

Available Programs Generic Baccalaureate.

Program Entrance Requirements Minimum overall college GPA of 2.0, CPR certification, health exam, health insurance, immunizations, interview, letters of recommendation, minimum high school GPA of 2.5, prerequisite course work.

Contact *Telephone:* 787-841-2000 Ext. 1604.

Universidad Adventista de las Antillas

Department of Nursing
Mayagüez, Puerto Rico

Founded in 1957

DEGREE • BSN

Nursing Program Faculty 11 (18% with doctorates).

Baccalaureate Enrollment 257
Women 69% **Men** 31% **Minority** 100% **International** 13% **Part-time** 1%

Nursing Student Activities Nursing club.

Nursing Student Resources Academic advising; academic or career counseling; assistance for students with disabilities; campus computer network; computer lab; computer-assisted instruction; e-mail services; employment services for current students; housing assistance; interactive nursing skills videos; Internet; learning resource lab; library services; nursing audiovisuals; remedial services; resume preparation assistance; skills, simulation, or other laboratory; tutoring; unpaid internships.

Library Facilities 2,488 volumes in health, 1,556 volumes in nursing; 29 periodical subscriptions health-care related.

BACCALAUREATE PROGRAMS

Degree BSN

Available Programs Generic Baccalaureate; RN Baccalaureate.
Study Options Full-time.

Program Entrance Requirements Minimum overall college GPA of 2.3, transcript of college record, health exam, health insurance, high school transcript, immunizations, interview, 2 letters of recommendation, minimum high school GPA of 2.5. Transfer students are accepted.

Advanced Placement Credit given for nursing courses completed elsewhere dependent upon specific evaluations.

Contact *Telephone:* 787-834-9595 Ext. 2209. *Fax:* 787-834-9597.

CONTINUING EDUCATION PROGRAM

Contact *Telephone:* 787-834-9595 Ext. 2284. *Fax:* 787-834-9597.

Universidad del Turabo

Nursing Program
Gurabo, Puerto Rico

Founded in 1972

DEGREE • BS

BACCALAUREATE PROGRAMS

Degree BS

Available Programs Generic Baccalaureate.

Contact *Telephone:* 787-743-7979.

Universidad Metropolitana

Department of Nursing
San Juan, Puerto Rico

http://www.suagm.edu/umet/umet_new_web/ escuelas/ciencias_tecnologia/ciencias_tecnologia. htm

Founded in 1980

DEGREE • BSN

Library Facilities 5,438 volumes in health; 110 periodical subscriptions health-care related.

BACCALAUREATE PROGRAMS

Degree BSN

Contact *Telephone:* 787-766-1717 Ext. 6422. *Fax:* 787-769-7663.

University of Puerto Rico at Arecibo

Department of Nursing
Arecibo, Puerto Rico

http://upra.edu/asuntosacademicos/enfermeria/ menu_enfe.htm

Founded in 1967

DEGREE • BSN

Nursing Program Faculty 21
Library Facilities 65,000 volumes; 3,660 periodical subscriptions.

BACCALAUREATE PROGRAMS

Degree BSN

Available Programs Generic Baccalaureate.
Contact *Telephone:* 787-878-2830. *Fax:* 787-880-4972.

University of Puerto Rico at Humacao

Department of Nursing
Humacao, Puerto Rico

http://cuhwww.upr.clu.edu/~enfe/

Founded in 1962

DEGREE • BS

Nursing Program Faculty 16 (12% with doctorates).
Nursing Student Activities Student Nurses' Association.
Nursing Student Resources Skills, simulation, or other laboratory.
Library Facilities 52,634 volumes; 136 periodical subscriptions.

BACCALAUREATE PROGRAMS

Degree BS

Available Programs Generic Baccalaureate.
Study Options Full-time and part-time.
Program Entrance Requirements Minimum overall college GPA, transcript of college record, health exam, health insurance, high school transcript, immunizations, minimum high school GPA of 2.0, minimum GPA in nursing prerequisites of 2.5. Transfer students are accepted.
Advanced Placement Credit by examination available. Credit given for nursing courses completed elsewhere dependent upon specific evaluations.
Contact *Telephone:* 787-850-9346. *Fax:* 787-850-9411.

University of Puerto Rico, Mayagüez Campus

Department of Nursing
Mayagüez, Puerto Rico

http://www.uprm.edu/enfe/

Founded in 1911

DEGREE • BSN

Nursing Program Faculty 21 (10% with doctorates).
Nursing Student Activities Nursing Honor Society, Sigma Theta Tau, Student Nurses' Association.
Nursing Student Resources Academic advising; academic or career counseling; assistance for students with disabilities; bookstore; campus computer network; career placement assistance; computer lab; computer-assisted instruction; e-mail services; employment services for current students; interactive nursing skills videos; Internet; learning resource lab; library services; nursing audiovisuals; paid internships; placement services for program completers; remedial services; resume preparation assistance; skills, simulation, or other laboratory; tutoring.
Library Facilities 921,392 volumes; 590,716 periodical subscriptions (68 health-care related).

BACCALAUREATE PROGRAMS

Degree BSN

Available Programs Generic Baccalaureate.
Study Options Full-time.
Program Entrance Requirements High school transcript, immunizations. Transfer students are accepted.
Advanced Placement Credit by examination available.
Contact *Telephone:* 787-263-3482. *Fax:* 787-832-3875.

CONTINUING EDUCATION PROGRAM

Contact *Telephone:* 787-265-3842. *Fax:* 787-832-3875.

University of Puerto Rico, Medical Sciences Campus

School of Nursing
San Juan, Puerto Rico

Founded in 1950

DEGREES • BSN • MSN

Nursing Program Faculty 37 (25% with doctorates).
Baccalaureate Enrollment 241
Women 85% **Men** 15% **Part-time** 12%
Graduate Enrollment 158
Women 79% **Men** 21% **Part-time** 6%
Nursing Student Activities Sigma Theta Tau, Student Nurses' Association.
Nursing Student Resources Academic advising; academic or career counseling; assistance for students with disabilities; computer lab; computer-assisted instruction; e-mail services; employment services for current students; interactive nursing skills videos; Internet; library services; nursing audiovisuals; skills, simulation, or other laboratory; tutoring.
Library Facilities 7,830 volumes in health, 1,143 volumes in nursing; 1,215 periodical subscriptions health-care related.

BACCALAUREATE PROGRAMS

Degree BSN

Available Programs ADN to Baccalaureate; Generic Baccalaureate.
Study Options Full-time and part-time.
Program Entrance Requirements Minimum overall college GPA of 2.0, transcript of college record, health exam, immunizations, interview, minimum high school GPA of 2.0, prerequisite course work. Transfer students are accepted.
Contact *Telephone:* 787-758-2525 Ext. 1984. *Fax:* 787-281-0721.

GRADUATE PROGRAMS

Contact *Telephone:* 787-758-2525 Ext. 3105. *Fax:* 787-281-0721.

MASTER'S DEGREE PROGRAM

Degree MSN

Available Programs Master's.
Concentrations Available Nurse anesthesia; nursing administration; nursing education. *Clinical nurse specialist programs in:* adult health, community health, critical care, gerontology, maternity-newborn, pediatric, psychiatric/mental health.
Site Options Mayaguez, PR.
Study Options Full-time and part-time.
Program Entrance Requirements Clinical experience, minimum overall college GPA of 2.5, transcript of college record, immunizations, interview, resume, statistics course, GRE or EXADEP.
Degree Requirements 48 total credit hours, thesis or project.

CONTINUING EDUCATION PROGRAM

Contact *Telephone:* 787-758-2525 Ext. 2102. *Fax:* 787-281-0721.

University of the Sacred Heart

Program in Nursing
San Juan, Puerto Rico

Founded in 1935

DEGREES • BSN • MSN

Nursing Student Resources Skills, simulation, or other laboratory.

BACCALAUREATE PROGRAMS

Degree BSN

Available Programs Generic Baccalaureate.
Contact *Telephone:* 787-728-1515. *Fax:* 787-727-1250.

University of the Sacred Heart (continued)
GRADUATE PROGRAMS
Contact *Telephone:* 787-728-1515 Ext. 2427. *Fax:* 787-727-1250.

MASTER'S DEGREE PROGRAM
Degree MSN

Available Programs Master's.

Concentrations Available *Nurse practitioner programs in:* occupational health.

Degree Requirements 37 total credit hours.

RHODE ISLAND

Rhode Island College
Department of Nursing
Providence, Rhode Island

http://www.ric.edu/nursing
Founded in 1854
DEGREES • BSN • MSN

Nursing Program Faculty 48 (40% with doctorates).

Baccalaureate Enrollment 432
Women 89% **Men** 11% **Minority** 24% **Part-time** 28%

Graduate Enrollment 22

Nursing Student Activities Sigma Theta Tau, Student Nurses' Association, nursing club.

Nursing Student Resources Academic advising; academic or career counseling; assistance for students with disabilities; bookstore; campus computer network; career placement assistance; computer lab; computer-assisted instruction; e-mail services; employment services for current students; housing assistance; interactive nursing skills videos; Internet; learning resource lab; library services; nursing audiovisuals; paid internships; remedial services; resume preparation assistance; skills, simulation, or other laboratory; tutoring.

Library Facilities 650,538 volumes (574 in nursing); 63 periodical subscriptions health-care related.

BACCALAUREATE PROGRAMS
Degree BSN

Available Programs Baccalaureate for Second Degree; Generic Baccalaureate; RN Baccalaureate.

Site Options Providence, RI; Pawtucket, RI.

Study Options Full-time and part-time.

Program Entrance Requirements Minimum overall college GPA of 2.7, CPR certification, health exam, health insurance, high school biology, high school chemistry, high school foreign language, 4 years high school math, 2 years high school science, high school transcript, immunizations, letters of recommendation, minimum GPA in nursing prerequisites of 2.0, prerequisite course work. Transfer students are accepted.

Advanced Placement Credit given for nursing courses completed elsewhere dependent upon specific evaluations.

Contact *Telephone:* 401-456-8014. *Fax:* 401-456-8206.

GRADUATE PROGRAMS
Contact *Telephone:* 401-456-9720. *Fax:* 401-456-8206.

MASTER'S DEGREE PROGRAM
Degree MSN

Available Programs Master's.

Concentrations Available *Clinical nurse specialist programs in:* acute care, community health, critical care.

Site Options Providence, RI; Pawtucket, RI.

Study Options Full-time and part-time.

Program Entrance Requirements Minimum overall college GPA of 3.0, transcript of college record, written essay, letters of recommendation, resume, statistics course.

Advanced Placement Credit given for nursing courses completed elsewhere dependent upon specific evaluations.

Degree Requirements 45 total credit hours, thesis or project.

Salve Regina University
Department of Nursing
Newport, Rhode Island

http://www.salve.edu/departments/nur/index.cfm
Founded in 1934
DEGREE • BS

Nursing Program Faculty 25 (16% with doctorates).

Baccalaureate Enrollment 141
Women 94% **Men** 6% **Minority** 4% **Part-time** 44%

Distance Learning Courses Available.

Nursing Student Activities Sigma Theta Tau, Student Nurses' Association, nursing club.

Nursing Student Resources Academic advising; academic or career counseling; assistance for students with disabilities; bookstore; campus computer network; career placement assistance; computer lab; computer-assisted instruction; e-mail services; housing assistance; interactive nursing skills videos; Internet; learning resource lab; library services; nursing audiovisuals; paid internships; resume preparation assistance; skills, simulation, or other laboratory; tutoring; unpaid internships.

Library Facilities 6,882 volumes in health, 1,081 volumes in nursing; 76 periodical subscriptions health-care related.

BACCALAUREATE PROGRAMS
Degree BS

Available Programs Generic Baccalaureate; RN Baccalaureate.

Site Options Pawtucket, RI; Warwick, RI; Providence, RI.

Study Options Full-time and part-time.

Program Entrance Requirements Minimum overall college GPA of 2.7, transcript of college record, written essay, high school biology, high school chemistry, high school foreign language, 3 years high school math, 3 years high school science, high school transcript, 2 letters of recommendation, minimum GPA in nursing prerequisites of 2.0, prerequisite course work. Transfer students are accepted. *Application deadline:* 2/1 (fall). Applications may be processed on a rolling basis for some programs. *Application fee:* $50.

Advanced Placement Credit by examination available. Credit given for nursing courses completed elsewhere dependent upon specific evaluations.

Expenses (2009–10) *Tuition:* full-time $29,800; part-time $993 per credit. *International tuition:* $29,800 full-time. *Room and board:* $10,950 per academic year. *Required fees:* full-time $200; part-time $40 per term.

Financial Aid 79% of baccalaureate students in nursing programs received some form of financial aid in 2008–09. *Gift aid (need-based):* Federal Pell, FSEOG, state, private, college/university gift aid from institutional funds. *Loans:* Federal Nursing Student Loans, FFEL (Subsidized and Unsubsidized Stafford PLUS), Perkins, college/university, alternative loans. *Work-study:* Federal Work-Study, part-time campus jobs. *Financial aid application deadline (priority):* 3/1.

Contact Mrs. Colleen Emerson, Dean of Undergraduate Admissions, Department of Nursing, Salve Regina University, 100 Ochre Point Avenue, Newport, RI 02840-4192. *Telephone:* 888-467-2583. *Fax:* 401-848-2823. *E-mail:* sruadmis@salve.edu.

CONTINUING EDUCATION PROGRAM
Contact Dr. Thomas Sabbagh, Dean, Continuing Education and Graduate Enrollment, Department of Nursing, Salve Regina University, Graduate Studies and Continuing Education Office, Newport, RI 02840-4192. *Telephone:* 800-637-0002. *Fax:* 401-341-2973. *E-mail:* thomas.sabbagh@salve.edu.

University of Rhode Island
College of Nursing
Kingston, Rhode Island

http://www.uri.edu/nursing

Founded in 1892

DEGREES • BS • MS • PHD

Nursing Program Faculty 47 (50% with doctorates).

Baccalaureate Enrollment 851
Women 87% **Men** 13% **Minority** 24% **International** 1% **Part-time** 10%
Graduate Enrollment 110
Women 95% **Men** 5% **Minority** 5% **International** 6% **Part-time** 75%
Nursing Student Activities Sigma Theta Tau, Student Nurses' Association.

Nursing Student Resources Academic advising; academic or career counseling; assistance for students with disabilities; bookstore; campus computer network; career placement assistance; computer lab; computer-assisted instruction; e-mail services; externships; housing assistance; interactive nursing skills videos; Internet; learning resource lab; library services; nursing audiovisuals; remedial services; resume preparation assistance; skills, simulation, or other laboratory; tutoring.

Library Facilities 1.2 million volumes; 7,926 periodical subscriptions.

BACCALAUREATE PROGRAMS

Degree BS

Available Programs ADN to Baccalaureate; Generic Baccalaureate; RN Baccalaureate.
Site Options Providence, RI.
Study Options Full-time and part-time.
Program Entrance Requirements Minimum overall college GPA of 2.5, transcript of college record, CPR certification, written essay, health exam, health insurance, high school foreign language, 3 years high school math, 2 years high school science, high school transcript, immunizations, 2 letters of recommendation, minimum high school rank 30%, minimum GPA in nursing prerequisites of 2.2. Transfer students are accepted.
Advanced Placement Credit given for nursing courses completed elsewhere dependent upon specific evaluations.
Expenses (2009–10) *Tuition, state resident:* full-time $9528. *Tuition, nonresident:* full-time $26,026. *Room and board:* $10,638 per academic year.
Financial Aid 70% of baccalaureate students in nursing programs received some form of financial aid in 2008–09. *Gift aid (need-based):* Federal Pell, FSEOG, state, private, college/university gift aid from institutional funds. *Loans:* Federal Nursing Student Loans, Federal Direct (Subsidized and Unsubsidized Stafford PLUS), Perkins, state, college/university. *Work-study:* Federal Work-Study. *Financial aid application deadline (priority):* 3/1.
Contact Undergraduate Admissions Office, College of Nursing, University of Rhode Island, Newman Hall, 14 Upper College Road, Kingston, RI 02881. *Telephone:* 401-874-7100.

GRADUATE PROGRAMS

Financial Aid 50% of graduate students in nursing programs received some form of financial aid in 2008–09.
Contact Dr. Mary Sullivan, Director of Graduate Programs, College of Nursing, University of Rhode Island, White Hall, Kingston, RI 02881. *Telephone:* 401-874-2766. *Fax:* 401-874-2061. *E-mail:* mcsullivan@uri.edu.

MASTER'S DEGREE PROGRAM

Degree MS

Available Programs Master's; RN to Master's.
Concentrations Available Clinical nurse leader; nursing administration; nursing education. *Clinical nurse specialist programs in:* gerontology, psychiatric/mental health. *Nurse practitioner programs in:* family health, gerontology.
Site Options Providence, RI.
Study Options Full-time and part-time.

Program Entrance Requirements Clinical experience, minimum overall college GPA of 3.0, transcript of college record, written essay, immunizations, 3 letters of recommendation, nursing research course, professional liability insurance/malpractice insurance, resume, statistics course.
Degree Requirements 41 total credit hours, thesis or project, comprehensive exam.

POST-MASTER'S PROGRAM

Areas of Study Nursing administration; nursing education. *Clinical nurse specialist programs in:* gerontology, psychiatric/mental health. *Nurse practitioner programs in:* family health, gerontology.

DOCTORAL DEGREE PROGRAM

Degree PhD

Available Programs Doctorate.
Areas of Study Nursing research, nursing science.
Program Entrance Requirements Clinical experience, minimum overall college GPA of 3.0, interview by faculty committee, 3 letters of recommendation, MSN or equivalent, scholarly papers, statistics course, vita, writing sample.
Degree Requirements 61 total credit hours, dissertation, oral exam, written exam, residency.

SOUTH CAROLINA

Charleston Southern University
Wingo School of Nursing
Charleston, South Carolina

http://www.csuniv.edu

Founded in 1964

DEGREES • BSN • MSN

Nursing Program Faculty 17 (29% with doctorates).

Baccalaureate Enrollment 95
Women 90% **Men** 10% **Minority** 25%
Graduate Enrollment 16
Distance Learning Courses Available.

Nursing Student Activities Sigma Theta Tau, Student Nurses' Association.

Nursing Student Resources Academic advising; academic or career counseling; assistance for students with disabilities; bookstore; campus computer network; career placement assistance; computer lab; computer-assisted instruction; e-mail services; externships; interactive nursing skills videos; Internet; learning resource lab; library services; nursing audiovisuals; remedial services; resume preparation assistance; skills, simulation, or other laboratory; tutoring.

Library Facilities 192,600 volumes (2,400 in health, 250 in nursing); 1,111 periodical subscriptions (55 health-care related).

BACCALAUREATE PROGRAMS

Degree BSN

Available Programs ADN to Baccalaureate; Generic Baccalaureate; RN Baccalaureate.
Study Options Full-time.
Program Entrance Requirements Minimum overall college GPA of 2.0, transcript of college record, CPR certification, written essay, health exam, health insurance, immunizations, minimum GPA in nursing prerequisites of 2.75, professional liability insurance/malpractice insurance, prerequisite course work. Transfer students are accepted. *Application deadline:* 3/15 (fall).
Advanced Placement Credit given for nursing courses completed elsewhere dependent upon specific evaluations.

Charleston Southern University (continued)

Expenses (2009–10) *Tuition:* full-time $19,238; part-time $400 per contact hour. *Room and board:* $7394 per academic year. *Required fees:* full-time $499.

Financial Aid 90% of baccalaureate students in nursing programs received some form of financial aid in 2008–09.

Contact Dr. Tara Hulsey, RN, Dean of Nursing, Wingo School of Nursing, Charleston Southern University, 9200 University Boulevard, PO Box 118087, Charleston, SC 29423-8087. *Telephone:* 843-863-7075. *Fax:* 843-863-7540. *E-mail:* thulsey@csuniv.edu.

GRADUATE PROGRAMS

Expenses (2009–10) *Tuition:* full-time $19,238; part-time $400 per credit hour. *Room and board:* $7394 per academic year. *Required fees:* full-time $100; part-time $100 per credit.

Financial Aid 95% of graduate students in nursing programs received some form of financial aid in 2008–09.

Contact Dr. Tara Hulsey, PhD, Dean, Wingo School of Nursing, Charleston Southern University, 9200 University Boulevard, PO Box 118087, Charleston, SC 29423. *Telephone:* 843-863-7075. *Fax:* 843-863-7540. *E-mail:* thulsey@csuniv.edu.

MASTER'S DEGREE PROGRAM

Degree MSN

Available Programs Master's; RN to Master's.
Concentrations Available Nursing education.
Study Options Full-time and part-time.
Online Degree Options Yes (online only).
Program Entrance Requirements Clinical experience, minimum overall college GPA of 3.0, transcript of college record, written essay, 3 letters of recommendation, resume. *Application deadline:* 6/31 (fall). *Application fee:* $20.
Advanced Placement Credit given for nursing courses completed elsewhere dependent upon specific evaluations.
Degree Requirements 39 total credit hours, thesis or project.

Clemson University
School of Nursing
Clemson, South Carolina

http://www.hehd.clemson.edu/nursing

Founded in 1889

DEGREES • BS • MS

Nursing Program Faculty 24 (71% with doctorates).

Baccalaureate Enrollment 402
Women 99% **Men** 1% **Minority** 11%

Graduate Enrollment 82
Women 96.3% **Men** 3.7% **Minority** 9.8% **Part-time** 65.9%

Nursing Student Activities Nursing Honor Society, Sigma Theta Tau, Student Nurses' Association.

Nursing Student Resources Academic advising; academic or career counseling; assistance for students with disabilities; bookstore; campus computer network; career placement assistance; computer lab; computer-assisted instruction; e-mail services; employment services for current students; externships; housing assistance; interactive nursing skills videos; Internet; learning resource lab; library services; nursing audiovisuals; other; remedial services; resume preparation assistance; skills, simulation, or other laboratory; tutoring; unpaid internships.

Library Facilities 1.2 million volumes (29,800 in health, 5,548 in nursing); 5,587 periodical subscriptions (877 health-care related).

BACCALAUREATE PROGRAMS

Degree BS

Available Programs Generic Baccalaureate; RN Baccalaureate.
Study Options Full-time and part-time.

Program Entrance Requirements Minimum overall college GPA of 2.5, transcript of college record, CPR certification, health insurance, high school biology, high school chemistry, 3 years high school math, 3 years high school science, high school transcript, immunizations, minimum high school GPA of 2.5, professional liability insurance/malpractice insurance, prerequisite course work. Transfer students are accepted.

Advanced Placement Credit by examination available. Credit given for nursing courses completed elsewhere dependent upon specific evaluations.

Contact *Telephone:* 864-656-5463. *Fax:* 864-656-2464.

GRADUATE PROGRAMS

Contact *Telephone:* 864-250-8881. *Fax:* 864-250-6711.

MASTER'S DEGREE PROGRAM

Degree MS

Available Programs Master's; RN to Master's.
Concentrations Available Nursing administration; nursing education. *Clinical nurse specialist programs in:* adult health, gerontology, maternity-newborn, parent-child, pediatric. *Nurse practitioner programs in:* adult health, family health, gerontology.
Study Options Full-time and part-time.
Program Entrance Requirements Clinical experience, computer literacy, minimum overall college GPA of 3.0, transcript of college record, CPR certification, 2 letters of recommendation, nursing research course, physical assessment course, professional liability insurance/malpractice insurance, prerequisite course work, resume, statistics course, GRE General Test.
Advanced Placement Credit by examination available. Credit given for nursing courses completed elsewhere dependent upon specific evaluations.
Degree Requirements 45 total credit hours, thesis or project, comprehensive exam.

POST-MASTER'S PROGRAM

Areas of Study Nursing administration; nursing education. *Clinical nurse specialist programs in:* adult health, gerontology, maternity-newborn, parent-child, pediatric. *Nurse practitioner programs in:* adult health, family health, gerontology.

CONTINUING EDUCATION PROGRAM

Contact *Telephone:* 864-656-3078. *Fax:* 864-656-1877.

Francis Marion University
Department of Nursing
Florence, South Carolina

http://www.fmarion.edu

Founded in 1970

DEGREE • BSN

Nursing Program Faculty 23 (9% with doctorates).

Baccalaureate Enrollment 156
Women 90% **Men** 10% **Minority** 26% **International** 1% **Part-time** 8%

Distance Learning Courses Available.

Nursing Student Activities Nursing Honor Society, Sigma Theta Tau, Student Nurses' Association.

Nursing Student Resources Academic advising; academic or career counseling; assistance for students with disabilities; bookstore; campus computer network; career placement assistance; computer lab; computer-assisted instruction; daycare for children of students; e-mail services; externships; housing assistance; interactive nursing skills videos; Internet; learning resource lab; library services; nursing audiovisuals; paid internships; placement services for program completers; remedial services; resume preparation assistance; skills, simulation, or other laboratory; tutoring; unpaid internships.

Library Facilities 396,526 volumes; 1,498 periodical subscriptions.

BACCALAUREATE PROGRAMS

Degree BSN

Available Programs ADN to Baccalaureate; Generic Baccalaureate.

Study Options Full-time.

Program Entrance Requirements Transcript of college record, CPR certification, written essay, health insurance, immunizations, 3 letters of recommendation, minimum GPA in nursing prerequisites of 3.0, prerequisite course work. Transfer students are accepted. *Application deadline:* 4/1 (fall), 11/1 (spring). Applications may be processed on a rolling basis for some programs. *Application fee:* $75.

Expenses (2009–10) *Tuition, state resident:* full-time $11,937; part-time $597 per credit hour. *Tuition, nonresident:* full-time $23,874; part-time $1194 per credit hour. *International tuition:* $23,874 full-time. *Room and board:* $6024; room only: $3524 per academic year. *Required fees:* full-time $175; part-time $12 per credit; part-time $30 per term.

Financial Aid 90% of baccalaureate students in nursing programs received some form of financial aid in 2008–09. *Gift aid (need-based):* Federal Pell, FSEOG, state, private, Academic Competitiveness Grant, National Smart Grant. *Loans:* FFEL (Subsidized and Unsubsidized Stafford PLUS), Perkins, state. *Work-study:* Federal Work-Study, part-time campus jobs. *Financial aid application deadline (priority):* 3/1.

Contact Mrs. Kristy Jones Padgett, Coordinator of Student Services, Nursing, Department of Nursing, Francis Marion University, PO Box 100547, Florence, SC 29502-0547. *Telephone:* 843-661-1226. *Fax:* 843-661-1696. *E-mail:* kpadgett@fmarion.edu.

Lander University
School of Nursing
Greenwood, South Carolina

http://www.lander.edu/nursing/
Founded in 1872
DEGREE • BSN

Nursing Program Faculty 21 (10% with doctorates).

Baccalaureate Enrollment 273
Women 92% **Men** 8% **Minority** 21% **Part-time** 16%

Distance Learning Courses Available.

Nursing Student Activities Sigma Theta Tau, Student Nurses' Association.

Nursing Student Resources Academic advising; academic or career counseling; assistance for students with disabilities; bookstore; campus computer network; career placement assistance; computer lab; computer-assisted instruction; e-mail services; externships; housing assistance; interactive nursing skills videos; Internet; learning resource lab; library services; nursing audiovisuals; resume preparation assistance; skills, simulation, or other laboratory.

Library Facilities 186,690 volumes (6,209 in health, 1,145 in nursing); 657 periodical subscriptions (36 health-care related).

BACCALAUREATE PROGRAMS
Degree BSN

Available Programs Accelerated Baccalaureate; Accelerated Baccalaureate for Second Degree; Accelerated RN Baccalaureate; Baccalaureate for Second Degree; Generic Baccalaureate; RN Baccalaureate.

Site Options Greenwood, SC.

Study Options Full-time and part-time.

Online Degree Options Yes.

Program Entrance Requirements Minimum overall college GPA of 2.6, transcript of college record, CPR certification, health exam, health insurance, immunizations, professional liability insurance/malpractice insurance, prerequisite course work. Transfer students are accepted. *Application deadline:* Applications may be processed on a rolling basis for some programs. *Application fee:* $35.

Advanced Placement Credit given for nursing courses completed elsewhere dependent upon specific evaluations.

Expenses (2009–10) *Tuition, state resident:* full-time $8760; part-time $365 per credit hour. *Tuition, nonresident:* full-time $16,560; part-time $690 per credit hour. *Room and board:* $6400; room only: $4000 per academic year.

Financial Aid 60% of baccalaureate students in nursing programs received some form of financial aid in 2008–09.

Contact Mrs. Jennifer M. Mathis, Director of Admissions, School of Nursing, Lander University, 320 Stanley Avenue, Greenwood, SC 29649-2099. *Telephone:* 864-388-8307. *Fax:* 864-388-8125. *E-mail:* jmathis@lander.edu.

Medical University of South Carolina
College of Nursing
Charleston, South Carolina

http://www.musc.edu/nursing
Founded in 1824
DEGREES • BSN • DNP • MSN • PHD

Nursing Program Faculty 41 (76% with doctorates).

Baccalaureate Enrollment 179
Women 84% **Men** 16% **Minority** 16% **Part-time** 1%

Graduate Enrollment 82
Women 96% **Men** 4% **Minority** 10% **Part-time** 60%

Distance Learning Courses Available.

Nursing Student Activities Sigma Theta Tau, Student Nurses' Association.

Nursing Student Resources Academic advising; bookstore; campus computer network; computer lab; computer-assisted instruction; e-mail services; housing assistance; interactive nursing skills videos; Internet; learning resource lab; library services; nursing audiovisuals; other; resume preparation assistance; skills, simulation, or other laboratory; tutoring.

Library Facilities 178,542 volumes (250,000 in health, 15,000 in nursing); 1,587 periodical subscriptions (6,000 health-care related).

BACCALAUREATE PROGRAMS
Degree BSN

Available Programs Accelerated Baccalaureate; Accelerated Baccalaureate for Second Degree.

Study Options Full-time.

Program Entrance Requirements Transcript of college record, CPR certification, written essay, health exam, health insurance, immunizations, 3 letters of recommendation, minimum GPA in nursing prerequisites of 3.0, prerequisite course work, RN licensure. Transfer students are accepted. *Application deadline:* 2/1 (fall), 9/15 (spring). *Application fee:* $85.

Advanced Placement Credit by examination available. Credit given for nursing courses completed elsewhere dependent upon specific evaluations.

Expenses (2009–10) *Tuition, state resident:* full-time $18,987; part-time $573 per credit hour. *Tuition, nonresident:* full-time $33,399; part-time $722 per credit hour. *Required fees:* full-time $555; part-time $330 per term.

Financial Aid 62% of baccalaureate students in nursing programs received some form of financial aid in 2008–09. *Gift aid (need-based):* Federal Pell, FSEOG, state, private, college/university gift aid from institutional funds, Federal Nursing, Scholarships for Disadvantaged Students (SDS). *Loans:* Federal Nursing Student Loans, FFEL (Subsidized and Unsubsidized Stafford PLUS), Perkins, state, Health Professions Loans, Loans for Disadvantaged Students program, Primary Care Loans, alternative loans. *Work-study:* Federal Work-Study.

Contact Mrs. Mardi Long, Program Coordinator, College of Nursing, Medical University of South Carolina, 99 Jonathan Lucas Street, MSC 160, Charleston, SC 29425-1600. *Telephone:* 843-792-6683. *Fax:* 843-792-9258. *E-mail:* longm@musc.edu.

GRADUATE PROGRAMS
Expenses (2009–10) *Tuition, state resident:* full-time $7005; part-time $722 per credit hour. *Tuition, nonresident:* full-time $11,601; part-time $1151 per credit hour. *Required fees:* full-time $1520; part-time $560 per term.

Medical University of South Carolina (continued)

Financial Aid 32% of graduate students in nursing programs received some form of financial aid in 2008–09. Federal Work-Study, scholarships, and traineeships available. Aid available to part-time students. *Financial aid application deadline:* 3/10.

Contact Dr. Robin L. Bissinger, Director of Graduate Programs, College of Nursing, Medical University of South Carolina, 99 Jonathan Lucas Street, Room 418, MSC 160, Charleston, SC 29425-1600. *Telephone:* 843-792-0531. *Fax:* 843-792-1741. *E-mail:* bissinrl@musc.edu.

MASTER'S DEGREE PROGRAM

Degree MSN

Available Programs Master's.

Concentrations Available Nursing administration; nursing education. *Nurse practitioner programs in:* adult health, family health, pediatric.

Study Options Full-time and part-time.

Online Degree Options Yes (online only).

Program Entrance Requirements Minimum overall college GPA of 3.0, transcript of college record, CPR certification, written essay, immunizations, 3 letters of recommendation, prerequisite course work, resume, statistics course. *Application deadline:* 2/1 (fall). *Application fee:* $85.

Advanced Placement Credit given for nursing courses completed elsewhere dependent upon specific evaluations.

Degree Requirements 58 total credit hours.

POST-MASTER'S PROGRAM

Areas of Study Nursing administration; nursing education.

DOCTORAL DEGREE PROGRAM

Degree DNP, PhD

Available Programs Doctorate; Post-Baccalaureate Doctorate.

Areas of Study Community health, family health, nursing administration, nursing education, nursing policy, nursing research.

Online Degree Options Yes (online only).

Program Entrance Requirements Minimum overall college GPA of 3.5, interview by faculty committee, interview, 3 letters of recommendation, MSN or equivalent, statistics course, vita, writing sample, GRE General Test (PhD). Application deadline: 2/1 (fall). Applications may be processed on a rolling basis for some programs. Application fee: $85.

Degree Requirements 62 total credit hours, dissertation, oral exam, written exam.

POSTDOCTORAL PROGRAM

Areas of Study Gerontology, nursing interventions, nursing research, vulnerable population.

Postdoctoral Program Contact Dr. William Basco, Program Director, College of Nursing, Medical University of South Carolina, Rutledge Towers, MSC 106, Charleston, SC 29425. *Telephone:* 843-876-6512. *Fax:* 843-876-8709. *E-mail:* bascob@musc.edu.

CONTINUING EDUCATION PROGRAM

Contact Ms. Carol Whelan, Administrative Assistant, College of Nursing, Medical University of South Carolina, 99 Jonathan Lucas Street, MSC 160, Charleston, SC 29425-1600. *Telephone:* 843-792-2651. *Fax:* 843-792-2104. *E-mail:* whelanc@musc.edu.

South Carolina State University

Department of Nursing
Orangeburg, South Carolina

Founded in 1896

DEGREE • BSN

Library Facilities 313,329 volumes; 3,031 periodical subscriptions.

BACCALAUREATE PROGRAMS

Degree BSN

Available Programs Generic Baccalaureate; RN Baccalaureate.

Program Entrance Requirements Minimum overall college GPA of 2.8, immunizations, minimum high school GPA of 2.8.

Contact *Telephone:* 803-536-7063. *Fax:* 803-536-8593.

University of South Carolina

College of Nursing
Columbia, South Carolina

http://www.sc.edu/nursing

Founded in 1801

DEGREES • BSN • MSN • MSN/MPH • PHD

Nursing Program Faculty 95 (30% with doctorates).

Baccalaureate Enrollment 1,005
Women 92% **Men** 8% **Minority** 23% **Part-time** 5%

Graduate Enrollment 170
Women 88% **Men** 12% **Minority** 16% **International** 1% **Part-time** 56%

Distance Learning Courses Available.

Nursing Student Activities Nursing Honor Society, Sigma Theta Tau, Student Nurses' Association.

Nursing Student Resources Academic advising; academic or career counseling; assistance for students with disabilities; bookstore; campus computer network; career placement assistance; computer lab; computer-assisted instruction; daycare for children of students; e-mail services; housing assistance; interactive nursing skills videos; Internet; learning resource lab; library services; nursing audiovisuals; remedial services; resume preparation assistance; skills, simulation, or other laboratory; tutoring.

Library Facilities 3.6 million volumes (97,703 in health, 10,578 in nursing); 51,540 periodical subscriptions (285 health-care related).

BACCALAUREATE PROGRAMS

Degree BSN

Available Programs Generic Baccalaureate.

Site Options Allendale, SC; Walterboro, SC; Lancaster, SC.

Study Options Full-time and part-time.

Program Entrance Requirements Minimum overall college GPA of 2.75, transcript of college record, high school biology, high school chemistry, high school foreign language, 1.5 years high school math, 1.5 years high school science, high school transcript, immunizations, minimum GPA in nursing prerequisites of 2.75. Transfer students are accepted. *Application deadline:* 12/1 (fall), 11/1 (spring), 5/1 (summer). *Application fee:* $50.

Advanced Placement Credit by examination available. Credit given for nursing courses completed elsewhere dependent upon specific evaluations.

Expenses (2009–10) *Tuition, state resident:* full-time $10,056; part-time $495 per hour. *Tuition, nonresident:* full-time $25,732; part-time $1215 per hour. *International tuition:* $25,732 full-time. *Room and board:* $7322; room only: $4850 per academic year. *Required fees:* full-time $2350; part-time $17 per credit; part-time $102 per term.

Financial Aid 90% of baccalaureate students in nursing programs received some form of financial aid in 2008–09.

Contact Mrs. Gail S. Vereen, Director of Recruitment and Undergraduate Advisement, College of Nursing, University of South Carolina, 1601 Greene Street, Columbia, SC 29208. *Telephone:* 803-777-2526. *Fax:* 803-777-0616. *E-mail:* gsveree@mailbox.sc.edu.

GRADUATE PROGRAMS

Expenses (2009–10) *Tuition, state resident:* full-time $11,288; part-time $559 per hour. *Tuition, nonresident:* full-time $23,080; part-time $1128 per hour. *International tuition:* $23,080 full-time. *Room and board:* room only: $990 per academic year. *Required fees:* full-time $2253; part-time $354 per credit; part-time $102 per term.

Financial Aid 61% of graduate students in nursing programs received some form of financial aid in 2008–09. 1 fellowship (averaging $1,200 per year), 3 research assistantships with partial tuition reimbursements available (averaging $2,790 per year), 11 teaching assistantships (averaging $5,533 per year) were awarded; scholarships, traineeships, and unspecified assistantships also available. *Financial aid application deadline:* 4/1.

Contact Ms. Cheryl Nelson, Student Services Coordinator, Graduate Programs, College of Nursing, University of South Carolina, 1601 Greene Street, Columbia, SC 29208. *Telephone:* 803-777-3754. *Fax:* 803-777-9080. *E-mail:* cyjackso@mailbox.sc.edu.

MASTER'S DEGREE PROGRAM

Degrees MSN; MSN/MPH

Available Programs Master's.

Concentrations Available Nursing administration. *Clinical nurse specialist programs in:* acute care, community health, psychiatric/mental health. *Nurse practitioner programs in:* acute care, adult health, family health, pediatric, psychiatric/mental health, women's health.

Study Options Full-time and part-time.

Program Entrance Requirements Minimum overall college GPA of 3.0, transcript of college record, written essay, immunizations, 2 letters of recommendation, resume, GRE General Test, MAT. *Application deadline:* 5/1 (fall). *Application fee:* $50.

Advanced Placement Credit given for nursing courses completed elsewhere dependent upon specific evaluations.

Degree Requirements 45 total credit hours.

POST-MASTER'S PROGRAM

Areas of Study *Nurse practitioner programs in:* acute care, adult health, family health, pediatric, psychiatric/mental health, women's health.

DOCTORAL DEGREE PROGRAM

Degree PhD

Available Programs Doctorate; Post-Baccalaureate Doctorate.

Areas of Study Health-care systems, individualized study.

Program Entrance Requirements Minimum overall college GPA of 3.0, interview by faculty committee, 3 letters of recommendation, scholarly papers, vita, writing sample, GRE General Test. Application deadline: 5/1 (fall). Application fee: $50.

Degree Requirements 61 total credit hours, dissertation, written exam, residency.

CONTINUING EDUCATION PROGRAM

Contact Ms. Lydia Zager, Director, Center for Nursing Leadership, College of Nursing, University of South Carolina, 1601 Greene Street, Columbia, SC 29208. *Telephone:* 803-777-7637. *Fax:* 803-777-6800. *E-mail:* lrzager@mailbox.sc.edu.

University of South Carolina Aiken

School of Nursing
Aiken, South Carolina

http://www.usca.edu/nursing/

Founded in 1961

DEGREE • BSN

Nursing Program Faculty 16 (50% with doctorates).

Baccalaureate Enrollment 250
Women 90% **Men** 10% **Minority** 30% **International** 1% **Part-time** 3%

Distance Learning Courses Available.

Nursing Student Activities Sigma Theta Tau, Student Nurses' Association.

Nursing Student Resources Academic advising; academic or career counseling; assistance for students with disabilities; bookstore; campus computer network; career placement assistance; computer lab; computer-assisted instruction; e-mail services; employment services for current students; housing assistance; interactive nursing skills videos; Internet; learning resource lab; library services; nursing audiovisuals; placement services for program completers; resume preparation assistance; skills, simulation, or other laboratory; tutoring.

Library Facilities 200 volumes in health, 100 volumes in nursing; 100 periodical subscriptions health-care related.

BACCALAUREATE PROGRAMS

Degree BSN

Available Programs ADN to Baccalaureate; Generic Baccalaureate; International Nurse to Baccalaureate; LPN to Baccalaureate; RN Baccalaureate.

Study Options Full-time and part-time.

Online Degree Options Yes.

Program Entrance Requirements CPR certification, written essay, health exam, immunizations, 3 letters of recommendation, minimum GPA in nursing prerequisites of 2.75, prerequisite course work. Transfer students are accepted. *Application deadline:* 3/15 (fall), 10/15 (spring).

Advanced Placement Credit by examination available. Credit given for nursing courses completed elsewhere dependent upon specific evaluations.

Financial Aid 50% of baccalaureate students in nursing programs received some form of financial aid in 2007–08.

Contact Ms. Kathy Simmons, Administrative Assistant, School of Nursing, University of South Carolina Aiken, 471 University Parkway, Aiken, SC 29801. *Telephone:* 803-648-3392. *Fax:* 803-641-3725. *E-mail:* kathers@usca.edu.

CONTINUING EDUCATION PROGRAM

Contact Dr. Julia Ball, RN, Dean of Nursing, School of Nursing, University of South Carolina Aiken, 471 University Parkway, Aiken, SC 29801. *Telephone:* 803-641-3263. *Fax:* 803-641-3725. *E-mail:* juliab@usca.edu.

University of South Carolina Beaufort

Nursing Program
Beaufort, South Carolina

Founded in 1959

DEGREE • BSN

Nursing Program Faculty 9 (43% with doctorates).

Baccalaureate Enrollment 80

Nursing Student Activities Student Nurses' Association.

Nursing Student Resources Academic advising; academic or career counseling; assistance for students with disabilities; bookstore; campus computer network; career placement assistance; computer lab; computer-assisted instruction; e-mail services; employment services for current students; externships; housing assistance; interactive nursing skills videos; Internet; learning resource lab; library services; nursing audiovisuals; paid internships; remedial services; resume preparation assistance; skills, simulation, or other laboratory; tutoring; unpaid internships.

Library Facilities 50,000 volumes; 395 periodical subscriptions.

BACCALAUREATE PROGRAMS

Degree BSN

Available Programs Generic Baccalaureate; RN Baccalaureate.

Contact *Telephone:* 843-208-8124. *E-mail:* Nursing@uscb.edu.

University of South Carolina Upstate

Mary Black School of Nursing
Spartanburg, South Carolina

http://www.uscs.edu/academics/mbsn/

Founded in 1967

DEGREE • BSN

Nursing Program Faculty 62 (18% with doctorates).

Baccalaureate Enrollment 448
Women 88% **Men** 12% **Minority** 20% **International** 1% **Part-time** 15%

University of South Carolina Upstate (continued)

Distance Learning Courses Available.

Nursing Student Activities Nursing Honor Society, Sigma Theta Tau, Student Nurses' Association.

Nursing Student Resources Academic advising; academic or career counseling; assistance for students with disabilities; bookstore; campus computer network; career placement assistance; computer lab; computer-assisted instruction; daycare for children of students; e-mail services; employment services for current students; externships; housing assistance; interactive nursing skills videos; Internet; learning resource lab; library services; nursing audiovisuals; paid internships; resume preparation assistance; skills, simulation, or other laboratory; tutoring; unpaid internships.

Library Facilities 201,237 volumes (214,998 in health, 23,359 in nursing); 27,405 periodical subscriptions.

BACCALAUREATE PROGRAMS

Degree BSN

Available Programs Generic Baccalaureate; RN Baccalaureate.

Site Options Greenville, SC.

Study Options Full-time and part-time.

Online Degree Options Yes.

Program Entrance Requirements Transcript of college record, health exam, immunizations, minimum GPA in nursing prerequisites of 2.5, professional liability insurance/malpractice insurance, prerequisite course work. Transfer students are accepted. *Application deadline:* 1/15 (fall), 5/15 (spring).

Advanced Placement Credit by examination available. Credit given for nursing courses completed elsewhere dependent upon specific evaluations.

Expenses (2009–10) *Tuition, state resident:* full-time $8062; part-time $467 per credit hour. *Tuition, nonresident:* full-time $16,404; part-time $992 per credit hour. *Room and board:* $4600; room only: $3500 per academic year. *Required fees:* full-time $1800; part-time $40 per credit.

Financial Aid 85% of baccalaureate students in nursing programs received some form of financial aid in 2008–09. *Gift aid (need-based):* Federal Pell, FSEOG, state, private, college/university gift aid from institutional funds. *Loans:* FFEL (Subsidized and Unsubsidized Stafford PLUS), Perkins, state, private loans. *Work-study:* Federal Work-Study, part-time campus jobs. *Financial aid application deadline (priority):* 3/1.

Contact Dr. Katharine M. Gibb, Interim Dean, Mary Black School of Nursing, University of South Carolina Upstate, 800 University Way, Spartanburg, SC 29303. *Telephone:* 864-503-5444. *Fax:* 864-503-5405. *E-mail:* kgibb@uscupstate.edu.

SOUTH DAKOTA

Augustana College

Department of Nursing
Sioux Falls, South Dakota

http://www.augie.edu

Founded in 1860

DEGREES • BA • MA

Nursing Program Faculty 16 (25% with doctorates).

Baccalaureate Enrollment 251
Women 87% **Men** 13% **Minority** 2% **Part-time** 2%

Graduate Enrollment 4
Women 100% **Part-time** 100%

Distance Learning Courses Available.

Nursing Student Activities Sigma Theta Tau, Student Nurses' Association.

Nursing Student Resources Academic advising; academic or career counseling; assistance for students with disabilities; bookstore; campus computer network; career placement assistance; computer lab; computer-assisted instruction; daycare for children of students; e-mail services;

employment services for current students; housing assistance; interactive nursing skills videos; Internet; learning resource lab; library services; nursing audiovisuals; remedial services; resume preparation assistance; skills, simulation, or other laboratory; tutoring; unpaid internships.

Library Facilities 203,804 volumes; 5,533 periodical subscriptions.

BACCALAUREATE PROGRAMS

Degree BA

Available Programs Generic Baccalaureate.

Study Options Full-time.

Program Entrance Requirements Minimum overall college GPA of 2.7, transcript of college record, CPR certification, written essay, health exam, health insurance, high school transcript, immunizations, 2 letters of recommendation, minimum high school GPA of 3.5, minimum GPA in nursing prerequisites of 2.7, prerequisite course work. Transfer students are accepted. *Application deadline:* 2/15 (fall). Applications may be processed on a rolling basis for some programs.

Advanced Placement Credit given for nursing courses completed elsewhere dependent upon specific evaluations.

Expenses (2009–10) *Tuition:* full-time $23,276. *Room and board:* $6414 per academic year. *Required fees:* full-time $373.

Financial Aid 98% of baccalaureate students in nursing programs received some form of financial aid in 2008–09. *Gift aid (need-based):* Federal Pell, FSEOG, state, private, college/university gift aid from institutional funds, need-linked special talent scholarships, minority scholarships. *Loans:* Federal Nursing Student Loans, FFEL (Subsidized and Unsubsidized Stafford PLUS), Perkins, college/university, Minnesota SELF Loans, alternative loans. *Work-study:* Federal Work-Study, part-time campus jobs. *Financial aid application deadline (priority):* 3/1.

Contact Debbie Anderson, Office Assistant, Department of Nursing, Augustana College, 2001 South Summit Avenue, Sioux Falls, SD 57197. *Telephone:* 605-274-4721. *Fax:* 605-274-4723. *E-mail:* debbie.anderson@augie.edu.

GRADUATE PROGRAMS

Expenses (2009–10) *Tuition:* part-time $330 per credit hour.

Contact Dr. Margot Nelson, Professor of Nursing, Department of Nursing, Augustana College, 2001 South Summit Avenue, Sioux Falls, SD 57197. *Telephone:* 605-274-4721. *Fax:* 605-274-4723. *E-mail:* margot.nelson@augie.edu.

MASTER'S DEGREE PROGRAM

Degree MA

Available Programs Master's.

Concentrations Available Clinical nurse leader.

Study Options Part-time.

Program Entrance Requirements Clinical experience, minimum overall college GPA of 3.0, transcript of college record, written essay, immunizations, 2 letters of recommendation, professional liability insurance/malpractice insurance, resume, statistics course. *Application deadline:* Applications may be processed on a rolling basis for some programs.

Advanced Placement Credit given for nursing courses completed elsewhere dependent upon specific evaluations.

Degree Requirements 39 total credit hours, thesis or project.

Mount Marty College

Nursing Program
Yankton, South Dakota

http://www.mtmc.edu

Founded in 1936

DEGREE • BSN

Nursing Program Faculty 13 (15% with doctorates).

Baccalaureate Enrollment 89
Women 89% **Men** 11% **Minority** 7% **Part-time** 2%

Nursing Student Activities Sigma Theta Tau, Student Nurses' Association, nursing club.

Nursing Student Resources Academic advising; academic or career counseling; assistance for students with disabilities; bookstore; campus computer network; career placement assistance; computer lab; computer-assisted instruction; daycare for children of students; e-mail services; employment services for current students; externships; housing assistance; interactive nursing skills videos; Internet; learning resource lab; library services; nursing audiovisuals; paid internships; placement services for program completers; remedial services; resume preparation assistance; skills, simulation, or other laboratory; tutoring; unpaid internships.

Library Facilities 76,571 volumes (8,750 in health, 5,350 in nursing); 424 periodical subscriptions (85 health-care related).

BACCALAUREATE PROGRAMS

Degree BSN

Available Programs ADN to Baccalaureate; Accelerated LPN to Baccalaureate; Generic Baccalaureate; International Nurse to Baccalaureate; LPN to Baccalaureate; LPN to RN Baccalaureate; RN Baccalaureate.

Site Options Watertown, SD.

Study Options Full-time and part-time.

Program Entrance Requirements Minimum overall college GPA of 2.7, transcript of college record, CPR certification, health exam, health insurance, high school transcript, immunizations, minimum GPA in nursing prerequisites of 2.0, prerequisite course work. Transfer students are accepted. *Application deadline:* Applications may be processed on a rolling basis for some programs.

Advanced Placement Credit given for nursing courses completed elsewhere dependent upon specific evaluations.

Expenses (2008–09) *Tuition:* full-time $16,420; part-time $410 per credit hour. *International tuition:* $16,420 full-time. *Room and board:* $5210 per academic year. *Required fees:* full-time $2475.

Financial Aid 100% of baccalaureate students in nursing programs received some form of financial aid in 2007–08. *Gift aid (need-based):* Federal Pell, FSEOG, state, private, college/university gift aid from institutional funds. *Loans:* Federal Nursing Student Loans, Federal Direct (Subsidized and Unsubsidized Stafford PLUS), FFEL (Subsidized and Unsubsidized Stafford PLUS), Perkins. *Work-study:* Federal Work-Study, part-time campus jobs. *Financial aid application deadline (priority):* 3/1.

Contact Dr. Jacqueline Ann Kelley, RN, Chair and Director, Division of Nursing, Nursing Program, Mount Marty College, 1105 West 8th Street, Yankton, SD 57078-3724. *Telephone:* 605-668-1594. *Fax:* 605-668-1607. *E-mail:* jacqueline.kelley@mtmc.edu.

National American University
School of Nursing
Rapid City, South Dakota

Founded in 1941

DEGREE • BSN

Library Facilities 31,018 volumes; 268 periodical subscriptions.

BACCALAUREATE PROGRAMS

Degree BSN

Available Programs Generic Baccalaureate.

Contact Dodie Serafini, RN, Nursing Program Chair, School of Nursing, National American University, Denver, CO 80222. *Telephone:* 303-876-7181. *Fax:* 303-876-7105. *E-mail:* dserafini@national.edu.

Presentation College
Department of Nursing
Aberdeen, South Dakota

http://www.presentation.edu

Founded in 1951

DEGREE • BSN

Nursing Program Faculty 21 (9% with doctorates).

Baccalaureate Enrollment 185

Women 95% **Men** 5% **Minority** 4% **Part-time** 24%

Distance Learning Courses Available.

Nursing Student Activities Nursing Honor Society, Sigma Theta Tau, Student Nurses' Association, nursing club.

Nursing Student Resources Academic advising; academic or career counseling; assistance for students with disabilities; bookstore; campus computer network; career placement assistance; computer lab; computer-assisted instruction; e-mail services; employment services for current students; externships; interactive nursing skills videos; Internet; learning resource lab; library services; nursing audiovisuals; placement services for program completers; remedial services; resume preparation assistance; skills, simulation, or other laboratory; tutoring; unpaid internships.

Library Facilities 40,000 volumes (378 in health, 353 in nursing); 430 periodical subscriptions (2,172 health-care related).

BACCALAUREATE PROGRAMS

Degree BSN

Available Programs ADN to Baccalaureate; Baccalaureate for Second Degree; Generic Baccalaureate; LPN to RN Baccalaureate; RN Baccalaureate.

Site Options Fargo, ND; Fairmont, MN.

Study Options Full-time and part-time.

Online Degree Options Yes.

Program Entrance Requirements Minimum overall college GPA of 2.5, transcript of college record, CPR certification, written essay, health exam, high school biology, high school chemistry, 2 years high school math, high school transcript, immunizations, 2 letters of recommendation, minimum high school GPA of 2.7, minimum GPA in nursing prerequisites of 2.5, prerequisite course work. Transfer students are accepted. *Application deadline:* 3/1 (fall).

Advanced Placement Credit by examination available. Credit given for nursing courses completed elsewhere dependent upon specific evaluations.

Expenses (2009–10) *Tuition:* full-time $14,250; part-time $525 per credit hour. *Room and board:* $5500; room only: $4100 per academic year. *Required fees:* full-time $1331; part-time $333 per term.

Financial Aid 91% of baccalaureate students in nursing programs received some form of financial aid in 2008–09.

Contact Ms. JoEllen Lindner, Dean of Admissions, Department of Nursing, Presentation College, 1500 North Main Street, Aberdeen, SD 57401. *Telephone:* 605-229-8492. *Fax:* 605-229-8489. *E-mail:* lindnerjo@presentation.edu.

South Dakota State University
College of Nursing
Brookings, South Dakota

http://www.sdstate.org/Academics/CollegeOfNursing/

Founded in 1881

DEGREES • BS • MS • PHD

Nursing Program Faculty 127 (22% with doctorates).

Baccalaureate Enrollment 553

Women 82% **Men** 18% **Minority** 4%

Graduate Enrollment 166

Women 96% **Men** 4% **Minority** 2% **Part-time** 100%

Distance Learning Courses Available.

Nursing Student Activities Sigma Theta Tau, Student Nurses' Association, nursing club.

Nursing Student Resources Academic advising; academic or career counseling; assistance for students with disabilities; bookstore; campus computer network; career placement assistance; computer lab; computer-assisted instruction; e-mail services; employment services for current students; externships; interactive nursing skills videos; Internet; learning resource lab; library services; nursing audiovisuals; paid internships;

South Dakota State University (continued)
placement services for program completers; remedial services; resume preparation assistance; skills, simulation, or other laboratory; tutoring.

Library Facilities 987,599 volumes (20,000 in health, 5,700 in nursing); 44,599 periodical subscriptions (4,402 health-care related).

BACCALAUREATE PROGRAMS

Degree BS

Available Programs Accelerated Baccalaureate; Generic Baccalaureate; RN Baccalaureate.

Site Options Rapid City, SD; Sioux Falls, SD.

Study Options Full-time.

Online Degree Options Yes.

Program Entrance Requirements Minimum overall college GPA of 2.7, transcript of college record, CPR certification, health exam, health insurance, immunizations, interview, minimum GPA in nursing prerequisites of 2.7, professional liability insurance/malpractice insurance, prerequisite course work. Transfer students are accepted. *Application deadline:* 1/25 (fall), 9/25 (spring).

Advanced Placement Credit given for nursing courses completed elsewhere dependent upon specific evaluations.

Expenses (2009–10) *Tuition, state resident:* part-time $92 per credit. *Tuition, nonresident:* part-time $291 per credit. *Room and board:* $5668; room only: $2540 per academic year. *Required fees:* part-time $236 per credit; part-time $460 per term.

Financial Aid 86% of baccalaureate students in nursing programs received some form of financial aid in 2008–09. *Gift aid (need-based):* Federal Pell, FSEOG, state, private, college/university gift aid from institutional funds, United Negro College Fund, Federal Nursing, Academic Competitiveness Grant, National Smart Grant, TEACH Grant, TRiO. *Loans:* Federal Nursing Student Loans, FFEL (Subsidized and Unsubsidized Stafford PLUS), Perkins, college/university, Health Professions Loans, private alternative loans. *Work-study:* Federal Work-Study, part-time campus jobs. *Financial aid application deadline (priority):* 3/11.

Contact Dr. Janet Lord, Undergraduate Department Head, College of Nursing, South Dakota State University, Box 2275, SNF 327, Brookings, SD 57007-0098. *Telephone:* 605-688-6153. *Fax:* 605-688-6523. *E-mail:* Janet. Lord@sdstate.edu.

GRADUATE PROGRAMS

Expenses (2009–10) *Tuition, state resident:* part-time $139 per credit. *Tuition, nonresident:* part-time $294 per credit. *Required fees:* part-time $123 per credit; part-time $185 per term.

Financial Aid 86% of graduate students in nursing programs received some form of financial aid in 2008–09. 2 fellowships, 1 research assistantship, 3 teaching assistantships were awarded; career-related internships or fieldwork, Federal Work-Study, scholarships, and unspecified assistantships also available.

Contact Dr. Sandra Bunkers, Department Head, College of Nursing, South Dakota State University, Box 2275, Rotunda Lane, NFA 217, Brookings, SD 57007-0098. *Telephone:* 605-688-4114. *Fax:* 605-688-5827. *E-mail:* sandra.bunkers@sdstate.edu.

MASTER'S DEGREE PROGRAM

Degree MS

Available Programs Master's; RN to Master's.

Concentrations Available Clinical nurse leader; nursing administration; nursing education. *Nurse practitioner programs in:* family health, neonatal health, psychiatric/mental health.

Site Options Rapid City, SD; Sioux Falls, SD.

Study Options Full-time and part-time.

Online Degree Options Yes.

Program Entrance Requirements Clinical experience, minimum overall college GPA of 3.0, transcript of college record, CPR certification, written essay, immunizations, 3 letters of recommendation, professional liability insurance/malpractice insurance, statistics course. *Application deadline:* 3/1 (fall). *Application fee:* $200.

Advanced Placement Credit given for nursing courses completed elsewhere dependent upon specific evaluations.

Degree Requirements 48 total credit hours, thesis or project, comprehensive exam.

POST-MASTER'S PROGRAM

Areas of Study Nursing education. *Nurse practitioner programs in:* family health.

DOCTORAL DEGREE PROGRAM

Degree PhD

Available Programs Doctorate.

Areas of Study Nursing research.

Site Options Sioux Falls, SD.

Program Entrance Requirements Minimum overall college GPA of 3.3, interview by faculty committee, 4 letters of recommendation, MSN or equivalent, scholarly papers, vita, writing sample. Application deadline: 3/1 (fall).

Degree Requirements 60 total credit hours, dissertation, oral exam, written exam.

CONTINUING EDUCATION PROGRAM

Contact Dr. Roberta K. Olson, Dean, College of Nursing, South Dakota State University, Box 2275, SNF 255, Brookings, SD 57007-0098. *Telephone:* 605-688-5178. *Fax:* 605-688-5745. *E-mail:* Roberta.Olson@sdstate.edu.

TENNESSEE

Aquinas College
Department of Nursing
Nashville, Tennessee

http://www.aquinas-tn.edu/nursing/index.htm

Founded in 1961

DEGREE • BSN

Nursing Student Resources Library services.

BACCALAUREATE PROGRAMS

Degree BSN

Available Programs RN Baccalaureate.

Program Entrance Requirements Interview, 2 letters of recommendation, RN licensure.

Advanced Placement Credit given for nursing courses completed elsewhere dependent upon specific evaluations.

Contact *Telephone:* 615-222-4038.

Austin Peay State University
School of Nursing
Clarksville, Tennessee

http://www.apsu.edu/nursing01

Founded in 1927

DEGREE • BSN

Nursing Program Faculty 20 (20% with doctorates).

Baccalaureate Enrollment 250

Nursing Student Activities Nursing Honor Society, Sigma Theta Tau, Student Nurses' Association.

Nursing Student Resources Academic advising; computer lab; computer-assisted instruction; interactive nursing skills videos; Internet; nursing audiovisuals; skills, simulation, or other laboratory.

Library Facilities 552,681 volumes (8,249 in health, 1,111 in nursing); 18,675 periodical subscriptions (146 health-care related).

BACCALAUREATE PROGRAMS

Degree BSN

Available Programs Generic Baccalaureate; RN Baccalaureate.

Study Options Full-time.

Program Entrance Requirements Minimum overall college GPA of 3.0, transcript of college record, CPR certification, health insurance, immunizations, minimum GPA in nursing prerequisites of 3.0, prerequisite course work. Transfer students are accepted. *Application deadline:* 5/1 (fall), 9/1 (spring).

Contact Ms. Debbie Cochener, Administrative Specialist/Pre-Nursing Advisor, School of Nursing, Austin Peay State University, PO Box 4658, Clarksville, TN 37044. *Telephone:* 931-221-7708. *Fax:* 931-221-7595. *E-mail:* cochenerd@apsu.edu.

Baptist College of Health Sciences
Nursing Division
Memphis, Tennessee

Founded in 1994

DEGREE • BSN

Nursing Program Faculty 40 (20% with doctorates).

Baccalaureate Enrollment 731
Women 89% **Men** 11% **Minority** 43% **Part-time** 45%

Distance Learning Courses Available.

Nursing Student Activities Sigma Theta Tau, Student Nurses' Association.

Nursing Student Resources Academic advising; academic or career counseling; assistance for students with disabilities; bookstore; campus computer network; computer lab; computer-assisted instruction; e-mail services; employment services for current students; externships; housing assistance; interactive nursing skills videos; Internet; learning resource lab; library services; nursing audiovisuals; paid internships; placement services for program completers; resume preparation assistance; skills, simulation, or other laboratory; tutoring.

Library Facilities 14,547 volumes (2,573 in health, 1,790 in nursing); 260 periodical subscriptions (213 health-care related).

BACCALAUREATE PROGRAMS
Degree BSN

Available Programs Generic Baccalaureate; LPN to Baccalaureate; RN Baccalaureate.

Study Options Full-time and part-time.

Program Entrance Requirements Minimum overall college GPA of 2.5, CPR certification, health exam, health insurance, 2 years high school math, 2 years high school science, high school transcript, immunizations, 3 letters of recommendation, minimum high school GPA of 2.75. Transfer students are accepted. *Application deadline:* 6/1 (fall), 11/1 (spring). *Application fee:* $25.

Expenses (2008–09) *Tuition:* part-time $274 per credit hour. *Room and board:* room only: $900 per academic year.

Financial Aid 91% of baccalaureate students in nursing programs received some form of financial aid in 2007–08.

Contact Ms. Lissa Morgan, Director of Admissions, Nursing Division, Baptist College of Health Sciences, 1003 Monroe, Memphis, TN 38104. *Telephone:* 901-572-2441. *Fax:* 901-572-2461. *E-mail:* lissa.morgan@bchs.edu.

Belmont University
School of Nursing
Nashville, Tennessee

http://www.belmont.edu/nursing

Founded in 1951

DEGREES • BSN • MSN

Nursing Program Faculty 65 (19% with doctorates).

Baccalaureate Enrollment 406
Women 84% **Men** 16% **Minority** 6% **International** 3% **Part-time** 8%

Graduate Enrollment 43
Women 98% **Men** 2% **Minority** 12% **International** 2% **Part-time** 63%

Nursing Student Activities Nursing Honor Society, Sigma Theta Tau, Student Nurses' Association.

Nursing Student Resources Academic advising; academic or career counseling; assistance for students with disabilities; bookstore; campus computer network; career placement assistance; computer lab; computer-assisted instruction; e-mail services; employment services for current students; externships; housing assistance; interactive nursing skills videos; Internet; learning resource lab; library services; nursing audiovisuals; placement services for program completers; remedial services; resume preparation assistance; skills, simulation, or other laboratory; tutoring.

Library Facilities 220,637 volumes (6,000 in health, 800 in nursing); 1,072 periodical subscriptions (7,500 health-care related).

BACCALAUREATE PROGRAMS
Degree BSN

Available Programs ADN to Baccalaureate; Accelerated Baccalaureate; Accelerated Baccalaureate for Second Degree; Baccalaureate for Second Degree; Generic Baccalaureate; LPN to RN Baccalaureate; RN Baccalaureate.

Study Options Full-time and part-time.

Program Entrance Requirements Minimum overall college GPA of 2.5, transcript of college record, CPR certification, written essay, health exam, health insurance, high school biology, high school chemistry, 3 years high school math, 3 years high school science, high school transcript, immunizations, 1 letter of recommendation, minimum high school GPA of 2.5, minimum GPA in nursing prerequisites of 3.0. Transfer students are accepted. *Application deadline:* Applications may be processed on a rolling basis for some programs. *Application fee:* $50.

Advanced Placement Credit by examination available. Credit given for nursing courses completed elsewhere dependent upon specific evaluations.

Expenses (2009–10) *Tuition:* full-time $21,270; part-time $820 per credit hour. *International tuition:* $21,270 full-time. *Room and board:* $8470; room only: $4600 per academic year. *Required fees:* full-time $1090; part-time $545 per term.

Financial Aid 85% of baccalaureate students in nursing programs received some form of financial aid in 2008–09. *Gift aid (need-based):* Federal Pell, FSEOG, state, private, college/university gift aid from institutional funds. *Loans:* Federal Direct PLUS), FFEL (Subsidized and Unsubsidized Stafford PLUS), Perkins, college/university. *Work-study:* Federal Work-Study. *Financial aid application deadline (priority):* 3/1.

Contact Mrs. Maren Bishop, Admissions Assistant, School of Nursing, Belmont University, 1900 Belmont Boulevard, Nashville, TN 37212-3757. *Telephone:* 615-460-6120. *Fax:* 615-460-6125. *E-mail:* maren.bishop@mail.belmont.edu.

GRADUATE PROGRAMS

Expenses (2009–10) *Tuition:* part-time $860 per credit hour. *Room and board:* $8470; room only: $4600 per academic year.

Financial Aid 95% of graduate students in nursing programs received some form of financial aid in 2008–09. Scholarships and traineeships available. *Financial aid application deadline:* 3/1.

Contact Dr. Leslie Higgins, Director, Graduate Program, School of Nursing, Belmont University, 1900 Belmont Boulevard, Nashville, TN 37212-3757. *Telephone:* 615-460-6027. *Fax:* 615-460-6125. *E-mail:* leslie.higgins@mail.belmont.edu.

MASTER'S DEGREE PROGRAM
Degree MSN

Available Programs Master's.

Concentrations Available Nursing education. *Nurse practitioner programs in:* family health.

Study Options Full-time and part-time.

Program Entrance Requirements Clinical experience, minimum overall college GPA of 3.0, transcript of college record, CPR certification, written essay, immunizations, interview, 2 letters of recommendation, resume, GRE. *Application fee:* $50.

Advanced Placement Credit given for nursing courses completed elsewhere dependent upon specific evaluations.

Degree Requirements 41 total credit hours, comprehensive exam.

Belmont University (continued)

POST-MASTER'S PROGRAM

Areas of Study Nursing education. *Nurse practitioner programs in:* family health.

Bethel University
Nursing Program
McKenzie, Tennessee

Founded in 1842

DEGREE • BSN

Nursing Program Faculty 10

Baccalaureate Enrollment 35

Nursing Student Activities Student Nurses' Association.

Nursing Student Resources Academic advising; academic or career counseling; assistance for students with disabilities; bookstore; campus computer network; computer lab; computer-assisted instruction; e-mail services; housing assistance; interactive nursing skills videos; Internet; learning resource lab; library services; nursing audiovisuals; remedial services; resume preparation assistance; skills, simulation, or other laboratory; tutoring.

Library Facilities 83,919 volumes; 255 periodical subscriptions.

BACCALAUREATE PROGRAMS

Degree BSN

Available Programs Generic Baccalaureate.

Study Options Full-time.

Program Entrance Requirements Minimum overall college GPA of 2.75, transcript of college record, minimum GPA in nursing prerequisites of 2.0, prerequisite course work. Transfer students are accepted. *Application deadline:* 3/1 (spring). *Application fee:* $25.

Advanced Placement Credit given for nursing courses completed elsewhere dependent upon specific evaluations.

Expenses (2009–10) *Tuition:* full-time $11,592. *Room and board:* $6926 per academic year. *Required fees:* full-time $1300.

Financial Aid 80% of baccalaureate students in nursing programs received some form of financial aid in 2008–09.

Contact Ms. Mary Bess Griffith, Director, Department of Nursing, Nursing Program, Bethel University, 325 Cherry Avenue, McKenzie, TN 38201. *Telephone:* 731-352-6768. *Fax:* 731-352-6772. *E-mail:* griffithmb@bethelu.edu.

Carson-Newman College
Division of Nursing
Jefferson City, Tennessee

http://www.cn.edu/nursing/

Founded in 1851

DEGREES • BSN • MSN

Nursing Program Faculty 15 (47% with doctorates).

Baccalaureate Enrollment 125
Women 90% **Men** 10% **Minority** 10% **International** 2%

Graduate Enrollment 46
Women 87% **Men** 13% **Minority** 4% **Part-time** 57%

Distance Learning Courses Available.

Nursing Student Activities Sigma Theta Tau, Student Nurses' Association.

Nursing Student Resources Academic advising; academic or career counseling; assistance for students with disabilities; bookstore; campus computer network; career placement assistance; computer lab; computer-assisted instruction; e-mail services; employment services for current students; externships; housing assistance; interactive nursing skills videos; Internet; learning resource lab; library services; nursing audiovisuals; placement services for program completers; remedial services; resume preparation assistance; skills, simulation, or other laboratory; tutoring; unpaid internships.

Library Facilities 218,371 volumes (6,497 in health, 5,419 in nursing); 3,966 periodical subscriptions (3,481 health-care related).

BACCALAUREATE PROGRAMS

Degree BSN

Available Programs Accelerated Baccalaureate; Generic Baccalaureate; LPN to RN Baccalaureate; RN Baccalaureate.

Study Options Full-time.

Program Entrance Requirements Minimum overall college GPA of 2.75, transcript of college record, health exam, high school transcript, immunizations, minimum GPA in nursing prerequisites of 2.75, prerequisite course work. Transfer students are accepted. *Application deadline:* 3/1 (fall), 9/1 (spring). Applications may be processed on a rolling basis for some programs.

Advanced Placement Credit given for nursing courses completed elsewhere dependent upon specific evaluations.

Expenses (2009–10) *Tuition:* full-time $17,850; part-time $745 per credit hour. *International tuition:* $17,850 full-time. *Room and board:* $7286; room only: $4010 per academic year. *Required fees:* full-time $882; part-time $311 per term.

Financial Aid 90% of baccalaureate students in nursing programs received some form of financial aid in 2008–09. *Gift aid (need-based):* Federal Pell, FSEOG, state, private, college/university gift aid from institutional funds. *Loans:* FFEL (Subsidized and Unsubsidized Stafford PLUS), Perkins, state, college/university, alternative loans. *Work-study:* Federal Work-Study, part-time campus jobs. *Financial aid application deadline (priority):* 4/1.

Contact Dr. Gregory A. Casalenuovo, Chair, Undergraduate Studies in Nursing, Division of Nursing, Carson-Newman College, 1646 Russell Avenue, C-N Box 71883, Jefferson City, TN 37760. *Telephone:* 865-471-3236. *Fax:* 865-471-4574. *E-mail:* gcasalenuovo@cn.edu.

GRADUATE PROGRAMS

Expenses (2009–10) *Tuition:* part-time $465 per credit hour. *Room and board:* $7286; room only: $4010 per academic year. *Required fees:* part-time $233 per term.

Financial Aid 100% of graduate students in nursing programs received some form of financial aid in 2008–09.

Contact Dr. Kimberly S. Bolton, Assistant Chair, Graduate Studies in Nursing, Division of Nursing, Carson-Newman College, 1646 Russell Avenue, C-N Box 71883, Jefferson City, TN 37760. *Telephone:* 865-471-4056. *Fax:* 865-471-4574. *E-mail:* kbolton@cn.edu.

MASTER'S DEGREE PROGRAM

Degree MSN

Available Programs Master's; RN to Master's.

Concentrations Available Nursing education. *Nurse practitioner programs in:* family health.

Study Options Full-time and part-time.

Program Entrance Requirements Minimum overall college GPA of 3.0, transcript of college record, written essay, interview, 3 letters of recommendation. *Application deadline:* 4/15 (fall), 10/15 (spring), 3/15 (summer). Applications may be processed on a rolling basis for some programs. *Application fee:* $50.

Advanced Placement Credit given for nursing courses completed elsewhere dependent upon specific evaluations.

Degree Requirements 45 total credit hours, thesis or project, comprehensive exam.

POST-MASTER'S PROGRAM

Areas of Study Nursing education. *Nurse practitioner programs in:* family health.

Cumberland University
Rudy School of Nursing and Health Professions
Lebanon, Tennessee

http://www.cumberland.edu/academics/nursing/index.html

Founded in 1842

DEGREE • BSN

Nursing Program Faculty 11 (30% with doctorates).

Baccalaureate Enrollment 214
Women 92% **Men** 8% **Minority** 6% **Part-time** .5%

Nursing Student Activities Nursing Honor Society, Student Nurses' Association.

Nursing Student Resources Academic advising; academic or career counseling; assistance for students with disabilities; bookstore; campus computer network; career placement assistance; computer lab; computer-assisted instruction; e-mail services; housing assistance; interactive nursing skills videos; Internet; learning resource lab; library services; nursing audiovisuals; remedial services; resume preparation assistance; skills, simulation, or other laboratory; tutoring.

Library Facilities 50,000 volumes (125 in health, 66 in nursing); 130 periodical subscriptions (25 health-care related).

BACCALAUREATE PROGRAMS

Degree BSN

Available Programs ADN to Baccalaureate; Accelerated Baccalaureate; Accelerated Baccalaureate for Second Degree; Baccalaureate for Second Degree; Generic Baccalaureate; LPN to Baccalaureate; LPN to RN Baccalaureate; RN Baccalaureate.

Site Options Mt. Juliet, TN.

Study Options Full-time and part-time.

Program Entrance Requirements Minimum overall college GPA of 2.8, transcript of college record, CPR certification, health exam, health insurance, high school transcript, immunizations, minimum high school GPA of 2.75, minimum GPA in nursing prerequisites of 2.8, professional liability insurance/malpractice insurance, prerequisite course work. Transfer students are accepted. *Application deadline:* 6/1 (fall), 10/1 (winter), 2/1 (summer). *Application fee:* $25.

Advanced Placement Credit by examination available. Credit given for nursing courses completed elsewhere dependent upon specific evaluations.

Expenses (2009–10) *Tuition:* full-time $8265; part-time $960 per credit hour. *Room and board:* $6250; room only: $2850 per academic year. *Required fees:* full-time $650; part-time $125 per credit; part-time $450 per term.

Financial Aid 95% of baccalaureate students in nursing programs received some form of financial aid in 2008–09.

Contact Dr. Carole Ann Bach, Professor and Dean, Rudy School of Nursing and Health Professions, Cumberland University, One Cumberland Square, McFarland Campus, Lebanon, TN 37087-3554. *Telephone:* 615-547-1200. *Fax:* 615-449-1368. *E-mail:* cbach@cumberland.edu.

East Tennessee State University
College of Nursing
Johnson City, Tennessee

http://www.etsu.edu/nursing

Founded in 1911

DEGREES • BSN • MSN • PHD

Nursing Program Faculty 69 (33% with doctorates).

Baccalaureate Enrollment 609
Women 90% **Men** 10% **Minority** 10% **Part-time** 11%

Graduate Enrollment 224
Women 91% **Men** 9% **Minority** 4% **Part-time** 44%

Distance Learning Courses Available.

Nursing Student Activities Sigma Theta Tau, Student Nurses' Association.

Nursing Student Resources Academic advising; academic or career counseling; assistance for students with disabilities; bookstore; campus computer network; career placement assistance; computer lab; computer-assisted instruction; daycare for children of students; e-mail services; employment services for current students; externships; housing assistance; interactive nursing skills videos; Internet; learning resource lab; library services; nursing audiovisuals; remedial services; resume preparation assistance; skills, simulation, or other laboratory; tutoring.

Library Facilities 1.1 million volumes; 3,714 periodical subscriptions.

BACCALAUREATE PROGRAMS

Degree BSN

Available Programs ADN to Baccalaureate; Accelerated Baccalaureate for Second Degree; Accelerated RN Baccalaureate; Generic Baccalaureate; LPN to Baccalaureate.

Site Options Pellissippi, TN; Sevierville, TN; Cleveland and Kingsport, TN.

Study Options Full-time and part-time.

Online Degree Options Yes.

Program Entrance Requirements Minimum overall college GPA of 2.6, transcript of college record, minimum GPA in nursing prerequisites of 2.6, prerequisite course work. Transfer students are accepted. *Application deadline:* 10/1 (fall), 2/1 (spring).

Advanced Placement Credit given for nursing courses completed elsewhere dependent upon specific evaluations.

Financial Aid *Gift aid (need-based):* Federal Pell, FSEOG, state, private, college/university gift aid from institutional funds, Federal Nursing. *Loans:* Federal Nursing Student Loans, Federal Direct (Subsidized and Unsubsidized Stafford PLUS), Perkins, college/university. *Work-study:* Federal Work-Study, part-time campus jobs. *Financial aid application deadline (priority):* 4/15.

Contact Mr. Scott Vaughn, Director, Student Services, College of Nursing, East Tennessee State University, PO Box 70664, Office of Student Services, Johnson City, TN 37614. *Telephone:* 423-439-4578. *Fax:* 423-439-4522. *E-mail:* admitnur@etsu.edu.

GRADUATE PROGRAMS

Financial Aid 6 research assistantships (averaging $5,500 per year), 4 teaching assistantships (averaging $5,500 per year) were awarded; career-related internships or fieldwork, traineeships, and unspecified assistantships also available.

Contact Ms. Amy Bower, Coordinator, College of Nursing, East Tennessee State University, PO Box 70664, Office of Student Services, Johnson City, TN 37614. *Telephone:* 423-439-4531. *Fax:* 423-439-4522. *E-mail:* bowera@etsu.edu.

MASTER'S DEGREE PROGRAM

Degree MSN

Available Programs Master's.

Concentrations Available Clinical nurse leader; nursing administration; nursing education. *Nurse practitioner programs in:* adult health, family health, gerontology, psychiatric/mental health.

Study Options Full-time and part-time.

Online Degree Options Yes.

Program Entrance Requirements Minimum overall college GPA of 3.0, transcript of college record, written essay, 3 letters of recommendation, GRE General Test. *Application deadline:* 12/1 (fall), 2/1 (spring), 7/1 (summer). *Application fee:* $35.

Advanced Placement Credit given for nursing courses completed elsewhere dependent upon specific evaluations.

Degree Requirements Comprehensive exam.

POST-MASTER'S PROGRAM

Areas of Study Health-care administration. *Nurse practitioner programs in:* adult health, family health, gerontology, psychiatric/mental health.

DOCTORAL DEGREE PROGRAM

Degree PhD

Available Programs Doctorate.

Areas of Study Individualized study.

East Tennessee State University (continued)
Program Entrance Requirements Clinical experience, minimum overall college GPA of 3.0, interview by faculty committee, 3 letters of recommendation, MSN or equivalent, statistics course, vita, writing sample. Application deadline: 2/1 (spring). Application fee: $35.
Degree Requirements 62 total credit hours, dissertation, written exam, residency.

King College
School of Nursing
Bristol, Tennessee

Founded in 1867
DEGREES • BSN • MSN • MSN/MBA

Nursing Program Faculty 31 (26% with doctorates).

Baccalaureate Enrollment 366
Women 96% **Men** 4% **Minority** 1% **International** 1%

Graduate Enrollment 35
Women 99% **Men** 1% **Minority** 1%

Distance Learning Courses Available.

Nursing Student Activities Student Nurses' Association.

Nursing Student Resources Academic advising; academic or career counseling; assistance for students with disabilities; bookstore; campus computer network; career placement assistance; computer lab; computer-assisted instruction; e-mail services; employment services for current students; externships; interactive nursing skills videos; Internet; learning resource lab; library services; nursing audiovisuals; paid internships; remedial services; resume preparation assistance; skills, simulation, or other laboratory; tutoring.

Library Facilities 113,933 volumes (929 in health, 158 in nursing); 468 periodical subscriptions (87 health-care related).

BACCALAUREATE PROGRAMS
Degree BSN
Available Programs Accelerated RN Baccalaureate; Generic Baccalaureate.
Site Options Kingsport, TN.
Study Options Full-time.
Program Entrance Requirements Minimum overall college GPA of 2.0, transcript of college record, CPR certification, written essay, health exam, health insurance, high school biology, high school chemistry, high school foreign language, 2 years high school math, 2 years high school science, high school transcript, immunizations, minimum high school GPA of 2.6, minimum high school rank 25%, minimum GPA in nursing prerequisites of 2.75. Transfer students are accepted. *Application deadline:* 6/1 (fall). *Application fee:* $100.
Expenses (2009–10) *Tuition:* full-time $21,880. *Room and board:* $7418; room only: $3726 per academic year. *Required fees:* full-time $600.
Financial Aid 90% of baccalaureate students in nursing programs received some form of financial aid in 2008–09.
Contact Dr. Jane E. Castle, Interim Dean and Professor, School of Nursing, King College, 1350 King College Road, Bristol, TN 37620. *Telephone:* 423-652-4841. *Fax:* 423-652-4833. *E-mail:* jecastle@king.edu.

GRADUATE PROGRAMS
Expenses (2009–10) *Tuition:* part-time $3300 per semester.
Financial Aid 100% of graduate students in nursing programs received some form of financial aid in 2008–09.
Contact Dr. Jane E. Castle, Interim Dean and Professor, School of Nursing, King College, 1350 King College Road, Bristol, TN 37620. *Telephone:* 423-652-4841. *Fax:* 423-652-4833. *E-mail:* jecastle@king.edu.

MASTER'S DEGREE PROGRAM
Degrees MSN; MSN/MBA
Available Programs Accelerated RN to Master's; Master's.
Concentrations Available *Clinical nurse specialist programs in:* acute care, adult health, oncology.
Study Options Full-time.

Program Entrance Requirements Clinical experience, computer literacy, minimum overall college GPA of 3.0, transcript of college record, CPR certification, written essay, immunizations, 2 letters of recommendation, nursing research course, physical assessment course, resume, statistics course. *Application deadline:* 4/15 (fall). *Application fee:* $100.
Degree Requirements 39 total credit hours, thesis or project.

Lincoln Memorial University
Department of Nursing
Harrogate, Tennessee

http://www.lmunet.edu/academics/undergrad/nursing/
Founded in 1897

DEGREE • BSN

Nursing Program Faculty 7 (57% with doctorates).

Nursing Student Activities Student Nurses' Association.

Nursing Student Resources Academic advising; academic or career counseling; bookstore; campus computer network; career placement assistance; computer lab; e-mail services; externships; interactive nursing skills videos; Internet; learning resource lab; library services; nursing audiovisuals; other; placement services for program completers; skills, simulation, or other laboratory; tutoring.

Library Facilities 199,892 volumes (1,230 in health, 630 in nursing); 334 periodical subscriptions (36 health-care related).

BACCALAUREATE PROGRAMS
Degree BSN
Available Programs RN Baccalaureate.
Site Options Knoxville, TN.
Program Entrance Requirements Minimum overall college GPA of 2.25, transcript of college record, CPR certification, immunizations, 3 letters of recommendation, professional liability insurance/malpractice insurance, prerequisite course work, RN licensure. Transfer students are accepted.
Advanced Placement Credit given for nursing courses completed elsewhere dependent upon specific evaluations.
Contact *Telephone:* 423-869-3611. *Fax:* 423-869-6444.

Lipscomb University
Department of Nursing
Nashville, Tennessee

Founded in 1891

DEGREE • BSN

Library Facilities 258,965 volumes; 809 periodical subscriptions.

BACCALAUREATE PROGRAMS
Degree BSN
Available Programs Generic Baccalaureate.
Contact Sonya Colvert, Department of Nursing, Lipscomb University, One University Park Drive, Nashville, TN 37204-3951. *Telephone:* 615-996-6650. *E-mail:* sonya.colvert@lipscomb.edu.

Martin Methodist College
Division of Nursing
Pulaski, Tennessee

Founded in 1870

DEGREE • BS

Nursing Program Faculty 7 (60% with doctorates).
Baccalaureate Enrollment 950

Nursing Student Activities Student Nurses' Association.

Nursing Student Resources Academic advising; academic or career counseling; bookstore; campus computer network; career placement assistance; computer lab; computer-assisted instruction; e-mail services; employment services for current students; housing assistance; interactive nursing skills videos; Internet; learning resource lab; library services; nursing audiovisuals; placement services for program completers; remedial services; resume preparation assistance; skills, simulation, or other laboratory; tutoring; unpaid internships.

Library Facilities 84,000 volumes (875 in nursing); 664 periodical subscriptions (400 health-care related).

BACCALAUREATE PROGRAMS

Degree BS

Available Programs Generic Baccalaureate.

Contact Dr. Kenneth R. Burns, RN, Professor and Chair, Division of Nursing, Martin Methodist College, 433 West Madison Street, Pulaski, TN 38478. *Telephone:* 931-424-7395. *Fax:* 931-363-9891. *E-mail:* kburns@martinmethodist.edu.

Middle Tennessee State University
School of Nursing
Murfreesboro, Tennessee

http://www.mtsu.edu/~nursing/

Founded in 1911

DEGREES • BSN • MSN

Nursing Program Faculty 45 (60% with doctorates).

Baccalaureate Enrollment 300
Women 85% **Men** 15% **Minority** 15%

Graduate Enrollment 100
Women 80% **Men** 20% **Minority** 15% **Part-time** 50%

Distance Learning Courses Available.

Nursing Student Activities Sigma Theta Tau, Student Nurses' Association.

Nursing Student Resources Academic advising; academic or career counseling; assistance for students with disabilities; bookstore; campus computer network; career placement assistance; computer lab; computer-assisted instruction; e-mail services; interactive nursing skills videos; Internet; learning resource lab; library services; nursing audiovisuals; remedial services; resume preparation assistance; skills, simulation, or other laboratory; tutoring.

Library Facilities 936,172 volumes (100 in health, 45 in nursing); 4,144 periodical subscriptions (100 health-care related).

BACCALAUREATE PROGRAMS

Degree BSN

Available Programs Generic Baccalaureate; LPN to RN Baccalaureate; RN Baccalaureate.

Study Options Full-time.

Online Degree Options Yes.

Program Entrance Requirements Minimum overall college GPA of 2.80, transcript of college record, CPR certification, health insurance, immunizations, interview, minimum GPA in nursing prerequisites of 2.0, professional liability insurance/malpractice insurance, prerequisite course work. Transfer students are accepted. *Application deadline:* 2/1 (fall), 10/1 (spring).

Advanced Placement Credit by examination available. Credit given for nursing courses completed elsewhere dependent upon specific evaluations.

Contact Dr. Lynn C. Parsons, RN, Professor and Director, School of Nursing, Middle Tennessee State University, PO Box 81, 1301 East Main Street, Murfreesboro, TN 37132-0001. *Telephone:* 615-898-2437. *Fax:* 615-898-5441. *E-mail:* lparsons@mtsu.edu.

GRADUATE PROGRAMS

Contact Lynn C. Parsons, RN, Professor and Director, School of Nursing, Middle Tennessee State University, PO Box 81, 1301 East Main Street, Murfreesboro, TN 37132-0001. *Telephone:* 615-898-2437. *Fax:* 615-898-5441. *E-mail:* lparsons@mtsu.edu.

MASTER'S DEGREE PROGRAM

Degree MSN

Available Programs Accelerated AD/RN to Master's; Master's.

Concentrations Available Nursing administration; nursing education; nursing informatics. *Nurse practitioner programs in:* family health.

Site Options multiple cities.

Study Options Full-time and part-time.

Online Degree Options Yes.

Program Entrance Requirements Minimum overall college GPA of 3.0, transcript of college record, 3 letters of recommendation, prerequisite course work, resume. *Application deadline:* Applications may be processed on a rolling basis for some programs.

Degree Requirements 43 total credit hours, thesis or project.

POST-MASTER'S PROGRAM

Areas of Study *Nurse practitioner programs in:* family health.

Milligan College
Department of Nursing
Milligan College, Tennessee

http://www.milligan.edu/BSN/

Founded in 1866

DEGREE • BSN

Nursing Program Faculty 8 (25% with doctorates).

Baccalaureate Enrollment 55
Women 90% **Men** 10% **Minority** 2%

Nursing Student Activities Nursing Honor Society, Student Nurses' Association.

Nursing Student Resources Academic advising; academic or career counseling; assistance for students with disabilities; bookstore; campus computer network; career placement assistance; computer lab; computer-assisted instruction; e-mail services; employment services for current students; externships; interactive nursing skills videos; Internet; learning resource lab; library services; nursing audiovisuals; placement services for program completers; remedial services; resume preparation assistance; skills, simulation, or other laboratory; tutoring; unpaid internships.

Library Facilities 145,605 volumes (2,430 in health, 184 in nursing); 11,097 periodical subscriptions (340 health-care related).

BACCALAUREATE PROGRAMS

Degree BSN

Available Programs ADN to Baccalaureate; Baccalaureate for Second Degree; Generic Baccalaureate; LPN to Baccalaureate; LPN to RN Baccalaureate; RN Baccalaureate.

Study Options Full-time and part-time.

Program Entrance Requirements Minimum overall college GPA of 2.5, transcript of college record, CPR certification, written essay, health exam, immunizations, minimum GPA in nursing prerequisites of 2.0, professional liability insurance/malpractice insurance, prerequisite course work. Transfer students are accepted. *Application deadline:* Applications may be processed on a rolling basis for some programs. *Application fee:* $30.

Advanced Placement Credit given for nursing courses completed elsewhere dependent upon specific evaluations.

Expenses (2009–10) *Tuition:* full-time $21,200; part-time $590 per credit hour. *International tuition:* $21,200 full-time. *Room and board:* $5650; room only: $2650 per academic year. *Required fees:* full-time $660; part-time $380 per credit.

Milligan College (continued)

Financial Aid 94% of baccalaureate students in nursing programs received some form of financial aid in 2008–09. *Gift aid (need-based):* Federal Pell, FSEOG, state, private, college/university gift aid from institutional funds. *Loans:* FFEL (Subsidized and Unsubsidized Stafford PLUS), Perkins, alternative loans. *Work-study:* Federal Work-Study, part-time campus jobs. *Financial aid application deadline (priority):* 3/1.

Contact Melinda K. Collins, Area Chair and Director of Nursing, Department of Nursing, Milligan College, Wilson Way, Suite 302, Milligan College, TN 37682. *Telephone:* 423-461-8655. *Fax:* 423-461-8982. *E-mail:* mcollins@milligan.edu.

South College
Department of Nursing
Knoxville, Tennessee

Founded in 1882

DEGREE • BSN

BACCALAUREATE PROGRAMS

Degree BSN

Available Programs Generic Baccalaureate.

Program Entrance Requirements Immunizations, minimum high school GPA of 2.5. Transfer students are accepted.

Contact *Telephone:* 865-251-1800.

Southern Adventist University
School of Nursing
Collegedale, Tennessee

http://nursing.southern.edu

Founded in 1892

DEGREES • BS • MSN • MSN/MBA

Nursing Program Faculty 18 (22% with doctorates).

Baccalaureate Enrollment 106
Women 80% **Men** 20% **Minority** 29% **International** 15% **Part-time** 37%

Graduate Enrollment 91
Women 85% **Men** 15% **Minority** 7% **Part-time** 45%

Nursing Student Activities Sigma Theta Tau, nursing club.

Nursing Student Resources Academic advising; academic or career counseling; assistance for students with disabilities; bookstore; campus computer network; computer lab; computer-assisted instruction; e-mail services; employment services for current students; housing assistance; interactive nursing skills videos; Internet; learning resource lab; library services; nursing audiovisuals; remedial services; resume preparation assistance; skills, simulation, or other laboratory; tutoring.

Library Facilities 7,795 volumes in health, 974 volumes in nursing; 1,750 periodical subscriptions (86 health-care related).

BACCALAUREATE PROGRAMS

Degree BS

Available Programs ADN to Baccalaureate.

Site Options Chattanooga, TN.

Study Options Full-time and part-time.

Program Entrance Requirements Minimum overall college GPA of 2.5, transcript of college record, CPR certification, health exam, high school transcript, immunizations, 2 letters of recommendation, minimum GPA in nursing prerequisites of 2.0, prerequisite course work, RN licensure. Transfer students are accepted. *Application deadline:* 2/1 (fall), 9/1 (winter). Applications may be processed on a rolling basis for some programs.

Advanced Placement Credit given for nursing courses completed elsewhere dependent upon specific evaluations.

Expenses (2009–10) *Tuition:* full-time $16,372; part-time $692 per hour. *International tuition:* $16,372 full-time.

Financial Aid 80% of baccalaureate students in nursing programs received some form of financial aid in 2008–09. *Gift aid (need-based):* Federal Pell, FSEOG, state, private, college/university gift aid from institutional funds. *Loans:* Federal Nursing Student Loans, FFEL (Subsidized and Unsubsidized Stafford PLUS), Perkins, college/university. *Work-study:* Federal Work-Study, part-time campus jobs. *Financial aid application deadline (priority):* 3/1.

Contact Mrs. Linda Marlowe, Admissions and Progression Coordinator, School of Nursing, Southern Adventist University, PO Box 370, Collegedale, TN 37315-0370. *Telephone:* 423-236-2941. *Fax:* 423-236-1940. *E-mail:* lmarlowe@southern.edu.

GRADUATE PROGRAMS

Expenses (2009–10) *Tuition:* full-time $13,149; part-time $487 per credit hour. *International tuition:* $13,149 full-time. *Room and board:* $10,500; room only: $7500 per academic year. *Required fees:* full-time $390.

Financial Aid 50% of graduate students in nursing programs received some form of financial aid in 2008–09.

Contact Mrs. Diane Proffitt, Applications Manager, School of Nursing, Southern Adventist University, PO Box 370, Collegedale, TN 37315-0370. *Telephone:* 423-236-2957. *Fax:* 423-236-1940. *E-mail:* dproffit@southern.edu.

MASTER'S DEGREE PROGRAM

Degrees MSN; MSN/MBA

Available Programs Accelerated RN to Master's; Master's.

Concentrations Available Nursing education. *Nurse practitioner programs in:* acute care, adult health, family health.

Study Options Full-time and part-time.

Program Entrance Requirements Clinical experience, minimum overall college GPA of 3.0, transcript of college record, CPR certification, written essay, immunizations, interview, 2 letters of recommendation, prerequisite course work, statistics course. *Application deadline:* 7/1 (fall), 11/1 (winter). *Application fee:* $25.

Advanced Placement Credit given for nursing courses completed elsewhere dependent upon specific evaluations.

Degree Requirements 46 total credit hours, thesis or project.

CONTINUING EDUCATION PROGRAM

Contact Mrs. Linda Marlowe, Admissions and Progression Coordinator, School of Nursing, Southern Adventist University, PO Box 370, Collegedale, TN 37315-0370. *Telephone:* 423-236-2941. *Fax:* 423-236-1940. *E-mail:* lmarlowe@southern.edu.

Tennessee State University
School of Nursing
Nashville, Tennessee

http://www.tnstate.edu/nurs

Founded in 1912

DEGREES • BSN • MSN

Nursing Program Faculty 37 (50% with doctorates).

Baccalaureate Enrollment 65
Women 90% **Men** 10% **Minority** 85% **Part-time** 19%

Graduate Enrollment 160
Women 91% **Men** 9% **Minority** 33% **Part-time** 97%

Nursing Student Activities Nursing Honor Society, Sigma Theta Tau, Student Nurses' Association.

Nursing Student Resources Academic advising; academic or career counseling; assistance for students with disabilities; bookstore; campus computer network; computer lab; e-mail services; interactive nursing skills videos; Internet; learning resource lab; library services; nursing audiovisuals; skills, simulation, or other laboratory; tutoring.

Library Facilities 630,890 volumes (50,000 in health, 25,000 in nursing); 300 periodical subscriptions health-care related.

BACCALAUREATE PROGRAMS

Degree BSN

Available Programs Generic Baccalaureate; LPN to Baccalaureate; RN Baccalaureate.

Site Options Nashville, TN.

Study Options Full-time and part-time.

Program Entrance Requirements Minimum overall college GPA of 2.8, transcript of college record, CPR certification, health exam, health insurance, immunizations, minimum GPA in nursing prerequisites of 2.8, professional liability insurance/malpractice insurance, prerequisite course work. Transfer students are accepted. *Application deadline:* 3/15 (fall).

Expenses (2009–10) *Tuition, area resident:* full-time $5414; part-time $241 per credit hour. *Tuition, nonresident:* full-time $17,342; part-time $738 per credit hour. *Room and board:* $5700; room only: $3160 per academic year.

Financial Aid 80% of baccalaureate students in nursing programs received some form of financial aid in 2008–09.

Contact Dr. Verla Vaughan, RN, Interim BSN Program Director, School of Nursing, Tennessee State University, 3500 John A. Merritt Boulevard, Box 9590, Nashville, TN 37209-1561. *Telephone:* 615-963-7615. *Fax:* 615-963-5593. *E-mail:* vvaughan@tnstate.edu.

GRADUATE PROGRAMS

Expenses (2009–10) *Tuition, area resident:* full-time $6990; part-time $338 per credit hour. *Tuition, nonresident:* full-time $17,910; part-time $904 per credit hour. *Room and board:* room only: $5000 per academic year.

Financial Aid 75% of graduate students in nursing programs received some form of financial aid in 2008–09. Research assistantships (averaging $6,500 per year), 3 teaching assistantships (averaging $6,500 per year) were awarded.

Contact Dr. Jane C. Norman, MSN Program Director, School of Nursing, Tennessee State University, 3500 John A. Merritt Boulevard, Box 9590, Nashville, TN 37209-1561. *Telephone:* 615-963-5255. *Fax:* 615-963-7614. *E-mail:* jnorman@tnstate.edu.

MASTER'S DEGREE PROGRAM

Degree MSN

Available Programs RN to Master's.

Concentrations Available Nursing education. *Clinical nurse specialist programs in:* family health. *Nurse practitioner programs in:* family health.

Site Options Nashville, TN.

Study Options Full-time and part-time.

Online Degree Options Yes.

Program Entrance Requirements Clinical experience, computer literacy, minimum overall college GPA of 3.0, transcript of college record, CPR certification, written essay, immunizations, interview, 3 letters of recommendation, physical assessment course, professional liability insurance/malpractice insurance, resume, statistics course, GRE General Test or MAT. *Application deadline:* 7/15 (fall), 3/15 (summer).

Advanced Placement Credit given for nursing courses completed elsewhere dependent upon specific evaluations.

Degree Requirements 43 total credit hours, thesis or project, comprehensive exam.

POST-MASTER'S PROGRAM

Areas of Study *Clinical nurse specialist programs in:* family health. *Nurse practitioner programs in:* family health.

Tennessee Technological University

School of Nursing
Cookeville, Tennessee

http://www.tntech.edu/nursing
Founded in 1915

DEGREES • BSN • M SC N • MSN

Nursing Program Faculty 23 (13% with doctorates).

Baccalaureate Enrollment 184

Women 87% **Men** 13% **Minority** 5%

Graduate Enrollment 41

Women 90% **Men** 10% **Minority** 5% **Part-time** 73%

Distance Learning Courses Available.

Nursing Student Activities Sigma Theta Tau, Student Nurses' Association.

Nursing Student Resources Academic advising; academic or career counseling; assistance for students with disabilities; bookstore; campus computer network; career placement assistance; computer lab; computer-assisted instruction; daycare for children of students; e-mail services; employment services for current students; externships; housing assistance; Internet; learning resource lab; library services; nursing audiovisuals; paid internships; placement services for program completers; remedial services; resume preparation assistance; skills, simulation, or other laboratory; tutoring; unpaid internships.

Library Facilities 693,169 volumes (312,892 in health, 11,893 in nursing); 1,636 periodical subscriptions (96 health-care related).

BACCALAUREATE PROGRAMS

Degree BSN

Available Programs ADN to Baccalaureate; Baccalaureate for Second Degree; Generic Baccalaureate; RN Baccalaureate.

Study Options Full-time.

Program Entrance Requirements Minimum overall college GPA of 2.5, transcript of college record, CPR certification, health exam, health insurance, high school biology, high school chemistry, high school foreign language, 3 years high school math, 2 years high school science, high school transcript, immunizations, minimum high school GPA of 3.0, minimum GPA in nursing prerequisites of 2.5, professional liability insurance/malpractice insurance, prerequisite course work. Transfer students are accepted. *Application deadline:* 2/1 (fall), 6/1 (spring).

Advanced Placement Credit given for nursing courses completed elsewhere dependent upon specific evaluations.

Expenses (2009–10) *Tuition, state resident:* full-time $5526; part-time $254 per credit hour. *Tuition, nonresident:* full-time $17,454; part-time $751 per credit hour. *International tuition:* $17,454 full-time. *Room and board:* $6908; room only: $3560 per academic year. *Required fees:* full-time $750.

Financial Aid 85% of baccalaureate students in nursing programs received some form of financial aid in 2008–09. *Gift aid (need-based):* Federal Pell, FSEOG, state, private, college/university gift aid from institutional funds, United Negro College Fund. *Loans:* Federal Direct (Subsidized and Unsubsidized Stafford PLUS), FFEL, Perkins, college/university. *Work-study:* Federal Work-Study, part-time campus jobs. *Financial aid application deadline (priority):* 3/15.

Contact Ms. Kristi L. Burris, Academic Advisor, School of Nursing, Tennessee Technological University, Box 5001, Cookeville, TN 38505-0001. *Telephone:* 931-372-3203. *Fax:* 931-372-6244. *E-mail:* nursing@tntech.edu.

GRADUATE PROGRAMS

Expenses (2009–10) *Tuition, state resident:* part-time $384 per credit hour. *Tuition, nonresident:* part-time $930 per credit hour. *International tuition:* $930 full-time.

Financial Aid 5% of graduate students in nursing programs received some form of financial aid in 2008–09.

Contact Ms. Kristi L. Burris, Academic Advisor, School of Nursing, Tennessee Technological University, Box 5001, Cookeville, TN 38505-0001. *Telephone:* 931-372-3203. *Fax:* 931-372-6244. *E-mail:* nursing@tntech.edu.

MASTER'S DEGREE PROGRAM

Degrees M Sc N; MSN

Available Programs Master's; Master's for Nurses with Non-Nursing Degrees.

Concentrations Available Health-care administration; nursing education; nursing informatics. *Nurse practitioner programs in:* family health.

Study Options Full-time and part-time.

Online Degree Options Yes (online only).

Program Entrance Requirements Computer literacy, minimum overall college GPA of 3.0, transcript of college record, CPR certification, immunizations, 3 letters of recommendation, professional liability insurance/malpractice insurance, resume. *Application deadline:* 8/1 (fall), 1/2 (spring), 5/1 (summer). Applications may be processed on a rolling basis for some programs. *Application fee:* $25.

Tennessee Technological University (continued)

Advanced Placement Credit given for nursing courses completed elsewhere dependent upon specific evaluations.

Degree Requirements 46 total credit hours, thesis or project.

Tennessee Wesleyan College

Fort Sanders Nursing Department
Knoxville, Tennessee

http://www.twcnet.edu/academics/nursing

Founded in 1857

DEGREE • BSN

Nursing Program Faculty 15 (20% with doctorates).

Baccalaureate Enrollment 101

Women 92% **Men** 8% **Minority** 3% **International** 2% **Part-time** 4%

Distance Learning Courses Available.

Nursing Student Activities Nursing Honor Society, Sigma Theta Tau, Student Nurses' Association.

Nursing Student Resources Academic advising; assistance for students with disabilities; bookstore; computer lab; Internet; library services; nursing audiovisuals; other; skills, simulation, or other laboratory.

Library Facilities 156,126 volumes (5,000 in health, 4,000 in nursing); 11,491 periodical subscriptions (135 health-care related).

BACCALAUREATE PROGRAMS

Degree BSN

Available Programs ADN to Baccalaureate; Generic Baccalaureate; RN Baccalaureate.

Site Options Knoxville, TN.

Study Options Full-time and part-time.

Program Entrance Requirements Minimum overall college GPA of 2.7, transcript of college record, CPR certification, written essay, health exam, high school transcript, immunizations, interview, prerequisite course work. Transfer students are accepted. *Application deadline:* 1/15 (fall). *Application fee:* $25.

Advanced Placement Credit given for nursing courses completed elsewhere dependent upon specific evaluations.

Expenses (2008–09) *Tuition:* full-time $16,500; part-time $690 per credit hour. *Room and board:* $7330 per academic year. *Required fees:* full-time $1650; part-time $69 per credit.

Financial Aid 95% of baccalaureate students in nursing programs received some form of financial aid in 2007–08.

Contact Nursing Contact, Fort Sanders Nursing Department, Tennessee Wesleyan College, 9821 Cogdill Road, Suite 2, Knoxville, TN 37932. *Telephone:* 865-777-5100. *Fax:* 865-777-5114.

Union University

School of Nursing
Jackson, Tennessee

http://www.uu.edu/academics/son/

Founded in 1823

DEGREES • BSN • MSN

Nursing Program Faculty 28 (36% with doctorates).

Baccalaureate Enrollment 285

Women 93% **Men** 7% **Minority** 27% **International** 2% **Part-time** 56%

Graduate Enrollment 55

Women 80% **Men** 20% **Minority** 25% **Part-time** 4%

Nursing Student Activities Nursing Honor Society, Sigma Theta Tau, Student Nurses' Association.

Nursing Student Resources Academic advising; academic or career counseling; assistance for students with disabilities; bookstore; campus computer network; career placement assistance; computer lab; computer-assisted instruction; e-mail services; employment services for current students; housing assistance; Internet; learning resource lab; library services; nursing audiovisuals; resume preparation assistance; skills, simulation, or other laboratory; tutoring.

Library Facilities 155,500 volumes (6,005 in nursing); 20,324 periodical subscriptions (1,284 health-care related).

BACCALAUREATE PROGRAMS

Degree BSN

Available Programs Accelerated Baccalaureate for Second Degree; Generic Baccalaureate; LPN to Baccalaureate; RN Baccalaureate.

Site Options Germantown, TN.

Study Options Full-time.

Program Entrance Requirements Minimum overall college GPA of 2.8, transcript of college record, CPR certification, health exam, immunizations, minimum GPA in nursing prerequisites of 2.8, prerequisite course work. Transfer students are accepted.

Advanced Placement Credit by examination available. Credit given for nursing courses completed elsewhere dependent upon specific evaluations.

Contact *Telephone:* 731-661-5538. *Fax:* 731-661-5504.

GRADUATE PROGRAMS

Contact *Telephone:* 731-661-5538. *Fax:* 901-661-5504.

MASTER'S DEGREE PROGRAM

Degree MSN

Available Programs Master's.

Concentrations Available Nurse anesthesia; nursing administration; nursing education. *Clinical nurse specialist programs in:* adult health, pediatric. *Nurse practitioner programs in:* family health.

Site Options Germantown, TN.

Study Options Full-time and part-time.

Program Entrance Requirements Minimum overall college GPA of 3.0, transcript of college record, CPR certification, written essay, immunizations, interview, 3 letters of recommendation, professional liability insurance/malpractice insurance, GRE.

Advanced Placement Credit given for nursing courses completed elsewhere dependent upon specific evaluations.

Degree Requirements 46 total credit hours.

POST-MASTER'S PROGRAM

Areas of Study Nursing administration; nursing education. *Clinical nurse specialist programs in:* adult health, pediatric. *Nurse practitioner programs in:* family health.

CONTINUING EDUCATION PROGRAM

Contact *Telephone:* 731-661-5152. *Fax:* 731-661-5504.

University of Memphis

Loewenberg School of Nursing
Memphis, Tennessee

http://nursing.memphis.edu

Founded in 1912

DEGREES • BSN • MSN

Nursing Program Faculty 65 (22% with doctorates).

Baccalaureate Enrollment 441

Women 91% **Men** 9% **Minority** 23% **Part-time** 15%

Graduate Enrollment 124

Women 92% **Men** 8% **Minority** 30% **Part-time** 75%

Distance Learning Courses Available.

Nursing Student Activities Sigma Theta Tau, Student Nurses' Association.

Nursing Student Resources Academic advising; academic or career counseling; assistance for students with disabilities; bookstore; campus computer network; career placement assistance; computer lab; computer-assisted instruction; daycare for children of students; e-mail services;

externships; housing assistance; interactive nursing skills videos; Internet; learning resource lab; library services; nursing audiovisuals; paid internships; remedial services; resume preparation assistance; skills, simulation, or other laboratory; tutoring.

Library Facilities 1.8 million volumes (74,513 in health); 9,500 periodical subscriptions (878 health-care related).

BACCALAUREATE PROGRAMS

Degree BSN

Available Programs ADN to Baccalaureate; Accelerated Baccalaureate; Accelerated Baccalaureate for Second Degree; Accelerated RN Baccalaureate; Baccalaureate for Second Degree; Generic Baccalaureate; RN Baccalaureate.

Site Options Jackson, TN.

Study Options Full-time.

Program Entrance Requirements Minimum overall college GPA of 2.7, transcript of college record, CPR certification, health exam, high school biology, high school chemistry, high school foreign language, 3 years high school math, 2 years high school science, high school transcript, immunizations, minimum high school GPA of 3.0, minimum GPA in nursing prerequisites of 2.4, prerequisite course work. Transfer students are accepted.

Advanced Placement Credit by examination available. Credit given for nursing courses completed elsewhere dependent upon specific evaluations.

Contact *Telephone:* 901-678-2003. *Fax:* 901-678-4906.

GRADUATE PROGRAMS

Contact *Telephone:* 901-678-2003. *Fax:* 901-678-4906.

MASTER'S DEGREE PROGRAM

Degree MSN

Available Programs Accelerated Master's for Nurses with Non-Nursing Degrees; Master's; Master's for Non-Nursing College Graduates; Master's for Nurses with Non-Nursing Degrees.

Concentrations Available Nursing administration; nursing education. *Nurse practitioner programs in:* family health.

Site Options Jackson, TN.

Study Options Full-time and part-time.

Online Degree Options Yes.

Program Entrance Requirements Minimum overall college GPA of 2.8, CPR certification, immunizations, 3 letters of recommendation, professional liability insurance/malpractice insurance.

Advanced Placement Credit given for nursing courses completed elsewhere dependent upon specific evaluations.

Degree Requirements 45 total credit hours, comprehensive exam.

POST-MASTER'S PROGRAM

Areas of Study *Nurse practitioner programs in:* family health.

The University of Tennessee
College of Nursing
Knoxville, Tennessee

http://www.nightingale.con.utk.edu
Founded in 1794

DEGREES • BSN • MSN • PHD

Nursing Program Faculty 61 (50% with doctorates).

Baccalaureate Enrollment 246
Women 87% **Men** 13% **Minority** 10% **International** 2.8% **Part-time** 8.9%

Graduate Enrollment 182
Women 89% **Men** 11% **Minority** 3.8% **International** 5.5% **Part-time** 25%

Distance Learning Courses Available.

Nursing Student Activities Sigma Theta Tau, Student Nurses' Association.

Nursing Student Resources Academic advising; academic or career counseling; assistance for students with disabilities; bookstore; campus computer network; computer lab; computer-assisted instruction; e-mail services; employment services for current students; externships; interactive nursing skills videos; Internet; learning resource lab; library services; nursing audiovisuals; remedial services; skills, simulation, or other laboratory; tutoring.

Library Facilities 3 million volumes (59,214 in health, 3,711 in nursing); 27,000 periodical subscriptions (572 health-care related).

BACCALAUREATE PROGRAMS

Degree BSN

Available Programs Accelerated RN Baccalaureate; Generic Baccalaureate.

Study Options Full-time and part-time.

Program Entrance Requirements Transcript of college record, CPR certification, written essay, health exam, health insurance, high school biology, high school chemistry, 3 years high school math, 2 years high school science, high school transcript, immunizations, interview, minimum high school GPA of 3.2, minimum GPA in nursing prerequisites of 3.2, professional liability insurance/malpractice insurance, prerequisite course work. Transfer students are accepted. *Application deadline:* 12/1 (fall), 12/1 (summer). Applications may be processed on a rolling basis for some programs. *Application fee:* $30.

Advanced Placement Credit given for nursing courses completed elsewhere dependent upon specific evaluations.

Expenses (2008–09) *Tuition, state resident:* full-time $5428; part-time $227 per credit hour. *Tuition, nonresident:* full-time $18,386; part-time $528 per credit hour. *International tuition:* $18,386 full-time. *Room and board:* $4477; room only: $2982 per academic year. *Required fees:* full-time $822; part-time $36 per credit.

Financial Aid 70% of baccalaureate students in nursing programs received some form of financial aid in 2007–08. *Gift aid (need-based):* Federal Pell, FSEOG, state, private, college/university gift aid from institutional funds, Federal Nursing. *Loans:* FFEL (Subsidized and Unsubsidized Stafford PLUS), Perkins, college/university. *Work-study:* Federal Work-Study. *Financial aid application deadline (priority):* 3/1.

Contact Director, Student Services, College of Nursing, The University of Tennessee, 1200 Volunteer Boulevard, Knoxville, TN 37996-4180. *Telephone:* 865-974-7606. *Fax:* 865-974-3569. *E-mail:* bbarret@utk.edu.

GRADUATE PROGRAMS

Expenses (2008–09) *Tuition, state resident:* full-time $6262; part-time $348 per credit hour. *Tuition, nonresident:* full-time $19,220; part-time $704 per credit hour. *Required fees:* full-time $812; part-time $36 per credit.

Financial Aid 75% of graduate students in nursing programs received some form of financial aid in 2007–08. 3 fellowships, 1 research assistantship were awarded; teaching assistantships, Federal Work-Study, institutionally sponsored loans, and unspecified assistantships also available. *Financial aid application deadline:* 2/1.

Contact Dr. Sandra L. McGuire, Chair, Masters Program, College of Nursing, The University of Tennessee, 1200 Volunteer Boulevard, Knoxville, TN 37996-4180. *Telephone:* 865-974-4151. *Fax:* 865-974-3569. *E-mail:* smcguire@utk.edu.

MASTER'S DEGREE PROGRAM

Degree MSN

Available Programs Accelerated Master's for Nurses with Non-Nursing Degrees; Accelerated RN to Master's; Master's; Master's for Non-Nursing College Graduates; Master's for Nurses with Non-Nursing Degrees; RN to Master's.

Concentrations Available Nurse anesthesia; nursing administration. *Clinical nurse specialist programs in:* adult health, gerontology, pediatric, psychiatric/mental health. *Nurse practitioner programs in:* adult health, family health, gerontology, pediatric, psychiatric/mental health.

Study Options Full-time.

Program Entrance Requirements Minimum overall college GPA of 3.0, transcript of college record, CPR certification, written essay, immunizations, 3 letters of recommendation, physical assessment course, professional liability insurance/malpractice insurance, prerequisite course work, statistics course, GRE General Test. *Application deadline:* 2/1 (fall), 10/1 (spring), 10/1 (summer). *Application fee:* $30.

The University of Tennessee (continued)

Advanced Placement Credit by examination available. Credit given for nursing courses completed elsewhere dependent upon specific evaluations.

Degree Requirements 41 total credit hours, thesis or project, comprehensive exam.

POST-MASTER'S PROGRAM

Areas of Study Nurse anesthesia; nursing administration; nursing education. *Clinical nurse specialist programs in:* adult health, gerontology, pediatric, psychiatric/mental health. *Nurse practitioner programs in:* adult health, family health, gerontology, pediatric, psychiatric/mental health.

DOCTORAL DEGREE PROGRAM

Degree PhD

Available Programs Doctorate; Post-Baccalaureate Doctorate.

Areas of Study Bio-behavioral research, biology of health and illness, faculty preparation, family health, health policy, health promotion/disease prevention, human health and illness, individualized study, neurobehavior, nursing administration, nursing education, nursing research, nursing science, women's health.

Online Degree Options Yes (online only).

Program Entrance Requirements Minimum overall college GPA of 3.0, interview by faculty committee, interview, 3 letters of recommendation, writing sample, GRE General Test. Application deadline: 10/1 (fall), 10/1 (summer). Application fee: $30.

Degree Requirements 67 total credit hours, dissertation, oral exam, written exam, residency.

CONTINUING EDUCATION PROGRAM

Contact Dr. Maureen Nalle, Coordinator, Continuing Education, College of Nursing, The University of Tennessee, 1200 Volunteer Boulevard, Knoxville, TN 37996-4180. *Telephone:* 865-974-7598. *Fax:* 865-974-3569. *E-mail:* mnalle@utk.edu.

The University of Tennessee at Chattanooga
School of Nursing
Chattanooga, Tennessee

http://www.utc.edu/~utcnurse/index.htm

Founded in 1886

DEGREES • BSN • MSN

Nursing Program Faculty 26 (42% with doctorates).

Baccalaureate Enrollment 129
Women 82% **Men** 18% **Minority** 8%

Graduate Enrollment 103
Women 79% **Men** 21% **Minority** 10% **Part-time** 49%

Distance Learning Courses Available.

Nursing Student Activities Sigma Theta Tau, Student Nurses' Association.

Nursing Student Resources Academic advising; academic or career counseling; assistance for students with disabilities; bookstore; campus computer network; computer lab; e-mail services; interactive nursing skills videos; Internet; learning resource lab; library services; nursing audiovisuals; skills, simulation, or other laboratory; tutoring.

Library Facilities 586,633 volumes (19,370 in health, 3,100 in nursing); 1,822 periodical subscriptions (200 health-care related).

BACCALAUREATE PROGRAMS

Degree BSN

Available Programs ADN to Baccalaureate; Baccalaureate for Second Degree; Generic Baccalaureate.

Study Options Full-time.

Program Entrance Requirements Minimum overall college GPA of 2.75, transcript of college record, CPR certification, health exam, health insurance, high school foreign language, 3 years high school math, high school transcript, immunizations, 2 letters of recommendation, minimum

high school GPA of 2.0, minimum GPA in nursing prerequisites of 2.5, professional liability insurance/malpractice insurance, prerequisite course work. Transfer students are accepted. *Application deadline:* 2/1 (fall), 9/1 (spring).

Advanced Placement Credit by examination available. Credit given for nursing courses completed elsewhere dependent upon specific evaluations.

Expenses (2008–09) *Tuition, state resident:* full-time $5310; part-time $304 per credit hour. *Tuition, nonresident:* full-time $15,870; part-time $744 per credit hour. *Room and board:* room only: $4000 per academic year.

Financial Aid 60% of baccalaureate students in nursing programs received some form of financial aid in 2007–08. *Gift aid (need-based):* Federal Pell, FSEOG, state, private, college/university gift aid from institutional funds, United Negro College Fund, Federal Nursing. *Loans:* FFEL (Subsidized and Unsubsidized Stafford PLUS), Perkins, college/university. *Work-study:* Federal Work-Study, part-time campus jobs. *Financial aid application deadline (priority):* 4/1.

Contact Dr. Katherine S. Lindgren, Director, School of Nursing, School of Nursing, The University of Tennessee at Chattanooga, 615 McCallie Avenue, Department 1051, Chattanooga, TN 37403-2598. *Telephone:* 423-425-4750. *Fax:* 423-425-4668. *E-mail:* Kay-Lindgren@utc.edu.

GRADUATE PROGRAMS

Expenses (2008–09) *Tuition, state resident:* full-time $6150; part-time $409 per credit hour. *Tuition, nonresident:* full-time $16,710; part-time $995 per credit hour. *Room and board:* room only: $4000 per academic year.

Financial Aid 70% of graduate students in nursing programs received some form of financial aid in 2007–08. Career-related internships or fieldwork, Federal Work-Study, institutionally sponsored loans, scholarships, and unspecified assistantships available. Aid available to part-time students. *Financial aid application deadline:* 4/1.

Contact Dr. Katherine S. Lindgren, Director, School of Nursing, School of Nursing, The University of Tennessee at Chattanooga, 615 McCallie Avenue, Department 1051, Chattanooga, TN 37403-2598. *Telephone:* 423-425-4750. *Fax:* 423-425-4668. *E-mail:* Kay-Lindgren@utc.edu.

MASTER'S DEGREE PROGRAM

Degree MSN

Available Programs Master's.

Concentrations Available Nurse anesthesia. *Nurse practitioner programs in:* family health.

Site Options Tupelo, MS.

Study Options Full-time and part-time.

Program Entrance Requirements Clinical experience, computer literacy, minimum overall college GPA of 3.0, transcript of college record, CPR certification, written essay, immunizations, interview, 3 letters of recommendation, nursing research course, physical assessment course, professional liability insurance/malpractice insurance, resume, statistics course, GRE General Test, MAT. *Application deadline:* 8/1 (summer).

Advanced Placement Credit given for nursing courses completed elsewhere dependent upon specific evaluations.

Degree Requirements 48 total credit hours, comprehensive exam.

POST-MASTER'S PROGRAM

Areas of Study Nurse anesthesia. *Nurse practitioner programs in:* family health.

CONTINUING EDUCATION PROGRAM

Contact Dr. Katherine S. Lindgren, Director, School of Nursing, School of Nursing, The University of Tennessee at Chattanooga, 615 McCallie Avenue, Department 1051, Chattanooga, TN 37403-2598. *Telephone:* 423-425-4750. *Fax:* 423-425-4668. *E-mail:* Kay-Lindgren@utc.edu.

The University of Tennessee at Martin
Department of Nursing
Martin, Tennessee

http://www.utm.edu

Founded in 1900

DEGREE • BSN

Nursing Program Faculty 15 (20% with doctorates).

Baccalaureate Enrollment 198
Women 88% **Men** 12% **Minority** 5% **International** 1% **Part-time** 18%

Distance Learning Courses Available.

Nursing Student Activities Nursing Honor Society, Sigma Theta Tau, Student Nurses' Association, nursing club.

Nursing Student Resources Academic advising; academic or career counseling; assistance for students with disabilities; bookstore; campus computer network; career placement assistance; computer lab; computer-assisted instruction; daycare for children of students; e-mail services; employment services for current students; housing assistance; interactive nursing skills videos; Internet; learning resource lab; library services; nursing audiovisuals; remedial services; resume preparation assistance; skills, simulation, or other laboratory; tutoring.

Library Facilities 533,854 volumes (1,772 in health, 1,645 in nursing); 1,203 periodical subscriptions (10,803 health-care related).

BACCALAUREATE PROGRAMS

Degree BSN

Available Programs ADN to Baccalaureate; Generic Baccalaureate; LPN to RN Baccalaureate.

Site Options Selmer, TN; Parsons, TN; Ripley, TN.

Study Options Full-time.

Program Entrance Requirements Minimum overall college GPA of 2.0, transcript of college record, CPR certification, health exam, health insurance, high school biology, high school chemistry, high school foreign language, 3 years high school math, 2 years high school science, high school transcript, immunizations, interview, minimum high school GPA of 3.0, minimum GPA in nursing prerequisites of 2.0, professional liability insurance/malpractice insurance, prerequisite course work. Transfer students are accepted. *Application deadline:* 2/1 (fall).

Advanced Placement Credit by examination available. Credit given for nursing courses completed elsewhere dependent upon specific evaluations.

Expenses (2009–10) *Tuition, state resident:* full-time $5675; part-time $238 per credit hour. *Tuition, nonresident:* full-time $17,169; part-time $715 per credit hour. *International tuition:* $17,169 full-time. *Room and board:* room only: $2300 per academic year. *Required fees:* full-time $1200; part-time $238 per credit; part-time $500 per term.

Financial Aid 95% of baccalaureate students in nursing programs received some form of financial aid in 2008–09. *Gift aid (need-based):* Federal Pell, FSEOG, state, private, college/university gift aid from institutional funds. *Loans:* FFEL (Subsidized and Unsubsidized Stafford PLUS), Perkins. *Work-study:* Federal Work-Study. *Financial aid application deadline (priority):* 3/1.

Contact Mrs. Brenda W. Campbell, Program Resource Specialist, Department of Nursing, The University of Tennessee at Martin, Gooch Hall 136J, Martin, TN 38238. *Telephone:* 731-881-7138. *Fax:* 731-881-7939. *E-mail:* brendac@utm.edu.

CONTINUING EDUCATION PROGRAM

Contact Dr. Victoria S. Seng, PhD, Interim Chair, Department of Nursing, The University of Tennessee at Martin, Gooch Hall 136H, 538 University Street, Martin, TN 38238. *Telephone:* 731-881-7140. *Fax:* 731-881-7939. *E-mail:* vseng@utm.edu.

The University of Tennessee Health Science Center

College of Nursing
Memphis, Tennessee

http://www.utmem.edu/nursing
Founded in 1911

DEGREES • DNP • MSN

Nursing Program Faculty 51 (87% with doctorates).

Graduate Enrollment 227
Women 85% **Men** 15% **Minority** 22%

Distance Learning Courses Available.

Nursing Student Activities Sigma Theta Tau, Student Nurses' Association.

Nursing Student Resources Academic advising; academic or career counseling; assistance for students with disabilities; bookstore; campus computer network; computer lab; computer-assisted instruction; e-mail services; housing assistance; interactive nursing skills videos; Internet; learning resource lab; library services; nursing audiovisuals; paid internships; remedial services; skills, simulation, or other laboratory; tutoring.

Library Facilities 165,200 volumes (198,936 in health, 8,061 in nursing); 1,784 periodical subscriptions (3,800 health-care related).

GRADUATE PROGRAMS

Expenses (2009–10) *Tuition, state resident:* full-time $9376; part-time $521 per credit hour. *Tuition, nonresident:* full-time $22,585; part-time $1254 per credit hour. *Required fees:* full-time $684.

Financial Aid 65% of graduate students in nursing programs received some form of financial aid in 2008–09. Fellowships with partial tuition reimbursements available, teaching assistantships, Federal Work-Study, institutionally sponsored loans, scholarships, and traineeships available. Aid available to part-time students. *Financial aid application deadline:* 2/28.

Contact Mr. Justin Casey, Assistant Director, Student Affairs, College of Nursing, The University of Tennessee Health Science Center, 877 Madison Avenue, Suite 637, Memphis, TN 38163. *Telephone:* 901-448-6139. *Fax:* 901-448-4121. *E-mail:* jcasey4@uthsc.edu.

MASTER'S DEGREE PROGRAM

Degree MSN

Available Programs Accelerated Master's for Non-Nursing College Graduates.

Concentrations Available Clinical nurse leader.

Study Options Full-time.

Program Entrance Requirements Computer literacy, minimum overall college GPA of 3.0, transcript of college record, CPR certification, written essay, immunizations, interview, 3 letters of recommendation, prerequisite course work, statistics course, GRE General Test. *Application deadline:* 1/15 (summer).

Degree Requirements 80 total credit hours.

POST-MASTER'S PROGRAM

Areas of Study Nurse anesthesia. *Clinical nurse specialist programs in:* acute care, critical care, family health, psychiatric/mental health, public health. *Nurse practitioner programs in:* acute care, family health, neonatal health, pediatric, primary care, psychiatric/mental health.

DOCTORAL DEGREE PROGRAM

Degree DNP

Available Programs Doctorate; Post-Baccalaureate Doctorate.

Areas of Study Addiction/substance abuse, advanced practice nursing, clinical practice, community health, critical care, family health, forensic nursing, gerontology, women's health.

Online Degree Options Yes (online only).

Program Entrance Requirements Minimum overall college GPA of 3.0, interview by faculty committee, interview, 3 letters of recommendation, writing sample. Application deadline: 2/1 (fall).

Degree Requirements Residency.

Vanderbilt University

School of Nursing
Nashville, Tennessee

http://www.nursing.vanderbilt.edu
Founded in 1873

DEGREES • DNP • MSN • MSN/MDIV • MSN/MTS

Nursing Program Faculty 133 (44% with doctorates).

Vanderbilt University (continued)
Graduate Enrollment 714
Women 90% **Men** 10% **Minority** 16% **International** 2% **Part-time** 47%
Distance Learning Courses Available.
Nursing Student Activities Sigma Theta Tau, Student Nurses' Association, nursing club.
Nursing Student Resources Academic advising; assistance for students with disabilities; bookstore; campus computer network; career placement assistance; computer lab; computer-assisted instruction; daycare for children of students; e-mail services; housing assistance; interactive nursing skills videos; Internet; library services; nursing audiovisuals; remedial services; resume preparation assistance; skills, simulation, or other laboratory.
Library Facilities 1.8 million volumes (195,900 in health); 26,885 periodical subscriptions (3,113 health-care related).

■ Vanderbilt University School of Nursing (VUSN) offers a Master of Science in Nursing (M.S.N.) program with multiple entry options: entry with a non-nursing degree*, with an associate degree in nursing, with a diploma in nursing, or with a baccalaureate degree in nursing. *Applicants without a bachelor's degree are considered on an individual basis. There is even an entry option for students who already have an M.S.N. degree but want a role change or role expansion. VUSN also offers a Doctor of Nursing Practice (D.N.P.) program, a Ph.D. in Nursing Science program, and beginning fall 2010, a Master of Science in Nutrition and Dietetics program. At Vanderbilt, faculty members are committed to the tradition of enhancing the quality of health-care delivery. VUSN's vast selection of specialties allows the School of Nursing to shape the careers of health-care leaders today in order to create professional excellence in the leaders of tomorrow.

GRADUATE PROGRAMS

Expenses (2009–10) *Tuition:* full-time $41,000; part-time $1030 per credit hour. *International tuition:* $41,000 full-time. *Required fees:* full-time $3032.
Financial Aid 89% of graduate students in nursing programs received some form of financial aid in 2008–09. 1 research assistantship (averaging $5,000 per year) was awarded; teaching assistantships, scholarships and tuition waivers also available. Aid available to part-time students. *Financial aid application deadline:* 3/15.
Contact Patricia Peerman, Assistant Dean of Enrollment Management, School of Nursing, Vanderbilt University, 207 Godchaux Hall, Nashville, TN 37240. *Telephone:* 615-322-3800. *Fax:* 615-343-0333. *E-mail:* Paddy. Peerman@vanderbilt.edu.

MASTER'S DEGREE PROGRAM

Degrees MSN; MSN/MDIV; MSN/MTS
Available Programs Accelerated AD/RN to Master's; Accelerated Master's; Accelerated Master's for Non-Nursing College Graduates; Accelerated Master's for Nurses with Non-Nursing Degrees; Accelerated RN to Master's; Master's; Master's for Non-Nursing College Graduates; Master's for Nurses with Non-Nursing Degrees; RN to Master's.
Concentrations Available Clinical nurse leader; health-care administration; nurse-midwifery; nursing administration; nursing informatics. *Clinical nurse specialist programs in:* adult health, medical-surgical, pediatric, psychiatric/mental health, women's health. *Nurse practitioner programs in:* acute care, adult health, family health, gerontology, neonatal health, pediatric, psychiatric/mental health, women's health.
Study Options Full-time and part-time.
Online Degree Options Yes.
Program Entrance Requirements Computer literacy, minimum overall college GPA of 3.0, transcript of college record, CPR certification, written essay, immunizations, 3 letters of recommendation, physical assessment course, prerequisite course work, statistics course, GRE General Test. *Application deadline:* Applications may be processed on a rolling basis for some programs.

Advanced Placement Credit by examination available. Credit given for nursing courses completed elsewhere dependent upon specific evaluations.
Degree Requirements 39 total credit hours.

POST-MASTER'S PROGRAM

Areas of Study Clinical nurse leader; health-care administration; nurse-midwifery; nursing administration; nursing informatics. *Clinical nurse specialist programs in:* adult health, medical-surgical, pediatric, psychiatric/mental health, women's health. *Nurse practitioner programs in:* acute care, adult health, family health, gerontology, neonatal health, pediatric, psychiatric/mental health, women's health.

DOCTORAL DEGREE PROGRAM

Degree DNP
Available Programs Doctorate.
Areas of Study Addiction/substance abuse, aging, biology of health and illness, clinical practice, community health, critical care, family health, gerontology, health policy, health promotion/disease prevention, health-care systems, human health and illness, information systems, maternity-newborn, nursing administration, nursing policy, oncology, women's health.
Program Entrance Requirements Clinical experience, minimum overall college GPA of 3.5, interview by faculty committee, interview, 3 letters of recommendation, MSN or equivalent, statistics course, vita, writing sample, GRE General Test. Application deadline: 1/15 (fall). Applications may be processed on a rolling basis for some programs. Application fee: $50.
Degree Requirements 74 total credit hours, oral exam.

POSTDOCTORAL PROGRAM

Areas of Study Individualized study.
Postdoctoral Program Contact Dr. Ann Minnick, Director, School of Nursing, Vanderbilt University, 415 Godchaux Hall, Nashville, TN 37240. *Telephone:* 615-343-2998. *Fax:* 615-343-5898. *E-mail:* ann.minnick@ vanderbilt.edu.

CONTINUING EDUCATION PROGRAM

Contact Ms. Ginny Moore, Director of Lifelong Learning, School of Nursing, Vanderbilt University, 461 21st Avenue South, Nashville, TN 37240. *Telephone:* 615-343-8493. *Fax:* 615-322-8816. *E-mail:* ginny.moore@ vanderbilt.edu.

See full description on page 536.

TEXAS

Abilene Christian University
Patty Hanks Shelton School of Nursing
Abilene, Texas

See description of programs under
Patty Hanks Shelton School of Nursing
(Abilene, Texas).

Angelo State University
Department of Nursing
San Angelo, Texas

http://www.angelo.edu/dept/nur/
Founded in 1928

DEGREES • BSN • MSN

Nursing Program Faculty 30 (5% with doctorates).
Baccalaureate Enrollment 99
Women 78% **Men** 22% **Minority** 20% **Part-time** 89%
Graduate Enrollment 118
Women 94% **Men** 6% **Minority** 16% **International** 1% **Part-time** 91%
Distance Learning Courses Available.
Nursing Student Activities Student Nurses' Association.

Nursing Student Resources Academic advising; academic or career counseling; bookstore; campus computer network; computer lab; computer-assisted instruction; e-mail services; housing assistance; interactive nursing skills videos; Internet; learning resource lab; library services; nursing audiovisuals; skills, simulation, or other laboratory; tutoring.

Library Facilities 590,221 volumes (7,560 in health, 762 in nursing); 33,585 periodical subscriptions (390 health-care related).

BACCALAUREATE PROGRAMS

Degree BSN

Available Programs RN Baccalaureate.
Online Degree Options Yes (online only).
Program Entrance Requirements Minimum overall college GPA of 2.5, transcript of college record, CPR certification, health insurance, immunizations, 2 letters of recommendation, RN licensure. Transfer students are accepted. *Application deadline:* 3/15 (fall), 10/15 (spring), 3/15 (summer).
Expenses (2009–10) *Tuition, state resident:* full-time $7900; part-time $498 per credit hour. *Tuition, nonresident:* full-time $17,800; part-time $773 per credit hour. *Room and board:* $7700; room only: $5200 per academic year. *Required fees:* full-time $1800; part-time $50 per credit; part-time $25 per term.
Financial Aid 30% of baccalaureate students in nursing programs received some form of financial aid in 2008–09. *Gift aid (need-based):* Federal Pell, FSEOG, state, private, college/university gift aid from institutional funds, Federal Nursing. *Loans:* Federal Nursing Student Loans, FFEL (Subsidized and Unsubsidized Stafford PLUS), Perkins, state, college/university, alternative loans. *Work-study:* Federal Work-Study, part-time campus jobs. *Financial aid application deadline (priority):* 4/1.
Contact Dr. Martha Ryder Sleutel, BSN Coordinator, Department of Nursing, Angelo State University, ASU Station #10902, San Angelo, TX 76909. *Telephone:* 325-942-2224. *Fax:* 325-942-2236. *E-mail:* martha.sleutel@angelo.edu.

GRADUATE PROGRAMS

Expenses (2009–10) *Tuition, state resident:* full-time $8800; part-time $501 per credit hour. *Tuition, nonresident:* full-time $18,900; part-time $778 per credit hour. *Room and board:* $7700; room only: $5200 per academic year. *Required fees:* full-time $1800; part-time $50 per credit; part-time $25 per term.
Financial Aid 75% of graduate students in nursing programs received some form of financial aid in 2008–09. Career-related internships or fieldwork, Federal Work-Study, and scholarships available. Aid available to part-time students. *Financial aid application deadline:* 3/1.
Contact Dr. Molly Walker, Graduate Adviser, MSN Program, Department of Nursing, Angelo State University, ASU Station #10902, San Angelo, TX 76909. *Telephone:* 325-942-2224. *Fax:* 325-942-2236. *E-mail:* molly.walker@angelo.edu.

MASTER'S DEGREE PROGRAM

Degree MSN

Available Programs Master's; Master's for Non-Nursing College Graduates; RN to Master's.
Concentrations Available Nursing education. *Clinical nurse specialist programs in:* adult health, medical-surgical.
Study Options Full-time and part-time.
Online Degree Options Yes (online only).
Program Entrance Requirements Computer literacy, minimum overall college GPA of 3.0, transcript of college record, CPR certification, immunizations, 2 letters of recommendation, physical assessment course, prerequisite course work, statistics course, GRE General Test. *Application deadline:* 8/1 (fall), 12/1 (spring).

Advanced Placement Credit given for nursing courses completed elsewhere dependent upon specific evaluations.
Degree Requirements 46 total credit hours, comprehensive exam.

Baylor University
Louise Herrington School of Nursing
Dallas, Texas

http://www.baylor.edu/nursing
Founded in 1845
DEGREES • BSN • DNP • MSN
Nursing Program Faculty 53 (24% with doctorates).
Baccalaureate Enrollment 260
Women 94.3% **Men** 5.7% **Minority** 24.6% **International** 1.5%
Graduate Enrollment 40
Women 95% **Men** 5% **Minority** 32.5% **Part-time** 70%
Nursing Student Activities Sigma Theta Tau, Student Nurses' Association.

Nursing Student Resources Academic advising; campus computer network; computer lab; e-mail services; housing assistance; interactive nursing skills videos; Internet; learning resource lab; library services; nursing audiovisuals; skills, simulation, or other laboratory.

Library Facilities 2.3 million volumes (6,000 in health, 5,000 in nursing); 8,429 periodical subscriptions (147 health-care related).

BACCALAUREATE PROGRAMS

Degree BSN

Available Programs Accelerated Baccalaureate for Second Degree; Generic Baccalaureate.
Study Options Full-time.
Program Entrance Requirements Minimum overall college GPA of 3.0, transcript of college record, CPR certification, written essay, health exam, immunizations, 3 letters of recommendation, minimum GPA in nursing prerequisites of 3.0, prerequisite course work. Transfer students are accepted. *Application deadline:* 1/15 (fall), 5/1 (spring).
Expenses (2008–09) *Tuition:* full-time $23,664; part-time $986 per credit hour. *International tuition:* $23,664 full-time. *Room and board:* $6600; room only: $3000 per academic year. *Required fees:* full-time $3100; part-time $50 per credit; part-time $1000 per term.
Financial Aid 91% of baccalaureate students in nursing programs received some form of financial aid in 2007–08. *Gift aid (need-based):* Federal Pell, FSEOG, state, college/university gift aid from institutional funds. *Loans:* Federal Nursing Student Loans, FFEL (Subsidized and Unsubsidized Stafford PLUS), Perkins, state, private loans—school will certify approved loan application. *Work-study:* Federal Work-Study, part-time campus jobs. *Financial aid application deadline (priority):* 3/1.
Contact Ms. Tina Glaspie, Academic Advisor, Louise Herrington School of Nursing, Baylor University, 3700 Worth Street, Dallas, TX 75246. *Telephone:* 214-214-4151. *Fax:* 214-820-3835. *E-mail:* tina_glaspie@baylor.edu.

GRADUATE PROGRAMS

Expenses (2008–09) *Tuition:* part-time $986 per credit hour. *Room and board:* $6600; room only: $3000 per academic year. *Required fees:* part-time $50 per credit; part-time $101 per term.
Financial Aid 100% of graduate students in nursing programs received some form of financial aid in 2007–08.
Contact Dr. Mary C. Brucker, Director, Graduate Program, Louise Herrington School of Nursing, Baylor University, 3700 Worth Street, Dallas, TX 75246. *Telephone:* 214-820-3361. *Fax:* 214-820-4770. *E-mail:* mary_brucker@baylor.edu.

MASTER'S DEGREE PROGRAM

Degree MSN

Available Programs Master's.
Concentrations Available *Nurse practitioner programs in:* family health, neonatal health.
Site Options Waco, TX.

Baylor University (continued)

Study Options Full-time and part-time.

Program Entrance Requirements Clinical experience, minimum overall college GPA of 3.0, transcript of college record, CPR certification, written essay, immunizations, 3 letters of recommendation, prerequisite course work, statistics course, GRE General Test. *Application deadline:* 6/1 (fall). *Application fee:* $40.

Advanced Placement Credit given for nursing courses completed elsewhere dependent upon specific evaluations.

Degree Requirements 39 total credit hours.

POST-MASTER'S PROGRAM

Areas of Study *Nurse practitioner programs in:* family health, neonatal health.

DOCTORAL DEGREE PROGRAM

Degree DNP

Available Programs Doctorate.

Areas of Study Maternity-newborn.

Program Entrance Requirements Clinical experience, minimum overall college GPA of 3, interview, 3 letters of recommendation, MSN or equivalent, vita, writing sample. Application deadline: 6/1 (fall). Application fee: $40.

Degree Requirements 75 total credit hours.

See display below.

East Texas Baptist University

Department of Nursing
Marshall, Texas

http://www.etbu.edu
Founded in 1912
DEGREE • BSN

Nursing Program Faculty 7 (2% with doctorates).

Baccalaureate Enrollment 35
Women 95% **Men** 5% **Minority** 5%

Nursing Student Activities Nursing Honor Society, Student Nurses' Association, nursing club.

Nursing Student Resources Academic advising; academic or career counseling; assistance for students with disabilities; bookstore; campus computer network; career placement assistance; computer lab; computer-assisted instruction; e-mail services; employment services for current students; housing assistance; interactive nursing skills videos; Internet; learning resource lab; library services; nursing audiovisuals; placement services for program completers; remedial services; resume preparation assistance; skills, simulation, or other laboratory; tutoring.

Library Facilities 229,006 volumes (568 in health, 291 in nursing); 21,000 periodical subscriptions (2,100 health-care related).

BACCALAUREATE PROGRAMS

Degree BSN

Available Programs Generic Baccalaureate.

Study Options Full-time.

Program Entrance Requirements Transcript of college record, CPR certification, written essay, health insurance, immunizations, 2 letters of recommendation, minimum GPA in nursing prerequisites of 2.8, prerequisite course work. Transfer students are accepted. *Application deadline:* 3/1 (fall).

Financial Aid 99% of baccalaureate students in nursing programs received some form of financial aid in 2008–09.

Contact Leslie Borcherding, Interim Dean of Nursing, Department of Nursing, East Texas Baptist University, 1209 North Grove Street, Marshall, TX 75670-1498. *Telephone:* 903-923-2210. *Fax:* 903-938-9225. *E-mail:* lborcherding@etbu.edu.

Hardin-Simmons University

Patty Hanks Shelton School of Nursing
Abilene, Texas

See description of programs under
Patty Hanks Shelton School of Nursing
(Abilene, Texas).

Houston Baptist University

College of Nursing
Houston, Texas

Founded in 1960

DEGREE • BSN

Nursing Program Faculty 23 (6% with doctorates).

Baccalaureate Enrollment 60
Women 90% **Men** 10% **Minority** 20% **International** 10%

Nursing Student Activities Nursing Honor Society, Sigma Theta Tau, Student Nurses' Association.

Nursing Student Resources Academic advising; academic or career counseling; assistance for students with disabilities; bookstore; career placement assistance; computer lab; e-mail services; employment services for current students; externships; housing assistance; interactive nursing skills videos; Internet; learning resource lab; library services; nursing audiovisuals; paid internships; placement services for program completers; remedial services; resume preparation assistance; skills, simulation, or other laboratory; tutoring; unpaid internships.

Library Facilities 235,973 volumes (4,276 in health, 1,200 in nursing); 59,855 periodical subscriptions (117 health-care related).

BACCALAUREATE PROGRAMS

Degree BSN

Site Options Houston, TX.

Study Options Full-time.

Program Entrance Requirements Minimum overall college GPA of 2.5, minimum GPA in nursing prerequisites of 2.5. Transfer students are accepted.

Advanced Placement Credit by examination available.

Contact *Telephone:* 281-649-3300. *Fax:* 281-649-3340.

Lamar University

Department of Nursing
Beaumont, Texas

http://dept.lamar.edu/nursing/

Founded in 1923

DEGREES • BSN • MSN • MSN/MBA

Nursing Program Faculty 39 (31% with doctorates).

Baccalaureate Enrollment 245
Women 84% **Men** 16% **Minority** 37% **International** 2% **Part-time** 1%

Graduate Enrollment 31
Women 87% **Men** 13% **Minority** 16% **International** 5% **Part-time** 84%

Distance Learning Courses Available.

Nursing Student Activities Sigma Theta Tau, Student Nurses' Association.

Nursing Student Resources Academic advising; academic or career counseling; assistance for students with disabilities; bookstore; campus computer network; career placement assistance; computer lab; computer-assisted instruction; daycare for children of students; e-mail services; employment services for current students; housing assistance; interactive nursing skills videos; Internet; learning resource lab; library services;

nursing audiovisuals; placement services for program completers; remedial services; resume preparation assistance; skills, simulation, or other laboratory; tutoring.

Library Facilities 698,285 volumes (6,825 in health, 3,160 in nursing); 2,900 periodical subscriptions (166 health-care related).

BACCALAUREATE PROGRAMS

Degree BSN

Available Programs ADN to Baccalaureate; Generic Baccalaureate; RN Baccalaureate.

Study Options Full-time.

Online Degree Options Yes.

Program Entrance Requirements Minimum overall college GPA of 2.0, transcript of college record, CPR certification, health exam, immunizations, minimum GPA in nursing prerequisites of 2.0, professional liability insurance/malpractice insurance, prerequisite course work. Transfer students are accepted. *Application deadline:* 3/1 (fall), 10/1 (spring). *Application fee:* $25.

Advanced Placement Credit given for nursing courses completed elsewhere dependent upon specific evaluations.

Expenses (2009–10) *Tuition, state resident:* full-time $6606. *Tuition, nonresident:* full-time $14,916. *Room and board:* $6290; room only: $4190 per academic year. *Required fees:* full-time $280.

Financial Aid 73% of baccalaureate students in nursing programs received some form of financial aid in 2008–09. *Gift aid (need-based):* Federal Pell, FSEOG, state, college/university gift aid from institutional funds. *Loans:* FFEL (Subsidized and Unsubsidized Stafford PLUS), Perkins, state, college/university. *Work-study:* Federal Work-Study, part-time campus jobs. *Financial aid application deadline (priority):* 4/1.

Contact Ms. Kaitlyn C. Brodnax, Academic Advisor, Department of Nursing, Lamar University, PO Box 10081, Beaumont, TX 77710. *Telephone:* 409-880-8868. *Fax:* 409-880-7736. *E-mail:* nursing@lamar.edu.

GRADUATE PROGRAMS

Expenses (2009–10) *Tuition, state resident:* full-time $6816; part-time $400 per credit hour. *Tuition, nonresident:* full-time $13,339; part-time $705 per credit hour. *International tuition:* $13,399 full-time. *Room and board:* $6290; room only: $4190 per academic year. *Required fees:* full-time $280; part-time $140 per term.

Financial Aid 43% of graduate students in nursing programs received some form of financial aid in 2008–09.

Contact Dr. Nancy Bume, Director of Graduate Nursing Studies, Department of Nursing, Lamar University, PO Box 10081, Beaumont, TX 77710. *Telephone:* 409-880-7720. *Fax:* 409-880-8698. *E-mail:* nancy.blume@lamar.edu.

MASTER'S DEGREE PROGRAM

Degrees MSN; MSN/MBA

Available Programs Master's.

Concentrations Available Nursing administration; nursing education.

Study Options Full-time and part-time.

Online Degree Options Yes (online only).

Program Entrance Requirements Computer literacy, minimum overall college GPA of 3.0, transcript of college record, immunizations, professional liability insurance/malpractice insurance, prerequisite course work, statistics course. *Application deadline:* Applications may be processed on a rolling basis for some programs. *Application fee:* $25.

Advanced Placement Credit given for nursing courses completed elsewhere dependent upon specific evaluations.

Degree Requirements 37 total credit hours, thesis or project, comprehensive exam.

POST-MASTER'S PROGRAM

Areas of Study Nursing administration; nursing education.

CONTINUING EDUCATION PROGRAM

Contact Dr. Cindy Stinson, RN, Coordinator of Continuing Education, Department of Nursing, Lamar University, PO Box 10081, Beaumont, TX 77710. *Telephone:* 409-880-8833. *Fax:* 409-880-1865. *E-mail:* cynthia.stinson@lamar.edu.

Lubbock Christian University
Department of Nursing
Lubbock, Texas

Founded in 1957

DEGREE • BSN

Nursing Program Faculty 5 (40% with doctorates).
Library Facilities 113,556 volumes; 545 periodical subscriptions.

BACCALAUREATE PROGRAMS

Degree BSN

Available Programs RN Baccalaureate.
Study Options Part-time.
Program Entrance Requirements Minimum overall college GPA of 2.5, transcript of college record, CPR certification, health exam, immunizations, interview, 2 letters of recommendation, minimum high school GPA, minimum GPA in nursing prerequisites of 2.5, professional liability insurance/malpractice insurance, prerequisite course work, RN licensure. Transfer students are accepted.

McMurry University
Patty Hanks Shelton School of Nursing
Abilene, Texas

See description of programs under
Patty Hanks Shelton School of Nursing
(Abilene, Texas).

Midwestern State University
Nursing Program
Wichita Falls, Texas

Founded in 1922

DEGREES • BSN • MN/MHSA • MSN • MSN/MHA

Nursing Program Faculty 22 (4.4% with doctorates).
Baccalaureate Enrollment 271
Women 82% **Men** 18% **Minority** 54% **International** 4% **Part-time** 1%
Graduate Enrollment 65
Women 86% **Men** 14% **Minority** 46% **International** 6% **Part-time** 70%
Nursing Student Activities Nursing Honor Society, Sigma Theta Tau, Student Nurses' Association.

Nursing Student Resources Academic advising; academic or career counseling; assistance for students with disabilities; bookstore; campus computer network; career placement assistance; computer lab; computer-assisted instruction; e-mail services; employment services for current students; externships; housing assistance; interactive nursing skills videos; Internet; learning resource lab; library services; nursing audiovisuals; other; paid internships; placement services for program completers; remedial services; resume preparation assistance; skills, simulation, or other laboratory; tutoring; unpaid internships.

Library Facilities 441,251 volumes (10,000 in health, 5,000 in nursing); 1,246 periodical subscriptions (200 health-care related).

BACCALAUREATE PROGRAMS

Degree BSN

Available Programs ADN to Baccalaureate; Generic Baccalaureate; RN Baccalaureate.
Study Options Full-time and part-time.

Program Entrance Requirements Transcript of college record, CPR certification, health exam, health insurance, high school transcript, immunizations, minimum GPA in nursing prerequisites of 3.0, professional liability insurance/malpractice insurance, prerequisite course work. Transfer students are accepted.
Advanced Placement Credit by examination available. Credit given for nursing courses completed elsewhere dependent upon specific evaluations.
Contact · *Telephone:* 940-397-4601. *Fax:* 940-397-4911.

GRADUATE PROGRAMS

Contact *Telephone:* 940-397-4601. *Fax:* 940-397-4911.

MASTER'S DEGREE PROGRAM

Degrees MN/MHSA; MSN; MSN/MHA

Available Programs Master's; RN to Master's.
Concentrations Available Health-care administration; nursing administration; nursing education. *Nurse practitioner programs in:* family health.
Study Options Full-time and part-time.
Program Entrance Requirements Clinical experience, computer literacy, minimum overall college GPA of 3.0, transcript of college record, CPR certification, immunizations, interview, nursing research course, physical assessment course, professional liability insurance/malpractice insurance, prerequisite course work, statistics course, GRE General Test or MAT.
Degree Requirements 36 total credit hours, thesis or project.

POST-MASTER'S PROGRAM

Areas of Study Nursing education. *Nurse practitioner programs in:* family health.

CONTINUING EDUCATION PROGRAM

Contact *Telephone:* 940-397-4048. *Fax:* 940-397-4513.

Patty Hanks Shelton School of Nursing
Patty Hanks Shelton School of Nursing
Abilene, Texas

http://www.aisn.edu/

DEGREES • BSN • MSN

Nursing Program Faculty 17 (33% with doctorates).
Baccalaureate Enrollment 130
Women 90% **Men** 10% **Minority** 15% **International** 4%
Graduate Enrollment 23
Women 75% **Men** 25% **Minority** 10%
Distance Learning Courses Available.
Nursing Student Activities Nursing Honor Society, Sigma Theta Tau, Student Nurses' Association.

Nursing Student Resources Academic advising; academic or career counseling; assistance for students with disabilities; bookstore; campus computer network; career placement assistance; computer lab; computer-assisted instruction; e-mail services; employment services for current students; externships; interactive nursing skills videos; Internet; learning resource lab; library services; nursing audiovisuals; remedial services; resume preparation assistance; skills, simulation, or other laboratory; tutoring.

Library Facilities 9,200 volumes in health, 1,300 volumes in nursing; 140 periodical subscriptions health-care related.

BACCALAUREATE PROGRAMS

Degree BSN

Available Programs Generic Baccalaureate; RN Baccalaureate.
Study Options Full-time.

Program Entrance Requirements Minimum overall college GPA of 3.0, transcript of college record, CPR certification, health exam, health insurance, immunizations, interview, 2 letters of recommendation, minimum GPA in nursing prerequisites of 3.0, professional liability insurance/malpractice insurance, prerequisite course work. Transfer students are accepted. *Application deadline:* 2/12 (fall). *Application fee:* $80.

Advanced Placement Credit by examination available. Credit given for nursing courses completed elsewhere dependent upon specific evaluations.

Financial Aid 80% of baccalaureate students in nursing programs received some form of financial aid in 2008–09.

Contact Mrs. Rachel King, Director, Learning and Student Development, Patty Hanks Shelton School of Nursing, 2149 Hickory Street, Abilene, TX 79601. *Telephone:* 325-671-2353. *Fax:* 325-671-2386. *E-mail:* rking@phssn. edu.

GRADUATE PROGRAMS

Financial Aid 50% of graduate students in nursing programs received some form of financial aid in 2008–09.

Contact Dr. Amy Roberts Toone, Director of the Graduate Program, Patty Hanks Shelton School of Nursing, 2149 Hickory Street, Abilene, TX 79601. *Telephone:* 325-671-2361. *Fax:* 325-671-2386. *E-mail:* atoone@phssn.edu.

MASTER'S DEGREE PROGRAM

Degree MSN

Available Programs Master's.

Concentrations Available Nursing administration; nursing education. *Nurse practitioner programs in:* family health.

Study Options Full-time and part-time.

Program Entrance Requirements Clinical experience, minimum overall college GPA of 3.5, transcript of college record, CPR certification, written essay, immunizations, interview, 3 letters of recommendation, physical assessment course, professional liability insurance/malpractice insurance, resume, statistics course.

Advanced Placement Credit given for nursing courses completed elsewhere dependent upon specific evaluations.

Degree Requirements 49 total credit hours.

POST-MASTER'S PROGRAM

Areas of Study *Nurse practitioner programs in:* family health.

CONTINUING EDUCATION PROGRAM

Contact Dr. Nina Ouimette, Dean and Associate Professor, Patty Hanks Shelton School of Nursing, 2149 Hickory Street, Abilene, TX 79601. *Telephone:* 325-671-2399. *Fax:* 325-671-2386. *E-mail:* nouimette@phssn. edu.

Prairie View A&M University

College of Nursing
Houston, Texas

http://dl.pvamu.edu/

Founded in 1878

DEGREES • BSN • MSN

Nursing Program Faculty 66 (26% with doctorates).

Baccalaureate Enrollment 447
Women 85% **Men** 15% **Minority** 38% **International** 2% **Part-time** 19%

Graduate Enrollment 103
Women 95% **Men** 5% **Minority** 25% **International** 2% **Part-time** 78%

Distance Learning Courses Available.

Nursing Student Activities Nursing Honor Society, Sigma Theta Tau, Student Nurses' Association, nursing club.

Nursing Student Resources Academic advising; academic or career counseling; assistance for students with disabilities; bookstore; campus computer network; career placement assistance; computer lab; computer-assisted instruction; e-mail services; employment services for current students; interactive nursing skills videos; Internet; learning resource lab;

library services; nursing audiovisuals; placement services for program completers; resume preparation assistance; skills, simulation, or other laboratory; tutoring.

Library Facilities 1.1 million volumes (355,707 in health, 7,899 in nursing); 39,724 periodical subscriptions (9,283 health-care related).

BACCALAUREATE PROGRAMS

Degree BSN

Available Programs Generic Baccalaureate; LPN to Baccalaureate; RN Baccalaureate.

Site Options Woodlands, TX; College Station, TX.

Study Options Full-time and part-time.

Program Entrance Requirements Minimum overall college GPA of 2.5, transcript of college record, CPR certification, health exam, immunizations, minimum GPA in nursing prerequisites of 2.0, professional liability insurance/malpractice insurance, prerequisite course work. Transfer students are accepted. *Application deadline:* 3/1 (fall), 10/1 (spring). *Application fee:* $25.

Advanced Placement Credit given for nursing courses completed elsewhere dependent upon specific evaluations.

Expenses (2009–10) *Tuition, area resident:* full-time $4232; part-time $163 per credit hour. *Tuition, nonresident:* full-time $11,435; part-time $440 per credit hour. *International tuition:* $11,435 full-time. *Required fees:* full-time $2181; part-time $272 per credit; part-time $864 per term.

Financial Aid 95% of baccalaureate students in nursing programs received some form of financial aid in 2008–09.

Contact Dr. Forest Smith, Director, Admissions and Student Services, College of Nursing, Prairie View A&M University, 6436 Fannin Street, Suite 109, Houston, TX 77030. *Telephone:* 713-797-7031. *Fax:* 713-797-7092. *E-mail:* fdsmith@pvamu.edu.

GRADUATE PROGRAMS

Expenses (2009–10) *Tuition, area resident:* full-time $6170; part-time $213 per credit hour. *Tuition, nonresident:* full-time $15,738; part-time $492 per credit hour. *International tuition:* $15,738 full-time. *Required fees:* full-time $3257; part-time $633 per credit; part-time $1086 per term.

Financial Aid 38% of graduate students in nursing programs received some form of financial aid in 2008–09. Career-related internships or fieldwork, Federal Work-Study, institutionally sponsored loans, scholarships, and traineeships available. Aid available to part-time students. *Financial aid application deadline:* 4/1.

Contact Dr. Jennifer Goodman, Director, College of Nursing, Prairie View A&M University, 6436 Fannin Street, Suite 1254, Houston, TX 77030. *Telephone:* 713-797-7015. *Fax:* 713-797-7011. *E-mail:* jjgoodman@pvamu. edu.

MASTER'S DEGREE PROGRAM

Degree MSN

Available Programs Master's.

Concentrations Available Nursing administration; nursing education. *Nurse practitioner programs in:* family health.

Study Options Full-time and part-time.

Program Entrance Requirements Clinical experience, minimum overall college GPA of 2.75, transcript of college record, CPR certification, immunizations, interview, 3 letters of recommendation, physical assessment course, prerequisite course work, resume, statistics course, MAT or GRE. *Application deadline:* 6/1 (fall), 10/1 (spring), 4/1 (summer). *Application fee:* $25.

Advanced Placement Credit by examination available. Credit given for nursing courses completed elsewhere dependent upon specific evaluations.

Degree Requirements 53 total credit hours, thesis or project.

POST-MASTER'S PROGRAM

Areas of Study Nursing administration; nursing education. *Nurse practitioner programs in:* family health.

Southwestern Adventist University

Department of Nursing
Keene, Texas

http://www.swau.edu
Founded in 1894

DEGREE • BS

Nursing Program Faculty 17 (12% with doctorates).

Baccalaureate Enrollment 95
Women 72% **Men** 28% **Minority** 70% **International** 12% **Part-time** .04%

Nursing Student Activities Nursing Honor Society, Sigma Theta Tau, Student Nurses' Association.

Nursing Student Resources Academic advising; academic or career counseling; assistance for students with disabilities; bookstore; campus computer network; computer lab; computer-assisted instruction; e-mail services; externships; interactive nursing skills videos; Internet; learning resource lab; library services; nursing audiovisuals; remedial services; resume preparation assistance; skills, simulation, or other laboratory; tutoring.

Library Facilities 108,481 volumes (6,575 in nursing); 457 periodical subscriptions (60 health-care related).

BACCALAUREATE PROGRAMS

Degree BS

Available Programs ADN to Baccalaureate; Accelerated LPN to Baccalaureate; Accelerated RN Baccalaureate; Generic Baccalaureate.

Study Options Full-time and part-time.

Program Entrance Requirements Transcript of college record, CPR certification, health exam, health insurance, immunizations, interview, 3 letters of recommendation, minimum GPA in nursing prerequisites of 2.75, prerequisite course work. *Application deadline:* 12/20 (spring). *Application fee:* $100.

Advanced Placement Credit by examination available.

Expenses (2009–10) *Tuition:* full-time $15,456; part-time $7728 per semester. *International tuition:* $15,456 full-time. *Room and board:* $7148; room only: $3128 per academic year. *Required fees:* full-time $600; part-time $150 per credit; part-time $300 per term.

Financial Aid 60% of baccalaureate students in nursing programs received some form of financial aid in 2008–09.

Contact Dr. Catherine A. Turner, RN, Chair of Nursing Department, Department of Nursing, Southwestern Adventist University, PO Box 567, Keene, TX 76059. *Telephone:* 817-645-3921 Ext. 519. *Fax:* 817-556-4713. *E-mail:* Turnerc@swau.edu.

Stephen F. Austin State University

Division of Nursing
Nacogdoches, Texas

http://www.fp.sfasu.edu/nursing/
Founded in 1923

DEGREE • BSN

Nursing Program Faculty 19 (16% with doctorates).

Baccalaureate Enrollment 128
Women 96% **Men** 4% **Minority** 1%

Nursing Student Activities Sigma Theta Tau, Student Nurses' Association.

Nursing Student Resources Academic advising; academic or career counseling; bookstore; computer lab; computer-assisted instruction; e-mail services; interactive nursing skills videos; Internet; library services; nursing audiovisuals; skills, simulation, or other laboratory; tutoring.

Library Facilities 732,286 volumes; 1,501 periodical subscriptions.

BACCALAUREATE PROGRAMS

Degree BSN

Available Programs RN Baccalaureate.

Site Options Lufkin, TX.

Study Options Full-time.

Program Entrance Requirements Minimum overall college GPA of 2.75, transcript of college record, CPR certification, health insurance, high school transcript, immunizations, minimum GPA in nursing prerequisites of 2.5, professional liability insurance/malpractice insurance, prerequisite course work. Transfer students are accepted.

Advanced Placement Credit given for nursing courses completed elsewhere dependent upon specific evaluations.

Contact *Telephone:* 936-468-3604. *Fax:* 936-468-1696.

Tarleton State University

Department of Nursing
Stephenville, Texas

http://www.tarleton.edu/~nursing
Founded in 1899

DEGREE • BSN

Nursing Program Faculty 19 (14% with doctorates).

Baccalaureate Enrollment 230
Women 95% **Men** 5% **Minority** 15% **International** 2% **Part-time** 25%

Nursing Student Activities Sigma Theta Tau, Student Nurses' Association.

Nursing Student Resources Academic advising; academic or career counseling; assistance for students with disabilities; bookstore; computer lab; computer-assisted instruction; daycare for children of students; e-mail services; employment services for current students; externships; learning resource lab; library services; nursing audiovisuals; remedial services; resume preparation assistance; skills, simulation, or other laboratory; tutoring; unpaid internships.

Library Facilities 400,000 volumes; 25,800 periodical subscriptions.

BACCALAUREATE PROGRAMS

Degree BSN

Available Programs ADN to Baccalaureate; Generic Baccalaureate; LPN to Baccalaureate.

Study Options Full-time and part-time.

Program Entrance Requirements Transcript of college record; CPR certification, written essay, health exam, high school transcript, immunizations, 3 letters of recommendation, minimum GPA in nursing prerequisites of 2.75, professional liability insurance/malpractice insurance, prerequisite course work. Transfer students are accepted.

Advanced Placement Credit by examination available. Credit given for nursing courses completed elsewhere dependent upon specific evaluations.

Contact *Telephone:* 254-968-9139. *Fax:* 254-968-9716.

CONTINUING EDUCATION PROGRAM

Contact *Telephone:* 325-649-8058. *Fax:* 325-649-8959.

Texas A&M International University

Canseco School of Nursing
Laredo, Texas

Founded in 1969

DEGREES • BSN • MSN

Nursing Program Faculty 18 (20% with doctorates).

Baccalaureate Enrollment 175
Women 70% **Men** 30% **Minority** 98% **International** 1% **Part-time** 25%

Graduate Enrollment 12

Women 75% **Men** 25% **Minority** 75% **Part-time** 100%

Nursing Student Activities Nursing Honor Society, Student Nurses' Association.

Nursing Student Resources Academic advising; academic or career counseling; assistance for students with disabilities; bookstore; campus computer network; career placement assistance; computer lab; computer-assisted instruction; daycare for children of students; e-mail services; employment services for current students; externships; housing assistance; interactive nursing skills videos; Internet; learning resource lab; library services; nursing audiovisuals; paid internships; placement services for program completers; remedial services; resume preparation assistance; skills, simulation, or other laboratory; tutoring.

Library Facilities 310,366 volumes (8,500 in nursing); 8,149 periodical subscriptions (80 health-care related).

BACCALAUREATE PROGRAMS

Degree BSN

Available Programs Generic Baccalaureate; RN Baccalaureate.

Study Options Full-time.

Program Entrance Requirements Minimum overall college GPA of 2.5, transcript of college record, written essay, health exam, immunizations, 2 letters of recommendation, minimum GPA in nursing prerequisites of 2.5, prerequisite course work. Transfer students are accepted. *Application deadline:* 9/1 (fall).

Advanced Placement Credit given for nursing courses completed elsewhere dependent upon specific evaluations.

Expenses (2009–10) *Tuition, state resident:* full-time $4740; part-time $288 per credit hour. *Tuition, nonresident:* full-time $11,386; part-time $564 per credit hour.

Financial Aid 85% of baccalaureate students in nursing programs received some form of financial aid in 2008–09.

Contact Dr. Regina C. Aune, RN, Dean, Canseco School of Nursing, Texas A&M International University, 5201 University Boulevard, Laredo, TX 78041-1900. *Telephone:* 956-326-2450. *Fax:* 956-326-2449. *E-mail:* regina.aune@tamiu.edu.

GRADUATE PROGRAMS

Expenses (2009–10) *Tuition, state resident:* full-time $4980; part-time $307 per credit hour. *Tuition, nonresident:* full-time $8634; part-time $558 per credit hour.

Financial Aid 85% of graduate students in nursing programs received some form of financial aid in 2008–09.

Contact Dr. Regina C. Aune, RN, Dean, Canseco School of Nursing, Texas A&M International University, 5201 University Boulevard, Laredo, TX 78041-1900. *Telephone:* 956-326-2450. *Fax:* 956-326-2449. *E-mail:* sbaker@tamiu.edu.

MASTER'S DEGREE PROGRAM

Degree MSN

Available Programs Master's; Master's for Nurses with Non-Nursing Degrees.

Concentrations Available *Nurse practitioner programs in:* family health.

Study Options Full-time and part-time.

Program Entrance Requirements Clinical experience, minimum overall college GPA of 3.0, transcript of college record, CPR certification, written essay, immunizations, interview, 2 letters of recommendation.

Advanced Placement Credit given for nursing courses completed elsewhere dependent upon specific evaluations.

Degree Requirements 45 total credit hours.

Texas A&M University–Corpus Christi

School of Nursing and Health Sciences
Corpus Christi, Texas

http://conhs.tamucc.edu/

Founded in 1947

DEGREES • BSN • MSN

Nursing Program Faculty 55 (45% with doctorates).

Baccalaureate Enrollment 425

Women 72% **Men** 28% **Minority** 52% **International** 1% **Part-time** 20%

Graduate Enrollment 345

Women 87% **Men** 13% **Minority** 38% **International** 1% **Part-time** 99%

Distance Learning Courses Available.

Nursing Student Activities Nursing Honor Society, Sigma Theta Tau, Student Nurses' Association.

Nursing Student Resources Academic advising; academic or career counseling; assistance for students with disabilities; bookstore; campus computer network; career placement assistance; computer lab; computer-assisted instruction; e-mail services; employment services for current students; housing assistance; interactive nursing skills videos; Internet; learning resource lab; library services; nursing audiovisuals; placement services for program completers; remedial services; resume preparation assistance; skills, simulation, or other laboratory; tutoring.

Library Facilities 731,586 volumes (500 in health, 350 in nursing); 1,901 periodical subscriptions (100 health-care related).

BACCALAUREATE PROGRAMS

Degree BSN

Available Programs ADN to Baccalaureate; Accelerated Baccalaureate for Second Degree; Baccalaureate for Second Degree; Generic Baccalaureate; RN Baccalaureate.

Study Options Full-time and part-time.

Online Degree Options Yes.

Program Entrance Requirements Minimum overall college GPA of 3.0, transcript of college record, CPR certification, immunizations, professional liability insurance/malpractice insurance, prerequisite course work. Transfer students are accepted. *Application deadline:* 2/16 (fall), 8/3 (spring), 12/1 (summer). *Application fee:* $25.

Advanced Placement Credit by examination available. Credit given for nursing courses completed elsewhere dependent upon specific evaluations.

Expenses (2009–10) *Tuition, area resident:* full-time $5317; part-time $141 per credit. *Tuition, state resident:* full-time $5317; part-time $144 per credit. *Tuition, nonresident:* full-time $16,276; part-time $422 per credit. *International tuition:* $16,276 full-time. *Room and board:* $1900; room only: $900 per academic year. *Required fees:* full-time $4376; part-time $150 per credit; part-time $1044 per term.

Financial Aid 70% of baccalaureate students in nursing programs received some form of financial aid in 2008–09.

Contact Ms. Angelica M. Santillan, Academic Advisor, School of Nursing and Health Sciences, Texas A&M University–Corpus Christi, 6300 Ocean Drive, Unit 5805, Corpus Christi, TX 78412. *Telephone:* 361-825-2461. *E-mail:* angelica.santillan@tamucc.edu.

GRADUATE PROGRAMS

Expenses (2009–10) *Tuition, area resident:* full-time $4103; part-time $70 per credit hour. *Tuition, state resident:* full-time $10,751; part-time $70 per credit hour. *Tuition, nonresident:* full-time $10,751; part-time $448 per credit hour. *International tuition:* $10,751 full-time. *Required fees:* full-time $1081; part-time $155 per credit; part-time $455 per term.

Financial Aid 20% of graduate students in nursing programs received some form of financial aid in 2008–09.

Contact Dr. Eve Layman, RN, Graduate Department Chair, School of Nursing and Health Sciences, Texas A&M University–Corpus Christi, 6300 Ocean Drive, Unit 5805, Corpus Christi, TX 78412. *Telephone:* 361-825-3781. *Fax:* 361-825-5853. *E-mail:* eve.layman@tamucc.edu.

MASTER'S DEGREE PROGRAM

Degree MSN

Available Programs Accelerated AD/RN to Master's; Accelerated RN to Master's; Master's.

Concentrations Available Nursing administration. *Clinical nurse specialist programs in:* adult health. *Nurse practitioner programs in:* family health.

Site Options Temple, TX.

Study Options Part-time.

Online Degree Options Yes (online only).

Texas A&M University–Corpus Christi (continued)

Program Entrance Requirements Computer literacy, minimum overall college GPA of 3.0, transcript of college record, CPR certification, written essay, immunizations, 3 letters of recommendation, nursing research course, resume, statistics course. *Application deadline:* 7/14 (fall), 11/15 (spring), 4/15 (summer). *Application fee:* $40.

Advanced Placement Credit given for nursing courses completed elsewhere dependent upon specific evaluations.

Degree Requirements 49 total credit hours.

POST-MASTER'S PROGRAM

Areas of Study Nursing administration; nursing education. *Clinical nurse specialist programs in:* adult health. *Nurse practitioner programs in:* family health.

CONTINUING EDUCATION PROGRAM

Contact Ms. Petra Martinez, Chair of Continuing Education Committee, School of Nursing and Health Sciences, Texas A&M University–Corpus Christi, 6300 Ocean Drive, ST 316, Corpus Christi, TX 78412. *Telephone:* 361-825-2353. *Fax:* 361-825-3491. *E-mail:* petra.martinez@tamucc.edu.

Texas A&M University–Texarkana
Nursing Department
Texarkana, Texas

http://www.tamut.edu/nursing/index.
php?pageid=13

Founded in 1971

DEGREES • BSN • MSN

Nursing Program Faculty 5 (60% with doctorates).

Baccalaureate Enrollment 31
Women 87% **Men** 13% **Minority** 23% **Part-time** 94%

Graduate Enrollment 26
Women 96% **Men** 4% **Minority** 15% **Part-time** 100%

Nursing Student Activities Nursing club.

Nursing Student Resources Academic advising; academic or career counseling; assistance for students with disabilities; bookstore; campus computer network; career placement assistance; computer lab; computer-assisted instruction; e-mail services; Internet; library services; nursing audiovisuals; resume preparation assistance.

Library Facilities 132,065 volumes (8,743 in health, 2,558 in nursing); 6,561 periodical subscriptions (80 health-care related).

BACCALAUREATE PROGRAMS

Degree BSN

Available Programs ADN to Baccalaureate.

Study Options Full-time and part-time.

Program Entrance Requirements Minimum overall college GPA of 2.0, transcript of college record, CPR certification, health exam, health insurance, immunizations, letters of recommendation, professional liability insurance/malpractice insurance, prerequisite course work, RN licensure. Transfer students are accepted. *Application deadline:* 7/15 (fall), 12/1 (spring), 4/1 (summer).

Advanced Placement Credit given for nursing courses completed elsewhere dependent upon specific evaluations.

Expenses (2009–10) *Tuition, state resident:* full-time $3900; part-time $130 per credit hour. *Tuition, nonresident:* full-time $12,210; part-time $407 per credit hour. *International tuition:* $12,210 full-time. *Required fees:* full-time $656; part-time $21 per credit.

Financial Aid 12% of baccalaureate students in nursing programs received some form of financial aid in 2008–09. *Gift aid (need-based):* Federal Pell, FSEOG, state, private, college/university gift aid from institutional funds. *Loans:* FFEL (Subsidized and Unsubsidized Stafford PLUS), college/university. *Work-study:* Federal Work-Study. *Financial aid application deadline (priority):* 5/1.

Contact Jo Kahler, EdD, Dean of the College of Health and Behavioral Sciences, Nursing Department, Texas A&M University–Texarkana, PO Box 5518, 2600 North Robison Road, Texarkana, TX 75501. *Telephone:* 903-223-3175. *Fax:* 903-223-3107. *E-mail:* Jo.Kahler@tamut.edu.

GRADUATE PROGRAMS

Expenses (2009–10) *Tuition, state resident:* full-time $3600; part-time $150 per credit hour. *Tuition, nonresident:* full-time $10,248; part-time $427 per credit hour. *International tuition:* $10,248 full-time. *Required fees:* full-time $532; part-time $20 per credit; part-time $9 per term.

Contact Dr. Jo Kahler, Dean, College of Health and Behavioral Sciences, Nursing Department, Texas A&M University–Texarkana, PO Box 5518, 2600 North Robison Road, Texarkana, TX 75505. *Telephone:* 903-223-3175. *E-mail:* jo.kahler@tamut.edu.

MASTER'S DEGREE PROGRAM

Degree MSN

Available Programs Master's.

Concentrations Available Nursing administration; nursing education.

Study Options Full-time and part-time.

Program Entrance Requirements Minimum overall college GPA of 3.0, transcript of college record, written essay, 3 letters of recommendation, resume. *Application deadline:* 7/15 (fall), 12/1 (spring), 4/1 (summer).

Degree Requirements 36 total credit hours.

Texas Christian University
Harris College of Nursing
Fort Worth, Texas

http://www.nursing.tcu.edu

Founded in 1873

DEGREES • BSN • DNP • MSN

Nursing Program Faculty 49 (59% with doctorates).

Baccalaureate Enrollment 600
Women 93.5% **Men** 6.5% **Minority** 24.5% **International** 1.5%

Graduate Enrollment 273
Women 63% **Men** 37% **Minority** 29% **International** 4% **Part-time** 9%

Distance Learning Courses Available.

Nursing Student Activities Sigma Theta Tau, Student Nurses' Association.

Nursing Student Resources Academic advising; academic or career counseling; assistance for students with disabilities; bookstore; campus computer network; career placement assistance; computer lab; computer-assisted instruction; e-mail services; externships; interactive nursing skills videos; Internet; learning resource lab; library services; nursing audiovisuals; other; remedial services; resume preparation assistance; skills, simulation, or other laboratory; tutoring.

Library Facilities 1.4 million volumes (18,590 in health, 3,144 in nursing); 32,935 periodical subscriptions (180 health-care related).

BACCALAUREATE PROGRAMS

Degree BSN

Available Programs Accelerated Baccalaureate for Second Degree; Generic Baccalaureate.

Site Options Fort Worth, TX.

Study Options Full-time and part-time.

Program Entrance Requirements Minimum overall college GPA of 2.5, transcript of college record, CPR certification, written essay, high school foreign language, 2 years high school math, 4 years high school science, high school transcript, immunizations, minimum high school GPA of 3.0, minimum GPA in nursing prerequisites of 2.5, prerequisite course work. Transfer students are accepted. *Application deadline:* 2/1 (fall), 10/1 (spring), 11/15 (summer). *Application fee:* $40.

Advanced Placement Credit by examination available. Credit given for nursing courses completed elsewhere dependent upon specific evaluations.

Expenses (2009–10) *Tuition:* full-time $28,250; part-time $980 per credit hour. *Room and board:* $6200; room only: $3600 per academic year. *Required fees:* full-time $600.

Financial Aid 80% of baccalaureate students in nursing programs received some form of financial aid in 2008–09. *Gift aid (need-based):* Federal Pell, FSEOG, state, private, college/university gift aid from institutional funds, United Negro College Fund. *Loans:* Federal Nursing Student Loans, FFEL (Subsidized and Unsubsidized Stafford PLUS), Perkins, state. *Work-study:* Federal Work-Study, part-time campus jobs. *Financial aid application deadline:* 5/1.

Contact Ms. Zoranna Jones, Assistant Director of Nursing Recruitment and Retention, Harris College of Nursing, Texas Christian University, TCU Box 298620, Fort Worth, TX 76129. *Telephone:* 817-257-7650. *Fax:* 817-257-7944. *E-mail:* z.jones@tcu.edu.

GRADUATE PROGRAMS

Expenses (2009–10) *Tuition:* full-time $28,636; part-time $980 per credit hour. *Required fees:* full-time $702.

Financial Aid 100% of graduate students in nursing programs received some form of financial aid in 2008–09.

Contact Ms. Sybil White, Assistant to Dean of Graduate Studies, Harris College of Nursing, Texas Christian University, TCU Box 298625, Fort Worth, TX 76129. *Telephone:* 817-257-6750. *Fax:* 817-257-6751. *E-mail:* s.white@tcu.edu.

MASTER'S DEGREE PROGRAM

Degree MSN

Available Programs Master's; RN to Master's.

Concentrations Available Clinical nurse leader; nurse anesthesia; nursing education. *Clinical nurse specialist programs in:* adult health, medical-surgical, pediatric.

Site Options Fort Worth, TX.

Study Options Full-time and part-time.

Online Degree Options Yes (online only).

Program Entrance Requirements Clinical experience, computer literacy, minimum overall college GPA of 3.0, transcript of college record, CPR certification, written essay, immunizations, 3 letters of recommendation, professional liability insurance/malpractice insurance, prerequisite course work, resume. *Application deadline:* 2/1 (spring). *Application fee:* $50.

Advanced Placement Credit given for nursing courses completed elsewhere dependent upon specific evaluations.

Degree Requirements 40 total credit hours, thesis or project.

POST-MASTER'S PROGRAM

Areas of Study Clinical nurse leader; nursing education. *Clinical nurse specialist programs in:* adult health, medical-surgical, pediatric.

DOCTORAL DEGREE PROGRAM

Degree DNP

Available Programs Doctorate; Post-Baccalaureate Doctorate.

Areas of Study Advanced practice nursing, nursing administration.

Site Options Fort Worth, TX.

Online Degree Options Yes (online only).

Program Entrance Requirements Clinical experience, minimum overall college GPA of 3.0, interview, 3 letters of recommendation, MSN or equivalent, vita, writing sample. Application deadline: 2/15 (fall). Application fee: $50.

Degree Requirements 30 total credit hours, oral exam, written exam.

CONTINUING EDUCATION PROGRAM

Contact Ms. Barbara Patten, RN, Program Planning and Continuing Nursing Education Coordinator, Harris College of Nursing, Texas Christian University, TCU Box 298620, Fort Worth, TX 76129. *Telephone:* 817-257-7368. *Fax:* 817-257-7944. *E-mail:* bapatten@tcu.edu.

Texas Tech University Health Sciences Center
School of Nursing
Lubbock, Texas

http://www.ttuhsc.edu∫on

Founded in 1969

DEGREES • BSC PN • DNP • MSN

Nursing Program Faculty 98 (53% with doctorates).

Baccalaureate Enrollment 928
Women 82.97% **Men** 17.03% **Minority** 37% **International** .32% **Part-time** 2.5%

Graduate Enrollment 389
Women 85% **Men** 15% **Minority** 29% **Part-time** 85.84%

Distance Learning Courses Available.

Nursing Student Activities Sigma Theta Tau, Student Nurses' Association.

Nursing Student Resources Academic advising; academic or career counseling; assistance for students with disabilities; bookstore; campus computer network; computer lab; e-mail services; Internet; learning resource lab; library services; nursing audiovisuals; other; skills, simulation, or other laboratory; tutoring.

Library Facilities 305,436 volumes in health, 11,000 volumes in nursing; 14,020 periodical subscriptions health-care related.

BACCALAUREATE PROGRAMS

Degree BSc PN

Available Programs Accelerated Baccalaureate; Accelerated Baccalaureate for Second Degree; Accelerated RN Baccalaureate; Generic Baccalaureate.

Site Options Odessa, TX; El Paso, TX; Marble Falls, TX.

Study Options Full-time.

Online Degree Options Yes (online only).

Program Entrance Requirements Minimum overall college GPA of 2.5, transcript of college record, written essay, immunizations, prerequisite course work. *Application deadline:* 2/1 (fall). Applications may be processed on a rolling basis for some programs. *Application fee:* $50.

Advanced Placement Credit given for nursing courses completed elsewhere dependent upon specific evaluations.

Expenses (2009–10) *Tuition, state resident:* full-time $5100. *Tuition, nonresident:* full-time $3300.

Financial Aid 82% of baccalaureate students in nursing programs received some form of financial aid in 2008–09.

Contact Dr. Cynthia ONeal, Department Chair of Traditional Undergraduate Studies, School of Nursing, Texas Tech University Health Sciences Center, 3601 4th Street, MS 6264, Lubbock, TX 79430. *Telephone:* 806-743-2730. *Fax:* 806-743-1648. *E-mail:* cynthia.oneal@ttuhsc.edu.

GRADUATE PROGRAMS

Expenses (2009–10) *Tuition, state resident:* full-time $3600. *Tuition, nonresident:* full-time $9486. *International tuition:* $9486 full-time. *Required fees:* full-time $2945.

Financial Aid 80% of graduate students in nursing programs received some form of financial aid in 2008–09. Institutionally sponsored loans, scholarships, and traineeships available. Aid available to part-time students. *Financial aid application deadline:* 12/1.

Contact Ms. Georgina Barrera, Graduate Program Coordinator, School of Nursing, Texas Tech University Health Sciences Center, 3601 4th Street, MS 6264, Lubbock, TX 79430. *Telephone:* 806-743-2762. *Fax:* 806-743-2324. *E-mail:* georgina.barrera@ttuhsc.edu.

MASTER'S DEGREE PROGRAM

Degree MSN

Available Programs Master's; RN to Master's.

Concentrations Available Nursing administration; nursing education. *Nurse practitioner programs in:* acute care, family health, gerontology, pediatric.

Site Options Odessa, TX; El Paso, TX; Marble Falls, TX.

Texas Tech University Health Sciences Center (continued)
Study Options Full-time and part-time.
Online Degree Options Yes (online only).
Program Entrance Requirements Clinical experience, computer literacy, minimum overall college GPA of 3.0, transcript of college record, CPR certification, written essay, immunizations, 3 letters of recommendation, nursing research course, statistics course. *Application deadline:* 5/1 (fall), 9/1 (spring). *Application fee:* $40.
Advanced Placement Credit given for nursing courses completed elsewhere dependent upon specific evaluations.
Degree Requirements 48 total credit hours, thesis or project, comprehensive exam.

POST-MASTER'S PROGRAM

Areas of Study *Nurse practitioner programs in:* acute care, family health, gerontology, pediatric.

DOCTORAL DEGREE PROGRAM

Degree DNP
Available Programs Doctorate.
Areas of Study Advanced practice nursing, nursing administration.
Program Entrance Requirements Clinical experience, minimum overall college GPA of 3.0, interview by faculty committee, interview, 3 letters of recommendation, MSN or equivalent, statistics course, vita, writing sample. Application deadline: 1/15 (summer). Application fee: $40.
Degree Requirements 48 total credit hours.

CONTINUING EDUCATION PROGRAM

Contact Ms. Shelley Burson, Director of Continuing Nursing Education, School of Nursing, Texas Tech University Health Sciences Center, 3601 4th Street, MS 6264, Lubbock, TX 79430. *Telephone:* 806-743-2732. *Fax:* 806-743-1198. *E-mail:* shelley.burson@ttuhsc.edu.

Texas Woman's University
College of Nursing
Denton, Texas

Founded in 1901
DEGREES • BS • MS • MSN/MHA • PHD

Nursing Program Faculty 175 (33% with doctorates).
Baccalaureate Enrollment 983
Women 90% **Men** 10% **Minority** 51% **International** 4% **Part-time** 14%
Graduate Enrollment 545
Women 94% **Men** 6% **Minority** 40% **International** 1% **Part-time** 85%
Distance Learning Courses Available.
Nursing Student Activities Sigma Theta Tau, Student Nurses' Association.
Nursing Student Resources Academic advising; academic or career counseling; assistance for students with disabilities; bookstore; campus computer network; career placement assistance; computer lab; computer-assisted instruction; e-mail services; employment services for current students; Internet; learning resource lab; library services; nursing audiovisuals; placement services for program completers; remedial services; skills, simulation, or other laboratory.
Library Facilities 643,323 volumes (250,000 in health, 26,463 in nursing); 3,500 periodical subscriptions (2,644 health-care related).

BACCALAUREATE PROGRAMS

Degree BS
Available Programs Accelerated Baccalaureate for Second Degree; Baccalaureate for Second Degree; Generic Baccalaureate; RN Baccalaureate.
Site Options Dallas, TX; Houston, TX.
Study Options Full-time and part-time.
Online Degree Options Yes.

Program Entrance Requirements Transcript of college record, CPR certification, high school transcript, immunizations, minimum GPA in nursing prerequisites of 3.0, professional liability insurance/malpractice insurance, prerequisite course work. Transfer students are accepted. *Application deadline:* 2/1 (fall), 9/1 (spring). *Application fee:* $30.
Advanced Placement Credit given for nursing courses completed elsewhere dependent upon specific evaluations.
Contact Teresa McDaniel, Nursing Admissions Coordinator, College of Nursing, Texas Woman's University, PO Box 425498, Denton, TX 76204. *Telephone:* 940-898-2412. *Fax:* 940-898-2437. *E-mail:* tmcdaniel1@mail. twu.edu.

GRADUATE PROGRAMS

Financial Aid 30% of graduate students in nursing programs received some form of financial aid in 2007–08. 37 fellowships (averaging $14,902 per year), 13 research assistantships (averaging $11,484 per year), 3 teaching assistantships (averaging $11,484 per year) were awarded; career-related internships or fieldwork, Federal Work-Study, institutionally sponsored loans, scholarships, traineeships, and unspecified assistantships also available. Aid available to part-time students. *Financial aid application deadline:* 3/1.
Contact Dr. Ruth Johnson, Associate Dean of the Graduate School, College of Nursing, Texas Woman's University, PO Box 425649, Denton, TX 76204. *Telephone:* 940-898-3415. *E-mail:* rjohnson@twu.edu.

MASTER'S DEGREE PROGRAM

Degrees MS; MSN/MHA
Available Programs Master's; RN to Master's.
Concentrations Available Nursing administration; nursing education. *Clinical nurse specialist programs in:* adult health, pediatric, women's health. *Nurse practitioner programs in:* acute care, adult health, family health, pediatric, women's health.
Site Options Dallas, TX; Houston, TX.
Study Options Full-time and part-time.
Online Degree Options Yes.
Program Entrance Requirements Clinical experience, minimum overall college GPA of 3.0, transcript of college record, CPR certification, immunizations, professional liability insurance/malpractice insurance, statistics course, GRE or MAT.
Advanced Placement Credit given for nursing courses completed elsewhere dependent upon specific evaluations.
Degree Requirements 48 total credit hours, thesis or project.

POST-MASTER'S PROGRAM

Areas of Study *Nurse practitioner programs in:* acute care, adult health, family health, pediatric, women's health.

DOCTORAL DEGREE PROGRAM

Degree PhD
Available Programs Doctorate.
Areas of Study Nursing research, nursing science, women's health.
Site Options Dallas, TX; Houston, TX.
Program Entrance Requirements Minimum overall college GPA of 3.5, 2 letters of recommendation, MSN or equivalent, statistics course, vita, GRE or MAT.
Degree Requirements 60 total credit hours, dissertation, oral exam, written exam.

University of Houston–Victoria
School of Nursing
Victoria, Texas

Founded in 1973
DEGREES • BSN • MSN

Library Facilities 50,000 volumes; 70,000 periodical subscriptions.

BACCALAUREATE PROGRAMS

Degree BSN

Available Programs Accelerated Baccalaureate for Second Degree; RN Baccalaureate.

Contact Baccalaureate programs, School of Nursing, University of Houston–Victoria, 3007 North Ben Wilson, Victoria, TX 77901. *Telephone:* 361-570-4848. *E-mail:* nursing@uhv.edu.

GRADUATE PROGRAMS

Contact Masters Programs, School of Nursing, University of Houston–Victoria, 3007 North Ben Wilson, Victoria, TX 77901. *Telephone:* 361-570-4848. *E-mail:* nursing@uhv.edu.

MASTER'S DEGREE PROGRAM

Degree MSN

Available Programs Master's; RN to Master's.

Concentrations Available Nursing administration; nursing education.

Program Entrance Requirements GRE or MAT.

University of Mary Hardin-Baylor
College of Nursing
Belton, Texas

http://www.umhb.edu

Founded in 1845

DEGREES • BSN • MSN

Nursing Program Faculty 22 (36% with doctorates).

Baccalaureate Enrollment 225
Women 94% **Men** 6% **Minority** 25% **Part-time** 1%

Graduate Enrollment 15
Women 100% **Minority** 40% **Part-time** 20%

Nursing Student Activities Sigma Theta Tau, Student Nurses' Association.

Nursing Student Resources Academic advising; academic or career counseling; assistance for students with disabilities; bookstore; campus computer network; career placement assistance; computer lab; e-mail services; employment services for current students; housing assistance; Internet; learning resource lab; library services; nursing audiovisuals; placement services for program completers; remedial services; resume preparation assistance; skills, simulation, or other laboratory; tutoring.

Library Facilities 7,769 volumes in health, 6,771 volumes in nursing; 120 periodical subscriptions health-care related.

BACCALAUREATE PROGRAMS

Degree BSN

Available Programs ADN to Baccalaureate; Generic Baccalaureate.

Study Options Full-time and part-time.

Program Entrance Requirements Minimum overall college GPA of 2.75, transcript of college record, CPR certification, written essay, health exam, health insurance, high school transcript, immunizations, minimum high school rank 50%, minimum GPA in nursing prerequisites of 2.75, professional liability insurance/malpractice insurance, prerequisite course work. Transfer students are accepted. *Application deadline:* 3/1 (fall), 10/1 (spring).

Advanced Placement Credit given for nursing courses completed elsewhere dependent upon specific evaluations.

Expenses (2009–10) *Tuition:* full-time $18,360; part-time $610 per credit. *Room and board:* $2675; room only: $2000 per academic year. *Required fees:* full-time $240; part-time $40 per credit.

Financial Aid 95% of baccalaureate students in nursing programs received some form of financial aid in 2008–09.

Contact Dr. Sharon Souter, RN, Dean and Professor, College of Nursing, University of Mary Hardin-Baylor, Box 8015, 900 College Street, Belton, TX 76513-2599. *Telephone:* 254-295-4665. *Fax:* 254-295-4141. *E-mail:* lpehl@umhb.edu.

GRADUATE PROGRAMS

Expenses (2009–10) *Tuition:* full-time $11,340; part-time $630 per credit hour. *Required fees:* full-time $1125; part-time $125 per credit.

Financial Aid 10% of graduate students in nursing programs received some form of financial aid in 2008–09.

Contact Dr. Margaret Prydun, RN, Director and Associate Professor, College of Nursing, University of Mary Hardin-Baylor, Box 8015, 900 College Street, Belton, TX 76513-2599. *Telephone:* 254-295-4674. *Fax:* 254-295-4141. *E-mail:* m.prydun@umhb.edu.

MASTER'S DEGREE PROGRAM

Degree MSN

Available Programs Master's.

Concentrations Available Clinical nurse leader; nursing education. *Clinical nurse specialist programs in:* adult health.

Study Options Full-time and part-time.

Program Entrance Requirements Clinical experience, computer literacy, minimum overall college GPA of 3.0, transcript of college record, CPR certification, written essay, immunizations, interview, 2 letters of recommendation, nursing research course, physical assessment course, professional liability insurance/malpractice insurance, prerequisite course work, resume, statistics course. *Application deadline:* 10/1 (fall).

Degree Requirements 36 total credit hours, comprehensive exam.

CONTINUING EDUCATION PROGRAM

Contact Dr. Ann Crawford, RN, Program Administrator, College of Nursing, University of Mary Hardin-Baylor, Box 8015, 900 College Street, Belton, TX 76513-2599. *Telephone:* 254-295-4671. *Fax:* 254-295-4141. *E-mail:* acrawford@umhb.edu.

The University of Texas at Arlington
School of Nursing
Arlington, Texas

http://www.uta.edu/nursing

Founded in 1895

DEGREES • BSN • MSN • MSN/MBA • MSN/MHA • MSN/MPH • PHD

Nursing Program Faculty 126 (34% with doctorates).

Baccalaureate Enrollment 2,243
Women 89% **Men** 11% **Minority** 40% **International** 10% **Part-time** 8%

Graduate Enrollment 542
Women 91% **Men** 9% **Minority** 22% **Part-time** 70%

Distance Learning Courses Available.

Nursing Student Activities Nursing Honor Society, Sigma Theta Tau, Student Nurses' Association, nursing club.

Nursing Student Resources Academic advising; campus computer network; computer lab; e-mail services; externships; interactive nursing skills videos; learning resource lab; nursing audiovisuals; skills, simulation, or other laboratory; tutoring.

Library Facilities 1.2 million volumes (36,000 in health, 23,300 in nursing); 58,417 periodical subscriptions (530 health-care related).

BACCALAUREATE PROGRAMS

Degree BSN

Available Programs Accelerated Baccalaureate; Accelerated Baccalaureate for Second Degree; Accelerated RN Baccalaureate; Baccalaureate for Second Degree; Generic Baccalaureate; RN Baccalaureate.

Site Options Fort Worth, TX; Dallas, TX; Waco, TX; Grayson, TX; Paris, TX; Kaufman, TX.

Study Options Full-time and part-time.

Online Degree Options Yes.

Program Entrance Requirements Minimum overall college GPA of 2.5, transcript of college record, CPR certification, health insurance, immunizations, minimum high school GPA of 2.5, minimum GPA in nursing prerequisites of 2.5, professional liability insurance/malpractice insurance, prerequisite course work. Transfer students are accepted. *Application deadline:* 1/2 (fall), 6/4 (spring).

The University of Texas at Arlington (continued)

Advanced Placement Credit given for nursing courses completed elsewhere dependent upon specific evaluations.

Expenses (2009–10) *Tuition, state resident:* full-time $8186; part-time $3125 per semester. *Tuition, nonresident:* part-time $5341 per semester. *International tuition:* $16,130 full-time. *Room and board:* $6400; room only: $3400 per academic year. *Required fees:* full-time $572; part-time $22 per credit; part-time $352 per term.

Financial Aid 90% of baccalaureate students in nursing programs received some form of financial aid in 2008–09. *Gift aid (need-based):* Federal Pell, FSEOG, state, private, college/university gift aid from institutional funds, United Negro College Fund. *Loans:* FFEL (Subsidized and Unsubsidized Stafford PLUS), Perkins, state. *Work-study:* Federal Work-Study, part-time campus jobs. *Financial aid application deadline (priority):* 5/15.

Contact Ms. Jean Ashwill, RN, Director, Undergraduate Student Services, School of Nursing, The University of Texas at Arlington, 411 South Nedderman Drive, Box 19407, Arlington, TX 76019-0407. *Telephone:* 817-272-2776. *Fax:* 817-272-5006. *E-mail:* nursing@uta.edu.

GRADUATE PROGRAMS

Expenses (2009–10) *Tuition, state resident:* full-time $7200; part-time $2500 per semester. *Tuition, nonresident:* full-time $12,186; part-time $4162 per semester. *International tuition:* $12,186 full-time. *Room and board:* $6400; room only: $3400 per academic year. *Required fees:* full-time $1656; part-time $92 per credit; part-time $552 per term.

Financial Aid 12% of graduate students in nursing programs received some form of financial aid in 2008–09. 24 fellowships with partial tuition reimbursements available (averaging $3,000 per year), 6 research assistantships (averaging $7,992 per year), 7 teaching assistantships (averaging $10,080 per year) were awarded; career-related internships or fieldwork and traineeships also available. *Financial aid application deadline:* 6/1.

Contact Dr. Mary Schira, Interim Associate Dean of Graduate Studies, School of Nursing, The University of Texas at Arlington, 411 South Nedderman Drive, Box 19407, Arlington, TX 76019-0407. *Telephone:* 817-272-7086. *Fax:* 817-272-5006. *E-mail:* schira@uta.edu.

MASTER'S DEGREE PROGRAM

Degrees MSN; MSN/MBA; MSN/MHA; MSN/MPH

Available Programs Master's.

Concentrations Available Health-care administration; nursing administration. *Nurse practitioner programs in:* acute care, adult health, family health, gerontology, pediatric, psychiatric/mental health.

Site Options Fort Worth, TX; Dallas, TX.

Study Options Full-time and part-time.

Program Entrance Requirements Computer literacy, minimum overall college GPA of 3.0, transcript of college record, CPR certification, written essay, immunizations, 3 letters of recommendation, physical assessment course, statistics course, GRE General Test. *Application deadline:* 6/15 (fall), 10/15 (spring). *Application fee:* $70.

Advanced Placement Credit given for nursing courses completed elsewhere dependent upon specific evaluations.

Degree Requirements 48 total credit hours, thesis or project, comprehensive exam.

POST-MASTER'S PROGRAM

Areas of Study Health-care administration. *Nurse practitioner programs in:* acute care, adult health, family health, gerontology, pediatric, psychiatric/mental health.

DOCTORAL DEGREE PROGRAM

Degree PhD

Available Programs Doctorate.

Areas of Study Faculty preparation, nursing education, nursing research.

Program Entrance Requirements Minimum overall college GPA of 3.0, interview, 3 letters of recommendation, MSN or equivalent, statistics course, GRE General Test. Application deadline: 6/15 (fall), 10/15 (spring). Application fee: $70.

Degree Requirements 58 total credit hours, dissertation, residency.

CONTINUING EDUCATION PROGRAM

Contact Ms. Toni McKenna, Director, School of Nursing, The University of Texas at Arlington, 411 South Nedderman Drive, Box 19407, Arlington, TX 76019-0407. *Telephone:* 817-272-0720. *Fax:* 817-272-5371. *E-mail:* tmckenna@uta.edu.

The University of Texas at Austin
School of Nursing
Austin, Texas

http://www.utexas.edu/nursing

Founded in 1883

DEGREES • BSN • MSN • MSN/MBA • PHD

Nursing Program Faculty 73 (62% with doctorates).

Baccalaureate Enrollment 701
Women 90.5% **Men** 9.5% **Minority** 33% **International** 1% **Part-time** 13%

Graduate Enrollment 222
Women 88% **Men** 12% **Minority** 27% **International** 9% **Part-time** 24%

Nursing Student Activities Nursing Honor Society, Sigma Theta Tau, Student Nurses' Association, nursing club.

Nursing Student Resources Academic advising; academic or career counseling; assistance for students with disabilities; bookstore; campus computer network; career placement assistance; computer lab; computer-assisted instruction; daycare for children of students; e-mail services; employment services for current students; externships; housing assistance; interactive nursing skills videos; Internet; learning resource lab; library services; nursing audiovisuals; other; paid internships; placement services for program completers; remedial services; resume preparation assistance; skills, simulation, or other laboratory; tutoring; unpaid internships.

Library Facilities 9 million volumes (100,000 in health, 80,000 in nursing); 504 periodical subscriptions health-care related.

BACCALAUREATE PROGRAMS

Degree BSN

Available Programs Generic Baccalaureate; RN Baccalaureate.

Study Options Full-time.

Program Entrance Requirements Minimum overall college GPA of 2.5, transcript of college record, CPR certification, written essay, 3 years high school math, 2 years high school science, high school transcript, immunizations, 3 letters of recommendation, minimum GPA in nursing prerequisites of 2.5, professional liability insurance/malpractice insurance, prerequisite course work. Transfer students are accepted.

Advanced Placement Credit by examination available. Credit given for nursing courses completed elsewhere dependent upon specific evaluations.

Contact *Telephone:* 512-232-4780. *Fax:* 512-232-4777.

GRADUATE PROGRAMS

Contact *Telephone:* 512-471-7927. *Fax:* 512-232-4777.

MASTER'S DEGREE PROGRAM

Degrees MSN; MSN/MBA

Available Programs Master's; Master's for Non-Nursing College Graduates; Master's for Nurses with Non-Nursing Degrees.

Concentrations Available Nursing administration. *Clinical nurse specialist programs in:* adult health, community health, medical-surgical, public health. *Nurse practitioner programs in:* family health, pediatric.

Study Options Full-time and part-time.

Program Entrance Requirements Clinical experience, minimum overall college GPA of 3.0, transcript of college record, CPR certification, written essay, immunizations, interview, 3 letters of recommendation, physical assessment course, professional liability insurance/malpractice insurance, prerequisite course work, resume, statistics course, GRE General Test.

Advanced Placement Credit given for nursing courses completed elsewhere dependent upon specific evaluations.

Degree Requirements 48 total credit hours.

POST-MASTER'S PROGRAM

Areas of Study *Nurse practitioner programs in:* family health, pediatric.

DOCTORAL DEGREE PROGRAM

Degree PhD

Available Programs Doctorate.

Areas of Study Aging, community health, faculty preparation, gerontology, health promotion/disease prevention, health-care systems, human health and illness, illness and transition, maternity-newborn, nursing administration, nursing research, women's health.

Program Entrance Requirements Minimum overall college GPA of 3.0, interview, 3 letters of recommendation, MSN or equivalent, statistics course, vita, GRE General Test.

Degree Requirements 64 total credit hours, dissertation, oral exam, written exam, residency.

POSTDOCTORAL PROGRAM

Areas of Study Women's health.

Postdoctoral Program Contact *Telephone:* 512-232-4751. *Fax:* 512-232-4777.

The University of Texas at Brownsville

Department of Nursing
Brownsville, Texas

http://www.ntmain.utb.edu/shs/nursing_dept.html
Founded in 1973
DEGREES • BSN • MSN

Nursing Program Faculty 25 (12% with doctorates).

Baccalaureate Enrollment 21
Women 90% **Men** 10% **Part-time** 70%

Graduate Enrollment 11
Women 90% **Men** 10% **Part-time** 80%

Nursing Student Resources Academic advising; academic or career counseling; assistance for students with disabilities; bookstore; campus computer network; career placement assistance; computer lab; computer-assisted instruction; daycare for children of students; e-mail services; employment services for current students; housing assistance; interactive nursing skills videos; Internet; learning resource lab; library services; nursing audiovisuals; remedial services; skills, simulation, or other laboratory; tutoring.

Library Facilities 174,660 volumes; 4,447 periodical subscriptions.

BACCALAUREATE PROGRAMS

Degree BSN

Available Programs ADN to Baccalaureate.

Study Options Full-time and part-time.

Program Entrance Requirements Minimum overall college GPA of 2.5, transcript of college record, CPR certification, immunizations, minimum GPA in nursing prerequisites of 2.5, professional liability insurance/malpractice insurance, prerequisite course work, RN licensure. Transfer students are accepted.

Advanced Placement Credit by examination available.

Contact *Telephone:* 956-882-5071. *Fax:* 956-882-5100.

GRADUATE PROGRAMS

Contact *Telephone:* 956-882-5079. *Fax:* 956-882-5100.

MASTER'S DEGREE PROGRAM

Degree MSN

Available Programs Master's.

Concentrations Available Nursing administration; nursing education. *Clinical nurse specialist programs in:* public health.

Study Options Full-time and part-time.

Program Entrance Requirements Minimum overall college GPA of 3.0, transcript of college record, immunizations, 2 letters of recommendation, professional liability insurance/malpractice insurance, statistics course.

Degree Requirements 37 total credit hours, thesis or project.

The University of Texas at El Paso

School of Nursing
El Paso, Texas

http://www.utep.edu/nursing
Founded in 1913
DEGREES • BSN • MSN

Nursing Program Faculty 64 (27% with doctorates).

Baccalaureate Enrollment 514
Women 76.5% **Men** 23.5% **Minority** 80.4% **International** 2.7% **Part-time** 58.8%

Graduate Enrollment 153
Women 81% **Men** 19% **Minority** 61.4% **International** 3.3% **Part-time** 78.4%

Distance Learning Courses Available.

Nursing Student Activities Nursing Honor Society, Sigma Theta Tau, Student Nurses' Association.

Nursing Student Resources Academic advising; academic or career counseling; assistance for students with disabilities; bookstore; campus computer network; career placement assistance; computer lab; computer-assisted instruction; e-mail services; employment services for current students; interactive nursing skills videos; Internet; learning resource lab; library services; nursing audiovisuals; remedial services; skills, simulation, or other laboratory; tutoring.

Library Facilities 1.3 million volumes (71,389 in health, 13,043 in nursing); 3,065 periodical subscriptions (314 health-care related).

BACCALAUREATE PROGRAMS

Degree BSN

Available Programs Accelerated Baccalaureate; Generic Baccalaureate; RN Baccalaureate.

Study Options Full-time and part-time.

Program Entrance Requirements Minimum overall college GPA of 2.0, transcript of college record, CPR certification, health exam, high school biology, high school math, high school science, high school transcript, immunizations, minimum GPA in nursing prerequisites of 2.5, professional liability insurance/malpractice insurance, prerequisite course work. Transfer students are accepted. *Application deadline:* 2/28 (fall), 9/30 (spring), 2/28 (summer).

Advanced Placement Credit by examination available. Credit given for nursing courses completed elsewhere dependent upon specific evaluations.

Expenses (2009–10) *Tuition, state resident:* full-time $4806; part-time $160 per credit hour. *Tuition, nonresident:* full-time $13,116; part-time $437 per credit hour. *International tuition:* $13,116 full-time. *Room and board:* room only: $4500 per academic year. *Required fees:* full-time $1631; part-time $46 per credit; part-time $178 per term.

Financial Aid 67% of baccalaureate students in nursing programs received some form of financial aid in 2008–09.

Contact Ms. Patricia Fowler, Assistant Dean, Undergraduate Education, School of Nursing, The University of Texas at El Paso, 1101 North Campbell Street, El Paso, TX 79902. *Telephone:* 915-747-7267. *Fax:* 915-747-8266. *E-mail:* pfowler@utep.edu.

GRADUATE PROGRAMS

Expenses (2009–10) *Tuition, state resident:* full-time $3928; part-time $218 per credit hour. *Tuition, nonresident:* full-time $8914; part-time $495 per credit hour. *International tuition:* $8914 full-time. *Room and board:* room only: $4500 per academic year. *Required fees:* full-time $1193; part-time $47 per credit; part-time $178 per term.

The University of Texas at El Paso (continued)

Financial Aid 34% of graduate students in nursing programs received some form of financial aid in 2008–09. Research assistantships with partial tuition reimbursements available (averaging $18,825 per year), teaching assistantships with partial tuition reimbursements available (averaging $18,000 per year) were awarded; fellowships with partial tuition reimbursements available, career-related internships or fieldwork, Federal Work-Study, institutionally sponsored loans, scholarships, and tuition waivers (partial) also available. Aid available to part-time students. *Financial aid application deadline:* 3/15.

Contact Dr. Kristynia Robinson, Assistant Dean, Graduate Education, School of Nursing, The University of Texas at El Paso, 1101 North Campbell Street, El Paso, TX 79902. *Telephone:* 915-747-7226. *Fax:* 915-747-8266. *E-mail:* krobinson@utep.edu.

MASTER'S DEGREE PROGRAM

Degree MSN

Available Programs Master's; RN to Master's.

Concentrations Available Nursing administration; nursing education. *Nurse practitioner programs in:* family health.

Study Options Full-time and part-time.

Online Degree Options Yes (online only).

Program Entrance Requirements Clinical experience, minimum overall college GPA of 3.0, transcript of college record, CPR certification, written essay, immunizations, interview, nursing research course, professional liability insurance/malpractice insurance, resume, statistics course, GRE General Test or MAT. *Application deadline:* 9/1 (fall), 2/1 (spring). Applications may be processed on a rolling basis for some programs. *Application fee:* $45.

Advanced Placement Credit given for nursing courses completed elsewhere dependent upon specific evaluations.

Degree Requirements 33 total credit hours, thesis or project, comprehensive exam.

POST-MASTER'S PROGRAM

Areas of Study Nursing administration; nursing education. *Nurse practitioner programs in:* family health.

The University of Texas at Tyler
Program in Nursing
Tyler, Texas

http://www.uttyler.edu/nursing

Founded in 1971

DEGREES • BSN • DNS • MSN • MSN/MBA

Nursing Program Faculty 65 (25% with doctorates).

Baccalaureate Enrollment 500
Women 70% **Men** 30% **Minority** 10% **International** 1% **Part-time** 15%

Graduate Enrollment 175
Women 88% **Men** 12% **Minority** 11% **Part-time** 88%

Nursing Student Activities Nursing Honor Society, Sigma Theta Tau, Student Nurses' Association, nursing club.

Nursing Student Resources Academic advising; academic or career counseling; assistance for students with disabilities; bookstore; campus computer network; career placement assistance; computer lab; computer-assisted instruction; e-mail services; employment services for current students; externships; interactive nursing skills videos; Internet; learning resource lab; library services; nursing audiovisuals; remedial services; resume preparation assistance; skills, simulation, or other laboratory; tutoring.

Library Facilities 486,895 volumes (11,000 in health, 5,500 in nursing); 525 periodical subscriptions (150 health-care related).

BACCALAUREATE PROGRAMS

Degree BSN

Available Programs ADN to Baccalaureate; Accelerated RN Baccalaureate; Generic Baccalaureate; International Nurse to Baccalaureate; LPN to Baccalaureate; LPN to RN Baccalaureate; RN Baccalaureate.

Site Options Palestine, TX; Longview, TX.

Study Options Full-time and part-time.

Online Degree Options Yes (online only).

Program Entrance Requirements Minimum overall college GPA of 2.75, transcript of college record, CPR certification, health exam, immunizations, minimum GPA in nursing prerequisites of 2.75, professional liability insurance/malpractice insurance, prerequisite course work. Transfer students are accepted. *Application deadline:* 2/15 (fall), 9/15 (spring).

Advanced Placement Credit given for nursing courses completed elsewhere dependent upon specific evaluations.

Financial Aid 70% of baccalaureate students in nursing programs received some form of financial aid in 2008–09. *Gift aid (need-based):* Federal Pell, FSEOG, state, private, college/university gift aid from institutional funds, Texas Grant, Institutional Grants (Education Affordability Prog). *Loans:* FFEL (Subsidized and Unsubsidized Stafford PLUS), state. *Work-study:* Federal Work-Study, part-time campus jobs. *Financial aid application deadline (priority):* 4/1.

Contact Ms. Renee Lampkin, Director of Marketing/Advising, Program in Nursing, The University of Texas at Tyler, 3900 University Boulevard, Tyler, TX 75799. *Telephone:* 903-565-5534. *Fax:* 903-565-5901. *E-mail:* rlampkin@uttyler.edu.

GRADUATE PROGRAMS

Financial Aid 60% of graduate students in nursing programs received some form of financial aid in 2008–09. 1 fellowship (averaging $10,000 per year), 3 research assistantships (averaging $2,200 per year) were awarded; institutionally sponsored loans and scholarships also available. *Financial aid application deadline:* 7/1.

Contact Ms. Renee Lampkin, Director of Marketing/Advising, Program in Nursing, The University of Texas at Tyler, 3900 University Boulevard, Tyler, TX 75799. *Telephone:* 903-565-5534. *Fax:* 903-565-5901. *E-mail:* rlampkin@uttyler.edu.

MASTER'S DEGREE PROGRAM

Degrees MSN; MSN/MBA

Available Programs Accelerated AD/RN to Master's; Accelerated RN to Master's; Master's; RN to Master's.

Concentrations Available Nursing administration; nursing education. *Nurse practitioner programs in:* acute care, adult health, family health, gerontology, pediatric, women's health.

Study Options Full-time and part-time.

Program Entrance Requirements Computer literacy, minimum overall college GPA of 3.0, transcript of college record, CPR certification, immunizations, 4 letters of recommendation, nursing research course, professional liability insurance/malpractice insurance, prerequisite course work, resume, statistics course, GRE General Test or MAT, GMAT.

Advanced Placement Credit given for nursing courses completed elsewhere dependent upon specific evaluations.

Degree Requirements 36 total credit hours, thesis or project, comprehensive exam.

POST-MASTER'S PROGRAM

Areas of Study Nursing administration; nursing education. *Nurse practitioner programs in:* acute care, adult health, family health, gerontology, pediatric, women's health.

DOCTORAL DEGREE PROGRAM

Degree DNS

Available Programs Doctorate.

Areas of Study Nursing science.

Program Entrance Requirements Minimum overall college GPA of 3.0, interview by faculty committee, 3 letters of recommendation, MSN or equivalent, scholarly papers, statistics course, vita, writing sample.

Degree Requirements 65 total credit hours, dissertation, written exam.

CONTINUING EDUCATION PROGRAM

Contact Dr. Pamela Martin, RN, Assistant Dean of Undergraduate Studies, Program in Nursing, The University of Texas at Tyler, 3900 University Boulevard, Tyler, TX 75799. *Telephone:* 903-566-7320. *Fax:* 903-565-5533. *E-mail:* pmartin@uttyler.edu.

The University of Texas Health Science Center at Houston

School of Nursing
Houston, Texas

http://son.uth.tmc.edu/

Founded in 1972

DEGREES • BSN • MSN • MSN/MPH • PHD

Nursing Program Faculty 96 (58% with doctorates).

Baccalaureate Enrollment 378
Women 86% **Men** 14% **Minority** 48% **International** 4% **Part-time** 30%

Graduate Enrollment 347
Women 85% **Men** 15% **Minority** 37% **International** 2% **Part-time** 66%

Distance Learning Courses Available.

Nursing Student Activities Sigma Theta Tau, Student Nurses' Association.

Nursing Student Resources Academic advising; academic or career counseling; assistance for students with disabilities; bookstore; campus computer network; computer lab; computer-assisted instruction; e-mail services; employment services for current students; housing assistance; interactive nursing skills videos; Internet; learning resource lab; library services; nursing audiovisuals; paid internships; remedial services; skills, simulation, or other laboratory; tutoring.

Library Facilities 339,062 volumes; 5,581 periodical subscriptions.

BACCALAUREATE PROGRAMS

Degree BSN

Available Programs ADN to Baccalaureate; Accelerated Baccalaureate for Second Degree; Generic Baccalaureate.

Site Options Houston, TX.

Study Options Full-time.

Program Entrance Requirements Transcript of college record, CPR certification, written essay, health exam, immunizations, interview, minimum GPA in nursing prerequisites of 2.75, prerequisite course work. Transfer students are accepted. *Application deadline:* 1/15 (fall), 9/1 (spring), 12/1 (summer). *Application fee:* $30.

Advanced Placement Credit given for nursing courses completed elsewhere dependent upon specific evaluations.

Expenses (2009–10) *Tuition, state resident:* full-time $7003. *Tuition, nonresident:* full-time $29,281. *International tuition:* $29,281 full-time. *Required fees:* full-time $1103.

Financial Aid 68% of baccalaureate students in nursing programs received some form of financial aid in 2008–09.

Contact Ms. Laurie Rutherford, Director of Student Affairs, School of Nursing, The University of Texas Health Science Center at Houston, 6901 Bertner Avenue, Suite 220, Houston, TX 77030. *Telephone:* 713-500-2101. *Fax:* 713-500-2107. *E-mail:* soninfo@uth.tmc.edu.

GRADUATE PROGRAMS

Expenses (2009–10) *Tuition, state resident:* full-time $4088. *Tuition, nonresident:* full-time $14,756. *International tuition:* $14,756 full-time. *Required fees:* full-time $1116.

Financial Aid 40% of graduate students in nursing programs received some form of financial aid in 2008–09. Research assistantships with tuition reimbursements available, teaching assistantships with tuition reimbursements available, institutionally sponsored loans, scholarships, traineeships, and tuition waivers (full) available. Aid available to part-time students.

Contact Ms. Laurie Rutherford, Director of Student Affairs, School of Nursing, The University of Texas Health Science Center at Houston, 6901 Bertner Avenue, Suite 220, Houston, TX 77030. *Telephone:* 713-500-2101. *Fax:* 713-500-2107. *E-mail:* soninfo@uth.tmc.edu.

MASTER'S DEGREE PROGRAM

Degrees MSN; MSN/MPH

Available Programs Master's.

Concentrations Available Nurse anesthesia; nursing administration; nursing education. *Clinical nurse specialist programs in:* acute care, adult health, critical care, gerontology. *Nurse practitioner programs in:* acute care, adult health, family health, gerontology, pediatric, psychiatric/mental health, women's health.

Study Options Full-time and part-time.

Program Entrance Requirements Clinical experience, minimum overall college GPA of 3.0, transcript of college record, CPR certification, immunizations, interview, 3 letters of recommendation, prerequisite course work, resume, statistics course, GRE or MAT. *Application deadline:* 4/15 (fall), 2/15 (summer). *Application fee:* $30.

Advanced Placement Credit given for nursing courses completed elsewhere dependent upon specific evaluations.

Degree Requirements 48 total credit hours, thesis or project.

POST-MASTER'S PROGRAM

Areas of Study Nursing administration; nursing education. *Clinical nurse specialist programs in:* acute care, adult health, critical care, gerontology, oncology. *Nurse practitioner programs in:* acute care, adult health, family health, gerontology, oncology, pediatric, psychiatric/mental health, women's health.

DOCTORAL DEGREE PROGRAM

Degree PhD

Available Programs Doctorate.

Areas of Study Addiction/substance abuse, advanced practice nursing, aging, bio-behavioral research, biology of health and illness, clinical practice, community health, critical care, ethics, faculty preparation, family health, gerontology, health policy, health promotion/disease prevention, health-care systems, human health and illness, illness and transition, individualized study, information systems, maternity-newborn, neurobehavior, nurse case management, nursing administration, nursing education, nursing policy, nursing research, nursing science, oncology, urban health, women's health.

Program Entrance Requirements Minimum overall college GPA of 3.0, interview by faculty committee, 3 letters of recommendation, MSN or equivalent, vita, writing sample, GRE. Application deadline: 4/1 (fall). Application fee: $30.

Degree Requirements 66 total credit hours, dissertation.

CONTINUING EDUCATION PROGRAM

Contact Dr. Vaunette P. Fay, RN, Associate Professor of Clinical Nursing, School of Nursing, The University of Texas Health Science Center at Houston, 6901 Bertner Avenue, Suite 846, Houston, TX 77030. *Telephone:* 713-500-2116. *Fax:* 713-500-2026. *E-mail:* vaunette.p.fay@uth.tmc.edu.

The University of Texas Health Science Center at San Antonio

School of Nursing
San Antonio, Texas

http://www.nursing.uthscsa.edu

Founded in 1976

DEGREES • BSN • MSN • MSN/MPH • PHD

Nursing Program Faculty 109 (39% with doctorates).

Baccalaureate Enrollment 508
Women 81% **Men** 19% **Minority** 52% **International** 1% **Part-time** 10%

Graduate Enrollment 212
Women 85% **Men** 15% **Minority** 47% **International** 1% **Part-time** 75%

Distance Learning Courses Available.

Nursing Student Activities Nursing Honor Society, Sigma Theta Tau, Student Nurses' Association, nursing club.

Nursing Student Resources Academic advising; academic or career counseling; assistance for students with disabilities; bookstore; campus computer network; career placement assistance; computer lab; computer-assisted instruction; e-mail services; housing assistance; interactive nursing

The University of Texas Health Science Center at San Antonio (continued)

skills videos; Internet; learning resource lab; library services; nursing audiovisuals; remedial services; resume preparation assistance; skills, simulation, or other laboratory; tutoring.

Library Facilities 205,641 volumes in health, 2,056 volumes in nursing; 250 periodical subscriptions health-care related.

BACCALAUREATE PROGRAMS

Degree BSN

Available Programs ADN to Baccalaureate; Accelerated Baccalaureate for Second Degree; Generic Baccalaureate.

Study Options Full-time and part-time.

Program Entrance Requirements Minimum overall college GPA of 2.5, transcript of college record, CPR certification, written essay, health insurance, immunizations, minimum GPA in nursing prerequisites of 2.5, professional liability insurance/malpractice insurance, prerequisite course work. Transfer students are accepted. *Application deadline:* 1/1 (fall), 7/1 (spring). *Application fee:* $45.

Advanced Placement Credit given for nursing courses completed elsewhere dependent upon specific evaluations.

Expenses (2009–10) *Tuition, state resident:* full-time $5000; part-time $165 per credit hour. *Tuition, nonresident:* full-time $15,000; part-time $500 per credit hour. *International tuition:* $15,000 full-time. *Required fees:* full-time $2110; part-time $120 per credit; part-time $916 per term.

Financial Aid 80% of baccalaureate students in nursing programs received some form of financial aid in 2008–09.

Contact Dr. Suzanne Yarbrough, RN, Associate Dean for Undergraduate Studies, School of Nursing, The University of Texas Health Science Center at San Antonio, 7703 Floyd Curl Drive, MC 7945, San Antonio, TX 78229-3900. *Telephone:* 210-567-5810. *Fax:* 210-567-3813. *E-mail:* yarbrough@uthscsa.edu.

GRADUATE PROGRAMS

Expenses (2009–10) *Tuition, state resident:* full-time $2400; part-time $50 per credit hour. *Tuition, nonresident:* full-time $7848; part-time $327 per credit hour. *International tuition:* $7848 full-time. *Required fees:* part-time $1818 per term.

Financial Aid 50% of graduate students in nursing programs received some form of financial aid in 2008–09. Research assistantships, teaching assistantships, institutionally sponsored loans and scholarships available. *Financial aid application deadline:* 4/1.

Contact Dr. Beverly Robinson, PhD, Associate Dean for Graduate Nursing Program, School of Nursing, The University of Texas Health Science Center at San Antonio, 7703 Floyd Curl Drive, MC 7945, San Antonio, TX 78229-3900. *Telephone:* 210-567-5815. *Fax:* 210-567-3813. *E-mail:* robinsonb@uthscsa.edu.

MASTER'S DEGREE PROGRAM

Degrees MSN; MSN/MPH

Available Programs Master's; RN to Master's.

Concentrations Available Nursing administration; nursing education; nursing informatics. *Clinical nurse specialist programs in:* critical care, medical-surgical. *Nurse practitioner programs in:* acute care, family health, pediatric, psychiatric/mental health.

Study Options Full-time and part-time.

Program Entrance Requirements Clinical experience, computer literacy, minimum overall college GPA of 3.0, transcript of college record, CPR certification, immunizations, interview, 3 letters of recommendation, physical assessment course, professional liability insurance/malpractice insurance, statistics course. *Application deadline:* 2/1 (fall), 9/1 (spring). *Application fee:* $45.

Advanced Placement Credit given for nursing courses completed elsewhere dependent upon specific evaluations.

Degree Requirements 47 total credit hours.

POST-MASTER'S PROGRAM

Areas of Study *Nurse practitioner programs in:* acute care, family health, pediatric, psychiatric/mental health.

DOCTORAL DEGREE PROGRAM

Degree PhD

Available Programs Doctorate; Post-Baccalaureate Doctorate.

Areas of Study Nursing education, nursing research, nursing science.

Program Entrance Requirements Clinical experience, minimum overall college GPA of 3.0, interview by faculty committee, interview, 3 letters of recommendation, statistics course, GRE, MAT. Application deadline: 2/1 (fall). Application fee: $45.

Degree Requirements 55 total credit hours, dissertation, oral exam, written exam.

CONTINUING EDUCATION PROGRAM

Contact Ms. Rosalie Tierney-Gumaer, Director of Nursing Continuing Education, School of Nursing, The University of Texas Health Science Center at San Antonio, 7703 Floyd Curl Drive, San Antonio, TX 78229-3900. *Telephone:* 210-567-5850. *Fax:* 210-567-5909. *E-mail:* tierneyguma@uthsca. edu.

The University of Texas Medical Branch
School of Nursing
Galveston, Texas

http://www.son.utmb.edu

Founded in 1891

DEGREES • BSN • MSN • MSN/PHD • PHD

Nursing Program Faculty 50 (62% with doctorates).

Baccalaureate Enrollment 347
Women 84% **Men** 16% **Minority** 33% **International** 1% **Part-time** 37%

Graduate Enrollment 280
Women 88% **Men** 12% **Minority** 28% **International** 36% **Part-time** 84%

Distance Learning Courses Available.

Nursing Student Activities Sigma Theta Tau, Student Nurses' Association.

Nursing Student Resources Academic advising; academic or career counseling; assistance for students with disabilities; bookstore; campus computer network; career placement assistance; computer lab; computer-assisted instruction; e-mail services; employment services for current students; housing assistance; interactive nursing skills videos; Internet; learning resource lab; library services; nursing audiovisuals; resume preparation assistance; skills, simulation, or other laboratory; tutoring.

Library Facilities 262,699 volumes in health, 6,053 volumes in nursing; 47,197 periodical subscriptions health-care related.

BACCALAUREATE PROGRAMS

Degree BSN

Available Programs Accelerated Baccalaureate for Second Degree; Generic Baccalaureate; RN Baccalaureate.

Study Options Full-time and part-time.

Online Degree Options Yes (online only).

Program Entrance Requirements Minimum overall college GPA of 2.75, transcript of college record, CPR certification, written essay, health exam, health insurance, immunizations, interview, minimum GPA in nursing prerequisites of 2.75, professional liability insurance/malpractice insurance, prerequisite course work. Transfer students are accepted. *Application deadline:* 1/15 (fall), 7/15 (spring). *Application fee:* $50.

Advanced Placement Credit by examination available. Credit given for nursing courses completed elsewhere dependent upon specific evaluations.

Expenses (2009–10) *Tuition, state resident:* full-time $5008; part-time $157 per credit hour. *Tuition, nonresident:* full-time $14,000; part-time $438 per credit hour. *Room and board:* $8436; room only: $4404 per academic year. *Required fees:* full-time $3855; part-time $273 per credit; part-time $1285 per term.

Financial Aid 60% of baccalaureate students in nursing programs received some form of financial aid in 2008–09.

Contact Dr. Linda Rath, Associate Professor and Director of Baccalaureate Programs, School of Nursing, The University of Texas Medical Branch, 301 University Boulevard, 3.630 SON/SAHS Building, Galveston, TX 77555-1029. *Telephone:* 409-772-8247. *Fax:* 409-772-3770. *E-mail:* lrath@utmb.edu.

GRADUATE PROGRAMS

Expenses (2009–10) *Tuition, state resident:* full-time $6300; part-time $210 per credit hour. *Tuition, nonresident:* full-time $14,730; part-time $491 per credit hour. *Room and board:* $8436; room only: $4404 per academic year. *Required fees:* full-time $2227; part-time $273 per credit; part-time $759 per term.

Financial Aid 32% of graduate students in nursing programs received some form of financial aid in 2008–09.

Contact Dr. Kathryn Fiandt, Professor and Masters Program Director, School of Nursing, The University of Texas Medical Branch, 301 University Boulevard, Galveston, TX 77555-1029. *Telephone:* 409-772-8297. *Fax:* 409-772-8215. *E-mail:* kfiandt@utmb.edu.

MASTER'S DEGREE PROGRAM

Degrees MSN; MSN/PhD

Available Programs Master's; RN to Master's.

Concentrations Available Nursing administration; nursing education. *Nurse practitioner programs in:* acute care, family health, gerontology, neonatal health, pediatric.

Study Options Full-time and part-time.

Online Degree Options Yes (online only).

Program Entrance Requirements Clinical experience, computer literacy, minimum overall college GPA of 3.0, transcript of college record, CPR certification, written essay, immunizations, interview, 3 letters of recommendation, professional liability insurance/malpractice insurance, prerequisite course work, statistics course. *Application deadline:* 4/1 (fall), 9/15 (spring). *Application fee:* $50.

Advanced Placement Credit given for nursing courses completed elsewhere dependent upon specific evaluations.

Degree Requirements 44 total credit hours, thesis or project.

POST-MASTER'S PROGRAM

Areas of Study Nursing administration; nursing education. *Nurse practitioner programs in:* acute care, family health, gerontology, neonatal health, pediatric.

DOCTORAL DEGREE PROGRAM

Degree PhD

Available Programs Doctorate; Post-Baccalaureate Doctorate.

Areas of Study Aging, bio-behavioral research, ethics, faculty preparation, gerontology, health policy, health promotion/disease prevention, human health and illness, individualized study, information systems, maternity-newborn, nursing education, nursing research, nursing science, women's health.

Online Degree Options Yes (online only).

Program Entrance Requirements Clinical experience, minimum overall college GPA of 3.0, interview by faculty committee, interview, 3 letters of recommendation, MSN or equivalent, statistics course, vita, writing sample. Application deadline: 3/1 (spring). Application fee: $50.

Degree Requirements 63 total credit hours, dissertation, oral exam, written exam, residency.

The University of Texas–Pan American

Department of Nursing
Edinburg, Texas

http://www.panam.edu

Founded in 1927

DEGREES • BSN • MSN

Nursing Program Faculty 23 (45% with doctorates).

Baccalaureate Enrollment 170
Women 78% **Men** 22% **Minority** 90%

Graduate Enrollment 65
Women 88% **Men** 12% **Minority** 88% **Part-time** 75%

Nursing Student Activities Sigma Theta Tau, Student Nurses' Association.

Nursing Student Resources Academic advising; academic or career counseling; assistance for students with disabilities; bookstore; campus computer network; career placement assistance; computer lab; computer-assisted instruction; daycare for children of students; e-mail services; employment services for current students; housing assistance; interactive nursing skills videos; Internet; learning resource lab; library services; nursing audiovisuals; remedial services; skills, simulation, or other laboratory; tutoring.

Library Facilities 598,008 volumes (230 in health, 200 in nursing); 35,004 periodical subscriptions (300 health-care related).

BACCALAUREATE PROGRAMS

Degree BSN

Available Programs ADN to Baccalaureate; Generic Baccalaureate; RN Baccalaureate.

Study Options Full-time.

Program Entrance Requirements Transcript of college record, CPR certification, immunizations, minimum GPA in nursing prerequisites of 2.5, professional liability insurance/malpractice insurance, prerequisite course work. Transfer students are accepted. *Application deadline:* 10/1 (fall), 10/1 (spring).

Expenses (2009–10) *Tuition, state resident:* full-time $5425; part-time $50 per credit hour. *Tuition, nonresident:* full-time $13,735; part-time $327 per credit hour. *International tuition:* $13,735 full-time. *Room and board:* $6456; room only: $4456 per academic year. *Required fees:* full-time $1033; part-time $15 per credit; part-time $162 per term.

Financial Aid 92% of baccalaureate students in nursing programs received some form of financial aid in 2008–09.

Contact Dr. Sandy M. Sánchez, BSN Program Coordinator, Department of Nursing, The University of Texas–Pan American, 1201 West University Drive, Edinburg, TX 78539. *Telephone:* 956-381-3491. *Fax:* 956-381-2875. *E-mail:* sandy@utpa.edu.

GRADUATE PROGRAMS

Expenses (2009–10) *Tuition, state resident:* full-time $4437; part-time $100 per credit hour. *Tuition, nonresident:* full-time $9423; part-time $377 per credit hour. *International tuition:* $9423 full-time. *Room and board:* $6984; room only: $4984 per academic year. *Required fees:* full-time $404; part-time $30 per credit; part-time $140 per term.

Financial Aid 50% of graduate students in nursing programs received some form of financial aid in 2008–09. Scholarships and traineeships available.

Contact Dr. Janice A. Maville, MSN Coordinator, Department of Nursing, The University of Texas–Pan American, 1201 West University Drive, Edinburg, TX 78539. *Telephone:* 956-381-3491. *Fax:* 956-381-2875. *E-mail:* jmaville@utpa.edu.

MASTER'S DEGREE PROGRAM

Degree MSN

Available Programs Master's.

Concentrations Available *Clinical nurse specialist programs in:* adult health. *Nurse practitioner programs in:* family health, pediatric.

Study Options Full-time and part-time.

Program Entrance Requirements Minimum overall college GPA of 2.75, transcript of college record, written essay, immunizations, 3 letters of recommendation, resume, statistics course. *Application deadline:* 7/1 (fall), 10/1 (winter), 4/1 (spring), 4/1 (summer).

Advanced Placement Credit given for nursing courses completed elsewhere dependent upon specific evaluations.

Degree Requirements 48 total credit hours, thesis or project.

POST-MASTER'S PROGRAM

Areas of Study *Clinical nurse specialist programs in:* adult health. *Nurse practitioner programs in:* family health, pediatric.

University of the Incarnate Word

Program in Nursing
San Antonio, Texas

Founded in 1881

University of the Incarnate Word (continued)
DEGREES • BSN • MSN • MSN/MBA

Nursing Program Faculty 35 (57% with doctorates).

Baccalaureate Enrollment 180
Women 88% **Men** 12% **Minority** 57%

Graduate Enrollment 70
Women 83% **Men** 17% **Minority** 59% **International** 10% **Part-time** 76%

Distance Learning Courses Available.

Nursing Student Activities Nursing Honor Society, Sigma Theta Tau, Student Nurses' Association.

Nursing Student Resources Academic advising; academic or career counseling; assistance for students with disabilities; bookstore; campus computer network; career placement assistance; computer lab; computer-assisted instruction; e-mail services; employment services for current students; externships; housing assistance; interactive nursing skills videos; Internet; learning resource lab; library services; nursing audiovisuals; paid internships; placement services for program completers; remedial services; resume preparation assistance; skills, simulation, or other laboratory; tutoring; unpaid internships.

Library Facilities 260,111 volumes (6,000 in health, 6,000 in nursing); 42,574 periodical subscriptions (3,048 health-care related).

BACCALAUREATE PROGRAMS

Degree BSN

Available Programs ADN to Baccalaureate; Baccalaureate for Second Degree; Generic Baccalaureate.

Study Options Full-time.

Online Degree Options Yes.

Program Entrance Requirements Minimum overall college GPA of 2.5, transcript of college record, CPR certification, health exam, health insurance, immunizations, minimum GPA in nursing prerequisites of 2.5, professional liability insurance/malpractice insurance, prerequisite course work. Transfer students are accepted. *Application deadline:* 2/1 (fall), 9/1 (spring).

Advanced Placement Credit given for nursing courses completed elsewhere dependent upon specific evaluations.

Expenses (2008–09) *Tuition:* full-time $19,400; part-time $640 per hour. *Room and board:* $7900 per academic year. *Required fees:* full-time $1750; part-time $800 per term.

Financial Aid 90% of baccalaureate students in nursing programs received some form of financial aid in 2007–08. *Gift aid (need-based):* Federal Pell, FSEOG, state, private, college/university gift aid from institutional funds, United Negro College Fund, Federal Nursing. *Loans:* Federal Nursing Student Loans, FFEL (Subsidized and Unsubsidized Stafford PLUS), Perkins, state, alternative loans. *Work-study:* Federal Work-Study, part-time campus jobs. *Financial aid application deadline (priority):* 4/1.

Contact Office of Admissions, Program in Nursing, University of the Incarnate Word, 4301 Broadway, San Antonio, TX 78209. *Telephone:* 210-829-6005.

GRADUATE PROGRAMS

Expenses (2008–09) *Tuition:* part-time $640 per credit hour. *Room and board:* $2500 per academic year. *Required fees:* part-time $100 per credit.

Financial Aid 75% of graduate students in nursing programs received some form of financial aid in 2007–08. Federal Work-Study, scholarships, and traineeships available. Aid available to part-time students.

Contact Dr. Sandra Strickland, Chair of Graduate Program, Program in Nursing, University of the Incarnate Word, 4301 Broadway, San Antonio, TX 78209. *Telephone:* 210-829-3988. *Fax:* 210-829-3174. *E-mail:* strickla@universe.uiwtx.edu.

MASTER'S DEGREE PROGRAM

Degrees MSN; MSN/MBA

Available Programs Master's.

Concentrations Available Clinical nurse leader. *Clinical nurse specialist programs in:* adult health.

Study Options Full-time and part-time.

Program Entrance Requirements Clinical experience, minimum overall college GPA of 2.5, transcript of college record, immunizations, 3 letters of recommendation, physical assessment course, professional liability insurance/malpractice insurance, statistics course. *Application deadline:* Applications may be processed on a rolling basis for some programs. *Application fee:* $20.

Advanced Placement Credit given for nursing courses completed elsewhere dependent upon specific evaluations.

Degree Requirements 36 total credit hours, thesis or project.

POST-MASTER'S PROGRAM

Areas of Study Clinical nurse leader.

West Texas A&M University
Division of Nursing
Canyon, Texas

http://www.wtamu.edu/nursing
Founded in 1909

DEGREES • BSN • MSN

Nursing Program Faculty 30 (23% with doctorates).

Baccalaureate Enrollment 380
Women 84% **Men** 16% **Minority** 27% **International** 1% **Part-time** 35%

Graduate Enrollment 54
Women 85% **Men** 15% **Minority** 9% **Part-time** 52%

Nursing Student Activities Sigma Theta Tau, Student Nurses' Association.

Nursing Student Resources Academic advising; academic or career counseling; assistance for students with disabilities; bookstore; campus computer network; career placement assistance; computer lab; computer-assisted instruction; daycare for children of students; e-mail services; employment services for current students; housing assistance; interactive nursing skills videos; Internet; learning resource lab; library services; nursing audiovisuals; placement services for program completers; remedial services; resume preparation assistance; skills, simulation, or other laboratory; tutoring.

Library Facilities 1.1 million volumes (17,000 in health, 10,000 in nursing); 19,022 periodical subscriptions (75 health-care related).

BACCALAUREATE PROGRAMS

Degree BSN

Available Programs ADN to Baccalaureate; Generic Baccalaureate; LPN to Baccalaureate.

Study Options Full-time and part-time.

Program Entrance Requirements Minimum overall college GPA of 2.5, transcript of college record, CPR certification, immunizations, minimum GPA in nursing prerequisites of 2.0, prerequisite course work. Transfer students are accepted.

Advanced Placement Credit given for nursing courses completed elsewhere dependent upon specific evaluations.

Contact *Telephone:* 806-651-2661. *Fax:* 806-651-2632.

GRADUATE PROGRAMS

Contact *Telephone:* 806-651-2637. *Fax:* 806-651-2632.

MASTER'S DEGREE PROGRAM

Degree MSN

Available Programs Master's; RN to Master's.

Concentrations Available Nursing administration; nursing education. *Nurse practitioner programs in:* family health.

Study Options Full-time and part-time.

Program Entrance Requirements Clinical experience, computer literacy, minimum overall college GPA of 3.0, transcript of college record, CPR certification, immunizations, nursing research course, prerequisite course work, statistics course, GRE General Test.

Advanced Placement Credit given for nursing courses completed elsewhere dependent upon specific evaluations.

Degree Requirements 39 total credit hours, thesis or project.

POST-MASTER'S PROGRAM

Areas of Study *Nurse practitioner programs in:* family health.

UTAH

Brigham Young University
College of Nursing
Provo, Utah

http://nursing.byu.edu

Founded in 1875

DEGREES • BS • MS

Nursing Program Faculty 47 (59% with doctorates).

Baccalaureate Enrollment 314
Women 92.4% **Men** 7.6% **Minority** 70% **International** 3.5%

Graduate Enrollment 30
Women 63% **Men** 37% **Minority** 6% **International** 1%

Nursing Student Activities Nursing Honor Society, Sigma Theta Tau, Student Nurses' Association.

Nursing Student Resources Academic advising; academic or career counseling; assistance for students with disabilities; bookstore; campus computer network; career placement assistance; computer lab; computer-assisted instruction; e-mail services; employment services for current students; housing assistance; interactive nursing skills videos; Internet; learning resource lab; library services; nursing audiovisuals; other; paid internships; resume preparation assistance; skills, simulation, or other laboratory; tutoring.

Library Facilities 3.5 million volumes (72,332 in health, 5,217 in nursing); 27,161 periodical subscriptions (10,500 health-care related).

BACCALAUREATE PROGRAMS

Degree BS

Available Programs RN Baccalaureate.

Study Options Full-time.

Program Entrance Requirements Minimum overall college GPA, transcript of college record, CPR certification, written essay, 2 letters of recommendation, minimum GPA in nursing prerequisites of 3.0, prerequisite course work. Transfer students are accepted. *Application deadline:* 5/31 (fall), 9/30 (winter).

Advanced Placement Credit given for nursing courses completed elsewhere dependent upon specific evaluations.

Expenses (2009–10) *Tuition:* full-time $5363; part-time $220 per credit hour. *International tuition:* $5363 full-time.

Financial Aid 33% of baccalaureate students in nursing programs received some form of financial aid in 2008–09.

Contact Dr. Mark E. White, Advisement Center Supervisor, College of Nursing, Brigham Young University, 550 SWKT, Provo, UT 84602-5532. *Telephone:* 801-422-7211. *Fax:* 801-422-0536. *E-mail:* mark_white@byu.edu.

GRADUATE PROGRAMS

Expenses (2009–10) *Tuition:* full-time $6775; part-time $301 per credit hour. *International tuition:* $6775 full-time.

Financial Aid 100% of graduate students in nursing programs received some form of financial aid in 2008–09. 2 research assistantships with full and partial tuition reimbursements available (averaging $10,000 per year), 3 teaching assistantships with full and partial tuition reimbursements available (averaging $10,000 per year) were awarded; institutionally sponsored loans, scholarships, tuition waivers (full), and unspecified assistantships also available. Aid available to part-time students. *Financial aid application deadline:* 2/1.

Contact Ms. Denise Gibbons Davis, Research Center and Graduate Program Secretary, College of Nursing, Brigham Young University, 400 SWKT, Provo, UT 84602-5532. *Telephone:* 801-422-4142. *Fax:* 801-422-0536. *E-mail:* denise_gibbons@byu.edu.

MASTER'S DEGREE PROGRAM

Degree MS

Available Programs Master's.

Concentrations Available *Nurse practitioner programs in:* family health.

Study Options Full-time and part-time.

Program Entrance Requirements Clinical experience, minimum overall college GPA of 3.0, transcript of college record, CPR certification, written essay, immunizations, interview, 3 letters of recommendation, prerequisite course work, resume, statistics course, GRE. *Application deadline:* 12/1 (spring). *Application fee:* $50.

Advanced Placement Credit given for nursing courses completed elsewhere dependent upon specific evaluations.

Degree Requirements 56 total credit hours, thesis or project.

POST-MASTER'S PROGRAM

Areas of Study *Nurse practitioner programs in:* family health.

Southern Utah University
Department of Nursing
Cedar City, Utah

http://www.suu.edu/sci/nursing

Founded in 1897

DEGREE • BSN

Nursing Program Faculty 9

Baccalaureate Enrollment 126
Women 70% **Men** 30% **Minority** 5% **International** 1%

Nursing Student Activities Student Nurses' Association, nursing club.

Nursing Student Resources Academic advising; academic or career counseling; assistance for students with disabilities; bookstore; campus computer network; career placement assistance; computer lab; computer-assisted instruction; e-mail services; employment services for current students; externships; housing assistance; interactive nursing skills videos; Internet; learning resource lab; library services; nursing audiovisuals; remedial services; skills, simulation, or other laboratory; tutoring.

Library Facilities 180,424 volumes (1,000 in health, 1,000 in nursing); 6,165 periodical subscriptions (5,000 health-care related).

BACCALAUREATE PROGRAMS

Degree BSN

Available Programs Generic Baccalaureate; LPN to Baccalaureate; RN Baccalaureate.

Study Options Full-time.

Program Entrance Requirements Minimum overall college GPA of 3.0, transcript of college record, CPR certification, written essay, health insurance, high school transcript, immunizations, 3 letters of recommendation, minimum GPA in nursing prerequisites of 3.0, prerequisite course work. Transfer students are accepted. *Application deadline:* 2/13 (fall), 9/11 (spring). *Application fee:* $20.

Advanced Placement Credit given for nursing courses completed elsewhere dependent upon specific evaluations.

Expenses (2009–10) *Tuition, state resident:* full-time $6000. *Tuition, nonresident:* full-time $12,000. *Room and board:* $4000; room only: $2000 per academic year. *Required fees:* full-time $800.

Financial Aid 90% of baccalaureate students in nursing programs received some form of financial aid in 2008–09.

Contact Vikki Robertson, Department Secretary, Department of Nursing, Southern Utah University, 351 West University Boulevard, GC 005, Cedar City, UT 84720. *Telephone:* 435-586-1906. *Fax:* 435-586-1984. *E-mail:* robertsonv@suu.edu.

University of Phoenix–Utah Campus

College of Health and Human Services
Salt Lake City, Utah

Founded in 1984

Nursing Program Faculty 2

Nursing Student Activities Sigma Theta Tau.

Nursing Student Resources Academic advising; academic or career counseling; assistance for students with disabilities; bookstore; campus computer network; computer lab; computer-assisted instruction; e-mail services; interactive nursing skills videos; Internet; learning resource lab; library services; nursing audiovisuals; remedial services; skills, simulation, or other laboratory; tutoring.

Library Facilities 16,871 periodical subscriptions (1,300 health-care related).

University of Utah

College of Nursing
Salt Lake City, Utah

http://www.nurs.utah.edu

Founded in 1850

DEGREES • BS • MS • PHD

Nursing Program Faculty 118 (52% with doctorates).

Baccalaureate Enrollment 319
Women 74% **Men** 26% **Minority** 7% **International** 6% **Part-time** 35%

Graduate Enrollment 244
Women 74% **Men** 26% **Minority** 7% **International** 6% **Part-time** 35%

Distance Learning Courses Available.

Nursing Student Activities Sigma Theta Tau, Student Nurses' Association.

Nursing Student Resources Academic advising; academic or career counseling; assistance for students with disabilities; bookstore; campus computer network; career placement assistance; computer lab; computer-assisted instruction; e-mail services; externships; interactive nursing skills videos; Internet; learning resource lab; library services; nursing audiovisuals; paid internships; remedial services; resume preparation assistance; skills, simulation, or other laboratory; unpaid internships.

Library Facilities 4.1 million volumes (197,845 in health, 8,000 in nursing); 45,830 periodical subscriptions (3,546 health-care related).

BACCALAUREATE PROGRAMS

Degree BS

Available Programs Accelerated Baccalaureate; Generic Baccalaureate; RN Baccalaureate.

Study Options Full-time.

Program Entrance Requirements Minimum overall college GPA of 2.8, transcript of college record, CPR certification, written essay, health exam, immunizations, 3 letters of recommendation, minimum GPA in nursing prerequisites of 3.0, professional liability insurance/malpractice insurance, prerequisite course work. Transfer students are accepted. *Application deadline:* 1/15 (fall).

Advanced Placement Credit by examination available. Credit given for nursing courses completed elsewhere dependent upon specific evaluations.

Expenses (2009–10) *Tuition, area resident:* full-time $6241. *Tuition, nonresident:* full-time $19,820. *International tuition:* $19,820 full-time. *Room and board:* $7359; room only: $3711 per academic year. *Required fees:* full-time $470.

Financial Aid 70% of baccalaureate students in nursing programs received some form of financial aid in 2008–09. *Gift aid (need-based):* Federal Pell, FSEOG, state, private, college/university gift aid from institutional funds, Federal Nursing. *Loans:* Federal Nursing Student Loans, FFEL (Subsidized and Unsubsidized Stafford PLUS), Perkins, college/university. *Work-study:* Federal Work-Study. *Financial aid application deadline (priority):* 3/15.

Contact Ms. Cynthia Weatbrook, Undergraduate Academic Advisor, College of Nursing, University of Utah, 10 South 2000 East, Salt Lake City, UT 84112-5880. *Telephone:* 801-581-3414. *Fax:* 801-585-9705. *E-mail:* cynthia.weatbrook@nurs.utah.edu.

GRADUATE PROGRAMS

Expenses (2009–10) *Tuition, area resident:* full-time $8014. *Tuition, nonresident:* full-time $15,465. *International tuition:* $15,465 full-time. *Room and board:* $7359; room only: $3711 per academic year. *Required fees:* full-time $700.

Financial Aid 72% of graduate students in nursing programs received some form of financial aid in 2008–09. Fellowships with partial tuition reimbursements available, research assistantships with partial tuition reimbursements available, teaching assistantships with partial tuition reimbursements available, scholarships available. *Financial aid application deadline:* 2/1.

Contact Ms. Lara Kandolin, Graduate Student Academic Advisor, College of Nursing, University of Utah, 10 South 2000 East, Salt Lake City, UT 84112-5880. *Telephone:* 801-585-6658. *Fax:* 801-585-9705. *E-mail:* lara.kandolin@nurs.utah.edu.

MASTER'S DEGREE PROGRAM

Degree MS

Available Programs Master's.

Concentrations Available Clinical nurse leader; nursing informatics. *Nurse practitioner programs in:* gerontology.

Site Options St. George, UT.

Study Options Full-time and part-time.

Program Entrance Requirements Clinical experience, computer literacy, minimum overall college GPA of 3.0, transcript of college record, CPR certification, written essay, immunizations, interview, 3 letters of recommendation, professional liability insurance/malpractice insurance, resume, statistics course, GRE General Test if undergraduate GPA is below 3.2. *Application deadline:* 1/15 (fall), 6/11 (spring), 11/30 (summer).

Advanced Placement Credit given for nursing courses completed elsewhere dependent upon specific evaluations.

Degree Requirements 35 total credit hours, thesis or project, comprehensive exam.

POST-MASTER'S PROGRAM

Areas of Study Nurse-midwifery. *Clinical nurse specialist programs in:* acute care, psychiatric/mental health, women's health. *Nurse practitioner programs in:* acute care, adult health, community health, family health, neonatal health, pediatric, primary care, psychiatric/mental health, women's health.

DOCTORAL DEGREE PROGRAM

Degree PhD

Available Programs Doctorate; Doctorate for Nurses with Non-Nursing Degrees; Post-Baccalaureate Doctorate.

Areas of Study Aging, bio-behavioral research, community health, ethics, faculty preparation, family health, gerontology, health policy, health promotion/disease prevention, health-care systems, human health and illness, illness and transition, individualized study, information systems, maternity-newborn, nursing administration, nursing education, nursing policy, nursing research, nursing science, oncology, women's health.

Program Entrance Requirements Clinical experience, minimum overall college GPA of 3.3, interview by faculty committee, interview, 3 letters of recommendation, vita, writing sample, GRE General Test. Application deadline: 1/15 (fall).

Degree Requirements 62 total credit hours, dissertation, oral exam, written exam, residency.

POSTDOCTORAL PROGRAM

Areas of Study Aging, cancer care, gerontology, nursing informatics, nursing interventions, nursing research, nursing science.

Postdoctoral Program Contact Dr. Ginette A. Pepper, Associate Dean for Research and PhD Programs, College of Nursing, University of Utah, 10 South 2000 East, Salt Lake City, UT 84112-5880. *Telephone:* 801-793-5733. *Fax:* 801-793-5701. *E-mail:* ginny.pepper@nurs.utah.edu.

Utah Valley University
Department of Nursing
Orem, Utah

http://www.uvsc.edu/nurs/

Founded in 1941

DEGREE • BSN

Nursing Program Faculty 22 (25% with doctorates).

Baccalaureate Enrollment 100
Women 60% **Men** 40% **Part-time** 99%

Nursing Student Activities Student Nurses' Association.

Nursing Student Resources Academic advising; academic or career counseling; assistance for students with disabilities; bookstore; campus computer network; career placement assistance; computer lab; computer-assisted instruction; daycare for children of students; e-mail services; employment services for current students; interactive nursing skills videos; Internet; learning resource lab; library services; nursing audiovisuals; resume preparation assistance; skills, simulation, or other laboratory; tutoring; unpaid internships.

Library Facilities 193,646 volumes (4,640 in health, 361 in nursing); 568 periodical subscriptions (200 health-care related).

BACCALAUREATE PROGRAMS

Degree BSN

Available Programs ADN to Baccalaureate.

Study Options Part-time.

Program Entrance Requirements CPR certification, health exam, health insurance, immunizations, minimum GPA in nursing prerequisites of 2.5, prerequisite course work, RN licensure. Transfer students are accepted.

Advanced Placement Credit by examination available.

Contact *Telephone:* 801-863-8199. *Fax:* 801-863-6093.

Weber State University
Program in Nursing
Ogden, Utah

Founded in 1889

DEGREES • BSN • MSN

Nursing Program Faculty 42 (5% with doctorates).

Baccalaureate Enrollment 250
Women 88% **Men** 12% **Minority** 3% **International** 1% **Part-time** 5%

Graduate Enrollment 17
Women 82% **Men** 18% **Minority** 1%

Distance Learning Courses Available.

Nursing Student Activities Sigma Theta Tau, Student Nurses' Association.

Nursing Student Resources Academic advising; academic or career counseling; assistance for students with disabilities; bookstore; campus computer network; career placement assistance; computer lab; computer-assisted instruction; daycare for children of students; e-mail services; employment services for current students; housing assistance; interactive nursing skills videos; Internet; learning resource lab; library services; nursing audiovisuals; placement services for program completers; resume preparation assistance; skills, simulation, or other laboratory; tutoring; unpaid internships.

Library Facilities 646,666 volumes (800 in health, 800 in nursing); 120 periodical subscriptions health-care related.

BACCALAUREATE PROGRAMS

Degree BSN

Available Programs ADN to Baccalaureate; Accelerated Baccalaureate.

Study Options Full-time and part-time.

Online Degree Options Yes.

Program Entrance Requirements Minimum overall college GPA of 3.0, transcript of college record, CPR certification, health insurance, immunizations, minimum GPA in nursing prerequisites of 3.0, prerequisite course work, RN licensure. Transfer students are accepted. *Application deadline:* 4/1 (fall), 11/1 (spring). *Application fee:* $25.

Advanced Placement Credit by examination available. Credit given for nursing courses completed elsewhere dependent upon specific evaluations.

Expenses (2009–10) *Tuition, state resident:* full-time $3400. *Tuition, nonresident:* full-time $10,800. *Required fees:* full-time $740.

Financial Aid 15% of baccalaureate students in nursing programs received some form of financial aid in 2008–09.

Contact Doug Watson, Academic Admissions Advisor, Program in Nursing, Weber State University, 3907 University Circle, Ogden, UT 84408-3907. *Telephone:* 801-626-6128. *Fax:* 801-626-6382. *E-mail:* dwatson@weber.edu.

GRADUATE PROGRAMS

Expenses (2009–10) *Tuition, state resident:* full-time $5200. *Required fees:* full-time $740.

Contact Mr. Robert W. Holt, Enrollment Director, Program in Nursing, Weber State University, 3903 University Circle, Ogden, UT 84408-3903. *Telephone:* 801-626-7774. *Fax:* 801-626-6397. *E-mail:* rholt@weber.edu.

MASTER'S DEGREE PROGRAM

Degree MSN

Available Programs Master's.

Concentrations Available Nursing administration; nursing education.

Study Options Full-time.

Program Entrance Requirements Clinical experience, minimum overall college GPA of 3.0, transcript of college record, CPR certification, written essay, immunizations, interview, 2 letters of recommendation, nursing research course, professional liability insurance/malpractice insurance, prerequisite course work, resume, statistics course. *Application deadline:* 3/1 (fall). *Application fee:* $70.

Degree Requirements 40 total credit hours, thesis or project.

Westminster College
School of Nursing and Health Sciences
Salt Lake City, Utah

http://www.westminstercollege.edu

Founded in 1875

DEGREES • BSN • MSN

Nursing Student Activities Sigma Theta Tau, Student Nurses' Association, nursing club.

Nursing Student Resources Academic advising; academic or career counseling; assistance for students with disabilities; bookstore; campus computer network; career placement assistance; computer lab; computer-assisted instruction; e-mail services; employment services for current students; housing assistance; interactive nursing skills videos; Internet; learning resource lab; library services; nursing audiovisuals; placement services for program completers; remedial services; resume preparation assistance; skills, simulation, or other laboratory; tutoring.

Library Facilities 181,319 volumes; 9,857 periodical subscriptions.

BACCALAUREATE PROGRAMS

Degree BSN

Available Programs Baccalaureate for Second Degree; Generic Baccalaureate; RN Baccalaureate.

Study Options Full-time.

Westminster College (continued)

Program Entrance Requirements Transcript of college record, written essay, 3 letters of recommendation, minimum GPA in nursing prerequisites of 2.5, prerequisite course work. Transfer students are accepted.

Contact *Telephone:* 801-832-2150. *Fax:* 801-832-3110.

GRADUATE PROGRAMS

Contact *Telephone:* 801-832-2150. *Fax:* 801-832-3110.

MASTER'S DEGREE PROGRAM

Degree MSN

Available Programs Master's.

Concentrations Available Nursing education. *Nurse practitioner programs in:* family health.

Program Entrance Requirements Transcript of college record, written essay, 3 letters of recommendation, resume, GRE.

Advanced Placement Credit given for nursing courses completed elsewhere dependent upon specific evaluations.

Degree Requirements 42 total credit hours, thesis or project.

POST-MASTER'S PROGRAM

Areas of Study *Nurse practitioner programs in:* family health.

VERMONT

Norwich University
Department of Nursing
Northfield, Vermont

http://www.norwich.edu/acad/nursing

Founded in 1819

DEGREE • BSN

Nursing Program Faculty 8 (10% with doctorates).

Baccalaureate Enrollment 90
Women 90% **Men** 10% **Minority** 10% **Part-time** 20%

Nursing Student Activities Student Nurses' Association, nursing club.

Nursing Student Resources Academic advising; academic or career counseling; assistance for students with disabilities; bookstore; campus computer network; career placement assistance; computer lab; e-mail services; employment services for current students; externships; housing assistance; interactive nursing skills videos; Internet; learning resource lab; library services; nursing audiovisuals; placement services for program completers; remedial services; resume preparation assistance; skills, simulation, or other laboratory; tutoring; unpaid internships.

Library Facilities 280,000 volumes; 904 periodical subscriptions.

BACCALAUREATE PROGRAMS

Degree BSN

Available Programs ADN to Baccalaureate; Generic Baccalaureate; RN Baccalaureate.

Site Options Rutland, VT.

Study Options Full-time and part-time.

Program Entrance Requirements Minimum overall college GPA of 2.5, transcript of college record, CPR certification, written essay, health exam, health insurance, high school biology, high school chemistry, 2 years high school math, 2 years high school science, high school transcript, immunizations, interview, 2 letters of recommendation, minimum GPA in nursing prerequisites of 2.5. Transfer students are accepted.

Advanced Placement Credit given for nursing courses completed elsewhere dependent upon specific evaluations.

Contact *Telephone:* 802-485-2008. *Fax:* 802-485-2032.

Southern Vermont College
Department of Nursing
Bennington, Vermont

http://www.svc.edu/academics/divisions/nursing.html

Founded in 1926

DEGREE • BSN

Nursing Program Faculty 7

Distance Learning Courses Available.

Nursing Student Resources Academic advising; academic or career counseling; assistance for students with disabilities; bookstore; computer lab; e-mail services; Internet; library services; resume preparation assistance; tutoring.

Library Facilities 26,000 volumes; 250 periodical subscriptions.

BACCALAUREATE PROGRAMS

Degree BSN

Available Programs ADN to Baccalaureate; RN Baccalaureate.

Advanced Placement Credit by examination available.

Expenses (2008–09) *Tuition:* full-time $8980; part-time $610 per credit. *Room and board:* $4250; room only: $2125 per academic year.

Contact Ms. Patricia G. Wrightsman, RN, Chair, Division of Nursing, Department of Nursing, Southern Vermont College, 982 Mansion Drive, Bennington, VT 05201. *Telephone:* 802-447-6335. *Fax:* 802-447-4652. *E-mail:* pwrightsman@svc.edu.

University of Vermont
Department of Nursing
Burlington, Vermont

http://www.uvm.edu/~cnhs/nursing

Founded in 1791

DEGREES • BS • MS

Nursing Program Faculty 37 (14% with doctorates).

Baccalaureate Enrollment 282
Women 95% **Men** 5% **Minority** 9%

Graduate Enrollment 78
Women 90% **Men** 10% **Minority** 9% **Part-time** 23%

Distance Learning Courses Available.

Nursing Student Activities Nursing Honor Society, Sigma Theta Tau, Student Nurses' Association.

Nursing Student Resources Academic advising; academic or career counseling; assistance for students with disabilities; bookstore; campus computer network; career placement assistance; computer lab; computer-assisted instruction; e-mail services; employment services for current students; interactive nursing skills videos; Internet; learning resource lab; library services; nursing audiovisuals; remedial services; resume preparation assistance; skills, simulation, or other laboratory; tutoring.

Library Facilities 2.6 million volumes (126,689 in health, 1,437 in nursing); 18,891 periodical subscriptions (5,084 health-care related).

BACCALAUREATE PROGRAMS

Degree BS

Available Programs ADN to Baccalaureate; Generic Baccalaureate.

Study Options Full-time and part-time.

Program Entrance Requirements Minimum overall college GPA of 3.0, transcript of college record, written essay, health insurance, high school biology, high school chemistry, high school foreign language, 3 years high school math, 2 years high school science, high school transcript, immunizations, letters of recommendation, minimum GPA in nursing prerequisites of 2.0. Transfer students are accepted. *Application deadline:* 1/15 (fall). *Application fee:* $55.

Advanced Placement Credit by examination available. Credit given for nursing courses completed elsewhere dependent upon specific evaluations.

Expenses (2009–10) *Tuition, state resident:* full-time $11,712; part-time $488 per credit hour. *Tuition, nonresident:* full-time $29,568; part-time $1232 per credit hour. *Room and board:* $9026 per academic year. *Required fees:* full-time $1812.

Financial Aid 87% of baccalaureate students in nursing programs received some form of financial aid in 2008–09.

Contact Ms. Erica S. Caloiero, Director of Student Services, Department of Nursing, University of Vermont, Rowell Building, Room 106, Burlington, VT 05405-0068. *Telephone:* 802-656-0968. *E-mail:* Erica.Caloiero@uvm.edu.

GRADUATE PROGRAMS

Expenses (2009–10) *Tuition, state resident:* full-time $8784; part-time $488 per credit hour. *Tuition, nonresident:* full-time $22,176; part-time $1232 per credit hour.

Financial Aid 36% of graduate students in nursing programs received some form of financial aid in 2008–09. *Application deadline:* 3/1.

Contact Ms. Miriam Harms, Graduate Program Assistant, Department of Nursing, University of Vermont, 216 Rowell Building, 106 Carrigan Drive, Burlington, VT 05405. *Telephone:* 802-656-2018. *Fax:* 802-656-8306. *E-mail:* Miriam.Harms@uvm.edu.

MASTER'S DEGREE PROGRAM

Degree MS

Available Programs Master's; Master's for Non-Nursing College Graduates; Master's for Nurses with Non-Nursing Degrees; RN to Master's.

Concentrations Available Nursing administration. *Nurse practitioner programs in:* adult health, family health, psychiatric/mental health.

Study Options Full-time and part-time.

Program Entrance Requirements Minimum overall college GPA of 3.0, transcript of college record, written essay, 3 letters of recommendation, physical assessment course, statistics course, GRE General Test. *Application deadline:* Applications may be processed on a rolling basis for some programs. *Application fee:* $40.

Advanced Placement Credit by examination available. Credit given for nursing courses completed elsewhere dependent upon specific evaluations.

Degree Requirements 57 total credit hours, thesis or project, comprehensive exam.

POST-MASTER'S PROGRAM

Areas of Study *Nurse practitioner programs in:* adult health, family health, psychiatric/mental health.

VIRGIN ISLANDS

University of the Virgin Islands
Division of Nursing
Saint Thomas, Virgin Islands

http://www.uvi.edu
Founded in 1962

DEGREE • BS

Nursing Program Faculty 10 (20% with doctorates).

Baccalaureate Enrollment 142
Women 97.3% **Men** 2.7% **Minority** 95% **International** 3% **Part-time** 20%

Distance Learning Courses Available.

Nursing Student Activities Student Nurses' Association.

Nursing Student Resources Academic advising; academic or career counseling; assistance for students with disabilities; bookstore; campus computer network; computer lab; computer-assisted instruction; e-mail services; employment services for current students; externships; housing

assistance; interactive nursing skills videos; Internet; learning resource lab; library services; nursing audiovisuals; paid internships; skills, simulation, or other laboratory; tutoring.

Library Facilities 106,361 volumes (95,000 in health, 600 in nursing); 113,623 periodical subscriptions (15 health-care related).

BACCALAUREATE PROGRAMS

Degree BS

Available Programs ADN to Baccalaureate; Generic Baccalaureate; LPN to Baccalaureate; RN Baccalaureate.

Site Options St. Croix, VI.

Study Options Full-time and part-time.

Program Entrance Requirements Minimum overall college GPA of 2.0, CPR certification, health exam, 2 years high school math, high school transcript, immunizations, minimum GPA in nursing prerequisites of 2.0, professional liability insurance/malpractice insurance, prerequisite course work. Transfer students are accepted. *Application deadline:* 10/15 (fall), 4/15 (spring). Applications may be processed on a rolling basis for some programs. *Application fee:* $25.

Advanced Placement Credit by examination available. Credit given for nursing courses completed elsewhere dependent upon specific evaluations.

Expenses (2009–10) *Tuition, state resident:* full-time $3600; part-time $120 per credit. *Tuition, nonresident:* full-time $10,800; part-time $360 per credit. *Room and board:* $3775; room only: $1610 per academic year. *Required fees:* full-time $846; part-time $395 per term.

Financial Aid 80% of baccalaureate students in nursing programs received some form of financial aid in 2008–09.

Contact Dr. Cheryl P. Franklin, Dean, Division of Nursing, Division of Nursing, University of the Virgin Islands, RR1 Box 10000, Kingshill, St. Croix, VI 00850-9781. *Telephone:* 340-778-1620 Ext. 4117. *Fax:* 340-693-1285. *E-mail:* cfrankl@uvi.edu.

VIRGINIA

Eastern Mennonite University
Department of Nursing
Harrisonburg, Virginia

Founded in 1917

DEGREE • BSN

Nursing Program Faculty 13 (23% with doctorates).

Baccalaureate Enrollment 146
Women 92.5% **Men** 7.5% **Minority** 8.2%

Nursing Student Activities Sigma Theta Tau, Student Nurses' Association.

Nursing Student Resources Academic advising; academic or career counseling; assistance for students with disabilities; bookstore; campus computer network; career placement assistance; computer lab; computer-assisted instruction; e-mail services; employment services for current students; externships; housing assistance; interactive nursing skills videos; Internet; learning resource lab; library services; nursing audiovisuals; placement services for program completers; remedial services; resume preparation assistance; skills, simulation, or other laboratory; tutoring.

Library Facilities 168,135 volumes (1,256 in health, 926 in nursing); 965 periodical subscriptions (33 health-care related).

BACCALAUREATE PROGRAMS

Degree BSN

Available Programs ADN to Baccalaureate; Baccalaureate for Second Degree; Generic Baccalaureate; LPN to Baccalaureate; RN Baccalaureate.

Site Options Lancaster, PA.

Study Options Full-time and part-time.

Eastern Mennonite University (continued)
Program Entrance Requirements Minimum overall college GPA of 2.6, transcript of college record, CPR certification, written essay, health exam, health insurance, high school chemistry, high school transcript, immunizations, 3 letters of recommendation, minimum high school GPA of 2.0, minimum GPA in nursing prerequisites of 2.8, professional liability insurance/malpractice insurance, prerequisite course work. Transfer students are accepted. *Application deadline:* 11/1 (fall), 4/1 (spring).

Advanced Placement Credit by examination available. Credit given for nursing courses completed elsewhere dependent upon specific evaluations.

Expenses (2009–10) *Tuition:* full-time $24,220; part-time $1010 per credit hour. *International tuition:* $24,220 full-time. *Required fees:* full-time $250.

Financial Aid 95% of baccalaureate students in nursing programs received some form of financial aid in 2008–09.

Contact Mrs. Stephanie C. Shafer, Director of Admissions, Department of Nursing, Eastern Mennonite University, 1200 Park Road, Harrisonburg, VA 22802. *Telephone:* 800-368-2665. *Fax:* 540-432-4118. *E-mail:* stephanie. schafer@emu.edu.

ECPI College of Technology
BSN Program
Virginia Beach, Virginia

Founded in 1966
DEGREE • BSN

Distance Learning Courses Available.

BACCALAUREATE PROGRAMS
Degree BSN

Available Programs RN Baccalaureate.
Online Degree Options Yes.
Contact Bachelors Degree Program, BSN Program, ECPI College of Technology, 5501 Greenwich Road, Suite 100, Virginia Beach, VA 23462. *Telephone:* 757-497-8400.

George Mason University
College of Health and Human Services
Fairfax, Virginia

http://cnhs.gmu.edu/
Founded in 1957
DEGREES • BSN • MSN • MSN/MBA • PHD

Nursing Program Faculty 39 (50% with doctorates).
Baccalaureate Enrollment 380
Women 89% **Men** 11% **Minority** 20% **International** 4% **Part-time** 6%
Graduate Enrollment 290
Women 96% **Men** 4% **Minority** 33% **International** 2% **Part-time** 86%
Distance Learning Courses Available.
Nursing Student Activities Nursing Honor Society, Sigma Theta Tau, Student Nurses' Association.
Nursing Student Resources Academic advising; computer lab; e-mail services; skills, simulation, or other laboratory.
Library Facilities 1.6 million volumes (16,172 in nursing); 388,085 periodical subscriptions (200 health-care related).

BACCALAUREATE PROGRAMS
Degree BSN

Available Programs Accelerated Baccalaureate for Second Degree; Generic Baccalaureate; LPN to Baccalaureate; RN Baccalaureate.
Study Options Full-time.

Program Entrance Requirements Minimum overall college GPA of 2.0, CPR certification, health exam, health insurance, immunizations, minimum GPA in nursing prerequisites of 3.0, prerequisite course work. Transfer students are accepted. *Application deadline:* 2/2 (fall).

Expenses (2008–09) *Tuition, state resident:* full-time $7512; part-time $313 per credit hour. *Tuition, nonresident:* full-time $22,476; part-time $937 per credit hour. *International tuition:* $22,476 full-time. *Room and board:* $10,770; room only: $7410 per academic year. *Required fees:* full-time $880.

Financial Aid 54% of baccalaureate students in nursing programs received some form of financial aid in 2007–08. *Gift aid (need-based):* Federal Pell, FSEOG, state, private, college/university gift aid from institutional funds. *Loans:* Federal Nursing Student Loans, FFEL (Subsidized and Unsubsidized Stafford PLUS), Perkins. *Work-study:* Federal Work-Study. *Financial aid application deadline (priority):* 3/1.

Contact Dr. Carol Urban, Assistant Dean, Division of Undergraduate Studies, School of Nursing, College of Health and Human Services, George Mason University, Mailstop 3C4, 4400 University Drive, Fairfax, VA 22030-4444. *Telephone:* 703-993-2991. *Fax:* 703-993-1949. *E-mail:* curban@gmu. edu.

GRADUATE PROGRAMS
Expenses (2008–09) *Tuition, state resident:* part-time $370 per credit hour. *Tuition, nonresident:* part-time $928 per credit hour.

Financial Aid Fellowships, research assistantships, teaching assistantships, tuition waivers (partial) and health care benefits (research or teaching assistantship recipients) available.

Contact Dr. Joyce Hahn, Assistant Dean for Graduate Programs, College of Health and Human Services, George Mason University, Mailstop 3C4, 4400 University Drive, Fairfax, VA 22030-4444. *Telephone:* 703-993-2335. *Fax:* 703-993-1949. *E-mail:* jhahn2@gmu.edu.

MASTER'S DEGREE PROGRAM
Degrees MSN; MSN/MBA

Available Programs Master's; RN to Master's.
Concentrations Available Clinical nurse leader; nursing administration; nursing education. *Clinical nurse specialist programs in:* acute care, adult health, cardiovascular, critical care, medical-surgical, oncology. *Nurse practitioner programs in:* adult health, family health, gerontology, primary care.
Site Options Loudoun County, VA; Prince William County, VA.
Study Options Full-time and part-time.
Program Entrance Requirements Clinical experience, minimum overall college GPA of 3.0, CPR certification, written essay, immunizations, 2 letters of recommendation, physical assessment course, statistics course. *Application deadline:* 4/15 (fall).
Degree Requirements 38 total credit hours, thesis or project.

POST-MASTER'S PROGRAM
Areas of Study Nursing administration; nursing education.

DOCTORAL DEGREE PROGRAM
Degree PhD

Available Programs Doctorate.
Areas of Study Individualized study, nursing administration, nursing education.
Program Entrance Requirements Clinical experience, minimum overall college GPA of 3.5, interview, 3 letters of recommendation, MSN or equivalent, statistics course, writing sample, MAT. Application deadline: 3/2 (spring). Application fee: $60.
Degree Requirements 58 total credit hours, dissertation, written exam.

POSTDOCTORAL PROGRAM
Postdoctoral Program Contact Mr. Jean Sorrell, Coordinator, College of Health and Human Services, George Mason University, Mailstop 3C4, 4400 University Drive, Fairfax, VA 22030-4444. *Telephone:* 703-993-1944. *Fax:* 703-993-1942. *E-mail:* jsorrell@gmu.edu.

CONTINUING EDUCATION PROGRAM
Contact Dr. Mona Ternus, Director, Academic Outreach, College of Health and Human Services, George Mason University, Mailstop 3C4, 4400 University Drive, Fairfax, VA 22030-4444. *Telephone:* 703-993-1910. *Fax:* 703-993-1622. *E-mail:* mternus@gmu.edu.

Hampton University
School of Nursing
Hampton, Virginia

http://www.hamptonu.edu/nursing/Index.htm

Founded in 1868

DEGREES • BS • MS • PHD

Nursing Program Faculty 35 (51% with doctorates).

Baccalaureate Enrollment 388
Women 91% **Men** 9% **Minority** 97% **International** 3% **Part-time** 3%

Graduate Enrollment 72
Women 86% **Men** 14% **Minority** 58% **Part-time** 35%

Nursing Student Activities Nursing Honor Society, Sigma Theta Tau, Student Nurses' Association.

Nursing Student Resources Academic advising; bookstore; computer lab; e-mail services; interactive nursing skills videos; Internet; library services; tutoring.

Library Facilities 336,092 volumes (4,000 in health, 2,000 in nursing); 1,414 periodical subscriptions (500 health-care related).

BACCALAUREATE PROGRAMS

Degree BS

Available Programs ADN to Baccalaureate; Accelerated Baccalaureate; Accelerated RN Baccalaureate; Baccalaureate for Second Degree; Generic Baccalaureate; LPN to Baccalaureate; LPN to RN Baccalaureate; RN Baccalaureate.

Site Options Virginia Beach, VA.

Study Options Full-time and part-time.

Program Entrance Requirements Minimum overall college GPA of 2.3, transcript of college record, CPR certification, written essay, health exam, health insurance, high school biology, high school chemistry, 3 years high school math, 2 years high school science, high school transcript, immunizations, 2 letters of recommendation, minimum high school GPA of 2.0, minimum high school rank 50%, minimum GPA in nursing prerequisites of 2.0, professional liability insurance/malpractice insurance. Transfer students are accepted.

Advanced Placement Credit by examination available. Credit given for nursing courses completed elsewhere dependent upon specific evaluations.

Contact *Telephone:* 757-727-5251. *Fax:* 757-727-5423.

GRADUATE PROGRAMS

Contact *Telephone:* 757-727-5251. *Fax:* 757-727-5423.

MASTER'S DEGREE PROGRAM

Degree MS

Available Programs Master's.

Concentrations Available Nursing administration; nursing education. *Clinical nurse specialist programs in:* adult health, community health, psychiatric/mental health. *Nurse practitioner programs in:* family health, gerontology, pediatric, women's health.

Study Options Full-time and part-time.

Program Entrance Requirements Clinical experience, minimum overall college GPA of 2.5, transcript of college record, CPR certification, immunizations, interview, 2 letters of recommendation, nursing research course, physical assessment course, professional liability insurance/malpractice insurance, prerequisite course work, resume, statistics course, GRE General Test.

Advanced Placement Credit given for nursing courses completed elsewhere dependent upon specific evaluations.

Degree Requirements 45 total credit hours, thesis or project, comprehensive exam.

POST-MASTER'S PROGRAM

Areas of Study *Nurse practitioner programs in:* family health.

DOCTORAL DEGREE PROGRAM

Degree PhD

Available Programs Doctorate.

Areas of Study Family health.

Program Entrance Requirements Clinical experience, minimum overall college GPA of 3.5, interview, 2 letters of recommendation, MSN or equivalent, scholarly papers, statistics course, vita, writing sample.

Degree Requirements 48 total credit hours, dissertation, oral exam, written exam, residency.

James Madison University
Department of Nursing
Harrisonburg, Virginia

http://www.nursing.jmu.edu

Founded in 1908

DEGREES • BSN • MSN

Nursing Program Faculty 35 (40% with doctorates).

Baccalaureate Enrollment 808
Women 95% **Men** 5% **Minority** 7%

Graduate Enrollment 47
Women 93% **Men** 7% **Minority** 5% **Part-time** 45%

Distance Learning Courses Available.

Nursing Student Activities Nursing Honor Society, Sigma Theta Tau, Student Nurses' Association.

Nursing Student Resources Academic advising; academic or career counseling; assistance for students with disabilities; bookstore; campus computer network; career placement assistance; computer lab; computer-assisted instruction; e-mail services; employment services for current students; externships; housing assistance; interactive nursing skills videos; Internet; learning resource lab; library services; nursing audiovisuals; paid internships; remedial services; resume preparation assistance; skills, simulation, or other laboratory; unpaid internships.

Library Facilities 788,639 volumes (67,716 in health, 12,054 in nursing); 17,078 periodical subscriptions.

BACCALAUREATE PROGRAMS

Degree BSN

Available Programs Accelerated RN Baccalaureate; Generic Baccalaureate.

Study Options Full-time and part-time.

Program Entrance Requirements Minimum overall college GPA of 2.8, transcript of college record, CPR certification, written essay, health exam, health insurance, immunizations, minimum GPA in nursing prerequisites of 2.0, prerequisite course work. Transfer students are accepted. *Application deadline:* Applications may be processed on a rolling basis for some programs.

Advanced Placement Credit given for nursing courses completed elsewhere dependent upon specific evaluations.

Expenses (2009–10) *Tuition, state resident:* full-time $7244. *Tuition, nonresident:* full-time $19,366. *Room and board:* $7386 per academic year. *Required fees:* full-time $532.

Financial Aid 37% of baccalaureate students in nursing programs received some form of financial aid in 2008–09. *Gift aid (need-based):* Federal Pell, FSEOG, state, private, college/university gift aid from institutional funds. *Loans:* FFEL (Subsidized and Unsubsidized Stafford PLUS), Perkins. *Work-study:* Federal Work-Study, part-time campus jobs. *Financial aid application deadline (priority):* 3/1.

Contact Ms. Kelly Brown, Administrative Assistant, Department of Nursing, James Madison University, 701 Carrier Drive, Health and Human Services Building, MSC 4305, Harrisonburg, VA 22807. *Telephone:* 540-568-6314. *Fax:* 540-568-7896. *E-mail:* brownkd@jmu.edu.

GRADUATE PROGRAMS

Expenses (2009–10) *Tuition, state resident:* part-time $305 per credit hour. *Tuition, nonresident:* part-time $890 per credit hour.

Financial Aid 95% of graduate students in nursing programs received some form of financial aid in 2008–09.

Contact Christy Comer, Administrative Assistant, Department of Nursing, James Madison University, 701 Carrier Drive, Health and Human Services Building, MSC 4305, Harrisonburg, VA 22807. *Telephone:* 540-568-6314. *Fax:* 540-568-7896. *E-mail:* comerca@jmu.edu.

James Madison University (continued)

MASTER'S DEGREE PROGRAM

Degree MSN

Available Programs Master's.

Concentrations Available Clinical nurse leader; nurse-midwifery; nursing administration. *Nurse practitioner programs in:* adult health, family health, gerontology.

Study Options Full-time and part-time.

Program Entrance Requirements Clinical experience, computer literacy, minimum overall college GPA of 2.8, transcript of college record, CPR certification, written essay, immunizations, 2 letters of recommendation, physical assessment course, prerequisite course work, resume, statistics course. *Application deadline:* Applications may be processed on a rolling basis for some programs.

Advanced Placement Credit given for nursing courses completed elsewhere dependent upon specific evaluations.

Degree Requirements 43 total credit hours.

POST-MASTER'S PROGRAM

Areas of Study Clinical nurse leader; nurse-midwifery; nursing administration. *Nurse practitioner programs in:* adult health, family health, gerontology.

Jefferson College of Health Sciences

Nursing Education Program
Roanoke, Virginia

http://www.jchs.edu

Founded in 1982

DEGREES • BSN • MSN

Nursing Program Faculty 24 (17% with doctorates).

Baccalaureate Enrollment 260
Women 93% **Men** 7% **Minority** 15% **Part-time** 47%

Graduate Enrollment 32
Women 91% **Men** 9% **Minority** 9% **Part-time** 3%

Distance Learning Courses Available.

Nursing Student Activities Nursing Honor Society, Sigma Theta Tau, Student Nurses' Association.

Nursing Student Resources Academic advising; academic or career counseling; assistance for students with disabilities; bookstore; campus computer network; computer lab; computer-assisted instruction; e-mail services; externships; housing assistance; interactive nursing skills videos; Internet; learning resource lab; library services; nursing audiovisuals; skills, simulation, or other laboratory; tutoring.

Library Facilities 10,533 volumes (4,403 in health, 1,422 in nursing); 376 periodical subscriptions (277 health-care related).

BACCALAUREATE PROGRAMS

Degree BSN

Available Programs ADN to Baccalaureate; Generic Baccalaureate; RN Baccalaureate.

Site Options Roanoke, VA.

Study Options Full-time and part-time.

Program Entrance Requirements Minimum overall college GPA of 2.0, transcript of college record, CPR certification, health exam, health insurance, high school biology, high school chemistry, 2 years high school math, 2 years high school science, high school transcript, immunizations, minimum high school GPA of 2.0, prerequisite course work. Transfer students are accepted.

Advanced Placement Credit by examination available. Credit given for nursing courses completed elsewhere dependent upon specific evaluations.

Contact *Telephone:* 540-985-9083. *Fax:* 540-224-6703.

GRADUATE PROGRAMS

Contact *Telephone:* 540-985-9083. *Fax:* 540-224-6703.

MASTER'S DEGREE PROGRAM

Degree MSN

Available Programs Master's; Master's for Nurses with Non-Nursing Degrees.

Concentrations Available Nursing administration; nursing education.

Site Options Roanoke, VA.

Study Options Full-time.

Program Entrance Requirements Clinical experience, computer literacy, transcript of college record, 2 letters of recommendation, nursing research course, resume, statistics course.

Degree Requirements 37 total credit hours, thesis or project.

CONTINUING EDUCATION PROGRAM

Contact *Telephone:* 540-767-6072.

Liberty University

Department of Nursing
Lynchburg, Virginia

http://www.liberty.edu

Founded in 1971

DEGREES • BSN • MSN

Nursing Program Faculty 25 (25% with doctorates).

Baccalaureate Enrollment 358
Women 93% **Men** 7% **Minority** 7% **International** 8%

Graduate Enrollment 280
Women 89% **Men** 11% **Minority** 29% **International** 3% **Part-time** 99%

Distance Learning Courses Available.

Nursing Student Activities Student Nurses' Association.

Nursing Student Resources Academic advising; academic or career counseling; assistance for students with disabilities; bookstore; campus computer network; career placement assistance; computer lab; e-mail services; externships; interactive nursing skills videos; Internet; learning resource lab; library services; nursing audiovisuals; resume preparation assistance; skills, simulation, or other laboratory; tutoring.

Library Facilities 291,243 volumes (3,632 in health, 3,000 in nursing); 67,234 periodical subscriptions (46 health-care related).

BACCALAUREATE PROGRAMS

Degree BSN

Available Programs Generic Baccalaureate; RN Baccalaureate.

Site Options Lynchburg, VA.

Study Options Full-time and part-time.

Program Entrance Requirements Minimum overall college GPA of 3.0, transcript of college record, CPR certification, written essay, immunizations, 2 letters of recommendation, minimum GPA in nursing prerequisites of 3.0, professional liability insurance/malpractice insurance, prerequisite course work. Transfer students are accepted. *Application deadline:* 2/11 (spring).

Advanced Placement Credit given for nursing courses completed elsewhere dependent upon specific evaluations.

Expenses (2008–09) *Tuition:* full-time $15,444; part-time $515 per credit hour. *International tuition:* $15,444 full-time. *Room and board:* $6400 per academic year. *Required fees:* full-time $1400.

Financial Aid 75% of baccalaureate students in nursing programs received some form of financial aid in 2007–08. *Gift aid (need-based):* Federal Pell, FSEOG, state, private, college/university gift aid from institutional funds, Academic Competitiveness Grant, National Smart Grant, TEACH Grant. *Loans:* FFEL (Subsidized and Unsubsidized Stafford PLUS). *Work-study:* Federal Work-Study, part-time campus jobs. *Financial aid application deadline:* 3/1.

Contact Dr. Deanna Britt, Chair, Department of Nursing, Liberty University, 1971 University Boulevard, Lynchburg, VA 24502. *Telephone:* 804-582-2519. *Fax:* 804-582-7035. *E-mail:* dbritt@liberty.edu.

GRADUATE PROGRAMS

Expenses (2008–09) *Tuition:* part-time $395 per credit hour. *Room and board:* room only: $5800 per academic year.

Financial Aid 65% of graduate students in nursing programs received some form of financial aid in 2007–08.

Contact Dr. Hila Spear, Director of Master Program, Department of Nursing, Liberty University, Lynchburg, VA 24502. *Telephone:* 804-582-2519. *E-mail:* hspear@liberty.edu.

MASTER'S DEGREE PROGRAM

Degree MSN
Available Programs Master's.
Concentrations Available Nursing education. *Clinical nurse specialist programs in:* acute care.
Site Options Lynchburg, VA.
Study Options Full-time and part-time.
Online Degree Options Yes (online only).
Program Entrance Requirements Clinical experience, computer literacy, minimum overall college GPA of 3.0, transcript of college record, CPR certification, written essay, immunizations, interview, 3 letters of recommendation, nursing research course, physical assessment course, prerequisite course work, resume, statistics course. *Application deadline:* Applications may be processed on a rolling basis for some programs. *Application fee:* $50.
Degree Requirements 36 total credit hours, thesis or project.

Lynchburg College
School of Health Sciences and Human Performance
Lynchburg, Virginia

http://www.lynchburg.edu/schools/NRSG.htm
Founded in 1903
DEGREE • BS

Nursing Program Faculty 14 (29% with doctorates).
Baccalaureate Enrollment 191
Women 85% **Men** 15% **Minority** 10%
Nursing Student Activities Sigma Theta Tau, Student Nurses' Association.
Nursing Student Resources Academic advising; academic or career counseling; assistance for students with disabilities; bookstore; campus computer network; career placement assistance; computer lab; computer-assisted instruction; e-mail services; employment services for current students; externships; Internet; learning resource lab; library services; nursing audiovisuals; resume preparation assistance; skills, simulation, or other laboratory; tutoring; unpaid internships.
Library Facilities 238,000 volumes (6,259 in health, 1,881 in nursing); 473 periodical subscriptions (65 health-care related).

BACCALAUREATE PROGRAMS
Degree BS
Available Programs Generic Baccalaureate.
Study Options Full-time and part-time.
Program Entrance Requirements Minimum overall college GPA of 2.7, transcript of college record, CPR certification, health exam, health insurance, 3 years high school math, immunizations, minimum GPA in nursing prerequisites of 2.7, prerequisite course work. Transfer students are accepted. *Application deadline:* 3/15 (fall), 10/15 (spring).
Advanced Placement Credit given for nursing courses completed elsewhere dependent upon specific evaluations.
Financial Aid 97% of baccalaureate students in nursing programs received some form of financial aid in 2008–09. *Gift aid (need-based):* Federal Pell, FSEOG, state, private, college/university gift aid from institutional funds. *Loans:* FFEL (Subsidized and Unsubsidized Stafford PLUS), Perkins. *Work-study:* Federal Work-Study, part-time campus jobs. *Financial aid application deadline (priority):* 3/5.
Contact Dr. Angela S. Taylor, Director of Nursing Program and Associate Professor, School of Health Sciences and Human Performance, Lynchburg College, 1501 Lakeside Drive, McMillan Nursing Building, Lynchburg, VA 24501-3199. *Telephone:* 434-544-8901. *Fax:* 434-544-8323. *E-mail:* taylor.a@lynchburg.edu.

Marymount University
School of Health Professions
Arlington, Virginia

http://www.marymount.edu/academic/healthprof/index.html
Founded in 1950
DEGREES • BSN • DNP • MSN

Nursing Program Faculty 18 (61% with doctorates).
Baccalaureate Enrollment 350
Women 90% **Men** 10% **Minority** 32% **International** 4% **Part-time** 17%
Graduate Enrollment 479
Women 91% **Men** 9% **Minority** 48% **International** 5% **Part-time** 84%
Distance Learning Courses Available.
Nursing Student Activities Sigma Theta Tau, Student Nurses' Association.
Nursing Student Resources Academic advising; academic or career counseling; assistance for students with disabilities; bookstore; campus computer network; career placement assistance; computer lab; computer-assisted instruction; e-mail services; externships; housing assistance; interactive nursing skills videos; Internet; learning resource lab; library services; nursing audiovisuals; paid internships; remedial services; resume preparation assistance; skills, simulation, or other laboratory; tutoring; unpaid internships.
Library Facilities 187,097 volumes (10,657 in health, 1,500 in nursing); 1,048 periodical subscriptions (100 health-care related).

BACCALAUREATE PROGRAMS
Degree BSN
Available Programs ADN to Baccalaureate; Accelerated Baccalaureate for Second Degree; Accelerated RN Baccalaureate; Baccalaureate for Second Degree; Generic Baccalaureate; RN Baccalaureate.
Site Options Arlington, VA.
Study Options Full-time and part-time.
Online Degree Options Yes.
Program Entrance Requirements Minimum overall college GPA of 2.5, health exam, health insurance, high school transcript, 2 letters of recommendation, minimum high school GPA of 2.5. Transfer students are accepted. *Application deadline:* Applications may be processed on a rolling basis for some programs. *Application fee:* $40.
Advanced Placement Credit by examination available. Credit given for nursing courses completed elsewhere dependent upon specific evaluations.
Expenses (2009–10) *Tuition:* full-time $22,370; part-time $725 per credit hour. *Room and board:* $9745 per academic year.
Financial Aid 84% of baccalaureate students in nursing programs received some form of financial aid in 2008–09. *Gift aid (need-based):* Federal Pell, FSEOG, state, private, college/university gift aid from institutional funds. *Loans:* FFEL (Subsidized and Unsubsidized Stafford PLUS), Perkins. *Work-study:* Federal Work-Study. *Financial aid application deadline (priority):* 3/1.
Contact Dr. Rosemarie Berman, Chair, School of Health Professions, Marymount University, 2807 North Glebe Road, Arlington, VA 22207-4299. *Telephone:* 703-284-1627. *Fax:* 703-284-3819. *E-mail:* rosemarie.berman@marymount.edu.

GRADUATE PROGRAMS
Expenses (2009–10) *Tuition:* part-time $725 per credit hour.
Financial Aid 57% of graduate students in nursing programs received some form of financial aid in 2008–09. Research assistantships with full and partial tuition reimbursements available, career-related internships or fieldwork, Federal Work-Study, scholarships, and unspecified assistantships available. Aid available to part-time students.
Contact Ms. Francesca Reed, Coordinator, Graduate Admissions, School of Health Professions, Marymount University, 2807 North Glebe Road, Arlington, VA 22207-4299. *Telephone:* 703-284-5906. *E-mail:* francesca.reed@marymount.edu.

Marymount University (continued)

MASTER'S DEGREE PROGRAM

Degree MSN

Available Programs Master's.

Concentrations Available Nursing education. *Nurse practitioner programs in:* family health.

Site Options Arlington, VA.

Study Options Full-time and part-time.

Program Entrance Requirements Minimum overall college GPA of 3.0, transcript of college record, CPR certification, immunizations, interview, 2 letters of recommendation, professional liability insurance/malpractice insurance, resume, statistics course, GRE, MAT. *Application deadline:* Applications may be processed on a rolling basis for some programs. *Application fee:* $40.

Advanced Placement Credit given for nursing courses completed elsewhere dependent upon specific evaluations.

Degree Requirements 40 total credit hours, comprehensive exam.

POST-MASTER'S PROGRAM

Areas of Study Nursing education. *Nurse practitioner programs in:* family health.

DOCTORAL DEGREE PROGRAM

Degree DNP

Available Programs Doctorate; Post-Baccalaureate Doctorate.

Areas of Study Advanced practice nursing.

Site Options Arlington, VA.

Program Entrance Requirements Clinical experience, minimum overall college GPA of 3.0, interview by faculty committee, interview, 2 letters of recommendation, MSN or equivalent, vita, GRE. Application deadline: 4/1 (fall). Application fee: $40.

Degree Requirements 32 total credit hours, residency.

Norfolk State University

Department of Nursing
Norfolk, Virginia

http://www.nsu.edu/schools/sciencetech/nursing/
Founded in 1935

DEGREE • BSN

Nursing Program Faculty 26 (40% with doctorates).

Baccalaureate Enrollment 133
Women 90% **Men** 10% **Minority** 85% **International** 15% **Part-time** 45%

Distance Learning Courses Available.

Nursing Student Activities Nursing Honor Society, Student Nurses' Association, nursing club.

Nursing Student Resources Academic advising; academic or career counseling; assistance for students with disabilities; bookstore; campus computer network; career placement assistance; computer lab; computer-assisted instruction; daycare for children of students; e-mail services; employment services for current students; externships; housing assistance; interactive nursing skills videos; Internet; learning resource lab; library services; nursing audiovisuals; paid internships; remedial services; resume preparation assistance; skills, simulation, or other laboratory; tutoring; unpaid internships.

Library Facilities 600 volumes in health, 300 volumes in nursing; 125 periodical subscriptions health-care related.

BACCALAUREATE PROGRAMS

Degree BSN

Available Programs Accelerated Baccalaureate for Second Degree; Accelerated LPN to Baccalaureate; RN Baccalaureate.

Site Options Virginia Beach, VA.

Study Options Full-time and part-time.

Program Entrance Requirements Minimum overall college GPA of 2.5, transcript of college record, CPR certification, health exam, health insurance, high school biology, high school chemistry, 2 years high school math, high school transcript, immunizations, minimum high school GPA of 2.5, minimum GPA in nursing prerequisites of 2.5, professional liability insurance/malpractice insurance, prerequisite course work. Transfer students are accepted. *Application deadline:* 8/1 (fall), 12/1 (winter), 2/1 (spring), 8/1 (summer).

Advanced Placement Credit by examination available. Credit given for nursing courses completed elsewhere dependent upon specific evaluations.

Expenses (2009–10) *Tuition, state resident:* full-time $2986; part-time $260 per credit hour. *Tuition, nonresident:* full-time $9016; part-time $662 per credit hour. *International tuition:* $9016 full-time. *Room and board:* $3665; room only: $2335 per academic year. *Required fees:* full-time $205.

Financial Aid 87% of baccalaureate students in nursing programs received some form of financial aid in 2008–09. *Gift aid (need-based):* Federal Pell, FSEOG, state, private, college/university gift aid from institutional funds. *Loans:* Federal Direct (Subsidized and Unsubsidized Stafford), FFEL, Perkins, state, alternative loans. *Work-study:* Federal Work-Study, part-time campus jobs. *Financial aid application deadline:* 5/31.

Contact Dr. Bennie L. Marshall, Department Head, Department of Nursing, Norfolk State University, 700 Park Avenue, Norfolk, VA 23504. *Telephone:* 757-823-9015. *Fax:* 757-823-2131. *E-mail:* blmarshall@nsu.edu.

Old Dominion University

Department of Nursing
Norfolk, Virginia

http://www.odu.edu/nursson
Founded in 1930

DEGREES • BSN • DNP • MSN

Nursing Program Faculty 27 (33% with doctorates).

Baccalaureate Enrollment 399
Women 91% **Men** 9% **Minority** 40% **Part-time** 46%

Graduate Enrollment 219
Women 92% **Men** 8% **Minority** 23% **Part-time** 47%

Distance Learning Courses Available.

Nursing Student Activities Sigma Theta Tau, Student Nurses' Association.

Nursing Student Resources Academic advising; academic or career counseling; assistance for students with disabilities; bookstore; campus computer network; career placement assistance; computer lab; computer-assisted instruction; e-mail services; externships; interactive nursing skills videos; Internet; learning resource lab; library services; nursing audiovisuals; paid internships; remedial services; resume preparation assistance; skills, simulation, or other laboratory; tutoring; unpaid internships.

Library Facilities 1.2 million volumes (44,144 in health, 3,622 in nursing); 17,967 periodical subscriptions (3,035 health-care related).

BACCALAUREATE PROGRAMS

Degree BSN

Available Programs Accelerated Baccalaureate; Generic Baccalaureate; RN Baccalaureate.

Site Options Olympia, WA; Yavapai, AZ.

Study Options Full-time.

Program Entrance Requirements Transcript of college record, CPR certification, immunizations, minimum GPA in nursing prerequisites of 2.5, prerequisite course work. Transfer students are accepted. *Application deadline:* 2/1 (fall). *Application fee:* $40.

Expenses (2008–09) *Tuition, area resident:* full-time $6720; part-time $224 per credit hour. *Tuition, state resident:* full-time $7200; part-time $240 per credit hour. *Tuition, nonresident:* full-time $18,390; part-time $613 per credit hour. *Room and board:* $18,500; room only: $13,500 per academic year. *Required fees:* full-time $250; part-time $150 per term.

Financial Aid 48% of baccalaureate students in nursing programs received some form of financial aid in 2007–08. *Gift aid (need-based):* Federal Pell, FSEOG, state, private, college/university gift aid from institutional funds, United Negro College Fund, Federal Nursing. *Loans:* Federal Nursing Student Loans, Federal Direct (Subsidized and Unsubsidized Stafford PLUS), Perkins, college/university. *Work-study:* Federal Work-Study. *Financial aid application deadline:* 3/15 (priority: 2/15).

Contact Ms. Phyllis D. Barham, Chief Academic Advisor, Department of Nursing, Old Dominion University, Norfolk, VA 23529-0500. *Telephone:* 757-683-5245. *Fax:* 757-683-5253. *E-mail:* pbarham@odu.edu.

GRADUATE PROGRAMS

Expenses (2008–09) *Tuition, area resident:* full-time $11,556; part-time $321 per credit hour. *Tuition, state resident:* full-time $12,600; part-time $350 per credit hour. *Tuition, nonresident:* full-time $28,656; part-time $796 per credit hour. *International tuition:* $28,656 full-time. *Room and board:* $18,500; room only: $13,500 per academic year. *Required fees:* full-time $1000; part-time $500 per term.

Financial Aid 42% of graduate students in nursing programs received some form of financial aid in 2007–08.

Contact Dr. Laurel Garzon, Graduate Program Director, Department of Nursing, Old Dominion University, Technology Building, Norfolk, VA 23529-0500. *Telephone:* 757-683-4298. *Fax:* 757-683-5253. *E-mail:* lgarzon@odu.edu.

MASTER'S DEGREE PROGRAM

Degree MSN

Available Programs Master's; RN to Master's.

Concentrations Available Nurse anesthesia; nurse-midwifery; nursing administration; nursing education. *Nurse practitioner programs in:* family health, women's health.

Site Options Athens, GA; Olympia, WA; Yavapai, AZ.

Study Options Full-time and part-time.

Online Degree Options Yes (online only).

Program Entrance Requirements Clinical experience, computer literacy, minimum overall college GPA of 3.0, transcript of college record, CPR certification, written essay, immunizations, interview, 3 letters of recommendation, physical assessment course, statistics course. *Application deadline:* 6/1 (fall), 12/1 (winter). *Application fee:* $40.

Advanced Placement Credit given for nursing courses completed elsewhere dependent upon specific evaluations.

Degree Requirements 47 total credit hours, comprehensive exam.

POST-MASTER'S PROGRAM

Areas of Study Nurse anesthesia; nurse-midwifery; nursing administration; nursing education. *Nurse practitioner programs in:* family health, women's health.

DOCTORAL DEGREE PROGRAM

Degree DNP

Available Programs Doctorate.

Areas of Study Advanced practice nursing.

Online Degree Options Yes (online only).

Program Entrance Requirements Clinical experience, minimum overall college GPA of 3.0, 3 letters of recommendation, MSN or equivalent, statistics course, vita, writing sample. Application deadline: 11/15 (fall), 11/15 (winter), 11/15 (spring).

Degree Requirements 36 total credit hours.

CONTINUING EDUCATION PROGRAM

Contact Mrs. Kimberly Curry-Lourenco, Senior Lecturer, Department of Nursing, Old Dominion University, 4608 Hampton Boulevard, Norfolk, VA 23529-0500. *Telephone:* 757-683-5261. *Fax:* 757-683-5253. *E-mail:* kcurrylo@odu.edu.

Radford University
School of Nursing
Radford, Virginia

http://www.radford.edu/nurs-web
Founded in 1910

DEGREES • BSN • DNP • MSN

Nursing Program Faculty 42 (5% with doctorates).

Baccalaureate Enrollment 280
Women 93% **Men** 7% **Minority** 9% **International** 3%

Graduate Enrollment 32
Women 100% **Minority** 5% **Part-time** 30%

Distance Learning Courses Available.

Nursing Student Activities Nursing Honor Society, Sigma Theta Tau, Student Nurses' Association.

Nursing Student Resources Academic advising; academic or career counseling; assistance for students with disabilities; bookstore; campus computer network; career placement assistance; computer lab; computer-assisted instruction; e-mail services; employment services for current students; externships; housing assistance; interactive nursing skills videos; Internet; learning resource lab; library services; nursing audiovisuals; resume preparation assistance; skills, simulation, or other laboratory; unpaid internships.

Library Facilities 382,048 volumes; 11,069 periodical subscriptions.

BACCALAUREATE PROGRAMS

Degree BSN

Available Programs Baccalaureate for Second Degree; Generic Baccalaureate; RN Baccalaureate.

Site Options Roanoke, VA; Martinsville, VA.

Study Options Full-time.

Online Degree Options Yes.

Program Entrance Requirements Minimum overall college GPA of 2.5, transcript of college record, CPR certification, written essay, health exam, health insurance, immunizations, minimum GPA in nursing prerequisites of 2.5, prerequisite course work. Transfer students are accepted. *Application deadline:* 11/15 (fall), 8/1 (spring).

Advanced Placement Credit given for nursing courses completed elsewhere dependent upon specific evaluations.

Financial Aid 50% of baccalaureate students in nursing programs received some form of financial aid in 2008–09. *Gift aid (need-based):* Federal Pell, FSEOG, state, private, college/university gift aid from institutional funds. *Loans:* Federal Nursing Student Loans, FFEL (Subsidized and Unsubsidized Stafford PLUS), Perkins, state, college/university. *Work-study:* Federal Work-Study, part-time campus jobs. *Financial aid application deadline (priority):* 3/1.

Contact Prof. Anthony Ray Ramsey, Undergraduate Program Coordinator, School of Nursing, Radford University, Box 6964, RU Station, Waldron Hall, Room 305, Radford, VA 24142. *Telephone:* 540-831-7700. *Fax:* 540-831-7716. *E-mail:* nurs-web@radford.edu.

GRADUATE PROGRAMS

Financial Aid 90% of graduate students in nursing programs received some form of financial aid in 2008–09. 1 research assistantship with partial tuition reimbursement available (averaging $8,000 per year), 6 teaching assistantships with partial tuition reimbursements available (averaging $8,700 per year) were awarded; career-related internships or fieldwork, Federal Work-Study, institutionally sponsored loans, scholarships, and unspecified assistantships also available. *Financial aid application deadline:* 3/1.

Contact Dr. Lisa Onega, PhD, Graduate Program Coordinator, School of Nursing, Radford University, Box 6964, RU Station, Waldron Hall, Radford, VA 24142. *Telephone:* 540-831-7647. *Fax:* 540-831-7716. *E-mail:* nurs-web@radford.edu.

MASTER'S DEGREE PROGRAM

Degree MSN

Available Programs Master's.

Concentrations Available Nurse-midwifery. *Clinical nurse specialist programs in:* adult health, gerontology. *Nurse practitioner programs in:* family health.

Study Options Full-time and part-time.

Program Entrance Requirements Clinical experience, computer literacy, minimum overall college GPA of 3.0, transcript of college record, CPR certification, written essay, immunizations, interview, 3 letters of recommendation, nursing research course, physical assessment course, professional liability insurance/malpractice insurance, prerequisite course work, resume, statistics course, GRE or MAT.

Radford University (continued)

Advanced Placement Credit given for nursing courses completed elsewhere dependent upon specific evaluations.

Degree Requirements 41 total credit hours, thesis or project.

POST-MASTER'S PROGRAM

Areas of Study *Clinical nurse specialist programs in:* gerontology. *Nurse practitioner programs in:* family health.

DOCTORAL DEGREE PROGRAM

Degree DNP

Available Programs Doctorate; Post-Baccalaureate Doctorate.

Areas of Study Advanced practice nursing, aging, clinical practice, faculty preparation, family health, gerontology, individualized study, maternity-newborn.

Online Degree Options Yes (online only).

Program Entrance Requirements Clinical experience, minimum overall college GPA of 3.0, interview by faculty committee, 3 letters of recommendation, vita, writing sample. Application deadline: 2/1 (fall).

Degree Requirements Residency.

Shenandoah University
Division of Nursing
Winchester, Virginia

http://www.su.edu/nursing/index.html

Founded in 1875

DEGREES • BSN • MSN

Nursing Program Faculty 44 (30% with doctorates).

Baccalaureate Enrollment 239
Women 97% **Men** 3% **Minority** 10% **International** 3% **Part-time** 15%

Graduate Enrollment 28
Women 97% **Men** 3% **Minority** 10% **Part-time** 25%

Nursing Student Activities Nursing Honor Society, Sigma Theta Tau, Student Nurses' Association.

Nursing Student Resources Academic advising; academic or career counseling; assistance for students with disabilities; bookstore; campus computer network; computer lab; daycare for children of students; e-mail services; interactive nursing skills videos; Internet; learning resource lab; library services; nursing audiovisuals; resume preparation assistance; skills, simulation, or other laboratory; tutoring.

Library Facilities 131,174 volumes (500 in health, 200 in nursing); 19,479 periodical subscriptions (250 health-care related).

BACCALAUREATE PROGRAMS

Degree BSN

Available Programs ADN to Baccalaureate; Accelerated Baccalaureate for Second Degree; Generic Baccalaureate; LPN to Baccalaureate; LPN to RN Baccalaureate; RN Baccalaureate.

Site Options Leesburg, VA.

Study Options Full-time and part-time.

Program Entrance Requirements Minimum overall college GPA of 2.5, transcript of college record, CPR certification, health exam, health insurance, high school biology, high school chemistry, 2 years high school math, high school transcript, immunizations, minimum high school GPA of 2.5, minimum GPA in nursing prerequisites of 2.0, prerequisite course work. Transfer students are accepted.

Advanced Placement Credit by examination available. Credit given for nursing courses completed elsewhere dependent upon specific evaluations.

Contact *Telephone:* 540-678-4381. *Fax:* 540-665-5519.

GRADUATE PROGRAMS

Contact *Telephone:* 540-665-5512. *Fax:* 540-665-5519.

MASTER'S DEGREE PROGRAM

Degree MSN

Available Programs Master's; RN to Master's.

Concentrations Available Nurse case management; nurse-midwifery. *Clinical nurse specialist programs in:* psychiatric/mental health. *Nurse practitioner programs in:* family health, psychiatric/mental health.

Study Options Full-time and part-time.

Program Entrance Requirements Clinical experience, computer literacy, minimum overall college GPA of 2.8, transcript of college record, CPR certification, immunizations, interview, 3 letters of recommendation, nursing research course, physical assessment course, professional liability insurance/malpractice insurance, prerequisite course work, resume, statistics course, GRE General Test.

Advanced Placement Credit given for nursing courses completed elsewhere dependent upon specific evaluations.

Degree Requirements 37 total credit hours, thesis or project.

POST-MASTER'S PROGRAM

Areas of Study Nurse-midwifery. *Nurse practitioner programs in:* family health, psychiatric/mental health.

CONTINUING EDUCATION PROGRAM

Contact *Telephone:* 540-665-4584.

Stratford University
School of Nursing
Falls Church, Virginia

Founded in 1976

DEGREE • BSN

Nursing Program Faculty 3 (33% with doctorates).

Baccalaureate Enrollment 14
Women 64% **Men** 36% **Minority** 79% **International** 7% **Part-time** 80%

Nursing Student Activities Student Nurses' Association.

Nursing Student Resources Academic advising; campus computer network; career placement assistance; computer lab; computer-assisted instruction; e-mail services; employment services for current students; interactive nursing skills videos; Internet; learning resource lab; library services; nursing audiovisuals; placement services for program completers; resume preparation assistance; skills, simulation, or other laboratory; tutoring; unpaid internships.

Library Facilities 1,800 volumes (120 in health, 110 in nursing); 75 periodical subscriptions (600 health-care related).

BACCALAUREATE PROGRAMS

Degree BSN

Available Programs Generic Baccalaureate.

Study Options Full-time and part-time.

Program Entrance Requirements Transcript of college record, written essay, high school transcript, 2 letters of recommendation. Transfer students are accepted. *Application deadline:* 9/30 (fall), 11/30 (winter), 2/28 (spring), 6/15 (summer). *Application fee:* $50.

Advanced Placement Credit by examination available.

Expenses (2009–10) *Tuition:* part-time $355 per credit hour.

Financial Aid 90% of baccalaureate students in nursing programs received some form of financial aid in 2008–09.

Contact Bachelor of Science in Nursing, School of Nursing, Stratford University, 7777 Leesburg Pike, Falls Church, VA 22043. *Telephone:* 703-821-8570.

University of Virginia
School of Nursing
Charlottesville, Virginia

http://www.nursing.virginia.edu

Founded in 1819

DEGREES • BSN • MSN • MSN/MBA • MSN/PHD • PHD

Nursing Program Faculty 103 (65% with doctorates).

Baccalaureate Enrollment 350
Women 95% **Men** 5% **Minority** 18% **International** 1% **Part-time** 5%

Graduate Enrollment 300
Women 90% **Men** 10% **Minority** 18% **International** 2% **Part-time** 40%

Distance Learning Courses Available.

Nursing Student Activities Nursing Honor Society, Sigma Theta Tau, Student Nurses' Association, nursing club.

Nursing Student Resources Academic advising; academic or career counseling; assistance for students with disabilities; bookstore; campus computer network; career placement assistance; computer-assisted instruction; e-mail services; housing assistance; interactive nursing skills videos; Internet; learning resource lab; library services; nursing audiovisuals; placement services for program completers; remedial services; resume preparation assistance; skills, simulation, or other laboratory; tutoring.

Library Facilities 5.5 million volumes (200,000 in health); 1,000 periodical subscriptions health-care related.

BACCALAUREATE PROGRAMS

Degree BSN

Available Programs ADN to Baccalaureate; Generic Baccalaureate; RN Baccalaureate.

Study Options Full-time.

Program Entrance Requirements Transcript of college record, written essay, health insurance, high school biology, 2 years high school math, 2 years high school science, high school transcript, immunizations, 1 letter of recommendation, minimum GPA in nursing prerequisites of 2.0. Transfer students are accepted. *Application deadline:* 1/1 (fall). *Application fee:* $60.

Advanced Placement Credit by examination available.

Expenses (2009–10) *Tuition, state resident:* full-time $9670. *Tuition, nonresident:* full-time $31,670. *International tuition:* $31,670 full-time.

Financial Aid 50% of baccalaureate students in nursing programs received some form of financial aid in 2008–09. *Gift aid (need-based):* Federal Pell, FSEOG, state, private, college/university gift aid from institutional funds, Federal Nursing. *Loans:* Federal Nursing Student Loans, FFEL (Subsidized and Unsubsidized Stafford PLUS), Perkins, college/university, alternative private loans. *Work-study:* Federal Work-Study. *Financial aid application deadline (priority):* 3/1.

Contact Dr. Theresa J. Carroll, Assistant Dean for Undergraduate Student Services, School of Nursing, University of Virginia, Claude Moore Nursing Education Building, PO Box 800826, Charlottesville, VA 22908. *Telephone:* 888-283-8703. *Fax:* 434-924-0528. *E-mail:* nur-osa@virginia.edu.

GRADUATE PROGRAMS

Expenses (2009–10) *Tuition, state resident:* full-time $12,645; part-time $565 per credit. *Tuition, nonresident:* full-time $22,645; part-time $1065 per credit. *International tuition:* $22,645 full-time. *Required fees:* full-time $17; part-time $9 per term.

Financial Aid 80% of graduate students in nursing programs received some form of financial aid in 2008–09. Fellowships, research assistantships, teaching assistantships, Federal Work-Study and scholarships available.

Contact Mr. Clay D. Hysell, Assistant Dean for Graduate Student Services, School of Nursing, University of Virginia, Claude Moore Nursing Education Building, PO Box 800826, Charlottesville, VA 22908. *Telephone:* 888-283-8703. *Fax:* 434-924-0528. *E-mail:* nur-osa@virginia.edu.

MASTER'S DEGREE PROGRAM

Degrees MSN; MSN/MBA; MSN/PhD

Available Programs Master's; Master's for Non-Nursing College Graduates; Master's for Nurses with Non-Nursing Degrees.

Concentrations Available Clinical nurse leader; nursing administration. *Clinical nurse specialist programs in:* acute care, adult health, community health, critical care, medical-surgical, psychiatric/mental health, public health. *Nurse practitioner programs in:* acute care, community health, family health, pediatric, primary care, psychiatric/mental health.

Study Options Full-time and part-time.

Program Entrance Requirements Minimum overall college GPA of 3.0, transcript of college record, written essay, 3 letters of recommendation, physical assessment course, prerequisite course work, resume, statistics course, GRE General Test, MAT. *Application deadline:* 4/1 (fall), 11/1 (spring), 4/1 (summer). Applications may be processed on a rolling basis for some programs. *Application fee:* $60.

Advanced Placement Credit given for nursing courses completed elsewhere dependent upon specific evaluations.

Degree Requirements 43 total credit hours.

POST-MASTER'S PROGRAM

Areas of Study Nursing administration. *Clinical nurse specialist programs in:* acute care, adult health, community health, critical care, medical-surgical, psychiatric/mental health, public health. *Nurse practitioner programs in:* acute care, family health, pediatric, primary care, psychiatric/mental health.

DOCTORAL DEGREE PROGRAM

Degree PhD

Available Programs Doctorate; Post-Baccalaureate Doctorate.

Areas of Study Advanced practice nursing, aging, bio-behavioral research, clinical practice, community health, critical care, ethics, faculty preparation, family health, forensic nursing, gerontology, health policy, health promotion/disease prevention, health-care systems, information systems, maternity-newborn, nursing administration, nursing education, nursing policy, nursing research, nursing science, oncology, women's health.

Program Entrance Requirements Minimum overall college GPA of 3.0, interview by faculty committee, interview, 3 letters of recommendation, statistics course, vita, writing sample, GRE General Test. Application deadline: 2/1 (fall). Applications may be processed on a rolling basis for some programs. Application fee: $60.

Degree Requirements 46 total credit hours, dissertation, written exam, residency.

POSTDOCTORAL PROGRAM

Areas of Study Nursing research, nursing science.

Postdoctoral Program Contact Mr. Clay D. Hysell, Assistant Dean for Graduate Student Services, School of Nursing, University of Virginia, McLeod Hall, PO Box 800782, Charlottesville, VA 22908. *Telephone:* 434-924-0141. *Fax:* 434-924-0528. *E-mail:* cdh6n@virginia.edu.

The University of Virginia's College at Wise
Department of Nursing
Wise, Virginia

http://www.uvawise.edu
Founded in 1954
DEGREE • BSN

Nursing Program Faculty 10 (20% with doctorates).

Baccalaureate Enrollment 47
Women 79% **Men** 21% **Minority** 15% **Part-time** 5%

Nursing Student Activities Sigma Theta Tau, Student Nurses' Association.

Nursing Student Resources Academic advising; academic or career counseling; assistance for students with disabilities; bookstore; campus computer network; computer lab; computer-assisted instruction; e-mail services; employment services for current students; externships; housing assistance; interactive nursing skills videos; Internet; learning resource lab; library services; nursing audiovisuals; resume preparation assistance; skills, simulation, or other laboratory; tutoring.

Library Facilities 143,260 volumes (4,654 in health, 2,761 in nursing); 3,155 periodical subscriptions (40 health-care related).

BACCALAUREATE PROGRAMS
Degree BSN

The University of Virginia's College at Wise (continued)

Available Programs ADN to Baccalaureate; Generic Baccalaureate; RN Baccalaureate.

Site Options Abingdon, VA.

Study Options Full-time.

Program Entrance Requirements Minimum overall college GPA of 2.7, transcript of college record, CPR certification, health exam, health insurance, immunizations, letters of recommendation, minimum GPA in nursing prerequisites of 2.5, professional liability insurance/malpractice insurance, prerequisite course work. Transfer students are accepted. *Application deadline:* 2/1 (fall). Applications may be processed on a rolling basis for some programs. *Application fee:* $25.

Advanced Placement Credit given for nursing courses completed elsewhere dependent upon specific evaluations.

Expenses (2008–09) *Tuition, state resident:* full-time $6439. *Tuition, nonresident:* full-time $18,313. *International tuition:* $18,313 full-time. *Room and board:* $6912; room only: $3944 per academic year.

Financial Aid 90% of baccalaureate students in nursing programs received some form of financial aid in 2007–08. *Gift aid (need-based):* Federal Pell, FSEOG, state, private, college/university gift aid from institutional funds. *Loans:* FFEL (Subsidized and Unsubsidized Stafford PLUS), Perkins, state, college/university. *Work-study:* Federal Work-Study. *Financial aid application deadline (priority):* 4/1.

Contact Dr. Debra Lynn Carter, Chair, Department of Nursing, The University of Virginia's College at Wise, One College Avenue, Wise, VA 24293-4400. *Telephone:* 276-376-1030. *Fax:* 276-376-4589. *E-mail:* dlc4e@uvawise.edu.

Virginia Commonwealth University

School of Nursing
Richmond, Virginia

http://www.nursing.vcu.edu

Founded in 1838

DEGREES • BS • MS • PHD

Nursing Program Faculty 137 (30% with doctorates).

Baccalaureate Enrollment 653
Women 91% **Men** 9% **Minority** 27% **International** 1% **Part-time** 44%

Graduate Enrollment 315
Women 92% **Men** 8% **Minority** 30% **International** 1% **Part-time** 55%

Distance Learning Courses Available.

Nursing Student Activities Sigma Theta Tau, Student Nurses' Association.

Nursing Student Resources Academic advising; academic or career counseling; assistance for students with disabilities; bookstore; campus computer network; career placement assistance; computer lab; computer-assisted instruction; daycare for children of students; e-mail services; employment services for current students; externships; housing assistance; interactive nursing skills videos; Internet; learning resource lab; library services; nursing audiovisuals; paid internships; placement services for program completers; remedial services; resume preparation assistance; skills, simulation, or other laboratory; tutoring.

Library Facilities 1.9 million volumes (476,122 in health, 15,562 in nursing); 23,800 periodical subscriptions (9,969 health-care related).

BACCALAUREATE PROGRAMS

Degree BS

Available Programs ADN to Baccalaureate; Accelerated Baccalaureate for Second Degree; Generic Baccalaureate.

Site Options Danville, VA; Fredericksburg, VA; Portsmouth, VA.

Study Options Full-time.

Program Entrance Requirements Minimum overall college GPA of 2.5, transcript of college record, CPR certification, written essay, health exam, immunizations, 3 letters of recommendation, minimum GPA in nursing prerequisites of 2.5, prerequisite course work. Transfer students are accepted. *Application deadline:* 1/15 (fall). *Application fee:* $40.

Advanced Placement Credit by examination available. Credit given for nursing courses completed elsewhere dependent upon specific evaluations.

Expenses (2009–10) *Tuition, state resident:* full-time $5185; part-time $217 per credit. *Tuition, nonresident:* full-time $18,409; part-time $768 per credit. *International tuition:* $18,409 full-time. *Room and board:* $9517; room only: $6267 per academic year. *Required fees:* full-time $1878; part-time $71 per credit.

Contact Mrs. Susan L. Lipp, RN, Assistant Dean of Enrollment and Student Services, School of Nursing, Virginia Commonwealth University, 1100 East Leigh Street, PO Box 980567, Richmond, VA 23298-0567. *Telephone:* 804-828-5171. *Fax:* 804-828-7743. *E-mail:* slipp@vcu.edu.

GRADUATE PROGRAMS

Expenses (2009–10) *Tuition, state resident:* full-time $8116; part-time $451 per credit. *Tuition, nonresident:* full-time $16,871; part-time $938 per credit. *International tuition:* $16,871 full-time. *Room and board:* $9517; room only: $6267 per academic year. *Required fees:* full-time $1878; part-time $71 per credit; part-time $7 per term.

Financial Aid Fellowships, research assistantships, teaching assistantships, career-related internships or fieldwork and institutionally sponsored loans available.

Contact Mrs. Susan L. Lipp, RN, Assistant Dean of Enrollment and Student Services, School of Nursing, Virginia Commonwealth University, 1100 East Leigh Street, PO Box 980567, Richmond, VA 23298-0567. *Telephone:* 804-828-5171. *Fax:* 804-828-7743. *E-mail:* slipp@vcu.edu.

MASTER'S DEGREE PROGRAM

Degree MS

Available Programs Accelerated Master's for Non-Nursing College Graduates; Master's; Master's for Nurses with Non-Nursing Degrees; RN to Master's.

Concentrations Available Clinical nurse leader; nursing administration; nursing education. *Clinical nurse specialist programs in:* acute care. *Nurse practitioner programs in:* acute care, adult health, family health, pediatric, primary care, women's health.

Study Options Full-time and part-time.

Program Entrance Requirements Computer literacy, minimum overall college GPA of 3.0, transcript of college record, CPR certification, written essay, immunizations, 3 letters of recommendation, prerequisite course work, resume, statistics course, GRE General Test. *Application deadline:* 2/1 (fall), 10/1 (spring). *Application fee:* $50.

Advanced Placement Credit given for nursing courses completed elsewhere dependent upon specific evaluations.

Degree Requirements 55 total credit hours.

POST-MASTER'S PROGRAM

Areas of Study Clinical nurse leader; nursing administration; nursing education. *Clinical nurse specialist programs in:* acute care. *Nurse practitioner programs in:* acute care, adult health, family health, pediatric, primary care, women's health.

DOCTORAL DEGREE PROGRAM

Degree PhD

Available Programs Doctorate; Post-Baccalaureate Doctorate.

Areas of Study Bio-behavioral research.

Program Entrance Requirements Minimum overall college GPA of 3.0, interview by faculty committee, interview, 3 letters of recommendation, MSN or equivalent, statistics course, vita, writing sample, GRE General Test. Application deadline: 2/1 (fall). Application fee: $50.

Degree Requirements 61 total credit hours, dissertation, written exam, residency.

POSTDOCTORAL PROGRAM

Postdoctoral Program Contact Ms. Susan L. Lipp, RN, Assistant Dean of Enrollment and Student Services, School of Nursing, Virginia Commonwealth University, 1100 East Leigh Street, PO Box 980567, Richmond, VA 23298-0567. *Telephone:* 804-828-5171. *Fax:* 804-828-7743. *E-mail:* slipp@vcu.edu.

WASHINGTON

Eastern Washington University
Intercollegiate College of Nursing/Washington State University
Cheney, Washington

See description of programs under
Intercollegiate College of Nursing/Washington State University (Spokane, Washington).

Gonzaga University
Department of Nursing
Spokane, Washington

http://www.gonzaga.edu/nursing
Founded in 1887
DEGREES • BSN • MSN

Nursing Program Faculty 24 (50% with doctorates).
Baccalaureate Enrollment 40
Women 86% **Men** 14% **Minority** 7% **Part-time** 50%
Graduate Enrollment 180
Women 94% **Men** 6% **Minority** 94% **International** 7%
Nursing Student Activities Sigma Theta Tau.
Nursing Student Resources Academic advising; assistance for students with disabilities; bookstore; computer lab; Internet; library services.
Library Facilities 305,517 volumes (35,000 in health, 950 in nursing); 32,106 periodical subscriptions (206 health-care related).

BACCALAUREATE PROGRAMS
Degree BSN
Available Programs ADN to Baccalaureate; RN Baccalaureate.
Program Entrance Requirements Transfer students are accepted.
Contact *Telephone:* 509-323-6643. *Fax:* 509-323-5827.

GRADUATE PROGRAMS
Contact *Telephone:* 509-323-6643. *Fax:* 509-323-5827.

MASTER'S DEGREE PROGRAM
Degree MSN
Available Programs Accelerated RN to Master's; Master's for Nurses with Non-Nursing Degrees; RN to Master's.
Concentrations Available Health-care administration; nurse case management; nursing administration; nursing education. *Clinical nurse specialist programs in:* adult health, critical care, gerontology, medical-surgical, psychiatric/mental health. *Nurse practitioner programs in:* family health, primary care, psychiatric/mental health.
Study Options Full-time and part-time.
Program Entrance Requirements Clinical experience, computer literacy, minimum overall college GPA of 3.0, transcript of college record, written essay, immunizations, 2 letters of recommendation, nursing research course, resume, statistics course, MAT.
Advanced Placement Credit given for nursing courses completed elsewhere dependent upon specific evaluations.
Degree Requirements 48 total credit hours, thesis or project.

POST-MASTER'S PROGRAM
Areas of Study Health-care administration; nursing administration; nursing education. *Clinical nurse specialist programs in:* adult health, critical care, gerontology, medical-surgical, psychiatric/mental health. *Nurse practitioner programs in:* family health, primary care, psychiatric/mental health.

CONTINUING EDUCATION PROGRAM
Contact *Telephone:* 509-323-3572. *Fax:* 509-323-5827.

Intercollegiate College of Nursing/Washington State University
Intercollegiate College of Nursing/Washington State University
Spokane, Washington

http://www.nursing.wsu.edu
DEGREES • BSN • MN • PHD

Nursing Program Faculty 114 (36% with doctorates).
Baccalaureate Enrollment 837
Women 85% **Men** 15% **Minority** 19% **International** 1% **Part-time** 34%
Graduate Enrollment 272
Women 86% **Men** 14% **Minority** 21% **Part-time** 76%
Distance Learning Courses Available.
Nursing Student Activities Nursing Honor Society, Sigma Theta Tau, Student Nurses' Association, nursing club.
Nursing Student Resources Academic advising; academic or career counseling; assistance for students with disabilities; bookstore; campus computer network; computer lab; computer-assisted instruction; e-mail services; interactive nursing skills videos; Internet; learning resource lab; library services; nursing audiovisuals; other; remedial services; resume preparation assistance; skills, simulation, or other laboratory; tutoring; unpaid internships.
Library Facilities 15,000 volumes in health, 7,000 volumes in nursing; 2,000 periodical subscriptions health-care related.

BACCALAUREATE PROGRAMS
Degree BSN
Available Programs Generic Baccalaureate; RN Baccalaureate.
Site Options Vancouver, WA; Yakima, WA; Richland, WA.
Study Options Full-time.
Program Entrance Requirements Minimum overall college GPA of 2.8, transcript of college record, CPR certification, health insurance, immunizations, interview, minimum GPA in nursing prerequisites of 2.8, professional liability insurance/malpractice insurance, prerequisite course work. Transfer students are accepted. *Application deadline:* 1/15 (fall), 8/5 (spring).
Advanced Placement Credit given for nursing courses completed elsewhere dependent upon specific evaluations.
Expenses (2009–10) *Tuition, state resident:* full-time $7600; part-time $380 per credit. *Tuition, nonresident:* full-time $18,676; part-time $934 per credit. *Required fees:* full-time $264.
Contact Ms. Renae J. Richter, Academic Coordinator, Intercollegiate College of Nursing/Washington State University, PO Box 1495, Spokane, WA 99210-1495. *Telephone:* 509-324-7337. *Fax:* 509-324-7336. *E-mail:* richre@wsu.edu.

GRADUATE PROGRAMS
Expenses (2009–10) *Tuition, state resident:* full-time $13,946; part-time $697 per credit. *Tuition, nonresident:* full-time $27,108. *Required fees:* full-time $264.
Contact Ms. Tamera Kelley, Principle Assistant, Intercollegiate College of Nursing/Washington State University, PO Box 1495, Spokane, WA 99210-1495. *Telephone:* 509-324-7334. *Fax:* 509-324-7336. *E-mail:* kelleyt@wsu.edu.

MASTER'S DEGREE PROGRAM
Degree MN
Available Programs Accelerated Master's for Nurses with Non-Nursing Degrees; Accelerated RN to Master's; Master's.
Concentrations Available Nurse case management; nursing administration; nursing education. *Clinical nurse specialist programs in:* community health. *Nurse practitioner programs in:* family health, psychiatric/mental health.

Intercollegiate College of Nursing/Washington State University (continued)

Site Options Vancouver, WA; Yakima, WA; Richland, WA.

Study Options Full-time and part-time.

Program Entrance Requirements Computer literacy, minimum overall college GPA of 3.0, transcript of college record, CPR certification, written essay, immunizations, interview, 3 letters of recommendation, physical assessment course, professional liability insurance/malpractice insurance, prerequisite course work, statistics course. *Application deadline:* 2/1 (fall), 10/1 (spring).

Advanced Placement Credit given for nursing courses completed elsewhere dependent upon specific evaluations.

Degree Requirements 45 total credit hours, thesis or project.

POST-MASTER'S PROGRAM

Areas of Study *Nurse practitioner programs in:* family health, psychiatric/mental health.

DOCTORAL DEGREE PROGRAM

Degree PhD

Available Programs Doctorate.

Areas of Study Nursing education, nursing research.

Program Entrance Requirements Minimum overall college GPA of 3.5, interview by faculty committee, 3 letters of recommendation, MSN or equivalent, scholarly papers, statistics course, vita. Application deadline: 1/10 (summer).

Degree Requirements 72 total credit hours, dissertation.

CONTINUING EDUCATION PROGRAM

Contact Ms. Carol Johns, Driector of Professional Development, Intercollegiate College of Nursing/Washington State University, PO Box 1495, Spokane, WA 99210-1495. *Telephone:* 509-324-7354. *Fax:* 509-324-7341. *E-mail:* cjohns@wsu.edu.

Northwest University
The Mark and Huldah Buntain School of Nursing
Kirkland, Washington

http://www.northwestu.edu/

Founded in 1934

DEGREE • BS

Nursing Program Faculty 24 (16% with doctorates).

Baccalaureate Enrollment 50
Women 87% **Men** 13% **Minority** 11%

Nursing Student Resources Academic advising; academic or career counseling; assistance for students with disabilities; bookstore; campus computer network; computer lab; computer-assisted instruction; e-mail services; employment services for current students; housing assistance; interactive nursing skills videos; Internet; learning resource lab; library services; nursing audiovisuals; other; remedial services; resume preparation assistance; skills, simulation, or other laboratory; tutoring; unpaid internships.

Library Facilities 129,721 volumes (1,922 in health, 387 in nursing); 12,458 periodical subscriptions (815 health-care related).

BACCALAUREATE PROGRAMS

Degree BS

Available Programs Generic Baccalaureate.

Study Options Full-time.

Program Entrance Requirements Minimum overall college GPA of 3.0, transcript of college record, CPR certification, written essay, health exam, health insurance, high school transcript, immunizations, 2 letters of recommendation, minimum GPA in nursing prerequisites of 3.0, prerequisite course work. Transfer students are accepted. *Application deadline:* 1/30 (fall). *Application fee:* $35.

Expenses (2008–09) *Tuition:* full-time $20,520; part-time $855 per credit hour. *International tuition:* $20,520 full-time. *Room and board:* $6578; room only: $3980 per academic year. *Required fees:* full-time $3395.

Financial Aid 99% of baccalaureate students in nursing programs received some form of financial aid in 2007–08. *Gift aid (need-based):* Federal Pell, FSEOG, state, private, college/university gift aid from institutional funds. *Loans:* FFEL (Subsidized and Unsubsidized Stafford PLUS), Perkins, state, alternative loans. *Work-study:* Federal Work-Study, part-time campus jobs. *Financial aid application deadline:* 8/1 (priority: 2/15).

Contact Dr. Carl N. Christensen, Dean, The Mark and Huldah Buntain School of Nursing, Northwest University, 5520 108th Avenue NE, PO Box 579, Kirkland, WA 98083. *Telephone:* 800-669-3781 Ext. 7822. *Fax:* 425-889-7822. *E-mail:* nursing@northwestu.edu.

Pacific Lutheran University
School of Nursing
Tacoma, Washington

http://www.plu.edu/~nurs/

Founded in 1890

DEGREES • BSN • MSN • MSN/MBA

Nursing Program Faculty 30 (40% with doctorates).

Baccalaureate Enrollment 238
Women 92% **Men** 8% **Minority** 24% **International** 2% **Part-time** 1%

Graduate Enrollment 70
Women 96% **Men** 4% **Minority** 15% **International** 1% **Part-time** 5%

Distance Learning Courses Available.

Nursing Student Activities Nursing Honor Society, Sigma Theta Tau, Student Nurses' Association, nursing club.

Nursing Student Resources Academic advising; academic or career counseling; assistance for students with disabilities; bookstore; campus computer network; career placement assistance; computer lab; computer-assisted instruction; e-mail services; employment services for current students; housing assistance; interactive nursing skills videos; Internet; learning resource lab; library services; nursing audiovisuals; resume preparation assistance; skills, simulation, or other laboratory; tutoring; unpaid internships.

Library Facilities 15,000 volumes in health, 6,500 volumes in nursing; 150 periodical subscriptions health-care related.

BACCALAUREATE PROGRAMS

Degree BSN

Available Programs ADN to Baccalaureate; Generic Baccalaureate; LPN to Baccalaureate.

Study Options Full-time and part-time.

Program Entrance Requirements Minimum overall college GPA of 3.0, transcript of college record, CPR certification, written essay, health exam, health insurance, 2 years high school math, high school transcript, immunizations, 2 letters of recommendation, minimum GPA in nursing prerequisites of 2.75, professional liability insurance/malpractice insurance, prerequisite course work. Transfer students are accepted. *Application deadline:* 2/1 (fall), 2/1 (spring), 2/1 (summer). Applications may be processed on a rolling basis for some programs. *Application fee:* $40.

Advanced Placement Credit by examination available. Credit given for nursing courses completed elsewhere dependent upon specific evaluations.

Expenses (2009–10) *Tuition:* full-time $28,100; part-time $880 per credit hour. *International tuition:* $28,100 full-time. *Room and board:* $8600; room only: $6000 per academic year. *Required fees:* full-time $400; part-time $200 per term.

Financial Aid 95% of baccalaureate students in nursing programs received some form of financial aid in 2008–09. *Gift aid (need-based):* Federal Pell, FSEOG, state, private, college/university gift aid from institutional funds, Federal Nursing. *Loans:* Federal Nursing Student Loans, FFEL (Subsidized and Unsubsidized Stafford PLUS), Perkins, state. *Work-study:* Federal Work-Study, part-time campus jobs. *Financial aid application deadline (priority):* 1/31.

Contact Dr. Amy S. Manoso, Admission, Retention, Recruitment Coordinator, School of Nursing, Pacific Lutheran University, 12180 Park Avenue South, Tacoma, WA 98447-0029. *Telephone:* 253-535-7672. *Fax:* 253-535-7590. *E-mail:* manosoas@plu.edu.

GRADUATE PROGRAMS

Expenses (2009–10) *Tuition:* part-time $888 per credit hour. *Required fees:* part-time $100 per term.

Financial Aid 50% of graduate students in nursing programs received some form of financial aid in 2008–09. Fellowships, Federal Work-Study, scholarships, and unspecified assistantships available. *Financial aid application deadline:* 3/1.

Contact Dr. Amy S. Manoso, PhD, Admissions Coordinator, School of Nursing, Pacific Lutheran University, 12180 Park Avenue South, Tacoma, WA 98447-0029. *Telephone:* 253-535-7672. *Fax:* 253-535-7590. *E-mail:* gradnurs@plu.edu.

MASTER'S DEGREE PROGRAM

Degrees MSN; MSN/MBA

Available Programs Accelerated Master's; Master's; Master's for Non-Nursing College Graduates; Master's for Nurses with Non-Nursing Degrees.

Concentrations Available Clinical nurse leader; health-care administration; nurse case management; nursing administration; nursing education. *Nurse practitioner programs in:* family health.

Study Options Full-time and part-time.

Program Entrance Requirements Clinical experience, computer literacy, minimum overall college GPA of 3.0, transcript of college record, CPR certification, written essay, immunizations, interview, 2 letters of recommendation, nursing research course, professional liability insurance/malpractice insurance, prerequisite course work, resume, statistics course, GRE General Test. *Application deadline:* 3/1 (fall), 11/15 (summer). Applications may be processed on a rolling basis for some programs. *Application fee:* $40.

Advanced Placement Credit given for nursing courses completed elsewhere dependent upon specific evaluations.

Degree Requirements 37 total credit hours, thesis or project.

CONTINUING EDUCATION PROGRAM

Contact Ms. Terry L. Bennett, Coordinator, Continuing Nursing Education and Clinical Placements, School of Nursing, Pacific Lutheran University, 12180 Park Avenue South, Tacoma, WA 98447-0029. *Telephone:* 253-535-7683. *Fax:* 253-535-7590. *E-mail:* bennettl@plu.edu.

Seattle Pacific University
School of Health Sciences
Seattle, Washington

http://www.spu.edu/depts/hsc

Founded in 1891

DEGREES • BS • MSN

Nursing Program Faculty 24 (38% with doctorates).

Baccalaureate Enrollment 98
Women 91% **Men** 9% **Minority** 21% **International** 2%

Graduate Enrollment 61
Women 89% **Men** 11% **Minority** 39% **Part-time** 49%

Nursing Student Activities Nursing Honor Society, Sigma Theta Tau, Student Nurses' Association, nursing club.

Nursing Student Resources Academic advising; academic or career counseling; assistance for students with disabilities; bookstore; campus computer network; career placement assistance; computer lab; computer-assisted instruction; e-mail services; employment services for current students; housing assistance; Internet; learning resource lab; library services; nursing audiovisuals; placement services for program completers; remedial services; resume preparation assistance; skills, simulation, or other laboratory; tutoring; unpaid internships.

Library Facilities 191,807 volumes (11,539 in health, 1,791 in nursing); 1,230 periodical subscriptions (274 health-care related).

BACCALAUREATE PROGRAMS

Degree BS

Available Programs Generic Baccalaureate; RN Baccalaureate.

Study Options Full-time.

Program Entrance Requirements Minimum overall college GPA of 2.75, transcript of college record, CPR certification, written essay, health exam, health insurance, high school transcript, immunizations, 1 letter of recommendation, minimum GPA in nursing prerequisites of 2.75, prerequisite course work. Transfer students are accepted. *Application deadline:* 1/15 (fall).

Advanced Placement Credit given for nursing courses completed elsewhere dependent upon specific evaluations.

Expenses (2009–10) *Tuition:* full-time $27,450. *Room and board:* $8544; room only: $4659 per academic year. *Required fees:* full-time $2515.

Financial Aid 94% of baccalaureate students in nursing programs received some form of financial aid in 2008–09. *Gift aid (need-based):* Federal Pell, FSEOG, state, private, college/university gift aid from institutional funds. *Loans:* Federal Nursing Student Loans, FFEL (Subsidized and Unsubsidized Stafford PLUS), Perkins, college/university. *Work-study:* Federal Work-Study, part-time campus jobs. *Financial aid application deadline (priority):* 4/1.

Contact Dr. Chris Henshaw, Associate Dean, School of Health Sciences, Seattle Pacific University, 3307 Third Avenue West, Marson Hall, Suite 106, Seattle, WA 98119-1922. *Telephone:* 206-281-2612. *Fax:* 206-281-2767. *E-mail:* chenshaw@spu.edu.

GRADUATE PROGRAMS

Expenses (2009–10) *Tuition:* part-time $568 per credit.

Financial Aid 60% of graduate students in nursing programs received some form of financial aid in 2008–09. 2 teaching assistantships were awarded; career-related internships or fieldwork and traineeships also available.

Contact Beth Van Camp, RN, MSN Admission Counselor, School of Health Sciences, Seattle Pacific University, 3307 Third Avenue West, Suite 111, Seattle, WA 98119-1922. *Telephone:* 206-281-2888. *Fax:* 206-378-5480. *E-mail:* beth.vancamp@spu.edu.

MASTER'S DEGREE PROGRAM

Degree MSN

Available Programs Master's; Master's for Nurses with Non-Nursing Degrees.

Concentrations Available Clinical nurse leader; nursing administration; nursing education. *Clinical-nurse specialist programs in:* acute care, adult health, community health, critical care, gerontology, medical-surgical, oncology, palliative care, parent-child, pediatric, women's health. *Nurse practitioner programs in:* adult health, family health, gerontology.

Study Options Full-time and part-time.

Program Entrance Requirements Clinical experience, computer literacy, minimum overall college GPA of 3.0, transcript of college record, CPR certification, written essay, immunizations, interview, 3 letters of recommendation, nursing research course, professional liability insurance/malpractice insurance, prerequisite course work, resume, statistics course, GRE General Test. *Application deadline:* 5/5 (fall). *Application fee:* $50.

Advanced Placement Credit given for nursing courses completed elsewhere dependent upon specific evaluations.

Degree Requirements 59 total credit hours, thesis or project, comprehensive exam.

POST-MASTER'S PROGRAM

Areas of Study Nursing education. *Nurse practitioner programs in:* adult health, family health, gerontology.

Seattle University
College of Nursing
Seattle, Washington

http://www.seattleu.edu/nurs

Founded in 1891

Seattle University (continued)

DEGREES • BSN • MSN

Nursing Program Faculty 81 (42% with doctorates).

Baccalaureate Enrollment 418
Women 90% **Men** 10% **Minority** 37% **International** 1%

Graduate Enrollment 110
Women 89% **Men** 11% **Minority** 18% **International** 1%

Distance Learning Courses Available.

Nursing Student Activities Sigma Theta Tau, Student Nurses' Association.

Nursing Student Resources Academic advising; academic or career counseling; assistance for students with disabilities; bookstore; campus computer network; career placement assistance; computer lab; computer-assisted instruction; e-mail services; employment services for current students; housing assistance; interactive nursing skills videos; Internet; learning resource lab; library services; nursing audiovisuals; paid internships; remedial services; resume preparation assistance; skills, simulation, or other laboratory; tutoring.

Library Facilities 141,478 volumes; 2,701 periodical subscriptions.

BACCALAUREATE PROGRAMS

Degree BSN

Available Programs Baccalaureate for Second Degree; Generic Baccalaureate.

Study Options Full-time.

Program Entrance Requirements Minimum overall college GPA of 2.75, transcript of college record, CPR certification, written essay, health insurance, high school biology, high school chemistry, high school foreign language, 3 years high school math, 2 years high school science, high school transcript, immunizations, minimum GPA in nursing prerequisites of 3.0, professional liability insurance/malpractice insurance, prerequisite course work. Transfer students are accepted. *Application deadline:* 1/5 (winter). *Application fee:* $50.

Expenses (2009–10) *Tuition:* full-time $29,340. *International tuition:* $29,340 full-time. *Room and board:* $8805 per academic year. *Required fees:* full-time $800.

Financial Aid 80% of baccalaureate students in nursing programs received some form of financial aid in 2008–09. *Gift aid (need-based):* Federal Pell, FSEOG, state, private, college/university gift aid from institutional funds, Federal Nursing. *Loans:* Federal Nursing Student Loans, Federal Direct (Subsidized and Unsubsidized Stafford PLUS), Perkins. *Work-study:* Federal Work-Study, part-time campus jobs. *Financial aid application deadline (priority):* 2/1.

Contact Rita Tower, Pre-Major Advisor, College of Nursing, Seattle University, 901 12th Avenue, PO Box 222000, Seattle, WA 98122-1090. *Telephone:* 206-296-2242. *Fax:* 206-296-5544. *E-mail:* rstower@seattleu.edu.

GRADUATE PROGRAMS

Financial Aid 81% of graduate students in nursing programs received some form of financial aid in 2008–09. Fellowships, research assistantships, career-related internships or fieldwork and Federal Work-Study available. Aid available to part-time students.

Contact Dr. Katherine Camacho Carr, Assistant Dean for Graduate Program, College of Nursing, Seattle University, 901 12th Avenue, PO Box 222000, Seattle, WA 98122-1090. *Telephone:* 206-296-5666. *Fax:* 206-296-5544. *E-mail:* kcarr@seattleu.edu.

MASTER'S DEGREE PROGRAM

Degree MSN

Available Programs Accelerated Master's for Nurses with Non-Nursing Degrees; Master's.

Concentrations Available *Clinical nurse specialist programs in:* community health. *Nurse practitioner programs in:* adult health, family health, psychiatric/mental health.

Study Options Full-time and part-time.

Program Entrance Requirements Clinical experience, computer literacy, minimum overall college GPA of 3.0, transcript of college record, CPR certification, written essay, immunizations, interview, 2 letters of recommendation, professional liability insurance/malpractice insurance, prerequisite course work, resume, statistics course, GRE General Test. *Application deadline:* 12/1 (fall), 4/1 (spring). *Application fee:* $55.

Advanced Placement Credit given for nursing courses completed elsewhere dependent upon specific evaluations.

Degree Requirements 108 total credit hours, thesis or project.

POST-MASTER'S PROGRAM

Areas of Study *Clinical nurse specialist programs in:* community health. *Nurse practitioner programs in:* adult health, family health, psychiatric/mental health.

University of Washington
School of Nursing
Seattle, Washington

---

http://www.son.washington.edu

Founded in 1861

DEGREES • BSN • MN • MN/MPH • PHD

Nursing Program Faculty 246 (78% with doctorates).

Baccalaureate Enrollment 497
Women 86% **Men** 14% **Minority** 23% **International** .8% **Part-time** 42%

Graduate Enrollment 598
Women 89% **Men** 11% **Minority** 21% **International** 4% **Part-time** 57%

Distance Learning Courses Available.

Nursing Student Activities Sigma Theta Tau, Student Nurses' Association.

Nursing Student Resources Academic advising; academic or career counseling; assistance for students with disabilities; bookstore; campus computer network; computer lab; computer-assisted instruction; e-mail services; employment services for current students; interactive nursing skills videos; Internet; learning resource lab; library services; nursing audiovisuals; skills, simulation, or other laboratory.

Library Facilities 5.8 million volumes (350,000 in health); 50,245 periodical subscriptions (2,400 health-care related).

BACCALAUREATE PROGRAMS

Degree BSN

Available Programs ADN to Baccalaureate; Accelerated Baccalaureate; Generic Baccalaureate.

Site Options Bothell, WA; Tacoma, WA.

Study Options Full-time.

Program Entrance Requirements Minimum overall college GPA of 2.0, transcript of college record, CPR certification, written essay, immunizations, 1 letter of recommendation, minimum GPA in nursing prerequisites of 2.8, prerequisite course work. Transfer students are accepted. *Application deadline:* 1/15 (fall).

Expenses (2009–10) *Tuition, area resident:* full-time $7692; part-time $257 per credit hour. *Tuition, nonresident:* full-time $24,369; part-time $812 per credit hour. *International tuition:* $24,369 full-time. *Room and board:* $7227; room only: $4617 per academic year. *Required fees:* full-time $300.

Financial Aid 9% of baccalaureate students in nursing programs received some form of financial aid in 2008–09. *Gift aid (need-based):* Federal Pell, FSEOG, state, private, college/university gift aid from institutional funds. *Loans:* Federal Nursing Student Loans, Federal Direct (Subsidized and Unsubsidized Stafford PLUS), Perkins, college/university. *Work-study:* Federal Work-Study, part-time campus jobs. *Financial aid application deadline (priority):* 2/28.

Contact Academic Services, School of Nursing, University of Washington, Box 357260, Health Sciences Building, Room T310, Seattle, WA 98195. *Telephone:* 206-543-8736. *Fax:* 206-543-3624. *E-mail:* sonas@u.washington.edu.

GRADUATE PROGRAMS

Expenses (2009–10) *Tuition, area resident:* full-time $15,819; part-time $753 per quarter hour. *Tuition, nonresident:* full-time $30,759; part-time $1465 per quarter hour. *International tuition:* $30,759 full-time. *Room and board:* $7227; room only: $4617 per academic year. *Required fees:* full-time $300.

Financial Aid 16% of graduate students in nursing programs received some form of financial aid in 2008–09. Fellowships with full tuition reimbursements available, research assistantships with partial tuition reimbursements available, teaching assistantships with partial tuition reimbursements available, Federal Work-Study, institutionally sponsored loans, scholarships, and traineeships available. *Financial aid application deadline:* 2/28.

Contact Academic Services, School of Nursing, University of Washington, Box 357260, Health Sciences Building, Room T310, Seattle, WA 98195. *Telephone:* 206-543-8736. *Fax:* 206-543-3624. *E-mail:* sonas@u. washington.edu.

MASTER'S DEGREE PROGRAM

Degrees MN; MN/MPH

Available Programs Master's; Master's for Nurses with Non-Nursing Degrees.

Concentrations Available Nurse-midwifery; nursing informatics. *Clinical nurse specialist programs in:* cardiovascular, community health, critical care, gerontology, maternity-newborn, medical-surgical, occupational health, oncology, palliative care, perinatal. *Nurse practitioner programs in:* acute care, adult health, family health, gerontology, neonatal health, oncology, pediatric, primary care, psychiatric/mental health.

Site Options Bothell, WA; Tacoma, WA.

Study Options Full-time and part-time.

Program Entrance Requirements Minimum overall college GPA of 3.0, transcript of college record, CPR certification, written essay, immunizations, 3 letters of recommendation, resume, statistics course, GRE. *Application deadline:* 1/15 (fall).

Advanced Placement Credit given for nursing courses completed elsewhere dependent upon specific evaluations.

Degree Requirements 38 total credit hours, thesis or project.

POST-MASTER'S PROGRAM

Areas of Study Nurse-midwifery; nursing education. *Clinical nurse specialist programs in:* cardiovascular, critical care, gerontology, medical-surgical, occupational health, oncology, palliative care. *Nurse practitioner programs in:* acute care, adult health, family health, gerontology, oncology, pediatric, primary care, psychiatric/mental health.

DOCTORAL DEGREE PROGRAM

Degree PhD

Available Programs Doctorate; Doctorate for Nurses with Non-Nursing Degrees; Post-Baccalaureate Doctorate.

Areas of Study Addiction/substance abuse, advanced practice nursing, aging, bio-behavioral research, biology of health and illness, clinical practice, community health, critical care, ethics, faculty preparation, family health, forensic nursing, gerontology, health policy, health promotion/disease prevention, health-care systems, human health and illness, illness and transition, individualized study, information systems, maternity-newborn, neuro-behavior, nurse case management, nursing administration, nursing education, nursing policy, nursing research, nursing science, oncology, urban health, women's health.

Program Entrance Requirements Minimum overall college GPA of 3.0, 3 letters of recommendation, scholarly papers, vita, GRE. Application deadline: 1/15 (fall).

Degree Requirements 93 total credit hours, dissertation, oral exam, written exam.

POSTDOCTORAL PROGRAM

Areas of Study Adolescent health, aging, cancer care, chronic illness, community health, family health, gerontology, health promotion/disease prevention, individualized study, infection prevention/skin care, neuro-behavior, nursing informatics, nursing interventions, nursing research, nursing science, outcomes, self-care, vulnerable population, women's health.

Postdoctoral Program Contact Academic Services, School of Nursing, University of Washington, Box 357260, Health Sciences Building, Room T310, Seattle, WA 98195. *Telephone:* 206-543-8736. *Fax:* 206-685-1613. *E-mail:* sonas@u.washington.edu.

CONTINUING EDUCATION PROGRAM

Contact Martha Duhamel, Assistant Dean for Continuing Nursing Education, School of Nursing, University of Washington, Box 359440, Seattle, WA 98195-9440. *Telephone:* 206-543-1047. *Fax:* 206-543-6953. *E-mail:* marthadu@u.washington.edu.

Walla Walla University
School of Nursing
College Place, Washington

http://www.wwc.edu/academics/department/ nursing

Founded in 1892

DEGREE • BS

Nursing Program Faculty 17 (17% with doctorates).

Baccalaureate Enrollment 150
Women 82% **Men** 18% **Minority** 14% **International** 1% **Part-time** 1%

Nursing Student Activities Nursing Honor Society, nursing club.

Nursing Student Resources Academic advising; assistance for students with disabilities; bookstore; campus computer network; computer lab; e-mail services; Internet; learning resource lab; library services; nursing audiovisuals; resume preparation assistance; skills, simulation, or other laboratory; tutoring.

Library Facilities 273,266 volumes (10,000 in health, 7,000 in nursing); 3,727 periodical subscriptions (450 health-care related).

BACCALAUREATE PROGRAMS

Degree BS

Available Programs ADN to Baccalaureate; Generic Baccalaureate; LPN to Baccalaureate; RN Baccalaureate.

Site Options Portland, OR.

Study Options Full-time.

Program Entrance Requirements Minimum overall college GPA of 2.75, transcript of college record, CPR certification, written essay, health exam, health insurance, high school biology, 3 years high school math, 2 years high school science, high school transcript, immunizations, 3 letters of recommendation, minimum high school GPA of 2.75, minimum GPA in nursing prerequisites of 2.75, prerequisite course work. Transfer students are accepted. *Application deadline:* 4/15 (fall), 2/1 (summer). *Application fee:* $40.

Advanced Placement Credit given for nursing courses completed elsewhere dependent upon specific evaluations.

Expenses (2009–10) *Tuition:* full-time $22,575; part-time $590 per quarter hour. *International tuition:* $22,575 full-time. *Room and board:* $5010; room only: $2760 per academic year. *Required fees:* full-time $819; part-time $25 per credit.

Financial Aid 96% of baccalaureate students in nursing programs received some form of financial aid in 2008–09.

Contact Jan Thurnhofer, RN, Student Program Advisor, School of Nursing, Walla Walla University, 10345 SE Market Street, Portland, OR 97216. *Telephone:* 503-251-6115 Ext. 7304. *Fax:* 503-251-6249. *E-mail:* JanT@wallawalla.edu.

Washington State University

Intercollegiate College of Nursing/Washington State University
Pullman, Washington

See description of programs under **Intercollegiate College of Nursing/Washington State University (Spokane, Washington).**

Whitworth College

Intercollegiate College of Nursing/Washington State University
Spokane, Washington

See description of programs under **Intercollegiate College of Nursing/Washington State University (Spokane, Washington).**

WEST VIRGINIA

Alderson-Broaddus College

Department of Nursing
Philippi, West Virginia

http://www.ab.edu
Founded in 1871
DEGREE • BSN

Nursing Program Faculty 11 (9% with doctorates).

Baccalaureate Enrollment 180
Women 94% **Men** 6% **Minority** 2% **International** 1% **Part-time** 2%

Nursing Student Activities Student Nurses' Association.

Nursing Student Resources Academic advising; academic or career counseling; assistance for students with disabilities; bookstore; campus computer network; career placement assistance; computer lab; computer-assisted instruction; e-mail services; employment services for current students; Internet; learning resource lab; library services; nursing audio-visuals; remedial services; resume preparation assistance; skills, simulation, or other laboratory; tutoring.

Library Facilities 100,000 volumes (6,000 in health, 1,000 in nursing); 11,000 periodical subscriptions (172 health-care related).

BACCALAUREATE PROGRAMS

Degree BSN

Available Programs Generic Baccalaureate; LPN to RN Baccalaureate; RN Baccalaureate.

Study Options Full-time.

Program Entrance Requirements Minimum overall college GPA of 2.0, transcript of college record, CPR certification, health exam, high school chemistry, high school transcript, immunizations, minimum GPA in nursing prerequisites of 2.25, professional liability insurance/malpractice insurance, prerequisite course work. Transfer students are accepted. *Application deadline:* 7/30 (fall), 1/5 (winter). Applications may be processed on a rolling basis for some programs. *Application fee:* $25.

Advanced Placement Credit by examination available. Credit given for nursing courses completed elsewhere dependent upon specific evaluations.

Expenses (2009–10) *Tuition:* full-time $19,830; part-time $660 per credit hour. *International tuition:* $19,830 full-time. *Room and board:* $6470 per academic year. *Required fees:* full-time $460.

Financial Aid 98% of baccalaureate students in nursing programs received some form of financial aid in 2008–09. *Gift aid (need-based):* Federal Pell, FSEOG, state, private, college/university gift aid from institutional funds, Federal Nursing, National Health Service Corp., Scholarship for Disadvantaged Students. *Loans:* Federal Nursing Student Loans, FFEL (Subsidized and Unsubsidized Stafford PLUS), Perkins. *Work-study:* Federal Work-Study, part-time campus jobs. *Financial aid application deadline (priority):* 3/1.

Contact Dr. Threasia L. Witt, Chairperson, Department of Nursing, Department of Nursing, Alderson-Broaddus College, 101 College Hill Drive, Philippi, WV 26416. *Telephone:* 304-457-6285. *Fax:* 304-457-6293. *E-mail:* witttl@ab.edu.

Bluefield State College

Program in Nursing
Bluefield, West Virginia

http://www.bluefieldstate.edu
Founded in 1895
DEGREE • BSN

Nursing Program Faculty 3 (30% with doctorates).

Baccalaureate Enrollment 36
Women 83% **Men** 17% **Minority** 6% **Part-time** 5%

Distance Learning Courses Available.

Nursing Student Activities Sigma Theta Tau, Student Nurses' Association.

Nursing Student Resources Academic advising; academic or career counseling; assistance for students with disabilities; bookstore; campus computer network; career placement assistance; computer lab; computer-assisted instruction; e-mail services; housing assistance; interactive nursing skills videos; Internet; learning resource lab; library services; nursing audiovisuals; resume preparation assistance; skills, simulation, or other laboratory; tutoring.

Library Facilities 75,942 volumes (5,649 in health, 1,250 in nursing); 22,292 periodical subscriptions (200 health-care related).

BACCALAUREATE PROGRAMS

Degree BSN

Available Programs ADN to Baccalaureate; RN Baccalaureate.
Site Options Beckley, WV.
Study Options Full-time and part-time.
Program Entrance Requirements Minimum overall college GPA of 2.5, transcript of college record, CPR certification, health exam, immunizations, letters of recommendation, minimum GPA in nursing prerequisites of 2.0, prerequisite course work, RN licensure. Transfer students are accepted. *Application deadline:* 4/15 (spring).
Expenses (2009–10) *Tuition, area resident:* full-time $2298; part-time $192 per credit hour. *Tuition, state resident:* full-time $3306; part-time $276 per credit hour. *Tuition, nonresident:* full-time $4500; part-time $375 per credit hour. *Required fees:* full-time $300; part-time $15 per credit.
Financial Aid 47% of baccalaureate students in nursing programs received some form of financial aid in 2008–09. *Gift aid (need-based):* Federal Pell, FSEOG, state. *Loans:* Federal Direct (Subsidized and Unsubsidized Stafford PLUS), Perkins. *Work-study:* Federal Work-Study, part-time campus jobs. *Financial aid application deadline (priority):* 3/1.
Contact Ms. Beth Pritchett, Director, Program in Nursing, Bluefield State College, 219 Rock Street, Bluefield, WV 24701. *Telephone:* 304-327-4139. *Fax:* 304-327-4219. *E-mail:* bpritchett@bluefieldstate.edu.

Fairmont State University

School of Nursing and Allied Health Administration
Fairmont, West Virginia

http://www.fscwv.edu

Founded in 1865

DEGREE • BSN

Nursing Program Faculty 3 (50% with doctorates).

Baccalaureate Enrollment 94
Women 97% **Men** 3% **Minority** 1% **International** 1% **Part-time** 40%

Nursing Student Activities Sigma Theta Tau, Student Nurses' Association.

Nursing Student Resources Academic advising; academic or career counseling; assistance for students with disabilities; bookstore; campus computer network; career placement assistance; computer lab; computer-assisted instruction; e-mail services; housing assistance; interactive nursing skills videos; Internet; learning resource lab; library services; nursing audiovisuals; placement services for program completers; remedial services; resume preparation assistance; skills, simulation, or other laboratory; tutoring.

Library Facilities 280,000 volumes (9,000 in health, 1,100 in nursing); 895 periodical subscriptions (50 health-care related).

BACCALAUREATE PROGRAMS
Degree BSN

Available Programs ADN to Baccalaureate; Accelerated RN Baccalaureate; LPN to RN Baccalaureate; RN Baccalaureate.

Study Options Full-time and part-time.

Program Entrance Requirements Minimum overall college GPA of 2.5, transcript of college record, CPR certification, health exam, high school chemistry, immunizations, letters of recommendation, minimum GPA in nursing prerequisites of 3.0, prerequisite course work, RN licensure. Transfer students are accepted. *Application deadline:* 8/15 (fall), 8/15 (winter), 1/2 (spring), 5/15 (summer). Applications may be processed on a rolling basis for some programs.

Advanced Placement Credit by examination available. Credit given for nursing courses completed elsewhere dependent upon specific evaluations.

Expenses (2009–10) *Tuition, state resident:* full-time $2512; part-time $210 per credit hour. *Tuition, nonresident:* full-time $5008; part-time $420 per credit hour. *International tuition:* $5008 full-time. *Room and board:* $5024; room only: $1640 per academic year. *Required fees:* full-time $84; part-time $4 per credit.

Financial Aid 80% of baccalaureate students in nursing programs received some form of financial aid in 2008–09.

Contact Dr. Mary M. Meighen, Professor, School of Nursing and Allied Health Administration, Fairmont State University, 1201 Locust Avenue, Fairmont, WV 26554. *Telephone:* 304-367-4761. *Fax:* 304-367-4268. *E-mail:* mmeighen@fairmontstate.edu.

CONTINUING EDUCATION PROGRAM
Contact Dr. Mary M. Meighen, Professor, School of Nursing and Allied Health Administration, Fairmont State University, 1201 Locust Avenue, Fairmont, WV 26554. *Telephone:* 304-367-4761. *Fax:* 304-367-4268. *E-mail:* mmeighen@fairmontstate.edu.

Marshall University

College of Health Professions
Huntington, West Virginia

http://www.marshall.edu/conhp

Founded in 1837

DEGREES • BSN • MSN

Nursing Program Faculty 35 (23% with doctorates).

Baccalaureate Enrollment 345
Women 80% **Men** 20% **Minority** 5% **Part-time** 35%

Graduate Enrollment 100
Women 90% **Men** 10% **Part-time** 60%

Nursing Student Activities Sigma Theta Tau, Student Nurses' Association, nursing club.

Nursing Student Resources Academic advising; academic or career counseling; assistance for students with disabilities; bookstore; campus computer network; career placement assistance; computer lab; computer-assisted instruction; daycare for children of students; e-mail services; employment services for current students; externships; housing assistance; interactive nursing skills videos; Internet; learning resource lab; library services; nursing audiovisuals; placement services for program completers; remedial services; resume preparation assistance; skills, simulation, or other laboratory; tutoring.

Library Facilities 1.6 million volumes (20,200 in health, 6,400 in nursing); 37,178 periodical subscriptions (500 health-care related).

BACCALAUREATE PROGRAMS
Degree BSN

Available Programs Accelerated RN Baccalaureate; Generic Baccalaureate.

Study Options Full-time and part-time.

Program Entrance Requirements Minimum overall college GPA of 2.5, transcript of college record, high school transcript, minimum high school GPA of 2.5. Transfer students are accepted.

Advanced Placement Credit given for nursing courses completed elsewhere dependent upon specific evaluations.

Contact *Telephone:* 304-696-2639. *Fax:* 304-696-6739.

GRADUATE PROGRAMS
Contact *Telephone:* 304-696-2639. *Fax:* 304-696-6739.

MASTER'S DEGREE PROGRAM
Degree MSN

Available Programs Master's.

Concentrations Available Nursing administration; nursing education. *Nurse practitioner programs in:* family health.

Study Options Full-time and part-time.

Program Entrance Requirements Minimum overall college GPA of 3.0, transcript of college record, nursing research course, resume, statistics course, GRE General Test.

Advanced Placement Credit given for nursing courses completed elsewhere dependent upon specific evaluations.

Degree Requirements 36 total credit hours, thesis or project.

POST-MASTER'S PROGRAM
Areas of Study Nursing administration; nursing education. *Nurse practitioner programs in:* family health.

Mountain State University

College of Nursing
Beckley, West Virginia

http://www.mountainstate.edu/majors/ onlinecatalogs/undergrad/programs/NursingBSN. aspx

Founded in 1933

DEGREES • BSN • MSN

Nursing Program Faculty 157 (6% with doctorates).

Baccalaureate Enrollment 699
Women 85% **Men** 15% **Minority** 24% **International** 16% **Part-time** 20%

Graduate Enrollment 143
Women 89% **Men** 11% **Minority** 6% **International** 1% **Part-time** 15%

Distance Learning Courses Available.

Mountain State University (continued)

Nursing Student Activities Nursing Honor Society, Student Nurses' Association.

Nursing Student Resources Academic advising; academic or career counseling; assistance for students with disabilities; bookstore; campus computer network; career placement assistance; computer lab; computer-assisted instruction; e-mail services; employment services for current students; externships; interactive nursing skills videos; Internet; learning resource lab; library services; nursing audiovisuals; placement services for program completers; remedial services; resume preparation assistance; skills, simulation, or other laboratory; tutoring.

Library Facilities 113,613 volumes (10,739 in health, 554 in nursing); 157 periodical subscriptions (4,266 health-care related).

BACCALAUREATE PROGRAMS

Degree BSN

Available Programs ADN to Baccalaureate; Accelerated Baccalaureate for Second Degree; Baccalaureate for Second Degree; Generic Baccalaureate; LPN to Baccalaureate; RN Baccalaureate; RPN to Baccalaureate.

Site Options Orlando, FL; Martinsburg, WV.

Study Options Full-time.

Program Entrance Requirements Minimum overall college GPA of 2.5, transcript of college record, CPR certification, health exam, health insurance, high school biology, 2 years high school science, high school transcript, immunizations, minimum high school GPA of 2.75. Transfer students are accepted. *Application deadline:* Applications may be processed on a rolling basis for some programs. *Application fee:* $25.

Advanced Placement Credit by examination available. Credit given for nursing courses completed elsewhere dependent upon specific evaluations.

Expenses (2009–10) *Tuition:* full-time $10,500; part-time $350 per credit hour. *International tuition:* $10,500 full-time. *Room and board:* $6116; room only: $3000 per academic year.

Financial Aid 55% of baccalaureate students in nursing programs received some form of financial aid in 2008–09.

Contact Dr. Judith Halle, Dean of the School of Health Sciences, College of Nursing, Mountain State University, PO Box 9003, Beckley, WV 25802-9003. *Telephone:* 304-929-1327. *Fax:* 304-929-1600. *E-mail:* jhalle@mountainstate.edu.

GRADUATE PROGRAMS

Expenses (2009–10) *Tuition:* full-time $4380; part-time $365 per credit hour. *International tuition:* $4380 full-time. *Room and board:* $6116; room only: $3000 per academic year.

Financial Aid 64% of graduate students in nursing programs received some form of financial aid in 2008–09.

Contact Dr. Judith Halle, Dean of the School of Health Sciences, College of Nursing, Mountain State University, PO Box 9003, Beckley, WV 25802-9003. *Telephone:* 304-929-1327. *Fax:* 304-929-1600. *E-mail:* jhalle@mountainstate.edu.

MASTER'S DEGREE PROGRAM

Degree MSN

Available Programs Master's.

Concentrations Available Nurse anesthesia; nursing administration; nursing education. *Nurse practitioner programs in:* family health.

Site Options Orlando, FL; Martinsburg, WV.

Study Options Full-time and part-time.

Program Entrance Requirements Clinical experience, computer literacy, minimum overall college GPA of 3.0, transcript of college record, CPR certification, written essay, immunizations, 3 letters of recommendation, nursing research course, physical assessment course, prerequisite course work, resume, statistics course. *Application deadline:* Applications may be processed on a rolling basis for some programs. *Application fee:* $25.

Advanced Placement Credit given for nursing courses completed elsewhere dependent upon specific evaluations.

Degree Requirements 35 total credit hours, thesis or project, comprehensive exam.

POST-MASTER'S PROGRAM

Areas of Study Nurse anesthesia; nursing administration; nursing education. *Nurse practitioner programs in:* family health.

Shepherd University
Department of Nursing Education
Shepherdstown, West Virginia

http://www.shepherd.edu/nurseweb/
Founded in 1871
DEGREE • BSN

Nursing Program Faculty 8 (50% with doctorates).

Baccalaureate Enrollment 144
Women 92% **Men** 8% **Minority** 18% **International** 4%

Nursing Student Activities Nursing Honor Society, Student Nurses' Association.

Nursing Student Resources Academic advising; academic or career counseling; assistance for students with disabilities; bookstore; campus computer network; career placement assistance; computer lab; computer-assisted instruction; e-mail services; interactive nursing skills videos; Internet; learning resource lab; library services; nursing audiovisuals; remedial services; resume preparation assistance; skills, simulation, or other laboratory; tutoring.

Library Facilities 183,509 volumes (4,997 in health, 462 in nursing); 14,483 periodical subscriptions (1,956 health-care related).

BACCALAUREATE PROGRAMS

Degree BSN

Available Programs ADN to Baccalaureate; Generic Baccalaureate; RN Baccalaureate.

Study Options Full-time.

Program Entrance Requirements Minimum overall college GPA of 2.5, transcript of college record, CPR certification, written essay, health exam, health insurance, immunizations, interview, minimum GPA in nursing prerequisites of 2.0, professional liability insurance/malpractice insurance, prerequisite course work. Transfer students are accepted. *Application deadline:* 3/1 (fall), 10/1 (spring).

Advanced Placement Credit by examination available. Credit given for nursing courses completed elsewhere dependent upon specific evaluations.

Expenses (2009–10) *Tuition, state resident:* full-time $2617; part-time $214 per credit. *Tuition, nonresident:* full-time $6787; part-time $561 per credit. *Room and board:* $3908 per academic year. *Required fees:* full-time $3000.

Financial Aid 86% of baccalaureate students in nursing programs received some form of financial aid in 2008–09. *Gift aid (need-based):* Federal Pell, FSEOG, state, private, college/university gift aid from institutional funds. *Loans:* Federal Direct (Subsidized and Unsubsidized Stafford PLUS), Perkins. *Work-study:* Federal Work-Study, part-time campus jobs. *Financial aid application deadline (priority):* 3/1.

Contact Dr. Sharon K. Mailey, Professor and Chair, Department of Nursing Education, Department of Nursing Education, Shepherd University, 301 North King Street, PO Box 5000, Shepherdstown, WV 25443. *Telephone:* 304-876-5341. *Fax:* 304-876-5169. *E-mail:* smailey@shepherd.edu.

CONTINUING EDUCATION PROGRAM

Contact Dr. Sharon K. Mailey, Professor and Chair, Department of Nursing Education, Department of Nursing Education, Shepherd University, 301 North King Street, PO Box 5000, Shepherdstown, WV 25443. *Telephone:* 304-876-5341. *Fax:* 304-876-5169. *E-mail:* smailey@shepherd.edu.

University of Charleston
Department of Nursing
Charleston, West Virginia

http://www.ucwv.edu/dhs/bsn
Founded in 1888
DEGREE • BSN

Nursing Program Faculty 8 (38% with doctorates).

Baccalaureate Enrollment 65
Women 97% **Men** 3% **Minority** 3% **International** 1% **Part-time** 1%
Nursing Student Activities Nursing Honor Society, Sigma Theta Tau, Student Nurses' Association, nursing club.

Nursing Student Resources Academic advising; academic or career counseling; assistance for students with disabilities; bookstore; campus computer network; career placement assistance; computer lab; computer-assisted instruction; e-mail services; employment services for current students; externships; housing assistance; interactive nursing skills videos; Internet; learning resource lab; library services; nursing audiovisuals; paid internships; placement services for program completers; remedial services; resume preparation assistance; skills, simulation, or other laboratory; tutoring; unpaid internships.

Library Facilities 164,457 volumes (3,900 in health, 1,550 in nursing); 14,192 periodical subscriptions (75 health-care related).

BACCALAUREATE PROGRAMS
Degree BSN

Available Programs Generic Baccalaureate.
Study Options Full-time and part-time.
Program Entrance Requirements Minimum overall college GPA of 2.75, transcript of college record, CPR certification, health exam, high school biology, 1 year of high school math, high school transcript, immunizations, minimum high school GPA of 2.25, minimum GPA in nursing prerequisites of 2.75, professional liability insurance/malpractice insurance, prerequisite course work. Transfer students are accepted. *Application deadline:* Applications may be processed on a rolling basis for some programs.
Advanced Placement Credit given for nursing courses completed elsewhere dependent upon specific evaluations.
Expenses (2009–10) *Tuition:* full-time $24,000; part-time $875 per credit. *Room and board:* $8937; room only: $4750 per academic year.
Financial Aid 90% of baccalaureate students in nursing programs received some form of financial aid in 2008–09.
Contact Office of Undergraduate Admissions, Department of Nursing, University of Charleston, 2300 MacCorkle Avenue SE, Charleston, WV 25304. *Telephone:* 304-357-4750. *Fax:* 304-357-4781. *E-mail:* admissions@ucwv.edu.

West Liberty University
Department of Health Sciences
West Liberty, West Virginia

http://www.westliberty.edu/nursing/index.htm
Founded in 1837
DEGREE • BSN

Nursing Program Faculty 8
Baccalaureate Enrollment 100
Women 88% **Men** 12% **Minority** 3%
Distance Learning Courses Available.
Nursing Student Activities Student Nurses' Association.
Nursing Student Resources Academic advising; academic or career counseling; assistance for students with disabilities; bookstore; campus computer network; career placement assistance; computer lab; computer-assisted instruction; e-mail services; externships; housing assistance; interactive nursing skills videos; Internet; learning resource lab; library services;

nursing audiovisuals; placement services for program completers; remedial services; resume preparation assistance; skills, simulation, or other laboratory; tutoring; unpaid internships.
Library Facilities 2,500 volumes in health, 750 volumes in nursing; 350 periodical subscriptions health-care related.

BACCALAUREATE PROGRAMS
Degree BSN
Available Programs Accelerated RN Baccalaureate; Generic Baccalaureate.
Site Options Tridelphia, WV; Wheeling, WV.
Study Options Full-time and part-time.
Program Entrance Requirements Minimum overall college GPA of 2.8, transcript of college record, health exam, minimum high school GPA of 3.0, prerequisite course work. Transfer students are accepted. *Application deadline:* 3/31 (fall), 3/31 (spring).
Advanced Placement Credit by examination available. Credit given for nursing courses completed elsewhere dependent upon specific evaluations.
Expenses (2009–10) *Tuition, area resident:* full-time $4880; part-time $203 per contact hour. *Tuition, state resident:* full-time $9560; part-time $398 per contact hour. *Tuition, nonresident:* full-time $11,950; part-time $498 per contact hour. *International tuition:* $11,950 full-time. *Room and board:* $6870; room only: $6870 per academic year.
Financial Aid 90% of baccalaureate students in nursing programs received some form of financial aid in 2008–09. *Gift aid (need-based):* Federal Pell, FSEOG, state, private, college/university gift aid from institutional funds. *Loans:* Federal Nursing Student Loans, Federal Direct (Subsidized and Unsubsidized Stafford PLUS), Perkins, alternative loans. *Work-study:* Federal Work-Study, part-time campus jobs. *Financial aid application deadline (priority):* 3/1.
Contact Ms. Sara E. Smith, RN, Nursing Program Director, Interim, Department of Health Sciences, West Liberty University, PO Box 295, CMC #140, West Liberty, WV 26074. *Telephone:* 304-336-8630. *Fax:* 304-336-5104. *E-mail:* ssmith1@westliberty.edu.

West Virginia University
School of Nursing
Morgantown, West Virginia

http://www.hsc.wvu.edu/son/
Founded in 1867
DEGREES • BSN • DNP • MSN • PHD

Nursing Program Faculty 85 (45% with doctorates).
Baccalaureate Enrollment 575
Women 88% **Men** 12% **Minority** 5.6% **International** 1% **Part-time** 21%
Graduate Enrollment 192
Women 97% **Men** 3% **Minority** 4.7% **Part-time** 80%
Distance Learning Courses Available.
Nursing Student Activities Nursing Honor Society, Sigma Theta Tau, Student Nurses' Association.
Nursing Student Resources Academic advising; academic or career counseling; assistance for students with disabilities; bookstore; campus computer network; career placement assistance; computer lab; computer-assisted instruction; e-mail services; employment services for current students; externships; housing assistance; interactive nursing skills videos; Internet; learning resource lab; library services; nursing audiovisuals; paid internships; remedial services; resume preparation assistance; skills, simulation, or other laboratory; tutoring.
Library Facilities 1.8 million volumes (211,803 in health, 2,663 in nursing); 9,592 periodical subscriptions (1,662 health-care related).

BACCALAUREATE PROGRAMS
Degree BSN
Available Programs Accelerated Baccalaureate for Second Degree; Generic Baccalaureate; RN Baccalaureate.
Site Options Charleston, WV; Montgomery, WV; Glenville/Keyser, WV.
Study Options Full-time.

West Virginia University (continued)

Online Degree Options Yes.

Program Entrance Requirements Minimum overall college GPA of 3.0, transcript of college record, CPR certification, high school chemistry, 3 years high school math, 3 years high school science, high school transcript, immunizations, interview, minimum high school GPA of 3.6, minimum GPA in nursing prerequisites of 3.0, prerequisite course work. Transfer students are accepted. *Application deadline:* 2/1 (fall). *Application fee:* $25.

Advanced Placement Credit by examination available. Credit given for nursing courses completed elsewhere dependent upon specific evaluations.

Expenses (2009–10) *Tuition, area resident:* full-time $5174; part-time $217 per credit hour. *Tuition, nonresident:* full-time $18,698; part-time $781 per credit hour. *Room and board:* $8240; room only: $5160 per academic year. *Required fees:* full-time $1472; part-time $199 per credit.

Financial Aid 92% of baccalaureate students in nursing programs received some form of financial aid in 2008–09. *Gift aid (need-based):* Federal Pell, FSEOG, state, private, college/university gift aid from institutional funds. *Loans:* Federal Direct (Subsidized and Unsubsidized Stafford PLUS), Perkins, college/university. *Work-study:* Federal Work-Study, part-time campus jobs. *Financial aid application deadline:* 3/1.

Contact Mr. Stuart R. Wells, Assistant Dean for Student Services, School of Nursing, West Virginia University, PO Box 9600, Morgantown, WV 26506-9600. *Telephone:* 304-293-1386. *Fax:* 304-293-2784. *E-mail:* swells@ hsc.wvu.edu.

GRADUATE PROGRAMS

Expenses (2009–10) *Tuition, area resident:* full-time $5842; part-time $327 per credit hour. *Tuition, nonresident:* full-time $19,674; part-time $1093 per credit hour. *Room and board:* $8240; room only: $5160 per academic year. *Required fees:* full-time $1172; part-time $66 per credit.

Financial Aid 25% of graduate students in nursing programs received some form of financial aid in 2008–09. 1 teaching assistantship with tuition reimbursement available (averaging $10,000 per year) was awarded; institutionally sponsored loans, tuition waivers (partial), and graduate administrative assistantships also available. *Financial aid application deadline:* 2/1.

Contact Mr. Stuart R. Wells, Assistant Dean for Student Services, School of Nursing, West Virginia University, 6415 Health Sciences Center South, PO Box 9600, Morgantown, WV 26506-9600. *Telephone:* 304-293-1386. *Fax:* 304-293-2784. *E-mail:* swells@hsc.wvu.edu.

MASTER'S DEGREE PROGRAM

Degree MSN

Available Programs Master's; RN to Master's.

Concentrations Available Nursing administration. *Nurse practitioner programs in:* family health, gerontology, neonatal health, pediatric, women's health.

Site Options Charleston, WV.

Study Options Full-time and part-time.

Online Degree Options Yes (online only).

Program Entrance Requirements Computer literacy, minimum overall college GPA of 3.0, transcript of college record, CPR certification, written essay, immunizations, 3 letters of recommendation, nursing research course, physical assessment course, resume, statistics course. *Application deadline:* 4/1 (fall). *Application fee:* $50.

Advanced Placement Credit by examination available. Credit given for nursing courses completed elsewhere dependent upon specific evaluations.

Degree Requirements 44 total credit hours.

POST-MASTER'S PROGRAM

Areas of Study Nursing administration. *Nurse practitioner programs in:* family health, gerontology, neonatal health, pediatric, women's health.

DOCTORAL DEGREE PROGRAM

Degree DNP, PhD

Available Programs Doctorate.

Areas of Study Nursing research.

Site Options Charleston, WV.

Program Entrance Requirements Minimum overall college GPA of 3.0, interview by faculty committee, interview, 3 letters of recommendation, MSN or equivalent, statistics course, vita, writing sample, GRE General Test (PhD). Application deadline: 1/4 (fall). Application fee: $50.

Degree Requirements 54 total credit hours, dissertation, oral exam, written exam.

CONTINUING EDUCATION PROGRAM

Contact Office of Extended Learning, School of Nursing, West Virginia University, PO Box 6800, Morgantown, WV 26506-6800. *Telephone:* 800-253-2762. *Fax:* 304-293-4233.

West Virginia Wesleyan College
Department of Nursing
Buckhannon, West Virginia

---

http://www.wvwc.edu

Founded in 1890

DEGREES • BSN • MSN

Nursing Program Faculty 7 (60% with doctorates).

Baccalaureate Enrollment 82
Women 93% **Men** 7% **Minority** 3%

Nursing Student Activities Sigma Theta Tau, Student Nurses' Association.

Nursing Student Resources Academic advising; academic or career counseling; assistance for students with disabilities; bookstore; campus computer network; career placement assistance; computer-assisted instruction; e-mail services; employment services for current students; externships; interactive nursing skills videos; Internet; learning resource lab; library services; nursing audiovisuals; placement services for program completers; remedial services; resume preparation assistance; skills, simulation, or other laboratory; tutoring.

Library Facilities 130,000 volumes (4,000 in health, 600 in nursing); 14,500 periodical subscriptions (90 health-care related).

BACCALAUREATE PROGRAMS

Degree BSN

Available Programs Generic Baccalaureate.

Study Options Full-time and part-time.

Program Entrance Requirements Minimum overall college GPA of 2.75, transcript of college record, CPR certification, health exam, health insurance, high school transcript, immunizations, interview, minimum high school GPA of 2.5, minimum GPA in nursing prerequisites of 2.0, prerequisite course work. Transfer students are accepted. *Application deadline:* 6/15 (fall), 12/15 (spring). Applications may be processed on a rolling basis for some programs.

Advanced Placement Credit by examination available. Credit given for nursing courses completed elsewhere dependent upon specific evaluations.

Financial Aid 95% of baccalaureate students in nursing programs received some form of financial aid in 2008–09. *Gift aid (need-based):* Federal Pell, FSEOG, state, private, college/university gift aid from institutional funds, Federal Nursing. *Loans:* Federal Nursing Student Loans, FFEL (Subsidized and Unsubsidized Stafford PLUS), Perkins, college/university. *Work-study:* Federal Work-Study, part-time campus jobs. *Financial aid application deadline (priority):* 2/15.

Contact Ms. Judith McKinney, EdD, Professor and Chairperson, Department of Nursing, West Virginia Wesleyan College, 59 College Avenue, Buckhannon, WV 26201-2995. *Telephone:* 304-473-8224. *Fax:* 304-473-8435. *E-mail:* mckinney@wvwc.edu.

GRADUATE PROGRAMS

Contact Dr. Sue Leight, Associate Professor and Director of MSN Program, Department of Nursing, West Virginia Wesleyan College, 59 College Avenue, Buckhannon, WV 26201. *Telephone:* 304-473-8228. *E-mail:* leight@wvwc.edu.

MASTER'S DEGREE PROGRAM

Degree MSN

Available Programs Master's.

Concentrations Available Nursing administration; nursing education.

Wheeling Jesuit University
Department of Nursing
Wheeling, West Virginia

http://www.wju.edu/academics/nursing/welcome. asp

Founded in 1954

DEGREES • BSN • MSN

Nursing Program Faculty 9 (50% with doctorates).

Library Facilities 144,242 volumes (5,065 in nursing); 456 periodical subscriptions (90 health-care related).

BACCALAUREATE PROGRAMS

Degree BSN

Study Options Full-time and part-time.

Program Entrance Requirements 2 Year (s) high school math, 1 year of high school science, high school transcript, minimum high school rank 50%. Transfer students are accepted.

Advanced Placement Credit by examination available. Credit given for nursing courses completed elsewhere dependent upon specific evaluations.

Contact *Telephone:* 304-243-2359. *Fax:* 304-243-2397.

GRADUATE PROGRAMS

Contact *Telephone:* 304-243-2344. *Fax:* 304-243-2608.

MASTER'S DEGREE PROGRAM

Degree MSN

Available Programs Master's.

Concentrations Available Nursing administration; nursing education. *Nurse practitioner programs in:* family health.

Study Options Full-time and part-time.

Program Entrance Requirements Computer literacy, minimum overall college GPA of 3.0, 3 letters of recommendation, statistics course, GRE General Test.

Advanced Placement Credit given for nursing courses completed elsewhere dependent upon specific evaluations.

Degree Requirements 42 total credit hours, comprehensive exam.

WISCONSIN

Alverno College
Division of Nursing
Milwaukee, Wisconsin

http://www.alverno.edu

Founded in 1887

DEGREES • BSN • MSN

Nursing Program Faculty 39 (5% with doctorates).

Baccalaureate Enrollment 763
Women 100% **Minority** 24% **Part-time** 22%

Graduate Enrollment 43
Women 96% **Men** 4% **Minority** 9% **Part-time** 62%

Nursing Student Activities Student Nurses' Association.

Nursing Student Resources Academic advising; academic or career counseling; assistance for students with disabilities; bookstore; campus computer network; career placement assistance; computer lab; computer-assisted instruction; daycare for children of students; e-mail services; employment services for current students; externships; housing assistance; interactive nursing skills videos; Internet; learning resource lab; library services; nursing audiovisuals; remedial services; resume preparation assistance; skills, simulation, or other laboratory; tutoring; unpaid internships.

Library Facilities 95,622 volumes; 3,932 periodical subscriptions.

BACCALAUREATE PROGRAMS

Degree BSN

Available Programs ADN to Baccalaureate; Baccalaureate for Second Degree; Generic Baccalaureate; LPN to Baccalaureate; RN Baccalaureate.

Study Options Full-time and part-time.

Program Entrance Requirements Minimum overall college GPA of 2.5, transcript of college record, written essay, high school biology, high school chemistry, 3 years high school math, 2 years high school science, high school transcript, minimum high school GPA of 2.0, prerequisite course work. Transfer students are accepted.

Advanced Placement Credit by examination available. Credit given for nursing courses completed elsewhere dependent upon specific evaluations.

Contact *Telephone:* 414-382-6276. *Fax:* 414-382-6279.

GRADUATE PROGRAMS

Contact *Telephone:* 414-382-6278. *Fax:* 414-382-6279.

MASTER'S DEGREE PROGRAM

Degree MSN

Available Programs Master's.

Concentrations Available Nursing education. *Clinical nurse specialist programs in:* adult health, gerontology, medical-surgical.

Study Options Full-time and part-time.

Program Entrance Requirements Clinical experience, transcript of college record, CPR certification, written essay, immunizations, 3 letters of recommendation, physical assessment course, statistics course.

Advanced Placement Credit given for nursing courses completed elsewhere dependent upon specific evaluations.

Degree Requirements 39 total credit hours, thesis or project.

CONTINUING EDUCATION PROGRAM

Contact *Telephone:* 414-382-6177. *Fax:* 414-382-6354.

Bellin College
Nursing Program
Green Bay, Wisconsin

http://www.bcon.edu

Founded in 1909

DEGREES • BSN • MSN

Nursing Program Faculty 20 (21% with doctorates).

Baccalaureate Enrollment 274
Women 92% **Men** 8% **Minority** 5% **International** 1% **Part-time** 9%

Graduate Enrollment 32
Women 93% **Men** 7% **Minority** 2% **Part-time** 81%

Distance Learning Courses Available.

Nursing Student Activities Sigma Theta Tau, Student Nurses' Association.

Nursing Student Resources Academic advising; academic or career counseling; assistance for students with disabilities; career placement assistance; computer lab; computer-assisted instruction; e-mail services; interactive nursing skills videos; Internet; learning resource lab; library services; nursing audiovisuals; resume preparation assistance; skills, simulation, or other laboratory; tutoring.

Bellin College (continued)

Library Facilities 7,000 volumes (7,000 in health, 4,000 in nursing); 225 periodical subscriptions (190 health-care related).

BACCALAUREATE PROGRAMS

Degree BSN

Available Programs Accelerated Baccalaureate; Accelerated Baccalaureate for Second Degree; Baccalaureate for Second Degree; Generic Baccalaureate.

Study Options Full-time and part-time.

Program Entrance Requirements Minimum overall college GPA of 2.7, transcript of college record, CPR certification, health exam, health insurance, high school biology, high school chemistry, 3 years high school math, 3 years high school science, high school transcript, immunizations, interview, 3 letters of recommendation, minimum high school GPA of 3.25, minimum GPA in nursing prerequisites of 2.7. Transfer students are accepted. *Application deadline:* Applications may be processed on a rolling basis for some programs. *Application fee:* $30.

Advanced Placement Credit by examination available. Credit given for nursing courses completed elsewhere dependent upon specific evaluations.

Expenses (2009–10) *Tuition:* full-time $18,500; part-time $884 per credit. *International tuition:* $18,500 full-time. *Required fees:* full-time $339; part-time $339 per credit.

Financial Aid 92% of baccalaureate students in nursing programs received some form of financial aid in 2008–09. *Gift aid (need-based):* Federal Pell, FSEOG, state, private, college/university gift aid from institutional funds. *Loans:* FFEL (Subsidized and Unsubsidized Stafford PLUS), state. *Work-study:* Federal Work-Study. *Financial aid application deadline (priority):* 3/1.

Contact Ms. Katie Klaus, Director of Admission, Nursing Program, Bellin College, 3201 Eaton Road, Green Bay, WI 54311. *Telephone:* 920-433-6651. *Fax:* 920-433-1922. *E-mail:* katie.klaus@bellincollege.edu.

GRADUATE PROGRAMS

Expenses (2009–10) *Tuition:* full-time $19,500; part-time $650 per credit. *International tuition:* $19,500 full-time. *Required fees:* full-time $500.

Financial Aid 63% of graduate students in nursing programs received some form of financial aid in 2008–09.

Contact Dr. Vera Dauffenbach, Director of Graduate Program, Nursing Program, Bellin College, 3201 Eaton Road, Green Bay, WI 54311. *Telephone:* 920-433-3624. *Fax:* 920-433-1922. *E-mail:* vera.dauffenbach@bellincollege.edu.

MASTER'S DEGREE PROGRAM

Degree MSN

Available Programs Master's.

Concentrations Available Nursing administration; nursing education.

Study Options Full-time and part-time.

Online Degree Options Yes.

Program Entrance Requirements Computer literacy, minimum overall college GPA of 3.0, transcript of college record, written essay, interview, 3 letters of recommendation, nursing research course, resume, statistics course. *Application deadline:* Applications may be processed on a rolling basis for some programs. *Application fee:* $50.

Advanced Placement Credit given for nursing courses completed elsewhere dependent upon specific evaluations.

Degree Requirements 38 total credit hours, thesis or project.

Cardinal Stritch University
Ruth S. Coleman College of Nursing
Milwaukee, Wisconsin

http://www.stritch.edu/nursing

Founded in 1937

DEGREES • BSN • MSN

Nursing Program Faculty 36 (11% with doctorates).

Baccalaureate Enrollment 98
Women 90% **Men** 10% **Minority** 17% **International** 6%

Graduate Enrollment 15
Women 100% **Minority** 13%

Nursing Student Activities Student Nurses' Association.

Nursing Student Resources Academic advising; academic or career counseling; assistance for students with disabilities; bookstore; campus computer network; career placement assistance; computer lab; e-mail services; employment services for current students; interactive nursing skills videos; Internet; learning resource lab; library services; nursing audiovisuals; remedial services; resume preparation assistance; skills, simulation, or other laboratory; tutoring.

Library Facilities 124,897 volumes (4,500 in health, 600 in nursing); 667 periodical subscriptions (1,500 health-care related).

BACCALAUREATE PROGRAMS

Degree BSN

Available Programs ADN to Baccalaureate.

Site Options Menomonee Falls, WI; Milwaukee, WI.

Study Options Full-time and part-time.

Program Entrance Requirements Minimum overall college GPA of 2.33, transcript of college record, RN licensure. Transfer students are accepted. *Application deadline:* Applications may be processed on a rolling basis for some programs.

Advanced Placement Credit by examination available. Credit given for nursing courses completed elsewhere dependent upon specific evaluations.

Expenses (2009–10) *Tuition:* full-time $13,920; part-time $580 per credit hour. *Room and board:* $6800; room only: $2190 per academic year. *Required fees:* full-time $510; part-time $205 per term.

Financial Aid 75% of baccalaureate students in nursing programs received some form of financial aid in 2008–09.

Contact Stacey Wegener, Nursing Admissions Counselor, Ruth S. Coleman College of Nursing, Cardinal Stritch University, 6801 North Yates Road, Milwaukee, WI 53217-3985. *Telephone:* 414-410-4966. *Fax:* 414-410-4049. *E-mail:* slwegener@stritch.edu.

GRADUATE PROGRAMS

Expenses (2009–10) *Tuition:* full-time $9100; part-time $650 per credit hour. *Required fees:* full-time $360; part-time $180 per term.

Financial Aid 53% of graduate students in nursing programs received some form of financial aid in 2008–09.

Contact Ms. Stacey Wegener, Nursing Admissions Counselor, Ruth S. Coleman College of Nursing, Cardinal Stritch University, 6801 North Yates Road, Milwaukee, WI 53217-3985. *Telephone:* 414-410-4966. *Fax:* 414-410-4049. *E-mail:* slwegener@stritch.edu.

MASTER'S DEGREE PROGRAM

Degree MSN

Available Programs Accelerated Master's.

Concentrations Available Nursing education.

Study Options Full-time.

Program Entrance Requirements Computer literacy, minimum overall college GPA of 3.0, transcript of college record, CPR certification, written essay, immunizations, interview, 3 letters of recommendation, nursing research course, resume, statistics course. *Application deadline:* Applications may be processed on a rolling basis for some programs.

Advanced Placement Credit given for nursing courses completed elsewhere dependent upon specific evaluations.

Degree Requirements 36 total credit hours, thesis or project.

Carroll University
Nursing Program
Waukesha, Wisconsin

Founded in 1846

DEGREE • BSN

Nursing Program Faculty 15 (6.6% with doctorates).

Baccalaureate Enrollment 290
Women 90% **Men** 10% **Minority** 15% **Part-time** 5%

Nursing Student Activities Sigma Theta Tau, Student Nurses' Association.

Nursing Student Resources Academic advising; academic or career counseling; assistance for students with disabilities; bookstore; campus computer network; computer lab; computer-assisted instruction; e-mail services; housing assistance; interactive nursing skills videos; Internet; learning resource lab; library services; nursing audiovisuals; skills, simulation, or other laboratory; tutoring.

Library Facilities 150,000 volumes; 18,000 periodical subscriptions.

BACCALAUREATE PROGRAMS

Degree BSN

Available Programs ADN to Baccalaureate; Generic Baccalaureate.
Study Options Full-time.

Program Entrance Requirements Minimum overall college GPA of 2.75, transcript of college record, written essay, health exam, health insurance, high school biology, high school chemistry, 3 years high school math, high school transcript, minimum high school GPA of 2.75. Transfer students are accepted. *Application deadline:* Applications may be processed on a rolling basis for some programs.

Expenses (2009–10) *Tuition:* full-time $22,470; part-time $345 per credit. *Room and board:* $3833 per academic year. *Required fees:* full-time $400.

Financial Aid 98% of baccalaureate students in nursing programs received some form of financial aid in 2008–09. *Gift aid (need-based):* Federal Pell, FSEOG, state, private, college/university gift aid from institutional funds. *Loans:* FFEL (Subsidized and Unsubsidized Stafford PLUS), Perkins, state, college/university. *Work-study:* Federal Work-Study, part-time campus jobs. *Financial aid application deadline:* Continuous.

Contact Ms. Angela Rose Brindowski, Chair, Department of Nursing, Nursing Program, Carroll University, 100 North East Avenue, Waukesha, WI 53186. *Telephone:* 262-524-7381. *E-mail:* abrindow@carrollu.edu.

Columbia College of Nursing
Columbia College of Nursing/Mount Mary College Nursing Program
Milwaukee, Wisconsin

See description of programs under
Columbia College of Nursing/Mount Mary College Nursing Program (Milwaukee, Wisconsin).

Columbia College of Nursing/ Mount Mary College Nursing Program
Columbia College of Nursing/Mount Mary College Nursing Program
Milwaukee, Wisconsin

---

http://www.mtmary.edu/nursing.htm
Founded in 2002
DEGREE • BSN

Nursing Program Faculty 20 (7% with doctorates).
Baccalaureate Enrollment 250
Women 95% **Men** 5% **Minority** 15% **Part-time** 20%
Nursing Student Activities Sigma Theta Tau, Student Nurses' Association.

Nursing Student Resources Academic advising; academic or career counseling; bookstore; campus computer network; career placement assistance; computer lab; computer-assisted instruction; daycare for children of students; e-mail services; employment services for current students; housing assistance; interactive nursing skills videos; Internet; learning resource lab; library services; nursing audiovisuals; resume preparation assistance; skills, simulation, or other laboratory; tutoring.

■ Columbia College of Nursing has a long history in nursing education dating back to 1901. Since 1913 Mount Mary College has been educating women in the liberal arts tradition. Jointly, Columbia College of Nursing and Mount Mary College offer a Bachelor of Science in Nursing degree. Nursing students combine nursing instruction with clinical placements, enabling them to meet the challenges of health care today and into the future. The nursing program is approved by the State of Wisconsin Board of Nursing and is accredited by the National League for Nursing Accrediting Commission. The nursing program recently introduced direct admission for qualified students, including transfer students. Students can find more information online at www.mtmary.edu and www.ccon.edu.

BACCALAUREATE PROGRAMS

Degree BSN

Available Programs Baccalaureate for Second Degree; Generic Baccalaureate; RN Baccalaureate.
Site Options Milwaukee, WI.
Study Options Full-time and part-time.

Program Entrance Requirements Minimum overall college GPA of 2.8, transcript of college record, health exam, health insurance, high school biology, high school chemistry, 2 years high school math, 2 years high school science, high school transcript, minimum high school GPA of 2.5, minimum high school rank 40%, minimum GPA in nursing prerequisites of 2.8, prerequisite course work. Transfer students are accepted.

Advanced Placement Credit by examination available. Credit given for nursing courses completed elsewhere dependent upon specific evaluations.

Expenses (2008–09) *Tuition:* full-time $19,950; part-time $575 per credit. *Room and board:* $6995 per academic year. *Required fees:* full-time $550; part-time $50 per credit.

Financial Aid 90% of baccalaureate students in nursing programs received some form of financial aid in 2007–08.

Contact Ms. Ronda Bond, Nursing Recruiter, Columbia College of Nursing/Mount Mary College Nursing Program, 2900 North Menomonee River Parkway, Milwaukee, WI 53222. *Telephone:* 414-256-1219 Ext. 193. *Fax:* 414-256-0180. *E-mail:* bondr@mtmary.edu.

See full description on page 484.

Concordia University Wisconsin
Program in Nursing
Mequon, Wisconsin

---

http://www.cuw.edu
Founded in 1881
DEGREES • BSN • DNP • MSN

Nursing Program Faculty 71 (1% with doctorates).
Baccalaureate Enrollment 329
Women 92% **Men** 8% **Minority** 10% **International** 1% **Part-time** 32%
Graduate Enrollment 337
Women 95% **Men** 5% **Minority** 8% **International** 1% **Part-time** 44%
Distance Learning Courses Available.
Nursing Student Activities Nursing Honor Society, Sigma Theta Tau, Student Nurses' Association.

Concordia University Wisconsin (continued)

Nursing Student Resources Academic advising; academic or career counseling; assistance for students with disabilities; bookstore; campus computer network; career placement assistance; computer lab; computer-assisted instruction; e-mail services; employment services for current students; externships; interactive nursing skills videos; Internet; learning resource lab; library services; nursing audiovisuals; paid internships; placement services for program completers; resume preparation assistance; skills, simulation, or other laboratory; tutoring.

Library Facilities 79,341 volumes (3,893 in health, 878 in nursing); 4,440 periodical subscriptions (922 health-care related).

BACCALAUREATE PROGRAMS

Degree BSN

Available Programs ADN to Baccalaureate; Generic Baccalaureate; LPN to RN Baccalaureate; RN Baccalaureate.

Site Options Milwaukee, WI.

Study Options Full-time.

Program Entrance Requirements Transcript of college record, CPR certification, health exam, health insurance, high school transcript, immunizations, minimum high school GPA of 2.75, minimum GPA in nursing prerequisites of 2.75, RN licensure. Transfer students are accepted. *Application deadline:* 7/15 (fall), 7/15 (winter), 10/15 (spring), 3/15 (summer). *Application fee:* $35.

Advanced Placement Credit given for nursing courses completed elsewhere dependent upon specific evaluations.

Expenses (2009–10) *Tuition:* full-time $20,900; part-time $870 per credit. *International tuition:* $20,900 full-time. *Room and board:* $3995; room only: $2345 per academic year. *Required fees:* part-time $10,450 per term.

Financial Aid 34% of baccalaureate students in nursing programs received some form of financial aid in 2008–09. *Gift aid (need-based):* Federal Pell, FSEOG, state, private, college/university gift aid from institutional funds. *Loans:* Federal Direct (Subsidized and Unsubsidized Stafford PLUS), state. *Work-study:* Federal Work-Study. *Financial aid application deadline (priority):* 4/1.

Contact Ms. Karen Jean Kentopp, Administrative Assistant, Nursing Depart, Program in Nursing, Concordia University Wisconsin, 12800 North Lake Shore Drive, Mequon, WI 53097. *Telephone:* 262-243-4374. *Fax:* 262-243-4466. *E-mail:* karen.kentopp@cuw.edu.

GRADUATE PROGRAMS

Expenses (2009–10) *Tuition:* part-time $520 per credit.

Financial Aid 57% of graduate students in nursing programs received some form of financial aid in 2008–09. *Application deadline:* 8/1.

Contact Dr. Teri Kaul, Director, Masters Program in Nursing and DNP, Program in Nursing, Concordia University Wisconsin, 12800 North Lake Shore Drive, Mequon, WI 53097. *Telephone:* 262-243-4538. *Fax:* 262-243-4506. *E-mail:* teri.kaul@cuw.edu.

MASTER'S DEGREE PROGRAM

Degree MSN

Available Programs Master's.

Concentrations Available Nursing education. *Nurse practitioner programs in:* family health, gerontology.

Site Options multiple cities and states.

Study Options Full-time and part-time.

Program Entrance Requirements Clinical experience, computer literacy, minimum overall college GPA of 3.0, transcript of college record, CPR certification, written essay, immunizations, interview, 2 letters of recommendation, physical assessment course, professional liability insurance/malpractice insurance, resume, statistics course. *Application deadline:* 7/15 (fall), 7/15 (winter), 10/15 (spring). *Application fee:* $35.

Advanced Placement Credit given for nursing courses completed elsewhere dependent upon specific evaluations.

Degree Requirements 44 total credit hours, thesis or project.

POST-MASTER'S PROGRAM

Areas of Study *Nurse practitioner programs in:* family health.

DOCTORAL DEGREE PROGRAM

Degree DNP

Available Programs Doctorate.

Areas of Study Family health, gerontology.

Site Options Mequon, WI.

Online Degree Options Yes (online only).

Program Entrance Requirements Clinical experience, minimum overall college GPA of 3.0, 2 letters of recommendation, MSN or equivalent, vita, writing sample. Application deadline: 4/1 (spring). Application fee: $35.

Degree Requirements 35 total credit hours, dissertation.

Edgewood College
Program in Nursing
Madison, Wisconsin

http://nursing.edgewood.edu

Founded in 1927

DEGREES • BS • MS • MSN/MBA

Nursing Program Faculty 36 (25% with doctorates).

Baccalaureate Enrollment 220
Women 90% **Men** 10% **Minority** 2% **International** 1% **Part-time** 35%

Graduate Enrollment 45
Women 86% **Men** 14% **Minority** 2% **Part-time** 100%

Distance Learning Courses Available.

Nursing Student Activities Sigma Theta Tau, Student Nurses' Association.

Nursing Student Resources Academic advising; academic or career counseling; assistance for students with disabilities; bookstore; campus computer network; career placement assistance; computer lab; computer-assisted instruction; e-mail services; employment services for current students; externships; housing assistance; interactive nursing skills videos; Internet; learning resource lab; library services; nursing audiovisuals; paid internships; remedial services; resume preparation assistance; skills, simulation, or other laboratory; tutoring; unpaid internships.

Library Facilities 107,873 volumes (4,500 in health, 1,000 in nursing); 164 periodical subscriptions (45 health-care related).

BACCALAUREATE PROGRAMS

Degree BS

Available Programs Accelerated Baccalaureate for Second Degree; Baccalaureate for Second Degree; Generic Baccalaureate.

Site Options Madison, WI.

Study Options Full-time and part-time.

Program Entrance Requirements Minimum overall college GPA of 2.75, transcript of college record, CPR certification, written essay, health exam, high school biology, high school chemistry, high school foreign language, high school math, high school transcript, immunizations, interview, minimum high school GPA of 2.75, minimum GPA in nursing prerequisites of 2.75, prerequisite course work. Transfer students are accepted. *Application deadline:* 1/15 (fall), 9/15 (spring). *Application fee:* $40.

Advanced Placement Credit given for nursing courses completed elsewhere dependent upon specific evaluations.

Expenses (2009–10) *Tuition:* full-time $21,042; part-time $662 per credit. *Room and board:* $6866 per academic year. *Required fees:* full-time $662.

Financial Aid 85% of baccalaureate students in nursing programs received some form of financial aid in 2008–09. *Gift aid (need-based):* Federal Pell, FSEOG, state, private, college/university gift aid from institutional funds. *Loans:* FFEL (Subsidized and Unsubsidized Stafford PLUS), Perkins, state, college/university. *Work-study:* Federal Work-Study, part-time campus jobs. *Financial aid application deadline (priority):* 3/1.

Contact Dr. Margaret C. Noreuil, Dean, School of Nursing, Program in Nursing, Edgewood College, 1000 Edgewood College Drive, Madison, WI 53711. *Telephone:* 608-663-2280. *Fax:* 608-663-2863. *E-mail:* mnoreuil@edgewood.edu.

GRADUATE PROGRAMS

Expenses (2009–10) *Tuition:* part-time $688 per credit.

Financial Aid 10% of graduate students in nursing programs received some form of financial aid in 2008–09.

Contact Dr. Margaret C. Noreuil, Dean, School of Nursing, Program in Nursing, Edgewood College, 1000 Edgewood College Drive, Madison, WI 53711. *Telephone:* 608-663-2280. *Fax:* 608-663-2863. *E-mail:* mnoreuil@edgewood.edu.

MASTER'S DEGREE PROGRAM

Degrees MS; MSN/MBA

Available Programs Master's.

Concentrations Available Nursing administration; nursing education.

Site Options Madison, WI.

Study Options Full-time and part-time.

Program Entrance Requirements Clinical experience, computer literacy, minimum overall college GPA of 3.0, transcript of college record, CPR certification, written essay, immunizations, interview, 2 letters of recommendation, nursing research course, prerequisite course work, resume, statistics course. *Application deadline:* Applications may be processed on a rolling basis for some programs.

Advanced Placement Credit given for nursing courses completed elsewhere dependent upon specific evaluations.

Degree Requirements 36 total credit hours, thesis or project.

Maranatha Baptist Bible College
Nursing Department
Watertown, Wisconsin

Founded in 1968

DEGREE • BSN

Baccalaureate Enrollment 58

Nursing Student Activities Student Nurses' Association.

Nursing Student Resources Academic advising; academic or career counseling; assistance for students with disabilities; bookstore; campus computer network; career placement assistance; computer lab; computer-assisted instruction; e-mail services; employment services for current students; housing assistance; interactive nursing skills videos; Internet; learning resource lab; library services; nursing audiovisuals; skills, simulation, or other laboratory; tutoring.

Library Facilities 122,251 volumes; 502 periodical subscriptions.

BACCALAUREATE PROGRAMS

Degree BSN

Available Programs RN Baccalaureate.

Program Entrance Requirements Minimum overall college GPA of 2.5, CPR certification, written essay, health exam, immunizations, interview, minimum high school GPA, minimum GPA in nursing prerequisites of 2.5, prerequisite course work. Transfer students are accepted. *Application deadline:* Applications may be processed on a rolling basis for some programs.

Contact Mrs. Kelly Ann Crum, RN, Chair, Department of Nursing, Nursing Department, Maranatha Baptist Bible College, 745 West Main Street, Watertown, WI 53094. *Telephone:* 920-206-4050. *E-mail:* kelly.crum@mbbc.edu.

Marian University
Nursing Studies Division
Fond du Lac, Wisconsin

http://www.mariancollege.edu

Founded in 1936

DEGREES • BSN • MSN

Baccalaureate Enrollment 221
Women 95% **Men** 5% **Minority** 1% **Part-time** 7%

Graduate Enrollment 39
Women 97% **Men** 3% **Part-time** 15%

Nursing Student Activities Student Nurses' Association.

Nursing Student Resources Academic advising; academic or career counseling; assistance for students with disabilities; bookstore; career placement assistance; computer lab; daycare for children of students; e-mail services; externships; interactive nursing skills videos; Internet; learning resource lab; library services; nursing audiovisuals.

Library Facilities 105,015 volumes (3,000 in health, 2,500 in nursing); 1,357 periodical subscriptions (91 health-care related).

BACCALAUREATE PROGRAMS

Degree BSN

Available Programs ADN to Baccalaureate; Generic Baccalaureate.

Site Options Appleton, WI; Beaver Dam, WI.

Study Options Full-time and part-time.

Program Entrance Requirements Transcript of college record, high school biology, high school chemistry, 3 years high school math, high school science, high school transcript, minimum high school GPA of 2.5. Transfer students are accepted.

Advanced Placement Credit given for nursing courses completed elsewhere dependent upon specific evaluations.

Contact *Telephone:* 920-923-8732. *Fax:* 920-923-8770.

GRADUATE PROGRAMS

Contact *Telephone:* 920-923-8094. *Fax:* 920-923-8094.

MASTER'S DEGREE PROGRAM

Degree MSN

Available Programs Master's.

Concentrations Available Nursing education. *Nurse practitioner programs in:* adult health.

Study Options Full-time and part-time.

Program Entrance Requirements Clinical experience, minimum overall college GPA of 3.0, transcript of college record, CPR certification, written essay, immunizations, 3 letters of recommendation, nursing research course, professional liability insurance/malpractice insurance, resume, statistics course.

Advanced Placement Credit given for nursing courses completed elsewhere dependent upon specific evaluations.

Degree Requirements 39 total credit hours, thesis or project.

POST-MASTER'S PROGRAM

Areas of Study Nursing education.

Marquette University
College of Nursing
Milwaukee, Wisconsin

http://www.marquette.edu/nursing

Founded in 1881

DEGREES • BSN • MSN • MSN/MBA • PHD

Nursing Program Faculty 35 (77% with doctorates).

Baccalaureate Enrollment 384
Women 94% **Men** 6% **Minority** 15% **Part-time** 3%

Graduate Enrollment 304
Women 93% **Men** 7% **Minority** 9% **Part-time** 62%

Distance Learning Courses Available.

Nursing Student Activities Nursing Honor Society, Sigma Theta Tau, Student Nurses' Association.

Nursing Student Resources Academic advising; academic or career counseling; assistance for students with disabilities; bookstore; campus computer network; career placement assistance; computer lab; computer-assisted instruction; daycare for children of students; e-mail services; employment services for current students; externships; housing assistance; interactive nursing skills videos; Internet; learning resource lab; library services; nursing audiovisuals; placement services for program completers; remedial services; resume preparation assistance; skills, simulation, or other laboratory; tutoring.

Marquette University (continued)

Library Facilities 1.6 million volumes (50,124 in health, 7,463 in nursing); 24,242 periodical subscriptions (3,250 health-care related).

BACCALAUREATE PROGRAMS

Degree BSN

Available Programs ADN to Baccalaureate; Generic Baccalaureate.

Study Options Full-time and part-time.

Program Entrance Requirements Minimum overall college GPA of 2.5, transcript of college record, written essay, high school biology, high school chemistry, 3 years high school math, high school transcript, 1 letter of recommendation, minimum high school GPA of 2.5, minimum high school rank 25%. *Application deadline:* 12/1 (fall).

Advanced Placement Credit given for nursing courses completed elsewhere dependent upon specific evaluations.

Expenses (2009–10) *Tuition:* full-time $28,680; part-time $835 per credit. *Room and board:* $9680 per academic year. *Required fees:* full-time $416.

Financial Aid 90% of baccalaureate students in nursing programs received some form of financial aid in 2008–09. *Gift aid (need-based):* Federal Pell, FSEOG, state, private, college/university gift aid from institutional funds. *Loans:* Federal Nursing Student Loans, Federal Direct (Subsidized and Unsubsidized Stafford PLUS), Perkins, state, college/university. *Work-study:* Federal Work-Study, part-time campus jobs. *Financial aid application deadline:* Continuous.

Contact Dr. Kerry Kosmoski-Goepfert, RN, Associate Dean for Undergraduate Programs, College of Nursing, Marquette University, Clark Hall, PO Box 1881, Milwaukee, WI 53201-1881. *Telephone:* 414-288-3809. *Fax:* 414-288-1597. *E-mail:* kerry.goepfert@marquette.edu.

GRADUATE PROGRAMS

Expenses (2009–10) *Tuition:* part-time $865 per credit.

Financial Aid 63% of graduate students in nursing programs received some form of financial aid in 2008–09. 6 research assistantships, 1 teaching assistantship were awarded; career-related internships or fieldwork, Federal Work-Study, institutionally sponsored loans, scholarships, and tuition waivers (full and partial) also available. Aid available to part-time students. *Financial aid application deadline:* 2/15.

Contact Dr. Kerry Kosmoski-Goepfert, Interim Associate Dean for Graduate Programs, College of Nursing, Marquette University, Clark Hall, PO Box 1881, Milwaukee, WI 53201-1881. *Telephone:* 414-288-3809. *Fax:* 414-288-1597. *E-mail:* kerry.goepfert@marquette.edu.

MASTER'S DEGREE PROGRAM

Degrees MSN; MSN/MBA

Available Programs Accelerated AD/RN to Master's; Accelerated Master's for Non-Nursing College Graduates; Accelerated RN to Master's; Master's; Master's for Non-Nursing College Graduates; Master's for Nurses with Non-Nursing Degrees; RN to Master's.

Concentrations Available Clinical nurse leader; nurse-midwifery; nursing administration. *Clinical nurse specialist programs in:* adult health, gerontology, pediatric. *Nurse practitioner programs in:* acute care, adult health, gerontology, pediatric.

Study Options Full-time and part-time.

Program Entrance Requirements Minimum overall college GPA of 3.0, transcript of college record, written essay, immunizations, 3 letters of recommendation, nursing research course, physical assessment course, resume, statistics course, GRE General Test. *Application deadline:* 8/1 (fall), 12/15 (spring).

Advanced Placement Credit given for nursing courses completed elsewhere dependent upon specific evaluations.

Degree Requirements 42 total credit hours, comprehensive exam.

POST-MASTER'S PROGRAM

Areas of Study Nurse-midwifery; nursing administration. *Clinical nurse specialist programs in:* adult health, gerontology, pediatric. *Nurse practitioner programs in:* acute care, adult health, gerontology, pediatric.

DOCTORAL DEGREE PROGRAM

Degree PhD

Available Programs Doctorate; Post-Baccalaureate Doctorate.

Areas of Study Aging, ethics, faculty preparation, health promotion/disease prevention, health-care systems, human health and illness, illness and transition, nursing administration, nursing education, nursing research, nursing science.

Program Entrance Requirements Minimum overall college GPA of 3.3, interview, 3 letters of recommendation, MSN or equivalent, statistics course, vita, writing sample. Application deadline: 2/15 (fall), 11/14 (spring). Applications may be processed on a rolling basis for some programs. Application fee: $50.

Degree Requirements 51 total credit hours, dissertation, oral exam, written exam, residency.

See full description on page 508.

Milwaukee School of Engineering
School of Nursing
Milwaukee, Wisconsin

http://www.msoe.edu/nursing

Founded in 1903

DEGREE • BSN

Nursing Program Faculty 29 (14% with doctorates).

Baccalaureate Enrollment 156

Nursing Student Activities Nursing Honor Society, Student Nurses' Association.

Nursing Student Resources Academic advising; academic or career counseling; assistance for students with disabilities; bookstore; campus computer network; career placement assistance; computer lab; computer-assisted instruction; e-mail services; externships; housing assistance; interactive nursing skills videos; Internet; learning resource lab; library services; nursing audiovisuals; placement services for program completers; remedial services; resume preparation assistance; skills, simulation, or other laboratory; tutoring.

Library Facilities 79,275 volumes (1,956 in health, 1,126 in nursing); 378 periodical subscriptions (116 health-care related).

BACCALAUREATE PROGRAMS

Degree BSN

Available Programs Generic Baccalaureate; RN Baccalaureate.

Study Options Full-time and part-time.

Program Entrance Requirements Minimum overall college GPA of 2.75, transcript of college record, CPR certification, health exam, health insurance, high school biology, high school chemistry, 3 years high school math, 3 years high school science, high school transcript, immunizations, minimum high school GPA of 2.8, professional liability insurance/malpractice insurance. Transfer students are accepted. *Application deadline:* 9/1 (fall), 12/1 (winter), 3/1 (spring). Applications may be processed on a rolling basis for some programs. *Application fee:* $25.

Advanced Placement Credit by examination available. Credit given for nursing courses completed elsewhere dependent upon specific evaluations.

Expenses (2009–10) *Tuition:* full-time $9555. *International tuition:* $9555 full-time. *Room and board:* $2670; room only: $1772 per academic year.

Financial Aid 100% of baccalaureate students in nursing programs received some form of financial aid in 2008–09.

Contact Dr. Debra L. Jenks, RN, Chair, School of Nursing, Milwaukee School of Engineering, 1025 North Broadway Street, Milwaukee, WI 53202-3109. *Telephone:* 414-277-4516. *Fax:* 414-277-4540. *E-mail:* jenks@msoe.edu.

Mount Mary College

Columbia College of Nursing/Mount Mary College Nursing Program
Milwaukee, Wisconsin

See description of programs under
Columbia College of Nursing/Mount Mary College Nursing Program (Milwaukee, Wisconsin).

Silver Lake College

Nursing Program
Manitowoc, Wisconsin

Founded in 1869

DEGREE • BSN

Nursing Program Faculty 12 (8% with doctorates).

Baccalaureate Enrollment 17

Distance Learning Courses Available.

Nursing Student Resources Academic advising; academic or career counseling; assistance for students with disabilities; bookstore; campus computer network; computer lab; computer-assisted instruction; e-mail services; Internet; library services; nursing audiovisuals; tutoring.

Library Facilities 62,465 volumes; 250 periodical subscriptions.

BACCALAUREATE PROGRAMS

Degree BSN

Available Programs ADN to Baccalaureate.

Site Options Wausau, WI.

Study Options Part-time.

Online Degree Options Yes.

Program Entrance Requirements Transcript of college record, health exam, 1 letter of recommendation, RN licensure. Transfer students are accepted. *Application deadline:* Applications may be processed on a rolling basis for some programs. *Application fee:* $50.

Advanced Placement Credit given for nursing courses completed elsewhere dependent upon specific evaluations.

Expenses (2009–10) *Tuition:* part-time $380 per credit.

Contact Kate Siegler, RN, BSN Completion Program Director, Nursing Program, Silver Lake College, 2406 South Alverno Road, Manitowoc, WI 54220. *Telephone:* 715-209-7828. *E-mail:* ksiegler@silver.sl.edu.

University of Wisconsin– Eau Claire

College of Nursing and Health Sciences
Eau Claire, Wisconsin

http://www.uwec.edu/conhs/index.htm

Founded in 1916

DEGREES • BSN • MSN

Nursing Program Faculty 43 (26% with doctorates).

Baccalaureate Enrollment 753
Women 91% **Men** 9% **Minority** 4% **International** .5% **Part-time** 25%

Graduate Enrollment 89
Women 93% **Men** 7% **Minority** 1% **Part-time** 62%

Distance Learning Courses Available.

Nursing Student Activities Sigma Theta Tau, Student Nurses' Association.

Nursing Student Resources Academic advising; academic or career counseling; assistance for students with disabilities; bookstore; campus computer network; career placement assistance; computer lab; computer-assisted instruction; daycare for children of students; e-mail services; employment services for current students; housing assistance; interactive nursing skills videos; Internet; learning resource lab; library services; nursing audiovisuals; other; placement services for program completers; remedial services; resume preparation assistance; skills, simulation, or other laboratory; tutoring.

Library Facilities 744,695 volumes (38,134 in health, 24,363 in nursing); 24,360 periodical subscriptions (3,593 health-care related).

■ The College of Nursing and Health Sciences has an excellent reputation for the high quality of its educational programs and its graduates. The College offers a bachelor's degree with traditional, accelerated, and BSN-completion options. The College also offers a master's degree in nursing, and, beginning in June 2010, a Doctor of Nursing Practice. Master's-level options include adult or family health specialization and advanced clinical practice (nurse practitioner, clinical nurse specialist), education, or administration role preparation. Baccalaureate-level students receive clinical experiences in a simulation lab in addition to receiving experiences in acute-care facilities, community health agencies, and other agencies. Through distance technology, the traditional bachelor's and some BSN completion and master's courses are available at a satellite in Marshfield, Wisconsin.

BACCALAUREATE PROGRAMS

Degree BSN

Available Programs ADN to Baccalaureate; Accelerated Baccalaureate for Second Degree; Generic Baccalaureate; RN Baccalaureate.

Site Options Marshfield, WI.

Study Options Full-time.

Program Entrance Requirements Minimum overall college GPA of 3.0, transcript of college record, CPR certification, written essay, health exam, high school biology, high school chemistry, high school foreign language, 3 years high school math, 3 years high school science, high school transcript, immunizations, minimum GPA in nursing prerequisites of 2.5, prerequisite course work. Transfer students are accepted. *Application deadline:* 7/1 (fall), 12/1 (spring). Applications may be processed on a rolling basis for some programs. *Application fee:* $44.

Advanced Placement Credit given for nursing courses completed elsewhere dependent upon specific evaluations.

Expenses (2009–10) *Tuition, state resident:* full-time $5527; part-time $230 per credit. *Tuition, nonresident:* full-time $13,100; part-time $546 per credit. *Room and board:* $5730; room only: $2830 per academic year. *Required fees:* full-time $1106; part-time $46 per credit; part-time $553 per term.

Financial Aid 66% of baccalaureate students in nursing programs received some form of financial aid in 2008–09.

Contact Dr. Mary Zwygart-Stauffacher, Interim Dean, College of Nursing and Health Sciences, University of Wisconsin–Eau Claire, 105 Garfield Avenue, Eau Claire, WI 54702-4004. *Telephone:* 715-836-5287. *Fax:* 715-836-5925. *E-mail:* zwygarmc@uwec.edu.

GRADUATE PROGRAMS

Expenses (2009–10) *Tuition, state resident:* full-time $7631; part-time $373 per credit. *Tuition, nonresident:* full-time $17,697; part-time $932 per credit. *Room and board:* $5730; room only: $2830 per academic year. *Required fees:* full-time $926; part-time $51 per credit; part-time $463 per term.

Financial Aid 57% of graduate students in nursing programs received some form of financial aid in 2008–09. *Application deadline:* 3/1.

Contact Dr. Mary Zwygart-Stauffacher, Interim Dean, College of Nursing and Health Sciences, University of Wisconsin–Eau Claire, 105 Garfield Avenue, Eau Claire, WI 54702-4004. *Telephone:* 715-836-5287. *Fax:* 715-836-5925. *E-mail:* zwygarmc@uwec.edu.

University of Wisconsin–Eau Claire (continued)

MASTER'S DEGREE PROGRAM

Degree MSN

Available Programs Master's; RN to Master's.

Concentrations Available Nursing administration; nursing education. *Clinical nurse specialist programs in:* adult health. *Nurse practitioner programs in:* adult health, family health.

Site Options Marshfield, WI.

Study Options Full-time and part-time.

Program Entrance Requirements Clinical experience, minimum overall college GPA of 3.0, transcript of college record, CPR certification, written essay, immunizations, 3 letters of recommendation, physical assessment course, professional liability insurance/malpractice insurance, statistics course, GRE. *Application deadline:* 7/1 (fall), 12/1 (spring). Applications may be processed on a rolling basis for some programs. *Application fee:* $56.

Advanced Placement Credit given for nursing courses completed elsewhere dependent upon specific evaluations.

Degree Requirements 42 total credit hours.

CONTINUING EDUCATION PROGRAM

Contact Ms. Peggy Ore, Program Manager, Nursing and Health Sciences, College of Nursing and Health Sciences, University of Wisconsin–Eau Claire, Continuing Education Department, Eau Claire, WI 54702-4004. *Telephone:* 715-836-5645. *Fax:* 715-836-5263. *E-mail:* orepd@uwec.edu.

University of Wisconsin–Green Bay

BSN–LINC Online RN–BSN Program
Green Bay, Wisconsin

http://www.bsnlinc.wisconsin.edu/

Founded in 1968

DEGREE • BSN

Nursing Program Faculty 7 (71% with doctorates).

Baccalaureate Enrollment 256
Women 89% **Men** 11% **Minority** 5% **International** 1% **Part-time** 96%

Distance Learning Courses Available.

Nursing Student Activities Sigma Theta Tau, Student Nurses' Association.

Nursing Student Resources Academic advising; academic or career counseling; assistance for students with disabilities; bookstore; campus computer network; career placement assistance; computer lab; computer-assisted instruction; e-mail services; employment services for current students; Internet; learning resource lab; library services; nursing audiovisuals; resume preparation assistance; skills, simulation, or other laboratory.

Library Facilities 360,795 volumes (1,000 in health, 675 in nursing); 4,452 periodical subscriptions (100 health-care related).

BACCALAUREATE PROGRAMS

Degree BSN

Available Programs RN Baccalaureate.

Site Options Marinette, WI; Rhinelander, WI.

Study Options Full-time and part-time.

Online Degree Options Yes.

Program Entrance Requirements Minimum overall college GPA of 2.5, transcript of college record, RN licensure. Transfer students are accepted. *Application fee:* $44.

Financial Aid 25% of baccalaureate students in nursing programs received some form of financial aid in 2008–09. *Gift aid (need-based):* Federal Pell, FSEOG, state, private, college/university gift aid from institutional funds. *Loans:* FFEL (Subsidized and Unsubsidized Stafford PLUS), Perkins. *Work-study:* Federal Work-Study, part-time campus jobs. *Financial aid application deadline (priority):* 4/15.

Contact Ms. Sharon Gajeski, Advisor, BSN–LINC Online RN–BSN Program, University of Wisconsin–Green Bay, 2420 Nicolet Drive, Green Bay, WI 54311-7001. *Telephone:* 920-465-2570. *Fax:* 920-465-2854. *E-mail:* gajeskis@uwgb.edu.

University of Wisconsin–Madison

School of Nursing
Madison, Wisconsin

http://www.son.wisc.edu

Founded in 1848

DEGREES • BS • DNP • PHD

Nursing Program Faculty 55 (35% with doctorates).

Baccalaureate Enrollment 384
Women 87% **Men** 13% **Minority** 11% **International** 2% **Part-time** 20%

Graduate Enrollment 206
Women 95% **Men** 5% **Minority** 7% **International** 4% **Part-time** 70%

Distance Learning Courses Available.

Nursing Student Activities Nursing Honor Society, Sigma Theta Tau, Student Nurses' Association, nursing club.

Nursing Student Resources Academic advising; academic or career counseling; assistance for students with disabilities; bookstore; campus computer network; computer lab; computer-assisted instruction; e-mail services; externships; interactive nursing skills videos; Internet; learning resource lab; library services; nursing audiovisuals; resume preparation assistance; skills, simulation, or other laboratory; tutoring.

Library Facilities 334,000 volumes in health, 8,300 volumes in nursing; 1,500 periodical subscriptions health-care related.

BACCALAUREATE PROGRAMS

Degree BS

Available Programs Generic Baccalaureate; RN Baccalaureate.

Site Options La Crosse, WI.

Study Options Full-time.

Program Entrance Requirements Minimum overall college GPA of 2.75, transcript of college record, CPR certification, written essay, high school chemistry, high school foreign language, 3 years high school math, 3 years high school science, high school transcript, immunizations, minimum GPA in nursing prerequisites of 2.75, prerequisite course work. Transfer students are accepted. *Application deadline:* 2/1 (fall). *Application fee:* $44.

Advanced Placement Credit by examination available. Credit given for nursing courses completed elsewhere dependent upon specific evaluations.

Expenses (2009–10) *Tuition, area resident:* full-time $8312; part-time $348 per credit. *Tuition, nonresident:* full-time $23,063; part-time $963 per credit. *Required fees:* full-time $1018; part-time $44 per credit; part-time $509 per term.

Financial Aid 65% of baccalaureate students in nursing programs received some form of financial aid in 2008–09.

Contact Nursing Admissions, School of Nursing, University of Wisconsin–Madison, 600 Highland Avenue, Room K6/146, Madison, WI 53792-2455. *Telephone:* 608-263-5202. *Fax:* 608-263-5296. *E-mail:* ugadmit@son.wisc.edu.

GRADUATE PROGRAMS

Expenses (2009–10) *Tuition, area resident:* full-time $10,516; part-time $659 per credit. *Tuition, nonresident:* full-time $25,072; part-time $1569 per credit. *Required fees:* full-time $1018; part-time $65 per credit; part-time $509 per term.

Financial Aid 55% of graduate students in nursing programs received some form of financial aid in 2008–09. 11 fellowships with full tuition reimbursements available (averaging $22,000 per year), 9 research assistantships with full tuition reimbursements available (averaging $20,000 per year), 8 teaching assistantships with full tuition reimbursements available (averaging $14,000 per year) were awarded; career-related internships or fieldwork, Federal Work-Study, institutionally sponsored loans, scholarships, traineeships, and unspecified assistantships also available. Aid available to part-time students. *Financial aid application deadline:* 6/1.

Contact Ms. Marcia Voss, Graduate Program Coordinator, School of Nursing, University of Wisconsin–Madison, 600 Highland Avenue, K6/140, Clinical Science Center, Madison, WI 53792-2455. *Telephone:* 608-263-5258. *Fax:* 608-263-5296. *E-mail:* mlvoss@wisc.edu.

DOCTORAL DEGREE PROGRAM

Degree DNP, PhD

Available Programs Doctorate; Post-Baccalaureate Doctorate.

Areas of Study Aging, bio-behavioral research, biology of health and illness, community health, faculty preparation, family health, gerontology, health policy, health promotion/disease prevention, human health and illness, information systems, nursing education, nursing research, oncology, women's health.

Program Entrance Requirements Minimum overall college GPA of 3.0, interview, 3 letters of recommendation, scholarly papers, vita, writing sample, GRE General Test. Application deadline: 1/15 (fall), 9/15 (spring). Application fee: $56.

Degree Requirements 60 total credit hours, dissertation, written exam, residency.

POSTDOCTORAL PROGRAM

Areas of Study Adolescent health, aging, cancer care, chronic illness, community health, family health, gerontology, health promotion/disease prevention, individualized study, nursing informatics, nursing interventions, nursing research, vulnerable population, women's health.

Postdoctoral Program Contact Carol Aspinwall, School of Nursing, University of Wisconsin–Madison, 600 Highland Avenue, Room K6/133, Madison, WI 53792-2455. *Telephone:* 608-263-9109. *Fax:* 608-263-5296. *E-mail:* caaspinwall@wisc.edu.

CONTINUING EDUCATION PROGRAM

Contact Ms. LeaRae Galarowicz, Clinical Professor, School of Nursing, University of Wisconsin–Madison, 600 Highland Avenue, H6/158, Clinical Science Center, Madison, WI 53792-2455. *Telephone:* 608-263-5336. *Fax:* 608-263-5332. *E-mail:* lbgalaro@facstaff.wisc.edu.

See full description on page 532.

University of Wisconsin–Milwaukee

College of Nursing
Milwaukee, Wisconsin

http://www.nursing.uwm.edu

Founded in 1956

DEGREES • BSN • MS • MS/MBA • PHD

Nursing Program Faculty 34 (100% with doctorates).

Baccalaureate Enrollment 1,172
Women 86% **Men** 14% **Minority** 17% **International** 1% **Part-time** 28%

Graduate Enrollment 310
Women 89% **Men** 11% **Minority** 14% **International** 1% **Part-time** 73%

Distance Learning Courses Available.

Nursing Student Activities Sigma Theta Tau, Student Nurses' Association.

Nursing Student Resources Academic advising; academic or career counseling; campus computer network; computer lab; computer-assisted instruction; e-mail services; interactive nursing skills videos; Internet; learning resource lab; library services; nursing audiovisuals; remedial services; skills, simulation, or other laboratory; tutoring.

Library Facilities 1.4 million volumes (330,089 in health, 179,089 in nursing); 8,240 periodical subscriptions (926 health-care related).

■ The University of Wisconsin–Milwaukee is a Carnegie Foundation–ranked Research Institution. The College of Nursing is nationally recognized for its faculty, programs, and alumni. Students are prepared as nurse leaders at the baccalaureate, master's, and doctoral levels for multiple roles in health care. Faculty members and students are involved in education, research, and service in more than 130 health-care settings. The College supports the Harriet H. Werley Center for Nursing Research and Evaluation, the Center for Cultural Diversity and Health, the Center for Nursing History, and the Nursing Learning Resource Center. The College also has two community nursing centers within its Institute for Urban Health Partnerships, which provides national and international leadership in health promotion and primary health care.

BACCALAUREATE PROGRAMS

Degree BSN

Available Programs Generic Baccalaureate; RN Baccalaureate.

Site Options Kenosha, WI; West Bend, WI.

Study Options Full-time and part-time.

Program Entrance Requirements Minimum overall college GPA of 2.5, transcript of college record, written essay, high school biology, high school chemistry, high school foreign language, 3 years high school math, 3 years high school science, high school transcript, minimum high school GPA of 2.0, minimum GPA in nursing prerequisites of 2.5, prerequisite course work. Transfer students are accepted. *Application deadline:* 1/15 (fall), 8/15 (spring).

Advanced Placement Credit given for nursing courses completed elsewhere dependent upon specific evaluations.

Expenses (2009–10) *Tuition, state resident:* full-time $7937; part-time $331 per credit. *Tuition, nonresident:* full-time $17,957; part-time $748 per credit. *International tuition:* $17,957 full-time. *Room and board:* $6437; room only: $3955 per academic year. *Required fees:* full-time $816; part-time $408 per term.

Financial Aid 70% of baccalaureate students in nursing programs received some form of financial aid in 2008–09. *Gift aid (need-based):* Federal Pell, FSEOG, state, private, college/university gift aid from institutional funds, Federal Nursing. *Loans:* Federal Nursing Student Loans, FFEL (Subsidized and Unsubsidized Stafford PLUS), Perkins, state, alternative loans. *Work-study:* Federal Work-Study. *Financial aid application deadline (priority):* 3/1.

Contact Ms. Donna Wier, Senior Advisor, College of Nursing, University of Wisconsin–Milwaukee, PO Box 413, Student Affairs, Milwaukee, WI 53201. *Telephone:* 414-229-5481. *Fax:* 414-229-5554. *E-mail:* ddw@uwm. edu.

GRADUATE PROGRAMS

Expenses (2009–10) *Tuition, state resident:* full-time $10,302; part-time $644 per credit. *Tuition, nonresident:* full-time $24,378; part-time $1524 per credit. *International tuition:* $24,378 full-time. *Room and board:* $6685; room only: $4202 per academic year. *Required fees:* full-time $816; part-time $408 per term.

Financial Aid 69% of graduate students in nursing programs received some form of financial aid in 2008–09. 10 teaching assistantships were awarded; career-related internships or fieldwork, Federal Work-Study, and unspecified assistantships also available. Aid available to part-time students. *Financial aid application deadline:* 4/15.

Contact Ms. Robin Jens, Director, Student Services, College of Nursing, University of Wisconsin–Milwaukee, PO Box 413, Student Affairs, Milwaukee, WI 53201. *Telephone:* 414-229-2494. *Fax:* 414-229-5554. *E-mail:* rjens@uwm.edu.

MASTER'S DEGREE PROGRAM

Degrees MS; MS/MBA

Available Programs Accelerated Master's for Nurses with Non-Nursing Degrees; Master's; RN to Master's.

Concentrations Available Health-care administration; nursing education. *Clinical nurse specialist programs in:* adult health, community health, parent-child, psychiatric/mental health, women's health. *Nurse practitioner programs in:* family health.

Site Options Kenosha, WI.

Study Options Full-time and part-time.

University of Wisconsin–Milwaukee (continued)

Program Entrance Requirements Minimum overall college GPA of 2.75, transcript of college record, written essay, interview, 3 letters of recommendation, prerequisite course work, statistics course, GRE General Test or MAT. *Application deadline:* 1/1 (fall), 9/1 (spring). *Application fee:* $56.

Advanced Placement Credit given for nursing courses completed elsewhere dependent upon specific evaluations.

Degree Requirements 46 total credit hours, thesis or project.

POST-MASTER'S PROGRAM

Areas of Study *Nurse practitioner programs in:* family health.

DOCTORAL DEGREE PROGRAM

Degree PhD

Available Programs Doctorate; Post-Baccalaureate Doctorate.

Areas of Study Individualized study, nursing research.

Online Degree Options Yes.

Program Entrance Requirements Minimum overall college GPA of 3.2, interview, 3 letters of recommendation, MSN or equivalent, scholarly papers, vita, writing sample, GRE. Application deadline: 1/1 (fall), 9/1 (spring), 11/1 (summer). Application fee: $56.

Degree Requirements 49 total credit hours, dissertation, oral exam, written exam.

University of Wisconsin–Oshkosh
College of Nursing
Oshkosh, Wisconsin

http://www.uwosh.edu/con

Founded in 1871

DEGREES • BSN • MSN

Nursing Program Faculty 69 (17% with doctorates).

Baccalaureate Enrollment 1,212
Women 91% **Men** 9% **Minority** 7% **Part-time** 14%

Graduate Enrollment 85
Women 91% **Men** 9% **Minority** 2% **Part-time** 81%

Distance Learning Courses Available.

Nursing Student Activities Sigma Theta Tau, Student Nurses' Association, nursing club.

Nursing Student Resources Academic advising; academic or career counseling; assistance for students with disabilities; bookstore; campus computer network; career placement assistance; computer lab; computer-assisted instruction; daycare for children of students; e-mail services; employment services for current students; externships; housing assistance; interactive nursing skills videos; Internet; learning resource lab; library services; nursing audiovisuals; other; paid internships; placement services for program completers; remedial services; resume preparation assistance; skills, simulation, or other laboratory; tutoring; unpaid internships.

Library Facilities 446,774 volumes; 5,219 periodical subscriptions.

BACCALAUREATE PROGRAMS

Degree BSN

Available Programs Accelerated Baccalaureate; Accelerated Baccalaureate for Second Degree; Accelerated RN Baccalaureate; Baccalaureate for Second Degree; Generic Baccalaureate; RN Baccalaureate.

Site Options Sheboygan, WI; Manitowoc, WI; Wausau, WI.

Study Options Full-time and part-time.

Online Degree Options Yes.

Program Entrance Requirements Minimum overall college GPA of 2.75, transcript of college record, CPR certification, written essay, health exam, 3 years high school math, 3 years high school science, immunizations, interview, minimum high school rank 50%, minimum GPA in nursing prerequisites of 2.75, prerequisite course work. Transfer students are accepted. *Application deadline:* 1/30 (fall), 8/30 (spring).

Advanced Placement Credit by examination available. Credit given for nursing courses completed elsewhere dependent upon specific evaluations.

Financial Aid *Gift aid (need-based):* Federal Pell, FSEOG, state, private, college/university gift aid from institutional funds, Federal Nursing. *Loans:* Federal Nursing Student Loans, FFEL (Subsidized and Unsubsidized Stafford PLUS), Perkins, state, college/university. *Work-study:* Federal Work-Study, part-time campus jobs. *Financial aid application deadline (priority):* 3/15.

Contact Dr. Suzanne Marnocha, RN, Undergraduate Program Director, College of Nursing, University of Wisconsin–Oshkosh, 800 Algoma Boulevard, Oshkosh, WI 54901-8660. *Telephone:* 920-424-1028. *Fax:* 920-424-0123. *E-mail:* marnocha@uwosh.edu.

GRADUATE PROGRAMS

Expenses (2008–09) *Tuition, state resident:* full-time $9288; part-time $404 per credit. *Tuition, nonresident:* part-time $979 per credit. *International tuition:* $22,507 full-time. *Room and board:* $7764; room only: $5164 per academic year.

Financial Aid 40% of graduate students in nursing programs received some form of financial aid in 2007–08. Fellowships, research assistantships with partial tuition reimbursements available, institutionally sponsored loans, scholarships, traineeships, tuition waivers (partial), and unspecified assistantships available. *Financial aid application deadline:* 3/15.

Contact Dr. Roxana Huebscher, Graduate Program Director, College of Nursing, University of Wisconsin–Oshkosh, 800 Algoma Boulevard, Oshkosh, WI 54901-8660. *Telephone:* 920-424-2106. *Fax:* 920-424-0123. *E-mail:* congrad@uwosh.edu.

MASTER'S DEGREE PROGRAM

Degree MSN

Available Programs Master's.

Concentrations Available Clinical nurse leader; nursing education. *Nurse practitioner programs in:* adult health, family health.

Study Options Full-time and part-time.

Program Entrance Requirements Computer literacy, minimum overall college GPA of 3.0, transcript of college record, CPR certification, written essay, immunizations, interview, 3 letters of recommendation, physical assessment course, prerequisite course work, resume, statistics course. *Application deadline:* 4/1 (fall). *Application fee:* $56.

Advanced Placement Credit given for nursing courses completed elsewhere dependent upon specific evaluations.

Degree Requirements 48 total credit hours, thesis or project.

POST-MASTER'S PROGRAM

Areas of Study Nursing education. *Nurse practitioner programs in:* adult health, family health.

CONTINUING EDUCATION PROGRAM

Contact Ms. Billie Gauthier, Director, Continuing Education and Extension, College of Nursing, University of Wisconsin–Oshkosh, 800 Algoma Boulevard, Oshkosh, WI 54901-8660. *Telephone:* 920-424-1129. *Fax:* 920-424-1803. *E-mail:* gauthier@uwosh.edu.

Viterbo University
School of Nursing
La Crosse, Wisconsin

http://www.viterbo.edu

Founded in 1890

DEGREES • BSN • MSN

Nursing Program Faculty 32 (8% with doctorates).

Baccalaureate Enrollment 674
Women 94% **Men** 6% **Minority** 3% **International** 1% **Part-time** 5%

Graduate Enrollment 54
Women 99% **Men** 1% **Minority** 1% **Part-time** 15%

Nursing Student Activities Sigma Theta Tau, Student Nurses' Association.

Nursing Student Resources Academic advising; academic or career counseling; assistance for students with disabilities; bookstore; campus computer network; career placement assistance; computer lab; computer-assisted instruction; e-mail services; interactive nursing skills videos;

Internet; learning resource lab; library services; nursing audiovisuals; remedial services; resume preparation assistance; skills, simulation, or other laboratory; tutoring.

Library Facilities 88,377 volumes (5,200 in health, 3,398 in nursing); 24,452 periodical subscriptions (312 health-care related).

BACCALAUREATE PROGRAMS

Degree BSN

Available Programs Generic Baccalaureate; RN Baccalaureate.

Site Options Madison, WI; Janesville, WI; Rochester, MN.

Study Options Full-time and part-time.

Program Entrance Requirements Minimum overall college GPA of 2.75, transcript of college record, CPR certification, health exam, high school chemistry, 2 years high school math, 2 years high school science, high school transcript, immunizations, minimum high school GPA of 3.0, minimum GPA in nursing prerequisites of 2.75, prerequisite course work. Transfer students are accepted. *Application deadline:* Applications may be processed on a rolling basis for some programs. *Application fee:* $25.

Advanced Placement Credit given for nursing courses completed elsewhere dependent upon specific evaluations.

Expenses (2009–10) *Tuition:* full-time $19,670. *Room and board:* $3830 per academic year. *Required fees:* full-time $245.

Financial Aid 88% of baccalaureate students in nursing programs received some form of financial aid in 2008–09.

Contact Dr. Roland Nelson, Director of Admission, School of Nursing, Viterbo University, 900 Viterbo Drive, La Crosse, WI 54601. *Telephone:* 608-796-3010. *Fax:* 608-796-3050. *E-mail:* adm.buzz@viterbo.edu.

GRADUATE PROGRAMS

Expenses (2009–10) *Tuition:* part-time $605 per credit.

Financial Aid 33% of graduate students in nursing programs received some form of financial aid in 2008–09.

Contact Dr. Bonnie Nesbitt, Director, School of Nursing, Viterbo University, 900 Viterbo Drive, La Crosse, WI 54601. *Telephone:* 608-796-3688. *Fax:* 608-796-3668. *E-mail:* bjnesbitt@viterbo.edu.

MASTER'S DEGREE PROGRAM

Degree MSN

Available Programs Master's.

Concentrations Available Nursing education. *Nurse practitioner programs in:* adult health, family health.

Study Options Full-time and part-time.

Program Entrance Requirements Clinical experience, computer literacy, minimum overall college GPA of 3.0, transcript of college record, CPR certification, written essay, immunizations, interview, 3 letters of recommendation, nursing research course, physical assessment course, resume, statistics course. *Application deadline:* 2/15 (fall). *Application fee:* $50.

Advanced Placement Credit given for nursing courses completed elsewhere dependent upon specific evaluations.

Degree Requirements 37 total credit hours, thesis or project.

POST-MASTER'S PROGRAM

Areas of Study Nursing education. *Nurse practitioner programs in:* adult health, family health.

CONTINUING EDUCATION PROGRAM

Contact Ms. Delayne Vogel, Continuing Education Coordinator, School of Nursing, Viterbo University, 900 Viterbo Drive, La Crosse, WI 54601. *Telephone:* 608-796-3686. *Fax:* 608-796-3668. *E-mail:* dgvogel@viterbo.edu.

Wisconsin Lutheran College
Nursing Program
Milwaukee, Wisconsin

Founded in 1973

DEGREE • BSN

Nursing Program Faculty 2

Baccalaureate Enrollment 14

Nursing Student Activities Student Nurses' Association.

Nursing Student Resources Academic advising; academic or career counseling; assistance for students with disabilities; bookstore; campus computer network; career placement assistance; computer lab; computer-assisted instruction; e-mail services; externships; housing assistance; interactive nursing skills videos; Internet; learning resource lab; library services; nursing audiovisuals; skills, simulation, or other laboratory; tutoring.

Library Facilities 78,107 volumes; 310 periodical subscriptions.

BACCALAUREATE PROGRAMS

Degree BSN

Available Programs Generic Baccalaureate.

Study Options Full-time.

Program Entrance Requirements Minimum overall college GPA of 2.75, transcript of college record, written essay, high school foreign language, interview, 3 letters of recommendation, minimum GPA in nursing prerequisites of 2.0, prerequisite course work. Transfer students are accepted. *Application deadline:* 3/15 (spring).

Expenses (2009–10) *Tuition:* full-time $27,000. *Room and board:* $10,000 per academic year.

Financial Aid 90% of baccalaureate students in nursing programs received some form of financial aid in 2008–09. *Gift aid (need-based):* Federal Pell, FSEOG, state, private, college/university gift aid from institutional funds. *Loans:* FFEL (Subsidized and Unsubsidized Stafford PLUS), private loans. *Work-study:* Federal Work-Study, part-time campus jobs. *Financial aid application deadline (priority):* 3/1.

Contact Admissions Office, Nursing Program, Wisconsin Lutheran College, 8800 West Bluemound Road, Milwaukee, WI 53226. *Telephone:* 414-443-8800.

CONTINUING EDUCATION PROGRAM

Contact School of Nursing, Nursing Program, Wisconsin Lutheran College, 8800 West Bluemound Road, Milwaukee, WI 53226. *Telephone:* 414-443-8800.

WYOMING

University of Wyoming
Fay W. Whitney School of Nursing
Laramie, Wyoming

http://www.uwyo.edu/nursing

Founded in 1886

DEGREES • BSN • MS

Nursing Program Faculty 33 (30% with doctorates).

Baccalaureate Enrollment 362
Women 90% **Men** 10% **Minority** 9% **International** 1% **Part-time** 58%

Graduate Enrollment 80
Women 89% **Men** 11% **Minority** 9% **Part-time** 69%

Distance Learning Courses Available.

Nursing Student Activities Sigma Theta Tau, Student Nurses' Association.

Nursing Student Resources Academic advising; academic or career counseling; assistance for students with disabilities; bookstore; campus computer network; career placement assistance; computer lab; computer-assisted instruction; e-mail services; employment services for current students; externships; housing assistance; interactive nursing skills videos; Internet; learning resource lab; library services; nursing audiovisuals; paid internships; remedial services; resume preparation assistance; skills, simulation, or other laboratory; tutoring; unpaid internships.

Library Facilities 1.4 million volumes (56,231 in health); 65,337 periodical subscriptions (1,689 health-care related).

University of Wyoming (continued)

BACCALAUREATE PROGRAMS

Degree BSN

Available Programs ADN to Baccalaureate; Accelerated Baccalaureate for Second Degree; Generic Baccalaureate.

Site Options Laramie, WY.

Study Options Full-time.

Online Degree Options Yes.

Program Entrance Requirements Transcript of college record, CPR certification, written essay, immunizations, 2 letters of recommendation, minimum GPA in nursing prerequisites of 2.75, professional liability insurance/malpractice insurance, prerequisite course work. Transfer students are accepted. *Application deadline:* 2/1 (fall). *Application fee:* $30.

Advanced Placement Credit given for nursing courses completed elsewhere dependent upon specific evaluations.

Expenses (2009–10) *Tuition, state resident:* part-time $94 per credit. *Tuition, nonresident:* part-time $358 per credit.

Contact Ms. Debbie A. Shoefelt, Credentials Analyst/Academic Advisor, Fay W. Whitney School of Nursing, University of Wyoming, Department 3065, 1000 East University Avenue, Laramie, WY 82071. *Telephone:* 307-766-4292. *Fax:* 307-766-4294. *E-mail:* basicbsn@uwyo.edu.

GRADUATE PROGRAMS

Expenses (2009–10) *Tuition, state resident:* part-time $183 per credit. *Tuition, nonresident:* part-time $523 per credit.

Financial Aid Research assistantships (averaging $10,062 per year), teaching assistantships (averaging $10,062 per year) were awarded; career-related internships or fieldwork, institutionally sponsored loans, scholarships, traineeships, and unspecified assistantships also available.

Contact Ms. Crystal McFadden, Office Associate, Fay W. Whitney School of Nursing, University of Wyoming, Department 3065, 1000 East University Avenue, Laramie, WY 82071. *Telephone:* 307-766-6568. *Fax:* 307-766-4294. *E-mail:* gradnurse@uwyo.edu.

MASTER'S DEGREE PROGRAM

Degree MS

Available Programs Master's; Master's for Nurses with Non-Nursing Degrees.

Concentrations Available Nursing education. *Nurse practitioner programs in:* family health, psychiatric/mental health.

Site Options Laramie, WY.

Study Options Full-time and part-time.

Online Degree Options Yes.

Program Entrance Requirements Minimum overall college GPA of 3.0, transcript of college record, CPR certification, written essay, immunizations, interview, 3 letters of recommendation, professional liability insurance/malpractice insurance, resume, statistics course, GRE General Test. *Application deadline:* 2/1 (fall). *Application fee:* $30.

Advanced Placement Credit given for nursing courses completed elsewhere dependent upon specific evaluations.

Degree Requirements 53 total credit hours, thesis or project.

POST-MASTER'S PROGRAM

Areas of Study Nursing education. *Nurse practitioner programs in:* family health, psychiatric/mental health.

CANADA

ALBERTA

Athabasca University
Centre for Nursing and Health Studies
Athabasca, Alberta

http://www.athabascau.ca/cnhs/

Founded in 1970

DEGREES • BN • MN • MN/MBA • MN/MHSA

Nursing Program Faculty 108 (43% with doctorates).

Baccalaureate Enrollment 3,335

Graduate Enrollment 1,226

Distance Learning Courses Available.

Nursing Student Activities Student Nurses' Association.

Nursing Student Resources Academic advising; academic or career counseling; assistance for students with disabilities; bookstore; campus computer network; computer lab; computer-assisted instruction; e-mail services; interactive nursing skills videos; Internet; library services; nursing audiovisuals; remedial services; skills, simulation, or other laboratory; tutoring.

Library Facilities 178,808 volumes; 32,619 periodical subscriptions.

BACCALAUREATE PROGRAMS

Degree BN

Available Programs Generic Baccalaureate; LPN to RN Baccalaureate; RN Baccalaureate.

Site Options Calgary, AB.

Study Options Full-time and part-time.

Program Entrance Requirements Minimum overall college GPA of 2.5, transcript of college record, CPR certification, high school biology, 3 years high school math, 3 years high school science, high school transcript, immunizations, minimum high school GPA of 2.0, minimum GPA in nursing prerequisites of 2.0, RN licensure. Transfer students are accepted. *Application deadline:* Applications may be processed on a rolling basis for some programs.

Advanced Placement Credit by examination available. Credit given for nursing courses completed elsewhere dependent upon specific evaluations.

Expenses (2009–10) *Tuition:* part-time CAN$639 per course. *International tuition:* CAN$1214 full-time.

Contact Gayle Deren-Purdy, Undergraduate Student Advisor, Centre for Nursing and Health Studies, Athabasca University, 1 University Drive, Athabasca, AB T9S 3A3. *Telephone:* 800-788-9041 Ext. 6446. *Fax:* 780-675-6468. *E-mail:* gayled@athabascau.ca.

GRADUATE PROGRAMS

Expenses (2009–10) *Tuition:* part-time CAN$1130 per course. *International tuition:* CAN$1330 full-time.

Contact Ms. Donna Dunn Hart, Graduate Student Advisor, Centre for Nursing and Health Studies, Athabasca University, 1 University Drive, Athabasca, AB T9S 3A3. *Telephone:* 800-788-9041 Ext. 6300. *Fax:* 780-675-6468. *E-mail:* donnad@athabascau.ca.

MASTER'S DEGREE PROGRAM

Degrees MN; MN/MBA; MN/MHSA

Available Programs Master's; Master's for Nurses with Non-Nursing Degrees.

Concentrations Available Nursing administration; nursing education. *Nurse practitioner programs in:* community health, family health, primary care.

Study Options Full-time and part-time.

Online Degree Options Yes.

Program Entrance Requirements Clinical experience, computer literacy, minimum overall college GPA of 3.0, transcript of college record, written essay, 3 letters of recommendation, resume. *Application deadline:* 3/1 (fall), 12/1 (spring). *Application fee:* CAN$200.

Advanced Placement Credit given for nursing courses completed elsewhere dependent upon specific evaluations.

Degree Requirements 33 total credit hours, thesis or project, comprehensive exam.

POST-MASTER'S PROGRAM

Areas of Study *Nurse practitioner programs in:* community health, family health.

University of Alberta
Faculty of Nursing
Edmonton, Alberta

Founded in 1906

DEGREES • BSCN • MN • PHD

Nursing Program Faculty 110 (50% with doctorates).

Baccalaureate Enrollment 1,600
Women 93% **Men** 7% **International** 1% **Part-time** 7%

Graduate Enrollment 221
Women 92% **Men** 8% **International** 11% **Part-time** 60%

Distance Learning Courses Available.

Nursing Student Activities Nursing Honor Society, Sigma Theta Tau, Student Nurses' Association.

Nursing Student Resources Academic advising; academic or career counseling; assistance for students with disabilities; bookstore; campus computer network; career placement assistance; computer lab; computer-assisted instruction; daycare for children of students; e-mail services; employment services for current students; housing assistance; interactive nursing skills videos; Internet; learning resource lab; library services; nursing audiovisuals; other; paid internships; remedial services; resume preparation assistance; skills, simulation, or other laboratory; tutoring; unpaid internships.

Library Facilities 9.7 million volumes (115,000 in health, 19,000 in nursing); 2,400 periodical subscriptions health-care related.

BACCALAUREATE PROGRAMS

Degree BScN

Available Programs Accelerated Baccalaureate for Second Degree; Generic Baccalaureate; RN Baccalaureate; RPN to Baccalaureate.

Site Options Red Deer, AB; Grande Prairie, AB; Fort McMurray, AB.

Study Options Full-time.

Program Entrance Requirements Minimum overall college GPA of 3.0, transcript of college record, CPR certification, health exam, high school biology, high school chemistry, 3 years high school math, 3 years high school science, high school transcript, immunizations, minimum high school GPA of 3.0, minimum high school rank 78%. Transfer students are accepted. *Application deadline:* 2/1 (fall). *Application fee:* CAN$115.

Advanced Placement Credit by examination available.

Expenses (2009–10) *Tuition, area resident:* full-time CAN$6800. *International tuition:* CAN$24,000 full-time. *Room and board:* CAN$8206; room only: CAN$4136 per academic year. *Required fees:* full-time CAN$1541.

Financial Aid 50% of baccalaureate students in nursing programs received some form of financial aid in 2008–09.

Contact Ms. Kristan Morin, Student Recruiter, Faculty of Nursing, University of Alberta, 2-143 Clinical Sciences Building, Edmonton, AB T6G 2G3. *Telephone:* 780-492-1242. *Fax:* 780-492-2551. *E-mail:* kristan.morin@ualberta.ca.

GRADUATE PROGRAMS

Expenses (2009–10) *Tuition, area resident:* full-time CAN$3588; part-time CAN$99 per credit. *International tuition:* CAN$7180 full-time. *Required fees:* full-time CAN$696; part-time CAN$216 per term.

Financial Aid 47% of graduate students in nursing programs received some form of financial aid in 2008–09. 12 fellowships with partial tuition reimbursements available (averaging $23,868 per year), 27 research assistantships with partial tuition reimbursements available (averaging $6,186 per year), 12 teaching assistantships with partial tuition reimbursements available (averaging $2,365 per year) were awarded; institutionally sponsored loans and scholarships also available.

Contact Barbara Dussault, Director, Graduate Services, Faculty of Nursing, University of Alberta, Clinical Sciences Building, 3rd Floor, Edmonton, AB T6G 2G3. *Telephone:* 780-492-3914. *Fax:* 780-492-2551. *E-mail:* barbara.dussault@ualberta.ca.

MASTER'S DEGREE PROGRAM

Degree MN

Available Programs Master's.

Concentrations Available *Nurse practitioner programs in:* adult health, gerontology, neonatal health, pediatric.

Study Options Full-time and part-time.

Program Entrance Requirements Clinical experience, computer literacy, minimum overall college GPA of 3.0, transcript of college record, CPR certification, 3 letters of recommendation, nursing research course, physical assessment course, resume, statistics course. *Application deadline:* 10/1 (fall).

Advanced Placement Credit given for nursing courses completed elsewhere dependent upon specific evaluations.

Degree Requirements 39 total credit hours, thesis or project.

POST-MASTER'S PROGRAM

Areas of Study *Nurse practitioner programs in:* adult health, gerontology, neonatal health, pediatric.

DOCTORAL DEGREE PROGRAM

Degree PhD

Available Programs Doctorate.

Areas of Study Aging, community health, ethics, family health, gerontology, health policy, health promotion/disease prevention, health-care systems, nursing education, nursing policy, nursing research.

Program Entrance Requirements Clinical experience, minimum overall college GPA of 3.0, 3 letters of recommendation, MSN or equivalent, scholarly papers, statistics course, vita, writing sample. Application deadline: 10/1 (fall).

Degree Requirements 36 total credit hours, dissertation, oral exam, written exam, residency.

POSTDOCTORAL PROGRAM

Postdoctoral Program Contact Dr. Phyllis Giovannetti, Associate Dean, Graduate Education, Faculty of Nursing, University of Alberta, Clinical Sciences Building, 3rd Floor, Edmonton, AB T6G 2G3. *Telephone:* 780-492-6764. *Fax:* 780-492-2551. *E-mail:* phyllis.giovannetti@ualberta.ca.

University of Calgary
Faculty of Nursing
Calgary, Alberta

http://www.ucalgary.ca/nu

Founded in 1945

DEGREES • BN • MN • PHD

Nursing Program Faculty 50 (85% with doctorates).

Baccalaureate Enrollment 930
Women 90% **Men** 10% **Minority** 5% **International** 1%

University of Calgary (continued)

Graduate Enrollment 110

Women 95% **Men** 5% **Minority** 1% **International** 1% **Part-time** 21%

Nursing Student Activities Student Nurses' Association.

Nursing Student Resources Academic advising; academic or career counseling; assistance for students with disabilities; bookstore; campus computer network; career placement assistance; computer lab; computer-assisted instruction; daycare for children of students; e-mail services; externships; housing assistance; interactive nursing skills videos; Internet; learning resource lab; library services; nursing audiovisuals; remedial services; resume preparation assistance; skills, simulation, or other laboratory; tutoring.

Library Facilities 3.3 million volumes; 37,285 periodical subscriptions.

BACCALAUREATE PROGRAMS

Degree BN

Available Programs Accelerated Baccalaureate; Accelerated Baccalaureate for Second Degree; Baccalaureate for Second Degree; Generic Baccalaureate; RN Baccalaureate.

Site Options Medicine Hat, AB.

Study Options Full-time.

Program Entrance Requirements Minimum overall college GPA of 3.3, transcript of college record, CPR certification, health exam, high school biology, high school chemistry, 3 years high school math, high school transcript, immunizations, minimum high school rank 78%. Transfer students are accepted.

Advanced Placement Credit by examination available. Credit given for nursing courses completed elsewhere dependent upon specific evaluations.

Contact *Telephone:* 403-220-4636. *Fax:* 403-284-4803.

GRADUATE PROGRAMS

Contact *Telephone:* 403-220-6241. *Fax:* 403-284-4803.

MASTER'S DEGREE PROGRAM

Degree MN

Available Programs Master's; RN to Master's.

Concentrations Available *Clinical nurse specialist programs in:* acute care, adult health, cardiovascular, community health, critical care, family health, gerontology, maternity-newborn, medical-surgical, parent-child, pediatric, perinatal, psychiatric/mental health, public health, rehabilitation, women's health. *Nurse practitioner programs in:* acute care, adult health, neonatal health.

Study Options Full-time and part-time.

Program Entrance Requirements Clinical experience, computer literacy, minimum overall college GPA of 3.0, transcript of college record, CPR certification, written essay, 3 letters of recommendation, nursing research course, statistics course.

Advanced Placement Credit given for nursing courses completed elsewhere dependent upon specific evaluations.

Degree Requirements 30 total credit hours, thesis or project, comprehensive exam.

POST-MASTER'S PROGRAM

Areas of Study *Nurse practitioner programs in:* acute care, adult health, neonatal health.

DOCTORAL DEGREE PROGRAM

Degree PhD

Available Programs Doctorate; Doctorate for Nurses with Non-Nursing Degrees.

Areas of Study Advanced practice nursing, aging, clinical practice, community health, critical care, ethics, family health, gerontology, health promotion/disease prevention, health-care systems, human health and illness, illness and transition, individualized study, maternity-newborn, neuro-behavior, nursing research, women's health.

Program Entrance Requirements Clinical experience, minimum overall college GPA of 3.0, 3 letters of recommendation, MSN or equivalent, scholarly papers, statistics course, vita, writing sample.

Degree Requirements Dissertation, oral exam, written exam.

University of Lethbridge
School of Health Sciences
Lethbridge, Alberta

http://home.uleth.ca/hlsc/

Founded in 1967

DEGREES • BN • M SC

Nursing Program Faculty 34 (15% with doctorates).

Baccalaureate Enrollment 599

Women 91% **Men** 9% **Part-time** 1%

Graduate Enrollment 21

Women 95% **Men** 5%

Nursing Student Activities Nursing club.

Nursing Student Resources Academic advising; academic or career counseling; assistance for students with disabilities; bookstore; campus computer network; computer lab; e-mail services; employment services for current students; housing assistance; interactive nursing skills videos; Internet; learning resource lab; library services; nursing audiovisuals; remedial services; resume preparation assistance; skills, simulation, or other laboratory; tutoring; unpaid internships.

Library Facilities 573,058 volumes (14,743 in health, 2,554 in nursing); 1,262 periodical subscriptions (11,168 health-care related).

BACCALAUREATE PROGRAMS

Degree BN

Available Programs Accelerated Baccalaureate for Second Degree; Accelerated RN Baccalaureate; Generic Baccalaureate; RN Baccalaureate.

Site Options Lethbridge, AB.

Study Options Full-time.

Program Entrance Requirements CPR certification, high school biology, high school chemistry, 3 years high school math, 3 years high school science, high school transcript, immunizations, minimum high school rank 70%. Transfer students are accepted. *Application deadline:* 3/1 (fall). *Application fee:* CAN$75.

Advanced Placement Credit given for nursing courses completed elsewhere dependent upon specific evaluations.

Financial Aid *Gift aid (need-based):* private, college/university gift aid from institutional funds. *Loans:* FFEL (Subsidized and Unsubsidized Stafford PLUS). *Financial aid application deadline:* Continuous.

Contact Mrs. Sherry Hogeweide, Academic Advisor, School of Health Sciences, University of Lethbridge, 4401 University Drive, Lethbridge, AB T1K 3M4. *Telephone:* 403-329-2220. *Fax:* 403-329-2668. *E-mail:* health.sciences@uleth.ca.

GRADUATE PROGRAMS

Contact Dr. David Gregory, Grad Studies Coordinator, School of Health Sciences, University of Lethbridge, 4401 University Drive, Lethbridge, AB T1K 3M4. *Telephone:* 403-329-2432. *Fax:* 403-329-2668. *E-mail:* health.sciences@uleth.ca.

MASTER'S DEGREE PROGRAM

Degree M Sc

Available Programs Master's.

Study Options Full-time and part-time.

Program Entrance Requirements Clinical experience, minimum overall college GPA of 3.0, transcript of college record, CPR certification, immunizations, interview. *Application deadline:* 3/1 (fall).

Advanced Placement Credit given for nursing courses completed elsewhere dependent upon specific evaluations.

Degree Requirements Thesis or project, comprehensive exam.

BRITISH COLUMBIA

British Columbia Institute of Technology
School of Health Sciences
Burnaby, British Columbia

http://www.health.bcit.ca/nursing/

Founded in 1964

DEGREE • BSN

Nursing Program Faculty 75 (.75% with doctorates).

Baccalaureate Enrollment 440
Women 90% **Men** 10%

Distance Learning Courses Available.

Nursing Student Activities Student Nurses' Association.

Nursing Student Resources Academic advising; academic or career counseling; assistance for students with disabilities; bookstore; campus computer network; computer lab; computer-assisted instruction; e-mail services; housing assistance; interactive nursing skills videos; Internet; learning resource lab; library services; nursing audiovisuals; resume preparation assistance; skills, simulation, or other laboratory; tutoring; unpaid internships.

Library Facilities 169,404 volumes (100 in health, 50 in nursing); 1,080 periodical subscriptions (100 health-care related).

BACCALAUREATE PROGRAMS

Degree BSN

Available Programs RN Baccalaureate; RPN to Baccalaureate.
Study Options Full-time.
Program Entrance Requirements Transcript of college record, CPR certification, written essay, high school biology, high school chemistry, 11 years high school math, 12 years high school science, high school transcript, immunizations, interview, 1 letter of recommendation, professional liability insurance/malpractice insurance, prerequisite course work. Transfer students are accepted. *Application deadline:* 1/31 (fall), 8/31 (winter). *Application fee:* CAN$60.
Advanced Placement Credit given for nursing courses completed elsewhere dependent upon specific evaluations.
Expenses (2009–10) *Tuition, area resident:* full-time CAN$5402. *Room and board:* room only: CAN$487 per academic year. *Required fees:* full-time CAN$237.
Financial Aid 70% of baccalaureate students in nursing programs received some form of financial aid in 2008–09. *Financial aid application deadline:* Continuous.
Contact Ms. Loreen Martin, Administrative Coordinator, School of Health Sciences, British Columbia Institute of Technology, 3700 Willingdon Avenue, SE12, Room 418, Burnaby, BC V5G 3H2. *Telephone:* 604-432-8884. *Fax:* 604-436-9590. *E-mail:* loreen_martin@bcit.ca.

CONTINUING EDUCATION PROGRAM

Contact Ms. Pauline O'Reilly, Program Head, School of Health Sciences, British Columbia Institute of Technology, 3700 Willingdon Avenue, SE12, Room 328, Burnaby, BC V5G 3H2. *Telephone:* 604-451-7115. *E-mail:* Pauline_O'Reilly@bcit.ca.

Kwantlen University College
Faculty of Community and Health Sciences
Surrey, British Columbia

http://www.kwantlen.ca

Founded in 1981

DEGREE • BSN

Nursing Program Faculty 60 (13% with doctorates).

Baccalaureate Enrollment 360
Women 90% **Men** 10% **Part-time** 13%

Nursing Student Activities Student Nurses' Association.

Nursing Student Resources Academic advising; academic or career counseling; assistance for students with disabilities; bookstore; campus computer network; career placement assistance; computer lab; computer-assisted instruction; e-mail services; employment services for current students; interactive nursing skills videos; Internet; learning resource lab; library services; nursing audiovisuals; remedial services; resume preparation assistance; skills, simulation, or other laboratory.

BACCALAUREATE PROGRAMS

Degree BSN

Available Programs Generic Baccalaureate; RN Baccalaureate.
Study Options Full-time.
Program Entrance Requirements CPR certification, health insurance, high school biology, high school chemistry, high school math, 2 years high school science, high school transcript, immunizations. Transfer students are accepted.
Advanced Placement Credit given for nursing courses completed elsewhere dependent upon specific evaluations.
Contact Ms. Theresa Abraniuk, Admissions Assistant, Faculty of Community and Health Sciences, Kwantlen University College, 12666 72nd Avenue, Surrey, BC V3W 2M8. *Telephone:* 604-599-2317. *E-mail:* theresa.abraniuk@kwantlen.ca.

Thompson Rivers University
School of Nursing
Kamloops, British Columbia

http://www.cariboo.bc.ca/nursing/index.html

Founded in 1970

DEGREE • BSN

Nursing Program Faculty 56

Library Facilities 273,900 volumes (7,326 in health, 2,275 in nursing); 13,709 periodical subscriptions (89 health-care related).

BACCALAUREATE PROGRAMS

Degree BSN

Study Options Full-time and part-time.
Program Entrance Requirements Minimum overall college GPA of 2.7, transcript of college record, CPR certification, health exam, high school biology, high school chemistry, high school foreign language, high school math, high school science, high school transcript, immunizations, interview, 2 letters of recommendation, minimum high school GPA of 2.3, minimum GPA in nursing prerequisites of 2.3. Transfer students are accepted.
Advanced Placement Credit given for nursing courses completed elsewhere dependent upon specific evaluations.
Contact *Telephone:* 250-828-5435. *Fax:* 250-828-5450.

CONTINUING EDUCATION PROGRAM

Contact *Telephone:* 250-828-5210. *Fax:* 250-371-5510.

Trinity Western University
Department of Nursing
Langley, British Columbia

Founded in 1962

DEGREE • BSCN

Nursing Program Faculty 9 (50% with doctorates).

Baccalaureate Enrollment 172
Women 91.9% **Men** 8.1% **Minority** 15.7% **International** 11.6%

Nursing Student Activities Student Nurses' Association.

Trinity Western University (continued)

Nursing Student Resources Academic advising; academic or career counseling; assistance for students with disabilities; bookstore; campus computer network; career placement assistance; computer lab; computer-assisted instruction; e-mail services; employment services for current students; housing assistance; interactive nursing skills videos; Internet; learning resource lab; library services; nursing audiovisuals; resume preparation assistance; skills, simulation, or other laboratory.

Library Facilities 190,565 volumes (2,500 in health, 800 in nursing); 11,000 periodical subscriptions (369 health-care related).

BACCALAUREATE PROGRAMS

Degree BScN

Available Programs Generic Baccalaureate.

Study Options Full-time.

Program Entrance Requirements Minimum overall college GPA of 2.0, CPR certification, health insurance, high school biology, high school chemistry, 1 year of high school math, 2 years high school science, high school transcript, immunizations, 2 letters of recommendation, minimum high school GPA of 2.7, minimum GPA in nursing prerequisites of 2.3. Transfer students are accepted. *Application deadline:* 2/28 (fall).

Advanced Placement Credit given for nursing courses completed elsewhere dependent upon specific evaluations.

Expenses (2008–09) *Tuition:* full-time CAN$17,460. *Room and board:* CAN$7380 per academic year.

Financial Aid 50% of baccalaureate students in nursing programs received some form of financial aid in 2007–08. *Gift aid (need-based):* private, college/university gift aid from institutional funds. *Loans:* FFEL (Subsidized and Unsubsidized Stafford PLUS), federal and provincial loans. *Financial aid application deadline (priority):* 2/28.

Contact Dr. Landa Terblanche, Director of Nursing, Department of Nursing, Trinity Western University, 7600 Glover Road, Langley, BC V2Y 1Y1. *Telephone:* 604-888-7511 Ext. 3268. *Fax:* 604-513-2018. *E-mail:* landa.terblanche@twu.ca.

The University of British Columbia

Program in Nursing
Vancouver, British Columbia

http://www.nursing.ubc.ca

Founded in 1915

DEGREES • BSN • MA/MSM • MSN • PHD

Nursing Program Faculty 48 (60% with doctorates).

Baccalaureate Enrollment 300

Graduate Enrollment 300

Nursing Student Activities Nursing Honor Society, Sigma Theta Tau, Student Nurses' Association.

Nursing Student Resources Academic advising; academic or career counseling; assistance for students with disabilities; bookstore; campus computer network; career placement assistance; computer lab; computer-assisted instruction; daycare for children of students; e-mail services; employment services for current students; housing assistance; interactive nursing skills videos; Internet; learning resource lab; library services; nursing audiovisuals; skills, simulation, or other laboratory.

Library Facilities 5.6 million volumes; 778,063 periodical subscriptions.

BACCALAUREATE PROGRAMS

Degree BSN

Available Programs Accelerated Baccalaureate; Accelerated Baccalaureate for Second Degree.

Study Options Full-time.

Program Entrance Requirements Minimum overall college GPA of 3.6, transcript of college record, CPR certification, written essay, health exam, health insurance, high school transcript, immunizations, interview, professional liability insurance/malpractice insurance, prerequisite course work.

Financial Aid *Gift aid (need-based):* private, college/university gift aid from institutional funds, provincial scholarships/grants, Federal Canada Study Grants. *Loans:* FFEL (Subsidized and Unsubsidized Stafford PLUS), college/university, Canadian student loans, provincial student loans. *Work-study:* part-time campus jobs. *Financial aid application deadline:* 9/15 (priority: 4/15).

Contact Nursing Programs, Program in Nursing, The University of British Columbia, T201-2211 Wesbrook Mall, Vancouver, BC V6T 2B5. *Telephone:* 604-822-7420. *Fax:* 604-822-7466. *E-mail:* information@nursing.ubc.ca.

GRADUATE PROGRAMS

Financial Aid 10% of graduate students in nursing programs received some form of financial aid in 2008–09. 4 fellowships (averaging $8,000 per year), 14 research assistantships (averaging $800 per year), 3 teaching assistantships were awarded.

Contact Peggy Faulkner, Graduate Records Officer, Program in Nursing, The University of British Columbia, T201-2211 Wesbrook Mall, Vancouver, BC V6T 2B5. *Telephone:* 604-822-7446. *Fax:* 604-822-7466. *E-mail:* gro@nursing.ubc.ca.

MASTER'S DEGREE PROGRAM

Degrees MA/MSM; MSN

Available Programs Master's.

Concentrations Available Nursing administration; nursing education. *Clinical nurse specialist programs in:* adult health, community health, family health, psychiatric/mental health, public health. *Nurse practitioner programs in:* family health, primary care.

Site Options Kamloops, BC.

Study Options Full-time and part-time.

Program Entrance Requirements Computer literacy, minimum overall college GPA of 3.3, transcript of college record, 3 letters of recommendation, resume, GRE.

Advanced Placement Credit given for nursing courses completed elsewhere dependent upon specific evaluations.

Degree Requirements 33 total credit hours, thesis or project.

DOCTORAL DEGREE PROGRAM

Degree PhD

Available Programs Doctorate.

Areas of Study Addiction/substance abuse, advanced practice nursing, aging, clinical practice, community health, ethics, faculty preparation, family health, gerontology, health policy, health promotion/disease prevention, health-care systems, human health and illness, illness and transition, individualized study, information systems, maternity-newborn, nursing administration, nursing education, nursing policy, nursing research, nursing science, oncology, urban health, women's health.

Program Entrance Requirements interview, 3 letters of recommendation, MSN or equivalent, vita, writing sample, GRE. Application deadline: 2/1 (fall).

Degree Requirements 18 total credit hours, dissertation, oral exam, written exam, residency.

POSTDOCTORAL PROGRAM

Areas of Study Addiction/substance abuse, adolescent health, aging, cancer care, chronic illness, community health, family health, gerontology, health promotion/disease prevention, individualized study, infection prevention/skin care, information systems, neuro-behavior, nursing informatics, nursing interventions, nursing research, nursing science, outcomes, self-care, vulnerable population, women's health.

Postdoctoral Program Contact Dr. Colleen Varcoe, Associate Director, Research, Program in Nursing, The University of British Columbia, T201-2211 Wesbrook Mall, Vancouver, BC V6T 2B5. *Telephone:* 604-827-3121. *Fax:* 604-822-7466. *E-mail:* Colleen.varcoe@nursing.ubc.ca.

University of Northern British Columbia

Nursing Programme
Prince George, British Columbia

http://www.unbc.ca/nursing/

Founded in 1994

DEGREES • BScN • M Sc N

Nursing Program Faculty 40 (18% with doctorates).

Baccalaureate Enrollment 600

Graduate Enrollment 60

Distance Learning Courses Available.

Nursing Student Activities Student Nurses' Association.

Nursing Student Resources Academic advising; academic or career counseling; assistance for students with disabilities; bookstore; campus computer network; computer lab; computer-assisted instruction; e-mail services; employment services for current students; externships; Internet; learning resource lab; library services; nursing audiovisuals; skills, simulation, or other laboratory.

Library Facilities 310,433 volumes (4,000 in health, 2,000 in nursing); 19,570 periodical subscriptions (300 health-care related).

BACCALAUREATE PROGRAMS

Degree BScN

Available Programs Generic Baccalaureate; RN Baccalaureate.

Site Options Prince George, BC; Quesnel, BC; Terrace, BC.

Study Options Full-time.

Program Entrance Requirements Minimum overall college GPA of 2.33, transcript of college record, CPR certification, health exam, high school biology, high school chemistry, 1 year of high school math, 4 years high school science, high school transcript, immunizations, minimum high school GPA of 2.3, minimum high school rank 65%, minimum GPA in nursing prerequisites of 2.0, professional liability insurance/malpractice insurance. Transfer students are accepted. *Application deadline:* 3/31 (fall). *Application fee:* CAN$35.

Advanced Placement Credit given for nursing courses completed elsewhere dependent upon specific evaluations.

Contact Mrs. Colleen Norish, Undergraduate Nursing Advisor, Nursing Programme, University of Northern British Columbia, 3333 University Way, Prince George, BC V2N 4Z9. *Telephone:* 250-960-5645. *E-mail:* norrisp@unbc.ca.

GRADUATE PROGRAMS

Contact Dr. Vincent L. Salyers, Chair, School of Nursing/Associate Professor, Nursing Programme, University of Northern British Columbia, 3333 University Way, Prince George, BC V2N 4Z9. *Telephone:* 250-960-5848. *Fax:* 250-960-6410. *E-mail:* salyers@unbc.ca.

MASTER'S DEGREE PROGRAM

Degree M Sc N

Available Programs Master's.

Concentrations Available *Nurse practitioner programs in:* family health.

Study Options Full-time and part-time.

Program Entrance Requirements Clinical experience, minimum overall college GPA of 3.0, transcript of college record, CPR certification, written essay, 3 letters of recommendation, nursing research course, professional liability insurance/malpractice insurance, prerequisite course work. *Application deadline:* 2/15 (fall). *Application fee:* CAN$75.

Advanced Placement Credit given for nursing courses completed elsewhere dependent upon specific evaluations.

Degree Requirements 51 total credit hours, thesis or project.

POSTDOCTORAL PROGRAM

Areas of Study Chronic illness, community health, family health, health promotion/disease prevention, individualized study, nursing interventions, nursing research, nursing science, outcomes, vulnerable population.

Postdoctoral Program Contact Dr. Martha MacLeod, Coordinator, Graduate Nursing Programs and Research, Nursing Programme, University of Northern British Columbia, 3333 University Way, Prince George, BC V2N 4Z9. *Telephone:* 250-960-6507. *Fax:* 250-960-6410. *E-mail:* macleod@unbc.ca.

University of Victoria
School of Nursing
Victoria, British Columbia

http://web.uvic.ca/nurs/

Founded in 1963

DEGREES • BSN • MN • PHD

Nursing Program Faculty 21 (95% with doctorates).

Baccalaureate Enrollment 1,100

Women 95% **Men** 5% **Part-time** 50%

Nursing Student Activities Student Nurses' Association.

Nursing Student Resources Academic advising; assistance for students with disabilities; bookstore; campus computer network; computer lab; e-mail services; employment services for current students; interactive nursing skills videos; Internet; library services; nursing audiovisuals; remedial services; resume preparation assistance; unpaid internships.

Library Facilities 1.8 million volumes; 14,000 periodical subscriptions.

BACCALAUREATE PROGRAMS

Degree BSN

Site Options Vancouver, BC.

Program Entrance Requirements Minimum overall college GPA of 3.5, transcript of college record, CPR certification, high school transcript, immunizations, prerequisite course work. Transfer students are accepted.

Contact *Telephone:* 250-721-7961. *Fax:* 250-721-6231.

GRADUATE PROGRAMS

Contact *Telephone:* 250-721-7961. *Fax:* 250-721-6231.

MASTER'S DEGREE PROGRAM

Degree MN

Available Programs Master's.

Site Options Victoria.

Study Options Full-time and part-time.

Program Entrance Requirements Clinical experience, transcript of college record, letters of recommendation.

Advanced Placement Credit given for nursing courses completed elsewhere dependent upon specific evaluations.

Degree Requirements 18 total credit hours, thesis or project.

DOCTORAL DEGREE PROGRAM

Degree PhD

Program Entrance Requirements Clinical experience, MSN or equivalent.

Degree Requirements Dissertation.

Vancouver Island University
Department of Nursing
Nanaimo, British Columbia

http://www.mala.bc.ca/www/discover/health/index.htm

Founded in 1969

DEGREE • BSCN

Nursing Program Faculty 42 (5% with doctorates).

Baccalaureate Enrollment 278

Women 98% **Men** 2% **Minority** 5.5%

Nursing Student Activities Student Nurses' Association.

Nursing Student Resources Academic advising; academic or career counseling; assistance for students with disabilities; bookstore; campus computer network; computer lab; computer-assisted instruction; daycare for children of students; e-mail services; employment services for current students; housing assistance; interactive nursing skills videos; Internet;

Vancouver Island University (continued)
learning resource lab; library services; nursing audiovisuals; remedial services; resume preparation assistance; skills, simulation, or other laboratory; tutoring; unpaid internships.

Library Facilities 9,475 volumes in health, 1,299 volumes in nursing; 800 periodical subscriptions health-care related.

BACCALAUREATE PROGRAMS

Degree BScN

Available Programs Generic Baccalaureate; RN Baccalaureate.

Study Options Full-time.

Program Entrance Requirements CPR certification, written essay, health insurance, high school biology, high school chemistry, 11 years high school math, high school transcript, immunizations, minimum GPA in nursing prerequisites of 3.0, prerequisite course work, RN licensure. Transfer students are accepted. *Application fee:* CAN$30.

Advanced Placement Credit given for nursing courses completed elsewhere dependent upon specific evaluations.

Expenses (2009–10) *Tuition, area resident:* full-time CAN$4800. *Room and board:* room only: CAN$3600 per academic year. *Required fees:* full-time CAN$400.

Financial Aid 65% of baccalaureate students in nursing programs received some form of financial aid in 2008–09. *Gift aid (need-based):* private, college/university gift aid from institutional funds. *Loans:* government student loans.

Contact Mrs. Madelene J. Heffel Ponting, RN, Chair of Bachelor of Science in Nursing Programs, Department of Nursing, Vancouver Island University, 900 Fifth Street, Nanaimo, BC V9R 5S5. *Telephone:* 250-740-6260. *Fax:* 250-740-6468. *E-mail:* Madelene.Heffelponting@viu.ca.

MANITOBA

Brandon University
School of Health Studies
Brandon, Manitoba

http://www.brandonu.ca/academic/health studies
Founded in 1899

DEGREE • BN

Nursing Program Faculty 20 (40% with doctorates).

Baccalaureate Enrollment 480
Women 95% **Men** 5% **Minority** 10% **Part-time** 25%

Distance Learning Courses Available.

Nursing Student Activities Nursing Honor Society, Sigma Theta Tau, Student Nurses' Association.

Nursing Student Resources Academic advising; academic or career counseling; assistance for students with disabilities; bookstore; campus computer network; career placement assistance; computer lab; computer-assisted instruction; e-mail services; employment services for current students; housing assistance; interactive nursing skills videos; Internet; library services; resume preparation assistance; skills, simulation, or other laboratory; tutoring.

Library Facilities 238,816 volumes; 1,699 periodical subscriptions.

BACCALAUREATE PROGRAMS

Degree BN

Available Programs Baccalaureate for Second Degree; Generic Baccalaureate; LPN to Baccalaureate; RN Baccalaureate.

Site Options Winnipeg, MB.

Study Options Full-time and part-time.

Program Entrance Requirements Minimum overall college GPA of 2.0, CPR certification, immunizations, minimum GPA in nursing prerequisites of 2.0, prerequisite course work. Transfer students are accepted. *Application deadline:* 5/1 (fall).

Advanced Placement Credit given for nursing courses completed elsewhere dependent upon specific evaluations.

Expenses (2009–10) *Tuition, area resident:* full-time CAN$3000. *Room and board:* CAN$3200 per academic year. *Required fees:* full-time CAN$3000.

Financial Aid 30% of baccalaureate students in nursing programs received some form of financial aid in 2008–09. *Gift aid (need-based):* college/university gift aid from institutional funds. *Loans:* provincial and federal student loans. *Financial aid application deadline (priority):* 6/30.

Contact Ms. Tracey Collyer, Instructional Associate/Student Advisor, School of Health Studies, Brandon University, 270 18th Street, Brandon, MB R7A 6A9. *Telephone:* 204-571-8567. *Fax:* 204-571-8568. *E-mail:* collyert@brandonu.ca.

University of Manitoba
Faculty of Nursing
Winnipeg, Manitoba

http://www.umanitoba.ca/faculties/nursing/
Founded in 1877

DEGREES • BN • MN • PHD

Nursing Program Faculty 51 (53% with doctorates).

Baccalaureate Enrollment 1,159
Women 88% **Men** 12% **Part-time** 29%

Graduate Enrollment 87
Women 92% **Men** 8% **Part-time** 61%

Distance Learning Courses Available.

Nursing Student Activities Nursing Honor Society, Sigma Theta Tau, Student Nurses' Association.

Nursing Student Resources Academic advising; academic or career counseling; assistance for students with disabilities; bookstore; campus computer network; computer lab; daycare for children of students; e-mail services; employment services for current students; housing assistance; interactive nursing skills videos; Internet; learning resource lab; library services; skills, simulation, or other laboratory; unpaid internships.

Library Facilities 1.6 million volumes (137,100 in health, 5,000 in nursing); 12,800 periodical subscriptions (2,208 health-care related).

BACCALAUREATE PROGRAMS

Degree BN

Available Programs Baccalaureate for Second Degree; Generic Baccalaureate; RN Baccalaureate.

Site Options The Pas, MB; Thompson, MB; Norway House, MB.

Study Options Full-time and part-time.

Program Entrance Requirements Minimum overall college GPA of 2.5, transcript of college record, CPR certification, high school chemistry, high school math, high school science, high school transcript, immunizations, minimum high school GPA of 2.5, prerequisite course work. Transfer students are accepted.

Advanced Placement Credit given for nursing courses completed elsewhere dependent upon specific evaluations.

Expenses (2009–10) *Tuition, state resident:* full-time CAN$3660; part-time CAN$122 per credit. *Tuition, nonresident:* full-time CAN$3660; part-time CAN$122 per credit.

Financial Aid *Gift aid (need-based):* state, private, college/university gift aid from institutional funds. *Loans:* Federal Direct (Subsidized and Unsubsidized Stafford PLUS), FFEL (Subsidized and Unsubsidized Stafford PLUS), Perkins, state, college/university, TERI Loans. *Work-study:* part-time campus jobs. *Financial aid application deadline (priority):* 10/1.

Contact Dr. Marion McKay, Associate Dean, Undergraduate Program, Faculty of Nursing, University of Manitoba, 277 Helen Glass Centre for Nursing, Winnipeg, MB R3T 2N2. *Telephone:* 204-474-6220. *Fax:* 204-474-7682. *E-mail:* marion_mckay@umanitoba.ca.

GRADUATE PROGRAMS

Expenses (2009–10) *Tuition, state resident:* full-time CAN$4177. *Tuition, nonresident:* full-time CAN$4177.

Contact Dr. Judith Scanlan, Associate Dean, Graduate Programs, Faculty of Nursing, University of Manitoba, 281-89 Curry Place, Winnipeg, MB R3T 2N2. *Telephone:* 204-474-9317. *Fax:* 204-474-7682. *E-mail:* judith_scanlan@ umanitoba.ca.

MASTER'S DEGREE PROGRAM

Degree MN

Available Programs Master's.

Concentrations Available Nursing administration. *Clinical nurse specialist programs in:* acute care, family health, gerontology, perinatal, women's health. *Nurse practitioner programs in:* primary care.

Study Options Full-time and part-time.

Program Entrance Requirements Clinical experience, minimum overall college GPA of 3.0, transcript of college record, written essay, 3 letters of recommendation, nursing research course, resume, statistics course.

Advanced Placement Credit given for nursing courses completed elsewhere dependent upon specific evaluations.

Degree Requirements 27 total credit hours, thesis or project, comprehensive exam.

DOCTORAL DEGREE PROGRAM

Degree PhD

Available Programs Doctorate.

Areas of Study Oncology.

Program Entrance Requirements Clinical experience, letters of recommendation, MSN or equivalent.

Degree Requirements 21 total credit hours, dissertation.

CONTINUING EDUCATION PROGRAM

Contact Dr. Dauna Crooks, Professor, Faculty of Nursing, University of Manitoba, 293 Helen Glass Centre for Nursing, Winnipeg, MB R3T 2N2. *Telephone:* 204-474-9201. *Fax:* 204-474-7500. *E-mail:* dauna_crooks@ umanitoba.ca.

NEW BRUNSWICK

Université de Moncton
School of Nursing
Moncton, New Brunswick

Founded in 1963

DEGREES • BSCN • M SC N

Nursing Program Faculty 24 (25% with doctorates).

Baccalaureate Enrollment 570
Women 90% **Men** 10% **International** 1%

Graduate Enrollment 8

Nursing Student Activities Student Nurses' Association.

Nursing Student Resources Academic or career counseling; assistance for students with disabilities; bookstore; campus computer network; career placement assistance; computer lab; computer-assisted instruction; daycare for children of students; e-mail services; externships; housing assistance; Internet; library services; nursing audiovisuals; placement services for program completers; resume preparation assistance; unpaid internships.

Library Facilities 789,046 volumes; 2,059 periodical subscriptions.

BACCALAUREATE PROGRAMS

Degree BScN

Available Programs RN Baccalaureate.

Site Options Moncton, NB; Edmundston, NB; Bathurst, NB.

Study Options Full-time and part-time.

Program Entrance Requirements Transcript of college record, CPR certification, high school biology, high school chemistry, 12 years high school math, high school science, high school transcript, immunizations, minimum high school rank 65%. Transfer students are accepted.

Advanced Placement Credit given for nursing courses completed elsewhere dependent upon specific evaluations.

Contact *Telephone:* 506-858-4443. *Fax:* 506-858-4544.

GRADUATE PROGRAMS

Contact *Telephone:* 506-858-4443. *Fax:* 506-858-4544.

MASTER'S DEGREE PROGRAM

Degree M Sc N

Available Programs Master's; RN to Master's.

Concentrations Available Health-care administration; nurse case management; nursing administration; nursing education. *Clinical nurse specialist programs in:* community health, family health, home health care, occupational health, pediatric, psychiatric/mental health, public health, school health. *Nurse practitioner programs in:* adult health, community health, family health, oncology, primary care.

Site Options Moncton, NB.

Study Options Full-time and part-time.

Program Entrance Requirements Minimum overall college GPA of 3.0, transcript of college record, CPR certification, written essay, 2 letters of recommendation, resume, statistics course.

Advanced Placement Credit given for nursing courses completed elsewhere dependent upon specific evaluations.

Degree Requirements 45 total credit hours, thesis or project.

CONTINUING EDUCATION PROGRAM

Contact *Telephone:* 506-858-4121.

University of New Brunswick Fredericton
Faculty of Nursing
Fredericton, New Brunswick

http://www.unbf.ca/nursing/

Founded in 1785

DEGREES • BN • MN

Nursing Program Faculty 75 (17% with doctorates).

Graduate Enrollment 51
Women 98% **Men** 2% **Part-time** 30%

Distance Learning Courses Available.

Nursing Student Activities Student Nurses' Association, nursing club.

Nursing Student Resources Academic advising; academic or career counseling; assistance for students with disabilities; bookstore; campus computer network; computer lab; computer-assisted instruction; daycare for children of students; e-mail services; interactive nursing skills videos; Internet; learning resource lab; library services; nursing audiovisuals; resume preparation assistance; skills, simulation, or other laboratory; tutoring.

Library Facilities 1.3 million volumes (12,547 in health, 1,910 in nursing); 22,564 periodical subscriptions (250 health-care related).

BACCALAUREATE PROGRAMS

Degree BN

Available Programs Accelerated Baccalaureate; Generic Baccalaureate.

Site Options Bathurst, NB; Moncton, NB.

Study Options Full-time.

Program Entrance Requirements Minimum overall college GPA of 3.0, transcript of college record, CPR certification, written essay, health exam, high school biology, high school chemistry, 60 years high school math, high school transcript, immunizations, interview, minimum high school rank 70%, prerequisite course work. Transfer students are accepted. *Application deadline:* 3/31 (winter). *Application fee:* CAN$45.

Advanced Placement Credit given for nursing courses completed elsewhere dependent upon specific evaluations.

University of New Brunswick Fredericton (continued)

Expenses (2009–10) *Tuition, area resident:* full-time CAN$5482; part-time CAN$548 per course. *International tuition:* CAN$11,912 full-time. *Room and board:* CAN$8159; room only: CAN$5051 per academic year. *Required fees:* part-time CAN$583 per credit.

Financial Aid 50% of baccalaureate students in nursing programs received some form of financial aid in 2008–09.

Contact Mr. Lee Heenan, Administrative Assistant, Faculty of Nursing, University of New Brunswick Fredericton, PO Box 4400, Fredericton, NB E3B 5A3. *Telephone:* 506-458-7670. *Fax:* 506-447-3374. *E-mail:* lheenan@unb.ca.

GRADUATE PROGRAMS

Expenses (2009–10) *Tuition, area resident:* full-time CAN$5482; part-time CAN$548 per course. *International tuition:* CAN$11,912 full-time. *Room and board:* CAN$8159; room only: CAN$5051 per academic year.

Financial Aid 10% of graduate students in nursing programs received some form of financial aid in 2008–09.

Contact Mr. Francis Perry, Graduate Assistant, Faculty of Nursing, University of New Brunswick Fredericton, PO Box 4400, Fredericton, NB E3B 5A3. *Telephone:* 506-451-6844. *Fax:* 506-447-3374. *E-mail:* fperry@unb.ca.

MASTER'S DEGREE PROGRAM

Degree MN

Available Programs Master's.

Concentrations Available Nurse case management; nursing administration; nursing education; nursing informatics. *Clinical nurse specialist programs in:* acute care, adult health, cardiovascular, community health, critical care, family health, gerontology, maternity-newborn, medical-surgical, oncology, parent-child, pediatric, psychiatric/mental health, public health, school health, women's health. *Nurse practitioner programs in:* acute care, adult health, community health, family health, gerontology, neonatal health, pediatric, primary care, psychiatric/mental health, women's health.

Study Options Full-time and part-time.

Program Entrance Requirements Clinical experience, computer literacy, minimum overall college GPA of 3.3, transcript of college record, written essay, 3 letters of recommendation, nursing research course, physical assessment course, prerequisite course work, statistics course. *Application deadline:* 1/2 (winter). *Application fee:* CAN$50.

Advanced Placement Credit given for nursing courses completed elsewhere dependent upon specific evaluations.

Degree Requirements 27 total credit hours, thesis or project.

CONTINUING EDUCATION PROGRAM

Contact Mr. Lee Heenan, Administrative Assistant, Faculty of Nursing, University of New Brunswick Fredericton, PO Box 4400, Fredericton, NB E3B 5A3. *Telephone:* 506-453-4642. *Fax:* 506-447-3057. *E-mail:* nursing@unb.ca.

NEWFOUNDLAND AND LABRADOR

Memorial University of Newfoundland

School of Nursing
St. John's, Newfoundland and Labrador

http://www.nurs.mun.ca

Founded in 1925

DEGREES • BN • MN

Nursing Program Faculty 42 (30% with doctorates).

Baccalaureate Enrollment 642
Women 92% **Men** 8% **International** 2% **Part-time** 50%

Graduate Enrollment 100
Women 91% **Men** 9% **International** 1% **Part-time** 82%

Nursing Student Activities Student Nurses' Association.

Nursing Student Resources Academic advising; academic or career counseling; assistance for students with disabilities; bookstore; campus computer network; computer lab; computer-assisted instruction; daycare for children of students; e-mail services; employment services for current students; externships; interactive nursing skills videos; Internet; learning resource lab; library services; nursing audiovisuals; remedial services; skills, simulation, or other laboratory; tutoring.

Library Facilities 1.7 million volumes (40,000 in health, 5,000 in nursing); 17,170 periodical subscriptions (3,800 health-care related).

BACCALAUREATE PROGRAMS

Degree BN

Available Programs Accelerated Baccalaureate for Second Degree; Generic Baccalaureate; LPN to Baccalaureate; RN Baccalaureate.

Study Options Full-time.

Online Degree Options Yes.

Program Entrance Requirements CPR certification, written essay, health exam, health insurance, high school biology, high school chemistry, high school math, high school science, high school transcript, immunizations, 2 letters of recommendation, minimum high school GPA. Transfer students are accepted. *Application deadline:* 3/1 (fall). *Application fee:* CAN$40.

Advanced Placement Credit given for nursing courses completed elsewhere dependent upon specific evaluations.

Expenses (2008–09) *Tuition, state resident:* full-time CAN$2890; part-time CAN$85 per credit hour. *Tuition, nonresident:* full-time CAN$2890; part-time CAN$85 per credit hour. *International tuition:* CAN$10,982 full-time. *Room and board:* CAN$5936; room only: CAN$2582 per academic year. *Required fees:* full-time CAN$200; part-time CAN$28 per term.

Financial Aid *Loans:* college/university. *Financial aid application deadline:* Continuous.

Contact Ms. Lena Clark, Consortium Coordinator, School of Nursing, Memorial University of Newfoundland, Registrar's Office, PO Box 4200, St. John's, NF A1C 5S7. *Telephone:* 709-737-6871. *Fax:* 709-737-3890. *E-mail:* nursingadmissions@mun.ca.

GRADUATE PROGRAMS

Expenses (2008–09) *Tuition, state resident:* full-time CAN$2199; part-time CAN$486 per semester. *Tuition, nonresident:* full-time CAN$2199; part-time CAN$486 per semester. *International tuition:* CAN$2859 full-time. *Room and board:* CAN$5936; room only: CAN$2582 per academic year. *Required fees:* full-time CAN$708.

Financial Aid 25% of graduate students in nursing programs received some form of financial aid in 2007–08. Fellowships, research assistantships, teaching assistantships available. *Financial aid application deadline:* 12/31.

Contact Dr. Shirley Solberg, Associate Director, Graduate Program and Research, School of Nursing, Memorial University of Newfoundland, 300 Prince Philip Drive, St. John's, NF A1B 3V6. *Telephone:* 709-777-6679. *Fax:* 709-777-7037. *E-mail:* ssolberg@mun.ca.

MASTER'S DEGREE PROGRAM

Degree MN

Available Programs Master's.

Concentrations Available *Clinical nurse specialist programs in:* acute care, adult health, community health, pediatric, psychiatric/mental health. *Nurse practitioner programs in:* acute care, psychiatric/mental health.

Study Options Full-time and part-time.

Online Degree Options Yes (online only).

Program Entrance Requirements Clinical experience, minimum overall college GPA of 3.0, transcript of college record, written essay, 3 letters of recommendation, nursing research course, professional liability insurance/malpractice insurance, resume, statistics course. *Application deadline:* 3/1 (fall). *Application fee:* CAN$40.

Advanced Placement Credit given for nursing courses completed elsewhere dependent upon specific evaluations.

Degree Requirements 34 total credit hours, thesis or project.

NOVA SCOTIA

Dalhousie University
School of Nursing
Halifax, Nova Scotia

http://www.dal.ca/nursing
Founded in 1818

DEGREES • BSCN • MN • MN/MHSA • PHD

Nursing Program Faculty 56 (31% with doctorates).

Baccalaureate Enrollment 518
Women 90% **Men** 10% **Minority** 18% **International** 3% **Part-time** 2%

Graduate Enrollment 109
Women 96% **Men** 4% **Minority** 4% **Part-time** 72%

Distance Learning Courses Available.

Nursing Student Activities Nursing Honor Society, Sigma Theta Tau, Student Nurses' Association.

Nursing Student Resources Academic advising; academic or career counseling; assistance for students with disabilities; bookstore; campus computer network; computer lab; computer-assisted instruction; daycare for children of students; e-mail services; employment services for current students; externships; housing assistance; interactive nursing skills videos; Internet; learning resource lab; library services; nursing audiovisuals; resume preparation assistance; skills, simulation, or other laboratory; tutoring.

Library Facilities 164 periodical subscriptions.

BACCALAUREATE PROGRAMS

Degree BScN

Available Programs Accelerated Baccalaureate; Accelerated Baccalaureate for Second Degree; Baccalaureate for Second Degree; Generic Baccalaureate; RN Baccalaureate.

Site Options Yarmouth, NS.

Study Options Full-time.

Program Entrance Requirements Minimum overall college GPA of 2.5, transcript of college record, high school biology, high school chemistry, 3 years high school math, high school transcript, immunizations, minimum high school rank 70%, minimum GPA in nursing prerequisites of 2.5, prerequisite course work. Transfer students are accepted.

Advanced Placement Credit given for nursing courses completed elsewhere dependent upon specific evaluations.

Contact *Telephone: 902-494-2004. Fax: 902-494-3487.*

GRADUATE PROGRAMS

Contact *Telephone: 902-494-2250. Fax: 902-494-3487.*

MASTER'S DEGREE PROGRAM

Degrees MN; MN/MHSA

Available Programs Master's.

Concentrations Available *Clinical nurse specialist programs in:* adult health, community health, family health, maternity-newborn, parent-child, pediatric, psychiatric/mental health, public health. *Nurse practitioner programs in:* adult health, family health, neonatal health, primary care.

Study Options Full-time and part-time.

Program Entrance Requirements Clinical experience, minimum overall college GPA of 3.0, transcript of college record, immunizations, interview, 3 letters of recommendation, nursing research course, prerequisite course work, statistics course.

Degree Requirements 36 total credit hours, thesis or project.

POST-MASTER'S PROGRAM

Areas of Study *Nurse practitioner programs in:* adult health, family health, neonatal health, primary care.

DOCTORAL DEGREE PROGRAM

Degree PhD

Available Programs Doctorate.

Areas of Study Advanced practice nursing, aging, community health, family health, health policy, health promotion/disease prevention, human health and illness, illness and transition, maternity-newborn, nursing policy, nursing research, nursing science, oncology, women's health.

Program Entrance Requirements Clinical experience, minimum overall college GPA of 3.3, interview, 3 letters of recommendation, MSN or equivalent, vita, writing sample.

Degree Requirements 27 total credit hours, dissertation, oral exam, written exam, residency.

St. Francis Xavier University
Department of Nursing
Antigonish, Nova Scotia

http://www.stfx.ca
Founded in 1853

DEGREE • BSCN

Nursing Program Faculty 67 (10% with doctorates).

Baccalaureate Enrollment 1,067
Women 90% **Men** 10% **Minority** 5% **International** 1% **Part-time** 40%

Nursing Student Activities Student Nurses' Association, nursing club.

Nursing Student Resources Academic advising; academic or career counseling; assistance for students with disabilities; bookstore; campus computer network; career placement assistance; computer lab; computer-assisted instruction; daycare for children of students; e-mail services; employment services for current students; externships; housing assistance; interactive nursing skills videos; Internet; learning resource lab; library services; nursing audiovisuals; other; paid internships; placement services for program completers; remedial services; resume preparation assistance; skills, simulation, or other laboratory; tutoring; unpaid internships.

Library Facilities 632,575 volumes (4,000 in health, 4,000 in nursing); 3,282 periodical subscriptions (1,015 health-care related).

BACCALAUREATE PROGRAMS

Degree BScN

Available Programs Accelerated Baccalaureate; Accelerated Baccalaureate for Second Degree; Accelerated LPN to Baccalaureate; Generic Baccalaureate; RN Baccalaureate.

Site Options Sydney, NS.

Study Options Full-time.

Program Entrance Requirements Transcript of college record, CPR certification, health exam, high school biology, high school chemistry, 2 years high school math, 2 years high school science, high school transcript, immunizations, minimum high school GPA, prerequisite course work. Transfer students are accepted.

Advanced Placement Credit given for nursing courses completed elsewhere dependent upon specific evaluations.

Contact *Telephone: 902-867-5386. Fax: 902-867-2329.*

CONTINUING EDUCATION PROGRAM

Contact *Telephone: 902-867-5186. Fax: 902-867-5154.*

ONTARIO

Brock University
Department of Nursing
St. Catharines, Ontario

http://www.brocku.ca/nursing/
Founded in 1964

Brock University (continued)
DEGREE • BSCN

Nursing Student Activities Student Nurses' Association, nursing club.

Nursing Student Resources Academic advising; academic or career counseling; assistance for students with disabilities; bookstore; campus computer network; computer lab; computer-assisted instruction; daycare for children of students; e-mail services; employment services for current students; housing assistance; interactive nursing skills videos; Internet; learning resource lab; library services; nursing audiovisuals; other; resume preparation assistance; skills, simulation, or other laboratory; tutoring.

Library Facilities 769,873 volumes.

BACCALAUREATE PROGRAMS

Degree BScN

Available Programs Generic Baccalaureate; RN Baccalaureate.
Study Options Full-time.
Program Entrance Requirements High school biology, high school chemistry.
Contact Dr. Linda Ritchie, RN, Chair and Assistant Professor, Department of Nursing, Brock University, 500 Glenridge Avenue, St. Catharines, ON L2S 3A1. *Telephone:* 905-688-5550 Ext. 4781. *E-mail:* lritchie@health.pec. brocku.ca.

Lakehead University
School of Nursing
Thunder Bay, Ontario

http://www.lakeheadu.ca
Founded in 1965
DEGREE • BSCN

Nursing Program Faculty 15 (20% with doctorates).
Baccalaureate Enrollment 575
Women 82% **Men** 18%

Distance Learning Courses Available.

Nursing Student Activities Student Nurses' Association.

Nursing Student Resources Academic advising; academic or career counseling; assistance for students with disabilities; bookstore; campus computer network; career placement assistance; computer lab; daycare for children of students; e-mail services; employment services for current students; externships; housing assistance; interactive nursing skills videos; Internet; library services; nursing audiovisuals; resume preparation assistance; skills, simulation, or other laboratory; tutoring; unpaid internships.

Library Facilities 613,047 volumes; 33,396 periodical subscriptions.

BACCALAUREATE PROGRAMS

Degree BScN

Available Programs Accelerated Baccalaureate; Generic Baccalaureate; RN Baccalaureate.
Study Options Full-time and part-time.
Online Degree Options Yes.
Program Entrance Requirements Transcript of college record, CPR certification, health insurance, high school biology, high school chemistry, 4 years high school math, high school transcript, immunizations, minimum high school GPA. Transfer students are accepted. *Application deadline:* 1/12 (winter). Applications may be processed on a rolling basis for some programs.
Advanced Placement Credit given for nursing courses completed elsewhere dependent upon specific evaluations.
Financial Aid *Loans:* college/university. *Work-study:* Federal Work-Study. *Financial aid application deadline:* 6/30.
Contact Prof. Karen Poole, Director, School of Nursing, Lakehead University, 955 Oliver Road, Thunder Bay, ON P7B 5E1. *Telephone:* 807-343-8439. *Fax:* 807-343-8246. *E-mail:* kpoole@lakeheadu.ca.

Laurentian University
School of Nursing
Sudbury, Ontario

Founded in 1960
DEGREE • BSCN

Nursing Program Faculty 20 (20% with doctorates).
Nursing Student Resources Internet.
Library Facilities 434,380 volumes; 37,122 periodical subscriptions.

BACCALAUREATE PROGRAMS

Degree BScN

Study Options Full-time and part-time.
Program Entrance Requirements CPR certification, health exam, high school biology, high school chemistry, high school transcript, immunizations, prerequisite course work. Transfer students are accepted.
Advanced Placement Credit given for nursing courses completed elsewhere dependent upon specific evaluations.
Contact *Telephone:* 705-675-1151 Ext. 3808. *Fax:* 705-675-4861.

CONTINUING EDUCATION PROGRAM

Contact *Telephone:* 705-675-1151 Ext. 3808. *Fax:* 705-675-4861.

McMaster University
School of Nursing
Hamilton, Ontario

http://www.fhs.mcmaster.ca/nursing
Founded in 1887
DEGREES • BSCN • M SC • MSN/PHD • PHD

Nursing Program Faculty 53 (47% with doctorates).
Baccalaureate Enrollment 548
Women 90% **Men** 10% **Part-time** 20%

Nursing Student Activities Student Nurses' Association.

Nursing Student Resources Academic advising; academic or career counseling; assistance for students with disabilities; bookstore; campus computer network; career placement assistance; computer lab; daycare for children of students; e-mail services; employment services for current students; housing assistance; Internet; learning resource lab; library services; nursing audiovisuals; placement services for program completers; remedial services; resume preparation assistance; skills, simulation, or other laboratory; tutoring.

Library Facilities 1.7 million volumes (150,446 in health); 57,487 periodical subscriptions (89,267 health-care related).

BACCALAUREATE PROGRAMS

Degree BScN

Available Programs Baccalaureate for Second Degree; Generic Baccalaureate; RN Baccalaureate.
Site Options Kitchener, ON.
Study Options Full-time and part-time.
Program Entrance Requirements CPR certification, health exam, high school biology, high school chemistry, 4 years high school math, 4 years high school science, high school transcript, immunizations, minimum high school GPA of 3.0, minimum high school rank 75%. Transfer students are accepted.
Advanced Placement Credit by examination available. Credit given for nursing courses completed elsewhere dependent upon specific evaluations.
Contact *Telephone:* 905-525-9140 Ext. 22232. *Fax:* 905-528-4727.

GRADUATE PROGRAMS

Contact *Telephone:* 905-525-9140 Ext. 22982. *Fax:* 905-546-1129.

MASTER'S DEGREE PROGRAM

Degrees M Sc; MSN/PhD

Available Programs Master's.

Concentrations Available *Clinical nurse specialist programs in:* perinatal. *Nurse practitioner programs in:* neonatal health.

Study Options Full-time and part-time.

Program Entrance Requirements Transcript of college record, written essay, 2 letters of recommendation.

Advanced Placement Credit given for nursing courses completed elsewhere dependent upon specific evaluations.

Degree Requirements Thesis or project.

DOCTORAL DEGREE PROGRAM

Degree PhD

Available Programs Doctorate.

Program Entrance Requirements 2 letters of recommendation, MSN or equivalent, vita.

Degree Requirements Dissertation, oral exam.

Nipissing University
Nursing Department
North Bay, Ontario

http://www.nipissingu.ca/nursing/

Founded in 1992

DEGREE • BSCN

Nursing Program Faculty 12 (3% with doctorates).

Baccalaureate Enrollment 248
Women 92% **Men** 8%

Nursing Student Activities Student Nurses' Association.

Nursing Student Resources Academic advising; academic or career counseling; assistance for students with disabilities; bookstore; campus computer network; career placement assistance; computer lab; computer-assisted instruction; e-mail services; employment services for current students; housing assistance; interactive nursing skills videos; Internet; learning resource lab; library services; nursing audiovisuals; placement services for program completers; remedial services; resume preparation assistance; skills, simulation, or other laboratory; tutoring; unpaid internships.

Library Facilities 187,000 volumes (2,800 in health, 1,820 in nursing); 19,115 periodical subscriptions (2,430 health-care related).

BACCALAUREATE PROGRAMS

Degree BScN

Available Programs Generic Baccalaureate.

Study Options Full-time.

Program Entrance Requirements Minimum overall college GPA of 3.0, transcript of college record, high school biology, high school chemistry, high school transcript, immunizations, minimum high school rank 70%. Transfer students are accepted. *Application deadline:* Applications may be processed on a rolling basis for some programs.

Expenses (2009–10) *Tuition, area resident:* full-time CAN$4130. *International tuition:* CAN$10,000 full-time. *Room and board:* room only: CAN$5460 per academic year.

Financial Aid 44% of baccalaureate students in nursing programs received some form of financial aid in 2008–09.

Contact Registrar's Office, Nursing Department, Nipissing University, 100 College Drive, PO Box 5002, North Bay, ON P1B 8L7. *Telephone:* 705-474-3450 Ext. 4521. *E-mail:* registrar@nipissingu.ca.

Queen's University at Kingston
School of Nursing
Kingston, Ontario

http://meds.queensu.ca/nursing

Founded in 1841

DEGREES • BNSC • M SC • PHD

Nursing Program Faculty 20 (80% with doctorates).

Baccalaureate Enrollment 400
Women 95% **Men** 5%

Graduate Enrollment 25
Women 95% **Men** 5%

Nursing Student Activities Student Nurses' Association.

Nursing Student Resources Academic advising; academic or career counseling; assistance for students with disabilities; bookstore; campus computer network; career placement assistance; computer lab; computer-assisted instruction; daycare for children of students; e-mail services; employment services for current students; housing assistance; interactive nursing skills videos; Internet; learning resource lab; library services; nursing audiovisuals; resume preparation assistance; skills, simulation, or other laboratory; tutoring; unpaid internships.

Library Facilities 3.5 million volumes (5,209 in health, 3,652 in nursing); 16,109 periodical subscriptions (1,054 health-care related).

BACCALAUREATE PROGRAMS

Degree BNSc

Available Programs Accelerated Baccalaureate; Generic Baccalaureate; RN Baccalaureate.

Study Options Full-time.

Program Entrance Requirements CPR certification, high school biology, high school chemistry, high school math, high school science, high school transcript, immunizations, minimum high school GPA, minimum high school rank. Transfer students are accepted.

Contact *Telephone:* 613-533-6000 Ext. 74743. *Fax:* 613-533-6770.

GRADUATE PROGRAMS

Contact *Telephone:* 613-533-6000 Ext. 74764. *Fax:* 613-533-6770.

MASTER'S DEGREE PROGRAM

Degree M Sc

Available Programs Master's.

Study Options Full-time.

Program Entrance Requirements Transcript of college record, 2 letters of recommendation, nursing research course, prerequisite course work, statistics course.

Degree Requirements Thesis or project.

DOCTORAL DEGREE PROGRAM

Degree PhD

Available Programs Doctorate.

Areas of Study Health promotion/disease prevention, human health and illness, illness and transition, nursing science.

Program Entrance Requirements Minimum overall college GPA of 3.0, interview, letters of recommendation, MSN or equivalent.

Degree Requirements 6 total credit hours, dissertation, oral exam, written exam, residency.

Ryerson University
Program in Nursing
Toronto, Ontario

http://www.ryerson.ca/nursing

Founded in 1948

DEGREES • BSCN • MN

Nursing Program Faculty 72 (22% with doctorates).

Ryerson University (continued)
Baccalaureate Enrollment 2,471
Women 92% **Men** 8% **International** 1%
Graduate Enrollment 84
Women 93% **Men** 7% **Part-time** 54%
Nursing Student Activities Sigma Theta Tau, Student Nurses' Association, nursing club.
Nursing Student Resources Academic advising; academic or career counseling; assistance for students with disabilities; bookstore; campus computer network; career placement assistance; computer lab; computer-assisted instruction; daycare for children of students; e-mail services; employment services for current students; housing assistance; interactive nursing skills videos; Internet; learning resource lab; library services; nursing audiovisuals; remedial services; resume preparation assistance; skills, simulation, or other laboratory; tutoring.
Library Facilities 487,361 volumes (70,000 in health, 7,000 in nursing); 28,075 periodical subscriptions (5,000 health-care related).

BACCALAUREATE PROGRAMS

Degree BScN

Available Programs Generic Baccalaureate; International Nurse to Baccalaureate; RN Baccalaureate; RPN to Baccalaureate.
Study Options Full-time.
Program Entrance Requirements Transcript of college record, CPR certification, health exam, health insurance, high school biology, high school chemistry, high school math, high school transcript, immunizations, minimum high school rank 75%.
Advanced Placement Credit given for nursing courses completed elsewhere dependent upon specific evaluations.
Financial Aid 45% of baccalaureate students in nursing programs received some form of financial aid in 2008–09. *Gift aid (need-based):* college/university gift aid from institutional funds. *Loans:* Federal Direct (Subsidized and Unsubsidized Stafford). *Financial aid application deadline:* 1/15.
Contact Richard Perras, Student Affairs Coordinator, Program in Nursing, Ryerson University, 350 Victoria Street, Room POD-474, Toronto, ON M5B 2K3. *Telephone:* 416-979-5000 Ext. 6318. *Fax:* 416-979-5332. *E-mail:* rperras@ryerson.ca.

GRADUATE PROGRAMS

Financial Aid 67% of graduate students in nursing programs received some form of financial aid in 2008–09.
Contact Mr. Gerry Warner, Program Administrator, Program in Nursing, Ryerson University, 350 Victoria Street, Toronto, ON M5B 2K3. *Telephone:* 416-979-5000 Ext. 7852. *Fax:* 416-979-5332. *E-mail:* g2warner@ryerson.ca.

MASTER'S DEGREE PROGRAM

Degree MN

Available Programs Master's.
Concentrations Available *Clinical nurse specialist programs in:* adult health, community health, family health, public health. *Nurse practitioner programs in:* primary care.
Study Options Full-time and part-time.
Program Entrance Requirements Minimum overall college GPA of 3.33, transcript of college record, written essay, 2 letters of recommendation, nursing research course, physical assessment course, resume. *Application deadline:* 1/15 (fall). *Application fee:* $90.
Advanced Placement Credit given for nursing courses completed elsewhere dependent upon specific evaluations.
Degree Requirements 11 total credit hours, thesis or project.

CONTINUING EDUCATION PROGRAM

Contact Paula Mastrilli, Program Manager, Program in Nursing, Ryerson University, 350 Victoria Street, Room CED, 515-Q, Toronto, ON M5B 2K3. *Telephone:* 416-979-5035 Ext. 2061. *Fax:* 416-979-5277. *E-mail:* pmastril@ryerson.ca.

Trent University
Nursing Program
Peterborough, Ontario

http://www.trentu.ca/nursing/
Founded in 1963
DEGREE • BSCN

Nursing Program Faculty 45 (10% with doctorates).
Baccalaureate Enrollment 523
Distance Learning Courses Available.
Nursing Student Activities Student Nurses' Association.
Nursing Student Resources Academic advising; academic or career counseling; assistance for students with disabilities; bookstore; campus computer network; computer lab; computer-assisted instruction; e-mail services; employment services for current students; housing assistance; interactive nursing skills videos; Internet; learning resource lab; library services; nursing audiovisuals; remedial services; resume preparation assistance; skills, simulation, or other laboratory; tutoring.
Library Facilities 740,653 volumes (6,393 in health, 1,281 in nursing); 1,464 periodical subscriptions (360 health-care related).

BACCALAUREATE PROGRAMS

Degree BScN

Available Programs Accelerated Baccalaureate; Generic Baccalaureate.
Site Options Peterborough, ON.
Study Options Full-time.
Program Entrance Requirements CPR certification, health exam, high school biology, high school chemistry, 4 years high school math, 4 years high school science, high school transcript, immunizations, minimum high school rank 70%. Transfer students are accepted.
Advanced Placement Credit given for nursing courses completed elsewhere dependent upon specific evaluations.
Contact *Telephone:* 705-748-1011 Ext. 7809. *Fax:* 705-748-1088.

University of Ottawa
School of Nursing
Ottawa, Ontario

http://www.health.uottawa.ca/sn/
Founded in 1848
DEGREES • BSCN • M SC N • PHD

Nursing Program Faculty 150 (20% with doctorates).
Baccalaureate Enrollment 1,485
Women 94% **Men** 6% **Part-time** 21%
Graduate Enrollment 140
Women 95% **Men** 5% **Part-time** 79%
Distance Learning Courses Available.
Nursing Student Activities Sigma Theta Tau, Student Nurses' Association.
Nursing Student Resources Academic advising; academic or career counseling; assistance for students with disabilities; bookstore; campus computer network; computer lab; e-mail services; employment services for current students; housing assistance; learning resource lab; library services; nursing audiovisuals; remedial services; skills, simulation, or other laboratory; tutoring.
Library Facilities 3.2 million volumes (54,000 in health, 7,000 in nursing); 48,398 periodical subscriptions (1,050 health-care related).

BACCALAUREATE PROGRAMS

Degree BScN

Available Programs Generic Baccalaureate; International Nurse to Baccalaureate; RN Baccalaureate; RPN to Baccalaureate.
Site Options Pembroke, ON; Kingston, PQ; Montreal, QC.

Study Options Full-time.

Program Entrance Requirements Transcript of college record, CPR certification, high school biology, high school chemistry, high school math, high school transcript, immunizations, minimum high school rank 70%. Transfer students are accepted.

Advanced Placement Credit given for nursing courses completed elsewhere dependent upon specific evaluations.

Contact *Telephone:* 613-562-5800 Ext. 5404. *Fax:* 613-562-5470.

GRADUATE PROGRAMS

Contact *Telephone:* 613-562-5800 Ext. 8422. *Fax:* 613-562-5473.

MASTER'S DEGREE PROGRAM

Degree M Sc N

Available Programs Master's.

Concentrations Available *Clinical nurse specialist programs in:* acute care, community health. *Nurse practitioner programs in:* primary care.

Study Options Full-time and part-time.

Online Degree Options Yes.

Program Entrance Requirements Clinical experience, minimum overall college GPA of 3.0, transcript of college record, written essay, immunizations, 3 letters of recommendation, nursing research course, physical assessment course, prerequisite course work, statistics course.

Advanced Placement Credit given for nursing courses completed elsewhere dependent upon specific evaluations.

Degree Requirements 24 total credit hours, thesis or project.

DOCTORAL DEGREE PROGRAM

Degree PhD

Available Programs Doctorate; Doctorate for Nurses with Non-Nursing Degrees.

Areas of Study Health promotion/disease prevention, health-care systems, nursing policy, nursing research, nursing science.

Program Entrance Requirements Minimum overall college GPA of 3.5, 3 letters of recommendation, MSN or equivalent, statistics course, vita, writing sample.

Degree Requirements 18 total credit hours, dissertation, oral exam, written exam, residency.

POSTDOCTORAL PROGRAM

Areas of Study Community health, nursing interventions.

Postdoctoral Program Contact *Telephone:* 613-562-5800.

University of Toronto
Faculty of Nursing
Toronto, Ontario

http://www.nursing.utoronto.ca/

Founded in 1827

DEGREES • BSCN • MN • PHD

Nursing Program Faculty 45 (58% with doctorates).

Baccalaureate Enrollment 300

Graduate Enrollment 360
Part-time 45%

Distance Learning Courses Available.

Nursing Student Activities Student Nurses' Association, nursing club.

Nursing Student Resources Academic advising; academic or career counseling; assistance for students with disabilities; bookstore; campus computer network; career placement assistance; computer lab; computer-assisted instruction; daycare for children of students; e-mail services; employment services for current students; externships; housing assistance; interactive nursing skills videos; Internet; learning resource lab; library services; nursing audiovisuals; skills, simulation, or other laboratory.

Library Facilities 13.4 million volumes; 77,145 periodical subscriptions.

BACCALAUREATE PROGRAMS

Degree BScN

Available Programs Accelerated Baccalaureate; Accelerated Baccalaureate for Second Degree; Accelerated RN Baccalaureate; Baccalaureate for Second Degree.

Study Options Full-time.

Program Entrance Requirements Minimum overall college GPA of 3.0, CPR certification, written essay, immunizations, 2 letters of recommendation, minimum GPA in nursing prerequisites of 3.0, prerequisite course work.

Contact *Telephone:* 416-978-2392. *Fax:* 416-978-8222.

GRADUATE PROGRAMS

Contact *Telephone:* 416-978-2392. *Fax:* 416-978-8222.

MASTER'S DEGREE PROGRAM

Degree MN

Available Programs Master's.

Concentrations Available Clinical nurse leader; health-care administration; nurse anesthesia; nursing administration; nursing education. *Clinical nurse specialist programs in:* acute care, adult health, community health, critical care, family health, gerontology, maternity-newborn, oncology, pediatric, psychiatric/mental health, public health, school health, women's health. *Nurse practitioner programs in:* acute care, adult health, family health, pediatric.

Study Options Full-time and part-time.

Online Degree Options Yes.

Program Entrance Requirements Clinical experience, minimum overall college GPA of 3.0, transcript of college record, CPR certification, written essay, 2 letters of recommendation, prerequisite course work, resume, statistics course.

Degree Requirements 9 total credit hours, thesis or project.

POST-MASTER'S PROGRAM

Areas of Study *Clinical nurse specialist programs in:* acute care, adult health, maternity-newborn, pediatric. *Nurse practitioner programs in:* acute care, adult health, pediatric.

DOCTORAL DEGREE PROGRAM

Degree PhD

Available Programs Doctorate.

Areas of Study Community health, ethics, family health, health policy, health-care systems, human health and illness, information systems, maternity-newborn, nursing administration, nursing education, nursing policy, nursing research, nursing science, oncology, women's health.

Program Entrance Requirements Minimum overall college GPA of 3.3, 2 letters of recommendation, MSN or equivalent, scholarly papers, statistics course, vita, writing sample.

Degree Requirements Dissertation, oral exam.

POSTDOCTORAL PROGRAM

Postdoctoral Program Contact *Telephone:* 416-978-8069.

The University of Western Ontario
School of Nursing
London, Ontario

http://www.uwo.ca/fhs/nursing

Founded in 1878

DEGREES • BSCN • M SC N • PHD

Nursing Program Faculty 101 (18% with doctorates).

Baccalaureate Enrollment 1,153
Women 93.24% Men 6.76% Part-time 13.53%

Graduate Enrollment 54
Women 89% Men 11% Part-time 28%

Nursing Student Activities Nursing Honor Society, Sigma Theta Tau, Student Nurses' Association.

The University of Western Ontario (continued)

Nursing Student Resources Academic advising; academic or career counseling; assistance for students with disabilities; bookstore; campus computer network; computer lab; computer-assisted instruction; daycare for children of students; e-mail services; employment services for current students; housing assistance; interactive nursing skills videos; Internet; learning resource lab; library services; nursing audiovisuals; resume preparation assistance; unpaid internships.

Library Facilities 3.5 million volumes (357,263 in health, 40 in nursing); 54,546 periodical subscriptions (250 health-care related).

BACCALAUREATE PROGRAMS

Degree BScN

Available Programs Accelerated Baccalaureate; Generic Baccalaureate; RN Baccalaureate.

Study Options Full-time.

Program Entrance Requirements CPR certification, high school biology, high school chemistry, 4 years high school math, high school science, high school transcript, immunizations, minimum high school rank 80%. Transfer students are accepted.

Advanced Placement Credit given for nursing courses completed elsewhere dependent upon specific evaluations.

Contact *Telephone:* 519-661-2111 Ext. 86564. *Fax:* 519-661-3928.

GRADUATE PROGRAMS

Contact *Telephone:* 519-661-3409. *Fax:* 519-661-3928.

MASTER'S DEGREE PROGRAM

Degree M Sc N

Available Programs Master's.

Concentrations Available Health-care administration; nursing administration; nursing education. *Clinical nurse specialist programs in:* acute care, adult health, community health, psychiatric/mental health, public health, women's health. *Nurse practitioner programs in:* community health.

Study Options Full-time and part-time.

Program Entrance Requirements Minimum overall college GPA of 3.5, transcript of college record, written essay, interview, 2 letters of recommendation, nursing research course, prerequisite course work, resume, statistics course.

Advanced Placement Credit given for nursing courses completed elsewhere dependent upon specific evaluations.

Degree Requirements 7 total credit hours, thesis or project.

DOCTORAL DEGREE PROGRAM

Degree PhD

Available Programs Doctorate.

Areas of Study Addiction/substance abuse, advanced practice nursing, aging, clinical practice, community health, faculty preparation, health policy, health promotion/disease prevention, health-care systems, human health and illness, individualized study, nurse case management, nursing administration, nursing education, nursing research, nursing science, women's health.

Program Entrance Requirements Clinical experience, minimum overall college GPA of 3.5, interview by faculty committee, interview, 2 letters of recommendation, MSN or equivalent, scholarly papers, statistics course, vita, writing sample.

Degree Requirements 4 total credit hours, dissertation, written exam.

POSTDOCTORAL PROGRAM

Areas of Study Addiction/substance abuse, community health, health promotion/disease prevention, vulnerable population, women's health.

Postdoctoral Program Contact *Telephone:* 519-661-2111 Ext. 86573.

University of Windsor
Faculty of Nursing
Windsor, Ontario

http://www.uwindsor.ca/nursing
Founded in 1857

DEGREES • BSCN • M SC

Nursing Program Faculty 23 (52% with doctorates).

Baccalaureate Enrollment 894
Women 85% **Men** 15% **International** .7% **Part-time** 10.9%

Graduate Enrollment 71
Women 93% **Men** 7% **Part-time** 60.6%

Distance Learning Courses Available.

Nursing Student Activities Nursing Honor Society, Sigma Theta Tau, Student Nurses' Association, nursing club.

Nursing Student Resources Academic advising; academic or career counseling; assistance for students with disabilities; bookstore; campus computer network; career placement assistance; computer lab; computer-assisted instruction; e-mail services; employment services for current students; externships; interactive nursing skills videos; Internet; learning resource lab; library services; nursing audiovisuals; remedial services; resume preparation assistance; skills, simulation, or other laboratory; tutoring; unpaid internships.

Library Facilities 2.8 million volumes (64,552 in nursing); 25,458 periodical subscriptions.

BACCALAUREATE PROGRAMS

Degree BScN

Available Programs Generic Baccalaureate.

Site Options Windsor, ON.

Study Options Full-time.

Program Entrance Requirements CPR certification, health exam, health insurance, high school biology, high school chemistry, high school math, 4 years high school science, high school transcript, immunizations, minimum high school rank 77%. Transfer students are accepted. *Application deadline:* 1/13 (fall). *Application fee:* CAN$115.

Advanced Placement Credit given for nursing courses completed elsewhere dependent upon specific evaluations.

Expenses (2009–10) *Tuition, area resident:* full-time CAN$4870; part-time CAN$742 per course. *International tuition:* CAN$19,109 full-time. *Room and board:* CAN$9797 per academic year. *Required fees:* full-time CAN$772; part-time CAN$580 per term.

Financial Aid 32% of baccalaureate students in nursing programs received some form of financial aid in 2008–09.

Contact Nursing Contact, Faculty of Nursing, University of Windsor, 401 Sunset Avenue, Windsor, ON N9B 3P4. *Telephone:* 519-253-3000 Ext. 2258. *Fax:* 519-973-7084. *E-mail:* nurse@uwindsor.ca.

GRADUATE PROGRAMS

Expenses (2009–10) *Tuition, area resident:* full-time CAN$4870; part-time CAN$487 per course. *International tuition:* CAN$17,630 full-time. *Room and board:* CAN$9797 per academic year. *Required fees:* full-time CAN$989; part-time CAN$12 per credit; part-time CAN$80 per term.

Financial Aid 11% of graduate students in nursing programs received some form of financial aid in 2008–09.

Contact Dr. Debbie Kane, Graduate Coordinator, Faculty of Nursing, University of Windsor, 401 Sunset Avenue, Windsor, ON N9B 3P4. *Telephone:* 519-253-3000 Ext. 2268. *Fax:* 519-973-7084. *E-mail:* dkane@uwindsor.ca.

MASTER'S DEGREE PROGRAM

Degree M Sc

Available Programs Master's.

Study Options Full-time and part-time.

Program Entrance Requirements Minimum overall college GPA of 3.0, transcript of college record, written essay, interview, 3 letters of recommendation, nursing research course, physical assessment course, statistics course. *Application deadline:* 1/15 (fall). *Application fee:* CAN$85.

Advanced Placement Credit given for nursing courses completed elsewhere dependent upon specific evaluations.

Degree Requirements 10 total credit hours, thesis or project.

CONTINUING EDUCATION PROGRAM

Contact Nursing Main Office, Faculty of Nursing, University of Windsor, 401 Sunset Avenue, Windsor, ON N9B 3P4. *Telephone:* 519-253-3000 Ext. 2258. *Fax:* 519-973-7084. *E-mail:* nurse@uwindsor.ca.

York University
School of Nursing, Atkinson Faculty of Liberal and Professional Studies
Toronto, Ontario

Founded in 1959

DEGREE • BSCN

Nursing Program Faculty 19 (79% with doctorates).

Baccalaureate Enrollment 850

Women 96% **Men** 4% **Minority** 30% **International** 1% **Part-time** 15%

Nursing Student Resources Academic advising; academic or career counseling; assistance for students with disabilities; bookstore; campus computer network; career placement assistance; computer lab; computer-assisted instruction; daycare for children of students; e-mail services; employment services for current students; housing assistance; interactive nursing skills videos; Internet; learning resource lab; library services; nursing audiovisuals; skills, simulation, or other laboratory; unpaid internships.

Library Facilities 6.1 million volumes; 540,000 periodical subscriptions.

BACCALAUREATE PROGRAMS

Degree BScN

Available Programs Generic Baccalaureate; RN Baccalaureate.

Site Options King City, ON; Barrie, ON; Oshawa, ON.

Study Options Full-time and part-time.

Program Entrance Requirements CPR certification, written essay, health exam, high school biology, high school chemistry, high school math, high school science, high school transcript, immunizations, 1 letter of recommendation, minimum high school GPA, minimum GPA in nursing prerequisites. Transfer students are accepted.

Advanced Placement Credit by examination available. Credit given for nursing courses completed elsewhere dependent upon specific evaluations.

Contact *Telephone:* 416-736-5271 Ext. 66351. *Fax:* 416-736-5714.

CONTINUING EDUCATION PROGRAM

Contact *Telephone:* 416-736-5271. *Fax:* 416-736-5714.

PRINCE EDWARD ISLAND

University of Prince Edward Island
School of Nursing
Charlottetown, Prince Edward Island

Founded in 1834

DEGREE • BSCN

Nursing Program Faculty 10 (2% with doctorates).

Baccalaureate Enrollment 211

Women 97% **Men** 3% **International** 1%

Nursing Student Activities Nursing Honor Society, Student Nurses' Association, nursing club.

Nursing Student Resources Academic advising; academic or career counseling; assistance for students with disabilities; bookstore; campus computer network; career placement assistance; computer lab; computer-assisted instruction; daycare for children of students; e-mail services; employment services for current students; housing assistance; interactive nursing skills videos; Internet; learning resource lab; library services; nursing audiovisuals; placement services for program completers; remedial services; resume preparation assistance; skills, simulation, or other laboratory; tutoring.

Library Facilities 402,808 volumes; 26,196 periodical subscriptions.

BACCALAUREATE PROGRAMS

Degree BScN

Available Programs Generic Baccalaureate.

Study Options Full-time and part-time.

Program Entrance Requirements Transcript of college record, CPR certification, high school chemistry, high school math, high school science, high school transcript, immunizations, minimum high school GPA of 3.0, minimum high school rank 75%, minimum GPA in nursing prerequisites of 3.0, prerequisite course work. Transfer students are accepted.

Advanced Placement Credit given for nursing courses completed elsewhere dependent upon specific evaluations.

Contact *Telephone:* 902-566-0733. *Fax:* 902-566-0777.

QUEBEC

McGill University
School of Nursing
Montréal, Quebec

http://www.nursing.mcgill.ca

Founded in 1821

DEGREES • BSCN • M SC • PHD

Nursing Program Faculty 163 (13% with doctorates).

Baccalaureate Enrollment 438

Women 90% **Men** 10% **International** 2% **Part-time** 25%

Graduate Enrollment 93

Women 90% **Men** 10% **International** 5% **Part-time** 26%

Nursing Student Activities Student Nurses' Association.

Nursing Student Resources Academic advising; academic or career counseling; assistance for students with disabilities; bookstore; campus computer network; career placement assistance; computer lab; e-mail services; Internet; learning resource lab; library services; nursing audiovisuals; skills, simulation, or other laboratory; tutoring; unpaid internships.

Library Facilities 4.2 million volumes; 49,433 periodical subscriptions.

BACCALAUREATE PROGRAMS

Degree BScN

Available Programs Accelerated RN Baccalaureate; Generic Baccalaureate; RN Baccalaureate.

Study Options Full-time.

Program Entrance Requirements Minimum overall college GPA of 3.0, transcript of college record, high school chemistry, 4 years high school math, 4 years high school science, high school transcript, minimum high school GPA of 3.3, minimum high school rank 25%. Transfer students are accepted. *Application deadline:* 1/15 (fall), 11/1 (winter). *Application fee:* CAN$85.

Advanced Placement Credit given for nursing courses completed elsewhere dependent upon specific evaluations.

Expenses (2009–10) *Tuition, state resident:* full-time CAN$1968; part-time CAN$66 per credit. *Tuition, nonresident:* full-time CAN$5501; part-time CAN$183 per credit. *International tuition:* CAN$15,420 full-time. *Room and board:* CAN$11,000 per academic year. *Required fees:* full-time CAN$1420.

Contact Ms. Celine Arseneault, Student Affairs Coordinator, Undergraduate Programs, School of Nursing, McGill University, 3506 University Street, Wilson Hall Building, Room 203, Montreal, QC H3A 2A7. *Telephone:* 514-398-3784. *Fax:* 514-398-8455. *E-mail:* undergraduate.nursing@mcgill.ca.

GRADUATE PROGRAMS

Expenses (2009–10) *Tuition, state resident:* full-time CAN$1968; part-time CAN$66 per credit. *Tuition, nonresident:* full-time CAN$5500; part-time CAN$183 per credit. *International tuition:* CAN$13,444 full-time. *Required fees:* full-time CAN$1534.

McGill University (continued)

Contact Ms. Anna Santandrea, Students Affairs Coordinator, Graduate and Post-Doctoral Studies, School of Nursing, McGill University, 3506 University Street, Montreal, QC H3A 2A7. *Telephone:* 514-398-4151. *Fax:* 514-398-8455. *E-mail:* anna.santandrea@mcgill.ca.

MASTER'S DEGREE PROGRAM

Degree M Sc

Available Programs Master's; Master's for Non-Nursing College Graduates.

Concentrations Available Nursing administration. *Clinical nurse specialist programs in:* acute care, adult health, cardiovascular, community health, critical care, family health, gerontology, home health care, maternity-newborn, medical-surgical, oncology, parent-child, pediatric, perinatal, psychiatric/mental health, public health, rehabilitation, women's health. *Nurse practitioner programs in:* neonatal health, primary care.

Study Options Full-time.

Program Entrance Requirements Clinical experience, minimum overall college GPA of 3.0, transcript of college record, CPR certification, written essay, immunizations, interview, 3 letters of recommendation, resume, statistics course. *Application deadline:* 1/15 (fall). *Application fee:* CAN$85.

Degree Requirements 53 total credit hours, thesis or project.

DOCTORAL DEGREE PROGRAM

Degree PhD

Available Programs Doctorate; Post-Baccalaureate Doctorate.

Areas of Study Family health, health-care systems, human health and illness, nursing administration, nursing research, oncology.

Program Entrance Requirements Minimum overall college GPA of 3.3, interview, 2 letters of recommendation, MSN or equivalent, statistics course, vita, writing sample. Application deadline: 1/15 (fall). Application fee: CAN$85.

Degree Requirements 90 total credit hours, dissertation, oral exam, written exam, residency.

POSTDOCTORAL PROGRAM

Areas of Study Cancer care, chronic illness.

Postdoctoral Program Contact Dr. C. Celeste Johnston, Associate Director, Research, School of Nursing, McGill University, 3506 University Street, Montreal, QC H3A 2A7. *Telephone:* 514-398-4157. *Fax:* 514-398-8455. *E-mail:* celeste.johnston@mcgill.ca.

Université de Montréal
Faculty of Nursing
Montréal, Quebec

http://www.scinf.umontreal.ca

Founded in 1920

DEGREES • BSCN • M SC • PHD

Nursing Program Faculty 54 (90% with doctorates).

Baccalaureate Enrollment 600
Women 70% **Men** 30% **Minority** 30% **International** 3% **Part-time** 20%

Graduate Enrollment 326
Women 75% **Men** 25% **Minority** 20% **International** 3%

Distance Learning Courses Available.

Nursing Student Activities Student Nurses' Association.

Nursing Student Resources Academic advising; academic or career counseling; assistance for students with disabilities; bookstore; campus computer network; career placement assistance; computer lab; computer-assisted instruction; daycare for children of students; e-mail services; employment services for current students; externships; housing assistance; interactive nursing skills videos; Internet; learning resource lab; library services; nursing audiovisuals; other; placement services for program completers; remedial services; resume preparation assistance; skills, simulation, or other laboratory; tutoring.

Library Facilities 4 million volumes (32,536 in health, 32,536 in nursing); 18,330 periodical subscriptions (1,319 health-care related).

BACCALAUREATE PROGRAMS

Degree BScN

Available Programs RN Baccalaureate.

Study Options Full-time and part-time.

Program Entrance Requirements Transfer students are accepted. *Application deadline:* 3/1 (fall). *Application fee:* CAN$70.

Contact Catherine Sarrazin, Assistant to Vice Dean, Faculty of Nursing, Université de Montréal, Faculté des sciences infirmières, Pav. Marg. d'Youville, CP 6128 Succursale Centre-Ville, Montreal, QC H3C 3J7. *Telephone:* 514-343-6439. *Fax:* 514-343-2306. *E-mail:* catherine.sarrazin@umontreal.ca.

GRADUATE PROGRAMS

Financial Aid Fellowships, research assistantships, teaching assistantships, career-related internships or fieldwork, Federal Work-Study, and institutionally sponsored loans available.

Contact Suzanne Pinel, Assistant to the Vice Dean of Studies, Faculty of Nursing, Université de Montréal, Faculté des sciences infirmières, Pav. Marg. d'Youville, CP 6128 Succursale Centre-Ville, Montreal, QC H3C 3J7. *Telephone:* 514-343-6111 Ext. 7098. *Fax:* 514-343-6111 Ext. 2705. *E-mail:* suzanne.pinel@umontreal.ca.

MASTER'S DEGREE PROGRAM

Degree M Sc

Available Programs Master's; RN to Master's.

Concentrations Available *Clinical nurse specialist programs in:* acute care, adult health, cardiovascular, community health, family health, gerontology, maternity-newborn, medical-surgical, occupational health, oncology, palliative care, parent-child, psychiatric/mental health, public health, rehabilitation, women's health. *Nurse practitioner programs in:* acute care, family health.

Study Options Full-time and part-time.

Program Entrance Requirements Transcript of college record, nursing research course, statistics course. *Application deadline:* 3/1 (fall).

Degree Requirements 45 total credit hours, thesis or project.

POST-MASTER'S PROGRAM

Areas of Study *Nurse practitioner programs in:* acute care, family health.

DOCTORAL DEGREE PROGRAM

Degree PhD

Available Programs Doctorate.

Program Entrance Requirements letters of recommendation, MSN or equivalent. Application deadline: 3/1 (fall).

Degree Requirements 90 total credit hours, dissertation, oral exam.

POSTDOCTORAL PROGRAM

Postdoctoral Program Contact Ms. Louise Berube, Assistant to the Vice Dean Research, Faculty of Nursing, Université de Montréal, Faculté des sciences infirmières, Pav. Marg. d'Youville, CP 6128 Succursale Centre-Ville, Montreal, QC H3C 3J7. *Telephone:* 514-343-6380. *Fax:* 514-343-2306. *E-mail:* louise.berube@umontreal.ca.

CONTINUING EDUCATION PROGRAM

Contact Ms. Jocelyne Labarre, Program Coordinator, Faculty of Nursing, Université de Montréal, Faculté des sciences infirmières, Pav. Marg. d'Youville, CP 6128 Succursale Centre-Ville, Montreal, QC H3C 3J7. *Telephone:* 514-343-7723. *Fax:* 514-343-2306. *E-mail:* jocyelyne.labarre@umontreal.ca.

Université de Sherbrooke
Department of Nursing
Sherbrooke, Quebec

http://www.usherbrooke.ca/scinf/

Founded in 1954

DEGREES • BSCN • M SC • PHD

Nursing Program Faculty 17 (76% with doctorates).

Baccalaureate Enrollment 482
Women 90% **Men** 10% **Minority** .5% **Part-time** 30%
Graduate Enrollment 61
Women 95% **Men** 5% **Part-time** 50%
Nursing Student Activities Student Nurses' Association.

Nursing Student Resources Academic advising; academic or career counseling; assistance for students with disabilities; bookstore; computer lab; computer-assisted instruction; e-mail services; externships; housing assistance; Internet; learning resource lab; library services; nursing audio-visuals; tutoring.

Library Facilities 1.2 million volumes (40,000 in health, 4,000 in nursing); 5,937 periodical subscriptions (3,000 health-care related).

BACCALAUREATE PROGRAMS

Degree BScN

Available Programs RN Baccalaureate.

Site Options Longueuil, QC.

Study Options Full-time and part-time.

Program Entrance Requirements Transcript of college record, high school chemistry, 4 years high school math, immunizations, professional liability insurance/malpractice insurance, RN licensure. Transfer students are accepted.

Advanced Placement Credit given for nursing courses completed elsewhere dependent upon specific evaluations.

Contact *Telephone:* 819-563-5355. *Fax:* 819-820-6816.

GRADUATE PROGRAMS

Contact *Telephone:* 819-564-5354. *Fax:* 819-820-6816.

MASTER'S DEGREE PROGRAM

Degree M Sc

Available Programs Master's.

Concentrations Available *Clinical nurse specialist programs in:* acute care, community health, family health, gerontology.

Site Options Longueuil, QC.

Study Options Full-time and part-time.

Program Entrance Requirements Transcript of college record, interview, 3 letters of recommendation, nursing research course, professional liability insurance/malpractice insurance, resume.

Degree Requirements 45 total credit hours, thesis or project.

DOCTORAL DEGREE PROGRAM

Degree PhD

Available Programs Doctorate.

Areas of Study Advanced practice nursing, aging, biology of health and illness, clinical practice, community health, critical care, family health, gerontology, health promotion/disease prevention, human health and illness, illness and transition, information systems, maternity-newborn, neuro-behavior, nurse case management, nursing administration, nursing education, nursing policy, nursing research, nursing science, oncology, women's health.

Site Options Longueuil, QC.

Program Entrance Requirements Clinical experience, interview, 3 letters of recommendation, MSN or equivalent, statistics course, vita, writing sample.

Degree Requirements 90 total credit hours, dissertation, oral exam, written exam.

POSTDOCTORAL PROGRAM

Postdoctoral Program Contact *Telephone:* 819-564-5355. *Fax:* 819-820-6816.

Université du Québec à Chicoutimi

Program in Nursing
Chicoutimi, Quebec

Founded in 1969

DEGREES • BNSC • MSN

Nursing Program Faculty 8 (25% with doctorates).
Baccalaureate Enrollment 600
Women 90% **Men** 10% **Minority** 5% **Part-time** 75%
Graduate Enrollment 30
Women 90% **Men** 10% **Minority** 2% **Part-time** 100%
Distance Learning Courses Available.

Nursing Student Activities Nursing Honor Society, Student Nurses' Association.

Nursing Student Resources Academic advising; academic or career counseling; assistance for students with disabilities; bookstore; campus computer network; computer lab; computer-assisted instruction; e-mail services; employment services for current students; externships; housing assistance; interactive nursing skills videos; Internet; learning resource lab; library services; nursing audiovisuals; resume preparation assistance; skills, simulation, or other laboratory; tutoring; unpaid internships.

Library Facilities 689,214 volumes (6,300 in nursing); 5,092 periodical subscriptions (5,250 health-care related).

BACCALAUREATE PROGRAMS

Degree BNSc

Available Programs Accelerated RN Baccalaureate; RN Baccalaureate.
Site Options Alma, QC; Sept-Iles, QC; St. Felicien, QC.
Study Options Full-time and part-time.

Program Entrance Requirements Transcript of college record, health exam, high school biology, high school chemistry, high school math, immunizations, interview. Transfer students are accepted. *Application deadline:* 3/1 (winter). *Application fee:* CAN$30.

Advanced Placement Credit given for nursing courses completed elsewhere dependent upon specific evaluations.

Expenses (2009–10) *Tuition, area resident:* part-time CAN$300 per course.

Financial Aid 5% of baccalaureate students in nursing programs received some form of financial aid in 2008–09. *Gift aid (need-based):* private, college/university gift aid from institutional funds. *Loans:* college/university. *Work-study:* part-time campus jobs.

Contact Mme. Anna Gauthier, Secretary, Program in Nursing, Université du Québec à Chicoutimi, 555 Boulevard de l'Universite, Saguenay (Chicoutimi), QC G7H 2B1. *Telephone:* 418-545-5011 Ext. 5315. *Fax:* 418-615-1205. *E-mail:* anna_gauthier@uqac.ca.

GRADUATE PROGRAMS

Expenses (2009–10) *Tuition:* part-time CAN$300 per course.

Financial Aid 2% of graduate students in nursing programs received some form of financial aid in 2008–09.

Contact Mrs. Francoise Courville, RN, Director of Masters Degree Program, Program in Nursing, Université du Québec à Chicoutimi, 555 Boulevard de l'Université, Chicoutimi, QC G7H 2B1. *Telephone:* 418-545-5011 Ext. 2374. *Fax:* 418-545-5012. *E-mail:* francoise_courville@uqac.ca.

MASTER'S DEGREE PROGRAM

Degree MSN

Available Programs Accelerated RN to Master's; RN to Master's.

Concentrations Available *Clinical nurse specialist programs in:* acute care, adult health, cardiovascular, community health, critical care, family health, gerontology, home health care, maternity-newborn, medical-surgical, occupational health, oncology, parent-child, pediatric, perinatal, psychiatric/mental health, public health, rehabilitation, school health, women's health.

Site Options Alma, QC; Sept-Iles, QC; St. Felicien, QC.
Study Options Full-time and part-time.

Program Entrance Requirements Clinical experience, minimum overall college GPA of 3.2, transcript of college record, written essay, interview, 3 letters of recommendation, nursing research course, professional liability insurance/malpractice insurance, resume, statistics course. *Application deadline:* 2/1 (fall), 11/1 (winter). *Application fee:* CAN$30.

Advanced Placement Credit given for nursing courses completed elsewhere dependent upon specific evaluations.

Degree Requirements 45 total credit hours, thesis or project.

Université du Québec à Rimouski
Program in Nursing
Rimouski, Quebec

http://www.uquebec.ca/mscinf/
Founded in 1973
DEGREES • BSCN • M SC N

Nursing Program Faculty 17 (53% with doctorates).

Baccalaureate Enrollment 750
Women 90% **Men** 10% **Part-time** 74%

Graduate Enrollment 24
Women 96% **Men** 4% **Part-time** 92%

Distance Learning Courses Available.

Nursing Student Activities Student Nurses' Association.

Nursing Student Resources Academic advising; academic or career counseling; assistance for students with disabilities; bookstore; campus computer network; career placement assistance; computer lab; daycare for children of students; e-mail services; employment services for current students; housing assistance; Internet; learning resource lab; library services; nursing audiovisuals; other; placement services for program completers; resume preparation assistance; skills, simulation, or other laboratory; tutoring.

Library Facilities 263,142 volumes (5,200 in health, 1,100 in nursing); 3,951 periodical subscriptions (1,300 health-care related).

BACCALAUREATE PROGRAMS

Degree BScN

Available Programs RN Baccalaureate.
Site Options Rimouski, QC; Lévis, QC.
Study Options Full-time and part-time.
Program Entrance Requirements Transcript of college record, professional liability insurance/malpractice insurance, prerequisite course work. Transfer students are accepted.
Advanced Placement Credit by examination available.
Financial Aid 8% of baccalaureate students in nursing programs received some form of financial aid in 2008–09. *Loans:* college/university.
Contact Mr. Mario Dube, Directeur du module des sciences de la sante, Program in Nursing, Université du Québec à Rimouski, 300, allee des Ursulines, Rimouski, QC G5L 3A1. *Telephone:* 418-723-1986 Ext. 1568. *Fax:* 418-724-1450. *E-mail:* Mario_Dube@uqar.qc.ca.

GRADUATE PROGRAMS

Financial Aid 17% of graduate students in nursing programs received some form of financial aid in 2008–09.
Contact Dr. Guy Belanger, Directeur, Program in Nursing, Université du Québec à Rimouski, 300, allee des Ursulines, Rimouski, QC G5L 3A1. *Telephone:* 418-723-1986 Ext. 1345. *Fax:* 418-724-1450. *E-mail:* Guy_Belanger@uqar.qc.ca.

MASTER'S DEGREE PROGRAM

Degree M Sc N
Available Programs Master's.
Concentrations Available *Clinical nurse specialist programs in:* community health, critical care, gerontology, psychiatric/mental health.
Site Options Rimouski, QC; Lévis, QC.
Study Options Full-time and part-time.
Program Entrance Requirements Clinical experience, transcript of college record, interview, 3 letters of recommendation, nursing research course, prerequisite course work, statistics course.
Advanced Placement Credit given for nursing courses completed elsewhere dependent upon specific evaluations.
Degree Requirements 45 total credit hours, thesis or project.

CONTINUING EDUCATION PROGRAM

Contact Mr. Richard Tremblay, Coordonnateur, Program in Nursing, Université du Québec à Rimouski, 300, allee des Ursulines, Rimouski, QC G5L 3A1. *Telephone:* 418-723-1986 Ext. 1818. *Fax:* 418-724-1525. *E-mail:* formationcontinue@uqar.qc.ca.

Université du Québec à Trois-Rivières
Program in Nursing
Trois-Rivières, Quebec

Founded in 1969
DEGREES • BSN • MSN

Nursing Program Faculty 28 (30% with doctorates).

Baccalaureate Enrollment 180
Women 95% **Men** 5% **Minority** 5% **International** 1% **Part-time** 75%

Graduate Enrollment 50
Women 97% **Men** 3% **Minority** 1% **Part-time** 90%

Distance Learning Courses Available.

Nursing Student Activities Student Nurses' Association.

Nursing Student Resources Academic advising; academic or career counseling; assistance for students with disabilities; bookstore; campus computer network; career placement assistance; computer lab; computer-assisted instruction; daycare for children of students; e-mail services; employment services for current students; externships; interactive nursing skills videos; Internet; learning resource lab; library services; nursing audiovisuals; placement services for program completers; resume preparation assistance; skills, simulation, or other laboratory; tutoring; unpaid internships.

Library Facilities 464,338 volumes (2,000 in health, 500 in nursing); 2,000 periodical subscriptions health-care related.

BACCALAUREATE PROGRAMS

Degree BSN

Available Programs Generic Baccalaureate; RN Baccalaureate.
Study Options Full-time and part-time.
Program Entrance Requirements Transcript of college record, CPR certification, high school biology, high school chemistry, prerequisite course work, RN licensure. Transfer students are accepted. *Application deadline:* 3/1 (fall). Applications may be processed on a rolling basis for some programs. *Application fee:* CAN$30.
Advanced Placement Credit given for nursing courses completed elsewhere dependent upon specific evaluations.
Financial Aid 50% of baccalaureate students in nursing programs received some form of financial aid in 2007–08. *Loans:* Perkins, state, college/university.
Contact Dr. Michele Côté, Directrice, Program in Nursing, Université du Québec à Trois-Rivieres, Casier Postal 500, Trois Rivieres, QC G9A 5H7. *Telephone:* 819-376-5011 Ext. 3471. *Fax:* 819-376-5048. *E-mail:* michele.cote@uqtr.ca.

GRADUATE PROGRAMS

Financial Aid 25% of graduate students in nursing programs received some form of financial aid in 2007–08.
Contact Michèle Côté, Program in Nursing, Université du Québec à Trois-Rivieres, Casier Postal 500, Trois Rivieres, QC G9A 5H7. *Telephone:* 819-376-5011 Ext. 3460. *E-mail:* Michele.Cote@uqtr.ca.

MASTER'S DEGREE PROGRAM

Degree MSN

Available Programs Master's.
Concentrations Available *Clinical nurse specialist programs in:* acute care, adult health, community health, critical care, family health, home health care, maternity-newborn, medical-surgical, pediatric, perinatal, psychiatric/mental health, public health. *Nurse practitioner programs in:* primary care.
Study Options Full-time and part-time.
Program Entrance Requirements Minimum overall college GPA of 3, transcript of college record, CPR certification, immunizations, 3 letters of recommendation, nursing research course, physical assessment course, prerequisite course work, statistics course. *Application deadline:* 8/29 (fall), 11/29 (winter), 4/29 (spring). Applications may be processed on a rolling basis for some programs. *Application fee:* CAN$30.

Advanced Placement Credit by examination available.
Degree Requirements 45 total credit hours, thesis or project.

Université du Québec en Abitibi-Témiscamingue
Département des sciences sociales et de la santé
Rouyn-Noranda, Quebec

http://www.uqat.uquebec.ca/gestac/prg/7855.asp

Founded in 1983

DEGREE • BN

Nursing Program Faculty 12

Baccalaureate Enrollment 78
Women 95% **Men** 5% **Part-time** 64%

Nursing Student Resources Academic advising; assistance for students with disabilities; bookstore; campus computer network; computer lab; computer-assisted instruction; housing assistance; Internet; library services; resume preparation assistance; skills, simulation, or other laboratory.

Library Facilities 135,882 volumes (3,239 in health, 715 in nursing); 302 periodical subscriptions (17 health-care related).

BACCALAUREATE PROGRAMS

Degree BN

Program Entrance Requirements Transfer students are accepted.
Contact *Telephone:* 819-762-0971 Ext. 2370. *Fax:* 819-797-4727.

Université du Québec en Outaouais
Département des Sciences Infirmières
Gatineau, Quebec

Founded in 1981

DEGREES • BSCN • M SC N

Nursing Program Faculty 13 (38% with doctorates).

Baccalaureate Enrollment 700
Women 90% **Men** 10% **Minority** 20% **Part-time** 40%

Graduate Enrollment 40
Women 99% **Men** 1% **Minority** 6% **Part-time** 100%

Nursing Student Activities Student Nurses' Association.

Nursing Student Resources Academic advising; academic or career counseling; bookstore; campus computer network; computer lab; daycare for children of students; e-mail services; employment services for current students; externships; housing assistance; Internet; learning resource lab; library services; nursing audiovisuals; placement services for program completers; skills, simulation, or other laboratory.

Library Facilities 230,910 volumes; 12,351 periodical subscriptions.

BACCALAUREATE PROGRAMS

Degree BScN

Available Programs Generic Baccalaureate; RN Baccalaureate.
Site Options St. Jerome, QC.
Study Options Full-time and part-time.
Program Entrance Requirements CPR certification, high school chemistry, immunizations, interview, RN licensure. Transfer students are accepted. *Application deadline:* 3/1 (fall). *Application fee:* CAN$30.
Advanced Placement Credit by examination available. Credit given for nursing courses completed elsewhere dependent upon specific evaluations.
Financial Aid *Loans:* college/university.

Contact Ms. Chantal Saint-Pierre, Directrice, Département des Sciences Infirmieres, Université du Québec en Outaouais, Office D-0414, Hull, QC J8X 3X7. *Telephone:* 819-595-3900 Ext. 2345. *Fax:* 819-595-3801. *E-mail:* chantal.st-pierre@uqo.ca.

GRADUATE PROGRAMS

Contact Ms. Chantal Saint-Pierre, Directrice, Département des Sciences Infirmieres, Université du Québec en Outaouais, CP 1250, Succursale Hull, Gatineau, QC J8X 3X7. *Telephone:* 819-595-3900 Ext. 2347. *Fax:* 819-595-2202. *E-mail:* chantal.st-pierre@uqo.ca.

MASTER'S DEGREE PROGRAM

Degree M Sc N

Available Programs Master's.

Concentrations Available Health-care administration. *Clinical nurse specialist programs in:* community health, critical care, psychiatric/mental health, rehabilitation. *Nurse practitioner programs in:* primary care.

Site Options St. Jerome, QC.

Study Options Full-time and part-time.

Program Entrance Requirements Computer literacy, 3 letters of recommendation, nursing research course, resume, statistics course. *Application deadline:* 5/1 (fall), 11/1 (winter), 3/1 (spring). *Application fee:* CAN$30.

Advanced Placement Credit given for nursing courses completed elsewhere dependent upon specific evaluations.

Degree Requirements 45 total credit hours, thesis or project.

Université Laval
Faculty of Nursing
Québec, Quebec

http://www.fsi.ulaval.ca

Founded in 1852

DEGREES • BSCN • MSN • PHD

Nursing Program Faculty 25 (64% with doctorates).

Baccalaureate Enrollment 798
Women 94% **Men** 6% **Minority** 18% **International** 12% **Part-time** 32%

Graduate Enrollment 116
Women 72% **Men** 28% **Minority** 32% **International** 24% **Part-time** 22%

Distance Learning Courses Available.

Nursing Student Activities Student Nurses' Association, nursing club.

Nursing Student Resources Academic advising; academic or career counseling; assistance for students with disabilities; bookstore; campus computer network; career placement assistance; computer lab; computer-assisted instruction; daycare for children of students; e-mail services; employment services for current students; externships; housing assistance; interactive nursing skills videos; Internet; learning resource lab; library services; nursing audiovisuals; placement services for program completers; resume preparation assistance; skills, simulation, or other laboratory; tutoring.

Library Facilities 3 million volumes (118,994 in health, 3,781 in nursing); 13,928 periodical subscriptions (624 health-care related).

BACCALAUREATE PROGRAMS

Degree BScN

Available Programs Accelerated Baccalaureate; Accelerated RN Baccalaureate; Generic Baccalaureate; RN Baccalaureate.

Study Options Full-time and part-time.

Program Entrance Requirements Transcript of college record, high school biology, high school chemistry, 5 years high school math, high school transcript, immunizations, minimum high school GPA. Transfer students are accepted.

Advanced Placement Credit given for nursing courses completed elsewhere dependent upon specific evaluations.

Contact *Telephone:* 418-656-2131 Ext. 7930. *Fax:* 418-656-7747.

GRADUATE PROGRAMS

Contact *Telephone:* 418-656-3356. *Fax:* 418-656-7304.

Université Laval (continued)

MASTER'S DEGREE PROGRAM

Degree MSN

Available Programs Accelerated Master's; Master's.

Concentrations Available Clinical nurse leader; health-care administration; nursing administration. *Clinical nurse specialist programs in:* acute care, adult health, cardiovascular, community health, critical care, family health, gerontology, oncology, palliative care, parent-child, pediatric, perinatal, psychiatric/mental health, public health, rehabilitation. *Nurse practitioner programs in:* adult health, primary care.

Study Options Full-time and part-time.

Program Entrance Requirements Clinical experience, transcript of college record, 2 letters of recommendation, nursing research course, resume, statistics course, French exam.

Advanced Placement Credit given for nursing courses completed elsewhere dependent upon specific evaluations.

Degree Requirements 45 total credit hours, thesis or project.

POST-MASTER'S PROGRAM

Areas of Study *Clinical nurse specialist programs in:* acute care, adult health, cardiovascular, community health, critical care, family health, gerontology, oncology, palliative care, parent-child, pediatric, perinatal, psychiatric/mental health, public health, rehabilitation. *Nurse practitioner programs in:* adult health, primary care.

DOCTORAL DEGREE PROGRAM

Degree PhD

Available Programs Doctorate.

Areas of Study Community health, nursing science.

Program Entrance Requirements Clinical experience, interview, 2 letters of recommendation, MSN or equivalent, scholarly papers, statistics course, vita, writing sample.

Degree Requirements 96 total credit hours, dissertation, oral exam, written exam.

POSTDOCTORAL PROGRAM

Areas of Study Aging, cancer care, community health, gerontology, health promotion/disease prevention, nursing interventions, nursing research, nursing science, outcomes.

Postdoctoral Program Contact *Telephone:* 418-656-3356. *Fax:* 418-656-7747.

CONTINUING EDUCATION PROGRAM

Contact *Telephone:* 418-656-2131 Ext. 6712. *Fax:* 418-656-7747.

SASKATCHEWAN

University of Saskatchewan

College of Nursing
Saskatoon, Saskatchewan

http://www.usask.ca/nursing/

Founded in 1907

DEGREES • BSN • MN • PHD

Nursing Program Faculty 134 (20% with doctorates).

Baccalaureate Enrollment 1,678
Women 93% **Men** 7% **Minority** 5% **Part-time** 17%

Graduate Enrollment 50
Women 94% **Men** 6% **Minority** 2% **Part-time** 62%

Distance Learning Courses Available.

Nursing Student Activities Student Nurses' Association.

Nursing Student Resources Academic advising; academic or career counseling; assistance for students with disabilities; bookstore; campus computer network; computer lab; computer-assisted instruction; daycare for children of students; e-mail services; employment services for current

students; interactive nursing skills videos; Internet; learning resource lab; library services; nursing audiovisuals; other; remedial services; resume preparation assistance; skills, simulation, or other laboratory; tutoring.

Library Facilities 2 million volumes (92,505 in health, 3,932 in nursing); 442,593 periodical subscriptions (3,069 health-care related).

BACCALAUREATE PROGRAMS

Degree BSN

Available Programs Accelerated Baccalaureate; Accelerated RN Baccalaureate; Baccalaureate for Second Degree; Generic Baccalaureate; RN Baccalaureate.

Site Options Regina, SK; Prince Albert, SK; Saskatoon, SK.

Study Options Full-time and part-time.

Program Entrance Requirements Transcript of college record, CPR certification, high school biology, high school chemistry, 4 years high school math, 4 years high school science, high school transcript, immunizations, minimum high school GPA of 2.0. Transfer students are accepted. *Application deadline:* 1/15 (fall). *Application fee:* CAN$90.

Advanced Placement Credit given for nursing courses completed elsewhere dependent upon specific evaluations.

Expenses (2009–10) *Tuition, area resident:* full-time CAN$5099; part-time CAN$168 per credit hour. *Required fees:* full-time CAN$695; part-time CAN$159 per credit.

Financial Aid 75% of baccalaureate students in nursing programs received some form of financial aid in 2008–09. *Gift aid (need-based):* private, college/university gift aid from institutional funds. *Loans:* FFEL (Subsidized and Unsubsidized Stafford PLUS), college/university, Canadian student loans, provincial loans. *Financial aid application deadline:* 3/15 (priority: 2/15).

Contact Ms. Shelley Bueckert, Academic Advisor and Admissions Officer, College of Nursing, University of Saskatchewan, 107 Wiggins Road, Saskatoon, SK S7N 5E5. *Telephone:* 306-966-6231. *Fax:* 306-966-6621. *E-mail:* shelley.bueckert@usask.ca.

GRADUATE PROGRAMS

Expenses (2009–10) *Tuition, area resident:* part-time CAN$500 per course. *Room and board:* room only: CAN$8151 per academic year. *Required fees:* part-time CAN$61 per credit.

Financial Aid 30% of graduate students in nursing programs received some form of financial aid in 2008–09. Fellowships, research assistantships, teaching assistantships available. *Financial aid application deadline:* 1/31.

Contact Dr. Lynnette Stamler, Assistant Dean, Graduate Studies, Continuing Education, and Information Technology, College of Nursing, University of Saskatchewan, 107 Wiggins Road, Saskatoon, SK S7N 5E5. *Telephone:* 306-966-1477. *Fax:* 306-966-6703. *E-mail:* lynnette.stamler@usask.ca.

MASTER'S DEGREE PROGRAM

Degree MN

Available Programs Master's.

Concentrations Available Nursing education. *Nurse practitioner programs in:* primary care.

Site Options Saskatoon, SK.

Study Options Full-time and part-time.

Program Entrance Requirements Minimum overall college GPA of 2.5, transcript of college record, 3 letters of recommendation, nursing research course, statistics course. *Application deadline:* 11/15 (fall). *Application fee:* CAN$75.

Advanced Placement Credit given for nursing courses completed elsewhere dependent upon specific evaluations.

Degree Requirements 24 total credit hours, thesis or project.

POST-MASTER'S PROGRAM

Areas of Study *Nurse practitioner programs in:* primary care.

DOCTORAL DEGREE PROGRAM

Degree PhD

Available Programs Doctorate.

Areas of Study Individualized study.

Site Options Saskatoon, SK.

Program Entrance Requirements Minimum overall college GPA of 4, 3 letters of recommendation, MSN or equivalent, statistics course, vita. Application deadline: 11/15 (fall). Application fee: CAN$75.

Degree Requirements 18 total credit hours, dissertation, oral exam, written exam.

CONTINUING EDUCATION PROGRAM

Contact Prof. Patricia Wall, Coordinator, College of Nursing, University of Saskatchewan, Continuing Nursing Education, Box 6000, RPO, Saskatoon, SK S7N 4J8. *Telephone:* 306-966-6261. *Fax:* 306-966-7673. *E-mail:* pat.wall@usask.ca.

CLOSE-UPS OF
NURSING PROGRAMS

Blessing-Rieman College of Nursing

Quincy, Illinois

THE COLLEGE

Blessing-Rieman College of Nursing (BRCN) prides itself on personal attention tailored to each student's needs and the high-quality nursing education it has offered for more than 115 years. Blessing Hospital School of Nursing, one of the first nursing schools in the state of Illinois, was founded in 1891 to train nurses for area health-care needs. Today, it is a small private college offering a Bachelor of Science in Nursing (B.S.N.) degree conferred jointly with a partner college, either Culver-Stockton College in Canton, Missouri, or Quincy University in Quincy, Illinois. This flexibility offers students many options not available from other programs while providing a high-quality college education and excellent nursing education at a regional medical center. Blessing-Rieman also offers an RN-to-B.S.N. track, an Advanced Placement track (for students with a bachelor's degree in another major), and a Master of Science in Nursing (M.S.N.) degree; none of these programs are joint programs.

Culver-Stockton College (C-SC) is an independent, private college with a scenic campus overlooking the Mississippi River in Canton, Missouri. The College offers music, theater, intercollegiate and intramural sports, student government, residence and dining halls, numerous clubs and organizations, and Greek life. Quincy University (QU) is an independent private institution rooted in the Catholic tradition. Cultural, social, and recreational opportunities include intercollegiate sports, a fitness center with an indoor pool, fine arts, student government, radio and TV studios, and housing options.

Blessing-Rieman is a member of the National League for Nursing, accredited by the Commission on Collegiate Nursing Education and the Higher Learning Commission (HLC) of the North Central Association of Colleges and Schools (NCA), and approved by the State Boards of Nursing in Illinois and Missouri. Students participate in the Student Nurse Organization and can act as representatives on College committees. The College offers apartments for upper-level students, a state-of-the-art child-care facility, a fitness center, and meal discounts at the hospital cafeteria.

To learn more about a career in nursing, receive more information on these programs, or to schedule a campus tour, students should contact the Admissions Office.

PROGRAM OF STUDY

Nursing courses are designed to help students acquire the knowledge, skills, and values needed to become professional nurses fully equipped to handle today's practice. Graduates are also prepared for leadership positions or further education in specialty fields. The joint Bachelor of Science in Nursing degree program for new college students is typically four years of study. Students are accepted into the nursing major during the sophomore year, after completing a successful freshman year. During the sophomore year, students take nursing classes on the Blessing-Rieman campus but continue to take general education courses on the partner campus. Nursing clinical experiences begin in the sophomore year at Blessing Hospital and other area health-care agencies. In the junior and senior years, students have usually completed most general education courses on the partner campus and may choose to live on the Blessing campus while focusing more on nursing courses and clinical experiences. Junior-level nursing instruction includes medical-surgical, psychiatric, obstetrical, and pediatric course work and clinicals.

Senior nursing courses include community health, acute-care nursing, professionalism, leadership, health policy, and research.

The joint-degree program with Culver-Stockton requires 124 semester hours, including English, speech, physical education, and religion core courses; computer science, fine arts, social science, and humanities general education courses; natural science, mathematics, psychology, and philosophy support courses; and 61 hours of nursing courses.

The joint-degree program with Quincy University requires 124 semester hours, including English, social sciences, humanities, fine arts, and theology courses; computer science and statistics tool courses; natural science and speech support courses; and 61 hours of nursing courses.

AFFILIATIONS WITH HEALTH-CARE FACILITIES

Blessing-Rieman is located on the campus of Blessing Hospital, a fully accredited regional medical facility serving the surrounding 100-mile radius. Blessing Hospital has state-of-the-art cancer and heart centers. Students have direct access to clinical areas of the hospital, with College instructors and hospital staff members providing guidance. Nearby clinics, health departments, nursing homes, and other health agencies offer additional clinical experiences.

ACADEMIC FACILITIES

Blessing-Rieman has computer-networked, air-conditioned classrooms and offices. A student lounge and locker room are adjacent to the classrooms. The Blessing Health Professions Library provides an extensive collection of books, online research databases, journals, and audiovisual teaching materials as well as study areas and a computer lab open to students that provides software, Internet access, and other resources. Students on the C-SC and QU campuses also have access to computers and libraries equipped with extensive resources.

Hands-on training in the College Skills Lab is provided prior to clinical experience. After demonstration by the Lab Coordinator, students use actual clinical equipment in a simulated hospital setting to practice nursing skills and clinical decision making. Skills Lab practice allows students to approach actual clinical experiences with confidence.

LOCATION

Blessing-Rieman College of Nursing is located in Quincy, Illinois, a city of around 45,000 people, on the bluff overlooking the Mississippi River in west-central Illinois. The city is known for its history, architecture, arts, and quality of life. Quincy has an Amtrak station, regional airport, TV and radio stations, convention center, numerous hotels and restaurants, shopping malls, theaters, and a symphony orchestra, and it is the site of fairs, festivals, and cultural events.

STUDENT SERVICES

One of the greatest benefits of the joint programs in nursing is that throughout their four-year concurrent enrollment, students enjoy all of the services and activities of Blessing-Rieman and the partnering institution as well as those of Blessing Hospital, whose state-of-the-art child-care center and fitness center are available for students.

THE NURSING STUDENT GROUP

Most students receive some form of financial aid. Many students choose to hold part-time jobs, including some who work in the

College as Student Assistants. Enrollment is approximately 200 students. Five to 10 percent of the students are men, and about 5 percent are members of minority groups. Of the graduates who seek employment, 100 percent have a position before graduation.

COSTS

According to the College's partnership agreements, tuition and fees for the first two years are set by the partner institutions, and the last two years are set by BRCN. Approximate tuition for the Culver-Stockton program is $22,250, and the Quincy University program is about $21,300. BRCN tuition is $16,275 for the junior and senior years. Students should check with the Admissions Office for current rates.

FINANCIAL AID

Significant scholarships and financial aid (federal, local, state, and private) are available at each institution, whether need-based and/or for academic achievement. Students should contact the financial aid office for further information.

APPLYING

Qualifications for acceptance as a freshman include a minimum 3.0 high school GPA, and a composite ACT score of at least 22 or an SAT combined score of at least 1020. High school courses must include 4 units of English; at least 2 units of science, including biology and chemistry; 3 units of social science; and 2 units of math, including 1 unit of algebra. Nontraditional students should contact the admissions office for requirements.

CORRESPONDENCE AND INFORMATION:

Blessing-Rieman College of Nursing
Broadway at 11th
Quincy, Illinois 62305-7005
Phone: 217-228-5520
        800-877-9140 Ext. 6949 (toll-free)
E-mail: admissions@brcn.edu
Web site: http://www.brcn.edu

Two Blessing-Rieman nursing students.

Columbia College of Nursing
Mount Mary College
Nursing Program
Milwaukee, Wisconsin

THE COLLEGES
In 1901, Columbia College of Nursing (CCON) began as part of the Knowlton Hospital and Training School. In 1909, the Columbia Hospital Corporation took over Knowlton Hospital and changed the name to the Columbia Hospital School of Nursing. In 1919, both hospital and school moved to their current location on Milwaukee's east side. By 1983, college-based nursing course work was replacing diploma nursing education. CCON joined with a college rooted in the liberal arts in order to confer an intercollegiate degree. In 2002, CCON and Mount Mary College entered into a partnership to confer the Bachelor of Science in Nursing degree.

Mount Mary College, an urban Catholic college for women sponsored by the School Sisters of Notre Dame, is located on the northwest side of Milwaukee. Mount Mary's roots are deep in the history of Wisconsin. St. Mary's Institute was founded in Prairie du Chien in 1872. In 1913, it extended its educational program to the postsecondary level and was chartered as St. Mary's College, a four-year Catholic college for women, the first in Wisconsin to grant degrees. Its academic standards were accepted by the North Central Association of Colleges in 1926. The institution changed its name to Mount Mary College when it moved to its present location on Milwaukee's northwest side in 1929.

THE INTERCOLLEGIATE NURSING PROGRAM
In 2002, Mount Mary College and the Columbia College of Nursing established a joint Bachelor of Science in Nursing (B.S.N.) degree program. The combination of Columbia's history of excellence with Mount Mary's highly respected tradition of a liberal arts-based education offers a program of high-quality preparation for a career in nursing. Nursing students combine nursing instruction with clinical placements, enabling them to meet the challenges of health care today and into the future. The nursing program is approved by the Wisconsin State Board of Nursing and the National League for Nursing Accrediting Commission. Both colleges are fully accredited by the North Central Association of Colleges and Schools.

PROGRAMS OF STUDY
Columbia College of Nursing and Mount Mary College offer a unique intercollegiate program leading to a Bachelor of Science in Nursing degree. A degree completion program leading to a Bachelor of Science in Nursing degree is also available for students who are registered nurses and have an associate degree or diploma in nursing.

AFFILIATIONS WITH HEALTH-CARE FACILITIES
Affiliations between Columbia College of Nursing and southeastern Wisconsin community clinical sites further guarantee that students, while experiencing the latest advances in nursing education, also remain on the cutting edge of today's changing health-care environment.

LOCATION
Columbia College of Nursing, located on Milwaukee's east side, is surrounded by residential neighborhoods and is easily accessible from the Interstate. The College is served by most of the city's major bus routes and is near a diverse assortment of shops, restaurants, and entertainment and recreational facilities.

Located on 80 acres on Milwaukee's northwest side, Mount Mary provides a park-like campus featuring stately stone buildings, gorgeous green lawns, and beautiful wooded areas in a residential area of Milwaukee.

STUDENT SERVICES
To broaden their cultural awareness, Columbia College of Nursing and Mount Mary encourage their students to take advantage of a variety of study-abroad opportunities. Accordingly, Mount Mary College sponsors trips to Rome, Peru, Guatemala, England, Ireland, Nicaragua, France, and China. Members of the nursing faculty accompanied nursing students to Arequipa, Peru, in 2007 for a community nursing clinical experience. Mount Mary College maintains affiliate relationships with numerous international colleges and universities, including the American College, Dublin, Ireland; the American Intercontinental University, London and Dubai; Nanzan College, Japan; Universidad Cathólica de Santa Maria (UCSM), Arequipa, Peru; and Notre Dame College, Kyoto, Japan.

Mount Mary College sponsors many social activities, including performances by musicians and comedians, dances, and picnics. These events are sponsored by the Mount Mary Programming and Activities Council (MMPAC), Student Government, Residence Hall Association, and other groups on campus. Other events include films, concerts, and lectures. Through participation in clubs/organizations, students have opportunities to develop leadership skills, collaborate with other clubs/organizations, network, and explore areas of interest. Special and professional interests are served by affiliates of national societies. Physical fitness and an interest in athletics are fostered through various activities, fitness programs, health and dance courses, and intercollegiate athletics. Mount Mary College is a member of NCAA Division III. The Blue Angels compete in basketball, cross-country, soccer, softball, tennis, and volleyball.

Academic and professional student services are available to all students. Services include tutoring and assistance with tests through the Academic Resource Center; advising, resume writing, and career planning through the Advising and Career Development Center; and personal counseling through the Counseling Center.

COSTS
For the 2009–10 academic year, tuition was $20,736 for full-time undergraduate study and $620 per credit for undergraduate nursing study. Various other fees are also applied. Room and board costs averaged $7280.

FINANCIAL AID
The Financial Aid Office at Mount Mary College develops a financial package on an individual basis for each qualified student. More than 90 percent of full-time Columbia/Mount Mary students receive some form of financial assistance. Students filing for financial aid should complete the Free Application for Federal Student Aid (FAFSA). Additional information on numerous merit-based scholarships, grants, and work-study opportunities is available for incoming first-year as well as transfer students. Students should contact the Admission Office for more information.

APPLYING
Candidates for admission are considered on the basis of academic preparation, scholarship, and evidence of the ability to do college work and benefit from it. Fifteen secondary school units are required for students entering directly from high school into the nursing program. The 15 units must consist of 2 in biology; 2 in chemistry; 2 in algebra; 3 in English; 4 in history, language, or social science; and 2 electives. Each applicant is reviewed individually. International students must take the Test of English as a Foreign Language (TOEFL). Early acceptance is available at Mount Mary College and advanced placement is honored. Mount Mary has a rolling admission policy. An admission decision is sent as soon as all required materials have been received and reviewed by the Admission Office. After notification of acceptance, students wishing to enroll must submit the $200 tuition deposit. There is a new direct admission policy for qualified students which applies to both transfer students and those entering directly from high school. Students make application for acceptance by Columbia College of Nursing to the nursing major upon completion of required college course work and demonstration of the required college grade point average. There is a separate application for the nursing program, along with course prerequisites. Neither Columbia College of Nursing nor Mount Mary discriminate

against any individual for reasons of race, color, religion, age, disability, or national or ethnic origin. The nursing program is open to both men and women.

CORRESPONDENCE AND INFORMATION

Admission Office
Mount Mary College
2900 North Menomonee River Parkway
Milwaukee, Wisconsin 53222-4597

Phone: 414-256-1219
       800-321-6265 (toll-free)
Web site: http://www.mtmary.edu

Columbia College of Nursing
Web site: http://www.ccon.edu

THE FACULTY OF COLUMBIA COLLEGE OF NURSING

Ann Aschenbrenner, Assistant Professor; M.S.N., Marquette, 2001. Adult nurse practitioner.

Virginia Bastian, Clinical Assistant Professor; M.S., Wisconsin–Milwaukee, 1996. Nurse practitioner, child and adolescent health.

Barbara Brenzel, Instructor; B.S.N., Wisconsin–Milwaukee, 1984. Foundations, medical-surgical nursing.

James Bumby, Clinical Instructor; M.S.N., Phoenix, 2007. Medical-surgical nursing.

Colleen Chamberlain, Clinical Instructor; B.S.N., Wisconsin–Milwaukee, 1982. Foundations, pediatric nursing.

Susan Cole, Assistant Professor; M.S, Marquette, 1991. Medical-surgical nursing.

Daniela Eichelberger, Assistant Professor; M.S.N., Marquette, 2004. Health-care systems.

Samuel Garland, Assistant Professor; M.S.N., Cardinal Stritch, 2007. Medical-surgical nursing.

Debra Johnson, Associate Professor; M.S.N., Wisconsin–Madison, 1977. Pediatrics.

Tammy Kasprovich, Assistant Professor; M.S.N., Cardinal Stritch, 2005. Emergency nursing.

Judy Kopka, Assistant Professor; M.S.N., Cardinal Stritch, 2002. Health promotion and mental health.

Kimberly Schuster, Clinical Assistant Professor; M.S.N., Northern Illinois, 1985. Medical-surgical nursing, oncology.

Gladys Simandl, Professor; Ph.D., Wisconsin–Milwaukee, 1990. Community nursing.

Giannina Vernon, Instructor; B.S.N., Concordia (Wisconsin), 2007. Medical-surgical nursing.

Jill Winters, Dean and C.E.O.; Ph.D., Wisconsin–Milwaukee, 1996. Biobehavioral interventions to improve outcomes in cardiovascular populations, telehealth, heart rate variability, exercise, therapeutic use of music, measurement.

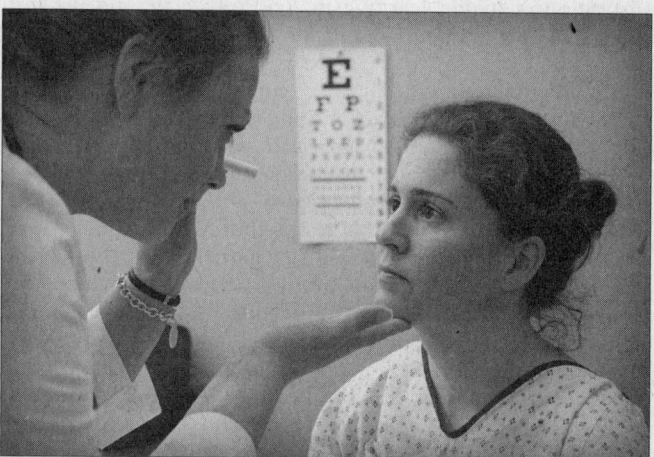

Nursing students in the state-of-the-art simulation center practice their newly learned techniques on each other.

Columbia University
School of Nursing
New York, New York

THE UNIVERSITY

By royal charter of King George III of England, Columbia University was founded in 1754 as King's College. It is the oldest institution of higher learning in New York State and the fifth oldest in the nation. A private, nonsectarian institution, Columbia University has, since its inception, addressed the issues of the moment, making important contributions to American life through teaching and research. It is organized into fifteen schools and is associated with more than seventy research and public service institutions and twenty-two scholarly journals. One of its most notable affiliations is with the research-oriented New York–Presbyterian Medical Center. The New York–Presbyterian Hospital, together with the Health Science Division of Columbia University, which includes the College of Physicians and Surgeons, College of Dental Medicine, School of Nursing, the Mailman School of Public Health, and programs in physical therapy, nutrition, and occupational therapy, constitute the Columbia University Medical Center. Total enrollment is close to 3,220 at the Health Science Campus and nearly 21,265 at the Morningside Campus.

THE SCHOOL OF NURSING

Founded in 1892 as the Presbyterian Hospital School of Nursing, the School first offered the baccalaureate degree when it joined Columbia University. In 1956, it became the first nursing program in the country to award a master's degree in a clinical nursing specialty. Today, the primary focus of the School is to educate advanced practice nurses: nurse practitioners, nurse midwives, and nurse anesthetists. This is done through the academic program at the graduate and advanced certificate levels. The School also offers two doctoral programs. The Ph.D. in Nursing is a research-intensive program that prepares nurse scholars to independently conduct research in outcomes and health policy. The Doctor of Nursing Practice (D.N.P.) prepares nurse clinicians with the knowledge and skills necessary for fully accountable practice with patients across sites and over time.

The curriculum is focused on preparing professional nurses who think critically, exercise technical competence, and make socially significant contributions to society through theory-based practice. The faculty members endeavor to provide knowledge, to stimulate learning, to define issues, and to serve as resource persons, clinicians, administrators, leaders, and innovators in nursing. A major strength of the School is that the faculty members maintain clinical practices in their advanced roles and incorporate students into these settings. One of these practices, Columbia Advanced Practice Nurse Associates (CAPNA), has gained national exposure as an innovative model of primary-care delivery by advanced practice nurses who are on the primary provider panels of several major managed-care organizations.

In addition to these programs, the School contains five academic centers: the Center for AIDS Research, the Center for Health Policy and Health Services Research, the Center for Evidence-Based Practice, the Center for Interdisciplinary Research to Reduce Antimicrobial Resistance, and the World Health Organization Collaborating Center for International Nursing Development in Advanced Practice. Columbia was the first nursing school to be awarded this World Health Organization designation, which makes the School an active participant in international exchange and collaborative research in advanced practice and health services research. It also facilitates the development of international study opportunities for its students.

PROGRAMS OF STUDY

The School of Nursing offers four levels of educational programs. The Combined B.S./M.S. (Entry to Practice) Program is an accelerated combined-degree program (B.S./M.S.) for non-nurse baccalaureate-prepared graduates, designed to prepare the student for a career as an advanced practice nurse. Academic studies are closely integrated with clinical experience. The prelicensure phase (B.S.) of the program consists of 60 credits, which are completed through full-time study. Upon completion, the student is eligible to take the professional nurse licensure examination in any state. In the specialty phase (postlicensure), the student follows the curriculum for a clinical specialty, which is described later in this section. Part-time study is available during the specialty phase.

The Graduate Program, leading to the M.S. degree, affords registered nurses with a bachelor's degree the opportunity to increase their knowledge in advanced nursing practice. The School currently offers eleven graduate majors: anesthesia, acute care, neonatal, psychiatric mental health nursing, midwifery, oncology, the primary-care specialties (adult, family, and pediatric), and women's health. The credit requirements range from 45 to 60 and are allocated among core, major, and elective courses. Cross-site curricula are available in selected programs. Joint degrees are available with the Schools of Public Health and Business.

The Advanced Certificate Program allows RNs with a master's degree in nursing to pursue an advanced practice program as a nurse practitioner. The credit requirements range from 23 to 36 credits.

The Ph.D. in Nursing Program is designed to prepare clinical nurse scholars to examine, shape, and refine the health-care delivery system. The program consists of 90 credits beyond the baccalaureate degree. Of these, 45 credits are credits earned at the master's level in a clinical specialist/nurse practitioner program.

The Doctor of Nursing Practice Program prepares nurses with the knowledge, skills, and attributes necessary for fully accountable practice with patients across sites and over time. The D.N.P. is the natural evolution and needed expansion of existing clinical degrees in nursing, the basic B.S. and the site-specific M.S. Currently, it is a 40-credit program designed for post-master's nurse practitioners.

AFFILIATIONS WITH HEALTH-CARE FACILITIES

The center of clinical activity at Columbia University Medical Center is the New York Presbyterian Medical Center, which includes a number of world-renowned facilities. Among the most notable are the Neurological Institute, the Eye Institute, Children's Hospital of New York, Sloane Hospital for Women, the Center for Geriatrics and Gerontology, the Organ Transplant Center, and the Center for Health Promotion and Disease Prevention. In addition, approximately 200 other sites in the tristate area are available for clinical education.

ACADEMIC FACILITIES

The Augustus C. Long Library is the fourth-largest academic medical library in the country and is part of the Columbia University Library system, which encompasses approximately forty libraries and more than 4 million volumes. The Long Library houses more than 400,000 volumes and receives more than 4,500 journals, most of which can be accessed through online computer search programs. The Media and Computer Center contains more than 3,000 audiovisual and computer-assisted instruction programs, including slides, videodiscs, tapes, and a wide variety of personal computer applications. Other services include microfilming, interlibrary loans, study and conference facilities, and photocopying services. The Special Collections Section houses several thousand rare works including the Florence Nightingale Collection, which is featured at exhibitions along with rare holdings of Freud and Webster.

The School of Nursing building houses two Technology Learning Centers (TLC). The TLCs include a mock hospital unit containing several patient units and an ambulatory-care area for practicing primary-care skills; it is used by graduate and undergraduate students for skills development, including physical assessment and state-of-the-art monitoring technology. There are also two informatics laboratories available to School of Nursing students.

LOCATION

The School of Nursing is part of the Columbia University Medical Center, a 20-acre campus overlooking the Hudson River on Manhattan's Upper West Side. Students can avail themselves of the recreational, cultural, and educational events and entertainment that have made New York City famous.

STUDENT SERVICES

The Office of Student Services is the hub of all student projects, programs, and services, and it coordinates activities with many other departments. Among the organizations and services provided are housing, health, athletic facilities, a Wellness Program, counseling and advisement, parking, shuttle bus, orientation, student records, Disability Services, and the International Student Office.

THE NURSING STUDENT GROUP

About 600 students are enrolled each year in the School of Nursing, and they represent a diverse group of nursing professionals. They come from all over the country, but most are from the tri-state area.

COSTS

During the 2009–10 academic year, tuition for undergraduates was $1118 per credit. For graduate students, tuition ranged from $1118 to $1522 per credit. Average housing costs at the Medical Center range from $4000 to $6000. Other expenses, including health fees, books, personal expenses, transportation, and uniforms, are estimated at $5000.

FINANCIAL AID

The goal of the School of Nursing Financial Aid Office is to provide as many students as possible with sufficient resources to meet their needs and to distribute funds to eligible students in a fair and equitable manner. Financial aid is met through a combination of scholarships, grants, work, and loans. Students should be able to meet all expenses for the academic year through a combination of these resources. The School of Nursing provides up to 99 percent of its students with financial assistance.

APPLYING

Columbia University School of Nursing has two semesters: one begins in September (fall semester) and the other in May (summer semester). All clinical sequences begin in the fall semester.

The Nurse Anesthesia Program enrolls once per year in May. Applications are due by November 1. The Post-Master's Certificate in Anesthesia Program enrolls in September, and applications are also due November 1. The Combined B.S./M.S. Program (Entry to Practice) enrolls once per year at the end of May. Applications are due by November 15. The Ph.D. enrolls once per year in September. Applications are due by February 1. The Doctor of Nursing Practice Program (D.N.P.) enrolls once per year in September. Applications are due by March 1. The University Statutory Certificate Program enrolls once per year in September. Applications can be submitted throughout the year and no later than June 1.

Admission is based on past academic and professional performance. Admission requirements include an online application form with a fee; a typed, double-spaced, 12-point font, a one-page personal statement describing professional goals and aspirations; three competed recommendation forms; official transcripts from all postsecondary schools; official GRE scores; a resume or CV; a copy of an RN license and current registration (if applicable); and an undergraduate course in statistics and in physical assessment. Students should consult the School of Nursing Web site for specific admission criteria.

CORRESPONDENCE AND INFORMATION

Columbia University School of Nursing
Office of Admissions
617 West 168th Street, Suite 134
New York, New York 10032

Phone: 800-899-8895
Fax: 212-305-3680
E-mail: nursing@columbia.edu
Web site: http://www.nursing.columbia.edu

Duke University
School of Nursing
Durham, North Carolina

THE UNIVERSITY

Since its founding in 1839 as the Union Institute, and later as Trinity College before incorporating in 1924, the basic principles of Duke University have remained constant. Through changing generations of students, the objective has been to encourage individuals to achieve, to the extent of their capacities, an understanding and appreciation of the world in which they live, their relationship to it, their opportunities, and their responsibilities. Today, Duke University has an enrollment of 12,800 from all fifty states and many foreign countries.

The School of Medicine, School of Nursing, and Duke Hospital and Health Network are the core institutions of the Duke University Medical Center and Health System, which ranks among the world's outstanding health-care providers. Duke Hospital, with 1,048 beds, is one of the most modern patient-care facilities available anywhere. The Health System's mission is to be a leader in world health care by maintaining superiority in its four primary functions: excellent patient care, dedication to educational programs, national and international distinction in the quality of research, and service to the region.

THE SCHOOL OF NURSING

Since the School's founding in 1930, Duke has prepared outstanding clinicians, educators, and researchers and is continuing this tradition. Using the intellectual and clinical resources of both Duke University Medical Center and Duke University, the School offers an Accelerated Bachelor of Science in Nursing degree (for second degree students), a Master of Science in Nursing degree, a Doctor of Nursing Practice, and a Ph.D. program.

Faculty members work closely with students to challenge and nurture them; students practice with state-of-the-art science and technology in the medical center and have opportunities to work in rural and underserved areas.

PROGRAMS OF STUDY

The School of Nursing offers a 58-credit-hour, full-time, Accelerated Bachelor of Science in Nursing (B.S.N.) degree program in a sixteen-month, intensive format. In addition, a flexible, 39- to 59-credit program leading to the Master of Science in Nursing (M.S.N.) degree is offered. There is a joint M.S.N./M.B.A. degree program in conjunction with the Fuqua School of Business. The School of Nursing also offers a collaborative arrangement with Meredith College in Raleigh, North Carolina, that facilitates completion of the M.S.N. degree in nursing and health-care leadership or clinical research management at the Duke School of Nursing and the M.B.A. at Meredith College. The School of Nursing also offers a post-master's certificate to students who have already earned an M.S.N. The purpose of the Master of Science in Nursing program is to prepare professional nurses for advanced practice in a clinical specialty, administration, or education. Graduates are prepared as clinical nurse specialists in gerontology, oncology, critical care, pediatrics, or neonatal care; as adult nurse practitioners (with specialization in primary care, acute care, cardiovascular care, or oncology/HIV); as gerontological nurse practitioners, family nurse practitioners, neonatal nurse practitioners, pediatric acute/chronic care nurse practitioners, pediatric nurse practitioners, or combined neonatal-pediatric nurse practitioners with an emphasis on rural health care; as nursing health-care leadership administrators and managers and clinical research managers; as nurse anesthetists; as advanced practice nurses prepared to serve faith communities; and as nurse educators. The clinical research management program, the nursing and health-care leadership program, the nursing education program, the nursing informatics program, and selected nurse practitioner core courses are available online to distance education students. The family nurse practitioner, adult nurse practitioner, and gerontological nurse practitioner programs are also available online. The integration of education, practice, and research is basic to the entire curriculum as well as to the activities of each student, and the program is designed to provide maximum flexibility for full-time or part-time study.

The School of Nursing is excited about its new Doctor of Nursing Practice (D.N.P.) program that was launched in the fall of 2008. The D.N.P. program is designed to prepare clinical scholars skilled in translating research and other evidence into clinical practice, measuring patient outcomes, and transforming health-care systems to ensure quality and safety. The program requires a minimum of 73 credits post-B.S.N.; full- and part-time options are available. Individuals with an earned master's degree in nursing in an advanced practice specialty can elect to pursue the Post-Master's D.N.P., which requires a minimum of 34 credits.

The School of Nursing also offers a Ph.D. in nursing. The Ph.D. program in nursing prepares nurse scientists to conduct nursing research in the broad area of trajectories of chronic illness and care systems. Graduates assume roles primarily in academic and research settings. The approach is to admit a small number of highly qualified applicants so every student can work closely with one or more faculty members in a series of mentored experiences supported by formal course work, to ensure socialization to the role of research scientist, ensure significant knowledge and skill acquisition for launching a successful program of independent postdoctorate research, and prepare for an entry-level role in an academic setting. The program requires a minimum of 54 credit hours of graduate course work (post-M.S.N.) prior to a dissertation. Students work on active research projects, and it is expected that most students graduate with a record of publication. Course work is structured with a substantial core (36 credits) of nursing science and research methods to be taken in the School of Nursing. This core is expanded with elected statistics, research methods, and minor area courses (18 credits) to be taken mainly outside of nursing in other Duke University departments. In addition to course work and a dissertation, the Ph.D. program in nursing includes two program-long structured activities that include mentored research and teaching experiences and development of the student's scholarly portfolio. Each student takes a comprehensive exam at the end of the second year or at the beginning of the third year of residence. The final requirement is the presentation of a dissertation. Students are expected to complete the program in four to five years. For more information and further details, students should inquire by e-mail at nursephd@notes.duke.edu.

AFFILIATIONS WITH HEALTH-CARE FACILITIES

As one of the leading national and international academic health systems, Duke University Health System has assembled and integrated a comprehensive range of health-care resources providing the very best in patient care, health education, and clinical research. The clinical faculty members of the School number more than 100 and represent all specialties. They actively participate in nursing education and practice nursing in hospitals and ambulatory settings. Cooperative teaching and clinical facilities, including health departments, retirement centers, and private practices in both urban and rural areas, are available to students mostly within the state of North Carolina. Occasionally, placements are arranged out-of-state or in other countries to accommodate the student's needs.

Nationally recognized centers with which the School of Nursing is affiliated include the Duke Heart Center, the Center for Aging and Human Development, the Comprehensive Cancer Center, the Comprehensive Sickle Cell Center, Alzheimer's Disease Research Center, Duke Hypertension Center, Duke–VA Center for Cerebrovascular Research, Cystic Fibrosis/Chest Center and Clinic, Sleep Disorders Center, the Eye Center, and the Geriatric Research, Education, and Clinical Center.

ACADEMIC FACILITIES

The goal of the Duke Nursing Research Center is to facilitate the conduct of clinical research by the students, faculty, and nursing staff. The center provides support for research through assistance with literature searches, development of research designs, the Institutional Review Board and/or the protection of human subjects consultation, data collection and data management, grant proposal development, and editorial review.

The Duke School of Nursing is a national leader in online education; all of the School's courses are enriched by the use of technology. The Center for Nursing Discovery includes two state-of-the art laboratories and an eighteen-station computer laboratory. The School also supports a Center for Instruction Technology and Distance Learning to provide technical support for online education and classroom technology.

The Medical Center Library, located in the Seeley G. Mudd Communications Center and Library Building, provides services and collections necessary to support educational, research, and clinical activities. The library has sizable holdings of nursing and health-care related books and journals. The Medical Center Library maintains a robust online presence (http://www.mclibrary.duke.edu/) that extends access to library resources and services, such as locally created and licensed databases, electronic books and journals, and online learning and reference tools.

LOCATION
Durham, a city of 257,947, is about 250 miles south of Washington, D.C. Durham and nearby Raleigh and Chapel Hill constitute the three points of the Research Triangle, one of the nation's foremost centers of research-oriented industries and government, research, and regulatory agencies.

STUDENT SERVICES
The University has many resources and activities to offer students. These include the Graduate and Professional Student Council, the Women's Center, the Mary Lou Williams Center for Black Culture, and the International House as well as the full programs of the Office of Cultural Affairs, the Duke University Campus Ministry, the Duke University Union, the Office of Student Activities, and recreational clubs.

THE NURSING STUDENT GROUP
Approximately 73 students are enrolled in the accelerated B.S.N. degree program, 358 students are enrolled in the M.S.N. and post-master's certificate programs, 26 students are enrolled in the D.N.P. program, and 11 students are enrolled in the Ph.D. program. About 10 percent are men, and 18 percent are members of minority groups.

COSTS
Tuition in 2009–10 was $1120 per credit hour for graduate nursing courses and $875 per credit hour for undergraduate nursing courses.

FINANCIAL AID
Merit and need-based scholarships, traineeships, and federal/state loan programs are generally available. Approximately 80 percent of School of Nursing students receive some form of financial aid.

APPLYING
Admission requirements for the Accelerated B.S.N. program include a bachelor's degree from an accredited college or university, a minimum 3.0 GPA (4.0 scale), three letters of recommendation, 1000 or greater on the GRE (scores not more than five years old), and completion of all required prerequisites. Admission requirements for the graduate program include a bachelor's degree with an upper-division nursing major from an NLNAC- or CCNE-accredited program, a preferred undergraduate scholastic average of 3.0 or better (4.0 scale), an introductory course in descriptive and inferential statistics, 1000 or greater on the GRE (scores not more than five years old), and RN licensure in North Carolina. An interview is requested; if distance prohibits, a telephone interview may be arranged. Exceptions to any of the above are considered on an individual basis.

Duke University does not discriminate on the basis of race, color, national and ethnic origin, handicap, sexual orientation or preference, gender, or age in the administration of educational policies, admission policies, financial aid, employment, or any other University program or activity. It admits qualified students to all the rights, privileges, programs, and activities generally accorded or made available to students.

CORRESPONDENCE AND INFORMATION
Office of Admissions and Student Services
Duke University School of Nursing
Box 3322 Medical Center
Durham, North Carolina 27710

Phone: 919-684-4248
      877-415-3853 (toll-free)
E-mail: SONAdmissions@mc.duke.edu
Web site: http://www.nursing.duke.edu

THE FACULTY
Ruth Anderson, Professor; Ph.D., Texas at Austin, 1987; RN.

Donald Bailey, Associate Professor; Ph.D., North Carolina at Chapel Hill, 2002; RN.

Julie V. Barroso, Associate Professor; Ph.D., Texas at Austin; RN, ANP, CS.

Shulamit L. Bernard, Associate Professor, Ph.D., North Carolina at Chapel Hill, 1994; RN, FHNC.

Jane Blood-Siegfried, Associate Professor; D.N.S., UCLA, 1995; RN, PNP.

Margaret Bowers, Assistant Clinical Professor; M.S.N., Duke, 1990; RN, FNP.

Wanda Bradshaw, Assistant Clinical Professor; M.S.N., Duke, 1996; RN, PNP, NNP.

Debra Brandon, Associate Professor; Ph.D., North Carolina at Chapel Hill, 2000; RN.

John Brion, Assistant Clinical Professor; Ph.D., Ohio State, 2007; RN.

Mary T. Champagne, Professor; Ph.D., Texas at Austin, 1981; RN.

Penny Cooper, Assistant Clinical Professor; M.S.N., Duke, 2002; RN.

Kirsten Corazzini, Assistant Professor; Ph.D., Massachusetts Boston, 2000.

Linda Davis, Professor; Ph.D., Maryland, 1984; RN.

Susan Denman, Assistant Professor; Ph.D., North Carolina at Chapel Hill, 1996; RN, FNP.

Sharron Docherty, Assistant Professor; Ph.D., North Carolina at Chapel Hill, 1999; RN, PNP.

Anthony T. Dren, Consulting Professor; Ph.D., Michigan, 1966.

Pamela Edwards, Associate Consulting Professor; M.S.N., Ed.D., North Carolina State, 1989; RN, BC.

Catherine Gilliss, Dean and Vice Chancellor for Nursing Affairs for Duke University Health System; D.N.Sc., California, San Francisco, 1983; RN.

Linda K. Goodwin, Associate Professor; Ph.D., Kansas, 1992; RN.

Helen Gordon, Assistant Clinical Professor; M.S., Utah, 1978; RN, CNM.

James Harmon, Clinical Associate Professor; M.S.N., Duke, 1997; RN.

Sharon Hawks, Assistant Professor; M.S.N., North Carolina at Greensboro, 1993; RN, CRNA.

Cristina Hendrix, Assistant Professor; D.N.Sc., LSU, 2001; RN, FNP.

Diane Holdtich-Davis, Professor; Ph.D., Connecticut, 1985; RN, FAAN.

Constance Johnson, Assistant Professor; Ph.D., Texas Health Science Center at Houston, 2003; RN.

Tracy Kelly, Assistant Clinical Professor; M.S.N.; RN, PNP.

Robin Knobel, Assistant Professor; Ph.D., North Carolina at Chapel Hill, 2006; RN, RNC, NNP.

Camille Lambe; Assistant Clinical Professor; Ph.D., North Carolina, 2006; RN, NP.

Lawrence Landerman, Associate Research Professor; Ph.D., Duke, 1979.

Janet Levy, Assistant Research Professor; Ph.D., Kansas, 1983.

Marcia S. Lorimer, Assistant Clinical Professor; M.S.N., Virginia, 1988; RN, PNP.

Michelle Martin, Assistant Professor; Ph.D., Case Western Reserve, 2001; RN.

Eleanor S. McConnell, Associate Research Professor; Ph.D., North Carolina at Chapel Hill, 1995; RN.

Mary Miller-Bell, Adjunct Associate Professor; Pharm.D., North Carolina at Chapel Hill, 1998.

Brenda M. Nevidjon, Clinical Professor and Chair of the M.S.N. Program; M.S.N., North Carolina at Chapel Hill, 1978; RN.

Holly Lieder Parker, Assistant Clinical Professor; M.S.N., Duke, 2000; RN, PNP.

Judith K. Payne, Assistant Professor; Ph.D., Iowa, 1998; RN, CS.

Katherine Pereira, Assistant Clinical Professor; M.S.N., Duke, 2002; RN, FNP.

Beth Phillips, Assistant Clinical Professor; M.S.N., Duke, 1993; RN.

Dorothy Powell, Clinical Professor; Ed.D., William and Mary, 1983; RN, FAAN.

Marva M. Price, Assistant Professor; Dr.P.H., North Carolina at Chapel Hill, 1994; RN, FNP, FAAN.

Michael Relf, Assistant Dean for Undergraduate Programs; Ph.D., Johns Hopkins, 2001; RN, ACNS-BC, AACRN.

Karen F. Ricker, Assistant Clinical Professor; M.S.N., North Carolina at Greensboro, 1993; CRNA, RRT.

Susan Schneider, Assistant Professor; Ph.D., Case Western Reserve, 1998; RN.

Nancy Short, Associate Clinical Professor and Chair of the Accelerated B.S.N. Program; Dr.P.H., North Carolina at Chapel Hill, 2003; RN.

Dori Sullivan, Associate Dean, Academic Affairs; Ph.D., Connecticut, 1990; RN, NE-BC, CNL, CPHQ.

Dierdre Thornlow; Assistant Professor; Ph.D., Virginia, 2007; RN.

J. Frank Titch, Assistant Clinical Professor; M.S.N.A., Virginia Commonwealth, 1994; RN, CRNA.

Kathryn Trotter, Assistant Clinical Professor; M.S.N., Kentucky, 1988; RN, FNP.

Barbara S. Turner, Professor and Director of the D.N.P. Program; D.N.Sc., California, San Francisco, 1984; RN, FAAN.

George H. Turner III, Assistant Clinical Professor; M.A., Webster, 1978; RPh.

Kathleen M. Turner, Assistant Clinical Professor and Associate Director of the Accelerated B.S.N. Program; M.S.N., Duke, 1993; RN.

Queen Utley-Smith, Assistant Professor; Ed.D., North Carolina State, 1999; RN.

Charles Vacchiano, Clinical Professor; Ph.D., Medical University of South Carolina, 1995; RN, CRNA.

Theresa Valiga, Director, Institute for Educational Excellence; Ed.D., NYU, 1981; RN, FAAN.

Kathryn A. Wood, Assistant Professor; Ph.D., California, San Francisco, 1996; RN.

Duquesne University

School of Nursing

Pittsburgh, Pennsylvania

THE UNIVERSITY

Duquesne University, located in Pittsburgh, Pennsylvania, America's renaissance city, is a private coeducational Catholic university with ten schools and an enrollment of more than 10,000 students. Currently, the University is experiencing a period of unprecedented growth, and nearly 100 nations and every state are represented in Duquesne's student body.

U.S. News & World Report's annual ranking of America's Best Colleges has moved Duquesne University into the top tier of more than 1,400 colleges surveyed. With a long tradition of scholarship and community service, Duquesne is among the top Catholic universities in the United States and has a well-deserved reputation for providing an education for the mind, heart, and spirit. The University offers a wide variety of activities and volunteer opportunities that complement the curriculum and provide a broad, well-balanced, and fully integrated education.

THE SCHOOL OF NURSING

Founded in 1937, the School of Nursing at Duquesne was the first nursing school in Pennsylvania to offer a baccalaureate program in nursing, and it was among the first in the nation to offer an online doctoral program in nursing. Continuing that tradition of innovation, Duquesne's School of Nursing offers a wide variety of online and traditional degree and certificate programs. The Doctor of Nursing Practice (D.N.P.) program began fall 2008. A leader in nursing education for generations, the School of Nursing at Duquesne maintains the highest standards of clinical competency, academic achievement, and dedication to helping others.

Duquesne University School of Nursing was recently recognized by the National League for Nursing as a Center of Excellence in Nursing Education for achievement in the area of student learning and professional development. Community service integrated with an unmatched educational experience is the hallmark of a nursing education at Duquesne. This commitment to service holds true for the faculty and staff, as well. Members of the School of Nursing's award-winning faculty have been widely recognized for their volunteer work as well as their clinical expertise, research accomplishments, and teaching skills.

Pittsburgh is home to a number of world-class medical centers that provide Duquesne nursing students with state-of-the-art clinical experiences. Duquesne faculty members teach all professional courses as well as guide and direct the clinical learning experiences.

Faculty members operate a number of Nurse-Managed Wellness Centers in underserved communities, where nurses and other health-care providers promote health and wellness and monitor chronic medical conditions. The clinics offer students an invaluable clinical learning experience and an ongoing opportunity for community service.

Established in 2006, the Center for Nursing Research is an outgrowth of the School's longstanding commitment to research and scholarship. Dedicated to building a community of scholars that includes faculty members and students, the center supports qualitative and quantitative methodologies with a particular emphasis on topics related to health disparities, cultural competence, and chronic deviations from health.

The School of Nursing offers students a transcultural perspective on health care. Through student/faculty exchange programs, collaborative international research projects, and hands-on training in other countries, students and faculty members are given a wide range of educational, research, and nursing leadership opportunities.

The Center for Health Care Diversity addresses health-care equity and diversity issues in minority populations through community-focused research, nursing education programs, health policy development, and community service.

PROGRAMS OF STUDY

The School of Nursing offers baccalaureate, master's, and doctoral degrees as well as a variety of professional certificates. School of Nursing students may enroll part-time or full-time. The undergraduate program of the School of Nursing leads to the degree of Bachelor of Science in Nursing (B.S.N.). At the undergraduate level, Duquesne offers a four-year B.S.N. and the Second Degree B.S.N. The B.S.N. program is designed to educate nurse generalists and usually requires four years of full-time study. The curriculum (130 credits) provides students with a strong foundation in the natural, biological, and behavioral sciences, most of which are taken during the first two years of study. Students receive an introduction to the nursing profession at the freshman level and begin clinical experience with clients and families during the sophomore year. The junior and senior years are devoted almost exclusively to clinical experience. More than 1,100 clinical hours are embedded in the community-based curriculum. Learning opportunities are provided in hospitals, schools, homes, health agencies, and in numerous community settings.

The Second Degree B.S.N. program allows the non-nurse with a baccalaureate degree to achieve a Bachelor of Science in Nursing degree in twelve months. After all requirements for the B.S.N. degree have been completed, students are eligible to take the state board examination for nursing licensure. The program begins in August and includes three semesters of intensive course work using traditional classroom instruction, creative Web-enhanced seminars for nonclinical courses, and more than 850 hours of clinical practice in leading health-care settings.

The M.S.N. program, which is offered entirely online, is based on the belief that specialization in nursing is acquired at the graduate level. This program is designed to meet the current and future needs of nurses who are likely to hold leadership positions. It educates nurses to plan, initiate, effect, and evaluate change; ensure high-quality patient care; and enhance the profession. Working nurses may continue their employment while undertaking this course of study through part-time enrollment, or course work may be undertaken on a full-time basis for all programs.

Three areas of specialization exist in the M.S.N. program: nursing education (39 credits), family nurse practitioner (46 credits), and forensic nursing (37 credits).

Post-master's certificates offered online give professional nurses the opportunity to learn skills and acquire information that may not have been offered in graduate programs. Course work in these nondegree programs is designed to prepare nurses for certification through applicable professional organizations. Duquesne offers the following post-master's certificates: nursing education (14 credits), family nurse practitioner (33 credits), forensic nursing (17 credits), and transcultural/international nursing (12 credits).

The online Doctor of Philosophy (Ph.D.) degree (58 credits) prepares nurses for a lifetime of intellectual inquiry and creative scholarship. This online program permits students to earn a doctoral degree in nursing using state-of-the-art distance education technology. Online courses are asynchronous, meaning that students can complete their work anytime and anywhere via the Internet. Mandatory fieldwork can be conducted near the student's home. Ph.D. students are required to be on campus for one week each spring during the completion of their required course work (a period that varies from two to four years). During that week, students meet with faculty advisers, attend lectures by visiting professors, participate in seminars for required courses, complete examinations, and participate in program evaluation.

The online Doctor of Nursing Practice (D.N.P.) program (33 credits) is for nurses with a nursing specialty who are seeking a terminal degree in nursing practice, and offers an alternative to research-focused doctoral programs. The D.N.P. program is also open to nurses whose long-range goals lie in nursing service or nursing education. The D.N.P. curriculum addresses dimensions of nursing practice with strong implications for service and education, as well as practice. The program was designed to provide nurses with the knowledge and skills to transform the health-care delivery system. Graduates are well prepared to judge organizational effectiveness and adapt to economic trends and new health-care policies, so they are able to design better models for patient-care services. The culminating capstone project demonstrates the candidate's ability to change health care in creative and innovative ways by seven developing systems, programs of evaluation, or nursing interventions that improve health outcomes for patient populations. Students are required to come to campus twice during the program of study.

ACADEMIC FACILITIES
Duquesne University's Gumberg Library houses extensive collections of digital research databases and electronic journals, books, and reference works that are accessible from remote locations. The library's facilities include DVD collections as well as numerous computers and multimedia learning tools. The School of Nursing has technologically advanced facilities, which include sophisticated educational tools and a realistic practice setting for learning clinical skills and procedures.

LOCATION
Duquesne's campus provides a comfortable and secure academic and social atmosphere that is just minutes from downtown Pittsburgh. The scenic hilltop campus is readily accessible to the city's business, cultural, entertainment, and shopping districts while still offering students the privacy and peaceful atmosphere of a self-contained 48-acre campus. Home to emerging technologies as well as established corporations and rated as one of the nation's most livable cities, Pittsburgh combines the best features of urban life with the charm, pace, and personality of small-town living. A new five-story recreation center provides student fitness facilities to meet increasing interest in health and wellness.

STUDENT SERVICES
Duquesne University offers a variety of services that help students achieve their academic and professional goals and grow socially, spiritually, and personally. Support services include student Health Service, the Office of Freshman Development and Special Student Services, Career Services Center, Comprehensive Student Advisement, University Counseling Center, Learning Skills Center, and Campus Ministry. In addition, the Office of International Programs assists students and scholars from other countries who are pursuing undergraduate and graduate studies at Duquesne.

THE NURSING STUDENT GROUP
The School of Nursing currently has an enrollment of more than 450 B.S.N. students. Ten percent are members of minority groups, and 10 percent are men. Doctoral students comprise 40 percent of the more than 250 graduate students. Duquesne's nursing students come from around the United States and the world. In addition to challenging clinical and classroom learning, Duquesne's nursing students are involved in a full range of campus activities, including student government, fraternities, sororities, and social and professional organizations (Alpha Tau Delta, Chi Eta Phi, Male Association of Nursing, Nurses Christian Fellowship, Sigma Theta Tau International Honor Society, and the Student Nurses Association of Pennsylvania). Nursing students have excelled in a number of competitive sports, including football, baseball, crew, volleyball, soccer, lacrosse, cross-country, swimming, and diving.

COSTS
For the 2009–10 academic year, undergraduate full-time students (12–18 credits) paid $26,468 per year for tuition and fees. Undergraduate room and board per semester were $4600 (double room). Undergraduate tuition and fees were $876 per credit for part-time students. Graduate tuition and fees (part-time or full-time) were $954 per credit. Other estimated undergraduate nursing school expenses each semester include books and supplies, $800; student liability insurance, $30; and uniforms, $150.

FINANCIAL AID
Tuition at Duquesne is among the lowest among private national universities, and competitive financial aid packages make a Duquesne education more affordable. Financial aid includes scholarships, grants, loans, and part-time employment awarded to help students meet the costs of education. Awards, both merit-based and need-based, come through a variety of sources, including programs administered by the federal and state government, private organizations, and the University. Duquesne is constantly developing resources for funding scholarships and providing financial assistance, and the School of Nursing maintains numerous listings of nursing funding sources for undergraduate and graduate nursing education, including federal, state, and private organizations and local hospital discounts. Students must apply for any awards by May 1 of each year.

APPLYING
Admission requirements for the undergraduate and graduate programs are specific for each degree option. Transfer and international applicants must fulfill all undergraduate or graduate admission requirements. A personal or telephone interview with a School of Nursing representative is highly recommended and may be required, depending on the program of study. Interested applicants should contact the School of Nursing or visit http://www.duq.edu/nursing for detailed information.

CORRESPONDENCE AND INFORMATION
Duquesne University School of Nursing
600 Forbes Avenue
Pittsburgh, Pennsylvania 15282-1760
Phone: 412-396-6550 (general information)
       412-396-4945 (program inquiries)
Fax: 412-396-6346
E-mail: nursing@duq.edu
Web site: http://www.duq.edu/nursing

D'Youville College
Department of Nursing
Buffalo, New York

THE COLLEGE

D'Youville College is a private, coeducational liberal arts and professional college offering students a high-quality education in more than thirty undergraduate and graduate degree programs. Founded in 1908 by the Grey Nuns as the first college for women in western New York to offer baccalaureate degrees to women, it was named for their founder, Saint Marguerite D'Youville. The current enrollment is 3,000 men and women. Students' learning is facilitated by the low 14:1 student-faculty ratio. The College is committed to helping its students grow not only academically but also in the social and personal areas of their college experience.

THE DEPARTMENT OF NURSING

D'Youville College has been educating and preparing professional nurses for careers since 1942; the first Bachelor of Science in Nursing (B.S.N.) class graduated in 1946. In 1957, the RN to B.S.N. degree program was initiated, offering a specialized curriculum for the working professional nurse. All programs offered by the nursing department are fully accredited by the Commission on Collegiate Nursing Education (CCNE) and approved by the New York State Education Department.

The nursing faculty members are committed, dedicated educators who pride themselves on providing individual attention. Faculty members, the majority of whom are prepared at the doctoral level, represent diverse backgrounds, both clinically and educationally, providing numerous specialty areas for the students to draw upon.

PROGRAMS OF STUDY

D'Youville College has been growing and attracting students from all over the world since 1908, playing a leadership role in the areas of professional health training. D'Youville offers a four-year Bachelor of Science in Nursing degree program, and students who are interested in pursuing careers in nursing also have the option of completing a dual-degree, five-year sequence to graduate with both a baccalaureate and a master's degree. It is a direct-entry program in which accepted students do not have to reapply or requalify for upper-division courses. The B.S.N. degree program combines a liberal arts foundation with professional nursing course work. Students begin their clinical experiences at area hospitals and health facilities in their sophomore year. Areas of clinical experience include geriatrics, pediatrics, OB/maternity, and medical/surgical nursing. To hone their clinical and research skills, students participate in internships during the summer of their junior year. The two-year RN to B.S.N. degree program includes an RN to B.S.N./M.S. option and an RN to B.S.N./M.S. in community health nursing option, in which RNs complete an additional year of study and graduate with both degrees. Convenient class scheduling provides working nursing professionals with the opportunity to study full-time by attending only two days a week. This alternative scheduling allows students to continue working in their professions while earning their degrees.

At the graduate level, nursing programs include the Master of Science (M.S.) in community health nursing, with concentrations in advanced clinical nursing, high-risk parents and children, nursing management, and nursing education; the M.S. in nursing, with choice of clinical focus; and the Master of Science in family nurse practitioner studies as well as a post-master's certificate in family nurse practitioner studies.

AFFILIATIONS WITH HEALTH-CARE FACILITIES

Specific facilities with which D'Youville has affiliations include Catholic Health System, which encompasses Mercy Hospital of Buffalo and Kenmore Mercy Hospital; Erie County Medical Center; WNY's Level I Trauma and Burn Center; Buffalo Psychiatric Center; Kaleida Health Care System, which comprises Women and Children's Hospital of Buffalo, Buffalo General Hospital, Millard Fillmore Hospital, and the Visiting Nurses Association of Western New York; BryLin Hospital; and the world-renowned Roswell Park Cancer Institute.

ACADEMIC FACILITIES

D'Youville's modern Library Resource Center, which was completed in 1999, contains 154,000 volumes, including microtext and software and subscriptions to 870 periodicals and newspapers. The multimillion-dollar Dr. Pauline M. Alt Building houses laboratories, including those for anatomy, organic chemistry, quantitative analysis, and computer science. It also houses classrooms, faculty offices, and development centers, including one for career development. In addition, an academic center opened in 2001.

LOCATION

D'Youville is situated on Buffalo's residential west side. The College is within minutes of many social attractions, including the downtown shopping center, the Kleinhans Music Hall, the Albright-Knox Art Gallery, two museums, and several theaters that offer stage productions. Seasonal changes in the area offer a variety of recreational opportunities. Buffalo is only 90 miles from Toronto and 25 minutes from Niagara Falls.

STUDENT SERVICES

The College offers a full range of student services. The D'Youville Freshman Experience (DFX) is designed to help make the students' first year exciting, fun, and challenging. At orientation, students are assigned a College mentor and register for the FOCUS Freshmen Seminar. There are also activities and leadership opportunities (D'Youville Leads) as well as a peer mentor program coordinated through the Leadership Development Institute. The College also has a Career Services Center, the Learning Center, the Multicultural Affairs Office, and the Personal Counseling Center. A new apartment residence opened in January 2005.

THE NURSING STUDENT GROUP

D'Youville has both traditional and nontraditional students from a variety of ethnic backgrounds in the nursing program, enhancing the educational and social experiences. Nursing organizations on campus include the National Student Nurse Association (NSNA), which is open to all nursing students. Students who excel academically may be invited to join the Society of Nursing, Sigma Theta Tau International.

COSTS

For 2009–10, tuition was $9900 per semester, and room and board cost $4900 per semester. A $230 general College fee is required and is based on credit hours taken. Graduate tuition for 2009–10 was $725 per credit hour. Students in the B.S.N./M.S. programs pay undergraduate tuition.

FINANCIAL AID

All students enrolled in the RN degree-completion program are offered a 50 percent tuition reduction. Ninety percent of

D'Youville freshmen receive financial aid. This includes nearly $2 million in grants and scholarships. Grants include Federal Pell Grants and Federal Supplemental Educational Opportunity Grants, the New York State Tuition Assistance Program, and the Aid for Part-Time Study Program. The Federal Work-Study Program, federally insured loans, and flexible payment plans are also available. All applicants are reviewed for academic scholarships at the time of acceptance. D'Youville's new Instant Scholarship Program offers scholarships with total values up to $62,000 for undergraduate and dual-degree programs.

APPLYING

D'Youville admits students on a rolling admission basis; therefore, applications are reviewed as they are received by the Admissions Office. Undergraduate applicants must submit a completed application along with a $25 processing fee; official high school transcripts or, for transfer students, official transcripts from colleges previously attended; SAT or ACT scores; and letters of recommendation.

Applicants to the master's program must present a baccalaureate degree in nursing from an accredited college or university program; a valid New York state or provincial license to practice nursing; evidence of an undergraduate course in statistics and an undergraduate course in computer science or its equivalent; and evidence of capability to succeed in a graduate program, as shown by an overall undergraduate GPA of at least 3.0 (based on a 4.0 system); an overall undergraduate GPA of at least 2.7, with a 3.0 or better in the upper half of undergraduate work; an overall undergraduate GPA of at least 2.7, with a 3.0 or better in the major field; or a baccalaureate degree in nursing plus a master's degree in another field from an accredited college or university with an overall GPA of at least 3.5. Candidates for the post-master's certificate program in family nurse practitioner studies must have a master's degree in nursing.

CORRESPONDENCE AND INFORMATION

Department of Nursing
D'Youville College
320 Porter Avenue
Buffalo, New York 14201-9985

Phone: 716-829-7613
Fax: 716-829-8159
E-mail: admissions@dyc.edu
Web site: http://www.dyc.edu

THE FACULTY

Patricia Bahn, M.S., RN. Adult health/nursing administration, holistic health/oncology.
Anna P. Caughill, M.S., Assistant Professor.
Rose De Rose, M.S., Emerita.
Denise Dunford, M.S., Assistant Professor, Nurse Practitioner Director.
Sandra Englert, M.S., Assistant Professor.
Lou Ann Gloekler, M.S., Assistant Professor.
Jennifer Guay, M.S., RN, Associate Professor.
Carol Gutt, Ed.D., RN, Associate Professor, Child health/curriculum/wellness.
Jennifer Jennings, M.S., FNP, Clinical Associate Professor.
Malena King-Jones, M.S., RN, Assistant Professor.
Judith H. Lewis, Ed.D., RN, Dean, School of Nursing.
Edith Malizia, Ed.D., RN, Associate Professor.
Sharon Mang, M.S., RN, Assistant Professor.
Kathleen Mariano, Ph.D., Assistant Professor.
Pamela Miller, M.S., RN, WHNP, Assistant Professor.
Abigail Mitchell, DH.Ed., M.S., RN, Assistant Professor.
Patricia Palumbo, Assistant Professor.
Karen Piotrowski, M.S., RN, Associate Professor.
Bernadette Pursel, M.S. Community health nursing.
Tina Sinatra-Wilhelm, M.S., RN, Assistant Professor.
Judith Stanley, Assistant Professor.

Emory University
Nell Hodgson Woodruff School of Nursing
Atlanta, Georgia

EMORY
NELL HODGSON
WOODRUFF
SCHOOL OF
NURSING

THE UNIVERSITY
Emory University, founded by the Methodist Church in 1836, has approximately 12,930 students and 2,860 faculty members who represent all regions of the United States and about ninety other nations. Emory has nine major academic divisions, numerous centers for advanced study, and a host of prestigious affiliated institutions. The University has a two-year and four-year undergraduate college of arts and sciences, a graduate school, and professional schools of medicine, theology, law, nursing, public health, and business.

THE SCHOOL OF NURSING
The Nell Hodgson Woodruff School of Nursing was founded in 1905 as the Training School for Nurses at Wesley Memorial Hospital in Atlanta. In 1922, the hospital and school of nursing were moved to the Emory University campus and functioned as a diploma school with a three-year hospital program. In 1944, the school became an integral part of Emory University, offering the Bachelor of Science in Nursing degree. The diploma program was offered concurrently until its discontinuation in 1949. The School of Nursing was named the Nell Hodgson Woodruff School of Nursing in 1968 in honor of Mrs. Woodruff, who supported the School of Nursing throughout her lifetime. The School offers undergraduate, graduate, and doctoral nursing education to nearly 400 students.

PROGRAMS OF STUDY
The Bachelor of Science in Nursing (B.S.N.) degree provides a strong academic foundation that focuses on connecting the theoretical basis of nursing with the development of critical-thinking and decision-making skills. The first two years of general education course work (including prerequisites) may be taken at any accredited college or university. Specific physical science, humanities, social science, and elective courses that total 60 semester hours are required for admission to the B.S.N. program at Emory. During the second year of prerequisite course work, students apply for admission to the School of Nursing. Qualified students are then admitted for the remaining two years of professional study. The four-semester, 60-semester-hour nursing program combines clinical and in-class experiences. The goals of the School of Nursing are to advance nursing knowledge, produce nurse leaders, and design new models of care.

Students who hold a bachelor's degree in another area but are interested in becoming nurses are eligible for the second degree B.S.N. program. Students enroll in the B.S.N. program and complete their nursing studies in four semesters (fall, spring, fall, spring) of full-time course work. Emory University also has two programs for non-nurses interested in becoming nurse practitioners or certified nurse midwives. The first is a B.S.N./M.S.N. Segue Option. Students must have a bachelor's degree in an area other than nursing to be eligible. This program provides a seamless course of study through admission into the B.S.N. program followed by direct entry into the M.S.N. program after receiving RN licensure. The second is an Accelerated B.S.N./M.S.N. option. Students must have a bachelor's degree in an area other than nursing to be eligible. This new program begins in summer 2010 and provides a seamless course of study through admission into the B.S.N. program followed by direct entry into the M.S.N. program after receiving RN licensure. The Accelerated B.S.N./M.S.N will be designed to build upon previous skills, education, and experience and to prepare students for the M.S.N. program by providing connections with M.S.N. faculty and students, and exposure to a variety of clinical settings. In doing so, the program will lay the foundation for advanced clinical and academic graduate study.

The degree programs at Emory University School of Nursing combine the advantages of outstanding facilities, a well-crafted curriculum, high-quality instruction, a prestigious and far-reaching reputation, and courses that are relevant to today's evolving practice environment. A wealth of clinical venues are available in the Atlanta metropolitan area, and clinical experiences are precisely geared to students' career focuses. Emory offers B.S.N., M.S.N., RN-M.S.N., Bridge, M.S.N./M.P.H., post-master's, and Ph.D. programs.

Programs of study leading to the Master of Science in Nursing (M.S.N.) include the following specialties: acute care nurse practitioner, adult nurse practitioner, emergency nurse practitioner, family nurse-midwife, family nurse practitioner, gerontological nurse practitioner, public-health nursing leadership, nurse-midwifery, pediatric nurse practitioner-acute care, pediatric nurse practitioner-primary care, women's health nurse practitioner, and women's health/adult health nurse practitioner. Length of the specialty programs ranges from three (one calendar year) to five consecutive semesters of full-time study. Part-time study is available. Students are eligible to sit for certification as nurse practitioners or certified nurse midwives.

The RN-M.S.N. bridge program provides an opportunity for associate degree or diploma-prepared nurses to obtain the Master of Science in Nursing. Students in the RN-M.S.N. program complete 17 semester hours of bridge course work prior to beginning the specialty curriculum of choice. In addition, a dual Master of Science in Nursing/Master of Public Health (M.S.N./M.P.H.) is available, and post-master's options are available in all graduate specialty areas except the Emergency Nurse Practitioner Program.

The Ph.D. in nursing offers flexible specialization options and is a four-year, full-time program. Students accepted to the program receive an annual stipend plus financial support to cover tuition for a maximum of four years.

AFFILIATIONS WITH HEALTH-CARE FACILITIES
The Nell Hodgson Woodruff School of Nursing maintains close ties with the Centers for Disease Control and Prevention (CDC) and the American Cancer Society. The School of Nursing at Emory is also the home of the Lillian Carter Center for International Nursing. Students at Emory have access to more than 200 diverse clinical learning sites.

ACADEMIC FACILITIES
In January 2001, the School of Nursing opened a state-of-the-art facility for nursing study and research. The building unites scholarship and teaching under one roof. The School of Nursing is part of the Robert W. Woodruff Health Sciences Center, a major provider of patient care and a national leader in clinical and research programs. Emory University is a close collaborator with the Carter Center, a nonprofit, nonpartisan public policy institute founded by former President Jimmy Carter and his wife, Rosalynn.

LOCATION
Emory University is located 6 miles northeast of downtown Atlanta. Emory is positioned along Clifton Road, which is also the home of the U.S. Centers for Disease Control and Prevention. With top-tier entertainment, cultural attractions, sports, and shopping, Atlanta has something for everyone.

STUDENT SERVICES
Nursing students at Emory enjoy a vibrant campus life. Opportunities for involvement on campus and within the nursing school are abundant. Emory students also have the opportunity to participate in student nursing organizations on the local, state, and national levels.

THE NURSING STUDENT GROUP
During the 2008–09 academic year, the School of Nursing enrolled 211 undergraduate students, 154 graduate students, and 14 doctoral students from across the nation and around the world.

COSTS
In 2009–10, full-time undergraduate tuition was $16,700 per semester. The student activity fee was $86 per semester or $5 per semester hour. The student athletic fee was $132 per semester or $40 for the summer semester.

Full-time graduate tuition was $16,700 per semester or $1392 per semester hour for part-time students (fewer than 12 semester hours). The student activity fee was $86 per semester or $5 per semester hour. The student athletic fee was $102 per semester or $40 for the summer semester.

FINANCIAL AID

Emory University and Nell Hodgson Woodruff School of Nursing are committed to providing a generous package of financial assistance to all who qualify. Currently, 96 percent of undergraduate nursing students and 95 percent of graduate nursing students receive financial assistance.

Students who apply for financial assistance at Emory University are considered for a combination of scholarships, grants, and low-interest loans. Merit-based scholarships are available at both the undergraduate and graduate levels.

APPLYING

All applicants to the School of Nursing are considered on an individual basis. Applications and supporting credentials should be submitted by January 15 for priority admission and scholarships; however, applications are reviewed as long as class space is available. The School of Nursing selects those applicants who are best qualified academically and have a strong desire of commitment to the field of nursing. After all application materials are received, the Admission Committee reviews the applicant's credentials and makes the decision to offer or deny admission. Final acceptance is contingent upon satisfactory completion of prerequisite course work.

CORRESPONDENCE AND INFORMATION

Office of Admission and Student Services
Emory University School of Nursing
1520 Clifton Road
Atlanta, Georgia 30322
Phone: 404-727-7980
      800-222-3879 (toll-free)
Fax: 404-727-8509
E-mail: admit@listserv.cc.
Web site: http://www.nursing.emory.edu

THE FACULTY

Corrine Abraham, Associate; M.N., Emory, 1985. Adult and elder health.

Susan Bauer-Wu, Associate Professor; D.N.Sc., Rush, 1997. Adult and elder health.

Kelly Brewer, Associate; M.S.N., Arkansas, 1992. Adult and elder health.

Carolyn Clevenger, Clinical Assistant Professor; D.N.P., Medical College of Georgia, 2007. Adult and elder health.

Caroline Coburn, Instructor; M.S., Emory, 1981. Adult and elder health.

Ann Connor, Clinical Assistant Professor; M.S.N., Alabama, 1980. Family and community nursing.

Safiya Dalmida, Assistant Professor; Ph.D., Emory, 2006. Family and community nursing.

Julie Davey, Instructor; M.S.N., Emory, 2001. Adult and elder health.

Madge M. Donnellan, Clinical Associate Professor; Ph.D., Tennessee, 1988. Family and community nursing.

Monica Donohue, Instructor; M.N., South Carolina, 1980. Family and community nursing.

Elizabeth Downes, Clinical Assistant Professor; M.S.N., Tennessee, 1986. Family and community nursing.

Sandra B. Dunbar, Coordinator of the Doctoral Program; D.S.N., Alabama at Birmingham, 1982. Adaptation to the stresses of acute and chronic cardiovascular illness.

Sara Edwards, Instructor; M.S.N./M.P.H., Emory, 1994. Family and community nursing.

Jennifer Foster, Assistant Professor; Ph.D., Massachusetts, 2003. Family and community nursing.

Sarah B. Freeman, Clinical Professor; Ph.D., Georgia State, 1989. Family and community nursing.

Rebecca Gary, Assistant Professor; Ph.D., North Carolina, 1979. Adult and elder health.

Maggie P. Gilead, Associate Professor; Ph.D., Emory, 1981. Adult and elder health.

Linda Grabbe, Instructor; Ph.D., Georgia State, 1992. Family and community nursing.

Kenneth Hepburn, Associate Dean for Research and Professor; Ph.D., Washington (Seattle), 1968.

Erin Hernadez, Instructor; M.S., Georgia State, 1995. Family and community nursing.

Leslie Holmes, Instructor; M.S.N., Medical University of South Carolina, 1993. Family and community nursing.

Marcia McDonnell Holstad, Assistant Professor; D.S.N., Alabama, 1996. Family and community nursing.

Maeve Howett, Clinical Assistant Professor; Ph.D., Emory, 2006. Family and community nursing.

Barbara Kaplan, Instructor; M.S.N., Emory, 1992. Family and community nursing.

Maureen A. Kelley, Clinical Associate Professor and Chair, Family and Community Nursing; Ph.D., Medical College of Georgia, 1993. Midwifery.

Joyce L. King, Clinical Assistant Professor; Ph.D., Emory, 1995. Family and community nursing.

Sally T. Lehr, Clinical Assistant Professor; Ph.D., Georgia State, 2001. Adult and elder health.

Marsha Lewis, Associate Dean for Education and Associate Professor; Ph.D., Minnesota, 1992.

Kathy Markowski, Associate; M.S.N., DePaul, 1980. Adult and elder health.

Jane E. Mashburn, Clinical Associate Professor and Interim Assistant Dean for the M.S.N. Program; M.N., Emory, 1978. Midwifery, family and community nursing.

Kathryn Matthews, Clinical Assistant Professor; D.N.P., Medical College of Georgia, 2007. Family and community nursing.

Linda McCauley, Dean and Professor; Director, Lillian Carter Center for International Nursing; Ph.D., Cincinnati, 1988.

Joyce P. Murray, Professor; Ed.D., Georgia, 1989. Adult and elder health.

Helen S. O'Shea, Professor Emerita; Ph.D., Georgia State, 1980. Adult health.

Quyen Phan, Instructor; M.S.N., Emory, 2003. Adult and elder health.

Marcene L. Powell, Professor; D.S.W., Utah, 1981. Family and community nursing.

Barbara D. Reeves, Clinical Assistant Professor; M.S.N., Vanderbilt, 1979. Family and community nursing.

Bethany D. Robertson, Clinical Assistant Professor; D.N.P., Medical College of Georgia, 2007. Family and community nursing.

Martha F. Rogers, Clinical Professor; M.D., Medical College of Georgia, 1976. Family and community nursing.

Deborah A. Ryan, Clinical Associate Professor and Interim Assistant Dean, B.S.N. Program; M.S.N., Marquette, 1981. Family and community nursing.

Lynn Sibley, Associate Professor; Ph.D., Colorado, 1993. Family and community nursing.

Linda Spencer, Clinical Associate Professor; Ph.D., Georgia State, 1988. Family and community nursing.

Ora Strickland, Professor; Ph.D., North Carolina at Greensboro, 1977. Family and community nursing.

Darla R. Ura, Clinical Associate Professor; M.A., Ball State, 1974. Adult and elder health.

Marylee Van Keuren, Instructor; M.S.N., Wayne State, 1987. Adult and elder health.

Catherine Vena, Assistant Professor; Ph.D., Emory, 2004. Adult and elder health.

Jeannie Weston, Instructor; M.S., Maryland, 1982. Family and community nursing.

Sandra White, Instructor; M.S.N., Emory, 2004. Adult and elder health.

Kathryn Woeber, Instructor; M.S.N./M.P.H., Emory, 1999. Family and community nursing.

Weihua Zhang, Clinical Assistant Professor; Ph.D., Georgia State, 2004. Adult and elder health.

Grand Canyon University
College of Nursing and Health Sciences
Phoenix, Arizona

THE UNIVERSITY
Grand Canyon University (GCU) is Arizona's only private, Christian university. Based in Phoenix, the regionally accredited, private, nondenominational Christian university offers online and campus-based bachelor's and master's degree programs through the Ken Blanchard College of Business, College of Education, College of Nursing and Health Sciences, and College of Liberal Arts. The school is ranked as one of the top online education programs by *Online Education Database (OEDb)* and as one of the top 5 online colleges for entrepreneurs by *Fortune* magazine. With a total enrollment of approximately 22,000 students, GCU emphasizes individual attention for both traditional undergraduate students as well as the working professional. For more information, students should visit http://www.gcu.edu/petersons.

THE COLLEGE OF NURSING AND HEALTH SCIENCES
Grand Canyon University's College of Nursing and Health Sciences is highly recognized throughout the nation. Not only are the academic and lab training standards extremely high, but GCU has one of the only programs that utilize human cadavers in its instruction. The challenging curriculum within the bachelor's and master's degree programs enhances intellectual knowledge and critical thinking skills that stay with students throughout their professional careers. Employers regard Grand Canyon University's premedical and nursing training as among the very best. Through small class sizes and mentoring by faculty members, Grand Canyon University provides a learning environment that is both challenging and nurturing.

Grand Canyon University is accredited by the Higher Learning Commission of the North Central Association. The Commission on Collegiate Nursing Education and the Arizona State Board of Nursing accredit the University for the Bachelor of Science in Nursing degree and the Master of Science in Nursing degree. The Commission on Accreditation of Athletic Training Education (CAATE) accredits the athletic training education program.

PROGRAMS OF STUDY
The College of Nursing and Health Sciences offers a wide range of degrees and professional health care programs. In order to meet the needs of its students, Grand Canyon University frequently adds new degree programs. For the most up-to-date list visit GCU's Web site at www.gcu.edu.

Students who plan to become professional registered nurses (RN) can enter as freshmen to begin the prerequisites (or come later with transfer hours) for the nursing major. They will earn a Bachelor of Science in Nursing (B.S.N.) degree. The College also has an accelerated evening program for nurses who are already licensed RNs, to enable them to complete their B.S.N. in as little as fifty-seven weeks. Grand Canyon University's traditional B.S.N. program includes five semesters of clinical coursework to develop the students' skills from the beginning to the professional health care level, and to instill and develop leadership skills appropriate to the role of nurse in today's health care system.

The Bachelor of Science in Nursing (B.S.N.; prelicensure) degree is designed to help students assess the individual, the family, and communities; utilize functional health patterns within a variety of clinical settings; formulate nursing diagnoses; plan and evaluate nursing interventions; and function as professionals within the health care team. The fast-track B.S.N. program allows students who have fulfilled all prerequisites to complete a degree in approximately twenty months.

The RN to B.S.N. program is designed for registered nurses with an associate's degree or diploma in nursing. The format and courses of the regionally accredited program are tailored to meet the needs of the adult learner RN, and to maximize strengths that the working RN possesses. A bridge course facilitates the transition of the working RN into the baccalaureate program. Courses are taught by experts in their respective fields who share knowledge and experience in areas of clinical patient care, healthcare management, and professional nursing practice and leadership. Opportunities are provided to apply concepts, theories, and research in the RN's clinical practice. Both the science and art of nursing are integral components of the program and are woven throughout. Graduates of the program are prepared to become leaders in the nursing profession.

The Registered Nurse to Master of Science in Nursing (RN/M.S.N.) program is a blend of the existing Registered Nurse to Bachelor of Science in Nursing and Master of Science–Nursing programs. The RN to B.S.N. curriculum will be truncated by several courses whose content will be covered in the master's materials. After the third semester in the course of study below, students will be eligible to transfer into other concentrations including clinical nurse specialist, clinical nurse specialist: education, family nurse practitioner, nursing education, and nursing leadership and health care systems.

The Master of Science–Nursing: Clinical Nurse Specialist (M.S.N./CNS) program prepares the professional nurse as an advance practice nurse. The CNS addresses health care needs in the three CNS spheres of influence: the patient/client, nurses and nursing practice, and systems and organizations. The dimensions of the CNS role include clinical judgment, clinical inquiry, facilitator of learning, collaboration, systems thinking, advocacy/moral agency, caring practices, and response to diversity.

The Master of Science–Nursing: Family Nurse Practitioner (M.S.N./FNP) prepares the advanced professional nurse for advance practice as a primary care provider. The FNP makes independent critical judgments in all levels of prevention including health promotion; health screening; illness prevention; and restoration and rehabilitation for individuals, families, communities, and populations. The FNP performs comprehensive health assessments, diagnoses, and prescribes pharmacologic and non-pharmacologic treatments to manage acute and chronic health problems to achieve quality cost-effective outcomes in a culturally sensitive context. The role of the nurse practitioner includes educating, consulting, collaborating, using research to make practice decisions, and influencing professional and public policies. Within various practice settings, the FNP provides health care throughout the life cycle, emphasizing care of the older adult. In preparation for the future, the FNP role synthesizes elements of the clinical nurse specialist practice role of assessing and addressing the needs not only of clients, but health care personnel and systems. This expanded role includes case management, marketing, business management, reimbursement, quality improvement, teaching of professionals, and broad-based consultation.

The Master of Science–Nursing: Nursing Education (M.S.N/NEd) prepares advanced professional nurses in the nursing role specialty of nursing education. The Nursing Education track addresses the expanding educational needs of the nursing profession. The nurse educator may practice in a variety of settings. The nurse educator will be prepared to practice in acute or chronic care settings as a staff-educator or in a role that is responsible for planning, implementing, and evaluating continuing education programs. The advanced professional nurse educator will also be prepared to assume a faculty position in a traditional college of nursing or in a non-traditional program that utilizes online technology as a teaching medium. Competencies of the professional practice nurse educator include assessing educational needs, planning programs to meet those needs, and evaluating the outcomes of their programs. This is accomplished in the context of an evidence-based practice model.

The College of Health Sciences has a wide range of undergraduate degrees to choose from. Students can earn a Bachelor of Science degree in biology, with an emphasis in premedicine, prepharmacy, pre–physician assistant, pre–physical therapy, or pre–occupational therapy. These degrees prepare the students to enter graduate schools to complete their medical education. Also available are Bachelor of Science degrees in athletic training, corporate fitness and wellness, and physical education and recreation. A Bachelor of Science in radiologic science is offered, along with B.S. degree completion programs for medical imaging, respiratory care, and health science. Among the newest programs, both a Bachelor of Science and a Master of Science are offered in addiction counseling and a Master of Science in professional counseling. Both the counseling programs and the medical imaging programs have several certificates of completion offered.

ACADEMIC FACILITIES

Grand Canyon University consists of thirty-six buildings on a 90-acre campus. The campus features the Fleming Library, which houses a collection of more than 166,000 volumes, 700 periodicals, newspapers, microfilm, and audiovisual materials. Library holdings are expanded by CD-ROM databases, computerized database searches, and interlibrary loans. Computers housed in the library have Internet access to assist students.

The College of Nursing and Health Sciences houses a fully equipped clinical skills lab. The lab consists of a simulated hospital room and three exam rooms, all appropriately equipped to enable students to practice and hone their clinical skills.

There are two computer labs on campus that offer Internet access and a host of applications for use outside of the classroom. Each student has an individual login, which includes secured space on a server to store personal files. In addition to the lab computers, wireless access is available for students with laptops.

LOCATION

Grand Canyon University is located in the heart of Phoenix, Arizona. With more than 300 days of sunshine a year, students have plenty of opportunities to venture outdoors and see Arizona's expansive parks, rivers, lakes, hiking trails, bike paths, and unbelievable sunsets.

Students have the opportunity to attend major league sporting events all year long, including football (Arizona Cardinals), baseball (Arizona Diamondbacks), hockey (Phoenix Coyotes), men's (Phoenix Suns) and women's basketball (Phoenix Mercury), and arena football (Arizona Rattlers) as well as NASCAR events at Phoenix International Raceway. Phoenix is also home to the annual FBR golf tournament and Parada Del Sol rodeo. In addition to sporting events, students have access to symphony orchestras, ballet and theater companies, and comedy clubs.

Phoenix is also less than a 6-hour drive from the beaches of Los Angeles, San Diego, and Rocky Point, Mexico.

THE NURSING STUDENT GROUP

The program's focus on leading, critical thinking, teaching, and meeting spiritual needs fosters quality development of each student. Approximately thirty students are admitted to the major each fall and spring and begin clinical practice in the very first semester with nurse faculty in groups of 10 or fewer.

COSTS

Tuition and related expenses at Grand Canyon University are among the lowest in the country for private colleges. In 2008–09, online undergraduate programs cost $395 per credit and nursing graduate (professional studies) courses cost $510 per credit. Low tuition, combined with GCU's financial aid programs, wide variety of degree offerings, quality education, and preparation for the future make Grand Canyon University one of America's best college buys.

FINANCIAL AID

Scholarships are available based on a student's previous academic work and need, and various loan and payment-option programs are available. Financial aid processing and advising are available through the University's Office of Financial Aid.

APPLYING

Grand Canyon University welcomes applications from qualified students who are at least 16 years of age. Although the University seeks to integrate Christian faith and practice into all aspects of campus life, no statement of faith or religious affiliation is required of prospective students. Applications for admission are considered primarily in light of the applicant's academic qualifications. Any qualified student willing to uphold the University's vision and mission and open to the possibility of spiritual as well as intellectual development is encouraged to apply. Grand Canyon University does not discriminate on the basis of age, race, color, national origin, gender, or handicap in its programs and activities.

First-year applicants with fewer than 24 transferable credits from an accredited, GCU-approved college, university, or program may be accepted to the University if they meet at least one of the following admission standards: secondary (high school) transcript, documenting no less than 75 percent of the coursework needed for degree completion, with an unweighted GPA of 2.75 or above; a degree-bearing, secondary (high school) transcript with an unweighted GPA of 2.75 or above; a post-secondary (college) transcript(s), including 6–23 credits with an unweighted GPA of 2.75 or above; passing scores of 520 on the GED (2002 Series or later) and transcripts of all credit-bearing course work; an average of 15 percent above the minimum passing scores on the GED (tests preceding the 2002 Series) and transcripts of all credit-bearing course work; a composite score of 19 or above on the ACT and a degree-bearing, secondary (high school and/or GED) transcript; or a composite SAT score of 920 or above and a degree-bearing, secondary (high school and/or GED) transcript. Applicants who do not meet one of these criteria may be admitted with specification. Applicants who cannot provide official copies of their secondary (high school) transcripts or of a completed GED and do not have any post-secondary transferable credits may complete the HS Self-Certification form, provided by their academic counselor. These students may also be admitted with specification.

Transfer applicants with 24 or more transferable credits from an accredited, GCU-approved college, university, or program may be accepted to the University if they meet at least one of the following admission standards: 24–59 undergraduate credits with an unweighted GPA of 2.25 or above; 60 or more undergraduate credits with an unweighted GPA of 2.25 or above; or a degree-bearing associate-level transcript with an unweighted GPA of 2.25 or above.

Applicants to the graduate programs may be accepted for admission by meeting one of the following criteria: an undergraduate degree from an accredited, GCU-approved college, university, or program with a GPA of 2.8 or better on the degree-bearing transcript; or a graduate degree from an accredited, GCU-approved college, university, or program. Some programs of study at Grand Canyon University, such as the graduate programs, require a higher GPA and/or other criteria to qualify for admission. A student desiring to be admitted into these programs should review the appropriate college section of the catalog for additional admission details.

CORRESPONDENCE AND INFORMATION:

Office of Admission
Grand Canyon University
3300 West Camelback Road
Phoenix, Arizona 85017

Phone: 800-800-9776 (toll-free)
E-mail: admissionsground@gcu.edu
Web site: http://www.gcu.edu

Hawai'i Pacific University
College of Nursing and Health Sciences
Kaneohe, Hawaii

THE UNIVERSITY

Hawai'i Pacific University (HPU) is a private, nonprofit university with an international student population of approximately 8,200 students. Founded in 1965, HPU prides itself on maintaining strong academic programs, small class sizes, individual attention to students, an experienced faculty, and a diverse student population. HPU is recognized as a "Best in the West" college by *The Princeton Review* and a College "Best Buy" by *Barron's*. HPU offers more than fifty acclaimed undergraduate programs and twelve distinguished graduate programs.

HPU is one of the most culturally diverse universities in America with students from all fifty U.S. states and more than 100 countries. The diversity of the student body stimulates learning about other cultures firsthand, both in and out of the classroom. There is no majority population at HPU. Students are encouraged to examine the values, customs, traditions, and principles of others to gain a clearer understanding of their own perspectives. HPU students develop friendships with students who are from cities throughout the United States and the world and make important connections for success in the global community of the twenty-first century.

THE NURSING PROGRAM

The nursing program at Hawai'i Pacific University has grown into the largest nursing program in the state of Hawaii, with more than 1,600 students in the baccalaureate and master's programs. Despite the program's size, the School maintains small class sizes where faculty members provide individual attention to students. Students receive high-quality instruction in multicultural classrooms consisting of 24 to 32 students and clinical groups consisting of 8 to 10 students.

The program emphasizes the qualities of humanism, caring, and collaboration as a foundation for the comprehensive study of the art and science of nursing. The program provides students with experience in the physical, mental, emotional, and spiritual care of clients from varied age groups and multiple ethnic backgrounds.

PROGRAMS OF STUDY

The baccalaureate nursing program offers four pathways toward a Bachelor of Science in Nursing degree. The first is the Basic Pathway for the beginning or transfer student with fewer than 45 college credits. Second is an LPN to B.S.N. Pathway for U.S. licensed practical nurses. Third, an RN to B.S.N. Pathway for licensed registered nurses from associate degree or diploma programs, and fourth, an International Nurse Pathway for persons who have graduated from a nursing program in another country and are not licensed in the United States.

HPU's graduate nursing program brings together theory and community-based practice. The M.S.N. program enables the registered nurse the opportunity to advance as a family nurse practitioner (FNP), or a community clinical nurse specialist (CNS). An RN to M.S.N. Pathway allows registered nurses without baccalaureate degrees in nursing to make the transition into the M.S.N. program. Students in the pathway are granted provisional admission status until all prerequisites are completed. Students interested in gaining a solid foundation in current business and management practice may pursue a joint M.S.N./M.B.A. degree program.

A post-master's certificate as a family nurse practitioner is also possible for nurses with master's degrees seeking to expand their practice. A certificate program in nursing education can be taken as part of the CNS concentration or as a stand-alone certificate.

AFFILIATIONS WITH HEALTH-CARE FACILITIES

The nursing program chooses health-care facilities that give students the best experience possible. Within these facilities, the choice of clinical units is made based upon the learning needs of the students. The majority of clinical faculty members are actively employed in the clinical specialties and/or facilities where they teach.

ACADEMIC FACILITIES

All nursing lecture and science laboratory classes are held on the suburban and residential windward Hawai'i Loa campus where life revolves around the Amos N. Starr and Juliette Montague Cooke Academic Center (AC). The AC houses classrooms; organic chemistry, nuclear magnetic resonance, and regular laboratories; faculty and staff offices; a theater; an art gallery; and the Atherton Library, which includes circulating and reference book collections in the areas of art, history, marine science, nursing, and Hawai'i and the Pacific. There are study rooms as well as computers available for library research and personal use. The library provides access to electronic books (e-books), online databases, and wireless internet for use by those with their own personal computers.

LOCATION

Hawai'i Pacific combines the excitement of an urban downtown campus with the serenity of the residential windward side of the island. The main campus is located in downtown Honolulu, the financial center of the Pacific, and is home to the College of Business Administration and the College of Humanities and Social Sciences. The Hawai'i Loa residential campus is 8 miles away in Kane'ohe at the base of the Ko'olau Mountains; it is the site of the College of Nursing and Health Sciences, the College of Natural and Computational Sciences, and a variety of other course offerings. The Oceanic Institute, an affiliate of the university, is an aquaculture research facility located on a 56-acre site, providing a global center for research and education in marine environmental and life sciences. The University also offers classes at six military locations on Oahu.

STUDENT SERVICES

The University has many services to meet student needs, including a professional staff of advisers who are available throughout the year to assist undergraduate students in advising and counseling matters. Other services include career placement programs; a cooperative education program; international student advising; various student organizations, including the Student Nurses' Association; and numerous honor societies, including Sigma Theta Tau International Nursing Honor Society. A director of student life and a residence life staff are actively involved in all aspects of student life.

HPU competes in NCAA Division II intercollegiate sports. Men's athletic programs include baseball, basketball, cheerleading, cross-country, golf, soccer, and tennis. Women's athletics include basketball, cheerleading, cross-country, soccer, softball, tennis, and volleyball.

The Housing Office at HPU offers many services and living options for students. On-campus residence halls with cafeteria service are available on the windward Hawai'i Loa campus, while off-campus apartments are available in the Honolulu and Waikiki area for those seeking more independent living arrangements.

THE NURSING STUDENT GROUP

The students in the School of Nursing are representative of the global community in terms of age, ethnicity, citizenship, gender, and professional experience. Students may attend either full- or part-time, with a substantial number of students choosing to accelerate the completion of their degree by studying during summer sessions. Various nursing courses are offered during summer sessions.

COSTS

Tuition for the 2009–10 academic year was $14,860. Part-time student tuition was $300 per unit for 1 to 6 credits and $620 per unit for 7 to 11 credits for freshmen and sophomores. The tuition for the nursing program (juniors and seniors only) was $21,760 for the academic year. For part-time juniors and seniors in the nursing program, the tuition was $905 per credit for 1 to 11 credits. Residence hall room and board were $11,094 and off-campus apartments rented between $2900 and $3300 per semester. (There was an additional $500 refundable security deposit required for residence halls and off-campus apartments.) Additional college-related expenses, including books, health insurance, technology fee, and student bus pass, were estimated at $2610.

FINANCIAL AID

The University provides financial aid for qualified students through institutional, state, and federal aid programs. Approximately 64 percent of the University's students receive financial aid. Among the forms of aid available are Federal Perkins Loans, Federal Stafford Student Loans, Guaranteed Parental Loans, Federal Pell Grants, and Federal Supplemental Educational Opportunity Grants. To apply for aid, students must submit the Free Application for Federal Student Aid (FAFSA). The FAFSA may be submitted at any time, but the priority deadline is March 1. Several local health-care agencies award low-interest loans to student nurses, which are forgiven for various lengths of service following successful completion of the NCLEX-RN examination.

APPLYING

Candidates are notified of admission decisions on a rolling basis, usually within two weeks of receipt of application materials. Early entrance and deferred entrance are available. HPU accepts the Common Application form.

CORRESPONDENCE AND INFORMATION

Office of Admissions
Hawai'i Pacific University
1164 Bishop Street, Suite 200
Honolulu, Hawaii 96813

Phone: 808-544-0238
　　　　866-CALL-HPU (toll-free)
Fax: 808-544-1136
E-mail: admissions@hpu.edu
Web site: http://www.hpu.edu/Petersons

The Johns Hopkins University
School of Nursing
Baltimore, Maryland

THE UNIVERSITY

Since its founding in 1876, Johns Hopkins University has been in the forefront of higher education. Originally established as an institution oriented toward graduate study and research, it is often called America's first true university. Today, Johns Hopkins' commitment to academic excellence continues in its nine academic divisions: Nursing, Medicine, Public Health, Arts and Science, Engineering, Education, Business, Advanced International Studies, and the Peabody Conservatory of Music. With a full-time enrollment of approximately 7,000 students, it is the smallest of the top-ranked universities in the United States and, by its own choice, remains small.

THE SCHOOL OF NURSING

The School of Nursing was established in 1983 by Johns Hopkins University. It is known worldwide for innovation and excellence in teaching, research, and patient care.

By choosing to attend Johns Hopkins University School of Nursing, students become leaders in the nursing profession. A Hopkins education provides a solid foundation on which to base a lifelong career in the ever-growing field of nursing. Hopkins students enjoy the advantages of an education at an institution with a worldwide reputation and an outstanding network of alumni who are willing to serve as guides and mentors. Students at the School of Nursing are given the opportunity to participate in designing an educational program tailored to their individual needs. A rigorous academic curriculum, which includes a strong scientific orientation, gives students the background to understand the health-care decisions they will make as professionals. Students learn in an atmosphere where excellence is expected, valued, and reinforced.

The School of Nursing emphasizes baccalaureate-level research. Its graduates are prepared for professional practice through an educational process that emphasizes clinical excellence, critical thinking, and intellectual curiosity.

PROGRAMS OF STUDY

Johns Hopkins University School of Nursing prepares students for professional nursing practice through an educational process that combines a strong academic curriculum with intensive clinical experience. The program is built on the University's commitment to research, teaching, patient service, educational innovation, and excellence in clinical practice. The School's mission is to prepare its students academically and technologically for challenges of the future and to graduate professional nurses who can participate in all aspects of modern health care.

The School of Nursing offers an NLNAC-accredited upper-division baccalaureate program leading to a Bachelor of Science degree with a major in nursing. College graduates with a degree in any major other than nursing are eligible to apply to either the 13½-month accelerated program, which begins annually in June, or to the twenty-one-month traditional program, which begins in the fall of each year.

The Johns Hopkins University School of Nursing is proud to offer the only Peace Corps Fellows Program in nursing. Returned Peace Corps Volunteers are eligible to participate in the Peace Corps Fellows program while enrolled in the School. This provides a unique opportunity for clinical education in community health nursing through the Community Outreach Program while meeting the human needs of low-income, underserved, and homeless families through preventive health services.

The School of Nursing also offers a Direct Entry to Combined B.S./M.S.N. option. In addition, an NLNAC-accredited master's program leading to the Master of Science in Nursing (M.S.N.) degree is offered. The goal of the master's program is to prepare nurse experts in advanced practice and/or management for leadership in professional nursing practice and patient-centered health-care delivery. Master's study and research opportunities are available in selected clinical areas, health policy, and management of nursing and health-care services. The program broadens the perspective of students by requiring them to take innovative interdisciplinary approaches to the resolution of health-care problems. Graduates are prepared to work throughout the health-care system in both the public and private sectors, including community-based primary care, acute care, sub-acute care, specialty care, and integrated systems of managed care.

Students planning a career path that focuses on nursing care for a specific population of patients may choose from several advanced practice nursing options. These include nurse practitioner in adult, family, pediatric primary care, or adult acute/critical care; health-systems management; clinical nurse specialist; clinical nurse specialist in women's health and a certificate of completion in midwifery, in collaboration with Shenandoah University Division of Nursing; or a combination of both management and clinical nurse specialist as a dual degree.

A master's specialty in health systems focuses on emergency preparedness and disaster response and prepares nurses for pivotal leadership roles during disaster and mass casualty incidents. The clinical nurse specialist role allows students to select a focus, such as forensic, geriatric, oncology, public health nursing, to name a few. Nurses with master's degrees in nursing are eligible to apply to the post-master's nurse practitioner option, which also includes an adult, family, or pediatric focus, as well as the accelerated adult acute-/critical-care nurse practitioner or the post-master's emergency preparedness/disaster response.

Other options include a joint M.S.N./M.P.H. degree program with the Bloomberg School of Public Health in public health nursing or a nurse practitioner role with a public health nursing focus and a joint M.S.N./M.B.A. and the Hopkins Business of Nursing certificate program for midlevel career nurses, which are both offered in conjunction with the Carey Business School and School of Education.

The Ph.D. program prepares nurse scholars to conduct original research that advances the theoretical foundation of nursing practice and health-care delivery. The School offers Ph.D. students the combination of a strong nursing science base, a broad range of faculty expertise, and unmatched opportunities for creative interdisciplinary collaboration. Course work includes nursing theory, research design and statistics, and required and supportive courses in the student's area of research. The length of the program is the equivalent of three to four years of full-time post-master's study.

The School of Nursing also has a Doctor of Nursing Practice (D.N.P.). The D.N.P. program is a practice-focused doctoral program designed to prepare expert nurse clinicians, administrators, and executive leaders to improve health and health-care outcomes. The 38-credit D.N.P. program is an executive-style post-master's option designed for professionals working full-time. The program can be completed in four semesters of full-time study, integrating approximately two weeks of on-site classes each semester with online and virtual learning experiences.

AFFILIATIONS WITH HEALTH-CARE FACILITIES

The Johns Hopkins Medical Institutions (JHMI) campus is part of a world-renowned academic health center that includes the

Schools of Nursing, Medicine, and Public Health; the Johns Hopkins Hospital; and the William H. Welch Medical Library.

The Johns Hopkins Health System includes, in addition to Johns Hopkins Hospital, three other hospital campuses, one of which houses the National Institute on Aging Gerontology Center and the National Institute on Drug Abuse Addiction Research Center.

ACADEMIC FACILITIES

The William H. Welch Medical Library provides the Johns Hopkins Medical Institutions and its affiliates with information services that advance research, teaching, and patient care. The Welch Library Gateway menu leads library users to remote and local online databases, including the JHMI Online Catalog and complete MEDLINE; a dynamic array of other databases, including WelchWeb and JHMI InfoNet; and a growing number of databases and full-text journals offered by the Milton S. Eisenhower Library. The Nursing Information Resource Center is managed by the Welch Library and maintains a core collection of books to support student course work.

The Center for Nursing Research provides support services to the School of Nursing faculty members and students, such as consultation on research design and conduct, including data management and analysis; information on funding sources and grant application processes; advice on career development and continuing education and research; and other resources.

The Nursing Research Laboratory is dedicated to research projects in nursing that incorporate basic biological science methods. The Research Laboratory consists of a dark room, microscopy facilities, tissue culture facilities, a core equipment area, an electrophysiologic lab, a vivarium, a cold room, a utility area, and bench space for research.

Three nursing practice labs are available to provide the student with an opportunity to gain experience and confidence in performing a wide variety of nursing technologies. Patient care stations in the laboratories, designed to closely approximate inpatient areas and stocked with necessary supplies, are available for students to practice both basic and advanced nursing technologies.

LOCATION

The School of Nursing is located on the campus of the Johns Hopkins Medical Institutions, including the School of Medicine, the Bloomberg School of Public Health, and the Johns Hopkins Hospital. Located 10 minutes away is the Homewood Campus of Johns Hopkins University, which is accessible to students via a free shuttle service.

STUDENT SERVICES

There are more than seventy student organizations within the University, including fraternities and sororities and social, religious, and cultural groups. Each class within the School of Nursing has a government board and a president. There is also the Student Government Association (SGA), which includes all divisions of the entire University. Each class has two representatives to the SGA, and anyone may attend the meetings. The Office of Admissions and Student Services is available to assist all students in matters ranging from orientation to graduation.

THE NURSING STUDENT GROUP

The School of Nursing attracts a national and international student body of 622 students, including baccalaureate and graduate students.

COSTS

For the 2009–10 academic year, baccalaureate tuition was $31,920, and master's tuition was $26,180. For the M.S.N./M.P.H., Ph.D., and D.N.P. programs, tuition was $46,452, $39,120, and $20,900, respectively.

FINANCIAL AID

Johns Hopkins University School of Nursing attempts to provide financial assistance to all eligible accepted students. The School of Nursing assists those students who qualify for need-based aid. Such assistance is usually in the form of loans, grants, scholarships, and work-study programs. While most of the financial aid received by students is based on financial need, many students also benefit from awards based on academic merit and achievement.

APPLYING

The School seeks individuals who will bring to the student body the qualities of scholarship, motivation, and commitment.

A complete baccalaureate and master's application consists of an application form and a nonrefundable $75 application fee. Doctoral applicants pay an application fee of $100.

Applicants to the baccalaureate program are required to have three recommendations, official college- or university-level transcripts, an official high school transcript (unless the applicant has already completed a college degree), and SAT or ACT scores, if they are not more than five years old and the student does not already hold a bachelor's degree. A grade point average above 3.0 (on a 4.0 scale) is recommended. Personal interviews may be requested.

Applicants to the master's program are required to have graduated from a baccalaureate or master's degree program in nursing with a GPA above 3.0 (on a 4.0 scale), a current Maryland state nursing license, academic and professional references, written expression of goals, and official transcripts from all previous colleges/universities attended. Personal interviews may be requested. Students interested in the Ph.D. or D.N.P. programs should contact the Office of Admissions and Student Services for individual counseling regarding entrance requirements.

International students whose native language is not English must submit official test score reports of the Test of English as a Foreign Language (TOEFL). In order to be considered for admission, nonpermanent residents must establish their ability to finance their education in the United States. International students must submit official records of all college- or university-level course work. To be considered for transfer toward a degree, any courses listed on an international transcript must be submitted by the student to the World Education Service (WES). International RN students may have their transcripts evaluated by the Commission on Graduates of Foreign Nursing Schools (CGFNS). Students should contact the Office of Admissions and Student Services for additional information regarding WES and CGFNS.

CORRESPONDENCE AND INFORMATION

Office of Admissions and Student Services, Suite 113
School of Nursing
The Johns Hopkins University
525 North Wolfe Street
Baltimore, Maryland 21205-2110

Phone: 410-955-7548
Fax: 410-614-7086
E-mail: jhuson@son.jhmi.edu
Web site: http://www.son.jhmi.edu

THE DEANS

Martha N. Hill, Dean, Professor, and Director of Center for Nursing Research; Ph.D., RN, FAAN.

Jerilyn Allen, Associate Dean for Research; Sc.D., RN, FAAN.

Sandra Angell, Associate Dean for Student Affairs; M.L.A., RN.

Claire Bogdanski, Associate Dean for Finance and Administration; M.B.A., CPA.

Fiona Newton, Associate Dean for Development and Alumni Relations; B.A., DipGM.

Jennifer Calhoun, Assistant Dean for Strategic Initiatives; M.S.

Kent State University
College of Nursing
Kent, Ohio

THE UNIVERSITY

Founded in 1910, Kent State University is classified among RU/H: Research Universities (high research activity) by the Carnegie Foundation and is one of the largest public universities in Ohio. The eight-campus system throughout northeastern Ohio enrolls nearly 34,000 students. The Kent campus offers baccalaureate, master's, and doctoral study in the Colleges of Arts and Science, Business Administration, Communication and Information, Education, Fine and Professional Arts, and Nursing and the School of Technology. Offered at the seven regional campuses are associate degrees in technical, business, and health fields as well as lower-division baccalaureate study.

The University's primary concern is the student. It has a commitment to providing an academic atmosphere and curricular and extracurricular activities that prepare for a vocation, stimulate curiosity, broaden perspective, enrich awareness, establish disciplined habits of thought, and help realize potential as an individual and as a responsible and informed citizen.

THE COLLEGE OF NURSING

The Kent State University College of Nursing, established in 1967, offers the most comprehensive program of study in nursing in Ohio, ranks in the 98th percentile in size in the nation, and enjoys a reputation for excellent academic performance, clinical knowledge, and leadership ability of its students and graduates. The associate degree in nursing program is accredited by the National League for Nursing Accrediting Commission. Both the Bachelor of Science in Nursing (B.S.N.) and Master of Science in Nursing (M.S.N.) programs are accredited by the Commission on Collegiate Nursing Education (CCNE).

Since its founding, nursing at Kent State University has enjoyed continued growth, and today it is the largest college of nursing in Ohio. The mission of Kent State University College of Nursing reflects a commitment to furthering nursing knowledge, to excellence in instruction, and to preparing graduates who are able to address changing societal needs. The College of Nursing offers an academic atmosphere that fosters intellectual curiosity, develops professional and personal values, and facilitates the acquisition, interpretation, utilization, and expansion of nursing knowledge for the discipline and for professional practice.

Kent State University's faculty members, skilled in the scholarship of teaching, discovery, application, and integration, foster the intellectual life of the University. The College of Nursing's faculty members, who number more than 123, are active and creative contributors to the advancement of nursing knowledge and to the improvement of health-care delivery through teaching, research, and service activities at the local, regional, national, and international levels.

PROGRAMS OF STUDY

The College of Nursing offers associate, baccalaureate, master's, and Ph.D. degree programs in nursing. The baccalaureate degree program accommodates general as well as second-degree, licensed practical nurse, and registered nurse students. In addition, an accelerated option is available for second-degree students. B.S.N. students who qualify may apply to the M.S.N. program and begin taking graduate-level courses in their junior year under the B.S.N.-to-M.S.N. Bridge Option. The master's degree nursing program offers clinical concentrations in nursing of adults, family, gerontology, psychiatric–mental health nursing, women's health, and pediatrics as well as functional concentrations in nurse practitioner clinical specialization and administration. Post-master's nurse practitioner certificate programs are also available in acute, family, gerontology, and primary care as well as women's health, pediatrics, and psychiatric–mental health nursing. A Web-based certificate program in nursing education is also offered. In addition, dual-degree M.S.N./M.P.A. and M.S.N./M.B.A. options are available. A Ph.D. in nursing program is offered jointly with the University of Akron's College of Nursing.

An associate degree in nursing program is offered at four regional campuses (Ashtabula, East Liverpool, Geauga, and Tuscarawas). The associate degree program prepares practitioners to assume responsibility for the provision of technical nursing care. For further information, students should contact the respective campus directly.

The baccalaureate nursing program is an undergraduate program leading to the B.S.N. degree and is offered at the main campus as well as four of the regional campuses. The curriculum includes courses in the humanities and biological and social sciences as well as theoretical knowledge and clinical practice in the discipline of nursing. Both generic students and nontraditional students (second-degree, RNs, and LPNs) are eligible for the program. Currently, nearly 1,500 students are enrolled in the baccalaureate program. An accelerated program is available for students who hold a non-nursing bachelor's degree.

The master's program is an accelerated graduate program leading to the M.S.N. degree. The purpose of this program is to prepare specialists for leadership and advanced practice roles in professional nursing. Enrollment in the master's program is more than 250, with approximately 85 percent of these students pursuing graduate study on a part-time basis.

The purpose of the Doctor of Philosophy (Ph.D.) degree program is to develop scholars in nursing who are informed about the many dimensions of scholarship with balance and synthesis among research, practice, and teaching. This program is conducted in collaboration with the University of Akron's College of Nursing and rests on the belief that strength can be achieved through strong linkages among faculty members and students and among the diverse units of both universities. The program consists of five components: nursing knowledge; research methods, designs, and statistics; cognates; health-care and nursing policy; and the dissertation. Both full- and part-time students are accommodated in this program.

A program of continuing nursing education is also offered. The College of Nursing is an Ohio Nurses Association–approved provider of continuing education and awards continuing education units (CEUs) for program offerings.

AFFILIATIONS WITH HEALTH-CARE FACILITIES

The College of Nursing has established affiliations with more than seventy-five health agencies throughout northeastern Ohio for clinical learning experiences. These include large urban medical centers, such as The Cleveland Clinic Foundation and University Hospitals of Cleveland, as well as small rural hospitals and clinics. The College of Nursing is also affiliated with a variety of long-term and community health-care agencies.

ACADEMIC FACILITIES

The College of Nursing is located in Henderson Hall. It contains a SIM lab, classrooms, faculty offices, conference rooms, study areas, nursing multipurpose and computer laboratories, a learning resource center, a nursing research center, and a 250-seat auditorium. In addition, the excellent services and resources of the entire University are available. The twelve-story open-stack library is a member of the Association of Research Libraries and holds more than 1.5 million volumes, including an extensive collection of nursing and medical references. The basic science complex of Northeastern Ohio Universities College of Medicine is located 6 miles from the Kent campus and is an integral part of Kent State.

LOCATION

Located in Kent, Ohio (population approximately 30,000), the Kent campus is situated on a beautiful 2,264-acre tree-covered area. Close by are the metropolitan areas of Cleveland (35 miles), Akron (15 miles), Canton (35 miles), and Youngstown (35 miles). The seven regional campuses are located in communities 35 to 80 miles from the Kent campus. The most populous of Ohio's four quadrants, northeastern Ohio is an area rich with cultural and recreational activities. Among these are Kent's Porthouse Theatre and Blossom Music Center, summer home of the Cleveland Orchestra.

STUDENT SERVICES

A comprehensive array of student services is available through the College of Nursing Office of Student Services and the University's Michael Schwartz Student Service Center. In addition to academic services, health services, counseling and guidance, career planning and placement, financial aid, residential service, recreation, and student activities programming are provided. More than 200 undergraduate and graduate student organizations on campus welcome members from throughout the University. Students can also participate in a variety of intercollegiate sports.

THE NURSING STUDENT GROUP

Kent serves a talented, culturally rich student body from Ohio and around the world, including historically underrepresented and nontraditional students. Students in nursing reflect a microcosm of the University student body.

Students for Professional Nursing (SPN) provides opportunities for development of leadership skills, promoting health-care activities on campus and facilitating socialization into the professional role. In addition, a chapter of the Ohio Nursing Students Association (ONSA) at Kent is active. Graduate students can take an active role in the University Graduate Student Senate and the Graduate Nurse Student Organization (GNSO).

COSTS

Kent State's tuition is set by the Board of Trustees. For current tuition information, students should visit the Bursar Office's Web site at http://www.kent.edu/bursar.

FINANCIAL AID

Kent State University has developed a financial aid program to assist students who lack the necessary funds for a college education. This program consists of scholarships, loans, grants-in-aid, and part-time employment. Registered nurses may find additional financial assistance through the clinical agencies with whom they are employed. Federal traineeships, graduate assistantships, scholarships, and special awards such as the Ohio Board of Regents Scholars program are additional sources of financial assistance for graduate students.

APPLYING

Applicants to the B.S.N. program need to submit a Kent State University application at http://www.kent.edu/admissions; a high school transcript and ACT or SAT scores (for students under 21 years of age); an official transcript from each college, university, or school attended; and a $30 application fee.

Students completing prenursing requirements with a GPA of 2.5 or higher and a 2.5 average or higher in the first-year science prerequisite courses are eligible to apply to the nursing sequence program, which begins in the second year. Registered nurses and persons holding a non-nursing degree are admitted directly to the College of Nursing after completing all prerequisites required by the College of Nursing.

Applicants to the master's program must have current Ohio licensure as a registered nurse, have a baccalaureate degree from an accredited program, achieve a grade point average of at least 3.0 on a 4.0 scale from the undergraduate program, and have completed an elementary course in research methodology. In addition to an application form, $30 application fee, and official transcripts, prospective students are asked to submit three letters of reference and an essay not exceeding 300 words describing previous education and experience, future professional goals, and reasons for seeking graduate nursing education. A satisfactory score on the Graduate Record Examinations is required for applicants with a GPA below 3.0. A preadmission interview is recommended.

Admission to the Joint Ph.D. in Nursing Program (JPDN) is determined by a review committee of JPDN faculty members. Each applicant must provide evidence of successful completion of a bachelor's degree in nursing and a master's degree in nursing or health-related field at an accredited program with a minimum grade point average of 3.0 on a 4.0 scale; evidence of current licensure in the United States or, for international students, evidence of legal ability to practice in their country of origin; acceptable scores on the Graduate Record Examinations within seven years of application; a statement of the applicant's clearly defined career goals; a sample of written work that indicates logic and writing skills (an essay, term paper, thesis, published article, or professional report); and three letters of reference from professionals or professors who can adequately evaluate the applicant's previous work and potential for success. The review committee may also request a personal interview to assess research interests and motivation for successful completion of doctoral study. A minimum score of 550 on the Test of English as a Foreign Language (TOEFL) is required for international students. Accepted applicants must register for courses within two years of acceptance into the JPDN.

CORRESPONDENCE AND INFORMATION

Office of Student Services
College of Nursing
216 Henderson Hall
Kent State University
P.O. Box 5190
Kent, Ohio 44242-0001

Phone: 330-672-7911
Fax: 330-672-2061
Web site: http://www.kent.edu/nursing

Long Island University, Brooklyn Campus
School of Nursing
Brooklyn, New York

THE UNIVERSITY AND THE CAMPUS
Celebrating its ninth decade of providing access to the American dream through excellence in higher education, Long Island University is one of the nation's largest, most comprehensive private universities. It offers 575 undergraduate, graduate, and doctoral-level degree programs and certificates. Over 650 full-time faculty members educate more than 24,000 students on seven metropolitan-area campuses in Brooklyn, Brookville (C.W. Post), Southampton, Brentwood, Rockland, Riverhead, and Westchester and at five overseas sites. The Arnold & Marie Schwartz College of Pharmacy and Health Sciences prepares students for successful careers in pharmacy and health care.

With more than 11,300 students and 256 certificate and undergraduate and graduate degree programs in the liberal arts and sciences, business, public administration, computer science, education, nursing, the health professions, and pharmacy, the Brooklyn Campus is distinguished by dynamic curricula reflecting the great urban community it serves. Students enjoy the benefits of living and learning in a multicultural environment that promotes growth and a progressive exchange of knowledge and ideas.

THE SCHOOL OF NURSING
The School of Nursing is exceptionally well positioned to fill the need for nursing professionals in the growing areas of health promotion; home care of the acutely, long-term, and chronically ill; and community health. The School offers the B.S. in nursing and an RN/B.S. Connection Program as well as the M.S. in adult nurse practitioner, family nurse practitioner, and geriatric nurse practitioner studies; the M.S. in Nursing: Executive Program for Nursing and Health Care Management; advanced certificates in adult nurse practitioner, family nurse practitioner, and geriatric nurse practitioner studies; a B.S./M.S. Accelerated Program in Nursing/Executive Program for Nursing and Health Care Management; a post-master's certificate in nursing education; and a B.S./M.S. Accelerated Program for Nursing/Adult Nurse Practitioners. Graduates of the bachelor's program are eligible to take the examination for licensure of registered professional nurses in New York State. Registered professional nurses who have earned a diploma or an associate degree at other institutions may apply credits toward completion of the Bachelor of Science degree through the RN/B.S. Connection Program.

PROGRAMS OF STUDY
The program leading to the B.S. in nursing is accredited by the Commission on Collegiate Nursing Education (CCNE). It is designed to prepare students who are beginning nursing studies to develop the competencies essential for professional nursing practice, to sit for the state licensure examination for registered nurses, and to build a foundation for graduate study. The program's proximity to Manhattan creates the opportunity for clinical experiences in some of the world's most prestigious hospitals and health-care agencies. Candidates must successfully complete 128 credits, including 4 credits in noncore freshman courses; 36 credits in the humanities, social sciences, sciences, and mathematics; 62 credits in nursing requirements; 7 credits in distribution; and 19 credits in ancillary requirements. Graduates are able to incorporate knowledge synthesized from the nursing, humanities, psychosocial, and biophysical curriculum into all aspects of professional nursing practice; use critical thinking, communication, and therapeutic intervention skills; embody the characteristics of humanism and caring in the practice of nursing; facilitate adaptive responses of individuals and families within the community in the promotion, maintenance, and restoration of health; and assume leadership roles in structured and unstructured health-care settings. The program

also is available to registered nurses seeking the baccalaureate degree through the RN/B.S. Connection Program. Registered nurses admitted into the program may receive up to 64 transfer credits, including required core curriculum, prerequisite, and distribution credits. Transferred credits also may include up to 31 credits in nursing courses for work previously completed. Flexible course schedules are available for the working professional.

The M.S. in adult nurse practitioner, M.S. in family nurse practitioner, and M.S. in geriatric nurse practitioner studies are designed to prepare advanced practice nurses in primary-care roles for adult and family populations. Clinical expertise is stressed, resulting in the graduates' ability to assess, diagnose, monitor, coordinate, and manage the health care of their clients in both primary- and acute-care settings; perform and interpret physical examinations and laboratory tests; select and prescribe appropriate drug therapy for common acute and chronic child and adult disorders; and articulate the role of the nurse practitioner as a collaborative member of the health team. Candidates for the degree must successfully complete 43 credits of theory, equivalent to 495 hours, and clinical laboratory work of 600 hours for the adult and geriatric programs and 49 credits and 900 clinical hours for the family nurse practitioner program.

An advanced certificate for adult nurse practitioners also is available for nurses who have earned a master's degree in nursing and are seeking clinical expertise in the advanced practice role for the care of adult clients. Candidates must successfully complete 35 credits of theory, equivalent to 360 hours, in addition to clinical laboratory work of 600 hours for the adult and geriatric programs and 41 credits and 900 clinical hours for the family nurse practitioner program.

The M.S. in Nursing: Executive Program for Nursing and Health Care Management provides a unique opportunity to educate the nurse executive with needed skills for today's complex health-care environment. The program combines both nursing and business courses, fulfilling the growing need for executive nurses who are responsible for multimillion-dollar budgets, cost-benefit analyses, reduction of overtime expenses, and staff. Graduates are prepared to assume leadership positions in hospitals, nursing homes, community health centers, HMOs, home-care agencies, consulting firms, and entrepreneurial ventures. Candidates must successfully complete 43 credits, including two semesters of internship experience in management of a nursing or health-care organization. The graduate programs are accredited by the Commission on Collegiate Nursing Education.

A post-master's certificate in nursing education is available for registered nurses who hold a master's degree in nursing and who wish to prepare themselves for teaching in schools of nursing and clinical education positions. It is a 12-credit program with additional hours in mentored teaching experience.

AFFILIATIONS WITH HEALTH-CARE FACILITIES
Due to the campus's proximity to New York City, students often have the opportunity to learn through clinical experiences and, after graduation, to obtain jobs in some of the top hospitals and health-care facilities in the world. The School's affiliates encompass a wide range of clinical health-care settings, including acute-care and community agencies, as well as prestigious hospitals, such as Beth Israel Medical Center, Montefiore Medical Center, New York Methodist Hospital, Maimonides Medical Center, and St. Luke's–Roosevelt Hospital Center.

ACADEMIC FACILITIES
Over the last five years, the campus has invested more than $72 million to construct and renovate buildings and academic facilities.

The William Zeckendorf Health Sciences Center houses state-of-the-art classrooms and labs for students in nursing, pharmacy, and the health professions. The campus's new $45-million Wellness, Recreation and Athletic Center offers members of the surrounding community free health-care services, including monitoring, health education, and counseling programs. It also provides hands-on learning experience for the campus's 3,000 students in health-related fields. In addition, the Harriet Rothkopf Heilbrunn B'32 Academic Nursing Center promotes healthy living with free programs for all members of the community and the Brooklyn Campus. The only center of its kind in Brooklyn, the Heilbrunn Center provides a comprehensive array of preventive care programs for adults at no charge.

LOCATION
The 11-acre Brooklyn Campus and King's County Hospital campus are located in the heart of downtown Brooklyn, only minutes from Manhattan. Some of Brooklyn's richest cultural and historic attractions are within walking distance, including the Brooklyn Academy of Music, known for its innovative drama, music, and dance productions; the Brooklyn Heights Promenade, featuring stunning panoramic views of the Manhattan skyline; the Brooklyn Bridge; and the Statue of Liberty. The campus is surrounded by neighborhoods the New York City Landmarks Preservation Commission recognizes as historic districts. Close to the campus are the Brooklyn Museum, Prospect Park, and the Brooklyn Botanic Garden.

STUDENT SERVICES
On any given day, students can participate in more than forty-five on-campus clubs and organizations. Nursing students also can join the Nursing Association. In addition, a wealth of services, including academic advising, financial aid advising, career counseling, job placement, tutoring, and computer-assisted instruction, are offered.

THE NURSING STUDENT GROUP
The undergraduate student body pursuing the B.S. in nursing is composed of students just beginning their nursing studies as well as practicing registered nurses who seek the baccalaureate degree. Upon completion of all requirements, these students are eligible to take the state licensure examination for registered professional nurses. The graduate student body pursuing the M.S. in nursing is composed of students preparing to become advanced practice nurses in primary-care roles. RN/B.S. students are normally registered nurses who already hold registered nurse licensure and are interested in earning the B.S. in nursing. Candidates for the M.S. in Nursing: Executive Program for Nursing and Health Care Management are nursing professionals interested in pursuing careers as nurse executives and administrators. The advanced certificate for adult nurse practitioners is available to nurses who have earned a master's degree and who are seeking clinical expertise in the advanced practice role for the care of adult clients.

COSTS
Brooklyn Campus undergraduate tuition rates for 2009–10 were $854 per credit. Graduate tuition was $930 per credit. These rates do not include University fees billed to students, including student activities and specific program fees. On-campus room and board charges averaged $6100 per semester.

FINANCIAL AID
Ninety percent of undergraduate students attending the Brooklyn Campus receive financial aid to help meet college expenses. Parental contributions, government aid programs, Long Island University Scholarships, student earnings, loans, and scholarships from outside sources are considered by the financial aid office when formulating a student's aid package. Full, partial, and transfer academic scholarships; Dean's Awards; and activity awards are available if the student qualifies. Complete details about all of these options are included in the Brooklyn Campus financial aid information publication, which is available through the admissions office. TAP and Pell grants also are available to those who qualify.

APPLYING
Before beginning the professional phase of the B.S. in nursing program, students must satisfy all proficiency requirements, complete all prerequisite courses, obtain a grade of 75 or above on the HESI A2 tests, and have a minimum grade point average (GPA) of 2.75. In addition, a personal interview may be required. Prior to entry into the first nursing course, students are responsible for obtaining certification in cardiopulmonary resuscitation (CPR).

An application for admission; an official high school transcript, evidence of graduation from high school, or GED scores; SAT or ACT test results; and a $30 application fee must be submitted to be considered for undergraduate admission. Transfer applicants must submit a completed transfer application form, an official transcript from all colleges previously attended, and a $30 application fee.

To qualify for admission into the RN/B.S. Connection Program, registered nurses must possess a current RN license, be a graduate of an accredited nursing program, demonstrate evidence of clinical competency, and have at least a 2.75 cumulative grade point average from previous academic studies.

Acceptance requirements for the M.S. in nurse practitioner studies include a B.S. degree from a CCNE- or NLNAC-accredited school of nursing, with a minimum 3.0 GPA in the nursing major and at least a 2.75 overall GPA; a New York State RN license; two years of recent clinical experience or the equivalent; three professional references; and a personal interview. Research, statistics, and health-assessment courses or certificate are also a prerequisite but may be completed during the first year of graduate work. Registered nurses with non-nursing baccalaureate degrees may be able to qualify for entrance to the graduate program by validation of knowledge through required tests.

Acceptance requirements for the advanced certificate program include an M.S. from a CCNE- or NLNAC-accredited school of nursing with a minimum 3.0 GPA, a New York State RN license, two years of recent clinical experience or equivalent, three professional references, and a personal interview.

Acceptance requirements for the M.S. in Nursing: Executive Program for Nursing and Health Care Management include a B.S. degree from a CCNE- or NLNAC-accredited school of nursing, with a minimum 3.0 GPA in the nursing major and at least a 2.75 overall GPA; a New York State RN license; two years of recent clinical experience or the equivalent; three professional references; a personal interview; and research and statistics prerequisites, which may be completed during the first year of graduate work.

CORRESPONDENCE AND INFORMATION:
Elizabeth Storinge, Dean of Admissions
Office of Admissions
Long Island University, Brooklyn Campus
1 University Plaza
Brooklyn, New York 11201-5372

Phone: 718-488-1011
Fax: 718-797-2399
E-mail: admissions@brooklyn.liu.edu
Web site: http://www.brooklyn.liu.edu

Dawn F. Kilts, Dean
School of Nursing, Room 401
Zeckendorf Health Sciences Center
Long Island University, Brooklyn Campus
1 University Plaza
Brooklyn, New York 11201-5372

Phone: 718-488-1059
Fax: 718-780-4019
E-mail: dawn.kilts@liu.edu
Web site: http://www.brooklyn.liu.edu/nursing

Luther College
Department of Nursing
Decorah, Iowa

THE COLLEGE

Luther College, founded in 1861, is a four-year, residential liberal arts college of the Evangelical Lutheran Church in America. The College, which was founded by Norwegian immigrants, is an academic community of faith and learning where students of promise from all beliefs and backgrounds have the freedom to learn, to express themselves, to perform, to compete, and to grow. The College, located in Decorah, Iowa, is home to 2,500 students from forty-one states and forty-seven countries around the world. Thirty-two percent of the students are from the state of Iowa; 87 percent come from the four-state area of Iowa, Minnesota, Wisconsin, and Illinois. Each year, approximately 125 international students (5 percent of the student body) choose to study at Luther. The College offers more than sixty majors and preprofessional programs leading to the Bachelor of Arts degree.

THE DEPARTMENT OF NURSING

The goals of Luther's nursing program are to prepare nurses to function autonomously and interdependently with individuals, families, groups, and communities to promote, maintain, and restore optimal health in a variety of health-care settings. The nursing major, therefore, offers an integrated program of liberal arts and fourteen professional nursing courses. The program gives students a broad approach to nursing, providing a base for graduate study or immediate entry into the nursing profession. Following graduation with a Bachelor of Arts in nursing, Luther nursing students may write the National Council Licensure Examination for Registered Nurses (NCLEX-RN).

PROGRAMS OF STUDY

It is Luther's mission to produce well-rounded and capable students. In the context of a Christian, liberal arts institution, student nurses explore the sciences and the humanities in addition to their nursing courses. The first year provides a foundation in the liberal arts.

Students entering the nursing program should have a solid background in English, math, biology, and chemistry.

Clinical nursing courses begin in the fall of the sophomore year. Nursing courses at this level emphasize health assessment throughout the life span in a variety of settings. These learning experiences develop new communication and interpersonal skills.

Third-year students engage in a concentrated study of nursing concepts through caring for children and adults with physical and emotional problems. The sites for the clinical experiences include Rochester Methodist Hospital and St. Mary's Hospital, affiliates of the Mayo Medical Center, as well as a variety of community-based health-care agencies in Rochester, Minnesota.

The senior year provides final preparation for entry into the practice of professional nursing. Courses focus on promoting health and preventing illness in childbearing families and in community groups.

AFFILIATIONS WITH HEALTH-CARE FACILITIES

Luther College conducts its clinical nursing experiences during the junior year at Mayo Medical Center facilities in Rochester, Minnesota, as well as a variety of community-based facilities. These affiliations afford students the opportunity for exposure to the most recent technical and personal strategies for effective nursing care. Additional clinical experiences occur with Winneshiek Medical Center, the Winneshiek County Public Health Nursing Service, and a variety of community-based agencies in northeast Iowa.

ACADEMIC FACILITIES

The 1,000-acre campus includes the Preus Library, housing 335,000 volumes, 831 periodicals, and the College art collection. The library offers five online indexes and ten commercial online services and provides access to more than 480 other libraries. Modern, well-equipped laboratories in the newly renovated Valders Hall of Science are supplemented by several other science-teaching facilities on campus, including the Sampson-Hoffland Laboratories, a planetarium, a greenhouse, an herbarium, a live-animal center, a human anatomy laboratory, a natural history museum, and a psychology sleep laboratory. The science facilities also include an extensive field study area and two electron microscopes. Within easy walking distance of the campus, the field study area offers an ideal setting for studies in aquatic biology, ecology, and field biology. Five ponds, two reestablished prairies, marshes, wooded areas, and agricultural lands are available for classwork and independent study. The College has a fiber-based campus network connecting a variety of PC and Macintosh computers (in several environments) to shared computing resources and to the Internet. More than 500 microcomputers and terminals are available for student use throughout the campus.

LOCATION

The College is located in Decorah, a city of 8,500 people in the scenic bluff country of northeast Iowa. The Upper Iowa River, which runs through the campus, is one of twenty-seven rivers throughout the country designated as a National Scenic and Recreational River. Rich in Scandinavian heritage, Decorah is a popular recreation area, providing opportunities for canoeing, fishing, hunting, cross-country skiing, camping, hiking, cycling, and spelunking. Three airports are located within a 75-mile radius of Decorah in Rochester, Minnesota; Waterloo, Iowa; and La Crosse, Wisconsin.

STUDENT SERVICES

Luther provides numerous student services in a setting that includes programming seven days a week. The Regents Center for recreation, the Centennial Union, and the Center for Faith and Life serve as hubs of student life activities. Students are involved in the governance of the College through involvement on college committees and student government organizations. Luther fields nineteen athletic teams and provides more than forty intramural activities. In addition, students from every academic department participate in the broad-based music program.

THE NURSING STUDENT GROUP

The Luther College nursing program enrolls approximately 140 students, with 35 to 40 students graduating annually. Enrollment is determined by faculty and clinical site availability. Since the program was established in 1978, the retention rate of nursing students from sophomore to senior year has typically been 90 percent. Nursing students are challenged in a very rigorous program that prepares them well for the profession or for graduate study. Nursing students must achieve a Luther College grade point average of at least 2.5 and earn grades of C or higher in all nursing and nursing support courses.

COSTS

For 2010–11, the comprehensive fee is $39,265, which includes tuition, general fees, facilities fees, room, board, and admission to College-supported concerts, lectures, and other events. A room telephone, cable TV, computer access from residence hall rooms, and a health-service program are also included. Private music lessons are $350 per semester. It is estimated that an additional $3000 is adequate for books, clothing, entertainment, and other personal expenses.

FINANCIAL AID

More than 97 percent of all Luther students receive some financial aid in the form of grants, such as the Federal Pell Grant, scholarships from Luther and other sources, loans, and jobs on campus. Luther awards Regent and Presidential scholarships to applicants demonstrating superior academic achievement. The amount of aid given is determined by the College's analysis of the Free Application for Federal Student Aid. The priority deadline for a financial aid application is March 1 each year. Students receive notification of their aid awards after their acceptance for admission. Junior-level nursing students benefit from the Bernice Fischer Cross and Bert S. Cross Perpetual Endowment for the Luther College Mayo Nursing Program and Health Sciences Program.

APPLYING

An application, SAT or ACT scores, an educator's reference, and a transcript of previous academic work are required for admission. On-campus interviews are recommended but not required. Admission is selective. An applicant must be a graduate of an accredited high school and have completed at least 4 units of English, 3 units of mathematics, 3 units of social science, and 2 units of natural science. It is strongly recommended that the applicant have at least two years of a foreign language.

CORRESPONDENCE AND INFORMATION

Admissions Office
Luther College
Decorah, Iowa 52101
Phone: 563-387-1287
            800-458-8437 (toll-free)
Fax: 563-387-2159
E-mail: admissions@luther.edu
Web site: http://www.luther.edu/academics/majors/nursing/

THE FULL-TIME FACULTY

Sheryl Juve, Department Head; Ed.D.; RN.
Donna Kubesh, Ph.D.; RN.
Corine Carlson, M.S.; RN.
Penny Leake, Ph.D.; RN.
Jayme Nelson, M.S.; RN.
Mary Overvold-Ronningen, Ph.D.; RN.
Amy Row Neal, M.S.; RN.

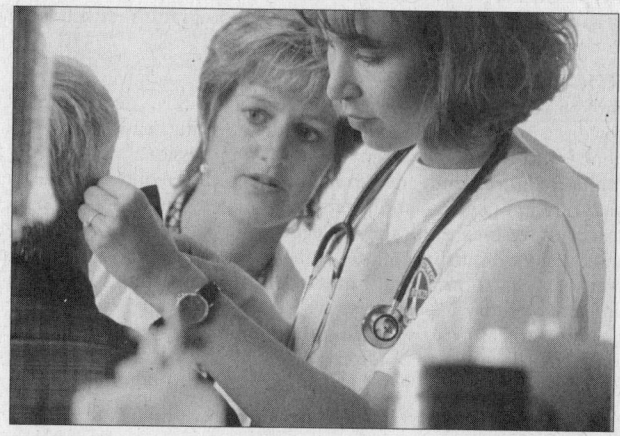

Luther College nursing students gain significant clinical experience in facilities associated with the Mayo Medical Center.

Marquette University
College of Nursing
Milwaukee, Wisconsin

THE UNIVERSITY
Established in 1881, Marquette University (MU) is recognized for its rigorous core curriculum and professional preparation in the Jesuit tradition. Marquette educates 7,600 undergraduates and enrolls 11,000 total students, including those in the dental, graduate, and law schools. Marquette students are richly diverse, as they come from all fifty states and eighty countries. Colleges and schools of the University include Arts and Sciences, Business Administration, Communication, Dental, Education, Engineering, Health Sciences, Law, Nursing, and Professional Studies. The location in the heart of Milwaukee affords students opportunities to apply learning in partnership with the dynamic urban community. The Marquette experience is personally transformational as it prepares graduates to transform society for the better.

THE COLLEGE OF NURSING
Marquette's College of Nursing has its roots in 1899 as St. Joseph's Hospital School of Nursing and established its baccalaureate program as Marquette University College of Nursing in 1936 and master's program in 1938. Established in 2003, the Ph.D. program has an emphasis on preparing teacher-scholars, with a focus on developing the body of knowledge related to vulnerable populations. The College focuses on excellence in clinical teaching and health care of the vulnerable, those at risk for adverse health outcomes. The graduate program is ranked among the top 20 percent in the nation.

PROGRAMS OF STUDY
The four-year Bachelor of Science in Nursing (B.S.N.) degree program provides a strong academic foundation in nursing, natural and social science, and humanities. Preparation for a professional nursing role is emphasized through the development of clinical, cognitive, and leadership skills and personal and professional values. Students are admitted directly as freshmen into the College of Nursing, which assures placement in clinical nursing courses. Nursing courses begin on the first day of enrollment. Clinical skills, introduced in the second year through clinical laboratory experiences, are developed through seven clinical rotations in health-care agencies in the junior and senior years. A low student-teacher ratio (8:1) affords personal attention in all clinical rotations, including adult care, maternity, mental health, pediatric, and community health and a synthesis course in a setting of the student's area of interest.

The 128-credit B.S.N. program includes courses in the humanities, physical-biological sciences, and social-behavioral sciences as well as electives and courses in the nursing major. A University Core of Common Studies is foundational for all majors at Marquette University. Lower-division nursing courses are Dimensions of Professional Nursing, Health Assessment, Foundations of Nursing Practice, Pathophysiology 1 and 2, and Pharmacotherapeutics. Upper-division courses include Nursing Research, Care of Adults*, Childbearing Family Nursing*, Mental Health Nursing*, Primary Health Care Concepts, Gerontological Nursing, Family Centered Nursing of Children*, Nursing of Communities*, Care of Acutely Ill Adults*, Nursing Synthesis*, and Nursing Leadership. The asterisk (*) denotes clinical practice courses.

Additional options for student in the B.S.N. program include a nursing/psychology double major and minors in Spanish for health professionals and family studies. ROTC programs are offered with the Army, Air Force, and Navy. Study-abroad options are also available in sixteen countries. Students may elect an internship at the Les Aspin Center for Government in Washington, D.C., in the area of health policy. The Advanced Nurse Scholar (ANS) program offers select freshmen entry into the nurse practitioner/clinical nurse specialist, health-care systems leadership, nurse midwifery, or clinical nurse leader M.S.N. programs.

The RN to B.S.N. program is available for ADN and diploma RNs. Prior course work is evaluated, and students may be awarded credits through credit transfer and a validation process.

Marquette University College of Nursing offers the Master of Science in Nursing (M.S.N.) degree and post-master's certificates that prepare graduates for advanced practice roles or leadership roles within health-care systems. Individuals may enter through four pathways: post-B.S.N.; Direct Entry (DE), a combined RN and M.S.N. for those with non-nursing bachelor's degrees; RN to B.S.N. to M.S.N.; and ADN-prepared nurses with bachelor's degrees in other disciplines. Graduates are academically eligible to seek formal professional certification as nurse practitioners, clinical nurse specialists, nurse midwives, or nurse administrators. Seven specialty options are available: health-care systems leadership, clinical nurse leader, and advanced practice programs in nurse midwifery, pediatrics, adults, older adults, and acute care. Full-time students complete the 33–45 credit programs in four semesters.

A 51-credit post-M.S.N./Ph.D. program to prepare teachers/scholars focuses on knowledge generation related to vulnerable populations.

A Doctor of Nursing Practice (D.N.P.) program began in fall 2008. The D.N.P. is another route to advanced practice or nursing administration and emphasizes translational research, epidemiology, informatics, health policy, statistics, and professional issues. All students complete a two-semester capstone clinical project. A residency course is also required.

AFFILIATIONS WITH HEALTH-CARE FACILITIES
The College is affiliated with more than eighty health-care agencies in Wisconsin and the surrounding states. These agencies include hospitals, clinics, home care facilities, public health departments, schools, parishes, long-term-care facilities, hospice, and clinics. Many of these agencies offer excellent student employment opportunities as well as financial aid and loan forgiveness programs once students graduate from the program.

ACADEMIC FACILITIES
Marquette is located on an 80-acre campus with excellent facilities. State-of-the-art libraries support student and faculty needs through their collections, services, and connections to worldwide resources. The Instructional Media Center provides a broad range of media support to faculty members and students. Information Technology Services offer voice and data communications and computer-based services to students all around campus, with Internet access from the residence hall rooms. The College of Nursing has many technology-enhanced classrooms and a well-equipped Simulation Technology and Learning Resource Center (STLRC), including SIM-MAN and many advanced simulation technology models for student learning. The STLRC provides computer access, media resources, and practice labs supplied with state-of-the-art models and equipment necessary to develop a solid foundation for clinical practice. Students participate in simulation exercises that are videotaped for maximal learning before entering into complex health-care systems.

LOCATION
The College is located in a metropolitan area on the shore of Lake Michigan with a population of more than 1 million people. The city of Milwaukee is known as the city of festivals and for the friendliness of its residents (the Germans call it *gemütlichkeit*). Students can enrich their lives with theater, music, art, major-league sports, and world-class dining.

STUDENT SERVICES
Students take advantage of a wide range of student services including individual advising with faculty members, student health services, a writing center, free tutoring services, a counseling center, 160 student organizations, and the University ministry with a staff dedicated to students' needs. Student development includes leadership and service opportunities. Marquette students, administrators, and faculty and staff members provide more than 100,000 hours of service per year. The University Task Force on Diversity attends to recruitment and the needs of a diverse group of students and faculty members and addresses multicultural appreciation.

THE NURSING STUDENT GROUP

Currently, more than 400 undergraduates are enrolled from throughout the U.S. Approximately 15 percent are students of color and about 15 percent are men. In the past five years, nursing students have earned local, regional, national, and University student leadership awards and have competed in varsity soccer, basketball, tennis, and track and cross-country as well as club sports.

In the current academic year, there are 330 (including DE) students in the M.S.N. program and 34 doctoral students enrolled in the College of Nursing. Approximately 20 percent are full-time students and most are employed while attending classes. Graduates from the M.S.N. programs are employed in various leadership positions that currently include hospital presidents, chief nursing officers of health-care systems, academic leaders, partners in group practices, nursing faculty members, clinical nurse specialists, nurse midwives, and nurse practitioners.

COSTS

The annual tuition for the undergraduate nursing program in 2009–10 was $28,680, and the cost for the graduate program was $865 per credit.

FINANCIAL AID

More than 90 percent of undergraduate students receive financial aid, including scholarships, grants, and low-interest loans. The rising demand for nurses has increased support for nursing education from federal and state sources as well as from health-care organizations. Applicants should complete the FAFSA (Free Application for Federal Student Aid) and work with the University's financial aid counselors to optimize support. Graduate student aid includes federal traineeships, teaching assistantships, research assistantships, Marquette University Tuition Scholarships, health-care agency tuition programs, and other option-specific dedicated scholarships.

APPLYING

Requirements for the prelicensure B.S.N. program include high school academic record; one year of algebra, geometry, biology, and chemistry; and ACT or SAT scores. Interested students are encouraged to visit in person or on the Web at http://www.marquette.edu/nursing. For detailed information, students should contact University Admissions toll-free at 800-222-6544.

Routes to admission to the M.S.N. program vary depending upon the student's background. Students with the following backgrounds are encouraged to apply for the M.S.N. program: those who have a bachelor's degree in nursing, those who have completed a non-nursing bachelor's degree, or those associate degree nurses who have completed a bachelor's degree in a discipline other than nursing. Admission requirements include the completed Marquette University Graduate School application (available online at http://www.grad.mu.edu), three completed reference forms, an up-to-date resume, a brief goal statement, GRE scores (only if the undergraduate GPA is equal to or less than 3.2), and an undergraduate GPA of 3.0 or better.

Direct Entry students are to have completed the following: bachelor's degree with a GPA of 3.0 or better; 5–6 credits in anatomy and physiology; 5–6 credits of another science, such as chemistry, biology, or microbiology; 3 credits of social science; and 3 credits of statistics.

The application deadline for the Direct Entry program is early January. Financial aid applications are due by February 15 for the following fall semester. DE students begin as a cohort in the last week in May and complete the pre-M.S.N. course work and an initial 9 graduate credits in fifteen months. At the completion of the pre-M.S.N. phase, they are eligible to take the professional licensing exam leading to licensure in the state of Wisconsin and, if successful, proceed into their desired graduate option.

Application requirements for the D.N.P. program include the MU Graduate School Application, a bachelor's degree in nursing with a GPA of 3.0 or higher on a 4.0 scale, GRE scores (General Test only, and this requirement is waived if the undergraduate GPA is 3.2 or greater), a goal statement that includes career intentions and practice focus, a curriculum vita, three letters of recommendation, and a professional license to practice nursing in Wisconsin and, for international applications, TOEFL scores or proof of English proficiency.

Application requirements for the Ph.D. program include the MU Graduate School Application, a bachelor's degree in nursing with a GPA of 3.0 or better, GRE scores (verbal, quantitative, and writing), three letters of recommendation, a goal statement, a curriculum vita, a writing sample and a personal interview.

CORRESPONDENCE AND INFORMATION

College of Nursing
Marquette University
P.O. Box 1881
Milwaukee, Wisconsin 53201

Phone: 414-288-3803
E-mail: kerry.goepfert@marquette.edu
Web site: http://www.marquette.edu/nursing

THE FACULTY

Lea Acord, Ph.D; RN. Educational administration.
Abir Bekhet, Ph.D., RN. Mental Health.
Ruth Ann Belknap, Ph.D.; APRN, BC. Family violence in Hispanic women.
Margaret Berner, M.S.N.; CNM, APNP. Nurse midwifery care.
Lesley Boaz, Ph.D., RN, APNP. Family health, spirituality in elders.
Kathleen Bobay Ph.D.; RN, CS, FNP. Health-care systems, measuring clinical nursing expertise.
Marilyn Bratt, Ph.D.; RN. Nurse residency programs.
Margaret Bull, Ph.D.; RN, FAAN. Continuity of care, community elder care.
Margaret Faut Callahan, Ph.D.; CRNA, FAAN. Nurse anesthesia, palliative and end-of-life care, pain management.
Diane Dressler, M.S.N.; RN, CCRN, CCTC. Critical care, heart transplant, heart failure.
Richard J. Fehring, Ph.D.; RN, CNFPP, CNFPE. Adult health, natural family planning.
Marilyn Frenn, Ph.D.; RN. Health promotion, adolescent health.
Kate Glasenap, M.S.N., ANP, BC-ADM, CDE. Diabetes management.
Kristin Haglund, Ph.D.; RN, FNP, PNP. Pediatric primary care, adolescent sexual behavior.
Lisa Hanson, Ph.D.; RN, CNM. Women's health, nurse midwifery care.
Kathryn Harrod, D.N.Sc.; RN, CNM. Nurse midwifery, caring behaviors in labor.
Kelli Jones, M.S.N.; RN. Community health.
Kerry Kosmoski-Goepfert, Ph.D.; RN; Associate Dean, Undergraduate Program. Critical care, health-care systems.
Judith Kowatsch, M.S.N.; RN-C. Maternal-child care.
Carolyn Laabs, Ph.D.; APRN-BC, FNP-C. Primary care, health-care ethics.
Mary Ann Lough, Ph.D.; RN. Community delivery systems, chronically ill elders.
Maureen O'Brien, Ph.D.; RN. Technology-dependent children.
Mary Paquette, M.S.N.; RN. Nursing administration, simulation technology in nursing education.
Linda Piacentine, M.S.; RN, APRN, CNRN. Spirituality in drug addicts.
Robin Poedel, B.S.N.,RN, Ph.D. candidate. Adolescent health.
Gloria Rhone, B.S.S.W., M.S.N.; RN. Adult nursing, nursing education.
Mary Ross, M.S., RN. Adult nursing, clinical simulation.
Kathryn Schroeter, Ph.D., RN, CNOR. Adult health, operating room.
Tracy Schweitzer, Ph.D.; RN. Adult nursing.
Margaret Sebern, Ph.D.; RN. Adults, informal caregivers, home health care.
Christine Shaw, Ph.D.; RN, BC, FNP, ANP. Primary care of underserved.
Leona VandeVusse, Ph.D.; RN, CNM. Primary care of women, birth stories.
Madeline Wake, Ph.D.; RN, FAAN. Nursing administration.
Marianne Weiss, D.N.Sc.; RN. Preterm labor, postpartum follow-up, health systems and outcomes.
Aimee Woda, M.S.N.; RN. Adult nursing.

Medical College of Georgia
School of Nursing
Augusta, Georgia

THE COLLEGE
The Medical College of Georgia (MCG), Georgia's health sciences university, is located at Georgia's eastern border on the Savannah River and is the state's primary institution to educate health-care professionals. It is the third largest of the thirty-four colleges and universities in the University System of Georgia, with approximately 2,500 students, interns, residents, and fellows. It is the largest single employer in the city of Augusta, with more than 5,000 faculty and staff members.

THE SCHOOL OF NURSING
In response to the wartime need for additional nurses, the University System of Georgia voted August 11, 1943, to offer courses in nursing education. This participation in the U.S. Cadet Nurse Corps paved the way for establishing a department of nursing at the University of Georgia the following fall. The program moved from Athens, Georgia, to Augusta in 1956 and became a part of the Medical College of Georgia. The first B.S.N. degrees were awarded in 1958. The School of Nursing, with a strong commitment to research, authorized a graduate program in nursing in 1966. The first Master of Science in Nursing degrees were conferred in 1969, and the first Ph.D. in nursing degrees were conferred in 1990.

In 1974, to meet Georgia's growing need for baccalaureate-prepared nurses, a free-standing, self-contained satellite campus was opened in Athens, Georgia. This campus, for more than thirty years, has consistently prepared one third of the graduates of the baccalaureate program each year. To assist faculty research, an essential component in graduate education, the Center for Nursing Research was established in 1987. In 1995, the Nursing Anesthesia Program was started. In 1996, an RN to B.S.N. program by distance learning was started in cooperation with Gordon College, located in Barnesville, Georgia. In 1999, a Family Nurse Practitioner program by distance learning was started in cooperation with Columbus State University, located in Columbus, Georgia. In 2000, an Adult Acute Care Clinical Nurse Specialist and a CRNA Completion program were approved for immediate implementation. In 2005, a Doctorate of Nursing program (DNP) was approved and implemented, and in 2006 a Clinical Nurse Leader program (CNL) was approved and implemented. In 2006, the School of Nursing and School of Allied Health Sciences moved into a state-of-the-art health sciences building, equipped with the latest technology available in patient care. In 2009, an online RN to M.S.N. program was approved and implemented.

The School of Nursing is accredited by the Commission on Colleges of the Southern Association of Colleges and Schools, and the Commission on Collegiate Nursing Education (CCNE) and is approved by the Georgia Board of Nursing. The School is a member of the Southern Regional Education Board (SREB) Council on Collegiate Education for Nursing.

PROGRAMS OF STUDY
Degrees offered are the Bachelor of Science in Nursing (B.S.N.), Master of Science in Nursing (M.S.N.) (clinical nurse leader, nurse practitioner, and nurse anesthesia), Doctor of Philosophy (Ph.D.) in nursing, and Doctor of Nursing Practice (D.N.P.). The baccalaureate program has a community-based curriculum that incorporates a wide variety of clinical experiences in inpatient, outpatient, and community settings.

The Master of Science in Nursing program offers specialties in acute care, clinical nurse leader, family and pediatric nurse practitioner studies, and nursing anesthesia. As part of the graduate program, an RN to M.S.N. completion program for registered nurses is offered online.

The Ph.D. program specialty is health care across the life span. The D.N.P. was one of the first ten such programs in the nation providing advanced practice education for nurse clinicians.

AFFILIATIONS WITH HEALTH-CARE FACILITIES
MCG's campus includes MCG Hospital, the Children's Medical Center, and more than eighty specialty clinics. The MCG Medical Center complex forms the core of MCG Health System's facilities and includes a 478-bed hospital, an Ambulatory Care Center with more than eighty outpatient clinics in one convenient setting, a Specialized Care Center housing a thirteen-county regional trauma center, and a 154-bed Children's Medical Center. The facility is a leading referral center for Georgia and the region. To meet the clinical learning needs of students and the baccalaureate program, more than 275 contracts exist between the School of Nursing and a variety of health-care agencies throughout Georgia and South Carolina.

ACADEMIC FACILITIES
The five-school campus of almost 90 acres includes forty-seven buildings, with construction of new buildings plus expansion and renovation of present buildings continuing the growth trend of the institution.

The University operates community outreach clinics in twenty-eight counties. Telemedicine sites are located throughout the state. The institution also has a satellite campus in Athens, Georgia, and delivers distance learning to students in Americus, Albany, Atlanta, Columbus, Morrow, and Valdosta. The University houses a large multimedia library that participates in the state library system, GALILEO, with MERLIN. GALILEO provides access to more than fifty databases and services pertinent to undergraduate studies. The library also offers an extensive public computing area with Macintosh and IBM-compatible microcomputers, terminals with access to MERLIN and GALILEO, and programs for word processing, spreadsheets, graphics, and other services. In addition, students have access to computers within their respective schools.

LOCATION
Augusta, the second-largest city in Georgia, is located on the south bank of the Savannah River, midway between the Great Smokey Mountains and the Atlantic Ocean. It is a growing and thriving city with a metropolitan-area population of around 200,000, and was recently ranked as the second most favorable place to live in Georgia. The area is known for its balmy climate, with an annual mean temperature of 64 degrees.

Founded in 1836 by General James Oglethorpe, Augusta is Georgia's second-oldest city. Augusta was Georgia's capital in 1778 and from 1785 to 1795. The city offers a wide array of cultural and recreational activities. Augusta has an impressive riverwalk, the site of many activities such as the Augusta Invitation Regatta, a national collegiate rowing event. The city also is a short drive from Lake Thurmond Reservoir, the site of such outdoor activities as waterskiing, swimming, boating, and camping. Augusta is world-renowned as the home of the Masters Golf Tournament.

Augusta has many associations dedicated to the performing and visual arts, including the Augusta Opera Association, the Augusta Ballet, the Augusta Players, the Augusta Children's Theatre, the Augusta Symphony, and the Augusta Art Association. The Medical College of Georgia, Augusta State University, and Paine College often bring prestigious films, speakers, and special events to the city.

Augusta offers exceptional shopping and features a downtown art and antiques district. The area's hundreds of restaurants range from fine to casual dining, featuring everything from ethnic specialties to burgers.

Augusta is within an easy 3-hour drive to Atlanta, the University of Georgia, the Atlantic Ocean, and the mountains.

Augusta is a leading health-care center of the Southeast and has a rapidly developing and diversified industrial base. The area's nine hospitals serve the Southeast and beyond.

STUDENT SERVICES

MCG's Student Health Services provides primary care for MCG students' medical, dental, and psychological needs. The Minority Academic Advisement Program ensures the recruitment and retention of minority students in schools through the University System of Georgia. The School of Nursing houses the Learning Resources Center and Simulation Center, where students train to manage emergencies in a safe, controlled, and replicable environment and learn psychomotor skills needed to practice nursing. Students also have access to computers, audiovisual materials, nursing journals, and classroom materials.

THE NURSING STUDENT GROUP

Student life at the Medical College of Georgia offers many learning experiences in a variety of settings. The School of Nursing has approximately 350 undergraduate students and 246 graduate students. Many student organizations are available to enhance the student's career, including the Georgia Association of Nursing Students (GANS); the IMHOTEP-Leadership Honor Society; MCG Student Government Association; Sigma Theta Tau, Beta Omicron Chapter; and Phi Chi Beta of Chi Eta Phi Sorority. The Augusta and Athens chapters of GANS are active on local, state, and national levels. Several students have held national offices.

COSTS

Full-time undergraduate tuition for 2009–10 was $3035 for in-state students and $12,140 for out-of-state students per semester. Part-time undergraduate tuitionwas $203 per credit hour for in-state students and $810 per credit hour for out-of-state students.

Full-time graduate tuition for 2009–10 for the Clinical Nurse Leader (CNL) program was $4450 for in-state students and $11,277 for out-of-state students per semester. Part-time graduate tuition for CNL was $371 per credit hour for in-state students and $940 per credit hour for out-of-state students. Full-time graduate tuition for the Certified Registered Nurse Anesthetist (CRNA) program was $5935 for in-state students and $12,727 for out-of-state students per semester. Part-time graduate tuition for the CRNA program was $495 per credit hour for in-state students and $1052 per credit hour for out-of-state students.

Full-time tuition for all other graduate nursing programs was $3823 for in-state students and $10,627 for out-of-state students per semester. Part-time tuition for all other graduate nursing programs was $319 per credit hour for in-state and $886 per credit hour for out-of-state students.

On-campus housing costs ranged from $1624 to $2464; off-campus room and board expenses ranged from $9000 to $13,000. Books, uniforms, and equipment fees were approximately $400 to $800 per academic year.

FINANCIAL AID

For a copy of the *Student Financial Aid Bulletin,* students should contact the Financial Aid Office (706-721-4901) or refer to the Web site (http://www.mcg.edu/students/finaid/). A limited number of part-time employment opportunities are available through the MCG Personnel Office.

APPLYING

Admission to the Medical College of Georgia School of Nursing is based on high school graduation or its equivalent; scores on the SAT or ACT; college graduate and GRE or MAT for graduate programs, cumulative GPA, with some preference given for outstanding grades in courses supporting nursing; completion of all prerequisite course work; and references.

CORRESPONDENCE AND INFORMATION

Office of Academic Admissions
AA-170 Kelly Building
Medical College of Georgia
Augusta, Georgia 30912

Phone: 706-721-2725
         800-519-3388 (toll-free)

Fax: 706-721-0186

E-mail: underadm@mail.mcg.edu
       gradadm@mail.mcg.edu

Web site: http://www.mcg.edu/son

The School of Nursing was founded in 1943 and serves as the University System of Georgia's flagship nursing school, meeting the challenges of an evolving health-care system.

New York University
College of Nursing
New York, New York

THE UNIVERSITY

New York University (NYU), one of the largest private universities in the country, was founded in 1831. NYU draws top students from every state and from over 130 countries. The University attracts a world-famous faculty and distinguished student body.

The University includes eighteen schools, colleges, and institutes. In NYU's College of Nursing, students have all the advantages and resources found only at a major research university, yet they are also part of a small college community that shares a commitment to the health and welfare of humanity. Exchanging ideas with scholars in health, education, and the arts assists nursing students' growth as professionals and people.

THE COLLEGE OF NURSING

Excellence has placed New York University's College of Nursing among the nation's top nursing programs, providing the foundation for tomorrow's nursing practice and scholarship. The intellectual energies of the faculty and students, the quality of the academic resources, and the rich interaction with a vibrant city provide a learning experience that is unique in its rigor and diversity. All programs—baccalaureate, master's, and doctoral—provide a dynamic balance between nursing theory and practice. These programs prepare graduates for leadership roles in direct care, administration, research, or teaching. They reflect the latest advances in knowledge and technology as well as today's modern health-care environment. When students graduate, in addition to a wealth of knowledge and skills, they take with them the ability to think analytically—the hallmark of a successful nursing career.

All of the College of Nursing's full-time, tenure-track faculty members are doctorally prepared. Full-time clinical faculty members are all master's- or doctorally prepared expert practitioners. Part-time faculty members hold at least a master's degree in their clinical specialty area.

NYU's College of Nursing alumni are in positions of leadership throughout the world, where they practice in diverse clinical, academic, and administrative settings. Many are making their mark through nursing science research. Others have forged new roles as entrepreneurs in private practice or as consultants to health insurers, pharmaceutical companies, and international health organizations.

The baccalaureate and master's programs at NYU College of Nursing are accredited by the Commission on Collegiate Nursing Education (CCNE), One Dupont Circle, NW, Suite 530, Washington, DC 20036, 202-887-6791.

PROGRAMS OF STUDY

The NYU College of Nursing offers B.S., M.S., post-master's certificate, D.N.P., and Ph.D. programs. Bachelor of Science programs include a traditional, four-year program; a B.S. program with a special sequence of courses for registered nurses; a college-graduate program, which may be completed in a regular track or fifteen-month accelerated track; and dual-degree B.S./M.S. programs, available to qualified NYU undergraduate nursing students. Nonclinical master's and post-master's certificate programs in nursing education, administration, or informatics are offered, and a dual-degree program (M.S. in nursing administration/Executive M.P.A. in management) is offered with the NYU Wagner Graduate School of Public Service. Clinical Master of Science and post-master's certificate programs are offered in advanced practice nursing with tracks in adult acute care, adult primary care, adult primary care/geriatrics, adult nurse practitioner/holistic nurse practitioner, adult nurse practitioner/palliative care nurse practitioner, geriatrics, mental health, nurse-midwifery, and pediatrics. There is also a dual-degree program offered in conjunction with NYU's Program in Global Public Health (M.S./M.P.H.). At the doctoral level, the College of Nursing offers the Doctor of Nursing Practice degree and the Florence S. Downs Ph.D. Program in Nursing Research and Theory Development.

The B.S. program in nursing prepares students to manage the full scope of nursing care responsibilities in today's complex health-care environment. The nursing science curricula emphasize a humanistic approach that examines the social, emotional, and environmental context in which wellness and illness occur. Students examine the growth and development of the family structure, patterns that characterize different age groups, human behavior in health and illness, and the effects of chronic illness. In the classroom, students learn nursing theories, nursing process, and relevant knowledge. Students apply these theories in practice through laboratory and clinical study. Students gain experience in all clinical areas, including maternal-child health, adult medical-surgical nursing, community/psychiatric nursing, geriatric nursing, and nursing leadership. Students work with all ages and cultures in a range of settings.

The M.S. programs in advanced education in nursing science prepare students for leadership roles in management, nursing education, informatics, and advanced nursing practice. They are unique programs that subscribe to a philosophy and vision of nursing reflecting a commitment to human values and the advancement of nursing as a profession. The programs emphasize critical thinking, the development and use of a theoretical base for advanced practice, the application of evidence-based practice to further nursing practice knowledge, and the promotion of a professional identity. The 45- to 48-point curricula include a core in nursing theory, a clinical advanced practice core, an area of concentration, and related cognates and electives. Graduates of the clinical programs are eligible to sit for ANCC and other certification examinations as nurse practitioners and/or clinical nurse specialists or are eligible for American College of Nurse-Midwives certification and licensure as professional midwives in New York State. All advanced practice nursing programs are registered by the state of New York as nurse practitioner programs. The post-M.S. advanced certificate programs require 12 to 30 points.

The D.N.P. (Doctor of Nursing Practice) is designed for nurse practitioners (N.P.) and nurse-midwives (C.N.M.) who seek to enhance their professional future and contribute to improving clinical outcomes and the context in which health care is delivered. The overarching goal of the D.N.P. program is to prepare graduates to be advanced practice nurse leaders in interdisciplinary health teams who work to improve systems of care, patient outcomes, quality, and safety. One will be guided in developing the skills and tools necessary to assess research evidence, evaluate the impact of research on practice, and implement practice changes that improve quality of care. The D.N.P. curriculum capitalizes on the research strengths of the faculty in gerontology/aging, chronic disease prevention and management, work force strategy and capacity, and infectious disease/global public health to promote development of one's clinically focused Capstone Project and practice scholarship portfolio. In addition, in select courses, students have the opportunity to interact with faculty experts at the Wagner Graduate School of Public Service and Steinhardt School of Culture, Education, and Human Development.

The Florence S. Downs Ph.D. Program in Nursing Research and Theory Development educates scholars in the critical and creative study of human beings and their environment and prepares leaders to examine issues in nursing and health care. The required course work of approximately 52 points is taken in the College of Nursing and other University departments on a full- or part-time basis. The curriculum is designed to provide a solid research foundation in quantitative and qualitative methods, which generates nursing knowledge and furthers theory development and substantive practice within the discipline.

AFFILIATIONS WITH HEALTH-CARE FACILITIES

The College of Nursing offers clinical and practicum experience at many of the nation's foremost hospitals, including NYU Langone Medical Center, Bellevue Hospital Center, Mount Sinai Medical Center, St. Vincent's Hospital, Beth Israel Medical Center, and more than fifty other acute-care hospitals. Students also gain significant experience in community settings, including the Visiting Nurse Service, the College's mobile health van, and other ambulatory and home-care settings.

ACADEMIC FACILITIES

NYU's Bobst Library is one of the largest open-stack research libraries in the world. Bobst is one of five NYU libraries, including the Langone Medical Center Library, to which nursing students have access. The College of Nursing provides on-campus clinical learning experiences that enable students to practice their nursing skills in a simulated hospital setting.

LOCATION

NYU is located in historic Greenwich Village, traditionally a community of artists and intellectuals. NYU's campus is within minutes of off-Broadway theaters, Little Italy, Chinatown, and renowned museums. As an international center of finance, culture, and communications, New York City offers unmatched educational, internship, and social opportunities.

STUDENT SERVICES

The University offers students a variety of services and resources, including the Student Resource Center, the Center for Multicultural Education and Programs, the Student Health Center, the Wasserman Center for Career Development, the Coles Sports and Recreation Center, the Palladium Sports Facility, Information Technology Services, and the Henry and Lucy Moses Center for Students with Disabilities.

THE NURSING STUDENT GROUP

The student body represents most of the fifty states and many other countries. This diversification affords opportunities for rich and lasting relationships. The average student is a mature, self-directed individual who assumes both professional and academic responsibilities, often in addition to family commitments.

COSTS

For the academic year 2009–10, the undergraduate tuition for full-time students was $36,586, plus nonrefundable registration and service fees of $2179; graduate tuition was $1239 per point (credit) per term, plus non-refundable registration and services fees of $403 for the first point in the fall term, $416 for the first point in the spring term, and $59 per point after the first point.

FINANCIAL AID

Financial aid at NYU comes from many sources. In order to meet an applicant's financial need, the University may offer a package of aid that includes scholarships or grants, loans, or work-study programs. NYU requires the submission of the Free Application for Federal Student Aid (FAFSA).

The College of Nursing offers a competitive financial aid program. Scholarships for full-time and part-time study are available. For master's and doctoral candidates, a number of fellowships and assistantships are available. Information on financial aid may be obtained from the NYU Office of Financial Aid at http://www.nyu.edu/financial.aid.

APPLYING

As baccalaureate program requirements differ for the traditional, RN, college graduate, and dual-degree B.S./M.S. programs, interested students should contact the College of Nursing Office of Student Affairs and Admissions for specific requirements (http://www.nyu.edu/info/nursing/guide; 212-998-5317). For admission to the M.S. program, a candidate must have a baccalaureate degree preferably in the major of nursing from an accredited nursing program or a baccalaureate degree in another field and an associate degree in nursing. A minimum overall GPA of 3.0, RN licensure, two professional letters of reference, and a goal statement are also required. TOEFL scores are required for students whose native language is not English. Students who have not met the prerequisites of basic statistics and nursing research may take them while in the program.

Admission requirements for the post-master's advanced certificate programs are a master's degree in nursing with a minimum 3.0 GPA. For admission to the Ph.D. program, the applicant must be a nurse with baccalaureate and master's degrees acceptable to NYU, with at least one degree in nursing. A minimum GPA of 3.0 on a scale of 4.0 and GRE scores of at least 1000 are required. In addition, the applicant must submit a resume, demonstration of professional performance/contribution to the nursing profession, two professional reference letters, a three- to five-page goal statement, copies of GRE scores, and transcripts of college-level work.

CORRESPONDENCE AND INFORMATION

New York University
Office of Student Affairs and Admissions
College of Nursing
726 Broadway, 10th Floor
New York, New York 10003-9502
Phone: 212-998-5317
E-mail: nursing.programs@nyu.edu
Web site: http://www.nyu.edu/info/nursing/petersons

THE FACULTY

Partial Faculty List
Carolyn Auerhahn, Clinical Assistant Professor, Ed.D., Columbia.
Babette Biesecker, Clinical Instructor, M.S., SUNY (Binghamton).
Marie Boltz, Assistant Professor, Ph.D., New York.
Mary Brennan, Clinical Assistant Professor, M.S., Boston College.
Elizabeth Capezuti, Associate Professor, Ph.D., Pennsylvania.
Edward Chung, Clinical Instructor, M.S., New York.

Deborah Chyun, Associate Professor, Ph.D., Yale.
Donna (Danuta) Clemmens, Assistant Professor, Ph.D., Connecticut.
Michele Crespo-Fierro, Clinical Instructor, M.S./M.P.H., Hunter College (CUNY).
James DeCarlo, Instructor, M.A., New York.
Victoria Vaughan Dickson, Assistant Professor, Ph.D., Pennsylvania.
May Dobal, Assistant Professor, Ph.D., Texas (Austin).
Caroline Dorsen, Adjunct Clinical Instructor, M.S.N., Yale.
Emerson E. Ea, Clinical Assistant Professor, D.N.P., Case Western Reserve.
Mei Fu, Assistant Professor, Ph.D., Missouri (Columbia).
Terry Fulmer, Erline Perkins McGriff Professor of Nursing and Dean, College of Nursing, Ph.D., Boston College.
Barbara Gallo, Clinical Professor, M.S., New York.
Leslie J. Goldfarb, B.S., M.S., Bridgeport.
Judith Haber, Professor and Associate Dean, Master's and Post-Master's Programs, College of Nursing, Ph.D., New York.
Donna Hallas, Clinical Associate Professor, Ph.D., Adelphi.
Katherine Hutchinson, Assistant Professor, Ph.D., Delaware.
Nancy Jackson, Clinical Associate Professor, Ed.D., Columbia.
Jill Kamen, Clinical Instructor, M.A., New York.
Christine Tassone Kovner, Professor, Ph.D., New York.
Barbara Krainovich-Miller, Clinical Professor, Ed.D., Columbia.
Betty Leef, Clinical Instructor, M.S.N., Phoenix.
Fidel Lim, Clinical Instructor, M.A., New York.
Diane O. McGivern, Professor, Ph.D., New York.
Gail D'Eramo Melkus, Professor, Ed.D., Columbia.
Mathy Mezey, Independence Foundation Professor of Nursing Education, Ed.D., Columbia.
Karla Mikhail, Clinical Instructor, M.S.N., Phoenix.
Madeline A. Naegle, Professor, Ph.D., New York.
Jamesetta A. Newland, Clinical Associate Professor, Ph.D., Pennsylvania.
Medel Paguirigan, Clinical Instructor, M.S., Wagner College.
Stephanie Perez, Clinical Instructor, B.S., Wagner College.
Hila Richardson, Clinical Professor and Associate Dean, Undergraduate Programs, College of Nursing, Dr.P.H., Columbia.
Mary Rosedale, Assistant Professor, Ph.D., New York.
Shiela Strauss, Associate Professor, Ph.D., CUNY (Graduate Center).
Rebecca A. Terranova, Instructor, M.A., New York.
Susan Vacca, Clinical Instructor, M.S.N., Seton Hall.
Nancy Van Devanter, Associate Professor, Dr.P.H., Columbia.

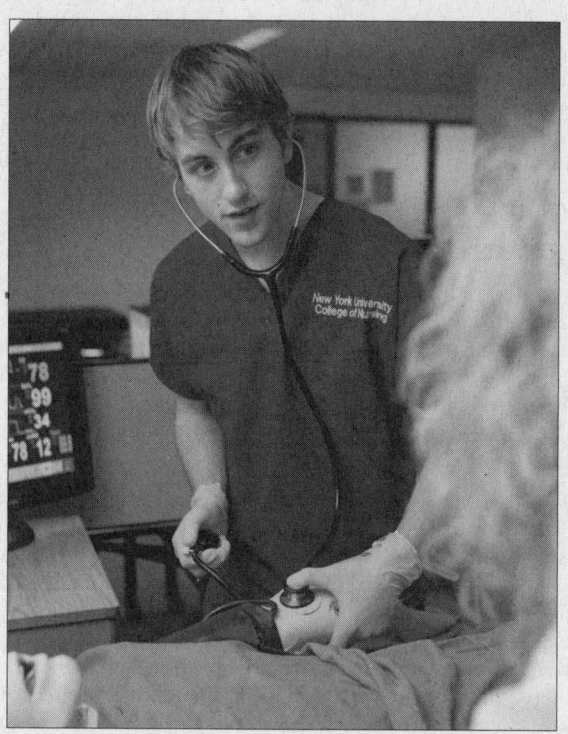

Students in the College of Nursing benefit from clinical and practicum experiences in a wide range of settings.

Regis College
School of Nursing and Health Professions
Weston, Massachusetts

THE COLLEGE

Regis College is a private, coeducational, Catholic liberal arts and sciences college. It was founded in 1927 by the Congregation of the Sisters of Saint Joseph of Boston with a desire to put their resources to use for the good of society through education. Regis College offers bachelor's degrees in a wide variety of majors; master's degrees in nursing, teaching, organizational and professional communication, leadership and organizational change, and health product regulation; and a doctoral program in nurse practice.

THE SCHOOL OF NURSING AND HEALTH PROFESSIONS

Established in 1983, the Division of Nursing began as a B.S. degree completion program for registered nurses. A weekend track was started in 1989 and was selected by the Army Nurse Corps as an educational pathway that would fulfill reserve nurses' military obligations while they earned a baccalaureate degree. The first military weekend group graduated in 1992. The programs are now housed in the School of Nursing and Health Professions and include a B.S.N. program, a master's program, and a Doctor of Nursing Practice (D.N.P.) program with a variety of traditional and accelerated formats. The nursing programs reflect the mission of Regis College—to educate individuals to attain personal and career goals while also addressing the changing needs of society. The faculty is dedicated to excellence in teaching and is committed to the integration of theory and practice in professional nursing. Students can expect a challenging educational experience in a supportive environment. The nursing programs are fully accredited by the National League for Nursing Accrediting Commission and offer flexible options for study on a full- or part-time basis.

PROGRAMS OF STUDY

The undergraduate program offers a B.S.N., a four-year course of study that prepares individuals for professional practice as registered nurses. This program integrates study in the liberal arts and sciences with professional nursing education. Students gain diverse clinical experiences within the greater Boston area and develop skills that prepare them to provide care to clients in a wide variety of health-care settings.

The graduate program offers a Master of Science (M.S.) with a focus in nursing leadership for diverse health-care systems, nurse practitioner, or clinical specialist in acute care. The nurse practitioner track offers three primary-care options: pediatric, family, and psychiatric–mental health nurse practitioner. An accelerated curriculum track is designed for non-nurses who hold a baccalaureate degree in a field other than nursing. This track requires the completion of certain prerequisite courses and requires three years, including two summers of study. Students take the NCLEX-RN exam after sixteen months, and a B.S.N. is awarded at the end of the second year. Students have the option of exiting the program with the B.S.N. At the completion of the third year, the M.S. is awarded, and students are eligible to take nurse practitioner certification examinations.

The RN to B.S.N. to M.S. Upward Mobility Track allows students with an associate degree or diploma in nursing to earn both the B.S.N. and M.S. within one curriculum. Students have the option of exiting the program with the B.S.N. Registered nurses who have a baccalaureate degree in a discipline other than nursing may enter this accelerated pathway as well. Classes are offered during the day, in the evening, on weekends, and during the summer. For RNs, post-master's certificates and certificates in nursing leadership and in nursing are also offered.

The Doctor of Nursing Practice program began in spring 2007 and offers tracks in nursing leadership and nursing education. The D.N.P. is offered in a weekend hybrid format to accommodate full-time working nurses. The Capstone Mentorship is self-designed and is customized to meet the professional goals of the student.

AFFILIATIONS WITH HEALTH-CARE FACILITIES

Students in the nursing programs at Regis College have clinical opportunities and experiences in a wide variety of health-care settings. Students are placed in ambulatory and acute-, subacute-, and long-term-care facilities; nurse-managed clinics in homeless shelters; elementary and secondary schools; and elderly and low-income housing in both urban and suburban settings. Qualified nurse practitioner students have the opportunity to complete a portion of the clinical requirement in approved national or international settings. The Graduate Nursing Program also offers on-site graduate courses for registered nurses employed in eight different hospitals in the greater Boston area.

ACADEMIC FACILITIES

The Regis College Library provides resources and services to meet the research and study needs of undergraduate and graduate students and faculty members. The library contains 140,000 volumes and 787 current periodical subscriptions in print. Regis College Library has approximately 115 nursing periodicals in paper format plus more than 600 nursing journal titles containing full-text articles that are available through the library's subscriptions to online nursing databases. The library also has thousands of nursing books, including a large reference collection and an extensive collection located in the library stacks.

LOCATION

Regis College is located on a beautiful 132-acre campus just 12 miles west of Boston, home to some of the world's leading educational, cultural, and health-care facilities. The College is easily accessible by major highways and is linked to metropolitan public transportation by a free campus shuttle.

STUDENT SERVICES

Regis College offers a wide range of student services, including the Fine Arts Center, which includes the 650-seat Eleanor Welch

Casey Theatre and the Carney Art Gallery. The Athletic Facility features a regulation 75-foot pool with outdoor patio and sun deck and a recently upgraded fitness center. The Student Union Building houses the main dining hall and College Café, the campus bookstore, and the post office. On-campus housing is available for undergraduates. Qualified nursing students are invited to join Sigma Theta Tau, the international nursing honor society. Regis also boasts more than thirty student clubs and organizations, and NCAA Division III men's and women's sports.

THE NURSING STUDENT GROUP

There are 150 undergraduate students, 450 graduate nursing students, and 50 doctoral students. Regis nursing graduates have gone on to hold distinguished positions in every area of the health-care industry, including administration, clinical practice, academia, and government.

COSTS

Undergraduate tuition for 2009–10 was $28,900; room and board were $12,190. Summer tuition depends on the number of credits carried. VISA, MasterCard, American Express, or Discover, as well as cash, checks, or money orders, may be used for tuition payment. A tuition payment plan is also available. The total cost of the program varies depending upon the number of credits transferred or granted by examination or articulation.

FINANCIAL AID

The Regis College Office of Financial Aid works with students on an individual basis in order to help them finance their education through the federal Direct Loan Program. This means that all student loans (subsidized and unsubsidized) are processed directly by Regis College through the government, providing for fewer forms to fill out, a lower interest rate, and the ability to consolidate loans after graduation. Financial aid is need-based and is awarded on a first-come, first-served basis. In addition, Regis College offers a comprehensive merit scholarship program. Contact the Office of Financial Aid for more information at 781-768-7180 or finaid@regiscollege.edu.

APPLYING

All undergraduate nursing applicants are processed through the Regis College Office of Admission and are considered on a rolling basis. Applicants must submit a completed application for admission (apply online at http://www.regiscollege.edu/apply), a $50 application fee, an essay, two letters of recommendation (one from a teacher and one from a guidance counselor), official transcripts, and SAT or ACT scores. Nonnative speakers of English must also submit TOEFL scores.

CORRESPONDENCE AND INFORMATION

Office of Admission
Regis College
235 Wellesley Street
Weston, Massachusetts 02493-1571
Phone: 781-768-7100
        866-GET-REGIS (438-7344) (toll-free)
Fax: 781-768-7071
E-mail: admission@regiscollege.edu
Web site: http://www.regiscollege.edu

THE FACULTY

Cynthia Bashaw, Assistant Professor of Nursing; M.S., Regis College.

Maureen Beirne-Streff, Associate Professor of Nursing; Ed.D., Boston University.

Michael Bilozur, Assistant Professor of Biology; Ph.D., Boston College.

Nancy Bittner, Associate Professor and Assistant Dean for Nursing; Ph.D., Rhode Island.

Patricia Ciarleglio, Lecturer in Nursing and Placement Coordinator; M.S., Regis College.

Karen Crowley, Assistant Professor of Nursing; M.S., Simmons; FNP.

Mary Crowley, Nursing Laboratory Coordinator; M.S., Boston University.

Joanne Dalton, Associate Professor of Nursing; Ph.D., Rhode Island.

Patricia Dardano, Associate Professor of Nursing; D.N.Sc., Boston University.

Kathleen Donahue, Associate Professor of Nursing; Ph.D., Massachusetts Boston.

Elisa Giaquinto, Assistant Professor of Nursing; M.S., Brown.

Penelope Glynn, Associate Professor of Nursing; Ph.D., Boston University.

Joanne Haynes, Assistant Professor of Nursing; M.S., Regis College.

Antoinette Hays, Associate Professor and Dean for Nursing; Ph.D., Brandeis.

Joanne Hyde, Lecturer in Nursing; M.S., Boston University.

Philip Jutras, Associate Professor of Management; Ed.M., Massachusetts Boston; Ph.D., Boston College.

Marylou Kelleher, Lecturer in Nursing; M.S., Regis College.

Mary Lombard, Professor of Biology; Ph.D., Boston College.

Margherite Matteis, Associate Professor of Nursing; Ph.D., NYU.

Luanne Nugent, Lecturer in Nursing; M.S., Boston University.

Joyce Oppenheimer, Associate Professor of Nursing; D.N.P, Case Western.

Marybeth Scanlon, Assistant Professor of Nursing; M.S., Regis College.

Mary Smalarz, Associate Professor of Nursing; Ed.D., Boston University.

Nancy Street, Assistant Professor; M.S., Boston College.

Diane Welsh, Assistant Professor of Nursing; D.N.Pc, Regis College.

Seton Hall University
College of Nursing
South Orange, New Jersey

THE UNIVERSITY

Seton Hall was founded in 1856 by Bishop James Roosevelt Bayley, the first bishop of Newark. The University is a private coeducational institution with approximately 10,000 enrolled students. Seton Hall's South Orange campus is home to seven schools and colleges: the College of Arts and Sciences, the College of Education and Human Services, the College of Nursing, the John C. Whitehead School of Diplomacy and International Relations, the School of Health and Medical Sciences, the Stillman School of Business, and Immaculate Conception Seminary School of Theology. Seton Hall's eighth school, the School of Law, is located in Newark, New Jersey. The University is accredited by the Middle States Commission on Higher Education.

THE COLLEGE OF NURSING

Since becoming the first university in New Jersey to offer a baccalaureate nursing program in 1937, Seton Hall's College of Nursing has firmly established itself as a leading center of scholarship, teaching, and practice in the profession. As part of Seton Hall University, one of the state's oldest academic institutions, the College is located on a picturesque campus in South Orange, New Jersey. It is only 14 miles from New York City and within easy reach of urban, suburban, and rural communities. Today the College is one of the largest and most respected nursing schools in the northeast, offering programs for nurses at every stage of their careers. At the heart of the College is its range of programs for students looking to become nurses, from the signature four-year baccalaureate degree, to the graduate clinical nurse leader program. Nursing programs are accredited by the Commission on Collegiate Nursing Education.

PROGRAMS OF STUDY

Whether applicants are nurses with many years of experience or poised to enter the profession, the College has a variety of options to help them develop academically and professionally.

There are three programs for prospective nurses. The four-year baccalaureate degree program lays the foundation for a successful career in nursing, combining in-depth theory, hands-on learning and extensive clinical practice exposure. The two-year B.S.N (second degree) program is designed for those already holding a non-nursing baccalaureate degree. And the 22-month clinical nurse leader program is New Jersey's only entry-level master's degree in nursing for high-caliber candidates with a baccalaureate degree in a non–nursing major.

The College has three programs for registered nurses. The RN to B.S.N. program is for experienced nurses who want to advance their education. It provides an affordable and accessible route to a baccalaureate degree. For registered nurses with non-nursing baccalaureate degrees, the Bridge to M.S.N. is a 12-week online program that provides students an opportunity to access any of the College's wide range of master's degree offerings. The College also offers certification programs, leading to certificates in school nursing, health systems administration, or case management.

The College's graduate nursing school is nationally recognized as a center for advanced education and is one of the top 100 schools in *U.S. News & World Report's* rankings. Graduate nurses may take part in a wide range of programs: M.S.N. nurse practitioner (pediatric, adult, or gerontological); M.S.N. in school nursing; M.S.N. in health systems administration; M.S.N. in health systems administration and case management; M.S.N. and M.B.A.; and M.A. in nursing education.

The College's Ph.D. program is designed to prepare nurse scholars for a lifetime of advanced research and helps shape the next generation of intellectual leadership in nursing. The College also offers a Doctor of Nursing Practice (D.N.P.) degree, which concentrates on improved delivery of care, patient outcomes, and clinical systems management. The D.N.P. curriculum is comprised of core course requirements in theory and research, as well as didactic and practice course requirements in either adult or pediatric advanced practice nursing, or health systems administration.

Post-master's certification programs are also available, leading to nurse practitioner, case management, or Lamaze childbirth educator certificates.

AFFILIATIONS WITH HEALTH-CARE FACILITIES

The College is affiliated with a variety of healthcare agencies to provide students with clinical practice experiences. Its convenient location allows students access to a wide range of placements, from the busiest inner-city general hospitals, to suburban healthcare centers. A current list of affiliations is available from the College upon request.

ACADEMIC FACILITIES

The College is based in the Caroline D. Schwartz nursing building on the University's main campus in South Orange, New Jersey. The building is divided between the academic areas and the laboratories, which are equipped with the latest patient-care simulation technology. In addition, there are extensive information technology facilities and a well-appointed student lounge. Students also benefit from the extensive academic and recreational facilities of the wider University.

LOCATION

Seton Hall University is located on a 58-acre campus in South Orange, New Jersey, a suburban area 14 miles southwest of

New York City. The town center is a 10-minute walk from the campus and features various bookstores, coffee shops and restaurants.

STUDENT SERVICES

Qualified nursing students are eligible to apply for membership in the Gamma Nu Chapter of Sigma Theta Tau International Honor Society of Nursing. The Gamma Nu Chapter presents scholarly programs throughout the academic year and also sponsors an annual research day. The honor society serves as a positive vehicle for dialogue among nurse scholars.

THE NURSING STUDENT GROUP

The College is home to around 500 undergraduate nursing students at any one time. Eleven percent of the nursing students are male.

COSTS

For the 2009–10 academic year, undergraduate full-time tuition (12 to 18 credits per semester) was $30,470. The individual cost per credit for undergraduate courses was $869. The latest information about tuition, fees, and room and board expenses can be found on the University Web site at http://www.shu.edu. The cost per credit for graduate nursing courses was $901.

FINANCIAL AID

Ninety percent of Seton Hall students receive some form of financial aid, and 72 percent of entering freshmen receive scholarships or grants directly from the University. Applicants are encouraged to contact the financial aid office at the earliest possible point to ensure that financial aid can be processed without delay.

APPLYING

Specific admissions criteria and application instructions for each of our programs can be obtained by visiting the College of Nursing Web site at http://nursing.shu.edu.

CORRESPONDENCE AND INFORMATION:

Dean Phyllis Hansell
College of Nursing
Seton Hall University
400 South Orange Avenue
South Orange, New Jersey 07079-2697

Phone: 973-761-9306
Fax: 973-761-9607
E-mail: nursing@shu.edu
Web site: http://nursing.shu.edu

THE FACULTY

The College of Nursing faculty members have a substantial record of academic achievement and are the key to delivering the unrivaled combination of evidence-based learning and hands-on expertise that has become the hallmark of a Seton Hall education. The College is led by Dean Phyllis Shanley Hansell Ed.D., RN, F.A.A.N. Further details and biographies can be found at http://nursing.shu.edu.

The College of Nursing has been educating high-caliber nursing students since 1937.

Thomas Edison State College
School of Nursing
Trenton, New Jersey

THE COLLEGE

Thomas Edison State College provides flexible, high-quality, collegiate learning opportunities for self-directed adults. Cited as "one of the brighter stars of higher learning" by the *New York Times* and identified by *Forbes* magazine as one of the top twenty colleges and universities in the nation in the use of technology to create learning opportunities for adults, Thomas Edison State College provides high-quality higher education to adults wherever they live and work. Founded in 1972, Thomas Edison State College enables adult students to complete associate, baccalaureate, and master's degrees through distance learning, using a variety of different methods of credit earning.

THE NURSING PROGRAM

The School of Nursing at Thomas Edison State College offers an RN-B.S.N./M.S.N. degree program that is designed for experienced RNs who want a high-quality education with the convenience and flexibility that an online program can provide. Admission is open and rolling; RNs can enroll any day of the year. The schedule is self-paced; there is no time limit for degree completion. There is no residency requirement. Maximum credit for prior learning is given, and multiple credit earning options are available. With highly interactive, asynchronous online group discussions, adult independent learners become part of a community of learners where experiences are shared and learning is enhanced. More than 1100 RNs from more than thirty states are currently enrolled in the School.

In the School of Nursing, experienced and academically qualified nurse educators from throughout the country fulfill the roles traditionally held by faculty members in campus-based programs. Known as mentors, these educators all have a minimum of a master's degree in nursing, with approximately 85 percent prepared at the doctoral level and many tenured at their home institution.

PROGRAMS OF STUDY

The Bachelor of Science in Nursing (B.S.N.) degree includes 9 graduate credits (three courses) that are applied to the School's Master of Science in Nursing (M.S.N.) degree program. There is no additional per-credit tuition charge if the student continues on for that degree. Initiated in 1983 as an examination-based program to provide for additional educational opportunities for RNs in New Jersey to attain a B.S.N. degree, the program transitioned to an online format in 2001, became the School of Nursing in 2003, and was opened to out-of-state RNs in 2004. The M.S.N. degree program opened in 2006.

The B.S.N. degree requires a minimum of 120 semester hours of credit—60 in general education, 48 in nursing, and 12 in free electives. RN graduates of an associate degree nursing program or a diploma program of nursing will have 20 credits from previous nursing course work applied toward the lower-division nursing requirement; an additional 12 nursing credits may be applied to free electives. A total of 80 credits may be accepted from a community college. Up to 60 credits, including the 20 credits used in the nursing requirement, may be awarded to diploma graduates based on current RN licensure valid in the U.S. There is no age restriction on credits transferred to Thomas Edison State College to meet general education requirements or lower-division nursing requirements. All credits transferred to Thomas Edison State College to satisfy upper-division nursing requirements must be from an accredited baccalaureate or higher-degree nursing program or from other Thomas Edison State College–approved credit-earning methods, must be newer than ten years, and must have a grade equivalent of C or better for the B.S.N. degree and B or better for the M.S.N. degree.

In addition to the 20-credit lower-division nursing requirement for the B.S.N. degree, there is a 28-credit upper-division nursing requirement. All eight requirements may be satisfied by twelve-week, online nursing courses offered quarterly by the School. All nursing courses are 3 credits each, with the exception of Community Health Nursing, which is 7 credits.

The M.S.N. degree program currently offers a Nurse Educator track which requires 36 credits with five core courses; five courses in the area of study, Nursing Education; and two elective courses. Two education practicums are included in the degree, one in on ground teaching and one in online teaching.

A Nurse Educator Certificate program is available to RNs with a master's degree in another area of nursing specialty. The program includes the three nursing education theory courses and the student's choice of one or both education Practicums for a total of 12–15 credits.

All nursing courses are independent learning, highly interactive courses that require student participation in asynchronous online group discussions at least three times weekly, in addition to readings and the online submission of written assignments. Assessment of learning by the online course mentors occurs via the online group discussion participation and written assignments; there are no proctored examinations. Graduations are quarterly.

There is no time limit for degree completion; however, students are required to complete a minimum of 3 credits that apply to degree requirements in each twelve-month period to remain on active status in the School. On completion of the B.S.N. degree, graduates who continue on for the M.S.N. degree have only an additional nine courses, or 27 of the required 36 credits, to complete the M.S.N. degree. The B.S.N. degree program is accredited by the National League for Nursing Accrediting Commission (NLNAC). The RN-B.S.N./M.S.N. degree program is accredited by the Commission on Collegiate Nursing Education (CCNE).

ACADEMIC FACILITIES

Thomas Edison State College uses state-of-the-art technology to deliver its academic program via the Internet. Students have access to the rich library research facilities of the New Jersey State Library, which is an affiliate of Thomas Edison State College. Students also have access to the Virtual Academic

Library Environment (VALE), a consortium of fifty-two New Jersey colleges and universities, which provides access to a network of research libraries.

LOCATION

Thomas Edison State College is located in the capital city of Trenton, New Jersey, but its reach is global. Students live and study in all fifty states and more than seventy other countries. The College's campus comprises the Kelsey Building at 101 West State Street and the adjacent Townhouse Complex, the Academic Center at 167 West Hanover Street, the Canal Banks Building at 221 West Hanover Street, and the Kuser Mansion at 315 West State Street. The College's state-of-the-art facilities, from electronic classrooms and computer labs to a corporate-style education conference room and other amenities, allow Thomas Edison State College to link students and mentors at dozens of colleges throughout the country and around the world.

STUDENT SERVICES

The Thomas Edison State College School of Nursing programs are distinctive in that they are completed entirely at a distance; therefore, students are provided access to the services needed primarily via online format. The College offers all core student services via the Internet through iTESC®, a suite of online services. Also through the Internet, students have access to such services as course and test registration and payment; displaying of registration schedules, course and mentor availability, and grades; displaying and updating of student information; online course and mentor evaluations; and other services.

In addition to technical support provided 24 hours a day, seven days a week by the College's Office of Management Information Systems (MIS) through Presidium Learning, a technical support mentor is embedded in the School's online nursing courses. This mentor answers questions and provides support for students and other mentors when any technological issue arises. Writing assistance is available in the online courses.

Online tutoring services in math, reading, writing and other subjects is made available to all students at the College free of charge through Smarthinking.com.

Enrolled students have access to all academic advisement services provided by the College, including the availability of an academic adviser for nursing. Enrolled students may access advisement services by the U.S. Postal Service, fax, Internet, e-mail, telephone, or in-person appointments. All College and program publications provided to students may also be accessed on the College Web site.

THE NURSING STUDENT GROUP

Students in the Thomas Edison State College School of Nursing are typically midcareer professionals with a wide variety of nursing practice and management experience. The average student is 43 years old. Of the approximately 1100 students enrolled in the 2009–10 academic year, nearly all are actively employed in nursing. Approximately 10 percent of the enrolled students are men, and the program enjoys a 23 percent diversity rate.

COSTS

The tuition for the 2009–10 academic year was $328 per credit for New Jersey residents and $386 per credit for out-of-state residents for the B.S.N. degree; $479 per credit for the M.S.N. degree. There is a $75 nonrefundable application fee and a one-time nonrefundable $300 B.S.N. credential-review fee. The estimated cost for books and supplies for the online nursing courses is $100 per course.

FINANCIAL AID

Nursing students support their study primarily with employer tuition aid and loans. Unsubsidized loans are available to all accepted applicants. The Thomas Edison State College Office of Financial Aid and Veterans' Affairs is available to assist students. Nursing scholarship information is posed on the School of Nursing page of the College Web site. Students are also encouraged to check the Johnson and Johnson Web site (http://www.discovernursing.com) for information on nursing scholarships.

APPLYING

Applicants to the School of Nursing must be RNs with a current and valid license in the United States and proficiency in using a computer, browsing the Web, and sending and receiving Internet mail, including attachments. They must also have access to, and a familiarity with, PowerPoint and Excel software for selected courses. Minimum system requirements to access an online course are access to the Internet; Internet browser, such as Firefox 1.X or newer or Microsoft Internet Explorer 6.0 or newer. All applicants to the School of Nursing must submit the completed School of Nursing application with the nonrefundable application fee; B.S.N. degree applicants must also submit the nonrefundable B.S.N. credential review fee. All applicants must submit a notarized copy of RN current license, valid in the U.S., to the College's Office of Admissions. Applicants should have all official college transcripts and college-level examination score reports sent to the College's Office of the Registrar.

CORRESPONDENCE AND INFORMATION

David Hoftiezer
Director of Admissions
Thomas Edison State College
101 West State Street
Trenton, New Jersey 08608-1176

Phone: 888-442-8372 (toll-free)
Fax: 609-984-8447
E-mail: nursinginfo@tesc.edu
Web site: http://www.tesc.edu

Thomas Jefferson University
School of Nursing
Philadelphia, Pennsylvania

THE UNIVERSITY

Jefferson School of Nursing is an integral part of Thomas Jefferson University, one of the nation's first academic health centers, which also includes Jefferson Medical College and Jefferson College of Graduate Studies. Jefferson has three other schools: a School of Health Professions (consisting of the Departments of Bioscience Technologies, General Studies, Couple and Family Therapy, Occupational Therapy, Physical Therapy, and Radiologic Sciences), a School of Pharmacy, and a School of Population Health.

Jefferson has a campuswide commitment to excellence in educating health-care professionals and discovering knowledge to define the future of clinical care. Scholarship and applied, collaborative, and interdisciplinary research are integral to generating this new health-care knowledge.

Jefferson School of Nursing is an upper-division school, meaning that students generally transfer into a program in their junior year. High school students can reserve a seat in a future class by applying to the Plan a College Education (PACE) program and attending an affiliated school for two years. An associate degree program in nursing for high school graduates is also available.

THE SCHOOL OF NURSING

For more than 100 years, Jefferson has been educating men and women for the nursing profession, first through a diploma program and now with a continuum of professional development opportunities, from associate degree to Doctor of Nursing Practice. Jefferson awards the Associate of Science in Nursing (A.S.N), the Bachelor of Science in Nursing (B.S.N.), the Master of Science in Nursing (M.S.N.), post-master's certificates, and the Doctor of Nursing Practice (D.N.P.). All nursing programs are fully accredited by the American Association of Colleges of Nursing Commission on Collegiate Nursing Education (CCNE) through 2011.

The majority of Jefferson's nursing faculty members are doctorally prepared. All faculty members have a deep commitment to their roles as teachers, and they work hard to develop professionalism within students. Undergraduate and graduate students have the opportunity to participate in faculty research, scholarly activities, and practice, as well as to collaborate in interdisciplinary University projects. In 2007–08, the School of Nursing enrolled 586 undergraduates, the majority of whom are full-time, and 302 graduate students, the majority of whom enroll on a part-time basis.

PROGRAMS OF STUDY

The first half of the A.S.N.-B.S.N. curriculum offered by the School of Nursing prepares students to serve as generalists in the role of caregiver in a hospital or in-patient setting. Students complete 68 credits of general education and nursing course work, completing the A.S.N. program in two academic years. Graduates may then progress to complete a bachelor's degree in two or more years. This program is offered at the Center City Philadelphia campus and the Geisinger Medical Center campus in Danville, Pennsylvania.

The B.S.N. curriculum is an upper-division program that emphasizes interdisciplinary education among students in the health professions. Students enter the nursing program at Jefferson after completing 59 lower-division credits in the sciences and humanities. The B.S.N. program balances liberal arts, sciences, and humanities with professional nursing preparation. It emphasizes health promotion, maintenance, and disease prevention as well as managing individuals and families coping with acute and chronic illness. Students complete 64 nursing credits at Jefferson. Full-time and part-time options are available. Graduates are prepared to practice professional nursing as generalists in a variety of health-care settings. The undergraduate program is among the most progressive in the United States.

The RN-B.S.N. program is designed to prepare registered nurses who graduated from diploma or associate degree nursing programs for an increased leadership role in nursing. Students complete 60 credits of sciences and humanities in lower-division courses prior to entering the nursing major at Jefferson. Up to thirty-five upper-division credits are awarded for previous nursing knowledge, and RN students have the unique opportunity to earn 10 of the remaining upper-division credits through a portfolio assessment of previous nursing knowledge. This enables RN students to begin the program in their senior year and complete the program in two semesters of full-time study or two years of part-time study. RNs can earn the B.S.N. completely online.

The RN-B.S.N./M.S.N. option allows RN students who have obtained their basic nursing education through either a diploma or associate degree program to qualify for admission to graduate nursing education through a combined B.S.N./M.S.N. program. With this option, RN students can earn the B.S.N. and M.S.N. degrees in a seamless integrated curriculum. Both degrees can be completed entirely online. An Accelerated Pathway option is available to RN students with a baccalaureate degree in a field other than nursing.

Two programs leading to the B.S.N. and M.S.N. degrees are available to highly motivated, academically talented students who hold a bachelor's degree in a field other than nursing. The Facilitated Academic Coursework Track (FACT) is a very intense program that enables prelicensure students to complete both degrees in two calendar years of full-time study. The Accelerated Pathway to the M.S.N. for Second-Degree Students is slower paced and enables students to earn both degrees in three academic years of full-time study.

The Master of Science in Nursing program prepares nurses for advanced and sophisticated clinical practice. The graduate program offers nurse practitioner, clinical nurse specialist, and post-master's certificate programs in acute care, adult health, community systems administration, family medicine, neonatal, nursing informatics, nurse anesthesia (CRNA), oncology, pediatrics, and women's health. A gerontology program is in development.

The Doctor of Nursing Practice (D.N.P.) provides academic preparation for professional nurses who will practice at the most advanced level of nursing, whether clinical practice, administration, education, or policy. This interprofessional educational experience offers students opportunities to take core courses with students from Jefferson Medical College, Jefferson College of Graduate Studies, Jefferson School of Health Professions, Jefferson School of Pharmacy, and Jefferson School of Population Health. The D.N.P. is offered in a mix of online and in-class courses. Full-time students who have an M.S.N. may complete the 36-credit program in one calendar year; part-time students complete the degree on their own timeline. A combined M.S.N./D.N.P. program enables students with a B.S.N. to complete both degrees in three calendar years of full-time study.

The curriculum is predicated on the School of Nursing's belief that professional nursing is an art and a science that incorporates theory, research, and clinical practice. The graduate curriculum is organized using a core curriculum concept. Most courses are available both in the classroom and via the Internet. All specialty areas except CRNA require 36 credits and can be completed part-time or full-time. The 74-credit CRNA program requires thirty months of full-time study.

AFFILIATIONS WITH HEALTH-CARE FACILITIES

The University shares its campus with Thomas Jefferson University Hospital, one of the nation's premier health-care facilities. The multi-institutional Jefferson Health System and other leading hospitals and agencies throughout the region offer outstanding learning opportunities in a broad array of health-care settings.

ACADEMIC FACILITIES

The Dorrance H. Hamilton Building is designed to create a team learning environment among doctors, nurses, occupational and physical therapists, scientists, and allied health professionals. The building features a state-of-the-art clinical-skills lab for nursing students to work with simulated patients and current medical equipment. Administrative and academic offices, as well as some classrooms, laboratories, and a Learning Resource Center, including a computer laboratory, are located in Jefferson's Edison Building. Jefferson Alumni Hall, a basic medical science/ student commons building, houses Jefferson College of Graduate Studies, basic science departments, classrooms, and research laboratories. The University library and administrative offices are located in the Scott Building. Clinical experience is acquired at Thomas Jefferson University Hospital or at more than 1,800 clinical affiliate sites.

Professional counseling services are available for all students who need assistance in resolving academic, vocational, and personal concerns.

LOCATION
Jefferson is in the center of Philadelphia, stretching from 8th to 11th Streets and from Chestnut to Locust Streets. In this prime location, a short walk takes students almost anywhere they need to go. Jefferson is four blocks from Independence Hall and the Liberty Bell, three blocks from Chinatown, seven blocks from South Street's funky shops and restaurants, and eight blocks from Rittenhouse Square's popular park and shopping area. Students may also use the bus (several lines run through the campus) or subway (only two blocks away) to get across town. Getting out of town is a breeze; the Market East regional rail station is two blocks away, Amtrak's 30th Street Station is less than a mile, and the Philadelphia International Airport is a 30-minute train ride.

Living on campus means that classes, the hospital, and the library are within easy walking distance. From studios to luxury three-bedroom apartments, Jefferson housing offers something to match almost any budget. The on-campus community includes students from the Schools of Nursing, Pharmacy, Health Professions, Population Health, Jefferson Medical College, and Jefferson College of Graduate Studies, as well as postdoctoral fellows and medical residents.

STUDENT SERVICES
The University's many resources and services include academic advising, counseling, housing, student health, tutoring, day care, fitness facilities, computing services, student organizations, and career services.

THE NURSING STUDENT GROUP
Students enrolled in the undergraduate and graduate programs represent a diverse group in terms of age, gender, ethnicity, cultural background, socioeconomic status, and religious orientation. In fall 2005, approximately 36 percent of the students indicated that they are members of ethnic minority groups. About 15 percent of the undergraduate students are registered nurses pursuing the B.S.N. Nursing students are active in University-wide student organizations and activities as well as nursing-specific organizations and activities. Jefferson's graduates are highly respected and recruited. The job placement rate for 2005 nursing graduates who pursued employment was 97 percent, with graduates often receiving multiple offers.

COSTS
Tuition for full-time A.S.N. to B.S.N. students for the 2009–10 academic year was $17,767. Tuition for full-time B.S.N. students was $25,739. Tuition for M.S.N. and D.N.P. students was $850 per credit. The twelve-month FACT fee was $32,947.

FINANCIAL AID
Jefferson is committed to meeting the financial needs of its students. More than 72 percent of the current students receive financial assistance. Aid can include Federal Pell Grants, National Direct Student Loans, the College Work-Study Program, Air Force ROTC scholarships, nursing scholarships, nursing loans, state grants, work scholarships, state-guaranteed loans, and academic scholarships. Completed applications must be received by the Financial Aid Office no later than May 1 to ensure the maximum award.

APPLYING
Jefferson School of Nursing uses the self-managed application process. The application, fee, recommendation letters, transcripts, and other documents must be returned to the Office of Admission in a single envelope and at the same time.

The application deadline for most undergraduate programs is July 15. FACT applicants must have all application materials submitted no later than April 1. Along with a completed application and nonrefundable application fee is $50 (reduced to $25 for online applications), applicants must submit transcripts for all college work, an essay, and two letters of recommendation. An interview is required for all academically eligible applicants. A high school transcript is required for PACE applicants. An evaluation of international transcripts by the World Education Service (WES) is required. All international students and U.S. permanent residents must demonstrate English language proficiency, as outlined by the Office of Admissions.

Applications to most M.S.N. programs are accepted until July 15. (The deadline for the CRNA program, which starts in January, is November 15.) For all programs except CRNA, full-time students begin the program in the summer semester. Part-time students may begin in the fall, spring, or summer semester. Admission requirements include RN licensure, a bachelor's degree in nursing or a nurse doctorate, a minimum GPA of 3.0 on a 4.0 scale, competitive scores on the GRE or MAT if the cumulative GPA from the B.S.N. is less than 3.2, undergraduate courses in statistics and nursing research, a course in basic physical assessment skills, computer literacy, two letters of reference, a resume, and an essay. CRNA applicants also need current ACLS and PALS certification, a resume that demonstrates a minimum of one year of experience in a critical-care nursing setting, and an interview with the CRNA program director. The CRNA program is a full-time program that begins in January.

The application deadline for the Doctor of Nursing Practice (D.N.P.) program is April 15, 2008. In addition to the requirements for the M.S.N. program, D.N.P. applicants must submit three letters of recommendation along with three attribute forms. In place of the application essay, a personal statement, including desired outcome goals for the program, is required.

CORRESPONDENCE AND INFORMATION
Office of Admissions
Edison Building, Suite 100
Thomas Jefferson University
130 South 9th Street
Philadelphia, Pennsylvania 19107-5233
Phone: 215-503-8890
      877-JEFF-247 (toll-free)
Fax: 215-503-7241
Web site: http://www.jefferson.edu/nursing

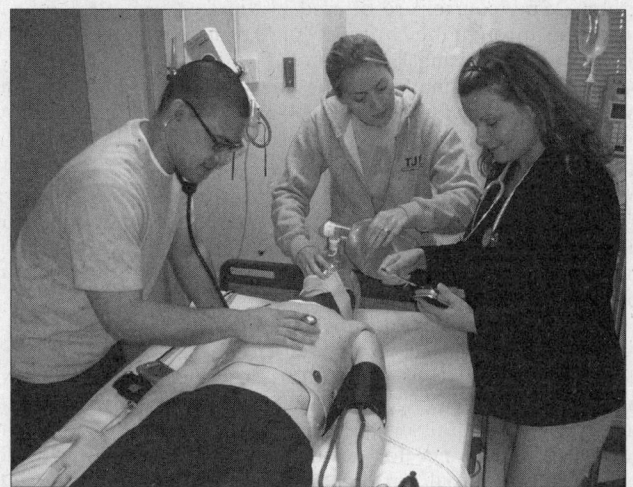

The University of Akron
College of Nursing
Akron, Ohio

THE UNIVERSITY

The University of Akron (UA) is the public research university for northern Ohio. *The Princeton Review* included The University of Akron among the "Best in the Midwest" institutions in its 2009 "Best Colleges: Region by Region" edition. The University has received national recognition and/or rankings in several areas, including business, chemistry, gerontological nursing, law, polymer science/engineering, and psychology.

The University of Akron is also a world leader in creating new materials for the new economy; a national leader in the development, protection, management, and commercialization of intellectual property; and a regional leader in information technology initiatives.

In 2008, the University of Akron and four other leading educational and medical institutions launched the BioInnovation Institute in Akron. This collaboration seeks to identify Akron as a nationally known center for medical products and procedures, health care training, and care for the medically underserved.

The University comprises a main campus in Akron, a regional campus in Wayne County, the Medina County University Center, and several other sites in Northeast Ohio. In 2000, UA launched the New Landscape for Learning initiative, an ongoing, major campus renovation campaign that has added five newly acquired or constructed buildings, 17 major additions and renovations to existing facilities, and 34 acres of new green space. InfoCision Stadium and Summa Field, a new on-campus stadium complex, opened in September 2009.

The 26,000 students enrolled at UA can choose from more than 200 undergraduate majors and areas of study, 170 master's degree programs and tracks, 29 doctoral degree programs and tracks, and a juris doctor program that includes seven specialties and tracks.

Working professionals interested in advancing their careers can select from a wide range of certificates, seminars, and workshops as well as associate, bachelor's, and graduate degree programs. Many courses are offered in the day, evenings, and on weekends through the University of Akron's Workforce Development and Continuing Education Division.

For more information about The University of Akron, visit http://www.uakron.edu or call 800-655-4884 (toll-free).

THE COLLEGE OF NURSING

Founded in 1967, the College has a long tradition of excellence. The College offers multiple educational programs designed to meet the needs of both students aspiring to become professional nurses and practicing professional nurses seeking career and professional advancement.

Located on the campus in Mary Gladwin Hall, the College offers the basic baccalaureate program (B.S.N.), an accelerated B.S.N. for students who hold at least a bachelor's degree in an area other than nursing, an RN/B.S.N. sequence for registered nurse graduates of associate degree and diploma programs, an LPN/B.S.N. sequence for licensed practical nurses aspiring to become professional nurses, the Master of Science in Nursing (M.S.N.) degree, and the RN/M.S.N. sequence for registered nurse graduates of associate degree and diploma programs who meet graduate standards. The University of Akron and Kent State University offer a Joint Ph.D. in Nursing (JPDN) program, a doctoral program with a single, unified doctoral nursing faculty and student body. The program prepares scholars in nursing with balanced preparation to be researchers, educators, administrators, consultants, or entrepreneurs. A Doctor of Nursing Practice (D.N.P.) program is currently under review.

The College employs faculty with a broad range of research and clinical backgrounds. There are 46 full-time and 45 part-time faculty members, of which 54 percent currently hold doctoral degrees. Several faculty members are in the latter stages of completing their doctoral studies. The remainder have master's degrees in nursing, with many having earned certification in advanced practice specialty areas.

The College offers clinical experiences for students in a wide variety of traditional and nontraditional settings and with diverse patient populations, including care of adults in hospitals, community agencies, and homes; care of well and ill elderly; care of newborns and children; care of persons with mental health problems in hospitals and community agencies; critical care; and extended care and rehabilitation.

The College is approved by the Ohio Board of Nursing and fully accredited by the Commission on Collegiate Nursing Education (CCNE).

International study in nursing through a summer elective course is often available.

PROGRAMS OF STUDY

The basic baccalaureate program leading to the B.S.N. degree and RN licensure is a four-year program that is balanced between nursing courses and University courses. Students enter the program after completing one year of prerequisite University courses. The nursing courses span three years, with clinical experiences in each semester of the program. The senior year features a senior practicum that is designed to give the student greater depth in an area of the student's choosing. A Cooperative Education Program is available to combine work and study.

A fifteen-month accelerated B.S.N. program is open to students who already hold a bachelor's degree and have completed prerequisite courses. All science courses must have been taken within the last five years.

The RN/B.S.N. sequence has been serving the educational needs of registered nurses since 1980. The sequence features learning contracts to allow flexible hours for clinical requirements and classroom time scheduled one day per week. Once students are admitted to the major, they can complete the sequence in one calendar year of full-time study; a part-time option is available. There is no testing required for admission. An outreach RN/B.S.N. sequence is offered at the Lorain County Community College campus, Wayne College, and Medina County University Center (MCUC).

The LPN/B.S.N. sequence was begun in 1990. The College was one of the first baccalaureate programs in the country to offer a sequence for LPNs. This sequence features testing for advanced placement and credit for prior learning. The LPN can finish the baccalaureate program in five semesters if advanced placement is earned.

The Master of Science in Nursing (M.S.N.) degree program prepares graduates for roles in advanced practice or advanced role preparation in administration. Within the advanced practice options, students may choose adult/gerontological health nursing, behavioral health nursing, child and adolescent health nursing, or nurse anesthesia tracks. Advanced practice options include preparation as a nurse practitioner or clinical nurse specialist. All M.S.N. graduate students take a common core and advanced practice or role options that include advanced clinical experiences.

The RN/M.S.N. sequence is designed for RN graduates of associate degree and diploma programs who meet graduate admission criteria. Students take three years to complete the sequence, which includes baccalaureate and master's course work. Through this program, the student may receive both the B.S.N. and M.S.N. degrees.

An M.P.H. consortium program exists with the Northeast Ohio University College of Medicine (NEOUCOM).

ACADEMIC FACILITIES

The College has a state-of-the-art learning resources center that includes simulated patient care areas and a computer laboratory. The College also has a Nursing Center for Community Health, which links the College to the community and is used by clients for health-care services and by the faculty and students as a practice and research site and provides a health care option for the underinsured and medically vulnerable populations in the area. The nursing library holdings are contained in the Science and Technology Library of the University. Nursing students have full access to all the facilities and services of the entire University.

LOCATION

Located in the northeast region of Ohio, Akron offers a wide variety of recreational, business, and cultural activities. The area is perfect for recreational activities that encompass all seasons. The University's presence in northeast Ohio provides numerous opportunities in major collegiate, amateur, and professional sports, concerts, cultural events, and commerce, all within easy driving distance and many accessible via public transportation. On campus, the Ohio Ballet, Emily Davis Art Gallery, University Orchestra, Opera/Musical Theatre, concerts, recitals, choral programs, Touring Arts Program, University Theatre, Repertory Dance Company, and professional artists performing at Edwin J. Thomas Performing Arts Hall contribute to the University's rich cultural environment.

Blossom Music Center, summer home of the Cleveland Orchestra, is located 20 minutes north of the campus. The city of Cleveland with all its fine recreational, sports, and cultural offerings is just 40 minutes from the University.

STUDENT SERVICES

The University has many resource and service offices to meet student needs. Campus resources include the Academic Advisement Center, Adult Resource Center, Sixty Plus Program, Placement Services, Student Employment, Career Placement Services, Student Volunteer Program, Counseling and Testing Center, Financial Aid Office, Student Health Services, Pan-African Center for Community Studies, Office of International Programs, Office of Multicultural Development, Peer Counseling Program, Office of Accessibility, Military Services Center, and writing, reading, and math developmental laboratories.

Undergraduate and graduate student organizations exist to involve students in the governance of the College. The Delta Omega chapter of Sigma Theta Tau, the international honor society of nursing, is housed within the College. The Student Nurses Association, which is open to all undergraduate students, is affiliated with the National Student Nurses Association. Other groups include Men in Nursing, Chi Eta Phi, Multicultural Student Nurses Association, and Intervarsity Nurses Christian Fellowship.

A new campus Student Recreation and Wellness Center and the Ocasek Natatorium are open to nursing students.

THE NURSING STUDENT GROUP

Enrollment in the undergraduate program is 602; it is 331 in the M.S.N. program and 32 in the joint Ph.D. program with Kent State. Full-time and part-time students are represented in all programs. Postbaccalaureate students, RNs, LPNs, transfer students, and new high school graduates are represented in the

College. About 15 percent of each entering B.S.N. class in the undergraduate program are men.

COSTS

Undergraduate tuition and fees for the 2009–10 academic year for Ohio residents were $308.27 per credit up to 11.5 credits or a $3609.24 flat fee per semester for 12 to 16 credits. Nonresidents paid a $308.27 per-credit surcharge.

Graduate tuition costs for the 2009–10 academic year were $397.55 per credit for Ohio residents. There was a $260 per-credit surcharge for nonresidents.

Additional costs include housing, transportation, books, course laboratory fees, immunizations, CPR certification, uniforms, and liability insurance.

FINANCIAL AID

Financial aid is available through the University as well as the College of Nursing. The University offers a variety of scholarships, grants, loans, student assistantships, work-study opportunities, and graduate assistantships. The College offers a variety of scholarships, graduate assistantships, and Federal Graduate Nurse Traineeships.

APPLYING

Students applying for the baccalaureate program must have completed one year of prerequisite college/university courses and have earned at least a 2.75 grade point average in those prerequisite courses. Applicants must be enrolled at The University of Akron for the spring semester prior to admission and are ranked according to grade point average in science prerequisite courses after completion of the spring semester. Each year, up to 160 students are admitted into the undergraduate program. Course work begins in the fall.

Students entering the LPN/B.S.N. sequence must hold a current Ohio LPN license and have completed two years of prerequisite college/university courses with a minimum prerequisite grade point average of 2.75. Course work begins in the spring semester.

Requirements for the RN/B.S.N. sequence include completion of prerequisite courses and current Ohio RN licensure. Course work begins in the summer.

Students applying to the M.S.N. program must hold a baccalaureate degree in nursing from an NLNAC-accredited nursing program; complete prerequisite courses; submit scores from the GRE taken within the last five years (CRNA program only), an essay, and three letters of reference; and hold a current Ohio RN license.

CORRESPONDENCE AND INFORMATION

Office of Student Affairs
College of Nursing
The University of Akron
Akron, Ohio 44325-3701

Phone: 888-477-7887 (toll-free)

Office of Undergraduate Admissions
The University of Akron
Akron, Ohio 44325-2001

Phone: 330-972-7100

Office of Graduate Admissions
The University of Akron
Akron, Ohio 44325-2101

Phone: 330-972-7663

Office of Financial Aid
The University of Akron
Akron, Ohio 44325-6211

Phone: 330-972-7032

Web site: http://www.uakron.edu

University of Phoenix
College of Nursing
Phoenix, Arizona

THE UNIVERSITY
University of Phoenix was established in 1976 with an innovative idea—to serve the largely unmet educational needs of working students and their employers. A commitment to educational excellence and unsurpassed student service has made University of Phoenix one of the nation's leading universities for working students. In fact, University of Phoenix is now the largest private university in North America with more than 200 campuses and learning centers as well as online courses available across the globe. University of Phoenix is accredited by the Higher Learning Commission and is a member of the North Central Association (ncahlc.org). In addition, the Bachelor of Science in Nursing (B.S.N.) and Master of Science in Nursing (M.S.N.) programs are accredited by the Commission on Collegiate Nursing Education (http://www.aacn.nche.edu).

Since 1983, University of Phoenix has offered professional nursing education and is proud to have graduated more than 25,000 RN to B.S.N. and M.S.N. students. University of Phoenix helps thousands of working students achieve a higher level of success every year.

In addition to nursing, University of Phoenix offers degree programs in business and management, criminal justice, education, health administration, information technology, and psychology at the associate, bachelor's, master's, and doctoral levels.

THE COLLEGE OF NURSING
University of Phoenix offers a comprehensive nursing program that provides convenience and flexibility for working nurses who seek to advance their credentials through an LPN/LVN to B.S.N., RN to B.S.N., M.S.N. or Ph.D. in nursing. A distinctive blend of established academic practices and innovative instructional delivery systems has helped build the University's growing network of campuses and learning centers throughout the United States. The curriculum is built upon a foundation of biological, physical, and social sciences that contribute to the science of nursing. The liberal arts components enhance the development of the intellectual, social, and cultural aspects of the professional nurse.

Faculty members are carefully selected based on their success in their own careers and for their ability and desire to effectively facilitate a challenging and rewarding learning environment. All degree programs are taught by faculty members who hold advanced degrees and have substantial experience in the fields they teach, so they bring academic and experiential insight to every course. Each instructor is trained in the unique craft of providing course instruction, direction, and feedback to students. This integration of advanced academic preparation, communications expertise, and current professional experience ensures that students learn current theory coupled with real-world application.

PROGRAMS OF STUDY
University of Phoenix nursing programs are designed in collaboration with academic leaders and industry professionals to ensure quality, relevance, and rigor. Depending upon the student's program of study, courses can be completed online or at a local campus. Some programs have additional requirements such as field experiences, clinical components or residencies. Not all programs are available in all states or in both online and on-campus formats. Students should contact a University enrollment adviser for further information.

A special sequence in the Bachelor of Science in Nursing program allows a currently Licensed Practical Nurse/Licensed Vocational Nurse (LPN/LVN) to achieve a B.S.N. degree. This program, offered at select campuses, builds on the basic education, skills, and experience of the practical nurse transitioning to the professional nursing role. Program content will focus on role transition, clinical skills, and critical thinking. Graduates of the program will be eligible to apply to take the National Council Licensure Examination for Registered Nurses.

The RN to Bachelor of Science in Nursing (RN to B.S.N.) program is designed to develop the professional knowledge and skills of working registered nurses. The program's behavioral objectives concentrate on the development of the nurse's role as caregiver, teacher, and leader. Using human caring as a framework, registered nurses are prepared as generalists who are able to apply critical thinking, professional skills, and knowledge to client outcomes. The RN to B.S.N. degree program is available online and through some on-campus locations. This program has a 41-credit required course of study and a 6-credit elective requirement.

The nursing program fulfills only part of the 120 minimum-credit requirement for bachelor's degree completion.

The Master of Science in Nursing (M.S.N.) program is designed for those nurses who want to pursue leadership roles in today's challenging health-care environment. Nursing theory and research provide the foundation for nurses to influence the future of nursing and health care in a variety of clinical, community, or academic settings. Thirty-nine credits are required for completion of this degree. Areas of concentration help students develop increased knowledge and/or skills in a specific area or particular role. University of Phoenix offers several M.S.N. specializations as well as programs that confer multiple master's-level degrees including the M.S.N./Master of Health Administration and M.S.N./Master of Business Administration/Master of Health Care Administration degrees. The M.S.N./nursing education specialization prepares a nurse to teach in a practice and/or academic setting. The M.S.N./informatics specialization provides course work in data management and information technology as they relate to nursing and the health-care setting. Generally the M.S.N. degrees with specializations may be completed in approximately two years; however, completion times vary depending on the program.

The Master of Science in Nursing/Master of Health Administration (M.S.N./M.H.A.) dual degree offers a unique blend of nursing and health care-related business skills—including finance, accounting, and economics—necessary to manage in today's evolving health care delivery systems. Essential elements from both programs provide students with the knowledge and skills needed to effectively examine and evaluate issues and trends impacting health care. The program consists of 54 credits and can generally be completed in less than three years.

The Master of Science in Nursing/Master of Business Administration/Health Care Management (M.S.N./M.B.A./H.C.M.) degree program combines essentials from each degree program to provide students with the knowledge and skills necessary to enhance and support patient services in a leadership position. The M.B.A./H.C.M. segment of the program emphasizes the identification, analysis, and solution of complex management problems that require technical understanding and balanced decision making. The M.S.N. section blends nursing theory with practice concepts necessary to successfully work within the structure, culture, and mission of any size health-care organization or educational setting. The M.S.N./M.B.A./H.C.M. program is 65 credits.

The M.S.N./Family Nurse Practitioner program, offered at select campuses, prepares advanced practice nurses to function in leadership roles in a practice or educational setting. Students complete 46 credits with core courses in advanced nursing content and process, then complete the family nurse practitioner sequence, which focuses on the health-care needs of people throughout their lives. Students also complete a 460-hour preceptorship in a primary care setting.

A Doctor of Philosophy (Ph.D.) in nursing is offered to help nurses improve the quality of health care as a researcher, educator and administrator. Offered through the University's School of Advanced Studies (SAS), the Ph.D. in nursing is designed to prepare scholars to conduct and interpret health care and educational research, advance the development and transformation of nursing education, and evaluate frameworks to guide ethical decision making. Special residency opportunities allow scholars to cultivate interprofessional relationships while completing the required doctoral dissertation.

ACADEMIC FACILITIES
At University of Phoenix, students can choose a learning format that fits their lifestyle and learning style. Depending upon the degree program, students can attend classes on campus or online. Some campuses offer a combined campus-based and online learning format. Local campus students attend class just once a week, in the evening or on weekends, and spend time completing additional assignments with their learning team. With the online learning format, students receive lectures, questions, and assignments from their instructors electronically and study them at their convenience. Students log in at least four days per week on days and times of their choosing. In both online and on-campus formats, classes are kept small for maximum interaction with both classmates and instructors.

LOCATION
University of Phoenix has more than 200 locations in thirty-nine states and the District of Columbia. Online courses are available in most countries around the world. Not all programs are available in all states or in both online and on-campus formats. Students should contact a University enrollment adviser for further information.

STUDENT SERVICES
University of Phoenix offers students exceptional customer service and support. From the first phone call through graduation, students receive guidance from dedicated advisers in enrollment, finance, and academics to make sure they are on track to graduate. Whether students attend class online or at a local campus, all administrative business can be conducted online, including registering for class, updating accounts, downloading textbooks and learning materials—even checking schedules and grades. And technical support is available 24/7, except on major holidays. With a phone call, a knowledgeable representative will answer questions or help solve technical issues.

University of Phoenix also offers an online library with a vast array of scholarly and professional research materials available anytime, from anywhere—even after students graduate. Although it's digitally updated and remotely accessible, the library has a full-time team of professional librarians and research specialists who oversee the online collection and are available to assist students with academic research.

Academic help is also available 24/7 through software tutorials, as well as online writing and math assistance. Specifically, the Center for Writing Excellence offers an automated system that can review students' papers for correct grammar and usage. Reviews by faculty members and other experts also are available, along with Web-based writing tutorials. Similarly, the Center for Mathematics Excellence provides online assistance to ease math anxiety and explain concepts. Supportive, easy-to-follow tutorials and exercises can give students the confidence they need to be successful in the classroom.

Many University of Phoenix locations also offer additional services to support students such as workshops, computers, Internet access, study rooms, and tutoring.

THE NURSING STUDENT GROUP
University courses are designed for students who have busy work schedules and full personal lives. The majority of students entering University of Phoenix nursing programs are age 30 and above with incomes greater than $50,000 annually. Nursing students come from a variety of backgrounds and nursing environments including urban and rural communities, magnet hospitals, and community health clinics.

COSTS
Undergraduate online nursing tuition is $450 per credit, and graduate online nursing tuition is $550 per credit. Tuition for campus-based courses varies by campus. Special tuition rates are available for military members and their spouses. Resource fees vary by course. Tuition and fees are subject to change at any time in the University's sole discretion.

FINANCIAL AID
University of Phoenix participates in many financial aid programs, including the Federal Stafford Student Loan, the Federal PLUS loan, and the Federal Pell Grant. The University does not charge students for processing financial aid applications. For further details about eligibility and to receive application forms, students should speak with a finance adviser.

APPLYING
Current employment in a nursing role is optimal, though not required, for application to University of Phoenix. However students must have access to a health-care environment to complete the necessary work-related assignments in each course. A current LPN/LVN license is necessary to apply to the LPN/LVN to B.S.N. program. Nurses applying to the RN to B.S.N. must have a diploma or associate's degree in nursing, with a cumulative GPA of at least 2.0 and a current, unencumbered and unrestricted RN license.

Graduate students must have an undergraduate degree from a regionally accredited college or university, with a cumulative GPA of at least 2.5. RNs who have a non-nursing bachelor's degree are required take three bridge courses from the B.S.N. program prior to being eligible for graduate nursing coursework.

To apply for admission, students may visit http://www.phoenix.edu or call 866-766-0766 (toll-free).

CORRESPONDENCE AND INFORMATION:
University of Phoenix
4615 E. Elwood St.
Phoenix, Arizona 85040

Phone: 877-611-3390 (toll-free in U.S.)
Fax: 602-387-6440
Web site: http://www.phoenix.edu

University of Pittsburgh
School of Nursing
Pittsburgh, Pennsylvania

THE UNIVERSITY

Founded in 1787 as a small private school, the Pittsburgh Academy was located in a log cabin near Pittsburgh's three rivers. In the 222 years since, the University has evolved into an internationally recognized center of learning and research. The University of Pittsburgh is the oldest institution of higher education west of the Allegheny Mountains. It is an independent, state-related, nonsectarian coeducational institution offering a variety of undergraduate and graduate programs. Total enrollment at the Pittsburgh campus is approximately 28,000, including nearly 10,000 graduate and professional students.

THE SCHOOL OF NURSING

Established in 1939 as an independent professional school of the University, the School of Nursing has a positive impact on the quality of health care for all segments of the population through its teaching, research, and service. It offers educational programs that anticipate and reflect the health-care needs of the region, state, and nation, resulting in the awarding of nearly 12,000 degrees to nursing students, including 8,341 baccalaureate degrees, 3,181 master's degrees, 189 doctoral degrees, and eighteen master's certificates. The current student nurse population is 1,028. Nursing students benefit from a low student-faculty ratio, small class sizes, and the extensive resources and enrichment opportunities of a research intensive university and a major metropolitan medical center.

The School is nationally known for the strengths of its clinical practice and research programs. Students hone clinical practice skills utilizing the strongest network of health-care providers in the nation, anchored by the University of Pittsburgh Medical Center. Clinical faculty members maintain their own professional clinical practice in order to enhance their skills and knowledge. Faculty members and students are engaged in multidisciplinary clinical and basic science research that aims to provide a scientific basis for the care of individuals across the life span.

PROGRAMS OF STUDY

The School of Nursing has undergraduate and graduate programs. There are three undergraduate curricula: the baccalaureate or prelicensure curriculum, the Accelerated 2nd Degree B.S.N., and the RN Options. All yield a Bachelor of Science in Nursing degree (B.S.N.) upon completion.

Baccalaureate students typically enter as freshmen unless they have completed all required freshman courses and are accepted into the sophomore class. The 124-credit curriculum emphasizes liberal arts and sciences courses during the first year and introduces clinical study in the second year. The last two years include a variety of clinical experiences culminating in a leadership/transition course where seniors work closely with professional nurse preceptors. Many undergraduates choose to complete an independent study with faculty mentors. Graduates are eligible to take the National Council Licensure Examination (NCLEX) to become registered nurses (RN).

The RN Options curriculum is designed for registered nurses, who obtained their nursing education through either a diploma or an associate degree program, to complete their nursing education with a Bachelor of Science in Nursing (B.S.N.) and offers them the opportunity to obtain an early admission to graduate nursing education to obtain a Master of Science in Nursing (M.S.N.).

The Accelerated 2nd Degree B.S.N. is designed to enable individuals with a baccalaureate degree in another discipline the ability to earn a Bachelor of Science degree in Nursing (B.S.N.) in three consecutive terms. Alternative schedules may be considered on an individual basis. At the completion, graduates are eligible to sit for the National Council Licensure Examination (NCLEX) to become registered nurses (RN). The curriculum is fast-paced and designed to build on the individual's previous education while providing the science and nursing content.

Admission to the Accelerated 2nd Degree B.S.N. program is highly competitive and is based upon proven academic achievement and grades earned in prerequisite courses.

Postbaccalaureate certificates include health-care genetics, research, and school nurse certification.

Graduate programs include master's and doctoral degrees. Professional nurses who wish to pursue a graduate degree have several choices at the School. The School of Nursing prepares advanced practice nurses for nurse anesthetist, nurse practitioner, or clinical nurse specialist roles. Nurse practitioner options include acute-care nurse practitioner with a concentration in adult health, cardiopulmonary, critical care, oncology, or a directed option. A primary-care nurse practitioner can specialize in adult, family, pediatrics, neonatal, or psychiatric roles. Another career path available is the role of the clinical nurse specialist. This area of concentration offers a choice of focus in medical/surgical or psychiatric nursing. Advanced specialist roles prepare nurses to become leaders in the areas of administration, clinical nurse leader, education, informatics, or research.

The Master of Science in Nursing (M.S.N) degree, consists of a variable number of credits depending on the major and area of concentration. Course work can be completed in full- or part-time study. The curriculum design includes core courses, advanced practice specialty course, and/or role development courses. Students in any major may also elect to earn a minor in nursing administration, nursing education, nursing informatics, nursing research, or healthcare genetics.

The Doctor of Philosophy (Ph.D.) program prepares scholars to extend scientific knowledge that advances the science and practice of nursing and to contribute to the scientific base of other disciplines. The curriculum includes courses in the history and philosophy of science, nursing theory development, the structure of nursing knowledge, issues influencing leadership and public policy in nursing and health, advanced statistics, quantitative research methods, research methodologies, instrumentation, and a research practicum with an experienced researcher. An area of research emphasis, which matches a faculty member's research emphasis, is selected by the student early in the program. Current faculty research initiatives include adolescent health, health-care outcomes, chronic disorders, critical care, health promotion, and mental health. The culminating requirement is a dissertation.

Two options exist for completing the Doctor of Philosophy program. The traditional M.S.N.-Ph.D. option is for students with a nursing master's degree. This option requires the completion of 64 credits. A one-term, full-time residency is required; however, the remainder of the degree requirements may be completed through either full- or part-time study. The B.S.N.-Ph.D. option, for nurses who wish to focus their career in research, does not require a master's degree. This option requires full-time study to complete 95–97 credits.

The Doctor of Nursing Practice (D.N.P.) is another doctoral program that is offered. This practice-focused doctoral program prepares nursing leaders for the highest level of clinical nursing practice beyond the initial preparation in the discipline. Throughout the program students develop the clinical, organizational, economic, and leadership skills to design and implement programs of care delivery that significantly impact health-care outcomes and have the potential to transform health-care delivery. Graduates with this terminal clinical degree are prepared for roles in direct care or indirect, systems-focused care. Advanced practice nurses practicing in today's health-care environment require complex clinical skills and sophisticated knowledge of the evidence-base for practice. Graduates of the D.N.P. program are able to affect the health-care delivery system by evaluating the evidence base for nursing practice, becoming leaders in the clinical arenas, establishing standards and policies, and meeting the needs of today's diverse health-care systems. Two options exist for completing the D.N.P., either the B.S.N. to D.N.P. or M.S.N. to D.N.P.

ACADEMIC FACILITIES

Nursing students have access to the University Library System, which is the twenty-sixth-largest academic research library in all of North America and the sixteenth-largest among the prestigious public libraries of the Association of American Universities. It provides a large array of innovative, world-class services. The School of Nursing Center for Innovation in Clinical Learning (CICL) provides technology and educational support to the students and faculty and staff members of the School. The department houses two computer labs, a quiet study area, videotape library and viewing area, a clinical lab, and a human simulation lab. In addition to providing distance education and technology support throughout the building, they support traditional instructional support for the classrooms.

LOCATION

The University's 132-acre campus is situated in Oakland, the heart of Pittsburgh's educational, medical, and cultural center. Within walking distance of the campus are theaters, art galleries, museums, libraries, and concert halls.

Pittsburgh has consistently been named one of the nation's most livable cities in various national surveys. Most students and many faculty members live within walking distance of the University, in Oakland, Squirrel Hill, or Shadyside. These areas abound in ethnic restaurants and in shops of all varieties, reflecting the cosmopolitan background of the residents. The city's industrial past has given way to an enterprising and vibrant present. Affordable living, distinctive neighborhoods, growing industries, and an abundance of leisure activities create a quality of life that is virtually unmatched. Most people find that Pittsburgh is a friendly, warm, active, exciting, and comfortable city in which to live.

STUDENT SERVICES

The University offers students a wide variety of services, including outpatient health care at the Student Health Service; career development, learning skills, and psychological services; veterans and disabled student services; numerous student activities; and child care.

THE NURSING STUDENT GROUP

In 2008–09, the School of Nursing enrolled 553 undergraduate students and 410 graduate students. Of the total student population, more than 50 percent were already registered nurses who were working toward B.S.N., M.S.N., D.N.P., or Ph.D. degrees in order to advance their career by assuming a new role or by changing career direction, or to increase their personal satisfaction.

COSTS

Undergraduate tuition per term in 2009–10 for full-time study was $8399 for in-state and $14,642 for out-of-state students. Tuition per credit for part-time study was $699 for in-state and $1220 for out-of-state students. Full-time student fees are approximately $984 per year. On-campus housing costs ranged from $1795 to $3495 per term. Available meal plan options varied from $410 to $2750 per term.

Graduate tuition per term in 2009–10 for full-time study was $9616 for in-state and $11,851 for out-of-state students. Tuition per credit for part-time study was $786 for in-state and $970 for out-of-state students. Full-time student fees are approximately $864 per year.

FINANCIAL AID

The University awards financial assistance to both undergraduate and graduate students through scholarships, loans, part-time employment, work-study, and School of Nursing awards. Freshman applicants should apply by March 1, continuing students by April 1, and graduate students by June 1.

Master's students receive a variety of financial aid through the School of Nursing, including Professional Nurse Traineeships for full-time study, University tuition aid for part-time study, specified scholarships, and loans.

Doctoral students also receive aid from the School. Out-of-state full-time students who meet specific criteria pay in-state tuition rates due to school-based scholarships. Many full-time doctoral students have graduate assistant, researcher, or teaching fellow positions, which are primarily merit-based, pay a stipend, and include a tuition scholarship and individual health insurance. These students work 10–20 hours per week, and many have excellent experiences on faculty research projects or teaching. Workshops on applying for predoctoral and postdoctoral training grant fellowships are provided. In addition, other scholarships and part-time tuition aid are available. Students should apply for all School-based aid by June 1 and should visit the Web site at http://www.nursing.pitt.edu.

APPLYING

Applicants to all programs should present appropriate transcripts, admission test scores, and other required material by the deadline date. For the latest and most complete admission information, applicants should visit the Web site at http://www.nursing.pitt.edu. High school applicants and those applying for transfer from another college or university should contact the University Office of Admissions and Financial Aid at 412-624-PITT or visit the Web site at http://www.pitt.edu to receive information and apply online. Admission decisions are made on a rolling basis, but applicants should apply as early as possible. Applicants are admitted on a rolling basis for all terms.

Undergraduate prelicensure applicants are evaluated primarily on the basis of their high school or previous college-level academic work, with an emphasis on performance in science courses. For high school applicants or transfer applicants with fewer than 24 credits, SAT scores as well as the student's high school record are considered.

Master's applicants must have a baccalaureate degree in nursing, a current license to practice, and one to two years of experience (for full-time study). Admission decisions are based upon a faculty interview, professional goals, previous academic performance, and GRE scores, if required by the program. Applications are due January 5 for the anesthesia program, for full-time and part-time study. Applications for full-time study for all other programs must be made by August 1 for fall term, December 1 for spring term, and April 1 for summer term. Applicants for part-time study may be admitted to any term on a rolling admissions basis as long as spaces are available. All applications can be submitted online at https://app.applyyourself.com/?id=up-nurs.

Doctoral applicants must have a baccalaureate degree in nursing, documentation of academic success in an appropriate master's program, evidence of competence in scholarly research and the ability to communicate in writing, and competitive GRE scores. Admission decisions are based upon previous academic performance, faculty interviews, professional and research goals, a match between the applicant's research interest and those of available faculty members, and GRE scores. Applications are accepted on a rolling basis and can be submitted online at https://app.applyyourself.com/?id=up-nurs.

CORRESPONDENCE AND INFORMATION

Student Services
School of Nursing
239 Victoria Building
University of Pittsburgh
3500 Victoria Street
Pittsburgh, Pennsylvania 15261

Phone: 412-624-4586
      888-747-0794 (toll-free)
Fax: 412-624-2409
E-mail: sao50@pitt.edu
Web site: http://www.nursing.pitt.edu

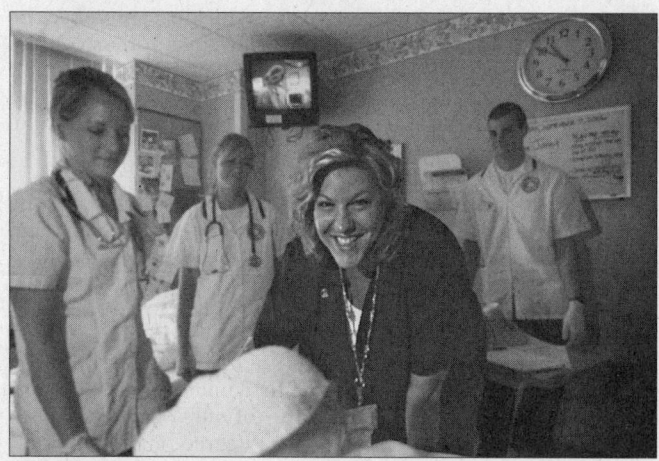

Students gain hands-on experience at the University of Pittsburgh School of Nursing.

University of Southern Indiana
College of Nursing and Health Professions
Evansville, Indiana

THE UNIVERSITY

The University of Southern Indiana (USI), established in 1965, is a comprehensive public university offering undergraduate and graduate degrees. The University is composed of five colleges—the Colleges of Nursing and Health Professions, Science and Engineering, Business, Education and Human Services, and Liberal Arts—and enrolls over 10,000 students.

The University of Southern Indiana has a strong tradition of commitment to low cost, accessible education excellence. In 1996, the University and the School of Nursing began offering Internet-based courses and programs for students. Undergraduate programs in nursing, health services, and imaging sciences and graduate programs in nursing, health administration, and occupational therapy are available online from the College of Nursing and Health Professions.

On-campus facilities include a students' fitness and health center, a bookstore, athletic facilities, a computer center, and a new comprehensive library that provides online reference materials.

THE SCHOOL OF NURSING

The School of Nursing was founded in 1988 as the first state-supported baccalaureate nursing program in southern Indiana. In 1996, the School initiated a master's degree program in nursing. The School also offers a post-master's nurse practitioner certificate program as well as other programs designed to meet the needs of practicing nurses in today's health-care environment. A Doctor in Nursing Practice (D.N.P.) program was implemented in August 2008.

Recognizing the complexity of health care, the School of Nursing has developed an undergraduate and graduate nursing curricula designed to prepare students for evidence-based practice. The curricula emphasize clinical nursing competence and uses a wide array of learning resources, including a Clinical Simulation Center.

The School of Nursing has been a leader in the development of distance education courses and programs. The RN-B.S.N., RN-M.S.N., and M.S.N. nursing programs may be completed online. The D.N.P. program combines on-campus intensives with online courses. In addition to these nursing programs, the College of Nursing and Health Professions offers online programs in health services, health administration, and radiologic and imaging sciences. Additional information may be obtained through the College's Web site at http://health.usi.edu.

PROGRAMS OF STUDY

The baccalaureate nursing program is designed to prepare the professional nurse to plan, implement, and evaluate health care for individuals, families, and groups in institutional and community settings. The nursing program is based on a planned progression of courses arranged to build upon previous knowledge and to develop skills and performance at an increasing level of competence. The 128 credits required for the degree include the University core curriculum courses supportive to the nursing major and 69 hours of nursing courses.

Registered nurses with an associate degree or diploma may obtain a baccalaureate degree in nursing through the RN-B.S.N. completion option. The nursing courses required for this option are provided online. The flexibility of the RN-B.S.N. option provides nurses with the opportunity to complete the course requirements in their own communities and on their own schedule with reasonable costs while receiving a quality education. The RN-B.S.N. curriculum is built upon a foundation of biological, physical, and social sciences and acknowledgment of previously learned nursing knowledge. No further testing of prior knowledge is required for nurses who hold a valid RN license and are in good standing in their current employment position.

The RN-M.S.N. program is designed for registered nurses with an associate degree or diploma who are interested in graduate nursing education and preparation for an advanced practice nursing role. The program builds on a student's prior learning and requires three years of current practice experience as a registered nurse. Students, in consultation with a faculty adviser, develop a plan of study that is based on prior learning and the student's selected graduate study major. After completion of University core courses, 20–25 hours of undergraduate nursing courses, and successful completion of 12 hours of graduate course credits, a Bachelor of Science in Nursing degree is awarded. At this point in their program of study, students are granted full admission into the graduate program. After completion of the remaining required graduate nursing courses, students are awarded an M.S.N. degree.

The Master of Science in Nursing is offered for nurses seeking advanced education in professional nursing. The graduate program prepares nurses for advanced practice as acute care nurse practitioners, family nurse practitioners, nurse educators, and nurse managers/leaders. The graduate degree is awarded upon the completion of 39 to 42 credits, dependent upon the graduate nursing specialty. Post-master's certificate programs are available for nurse practitioner, nursing management and leadership, and nursing education.

The baccalaureate and graduate nursing programs are fully accredited by the Commission on Collegiate Nursing Education. The 25 members of the nursing faculty represent diverse areas of teaching, practice, and research. Faculty members have expertise and strong clinical practice backgrounds in their areas of teaching.

The Doctor of Nursing Practice (D.N.P.) is a 78 credit hour post-master's program. A maximum of 42 credit hours from the master's degree may be applied to the D.N.P. degree. The D.N.P. program prepares experts in advanced nursing with emphasis placed on innovative, evidence-based practice that reflects the application of credible research findings. The expanded knowledge base in nursing will broaden the D.N.P. graduate's ability to translate that knowledge quickly and effectively to benefit patients, improve outcomes, and contribute to the profession. The curriculum consists of two to three years of doctoral-level course work which culminates in the completion of an evidence-based capstone project.

AFFILIATIONS WITH HEALTH-CARE FACILITIES

The School of Nursing is affiliated with a variety of clinical facilities, including hospitals, community agencies, physician practice groups, HMOs, schools, clinics, home health agencies, senior centers, and day-care centers that are used throughout the program of study. Written agreements are established with preceptors and health-care facilities located conveniently in a student's home community.

ACADEMIC FACILITIES

The David L. Rice Library houses about 340,000 volumes, 6,000 listening and viewing materials, and 575,000 items in microformat and subscribes to 57 electronic online databases with more than 19,000 full-text online journals. The library is fully automated for literature searches and online full-text journal searches. More than 2,000 online nursing and health-care journals are available for enrolled students.

The Computer Center has campus labs throughout the University and dedicated equipment for online learning. Technical assistance and a variety of color graphics, database management systems, simulations, and software are available for students. The University and College technology teams are also available to assist students enrolled in distance education courses.

The Charles E. Day Learning Resource Center, located in the College of Nursing and Health Professions, includes a learning laboratory with the latest technology. The Clinical Simulation Center provides students with hands-on learning prior to practice in hospitals and community settings and advance clinical decision making for acute care patients.

LOCATION

Evansville, Indiana, with a population of approximately 135,000, is home to the University of Southern Indiana. Evansville is big enough to provide metropolitan amenities but small enough to have small-town charm and hospitality. Located at a horseshoe bend on the Ohio River, Evansville has a long and colorful history. The campus is conveniently located 7 miles from downtown Evansville.

STUDENT LIFE

A wide variety of organizations and activities contribute to the total education of the on-campus student. More than eighty student organizations provide activities that include student government, leadership academy, career organizations, multicultural center, athletics, student publications, and a student-operated radio station.

The USI Association of Nursing Students and the Omicron Psi chapter of Sigma Theta Tau International Nursing Honor Society provide students with the opportunity to develop leadership skills; to participate in local, regional, and national nursing forums; and to work collaboratively with nursing school faculty members.

THE NURSING STUDENT GROUP

The School of Nursing enrolls more than 400 undergraduate, 300 graduate, and 30 doctoral nursing students. The diversity of the nursing student population is representative of the general population of the geographic regional area.

COSTS

In 2009–10, undergraduate tuition for in-state students was $177 per credit hour or $2650 per semester for full-time study (15 hours). For graduate students, in-state tuition was $255 per credit or $2300 per semester for full-time study (9 hours). University fees ranged from $200 to $400 per semester. Other fees and housing costs are determined on an individual basis.

FINANCIAL AID

USI offers a wide variety of financial assistance programs through various federal and state programs. Additional scholarships are offered through contributions made to the School by alumni and patrons. The amounts and types of financial assistance that a student receives include full tuition and living expenses as well as other scholarships that are determined by the eligibility of the applicant for the respective nursing program.

APPLYING

Applicants for the B.S.N. program must first be admitted to the University. A second application is then submitted to the nursing program.

Admission to the undergraduate nursing program may occur prior to matriculation to the University for high school students with outstanding high school achievement and high SAT/ACT scores. The larger proportion of students are evaluated and admitted after the fall semester of their second year or when required credit hours are completed.

Criteria for admission to the nursing program (guaranteed admission) for high school students prior to the fall semester of their second year includes admission to the University; completion of the nursing application; a minimum high school GPA of 3.5 on a 4.0 scale and a combined SAT score of at least 1800 or equivalent ACT score. To maintain this guaranteed admission status and begin nursing courses in their second year, students must maintaining a college GPA of at least 3.0 on a 4.0 scale during the first 30 credit hours with a grade of C or better in all science courses, Nutrition 376, English 101, English 201, CMST (Communications) 101/107, Psychology 201, and Sociology 121.

Admission to the program for all other students is competitive and based upon the following criteria: admission to the University; completion of the nursing application; college GPA; a grade of C or better in all science courses, Nutrition 376, English 101, English 201, CMST 101/107, Psychology 201, and Sociology 121; and a combined SAT score of at least 1500 or equivalent ACT score.

All students selected for admission to the nursing program must also meet clinical agency requirements, present evidence of satisfactory health status, be eligible for RN licensure, be capable of fulfilling clinical practice requirements, and submit a satisfactory drug screen and criminal record check.

RN-B.S.N. applicants must hold a current unencumbered registered nurse license in one of the fifty states or territories, meet general University requirements for admission, and have graduated from an accredited nursing program with a minimum GPA of 2.7. RN-M.S.N. applicants must have three years experience as a registered nurse, hold a current, unencumbered RN license, and must have a minimum GPA of 3.0.

Applicants to the master's and post-master's degree programs are required to have a current license as a registered nurse in one of the fifty states or territories, hold an earned B.S. or M.S. degree in nursing from an accredited school, have a minimum GPA of 3.0, and provide letters of reference. Practice as an RN is highly recommended prior to admission to the graduate nursing program.

Applicants to the D.N.P. program must have completed a master's degree in nursing with a GPA of 3.25 and at least one research course completed with a grade of B or above. Three letters of reference are required as well as a written goal statement.

Admission and enrollment information is available online at the College's Web site (http://health.usi.edu).

CORRESPONDENCE AND INFORMATION

Admissions and Advising Coordinator
College of Nursing and Health Professions
University of Southern Indiana
8600 University Boulevard
Evansville, Indiana 47712

Phone: 812-465-1150
E-mail: cnhpadmissions@usi.edu
Web site: http://health.usi.edu

The University of Tampa
Department of Nursing
Tampa, Florida

The University Of
TAMPA

THE UNIVERSITY

The University of Tampa (UT), founded in 1931, is a medium-sized, residential, private university that integrates the richness of the liberal arts tradition with twenty-first-century technology and innovative teaching strategies. More than 120 fields of study and preprofessional programs are offered. Graduate programs in business, teaching, and nursing and an Evening College complement the curriculum.

The 237 full-time faculty members include distinguished scholars, authors, artists, and educators who promote student- and community-responsive learning opportunities. The 5,800 currently enrolled students experience classes in small, personalized settings that balance "learning by thinking" with "learning by doing."

In an innovative first-year program, students explore global issues and cultures, examine career possibilities, and refine their critical-thinking and communication skills. Students, representing fifty states and territories and over 100 countries, find their academic experience at UT to be an enriching one that encourages a global perspective, provides opportunities to apply their skills and knowledge throughout the curriculum, and prepares them for future career challenges. For qualifying students, the Honors Program offers expanded opportunities for instruction, internships, and study abroad.

Seventy percent of all full-time students live on campus. The Vaughn Center and residence hall complex serves as the hub of campus life.

UT has one of the best NCAA Division II sports programs. Spartan athletes compete on fourteen men's and women's varsity teams. The swimming pool, tennis courts, jogging track, outdoor volleyball and basketball courts, crew training facility, and modern fitness center are enjoyed by all, making sunshine, sports, and fitness hallmarks of the UT experience.

The University of Tampa is accredited by the Southern Association of Colleges and Schools to award associate, baccalaureate, and master's degrees. In addition, the University is accredited for teacher education by the Florida State Board of Education. The Florida State Approving Agency for Veterans' Training recognizes the University with approval for veterans' educational benefits. The University is an associate member of the Council of International Schools (CIS), an international accrediting association. All nursing programs are accredited by the National League for Nursing Accrediting Commission (NLNAC), and the University is a member of the American Association of Colleges of Nursing and the National Organization of Nurse Practitioner Faculties.

THE DEPARTMENT OF NURSING

The Department of Nursing admitted its first class in 1981 and graduated its charter class in 1984. The B.S.N. completion program gained accreditation from the National League for Nursing Accrediting Commission (NLNAC) in 1986. The Master of Science in Nursing (M.S.N.) degree program was awarded NLNAC accreditation in 1998. Master's degree options include family and adult nurse practitioner studies and nursing education. Post-master's certificates may be earned in each of these concentrations.

PROGRAMS OF STUDY

In 2002, UT began a traditional four-year Bachelor of Science in Nursing (B.S.N.) program (accredited by the NLNAC in 2003),

helping to round out a slate of offerings that already included RN to B.S.N. completion and RN/B.S.N./M.S.N. tracks. The RN to B.S.N. program allows RN graduates of diploma and associate degree programs to complete the B.S.N. degree, and it provides a foundation for graduate education. RNs with associate degrees who seek a Master of Science in Nursing (M.S.N.) degree enroll in the RN to B.S.N./M.S.N. option, enabling the qualified RN to complete both the B.S.N. and M.S.N. degrees more rapidly than in traditional programs. Certain undergraduate courses are then replaced by graduate-level courses. Students formally apply to the M.S.N. program and complete the GRE during the progression of the B.S.N. program. In this option, when required undergraduate courses are completed, students are awarded the B.S.N.

The master's degree program offers family nurse practitioner and adult nurse practitioner concentrations. UT's graduate nursing education concentration responds to the critical shortage of nurse educators throughout the nation. It is the only nursing education program in west central Florida.

Many nurses seeking graduate degrees choose one of the nurse practitioner concentrations because of the opportunity to impact patient care decisions and health-care policy with greater autonomy. UT's nursing education concentration is poised to add significantly to the number of nurse educators who will have positive effects on the nursing shortage.

All of these programs recognize that nursing is a very different career than it was prior to the explosion of new information, new technology, new pharmacology, and the demands of a burgeoning health-care consumer population. Along with judgment and critical thinking, UT's nursing programs prepare graduates who are superbly educated, empowered, ethical, and politically articulate. Nurses are educated to have authority—not only when they occupy high-level positions, but at the bedside.

AFFILIATIONS WITH HEALTH-CARE FACILITIES

In keeping with the University's commitment to hands-on, real-world learning, UT's nursing programs enjoy affiliations with more than 120 Tampa Bay–area clinical facilities. There are twenty-five hospitals and nearly 1,000 doctor's offices in Hillsborough County alone. Tampa General Hospital, a 958-bed acute-care facility and level one trauma center, has established a partnership with UT's four-year B.S.N. program. State-of-the-art clinical laboratories utilizing computer-generated simulations as well as simulated human models are available for UT nursing students at Tampa General Hospital and on campus. These laboratories provide students with opportunities to learn and practice their nursing skills with the latest technology available.

The Tampa Bay area is rich in clinical experience opportunities. Specialty facilities and expert health-care professionals enrich the education of UT nursing students through their willingness to precept, mentor, and teach in the University's programs. Myriad opportunities for challenging positions in all aspects of health await those graduates who choose to remain in Florida following graduation.

ACADEMIC FACILITIES

For nursing and all students, the Macdonald-Kelce Library is well-equipped to meet the diversified needs of college students. It has more than 275,000 bound volumes and some 16,000 periodicals. In addition, the library is a member of the Tampa Bay Library Consortium, which provides delivery of books and research materials from a variety of member libraries. UTOPIA, an electronic online catalog, allows patrons to search other libraries and databases, check the status of their accounts, and even read government documents. Students can access UTOPIA from home, residence hall, office, or anywhere an online computer can be found.

Many of UT's classrooms are tech supported, but the Computer Resources Center is the technological center of the University. It offers hands-on experience in a laboratory environment, combining practical application with theoretical instruction. The entire campus is linked by a high-speed campus computer network and many areas are wireless. All members of the UT community have free Internet access and e-mail. All students in every residence hall have their own computer jacks, and they may use one of the many computer labs located in convenient areas on campus.

LOCATION

Surrounding the UT campus is Tampa, a vibrant, ethnically and culturally diverse, modern city located on the west central coast of Florida. Once a sleepy southern town, Tampa's boom began in the 1950s and continues unabated in the 2000s. An imposing skyline continues to burst into bloom over a cityscape that was almost entirely flat just two decades ago. Tampa is just an hour west of Orlando's Disney attractions and 30 minutes from beautiful gulf beaches.

More than a million residents now inhabit the city and surrounding Hillsborough County, with more than 2.6 million in the four-county Tampa–St. Petersburg–Clearwater metroplex (commonly referred to simply as "Tampa Bay") and 4 million in the eleven-county region. Tampa is the educational, medical, cultural, economic, business, shipping, entertainment, and legal center of it all, and the community is involved with its premier private university. More than 700 Tampa Bay community leaders serve on University boards and advisory groups.

STUDENT SERVICES

Leadership opportunities abound in an atmosphere of individual discovery and development fostered by the University's active campus life, including Greek life, more than 140 student clubs and organizations, and service learning opportunities. A cocurricular transcript option gives UT graduates a resume-enhancing edge with prospective employers and graduate schools. Professionals in the Academic Center for Excellence (ACE), the Saunders Writing Center, and the Academic Advising and Career Services offices help students stay on track academically.

THE NURSING STUDENT GROUP

There are 352 students currently enrolled in UT nursing programs: 21 in the B.S.N. completion program, 112 in the M.S.N. and postgraduate certificate programs, and 219 in the Department's four-year B.S.N program. The B.S.N. completion and graduate programs are designed for adult learners who attend part-time. The majority are already working in various health-care settings in the Tampa Bay community. Applying from many parts of the country, most four-year students are residential and attend full-time during the day. Because of the critical shortage of nurses to serve a growing population of acutely ill and elderly patients, many graduates select employment in Florida, where they receive excellent salaries and benefits.

COSTS

Undergraduate tuition and fee costs for the 2009–10 academic year were $22,482 for full-time study. Room and board charges averaged $8296 for a double room for the academic year. RN to B.S.N. tuition was $455 per credit hour. Graduate tuition (for graduate-level courses only) was $488 per credit hour. Additional fees for books, supplies, lab fees, etc., also apply, and vary by semester.

FINANCIAL AID

Special Florida and federal financial aid incentives are in place to encourage students to pursue nursing degrees. UT awards institutional financial aid based on merit and need to full-time undergraduate students. Some graduate assistantships and federal traineeships are awarded to M.S.N. students each year. Students are encouraged to explore outside funding sources such as employers and health-related agencies. All students pursuing at least half-time study are eligible for loans. Information on financial assistance is available online at http://www.ut.edu/financialaid or by contacting the Financial Aid Office at 813-253-6219 or finaid@ut.edu.

APPLYING

University admission application forms are available on the University's Web site for downloading or completion online. Applications for admission to the RN to B.S.N. and M.S.N. programs are evaluated on a rolling basis, and students may enter in the fall, spring, or summer terms.

Undergraduate students apply to the four-year baccalaureate nursing program by first applying to the University, completing the regular UT undergraduate admissions application. Official transcripts from all schools attended, SAT or ACT scores, an essay, and a recommendation from a guidance counselor or teacher are required. Acceptance to the University does not constitute admission to the nursing program. Separate application is made to the nursing program once pre-nursing requirements have been met. Meeting minimal requirements does not guarantee admission to this high-demand, limited-enrollment program. Four-year B.S.N. students are admitted to the nursing program each fall for the spring term only.

Admission to the RN to B.S.N. program requires the applicant to be currently licensed in Florida as a registered nurse. Applicants who provide proof of eligibility for licensure may attend the first semester, but they must have obtained a Florida RN license by the end of that semester to continue in the program. Applicants to this program must submit the regular undergraduate admission application and provide official transcripts from each college attended. Admission to the M.S.N. program requires a graduate M.S.N. application, current Florida licensure as an RN, a GPA of 3.0 or higher in the last 60 credit hours of college/university courses, a computer course, a statistics course, and successful completion of the GRE. Two professional letters of reference and a resume are also required. Applicants with a Florida license and a baccalaureate degree in a discipline other than nursing may enroll in the pre-M.S.N. program to complete additional course work prior to full admission to the M.S.N. degree program.

CORRESPONDENCE AND INFORMATION:

Admissions Office
University of Tampa
401 West Kennedy Boulevard
Tampa, Florida 33606

Phone: 813-253-6273
Fax: 813-258-7398
E-mail: nursing@ut.edu
Web site: http://www.ut.edu

University of Wisconsin–Madison
School of Nursing
Madison, Wisconsin

THE UNIVERSITY

In achievement and prestige, the University of Wisconsin–Madison (UW–Madison) has long been recognized as one of America's great universities. Founded in 1849, it is today one of the nation's largest public land-grant institutions, with an international reputation as a leading teaching and research university. As stated in the *Vision for the Future*, the University's mission is "to create, integrate, transfer and apply knowledge." The University offers a complete spectrum of liberal arts studies, professional programs, and student activities. With more than 40,000 students, the student body is diverse and cosmopolitan.

THE SCHOOL OF NURSING

The School of Nursing has had a strong commitment to enhancing health care since its beginning in 1924. Consistently ranked among top nursing schools for graduate education and research, the School is an integral part of the UW–Madison health sciences complex. Members of the faculty are academically well prepared and recognized as scholars, researchers, expert clinicians and teachers, and leaders in the profession.

The School offers a Bachelor of Science degree in nursing, a Doctor of Nursing Practice (D.N.P.) degree, a Doctor of Philosophy degree with a major in nursing, and opportunities for postdoctoral research. The School is no longer admitting students to the Master of Science degree program. In fall 2009, the School enrolled 317 students in the baccalaureate nursing major, 68 returning RN students, 164 students in the M.S. program, 7 students in post-master's nurse practitioner options, and 35 students in the Ph.D. and postdoctoral programs.

PROGRAMS OF STUDY

The Bachelor of Science program in nursing prepares men and women for entry-level positions in professional practice and provides a basis for leadership roles and graduate study. The 124-credit curriculum comprises course work in general education, nursing practice, and electives. Students are admitted to the nursing major in the junior year. An honors program is offered, providing opportunities for high-ability students who seek greater depth and challenge in their educational experience. Students have the opportunity to complete the nursing component of the program either at the UW–Madison campus or the Western Campus for Nursing located at Gundersen Lutheran Medical Center in LaCrosse, Wisconsin. An Early Entry Ph.D. option is designed for undergraduate students who are interested in research careers in nursing.

The BSN@Home Program, of which the UW–Madison School of Nursing is a partner, is offered for registered nurse students seeking a baccalaureate degree. The program is offered to Wisconsin residents via the Internet and the combined resources of five University of Wisconsin System nursing schools.

The purpose of the D.N.P. program is to prepare nurses for leadership roles in advanced nursing practice. Students prepare for roles as clinical nurse specialists or nurse practitioners in their selected population focus. Those interested in dual preparation as an advanced practice nurse and nurse educator may add a nursing education focus. Three population foci are available in the program: adult/gerontology, pediatrics, and psychiatric–mental health. Students in the adult/gerontology population focus will have the option to select between acute care and primary care. The curriculum is organized around three core components: systematic evaluation of practice, leadership/policy, and practice. These core components prepare graduates with the requisite knowledge and skills to influence health-care practice for the future.

The Ph.D. program in nursing is characterized by an early and continuous training in research, a strong scientific base in nursing, and a minor in a related discipline. The purpose of the program is to prepare nurses to assume major roles in the development, evaluation, and dissemination of knowledge about phenomena of interest in nursing. Graduates become the scholars and teachers who move the nursing profession forward through systematic inquiry into nursing issues. The curriculum leading to the doctorate includes seven components: existing and evolving knowledge in nursing, methods of nursing inquiry, research ethics, nursing doctoral seminars, course work in a minor field, teaching and learning, and research/dissertation credits. Graduates of the program have assumed faculty positions at major universities in the United States, Canada, and many other countries and have been awarded postdoctoral fellowships to further their research. Doctoral and postdoctoral funding is available as part of an NINR-funded training program in patient-centered interventions.

AFFILIATIONS WITH HEALTH-CARE FACILITIES

Faculty and staff members maintain affiliations with many health, education, and social service agencies throughout urban and rural Wisconsin, including the Wisconsin Department of Health and Family Services and many public health departments, schools, and hospitals. The School is especially committed to performing research and providing student clinical experiences in health professional shortage areas, as exemplified by participation in the Area Health Education Centers (AHEC) of Wisconsin.

ACADEMIC FACILITIES

The Health Sciences Learning Center provides the Schools of Medicine, Nursing, and Pharmacy with state-of-the-art classrooms, computer resources, and distance education facilities as well as a comprehensive health sciences library. Educational resources for both on-campus and distance students include online access to library journals, Web-based course materials, and videoconferencing technologies. Collaborative arrangements with a number of campus departments expand the practice, education, and research experiences open to students.

LOCATION

Madison, situated on an isthmus between Lakes Mendota and Monona, is a midsize city with a population of about 225,000, known for its natural beauty. With its good economy, low crime rate, and abundance of cultural and recreational activities, Madison ranks consistently among the top cities in the country. Its central location, 90 miles from Milwaukee, 120 miles from Chicago, and 250 miles from Minneapolis, places it within easy driving distance of these major metropolitan areas.

STUDENT SERVICES

Advisers are available in the B.S. program to help students interpret curriculum and academic requirements and plan a balanced program. They also assist with academic problems and acquaint students with campus resources. At the graduate level, students may select, or are assigned, a faculty adviser with whom they plan their program of study. A writing course is taught in the School for graduate students. Career services are also available for students. The campus offers a wide variety of other support services for students, including the International Student Services Office, the McBurney Disability Resource Center, the Multicultural Student Center, the Writing Center, and many others.

THE NURSING STUDENT GROUP

The student body comprises students from throughout the U.S. and abroad. The School is committed to recruitment, admission, retention, and graduation of students who are members of minority groups. The student view is welcomed and important. Students serve as voting members on School of Nursing committees.

COSTS

For 2009–10, full-time tuition and fees for resident undergraduate students were $8312; they were $23,064 for nonresidents. Full-time tuition and fees for resident graduate students were $10,518; they were $25,072 for nonresidents.

FINANCIAL AID

The campus Office of Student Financial Services awards financial aid based on need. Financial aid packages consist of loans, grants, and work-study assistance. The School of Nursing administers a number of scholarships to qualified nursing students. Scholarships in varying amounts are awarded annually, and some are renewable as long as the recipient is in good academic standing. Several forms of financial aid are available for graduate students. These include traineeships, fellowships, scholarships, research and teaching assistantships, and loans. Advanced Opportunity Fellowships are available for qualified minority or economically disadvantaged students. The School is committed to funding full-time students in the Ph.D. program.

APPLYING

Admission to the nursing major is available in the fall semester only. The deadline for applying is February 1. Individuals may be considered for admission as prenursing students in the fall, spring, and summer sessions, provided they are entering as beginning freshmen or transfer students with more than 24 college credits. The deadline for freshmen and prenursing transfer students is February 1 for summer and fall and October 1 for spring. Admission to the prenursing classification is no guarantee of admission to the nursing major.

Graduate application deadlines depend on the program of interest. Master's and post-master's applications are due March 1 for fall enrollment and October 1 for spring semester enrollment. For the Ph.D. program, applications are due January 15 for fall enrollment and September 15 for spring enrollment.

Prospective students are encouraged to visit the School of Nursing's Web site (http://www.son.wisc.edu) for more detailed information about admission requirements.

CORRESPONDENCE AND INFORMATION

School of Nursing
University of Wisconsin–Madison
600 Highland Avenue
Madison, Wisconsin 53792-2455
Fax: 608-263-5296
Web site: http://www.son.wisc.edu

Undergraduate Admissions, Office K6/146

Phone: 608-263-5202
E-mail: ugadmin@wisc.edu

Graduate Admissions, Office K6/145B

Phone: 608-263-5180
E-mail: gradadmit@son.wisc.edu
Web site: http://www.son.wisc.edu

The Health Sciences Learning Center on the UW–Madison campus.

Ursuline College
The Breen School of Nursing
Pepper Pike, Ohio

THE COLLEGE
Ursuline College is a Catholic liberal arts college offering baccalaureate and graduate programs. Although Ursuline was founded as a women's college in 1871 and remains a women's college, men are welcome and represent 7 percent of the students who are enrolled in nursing. Most students come from Ohio and surrounding states and represent different ethnic, racial, cultural, religious, and economic backgrounds. Currently, The Breen School of Nursing has approximately 450 undergraduate and 100 graduate students.

Ursuline's nationally recognized core curriculum encourages students to explore their identities and life goals. Ursuline takes a holistic approach to learning, encouraging students to rely on their studies not only as a means for launching a successful career but also for enjoying a happy and meaningful life. This integrated approach is truly reflective of a new generation of students who, along with the faculty members, serve as catalysts for the dynamic learning environment at Ursuline. That culture and small classes provide more than 1,600 students with individual attention and special care.

THE SCHOOL OF NURSING
Nursing has been a vital program at Ursuline College since 1975. Today, The Breen School of Nursing has the largest academic program on campus. The School offers B.S.N. and M.S.N. degree programs and post-master's certificates. B.S.N. graduates typically score higher than the national average on the NCLEX exam. The M.S.N. program offers the following Advanced Practice Registered Nurse (APRN) role and population-focused educational tracks: adult health clinical nurse specialist studies, adult nurse practitioner studies, and family nurse practitioner studies. Nursing education and palliative care are also offered as subspecialties. The palliative care subspecialty was the first of its kind to be offered to nurses in this country and is currently being designed with an increasingly global focus.

The Breen School of Nursing offers its professional programs within Ursuline's values-based learning environment. An individualized approach enables students to enjoy personal instruction, learn material in greater depth, and gain experience in a wide variety of health-care environments. The Breen School's graduates are sought by employers, who find them to be well prepared and flexible in adapting to new settings. The School has more than 2,000 graduates, many of whom hold leadership positions. In addition to a highly qualified full-time faculty, the M.S.N. program has visiting professors who are nationally recognized leaders in nursing.

PROGRAMS OF STUDY
The Breen School offers programs that prepare nurses for the health-care marketplace of the future, at both the basic (B.S.N.) and advanced practice (M.S.N.) levels.

The B.S.N. program provides a broad foundation by combining Ursuline's liberal studies core with an intensive three-year sequence in the nursing major. Qualified students are admitted directly into nursing. The B.S.N. program (129 credits, 58 of which are in nursing) can be completed in four years. Unique classroom and clinical assignments enable students to develop critical-thinking, communication, technical, and leadership skills. Students complete clinical rotations in world-renowned health-care institutions in the greater Cleveland area. The School's holistic and values-based nursing program provides a framework for students to learn about the caring and ethical side of health care, pass the NCLEX licensing exam, and adapt to practice in the twenty-first century. There are accelerated tracks for RNs, LPNs, and for those who have earned a bachelor's degree or higher in another discipline.

The emphasis for nursing education at the graduate level is on refining analytical skills, developing a clearer ability to connect theory to practice, and enhancing professional skills. All programs have a strong clinical component where caring, communication, and critical thinking are emphasized. The number of credit hours required for the M.S.N. degree is 39, with the exception of the family nurse practitioner studies track, which requires 42 credit hours. Courses are offered in the evenings and on Saturdays in an accelerated model. Students may choose to complete the clinical practicum in the greater Cleveland area or at an alternate location. The palliative care post-M.S.N. track is available via distance learning, and adult/family nurse practitioner post-M.S.N. programs are available on campus. All M.S.N. graduates are eligible to take advanced practice certification exams.

AFFILIATIONS WITH HEALTH-CARE FACILITIES
The Breen School of Nursing is affiliated with numerous internationally renowned and community-based health-care agencies throughout the greater Cleveland area. M.S.N. students may elect to do their practicum in another state or country.

ACADEMIC FACILITIES
Ursuline's library, well-known to health professionals in the area, houses more than 125,400 volumes, 369 periodical subscriptions, and 3,641 electronic subscriptions. Membership in OhioLINK and a comprehensive media collection provide access to thousands of additional resources. One of the reference librarians is a liaison with the School of Nursing. Other campus resources include media and computer centers. The College has five dedicated rooms for computers, plus individual computers in numerous locations, including the residence halls. Students enjoy classes in the Bishop Anthony M. Pilla Student Learning Center, which houses a state-of-the-art nursing skills lab.

LOCATION
Ursuline College is located on a beautiful campus in Pepper Pike, a residential suburb 12 miles from downtown Cleveland. The surrounding area has many restaurants and stores, including a large mall just 10 minutes from campus. The Cleveland area offers a multitude of activities such as music, art, science, parks, and sports. Ursuline is easily accessible from Route 271 via public or personal transportation. For students looking to combine a quiet but serious academic life with the cultural excitement of a major city, Ursuline College provides these unique advantages.

STUDENT SERVICES
In addition to sports, the College provides a fitness center, personal and career counseling, mentoring and cooperative education programs, campus ministry, and an Office for Multicultural Affairs. The Academic Support and Learning

Disabilities Center provides academic support services for all students, including assistance with study, testing, and writing skills. Tutoring is available in reading, writing, math, and science. The Program for Academic Success (PAS) was designed to help students who are not prepared for college-level work, especially in math and science.

COSTS

Tuition for the 2009–10 academic year was $759 per credit hour. Full-time students usually carry 12 to 16 credits. Graduate tuition was $808 per credit hour.

FINANCIAL AID

The Office of Financial Aid administers a number of institutional, state, and federal programs. Financial assistance may include a combination of scholarships, loans, grants, and work-study opportunities. To apply for financial aid, students must complete the Free Application for Federal Student Aid (FAFSA) and the Ursuline College Financial Aid Application. Approximately 85 percent of undergraduates in nursing receive financial aid.

APPLYING

Undergraduate applications are accepted on a rolling basis. Graduate applications must be received by April 1 of every year.

Admission to the B.S.N. program is through the Office of Admission. In addition to meeting the criteria for clear admission to the College, applicants seeking admission to the B.S.N. program directly from high school need to have 2.75 or higher GPAs and minimum ACT scores of 20 or SAT composite scores of 1000. Also, they must demonstrate proficiency by achieving a grade of at least C+ in algebra 1, biology with lab, and chemistry with lab. Transfer students need a strong recommendation from a counselor or teacher and at least a 2.5 cumulative GPA average in all completed college work. Applicants who are or have attended other nursing programs must also submit a letter of good standing from that program's dean or program director.

For admission to the RN-B.S.N. program, students must meet the criteria for clear admission to the College, have graduated from an accredited associate or diploma program, and hold an active RN license in the state of Ohio.

For admission to the LPN-B.S.N. program, students must meet the criteria for clear admission to the College, have graduated from an accredited LPN program, and hold an active LPN license in the state of Ohio.

Second-degree students seeking admission to the Accelerated Program for Second Degree Students must be accepted to Ursuline College; supply proof of a degree from an accredited college or university; and have earned a minimum GPA of 2.5 in their first degree program. Admission to the M.S.N. program is through The Breen School of Nursing. Admission criteria include an official transcript verifying completion of an accredited baccalaureate program in nursing and showing evidence of the applicant's ability to do graduate work, as indicated by a GPA of at least 3.0. The MAT or GRE may be required of applicants whose GPA is less than 3.0. In addition, applicants must submit three letters of recommendation from professionals attesting to the suitability of the applicant for graduate work in the particular program and provide proof of current licensure or eligibility for licensure as a registered nurse in Ohio. An interview with the program director and/or a graduate faculty member may be required.

CORRESPONDENCE AND INFORMATION

For the Undergraduate Program:
Kimberly A. T. Shepherd
Director of Admission
Ursuline College
2550 Lander Road
Pepper Pike, Ohio 44124-4398

Phone: 440-449-4203
　　　　888-URSULINE (toll-free)
Fax: 440-684-6138
Web site: http://www.ursuline.edu

For the Graduate Program:
Janet Baker, D.N.P., APRN, BC, CNS
Director, Graduate Program
The Breen School of Nursing
Ursuline College
2550 Lander Road
Pepper Pike, Ohio 44124-4398

Phone: 440-646-8172
Fax: 440-684-6053
E-mail: jbaker@ursuline.edu
Web site: http://www.ursuline.edu/academics/breen/

Located on 112 scenic acres in Pepper Pike, Ohio—just 12 miles east of Cleveland—the Breen School of Nursing is a student's pathway to success.

Vanderbilt University
School of Nursing
Nashville, Tennessee

THE UNIVERSITY

Vanderbilt University was established in 1873 through a $1-million donation by Commodore Cornelius Vanderbilt. Vanderbilt University offers a full range of undergraduate programs, as well as fifty-four master's degree programs and forty-six Ph.D. programs. Vanderbilt also offers professional degrees in business administration, divinity, education and human development, engineering, law, management, medicine, nursing, and public policy. There are 2,997 full-time faculty members and a diverse student population of 12,000.

THE SCHOOL OF NURSING

For over 100 years, Vanderbilt University School of Nursing (VUSN) has been providing innovative educational opportunities for its students. The School's proudest tradition is educating nurses who are impassioned professionals capable of meeting—and exceeding—the demands of a constantly evolving profession. By 1926, the School had grown from its initiation as the Vanderbilt Hospital Training School (1909) to a school of nursing, offering a diploma in nursing combined with studies in arts and sciences, leading to a B.S. degree. In 1933, VUSN offered the first B.S.N. in Tennessee and became a charter member of the Association of Collegiate Schools of Nursing (ACSN), which later became the National League for Nursing Accrediting Commission (NLNAC), under which the program is currently accredited. The nurse-midwifery program is accredited by the American College of Nurse-Midwives. In 1985, VUSN introduced the Prespecialty Pathway to the master's program, replacing the B.S.N. degree program. The Prespecialty Pathway offers multiple entry options for students seeking to become advanced practice nurses, including those with a bachelor's degree in a field other than nursing (applicants without a bachelor's degree will be considered on an individual basis), an associate degree or diploma in nursing and 78 hours of college credit, or a B.S.N. Recognizing that some nurses who may have earned master's degrees in nursing would like additional or different specialties, VUSN offers a post-master's option. In 1993, the Ph.D. in Nursing Science program was established. In 2008, the Doctor of Nursing Practice (D.N.P.) program was established. Beginning fall 2010, the School of Nursing is adding a Master of Science in Nutrition and Dietetics program. The program offers two unique specialty tracks: nutrition informatics and nutrition management in health-care systems.

PROGRAMS OF STUDY

Vanderbilt University School of Nursing offers a Master of Science in Nursing (M.S.N.) with multiple entry options. Applicants with a Bachelor of Science in Nursing, an associate degree in nursing and 78 semester hours of college credit, a diploma in nursing and 78 semester hours of college credit, or a bachelor's degree in another field are eligible to apply to the program. Applicants without a bachelor's degree will be considered on an individual basis.

The M.S.N. degree is offered with the following specialties: clinical nurse leader, clinical nurse specialist, emergency nurse practitioner, women's health nurse practitioner/adult nurse practitioner dual certification, nurse midwifery/family nurse practitioner dual certification, health-systems management, nurse midwifery, nursing informatics, primary-care nurse practitioner (adult, adult/gerontology dual certification, family, pediatric, or women's health), specialty-care nurse practitioner (acute care, neonatal, pediatric acute care, or psychiatric–mental health), and joint degrees combining the Master of Science in Nursing with the Master of Divinity (M.S.N./M.Div. dual degree), and Master of Theological Studies (M.S.N./M.T.S. dual degree). The School offers numerous focus areas, including cardiovascular disease management, clinical research management, forensic nursing, oncology, palliative care, transplant services, trauma, and urogynecology. Many of the programs are delivered in a modified distance format to accommodate individuals who work full-time and/or maintain residence outside middle Tennessee.

Applicants with a Bachelor of Science in Nursing (B.S.N.) from a CCNE- or an NLNAC-accredited program are admitted directly to the specialty year for a 39- or 40-semester-hour (three semesters full-time) program of studies. Nurse-midwifery, dual concentrations, and joint degree programs require additional semester hours. Admission to the School of Nursing without a B.S.N. degree is possible through the generalist nursing Prespecialty/M.S.N. program. Students with an associate degree in nursing and 78 semester hours of college credit or a diploma in nursing and 78 semester hours of college credit may enter the program and earn the Master of Science in Nursing degree in five semesters of full-time study. Students with a baccalaureate degree in another field may enter the program and earn an M.S.N. degree in six semesters of full-time study.

The Doctor of Nursing Practice (D.N.P.) program is built upon Vanderbilt School of Nursing's internationally recognized advanced practice nursing programs. The D.N.P. program provides an alternative to a research-focused doctorate with education in evidence-based practice, quality improvement, and systems thinking.

The Ph.D. in Nursing Science program prepares scholars for research and teaching careers at major universities and for research positions in public or private sectors of health care. Graduates of the program conduct and disseminate research that addresses regional and national needs and extends the knowledge base in the discipline of nursing.

Two tracks of study are available: clinical research and health services research. These areas of study are reflective of the overall research interests and expertise of School of Nursing faculty members and the resources available in the medical center, the University, the School of Nursing nurse-managed and interdisciplinary care delivery centers, and the Veterans Affairs Tennessee Valley Healthcare System (Nashville campus).

The Master of Science in Nutrition and Dietetics program offers advanced education and training to prepare nutrition and dietetics practitioners who will create new ways to deliver safe, appropriate, diverse, and cost-effective nutrition care. Two tracks of study are available: nutrition informatics and nutrition management in health-care systems. This program builds upon Vanderbilt's leadership in nursing management to prepare dietitians for new roles in disease management and administration in various health-care settings and systems.

The faculty of VUSN is committed to the educational preparation of a group of nurse scholars who can lead the nation in demonstrating how well-conceived, theory-based nursing research verifies and extends the body of nursing knowledge. Students work with faculty mentors who guide and oversee their educational programs from admission through the completion of degree requirements. They participate in intensive research experiences connected with faculty research projects and are exposed to a variety of research designs and analysis techniques.

AFFILIATIONS WITH HEALTH-CARE FACILITIES

Vanderbilt University School of Nursing offers its students opportunities to complete clinical courses, conduct inquiry, and learn in diverse settings. The School maintains more than 1,000 contracts with clinical practices in hospitals, communities, health departments, private practices, clinics, outpatient facilities, home-health agencies, skilled-care facilities, nursing homes, schools, and industries. These sites are in urban settings in Nashville, rural areas of Tennessee, and in other areas across the country. The Vanderbilt University Medical Center maintains a reputation for excellence in teaching, practice, and research and provides students with a tertiary academic setting, where patients receive exemplary care from creative health-care teachers and scholars.

ACADEMIC FACILITIES

The Jean and Alexander Heard Library is the collective name for all of the libraries at Vanderbilt, which have a combined collection of more than 3 million volumes. In addition to the Central library, the Biomedical, Divinity, Education, Law, Management, and Science libraries serve their respective schools and disciplines. The state-of-the-art Annette and Irwin Eskind Biomedical Library provide students with access to worldwide information through the very best in informatic retrieval and management technology. Traditional library services, book stacks, and comfortable reading areas are also provided along with technology training assistance.

The focal point of scholarship at the School of Nursing is the Center for Research Development and Scholarship (CRDS), which is housed in Godchaux Hall. Although research and scholarship activities occur throughout the School and are interwoven into all aspects of academic life at Vanderbilt, the center serves as the central resource, repository, and facilitator of faculty member, student, and nursing staff member scholarship. CRDS assists with grant proposal development, Institutional Review Board application, paper and poster presentation, database management, instrument development, use of computers, literature searches, reference retrieval, and manuscript preparation.

LOCATION

Vanderbilt is located on a 333-acre parklike campus approximately 1½ miles from downtown Nashville, providing a peaceful setting within an urban environment. Long known as a center of banking, finance, and publishing, this capital city of Tennessee is a unique blend of Southern hospitality and cosmopolitan diversity that ranks high in the quality-of-life surveys. Nashville has an international airport and is easily accessible from interstate highways.

STUDENT SERVICES

Vanderbilt provides its students with a comprehensive list of services, including the Career Center; Psychological and Counseling Services; Student Health Center; the Office of International Services; the Child Care Center; the Bishop Joseph Johnson Black Cultural Center; the Office of Lesbian, Gay, Bisexual, Transgender, Queer, and Intersex Life; and the Margaret Cuninggim Women's Center, as well as security escort services and shuttle bus services.

THE NURSING STUDENT GROUP

Vanderbilt University School of Nursing has been successful in attracting students from diverse educational backgrounds and work experiences. Approximately 40 percent of the M.S.N. class began the program in the 2009 academic year without a background in nursing. These individuals will enter the nursing profession prepared as advanced practice nurses after two full calendar years (six semesters) of study. Ages of class members range from 20 to 60, and 11 percent of the students are men. The School's diverse student body includes Asian Americans, African Americans, American Indians, and Hispanic students, in addition to international students.

COSTS

Tuition for the M.S.N. program for the 2009–10 academic year was $1030 per semester hour for all students. Tuition for the Ph.D. in Nursing Science program was $1568 per semester hour. Tuition for both programs is subject to change.

Expenses for books and supplies vary according to specialty. Equipment such as PDA (personal digital assistant), tape recorders and diagnostic tools is required for certain specialties. Other charges include laboratory fees, student activities and recreation fees, liability insurance coverage, and hospitalization insurance.

FINANCIAL AID

Financial aid is available from several sources for full-time M.S.N. students. All students who wish to apply for financial aid and scholarships must apply to the School of Nursing no later than March 15 for the next academic year. Information about financial aid for M.S.N. students can be obtained from the School of Nursing Admissions Office Web site, http://www.nursing.vanderbilt.edu/msn/admissions/financial_aid.html.

Information about financial aid for D.N.P., Ph.D., and M.S. in nutrition and dietetics students can be obtained from the Director, Student Financial Services, 208 Godchaux Hall, 461 21st Avenue South, Nashville, Tennessee 37240 or http://www.nursing.vanderbilt.edu/phd/financial.html and http://www.nursing.vanderbilt.edu/dnp/financial.html.

APPLYING

The School of Nursing host campus visits in October and March each year. Applicants are strongly encouraged to attend to learn more about programs offered at the School of Nursing. Admission requirements for the MSN program along with the online application are found online at http://www.nursing.vanderbilt.edu/msn/admissions/admission_req.html. Admission requirements for the D.N.P. program along with the online application are found online at http://www.nursing.vanderbilt.edu/dnp/index.html.

Admission to the Ph.D. in Nursing Science program is through the University's Graduate School, which has oversight responsibility for all doctoral programs in the University. Application materials are found online at http://www.nursing.vanderbilt.edu/phd/welcome.html.

Successful applicants to the Ph.D. in Nursing Science program are those whose previous academic performance, letters of reference, Graduate Record Examinations (GRE) scores, and personal statement meet admission standards for the School of Nursing and the University Graduate School. In addition, because of the importance of research oversight in doctoral education, only students whose research and career goals fit with the School's areas of concentration are considered for admission. All applicants are interviewed by the Director of the Doctoral Program and 2 doctoral faculty members.

Admission requirements for the M.S. in Nutrition and Dietetics program along with the online application are found online at http://www.nursing.vanderbilt.edu/nutrition/admissions.html.

CORRESPONDENCE AND INFORMATION:

For information on the M.S.N, D.N.P., and Ph.D. in Nursing Science programs:

Admissions Office
Vanderbilt University School of Nursing
Godchaux Hall Room 207
461 21st Avenue South
Nashville, Tennessee 37240

Phone: 615-322-3800
     888-333-9192 (toll-free)
Fax: 615-343-0333
E-mail: vusn-admissions@vanderbilt.edu
Web site: http://www.nursing.vanderbilt.edu

For information on the M.S. in Nutrition and Dietetics programs:

Admissions Office
Vanderbilt University School of Nursing
Godchaux Hall Room 207
461 21st Avenue South
Nashville, Tennessee 37240

Phone: 615-322-3800
     888-333-9192 (toll-free)
Fax: 615-343-0333
E-mail: vusn-nutrition@vanderbilt.edu
Web site: http://www.nutrition.vanderbilt.edu

INDEXES

BACCALAUREATE PROGRAMS

ACCELERATED BACCALAUREATE

U.S. AND U.S. TERRITORIES

Alabama

University of South Alabama, College of Nursing, *Mobile* (BSN)

Arizona

Grand Canyon University, College of Nursing and Health Sciences, *Phoenix* (BSN)

University of Phoenix, Online Campus, *Phoenix* (BSN)

University of Phoenix-Phoenix Campus, College of Health and Human Services, *Phoenix* (BSN)

University of Phoenix-Southern Arizona Campus, College of Health and Human Services, *Tucson* (BSN)

California

Azusa Pacific University, School of Nursing, *Azusa* (BSN)

California State University, East Bay, Department of Nursing and Health Sciences, *Hayward* (BS)

California State University, Northridge, Nursing Program, *Northridge* (BSN)

California State University, San Marcos, School of Nursing, *San Marcos* (BSN)

Mount St. Mary's College, Department of Nursing, *Los Angeles* (BSN, BSc PN)

National University, Department of Nursing, *La Jolla* (BSN)

Samuel Merritt University, School of Nursing, *Oakland* (BSN)

University of Phoenix-Bay Area Campus, College of Health and Human Services, *Pleasanton* (BSN)

University of Phoenix-Sacramento Valley Campus, College of Health and Human Services, *Sacramento* (BSN)

University of Phoenix-San Diego Campus, College of Health and Human Services, *San Diego* (BSN)

University of Phoenix-Southern California Campus, College of Health and Human Services, *Costa Mesa* (BSN)

Colorado

Platt College, School of Nursing, *Aurora* (BSN)

Regis University, School of Nursing, *Denver* (BSN)

University of Northern Colorado, School of Nursing, *Greeley* (BS)

University of Phoenix-Denver Campus, College of Health and Human Services, *Lone Tree* (BSN)

Connecticut

Southern Connecticut State University, Department of Nursing, *New Haven* (BS)

District of Columbia

The Catholic University of America, School of Nursing, *Washington* (BSN)

Florida

Barry University, School of Nursing, *Miami Shores* (BSN)

Florida State University, College of Nursing, *Tallahassee* (BSN)

Jacksonville University, School of Nursing, *Jacksonville* (BSN)

University of Phoenix-Central Florida Campus, College of Health and Human Services, *Maitland* (BSN)

University of Phoenix-North Florida Campus, College of Health and Human Services, *Jacksonville* (BSN)

University of Phoenix-West Florida Campus, College of Health and Human Services, *Temple Terrace* (BSN)

Georgia

Kennesaw State University, School of Nursing, *Kennesaw* (BSN)

Hawaii

University of Phoenix-Hawaii Campus, College of Health and Human Services, *Honolulu* (BSN)

Illinois

Loyola University Chicago, Marcella Niehoff School of Nursing, *Maywood* (BSN)

Southern Illinois University Edwardsville, School of Nursing, *Edwardsville* (BS)

West Suburban College of Nursing, *Oak Park* (BSN)

Indiana

Saint Mary's College, Department of Nursing, *Notre Dame* (BS)

Valparaiso University, College of Nursing, *Valparaiso* (BSN)

Iowa

Allen College, Program in Nursing, *Waterloo* (BSN)

Kansas

MidAmerica Nazarene University, Division of Nursing, *Olathe* (BSN)

Wichita State University, School of Nursing, *Wichita* (BSN)

Louisiana

University of Louisiana at Monroe, Nursing, *Monroe* (BS)

University of Phoenix-Louisiana Campus, College of Health and Human Services, *Metairie* (BSN)

Maine

University of Maine at Fort Kent, Department of Nursing, *Fort Kent* (BSN)

Maryland

Bowie State University, Department of Nursing, *Bowie* (BSN)

Massachusetts

Massachusetts College of Pharmacy and Health Sciences, School of Nursing, *Boston* (BSN)

MGH Institute of Health Professions, School of Nursing, *Boston* (BSN)

Regis College, School of Nursing and Health Professions, *Weston* (BSN)

Simmons College, Department of Nursing, *Boston* (BS)

Michigan

Northern Michigan University, College of Nursing and Allied Health Science, *Marquette* (BSN)

University of Phoenix-Metro Detroit Campus, College of Health and Human Services, *Southfield* (BSN)

Missouri

Cox College of Nursing and Health Sciences, Department of Nursing, *Springfield* (BSN)

Goldfarb School of Nursing at Barnes-Jewish College, *St. Louis* (BSN)

Graceland University, School of Nursing, *Independence* (BSN)

Maryville University of Saint Louis, Nursing Program, School of Health Professions, *St. Louis* (BSN)

Research College of Nursing, College of Nursing, *Kansas City* (BSN)

Saint Louis University, School of Nursing, *St. Louis* (BSN)

University of Missouri-Columbia, Sinclair School of Nursing, *Columbia* (BSN)

University of Missouri-Kansas City, School of Nursing, *Kansas City* (BSN)

University of Missouri-St. Louis, College of Nursing, *St. Louis* (BSN)

William Jewell College, Department of Nursing, *Liberty* (BS)

Nebraska

University of Nebraska Medical Center, College of Nursing, *Omaha* (BSN)

Nevada

Touro University, School of Nursing, *Henderson* (BSN)

University of Nevada, Las Vegas, School of Nursing, *Las Vegas* (BSN)

University of Nevada, Reno, Orvis School of Nursing, *Reno* (BSN)

New Mexico

University of Phoenix-New Mexico Campus, College of Health and Human Services, *Albuquerque* (BSN)

New York

Columbia University, School of Nursing, *New York* (BS)

Hartwick College, Department of Nursing, *Oneonta* (BS)

Mount Saint Mary College, Division of Nursing, *Newburgh* (BSN)

New York University, College of Nursing, *New York* (BS)

The Sage Colleges, Department of Nursing, *Troy* (BS)

Stony Brook University, State University of New York, School of Nursing, *Stony Brook* (BS)

North Carolina

Queens University of Charlotte, Presbyterian School of Nursing, *Charlotte* (BSN)

Western Carolina University, School of Nursing, *Cullowhee* (BSN)

Ohio

Kent State University, College of Nursing, *Kent* (BSN)

MedCentral College of Nursing, *Mansfield* (BS)

University of Phoenix-Cleveland Campus, College of Health and Human Services, *Independence* (BSN)

Walsh University, Department of Nursing, *North Canton* (BSN)

Oklahoma

Northwestern Oklahoma State University, Division of Nursing, *Alva* (BSN)

BACCALAUREATE PROGRAMS
Accelerated Baccalaureate

Oregon
Oregon Health & Science University, School of Nursing, *Portland* (BS)

Pennsylvania
DeSales University, Department of Nursing and Health, *Center Valley* (BSN)

Edinboro University of Pennsylvania, Department of Nursing, *Edinboro* (BS)

Holy Family University, School of Nursing and Allied Health Professions, *Philadelphia* (BSN)

Thomas Jefferson University, Department of Nursing, *Philadelphia* (BSN)

University of Pennsylvania, School of Nursing, *Philadelphia* (BSN)

Waynesburg University, Department of Nursing, *Waynesburg* (BSN)

Puerto Rico
Inter American University of Puerto Rico, Metropolitan Campus, Carmen Torres de Tiburcio School of Nursing, *San Juan* (BSN)

South Carolina
Lander University, School of Nursing, *Greenwood* (BSN)

Medical University of South Carolina, College of Nursing, *Charleston* (BSN)

South Dakota
South Dakota State University, College of Nursing, *Brookings* (BS)

Tennessee
Belmont University, School of Nursing, *Nashville* (BSN)

Carson-Newman College, Division of Nursing, *Jefferson City* (BSN)

Cumberland University, Rudy School of Nursing and Health Professions, *Lebanon* (BSN)

University of Memphis, Loewenberg School of Nursing, *Memphis* (BSN)

Texas
Texas Tech University Health Sciences Center, School of Nursing, *Lubbock* (BSc PN)

The University of Texas at Arlington, School of Nursing, *Arlington* (BSN)

The University of Texas at El Paso, School of Nursing, *El Paso* (BSN)

Utah
University of Utah, College of Nursing, *Salt Lake City* (BS)

Weber State University, Program in Nursing, *Ogden* (BSN)

Virginia
Hampton University, School of Nursing, *Hampton* (BS)

Old Dominion University, Department of Nursing, *Norfolk* (BSN)

Washington
University of Washington, School of Nursing, *Seattle* (BSN)

Wisconsin
Bellin College, Nursing Program, *Green Bay* (BSN)

University of Wisconsin–Oshkosh, College of Nursing, *Oshkosh* (BSN)

CANADA

Alberta
University of Calgary, Faculty of Nursing, *Calgary* (BN)

British Columbia
The University of British Columbia, Program in Nursing, *Vancouver* (BSN)

New Brunswick
University of New Brunswick Fredericton, Faculty of Nursing, *Fredericton* (BN)

Nova Scotia
Dalhousie University, School of Nursing, *Halifax* (BScN)

St. Francis Xavier University, Department of Nursing, *Antigonish* (BScN)

Ontario
Lakehead University, School of Nursing, *Thunder Bay* (BScN)

Queen's University at Kingston, School of Nursing, *Kingston* (BNSc)

Trent University, Nursing Program, *Peterborough* (BScN)

University of Toronto, Faculty of Nursing, *Toronto* (BScN)

The University of Western Ontario, School of Nursing, *London* (BScN)

Quebec
Université Laval, Faculty of Nursing, *Québec* (BScN)

Saskatchewan
University of Saskatchewan, College of Nursing, *Saskatoon* (BSN)

ACCELERATED BACCALAUREATE FOR SECOND DEGREE

U.S. AND U.S. TERRITORIES

Arizona
Arizona State University at the Downtown Phoenix Campus, College of Nursing, *Phoenix* (BSN)

Northern Arizona University, School of Nursing, *Flagstaff* (BSN)

The University of Arizona, College of Nursing, *Tucson* (BSN)

Arkansas
University of Arkansas for Medical Sciences, College of Nursing, *Little Rock* (BSN)

California
Loma Linda University, School of Nursing, *Loma Linda* (BS)

San Diego State University, School of Nursing, *San Diego* (BSN)

Colorado
Colorado State University–Pueblo, Department of Nursing, *Pueblo* (BSN)

University of Colorado at Colorado Springs, Beth-El College of Nursing and Health Sciences, *Colorado Springs* (BSN)

Connecticut
Fairfield University, School of Nursing, *Fairfield* (BS)

Quinnipiac University, Department of Nursing, *Hamden* (BSN)

Saint Joseph College, Department of Nursing, *West Hartford* (BS)

Delaware
University of Delaware, School of Nursing, *Newark* (BSN)

District of Columbia
The Catholic University of America, School of Nursing, *Washington* (BSN)

Georgetown University, School of Nursing & Health Studies, *Washington* (BSN)

Howard University, Division of Nursing, *Washington* (BSN)

Florida
Barry University, School of Nursing, *Miami Shores* (BSN)

Florida Atlantic University, Christine E. Lynn College of Nursing, *Boca Raton* (BS)

Florida International University, Nursing Program, *Miami* (BSN)

Jacksonville University, School of Nursing, *Jacksonville* (BSN)

University of Central Florida, School of Nursing, *Orlando* (BSN)

University of Florida, College of Nursing, *Gainesville* (BSN)

University of Miami, School of Nursing and Health Studies, *Coral Gables* (BSN)

University of North Florida, School of Nursing, *Jacksonville* (BSN)

University of South Florida, College of Nursing, *Tampa* (BS)

Georgia
Albany State University, College of Sciences and Health Professions, *Albany* (BSN)

Georgia Southwestern State University, School of Nursing, *Americus* (BSN)

Kennesaw State University, School of Nursing, *Kennesaw* (BSN)

Idaho
Idaho State University, Department of Nursing, *Pocatello* (BSN)

Illinois
Blessing-Rieman College of Nursing, *Quincy* (BSN)

Illinois State University, Mennonite College of Nursing, *Normal* (BSN)

Lewis University, Program in Nursing, *Romeoville* (BSN)

Methodist College of Nursing, *Peoria* (BSN)

Trinity College of Nursing and Health Sciences, *Rock Island* (BSN)

West Suburban College of Nursing, *Oak Park* (BSN)

Indiana
Ball State University, School of Nursing, *Muncie* (BS)

Indiana University–Purdue University Indianapolis, School of Nursing, *Indianapolis* (BSN)

Indiana University South Bend, Division of Nursing and Health Professions, *South Bend* (BSN)

Indiana Wesleyan University, School of Nursing, *Marion* (BSN)

Marian University, Department of Nursing and Nutritional Science, *Indianapolis* (BSN)

Purdue University, School of Nursing, *West Lafayette* (BS)

Purdue University Calumet, School of Nursing, *Hammond* (BS)

University of Indianapolis, School of Nursing, *Indianapolis* (BSN)

Iowa
Allen College, Program in Nursing, *Waterloo* (BSN)

Kansas
MidAmerica Nazarene University, Division of Nursing, *Olathe* (BSN)

Wichita State University, School of Nursing, *Wichita* (BSN)

Kentucky
Bellarmine University, Donna and Allan Lansing School of Nursing and Health Sciences, *Louisville* (BSN)

Northern Kentucky University, Department of Nursing, *Highland Heights* (BSN)

Spalding University, School of Nursing, *Louisville* (BSN)

University of Louisville, School of Nursing, *Louisville* (BSN)

Louisiana

Louisiana State University Health Sciences Center, School of Nursing, *New Orleans* (BSN)

Southeastern Louisiana University, School of Nursing, *Hammond* (BS)

University of Louisiana at Lafayette, College of Nursing, *Lafayette* (BSN)

Maine

University of Southern Maine, College of Nursing and Health Professions, *Portland* (BS)

Maryland

The Johns Hopkins University, School of Nursing, *Baltimore* (BS)

Salisbury University, Program in Nursing, *Salisbury* (BS)

Stevenson University, Nursing Division, *Stevenson* (BS)

Massachusetts

Curry College, Division of Nursing, *Milton* (BS)

Massachusetts College of Pharmacy and Health Sciences, School of Nursing, *Boston* (BSN)

Regis College, School of Nursing and Health Professions, *Weston* (BSN)

Salem State College, Program in Nursing, *Salem* (BSN)

Simmons College, Department of Nursing, *Boston* (BS)

University of Massachusetts Amherst, School of Nursing, *Amherst* (BS)

University of Massachusetts Boston, College of Nursing and Health Sciences, *Boston* (BS)

Michigan

Ferris State University, School of Nursing, *Big Rapids* (BSN)

Grand Valley State University, Kirkhof College of Nursing, *Allendale* (BSN)

Michigan State University, College of Nursing, *East Lansing* (BSN)

Saginaw Valley State University, Crystal M. Lange College of Nursing and Health Sciences, *University Center* (BSN)

University of Detroit Mercy, McAuley School of Nursing, *Detroit* (BSN)

University of Michigan, School of Nursing, *Ann Arbor* (BSN)

University of Michigan-Flint, Department of Nursing, *Flint* (BSN)

Wayne State University, College of Nursing, *Detroit* (BSN)

Minnesota

The College of St. Scholastica, Department of Nursing, *Duluth* (BS)

Concordia College, Department of Nursing, *Moorhead* (BA)

Minnesota State University Mankato, School of Nursing, *Mankato* (BS)

Mississippi

University of Mississippi Medical Center, Program in Nursing, *Jackson* (BSN)

Missouri

Cox College of Nursing and Health Sciences, Department of Nursing, *Springfield* (BSN)

Goldfarb School of Nursing at Barnes-Jewish College, *St. Louis* (BSN)

Graceland University, School of Nursing, *Independence* (BSN)

Research College of Nursing, College of Nursing, *Kansas City* (BSN)

Saint Louis University, School of Nursing, *St. Louis* (BSN)

University of Missouri-Columbia, Sinclair School of Nursing, *Columbia* (BSN)

Nebraska

Creighton University, School of Nursing, *Omaha* (BSN)

Nebraska Methodist College, Department of Nursing, *Omaha* (BSN)

University of Nebraska Medical Center, College of Nursing, *Omaha* (BSN)

Nevada

Nevada State College at Henderson, Nursing Program, *Henderson* (BSN)

Touro University, School of Nursing, *Henderson* (BSN)

New Jersey

Fairleigh Dickinson University, Metropolitan Campus, Henry P. Becton School of Nursing and Allied Health, *Teaneck* (BSN)

New Jersey City University, Department of Nursing, *Jersey City* (BSN)

Rutgers, The State University of New Jersey, College of Nursing, *Newark* (BS)

Seton Hall University, College of Nursing, *South Orange* (BSN)

University of Medicine and Dentistry of New Jersey, School of Nursing, *Newark* (BSN)

William Paterson University of New Jersey, Department of Nursing, *Wayne* (BSN)

New Mexico

New Mexico State University, School of Nursing, *Las Cruces* (BSN)

University of New Mexico, College of Nursing, *Albuquerque* (BSN)

New York

Adelphi University, School of Nursing, *Garden City* (BS)

The College of New Rochelle, School of Nursing, *New Rochelle* (BSN)

Columbia University, School of Nursing, *New York* (BS)

Dominican College, Department of Nursing, *Orangeburg* (BSN)

Hartwick College, Department of Nursing, *Oneonta* (BS)

New York University, College of Nursing, *New York* (BS)

Pace University, Lienhard School of Nursing, *New York* (BS)

The Sage Colleges, Department of Nursing, *Troy* (BS)

State University of New York Downstate Medical Center, College of Nursing, *Brooklyn* (BS)

University at Buffalo, the State University of New York, School of Nursing, *Buffalo* (BS)

University of Rochester, School of Nursing, *Rochester* (BS)

North Carolina

Duke University, School of Nursing, *Durham* (BSN)

Queens University of Charlotte, Presbyterian School of Nursing, *Charlotte* (BSN)

The University of North Carolina at Chapel Hill, School of Nursing, *Chapel Hill* (BSN)

North Dakota

University of North Dakota, College of Nursing, *Grand Forks* (BSN)

Ohio

Capital University, School of Nursing, *Columbus* (BSN)

Cleveland State University, School of Nursing, *Cleveland* (BSN)

Kent State University, College of Nursing, *Kent* (BSN)

Mount Carmel College of Nursing, Nursing Programs, *Columbus* (BSN)

The University of Akron, College of Nursing, *Akron* (BSN)

University of Cincinnati, College of Nursing, *Cincinnati* (BSN)

Ursuline College, The Breen School of Nursing, *Pepper Pike* (BSN)

Walsh University, Department of Nursing, *North Canton* (BSN)

Wright State University, College of Nursing and Health, *Dayton* (BSN)

Oklahoma

Oklahoma City University, Kramer School of Nursing, *Oklahoma City* (BSN)

University of Oklahoma Health Sciences Center, College of Nursing, *Oklahoma City* (BSN)

Oregon

Linfield College, School of Nursing, *McMinnville* (BSN)

Pennsylvania

Drexel University, College of Nursing and Health Professions, *Philadelphia* (BSN)

Duquesne University, School of Nursing, *Pittsburgh* (BSN)

Edinboro University of Pennsylvania, Department of Nursing, *Edinboro* (BS)

Temple University, Department of Nursing, *Philadelphia* (BSN)

Thomas Jefferson University, Department of Nursing, *Philadelphia* (BSN)

University of Pennsylvania, School of Nursing, *Philadelphia* (BSN)

University of Pittsburgh, School of Nursing, *Pittsburgh* (BSN)

Villanova University, College of Nursing, *Villanova* (BSN)

Waynesburg University, Department of Nursing, *Waynesburg* (BSN)

Wilkes University, Department of Nursing, *Wilkes-Barre* (BS)

South Carolina

Lander University, School of Nursing, *Greenwood* (BSN)

Medical University of South Carolina, College of Nursing, *Charleston* (BSN)

Tennessee

Belmont University, School of Nursing, *Nashville* (BSN)

Cumberland University, Rudy School of Nursing and Health Professions, *Lebanon* (BSN)

East Tennessee State University, College of Nursing, *Johnson City* (BSN)

Union University, School of Nursing, *Jackson* (BSN)

University of Memphis, Loewenberg School of Nursing, *Memphis* (BSN)

Texas

Baylor University, Louise Herrington School of Nursing, *Dallas* (BSN)

Texas A&M University-Corpus Christi, School of Nursing and Health Sciences, *Corpus Christi* (BSN)

Texas Christian University, Harris College of Nursing, *Fort Worth* (BSN)

Texas Tech University Health Sciences Center, School of Nursing, *Lubbock* (BSc PN)

Texas Woman's University, College of Nursing, *Denton* (BS)

University of Houston-Victoria, School of Nursing, *Victoria* (BSN)

The University of Texas at Arlington, School of Nursing, *Arlington* (BSN)

The University of Texas Health Science Center at Houston, School of Nursing, *Houston* (BSN)

The University of Texas Health Science Center at San Antonio, School of Nursing, *San Antonio* (BSN)

The University of Texas Medical Branch, School of Nursing, *Galveston* (BSN)

Virginia

George Mason University, College of Health and Human Services, *Fairfax* (BSN)

Marymount University, School of Health Professions, *Arlington* (BSN)

Norfolk State University, Department of Nursing, *Norfolk* (BSN)

Shenandoah University, Division of Nursing, *Winchester* (BSN)

Virginia Commonwealth University, School of Nursing, *Richmond* (BS)

West Virginia

Mountain State University, College of Nursing, *Beckley* (BSN)

West Virginia University, School of Nursing, *Morgantown* (BSN)

Wisconsin

Bellin College, Nursing Program, *Green Bay* (BSN)

Edgewood College, Program in Nursing, *Madison* (BS)

University of Wisconsin-Eau Claire, College of Nursing and Health Sciences, *Eau Claire* (BSN)

University of Wisconsin-Oshkosh, College of Nursing, *Oshkosh* (BSN)

Wyoming

University of Wyoming, Fay W. Whitney School of Nursing, *Laramie* (BSN)

CANADA

Alberta

University of Alberta, Faculty of Nursing, *Edmonton* (BScN)

University of Calgary, Faculty of Nursing, *Calgary* (BN)

University of Lethbridge, School of Health Sciences, *Lethbridge* (BN)

British Columbia

The University of British Columbia, Program in Nursing, *Vancouver* (BSN)

Newfoundland and Labrador

Memorial University of Newfoundland, School of Nursing, *St. John's* (BN)

Nova Scotia

Dalhousie University, School of Nursing, *Halifax* (BScN)

St. Francis Xavier University, Department of Nursing, *Antigonish* (BScN)

Ontario

University of Toronto, Faculty of Nursing, *Toronto* (BScN)

ACCELERATED LPN TO BACCALAUREATE

U.S. AND U.S. TERRITORIES

California

San Francisco State University, School of Nursing, *San Francisco* (BSN)

Kansas

MidAmerica Nazarene University, Division of Nursing, *Olathe* (BSN)

New York

Dominican College, Department of Nursing, *Orangeburg* (BSN)

Ohio

Ursuline College, The Breen School of Nursing, *Pepper Pike* (BSN)

Oklahoma

Northwestern Oklahoma State University, Division of Nursing, *Alva* (BSN)

Pennsylvania

The University of Scranton, Department of Nursing, *Scranton* (BS)

Wilkes University, Department of Nursing, *Wilkes-Barre* (BS)

South Dakota

Mount Marty College, Nursing Program, *Yankton* (BSN)

Texas

Southwestern Adventist University, Department of Nursing, *Keene* (BS)

Virginia

Norfolk State University, Department of Nursing, *Norfolk* (BSN)

CANADA

Nova Scotia

St. Francis Xavier University, Department of Nursing, *Antigonish* (BScN)

ACCELERATED RN BACCALAUREATE

U.S. AND U.S. TERRITORIES

Arizona

Arizona State University at the Downtown Phoenix Campus, College of Nursing, *Phoenix* (BSN)

Arkansas

University of Arkansas for Medical Sciences, College of Nursing, *Little Rock* (BSN)

California

Azusa Pacific University, School of Nursing, *Azusa* (BSN)

California Baptist University, School of Nursing, *Riverside* (BSN)

Loma Linda University, School of Nursing, *Loma Linda* (BS)

West Coast University, Nursing Programs, *North Hollywood* (BSN)

Colorado

Colorado State University-Pueblo, Department of Nursing, *Pueblo* (BSN)

Delaware

Wilmington University, College of Health Professions, *New Castle* (BSN)

Georgia

Albany State University, College of Sciences and Health Professions, *Albany* (BSN)

Thomas University, Division of Nursing, *Thomasville* (BSN)

Idaho

Boise State University, Department of Nursing, *Boise* (BS)

Illinois

Benedictine University, Department of Nursing, *Lisle* (BSN)

DePaul University, Department of Nursing, *Chicago* (BS)

Lakeview College of Nursing, *Danville* (BSN)

Lewis University, Program in Nursing, *Romeoville* (BSN)

Olivet Nazarene University, Division of Nursing, *Bourbonnais* (BSN)

Saint Francis Medical Center College of Nursing, Baccalaureate Nursing Program, *Peoria* (BSN)

University of St. Francis, College of Nursing and Allied Health, *Joliet* (BSN)

West Suburban College of Nursing, *Oak Park* (BSN)

Indiana

Indiana University Kokomo, Indiana University School of Nursing, *Kokomo* (BSN)

Purdue University Calumet, School of Nursing, *Hammond* (BS)

Iowa

Allen College, Program in Nursing, *Waterloo* (BSN)

Mount Mercy College, Department of Nursing, *Cedar Rapids* (BSN)

Kansas

MidAmerica Nazarene University, Division of Nursing, *Olathe* (BSN)

Southwestern College, Nursing Program, *Winfield* (BSN)

Tabor College, Department of Nursing, *Hillsboro* (BSN)

Kentucky

Bellarmine University, Donna and Allan Lansing School of Nursing and Health Sciences, *Louisville* (BSN)

Eastern Kentucky University, Department of Baccalaureate and Graduate Nursing, *Richmond* (BSN)

Midway College, Program in Nursing (Baccalaureate), *Midway* (BSN)

Spalding University, School of Nursing, *Louisville* (BSN)

Louisiana

Southeastern Louisiana University, School of Nursing, *Hammond* (BS)

Maine

University of New England, Department of Nursing, *Biddeford* (BSN)

Maryland

College of Notre Dame of Maryland, Department of Nursing, *Baltimore* (BS)

Columbia Union College, Nursing Department, *Takoma Park* (BS)

Coppin State University, Helene Fuld School of Nursing, *Baltimore* (BSN)

Stevenson University, Nursing Division, *Stevenson* (BS)

Massachusetts

Regis College, School of Nursing and Health Professions, *Weston* (BSN)

University of Massachusetts Amherst, School of Nursing, *Amherst* (BS)

Missouri

Chamberlain College of Nursing, *St. Louis* (BSN)

Graceland University, School of Nursing, *Independence* (BSN)

Maryville University of Saint Louis, Nursing Program, School of Health Professions, *St. Louis* (BSN)

Missouri State University, Department of Nursing, *Springfield* (BSN)

Nebraska

Clarkson College, Master of Science in Nursing Program, *Omaha* (BSN)

Nebraska Wesleyan University, Department of Nursing, *Lincoln* (BSN)

University of Nebraska Medical Center, College of Nursing, *Omaha* (BSN)

Nevada

Touro University, School of Nursing, *Henderson* (BSN)

New Jersey

College of Saint Elizabeth, Department of Nursing, *Morristown* (BSN)

Rutgers, The State University of New Jersey, Camden College of Arts and Sciences, Department of Nursing, *Camden* (BS)

New York

The College at Brockport, State University of New York, Department of Nursing, *Brockport* (BSN)

The College of New Rochelle, School of Nursing, *New Rochelle* (BSN)

Columbia University, School of Nursing, *New York* (BS)

Daemen College, Department of Nursing, *Amherst* (BS)

Dominican College, Department of Nursing, *Orangeburg* (BSN)

Keuka College, Division of Nursing, *Keuka Park* (BS)

Lehman College of the City University of New York, Department of Nursing, *Bronx* (BS)

Medgar Evers College of the City University of New York, Department of Nursing, *Brooklyn* (BSN)

Mercy College, Program in Nursing, *Dobbs Ferry* (BS)

Molloy College, Department of Nursing, *Rockville Centre* (BS)

Mount Saint Mary College, Division of Nursing, *Newburgh* (BSN)

Roberts Wesleyan College, Division of Nursing, *Rochester* (BScN)

St. John Fisher College, Advanced Practice Nursing Program, *Rochester* (BS)

State University of New York at Binghamton, Decker School of Nursing, *Binghamton* (BS)

State University of New York Institute of Technology, School of Nursing and Health Systems, *Utica* (BS)

Stony Brook University, State University of New York, School of Nursing, *Stony Brook* (BS)

University of Rochester, School of Nursing, *Rochester* (BS)

North Carolina

Winston-Salem State University, Department of Nursing, *Winston-Salem* (BSN)

North Dakota

University of North Dakota, College of Nursing, *Grand Forks* (BSN)

Ohio

Ashland University, Department of Nursing, *Ashland* (BSN)

College of Mount St. Joseph, Department of Nursing, *Cincinnati* (BSN)

Kent State University, College of Nursing, *Kent* (BSN)

The Ohio State University, College of Nursing, *Columbus* (BSN)

Otterbein College, Department of Nursing, *Westerville* (BSN)

Ursuline College, The Breen School of Nursing, *Pepper Pike* (BSN)

Oklahoma

Bacone College, Department of Nursing, *Muskogee* (BSN)

Northeastern State University, Department of Nursing, *Tahlequah* (BSN)

Northwestern Oklahoma State University, Division of Nursing, *Alva* (BSN)

Oklahoma Wesleyan University, Division of Nursing, *Bartlesville* (BSN)

Pennsylvania

Carlow University, School of Nursing, *Pittsburgh* (BSN)

DeSales University, Department of Nursing and Health, *Center Valley* (BSN)

Eastern University, Program in Nursing, *St. Davids* (BSN)

Gwynedd-Mercy College, School of Nursing, *Gwynedd Valley* (BSN)

Immaculata University, Department of Nursing, *Immaculata* (BSN)

La Roche College, Department of Nursing and Nursing Management, *Pittsburgh* (BSN)

Misericordia University, Department of Nursing, *Dallas* (BSN)

Mount Aloysius College, Department of Nursing, *Cresson* (BSN)

Thomas Jefferson University, Department of Nursing, *Philadelphia* (BSN)

University of Pennsylvania, School of Nursing, *Philadelphia* (BSN)

West Chester University of Pennsylvania, Department of Nursing, *West Chester* (BSN)

Wilkes University, Department of Nursing, *Wilkes-Barre* (BS)

South Carolina

Lander University, School of Nursing, *Greenwood* (BSN)

Tennessee

East Tennessee State University, College of Nursing, *Johnson City* (BSN)

King College, School of Nursing, *Bristol* (BSN)

University of Memphis, Loewenberg School of Nursing, *Memphis* (BSN)

The University of Tennessee, College of Nursing, *Knoxville* (BSN)

Texas

Southwestern Adventist University, Department of Nursing, *Keene* (BS)

Texas Tech University Health Sciences Center, School of Nursing, *Lubbock* (BSc PN)

The University of Texas at Arlington, School of Nursing, *Arlington* (BSN)

The University of Texas at Tyler, Program in Nursing, *Tyler* (BSN)

Virginia

Hampton University, School of Nursing, *Hampton* (BS)

James Madison University, Department of Nursing, *Harrisonburg* (BSN)

Marymount University, School of Health Professions, *Arlington* (BSN)

West Virginia

Fairmont State University, School of Nursing and Allied Health Administration, *Fairmont* (BSN)

Marshall University, College of Health Professions, *Huntington* (BSN)

West Liberty University, Department of Health Sciences, *West Liberty* (BSN)

Wisconsin

University of Wisconsin–Oshkosh, College of Nursing, *Oshkosh* (BSN)

CANADA

Alberta

University of Lethbridge, School of Health Sciences, *Lethbridge* (BN)

Ontario

University of Toronto, Faculty of Nursing, *Toronto* (BScN)

Quebec

McGill University, School of Nursing, *Montréal* (BScN)

Université du Québec à Chicoutimi, Program in Nursing, *Chicoutimi* (BNSc)

Université Laval, Faculty of Nursing, *Québec* (BScN)

Saskatchewan

University of Saskatchewan, College of Nursing, *Saskatoon* (BSN)

ADN TO BACCALAUREATE

U.S. AND U.S. TERRITORIES

Alabama

Troy University, School of Nursing, *Troy* (BSN)

Tuskegee University, Program in Nursing, *Tuskegee* (BSN)

University of Mobile, School of Nursing, *Mobile* (BSN)

University of South Alabama, College of Nursing, *Mobile* (BSN)

Arizona

Grand Canyon University, College of Nursing and Health Sciences, *Phoenix* (BSN)

Arkansas

Arkansas Tech University, Program in Nursing, *Russellville* (BSN)

Harding University, College of Nursing, *Searcy* (BSN)

Henderson State University, Department of Nursing, *Arkadelphia* (BSN)

Southern Arkansas University–Magnolia, Department of Nursing, *Magnolia* (BSN)

University of Arkansas at Fort Smith, Carol McKelvey Moore School of Nursing, *Fort Smith* (BSN)

University of Arkansas at Monticello, School of Nursing, *Monticello* (BSN)

University of Arkansas for Medical Sciences, College of Nursing, *Little Rock* (BSN)

University of Central Arkansas, Department of Nursing, *Conway* (BSN)

California

Azusa Pacific University, School of Nursing, *Azusa* (BSN)

Biola University, Department of Nursing, *La Mirada* (BSN)

BACCALAUREATE PROGRAMS
ADN to Baccalaureate

California Baptist University, School of Nursing, *Riverside* (BSN)

California State University, Chico, School of Nursing, *Chico* (BSN)

California State University, East Bay, Department of Nursing and Health Sciences, *Hayward* (BS)

California State University, Fresno, Department of Nursing, *Fresno* (BSN)

California State University, Fullerton, Department of Nursing, *Fullerton* (BSN)

California State University, Long Beach, Department of Nursing, *Long Beach* (BSN)

California State University, Northridge, Nursing Program, *Northridge* (BSN)

California State University, Sacramento, Division of Nursing, *Sacramento* (BSN)

California State University, Stanislaus, Department of Nursing, *Turlock* (BSN)

Humboldt State University, Department of Nursing, *Arcata* (BSN)

Loma Linda University, School of Nursing, *Loma Linda* (BS)

Mount St. Mary's College, Department of Nursing, *Los Angeles* (BSN, BSc PN)

Pacific Union College, Department of Nursing, *Angwin* (BSN)

Point Loma Nazarene University, School of Nursing, *San Diego* (BSN)

San Diego State University, School of Nursing, *San Diego* (BSN)

San Francisco State University, School of Nursing, *San Francisco* (BSN)

Sonoma State University, Department of Nursing, *Rohnert Park* (BSN)

University of California, Los Angeles, School of Nursing, *Los Angeles* (BS)

Colorado

Colorado State University-Pueblo, Department of Nursing, *Pueblo* (BSN)

Mesa State College, Department of Nursing and Radiologic Sciences, *Grand Junction* (BSN)

Metropolitan State College of Denver, Department of Health Professions, *Denver* (BS)

Connecticut

Sacred Heart University, Program in Nursing, *Fairfield* (BS)

Southern Connecticut State University, Department of Nursing, *New Haven* (BS)

University of Hartford, College of Education, Nursing, and Health Professions, *West Hartford* (BSN)

Florida

Barry University, School of Nursing, *Miami Shores* (BSN)

Florida Gulf Coast University, School of Nursing, *Fort Myers* (BSN)

Florida Southern College, Department of Nursing, *Lakeland* (BSN)

Jacksonville University, School of Nursing, *Jacksonville* (BSN)

St. Petersburg College, Department of Nursing, *St. Petersburg* (BSN)

University of South Florida, College of Nursing, *Tampa* (BS)

The University of Tampa, Department of Nursing, *Tampa* (BSN)

University of West Florida, Department of Nursing, *Pensacola* (BSN)

Georgia

Albany State University, College of Sciences and Health Professions, *Albany* (BSN)

Armstrong Atlantic State University, Program in Nursing, *Savannah* (BSN)

Brenau University, School of Health and Science, *Gainesville* (BSN)

Georgia Southern University, School of Nursing, *Statesboro* (BSN)

Kennesaw State University, School of Nursing, *Kennesaw* (BSN)

Macon State College, School of Nursing and Health Sciences, *Macon* (BSN)

North Georgia College & State University, Department of Nursing, *Dahlonega* (BSN)

Thomas University, Division of Nursing, *Thomasville* (BSN)

Guam

University of Guam, College of Nursing and Health Sciences, *Mangilao* (BSN)

Hawaii

University of Hawaii at Hilo, Department in Nursing, *Hilo* (BSN)

University of Hawaii at Manoa, School of Nursing and Dental Hygiene, *Honolulu* (BSN)

Idaho

Idaho State University, Department of Nursing, *Pocatello* (BSN)

Lewis-Clark State College, Division of Nursing and Health Sciences, *Lewiston* (BSN)

Illinois

MacMurray College, Department of Nursing, *Jacksonville* (BSN)

McKendree University, Department of Nursing, *Lebanon* (BSN)

Northern Illinois University, School of Nursing and Health Studies, *De Kalb* (BS)

Rockford College, Department of Nursing, *Rockford* (BSN)

Southern Illinois University Edwardsville, School of Nursing, *Edwardsville* (BS)

Trinity College of Nursing and Health Sciences, *Rock Island* (BSN)

University of Illinois at Chicago, College of Nursing, *Chicago* (BSN)

West Suburban College of Nursing, *Oak Park* (BSN)

Indiana

Bethel College, Department of Nursing, *Mishawaka* (BSN)

Indiana University East, School of Nursing, *Richmond* (BSN)

Indiana University-Purdue University Indianapolis, School of Nursing, *Indianapolis* (BSN)

Purdue University, School of Nursing, *West Lafayette* (BS)

Purdue University North Central, Department of Nursing, *Westville* (BS)

University of Indianapolis, School of Nursing, *Indianapolis* (BSN)

Iowa

Allen College, Program in Nursing, *Waterloo* (BSN)

Briar Cliff University, Department of Nursing, *Sioux City* (BSN)

Iowa Wesleyan College, Division of Health and Natural Sciences, *Mount Pleasant* (BSN)

Luther College, Department of Nursing, *Decorah* (BA)

Mercy College of Health Sciences, Division of Nursing, *Des Moines* (BSN)

Kansas

Emporia State University, Newman Division of Nursing, *Emporia* (BSN)

Kansas Wesleyan University, Department of Nursing Education, *Salina* (BSN)

MidAmerica Nazarene University, Division of Nursing, *Olathe* (BSN)

Tabor College, Department of Nursing, *Hillsboro* (BSN)

The University of Kansas, School of Nursing, *Kansas City* (BSN)

Washburn University, School of Nursing, *Topeka* (BSN)

Wichita State University, School of Nursing, *Wichita* (BSN)

Kentucky

Kentucky State University, School of Nursing, *Frankfort* (BSN)

Midway College, Program in Nursing (Baccalaureate), *Midway* (BSN)

Morehead State University, Department of Nursing, *Morehead* (BSN)

Louisiana

McNeese State University, College of Nursing, *Lake Charles* (BSN)

Northwestern State University of Louisiana, College of Nursing, *Shreveport* (BSN)

University of Louisiana at Lafayette, College of Nursing, *Lafayette* (BSN)

University of Louisiana at Monroe, Nursing, *Monroe* (BS)

Maine

University of Southern Maine, College of Nursing and Health Professions, *Portland* (BS)

Maryland

Salisbury University, Program in Nursing, *Salisbury* (BS)

Stevenson University, Nursing Division, *Stevenson* (BS)

Massachusetts

Anna Maria College, Department of Nursing, *Paxton* (BSN)

Atlantic Union College, Department of Nursing, *South Lancaster* (BS)

Fitchburg State College, Department of Nursing, *Fitchburg* (BS)

Framingham State College, Department of Nursing, *Framingham* (BS)

Regis College, School of Nursing and Health Professions, *Weston* (BSN)

Salem State College, Program in Nursing, *Salem* (BSN)

Simmons College, Department of Nursing, *Boston* (BS)

Michigan

Andrews University, Department of Nursing, *Berrien Springs* (BS)

Davenport University, Division of Nursing, *Grand Rapids* (BSN)

Grand Valley State University, Kirkhof College of Nursing, *Allendale* (BSN)

Lake Superior State University, Department of Nursing, *Sault Sainte Marie* (BSN)

Madonna University, College of Nursing and Health, *Livonia* (BSN)

Spring Arbor University, Program in Nursing, *Spring Arbor* (BSN)

Western Michigan University, College of Health and Human Services, *Kalamazoo* (BSN)

Minnesota

Augsburg College, Program in Nursing, *Minneapolis* (BS)

The College of St. Scholastica, Department of Nursing, *Duluth* (BS)

Minnesota State University Moorhead, School of Nursing and Healthcare Leadership, *Moorhead* (BSN)

Mississippi

Delta State University, School of Nursing, *Cleveland* (BSN)

Mississippi University for Women, College of Nursing and Speech-Language Pathology, *Columbus* (BSN)

University of Southern Mississippi, School of Nursing, *Hattiesburg* (BSN)

William Carey University, School of Nursing, *Hattiesburg* (BSN)

Missouri

Chamberlain College of Nursing, *St. Louis* (BSN)

Cox College of Nursing and Health Sciences, Department of Nursing, *Springfield* (BSN)

Goldfarb School of Nursing at Barnes-Jewish College, *St. Louis* (BSN)

Graceland University, School of Nursing, *Independence* (BSN)

Missouri Southern State University, Department of Nursing, *Joplin* (BSN)

Missouri State University, Department of Nursing, *Springfield* (BSN)

University of Missouri–Columbia, Sinclair School of Nursing, *Columbia* (BSN)

Webster University, Department of Nursing, *St. Louis* (BSN)

Montana

Montana State University–Northern, College of Nursing, *Havre* (BSN)

Nebraska

Clarkson College, Master of Science in Nursing Program, *Omaha* (BSN)

College of Saint Mary, Division of Health Care Professions, *Omaha* (BSN)

Midland Lutheran College, Department of Nursing, *Fremont* (BSN)

Nebraska Methodist College, Department of Nursing, *Omaha* (BSN)

Nebraska Wesleyan University, Department of Nursing, *Lincoln* (BSN)

Union College, Division of Health Sciences, *Lincoln* (BSN)

University of Nebraska Medical Center, College of Nursing, *Omaha* (BSN)

Nevada

University of Nevada, Reno, Orvis School of Nursing, *Reno* (BSN)

New Hampshire

Franklin Pierce University, Master of Science in Nursing, *Rindge* (BS)

Rivier College, Division of Nursing, *Nashua* (BS)

New Jersey

College of Saint Elizabeth, Department of Nursing, *Morristown* (BSN)

Kean University, Department of Nursing, *Union* (BSN)

Monmouth University, Marjorie K. Unterberg School of Nursing, *West Long Branch* (BSN)

Saint Peter's College, Nursing Program, *Jersey City* (BSN)

William Paterson University of New Jersey, Department of Nursing, *Wayne* (BSN)

New York

Adelphi University, School of Nursing, *Garden City* (BS)

The College at Brockport, State University of New York, Department of Nursing, *Brockport* (BSN)

College of Mount Saint Vincent, Department of Nursing, *Riverdale* (BS)

College of Staten Island of the City University of New York, Department of Nursing, *Staten Island* (BS)

Daemen College, Department of Nursing, *Amherst* (BS)

Elmira College, Program in Nursing Education, *Elmira* (BS)

Le Moyne College, Nursing Programs, *Syracuse* (BS)

Medgar Evers College of the City University of New York, Department of Nursing, *Brooklyn* (BSN)

The Sage Colleges, Department of Nursing, *Troy* (BS)

St. Francis College, Department of Nursing, *Brooklyn Heights* (BS)

St. John Fisher College, Advanced Practice Nursing Program, *Rochester* (BS)

State University of New York at Plattsburgh, Department of Nursing, *Plattsburgh* (BS)

State University of New York Institute of Technology, School of Nursing and Health Systems, *Utica* (BS)

State University of New York Upstate Medical University, College of Nursing, *Syracuse* (BS)

University of Rochester, School of Nursing, *Rochester* (BS)

York College of the City University of New York, Program in Nursing, *Jamaica* (BS)

North Carolina

Appalachian State University, Department of Nursing, *Boone* (BSN)

East Carolina University, College of Nursing, *Greenville* (BSN)

Lees-McRae College, Nursing Program, *Banner Elk* (BSN)

Lenoir-Rhyne University, Program in Nursing, *Hickory* (BS)

Queens University of Charlotte, Presbyterian School of Nursing, *Charlotte* (BSN)

The University of North Carolina at Chapel Hill, School of Nursing, *Chapel Hill* (BSN)

The University of North Carolina at Charlotte, School of Nursing, *Charlotte* (BSN)

The University of North Carolina at Greensboro, School of Nursing, *Greensboro* (BSN)

Winston-Salem State University, Department of Nursing, *Winston-Salem* (BSN)

North Dakota

Dickinson State University, Department of Nursing, *Dickinson* (BSN)

North Dakota State University, Department of Nursing, *Fargo* (BSN)

University of North Dakota, College of Nursing, *Grand Forks* (BSN)

Ohio

Ashland University, Department of Nursing, *Ashland* (BSN)

Capital University, School of Nursing, *Columbus* (BSN)

Case Western Reserve University, Frances Payne Bolton School of Nursing, *Cleveland* (BSN)

Kent State University, College of Nursing, *Kent* (BSN)

Malone University, School of Nursing, *Canton* (BSN)

Mercy College of Northwest Ohio, Division of Nursing, *Toledo* (BSN)

Miami University, Department of Nursing, *Hamilton* (BSN)

Shawnee State University, Department of Nursing, *Portsmouth* (BSN)

The University of Akron, College of Nursing, *Akron* (BSN)

University of Cincinnati, College of Nursing, *Cincinnati* (BSN)

The University of Toledo, College of Nursing, *Toledo* (BSN)

Oklahoma

East Central University, Department of Nursing, *Ada* (BS)

Northwestern Oklahoma State University, Division of Nursing, *Alva* (BSN)

Oklahoma Baptist University, School of Nursing, *Shawnee* (BSN)

Oklahoma City University, Kramer School of Nursing, *Oklahoma City* (BSN)

Oklahoma Panhandle State University, Bachelor of Science in Nursing Program, *Goodwell* (BSN)

Oklahoma Wesleyan University, Division of Nursing, *Bartlesville* (BSN)

Oral Roberts University, Anna Vaughn School of Nursing, *Tulsa* (BSN)

Rogers State University, Nursing Program, *Claremore* (BSN)

Southern Nazarene University, School of Nursing, *Bethany* (BS)

Southwestern Oklahoma State University, Division of Nursing, *Weatherford* (BSN)

University of Oklahoma Health Sciences Center, College of Nursing, *Oklahoma City* (BSN)

Oregon

Linfield College, School of Nursing, *McMinnville* (BSN)

Pennsylvania

Bloomsburg University of Pennsylvania, Department of Nursing, *Bloomsburg* (BSN)

Clarion University of Pennsylvania, School of Nursing, *Oil City* (BSN)

DeSales University, Department of Nursing and Health, *Center Valley* (BSN)

Drexel University, College of Nursing and Health Professions, *Philadelphia* (BSN)

Edinboro University of Pennsylvania, Department of Nursing, *Edinboro* (BS)

Gannon University, Villa Maria School of Nursing, *Erie* (BSN)

Gwynedd-Mercy College, School of Nursing, *Gwynedd Valley* (BSN)

Holy Family University, School of Nursing and Allied Health Professions, *Philadelphia* (BSN)

Marywood University, Department of Nursing, *Scranton* (BSN)

Mount Aloysius College, Department of Nursing, *Cresson* (BSN)

Penn State University Park, School of Nursing, *State College, University Park* (BS)

Slippery Rock University of Pennsylvania, Department of Nursing, *Slippery Rock* (BSN)

Thomas Jefferson University, Department of Nursing, *Philadelphia* (BSN)

University of Pennsylvania, School of Nursing, *Philadelphia* (BSN)

Villanova University, College of Nursing, *Villanova* (BSN)

Widener University, School of Nursing, *Chester* (BSN)

Wilkes University, Department of Nursing, *Wilkes-Barre* (BS)

Puerto Rico

Inter American University of Puerto Rico, Metropolitan Campus, Carmen Torres de Tiburcio School of Nursing, *San Juan* (BSN)

BACCALAUREATE PROGRAMS
ADN to Baccalaureate

University of Puerto Rico, Medical Sciences Campus, School of Nursing, *San Juan* (BSN)

Rhode Island
University of Rhode Island, College of Nursing, *Kingston* (BS)

South Carolina
Charleston Southern University, Wingo School of Nursing, *Charleston* (BSN)
Francis Marion University, Department of Nursing, *Florence* (BSN)
University of South Carolina Aiken, School of Nursing, *Aiken* (BSN)

South Dakota
Mount Marty College, Nursing Program, *Yankton* (BSN)
Presentation College, Department of Nursing, *Aberdeen* (BSN)

Tennessee
Belmont University, School of Nursing, *Nashville* (BSN)
Cumberland University, Rudy School of Nursing and Health Professions, *Lebanon* (BSN)
East Tennessee State University, College of Nursing, *Johnson City* (BSN)
Milligan College, Department of Nursing, *Milligan College* (BSN)
Southern Adventist University, School of Nursing, *Collegedale* (BS)
Tennessee Technological University, School of Nursing, *Cookeville* (BSN)
Tennessee Wesleyan College, Fort Sanders Nursing Department, *Knoxville* (BSN)
University of Memphis, Loewenberg School of Nursing, *Memphis* (BSN)
The University of Tennessee at Chattanooga, School of Nursing, *Chattanooga* (BSN)
The University of Tennessee at Martin, Department of Nursing, *Martin* (BSN)

Texas
Lamar University, Department of Nursing, *Beaumont* (BSN)
Midwestern State University, Nursing Program, *Wichita Falls* (BSN)
Southwestern Adventist University, Department of Nursing, *Keene* (BS)
Tarleton State University, Department of Nursing, *Stephenville* (BSN)
Texas A&M University-Corpus Christi, School of Nursing and Health Sciences, *Corpus Christi* (BSN)
Texas A&M University-Texarkana, Nursing Department, *Texarkana* (BSN)
University of Mary Hardin-Baylor, College of Nursing, *Belton* (BSN)
The University of Texas at Brownsville, Department of Nursing, *Brownsville* (BSN)
The University of Texas at Tyler, Program in Nursing, *Tyler* (BSN)
The University of Texas Health Science Center at Houston, School of Nursing, *Houston* (BSN)
The University of Texas Health Science Center at San Antonio, School of Nursing, *San Antonio* (BSN)
The University of Texas-Pan American, Department of Nursing, *Edinburg* (BSN)
University of the Incarnate Word, Program in Nursing, *San Antonio* (BSN)
West Texas A&M University, Division of Nursing, *Canyon* (BSN)

Utah
Utah Valley University, Department of Nursing, *Orem* (BSN)
Weber State University, Program in Nursing, *Ogden* (BSN)

Vermont
Norwich University, Department of Nursing, *Northfield* (BSN)
Southern Vermont College, Department of Nursing, *Bennington* (BSN)
University of Vermont, Department of Nursing, *Burlington* (BS)

Virgin Islands
University of the Virgin Islands, Division of Nursing, *Saint Thomas* (BS)

Virginia
Eastern Mennonite University, Department of Nursing, *Harrisonburg* (BSN)
Hampton University, School of Nursing, *Hampton* (BS)
Jefferson College of Health Sciences, Nursing Education Program, *Roanoke* (BSN)
Marymount University, School of Health Professions, *Arlington* (BSN)
Shenandoah University, Division of Nursing, *Winchester* (BSN)
University of Virginia, School of Nursing, *Charlottesville* (BSN)
The University of Virginia's College at Wise, Department of Nursing, *Wise* (BSN)
Virginia Commonwealth University, School of Nursing, *Richmond* (BS)

Washington
Gonzaga University, Department of Nursing, *Spokane* (BSN)
Pacific Lutheran University, School of Nursing, *Tacoma* (BSN)
University of Washington, School of Nursing, *Seattle* (BSN)
Walla Walla University, School of Nursing, *College Place* (BS)

West Virginia
Bluefield State College, Program in Nursing, *Bluefield* (BSN)
Fairmont State University, School of Nursing and Allied Health Administration, *Fairmont* (BSN)
Mountain State University, College of Nursing, *Beckley* (BSN)
Shepherd University, Department of Nursing Education, *Shepherdstown* (BSN)

Wisconsin
Alverno College, Division of Nursing, *Milwaukee* (BSN)
Cardinal Stritch University, Ruth S. Coleman College of Nursing, *Milwaukee* (BSN)
Carroll University, Nursing Program, *Waukesha* (BSN)
Concordia University Wisconsin, Program in Nursing, *Mequon* (BSN)
Marian University, Nursing Studies Division, *Fond du Lac* (BSN)
Marquette University, College of Nursing, *Milwaukee* (BSN)
Silver Lake College, Nursing Program, *Manitowoc* (BSN)
University of Wisconsin-Eau Claire, College of Nursing and Health Sciences, *Eau Claire* (BSN)

Wyoming
University of Wyoming, Fay W. Whitney School of Nursing, *Laramie* (BSN)

BACCALAUREATE FOR SECOND DEGREE

U.S. AND U.S. TERRITORIES

Alabama
Samford University, Ida V. Moffett School of Nursing, *Birmingham* (BSN)
Spring Hill College, Division of Nursing, *Mobile* (BSN)
The University of Alabama, Capstone College of Nursing, *Tuscaloosa* (BSN)
The University of Alabama at Birmingham, School of Nursing, *Birmingham* (BSN)
The University of Alabama in Huntsville, College of Nursing, *Huntsville* (BSN)

Arizona
Arizona State University at the Downtown Phoenix Campus, College of Nursing, *Phoenix* (BSN)

Arkansas
University of Arkansas for Medical Sciences, College of Nursing, *Little Rock* (BSN)

California
California State University, Chico, School of Nursing, *Chico* (BSN)
California State University, Dominguez Hills, Program in Nursing, *Carson* (BSN)
California State University, Fullerton, Department of Nursing, *Fullerton* (BSN)
California State University, Long Beach, Department of Nursing, *Long Beach* (BSN)
California State University, Sacramento, Division of Nursing, *Sacramento* (BSN)
Dominican University of California, Program in Nursing, *San Rafael* (BSN)
Humboldt State University, Department of Nursing, *Arcata* (BSN)
Sonoma State University, Department of Nursing, *Rohnert Park* (BSN)
University of San Francisco, School of Nursing, *San Francisco* (BSN)

Colorado
Colorado State University-Pueblo, Department of Nursing, *Pueblo* (BSN)

Connecticut
Saint Joseph College, Department of Nursing, *West Hartford* (BS)

District of Columbia
Howard University, Division of Nursing, *Washington* (BSN)

Florida
Barry University, School of Nursing, *Miami Shores* (BSN)
Jacksonville University, School of Nursing, *Jacksonville* (BSN)
University of Miami, School of Nursing and Health Studies, *Coral Gables* (BSN)

Georgia
Armstrong Atlantic State University, Program in Nursing, *Savannah* (BSN)
Emory University, Nell Hodgson Woodruff School of Nursing, *Atlanta* (BSN)
Georgia Southwestern State University, School of Nursing, *Americus* (BSN)

Kennesaw State University, School of Nursing, *Kennesaw* (BSN)

Illinois
MacMurray College, Department of Nursing, *Jacksonville* (BSN)
Saint Anthony College of Nursing, Saint Anthony College of Nursing, *Rockford* (BSN)
University of Illinois at Chicago, College of Nursing, *Chicago* (BSN)
Western Illinois University, School of Nursing, *Macomb* (BSN)
West Suburban College of Nursing, *Oak Park* (BSN)

Indiana
Ball State University, School of Nursing, *Muncie* (BS)
Indiana University Bloomington, Department of Nursing-Bloomington Division, *Bloomington* (BSN)
Indiana University Northwest, School of Nursing and Health Professions, *Gary* (BSN)
Purdue University, School of Nursing, *West Lafayette* (BS)

Iowa
Allen College, Program in Nursing, *Waterloo* (BSN)
Clarke College, Department of Nursing and Health, *Dubuque* (BS)
Iowa Wesleyan College, Division of Health and Natural Sciences, *Mount Pleasant* (BSN)
Morningside College, Department of Nursing Education, *Sioux City* (BSN)

Kansas
Washburn University, School of Nursing, *Topeka* (BSN)

Kentucky
Bellarmine University, Donna and Allan Lansing School of Nursing and Health Sciences, *Louisville* (BSN)
Eastern Kentucky University, Department of Baccalaureate and Graduate Nursing, *Richmond* (BSN)
University of Kentucky, Graduate School Programs in the College of Nursing, *Lexington* (BSN)

Maryland
Coppin State University, Helene Fuld School of Nursing, *Baltimore* (BSN)
The Johns Hopkins University, School of Nursing, *Baltimore* (BS)

Massachusetts
Regis College, School of Nursing and Health Professions, *Weston* (BSN)
Simmons College, Department of Nursing, *Boston* (BS)

Michigan
Eastern Michigan University, School of Nursing, *Ypsilanti* (BSN)
Grand Valley State University, Kirkhof College of Nursing, *Allendale* (BSN)
Madonna University, College of Nursing and Health, *Livonia* (BSN)
Saginaw Valley State University, Crystal M. Lange College of Nursing and Health Sciences, *University Center* (BSN)
University of Michigan-Flint, Department of Nursing, *Flint* (BSN)
Western Michigan University, College of Health and Human Services, *Kalamazoo* (BSN)

Minnesota
St. Catherine University, Department of Nursing, *St. Paul* (BS)

Missouri
Cox College of Nursing and Health Sciences, Department of Nursing, *Springfield* (BSN)
Missouri Southern State University, Department of Nursing, *Joplin* (BSN)
Research College of Nursing, College of Nursing, *Kansas City* (BSN)

Nebraska
University of Nebraska Medical Center, College of Nursing, *Omaha* (BSN)

Nevada
Touro University, School of Nursing, *Henderson* (BSN)

New Jersey
Rutgers, The State University of New Jersey, Camden College of Arts and Sciences, Department of Nursing, *Camden* (BS)
Rutgers, The State University of New Jersey, College of Nursing, *Newark* (BS)
Seton Hall University, College of Nursing, *South Orange* (BSN)

New York
Adelphi University, School of Nursing, *Garden City* (BS)
College of Mount Saint Vincent, Department of Nursing, *Riverdale* (BS)
The College of New Rochelle, School of Nursing, *New Rochelle* (BSN)
Concordia College-New York, Nursing Program, *Bronxville* (BSN)
Lehman College of the City University of New York, Department of Nursing, *Bronx* (BS)
Molloy College, Department of Nursing, *Rockville Centre* (BS)
New York University, College of Nursing, *New York* (BS)
The Sage Colleges, Department of Nursing, *Troy* (BS)
St. John Fisher College, Advanced Practice Nursing Program, *Rochester* (BS)
Wagner College, Department of Nursing, *Staten Island* (BS)

North Carolina
Queens University of Charlotte, Presbyterian School of Nursing, *Charlotte* (BSN)
The University of North Carolina at Greensboro, School of Nursing, *Greensboro* (BSN)
Winston-Salem State University, Department of Nursing, *Winston-Salem* (BSN)

North Dakota
University of North Dakota, College of Nursing, *Grand Forks* (BSN)

Ohio
Ashland University, Department of Nursing, *Ashland* (BSN)
Kent State University, College of Nursing, *Kent* (BSN)
Wright State University, College of Nursing and Health, *Dayton* (BSN)

Oklahoma
Northwestern Oklahoma State University, Division of Nursing, *Alva* (BSN)
Oklahoma Baptist University, School of Nursing, *Shawnee* (BSN)
Oklahoma Wesleyan University, Division of Nursing, *Bartlesville* (BSN)
Southern Nazarene University, School of Nursing, *Bethany* (BS)

Oregon
Linfield College, School of Nursing, *McMinnville* (BSN)

Pennsylvania
Bloomsburg University of Pennsylvania, Department of Nursing, *Bloomsburg* (BSN)
Carlow University, School of Nursing, *Pittsburgh* (BSN)
Cedar Crest College, Department of Nursing, *Allentown* (BS)
DeSales University, Department of Nursing and Health, *Center Valley* (BSN)
Eastern University, Program in Nursing, *St. Davids* (BSN)
Edinboro University of Pennsylvania, Department of Nursing, *Edinboro* (BS)
Gannon University, Villa Maria School of Nursing, *Erie* (BSN)
Indiana University of Pennsylvania, Department of Nursing and Allied Health, *Indiana* (BSN)
La Salle University, School of Nursing and Health Sciences, *Philadelphia* (BSN)
Misericordia University, Department of Nursing, *Dallas* (BSN)
Neumann University, Program in Nursing and Health Sciences, *Aston* (BS)
Robert Morris University, School of Nursing and Health Sciences, *Moon Township* (BSN)
Thomas Jefferson University, Department of Nursing, *Philadelphia* (BSN)
University of Pennsylvania, School of Nursing, *Philadelphia* (BSN)
The University of Scranton, Department of Nursing, *Scranton* (BS)
Villanova University, College of Nursing, *Villanova* (BSN)

Rhode Island
Rhode Island College, Department of Nursing, *Providence* (BSN)

South Carolina
Lander University, School of Nursing, *Greenwood* (BSN)

South Dakota
Presentation College, Department of Nursing, *Aberdeen* (BSN)

Tennessee
Belmont University, School of Nursing, *Nashville* (BSN)
Cumberland University, Rudy School of Nursing and Health Professions, *Lebanon* (BSN)
Milligan College, Department of Nursing, *Milligan College* (BSN)
Tennessee Technological University, School of Nursing, *Cookeville* (BSN)
University of Memphis, Loewenberg School of Nursing, *Memphis* (BSN)
The University of Tennessee at Chattanooga, School of Nursing, *Chattanooga* (BSN)

Texas
Texas A&M University-Corpus Christi, School of Nursing and Health Sciences, *Corpus Christi* (BSN)
Texas Woman's University, College of Nursing, *Denton* (BS)
The University of Texas at Arlington, School of Nursing, *Arlington* (BSN)
University of the Incarnate Word, Program in Nursing, *San Antonio* (BSN)

Utah
Westminster College, School of Nursing and Health Sciences, *Salt Lake City* (BSN)

Virginia
Eastern Mennonite University, Department of Nursing, *Harrisonburg* (BSN)

BACCALAUREATE PROGRAMS
Baccalaureate for Second Degree

Hampton University, School of Nursing, *Hampton* (BS)

Marymount University, School of Health Professions, *Arlington* (BSN)

Radford University, School of Nursing, *Radford* (BSN)

Washington

Seattle University, College of Nursing, *Seattle* (BSN)

West Virginia

Mountain State University, College of Nursing, *Beckley* (BSN)

Wisconsin

Alverno College, Division of Nursing, *Milwaukee* (BSN)

Bellin College, Nursing Program, *Green Bay* (BSN)

Columbia College of Nursing/Mount Mary College Nursing Program, *Milwaukee* (BSN)

Edgewood College, Program in Nursing, *Madison* (BS)

University of Wisconsin-Oshkosh, College of Nursing, *Oshkosh* (BSN)

CANADA

Alberta

University of Calgary, Faculty of Nursing, *Calgary* (BN)

Manitoba

Brandon University, School of Health Studies, *Brandon* (BN)

University of Manitoba, Faculty of Nursing, *Winnipeg* (BN)

Nova Scotia

Dalhousie University, School of Nursing, *Halifax* (BScN)

Ontario

McMaster University, School of Nursing, *Hamilton* (BScN)

University of Toronto, Faculty of Nursing, *Toronto* (BScN)

Saskatchewan

University of Saskatchewan, College of Nursing, *Saskatoon* (BSN)

GENERIC BACCALAUREATE

U.S. AND U.S. TERRITORIES

Alabama

Auburn University, School of Nursing, *Auburn University* (BSN)

Auburn University Montgomery, School of Nursing, *Montgomery* (BSN)

Jacksonville State University, College of Nursing and Health Sciences, *Jacksonville* (BSN)

Oakwood University, Department of Nursing, *Huntsville* (BS)

Samford University, Ida V. Moffett School of Nursing, *Birmingham* (BSN)

Spring Hill College, Division of Nursing, *Mobile* (BSN)

Troy University, School of Nursing, *Troy* (BSN)

Tuskegee University, Program in Nursing, *Tuskegee* (BSN)

The University of Alabama, Capstone College of Nursing, *Tuscaloosa* (BSN)

The University of Alabama at Birmingham, School of Nursing, *Birmingham* (BSN)

The University of Alabama in Huntsville, College of Nursing, *Huntsville* (BSN)

University of Mobile, School of Nursing, *Mobile* (BSN)

University of North Alabama, College of Nursing and Allied Health, *Florence* (BSN)

University of South Alabama, College of Nursing, *Mobile* (BSN)

Alaska

University of Alaska Anchorage, School of Nursing, *Anchorage* (BS)

Arizona

Arizona State University at the Downtown Phoenix Campus, College of Nursing, *Phoenix* (BSN)

Grand Canyon University, College of Nursing and Health Sciences, *Phoenix* (BSN)

Northern Arizona University, School of Nursing, *Flagstaff* (BSN)

The University of Arizona, College of Nursing, *Tucson* (BSN)

Arkansas

Arkansas State University, Department of Nursing, *Jonesboro, State University* (BSN)

Arkansas Tech University, Program in Nursing, *Russellville* (BSN)

Harding University, College of Nursing, *Searcy* (BSN)

Henderson State University, Department of Nursing, *Arkadelphia* (BSN)

Southern Arkansas University-Magnolia, Department of Nursing, *Magnolia* (BSN)

University of Arkansas, Eleanor Mann School of Nursing, *Fayetteville* (BSN)

University of Arkansas at Fort Smith, Carol McKelvey Moore School of Nursing, *Fort Smith* (BSN)

University of Arkansas at Monticello, School of Nursing, *Monticello* (BSN)

University of Arkansas at Pine Bluff, Department of Nursing, *Pine Bluff* (BSN)

University of Arkansas for Medical Sciences, College of Nursing, *Little Rock* (BSN)

University of Central Arkansas, Department of Nursing, *Conway* (BSN)

California

Azusa Pacific University, School of Nursing, *Azusa* (BSN)

Biola University, Department of Nursing, *La Mirada* (BSN)

California Baptist University, School of Nursing, *Riverside* (BSN)

California State University, Bakersfield, Program in Nursing, *Bakersfield* (BSN)

California State University Channel Islands, Nursing Program, *Camarillo* (BSN)

California State University, Chico, School of Nursing, *Chico* (BSN)

California State University, East Bay, Department of Nursing and Health Sciences, *Hayward* (BS)

California State University, Fresno, Department of Nursing, *Fresno* (BSN)

California State University, Fullerton, Department of Nursing, *Fullerton* (BSN)

California State University, Long Beach, Department of Nursing, *Long Beach* (BSN)

California State University, Los Angeles, School of Nursing, *Los Angeles* (BSN)

California State University, Sacramento, Division of Nursing, *Sacramento* (BSN)

California State University, San Bernardino, Department of Nursing, *San Bernardino* (BSN)

California State University, San Marcos, School of Nursing, *San Marcos* (BSN)

California State University, Stanislaus, Department of Nursing, *Turlock* (BSN)

Dominican University of California, Program in Nursing, *San Rafael* (BSN)

Humboldt State University, Department of Nursing, *Arcata* (BSN)

Loma Linda University, School of Nursing, *Loma Linda* (BS)

Mount St. Mary's College, Department of Nursing, *Los Angeles* (BSN, BSc PN)

National University, Department of Nursing, *La Jolla* (BSN)

Point Loma Nazarene University, School of Nursing, *San Diego* (BSN)

Samuel Merritt University, School of Nursing, *Oakland* (BSN)

San Diego State University, School of Nursing, *San Diego* (BSN)

San Francisco State University, School of Nursing, *San Francisco* (BSN)

San Jose State University, School of Nursing, *San Jose* (BS)

Sonoma State University, Department of Nursing, *Rohnert Park* (BSN)

University of California, Irvine, Program in Nursing Science, *Irvine* (BS)

University of California, Los Angeles, School of Nursing, *Los Angeles* (BS)

University of San Francisco, School of Nursing, *San Francisco* (BSN)

Colorado

Colorado State University-Pueblo, Department of Nursing, *Pueblo* (BSN)

Mesa State College, Department of Nursing and Radiologic Sciences, *Grand Junction* (BSN)

Regis University, School of Nursing, *Denver* (BSN)

University of Colorado at Colorado Springs, Beth-El College of Nursing and Health Sciences, *Colorado Springs* (BSN)

University of Colorado Denver, College of Nursing, *Denver* (BS)

University of Northern Colorado, School of Nursing, *Greeley* (BS)

Connecticut

Central Connecticut State University, Department of Nursing, *New Britain* (BSN)

Fairfield University, School of Nursing, *Fairfield* (BS)

Quinnipiac University, Department of Nursing, *Hamden* (BSN)

Sacred Heart University, Program in Nursing, *Fairfield* (BS)

Saint Joseph College, Department of Nursing, *West Hartford* (BS)

Southern Connecticut State University, Department of Nursing, *New Haven* (BS)

University of Connecticut, School of Nursing, *Storrs* (BS)

Western Connecticut State University, Department of Nursing, *Danbury* (BS)

Delaware

Delaware State University, Department of Nursing, *Dover* (BSN)

University of Delaware, School of Nursing, *Newark* (BSN)

Wesley College, Nursing Program, *Dover* (BSN)

District of Columbia

The Catholic University of America, School of Nursing, *Washington* (BSN)

Georgetown University, School of Nursing & Health Studies, *Washington* (BSN)

Howard University, Division of Nursing, *Washington* (BSN)

Trinity (Washington) University, Nursing Program, *Washington* (BSN)

Florida

Barry University, School of Nursing, *Miami Shores* (BSN)

Bethune-Cookman University, School of Nursing, *Daytona Beach* (BSN)

Florida Agricultural and Mechanical University, School of Nursing, *Tallahassee* (BSN)

Florida Atlantic University, Christine E. Lynn College of Nursing, *Boca Raton* (BS)

Florida Gulf Coast University, School of Nursing, *Fort Myers* (BSN)

Florida Hospital College of Health Sciences, Department of Nursing, *Orlando* (BS)

Florida International University, Nursing Program, *Miami* (BSN)

Florida Southern College, Department of Nursing, *Lakeland* (BSN)

Florida State University, College of Nursing, *Tallahassee* (BSN)

Jacksonville University, School of Nursing, *Jacksonville* (BSN)

Nova Southeastern University, College of Allied Health and Nursing, *Fort Lauderdale* (BSN)

South University, Nursing Program, *West Palm Beach* (BSN)

University of Central Florida, School of Nursing, *Orlando* (BSN)

University of Florida, College of Nursing, *Gainesville* (BSN)

University of Miami, School of Nursing and Health Studies, *Coral Gables* (BSN)

University of North Florida, School of Nursing, *Jacksonville* (BSN)

University of South Florida, College of Nursing, *Tampa* (BS)

The University of Tampa, Department of Nursing, *Tampa* (BSN)

University of West Florida, Department of Nursing, *Pensacola* (BSN)

Georgia

Albany State University, College of Sciences and Health Professions, *Albany* (BSN)

Armstrong Atlantic State University, Program in Nursing, *Savannah* (BSN)

Brenau University, School of Health and Science, *Gainesville* (BSN)

Clayton State University, Department of Nursing, *Morrow* (BSN)

Columbus State University, Nursing Program, *Columbus* (BSN)

Emory University, Nell Hodgson Woodruff School of Nursing, *Atlanta* (BSN)

Georgia Baptist College of Nursing of Mercer University, Department of Nursing, *Atlanta* (BSN)

Georgia College & State University, College of Health Sciences, *Milledgeville* (BSN)

Georgia Southern University, School of Nursing, *Statesboro* (BSN)

Georgia Southwestern State University, School of Nursing, *Americus* (BSN)

Georgia State University, Byrdine F. Lewis School of Nursing, *Atlanta* (BS)

Kennesaw State University, School of Nursing, *Kennesaw* (BSN)

LaGrange College, Department of Nursing, *LaGrange* (BSN)

Macon State College, School of Nursing and Health Sciences, *Macon* (BSN)

Medical College of Georgia, School of Nursing, *Augusta* (BSN)

Piedmont College, School of Nursing, *Demorest* (BSN)

University of West Georgia, School of Nursing, *Carrollton* (BSN)

Valdosta State University, College of Nursing, *Valdosta* (BSN)

Guam

University of Guam, College of Nursing and Health Sciences, *Mangilao* (BSN)

Hawaii

Hawai'i Pacific University, College of Nursing and Health Sciences, *Honolulu* (BSN)

University of Hawaii at Hilo, Department in Nursing, *Hilo* (BSN)

University of Hawaii at Manoa, School of Nursing and Dental Hygiene, *Honolulu* (BSN)

Idaho

Boise State University, Department of Nursing, *Boise* (BS)

Idaho State University, Department of Nursing, *Pocatello* (BSN)

Lewis-Clark State College, Division of Nursing and Health Sciences, *Lewiston* (BSN)

Northwest Nazarene University, School of Health and Science, *Nampa* (BSN)

Illinois

Aurora University, School of Nursing, *Aurora* (BSN)

Blessing-Rieman College of Nursing, *Quincy* (BSN)

Bradley University, Department of Nursing, *Peoria* (BSN, BSc PN)

Chicago State University, College of Nursing and Allied Health Professions, *Chicago* (BSN)

Elmhurst College, Deicke Center for Nursing Education, *Elmhurst* (BS)

Illinois State University, Mennonite College of Nursing, *Normal* (BSN)

Illinois Wesleyan University, School of Nursing, *Bloomington* (BSN)

Lakeview College of Nursing, *Danville* (BSN)

Lewis University, Program in Nursing, *Romeoville* (BSN)

Loyola University Chicago, Marcella Niehoff School of Nursing, *Maywood* (BSN)

MacMurray College, Department of Nursing, *Jacksonville* (BSN)

Millikin University, School of Nursing, *Decatur* (BSN)

Northern Illinois University, School of Nursing and Health Studies, *De Kalb* (BS)

North Park University, School of Nursing, *Chicago* (BS)

Olivet Nazarene University, Division of Nursing, *Bourbonnais* (BSN)

Rockford College, Department of Nursing, *Rockford* (BSN)

Saint Anthony College of Nursing, Saint Anthony College of Nursing, *Rockford* (BSN)

Saint Francis Medical Center College of Nursing, Baccalaureate Nursing Program, *Peoria* (BSN)

St. John's College, Department of Nursing, *Springfield* (BSN)

Saint Xavier University, School of Nursing, *Chicago* (BSN)

Southern Illinois University Edwardsville, School of Nursing, *Edwardsville* (BS)

Trinity Christian College, Department of Nursing, *Palos Heights* (BSN)

University of Illinois at Chicago, College of Nursing, *Chicago* (BSN)

University of St. Francis, College of Nursing and Allied Health, *Joliet* (BSN)

Western Illinois University, School of Nursing, *Macomb* (BSN)

Indiana

Ball State University, School of Nursing, *Muncie* (BS)

Bethel College, Department of Nursing, *Mishawaka* (BSN)

Goshen College, Department of Nursing, *Goshen* (BSN)

Huntington University, Department of Nursing, *Huntington* (BSN)

Indiana State University, Department of Nursing, *Terre Haute* (BS)

Indiana University Bloomington, Department of Nursing–Bloomington Division, *Bloomington* (BSN)

Indiana University East, School of Nursing, *Richmond* (BSN)

Indiana University Kokomo, Indiana University School of Nursing, *Kokomo* (BSN)

Indiana University Northwest, School of Nursing and Health Professions, *Gary* (BSN)

Indiana University–Purdue University Fort Wayne, Department of Nursing, *Fort Wayne* (BS)

Indiana University–Purdue University Indianapolis, School of Nursing, *Indianapolis* (BSN)

Indiana University South Bend, Division of Nursing and Health Professions, *South Bend* (BSN)

Indiana University Southeast, Division of Nursing, *New Albany* (BSN)

Indiana Wesleyan University, School of Nursing, *Marion* (BSN)

Marian University, Department of Nursing and Nutritional Science, *Indianapolis* (BSN)

Purdue University, School of Nursing, *West Lafayette* (BS)

Purdue University Calumet, School of Nursing, *Hammond* (BS)

Saint Mary's College, Department of Nursing, *Notre Dame* (BS)

University of Evansville, Department of Nursing, *Evansville* (BSN)

University of Indianapolis, School of Nursing, *Indianapolis* (BSN)

University of Saint Francis, Department of Nursing, *Fort Wayne* (BSN)

University of Southern Indiana, College of Nursing and Health Professions, *Evansville* (BSN)

Valparaiso University, College of Nursing, *Valparaiso* (BSN)

Iowa

Allen College, Program in Nursing, *Waterloo* (BSN)

Briar Cliff University, Department of Nursing, *Sioux City* (BSN)

Clarke College, Department of Nursing and Health, *Dubuque* (BS)

Coe College, Department of Nursing, *Cedar Rapids* (BSN)

Dordt College, Nursing Program, *Sioux Center* (BSN)

Grand View University, Division of Nursing, *Des Moines* (BSN)

Iowa Wesleyan College, Division of Health and Natural Sciences, *Mount Pleasant* (BSN)

Luther College, Department of Nursing, *Decorah* (BA)

Morningside College, Department of Nursing Education, *Sioux City* (BSN)

Mount Mercy College, Department of Nursing, *Cedar Rapids* (BSN)

Northwestern College, Nursing Program, *Orange City* (BSN)

St. Ambrose University, Program in Nursing (BSN), *Davenport* (BSN)

BACCALAUREATE PROGRAMS
Generic Baccalaureate

The University of Iowa, College of Nursing, *Iowa City* (BSN)

Kansas

Baker University, School of Nursing, *Topeka* (BSN)

Bethel College, Department of Nursing, *North Newton* (BSN)

Emporia State University, Newman Division of Nursing, *Emporia* (BSN)

Fort Hays State University, Department of Nursing, *Hays* (BSN)

Kansas Wesleyan University, Department of Nursing Education, *Salina* (BSN)

MidAmerica Nazarene University, Division of Nursing, *Olathe* (BSN)

Newman University, Division of Nursing, *Wichita* (BSN)

Pittsburg State University, Department of Nursing, *Pittsburg* (BSN)

Southwestern College, Nursing Program, *Winfield* (BSN)

The University of Kansas, School of Nursing, *Kansas City* (BSN)

University of Saint Mary, Bachelor of Science in Nursing Program, *Leavenworth* (BSN)

Washburn University, School of Nursing, *Topeka* (BSN)

Wichita State University, School of Nursing, *Wichita* (BSN)

Kentucky

Bellarmine University, Donna and Allan Lansing School of Nursing and Health Sciences, *Louisville* (BSN)

Berea College, Department of Nursing, *Berea* (BS)

Eastern Kentucky University, Department of Baccalaureate and Graduate Nursing, *Richmond* (BSN)

Kentucky Christian University, School of Nursing, *Grayson* (BSN)

Morehead State University, Department of Nursing, *Morehead* (BSN)

Murray State University, Program in Nursing, *Murray* (BSN)

Northern Kentucky University, Department of Nursing, *Highland Heights* (BSN)

Spalding University, School of Nursing, *Louisville* (BSN)

Thomas More College, Program in Nursing, *Crestview Hills* (BSN)

University of Kentucky, Graduate School Programs in the College of Nursing, *Lexington* (BSN)

University of Louisville, School of Nursing, *Louisville* (BSN)

Louisiana

Dillard University, Division of Nursing, *New Orleans* (BSN)

Grambling State University, School of Nursing, *Grambling* (BSN)

Louisiana College, Department of Nursing, *Pineville* (BSN)

Louisiana State University Health Sciences Center, School of Nursing, *New Orleans* (BSN)

McNeese State University, College of Nursing, *Lake Charles* (BSN)

Nicholls State University, Department of Nursing, *Thibodaux* (BSN)

Northwestern State University of Louisiana, College of Nursing, *Shreveport* (BSN)

Our Lady of Holy Cross College, Division of Nursing, *New Orleans* (BSN)

Southeastern Louisiana University, School of Nursing, *Hammond* (BS)

Southern University and Agricultural and Mechanical College, School of Nursing, *Baton Rouge* (BSN)

University of Louisiana at Lafayette, College of Nursing, *Lafayette* (BSN)

University of Louisiana at Monroe, Nursing, *Monroe* (BS)

Maine

Husson University, School of Nursing, *Bangor* (BSN)

Saint Joseph's College of Maine, Department of Nursing, *Standish* (BSN)

University of Maine, School of Nursing, *Orono* (BSN)

University of Maine at Fort Kent, Department of Nursing, *Fort Kent* (BSN)

University of Southern Maine, College of Nursing and Health Professions, *Portland* (BS)

Maryland

Bowie State University, Department of Nursing, *Bowie* (BSN)

Columbia Union College, Nursing Department, *Takoma Park* (BS)

Coppin State University, Helene Fuld School of Nursing, *Baltimore* (BSN)

The Johns Hopkins University, School of Nursing, *Baltimore* (BS)

Salisbury University, Program in Nursing, *Salisbury* (BS)

Stevenson University, Nursing Division, *Stevenson* (BS)

Towson University, Department of Nursing, *Towson* (BS)

University of Maryland, Baltimore, Master's Program in Nursing, *Baltimore* (BSN)

Massachusetts

American International College, Division of Nursing, *Springfield* (BSN)

Boston College, William F. Connell School of Nursing, *Chestnut Hill* (BS)

Curry College, Division of Nursing, *Milton* (BS)

Elms College, Division of Nursing, *Chicopee* (BS)

Endicott College, Major in Nursing, *Beverly* (BS)

Northeastern University, School of Nursing, *Boston* (BSN)

Regis College, School of Nursing and Health Professions, *Weston* (BSN)

Salem State College, Program in Nursing, *Salem* (BSN)

Simmons College, Department of Nursing, *Boston* (BS)

University of Massachusetts Amherst, School of Nursing, *Amherst* (BS)

University of Massachusetts Boston, College of Nursing and Health Sciences, *Boston* (BS)

University of Massachusetts Dartmouth, College of Nursing, *North Dartmouth* (BSN)

University of Massachusetts Lowell, Department of Nursing, *Lowell* (BS)

Worcester State College, Department of Nursing, *Worcester* (BS)

Michigan

Andrews University, Department of Nursing, *Berrien Springs* (BS)

Calvin College, Department of Nursing, *Grand Rapids* (BSN)

Davenport University, Division of Nursing, *Grand Rapids* (BS)

Eastern Michigan University, School of Nursing, *Ypsilanti* (BSN)

Ferris State University, School of Nursing, *Big Rapids* (BSN)

Finlandia University, College of Professional Studies, *Hancock* (BSN)

Grand Valley State University, Kirkhof College of Nursing, *Allendale* (BSN)

Hope College, Department of Nursing, *Holland* (BSN)

Lake Superior State University, Department of Nursing, *Sault Sainte Marie* (BSN)

Madonna University, College of Nursing and Health, *Livonia* (BSN)

Michigan State University, College of Nursing, *East Lansing* (BSN)

Northern Michigan University, College of Nursing and Allied Health Science, *Marquette* (BSN)

Oakland University, School of Nursing, *Rochester* (BSN)

Saginaw Valley State University, Crystal M. Lange College of Nursing and Health Sciences, *University Center* (BSN)

University of Detroit Mercy, McAuley School of Nursing, *Detroit* (BSN)

University of Michigan, School of Nursing, *Ann Arbor* (BSN)

University of Michigan–Flint, Department of Nursing, *Flint* (BSN)

Wayne State University, College of Nursing, *Detroit* (BSN)

Western Michigan University, College of Health and Human Services, *Kalamazoo* (BSN)

Minnesota

Bemidji State University, Department of Nursing, *Bemidji* (BS)

Bethel University, Department of Nursing, *St. Paul* (BSN)

College of Saint Benedict, Department of Nursing, *Saint Joseph* (BS)

The College of St. Scholastica, Department of Nursing, *Duluth* (BS)

Concordia College, Department of Nursing, *Moorhead* (BA)

Crown College, Nursing Department, *St. Bonifacius* (BSN)

Globe University, Bachelor of Science in Nursing, *Woodbury* (BS)

Gustavus Adolphus College, Department of Nursing, *St. Peter* (BA)

Minnesota Intercollegiate Nursing Consortium, *Northfield* (BA)

Minnesota State University Mankato, School of Nursing, *Mankato* (BS)

Minnesota State University Moorhead, School of Nursing and Healthcare Leadership, *Moorhead* (BSN)

St. Catherine University, Department of Nursing, *St. Paul* (BS)

St. Cloud State University, Department of Nursing Science, *St. Cloud* (BS)

St. Olaf College, Department of Nursing, *Northfield* (BA)

University of Minnesota, Twin Cities Campus, School of Nursing, *Minneapolis* (BSN)

Winona State University, College of Nursing and Health Sciences, *Winona* (BS)

Mississippi

Alcorn State University, School of Nursing, *Natchez* (BSN)

Delta State University, School of Nursing, *Cleveland* (BSN)

Mississippi College, School of Nursing, *Clinton* (BSN)

Mississippi University for Women, College of Nursing and Speech-Language Pathology, *Columbus* (BSN)

University of Mississippi Medical Center, Program in Nursing, *Jackson* (BSN)

University of Southern Mississippi, School of Nursing, *Hattiesburg* (BSN)

William Carey University, School of Nursing, *Hattiesburg* (BSN)

Missouri

Avila University, School of Nursing, *Kansas City* (BSN)

Central Methodist University, College of Liberal Arts and Sciences, *Fayette* (BN)

Chamberlain College of Nursing, *St. Louis* (BSN)

Cox College of Nursing and Health Sciences, Department of Nursing, *Springfield* (BSN)

Goldfarb School of Nursing at Barnes-Jewish College, *St. Louis* (BSN)

Graceland University, School of Nursing, *Independence* (BSN)

Maryville University of Saint Louis, Nursing Program, School of Health Professions, *St. Louis* (BSN)

Missouri Southern State University, Department of Nursing, *Joplin* (BSN)

Missouri State University, Department of Nursing, *Springfield* (BSN)

Missouri Western State University, Department of Nursing, *St. Joseph* (BSN)

Research College of Nursing, College of Nursing, *Kansas City* (BSN)

Saint Louis University, School of Nursing, *St. Louis* (BSN)

Saint Luke's College, Nursing College, *Kansas City* (BSN)

Southeast Missouri State University, Department of Nursing, *Cape Girardeau* (BSN)

Truman State University, Program in Nursing, *Kirksville* (BSN)

University of Central Missouri, Department of Nursing, *Warrensburg* (BS)

University of Missouri–Columbia, Sinclair School of Nursing, *Columbia* (BSN)

University of Missouri–Kansas City, School of Nursing, *Kansas City* (BSN)

University of Missouri–St. Louis, College of Nursing, *St. Louis* (BSN)

William Jewell College, Department of Nursing, *Liberty* (BS)

Montana

Carroll College, Department of Nursing, *Helena* (BA)

Montana State University, College of Nursing, *Bozeman* (BSN)

Nebraska

BryanLGH College of Health Sciences, School of Nursing, *Lincoln* (BSc PN)

College of Saint Mary, Division of Health Care Professions, *Omaha* (BSN)

Creighton University, School of Nursing, *Omaha* (BSN)

Midland Lutheran College, Department of Nursing, *Fremont* (BSN)

Nebraska Methodist College, Department of Nursing, *Omaha* (BSN)

Union College, Division of Health Sciences, *Lincoln* (BSN)

University of Nebraska Medical Center, College of Nursing, *Omaha* (BSN)

Nevada

Nevada State College at Henderson, Nursing Program, *Henderson* (BSN)

Touro University, School of Nursing, *Henderson* (BSN)

University of Nevada, Las Vegas, School of Nursing, *Las Vegas* (BSN)

University of Nevada, Reno, Orvis School of Nursing, *Reno* (BSN)

University of Southern Nevada, College of Nursing, *Henderson* (BSN)

New Hampshire

Colby-Sawyer College, Department of Nursing, *New London* (BSN)

University of New Hampshire, Department of Nursing, *Durham* (BS)

New Jersey

Bloomfield College, Division of Nursing, *Bloomfield* (BS)

The College of New Jersey, School of Nursing, Health and Exercise Science, *Ewing* (BSN)

Fairleigh Dickinson University, Metropolitan Campus, Henry P. Becton School of Nursing and Allied Health, *Teaneck* (BSN)

Felician College, Division of Nursing and Health Management, *Lodi* (BSN)

Ramapo College of New Jersey, Master of Science in Nursing Program, *Mahwah* (BSN)

Rutgers, The State University of New Jersey, Camden College of Arts and Sciences, Department of Nursing, *Camden* (BS)

Rutgers, The State University of New Jersey, College of Nursing, *Newark* (BS)

Saint Peter's College, Nursing Program, *Jersey City* (BSN)

Seton Hall University, College of Nursing, *South Orange* (BSN)

William Paterson University of New Jersey, Department of Nursing, *Wayne* (BSN)

New Mexico

New Mexico State University, School of Nursing, *Las Cruces* (BSN)

University of New Mexico, College of Nursing, *Albuquerque* (BSN)

New York

Adelphi University, School of Nursing, *Garden City* (BS)

The College at Brockport, State University of New York, Department of Nursing, *Brockport* (BSN)

College of Mount Saint Vincent, Department of Nursing, *Riverdale* (BS)

The College of New Rochelle, School of Nursing, *New Rochelle* (BSN)

Dominican College, Department of Nursing, *Orangeburg* (BSN)

D'Youville College, Department of Nursing, *Buffalo* (BSN)

Elmira College, Program in Nursing Education, *Elmira* (BS)

Hartwick College, Department of Nursing, *Oneonta* (BS)

Hunter College of the City University of New York, Hunter-Bellevue School of Nursing, *New York* (BS)

Lehman College of the City University of New York, Department of Nursing, *Bronx* (BS)

Long Island University, Brooklyn Campus, School of Nursing, *Brooklyn* (BS)

Molloy College, Department of Nursing, *Rockville Centre* (BS)

Mount Saint Mary College, Division of Nursing, *Newburgh* (BSN)

Nazareth College of Rochester, Department of Nursing, *Rochester* (BS)

New York University, College of Nursing, *New York* (BS)

Pace University, Lienhard School of Nursing, *New York* (BS)

Roberts Wesleyan College, Division of Nursing, *Rochester* (BScN)

The Sage Colleges, Department of Nursing, *Troy* (BS)

St. John Fisher College, Advanced Practice Nursing Program, *Rochester* (BS)

State University of New York at Binghamton, Decker School of Nursing, *Binghamton* (BS)

State University of New York at Plattsburgh, Department of Nursing, *Plattsburgh* (BS)

University at Buffalo, the State University of New York, School of Nursing, *Buffalo* (BS)

Utica College, Department of Nursing, *Utica* (BS)

Wagner College, Department of Nursing, *Staten Island* (BS)

North Carolina

Barton College, School of Nursing, *Wilson* (BSN)

East Carolina University, College of Nursing, *Greenville* (BSN)

Fayetteville State University, Program in Nursing, *Fayetteville* (BS)

Lenoir-Rhyne University, Program in Nursing, *Hickory* (BS)

North Carolina Agricultural and Technical State University, School of Nursing, *Greensboro* (BSN)

North Carolina Central University, Department of Nursing, *Durham* (BSN)

Queens University of Charlotte, Presbyterian School of Nursing, *Charlotte* (BSN)

The University of North Carolina at Chapel Hill, School of Nursing, *Chapel Hill* (BSN)

The University of North Carolina at Charlotte, School of Nursing, *Charlotte* (BSN)

The University of North Carolina at Greensboro, School of Nursing, *Greensboro* (BSN)

The University of North Carolina at Pembroke, Nursing Program, *Pembroke* (BSN)

The University of North Carolina Wilmington, School of Nursing, *Wilmington* (BS)

Western Carolina University, School of Nursing, *Cullowhee* (BSN)

Winston-Salem State University, Department of Nursing, *Winston-Salem* (BSN)

North Dakota

Minot State University, Department of Nursing, *Minot* (BSN)

North Dakota State University, Department of Nursing, *Fargo* (BSN)

University of Mary, Division of Nursing, *Bismarck* (BS)

University of North Dakota, College of Nursing, *Grand Forks* (BSN)

Ohio

Capital University, School of Nursing, *Columbus* (BSN)

Case Western Reserve University, Frances Payne Bolton School of Nursing, *Cleveland* (BSN)

Cleveland State University, School of Nursing, *Cleveland* (BSN)

College of Mount St. Joseph, Department of Nursing, *Cincinnati* (BSN)

Franciscan University of Steubenville, Department of Nursing, *Steubenville* (BSN)

Kent State University, College of Nursing, *Kent* (BSN)

Lourdes College, Nursing Department, *Sylvania* (BSN)

Malone University, School of Nursing, *Canton* (BSN)

Mercy College of Northwest Ohio, Division of Nursing, *Toledo* (BSN)

Miami University, Department of Nursing, *Hamilton* (BSN)

Mount Carmel College of Nursing, Nursing Programs, *Columbus* (BSN)

Muskingum University, Department of Nursing, *New Concord* (BSN)

BACCALAUREATE PROGRAMS
Generic Baccalaureate

Notre Dame College, Nursing Department, *South Euclid* (BSN)

The Ohio State University, College of Nursing, *Columbus* (BSN)

Ohio University, School of Nursing, *Athens* (BSN)

Otterbein College, Department of Nursing, *Westerville* (BSN)

The University of Akron, College of Nursing, *Akron* (BSN)

University of Cincinnati, College of Nursing, *Cincinnati* (BSN)

The University of Toledo, College of Nursing, *Toledo* (BSN)

Ursuline College, The Breen School of Nursing, *Pepper Pike* (BSN)

Walsh University, Department of Nursing, *North Canton* (BSN)

Wright State University, College of Nursing and Health, *Dayton* (BSN)

Xavier University, Department of Nursing, *Cincinnati* (BSN)

Oklahoma

East Central University, Department of Nursing, *Ada* (BS)

Langston University, School of Nursing and Health Professions, *Langston* (BSN)

Northwestern Oklahoma State University, Division of Nursing, *Alva* (BSN)

Oklahoma Baptist University, School of Nursing, *Shawnee* (BSN)

Oklahoma Christian University, Nursing Program, *Oklahoma City* (BSN)

Oklahoma City University, Kramer School of Nursing, *Oklahoma City* (BSN)

Oklahoma Wesleyan University, Division of Nursing, *Bartlesville* (BSN)

Oral Roberts University, Anna Vaughn School of Nursing, *Tulsa* (BSN)

Southern Nazarene University, School of Nursing, *Bethany* (BS)

Southwestern Oklahoma State University, Division of Nursing, *Weatherford* (BSN)

University of Central Oklahoma, Department of Nursing, *Edmond* (BS)

University of Oklahoma Health Sciences Center, College of Nursing, *Oklahoma City* (BSN)

University of Tulsa, School of Nursing, *Tulsa* (BSN)

Oregon

Concordia University, Nursing Program, *Portland* (BSN)

George Fox University, Nursing Department, *Newberg* (BSN)

Linfield College, School of Nursing, *McMinnville* (BSN)

Oregon Health & Science University, School of Nursing, *Portland* (BS)

University of Portland, School of Nursing, *Portland* (BSN)

Pennsylvania

Alvernia University, Nursing, *Reading* (BSN)

Bloomsburg University of Pennsylvania, Department of Nursing, *Bloomsburg* (BSN)

Carlow University, School of Nursing, *Pittsburgh* (BSN)

Cedar Crest College, Department of Nursing, *Allentown* (BS)

DeSales University, Department of Nursing and Health, *Center Valley* (BSN)

Drexel University, College of Nursing and Health Professions, *Philadelphia* (BSN)

Duquesne University, School of Nursing, *Pittsburgh* (BSN)

Eastern University, Program in Nursing, *St. Davids* (BSN)

East Stroudsburg University of Pennsylvania, Department of Nursing, *East Stroudsburg* (BS)

Edinboro University of Pennsylvania, Department of Nursing, *Edinboro* (BS)

Gannon University, Villa Maria School of Nursing, *Erie* (BSN)

Holy Family University, School of Nursing and Allied Health Professions, *Philadelphia* (BSN)

Indiana University of Pennsylvania, Department of Nursing and Allied Health, *Indiana* (BSN)

La Salle University, School of Nursing and Health Sciences, *Philadelphia* (BSN)

Mansfield University of Pennsylvania, Robert Packer Department of Health Sciences, *Mansfield* (BSN)

Marywood University, Department of Nursing, *Scranton* (BSN)

Messiah College, Department of Nursing, *Grantham* (BSN)

Misericordia University, Department of Nursing, *Dallas* (BSN)

Moravian College, St. Luke's School of Nursing, *Bethlehem* (BS)

Neumann University, Program in Nursing and Health Sciences, *Aston* (BS)

Penn State University Park, School of Nursing, *State College, University Park* (BS)

Robert Morris University, School of Nursing and Health Sciences, *Moon Township* (BSN)

Saint Francis University, Department of Nursing, *Loretto* (BSN)

Temple University, Department of Nursing, *Philadelphia* (BSN)

Thomas Jefferson University, Department of Nursing, *Philadelphia* (BSN)

University of Pennsylvania, School of Nursing, *Philadelphia* (BSN)

University of Pittsburgh, School of Nursing, *Pittsburgh* (BSN)

University of Pittsburgh at Bradford, Department of Nursing, *Bradford* (BSN)

The University of Scranton, Department of Nursing, *Scranton* (BSN)

Villanova University, College of Nursing, *Villanova* (BSN)

Waynesburg University, Department of Nursing, *Waynesburg* (BSN)

West Chester University of Pennsylvania, Department of Nursing, *West Chester* (BSN)

Widener University, School of Nursing, *Chester* (BSN)

Wilkes University, Department of Nursing, *Wilkes-Barre* (BS)

York College of Pennsylvania, Department of Nursing, *York* (BS)

Puerto Rico

Inter American University of Puerto Rico, Arecibo Campus, Nursing Program, *Arecibo* (BS)

Inter American University of Puerto Rico, Metropolitan Campus, Carmen Torres de Tiburcio School of Nursing, *San Juan* (BSN)

Pontifical Catholic University of Puerto Rico, Department of Nursing, *Ponce* (BSN)

Universidad Adventista de las Antillas, Department of Nursing, *Mayagüez* (BSN)

Universidad del Turabo, Nursing Program, *Gurabo* (BS)

University of Puerto Rico at Arecibo, Department of Nursing, *Arecibo* (BSN)

University of Puerto Rico at Humacao, Department of Nursing, *Humacao* (BS)

University of Puerto Rico, Mayagüez Campus, Department of Nursing, *Mayagüez* (BSN)

University of Puerto Rico, Medical Sciences Campus, School of Nursing, *San Juan* (BSN)

University of the Sacred Heart, Program in Nursing, *San Juan* (BSN)

Rhode Island

Rhode Island College, Department of Nursing, *Providence* (BSN)

Salve Regina University, Department of Nursing, *Newport* (BS)

University of Rhode Island, College of Nursing, *Kingston* (BS)

South Carolina

Charleston Southern University, Wingo School of Nursing, *Charleston* (BSN)

Clemson University, School of Nursing, *Clemson* (BS)

Francis Marion University, Department of Nursing, *Florence* (BSN)

Lander University, School of Nursing, *Greenwood* (BSN)

South Carolina State University, Department of Nursing, *Orangeburg* (BSN)

University of South Carolina, College of Nursing, *Columbia* (BSN)

University of South Carolina Aiken, School of Nursing, *Aiken* (BSN)

University of South Carolina Beaufort, Nursing Program, *Beaufort* (BSN)

University of South Carolina Upstate, Mary Black School of Nursing, *Spartanburg* (BSN)

South Dakota

Augustana College, Department of Nursing, *Sioux Falls* (BA)

Mount Marty College, Nursing Program, *Yankton* (BSN)

National American University, School of Nursing, *Rapid City* (BSN)

Presentation College, Department of Nursing, *Aberdeen* (BSN)

South Dakota State University, College of Nursing, *Brookings* (BS)

Tennessee

Austin Peay State University, School of Nursing, *Clarksville* (BSN)

Baptist College of Health Sciences, Nursing Division, *Memphis* (BSN)

Belmont University, School of Nursing, *Nashville* (BSN)

Bethel University, Nursing Program, *McKenzie* (BSN)

Carson-Newman College, Division of Nursing, *Jefferson City* (BSN)

Cumberland University, Rudy School of Nursing and Health Professions, *Lebanon* (BSN)

East Tennessee State University, College of Nursing, *Johnson City* (BSN)

King College, School of Nursing, *Bristol* (BSN)

Lipscomb University, Department of Nursing, *Nashville* (BSN)

Martin Methodist College, Division of Nursing, *Pulaski* (BS)

Middle Tennessee State University, School of Nursing, *Murfreesboro* (BSN)

Milligan College, Department of Nursing, *Milligan College* (BSN)

South College, Department of Nursing, *Knoxville* (BSN)

Tennessee State University, School of Nursing, *Nashville* (BSN)

Tennessee Technological University, School of Nursing, *Cookeville* (BSN)

Tennessee Wesleyan College, Fort Sanders Nursing Department, *Knoxville* (BSN)

Union University, School of Nursing, *Jackson* (BSN)

University of Memphis, Loewenberg School of
Nursing, *Memphis* (BSN)
The University of Tennessee, College of
Nursing, *Knoxville* (BSN)
The University of Tennessee at Chattanooga,
School of Nursing, *Chattanooga* (BSN)
The University of Tennessee at Martin,
Department of Nursing, *Martin* (BSN)

Texas
Baylor University, Louise Herrington School of
Nursing, *Dallas* (BSN)
East Texas Baptist University, Department of
Nursing, *Marshall* (BSN)
Lamar University, Department of Nursing,
Beaumont (BSN)
Midwestern State University, Nursing Program,
Wichita Falls (BSN)
Patty Hanks Shelton School of Nursing, *Abilene*
(BSN)
Prairie View A&M University, College of
Nursing, *Houston* (BSN)
Southwestern Adventist University, Department
of Nursing, *Keene* (BS)
Tarleton State University, Department of
Nursing, *Stephenville* (BSN)
Texas A&M International University, Canseco
School of Nursing, *Laredo* (BSN)
Texas A&M University-Corpus Christi, School
of Nursing and Health Sciences, *Corpus
Christi* (BSN)
Texas Christian University, Harris College of
Nursing, *Fort Worth* (BSN)
Texas Tech University Health Sciences Center,
School of Nursing, *Lubbock* (BSc PN)
Texas Woman's University, College of Nursing,
Denton (BS)
University of Mary Hardin-Baylor, College of
Nursing, *Belton* (BSN)
The University of Texas at Arlington, School of
Nursing, *Arlington* (BSN)
The University of Texas at Austin, School of
Nursing, *Austin* (BSN)
The University of Texas at El Paso, School of
Nursing, *El Paso* (BSN)
The University of Texas at Tyler, Program in
Nursing, *Tyler* (BSN)
The University of Texas Health Science Center
at Houston, School of Nursing, *Houston*
(BSN)
The University of Texas Health Science Center
at San Antonio, School of Nursing, *San
Antonio* (BSN)
The University of Texas Medical Branch,
School of Nursing, *Galveston* (BSN)
The University of Texas-Pan American,
Department of Nursing, *Edinburg* (BSN)
University of the Incarnate Word, Program in
Nursing, *San Antonio* (BSN)
West Texas A&M University, Division of
Nursing, *Canyon* (BSN)

Utah
Southern Utah University, Department of
Nursing, *Cedar City* (BSN)
University of Utah, College of Nursing, *Salt
Lake City* (BS)
Westminster College, School of Nursing and
Health Sciences, *Salt Lake City* (BSN)

Vermont
Norwich University, Department of Nursing,
Northfield (BSN)
University of Vermont, Department of Nursing,
Burlington (BS)

Virgin Islands
University of the Virgin Islands, Division of
Nursing, *Saint Thomas* (BS)

Virginia
Eastern Mennonite University, Department of
Nursing, *Harrisonburg* (BSN)
George Mason University, College of Health
and Human Services, *Fairfax* (BSN)
Hampton University, School of Nursing,
Hampton (BS)
James Madison University, Department of
Nursing, *Harrisonburg* (BSN)
Jefferson College of Health Sciences, Nursing
Education Program, *Roanoke* (BSN)
Liberty University, Department of Nursing,
Lynchburg (BSN)
Lynchburg College, School of Health Sciences
and Human Performance, *Lynchburg* (BS)
Marymount University, School of Health
Professions, *Arlington* (BSN)
Old Dominion University, Department of
Nursing, *Norfolk* (BSN)
Radford University, School of Nursing, *Radford*
(BSN)
Shenandoah University, Division of Nursing,
Winchester (BSN)
Stratford University, School of Nursing, *Falls
Church* (BSN)
University of Virginia, School of Nursing,
Charlottesville (BSN)
The University of Virginia's College at Wise,
Department of Nursing, *Wise* (BSN)
Virginia Commonwealth University, School of
Nursing, *Richmond* (BS)

Washington
Intercollegiate College of Nursing/Washington
State University, *Spokane* (BSN)
Northwest University, The Mark and Huldah
Buntain School of Nursing, *Kirkland* (BS)
Pacific Lutheran University, School of Nursing,
Tacoma (BSN)
Seattle Pacific University, School of Health
Sciences, *Seattle* (BS)
Seattle University, College of Nursing, *Seattle*
(BSN)
University of Washington, School of Nursing,
Seattle (BSN)
Walla Walla University, School of Nursing,
College Place (BS)

West Virginia
Alderson-Broaddus College, Department of
Nursing, *Philippi* (BSN)
Marshall University, College of Health
Professions, *Huntington* (BSN)
Mountain State University, College of Nursing,
Beckley (BSN)
Shepherd University, Department of Nursing
Education, *Shepherdstown* (BSN)
University of Charleston, Department of
Nursing, *Charleston* (BSN)
West Liberty University, Department of Health
Sciences, *West Liberty* (BSN)
West Virginia University, School of Nursing,
Morgantown (BSN)
West Virginia Wesleyan College, Department of
Nursing, *Buckhannon* (BSN)

Wisconsin
Alverno College, Division of Nursing,
Milwaukee (BSN)
Bellin College, Nursing Program, *Green Bay*
(BSN)
Carroll University, Nursing Program, *Waukesha*
(BSN)
Columbia College of Nursing/Mount Mary
College Nursing Program, *Milwaukee* (BSN)
Concordia University Wisconsin, Program in
Nursing, *Mequon* (BSN)
Edgewood College, Program in Nursing,
Madison (BS)

Marian University, Nursing Studies Division,
Fond du Lac (BSN)
Marquette University, College of Nursing,
Milwaukee (BSN)
Milwaukee School of Engineering, School of
Nursing, *Milwaukee* (BSN)
University of Wisconsin-Eau Claire, College of
Nursing and Health Sciences, *Eau Claire*
(BSN)
University of Wisconsin-Madison, School of
Nursing, *Madison* (BS)
University of Wisconsin-Milwaukee, College of
Nursing, *Milwaukee* (BSN)
University of Wisconsin-Oshkosh, College of
Nursing, *Oshkosh* (BSN)
Viterbo University, School of Nursing, *La
Crosse* (BSN)
Wisconsin Lutheran College, Nursing Program,
Milwaukee (BSN)

Wyoming
University of Wyoming, Fay W. Whitney School
of Nursing, *Laramie* (BSN)

CANADA

Alberta
Athabasca University, Centre for Nursing and
Health Studies, *Athabasca* (BN)
University of Alberta, Faculty of Nursing,
Edmonton (BScN)
University of Calgary, Faculty of Nursing,
Calgary (BN)
University of Lethbridge, School of Health
Sciences, *Lethbridge* (BN)

British Columbia
Kwantlen University College, Faculty of
Community and Health Sciences, *Surrey*
(BSN)
Trinity Western University, Department of
Nursing, *Langley* (BScN)
University of Northern British Columbia,
Nursing Programme, *Prince George* (BScN)
Vancouver Island University, Department of
Nursing, *Nanaimo* (BScN)

Manitoba
Brandon University, School of Health Studies,
Brandon (BN)
University of Manitoba, Faculty of Nursing,
Winnipeg (BN)

New Brunswick
University of New Brunswick Fredericton,
Faculty of Nursing, *Fredericton* (BN)

Newfoundland and Labrador
Memorial University of Newfoundland, School
of Nursing, *St. John's* (BN)

Nova Scotia
Dalhousie University, School of Nursing,
Halifax (BScN)
St. Francis Xavier University, Department of
Nursing, *Antigonish* (BScN)

Ontario
Brock University, Department of Nursing, *St.
Catharines* (BScN)
Lakehead University, School of Nursing,
Thunder Bay (BScN)
McMaster University, School of Nursing,
Hamilton (BScN)
Nipissing University, Nursing Department,
North Bay (BScN)
Queen's University at Kingston, School of
Nursing, *Kingston* (BNSc)
Ryerson University, Program in Nursing,
Toronto (BScN)

BACCALAUREATE PROGRAMS
Generic Baccalaureate

Trent University, Nursing Program, *Peterborough* (BScN)

University of Ottawa, School of Nursing, *Ottawa* (BScN)

The University of Western Ontario, School of Nursing, *London* (BScN)

University of Windsor, Faculty of Nursing, *Windsor* (BScN)

York University, School of Nursing, Atkinson Faculty of Liberal and Professional Studies, *Toronto* (BScN)

Prince Edward Island
University of Prince Edward Island, School of Nursing, *Charlottetown* (BScN)

Quebec
McGill University, School of Nursing, *Montréal* (BScN)

Université du Québec à Trois-Rivières, Program in Nursing, *Trois-Rivières* (BSN)

Université du Québec en Outaouais, Département des Sciences Infirmières, *Gatineau* (BScN)

Université Laval, Faculty of Nursing, *Québec* (BScN)

Saskatchewan
University of Saskatchewan, College of Nursing, *Saskatoon* (BSN)

INTERNATIONAL NURSE TO BACCALAUREATE

U.S. AND U.S. TERRITORIES

Delaware
Wesley College, Nursing Program, *Dover* (BSN)

Wilmington University, College of Health Professions, *New Castle* (BSN)

Hawaii
Hawai'i Pacific University, College of Nursing and Health Sciences, *Honolulu* (BSN)

Iowa
Morningside College, Department of Nursing Education, *Sioux City* (BSN)

Massachusetts
Salem State College, Program in Nursing, *Salem* (BSN)

Nebraska
Nebraska Wesleyan University, Department of Nursing, *Lincoln* (BSN)

University of Nebraska Medical Center, College of Nursing, *Omaha* (BSN)

New Jersey
College of Saint Elizabeth, Department of Nursing, *Morristown* (BSN)

New York
College of Mount Saint Vincent, Department of Nursing, *Riverdale* (BS)

Daemen College, Department of Nursing, *Amherst* (BS)

Lehman College of the City University of New York, Department of Nursing, *Bronx* (BS)

Long Island University, Brooklyn Campus, School of Nursing, *Brooklyn* (BS)

The Sage Colleges, Department of Nursing, *Troy* (BS)

St. Francis College, Department of Nursing, *Brooklyn Heights* (BS)

North Dakota
University of North Dakota, College of Nursing, *Grand Forks* (BSN)

Oklahoma
Oklahoma Wesleyan University, Division of Nursing, *Bartlesville* (BSN)

Pennsylvania
Eastern University, Program in Nursing, *St. Davids* (BSN)

Edinboro University of Pennsylvania, Department of Nursing, *Edinboro* (BS)

Gannon University, Villa Maria School of Nursing, *Erie* (BSN)

Holy Family University, School of Nursing and Allied Health Professions, *Philadelphia* (BSN)

Marywood University, Department of Nursing, *Scranton* (BSN)

Neumann University, Program in Nursing and Health Sciences, *Aston* (BS)

Villanova University, College of Nursing, *Villanova* (BSN)

South Carolina
University of South Carolina Aiken, School of Nursing, *Aiken* (BSN)

South Dakota
Mount Marty College, Nursing Program, *Yankton* (BSN)

Texas
The University of Texas at Tyler, Program in Nursing, *Tyler* (BSN)

CANADA

Ontario
Ryerson University, Program in Nursing, *Toronto* (BScN)

University of Ottawa, School of Nursing, *Ottawa* (BScN)

LPN TO BACCALAUREATE

U.S. AND U.S. TERRITORIES

Arizona
University of Phoenix-Phoenix Campus, College of Health and Human Services, *Phoenix* (BSN)

University of Phoenix-Southern Arizona Campus, College of Health and Human Services, *Tucson* (BSN)

Arkansas
Arkansas State University, Department of Nursing, *Jonesboro, State University* (BSN)

Arkansas Tech University, Program in Nursing, *Russellville* (BSN)

Harding University, College of Nursing, *Searcy* (BSN)

University of Arkansas, Eleanor Mann School of Nursing, *Fayetteville* (BSN)

University of Arkansas at Monticello, School of Nursing, *Monticello* (BSN)

University of Arkansas for Medical Sciences, College of Nursing, *Little Rock* (BSN)

University of Central Arkansas, Department of Nursing, *Conway* (BSN)

California
Biola University, Department of Nursing, *La Mirada* (BSN)

California State University, Chico, School of Nursing, *Chico* (BSN)

California State University, Long Beach, Department of Nursing, *Long Beach* (BSN)

California State University, San Bernardino, Department of Nursing, *San Bernardino* (BSN)

California State University, Stanislaus, Department of Nursing, *Turlock* (BSN)

Dominican University of California, Program in Nursing, *San Rafael* (BSN)

Loma Linda University, School of Nursing, *Loma Linda* (BS)

National University, Department of Nursing, *La Jolla* (BSN)

University of Phoenix-Sacramento Valley Campus, College of Health and Human Services, *Sacramento* (BSN)

Colorado
Colorado State University-Pueblo, Department of Nursing, *Pueblo* (BSN)

Mesa State College, Department of Nursing and Radiologic Sciences, *Grand Junction* (BSN)

University of Phoenix-Denver Campus, College of Health and Human Services, *Lone Tree* (BSN)

Delaware
Delaware State University, Department of Nursing, *Dover* (BSN)

Wesley College, Nursing Program, *Dover* (BSN)

District of Columbia
Howard University, Division of Nursing, *Washington* (BSN)

Florida
Barry University, School of Nursing, *Miami Shores* (BSN)

Georgia
Armstrong Atlantic State University, Program in Nursing, *Savannah* (BSN)

Piedmont College, School of Nursing, *Demorest* (BSN)

Hawaii
Hawai'i Pacific University, College of Nursing and Health Sciences, *Honolulu* (BSN)

University of Phoenix-Hawaii Campus, College of Health and Human Services, *Honolulu* (BSN)

Idaho
Boise State University, Department of Nursing, *Boise* (BS)

Idaho State University, Department of Nursing, *Pocatello* (BSN)

Lewis-Clark State College, Division of Nursing and Health Sciences, *Lewiston* (BSN)

Illinois
Blessing-Rieman College of Nursing, *Quincy* (BSN)

Bradley University, Department of Nursing, *Peoria* (BSN, BSc PN)

Chicago State University, College of Nursing and Allied Health Professions, *Chicago* (BSN)

Indiana
Ball State University, School of Nursing, *Muncie* (BS)

Indiana State University, Department of Nursing, *Terre Haute* (BS)

Marian University, Department of Nursing and Nutritional Science, *Indianapolis* (BSN)

Iowa
Allen College, Program in Nursing, *Waterloo* (BSN)

Briar Cliff University, Department of Nursing, *Sioux City* (BSN)

Iowa Wesleyan College, Division of Health and Natural Sciences, *Mount Pleasant* (BSN)

Morningside College, Department of Nursing Education, *Sioux City* (BSN)

Kansas
Bethel College, Department of Nursing, *North Newton* (BSN)

Emporia State University, Newman Division of Nursing, *Emporia* (BSN)

Newman University, Division of Nursing, *Wichita* (BSN)

Southwestern College, Nursing Program, *Winfield* (BSN)

Washburn University, School of Nursing, *Topeka* (BSN)

Louisiana

McNeese State University, College of Nursing, *Lake Charles* (BSN)

Nicholls State University, Department of Nursing, *Thibodaux* (BSN)

Northwestern State University of Louisiana, College of Nursing, *Shreveport* (BSN)

Southeastern Louisiana University, School of Nursing, *Hammond* (BS)

University of Louisiana at Lafayette, College of Nursing, *Lafayette* (BSN)

University of Louisiana at Monroe, Nursing, *Monroe* (BS)

University of Phoenix–Louisiana Campus, College of Health and Human Services, *Metairie* (BSN)

Massachusetts

Salem State College, Program in Nursing, *Salem* (BSN)

Simmons College, Department of Nursing, *Boston* (BS)

Michigan

Lake Superior State University, Department of Nursing, *Sault Sainte Marie* (BSN)

Madonna University, College of Nursing and Health, *Livonia* (BSN)

Northern Michigan University, College of Nursing and Allied Health Science, *Marquette* (BSN)

Missouri

Cox College of Nursing and Health Sciences, Department of Nursing, *Springfield* (BSN)

Maryville University of Saint Louis, Nursing Program, School of Health Professions, *St. Louis* (BSN)

Missouri Southern State University, Department of Nursing, *Joplin* (BSN)

Missouri State University, Department of Nursing, *Springfield* (BSN)

Montana

Montana State University, College of Nursing, *Bozeman* (BSN)

Nebraska

Clarkson College, Master of Science in Nursing Program, *Omaha* (BSN)

Nebraska Methodist College, Department of Nursing, *Omaha* (BSN)

Union College, Division of Health Sciences, *Lincoln* (BSN)

University of Nebraska Medical Center, College of Nursing, *Omaha* (BSN)

New Jersey

William Paterson University of New Jersey, Department of Nursing, *Wayne* (BSN)

New York

Adelphi University, School of Nursing, *Garden City* (BS)

College of Mount Saint Vincent, Department of Nursing, *Riverdale* (BS)

Dominican College, Department of Nursing, *Orangeburg* (BSN)

Molloy College, Department of Nursing, *Rockville Centre* (BS)

Nazareth College of Rochester, Department of Nursing, *Rochester* (BS)

The Sage Colleges, Department of Nursing, *Troy* (BS)

North Carolina

North Carolina Agricultural and Technical State University, School of Nursing, *Greensboro* (BSN)

The University of North Carolina at Greensboro, School of Nursing, *Greensboro* (BSN)

Winston-Salem State University, Department of Nursing, *Winston-Salem* (BSN)

North Dakota

Dickinson State University, Department of Nursing, *Dickinson* (BSN)

North Dakota State University, Department of Nursing, *Fargo* (BSN)

University of Mary, Division of Nursing, *Bismarck* (BS)

University of North Dakota, College of Nursing, *Grand Forks* (BSN)

Ohio

Kent State University, College of Nursing, *Kent* (BSN)

Lourdes College, Nursing Department, *Sylvania* (BSN)

MedCentral College of Nursing, *Mansfield* (BS)

Otterbein College, Department of Nursing, *Westerville* (BSN)

The University of Akron, College of Nursing, *Akron* (BSN)

Oklahoma

Langston University, School of Nursing and Health Professions, *Langston* (BSN)

Northwestern Oklahoma State University, Division of Nursing, *Alva* (BSN)

Oklahoma Baptist University, School of Nursing, *Shawnee* (BSN)

Oklahoma Wesleyan University, Division of Nursing, *Bartlesville* (BSN)

Southern Nazarene University, School of Nursing, *Bethany* (BS)

University of Central Oklahoma, Department of Nursing, *Edmond* (BSN)

Pennsylvania

Alvernia University, Nursing, *Reading* (BSN)

Cedar Crest College, Department of Nursing, *Allentown* (BS)

East Stroudsburg University of Pennsylvania, Department of Nursing, *East Stroudsburg* (BS)

Holy Family University, School of Nursing and Allied Health Professions, *Philadelphia* (BSN)

Indiana University of Pennsylvania, Department of Nursing and Allied Health, *Indiana* (BSN)

La Salle University, School of Nursing and Health Sciences, *Philadelphia* (BSN)

Marywood University, Department of Nursing, *Scranton* (BSN)

Waynesburg University, Department of Nursing, *Waynesburg* (BSN)

South Carolina

University of South Carolina Aiken, School of Nursing, *Aiken* (BSN)

South Dakota

Mount Marty College, Nursing Program, *Yankton* (BSN)

Tennessee

Baptist College of Health Sciences, Nursing Division, *Memphis* (BSN)

Cumberland University, Rudy School of Nursing and Health Professions, *Lebanon* (BSN)

East Tennessee State University, College of Nursing, *Johnson City* (BSN)

Milligan College, Department of Nursing, *Milligan College* (BSN)

Tennessee State University, School of Nursing, *Nashville* (BSN)

Union University, School of Nursing, *Jackson* (BSN)

Texas

Prairie View A&M University, College of Nursing, *Houston* (BSN)

Tarleton State University, Department of Nursing, *Stephenville* (BSN)

The University of Texas at Tyler, Program in Nursing, *Tyler* (BSN)

West Texas A&M University, Division of Nursing, *Canyon* (BSN)

Utah

Southern Utah University, Department of Nursing, *Cedar City* (BSN)

Virgin Islands

University of the Virgin Islands, Division of Nursing, *Saint Thomas* (BS)

Virginia

Eastern Mennonite University, Department of Nursing, *Harrisonburg* (BSN)

George Mason University, College of Health and Human Services, *Fairfax* (BSN)

Hampton University, School of Nursing, *Hampton* (BS)

Shenandoah University, Division of Nursing, *Winchester* (BSN)

Washington

Pacific Lutheran University, School of Nursing, *Tacoma* (BSN)

Walla Walla University, School of Nursing, *College Place* (BS)

West Virginia

Mountain State University, College of Nursing, *Beckley* (BSN)

Wisconsin

Alverno College, Division of Nursing, *Milwaukee* (BSN)

CANADA

Manitoba

Brandon University, School of Health Studies, *Brandon* (BN)

Newfoundland and Labrador

Memorial University of Newfoundland, School of Nursing, *St. John's* (BN)

LPN TO RN BACCALAUREATE

U.S. AND U.S. TERRITORIES

Arkansas

Harding University, College of Nursing, *Searcy* (BSN)

University of Arkansas, Eleanor Mann School of Nursing, *Fayetteville* (BSN)

University of Central Arkansas, Department of Nursing, *Conway* (BSN)

California

California State University, Los Angeles, School of Nursing, *Los Angeles* (BSN)

California State University, Sacramento, Division of Nursing, *Sacramento* (BSN)

Dominican University of California, Program in Nursing, *San Rafael* (BSN)

BACCALAUREATE PROGRAMS
LPN to RN Baccalaureate

Loma Linda University, School of Nursing, *Loma Linda* (BS)

Point Loma Nazarene University, School of Nursing, *San Diego* (BSN)

Colorado

Colorado State University–Pueblo, Department of Nursing, *Pueblo* (BSN)

Mesa State College, Department of Nursing and Radiologic Sciences, *Grand Junction* (BSN)

Florida

Barry University, School of Nursing, *Miami Shores* (BSN)

Georgia

Georgia Southern University, School of Nursing, *Statesboro* (BSN)

Georgia Southwestern State University, School of Nursing, *Americus* (BSN)

Illinois

MacMurray College, Department of Nursing, *Jacksonville* (BSN)

Saint Xavier University, School of Nursing, *Chicago* (BSN)

Indiana

Indiana State University, Department of Nursing, *Terre Haute* (BS)

Indiana University–Purdue University Fort Wayne, Department of Nursing, *Fort Wayne* (BS)

Iowa

Iowa Wesleyan College, Division of Health and Natural Sciences, *Mount Pleasant* (BSN)

Kansas

Wichita State University, School of Nursing, *Wichita* (BSN)

Louisiana

Dillard University, Division of Nursing, *New Orleans* (BSN)

Grambling State University, School of Nursing, *Grambling* (BSN)

McNeese State University, College of Nursing, *Lake Charles* (BSN)

University of Louisiana at Monroe, Nursing, *Monroe* (BS)

Massachusetts

Salem State College, Program in Nursing, *Salem* (BSN)

Michigan

Lake Superior State University, Department of Nursing, *Sault Sainte Marie* (BSN)

Missouri

Chamberlain College of Nursing, *St. Louis* (BSN)

Cox College of Nursing and Health Sciences, Department of Nursing, *Springfield* (BSN)

Nebraska

Clarkson College, Master of Science in Nursing Program, *Omaha* (BSN)

Midland Lutheran College, Department of Nursing, *Fremont* (BSN)

University of Nebraska Medical Center, College of Nursing, *Omaha* (BSN)

New York

Adelphi University, School of Nursing, *Garden City* (BS)

College of Mount Saint Vincent, Department of Nursing, *Riverdale* (BS)

North Carolina

North Carolina Agricultural and Technical State University, School of Nursing, *Greensboro* (BSN)

The University of North Carolina at Greensboro, School of Nursing, *Greensboro* (BSN)

North Dakota

Dickinson State University, Department of Nursing, *Dickinson* (BSN)

University of North Dakota, College of Nursing, *Grand Forks* (BSN)

Ohio

Kent State University, College of Nursing, *Kent* (BSN)

Oklahoma

Northwestern Oklahoma State University, Division of Nursing, *Alva* (BSN)

University of Oklahoma Health Sciences Center, College of Nursing, *Oklahoma City* (BSN)

University of Tulsa, School of Nursing, *Tulsa* (BSN)

Pennsylvania

Alvernia University, Nursing, *Reading* (BSN)

Bloomsburg University of Pennsylvania, Department of Nursing, *Bloomsburg* (BSN)

Gannon University, Villa Maria School of Nursing, *Erie* (BSN)

Holy Family University, School of Nursing and Allied Health Professions, *Philadelphia* (BSN)

The University of Scranton, Department of Nursing, *Scranton* (BS)

Wilkes University, Department of Nursing, *Wilkes-Barre* (BS)

York College of Pennsylvania, Department of Nursing, *York* (BS)

South Dakota

Mount Marty College, Nursing Program, *Yankton* (BSN)

Presentation College, Department of Nursing, *Aberdeen* (BSN)

Tennessee

Belmont University, School of Nursing, *Nashville* (BSN)

Carson-Newman College, Division of Nursing, *Jefferson City* (BSN)

Cumberland University, Rudy School of Nursing and Health Professions, *Lebanon* (BSN)

Middle Tennessee State University, School of Nursing, *Murfreesboro* (BSN)

Milligan College, Department of Nursing, *Milligan College* (BSN)

The University of Tennessee at Martin, Department of Nursing, *Martin* (BSN)

Texas

The University of Texas at Tyler, Program in Nursing, *Tyler* (BSN)

Virginia

Hampton University, School of Nursing, *Hampton* (BS)

Shenandoah University, Division of Nursing, *Winchester* (BSN)

West Virginia

Alderson-Broaddus College, Department of Nursing, *Philippi* (BSN)

Fairmont State University, School of Nursing and Allied Health Administration, *Fairmont* (BSN)

Wisconsin

Concordia University Wisconsin, Program in Nursing, *Mequon* (BSN)

CANADA

Alberta

Athabasca University, Centre for Nursing and Health Studies, *Athabasca* (BN)

RN BACCALAUREATE

U.S. AND U.S. TERRITORIES

Alabama

Auburn University Montgomery, School of Nursing, *Montgomery* (BSN)

Jacksonville State University, College of Nursing and Health Sciences, *Jacksonville* (BSN)

Oakwood University, Department of Nursing, *Huntsville* (BS)

Tuskegee University, Program in Nursing, *Tuskegee* (BSN)

The University of Alabama, Capstone College of Nursing, *Tuscaloosa* (BSN)

The University of Alabama at Birmingham, School of Nursing, *Birmingham* (BSN)

The University of Alabama in Huntsville, College of Nursing, *Huntsville* (BSN)

University of Mobile, School of Nursing, *Mobile* (BSN)

University of North Alabama, College of Nursing and Allied Health, *Florence* (BSN)

University of South Alabama, College of Nursing, *Mobile* (BSN)

Alaska

University of Alaska Anchorage, School of Nursing, *Anchorage* (BS)

Arizona

Arizona State University at the Downtown Phoenix Campus, College of Nursing, *Phoenix* (BSN)

Grand Canyon University, College of Nursing and Health Sciences, *Phoenix* (BSN)

Northern Arizona University, School of Nursing, *Flagstaff* (BSN)

Arkansas

Arkansas State University, Department of Nursing, *Jonesboro, State University* (BSN)

Arkansas Tech University, Program in Nursing, *Russellville* (BSN)

Harding University, College of Nursing, *Searcy* (BSN)

Southern Arkansas University–Magnolia, Department of Nursing, *Magnolia* (BSN)

University of Arkansas, Eleanor Mann School of Nursing, *Fayetteville* (BSN)

University of Arkansas at Monticello, School of Nursing, *Monticello* (BSN)

University of Arkansas for Medical Sciences, College of Nursing, *Little Rock* (BSN)

University of Central Arkansas, Department of Nursing, *Conway* (BSN)

California

Biola University, Department of Nursing, *La Mirada* (BSN)

California State University, Bakersfield, Program in Nursing, *Bakersfield* (BSN)

California State University Channel Islands, Nursing Program, *Camarillo* (BSN)

California State University, Chico, School of Nursing, *Chico* (BSN)

California State University, Dominguez Hills, Program in Nursing, *Carson* (BSN)

California State University, Los Angeles, School of Nursing, *Los Angeles* (BSN)

California State University, San Bernardino, Department of Nursing, *San Bernardino* (BSN)

Dominican University of California, Program in Nursing, *San Rafael* (BSN)

Fresno Pacific University, RN to BSN Program, *Fresno* (BSN)

Holy Names University, Department of Nursing, *Oakland* (BSN)

Humboldt State University, Department of Nursing, *Arcata* (BSN)

Loma Linda University, School of Nursing, *Loma Linda* (BS)

National University, Department of Nursing, *La Jolla* (BSN)

Point Loma Nazarene University, School of Nursing, *San Diego* (BSN)

San Diego State University, School of Nursing, *San Diego* (BSN)

San Francisco State University, School of Nursing, *San Francisco* (BSN)

Sonoma State University, Department of Nursing, *Rohnert Park* (BSN)

University of Phoenix-Central Valley Campus, College of Health and Human Services, *Fresno* (BSN)

West Coast University, Nursing Programs, *North Hollywood* (BSN)

Colorado

Adams State College, Nursing Program, *Alamosa* (BSN)

Colorado State University-Pueblo, Department of Nursing, *Pueblo* (BSN)

Mesa State College, Department of Nursing and Radiologic Sciences, *Grand Junction* (BSN)

Metropolitan State College of Denver, Department of Health Professions, *Denver* (BS)

Regis University, School of Nursing, *Denver* (BSN)

University of Colorado at Colorado Springs, Beth-El College of Nursing and Health Sciences, *Colorado Springs* (BSN)

University of Colorado Denver, College of Nursing, *Denver* (BS)

University of Northern Colorado, School of Nursing, *Greeley* (BS)

Connecticut

Central Connecticut State University, Department of Nursing, *New Britain* (BSN)

Fairfield University, School of Nursing, *Fairfield* (BS)

Sacred Heart University, Program in Nursing, *Fairfield* (BS)

Southern Connecticut State University, Department of Nursing, *New Haven* (BS)

University of Hartford, College of Education, Nursing, and Health Professions, *West Hartford* (BSN)

Western Connecticut State University, Department of Nursing, *Danbury* (BS)

Delaware

University of Delaware, School of Nursing, *Newark* (BSN)

Wilmington University, College of Health Professions, *New Castle* (BSN)

District of Columbia

The Catholic University of America, School of Nursing, *Washington* (BSN)

Howard University, Division of Nursing, *Washington* (BSN)

Trinity (Washington) University, Nursing Program, *Washington* (BSN)

University of the District of Columbia, Nursing Education Program, *Washington* (BSN)

Florida

Barry University, School of Nursing, *Miami Shores* (BSN)

Bethune-Cookman University, School of Nursing, *Daytona Beach* (BSN)

Florida Atlantic University, Christine E. Lynn College of Nursing, *Boca Raton* (BS)

Florida Hospital College of Health Sciences, Department of Nursing, *Orlando* (BS)

Florida International University, Nursing Program, *Miami* (BSN)

Florida State University, College of Nursing, *Tallabassee* (BSN)

Indian River State College, Bachelor of Science in Nursing Program, *Fort Pierce* (BSN)

Nova Southeastern University, College of Allied Health and Nursing, *Fort Lauderdale* (BSN)

Palm Beach Atlantic University, School of Nursing, *West Palm Beach* (BSN)

St. Petersburg College, Department of Nursing, *St. Petersburg* (BSN)

South University, Nursing Program, *West Palm Beach* (BSN)

University of Central Florida, School of Nursing, *Orlando* (BSN)

University of Miami, School of Nursing and Health Studies, *Coral Gables* (BSN)

University of North Florida, School of Nursing, *Jacksonville* (BSN)

University of Phoenix-South Florida Campus, College of Health and Human Services, *Fort Lauderdale* (BSN)

The University of Tampa, Department of Nursing, *Tampa* (BSN)

Georgia

Albany State University, College of Sciences and Health Professions, *Albany* (BSN)

Armstrong Atlantic State University, Program in Nursing, *Savannah* (BSN)

Brenau University, School of Health and Science, *Gainesville* (BSN)

Clayton State University, Department of Nursing, *Morrow* (BSN)

Georgia Baptist College of Nursing of Mercer University, Department of Nursing, *Atlanta* (BSN)

Georgia College & State University, College of Health Sciences, *Milledgeville* (BSN)

Georgia Southwestern State University, School of Nursing, *Americus* (BSN)

Kennesaw State University, School of Nursing, *Kennesaw* (BSN)

LaGrange College, Department of Nursing, *LaGrange* (BSN)

Piedmont College, School of Nursing, *Demorest* (BSN)

Shorter College, School of Nursing, *Rome* (BSN)

Thomas University, Division of Nursing, *Thomasville* (BSN)

University of West Georgia, School of Nursing, *Carrollton* (BSN)

Valdosta State University, College of Nursing, *Valdosta* (BSN)

Guam

University of Guam, College of Nursing and Health Sciences, *Mangilao* (BSN)

Hawaii

Hawai'i Pacific University, College of Nursing and Health Sciences, *Honolulu* (BSN)

University of Hawaii at Hilo, Department in Nursing, *Hilo* (BSN)

University of Hawaii at Manoa, School of Nursing and Dental Hygiene, *Honolulu* (BSN)

Idaho

Boise State University, Department of Nursing, *Boise* (BS)

Illinois

Aurora University, School of Nursing, *Aurora* (BSN)

Blessing-Rieman College of Nursing, *Quincy* (BSN)

Bradley University, Department of Nursing, *Peoria* (BSN, BSc PN)

Chicago State University, College of Nursing and Allied Health Professions, *Chicago* (BSN)

Eastern Illinois University, Nursing Program, *Charleston* (BSN)

Elmhurst College, Deicke Center for Nursing Education, *Elmhurst* (BS)

Governors State University, College of Health and Human Services, *University Park* (BS)

Illinois State University, Mennonite College of Nursing, *Normal* (BSN)

Lakeview College of Nursing, *Danville* (BSN)

Loyola University Chicago, Marcella Niehoff School of Nursing, *Maywood* (BSN)

MacMurray College, Department of Nursing, *Jacksonville* (BSN)

Methodist College of Nursing, *Peoria* (BSN)

Millikin University, School of Nursing, *Decatur* (BSN)

Northern Illinois University, School of Nursing and Health Studies, *De Kalb* (BS)

North Park University, School of Nursing, *Chicago* (BS)

Rockford College, Department of Nursing, *Rockford* (BSN)

Saint Anthony College of Nursing, Saint Anthony College of Nursing, *Rockford* (BSN)

Saint Xavier University, School of Nursing, *Chicago* (BSN)

Trinity Christian College, Department of Nursing, *Palos Heights* (BSN)

Trinity College of Nursing and Health Sciences, *Rock Island* (BSN)

University of Illinois at Chicago, College of Nursing, *Chicago* (BSN)

Western Illinois University, School of Nursing, *Macomb* (BSN)

West Suburban College of Nursing, *Oak Park* (BSN)

Indiana

Anderson University, School of Nursing, *Anderson* (BSN)

Ball State University, School of Nursing, *Muncie* (BS)

Bethel College, Department of Nursing, *Mishawaka* (BSN)

Goshen College, Department of Nursing, *Goshen* (BSN)

Huntington University, Department of Nursing, *Huntington* (BSN)

Indiana State University, Department of Nursing, *Terre Haute* (BS)

Indiana University Bloomington, Department of Nursing-Bloomington Division, *Bloomington* (BSN)

Indiana University East, School of Nursing, *Richmond* (BSN)

Indiana University Northwest, School of Nursing and Health Professions, *Gary* (BSN)

Indiana University-Purdue University Fort Wayne, Department of Nursing, *Fort Wayne* (BS)

Indiana University-Purdue University Indianapolis, School of Nursing, *Indianapolis* (BSN)

Indiana University South Bend, Division of Nursing and Health Professions, *South Bend* (BSN)

Indiana University Southeast, Division of Nursing, *New Albany* (BSN)

Indiana Wesleyan University, School of Nursing, *Marion* (BSN)

Marian University, Department of Nursing and Nutritional Science, *Indianapolis* (BSN)

Purdue University, School of Nursing, *West Lafayette* (BS)

Purdue University Calumet, School of Nursing, *Hammond* (BS)

Purdue University North Central, Department of Nursing, *Westville* (BS)

University of Evansville, Department of Nursing, *Evansville* (BSN)

University of Southern Indiana, College of Nursing and Health Professions, *Evansville* (BSN)

Valparaiso University, College of Nursing, *Valparaiso* (BSN)

Vincennes University, Department of Nursing, *Vincennes* (BSN)

Iowa

Allen College, Program in Nursing, *Waterloo* (BSN)

Briar Cliff University, Department of Nursing, *Sioux City* (BSN)

Clarke College, Department of Nursing and Health, *Dubuque* (BS)

Coe College, Department of Nursing, *Cedar Rapids* (BSN)

Grand View University, Division of Nursing, *Des Moines* (BSN)

Iowa Wesleyan College, Division of Health and Natural Sciences, *Mount Pleasant* (BSN)

Morningside College, Department of Nursing Education, *Sioux City* (BSN)

St. Ambrose University, Program in Nursing (BSN), *Davenport* (BSN)

University of Dubuque, School of Professional Programs, *Dubuque* (BSN)

The University of Iowa, College of Nursing, *Iowa City* (BSN)

Upper Iowa University, RN-BSN Nursing Program, *Fayette* (BSN)

Kansas

Baker University, School of Nursing, *Topeka* (BSN)

Bethel College, Department of Nursing, *North Newton* (BSN)

Emporia State University, Newman Division of Nursing, *Emporia* (BSN)

Fort Hays State University, Department of Nursing, *Hays* (BSN)

Kansas Wesleyan University, Department of Nursing Education, *Salina* (BSN)

MidAmerica Nazarene University, Division of Nursing, *Olathe* (BSN)

Newman University, Division of Nursing, *Wichita* (BSN)

Pittsburg State University, Department of Nursing, *Pittsburg* (BSN)

Southwestern College, Nursing Program, *Winfield* (BSN)

The University of Kansas, School of Nursing, *Kansas City* (BSN)

University of Saint Mary, Bachelor of Science in Nursing Program, *Leavenworth* (BSN)

Washburn University, School of Nursing, *Topeka* (BSN)

Wichita State University, School of Nursing, *Wichita* (BSN)

Kentucky

Bellarmine University, Donna and Allan Lansing School of Nursing and Health Sciences, *Louisville* (BSN)

Eastern Kentucky University, Department of Baccalaureate and Graduate Nursing, *Richmond* (BSN)

Midway College, Program in Nursing (Baccalaureate), *Midway* (BSN)

Morehead State University, Department of Nursing, *Morehead* (BSN)

Murray State University, Program in Nursing, *Murray* (BSN)

Northern Kentucky University, Department of Nursing, *Highland Heights* (BSN)

University of Kentucky, Graduate School Programs in the College of Nursing, *Lexington* (BSN)

University of Louisville, School of Nursing, *Louisville* (BSN)

Louisiana

Dillard University, Division of Nursing, *New Orleans* (BSN)

Grambling State University, School of Nursing, *Grambling* (BSN)

Louisiana State University Health Sciences Center, School of Nursing, *New Orleans* (BSN)

Loyola University New Orleans, School of Nursing, *New Orleans* (BSN)

Nicholls State University, Department of Nursing, *Thibodaux* (BSN)

Northwestern State University of Louisiana, College of Nursing, *Shreveport* (BSN)

Our Lady of the Lake College, Division of Nursing, *Baton Rouge* (BSN)

Southeastern Louisiana University, School of Nursing, *Hammond* (BS)

University of Louisiana at Monroe, Nursing, *Monroe* (BS)

Maine

Saint Joseph's College of Maine, Department of Nursing, *Standish* (BSN)

University of Maine, School of Nursing, *Orono* (BSN)

University of Maine at Fort Kent, Department of Nursing, *Fort Kent* (BSN)

University of New England, Department of Nursing, *Biddeford* (BSN)

University of Southern Maine, College of Nursing and Health Professions, *Portland* (BS)

Maryland

Bowie State University, Department of Nursing, *Bowie* (BSN)

College of Notre Dame of Maryland, Department of Nursing, *Baltimore* (BS)

Coppin State University, Helene Fuld School of Nursing, *Baltimore* (BSN)

The Johns Hopkins University, School of Nursing, *Baltimore* (BS)

Salisbury University, Program in Nursing, *Salisbury* (BS)

Stevenson University, Nursing Division, *Stevenson* (BS)

Towson University, Department of Nursing, *Towson* (BS)

University of Maryland, Baltimore, Master's Program in Nursing, *Baltimore* (BSN)

Massachusetts

American International College, Division of Nursing, *Springfield* (BSN)

Anna Maria College, Department of Nursing, *Paxton* (BSN)

Atlantic Union College, Department of Nursing, *South Lancaster* (BS)

Curry College, Division of Nursing, *Milton* (BS)

Elms College, Division of Nursing, *Chicopee* (BS)

Emmanuel College, Department of Nursing, *Boston* (BSN)

Endicott College, Major in Nursing, *Beverly* (BS)

Fitchburg State College, Department of Nursing, *Fitchburg* (BS)

Northeastern University, School of Nursing, *Boston* (BSN)

Regis College, School of Nursing and Health Professions, *Weston* (BSN)

Simmons College, Department of Nursing, *Boston* (BS)

University of Massachusetts Boston, College of Nursing and Health Sciences, *Boston* (BS)

University of Massachusetts Dartmouth, College of Nursing, *North Dartmouth* (BSN)

University of Massachusetts Lowell, Department of Nursing, *Lowell* (BS)

Worcester State College, Department of Nursing, *Worcester* (BS)

Michigan

Davenport University, Division of Nursing, *Grand Rapids* (BSN)

Eastern Michigan University, School of Nursing, *Ypsilanti* (BSN)

Ferris State University, School of Nursing, *Big Rapids* (BSN)

Finlandia University, College of Professional Studies, *Hancock* (BSN)

Grand Valley State University, Kirkhof College of Nursing, *Allendale* (BSN)

Lake Superior State University, Department of Nursing, *Sault Sainte Marie* (BSN)

Madonna University, College of Nursing and Health, *Livonia* (BSN)

Michigan State University, College of Nursing, *East Lansing* (BSN)

Northern Michigan University, College of Nursing and Allied Health Science, *Marquette* (BSN)

Oakland University, School of Nursing, *Rochester* (BSN)

Saginaw Valley State University, Crystal M. Lange College of Nursing and Health Sciences, *University Center* (BSN)

University of Detroit Mercy, McAuley School of Nursing, *Detroit* (BSN)

University of Michigan, School of Nursing, *Ann Arbor* (BSN)

University of Michigan–Flint, Department of Nursing, *Flint* (BSN)

Western Michigan University, College of Health and Human Services, *Kalamazoo* (BSN)

Minnesota

Bemidji State University, Department of Nursing, *Bemidji* (BS)

Bethel University, Department of Nursing, *St. Paul* (BSN)

Minnesota State University Mankato, School of Nursing, *Mankato* (BS)

Minnesota State University Moorhead, School of Nursing and Healthcare Leadership, *Moorhead* (BSN)

St. Catherine University, Department of Nursing, *St. Paul* (BS)

Winona State University, College of Nursing and Health Sciences, *Winona* (BS)

Mississippi

Alcorn State University, School of Nursing, *Natchez* (BSN)

Mississippi College, School of Nursing, *Clinton* (BSN)

Mississippi University for Women, College of Nursing and Speech-Language Pathology, *Columbus* (BSN)

Missouri

Chamberlain College of Nursing, *St. Louis* (BSN)

College of the Ozarks, Armstrong McDonald School of Nursing, *Point Lookout* (BSN)

Cox College of Nursing and Health Sciences, Department of Nursing, *Springfield* (BSN)

Goldfarb School of Nursing at Barnes-Jewish College, *St. Louis* (BSN)

Graceland University, School of Nursing, *Independence* (BSN)

Lincoln University, Department of Nursing, *Jefferson City* (BSN)

Maryville University of Saint Louis, Nursing Program, School of Health Professions, *St. Louis* (BSN)

Missouri Southern State University, Department of Nursing, *Joplin* (BSN)

Missouri State University, Department of Nursing, *Springfield* (BSN)

Saint Louis University, School of Nursing, *St. Louis* (BSN)

Southeast Missouri State University, Department of Nursing, *Cape Girardeau* (BSN)

Southwest Baptist University, College of Nursing, *Bolivar* (BSN)

University of Central Missouri, Department of Nursing, *Warrensburg* (BS)

University of Missouri–Columbia, Sinclair School of Nursing, *Columbia* (BSN)

University of Missouri–Kansas City, School of Nursing, *Kansas City* (BSN)

University of Missouri–St. Louis, College of Nursing, *St. Louis* (BSN)

Webster University, Department of Nursing, *St. Louis* (BSN)

Montana

Montana State University–Northern, College of Nursing, *Havre* (BSN)

Salish Kootenai College, Nursing Department, *Pablo* (BS)

Nebraska

BryanLGH College of Health Sciences, School of Nursing, *Lincoln* (BSc PN)

Clarkson College, Master of Science in Nursing Program, *Omaha* (BSN)

Creighton University, School of Nursing, *Omaha* (BSN)

Midland Lutheran College, Department of Nursing, *Fremont* (BSN)

Nebraska Wesleyan University, Department of Nursing, *Lincoln* (BSN)

University of Nebraska Medical Center, College of Nursing, *Omaha* (BSN)

Nevada

Great Basin College, BSN Program, *Elko* (BSN)

Nevada State College at Henderson, Nursing Program, *Henderson* (BSN)

Touro University, School of Nursing, *Henderson* (BSN)

University of Nevada, Reno, Orvis School of Nursing, *Reno* (BSN)

New Hampshire

Franklin Pierce University, Master of Science in Nursing, *Rindge* (BS)

Rivier College, Division of Nursing, *Nashua* (BS)

Saint Anselm College, Department of Nursing, *Manchester* (BSN)

University of New Hampshire, Department of Nursing, *Durham* (BS)

New Jersey

Bloomfield College, Division of Nursing, *Bloomfield* (BS)

College of Saint Elizabeth, Department of Nursing, *Morristown* (BSN)

Fairleigh Dickinson University, Metropolitan Campus, Henry P. Becton School of Nursing and Allied Health, *Teaneck* (BSN)

Kean University, Department of Nursing, *Union* (BSN)

Monmouth University, Marjorie K. Unterberg School of Nursing, *West Long Branch* (BSN)

New Jersey City University, Department of Nursing, *Jersey City* (BSN)

Ramapo College of New Jersey, Master of Science in Nursing Program, *Mahwah* (BSN)

The Richard Stockton College of New Jersey, Program in Nursing, *Pomona* (BSN)

Rutgers, The State University of New Jersey, Camden College of Arts and Sciences, Department of Nursing, *Camden* (BS)

Rutgers, The State University of New Jersey, College of Nursing, *Newark* (BS)

Saint Peter's College, Nursing Program, *Jersey City* (BSN)

Seton Hall University, College of Nursing, *South Orange* (BSN)

Thomas Edison State College, School of Nursing, *Trenton* (BSN)

University of Medicine and Dentistry of New Jersey, School of Nursing, *Newark* (BSN)

William Paterson University of New Jersey, Department of Nursing, *Wayne* (BSN)

New Mexico

Eastern New Mexico University, Department of Allied Health-Nursing, *Portales* (BSN)

New Mexico State University, School of Nursing, *Las Cruces* (BSN)

University of New Mexico, College of Nursing, *Albuquerque* (BSN)

Western New Mexico University, Nursing Department, *Silver City* (BSN)

New York

Adelphi University, School of Nursing, *Garden City* (BS)

College of Mount Saint Vincent, Department of Nursing, *Riverdale* (BS)

The College of New Rochelle, School of Nursing, *New Rochelle* (BSN)

College of Staten Island of the City University of New York, Department of Nursing, *Staten Island* (BS)

Daemen College, Department of Nursing, *Amherst* (BS)

Dominican College, Department of Nursing, *Orangeburg* (BSN)

D'Youville College, Department of Nursing, *Buffalo* (BSN)

Elmira College, Program in Nursing Education, *Elmira* (BS)

Excelsior College, School of Nursing, *Albany* (BS)

Hartwick College, Department of Nursing, *Oneonta* (BS)

Hunter College of the City University of New York, Hunter-Bellevue School of Nursing, *New York* (BS)

Lehman College of the City University of New York, Department of Nursing, *Bronx* (BS)

Le Moyne College, Nursing Programs, *Syracuse* (BS)

Long Island University, Brooklyn Campus, School of Nursing, *Brooklyn* (BS)

Long Island University, C.W. Post Campus, Department of Nursing, *Brookville* (BS)

Mercy College, Program in Nursing, *Dobbs Ferry* (BS)

Molloy College, Department of Nursing, *Rockville Centre* (BS)

Mount Saint Mary College, Division of Nursing, *Newburgh* (BSN)

Nazareth College of Rochester, Department of Nursing, *Rochester* (BS)

New York City College of Technology of the City University of New York, Department of Nursing, *Brooklyn* (BS)

New York University, College of Nursing, *New York* (BS)

Niagara University, Department of Nursing, *Niagara Falls, Niagara University* (BS)

Roberts Wesleyan College, Division of Nursing, *Rochester* (BScN)

The Sage Colleges, Department of Nursing, *Troy* (BS)

St. John Fisher College, Advanced Practice Nursing Program, *Rochester* (BS)

St. Joseph's College, New York, Department of Nursing, *Brooklyn* (BSN)

State University of New York at Plattsburgh, Department of Nursing, *Plattsburgh* (BS)

State University of New York College of Agriculture and Technology at Morrisville, Division of Nursing, *Morrisville* (BS)

State University of New York Downstate Medical Center, College of Nursing, *Brooklyn* (BS)

State University of New York Empire State College, Bachelor of Science in Nursing Program, *Saratoga Springs* (BS)

State University of New York Institute of Technology, School of Nursing and Health Systems, *Utica* (BS)

Stony Brook University, State University of New York, School of Nursing, *Stony Brook* (BS)

University of Rochester, School of Nursing, *Rochester* (BS)

Utica College, Department of Nursing, *Utica* (BS)

York College of the City University of New York, Program in Nursing, *Jamaica* (BS)

North Carolina

Barton College, School of Nursing, *Wilson* (BSN)

Cabarrus College of Health Sciences, Louise Harkey School of Nursing, *Concord* (BSN)

Fayetteville State University, Program in Nursing, *Fayetteville* (BS)

Gardner-Webb University, School of Nursing, *Boiling Springs* (BSN)

North Carolina Agricultural and Technical State University, School of Nursing, *Greensboro* (BSN)

Queens University of Charlotte, Presbyterian School of Nursing, *Charlotte* (BSN)

The University of North Carolina at Chapel Hill, School of Nursing, *Chapel Hill* (BSN)

The University of North Carolina at Charlotte, School of Nursing, *Charlotte* (BSN)

The University of North Carolina at Greensboro, School of Nursing, *Greensboro* (BSN)

The University of North Carolina at Pembroke, Nursing Program, *Pembroke* (BSN)

The University of North Carolina Wilmington, School of Nursing, *Wilmington* (BS)

Western Carolina University, School of Nursing, *Cullowhee* (BSN)

Winston-Salem State University, Department of Nursing, *Winston-Salem* (BSN)

North Dakota

Dickinson State University, Department of Nursing, *Dickinson* (BSN)

Medcenter One College of Nursing, Medcenter One College of Nursing, *Bismarck* (BSN)

Minot State University, Department of Nursing, *Minot* (BSN)

University of Mary, Division of Nursing, *Bismarck* (BS)

University of North Dakota, College of Nursing, *Grand Forks* (BSN)

Ohio

Ashland University, Department of Nursing, *Ashland* (BSN)

Capital University, School of Nursing, *Columbus* (BSN)

Case Western Reserve University, Frances Payne Bolton School of Nursing, *Cleveland* (BSN)

Cedarville University, Department of Nursing, *Cedarville* (BSN)

Cleveland State University, School of Nursing, *Cleveland* (BSN)

Franciscan University of Steubenville, Department of Nursing, *Steubenville* (BSN)

Kent State University, College of Nursing, *Kent* (BSN)

Kettering College of Medical Arts, Division of Nursing, *Kettering* (BSN)

Lourdes College, Nursing Department, *Sylvania* (BSN)

Malone University, School of Nursing, *Canton* (BSN)

MedCentral College of Nursing, *Mansfield* (BS)

Mercy College of Northwest Ohio, Division of Nursing, *Toledo* (BSN)

Miami University, Department of Nursing, *Hamilton* (BSN)

Mount Carmel College of Nursing, Nursing Programs, *Columbus* (BSN)

Mount Vernon Nazarene University, School of Nursing and Health Sciences, *Mount Vernon* (BSN)

Notre Dame College, Nursing Department, *South Euclid* (BSN)

Ohio Northern University, Nursing Program, *Ada* (BSN)

Ohio University, School of Nursing, *Athens* (BSN)

Otterbein College, Department of Nursing, *Westerville* (BSN)

Shawnee State University, Department of Nursing, *Portsmouth* (BSN)

The University of Akron, College of Nursing, *Akron* (BSN)

University of Cincinnati, College of Nursing, *Cincinnati* (BSN)

University of Rio Grande, Holzer School of Nursing, *Rio Grande* (BSN)

Urbana University, BSN Completion Program, *Urbana* (BSN)

Walsh University, Department of Nursing, *North Canton* (BSN)

Wright State University, College of Nursing and Health, *Dayton* (BSN)

Oklahoma

Langston University, School of Nursing and Health Professions, *Langston* (BSN)

Northeastern State University, Department of Nursing, *Tahlequah* (BSN)

Northwestern Oklahoma State University, Division of Nursing, *Alva* (BSN)

Oklahoma Baptist University, School of Nursing, *Shawnee* (BSN)

Oklahoma Wesleyan University, Division of Nursing, *Bartlesville* (BSN)

Oral Roberts University, Anna Vaughn School of Nursing, *Tulsa* (BSN)

University of Central Oklahoma, Department of Nursing, *Edmond* (BSN)

University of Tulsa, School of Nursing, *Tulsa* (BSN)

Oregon

Oregon Health & Science University, School of Nursing, *Portland* (BS)

Pennsylvania

Alvernia University, Nursing, *Reading* (BSN)

Bloomsburg University of Pennsylvania, Department of Nursing, *Bloomsburg* (BSN)

California University of Pennsylvania, Department of Nursing, *California* (BSN)

Cedar Crest College, Department of Nursing, *Allentown* (BS)

Chatham University, Program in Nursing, *Pittsburgh* (BSN)

Clarion University of Pennsylvania, School of Nursing, *Oil City* (BSN)

DeSales University, Department of Nursing and Health, *Center Valley* (BSN)

Drexel University, College of Nursing and Health Professions, *Philadelphia* (BSN)

East Stroudsburg University of Pennsylvania, Department of Nursing, *East Stroudsburg* (BS)

Gannon University, Villa Maria School of Nursing, *Erie* (BSN)

Gwynedd-Mercy College, School of Nursing, *Gwynedd Valley* (BSN)

Holy Family University, School of Nursing and Allied Health Professions, *Philadelphia* (BSN)

Indiana University of Pennsylvania, Department of Nursing and Allied Health, *Indiana* (BSN)

Kutztown University of Pennsylvania, Department of Nursing, *Kutztown* (BSN)

La Roche College, Department of Nursing and Nursing Management, *Pittsburgh* (BSN)

La Salle University, School of Nursing and Health Sciences, *Philadelphia* (BSN)

Mansfield University of Pennsylvania, Robert Packer Department of Health Sciences, *Mansfield* (BSN)

Marywood University, Department of Nursing, *Scranton* (BSN)

Millersville University of Pennsylvania, Department of Nursing, *Millersville* (BSN)

Misericordia University, Department of Nursing, *Dallas* (BSN)

Moravian College, St. Luke's School of Nursing, *Bethlehem* (BS)

Neumann University, Program in Nursing and Health Sciences, *Aston* (BS)

Penn State University Park, School of Nursing, *State College, University Park* (BS)

Pennsylvania College of Technology, School of Health Sciences, *Williamsport* (BSN)

Saint Francis University, Department of Nursing, *Loretto* (BSN)

Slippery Rock University of Pennsylvania, Department of Nursing, *Slippery Rock* (BSN)

Temple University, Department of Nursing, *Philadelphia* (BSN)

Thomas Jefferson University, Department of Nursing, *Philadelphia* (BSN)

University of Pennsylvania, School of Nursing, *Philadelphia* (BSN)

University of Pittsburgh, School of Nursing, *Pittsburgh* (BSN)

University of Pittsburgh at Bradford, Department of Nursing, *Bradford* (BSN)

The University of Scranton, Department of Nursing, *Scranton* (BS)

Villanova University, College of Nursing, *Villanova* (BSN)

Widener University, School of Nursing, *Chester* (BSN)

Wilkes University, Department of Nursing, *Wilkes-Barre* (BS)

York College of Pennsylvania, Department of Nursing, *York* (BS)

Puerto Rico

Universidad Adventista de las Antillas, Department of Nursing, *Mayagüez* (BSN)

Rhode Island

Rhode Island College, Department of Nursing, *Providence* (BSN)

Salve Regina University, Department of Nursing, *Newport* (BS)

University of Rhode Island, College of Nursing, *Kingston* (BS)

South Carolina

Charleston Southern University, Wingo School of Nursing, *Charleston* (BSN)

Clemson University, School of Nursing, *Clemson* (BS)

Lander University, School of Nursing, *Greenwood* (BSN)

South Carolina State University, Department of Nursing, *Orangeburg* (BSN)

University of South Carolina Aiken, School of Nursing, *Aiken* (BSN)

University of South Carolina Beaufort, Nursing Program, *Beaufort* (BSN)

University of South Carolina Upstate, Mary Black School of Nursing, *Spartanburg* (BSN)

South Dakota

Mount Marty College, Nursing Program, *Yankton* (BSN)

Presentation College, Department of Nursing, *Aberdeen* (BSN)

South Dakota State University, College of Nursing, *Brookings* (BS)

Tennessee

Aquinas College, Department of Nursing, *Nashville* (BSN)

Austin Peay State University, School of Nursing, *Clarksville* (BSN)

Baptist College of Health Sciences, Nursing Division, *Memphis* (BSN)

Belmont University, School of Nursing, *Nashville* (BSN)

Carson-Newman College, Division of Nursing, *Jefferson City* (BSN)

Cumberland University, Rudy School of Nursing and Health Professions, *Lebanon* (BSN)

Lincoln Memorial University, Department of Nursing, *Harrogate* (BSN)

Middle Tennessee State University, School of Nursing, *Murfreesboro* (BSN)

Milligan College, Department of Nursing, *Milligan College* (BSN)

Tennessee State University, School of Nursing, *Nashville* (BSN)

Tennessee Technological University, School of Nursing, *Cookeville* (BSN)

Tennessee Wesleyan College, Fort Sanders Nursing Department, *Knoxville* (BSN)

Union University, School of Nursing, *Jackson* (BSN)

University of Memphis, Loewenberg School of Nursing, *Memphis* (BSN)

Texas

Angelo State University, Department of Nursing, *San Angelo* (BSN)

Lamar University, Department of Nursing, *Beaumont* (BSN)

Lubbock Christian University, Department of Nursing, *Lubbock* (BSN)

Midwestern State University, Nursing Program, *Wichita Falls* (BSN)

Patty Hanks Shelton School of Nursing, *Abilene* (BSN)

Prairie View A&M University, College of Nursing, *Houston* (BSN)

Stephen F. Austin State University, Division of Nursing, *Nacogdoches* (BSN)

Texas A&M International University, Canseco School of Nursing, *Laredo* (BSN)

Texas A&M University-Corpus Christi, School of Nursing and Health Sciences, *Corpus Christi* (BSN)

Texas Woman's University, College of Nursing, *Denton* (BS)

University of Houston-Victoria, School of Nursing, *Victoria* (BSN)

The University of Texas at Arlington, School of Nursing, *Arlington* (BSN)

The University of Texas at Austin, School of Nursing, *Austin* (BSN)

The University of Texas at El Paso, School of Nursing, *El Paso* (BSN)

The University of Texas at Tyler, Program in Nursing, *Tyler* (BSN)

The University of Texas Medical Branch, School of Nursing, *Galveston* (BSN)

The University of Texas-Pan American, Department of Nursing, *Edinburg* (BSN)

Utah

Brigham Young University, College of Nursing, *Provo* (BS)

Southern Utah University, Department of Nursing, *Cedar City* (BSN)

University of Utah, College of Nursing, *Salt Lake City* (BS)

Westminster College, School of Nursing and Health Sciences, *Salt Lake City* (BSN)

Vermont

Norwich University, Department of Nursing, *Northfield* (BSN)

Southern Vermont College, Department of Nursing, *Bennington* (BSN)

Virgin Islands

University of the Virgin Islands, Division of Nursing, *Saint Thomas* (BS)

Virginia

Eastern Mennonite University, Department of Nursing, *Harrisonburg* (BSN)

ECPI College of Technology, BSN Program, *Virginia Beach* (BSN)

George Mason University, College of Health and Human Services, *Fairfax* (BSN)

Hampton University, School of Nursing, *Hampton* (BS)

Jefferson College of Health Sciences, Nursing Education Program, *Roanoke* (BSN)

Liberty University, Department of Nursing, *Lynchburg* (BSN)

Marymount University, School of Health Professions, *Arlington* (BSN)

Norfolk State University, Department of Nursing, *Norfolk* (BSN)

Old Dominion University, Department of Nursing, *Norfolk* (BSN)

Radford University, School of Nursing, *Radford* (BSN)

Shenandoah University, Division of Nursing, *Winchester* (BSN)

University of Virginia, School of Nursing, *Charlottesville* (BSN)

The University of Virginia's College at Wise, Department of Nursing, *Wise* (BSN)

Washington

Gonzaga University, Department of Nursing, *Spokane* (BSN)

Intercollegiate College of Nursing/Washington State University, *Spokane* (BSN)

Seattle Pacific University, School of Health Sciences, *Seattle* (BS)

Walla Walla University, School of Nursing, *College Place* (BS)

West Virginia

Alderson-Broaddus College, Department of Nursing, *Philippi* (BSN)

Bluefield State College, Program in Nursing, *Bluefield* (BSN)

Fairmont State University, School of Nursing and Allied Health Administration, *Fairmont* (BSN)

Mountain State University, College of Nursing, *Beckley* (BSN)

Shepherd University, Department of Nursing Education, *Shepherdstown* (BSN)

West Virginia University, School of Nursing, *Morgantown* (BSN)

Wisconsin

Alverno College, Division of Nursing, *Milwaukee* (BSN)

Columbia College of Nursing/Mount Mary College Nursing Program, *Milwaukee* (BSN)

Concordia University Wisconsin, Program in Nursing, *Mequon* (BSN)

Maranatha Baptist Bible College, Nursing Department, *Watertown* (BSN)

Milwaukee School of Engineering, School of Nursing, *Milwaukee* (BSN)

University of Wisconsin-Eau Claire, College of Nursing and Health Sciences, *Eau Claire* (BSN)

University of Wisconsin-Green Bay, BSN-LINC Online RN-BSN Program, *Green Bay* (BSN)

University of Wisconsin-Madison, School of Nursing, *Madison* (BS)

University of Wisconsin-Milwaukee, College of Nursing, *Milwaukee* (BSN)

University of Wisconsin-Oshkosh, College of Nursing, *Oshkosh* (BSN)

Viterbo University, School of Nursing, *La Crosse* (BSN)

CANADA

Alberta

Athabasca University, Centre for Nursing and Health Studies, *Athabasca* (BN)

University of Alberta, Faculty of Nursing, *Edmonton* (BScN)

University of Calgary, Faculty of Nursing, *Calgary* (BN)

University of Lethbridge, School of Health Sciences, *Lethbridge* (BN)

British Columbia

British Columbia Institute of Technology, School of Health Sciences, *Burnaby* (BSN)

Kwantlen University College, Faculty of Community and Health Sciences, *Surrey* (BSN)

University of Northern British Columbia, Nursing Programme, *Prince George* (BScN)

Vancouver Island University, Department of Nursing, *Nanaimo* (BScN)

Manitoba

Brandon University, School of Health Studies, *Brandon* (BN)

University of Manitoba, Faculty of Nursing, *Winnipeg* (BN)

New Brunswick

Université de Moncton, School of Nursing, *Moncton* (BScN)

Newfoundland and Labrador

Memorial University of Newfoundland, School of Nursing, *St. John's* (BN)

Nova Scotia

Dalhousie University, School of Nursing, *Halifax* (BScN)

St. Francis Xavier University, Department of Nursing, *Antigonish* (BScN)

Ontario

Brock University, Department of Nursing, *St. Catharines* (BScN)

Lakehead University, School of Nursing, *Thunder Bay* (BScN)

McMaster University, School of Nursing, *Hamilton* (BScN)

Queen's University at Kingston, School of Nursing, *Kingston* (BNSc)

Ryerson University, Program in Nursing, *Toronto* (BScN)

University of Ottawa, School of Nursing, *Ottawa* (BScN)

The University of Western Ontario, School of Nursing, *London* (BScN)

York University, School of Nursing, Atkinson Faculty of Liberal and Professional Studies, *Toronto* (BScN)

Quebec

McGill University, School of Nursing, *Montréal* (BScN)

Université de Montréal, Faculty of Nursing, *Montréal* (BScN)

Université de Sherbrooke, Department of Nursing, *Sherbrooke* (BScN)

Université du Québec à Chicoutimi, Program in Nursing, *Chicoutimi* (BNSc)

Université du Québec à Rimouski, Program in Nursing, *Rimouski* (BScN)

Université du Québec à Trois-Rivières, Program in Nursing, *Trois-Rivières* (BSN)

Université du Québec en Outaouais, Département des Sciences Infirmières, *Gatineau* (BScN)

Université Laval, Faculty of Nursing, *Québec* (BScN)

Saskatchewan

University of Saskatchewan, College of Nursing, *Saskatoon* (BSN)

RPN TO BACCALAUREATE

U.S. AND U.S. TERRITORIES

California

San Jose State University, School of Nursing, *San Jose* (BS)

Maryland

Towson University, Department of Nursing, *Towson* (BS)

Massachusetts

Curry College, Division of Nursing, *Milton* (BS)

Michigan

Lake Superior State University, Department of Nursing, *Sault Sainte Marie* (BSN)

Nebraska

University of Nebraska Medical Center, College of Nursing, *Omaha* (BSN)

BACCALAUREATE PROGRAMS
RPN to Baccalaureate

New York

St. Francis College, Department of Nursing, *Brooklyn Heights* (BS)

Ohio

Franciscan University of Steubenville, Department of Nursing, *Steubenville* (BSN)

West Virginia

Mountain State University, College of Nursing, *Beckley* (BSN)

CANADA

Alberta

University of Alberta, Faculty of Nursing, *Edmonton* (BScN)

British Columbia

British Columbia Institute of Technology, School of Health Sciences, *Burnaby* (BSN)

Ontario

Ryerson University, Program in Nursing, *Toronto* (BScN)

University of Ottawa, School of Nursing, *Ottawa* (BScN)

MASTER'S DEGREE PROGRAMS

ACCELERATED AD/RN TO MASTER'S

U.S. AND U.S. TERRITORIES

Alabama
Spring Hill College, Division of Nursing, *Mobile* (MSN)

California
California State University, Fullerton, Department of Nursing, *Fullerton* (MSN)
University of San Francisco, School of Nursing, *San Francisco* (MSN)
Western University of Health Sciences, College of Graduate Nursing, *Pomona* (MSN)

Delaware
Wesley College, Nursing Program, *Dover* (MSN)
Wilmington University, College of Health Professions, *New Castle* (MSN, MSN/MBA, MSN/MS)

Florida
Florida International University, Nursing Program, *Miami* (MSN)
Florida Southern College, Department of Nursing, *Lakeland* (MSN)

Georgia
Albany State University, College of Sciences and Health Professions, *Albany* (MSN)
Brenau University, School of Health and Science, *Gainesville* (MSN)

Idaho
Idaho State University, Department of Nursing, *Pocatello* (MS)

Kansas
The University of Kansas, School of Nursing, *Kansas City* (MS, MS/MHSA, MS/MPH)

Kentucky
Frontier School of Midwifery and Family Nursing, Nursing Degree Programs, *Hyden* (MSN)

Massachusetts
Regis College, School of Nursing and Health Professions, *Weston* (MSN)
Simmons College, Department of Nursing, *Boston* (MS)

Michigan
Ferris State University, School of Nursing, *Big Rapids* (MSN, MSN/MBA)
Madonna University, College of Nursing and Health, *Livonia* (MSN, MSN/MBA)
University of Detroit Mercy, McAuley School of Nursing, *Detroit* (MSN)

Mississippi
University of Mississippi Medical Center, Program in Nursing, *Jackson* (MSN)

Missouri
Missouri State University, Department of Nursing, *Springfield* (MSN)

Nebraska
Nebraska Wesleyan University, Department of Nursing, *Lincoln* (MSN)

New York
Daemen College, Department of Nursing, *Amherst* (MS)

State University of New York Institute of Technology, School of Nursing and Health Systems, *Utica* (MS)
University of Rochester, School of Nursing, *Rochester* (MS, MSN/PhD)

Ohio
Case Western Reserve University, Frances Payne Bolton School of Nursing, *Cleveland* (MSN, MSN/MA, MSN/MBA, MSN/MPH)

Pennsylvania
DeSales University, Department of Nursing and Health, *Center Valley* (MSN, MSN/MBA)
Gannon University, Villa Maria School of Nursing, *Erie* (MSN)
University of Pennsylvania, School of Nursing, *Philadelphia* (MSN, MSN/MPH, MSN/PhD)
The University of Scranton, Department of Nursing, *Scranton* (MS)
Wilkes University, Department of Nursing, *Wilkes-Barre* (MS)

Tennessee
Middle Tennessee State University, School of Nursing, *Murfreesboro* (MSN)
Vanderbilt University, School of Nursing, *Nashville* (MSN, MSN/MDIV, MSN/MTS)

Texas
Texas A&M University–Corpus Christi, School of Nursing and Health Sciences, *Corpus Christi* (MSN)
The University of Texas at Tyler, Program in Nursing, *Tyler* (MSN, MSN/MBA)

Wisconsin
Marquette University, College of Nursing, *Milwaukee* (MSN, MSN/MBA)

ACCELERATED MASTER'S

U.S. AND U.S. TERRITORIES

Alabama
University of South Alabama, College of Nursing, *Mobile* (MSN)

California
California State University, Fresno, Department of Nursing, *Fresno* (MSN)
California State University, Long Beach, Department of Nursing, *Long Beach* (MSN, MSN/MPH)
University of Phoenix-Sacramento Valley Campus, College of Health and Human Services, *Sacramento* (MSN, MSN/MHA)
Western University of Health Sciences, College of Graduate Nursing, *Pomona* (MSN)

Georgia
Albany State University, College of Sciences and Health Professions, *Albany* (MSN)
Medical College of Georgia, School of Nursing, *Augusta* (MSN)

Hawaii
University of Hawaii at Manoa, School of Nursing and Dental Hygiene, *Honolulu* (MS, MSN/MBA)

Illinois
Benedictine University, Department of Nursing, *Lisle* (MSN)

Lewis University, Program in Nursing, *Romeoville* (MSN, MSN/MBA)

Massachusetts
Boston College, William F. Connell School of Nursing, *Chestnut Hill* (MS, MSN/MA, MSN/MBA, MSN/PhD)
Regis College, School of Nursing and Health Professions, *Weston* (MSN)
Simmons College, Department of Nursing, *Boston* (MS)
University of Massachusetts Lowell, Department of Nursing, *Lowell* (MS)

Nebraska
Nebraska Wesleyan University, Department of Nursing, *Lincoln* (MSN)

New York
Roberts Wesleyan College, Division of Nursing, *Rochester* (M Sc N)
The Sage Colleges, Department of Nursing, *Troy* (MS)

Ohio
Ursuline College, The Breen School of Nursing, *Pepper Pike* (MSN)

Oklahoma
Southern Nazarene University, School of Nursing, *Bethany* (MS)

Pennsylvania
Carlow University, School of Nursing, *Pittsburgh* (MSN)
Thomas Jefferson University, Department of Nursing, *Philadelphia* (MSN)
Villanova University, College of Nursing, *Villanova* (MSN)
Waynesburg University, Department of Nursing, *Waynesburg* (MSN, MSN/MBA)

Tennessee
Vanderbilt University, School of Nursing, *Nashville* (MSN, MSN/MDIV, MSN/MTS)

Washington
Pacific Lutheran University, School of Nursing, *Tacoma* (MSN, MSN/MBA)

Wisconsin
Cardinal Stritch University, Ruth S. Coleman College of Nursing, *Milwaukee* (MSN)

CANADA

Quebec
Université Laval, Faculty of Nursing, *Québec* (MSN)

ACCELERATED MASTER'S FOR NON-NURSING COLLEGE GRADUATES

U.S. AND U.S. TERRITORIES

Alabama
The University of Alabama at Birmingham, School of Nursing, *Birmingham* (MSN, MSN/MPH)

California
Azusa Pacific University, School of Nursing, *Azusa* (MSN)
California State University, Fullerton, Department of Nursing, *Fullerton* (MSN)

MASTER'S DEGREE PROGRAMS
Accelerated Master's for Non-Nursing College Graduates

Loma Linda University, School of Nursing, *Loma Linda* (MS, MS/MA, MS/MPH)
San Francisco State University, School of Nursing, *San Francisco* (MSN)
Sonoma State University, Department of Nursing, *Rohnert Park* (MSN)
University of San Diego, Hahn School of Nursing and Health Science, *San Diego* (MSN, MSN/MBA)
University of San Francisco, School of Nursing, *San Francisco* (MSN)
Western University of Health Sciences, College of Graduate Nursing, *Pomona* (MSN)

Georgia
Medical College of Georgia, School of Nursing, *Augusta* (MSN)

Illinois
Millikin University, School of Nursing, *Decatur* (MSN)

Indiana
University of Indianapolis, School of Nursing, *Indianapolis* (MSN, MSN/MBA)

Maryland
University of Maryland, Baltimore, Master's Program in Nursing, *Baltimore* (MS, MSN/MBA, MSN/MPH, MSN/JD)

Massachusetts
Boston College, William F. Connell School of Nursing, *Chestnut Hill* (MS, MSN/MA, MSN/MBA, MSN/PhD)
Northeastern University, School of Nursing, *Boston* (MS, MSN/MBA)
Regis College, School of Nursing and Health Professions, *Weston* (MSN)
Salem State College, Program in Nursing, *Salem* (MSN, MSN/MBA)
Simmons College, Department of Nursing, *Boston* (MS)
University of Massachusetts Worcester, Graduate School of Nursing, *Worcester* (MS)

New York
Columbia University, School of Nursing, *New York* (MS, MSN/MBA, MSN/MPH)
Mercy College, Program in Nursing, *Dobbs Ferry* (MS)
University of Rochester, School of Nursing, *Rochester* (MS, MSN/PhD)

North Carolina
East Carolina University, College of Nursing, *Greenville* (MSN)

Ohio
College of Mount St. Joseph, Department of Nursing, *Cincinnati* (MN)
The Ohio State University, College of Nursing, *Columbus* (MS, MS/MPH)
University of Cincinnati, College of Nursing, *Cincinnati* (MSN, MSN/MBA, MSN/PhD)

Pennsylvania
University of Pennsylvania, School of Nursing, *Philadelphia* (MSN, MSN/MPH, MSN/PhD)

Tennessee
The University of Tennessee Health Science Center, College of Nursing, *Memphis* (MSN)
Vanderbilt University, School of Nursing, *Nashville* (MSN, MSN/MDIV, MSN/MTS)

Virginia
Virginia Commonwealth University, School of Nursing, *Richmond* (MS)

Wisconsin
Marquette University, College of Nursing, *Milwaukee* (MSN, MSN/MBA)

ACCELERATED MASTER'S FOR NURSES WITH NON-NURSING DEGREES

U.S. AND U.S. TERRITORIES

California
Azusa Pacific University, School of Nursing, *Azusa* (MSN)
California State University, Los Angeles, School of Nursing, *Los Angeles* (MSN)
San Francisco State University, School of Nursing, *San Francisco* (MSN)

Connecticut
University of Connecticut, School of Nursing, *Storrs* (MS, MS/MBA)

Illinois
Bradley University, Department of Nursing, *Peoria* (MSN)
Lewis University, Program in Nursing, *Romeoville* (MSN, MSN/MBA)
West Suburban College of Nursing, *Oak Park* (MSN)

Massachusetts
Boston College, William F. Connell School of Nursing, *Chestnut Hill* (MS, MSN/MA, MSN/MBA, MSN/PhD)
Regis College, School of Nursing and Health Professions, *Weston* (MSN)
Simmons College, Department of Nursing, *Boston* (MS)

Mississippi
Delta State University, School of Nursing, *Cleveland* (MSN)

New Jersey
Kean University, Department of Nursing, *Union* (MSN, MSN/MPA)
Seton Hall University, College of Nursing, *South Orange* (MSN, MSN/MA, MSN/MBA)

New York
Columbia University, School of Nursing, *New York* (MS, MSN/MBA, MSN/MPH)
Mercy College, Program in Nursing, *Dobbs Ferry* (MS)
Roberts Wesleyan College, Division of Nursing, *Rochester* (M Sc N)

Oklahoma
Southern Nazarene University, School of Nursing, *Bethany* (MS)

Pennsylvania
Waynesburg University, Department of Nursing, *Waynesburg* (MSN, MSN/MBA)

Tennessee
University of Memphis, Loewenberg School of Nursing, *Memphis* (MSN)
The University of Tennessee, College of Nursing, *Knoxville* (MSN)
Vanderbilt University, School of Nursing, *Nashville* (MSN, MSN/MDIV, MSN/MTS)

Washington
Intercollegiate College of Nursing/Washington State University, *Spokane* (MN)
Seattle University, College of Nursing, *Seattle* (MSN)

Wisconsin
University of Wisconsin–Milwaukee, College of Nursing, *Milwaukee* (MS, MS/MBA)

ACCELERATED RN TO MASTER'S

U.S. AND U.S. TERRITORIES

California
California State University, Los Angeles, School of Nursing, *Los Angeles* (MSN)

Delaware
Wesley College, Nursing Program, *Dover* (MSN)

Georgia
Brenau University, School of Health and Science, *Gainesville* (MSN)

Illinois
Lewis University, Program in Nursing, *Romeoville* (MSN, MSN/MBA)

Indiana
Purdue University Calumet, School of Nursing, *Hammond* (MS)

Iowa
The University of Iowa, College of Nursing, *Iowa City* (MSN, MSN/MBA, MSN/MPH)

Kentucky
Spalding University, School of Nursing, *Louisville* (MSN)

Massachusetts
Regis College, School of Nursing and Health Professions, *Weston* (MSN)
Simmons College, Department of Nursing, *Boston* (MS)
University of Massachusetts Lowell, Department of Nursing, *Lowell* (MS)

Michigan
Madonna University, College of Nursing and Health, *Livonia* (MSN, MSN/MBA)
University of Michigan, School of Nursing, *Ann Arbor* (MS, MSN/MBA, MSN/MPH)

Minnesota
Minnesota State University Mankato, School of Nursing, *Mankato* (MSN, MSN/MS)

Missouri
Maryville University of Saint Louis, Nursing Program, School of Health Professions, *St. Louis* (MSN)

Nebraska
Nebraska Wesleyan University, Department of Nursing, *Lincoln* (MSN)

New Jersey
Fairleigh Dickinson University, Metropolitan Campus, Henry P. Becton School of Nursing and Allied Health, *Teaneck* (MSN)
Felician College, Division of Nursing and Health Management, *Lodi* (MSN, MA/MSM)
Monmouth University, Marjorie K. Unterberg School of Nursing, *West Long Branch* (MSN)

New York
Daemen College, Department of Nursing, *Amherst* (MS)
Mercy College, Program in Nursing, *Dobbs Ferry* (MS)
The Sage Colleges, Department of Nursing, *Troy* (MS)

State University of New York Institute of Technology, School of Nursing and Health Systems, *Utica* (MS)

State University of New York Upstate Medical University, College of Nursing, *Syracuse* (MS)

University of Rochester, School of Nursing, *Rochester* (MS, MSN/PhD)

North Carolina

Queens University of Charlotte, Presbyterian School of Nursing, *Charlotte* (MSN, MSN/MBA)

Ohio

Kent State University, College of Nursing, *Kent* (MSN, MSN/MBA, MSN/MPA)

Pennsylvania

Gannon University, Villa Maria School of Nursing, *Erie* (MSN)

Thomas Jefferson University, Department of Nursing, *Philadelphia* (MSN)

University of Pennsylvania, School of Nursing, *Philadelphia* (MSN, MSN/MPH, MSN/PhD)

The University of Scranton, Department of Nursing, *Scranton* (MS)

Waynesburg University, Department of Nursing, *Waynesburg* (MSN, MSN/MBA)

Wilkes University, Department of Nursing, *Wilkes-Barre* (MS)

Tennessee

King College, School of Nursing, *Bristol* (MSN, MSN/MBA)

Southern Adventist University, School of Nursing, *Collegedale* (MSN, MSN/MBA)

The University of Tennessee, College of Nursing, *Knoxville* (MSN)

Vanderbilt University, School of Nursing, *Nashville* (MSN, MSN/MDIV, MSN/MTS)

Texas

Texas A&M University-Corpus Christi, School of Nursing and Health Sciences, *Corpus Christi* (MSN)

The University of Texas at Tyler, Program in Nursing, *Tyler* (MSN, MSN/MBA)

Washington

Gonzaga University, Department of Nursing, *Spokane* (MSN)

Intercollegiate College of Nursing/Washington State University, *Spokane* (MN)

Wisconsin

Marquette University, College of Nursing, *Milwaukee* (MSN, MSN/MBA)

CANADA

Quebec

Université du Québec à Chicoutimi, Program in Nursing, *Chicoutimi* (MSN)

JOINT DEGREES

U.S. AND U.S. TERRITORIES

Alabama

Samford University, Ida V. Moffett School of Nursing, *Birmingham* (MSN, MSN/MBA)

The University of Alabama, Capstone College of Nursing, *Tuscaloosa* (MSN, MSN/MA, MSN/Ed D)

The University of Alabama at Birmingham, School of Nursing, *Birmingham* (MSN, MSN/MPH)

Arizona

Arizona State University at the Downtown Phoenix Campus, College of Nursing, *Phoenix* (MS, MS/MPH)

Grand Canyon University, College of Nursing and Health Sciences, *Phoenix* (MS, MS/MBA)

University of Phoenix, Online Campus, *Phoenix* (MSN, MSN/MBA, MSN/MHA)

University of Phoenix-Phoenix Campus, College of Health and Human Services, *Phoenix* (MSN, MSN/MBA, MSN/MHA)

California

California State University, Long Beach, Department of Nursing, *Long Beach* (MSN, MSN/MPH)

Holy Names University, Department of Nursing, *Oakland* (MSN, MSN/MBA)

Loma Linda University, School of Nursing, *Loma Linda* (MS, MS/MA, MS/MPH)

University of California, Los Angeles, School of Nursing, *Los Angeles* (MSN, MSN/MBA)

University of Phoenix-Bay Area Campus, College of Health and Human Services, *Pleasanton* (MSN, MSN/MBA, MSN/MHA)

University of Phoenix-Sacramento Valley Campus, College of Health and Human Services, *Sacramento* (MSN, MSN/MHA)

University of Phoenix-Southern California Campus, College of Health and Human Services, *Costa Mesa* (MSN, MSN/MBA, MSN/MHA)

University of San Diego, Hahn School of Nursing and Health Science, *San Diego* (MSN, MSN/MBA)

Colorado

University of Phoenix-Denver Campus, College of Health and Human Services, *Lone Tree* (MSN, MSN/MHA, MSN/Ed D)

Connecticut

Sacred Heart University, Program in Nursing, *Fairfield* (MSN, MSN/MBA)

University of Connecticut, School of Nursing, *Storrs* (MS, MS/MBA)

University of Hartford, College of Education, Nursing, and Health Professions, *West Hartford* (MSN, MSN/MSOB)

Yale University, School of Nursing, *New Haven* (MSN, MSN/MPH, MSN/MDIV)

Delaware

Wilmington University, College of Health Professions, *New Castle* (MSN, MSN/MBA, MSN/MS)

District of Columbia

The Catholic University of America, School of Nursing, *Washington* (MSN, MA/MSM)

Florida

Barry University, School of Nursing, *Miami Shores* (MSN, MSN/MBA)

Florida Atlantic University, Christine E. Lynn College of Nursing, *Boca Raton* (MS, MSN/MBA)

Jacksonville University, School of Nursing, *Jacksonville* (MSN, MSN/MBA)

Nova Southeastern University, College of Allied Health and Nursing, *Fort Lauderdale* (MSN, MSN/MBA)

University of Florida, College of Nursing, *Gainesville* (MSN, MSN/PhD)

University of Phoenix-North Florida Campus, College of Health and Human Services, *Jacksonville* (MSN, MSN/MHA, MSN/Ed D)

University of Phoenix-South Florida Campus, College of Health and Human Services, *Fort Lauderdale* (MSN, MSN/MBA, MSN/MHA)

University of South Florida, College of Nursing, *Tampa* (MS, MS/MPH)

Georgia

Armstrong Atlantic State University, Program in Nursing, *Savannah* (MSN, MS/MHSA)

Emory University, Nell Hodgson Woodruff School of Nursing, *Atlanta* (MSN, MSN/MPH)

Georgia College & State University, College of Health Sciences, *Milledgeville* (MSN, MSN/MBA)

Thomas University, Division of Nursing, *Thomasville* (MSN, MSN/MBA)

Hawaii

Hawai'i Pacific University, College of Nursing and Health Sciences, *Honolulu* (MSN, MSN/MBA)

University of Hawaii at Manoa, School of Nursing and Dental Hygiene, *Honolulu* (MS, MSN/MBA)

Idaho

Boise State University, Department of Nursing, *Boise* (MSN, MSN/MS)

Illinois

Elmhurst College, Deicke Center for Nursing Education, *Elmhurst* (MS, MS/MBA)

Lewis University, Program in Nursing, *Romeoville* (MSN, MSN/MBA)

Loyola University Chicago, Marcella Niehoff School of Nursing, *Maywood* (MSN, MSN/MBA, MSN/MDIV)

Northern Illinois University, School of Nursing and Health Studies, *De Kalb* (MS, MSN/MPH)

North Park University, School of Nursing, *Chicago* (MS, MSN/MA, MSN/MBA, MSN/MM)

Saint Xavier University, School of Nursing, *Chicago* (MSN, MSN/MBA)

University of Illinois at Chicago, College of Nursing, *Chicago* (MS, MS/MBA, MS/MPH)

Indiana

Anderson University, School of Nursing, *Anderson* (MSN, MSN/MBA)

Indiana University-Purdue University Indianapolis, School of Nursing, *Indianapolis* (MSN, MSN/MPH)

University of Indianapolis, School of Nursing, *Indianapolis* (MSN, MSN/MBA)

Valparaiso University, College of Nursing, *Valparaiso* (MSN, MSN/MBA)

Iowa

The University of Iowa, College of Nursing, *Iowa City* (MSN, MSN/MBA, MSN/MPH)

Kansas

The University of Kansas, School of Nursing, *Kansas City* (MS, MS/MHSA, MS/MPH)

Wichita State University, School of Nursing, *Wichita* (MSN, MSN/MBA)

Kentucky

Bellarmine University, Donna and Allan Lansing School of Nursing and Health Sciences, *Louisville* (MSN, MSN/MBA)

Maine

Saint Joseph's College of Maine, Department of Nursing, *Standish* (MSN, MSN/MHA)

University of Southern Maine, College of Nursing and Health Professions, *Portland* (MS, MS/MBA)

MASTER'S DEGREE PROGRAMS
Joint Degrees

Maryland

The Johns Hopkins University, School of Nursing, *Baltimore* (MSN, MSN/MBA, MSN/MPH, MSN/PhD)

University of Maryland, Baltimore, Master's Program in Nursing, *Baltimore* (MS, MSN/MBA, MSN/MPH, MSN/JD)

Massachusetts

Boston College, William F. Connell School of Nursing, *Chestnut Hill* (MS, MSN/MA, MSN/MBA, MSN/PhD)

Northeastern University, School of Nursing, *Boston* (MS, MSN/MBA)

Salem State College, Program in Nursing, *Salem* (MSN, MSN/MBA)

Michigan

Ferris State University, School of Nursing, *Big Rapids* (MSN, MSN/MBA)

Madonna University, College of Nursing and Health, *Livonia* (MSN, MSN/MBA)

Spring Arbor University, Program in Nursing, *Spring Arbor* (MSN, MSN/MBA)

University of Michigan, School of Nursing, *Ann Arbor* (MS, MSN/MBA, MSN/MPH)

Minnesota

Minnesota State University Mankato, School of Nursing, *Mankato* (MSN, MSN/MS)

University of Minnesota, Twin Cities Campus, School of Nursing, *Minneapolis* (MS, MS/MPH)

Missouri

Saint Louis University, School of Nursing, *St. Louis* (MSN, MSN/MPH)

University of Missouri–Columbia, Sinclair School of Nursing, *Columbia* (MSN, MSN/PhD)

Nevada

University of Nevada, Reno, Orvis School of Nursing, *Reno* (MSN, MSN/MPH)

New Jersey

Felician College, Division of Nursing and Health Management, *Lodi* (MSN, MA/MSM)

Kean University, Department of Nursing, *Union* (MSN, MSN/MPA)

Rutgers, The State University of New Jersey, College of Nursing, *Newark* (MS, MS/MPH)

Seton Hall University, College of Nursing, *South Orange* (MSN, MSN/MA, MSN/MBA)

University of Medicine and Dentistry of New Jersey, School of Nursing, *Newark* (MSN, MSN/MPH)

New Mexico

University of New Mexico, College of Nursing, *Albuquerque* (MSN, MSN/MALAS, MSN/MPA, MSN/MPH)

New York

Adelphi University, School of Nursing, *Garden City* (MS, MS/MBA)

Columbia University, School of Nursing, *New York* (MS, MSN/MBA, MSN/MPH)

Hunter College of the City University of New York, Hunter-Bellevue School of Nursing, *New York* (MS, MS/MPH)

Long Island University, C.W. Post Campus, Department of Nursing, *Brookville* (MS, MSN/MA, MSN/MBA)

New York University, College of Nursing, *New York* (MS, MSN/MPH)

State University of New York Downstate Medical Center, College of Nursing, *Brooklyn* (MS, MS/MPH)

University of Rochester, School of Nursing, *Rochester* (MS, MSN/PhD)

North Carolina

Duke University, School of Nursing, *Durham* (MSN, MSN/MBA)

Gardner-Webb University, School of Nursing, *Boiling Springs* (MSN, MSN/MBA)

Queens University of Charlotte, Presbyterian School of Nursing, *Charlotte* (MSN, MSN/MBA)

The University of North Carolina at Chapel Hill, School of Nursing, *Chapel Hill* (MSN, MSN/MS)

The University of North Carolina at Greensboro, School of Nursing, *Greensboro* (MSN, MSN/MBA)

North Dakota

University of Mary, Division of Nursing, *Bismarck* (MSN, MSN/MBA)

Ohio

Capital University, School of Nursing, *Columbus* (MSN, MN/MBA, MSN/JD, MSN/MDIV)

Case Western Reserve University, Frances Payne Bolton School of Nursing, *Cleveland* (MSN, MSN/MA, MSN/MBA, MSN/MPH)

Cleveland State University, School of Nursing, *Cleveland* (MSN, MSN/MBA)

Kent State University, College of Nursing, *Kent* (MSN, MSN/MBA, MSN/MPA)

The Ohio State University, College of Nursing, *Columbus* (MS, MS/MPH)

University of Cincinnati, College of Nursing, *Cincinnati* (MSN, MSN/MBA, MSN/PhD)

Wright State University, College of Nursing and Health, *Dayton* (MS, MS/MBA)

Xavier University, Department of Nursing, *Cincinnati* (MSN, MSN/MBA)

Oklahoma

Oklahoma City University, Kramer School of Nursing, *Oklahoma City* (MSN, MSN/MBA)

Oregon

Oregon Health & Science University, School of Nursing, *Portland* (MS, MSN/MPH)

Pennsylvania

Bloomsburg University of Pennsylvania, Department of Nursing, *Bloomsburg* (MSN, MSN/MBA)

DeSales University, Department of Nursing and Health, *Center Valley* (MSN, MSN/MBA)

La Salle University, School of Nursing and Health Sciences, *Philadelphia* (MSN, MSN/MBA)

Marywood University, Department of Nursing, *Scranton* (MSN, MSN/MPH)

Penn State University Park, School of Nursing, *State College, University Park* (MS, MSN/PhD)

University of Pennsylvania, School of Nursing, *Philadelphia* (MSN, MSN/MPH, MSN/PhD)

Waynesburg University, Department of Nursing, *Waynesburg* (MSN, MSN/MBA)

Widener University, School of Nursing, *Chester* (MSN, MSN/PhD)

South Carolina

University of South Carolina, College of Nursing, *Columbia* (MSN, MSN/MPH)

Tennessee

King College, School of Nursing, *Bristol* (MSN, MSN/MBA)

Southern Adventist University, School of Nursing, *Collegedale* (MSN, MSN/MBA)

Vanderbilt University, School of Nursing, *Nashville* (MSN, MSN/MDIV, MSN/MTS)

Texas

Lamar University, Department of Nursing, *Beaumont* (MSN, MSN/MBA)

Midwestern State University, Nursing Program, *Wichita Falls* (MSN, MN/MHSA, MSN/MHA)

Texas Woman's University, College of Nursing, *Denton* (MS, MSN/MHA)

The University of Texas at Arlington, School of Nursing, *Arlington* (MSN, MSN/MBA, MSN/MHA, MSN/MPH)

The University of Texas at Austin, School of Nursing, *Austin* (MSN, MSN/MBA)

The University of Texas at Tyler, Program in Nursing, *Tyler* (MSN, MSN/MBA)

The University of Texas Health Science Center at Houston, School of Nursing, *Houston* (MSN, MSN/MPH)

The University of Texas Health Science Center at San Antonio, School of Nursing, *San Antonio* (MSN, MSN/MPH)

The University of Texas Medical Branch, School of Nursing, *Galveston* (MSN, MSN/PhD)

University of the Incarnate Word, Program in Nursing, *San Antonio* (MSN, MSN/MBA)

Virginia

George Mason University, College of Health and Human Services, *Fairfax* (MSN, MSN/MBA)

University of Virginia, School of Nursing, *Charlottesville* (MSN, MSN/MBA, MSN/PhD)

Washington

Pacific Lutheran University, School of Nursing, *Tacoma* (MSN, MSN/MBA)

University of Washington, School of Nursing, *Seattle* (MN, MN/MPH)

Wisconsin

Edgewood College, Program in Nursing, *Madison* (MS, MSN/MBA)

Marquette University, College of Nursing, *Milwaukee* (MSN, MSN/MBA)

University of Wisconsin–Milwaukee, College of Nursing, *Milwaukee* (MS, MS/MBA)

CANADA

Alberta

Athabasca University, Centre for Nursing and Health Studies, *Athabasca* (MN, MN/MHSA, MN/MBA)

British Columbia

The University of British Columbia, Program in Nursing, *Vancouver* (MSN, MA/MSM)

Nova Scotia

Dalhousie University, School of Nursing, *Halifax* (MN, MN/MHSA)

Ontario

McMaster University, School of Nursing, *Hamilton* (M Sc, MSN/PhD)

MASTER'S

U.S. AND U.S. TERRITORIES

Alabama

Auburn University, School of Nursing, *Auburn University* (MSN)

Auburn University Montgomery, School of Nursing, *Montgomery* (MSN)

Jacksonville State University, College of Nursing and Health Sciences, *Jacksonville* (MSN)

Samford University, Ida V. Moffett School of Nursing, *Birmingham* (MSN, MSN/MBA)

Spring Hill College, Division of Nursing, *Mobile* (MSN)

Troy University, School of Nursing, *Troy* (MSN)

The University of Alabama, Capstone College of Nursing, *Tuscaloosa* (MSN, MSN/MA, MSN/Ed D)

The University of Alabama at Birmingham, School of Nursing, *Birmingham* (MSN, MSN/MPH)

The University of Alabama in Huntsville, College of Nursing, *Huntsville* (MSN)

University of Mobile, School of Nursing, *Mobile* (MSN)

University of North Alabama, College of Nursing and Allied Health, *Florence* (MSN)

University of South Alabama, College of Nursing, *Mobile* (MSN)

Alaska

University of Alaska Anchorage, School of Nursing, *Anchorage* (MS)

Arizona

Arizona State University at the Downtown Phoenix Campus, College of Nursing, *Phoenix* (MS, MS/MPH)

Grand Canyon University, College of Nursing and Health Sciences, *Phoenix* (MS, MS/MBA)

Northern Arizona University, School of Nursing, *Flagstaff* (MS)

University of Phoenix, Online Campus, *Phoenix* (MSN, MSN/MBA, MSN/MHA)

University of Phoenix–Phoenix Campus, College of Health and Human Services, *Phoenix* (MSN, MSN/MBA, MSN/MHA)

University of Phoenix–Southern Arizona Campus, College of Health and Human Services, *Tucson* (MSN)

Arkansas

Arkansas State University, Department of Nursing, *Jonesboro, State University* (MSN)

Arkansas Tech University, Program in Nursing, *Russellville* (MSN)

University of Arkansas, Eleanor Mann School of Nursing, *Fayetteville* (MSN)

University of Arkansas for Medical Sciences, College of Nursing, *Little Rock* (MN Sc)

University of Central Arkansas, Department of Nursing, *Conway* (MSN)

California

Azusa Pacific University, School of Nursing, *Azusa* (MSN)

California State University, Chico, School of Nursing, *Chico* (MSN)

California State University, Dominguez Hills, Program in Nursing, *Carson* (MS)

California State University, Fresno, Department of Nursing, *Fresno* (MSN)

California State University, Fullerton, Department of Nursing, *Fullerton* (MSN)

California State University, Long Beach, Department of Nursing, *Long Beach* (MSN, MSN/MPH)

California State University, Los Angeles, School of Nursing, *Los Angeles* (MSN)

California State University, Sacramento, Division of Nursing, *Sacramento* (MS)

California State University, San Bernardino, Department of Nursing, *San Bernardino* (MSN)

Dominican University of California, Program in Nursing, *San Rafael* (MSN)

Holy Names University, Department of Nursing, *Oakland* (MSN, MSN/MBA)

Loma Linda University, School of Nursing, *Loma Linda* (MS, MS/MA, MS/MPH)

Mount St. Mary's College, Department of Nursing, *Los Angeles* (MSN)

Point Loma Nazarene University, School of Nursing, *San Diego* (MSN)

Samuel Merritt University, School of Nursing, *Oakland* (MSN)

San Diego State University, School of Nursing, *San Diego* (MSN)

San Francisco State University, School of Nursing, *San Francisco* (MSN)

San Jose State University, School of Nursing, *San Jose* (MS)

Sonoma State University, Department of Nursing, *Rohnert Park* (MSN)

University of California, Los Angeles, School of Nursing, *Los Angeles* (MSN, MSN/MBA)

University of California, San Francisco, School of Nursing, *San Francisco* (MS)

University of Phoenix–Bay Area Campus, College of Health and Human Services, *Pleasanton* (MSN, MSN/MBA, MSN/MHA)

University of Phoenix–San Diego Campus, College of Health and Human Services, *San Diego* (MSN, MSN/Ed D)

University of Phoenix–Southern California Campus, College of Health and Human Services, *Costa Mesa* (MSN, MSN/MBA, MSN/MHA)

University of San Diego, Hahn School of Nursing and Health Science, *San Diego* (MSN, MSN/MBA)

Western University of Health Sciences, College of Graduate Nursing, *Pomona* (MSN)

Colorado

Colorado State University–Pueblo, Department of Nursing, *Pueblo* (MS)

Regis University, School of Nursing, *Denver* (MS)

University of Colorado at Colorado Springs, Beth-El College of Nursing and Health Sciences, *Colorado Springs* (MSN)

University of Colorado Denver, College of Nursing, *Denver* (MS)

University of Northern Colorado, School of Nursing, *Greeley* (MS)

University of Phoenix–Denver Campus, College of Health and Human Services, *Lone Tree* (MSN, MSN/MHA, MSN/Ed D)

Connecticut

Fairfield University, School of Nursing, *Fairfield* (MSN)

Quinnipiac University, Department of Nursing, *Hamden* (MSN)

Sacred Heart University, Program in Nursing, *Fairfield* (MSN, MSN/MBA)

Saint Joseph College, Department of Nursing, *West Hartford* (MS)

Southern Connecticut State University, Department of Nursing, *New Haven* (MSN)

University of Connecticut, School of Nursing, *Storrs* (MS, MS/MBA)

University of Hartford, College of Education, Nursing, and Health Professions, *West Hartford* (MSN, MSN/MSOB)

Western Connecticut State University, Department of Nursing, *Danbury* (MS)

Yale University, School of Nursing, *New Haven* (MSN, MSN/MPH, MSN/MDIV)

Delaware

University of Delaware, School of Nursing, *Newark* (MSN)

Wesley College, Nursing Program, *Dover* (MSN)

Wilmington University, College of Health Professions, *New Castle* (MSN, MSN/MBA, MSN/MS)

District of Columbia

The Catholic University of America, School of Nursing, *Washington* (MSN, MA/MSM)

Georgetown University, School of Nursing & Health Studies, *Washington* (MS)

Howard University, Division of Nursing, *Washington* (MSN)

Florida

Barry University, School of Nursing, *Miami Shores* (MSN, MSN/MBA)

Florida Agricultural and Mechanical University, School of Nursing, *Tallahassee* (MSN)

Florida Atlantic University, Christine E. Lynn College of Nursing, *Boca Raton* (MS, MSN/MBA)

Florida Gulf Coast University, School of Nursing, *Fort Myers* (MSN)

Florida International University, Nursing Program, *Miami* (MSN)

Florida Southern College, Department of Nursing, *Lakeland* (MSN)

Florida State University, College of Nursing, *Tallahassee* (MSN)

Jacksonville University, School of Nursing, *Jacksonville* (MSN, MSN/MBA)

Nova Southeastern University, College of Allied Health and Nursing, *Fort Lauderdale* (MSN, MSN/MBA)

South University, Nursing Program, *West Palm Beach* (MSN)

University of Central Florida, School of Nursing, *Orlando* (MSN)

University of Florida, College of Nursing, *Gainesville* (MSN, MSN/PhD)

University of Miami, School of Nursing and Health Studies, *Coral Gables* (MSN)

University of North Florida, School of Nursing, *Jacksonville* (MSN)

University of Phoenix–Central Florida Campus, College of Health and Human Services, *Maitland* (MSN, MSN/Ed D)

University of Phoenix–North Florida Campus, College of Health and Human Services, *Jacksonville* (MSN, MSN/MHA, MSN/Ed D)

University of Phoenix–South Florida Campus, College of Health and Human Services, *Fort Lauderdale* (MSN, MSN/MBA, MSN/MHA)

University of South Florida, College of Nursing, *Tampa* (MS, MS/MPH)

The University of Tampa, Department of Nursing, *Tampa* (MSN)

Georgia

Albany State University, College of Sciences and Health Professions, *Albany* (MSN)

Armstrong Atlantic State University, Program in Nursing, *Savannah* (MSN, MS/MHSA)

Brenau University, School of Health and Science, *Gainesville* (MSN)

Clayton State University, Department of Nursing, *Morrow* (MSN)

Emory University, Nell Hodgson Woodruff School of Nursing, *Atlanta* (MSN, MSN/MPH)

Georgia Baptist College of Nursing of Mercer University, Department of Nursing, *Atlanta* (MSN)

Georgia College & State University, College of Health Sciences, *Milledgeville* (MSN, MSN/MBA)

Georgia Southern University, School of Nursing, *Statesboro* (MSN)

Georgia State University, Byrdine F. Lewis School of Nursing, *Atlanta* (MSN)

Kennesaw State University, School of Nursing, *Kennesaw* (MSN)

Medical College of Georgia, School of Nursing, *Augusta* (MSN)

North Georgia College & State University, Department of Nursing, *Dahlonega* (MS)

Thomas University, Division of Nursing, *Thomasville* (MSN, MSN/MBA)

University of West Georgia, School of Nursing, *Carrollton* (MSN)

Valdosta State University, College of Nursing, *Valdosta* (MSN)

Hawaii

Hawai'i Pacific University, College of Nursing and Health Sciences, *Honolulu* (MSN, MSN/MBA)

University of Hawaii at Manoa, School of Nursing and Dental Hygiene, *Honolulu* (MS, MSN/MBA)

University of Phoenix-Hawaii Campus, College of Health and Human Services, *Honolulu* (MSN, MSN/Ed D)

Idaho

Boise State University, Department of Nursing, *Boise* (MSN, MSN/MS)

Idaho State University, Department of Nursing, *Pocatello* (MS)

Northwest Nazarene University, School of Health and Science, *Nampa* (MSN)

Illinois

Aurora University, School of Nursing, *Aurora* (MSN)

Benedictine University, Department of Nursing, *Lisle* (MSN)

Blessing-Rieman College of Nursing, *Quincy* (MSN)

Bradley University, Department of Nursing, *Peoria* (MSN)

DePaul University, Department of Nursing, *Chicago* (MS)

Elmhurst College, Deicke Center for Nursing Education, *Elmhurst* (MS, MS/MBA)

Governors State University, College of Health and Human Services, *University Park* (MS)

Illinois State University, Mennonite College of Nursing, *Normal* (MSN)

Loyola University Chicago, Marcella Niehoff School of Nursing, *Maywood* (MSN, MSN/MBA, MSN/MDIV)

McKendree University, Department of Nursing, *Lebanon* (MSN)

Millikin University, School of Nursing, *Decatur* (MSN)

Northern Illinois University, School of Nursing and Health Studies, *De Kalb* (MS, MSN/MPH)

North Park University, School of Nursing, *Chicago* (MS, MSN/MA, MSN/MBA, MSN/MM)

Olivet Nazarene University, Division of Nursing, *Bourbonnais* (MSN)

Rush University, College of Nursing, *Chicago* (MSN)

Saint Anthony College of Nursing, Saint Anthony College of Nursing, *Rockford* (MSN)

Saint Francis Medical Center College of Nursing, Baccalaureate Nursing Program, *Peoria* (MSN)

Saint Xavier University, School of Nursing, *Chicago* (MSN, MSN/MBA)

Southern Illinois University Edwardsville, School of Nursing, *Edwardsville* (MS)

University of Illinois at Chicago, College of Nursing, *Chicago* (MS, MS/MBA, MS/MPH)

University of St. Francis, College of Nursing and Allied Health, *Joliet* (MSN)

West Suburban College of Nursing, *Oak Park* (MSN)

Indiana

Anderson University, School of Nursing, *Anderson* (MSN, MSN/MBA)

Ball State University, School of Nursing, *Muncie* (MS)

Bethel College, Department of Nursing, *Mishawaka* (MSN)

Indiana State University, Department of Nursing, *Terre Haute* (MSN)

Indiana University-Purdue University Fort Wayne, Department of Nursing, *Fort Wayne* (MS)

Indiana University-Purdue University Indianapolis, School of Nursing, *Indianapolis* (MSN, MSN/MPH)

Indiana University South Bend, Division of Nursing and Health Professions, *South Bend* (MSN)

Indiana Wesleyan University, School of Nursing, *Marion* (MSN)

Purdue University, School of Nursing, *West Lafayette* (MS)

Purdue University Calumet, School of Nursing, *Hammond* (MS)

University of Indianapolis, School of Nursing, *Indianapolis* (MSN, MSN/MBA)

University of Saint Francis, Department of Nursing, *Fort Wayne* (MSN)

University of Southern Indiana, College of Nursing and Health Professions, *Evansville* (MSN)

Valparaiso University, College of Nursing, *Valparaiso* (MSN, MSN/MBA)

Iowa

Allen College, Program in Nursing, *Waterloo* (MSN)

Briar Cliff University, Department of Nursing, *Sioux City* (MSN)

Clarke College, Department of Nursing and Health, *Dubuque* (MSN)

St. Ambrose University, Program in Nursing (BSN), *Davenport* (MSN)

The University of Iowa, College of Nursing, *Iowa City* (MSN, MSN/MBA, MSN/MPH)

Kansas

Fort Hays State University, Department of Nursing, *Hays* (MSN)

Pittsburg State University, Department of Nursing, *Pittsburg* (MSN)

The University of Kansas, School of Nursing, *Kansas City* (MS, MS/MHSA, MS/MPH)

Washburn University, School of Nursing, *Topeka* (MSN)

Wichita State University, School of Nursing, *Wichita* (MSN, MSN/MBA)

Kentucky

Bellarmine University, Donna and Allan Lansing School of Nursing and Health Sciences, *Louisville* (MSN, MSN/MBA)

Eastern Kentucky University, Department of Baccalaureate and Graduate Nursing, *Richmond* (MSN)

Murray State University, Program in Nursing, *Murray* (MSN)

Northern Kentucky University, Department of Nursing, *Highland Heights* (MSN)

Spalding University, School of Nursing, *Louisville* (MSN)

University of Kentucky, Graduate School Programs in the College of Nursing, *Lexington* (MSN)

University of Louisville, School of Nursing, *Louisville* (MSN)

Louisiana

Grambling State University, School of Nursing, *Grambling* (MSN)

Louisiana State University Health Sciences Center, School of Nursing, *New Orleans* (MN)

Loyola University New Orleans, School of Nursing, *New Orleans* (MSN)

McNeese State University, College of Nursing, *Lake Charles* (MSN)

Northwestern State University of Louisiana, College of Nursing, *Shreveport* (MSN)

Our Lady of the Lake College, Division of Nursing, *Baton Rouge* (MSN)

Southeastern Louisiana University, School of Nursing, *Hammond* (MSN)

Southern University and Agricultural and Mechanical College, School of Nursing, *Baton Rouge* (MSN)

University of Louisiana at Lafayette, College of Nursing, *Lafayette* (MSN)

Maine

Husson University, School of Nursing, *Bangor* (MSN)

Saint Joseph's College of Maine, Department of Nursing, *Standish* (MSN, MSN/MHA)

University of Maine, School of Nursing, *Orono* (MSN)

University of Southern Maine, College of Nursing and Health Professions, *Portland* (MS, MS/MBA)

Maryland

Bowie State University, Department of Nursing, *Bowie* (MSN)

Coppin State University, Helene Fuld School of Nursing, *Baltimore* (MSN)

The Johns Hopkins University, School of Nursing, *Baltimore* (MSN, MSN/MBA, MSN/MPH, MSN/PhD)

Salisbury University, Program in Nursing, *Salisbury* (MS)

Towson University, Department of Nursing, *Towson* (MS)

University of Maryland, Baltimore, Master's Program in Nursing, *Baltimore* (MS, MSN/MBA, MSN/MPH, MSN/JD)

Massachusetts

American International College, Division of Nursing, *Springfield* (MSN)

Boston College, William F. Connell School of Nursing, *Chestnut Hill* (MS, MSN/MA, MSN/MBA, MSN/PhD)

Curry College, Division of Nursing, *Milton* (MSN)

Elms College, Division of Nursing, *Chicopee* (MSN)

Endicott College, Major in Nursing, *Beverly* (MSN)

Fitchburg State College, Department of Nursing, *Fitchburg* (M Sc N)

Framingham State College, Department of Nursing, *Framingham* (MSN)

MGH Institute of Health Professions, School of Nursing, *Boston* (MS)

Northeastern University, School of Nursing, *Boston* (MS, MSN/MBA)

Regis College, School of Nursing and Health Professions, *Weston* (MSN)

Salem State College, Program in Nursing, *Salem* (MSN, MSN/MBA)

Simmons College, Department of Nursing, *Boston* (MS)

University of Massachusetts Amherst, School of Nursing, *Amherst* (MS)

University of Massachusetts Boston, College of Nursing and Health Sciences, *Boston* (MS)

University of Massachusetts Dartmouth, College of Nursing, *North Dartmouth* (MS)

University of Massachusetts Lowell, Department of Nursing, *Lowell* (MS)

University of Massachusetts Worcester, Graduate School of Nursing, *Worcester* (MS)

Worcester State College, Department of Nursing, *Worcester* (MS)

Michigan
Andrews University, Department of Nursing, *Berrien Springs* (MS)
Eastern Michigan University, School of Nursing, *Ypsilanti* (MSN)
Ferris State University, School of Nursing, *Big Rapids* (MSN, MSN/MBA)
Grand Valley State University, Kirkhof College of Nursing, *Allendale* (MSN)
Madonna University, College of Nursing and Health, *Livonia* (MSN, MSN/MBA)
Michigan State University, College of Nursing, *East Lansing* (MSN)
Northern Michigan University, College of Nursing and Allied Health Science, *Marquette* (MSN)
Oakland University, School of Nursing, *Rochester* (MSN)
Saginaw Valley State University, Crystal M. Lange College of Nursing and Health Sciences, *University Center* (MSN)
Spring Arbor University, Program in Nursing, *Spring Arbor* (MSN, MSN/MBA)
University of Detroit Mercy, McAuley School of Nursing, *Detroit* (MSN)
University of Michigan, School of Nursing, *Ann Arbor* (MS, MSN/MBA, MSN/MPH)
University of Phoenix-Metro Detroit Campus, College of Health and Human Services, *Southfield* (MSN)
Wayne State University, College of Nursing, *Detroit* (MSN)

Minnesota
Augsburg College, Program in Nursing, *Minneapolis* (MA)
Bethel University, Department of Nursing, *St. Paul* (MA)
The College of St. Scholastica, Department of Nursing, *Duluth* (MA)
Concordia College, Department of Nursing, *Moorhead* (MS)
Minnesota State University Mankato, School of Nursing, *Mankato* (MSN, MSN/MS)
Minnesota State University Moorhead, School of Nursing and Healthcare Leadership, *Moorhead* (MS)
St. Catherine University, Department of Nursing, *St. Paul* (MA)
University of Minnesota, Twin Cities Campus, School of Nursing, *Minneapolis* (MS, MS/MPH)
Winona State University, College of Nursing and Health Sciences, *Winona* (MS)

Mississippi
Alcorn State University, School of Nursing, *Natchez* (MSN)
Delta State University, School of Nursing, *Cleveland* (MSN)
Mississippi University for Women, College of Nursing and Speech-Language Pathology, *Columbus* (MSN)
University of Mississippi Medical Center, Program in Nursing, *Jackson* (MSN)
University of Southern Mississippi, School of Nursing, *Hattiesburg* (MSN)
William Carey University, School of Nursing, *Hattiesburg* (MSN)

Missouri
Central Methodist University, College of Liberal Arts and Sciences, *Fayette* (MSN)
Goldfarb School of Nursing at Barnes-Jewish College, *St. Louis* (MSN)
Graceland University, School of Nursing, *Independence* (MSN)

Maryville University of Saint Louis, Nursing Program, School of Health Professions, *St. Louis* (MSN)
Missouri Southern State University, Department of Nursing, *Joplin* (MSN)
Missouri State University, Department of Nursing, *Springfield* (MSN)
Research College of Nursing, College of Nursing, *Kansas City* (MSN)
Saint Louis University, School of Nursing, *St. Louis* (MSN, MSN/MPH)
Southeast Missouri State University, Department of Nursing, *Cape Girardeau* (MSN)
University of Central Missouri, Department of Nursing, *Warrensburg* (MS)
University of Missouri-Columbia, Sinclair School of Nursing, *Columbia* (MSN, MSN/PhD)
University of Missouri-Kansas City, School of Nursing, *Kansas City* (MSN)
University of Missouri-St. Louis, College of Nursing, *St. Louis* (MSN)
Webster University, Department of Nursing, *St. Louis* (MSN)

Montana
Montana State University, College of Nursing, *Bozeman* (MN)

Nebraska
BryanLGH College of Health Sciences, School of Nursing, *Lincoln* (MS)
Clarkson College, Master of Science in Nursing Program, *Omaha* (MSN)
Creighton University, School of Nursing, *Omaha* (MSN)
Nebraska Methodist College, Department of Nursing, *Omaha* (MSN)
Nebraska Wesleyan University, Department of Nursing, *Lincoln* (MSN)
University of Nebraska Medical Center, College of Nursing, *Omaha* (MSN)

Nevada
Touro University, School of Nursing, *Henderson* (MSN)
University of Nevada, Las Vegas, School of Nursing, *Las Vegas* (MSN)
University of Nevada, Reno, Orvis School of Nursing, *Reno* (MSN, MSN/MPH)

New Hampshire
Franklin Pierce University, Master of Science in Nursing, *Rindge* (MSN)
Rivier College, Division of Nursing, *Nashua* (MS)
University of New Hampshire, Department of Nursing, *Durham* (MS)

New Jersey
The College of New Jersey, School of Nursing, Health and Exercise Science, *Ewing* (MSN)
Fairleigh Dickinson University, Metropolitan Campus, Henry P. Becton School of Nursing and Allied Health, *Teaneck* (MSN)
Felician College, Division of Nursing and Health Management, *Lodi* (MSN, MA/MSM)
Kean University, Department of Nursing, *Union* (MSN, MSN/MPA)
Monmouth University, Marjorie K. Unterberg School of Nursing, *West Long Branch* (MSN)
Ramapo College of New Jersey, Master of Science in Nursing Program, *Mahwah* (MSN)
Rutgers, The State University of New Jersey, College of Nursing, *Newark* (MS, MS/MPH)
Saint Peter's College, Nursing Program, *Jersey City* (MSN)
Seton Hall University, College of Nursing, *South Orange* (MSN, MSN/MA, MSN/MBA)

Thomas Edison State College, School of Nursing, *Trenton* (MSN)
University of Medicine and Dentistry of New Jersey, School of Nursing, *Newark* (MSN, MSN/MPH)
William Paterson University of New Jersey, Department of Nursing, *Wayne* (MSN)

New Mexico
New Mexico State University, School of Nursing, *Las Cruces* (MSN)
University of New Mexico, College of Nursing, *Albuquerque* (MSN, MSN/MALAS, MSN/MPA, MSN/MPH)
University of Phoenix-New Mexico Campus, College of Health and Human Services, *Albuquerque* (MSN, MSN/Ed D)

New York
Adelphi University, School of Nursing, *Garden City* (MS, MS/MBA)
College of Mount Saint Vincent, Department of Nursing, *Riverdale* (MSN)
The College of New Rochelle, School of Nursing, *New Rochelle* (MS)
College of Staten Island of the City University of New York, Department of Nursing, *Staten Island* (MS)
Columbia University, School of Nursing, *New York* (MS, MSN/MBA, MSN/MPH)
Daemen College, Department of Nursing, *Amherst* (MS)
Dominican College, Department of Nursing, *Orangeburg* (M Sc N)
D'Youville College, Department of Nursing, *Buffalo* (MS)
Excelsior College, School of Nursing, *Albany* (MS)
Hunter College of the City University of New York, Hunter-Bellevue School of Nursing, *New York* (MS, MS/MPH)
Lehman College of the City University of New York, Department of Nursing, *Bronx* (MS)
Le Moyne College, Nursing Programs, *Syracuse* (MS)
Long Island University, Brooklyn Campus, School of Nursing, *Brooklyn* (MS)
Long Island University, C.W. Post Campus, Department of Nursing, *Brookville* (MS, MSN/MA, MSN/MBA)
Mercy College, Program in Nursing, *Dobbs Ferry* (MS)
Molloy College, Department of Nursing, *Rockville Centre* (MS)
Mount Saint Mary College, Division of Nursing, *Newburgh* (MS)
Nazareth College of Rochester, Department of Nursing, *Rochester* (MS)
New York University, College of Nursing, *New York* (MS, MSN/MPH)
Pace University, Lienhard School of Nursing, *New York* (MS)
The Sage Colleges, Department of Nursing, *Troy* (MS)
St. John Fisher College, Advanced Practice Nursing Program, *Rochester* (MS)
St. Joseph's College, New York, Department of Nursing, *Brooklyn* (MS)
State University of New York at Binghamton, Decker School of Nursing, *Binghamton* (MS)
State University of New York Downstate Medical Center, College of Nursing, *Brooklyn* (MS, MS/MPH)
State University of New York Institute of Technology, School of Nursing and Health Systems, *Utica* (MS)
State University of New York Upstate Medical University, College of Nursing, *Syracuse* (MS)

MASTER'S DEGREE PROGRAMS
Master's

Stony Brook University, State University of New York, School of Nursing, *Stony Brook* (MS)

University at Buffalo, the State University of New York, School of Nursing, *Buffalo* (MS)

University of Rochester, School of Nursing, *Rochester* (MS, MSN/PhD)

North Carolina

Duke University, School of Nursing, *Durham* (MSN, MSN/MBA)

East Carolina University, College of Nursing, *Greenville* (MSN)

Gardner-Webb University, School of Nursing, *Boiling Springs* (MSN, MSN/MBA)

Queens University of Charlotte, Presbyterian School of Nursing, *Charlotte* (MSN, MSN/MBA)

The University of North Carolina at Charlotte, School of Nursing, *Charlotte* (MSN)

The University of North Carolina at Greensboro, School of Nursing, *Greensboro* (MSN, MSN/MBA)

The University of North Carolina Wilmington, School of Nursing, *Wilmington* (MSN)

Western Carolina University, School of Nursing, *Cullowhee* (MS)

Winston-Salem State University, Department of Nursing, *Winston-Salem* (MSN)

North Dakota

North Dakota State University, Department of Nursing, *Fargo* (MS)

University of Mary, Division of Nursing, *Bismarck* (MSN, MSN/MBA)

University of North Dakota, College of Nursing, *Grand Forks* (MS)

Ohio

Capital University, School of Nursing, *Columbus* (MSN, MN/MBA, MSN/JD, MSN/MDIV)

Case Western Reserve University, Frances Payne Bolton School of Nursing, *Cleveland* (MSN, MSN/MA, MSN/MBA, MSN/MPH)

Cleveland State University, School of Nursing, *Cleveland* (MSN, MSN/MBA)

Franciscan University of Steubenville, Department of Nursing, *Steubenville* (MSN)

Kent State University, College of Nursing, *Kent* (MSN, MSN/MBA, MSN/MPA)

Malone University, School of Nursing, *Canton* (MSN)

Mount Carmel College of Nursing, Nursing Programs, *Columbus* (MS)

The Ohio State University, College of Nursing, *Columbus* (MS, MS/MPH)

Ohio University, School of Nursing, *Athens* (MSN)

Otterbein College, Department of Nursing, *Westerville* (MSN)

The University of Akron, College of Nursing, *Akron* (MSN)

University of Cincinnati, College of Nursing, *Cincinnati* (MSN, MSN/MBA, MSN/PhD)

University of Phoenix–Cleveland Campus, College of Health and Human Services, *Independence* (MSN)

The University of Toledo, College of Nursing, *Toledo* (MSN)

Urbana University, BSN Completion Program, *Urbana* (MSN)

Ursuline College, The Breen School of Nursing, *Pepper Pike* (MSN)

Wright State University, College of Nursing and Health, *Dayton* (MS, MS/MBA)

Xavier University, Department of Nursing, *Cincinnati* (MSN, MSN/MBA)

Oklahoma

Oklahoma Baptist University, School of Nursing, *Shawnee* (MSN)

Oklahoma City University, Kramer School of Nursing, *Oklahoma City* (MSN, MSN/MBA)

University of Oklahoma Health Sciences Center, College of Nursing, *Oklahoma City* (MS)

Oregon

Oregon Health & Science University, School of Nursing, *Portland* (MS, MSN/MPH)

University of Portland, School of Nursing, *Portland* (MS)

Pennsylvania

Bloomsburg University of Pennsylvania, Department of Nursing, *Bloomsburg* (MSN, MSN/MBA)

Carlow University, School of Nursing, *Pittsburgh* (MSN)

Cedar Crest College, Department of Nursing, *Allentown* (MSN)

Chatham University, Program in Nursing, *Pittsburgh* (MSN)

Clarion University of Pennsylvania, School of Nursing, *Oil City* (MSN)

DeSales University, Department of Nursing and Health, *Center Valley* (MSN, MSN/MBA)

Drexel University, College of Nursing and Health Professions, *Philadelphia* (MSN)

Duquesne University, School of Nursing, *Pittsburgh* (MSN)

Gannon University, Villa Maria School of Nursing, *Erie* (MSN)

Gwynedd-Mercy College, School of Nursing, *Gwynedd Valley* (MSN)

Holy Family University, School of Nursing and Allied Health Professions, *Philadelphia* (MSN)

Immaculata University, Department of Nursing, *Immaculata* (MSN)

Indiana University of Pennsylvania, Department of Nursing and Allied Health, *Indiana* (MS)

Kutztown University of Pennsylvania, Department of Nursing, *Kutztown* (MSN)

La Roche College, Department of Nursing and Nursing Management, *Pittsburgh* (MSN)

La Salle University, School of Nursing and Health Sciences, *Philadelphia* (MSN, MSN/MBA)

Mansfield University of Pennsylvania, Robert Packer Department of Health Sciences, *Mansfield* (MSN)

Marywood University, Department of Nursing, *Scranton* (MSN, MSN/MPH)

Millersville University of Pennsylvania, Department of Nursing, *Millersville* (MSN)

Misericordia University, Department of Nursing, *Dallas* (MSN)

Moravian College, St. Luke's School of Nursing, *Bethlehem* (MS)

Neumann University, Program in Nursing and Health Sciences, *Aston* (MS)

Penn State University Park, School of Nursing, *State College, University Park* (MS, MSN/PhD)

Robert Morris University, School of Nursing and Health Sciences, *Moon Township* (MSN)

Temple University, Department of Nursing, *Philadelphia* (MSN)

Thomas Jefferson University, Department of Nursing, *Philadelphia* (MSN)

University of Pennsylvania, School of Nursing, *Philadelphia* (MSN, MSN/MPH, MSN/PhD)

University of Pittsburgh, School of Nursing, *Pittsburgh* (MSN)

The University of Scranton, Department of Nursing, *Scranton* (MS)

Villanova University, College of Nursing, *Villanova* (MSN)

West Chester University of Pennsylvania, Department of Nursing, *West Chester* (MSN)

Widener University, School of Nursing, *Chester* (MSN, MSN/PhD)

Wilkes University, Department of Nursing, *Wilkes-Barre* (MS)

York College of Pennsylvania, Department of Nursing, *York* (MS)

Puerto Rico

University of Puerto Rico, Medical Sciences Campus, School of Nursing, *San Juan* (MSN)

University of the Sacred Heart, Program in Nursing, *San Juan* (MSN)

Rhode Island

Rhode Island College, Department of Nursing, *Providence* (MSN)

University of Rhode Island, College of Nursing, *Kingston* (MS)

South Carolina

Charleston Southern University, Wingo School of Nursing, *Charleston* (MSN)

Clemson University, School of Nursing, *Clemson* (MS)

Medical University of South Carolina, College of Nursing, *Charleston* (MSN)

University of South Carolina, College of Nursing, *Columbia* (MSN, MSN/MPH)

South Dakota

Augustana College, Department of Nursing, *Sioux Falls* (MA)

South Dakota State University, College of Nursing, *Brookings* (MS)

Tennessee

Belmont University, School of Nursing, *Nashville* (MSN)

Carson-Newman College, Division of Nursing, *Jefferson City* (MSN)

East Tennessee State University, College of Nursing, *Johnson City* (MSN)

King College, School of Nursing, *Bristol* (MSN, MSN/MBA)

Middle Tennessee State University, School of Nursing, *Murfreesboro* (MSN)

Southern Adventist University, School of Nursing, *Collegedale* (MSN, MSN/MBA)

Tennessee Technological University, School of Nursing, *Cookeville* (MSN, M Sc N)

Union University, School of Nursing, *Jackson* (MSN)

University of Memphis, Loewenberg School of Nursing, *Memphis* (MSN)

The University of Tennessee, College of Nursing, *Knoxville* (MSN)

The University of Tennessee at Chattanooga, School of Nursing, *Chattanooga* (MSN)

Vanderbilt University, School of Nursing, *Nashville* (MSN, MSN/MDIV, MSN/MTS)

Texas

Angelo State University, Department of Nursing, *San Angelo* (MSN)

Baylor University, Louise Herrington School of Nursing, *Dallas* (MSN)

Lamar University, Department of Nursing, *Beaumont* (MSN, MSN/MBA)

Midwestern State University, Nursing Program, *Wichita Falls* (MSN, MN/MHSA, MSN/MHA)

Patty Hanks Shelton School of Nursing, *Abilene* (MSN)

Prairie View A&M University, College of Nursing, *Houston* (MSN)

Texas A&M International University, Canseco School of Nursing, *Laredo* (MSN)

Texas A&M University-Corpus Christi, School of Nursing and Health Sciences, *Corpus Christi* (MSN)

Texas A&M University-Texarkana, Nursing Department, *Texarkana* (MSN)

Texas Christian University, Harris College of Nursing, *Fort Worth* (MSN)

Texas Tech University Health Sciences Center, School of Nursing, *Lubbock* (MSN)

Texas Woman's University, College of Nursing, *Denton* (MS, MSN/MHA)

University of Houston-Victoria, School of Nursing, *Victoria* (MSN)

University of Mary Hardin-Baylor, College of Nursing, *Belton* (MSN)

The University of Texas at Arlington, School of Nursing, *Arlington* (MSN, MSN/MBA, MSN/MHA, MSN/MPH)

The University of Texas at Austin, School of Nursing, *Austin* (MSN, MSN/MBA)

The University of Texas at Brownsville, Department of Nursing, *Brownsville* (MSN)

The University of Texas at El Paso, School of Nursing, *El Paso* (MSN)

The University of Texas at Tyler, Program in Nursing, *Tyler* (MSN, MSN/MBA)

The University of Texas Health Science Center at Houston, School of Nursing, *Houston* (MSN, MSN/MPH)

The University of Texas Health Science Center at San Antonio, School of Nursing, *San Antonio* (MSN, MSN/MPH)

The University of Texas Medical Branch, School of Nursing, *Galveston* (MSN, MSN/PhD)

The University of Texas-Pan American, Department of Nursing, *Edinburg* (MSN)

University of the Incarnate Word, Program in Nursing, *San Antonio* (MSN, MSN/MBA)

West Texas A&M University, Division of Nursing, *Canyon* (MSN)

Utah

Brigham Young University, College of Nursing, *Provo* (MS)

University of Utah, College of Nursing, *Salt Lake City* (MS)

Weber State University, Program in Nursing, *Ogden* (MSN)

Westminster College, School of Nursing and Health Sciences, *Salt Lake City* (MSN)

Vermont

University of Vermont, Department of Nursing, *Burlington* (MS)

Virginia

George Mason University, College of Health and Human Services, *Fairfax* (MSN, MSN/MBA)

Hampton University, School of Nursing, *Hampton* (MS)

James Madison University, Department of Nursing, *Harrisonburg* (MSN)

Jefferson College of Health Sciences, Nursing Education Program, *Roanoke* (MSN)

Liberty University, Department of Nursing, *Lynchburg* (MSN)

Marymount University, School of Health Professions, *Arlington* (MSN)

Old Dominion University, Department of Nursing, *Norfolk* (MSN)

Radford University, School of Nursing, *Radford* (MSN)

Shenandoah University, Division of Nursing, *Winchester* (MSN)

University of Virginia, School of Nursing, *Charlottesville* (MSN, MSN/MBA, MSN/PhD)

Virginia Commonwealth University, School of Nursing, *Richmond* (MS)

Washington

Intercollegiate College of Nursing/Washington State University, *Spokane* (MN)

Pacific Lutheran University, School of Nursing, *Tacoma* (MSN, MSN/MBA)

Seattle Pacific University, School of Health Sciences, *Seattle* (MSN)

Seattle University, College of Nursing, *Seattle* (MSN)

University of Washington, School of Nursing, *Seattle* (MN, MN/MPH)

West Virginia

Marshall University, College of Health Professions, *Huntington* (MSN)

Mountain State University, College of Nursing, *Beckley* (MSN)

West Virginia University, School of Nursing, *Morgantown* (MSN)

West Virginia Wesleyan College, Department of Nursing, *Buckhannon* (MSN)

Wheeling Jesuit University, Department of Nursing, *Wheeling* (MSN)

Wisconsin

Alverno College, Division of Nursing, *Milwaukee* (MSN)

Bellin College, Nursing Program, *Green Bay* (MSN)

Concordia University Wisconsin, Program in Nursing, *Mequon* (MSN)

Edgewood College, Program in Nursing, *Madison* (MS, MSN/MBA)

Marian University, Nursing Studies Division, *Fond du Lac* (MSN)

Marquette University, College of Nursing, *Milwaukee* (MSN, MSN/MBA)

University of Wisconsin-Eau Claire, College of Nursing and Health Sciences, *Eau Claire* (MSN)

University of Wisconsin-Milwaukee, College of Nursing, *Milwaukee* (MS, MS/MBA)

University of Wisconsin-Oshkosh, College of Nursing, *Oshkosh* (MSN)

Viterbo University, School of Nursing, *La Crosse* (MSN)

Wyoming

University of Wyoming, Fay W. Whitney School of Nursing, *Laramie* (MS)

CANADA

Alberta

Athabasca University, Centre for Nursing and Health Studies, *Athabasca* (MN, MN/MHSA, MN/MBA)

University of Alberta, Faculty of Nursing, *Edmonton* (MN)

University of Calgary, Faculty of Nursing, *Calgary* (MN)

University of Lethbridge, School of Health Sciences, *Lethbridge* (M Sc)

British Columbia

The University of British Columbia, Program in Nursing, *Vancouver* (MSN, MA/MSM)

University of Northern British Columbia, Nursing Programme, *Prince George* (M Sc N)

University of Victoria, School of Nursing, *Victoria* (MN)

Manitoba

University of Manitoba, Faculty of Nursing, *Winnipeg* (MN)

New Brunswick

Université de Moncton, School of Nursing, *Moncton* (M Sc N)

University of New Brunswick Fredericton, Faculty of Nursing, *Fredericton* (MN)

Newfoundland and Labrador

Memorial University of Newfoundland, School of Nursing, *St. John's* (MN)

Nova Scotia

Dalhousie University, School of Nursing, *Halifax* (MN, MN/MHSA)

Ontario

McMaster University, School of Nursing, *Hamilton* (M Sc, MSN/PhD)

Queen's University at Kingston, School of Nursing, *Kingston* (M Sc)

Ryerson University, Program in Nursing, *Toronto* (MN)

University of Ottawa, School of Nursing, *Ottawa* (M Sc N)

University of Toronto, Faculty of Nursing, *Toronto* (MN)

The University of Western Ontario, School of Nursing, *London* (M Sc N)

University of Windsor, Faculty of Nursing, *Windsor* (M Sc)

Quebec

McGill University, School of Nursing, *Montréal* (M Sc)

Université de Montréal, Faculty of Nursing, *Montréal* (M Sc)

Université de Sherbrooke, Department of Nursing, *Sherbrooke* (M Sc)

Université du Québec à Rimouski, Program in Nursing, *Rimouski* (M Sc N)

Université du Québec à Trois-Rivières, Program in Nursing, *Trois-Rivières* (MSN)

Université du Québec en Outaouais, Département des Sciences Infirmières, *Gatineau* (M Sc N)

Université Laval, Faculty of Nursing, *Québec* (MSN)

Saskatchewan

University of Saskatchewan, College of Nursing, *Saskatoon* (MN)

MASTER'S FOR NON-NURSING COLLEGE GRADUATES

U.S. AND U.S. TERRITORIES

California

California State University, Dominguez Hills, Program in Nursing, *Carson* (MS)

California State University, Long Beach, Department of Nursing, *Long Beach* (MSN, MSN/MPH)

California State University, Los Angeles, School of Nursing, *Los Angeles* (MSN)

Samuel Merritt University, School of Nursing, *Oakland* (MSN)

San Francisco State University, School of Nursing, *San Francisco* (MSN)

University of California, Los Angeles, School of Nursing, *Los Angeles* (MSN, MSN/MBA)

University of California, San Francisco, School of Nursing, *San Francisco* (MS)

Connecticut

Yale University, School of Nursing, *New Haven* (MSN, MSN/MPH, MSN/MDIV)

District of Columbia

Georgetown University, School of Nursing & Health Studies, *Washington* (MS)

MASTER'S DEGREE PROGRAMS
Master's for Non-Nursing College Graduates

Florida
University of Miami, School of Nursing and Health Studies, *Coral Gables* (MSN)

Hawaii
University of Hawaii at Manoa, School of Nursing and Dental Hygiene, *Honolulu* (MS, MSN/MBA)

Illinois
DePaul University, Department of Nursing, *Chicago* (MS)
Rush University, College of Nursing, *Chicago* (MSN)
University of Illinois at Chicago, College of Nursing, *Chicago* (MS, MS/MBA, MS/MPH)

Maine
University of Southern Maine, College of Nursing and Health Professions, *Portland* (MS, MS/MBA)

Massachusetts
MGH Institute of Health Professions, School of Nursing, *Boston* (MS)
Regis College, School of Nursing and Health Professions, *Weston* (MSN)
Simmons College, Department of Nursing, *Boston* (MS)

Nebraska
University of Nebraska Medical Center, College of Nursing, *Omaha* (MSN)

New York
Columbia University, School of Nursing, *New York* (MS, MSN/MBA, MSN/MPH)
Mercy College, Program in Nursing, *Dobbs Ferry* (MS)

Ohio
The Ohio State University, College of Nursing, *Columbus* (MS, MS/MPH)
The University of Toledo, College of Nursing, *Toledo* (MSN)

Oklahoma
University of Oklahoma Health Sciences Center, College of Nursing, *Oklahoma City* (MS)

Oregon
Oregon Health & Science University, School of Nursing, *Portland* (MS, MSN/MPH)
University of Portland, School of Nursing, *Portland* (MS)

Pennsylvania
Thomas Jefferson University, Department of Nursing, *Philadelphia* (MSN)
Wilkes University, Department of Nursing, *Wilkes-Barre* (MS)

Tennessee
University of Memphis, Loewenberg School of Nursing, *Memphis* (MSN)
The University of Tennessee, College of Nursing, *Knoxville* (MSN)
Vanderbilt University, School of Nursing, *Nashville* (MSN, MSN/MDIV, MSN/MTS)

Texas
Angelo State University, Department of Nursing, *San Angelo* (MSN)
The University of Texas at Austin, School of Nursing, *Austin* (MSN, MSN/MBA)

Vermont
University of Vermont, Department of Nursing, *Burlington* (MS)

Virginia
University of Virginia, School of Nursing, *Charlottesville* (MSN, MSN/MBA, MSN/PhD)

Washington
Pacific Lutheran University, School of Nursing, *Tacoma* (MSN, MSN/MBA)

Wisconsin
Marquette University, College of Nursing, *Milwaukee* (MSN, MSN/MBA)

CANADA

Quebec
McGill University, School of Nursing, *Montréal* (M Sc)

MASTER'S FOR NURSES WITH NON-NURSING DEGREES

U.S. AND U.S. TERRITORIES

Alabama
University of South Alabama, College of Nursing, *Mobile* (MSN)

Arizona
University of Phoenix, Online Campus, *Phoenix* (MSN, MSN/MBA, MSN/MHA)

Arkansas
Arkansas Tech University, Program in Nursing, *Russellville* (MSN)

California
California State University, Dominguez Hills, Program in Nursing, *Carson* (MS)
California State University, Fresno, Department of Nursing, *Fresno* (MSN)
California State University, Sacramento, Division of Nursing, *Sacramento* (MS)
Dominican University of California, Program in Nursing, *San Rafael* (MSN)
Holy Names University, Department of Nursing, *Oakland* (MSN, MSN/MBA)
Samuel Merritt University, School of Nursing, *Oakland* (MSN)
San Francisco State University, School of Nursing, *San Francisco* (MSN)
Sonoma State University, Department of Nursing, *Rohnert Park* (MSN)
University of California, San Francisco, School of Nursing, *San Francisco* (MS)
University of San Diego, Hahn School of Nursing and Health Science, *San Diego* (MSN, MSN/MBA)
University of San Francisco, School of Nursing, *San Francisco* (MSN)

Connecticut
Fairfield University, School of Nursing, *Fairfield* (MSN)
Saint Joseph College, Department of Nursing, *West Hartford* (MS)
University of Hartford, College of Education, Nursing, and Health Professions, *West Hartford* (MSN, MSN/MSOB)
Yale University, School of Nursing, *New Haven* (MSN, MSN/MPH, MSN/MDIV)

Delaware
University of Delaware, School of Nursing, *Newark* (MSN)

Florida
Florida Atlantic University, Christine E. Lynn College of Nursing, *Boca Raton* (MS, MSN/MBA)
Florida International University, Nursing Program, *Miami* (MSN)
Florida Southern College, Department of Nursing, *Lakeland* (MSN)

University of South Florida, College of Nursing, *Tampa* (MS, MS/MPH)

Georgia
Thomas University, Division of Nursing, *Thomasville* (MSN, MSN/MBA)

Illinois
DePaul University, Department of Nursing, *Chicago* (MS)
Rush University, College of Nursing, *Chicago* (MSN)
Saint Francis Medical Center College of Nursing, Baccalaureate Nursing Program, *Peoria* (MSN)
Saint Xavier University, School of Nursing, *Chicago* (MSN, MSN/MBA)
University of Illinois at Chicago, College of Nursing, *Chicago* (MS, MS/MBA, MS/MPH)
University of St. Francis, College of Nursing and Allied Health, *Joliet* (MSN)
West Suburban College of Nursing, *Oak Park* (MSN)

Indiana
University of Saint Francis, Department of Nursing, *Fort Wayne* (MSN)

Iowa
Allen College, Program in Nursing, *Waterloo* (MSN)
The University of Iowa, College of Nursing, *Iowa City* (MSN, MSN/MBA, MSN/MPH)

Kansas
Wichita State University, School of Nursing, *Wichita* (MSN, MSN/MBA)

Kentucky
Bellarmine University, Donna and Allan Lansing School of Nursing and Health Sciences, *Louisville* (MSN, MSN/MBA)

Louisiana
Loyola University New Orleans, School of Nursing, *New Orleans* (MSN)

Maine
Husson University, School of Nursing, *Bangor* (MSN)
Saint Joseph's College of Maine, Department of Nursing, *Standish* (MSN, MSN/MHA)
University of Southern Maine, College of Nursing and Health Professions, *Portland* (MS, MS/MBA)

Massachusetts
MGH Institute of Health Professions, School of Nursing, *Boston* (MS)
Regis College, School of Nursing and Health Professions, *Weston* (MSN)
Salem State College, Program in Nursing, *Salem* (MSN, MSN/MBA)
Simmons College, Department of Nursing, *Boston* (MS)

Michigan
University of Detroit Mercy, McAuley School of Nursing, *Detroit* (MSN)

Minnesota
Metropolitan State University, College of Nursing and Health Sciences, *St. Paul* (MSN)
Minnesota State University Mankato, School of Nursing, *Mankato* (MSN, MSN/MS)
Minnesota State University Moorhead, School of Nursing and Healthcare Leadership, *Moorhead* (MS)
Winona State University, College of Nursing and Health Sciences, *Winona* (MS)

Missouri

Saint Louis University, School of Nursing, *St. Louis* (MSN, MSN/MPH)

Nebraska

BryanLGH College of Health Sciences, School of Nursing, *Lincoln* (MS)

Nebraska Methodist College, Department of Nursing, *Omaha* (MSN)

Nevada

Touro University, School of Nursing, *Henderson* (MSN)

New Hampshire

Franklin Pierce University, Master of Science in Nursing, *Rindge* (MSN)

Rivier College, Division of Nursing, *Nashua* (MS)

University of New Hampshire, Department of Nursing, *Durham* (MS)

New Jersey

The College of New Jersey, School of Nursing, Health and Exercise Science, *Ewing* (MSN)

Fairleigh Dickinson University, Metropolitan Campus, Henry P. Becton School of Nursing and Allied Health, *Teaneck* (MSN)

Kean University, Department of Nursing, *Union* (MSN, MSN/MPA)

Saint Peter's College, Nursing Program, *Jersey City* (MSN)

Seton Hall University, College of Nursing, *South Orange* (MSN, MSN/MA, MSN/MBA)

University of Medicine and Dentistry of New Jersey, School of Nursing, *Newark* (MSN, MSN/MPH)

William Paterson University of New Jersey, Department of Nursing, *Wayne* (MSN)

New York

College of Mount Saint Vincent, Department of Nursing, *Riverdale* (MSN)

Columbia University, School of Nursing, *New York* (MS, MSN/MBA, MSN/MPH)

Lehman College of the City University of New York, Department of Nursing, *Bronx* (MS)

Le Moyne College, Nursing Programs, *Syracuse* (MS)

Long Island University, C.W. Post Campus, Department of Nursing, *Brookville* (MS, MSN/MA, MSN/MBA)

Mercy College, Program in Nursing, *Dobbs Ferry* (MS)

Pace University, Lienhard School of Nursing, *New York* (MS)

State University of New York Upstate Medical University, College of Nursing, *Syracuse* (MS)

North Carolina

The University of North Carolina at Chapel Hill, School of Nursing, *Chapel Hill* (MSN, MSN/MS)

Ohio

The Ohio State University, College of Nursing, *Columbus* (MS, MS/MPH)

The University of Toledo, College of Nursing, *Toledo* (MSN)

Wright State University, College of Nursing and Health, *Dayton* (MS, MS/MBA)

Xavier University, Department of Nursing, *Cincinnati* (MSN, MSN/MBA)

Oregon

Oregon Health & Science University, School of Nursing, *Portland* (MS, MSN/MPH)

Pennsylvania

Bloomsburg University of Pennsylvania, Department of Nursing, *Bloomsburg* (MSN, MSN/MBA)

Drexel University, College of Nursing and Health Professions, *Philadelphia* (MSN)

Indiana University of Pennsylvania, Department of Nursing and Allied Health, *Indiana* (MS)

Thomas Jefferson University, Department of Nursing, *Philadelphia* (MSN)

Widener University, School of Nursing, *Chester* (MSN, MSN/PhD)

Tennessee

Tennessee Technological University, School of Nursing, *Cookeville* (MSN, M Sc N)

University of Memphis, Loewenberg School of Nursing, *Memphis* (MSN)

The University of Tennessee, College of Nursing, *Knoxville* (MSN)

Vanderbilt University, School of Nursing, *Nashville* (MSN, MSN/MDIV, MSN/MTS)

Texas

Texas A&M International University, Canseco School of Nursing, *Laredo* (MSN)

The University of Texas at Austin, School of Nursing, *Austin* (MSN, MSN/MBA)

Vermont

University of Vermont, Department of Nursing, *Burlington* (MS)

Virginia

Jefferson College of Health Sciences, Nursing Education Program, *Roanoke* (MSN)

University of Virginia, School of Nursing, *Charlottesville* (MSN, MSN/MBA, MSN/PhD)

Virginia Commonwealth University, School of Nursing, *Richmond* (MS)

Washington

Gonzaga University, Department of Nursing, *Spokane* (MSN)

Pacific Lutheran University, School of Nursing, *Tacoma* (MSN, MSN/MBA)

Seattle Pacific University, School of Health Sciences, *Seattle* (MSN)

University of Washington, School of Nursing, *Seattle* (MN, MN/MPH)

Wisconsin

Marquette University, College of Nursing, *Milwaukee* (MSN, MSN/MBA)

Wyoming

University of Wyoming, Fay W. Whitney School of Nursing, *Laramie* (MS)

CANADA

Alberta

Athabasca University, Centre for Nursing and Health Studies, *Athabasca* (MN, MN/MHSA, MN/MBA)

RN TO MASTER'S

U.S. AND U.S. TERRITORIES

Alabama

Samford University, Ida V. Moffett School of Nursing, *Birmingham* (MSN, MSN/MBA)

Spring Hill College, Division of Nursing, *Mobile* (MSN)

Troy University, School of Nursing, *Troy* (MSN)

The University of Alabama, Capstone College of Nursing, *Tuscaloosa* (MSN, MSN/MA, MSN/Ed D)

The University of Alabama at Birmingham, School of Nursing, *Birmingham* (MSN, MSN/MPH)

The University of Alabama in Huntsville, College of Nursing, *Huntsville* (MSN)

Arizona

Grand Canyon University, College of Nursing and Health Sciences, *Phoenix* (MS, MS/MBA)

Arkansas

Arkansas Tech University, Program in Nursing, *Russellville* (MSN)

University of Arkansas for Medical Sciences, College of Nursing, *Little Rock* (MN Sc)

University of Central Arkansas, Department of Nursing, *Conway* (MSN)

California

Loma Linda University, School of Nursing, *Loma Linda* (MS, MS/MA, MS/MPH)

Mount St. Mary's College, Department of Nursing, *Los Angeles* (MSN)

Point Loma Nazarene University, School of Nursing, *San Diego* (MSN)

University of San Francisco, School of Nursing, *San Francisco* (MSN)

Colorado

Regis University, School of Nursing, *Denver* (MS)

University of Colorado Denver, College of Nursing, *Denver* (MS)

Connecticut

Sacred Heart University, Program in Nursing, *Fairfield* (MSN, MSN/MBA)

Southern Connecticut State University, Department of Nursing, *New Haven* (MSN)

University of Connecticut, School of Nursing, *Storrs* (MS, MS/MBA)

Delaware

University of Delaware, School of Nursing, *Newark* (MSN)

Wesley College, Nursing Program, *Dover* (MSN)

Florida

Florida Atlantic University, Christine E. Lynn College of Nursing, *Boca Raton* (MS, MSN/MBA)

Jacksonville University, School of Nursing, *Jacksonville* (MSN, MSN/MBA)

South University, Nursing Program, *West Palm Beach* (MSN)

University of Central Florida, School of Nursing, *Orlando* (MSN)

University of North Florida, School of Nursing, *Jacksonville* (MSN)

University of South Florida, College of Nursing, *Tampa* (MS, MS/MPH)

The University of Tampa, Department of Nursing, *Tampa* (MSN)

Georgia

Albany State University, College of Sciences and Health Professions, *Albany* (MSN)

Armstrong Atlantic State University, Program in Nursing, *Savannah* (MSN, MS/MHSA)

Brenau University, School of Health and Science, *Gainesville* (MSN)

Emory University, Nell Hodgson Woodruff School of Nursing, *Atlanta* (MSN, MSN/MPH)

Georgia College & State University, College of Health Sciences, *Milledgeville* (MSN, MSN/MBA)

Georgia Southern University, School of Nursing, *Statesboro* (MSN)

Georgia State University, Byrdine F. Lewis School of Nursing, *Atlanta* (MSN)

Medical College of Georgia, School of Nursing, *Augusta* (MSN)

Valdosta State University, College of Nursing, *Valdosta* (MSN)

MASTER'S DEGREE PROGRAMS
RN to Master's

Hawaii

Hawai'i Pacific University, College of Nursing and Health Sciences, *Honolulu* (MSN, MSN/MBA)

University of Hawaii at Manoa, School of Nursing and Dental Hygiene, *Honolulu* (MS, MSN/MBA)

Idaho

Northwest Nazarene University, School of Health and Science, *Nampa* (MSN)

Illinois

DePaul University, Department of Nursing, *Chicago* (MS)

Lewis University, Program in Nursing, *Romeoville* (MSN, MSN/MBA)

Loyola University Chicago, Marcella Niehoff School of Nursing, *Maywood* (MSN, MSN/MBA, MSN/MDIV)

McKendree University, Department of Nursing, *Lebanon* (MSN)

North Park University, School of Nursing, *Chicago* (MS, MSN/MA, MSN/MBA, MSN/MM)

Rush University, College of Nursing, *Chicago* (MSN)

Saint Francis Medical Center College of Nursing, Baccalaureate Nursing Program, *Peoria* (MSN)

West Suburban College of Nursing, *Oak Park* (MSN)

Indiana

Ball State University, School of Nursing, *Muncie* (MS)

Indiana University–Purdue University Indianapolis, School of Nursing, *Indianapolis* (MSN, MSN/MPH)

University of Southern Indiana, College of Nursing and Health Professions, *Evansville* (MSN)

Valparaiso University, College of Nursing, *Valparaiso* (MSN, MSN/MBA)

Iowa

Allen College, Program in Nursing, *Waterloo* (MSN)

Kansas

The University of Kansas, School of Nursing, *Kansas City* (MS, MS/MHSA, MS/MPH)

Wichita State University, School of Nursing, *Wichita* (MSN, MSN/MBA)

Kentucky

Bellarmine University, Donna and Allan Lansing School of Nursing and Health Sciences, *Louisville* (MSN, MSN/MBA)

University of Kentucky, Graduate School Programs in the College of Nursing, *Lexington* (MSN)

Louisiana

Loyola University New Orleans, School of Nursing, *New Orleans* (MSN)

University of Louisiana at Lafayette, College of Nursing, *Lafayette* (MSN)

Maine

Saint Joseph's College of Maine, Department of Nursing, *Standish* (MSN, MSN/MHA)

University of Maine, School of Nursing, *Orono* (MSN)

University of Southern Maine, College of Nursing and Health Professions, *Portland* (MS, MS/MBA)

Maryland

Salisbury University, Program in Nursing, *Salisbury* (MS)

University of Maryland, Baltimore, Master's Program in Nursing, *Baltimore* (MS, MSN/MBA, MSN/MPH, MSN/JD)

Massachusetts

Boston College, William F. Connell School of Nursing, *Chestnut Hill* (MS, MSN/MA, MSN/MBA, MSN/PhD)

Curry College, Division of Nursing, *Milton* (MSN)

Elms College, Division of Nursing, *Chicopee* (MSN)

MGH Institute of Health Professions, School of Nursing, *Boston* (MS)

Northeastern University, School of Nursing, *Boston* (MS, MSN/MBA)

Regis College, School of Nursing and Health Professions, *Weston* (MSN)

Salem State College, Program in Nursing, *Salem* (MSN, MSN/MBA)

Simmons College, Department of Nursing, *Boston* (MS)

Michigan

Saginaw Valley State University, Crystal M. Lange College of Nursing and Health Sciences, *University Center* (MSN)

University of Michigan, School of Nursing, *Ann Arbor* (MS, MSN/MBA, MSN/MPH)

Minnesota

Metropolitan State University, College of Nursing and Health Sciences, *St. Paul* (MSN)

Minnesota State University Mankato, School of Nursing, *Mankato* (MSN, MSN/MS)

Winona State University, College of Nursing and Health Sciences, *Winona* (MS)

Mississippi

University of Mississippi Medical Center, Program in Nursing, *Jackson* (MSN)

University of Southern Mississippi, School of Nursing, *Hattiesburg* (MSN)

Missouri

Graceland University, School of Nursing, *Independence* (MSN)

Maryville University of Saint Louis, Nursing Program, School of Health Professions, *St. Louis* (MSN)

Missouri State University, Department of Nursing, *Springfield* (MSN)

Saint Louis University, School of Nursing, *St. Louis* (MSN, MSN/MPH)

Webster University, Department of Nursing, *St. Louis* (MSN)

Nebraska

Clarkson College, Master of Science in Nursing Program, *Omaha* (MSN)

Nebraska Wesleyan University, Department of Nursing, *Lincoln* (MSN)

University of Nebraska Medical Center, College of Nursing, *Omaha* (MSN)

New Hampshire

Franklin Pierce University, Master of Science in Nursing, *Rindge* (MSN)

Rivier College, Division of Nursing, *Nashua* (MS)

New Jersey

The College of New Jersey, School of Nursing, Health and Exercise Science, *Ewing* (MSN)

Fairleigh Dickinson University, Metropolitan Campus, Henry P. Becton School of Nursing and Allied Health, *Teaneck* (MSN)

Seton Hall University, College of Nursing, *South Orange* (MSN, MSN/MA, MSN/MBA)

Thomas Edison State College, School of Nursing, *Trenton* (MSN)

New York

The College of New Rochelle, School of Nursing, *New Rochelle* (MS)

Daemen College, Department of Nursing, *Amherst* (MS)

D'Youville College, Department of Nursing, *Buffalo* (MS)

Excelsior College, School of Nursing, *Albany* (MS)

Long Island University, Brooklyn Campus, School of Nursing, *Brooklyn* (MS)

New York University, College of Nursing, *New York* (MS, MSN/MPH)

Pace University, Lienhard School of Nursing, *New York* (MS)

St. John Fisher College, Advanced Practice Nursing Program, *Rochester* (MS)

State University of New York Upstate Medical University, College of Nursing, *Syracuse* (MS)

Stony Brook University, State University of New York, School of Nursing, *Stony Brook* (MS)

North Carolina

Duke University, School of Nursing, *Durham* (MSN, MSN/MBA)

East Carolina University, College of Nursing, *Greenville* (MSN)

Gardner-Webb University, School of Nursing, *Boiling Springs* (MSN, MSN/MBA)

Queens University of Charlotte, Presbyterian School of Nursing, *Charlotte* (MSN, MSN/MBA)

The University of North Carolina at Chapel Hill, School of Nursing, *Chapel Hill* (MSN, MSN/MS)

The University of North Carolina at Charlotte, School of Nursing, *Charlotte* (MSN)

The University of North Carolina Wilmington, School of Nursing, *Wilmington* (MSN)

North Dakota

University of Mary, Division of Nursing, *Bismarck* (MSN, MSN/MBA)

University of North Dakota, College of Nursing, *Grand Forks* (MS)

Ohio

Capital University, School of Nursing, *Columbus* (MSN, MN/MBA, MSN/JD, MSN/MDIV)

Case Western Reserve University, Frances Payne Bolton School of Nursing, *Cleveland* (MSN, MSN/MA, MSN/MBA, MSN/MPH)

Franciscan University of Steubenville, Department of Nursing, *Steubenville* (MSN)

The University of Akron, College of Nursing, *Akron* (MSN)

Xavier University, Department of Nursing, *Cincinnati* (MSN, MSN/MBA)

Oregon

University of Portland, School of Nursing, *Portland* (MS)

Pennsylvania

Bloomsburg University of Pennsylvania, Department of Nursing, *Bloomsburg* (MSN, MSN/MBA)

Carlow University, School of Nursing, *Pittsburgh* (MSN)

Clarion University of Pennsylvania, School of Nursing, *Oil City* (MSN)

DeSales University, Department of Nursing and Health, *Center Valley* (MSN, MSN/MBA)

Drexel University, College of Nursing and Health Professions, *Philadelphia* (MSN)

Gannon University, Villa Maria School of Nursing, *Erie* (MSN)

Gwynedd-Mercy College, School of Nursing, *Gwynedd Valley* (MSN)

La Roche College, Department of Nursing and Nursing Management, *Pittsburgh* (MSN)

La Salle University, School of Nursing and Health Sciences, *Philadelphia* (MSN, MSN/MBA)

Misericordia University, Department of Nursing, *Dallas* (MSN)

Neumann University, Program in Nursing and Health Sciences, *Aston* (MS)

Thomas Jefferson University, Department of Nursing, *Philadelphia* (MSN)

University of Pittsburgh, School of Nursing, *Pittsburgh* (MSN)

The University of Scranton, Department of Nursing, *Scranton* (MS)

Villanova University, College of Nursing, *Villanova* (MSN)

Wilkes University, Department of Nursing, *Wilkes-Barre* (MS)

York College of Pennsylvania, Department of Nursing, *York* (MS)

Rhode Island

University of Rhode Island, College of Nursing, *Kingston* (MS)

South Carolina

Charleston Southern University, Wingo School of Nursing, *Charleston* (MSN)

Clemson University, School of Nursing, *Clemson* (MS)

South Dakota

South Dakota State University, College of Nursing, *Brookings* (MS)

Tennessee

Carson-Newman College, Division of Nursing, *Jefferson City* (MSN)

Tennessee State University, School of Nursing, *Nashville* (MSN)

The University of Tennessee, College of Nursing, *Knoxville* (MSN)

Vanderbilt University, School of Nursing, *Nashville* (MSN, MSN/MDIV, MSN/MTS)

Texas

Angelo State University, Department of Nursing, *San Angelo* (MSN)

Midwestern State University, Nursing Program, *Wichita Falls* (MSN, MN/MHSA, MSN/MHA)

Texas Christian University, Harris College of Nursing, *Fort Worth* (MSN)

Texas Tech University Health Sciences Center, School of Nursing, *Lubbock* (MSN)

Texas Woman's University, College of Nursing, *Denton* (MS, MSN/MHA)

University of Houston–Victoria, School of Nursing, *Victoria* (MSN)

The University of Texas at El Paso, School of Nursing, *El Paso* (MSN)

The University of Texas at Tyler, Program in Nursing, *Tyler* (MSN, MSN/MBA)

The University of Texas Health Science Center at San Antonio, School of Nursing, *San Antonio* (MSN, MSN/MPH)

The University of Texas Medical Branch, School of Nursing, *Galveston* (MSN, MSN/PhD)

West Texas A&M University, Division of Nursing, *Canyon* (MSN)

Vermont

University of Vermont, Department of Nursing, *Burlington* (MS)

Virginia

George Mason University, College of Health and Human Services, *Fairfax* (MSN, MSN/MBA)

Old Dominion University, Department of Nursing, *Norfolk* (MSN)

Shenandoah University, Division of Nursing, *Winchester* (MSN)

Virginia Commonwealth University, School of Nursing, *Richmond* (MS)

Washington

Gonzaga University, Department of Nursing, *Spokane* (MSN)

West Virginia

West Virginia University, School of Nursing, *Morgantown* (MSN)

Wisconsin

Marquette University, College of Nursing, *Milwaukee* (MSN, MSN/MBA)

University of Wisconsin–Eau Claire, College of Nursing and Health Sciences, *Eau Claire* (MSN)

University of Wisconsin–Milwaukee, College of Nursing, *Milwaukee* (MS, MS/MBA)

CANADA

Alberta

University of Calgary, Faculty of Nursing, *Calgary* (MN)

New Brunswick

Université de Moncton, School of Nursing, *Moncton* (M Sc N)

Quebec

Université de Montréal, Faculty of Nursing, *Montréal* (M Sc)

Université du Québec à Chicoutimi, Program in Nursing, *Chicoutimi* (MSN)

CASE MANAGEMENT

Boise State University, ID
Carlow University, PA
DePaul University, IL
Duke University, NC
Gonzaga University, WA
Intercollegiate College of Nursing/Washington State University, WA
The Johns Hopkins University, MD
Kent State University, OH
Lewis University, IL
Loyola University New Orleans, LA
Pacific Lutheran University, WA
Regis College, MA
Saint Peter's College, NJ
Samuel Merritt University, CA
San Francisco State University, CA
Seton Hall University, NJ
Shenandoah University, VA
Université de Moncton, NB
The University of Alabama, AL
University of Central Florida, FL
University of Kentucky, KY
University of Nebraska Medical Center, NE
University of New Brunswick Fredericton, NB
The University of North Carolina at Chapel Hill, NC
Ursuline College, OH
Valdosta State University, GA

CLINICAL NURSE LEADER

Augustana College, SD
Boise State University, ID
Brenau University, GA
California State University, Dominguez Hills, CA
Cleveland State University, OH
Creighton University, NE
Curry College, MA
East Tennessee State University, TN
Elmhurst College, IL
Fairfield University, CT
Florida Atlantic University, FL
George Mason University, VA
Idaho State University, ID
Illinois State University, IL
James Madison University, VA
Kutztown University of Pennsylvania, PA
Marquette University, WI
Medical College of Georgia, GA
Millikin University, IL
Montana State University, MT
Moravian College, PA
The Ohio State University, OH
Pacific Lutheran University, WA
Pittsburg State University, KS
Queens University of Charlotte, NC
Regis College, MA
Rush University, IL
Sacred Heart University, CT
Saint Anthony College of Nursing, IL
Saint Francis Medical Center College of Nursing, IL
Saint Xavier University, IL
Salem State College, MA
Seattle Pacific University, WA
Seton Hall University, NJ
Sonoma State University, CA
South Dakota State University, SD
Southern Connecticut State University, CT

Spring Hill College, AL
Texas Christian University, TX
Université Laval, QC
The University of Alabama, AL
The University of Alabama at Birmingham, AL
The University of Alabama in Huntsville, AL
University of California, Los Angeles, CA
University of Connecticut, CT
University of Florida, FL
University of Mary Hardin-Baylor, TX
University of Maryland, Baltimore, MD
University of Massachusetts Amherst, MA
University of Medicine and Dentistry of New Jersey, NJ
University of Nevada, Reno, NV
The University of North Carolina at Chapel Hill, NC
University of Oklahoma Health Sciences Center, OK
University of Pittsburgh, PA
University of Portland, OR
University of Rhode Island, RI
University of Rochester, NY
University of San Diego, CA
University of San Francisco, CA
University of Southern Maine, ME
University of South Florida, FL
The University of Tennessee Health Science Center, TN
University of the Incarnate Word, TX
The University of Toledo, OH
University of Toronto, ON
University of Utah, UT
University of Virginia, VA
University of West Georgia, GA
University of Wisconsin-Oshkosh, WI
Vanderbilt University, TN
Virginia Commonwealth University, VA
Western University of Health Sciences, CA
West Suburban College of Nursing, IL
Wright State University, OH
Xavier University, OH

CLINICAL NURSE SPECIALIST PROGRAMS

Acute Care

Arizona State University at the Downtown Phoenix Campus, AZ
California State University, Fresno, CA
Colorado State University-Pueblo, CO
George Mason University, VA
Georgetown University, DC
Georgia Baptist College of Nursing of Mercer University, GA
Indiana University-Purdue University Indianapolis, IN
The Johns Hopkins University, MD
Kent State University, OH
King College, TN
Liberty University, VA
Loyola University Chicago, IL
McGill University, QC
Memorial University of Newfoundland, NL
MGH Institute of Health Professions, MA
Regis College, MA
Rhode Island College, RI
The Sage Colleges, NY
Seattle Pacific University, WA
Thomas Jefferson University, PA

Université de Montréal, QC
Université de Sherbrooke, QC
Université du Québec à Chicoutimi, QC
Université du Québec à Trois-Rivières, QC
Université Laval, QC
University of Arkansas, AR
University of Arkansas for Medical Sciences, AR
University of Calgary, AB
University of California, Los Angeles, CA
University of Central Florida, FL
University of Connecticut, CT
University of Illinois at Chicago, IL
University of Kentucky, KY
University of Manitoba, MB
University of Maryland, Baltimore, MD
University of Massachusetts Boston, MA
University of Missouri-Columbia, MO
University of Nebraska Medical Center, NE
University of New Brunswick Fredericton, NB
University of Oklahoma Health Sciences Center, OK
University of Ottawa, ON
University of San Diego, CA
University of South Alabama, AL
University of South Carolina, SC
The University of Texas Health Science Center at Houston, TX
University of Toronto, ON
University of Virginia, VA
The University of Western Ontario, ON
Virginia Commonwealth University, VA
Wayne State University, MI
Wichita State University, KS

Adult Health

Alverno College, WI
Angelo State University, TX
Arizona State University at the Downtown Phoenix Campus, AZ
Arkansas State University, AR
Armstrong Atlantic State University, GA
Auburn University, AL
Auburn University Montgomery, AL
Azusa Pacific University, CA
Ball State University, IN
Bloomsburg University of Pennsylvania, PA
Boston College, MA
California State University, Chico, CA
California State University, Long Beach, CA
California State University, Sacramento, CA
The Catholic University of America, DC
Clemson University, SC
College of Mount Saint Vincent, NY
The College of New Jersey, NJ
The College of St. Scholastica, MN
College of Staten Island of the City University of New York, NY
Creighton University, NE
Dalhousie University, NS
DeSales University, PA
East Carolina University, NC
Eastern Michigan University, MI
Florida Southern College, FL
George Mason University, VA
Georgia College & State University, GA
Georgia State University, GA
Gonzaga University, WA
Governors State University, IL
Grambling State University, LA
Grand Canyon University, AZ
Hampton University, VA
Idaho State University, ID

CONCENTRATIONS WITHIN MASTER'S DEGREE PROGRAMS
Clinical Nurse Specialist Programs

Indiana University-Purdue University
  Indianapolis, IN
The Johns Hopkins University, MD
Kennesaw State University, GA
Kent State University, OH
King College, TN
La Salle University, PA
Lehman College of the City University of New
  York, NY
Loma Linda University, CA
Long Island University, C.W. Post Campus, NY
Louisiana State University Health Sciences
  Center, LA
Malone University, OH
Marquette University, WI
McGill University, QC
McNeese State University, LA
Memorial University of Newfoundland, NL
MGH Institute of Health Professions, MA
Minnesota State University Mankato, MN
Minnesota State University Moorhead, MN
Misericordia University, PA
Molloy College, NY
Mount Carmel College of Nursing, OH
Mount Saint Mary College, NY
Mount St. Mary's College, CA
Murray State University, KY
North Dakota State University, ND
Northern Illinois University, IL
Northwestern State University of Louisiana, LA
The Ohio State University, OH
Otterbein College, OH
Penn State University Park, PA
Purdue University Calumet, IN
Radford University, VA
Rutgers, The State University of New Jersey,
  College of Nursing, NJ
Ryerson University, ON
The Sage Colleges, NY
Saint Anthony College of Nursing, IL
St. John Fisher College, NY
St. Joseph's College, New York, NY
Saint Louis University, MO
San Diego State University, CA
San Francisco State University, CA
Seattle Pacific University, WA
Southeastern Louisiana University, LA
Southeast Missouri State University, MO
State University of New York Downstate
  Medical Center, NY
Stony Brook University, State University of
  New York, NY
Texas A&M University-Corpus Christi, TX
Texas Christian University, TX
Texas Woman's University, TX
Thomas Jefferson University, PA
Troy University, AL
Union University, TN
Université de Montréal, QC
Université du Québec à Chicoutimi, QC
Université du Québec à Trois-Rivières, QC
Université Laval, QC
University at Buffalo, the State University of
  New York, NY
The University of Akron, OH
The University of Alabama at Birmingham, AL
The University of Alabama in Huntsville, AL
University of Arkansas for Medical Sciences, AR
The University of British Columbia, BC
University of Calgary, AB
University of California, Los Angeles, CA
University of Cincinnati, OH
University of Colorado at Colorado Springs, CO
University of Colorado Denver, CO
University of Delaware, DE
University of Illinois at Chicago, IL
The University of Iowa, IA
The University of Kansas, KS

University of Kentucky, KY
University of Louisiana at Lafayette, LA
University of Mary Hardin-Baylor, TX
University of Massachusetts Dartmouth, MA
University of Minnesota, Twin Cities Campus,
  MN
University of Missouri-Columbia, MO
University of Nebraska Medical Center, NE
University of New Brunswick Fredericton, NB
University of New Hampshire, NH
University of North Florida, FL
University of Pennsylvania, PA
University of Puerto Rico, Medical Sciences
  Campus, PR
University of St. Francis, IL
University of San Diego, CA
The University of Scranton, PA
University of Southern Mississippi, MS
The University of Tennessee, TN
The University of Texas at Austin, TX
The University of Texas Health Science Center
  at Houston, TX
The University of Texas-Pan American, TX
University of the Incarnate Word, TX
The University of Toledo, OH
University of Toronto, ON
University of Virginia, VA
The University of Western Ontario, ON
University of Wisconsin-Eau Claire, WI
University of Wisconsin-Milwaukee, WI
Ursuline College, OH
Valdosta State University, GA
Valparaiso University, IN
Vanderbilt University, TN
Western Connecticut State University, CT
Widener University, PA
Winona State University, MN
Wright State University, OH
York College of Pennsylvania, PA

Cardiovascular
Creighton University, NE
George Mason University, VA
The Johns Hopkins University, MD
Kent State University, OH
Loyola University Chicago, IL
McGill University, QC
The Ohio State University, OH
The Sage Colleges, NY
Université de Montréal, QC
Université du Québec à Chicoutimi, QC
Université Laval, QC
University of Calgary, AB
University of California, San Francisco, CA
University of Illinois at Chicago, IL
University of Missouri-Columbia, MO
University of Nebraska Medical Center, NE
University of New Brunswick Fredericton, NB
University of North Florida, FL
University of Washington, WA
Yale University, CT

Community Health
Arizona State University at the Downtown
  . Phoenix Campus, AZ
Augsburg College, MN
Bloomsburg University of Pennsylvania, PA
Boston College, MA
California State University, Fresno, CA
California State University, Sacramento, CA
California State University, San Bernardino, CA
The Catholic University of America, DC
Cleveland State University, OH
Dalhousie University, NS
DePaul University, IL
D'Youville College, NY
Georgia Southern University, GA
Hampton University, VA

Hawai'i Pacific University, HI
Holy Family University, PA
Hunter College of the City University of New
  York, NY
Indiana University-Purdue University
  Indianapolis, IN
Intercollegiate College of Nursing/Washington
  State University, WA
Jacksonville State University, AL
The Johns Hopkins University, MD
Kean University, NJ
La Roche College, PA
Louisiana State University Health Sciences
  Center, LA
McGill University, QC
Memorial University of Newfoundland, NL
Mount St. Mary's College, CA
New Mexico State University, NM
Northern Illinois University, IL
North Park University, IL
The Ohio State University, OH
Penn State University Park, PA
Rhode Island College, RI
Rush University, IL
Rutgers, The State University of New Jersey,
  College of Nursing, NJ
Ryerson University, ON
The Sage Colleges, NY
Salem State College, MA
San Diego State University, CA
Seattle Pacific University, WA
Seattle University, WA
State University of New York at Binghamton,
  NY
Stony Brook University, State University of
  New York, NY
Thomas Jefferson University, PA
Université de Moncton, NB
Université de Montréal, QC
Université de Sherbrooke, QC
Université du Québec à Chicoutimi, QC
Université du Québec à Rimouski, QC
Université du Québec à Trois-Rivières, QC
Université du Québec en Outaouais, QC
Université Laval, QC
University of Alaska Anchorage, AK
The University of British Columbia, BC
University of Calgary, AB
University of California, San Francisco, CA
University of Connecticut, CT
University of Illinois at Chicago, IL
The University of Iowa, IA
University of Kentucky, KY
University of Maryland, Baltimore, MD
University of Massachusetts Dartmouth, MA
University of Michigan, MI
University of Missouri-Columbia, MO
University of Nebraska Medical Center, NE
University of New Brunswick Fredericton, NB
The University of North Carolina at Charlotte,
  NC
University of North Dakota, ND
University of North Florida, FL
University of Ottawa, ON
University of Puerto Rico, Medical Sciences
  Campus, PR
University of South Alabama, AL
University of South Carolina, SC
University of Southern Mississippi, MS
The University of Texas at Austin, TX
University of Toronto, ON
University of Virginia, VA
University of Washington, WA
The University of Western Ontario, ON
University of Wisconsin-Milwaukee, WI
Wayne State University, MI
Wesley College, DE
West Chester University of Pennsylvania, PA

Widener University, PA
William Paterson University of New Jersey, NJ
Worcester State College, MA
Wright State University, OH

Critical Care

California State University, Fresno, CA
Duke University, NC
George Mason University, VA
Georgetown University, DC
Georgia Baptist College of Nursing of Mercer University, GA
Gonzaga University, WA
Indiana University–Purdue University Indianapolis, IN
The Johns Hopkins University, MD
Kent State University, OH
McGill University, QC
Murray State University, KY
Northwestern State University of Louisiana, LA
Purdue University Calumet, IN
Rhode Island College, RI
Rush University, IL
The Sage Colleges, NY
San Diego State University, CA
Seattle Pacific University, WA
Stony Brook University, State University of New York, NY
Thomas Jefferson University, PA
Université du Québec à Chicoutimi, QC
Université du Québec à Rimouski, QC
Université du Québec à Trois-Rivières, QC
Université du Québec en Outaouais, QC
Université Laval, QC
University of Calgary, AB
University of California, San Francisco, CA
University of Central Florida, FL
University of Cincinnati, OH
University of Kentucky, KY
University of Maryland, Baltimore, MD
University of Massachusetts Boston, MA
University of Missouri–Columbia, MO
University of Nebraska Medical Center, NE
University of New Brunswick Fredericton, NB
University of North Florida, FL
University of Puerto Rico, Medical Sciences Campus, PR
The University of Texas Health Science Center at Houston, TX
The University of Texas Health Science Center at San Antonio, TX
University of Toronto, ON
University of Virginia, VA
University of Washington, WA
Wayne State University, MI
Widener University, PA
Yale University, CT

Family Health

California State University, Sacramento, CA
College of Mount Saint Vincent, NY
Creighton University, NE
Dalhousie University, NS
The Johns Hopkins University, MD
Loma Linda University, CA
McGill University, QC
MGH Institute of Health Professions, MA
Minnesota State University Mankato, MN
Missouri Southern State University, MO
Pittsburg State University, KS
Point Loma Nazarene University, CA
Ryerson University, ON
The Sage Colleges, NY
Saint Joseph College, CT
Southern University and Agricultural and Mechanical College, LA
State University of New York at Binghamton, NY

Stony Brook University, State University of New York, NY
Tennessee State University, TN
Université de Moncton, NB
Université de Montréal, QC
Université de Sherbrooke, QC
Université du Québec à Chicoutimi, QC
Université du Québec à Trois-Rivières, QC
Université Laval, QC
The University of British Columbia, BC
University of Calgary, AB
University of Illinois at Chicago, IL
University of Manitoba, MB
University of Nebraska Medical Center, NE
University of New Brunswick Fredericton, NB
University of Northern Colorado, CO
University of South Alabama, AL
University of Toronto, ON
Valdosta State University, GA
Webster University, MO

Forensic Nursing

Boston College, MA
Cleveland State University, OH
Duquesne University, PA
Fairleigh Dickinson University, Metropolitan Campus, NJ
Fitchburg State College, MA
The Johns Hopkins University, MD
Monmouth University, NJ
Xavier University, OH

Gerontology

Alverno College, WI
Auburn University, AL
Auburn University Montgomery, AL
Boston College, MA
California State University, Dominguez Hills, CA
Case Western Reserve University, OH
Clemson University, SC
College of Mount Saint Vincent, NY
The College of St. Scholastica, MN
College of Staten Island of the City University of New York, NY
Creighton University, NE
Dominican University of California, CA
Duke University, NC
Gonzaga University, WA
Gwynedd-Mercy College, PA
The Johns Hopkins University, MD
Kent State University, OH
Lehman College of the City University of New York, NY
Marquette University, WI
McGill University, QC
MGH Institute of Health Professions, MA
Neumann University, PA
Penn State University Park, PA
Point Loma Nazarene University, CA
Radford University, VA
Rush University, IL
The Sage Colleges, NY
St. John Fisher College, NY
Saint Louis University, MO
San Diego State University, CA
San Jose State University, CA
Seattle Pacific University, WA
State University of New York at Binghamton, NY
Université de Montréal, QC
Université de Sherbrooke, QC
Université du Québec à Chicoutimi, QC
Université du Québec à Rimouski, QC
Université Laval, QC
The University of Akron, OH
University of Calgary, AB
University of California, Los Angeles, CA

University of California, San Francisco, CA
University of Cincinnati, OH
University of Illinois at Chicago, IL
The University of Iowa, IA
The University of Kansas, KS
University of Kentucky, KY
University of Manitoba, MB
University of Michigan, MI
University of Minnesota, Twin Cities Campus, MN
University of Nebraska Medical Center, NE
University of New Brunswick Fredericton, NB
University of North Dakota, ND
University of North Florida, FL
University of Puerto Rico, Medical Sciences Campus, PR
University of Rhode Island, RI
University of South Alabama, AL
The University of Tennessee, TN
The University of Texas Health Science Center at Houston, TX
University of Toronto, ON
University of Washington, WA
Valparaiso University, IN
Wilkes University, PA

Home Health Care

Carlow University, PA
McGill University, QC
Thomas Jefferson University, PA
Université de Moncton, NB
Université du Québec à Chicoutimi, QC
Université du Québec à Trois-Rivières, QC
University of Michigan, MI
University of Missouri–Columbia, MO

Maternity-Newborn

Clemson University, SC
Creighton University, NE
Dalhousie University, NS
Duke University, NC
Grambling State University, LA
The Johns Hopkins University, MD
Loma Linda University, CA
McGill University, QC
San Diego State University, CA
State University of New York Downstate Medical Center, NY
Troy University, AL
Université de Montréal, QC
Université du Québec à Chicoutimi, QC
Université du Québec à Trois-Rivières, QC
University of Calgary, AB
University of Connecticut, CT
University of Illinois at Chicago, IL
University of Missouri–Columbia, MO
University of Nebraska Medical Center, NE
University of New Brunswick Fredericton, NB
The University of North Carolina at Chapel Hill, NC
University of North Florida, FL
University of Puerto Rico, Medical Sciences Campus, PR
University of South Alabama, AL
University of Toronto, ON
University of Washington, WA

Medical-Surgical

Alverno College, WI
Angelo State University, TX
Azusa Pacific University, CA
Case Western Reserve University, OH
DePaul University, IL
Gannon University, PA
George Mason University, VA
Gonzaga University, WA
Hunter College of the City University of New York, NY

CONCENTRATIONS WITHIN MASTER'S DEGREE PROGRAMS
Clinical Nurse Specialist Programs

The Johns Hopkins University, MD
Kent State University, OH
Loma Linda University, CA
Malone University, OH
McGill University, QC
Murray State University, KY
New Mexico State University, NM
Point Loma Nazarene University, CA
Rush University, IL
The Sage Colleges, NY
Saint Francis Medical Center College of
    Nursing, IL
Seattle Pacific University, WA
State University of New York Upstate Medical
    University, NY
Texas Christian University, TX
Thomas Jefferson University, PA
Université de Montréal, QC
Université du Québec à Chicoutimi, QC
Université du Québec à Trois-Rivières, QC
University at Buffalo, the State University of
    New York, NY
University of Arkansas, AR
University of Calgary, AB
University of Central Arkansas, AR
University of Cincinnati, OH
University of Illinois at Chicago, IL
University of Kentucky, KY
University of Michigan, MI
University of Nebraska Medical Center, NE
University of New Brunswick Fredericton, NB
University of North Florida, FL
University of Pittsburgh, PA
University of San Diego, CA
University of Southern Maine, ME
The University of Texas at Austin, TX
The University of Texas Health Science Center
    at San Antonio, TX
University of Virginia, VA
University of Washington, WA
Vanderbilt University, TN

Occupational Health

Université de Moncton, NB
Université de Montréal, QC
Université du Québec à Chicoutimi, QC
University of California, San Francisco, CA
University of Cincinnati, OH
University of Illinois at Chicago, IL
The University of Iowa, IA
University of Michigan, MI
University of Washington, WA

Oncology

Creighton University, NE
Duke University, NC
George Mason University, VA
Gwynedd-Mercy College, PA
Indiana University-Purdue University
    Indianapolis, IN
The Johns Hopkins University, MD
Kent State University, OH
King College, TN
Loyola University Chicago, IL
McGill University, QC
Rutgers, The State University of New Jersey,
    College of Nursing, NJ
The Sage Colleges, NY
Seattle Pacific University, WA
Thomas Jefferson University, PA
Université de Montréal, QC
Université du Québec à Chicoutimi, QC
Université Laval, QC
University of California, Los Angeles, CA
University of California, San Francisco, CA
University of Kentucky, KY
University of Missouri-Columbia, MO
University of Nebraska Medical Center, NE

University of New Brunswick Fredericton, NB
University of Toronto, ON
University of Washington, WA
Yale University, CT

Palliative Care

Boston College, MA
Daemen College, NY
D'Youville College, NY
The Johns Hopkins University, MD
The Sage Colleges, NY
Seattle Pacific University, WA
Université de Montréal, QC
Université Laval, QC
University of Missouri-Columbia, MO
University of Washington, WA
Ursuline College, OH

Parent-Child

Azusa Pacific University, CA
California State University, Dominguez Hills,
    CA
California State University, Sacramento, CA
Clemson University, SC
Dalhousie University, NS
Hunter College of the City University of New
    York, NY
The Johns Hopkins University, MD
Lehman College of the City University of New
    York, NY
Loma Linda University, CA
Louisiana State University Health Sciences
    Center, LA
McGill University, QC
The Ohio State University, OH
Rutgers, The State University of New Jersey,
    College of Nursing, NJ
Saint Francis Medical Center College of
    Nursing, IL
Seattle Pacific University, WA
Stony Brook University, State University of
    New York, NY
Université de Montréal, QC
Université du Québec à Chicoutimi, QC
Université Laval, QC
University of Calgary, AB
University of Kentucky, KY
University of Nebraska Medical Center, NE
University of New Brunswick Fredericton, NB
University of Wisconsin-Milwaukee, WI

Pediatric

Arizona State University at the Downtown
    Phoenix Campus, AZ
Auburn University, AL
Auburn University Montgomery, AL
Azusa Pacific University, CA
Boston College, MA
California State University, Fresno, CA
California State University, Sacramento, CA
The Catholic University of America, DC
Clemson University, SC
Creighton University, NE
Dalhousie University, NS
Duke University, NC
Georgia State University, GA
Grambling State University, LA
Gwynedd-Mercy College, PA
Indiana University-Purdue University
    Indianapolis, IN
The Johns Hopkins University, MD
Kent State University, OH
Loma Linda University, CA
Marquette University, WI
McGill University, QC
Memorial University of Newfoundland, NL
MGH Institute of Health Professions, MA
Minnesota State University Mankato, MN

Rush University, IL
St. John Fisher College, NY
Saint Louis University, MO
Seattle Pacific University, WA
Stony Brook University, State University of
    New York, NY
Texas Christian University, TX
Texas Woman's University, TX
Thomas Jefferson University, PA
Union University, TN
Université de Moncton, NB
Université du Québec à Chicoutimi, QC
Université du Québec à Trois-Rivières, QC
Université Laval, QC
The University of Akron, OH
University of Arkansas for Medical Sciences, AR
University of Calgary, AB
University of California, Los Angeles, CA
University of California, San Francisco, CA
University of Delaware, DE
University of Illinois at Chicago, IL
University of Kentucky, KY
University of Maryland, Baltimore, MD
University of Minnesota, Twin Cities Campus,
    MN
University of Missouri-Columbia, MO
University of Nebraska Medical Center, NE
University of New Brunswick Fredericton, NB
The University of North Carolina at Chapel
    Hill, NC
University of North Florida, FL
University of Pennsylvania, PA
University of Puerto Rico, Medical Sciences
    Campus, PR
University of South Alabama, AL
The University of Tennessee, TN
University of Toronto, ON
Vanderbilt University, TN
Wright State University, OH

Perinatal

California State University, Sacramento, CA
Georgia State University, GA
The Johns Hopkins University, MD
McGill University, QC
McMaster University, ON
San Francisco State University, CA
Stony Brook University, State University of
    New York, NY
Université du Québec à Chicoutimi, QC
Université du Québec à Trois-Rivières, QC
Université Laval, QC
University of Calgary, AB
University of California, San Francisco, CA
University of Illinois at Chicago, IL
University of Kentucky, KY
University of Manitoba, MB
University of Nebraska Medical Center, NE
University of Washington, WA

Psychiatric/Mental Health

Arizona State University at the Downtown
    Phoenix Campus, AZ
Boston College, MA
California State University, Fresno, CA
California State University, Los Angeles, CA
California State University, Sacramento, CA
Case Western Reserve University, OH
Colorado State University-Pueblo, CO
Dalhousie University, NS
Georgia State University, GA
Gonzaga University, WA
Hampton University, VA
Hunter College of the City University of New
    York, NY
Husson University, ME
Indiana University-Purdue University
    Indianapolis, IN

Kent State University, OH
Louisiana State University Health Sciences Center, LA
McGill University, QC
McNeese State University, LA
Memorial University of Newfoundland, NL
MGH Institute of Health Professions, MA
New Mexico State University, NM
Northeastern University, MA
The Ohio State University, OH
Point Loma Nazarene University, CA
Rivier College, NH
Rush University, IL
Rutgers, The State University of New Jersey, College of Nursing, NJ
The Sage Colleges, NY
Saint Joseph College, CT
Saint Louis University, MO
Shenandoah University, VA
Southeastern Louisiana University, LA
Stony Brook University, State University of New York, NY
Temple University, PA
Université de Moncton, NB
Université de Montréal, QC
Université du Québec à Chicoutimi, QC
Université du Québec à Rimouski, QC
Université du Québec à Trois-Rivières, QC
Université du Québec en Outaouais, QC
Université Laval, QC
The University of Akron, OH
University of Alaska Anchorage, AK
The University of British Columbia, BC
University of Calgary, AB
University of California, San Francisco, CA
University of Delaware, DE
University of Florida, FL
University of Hawaii at Manoa, HI
University of Illinois at Chicago, IL
The University of Iowa, IA
University of Kentucky, KY
University of Louisiana at Lafayette, LA
University of Louisville, KY
University of Maryland, Baltimore, MD
University of Massachusetts Lowell, MA
University of Medicine and Dentistry of New Jersey, NJ
University of Michigan, MI
University of Minnesota, Twin Cities Campus, MN
University of Nebraska Medical Center, NE
University of New Brunswick Fredericton, NB
The University of North Carolina at Chapel Hill, NC
University of North Dakota, ND
University of North Florida, FL
University of Pennsylvania, PA
University of Pittsburgh, PA
University of Puerto Rico, Medical Sciences Campus, PR
University of Rhode Island, RI
University of South Alabama, AL
University of South Carolina, SC
University of Southern Maine, ME
University of Southern Mississippi, MS
The University of Tennessee, TN
The University of Toledo, OH
University of Toronto, ON
University of Virginia, VA
The University of Western Ontario, ON
University of Wisconsin-Milwaukee, WI
Valdosta State University, GA
Vanderbilt University, TN
Wayne State University, MI
Widener University, PA
Wilkes University, PA
Yale University, CT

Public Health

Bloomsburg University of Pennsylvania, PA
California State University, Fresno, CA
Case Western Reserve University, OH
Dalhousie University, NS
Eastern Kentucky University, KY
Emory University, GA
The Johns Hopkins University, MD
La Salle University, PA
McGill University, QC
The Ohio State University, OH
Rush University, IL
Ryerson University, ON
Salem State College, MA
San Francisco State University, CA
Thomas Jefferson University, PA
Université de Moncton, NB
Université de Montréal, QC
Université du Québec à Chicoutimi, QC
Université du Québec à Trois-Rivières, QC
Université Laval, QC
The University of British Columbia, BC
University of Calgary, AB
University of Cincinnati, OH
University of Florida, FL
University of Hartford, CT
University of Illinois at Chicago, IL
University of Kentucky, KY
University of Maryland, Baltimore, MD
University of Missouri-Columbia, MO
University of Nebraska Medical Center, NE
University of New Brunswick Fredericton, NB
University of North Dakota, ND
The University of Texas at Austin, TX
The University of Texas at Brownsville, TX
University of Toronto, ON
University of Virginia, VA
The University of Western Ontario, ON
Worcester State College, MA
Wright State University, OH

Rehabilitation

McGill University, QC
Salem State College, MA
Université de Montréal, QC
Université du Québec à Chicoutimi, QC
Université du Québec en Outaouais, QC
Université Laval, QC
University of Calgary, AB
University of Missouri-Columbia, MO

School Health

Azusa Pacific University, CA
Bloomsburg University of Pennsylvania, PA
California State University, Fullerton, CA
California State University, Sacramento, CA
Kean University, NJ
Kent State University, OH
Monmouth University, NJ
San Diego State University, CA
San Jose State University, CA
Seton Hall University, NJ
Université de Moncton, NB
Université du Québec à Chicoutimi, QC
University of Delaware, DE
University of Illinois at Chicago, IL
University of Missouri-Columbia, MO
University of Nevada, Reno, NV
University of New Brunswick Fredericton, NB
University of Toronto, ON
Wright State University, OH
Xavier University, OH

Women's Health

Drexel University, PA
Georgia State University, GA
The Johns Hopkins University, MD
McGill University, QC

St. John Fisher College, NY
San Diego State University, CA
Seattle Pacific University, WA
Stony Brook University, State University of New York, NY
Texas Woman's University, TX
Université de Montréal, QC
Université du Québec à Chicoutimi, QC
University of Calgary, AB
University of Illinois at Chicago, IL
University of Kentucky, KY
University of Manitoba, MB
University of Missouri-Columbia, MO
University of Nebraska Medical Center, NE
University of New Brunswick Fredericton, NB
The University of North Carolina at Chapel Hill, NC
University of North Florida, FL
University of South Alabama, AL
University of Toronto, ON
The University of Western Ontario, ON
University of Wisconsin-Milwaukee, WI
Valparaiso University, IN
Vanderbilt University, TN
Wesley College, DE

HEALTH-CARE ADMINISTRATION

Adelphi University, NY
Boise State University, ID
California State University, Long Beach, CA
Cleveland State University, OH
The College of New Rochelle, NY
Daemen College, NY
Duke University, NC
Fairfield University, CT
Gannon University, PA
Georgetown University, DC
Gonzaga University, WA
Grand Canyon University, AZ
Holy Family University, PA
The Johns Hopkins University, MD
Kean University, NJ
Kent State University, OH
La Roche College, PA
Loma Linda University, CA
Louisiana State University Health Sciences Center, LA
Loyola University New Orleans, LA
McNeese State University, LA
Mercy College, NY
Midwestern State University, TX
The Ohio State University, OH
Pacific Lutheran University, WA
Quinnipiac University, CT
Regis College, MA
Regis University, CO
The Sage Colleges, NY
Salisbury University, MD
Seton Hall University, NJ
Southern Illinois University Edwardsville, IL
Southern University and Agricultural and Mechanical College, LA
Tennessee Technological University, TN
Thomas University, GA
Towson University, MD
Université de Moncton, NB
Université du Québec en Outaouais, QC
Université Laval, QC
The University of Alabama at Birmingham, AL
The University of Alabama in Huntsville, AL
University of Alaska Anchorage, AK
University of Delaware, DE
University of Illinois at Chicago, IL
The University of Kansas, KS

CONCENTRATIONS WITHIN MASTER'S DEGREE PROGRAMS
Health-Care Administration

University of Louisiana at Lafayette, LA
University of Maine, ME
University of Michigan, MI
University of Nebraska Medical Center, NE
University of Oklahoma Health Sciences
  Center, OK
University of Pennsylvania, PA
University of Phoenix, AZ
University of Phoenix-Bay Area Campus, CA
University of Phoenix-Hawaii Campus, HI
University of Phoenix-Metro Detroit Campus,
  MI
University of Phoenix-North Florida Campus,
  FL
University of Phoenix-Phoenix Campus, AZ
University of Phoenix-Sacramento Valley
  Campus, CA
University of Phoenix-San Diego Campus, CA
University of Phoenix-Southern Arizona
  Campus, AZ
University of Phoenix-Southern California
  Campus, CA
University of Phoenix-South Florida Campus,
  FL
University of Rochester, NY
The University of Texas at Arlington, TX
University of Toronto, ON
The University of Western Ontario, ON
University of Wisconsin-Milwaukee, WI
Vanderbilt University, TN
Villanova University, PA
West Suburban College of Nursing, IL
Wright State University, OH

LEGAL NURSE CONSULTANT

Capital University, OH
Cleveland State University, OH
Wilmington University, DE

NURSE ANESTHESIA

Arkansas State University, AR
Bloomsburg University of Pennsylvania, PA
Boston College, MA
Bradley University, IL
BryanLGH College of Health Sciences, NE
California State University, Fullerton, CA
Case Western Reserve University, OH
Columbia University, NY
DePaul University, IL
Drexel University, PA
Duke University, NC
East Carolina University, NC
Fairfield University, CT
Florida Gulf Coast University, FL
Florida International University, FL
Gannon University, PA
Georgetown University, DC
Goldfarb School of Nursing at Barnes-Jewish
  College, MO
La Salle University, PA
Louisiana State University Health Sciences
  Center, LA
Medical College of Georgia, GA
Michigan State University, MI
Mountain State University, WV
Murray State University, KY
Northeastern University, MA
Oakland University, MI
Old Dominion University, VA
Oregon Health & Science University, OR
Our Lady of the Lake College, LA
Rush University, IL
Samford University, AL
Samuel Merritt University, CA

Southern Illinois University Edwardsville, IL
State University of New York Downstate
  Medical Center, NY
Texas Christian University, TX
Thomas Jefferson University, PA
Union University, TN
University at Buffalo, the State University of
  New York, NY
The University of Akron, OH
University of Cincinnati, OH
The University of Iowa, IA
University of Maryland, Baltimore, MD
University of Medicine and Dentistry of New
  Jersey, NJ
University of Miami, FL
University of Minnesota, Twin Cities Campus,
  MN
The University of North Carolina at Charlotte,
  NC
The University of North Carolina at
  Greensboro, NC
University of North Dakota, ND
University of Pennsylvania, PA
University of Pittsburgh, PA
University of Puerto Rico, Medical Sciences
  Campus, PR
The University of Scranton, PA
University of South Florida, FL
The University of Tennessee, TN
The University of Tennessee at Chattanooga,
  TN
The University of Texas Health Science Center
  at Houston, TX
University of Toronto, ON
Villanova University, PA
Western Carolina University, NC
York College of Pennsylvania, PA
Youngstown State University, OH

NURSE-MIDWIFERY

California State University, Fullerton, CA
Case Western Reserve University, OH
Columbia University, NY
East Carolina University, NC
Emory University, GA
Georgetown University, DC
James Madison University, VA
The Johns Hopkins University, MD
Loyola University Chicago, IL
Marquette University, WI
The Ohio State University, OH
Old Dominion University, VA
Oregon Health & Science University, OR
Radford University, VA
San Diego State University, CA
Shenandoah University, VA
State University of New York Downstate
  Medical Center, NY
Stony Brook University, State University of
  New York, NY
University of California, San Francisco, CA
University of Cincinnati, OH
University of Colorado Denver, CO
University of Florida, FL
University of Illinois at Chicago, IL
University of Indianapolis, IN
The University of Kansas, KS
University of Medicine and Dentistry of New
  Jersey, NJ
University of Michigan, MI
University of Minnesota, Twin Cities Campus,
  MN
University of New Mexico, NM
University of Pennsylvania, PA
University of Washington, WA
Vanderbilt University, TN

Wayne State University, MI
Wichita State University, KS
Yale University, CT

NURSE PRACTITIONER PROGRAMS

Acute Care

Allen College, IA
Arizona State University at the Downtown
  Phoenix Campus, AZ
Barry University, FL
California State University, Los Angeles, CA
Case Western Reserve University, OH
The Catholic University of America, DC
Colorado State University-Pueblo, CO
Columbia University, NY
Creighton University, NE
Drexel University, PA
Duke University, NC
Emory University, GA
Florida Gulf Coast University, FL
Georgetown University, DC
Goldfarb School of Nursing at Barnes-Jewish
  College, MO
Indiana University-Purdue University
  Indianapolis, IN
The Johns Hopkins University, MD
Kent State University, OH
Loyola University Chicago, IL
Marquette University, WI
Memorial University of Newfoundland, NL
MGH Institute of Health Professions, MA
New York University, NY
Northeastern University, MA
Northwestern State University of Louisiana, LA
Rush University, IL
Rutgers, The State University of New Jersey,
  College of Nursing, NJ
The Sage Colleges, NY
Saint Louis University, MO
San Diego State University, CA
Southern Adventist University, TN
Texas Tech University Health Sciences Center,
  TX
Texas Woman's University, TX
Thomas Jefferson University, PA
Université de Montréal, QC
The University of Alabama at Birmingham, AL
The University of Alabama in Huntsville, AL
University of Arkansas for Medical Sciences, AR
University of Calgary, AB
University of California, Los Angeles, CA
University of California, San Francisco, CA
University of Connecticut, CT
University of Florida, FL
University of Illinois at Chicago, IL
University of Kentucky, KY
University of Maryland, Baltimore, MD
University of Massachusetts Worcester, MA
University of Medicine and Dentistry of New
  Jersey, NJ
University of Miami, FL
University of Michigan, MI
University of Mississippi Medical Center, MS
University of Nebraska Medical Center, NE
University of New Brunswick Fredericton, NB
University of New Mexico, NM
University of Pennsylvania, PA
University of Pittsburgh, PA
University of Rochester, NY
University of South Alabama, AL
University of South Carolina, SC
University of Southern Indiana, IN
The University of Texas at Arlington, TX
The University of Texas at Tyler, TX

The University of Texas Health Science Center at Houston, TX
The University of Texas Health Science Center at San Antonio, TX
The University of Texas Medical Branch, TX
University of Toronto, ON
University of Virginia, VA
University of Washington, WA
Vanderbilt University, TN
Virginia Commonwealth University, VA
Wayne State University, MI
Wichita State University, KS
Wright State University, OH
Yale University, CT

Adult Health
Adelphi University, NY
Allen College, IA
Arizona State University at the Downtown Phoenix Campus, AZ
Armstrong Atlantic State University, GA
Azusa Pacific University, CA
Ball State University, IN
Bloomsburg University of Pennsylvania, PA
Boston College, MA
California State University, Long Beach, CA
California State University, Los Angeles, CA
Case Western Reserve University, OH
The Catholic University of America, DC
Clarkson College, NE
Clemson University, SC
College of Mount Saint Vincent, NY
The College of St. Scholastica, MN
College of Staten Island of the City University of New York, NY
Columbia University, NY
Creighton University, NE
Daemen College, NY
Dalhousie University, NS
DePaul University, IL
Duke University, NC
East Carolina University, NC
East Tennessee State University, TN
Emory University, GA
Fairleigh Dickinson University, Metropolitan Campus, NJ
Felician College, NJ
Florida Agricultural and Mechanical University, FL
Florida Atlantic University, FL
Florida Gulf Coast University, FL
Florida International University, FL
Florida Southern College, FL
George Mason University, VA
Georgia State University, GA
Goldfarb School of Nursing at Barnes-Jewish College, MO
Gwynedd-Mercy College, PA
Hunter College of the City University of New York, NY
Indiana University-Purdue University Fort Wayne, IN
Indiana University-Purdue University Indianapolis, IN
James Madison University, VA
The Johns Hopkins University, MD
Kennesaw State University, GA
Kent State University, OH
La Salle University, PA
Lewis University, IL
Loma Linda University, CA
Long Island University, Brooklyn Campus, NY
Loyola University Chicago, IL
Loyola University New Orleans, LA
Madonna University, MI
Marian University, WI
Marquette University, WI
Maryville University of Saint Louis, MO

McNeese State University, LA
Medical University of South Carolina, SC
Metropolitan State University, MN
MGH Institute of Health Professions, MA
Michigan State University, MI
Molloy College, NY
Monmouth University, NJ
Montana State University, MT
Mount Saint Mary College, NY
New York University, NY
Northeastern University, MA
Northern Illinois University, IL
Northern Kentucky University, KY
North Park University, IL
Oakland University, MI
The Ohio State University, OH
Otterbein College, OH
Penn State University Park, PA
Purdue University, IN
Quinnipiac University, CT
Regis College, MA
The Richard Stockton College of New Jersey, NJ
Rush University, IL
Rutgers, The State University of New Jersey, College of Nursing, NJ
The Sage Colleges, NY
St. Catherine University, MN
Saint Louis University, MO
Saint Peter's College, NJ
San Diego State University, CA
Seattle Pacific University, WA
Seattle University, WA
Seton Hall University, NJ
Southeastern Louisiana University, LA
Southern Adventist University, TN
Spalding University, KY
Spring Arbor University, MI
State University of New York Institute of Technology, NY
State University of New York Upstate Medical University, NY
Stony Brook University, State University of New York, NY
Temple University, PA
Texas Woman's University, TX
Thomas Jefferson University, PA
Université de Moncton, NB
Université Laval, QC
University at Buffalo, the State University of New York, NY
The University of Akron, OH
The University of Alabama at Birmingham, AL
University of Alberta, AB
University of Calgary, AB
University of California, Los Angeles, CA
University of California, San Francisco, CA
University of Central Arkansas, AR
University of Central Florida, FL
University of Cincinnati, OH
University of Colorado at Colorado Springs, CO
University of Colorado Denver, CO
University of Delaware, DE
University of Florida, FL
University of Hawaii at Manoa, HI
University of Illinois at Chicago, IL
The University of Iowa, IA
The University of Kansas, KS
University of Kentucky, KY
University of Louisiana at Lafayette, LA
University of Louisville, KY
University of Maryland, Baltimore, MD
University of Massachusetts Boston, MA
University of Massachusetts Dartmouth, MA
University of Medicine and Dentistry of New Jersey, NJ
University of Michigan, MI
University of Missouri-Kansas City, MO

University of Missouri-St. Louis, MO
University of Nebraska Medical Center, NE
University of New Brunswick Fredericton, NB
University of New Hampshire, NH
The University of North Carolina at Chapel Hill, NC
The University of North Carolina at Charlotte, NC
The University of North Carolina at Greensboro, NC
University of Oklahoma Health Sciences Center, OK
University of Pennsylvania, PA
University of Pittsburgh, PA
University of Rochester, NY
University of St. Francis, IL
University of San Diego, CA
University of South Carolina, SC
University of Southern Maine, ME
University of South Florida, FL
The University of Tampa, FL
The University of Tennessee, TN
The University of Texas at Arlington, TX
The University of Texas at Tyler, TX
The University of Texas Health Science Center at Houston, TX
The University of Toledo, OH
University of Toronto, ON
University of Vermont, VT
University of Washington, WA
University of Wisconsin-Eau Claire, WI
University of Wisconsin-Oshkosh, WI
Ursuline College, OH
Vanderbilt University, TN
Villanova University, PA
Virginia Commonwealth University, VA
Viterbo University, WI
Washburn University, KS
Western Connecticut State University, CT
William Paterson University of New Jersey, NJ
Wilmington University, DE
Winona State University, MN
Yale University, CT
York College of Pennsylvania, PA

Community Health
Athabasca University, AB
DePaul University, IL
The Ohio State University, OH
The Sage Colleges, NY
State University of New York at Binghamton, NY
Université de Moncton, NB
University of Hawaii at Manoa, HI
University of Medicine and Dentistry of New Jersey, NJ
University of Nebraska Medical Center, NE
University of New Brunswick Fredericton, NB
University of Saint Francis, IN
University of Virginia, VA
The University of Western Ontario, ON

Family Health
Albany State University, GA
Alcorn State University, MS
Allen College, IA
Arizona State University at the Downtown Phoenix Campus, AZ
Athabasca University, AB
Azusa Pacific University, CA
Ball State University, IN
Barry University, FL
Baylor University, TX
Belmont University, TN
Boston College, MA
Bowie State University, MD
Brenau University, GA
Briar Cliff University, IA

CONCENTRATIONS WITHIN MASTER'S DEGREE PROGRAMS
Nurse Practitioner Programs

Brigham Young University, UT
California State University, Dominguez Hills, CA
California State University, Fresno, CA
California State University, Long Beach, CA
California State University, Los Angeles, CA
California State University, Sacramento, CA
Carlow University, PA
Carson-Newman College, TN
Case Western Reserve University, OH
The Catholic University of America, DC
Clarion University of Pennsylvania, PA
Clarke College, IA
Clarkson College, NE
Clemson University, SC
College of Mount Saint Vincent, NY
The College of New Jersey, NJ
The College of New Rochelle, NY
The College of St. Scholastica, MN
Colorado State University-Pueblo, CO
Columbia University, NY
Concordia University Wisconsin, WI
Coppin State University, MD
Creighton University, NE
Dalhousie University, NS
Delta State University, MS
DePaul University, IL
DeSales University, PA
Dominican College, NY
Drexel University, PA
Duke University, NC
Duquesne University, PA
D'Youville College, NY
East Carolina University, NC
Eastern Kentucky University, KY
East Tennessee State University, TN
Emory University, GA
Fairfield University, CT
Fairleigh Dickinson University, Metropolitan Campus, NJ
Felician College, NJ
Florida Atlantic University, FL
Florida Gulf Coast University, FL
Florida International University, FL
Fort Hays State University, KS
Franciscan University of Steubenville, OH
Gannon University, PA
George Mason University, VA
Georgetown University, DC
Georgia College & State University, GA
Georgia Southern University, GA
Georgia State University, GA
Gonzaga University, WA
Graceland University, IA
Grambling State University, LA
Grand Canyon University, AZ
Grand Valley State University, MI
Hampton University, VA
Hawai'i Pacific University, HI
Holy Names University, CA
Howard University, DC
Husson University, ME
Idaho State University, ID
Illinois State University, IL
Indiana State University, IN
Indiana University-Purdue University Indianapolis, IN
Indiana University South Bend, IN
Indiana Wesleyan University, IN
Intercollegiate College of Nursing/Washington State University, WA
Jacksonville University, FL
James Madison University, VA
The Johns Hopkins University, MD
Kennesaw State University, GA
Kent State University, OH
La Salle University, PA
Loma Linda University, CA

Long Island University, Brooklyn Campus, NY
Long Island University, C.W. Post Campus, NY
Loyola University Chicago, IL
Loyola University New Orleans, LA
Malone University, OH
Marshall University, WV
Marymount University, VA
Maryville University of Saint Louis, MO
Medical College of Georgia, GA
Medical University of South Carolina, SC
Metropolitan State University, MN
MGH Institute of Health Professions, MA
Michigan State University, MI
Middle Tennessee State University, TN
Midwestern State University, TX
Millersville University of Pennsylvania, PA
Minnesota State University Mankato, MN
Misericordia University, PA
Mississippi University for Women, MS
Missouri State University, MO
Molloy College, NY
Monmouth University, NJ
Montana State University, MT
Mountain State University, WV
Murray State University, KY
North Dakota State University, ND
Northeastern University, MA
Northern Arizona University, AZ
Northern Illinois University, IL
Northern Kentucky University, KY
Northern Michigan University, MI
North Georgia College & State University, GA
North Park University, IL
Northwestern State University of Louisiana, LA
Oakland University, MI
The Ohio State University, OH
Ohio University, OH
Old Dominion University, VA
Oregon Health & Science University, OR
Otterbein College, OH
Pace University, NY
Pacific Lutheran University, WA
Patty Hanks Shelton School of Nursing, TX
Penn State University Park, PA
Pittsburg State University, KS
Prairie View A&M University, TX
Purdue University Calumet, IN
Quinnipiac University, CT
Radford University, VA
Regis College, MA
Regis University, CO
Research College of Nursing, MO
Rivier College, NH
Rush University, IL
Rutgers, The State University of New Jersey, College of Nursing, NJ
Sacred Heart University, CT
The Sage Colleges, NY
Saginaw Valley State University, MI
St. John Fisher College, NY
Saint Joseph College, CT
Saint Louis University, MO
Saint Xavier University, IL
Salisbury University, MD
Samford University, AL
Samuel Merritt University, CA
San Francisco State University, CA
San Jose State University, CA
Seattle Pacific University, WA
Seattle University, WA
Shenandoah University, VA
Simmons College, MA
Sonoma State University, CA
South Dakota State University, SD
Southeast Missouri State University, MO
Southern Adventist University, TN
Southern Connecticut State University, CT
Southern Illinois University Edwardsville, IL

Southern University and Agricultural and Mechanical College, LA
Spalding University, KY
State University of New York at Binghamton, NY
State University of New York Downstate Medical Center, NY
State University of New York Institute of Technology, NY
State University of New York Upstate Medical University, NY
Stony Brook University, State University of New York, NY
Temple University, PA
Tennessee State University, TN
Tennessee Technological University, TN
Texas A&M International University, TX
Texas A&M University-Corpus Christi, TX
Texas Tech University Health Sciences Center, TX
Texas Woman's University, TX
Thomas Jefferson University, PA
Troy University, AL
Union University, TN
Université de Moncton, NB
Université de Montréal, QC
University at Buffalo, the State University of New York, NY
The University of Alabama at Birmingham, AL
The University of Alabama in Huntsville, AL
University of Alaska Anchorage, AK
University of Arkansas for Medical Sciences, AR
The University of British Columbia, BC
University of California, Los Angeles, CA
University of California, San Francisco, CA
University of Central Arkansas, AR
University of Central Florida, FL
University of Central Missouri, MO
University of Cincinnati, OH
University of Colorado at Colorado Springs, CO
University of Colorado Denver, CO
University of Delaware, DE
University of Detroit Mercy, MI
University of Florida, FL
University of Hawaii at Manoa, HI
University of Illinois at Chicago, IL
University of Indianapolis, IN
The University of Iowa, IA
The University of Kansas, KS
University of Kentucky, KY
University of Louisville, KY
University of Maine, ME
University of Mary, ND
University of Maryland, Baltimore, MD
University of Massachusetts Boston, MA
University of Massachusetts Lowell, MA
University of Massachusetts Worcester, MA
University of Medicine and Dentistry of New Jersey, NJ
University of Memphis, TN
University of Miami, FL
University of Michigan, MI
University of Minnesota, Twin Cities Campus, MN
University of Mississippi Medical Center, MS
University of Missouri-Columbia, MO
University of Missouri-Kansas City, MO
University of Missouri-St. Louis, MO
University of Nebraska Medical Center, NE
University of Nevada, Las Vegas, NV
University of Nevada, Reno, NV
University of New Brunswick Fredericton, NB
University of New Hampshire, NH
University of New Mexico, NM
The University of North Carolina at Chapel Hill, NC
The University of North Carolina at Charlotte, NC

The University of North Carolina Wilmington, NC
University of North Dakota, ND
University of Northern British Columbia, BC
University of Northern Colorado, CO
University of North Florida, FL
University of Oklahoma Health Sciences Center, OK
University of Pennsylvania, PA
University of Phoenix, AZ
University of Phoenix–Hawaii Campus, HI
University of Phoenix–Phoenix Campus, AZ
University of Phoenix–Sacramento Valley Campus, CA
University of Phoenix–Southern Arizona Campus, AZ
University of Phoenix–Southern California Campus, CA
University of Pittsburgh, PA
University of Rhode Island, RI
University of Rochester, NY
University of St. Francis, IL
University of Saint Francis, IN
University of San Diego, CA
The University of Scranton, PA
University of South Alabama, AL
University of South Carolina, SC
University of Southern Indiana, IN
University of Southern Maine, ME
University of Southern Mississippi, MS
University of South Florida, FL
The University of Tampa, FL
The University of Tennessee, TN
The University of Tennessee at Chattanooga, TN
The University of Texas at Arlington, TX
The University of Texas at Austin, TX
The University of Texas at El Paso, TX
The University of Texas at Tyler, TX
The University of Texas Health Science Center at Houston, TX
The University of Texas Health Science Center at San Antonio, TX
The University of Texas Medical Branch, TX
The University of Texas–Pan American, TX
The University of Toledo, OH
University of Toronto, ON
University of Vermont, VT
University of Virginia, VA
University of Washington, WA
University of Wisconsin–Eau Claire, WI
University of Wisconsin–Milwaukee, WI
University of Wisconsin–Oshkosh, WI
University of Wyoming, WY
Ursuline College, OH
Vanderbilt University, TN
Villanova University, PA
Virginia Commonwealth University, VA
Viterbo University, WI
Wagner College, NY
Washburn University, KS
Western Carolina University, NC
Western University of Health Sciences, CA
Westminster College, UT
West Texas A&M University, TX
West Virginia University, WV
Wheeling Jesuit University, WV
Wichita State University, KS
Widener University, PA
William Paterson University of New Jersey, NJ
Wilmington University, DE
Winona State University, MN
Winston-Salem State University, NC
Wright State University, OH
Yale University, CT

Gerontology
Allen College, IA

Boston College, MA
California State University, Long Beach, CA
Case Western Reserve University, OH
The Catholic University of America, DC
Clemson University, SC
The College of St. Scholastica, MN
College of Staten Island of the City University of New York, NY
Columbia University, NY
Concordia University Wisconsin, WI
Creighton University, NE
Delta State University, MS
Duke University, NC
East Tennessee State University, TN
Emory University, GA
Florida Agricultural and Mechanical University, FL
Florida Atlantic University, FL
George Mason University, VA
Hampton University, VA
Hunter College of the City University of New York, NY
Illinois State University, IL
James Madison University, VA
Kent State University, OH
Long Island University, Brooklyn Campus, NY
Marquette University, WI
MGH Institute of Health Professions, MA
Mississippi University for Women, MS
Nazareth College of Rochester, NY
Neumann University, PA
New York University, NY
Northern Kentucky University, KY
Oakland University, MI
Rush University, IL
The Sage Colleges, NY
St. Catherine University, MN
Saint Louis University, MO
San Diego State University, CA
Seattle Pacific University, WA
Seton Hall University, NJ
Spring Arbor University, MI
State University of New York at Binghamton, NY
Texas Tech University Health Sciences Center, TX
The University of Akron, OH
The University of Alabama at Birmingham, AL
University of Alberta, AB
University of Arkansas for Medical Sciences, AR
University of California, Los Angeles, CA
University of California, San Francisco, CA
University of Hawaii at Manoa, HI
University of Illinois at Chicago, IL
University of Indianapolis, IN
The University of Iowa, IA
The University of Kansas, KS
University of Kentucky, KY
University of Maryland, Baltimore, MD
University of Massachusetts Boston, MA
University of Massachusetts Lowell, MA
University of Massachusetts Worcester, MA
University of Medicine and Dentistry of New Jersey, NJ
University of Michigan, MI
University of Minnesota, Twin Cities Campus, MN
University of Mississippi Medical Center, MS
University of Missouri–Columbia, MO
University of Nebraska Medical Center, NE
University of New Brunswick Fredericton, NB
The University of North Carolina at Greensboro, NC
University of North Dakota, ND
University of Pennsylvania, PA
University of Rhode Island, RI
University of Rochester, NY
University of South Alabama, AL

The University of Tennessee, TN
The University of Texas at Arlington, TX
The University of Texas at Tyler, TX
The University of Texas Health Science Center at Houston, TX
The University of Texas Medical Branch, TX
University of Utah, UT
University of Washington, WA
Vanderbilt University, TN
Villanova University, PA
Wayne State University, MI
West Virginia University, WV
Wilmington University, DE
Yale University, CT

Neonatal Health
Arizona State University at the Downtown Phoenix Campus, AZ
Baylor University, TX
Case Western Reserve University, OH
The College of New Jersey, NJ
Columbia University, NY
Creighton University, NE
Dalhousie University, NS
Duke University, NC
East Carolina University, NC
Indiana University–Purdue University Indianapolis, IN
Louisiana State University Health Sciences Center, LA
McGill University, QC
McMaster University, ON
Northeastern University, MA
Northwestern State University of Louisiana, LA
The Ohio State University, OH
Regis University, CO
Rush University, IL
St. Catherine University, MN
Saint Francis Medical Center College of Nursing, IL
South Dakota State University, SD
Stony Brook University, State University of New York, NY
Thomas Jefferson University, PA
The University of Alabama at Birmingham, AL
University of Alberta, AB
University of Calgary, AB
University of California, San Francisco, CA
University of Cincinnati, OH
University of Connecticut, CT
University of Florida, FL
The University of Iowa, IA
University of Louisville, KY
University of Missouri–Kansas City, MO
University of Missouri–St. Louis, MO
University of Nebraska Medical Center, NE
University of New Brunswick Fredericton, NB
The University of North Carolina at Chapel Hill, NC
University of Oklahoma Health Sciences Center, OK
University of Pennsylvania, PA
University of Pittsburgh, PA
University of Rochester, NY
University of South Alabama, AL
The University of Texas Medical Branch, TX
University of Washington, WA
Vanderbilt University, TN
Wayne State University, MI
West Virginia University, WV

Occupational Health
The University of Alabama at Birmingham, AL
University of California, Los Angeles, CA
University of California, San Francisco, CA
University of Cincinnati, OH
University of Illinois at Chicago, IL
University of South Florida, FL

CONCENTRATIONS WITHIN MASTER'S DEGREE PROGRAMS
Nurse Practitioner Programs

University of the Sacred Heart, PR

Oncology
Case Western Reserve University, OH
Columbia University, NY
Creighton University, NE
Duke University, NC
Thomas Jefferson University, PA
Université de Moncton, NB
University of California, Los Angeles, CA
University of Nebraska Medical Center, NE
The University of North Carolina at Chapel Hill, NC
University of South Florida, FL
University of Washington, WA
Yale University, CT

Pediatric
Arizona State University at the Downtown Phoenix Campus, AZ
Azusa Pacific University, CA
Boston College, MA
California State University, Fresno, CA
California State University, Long Beach, CA
California State University, Los Angeles, CA
Case Western Reserve University, OH
The Catholic University of America, DC
The College of St. Scholastica, MN
Colorado State University-Pueblo, CO
Columbia University, NY
Creighton University, NE
DePaul University, IL
Drexel University, PA
Duke University, NC
Emory University, GA
Florida International University, FL
Georgia State University, GA
Grambling State University, LA
Gwynedd-Mercy College, PA
Hampton University, VA
Hunter College of the City University of New York, NY
Indiana University-Purdue University Indianapolis, IN
The Johns Hopkins University, MD
Kent State University, OH
Lehman College of the City University of New York, NY
Loma Linda University, CA
Loyola University Chicago, IL
Marquette University, WI
Medical College of Georgia, GA
Medical University of South Carolina, SC
MGH Institute of Health Professions, MA
Mississippi University for Women, MS
Molloy College, NY
New York University, NY
Northeastern University, MA
Northern Kentucky University, KY
Northwestern State University of Louisiana, LA
The Ohio State University, OH
Purdue University, IN
Regis College, MA
Rush University, IL
Rutgers, The State University of New Jersey, College of Nursing, NJ
St. Catherine University, MN
Saint Louis University, MO
Seton Hall University, NJ
Spalding University, KY
State University of New York Upstate Medical University, NY
Stony Brook University, State University of New York, NY
Temple University, PA
Texas Tech University Health Sciences Center, TX
Texas Woman's University, TX

Thomas Jefferson University, PA
University at Buffalo, the State University of New York, NY
The University of Akron, OH
The University of Alabama at Birmingham, AL
University of Alberta, AB
University of Arkansas for Medical Sciences, AR
University of California, Los Angeles, CA
University of California, San Francisco, CA
University of Central Florida, FL
University of Cincinnati, OH
University of Colorado Denver, CO
University of Florida, FL
University of Hawaii at Manoa, HI
University of Illinois at Chicago, IL
The University of Iowa, IA
University of Kentucky, KY
University of Maryland, Baltimore, MD
University of Michigan, MI
University of Minnesota, Twin Cities Campus, MN
University of Missouri-Columbia, MO
University of Missouri-Kansas City, MO
University of Missouri-St. Louis, MO
University of Nebraska Medical Center, NE
University of Nevada, Las Vegas, NV
University of New Brunswick Fredericton, NB
University of New Mexico, NM
The University of North Carolina at Chapel Hill, NC
University of Oklahoma Health Sciences Center, OK
University of Pittsburgh, PA
University of Rochester, NY
University of San Diego, CA
University of South Alabama, AL
University of South Carolina, SC
University of South Florida, FL
The University of Tennessee, TN
The University of Texas at Arlington, TX
The University of Texas at Austin, TX
The University of Texas at Tyler, TX
The University of Texas Health Science Center at Houston, TX
The University of Texas Health Science Center at San Antonio, TX
The University of Texas Medical Branch, TX
The University of Texas-Pan American, TX
The University of Toledo, OH
University of Toronto, ON
University of Virginia, VA
University of Washington, WA
Vanderbilt University, TN
Villanova University, PA
Virginia Commonwealth University, VA
Wayne State University, MI
West Virginia University, WV
Wichita State University, KS
Wright State University, OH
Yale University, CT

Primary Care
Arkansas State University, AR
Athabasca University, AB
Azusa Pacific University, CA
California State University, Los Angeles, CA
California State University, Sacramento, CA
Dalhousie University, NS
Duke University, NC
Emory University, GA
George Mason University, VA
Gonzaga University, WA
The Johns Hopkins University, MD
Kennesaw State University, GA
Kent State University, OH
Loma Linda University, CA
Louisiana State University Health Sciences Center, LA

Madonna University, MI
McGill University, QC
MGH Institute of Health Professions, MA
Montana State University, MT
New York University, NY
Northeastern University, MA
The Ohio State University, OH
Regis College, MA
Ryerson University, ON
Samford University, AL
Simmons College, MA
State University of New York at Binghamton, NY
Université de Moncton, NB
Université du Québec à Trois-Rivières, QC
Université du Québec en Outaouais, QC
Université Laval, QC
The University of Alabama at Birmingham, AL
The University of British Columbia, BC
University of Connecticut, CT
University of Manitoba, MB
University of Maryland, Baltimore, MD
University of Massachusetts Worcester, MA
University of Michigan, MI
University of Missouri-Columbia, MO
University of Nebraska Medical Center, NE
University of New Brunswick Fredericton, NB
The University of North Carolina at Chapel Hill, NC
University of North Florida, FL
University of Ottawa, ON
University of Pennsylvania, PA
University of Saskatchewan, SK
University of Virginia, VA
University of Washington, WA
Virginia Commonwealth University, VA
Wayne State University, MI
Western Kentucky University, KY
Yale University, CT

Psychiatric/Mental Health
Allen College, IA
Arizona State University at the Downtown Phoenix Campus, AZ
Boston College, MA
California State University, Long Beach, CA
California State University, Los Angeles, CA
Case Western Reserve University, OH
The College of St. Scholastica, MN
Columbia University, NY
Creighton University, NE
Delta State University, MS
Drexel University, PA
Eastern Kentucky University, KY
East Tennessee State University, TN
Fairfield University, CT
Fairleigh Dickinson University, Metropolitan Campus, NJ
Georgia State University, GA
Gonzaga University, WA
Intercollegiate College of Nursing/Washington State University, WA
Kent State University, OH
Loma Linda University, CA
McNeese State University, LA
Memorial University of Newfoundland, NL
MGH Institute of Health Professions, MA
Mississippi University for Women, MS
Molloy College, NY
Monmouth University, NJ
Montana State University, MT
New Mexico State University, NM
New York University, NY
Northeastern University, MA
The Ohio State University, OH
Oregon Health & Science University, OR
Regis College, MA
Rivier College, NH

Rush University, IL
Rutgers, The State University of New Jersey, College of Nursing, NJ
The Sage Colleges, NY
Saint Louis University, MO
Seattle University, WA
Shenandoah University, VA
South Dakota State University, SD
Southeastern Louisiana University, LA
State University of New York Upstate Medical University, NY
Stony Brook University, State University of New York, NY
University at Buffalo, the State University of New York, NY
The University of Akron, OH
The University of Alabama at Birmingham, AL
University of Alaska Anchorage, AK
University of Arkansas for Medical Sciences, AR
University of California, San Francisco, CA
University of Colorado Denver, CO
University of Florida, FL
University of Illinois at Chicago, IL
The University of Iowa, IA
The University of Kansas, KS
University of Kentucky, KY
University of Louisiana at Lafayette, LA
University of Louisville, KY
University of Maryland, Baltimore, MD
University of Massachusetts Lowell, MA
University of Medicine and Dentistry of New Jersey, NJ
University of Michigan, MI
University of Mississippi Medical Center, MS
University of Missouri-Columbia, MO
University of Nebraska Medical Center, NE
University of New Brunswick Fredericton, NB
The University of North Carolina at Chapel Hill, NC
University of North Dakota, ND
University of Pennsylvania, PA
University of Pittsburgh, PA
University of Rochester, NY
University of South Alabama, AL
University of South Carolina, SC
University of Southern Maine, ME
University of Southern Mississippi, MS
University of South Florida, FL
The University of Tennessee, TN
The University of Texas at Arlington, TX
The University of Texas Health Science Center at Houston, TX
The University of Texas Health Science Center at San Antonio, TX
University of Vermont, VT
University of Virginia, VA
University of Washington, WA
University of Wyoming, WY
Vanderbilt University, TN
Wayne State University, MI
Wichita State University, KS
Winston-Salem State University, NC
Yale University, CT

School Health

La Roche College, PA
The Ohio State University, OH
Seton Hall University, NJ
University of Illinois at Chicago, IL

Women's Health

Arizona State University at the Downtown Phoenix Campus, AZ
Boston College, MA
California State University, Fullerton, CA
California State University, Long Beach, CA
Case Western Reserve University, OH
Columbia University, NY

DePaul University, IL
Drexel University, PA
Emory University, GA
Florida Agricultural and Mechanical University, FL
Georgetown University, DC
Georgia State University, GA
Hampton University, VA
Indiana University-Purdue University Fort Wayne, IN
Indiana University-Purdue University Indianapolis, IN
Kent State University, OH
Loyola University Chicago, IL
MGH Institute of Health Professions, MA
Northwestern State University of Louisiana, LA
The Ohio State University, OH
Old Dominion University, VA
Regis College, MA
Rutgers, The State University of New Jersey, College of Nursing, NJ
San Diego State University, CA
State University of New York Downstate Medical Center, NY
Stony Brook University, State University of New York, NY
Texas Woman's University, TX
University at Buffalo, the State University of New York, NY
The University of Alabama at Birmingham, AL
University of Arkansas for Medical Sciences, AR
University of Cincinnati, OH
University of Colorado Denver, CO
University of Illinois at Chicago, IL
University of Indianapolis, IN
University of Medicine and Dentistry of New Jersey, NJ
University of Minnesota, Twin Cities Campus, MN
University of Missouri-Kansas City, MO
University of Missouri-St. Louis, MO
University of Nebraska Medical Center, NE
University of New Brunswick Fredericton, NB
The University of North Carolina at Chapel Hill, NC
University of Pennsylvania, PA
University of South Alabama, AL
University of South Carolina, SC
The University of Texas at Tyler, TX
The University of Texas Health Science Center at Houston, TX
Vanderbilt University, TN
Virginia Commonwealth University, VA
Wayne State University, MI
West Virginia University, WV
Yale University, CT

NURSING ADMINISTRATION

Adelphi University, NY
Allen College, IA
American International College, MA
Anderson University, IN
Arkansas Tech University, AR
Armstrong Atlantic State University, GA
Athabasca University, AB
Aurora University, IL
Azusa Pacific University, CA
Ball State University, IN
Barry University, FL
Bellarmine University, KY
Bellin College, WI
Bethel College, IN
Bethel University, MN
Blessing-Rieman College of Nursing, IL
Bloomsburg University of Pennsylvania, PA
Boise State University, ID

Bradley University, IL
California State University, Dominguez Hills, CA
California State University, Fullerton, CA
California State University, Los Angeles, CA
California State University, Sacramento, CA
California State University, San Bernardino, CA
Capital University, OH
Carlow University, PA
Chatham University, PA
Clarkson College, NE
Clayton State University, GA
Clemson University, SC
Cleveland State University, OH
College of Mount Saint Vincent, NY
The College of New Jersey, NJ
The College of New Rochelle, NY
The College of St. Scholastica, MN
Creighton University, NE
Delta State University, MS
DePaul University, IL
DeSales University, PA
Drexel University, PA
Duke University, NC
East Carolina University, NC
East Tennessee State University, TN
Edgewood College, WI
Elms College, MA
Endicott College, MA
Excelsior College, NY
Fairleigh Dickinson University, Metropolitan Campus, NJ
Ferris State University, MI
Florida Atlantic University, FL
Florida International University, FL
Fort Hays State University, KS
Framingham State College, MA
Franklin Pierce University, NH
Gannon University, PA
Gardner-Webb University, NC
George Mason University, VA
Georgia College & State University, GA
Goldfarb School of Nursing at Barnes-Jewish College, MO
Gonzaga University, WA
Hampton University, VA
Holy Names University, CA
Idaho State University, ID
Illinois State University, IL
Immaculata University, PA
Indiana State University, IN
Indiana University of Pennsylvania, PA
Indiana University-Purdue University Fort Wayne, IN
Indiana University-Purdue University Indianapolis, IN
Indiana Wesleyan University, IN
Intercollegiate College of Nursing/Washington State University, WA
Jacksonville University, FL
James Madison University, VA
Jefferson College of Health Sciences, VA
The Johns Hopkins University, MD
Kean University, NJ
Kent State University, OH
Lamar University, TX
La Roche College, PA
La Salle University, PA
Lehman College of the City University of New York, NY
Le Moyne College, NY
Lewis University, IL
Loma Linda University, CA
Long Island University, Brooklyn Campus, NY
Louisiana State University Health Sciences Center, LA
Loyola University Chicago, IL
Madonna University, MI

CONCENTRATIONS WITHIN MASTER'S DEGREE PROGRAMS
Nursing Administration

Mansfield University of Pennsylvania, PA
Marquette University, WI
Marshall University, WV
Marywood University, PA
McGill University, QC
McKendree University, IL
McNeese State University, LA
Medical University of South Carolina, SC
Mercy College, NY
Metropolitan State University, MN
Middle Tennessee State University, TN
Midwestern State University, TX
Molloy College, NY
Monmouth University, NJ
Moravian College, PA
Mountain State University, WV
Mount St. Mary's College, CA
Nebraska Methodist College, NE
Nebraska Wesleyan University, NE
New Mexico State University, NM
New York University, NY
Northeastern University, MA
Northern Kentucky University, KY
North Park University, IL
Northwestern State University of Louisiana, LA
Nova Southeastern University, FL
The Ohio State University, OH
Ohio University, OH
Oklahoma City University, OK
Old Dominion University, VA
Otterbein College, OH
Our Lady of the Lake College, LA
Pacific Lutheran University, WA
Patty Hanks Shelton School of Nursing, TX
Penn State University Park, PA
Pittsburg State University, KS
Prairie View A&M University, TX
Purdue University Calumet, IN
Queens University of Charlotte, NC
Regis College, MA
Regis University, CO
Research College of Nursing, MO
Roberts Wesleyan College, NY
Sacred Heart University, CT
The Sage Colleges, NY
Saginaw Valley State University, MI
St. Ambrose University, IA
Saint Joseph's College of Maine, ME
Saint Peter's College, NJ
Saint Xavier University, IL
Salem State College, MA
Samford University, AL
San Diego State University, CA
San Francisco State University, CA
San Jose State University, CA
Seattle Pacific University, WA
Seton Hall University, NJ
Simmons College, MA
Sonoma State University, CA
South Dakota State University, SD
Southeastern Louisiana University, LA
Southern Nazarene University, OK
Spalding University, KY
State University of New York at Binghamton, NY
State University of New York Institute of Technology, NY
Texas A&M University-Corpus Christi, TX
Texas A&M University-Texarkana, TX
Texas Tech University Health Sciences Center, TX
Texas Woman's University, TX
Thomas University, GA
Troy University, AL
Union University, TN
Université de Moncton, NB
Université Laval, QC
The University of Akron, OH

The University of Alabama, AL
The University of Alabama at Birmingham, AL
University of Arkansas for Medical Sciences, AR
The University of British Columbia, BC
University of California, Los Angeles, CA
University of California, San Francisco, CA
University of Central Florida, FL
University of Cincinnati, OH
University of Connecticut, CT
University of Detroit Mercy, MI
University of Hartford, CT
University of Hawaii at Manoa, HI
University of Houston-Victoria, TX
University of Illinois at Chicago, IL
University of Indianapolis, IN
The University of Iowa, IA
The University of Kansas, KS
University of Kentucky, KY
University of Louisiana at Lafayette, LA
University of Manitoba, MB
University of Mary, ND
University of Maryland, Baltimore, MD
University of Memphis, TN
University of Michigan, MI
University of Minnesota, Twin Cities Campus, MN
University of Mississippi Medical Center, MS
University of Missouri-Columbia, MO
University of Mobile, AL
University of Nebraska Medical Center, NE
University of New Brunswick Fredericton, NB
University of New Mexico, NM
University of North Alabama, AL
The University of North Carolina at Chapel Hill, NC
The University of North Carolina at Charlotte, NC
The University of North Carolina at Greensboro, NC
University of Pennsylvania, PA
University of Phoenix, AZ
University of Phoenix-Bay Area Campus, CA
University of Phoenix-Central Florida Campus, FL
University of Phoenix-Cleveland Campus, OH
University of Phoenix-Denver Campus, CO
University of Phoenix-Hawaii Campus, HI
University of Phoenix-Metro Detroit Campus, MI
University of Phoenix-New Mexico Campus, NM
University of Phoenix-North Florida Campus, FL
University of Phoenix-Phoenix Campus, AZ
University of Phoenix-Sacramento Valley Campus, CA
University of Phoenix-San Diego Campus, CA
University of Phoenix-Southern Arizona Campus, AZ
University of Phoenix-Southern California Campus, CA
University of Phoenix-South Florida Campus, FL
University of Pittsburgh, PA
University of Puerto Rico, Medical Sciences Campus, PR
University of Rhode Island, RI
University of San Diego, CA
University of South Alabama, AL
University of South Carolina, SC
University of Southern Indiana, IN
University of Southern Mississippi, MS
The University of Tennessee, TN
The University of Texas at Arlington, TX
The University of Texas at Austin, TX
The University of Texas at Brownsville, TX
The University of Texas at El Paso, TX
The University of Texas at Tyler, TX

The University of Texas Health Science Center at Houston, TX
The University of Texas Health Science Center at San Antonio, TX
The University of Texas Medical Branch, TX
University of Toronto, ON
University of Vermont, VT
University of Virginia, VA
The University of Western Ontario, ON
University of West Georgia, GA
University of Wisconsin-Eau Claire, WI
Urbana University, OH
Valdosta State University, GA
Vanderbilt University, TN
Virginia Commonwealth University, VA
Washburn University, KS
Waynesburg University, PA
Weber State University, UT
Webster University, MO
Western Carolina University, NC
Western Kentucky University, KY
Western University of Health Sciences, CA
West Suburban College of Nursing, IL
West Texas A&M University, TX
West Virginia University, WV
West Virginia Wesleyan College, WV
Wheeling Jesuit University, WV
Wilkes University, PA
William Paterson University of New Jersey, NJ
Wilmington University, DE
Winona State University, MN
Wright State University, OH
Xavier University, OH
Yale University, CT
York College of Pennsylvania, PA

NURSING EDUCATION

Adelphi University, NY
Albany State University, GA
Alcorn State University, MS
Allen College, IA
Alverno College, WI
American International College, MA
Andrews University, MI
Angelo State University, TX
Arkansas State University, AR
Athabasca University, AB
Auburn University, AL
Auburn University Montgomery, AL
Aurora University, IL
Azusa Pacific University, CA
Ball State University, IN
Barry University, FL
Bellarmine University, KY
Bellin College, WI
Belmont University, TN
Bethel College, IN
Bethel University, MN
Blessing-Rieman College of Nursing, IL
Boise State University, ID
Bowie State University, MD
Brenau University, GA
Briar Cliff University, IA
California State University, Chico, CA
California State University, Dominguez Hills, CA
California State University, Fresno, CA
California State University, Fullerton, CA
California State University, Long Beach, CA
California State University, Los Angeles, CA
California State University, Sacramento, CA
California State University, San Bernardino, CA
Capital University, OH
Cardinal Stritch University, WI
Carlow University, PA
Carson-Newman College, TN

The Catholic University of America, DC
Charleston Southern University, SC
Chatham University, PA
Clarion University of Pennsylvania, PA
Clarke College, IA
Clarkson College, NE
Clayton State University, GA
Clemson University, SC
Cleveland State University, OH
College of Mount Saint Vincent, NY
The College of New Rochelle, NY
Colorado State University–Pueblo, CO
Concordia College, MN
Concordia University Wisconsin, WI
Creighton University, NE
Daemen College, NY
Delta State University, MS
DePaul University, IL
DeSales University, PA
Dominican University of California, CA
Drexel University, PA
Duke University, NC
Duquesne University, PA
D'Youville College, NY
East Carolina University, NC
Eastern Kentucky University, KY
East Tennessee State University, TN
Edgewood College, WI
Elmhurst College, IL
Elms College, MA
Endicott College, MA
Excelsior College, NY
Fairleigh Dickinson University, Metropolitan
    Campus, NJ
Felician College, NJ
Ferris State University, MI
Florida Atlantic University, FL
Florida Gulf Coast University, FL
Florida International University, FL
Florida Southern College, FL
Florida State University, FL
Fort Hays State University, KS
Framingham State College, MA
Franciscan University of Steubenville, OH
Franklin Pierce University, NH
Gannon University, PA
Gardner-Webb University, NC
George Mason University, VA
Georgetown University, DC
Georgia Baptist College of Nursing of Mercer
    University, GA
Georgia College & State University, GA
Goldfarb School of Nursing at Barnes-Jewish
    College, MO
Gonzaga University, WA
Graceland University, IA
Grambling State University, LA
Grand Canyon University, AZ
Grand Valley State University, MI
Hampton University, VA
Hawai'i Pacific University, HI
Holy Family University, PA
Holy Names University, CA
Husson University, ME
Idaho State University, ID
Immaculata University, PA
Indiana State University, IN
Indiana University of Pennsylvania, PA
Indiana University–Purdue University Fort
    Wayne, IN
Indiana Wesleyan University, IN
Intercollegiate College of Nursing/Washington
    State University, WA
Jacksonville University, FL
Jefferson College of Health Sciences, VA
Kent State University, OH
Kutztown University of Pennsylvania, PA
Lamar University, TX

La Roche College, PA
Lehman College of the City University of New
    York, NY
Le Moyne College, NY
Lewis University, IL
Liberty University, VA
Loma Linda University, CA
Long Island University, Brooklyn Campus, NY
Long Island University, C.W. Post Campus, NY
Louisiana State University Health Sciences
    Center, LA
Mansfield University of Pennsylvania, PA
Marian University, WI
Marshall University, WV
Marymount University, VA
Maryville University of Saint Louis, MO
McKendree University, IL
McNeese State University, LA
Medical University of South Carolina, SC
Mercy College, NY
MGH Institute of Health Professions, MA
Michigan State University, MI
Middle Tennessee State University, TN
Midwestern State University, TX
Millersville University of Pennsylvania, PA
Millikin University, IL
Minnesota State University Mankato, MN
Minnesota State University Moorhead, MN
Misericordia University, PA
Missouri Southern State University, MO
Missouri State University, MO
Molloy College, NY
Monmouth University, NJ
Moravian College, PA
Mountain State University, WV
Mount Carmel College of Nursing, OH
Mount St. Mary's College, CA
Nebraska Methodist College, NE
Nebraska Wesleyan University, NE
Neumann University, PA
New York University, NY
North Dakota State University, ND
Northern Arizona University, AZ
Northern Illinois University, IL
Northern Kentucky University, KY
North Georgia College & State University, GA
Northwestern State University of Louisiana, LA
Northwest Nazarene University, ID
Nova Southeastern University, FL
Oakland University, MI
Ohio University, OH
Oklahoma Baptist University, OK
Oklahoma City University, OK
Old Dominion University, VA
Oregon Health & Science University, OR
Otterbein College, OH
Our Lady of the Lake College, LA
Pace University, NY
Pacific Lutheran University, WA
Patty Hanks Shelton School of Nursing, TX
Pittsburg State University, KS
Point Loma Nazarene University, CA
Prairie View A&M University, TX
Queens University of Charlotte, NC
Ramapo College of New Jersey, NJ
Regis College, MA
Regis University, CO
Research College of Nursing, MO
Rivier College, NH
Robert Morris University, PA
Roberts Wesleyan College, NY
The Sage Colleges, NY
Saginaw Valley State University, MI
Saint Anthony College of Nursing, IL
St. Catherine University, MN
Saint Francis Medical Center College of
    Nursing, IL
St. John Fisher College, NY

Saint Joseph College, CT
St. Joseph's College, New York, NY
Saint Joseph's College of Maine, ME
Saint Louis University, MO
Salem State College, MA
Salisbury University, MD
Samford University, AL
San Diego State University, CA
San Jose State University, CA
Seattle Pacific University, WA
Seton Hall University, NJ
Sonoma State University, CA
South Dakota State University, SD
Southeastern Louisiana University, LA
Southeast Missouri State University, MO
Southern Adventist University, TN
Southern Connecticut State University, CT
Southern Illinois University Edwardsville, IL
Southern Nazarene University, OK
Southern University and Agricultural and
    Mechanical College, LA
South University, FL
Spalding University, KY
Spring Arbor University, MI
State University of New York at Binghamton,
    NY
Temple University, PA
Tennessee State University, TN
Tennessee Technological University, TN
Texas A&M University-Texarkana, TX
Texas Christian University, TX
Texas Tech University Health Sciences Center,
    TX
Texas Woman's University, TX
Thomas Jefferson University, PA
Thomas University, GA
Towson University, MD
Troy University, AL
Union University, TN
Université de Moncton, NB
The University of Alabama, AL
University of Alaska Anchorage, AK
University of Arkansas, AR
University of Arkansas for Medical Sciences, AR
The University of British Columbia, BC
University of Central Arkansas, AR
University of Central Florida, FL
University of Central Missouri, MO
University of Detroit Mercy, MI
University of Hartford, CT
University of Hawaii at Manoa, HI
University of Houston-Victoria, TX
University of Indianapolis, IN
The University of Iowa, IA
University of Louisiana at Lafayette, LA
University of Maine, ME
University of Mary, ND
University of Mary Hardin-Baylor, TX
University of Massachusetts Worcester, MA
University of Medicine and Dentistry of New
    Jersey, NJ
University of Memphis, TN
University of Miami, FL
University of Mississippi Medical Center, MS
University of Missouri-Columbia, MO
University of Missouri-Kansas City, MO
University of Missouri-St. Louis, MO
University of Mobile, AL
University of Nebraska Medical Center, NE
University of Nevada, Las Vegas, NV
University of Nevada, Reno, NV
University of New Brunswick Fredericton, NB
University of New Mexico, NM
University of North Alabama, AL
The University of North Carolina at Chapel
    Hill, NC
The University of North Carolina at Charlotte,
    NC

CONCENTRATIONS WITHIN MASTER'S DEGREE PROGRAMS
Nursing Education

The University of North Carolina at Greensboro, NC
The University of North Carolina Wilmington, NC
University of North Dakota, ND
University of Northern Colorado, CO
University of Oklahoma Health Sciences Center, OK
University of Phoenix, AZ
University of Phoenix-Bay Area Campus, CA
University of Phoenix-Central Florida Campus, FL
University of Phoenix-Denver Campus, CO
University of Phoenix-Hawaii Campus, HI
University of Phoenix-Metro Detroit Campus, MI
University of Phoenix-New Mexico Campus, NM
University of Phoenix-North Florida Campus, FL
University of Phoenix-Phoenix Campus, AZ
University of Phoenix-Sacramento Valley Campus, CA
University of Phoenix-San Diego Campus, CA
University of Phoenix-Southern Arizona Campus, AZ
University of Phoenix-Southern California Campus, CA
University of Phoenix-South Florida Campus, FL
University of Pittsburgh, PA
University of Puerto Rico, Medical Sciences Campus, PR
University of Rhode Island, RI
University of St. Francis, IL
University of San Diego, CA
University of Saskatchewan, SK
The University of Scranton, PA
University of South Alabama, AL
University of Southern Indiana, IN

University of South Florida, FL
The University of Texas at Brownsville, TX
The University of Texas at El Paso, TX
The University of Texas at Tyler, TX
The University of Texas Health Science Center at Houston, TX
The University of Texas Health Science Center at San Antonio, TX
The University of Texas Medical Branch, TX
The University of Toledo, OH
University of Toronto, ON
The University of Western Ontario, ON
University of West Georgia, GA
University of Wisconsin-Eau Claire, WI
University of Wisconsin-Milwaukee, WI
University of Wisconsin-Oshkosh, WI
University of Wyoming, WY
Urbana University, OH
Valdosta State University, GA
Villanova University, PA
Virginia Commonwealth University, VA
Viterbo University, WI
Wagner College, NY
Waynesburg University, PA
Weber State University, UT
Webster University, MO
Western Carolina University, NC
Western Kentucky University, KY
Westminster College, UT
West Suburban College of Nursing, IL
West Texas A&M University, TX
West Virginia Wesleyan College, WV
Wheeling Jesuit University, WV
Widener University, PA
Wilkes University, PA
William Carey University, MS
William Paterson University of New Jersey, NJ
Wilmington University, DE
Winona State University, MN
Winston-Salem State University, NC

Xavier University, OH
York College of Pennsylvania, PA
Youngstown State University, OH

NURSING INFORMATICS

Case Western Reserve University, OH
Duke University, NC
Excelsior College, NY
Fairleigh Dickinson University, Metropolitan Campus, NJ
Ferris State University, MI
Georgia College & State University, GA
Georgia State University, GA
Middle Tennessee State University, TN
Molloy College, NY
New York University, NY
Saginaw Valley State University, MI
Tennessee Technological University, TN
Thomas Jefferson University, PA
Troy University, AL
The University of Alabama at Birmingham, AL
University of Colorado Denver, CO
University of Illinois at Chicago, IL
The University of Iowa, IA
The University of Kansas, KS
University of Maryland, Baltimore, MD
University of Medicine and Dentistry of New Jersey, NJ
University of Michigan, MI
University of Nebraska Medical Center, NE
University of New Brunswick Fredericton, NB
The University of North Carolina at Chapel Hill, NC
University of Pittsburgh, PA
The University of Texas Health Science Center at San Antonio, TX
University of Utah, UT
University of Washington, WA
Vanderbilt University, TN
Xavier University, OH

Doctoral Programs

U.S. AND U.S. TERRITORIES

Alabama

Samford University, Ida V. Moffett School of Nursing, *Birmingham* (DNP)

The University of Alabama, Capstone College of Nursing, *Tuscaloosa* (DNP)

The University of Alabama at Birmingham, School of Nursing, *Birmingham* (DNP, PhD)

The University of Alabama in Huntsville, College of Nursing, *Huntsville* (DNP)

Arizona

Arizona State University at the Downtown Phoenix Campus, College of Nursing, *Phoenix* (DNP)

The University of Arizona, College of Nursing, *Tucson* (PhD)

University of Phoenix, Online Campus, *Phoenix* (PhD)

Arkansas

University of Arkansas for Medical Sciences, College of Nursing, *Little Rock* (PhD)

California

Azusa Pacific University, School of Nursing, *Azusa* (PhD)

Loma Linda University, School of Nursing, *Loma Linda* (DNP, PhD)

University of California, Los Angeles, School of Nursing, *Los Angeles* (PhD)

University of California, San Francisco, School of Nursing, *San Francisco* (PhD)

University of San Diego, Hahn School of Nursing and Health Science, *San Diego* (PhD)

University of San Francisco, School of Nursing, *San Francisco* (DNP)

Western University of Health Sciences, College of Graduate Nursing, *Pomona* (DNP)

Colorado

University of Colorado at Colorado Springs, Beth-El College of Nursing and Health Sciences, *Colorado Springs* (DNP)

University of Colorado Denver, College of Nursing, *Denver* (PhD)

University of Northern Colorado, School of Nursing, *Greeley* (PhD)

Connecticut

Sacred Heart University, Program in Nursing, *Fairfield* (DNP)

University of Connecticut, School of Nursing, *Storrs* (PhD)

Yale University, School of Nursing, *New Haven* (PhD)

District of Columbia

The Catholic University of America, School of Nursing, *Washington* (PhD)

Florida

Barry University, School of Nursing, *Miami Shores* (PhD)

Florida Agricultural and Mechanical University, School of Nursing, *Tallahassee* (PhD)

Florida Atlantic University, Christine E. Lynn College of Nursing, *Boca Raton* (PhD)

Florida International University, Nursing Program, *Miami* (PhD)

Florida State University, College of Nursing, *Tallahassee* (DNP)

University of Central Florida, School of Nursing, *Orlando* (PhD)

University of Florida, College of Nursing, *Gainesville* (PhD)

University of Miami, School of Nursing and Health Studies, *Coral Gables* (DSN)

University of South Florida, College of Nursing, *Tampa* (DNP, PhD)

Georgia

Emory University, Nell Hodgson Woodruff School of Nursing, *Atlanta* (PhD)

Georgia Baptist College of Nursing of Mercer University, Department of Nursing, *Atlanta* (PhD)

Georgia Southern University, School of Nursing, *Statesboro* (DNP)

Georgia State University, Byrdine F. Lewis School of Nursing, *Atlanta* (PhD)

Medical College of Georgia, School of Nursing, *Augusta* (DNP, PhD)

Hawaii

University of Hawaii at Manoa, School of Nursing and Dental Hygiene, *Honolulu* (PhD)

Illinois

Illinois State University, Mennonite College of Nursing, *Normal* (PhD)

Loyola University Chicago, Marcella Niehoff School of Nursing, *Maywood* (PhD)

Rush University, College of Nursing, *Chicago* (DNP)

Saint Francis Medical Center College of Nursing, Baccalaureate Nursing Program, *Peoria* (DNP)

University of Illinois at Chicago, College of Nursing, *Chicago* (PhD)

University of St. Francis, College of Nursing and Allied Health, *Joliet* (DNP)

Indiana

Ball State University, School of Nursing, *Muncie* (DNP)

Indiana University–Purdue University Indianapolis, School of Nursing, *Indianapolis* (PhD)

Purdue University, School of Nursing, *West Lafayette* (DNP)

University of Southern Indiana, College of Nursing and Health Professions, *Evansville* (DNP)

Iowa

The University of Iowa, College of Nursing, *Iowa City* (PhD)

Kansas

The University of Kansas, School of Nursing, *Kansas City* (PhD)

Wichita State University, School of Nursing, *Wichita* (DNP)

Kentucky

Frontier School of Midwifery and Family Nursing, Nursing Degree Programs, *Hyden* (DNP)

University of Kentucky, Graduate School Programs in the College of Nursing, *Lexington* (PhD)

University of Louisville, School of Nursing, *Louisville* (PhD)

Louisiana

Louisiana State University Health Sciences Center, School of Nursing, *New Orleans* (DNS)

Southern University and Agricultural and Mechanical College, School of Nursing, *Baton Rouge* (PhD)

Maryland

The Johns Hopkins University, School of Nursing, *Baltimore* (PhD)

University of Maryland, Baltimore, Master's Program in Nursing, *Baltimore* (DNP)

Massachusetts

Boston College, William F. Connell School of Nursing, *Chestnut Hill* (PhD)

MGH Institute of Health Professions, School of Nursing, *Boston* (DNP)

Northeastern University, School of Nursing, *Boston* (PhD)

Regis College, School of Nursing and Health Professions, *Weston* (DNP)

Simmons College, Department of Nursing, *Boston* (DNP)

University of Massachusetts Amherst, School of Nursing, *Amherst* (PhD)

University of Massachusetts Boston, College of Nursing and Health Sciences, *Boston* (DNP, PhD)

University of Massachusetts Dartmouth, College of Nursing, *North Dartmouth* (PhD)

University of Massachusetts Lowell, Department of Nursing, *Lowell* (PhD)

University of Massachusetts Worcester, Graduate School of Nursing, *Worcester* (PhD)

Michigan

Grand Valley State University, Kirkhof College of Nursing, *Allendale* (DNP)

Michigan State University, College of Nursing, *East Lansing* (PhD)

University of Michigan, School of Nursing, *Ann Arbor* (PhD)

University of Michigan-Flint, Department of Nursing, *Flint* (DNP)

Wayne State University, College of Nursing, *Detroit* (DNP, PhD)

Minnesota

The College of St. Scholastica, Department of Nursing, *Duluth* (DNP)

Minnesota State University Mankato, School of Nursing, *Mankato* (DNP)

Minnesota State University Moorhead, School of Nursing and Healthcare Leadership, *Moorhead* (DNP)

St. Catherine University, Department of Nursing, *St. Paul* (DNP)

University of Minnesota, Twin Cities Campus, School of Nursing, *Minneapolis* (PhD)

Winona State University, College of Nursing and Health Sciences, *Winona* (DNP)

Mississippi

University of Mississippi Medical Center, Program in Nursing, *Jackson* (PhD)

University of Southern Mississippi, School of Nursing, *Hattiesburg* (PhD)

Missouri

Goldfarb School of Nursing at Barnes-Jewish College, *St. Louis* (DNP, PhD)

Saint Louis University, School of Nursing, *St. Louis* (PhD)

University of Missouri–Columbia, Sinclair School of Nursing, *Columbia* (PhD)

University of Missouri–Kansas City, School of Nursing, *Kansas City* (PhD)

University of Missouri–St. Louis, College of Nursing, *St. Louis* (DNP)

Nebraska

Creighton University, School of Nursing, *Omaha* (DNP)

University of Nebraska Medical Center, College of Nursing, *Omaha* (PhD)

Nevada

Touro University, School of Nursing, *Henderson* (DNP)

University of Nevada, Las Vegas, School of Nursing, *Las Vegas* (PhD)

New Jersey

Fairleigh Dickinson University, Metropolitan Campus, Henry P. Becton School of Nursing and Allied Health, *Teaneck* (DNP)

Rutgers, The State University of New Jersey, College of Nursing, *Newark* (DNP, PhD)

Seton Hall University, College of Nursing, *South Orange* (DNP, PhD)

University of Medicine and Dentistry of New Jersey, School of Nursing, *Newark* (DNP)

New Mexico

University of New Mexico, College of Nursing, *Albuquerque* (PhD)

New York

Adelphi University, School of Nursing, *Garden City* (PhD)

Columbia University, School of Nursing, *New York* (DNP)

Daemen College, Department of Nursing, *Amherst* (DNP)

Lehman College of the City University of New York, Department of Nursing, *Bronx* (DNS)

New York University, College of Nursing, *New York* (PhD)

Pace University, Lienhard School of Nursing, *New York* (DNP)

The Sage Colleges, Department of Nursing, *Troy* (DNS)

St. John Fisher College, Advanced Practice Nursing Program, *Rochester* (DNP)

State University of New York at Binghamton, Decker School of Nursing, *Binghamton* (PhD)

Teachers College, Columbia University, Department of Health and Behavioral Studies, *New York* (EdD)

University at Buffalo, the State University of New York, School of Nursing, *Buffalo* (PhD)

University of Rochester, School of Nursing, *Rochester* (DNP, PhD)

North Carolina

Duke University, School of Nursing, *Durham* (PhD)

East Carolina University, College of Nursing, *Greenville* (PhD)

The University of North Carolina at Chapel Hill, School of Nursing, *Chapel Hill* (PhD)

The University of North Carolina at Greensboro, School of Nursing, *Greensboro* (PhD)

North Dakota

North Dakota State University, Department of Nursing, *Fargo* (DNP)

University of North Dakota, College of Nursing, *Grand Forks* (PhD)

Ohio

Case Western Reserve University, Frances Payne Bolton School of Nursing, *Cleveland* (PhD)

Kent State University, College of Nursing, *Kent* (PhD)

The Ohio State University, College of Nursing, *Columbus* (DNP)

The University of Akron, College of Nursing, *Akron* (PhD)

University of Cincinnati, College of Nursing, *Cincinnati* (PhD)

The University of Toledo, College of Nursing, *Toledo* (DNP)

Wright State University, College of Nursing and Health, *Dayton* (DNP)

Oklahoma

Oklahoma City University, Kramer School of Nursing, *Oklahoma City* (PhD)

University of Oklahoma Health Sciences Center, College of Nursing, *Oklahoma City* (PhD)

Oregon

Oregon Health & Science University, School of Nursing, *Portland* (PhD)

University of Portland, School of Nursing, *Portland* (DNP)

Pennsylvania

Chatham University, Program in Nursing, *Pittsburgh* (DNP)

Drexel University, College of Nursing and Health Professions, *Philadelphia* (Dr NP)

Duquesne University, School of Nursing, *Pittsburgh* (PhD)

Indiana University of Pennsylvania, Department of Nursing and Allied Health, *Indiana* (PhD)

Penn State University Park, School of Nursing, *State College, University Park* (PhD)

Robert Morris University, School of Nursing and Health Sciences, *Moon Township* (DNP)

Thomas Jefferson University, Department of Nursing, *Philadelphia* (DNP)

University of Pennsylvania, School of Nursing, *Philadelphia* (PhD)

University of Pittsburgh, School of Nursing, *Pittsburgh* (PhD)

Villanova University, College of Nursing, *Villanova* (PhD)

Waynesburg University, Department of Nursing, *Waynesburg* (DNP)

Widener University, School of Nursing, *Chester* (PhD)

Rhode Island

University of Rhode Island, College of Nursing, *Kingston* (PhD)

South Carolina

Medical University of South Carolina, College of Nursing, *Charleston* (DNP, PhD)

University of South Carolina, College of Nursing, *Columbia* (PhD)

South Dakota

South Dakota State University, College of Nursing, *Brookings* (PhD)

Tennessee

East Tennessee State University, College of Nursing, *Johnson City* (PhD)

The University of Tennessee, College of Nursing, *Knoxville* (PhD)

The University of Tennessee Health Science Center, College of Nursing, *Memphis* (DNP)

Vanderbilt University, School of Nursing, *Nashville* (DNP)

Texas

Baylor University, Louise Herrington School of Nursing, *Dallas* (DNP)

Texas Christian University, Harris College of Nursing, *Fort Worth* (DNP)

Texas Tech University Health Sciences Center, School of Nursing, *Lubbock* (DNP)

Texas Woman's University, College of Nursing, *Denton* (PhD)

The University of Texas at Arlington, School of Nursing, *Arlington* (PhD)

The University of Texas at Austin, School of Nursing, *Austin* (PhD)

The University of Texas at Tyler, Program in Nursing, *Tyler* (DNS)

The University of Texas Health Science Center at Houston, School of Nursing, *Houston* (PhD)

The University of Texas Health Science Center at San Antonio, School of Nursing, *San Antonio* (PhD)

The University of Texas Medical Branch, School of Nursing, *Galveston* (PhD)

Utah

University of Utah, College of Nursing, *Salt Lake City* (PhD)

Virginia

George Mason University, College of Health and Human Services, *Fairfax* (PhD)

Hampton University, School of Nursing, *Hampton* (PhD)

Marymount University, School of Health Professions, *Arlington* (DNP)

Old Dominion University, Department of Nursing, *Norfolk* (DNP)

Radford University, School of Nursing, *Radford* (DNP)

University of Virginia, School of Nursing, *Charlottesville* (PhD)

Virginia Commonwealth University, School of Nursing, *Richmond* (PhD)

Washington

Intercollegiate College of Nursing/Washington State University, *Spokane* (PhD)

University of Washington, School of Nursing, *Seattle* (PhD)

West Virginia

West Virginia University, School of Nursing, *Morgantown* (DNP, PhD)

Wisconsin

Concordia University Wisconsin, Program in Nursing, *Mequon* (DNP)

Marquette University, College of Nursing, *Milwaukee* (PhD)

University of Wisconsin–Madison, School of Nursing, *Madison* (DNP, PhD)

University of Wisconsin–Milwaukee, College of Nursing, *Milwaukee* (PhD)

CANADA

Alberta

University of Alberta, Faculty of Nursing, *Edmonton* (PhD)

University of Calgary, Faculty of Nursing, *Calgary* (PhD)

British Columbia

The University of British Columbia, Program in Nursing, *Vancouver* (PhD)

University of Victoria, School of Nursing, *Victoria* (PhD)

Manitoba

University of Manitoba, Faculty of Nursing, *Winnipeg* (PhD)

Nova Scotia

Dalhousie University, School of Nursing, *Halifax* (PhD)

Ontario

McMaster University, School of Nursing, *Hamilton* (PhD)

Queen's University at Kingston, School of Nursing, *Kingston* (PhD)

University of Ottawa, School of Nursing, *Ottawa* (PhD)

University of Toronto, Faculty of Nursing, *Toronto* (PhD)

The University of Western Ontario, School of Nursing, *London* (PhD)

Quebec

McGill University, School of Nursing, *Montréal* (PhD)

Université de Montréal, Faculty of Nursing, *Montréal* (PhD)

Université de Sherbrooke, Department of Nursing, *Sherbrooke* (PhD)

Université Laval, Faculty of Nursing, *Québec* (PhD)

Saskatchewan

University of Saskatchewan, College of Nursing, *Saskatoon* (PhD)

POSTDOCTORAL PROGRAMS

U.S. AND U.S. TERRITORIES

Arizona
The University of Arizona, College of Nursing, *Tucson*

Arkansas
University of Arkansas for Medical Sciences, College of Nursing, *Little Rock*

California
University of California, Los Angeles, School of Nursing, *Los Angeles*
University of California, San Francisco, School of Nursing, *San Francisco*

Colorado
University of Colorado Denver, College of Nursing, *Denver*

Connecticut
Yale University, School of Nursing, *New Haven*

Illinois
University of Illinois at Chicago, College of Nursing, *Chicago*

Indiana
Indiana University-Purdue University Indianapolis, School of Nursing, *Indianapolis*

Iowa
The University of Iowa, College of Nursing, *Iowa City*

Kansas
The University of Kansas, School of Nursing, *Kansas City*

Kentucky
University of Louisville, School of Nursing, *Louisville*

Maryland
The Johns Hopkins University, School of Nursing, *Baltimore*

Michigan
University of Michigan, School of Nursing, *Ann Arbor*
Wayne State University, College of Nursing, *Detroit*

Nebraska
University of Nebraska Medical Center, College of Nursing, *Omaha*

New York
Columbia University, School of Nursing, *New York*
University of Rochester, School of Nursing, *Rochester*

North Carolina
The University of North Carolina at Chapel Hill, School of Nursing, *Chapel Hill*

Ohio
Case Western Reserve University, Frances Payne Bolton School of Nursing, *Cleveland*

Oregon
Oregon Health & Science University, School of Nursing, *Portland*

Pennsylvania
Penn State University Park, School of Nursing, *State College, University Park*
University of Pennsylvania, School of Nursing, *Philadelphia*
University of Pittsburgh, School of Nursing, *Pittsburgh*

South Carolina
Medical University of South Carolina, College of Nursing, *Charleston*

Tennessee
Vanderbilt University, School of Nursing, *Nashville*

Texas
The University of Texas at Austin, School of Nursing, *Austin*

Utah
University of Utah, College of Nursing, *Salt Lake City*

Virginia
University of Virginia, School of Nursing, *Charlottesville*
Virginia Commonwealth University, School of Nursing, *Richmond*

Washington
University of Washington, School of Nursing, *Seattle*

Wisconsin
University of Wisconsin-Madison, School of Nursing, *Madison*

CANADA

British Columbia
The University of British Columbia, Program in Nursing, *Vancouver*
University of Northern British Columbia, Nursing Programme, *Prince George*

Ontario
University of Ottawa, School of Nursing, *Ottawa*
The University of Western Ontario, School of Nursing, *London*

Quebec
McGill University, School of Nursing, *Montréal*
Université de Montréal, Faculty of Nursing, *Montréal*
Université de Sherbrooke, Department of Nursing, *Sherbrooke*
Université Laval, Faculty of Nursing, *Québec*

ONLINE BACCALAUREATE PROGRAMS

Albany State University, GA
Alcorn State University, MS
Angelo State University, TX
Arkansas Tech University, AR
Ashland University, OH
Ball State University, IN
Blessing-Rieman College of Nursing, IL
Boise State University, ID
Brenau University, GA
California State University, Dominguez Hills, CA
Chamberlain College of Nursing, MO
Chatham University, PA
Clarion University of Pennsylvania, PA
Clarkson College, NE
Clayton State University, GA
Cleveland State University, OH
The College of St. Scholastica, MN
Creighton University, NE
Davenport University, MI
Delta State University, MS
East Carolina University, NC
Eastern New Mexico University, NM
East Tennessee State University, TN
ECPI College of Technology, VA
Edinboro University of Pennsylvania, PA
Ferris State University, MI
Finlandia University, MI
Florida Gulf Coast University, FL
Florida International University, FL
Florida State University, FL
Fort Hays State University, KS
Georgia Southern University, GA
Georgia Southwestern State University, GA
Grand Canyon University, AZ
Illinois State University, IL
Indiana State University, IN
Jacksonville State University, AL
Jacksonville University, FL
Kutztown University of Pennsylvania, PA
Lakehead University, ON
Lamar University, TX
Lander University, SC
Lehman College of the City University of New York, NY
Marymount University, VA
Memorial University of Newfoundland, NL
Mercy College, NY
Mercy College of Northwest Ohio, OH
Mesa State College, CO
Michigan State University, MI
Middle Tennessee State University, TN
Minot State University, ND
Mississippi College, MS
Mississippi University for Women, MS
Missouri State University, MO
Montana State University-Northern, MT
Morehead State University, KY
Northeastern State University, OK
Northern Arizona University, AZ
North Georgia College & State University, GA
Northwestern State University of Louisiana, LA
Ohio University, OH
Oklahoma Panhandle State University, OK
Penn State University Park, PA
Pittsburg State University, KS
Presentation College, SD
Purdue University Calumet, IN
Queens University of Charlotte, NC

Radford University, VA
Ramapo College of New Jersey, NJ
Rivier College, NH
Sacred Heart University, CT
Saint Louis University, MO
St. Petersburg College, FL
San Diego State University, CA
Silver Lake College, WI
Slippery Rock University of Pennsylvania, PA
South Dakota State University, SD
Southeastern Louisiana University, LA
South University, FL
Southwest Baptist University, MO
Southwestern College, KS
Southwestern Oklahoma State University, OK
State University of New York at Plattsburgh, NY
State University of New York Empire State College, NY
Tabor College, KS
Texas A&M University-Corpus Christi, TX
Texas Tech University Health Sciences Center, TX
Texas Woman's University, TX
Touro University, NV
University of Arkansas at Fort Smith, AR
University of Arkansas for Medical Sciences, AR
University of Central Missouri, MO
University of Colorado at Colorado Springs, CO
University of Colorado Denver, CO
University of Illinois at Chicago, IL
University of Louisiana at Lafayette, LA
University of Louisiana at Monroe, LA
University of Maine at Fort Kent, ME
University of Mary, ND
University of Maryland, Baltimore, MD
University of Massachusetts Amherst, MA
University of Massachusetts Boston, MA
University of Michigan-Flint, MI
University of Missouri-Columbia, MO
University of Missouri-St. Louis, MO
University of North Alabama, AL
The University of North Carolina Wilmington, NC
University of North Dakota, ND
University of Phoenix, AZ
University of Phoenix-Phoenix Campus, AZ
University of Phoenix-Sacramento Valley Campus, CA
University of Phoenix-Southern Arizona Campus, AZ
University of Phoenix-South Florida Campus, FL
University of Phoenix-West Florida Campus, FL
University of St. Francis, IL
University of Saint Mary, KS
University of South Carolina Aiken, SC
University of South Carolina Upstate, SC
University of Southern Indiana, IN
University of Southern Mississippi, MS
The University of Texas at Arlington, TX
The University of Texas at Tyler, TX
The University of Texas Medical Branch, TX
University of the Incarnate Word, TX
The University of Toledo, OH
University of West Florida, FL
University of Wisconsin-Green Bay, WI
University of Wisconsin-Oshkosh, WI
University of Wyoming, WY
Weber State University, UT
Western Carolina University, NC
Western Illinois University, IL

West Virginia University, WV
Wichita State University, KS
Wilmington University, DE

ONLINE ONLY BACCALAUREATE PROGRAMS

Angelo State University, TX
Ashland University, OH
Chamberlain College of Nursing, MO
Chatham University, PA
Clarion University of Pennsylvania, PA
Eastern New Mexico University, NM
Georgia Southwestern State University, GA
Mississippi College, MS
Montana State University-Northern, MT
Northern Arizona University, AZ
North Georgia College & State University, GA
Oklahoma Panhandle State University, OK
Rivier College, NH
Saint Louis University, MO
Slippery Rock University of Pennsylvania, PA
State University of New York Empire State College, NY
Tabor College, KS
Texas Tech University Health Sciences Center, TX
University of Arkansas at Fort Smith, AR
University of Louisiana at Monroe, LA
University of North Alabama, AL
University of Saint Mary, KS
The University of Texas at Tyler, TX
The University of Texas Medical Branch, TX

ONLINE MASTER'S DEGREE PROGRAMS

Albany State University, GA
Allen College, IA
Angelo State University, TX
Athabasca University, AB
Ball State University, IN
Bellin College, WI
Benedictine University, IL
California State University, Chico, CA
California State University, Dominguez Hills, CA
California State University, Fullerton, CA
California State University, Sacramento, CA
Charleston Southern University, SC
Clarkson College, NE
Cleveland State University, OH
Delta State University, MS
Drexel University, PA
Duke University, NC
Duquesne University, PA
East Carolina University, NC
East Tennessee State University, TN
Excelsior College, NY
Felician College, NJ
Ferris State University, MI
Fitchburg State College, MA
Florida Atlantic University, FL
Florida State University, FL
Fort Hays State University, KS
Graceland University, IA
Grand Canyon University, AZ
Idaho State University, ID

ONLINE PROGRAMS
Online Master's Degree Programs

Indiana State University, IN
Indiana Wesleyan University, IN
Jacksonville State University, AL
Kutztown University of Pennsylvania, PA
Lamar University, TX
La Roche College, PA
Lewis University, IL
Liberty University, VA
Mansfield University of Pennsylvania, PA
McNeese State University, LA
Medical College of Georgia, GA
Medical University of South Carolina, SC
Memorial University of Newfoundland, NL
Mercy College, NY
Michigan State University, MI
Middle Tennessee State University, TN
Missouri State University, MO
Nebraska Methodist College, NE
Northern Arizona University, AZ
Northern Kentucky University, KY
Northwest Nazarene University, ID
Old Dominion University, VA
Penn State University Park, PA
Purdue University Calumet, IN
Ramapo College of New Jersey, NJ
Regis University, CO
Research College of Nursing, MO
Rush University, IL
Sacred Heart University, CT
Saint Francis Medical Center College of
    Nursing, IL
Saint Joseph's College of Maine, ME
Saint Louis University, MO
Saint Xavier University, IL
Samuel Merritt University, CA
Seton Hall University, NJ
Simmons College, MA
Sonoma State University, CA
South Dakota State University, SD
South University, FL
Spring Arbor University, MI
Spring Hill College, AL
Tennessee State University, TN
Tennessee Technological University, TN
Texas A&M University-Corpus Christi, TX
Texas Christian University, TX
Texas Tech University Health Sciences Center,
    TX
Texas Woman's University, TX
Touro University, NV
The University of Alabama, AL
The University of Alabama at Birmingham, AL
The University of Alabama in Huntsville, AL
University of Arkansas, AR
University of Central Arkansas, AR
University of Central Missouri, MO
University of Cincinnati, OH
University of Colorado at Colorado Springs, CO
University of Colorado Denver, CO
University of Florida, FL
University of Hawaii at Manoa, HI
University of Indianapolis, IN
The University of Kansas, KS
University of Louisiana at Lafayette, LA
University of Mary, ND
University of Maryland, Baltimore, MD
University of Medicine and Dentistry of New
    Jersey, NJ
University of Memphis, TN
University of Missouri-Columbia, MO
University of Missouri-Kansas City, MO
University of Missouri-St. Louis, MO
University of Nevada, Las Vegas, NV
University of New Mexico, NM
University of North Alabama, AL
The University of North Carolina at Charlotte,
    NC

The University of North Carolina Wilmington,
    NC
University of North Dakota, ND
University of Northern Colorado, CO
University of Oklahoma Health Sciences
    Center, OK
University of Ottawa, ON
University of Phoenix, AZ
University of Phoenix-New Mexico Campus,
    NM
University of Phoenix-Phoenix Campus, AZ
University of Phoenix-Southern Arizona
    Campus, AZ
University of Phoenix-South Florida Campus,
    FL
University of Pittsburgh, PA
University of Rochester, NY
University of St. Francis, IL
University of Southern Indiana, IN
The University of Texas at El Paso, TX
The University of Texas Medical Branch, TX
University of Toronto, ON
University of Wyoming, WY
Vanderbilt University, TN
Wesley College, DE
Western Carolina University, NC
Western University of Health Sciences, CA
West Virginia University, WV
Wright State University, OH
Yale University, CT

ONLINE ONLY MASTER'S DEGREE PROGRAMS

Albany State University, GA
Angelo State University, TX
Ball State University, IN
Benedictine University, IL
California State University, Chico, CA
California State University, Sacramento, CA
Charleston Southern University, SC
Clarkson College, NE
Cleveland State University, OH
Delta State University, MS
Duquesne University, PA
Excelsior College, NY
Felician College, NJ
Ferris State University, MI
Fitchburg State College, MA
Florida State University, FL
Graceland University, IA
Idaho State University, ID
Indiana State University, IN
Jacksonville State University, AL
Kutztown University of Pennsylvania, PA
Lamar University, TX
La Roche College, PA
Lewis University, IL
Liberty University, VA
Mansfield University of Pennsylvania, PA
McNeese State University, LA
Medical University of South Carolina, SC
Memorial University of Newfoundland, NL
Missouri State University, MO
Nebraska Methodist College, NE
Northern Arizona University, AZ
Northwest Nazarene University, ID
Old Dominion University, VA
Ramapo College of New Jersey, NJ
Saint Francis Medical Center College of
    Nursing, IL
Saint Joseph's College of Maine, ME
Saint Louis University, MO
Seton Hall University, NJ
Spring Arbor University, MI
Spring Hill College, AL

Tennessee Technological University, TN
Texas A&M University-Corpus Christi, TX
Texas Christian University, TX
Texas Tech University Health Sciences Center,
    TX
Touro University, NV
The University of Alabama, AL
The University of Alabama at Birmingham, AL
University of Central Arkansas, AR
University of Central Missouri, MO
University of Colorado at Colorado Springs, CO
University of Louisiana at Lafayette, LA
University of Maryland, Baltimore, MD
University of Missouri-Columbia, MO
University of Missouri-Kansas City, MO
University of Nevada, Las Vegas, NV
University of New Mexico, NM
University of North Alabama, AL
University of Northern Colorado, CO
University of Southern Indiana, IN
The University of Texas at El Paso, TX
The University of Texas Medical Branch, TX
Western University of Health Sciences, CA
West Virginia University, WV

ONLINE DOCTORAL DEGREE PROGRAMS

Ball State University, IN
The Catholic University of America, DC
Chatham University, PA
Concordia University Wisconsin, WI
Duquesne University, PA
Georgia Southern University, GA
Medical University of South Carolina, SC
Minnesota State University Moorhead, MN
North Dakota State University, ND
Old Dominion University, VA
Radford University, VA
Rush University, IL
Saint Francis Medical Center College of
    Nursing, IL
Seton Hall University, NJ
Simmons College, MA
Texas Christian University, TX
Touro University, NV
The University of Alabama, AL
The University of Alabama in Huntsville, AL
The University of Arizona, AZ
University of Colorado at Colorado Springs, CO
University of Florida, FL
University of Hawaii at Manoa, HI
The University of Kansas, KS
University of Michigan-Flint, MI
University of Missouri-Kansas City, MO
University of Nevada, Las Vegas, NV
University of Northern Colorado, CO
University of Phoenix, AZ
The University of Tennessee, TN
The University of Tennessee Health Science
    Center, TN
The University of Texas Medical Branch, TX
The University of Toledo, OH
University of Wisconsin-Milwaukee, WI
Western University of Health Sciences, CA
Winona State University, MN
Wright State University, OH

ONLINE ONLY DOCTORAL DEGREE PROGRAMS

Ball State University, IN
Chatham University, PA
Concordia University Wisconsin, WI
Duquesne University, PA

Georgia Southern University, GA
Medical University of South Carolina, SC
Minnesota State University Moorhead, MN
Old Dominion University, VA
Radford University, VA
Rush University, IL
Saint Francis Medical Center College of
  Nursing, IL
Seton Hall University, NJ
Simmons College, MA

Texas Christian University, TX
Touro University, NV
The University of Alabama, AL
The University of Alabama in Huntsville, AL
The University of Arizona, AZ
University of Colorado at Colorado Springs, CO
University of Hawaii at Manoa, HI
University of Michigan-Flint, MI
University of Missouri-Kansas City, MO
University of Nevada, Las Vegas, NV

University of Northern Colorado, CO
University of Phoenix, AZ
The University of Tennessee, TN
The University of Tennessee Health Science
  Center, TN
The University of Texas Medical Branch, TX
The University of Toledo, OH
Western University of Health Sciences, CA
Winona State University, MN
Wright State University, OH

CONTINUING EDUCATION PROGRAMS

U.S. AND U.S. TERRITORIES

Alabama

Jacksonville State University, College of Nursing and Health Sciences, *Jacksonville*

Samford University, Ida V. Moffett School of Nursing, *Birmingham*

The University of Alabama in Huntsville, College of Nursing, *Huntsville*

University of Mobile, School of Nursing, *Mobile*

University of North Alabama, College of Nursing and Allied Health, *Florence*

Arizona

Arizona State University at the Downtown Phoenix Campus, College of Nursing, *Phoenix*

Grand Canyon University, College of Nursing and Health Sciences, *Phoenix*

University of Phoenix, Online Campus, *Phoenix*

University of Phoenix-Phoenix Campus, College of Health and Human Services, *Phoenix*

University of Phoenix-Southern Arizona Campus, College of Health and Human Services, *Tucson*

Arkansas

Harding University, College of Nursing, *Searcy*

University of Arkansas, Eleanor Mann School of Nursing, *Fayetteville*

University of Arkansas for Medical Sciences, College of Nursing, *Little Rock*

California

Azusa Pacific University, School of Nursing, *Azusa*

California State University, Bakersfield, Program in Nursing, *Bakersfield*

California State University, Chico, School of Nursing, *Chico*

California State University, Dominguez Hills, Program in Nursing, *Carson*

California State University, Fresno, Department of Nursing, *Fresno*

California State University, Fullerton, Department of Nursing, *Fullerton*

Dominican University of California, Program in Nursing, *San Rafael*

Pacific Union College, Department of Nursing, *Angwin*

Point Loma Nazarene University, School of Nursing, *San Diego*

San Diego State University, School of Nursing, *San Diego*

San Francisco State University, School of Nursing, *San Francisco*

University of California, Los Angeles, School of Nursing, *Los Angeles*

University of Phoenix-Sacramento Valley Campus, College of Health and Human Services, *Sacramento*

University of Phoenix-Southern California Campus, College of Health and Human Services, *Costa Mesa*

Colorado

University of Colorado at Colorado Springs, Beth-El College of Nursing and Health Sciences, *Colorado Springs*

University of Colorado Denver, College of Nursing, *Denver*

Connecticut

Fairfield University, School of Nursing, *Fairfield*

Quinnipiac University, Department of Nursing, *Hamden*

University of Connecticut, School of Nursing, *Storrs*

University of Hartford, College of Education, Nursing, and Health Professions, *West Hartford*

Delaware

Wesley College, Nursing Program, *Dover*

Florida

Florida Agricultural and Mechanical University, School of Nursing, *Tallahassee*

Florida Atlantic University, Christine E. Lynn College of Nursing, *Boca Raton*

Florida Gulf Coast University, School of Nursing, *Fort Myers*

Florida Southern College, Department of Nursing, *Lakeland*

St. Petersburg College, Department of Nursing, *St. Petersburg*

University of Miami, School of Nursing and Health Studies, *Coral Gables*

University of South Florida, College of Nursing, *Tampa*

The University of Tampa, Department of Nursing, *Tampa*

Georgia

Brenau University, School of Health and Science, *Gainesville*

Kennesaw State University, School of Nursing, *Kennesaw*

Valdosta State University, College of Nursing, *Valdosta*

Illinois

Lewis University, Program in Nursing, *Romeoville*

Rush University, College of Nursing, *Chicago*

Saint Xavier University, School of Nursing, *Chicago*

Southern Illinois University Edwardsville, School of Nursing, *Edwardsville*

University of Illinois at Chicago, College of Nursing, *Chicago*

Indiana

Indiana State University, Department of Nursing, *Terre Haute*

Indiana University Kokomo, Indiana University School of Nursing, *Kokomo*

Indiana University-Purdue University Fort Wayne, Department of Nursing, *Fort Wayne*

Indiana University-Purdue University Indianapolis, School of Nursing, *Indianapolis*

Purdue University, School of Nursing, *West Lafayette*

University of Indianapolis, School of Nursing, *Indianapolis*

University of Southern Indiana, College of Nursing and Health Professions, *Evansville*

Valparaiso University, College of Nursing, *Valparaiso*

Iowa

Allen College, Program in Nursing, *Waterloo*

Briar Cliff University, Department of Nursing, *Sioux City*

Clarke College, Department of Nursing and Health, *Dubuque*

Grand View University, Division of Nursing, *Des Moines*

Luther College, Department of Nursing, *Decorah*

Mount Mercy College, Department of Nursing, *Cedar Rapids*

The University of Iowa, College of Nursing, *Iowa City*

Kansas

MidAmerica Nazarene University, Division of Nursing, *Olathe*

Pittsburg State University, Department of Nursing, *Pittsburg*

The University of Kansas, School of Nursing, *Kansas City*

Washburn University, School of Nursing, *Topeka*

Kentucky

Bellarmine University, Donna and Allan Lansing School of Nursing and Health Sciences, *Louisville*

Berea College, Department of Nursing, *Berea*

Kentucky Christian University, School of Nursing, *Grayson*

Midway College, Program in Nursing (Baccalaureate), *Midway*

Murray State University, Program in Nursing, *Murray*

Spalding University, School of Nursing, *Louisville*

University of Kentucky, Graduate School Programs in the College of Nursing, *Lexington*

University of Louisville, School of Nursing, *Louisville*

Western Kentucky University, Department of Nursing, *Bowling Green*

Louisiana

Louisiana State University Health Sciences Center, School of Nursing, *New Orleans*

McNeese State University, College of Nursing, *Lake Charles*

Nicholls State University, Department of Nursing, *Thibodaux*

Northwestern State University of Louisiana, College of Nursing, *Shreveport*

Our Lady of the Lake College, Division of Nursing, *Baton Rouge*

University of Louisiana at Lafayette, College of Nursing, *Lafayette*

University of Louisiana at Monroe, Nursing, *Monroe*

Maine

Saint Joseph's College of Maine, Department of Nursing, *Standish*

University of New England, Department of Nursing, *Biddeford*

University of Southern Maine, College of Nursing and Health Professions, *Portland*

Maryland

The Johns Hopkins University, School of Nursing, *Baltimore*

University of Maryland, Baltimore, Master's Program in Nursing, *Baltimore*

Massachusetts

Anna Maria College, Department of Nursing, *Paxton*

CONTINUING EDUCATION PROGRAMS

Boston College, William F. Connell School of Nursing, *Chestnut Hill*

Endicott College, Major in Nursing, *Beverly*

Framingham State College, Department of Nursing, *Framingham*

Massachusetts College of Pharmacy and Health Sciences, School of Nursing, *Boston*

Northeastern University, School of Nursing, *Boston*

Regis College, School of Nursing and Health Professions, *Weston*

Salem State College, Program in Nursing, *Salem*

University of Massachusetts Amherst, School of Nursing, *Amherst*

University of Massachusetts Boston, College of Nursing and Health Sciences, *Boston*

University of Massachusetts Dartmouth, College of Nursing, *North Dartmouth*

University of Massachusetts Worcester, Graduate School of Nursing, *Worcester*

Michigan

Grand Valley State University, Kirkhof College of Nursing, *Allendale*

Madonna University, College of Nursing and Health, *Livonia*

Michigan State University, College of Nursing, *East Lansing*

Northern Michigan University, College of Nursing and Allied Health Science, *Marquette*

Oakland University, School of Nursing, *Rochester*

Saginaw Valley State University, Crystal M. Lange College of Nursing and Health Sciences, *University Center*

University of Michigan-Flint, Department of Nursing, *Flint*

Wayne State University, College of Nursing, *Detroit*

Minnesota

Bemidji State University, Department of Nursing, *Bemidji*

Minnesota State University Mankato, School of Nursing, *Mankato*

University of Minnesota, Twin Cities Campus, School of Nursing, *Minneapolis*

Mississippi

University of Mississippi Medical Center, Program in Nursing, *Jackson*

Missouri

Cox College of Nursing and Health Sciences, Department of Nursing, *Springfield*

Missouri State University, Department of Nursing, *Springfield*

Saint Louis University, School of Nursing, *St. Louis*

University of Missouri-Columbia, Sinclair School of Nursing, *Columbia*

University of Missouri-Kansas City, School of Nursing, *Kansas City*

University of Missouri-St. Louis, College of Nursing, *St. Louis*

Nebraska

Clarkson College, Master of Science in Nursing Program, *Omaha*

Nebraska Methodist College, Department of Nursing, *Omaha*

University of Nebraska Medical Center, College of Nursing, *Omaha*

Nevada

Touro University, School of Nursing, *Henderson*

University of Nevada, Las Vegas, School of Nursing, *Las Vegas*

New Hampshire

Saint Anselm College, Department of Nursing, *Manchester*

New Jersey

College of Saint Elizabeth, Department of Nursing, *Morristown*

Fairleigh Dickinson University, Metropolitan Campus, Henry P. Becton School of Nursing and Allied Health, *Teaneck*

Kean University, Department of Nursing, *Union*

Monmouth University, Marjorie K. Unterberg School of Nursing, *West Long Branch*

Ramapo College of New Jersey, Master of Science in Nursing Program, *Mahwah*

Rutgers, The State University of New Jersey, College of Nursing, *Newark*

Seton Hall University, College of Nursing, *South Orange*

University of Medicine and Dentistry of New Jersey, School of Nursing, *Newark*

New Mexico

New Mexico State University, School of Nursing, *Las Cruces*

New York

Adelphi University, School of Nursing, *Garden City*

Columbia University, School of Nursing, *New York*

Elmira College, Program in Nursing Education, *Elmira*

Hunter College of the City University of New York, Hunter-Bellevue School of Nursing, *New York*

Molloy College, Department of Nursing, *Rockville Centre*

Nazareth College of Rochester, Department of Nursing, *Rochester*

New York University, College of Nursing, *New York*

The Sage Colleges, Department of Nursing, *Troy*

State University of New York at Binghamton, Decker School of Nursing, *Binghamton*

State University of New York Downstate Medical Center, College of Nursing, *Brooklyn*

State University of New York Institute of Technology, School of Nursing and Health Systems, *Utica*

State University of New York Upstate Medical University, College of Nursing, *Syracuse*

Stony Brook University, State University of New York, School of Nursing, *Stony Brook*

University of Rochester, School of Nursing, *Rochester*

North Carolina

Queens University of Charlotte, Presbyterian School of Nursing, *Charlotte*

The University of North Carolina at Chapel Hill, School of Nursing, *Chapel Hill*

The University of North Carolina Wilmington, School of Nursing, *Wilmington*

Winston-Salem State University, Department of Nursing, *Winston-Salem*

Ohio

Case Western Reserve University, Frances Payne Bolton School of Nursing, *Cleveland*

Cleveland State University, School of Nursing, *Cleveland*

Kent State University, College of Nursing, *Kent*

Mercy College of Northwest Ohio, Division of Nursing, *Toledo*

Otterbein College, Department of Nursing, *Westerville*

Shawnee State University, Department of Nursing, *Portsmouth*

The University of Akron, College of Nursing, *Akron*

University of Cincinnati, College of Nursing, *Cincinnati*

The University of Toledo, College of Nursing, *Toledo*

Wright State University, College of Nursing and Health, *Dayton*

Oklahoma

Oklahoma City University, Kramer School of Nursing, *Oklahoma City*

University of Oklahoma Health Sciences Center, College of Nursing, *Oklahoma City*

Oregon

Linfield College, School of Nursing, *McMinnville*

Oregon Health & Science University, School of Nursing, *Portland*

Pennsylvania

Alvernia University, Nursing, *Reading*

Bloomsburg University of Pennsylvania, Department of Nursing, *Bloomsburg*

Carlow University, School of Nursing, *Pittsburgh*

DeSales University, Department of Nursing and Health, *Center Valley*

Drexel University, College of Nursing and Health Professions, *Philadelphia*

Duquesne University, School of Nursing, *Pittsburgh*

Holy Family University, School of Nursing and Allied Health Professions, *Philadelphia*

La Roche College, Department of Nursing and Nursing Management, *Pittsburgh*

La Salle University, School of Nursing and Health Sciences, *Philadelphia*

Marywood University, Department of Nursing, *Scranton*

Millersville University of Pennsylvania, Department of Nursing, *Millersville*

Moravian College, St. Luke's School of Nursing, *Bethlehem*

Mount Aloysius College, Department of Nursing, *Cresson*

Penn State University Park, School of Nursing, *State College, University Park*

Thomas Jefferson University, Department of Nursing, *Philadelphia*

University of Pennsylvania, School of Nursing, *Philadelphia*

University of Pittsburgh, School of Nursing, *Pittsburgh*

Villanova University, College of Nursing, *Villanova*

Wilkes University, Department of Nursing, *Wilkes-Barre*

Puerto Rico

Universidad Adventista de las Antillas, Department of Nursing, *Mayagüez*

University of Puerto Rico, Mayagüez Campus, Department of Nursing, *Mayagüez*

University of Puerto Rico, Medical Sciences Campus, School of Nursing, *San Juan*

Rhode Island

Salve Regina University, Department of Nursing, *Newport*

South Carolina

Clemson University, School of Nursing, *Clemson*

Medical University of South Carolina, College of Nursing, *Charleston*

University of South Carolina, College of Nursing, *Columbia*

University of South Carolina Aiken, School of Nursing, *Aiken*

South Dakota

South Dakota State University, College of Nursing, *Brookings*

Tennessee

Southern Adventist University, School of Nursing, *Collegedale*

Union University, School of Nursing, *Jackson*

The University of Tennessee, College of Nursing, *Knoxville*

The University of Tennessee at Chattanooga, School of Nursing, *Chattanooga*

The University of Tennessee at Martin, Department of Nursing, *Martin*

Vanderbilt University, School of Nursing, *Nashville*

Texas

Lamar University, Department of Nursing, *Beaumont*

Midwestern State University, Nursing Program, *Wichita Falls*

Patty Hanks Shelton School of Nursing, *Abilene*

Tarleton State University, Department of Nursing, *Stephenville*

Texas A&M University-Corpus Christi, School of Nursing and Health Sciences, *Corpus Christi*

Texas Christian University, Harris College of Nursing, *Fort Worth*

Texas Tech University Health Sciences Center, School of Nursing, *Lubbock*

University of Mary Hardin-Baylor, College of Nursing, *Belton*

The University of Texas at Arlington, School of Nursing, *Arlington*

The University of Texas at Tyler, Program in Nursing, *Tyler*

The University of Texas Health Science Center at Houston, School of Nursing, *Houston*

The University of Texas Health Science Center at San Antonio, School of Nursing, *San Antonio*

Virginia

George Mason University, College of Health and Human Services, *Fairfax*

Jefferson College of Health Sciences, Nursing Education Program, *Roanoke*

Old Dominion University, Department of Nursing, *Norfolk*

Shenandoah University, Division of Nursing, *Winchester*

Washington

Gonzaga University, Department of Nursing, *Spokane*

Intercollegiate College of Nursing/Washington State University, *Spokane*

Pacific Lutheran University, School of Nursing, *Tacoma*

University of Washington, School of Nursing, *Seattle*

West Virginia

Fairmont State University, School of Nursing and Allied Health Administration, *Fairmont*

Shepherd University, Department of Nursing Education, *Shepherdstown*

West Virginia University, School of Nursing, *Morgantown*

Wisconsin

Alverno College, Division of Nursing, *Milwaukee*

University of Wisconsin-Eau Claire, College of Nursing and Health Sciences, *Eau Claire*

University of Wisconsin-Madison, School of Nursing, *Madison*

University of Wisconsin-Oshkosh, College of Nursing, *Oshkosh*

Viterbo University, School of Nursing, *La Crosse*

Wisconsin Lutheran College, Nursing Program, *Milwaukee*

CANADA

British Columbia

British Columbia Institute of Technology, School of Health Sciences, *Burnaby*

Thompson Rivers University, School of Nursing, *Kamloops*

Manitoba

University of Manitoba, Faculty of Nursing, *Winnipeg*

New Brunswick

Université de Moncton, School of Nursing, *Moncton*

University of New Brunswick Fredericton, Faculty of Nursing, *Fredericton*

Nova Scotia

St. Francis Xavier University, Department of Nursing, *Antigonish*

Ontario

Laurentian University, School of Nursing, *Sudbury*

Ryerson University, Program in Nursing, *Toronto*

University of Windsor, Faculty of Nursing, *Windsor*

York University, School of Nursing, Atkinson Faculty of Liberal and Professional Studies, *Toronto*

Quebec

Université de Montréal, Faculty of Nursing, *Montréal*

Université du Québec à Rimouski, Program in Nursing, *Rimouski*

Université Laval, Faculty of Nursing, *Québec*

Saskatchewan

University of Saskatchewan, College of Nursing, *Saskatoon*

ALPHABETICAL LISTING OF INSTITUTIONS

Peterson's
Book Satisfaction Survey

Give Us Your Feedback

Thank you for choosing Peterson's as your source for personalized solutions for your education and career achievement. Please take a few minutes to answer the following questions. Your answers will go a long way in helping us to produce the most user-friendly and comprehensive resources to meet your individual needs.

When completed, please tear out this page and mail it to us at:

Publishing Department
Peterson's, a Nelnet company
2000 Lenox Drive
Lawrenceville, NJ 08648

You can also complete this survey online at **www.petersons.com/booksurvey.**

1. **What is the ISBN of the book you have purchased? (The ISBN can be found on the book's back cover in the lower right-hand corner.)** _____

2. **Where did you purchase this book?**
   ❑ Retailer, such as Barnes & Noble
   ❑ Online reseller, such as Amazon.com
   ❑ Petersons.com
   ❑ Other (please specify) _____

3. **If you purchased this book on Petersons.com, please rate the following aspects of your online purchasing experience on a scale of 4 to 1 (4 = Excellent and 1 = Poor).**

	4	3	2	1
Comprehensiveness of Peterson's Online Bookstore page	❑	❑	❑	❑
Overall online customer experience	❑	❑	❑	❑

4. **Which category best describes you?**
   ❑ High school student
   ❑ Parent of high school student
   ❑ College student
   ❑ Graduate/professional student
   ❑ Returning adult student

   ❑ Teacher
   ❑ Counselor
   ❑ Working professional/military
   ❑ Other (please specify) _____

5. **Rate your overall satisfaction with this book.**

Extremely Satisfied	Satisfied	Not Satisfied
❑	❑	❑

6. Rate each of the following aspects of this book on a scale of 4 to 1 (4 = Excellent and 1 = Poor).

	4	3	2	1
Comprehensiveness of the information	❑	❑	❑	❑
Accuracy of the information	❑	❑	❑	❑
Usability	❑	❑	❑	❑
Cover design	❑	❑	❑	❑
Book layout	❑	❑	❑	❑
Special features (e.g., CD, flashcards, charts, etc.)	❑	❑	❑	❑
Value for the money	❑	❑	❑	❑

7. This book was recommended by:
- ❑ Guidance counselor
- ❑ Parent/guardian
- ❑ Family member/relative
- ❑ Friend
- ❑ Teacher
- ❑ Not recommended by anyone—I found the book on my own
- ❑ Other (please specify) _____

8. Would you recommend this book to others?

Yes	Not Sure	No
❑	❑	❑

9. Please provide any additional comments.

_____

_____

_____

_____

_____

Remember, you can tear out this page and mail it to us at:

Publishing Department
Peterson's, a Nelnet company
2000 Lenox Drive
Lawrenceville, NJ 08648

or you can complete the survey online at **www.petersons.com/booksurvey**.

Your feedback is important to us at Peterson's, and we thank you for your time!

If you would like us to keep in touch with you about new products and services, please include your e-mail address here: _____